COMPANION TO
THEATRE
IN AUSTRALIA

Companion to
THEATRE
in Australia

General editor Philip Parsons
with Victoria Chance

CURRENCY PRESS · SYDNEY
in association with

Companion to Theatre in Australia
First published in 1995 by Currency Press Pty Ltd ACN 000 938 929,
PO Box 452, Paddington NSW 2021, Australia.
Copyright © Currency Press Pty Ltd 1995.
This book is copyright. Apart from fair dealing for the purpose of private study, reseach or
review as permitted under the Copyright Act, no part may be reproduced by any process
without written permission. Enquiries should be addressed to the publisher.

Conceived, edited and designed by Ampersand Editions Pty Ltd, Sydney.
Printed in Australia by Southwood Press Pty Ltd, Sydney.

The project has been assisted by the Commonwealth Government through the Australia Council, its arts-funding and advisory body.

This publication has been partially funded by the Australian Bicentennial Authority to celebrate Australia's bicentenary in 1988.

Published outside Australia by the Press Syndicate of the University of Cambridge
The Pitt Building, Trumpington Street, Cambridge CB2 1RP, United Kingdom
40 West 20th Street, New York, NY 10011-4211, USA.

National Library of Australia cataloguing-in-publication data
Companion to theatre in Australia

Bibliography.
Includes index.
ISBN 0 86819 357 7.

1. Theater - Australia - History. 2. Actors - Australia ; Biography. 3. Theater - Australia - Biography.
I. Parsons, Philip, 1926–1993. II. Chance, Victoria

792.0994

Library of Congress Cataloging-in-Publication Data
A companion to theatre in Australia / edited by Philip Parsons with Victoria Chance
    p.   cm.
Includes bibliographical references and index.
ISBN 0–86819–357–7 (Currency Press). — ISBN 0–521–34528–6 (Cambridge University Press)
1. Theater—Australia—Encyclopedias. 2. Performing arts—Australia—Encyclopedias. 3. Theater—Australia—Biography—Dictionaries. 4. Performing arts—Australia—Biography—Dictionaries. I. Parsons, Philip. II. Chance, Victoria.
PN3011.C66 1995
792'.0994—dc20   95–119287
                                                                                                       CIP

A catalogue record for this book is available from the British Library.
Currency Press ISBN 0 86819 357 7 Hardback
Cambridge University Press ISBN 0 521 34528 6 Hardback

PREFACE

It grieves us all that Philip Parsons, general editor of this work, did not live to see it in print. He died in Sydney on 20 June 1993, seven years after laying the foundations of the project, and a few weeks after receiving the last contribution. While he was not responsible for the final text or the many hard decisions involved in concentrating a mountain of research into a practicable space, he did provide a powerful framework within which the task was accomplished. The book embodies the broad perspective, high critical standards and deep understanding that he brought to it.

Companion to Theatre in Australia is unique in this country and works of its scope are rare elsewhere. The designation 'theatre' covers all theatrical forms, including circus, mime, puppetry, vaudeville, pantomime, revue, and musical theatre except opera and dance, which were ceded to the forthcoming *Companion to Music and Dance in Australia*. Within these limits, the primary aim of the present book is to cover every major development and every significant figure in theatre in Australia, from earliest colonial times to the present. This book is a companion, not an encyclopedia, and this implies a certain selectivity. Further, it is about theatre in Australia, not Australian theatre. This recognises the procession of visiting stars and companies, from Edwin Booth to the Royal Shakespeare Company, who have set fresh standards and broadened taste, especially in the flourishing colonial theatre. There are articles on individuals and companies who were resident for a period or made an extensive working visit; or made a notable contribution to the development of some aspect of theatre here; or, as in the case of Sarah Bernhardt, simply left a legend behind.

So while the subjects are not all Australian, all have been historically significant in the development of some aspect of theatre in Australia. Articles on notable expatriates such as Judith Anderson and Oscar Asche are confined as far as possible to the Australian aspects of their careers. The more substantial treatment is accorded to those who have lived and worked here.

Companion to Theatre in Australia is not a Who's Who in Australian Theatre and many a contemporary figure who might be found in one is not the subject of a separate article here. Resident individuals are subjects of articles because they have made a notable contribution to the theatre in Australia or have served for an extended period at a senior level. These criteria may have been met nationally or locally, for Australia has no single metropolitan theatre centre and significant careers have not always spanned the length and breadth of this vast country. Constraints of space made the long-service category increasingly selective. The contemporary scene, more densely populated than ever before, caused the greatest debate. A further criterion of at least 15 years on the professional stage was introduced, and some borderline cases were settled by the question: 'Would you expect to find this name in this book?' Screen actors will appear fully in the forthcoming *Companion to Australian Film, Radio and Television*.

For Australian works, three criteria applied: a substantial critical or artistic impact on first performance; continuing attention over a substantial period, either through revivals or critical discussion; some significant association or aspect, such as an outstanding star performance. Many works that met none of these criteria are mentioned in articles on their authors. Non-Australian works rarely rate attention unless they have been landmark events in a sense other than a long run.

Articles on individuals give essential biographical detail and landmark events, but the emphasis is upon informed opinion and a lively account of a person's contribution to theatre. Thematic articles emphasise the history, nature and public reception of the subject and its significance in retrospect. When the person best qualified to write on a contemporary subject—the history of a company, for example—was someone who had been involved we have not denied ourselves their authority. In such cases, where reference to 'the present writer' would be intrusive in simple factual information the contributor's name has been retained in the text.

A subsidiary but important function of this book is to encourage research by revealing gaps in theatrical history. Coverage of important towns, for example, is not comprehensive—there is an article on Newcastle (NSW) but none on Geelong (Vic.). Amateur theatre deserves much more exploration, even though this book has gone farther than any other in acknowledging a debt, so often ignored, to those innovators who kept theatre alive when the profession was moribund. Various theses have proved valuable resources; and areas awaiting further research have been noted.

Overseas influences are erratically covered. We have published what has been achieved by research, but much work is still needed—for example, on immigrant communities, especially early in the 20th century. There is no article on Jewish influence, even though the Jewish merchant Barnett Levey was the 'father' of theatre in Australia. Nor has Irish influence been fully documented. These must await the next edition. This first edition reflects the state of the art. We hope that researchers will find in the book fresh fields of interest and keep us advised of their work. For the companions are more than a three-volume series: they are an encyclopedic bank that we plan to keep current.

Some 200 writers have contributed articles, ranging in length from 100 to 10 000 words. Most are by academics and professional workers in the field, and others are by librarians, archivists, practitioners who have taken up the task of recording their experiences and other private researchers. To all of them I express our deep gratitude for their labours, their patience with the gruelling editorial process and the wearing demands of historical accuracy. Their reward will lie, we hope, in the knowledge that they have played a part in building a unique and indispensable reference text.

I would also like to acknowledge those who have given time and dedication to the work beyond the call of duty. The burden of editorial administration fell upon Victoria Chance, Philip Parsons's associate editor, and she managed it with supreme skill and discretion. Specialist editors, advisers and major contributors gave generously of their time, energy and expertise. Richard Fotheringham not only undertook the tasks of regional editor for Queensland and specialist editor for 1850–1920 but contributed the majority of articles on that period. Other regional editors helped to determine the essential topics in their field, sought out potential contributors and often researched and wrote a great deal themselves: Gillian Winter in Tasmania, Bill Dunstone and Maurice Jones in Western Australia, Jo Peoples in South Australia and Sally Dawes in Victoria helped to make this book truly national in outlook. As specialist editor for the period to 1850, Elizabeth Webby shared her extensive research into early colonial theatre. We owe a massive debt of gratitude to John West, whose knowledge of Australian show business is encyclopedic.

Other major contributors are Richard Bradshaw, whose excavations into the history of puppetry have revealed many surprises; Veronica Kelly, whose work on pantomime is highly illuminating; Harold Love, who gave freely of his profound knowledge of Melbourne's colonial theatre; John McCallum, who contributed substantially on playwriting; Lynne Murphy and Richard Lane, whose interest in preserving the records of theatre from the 1940s to the 1960s we have exploited unreservedly; Mark St Leon, Australia's premier historian of the circus; and Ross Thorne, whose research into theatre buildings is unceasing.

We are grateful too for the existence of the performing-arts collections and the enthusiasm of their curators and researchers: the indefatigable Ivan King at the Perth Theatre Trust's Theatre Collection; Jo Peoples at the Colin Ballantyne Performing Arts Collection in Adelaide; Frank Van Straten at the Performing Arts Museum in Melbourne; and Paul Bentley at the Dennis Wolanski Library of the Performing Arts at the Sydney Opera House. The many private collections preserved by the Australian National Library and state libraries have been intrinsic to contributors' work.

Without financial support Currency Press would not have survived the call upon its resources represented by this project. The proposal from which the companions sprang came from the Australian Bicentennial Authority in 1986 with a grant of $110 000. Philip Parsons himself contributed substantially; and in 1991 the Australia Council agreed to invest in the work. This injection of funds enabled *Companion to Theatre in Australia* to reach completion. The book is a co-edition with Cambridge University Press, which will distribute it within Australia and around the world. To this wealth of investment of time, money, dedication and persistence this book is a monument.

Katharine Brisbane, Publisher

Contributors

Meg Abbie-Denton is a former dancer, teacher and dance notator who has studied the theatrical history of Adelaide.

Thelma Afford began designing for the theatre in Adelaide in the early 1930s and designed for Independent Theatre and Whitehall Theatrical Productions in Sydney in the 1940s.

May-Brit Akerholt is a dramaturge and artistic director of the Australian National Playwrights' Centre in Sydney.

Christopher Allen is theatre project co-ordinator at the Centre for Performance Studies at the University of Sydney.

John Andrews wrote his PhD thesis on subsidy in the performing arts in Australia between 1942 and 1970.

Delyse Anthony teaches literature and drama at the Australian Catholic University, Queensland.

Allan Ashbolt is a writer, broadcaster, drama critic and theatre historian.

The late **Frank Baden-Powell** was a founder of the Hole in the Wall Theatre in Perth and owner of a chain of theatre-restaurants.

Annette Bain is a Sydney barrister and theatre lover.

Michelle Ballard is a Sydney researcher into Australian theatrical history who studied the entrepreneur Kate Howarde for an honours degree.

Peter Banki is a Sydney solicitor who specialises in copyright law.

Tom Bannerman is a freelance designer in Sydney with an MA in theatre studies from the University of NSW.

John Barnes teaches Australian literature at La Trobe University in Melbourne.

Don Batchelor has been an actor, director, administrator and writer in Queensland theatre since 1964. He teaches drama at the Academy of the Arts in the Queensland University of Technology, Brisbane.

The late **Tom Bencke** co-founded the Rockhampton Little Theatre with Graham Macdonald, a fellow insurance agent, in 1945 and acted, directed or stage-managed almost every production for nearly 40 years. He was also a long-serving city councillor. He died in 1993.

Paul Bentley is librarian of the Dennis Wolanski Library of the Performing Arts at the Sydney Opera House.

Felicity Biggins is a journalist and theatre worker. She wrote about John O'Donoghue for a thesis in drama at the University of Newcastle (NSW).

Marjorie Biggins was drama critic for ABC radio in Newcastle from 1964 to 1990.

Frank Bladwell is principal of Maroubra High School, Sydney.

Bill Blaikie teaches at Charles Sturt University in Bathurst (NSW).

Ron Blair is a playwright and head of scriptwriting at the Australian Film, Television and Radio School in Sydney. He was a co-founder of the Nimrod Theatre Company.

Jennifer Blocksidge is an actor and teacher in Brisbane.

David Bradley was professor of English at Monash University in Melbourne from 1970 to 1989.

Richard Bradshaw AO is a freelance puppeteer.

Murray Bramwell has reviewed theatre for the *Australian*, the *National Times*, the *Adelaide Advertiser* and other journals. He teaches drama at Flinders University in Adelaide.

Errol Bray is a director and writer who specialises in young people's theatre. He was a co-founder of Shopfront Theatre in Sydney.

Benita Brebach was formerly an actor with Independent Theatre in Sydney and is conducting private research into the period.

Nicky Bricknell was a founding member of the Queensland Theatre of the Deaf and its artistic director for three years.

Katharine Brisbane AM is publisher of Currency Press and a former theatre critic.

Alan Brissenden is a critic and historian of theatre and dance, a Shakespearean scholar and honorary research fellow in English at the University of Adelaide.

Alison Broinowski is a writer on Asian affairs. She has lived and worked in Asian countries for more than 15 years.

The late **Tom Brown** was a director and theatre consultant and head of the National Institute of Dramatic Art in Sydney from 1963 to 1969.

Jeff Brownrigg is senior manager, corporate relations branch, of the National Film and Sound Archive in Canberra.

Tom Burvill teaches theatre and cultural studies at Macquarie University in Sydney. He has a long association with Sidetrack Performance Group.

Alwyn Capern is a theatre researcher and author of a biography of his lifelong friend Gladys Moncrieff.

Dennis Carroll is professor and chair of theatre and dance at the University of Hawaii at Manoa. He is author of *Australian Contemporary Drama* and *David Mamet*.

Victoria Chance is an editor who has written a BA honours thesis on Australian vaudeville in the 1930s.

Christopher Chapman is assistant curator of Australian drawings at the National Gallery of Australia in Canberra.

John Clark AM is director of the National Institute of Dramatic Art in Sydney.

Mimi Colligan is a historian with a special interest in 19th-century theatre and scenic design.

Coralie Condon is an actor, writer and director in Perth, who specialises in musicals and music-hall.

Joan Massey Cook is a speech and drama teacher in Brisbane who has written a history of the Speech and Drama Association of Queensland.

Bronwyn Coy is a PhD student and a tutor in the School of Theatre and Film Studies at the University of NSW in Sydney. She has written an honours thesis on amateur theatre in Sydney in the 1930s.

Terry Craig is a business manager who for 25 years was general manager of the West Australian Opera Company.

Sue Cullen is at Southern Cross University (NSW). She wrote a thesis on Brisbane Repertory Theatre at La Boîte. She has been a research assistant for the Australian Drama Bibliography Project at the University of Queensland.

Jim Davis is head of the School of Theatre and Film Studies at the University of NSW in Sydney.

Miriam Davis is a Sydney journalist who specialises in theatre and film criticism.

The late **Dennis Davison** was a critic, playwright, director, poet, author, publisher and academic. He reviewed theatre for the *Australian* and the Melbourne *Sunday Herald*. He died in 1994.

Remy Davison is a playwright, director and producer. He teaches political science at the University of Melbourne.

Sally Dawes studied history of art at London University and spent 12 years with the Performing Arts Museum in Melbourne, where she researched and curated many exhibitions.

Ian Dicker was chairman of general studies of the NSW State Conservatorium of Music from 1973 to 1989.

Peter Douglas is an actor, director, writer, producer, musician and academic.

Peter Downes has researched and written widely on the history of the performing arts in New Zealand. A retired broadcaster, he lives near Wellington.

John du Feu, an actor, director and dramaturge, is manager of the Civic Theatre at Townsville (Qld).

Bill Dunstone teaches at the University of Western Australia in Perth.

Ann Edgeworth is a director, tutor, community educator and writer in Canberra.

Victor Emeljanow is professor of drama at the University of Newcastle (NSW).

Nick Enright is a playwright and actor.

Bob Evans was a theatre critic for the *Sydney Morning Herald* from 1985 and principal critic from 1989 to 1994.

CONTRIBUTORS

Michael FitzGerald AM is an arts consultant and world president of the International Association of Theatre for Children and Young People.

Peter Fitzpatrick is associate professor of English at Monash University and director of the Centre for Drama and Theatre.

Richard Fotheringham is senior lecturer in drama in the English department of the University of Queensland in Brisbane.

Arthur Frame is an actor, director and deputy general manager of the Queensland Arts Council.

L. E. Fredman is a former associate professor of history at the University of Newcastle (NSW).

Larry Galbraith is a critic, journalist and playwright in Sydney.

Barbara Garlick, a lecturer in English at the University of Queensland in Brisbane, researched early Australian travelling theatre for her PhD.

Gregory Gesch is an actor, director and playwright. He was resident director of the Queensland Theatre Company from 1983 to 1989 and became artistic director of the New England Theatre Company in 1990.

Helen Gilbert has published numerous articles on contemporary Australian drama. She teaches at the University of Queensland.

Hilary Glow works as a dramaturge and has had a long collaboration with the playwright Hannie Rayson. She manages the women's program at the Australian Film Commission in Melbourne.

Ray Goodlass teaches acting for stage and screen at the School of Visual and Performing Arts at Charles Sturt University in Wagga Wagga (NSW). He is resident director for the University Theatre Ensemble.

Clem Gorman is a playwright and dramaturge. He teaches at the University of Wollongong (NSW).

Charles Grahame is a writer and broadcaster on entertainment.

Stephen Gray is a South African novelist, poet and academic who has published widely on South African theatre and literature.

Janet Greason is a freelance writer who lives in Melbourne.

Ron Haddrick MBE is an actor who lives in Sydney

J. D. Hainsworth was professor of English at the University of New England in Armidale (NSW) until his retirement. His writings for and about the theatre include a book on Jack Hibberd's plays.

Sara Hardy is a playwright who lives in Melbourne.

Wayne Harrison is director of the Sydney Theatre Company.

Jon Hawkes is director of the Australian Centre of the International Theatre Institute in Sydney. He was a founder-member of the Australian Performing Group and Circus Oz.

Ken Healey has been literary manager at the National Institute of Dramatic Art since 1987. He has been a regular reviewer of performing arts for many years, mainly in the *Canberra Times* (1971–86) and in the Sydney *Sun-Herald* since 1987.

Rachel Healy is an arts manager who has worked as an arts editor and a freelance journalist.

Paul Herlinger is an actor, director and teacher of English. He is researching a PhD on New Theatre.

Robert Hewett is a playwright who lives in Melbourne.

Susan Hogan is a Sydney researcher in Australian history.

Simon Hopkinson is a playwright who now concentrates on writing for the screen, with occasional forays into directing in the commercial theatre.

Ros Horin is artistic director of the Griffin Theatre Company in Sydney.

David Hough is a writer on theatre, the arts and business. He manages the international program of the faculty of business at Edith Cowan University in Perth.

Richard Hunter is assistant program manager of the Sydney Opera House.

Barbara James is a writer in Darwin.

Barry Jones MHR is a parliamentarian, historian and writer. He was a member of the Australian Council for the Arts in 1969–73 and sits on the executive board of UNESCO. He was federal Science Minister from 1983 to 1990.

Maurice Jones studied drama under Jeana Bradley in Perth and designed décor for her productions.

Melinda Jones teaches law at the University of NSW in Sydney.

Rob Jordan is professor of drama in the School of Theatre and Film Studies at the University of NSW in Sydney.

Bruce Keller is an actor, director, dramaturge and playwright. He was co-founder of Australian Nouveau Theatre in Melbourne. He now works with the Entr'acte Theatre Company in Sydney and Jigsaw Theatre in Canberra.

The late **Paul Kelly** was general manager and a board member of the Arts Council of New South Wales.

Veronica Kelly teaches at the University of Queensland in Brisbane and has published widely on colonial and contemporary theatre and drama.

Patricia Kennedy OBE is an actor.

Adrian Kiernander is a director, critic and professor of theatre studies at the University of New England in Armidale (NSW).

Ivan King is a theatre historian working at the Western Australian Performing Arts Museum at His Majesty's Theatre in Perth.

Jacqueline Kott is an actor, director and administrator in Sydney.

Maria Kreisler is a retired lecturer in theatre studies. She lives in NSW.

Deslye Kruck is a retired drama teacher who taught at the Brisbane College of Advanced Education, now the Queensland University of Technology.

Axel Kruse teaches in the English department of the University of Sydney. He has published studies of Shakespeare, George Bernard Shaw and Patrick White.

Nigel Lampe is the principal of one of Australia's leading entertainment agencies.

Laurie Landray was a performing-arts critic in Melbourne from 1963 to 1985.

Josephine Landsberg was the research officer at the Performing Arts Collection of South Australia in Adelaide.

Richard Lane has written widely for radio and television and is author of *The Golden Age of Australian Radio Drama*.

Peter Lavery is head of the Academy of Arts at Queensland University of Technology in Brisbane. He has worked as a professional actor and has been involved with development of drama curricula for many years.

Phillip Lawton is a Sydney historian.

Vic Lloyd is a retired Brisbane academic with a longstanding interest in Dympha Cusack's writings.

Mary Lord is an author who has lectured in English and Australian literature. Her most recent book is *Hal Porter—Man of many parts*.

Harold Love is a reader in English at Monash University in Melbourne and the author of a biography of J. E. Neild.

Rodney Lumer was president of Playlab from 1974 to 1978 and from 1978 founding editor of Playlab Press in Brisbane.

Tony MacGregor is a Sydney writer and sound designer for installation and performance. He is a producer of the ABC radio program *The Listening Room*.

The late **Peter Mann** was an actor, director and teacher in Perth.

F. H. Mares taught English at the University of Adelaide until he retired in 1984. His special interest is Shakespeare. He was a member of the board of the South Australian Theatre Company.

Joan Maslen specialised in theatrical history as a librarian at the La Trobe Library of the State Library of Victoria in Melbourne until she retired.

Anne Mayor is Beryl Bryant's daughter. She lives in Adelaide.

Bob Maza AM is a playwright, director and actor who has been influential in Aboriginal theatre in Sydney.

CONTRIBUTORS

John McCallum is Sydney theatre critic of the *Australian*. He teaches in the School of Theatre and Film Studies at the University of NSW in Sydney.

Greg McCart is head of the department of music, theatre and visual arts at the University of Southern Queensland.

Patsy McCarthy is an actor and teacher. She lectures in speech communication at the Queensland University of Technology in Brisbane.

Andrew McCredie is a musicologist who holds a personal chair at the University of Adelaide.

Frances McDonald was a theatrical agent with a leading Sydney agency for six years before she began working in the film industry.

Paul McGillick is the author of *Jack Hibberd* and performing arts critic for the *Australian Financial Review*.

Aubrey Mellor OAM is artistic director of the Playbox Theatre Centre in Melbourne.

Lydia Miller is executive officer of the Aboriginal and Torres Strait Islander arts board of the Australia Council.

Geoffrey Milne is a theatre critic for ABC radio 3LO and head of the theatre and drama department at La Trobe University in Melbourne.

Irene Mitchell MBE was a director of the Little Theatre in Melbourne and is still involved with its successor, the St Martin's Youth Arts Centre. She is an archivist with the Performing Arts Museum.

Tony Mitchell is senior lecturer in performance studies at the University of Technology in Sydney.

Ray Mooney is a playwright, novelist and screenwriter. He began writing in prison and is now co-ordinator of the theatre technology course and lecturer in writing at Holmsglen College of Technology in Melbourne.

Anne C. Murch is a retired lecturer in French, formerly at Monash University in Melbourne.

Richard Murphet is a director and playwright who is head of the department of directing, writing and animating at the School of Drama of the Victorian College of the Arts in Melbourne.

Lynne Murphy is an actor, researcher and writer. She began her career with Metropolitan Theatre in Sydney.

Helen Musa is theatre critic of the *Canberra Times* and editor of *Muse* magazine. She has researched and written widely on Australian theatrical history.

Jessica Noad is an actor who began her career with Independent Theatre in Sydney.

Louis Nowra is a playwright, screenwriter, radio dramatist and novelist. He lives in Sydney.

Mudrooroo Nyoongar is an author and chair of the Aboriginal and Torres Strait Islander program at Murdoch University in Perth.

Angela O'Brien teaches Australian theatre at the School of Visual and Performing Arts Education at the University of Melbourne. She has a special interest in the New Theatre movement.

Colm O'Doherty is an actor who worked with the Anew McMaster Company from 1944 to 1949.

Bruce Parr has had 25 years' experience in Queensland as actor, director, arts administrator and teacher.

George Parsons teaches economic and social history at Macquarie University in Sydney. He is trying to rewrite the history of early Australia.

Michael Pate is an actor, director, producer and writer. He has written a history of the 1st Australian Army Entertainment Unit, in which he served from 1942 until 1946.

Pamela Payne is senior theatre critic for the Sydney *Sun-Herald*.

Jo Peoples is curator of the Performing Arts Collection of South Australia at the Adelaide Festival Centre.

Elizabeth Perkins is associate professor of English at James Cook University of North Queensland.

Louise Permezel is artistic director of Zootango Theatre Company in Hobart.

Carolyn Pickett teaches drama in the School of Arts and Media at La Trobe University in Melbourne.

Simon Plant is arts editor of the *Herald-Sun* in Melbourne and a member of the Goodfa Business Theatre Company.

Joan Pope is founder of the Children's Activities Times Society (CATS) in Perth and a part-time lecturer in education and community arts.

Michelle Potter is a freelance arts writer and researcher. In 1988–90 she was Esso research fellow in the performing arts at the National Library of Australia in Canberra.

John Preston is an actor, director and lecturer in performing arts at Swinburne University of Technology in Melbourne.

Will Quekett is general manager of the Grand Theatre at Blackpool (England). He was administrator of the Festival of Perth from 1977 to 1988 and programming director for the Perth Theatre Trust from 1988 to 1993.

Jennifer Radbourne researches and writes on strategic planning and marketing in the arts. She co-ordinates the graduate program in arts administration and teaches in the faculty of business at the Queensland University of Technology in Brisbane.

Leonard Radic is a playwright and critic. He was theatre critic for the *Age* in Melbourne from 1974 to 1994.

Collette Rayment is a National Institute of Dramatic Art graduate in directing.

Leslie Rees AM is a critic, dramatist and theatre historian. For many years he was the Australian Broadcasting Commission's federal drama editor and chairman of the Playwrights' Advisory Board.

Don Reid is an actor and lecturer on drama. He was a permanent member of the Ensemble Theatre Company in Sydney from 1960 to 1984.

Paul Richardson is senior lecturer in education at Monash University in Melbourne

John Rickard spent some years working in the theatre as an actor and singer. He has written widely on Australian theatrical history and is reader in history at Monash University in Melbourne.

Robyn Riddett is an architectural historian and interior designer specialising in restoration. She worked on the restoration of the Princess Theatre.

Malcolm Robertson is an actor, director, producer, writer and literary manager of the Playbox Theatre Centre in Melbourne.

Phyllis Jane Rose teaches performance and gender in the drama department of Flinders University in Adelaide.

Tim Rowse works in the department of government and administration at the University of Sydney.

Donna Sadka was theatre critic for the *West Australian* newspaper in Perth from 1963 to 1985.

Maurice Scott is senior lecturer in English and media studies at the University of Wollongong (NSW).

Fiona Scott-Norman is an arts writer in Melbourne and theatre critic for the *Bulletin* and *Inpress*.

Brett Sheehy is assistant general manager of the Sydney Theatre Company.

Tony Sheldon is an actor, singer and writer with a special interest in the history of Australian musical theatre.

Guy Sherborne teaches in the School of Applied and Performing Arts at the University of NSW in Sydney.

Adam Shoemaker has worked closely with Aboriginal playwrights and authors since 1980. He has written books on their work and he was co-editor of the first national anthology of Aboriginal writing.

Marie Simmons is a journalist in Perth who has researched a history of the Repertory Club.

D. C. S. Sissons is formerly of the Research School of Pacific Studies at the Australian National University.

Kim Spinks is a dramaturge and artistic counsel to the Sydney Theatre Company. She was a co-founder of Death Defying Theatre.

CONTRIBUTORS

Suzanne Spunner, who lives in Darwin, is a playwright, designer, dramaturge, critic and film maker. In Melbourne, she was a founder of the Home Cooking Theatre Company and *Lip* magazine, and a member of the Women's Theatre Group.

Mark St Leon has researched and written on circus in Australia, in which his family has been involved from the outset.

Naomi Steer is NSW state secretary of the Media Entertainment and Arts Alliance.

Lurline Stuart is a research associate at the National Centre for Australian Studies at Monash University in Melbourne. She has written a biography of James Smith.

Walter Sullivan is film and television critic of the *Telegraph Mirror* in Sydney and a former actor.

The late **Alrene Sykes** was senior lecturer in the English department of the University of Queensland in Brisbane.

George Michael Tallis is the grandson of Sir George Tallis and honorary research fellow in mathematics at the University of Adelaide.

David Taranto is a journalist, producer and comedy consultant. He is in his second decade of presenting *The Cheese Shop*, a comedy magazine program, on Melbourne radio.

Gerald Taylor is a magician, inventor of magical effects, and historian of magic.

Daniel Thomas AM is director emeritus of the South Australian Art Gallery.

Pauline Thomas is a journalist and public-relations consultant in Melbourne. She studied drama with Marjorie McLeod and performed in her formative Swan Hill National Theatre productions.

John Thomson lectures in English at the Victoria University of Wellington in New Zealand.

Ross Thorne is associate professor of architecture at the University of Sydney. He has researched theatre buildings for three decades.

David Throsby is professor of economics at Macquarie University in Sydney and author of several economic reports for the Australia Council.

Christine Tilley teaches in the faculty of information technology at the Queensland Institute of Technology in Brisbane.

John Timlin is a literary agent with the Almost Managing Company, a Melbourne conglomerate of concerned, witty people.

Richard Tulloch is a full-time writer of books for young people and plays for young audiences in theatre and television.

Frank Van Straten was director of the Performing Arts Museum at the Victorian Arts Centre in Melbourne from 1984 to 1993.

Maeve Vella has worked professionally in puppetry since 1977, primarily as a performer. She was a founding member of the Handspan Theatre Company and founding editor of the puppetry journal *Manipulation*.

Caroline von Oppeln was Crowther Librarian in the special collections of the State Library of Tasmania in Hobart from 1974 to 1984.

James Waites, a freelance writer and theatre critic, is a reviewer for the *Sydney Morning Herald*.

Roma Wallis is author of a history of the Prince of Wales Opera House in Gulgong (NSW).

Lisa Warrington teaches theatre studies at the University of Otago in Dunedin (New Zealand). She has directed many professional and university productions.

Richard Waterhouse, associate professor of history at the University of Sydney, is author of a book on the Australian popular stage from 1788 to 1914.

David Watt teaches in the department of drama at the University of Newcastle (NSW). He has published predominantly on community and political theatre.

Elizabeth Webby has researched and written on the theatrical and literary culture of 19th-century for 28 years. She is professor of Australian literature at the University of Sydney and editor of the quarterly *Southerly*.

John West is a broadcaster and theatre historian. He lives in Sydney.

George Whaley is an actor, director, teacher and writer in theatre, film and television.

Margaret Williams was a member of the Australian Performing Group and is now a senior lecturer in theatre and film studies at the University of NSW in Sydney.

Ken Willis teaches in the School of Language Education at Edith Cowan University in Perth.

Rose Wilson is librarian and dramaturge with State Theatre in Adelaide.

Gillian Winter is a librarian at the State Library of Tasmania. She has published articles on Tasmanian social history.

Rod Wissler is an actor and director. He is director of the Centre for Innovation in the Arts at Queensland University of Technology.

Guthrie Worby is associate professor in cultural studies and head of the School of Cultural Studies at Flinders University in Adelaide.

The late **Elizabeth Wright** wrote a BA honours thesis on Duncan McDougall.

Tony Youlden has worked for 30 years as a lighting designer and administrator.

Penny Young is an arts administrator. She manages the Barking Gecko Theatre Company in Perth.

Pamela Zeplin is a writer, artist and senior lecturer in visual arts theory at the University of South Australia in Adelaide.

How this book works

Articles are arranged in alphabetical order of their subjects, with surnames given last in headings. In deference to computer technology, names beginning with Mac or Mc appear in strict alphabetical order and apostrophes in names are ignored.

In articles about persons and most companies the main text is preceded by a synopsis of the principal facts.

Foreign places are identified by the name they bore and the country in which they were at the time. An example comes from Eastern Europe: at the onset of the First World War the capital of the Austrian province of Galicia was called Lemberg, but by 1913, when the designer Wladyslaw Dutkiewicz was born there, the city was in newly independent Ukraine and called Lviv in Ukrainian. In 1921 it was incorporated in Poland and became Lwów. Ceded to the Soviet Union in 1945, it gained the Russian name of Lvov. Now Ukraine is again independent and the city is Lviv.

A date in parenthesis after a work is the date of its first performance anywhere.

'The Firm' and 'J. C. Williamson's' both designate J. C. Williamson Ltd or any of the corporate entities that succeeeded this company.

Similarly, 'the Trust' refers to the Australian Elizabethan Theatre Trust. In the main text of articles small capitals indicate that a topic is the subject of a separate article.

A comma separating the names of two contributors indicates that their contributions have been combined editorially.

Where appropriate, further reading is suggested. Some works were recommended so frequently that mention of them has been largely restricted to the list of sources for reference given in the article on Research and scholarship (pp. 494–99). Outstanding among them are works by the pioneers of Australian theatre research: the unpublished work on colonial theatre by the late Helene Oppenheim; *Theatre in Australia* by John West; the documentary history edited by Harold Love; the two-volume history of Australian drama by Leslie Rees and the history of recent playwriting by Leonard Radic; the five books on the colonial period by the late Eric Irvin; the meticulous research into colonial theatres by Ross Thorne; and the book on colonial playwrights by Margaret Williams. The publisher gratefully acknowledges these sterling works.

A comprehensive index begins on p. 656. It includes libraries and other collections cited as sources of manuscripts and other references.

Abbreviations
ABC: Australian Broadcasting Corporation, later Australian Broadcasting Commission.
ACT: Australian Capital Territory.
NIDA: National Institute of Dramatic Art.
NSW: New South Wales.
NT: Northern Territory.
Qld: Queensland.
SA: South Australia.
Tas.: Tasmania.
Vic.: Victoria.
WA: Western Australia.

Ab Intra Studio Theatre

Amateur dramatic company in Adelaide, founded in 1931 by Kester Baruch and Alan Harkness. Closed 1935. **venues** North Terrace. King William Street South. **first production** *Demon's Mask* translated by Arthur Waley, 23 December 1931. Cast: Alan Harkness, Kester Baruch. Choreography: Mina Bauer. **landmark productions** *The Poetasters of Ispahan* by Clifford Bax and *Suilven and the Eagle* by Gordon Bottomley, July 1934.

During the Great Depression ALAN HARKNESS and KESTER BARUCH founded Ab Intra—Latin meaning 'from within'— and gave a new visual emphasis to theatrical production in Adelaide. Harkness, an actor, had been trained as a painter and he believed in visual communication with an audience. Baruch was a writer and lighting designer. They put their theories into practice in a large, empty drapery store in King William Street South. Upstairs they turned the largest showroom into a small theatre with black hessian curtains and a few wooden structures forming a small stage without a proscenium. They also improvised living quarters and a workshop. In a larger space on the ground floor, coffee was served during intervals.

Baruch devised lighting and scenic effects, and Harkness was designer and director. Both men also acted. Other actors included AGNES DOBSON, PATRICIA HACKETT and ROBERT HELPMANN. There were also dancers—Mina Bauer, Walter Dasborough and Joan Joske from Melbourne. Ab Intra, operating as a club, mostly presented one-act plays or dramatisations of poems by European writers. Its first production, *Demon's Mask*, was a one-act Japanese *noh* play. In August 1931 they presented another, *The Robe of Yama*, after a year's preparation. It had music especially written by Spruhan Kennedy, and created an appropriate sensation. Douglas Loan wrote in *Town Topics* magazine that in its Oriental splendour and visual symbolism the production's 'sheer plunge into the icy waters of unorthodoxy' left him breathless. 'Every movement of the finger is a lyric poem in itself', he wrote. 'Ab Intra is not a hothouse of fanatics … whatever be its faults—and there are many—it cannot be fairly accused of being a stunt.'

Much of the company's work included dance and mime, sometimes to the accompaniment of poetry. There is a vivid account of the style in Lilias Gordon's down-to-earth review in *Adelaide Truth*: 'How on earth Kester Baruch and Alan Harkness achieve their lighting effects with the aid of ingenuity and jam tins, would earn them positions with any electric power company. Joan Joske makes up her dances as she goes. There are times when she looked like an Egyptian traffic cop, and there are others when she appears like an underwater shot of Undine. There is something strange and almost terrifying in her lean brown hands and arms, that are as sinuous as a Javanese dancer's …'.

Ab Intra's repertoire had a strong symbolist bias. It included plays by Leonid Andreyev, Clifford Bax, Jacques Copeau, Nikolai Evreinov, Luigi Pirandello, August Strindberg and Thornton Wilder. Late in 1934 Ab Intra and PATRICIA HACKETT's Torch Theatre joined in a season of short classics. In 1934 Ab Intra produced two long plays, *The House into Which We Are Born* by Copeau and *Martine* by Jean-Jacques Bernard. In March 1935 Baruch and Harkness gave two benefit performances in the home of the Lady Mayoress, Mrs J. L. Bonython, and then left for England.
❧*Thelma Afford*

Robert Helpmann as a monk in Ab Intra Studio Theatre's production of The Aspen Tree

Aborigines and theatre

One of the first known plays concerning Aborigines and Australia was performed at the Théâtre des Amis de la Patrie in Paris in 1792. It was *Les Emigrés aux terres australes*, a politico-propagandist comedy written amid the turmoil of the French Revolution by a Jacobin playwright, Citizen Gamas. Its portrayal of the colony is melodramatic and romantic. Transported unpatriotic Emigrés of Nobility, financiers, judges and clergy are confronted by vanguard egalitarianism in the form of a labourer, Mathurin, and the colony's 'savage chief' Oziambo. Speaking fluent French, Oziambo omnicompetently adjudicates upon them, meting out justice to befit a proletarian Danton. He was doubtless played by a Frenchman.

In Edinburgh in 1829, the Caledonian Theatre performed THE BUSHRANGERS, a first-hand attempt to address the realities of the colony by DAVID BURN, a Scottish settler who was on his first trip home. His play is a semi-factual adventure tale in which the heroes are honest highwaymen and hardworking settlers who reject tyrannical officialdom. The attitude of the settlers towards the indigenes, eloquently noted by William Hiener in his foreword to the 1971 publication of the play, is 'indicative of the sense of moral superiority and contempt felt by the settlers at the time. By stressing the comic barbarity and avarice of the Aborigines in contrast to the magnanimity of the settlers, who had long been a source of unstinting generosity, Burn could vindicate the colonists' apparent lack of tolerance and impatience.'

Here are some samples of Burn's treatment of Aboriginal characters: 'Settlers are surrounded by villainous natives who demand "de poff poff" [tobacco] and exclaim "Corobbora, Corobbora" performing rude dances and throwing their arms about in an extravagant manner'. The bushranger Matthew Brady and his party rescue the settlers, shooting the natives and disposing of their bodies in the river as 'black carrion'. Burn, perhaps by luck more than design, was the first white writer to acknowledge the dance of the Aborigines in corroboree, although his way of presenting it was quite different from theirs.

Corroboree presented by Aborigines—who had no other theatrical experience—was a major form of entertainment in Australia at that time. The *Perth Gazette* of 16 March 1833 wrote glowingly of a corroboree held by Swan River and King George's River tribesmen to honour the Lieutenant-Governor of Western Australia. The article accorded the tribal dances a description befitting a court ballet. Perth dignitaries were present and Yagan, a respected Aboriginal leader, was master of ceremonies. A few weeks later, however, Yagan was declared an outlaw by the governor and shot. His body was beheaded and his head was put on public display in Sydney and London. Scarred skin from his back was made into a belt.

In England in 1831 *Van Dieman's* [sic] *Land*, a play by W. T. Moncrieff, showed Australian Aborigines as something of a mixture of the inhabitants of India and Polynesia —Tahitians had been in vogue since the 1790s, when plays about the adventures of the navigators James Cook and William Bligh in the Pacific Ocean were performed in London. Solo songs and choruses are interspersed through the play, which relates adventures of free settlers, convicts, natives called Caffres and the bushranger Michael Howe. The scene, Wild Beast Wood, is inhabited by lions, tigers, wild boars and the like. The leading Caffre, Benni-long, wears white shirt, short trunks, scarf and Indian headdress. This world-travelled character addresses his untutored Caffre sister Kangaree in terms such as: 'Aye, let the colourless strangers fear! That have usurped our plains and would fain extirpate our race'.

In April 1834 Henry Melville, a newspaper publisher, wrote THE BUSHRANGERS in Hobart and it was staged there in in May and in Launceston in November. It tells of a bushranger's attack on the home of a settler. He is saved by a prospective son-in-law and his Aboriginal companion, who is treated reasonably by the standards of the period.

There is no Aboriginal character in Edward Geoghegan's ballad opera THE CURRENCY LASS, which appeared in Sydney in 1844, but the convict playwright does address racial snobbery. A rich uncle, learning that his nephew is to marry a 'native' girl, or currency lass, mistakenly pictures himself as the grandfather of a string of piccaninnies.

Comic stock characters

The popular comedies and melodramas of the second half of the 19th century were rich in comic Aboriginal stock characters. One of the earliest was Warren Warren in J. R. McLachlan's *Arabin—or, The Adventures of a Settler*, published in London in 1845. Warren Warren is an enterprising fellow who expounds in a form of pidgin on the superiority of bush life in the manner of a noble savage, and then laughingly deserts his helpless new chum in the wilds. The typical stage Aborigine was humorous, resourceful, quick-witted and there to resolve the plot or save the deserving. One of the better examples is Warrigal, faithful friend of the outlaw Captain Starlight in the adaptation of ROBBERY UNDER ARMS (1890) by Alfred Dampier and Garnet Walch.

In 1893 GEORGE RIGNOLD presented a dramatisation of Fergus Hume's novel *The Mystery of a Hansom Cab*, which includes Aboriginal characters, although they are little more than part of the backdrop. In the same year Rignold produced *It's Never Too Late to Mend*, from Charles Reade's novel, as a lavish spectacle with real waterfalls. Forty Queensland Aborigines appeared in 'primitive wild Australian' scenes, with such enthusiasm that on the first night lighted spears singed two property men.

In 1896 THE DUCHESS OF COOLGARDIE by Euston Leigh and Cyril Clare was produced in London. Set on the goldfields of Western Australia, the story revolves around Sybil, who is cruelly separated from her beloved. After many turns of events the sweethearts are reunited and their Cupid turns out to be their loyal Aboriginal friend Wallaroo.

In the early 1900s Australians acclaimed dramas with 'true' Australian content from writers like BERT BAILEY, C. J. Dennis and STEELE RUDD. In the 1930s and 1940s, this type of drama, especially on radio, was the greatest single dramatic influence on Aboriginal Australia and, no doubt, on the rest of the rural community. In a time of widespread hardship everyone could easily identify with Rudd's characters. LOUIS ESSON criticised Rudd's works as farcical. In one of Esson's own plays, THE DROVERS, a tragedy about the death of a drover, there is particular interest in the epitaph given by his companion, the old Aborigine Pidgeon. Another Esson play, *Andeganora* deals with the treatment of Aborigines at the hands of a brumby-runner.

Justine Saunders as Ruby and Brian Syron as Sweet William in The Cake Man *at the Bondi Pavilion Theatre in Sydney in 1977. Saunders created the role of Ruby in the premiere production of Robert J. Merritt's play by Black Theatre in 1975. She and Syron were the stars of all productions of* The Cake Man *in the 1980s*

In 1927 Katharine Susannah Prichard won the *Triad* magazine prize for her play BRUMBY INNES, probably the first drama to attack the brutal realities of black–white relations in the outback. Prichard was followed by George Landen Dann, who wrote several realist plays that sought to understand dramatically the black outlook. The chief of these is FOUNTAINS BEYOND (1942), a tragedy about the treatment of reserve Aborigines by a town council.

At this time, too, the NEW THEATRE movement in Melbourne took up the issue of black–white relations. Black actors performed for New Theatre in a work called *White Justice*. This collaboration was probably the first of its kind in the modern theatre. New Theatre's resident writer, ORIEL GRAY was among those who took up the theme. Her play BURST OF SUMMER, suggested by the story of Ngarla Kunoth, who returned to her country-town origins after starring in the film *Jedda*, won a J. C. Williamson's prize in 1959.

In 1970, when the Nindethana Theatre group was formed in Melbourne, Jack Charles performed *The Blood Knot*, a monodrama by the South African writer Athol Fugard, for New Theatre. Later an ensemble of black actors performed a revue, *Jack Charles is Up and Fighting*. In 1972, Jack Charles created the role of Jack in JOHN ROMERIL's *Bastardy*, a play about fringe-dwellers, for the AUSTRALIAN PERFORMING GROUP. In 1972 Nindethana joined the APG at the Pram Factory to perform the premiere of *Brumby Innes*. The production was broadcast on 0–10 television in 1973.

Some modern plays by reputable white Australian writers are notable because they attack the habit of stigmatising anything Aboriginal as 'third rate', and because they notice Aborigines and appreciate them. BILL REED's *Truganinni*, produced in Melbourne in 1970, gave great insight into the Tasmanian Aborigines. About the same time at the same theatre, in RODNEY MILGATE's *A Refined Look at Existence*, Aboriginal actors played roles for the first time, though the parts that Jack Charles and Zac Martin played were not Aborigines. Charles and Martin were seasoned actors by the time they and young David Gulpilil appeared in leading parts in the OLD TOTE THEATRE COMPANY's production of *The Cradle of Hercules*, a clever play by MICHAEL BODDY about the early Sydney colony, complete with Captain Phillip and Benelong. Plays with Aboriginal content began to enter the mainstream theatre in the 1980s, with THOMAS KENEALLY's *Bullie's House*, TONY STRACHAN's *State of Shock* and DAVID WILLIAMSON's *Celluloid Heroes*.

International black theatre

In the late 1950s orators like Martin Luther King, Anwar el-Sadat, Julius Nyerere and Malcolm X preached a new outlook for the indigenes of colonised countries. 'Black is beautiful' became the catchcry in self-awakening Aboriginal Australia. Many Aborigines had their first experience of overseas black theatre in 1976, when the South African actors John Kani and Winston Ntshona appeared in Australia in Athol Fugard's productions of his plays *The Island* and *Sizwe Bansi is Dead*, which they had helped to create.

Aborigines were able to feast on a cultural banquet when the National Theatre of Papua New Guinea presented plays in Motu (a national language), Pidgin and English in Australia in 1978. All the productions were extremely professional and entertaining and the message of self-determination was loud and clear. In 1972 Australia saw its indigenes demonstrating for land rights with a 'Tent Embassy' in Canberra. From that incident were born National Black Theatre in Sydney, Task Force in Adelaide, Nindethana Theatre in Melbourne, and Noongar Theatre in Perth. Aborigines in other states quickly followed suit.

In the forefront of the Aboriginal literary movement were JACK DAVIS, Kevin Gilbert and Kath Walker (Oodgeroo Noonuccal), who wrote poetry, prose and plays that have been produced in Australia and overseas—THE DREAMERS and *Kullark* by Davis, THE CHERRY PICKERS by Gilbert and *Burrum* by Walker. Other Aboriginal playwrights who came out of this period were Gerald Bostock (*Here Comes the Nigger*), BOB MAZA (*Mereki*) and Robert J. Merritt (THE CAKE MAN).

In January 1987 the First National Black Playwrights' Conference was held in Canberra. Aboriginal plays of great substance were produced daily in workshops and new playwrights developed, among them Jimmy Everett, Eva Johnson, Mudrooroo Nyoongar, Vivian Walker, Richard Walley and Archie Weller. National Black Theatre developed a revue, *Basically Black*, from workshops presented at the Nimrod Street Theatre in Sydney in 1972. Aboriginal Islander Dance Theatre and other companies have also developed works from skeleton scripts and ideas formulated at workshops. Many Aboriginal playwrights work in several media. Mudrooroo and Weller are established novelists. Bostock, Maza and Merritt are film-makers.

Traditional Aboriginal companies now perform at home and overseas. In the far north there are groups like Aborigines Woomera from Mornington Island (Qld), David Gulpilil's Arnhem Land Dancers from Yirrkala (NT) and Soft Sands from Elcho Island (NT). The Elcho Islanders perform both traditional dances and country and western music. Traditional theatre of the Torres Strait Islands is represented by groups like the Torres Strait Island Dance Company, based in Sydney, and the Meriamie Company in Townsville (Qld). Other urban-based traditional groups, such as Middar from Perth and the Idinji Dancers from Cairns (Qld), are appearing in theatres around the world.

Aboriginal dramatists' methods

Much early work by black playwrights has been criticised for being stereotyped, lacking depth or being oversimplified, but beauty lies in the eye of the beholder. Aboriginal writers at present are concerned with creating awareness in the Aboriginal community of virtues such as pride, respect, self-esteem and motivation. In order to communicate these values effectively the mode must be familiar to the writer's chosen audience. The writer will use a familiar environment so that backdrops will not distract from the message. Jack Davis's *No Sugar* is an ambulatory work. As the audience, black and white, moves from one scene to another its members are able to communicate with one another. People used to hiding anonymously in the audience have to talk to strangers—and they enjoy it. The play has proved successful not only as an art form but as a social exercise. On those occasions all members of the audience learned some valuable things about one another. This open-mindedness is highly characteristic of an Aboriginal community and Jack Davis put it to good use.

Characters in black plays are all too quickly branded as stereotypes by non-Aborigines, yet they are precisely what the black writers require. Any less would not be genuine. In Richard Walley's play *Coordah* nearly all the male characters are drunk, unemployed and wasters, yet every Aborigine who saw the play identified with and was moved by these characters because they were their own, warts and all. Aborigines see them not as stereotypes but as victims. A noted white writer once remarked that Aboriginal plays reminded him of the old 'Negro' plays of the *Uncle Tom's Cabin* type with black folks singin' and dancin'. My reply was to thank him very much because I did not think we had reached that standard of storytelling yet. He was a little perturbed when I said the dream of many black writers was to be able to tell stories like our old people did, about mundane things like honesty, trust and respect for one another, instead of greed, lust and other deadly sins that are today's criteria for good theatre.

Possibly the greatest difference between black writers and white writers in Australia is ideology. In the main white writers are preoccupied with justifying and qualifying their existence in this land, even to the point of attempting to clone European theatre, which is steeped in many centuries of culture. Unfortunately, Australian white theatre, undergoing an identity crisis, is still standing outside, peeping through the fence. Black writers, on the other hand, do not have theatre to clone from, so standards and procedures do not inhibit free flight and black theatre is exploring new heights. ❦*Robert L. Maza*

Nyungar theatre

In contemporary Aboriginal theatre Western Australia has been particularly significant in providing writers and actors. Themes and structures of Aboriginal culture from Nyungars, Yamadjis, Wonghis and other communities are strongly present in theatre and dance. This is because of the strength of the strands of the Dreaming Tracks of our ancestors, our ceremonies, and the vitality of our oral storytelling traditions—which can be easily translated onto the stage or into the theatre rather than be rendered down into the pages of a book. Jack Davis, for example, in his monodrama *Wahngin Country* (1993) used Stephen Albert from

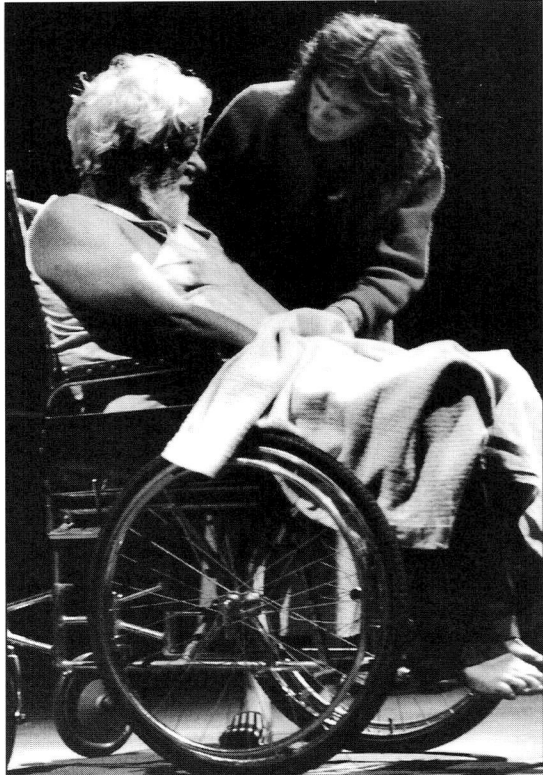

Jack Davis played Uncle Worru when the Western Australian Theatre Company produced his play The Dreamers *in Perth in 1982. With him is Lynette Narkle as Dolly. Davis has emerged as a major dramatist since he wrote his first full-length play at the age of 61*

Broome in the character of a storyteller, and the director, Andrew Ross, took the action away from the conventional theatre building out into the grounds of the University of Western Australia. It is the vitality of Nyungar culture plus the proximity of more traditional Aboriginal culture from other communities that enables us to utilise Aboriginal motifs and structures in our theatre.

As Nyungars live in the southwest of Western Australia and part of their country is Perth, we are host to many communities in Western Australia. These enter into our drama and there is an exchange between us to produce a vibrant theatre within our country and culture. An example of this interchange is Jimmy Chi's musical *Bran Nue Dae*, in which the action ranges from Perth to Broome. Another example was a performance of *Women's Dreaming* in Adelaide in 1990 by a group of women from Central Australia. This had all the quiet dignity and formalism of a Japanese *noh* play together with the studied informality of some folk theatre. The actors decided to do a piece—usually a dance—did it, talked a while, then performed another piece.

The vitality of our traditions could be seen again at the 1993 Festival of Perth, where a Nyungar-culture dramatic piece, *My Spiritual Dreaming* by Eddie Bennell, was staged in the open air at the University of Western Australia. It was a post-colonial work for voices and dance in which Aborigines reached beyond the initial conventional production standards and took control, improving the performance evening by evening, to present a more authentic expression of contemporary Nyungar life. In reaching towards this Aboriginality of theatrical expression, in *My Spiritual Dreaming* the songman held central place and directed the action as in ceremonial business. If, as it is said, European theatre developed out of ritual, then Nyungar theatre may be said to be seeking to deconstruct European theatre back into ritual, into ceremony in which the story teller, the songman, the director of ceremonies, holds central place and controls the drama.

Aboriginal theatre, especially Nyungar theatre that is close to its cultural roots, is often criticised for stereotyping of character and a lack of dramatic movement; but critics often miss the Aboriginality of form and content. Such a lack of cultural awareness can only be overcome by acknowledging that the roots of Nyungar theatre do not lie in the European theatrical tradition. If the Nyungar language, not English, were employed acceptance of difference might be ensured, and divergences from European theatrical traditions put down correctly as cultural differences of which the critic and the audience must be aware.

Mudrooroo Nyoongar

further reading
BURN, DAVID. *The Bushrangers*. Melbourne: Heinemann 1971.
CHI, JIMMY and KUCKLES. *Bran Nue Dae*. Broome: Magabala Books 1991. Sydney: Currency Press 1991.
DAMPIER, ALFRED and GARNET WALCH. *Robbery Under Arms*. Sydney: Currency Press 1985.
DANN, GEORGE LANDEN. *Fountains Beyond*. Sydney: Australasian 1944.
DAVIS, JACK. *Barungin*. Sydney: Currency Press 1989.
DAVIS, JACK. *The Dreamers* (revised 1984). Sydney: Currency Press 1989 in *Plays from Black Australia*.
DAVIS, JACK. *In Our Town*. Sydney: Currency Press 1992.
DAVIS, JACK. *Kullark* and *The Dreamers*. Sydney: Currency Press 1982.
DAVIS, JACK. *No Sugar*. Sydney: Currency Press 1986.
ESSON, LOUIS. *Andeganora*. Sydney: Angus and Robertson 1937 in *Best Australian One-Act Plays*.
ESSON, LOUIS. *The Drovers*. London: Henderson 1920 in *Dead Timber and Other Plays*. Sydney: Mulga 1944 in *Six One-Act Australian Plays*. Brisbane: University of Queensland Press 1977 in *Five Plays for Stage, Radio and TV*.
FRANCIS, GORDON. *God's Best Country*. Sydney: Currency Press 1988.
GILBERT, KEVIN. *The Cherry Pickers*. Canberra: Burrambinga Books, revised 1988.
JOHNSON, EVA. *Murras*. Sydney: Currency Press 1989 in *Plays from Black Australia*.
KENEALLY, THOMAS. *Bullie's House*. Sydney: Currency Press 1981.
MAZA, BOB. *The Keepers*. Sydney: Currency Press 1989 in *Plays from Black Australia*.
MELVILLE, HENRY. *The Bushrangers*. Hobart: April 1834 in *Hobart Town Magazine*.
MERRITT, ROBERT J. *The Cake Man*. Sydney: Currency Press 1983.
MILGATE, RODNEY. *A Refined Look at Existence*. London: Methuen 1968.
PRICHARD, KATHARINE SUSANNAH. *Brumby Innes*. Perth: Paterson 1940. Sydney: Currency Press 1983.
REED, BILL. *Truganinni*. Melbourne: Heinemann 1977.
ROMERIL, JOHN. *Bastardy*. Melbourne: Yackandandah 1982.
STRACHAN, TONY. *State of Shock*. Sydney: Currency Press 1986.
WALLEY, RICHARD. *Coordah*. Sydney: Currency Press 1989 in *Plays from Black Australia*.

reference
The manuscripts of *Les Emigrés aux terres australes* by Citizen Gamas, *Arabin* by J. M. McLachlan and *Van Dieman's Land* by W. T. Moncrieff are in the Mitchell Library (Sydney).

Janet Achurch

English actor, 1864–1916. Originally Janet Sharp. With second husband Charles Charrington gave first English-language performance of Henrik Ibsen's *A Doll's House*, in London, June 1889. Toured Australia and New Zealand with Charrington from September 1889 to August 1891. Became leading interpreter of Ibsen and George Bernard Shaw in London in 1890s.

Modern drama began when Ibsen's *A Doll's House* had its premiere in Copenhagen in 1879. In it Nora, a strong and financially astute woman who for her husband's benefit acts the role of a childish and scatterbrained wife, realises the hollowness of her marriage and, leaving her children in a nanny's care, walks out of the house, slamming the door behind her. An 'Ibsen controversy' raged in Europe, but the play was not seen in England until 1884, when a travesty called *Breaking a Butterfly*, in which the wife blames herself and asks her husband's forgiveness, was staged. Nine years after the premiere the real play still had not been performed in English. Then two young actors, Janet Achurch and her husband Charles Charrington, commissioned a translation from the Scottish critic William Archer, who had learned Norwegian and met Ibsen in Norway. Archer's world travels had also included Australia, where his parents were pioneers near Rockhampton (Qld).

Achurch and Charrington had signed a contract with WILLIAMSON, GARNER AND MUSGROVE to tour Australia for two years. They mortgaged their future salaries and raised enough money to give seven performances of *A Doll's House* at a minor London theatre in June 1889. Achurch, drawing on memories of her own disastrous first marriage, was an overnight success as Nora, and the season was extended by 17 performances—delaying the couple's departure for Australia by three weeks, to the annoyance of the triumvirate. But London, suddenly aware of the 'Ibsen controversy', was abruptly deprived of the Achurch-Charrington production. For the next two years it was played throughout Australia and New Zealand.

The stars were known in Australia only through sensational press reports that arrived at the same time and they had a hostile reception. Typical was an editorial on 'Ibsenism' in the Melbourne theatrical newspaper *Lorgnette* on 31 August 1889, quoting the most vituperative London critic, Clement Scott. He saw the play as 'flinging upon the stage a congregation of men and women without one spark of nobility in their natures, men without conscience and women without affection, an unlovable, unlovely and detestable crew'. However, the *Lorgnette* thought Australians were too 'level-headed' to take to Ibsen.

Rowdy scenes marked the first night of *A Doll's House* at the Princess Theatre in Melbourne on 14 September 1889, and reviews were negative, although Achurch was generally praised for refined and artistic acting. J. C. WILLIAMSON objected to the ending and proposed a different one in which Nora would stay for her children's sake. He even suggested a final line: 'My darlings, I cannot leave you!' Achurch refused to alter Ibsen's text, although, according to the *Bulletin* on 28 September, some cuts were made after the opening night, including the erroneously hopeful last line of the husband Helmer: 'The miracle?'

Achurch and Charrington had an extensive repertoire which included sensational melodramas, comedies and historical dramas. They went to Adelaide in November and returned to Melbourne at the end of 1889, when the Ibsen play was more favourably received. After touring they opened a three-month season at the Criterion Theatre in Sydney on 4 July 1890. Miriam Franc claimed (in her *Ibsen in England* in 1915) that the audience had hissed Nora's famous exit on the opening night of *A Doll's House* on 12 July, but the Australian reviews reported rioting at the beginning rather than the end of the performance. The *Bulletin* said the performance was disrupted by 'the noisiest gallery ever gathered in this house but after the ejection of one or two deities—the overslop from the Royal, thirsting for bouffe business—things quietened down, and from thence mind triumphed over matter and the actress, scarcely ever off stage, had them in her power'.

The *Sydney Morning Herald* on 14 July was outraged. 'Certainly, *A Doll's House* is not a play that is acceptable to a crowd of roughs, but Miss Achurch is entitled to a fair hearing for three sound reasons—she is a woman, she is an actress of merit and reputation, and she is a stranger in our midst', it declared. The paper later published responses to the play, including 'A Woman's View', 'A Man's View' and 'A Wife's View'. The most positive was the woman's view, on 2 August 1890, which ended: '… Miss Achurch will always be gratefully remembered by every true woman whose heart has throbbed in response to the ringing tones of her noble utterances; gratefully remembered as one who has dared to defy conventional thought and helped her sisters to recognise their mournful shortcoming and their glorious potentialities; gratefully remembered by one woman at least, as the most soul-stirring, sympathetic, subtle actress it has been my lot to watch in Australia.'

After visiting New Zealand, the Achurch–Charrington company went to Brisbane, where a warm reception for *A Doll's House* was offset by a controversy over *Camille*. It was advertised that the performance of this version of *La Dame aux camélias* by Alexandre Dumas *fils* would be under the patronage and in the presence of the Acting Governor, but he declared the story of the reformed prostitute Marguerite Gautier to be immoral, and refused to attend.

After Brisbane the couple made farewell appearances in Melbourne in February-April 1891 and Sydney in May and June. The farewell Melbourne season at the small Bijou Theatre was a success. 'Melbourne emphatically endorses the London verdict regarding the sterling merits of this wonderful play and the unrivalled impersonation of Janet Achurch as Nora Helmer', advertisements claimed. The last Sydney season was less well received by the public, but distinguished by a remarkable benefit matinée of *A Doll's House* that raised £200 for the Women's College at the University of Sydney.

Achurch and Charrington left Australia by way of Goulburn, Wagga Wagga, Albury, Geelong, Adelaide, Broken Hill and Perth. During this period they produced *Devil Caresfoot*, an adaptation of H. Rider Haggard's *Dawn* by the expatriate Australian C. Haddon Chambers. Other plays Achurch and Charrington performed in Australia included *The Merchant of Venice*, Wilkie Collins's *The New Magdalen*, and Ibsen's *Hedda Gabler* once (in Brisbane on 31 October 1891). They performed in India and Egypt on the way home. Some critics, including her friend and admirer George Bernard Shaw, thought Achurch had coarsened her performance in pandering to colonial tastes, but she quickly re-established herself as a leading interpreter of Ibsen and Shaw in London. She revived *A Doll's House* in London in 1892 and 1897 and played Nora in New York in 1895. Her other Ibsen roles included Hedda Gabler, Mrs Alving in *Ghosts* and Rita in *Little Eyolf*. She financed and directed a production of *Little Eyolf* which was so successful that it was taken up commercially with the more popular Mrs Patrick Campbell in Achurch's role. Achurch created the title-role in Shaw's *Candida* in 1893. Shaw said in *Our Theatres in the Nineties* that she was 'the only tragic actress of genius we now possess'. In later years Achurch suffered from morphine addiction, brought on by poor medical treatment, but she was still an actor of distinction in *Ghosts* in 1907. Sources differ on the date of her retirement. ❦*Richard Fotheringham, with Noela Beith*

further reading
CAMPBELL, DEBORAH. *A Doll's House*—The colonial response. *Nellie Melba, Ginger Meggs and Friends*. Malinsbury: Kibble 1982.

Acrobatics

An acrobat is strictly a tumbler who, unlike a gymnast, performs without the aid of appliances such as bars or teeterboard. In practice, however, the distinction between acrobatics and gymnastics has become increasingly blurred. Vaulting exercises were exhibited at the Governor's Arms Inn, near Parramatta (NSW) on 5 March 1835. The company of LUIGI DALLE CASE, which opened at the Royal Victoria Theatre in Sydney on 13 August 1841, included 'the Man Tortoise and Mr King, both of whom are really wonderful in their acrobatic exercises', according to the *Sydney Herald* of 5 March 1842. In the *Cornwall Chronicle* of 29 December 1847 the earliest bill for the first CIRCUS, the Royal Circus in Launceston (Tas.), listed 'Gymnastic Feats … performed by the Four Wonderful Acrobats'. Acrobats thereafter were common in the Australian circus.

The most famous acrobatic troupe the Australian circus has produced was the SEVEN ASHTONS. They were specialists in the Risley act, in which one or more performers lie on their backs to juggle smaller members of the troupe with their feet. This act was named after its originator, Richard Risley Carlisle, a renowned American-born acrobat. He travelled widely and visited East Asia, so he may have been the 'Mr Risley' who performed as an acrobat at Ashton's Royal Amphitheatre in Launceston in 1851. Three sons of the Australian circus proprietor Gus St Leon developed a polished act in the USA with 'Mo' Aarons, a Jewish 'knockabout' acrobat from New York, and young Georgie Smith, the 'topmounter'. They all came to Australia in 1908 as the Five St Leons. The Martinettis, an acrobatic troupe drawn from a branch of the Ashton circus family, toured England before the Second World War.

The Nanjing Acrobatic Troupe from China rekindled interest in acrobatics when it visited Australia in 1983–84, sponsored by CIRCUS OZ and the FLYING FRUIT FLY CIRCUS. ❦*Mark St Leon*

Acting

In the 140 years before professional theatre collapsed in 1930 Australian actors and acting followed the London stage through three major aesthetic revolutions, at a respectful distance and sometimes unenthusiastically. At the end of the 18th century, when convicts were acting in SIDAWAY'S THEATRE in Sydney, John Philip Kemble and Sarah Siddons brought English stage classicism to its peak with 'noble simplicity and quiet grandeur'. The actor moved little, concentrated on a dignified posture, and gestured with one arm only, while retaining a balanced vertical line through the body. Siddons's mild innovation of not carrying a candle for Lady Macbeth's sleepwalking scene—so that she could wring her hands at 'Out, damned spot'—was a shocking but successful departure from tradition. Kemble employed little facial expression, but critics noted how Siddons's eyes, shoulders and hands indicated her character's passions before she spoke.

By the time continuous professional theatre began in Sydney and Hobart in the 1830s the romantic movement in acting—associated particularly with Edmund Kean—and the trend to melodrama in performance had established an alternative approach. This was long favoured by provincial audiences and less sophisticated theatregoers in the colonies. They thrilled to violent expressions of emotion, flamboyant studied gestures, and stentorian voices that went from a whisper to a shout in a second. The *Dramatic Year Book* for 1891 quotes an old-timer lamenting the passing of actors like the 1840s Sydney star FRANCIS NESBITT, who could be heard 't'other side o' the Racecourse, half-a-mile away'. Actors often declaimed to the audience rather than to the other characters, and after a fine speech or sequence applause sometimes brought the actor out of character to bow acknowledgment, much to the disgust of mid-century reformers. The 'old school', with its elocution, posturing and flamboyance, retained admirers throughout the 19th century. Actors who came to Australia after their style of performance had fallen from favour in England—such as WILLIAM CRESWICK—helped to perpetuate 'the robust school of acting' in the colonies.

As theatres grew larger and then smaller again, as lighting changed from candles to gaslight to limelight to electricity, so actors enlarged and then refined their tools of communication—voice, gesture, posture, expression, costume, make-up. As musical accompaniment and scenic spectacle interacted with speech to point character reactions and make human preoccupations visible, so interpretations of the great acting roles changed. In 1863 CHARLES KEAN brought fussy, detailed domestic sets and props to Australia for his production of *The Merchant of Venice*, inviting an interpretation of Shylock as a family man who cared more about the loss of his daughter than his money.

Unlike the stars of magnificent productions in vast theatres in London, early players in Australia were all too often poorly rehearsed, underpaid, technically inept and resigned to makeshift buildings. Benefit nights were essential for the actor to make a living, and they supplemented generally low rates of pay for most of the 19th century. Long after competent professional standards had been achieved in the 1850s, actors told of the inadequacies of colonial stages, particularly in the bush, where many companies consisted solely of that quintessentially Australian trio—man, wife, and mate. In *Harry Emmet's Theatrical Holiday Book* in 1885 W. G. Carey tells of touring with such a troupe, doing scenes from Shakespeare in venues 'more remarkable for their originality than for their comfort'. At one they performed in a skittle alley on a stage made from gin cases with six candles stuck in nails for footlights, with Carey doubling as Hamlet and the orchestra, playing a borrowed violin. As Macbeth, Carey was obliged to halt the performance to evict an offensive drunk. Back on the stage, he resumed with 'Sweet love, Duncan comes here tonight'. 'Then he'll have to behave himself', interjected an onlooker.

In the major cities, however, standards quickly rose to comparability with those of the English provinces. Adoption of the STAR SYSTEM and the stock company encouraged a style of virtuoso performing. *Delirium tremens* scenes and Rip Van Winkle waking after his long sleep were particular favourites. By the 1880s entire touring casts, such as the LONDON COMEDY COMPANY, in long-running seasons of major plays had begun to replace the stock company, and solo star acting had given way to more developed character interactions and psychological subtlety.

Realism was the key particularly in the second half of the 19th century, when French acting styles began to find favour in drama and light comedy, rehearsals were more thorough, and staging began to emphasise antiquarian accuracy in historical plays and photographic detail in melodramas of contemporary life. Increasingly 'natural' behaviour and settings marked 'new-style' acting and production methods—attributed initially to Mme Vestris, CHARLES MATHEWS, Charles Kean and later Squire Bancroft and Marie Wilton. The earliest surviving sound recordings and films, however, show that 50 years later, after several generations of performers had each been acclaimed as more 'realistic' than the last, the acting was still far from what a modern audience would consider realistic, while stage speech was close to song in its linearity.

Many stars toured Australia between the gold rushes of the 1850s and the Great Depression of the 1930s—among them Wilson Barrett, SARAH BERNHARDT, DION BOUCICAULT, JOSEPH JEFFERSON, Kean, Mathews, ADELAIDE RISTORI and BARRY SULLIVAN—and local performers watched them closely for evidence of innovations in staging and acting style. Comic acting went from 'Liston school' broad characterisation—copied by GEORGE COPPIN, whose famous Paul Pry in the play of the same name by John Poole had been John Liston's best-known role in London in the 1820s—to a lighter gentlemanly style. Charles Mathews's tour in 1870, memorable in particular for his doubled roles of Sir Fretful Plagiary and Mr Puff in R. B. Sheridan's *The Critic*, set the trend. The name of one of his earlier characters, Patter, aptly described the quicker, less-inflected vocal style appropriate to his witty, urbane roles. Australian-based performers like ROBERT BROUGH, MRS ROBERT BROUGH, BLAND HOLT and GEORGE LAURI followed this trend in the 1880s and 1890s. Comedians who learned their trade in lower-class and provincial companies in the colonies—like BERT BAILEY, KATE HOWARDE, FRED MACDONALD and Tal Ordell—retained a broader style of characterisation, which re-established itself in bush comedy after 1912. Those whose tastes ran to subtler approaches particularly admired GEORGE S. TITHERADGE, master of the dramatic pause, among the new-

Robert and Florence Brough brought witty, urbane acting to plays by J. M. Barrie, Arthur Wing Pinero and Oscar Wilde

style serious actors. He, the Broughs and DION BOUCICAULT JNR experimented with ideas of ensemble playing and autocratic direction that they had learned from W. S. Gilbert.

As well as the genuine stars who toured the colonies lesser performers made names for themselves in Australia by imitating actors with whom they had worked in London. So WALTER MONTGOMERY's Hamlet was allegedly copied from Charles Fechter's, GEORGE RIGNOLD's Henry V from Charles Calvert's and ALFRED DAMPIER's Shylock from Henry Irving's. The same was true of Australian-based performers who travelled to London. From the 1880s these travellers also took an interest in the American stage. FLORENCE YOUNG and many others returned to Australia by way of New York. ESSIE JENYNS based her many Shakespearean heroines on the interpretations of the American star Mary Anderson.

Tradition was highly valued on the professional stage in Australia, and actors learnt their craft by imitating gestures, attitudes, vocal emphasis and 'points'—actions and reactions that illuminated character. Points were considered as essential to meaning as the heavily cut and bowdlerised text. Hamlet's 'take' on seeing the ghost went back to David Garrick. It was also traditional for Hamlet to return to kiss Ophelia's hand after the 'Get thee to a nunnery' scene. Actor-managers apparently believed that Shakespeare had insufficiently emphasised Hamlet's love as against his revulsion. Edmund Kean's Richard III absent-mindedly drew lines on the ground with his sword as he meditated before Bosworth Field. Henry Irving's Mathias in *The Bells* slowly picked imaginary cork from his wine glass when he heard a chance reference to the man he had murdered many years earlier. The first actor to come to the colonies with such business had a decided advantage. This global tradition of borrowing and imitation also meant that by the 1890s many Australian performers were able to audition successfully for roles on the London stage. The profession had its own character 'texts', which were known throughout the English-speaking world.

Throughout the second half of the 19th century the actor in England rose in social status from vagabond to knight. Irving finally accepted a knighthood in 1895; by 1910 at least six other British actors had been similarly honoured. It was often observed, however, that the actor in Australia was not so well regarded. As late as 1880 the prominent Ella Carrington was arrested, charged with infanticide and imprisoned along with her fellow players solely because a child's body had been found while they were playing in western Victoria. Questions were asked in parliament on her behalf, but acting remained a dubious profession for many years, particularly for women. Many early amateur theatrical societies consisted of men only because no 'respectable' woman would appear on the stage. The female roles were played by professional actresses or men.

Actors tried to win public standing by performing Shakespeare rather than more profitable melodramas, playing cricket matches against local teams, and obtaining the patronage of state governors and the clergy. In most cases, however, only those who took public office or became primarily financiers and producers escaped the general stigma against the profession. To speak the thing was to be tainted by it. A critic in 1870 lamented the certain 'pernicious effect' of the courtesan drama *Formosa—or, The Railroad to Ruin* on the morals of the actresses playing in it.

Actors were not unionised and each had to negotiate a wage according to reputation and experience and the economic climate of the day. The GEORGE LEITCH papers in the Mitchell Library, Sydney, offer much information on such bargaining at the end of the 19th century. Leitch's standard contract would include a week's rehearsal at no pay, and half-pay if a second week was required. In the boom 1880s a leading actor could expect to receive up to £15 a week; in the bust 1890s Leitch—as long as he supplied the costume—could beat even a seasoned performer down to £7. Colonial actors, unlike their counterparts on the English stage, usually still had to provide all their own stage clothes, and an actress's wardrobe was her most valued asset.

By the beginning of the 20th century the tendency of J. C. WILLIAMSON to import complete London or New York casts made times hard for local performers. Most of them found work only in minor provincial companies. Such troupes were notorious for never paying their bills before leaving town, and apocryphal stories abound of properties being smuggled out the stage door while the star entertained the bailiffs inside, or of him leaving the theatre disguised in petticoats. Conversely, after a successful season the profession's probity would be emphasised by advertisements like this one in the *Brisbane Courier* after E. I. Cole's Ned Kelly play *Hands Up!* in Brisbane in 1900: 'All accounts owing by the Bohemian and Texas Jack Company must be sent in before 17 January, as their partnership terminates'.

After the decline of the stock-company system many companies again became extended family groups who travelled with plays written, cut or pasted to suit their forces. In other companies productions would be prepared and then toured as a complete unit, with musicians, technicians and supernumeraries being quickly rehearsed in each town. In the 1860s and 1870s the aspiring actor had been expected to master several hundred roles from the standard repertoire, including stock moves for scenes like the duelling sequences in *Hamlet* or *The Corsican Brothers*, and to be able to play them at very short notice. This changed as new staging techniques, greater emphasis on pictorial groupings of characters, and the breakdown of 'stock' stage positions and business made performances less predictable and required greater time and effort in rehearsal.

American innovations also started to influence a profession that looked predominantly towards London. When J. C. Williamson toured two American actors in modern dramas in 1903, the *Brisbane Courier* noted of David Belasco's *The Girl I Left Behind Me*: 'A peculiar thing in this play and in the playing of it was the obscuring of the principals at times. Mr Frawley and Miss Van Buren avoided conspicuous positions and those old stage tricks which have always been regarded as "the right of the star". They are never obtrusive, they do not attempt to work up "situations" … Without desiring to enter upon a disquisition of art ethics, we may ask whether [their] methods … are not entitled to a large amount of respect?'

There was no formal acting school of the kind known today. As late as 1907 J. C. Williamson advised 'every humble performer' to 'make his closet his college and tutor himself'. In fact, many old actors had run private classes in singing, dancing, elocution and stagecraft during the 19th century. PHILIP LYTTON in Sydney and Mrs G. B. W. Lewis in Melbourne were perhaps the best known and most enduring teachers. Early in the 20th century GREGAN MCMAHON in Sydney and Agnes Rahilly in Brisbane supplemented such work by forming training companies, whose members played everything from Shakespeare to *East Lynne*. Williamson nevertheless continued loud and often in his complaint that Australian male actors were lazy, though he thought the women worked harder and that there were 'no brighter children on the stage to be found anywhere'. By the 1920s the Williamson firm and its few rivals had their own trainers for dancers in operettas.

Outside the profession, freelance elocution teachers were beginning to appear in major towns and to associate themselves with the emerging repertory movement. ARTHUR H. ADAMS, LEON BRODZKY, LOUIS ESSON and others had seen the work of the Irish National Theatre, the seasons given by John Vedrenne and Harley Granville-Barker at the Royal Court Theatre in London or Annie Horniman's Repertory Company in Manchester, and ideas about ensemble and more intimate performing styles and spaces for non-commercial drama were beginning to be applied, though not always completely understood, by professional directors like McMahon. ❦*Richard Fotheringham*

Naturalism ascendant

From the 1920s to the mid-1950s there was no singular or overriding style of acting. There was, as in any era, a range of styles determined partly by techniques inherited from the past, partly by learning through example and instruction and partly by the pressures of giving life and substance to new works by contemporary dramatists. Most notably, colonial cringe in actors was gradually replaced by eclectic awareness of theatrical ideas, movements, fashions and methods throughout the world. Until the late 1940s theatre in Australia remained peculiarly colonial, deriving its performance standards mainly from London, the centre of imperial culture. The Australian accent was regarded as a crippling handicap and most actors laboured to rid themselves of it. Promising actors constantly emigrated to England and British luminaries—varying in brilliance from fast-fading to brightly shining—fairly constantly flowed in on the colonial tours. Dependence upon English and to some extent American drama was almost total, and acting styles were likewise imported. Only in revue and bush comedy—such as *ON OUR SELECTION*—was there much attempt to develop an indigenous approach and manner.

In 1949 the English director Tyrone Guthrie was invited here to advise the federal government on how to set up a national theatre. He surveyed the scene and concluded that the most efficient solution would be to establish a company in England, consisting largely of emigré Australian actors. Such a company would be welded together in performances overseas and eventually brought to Australia. The GUTHRIE REPORT was the sort of patronising assessment that Australian actors and directors had by then come to expect.

In 1920 Australia lagged behind England in style by about ten to 15 years. The flamboyant, broad-gestured, declamatory acting extensively used in England for melodrama in the 19th century had not yet vanished from Australian playhouses. VANCE PALMER offered this pertinent analysis of George Dawe, leading man for the PIONEER PLAYERS in Melbourne in 1920–26: '… a born actor of great power and vitality, with a gift for mimetics, a rich, fluty voice and a commanding presence on stage. He had a dim awareness that he had wasted his gifts barnstorming around the back streets of two continents, and he was ready to give himself to a movement that seemed to have some national significance. But his technique had been formed in the old-fashioned school in which the leading actor entered to a blare of trumpets and kept his place very emphatically in the centre of the stage till his exit, and he was a little bothered by our demands for a natural style that subordinated the personalities of individual characters to the general intentions of the play.'

Virtuoso actors of 'the old school'—often more capable of striking attitudes than of illuminating dramatic texts—lingered on until the 1930s, frequently by taking refuge in Shakespeare. In 1922–24 OSCAR ASCHE, a London celebrity, made the last of his three tours of his homeland with *Julius Caesar*, *Othello* and his own spectacles *Cairo* and *The Spanish Main*. But between 1916 and the Depression, the most prominent Shakespearean was the English actor-manager ALLAN WILKIE, whose itinerant troupe was optimistically designated 'permanent'. Wilkie was not much admired by perceptive critics—one of whom considered his initial production of *As You Like It* 'shamelessly melodramatised'—but his grit and persistent energy gained him steady public support for 15 years. Old-school acting was revived as late as 1949–50, when the Irish actor-manager ANEW MCMASTER took Shakespeare to Perth, Melbourne and rural Victoria.

Larger-than-life bravura acting was not necessarily pretentious, cliché-ridden and bombastic. McMaster could be an excellent Shylock, for example. Nor was it suddenly supplanted by restrained forms of modern realism. There was no clear shift, but as melodrama in all its fruity variants became less credible to audiences, acting techniques changed to accommodate new kinds of drama that were more firmly grounded in observable social behaviour. The drawing-room drama of Noël Coward, John Galsworthy, Somerset Maugham, A. A. Milne, J. B. Priestley and, later,

Terence Rattigan required the less expansive, less spacious style that came to be known as naturalistic. Actors tried to look and sound as though they belonged to the real, everyday world rather than the romantic world of melodramatic imagination. Voices of rolling thunder had no place in these plays, but strict attention was still paid to diction and resonance, if only because it was important to be heard at the back of the upper circle. The polite, upper-middle-class atmosphere of most drawing-room drama, however, encouraged a quiet, controlled and emotionally confined style which virtually imprisoned acting in a bourgeois straitjacket. The robust expressiveness that had distinguished the old school was lost over the years—perhaps somewhere between Milne and Rattigan.

The limits imposed by radio acting contributed to this falling away of traditional skills. With the closing of many playhouses during the Great Depression and the spread of broadcast entertainment reaching directly into the home, professional actors turned to the air waves for their living. Radio work demanded unusual vocal flexibility and tonal colour, but actors became accustomed to moving only towards and around a microphone. There was little opportunity to build physical characterisation beyond the voice. Furthermore, dialogue in radio drama was generally restricted to the rhythms and vocabularies of ordinary speech and conversation. Thus the naturalism fostered by radio tended to leave actors ill-equipped for the more heightened, physically expressive style needed on stage. The finest radio actor of the period, PETER FINCH, certainly conveyed a strong impact in the theatre, but he had a valuable pre-radio background in travelling tent companies and in revue. From 1930 to 1945 revue was, indeed, almost the sole repository of histrionic sweep and vigour.

Talking pictures reinforced the general ascendancy of naturalism. Films from England, America and Europe confirmed it as the dominant style. Acting standards were perhaps more effectively preserved in AMATEUR THEATRE rather than in professional enterprises during 1930–45. In March 1941, for instance, a *Bulletin* critic rated the Melbourne University Dramatic Club's presentation of Patrick Hamilton's *Rope* as 'considerably better' than the professional production some years previously. Of course, the word 'amateur' was in some respects a misnomer, because amateur groups —such as the GREGAN MCMAHON PLAYERS, ADELAIDE REPERTORY THEATRE, the REPERTORY CLUB in Perth, INDEPENDENT THEATRE in Sydney and the Melbourne Little Theatre Company—often used professional actors who earned an income in radio. But no amateur organisation, however important as a training ground, was ever able to establish consistent quality or to achieve a distinctive ensemble style.

One exception may have been the Dolia Ribush Players, whose four productions in Melbourne between 1937 and 1944 were rigorously rehearsed, highly disciplined and often demonstrated a rare artistic sensibility. DOLIA RIBUSH, a Russian immigrant, drew his theories of acting primarily from Konstantin Stanislavsky and to that extent he introduced into theatrical culture a fresh view that owed nothing to English influence or tradition. His discussions with Peter Finch in Melbourne in 1944 helped the rising actor to adopt the psycho-technique, and to teach it at the Mercury Theatre School in Sydney in 1946–48. Stanislavsky began to be read and studied more widely about that time, though it was another two decades before ruling orthodoxies incorporated his methods. But this growing interest in Stanislavsky during the 1940s signified an irreparable break with the provincialism of the past and brought new seriousness to acting. It started to throw off the taint of exhibitionism and to seek the dignity of art.

Viewed historically, 1948 was a crucial year. Laurence Olivier's visit at the head of the OLD VIC THEATRE COMPANY can now be looked upon as the last genuinely influential colonial tour. His Richard III, in the sheer athleticism of its creative drive and subtlety of its interpretation, set a benchmark for the rising generation of actors. Evidence that the new seriousness was making progress came when Olivier praised the MERCURY THEATRE production of Molière's *The Imaginary Invalid*. He later called it 'as expert a production as could be imagined'. Another portent of hope in 1948 was the Independent Theatre production of Sumner Locke Elliott's RUSTY BUGLES, which gave tremendous impetus to the legitimising of the Australian idiom and a characteristically Australian mode of acting. With the arrival in 1955 of Ray Lawler's SUMMER OF THE SEVENTEENTH DOLL, the legitimation was almost complete. The fact the subsidised UNION THEATRE REPERTORY COMPANY, housed at the University of Melbourne since 1953, gave the first performance was further indication that a sense of confident, nationally conscious theatrical maturing was taking hold. *Allan Ashbolt*

Acting in the television age

With the advent of television in 1956, commercial radio production began to dry up, eroding the economic base of a generation of actors. The Australian Broadcasting Commission, however, remained committed to radio drama and features, providing dignity and even stability for some actors. Large-scale commercial theatre withered as it lost audiences to television and CLUB ENTERTAINMENT. The TIVOLI CIRCUIT died. The lively PHILLIP STREET REVUES in Sydney— which had nurtured such talents as GORDON CHATER, RUTH CRACKNELL, BARRY CREYTON, BARRY HUMPHRIES, MARGO LEE, JUNE SALTER and Charles Tingwell—moved elsewhere in 1961 and the theatre was demolished. The actors gradually shifted their allegiances or went abroad. The sale and demolition of many old metropolitan theatres signalled the end of a vital popular tradition.

The foundation of the AUSTRALIAN ELIZABETHAN THEATRE TRUST in 1954 foreshadowed the growth of the state as employer of actors. After a brief period of national touring by the TRUST PLAYERS, the Trust helped to establish state theatre companies and, in 1959, the first full-time professional theatre school, the NATIONAL INSTITUTE OF DRAMATIC ART. These modestly funded initiatives resulted in the training of a new generation of actors and enhanced non-commercial play production, in which professional actors had previously engaged for love or out-of-pocket expenses.

The film industry was largely dormant but local television drama slowly and steadily increased in quantity and quality, providing livelihoods for a growing number of actors, and even popular recognition for a few. As governments answered a growing need for national self-definition through the arts by significantly increasing funds for theatre and film, regional theatre companies were established and existing groups were subsidised. Metropolitan and provincial PERFORMING-ARTS CENTRES proliferated, providing

Edna Everage in 1959. Barry Humphries created the character in 1955, when he was an actor in the Union Theatre Repertory Company. She remains the most famous of the characters through whom Humphries expounds his view of the world

new theatres that varied widely in size and quality but improved working conditions and emphasised civic involvement in the performing arts.

Subsidy and private initiative revitalised the film industry, which was fed by new schools and courses in film and video. The growth of theatre-in-education and community theatre, a new vogue for THEATRE-RESTAURANTS and cabarets, and quotas for Australian content in television drama all made more work for actors. Film and television roles and seasons in successful subsidised theatres brought leading actors rising status—and, for some, rising incomes—the possibility of critical recognition, public following and occasionally the beginning of an international career.

A larger profession with a bigger collective earning capacity made for more vigorous union activity, and thus for some betterment of working conditions. For example, niggardly touring allowances were gradually raised, protection against defaulting entrepreneurs was increased, and decent minimum rates for screen work were won. Award rates for theatrical workers—dancers and chorus especially—have remained markedly below general community levels, however. But the most apparent progress was that towards a recognisably Australian style of performance. When commercial touring companies predominated, regional distinctions were largely confined to amateur theatre and individual drama teachers. But the contemporary theatre has seen the rise in Sydney and Melbourne of distinctive acting cultures that have influenced national consciousness. Throughout the changes from 1954 Sydney largely retained the scripted drama and hierarchy of the English repertory company while Melbourne divided itself between the traditional values of the Union Theatre Repertory Company and a movement in favour of democratic, non-analytic forms in which text was secondary.

In Sydney the personalities who established the Trust were British-trained or came from the amateur repertory movement. The Trust Players were set up in 1959 in this manner and carried the tradition forward into the structure of NIDA and a decade later into state theatre companies. The rebellion begun in the late 1960s by the early work of the directors JOHN BELL, REX CRAMPHORN, JIM SHARMAN, BRIAN SYRON and JOHN TASKER concerned itself in diverse ways with actor's energy, danger, economy and an intimate relationship between actor and audience, but only marginally with company structure. To a large extent these directors, like their predecessors, were creating a director's theatre, aimed at perfectibility in performance.

The 1960s and 1970s introduced Sydney audiences to the open stage. And in the first decade they met a rugged new kind of actor—not from NIDA—with a closer affinity to the larrikin new-wave plays to be seen at the Nimrod Street Theatre and the Ensemble Theatre. Some who rejected the traditional style of acting were MAX CULLEN, GLORIA DAWN, JOHN GADEN, JANE HARDERS, John Hargreaves, MARTIN HARRIS, CHRIS HAYWOOD, GILLIAN JONES, MAGGIE KIRKPATRICK and Max Phipps. So did Jim Sharman's 1969 production of the musical *Hair*, which was largely cast from outside the profession. Today, with the benefit of 30 years' steady evolution at NIDA—which has produced most of Sydney's leading actors—Sydney theatre has a skilled and unselfconsciously Australian workforce. Most of the agents, casting directors, writers and freelance directors are based in Sydney. But the structure of the industry has changed little in New South Wales, or in Queensland and South Australia, where mainstream theatre is closely tied to Sydney; or in Western Australia, where the English connection remains as strong as ever. The method of hiring and firing actors is much as it has ever been.

Ron Haddrick turned his back on an English career to act in his homeland. His performance as Jock (above) in the Nimrod Theatre Company production of The Club *by David Williamson took him back to London in 1977–78*

On the other hand, Melbourne's rebellion, which dated almost from the foundation of the Union Theatre Repertory Company, has radically affected actors in Victoria and the works they have generated. For the best part of 20 years Melbourne actors outside this company—and its successor, the MELBOURNE THEATRE COMPANY—rejected the ideas of the director's authority, analysis and interpretation of text in favour of exploring process, ideas, improvisation and worker-participation. UNIVERSITIES have influenced Australian theatre and the Melbourne new wave was inspired by drama-in-education courses aimed not at dramaturgy or acting skills but at training student teachers in communication and self-expression.

The beginnings were seen at the University of Melbourne in the late 1950s, when student productions at Union Hall began to show renewed interest in the methods of Stanislavsky and BERTOLT BRECHT, and the ideal of the ensemble. GEORGE OGILVIE, an actor who was beginning as a director, later transferred these ideas to the Melbourne and South Australian Theatre Companies. Another influential young mind on campus at that time was WAL CHERRY, who at 23 in 1956 took over the Union Theatre Repertory Company from JOHN SUMNER until 1959. Cherry's productions introduced Melbourne to new writing and new theory, which he pursued in the EMERALD HILL THEATRE COMPANY from 1962 to 1966 and then with his students at Flinders University in Adelaide.

While Sumner's company was establishing itself in the traditional style of repertory—with actors like ZOË CALDWELL, PATRICIA CONOLLY, NOEL FERRIER, Stewart Ginn, Alex Scott and Maree Tomasetti, some of whom soon went abroad on Trust scholarships—opposing ideas fermented in student culture. The first centre was the Secondary Teachers' College—later Melbourne State College—where Ron Danielson began a small communications-skills unit which was expanded into a three-year drama course in 1964. Principals in this were John and Lois Ellis, and later LINDY DAVIES, Claire Dobbin, MAX GILLIES, EVELYN KRAPE and TONY TAYLOR, who became active in establishing the La Mama Company and the AUSTRALIAN PERFORMING GROUP.

Student teachers under John Ellis earned credits by creating community projects in country towns, and so from the start the course began to disseminate the idea of self-generating and self-expressive COMMUNITY THEATRE. In 1966 the Ellises moved to Monash Teachers' College—later Rusden State College and now part of Deakin University—and expanded the process further. The intimate space at the LA MAMA THEATRE, where actors and audience rubbed knees, led to a rapid rethinking of the techniques of acting and a discarding of illusion. There was steady exchange of theory and practice between the open stages of La Mama, the Australian Performing Group's Pram Factory and the Open Stage at the Secondary Teachers' College—all in the inner suburb of Carlton. The members of the companies were students and staff from the college and the University of Melbourne. A further influence was Ellis's Melbourne Youth Theatre, which presented classic and modern plays from 1956 to 1971, and nurtured talents like the director and designer Elijah Moshinsky and the actors Peter Curtin, Max Gillies, Wendy Hughes, Robert Meldrum and BRUCE SPENCE. These practices were given further weight by Peter Oyston and James McCaughey in the 1970s. Oyston was founding head of the VICTORIAN COLLEGE OF THE ARTS, which opened in 1976. He aimed to establish community cultural centres throughout the country, and his graduates were especially active in this work in the 1980s. Robert Perrier's MURRAY RIVER PERFORMING GROUP has been the most enduring result. McCaughey, a classicist and drama academic, established the MILL THEATRE COMPANY in Geelong under the umbrella of the new Deakin University in 1978. It was the first of the professional community theatres that proliferated in Victoria from 1979. It failed to bind itself to the community and it closed in 1988 but McCaughey's developmental process of creating work with local reference, and his creative use of unconventional space, sound and light, left a lasting impression upon the Melbourne actors of the period and set a pattern. Richard Murphet's work at the Victorian College of the Arts, and THEATREWORKS, directed by Robert Draffin, are examples.

Common to all these ventures was the idea that theatre need not be harnessed to the play. Their activities included street theatre, dance drama, PERFORMANCE ART, circus and STAND-UP COMEDY. Nothing like this variety was to be found in other parts of the country, although South Australia produced some similar results through its own drama-in-education courses and its proximity to Victoria.

Café culture in Melbourne

In 1975 the Australian Performing Group created THE HILLS FAMILY SHOW and contributed to the formation of CIRCUS OZ. By 1977 Melbourne had created a café culture unique in Australia. From Rusden and the Victorian College of the Arts were coming eccentric comic performers like Los Trios Ringbarkus and the Wogs Out of Work team and individual artists like Geoff Hooke, Jenny Kemp and the comedian Jean Kittson. A concert producer, JOHN PINDER began to promote the comedians by opening eating places with performing spaces in the Melbourne suburb of Fitzroy. By the mid-1980s, however, the café culture had transferred its energies to television.

The role of the director began to re-emerge, but the leading figures in Melbourne continued to be revered for their ideas and their methodology, ahead of the goal of a finished performance. In this climate European influences have been significant, most recently through the directors Jean-Pierre Mignon, founder of AUSTRALIAN NOUVEAU THEATRE, and Barrie Kosky, founder of the Jewish company Gilgul. La Mama has remained an experimental venue for the avant-garde and has been largely responsible for the steady output of artists for which Melbourne is noted.

Despite the changes, some actors in the 1970s continued to seek work abroad and established careers in the United Kingdom frequently and in the USA or Canada occasionally. Many more stayed in Australia, sometimes in their own cities. Financial and artistic rewards grew in Melbourne and Sydney, and Adelaide, Brisbane and Perth sustained small bodies of actors. Good training became more readily available. A healthy 'fringe' theatre was visible in most capitals. The profession began at last to reflect the diversity of the society. Throughout the 1970s emigré Australian actors returned, enriching the available talent, but the loss of a generation through attrition or emigration showed in a marked shortage of senior leading men. All these changes, supported from 1968 by public funding, led to the collapses of the J. C. Williamson's empire in 1976 and the OLD TOTE THEATRE COMPANY, surpassed in vigour by the NIMROD THEATRE COMPANY, in 1978. The end of the Firm made way for energetic new producers who provide steady work in plays, musicals and dance shows.

The 1980s was an anxious decade for actors. The real value of government funding declined and the security and status of the film industry were still regularly threatened by the spectre of an 'open-door' policy in film and television. The older actors remembered when an open door in the heyday of commercial theatre had admitted a steady succession of 'stars' to major roles. Anomalies abounded in the late 1980s. Training and diversity of challenge had raised general levels of skill, but much hasty and inept production, and the marketplace emphasis on raw youth that had been typical of theatre companies in the 1970s, now maintained low performance standards in most long-running television series and serials. The theatre and, notoriously, film and television still neglected women as central subjects and as performers, despite some successful promotion of women's theatre and some women's screen projects. The depth and range of female talent in all kinds of performance was remarkable, yet the industry still provided substantially more opportunities for male actors, mainly by focusing on traditional male endeavours.

Anomalies, fears and anxieties among actors could not, however, obscure the advances of the previous three or four decades, and towards the end of the 1980s there were some of the periodic signs of hope that encourage a resilient profession. There was a renewal of small-scale commercial production and the incorporation of Australia into the Cameron Mackintosh multinational empire offered long-term stage employment and opened channels to performance abroad for some. Writers were maturing and beginning to provide Australian actors with substantial roles, which occasionally took them overseas too. Dim reflections of the extraordinary diversity of Australian society were to be seen in writing and performance. There was even occasional acknowledgment by society of the importance and value of the Australian actor; and some improvements in working conditions and in average earnings.

Most serious playmaking until the advent of subsidy had been an essentially amateur activity in which the finest and the rawest talents might play side by side. The increase in Australian writing for stage and screen, however, has strongly influenced actors' self-image. Theatrical practice itself has been modified by visits of foreign directors and companies and freer exchange of ideas, artists and teachers in the age of festivals, air travel and video-tape.

The range of employment has widened with the general growth in production, but the profession has grown too. In the middle 1950s there were probably fewer than 2000 ACTORS' EQUITY members seeking work; 10 300 performers were union members in 1993. But while film and television have given the actor a public profile, the rising status of state theatre companies and the new audiences generated by long-running musicals have restored some stage actors to the senior status that the actor–manager once had. John Bell and ANNA VOLSKA founded the Bell Shakespeare Company in 1990. JOHN GADEN and ROBYN NEVIN have made names as directors as well as leading actors; honours have been conferred on veterans like RUTH CRACKNELL and RON HADDRICK. Actor-singers like DENNIS OLSEN, Philip Quast and John Diedrich have repeated their performances in London. Barry Humphries and ROBYN ARCHER have generated their own international careers.

The aspirations of a previous generation towards a kind of Englishness necessitated by most stage or radio material have been replaced by a sense of national identity that, for example, makes it acceptable to perform classical texts with Australian accents and even in Australian contexts. The generation reared in and for the theatre rather than radio and trained in tertiary institutions works with more physical attack and resourcefulness than its elders, often manifesting other performing skills in accord with the demands of new writing and new ideas. The actor in a subsidised company is also now more likely to participate in some measure in writing and production, chiefly in the development—sometimes the devising—of new works. Actors are increasingly reflecting the diversity of their skills and experience in creating their own employment. This ranges from solo entertainments to multi-skill groups and actor-based drama, film and television companies. Each of these points can be contested. All that can confidently be asserted is that despite the uncertainties of an overcrowded underpaid profession, Australia now rejoices in a large body of gifted home-bred actors. *Katharine Brisbane*, Nick Enright

further reading
ASHBOLT, ALLAN. Courage, contradiction and compromise—Gregan McMahon 1874–1941. *Meanjin* 37/3 (Melbourne 1978).
EMMET, HARRY. *Harry Emmet's Theatrical Holiday Book*. Melbourne: Rae 1885.
FRANCISCO, VIRGINIA R. Mr Charles Kean, actor—a re-evaluation. *Theatre History Studies* 9 (1989).
KIERNANDER, ADRIAN. Introduction. The *Land of the Moa* by George Leitch. Wellington (New Zealand): Victoria University Press 1990.
MCMAHON, MORGAN. Players of the past. *Lone Hand* (Sydney) 1 July 1909.
MILNE, GEOFFREY. Wanted (presumed dead)—community theatre in Victoria. *Australasian Drama Studies* 23 (Brisbane, October 1993).
SUMNER, JOHN. *Recollections at Play—A life in Australian theatre*. Melbourne: University Press 1993.

Actors' Equity

Trade union of performing artists. Founded in 1920 as Actors' Federation of Australia. Reorganised as Actors' and Announcers' Equity Association of Australia 1939. Amalgamated with Australian Journalists' Association and Australian Theatrical and Amusement Employees' Association as Media, Entertainment and Arts Alliance in 1992.

Since actors went on strike against J. C. WILLIAMSON'S in 1944 Actors' Equity has dominated INDUSTRIAL RELATIONS in the theatre. The union has achieved nearly 100 per cent membership in the entertainment industry and used its collective strength to pursue its objectives of lobbying, campaigning for and protecting work opportunities; and setting and enforcing acceptable minimum rates of pay and conditions. Some of its recent achievements include: regulation of the number of overseas artists who can work in Australia; introduction of standard contracts in all parts of the industry; averaging of income for tax; payment of repeat and residual fees; establishment of the world's first superannuation scheme for performers; minimum rates in all fields of work; and free legal advice. The union has influenced governments to fund the arts and to ensure that professional Australian theatre remains viable. It has fought for a fair deal for Australian performers by lobbying for Australian-content quotas in film and television.

Hal Alexander, who led the reorganisation of the union in 1939, was general secretary of Equity until 1971, when he was replaced by his son Bob Alexander. He held the position until 1983 and was followed by Michael Crosby until 1991. In 1993 Anne Britton was the joint federal secretary of the Media, Entertainment and Arts Alliance, into which Equity merged in 1992 as a result of a federal government initiative for amalgamation of small unions. The speciality dancer Hal Lashwood, who joined Equity in 1936 at the age of 16, was president from 1951 to 1976, and the actor Don Crosby was president from 1978 to 1986. Other past presidents include the actors Lloyd Lamble, Geraldine Turner and Rowena Wallace. ❦*Katharine Brisbane, Naomi Steer*

reference
Actors' Equity papers, ANU Archives of Business and Labour, in National Library of Australia (Canberra).
Hal Lashwood, De Berg tapes no. 652 in National Library of Australia.

Arthur H. Adams

Dramatist. Born 6 June 1872 at Lawrence (New Zealand). Graduated from University of Otago (Dunedin) 1894. Journalist on Wellington *Evening Post*. Covered Boxer rebellion for *Sydney Morning Herald* 1900. Wrote libretti for Alfred Hill, novels and poetry. Edited Red Page of Sydney *Bulletin* 1906–09. Edited *Lone Hand* 1909–11. Impoverished by 1930. Granted Commonwealth Literary Fund assistance 1933. Died 4 March 1936 in Sydney.

Arthur H. Adams was the most vigorous supporter of Australian playwrights early in the 20th century and a successful one himself. About 1897 he wrote the libretto of *Tapu*, an operetta on a Maori subject, for the Wellington composer Alfred Hill. This gained Adams work for two years in Sydney in 1898–1900 as J. C. Williamson's literary secretary, though he was not pleased when Williamson rewrote and staged the operetta during his absence in England. In the *Lone Hand* and *Theatre* magazine he described this and other attempts to have his plays performed, attacked the indifference to local writers of the great actor-managers who controlled Australian theatre, and gave aspiring playwrights good advice on learning their craft: 'Get your play produced. Failing the Managers, get it done by amateurs'.

Adams took his own advice, with success. *Pierrot in Australia* in Sydney in 1910 and in London in 1912, *The Tame Cat*, *The Wasters*, Mrs Pretty and the Premier and other plays received amateur production. A professional management in England took up *Mrs Pretty and the Premier*. Adams noted in an introduction to his *Three Plays for the Australian Stage—The Wasters*, *Mrs Pretty* and *Galahad Jones*—in 1914: 'One of the many drawbacks to their production is that there is no Australian stage'. He described the unperformed *Galahad Jones*, adapted from his own novel, as 'a comedy with a tragic tang', since the leading female character dies at the end. Insisting that it was a play for production in the professional theatre as well as for amateurs, Adams added a postscript: 'Should the theatrical manager demand his pound of flesh, the author has written, much against his will, an alternative "happy ending" in which Sybil recovers'.

Adams's last play, *Gallipoli Bill*, is his most original. Set during the last days of the First World War, it concerns two ANZAC soldiers. While recovering from wounds, Bill and Jim spend a few weeks in romantic dalliance at an English country mansion. The English lord and lady, their officer son and a silly chappie from the War Office are conventional, but the two soldiers, a lecherous old dowager aunt, the lord's daughter, who works in a munitions factory, and her Australian girl friend, who is equal to Bill's love-them-and-leave-them flirtations, are vigorous and cleverly written. Bill has a long, hilarious drunk scene which obviously appealed to the actor-manager Tal Ordell, who cast himself in the role for a season in suburban Sydney in 1926. There are reports of other performances in 1928. In February 1929 Adams sold the stage and film rights to Bert Bailey, who revised the script, but the Great Depression prevented further performance. ❦*Richard Fotheringham*

published plays
Doctor Death. In *Lone Hand* 5/27 (Sydney 1909).
Galahad Jones. Sydney: Brooks 1914 in *Three Plays for the Australian Stage*.
Mrs Pretty and the Premier. Sydney: Brooks 1914 in *Three Plays for the Australian Stage*.
The Wasters. Sydney: Brooks 1914 in *Three Plays for the Australian Stage*.

further reading
Andrews, B. G. and Ann Mari Jordens. Arthur H. Adams. *Australian Dictionary of Biography* 7. Melbourne University Press 1979.
Thomson, John M. *A Distant Music*. Auckland (New Zealand): Oxford University Press 1980.
Theatre (Sydney) 1 March 1915.

Harvey Adams

Actor, director. Born c.1893 in England. Trained in Shakespeare with Frank Benson. With Liverpool Repertory before First World War. Shakespeare Memorial Theatre (Stratford-Upon-Avon) 1921. Toured South America. Acted in London West End. Came to Australia for J. C. Williamson's 1928. Acted on radio from 1930s. Died 1960 in Melbourne.

A prominent actor and director in Australia for three decades, Harvey Adams came here from England as director and actor in leading roles on Muriel Starr's final visit for J. C. Williamson's in 1928. He had a solid background of classical and popular theatre which included working with Arthur Bourchier and Nigel Playfair. During the 1930s he acted continually for J. C. Williamson's, notably as Osbourne in R. C. Sherriff's *Journey's End* and in two sophisticated comedies, *Let Us Be Gay* by Rachel Crothers and *While Parents Sleep* by Anthony Kimmins. In 1940 he directed Terence Rattigan's *French Without Tears* at the Minerva Theatre in Sydney, and next year in Alec Coppel's *Mr Smart Guy* he made the first of many appearances as an actor at that theatre. In 1946 Adams directed *They Walk Alone* by Max Catto at Bryant's Playhouse in Sydney for the short-lived Radio Players. This was also one of four plays he directed for Independent Theatre in 1948. He directed a fine production of Eugene O'Neill's *Anna Christie* for the John Alden Company in 1951. ❦*Richard Lane*

Adelaide

When the colony of South Australia was founded in 1836 there was already in Australia a corps of professional actors, mostly from England. They encompassed a wide range of styles, because they had to perform in tragedy, melodrama, comedy and farce. Most could also sing and dance, so they were well equipped to entertain audiences at a time when a typical performance consisted of two or even three plays interspersed with divertissements such as songs and dances, plus perhaps a curtainraiser and an afterpiece.

On 28 May 1838, the first theatre opened in Adelaide, capital of 17-month-old South Australia. The 100-seat Theatre Royal, a room above the Adelaide Tavern in Franklin Street, was under the management of GEORGE BUCKINGHAM, an experienced actor from Sydney. The theatre was well-attended apparently—Edward John Eyre, visiting the town, complained that he was crowded out—but it closed in June because there was a severe housing shortage and the room was needed as a dormitory for immigrants. A successor, the Victoria Theatre, opened in a room in a warehouse on North Terrace on 27 November 1839. SAMSON CAMERON was the manager and the performers included Buckingham and EDWARD OPIE, who also worked as a scene-painter. After five months the theatre was closed for renovation.

In May 1840 Buckingham opened the Argyle Rooms in Gilles Arcade and the Victoria reopened as the Royal Victoria Theatre. Both these theatres closed in December 1840 and were replaced by the fine QUEEN'S THEATRE, also in Gilles Arcade, which opened on 11 January 1841 with *Othello*. Its joint owner, EMANUEL SOLOMON gave Adelaide a strong company. He brought several performers from Sydney, including the actor-manager JOHN LAZAR. Professional performers had full-time work until 1841, when the South Australian economy turned sharply downwards. Solomon strove to keep the Queen's Theatre open but he finally leased the building to the government for use as a law court. Moralists applauded the closure of the theatre.

Prosperity returned to South Australia in the mid-1840s and new theatres were opened. In September 1845 the first performance was given at the Pavilion Theatre in the Southern Cross Hotel in Currie Street. The Pavilion lasted until November. The Royal Adelaide Theatre, managed by Henry Deering, opened on 22 June 1846 on the premises of the Bush Club House in Franklin Street. The Queen's Theatre was still leased to the government in September 1846, when GEORGE COPPIN arrived in Adelaide, but he negotiated with Solomon to convert the large billiards room of the adjacent Temple Tavern into the New Queen's Theatre, seating 700 in a pit and a row of boxes above. Coppin made his Adelaide debut when the theatre opened on 2 November 1846. They plays presented were *The King and the Comedian* and a farce, *The Spectre Bridegroom*. Various songs and dances followed and *The Turnpike Gate* concluded the program. Coppin engaged the best local actors, and brought performers from other colonies. Early in 1848 he handed the management of the New Queen's Theatre to John Lazar, but soon after the death of his companion Maria on 10 August he returned in partnership with Lazar. In April 1850 he closed the little theatre.

Early in 1850 John Lewis Jacobs opened the Dramatic Hall above the Black Horse Hotel in Leigh Street. It was described as a vaudeville theatre that offered 'singing of a superior description, and dancing, under the direction of Mr Jacobs'. Members of the Dramatic Hall troupe attempted to discredit the rival company at the New Queen's Theatre by accusing Lazar of improprieties in performances of *Box and Cox* by J. M. Morton, *Othello Transvestie* and other plays. Lazar won a libel action and celebrated his victory by giving himself a benefit. Jacobs was charged with perjury and the Dramatic Hall was closed. Solomon refurbished the Queen's Theatre after the government's lease expired and reopened it as the Royal Victoria Theatre in December 1850. In October 1850 the Circus Royal opened in Currie Street. As well as the usual circus routines, it provided a pantomime and vaudeville acts, some of which were taken into productions at the Royal Victoria Theatre. After renovations, it was renamed Taylor's Royal Amphitheatre in January 1851 and Olympic Circus in September 1851. It closed about December 1851.

Coppin built the Port Adelaide Theatre, which shared performers with the Royal Victoria Theatre. From June 1851 the two houses together provided entertainment every night of the week, but by December performers and audience were joining the rush to the goldfields in NSW and Victoria. After 1851 Adelaide was unable to support local professional performers for the rest of the 19th century but it was part of the regular touring circuit embracing Melbourne, Sydney and the goldfields.

A new theatre, White's Rooms, opened in King William Street in 1856. It survived under various names until 1916, when it was rebuilt as the MAJESTIC THEATRE. Coppin returned in 1868 and fitted up the two-year-old Adelaide Town Hall as a theatre. He opened with the tragedian James Anderson on 2 March 1868. 'Hard times, hot weather and bad acoustics' prevented success, according to the *South Australian Register*. Coppin modified the acoustics but attendances remained poor and the city council released him from his three-month contract.

Coppin then became the first lessee and director of the new THEATRE ROYAL, which opened in Hindley Street on 13 April 1868. This superseded the Royal Victoria Theatre as a venue for visiting companies—other than vaudeville troupes, which had their own theatres. The Academy of Music, described as a 'beautiful little bijou amusement resort', opened on 2 June 1879 and presented small shows.

George Coppin, an English comic actor—here depicted singing the Cockney music-hall song 'Villikins and his Dinah'—moved to Adelaide in 1846. He ran theatres and hotels until 1851, when he could not withstand the loss of performers and audience to the Victorian goldfields. Coppin, insolvent, followed them. He returned to Adelaide in 1868, after recouping his losses on the goldfields and elsewhere, and leased a new theatre

The Victorian style of auditorium, with a proscenium designed like a picture frame, made one of its early appearances in Australia when the Theatre Royal in Adelaide was rebuilt in 1878. The three-level, gaslit auditorium seated 3000 persons. J. C. Williamson and the firms founded by him presented major productions in the theatre until 1959

It was destroyed by fire in January 1884, January 1885 and December 1886, and was not rebuilt after the third blaze. For an international exhibition celebrating the half-century of South Australia, the Exhibition Building was opened on North Terrace in 1887. It was later used as a skating rink, a circus and a concert hall. *Meg Abbie-Denton*

1901–30

In 1901 Harry Rickards bought the Tivoli Theatre—originally White's Rooms—renamed it the New Tivoli Theatre and presented famous London artists such as Lottie Collins and Marie Lloyd. It became the place for aspiring comics and singers. The other leading venue of the early 1900s was the Theatre Royal, which had been rebuilt in 1878. It presented WIRTHS' CIRCUS and Lancelot Booth's play *Outlaw Kelly* in 1901, the LONDON GAIETY COMPANY in 1904, and BLAND HOLT's productions of *The Breaking of the Drought* and *The Great Rescue* in 1908.

Thriving local amateur groups as well as visiting professional performers characterised Adelaide theatre between 1901 and 1930. At the Elder Conservatorium BRYCESON TREHARNE from the United Kingdom introduced the drive for more 'intelligent' theatre to Australia. Play readings by his students in 1908 led to the formation of Adelaide Literary Theatre. It began with productions in a concert hall of plays by George Bernard Shaw and W. B. Yeats. It produced two works by ARTHUR H. ADAMS of Sydney—*The Minstrel*, a one act-play, and *The Wasters*, a full-length play which closed after one scandalous performance in 1910. In 1911 the group became ADELAIDE REPERTORY THEATRE, with high intellectual standards and a determination to perform Australian plays. Theatre was flourishing, in spite of cinemas. Several open-air companies formed in the summer, and there was increasing investment in theatre buildings farther from the city centre than previously.

Theatrical highlights during the First World War included a lecture tour by ALLAN WILKIE in 1915 and NANCYE STEWART in *The Thirteenth Chair*, a thriller by Bayard Veiller, in 1918. In 1927 JUDITH ANDERSON returned to her native city as the star of Michael Arlen's *The Green Hat*. ❧*Rose Wilson*

1930s amateur theatre

By the 1930s the work begun by Treharne had spread beyond Adelaide Repertory Theatre into a remarkable variety of amateur groups. Many were run by actors and teachers thrown out of work by the Great Depression. Young people founded the Workers' Educational Association Dramatic Society in 1926 and began producing one-act plays for members only. COLIN BALLANTYNE was its electrician. By 1930 this group was known as WEA Little Theatre and was publicly producing three-act plays. Its actors included Ballantyne, AGNES DOBSON and Reginald Goldsworthy. Ballantyne also directed and his play *Harvest* was one production. Others were *The Ascent of F6* by W. H. Auden and Christopher Isherwood, *Children in Uniform* by Christie Winsloe, *The Green Bay Tree* by Mordaunt Shairp, *Noah* by André Obey and *Winterset* by Maxwell Anderson. The society was later renamed Little Theatre.

Agnes Dobson, a professional actor, director and dramatist, was an indomitable creative force and unorthodox methods sometimes gave originality to her productions. She directed for WEA Little Theatre in the 1930s and in 1936 founded Independent Repertory Theatre, which performed her play *Dark Brother*. It also staged notable productions of *Antony and Cleopatra*, *Dragon's Teeth* by Shirland Quin, *The Playboy of the Western World* by J. M. Synge, *Strange Orchestra* by Rodney Ackland and *Till the Day I Die* by Clifford Odets. The group lasted until 1940.

Dobson also acted with AB INTRA STUDIO THEATRE, which from 1931 to 1934 offered Adelaide experimental productions that communicated interpretation through visual effect. Another actor who supported Ab-Intra was PATRICIA HACKETT, the first woman in Adelaide to own a little theatre. She operated her first Torch Theatre in 1934–35, and her second from 1952 to 1960. Her productions were creative, unconventional and visual, and mostly employed dramatic material not previously produced in Adelaide.

Father Patrick O'Doherty, an Australian priest trained in Ireland and Rome, founded the Calaroga Players in the late 1920s for Catholics. He wrote and produced *King Hal's Divorce*, *Mary Queen of Scots*, *St Thomas More* and *The True St Joan* before the group came to an end in the 1930s.

LLOYD PRIDER began Playbox Theatre in 1932 as a tiny amateur dramatic society in a hall in the inner suburb of Burnside, but by 1935 he had transferred his productions to the larger Australia Hall in Angus Street. Many amateur groups presented their productions there in the 1930s and 1940s. Prider directed all Playbox productions. The yearly program of seven always included one musical, and sometimes a second in midyear, created entirely by local talent. The first musical, *The Schemers*, in 1935 had a chorus of only 12. The last, *Girls Please*, had 13 principals, a chorus of 40 men and women and a ballet of ten. Prider acted, designed costumes and sets, adapted straight plays into musicals and directed uncomplicated, entertaining productions concerned with colour, light and visual presentation.

A group of earnest, conventional young actors founded the Tree Players in 1937. As they hoped, Adelaide Repertory Theatre directors and actors worked with them in English and American plays. They produced five plays annually in Stow Hall, including *The Barretts of Wimpole Street* by Rudolf Bester and *Journey's End* by R. C. Sherriff. JEAN MARSHALL directed her own adaptation of Louisa M. Alcott's novel *Little Women*. Among the actors in the group, which faded away in the early 1940s, were Bettie Dickson and FRANK WATERS.

Brenda Kekwick, an actor, director and playwright, founded Junior Theatre in 1934. She developed an individual technique of using children's power of make-believe to stimulate initiative, imagination and creative ability in dramatic form. Her productions included three of her own works. She died in 1936, aged 28.

Academics who aimed to study the theatre arts founded the ADELAIDE UNIVERSITY THEATRE GUILD in 1938. It was innovative, had wide-ranging tastes and produced a diversity of Australian plays. ❧*Thelma Afford*

Professional theatre in 1930s

Many and varied professional companies visited Adelaide in the 1930s, but productions by J. C. Williamson's predominated. The Firm presented a season of Gilbert and Sullivan operettas with the comedian IVAN MENZIES and a stream of comedies and dramas with imported stars, including Sybil Thorndike and Lewis Casson in 1932.

The local song-writing team of Tom King and Jack Fewster had great successes with four musicals presented at the Theatre Royal to raise money for charity. Revue flourished. In 1933 ERIC EDGLEY and Clem Dawe presented *Midnight Frolics* with Tom King and Alec Regan in a company that toured Australia. ERNEST C. ROLLS, described in the program as 'the genius responsible for the most brilliant Revues and Musical Comedies on stage in Australia', presented ROY RENE and STRELLA WILSON in *Vogues of 1935* at West's Theatre. At the Theatre Royal in 1938, the American actor Ruth Draper astounded audiences with her solo performance. ❧*Jo Peoples*

1940–65

Amateur theatre was at its strongest between 1940 and 1965. Adelaide Repertory Theatre continued to present productions of high quality during the Second World War. Playbox Theatre produced occasional musicals until October 1946, when Lloyd Prider directed *Girls Please*, his last musical in Adelaide. KEITH MICHELL designed the sets. Playbox closed in 1947, when Prider went to London. Performers with Playbox included RON HADDRICK and Michell.

The Therry Dramatic Society, formed in 1944 and still operating, was named after Father Joseph Therry, the first official Roman Catholic priest in Australia. It presented four plays a year, always strong commercial successes with a moral message. Its productions have included *A Man for All Seasons* by Robert Bolt, *The First Born* by Christopher Fry, *Long Day's Journey into Night* by Eugene O'Neill, *Saint Joan* by Shaw and *The Merchant of Venice*. Among its actors have been KATE FITZPATRICK and DENNIS OLSEN.

The ADELAIDE THEATRE GROUP, founded in 1946 by Francis Flanagan and others, introduced European playwrights to Adelaide and promoted Australian plays in sincere, intelligent productions. It closed in 1958. RON HADDRICK acted occasionally with the group. He had previously acted with Tapestry Theatre, which was established in 1947 by some former members of the Tree Players and other amateur groups. Its productions included such standard works as *Acacia Avenue* by Mabel Costanduros, *George and Margaret* by Gerald Savory, *The Ghost Train* by Arnold Ridley and *The Playboy of the Western World*. In 1948 it amalgamated with Little Theatre, which had produced few plays in the 1940s, to become Theatres Associated.

The touring OLD VIC THEATRE COMPANY played capacity business at the Theatre Royal in 1948 in *Richard III* and Thornton Wilder's *The Skin of Our Teeth*. At the Majestic and Tivoli Theatres the comedians Edgley and Dawe, Roy Rene, Tommy Trinder and GEORGE WALLACE appeared in various revues. In the late 1940s the Adelaide Musical Comedy Company, with the backing of J. C. Williamson's and Alan Chapman as director, gave professional work to local actors, including Ron Beck, Rae Cocking and Phyl Skinner. Expatriate Adelaide stars returned on tour during the 1950s—Keith Michell with the Shakespeare Memorial Theatre Company in 1953, Robert Helpmann heading the OLD VIC THEATRE COMPANY with Katharine Hepburn in 1955, and JUDITH ANDERSON for the AUSTRALIAN ELIZABETHAN THEATRE TRUST in the same year.

Audiences were seeing excellent amateur productions at the time. Colin Ballantyne, with the Arts Council of South Australia as sponsor and guarantor, directed a cycle of Shakespeare between 1947 and 1951. EDWIN HODGEMAN and William Job were among the actors. 'He is the only producer here and now who is capable of taking good plays and stamping the production with a unique personal interpretation', Max Harris wrote of Ballantyne in 1951. With a small group of poets Ballantyne established the Company of Players in 1955, presenting three plays by the South Australian authors John Bray, Charles Jury and Brian Medlin.

In 1952 Patricia Hackett formed her second Torch Theatre in the basement of her home. In this salon theatre she built up a small, select audience. Critics were banned, with the exception of the Hon. H. Stafford Northcote, son of the former Governor-General Lord Northcote.

The University of Adelaide Theatre Guild formed an association with the Elizabethan Trust in the late 1950s and staged professional productions, including T. S. Eliot's *Murder in the Cathedral* for the first ADELAIDE FESTIVAL OF ARTS in 1960. In the 1962 festival it performed Shaw's *Saint Joan* with the visiting star ZOË CALDWELL. In the following year the guild performed the premiere of Patrick White's THE HAM FUNERAL, which the festival had rejected. It later gave the first performances of his *The Season at Sarsaparilla* (1962) and *Night on Bald Mountain* (1964).

The Adelaide Theatre Group became one of the most influential amateur companies. Jean Marshall, a director and teacher of great influence, directed the world premiere of Alan Seymour's play THE ONE DAY OF THE YEAR—also rejected by the festival—for the group in 1960. Other influences on amateur theatre were the Polish artist and director WŁADYSŁAW DUTKIEWICZ, who formed the Art Studio Players, and the local actor and playwright Betty Quin.

By 1960 there was dissatisfaction in theatrical circles with the standard of touring professional shows. Rosemary Burden expressed it, asking in *Mary's Own Paper*: '… if it were not for the energy and imagination of the various groups here in this little smug city, what on earth would we have seen of serious contemporary theatre in the last X number of years?' In 1962 the English actor and director John Edmund opened Adelaide's first professional company in the 20th century, THEATRE '62, with his own adaptation of Charles Dickens's novel *Great Expectations*.
❧*Thelma Afford, Jo Peoples*

Since 1965

There were still many amateur groups in 1965. The Adelaide Theatre Group played at the Sheridan Theatre. Jean Marshall was still Adelaide's leading female director. Theatre '62 and Adelaide Repertory Theatre in its Arts Theatre both provided important venues for the Adelaide Festival. The Adelaide University Theatre Guild was a valuable training ground for artists under Harry Medlin. One of its 1965 highlights, *Tata Goonight Goonight*, featured a law student named John Bannon. Like another amateur thespian, Don Dunstan, he later became a Labor Premier of South Australia and Minister for the Arts.

The cultural atmosphere in South Australia was changing. Musical comedy still seemed more popular than drama, but the achievements of three Adelaide Festivals were having an effect. Adelaide people adopted the phrase 'the Athens of the South' on the grounds of the festivals' innovation and pursuit of excellence, but they retained a huge respect for everything British.

When the South Australian Theatre Company became a statutory body in 1972 its chairman was Colin Ballantyne, the doyen of the dedicated amateurs who had kept theatre alive in Adelaide. The first artistic director was GEORGE OGILVIE. After years of working in a variety of venues, mainly within the University of Adelaide, the company moved into the Playhouse in the ADELAIDE FESTIVAL CENTRE in 1974. It had a steady turnover of artistic directors and it reached a peak of popularity under Colin George, from the United Kingdom, who stayed from 1977 to 1980. It was not until JOHN GADEN was artistic director from 1986 to 1989, that the company, renamed the State Theatre Company of South Australia in 1979, again enjoyed such popularity. JIM SHARMAN, artistic director in 1983–84, received critical acclaim for artistically challenging work. The company was renamed STATE THEATRE in 1994.

Meanwhile some other groups emerged. In 1970 Betty and Don Quin opened the amateur Q Theatre to produce

Joan Bruce from Perth and Hedley Cullen played Mr and Mrs Lusty in the world premiere of The Ham Funeral *by Patrick White. The Adelaide University Theatre Guild staged the play in 1961 after the Adelaide Festival of Arts had rejected it as too difficult for the general public. Audiences and critics acclaimed the production, which was directed by John Tasker. He later directed the guild in two more plays by White*

the plays of Betty Quin and other Australians. Bruno Knez's enterprising La Mama Cellar Theatre had a short life from 1973. In 1976 a group from Salisbury Teachers' College established TROUPE with DAVID ALLEN's production of John Arden's *Serjeant Musgrave's Dance* in a converted building in Angas Street that they named the Red Shed. Troupe was a subsidised left-wing collective. Its work was sometimes too didactic for general taste, but it was noted for presenting the early plays of DAVID ALLEN and DOREEN CLARKE. Troupe's fortunes rose and fell; it expanded to the Unley Town Hall but eventually closed in 1987. A new collective, the RED SHED COMPANY, emerged to work at the Red Shed. It consisted of graduates from the Flinders University Drama Centre and worked under the influence of Julie Holledge, who had come from England to teach at the university. Red Shed presented *Frankenstein's Children* by David Carlin in the 1990 Adelaide Festival.

A third subsidised company, the STAGE COMPANY was established in 1977. At that time local artists had few opportunities for employment by the State Theatre Company of South Australia, so the Stage Company, resident at the Space in the Adelaide Festival Centre, provided a welcome alternative, offering such highlights as *Percy and Rose* by the Adelaide writer ROB GEORGE. It was disbanded in 1986 after the withdrawal of federal and state funding.

Roger Chapman, founder of the MAGPIE THEATRE COMPANY, the theatre-in-education team of State Theatre, created the flagship of Australian youth theatre at CARCLEW YOUTH ARTS CENTRE, an administrative centre which has also become the home of the COME OUT YOUTH ARTS FESTIVAL. Successful theatre groups now active are the PATCH THEATRE COMPANY, UNLEY YOUTH THEATRE, the JUNCTION THEATRE COMPANY and VITALSTATISTIX. The bilingual DOPPIO TEATRO began performing in Italian and English in 1983.

The Independent Theatre Company, led by Rob Croser, and Theatre Exchange, led by Warwick Cooper, have provided good semiprofessional productions of classics in recent years. Adelaide's most avant-garde theatre has come from Nicholas Tsoutas, whose All Out Ensemble performed at the 1982 Adelaide Festival before moving to Sydney. It is always a problem for South Australia that its artists reach a degree of success and then depart for eastern states where larger populations offer more opportunities. David Allen and Betty Quin are other examples. The performing arts now thrive in Adelaide, however. About half the artists State Theatre employs are locals and CHRIS WESTWOOD, a native of Adelaide, returned from Sydney as executive producer in 1993. Women make a strong contribution to theatre in Adelaide and VITALSTATISTIX specialises in women's issues. The Third International Women Playwrights' Conference was held in the city in 1994. At every Adelaide Festival the Fringe edges closer to the limelight as performers beat a path to Adelaide. ❦*Rose Wilson*

further reading
DEPASQUALE, PAUL. *The Writing of Plays in South Australia to 1950*. Adelaide: Pioneer 1977.
FISCHER, GERALD. The professional theatre in Adelaide 1838–1922. *Australian Letters* 2/4 (Adelaide, March 1960).
VAVERE, A. A history of Adelaide Literary/Repertory Theatre. Flinders University (Adelaide) MA thesis 1978.
WARD, PETER. *A Singular Act—Twenty-five years of the State Theatre Company of South Australia*. Adelaide: State Theatre Company/Wakefield Press 1992.

WHITELOCK, DEREK. *Festival!—The story of the Adelaide Festival of Arts*. Adelaide: Derek Whitelock 1980.
WORBY, GUS. A theatre now and then. *From Colonel Light into the Footlights* (ed. Andrew D. McCredie). Adelaide: Pagel 1988.
The Adelaide Theatre Group. *On Stage* (Adelaide) 1/2 (May 1955).
Company of Players. *On Stage* 1/1 (April 1955).
That nice Mr Eliot and his Cocktail Party. *Mary's Own Paper* (Adelaide) October 1960.
A valentine for Ballantyne. *Mary's Own Paper* April 1951.

Adelaide Festival Centre
Performing-arts centre in King William Street, Adelaide. Architect: Hassell Pty Ltd. Includes **Festival Theatre**, opened 1973; **Playhouse** 1974; **Space** 1974; **Amphitheatre** 1977.

The Adelaide Festival Centre has provided an optimal combination of low cost, workability and audience enjoyment. The idea for it emerged in 1960, the year of the first ADELAIDE FESTIVAL OF ARTS, when it became clear that future festivals would need a first-class venue for leading attractions. The Adelaide City Council set up a cultural committee in 1963 to consider the city's needs, and the state government announced that it would join in financing a hall. An act passed in 1964 incorporated the Festival Hall and provided for the council to construct and operate it.

A design was produced in 1965 but inadequate finance delayed the project. There were fundamental objections that the hall could not be used for ballet or opera, and after talks with performing-arts groups the council proposed a multipurpose hall with full stage facilities. A New York consultant, Thomas De Gaetani reviewed the scheme and recommended that a drama theatre, experimental theatre and workshop be attached. The council instructed Hassell Pty Ltd to design a multipurpose theatre, remembering that the project could be extended as proposed.

Building of the Festival Theatre began in 1970 on the northern edge of the central business district, facing Elder Park and the Torrens River. In August 1971 the South Australian Premier, Don Dunstan, announced that the drama theatre and the experimental theatre would be added in a separate building. At the end of 1971 the government and the city council agreed that the ADELAIDE FESTIVAL CENTRE TRUST should be set up to operate the centre.

The Festival Theatre, completed first, is a lyric theatre with a proscenium stage and a fly tower. With a removable orchestra shell and an organ, it is convertible to a concert hall. It seats up to 1978 on three levels. The second stage was the Playhouse and the Space. The Playhouse, seating up to 612 on two levels, has a semi-thrust proscenium stage and a fly tower, with flying over the full stage, including the thrust. The Space is a square, flat-floored flexible space with pull-out bleacher seating for up to about 350 in theatre-in-the-round configuration, and fewer in thrust-stage, corner-stage, or end-stage configuration.

The centre, which cost $21 million, was completed in 1977 with the plaza and the car park. The Playhouse and Space building appears to be connected to the Festival Theatre beneath the plaza. Entrances from car 'drop-off' points here and from the car park are rather bleak, but seem to be the only disadvantages of the centre. In 1978 work began on adding a restaurant, a banqueting room, a brasserie and a piano bar at a cost of $2 million. Allowing for inflation and the lack of a separate concert hall, the cost of the centre, facility for facility, was one-quarter to one-third the cost of the SYDNEY OPERA HOUSE and about half the cost of the VICTORIAN ARTS CENTRE to its second stage.

The Festival Centre functions better than the Sydney Opera House in several ways. There are some disadvantages in attempting to produce an auditorium that can double as lyric theatre and concert hall, such as the Festival Theatre, but it was wise to build a good, large lyric theatre that can be converted to a concert hall by constructing a heavy acoustic shell within the proscenium stage. The acoustic shell can be removed and the proscenium adjusted to the lyric-theatre format within three hours. Reverberation times are changed as required for theatrical or concert modes by positioning acoustic curtains and banners. A 13-tonne pipe organ can be moved to the front of the stage for organ recitals, to the rear for orchestral or choral performances, or backstage for use in an opera. The stage—the largest in Australia until the State Theatre of the Victorian Arts Centre was built—is very workable with ample wing and rear space. The auditorium combines the rectangular plan of a traditional concert hall with the three tiers and side boxes of a traditional theatre.

Intimate theatre

The Playhouse is also cleverly designed, with a wide auditorium crouching over the stage for an intimate actor-audience relationship. The design maximises the combined effectiveness of a thrust stage and a proscenium stage. Stage entrances surmounted by Juliet balconies in front of the proscenium wall on each side permit a performance style approaching that practised in the Georgian, Regency and early Victorian eras.

The Space was the first square, boxlike space built in Australia for experimental or alternative theatre. At 21 metres square it is as large as this type of theatre can be and still have satisfactory acoustics. The room echoed until absorbent banners were hung above the surrounding walkway balcony. Between the Festival Theatre and the Playhouse is the Amphitheatre, an outdoor thrust-stage theatre with stepped seating for 800. An overflow crowd of 400 can be accommodated on the steps and walkways above the Amphitheatre. At the back of the stage there are vine-covered fences, trees and shrubs. On the eastern and southern sides of the two buildings is an open plaza 1·4 hectares in area.

STATE THEATRE is resident in the Playhouse, which is also used annually by Australian Dance Theatre and for a summer comedy season. The Festival Theatre is used by the Australian Broadcasting Corporation for concerts, by the Australian Ballet, and by touring opera and modern-dance companies. The Space is used regularly by the STAGE COMPANY and for alternative-theatre productions from other states, chamber music and children's theatre. The trust also conducts community-arts activities in the Plaza and the Amphitheatre, particularly in summer. ❦*Ross Thorne*

further reading

BROWN, IAN. Adelaide Festival Centre review. *Architecture Australia* 66/5 (November 1977).
SAUNDERS, D. Sense and non-sense at the Adelaide Festival Theatre. *Architecture Australia* 72/6 (December 1973).
WARD, PETER. *A Singular Act*. Adelaide: Wakefield Press 1992.

Adelaide Festival Centre Trust

Set up to manage the ADELAIDE FESTIVAL CENTRE and to encourage the arts in South Australia, the Adelaide Festival Centre Trust has promoted all art forms and offered popular and artistically adventurous programs. The South Australian Parliament legislated in 1971 to establish the trust, which was initially concerned with managing the theatres in the centre. It also oversaw the running of HER MAJESTY'S THEATRE. In 1980 it began co-production, staging the musical *Evita* with Robert Stigwood. Since then it has co-produced musicals with Cameron Mackintosh. The sets for all his major Australian productions have been built at the trust's workshops near Adelaide. The success of commercial ventures such as the musicals *Cats*, *The King and I*, *My Fair Lady* and *The Phantom of the Opera* has increasingly subsidised more specialised productions, the trust's education program and other arts developments. The general managers of the trust have been, successively, ANTHONY STEEL, Kevin Earle and Tim Macfarlane. ❦*Murray Bramwell*

Adelaide Festival of Arts

Biennial festival of arts in Adelaide. Founded 1960. **directors** 1960–64 John Bishop. 1966, 1968 Max Lamshed. 1970 Robert Helpmann. 1972 Louis van Eyssen. 1974, 1978 Anthony Steel. 1980 Christopher Hunt. 1982 Jim Sharman. 1984, 1986 Anthony Steel. 1988 Lord Harewood. 1990 Clifford Hocking. 1992 Rob Brookman. 1994 Christopher Hunt.

A combination of vision, location, benevolent climate, civic layout and services, and intelligent marketing has won the Adelaide Festival of Arts a reputation in Australia and overseas as an influential forum for artists. Held for two or three weeks in March every second year since 1960, the festival has been a force in Australian theatre. It has given local actors opportunities in noteworthy productions of classics by Anton Chekhov, T. S. Eliot, Shakespeare and George Bernard Shaw, given commissions to Australian playwrights, and served as a showcase for readings and performances of works created independently of its patronage. MICHAEL GOW, STEPHEN SEWELL and PATRICK WHITE have written specially for the occasion. The AUSTRALIAN PERFORMING GROUP, the Marli Biyol Company, the MELBOURNE THEATRE COMPANY and the NIMROD THEATRE COMPANY have presented plays by RON BLAIR, ALEX BUZO, JACK DAVIS and JACK HIBBERD, and CIRCUS OZ has maintained a long association with the festival. The festival has also encouraged public discussion on the status and significance of the arts in Australia and elsewhere.

Its influence on South Australia is equally important, financially, aesthetically and professionally. STATE THEATRE is now central to any program. This company is said to have come of age with festival productions by Colin George of Sophocles's *Oedipus the King* in 1978 and the Wakefield mystery plays in 1980. Smaller companies have contributed since 1970 to the main program, to the unofficial Fringe from 1960 to 1975 or to the partially funded Focus since 1975. The ADELAIDE FESTIVAL CENTRE, opened in 1973–74, permanently expresses the commitment of South Australia, which styles itself 'the Festival State', to promoting the arts. This complex of indoor and outdoor theatres, galleries and restaurants caters for all kinds of cultural activities. It gave the festival a much-needed focal point and helped to subdue criticism of venues—from university campus to agricultural showgrounds—that had not done justice to theatrical or musical performances. It set a standard and precedent for new arts and entertainment centres.

The 1994 festival attracted 118 299 attendances for 344 performances of 34 events involving 951 artists from 15 countries. Forty-two works were given their first Australian performance. Adelaide Festival Inc. gained income of $8·5 million, including grants of $3·5 million, and spent $8·7 million. By contrast, £45 000 was raised for the first festival in 1960 in private pledges, through public appeal and by civic, state and federal government grants to guarantee some 74 performances to 340 000 patrons. The South Australian government, the federal government through the Australia Council and other agencies, and the Adelaide City Council and Corporation of the City of Adelaide are the principal supporters of the festival. The guarantee system lapsed in 1980 and since then events have been 'sold' to sponsors, and they are shared with other festivals.

The Adelaide Festival resulted from discussions between John Bishop, professor of music at the University of Adelaide, and Sir Lloyd Dumas, managing director of the *Advertiser* newspaper. Their idealism and enterprise satisfied a long-felt civic need for recognition, development and cultural contact with a wider world, and Europe in particular. The first festival was staffed primarily by volunteers. Bishop served as honorary director, responsible, like all later directors, to a board of governors. He was supported by 90 persons on 14 committees, and by the administrator of the Edinburgh Festival, Ian Hunter, on secondment. Until 1994 membership of the board was attained by ministerial recommendation with the endorsement of the board. Now membership is by ministerial appointment on the recommendation of the Department for the Arts and Cultural Development, after public advertisement.

When Bishop died in 1964, he had assured the festival's future and seen the emergence of now-familiar features—promotion of a range of cultures, commitment to outdoor popular performance and parades, a fringe, overseas press coverage and controversy. This last aspect emerged with the board's rejections of Alan Seymour's THE ONE DAY OF THE YEAR in 1960 and Patrick White's THE HAM FUNERAL in 1962. Struggles between boards, administrators, directors and press over artistic policy, censorship and expenditure became a feature in themselves until the early 1980s.

Growth of the Fringe
The Fringe, never an official part of the festival, is also partly funded by the state and federal governments. Since 1988 it has had a home in the Living Arts Centre. It has developed in response to a need for flexible and unrestricted programming and taken on a life of its own, providing fairly cheap, often untried but exciting alternative entertainment. There is no selection for the Fringe. Participants find their own venues and audiences and register with the Focus organisation, which promotes the overall event. The Fringe begins with a street party a week before the festival and accentuates popular and particularly Australian entertainment—with a dash of imported brilliance. Fringe performances are to be found in the smaller theatres, clubs, converted spaces and open-air venues throughout the city.

The popularity of the Fringe has increased as the festival's costs and prices have risen. In 1994 booking schedules and attendances for the Fringe compared so favourably with those of the festival proper that there was debate about the roles and prospects of the two events. Their administrators and directors insist that they are complementary.

Since 1960 ten directors or administrators have directed 18 Adelaide Festivals. They have favoured five different approaches to programming. Bishop built cultural 'bridges'. ROBERT HELPMANN and Lord Harewood promoted high art. ANTHONY STEEL successfully championed experiment and eclecticism. Christopher Hunt tried to reconcile old and new cultures. JIM SHARMAN made what he saw as a personal and collective attempt to reconcile residual Eurocentrism with a growing need to redefine 'home' and to the build an appropriate new civilisation in a land that both fascinated and repelled its immigrants. In the process he contrived a watershed festival that questioned the canons of taste and tolerance in almost all art forms.

Successful festivals have followed most of the principles outlined by Bishop and Steel: break new ground, look to present trends, use criticism wisely, be sure of artistic focus, lead by example, encourage local artists, appeal to a cross-section of patrons but not to everyone. The last criterion has provoked debate and charges of elitism. Theatregoers have come to expect variety of fare and achievement from both local and imported productions. They look for a balance between acknowledged centrepieces, experiments, folk or traditional performances and popular theatre. Solo performances have also proved attractive. More recently, thematic festivals have been attempted. Rob Brookman's 'big issues' Eastern Europe festival in its way marked the fall of the Berlin wall. In 1994 Christopher Hunt presented an Asian festival, with a purpose-built Open Roof performance space next to the Festival Centre in Elder Park.

Local companies provided features of early festivals, especially the ADELAIDE UNIVERSITY THEATRE GUILD with Eliot's *Murder in the Cathedral* in 1960 and Shaw's *Saint Joan* in 1962. The Black Theatre of Prague performed at the festival in 1964 and JUDITH ANDERSON gave problematic recitals from *Macbeth* and Euripides's *Medea* in 1966. Influential ROYAL SHAKESPEARE COMPANY productions of *The Winter's Tale* and *Twelfth Night* marked 1970, when there was an increase in the number of large-scale imported productions. In later years this policy has yielded the Kabuki and Noh Theatres from Japan in 1978 and 1983 respectively, Peter Brook's open-air productions of *Conference of the Birds* in 1980 and the night-long *Mahabarata* in 1988, Pina Bausch's provocative *Kontakthof* and *Blue Beard* in 1982, Macunaima from Brazil in 1984, and brilliant adaptations of Bertolt Brecht and Shakespeare from Georgia's Shota Rustaveli Company in 1986. This trend continued in 1992 with Hungary's Katona Joseph Theatre in *The Governor General* and the State Theatre of Lithuania production of Anton Chekhov's *Uncle Vanya*.

The range of cultural and creative influences over three decades is suggested by experimental works such as Cricot 2's *The Dead Class* in 1978 and Jan Fabre's *The Power of Theatrical Madness* in 1986; the mesmeric *bhuto* dance of Sankai Juku from Japan in 1988; the political force of Athol Fugard's plays in 1976 and *Bopha* by the Earth Players of Johannesburg in 1988; the vibrancy and charm of Raun

Raun, Papua New Guinea's folk opera company from Goroka, in 1984; and the Vietnamese Water Puppets in 1988. The return of the Bunraku Puppet Theatre from Japan in 1994 after 20 years and the inclusion of Circus Archaos in 1990 and the Japanese performance-art group Dumb Type in 1994 continued the juxtaposition of traditional and contemporary experimental art. In response stands the work of Australian artists such as the directors NEIL ARMFIELD, Teresa Crea, Glenn Elston, JIM SHARMAN and JOHN TASKER; the actors ROBYN ARCHER, JOHN BELL, EDWIN HODGEMAN, EVELYN KRAPE, ROBYN NEVIN, DENNIS OLSEN, PETER O'SHAUGHNESSY and Carol Skinner; the playwrights Roger Bennett, ROB GEORGE, Paul Kelly, PETER KENNA and Sally Morgan, the solo performer REG LIVERMORE; and pioneering companies such as AUSTRALIAN NOUVEAU THEATRE, the Australian Performing Group, DOPPIO TEATRO, Nimrod, the RED SHED COMPANY and Thalia. Designers from STANISLAUS OSTOJA-KOTKOWSKI to STEPHEN CURTIS, Mary Moore, Mark Thompson and BRIAN THOMSON have also made their mark. ❦*Gus Worby*

further reading
McCREDIE, ANDREW D. (ed.). *From Colonel Light into the Footlights*. Adelaide: Pagel 1988.
SYMONS, CHRISTOPHER. *John Bishop—A life for music*. Melbourne: Hyland House 1989.
WHITELOCK, DEREK. *Festival!—The story of the Adelaide Festival of Arts*. Adelaide: Derek Whitelock 1980.

Adelaide Repertory Theatre

Amateur dramatic society in Adelaide, founded in 1908 at Elder Conservatorium as Bryceson Treharne's Class. Renamed Adelaide Literary Theatre 1910, Adelaide Repertory Theatre 1911. **venues** 1916–22 Unley Town Hall, Walkerville Hall, Queen's Hall, Victoria Hall, King's Theatre and Tivoli Theatre. 1923–29 Victoria Hall. 1930–63 Australia Theatre and Tivoli Theatre. 1963– Arts Theatre. **first productions** *The Man of Destiny* by George Bernard Shaw and *The Land of Heart's Desire* by W. B. Yeats, 24 September 1908 at Elder Conservatorium. **landmark productions** *Colonel Light—The Founder* by Max Afford. *Faust* by Johann von Goethe. *I Killed the Count* by Alec Coppel. *Interval* by Sumner Locke Elliott. *The Lilies of the Field* by Hastings Turner. *Major Barbara* by Shaw. *The Touch of Silk* by Betty Roland. *The Wind and the Rain* by Merton Hodge.

One of the oldest theatrical organisations in Australia had its origin in 1902, when BRYCESON TREHARNE, a 23-year-old Welsh piano teacher at the Elder Conservatorium, gathered a group of students interested in singing, literature and drama. This group, known as Bryceson Treharne's Class, in 1908 mounted its first productions before an audience, which was asked to pay sixpence for a program to assist in defraying expenses. It performed at the conservatorium, in a hall that had no real stage equipment and was little better than a large room. Sets and visual effects were difficult to obtain and the players had to rely on the text and merits of the plays.

In 1910 the group called itself Adelaide Literary Theatre, after Irish Literary Theatre in Dublin, and gave its first production in the Walkerville Hall. One of the plays was John Galsworthy's *The Silver Box*. In 1911 Adelaide Literary Theatre produced *The Woman Tamer* by LOUIS ESSON and *The Web of Steel* by Wilfred Neill. Treharne left Australia in 1911, and the group became Adelaide Repertory Theatre. It felt Treharne's influence for many decades in its concern for serious drama, though it was not experimental. In November 1924 Royston Marcus directed Hastings Turner's *The Lilies of the Field* in the Victoria Hall and later in the month radio 5DN broadcast the production—the first three-act play broadcast in South Australia. One of the society's greatest adventures was a large-scale production of Goethe's *Faust* in 1934, directed by THEO SHALL, a visiting J. C. Williamson's star.

Adelaide Repertory Theatre has consistently encouraged Australian playwrights, holding competitions and producing plays by established and new writers. Those whose work the group produced up to 1950 included MAX AFFORD, Catherine Brownhill, ALEC COPPEL, DYMPHNA CUSACK, HENRIETTA DRAKE-BROCKMAN, SUMNER LOCKE ELLIOTT, FRANK HARVEY, BETTY ROLAND, Alex Somerville and Alex Symons. In 1963 the society built its own Arts Theatre at a cost of £45 000, on land it owned in the city centre. It still performs a yearly program, usually of five plays. ❦*Thelma Afford*

further reading
VAVERE, A. *A history of Adelaide Literary/Repertory Theatre*. Flinders University (Adelaide) MA thesis 1978.

Adelaide Theatre Group

Amateur dramatic company, founded in 1946 by Francis Flanagan, Margaret Day, Douglas Calder and Lewis Burgess. Closed 1984. **venues** 1946–62 various. 1963–84 Sheridan Theatre. **directors** 1946–58 Francis Flanagan. 1963–72 Colin Ballantyne. 1980–83 Doug Leonard. **first production** *No Triangle This* by Douglas Calder, 1946 in Stow Hall. Designer: Jacqueline Hick. Director: Phyllis Orphel. **landmark productions** *The Night of the Iguana* by Tennessee Williams, 1964. *Three Sisters* by Anton Chekhov, 1966 Adelaide Festival. *Macbird* by Barbara Garson, 1968 Adelaide Festival. *Pacific Rape* by Colin Ballantyne, 1970. *Jack the Ripper* by Ron Pember and Dennis Di Marne, 1977.

During the decade from 1963 the Adelaide Theatre Group enjoyed high achievement and popularity in the intimate and unconventional Sheridan Theatre in North Adelaide. Experimenting in form and content, it became the wellspring for professional theatre in Adelaide. The group opened in 1946 with a comedy by Douglas Calder, one of its members, although it was established to present plays written or translated from French by South Australians. French theatre was the particular interest of Francis Flanagan, the principal early director and designer.

On 20 July 1960 the Adelaide Theatre Group came to national attention when it presented the premiere of Alan Seymour's *THE ONE DAY OF THE YEAR*, after its controversial rejection by the Adelaide Festival board. JEAN MARSHALL directed the production. In 1963 the group converted a colonial house in North Adelaide into the Sheridan Theatre. It was intimate and flexible, without fixed seating, and the audience often sat at tables. The group opened at the Sheridan with *Trio in Gunshot*, three one-act plays written for the occasion by COLIN BALLANTYNE, who became the major director at that time. The group's repertoire was solidly advanced, if not avant-garde: new English, American and European plays and some Australian works.

The 1960s were the group's most fruitful period and by 1980 it had largely dispersed. Doug Leonard attempted to revive it over the next three years with productions of

Shakespeare and other classics, but problems associated with the Sheridan Theatre defeated him and the Adelaide Theatre Group ceased to exist in 1984. Well-known actors who worked for it included RON HADDRICK, ALEXANDER HAY and EDWIN HODGEMAN. In the early days leading local painters such as WLADYSLAW DUTKIEWICZ, Doug Roberts and Jeffrey Smart designed the sets. ❧*Jo Peoples*

Adelaide University Theatre Guild

Amateur dramatic company, founded in 1938 by staff of University of Adelaide. **venues** 1938–58 Little Hut. 1958– Union Hall. **first production** *Prelude and Fugue* by Clifford Bax, *Fame and the Poet* by Lord Dunsany and *The Dark Lady of the Sonnets* by George Bernard Shaw, 28 September 1938 in Little Hut. **landmark productions** *The Ham Funeral* by Patrick White, 1961. *The Season at Sarsaparilla* by Patrick White, 1962. *Night on Bald Mountain* by Patrick White, 1964.

The Adelaide University Theatre Guild was established not as an undergraduate group but as 'an amateur group with a university tie-up' aimed at cultural improvement. From the start its membership was a mixture of professionals and amateurs and it received financial assistance from the university. Its object was 'the study of drama, through the practice of the arts and crafts of the theatre … The activities would be play-reading and study, the acting and producing of plays, design of stage settings and costumes, also the study of radio technique'. In 1938 radio drama was a new art form, which many diehards barely recognised. The guild began playing in September 1938 in the Little Hut, a timber hall with a platform stage at one end. Members converted the platform into a workable stage and added dressing rooms, make-up rooms, shower and toilet. The guild used the hall until 1958, when it moved into a new theatre on campus, the Union Hall.

The guild's repertoire stretched from Greek drama to contemporary overseas and Australian plays. During its first year the eurhythmics specialist Heather Gell and Frank Johnston directed John Masefield's poetic drama *The Coming of Christ*. 'It was an appropriate play for the guild to express their policy of combining all the arts of the theatre', said a critic in the *Advertiser* on 29 November. True to this aim, the first year's program included ballet, films, an opera, singing, poetry readings and instrumental music as well as drama.

Professor Innes Stewart was the president and other board members included Professor E. Harold Davies of the Elder Conservatorium, Heather Gell, Dr Charles Fenner, and Eugene McLaughlin and Thomas Campbell, academics who also designed stage sets and lighting for other amateur groups.

In the 1960s the guild formed an association with the AUSTRALIAN ELIZABETHAN THEATRE TRUST to present semi-professional productions of plays by Patrick White—*THE HAM FUNERAL* in 1961, *THE SEASON AT SARSAPARILLA* in 1962 and *Night on Bald Mountain* in 1964, together with Bertolt Brecht's *The Good Woman of Setzuan* in 1962 and Sophocles's *Oedipus Rex* in 1963. The association, under the guidance of the chairman of the guild, Harry Medlin, led to the Trust creating the South Australian Theatre Company in 1965 with JOHN TASKER as its first director. In the late 1970s the guild produced *Romeo and Juliet*, *A Midsummer Night's Dream*, Brecht's *The Caucasian Chalk Circle* and Ödön von Horváth's *Tales from the Vienna Woods*. It still produces plays in the Union Hall. ❧*Thelma Afford*

Max Afford

Dramatist. Born 12 April 1906 in Adelaide. Journalist until 1932. Involved in amateur theatre in Adelaide. Wrote radio plays and serials and adapted many stage plays, 1929–54. Won Adelaide *Advertiser* play competition 1936. Moved to Sydney for ABC 1936. Died 1954 in Sydney. Husband of designer Thelma Afford.

During the 1940s, when Max Afford was the foremost writer of commercial radio serials in Australia, he diligently wrote stage plays and had commercial successes at a time when it was almost unknown for an Australian management to produce a local play. At the Theatre Royal in Sydney in 1944 J. C. WILLIAMSON'S produced his comedy-thriller *LADY IN DANGER* and his *Mischief in the Air*, a comedy set in Sydney commercial radio. *Lady in Danger* was also presented in New York City in 1944. In 1947 INDEPENDENT THEATRE in Sydney presented Afford's *AWAKE MY LOVE*, a rewriting of his *Colonel Light—The Founder*, which won the Adelaide *Advertiser*'s first prize for a play to celebrate the centenary of South Australia in 1936. His last play, *Dark Enchantment*, was produced at the MINERVA THEATRE in Sydney in 1949, and in 1950 it began a tour in England. ❧*Richard Lane*

published plays
Awake My Love (1947). Brisbane: University of Queensland Press 1974.
Lady in Danger (1942). Sydney: Mulga Press 1944.
Mischief in the Air (1944). Brisbane: University of Queensland Press 1974.

further reading
TOLLEY, MICHAEL J. Malcolm (Max) Afford. *Australian Dictionary of Biography* 13. Melbourne University Press 1994.

reference
The Max and Thelma Afford Collection in the Fryer Library at the University of Queensland (Brisbane) contains many of Max Afford's plays and other writings and his press books.

Thelma Afford

Actor, designer. Born 1 December 1908 at Broken Hill (NSW). Originally Thelma Thomas. Trained in art in Adelaide. First worked as designer with Ab Intra Studio Theatre (Adelaide). Designed costumes for commemorative pageants in Melbourne 1934, Adelaide 1936 and Sydney 1938. Worked in Sydney from 1937. Designed costumes for Independent Theatre (Sydney) 1941–47. Designer at Minerva Theatre (Sydney) 1946–49. Also designed for film and television. Secondary school art teacher 1955–78. Married to dramatist Max Afford.

Adelaide's avant-garde AB-INTRA STUDIO THEATRE, celebrated for its strikingly original Oriental and symbolic visual effects was the major early influence upon Thelma Afford. She worked as actor and designer during the company's short life. At a time when the professional theatre automatically imported setting and costume designs, she received three major commissions—for the Melbourne centennial pageant in 1934, three Adelaide centennial pageants and Max Afford's play *Colonel Light—The Founder* in 1936, and the main NSW sesquicentennial pageants in Sydney in 1938. In the style of the time, the costumes were historical or spectacular symbols of the produce of the celebrating states. In 1938 she married Afford and settled in Sydney.

She designed costumes for INDEPENDENT THEATRE productions, including Max Afford's AWAKE MY LOVE, The Insect Play by Karel and Josef Capek, and The Little Round House. As resident designer at the MINERVA THEATRE she designed costumes and decor for Dark Enchantment by Max Afford, Ah, Wilderness! by Eugene O'Neill and other plays. She designed the costumes for the pantomime Cinderella at the Elizabethan Theatre in Sydney in 1957. She was costume designer for several early ABC television productions of plays, including J. M. Barrie's The Twelve Pound Look in 1956, the first play on Australian television. ❦Leslie Rees

reference
Three libraries hold major collections of Thelma Afford's designs. The Mortlock Library (Adelaide) has 90, the Mitchell Library (Sydney) has 200 and the Fryer Library of the University of Queensland (Brisbane) has 200 in the Max and Thelma Afford Collection, together with a lengthy manuscript in which she describes Adelaide amateur theatre in the 1930s.

Agents

As Australian theatre and film have grown since 1960s so have the number and influence of agents who nurture and guide the creative lives of artists. Agents are essential in any sophisticated theatre and film industry and they depend upon its success. They involve themselves in a blend of art, business and diplomacy. Successful artists' agents agree that their relationship with their clients must necessarily be close. Many of them have had experience in some aspect of film or theatre production, while the various backgrounds of others include the legal profession.

Agents advise clients on all matters regarding advancement of their careers. They seek work for them, negotiate terms and conditions, and promote clients and their work within the industry and to the public. The final decision on any career move ultimately rests with the client, however. While the Media, Entertainment and Arts Alliance and the AUSTRALIAN WRITERS' GUILD continue to negotiate basic minimum terms and conditions that benefit theatrical workers generally, agents have achieved new standards for artists at the top of the profession. These benefits flow down to colleagues. Before the First World War entrepreneurs mounted big productions with overseas stars whom they treated well, and many stars were happy to negotiate their own contracts. Others were represented by agents in the USA or England. The players of smaller parts had to work their way up through the ranks of the industry.

By the 1930s there were agents resembling today's booking agents. They usually came from the theatre and took on small stables of performers. Agents would represent only working actors and they operated on a system of giving and owing favours to producers. By providing a small act cheaply an agent could seek better conditions for another client. The main employment opportunities were in radio and revue, and there were small parts in big productions mounted by J. C. WILLIAMSON'S and other entrepreneurs. Agents were responsible for improvements in actors' and playwrights' conditions, including reasonable billing, royalties, options and buy-out clauses. Agents and actors were known to gather at certain pubs and restaurants. In Sydney the Criterion Hotel, on the corner of Pitt and Park Streets—better known as POVERTY POINT—was a particular favourite.

Ted James and Bill Sadler were busy agents in Sydney and BRETT RANDALL operated in Melbourne.

In the early 1960s Gloria Payten, who was casting films for overseas production companies, recognised that Australian actors desperately needed professional representation. She set up the International Casting Service in Sydney in 1962 with a stable of about 40 actors. Faith Martin began representing actors in the mid-1960s with Martin Artists. Bill Shanahan joined her in 1976 to form Martin and Shanahan, which became Shanahan Management in 1979. Today this company represents more than 150 actors working in theatre, film and television, as well as writers, directors and choreographers. Other highly regarded Sydney agencies representing chiefly actors include Barbara Leane and Associates (founded in 1980), Kevin Palmer Management (1983) and Robyn Gardiner (1984). Each includes directors and other theatre and film personnel on its books.

The London literary agency Curtis Brown foresaw an expansion in Australian writing and in 1971 established an office in Sydney under Peter Gross. Tim Curnow took over the branch in 1976. Most of the agency's clients are novelists but it also represents playwrights and screenwriters.

Hilary Linstead and Liz Mullinar set up the consultancy M and L Casting in 1970, casting large-scale theatrical productions and films. When the directors of the NIMROD THEATRE COMPANY, John Bell and Richard Wherrett, asked Linstead to consider representing RON BLAIR and other emerging playwrights in Sydney the first agency in Australia to represent production personnel was established. With directors and designers also increasingly requesting representation, the agency arm of M and L expanded. In 1985 Linstead set up Hilary Linstead and Associates. The clientele has widened to include composers, choreographers, script editors, cinematographers and entertainers as well as writers, designers and directors.

Jane Cameron, intending to develop a more eclectic agency than those already established, began Cameron's Management in 1976, with eight models, one actor and one theatre director. It now represents high-fashion models, directors, composers and opera singers. Cameron and the literary agent Rose Creswell merged in 1991 to create a second company, the Cameron Creswell Agency, which manages scriptwriters, authors, designers and directors. Other Sydney agencies representing a variety of theatrical personnel and writers are Anthony A. Williams Management, William Street Management, Hickson Associates and Rick Raftos Management.

In Melbourne the existence of Crawford Productions, which began to provide work in television for actors in the early 1960s, stimulated the establishment of agencies. Theatrical companies, however, resisted working through agents, believing they would ultimately push up artists' fees. Frances McDonald (not the present writer) set up an early agency, Frog Promotions, in 1965. It was followed soon afterwards by Woods Theatrical Agency, now Barbara Gange Management. Both represent actors working in theatre, film and television. Active Casting has diversified into the management of bands and celebrities, and owns a recording studio and a record label. Since it was formed in 1966 it has changed hands three times and now incorporates Selective Artists Management. John Timlin founded the Almost Managing Company in 1981. He began representing MAX GILLIES and other performers who lost their usual avenues of work when the AUSTRALIAN PERFORMING GROUP closed. He also took on JOHN ROMERIL and other playwrights who had been in the group. The result was a company renowned for initiating projects to exploit the skills of specific clients. Performers' Management was set up in 1984 in association with Hocking and Woods, owners of the Universal Theatre in Melbourne. It handles only writers, actors, composers and conductors. Other well-known Melbourne agents include MAM (established in 1972), the Actors' Agency (1980) and Stacey Testro Management (1985), which has branches in NSW and New Zealand. These agents primarily represent actors but have directors, writers and singers as clients from time to time.

Outside Sydney and Melbourne, agencies have arisen because increased government and private investment in film production and the establishment of studios in Queensland, South Australia and Western Australia have created a need for artists to have local representation. Agents in these states must still diversify their operations to run profitably and they tend to combine agency and casting services. In Adelaide Anne Peters is one of the best-known agents and in Perth the largest is an offshoot of Melbourne's Frog Promotions. There are also a few agents, such as HARRY M. MILLER and Peter Rix Management in Sydney, who specialise in managing conspicuous media personalities, taking care of their business and professional affairs and their public image. ❦*Frances McDonald*

W. M. Akhurst

Critic, dramatist. Born 29 December 1822. Wrote two stage pieces in London. Arrived in Adelaide 1849. Worked as journalist. Moved to Melbourne as music and drama critic of *Herald* 1853. Wrote 40 known stage pieces, usually containing music, to 1869. Returned to London 1870. Wrote 16 more theatre pieces. Died 6 June 1878, aboard ship bound for Melbourne.

The outstanding pioneer of professional writing for the colonial theatre was William Mower Akhurst. In 20 years in Australia, working principally in Melbourne, he established the practicability of his profession by writing at least 40 stage pieces—pantomimes, burlesques, musical farces, some dramas and an operetta. Most of his abundant output was 'localisation'—adaptations or translations of foreign works. Much of his work involved arranging or writing material for musical artists, and he himself composed songs for specific performers. Akhurst's first plays in Melbourne were musical farces for Sydney Nelson and GEORGE BUCKINGHAM and their families. In 1854 Akhurst collaborated with F. M. SOUTTEN in a topical farce, *The Battle of Melbourne*. He provided a vehicle for GEORGE COPPIN's parodies and impersonations, including *Coppin in Cairo*, in 1858. *We've Taken Gardiner* in 1862 was a forerunner of many bushranger farces featuring comically incompetent police.

Akhurst began writing pantomimes at least as early as 1855, and he steadily produced them—all with strong topical interest—until he left Melbourne. He provided *Harlequin Valentine and Orson* for the actors Sir William and Lady Don in 1861 and *The Last of the Ogres* for Lady Don in 1864. He devised *Harlequin Arabian Nights* for W. S. LYSTER's Royal English and Italian Opera Company in 1862. Many of Akhurst's pantomimes, culminating in *Tom Tom, the Piper's Son* in 1867, advocated free, secular and compulsory education, which came to Victoria in 1873. *Gulliver on his Travels* in 1866 was an original script. Like *Harlequin Jack Sheppard* of 1869, it indicates ingenious comic staging with circus routines, flying effects and sight gags. Akhurst concentrated on local content in *Harlequin Robinson Crusoe* in 1868. He developed this trend in 1869 in *The House that Jack Built*, an original pantomime with an allegorical plot that perhaps provided a model for GARNET WALCH's *Australia Felix*. The use of local themes became common at that time.

Akhurst's first-long-running burlesque was an adaptation of F. C. Burnand's *Ixion*, starring TILLY EARLE and John Dunn. It ran initially for 47 performances at the Princess's Theatre in Melbourne in 1866, but was outrun by a lavish production of Akhurst's own *Paris the Prince and Helen the Fair* at the Theatre Royal in 1868. Later it toured country districts and it was retitled *The Siege of Troy*. *King Arthur* in 1868 was the farewell to the stage of Marian Dunn, Marcus Clarke's wife. These burlesques, with *The Battle of Hastings* in 1869, established a strong taste in Melbourne for extravagant musical theatre. In the mid-1860s Akhurst provided operatic burlesques for a blackface troupe called Christy's Minstrels. He adapted the libretto of Jacques Offenbach's 1859 *opéra-bouffe Un Mari à la porte* for performance in Melbourne in 1868 as *The Wrong Side of the Door*.

Hippodrama was another early interest of Akhurst. He wrote *The Battle of Inkermann* in 1855 for George Lewis's Royal Amphitheatre in Melbourne. It was not performed there but was eventually performed as an equestrian spectacle titled *The Fall of Sebastopol* at the Theatre Royal in 1857. On his return to London Akhurst provided equestrian spectacles for 'Lord' George Sanger at the former Astley's Amphitheatre. The only other dramatic piece he had performed was *The Poor of Melbourne*, an adaptation of Dion Boucicault's *The Poor of New York*, in 1863. ❦*Veronica Kelly*

published plays

The Battle of Hastings—or, The Duke, the Earl, the Witch, the Why and the Wherefore burlesque (1869). Melbourne: Bell 1869.

Gulliver on his Travels—or, Harlequin Old Father Christmas and the Fairy Queen of the Silver Acacias pantomime (1866). Melbourne: Abbott 1866.

Harlequin Jack Sheppard—or, The Disreputable Detective, the Clever Kleptomaniac, and the Plot of the Piebald Goblin pantomime (1869). Melbourne: Abbott 1869.

Harlequin Robinson Crusoe—or, The Nimble Naiad, the Lonely Squatter and the Lively Aboriginal pantomime (1868). Melbourne: Bell 1868.

The House that Jack Built—or, Harlequin Progress and the Loves, Laughs, Laments and Labours of Jack Melbourne and Little Victoria pantomime (1869). Melbourne: Cordell 1869.

King Arthur—or, Lancelot the Goose, Gin-ever the Square and the Nights of the Round Table and Other Furniture burlesque extravaganza (1868). Melbourne: Bell 1868.

Paris the Prince and Helen the Fair—or, The Giant Horse and the Siege of Troy burlesque extravaganza, also known as *The Siege of Troy* (1868). Melbourne: Bell 1869.

Tom Tom, the Piper's Son, and Mary Mary Quite Contrary—or, Harlequin Piggy Wiggy and the Good Child's History of England pantomime (1867). Melbourne: Bell 1867.

further reading

IRVIN, ERIC. Nineteenth-century English dramatists in Australia. *Theatre Notebook* 30/1 (London, 1976).

RICHARDSON, PAUL. Harlequin in the Antipodes. *Southerly* 42/2 (Sydney, June 1982).

John Alden

Actor, director. Born 1907 near Taree (NSW). Originally Gordon Buchanan. Schoolteacher for ten years. Played in 12 Independent Theatre productions in Sydney 1934–37. Worked in stock companies, repertory and Old Vic Theatre Company in England from 1937. Leading radio actor in Sydney during Second World War. Played to allied forces in Japan after war. Produced Shakespeare for Independent Theatre 1948–50. Formed John Alden Company in Sydney 1950. Turned company professional and toured all states 1952–53. Acted and directed for Independent Theatre 1957–59. Artistic director of J. C. Williamson Shakespeare Company 1959–60. Gave Shakespeare season for Australian Elizabethan Theatre Trust in 1961. Died 1962 in Sydney.

The last Australian actor-manager in the Victorian tradition, John Alden founded the first indigenous classical company to tour Australia since the ALLAN WILKIE SHAKESPEAREAN COMPANY in the 1920s. The unsubsidised JOHN ALDEN COMPANY gave Shakespeare seasons in capital cities in 1952 for professional managements. Drive and ambition enabled Alden to convince these organisations and private guarantors to sponsor the professional development of the company. It provided impetus for the establishment of the AUSTRALIAN ELIZABETHAN THEATRE TRUST in 1954.

Alden thought of forming a permanent company to present Shakespeare when he returned to Australia after playing to occupation forces in Japan. His first production was *Measure for Measure* on 1 December 1948 in Sydney for INDEPENDENT THEATRE, for which he had acted before the Second World War. *The Merry Wives of Windsor*, *The Tempest*, *The Winter's Tale* and *The Merchant of Venice* followed. In 1950, he moved the company to St James Hall and called it the John Alden Company.

Alden was volatile, autocratic and impatient and his style of direction was simple and direct. His most imaginative production was *The Tempest* for Independent Theatre in 1949. He was a clever actor, at his best when he could draw upon his intellectual rather than emotional resources. His style suited rich villainy and conspiracy better than roles that required emotional depth and veracity. In April 1955, he appeared in *My Three Angels* by Sam and Bella Spewack for J. C. WILLIAMSON'S in Sydney and Melbourne. He was invited to play Creon in Euripides's *Medea* by the Trust. On the first night of the Melbourne season, 20 December 1955, he suffered a heart attack and was forced to withdraw from the national tour. Alden returned to Independent Theatre in February 1957 to direct James Bridie's *Tobias and the Angel*. In April he directed a revival of *The Merchant of Venice*, with Owen Weingott as Shylock. Next year he directed and played the title-role in *Titus Andronicus*, his first new production since 1953. In 1959 he directed and played in a revival of *A Midsummer Night's Dream* for Independent Theatre in March and he was artistic director of the J. C. Williamson Shakespeare Company, which toured *King Lear*, *A Midsummer Night's Dream* and *The Winter's Tale*. Alden shared the leading roles with the Scottish actor John Laurie and PETER O'SHAUGHNESSY.

In July and August 1961, Alden's Shakespeare Productions Ltd, assisted by the Trust, presented *Othello*, *The Merchant of Venice* and *Macbeth* in the First Sydney Shakespeare Festival, at the Elizabethan Theatre, the NSW State Conservatorium of Music and the Orpheum cinema in Cremorne. Among actors who worked with Alden were RUTH CRACKNELL, RON GRAHAM, JOHN MEILLON, DINAH SHEARING, LEONARD TEALE and the present writer. ❦*Malcolm Robertson*

further reading
BRISBANE, KATHARINE (ed.). *Entertaining Australia*. Sydney: Currency Press 1991.
FITTON, DORIS. *Not Without Dust and Heat*. Sydney: Harper and Row 1981.
RICKARD, JOHN. John Alden. *Australian Dictionary of Biography* 13. Melbourne University Press 1994.

All for Gold

—*or, Fifty Millions of Money*. Play in three acts by F. R. C. Hopkins from *Le Juif errant*, novel by Eugène Sue. **premiere** 10 March 1877, Royal Victoria Theatre, Sydney. Cast: Mr Alexander, Mr Bartlett, Alfred Dampier, Lily Dampier, Rose Dampier, B. N. Jones, Mr Seagrave. Director: Alfred Dampier.

The actor-manager ALFRED DAMPIER launched his reputation as the major supporter of Australian dramatists when he took *All for Gold* into his repertoire. It was the first of five plays by F. R. C. HOPKINS that he staged. Dampier had just set up his own company and was looking for starring roles for himself and his little daughters Lily and Rose. Hopkins obligingly dramatised parts of Eugène Sue's popular 32-year-old novel about the Wandering Jew—although the Jew himself was rendered irrelevant to the plot.

Dampier played Dagobert, an old soldier entrusted with taking a general's two young daughters to Paris, where they are due to inherit a fortune if they appear at the reading of a will. Dagobert's 'honesty of purpose and indomitable courage' overcome the obstacles of a Mafia-like secret society, a double-dealing lion tamer and a character known only as 'the Thug'. The play was staged with great care and remarkably fine ensemble acting, said the *Sydney Mail* on 17 March 1877. The acting of nine-year-old LILY DAMPIER was central to the initial success of the play. Dampier presented it in Australia, New Zealand and the USA in 1877 and in England in 1878. He was still dusting it off—with new child actors—as late as 1892. ❦*Richard Fotheringham*

reference
A script of *All for Gold* is in the Lord Chamberlain's collection in the British Library (London).

Allan Wilkie Shakespearean Company

Professional touring dramatic company, founded in 1920 by Allan Wilkie. Disbanded 11 October 1930. **first production** *Macbeth*, 11 September 1920, at Princess Theatre, Melbourne.

The first permanent touring Shakespeare company in Australia, the Allan Wilkie Shakespearean Company visited every state over a decade. ALLAN WILKIE officially launched the company with *Macbeth* in Melbourne in 1920 and then took *Macbeth* and six other plays on tour to Adelaide, Sydney, Hobart and various country towns. In Sydney it played in the Grand Opera House. Wilkie had previously produced Shakespeare for its lessee, GEORGE MARLOW. In 1921 the company made its first full-scale tour of Australia and New Zealand, visiting all the capitals and many other towns. It often found its greatest support in towns where Shakespeare and legitimate drama were not commonly seen. Wilkie wanted to popularise Shakespeare, and his company generally performed in a broad style, emphasising the low comedy in *Henry V*, for example, and frequently employing traditional stage business. The productions pivoted on Wilkie and his wife Frediswyde Hunter-Watts. Scenes would be cut and rearranged to ensure a curtain line for Wilkie's character.

Critics were disposed to be generous to the company at first, though there was diversity of opinion on Wilkie's own skills as an actor, especially in such roles as Macbeth and Hamlet. There was often comment on an excessive breadth of humour that tended to unbalance such plays as *A Midsummer Night's Dream* or *As You Like It*. In general it was agreed the Wilkie company's productions might not be perfect but its honest attempts to bring Shakespeare to life on the stage were a matter for congratulation. Its early productions had to suffer comparison with touring ventures boasting splendour to which Wilkie could not aspire, such as the company headed by Oscar Asche in 1922. The Wilkie company's settings in its early years were simple arrangements of green curtains, backcloths and furniture which were intended to streamline the continuity of action and to facilitate extensive touring. Wilkie's designer, Arthur Goodsall, had worked in England with William Poel and the Elizabethan Stage Society.

Wilkie at first had difficulty in finding actors with any training in the classics, but by 1923 he had a company with a useful blend of older, experienced actors and young talents for whom it provided a training ground. The 30-odd members varied from year to year, but some were long serving, including Lorna Forbes from 1920 to 1929; Augustus Neville, good in comedy, from 1921 to 1925; and Bradshaw Major, musical director from 1921 to 1930. The young actors included Ellis Irving and Irene Webb. Wilkie employed some English actors, including J. Plumpton Wilson, who played character roles; Dennis Barry, who played romantic leads; and Frank D. Clewlow, who took such roles as Henry VIII, designed the lighting and advised on staging.

Touring with a large company was a precarious business at the best of times. A season of poor attendances could wipe out capital, and Wilkie often struggled to make ends meet. In 1922 a poor season in New Zealand—where there was a recession—nearly put an end to the company, and Wilkie did not return there until 1927. Transport strikes were another hazard. A policy of reduced prices for schoolchildren and university students also took its toll. In 1923 Wilkie requested government concessions on freight, since his productions served an educational purpose, and by 1927 he had been granted completely free transport over the entire railway systems of Australia and New Zealand for his company, properties and effects. Wilkie was adept at securing the patronage of leading citizens in each state, and his company numbered governors, premiers, mayors and university vice-chancellors amongst its supporters. Their presence in the audience ensured social and academic respectability. S. M. Bruce, Prime Minister of Australia from 1923 to 1929, and other politicians supported the company by praising its efforts.

As J. C. Williamson's consolidated its monopoly, the independent Wilkie found increasing difficulty in booking theatres in central Sydney and Melbourne, and he turned to smaller theatres in less fashionable districts, such as the Majestic Theatre in Newtown, Sydney. There was a major disaster in June 1926, when fire in a makeshift theatre in Geelong destroyed the company's costumes, sets and props, which were worth an estimated £4000 and were not insured. The company was regarded as a national institution, and a rallying of support around the country led to a public appeal for funds. This helped to restart the company in January 1927. It emphasised costumes, attractive scenery and lighting effects, in an attempt to win back audiences. Wilkie added R. B. Sheridan and other playwrights to the repertoire from 1927. His Shakespeare productions were exempted from federal Entertainments tax from 1929 but this was not enough to offset the effects of fluctuating attendances and the Great Depression, and the company disbanded after performing Doris Egerton Jones's *Governor Bligh* in Melbourne in 1930. ❦*Lisa Warrington*

further reading
Warrington, Lisa J. Allan Wilkie in Australia—The work of a Shakespearean actor–manager. University of Tasmania MA thesis 1981.

David Allen

Dramatist. Born 4 January 1936 in Birmingham (England). Educated at Liverpool and Manchester Universities. Taught English and drama in schools 1958–66. Married Marilyn Allen, actor and dramatist, 1960. Education officer in Uganda 1966-1970; founded Theatre Ltd with Robert Serumaga. Directed at National Theatre of Uganda. Studied theatre direction under Hugh Hunt in Manchester 1970–72. Lectured in drama at Salisbury College of Advanced Education (Adelaide) 1972–80. Co-founded and directed extensively for Troupe (Adelaide) 1976–80. Became full-time writer 1980. Moved to Sydney 1982. Australian Writers' Guild Awgie award 1984 for *Manila Yellow*. Green Room Award 1984 and Victorian Premier's Award 1986 for *Cheapside*. Also writes for film, radio and television. Father of Elizabeth Allen, designer.

David Allen is unique in contemporary Australian theatre because he deliberately writes as an outsider. He was mature when he arrived in Australia and many of his plays —especially *Upside Down at the Bottom of the World* (1980), *Cheapside* (1984), *Pommies* (1986) and *Modest Expectations* (1990)—deal with the relationship and contrasts between English and Australian cultures. This may account for his plays being performed outside Australia more than those of most of his contemporaries. He has had plays produced in Canada, England, Germany, Ireland, the Netherlands and the USA as well as in every Australian state and territory. Allen's work is exuberantly theatrical and effervescent in its language. He rarely draws on his personal or social background but he has often used historical figures—D. H. Lawrence, Robert Greene, Stan Laurel and Charles Dickens—as the main characters in his plays and treated the past as a paradigm for the present. Until 1980 all Allen's plays were first produced by Troupe and directed by him. ❦*Simon Hopkinson*

published plays
Cheapside (1984). Sydney: Currency Press (1985).
Gone with Hardy (1978). *Theatre Australia* 3/4 and 5 (Sydney 1978).
Karen (1982). Melbourne: Heinemann. 1982
Modest Expectations (1990). Sydney: Currency Press 1990.
One-Act Plays series 2. Melbourne: Heinemann 1983.
Upside Down at the Bottom of the World (1980). Melbourne: Heinemann 1981.

Amateur theatre

The contemporary Australian theatre, reflecting as it does the taste, preoccupations and patronage largely of middle-class people, is the legacy of the 'serious' minds within the amateur theatre movement. The contribution of amateur theatre to national development remains to be recognised by historians though it has been the subject of students' theses and has been debated in literary journals since the beginning of the 20th century. In each generation amateur theatre has reflected the need for self-expression and the aspirations of the community, sometimes in spite of an alien world. Amateur theatre has supplied solace in times of depression and in isolation. It has pointed to the need for change and has argued for the civilising and the spiritual when the country's ambitions were at their most material. It has concerned itself with national identity, with innovation and with self-confidence at times when the nation was least nationalistic, least imaginative and least assured. The amateur arts largely prepared the ground for the Australian Council for the Arts in 1968, and in doing so generated a radical alternative—a true repertory theatre, amateur in its educational aims but professional in execution.

When the colonies began all theatre was amateur. It was a social pastime that relieved the pain of penal servitude for convicts and the tedium of exile for the military. Music and sketches that reminded them of home were softening and civilising influences in an unforgiving environment. To answer these needs Barnett Levey opened a theatre in Sydney in 1832. He advertised his performances as 'amateur theatricals', not just to satisfy the licensing requirements—amateur and professional theatre alike came under censorship in NSW in 1832—but to imply a respectability that the professional theatre did not then have. Until the end of the 19th century performers in Great Britain were legally 'rogues and vagabonds'. There were no 'respectable' acting schools. Acting was a matter of using one's wits. Many performers made a living with a song and a story in public houses and free-and-easies before they found themselves unwilling emigrants to NSW. The small population of the colony and the improvised nature of its society inevitably compelled amateurs and professionals to inhabit the same theatrical world.

Private theatricals of the kind described by Jane Austen in *Mansfield Park* in 1814 had become increasingly popular in England among the aristocracy and middle classes, who performed mainly romantic comedy for charity or for their own amusement. Austen's Tom Bertram spoke for the younger generation when he said: 'I can see no greater harm or danger to any of us in conversing in the elegant written language of some respectable author than in chattering words of our own.' Groups thrown together in outposts of empire such as military garrisons and colonial settlements commonly turned to performance as a pastime. By the mid-19th century some of England's most influential amateur groups had been founded, including the Manchester Athenaeum Dramatic Society in 1846 and Cambridge University's Amateur Dramatic Club in 1855. Not until 1889 was there was a university society in Australia—the SYDNEY UNIVERSITY DRAMATIC SOCIETY.

The colonists who founded the Swan River Colony in 1829 were from the world of Jane Austen. They had amateur theatricals from 16 July 1839, when 'a few gentlemen and ladies' of the colony who formed the Amateur Theatricals performed *Love à la Militaire*, an operetta of unknown provenance by a Major Hort, at Leeder's Hotel in Perth. Their three seasons in 1839 were genteel affairs but they ran into opprobrium for exposing females to indelicate sentiments. A group of 'tradesmen and mechanics of the town', performed the first melodrama in Perth, Edward Fitzball's *The Inchcape Bell*, at Hodge's Hotel in December 1842. It is revealing of the class structure in Perth that efforts to join the two groups came to nothing.

Repertoire depended largely upon published scripts of plays that were standard in the British theatre of the time, like Isaac Pocock's *The Miller and His Men*. Acting editions of British plays were widely disseminated throughout the British Empire. Copyright in these plays lay with the publisher, not the author. The comprehensive *Amateur's Handbook and Guide to Home or Drawing Room Theatricals*, published in 1866, and other manuals of acting were also available in the colonies. European comedies and Gothic dramas appeared occasionally by way of the English stage but continental European influence was not apparent until the start of the 20th century, when the amateur theatre began to take drama seriously as a medium of education.

Amateur theatres appeared rapidly in goldrush towns in Victoria in the 1850s. In 1856 Ballarat, Bendigo and Castlemaine all had healthy amateur dramatic societies. The Ballarat amateurs performed in the Montezuma Theatre, a wooden-framed canvas structure. There was a Sandhurst Amateur Dramatic Club in Bendigo. As these towns grew, touring theatre companies augmented the amateurs, and in the free-and-easies local amateurs augmented visiting performers. In settlements where the gold did not run out professional services were soon supplied as the demand arose for a more settled life and more refined pursuits. Bendigo's first theatre, the Theatre Royal, was proclaimed to provide 'respectable and rational entertainment', while the Queen's Theatre at Ballarat would be 'intellectual and amusing'. At Chiltern the Garrick Club would 'evince its utility by aiding the process of humanising and elevating'.

As the colonies prospered from gold the influx of professional troupes became rapid and regular and amateur theatre became less evident, but wherever professional theatre was not established amateurs met the need. In South Australia, for example, groups such as the Amateur Comedy Company, founded in 1881, the Yorricks (1882), the Royalists (1891) and the Garrick Club (1892) aimed their performances of popular English fare at ladies and gentlemen of the colony, even travelling to country towns by train like professional troupes. Amateurs contributed theatre to Western Australia until the discovery of gold in the 1890s brought with it theatre buildings and touring companies. Where professionals were absent even the leaders of society took part in amateur performances. Sir William Robinson, three times governor between 1875 and 1895, was an exceptional patron of the performing arts.

The repertory movement

In the 1880s professional theatre in Great Britain was centred in London and increasingly American-backed. There was nothing like the provincial theatres that received subvention to maintain artistic standards and played round repertoire—several plays in turn—in other parts of Europe. The professional theatre took little account of the new literary drama and the emerging realist movement. A movement for change began in London in 1891, when J. T. Grein founded the Independent Theatre Club, which produced the plays of Henrik Ibsen and George Bernard Shaw. It spread to the regions through the patronage of Annie Horniman, a wealthy Englishwoman who had been secretary to W. B. Yeats. She established resident companies at the Abbey Theatre in Dublin, which she built in 1904, and the Gaiety Theatre in Manchester, which she opened in 1908. In 1904 the actor, director and playwright Harley Granville-Barker joined John Vedrenne at London's Royal Court Theatre, where they continued Grein's work and introduced the plays of John Galsworthy.

This breakaway to 'serious' theatre spread overseas and in Australia was taken up by professionals, who pragmatically turned to the amateur movement for realisation. This has led to terminological confusion about the purpose of theatrical societies, in which the word 'amateur' has taken on a pejorative implication of light entertainment for personal enjoyment. While the repertory movement in Britain was wholly professional the Australian 'repertory' society was amateur. Australian amateurs typically played in seasons of plays, not in round repertoire

'Repertory' societies shared aims of cultural improvement by interpreting dramatic literature—the classics, serious modern plays and the work of Australians. In some the study of style and dramatic theory and the translation of key foreign-language plays were significant. The 'repertory' movement came to Australia in 1904, when the journalist LEON BRODZKY started the Australian Theatre Society in Melbourne. He wanted to produce the works of Ibsen, Maurice Maeterlinck, Shaw and Yeats, but the society dwindled into a play-reading group. It was succeeded by WILLIAM MOORE's Annual Drama Nights in 1909–12.

The repertory movement began in earnest in Adelaide. On the initiative of BRYCESON TREHARNE, a Welsh piano teacher, Shaw's *The Man of Destiny* and Yeats's *The Land of Heart's Desire* were performed in a hall at the Elder Conservatorium in 1908. From this grew Adelaide Literary Theatre, which proposed to produce plays of literary and artistic value—'poetic and symbolic dramas, plays bearing directly on the actual problems of life, translations from the

In the Australian colonies as in England, amateur theatricals were a popular amusement for the gentry. In the early 1880s Robert Barr Smith built a theatre on his Torrens Park estate, near Adelaide. In it some of his family and friends—including the daughter of Governor Sir William Jervois (seated)—staged this Lochinvar tableau, based on Walter Scott's poem

AMATEUR THEATRE

Amateurs provided the only theatrical entertainment in many outback towns. This group performed at the Bijou Theatre in Bourke, northwestern NSW, in 1900

works of German, French and Russian Dramatists, plays by Australian writers'. According to Paul McGuire, the group regarded the 'Pinero–Sutro' type of play as 'neurotic', and it saw the theatre as comparable to the pulpit in its social purpose. The ambitions of most repertory groups in the following half-century broadly matched these aims. Moral purpose was clearest in the aims of the many Catholic dramatic societies. Treharne left Adelaide in 1911 but the society he initiated continued to flourish as ADELAIDE REPERTORY THEATRE, retaining an exclusive tone and gaining with the years a comfortable membership of well-established citizens. Its repertoire largely comprised popular classics and comedies but was occasionally adventurous.

The central figure in the repertory movement was GREGAN MCMAHON, a character actor who founded the MELBOURNE REPERTORY THEATRE COMPANY in 1911 to follow in the footsteps of Grein and Granville-Barker. This amateur company achieved a notable standard, and its early seasons included works by Anton Chekhov, Granville-Barker, Gerhart Hauptmann, Ibsen, Luigi Pirandello and Shaw.

Little theatre

The composer ALFRED HILL and Downs Johnstone founded the Sydney Repertory Theatre Society in 1913. The First World War ended both this venture and LITTLE THEATRE, which Hugh Buckler and his wife Violet Paget established in Sydney in 1913. Little Theatre was a professional company but its name came from an amateur movement that began in the USA beyond New York City about 1910 as a protest against the domination of Broadway. It called itself 'little theatre' to distinguish it from the pastime of amateur performance. Most American little theatres were professionally managed but used amateur actors —often people who might have been professionals had work been available—and most amateur theatres in Australian cities adopted this relationship. Many disputes about policy and repertoire ensued.

The high point of 'little theatre' activity was from the 1920s to the 1940s, when the professional legitimate theatre was at its lowest ebb. Necessity drew the amateur and the professional much closer together than either would have preferred in other circumstances. Amateur theatres began to assume the role filled by professional repertory theatres in other countries. Actors could train on the public platform only in amateur theatre until the NATIONAL INSTITUTE OF DRAMATIC ART was founded in 1958.

The 1920s and 1930s saw amateur theatre move from private entertainment to become a force in national consciousness, advancing questions of community and cultural improvement, social and moral justice, and the need for Australia's own playwrights and actors. Repertoires of this time were particularly influenced by European forces— Konstantin Stanislavsky, Max Reinhardt, Vsevolod Meyerhold, the Abbey Theatre, the Théâtre Antoine, Théâtre Libre—and American experiments like the Living Newspaper. These opened the way to some remarkable advances in STAGE DESIGN and ACTING theory. New publications from Europe and the USA broke the imperial hold on amateur theatre that dissemination of acting editions had given the British. The books and manuscripts of the Playwrights' Advisory Board loosened it further from 1938.

In 1920, while working for J. C. WILLIAMSON'S in Sydney, Gregan McMahon persuaded J. AND N. TAIT LTD, which had taken charge of the Firm, to support his founding of a new SYDNEY REPERTORY THEATRE SOCIETY. This was a socially influential group, whose members acted only in minor roles. The principals in McMahon's productions for the society were, like him, on the Williamson payroll.

DUNCAN MACDOUGALL's Playbox Society and the Sydney Players' Club, both founded in Sydney in 1923, claimed inspiration from the 'art theatre of Europe'. Playbox had the greater claim, producing expressionist plays from Europe and the USA and campaigning for a national theatre. In 1925 the *Evening News* described the group as 'in germ what the Moscow Art Theatre is to Moscow'.

In Melbourne J. BERESFORD FOWLER, an actor impeded by advancing deafness, directed amateur productions and in

1925 established the Art Theatre Players Company at the small Queen's Hall. His repertoire resembled McMahon's, with the addition of Shakespeare and occasionally Noël Coward and Arthur Wing Pinero; but the quality varied and in the later years suffered from lack of resources. In 1927 Fowler produced Hermann Sudermann's historical drama *The Fires of St John*, which had been denounced as 'an open drain' when J. C. WILLIAMSON presented it in Melbourne in 1905, because of a bedroom scene between illicit lovers. Fowler's interpretation of the scene received only favourable comment—a reflection of changing community standards and growing respect for 'serious' intent.

In response to the growing amateur movement in southern capitals, BARBARA SISLEY, an English-trained actor, founded the BRISBANE REPERTORY THEATRE SOCIETY in 1925 to 'foster the love of drama in the community'. A. A. Milne and J. M. Barrie appeared not infrequently in its early repertoire, but it generally followed McMahon's lead in producing plays by Galsworthy, Ibsen, Shaw and Yeats. It also had a policy of presenting Australian works. Brisbane Repertory has probably made the most substantial contribution to the community of all the major groups. In Tasmania, the HOBART REPERTORY THEATRE SOCIETY was founded in 1926 and the Launceston Players were founded in 1927. The leading figure in the founding of the Hobart society was OLIVE WILTON, an English actor who had made a name in plays by Pinero and Hall Caine in London and New York. Hobart Repertory opened its own 350-seat Playhouse in 1938. A key figure in the performing arts in South Australia, COLIN BALLANTYNE was a leading member of the Workers' Educational Association Dramatic Society in Adelaide, founded in 1926.

Amateur drama began in Canberra in 1926 with the only production of the Community Players. Next year the Society for Arts and Literature was founded. An energetic and hot-tempered amateur actor and director, Lewis Nott, recklessly expanded its dramatic activities into full-blown popular theatre. He resigned in 1932 and with followers formed the CANBERRA REPERTORY SOCIETY. The federal capital had only 11 000 inhabitants by 1938 but a high proportion were educated, travelled and influential. This was reflected within the society in frequent disputes and strong views on performance standards.

The Sydney Repertory Theatre Society collapsed in 1928 after J. C. Williamson's proposed that it become fully professional. McMahon went back to Melbourne and in 1929 founded his own semi-professional company, the GREGAN MCMAHON PLAYERS. In 1928 DON FINLEY founded Turret Theatre on the north side of Sydney Harbour. It lasted barely two years but in 1929 it was home to possibly the first amateur drama festival. This attracted 17 companies around Sydney and full houses. CARRIE TENNANT created an Australian author's theatre in the basement of a Sydney church hall in 1929. In its first year Community Theatre presented 30 one-act plays and four three-act plays, including works by Rex Rienits, Marguerite Dale and Dora Wilcox and its major discovery, LESLIE HAYLEN's *Two Minutes' Silence*.

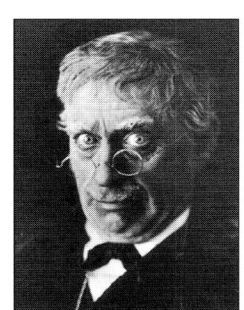

Gregan McMahon, a professional actor and director, strove throughout a long career to present serious plays with amateur actors. Here he plays a character role, about 1910, the year before he founded the Melbourne Repertory Theatre Company

Community Theatre lasted until 1933 but in 1931 Tennant moved it out of its tiny theatre. This became BRYANT's PLAYHOUSE, run by the actor and teacher BERYL BRYANT and her father, the actor GEORGE BRYANT, to serve their acting school. Many strong theatrical personalities were thrown on their own resources in 1929–31—the early years of Great Depression, when many live theatres were closed or became cinemas—and the serious amateur movement provided a hazardous living. Most amateur groups lasted only until their founders moved on, but INDEPENDENT THEATRE, started in Sydney in 1930, lasted for 47 years. Its founder was DORIS FITTON, an actor who had been a student of McMahon and secretary of Turret Theatre. She was a follower of Stanislavsky and the aims of J. T. Grein and she started Independent Theatre to present 'the world's best plays'. This was its masthead to the end, but economics dictated that its basic fare remained polite comedy and classic drama, with grittier material occasionally and a courageous proportion of new Australian works. Notable among the latter were HUGH McRAE's poetic fantasy *The Ship of Heaven* with music by Alfred Hill in 1933; and Sumner Locke Elliott's RUSTY BUGLES in 1948.

The company's early quality was indicated by the success of its production of *The Constant Nymph* by Margaret Kennedy and Basil Dean, which J. C. Williamson's transferred to the Palace Theatre for a month in 1932. Olive Wilton's 17-year-old daughter Junee Cornell played Tessa. Later she gave Hal Porter an insight into the semi-professional world of the time: 'I was sometimes paid as a guest artist, sometimes not, according to a peculiar method all the Independent's own.'

Scott Alexander resumed McMahon's work with the New Sydney Repertory Society in 1931, but this group showed a marked preference for Grand Guignol. Alexander did more substantial work in Sydney as director of the innovative Kursaal Theatre in 1934–38. Its repertoire included plays by Chekhov, Ibsen and Shakespeare and works by its club members.

There was strong continental European influence on Impressionist Theatre, founded in Sydney by Raoul Cardamatis. It appeared briefly in 1933 and gave occasional performances with great emphasis upon the visual. Gerhart Hauptmann's *Hanneles Himmelfahrt* and Edmond Rostand's *Cyrano de Bergerac* were two of its productions. The year 1933 also saw a notable production at the Savoy Theatre of Rostand's *L'Aiglon*, by the Sydney University Dramatic Society, It was directed by MAY HOLLINWORTH, who had revived the society.

In Melbourne, DOLIA RIBUSH, a Russian immigrant, introduced the traditions of the Moscow Art Theatre to the amateur movement, and Louise Dunn ran an eccentric all-female Shakespeare company as part of her acting school. The first attempt to unify the amateur movement was made in Sydney in 1933 by Richard Windeyer, a barrister who was president of the Players' Club, a social group with members of some distinction. He moved to form 'a united organisation of repertory theatres' with the aim of 'great productions worthy of the city'. A committee was formed to create an Australian Drama League on the lines of the British Drama League, to provide a script library, a drama festival, lectures and receptions. These plans were not realised but BEATRICE TILDESLEY founded a branch of the British Drama League in 1937.

Doris Fitton founded Independent Theatre in Sydney in 1930 and remained its artistic director for 47 years. Here she plays Madame Arkadina in Independent Theatre's 1965 production of The Seagull *by Anton Chekhov*

The work of the REPERTORY CLUB in Perth, founded in 1919, became more serious in the 1930s. Its early aims had been largely social—elegant young women would pose in character for studio portraits for the social columns—but between 1932 and 1942 it presented 30 new Australian plays, including works by DYMPHNA CUSACK, HENRIETTA DRAKE-BROCKMAN and ALEXANDER TURNER. It also began to co-ordinate the work of country and suburban groups, and earned affiliations with 19 of them. The club and the *West Australian* backed the first annual Western Australian Drama Festival, which was organised in 1937 by PAUL HASLUCK, an active member of the club and drama reviewer for the newspaper. After four years the festivals ceased in favour of the war effort, but the Theatre Council of Western Australia revived them in 1949. Other groups established in Perth before the war included the Independent Players, GARRICK THEATRE, the Mercury Players, Q Theatre, the University Players and the WORKERS' ART GUILD.

Workers' theatre groups, which united as the NEW THEATRE movement, were the amateur theatre's strong socialist conscience amid the predominant middle-class influence. They were particularly evident during the Spanish Civil War. The New Theatre League was among as many as 17 amateur theatre groups that met in metropolitan Adelaide in the 1930s. The city had particularly strong and forward-looking amateur theatre. Some groups, like LLOYD PRIDER's Playbox Theatre, presented musical entertainment, others enlarged their horizons. Probably the most avant-garde little theatre in Australia was AB INTRA STUDIO THEATRE, a breakaway from Adelaide Repertory Theatre founded in 1931. It produced esoteric and highly visual work with a strong symbolist bias that paralleled the theories of Michael Chekhov and Sergey Diaghilev.

The mantle of Ab Intra fell upon PATRICIA HACKETT, a lawyer who sought self-expression with visually compelling productions of classics and poetic plays in her tiny Torch Theatres in 1934–35 and 1952–60. Her style, influenced by the work of Ab Intra, was strongly anti-naturalistic. As a personality Hackett attracted criticism, though at her best she was a considerable actor, director and designer.

AGNES DOBSON, a professional actor, turned to teaching, broadcasting and working with the WEA Dramatic Society in Adelaide when the Great Depression closed the theatres. She opened her Independent Repertory Theatre in 1936 and in the next year produced the *Oresteia* trilogy by Aeschylus and classics by Molière, Pirandello, Algernon Swinburne and J. M. Synge.

Melbourne's third influential theatre club opened in 1931 when two out-of-work actors, BRETT RANDALL and Hal Percy, sought to employ themselves gainfully by setting up the Little Theatre Laboratory of Dramatic Art. It became Melbourne Little Theatre in February 1934, when Randall opened a disused church in South Yarra as the Little Theatre with his most ambitious production, Georg Kaiser's expressionist drama *From Morning to Midnight*. In his early repertoire Randall advanced from McMahon, essaying translations of Valentin Katayev, Pedro Calderón and Ernest Vajda and the Chinese classic *The Circle of Chalk* as well as plays by Ashley Dukes, Lillian Hellman and A. A. Milne. As with the majority of little theatres, the choice was assisted by two magazines that published the texts of the most recent successes, *Plays and Players* from the United Kingdom and *Theatre Arts* from the USA, and French's Acting Editions. Since 1926 Randall had been a rights agent—the first in Australia—and he built up a library of some 3500 playscripts for hire by amateur groups.

By the mid-1930s the forces of actor-management and social expression were giving way to a perceived need for education. One of the national movements that came into being was Catholic theatre groups, notably the Therry dramatic societies, founded in Melbourne in 1936 to 'provide education in liturgy, drama and the arts' and 'aim at restoring active entertainment in the home as a major necessity of Christian living'. Allied societies followed in Adelaide in 1943 and Perth in 1944. The Sydney equivalent is the Genesians, an influential group with a small theatre in Kent Street, provided by the archdiocese. In Brisbane, the Villanova Players were founded in 1948 by Father Hanrahan, an Augustinian priest, and Donagh McDonagh, editor of the *Catholic Leader*. The group became the official theatre of the archdiocese of Brisbane in 1955, and in the 1960s it was particularly noted for its presentations of the work of the Brisbane playwright BARBARA STELLMACH.

As part of the new mood in the 1930s, the elocutionist began to displace the actor–manager in amateur drama. The subject needs further research, but there is evidence that a remedy was sought in speech, drama and ballet studios for the inferiority complex that came to be dubbed the 'cultural cringe'. Rising prosperity and advances in secondary education also contributed to the popularity of these institutions and of the work of the Australian Music Examinations Board. The AMEB was established in 1918 and it extended its activities, in speech and drama as well as music, to the farthest parts of the country by the 1950s.

The proliferating speech and drama schools soon sought outlets for performance and nowhere was their influence more apparent than in Brisbane. JEAN TRUNDLE, a speech and drama teacher, had her own student group, the Jean Trundle Players, and from that evolved Brisbane Amateur Theatres in 1936. The plural name related to an intention to co-ordinate the work of the existing little theatres in Brisbane. Trundle's husband Vic Hardgreaves, was principal producer of the group, which became BRISBANE ARTS THEATRE in 1947. It has been remarkably consistent. The group was established with avowedly conservative aims and, while it emphasised entertainment in the choice of play, it encouraged local writers of comedies and thrillers.

Another speech and drama teacher with her own studio, RHODA FELGATE sought expansion for her students and herself and formed TWELFTH NIGHT THEATRE in 1936. The aim of this breakaway from Brisbane Repertory was to produce 'worthwhile' plays, which proved in practice to be the most successful new overseas plays available to amateurs, but the emphasis was upon developing the skills of a small group by study and performance. The repertoire was eclectic, including Shakespeare and modern plays like Emlyn Williams's *The Corn is Green* and Jean Cocteau's *The Eagle Has Two Heads*, chosen with an eye to acting opportunities rather than argument.

Ida and Edward Beeby founded PATCH THEATRE in Perth as a speech and drama studio in 1939. They were musicians and modern-dance enthusiasts and the theatre acquired a reputation for daring, for choreography and for Edward Beeby's striking stage lighting. The repertoire ranged from children's work to the avant garde. Dance became less evident after the Beebys retired in 1952.

Postwar expansion
The Second World War nearly destroyed the quality of theatre at every level, but straitened circumstances and broadened horizons combined to raise a renewed interest in cultural as well as economic development. The remainder of the 1940s was a period of enormous expansion for amateur theatre. The March 1946 edition of Melbourne Little Theatre's journal, *Foyer*—a de facto national magazine for a time—quotes Lindsey Browne, theatre and music critic of the *Sydney Morning Herald*: 'L.B. points out that of the 65 plays reviewed by his paper during 1945, fewer than a dozen were professional productions, "and even in some of those dozen professional plays, the players were mostly paid amateurs. 'Professional' plays", he continues, "are most often under-prepared, dull, imprecise, and unimaginative in production. It is even suggested by some of the most ardent amateur theatre people that the two existing professional theatres have alienated professional audiences by mediocre productions of mediocre plays, which they fully expect to get by at the box office because of the hundreds of thousands of people whose taste has already been corrupted by poor theatre over the years."'

Concerned parties set about redressing the balance. The wartime Council for the Encouragement of Music and the Arts became the ARTS COUNCIL OF AUSTRALIA, with state branches, in 1947. Adult education and workers' education bodies also attested to new aspirations. Backed by the state arts councils and adult education boards, professional touring companies, with actors drawn largely from the little theatres, began extensive tours of country towns, encouraging the work of amateurs. Professional directors and teachers were also supplied to amateur groups. Many groups became affiliated with the NATIONAL THEATRE MOVEMENT or the Victorian Drama League, established in Melbourne in 1952, or the British Drama League in Sydney. The leagues provided lending libraries of acting scripts and training workshops. Amateur drama festivals proliferated.

For the jubilee of the Commonwealth of Australia in 1951 there was an amateur drama festival with state heats.

Melbourne Little Theatre presented 14 Australian plays between 1945 and 1950, by writers including SUMNER LOCKE ELLIOTT, HAL PORTER and Archie Menzies. It had a success in 1947 with *Enduring as the Camphor Tree*, a Chinese fantasy by RUSSELL OAKES, perhaps inspired by the success of *The Circle of Chalk*. It was subsequently produced by most of the major amateur groups in Australia.

Sydney's Independent Theatre gained a wide reputation for professional standards in 1946 when its production of Eugene O'Neill's *Mourning Becomes Electra* was transferred to the Comedy Theatre in Melbourne. It was directed by ROBERT QUENTIN, on leave from the British navy. Quentin, later an officer of the Australian Elizabethan Theatre Trust and founder of the National Institute of Dramatic Art, played a key role in the transition from amateur to professional theatre in Sydney. Independent Theatre ran a school and employed professional directors and performers from time to time. It also had an informal partnership with the JOHN ALDEN COMPANY between 1948 and 1959 and affiliations with immigrant groups. Atzala, a Lithuanian group, performed at its theatre in 1955, and G. R. Feber founded the German-speaking Kammerspiele within Independent Theatre in 1958. Immigrants enriched amateur theatre after the war by joining established groups and by creating groups to perform in their own languages. The latter field remains to be researched.

With a professional repertory company in view, May Hollinworth founded the amateur METROPOLITAN THEATRE in Sydney in 1946. Hollinworth, undeterred by the restrictions of a tiny 70-seat theatre, presented plays like *Othello*, Maxwell Anderson's *Winterset* and William Wycherley's risqué *The Country Wife*, for which entrance rules were restricted. Another small landmark in Sydney was Norman McVicker's POCKET PLAYHOUSE at Sydenham, which held only 60 people. It opened in 1947. It encouraged Australian writers and served a need in inner southern Sydney but it closed in 1972, unable to survive competition from the new subsidised theatres.

The ADELAIDE THEATRE GROUP grew out of WEA Little Theatre—originally the Workers' Educational Association Dramatic Society—in 1946. The group's aims were, according to Peter Ward, 'to produce Australian plays exclusively and redevelop the "regional" theatre which had been lost when Ab Intra closed. The method employed was not as exotic as Ab Intra, but they did develop their own playwrights and translators, who for a year or so, made their own translations of French, German and Russian drama'.

In 1948 Laurence Olivier and Vivien Leigh led the OLD VIC THEATRE COMPANY on a tour of Australia. The stars visited the major amateur companies in each state. The Old Vic was heady stuff in the postwar drought and the amateur theatre and government instrumentalities both took it as a recipe for what theatre ought to be. It followed therefore, that in the heart of government, the Canberra Repertory Society became one of the earliest amateur groups to nurture aspirations to professionalism. In 1949 the Prime Minister, Ben Chifley, established a Committee for Cultural Development in Canberra and part of its annual grant was allotted to Canberra Repertory for a director and a part-time secretary.

In Brisbane in 1949 a move began for the city's little theatres to affiliate into a national theatre for mutual development and encouragement of local drama. The playwright and director Eunice Hanger, a member of Twelfth Night, was central to the idea. It led to a drama festival but after Tyrone Guthrie visited Brisbane the arguments were subsumed by the Guthrie report to Chifley on national theatre, and in due course by the establishment of the Australian Elizabethan Theatre Trust.

In Perth, David Lopian became the first postwar professional director of the Repertory Club in 1950 and began the stirring toward professionalism. As part of the move to provide theatre in country towns the professional Company of Four, employing leading Repertory Club personalities, was established in 1950 under the aegis of the Adult Education Board. Another initiative of the board was an annual summer school at the University of Western Australia; and in 1953 it initiated the first Festival of Perth, in which amateurs participated until the 1970s. The Company of Four merged with the Repertory Club in 1956 to establish the semiprofessional National Theatre Company. The company became fully professional in 1960 but the conflicting priorities of established amateurs and imported professionals created a turbulence that took many years to subside.

Preparing for professionalism

Australia's first public patron of the arts, the Australian Elizabethan Theatre Trust, established in 1954, was essentially an initiative of the amateur theatre—of concerned parties who were aware in the prosperous 1950s that the country lacked civilised pursuits and who sought to engineer change from outside the profession. The Trust's avowed aims were much in sympathy with those at the start of the repertory movement. It de facto undertook the task of transforming the arts community's largely amateur outlook into a professional one. Its progress was uneven and often struck rocky and unyielding ground, but by the time the Trust was displaced by the Australian Council for the Arts in 1968 it had prepared fertile soil.

In 1961 the Trust assisted the University of Adelaide Theatre Guild in a production of Patrick White's The Ham Funeral after the Adelaide Festival had discarded it. This was the first of three premieres of plays by White that the guild gave under John Tasker's direction in 1961–64. A continuing informal relationship between the two organisations led in 1964 to the Trust assigning Tasker to establish the South Australian Theatre Company under its umbrella. The stamina required, and the disputes surrounding the establishment of a professional company, the fledgling festival and the building of the Adelaide Festival Centre, absorbed the energies of the major figures in the amateur movement in South Australia from then. Small initiatives continued for a time. The actor-manager John Edmund's semiprofessional Theatre '62, founded in 1962 with the John Edmund Academy to 'bridge the gap between the amateur and professional', produced some notable work in its early years. In 1974 the building and management were taken over by the South Australian Education Department.

In 1964 Peter Batey began steering the Canberra Repertory Society towards all-professional theatre, but resistance within the society was strong and the Playhouse in the new Canberra Theatre Centre proved unsuitable for amateur production. Since then amateur, semiprofessional and professional groups have struggled to survive in Canberra, but disparate interests have militated against united support.

The Brisbane Repertory Theatre Society moved towards professionalism apparently with less trauma than some groups, perhaps because it adhered to the McMahon–Sisley principles of solid, challenging theatre and strong, dedicated personalities always controlled its activities. This was acknowledged when Babette Stephens was given the title of director in 1961. She was an honorary director, as was Joan Whalley, who succeeded Rhoda Felgate as director of Twelfth Night Theatre in the same year. Whalley had been a teacher for Twelfth Night in the 1950s. Twelfth Night conducted a full annual program of classics and modern work and encouraged a variety of directors. Brisbane Arts Theatre, which opened its Arts Theatre in 1961, strove to produce Australian plays.

In 1966 Stefan Haag, executive director of the Trust, approached Brisbane Arts Theatre, proposing that the Trust set up a state company, created out of the three major little theatres, at the Arts Theatre. 'All of the groups stood to gain something by combining for the formation of a professional company', he claimed. Brisbane Arts Theatre saw no gain. It was the strongest of the three, playing regularly six nights a week, with a $100 000 bank balance. The debate was pressing. In a long article in the *Courier–Mail* Bob Hart argued: 'In the hands of the Arts has been placed not only their own future, but the future of all theatre in this city. Brisbane has waited a long time for a professional theatre company. We have insisted that we are worthy of one and we are about to be given a chance to prove it—a chance that must be taken.' In the event all three groups declined the offer, and three years later the state government decided to establish the Queensland Theatre Company.

All three amateur groups built their own theatres in the late 1960s. Twelfth Night had expanded beyond Gowrie Hall and in 1966 it announced plans for a new theatre. It built the Twelfth Night Complex in 1970 but the final cost left the group with a $150 000 debt. The burden pushed it into becoming a professional theatre supported by a school and a club bar; and ultimately to its downfall.

Brisbane Repertory opened its La Boîte theatre in 1967. Jennifer Blocksidge, an actor and director with the society, succeeded Stephens as its honorary director in 1968 and undertook a steady revolution, seeking funding and local support for youth programs, workshops on new scripts, and presenting the challenging new writing of the time. In this she was aided by the in-the-round auditorium of La Boîte, which gave a shock of intimacy similar to that of the recently-created La Mama Theatre in Melbourne. The style developed over her period in office was confirmed by the opening of a new 200-seat in-the-round La Boîte in 1972. Blocksidge resigned in favour of a paid director in 1976, and Rick Billinghurst was appointed. By that time the existence of the state theatre company had irrevocably altered the outlooks of performers and audiences on amateur theatre. Brisbane Arts retains its Arts Theatre—rebuilt after a fire in 1964—and its amateur status but it has been displaced as a major force in Brisbane theatre.

In Victoria, Harold Baigent, administrator of the Victorian Drama League, complained in 1964: 'An adventurous spirit is lacking in the amateur movement. They prefer to fall back on the well-tried formula play that has achieved success overseas. The "avant garde" play is ignored in Victoria, or left to the semiprofessional theatres such as the St Martin's Theatre or the Union Theatre Repertory Company.' The arrival of television in Melbourne and Sydney in 1956 partly accounted for the loss of creativity and concentration upon the box office. But a new student movement swiftly revolted against the 'well-tried formula'. In the Emerald Hill Theatre, the Secondary Teachers' College and La Mama Theatre in Melbourne, the Schonell Theatre at the University of Queensland, the Sheridan Theatre in Adelaide, and the Ensemble and Nimrod Street Theatres in Sydney the avant garde emerged in HAPPENINGS, new forms of theatre and new writing.

Semiprofessionalism eclipsed

A secure profession began to become established with the aid of the Australian Council for the Arts after 1968. But while this happened the fragile financial structure of the 'semiprofessional' movement was rapidly eroded. Some companies with their own buildings metamorphosed by degrees into professional companies, with new corporate structures. Government requirements of public accountability, non-profitability and boards of directors, did away with the last of the old private managements. And ACTORS' EQUITY had grown in strength and was militating against the semiprofessional concept. Since that time amateur theatre has had no influence upon the direction of dramatic taste and thought.

Independent Theatre in Sydney made a short-lived attempt to run a professional company in round repertoire with government funding in 1968. The group's character and shaky financial structure, however, precluded transformation into a major subsidised theatre. It closed in 1977.

The MELBOURNE THEATRE COMPANY was nominated as the official state theatre company of Victoria in 1968. The ST MARTIN'S THEATRE COMPANY closed in 1973. IRENE MITCHELL, artistic director of St Martin's from 1956 to 1973, summed up the changed world in an interview with Jennifer Radbourne in 1977: 'There was happiness in that theatre until the money came into it from the government ... Money had to go to non-profit making organisations which we weren't. We couldn't be because we had to pay back the money to our subscribers. The theatre was built on ten-pound debentures from patrons.'

In the 1970s government funding began to produce alternative theatre groups of a new kind. These groups, which sprang up to expand beyond the established formal city theatres, roughly come under the title of COMMUNITY THEATRE. They have been particularly important in spreading theatre to country towns, particularly in South Australia, Victoria and Queensland. In Adelaide they formed an Association of Fringe Theatres as an adjunct to the Adelaide Festival. These groups fluctuate between amateur and professional only in regard to salaries; but their purposes are no longer the middle-class cultural education and entertainment espoused by the repertory-theatre and little-theatre movements.

In the 1990s amateur theatre and theatre competitions still exist healthily in the country and the outer suburbs in answer to the need for self-expression. Many municipal councils have been persuaded to build multipurpose halls for the use of drama companies. But the motivation for amateur theatre today remains social and educational, as it was in the early colonies. Ross Thorne surveyed country drama groups in 1970 and concluded that the members were apt to be middle-class, of above average education and living on average 11 km from the theatre. Nevertheless, in rural areas where local and community theatre thrive, particularly in north Queensland and the Northern Territory, much greater distances are involved and ingenuity may be needed. In 1982 a cast of 20 from outback cattle stations in the Northern Territory rehearsed Jack Hibberd's popular comedy *Dimboola* over party-radio. They came together for performances in Katherine. The AUSTRALIA COUNCIL acknowledges the needs and complexities of life outside the capital cities by funding the DARWIN THEATRE COMPANY. No other semiprofessional group regularly receives such funding. ❦*Katharine Brisbane*

further reading

BADGER, COLIN. Rural theatre in relation to the rest of the community. *UNESCO Conference on Repertory Theatre.* Adelaide: 1966.

BAIGENT, HAROLD. *The Amateur Theatre in Victoria—A survey.* Melbourne: Victorian Drama League 1964.

BRODZKY, LEON. Towards an Australian Drama. *Lone Hand* (Sydney) 1 June 1908.

CAMPBELL, JEAN. Nonprofessional theatre in Australia. Arts in Australia (Sydney) 1948. Manuscript in Mitchell Library (Sydney).

CARRUTHERS, VIRGINIA. The development of Australian theatre and drama 1788–1964. Duke University (South Carolina, USA) PhD thesis 1969.

COY, BRONWYN. The significance of the little theatre movement in Australia in the 1930s with particular reference to the Independent Theatre. University of NSW (Sydney) honours thesis 1990.

DUNSTONE, BILL. Imperialist discourses—Amateur theatrical performances in Perth to 1854. *Australasian Drama Studies* (Brisbane) October 1993.

EDGEWORTH, ANNE. *The Cost of Jazz Garters—A history of Canberra Repertory Society 1932-1982.* Canberra Repertory Society 1992.

FOWLER, J. BERESFORD. *Stars in My Backyard.* Ilfracombe (England): Arthur H. Stockwell 1962.

GOERS, PETER. With no regrets—Colin Ballantyne interviewed. *From Colonel Light to the Footlights—The performing arts in South Australia from 1836 to the present* (ed. Andrew D. McCredie). Adelaide: Pagel 1988.

HART, BOB. Brisbane to have a professional theatre company? *Courier-Mail* (Brisbane) 24 August 1966.

HOWELL, EDWARD. The little theatre movement—what impedes it? *Harmony* (Sydney) 17 February 1934.

MCMAHON, GREGAN. *Table Talk* (Melbourne) 2 May 1935.

ROBERTS, SUSAN INGRID. Some aspects of 'rough' and 'refined' theatre on the Victorian goldfields in the 1850s. University of NSW (Sydney) BA (hons) thesis 1978.

SORRELL, W. J. *The Amateur's Hand-Book and Guide to Home or Drawing Room Theatricals—How to get them up and to act in them.* London: T. H. Lacy 1866.

THORNE, ROSS. Community (amateur) theatre. University of Sydney Faculty of Architecture research paper 1970.

TILDESLEY, BEATRICE. The little theatre movement in Sydney. *Manuscripts* 4 (February 1933).

TOYNE, GABRIEL. The repertory theatre's place in the thought of a nation. *Playbill* April 1935.

VAVERE, A. History of Adelaide Literary/Repertory Theatre. Flinders University (Adelaide) MA thesis 1978.

WARD, PETER. Theatre in Adelaide 1920 to 1960. *Australian Letters* 2/4 (Adelaide, March 1960).

WORBY, GUS. A theatre now and then. *From Colonel Light into the Footlights* (ed. Andrew D. McCredie). Adelaide: Pagel 1988.

American influences

There has been greater American influence on Australian theatre than many Australian commentators have liked to acknowledge. The American and Australian theatres first made contact when performers from California arrived in Australia during the gold rushes in 1853. American influences through repertoire, genres, and techniques of performance came later in the 19th century, but remained slight compared with the influences of English theatre. They perceptibly increased just before the First World War, became strong in the 1920s, eased off during the Great Depression, picked up again during the Second World War, and reached an all-time high in the 1950s.

Between the gold rushes and the end of the First World War, the most influential American in Australian theatre was J. C. WILLIAMSON. He arrived in 1874, already versed in the difficulties of touring companies over vast distances. He was the first in Australia to perfect the technique of running big productions concurrently in the capital cities for maximum profit. He usually had an unerring sense of what Australians wanted to see—and he was convinced that it was not Australian plays. But, even though he was American, he regarded American plays as secondary imports.

Nevertheless, American influence did gain strength in the period 1853–1918, for several reasons. The newly emergent genre of musical comedy was less characteristically American at the time than ethnic comedy but it proved its potency in 1899, when Williamson's partner GEORGE MUSGROVE made a personal fortune from the success in London of an American show, *The Belle of New York*. From that time an increased commitment to musical comedy became apparent in Australia.

Another reason for the rise of American influence was the popularity of American silent films, which may well have enlarged the appetite for other kinds of American entertainment during the first years of the 20th century. Yet another was geographical: during the disruptions of the First World War the theatrical world of New York was more accessible than London. One of the Williamson firm's rivals, J. AND N. TAIT LTD set up a permanent office in New York at the end of the war, and entered into keen competition in buying American musicals and plays. This opened the way to still more American influence in the jazz age.

Goldrush visitors

When the gold rushes began the American company of C. B. Thorne was already here, and the first visitors the boom drew to Australia were the American tragedians Sarah and James Stark in 1853. They left in 1854 with £20 000 profit, earned partly by their wildly histrionic acting style, which was novel in Australia and definitely in accord with the national mood at the time. They were followed by young EDWIN BOOTH and LAURA KEENE, later famous in their own country. In Australia, however, they were comparative failures, because of their restrained style.

These first American visitors were put down in some sections of the press for American 'peculiarities' of enunciation and intonation. Other notable early visitors included the tragedians Daniel and Emma Waller in 1855 and McKean Buchanan a year later; Marie Provost, who stayed for two years from 1859 and played in *Camille* by Alexandre Dumas *fils* and other serious plays; and Avonia Jones, who opened in Sydney in *Medea* in 1859. All these visitors had a fairly standard repertoire of Edward Bulwer-Lytton, Friedrich von Kotzebue, Shakespeare and melodrama, which had little relationship to their nationality.

The American comic actor JOSEPH JEFFERSON arrived in 1862 with a newer repertoire dealing with more American subject matter. It included Tom Taylor's *Our American Cousin* (1858), which is set in England but has an important role of an American suitor; an early version of Jefferson's later hit *Rip Van Winkle*; and Dion Boucicault's new melodrama *The Octoroon* (1859) set in Louisiana. Jefferson, who stayed until 1865, was so popular that he played Melbourne three times and Sydney twice, and visited all the other major centres and New Zealand.

In the 1870s, MINSTRELS had a strong impact. As early as the 1850s five American minstrel troupes played in Australia and by 1865 they included black—as distinct from blackface—performers. Communication between Australia and the west coast of North America was much improved by a regular steamship connection by the 1870s.

Two young Americans on the threshold of stardom at home, Edwin Booth and Laura Keene toured Australia in 1854. Their restrained style was not appreciated and they suffered financial failure

The first major visiting troupe in that decade was Billy Emerson's California Minstrels. It was in turn eclipsed by CHARLES B. HICKS's Georgia Minstrels, who arrived in 1877. This all-black company had a huge success with a three-part program, which had then become usual for minstrel shows. Part one consisted of sentimental songs, part two comprised variety acts, and part three was a potted version of a current musical success. Part three often inculcated antislavery sentiments in the audience. In 1878 Hicks's troupe and the L. M. Bayless Dramatic Company combined to present *Uncle Tom's Cabin*, and this was the most successful version of Harriet Beecher Stowe's novel ever to play in Australia. By 1880 the craze for minstrelsy had passed. Hicks visited Australia again—as a leading light in the Hicks-Sawyer Minstrels from 1881 to 1891—but did not repeat his success of the 1870s. Minstrels often played in venues other than theatres and appealed especially to working-class audiences. Later, negative 'coon' stereotypes fostered in minstrel programs began to be applied to Aborigines and tended to encourage racism.

In the 1870s too, American influence manifested itself through visiting performers in two other notable ways. Circus influence began first and lasted until about 1900. And, with the visit of the famous midget General Tom Thumb in 1872, American-style promotion techniques arrived in Australia. Tom Thumb and his equally diminutive wife had been developed as a performing attraction in the USA by Phineas T. Barnum. The Barnum publicity technique made the couple a considerable box-office attraction in Australia, particularly in country towns. Otherwise the American performers to make the greatest impact in the 1870s were comic actors, who introduced a distinctively American kind of ethnic comedy. The first was Williamson in 1874 in his hit *Struck Oil*, which caught on in spite of a German dialect, the so-called Pennsylvania Dutch. Then in 1876 came the 'father of German-American comedy', Joseph Emmett, with another big hit, Charles Gayler's *Fritz Our Cousin German*. An Irish-American company headed by Wallace and Firmin came in 1878, and the Irish-American comedian Grattan Riggs in 1880. Other types of American comic material appeared over the next few years. In 1895 Mark Twain was a success in *At Home*, an idiosyncratic, folksy presentation of contrasting short comic stories.

In the early 20th century a slightly more aggressive type of American farce comedy was introduced, often with 'ethnic' elements. At first it bothered the audience, apparently because of its pace and style. The throwaway techniques of Willie Collier, a New York star, were not appreciated in 1906. But in 1912 Fred Niblo and his wife Josephine Cohan came and conquered until 1914. 'He has given American comedy a brilliant reputation here', the Sydney *Sun* said of Niblo on 1 June 1913. The Taits scored an even bigger success and made a fortune two years later by presenting *Peg o' My Heart*, an 'Irish' tearjerker by an American, J. Hartley Manners. It starred Sara Allgood, from the Abbey Theatre in Dublin.

More and more operettas were played in Australia from the beginning of the 20th century, but the distinctively American form of the musical was not yet indelibly established and the public seems not to have strongly associated the genre with the USA.

Meanwhile the parade of more serious American performers, with a more Europeanised repertoire, continued. Some of the more notable visitors included Mr and Mrs F. M. Bates in 1874; George D. Chaplin and Hattie Roche in 1877; Louise Pomeroy in 1881; the W. E. Sheridan company in 1882; Nance O'Neil in Ibsen in 1905; MINNIE TITTELL BRUNE from 1904 to 1909; and John Barrymore in 1906.

In early Australian VAUDEVILLE it was American genres rather than performers that made an important mark. In 1894 HARRY RICKARDS, founder of the first TIVOLI CIRCUIT, made use of four minstrel 'end men' as a prelude and as a frame for the vaudeville acts that made up the second part of his bills. Minstrel music was succeeded by the ragtime craze, which reached Australia in 1899 with ORPHEUS McADOO's Georgia Minstrels and Alabama Cakewalkers.

Notable Americans appeared on Rickards's bills—W. C. Fields as a comic juggler in 1903, the black boxer Jack Johnson in 1908, and the magician Harry Houdini and

The most influential American in the history of theatre in Australia was J. C. Williamson, an actor who founded the largest theatrical organisation in the world

Minnie Tittell Brune, a New Yorker, was a drawcard for J. C. Williamson. After five years in Australia she went to London and called herself Australian. Here, in the title-role of Edmond Rostand's L'Aiglon, she plays young Napoleon II, who was proclaimed Emperor of France but deposed after five days

End-men, a feature of the American blackface minstrel show in the middle of the 19th century, survived in Australian vaudeville into the second decade of the 20th century

Walter C. Kelly (uncle of Princess Grace of Monaco) in 1910—but most of his acts were English. Rickards died in 1911 and next year his heirs sold control of the Tivoli circuit to HUGH D. MCINTOSH, a sporting entrepreneur. McIntosh dropped Rickards's minstrel-show first part and the bill now resembled the American vaudeville formula. More star acts were needed to fill it and McIntosh recruited these from New York until the First World War cut off the supply of imported stars. Then McIntosh switched to musicals and revue. During the war burlesque of the American kind was epitomised by Bert Le Blanc, an American, who cemented its popularity through the FULLERS' management. Whereas English BURLESQUE developed out of a tradition of 'pantomime for elders'—a leg, costume and scenic show designed to titillate and relax—the American form was more robust and tartly satirical and developed from a tradition of afterpiece travesties. There were also many visitors who played a more idiosyncratic and informal American repertoire. They included juvenile actors and troupes; versatile solo acts with a gimmick, like Nell the California Diamond in 1876; female impersonators; and sister acts who performed light comedy and mildly erotic burlesque, like Adelaide and JOEY GOUGENHEIM from 1856 and the three Zavistowski Sisters in 1871.

It is tempting to conclude that Australians recognised an American performance style before the end of the First World War. In 1913 an obituary of J. C. Williamson claimed that as an actor he had introduced audiences to 'naturalness'. But even earlier, Jefferson and other performers had been praised for a low-key, 'naive' approach. In 1913 MURIEL STARR, in Bayard Veiller's courtroom drama *Within the Law*, was complimented for her 'naturalness' in weeping, which made it 'very powerful and real.' It seems that the bombast and large effects common with English performers were less usual with Americans.

American plays

Most of the distinctively American plays performed before the end of the First World War seem to have been given by American visitors. Australian performers apparently felt more comfortable with melodrama, the dominant and most international genre of the period. This may have been partly because most hit melodramas were localised and sometimes suitably retitled. Yet melodramas with American subject-matter that made localisation impossible were popular with Australian companies. These melodramas included *The Octoroon* and several pirated versions of *Uncle Tom's Cabin*, one of the most popular plays on the Australian stage in the 19th century.

Some American plays caught the public's fancy when done by Australians but others did not. For example, GEORGE DARRELL toured *Rube Redmond*, a pirated version of the Davy Crockett story, for years, but its success with local audiences was limited. On the other hand, NELLIE STEWART reached the height of her popularity in *Sweet Nell of Old Drury*, Paul Kester's sentimental romance about Nell Gwyn and King Charles II, which she first played in 1902.

There has been little research on American influence on early Australian plays. Margaret Williams has suggested that WALTER COOPER's *Fuss* (1888) may have owed something to the 'contrast' fable of early American drama, in which the old and new worlds are set against each other to the advantage of the new. Also, Cooper wrote his *Hazard* (1902) partly as a vehicle for his friend Frank Hussey, an experienced blackface performer. There is evidence that JO SMITH in his later plays like THE BUSHWOMAN (1909) was influenced by a more restrained new American drama which stressed the homely details of country life.

Australian actor-managers such as Darrell and ALFRED DAMPIER sometimes made adaptations, authorised or not, of American material. Cooper, Darrell, Dampier and other Australian actor-managers who toured the USA—with indifferent results—professed to have learnt a lot about up-to-date techniques of presentation. Greater awareness of the overseas theatre must also have made adaptation easier. For example, the first Australian play to be staged in New York—by the Dampier company on the way to London in 1878—was Garnet Walch's HELEN'S BABIES, but it was an adaptation of an American novel.

Williams has also drawn attention to the fact that the Australian bushranging melodrama accorded well with motifs from the American frontier myth and the Wild West shows. Dampier's THE SCOUT and *The Trapper* both utilised these strongly. *The Scout*, staged in 1891, had an American champion sharpshooter, W. F. CARVER, as its star, together with his Wild America troupe. The production sported spectacular action and tableaux that 'precluded any real need for acting,' as *Table Talk* put it on 15 May 1891.

In the next decade, E. I. Cole's BOHEMIAN DRAMATIC COMPANY had its own Wild West show which toured the outback under tents before settling down in Sydney. Cole's earliest season there began with *The Prairie Scout*, a western play that blended drama and Wild West show spectacle. The American plays that the company first produced must have influenced the later Australian plays it performed.

Managements look to USA

In the years between the world wars, American influence in theatre was more clearly than before tied in with world events—the exuberance of the 1920s, the impact of the Great Depression and the inexorable move towards the Second World War. Periods of prosperity, privation and recovery affected the importation of both performers and new repertoire. But in these years American influence was also affected by the taste and initiative of the heads of the commercial managements. These were still dominated by J. C. WILLIAMSON'S, which amalgamated with J. and N. Tait Ltd in 1920. GEORGE TALLIS, a major power in the Williamson firm, wanted to build an empire overseas, both

AMERICAN INFLUENCES

The Marcus Show came to Australia from the USA for J. C. Williamson's in 1937. It combined 'elements of Parisian and American revues in a manner probably unprecedented in Australian stage annals', said the Sydney Morning Herald

in London and New York—but he was frustrated by some production failures, the TAIT BROTHERS' caution, and the Great Depression. In 1929 he formed an alliance with three New York impresarios—Florenz Ziegfeld, Charles Dillingham and Abe Erlanger—for a joint Broadway production of *Josef Süss*, an adaptation by Ashley Dukes of Lion Feuchtwanger's novel *Jew Süss*. It starred the Russian-Jewish actor MAURICE MOSCOVITCH, who had recently toured Australia, but the venture failed. An American-style entrepreneur, ERNEST C. ROLLS, active as a producer–director from 1926 in Australia, propelled himself into a position of power after control of the Williamson firm shifted to New Zealand interests in 1937. Rolls was addicted to making grandiose promises about forthcoming stars, but before he was forced out in 1939 he brought out two major American shows with largely imported casts—the musical *I Married An Angel* and a quite daring choice in those times, Clare Boothe's *The Women*. The musical, in which an elevator stage was used for the first time in Australia, failed disastrously, but the controversial play toured for six months all over Australia and New Zealand.

Rolls also engaged a New York producer-director, Rowland G. Edwards, and his wife Doris Packer. The latter headed a stock company—along the lines of the New York Theatre Guild and the Group Theatre—organised by Frederick Blackman at the new MINERVA THEATRE in Sydney in 1939 and 1940. In a newspaper story Packer and Blackman made enthusiastic comparisons with the New York models, but the venture did not survive.

Three Americans played major managerial roles in variety in the interwar years. One was MIKE CONNORS, who with his Australian wife QUEENIE PAUL successfully instituted an amalgamation with the struggling Tivoli circuit in the depths of the Great Depression, relying on Australian artists and low prices to see them through. Later, WILL MAHONEY and EVIE HAYES, Americans originally brought out by the Tivoli, took over the management of the Cremorne Theatre in Brisbane and later the Theatre Royal. The management was popular with the American armed forces, who were more numerous in Brisbane than any other Australian city during the Second World War. During 1943-45 their performances, often with specially imported American artists, were open only to the American and Australian forces.

Visitors and repertoires 1919–46

Imported American 'stars' were more numerous between the wars, especially in the prosperous 1920s. Some of the more notable included Lilian Tucker in 1918; Dorothy South in 1920; Louis Benison, who had risen to fame in a cowboy role on Broadway, in 1921-24; the Canadian Muriel Starr, who came four times up to 1930; Gertrude Elliott (Lady Forbes-Robertson) in 1923; Joseph Coyne in 1921; John D. O'Hara in 1921–24; Maude Hanaford in 1921; Guy Bates Post in 1917 and 1924; Thurston Hall in 1924; Pauline Frederick in 1925; and Olsen and Johnson in 1928. In the 1930s American visitors included Robert Coote and the comic silent-film star Harold Langdon in 1936; Robert Halliday in 1937; Ruth Draper in 1938, Charlotte Greenwood in 1939; and Pauline Lord for two weeks in Melbourne in 1939. But it is difficult to discern a significant linkage between these performers and American material, except in the case of those who played in comedy. Quite often British or Australian performers played in American repertoire, and sometimes American imports relied on British plays and musicals.

American musical theatre became more characteristically American and a more conspicuous import between the wars. Jerome Kern was represented by the musical comedies *Oh, Lady! Lady!!* in 1921, *Sally* in 1923, *Good Morning Dearie* in 1924, *Leave It to Jane* and *The Cabaret Girl* in 1925, *Sunny* in 1927 and *Roberta* in 1935. But the most important Kern work *Show Boat* was not a success in Australia in 1928. To make the production more authentic, the Tait brothers urged the importation of 20 black actors. In the event only eight were used and even they were deemed by Tallis to be 'scraggy, ugly and unnecessary'. The Taits were held responsible for the box-office debacle.

Two Sigmund Romberg operettas, *The Desert Song* in 1927 and *The Student Prince* in 1928, proved significant later for revival seasons. There were three George Gershwin musical comedies: *Primrose* in 1925, *Tip-Toes* in 1928 and *Funny Face* in 1931. Likewise there were three from Cole Porter: *Gay Divorce* in 1934, *Anything Goes* in 1936 and *Let's Face It!* in 1942. The librettist Lorenz Hart and the composer Richard Rodgers were represented by *The Girl Friend* in 1928, *Dearest Enemy* in 1931 and *I Married an Angel* in 1938. In addition, there were several operettas with libretto or lyrics by Oscar Hammerstein II, including Rudolf Friml's perennial *Rose-Marie* in 1928. Quite often, choreographers and speciality dancers were imported from America to lend authenticity and style to the dancing, which was already of major importance in the genre.

In the early 1920s, the press associated the USA with the 'bedroom' plays—slightly salacious comedies with risqué scenes—and 'crook' plays, whodunits with melodramatic elements. So many plays of these kinds were offered that by 1921 the Sydney *Daily Telegraph* complained that American plays were being favoured over the better British ones. The paper was particularly offended by a Maude Hanaford vehicle, *Scandal*, which the Taits had milked with salacious advertising. It protested: 'This, if you please, is dramatic art as practised in that land of imitation Corots, vulgar dancing, and nigger music—America'.

A worthwhile play was occasionally staged—in 1928 the Moscovitch company presented Sidney Howard's *They Knew What They Wanted*—but the professional managements preferred innocuous middlebrow plays by now largely forgotten playwrights such as Rachel Crothers, Frank Craven and J. C. and Elliott Nugent. The most vital were farces by George M. Cohan and ethnic plays of Irish-American subject matter which were brought here by John D. O'Hara and Allen Doone.

In the late 1930s, more challenging American plays were attempted and they were more consistently cast with American stars. There are few signs in reviews of the public being aware of especially 'American' qualities of performance, although speed of delivery and 'low-key' acting could still be problems for Australian audiences. Some of these difficulties could be traced to many visitors having more of a Hollywood than a New York name. For instance, Mary Dees, a star of *The Women*, had no stage experience, but she had been Jean Harlow's stand-in and after her death had been used in the completion of the film *Saratoga*.

A 'Hollywood personality', Lina Basquette starred in Robert Sherwood's anti-Fascist play *Idiot's Delight*, which caused a stir in Melbourne and Sydney in 1939. In Sydney in 1939 Doris Packer, with more substantial stage experience, played in Maxwell Anderson's *Elizabeth the Queen* in 1939 at the M̦inerva Theatre, where a number of substantial American plays were done during the war, though with fewer American performers. The biggest success was George S. Kaufman and Moss Hart's *The Man Who Came to Dinner* in 1941–42. One of its stars was Diana Parnham, a glamorous American who, according to Viola Tait, needed American marines to protect her from past and present lovers when entering the theatre. Other American plays performed at the Minerva included Kaufman and Edna Ferber's *Dinner at Eight* in 1939, John Steinbeck's *Of Mice and Men* in 1940, and Lillian Hellman's *Watch on the Rhine* and Kaufman and Hart's *You Can't Take it with You* in 1942.

In the 1920s there were several imported American acts in vaudeville, including whole jazz bands, but during the Great Depression local performers dominated the bill. During the recovery Frank Neil, head of the Tivoli circuit, returned to a policy of importations, and the Americans included Mahoney and Hayes, and Billy Costello (the screen voice of Popeye the Sailor), Adriana Caselotti (the voice of Snow White), the Mills Brothers, and the female impersonator Lea Sonia.

Amateur theatre

The so-called 'repertory' theatres of the 1910s and 1920s rarely staged American plays. But one amateur group, the Playbox Society in Sydney, did produce significant American works. Its director, Duncan MacDougall, had worked on the first Eugene O'Neill play to be staged in New York, in 1916, and managed the small Barn Theatre in Greenwich Village for some years. Playbox began with O'Neill's *The Hairy Ape* in 1923, and the *Sydney Morning Herald* called the play 'crude drivel.' In 1926 Playbox produced Susan Glaspell and George Cram Cook's *Suppressed Desires*, Elmer Rice's *The Adding Machine* and O'Neill's *The Emperor Jones*. Maurine Dallas Watkins's *Chicago* followed in 1928.

The amateur theatres that emerged in the 1930s—the longest lasting were the Melbourne Little Theatre Company and Independent Theatre in Sydney—did few challenging American plays at that time. Melbourne Little Theatre, for example, did only three important American plays up to 1945—Lillian Hellman's *The Children's Hour* in 1936 and *The Little Foxes* in 1944, and Clare Boothe's *The Women* in 1945. Independent Theatre on average produced only two or three plays annually from 1930 to 1946 and they were mostly lightweight. There were four plays by Kaufman and Hart; three each by S. N. Behrman, Kaufman and Ferber, and Elmer Rice; two by Thornton Wilder; and one each by Maxwell Anderson, Robert Ardrey, Sidney Howard, Clifford Odets, O'Neill, William Saroyan, and James Thurber and Elliott Nugent. Neither did Gregan McMahon do any significant American plays towards the end of his career in the 1930s, with the possible exception of O'Neill's flawed *Days Without End*.

The American repertoire was of more importance to the socialist-oriented New Theatre movement, which began in 1932 and was named after the New Theatre League in the USA. Odets's *Waiting for Lefty* had enormous impact when

AMERICAN INFLUENCES

The Broadway sensation of 1943, Oklahoma! *came to Australia in 1949. Ten American principals performed the words of Oscar Hammerstein II, the music of Richard Rodgers and the choreography of Agnes de Mille*

first staged in 1936, as much for its unusual form as for its content, and it became a staple for the groups. Odets's anti-Fascist play *Till the Day I Die* incurred CENSORSHIP in two states in 1936, but some New Theatre performances were given among enormous controversy and publicity. This decided New Theatre groups to cement themselves to the Group Theatre model and repertoire, and to ally themselves more formally with the New Theatre League. Productions of further plays by Odets and Irwin Shaw were successful. New Theatre Melbourne took the 'Living Newspaper' form pioneered by the Federal Theatre project as a model for *Thirteen Dead*, a play about a mining disaster at Wonthaggi (Vic.).

Some pioneer Australian playwrights of the 1920s show some influences from O'Neill, whose works were then in print. Louis Esson greatly admired O'Neill and followed his development with interest, but an O'Neill-style abrupt development of dramatic action and melodramatic extremism of situation are not apparent until Esson's late unpublished plays *Shipwreck*, written in 1924–28, and *The Quest* of 1929–30. KATHARINE SUSANNAH PRICHARD's three plays of the 1920s—*The Great Man*, *Bid Me to Love* and BRUMBY INNES—reveal clearer traces of O'Neill in highly charged domestic and sexual confrontations and especially in the expressionist compression of the standard three-act play structure, which was evident in O'Neill plays of the 1920s.

Many Australian plays of the 1930s show similarities to the social-realist playwriting model as described by the American playwright John Howard Lawson in his influential study *The Theory and Technique of Playwriting*, first published in 1936. In this model, action and character were shaped specifically to drive home a social message. DYMPHNA CUSACK, for example, reveals this kind of schematisation in plays like *Comets Soon Pass* (1950) and *Morning Sacrifice* (1943) and the latter has overtones of Lillian Hellman. But GEORGE LANDEN DANN sometimes escapes this constriction and also reveals similarities with O'Neill in the lyricism and discursiveness of some of his plays, especially *In Beauty it is Finished* (1931) and *Fountains Beyond* (1942).

Two playwrights of the 1940s also show assimilated American influence. DOUGLAS STEWART, whose *The Fire on the Snow* was first performed on radio in 1941, admitted a debt to Archibald MacLeish and his 1937 radio play *The Fall of a City*. SUMNER LOCKE ELLIOTT, in *Invisible Circus* (1946) and his greatest success *Rusty Bugles* (1948), shows traces of Broadway comedies of the kind Independent Theatre was staging in the late 1930s. Elliott emigrated to the USA before the production of *Rusty Bugles*, depriving Australia of perhaps its first major modern playwright.

Changing attitudes to USA

During the Second World War, Australians were grateful for the defence support of the USA at a time when the United Kingdom could give little and afterwards Australia was more receptive than ever before to American influence. In the 1950s, there was accord in foreign policy, strengthened by the ANZUS Treaty in 1951, and economic reliance on massive imports of American secondary goods.

The decade saw the greatest exposure to American popular culture in Australian history, largely because television, introduced in 1956, needed American programs at first. Revue declined in importance in the face of television and big American names imported for concerts, although Americans were not especially favoured when the Tivoli circuit resumed its policy of importing overseas acts.

Meanwhile the musical had matured into the most inimitable and dynamic American genre. Unfavourable American and Australian tax laws delayed its invasion of Australia until 1947 but it dominated professional theatre in Australia through the 1950s. The leading American playwrights of the time, Tennessee Williams and Arthur Miller, were popular in the amateur theatre.

During the next decade, however, things turned increasingly sour. By 1967, many were castigating the USA for its dominance of Australia's foreign policy and economy, and American musicals were seen as one of the foreign influences that were preventing the Australian theatre from finding its own individuality. During the Vietnam War, the rising Australian alternative-theatre movement used American guerrilla-theatre techniques to attack American influences and policies.

From the 1970s American influence in Australian drama and theatre has declined further. In the 1950s, Rodgers and Hammerstein perfected what has been called the integrated musical, in which the musical numbers emerge unobtrusively from an evolving plot. This form developed on Broadway, but ossified in the 1960s, to be replaced in the early 1970s by the 'concept musical' in which a theme or image, rather than a plot, determined the use and placement of the musical numbers. Though usually associated with Stephen Sondheim and the director Harold Prince in several musicals, beginning with *Company* in 1970, the form quickly became internationalised and has never seemed as inimitably American as its predecessor.

Other overseas influences, including those of various British and European playwrights, have been on the rise. In addition, the decline of the commercial theatre and the rise of subsidised professional theatre in each state has reduced interstate touring productions with imported stars. Unable to adapt to these changes, and after an unsuccessful attempt in 1964 to merge with the Music Corporation of America, J. C. Williamson's collapsed in 1977, only to reconstitute itself a little later by selling off some theatres and allying itself with rival managements. Some of these rivals—headed by entrepreneurs like KENN BRODZIAK, GARNET H. CARROLL, MICHAEL EDGLEY, HARRY M. MILLER and HARRY WREN—had been a little more adventurous than Williamson's in choosing and casting American material.

Australian theatre traffic to the USA has not been notable, although more and more state companies have taken productions to second-string venues and festivals. Broadway productions of Ray Lawler's SUMMER OF THE SEVENTEENTH DOLL in 1958 and David Williamson's THE CLUB—as *The Players*—20 years later during a newspaper strike made little impact. Lawler's play, however, has had several New York revivals in smaller houses. Other Australian plays have been produced in smaller off-Broadway theatres and beyond New York City.

American musicals

The American musical deluge began with *Annie Get Your Gun* in 1947, starring an American immigrant, EVIE HAYES. *Oklahoma!* by Rodgers and Hammerstein followed in 1948, and both had long runs in all major centres. Hammerstein, married to an Australian, took a special interest in *Oklahoma!* His cousin Ted Hammerstein directed the production, for which ten American principals were imported. The majority of the musicals that followed had leading players who were either specially imported from the USA—where they were not true stars—or were Australian residents of American origin. Such musicals and players included—*Brigadoon* with Ken Cantril in 1951; *Kiss Me, Kate* with HAYES GORDON in 1952; *South Pacific* with Mary La Roche, Virginia Paris and Leonard Stone in 1953; *Call Me Madam* with Evie Hayes and Hayes Gordon in 1954. These were all J. C. Williamson's productions, and the line also included *Can-Can* in 1956, *My Fair Lady*, the biggest success of all, in 1959, *Camelot* and *How to Succeed in Business without Really Trying* in 1963, *Bye Bye Birdie* in 1964, *A Funny Thing Happened on the Way to the Forum* in 1964, *Fiddler on the Roof* in 1967 and *Promises, Promises* in 1973.

J. C. Williamson's broke with postwar precedent in 1957 and used two Australian leads in *The Pajama Game*, but this did not lead to a consistent new policy. JOHN McCALLUM, briefly head of the Firm in the mid-1960s, clashed with the board in insisting that an Australian, JILL PERRYMAN, play the lead in *Funny Girl* in 1966. Americans often directed the musicals. By 1970 FRED HEBERT had directed 12 Australian productions, mostly musicals, though his credits were chiefly those of a production stage manager. Hebert's career epitomised a habit in the Australian commercial theatre of the 1950s and 1960s of reproducing the Broadway production in detail. Several influential musicals were done by other managements. Garnet H. Carroll, working with the Tivoli circuit, presented *The Music Man* and *West*

Evie Hayes and Hayes Gordon, both Americans, headed the cast in Kiss Me, Kate *in 1952. Gordon came from New York for the J. C. Williamson's production. He remained in Sydney, where he became an influential teacher of Method acting and founded the Ensemble Theatre Company. Hayes performed in revue in Australia from 1938 and after the war she starred in a string of American musicals*

Side Story in 1960, *The King and I* and *The Sound of Music* in 1962, and *Carousel* in 1964. The most artistically important production, *West Side Story* was credited to the original director, Jerome Robbins. It had an almost entirely imported company and a revelatory dance ensemble but it failed at the box office. More popular and influential was the rock musical *Hair*, which was staged from 1969 to 1973. Its subject matter and style had far-reaching effects on the established theatre in Australia and familiarised thousands with American alternative-theatre devices in a palatable and effective fashion. *Hair* was produced by HARRY M. MILLER, with six black Americans in a mostly Australian cast, and given a wholly original direction by JIM SHARMAN.

The outstanding American musical of the later 1970s was *A Chorus Line* in 1977, which made the 'new' J. C. Williamson's financially viable. None of the many musicals staged in the 1980s had comparable influence, though there were several successes. One was *Chicago* in 1981, which the SYDNEY THEATRE COMPANY transferred to a commercial theatre and played in Melbourne, Adelaide and Hong Kong. The sources of imported stars were a little more varied after 1977, and more Australians were cast.

American drama

The 1950s marked a peak of popularity for American drama in Australia. The Method, as taught at the Actors' Studio in New York City was introduced to Australia by HAYES GORDON, who settled in Sydney and founded a revolutionary new style of theatre. The first productions of his ENSEMBLE THEATRE COMPANY exemplified the Method to stunning effect in 1957–58. This kind of acting training caught on elsewhere and began to displace the British-based methods which had been the norm in drama schools and academies in Australia. The realist American drama of the 1950s provided its ideal medium.

Australia's most gifted young directors of the time—WAL CHERRY, ROBIN LOVEJOY and Peter Summerton—and later JOHN TASKER were all consistently associated with American plays. The first three were responsible for important and successful productions—Cherry for the Union Theatre Repertory Company in Melbourne, Lovejoy for the TRUST PLAYERS and Summerton for Independent Theatre in Sydney. The last company performed no less than 18 American plays—including four by Tennessee Williams and two each by Arthur Miller, Thornton Wilder and William Inge—in seasons from 1954 to 1958.

The professional theatre did not neglect American plays. The OLD VIC THEATRE COMPANY's successful tour in 1948 included Thornton Wilder's demanding *The Skin of Our Teeth*. J. C. Williamson's avoided what Viola Tait called the 'kitchen-sink type of play'. This term encompassed the work of Eugene O'Neill, Tennessee Williams and Edward Albee, but Williams's *A Streetcar Named Desire* was somehow an exception in 1950, with three imported Americans. So was Robert Anderson's controversial *Tea and Sympathy* in 1956. Conventional comedies like Mary Chase's *Harvey* with Joe E. Brown in 1950, John Patrick's *The Teahouse of the August Moon* in 1955 and Howard Lindsay and Russel Crouse's *The Great Sebastians* in 1958 were the order of the day, however. Other managements were sometimes more adventurous, as was the case with WHITEHALL THEATRICAL PRODUCTIONS in Sydney in the late 1940s, the Carroll–Fuller Theatre Company with F. Hugh Herbert's risqué *The Moon is Blue* in 1952, and HARRY WREN with Herman Wouk's *The Caine Mutiny Court Martial* in 1954. But often such daring was paid for with financial failure.

The popularity of American drama declined steadily through the 1960s. New Theatre in Sydney produced Jean-Claude van Itallie's *America Hurrah!* in 1968, sparking a censorship battle. The Ensemble Theatre Company did more American plays than any other company in Australia. Of the total of 37 plays it produced from 1960 to 1968, 22 were American. Sydney's NIMROD THEATRE COMPANY staged important new American plays in the 1970s; so did the Playbox Theatre Company in Melbourne in the early 1980s, particularly works by Christopher Durang, David Mamet and Sam Shepard.

Important commercial productions of American plays in later years included Harry M. Miller's presentation of Mart Crowley's *The Boys in the Band*, which was at the centre of an Australian censorship battle in 1968–70, and a 1976–78 tour by an imported company in Ntozake Shange's highly regarded black feminist play *for colored girls who have considered suicide when the rainbow is enuf*.

Records show that some of the larger state-subsidised theatres that became well established from the 1970s—especially the SYDNEY THEATRE COMPANY, the QUEENSLAND THEATRE COMPANY, STATE THEATRE in Adelaide and the Tasmanian Theatre Company—rarely chose to stage important new American plays but there has been no lack of reverent revivals of 'classic' American plays of the 1950s and earlier. The most popular American play in Australia has been Tennessee Williams's *The Glass Menagerie* with 30 major productions all over the country since it was first done at the Minerva Theatre with an American cast and director in 1947. The Broadway comedies of Neil Simon, Bernard Slade and Leonard Gershe (*Butterflies are Free*) have been ubiquitously produced by professional and amateur companies alike, whereas seminal works by Durang, Mamet, David Rabe and Shepard have sometimes had only one or two productions in Sydney or Melbourne.

Contemporary influences on repertoire

By their own admission, RAY LAWLER and PETER KENNA, two Australian playwrights who first came to public notice in the 1950s, were heavily influenced by Tennessee Williams and Arthur Miller, mostly in technique and tone. For example, Lawler's *Summer of the Seventeenth Doll* reveals its debt to Williams in a salving lyricism in potentially 'sordid' subject matter, a heavy reliance on props as symbols, and a setting in the style of the American designer Jo Mielziner, with several rooms seen in cutaway section and area lighting to soften kitchen-sink literalness. Another influence from the Americans was a tendency to stress sensational violence and sexual strong-arm tactics. Some felt this was not a true reflection of the source, and in lesser playwrights of the 1950s it produced corny derivation.

In the 1960s, American influence clearly receded. A looser, more episodic kind of structure than the American realists of the 1940s and 1950s used was more evident in Australian plays. It derived more from the theatre of Brecht, the Theatre of the Absurd, and some of the younger English playwrights. The Australian alternative-theatre movement of the late 1960s and early 1970s owed a lot to the concurrent movement in American theatre. Betty Burstall's LA MAMA THEATRE in Melbourne took much inspiration as well as its title from Ellen Stewart's New York venue. The AUSTRALIAN PERFORMING GROUP, founded in 1970, had a similar title to Richard Schechner's American Performance Group, founded a couple of years earlier. Members of the Australian Performing Group read *Drama Review*, an important American publication which gave much space to the activities of the American radical theatre, and they knew of such techniques as the 'transformational' acting exercises of the Open Theatre in New York.

JOHN ROMERIL's agitational plays *Mr Big the Big Big Pig* and *The American Independence Hour* and the concomitant parade and demonstration at the American consulate in Melbourne in 1969 owed a debt to the American street-theatre and guerrilla-theatre movements of the time, and to the mask and puppet techniques of the Bread and Puppet Theatre. Paradoxically, American models were used to express Australian nationalist and anti-American content. There were, of course, other influences from elsewhere, notably from Jerzy Grotowski's Laboratory Theatre in Poland and the Open Space Theatre in London.

If American influence has been negligible in recent Australian drama, the depiction of the USA is overridingly negative. Fears of American domination of Australia had already been apparent in some plays of the 1960s, such as RIC THROSSELL's *Dr Homer Speaks* (1962) or RODNEY MILGATE's *A Refined Look at Existence* (1968). Later, two plays by Romeril—*Chicago, Chicago* (1969) and *He Can Swagger Sitting Down* (1972)—were entirely set in a mythicised and predatory America as a metaphorical warning of what Australia could become. Other playwrights recently have often presented the USA as a sinister power undermining Australia's economic and political independence—STEPHEN SEWELL, for example, in *The Blind Giant is Dancing* (1983).

The permanent legacy of all these American influences is probably less than the sum of its parts. The model of commercial entrepreneurship, which some have identified as typically American, has also been practised in the United Kingdom and other countries in the 20th century. The volatile emotional realism of the Method, which seemed so all-embracingly valid and truthful 30 years ago, has given way to wider-ranging acting methods more suitable for surreal and presentational forms of theatre. The American musical, once so internationally influential, is now internationally property—though Australia has yet to utilise it to real effect. Given the confident state of Australian theatre and the strength of contemporary Australian drama, it seems unlikely that American imported stars and material will ever regain the hegemony they had in the heyday of unsubsidised commercial theatre. Australian productions of American repertoire have never been really accurate in rhythm or intonation, but Australians rarely notice. The influence of American playwriting techniques and models on Australian drama up to 1960 seems likely to remain apparent whenever these plays are studied, admired and revived in production. ❦*Dennis Carroll*

further reading

CARROLL, DENNIS. *Australian Contemporary Drama*. Sydney: Currency Press 1994.

WATERHOUSE, RICHARD. *From Minstrel Show to Vaudeville*. Sydney: University of NSW Press 1990.

Judith Anderson AC DBE

Actor. Born 10 February 1898 in Adelaide. Originally Frances Margaret Anderson-Anderson. Acted in Julius Knight company during First World War. Acted mainly in USA from 1918. Performed in Australia 1927, 1955, 1966. Died 3 January 1992 in Santa Barbara (California, USA). DBE 1960. AC 1991.

Before she was 20 Judith Anderson was acting for J. C. WILLIAMSON'S in crowd-pleasers like Wilson Barrett's *The Sign of the Cross* and Booth Tarkington's *Monsieur Beaucaire* in a company led by JULIUS KNIGHT. 'Dear Julius Knight', she once said, 'he was so marvellous to me—he gave me the foundation of everything I know in the professional theatre'. It was perhaps this foundation that made critics find some of her acting too full-blooded when she returned to Australia for the newly formed AUSTRALIAN ELIZABETHAN THEATRE TRUST in 1955 in her greatest success, the version of Euripides's *Medea* by the American poet Robinson Jeffers. She also received indifferent reviews in 1966 when she appeared at the Adelaide Festival in a program of excerpts in an unsuitable venue. In the USA, where she made the bulk of her career from 1918, Anderson was seen in *Medea* as late as 1982, but as the Nurse, not in the leading role. Another of her American successes was Iris in Michael Arlen's *The Green Hat*, in which she returned briefly to Australia in 1927. ❦*John West*

further reading

HARTNOLL, PHYLLIS and PETER FOUND (eds). *The Concise Oxford Companion to the Theatre*. Oxford (UK): Oxford University Press 1993.

HERBERT, IAN (ed.). *Who's Who in the Theatre* 16th edn. London: Pitman 1977.

William Anderson

Entrepreneur. Born 14 January 1868 at Bendigo (Vic.). Theatrical manager in Bendigo c.1889–96. Married actor Eugenie Duggan 1898. Staged Australian plays by her brother Edmund Duggan and others 1905–c.1932. Built Wonderland City funfair in Sydney 1906. Built King's Theatre, Melbourne, 1908. Based in Adelaide c.1915–c.1930. Separated from wife in 1920s. Died 16 August 1940 in Melbourne. Father of actor Mary Anderson (1900–83).

From about 1897 to 1911 William Anderson was a major theatrical entrepreneur in eastern Australia, and he remained a manager of lesser prominence until 1939. The son of a Victorian gold-miner, Anderson claimed to have been stagestruck early in life, tried to run away with a circus, and played a robin in a pantomime. In fact he was unusual among his counterparts in that he never appeared on stage. He was solely a business promoter who learned his trade by posting bills and selling tickets at the Princess's Theatre in Bendigo and later by acting as agent for touring theatrical companies, arranging hire of theatres, orchestras and support staff, and advertising.

His marriage to EUGENIE DUGGAN led to the formation of a strong company. She was leading lady and her brother EDMUND DUGGAN played mostly villains and comic Irishmen. Other actors came from the Duggan and Holloway companies, which Anderson had presented in Bendigo. The new organisation played long and successful seasons in Sydney and Melbourne for many years, specialising in popular sensation melodramas such as *The Beggar Maid*,

Between Two Women, *East Lynne* and *The Face at the Window*. In 1902, persuaded by his wife, he presented a Sydney season of Edmond Rostand's *Cyrano de Bergerac*. After only a week it was replaced by *The Worst Woman in London*. In 1902 Anderson also formed a second company, which toured the eastern states and New Zealand.

One of Anderson's competitors, BLAND HOLT, had begun localising English plays with success since 1898. Anderson, after initial doubts, followed suit in 1905 with *Thunderbolt*, a bushranging drama by A. S. Joseph and Ambrose Pratt. His faith in local playwrights was rewarded in 1907, when Edmund Duggan and a leading comedian in his company, BERT BAILEY, gave him a spectacular success, THE SQUATTER'S DAUGHTER. Sceptical reviewers pointed out that it was a patchwork of localised scenes from English and American plays, but its flock of real sheep, shearing contest, horse-riding heroine, comic Scottish new chum, Ben Hall the evil bushranger, and spectacular bush scenery convinced audiences. Its Sydney season ran for a near-record 11 weeks. It was followed by other successful plays about Australian bush life, including in 1909 *The Man from Outback* by Bailey and Duggan and THE BUSHWOMAN by Jo Smith.

In Melbourne in 1910 Anderson staged a Melbourne Cup play, THE WINNING TICKET, which he had written with Temple Harrison, another of his actors, plagiarising much of the story and several visual sensations from an English play. Anderson also collaborated with the actor ROY REDGRAVE on *By Wireless Telegraphy*, a murder mystery based on the Crippen case. It had limited success.

At the time of his ventures into localised plays, Anderson began diversifying his investments. In Sydney on 1 December 1906 he opened Wonderland City at Tamarama Bay. It had three theatres, a switchback railway, a helter-skelter, a circus hippodrome, a maze, a Katzenjammer Castle, waxworks and many other attractions. When MEYNELL AND GUNN outbid Anderson for a new lease on the Theatre Royal in Melbourne he responded by building the KING'S THEATRE. In 1909–10 he began to invest in production and distribution of Australian films. Losses on Wonderland City caused him to go into partial retirement in 1912, leaving play production in the capable hands of Bert Bailey. In 1917 Edmund Duggan, who had remained with Bailey, rejoined Anderson and until the Depression they based their activities in Adelaide.

Anderson's daughter Mary starred in his Adelaide productions in the 1920s. He retained interests in many ventures and occasionally attempted seasons of plays from his old repertoire in Sydney in 1917 and in Melbourne in 1917, 1928 and 1929, with mixed success. In 1928 he presented Duggan as director and star of *The Rudd Family* by STEELE RUDD. This apparently rescued Anderson from bankruptcy and helped him through the Depression years, during which he returned to Melbourne. ❦*Richard Fotheringham*

further reading
WILLIAMS, MARGARET. The Barnum of Australia. *Australasian Drama Studies* 2/2 (Brisbane, April 1984).
WILLIAMS, MARGARET. William Anderson. *Australian Dictionary of Biography* 7. Melbourne University Press 1979.

reference
The Anderson collections of Australian playscripts, in the Mitchell Library (Sydney) and the La Trobe Library (Melbourne), constitute a major record of the Australian stage at the beginning of the 20th century.

William Andrews

Actor. Born 1836 in Sydney. Debut at Royal Victoria Theatre, Sydney, 1855. Went to Melbourne with G. V. Brooke 1855. Joined Barry Sullivan's company in Melbourne 1863. Died 1878 in Sydney.

The first actor trained in the colonies to spend his acting career on the Australian stage was William Andrews. He specialised in low comedy. The Sydney *Town and Country Journal* called him 'Australia's best comedian' and noted that 'the fame he acquired during his twenty-three years' association with the stage in Australia entitles him to the first place among Australian comedians'. His most successful comic roles were in two plays by WALTER COOPER—Joseph Grudge in COLONIAL EXPERIENCE in 1868 and Sponge Loafer in *Hazard* in 1872. He performed the drag role of Judy O'Brien in Garnet Walch's pantomime *Trookulentos, the Tempter* in 1871. He acted in Shakespeare but was better known for his roles in popular melodramas, including Mark Medal in Dion Boucicault's *London Assurance*. In his later years he was best known for Deacon Skinner in J. C. WILLIAMSON's production of *Struck Oil*. His final appearance was as Scrubs in *Rory O'More* at the Queen's Theatre in Sydney in 1878. ❦*Delyse Anthony*

further reading
Town and Country Journal (Sydney) 5 October 1878.

Julie Anthony

Singer. Born 24 August 1949 in Lamaroo (SA). Originally Julie Lush. Grew up on farm at Galga (SA). Began singing with band in local pub. Won television talent quest in Adelaide 1970. Sang in clubs and on television. Title-role in *Irene* in Sydney 1974 and London 1976. Vocal problems 1977–79. Club and television work in Australia and USA. Maria in *The Sound of Music* 1983.

After she had auditioned unsuccessfully for *A Little Night Music*, J. C. WILLIAMSON's cast 25-year-old Julie Anthony in the leading role of Irene O'Dare in the 1974 revival of the 1919 musical comedy *Irene*. Her youthful charm exactly suited the role and she was again the star of *Irene* two years later, when Williamson's joined the impresario Harold Fielding in a London production. After a year, throat problems forced her to return to Australia, where she rejoined the club circuit. She was booked to appear in London at Christmas 1977 but on opening her voice failed. In February 1979 she underwent a curative operation in Germany. After that she worked in clubs and television and became a regular singer at great public events, indoor and outdoor. A newspaper columnist has hailed her as the only person in Australia with the documented ability to sing *Advance Australia Fair* past the chorus. ❦*John West*

Gustavus Arabin

Actor, dramatist. Arrived in Hobart from London, November 1836. Australian debut at Theatre Royal, Hobart, 23 November 1836. Debut in Sydney at opening of Royal Victoria Theatre, 26 March 1838. In opening cast at Queen's Theatre, Adelaide, 11 January 1841. Stage manager at Olympic Theatre, Launceston (Tas.), 1842 to 1843. Married actor Frances Mackay.

Like other early stars of the Australian theatre, Gustavus Arabin followed his fortune. He started in Hobart, advertised as from 'The Theatres Royal, London and York,' as Jaffier in Thomas Otway's *Venice Preserv'd* at the Theatre Royal in November 1836, and quickly established himself as a favourite. His strength in melodrama and Walter Scott won him the *Tasmanian*'s praise on 23 December but the *Colonial Times* said on 13 January 1837 that he had 'mistaken his forte' as Othello. The *Sydney Gazette* also criticised his Othello when he played the part at the opening of the ROYAL VICTORIA THEATRE on 26 March 1838, but he became popular there. When the proprietor, JOSEPH WYATT, refused to raise salaries in November 1840 Arabin left for Adelaide, where he acted at the opening of the QUEEN'S THEATRE.

Arabin did little for his career by marrying the untalented actor FRANCES MACKAY in 1836. She provoked Arabin to 'imprudent behaviour' in Launceston (Tas.), when she eloped with an insane actor named Boyd. Arabin was forced to apologise for his behaviour in the Launceston press on 10 September 1842. In June 1843 he played Iago at the Olympic Theatre in Launceston and his loyal supporters preferred him to FRANCIS NESBITT, the Othello. Arabin took to writing plays, notably *Malavolti* which was submitted to the NSW Colonial Secretary in July 1845 and still performed as late as 17 June 1850 at the Royal Victoria in Sydney. He acted in Shakespeare with ELIZA WINSTANLEY at the Royal Victoria from October 1845 and stayed through 1846. Thereafter little is heard of him. ❦*Helen Musa*

Alexander Archdale

Actor, director. Born 1905 in India. Educated in England and Canada. Trained on tour with Henry Ainley. Acted in English repertory for five years. In West End theatres in London from 1932. In Royal Navy during Second World War. Came to Australia 1951. Australian debut with Mercury Theatre (Sydney) 1952. Sydney Critics' Circle Award for best actor 1952, 1962. Founding director of Community Theatre Company (Sydney) 1965–70. Also worked in radio and television drama. Died May 1986 in Sydney.

An actor of great skill and command, Alexander Archdale had the range to encompass the elegiac cadences of the old man remembering in Samuel Beckett's *Krapp's Last Tape* and the cynical worldliness of the Earl of Warwick in George Bernard Shaw's *Saint Joan*. He also had the vision and tenacity to found the Community Theatre Company— later the MARIAN STREET THEATRE COMPANY—and the director's ability to carry it through its first years. Archdale had the idea of starting a professional repertory company in Sydney in 1961, while he was recuperating from illness in England. He finally launched Community Theatre in October 1965, by directing a double bill of his own performance of *Krapp's Last Tape* and Christopher Fry's *A Phoenix Too Frequent*. He remained director of the company until a car accident and recurring illness made him retire in 1970.

Archdale came to Sydney in 1951 to join his sister, the educationist Betty Archdale, and soon commanded attention with brilliant performances for MERCURY THEATRE as the Father in Jean Anouilh's *Point of Departure* and in the title-role of August Strindberg's *The Father*. He also directed and acted in *The Man with a Load of Mischief* by Ashley Dukes and *Love from a Stranger* by Frank Vosper on an Arts Council tour of NSW in 1953; and in Frank Harvey jnr's *The Poltergeist* for METROPOLITAN THEATRE. In 1954 he toured in *Dear Charles* by Alan Melville for J. C. Williamson's. For the AUSTRALIAN ELIZABETHAN THEATRE TRUST he directed Brandon Thomas's *Charley's Aunt* in 1960, and played Warwick in *Saint Joan* with ZOË CALDWELL at the 1962 Adelaide Festival. He later redirected *Saint Joan* for a tour to Melbourne. In 1963 he played Molière's *The Miser* in the Festival of Perth, and in Sydney the lead in Friedrich Dürrenmatt's *The Visit* for INDEPENDENT THEATRE and *Krapp's Last Tape* for Q Theatre. After Archdale retired from Community Theatre he worked in television and film. He toured England with the Ralph Richardson company in 1973, and acted in Sydney for the OLD TOTE THEATRE COMPANY. In association with the Festival of Sydney in January 1977 Archdale devised a solo show, *Time's Wing'd Chariot*. The first half was a potpourri of poetry and character roles and the second his performance of *Krapp's Last Tape*. ❦*Lynne Murphy*

Robyn Archer

Director, singer, writer. Born 18 June 1948 in Adelaide. Originally Robyn Smith. Educated at University of Adelaide. Taught in secondary schools 1973–74. Wrote first theatre piece *The Live-Could-Possibly-Be-True-One-Day Adventures of Superwoman* 1975. Gave Brecht–Weill recitals in Australia, Hong Kong and United Kingdom during 1970s and 1980s. Began writing political cabarets and solo shows 1978. National concert tours 1980–89. In artistic directorate of Belvoir Street Theatre (Sydney) from 1986. Australian Artist Creative Fellowship 1991–93. Director of National Festival of Australian Theatre (Canberra) 1993–.

In a multifaceted career, Robyn Archer has used many forms of music-theatre as vehicles for protest and trenchant comment on political and social issues, especially those affecting women. In Australia and London in the late 1970s and throughout the 1980s she established herself with singular success as a satirist of established behaviour by writing, directing and performing in political cabaret that examined attitudes to sex, politics and feminist thought.

Archer began singing folk songs to her own guitar while she was at high school. In 1964–65 she was on contract to the television pop music show *Bandstand*. At the University of Adelaide she sang jazz, folk music and rock 'n' roll, performed in revue and drama, worked in children's theatre, music-hall and television, and formed her first band. After graduation she taught English, worked in hotels and clubs and performed in pantomime and revue, in Adelaide, Melbourne and Sydney. She sang as Annie I in *The Seven Deadly Sins*, a ballet with words by Bertolt Brecht and music by Kurt Weill, in Adelaide in 1974 . Next year she appeared in the same authors' *The Threepenny Opera* and she has since become an acclaimed interpreter of music of Germany during the Weimar republic, and particularly of Weill in his collaborations with Brecht. Early 20th-century Viennese cabarets inspired her satirical *Cafe Fledermaus* in 1990.

In her writing, performing and directing Archer has consistently addressed political and sexual issues. In the late 1970s and throughout the 1980s, working in London and Australia, she wrote, directed and performed in cabaret shows including *Kold Komfort Kaffee* in 1978, *A Star is Torn* in 1979, *Tonight Lola Blau* in 1979, THE PACK OF WOMEN in 1981, *Cabaret Passé* in 1983, *Cut and Thrust* in 1983 and *Scandals* in 1985. *A Star is Torn* opened at the Universal Theatre in Melbourne, toured nationally in 1980 and opened in London in 1982; it transferred to the West End. In 1983 it returned for seasons at the Princess Theatre in Melbourne and Her Majesty's Theatre in Sydney. All these shows examined attitudes to sex, politics and feminist thinking and established Archer's willingness to confront established behaviour through satirical theatre. ❦*Michelle Potter*

published works
Cafe Fledermaus (1990). Sydney: Currency Press 1990.
The Robyn Archer Songbook. Melbourne: McPhee Gribble 1980.

further reading
MITCHELL, SUSAN. *Tall Poppies*. Melbourne: Penguin 1992.

Arena Theatre Company

Professional theatre-in-education company in Melbourne. Began as Toorak Players Children's Theatre 1966. Became fully professional as CAT (Children's Arena Theatre) 1968. Adopted present name 1982. **venues** 1966–72 converted hall in Armadale. 1972–91 converted hall in South Yarra. 1992– Napier Street Theatre, South Melbourne. **directors** 1968–70 Be Colchin, 1968–73 Elaine Clark, Naomi Marks, Robin Ramsey, 1970–73 Phillipa Metz. 1973–75 David Young, 1976–77 John O'May, 1977–80 Peter Tulloch, 1980–85 Peter Charlton, 1985–88 Angela Chaplin, 1988–92 Barbara Ciszewska, 1993– David Carlin.

Melbourne's major and oldest professional producer of theatre-in-education, the Arena Theatre Company typically tours four plays a year to schools in the metropolis and other parts of Victoria. Vigorous commissioning of new works from prominent local writers and employment of experienced designers enable it to create engaging plays of direct relevance to children in specific age groups.

Since 1980 Arena, performing almost entirely works written in Australia, has developed a distinctive, intellectually stimulating and aesthetically enriching style. It is visual, physical, musical and, above all, non-naturalistic and increasingly non-didactic. Arena's work during the 1980s tended to focus away from curriculum topics to fictional themes and wider social issues. Peter Charlton's *Wolf Boy* in 1982 was a fantasy about a boy growing up among wolves. Julianne O'Brien's *The Rainbow Warrior* in 1988 portrayed the sinking of the Greenpeace ship by French saboteurs in New Zealand. Ernie Gray's *Fix It, Alice* in 1989 was about a woman working in male-dominated vehicle-building. Other important works dealt with sex education (Gilly Farrelly's *Dancing in the Dark* in 1990), mathematics (Peter Dickinson's *Your Number's Up* in 1989) and multiculturalism (TES LYSSIOTIS's *Zac's Place* in 1991). Another play by Julianne O'Brien, *The Women There*, was performed at the Come Out Festival in Adelaide in 1987 and the Vancouver Children's Festival in 1988.

The company originated in the amateur Toorak Players Children's Theatre, for which Naomi Marks produced plays by the British educational writer Brian Way. In consequence, the company's repertoire was mainly British until 1980. It commissioned its first Australian play, *The Incredible Mind-Blowing Journey of Jack Smith* by HELMUT BAKAITIS in 1971. John O'May presented the first all-Australian season in 1976. Its South Yarra theatre was converted for three-sided arena staging and renamed the Arena Theatre in 1974. Since 1993 Arena's repertoire has alternated between commissioned 'in-theatre' works and plays in schools. It no longer employs a permanent acting ensemble. ❦*Geoffrey Milne*

Argyle Assembly Rooms

Theatre in assembly rooms at corner of Argyle and Liverpool Streets, Hobart. Opened as **Theatre Royal**, seating 500, on 29 May 1834. Renamed **Albert Theatre** 1842. Used until late 1840s.

The main theatrical venue in Hobart between the first season at the FREEMASON'S TAVERN in 1834 and the opening of the New THEATRE ROYAL in 1837, was the Argyle Assembly Rooms. John Mezger, a successful businessman, built the Argyle Rooms alongside his Bird in Hand Hotel. His first tenant was the entrepreneur and musician J. P. DEANE, who began giving musical soirées in February 1834. These ended with short pantomime pieces, which proved successful, and Deane fitted up the assembly rooms as the Theatre Royal. It opened with Henry Melville's play THE BUSHRANGERS. The theatre had fine acoustics, a splendid chandelier and, a report said, 'abundant stage room and a division of the audience ... of all classes'.

The actor–manager SAMSON CAMERON leased the theatre late in 1834 and altered the seating. Another actor–manager, JOHN MEREDITH altered it again in 1836. 'Instead of a continuous line of seats, there are now stage boxes, pit, back pit and above these there are the boxes and private boxes', the *Colonial Times* reported on 5 April 1836. The theatre could not withstand the competition of the New Theatre Royal, which opened in March 1837, but it was an alternative during the 1840s.

ANNE CLARKE called it the Albert Theatre in 1842, when she launched her company from England. LUIGI DALLE CASE's company performed in it in 1843. A newspaper called it 'a neat little theatre' in 1848 but it was probably too small for the increasingly complex scenery and machinery required for new plays and the greater realism demanded by later playgoers. ❦*Gillian Winter*

Neil Armfield

Director. Born 22 April 1955 in Sydney. Began directing for Sydney University Dramatic Society. Graduated 1977. First professional production for Nimrod Theatre Company (Sydney) 1979. Artistic co-director of Nimrod Theatre Company 1980–82. Associate director of Lighthouse Company (Adelaide) 1983. Has directed especially for Belvoir Street Theatre (Sydney), State Theatre Company of South Australia (Adelaide) and Sydney Theatre Company. On board of Company B at Belvoir Street Theatre 1984–. Also directs opera, film and television. Churchill Fellowship 1984. Sidney Myer Performing Arts Award 1989 for outstanding individual achievement. Sydney Critics' Circle Awards 1986 (*Glengarry Glen Ross* by David Mamet), 1988 (*Ghosts* by Henrik Ibsen), 1989 (*Diary of a Madman* and special award for an outstanding year's contribution), 1990 (*The Tempest*), 1992 (*Uncle Vanya* by Anton Chekhov). Green Room Award 1987 (*Away* by Michael Gow), 1988 (*Hate* by Stephen Sewell). Australian Artist Creative Fellowship 1992–94.

A steady creative—even familial—bond with playwrights and actors has made Neil Armfield one of Australia's most valued stage interpreters. His work is alert and startling, and originates in a belief that the theatre has a responsibility to surprise. His inventive and original productions of the classics make characters and stories from all ages and all cultures speak to Australia today. 'You took me up into high mountains where I could see all the kingdoms of this world', the historian Manning Clark wrote to Armfield about his production of Henrik Ibsen's *Master Builder* at the BELVOIR STREET THEATRE in 1991.

Armfield's production of Barrie Keefe's *Gimme Shelter* for the SYDNEY UNIVERSITY DRAMATIC SOCIETY in 1979 brought him an invitation to be a guest director with the NIMROD THEATRE COMPANY. His first professional production, DAVID ALLEN's *Upside Down at the Bottom of the World*, was invited to the 1980 Edinburgh Festival. Armfield's Nimrod productions in 1980 included a dynamic staging of STEPHEN SEWELL's *Traitors* and the premiere of LOUIS NOWRA's *Inside the Island*. Other premieres directed by Armfield include Nowra's *Whitsunday* (1988); Sewell's *Welcome the Bright World* (1982), *THE BLIND GIANT IS DANCING* (1983), *Dreams in an Empty City* (Adelaide Festival 1986) and *Hate* (Melbourne 1988); Patrick White's *Signal Driver* (1982) and *Shepherd on the Rocks* (1987). He also directed revivals of White's *THE SEASON AT SARSAPARILLA* in 1983 and *THE HAM FUNERAL* in 1989.

Armfield's production of *Twelfth Night* in a Caribbean setting for the Lighthouse Company in Adelaide in 1983 was highly popular. It transferred to the 1984 Sydney Festival and was later filmed. He added to his reputation as an author's director with two successful David Mamet plays for Gary Penny Productions, *Glengarry Glen Ross* in 1986 and *Speed the Plow* in 1989. In recent years he has turned to classics and opera. His Belvoir Street production of DAVID HOLMAN's adaptation of Nikolai Gogol's *Diary of a Madman* toured to Russia and Georgia in 1992. Armfield has been a member of the board of Company B, the artistic body at Belvoir Street, since its inception and since 1994 artistic director. ❦*May-Brit Akerholt*

Army entertainment units

Isolated military units have long resorted occasionally to theatrical entertainment to ward off boredom and raise morale, but the organised concert party or entertainment unit is of comparatively recent origin. Australia's earliest attempts at entertaining the troops appear to date from the First World War. In the Gallipoli, Sinai and Palestine campaigns against Turkey and the later campaigns against the Germans in Belgium and France the very nature of the terrain precluded entertainment of Australian troops, official or otherwise. In November–December 1916 officials of the Australian Comforts Fund hired a large barn in a French village and arranged concerts for units of the Australian and New Zealand Army Corps.

The Australian divisions began organising their own divisional concert parties. The concert party of the 4th Australian Division, known as the Smart Set, was preparing to perform at Allonville on 31 May 1918 when two shells hit a barn alongside the theatre. The entertainers survived unscathed but 87 men of the 4th Brigade billeted in the barn were killed or wounded. The Smart Set Diggers and other all-male concert parties that had given shows in France toured Australia and New Zealand after the war as DIGGER COMPANIES.

It was different at the start of the Second World War. Commanding officers established units to entertain brigades, then divisions. Later in the war Army Amenities organised units and the 1st Australian Army Entertainment Unit was established under the command of Lieutenant-Colonel Jim Davidson, a famous bandleader. These units and many more entertained Australian and Allied forces throughout the Middle East and the South West Pacific Area. Sometime the audience would be as small as a few dozen men in a couple of gunpits on a battle perimeter, but at the end of the Pacific war audiences of 15 000–20 000 were commonplace in the back areas.

During the six years of the Second World War the men and women of the Australian armed forces were entertained at home and overseas by the greatest collection of musicians, comedians, dancers, singers, female impersonators, jugglers, acrobats, straight men, speciality acts, ventriloquists, magicians and technicians in the history of Australian show business.

Memories of their performances linger with men and women who often sat in mud, in blinding rain, in sandstorms, in blazing heat or under attack by enemy forces, to see a few hours of world-class entertainment. By the end of the war there were more than 20 concert parties and detachments in the 1st Australian Army Entertainment Unit and each gave hundreds of shows. More than 12 000 performances were given in North Africa, Syria, Palestine, Dutch New Guinea, Papua and New Guinea, Bougainville, New Britain and Borneo.

Men gathered from the 16th Brigade of the 6th Australian Division at a camp at Ingleburn, outside Sydney, formed the first concert party of the Second Australian Imperial Force. A member of a theatrical family, Corporal John Harris, was the driving force behind the organisation of the concert party, which gave its first concert, called 'Aussies on Parade', at the camp on 9 November 1939. The 6th Division Concert Party later performed in Libya, Greece and Crete, northern Australia and Borneo.

Other divisions formed concert parties while on service in the Middle East and Malaya in the early years of the war. In late 1940, the famous comedian JIM GERALD, with the rank of lieutenant-colonel, and Jim Davidson, with the rank of lieutenant, recruited about 70 entertainers, musicians and stage technicians at Victoria Barracks in Sydney. They arrived in Egypt in September 1941, where civilian female musicians and showgirls joined the concert party. Its first show, 'All in Fun', had a gala opening night on 16 December 1941 near Gaza in Palestine. The Middle East (HQ) Concert Party was formed shortly afterwards.

Concert parties in the Pacific

Other divisional and lines-of-communication area concert parties came into being in Australia from the end of 1941, when Japan widened the war in the Pacific and men were called into the five divisions that comprised the Australian Military Forces. The 30 Club Concert Party came out of the 30th Brigade, which was rushed to Port Moresby in the desperate early days of 1942.

Several other units were formed in 1942 and did early service in the Pacific islands. A small group of men who were posted to Milne Bay in New Guinea as transport drivers became the Milne Bay Force Concert Party because of their musical and other talents.

The 1st Division Concert Party, known as the Boomerang Show and more often as the Crazy Days Show, was formed in Melbourne soon after Australia went to war with Japan. 'Happy' Hammond was the producer and comedian and Keith Glover was the compere and straight man. The commander was Lieutenant Noel Waterworth, who had organised the 7th Division Concert Party in Syria.

The 2nd Division Concert Party, better known as the Islanders, was formed in midsummer 1941–42 and gave its first shows in a deroped boxing ring at Walgrove Camp, west of Sydney. It did tours of duty in Western Australia, Dutch New Guinea, north Queensland, the Torres Strait Islands, New Britain and New Guinea and, after the war, Victoria, NSW and Queensland. George Wallace jnr was the producer and comedian. The present writer served as compere, straight man, character actor and writer. Doug Cross was musical director, followed by Wally Nash and Neville Chynoweth.

Just before the war ended the Islanders were posted to Lae in New Guinea, where their last concert was in support of the English comedian Gracie Fields in front of 25 000 troops. For most of the war the Islanders were commanded by Lieutenant Fred Hughes, a distinguished actor-manager before the war.

The 3rd Division Concert Party was formed in June 1942 and gave its first show at Maryborough (Qld) on 1 October 1942. Until the end of 1945, it presented five different shows in Queensland and the Northern Territory and three in New Guinea.

The 4th Division Concert Party did a tour of duty through the backblocks of Western Australia as far north as Geraldton, an area in which many Australian troops were stationed, waiting for a Japanese invasion. After several tours of duty through the Australian hinterland, the concert party found itself at Cape York, on the Torres Strait Islands and in Dutch New Guinea. Les Dixon was the musical director and BILL KERR was the comedian.

The 5th Division Concert Party, one of the first officially organised, called itself the Divvy Show and gave its first performance at the Theatre Royal in Townsville (Qld) towards the end of 1942. In May 1943 it went to Milne Bay to relieve the New Guinea Force Concert Party. Then it toured the islands until June 1944 and returned to Brisbane.

The 6th Division Concert Party served in the Western Desert, Greece and Crete. It was inspirational in the evacuation of Crete, singing song after song to rally the retreating troops. A member of the concert party was the female impersonator Eric Paige, who had been a member of the Smart Set Diggers in France during the First World War.

The 7th Division Concert Party was formed in Syria and performed there before returning to Australia. After a tour of southern Queensland, in October 1943 its members found themselves playing to Australian and US troops in the Ramu Valley in New Guinea, during one of the most brutal battles fought in the New Guinea campaign .

The 8th Division Concert Party was formed in Malaya, where seven of its members were killed in action against the Japanese. The remainder were incarcerated at the infamous Changi Prison in Singapore where they settled down and organised entertainment for the other prisoners of war.

The 9th Division Concert Party was formed in Libya and returned to Australia after service at the siege of Tobruk. At the end of 1944, as the division went into action in New Guinea, the concert party presented a new show, called *22 Hits and a Miss*, at Townsville. COLIN CROFT and the bandleader Frank Coughlan were later seconded from the concert party to a detachment called the Ramblers which did a tour of duty in Bougainville in the latter months of 1945.

The 11th Division Concert Party was assembled originally in Melbourne. Various elements of it formed the New Guinea Force Concert Party. In 1943 Major Jim Davidson formed the 50-50 Show in the Port Moresby area. It comprised 30 members from the Australian Army, six from the Royal Australian Air Force and 21 from the US Army. Personnel of the show included Leigh Bridson, Joe Latona, Royston MacGregor, JOHN MCCALLUM, Charles Munro and RALPH PETERSON. Davidson produced the show.

The lines-of-communication areas—basically the capital cities—provided other concert parties to entertain the troops throughout the Australian mainland and the Pacific islands. In the NSW LOC area the Waratahs gave their first concert at Ingleburn Army Camp on 21 September 1942 and many shows in Australia before being posted to New Guinea in 1944. Their last performance in New Guinea was at Wewak in late 1945, supporting Gracie Fields. Buster Noble was the comedian. The concert party was commanded at first by Lieutenant Robin Wood, a classical pianist, and later by Albert Chappelle, a well-known baritone in prewar musical theatre.

A concert party known variously as the Digger Dandies and the Queenslanders, formed in the Queensland LOC area, toured continually around Australia and served for some time in the Port Moresby area.

In the Tasmanian LOC area, a concert party known as the Tasmaniacs was formed in Hobart and for some time performed a revue called *The Lights of London* with a chorus line of extremely pretty girls, some local, some from other states and most of them professional. The concert party was eventually posted overseas and saw service in New Guinea and Bougainville.

In the Victorian LOC area the Yarraroos, later known as the Kookaroos, first performed as a concert party on 14 September 1942 at an anti-aircraft station at Coode Island. Max Reddy was the comedian, John Storr was the straight man and Smokey Dawson provided his brand of country music. After a tour of duty in north Queensland, the concert party was posted to Bougainville from May 1945 until the end of the year.

In the Western Australian LOC area the WALOCS concert party was formed in mid-1942 and served mainly in the west. Various members of the original troupe, including John Lennigan, Kevin Caporn and Eddie Smith, were transferred to other concert parties during the war.

Army Entertainment Unit

Towards the end of the war other units were created under the umbrella of the 1st Australian Army Entertainment Unit, which was officially formed in early April 1945. It comprised some 450 men and women under the command of Lieutenant-Colonel Jim Davidson. He put Sergeant PETER FINCH in charge of forming the Army Theatre Company at the Army Entertainment Unit headquarters at Pagewood in Sydney. On 18 June 1945 it moved out to tour army camps in NSW and Victoria in two plays by Terence Rattigan, *While the Sun Shines* and *French Without Tears*. In late September the company was shipped to New Guinea. After tours of duty there and in New Britain it returned to Sydney on 8 May 1946.

Thirty of the finest musicians in Australia were seconded from their units to form the Army Concert Orchestra at Pagewood. The orchestra, which was in operation shortly before the theatre company, was conducted at various times by Ken Macpherson, Anton Sorgato and Charles Munro. Essentially a smaller version of the ABC orchestras in Melbourne and Sydney, it played classics and lighter works on tours throughout Victoria, NSW and Queensland for most of 1945.

Troubadour concert parties were formed to entertain combat troops in Bougainville and throughout the Borneo campaign. They had minimal personnel and would often give shows under gunfire.

In February 1946 the Army Musical Comedy Company, under the command of the newly commissioned Lieutenant Albert Chappelle, was posted to Rabaul in New Britain to present *The Maid of the Mountains*. There was no theatre in the town but, with the support of the area commander, Chappelle drew up plans for one. These were given to a captured Japanese engineer and within nine hours the theatre was ready for Chappelle and his company to begin performing *The Maid of the Mountains*. Chappelle played Beppo and Sid Ellwood conducted the orchestra. The company returned to Pagewood for demobilisation on 2 May 1946. The entry in the War Diary/Intelligence Report of the 1st Australian Army Entertainment Unit (1–31 May 1946) reads for 3 May: 'Pagewood —0900 hrs—Lieut. A. E. Chappelle posted as O.C. Entertainment Unit.' Chappelle was the last officer commanding the 1st Australian Army Entertainment Unit and he supervised its disbandment in July 1946. ❦*Michael Pate*

further reading
Pate, Michael. *An Entertaining War*. Sydney: Dreamweaver Books 1986.

Linda Aronson

Dramatist. Born 20 March 1950 in London. Educated at New University of Ulster and Oxford University. Emigrated to Australia 1973. Australia Council Young Writer's Fellowship 1979. Consultant scriptwriter with Australian Film Television and Radio School 1981–82. Has written for stage, radio, television and film. Sydney Theatre Company Short Play Prize 1984 and Australian Elizabethan Theatre Trust biennial play award 1985 for *Reginka's Lesson*. NSW Women and Arts Fellowship 1987.

Linda Aronson's six stage plays engage the audience with wry humour while they explore the problematical interaction between the social and personal conditions of the characters. The two most successful are *Dinkum Assorted*, which examines the social position of women working in a wartime biscuit factory, and *Reginka's Lesson*, concerned with a woman's attempts to cope with isolation, as her friends and relatives die or move away. ❦*Carolyn Pickett*

published plays
Dinkum Assorted (1988). Sydney: Currency Press 1990.
Reginka's Lesson (1986). Sydney: Currency Press 1990.

Arrow Theatre

Amateur dramatic company in Melbourne, founded in 1951 by Frank Thring. Closed 1954. **venue** Arrow Theatre, Middle Park. **artistic director** Frank Thring. **first production** *Salome* by Oscar Wilde and *A Phoenix Too Frequent* by Christopher Fry. Director: Irene Mitchell.

Frank Thring brought amateur and professional experience and the necessary finance to the Arrow Theatre. He renamed the 200-seat theatre of the defunct Melbourne Repertory Theatre and spared no expense in production. As actor-manager he aimed to present the best plays of present and past, and he staged at least one Australian play, *The Square Ring* by Ralph Peterson. But the inner-suburban location was a drawback. The theatre lacked public support and heavy financial loss forced Thring to close it. He went to England and other Arrow Theatre actors—including Bunney Brooke, Zoë Caldwell and Moira Carleton—found professional work with the Union Theatre Repertory Company. ❦*Joan Maslen*

further reading
Arrow Theatre Souvenir Programme 1951–53.
Thring, Frank and Roland Rocheccioli. *The Actor Who Laughed*. Melbourne: Hutchinson 1985.

Artrage

Known unofficially as 'the spring festival', Artrage has become a well-established annual event in Perth. It began in 1983, when a loose confederation of West Australian artists formed the Perth Festival Fringe Society to provide a program of visual and performing arts as an alternative to the Festival of Perth. The Fringe Festival was held simultaneously with the main festival during February and March until 1987. In 1988 its title was changed to Artrage and since then it has been held in October—before Christmas and the summer holidays drain the public's wallet. Artrage is funded annually by the Western Australian Department of the Arts and half goes directly to participating artists. Administrative costs are carefully managed and Artrage has advertised effectively since it began.

Artrage is a platform for innovation and experimentation in many arts. Theatre has been prominent, with playwrights, directors and actors taking risks not possible in the mainstream. Plays given first performances at Artrage include John Aitken's *Watershed*, David Britton's *Landlovers*, Larry Buttrose's *Pallas*, Paige Gibbs's *Something Blue*, Sally Richardson's *Picasso and Françoise* and Maree Walk's *A Lone Woman* and *Casualty*. Among many challenging plays from overseas given world premieres at Artrage have been Harvey Fierstein's *Safe Sex*, Catherine Hayes's *Skirmishes*, Slawomir Mrozek's *The Emigrants* and John Patrick Shanley's *Danny and the Deep Blue Sea*. Perhaps the most memorable Artrage production has been Jack Hibberd's *A Stretch of the Imagination*, directed by Simon Phillips in 1987 with Bill McCluskey as Monk O'Neill. A great critical success, it was invited to World Expo '88 in Brisbane. ❦*Maurice Jones*

Arts Council of Australia

One of the oldest continuously functioning arts bodies in the country, the Arts Council of Australia operates through committees of local volunteers, arranging performances, exhibitions, training workshops and community arts projects, mainly outside capital cities. Funded by all levels of government, it is a communal organisation with autonomous state branches and councils. It was founded in 1943 by DOROTHY HELMRICH, a lieder singer. At an age when most people consider retirement, Helmrich, a woman of determination, enthusiasm and drive, set about ensuring access to the arts for all Australians and particularly those who lived outside the capital cities. She called it the Council for the Encouragement of Music and the Arts (CEMA), the same name as a British government organisation for which she had sung. In 1946, the British CEMA was reconstituted as the Arts Council, and the Australian CEMA followed suit in 1947, becoming the Arts Council of Australia.

The early years were difficult. There was no government money for arts organisations and there was only a handful of professional and semiprofessional performing companies. J. C. WILLIAMSON'S dominated the theatrical scene. The Arts Council mounted performances by drawing on amateur theatre companies such as INDEPENDENT THEATRE in Sydney, dance schools and individual singers and instrumentalists. Helmrich gathered around her committees of volunteers from the arts, business and education. Performances were possible only because people in the Arts Council gave personal guarantees against loss. The publishing magnate Sir Frank Packer provided the guarantee against loss when the Arts Council Ballet performed *Corroboree* at a gala in the presence of Queen Elizabeth II in Sydney on 6 February 1954, but the members of the Arts Council's executive committee paid for the costumes and production. The second phase of the Arts Council's development came in 1948 with federal and state government funding. It became a nationwide organisation with divisions in each state and branches in most country towns.

Funding led to important differences in the operations of the Arts Council's divisions because each needed to find a niche in the overall arts policies of its state. The NSW council has ceased entrepreneurial activity in favour of helping local arts councils with projects and funding. It also employs regional staff. Queensland, Tasmania, the Northern Territory and Victoria engage in considerable touring of performances to the country areas and into metropolitan and country schools. In South Australia the function of the Arts Council has been now subsumed by the South Australian Country Arts Trust, though local councils are still active. In Western Australia the Arts Council, which had been absorbed into the Arts Ministry, has emerged as an independent body. The ACT Arts Council has ceased operation. The arts councils share their entrepreneurial role with their branches and local arts councils in varying proportions. The Arts Council of Australia is now a co-ordinating body, lobbyist and organiser of a biennial conference of the state and territory councils. ❦*Paul Kelly*

further reading
HELMRICH, DOROTHY. *The First Twenty-Five Years—A study of the Arts Council of Australia*. Sydney: Arts Council of Australia, NSW division 1968.

Oscar Asche

Actor, dramatist, manager. Born 24 January 1871 at Geelong (Vic.). Developed interest in theatre from actors visiting his Norwegian father's hotel in Sydney. Trained in Kristiana (Sweden) under actor-manager Björn Bjørnson and in London. Made London debut in *Man and Woman* at Opéra Comique Theatre, March 1893. Married actor Lily Brayton 1899. Toured Australia with companies 1909–10, 1912–13, 1922–24. Staged unsuccessful last show, *The Good Old Days of England,* in London 1928. Published autobiography 1929 and two novels 1930. Directed Brayton's last stage appearance 1932. Died 23 March 1936 at Bisham (England).

A huge man with a dominating stage presence, Oscar Asche brought plays, Oriental musical extravaganzas and memorable Shakespeare to his homeland in productions that had already succeeded in London. It was there that he first gained attention, working with F. R. Benson in 1894–1902 and Herbert Beerbohm Tree in 1902–04 before moving into management at the Adelphi Theatre. Later he was at His Majesty's Theatre. With his wife he formed the Oscar Asche–Lily Brayton Company, which they brought to Australia in 1909 for Clarke, Meynell and Gunn. At a time when productions of Shakespeare were rare here, their repertoire included *As You Like It*, *The Merchant of Venice*, *Othello*, *The Taming of the Shrew* and Asche's own dramatisation of Stanley Wyman's book *Count Hannibal*. Asche first appeared in Australia in *The Taming of the Shrew* at the Theatre Royal in Melbourne in 1909. The company played two seasons in Sydney and three in Melbourne and Asche declared that its success vindicated Australian taste.

The Melbourne *Argus* on 10 January 1910 found *Count Hannibal* to be a 'bustling, moving play' in which Asche gave a 'powerful, breezy and commanding rendering' of the title-role. In Sydney, *Theatre* magazine admired Asche's strength, intelligence and technical knowledge, but criticised his limited vocal range and inflexions. It thought his most finished performance was Christopher Sly in *The Taming of the Shrew* and said he lacked the requisite tenderness in scenes of grief in *Othello*.

Back in London, Asche mounted Edward Knoblock's play *Kismet*, which ran for two years before he brought it to Australia in 1912–13 with more Shakespeare, including *Antony and Cleopatra*. During this visit, Asche met the novelist H. Rider Haggard in Brisbane and subsequently dramatised his *A Child of the Storm* as *Mameena*. It was produced in London in 1914, without great success

Asche's biggest success was *Chu Chin Chow*, a musical comedy with a score by Frederic Norton. It ran in London for five years from 31 August 1916, a run that was not surpassed until Agatha Christie's *The Mousetrap*. The record-breaking production was said to have cost only £3000, so Asche must have created his extravagant effects with technical skill rather than money. HUGH D. MCINTOSH said the first Australian production cost him £20 000 in 1921.

J. C. WILLIAMSON'S contracted Asche for an Australian tour from July 1922. This time his wife did not join him. The repertoire included Asche's own shows *Chu Chin Chow*, *Cairo* and *The Spanish Main*; Shakespeare, including *Julius Caesar*; John Galsworthy's *The Skin Game* and Arthur Wing Pinero's *Iris*. Asche also directed the Williamson's production of the musical comedy *A Southern Maid* in Melbourne in January 1923.

In Sydney Asche judged the *Daily Telegraph*'s 1923 play competition. The editor of the newspaper, W. Farmer Whyte, and Mungo MacCallum supported Louis Stone's *Lap of the Gods*, but Asche persuaded Whyte to change his allegiance by promising a London production of Betty Hiscock's *Desire of Spring*, whose Indian setting appealed to him. Local critics ridiculed the idea of a play set in India winning an Australian competition and the promised production never happened.

Throughout the tour, relations between Asche and J. C. Williamson's were uneasy and after a quarrel in 1924 the Firm terminated his contract. Asche publicly criticised the Firm on stage on his last night. Back in London his success dwindled and he found himself in debt. Asche's last show, *The Good Old Days of England*, produced with the help of his now-estranged wife, was a flop and he died in poverty.

Asche thought his finest work as an actor was in *Othello* and as a producer and manager in *Chu Chin Chow*. He was extremely theatrical, though he maintained that the essence of drama was 'two boards and a passion'. He was innovative in his Shakespearean interpretations and his use of lighting techniques, particularly in *Kismet*. Asche was big—athletic in youth but obese in later years—and famed for the 'vilest temper in show business'. Distinguished by his sheer physical power, he was often extremely violent on stage and was criticised for lacking tenderness and subtlety. ❦*Victoria Chance*

published plays
Cairo (1921). London: Ascherberg, Hopwood and Crew c.1920.
Chu Chin Chow (1916). London: Samuel French 1931.
Mameera. London 1914.
Shakespeare's Comedy As You Like It arranged by Oscar Asche. London: Constable 1907.

other writings
Oscar Asche—His life by himself. London: Hurst and Blackett 1929.

further reading
BEVAN, IAN. *The Story of the Theatre Royal*. Sydney: Currency Press 1993.
BLAKE, L. J. Thomas Stange Heiss Oscar Asche. *Australian Dictionary of Biography* 7. Melbourne University Press 1979.
Argus (Melbourne) 17 January 1910.
Argus (Melbourne) 8 November 1910.
Theatre (Sydney) January 1910.

James Henry Ashton

Circus proprietor, equestrian. Born c.1818 at or near Beddow (Essex, England).Gave first equestrian performances at Royal Circus, Hobart, 1848. Founded circus in Sydney 1852. Died 17 January 1889 near Gladstone (Qld).

The founder of ASHTON'S CIRCUS, James Henry Ashton may have come from a family of tinkers. The *Bulletin* of 26 December 1891 described Ashton's speech as marked by 'a little Romany articulation etymology à la St Giles'—a reference to an infamous London quarter. As an itinerant, Ashton may have acquired circus skills by associating with the fairground and show folk of rural England at an early age. His obituary said he had served an equestrian apprenticeship in English provincial circuses. It seems unlikely that his well-documented equestrian prowess could have been nurtured in Australia.

On 6 December 1848 the *Hobart Town Courier* announced the forthcoming appearance of 'a Mr Ashton' at ROBERT RADFORD's Royal Circus. By 20 January 1849, the *Cornwall Chronicle* could report that Ashton's 'bold and fearless style of riding surpassed anything of the kind ever seen in the colony'. On 25 January 1851 he applied to the Colonial Secretary of Van Diemen's Land for permission to give equestrian performances in the Royal Circus in Launceston. The request granted, Ashton gave a few performances with his company. Then he suddenly fled, 'leaving numerous creditors to deplore his exit', according to the *Cornwall Chronicle* of 19 April 1851. Ashton and his wife found their way to Sydney where, on 29 August 1851, he made his debut at Malcom's Royal Australian Circus. Next year Ashton's wife died after childbirth. He married again in 1853 and this marriage produced 12 children. Most of those who survived infancy were brought up as performers in ASHTON'S CIRCUS. His son Freddy was a rider in Hyland's Vice-Regal Circus in Melbourne in September 1899. Ashton travelled with the company until his death. His fourth, fifth and sixth generation descendants form the Ashton circus family today. ❦*Mark St Leon*

Ashton's Circus

The oldest circus in the English-speaking world is probably Ashton's Circus, which can date its foundation back to equestrian performances given by JAMES HENRY ASHTON in the Royal Circus at Launceston (Tas.) in 1851. A circus under the Ashton name appears to have existed almost continuously in Australia since 23 February 1852, when Ashton and another equestrian, Signor Cardoza, reopened the Olympic Circus in Sydney.

Ashton's Circus was one of the larger and more popular troupes during the second half of the 19th century. It largely confined its activities to the outback in the eastern colonies, particularly northern NSW and Queensland. Ashton and his 12 children formed the nucleus of the company, but he employed other artists from time to time. These included Mongo Mongo, Combo Combo and Master Callaghan and other Aboriginal equestrians trained by Ashton; the clown Jack Howe; the English clown Reuben Cousins, who in 1865 took his own circus on an abortive tour of India; Annie Yeamans, a young equestrian who later won fame as an actor in the USA; and the family of musicians who founded WIRTHS' CIRCUS. Beyond its talented company the circus owed much of its popularity to the generosity of Ashton in donating his takings to local building, charity and flood-relief funds of outback towns.

In the early 1880s Ashton relinquished the management to his son James but he travelled with the circus until he died in 1889. James and his brother Fred operated the circus until they gradually drifted apart. Fred Ashton became a rider with Hyland's Circus in Melbourne late in 1898. The James Ashton family was engaged by FITZGERALD BROTHERS' CIRCUS for the 1904–05 season and a New Zealand tour. During 1906–07, the James Ashton and Walter St Leon families formed Ashton and St Leon's Combined Circus to tour NSW and Queensland. The James Ashton circus that started out from Mildura (Vic.) early in 1913 included CON COLLEANO and his family. Members of the James Ashton family became closely associated with Barton's Circus from about 1914. James Ashton drowned in the Macquarie River at Dubbo (NSW) in May 1918, while engaged with the Eroni and Sole combined circus.

By the mid-1920s most of James Ashton's family had left circus work for vaudeville or a settled life. His second daughter, Ethel, married Roy Barton in 1914 and with his family ran Barton's Follies, a popular travelling variety company, until after the Second World War. Since about 1918 there have been circuses under the name of Ashton, organised by Fred Ashton, who died in Sydney in 1941, his son Joe, and Joe's son Doug (1920–). Joe Ashton's circus reached its peak in 1937, when it comprised as many as 70 people. The circus was laid up during the war years, and reorganised in 1949. Ashton's Circus has travelled Australia, New Zealand and Papua almost continuously ever since. Between the wars another son of Fred Ashton, known as 'Captain' Fred Ashton, organised his own circus and called it Goldwyn Brothers' Circus. ❦*Mark St Leon*

further reading
FERNANDEZ, NATALIE. *Circus Saga*. Sydney: Ashton's Circus 1971.
ST LEON, MARK. An Australian Circus: The origins of Ashton's Circus and a brief record of its travels in Australia until 1918. Ms in Mitchell Library (Sydney).

Asia and the Australian theatre

Since colonial times theatre in Australia has revealed and inculcated popular perceptions of Asia. In the 19th century CHINESE and JAPANESE PERFORMERS appeared in the cities and on the goldfields, often meeting condescension from critics. Between 1845 and 1929 Australian theatres confirmed a European view of 'the East' in some 50 productions, from operetta to melodrama. Asia was popular in the theatre because it offered scope for exotic settings, spectacular costumes, comic stereotypes, melodramatic seductions, political controversy and Oriental fantasy.

Stage orientalism was a magnificent invention that gratified the colonial audience's desire for a more richly expressed existence than the social and sexual constrictions of industrialised life allowed. It also permitted racist humour. Some titles give the flavour: *Pong Wong the Mandarin*, *Bluebeard and the Heathen Chinese*, *Djin Djin the Japanese Bogie Man*, *The Geisha—or, A Story of a Tea House, East of Suez*. Theatrical names for Asians—from the Middle East, Japan, or China—included Cheekee, Chop Chop, Hang Lo, Hang Hi, Gay-Jay, So-So, Washee Washee, Tiddli Hi Ti, the Damio of Kissi-Kissi, and Kissi-me, his daughter. Names again reveal the attitude in W. S. Gilbert's libretto for *The Mikado*—Nanki Poo, Pooh-Bah, Yum-Yum, Pitti-Sing, Peep-Bo, and the Town of Titipu (probably a corruption of *Chichibu*, a Japanese ship that visited England just before Gilbert and Sullivan completed the operetta). *The Mikado* exposed large Australian audiences in the 1880s to the Orientalist mock-Asia tradition. They trivialised the fantasy Far East, and satirised its admirers. In western plays set in 'the East' and in newspaper reports references to 'mousmees' (*musume*—daughter, young girl), *maiko* (apprentice geisha), and teahouses (brothels) were broad hints about the sexual subtext.

Local Chinese occasionally appeared in supporting casts but Asian leading roles were commonly played by Europeans, such as MAGGIE MOORE in *The Chinese Question* in 1879. The theatrical historian F. C. Brewer wrote in *The Drama and Music of New South Wales* that in 1862 Frederick Younge's 'make-up and action as a Chinaman were remarkable; and when he presented "John" on the stage none laughed at him more heartily than the "Chinkies" who frequently formed a goodly portion of the audience'. Countless Ali Babas and Aladdins kept the Eastern theme alive in pantomime and burlesque. G. V. BROOKE's production of Byron's *Sardanapulus* in Melbourne in 1857 deployed lavish archeologically inspired scenery and costumes, such as Charles Kean had used in his recent London revival of the play. Shylock became a noble 'Oriental' figure in ALFRED DAMPIER's version of the *Merchant of Venice*.

Plays legitimised contemporary Western views—either hostile and racist or trivialising and condescending—of a generalised Asia. Most of the plays were imported from England and America but some were written by Australian dramatists, who were preoccupied with the possibility of Chinese or Japanese invasion. *Besieged at Port Arthur*, an Australianised drama presented by BLAND HOLT in 1905, and Randolph Bedford's WHITE AUSTRALIA (1909) are examples. Another is F. R. C. HOPKINS's *Reaping the Whirlwind*, published in 1909 but not performed.

At the end of the 19th century *Antony and Cleopatra* developed into a vehicle for Oriental opulence and spectacle. OSCAR ASCHE, an all-round master of what a contemporary called Ali-Babarism, toured his magnificent production of this play—starring himself and his wife Lily Brayton—and Edward Knoblock's *Kismet* to Australia in 1912. The Sydney *Bulletin*, sceptical about Asche's aspirations to high art, proclaimed of *Kismet* on 18 April 1912: 'Behold! the bellowdrama that is clothed in gladrag and located in Baghdad, the garnishings whereof are as glorious as the midnight sunset on a silver sea, and whose story has all the hues of the rainbow, not to mention the peacock's tail—behold! it reigneth at the Melbourne Royal …'. Asche's musical comedy *Chu Chin Chow* presented a dignified prince, but more often Asians were characterised either as devious, dirty, lazy, conniving and salacious, or as artistic, quaint, comical and industrious.

Contemporary theatre

From 1968 theatre reflected changing attitudes to Asia in Australia. In 1968 Alex Buzo's NORM AND AHMED broke new ground, not by considering an encounter between an Australian racist and an Asian—that was a long tradition in Australian theatre—but by sympathising with a Pakistani student. In later plays Buzo showed Australians as marginal people in Asian and South Pacific ports. In THE FLOATING WORLD, *The Imposter*, *Lost Weekend*, *Top End* and other plays JOHN ROMERIL considered Australians' move towards accommodation with Asia—and his own. LOUIS NOWRA and THÉRÈSE RADIC examined the human condition through historical episodes in China or Japan. Nowra, Margaret Barr, RON BLAIR, ROGER PULVERS, LEONARD RADIC, John Summons, DAVID WILLIAMSON and others wrote plays with the Vietnam war as the background. In *Shimada* (1987) JILL SHEARER returned to the perennial Australian fear of becoming the poor white trash of Asia, conquered by the Japanese, in her study of the prejudices underlying trade relations. The play was presented briefly on Broadway in 1992 by a producer who sought to exploit a similar fear in the USA. NIGEL TRIFFITT did the same with more phantasmagoria in *The Fall of Singapore*. Recent plays and music-theatre produced in DARWIN have begun interesting explorations of the complexities of Timor and northern Australian society. They include *Death at Balibo*, a play by Maria Alice Casimiro, Jose Monteiro and Graham Pitts about the killing of Australian television journalists in East Timor, and audiovisual works by Martin Wesley-Smith. The patchwork-quilt northern Australian society was also the launching pad for Jimmy

Chi's musical *Bran Nue Dae* in 1990. Tony Strachan's *The Eyes of the Whites* in 1983 dealt with identity crises on both sides in newly independent Papua New Guinea.

Most of these plays highlighted cultural differences between Australia and Asia. The sexual subtext and the perennial view of Asian women as seducers or victims, perpetuated by Hal Porter in *The Professor* in 1966, were still in evidence in 1978 in Daniel Keene's *Cho Cho San*—an Australian version of the Madam Butterfly theme—in Michael Gurr's *Sex Diary of an Infidel* (1992), as they were in films and novels of the 1980s and 1990s.

But as Asian-Australian dramatists emerged—among them John Lee Joo For and Ernest MacIntyre—they began to exploit and interpret the very East-West dichotomy that other Australians were trying to eliminate. Dance-drama by Kai Tai Chan's One Extra Dance Theatre and by the Bharatam Dance Company reflected worldwide moves towards internationalisation of theme, technique, and cast. At the National Institute of Dramatic Art, John Clark established connections with Indian theatre, and at the University of Sydney music and drama students were taught Japanese *noh* dance in the 1980s. In the 1980s Tess de Quincy, Julie Drysdale, Carrillo Gantner, Nigel Kellaway, Richard Moore and many others went to Japan and studied the avant-garde performance genre *butoh* with Japanese masters. These Australians and those who more recently discovered *kyogen* and the dance-drama techniques of Tadashi Suzuki were exploring new sources of stimulus.

Bali, with its idyllic beauty, its communal artistry and its *wayang* tradition has had an apparently magnetic attraction for dramatists. Kai Tai Chan co-produced *Dancing Demons* there in 1991 and Graham Shiel's *Bali: Adat* in 1991 combined Balinese music and dance with a drama about Dutch colonialism. Gamelan, which accompanies traditional performance, has been studied at Monash and Sydney Universities for two decades and at the University of Western Australia, and Australian student productions of W. S. Rendra's *The History of the Naga Tribe* have proliferated. Kerry Walker, after undertaking research on Asian theatre, introduced Nano Riantiarno's *The Cockroach Opera* from Java to Sydney in 1992, in an English translation by John H. McGlynn. A cast of Asian, Aboriginal and other Australians played the roles of Indonesian transvestites and prostitutes, government officials and police. Australian interest in Indonesian performance therefore ranged from the traditional, as practised both in Australia and in various places in Indonesia, to the contemporary, with Australia offering venues for work that might be considered subversive in Indonesia.

Because of its proximity to Asia, and because growing numbers of Australians are of Asian origin or ancestry, Australia could become the first country to achieve real cross-cultural fertilisation in theatre, in both theme and technique. Yet few Asian-Australians have appeared in theatre outside dance-drama, and few have entered drama schools. In 1992 a Chinese and a Japanese actor played leading roles in Michael Gurr's *Sex Diary of an Infidel* and *Tokyo Two* by Keith Gallasch and Virginia Baxter. In 1993 Miki Oikawa appeared in Thérèse Radic's *The Emperor Regrets* and played opposite Anna Broinowski in Broinowski's bilingual play, *The Gap*, which had a season in Japan in 1994. When more Asian-Australians find places in the theatre, the East–West, us–them gap that playwrights have exploited for centuries will belong to the past in Australia. ❦*Alison Broinowski, Veronica Kelly*

further reading
Asche, Oscar. *Oscar Asche—His life by himself*. London: Hurst and Blackett 1929.
Broinowski, Alison. *The Yellow Lady—Australian impressions of Asia*. Melbourne: Oxford University Press 1992.
Fitzpatrick, Peter. Asian stereotypes in recent Australian plays. *Australian Literary Studies* 12/1 (Brisbane, 1985).
Kelly, Veronica. Orientalism in early Australian theatre. *New Literatures Review* 26 (Wollongong 1993).
Love, Harold. Chinese theatre on the Victorian goldfields 1858–1870. *Australasian Drama Studies* 3/2 (Brisbane 1985).
Milne, Geoffrey. *Cho Cho San*—A triumph of collaboration. *Australasian Drama Studies* 12/13 (1988).
Said, Edward. *Orientalism*. London: Peregrine 1985.

Athenaeum Theatre

Theatre in Collins Street, Melbourne, opened as Melbourne Mechanics' Institute and Hall of Arts 1843. Rebuilt in 1885–86 and renamed **Athenaeum Hall**. Rebuilt as 880-seat, three-level **Athenaeum Theatre**, designed by Henry E. White for Frank Talbot, 1922–24. Used as cinema 1929–70 and 1970–77. Includes small hall converted to 100-seat **Athenaeum 2** studio theatre in 1977 and to 150-seat end-stage theatre in 1987.

A few master builders in embryonic Melbourne formed a mechanics' institute on 4 October 1839. The institute erected a two-storeyed building in Collins Street on a 19·8-metre-wide block extending to Little Collins Street. It had a library and reading room downstairs and a 'hall of arts' upstairs, where the town council met and lectures were given. The present hall was built in 1872 on the vacant rear half of the site to house concerts and occasional theatricals.

After major rebuilding on the front portion in 1885–86, the Mechanics' Institute building was renamed the Athenaeum Hall. Like any institutional or town hall, it had an end stage and a small gallery at the opposite end. A smaller hall was on the top floor in the three-storey front section of the building. In 1882 the Athenaeum Hall became one of the first public spaces connected to electricity.

In 1924 Henry E. White completed alterations to produce a Bijou-style drama theatre with fly-tower stage, stalls, circle and gallery. White used his current Adam style of decoration, but in a more austere manner than in his larger theatres. After five years of plays the Athenaeum Theatre began showing films with Al Jolson's *The Jazz Singer*.

There was an interlude of live drama for six months in 1970 but the theatre did not permanently return to its origins until the Melbourne Theatre Company took it over in 1977. The company at first presented classics in the theatre. Then it modified the small hall at the front of the building to make a studio theatre, Athenaeum 2. After the Melbourne Theatre Company moved to the new Victorian Arts Centre in 1984, Athenaeum 1 continued as a live theatre, beginning a new era which included its longest-running show, *Wogs Out of Work*. In 1987 the lessees, Elston, Hocking and Woods, refurbished Athenaeum 2 as an end-stage theatre. In 1991 the remainder of the building was refurbished as a heritage conservation project, with larger foyer and bar spaces, and restored auditorium. It reopened with a revival of *Hair*. ❦*Ross Thorne*

Audiences

In 18th-century England people of all ranks and classes shared their pastimes. The aristocracy and the gentry saw it as a duty to organise and patronise activities such as fairs and wakes. Despite this elite patronage, such events were essentially expressions of the shared values and meanings of the common people, and therefore often occasions for articulation of opposition to the moral and legal order. The theatre shared these characteristics. The audience was always a mixture of classes, although particular social groups tended to be prominent on particular days and for particular programs. Wednesday, for example, was traditionally a day on which the lower orders went to the theatre. The poorer people were also the most likely to attend Christmas and Easter pantomimes. Disorder was common in playhouses. Dissatisfied theatregoers threw fruit and other missiles almost as a matter of course. Sometimes disorder became outright violence. On one occasion upper-class theatregoers invaded the stage and attacked the scenery with their swords. In London in 1776 a crowd disappointed by atrocious acting in *The Blackamoor Wash'd White* broke up the theatre.

The early performances at BARNETT LEVEY'S THEATRE ROYAL in Sydney in 1833 attracted not only the lower orders but also the 'very respectable' members of the community, according to the *Sydney Gazette*. There was 'a dazzling display of beauty' in the boxes and the officer class was usually out in force. Initially, at least, the Sydney audience comprised a microcosm of the society. Within a year, however, its composition had changed. The 'best' people no longer patronised the stage. The audience now most noticeably consisted of 'courtesans', or 'women of a certain sort' and 'young men about town'. Those who were careful of their social reputation no longer took themselves to the playhouse. The well-to-do and 'respectable' colonists withdrew their patronage in the first place because the 'general good order' of the early audiences had given way to rowdy and exaggerated behaviour. In keeping with English tradition, Sydney theatregoers had begun throwing fruit and hissing at performers who displeased them. In the 1840s Melbourne playgoers were even more demonstrative and violent. In 1844, Irish settlers objected to the appearance of an altar and a priest in a play and a waddy was heaved at an actress on stage. Three years later, a 'Yankee' failed to appear as advertised to perform at the QUEEN'S THEATRE ROYAL and the audience responded by destroying lamps and mouldings in the auditorium.

The behaviour of actors also helped to drive the upper class out of the theatre. George Bennett, a visiting surgeon, claimed that performers at Levey's Theatre Royal 'too often mistook indecency for wit'. Actors at the Royal Pavilion Saloon in Melbourne performed what the *Port Phillip Herald* called their own 'indelicate composition'. 'Decent' colonists also increasingly objected to the repertoire. The government of the colony intended the theatre to serve as a medium of moral and intellectual instruction but managers staged many plays that flew in the face of notions of 'rational recreation'. For example, William Moncrieff's stage adaptation of Pierce Egan's novel *Tom and Jerry—or, Life in London* was produced at Sydney's Theatre Royal in 1834. The story centres on the progress of two upper-class rakes through the slums of London. The colonial performance caused a furore. The press denounced it as immoral, and 'respectable' citizens stayed away from the playhouse, leaving it in possession of a 'rabble'.

In Sydney and Hobart in the 1840s and in Melbourne a decade later, the colonial stage, or at least sections of it, began to adopt and reflect the moral and cultural values of a culture of reason. In all three cities managers began to stage a higher proportion of opera and Shakespeare and other serious English plays. Respectable and orderly audiences returned to the theatre as a result. In Sydney, for example, the Governor of NSW was a periodic visitor to the Royal Victoria Theatre in the 1840s. When the Royal City Theatre opened in 1843 it provided private family boxes to attract the 'higher classes'. At the same time those most likely to cause disruption, the lower orders, were increasingly attracted to the emergent specialised venues—music halls and circus amphitheatres. Here was a sign that the theatre, and indeed colonial culture as a whole, was losing pre-industrial homogeneity and taking on modern and specialised characteristics. *Richard Waterhouse*

Gold rushes to 1920s

Between the gold rushes of the 1850s and the First World War Australia received huge influxes of people from Europe, America, and Asia, and periods of great prosperity, such as the 1880s, alternated with severe recessions and unemployment. Theatre attendances were extremely sensitive to the booms and busts. Even as late as 1892 all the theatres in Melbourne, then the largest city in Australia, were closed during the worst months of a depression.

The most money was to be made from the rising middle classes. Hence the Grand World Circus advertising in the respectable Melbourne *Argus* in 1866: 'So cautious has and will be the selection that the tender father, the affectionate husband, or admiring lover need not fear that the blush of modesty will be affected by any exhibition within the arena'. Although respectability and decorum eventually prevailed, audiences throughout this period still endured overcrowding, poor ventilation, narrow stairways, and filthy or nonexistent toilets.

Behaviour and the adequacy of facilities were greatly determined by the sale of liquor. Earlier in the 19th century a good proportion of the audience had access to alcohol between acts and during performances, but the licensing laws later restricted liquor sales to intervals. By the end of the century patrons had to leave the theatre and go the hotel next door for a drink. In many theatres dress-circle patrons, who it was assumed drank in moderation or could hold their liquor, had their own saloons, where tea and coffee were also available. Something of the old rough and tumble returned after Federation with the tent theatres of E. I. Cole's BOHEMIAN DRAMATIC COMPANY, PHILIP LYTTON and others. Seats were unreserved and food and drink were never far away. However, even these managers, acknowledging the financial value of 'better class' patronage and their own dubious social status, attempted to control—but not remove—the larrikin element.

Reviewers commonly used the phrase 'pit, box, and gallery' to suggest that all the social classes in the playhouse had responded favourably to the entertainment. The major theatrical forms—pantomime and melodrama—attempted to reflect the social classes and to provide something for everyone. This unification incorporated changing social needs. As general audience behaviour improved, large and prominent dress circles replaced private boxes and allowed the better-dressed playgoer to be seen and to see. Darkened auditoria induced a more passive role in the audience, but roughs in the gallery remained proudly defiant. They no longer urinated on those below, but spat occasionally.

Popular entertainment attempted to incorporate these varied interests and codes of behaviour. The horse-racing melodramas staged by BLAND HOLT are a supreme example. The story would concern the English upper classes, and for upper-class Englishmen there would be scenes of high-class gambling and financial speculation. Often there was jingoistic military imperialism as well, which the colonial governor and his entourage would witness at a special performance with silk playbills. The play would be set in contemporary society, and would attract female playgoers by parading actresses in the latest fashions imported from London and Paris—day frocks at the racecourse and evening gowns at the ball afterwards. A variety sequence would allow blackface minstrels, acrobats, trick cyclists, and other lower-class acts to appear; a betting scene would allow the gallery to shout odds and witticisms to the 'bookmakers' on the stage, and the race itself would exploit sensational staging techniques to which all could thrill.

Major divisions of the audience emerged between theatrical forms rather than within the one play or playhouse, and they were divisions not of class but of ethnicity and sex. Anglophone historians know little of the many occasions when performances were given in languages other than English for specific ethnic groups. Well-behaved Chinese audiences expressed approval of visiting Chinese opera companies in the 1850s and 1860s by hammering with their feet and shouting what the Bendigo *Advertiser* took to be Asian equivalents of 'bravo!' The Chinese proprietors' main concern was disturbances by non-Chinese youths. In other non-Anglophone communities theatre functioned as a form of ghetto solidarity. Here ethnic pride demanded good behaviour and perhaps passionate identification with stories of 'home' in Europe. Within the main Anglophone community the tastes and interests of bourgeois women led in the 1860s to the rise of commercially successful European opera and later to dance companies and forms of theatre that were less attractive to men.

From 1900 to the end of the First World War the best seats in the Theatre Royal or Her Majesty's Theatre in Sydney cost two to five shillings, according to the type of show. Some managements arranged ticket prices to determine the composition of audiences. The BROUGH-BOUCICAULT COMEDY COMPANY, for example, used smaller theatres, often built without galleries, and charged at least one shilling and sixpence. Populists like GEORGE DARRELL and ALFRED DAMPIER sometimes halved the gallery charge for melodrama to sixpence in order to ensure a large male house, even if it was less remunerative. Some overt melodramas—particularly Frank Harvey's *The World Against Her* and dramatisations of Mrs Henry Wood's *East Lynne*, and Elizabeth Braddon's *Lady Audley's Secret*—were specifically advertised as 'the ladies' drama' and may have attracted working women, but it was musical and 'society' comedies and dramas, with their parade of contemporary fashions, light classical orchestral music, and representations of the joys and problems of upper middle-class life, that marked the first major split in public taste.

MUSICAL THEATRE attempted with scantily clad dancers to appeal to men but gradually became biased towards women of the upper classes as young working men were drawn away to burlesque, revue and film. VAUDEVILLE, a new attraction from the 1890s, is often mistakenly classed as working-class culture, but in fact it was set in opposition to less refined variety entertainment and it attracted high-class patronage, at least until the First World War. By the end of that war film had largely swept away melodrama as a popular art form, vaudeville was struggling, and operetta was consolidated as the major means by which women and the *haute bourgeoisie* defined the dimensions of a different and for some better way of life. ❦Richard Fotheringham

Between the wars

Audiences changed profoundly in size and composition between the two world wars. When the 1920s began film was so popular that screenings outnumbered live performances by 6692 to 3456 in NSW in 1921. Films competed increasingly with live theatre but not until the end of the 1920s did they inhibit its growth. New theatres opened or were refurbished in Sydney and Melbourne as late as 1927 and, although theatrical managements had been appealing to the rising middle class for some time, the audience was large and diverse. Men in the stalls of the Criterion Theatre in Sydney wore dinner suits, but policemen attended some of the rowdier suburban vaudeville houses to control outbreaks of fighting.

The audience was still broad enough for the two major managements to encroach upon each other's territory. In 1924 J. C. WILLIAMSON'S took control of the TIVOLI CIRCUIT and moved into vaudeville. FULLERS' began to tackle the Firm on its own ground, recruiting HUGH J. WARD and producing musicals and other commercial fare, at its new St James Theatre in Sydney in 1926. Another feature of the decade was the ALLAN WILKIE SHAKESPEAREAN COMPANY.

Some of the middle-class theatre audience gravitated towards socially prestigious amateur groups which, often with viceregal patronage, offered more literary plays. J. C. Williamson's showed that it was keen to cater to this audience by supporting matinees of serious drama presented by GREGAN McMAHON. But the Firm was often regarded with suspicion, as McMahon found when he failed to persuade his amateur SYDNEY REPERTORY THEATRE SOCIETY to become professional under the Williamson banner.

The 1920s, a time of relative prosperity before the Great Depression, saw ticket prices more than double at major city theatres. Gallery prices—and the gallery itself, when some theatres were remodelled—disappeared. This widened the split between the middle-class live theatre and the working-class cinema in the first half of the 1920s, and led to the building of picture palaces in the second half as film exhibitors took their industry up market. The new picture palaces were glamorous, clean, warm and comfortable, in contrast to the flea-ridden, draughty old live theatres. Those who liked a little live entertainment could have that at the cinema too. As part of the ballyhoo promoting new films, there would be perhaps an organist accompanying community singing and lucky door prizes—sometimes food hampers. Otherwise there would be a vaudeville act as a curtainraiser. Vaudeville lost the battle for the audience first. Fullers' abandoned vaudeville in 1927 and J. C. Williamson's in 1929. Fullers' was also forced to give up REVUE and musical comedy in 1929. Popular theatre disappeared from city centres and slowly declined in the suburbs and in the country, where J. Clarence Lee's *Out on the Castlereagh*, the Bohemian Dramatic Company's *The Sport from Hollowlog Flat* and other comedy-melodramas could still command audiences during the 1920s. But even Bert Bailey's staging of *On Our Selection* had come off the road before the stock market crashed in 1929.

The year when the Great Depression began was also the year when sound films arrived and gave a new impetus to cinema-going. Competition intensified when Hollywood began to make films of musicals. Worse still, a film and a live production of the same show occasionally ran at the same time. For example, in Sydney in 1929 the talkie *Showboat* was on screen at the St James Theatre while Jerome Kern's *Show Boat* was playing live at Her Majesty's Theatre. The cheapness and novelty of talking pictures crippled live theatre. At first-release city cinemas ticket prices ranged from one shilling up to two shillings and sixpence. At the same time, theatre tickets began at two and sixpence and rose to about 11 shillings and sixpence for overseas stars, such as Sybil Thorndike and Lewis Casson in 1932.

Theatre prices were unchanged throughout the 1930s, but some state governments introduced taxes on entertainment. These taxes compounded an existing federal tax and particularly affected live theatre, since cinema tickets were generally under the tax threshold. According to records compiled in connection with the federal tax, 2 460 000 tickets costing two and sixpence or more were sold across Australia in 1929 but by 1934 the total had fallen to 166 000.

Ten live theatres were operational in downtown Sydney at the beginning of 1929. In 1935 one had been rebuilt as a cinema and five had been wired for talking pictures. Only the Tivoli Theatre and the Theatre Royal were live theatres. The Tivoli housed a renascence of revue during the Great Depression. Many of the performers were Australians who provided a topical and local style of humour. Moreover, the prices of tickets to revues—starting at one shilling— compared favourably with cinema prices.

Meanwhile, cost-cutting by J. C. Williamson's turned the Firm's once-renowned operettas into minimalist shows. Old productions such as *The Maid of the Mountains* were revamped, with recycled costumes and a greatly reduced ballet. This was not attractive to people who had previously seen the more elaborate show. J. C. Williamson's also produced thrillers and comedies, aimed increasingly at the moneyed classes. In response to the irrelevance of this kind of theatre AMATEUR THEATRE grew during the Depression. Amateur groups wanted to produce plays of substance.

Perhaps the most formidable competitor with professional theatre was RADIO. By the end of the 1930s it was estimated that every home had at least a crystal set. Radio stations broadcast most theatrical entertainments—drama, variety and comedy—and much more. By 1935 in Sydney eight vigorous radio stations outnumbered the two major live theatres. Some had auditoria where audiences— dressed formally, like the actors—could see and hear their favourite program performed.

By the outbreak of the Second World War professional theatre still drew a broad audience, but it was vastly diminished and increasingly middle class. Replacement of old suburban halls by cinemas had eliminated local theatre, the first stop for performers and audiences alike. Now it was in tiny amateur and semiprofessional theatres that actors learned their craft. It was there that the future of the Australian theatre was debated and experiments in dramatic theory were made. The actors and audiences in these theatres were to have the most profound effect upon postwar reconstruction of the entertainment industry— and eventually to change the pattern for ever. *Annette Bain, Richard Fotheringham*

Since the Second World War

By the late 1930s critics were already arguing that theatre should be more democratic in audience, national in subject, and intellectually challenging in intention. The butt of this criticism was J. C. Williamson's and its repertoire of ballet, operetta and West End and Broadway hits. Some saw the Firm as nurturing complacency in the audience. Allan Aldous called the Williamson audience the 'upper crust' and urged other theatre workers to stimulate patrons out of their stuffiness. He instanced Eugene O'Neill's *Mourning Becomes Electra*, which was a success for INDEPENDENT THEATRE in Sydney in 1945 but unpopular when presented by Williamson's at the Comedy Theatre in Melbourne in 1946. Only two per cent of the Firm's regular patrons were serious theatregoers, Aldous suggested. An anonymous historian of NEW THEATRE in 1948 said J. C. Williamson's had fostered an 'abyss of commercial decadence' and specified the Firm's failure to train staff and audience. Nevertheless, from 1947 the Firm took on a new lease of life with its postwar musicals, including *Kiss Me, Kate* and, particularly, *Annie Get Your Gun*, which made EVIE HAYES a new star. Audiences captured by the energy of the American mass culture they had seen at first hand during the war, and starved of colour and spectacle, poured into the theatres.

The experiments of New Theatre and other amateur groups, such as Independent Theatre and the Melbourne Little Theatre Company heartened reformers like Aldous. These groups' low production costs afforded them experimental licence to appeal at first to small audiences that were critical of Australian society or interested in a different kind of theatrical fare.

The end of the war intensified the demand for reshaped relationships between the arts and audiences, 'to bring opportunities for culture to people everywhere', as the Council for the Encouragement of Music and the Arts proclaimed, reflecting the worldwide view that cultural exchange was the path to lasting peace. But visions of the new relationship showed important practical differences. CEMA and its successor, the ARTS COUNCIL OF AUSTRALIA, planned to expose inhabitants of country towns and outlying suburbs to the performances enjoyed by people of the more affluent parts of the capital cities. It wished to broaden distribution and access to 'the best' but did not question the nature of 'culture'.

The OLD VIC THEATRE COMPANY toured with spectacular success in 1948 and showed Australian audiences what culture could be. In the GUTHRIE REPORT of 1949 the English director Tyrone Guthrie advised the government that the time was not ripe for a state-sponsored national company. Australian audiences needed Australian actors trained in English productions on English stages, he said. LESLIE REES argued that this loyal dominion model would downgrade not stimulate local culture. Audiences must be allowed to realise that Australian scripts and accents were as worthy of being called culture as Guthrie's examples. 'Indigenous plays are surely the type ... [Australians] ... will demand, with consequently more and more failures among the importations', wrote Rees in 1953.

There was little consensus on what this theatre and its emerging new audience should be. Some saw an intelligentsia and a working class critical of capitalism; others envisaged a people ever more conscious of its national identity. Differences between these two notions of the audience were obscured, however, by common adversaries. One was respectability. In 1948 the NSW Chief Secretary, J. M. Baddeley banned Sumner Locke Elliott's RUSTY BUGLES until 'Cripes!' replaced 'Christ!' and 'mug' or 'stinker' supplanted 'bastard'. The reformers derided his implicit image of the audience, boosting their own confidence and renewing their dislike of parsonical gentility in theatrical culture. In the event the expletives were restored by the actors and the play had a hugely popular professional tour. Ray Lawler's SUMMER OF THE SEVENTEENTH DOLL received similar criticism for the irregular nature of its love affairs.

What was 'Australian' and how popular it would be with theatregoers remained a perplexing issue, especially when the 1955 success of *Summer of the Seventeenth Doll* was followed by commercial failures of other Australian plays. These results disappointed and confused J. C. Williamson's and the AUSTRALIAN ELIZABETHAN THEATRE TRUST, which had seen the *Doll* as announcing a new audience.

Challenges to taste

WAL CHERRY, director of the UNION THEATRE REPERTORY COMPANY in 1956–59, denounced the audience's gentility and chose plays that he thought would challenge it. When JOHN SUMNER returned as director of the company in 1960 he warned subscribers that Shelagh Delaney's *A Taste of Honey* might offend them. And when he presented Joe Orton's *Entertaining Mr Sloane* the University of Melbourne temporarily withdrew its support. Cultural elites in Adelaide also sought to protect the audience. Rather than offend the Returned Services League, the governors of the ADELAIDE FESTIVAL OF ARTS declined to stage Alan Seymour's THE ONE DAY OF THE YEAR in 1960. Two years later they rejected Patrick White's THE HAM FUNERAL, maintaining, Max Harris said, that it was 'an abstract play which the general public will find difficult and impossible to understand'.

Controversy over the right of the audience to be entertained rather than affronted indicated a broader ambiguity in the relationship of UNIVERSITIES with their upper-middle-class public. By 1960, universities had become an integral part of the movement for self-improvement that the little theatres had begun, and emerged as the most important agent of regeneration of the theatrical audience. Noting in 1960 that most universities were building theatres or supporting companies, ROBERT QUENTIN, director of the National Institute of Dramatic Art, declared their mission to be equipping 'a man to take up arms against a sea of rubbish'. He could well have been referring to television, which from 1956 had, like cinema, exemplified 'popular entertainment' in contrast to the 'performing arts'.

In Sydney the University of Technology, which became the University of NSW, accepted responsibility for the NATIONAL INSTITUTE OF DRAMATIC ART in 1958, gave a building to the OLD TOTE THEATRE COMPANY in 1963 and helped to start the JANE STREET THEATRE in 1966. Other universities—particularly Adelaide, Queensland and Western Australia—built venues, inspired students to perform and encouraged campus audiences. The Universities of Melbourne and Sydney declined to teach drama but they nurtured it in other ways, officially and unofficially. Universities both served the social elevation of an increasingly numerous credentialled class and protected and encouraged its intellectually and morally dissident members. Passions aroused by the Vietnam War increased the tension of this duality.

The entrepreneur HARRY M. MILLER cashed in on the new dissidence with productions of Mart Crowley's *The Boys in the Band* and the rock musical *Hair* in 1969, and *Jesus Christ Superstar* in 1972. All confirmed that a substantial sector of the middle class had emerged as a morally and politically tolerant audience that needed more than the declining J. C. Williamson's could offer. With an aged and increasingly remote board that was unable to come to terms with the rapid changes of the 1960s, the Firm lost ground to a rash of young entrepreneurs and finally left the stage in 1976.

But the audience appeal of 'Australianness' remained ambiguous. Rees never seems to have doubted that Australians, through a shared 'national character', enjoyed dramas of 'ordinary, uneducated, wholesome, battling people depicted from their own point of view'. Other critics saw a more complex relationship between middle-class audiences and representations of Australia. Explaining the box-office failure of Lawler's *The Piccadilly Bushman*, which examined middle-class pretentiousness, EUNICE HANGER suggested in 1961 that the play did not please 'Australians who want to get rid of their Australianness'. Theatre audiences and church congregations, like university students, 'laugh understandingly when Australian speech and slang of an obvious kind is used ... but listen reverently to any overseas lecturer', she said. H. G. Kippax argued in 1965 that recent successful Australian plays 'are set in working class or slum suburbs because ... working class characters permit comic exploitation of the vernacular ...', a too easy and condescending position from which middle-class audiences could warm to Australian material.

In 1970 Michael Boddy and Bob Ellis's THE LEGEND OF KING O'MALLEY boldly confronted anxiety about Australianness by addressing their audience in the style of Tivoli revues. They pushed the comic possibilities of Australianness to vaudevillian limits while inviting serious attention to political history. Companies such as the NIMROD THEATRE COMPANY and the AUSTRALIAN PERFORMING GROUP were now fostering new writing and audiences which saw no conflict between larrikinism and intellectual purpose.

But the renascence in Australian drama was not led by a change in the theatre audience as a whole. When the Melbourne Theatre Company asked 10 000 subscribers to nominate their five favourite plays of 1958–68, no Australian play made the list. An AUSTRALIA COUNCIL survey in 1975 found that theatre subscribers wanted 'comedy and farce', 'enlargement of appreciation of famous plays' and a 'sense of relaxation and effortless enjoyment'—no specifically nationalist preferences. Another Australia Council survey in 1980 found that a smaller proportion attended Australian plays than attended 'English and American comedies' and 'musicals like *Annie*'. A Victorian survey found in 1980 that both subsidised and commercial theatres attracted middle-class audiences, though the subsidised audience was younger, more likely to be unmarried and to be from better-educated households.

If the new commitment to Australianism afforded by increased subsidy has been so easily appropriated to enhance an ever-prospering middle-class lifestyle, then the refashioning of theatrical culture may have found its social limits. The vernacular voice, however 'extrovert, athletic, rough and impudent'—KATHARINE BRISBANE's phrase—has become respectable. As this became evident in the late 1970s, COMMUNITY THEATRE began to seek a new audience. Rejoicing in the plurality of Australian society, these intensely local groups have forced all concerned with theatre to question the assumption that audience re-education is needed, that there can be such things as *national* companies (perhaps touring the provinces) and *centres* of excellence expressing *national* culture. *Tim Rowse*

Australia Council

The presence of scores of adult and youth professional theatre companies across Australia today is in large measure due to the policies of the Australia Council, the federal government's funding and advisory body for the arts. At a time when the theatre consisted mostly of commercial entrepreneurs presenting imported popular entertainment and amateur companies run by actor–managers, the council reconstructed an industry of non-profit organisations providing local employment. It established major state companies and consolidated others, and made grants to individual artists. More recently, its community-arts board, formed in 1978, and programs of access and participation —such as Art and Working Life, youth arts and multicultural arts—have expanded the horizons of the performing arts. Equally, the Aboriginal arts board has promoted a huge increase in appreciation of performance as part of indigenous culture, as well as providing opportunities for Aboriginal performers to develop their craft in parallel with European dance and theatrical practice.

In response to growing nationalism engendered by a postwar generation that no longer tolerated the derivative nature of Australian culture, John Gorton's Liberal–Country government established the Australian Council for the Arts in 1968, to subsidise the performing arts. The council's founding chair was H. C. COOMBS and its other members were Betty Archdale, JEANA BRADLEY, Peter Coleman, Geoffrey Dutton, Joan Erwin, Mary Houghton, Barry Jones, Karl Langer and Kay Masterman. Jean Battersby was executive officer.

A drama committee to oversee and subsidise theatrical companies and activities met for the first time on 30 September 1968. Its members were Geoffrey Dutton (chair), Mary Houghton, KEITH MACARTNEY, Kay Masterman, Patricia Rolfe, JIM SHARMAN, JOHN SUMNER, Marlis Thiersch and the present writer. Early in 1969 the drama committee made a historic report to the council and set the pattern for much Australian theatre since. Rejecting the notion of a national theatre company, it concentrated on building up subsidised companies in state capitals—the MELBOURNE THEATRE COMPANY, the NATIONAL THEATRE Company in Perth, the OLD TOTE THEATRE COMPANY in Sydney, the SOUTH AUSTRALIAN THEATRE COMPANY in Adelaide, and, later, the QUEENSLAND THEATRE COMPANY in Brisbane. The council emphasised professionalism and training over support for amateurs and capital works but excluded commercially structured organisations. It initiated funding to children's theatre and to playwrights.

Through a special projects fund it began to subsidise innovative theatre and dance, commissioning new works and productions of Australian plays. Among the beneficiaries were the La Mama Company and the AUSTRALIAN PERFORMING GROUP in Melbourne and the Australian Drama Foundation at the University of NSW in Sydney. These became cradles of new Australian drama.

Before the council existed, commonwealth and state funding—and private donations—had been channelled through the AUSTRALIAN ELIZABETHAN THEATRE TRUST, which funded the NATIONAL INSTITUTE OF DRAMATIC ART and the country's major performing-arts institutions. In 1968 it received $1 million from the commonwealth and $550 000 from the states for this purpose. The council now took over the responsibility for commonwealth funding and the Trust became an applicant as an industry service organisation and temporary administrative umbrella for small organisations like the MARIONETTE THEATRE OF AUSTRALIA, the Theatre of the Deaf in NSW, the International Theatre Institute, the AUSTRALIAN NATIONAL PLAYWRIGHTS' CONFERENCE and later the SYDNEY THEATRE COMPANY. It also funded the state divisions of the ARTS COUNCIL OF AUSTRALIA, enabling city companies to tour country towns. Government funding to the council began modestly at $1·7 million but grew to $3·85 million in the 1970–71 budget and to $4·7 million in 1972–73.

Statutory authority

The Council for the Arts was subject to much controversy and debate over its lay membership and there were constant questions in parliament about individual grants. After Gough Whitlam became Prime Minister in 1972 he sought to give the council autonomy by making it a statutory body 'to safeguard the integrity of our artists and their works'. Under his Labor government the administration of the council was separated from the Prime Minister's Department—though he remained the minister responsible. The methods of appointment to the council and its boards proved as autocratic as ever but from that time artists began to constitute the majority of appointees. In 1973–74, the first year of funding for the expanded council, the support budget was almost doubled to $14 million.

The Whitlam government brought all commonwealth funding for the arts together under the council—renamed the Australia Council—as a statutory authority in 1975. Peter Karmel, who had succeeded Coombs in 1974, remained in the chair until 1977. In 1976 Malcolm Fraser's Liberal–Country government appointed John Cameron, then controller of ABC television, as the council's general manager, effectively removing Battersby from administrative control. The council had seven art-form boards.

The board for theatre arts, including dance, comprised Theodore Bray, TOM BROWN, Colin Cave, DON CROSBY, RON HADDRICK, Peter Hall (chair), Joan Hammond, Mary Houghton, Garrie Hutchinson, Marilyn Jones, ANTHONY STEEL, John Stoddart and Patricia Wynn. An innovation was the Aboriginal arts board, which created opportunities for traditional and urban Aboriginal performers.

Funding rose to $19·7 in 1975–76 but was quickly eroded by galloping inflation. Across-the-board budgetary constraints under the Fraser government from 1976 kept the figure at $23 million to 1980–81. From 1977–78 to 1982–83 the government itself determined the grants to the largest clients—the Australian Ballet, the Australian Opera, the two Elizabethan Trust orchestras and NIDA—while funding declined, reaching its lowest point in 1981–82. The picture brightened slightly in 1982–83.

Changes in structure and emphasis

During the 1980s the bureaucracy grew and successive ministers restructured the council internally and clashed with personalities. In 1981 the government appointed Timothy Pascoe, a management consultant, to the combined post of chair—in succession to Geoffrey Blainey—and chief executive, and sent Cameron on 18 months' leave before his retirement. The council now began to place more emphasis on individual artists, ethnic diversity and community arts. Pascoe's role was to develop sponsorship but this failed. In 1982 the chair of the theatre board, Elizabeth Butcher, announced that the larger drama companies' funds would be further cut by 10 per cent and that a challenge grant scheme, offering companies $1 for every $3 they raised, would be introduced as an incentive to seek sponsorship. These moves led to a Stage Crisis Day on 19 November 1982, when all levels of the performing arts joined in protest. It resulted in a $809 000 supplementary grant to the Australia Council.

The challenge grant scheme was only moderately successful in attracting new patrons, despite a grant to the Confederation of Australian Professional Performing Arts to mount a national fund-raising campaign. Of the supplementary grant the theatre board received $193 000 and was able to restore funding to some of the small companies—the BRISBANE REPERTORY THEATRE SOCIETY, the ENSEMBLE THEATRE COMPANY in Sydney, the HOLE-IN-THE-WALL THEATRE COMPANY in Perth, and the STAGE COMPANY in Adelaide.

Pascoe radically reconstructed the management into five departments related to administration instead of art form. The boards' staff were gathered under 'client services'. This proved disruptive to both the organisation and the clients. Only the policy and planning unit survived Pascoe's period in office, which ended in 1984. He was followed as as general manager by Di Yerbury in 1984 and as chair by Donald Horne from 1985 to 1991. Yerbury's incumbency proved to be as stormy as Pascoe's, aggravated by a fundamental divergence of outlook between her and Horne. The situation became more settled in 1987 with the appointment of Max Bourke, a public servant from the Prime Minister's Department, as general manager. It was feared that he had been appointed to dismantle the council, but he proved to be a steady lobbyist and liaison for the council in Canberra. In 1987 the music and theatre boards were merged to form a performing-arts board with specialist art-form committees. Horne's successors were Rodney Hall in 1991–94 and Hilary McPhee from 1994. Michael Lynch succeeded Bourke in 1994.

From 1982-83 the government's allocation to the Australia Council was no more than indexed. A decade later it was $61 million and a 41 per cent increase would have been needed to restore parity with the 1974–75 figure.

On 18 October 1994, the Prime Minister, Paul Keating, in 'the first cultural policy in our history', announced funding totalling $252 billion over four years. The Australia Council's 1994–95 allocation of $59.2 million was boosted by a further $25 million over four years. The statement, entitled 'Creative Nation', confirmed the council as the primary arts-support body, but commented that financial support had failed to keep pace with the growth of clients. It also confirmed the council's principles of arms-length funding and peer assessment of applications; but asked that it simplify the process and address the current definition of 'peer'. The report emphasised the growing interdependence of art forms and the potential of new communications technology; and confirmed that the council should take responsibility for export marketing strategies and audience development.

The government undertook to provide triennial funding for the council, to establish a major organisations board to facilitate forward planning; to increase funding to individual artists and establish junior creative fellowships on a par with the senior Australian Artists' Creative Fellowships. It would hand responsibility for the Foundation for Australian Cultural Development to the council; and the chair of the council would be made a full-time executive position. ♥*Katharine Brisbane*

further reading
MACDONNELL, JUSTIN. *Arts, Minister?* Sydney: Currency Press 1992.
PARSONS, PHILIP (ed.). *Shooting the Pianist—The role of government in the arts*. Sydney: Currency Press 1987.
ROWSE, TIM. *Arguing the Arts—The funding of arts in Australia*. Melbourne: Penguin 1985.

reference
H. C. Coombs papers, M448/1 in Australian Archives, Canberra.

Australia Felix
—*or, Harlequin Laughing Jackass and the Magic Bat*. Pantomime in two acts by Garnet Walch. **premiere**: 26 December 1873, Prince of Wales Opera House, Melbourne, by W. S. Lyster's *opéra-bouffe* company. Cast: Lydia Howarde, J. E. Kitts, Charles Lascelles, George Leopold, Jeanie Winston, Alice Wooldridge. Music: arranged by F. Zeplin. Scenery: Alexander Habbe. **published** Melbourne: Azzopardi, Hildreth 1873. Brisbane: University of Queensland Press 1988.

The most successful colonial pantomime to use Australian characters and topics in a fantasia based on the conventions of the form was *Australia Felix*. GARNET WALCH partly reworked his own 1871 Sydney pantomime *Trookulentos. the Tempter* for the plot and his literary model appears to have been W. M. AKHURST's 1869 Melbourne pantomime *The House that Jack Built*. *Australia Felix* involves rivalry between Mirth and Mischief for the rule of Australia, supervised by the Demon King Kantankeros, who wishes to import English gloom. Young Australia Felix is given a magic cricket bat to play for a Victorian XVIII against W. G. Grace's All-England XI. The real match—which the Victorians won—began on the very day of the pantomime's premiere, and Walch includes it in the offstage action. Felix gambles away the bat but it is recovered through the agency of a kookaburra and other helpful characters, and Kantankeros is defeated. The *Australasian* praised the 'ingenious consistency' of the piece on 27 December 1873. The local points were harmoniously brought in and the allegorical character was well preserved, it said. The *Leader* on 3 January 1874 found 'a dramatic unity and completeness in the pantomime that fixes the attention and excites the interest'. ❧*Veronica Kelly*

The Australian Bunyips

—*or, Life in the City and the Bush*. Melodrama in four acts by Monsieur Richard. **premiere** 26 January 1857, Our Lyceum Theatre, Sydney.

Aborigines probably first appeared on stage in *The Australian Bunyips*, performing war dances and a corroboree. Novel touches in local scenery and effects in this melodrama were accompanied, however, by poorly developed characterisation, according to reviews. No script survives but reviewers' plot summaries show the characters to have been the usual melodramatic types, even to their names. Rookly, a villainous wealthy squatter, plots to marry off his stepdaughter Flora, to another evil crony, Crafty. He also employs Trapp, a bushranger, to destroy the hero, Lawrence, by causing him to fall off a bridge into the Bunyip's Glen. Lawrence is, however, saved by a helpful and loyal Aborigine, King Billy (played by a white actor). All ends happily with the death of the villain and the uniting of Flora and Lawrence. ❧*Elizabeth Webby*

Australian Contemporary Theatre Company

Professional alternative-theatre company in Melbourne founded in 1983 by John and Lois Ellis. Closed February 1990. **venue** The Church, Hawthorn. **directors** 1983–85 John and Lois Ellis. 1985–89 John Ellis. **first production** *Dance in the Ashes* by Sandy McCutcheon, 1983. **landmark productions** *The Comedy of Errors*, 1987. *The Pathfinder* by Darryl Emmerson, 1986. *Call of the Wild* by Jenny Kemp, 1989.

In its seven-year life the Australian Contemporary Theatre Company—also known as the Church after its theatre—presented 50 productions or co-productions with itinerant alternative groups, mostly of plays by contemporary Australian playwrights. There were challenging works, including some excellent music-theatre, by lesser-known local playwrights and by some better-known Australian and overseas writers who were largely ignored elsewhere in Melbourne. The Church also housed some splendidly staged plays for children, especially Dorothy Hewett's *Golden Valley* and adaptations of children's classics by Ernie Gray. The lofty spaces and flexible seating of the old church, formerly home of Pilgrim Puppet Theatre, encouraged visual excitement in production and generally more interesting actor–audience relationships than in most mainstream theatres. The chronically underfunded company closed down in February 1990, when state and federal government subsidies were withdrawn. ❧*Geoffrey Milne*

Australian drama in school curricula

The upsurge in writing for the theatre in the 1960s was by the mid-1970s reflected in the syllabuses of universities, colleges and secondary schools. Students of literature began to encounter Australian playwrights alongside poets and novelists. Now school-leavers are more likely to have met David Williamson or Peter Kenna in their senior studies than they are earlier writers such as Henry Lawson or Vance Palmer. Acquaintance with dramatists' stage plays is reinforced by television and film. In addition, drama is now a separate examination study in most states.

Playscripts become textbooks when they are set for study for public examinations—except in Queensland, where texts are not prescribed. Plays selected for study enter the teaching repertoire and occasionally receive student productions. The prescriptions are revised every two years but the books remain in schools. Inclusion of plays in syllabuses has increasingly influenced the repertoires of theatre companies, and students are likely to be able to see professional productions of texts they study.

The first Australian play prescribed was Alex Buzo's *Macquarie*, set as an option in the third-level NSW Higher School Certificate course in 1973. It was safe—historical, solid and noncontroversial—and it was not widely chosen by students and teachers. Ray Lawler's Summer of the Seventeenth Doll, taken up in in 1978, has remained a staple in school courses nationally for nearly 20 years.

As the examiners grew more adventurous, several new plays were deemed appropriate for 17-year-olds to study at school. In 1978 Williamson's The Removalists was considered a lively contemporary option for the less academic. The Club by Williamson was the first contemporary Australian play to reach the Victorian syllabus. It has been regularly prescribed in most states, and more than 100 000 copies have been sold. Other durable selections have been Peter Kenna's A Hard God—in Catholic and other schools —Alan Seymour's The One Day of the Year, Kenneth Ross's *Breaker Morant* and Williamson's *Don's Party*. Syllabus committees have sometimes adopted plays rapidly; Michael Gow's *Away* and Louis Nowra's *Così* were adopted within a year of two.

Students in specialised courses, such as the contemporary Australian drama option in three-unit English in the NSW HSC, have had access to a broad range of texts. Plays such as Ron Blair's The Christian Brothers, John Romeril's The Floating World, Dorothy Hewett's The Chapel Perilous, George Hutchinson's *No Room for Dreamers* and Patrick White's *Signal Driver* have challenged advanced students. Jack Davis's *The Dreamers* and *No Sugar* have represented Aboriginal viewpoints.

Proliferation of tertiary courses in Australian literature has produced a demand that has been met by several of the above plays, by Jack Hibberd's A Stretch of the Imagination, and by plays of historical significance, including George Darrell's The Sunny South and Louis Esson's The Time is Not Yet Ripe. Adult themes and graphic language render many contemporary plays unsuitable for classroom study and ensure that others are controversial choices. However, new writers within young people's theatre have extended the range of Australian drama for school study. ❧*Frank Bladwell*

Australian Elizabethan Theatre Trust

The first public body for the performing arts was the Australian Elizabethan Theatre Trust, founded in September 1954 as a non-profit public company limited by guarantee. It made its mark as the seeding and founding body for the NATIONAL INSTITUTE OF DRAMATIC ART, the Theatre of the Deaf and the MARIONETTE THEATRE OF AUSTRALIA, the Australian Ballet and the Australian Opera. As an entrepreneur it was most significant in sending productions of major plays like Ray Lawler's SUMMER OF THE SEVENTEENTH DOLL and Alan Seymour's THE ONE DAY OF THE YEAR on tour overseas.

The Trust was the forerunner of the present arts-funding bodies, but was set up with a far wider brief. The founders, H. C. COOMBS, governor of the Commonwealth Bank, Sir Charles Moses, general manager of the Australian Broadcasting Commission, and John Douglas Pringle, editor of the *Sydney Morning Herald*, raised £100 000 through public appeal. The aim was to establish national drama, opera and ballet companies, employing local artists. More idealistically, it was to 'make the theatre in Australia the same vigorous and significant force in our national life that it was in the reign of the first Elizabeth'. The Trust was named to commemorate the recent visit to Australia of Queen Elizabeth II.

In March 1955 the Trust leased the old 1500-seat Majestic Theatre in Newtown, Sydney, and reopened it as the ELIZABETHAN THEATRE on 27 July 1955 with Terence Rattigan's *The Sleeping Prince*. This production, by GARNET H. CARROLL and H. M. Tennent, starred the English actors Lewis Casson, Meriel Forbes, Ralph Richardson and Sybil Thorndike. The next play was Rattigan's *Separate Tables*. In Canberra in October the expatriate JUDITH ANDERSON starred in Robinson Jeffers's version of Euripides's *Medea*, launching the Australian Drama Company. It toured for six months.

The Trust made its most exciting contributions to national drama under its first executive director, HUGH HUNT, an Englishman who was often seen as aloof from Australian concerns. Under Hunt there was a flurry of stage activities and fund-raising in the 1950s. In 1955 the Trust took over *Summer of the Seventeenth Doll* from the Union Theatre Repertory Company in Melbourne and presented it in Sydney to packed houses. *The Doll* became a solid source of revenue as it toured the country. The Trust launched the TRUST PLAYERS and PETER SCRIVEN's puppets in THE TINTOOKIES. It also gave financial assistance to amateur groups in Canberra and most state capitals. The Trust received funding from state and municipal governments, and a promise of increased federal funding.

Productions of Richard Beynon's THE SHIFTING HEART in 1957, the musical LOLA MONTEZ in 1958, Peter Kenna's THE SLAUGHTER OF ST TERESA'S DAY in 1959, THE ONE DAY OF THE YEAR in 1961 and Patrick White's THE HAM FUNERAL in 1962 were evidence of the Trust's prolific support and encouragement of indigenous plays, even when it did not actually initiate productions. From 1958 the Trust administered an annual theatre award by General Motors Holden. It was first won by Kenna with *The Slaughter of St Teresa's Day*.

The Trust set up a young Shakespearean company, the Young Elizabethan Players, which from 1958 toured abridged plays throughout Australia under the title 'Shakespeare in Jeans'. In co-operation with the University of NSW and the ABC, the Trust founded the NATIONAL INSTITUTE OF DRAMATIC ART in Sydney in 1958. Hiring costumes, props, lighting and scenery brought the Trust into contact with schools and amateurs throughout NSW.

With Neil Hutchison as director, the Trust saw the early 1960s as a time for joint ventures with entrepreneurs and an emphasis on lighter pieces. The Trust Players, worn out by national tours and playing serious drama in the big Elizabethan Theatre, were disbanded in 1962. Stefan Haag became executive director in that year. Kevon Kemp, H. G. KIPPAX and DOUGLAS STEWART, all writing in *Meanjin* in the third quarter of 1964, testify to the quantity of the Trust's activities in the 1960s but charge that when box-office receipts fell it too readily took off Australian works instead of standing the losses.

Haag's term as executive director ended in 1967. He was followed by Stephen Hall, with Donald McDonald as general manager. Establishment of the Australian Council for the Arts, supported by the federal government, displaced the Trust as a funding body in 1968. This led the Trust into more diverse activities than its founders had envisaged. Problems of definition and direction plagued it, although it continued to provide office facilities and shelter to groups as diverse in aim as the AUSTRALIAN NATIONAL PLAYWRIGHTS' CONFERENCE and the SYDNEY THEATRE COMPANY.

The 1980s saw the Trust continue entrepreneurial activity, including the importing of major Japanese drama and puppet companies. Its funding was greatly reduced but it made innovations, such as an Australian-content department under the direction of WENDY BLACKLOCK and a superannuation scheme for artists. The Trust now moved more certainly into supporting artists as well as the arts. In 1988 it administered the BP Australian Playwriting Award and demonstrated the broadened purpose by establishing promotional facilities for artists. The Trust was eligible to receive tax-deductible donations, and by arrangement with the Australian Taxation Office it was able to receive donations to other cultural organisations and pass them on less an administrative charge. ❦*Helen Musa*

further reading
PAGE, ROBERT. A position of trust. *Theatre Australia* 6 (September 1981).
SUMNER, JOHN. *Recollections at Play—A life in Australian theatre*. Melbourne: University Press 1993.

reference
Australian Elizabethan Theatre Trust papers, MS 7003 in National Library of Australia (Canberra).
H. C. Coombs papers, M448/1 in Australian Archives (Canberra.)

Australian National Playwrights' Conference

The only annual event that attracts theatrical workers from all over the country is the Australian National Playwrights' Conference, a residential dramaturgical workshop and forum held in Canberra since 1973. It has been a function of the Australian National Playwrights' Centre in Sydney since 1986. It is held over two weeks at Burgmann College and the Arts Centre on the Australian National University campus in the September vacation. It comprises development of selected scripts through workshops and public readings conducted by a team of actors, directors and dramaturges, and forum discussions on matters of concern to the theatre industry. The number of scripts chosen has varied from seven to 21.

The conference was the idea of the director BRIAN SYRON, who had worked at the American National Playwrights' Conference at the Eugene O'Neill Memorial Center at Waterford (Connecticut). He gained the support of Amy McGrath and her husband Judge Frank McGrath, who were conducting Sunday play readings in a private theatre in their home in Sydney. A meeting at the McGraths' house on 13 January 1972 established the aims of the conference: to promote and encourage the writing of plays by Australians and their production by professional companies; to hold an annual conference of rehearsed readings; and to offer dramaturgical assistance to playwrights.

The founding chair was the screenwriter Lance Peters, then president of the AUSTRALIAN WRITERS' GUILD. The other members were the actor Jeff Ashby; the playwright ALEX BUZO; the actor COLIN CROFT; Lorna Curtin, a member of the AUSTRALIAN ELIZABETHAN THEATRE TRUST board; the actor JACQUELINE KOTT (the first treasurer and later co-ordinator); the film maker Joan Long; the director AARNE NEEME; the actor Don Reid; and David Whitaker, a film-script adviser; and the present writer. The inaugural conference was held in March 1973 in Canberra at University House and Childers Hall. The scripts selected were by ALMA DE GROEN, Stuart Dickson, the New Zealand playwright Robert Lord, Finola Moorhead, Ru Pullen, Mark O'Connor and ALAN SEYMOUR (brought from London for the occasion). The first artistic director was Robert Levis and the first administrator was the actor Lew Luton.

Initially the structure followed that of the American conference, reintroducing to Australia the concept of playwrights' workshops—actors and director working over a text on the floor as a preliminary to rehearsal. This process had been lost since the days of the actor-playwright but is now customary in most Australian theatre companies that present untried work. The conference also introduced to the Australian theatre the dramaturge, a person who works closely with an author or director on the detail, interpretation and background of a text or a production.

Admission of public
However, it soon became clear that development was needed in many areas of theatre, because of the growth that had followed the establishment of the Australian Council for the Arts in 1968. A condition of the council's first grant to the conference in 1974 was admission of the public; this was the first measure to move it away from the exclusive, hierarchical American model. The second measure was a consensus that appointments should not extend beyond a year; that the artistic direction should be fluid and respond to the climate of the time. The rotating nature of the committee, short-term employment of staff and the changing nature of the theatre led to many robust debates, takeovers, and advocacy of widely varying styles of theatre, some challenging the supremacy of the textual work.

A committee of volunteers ran the conference until 1984, when the artistic director, Anne Harvey, and administrator, Michael Haeburn-Little, were appointed for a further three years to develop the group into a professional centre providing year-round script assessment and dramaturgical support. TERENCE CLARKE was appointed director of script assessment. The organisation was then incorporated as the Australian National Playwrights' Centre. Until then the committee had sheltered variously under the umbrellas of the AUSTRALIAN ELIZABETHAN THEATRE TRUST, the International Theatre Institute and the Theatre Workshop of the University of Sydney. In 1988 it achieved its first home, a cottage in Woolloomooloo; and in 1991 it moved to the NSW Writers' Centre, newly established by the state government in Rozelle. Harvey was succeeded by Kingston Anderson 1989–92 and by May-Brit Akerholt in 1993.

Among the playwrights who have gained attention for their work are DAVID ALLEN, LINDA ARONSON, JANIS BALODIS, Richard Barrett, MONA BRAND, MICHAEL GOW, DOROTHY HEWETT, RODNEY MILGATE, Heather Nimmo, Debra Oswald, JILL SHEARER and JOHN UPTON, and the New Zealanders Robert Lord and Greg McGee. Many of the selected writers have subsequently moved from the theatre into the television and film industries. Most Australian theatre directors have at one time worked at the conference and actors who like the opportunity to contribute to new work and the hard labour involved return again and again. Chairs of the conference have included the present writer (1977, 1985–90), the critics NORMAN KESSELL (1974–76) and Ken Healey (1984–85), and the playwrights DAVID WILLIAMSON (1980–82) and JANIS BALODIS (1991–92).

Guests at conferences
The official guest at the first conference was George White, administrator of the American conference. Others have been Lloyd Richards, permanent artistic director of the American conference; Arthur Ballet, an American dramaturge; and the British critic Martin Esslin (1974); the international entrepreneur Helen Montagu (1975, 1977); the American scriptwriter and play-doctor Irvin Bauer (1976), the British playwrights Snoo Wilson and John Osborne (1977), Trevor Griffiths (1983) and John McGrath (1985). The conference has also been attended by playwrights from Canada, Japan and other Pacific countries.

The history of the Australian National Playwrights' Conference has been turbulent and, its work being concerned largely with early development, the benefits have been intangible. It has been funded annually by the AUSTRALIA COUNCIL, state ministries, and private donation but its finances have always been shaky and the organisers have been caught between the need to provide privacy and supportive conditions for the untried playwright and the need to demonstrate publicly the value of the work for sponsors. From 1984 the Australian National Playwrights' Centre began systematically to initiate developments and to demonstrate through the conference the potential of such aspects of theatre as new form, radio drama, translation and the employment of bilingual actors and black actors. It has made links with the New Zealand Playwrights' Conference and the Australian National Black Playwrights' Conference. The latter met in 1987 in Canberra and in 1989 at Macquarie University in Sydney, supported by the Aboriginal arts board of the Australia Council and other sponsors. In 1992 the Australian and New Zealand conferences held a joint conference in Canberra, and in 1993 the black conference joined the Canberra event.

Today script assessment is provided year-round and the centre conducts regular weekend courses and seminars.

The first script-assessment service of this kind in Australia was provided from 1936 by the Australian Broadcasting Commission's federal drama department under LESLIE REES and MAX AFFORD. Although the scripts were for radio, many stage writers benefited from their advice on dramatic structure. Rees employed his skills in a voluntary capacity with the PLAYWRIGHTS' ADVISORY BOARD, which provided help to writers for 25 years from 1938. A similar, informal service was offered at the Melbourne Theatre Company from the late 1960s to the 1980s, by the excellent editor Carmel Dunn and later by RAY LAWLER.

Other sources of development
The Australian National Playwright's Conference is no longer the only source of play development. Most states have small writers' groups. The oldest is Playlab (Queensland Playwrights' Laboratory), a self-help writers' organisation which offers readings and an advisory service. It was founded in 1972 by a group of playwrights led by BARBARA STELLMACH. In 1978 Rodney Lumer set up Playlab Press to publish the work of Queensland playwrights and he has remained its editor. By 1993 it had published 34 volumes of plays. Melbourne Writers' Theatre, founded by JACK HIBBERD, Dinny O'Hearn and others in 1982, has its own workshop theatre, the Courthouse, and holds monthly meetings for readings and dramaturgical advice. Playworks was established by the director Ros Horin in 1985 with a national brief and headquarters in Sydney. It conducts extensive workshops on the work of female playwrights; Katherine Thomson's *Diving for Pearls* (1992) is its most successful product. The Western Australian Playwrights' Consortium, known as Stages, was founded in 1991 to offer a script assessment service and dramaturgical assistance and workshops to theatre companies in the state. Its founding director is Steve Agnew. All these organisations receive some state or federal funding. South Australia also has a small voluntary Writers' Theatre and a female writers' group. The work of all these groups is challenged by new needs as theatre companies absorb dramaturgy into play development. ❦*Katharine Brisbane*

further reading
PARSONS, HARRIET. *Australian National Playwrights' Conference—A retrospective*. Sydney: Currency Press 1988.
THOMAS, MARGARET. A shocking misuse of power. *ArtsWest* (Perth) November–December 1992.
Playlab, enriching and noticing what we have. *Performing Arts* (Brisbane) November 1987.

Australian Nouveau Theatre

Professional dramatic company in Melbourne, founded on 12 August 1981 by Bruce Keller and Jean-Pierre Mignon. Also known as ANT and Anthill. Folded 1994. **venues** 1981–92 Anthill Theatre, South Melbourne. 1992–94 Gasworks. **artistic director** Jean-Pierre Mignon. **first production** three short plays by Samuel Beckett, performed by Bruce Keller, Jean-Pierre Mignon and Marilyn O'Donnell at La Mama Theatre, January 1980. **landmark productions** Chekhov Triptych (*The Cherry Orchard*, *Three Sisters*, *Uncle Vanya*). *Kidstuff* by Raymond Cousse. *Summer of the Seventeenth Doll* by Ray Lawler. *Tartuffe* by Molière.

By developing a style of performance at odds with the prevailing naturalism, the small Australian Nouveau Theatre company made a strong impact in Melbourne. In most productions it favoured stylisation and theatricality, sometimes in extreme forms. It began when Jean-Pierre Mignon, an actor and director from France who had met closed doors in Melbourne, and Bruce Keller, a local actor and writer, set up a company of young trained performers who were prepared to work without pay. They aimed to tour in Australia, staging plays from the international repertoire, emphasising contemporary drama from Europe and great classical texts that treat universal themes. European playwrights staged by the company include Antonin Artaud, Samuel Beckett, Mikhail Bulgakov, Anton Chekhov, Raymond Cousse, Jean Genet, Peter Handke, Henrik Ibsen, Bernard-Marie Koltes, Molière, Slawomir Mrozek, Heiner Müller, Roland Tpor and Stanislaw Witkiewicz. The company performed throughout Australia and had successful seasons in Asia and in Europe.

The company's main thrust was towards longer and more thorough rehearsals and workshops to give the actor's powers of expression precedence over other stage effects. This and economic constraints led to minimalist staging and 'poor theatre'. Lack of money precluded a permanent ensemble but the company had a circle of performers and other workers who shared its philosophy. It encouraged actors from ethnic minorities to use their individual qualities, verbal and nonverbal, in new ways rather than hide their origins to win acceptance in the mainstream. ❦*Anne C. Murch*

Australian Performing Group

Co-operative theatre company in Melbourne, formed in 1968 as amateur La Mama Company. Renamed as professional group 1970. Disbanded 1981. **venues** 1968–70 La Mama Theatre. 1970–81 Pram Factory. **first production** *Marvellous Melbourne* by Jack Hibberd and John Romeril, 11 December 1970, Pram Factory. **landmark productions** *Don's Party* by David Williamson. *The Feet of Daniel Mannix* by Barry Oakley. *The Floating World* by Romeril. *The Hills Family Show*. *Marvellous Melbourne*. *A Stretch of the Imagination* by Hibberd. *A Toast to Melba* by Hibberd. *Traitors* by Stephen Sewell.

Some of the most exciting and important theatrical developments in the 1970s came from the Australian Performing Group. It began life in 1968 at LA MAMA THEATRE in Carlton, where writers, actors, designers and directors—most of them from the University of Melbourne or Monash University—joined forces to create the La Mama Company, with a firm commitment to Australian plays. Early members included the actor–director GRAEME BLUNDELL; the playwrights JACK HIBBERD, JOHN ROMERIL and DAVID WILLIAMSON; the actors PETER CUMMINS, LINDY DAVIES, Kerry Dwyer, Bill Garner, MAX GILLIES, EVELYN KRAPE, Fay Mokotow and BRUCE SPENCE; and the manager John Timlin.

From the start the group was interested in the new and local rather than the tested import. It intended to develop drama that 'eschewed taste-following for taste-making' and 'to innovate rather than duplicate'. In its early years some 90 per cent of its productions were by Australian writers, mostly its own members. Reacting against the refined, elocutionary and highly artificial style favoured by visiting English actors, the La Mama Company developed its own style. It was raw, vital, strongly physical and mostly comic, with realism exaggerated for effect. It grew out of Hibberd's early plays, which mixed surface naturalism and larger-than-life characters. But it was also the product of the intimate La Mama Theatre.

The group's importance was first publicly recognised when it was invited to perform at the 1970 FESTIVAL OF PERTH. Taking the plunge, the group declared itself professional and headed west with two plays by Hibberd, one by Romeril and one by ALEX BUZO. On its return the company presented the four plays in a season divided between La Mama and the University of Melbourne.

The Australian Performing Group, which grew out of the La Mama Company, was established as a collective with a firm commitment to participatory democracy and worker control. The members, who numbered about 50, were expected to contribute to the practical running of the theatre, writers included. Strong political bias and radicalism distinguished the group's work from the start. Apart from performing in the theatre, it regularly went to schools, universities, factories and prisons and took part in public protests on issues such as censorship.

In May 1970 the group found more suitable, larger premises around the corner in Drummond Street, in an old livery stable where Paramount prams had been made later. This became the Pram Factory. The main stage was in the upstairs Front Theatre, which seated up to 150 people. In 1973 the group opened the 75-seat Back Theatre for more specialised and smaller-scale work. The Front Theatre opened in December 1970 with MARVELLOUS MELBOURNE, a fast-moving larrikin piece that offered a cartoon view of Melbourne in the 1880s land boom. After eight tryout performances and reworking it was presented with considerable success in March 1971.

Marvellous Melbourne was written by Hibberd and Romeril, who between them supplied the bulk of the Pram Factory's output over the next few years. Other playwrights whose work the collective staged in this incredibly fertile and vigorous period included BARRY OAKLEY, TIM ROBERTSON and Williamson. The company also did group-devised shows on political or feminist themes, including *Betty Can Jump* in 1972. This was devised by female members of the APG, including Kerry Dwyer and Evelyn Krape, in reaction to what they saw as stereotypic and unconvincing roles supplied by the men. THE HILLS FAMILY SHOW, first staged in 1975 and revived several times, was the most popular and successful group-devised show.

From 1976 there was increasing pressure within the group to widen the repertoire to include interesting overseas writers. By 1978 the group was fragmenting, with members hiving off to form their own companies, including CIRCUS OZ and the Women's Theatre Group. It had become difficult to sustain the energy of the early years, the quality of new plays had appreciably declined, and audiences were falling away. In 1980 the Pram Factory was sold to a development company. It was the death-knell for both the theatre and the company, although a five-play season was mounted in 1981, using guest directors and casts drawn from the general pool of actors and not the Australian Performing Group itself. The last play in that season, *The Bedbug Celebration*, a futuristic satire by John Blay, was the last staged at the Pram Factory. Soon afterwards the wreckers moved in. A public campaign to save the building was mounted, but a supermarket now occupies the site.

Like the NIMROD THEATRE COMPANY in Sydney, the APG helped to shift the balance from the imported theatrical product to the local. In its early years, when established companies were content to do the occasional Australian play, the APG did little else. Whereas established companies largely restricted themselves to conventional presentation of straight plays, the APG went further and worked up shows for all occasions. In the process it developed a distinctly Australian playing style with emphasis on physicality and strong overtones of variety. The APG thought of itself as a performer's theatre, but it was its writers—particularly Hibberd, Oakley, Robertson, Romeril and Williamson—who gave it its original reputation, and provided it with its best and most exciting plays or shows. Several plays first performed at the Pram Factory are still in the repertoire, including DON'S PARTY, A STRETCH OF THE IMAGINATION and THE FLOATING WORLD. ❦*Leonard Radic*

further reading
BRISBANE, KATHARINE. Death of the Pram Factory. *National Times* (Sydney) 6–12 September 1981.

reference
APG papers are held at the Performing Arts Museum and the La Trobe Library (Melbourne) and at the Defence Forces Academy (Canberra).

Australian Theatre for Young People

Youth-theatre company in Sydney, founded in 1963. **artistic directors** Antoinette Blaxland, Mark Gaal, Colette Rayment, Jane Westbrook.

Australian Theatre for Young People introduces young people, aged from eight to 25 years, to a wide range of theatrical work—acting, performance-making, music, street theatre, acting for the camera, dramatic writing, set and costume design, and production assistance, including stage management and lighting. Concern that children lacked opportunities for theatrical experience led enthusiastic young professional actors to found it as a professional troupe that essentially toured to entertain children. Many of its members were associated with ROBIN LOVEJOY and the OLD TOTE THEATRE COMPANY, which assisted the fledgling company. When the Old Tote company folded in 1978, the directors of Australian Theatre for Young People, led by Diana Sharpe, secured its future by disentangling it. Then its function changed. The young were no longer merely audience but actors, directors, technicians and writers.

Professional actors, technicians, designers and directors lead the young people in workshops and in a few productions each year. One production goes on tour. Australian Theatre for Young People is a non-profit organisation. It raises most of its income from fees and box-office but it is well supported by the NSW Ministry for the Arts, the AUSTRALIA COUNCIL and corporate sponsors. ❦*Colette Rayment*

reference
The company's archives are in the Australian National Library (Canberra).

Australian Writers' Guild

The national professional association for writers of dramatic scripts in all media, the Australian Writers' Guild has been a force in establishing minimum award agreements for playwrights and encouraging the production of Australian plays, as part of its advocacy. Writers led by Don Houghton founded it in Sydney on 2 May 1962, as the Australian Radio, Television and Screen Writers' Guild. Houghton became its first president and Ric Aspinall drew up its first constitution. The radio writer John Abbott and the actor and playwright ALAN HOPGOOD established a Victorian chapter later in 1962 and eventually the guild became a national organisation, though it was registered as a trade union only in NSW.

The guild changed its name in the mid-1960s to reflect its widening membership, but it was only in the late 1970s that it began to represent and develop policies for playwrights. The first stage writers' subcommittee was convened in 1979, with RON BLAIR in the chair. Negotiation of a basic award agreement on original non-commissioned plays guaranteed playwrights a set royalty and much greater control over the regional licensing of their plays. All major theatre companies signed the agreement. The committee also set minimum rates for theatre-in-education, public readings and amateur productions. By 1982 it had begun to establish guidelines for the commissioning of stage plays, the role of the literary adviser, or dramaturge, and the terms and conditions of playwright-in-residence schemes.

The guild has also lobbied the AUSTRALIA COUNCIL for schemes to encourage theatre companies to maintain quotas of Australian works and it has supported companies with proven commitment to Australian drama. It provided the impetus for the short-lived but vigorous Writers' Theatre movement in Sydney, Melbourne and Adelaide and has been involved with the AUSTRALIAN NATIONAL PLAYWRIGHTS' CONFERENCE since that began in 1972.

A campaign in the early 1980s for quicker responses to Australian works sent to theatre companies resulted in a regularly updated publication, *The Market for Stage Plays*. In addition to reporting market opportunities for its 2600 members, the guild mediates disputes, fights for grants, holds seminars and craft weekends and produces the monthly newsletter *Viewpoint*. Since 1968 it has honoured writers with the annual Awgie AWARDS for the best stage, radio, film and television scripts. In 1971 THE LEGEND OF KING O'MALLEY by Michael Boddy and Bob Ellis became the first stage play to win the major award, which is for the best script in any medium. ❦*Victoria Chance*

Awake My Love

Play in three acts by Max Afford. **premiere** 4 September 1947, Independent Theatre, Sydney. Cast: Paul O'Loughlin, Kevin Brennan. Designer: Thelma Afford. Director: Doris Fitton. **published** Brisbane: University of Queensland Press 1974.

With this play, originally titled *Colonel Light—The Founder*, MAX AFFORD won the Adelaide *Advertiser* newspaper's first prize for a play to celebrate South Australia's centenary in 1936. He rewrote it as *Awake My Love*, incorporating love interest into a historical drama based on the life of Colonel William Light, the first Surveyor-General of South Australia. The play is set in the years 1837–39 and deals mainly with the conflict between Light and autocratic Governor Hindmarsh over the site of the city of Adelaide. The playwright's wife, THELMA AFFORD designed the decor and costumes. ❦*Richard Lane*

Awards

Awards for excellence have been important in conferring status on indigenous theatre. In most state capitals awards have helped to establish the credentials of the theatrical profession and to distinguish its eminent members. The Erik Kuttner Awards for best actor and best actress were the first. They commemorate a refugee German actor who came to Melbourne in the 1930s and shared his knowledge and love of theatre, although he was unable to secure stable employment as actor or teacher. His death in relative obscurity in 1954 prompted the actors Hanna and George Pravda to initiate the awards, known as the Eriks. Judged by a panel of Melbourne critics, the first awards went to Stewart Ginn and ZOË CALDWELL, in May 1955. The Eriks later included the DOLIA RIBUSH Award for best director, the IRENE MITCHELL Award for best stage design, the Rosa Ribush Awards for best supporting actor and actress, an award for the best new Australian play and an occasional special award for services to Australian theatre.

In Sydney in the late 1960s the critic NORMAN KESSELL founded the Glugs, a name drawn from C. J. Dennis's book *The Glugs of Gosh*. They are a luncheon group of regular theatregoers who annually vote for contributors to the quality of Sydney theatre. The original award for an outstanding performance was renamed in Kessell's honour after his death in 1986. Other Glugs include the Jeffrey Joynton-Smith Award (since 1992) for a newcomer and the Chief Glugs' Award (since 1993) for someone behind the scenes. A lifetime achievement award is sometimes made.

The Australian Variety Artistes' Association first voted on the Mo Awards for variety and comedy performers in 1976. Since 1989 these have been known as the Australian Entertainment 'Mo' Awards. Specialists around Australia elect the winners of 44 statuettes of the comedian ROY RENE in character as Mo, for excellence in live performance in comedy, variety, musical theatre, circus and other fields. The major award is a platinum statuette for Australian performer of the year.

In 1975 the AUSTRALIA COUNCIL initiated the National Critics' Circle, which aimed to redress insularity and to improve the standard of criticism. It paid for critics from metropolitan newspapers—and later national radio—to travel to see productions, meet colleagues semi-informally and vote for nominations for annual awards in each state. The industry at large voted on these nominations to determine the National Professional Theatre Awards, which were presented at the AUSTRALIAN NATIONAL PLAYWRIGHTS' CONFERENCE in 1977 and 1978.

The Australia Council withdrew its funding in 1979 after criticism of the scheme. In its wake, Sydney critics established the annual Sydney Critics' Circle Award in the form of a trophy for the most significant contribution to Sydney theatre, voted and initially funded by the critics. After gaining sponsorship in the mid-1980s, the awards expanded to six, generally two to performers and the rest according to voting in about ten categories. Since 1989 the JOHN TASKER Memorial Award for a freelance director has also been included.

In Melbourne, the Eriks petered out in the early 1970s, and were replaced by the Green Room Awards in 1984. The committee of the Green Room Awards Association determines nominations in opera, dance, music-theatre and drama, which are voted on by several hundred theatre professionals and theatregoers. The committee itself makes further awards, for lifetime achievement and outstanding technical achievement, when appropriate. Current awards in other states include five annual Matilda Awards, judged by Brisbane critics. They were established in 1988 with funding from the arts division of the Queensland Premier's Department and for three years were worth $2000 each, but funding was withdrawn in 1992. The Swan Gold Theatre Awards have been presented in Perth since 1989 and the Canberra Critics' Circle Awards since 1991. In Adelaide there is no award.

The richest awards, the Australian Artists' Creative Fellowships, were introduced by Paul Keating when he was federal Treasurer in 1989, in recognition of the fact that leading professionals earn much less in the arts than in other occupations. Artists at the top of their profession, including performing artists, compete annually for fellowships of $55 000 a year for three to five years. Also richly endowed are the Sidney Myer Performing Arts Awards, which were created in 1984 to commemorate the Melbourne businessman and to pay tribute to outstanding achievement in the performing arts with awards of $20 000 and $30 000 to an individual and a group respectively. The playwright JACK DAVIS won the first individual award.

The most significant theatre award won overseas by Australians is the George Devine Award, which in 1971 left the United Kingdom for the first time to go to the Nimrod Theatre Company for its Sydney production of David Williamson's play THE REMOVALISTS. ❧Victoria Chance

Away

Play in two acts by Michael Gow. **premiere** 7 January 1986, Stables Theatre, Sydney by Griffin Theatre Company. Cast: Vanessa Downing, Benjamin Franklin, Julie Godfrey, Christian Hodge, David Lynch, Andrea Moor, Geoff Morrell, Angela Toohey. Designer: Robert Kemp. Director: Peter Kingston. **published** Sydney: Currency Press 1986.

One of the most frequently revived Australian plays, *Away* opens with the close of Shakespeare's *A Midsummer Night's Dream* and closes with the opening of *King Lear*. These reference points, together with extracts from Felix Mendelssohn's incidental music for the *Dream*, contribute importantly to the play's structure and atmosphere. The first act begin like yet another satire on suburban banality as three families at a school play look forward to the summer holidays. Behind it, however, is nostalgia for the innocently booming Australia of the 1960s.

In the second act the play becomes a different kind of comedy. Couples who are locked into ritual and pretence at home are freed by the experience of being 'away' on the northeast coast to evolve new understandings that may prove to be durable. Harry and Vic, an English couple whose son Tom is dying of leukaemia, are less a target for satire than the others. Gow's major satiric objects are Jim and Gwen, parents of Tom's friend Meg. Gwen is obsessed with keeping up appearances. But all the parents in *Away* have much to learn.

The transformations are partly attributable to relocation, to a storm that exposes everyone to the elements on an unknown beach, and to confrontation with Tom's real tragedy. However they also stem from a shift in mode. *Away* relies less on dialogue as it moves away from familiar places and familiar ways of looking at them. Anti-realist staging of the storm with the fairies from the opening scene, the romantic suggestiveness of the music, a strange play that Tom and Coral stage for the campers, as well as Shakespeare's verse, all gesture toward an order of knowledge that resists common sense. The couples' final reconciliations are all wordless.

Away becomes comedy of the Shakespearean kind, in which harmony is established where only discord had seemed possible. Gow seems to achieve that against all odds when Tom at the end begins to read from *King Lear*. There is cruel irony in the boy, who is about to die, speaking the words of the octogenarian Lear. Gow refuses to be embarrassed about those kinds of emotional claims, and makes them real and memorable. In 1992, when Gow directed the play in Sydney he gave Meg the final reading, making Tom's death tangible. This version has been adopted in subsequent productions. ❧*Peter Fitzpatrick*

Frank Baden-Powell

Actor, director, entrepreneur. Born 14 August 1929 in Perth. Involved with Independent Players and Therry Society in Perth. Acted in repertory companies in United Kingdom 1950–55. Toured Australia for Australian Elizabethan Theatre Trust 1955. Artistic director of National Theatre Company (Perth) 1956–60. Founded Hole-in-the-Wall Theatre Company (Perth) with John Gill 1961. Began Music Hall Company chain of theatre-restaurants by opening Old Time Music Hall in Perth 1967. Perth city councillor 1969–82. Retired from Music Hall Company 1987. Died 16 May 1992 in Sydney. Married and divorced actors Joan Bruce and, second, Eileen Colocott.

Frank Baden-Powell supervised the establishment of the first professional theatre company in Perth and founded the city's first theatre-in-the-round and the first of its THEATRE-RESTAURANTS. After working with two amateur groups, he left Perth in December 1949 to become a professional actor in the United Kingdom. He returned in 1955 and toured in the company headed by Lewis Casson, Ralph Richardson and Sybil Thorndike that gave the first production for the AUSTRALIAN ELIZABETHAN THEATRE TRUST. After the tour he returned to Perth to co-ordinate the establishment of the professional NATIONAL THEATRE COMPANY and the building of its Playhouse theatre.

While artistic director of the company Baden-Powell directed some 15 major productions, including successful presentations of *Johnny Belinda* by Elmer Harris and *Our Hearts were Young and Gay* by Cornelia Otis Skinner and Emily Kimbrough and the first performance of DOROTHY HEWETT's early play, *This Old Man Comes Rolling Home*. He also acted in many productions, including Sam and Bella Spewack's *My Three Angels*, T. S. Eliot's *Murder in the Cathedral* and Arthur Miller's *A View from the Bridge*.

Baden-Powell left the Playhouse in December 1960 and in July 1961 founded Perth's first theatre-in-the-round, Theatre 61. It became better known as the Hole-in-the-Wall Theatre. After arranging a move to a new location in 1967 he ceased active involvement with the HOLE-IN-THE-WALL COMPANY. In partnership with the present writer, he opened the Old Time Music Hall, the first theatre-restaurant in Perth. From this developed a nationwide chain of theatre-restaurants which became the largest in Australia, with companies in all states except Tasmania. ❧*Coralie Condon*

Bert Bailey

Actor, dramatist, manager. Born 11 June 1868 in Auckland (New Zealand). Emigrated to Australia with mother c.1879. Educated in Sydney. Worked in skating rink, as telegram boy, as tambourine player and singer in music-hall. Toured outback towns in melodrama companies 1889–1900. Joined William Anderson's company as comic lead 1900. Married actor Ivy Gorrick 11 February 1902. Wrote plays with Edmund Duggan 1907–12. In two silent films, 1910–11. Began partnership with Julius Grant at King's Theatre, Melbourne, 1912. Wrote and starred in *On Our Selection* 1912. Played in *On Our Selection* in London from 19 August 1920. Retired 1929. Began making sound films 1932, year of wife's death. Retired 1940. Died 30 March 1953 in Sydney. Daughter 'Tim', writer for children, was his secretary.

The archetypal Dad in dramatisations of the stories of STEELE RUDD, Bert Bailey enjoyed mass recognition of his work for several generations. He joined Edmund Duggan and Beaumont Smith's theatre company in 1889 and toured country towns throughout NSW, Victoria and Queensland, playing in melodramas, especially those of WALTER COOPER, GEORGE DARRELL and BLAND HOLT. Later he toured to the Gulf of Carpentaria, Thursday Island and Perth in companies run by KATE HOWARDE, Irve Hyman and others. In WILLIAM ANDERSON's company in 1907 Bailey and DUGGAN wrote a melodrama, THE SQUATTER'S DAUGHTER. It was a great success and the two actors, whose collaboration was attributed to 'Albert Edmunds', collaborated in two more sensation plays, *The Man from Outback* and *The Native Born*.

In 1912 Bailey began a partnership with Julius Grant at the King's Theatre in Melbourne, first as Bailey and Grant, and later as the Bert Bailey Dramatic Company, in which shareholders were Bailey, Grant, Duggan and Anderson. It tried everything from Shakespeare to pantomime for 17 years. Bailey made his name as Dad Rudd in ON OUR SELECTION, his rewriting of a dramatisation of Rudd's short stories that had been made by Rudd and BEAUMONT SMITH and rejected by J. C. WILLIAMSON's. Actors' parts in the National Library of Australia show that much of the acting script was Bailey's invention, and there was minor input from Duggan. In an interview in *Theatre* magazine of 1 June 1912 Rudd said that except for 60 per cent of the dialogue taken straight from the short stories, 'I could not recognise anything of the dramatisation as originally done by Mr Smith and me'. Bailey's original inclusion of Smith's name in the program was a sign of his generosity, Rudd said. Correspondence between Rudd and Bailey on the subject shows a direct and generally cordial relationship.

In 1922 Bailey produced for DAN AND E. J. CARROLL the original stage adaptation of C. J. Dennis's verses *The Sentimental Bloke*. He later acted the role of Ginger Mick in the play. Typically, Bailey saw that films made it time for him to get out of the theatre and in 1929, after touring Barry Connor's play *The Patsy* to 110 towns, he retired. In 1932 he came out of retirement to win new fame in a film of *On Our Selection*, the first of four Rudd family films for Ken G. Hall. He also assisted Hall as acting coach in early talkies. His films show his own acting style becoming more subdued as he acquires a film technique. The earliest films show just how studied the theatrical style of his time must have been. Bailey was clearly a stylish but exaggerated comic actor who learned to tone it down.

In some ways Bailey himself was a larger-than-life 'character', given to exaggerated storytelling. 'Life is melodrama', he once said, and on this principle he based most of his writing and choices of repertoire. Hall believed that Bailey's addiction to melodrama limited him, but he judiciously blended it with his comic forte to suit his public. Bailey's aspirations to be recognised as a patriotic Australian playwright were thwarted by criticisms such as the *Bulletin*'s judgment of THE SQUATTER'S DAUGHTER as 'an English bellowdrama Australianised'.

Bailey combined adventuring with hardheaded theatrical and business practices. He despised refinement and 'culture' in the theatre and he bore a characteristic Australian inverted snobbery. A practical director who would run a play half an hour faster to an unresponsive audience, he advised actors to try for laughs and immediate effects all the time. His efforts at local colour were often obvious. 'We'll spray the bloody theatre with eucalyptus and make them think they're in the bush', he once said. A critic noted a high head count of native fauna in Bailey's local plays. But an examination of scripts shows Bailey—and Duggan to a degree—to have been an expert theatrical craftsman with a good sense of timing and humour. His more serious writing remains superficial in the melodramatic subplots invented to hold together *The Squatter's Daughter* and *On Our Selection*, but in this he was a creature of his time and his huge success on the stage shows that he understood his audience's expectations of the theatre. His grasp of contemporary issues is seen in the way he often opposed the cynical squatter to the struggling selector or working man.

Bailey was judge, jury and Privy Council in his theatres. He forced good work out of actors, who characteristically used words like 'adamant' and 'dominant' to describe his methods. Bailey threw people out for being late to rehearsals and manoeuvred himself into the limelight. At the same time he knew how to surround himself with talent, so that his Dad and Dave plays were well known to have depended as much upon the abilities of FRED MACDONALD, who created the stage and film Dave, as upon his own.

Bailey grew up in prosperity. His mother ran McCathie's drapery store in Sydney. He married the daughter of a Newcastle solicitor. His private circumstances hint at the gradual infiltration of the middle-class into the acting profession which, by the time Bailey finally retired, was far more respectable than it had ever been in the 19th century. ❧*Helen Musa*

published play
On Our Selection with Edmund Duggan, Steele Rudd and Beaumont Smith (ed. Helen Musa). Sydney: Currency Press 1984.

further reading
PIKE, ANDREW. Bert Bailey. *Australian Dictionary of Biography* 7. Melbourne University Press 1979.
PIKE, ANDREW. Dad and Dave in the cinema. In *On Our Selection* by Bert Bailey. Sydney: Currency Press 1984.

reference
Bert and Tim Bailey manuscript collection (MS 6141), National Library of Australia (Canberra). Bert Bailey papers in Mitchell Library (Sydney).

J. C. Bain

Manager. Born c.1873 in Ispwich (Qld). At Temperance Hall, Hobart, 1903–06. National Amphitheatre, Sydney, 1907–11. Presented vaudeville companies in Sydney suburbs from 1911. Died 24 May 1946 in Brisbane.

An old-time manager of second-rank variety entertainment, Jimmy Bain was variously described as business manager and general manager for JAMES BRENNAN at the National Amphitheatre in Sydney. After Brennan teamed up with FULLERS' in 1911, Bain ran the small Princess Theatre in Railway Square with his own Advanced Vaudeville Entertainers. By early 1912 he also had touring companies at the Coliseum in North Sydney, the Coronation Theatre at Bondi Junction and the Acme Theatre at Rockdale.

After the First World War began in 1914, Bain, according to *Australian Variety* magazine 'found the fight too strenuous, with the result that he has dropped the reins of proprietorship of the Princess and the house reverts to the Fuller-Brennan people'. Bain, however, continued in show business at venues like the Gaiety Theatre in Oxford Street. In 1924 he was presenting vaudeville at the Hippodrome when it was not required by WIRTHS' CIRCUS. When the Tivoli Theatre in Sydney closed in 1929, Bain was among the veteran performers who appeared in the final show. In 1931 he was doing front-of-house duties at the Palace Theatre in Sydney before it became a cinema. ❦*John West*

Helmut Bakaitis

Actor, director, dramatist. Born 26 September 1944 in Dresden (Germany) of Lithuanian parents. Graduated from National Institute of Dramatic Art (Sydney) 1965. Resident actor with Melbourne Theatre Company 1966–71. Director of youth activities for South Australian Theatre Company (Adelaide) 1972–76. Director of youth programming for Adelaide Festival 1972. Artistic director of St Martin's Youth Arts Centre (Melbourne) 1978–84. Artistic director of New Moon Theatre Company (Townsville, Qld) 1984–86. Artistic director of Q Theatre Company (Penrith NSW) 1989–. Has written many scripts for youth theatre companies. Has acted in film and television.

In a long and varied career Helmut Bakaitis has been most noted as a director, principally in theatre for young people. In the 1970s he had a far-reaching influence in Adelaide. Each of the organisations he helped to establish—including the theatre-in-education MAGPIE THEATRE COMPANY, CARCLEW YOUTH ARTS CENTRE and the COME OUT FESTIVAL—is now essential to Australia's youth arts infrastructure. Similarly, much of the style of his pioneering work remains entrenched at the ST MARTIN'S YOUTH ARTS CENTRE, especially the emphasis upon topical, large-cast shows with music, of which he developed many with the young performers. His production of Allan Mackay's *Cain's Head* was particularly successful and toured to the Nimrod Theatre in Sydney in 1981. As a director of provincial theatres in Queensland and NSW, Bakaitis has included energetic, purpose-made new works—such as the rock musical *Beach Blanket Tempest* for the NEW MOON THEATRE COMPANY in 1984—in judiciously blended artistic programs. He has brought new energy to Q Theatre with musicals like *Better Known as Bee* in 1992 and *Kenny's Coming Home* in 1991. While with the MELBOURNE THEATRE COMPANY he began writing plays for MTC Youth Theatre—*The Pageant of the Love Tree* (1966) and *The Little Lady Steps Out* (1969). In Sydney, the NIMROD THEATRE COMPANY presented his *Shadows of Blood* in 1972. For the first Come Out Festival in 1975 he wrote and presented *The Lay of Sir Orfeo* and for the 1977 festival *Carlotta and Maximilian*. ❦*Geoffrey Milne*

published play
The Incredible Mind-Blowing Trial of Jack Smith (1971). Melbourne: Heinemann 1971.

The Ballad of Angel's Alley

Musical. **libretto** Jeff Underhill. **music** Bruce George. **premiere** 26 December 1958, New Theatre, Flinders Street, Melbourne. Director: Jeff Underhill. Producer: William Jeffries. **revivals** 1962, Russell Street Theatre, Melbourne, by Melbourne Theatre Company. 9 January 1965 and 8 December 1973 by New Theatre Sydney.

A Melbourne counterpart of John Gay's *The Beggar's Opera*, *Angel's Alley* is based on the 'push' wars of the 1890s. The libretto of *Angel's Alley* is robust but charming, and the caricatured vernacular is fast-moving good fun. Frank Murphy acclaimed the musical in the *Advocate* in January 1959 as 'a delicious extravaganza, written in a mock serious style that capitally captures and sustains the old ballad melodramas', but it failed to capture any of the public interest generated by New Theatre's production of the folk musical REEDY RIVER five years earlier. William Jeffries produced *Angel's Alley* with financial assistance from the AUSTRALIAN ELIZABETHAN THEATRE TRUST, while New Theatre Melbourne provided the theatre, costuming, set design and construction, stage direction, lighting and some actors. ❦*Angela O'Brien*

Colin Ballantyne CMG

Director. Born 12 July 1908 in Adelaide. Worked as photographer for Adelaide *Register* 1927–31; later in own business. Acted with Adelaide Repertory Theatre 1927–33. Joined WEA Little Theatre as actor 1928. Married Gwenneth Richmond, actor and drama teacher, 1934; produced many plays with her in 1930s. Directed for Adelaide University Theatre Guild in 1940s and 1950s; Adelaide Theatre Group in 1950s and 1960s; Company of Players 1955. Federal director of Arts Council of Australia 1966–75. Founding chairman of State Theatre Company of South Australia 1972–78. Federal president of Arts Council of Australia 1974–77. Chairman of Performing Arts Collection of South Australia 1980–88. Died 2 July 1988 in Adelaide. CMG 1971. Father of actor Elspeth Ballantyne, film producer Jane Ballantyne and television producer Guy Ballantyne.

At a time when there was little professional theatre in South Australia Colin Ballantyne made it happen. Between 1948 and 1971 he produced or directed more than 100 plays, including major productions for the ADELAIDE FESTIVAL OF ARTS. 'The years in which he was most active in encouraging a vigorous theatre life in South Australia were those that saw the performing arts in other Australian centres struggling to offset dwindling audiences and returns', said his CMG citation in 1971. 'By contrast, South Australian theatre audiences were able to enjoy a continuing and vital theatre activity, much of which came as a result of his enthusiasm, leadership, talent and vision.'

During wartime military service in Darwin Ballantyne studied the Stanislavsky method and introduced it to

Adelaide in the 1940s and 1950s, when he directed classics and modern works for the ADELAIDE UNIVERSITY THEATRE GUILD. For the Arts Council of South Australia he directed notable productions of *Macbeth* in 1948, *Twelfth Night* in 1949 and *As You Like It* in 1951—the last adventurously in a three-quarter-round outdoor venue. After spending much of the 1950s directing for the Arts Council, Ballantyne was a leading force in the ADELAIDE THEATRE GROUP in the 1960s. He was also director of the Company of Players, formed in 1955 to perform blank-verse plays by the Adelaide poets Charles Jury, John Bray and Brian Medlin.

A Fabian socialist in a city where amateur performance was largely a middle-class affair, Ballantyne exercised a wide-ranging anti-establishment influence through his repertoire and the monthly open house he held at his North Adelaide home. He and his wife Gwenneth were largely responsible for creating the climate for intellectual radicalism that emerged in Adelaide in the 1960s. Among his actor protegés were the theatre consultant TOM BROWN, the actor EDWIN HODGEMAN and Don Dunstan, who became Premier of South Australia in 1970. During Dunstan's Labor regime Ballantyne was influential in the formation of the STATE THEATRE Company of South Australia as a statutory body and in guiding its direction.

Ballantyne's strong views, dynamic personality and impatience often led to confrontation, but his persistent demand for innovation and excellence in performance and tireless work towards establishment of systems of state and federal subvention, made him an enduring figure. He gave his theatre photographs to the Performing Arts Collection of South Australia. After his death this was renamed the Colin and Gwynneth Ballantyne Performing Arts Collection. ❦*Katharine Brisbane*

further reading
Ward, Peter. *A Singular Act—Twenty-five years of the State Theatre Company of South Australia.* Adelaide: Wakefield Press 1992.
Who's Who in Australia, 1985. Melbourne: Information Australia.
Adelaide Review August 1988. Obituary.
Advertiser (Adelaide) 5 July 1988. Obituary.
Australian 5 July 1988. Obituary.
Variety (New York) 27 July 1988. Obituary.

Janis Balodis

Director, dramatist. Born 21 September 1950 in Tully (Qld). Primary-school teacher 1971–72. Assistant stage manager in Queensland Theatre Company 1974. Attended E15 Acting School (London) 1975–79. First play produced 1980. Collaborated with Darwin Theatre Group 1982 and TN Theatre Company (Brisbane), 1982 and 1984. Associate director of Melbourne Theatre Company 1988–93. Writes for radio and television.

A mainstream playwright, Janis Balodis writes in theatrical and non-naturalistic styles of the immigrant experience—he is of Latvian parentage—and of contemporary relationships, frequently set against the landscape and cyclic rhythms of nature. His plays also examine Australian sexual relationships, with prominent female characters. *Too Young for Ghosts* (1985) concerns the experience of the first generation of postwar immigrants in the late 1940s. Balodis's best-known play, it has been produced throughout the country. Balodis continues the story of its characters in *No Going Back*, the second play in a planned trilogy The MELBOURNE THEATRE COMPANY produced it in 1993.

Balodis's first play, *Backyard* (1980) is a wry picture of 1960s small-town life in a largely realistic style with black-comedy overtones. He provided the Darwin Theatre Group and the TN THEATRE COMPANY with *Happily Never After* (1982) and *Summerland* (1984) respectively. Based on Grimms' fairy tales, they are comic musical fantasies dealing with media imagery and the quest for personal fulfilment. *Beginning of the End* (1984) is a highly theatrical comic fantasia on the doomed Port Essington settlement in tropical northern Australia. *Wet and Dry* (1986), a comedy of contemporary manners, examines childlessness and family bonds, contrasting the physical, spiritual and cultural climates of Darwin and Sydney. It was performed in Darwin and Melbourne in 1986. The Melbourne Theatre Company produced Balodis's *Heart for the Future* as its 500th production in 1989. This play juxtaposes video and live performance to deal with sport and female ambition, control of imagery by the electronic media, and the implications of the Maralinga nuclear-weapons test site. ❦*Veronica Kelly*

published plays
Too Young for Ghosts (1985). Sydney: Currency Press 1985.
Wet and Dry (1986). Sydney: Currency Press 1991.

further reading
BRISBANE, KATHARINE. In *Contemporary Dramatists* (ed. K. A. Berney) 5th edn. London: St James Press 1993.
KELLY, VERONICA. Falling between stools—The theatre of Janis Balodis. *Ariel* 23/1 (Calgary, Canada, January 1992.)
KELLY, VERONICA. Projecting the inner world onto an existing landscape. *Australasian Drama Studies* 17 (Brisbane, October 1990). Interview with Balodis.
KRAUSMAN, RUDI. Interview with Balodis. *Aspect* 32–35 (Sydney, 1985).

Bandicoot on a Burnt Ridge

Play in three acts by Marien Dreyer. **premiere** 5 June 1965, Russell Street Theatre, Melbourne, by Melbourne Theatre Company. Cast: Alan Hopgood, Roma Johnson. Director: Richard Campion.

A two-hander notable for dramatic use of urban sounds and strong use of local vernacular, Marien Dreyer's *Bandicoot on a Burnt Ridge* won the Sydney Journalists' Club 1963–64 play award of £1000. When produced by Studio 228 in Sydney in the NSW Arts Council's 1965 Drama Festival it also won awards for best Australian play and best city play. The play is set in Kings Cross, Sydney, in a run-down flat inhabited by an angry and disillusioned middle-aged couple who live vicariously upon their observations of the noisy life around them. A serial killer is loose and they come to believe that the house opposite is being watched by police on their roof. With mounting excitement, they gather friends and the press to their balcony to watch the expected arrest. But the tension, the waiting and the drink uncover long-held memories, lies and resentments. When finally the watchers miss the arrest, and lose the chance of momentary fame, anger explodes into despairing violence. The play's professional premiere in Melbourne was delayed by the collapse of the leading lady and the season closed early. ❦*Katharine Brisbane*

reference
A carbon copy of the manuscript, including stage directions by the author, is in the Currency Press collection.

The Bandit of the Rhine

Melodrama in three acts by Evan Henry Thomas. **premiere** 14 October 1835 at theatre in British Hotel, Launceston, by Samson Cameron's company. Cast: Cordelia Cameron, J. H. S. Lee, John Meredith, Dinah Murray. **revived** 22 October 1836, Theatre Royal in Argyle Rooms, Hobart. **published** Hobart October 1835.

Evan Henry Thomas, an Irishman despite his name, advertised in Hobart and Launceston in October 1834 for subscribers to 100 copies to enable him to publish his full-length play *The Bandit of the Rhine*. In October 1835 it was published in Hobart and performed in Launceston. Thomas, a keen supporter of the Amateur Dramatic Association in Launceston, was perhaps a more enthusiastic than able playwright. The 'bumper house' and applause for the premiere probably owed more to the novelty of local authorship than the intrinsic worth of the play. No copy of the text exists. A later work by Thomas, *The Rose of the Wilderness—or, Emily the Maniac*, attracted insufficient subscribers to permit publication. Thomas was a lawyer who followed diverse occupations, including editorship of the *Hobart Town Gazette* in 1824–25. ❦Gillian Winter

further reading
FLINN, E. Evan Henry Thomas. *Australian Dictionary of Biography* 2. Melbourne University Press 1967.
MILLER, E. M. *Pressmen and Governors*. Sydney University Press 1973.

Fifi Banvard

Actor, producer. Born 25 December 1901 in California (USA). Originally Yvonne Banvard. Began acting at seven. Came to Australia 1920. Three years dramatic stock in Brisbane, then comedy, musicals and vaudeville through 1920s and 1930s. Comedian, actor, producer in radio in 1940s. Acted at Minerva Theatre, Sydney, in early 1940s. Directed at Minerva Theatre 1947–50. Ran own production company at Theatre Royal, Hobart, 1950–52. Acted on stage and radio and produced radio in Sydney from 1954. Died 1962 in Sydney.

Fifi Banvard brought energy, determination and a degree of extravagance to many forms of theatrical endeavour. Her career began at the age of seven in one of the POLLARD OPERA COMPANIES. She played Fifi Fricor in *The Belle of New York* so often that the name Fifi stuck to her. When she was 17 she played the title-role in John N. Raphael's *Madame X* for David Belasco in New York City. She began in Australia with three years in stock at the Theatre Royal in Brisbane, in roles ranging from the heroine of Bayard Veiller's *Within the Law* to the title-role in J. Hartley Manners's *Peg o' My Heart*. She toured for FULLERS' vaudeville in a song-and-dance act with her husband, Eddie de Tisne. For J. C. WILLIAMSON'S she was Lady Jane in the operetta *Rose-Marie* in 1926 and 1928. Through the 1930s she played throughout Australia in comedies, revue and musicals, but by the 1940s she was increasingly working in Sydney radio and turning towards straight roles and directing. After acting at the Minerva Theatre, she began four years there as director with Eugene O'Neill's *Ah, Wilderness!* She directed plays performed by a WHITEHALL THEATRICAL PRODUCTIONS company for occupation forces in Japan in 1948–49, and in 1950 she directed the last play at the Minerva—Elmer Rice's *Dream Girl*. With Gwen Friend she then leased the THEATRE ROYAL in Hobart and formed Fifi Banvard Productions. With leading mainland actors and local artists, they presented modern comedies and dramas for three years. Banvard played Mrs Branson in Emlyn Williams's *Night Must Fall* and Sadie Thompson in a dramatic adaptation of Somerset Maugham's *Rain*. After losing more than £100 000 the partners abandoned the venture and returned to Sydney, where Banvard acted in more stage plays, including Noël Coward's *Nude with Violin*. ❦Richard Lane

further reading
GAUDRY, ANNE-MARIE. Fifi Banvard. *Australian Dictionary of Biography* 13. Melbourne University Press 1994.

Lyndall Barbour

Actor. Born 19 May 1916 in Egypt to Australian parents. Began acting with Sydney University Dramatic Society 1935. Radio actor 1937–80. Graduated 1938. On stage for Metropolitan Players, Radio Players, Minerva Theatre, Independent Theatre, John Alden Company, Mercury Theatre, Australian Elizabethan Theatre Trust from 1944. Sydney Theatre Critics' Award 1956 (*The Rose Tattoo* by Tennessee Williams). Died 10 October 1986 in Sydney.

A great radio actor, Lyndall Barbour also gave stellar performances on the stage from the mid-1940s to the 1960s. She made her mark in leading roles in many SYDNEY UNIVERSITY DRAMATIC SOCIETY productions and began her radio career before she graduated. Established as radio's most popular actress, she returned to the stage in the early 1940s, working with the director MAY HOLLINWORTH in Clemence Dane's *Granite* and Philip Barry's *Hotel Universe*. She showed her great emotional range in two plays directed by HARVEY ADAMS, Max Catto's *They Walk Alone* in 1946 and 1948 and in Eugene O'Neill's *Anna Christie* in 1951. She was at her peak in dramatic roles in the 1950s. She starred in O'Neill's *SS Glencairn*, William Inge's *Come Back Little Sheba* and Tennessee Williams's *The Rose Tattoo* for INDEPENDENT THEATRE. In 1957 she played Mamma Bianchi in the world premiere of Richard Beynon's THE SHIFTING HEART. Barbour displayed her wit most happily as Madame Desmermortes in Jean Anouilh's *Ring Round the Moon* for MERCURY THEATRE in 1953, and in Arthur Kopit's black comedy *Oh Dad, Poor Dad, Mama's Hung You in the Closet and I'm Feelin' So Sad* for Independent Theatre in 1963. ❦Richard Lane

Don Barker

Actor. Born 18 March 1940 in Adelaide. Began professional acting 1963. South Australian Theatre Company 1968–73. State Theatre Company of South Australia 1973–. Co-founder of Stage Company (Adelaide) 1977. Has also acted in television drama series.

Burly Don Barker has been a mainstay of Adelaide theatre since he made his professional debut for the ADELAIDE UNIVERSITY THEATRE GUILD in Patrick White's THE SEASON AT SARSAPARILLA in 1963. A handy ensemble member, he has acted in classical plays and contemporary works by Harold Pinter, STEPHEN SEWELL and DAVID WILLIAMSON. In 1991 he appeared as Sergeant Simmonds in the STATE THEATRE Company of South Australia's revival of Williamson's THE REMOVALISTS and in the title-role in its successful *Julius Caesar*. In 1993 he appeared in State Theatre productions of R. B. Sheridan's *The School for Scandal*, LOUIS NOWRA's *Così* and Dylan Thomas's *Under Milk Wood*. ❦Murray Bramwell

Barr Smith Theatre

Private theatre in Torrens Park, Adelaide, built by Robert Barr Smith 1882–85. Used as military hospital ward 1915–18. Bought by Scotch College 1919. Restored 1980–81, with historical research by K. Preiss and conservation design by architect R. A. Danvers.

The only theatre in Australia with remnants of its original gas lighting, this rare private theatre was built onto a large homestead. It seems to have been designed by Robert Barr Smith, much guided by correspondence from an architect in London. The exterior is in Gothic Revival style, with steeply pitched roofs, fretwork bargeboard gable ends, and walls of stone rubble with dressed-stone window trims and quoins. Four small oval windows about halfway up the side walls are stylistically incompatible but they are integral to the Victorian classical style of the flat-floored hall within. This is almost 18 metres long by about 9.25 metres wide by seven metres high, divided lengthwise into five arcaded bays delineated by fluted pilasters and false ceiling beams beneath the roof trusses. The whole is decorated with richly modelled plasterwork, designed by the English architect W. Neville Ashbee, in its original colours and gilding. Gas brackets on the walls have been replaced by electrical fittings in the same style, but in the ceiling the two original sun-burners, each giving 81 flames, have been restored to working order. Behind the rear wall, a spiral stair leads up to two recessed private boxes.

At the opposite end is a high stage with a five-metre-wide proscenium containing doors opening onto a small stage apron in front of a typical 19th-century green baize curtain. The whole stage, including its two commodious wings is about 19 metres wide and six metres from the proscenium to the cyclorama. The floor is raked, consistent with 19th-century practice, and the flies are high enough only for raising borders. The actor WYBERT REEVE planned the stage arrangements and occasionally performed at the theatre. The first known performance comprised the balcony scene from *Romeo and Juliet* played by Mabel and Joanna Barr Smith, followed by *Checkmate*, a two-act comedy acted by members of the Barr Smith family and friends. *Tableaux vivants*, with elaborate costumes and scenery, were staged at the theatre as well as plays, particularly during its first 17 years. Since the theatre has been restored, the stage has been improved for use by drama students at Scotch College. ❦*Ross Thorne*

further reading
PREISS, KEN and PAMELA OBORN. *The Torrens Park Estate—A social and architectural history*. Adelaide: K. Preiss and P. Oborn 1991.

Ray Barrett

Actor. Born 2 May 1927 in Brisbane. Elocution lessons from 1937. Made professional debut as ABC radio actor, Brisbane 1939. ABC first contract actor 1950–51. Stage debut with Brisbane Repertory Theatre Society 1952. Worked in drama, intimate revue and radio in Sydney 1954–58. Revue, theatre, film and television in United Kingdom 1959–75. Returned to Australia in 1976 and has since appeared in plays, films and television.

Best known for creating tough, crusty characters with hidden vulnerability, Ray Barrett made his professional debut as a 12-year-old radio actor. At 15 he joined 4BH Brisbane as an office boy and within a year he was presenting his own program. By 1954 he had a popular radio revue program in Sydney. He also appeared in PHILLIP STREET REVUES, toured with Margaret Rutherford and played Jimmy Porter in John Osborne's *Look Back in Anger* for the AUSTRALIAN ELIZABETHAN THEATRE TRUST. He worked extensively in England, where *Mogul*—also called *The Troubleshooters*—on television in 1965–72 made him well known. Since returning to Australia, he has created roles in plays by DAVID WILLIAMSON—the Premier in the Melbourne Theatre Company's production of *Sons of Cain* in 1985 and the feckless father Brian in the Queensland Theatre Company's *Brilliant Lies* in 1993. When Michael Noonan adapted his novel *A Different Drummer* for the latter company in 1988 he wrote the role of E. J. Banfield for Barrett. ❦*Gregory Gesch*

further reading
ATTERTON, MARGARET (ed.) *The Illustrated Encyclopedia of Australian Showbiz*. Sydney: Sunshine Books 1984.

Dan Barry

Actor, manager. Born 1851 in Dublin (Ireland). Originally John Ringrose Atkins. Son of barrister who emigrated to Melbourne. Worked briefly as a journalist. Adopted name Dan Barry and took to acting and production in outback. Organised 'Paradise', moving-picture and concert entertainment, at St Kilda Beach, Melbourne, 1907. Died 1 July 1908 in Melbourne.

A notorious eccentric, Dan Barry was famous from Bourke to Melbourne as the country's leading outback manager. He barnstormed around the inland, once touring from Melbourne to Launceston (Tas.) by way of Narrandera (NSW). His fame derives from his commercial success, his famous hoaxes, and his pet bulldog Paddy, which stole the show in *The Rainhill Murders* by finding corpses. His taste lay in popular theatre, with streaks of pantomime and vaudeville through most of his work, though his education—Melbourne Grammar School and, he claimed, the University of Melbourne—and training set him apart from his theatrical contemporaries. Once described as a 'sweet actor', Barry played both clergymen and villains with understatement. His bold seizure of any newsworthy subject or trend ensured few failures. From January to April 1898 he treated Melbourne to a feast of grisly contemporary dramas—*The Days of the Land Boom*, *Factory Girls of Melbourne* and Reg Rede's *The Kelly Gang*, in which he played the hero as 'an amiable sort of murderer' to a huge profit. A later KELLY GANG play by Arnold Denham contains a character called Danbarri Sullivani, and how much of the piece is really Barry's remains to be established.

Barry's triumphant Melbourne sojourns often saved the fortunes of the Alexandra Theatre, normally used for the more tasteful fare of ALFRED DAMPIER. A publicist ahead of his time, Barry amused the *Argus* critic with such catchy descriptions as 'Frenzied With the Fierce Financial Fever of the Day', and with his habit of attributing his works to such unlikely authors as General Booth. His managerial skills were said to be the envy of J. C. WILLIAMSON. His leading man was J. P. O'Neill, one of the better known comics of the Australian stage. Barry's abstemiousness, thrift in paying actors, bachelor status and clever managerial sense reputedly made him a huge personal fortune. His death in 1908 was marked by an outburst of Dan Barry anecdotes, apocryphal and otherwise. ❦*Helen Musa*

further reading
O'RELL, MAX. *John Bull and Co.* London 1894.
VAN DER POORTEN, HELEN. John Ringrose Atkins. *Australian Dictionary of Biography* 3. Melbourne University Press 1969.
Argus (Melbourne) 1898.
Liber Melburniensis centenary number, 4th edn. Melbourne Church of England Grammar School 1965.
Lorgnette (Melbourne) 2 November 1878.
Melbourne Punch 24 April 1891.
Table Talk (Melbourne) 17 January 1896.
Tatler (Melbourne) January 1898.

Kester Baruch

Designer, director, dramatist. Born 1903 in Adelaide. Originally Frank Perkins. Began to write for newspapers and changed name in late 1920s. Co-founded Ab Intra Studio Theatre (Adelaide) 1931. Joined Chekhov Studio Theatre in England 1935. Changed name to Kester Berwick during Second World War. In Australia 1945–52. Lived in Greece until death on Corfu in 1992.

With ALAN HARKNESS, Kester Baruch established the experimental AB INTRA STUDIO THEATRE in Adelaide in 1931. He designed sets and lighting and wrote plays and poems for performance. His plays *Archway Motif*, *Judgement Day* and *Fulfilment* were well received. In 1935 Baruch and Harkness began working with the Chekhov Studio Theatre at Dartington Hall in England, studying with the Russian actor Michael Chekhov—a nephew of Anton Chekhov—and sharing his views on the importance of the visual in the theatre. Chekhov moved his company to the USA at the outbreak of the Second World War but Baruch remained in England, and changed his surname to Berwick, which did not sound German. In 1945 he returned to Adelaide to teach and produce drama for the Workers' Educational Association. He also directed August Strindberg's *The Stronger* for the ADELAIDE UNIVERSITY THEATRE GUILD in 1945, and two plays for the WEA at Newcastle (NSW) in 1951. He published his first novel, *Head of Orpheus Singing*, in 1973, when he was 70. ❦*Thelma Afford*

reference
Several of Baruch's plays (under the surname Berwick) are in the Fryer Library, University of Queensland (Brisbane). They include *Archway Motif*, *Judgement Day* and *Woman Song*.

Peter Batey

Actor, director, dramatist, lighting designer. Born 4 August 1933 at Benalla (Vic.). Trained at University of Melbourne Conservatorium drama school. Began professional acting for National Theatre Movement, Victoria 1951. Founding member of Union Theatre Repertory Company (Melbourne) 1953–57; associate director 1957. Resident director of National Theatre Company (Perth) 1959–62. Director–manager of Canberra Repertory Society 1964–67. Artistic director of South Australian Theatre Company (Adelaide) 1970–72. Inaugural director of Victorian Arts Council 1973–75. Collaborated with Reg Livermore in revues from 1975.

The career of Peter Batey has spanned rapid and fundamental changes in Australian theatre. Above all, he has made his living in commercial theatre since the demise of J. C. WILLIAMSON'S. His career also reflects the pioneering spirit of the young, unestablished subsidised companies, the striving towards Australian-made theatre, the nurturing of rising young talent and the eventual acceptance by the popular audience of an Australian theatrical idiom. Batey was a founding member of the Union Repertory Theatre Company in Melbourne. He played many roles and assisted a colleague, BARRY HUMPHRIES, in writing the first Edna Everage sketches and co-directed the 1956 revue *Return Fare*, in which Edna first appeared. In Perth, Batey was involved in the NATIONAL THEATRE COMPANY's moves to professional structure and performance. As well as directing and designing productions, he wrote a bush comedy, *The No-Hopers* which had a successful season with Joan Macarthur in the leading role and made a tour of Western Australia. He returned to the Union Theatre Repertory Company in 1962 to direct a new production of *The No-Hopers* which toured throughout Victoria and was presented at the Theatre Royal in Hobart.

As director–manager of the CANBERRA REPERTORY SOCIETY Batey encouraged presentation of new Australian works, but the membership opposed the society becoming, as he had hoped, Canberra's first professional company, He opened the Playhouse at the CANBERRA THEATRE CENTRE with Peter Ustinov's *Romanoff and Juliet*, followed by Edward Albee's *The Ballad of the Sad Café*, John Osborne's *Inadmissible Evidence*, Rolf Hochhuth's *The Representative* and R. B. Sheridan's *The School for Scandal*. He directed and designed all of them. In 1968 he directed *… But I Wouldn't Want to Live There* a revue by John McKellar, with the Phillip Theatre stars RUTH CRACKNELL, GLORIA DAWN and Lyle O'Hara. It later had a successful Sydney season.

Australia's official presentation at World Expo '70 in Osaka (Japan) was Batey's AUSTRALIAN MARIONETTE THEATRE production of *The Magic Pudding*. It was seen by 12 million Japanese television viewers and it later toured southeast Asia and Australia. While Batey was director of the Victorian Arts Council he wrote and directed *From Smike to Bulldog*, an adaptation of the letters of Arthur Streeton to Tom Roberts, which was performed throughout Victoria.

As artistic director of the SOUTH AUSTRALIAN THEATRE COMPANY Batey introduced stability in a period of confusion as the formerly homeless 'gipsy troupe' adapted to occupancy of the ADELAIDE FESTIVAL CENTRE. He extended its activities to a year-round program and wide touring.

In 1975 Batey began a collaboration with REG LIVERMORE, his understudy in the Phillip Street revue *Cross Section* in Sydney in 1957. Batey co-devised and directed Livermore's first major success, *THE BETTY BLOKK BUSTER FOLLIES*. He also designed spectacular lighting, which was a feature of this and later Livermore shows—*Wonder Woman* (1976), *Sacred Cow* (1979), *Sacred Cow II* (1982) and *Firing Squad* (1983). He was director of productions for Livermore's producer Eric Dare, and he was responsible for the Australian tours of the Lindsay Kemp Mime Company in 1975 and Steven Berkoff's London Theatre Group in 1978. In 1990 he once more worked with Livermore, on his musical play *Big Sister* at the Riverside Theatres at Parramatta. Batey has also collaborated with the composer John Mulder. Their rock opera *Ecstasies* received a concert performance at the Bijou Theatre; and in 1979 they wrote a musical biography, *Songs My Mother Didn't Teach Me*, which Batey directed at the Bondi Pavilion Theatre. ❦*Katharine Brisbane*

further reading
WARD, PETER. *A Singular Act*. Adelaide: Wakefield Press 1992.

Syd Beck

Comedian. Born 1898 in Sydney. Stage debut in Fullers' vaudeville 1924. Died 11 March 1948 in Brisbane.

From 1926, when he first played the TIVOLI CIRCUIT, until the early 1940s, Syd Beck was a popular variety comedian. He was short and pug-nosed, and had a repertoire of quaint novelty songs and characterisations, including a perennially popular Egyptian mummy sketch. In his youth, Beck was a versatile and successful swimmer. He was noted for his comic performances at Manly Life-Saving Club benefits. He won a place as the funny man in a NSW diving troupe, where BENJAMIN FULLER spotted him. In his later years Beck lost a battle with alcohol, and he died destitute. ❦*Frank Van Straten*

further reading
Daily Mirror (Sydney) 3 February 1973.
Parade August 1973.

Randolph Bedford

Dramatist. Born 27 June 1868 in Sydney. Travelled briefly as actor with Edmund Duggan Theatre Company in mid-1880s. Became newspaper journalist. Ran *Clarion*, literary and mining journal, 1896–1909. Speculated on mines. Had three novels published 1903–12. Wrote short stories for *Bulletin* and plays, 1909–15. Labor member of Queensland parliament 1917–41. Died bankrupt, 7 July 1941 in Brisbane. Father of singer and composer Vera Bedford.

A larger-than-life eccentric, raconteur and speculator, Randolph Bedford wrote two plays that succeeded, two that failed and at least three that remain unperformed. He filled his plays with vivid stories, bold characters and a profusion of incident but marred them with his avowed white-Australian racism and hasty, careless writing. His first play, *For Australia—or, The White Man's Land* succeeded as theatre and propaganda when staged spectacularly as WHITE AUSTRALIA in 1909. Bedford's other success was *The Boss Cocky*, written in 1914 as *Aladdin and the Boss Cocky* and first staged in 1920, in Newcastle (NSW). It subsequently toured the eastern states, attracting large audiences. ❦*Richard Fotheringham*

writings
Naught to Thirty-Three. Melbourne University Press 1976.
    Autobiography

further reading
BOLAND, RODNEY G. Randolph Bedford. *Australian Dictionary of Biography* 7. Melbourne University Press 1979.

reference
Scripts of all Bedford's plays are held among copyright applications in the Australian Archives (Canberra).

Francis Belfield

Actor, dramatist. Active in Melbourne and Sydney 1840s to 1860s.

By adapting well-worn dramatic themes or popular fiction, Francis Belfield wrote undistinguished plays, most of them apparently for performance at his benefit nights. *The Mysteries of Sydney*, for example, played for his benefit at the Royal Victoria Theatre in Sydney in 1853, was 'founded on that well-known work which has appeared in *Bell's Life in Sydney*'. In it Belfield played the comic role of Mr Corney O'Pratie, which, along with the titles of some of his other plays, suggests that he specialised in Irish roles. He himself appears to have been Irish, if he was the Francis Belfield O'Brien who was licensed to perform at Singleton (NSW) in December 1846 and then given a 12-month licence for 1847. In 1848 he received a six-month licence to perform at Goulburn (NSW). ❦*Elizabeth Webby*

John Bell AM OBE

Actor, director. Born 1 November 1940 at Maitland (NSW). Educated at University of Sydney. Acted with Sydney University Dramatic Society. Professional debut with Old Tote Theatre Company (Sydney) 1963. Trained and worked in England with Royal Shakespeare Company, Lincoln Repertory Company and Bristol Old Vic from 1965. Returned to Sydney as tutor at National Institute of Dramatic Art 1970. Co-founded Nimrod Theatre Company (Sydney) 1970; artistic director, director and principal actor until 1985. Founded Bell Shakespeare Company 1990. Married actor Anna Volska 1965. Father of Hilary Bell, dramatist, and Lucy Bell, actor. OBE 1978. AM 1987. Australian Artists' Creative Fellowship 1993–94. HonDLitt (University of Newcastle) 1994.

Probably the best-known stage name in the contemporary Australian theatre, John Bell has curiously spanned the worlds of campaigner for new works and classical actor in the English mould. Upon leaving the University of Sydney in 1962 he immediately hired the Genesian Theatre for a solo performance of excerpts from Shakespeare, *This Sceptred Isle*. He drew praise from Sydney critics, the *Sydney Morning Herald* calling him 'a possible Olivier of the future'. In 1963 he joined the OLD TOTE THEATRE COMPANY and played Trofimov in its first production, Anton Chekhov's *The Cherry Orchard*. Later in the year he played Hamlet. He gained national attention in 1964 as Henry V, with ANNA VOLSKA as Katherine, in a production mounted in a tent at the Adelaide Festival by the AUSTRALIAN ELIZABETHAN THEATRE TRUST to celebrate Shakespeare's quatercentenary. Bell was hailed as a bright but untutored young talent. Margaret Jones in the *Sydney Morning Herald* on 12 February 1973 recalled critics' accounts of his Hamlet: 'a lithe and virile actor with a face of sculptured mobility and a manner of immediate command'.

In 1965 Bell set out for England, with a scholarship to the Bristol Old Vic School, to gain the classical skills. After three months in Bristol he was transferred to the Royal Shakespeare Company at Stratford-upon-Avon, where he in due course became an associate artist. Bell's preferences remain in that world. Nevertheless, his recognition of untapped theatrical energies within the movement for cultural independence in the late 1960s led to his seminal revue-style production of THE LEGEND OF KING O'MALLEY in 1970 and in great part to the establishment of the NIMROD THEATRE COMPANY. His experience with the small, egalitarian Lincoln Repertory Company in England was also significant in the creation of the Nimrod style and structure.

Energy, colour and a certain felicitous vulgarity have characterised much of his work as a director, particularly his Shakespeare productions. For Nimrod they included an uneven but hypnotic *Macbeth* in 1971, presented in the form of a ritual black mass, and *Much Ado About Nothing* in 1975, played with low-comedy Sicilian accents. He applied the same outrageousness to such Nimrod productions as a dramatic adaptation of Laurence Sterne's *Tristram Shandy* in

1982, THE VENETIAN TWINS, a musical after Carlo Goldoni, and the musical *Candide* in 1982.

Bell's aggressive production of David Williamson's THE REMOVALISTS in 1971 gained widespread attention when it transferred to a commercial theatre and won Nimrod the George Devine Award in London. He has directed other Williamson plays, including THE CLUB in 1977, which toured to London, and the premiere of TRAVELLING NORTH in 1979. He also directed with distinction for Nimrod the premieres of Peter Kenna's A HARD GOD in 1970, JIM MCNEIL's *How Does Your Garden Grow* in 1974 and Ron Blair's THE CHRISTIAN BROTHERS in 1976.

As an actor Bell retains a love of the big role and the big gesture. Though a romantic figure, he is not a romantic actor but shines most in character roles that hint at hidden emotion or danger or that call for classical showmanship. Naturalism is not his forte, although he excels at Chekhov. He was reputed never to have appeared on stage in modern dress until he played in Tom Stoppard's *The Real Thing* in 1985. His second such role was Colin in Williamson's *EMERALD CITY* for the Sydney Theatre Company in 1986.

Bell's most memorable performances—for Nimrod unless otherwise ascribed—include the title-role in Bertolt Brecht's *The Resistible Rise of Arturo Ui* for the Old Tote 1971 and Nimrod in 1985; Hamlet in 1973; Trigorin in Chekhov's *The Seagull* in 1974; Satin in an outstanding production of Maxim Gorky's *The Lower Depths* by the Romanian director Liviu Ciulei for the Old Tote in 1977; Prince Hal in a conflation of both parts of *Henry IV* in 1978; the title-role in Ben Jonson's *Volpone* in 1980; a brittle, quixotic Cyrano de Bergerac for the Sydney Theatre Company in an extravagant production of Edmond Rostand's play mounted by Richard Wherrett as a tribute to Bell in 1980; Vershinin in Chekhov's *Three Sisters* in 1981; an engaging Platonov in Michael Frayn's *Wild Honey* in 1986; and a foolishly proper Pastor Manders in Henrik Ibsen's *Ghosts* at the Belvoir Street Theatre in 1988. Essentially a stage actor, Bell has rarely appeared on film or television.

Bell played his first major role in a musical as Duke in *Big River* at Her Majesty's Theatre in Sydney and on tour in 1989 for Essington Entertainment and the GORDON FROST ORGANISATION. This role, a delightfully athletic parody of the classical actor, also introduced him to large-scale commercial production. This experience may have encouraged him to accept an invitation from Tony Gilbert, a Shakespeare-loving businessman, to establish a national touring organisation presenting Shakespeare in a popular style. The Bell Shakespeare Company as was launched in 1990 under the aegis of the AUSTRALIAN ELIZABETHAN THEATRE TRUST. The bankruptcy of the Trust a few months later set back the company but it reformed in 1991 and continued its tour. Its first productions were *Hamlet* and *The Merchant of Venice* (in which Bell played Shylock), followed by *Richard III* with Bell in the title-role and *Romeo and Juliet*. In 1993 the federal government matched a challenge grant of $250 000 from Gilbert to establish the company on a firm footing.

In the same year Science Press published its first Bell Shakespeare text for the study of Shakespeare in Australia. ❦*Katharine Brisbane*

further reading
BOGLE, DEBORAH. The Bell enigma. *Australian Magazine* 9–10 April 1994.

COLMAN, ADRIAN (ed.). *Romeo and Juliet* in Bell Shakespeare series. Sydney: Science Press 1993.
JONES, MARGARET. Favoured child of the stage. *Sydney Morning Herald* 12 February 1973.

James Belmore

Manager, theatrical machinist. Trained in London theatres. Began working at Theatre Royal, Sydney, April 1835. Theatre manager, acting manager and publican in Sydney and Hobart. Died 3 October 1843 in Sydney. Married to English actor.

At a time when the demand for spectacle made the machinist's skill perhaps more vital than the actor's talent, James Belmore claimed that his training, which included eight years at the Queen's Theatre in London, was unique in Australia. In 1835, his first year at the Theatre Royal in Sydney, he created a cascading waterfall in *Heart of Midlothian* and a moving panorama of a regatta on the Thames in *The Cedar Chest*. Early in 1836 Belmore was in Hobart, working with John Meredith at the ARGYLE ROOMS. He installed machinery that enabled more ambitious productions to be undertaken. Later in 1836 he joined Samson Cameron at the almost completed THEATRE ROYAL. His craftsmanship in installing the machinery there was also considered to be exceptional. In April 1838 he became one of the managers of the Theatre Royal and by August the licensee of the Shades Tavern beneath it. During 1838 Mrs Belmore, 'from the Theatre Royal, London', made her first appearance on the colonial stage. By October 1838 Belmore had returned to Sydney after substantial losses in Hobart. He was co-proprietor with JOSEPH SIMMONS and machinist of the Royal City Theatre in Sydney in 1843. ❦*Gillian Winter*

Belvoir Street Theatre

Theatre in Surry Hills, Sydney. Converted from factory by Nimrod Theatre Company. Main theatre, seating 320 persons, opened 1 June 1974 as **Nimrod Theatre**. **Downstairs** theatre, seating 110, opened 7 February 1976. Building bought on 19 June 1984 by syndicate now called Belvoir Street Theatre Ltd and renamed **Belvoir Street Theatre**.

When the NIMROD THEATRE COMPANY needed a theatre larger than the Nimrod Street Theatre—now the STABLES THEATRE—a developer offered it rent-free leasehold of a two-storey factory on a site for which low-rise office buildings were planned. The architect VIVIAN FRASER designed a theatre occupying the whole top floor, using the diagonal of the plan as the axis for a corner thrust stage and wide fan of seating around it. The lower floor contained a rehearsal room, dressing rooms, offices and a foyer and bar in which poster-covered walls and brick paving hinted at the informality of Nimrod Street. The rehearsal room was opened in 1976 as Downstairs, an open-space theatre which has been used in several formats. ROBYN ARCHER used it as a cabaret for her *Kold Komfort Kaffee* and Gordon Chater performed Steve J. Spears's *THE ELOCUTION OF BENJAMIN FRANKLIN* on an end stage. For a decade the theatre stood alone on a large cleared site. In 1982 the Nimrod company converted its 15-year lease to ownership of the building and one metre of land around it for $1. In 1984, the company, facing insolvency, decided to sell its theatre and move to the SEYMOUR THEATRE CENTRE. ❦*Ross Thorne*

Company B

Over a weekend in August 1984 CHRIS WESTWOOD and Sue Hill, partners in a holding company called Understudies Pty Ltd, drummed up a $50 000 as a deposit on the Nimrod Theatre and then within six months raised the balance of $450 000 needed to buy it. A syndicate of workers in theatre, film and television bought $1000 shares. This became Company A and was later incorporated as Belvoir Street Theatre Ltd. Members of the syndicate formed Company B, a non-profit organisation, to manage the theatre and produce the shows. Company B had a policy of presenting productions ranging from 'radical interpretations of classics to newly commissioned plays, the work and expression of ideas by women, Aboriginal theatre and new forms of theatre'. Until 1994 the company's members annually elected up to nine artistic directors, who appoint a general manager. Westwood and Hill held the position jointly in 1984–85, followed by Westwood alone in 1985–88, Robyn Kershaw in 1989–94 and Louise O'Halloran in 1994. NEIL ARMFIELD was appointed sole artistic director in 1994.

In the Upstairs theatre Company B presents an annual subscription program of five productions. The first was *Ha Ha Performing Human Beings* in March 1985 and in September 1985 Robyn Archer's *Scandals* opened the Downstairs theatre. This is hired out to groups in sympathy with Belvoir's artistic aims. The Upstairs theatre is regularly let to the Festival of Sydney, the Gay and Lesbian Mardi Gras and the Aboriginal Islander Dance Theatre.

One or two productions a year tour nationally and in 1991 the Belvoir company toured Russia—the first Australian theatre company to do so—with GEOFFREY RUSH in Nikolai Gogol's *The Diary of a Madman*, directed by Neil Armfield. It has also had box-office successes with *The Tempest* and plays by Henrik Ibsen, in particular *Ghosts* and *Master Builder* directed by Armfield and *A Doll's House* directed by Gale Edwards.

Company B has produced new works by Robyn Archer, LOUIS NOWRA, STEPHEN SEWELL, KATHERINE THOMSON and PATRICK WHITE. A political revue by John Clarke and Ross Stevenson, *The Royal Commission into the Australian Economy*, was a big hit in 1991. The theatre's annual turnover is $2 million and there is a full-time staff of ten, all of whom are paid the same wage. ❦*Ron Blair*

further reading
LEWIS, BERWYN. The miracle of Belvoir Street. *Weekend Australian* 29 November 1986.

Sarah Bernhardt

French actor 1844–1923. Originally Rosine Bernard. At Comédie-Française (Paris) 1862–80. Began touring 1879. Performed in Melbourne, Adelaide and Sydney 1891.

Sarah Bernhardt's visit to Australia in 1891, at the height of her career, was the theatrical and social event of the decade. It soothed colonial feelings of cultural isolation and inferiority. Her performances had the effect of raising local standards and allowing Australians to boast of a theatre which, under the daring entrepreneurial talents of J. C. WILLIAMSON, billed the world's greatest stars. Bringing Bernhardt to Australia was a risky venture for WILLIAMSON, GARNER AND Co., in view of the little tested response of Australian audiences to serious drama in a foreign language. Williamson began arousing public anticipation in October 1890 and on 25 May 1891 he staged a triumphant welcome to Bernhardt, who drove through decorated Sydney streets to a viceregal welcome at Government House.

Bernhardt brought with her a supporting cast of 40 and more than 200 tonnes of luggage, including stage costumes and sets. She travelled to Melbourne in a specially fitted train and opened at the Princess's Theatre in *La Dame aux camélias* by Alexandre Dumas *fils*. Even with admission prices doubled—to ten shillings for the best seats—the theatre was packed and scalpers were seeking five guineas a ticket. The night was hailed as an artistic triumph. 'For once fulfilment has outrun expectation, immoderate as this was …', declared the *Argus*.

Bernhardt offered a substantial repertoire. Besides *La Dame aux camélias*, she acted in *Cléopâtre*, *Fédora*, *Théodora* and *La Tosca* by Victorien Sardou, *Pauline Blanchard* by Darmont, *Adrienne Lecouvreur* by Eugène Scribe and Ernest Legouvé, *Frou Frou* by Henri Meilhac and Ludovic Halévy, and *Jeanne d'Arc* by Jules Barbier. The auditorium was kept lit during performance so that the audience could follow a translation of the French text. This disturbed Bernhardt. 'The white glimmer of the books and the regular turn of the pages, like so many birds settling, well nigh paralysed my energies', she complained in a letter.

Melbourne audiences, on the other hand, were irritated by frequent and excessively long intervals, which meant curtains long after midnight and missed last trains. During at least one interval Bernhardt slipped away to the Alexandra Theatre to see spectacular aquatic effects staged by Alfred Dampier in *The Scout*. In Adelaide, Bernhardt played six different roles over six nights and received a favourable though not ecstatic response, perhaps because of the smaller staging and musical resources there.

In Sydney, Bernhardt limited the length of intermissions, to the relief of audiences. She opened on 8 July in *La Dame aux camélias* and the *Sydney Mail*, three days later, concluded: '… criticism stands aside shamefaced at the idea of analysing or judging so complete a whole'. Bernhardt thrilled the city by performing the world premiere of *Pauline Blanchard*, written especially for her by M. Darmont, the *jeune premier* of her company. 'The gracefulness of this compliment will be the more appreciated by the people of Sydney when it is remembered that of all the cities she has visited heretofore, only Paris, London and New York have witnessed her debut in a new play, and that such an event excites the deepest interest throughout the artistic world', remarked the *Sydney Morning Herald*. Stalls and circle were fully booked for the entire season, but gallery attendance declined after the first week. On her last night, however, a packed audience cheered itself hoarse and showered the stage with flowers.

Bernhardt cancelled a one-week Brisbane season on the grounds of excessive fatigue, and sailed from Sydney on 8 August 1891. Her two and a half months in Australia constituted part of a world tour which lasted two years and eight months and yielded her a net profit of 3·5 million gold francs. ❦*Ian G. Dicker*

further reading
COLE, TOBY and HELEN K. CHINOY. *Actors on Acting*. New York: Crown 1965.
RICHARDSON, JOANNE. *Sarah Bernhardt*. London: Reinhardt 1959.

The Betty Blokk Buster Follies

Revue by Reg Livermore, originally titled *Reg's Show*. **premiere** 16 April 1975, Balmain Bijou Theatre, Sydney. Cast: Reg Livermore, with Reginas singing trio and Baxter Funt band. Director: Peter Batey. Musical director: Mike Wade. Producer: Eric Dare.

A showcase for the spectacularly gifted REG LIVERMORE, *The Betty Blokk Buster Follies* was an overwhelming experience. Among Livermore's unforgettable creations were Betty B, herself, a wicked, bare-bottomed Third Reich peasant girl; a shambling old man, half Fagin, half ROY RENE; and Vaseline Amalnitrate, an astoundingly foul-mouthed footballer, half in a football jersey, half in a tutu. Sexual confusion was not rare in this show, which played for ten months in Balmain and toured nationally. ❦*John West*

Richard Beynon

Actor, dramatist. Born 1927. Acted in radio serials as schoolboy. Professional stage debut at 17. Left Australia 1947. Successful as actor in England. Returned to Australia in touring company 1954. Won first prize in Sydney Journalists' Club 1956 playwriting competition with *The Shifting Heart*. Has since lived in London, working primarily for BBC as script editor and television producer. Guest lecturer at Australian Film, Radio and Television School (Sydney) 1984; writer-in-residence 1986.

Richard Beynon's THE SHIFTING HEART (1957) is customarily grouped with Ray Lawler's SUMMER OF THE SEVENTEENTH DOLL (1955) and Alan Seymour's THE ONE DAY OF THE YEAR (1960) as one of the naturalist plays that brought Australian language, issues and images successfully to the stage in the late 1950s. There was the same commitment to the naturalism in Beynon's *Summer Shadows*, which was performed during the 1986 Spoleto Festival in Melbourne. Like Lawler's return, after 20 years, to the lives of his characters in the *Doll*, Beynon's return to writing for the stage, with a play set in 1927, was rooted in cultural nostalgia and the experiences of his own early life. ❦*Peter Fitzpatrick*

published plays
The Shifting Heart (1957). Sydney: Angus and Robertson 1960.
Simpson, J. 202 (1990). Sydney: Currency Press 1991.
Summer Shadows (1986). Sydney: Currency Press 1986.

further reading
CARROLL, DENNIS. *Australian Contemporary Drama from 1909* 2nd edn. Sydney: Currency Press 1995.

Big Toys

Play in three acts by Patrick White. **premiere** 27 July 1977, Parade Theatre, Sydney, by Old Tote Theatre Company. Cast: Max Cullen, Arthur Dignam, Kate Fitzpatrick. Director: Jim Sharman.
published Sydney: Currency Press 1978.

A revival of PATRICK WHITE's *The Season at Sarsaparilla* directed by Jim Sharman in 1976 inspired the author to return to the theatre after more than 13 years' absence. He wrote *Big Toys* for two of the actors in SHARMAN's production, Max Cullen and Kate Fitzpatrick. *Big Toys* is a scathing attack on power-mongers without heart, conscience or spiritual values, who govern our fragile, nuclear-threatened world. More conventional in form than his previous plays, it is an ambitious drama in which mannered rituals are a cover for social and political exploitation and personal corruption.

'A comedy of radical chic manners', Sharman called it. As the layers of comedy are pared down, the action reveals human pawns manipulated in dangerous games. The characters are both the victims and the perpetrators, caught in a society they have themselves created.

The setting is a luxurious harbourside apartment, with a sumptuous bed as the central feature. The back of the stage is covered by a screen which opens to reveal the glittering panorama of city and harbour, both seductive and threatening. The city is also, paradoxically, a void, whose 'black nor'wester' preys on the characters' minds, blowing nothingness into their souls and hearts. The core of the city is dead; its people are the minions of its overlords, the power brokers who control industry, politics, media and perhaps even its culture.

The play is realistic in its structure, with a gradual exposition of past experience, and highly symbolic in dialogue and action. The balance of satire, elegant wit and serious drama is skilfully sustained. The language emphasises the characters' social games and reveals their underlying motives. The bleak final vision is ironically tempered throughout the play by Mozart's music, subtle parody of stock figures in Australian life, and colourful and comical visual effects.

Critics' opinions were divided, but the production aroused great public interest and was successfully transferred to Melbourne. Kate Fitzpatrick and Arthur Dignam played the rich and powerful Bosanquets and Max Cullen the powerful trade-union man Terry Legge. White adapted *Big Toys* for television and the ABC showed it in August 1980. ❦*May-Brit Akerholt*

further reading
HOAD, BRIAN. White's icy look at our urban chic. *Bulletin* (Sydney) 6 August 1977.

Bijou Theatre

Theatre above Victoria Arcade, opened as **Academy of Music** 6 November 1876. Architects: Read and Barnes. Renamed **Bijou Theatre** 1880. Destroyed by fire 22 April 1889. Rebuilt and opened 5 April 1890. Architect: George Johnson. Demolished 1934.

The Bijou Theatre, always praised as comfortable and intimate, was above the Victoria Arcade, which ran from Bourke Street to Little Collins Street. Stairs rose from an entrance in Bourke Street to a gallery, 36 metres long by 5.7 metres wide, that gave access to the theatre. Along the full length of the gallery, overlooking Royal Lane, was a 19th-century version of a glass curtain wall in arches and filigree cast-iron. The opposite wall repeated the arch motif in mirrors. The space was replete with statuary, urns, tessellated floor and large basket chandeliers on the ceiling. Next to the gallery was an even longer billiards saloon.

The theatre appears to have been a three-and-a-half-level house, seating up to 1500 persons, with a modest stage, which backed onto Little Collins Street. There was no pit, but only stalls surrounded by a dress circle at stage level— half a level above the stalls floor. Posts supported a family circle and a gallery above. An alderman, Joseph Aarons, built the theatre and leased it to the entrepreneur George Lewis, who managed it as the Academy of Music. The Italian actor EDUARDO MAJERONI took it over and renamed it the Bijou Theatre in 1880. The theatre was the BROUGH-

BOUCICAULT COMEDY COMPANY's Melbourne home until fire reduced it to bare walls. After a coroner's inquest into two deaths caused falling bricks, *Lorgnette* magazine attacked the Victorian Board of Health, which licensed theatres. It also condemned fire brigades for 'their petty squabbles, their concentrated detestation of each other, their puerile punctiliousness, their contemptible intriguing, their peculiar appropriation of funds granted by Government, their drunkenness, thievery and insubordination'. All this indicates why fires were rarely brought under control.

The Brough-Boucicault company returned to the rebuilt theatre, which seems largely to have retained its original features, though the auditorium was now on three levels, with the stalls extending beneath the dress circle, and the capacity was 1700–1900 persons. The proscenium was 9 metres wide by 13·8 metres deep, with small dressing rooms in the flies. The old groove system of scenery, with its many ropes and pulleys, had been discarded.

In the early 20th century the Bijou had no long-term lessee until FULLERS' took it over, together with the smaller Gaiety Theatre in the same building. Fullers' decided in 1929 to convert both theatres to cinemas, with the aim of eventually demolishing them and building one or more new theatres. Then a company of unemployed actors performed at the Bijou until it was demolished in 1934. No theatre was built on the site. ❦*Ross Thorne*

'Billy Barlow'

Originally mentioned in an English comic song of the 1820s, Billy Barlow was apparently a real London street character, known for eccentric and 'simple' behaviour. After his death in a Whitechapel workhouse in the early 19th century the comic song was written about him and taken up by performers who dressed in ragged costumes. One of them was GEORGE COPPIN, who performed an adaptation, 'Billy Barlow in Dublin', in the Irish capital in 1841. He performed another localised version in Cape Town on his way to Sydney in 1843.

In Sydney Coppin introduced 'Billy Barlow' at the Royal Victoria Theatre on 13 March 1843 and it became enormously popular. At the Royal Victoria on 12 October 1843 Coppin appeared in *The Barlow Family*, a farce written for him and Maria Coppin by Charles Alexander Dibdin. Coppin also performed popular local versions of 'Billy Barlow' in Adelaide, Hobart, Launceston and Melbourne during the 1840s and 1850s.

Others soon took up 'Billy Barlow' too. 'Billy Barlow in Australia', apparently by a local man, Benjamin Griffin, was sung during an amateur theatrical night at Maitland (NSW) on 28 August 1843. On 27 June 1846 HENRY DEERING sang 'Billy Barlow's Visit to Adelaide' at the Royal Adelaide Theatre. At Launceston in October 1850 a new version of 'Billy Barlow' was said to have included comments on such topical issues as opposition to transportation and 'tea-totallers'. ❦*Elizabeth Webby*

further reading
ANDERSON, HUGH. *Songs of Billy Barlow*. Ferntree Valley (Vic.): Ram's Skull Press 1956.
DEVER, M. *Billy Barlow* by C. A. Dibdin. *Australasian Drama Studies* 14 (Brisbane, April 1989). Includes text of *The Barlow Family*.

reference
The manuscript of Dibdin's *The Barlow Family* is held in the Colonial Secretary's Papers in the NSW Archives under the title *Billy Barlow, an Eccentric Farce*.

Wendy Blacklock

Actor, administrator. Born in Sydney. Studied acting at Rathbone School of Dramatic Art (Sydney). Began two years in repertory in England 1950. On return to Australia worked for J. C. Williamson's and in radio drama. In Phillip Street revues in Sydney from 1955. Acted in England again. Returned to Australia 1959 and acted on stage and television. Headed Australian content department of Australian Elizabethan Theatre Trust 1982–90. General manager of Performing Lines Ltd 1990–.

In eight years under Wendy Blacklock the AUSTRALIAN ELIZABETHAN THEATRE TRUST's Australian content department, set up to encourage new Australian theatrical writing and performance, produced or toured more than 40 shows at home and overseas. In July 1990 the department was incorporated as Performing Lines Ltd, an autonomous, non-profit company funded by the AUSTRALIA COUNCIL and private sponsors, to pursue the same ends. Blacklock was made general manager.

Before she turned to administration her stage appearances in Sydney included the PHILLIP STREET REVUES *Two to One* (1955), *Around the Loop* (1956–57) and *Phillip Street Revue* (1960–61); Pegeen in J. M. Synge's *The Playboy of the Western World* for the OLD TOTE THEATRE COMPANY in 1963; Honey in the first Australian production of Edward Albee's *Who's Afraid of Virginia Woolf?* in 1964; and Jody the toffee-nosed Liberal in David Williamson's DON'S PARTY at the Jane Street Theatre in 1972. ❦*John West*

Ron Blair

Dramatist. Born 14 October 1942 in Sydney. In dramatic societies at University of Sydney. Helped to found Nimrod Theatre Company 1970. Assistant director of South Australian Theatre Company (Adelaide) 1976–78. Broadcaster, writer, editor and producer for ABC radio. Has written for television.

Literacy, wit and rhetorical energy characterise the work of Ron Blair. In his monodrama THE CHRISTIAN BROTHERS (1975) he created an archetype of Australian drama—the lonely, ageing teacher of a generation of Catholic boys who enter a world that is as unknown to him as it is to them. Blair himself was educated by the Christian Brothers. Then at the University of Sydney he worked in dramatic societies with Ken Horler, whom he later helped to found the NIMROD THEATRE COMPANY. Blair's first stage works, seen at the Nimrod Street Theatre in 1970–71, were contributions to the seasonal romps *Biggles* (1970) and HAMLET ON ICE (1971) and *Flash Jim Vaux* (1971).

Based on the memoirs of James Hardy Vaux, an Englishman who was transported to Australia as a convict no less than three times, *Flash Jim Vaux* is a ballad opera in which traditional airs are interspersed with songs by TERENCE CLARKE and Charles Colman. Six actors portray 25 characters. *Flash Jim Vaux* has received productions throughout Australia—including a revival at the Nimrod Theatre in Sydney in 1982—and at the Hampstead Theatre Club in London. The teasing title of another success at Nimrod

Street, *President Wilson in Paris* (1973), masked a black comedy of murderous *folie à deux*.

There was less acclaim for Blair's treatment of a genuine historical subject, the British in Afghanistan, in the ambitious epic *Kabul* (1973) commissioned and performed by the OLD TOTE THEATRE COMPANY. *The Christian Brothers*, Blair's most widely performed work, marked a triumphant return to Nimrod in 1975.

A stint as assistant director of the SOUTH AUSTRALIAN THEATRE COMPANY led to Adelaide premieres of Blair's one-act *A Place in the Present* (1977) and two major works—*Last Day in Woolloomooloo* (1976), a dark and often surreal contemporary comedy, and *Marx* (1978), scenes from the philosopher's life in London. Other works in the productive 1970s included *Perfect Strangers* (1976), a short study of the aftermath of a marriage, and *Mad, Bad and Dangerous to Know* (1976), a one-man portrait of Lord Byron for JOHN BELL. ❦*Nick Enright, Tony Sheldon*

published plays
The Christian Brothers (1975). Sydney: Currency–Methuen 1975.
Last Day in Woolloomooloo (1976). Sydney: Alternative Publishing Cooperative 1983.
Mad, Bad and Dangerous to Know (1976). In *Quadrant* (Sydney) October 1976.
Marx (1978). Sydney: Currency Press 1983.
A Place in the Present (1977). Sydney: Currency Press 1985 in *Popular Short Plays*.
President Wilson in Paris (1973). Sydney: Currency Press 1974.

Leila Blake

Actor, director, dramatist. Born 1931 in England. Trained at London Academy of Music and Dramatic Art. Came to Australia 1950. Directed for Mercury Theatre (Sydney) 1953. Formed Intimate Theatre (Sydney) 1956. Directed premiere of Harold Pinter's *A Night Out* at Comedy Theatre, London, 1960. Returned to Australia 1965. Founded Wayside Theatre (Sydney) 1967. South Australian Theatre Company (Adelaide) 1967. Melbourne Theatre Company 1968–69. Co-founded Claremont Theatre (Melbourne) 1972. Acted in New York in late 1970s. Returned to Sydney 1979. Died 10 November 1991 in Sydney. Mother of actor Lisa Peers.

Leila Blake had the energy, talent and enterprise to create much of her own work and to contribute richly to the stage in Sydney and Melbourne. She founded Sydney's first theatre-in-the-round, the Intimate Theatre, and the Wayside Theatre in Kings Cross, where she played Winnie in the Australian premiere of Samuel Beckett's *Happy Days* in 1967. She played the role again at the Arts Theatre in Melbourne in 1968. While in Melbourne in 1968–1969 she also formed Studio Australia, an experimental and developmental company for actors and writers, and co-founded Claremont Theatre in South Yarra.

During 1970–73 Blake performed Jean Cocteau's monodrama *The Human Voice* in lunch-hour theatre in Sydney and Melbourne. In Sydney, Q THEATRE presented her one-act plays *Prey* and *Fair Go* and at the Independent Theatre in 1971 she performed *Feminine Gender*, a solo show she had devised from her favourite women in Shakespeare. She followed it in 1972 with *Women of Importance* from the female characters of Oscar Wilde, and in Sydney in 1973 she combined these entertainments into *Feminine Plural*. She later performed this program on tour in NSW for the AUSTRALIAN ELIZABETHAN THEATRE TRUST, in Dublin and in England and the USA. In 1974 the *Sydney Morning Herald* named Blake actress of the year for her performance in Athol Fugard's *Hello and Goodbye* in Sydney and at the Adelaide Festival. On return to Sydney from New York in 1979 she acted in her own *I Love, You Love*, three one-act plays on love in three stages of life. As part of the Women and Arts Festival in 1982 Blake directed her daughter Lisa Peers in Sandy McCutcheon's *The Truce* at the Wayside Theatre. Later Peers directed her in BARRY DICKINS's *The Death of Minnie*. ❦*Lynne Murphy*

published play
Prey (1973). Brisbane: University of Queensland Press 1978, in *Can't You Hear Me Talking to You?*

reference
Manuscripts of *Fair Go*, *Prey* and *The Stirrer* are held in the Fryer Library, University of Queensland (Brisbane).

Michael Blakemore

Actor, director. Born 18 June 1928 in Sydney. Studied medicine at University of Sydney for three years. Press agent for Robert Morley on Australian tour 1949. Studied acting at Royal Academy of Dramatic Art (London) 1950–52. Worked in repertory. Married actor Shirley Bush 1960; later divorced. Joined Glasgow Citizens' Theatre and began directing plays 1966. Associate director at National Theatre (London) 1971–76. Married stage designer Tanya McCallin 1986. New York Outer Critics Circle Award for outstanding director 1990.

Respect for the text and the actors' contributions and apparent absence of directorial imposition characterise the productions of Michael Blakemore, who is probably the outstanding Australian director working abroad. 'While he contributed to every aspect of the production ... we never felt that one suggestion he made, not one of his rare demands, was based on ego', the author Larry Gelbart wrote in his introduction to *City of Angels*. 'Whatever glory he sought was for the show, not for himself. He put his hand to everything without leaving a single fingerprint.' Blakemore is known in the profession as an actors' director, perhaps because of his origins as an actor. The son of a medical specialist, he deserted medicine for the stage and, encouraged by Robert Morley, went to London. Blakemore vividly describes the actor's vulnerability in his novel, written at a turning point in his life.

His first break as a director came with his friend Peter Nichols's autobiographical play *A Day in the Death of Joe Egg*. His Glasgow Citizens' Theatre production transferred to London in 1967 and to New York in 1968. In the 1980s Blakemore collaborated similarly with the writer Michael Frayn. He has been equally supportive of DAVID WILLIAMSON. He directed his DON'S PARTY in London in 1975, THE CLUB under the title *Players* in Washington DC and on Broadway in 1977, TRAVELLING NORTH in London in 1980 and *Money and Friends* in Los Angeles in 1992.

Blakemore's productions at the National Theatre in London included Ben Hecht and Charles MacArthur's *The Front Page* with Denis Quilley in 1972; it toured to Australia. His first Australian production was Ira Levin's thriller *Deathtrap*, for a national tour after his London production in 1978. He directed Eugene O'Neill's *Mourning Becomes Electra* for the MELBOURNE THEATRE COMPANY in 1981. ❦*Katharine Brisbane*

writings
Next Season. London: Weidenfeld and Nicholson, 1969. Novel.
further reading
BRADDON, RUSSELL. *Australia Fair?* Sydney: Methuen 1984. Anthology based on *A Personal History of the Australian Surf*, Blakemore's 1981 film about his memories of Bondi Beach.
BRISBANE, KATHARINE. Watch this man; he's a comer. *Australian* 19 July 1969.
O'DONNELL, OWEN. *Contemporary Theatre, Film and Television* 8th edn. Detroit (USA): Gale 1990.

Dorothy Blewett

Dramatist. Born July 1898 in Melbourne. Worked as secretary in travel agency. Won Western Australian Drama Festival prize with *Quiet Night* 1941. Won Playwrights' Advisory Board competition with *The First Joanna* 1947. Went to London. Returned to Melbourne 1960. Established literary agency. Wrote radio plays and novels. Died 17 September 1965 in Melbourne.

Dorothy Blewett's major play, *The First Joanna* is an early and progressive plea to the narrow-minded middle-classes to face their origins. A young English war bride in an unsympathetic pastoral community is suffocated by the provincialism of her new family. Presented with a chair that had belonged to the 'first Joanna', she rips the upholstery in a rage and finds the woman's diaries inside. They reveal that the family seat had been established by no pillar of Victorian values but a gritty convict girl who escaped from a Tasmanian jail with her lover and shot a villain to save her secret. The play was performed first in Sydney in February 1948, directed by MAY HOLLINWORTH for Metropolitan Theatre, and then in other states. A London management bought the rights but let them lapse, although Blewett went to London in pursuit of the promised production. Her earlier *Quiet Night* was staged by the Melbourne Little Theatre Company on 8 March 1941 and thereafter performed regularly by amateurs in Australia and occasionally overseas. A comedy set in the service section of a hospital ward, it 'hasn't anything important to say but the hospital atmosphere is excellent ... and the dialogue has the ring of life', says Leslie Rees. ❦*Katharine Brisbane*

published play
Quiet Night (1941). Sydney: Australasian 1944.
further reading
Age (Melbourne) 20 September 1965. Obituary.
reference
A script of *The First Joanna* is held in the Fryer Library, University of Queensland (Brisbane).

The Blind Giant is Dancing

Play in three acts by Stephen Sewell. **premiere** 15 October 1983, Playhouse, Adelaide Festival Centre, by Lighthouse Company. Cast: Robynne Bourne, Peter Cummins, Robert Grubb, Gillian Jones, Melita Jurisic, Russell Kiefel, Stuart McCreery, Jacqy Phillips, Geoffrey Rush, Igor Sas, Kerry Walker, John Wood. Designer: Stephen Curtis. Director: Neil Armfield. Music: Alan John.
published Sydney: Currency Press 1983, revised edition 1985.

In *The Blind Giant is Dancing* STEPHEN SEWELL first turned to contemporary Australian life with his analysis of the interaction between individual actions and the political events that help to control them. It evokes linked worlds of politics and crime in NSW in studying an idealistic politician who faces the dilemma of maintaining his ideals and losing power or gaining power through corruption and so betraying the principles that drove him to seek it. The politician, Allen Fitzgerald, has intimate links with the idealistic left that has nurtured him, and connections with the right-wing party machine, which he discovers is corrupt. The farther he goes into 'pragmatic' power politics the more he faces pressure in his personal life as his relationship with his wife reflects the corruption in his public life. He has an ambivalent affair with a mysterious woman, Rose Draper, who herself embodies the savage nexus of personal and political idealism and cynicism. The study of Fitzgerald's descent into moral madness in parallel with his ascent to political power gave the play topical impact when it appeared in 1983, a time of public controversy about a new turn towards pragmatism in the Australian Labor Party. DAVID WILLIAMSON's *Sons of Cain*, a much gentler and more individualistic play about political corruption, appeared in the same year and comparison between the two plays said a great deal about the different styles of two generations of playwrights. ❦*John McCallum*

Jennifer Blocksidge

Actor, director. Born 1932 in Karachi (India). Educated in India and England. Trained at Central School of Speech and Drama, London. Taught drama in Armidale (NSW), 1953–56. Honorary artistic director of Brisbane Repertory Theatre Society 1968–75. On Australia Council's community arts board 1981–85. Founding member of Brisbane Theatre Company 1989. Appointed to board of Queensland Theatre Company in May 1990.

With Jennifer Blocksidge as its artistic director, the amateur BRISBANE REPERTORY THEATRE SOCIETY allowed audiences to see new plays that were performed professionally in other states. Blocksidge presented Australian plays, innovative plays from overseas and the classics. She and her husband, Bruce Blocksidge, president of the society in the late 1960s, were instrumental in establishing its La Boîte theatre-in-the-round. In 1975, she helped to establish the Early Childhood Drama Project, the first fully professional arm of La Boîte. She also introduced classes for all ages and a teenage group called Middle Stages. Blocksidge's work as a director at La Boîte included *Romeo and Juliet* in 1977 and two plays by the Australian playwright Lorna Bol, *Treadmill* in 1977 and *But I'm Still Here* in 1986. Notable roles in her career include Maxine Charlesworth in HAL PORTER's *Eden House* for Brisbane Repertory in 1970, Gertrude in *Hamlet* and Mother Courage in Bertolt Brecht's *Mother Courage and Her Children* for TWELFTH NIGHT THEATRE and Melanie Klein in Nicholas Wright's *Mrs Klein* for the QUEENSLAND THEATRE COMPANY in 1991. ❦*Delyse Anthony*

Blue Mountain Melody

Musical comedy. **book** J. C. Bancks. **lyrics and music** Charles Zwar. **premiere** 22 September 1934, Theatre Royal, Sydney. Cast: Gus Bluett, Madge Elliott, Cyril Ritchard, Athol Tier. Director: Frederick Blackman. Musical director: Andrew MacCunn. Producer: J. C. Williamson's.

Tuneful music, a revolving stage and spectacular scenery ranging from Palm Beach to the Blue Mountains distinguished *Blue Mountain Melody*, a musical comedy that was perhaps the J. C. WILLIAMSON'S answer to F. W. THRING'S COLLITS' INN. The book by J. C. Bancks, creator of the Ginger Meggs comic strip, presented such characters as a sheep and cattle king played by CYRIL RITCHARD, a cafe singer and dancer played by MADGE ELLIOTT, a boxer played by GUS BLUETT and a life-saver played by Athol Tier. There were choruses of hikers, guests, bathing girls and boxing girls. The music was the first professional work of young Charles Zwar, who went to London in 1937 and became a successful composer and musical director in revue and musical comedy. The show ran for six weeks in Sydney and seven in Melbourne, but toured no farther. ❦Lynne Murphy

Fred Bluett

Comedian. Born 1876 in London. Came to Australia 1892. Died 3 December 1942 in Sydney. Father of comedians Gus and Kitty Bluett.

Fred Bluett's father and great-grandfather had been comedians, and young Fred was three when he made his stage debut. In 1891 he went with a small company to New Zealand, where he developed a solo act that led to bookings on the Fullers' vaudeville circuit there. Bluett made his first appearance in Australia on the TIVOLI CIRCUIT in 1902. He was a genial, robust knockabout comedian, equally at home as a pantomime dame. In 1909 he introduced a sketch in which he was a scoutmaster with a line of youngsters, including his five-year-old son Gus. He took this act to London with great success. He later returned to solo work. He performed regularly in Tivoli theatres, and in 1926 he teamed with ROY RENE in a sketch called *The Admiral and the Sailor*. They also appeared together in the pantomime *Aladdin* at the Grand Opera House in Sydney in 1926. Bluett died in his sleep in 1942 after playing in a radio drama. ❦Frank Van Straten

further reading
GIBBNEY, H. J. and ANNE G. SMITH. *A biographical register 1788–1939*. Canberra: Australian Dictionary of Biography 1987.

Gus Bluett

Comedian. Born 1904 in Australia. Son of Fred Bluett. Died 13 March 1936 in Sydney.

When he died, aged 32, Gus Bluett was considered to be the best light comedian Australia had produced. He began on stage as a tiny boy scout in the comedy act of his father, FRED BLUETT. His big break came in 1922 when he played Buttons to his father's Dame in the pantomime *Cinderella* at the Theatre Royal in Sydney. The next Christmas he had a featured role in ADA REEVE's production of *Aladdin*. He occasionally acted in plays, but he was best known in J. C. WILLIAMSON'S musical productions. ❦Frank Van Straten

further reading
GIBBNEY, H. J. and ANNE G. SMITH. *A biographical register 1788–1939*. Canberra: Australian Dictionary of Biography 1987.

Kitty Bluett

Actor, comedian. Born 1918 in London. Daughter of comedian Fred Bluett. On stage from childhood. Acted on stage and radio in Sydney 1941–48. She entertained troops in New Guinea 1943. Radio comedian in United Kingdom from 1949.

A popular radio performer in the 1940s, Kitty Bluett played her first dramatic stage role in Noël Coward's *Point Valaine* at the MINERVA THEATRE in Sydney, in 1945. Roles in other plays followed. Born during the Bluett family's sojourn in the United Kingdom in 1918, she had been on the stage since she joined her brother Gus and sister Belle (born 1911) in their father's scouting sketch at two and a half years of age. She performed intermittently as a child, and appeared with Gus in the musical *Nice Goings On* in 1935. In the late 1930s she danced in musicals for J. C. WILLIAMSON'S, then for nearly a year played cabaret with Sam Babicci in Sydney. After a successful audition for the radio star Jack Davey in 1941 she became a familiar broadcaster in comedy, variety, straight plays and as a vocalist. In 1948 she starred in the film *A Son is Born*. She moved to London, where in April 1949 she began a long-running radio comedy series with Ted Ray, *Ray's a Laugh*. ❦Frank Van Straten

Graeme Blundell

Actor, director. Born 1945 in Melbourne. Founding director of La Mama Company (later Australian Performing Group) 1967–73. Founding director of Hoopla Productions (later Playbox Theatre Company) 1976–80. Artistic director of Australian National Playwrights' Conference 1981. Associate director of Melbourne Theatre Company 1982–85. Artistic director of Kinsela's Cabaret Theatre (Sydney) 1985–87. Many film and television roles.

In a long acting career, Graeme Blundell is best remembered for his flamboyant portrayals of larrikin characters in the 'new wave' of Australian drama in the late 1960s and early 1970s. Since the 1980s he has had success playing more mature characters on stage. He was an energetic leader of the movement that produced important alternative-theatre organisations, such as the La Mama Company, the AUSTRALIAN PERFORMING GROUP, Playbox Theatre Company and KINSELA'S CABARET THEATRE. He has written numerous articles about Australian drama and introductions to plays. ❦Geoffrey Milne

writings
Introduction. *Penguin Plays—Buzo, Hibberd, Romeril*. Melbourne: Penguin 1970.

Michael Boddy

Actor, director, dramatist. Born 8 March 1934 in England. Educated at Cambridge University. Emigrated to Tasmania 1959. Later settled in NSW. Wrote and directed for Music Hall Theatre Restaurant, Sydney, 1977–79. Has written for and acted in theatre, film, television and radio. Also author, publisher, newspaper food and wine columnist, and farmer. Erik Kuttner Award 1965. Won James Cook Bicentennial Play Competition 1970 with *The Legend of King O'Malley* Two Australian Writers' Guild Awgie awards 1971 (for *The Legend of King O'Malley*). Producers and Directors Guild of Australia Award 1971.

The output of versatile Michael Boddy has been prodigious. In the theatre, he has been acclaimed most for THE LEGEND OF KING O'MALLEY, which he wrote in collaboration with BOB ELLIS. He collaborated with RON BLAIR and Marcus Cooney in writing and producing *Biggles* for the opening of the Nimrod Street Theatre in 1970 and in writing the book for HAMLET ON ICE for the Nimrod company in 1971. In the 1970s he also wrote historical plays and melodramas and—

with Cooney—a musical revue *Cash!* (1972). Boddy's *Cradle of Hercules* for the Old Tote Theatre Company in Sydney in 1974 gave Jack Charles as Bennelong one of first contemporary roles for an Aboriginal actor. ❦*Gillian Winter*

published play
The Legend Of King O'Malley with Bob Ellis (1970). Sydney: Angus and Robertson 1974. Sydney: Currency Press 1987.

further reading
Who's Who of Australian Writers. Melbourne: Thorpe 1991.

Bohemian Dramatic Company

Touring tent-theatre company, founded by E. I. Cole in 1900. Closed 1947. **directors** 1900–21 E. I. Cole. 1921–47 W. J. Ayr.

For nearly half a century the Bohemian Dramatic Company presented melodrama, WILD WEST SHOWS and variety throughout eastern Australia. It was founded by Edward Irham 'Bohemian' Cole, who was born in London in late 1859 or 1860 and came to Australia when he was about 12. At one time he was a coachman in Adelaide, supposedly at Government House. During the 1890s he went on the road as a lecturer, cheapjack and 'painless' dentist. In 1898 he joined the craze for writing Kelly Gang plays with *Hands Up!*, first performed in Armidale (NSW) on 27 September. It may have begun as more of an illustrated lecture than the full-blooded bushranging dramas with horses and Cobb and Co. coaches that Cole later played around Australia.

For a time Cole teamed with an American cowboy, 'Texas Jack', and his Wild West Dramatic Company. Their partnership dissolved in January 1900 after a season in Brisbane. Cole took over the organisation, cowboys, Indians, sharpshooters, lassoers, horses, 'spacious tent' and all. He grew his hair to resemble 'Buffalo Bill' Cody. He expanded his repertoire to include cowboy plays; *Dick Turpin*, *Thunderbolt* and *Captain Moonlight*; stock melodramas like *Uncle Tom's Cabin* and *East Lynne*; Irish plays, including *Shamus O'Brien*, *The Parish Priest* and *Irish Pluck*; and much more.

In 1905 Cole married 26-year-old Vene Linden, who became the company's leading actress, and for the next 40 years the troupe was a large extended-family affair. In 1906 Cole split the company in two, after three years on and off in his Hippodrome—a tent holding up to 3000 persons—in Sydney's Haymarket. He left Bill Ogle, his wife's sister's husband and his chief mechanist, in charge while he set up a second tent Hippodrome in Melbourne. By the middle of 1907 newspapers were calling Cole an 'Australian Barnum'. He dabbled in film-making as well as presenting plays and circus acts.

Cole's publicity emphasised the comfort of his theatres and the respectability of his audiences. A critic who wrote in the *Bulletin* on 26 April 1906 was not impressed when he went to review E. W. O'Sullivan's Ben Hall play COO-EE: 'Out of George-street into Hay-street; drop at once into one of the most unlovely parts of Sydney, and in a hundred years you come to the vast tent in which "The People's Theatre" is housed. … The ushering arrangements are simple; you help yourself. Away back in the dim distance rise the sixpenny planks, tier on tier. In the middle of the stalls, forms; flanking them, more tiers. The planks are best; and you can bring a cushion yourself. … The band bursts in and turns itself into an orchestra; and up and down …

moves the "boss", his black hair flowing down his back; on his head 3 ft of hat; in his hand his badge of authority, a whip with a whistle in the handle. He blows the whistle, and up creeps the curtain.'

Cole's company later toured eastern Australia in horse-drawn caravans and hired trains, with long seasons in Bendigo (Vic.) in 1909, Geelong (Vic.) in 1911, Hobart in 1912, Adelaide in 1914 and Brisbane in 1918–19. In the 55-week Brisbane season Cole abandoned the tent for the Theatre Royal. Vene Linden's 'two beautiful boudoir cars' caused comment wherever they went. The larger, 9 metres long by 2·5 metres wide, had two large rooms with plate-glass sliding panels, folding sofas which changed to 'comfortable bedheads' at night, opulent mirrors, pot plants and paintings on the walls, and it was finished in 'polished cedar and elegantly upholstered in gold and red velvet'. Cole supposedly staged plays with great attention to realistic detail. He claimed to be a collector of antiques, including the gold escort coach that Frank Gardiner and his gang had robbed and the rope by which Ned Kelly was hanged. Some believed him.

Cole himself retired in 1921 and set up a factory in Sydney to produce Buffalo Bill costumes 'made by Australians for Young Australians'. His son-in-law Bill Ayr took charge of the theatre company, and one of their actors, FRANK NEIL, branched out on his own. During the 1920s the company, still trading on the Cole name, continued to present new Australian plays. The Depression, the talking pictures and double ENTERTAINMENTS TAX in some states, however, caused a major shift of emphasis back to circus and variety acts. The company, increasingly known as Bill Ayr's Bush Players, was reduced to following the show circuit, travelling in motor buses. It is supposed to have given its last performance in 1947 at Maroubra, Sydney. ❦*Richard Fotheringham*

further reading
GARLICK, BARBARA. The problem of sources—The 'Bohemian' Cole collection. *Australasian Drama Studies* (Brisbane, October 1993).
Newsletter 14 August 1907.
Referee (Sydney) 22 July 1931.

reference
'Bohemian' Cole collection ML 5497 in Mitchell Library (Sydney).

Edwin Booth

American actor, 1833–93. Toured Australia with Laura Keene and D. J. Anderson 1854. Parted with Keene in Honolulu and returned to USA with Anderson. Became leading American actor of his time.

Edwin Booth visited Australia before he rose to become the foremost American tragedian of his time. After the death of his father, the famous actor Junius Brutus Booth, the 20-year-old Booth sailed from California for Australia in 1854 with the actors LAURA KEENE and D. J. Anderson. They arrived in Sydney on 11 October 1854 and opened in Edward Bulwer-Lytton's *The Lady of Lyons* at the Royal Victoria Theatre on 23 October.

Sydney critics recognised Booth's talents, with the *Sydney Morning Herald* describing his visit as 'quite an event' and the *Empire* praising his Claude Melnotte in *The Lady of Lyons* as 'fiery and intelligent.' His Hamlet was praised for sensitive elocution, his Benedick in *Much Ado About Nothing* for heartless cynicism. Inevitably his interpretations were based in the Edmund Kean tradition he had inherited from his father. 'So-so business' in Sydney led to fortune-hunting in the Melbourne season. Booth's first act was to stage an inebriate celebration of his 21st birthday, hoisting the American flag at his hotel. After difficulty in finding a theatre, he opened at the Queen's Theatre Royal on 20 November in *Much Ado About Nothing*. There was a large audience, eager to see 'the son of Edmund Kean's rival', but later he had poor houses. The *Argus* critic objected to Booth's 'national peculiarities of intonation' and his 'disagreeable intonation of voice'.

The tour was a dismal financial failure but it gave Booth his first chance to play Shylock, whom he interpreted as totally evil, his first taste of adult performance standards away from his native environment and a dose of stern 'old country' criticism. He also experienced excess, which he later noted in a comment on 'all the accumulated vices I had acquired in the wilds of California and Australia'. In 1865 the *Empire* recalled Booth's visit when news that his younger brother John Wilkes Booth had assassinated President Lincoln reached Sydney. ❦*Helen Musa*

further reading

BOOTH CLARKE, ASIA. *The Elder and the Younger Booths*. 1882.
BOOTH GROSSMAN, EDWINA. *Edwin Booth*. 1894.
RUGGLES, E. *Prince of Players*. London 1953.
VAN DER POORTEN, HELEN M. Edwin Booth. *Australian Dictionary of Biography* 3. Melbourne University Press 1978.
WINTER, WILLIAM. *The Life and Art of Edwin Booth*. Boston 1893.
Dictionary of American Biography. New York 1927.

Harry Borradale

Director, manager, reciter, speech teacher. Born 1883 in Melbourne. Grew up in Burnie (Tas.). Went to Brisbane about 1916. Began teaching 1917. Formed and toured Dandies variety group 1918. Formed semiprofessional Sparklers variety group, playing at Palace Gardens, 1921. Formed Brisbane Repertory Society 1922. Died 1957 in Brisbane.

A pioneer in Brisbane's amateur theatre between the world wars, Harry Borradale directed programs for the Brisbane Shakespeare Society, the Queensland University Dramatic Society and the Dickens Fellowship. For the Shakespeare Society he directed *The Merchant of Venice* and *Othello* in Centennial Hall in October and November 1920 respectively. In 1922 he formed the short-lived Brisbane Repertory Society, which played at the Elite Theatre in 1923. At the same theatre on 11 December 1924 Borradale directed a performance of STEELE RUDD's *On Grubb's Selection* for the Authors and Artists' Association. A popular reciter, Borradale performed regularly at the annual free Sunday concerts of the Masonic United Grand Lodge of Queensland in the Brisbane City Hall. He became grand master of the lodge in 1938. He adjudicated at eisteddfods as late as 1951. ❦*Joan Massey Cook*

Dion Boucicault

Irish actor, dramatist, 1820–90. Originally Dionysius Lardner Boursiquot. Began theatrical career 1838 as Lee Moreton. Altered name to Bourçicault 1841. Married actor Agnes Robertson, second wife, 1853. Separated 1879. Brought to Melbourne and Sydney by J. C. Williamson 1885. Bigamously married Louise Thorndyke in Sydney, 9 September 1885. Died 18 September 1890 in USA. His six children included actors Dion jnr and Nina.

The most prolific and successful playwright of mid-19th century was Dion Boucicault. He pioneered 'sensation' melodrama with *The Poor of New York* in 1857, Irish comedies with *The Colleen Bawn* in 1860 and Irish political dramas with *The Shaughraun* in 1874. These three plays, another the Irish drama *Arrah-na-pogue* and the horse-racing play *Flying Scud* were his best-known and longest-lasting successes. From the 1860s virtually every Australian professional company had at least one of them in its repertoire. They were still revived in the 1930s. Boucicault also promoted copyright law and fire safety in theatres.

He was the great stage Irishman of his time, but when J. C. Williamson invited him to visit Australia in 1885 he was, according to his biographer Richard Fawkes, 'an eccentric relic from a former age'. Boucicault and his eldest surviving son, DION BOUCICAULT JNR, known as 'Dot', were then playing in New York, and they had recently been joined by his daughter NINA BOUCICAULT. In May 1885 Boucicault, his children and another young actor, Louise Thorndyke, played a four-week season in San Francisco which included the world premiere of *The Jilt*, his last success as a dramatist. Then they sailed to Australia and opened in Melbourne on 11 July, with Boucicault playing his most famous Irish role, Conn the Shaughraun. Williamson staged Boucicault's plays with great expense and the box-office returns in Melbourne were outstanding. Critics, however, were decidedly lukewarm about the acting of the star and about *The Jilt*, which was misrepresented as a world premiere. The *Leader* of 1 August thought it was the 'weakest product of his experienced and fertile pen'.

Boucicault in turn thought Australian theatregoers were uncultivated and the THEATRE ROYAL was 'large, dusty' and 'primitive'. He also complained that Melbourne audiences were 'overrun with the rowdy element', though it was not prominent in Sydney. This, he presumed, was because the cheapest ticket in Sydney was two shillings, twice the price of the Melbourne gallery. Perhaps Williamson had learnt from the Melbourne season—the plays Boucicault brought with him were society dramas and character pieces rather than the sensation melodramas for which he was principally acclaimed in Australia.

The Sydney Irish invited Boucicault to be guest of honour at a picnic. They saw him as a champion because in 1876 he had publicly written to the British Prime Minister, Benjamin Disraeli, denouncing the holding of Irish political prisoners in England and Australia. Then the 64-year-old Boucicault married the 21-year-old Thorndyke in a registry office and caused an international sensation. He claimed never to have been legally married to his estranged wife in England, the actor Agnes Robertson. Dot and Nina, siding with their mother, left the company and stayed in Australia when their father ended his engagement in October and left for New Zealand. In the incident there was a curious echo of Dion Boucicault's own parentage. His mother was the wife of Samuel Boursiquot, a wine-merchant, but her lover Dr Dionysus Lardner, a lecturer at Trinity College, Dublin, is believed to have been father of the playwright.

Boucicault published an account of his tour, in which he said he had been an unprecedented success but expenses were so heavy that no 'first class star' would be induced to make the journey. He thought there was enough intelligence in Australia to make a critical public to support 'plays of the higher class'. His estranged son validated this claim during the next decade. ❦*Richard Fotheringham*

further reading
BEVAN, IAN. *The Story of the Theatre Royal*. Sydney: Currency Press 1993.
BOUCICAULT, DION. *Plays by Dion Boucicault* (ed. Peter Fawkes). London: Quartet 1979.
COLE, TOBY and HELEN K. CHINOY. *Actors on Acting*. New York: Crown 1965.

Dion Boucicault jnr

Actor, director, manager. Born 23 May 1859 in USA. Originally Darley George Boucicault. Son of actors Dion Boucicault and Agnes Robertson. Stage debut in New York City 1874. Came to Australia with father 1885. Co-founded Brough-Boucicault Comedy Company in Sydney 1886. Returned to England 1895. Married actor Irene Vanbrugh 2 July 1901. Founded Vanbrugh–Boucicault Company, which toured Australia 1923–25 and 1927–28. Died 25 June 1929 in England.

The first person in British theatre who was employed as an artistic director, but was not required to act as well, was supposedly Dion Boucicault jnr. He set standards in Australian professional theatre in design, props, costuming and orchestral accompaniment for plays that made him a legend for a generation. He was still serving his stage apprenticeship when he first came to Australia in 1885 with his sister NINA BOUCICAULT and their celebrated father DION BOUCICAULT. At his father's request he had called himself Dion Boucicault jnr after his elder brother Dion William died in a train crash in 1876, but he was widely known as 'Dot'. He and Nina were outraged when their father bigamously remarried in Sydney in 1885. They left the company and J. C. WILLIAMSON gave Dot a job managing the tour of a visiting English comedian, ROBERT BROUGH.

In 1886 Dot and Brough formed the BROUGH-BOUCICAULT COMEDY COMPANY, with productions 'under the sole direction of Mr Boucicault'. From the first he concentrated on directing the other actors and demanding standards of production that astonished reviewers. The plays of the English dramatist Arthur Wing Pinero, who was a personal friend of Boucicault, were the backbone of the company's repertoire. Leasing and refurbishing smaller, more luxurious theatres than those used by the popular melodrama companies, Brough and Boucicault usually attracted the cream of colonial society, including governors, to their opening nights in each capital city. They seemed destined for great prosperity until a disastrous fire at the BIJOU THEATRE in Melbourne in 1889 and a severe financial depression in the 1890s jolted their careers. In 1895 Brough and his wife separated from the company for a time and Boucicault's 12-week Melbourne season was a financial flop.

Soon afterwards Boucicault returned to England, claiming to have been exhausted by the struggle to keep 'quality' theatre alive in Australia. However, he had also announced his engagement to the Australian actor PATTIE BROWNE, who was at the Theatre Royal, Drury Lane, in London. Marriage did not eventuate and in 1901 Boucicault married Irene Vanbrugh, a distinguished actor who had created the role of Gwendolyn in Oscar Wilde's *The Importance of Being Earnest* in 1895. They formed the VANBRUGH–BOUCICAULT COMPANY and became one of the most celebrated acting teams of their day. Boucicault directed at the Duke of York's Theatre until 1915. The world premiere of J. M. Barrie's *Peter Pan* in 1904 was one of his productions.

In 1923, soon after a royal command performance at Buckingham Palace, J. C. Williamson's brought Boucicault and Vanbrugh to Australia. They opened triumphantly in Melbourne in *His House in Order*, supposedly written for them by Pinero many years before. Boucicault added only works by Somerset Maugham and Frederick Lonsdale to the kind of plays he had produced in Australia 30 years previously. He had no sympathy for 'newer' playwrights like Anton Chekhov, Henrik Ibsen, George Bernard Shaw or even John Galsworthy. Lonsdale's farce *Aren't We All?* was the popular success of the tour.

Another Vanbrugh-Boucicault tour in 1927-28 was less notable. Boucicault's physical and mental powers were failing and his stage mannerisms becoming more pronounced. A season at the Comedy Theatre in Melbourne ended with Lonsdale's *On Approval* on 17 November 1928 and he left for New Zealand. There were no major farewells as he intended to return to Australia in 1929. But after the New Zealand tour, his health still declining, Boucicault went directly to London, where he died in June 1929. Vanbrugh continued her career. ❦*Richard Fotheringham*

further reading
VAN DER POORTEN, HELEN. Dionysius George Boucicault. *Australian Dictionary of Biography* 3. Melbourne University Press 1978.

Nina Boucicault

English actor, 1867–1950. Daughter of actors Dion Boucicault and Agnes Robertson. Stage debut c.1885. In Australia 1885–88. London career c.1891–1936. Sister of Dion Boucicault jnr.

Only 18 when she came to Australia with her father DION BOUCICAULT for a short tour, Nina Boucicault stayed for nearly three years after spurning him when he claimed that he had never been legally married to her mother and bigamously married the actress Louise Thorndyke. Her eldest brother DION BOUCICAULT JNR also left and co-founded the BROUGH-BOUCICAULT COMEDY COMPANY. Nina appeared in most of its earliest productions, though seldom in starring roles. In Mark M. Alford's *Turned Up*, remarked the Melbourne *Age* on 11 October 1886, 'Miss Boucicault had little more to do as the general's daughter than present an attractive appearance, and this cost her no effort'.

In March 1888 she went to try her luck in the USA, where she represented the estranged family at her father's funeral in 1890. She then began a long and successful stage career in England, creating the role of Kitty Verdun in Brandon Thomas's *Charley's Aunt* in 1892 and the title-role in J. M. Barrie's *Peter Pan* in 1904. ❦*Richard Fotheringham*

Andrew Bovell

Dramatist. Born 23 November 1962 in Kalgoorlie (WA). Educated at University of Western Australia (Perth) and Victorian College of the Arts (Melbourne). Associated with Melbourne Workers' Theatre. Also writes for television and film.

In a brief career, Andrew Bovell has shown impressive facility in writing in a variety styles and contexts and for performance in a wide range of venues. His best-known work, *After Dinner* was first performed at LA MAMA THEATRE in Melbourne in 1988, and by 1991 it had had 12 more productions in Australia and New Zealand. It is an exuberant farce set in the bistro of a typical Australian hotel. Two sexually dysfunctional male social cripples and three lonely, unhappy women play out clumsy courting rituals during a night of increasing drunkenness and social tension. The play shows Bovell's firm sense of character, ear for dialogue, and facility with popular comedy, but it lacks the ambition and social concern of his lesser-known work.

Bovell's social and political concern is clearest in two plays he wrote for workplace performance by MELBOURNE WORKERS' THEATRE, *State of Defence* (1987) and *The Ballad of Lois Ryan* (1988). They explore the intersections of the public and the private in the lives of trade-union activists. In a social-realist mode that is the bedrock of Bovell's developing style, both plays tell powerful stories in a deceptively simple style. *The Ballad of Lois Ryan*, based on the broad issue of industrial health and safety, has gone on to two further productions in Australia and one in New Zealand.

Bovell overlays his social-realist writing with metaphor. In *State of Defence* the Gordian knot is a metaphoric means of capturing the conflict between self-interest and union solidarity in a recession. The technique is more expansive in *Ship of Fools* (1988), in which a small cast alternates doubled roles in parallel tales. One portrays the setting loose of a crew of social outcasts in a boat on the Rhine from Basel in 1492, and the other a similar motley crew sent by the Department of Social Security by bus into central Australia on a work-for-the-dole scheme. The device enlarges and dignifies the tiny particularities of social life that form the core of Bovell's plays. *Gulliver's Travels*, a huge adaptation of Jonathan Swift's novel, married the resources of the MELBOURNE THEATRE COMPANY and the skills of HANDSPAN THEATRE COMPANY in 1992. It was not received particularly well but it indicated Bovell's theatrical courage. ❦*David Watt*

published plays
After Dinner. Sydney: Currency Press, 1989.
The Ballad of Lois Ryan. In *Australasian Drama Studies* 17 (Brisbane, October 1990).

further reading
WATT, DAVID. The trade union movement, Art and Working Life and Melbourne Workers' Theatre. *Australasian Drama Studies* 14 (Brisbane, April 1989).
WATT, DAVID. Art and working life: Australian trades unions and theatre. *New Theatre Quarterly* 6/22 (Cambridge, England, May 1990).
WATT, DAVID. Introduction to *The Ballad of Lois Ryan*. *Australasian Drama Studies* 17 (Brisbane, October 1990).

Harald Bowden

Manager. Born 10 July 1886 in Sydney. Educated at St Andrew's Cathedral School (Sydney). Cathedral choirmaster for three years from 1909. Joined J. and N. Tait Ltd as New York representative 1918. Represented J. C. Williamson's in New York 1926–33. Returned to Australia 1934. General manager of J. C. Williamson Theatres Ltd 1940–67. Died 23 August 1970 in Sydney.

Harald Bowden developed a remarkable flair for choosing successful shows while they were still on the road, before they reached Broadway. While in New York for J. C. Williamson's, he bought the rights to the operettas *The Desert Song* and *The New Moon*, the musical comedy *Dearest Enemy* and Barry Connor's play *The Patsy*. As general manager of the firm he bought rights to the musicals *Funny Girl*, *My Fair Lady* and *South Pacific*. ❦*Alwyn Capern*

further reading
GIBBNEY, H. J. and ANNE G. SMITH. *A biographical register 1788–1939*. Canberra: Australian Dictionary of Biography 1987.

Boys' Own McBeth

—*A really rotten tragedy*. Comic musical play. **libretto** Grahame Bond and Jim Burnett. **music** composed by Grahame Bond and arranged by Rory O'Donoghue. **premiere** 11 July 1979, Kirk Gallery, Sydney. Cast: Grahame Bond, Paul Johnstone, Nicos Lathouris, Nicolas Lyon, Rory O'Donoghue, Bjarne Ohlin, Elizabeth Wilder. Directors: Grahame Bond and Mark Gould. Design: settings by Kosta Akon and Pio Calone; costumes by Melody Cooper. **published** Sydney: Currency Press 1980.

A comic send-up of schoolboy exploitation and the fear of leaving school, *Boys' Own McBeth* was a watershed between the celebratory iconoclasm of the 1960s and 1970s, and the swift and sudden changes to come. In the event it proved an accurate indicator of the emotional climate that created the extremes of the 1980s. An absurd plot is centred on the end-of-year play at Dunsinane, a not-so-great public school. The protagonist is Terry Shakespeare (originally played by Grahame Bond), a 42-year-old schoolboy who has married the tuckshop owner and endowed the school. His anarchic reign ends when the school is converted into a *schule* and the extravagantly gay English master wins the headship after a lightning conversion to Judaism.

The play has all the childish innocence, cruelty, prejudice and engagement inherent in Bond's own comic characters Aunty Jack and Kev Kavanagh. Its extravagant satire, energy and memorable pastiche songs gained it a popularity amounting to a cult. After being forced out of the Kirk Gallery by fire regulations, it went to Newcastle (NSW); spent a year in Sydney at the Paris Theatre (the last show before the building was demolished); then toured Melbourne, Adelaide and country centres before opening in Los Angeles at the Westwood Playhouse in 1981. It returned to a tour of larger theatres, including the Comedy Theatre in Melbourne, the Opera Theatre in Adelaide and closed at the Regal in Perth. It is regularly revived by schools and amateurs. ❦*Katharine Brisbane*

Jeana Bradley

Director. Born at Wiluna (WA). Originally Jeana Tweedie. Taught in private schools 1932–46 and at University of Western Australia (Perth) 1947–71. Studied in England 1951–52. Member of Australian Council for Arts 1969–74. Directed productions in schools, at University of Western Australia and Western Australian Institute of Technology, and for National Theatre Company, Old Mill Theatre and Western Australian Opera Company. Died 29 December 1991.

Largely because of Jeana Bradley, the University of Western Australia has probably the largest range of theatres in any Australian university. She began directing an annual summer season of a classic play with students in the open-air Sunken Garden of the university in 1948 and these popular seasons contributed to the decision to establish the FESTIVAL OF PERTH in 1953. In 1959, with David Bradley, her husband and colleague in the English department, and Allen Edwards, professor of English, she had disused engineering workshops on the campus converted into the Dolphin Theatre, which had doors in its proscenium arch. It was replaced in the 1970s by a theatre designed by PETER PARKINSON. Jeana Bradley and Edwards were involved in planning other theatres at the university, including the Elizabethan-style NEW FORTUNE THEATRE, which opened with her production of *Hamlet* in 1964. They worked with TYRONE GUTHRIE and Parkinson to create the OCTAGON THEATRE, a lecture hall and theatre. On 11 March 1989 a new rehearsal room for the Dolphin and Octagon Theatres was officially named the Bradley Studio in her presence.

Bradley was associated with most personalities in Western Australian theatre and many performers, directors, designers and other workers began with her. She was a director who demanded total loyalty from her actors and she brought out their potential. Her busiest years were at the university, directing the UNIVERSITY OF WESTERN AUSTRALIA DRAMATIC SOCIETY, the University of Western Australia Graduate Dramatic Society, Bankside Theatre Productions and the Swan Players.

She was Catholic in her taste, and she did her best work in Sophocles, Elizabethan and Jacobean playwrights, Henrik Ibsen and Anton Chekhov. In the university's Sunken Garden Theatre in 1948 her production of Sophocles's *Oedipus Rex* drew praise from Laurence Olivier. At Winthrop Hall she staged *The Taming of the Shrew* in the round and *Two Gentlemen of Verona*, *Romeo and Juliet* and *Richard II* with an Elizabethan-style stagehouse. She used the hall's wide platform stage for effects of epic grandeur in *King Lear*, *Antony and Cleopatra* and Euripides's *The Trojan Women* between 1951 and 1958. She was not a lover of the bare boards style and her productions were always visually attractive. ❦*Maurice Jones*

Richard Bradshaw AO

Director, dramatist, puppeteer. Born 28 December 1938 in Sydney. Trained at Clovelly Puppet Theatre from 1952. Graduated in science from University of Sydney 1959. Taught secondary-school mathematics and science while developing as puppeteer. Performed solo at festivals and worked as assistant puppeteer and actor in England and Europe 1964–66. Toured solo show for schoolchildren 1969. Seasons at Nimrod Street Theatre, Sydney, 1971. Tours in Australia, Europe and USA. Artistic director of Australian Puppet Festival 1975. Artistic director of Marionette Theatre of Australia (Sydney) 1976–84. Toured solo show in Australasia, Europe, Japan, India and North America. Resumed full-time solo career 1984. AO 1986. Joint winner of Sidney Myer Performing Arts Award 1987.

Recognised around the world as a leading exponent of shadow puppetry, Richard Bradshaw performs regularly in Australia and abroad. He writes, designs and constructs his own material for short sketches—some barbed with political satire, others purely whimsical. He cuts his puppets from cardboard and acetate with deft, uncluttered line, and designs simple shows with minimal scenery. He performed his first program of shadow items, to critical enthusiasm, at the 1964 Karlovy-Vary Puppet Festival in Bohemia. He was assisted in this by EDITH MURRAY, his early mentor. One of the first productions in which he participated at her Clovelly Puppet Theatre was a shadow play inspired by the shadow puppets of the German puppeteer and film-maker Lotte Reiniger, which had recently been seen in Sydney. In 1967 Bradshaw recorded a shadow item for *Playschool* on ABC television. He left schoolteaching in 1969 to tour a solo show for schoolchildren with JOAN AND BETTY RAYNER's Australian Children's Theatre. By 1975 he was touring on local and international circuits, playing in theatres, schools and festivals and enjoying success with adult and child audiences. He recorded a shadow item for the television *Muppet Show* in London in 1976.

As artistic director of the MARIONETTE THEATRE OF AUSTRALIA from 1976 to 1984, Bradshaw steered its style away from string puppets to rod puppets, and employed staging techniques including screens, tabletop, black theatre, puppeteer-in-view and puppets with actors. He diversified the company's output, producing work for schools, television and adult audiences as well as regular children's theatre seasons. He wrote and directed *Roos* in 1976, *Puppet Power* in 1978 and *Buried Treasure* in 1984, and *Pure Puppet Adultery* in 1985 for the Sydney Puppet Theatre. He directed *Captain Lazar and His Earthbound Circus* in 1980, *The Magic Pudding* in 1981, *Smiles Away* in 1982, and *Bear Dinkum* in 1983. ❦*Maeve Vella*

published play
Bananas. Sydney and London: Currency–Methuen 1976.
other writings
Merlin of the south. *Australasian Drama Studies* 7 (Brisbane, October 1985)
Merlin. *Manipulation* 6/2 (1986).

Nellie Bramley

Actor, manager. Born 4 February 1890 in Melbourne. Studied voice production and dramatic technique with Daisy Belmore. Began acting as teenager. Major supporting roles by 1911. Leading roles in Fullers' dramatic companies from 1917. Star of her own company in long seasons in Brisbane and other cities in 1920s. Bankrupt 1934. Died 9 June 1982 in Sydney. Sister of actor Marguerite Adele.

Nellie Bramley was foremost among the stars of the popular weekly-change theatres, which until the Great Depression provided entertainment of the sort now provided by television—situation comedies and action thrillers. The actor CAMPBELL COPELIN described her as 'one of the smoothest performers to work with … a trouper'. She was stage-struck at an early age and at 14 she made her debut as a maid in *East Lynne*. Further roles included the daughter of the demented innkeeper in a silent film of Leopold Lewis's play *The Bells* in 1911. During the First World War FULLERS' created dramatic companies for some of their theatres, and Bramley and Austin Milroy led the company at the Palace Theatre in Melbourne from 1917 to 1921. It provided popular plays with titles such as *The Broken Home*, *A Girl's Good Luck*, *Is the Girl to Blame?* and *Margaret of the Red Cross*.

With her own company, from about 1925, Bramley specialised in a long run in one theatre and in the 1920s she had several. In 1928-29 she ran for 85 weeks in Brisbane at Her Majesty's Theatre and the Theatre Royal. She also had further seasons in Melbourne and toured Australia and

New Zealand. By the 1930s the standard of Bramley's plays had improved but those were terrible times for live theatre and 1934 saw her in the bankruptcy court. She owed £3255, principally to theatrical managements and the Commissioner of Taxation, and her assets were £700. She told the court she had been successful in Brisbane but had lost in North Queensland and at the Palace Theatre and the Grand Opera House in Sydney. She had then tried Western Australia for a year—'a dreadful experience', she said grimly. After further losses in Adelaide and Broken Hill came Melbourne where, after a shaky start, she had run 67 weeks for a profit of £2000, which was absorbed in paying off debts.

The Depression and talking pictures had changed theatre, and weekly-change drama and comedy were no longer needed. Bramley slipped from sight. Her last stage appearance was in a supporting role at the Minerva Theatre in Sydney in March 1947. Her much younger sister Adele, who had married advantageously and become a Sydney society matron, cared for her until she died. ❦*John West*

further reading
People (Sydney) 13 September 1950.

Bran Nue Dae

Musical in two acts by Jimmy Chi and Kuckles band. **premiere** 1 March 1990, Octagon Theatre, Perth. Cast: Stephen Albert, Rohanna Angus, Alan Charlton, Sylvia Clarke, Jimmy Edgar, Robert Faggetter, John Moore, Lynda Nutter, plus Kuckles band, singers and dancers. Choreography: Michael Leslie. Costumes: Cordula Albrecht. Director: Andrew Ross. Lighting: Duncan Ord. Musical director: Michael Manolis. Sets: Robert Juniper. **published** Broome: Magabala Books 1991. Sydney: Currency Press 1991.

The first major Aboriginal musical, *Bran Nue Dae* emerged from the black cultural revival in Western Australia. It tells of Willie, who, expelled from the missionary school in Broome (WA), travels to Perth and finds his Uncle Tadpole. Together they journey back to Broome, riding with a hippie and a German tourist. Willy discovers sex and true love; and their adventures end in the revelation that all the principal characters are related to one another. The whole is a celebration of the multicultural life of Broome and of failures by government and church to make the black population assimilate and conform. Music is central to life in Broome and the play's eclectic mixture of country, gospel, reggae, torch and all the popular-music styles beamed in by radio combines with lyrics of often startlingly critical wit to make a work that is engaging in its welcome and uncompromising in its message.

Its origins lie in songs by Jimmy Chi, a self-taught musician, which the Kuckles band began to perform in the 1980s. In 1986, when the musical was still an idea and a few songs, the Aboriginal Writers', Oral Literature and Dramatists' Association staged a workshop in Perth. Chi was encouraged to continue work by the playwright JACK DAVIS, Marita Darcy in Broome, and Peter Bibby, editor of Magabala, a newly formed Aboriginal publishing company in Broome. In 1989 the Aboriginal National Theatre Trust included the developing script in its national playwrights' conference and workshop in Sydney. Bran Nue Dae Productions and the Western Australian Theatre Company presented the show at the 1990 Festival of Perth.

It was immediately successful. Then it toured north Western Australia and to Canberra, Brisbane and Darwin in 1990, and to the Festival of Sydney in 1991. It was revived in 1992–93 and a cabaret version was devised to travel to Fiji and elsewhere. ❦*Katharine Brisbane*

Mona Brand

Dramatist. Born 22 October 1915 in Sydney. Published three collections of verse 1938–46. Has had 24 plays, mostly full-length, performed on stage, in Australia, England, Eastern Europe, India and China since 1948. Married Len Fox, journalist, poet, labour historian, 1955. Also writes for radio and television.

Mona Brand has written on a wide variety of topics, usually of social relevance. Her topics have often been new to Australian playwriting, from Australian race relations with Aboriginal and Asian people in her first play, *Here Under Heaven* (1948), to Australian communists and ex-communists living in London in the late 1940s and 1970s in the comedy-drama *Down Under Chelsea* (1991). British colonialism in Malaya was the subject of *Strangers in the Land*, first performed in 1952 in London. *Here Under Heaven* had seasons in 18 East German towns between 1954 and 1968. Brand's work is often satirical and since early 1954 she has contributed many satirical sketches to social and political revues staged by NEW THEATRE Sydney and to other outlets, including street theatre. In 1967 she helped New Theatre to pioneer Australian historical 'total theatre' by writing *On Stage Vietnam* with Pat Barnett. ❦*Christine Tilley*

published plays
Here Comes Kisch! (1984). Melbourne: Yackandandah Playscripts 1983.
Here Under Heaven (1948). Melbourne: Yackandandah Playscripts 1989.
Flying Saucery—Three plays for young people. Sydney: APCOL 1989.
For Richer, For Poorer. Sydney: Pascal Press 1989
reference
Some unpublished scripts can be seen in the New Theatre collection at the Mitchell Library (Sydney) or by application to the author.

Breakfast with Julia

Play in two acts by Burton Graham. **premiere** 27 November 1963, St Martin's Theatre, Melbourne. Cast: Julia Blake, Ian Boyce, Terry Norris, Marie Redshaw. Director: Irene Mitchell. **revived** 29 July 1964, Phillip Theatre, Sydney. Cast: Glenna Brydon, James Condon, James Mellen, Marie Redshaw. Director: Irene Mitchell.

A big success in Melbourne in 1963, *Breakfast with Julia* is a four-hander with many familiar comic twists, set in an apartment in Kings Cross, Sydney. An apparently compromised wife, Julia is pursued by an American naval officer. The other characters are the obligatory bemused husband and Conchita, a Spanish charmer. GARNET H. CARROLL picked up the play and presented it in Sydney. It ran for six weeks but did not repeat its southern success. There were later productions in other Australian states, and in 1966 a West German production toured extensively. The success of *Breakfast with Julia*, and its reported sale in London and for a film starring Shirley Maclaine and Jack Lemmon, encouraged the 52-year-old Burton Graham to leave public relations work to become a full-time writer.

The film was never made, however, and the provincial English tour of the play was not encouraging. Later plays by Graham, who lived overseas from 1968 to 1980, include *And So To Bedlam*, *Killer*, *Nightfall*, *Sitting Ducks* and *These Cats Are Dangerous*. He began writing for the theatre at 16 and his mother produced his first efforts, at Northam (WA) in the 1920s. Later he acted for the distinguished drama teacher Thea Rowe in Perth at the Five Arts Club, where one of his plays was produced. ❦*John West*

The Breaking of the Drought

Play in four acts by Edward Dyson, adapted from *The Boom of Big Ben* by Arthur Shirley. **premiere** 26 December 1902, Lyceum Theatre, Sydney. Cast: Walter E. Baker, Alfred Harford, Bland Holt, Harrie Ireland, Minnie Livingstone, Max Maxwell, Albert Norman, Frances Ross, Frances Ruttledge, Arthur Styan. Designer: John Brunton. Director: Bland Holt.

One of the biggest successes of the Australian stage in the Edwardian age was *The Breaking of the Drought*. The long drought of 1895-1902 was ending when BLAND HOLT, the 'king of melodrama', decided to localise an English play about a country squire facing bankruptcy on his estate while his medical student son is neglecting his studies and living high in London. Holt asked EDWARD DYSON to substitute local place names for English ones, excise obviously foreign references and insert a few topical local jokes. Dyson also suggested the title *The Breaking of the Drought*, since he had 'made the old man look upon his troubles as a protracted drought and speak of the dawning of better times as the passing of the dry spell'.

Holt took up this idea in his staging and provided real crows pecking at the carcasses of dead cattle during the drought; a bushfire, during which he gallantly rode to rescue the prodigal son; and swimmers and divers performing in a tank of water which represented the Little Coogee baths in Sydney. In the 1903 Melbourne season the champion swimmer ANNETTE KELLERMANN dived and did trick swimming. During one performance she was nearly killed when she foolishly stayed in the tank while huge pumps were emptying it.

The premiere season in Sydney opened just after the first good rains had fallen, and the advertising ran:

> *The Drought is Broken, peace has come again,*
> *And hearts are cleansed as by the fruitful rain.*

JOHN BRUNTON, noted for his use of photographs and on-location sketches, brilliantly captured the look of Sydney and the bush in his stage designs, but the storyline was not changed from the English original. Australian society was represented as an exact reflection of English society. The county manor became a squatter's outback station, while London's seamy side became a tour of Woolloomooloo, Coogee, Paddy's Market, and Mosman's Bay. This celebration of the bunyip aristocracy was not accepted uncritically by reviewers, and the *Bulletin* of 10 January 1903 scoffed at a scene at the Hurricane Club: 'The audience is thrilled by allusions to Sydney as a city of terrible and beautiful temptations and much romance. The average Sydneyite has usually regarded it as a place where he is liable to be run over by tramcars at any moment, and its really high-class sins are not so well known as might be expected.' But, whatever the critics thought, Holt had a major hit on his hands. The noble squatter, his spirited daughter, and his loyal servant-rouseabouts became regular characters in many similar imitations or localisations of English stories. Until about 1912 they all sided with aristocratic land-owners against middle-class financiers and opportunists, and represented a Tory Australian working class fiercely devoted to 'the boss', whatever his faults and failings. These pseudo-Australian stories later began to look ridiculous and quickly fell from favour. ❦*Richard Fotheringham*

Bertolt Brecht

In the political climate of the 1930s Australian amateurs were not slow in recognising the influence of Bertolt Brecht. NEW THEATRE in Sydney gave the first known Australian production of a Brecht play, *Señora Carrar's Rifles*, in 1939 and followed it in 1941 with *The Informer*. In 1935 New Theatre also did a rare production of the prologue of Ernst Toller's *Oopla, We Live!*, a play made famous by Brecht's teacher Erwin Piscator.

It was not until the subsidised theatres were established, however, that Brecht began to enter the repertoire. Between 1960 and 1979 there were no fewer than 60 productions of Brecht's plays in Australia, according to WAL CHERRY. 'Brecht was never in Australia in body and seldom in spirit', he writes. '... Any old translation, adaptation, will do and any old shoddy staging can be justified in terms of something called "Brecht's theories" ... This is not to say there have been no excellent productions of Brecht in Australia.' Cherry himself directed Brecht plays in Melbourne and Adelaide, including *The Threepenny Opera* in the translation by the British scholar John Willett, with ROBYN ARCHER as Jenny in 1975 and with Willett as co-director in 1977. During Willett's sojourns in Australia in 1975 and 1977 he was influential when he worked on an Australian adaptation of *Puntila* and co-ordinated readings of *Days of the Commune*, *Man is Man* and *The Threepenny Opera* with the AUSTRALIAN PERFORMING GROUP. He worked with Archer as translator and dramaturge of Brecht songs in a program at the Old Vic Theatre in London and on recordings she made in 1983 and 1984.

Other productions of works by Brecht include:

The Caucasian Chalk Circle by the OLD TOTE THEATRE COMPANY in 1964, the MELBOURNE THEATRE COMPANY in 1970, the QUEENSLAND THEATRE COMPANY in 1971 and the NATIONAL INSTITUTE OF DRAMATIC ART in 1979.

The Life of Galileo by INDEPENDENT THEATRE in 1961, the Melbourne Theatre Company in 1971 and the NIMROD THEATRE COMPANY in 1979.

Mother Courage and Her Children by New Theatre Sydney in 1966, by the ADELAIDE UNIVERSITY THEATRE GUILD in 1966, by the Melbourne Theatre Company in 1973, and by NIDA in 1978. Joachim Tenschert was brought from Germany to direct the Melbourne Theatre Company production, in which GLORIA DAWN played the title-role.

The Resistible Rise of Arturo Ui by the Old Tote company in 1971, Nimrod in 1986 and the Melbourne Theatre Company in 1978.

The Threepenny Opera in an Australian setting, directed by JIM SHARMAN in Sydney in 1973.

Hoopla in Melbourne performed Roger Pulvers's play *Bertolt Brecht Leaves Los Angeles* in 1979. In addition to Robyn Archer's Brechtian cabarets, works by playwrights such as MONA BRAND, JACK DAVIS, NICK ENRIGHT, DOROTHY HEWETT, JACK HIBBERD, Alison Lyssa, LOUIS NOWRA, JOHN ROMERIL and STEPHEN SEWELL have at least a superficial Brechtian influence. JAN FRIEDL performed *Kurt, Bert and Jan*, a compelling evening of Brecht–Weill songs, in Melbourne in 1987. ❦*Tony Mitchell*

further reading
CHERRY, WAL. Bertolt Brecht production in Australia. *Theatre Australia* 3/11 (Sydney, June 1979).
Willett, John. Brecht's *The Threepenny Opera* at the Adelaide Festival Centre. *Theatre Quarterly* 7/26 (summer 1977).
WILLETT, JOHN. The transportation of Jack Punt. *Theatre Australia* 3/11 (June 1979).

Marie Bremner
Actor, soprano singer. Born 13 April 1904 in Melbourne. Trained at Albert Street Conservatorium (Melbourne). Rose from J. C. Williamson's chorus to leading roles in operetta. Retired from stage in late 1930s. Died 20 December 1981 in Melbourne.

One of the last Australian operetta stars to rise from the chorus, attractive Marie Bremner was a good actor and had vocal gifts that brought her a Nellie Melba scholarship at 17. The great soprano believed that Bremner lacked the stamina for opera and advised a career on the concert platform or the operetta stage. After a short time in the J. C. WILLIAMSON'S chorus, Bremner played second lead in *Lilac Time* in 1924. Then she headed a company touring South Africa in *Rose-Marie* in 1926.

In spite of the successes of local artists such as JOSIE MELVILLE and GLADYS MONCRIEFF, the Firm began importing performers to head its operetta companies. Many were disastrous, such as Virginia Perry, an American who played only the opening Melbourne season in *The Desert Song* in 1928. Bremner successfully took over the lead for the rest of the Australian tour. In the early 1930s Bremner starred in two Gilbert and Sullivan seasons and played the lead in *The New Moon* and revivals, including *The Belle of New York* and *Miss Hook of Holland*. When the Great Depression and internal upheavals almost brought J. C. Williamson's to its knees Bremner retired from the stage after marrying Ewart Chapple, concert manager of the ABC. She gave some recitals on ABC radio during the Second World War. ❦*Alwyn Capern*

Brennan vaudeville circuit
A strong force in show business, particularly vaudeville, began to emerge in Sydney on Boxing Night 1906, when James Brennan presented the Charles and Will Bovis Mammoth Entertainers to open a new vaudeville house virtually next door to HARRY RICKARDS's Tivoli Theatre in Castlereagh Street. The National Amphitheatre boasted 'Australian Artists and Prices for Australian People'. Those prices were low enough, ranging from sixpence to one shilling and sixpence. Brennan was the sole proprietor of the 'Nash', as the National Amphitheatre became popularly known. While the Bovis brothers saw to the entertainment, J. C. BAIN ran the place from day to day as business manager. Brennan's brother Harry was his private secretary and treasurer. Brennan leased the small Gaiety Theatre in Melbourne and began to present vaudeville there on 19 October 1907. Success encouraged him to lease theatres in Hobart and Brisbane and to build a much bigger theatre in Melbourne. In 1911 Brennan's Amphitheatres Ltd floated a public company with 100 000 £1 shares. The float was immediately oversubscribed by £35 000. Brennan's Amphitheatre opened in Bourke Street on 6 April 1912. Brennan may have overreached himself financially. He had a working arrangement in New Zealand with the FULLERS' vaudeville organisation, which was keen to graze in the greener pastures of Australia. In April 1912 advertisements in the *Sunday Times* told an interesting story: on 7 April the sole proprietor of the National Amphitheatre in Sydney was Brennan's Amphitheatres Ltd, 'governing director James Brennan'. There was no advertisement on 14 April, but on 21 April the owner was Brennan–Fullers Vaudeville Circuit, managing director Ben J. Fuller. Brennan's Amphitheatre became the National Amphitheatre.

The Brennan-Fuller banner was allowed to fly until the end of the First World War. Between August 1918 and March 1919, Fuller Brothers extensively renovated the Sydney 'Nash' and renamed it FULLERS' NATIONAL THEATRE. Brennan's name slipped off the bill at the same time as Fullers' assumed full control. Brennan's original slogan 'Australian Artists and Prices for Australian People' remained the watchword of the Fuller management, a nice contrast to the Tivoli's overseas stars. ❦*John West*

Nancye Bridges OAM
Variety artist. Born in Wanganui (New Zealand). Began performing in charity concerts with elder brother Cliff (pianist) and younger sister Babe (marimba) as Bridges Trio. Played in variety in Australia. OAM 1986.

The Bridges Trio—Nancye, Babe and Cliff—was a fixture in Australian variety, playing in every imaginable venue. They were brought up in Wanganui in a musical family, though their father died before Babe was born. Their mother imported the largest possible marimba and Babe was trained to play it. All three would attack the marimba as a climax to their act. Bent on a professional career, they arrived in Australia with a letter of introduction from the Prime Minister of New Zealand to a fellow New Zealander, the wife of the entrepreneur BENJAMIN FULLER. He facilitated their entry into Australian show business.

During the Second World War Cliff was in the air force, but his sisters continued with another pianist. He returned to the trio after the war, but soon joined ABC radio and became a music producer. Nancye and Babe continued as a duo and in the 1950s spent four years playing in England and Europe. The act ended in 1975, when Nancye began organising Old Fashioned Shows with expert artists from the old TIVOLI CIRCUIT days, at the Sydney Opera House and later in other states. She then began taking entertainment into hospitals and nursing homes. ❦*John West*

writings
Curtain Call (with Frank Crook). Sydney: Cassell Australia 1980. Entertaining history of Australian music and variety from 1920s to 1960s.
Wonderful Wireless (with Frank Crook). Sydney: Methuen 1983.

Brisbane

The Moreton Bay colony, founded as a penal settlement in 1824 and opened to free settlers in 1842, saw its first show on 26 April 1847 when George Croft, a tightrope dancer, opened an amphitheatre in South Brisbane. He balanced on his head atop a three-metre-high pole surrounded by fireworks, and later sang an 'obscene' song. Circuses, the Flying Pieman and other performers of feats of endurance or strength, and minstrel shows followed at infrequent intervals. M. D. Finucan's Licensed Travelling Theatre, possibly the first visiting theatrical company, arrived in May 1856. It found the School of Arts Hall, built in 1851, to be unsuitable but by 4 August it had opened its own improvised theatre with a three-act melodrama, *Blanche—or, The Brigand's Bride*, and two short farces.

About the same time there was a debate at the School of Arts on the topic 'Has the legitimate stage a moral or immoral tendency?' The latter alternative was favoured and this belief often resurfaced over the years in opposition to theatres and performances. Nevertheless, amateurs formed a dramatic society in 1861 and before it disbanded they performed W. B. Rhodes's musical burletta *Bombastes Furioso* and the farce *Locomotion*. In 1864 Frederick Younge, a professional comedian who had converted several halls into temporary theatres, was hailed as 'the pioneer of drama in Queensland'. His brother Richard Younge, lessee of the Royal Hotel, also took part in theatricals. He had played Iago to G. V. Brooke's Othello.

The Younges probably started the New Dramatic Company, which performed in the old Armoury until it opened Mason's Concert Hall with the farce *Poor Pillicoddy*. on 25 January 1865. This theatre was built in Elizabeth Street by George B. Mason, music and dance teacher, pianist and lessee of the Victoria Hotel. In March the company staged *The Belle of Brisbane—or, The Lady of Queensland* by Myers David Isaacs, a local playwright.

Next year W. S. Lyster's Royal English and Italian Opera Company gave 15 operas. The theatre was renamed the Royal Victoria, but poor business soon led to Mason's departure. A rival hotelier, James Dinsdale, improved the Oxford Music Hall in Edward Street and opened it as the Royal Alexandra Theatre on 24 November 1866. This smaller, rougher theatre was more successful than its rival for about five years, although several actors defected to the Royal Victoria when Dinsdale staged J. B. Buckstone's *Jack Sheppard* and other scurrilous pieces. The Alexandra later declined and was not used after about 1880.

The West Indian tragedian Morton Tavares visited Brisbane in 1873 and returned next year as lessee of the Royal Victoria Theatre, which he refurbished and renamed the Queensland Theatre. William Creswick, George Darrell, Lady Don, Lydia Howarde, Eduardo and Giulia Majeroni and other major artists visited it during the 1870s. The tiny stage, heat, mosquitoes, and rain on the iron roof made it unpleasant, however, and it was pulled down with few regrets in 1880. Just before its demise the French writer Edmond Marin la Meslée visited it, and in 1883 he wrote in *The New Australia*: 'Shakespeare's masterpieces were performed on a stage three yards square, and the ghost of the King of Denmark could be seen making his exit behind a backdrop representing Mount Vesuvius in eruption. Hamlet, dressed like an undertaker's mute, philosophised on the vanity of the human condition, while contemplating a hollowed out pumpkin, in which an artist had cut out the jawbone, the nose, and two huge round eyes.'

A boom fuelled by gold discoveries in Queensland saw the population of Brisbane almost double to about 100 000 in the 1870s and the demand for entertainment increased. The Queensland Theatre was rebuilt as the larger, better-equipped Theatre Royal. This 1350-seat theatre opened on 18 April 1881 with H. J. Byron's comedy *Our Girls* and it lasted until 1959. However, professional theatre was dominated for nearly 100 years by Her Majesty's Theatre, in Queen Street. It was called Her Imperial Majesty's Opera House when it opened with William Gillette's *Held by the Enemy* on 2 April 1888. Seating about 2200 people, it was large enough to stage spectacular shows, such as *Chu Chin Chow* in 1922. A 700-seat Princess Theatre was also built in 1888, on the other side of the Brisbane River. It suffered after a flood in 1893 swept away the only bridge connecting it to the more populous and prosperous northern suburbs.

In 1888 Sydney and Brisbane were joined by rail and the major dramatic and operatic companies began to include Brisbane in their tours. J. C. Williamson, George Musgrove, Bland Holt, Alfred Dampier, Meynell and Gunn and smaller provincial managers like Dan Barry and the Majeronis all offered regular seasons. The agricultural show in August attracted the year's peak offerings and there was a

Her Imperial Majesty's Opera House—later called Her Majesty's Theatre—was Brisbane's principal theatre from 1888 to 1983. This photograph was taken during Pattie Browne's 1898 season of J, M. Barrie's The Little Minister

The Tivoli Theatre, opened by Hugh D. McIntosh in 1915, seated 1800 persons. Above it was the Roof-Garden Theatre, where 1200 could sit in open air. The main auditorium, seen here in 1918, was reconstructed as a two-level cinema in 1927

scramble for venues, which several companies avoided by performing in tents. PHILIP LYTTON brought His Majesty's Moving Theatre in 1907. WILLIAM ANDERSON brought the Grand Pavilion Theatre and the New Dan Barry Company played in the Hippodrome opposite the Theatre Royal in 1909, and Cole's Players brought their Marquee in 1929. But only Her Majesty's Theatre was needed regularly, and the Theatre Royal became predominantly a vaudeville house, particularly after Ted Holland became regular lessee in the 1900s. Holland presented in Queensland the acts that Harry Rickards brought to the southern states for his TIVOLI CIRCUIT. In the 1910s four new theatres opened within four years. The Cremorne—initially an open-air theatre—the Empire and the Palace Gardens (converted from the Centennial Hall) were built in 1911, and the TIVOLI THEATRE in 1915. All were used primarily for revue and variety, with occasional seasons of legitimate drama.

Some smaller managers attempted to make Brisbane their permanent base. Philip Agnew wrote and staged his own melodramas in the 1880s, and C. E. King's company revived legitimate plays at the Theatre Royal in 1913–14 and at the Tivoli Theatre in 1916. In the 1920s the actor–managers FIFI BANVARD and NELLIE BRAMLEY each ran long seasons of plays. Bramley began at Her Majesty's in April 1928 and then moved to the Theatre Royal. She stayed there, except for short country tours, until November 1930, performing more than 60 different plays, from *When Wives Walk Out* to *Kitty Walks In*. She also offered 'the all-Queensland tale' *Drought*.

The time at which performances ended concerned Brisbane playgoers for many years. At the Theatre Royal in 1881 advertisements stated: 'Omnibuses leave the Theatre for all suburbs immediately after the performance'. By August 1892, when Henry Towle Harrison's original comic opera *Bulbo* had its premiere in Brisbane, this had become a local joke. The finale concluded:

> Tho' our joys unending,
> We must not be sending
> People home too late, you know.

For many years special trains ran to and from Sandgate and Ipswich, and ferry services crossed the Brisbane River, but in June 1914 a late finish to *Uncle Tom's Cabin* had patrons hurrying for the door throughout Uncle Tom's death scene.

Good times were always needed to encourage companies to visit Brisbane, one of the smaller capitals. A tramway strike from January to March 1912 meant there were only 25 opening nights in the whole year. In 1919 the influenza epidemic caused havoc. Many theatres were closed, and the Theatre Royal and others were disinfected daily. An advertisement promised that 'during the performances the audience and the atmosphere will be sprinkled with a strong germicide delightfully blended with perfume'. Courting couples vigorously opposed an instruction to sit in every second seat.

During the prosperous 1920s there were at least 70 opening nights each year, with a peak of more than 100 in 1923. This level was maintained until the Great Depression, when even Her Majesty's Theatre was wired for talking pictures. By 1931 it was also being used for mini-golf. The Cremorne Theatre was rebuilt with a roof and wired for sound, and the Empire Theatre became the St James cinema. J. C. WILLIAMSON'S still gave occasional seasons of Gilbert and Sullivan and other operetta, and variety shows were revived for the forces during the Second World War. But drama teachers' groups and other AMATEUR THEATRE provided the most significant developments for many years.

At least as early as 1907 Agnes Rahilly was teaching speech and drama, and using her students in productions of plays from *Little Lord Fauntleroy* to *The Kelly Gang*. BARBARA SISLEY and HARRY BORRADALE, began teaching elocution in 1916 and 1917 respectively. Sisley founded the BRISBANE REPERTORY THEATRE SOCIETY in 1925, and with Maibry Wragge founded the Art of Speech Association in 1939. Two little theatres broke away from Brisbane Repertory in 1936—Brisbane Amateur Theatres (later BRISBANE ARTS THEATRE), founded by JEAN TRUNDLE and VIC HARDGREAVES, and TWELFTH NIGHT THEATRE, established by RHODA FELGATE. These groups used All Saints' Hall, Albert Hall, and the Cremorne, Empire and Princess Theatres at different times for seasons of Shakespeare, literary dramas and comedies and a respectable proportion of Australian plays. Through them the European 'theatre of the absurd', works of Bertolt Brecht, and modern British plays from John Osborne's *Look Back in Anger* onwards were introduced to Brisbane audiences. In 1959 the COLLEGE PLAYERS, a university group directed by Bryan Nason, began a bold program of semi-professional work that lasted until 1969.

Brisbane Arts Theatre opened its own 157-seat theatre in 1961, and it has steadily presented amateur actors in light-weight plays. The other groups saw the probability of state and federal support for professional and semiprofessional work. New theatres were being built, including the 600-seat State Government Insurance Office Theatre (later the Suncorp Theatre) in Turbot Street in 1969 and the 400-seat Schonell Theatre at the University of Queensland in 1970. Bryan Nason directed the inaugural production of the QUEENSLAND THEATRE COMPANY, Peter Shaffer's *The Royal Hunt of the Sun*, at the SGIO Theatre and he wrote and directed the first show at the Schonell, *Bacchoi*.

Twelfth Night built its own 450-seat theatre and restaurant in the inner suburb of Bowen Hills, and under Joan Whalley's direction tried to compete with the Queensland Theatre Company. This led to financial ruin and the sale of the site to the state government. Trading as the TN Theatre Company from 1979, the company used a church hall in Fortitude Valley in 1982–85, and in 1986 went to the Princess Theatre in South Brisbane, the only colonial playhouse surviving since the demolition of Her Majesty's in 1983 and the Theatre Royal in 1987. A program of radical and sometimes controversial classics, such as Caryl Churchill's *Cloud Nine*, and original Australian works, including plays by JANIS BALODIS, briefly reinvigorated the moribund company, which closed permanently in 1991.

The Brisbane Repertory Theatre Society opened a small 200-seat theatre-in-the-round, La Boîte, in 1972. It has combined cautious semi-professionalism with a central dedication to new Australian plays. It gave the world premiere of STEPHEN SEWELL's first play, *The Father We Loved on a Beach by the Sea*, in 1978. Alternative and community-theatre groups —among them the professional POPULAR THEATRE TROUPE in 1975–82, the STREET ARTS THEATRE COMPANY from 1983 and Rock 'n' Roll Circus from 1986—have provided wide diversity in performance styles, subjects, and locations. Several

The Queensland Theatre Company's premiere production of David Williamson's Money and Friends, *directed by Aubrey Mellor, went on national tour after the Brisbane season in 1992. The actors here are, from left, Don Barker as Conrad, Robyn Nevin as Margaret, Sally McKenzie as Vicki, Brandon Burke as Alex, Peter Carroll as Stephen and Barbara Stephens as Penny*

other small and short-lived professional groups such as the BRISBANE ACTORS' COMPANY in 1976–81 and the Brisbane Theatre Company from 1989 have done interesting work.

The Queensland Theatre Company has tended to dominate Brisbane theatre since it began regular performance in 1970. Alan Edwards's 19 years as artistic director of the company saw it established artistically and financially, and between 1989 and 1993 his successor Aubrey Mellor took it to national prominence. It has been heavily funded by comparison with all other groups, and from the mid-1970s it has attracted audiences through a large subscription scheme. Annual spring performances of Shakespeare in Albert Park led to the building of an open-air auditorium for the purpose in 1982. Commercial theatre began to revive, especially after the opening in 1985 of the 2000-seat Lyric Theatre in the new QUEENSLAND PERFORMING ARTS COMPLEX on the South Bank.

In 1988 a 'World Expo on Stage' Festival, featuring major international companies, affected all local groups. At the same time the small Cremorne Theatre—named after the old theatre destroyed by fire in 1954—in the Performing Arts Complex was host to a remarkable series of Australian plays performed by companies from across the country. This was one of the most significant national theatrical events of the 1980s. *Richard Fotheringham*

further reading

MCKEAN, KATE. Brisbane's first theatre. University of NSW thesis 1980.
RADBOURNE, JENNIFER. Little Theatre—its development since World War II in Australia, with particular reference to Queensland. University of Queensland MA thesis 1978.

Katharine Brisbane AM

Critic, publisher. Born 7 January 1932 in Singapore. Came to Australia 1932. Educated at University of Western Australia. Directed plays for University Dramatic Society and Graduate Dramatic Society. Reporter on *West Australian* 1954–55, 1957–60. Theatre critic of *West Australian* 1959–61, 1962–65. National theatre critic for *Australian* 1967–74. Member of first drama committee of

Australian Council for the Arts 1968. Founded Currency Press with husband Philip Parsons 1971. Founding member of Australian National Playwrights' Conference 1972. Sydney theatre critic of *Australian* 1978–80. National theatre writer for *National Times* 1981–82. Chair of Australian National Playwrights' Centre 1984–90. Australian Writers' Guild Dorothy Crawford Award 1985. Sydney Critics' Circle Major Award for services to Australian theatre, with Philip Parsons, 1992. AM 1993. HonDLitt (University of NSW) for work as critic 1994. Gold medal of National Book Council 1994. Mother of Nicholas Parsons, dramatist and director.

Since the late 1960s Katharine Brisbane has been 'den mother' of Australian playwrights. As national reviewer for the *Australian* from 1967 to 1974 she was in a unique position to comment on and support the nationalistic revival that is still often called the 'new wave' of Australian theatre. She became a vociferous and enthusiastic champion of Australian plays, and an articulate chronicler of the 'larrikin' theatrical style of the early 1970s, which she saw as distinctively Australian. For 30 years she been influential in setting the agenda for critical debate about Australian theatre, through many contributions to standard reference works and critical introductions to plays published by Currency Press. ❦*John McCallum*

writings
Australian drama. *The Literature of Australia* (ed. Geoffrey Dutton). Melbourne: Penguin 1976.
Chapters in *Contemporary Australian Drama* (ed. Peter Holloway). Sydney: Currency Press 1987.
Investing in authors—A history of Currency Press. *Voices* (Canberra) spring 1993.

Brisbane Actors' Company

Professional dramatic company in Brisbane, founded in 1976 as Actors' Theatre by David Clendinning and Bruce Parr. Renamed Brisbane Actors' Company 1978. Last production 1981. Dissolved 1983. **artistic director** David Clendinning. **first production** *The Misanthrope* by Molière, 1976, at Conservatorium Theatre. Designer and director: David Clendinning.

Brisbane's third professional company mounted ten productions in four years with early success. It was founded to provide employment for actors by DAVID CLENDINNING and the present writer, an actor and teacher who became it administrator. The company's second production—and first as the Brisbane Actors' Company—was a double bill of Eugène Ionesco's *The Chairs* and Anton Chekhov's *The Proposal* (translated by Clendinning) performed by Clendinning, JENNIFER FLOWERS and the present writer in March 1978. Critical and box-office success led to the company being registered as a co-operative in May 1979.

In early programs the company reiterated its simple philosophy: '… to present quality theatre, spiced with joy, excitement and imagination'. This was to be achieved by close analysis of texts, the 'star' being the play itself, and meticulous attention to detail. David Storey's *Home*, directed by John Milson in February 1981, was described by Jeremy Ridgman in *Theatre Australia* in April 1981 as 'a rare and memorable production, a perfect vehicle for the company, at last defining an area they might profitably quarry in future'. However, increasing difficulties with funding and sustaining a third professional company in Brisbane made this the company's last production. ❦*Bruce Parr*

Brisbane Arts Theatre

Amateur dramatic society founded in 1936 by Jean Trundle and Vic Hardgreaves as Brisbane Amateur Theatres. Renamed Brisbane Arts Theatre 1947. **venues** 1930s and 1940s All Saints' Hall, Princess Theatre, Theatre Royal. 1950s Albert Hall. 1961– Arts Theatre. **first production** *Tell Me the Truth* by Leslie Howard, at All Saints' Hall, 28 May 1936. Director: Jean Trundle.

Amid competition from professional companies and exciting amateur groups rising and falling, Brisbane Arts Theatre, a 'little theatre' in the city centre, has maintained artistic viability and financial solidity from box-office receipts, apart from a small annual state government grant from 1969 to 1992. It does not test its audiences with experiment, but offers comedies, mysteries, thrillers and modern classics. A strong tradition of Saturday youth productions and workshops has resulted in a constant inflow of amateur actors, directors, technicians and stage crew. Administrative and costume-hire staff are employed full time.

The society made its debut with *A Night with A. A. Milne* on 8 April 1936—before the official opening production in May. It announced that it intended 'to be an instrument of self-expression in histrionic art', to present 'plays with popular appeal and entertainment value' and 'to revive and retain the atmosphere and tradition of the theatre'. The founders were JEAN TRUNDLE, a speech and drama teacher who had performed with the BRISBANE REPERTORY THEATRE SOCIETY since 1926, and her husband VIC HARDGREAVES. In 1939 there was an extended press debate in the Brisbane *Telegraph* over its account of the group's disappointing performance standards. During the late 1930s and the 1940s the society encouraged local playwrights. Of 17 three-act plays staged in 1940–42 eight were by Australians—David Cahill, Constance Cummins, SUMNER LOCKE ELLIOTT, Bobby Mack and GWEN MEREDITH.

In 1959, when the society was presenting major productions in the Albert Hall, it bought an old building in Petrie Terrace for £600 and, with a £1000 loan garnered from members, gradually converted it into club rooms and the two-tiered 170-seat Arts Theatre. This opened in 1961 with a production of BARBARA VERNON'S *The Multi-Coloured Umbrella*, directed by Trundle and Hardgreaves. The society invited submissions of plays and set up a 'playwrights' theatre', playing four-week seasons from Monday to Wednesday. In 1964 it sponsored an annual play competition with the Warana Festival. Queensland playwrights whose work the society has assisted include Ian Austin, Helen Haenke, Russell Jarrett, Paul Sherman and BARBARA STELLMACH. In 1964 the theatre was destroyed by fire and rebuilt and improved by its dedicated members. All the society's productions have been staged there since 1968. In 1965 Brisbane Arts Theatre represented Australia at the Monaco Theatre Festival with *Manly Ferry* by Vince Moran. Jean Trundle's sudden death in the same year ended the company's period of greatest achievement.

During the 1960s Brisbane Arts Theatre performed six nights a week, mounted touring productions and long-running late-night revues. It fostered many actors, designers and directors for the professional theatre, including Brian Blain, Carol Burns, DAVID CLENDINNING, Penny Downey, Ray Dunlop, Russell Jarrett, Gerard Kennedy, Bernard King, Ken Lord, Brian Moll, BARRY OTTO, Shane

Porteous, Kevin Radbourne, JOHN STANTON, Garth Welch (the dancer) and Bryon Williams. ❦*Jennifer Radbourne*

further reading
RADBOURNE, JENNIFER. Little Theatre—Its development since WW2 in Australia, with particular reference to Queensland. University of Queensland MA thesis 1978.
RADBOURNE, JENNIFER (ed.). *Brisbane Arts Theatre—The first 50 years 1936–86*. Brisbane Arts Theatre 1987.

Brisbane Repertory Theatre Society

Professional dramatic society in Brisbane, founded in 1925 by Barbara Sisley and J. J. Stable as amateur society. Also known as La Boîte Theatre since 1976. Became fully professional 1 January 1993. **venues** 1934–41 Princess Theatre, 1942–66 Albert Hall, 1967– La Boîte. **artistic directors** 1960–68 Babette Stephens. 1968–75 Jennifer Blocksidge. 1976–79 Rick Billinghurst. 1979–82 Malcolm Blaylock. 1982–84 Andrew Ross. 1984–86 Mary Hickson and Michael Bridges. 1986–89 Jim Vile. 1990 Patrick Mitchell. 1991–92 David Bell. 1993– Sue Rider. **first production** *The Dover Road* by A. A. Milne, 31 July 1925, Theatre Royal. Director: Barbara Sisley.

The first amateur major dramatic society in Brisbane and the fount of most subsequent amateur theatre there was the Brisbane Repertory Theatre Society. BARBARA SISLEY, an English-trained actor who ran a speech and drama studio, founded it with J. J. Stable, professor of English at the University of Queensland, and others from the university. Sisley directed many of the society's major productions until 1945. Other early directors included Gloria Birdwood-Smith, RHODA FELGATE and JEAN TRUNDLE. BABETTE STEPHENS, later a principal director, was an early member. Those who trained for the professional stage with the society included the actors Judith Arthy, RAY BARRETT, JOHN McCALLUM and LEONARD TEALE and the director CARRIE TENNANT.

The society's initial policy was to produce plays of literary merit that had been overlooked by others, but until the late 1960s it frequently presented plays solely for their popular appeal. It encouraged Australian drama in 1931 with a national playwriting competition, which was won by George Landen Dann's *IN BEAUTY IT IS FINISHED*. Other works by Dann, VANCE PALMER's *Happy Valley* and Betty Roland's *THE TOUCH OF SILK* were among early productions.

The society was at its peak during the 1950s and 1960s. In the 1950s it bought a pair of cottages in Hale Street, Milton, as club rooms. In 1960 it appointed its first director. It performed in the Albert Hall. This was demolished in 1966 to make way for the State Government Insurance Office, so the society converted the cottages into Brisbane's first theatre-in-the-round, La Boîte. With Babette Stephens as artistic director, a more innovative style and Australian and experimental plays emerged in this intimate theatre. All this continued when a new 200-seat brick La Boîte replaced the cottages in 1972. This building strengthened identification with theatre-in-the-round, and since it opened the society has been popularly known as La Boîte. The first production there was RODNEY MILGATE's *A Refined Look at Existence*, directed by JENNIFER BLOCKSIDGE, who had a policy of producing Australian plays.

In 1976 the AUSTRALIA COUNCIL provided money for a salaried artistic director. The first, Rick Billinghurst, and his successor, Malcolm Blaylock, continued Blocksidge's policy. There were major productions of 56 Australian plays, including 21 premieres, from 1972 to 1981. By the late 1970s Australian plays had entered the mainstream. To remain innovative Brisbane Repertory had to seek more unusual approaches or lesser-known Australian works. It staged, for example, a season of three Queensland playwrights in 1977, an all-Australian season of five plays in 1980, and five Australian plays with music in 1982. The society sold some of its property in 1992 to overcome serious financial problems. It is now generously supported by the federal and Queensland governments. In addition to main-house productions it stages theatre-in-education, late-night cabaret and Theatresports. ❦*Sue Cullen*

further reading
CULLEN, SUE. A history of Brisbane Repertory Theatre at La Boîte June 1972 to June 1982. University of Queensland honours thesis 1982.

Aileen Britton

Actor. Born 1916 in Inverell (NSW). Acted at Minerva Theatre, Sydney, and for J. C. Williamson's from 1939. Mainly with Independent Theatre (Sydney) in 1950s and 1960s. Then largely television and film work. Died 1986 in Sydney.

More than any other woman on the Australian professional stage in the 1940s, tall, dark-haired Aileen Britton represented healthy, attractive, no-nonsense young womanhood. Later she played older women of considerable strength. She came to notice in the Cinesound film *Tall Timbers* in 1937, but quickly gravitated to the stage. At the Minerva Theatre in Sydney from 1939 she acted in Clare Boothe's *The Women*, Rachel Crothers's *Susan and God* and George S. Kaufman and Moss Hart's *You Can't Take it with You*. For J. C. WILLIAMSON's in Sydney in 1944 she acted in Max Afford's *Mischief in the Air* and Jane Cowl's *Smilin' Through*. In Melbourne she was in Lillian Hellman's *Watch on the Rhine* in 1943. Britton switched to middle-aged roles in the 1950s. She was outstanding as Willy Loman's wife in Arthur Miller's *Death of a Salesman* for INDEPENDENT THEATRE in 1953. In the Independent's professional repertory company in 1967–68, she was chillingly hilarious as a grotesquely malevolent matriarch with a tailored black eye-patch in Bill McIlwraith's black comedy *The Anniversary*. In 1970 she co-starred with RIC HUTTON and Gillian Owen in Noël Coward's trilogy *A Suite in Three Keys*. ❦*Richard Lane*

Kenn Brodziak

Entrepreneur. Born 31 May 1913 in Sydney. Studied law. Served overseas in air force during Second World War. Founded Aztec Services Pty Ltd in 1946. Managing director of J. C. Williamson Productions Ltd 1976–80.

In a long career, Kenn Brodziak produced or co-produced *The Black and White Minstrel Show*, *Charlie Girl*, *A Chorus Line*, *Dracula*, *Godspell* and other notable shows and he imported some celebrated performers. His greatest coup was to engage the Beatles before they were world famous. He presented them in Australia in 1964, for a fraction of the fee they commanded elsewhere. In London while on military service in 1945 Brodziak saw a revue called *Get a Load of This*, and on his return to Australia he recommended it to DAVID N. MARTIN, head of the Tivoli circuit. Martin invited him to become assistant producer for the show. A year later

Brodziak set up Aztec Services Pty Ltd to bring stars to Australia. He usually presented his actors and pop musicians in association with other Australian producers. After the J. C. WILLIAMSON's empire broke up in 1976, Brodziak secured the right to the historic name and set up J. C. Williamson Productions Ltd. He was managing director of the new company, in which Aztec was a major shareholder, until he retired in May 1980. He remained chairman or, later, deputy chairman of the company until the mid-1980s. ❦*John West*

further reading
BEVAN, IAN. *The Story of the Theatre Royal*. Sydney: Currency Press 1993.

Leon Brodzky

Dramatic critic, dramatist. Born 29 August 1883 in Melbourne. Wrote as Spencer Brodney. Son of journalist Maurice Brodzky, founder of *Table Talk*. Educated at University of Melbourne. Began career as journalist with *Table Talk*. Critic for *Table Talk* and *The Lone Hand*. Founded Australian Theatre Society in Melbourne 1904. Lived mainly overseas from 1914. Died 1973.

As a critic and exuberant publicist Leon Brodzky argued for a national theatre that would be exclusively committed to indigenous writing and would seek distinctively Australian mythology in the experience of the rural battler. Like LOUIS ESSON, he became committed to a model of national drama that was deeply influenced by the Irish dramatists J. M. Synge and W. B. Yeats. Esson was Brodzky's friend from Melbourne University, and introduced him to socialism. They went to Dublin to see the Abbey Theatre in 1905, after the Australian Theatre Society had failed to realise Brodzky's aims. 'When I set out on the Melbourne experiment', he wrote in 1908, 'I wanted a society to produce plays, like the Stage Society here in London, or, better still, the Irish Theatre in Dublin. But at the time I knew hardly anything about those institutions; and as those who responded to my call were cultivated people interested in good plays rather than people in earnest about building up something new, I was forced to let the society be turned into a sort of pleasant social institution for the reading of plays over the tea-cups, and for the reception of leading actors. To such a body there is not the least objection. But it is quite outside our purpose and no real concern of those who want to see Australian plays produced and the foundations laid of an Australian national drama. Ours is a serious affair, and a task sooner or later to be undertaken.'

In 1914 Lord Northcliffe appointed Brodzky editor of the London *Weekly Dispatch*, with the proviso that he change his name to one less Jewish-sounding. He called himself Spencer Brodney and thereafter spent most of his time overseas, particularly in New York. During a brief return to Australia in the early 1920s he wrote *Rebel Smith* in Brisbane. The Pioneer Players considered but did not produce *Rebel Smith*, which is set in the turbulence of international unionism with appropriate echoes of Eugene O'Neill. It was published but never produced in Brodzky's lifetime. Another play, *Grand Chief*, was similarly admired but neither performed nor published. ❦*Peter Fitzpatrick*

published play
Rebel Smith (as Spencer Brodney). New York: Siebel 1925.

Brolgas

Touring theatre-in-education company in Queensland, founded in 1970 by Queensland Theatre Company as Young Elizabethan Players. Called Roadwork 1981–88. **director** Janet Robertson 1990–.

The QUEENSLAND THEATRE COMPANY's youth arm, Brolgas presents strong, innovative theatre to more than 50 000 Queensland school pupils in an average year. It believes in presenting plays that reflect the diversity and needs of young people and seeks to encourage them to question the world around them. Since the Queensland Theatre Company was founded in 1970 it has allowed young people throughout the state to see plays in schools, to attend special main-house performances, to take part in youth theatre in Brisbane and to attend annual residential schools in theatrical techniques. It has often given students in remote places their first experience of live theatre. In 1970 it appointed Murray Foy as education officer and toured with *A Cloak, a Crown and a Sword* by MICHAEL BODDY, *Meet Mr Brutus* by Boddy and BOB ELLIS, and *Poetry is People*, arranged by Foy. The company, choosing plays to complement the curriculum, has also performed works by Don Batchelor, BILLE BROWN, Richard Fotheringham, GEOFFREY RUSH and Kate Wilson.

In 1981 the company registered the name Roadwork for its touring team, which played to adult audiences as well as to schools. The Australia Council withdrew funding for theatre-in-education in 1986 but touring continued, helped by the secondment of Christine Campbell from the state Department of Education as education officer. AUBREY MELLOR, who became artistic director of the company in 1988, chose the name Brolgas for the team. Brolgas also devises programs and commissions plays, and in 1992 it launched an annual playwriting competition. It aims to develop artists by giving work experience to students and employing Queensland graduates. It tours in conjunction with the Queensland Arts Council. ❦*Jennifer Blocksidge*

further reading
HEDGE, DOUGLAS. *The Company We Keep—The first 10 years of QTC*. Brisbane: Queensland Theatre Company 1980.

June Bronhill OBE

Actor, soprano singer. Born 26 June 1929 in Broken Hill (NSW). Originally June Gough. Studied singing with Marianne Mathy in Sydney and Dino Borgioli in London. In Sadler's Wells Opera Company (London) 1954-64. Toured Australia with Sadler's Wells 1960. In Australia in *Robert and Elizabeth* 1966. In musicals, plays, television comedy and concerts in Australia from 1975. OBE 1977.

June Bronhill's impish sense of fun marks her characterisations in many fields. She sang opera in London at Covent Garden and Sadler's Wells, but her greatest fame came from operetta roles for the SADLER'S WELLS OPERA COMPANY, which brought her back to Australia in *The Merry Widow* in 1960. Next year she played Maria in GARNET H. CARROLL's production of *The Sound of Music*. She enlarged her fame in London in 1964 in the leading role in *Robert and Elizabeth*— opposite KEITH MICHELL—and she repeated it in Australia. Since 1975 she has made much of her career here. She returned to London to sing the Abbess in *The Sound of Music* in 1981. In 1984 she sang Ruth in the Victoria State Opera's touring Broadway version of *The Pirates of*

Penzance. Increasing deafness made singing on stage difficult and she turned more to acting in comedy, notably as Abbie in Joseph Kesselring's *Arsenic and Old Lace* in 1991 and as Vera in *Straight and Narrow* in 1994. Bronhill's stage surname is elided from the name of her native town, where her soprano voice had its first training. ❦*John West*

writings
The Merry Bronhill. Melbourne: Methuen Haynes 1987.

Bunney Brooke

Actor. Born 9 January 1921 at Golden Square (Vic.). Began acting with Melbourne Repertory Theatre, Melbourne Little Theatre and Arrow Theatre in early 1950s. Professional debut in repertory in England. Union Theatre Repertory Company 1961–62, 1964–66. Erik Kuttner Award for best actress 1962 (Dot in Alan Seymour's *The One Day of the Year*). Many roles in film and television.

Bunney Brooke's ability to reveal deep humanity and vulnerability in characters earned her a leading place in Melbourne theatre in the 1960s. She had begun acting as an amateur in Melbourne in the early 1950s and after three years' professional work in repertory theatre, radio and television in England she returned in 1961 to play in the J. C. WILLIAMSON'S production of John Chapman's *Simple Spymen* and Dot in THE ONE DAY OF THE YEAR.

After two years in television, Brooke returned to the Union Theatre Repertory Company in ALAN HOPGOOD's *The Golden Legion of Cleaning Women*. She drew warm praise for outstanding performances as Martha in Edward Albee's *Who's Afraid of Virginia Woolf?* and in the title-role in Frank Marcus's *The Killing of Sister George*. In 1965 she acted opposite FRANK THRING in Noël Coward's *Present Laughter* as the long-suffering secretary Monica Reed, a role she had first played at Thring's ARROW THEATRE in 1953. In 1966 Brooke went to Tokyo to play Dot in *The One Day of the Year* at the English Language Theatre. She repeated the role for INDEPENDENT THEATRE in Sydney in 1970.

Brooke became deeply interested in theatre for children. She directed *The Wizard of Oz* and one of her own plays, *Trumbo*, for Independent Children's Theatre in 1970. In 1975 she played the drug addict mother in Mart Crowley's *Breeze from the Gulf* at the Australian Theatre in Newtown, Sydney. After many years in television Brooke returned to the stage as the crusty Norma in JOHN ROMERIL's *Top End* for the Melbourne Theatre Company in 1989. ❦*Lynne Murphy*

G. V. Brooke

Actor, manager. Born 25 April 1818, into Irish protestant family of 'independent property'. Stage debut at Theatre Royal, Dublin, 1833. Toured USA 1851–53. New York debut at Broadway Theatre, 15 December 1851. Signed agreement to go to Australia for George Coppin in Dublin, 13 September 1854. Arrived 1855. Debut at Queen's Theatre Royal, Melbourne, 26 February 1855. Partner of Coppin 1857–59. Managed Theatre Royal, Melbourne, 1859–60. Left Australia 1861. Acted in England 1861–65. Died January 1866, at sea on way to Australia.

During six years in Australia Gustavus Vaughan Brooke experienced professional and personal triumph and utter failure. He came after a substantial provincial career in the British Isles and successes in London and the USA. His London debut at the Olympic Theatre on 3 January 1848 brought him favourable comparison with Edmund Kean as Othello. On his debut in New York City he was considered to be a fine exponent of the old school. The Melbourne critic James Smith, who saw Brooke's London debut, believed that in response to the climate and atmosphere in Australia, he reached the height of his powers as an actor, surpassing William Macready as Othello and Richelieu.

Versatility ensured Brooke's success in Australia. He was at home in domestic drama, tragedy, comedy and farce as well as Shakespeare, 23 of whose plays he performed. His Othello set a benchmark that remained long after his death. *Coriolanus*, *Macbeth*, *The Merchant of Venice* and *Richard III* in Colley Cibber's version also suited his grand declamatory style. When supported by an audience in a large theatre Brooke responded with the inspiration of the moment and the spark of genius. He extended his repertoire each season until it included more than 50 plays in addition to Shakespeare. His appearance in W. Bayle Bernard's farce *His Last Legs* (written in 1839) 'only served to show that Mr Brooke's genius is as diversified as it is commanding', said the *Illustrated Sydney News* on 23 June 1855. Other plays in which he was popular were Morris Barnett's *The Serious Family*, Bernard's *The Irish Attorney* (1840), Dion Boucicault's *Louis XI* (1855), Edward Bulwer-Lytton's *The Lady of Lyons* (1838) and *Richelieu* (1839), Edward Fitzball's *Azael the Prodigal* (1851), and Sheridan Knowles's *The Hunchback* (1832) and *Virginius* (1820).

Brooke earned considerable fortunes for himself and GEORGE COPPIN and in 1857 they entered into a partnership to operate the THEATRE ROYAL, the OLYMPIC THEATRE, Astley's Amphitheatre, the CREMORNE GARDENS and four large hotels in Melbourne. Brooke, a failure as a manager in New York, found this partnership financially distressing and it was dissolved in February 1859. Brooke disposed of his remaining money by managing the Theatre Royal in his own name. In 1860 he strained his friendships and his marriage by becoming infatuated with Avonia Jones, an attractive young American actor. He departed for England with her in May 1861, after much leave-taking and warnings from the press that the public would no longer stand for his farewells. He was forced to borrow £110 from James Smith to pay for his passage.

The decline of Brooke's career continued exponentially in England. Neither he nor Avonia Jones had the success they expected and they were forced to seek work separately. Brooke was increasingly affected by alcohol on and off the stage, his failures mounted and he was jailed for debt. But in November 1865 Coppin signed Brooke to perform in Australia again for two years, despite his alcoholism and the bad impressions left by his last years in Melbourne. Brooke sailed on a ship that sank in the Bay of Biscay in January 1866. He did not leave with the lifeboats and it was reported in the British press that his parting words were: 'If you succeed in saving yourself, give my farewell to the people of Melbourne'. News of his death aroused genuine sorrow and subscriptions were received in Melbourne for a memorial. A marble bust of Brooke is in the foyer of the State Library of Victoria. ❦*Paul Richardson*

further reading
OPPENHEIM, H. L. Gustavus Vaughan Brooke. *Australian Dictionary of Biography* 3. Melbourne University Press 1978.

Mrs Robert Brough

Actor. Born c.1860 in England. Originally Florence Trevelyan Major. Began performing as Florence Trevelyan. Married Robert Brough 1881. Acted and sang in Gilbert and Sullivan operettas and played leading roles in Brough's Australian companies 1886–1906. Went to England c.1914. Returned to Australia 1920. Died 7 January 1932 in Sydney.

Florence Trevelyan, known as Mrs Robert Brough for most of her long Australian career, came here in 1885 to play the Queen of the Fairies in *Iolanthe*. The Melbourne *Age* of 11 May thought she made 'an excellent impression' in the operetta, although her singing voice was weak. Not an 'emotional actress' either, she preferred witty and dramatic speaking parts and became one of the finest actors on the colonial stage. She created many roles in Australia, including Mrs Erlynne in Oscar Wilde's *Lady Windermere's Fan* and Paula Tanqueray in Arthur Wing Pinero's *The Second Mrs Tanqueray* in 1894, and the title-role in Wilde's *A Woman of No Importance* in 1897. She usually played opposite GEORGE S. TITHERADGE in drama or her husband, ROBERT BROUGH, in comedy. After Brough's death in 1906 she continued her Australian career, starring for J. C. WILLIAMSON in *Brewster's Millions* by Byron Ongley and Winchell Smith in 1908 and reviving *The Second Mrs Tanqueray* for the Plimmer-Denniston Company in 1911. After about six years in England, she returned to Australia in 1920 in the J. C. WILLIAMSON'S cast of *Tilly of Bloomsbury* by Ian Hay. She was still active in Sydney in 1924. ❧Richard Fotheringham

Robert Brough

Actor-manager. Born 1857 in England. Originally Lionel Barnabas Brough. Son of playwright Robert Barnabas Brough and actor Elizabeth Romer. Brother of actor Fanny Whiteside Brough. Nephew of comedian Lionel Brough. Made English stage debut as Robert Brough 1870. Joined D'Oyly Carte Opera Company as comic actor in Gilbert and Sullivan operettas. Married co-star Florence Trevelyan 1881. Toured Australia 1885. Returned with own company of London actors 1886. Co-founded Brough–Boucicault Comedy Company 1886. Co-founded Brough Comedy Company 1896. Toured India, China, England, South Africa. Returned to Australia in ill-health 1905. Formed Brough–Flemming Company. Died 20 April 1906 in Sydney.

So strong was Robert Brough's impact on Australian theatre from 1885 that in 1906, after nearly four years overseas, he was still third in *Theatre Magazine*'s survey of Australia's best-loved actors. His father and grandfather were both successful London playwrights. His mother and his sister were noted actors, and his uncle Lionel Brough was a favourite comedian. After 15 years in light comedy and Gilbert and Sullivan Brough came to Australia in 1885 with his equally talented wife to star in the premiere season of *Iolanthe* for J. C. WILLIAMSON. The Melbourne *Age* of 11 May thought Brough 'irresistibly funny' in Lord Chancellor's *Faint heart never won fair lady*.

There was a subsequent tour of comedies and farces in which the company was managed by DION BOUCICAULT JNR. After visiting England briefly to recruit actors, including his mother, Brough co-founded the BROUGH–BOUCICAULT COMEDY COMPANY in 1886. Boucicault and, later, Brough limited their own stage appearances in order to concentrate on directing plays and setting technical standards unequalled in their day. They specialised in 'better-quality' plays and made themselves favourites with both intellectuals and the social elite. Boucicault departed for London in the mid-1890s but Brough remained here until 1901.

After touring overseas for four years, he formed a new Australian company with HERBERT FLEMMING. Early in 1906 he opened a new season in Sydney but he died in April. On 12 July the *Bulletin* remarked of an actor in Adelaide that he was 'playing effectively a part that one can "see" Brough in. That is the trouble just now; one looks for Brough everywhere.' In a long appreciation of Brough's contribution to the Australian stage published in *Steele Rudd's Magazine* in October and November 1906 the actor and journalist BEAUMONT SMITH described him as 'the greatest actor-manager Australia has known'. In its obituary of Brough on 26 April 1906 the *Bulletin* said: 'In the course of a long career, he never … quite lost sight of the duty of the theatre to Art'. Art had not enriched his pocket, however, since he left an unexpectedly meagre estate of £2700 to his wife. ❧Richard Fotheringham

further reading
BROUGH, J. W. *Prompt Copy*. London: 1952.

Brough–Boucicault Comedy Company

For 20 years after its debut in 1886 the company founded by ROBERT BROUGH and DION BOUCICAULT JNR was the toast of Australia's literary intellectuals and social elite. Brough and Boucicault set out to create a market for both elegant 'society' comedy and what was then considered serious drama. They avoided popular sensation melodrama, set high admission prices to keep out the gallery roughs and when possible performed in the smaller, more luxurious theatres in the colonial capitals. Their repertoire included comedies and dramas by J. M. Barrie, Sydney Grundy, Jerome K. Jerome, Henry Arthur Jones, Arthur Wing Pinero and Oscar Wilde.

It was a family company. Florence Brough, billed as MRS ROBERT BROUGH, was the regular star and Brough was the leading comedian. Supporting actors were Dion and NINA BOUCICAULT; Brough's mother Elizabeth Romer; her daughter by a second marriage, Brenda Gibson; and Mrs Brough's sisters Emma Temple and Bessie Major. The only long-term member of the company not related to either family was the leading English actor GEORGE S. TITHERADGE, though two of his children later joined. Brough imported for the company a scenic artist, W. B. Spong, and a composer and conductor, F. Stanislaus.

With Boucicault supervising nearly all the productions in a manner closer to the modern director than the 19th-century stage manager, the company astonished Australian critics and audiences with the sheer professionalism of its presentations and its subtle, 'natural' ensemble acting. The Melbourne *Age* on 11 October 1886 said the company's first production, Mark M. Alford's farce *Turned Up*, had succeeded 'not so much on what is said but what is done'. Critics regularly confirmed that the acting was polished and entirely believable, the overtures and musical interludes revelatory in their conception and playing, the settings luxurious and appropriate, and the furnishings perfect. Both Brough and Boucicault believed in meticulous rehearsal and they sometimes prepared productions without acting in them. They can probably be credited with introducing to the Australian professional theatre the idea of the non-acting artistic director whose vision interprets and unifies a production.

Disaster struck the company on 22 April 1889 when the BIJOU THEATRE in Melbourne burned to the ground. Some scenery and properties were saved but 'the salvage was as nothing to the actual destruction', said the *Age* on 23 April. Aided by benefit performances and charity sporting events, the company slowly returned to relative prosperity but, along with the rest of the profession, it was badly affected by the financial depression and bank closures of 1891–92. Several difficult years followed, but by 1894 the company seemed to have recovered. A successful season of 'the latest London novelties' at the Lyceum Theatre in Sydney included the Australian premieres of Pinero's *The Second Mrs Tanqueray*, Jones's *The Bauble Shop* and Wilde's *Lady Windermere's Fan*. Pinero's *The Amazons*, *Dandy Dick* and *The Cabinet Minister* dominated the rest of the season.

The company's attempts to introduce Wilde to the Australian public encountered some hostility. The *Bulletin* savaged *Lady Windermere's Fan* on 26 May 1894 for its 'faint odour of tired-out cynicism' and characters who 'lie around wearily amid much costly furniture, smoking cigarettes and blasting other people's character, and uttering that kind of morally-diseased wit which is based on the assumption that everybody is tired and dirty of soul'. At the time of Wilde's trials and imprisonment, the company presented *An Ideal Husband* in Sydney on 13 April 1895. The daily newspapers refused to mention his name in the advertisements. The public stayed away, although the *Bulletin* thought 'the play is sufficiently healthy in its tone ... Oscar Wilde's second-best wit is far above the best of most playwrights ... [and] the author deserved a longer start of the police than he got'.

The Importance of Being Earnest in Melbourne in August 1895 was no more successful, although the *Age* on 10 August declared it to be 'the most delightful and innocently amusing satire upon London fashionable life' and as difficult to describe 'as to bottle a sunbeam'. The Governor of Victoria, Sir John Madden, thought it respectable enough to attend the opening night with his wife. The Broughs were for some reason absent during this Melbourne season, and the *Age* on 24 August noted: 'Despite the production of the latest London successes, in a manner perfect both in respect of acting and equipment, audiences have been small'. Soon afterwards Boucicault decided to return to England, possibly for personal reasons, but he was undoubtedly discouraged by colonial indifference.

The organisation resumed operations in July 1896 as the Brough Comedy Company with a season in Brisbane. Vice-regal approval was again forthcoming, Lord Lamington attending the opening night of *Niobe* by Harry and Edward Paulton on 3 July. This comedy was one of the company's biggest successes. After its premiere in Sydney in 1893 it ran for six weeks, with Robert and Florence Brough playing foils to one another and raising 'roars of laughter', according to the *Sydney Morning Herald* on 2 April 1894.

The Australian actor and director GREGAN McMAHON learned his craft with the Broughs. He joined the company as a young actor about 1900 and accompanied them on a tour of India and China in 1901. After several years touring the world, Brough returned to Australia in 1905 and started the company again with a new partner, HERBERT FLEMMING. But he was in poor health and he died next year during a Sydney season which included Grundy's *A Village Priest* and Barrie's *Quality Street*. 'When they are played as only a Brough company can play them they are an intellectual delight', the *Bulletin* enthused on 19 April 1906, the day before Brough died. Flemming, Mrs Brough and McMahon tried to keep the company afloat, but it ceased operation in the same year. ❦*Richard Fotheringham*

Bille Brown

Actor, director, dramatist. Born 11 January 1952 at Biloela (Qld). Originally William Gerard Brown. Educated at University of Queensland. Acted at university and with Brisbane Repertory Theatre Society. Professional debut with Queensland Theatre Company 1971. Went to England 1975. Member of Royal Shakespeare Company 1976–82. Lived in New York City 1982–89. Artist-in-residence at State University of New York 1982. Visited Australia to perform with Queensland Theatre Company 1984, 1985, 1987. Resident in Australia 1989–94. Returned to Royal Shakespeare Company.

A charismatic actor, Bille Brown has gained a large following from his appearances with the QUEENSLAND THEATRE COMPANY. On visits to Australia he gave braggadocio performances in open-air Shakespeare—as Henry V in 1984, Benedick in 1985 and Falstaff in 1987—and while resident in 1989–94 he enhanced his reputation for theatrically perceptive and powerful acting. While Brown was with the company in 1975 its theatre-in-education wing produced his first play, *Springle*. This began a trilogy that he completed with *tufff...* in 1976 and *Prunes* in 1977. The former toured Queensland schools for more than a decade and was performed in London in 1977. Brown was the first actor the Royal Shakespeare Company had commissioned to write and perform in their own work—a pantomime, *The Swan Down Gloves*. This opened the Barbican centre in London with a royal command performance in 1981. In New York City Brown made his Broadway debuts as a playwright with *A Christmas Carol* in 1984 and as an actor in Michael Frayn's *Wild Honey* in 1986. ❦*Gregory Gesch*

published play
tufff.... Brisbane: Playlab Press 1990 in *Two Plays for Primary School*.

further reading
DANIELL, DAVID. *Coriolanus in Europe*. London: Athlone Press 1980.
FINDLATER, RICHARD (ed.). *At the Royal Court*. New York: Grove Press 1981.
MORLEY, SHERIDAN. *Spread a Little Happiness*. London: Thames and Hudson 1987.

Paul Brown

Administrator, dramatist. Born 21 January 1952 in Sydney. Street performer in Cartwheel Theatre in mid-1970s. Founder-member of Death Defying Theatre 1981–84. Studied screenwriting at Australian Film, Television and Radio School (Sydney) 1984. Began writing for theatre, television and film 1985. Community arts officer in Melbourne 1985–86. Administrator of Australia Council community cultural development unit 1988–89. Ecological strategies manager for Greenpeace 1992–93. Member of theatre committee of NSW arts ministry 1992–94.

Paul Brown uses theatre for cultural and political activism and he has created rich and resonant events in community theatre, but his work has been little seen beyond the communities through which it was generated. His experiences in documentary film and street performances in DEATH DEFYING THEATRE have given him an ease in employing research-derived material and popular-theatre styles that has led to some spectacular outdoor shows. He combined these facilities in 1985 in *Coal Town* on the history and character of Collinsville, a Queensland mining town. This influential Art and Working Life project was designed for performance on a football oval. Brown extended this model in two works for large community casts for the MURRAY RIVER PERFORMING GROUP—*Murray River Story* (1988), a historical show about environmental issues performed on the riverbanks, and *Two Cities* (1990), an incisive and controversial piece on the recent growth of Albury–Wodonga.

Two 1991 projects exemplified Brown's research and editorial skills and his attention to the needs and aspirations of particular communities, which he learned through the community-arts movement. The Gulf War gave rise to *Cafe Hakawati*, which Brown wrote for Death Defying Theatre. Among Arab communities in western Sydney he gathered material on the effects upon their members of Australia's involvement in the war. Then he shaped stories and interviews into a performance—unlike conventional European theatre—that was appropriate to their culture. Brown based *Aftershocks* entirely on edited transcripts of interviews with staff and members of the Newcastle Workers' Club, where nine persons died in the 1989 earthquake. He generated the play through consultation with a steering committee convened by the workers' cultural action committee of Newcastle Trades Hall Council. A production at the Belvoir Street Theatre in Sydney in 1993 drew wider attention to his work. ❦*David Watt*

published play
Aftershocks (1991). Sydney: Currency Press 1993.
further reading
BROWN, PAUL. Making *Coal Town*. *Meanjin* 46/4 (Melbourne 1987).

Tom Brown

Theatre consultant. Born 23 March 1924 in Adelaide. Studied in London at Old Vic School and Ballet Rambert School. Member of Metropolitan Ballet, Young Vic and Old Vic Companies in London. Assistant to Tyrone Guthrie at Shakespeare Festival Theatre, Stratford (Ontario, Canada). Artistic co-director of Old Tote Theatre Company (Sydney) 1965–68. Deputy director of National Institute of Dramatic Art (Sydney) 1961–63; director 1963–69. Died 17 March 1995 in Sydney.

For two decades Tom Brown was the foremost theatre consultant in Australia. He was consultant on all the PERFORMING-ARTS CENTRES built during a golden period. His expertise came from practical experience after 1950 as actor, choreographer, dancer, director, and head of the NATIONAL INSTITUTE OF DRAMATIC ART. He began acting for Colin Ballantyne in the ADELAIDE UNIVERSITY THEATRE GUILD, playing Sebastian in *Twelfth Night* in 1945 and in other classics. In 1968 he began an association with the architects Hassell Pty Ltd with consultation on the ADELAIDE FESTIVAL CENTRE, and continued with the design of performing-arts centres at Mount Gambier (SA), Port Pirie (SA), Whyalla (SA), Alice Springs (NT) and Wollongong (NSW). Other major centres among some 30 performing-arts buildings on which Brown was consulted are the VICTORIAN ARTS CENTRE in Melbourne, the QUEENSLAND PERFORMING ARTS COMPLEX in Brisbane, the 12 000-seat Sydney Entertainment Centre, and the Aotea Centre in Auckland (New Zealand). Major city theatres include the THEATRE ROYAL in Sydney and HIS MAJESTY'S THEATRE in Perth. At the other end of the scale is the small Town Hall in Albany (WA), which was recycled into an intimate theatre. Although Brown was principally concerned with the technicalities of production and the audience seeing the stage, he believed that the whole theatrical environment should provide patrons with excitement and magic through contemporary architectural design that acknowledges theatrical history. ❦*Ross Thorne*

Coral Browne

Actor. Born 23 July 1913 in Melbourne. Originally Coral Brown. Studied at National Gallery Art School (Melbourne). Made amateur debut for Melbourne Repertory Theatre Company 1930. Acted professionally for J. C. Williamson's 1931–32. Gregan McMahon Players 1933. London debut at Vaudeville Theatre, October 1934. Old Vic from 1951. Tours of USA and Russia. Also acted in film and television. Married American film actor Vincent Price. Died 30 May 1991 in Los Angeles (USA).

Beautiful, striking in personality, stylish in presence and able to shine equally in light comedy and drama, Coral Browne from an early age impressed all who saw her perform. She made her amateur debut at 17 for the MELBOURNE REPERTORY THEATRE COMPANY as Gloria in George Bernard Shaw's *You Never Can Tell*. The director, FRANK D. CLEWLOW, called her a 'rare find'. He introduced her to GREGAN MCMAHON, who cast her in John Galsworthy's *The Roof* with great success. McMahon also directed Galsworthy's *Loyalties*, in which Browne made her professional debut in Melbourne in May 1931. McMahon predicted that 'she could not escape success'. Many years later she said he had taught her all she knew and ensured her triumph. Touring under contract to J. C. WILLIAMSON'S, Browne played vamps and wicked adventuresses with maturity and poise beyond her years and she was praised for vivid characterisation of a Cockney girl in *My Lady's Dress*. Under McMahon's direction in Melbourne in 1933 Browne was highly praised in Christie Winsloe's *Children in Uniform* and in the title-role of Henrik Ibsen's *Hedda Gabler*. In London from 1934, she became famous for her outrageous wit as well as for her acting and beauty. She shared a deep interest in painting with her husband Vincent Price, whom she met while making a horror film in 1971. ❦*Lynne Murphy*

Lindsey Browne

Critic. Born 6 October 1915 in Melbourne. Worked as clerk and on Melbourne *Star*. Joined *Sydney Morning Herald* 1935. Film, music and theatre critic 1946–60. On *Bulletin* 1961. Co-ordinator of promotion for Australian Elizabethan Theatre Trust 1963–71. Compiled column on music for Sydney *Sun-Herald* 1971–81.

Lindsey Browne's career marked the shift in the quality and emphasis of arts journalism between the 1930s and the 1960s. This was brought about by social changes and an increase in professional performances. When he began in 1936 musical and theatrical performances were largely amateur and he was one of a handful of reporters who volunteered to report them on Saturday nights for twopence a line. 'You didn't even have to express an opinion', he says. During the Second World War, however, musical life was enlarged by touring artists who settled in Australia. The English critic Neville Cardus joined the *Sydney Morning Herald* and brought a new standard of music criticism to the daily press. Browne was recalled from the *Herald*'s New York bureau in 1946 to replace Cardus and he inherited his status.

As full-time arts reviewer Browne exerted, with his incisive style and constructive commentary, a powerful influence upon the musical and theatre-going public until he resigned for family reasons in 1960. He retained the approach of a fair reporter and in retrospect he claimed that it was his early years among the amateurs, observing artists develop, that taught him to discriminate and to define constructively the widely varying qualities of the performances he covered. His reviews of the 1948–49 OLD VIC THEATRE COMPANY tour and the early performances of Ray Lawler's SUMMER OF THE SEVENTEENTH DOLL were notable.

As a cadet reporter Browne learned to devise cryptic crossword puzzles, and he began to supply the *Sydney Morning Herald*'s weekly puzzle in 1939. This market expanded to other journals and in his latter years has provided his principal income. ❦*Katharine Brisbane*

Pattie Browne

Actor. Born 10 May 1869 in Sydney. Debut in 1882 for Williamson and Musgrove. Played with Brough–Boucicault Comedy Company. Went to England in early 1890s. Toured Australia 1898. Acted overseas until about 1925.

When Pattie Browne toured Australia for HARRY RICKARDS in light comedies and French farces like *The Dovecote* in 1898, the *Sydney Morning Herald* hailed her on 4 November as 'Australia's greatest comedienne'. She had been only a minor player when she left Australia for England in the early 1890s. She was briefly engaged to DION BOUCICAULT JNR and probably used his friendship with the playwright Arthur Wing Pinero to gain entry to London theatre. Her first appearance in England was in Pinero's *The Amazons* at the Royal Court Theatre in 1893. She also played in his *Trelawney of the 'Wells'* in 1898. In England in 1902 she created the show-stealing role of the maid Tweeny in J. M. Barrie's *The Admirable Crichton*. ❦*Richard Fotheringham*

Joan Bruce

Actor. Born 29 February 1928. Originally Joan Thompson. Trained at London Academy of Dramatic Art. Worked in repertory, mainly in northern England, for six years from 1948. Came to Australia to tour in Australian Elizabethan Theatre Trust company 1955. Worked in Perth theatre, radio and television 1956–68. Community Theatre (Sydney) repertory company 1968–69. Married to and divorced from Frank Baden-Powell, actor, director and entrepreneur.

A special quality of restrained power and a graceful earthiness in a wide variety of theatre made Joan Bruce a favourite with audiences during her 12 years as a leading actor in Perth. She is best remembered for her performances in Bill McIlwraith's *The Anniversary*, Joe Orton's *Entertaining Mr Sloane*, as Martha in Edward Albee's *Who's Afraid of Virginia Woolf?*, the musicals *Mame* and *Oh, What a Lovely War!*, and three intimate revues with the NATIONAL THEATRE COMPANY. She visited Adelaide to play Mrs Lusty in the world premiere of Patrick White's THE HAM FUNERAL in 1961. H. G. KIPPAX wrote in *Nation*: 'Joan Bruce would not be bettered in the east. Her landlady had the *weight* which this monumental character demands, and a surging vitality'. She repeated the performance in Sydney and the critics there chose her as best actress of the year.

Bruce also visited Sydney to play Miriam Sword in White's *Night on Bald Mountain* in 1964, Canberra for Albee's *The Ballad of the Sad Café* in 1965, and Melbourne for Arthur Miller's *Death of a Salesman* in 1967. Among her notable roles since she left Perth have been Mrs Warren in George Bernard Shaw's *Mrs Warren's Profession* for Community Theatre in Sydney in 1970; Frances in David Williamson's *Travelling North* for the QUEENSLAND THEATRE COMPANY in 1980 and the MARIAN STREET THEATRE COMPANY in Sydney in 1984; Mrs Nickleby in David Edgar's *The Life and Adventures of Nicholas Nickleby* and Nurse Guinness in Shaw's *Heartbreak House* for the SYDNEY THEATRE COMPANY in 1983–84 and 1985 respectively. ❦*Maurice Jones*

Brumby Innes

Drama in three acts by Katharine Susannah Prichard. **premiere** 1 November 1972, Pram Factory, Melbourne by Australian Performing Group and Nindethana Theatre. Cast: Marcia Briggs, Peter Cummins, Lynette Curran, Elizabeth Hoffman, Monica Hoffman, Vic Marsh, Dennis Miller, Val Power. Designer: Helen Pitt. Director: John Smythe. **published** Perth: Paterson 1940. Sydney and London: Currency Methuen 1974. Sydney: Currency Press 1983.

When KATHARINE SUSANNAH PRICHARD won the *Triad* magazine's play competition in 1927 with *Brumby Innes* GREGAN MCMAHON wrote in his judge's report: 'I consider *Brumby Innes* to be in a class by itself. In originality of subject, atmosphere, characterisation, virility and technique, it is a very remarkable work, comparable to some of the best of Eugene O'Neill's; and it is, moreover, essentially Australian.' An amalgam of poetry and dramatic realism makes *Brumby Innes* a work of extraordinary integrity. It was written without resort to the theatre and against the climate of the time. 'But the thing wrote itself. I couldn't help it', Prichard wrote to VANCE PALMER on 23 June 1927. She drafted the play at Turee Creek Station, in Western Australia's far northwest, and it savagely contrasts the nice morality of the city with the extreme conditions of the north, where sexuality is as harsh as nature and as demanding. Brumby Innes is a station owner, accustomed to using black women as he pleases. May Hallinan is a city girl come to see 'life' on a neighbouring station. Brumby takes her flirting for sexual need and rapes her. She marries him but soon finds herself 'one of Brumby's mares'.

Victory in the *Triad* competition was to have brought the play a production by McMahon for J. C. WILLIAMSON's, but this did not eventuate. Prichard soon translated *Brumby Innes* into her 1928 novel *Coonardoo*, but the play, though published in 1940, remained unperformed until 1972. The premiere production was broadcast in 1973 by ATV–0 television in Melbourne, but the play still awaits a mainstage production. ❦*Katharine Brisbane*

Dorothy Brunton

Actor, singer. Born in early 1890s in Melbourne. Daughter of scene-painter John Brunton. Began singing principal roles in musical comedy 1914. London debut 1918. Returned to Australia 1920. Acted in London and toured South Africa in late 1920s. Returned to Australia and married businessman 1931. Retired from stage 1934. Died 5 June 1977 in Sydney.

During a career that was shorter than most, Dorothy Brunton more than held her own against vigorous competition. 'GLADYS MONCRIEFF—the best comic opera singer; Dorothy Brunton—the best musical comedy actress' was a succinct summing-up of the two favourites by Johnny Farrell, an executive of J. C. WILLIAMSON's. Brunton played her first roles for actor-managers of the calibre of BLAND HOLT, but her musical talent took her to Williamson's. By 1912 the *Bulletin* had noted her emergence from understudy roles. In June 1913 she was in the first Australian production of *Autumn Manoeuvres*, which starred FLORENCE YOUNG. A year later Brunton had a more important role in *Gypsy Love*. By the beginning of the First World War she was a star in operettas such as *The Girl in the Taxi*, *The Girl on the Film* and *High Jinks*. Just before the end of the war she made her London debut at the Theatre Royal, Drury Lane, in a spectacular operetta, *Shanghai*, and in 1919 she was in *Her Soldier Boy* at the same theatre. 'At the first night at Drury Lane of *Her Soldier Boy*, at the first entrance of Dot Brunton, the Australians there stopped the show', wrote an eyewitness many years later.

Back in Australia by 1920, she revived old shows and played in new ones. In 1920 she was in *Yes, Uncle!*, in 1921 *Oh, Lady! Lady!!* In the mid-1920s she exploited her dramatic abilities as co-star with the American actor Guy Bates Post in *The Climax* by Edward J. Locke in Australia and in London. In Australia in 1931 she played Betsy Burke in the musical *Dearest Enemy*. In 1933 she played Kitty Hamble in Walter Hackett's modern play *Road House*. It included a flashback scene set in 1899, which gave Brunton a chance to exercise her strong sense of comedy as a Victorian barmaid. After 1949, Brunton, widowed and afflicted by Parkinson's disease, lived in obscurity until her death. ❦*John West*

further reading
RUTLEDGE, MARTHA. Dorothy Brunton. *Australian Dictionary of Biography* 13. Melbourne University Press 1994.

John Brunton

Scene-painter. Born 15 May 1849. Studied scene-painting under William Glover in Glasgow, 1861–68. Scene-painter at Theatre Royal, Plymouth, 1869–70; Old Theatre Royal, Edinburgh, for four years; Alexandra Theatre, Liverpool, for nine years. Exhibited easel-paintings at Royal Academy, London, 1886. Came to Australia 1886. Scene-painter in Melbourne and Sydney for Arthur Garner, Bland Holt, George Rignold and J. C. Williamson's and other managements. Died 22 July 1909 in Sydney.

At the end of the 19th century John Brunton was the Steven Spielberg of the Australian stage. He used live animals, real vehicles, water and three-dimensional scenery. Public and press acclaimed his breathtaking stagecraft in *A Midsummer Night's Dream* and *Joseph of Canaan* for GEORGE RIGNOLD and in melodramas for BLAND HOLT, including *The White Heather*, *The Great Ruby* and THE BREAKING OF THE DROUGHT. Holt's later successes depended greatly upon Brunton's extravagant spectacles. These included a balloon ascent, a bicycle race, a flooded mine, a sinking ship and a variety of *trompe l'oeil* locales, including his speciality, the Scottish Highlands. Before he emigrated, Brunton was recognised throughout Great Britain as a worthy successor to such scene-painters as Clarkson Stanfield and William Roxby Beverley. He was an accomplished landscape painter. Brunton was also a boxer and fencer, and on the Edinburgh stage he and his teacher William Glover fought with broadswords in Isaac Pocock's *Rob Roy*. ❦*Pamela Zeplin*

further reading
SOUTER, D. H. John Brunton. *Journal of Institute of Architects of NSW* (Sydney) July-August 1909.
Table Talk (Melbourne) 20 September 1889.

Beryl Bryant

Actor, director, manager. Born 9 January 1893 in New York City. Daughter of actor George Bryant. Came to Australia with parents 1906. Began acting in films 1911. Stage debut 1917. Toured in J. C. Williamson productions 1918–21. Married and retired from theatre 1921. Returned to stage 1923. Retired 1925–31. Founded Bryant's Playhouse with father 1932. Widely active in Sydney theatre in 1930s. Worked in theatre for Moral Rearmament from 1941. Died 31 May 1973 in Melbourne.

Reviewers praised the naturalness, intensity and intelligence of Beryl Bryant's acting. For example, the Melbourne *EveningSun* on 16 June 1923 called her performance in *The Faithful Heart* by Monckton Hoffe 'a sketch so close to perfection in its gripping poignancy and naturalness that it is impossible to find a fault'. She began acting in a film directed by her father, GEORGE BRYANT, in 1911 and appeared in several more films until 1913. Her stage career began only in May 1917, when she appeared in Hubert Henry Davies's *Outcast* in Melbourne. She toured for J. C. WILLIAMSON's in productions including *L'Aiglon* by Edmond Rostand in 1918, *Romance* by Edward Sheldon in New Zealand in 1918, *Peg o' My Heart* by J. Hartley Manners in 1920 and *His Lady Friends* by Emile Nyitray and Frank Mandel in 1921. Then she married, settled in Sydney and left the stage until 1923. She returned in *The Faithful Heart* in Melbourne. In 1924 she took over the romantic lead at short notice opposite the English star Seymour Hicks in his own play *The Man in Dress Clothes* in Sydney.

After another retirement, Bryant became widely active in Sydney theatre from 1931. With her father, she founded BRYANTS' PLAYHOUSE, for which she acted, taught acting and directed productions. She also directed revues and acted in radio plays. In 1941 she played Calpurnia in *Julius Caesar* for J. C. Williamson's. In 1943 her health worsened. From January 1946 she was increasingly involved with drama productions for Moral Rearmament, including visits to Switzerland in 1947, New Zealand in 1950 and Asia in 1958. ❦*Axel Kruse with E. A. Mayor*

further reading
PIKE, ANDREW and ROSS COOPER. *Australian Film 1900–1977*. Melbourne: Oxford University Press 1980.
RADI, HEATHER. Beryl Bryant. *Australian Dictionary of Biography* 13. Melbourne University Press 1994.

George Bryant

Actor, director. Born 27 November 1862 near Queenscliff (Vic.). Worked at Melbourne Botanical Gardens. Began to act at 20. Went to USA 1890. Leading actor in New York and in touring companies 1890–1906. Returned to Australia 1906. Acted in many productions until his seventies. Acted in films 1911–36. Founded Bryant's Playhouse in Sydney with daughter Beryl Bryant, 1932. Died 26 November 1943 in Melbourne.

One of the great villains of melodrama in Australia was Cash Hawkins in Milton Royle's *The Squaw Man* as portrayed by George Bryant. He returned to Australia in 1906 to play this part after more than 15 years in the USA. He had become widely experienced in the international style of acting, in drama from Shakespeare to melodrama and in parts ranging from romantic leads to villains.

Bryant was with the Louise Pomeroy company in 1883. He played Sergeant Lugg in a WILLIAMSON, GARNER AND MUSGROVE production of Arthur Wing Pinero's *The Magistrate*, with ROBERT BROUGH and DION BOUCICAULT JNR in the leading parts, in Melbourne in November 1885. This was a golden time for management but dissatisfaction was widespread among actors. They had a saying: 'If you want to stay in the country get out of the business, if you want to stay in the business get out of the country'. Bryant had a disagreement with J. C. WILLIAMSON about working conditions and went to the USA. There, Bryant claimed, he found that Williamson, an American, had blackballed him with major companies on the west coast. He paid his way to New York by drawing on his early experience in the Melbourne Botanical Gardens. He advertised himself as a distinguished New Zealand botanist, and gave public lectures on life and nature in Australia, including shooting rapids on the Murray River.

In New York and in touring companies Bryant became a leading actor. He acted in Shakespeare with Kyrle Bellew and Cora Brown Potter. He was in productions managed by David Belasco and by Daniel and Charles Frohman. In E. H. Sothern's company in New York in 1899 he played Aramis in Robert Loraine's *The Three Musketeers*. In 1901–03 in New York he acted in melodrama, farce and literary classics with a weekly repertory company, the F. F. Proctor Big Stock Company. He was in the New York production of George Ade's *The College Widow* in 1904.

Bryant returned to Australia in 1906 at the invitation of J. C. Williamson to direct *The Squaw Man*—and play Cash Hawkins—and a dramatisation of Owen Wister's novel *The Virginian*. Only when rehearsals began, Bryant said, did Williamson realise that this was the actor he had blackballed in 1890. Bryant acted in a wide range of companies and plays in Australia. He played the sheriff Jack Rance in David Belasco's *The Girl of the Golden West* in 1910. Bryant played another sheriff in *For A Woman's Sake*, a film he directed in 1911. He acted in 11 more feature films, especially for W. J. Lincoln, until 1936. One of his most successful later stage performances was the title-role in John Drinkwater's *Abraham Lincoln* in productions by GREGAN McMAHON in March 1924 for the Sydney Repertory Theatre Society and in December 1936 for the Gregan McMahon Players. In 1932 he helped his daughter BERYL BRYANT to found BRYANT'S PLAYHOUSE. He appeared for this amateur group as Shylock in *The Merchant of Venice* in May and June 1938, in George Bernard Shaw's *The Doctor's Dilemma* in October 1939 and *You Never Can Tell* in December 1939, and in Henrik Ibsen's *Peer Gynt* in March 1940. ❦*Axel Kruse with E. A. Mayor*

further reading
PIKE, ANDREW and ROSS COOPER. *Australian Film 1900–1977*. Melbourne: Oxford University Press 1980.

Bryant's Playhouse

Amateur theatrical group in Sydney founded on 16 July 1932 by Beryl and George Bryant. Closed 1945. **venues** Bryant's Playhouse, Forbes Street. Bryant's Playhouse, 5 Phillip Street. **directors** 1932–c.1943 Beryl Bryant. c.1938–1945 Dorothy Hemingway.

A leader in the amateur movement in Sydney in the 1930s, Bryant's Playhouse was founded to answer the needs of BERYL BRYANT's students. The group developed under her leadership and the patronage of some Sydney socialites and their families. It was a school of voice production and acting; a club with membership fees, special performances and functions such as dinners and lectures; and an amateur and semiprofessional company which provided public performances once or twice a week in the basement of St Peter's Church hall in Forbes Street, Darlinghurst. This, previously CARRIE TENNANT's Community Playhouse, seated 82 persons in tiers facing a miniature stage and was said to be the smallest licensed theatre in Australia.

The public seasons included contemporary London and New York drama and showed strong commitment to literary drama and new Australian plays. LESLIE REES has described Beryl Bryant's choice of plays as 'boldly, almost recklessly, courageous ... plays of challenge or experiment, most given with drive, wit and fluency'. There were annual one-act play competitions and plays by members and friends. The January–March 1935 season included *Bread and Butter Women* by young PATRICK WHITE, with his sister Suzanne in the cast. His mother, Ruth White, was in charge of the group's finances. His one-act play *School for Friends* was performed in a competition in April–May 1937. Other Australian writers who had works performed were John Cazabon, DULCIE DEAMER, Margot and Neville Goyder, and Bobby Mack (Robert McCaughren).

The success of the company depended upon a strong group identity, the idea that it was a joint workshop, and the work of leading members, such as 'Tookie' Lipscombe Hannam, who looked after the costumes, and Dorothy Hemingway, who acted and directed.

Successful public seasons in 1939–41 included George Bernard Shaw's *The Millionairess* and his complete *Man and Superman*, and open-air productions of Henrik Ibsen's *Peer Gynt* and *Brand* at Beryl Bryant's home in Vaucluse. In February 1942 Bryant's Playhouse moved to a larger theatre, previously the Little Theatre, in Phillip Street, near Circular Quay. Beryl Bryant withdrew in 1942–43 as a result of ill-health but in June 1944 she contributed to *Thérèse Raquin*, a stage version of Emile Zola's novel newly translated by

Margaret Blair and Robin Jansen. The company continued to present significant productions with the actor ENID LORIMER, the director ROBERT QUENTIN, the designer LOUDON SAINTHILL and other notable theatrical workers until the end of 1945. In 1946 the theatre, still known as Bryant's Playhouse, was used by Theatre Arts Productions, directed by Adrian Borzell, and by the Radio Players, who included JOHN ALDEN, Allan Cuthbertson and LEONARD TEALE. ❦*Axel Kruse with E. A. Mayor*

George Buckingham

Actor, manager. Born *c.*1800. Came to Australia from United Kingdom as convict. Member of company at Theatre Royal, Sydney, from opening in 1832. Married Anne Jessop in Sydney, 21 July 1834. Pioneered theatre in Adelaide, Melbourne and New Zealand. Died before 1861 in Auckland (New Zealand).

A pioneer actor-manager in Australia and New Zealand, George Buckingham was praised in the *Sydney Monitor* on 19 October 1833 as 'an industrious, clever actor' who, unlike most others then in Sydney, never came on stage without a good knowledge of his part. Nothing is known about Buckingham's early life. He was an emancipist when he joined BARNETT LEVEY's company in 1832, so he must have been transported no later than the early 1820s. His name does not appear in the convict records, so he may have changed it when he became an actor.

Buckingham, playing the villain Doggrass in Douglas Jerrold's *Black-Eyed Susan*, had the honour of being the first to step on stage for opening night in the fit-up theatre in Levey's Royal Hotel. He acted at the THEATRE ROYAL until 1837, despite various dismissals by Levey for campaigning for better pay. He was so popular that Levey was forced to reinstate him, and eventually to raise his wage to £2 from about 30 shillings, which Buckingham earned as an emancipist. Immigrant actors were paid about £3. In September 1837 Buckingham took a farewell benefit and became a publican, running the Oddfellows' Arms on the corner of Park and Elizabeth Streets. He instituted a glee club there in October and advertised a grand carnival for Christmas 1838. He transferred his licence on 12 February 1839, and at the end of that year he was named with CORDELIA CAMERON and J. H. S. LEE in a group of 'runaway actors' who had 'bolted' to Adelaide, leaving large debts. Buckingham and Mrs Cameron actually played a short season in Launceston early in 1840 before joining SAMSON CAMERON in Adelaide late in January. Buckingham was Cameron's stage manager and played second leads at his Theatre Royal.

In May 1840, while the Theatre Royal was closed for renovations, Buckingham opened the Argyle Rooms in Gillies Arcade, playing Mondays and Saturdays. When Cameron reopened his theatre as the Royal Victoria later in the month he played Mondays, Wednesdays and Saturdays. In the *South Australian Register* on 20 June 1840 Buckingham advertised for actors at £3 a week, indicating that some of his company had joined Cameron. Nevertheless his theatre continued until the end of 1840. Then the rival companies united to open the new QUEEN'S THEATRE in January 1841. Buckingham and his wife were listed as responsible for costumes and stage properties.

In May 1841 Buckingham took a farewell benefit—in the Royal Victoria Theatre—before departing for Melbourne. There he worked as stage manager and actor at the Royal Pavilion Saloon, which was renamed the Theatre Royal and licensed in early 1842. Buckingham was still in charge of the theatre when it reopened as the ROYAL VICTORIA THEATRE in August 1842. On 17 January 1843 the *Port Phillip Herald* complained of his mismanagement and poor behaviour. It cited 'his habits of improperly addressing and taking other liberties with the audience' and his 'proverbially bad' temper. 'It would be altogether better for the interests of the proprietors and the public that the management … should be put into other hands', the paper said. In July the licence was given to CONRAD KNOWLES.

After an unsuccessful attempt to establish a theatre at Geelong, Buckingham and his family left for New Zealand, where he opened the first theatre in Auckland in the long room of the Royal Hotel on 26 December 1843. On 25 March 1854 the *Illustrated Sydney News* published a portrait of the Buckingham Family Entertainers—husband, wife, two boys and two girls—who had been giving concerts in Sydney and were about to depart for Melbourne. They later returned to New Zealand, where Buckingham came out of retirement in 1855 to join Mrs W. H. Foley in plays in Auckland. ❦*Elizabeth Webby*

further reading

DOWNES, PETER. George Buckingham. *The Dictionary of New Zealand Biography* 1. Wellington (NZ): Allen and Unwin 1990.

Arthur Buckley

Magician. Born 15 December 1890 in Brisbane. Joined touring show 1908. Performed in capital cities from 1910. Went to USA as feature act on Orpheum circuit 1918. Returned to Australia in mid-1920s. Returned to USA 1934. Died 20 February 1953 in Chicago (USA).

Arthur Buckley and his wife Helena broke records with a mental telepathy act during the late 1920s and early 1930s. Buckley began performing before an audience with a coin-manipulation and card-effects act in a touring company in far north Queensland and Thursday Island from 1908. He returned to Brisbane as a headliner at the Theatre Royal in 1910 and from then he performed in other capital cities until he went to the USA in 1918. He returned to Australia in the mid-1920s, initially on the TIVOLI CIRCUIT. Later he worked for FULLERS'. A man of many talents, Buckley returned to the USA in 1934 as an electronic and communications engineer, and developed many patents with commercial success. He wrote three books which place him at the pinnacle of knowledge of magic. He was performing on American television a few weeks before he died of a heart attack. ❦*Gerald Taylor*

writings

Card Control. USA: Arthur Buckley 1946.
Gems of Mental Magic. USA: Arthur Buckley 1947.
Principles and Deceptions. USA: Arthur Buckley 1948; Gamblers' Book Club 1973.

Bullen Brothers' Circus

Australia's last large circus had its origins early in the 1920s, when Percy Bullen left his job as a reporter on a Wollongong (NSW) newspaper and became a vagabond, travelling the country shows. An out-of-luck showman sold him a performing sheep and pony. Bullen and his wife, a former vaudeville dancer, dreamed of owning their own circus. At times Bullen, billing himself as Captain Alfredo, played the sideshows with a single performing lion. The Bullens clung to their dream despite the Great Depression and by the Second World War they had built a large circus. During the war Bullen Brothers' Circus was stranded at Yeppoon (Qld), where a large audience of American servicemen gave the Bullens their first major financial success. By then, their eldest son, Stafford, was an accomplished wirewalker and two younger sons, Gregory and Ken, assisted in managing and operating the circus.

Shortly after the war, the circus gained further financial success by touring New Zealand. Then the Bullen family built a large and exciting circus which rivalled and eventually surpassed the famous WIRTHS' CIRCUS in size and popularity. Some members of the family performed in the ring. Other performers, some imported, were engaged from year to year. At its peak in the late 1950s and the early 1960s, Bullen Brothers' Circus included a menagerie, 13 performing elephants, and a wild west show in Davy Crockett or Buffalo Bill style as well as the usual circus program. The performance was accompanied by recorded music except in large cities, when a band was engaged.

Bullen Brothers' Circus travelled extensively throughout Australia and New Zealand. When Wirths' Circus closed in 1963, Bullen's was the largest circus left in Australia. The ever-increasing popularity of television, however, led the Bullen family to close their circus and open a string of lion safari parks. They had closely observed the popularity of these parks in the United Kingdom. The circus gave its last performance at Parramatta, Sydney, in 1969. The Bullen family has collaborated with the entrepreneur MICHAEL EDGLEY in bringing the Great Moscow Circus to Australia regularly since the early 1960s. ❦*Mark St Leon*

further reading
ST LEON, MARK VALENTINE. Alfred Percy and Lilian Ethel Bullen. *Australian Dictionary of Biography* 13. Melbourne University Press 1994.

The Bunyip

Pantomime. **text** Ella Airlie and Nat Phillips. **music** Ella Airlie, Herbert de Pinna. **premiere** December 1916, Grand Opera House, Sydney. **cast** Villiers Arnold, Vince Courtney, Nellie Kolle, Pearl Ladd, Daisy Merritt, Queenie Paul, Roy Rene.

A huge success throughout Australia and New Zealand, *The Bunyip* was considered the best and most original Australian pantomime. It was perhaps closer to the BURLESQUES of GARNET WALCH and others than to traditional pantomime. It began as a revue for five people, written in 1908 by Ella Airlie, a young Ballarat-born composer, pianist and singer. Over the next eight years she considerably altered the script in collaboration with the vaudeville comedian NAT PHILLIPS before FULLERS' produced it as the 1916 Christmas attraction at the Grand Opera House in Sydney.

The characters include the King and Queen of Fairyland and their daughter Princess Wattleblossom, and the evil King of the Bush Gnomes, who casts a spell on the princess and changes her into a fearsome bunyip. She regains her true identity after various sensations—an Aboriginal corroboree, a bush fire in which the Gnome King is killed when a burning tree falls on him, scenes in the Blue Mountains and the Snowy Mountains, masses of wattle trees, a Tree of Truth, and a finale of Australian characters. These include Ned Kelly, who was played by ROY RENE, Phillips's partner in the Stiffy and Mo team. Phillips's wife, Daisy Merritt played the Dame and the principal boy was QUEENIE PAUL. *The Bunyip* gained notoriety after an advertisement in the *Brisbane Courier* asked prospective ballet girls to supply a photograph in bathing suit. Archbishop Duhig of Brisbane announced that church sacraments would be refused any Roman Catholic girl who answered it. The author of such an advertisement once would have been horsewhipped, he said. ❦*Alwyn Capern*

Charles Burford

Actor, dramatist. Born 1820 in London. Began career in London. Arrived in Australia 1853. In Barry Sullivan's company in Melbourne in 1860s. Ended career as stage-door keeper. Died 1899.

A deep-voiced old-school actor who looked like the Duke of Wellington, Charles Burford specialised in melodrama. He had his first major success in Australia as Baradas in Edward Bulwer-Lytton's *Richelieu* at the Royal Victoria Theatre in Sydney in 1853. In 1863 he played a 'darky' bushranger in *Canowindra* and was praised by the Sydney *Empire* for not portraying him as a hero. As Peter Shrivel in Walter Cooper's COLONIAL EXPERIENCE Burford was one of the few actors called before the curtain on opening night in 1868. Other local plays in which he acted included Edward Reeve's RAYMOND, LORD OF MILAN in 1863, and *Anniversary Day* by J. G. Marwick in 1868. He also acted in his own *London after Dark* (1872) and wrote *The Drunkard—or, Scenes of Colonial Life* (1865) and *The Mysteries of Sydney—or, Startling Revelations* (1882). ❦*Delyse Anthony*

Marie Burke

Actor, singer. Born 1894 in England. Trained for opera in Italy but made debut in musical comedy and graduated to leading roles. In Tivoli vaudeville and J. C. Williamson's musicals in Australia 1924–28. Returned to Australia 1939. Leading roles at Minerva Theatre, Sydney, 1941–42. Subsequent career in England. First husband was English operatic tenor Tom Burke. Mother of actor Patricia Burke.

Dazzling talent as singer and actor combined with vivid dark beauty gained Marie Burke immense and lasting popularity as a star of operetta in the 1920s. Her warmth and charm in hundreds of concerts for the Red Cross during the Second World War further endeared her to Australians. She came to Australia for the TIVOLI CIRCUIT, but J. C. WILLIAMSON'S gave her a big break in the operetta *The Cousin From Nowhere* in 1924. She had her first triumph as the fiery heroine of *Wildflower* in Sydney in 1925. *Katja, the Dancer* followed in 1926, and in May 1927 she opened in perhaps her greatest success, *Frasquita*, at the Theatre Royal in Sydney. *Theatre* magazine said: 'Marie Burke as the passionate Spanish gypsy not only sang all the music with artistic judgement but gave due colour and life to the fiery impetuous character of Frasquita'. Burke toured widely in these operettas and appeared in *The Whole Town's Talking*, a farce by John Emerson and Anita Loos, in Sydney in 1928, before she left to play Julie in the London premiere of *Show Boat*.

Burke returned to live in Australia with her second husband, a New Zealander, in 1939. In 1941 she played the title-role in *Robert's Wife* by St John Ervine at the MINERVA THEATRE. Next year she played the leading role in Noël Coward's *Point Valaine*. ❦*Lynne Murphy*

Burlesque

Music, lively dancing, comedy, glamorous women wearing tights and daring costumes, cross-casting and vibrant energy were the elements of burlesque. The libretti were written in rhyming couplets, with puns galore. Countless musically gifted actors, plus legs and managerial expenditure, established the drawing power of burlesque in England, where it originated. The leading English writers were Edward Leman Blanchard, the brothers William and Robert Barnabas Brough, F. C. Burnand, H. J. Byron, W. S. Gilbert and J. R. Planché, who is commonly seen as the founder of 19th-century burlesque. Plays by all of them were popular in Australia, where burlesque was in its heyday in the 1860s.

Early burlesques spoofed classical, historical or legendary subjects, but most plots were largely parasitic on theatre itself. As long as it was topical and popular, any and every style from Shakespeare, opera or tragedy to minstrel shows or circus was burlesqued. MELODRAMA was a beloved target of colonial burlesque in the 1860s. Specific works, actors and productions were spoofed as well as the general characteristics of theatrical forms. The brilliant mimic GEORGE FAWCETT impersonated well-known civic and theatrical individuals in topical Melbourne pieces in the 1860s. In 19th-century Australia burlesque did not mutate into a seedy girlie show, as in the USA, but stayed close to the English format while developing strong local colouring.

The principal Australian writer of burlesques was W. M. AKHURST. He began his association with the form when he adapted Burnand's *Ixion* in 1866 and in 1868 he consolidated the Theatre Royal's dominance in burlesque in Melbourne with his original work *The Siege of Troy*. Like MARCUS CLARKE's *Alfred the Great*, produced in Melbourne in 1878, it exemplifies the prevalence of classical and historical themes. The annals of 19th-century theatre are replete with titles—such as *HMS Pun-no-fear*—of burlesques of popular works, both serious and comic. Sometimes burlesques appeared within days of their originals. Akhurst's *L'Africaine—or, The Fickle Geographer and the Fair Aboriginal*, for example, appeared in Melbourne in 1866, soon after *L'Africaine*, Giacomo Meyerbeer's opera about Vasco da Gama.

Burlesque was close in style and content to EXTRAVAGANZA and the two frequently became interchangeable. Both in turn infiltrated PANTOMIME and in contemporary practice the forms were seen as closely interrelated, as a description such as 'a burlesque extravaganza opening to pantomime' indicates. Like pantomime, extravaganza and 19th-century theatre generally, burlesque loved to be topical so it readily acclimatised to the colonial scene. The titles of many shows of the 1850s or 1860s give no indication of the generous amounts of local reference and satire that reviews reveal to have been introduced, by nameless adaptors or by the improvised gagging of actors.

Pirating of Jacques Offenbach's music greatly enhanced the success of local scripts and in the 1870s his *opérasbouffes*, with all the original music rather than arrangements of familiar tunes, complemented burlesque in popularity. Sterner rivals were the GILBERT AND SULLIVAN operettas, which dominated from the 1880s. By the 1890s burlesque was all but extinct, ousted by musical comedy. ❦*Veronica Kelly*

further reading
ADAMS, W. D. *A Book of Burlesque*. London: Henry 1862.
BOOTH, MICHAEL (ed.). *English Plays of the Nineteenth Century* 5. Oxford: Clarendon Press 1976.
CLINTON-BADDELEY, V. C. *The Burlesque Tradition in the English Theatre after 1660*. London: Methuen 1952.
HOLLINGSHEAD, JOHNS. *Gaiety Chronicles*. London: Archibald Constable 1898.
LEECH, CLIFFORD and C. W. CRAIK (eds). *The Revels History of Drama in English* 6. London: Methuen 1975.
NICOLL, ALLARDYCE. *A History of English Drama 1660–1900* 6 vols revised. Cambridge University Press 1952-59.
PLANCHÉ, J. R. *The Recollections and Reflections* 2 vols. London: Tinsley Brothers 1872.

David Burn

Dramatist. Born *c*.1799 in Scotland. Spent some time in navy. Emigrated to join mother in Tasmania in 1826. Returned to Scotland for divorce 1828. Returned to Tasmania 1830. Bought land near New Norfolk and remarried. Later lived briefly in Sydney. Moved to New Zealand 1847. Died 14 June 1875 in Auckland (New Zealand).

The first play David Burn wrote, *THE BUSHRANGERS*, was one of the first plays about life in Australia. It was not performed in Australia but Burn saw it staged in Edinburgh in 1829. He was also author of *Plays, and Fugitive Pieces in Prose*, which came out in 1842 in Hobart. The first collection of plays published in Australia, it included three tragedies, a romantic drama and a farce, all set outside Australia. The tragedies, like most written in 19th-century Australia, were historical pieces showing strong Shakespearean influence. Burn himself described his five-act tragedy *Regulus* as 'ill adapted for stage representation' and much the same could have been said of his three-act historical tragedy *De Rullecourt* and three-act romantic drama *Loreda*.

More command of characterisation and dramatic effect is seen in the five-act tragic play *The Queen's Love*, which was performed on 29 September 1845 at the Royal Victoria Theatre in Sydney and at the Queen's Theatre Royal in Melbourne in the same year. Even more successful was *Our First Lieutenant*, a two-act farce, which Burn claimed received many performances after its premiere at the Caledonian Theatre in Edinburgh on 6 January 1830. It was performed in Hobart at the Royal Victoria Theatre on 5 July 1843 and in Sydney at the Royal Victoria Theatre on 27 and 30 November 1844. Burn's final play, *Sydney Delivered*, was a burlesque that satirised topical targets—French imperialism in Tahiti and the Sydney City Council—through comic songs and the usual literary parody, especially of *Macbeth* and *Richard III*. Local reviewers received it well but, like *The Bushrangers*, it had no Australian production for fear of political censorship.

Little is known about Burn's early life, though he clearly received a good general education. His mother was the first woman to be granted land in Tasmania. ❦*Elizabeth Webby*

published plays
The Bushrangers. Melbourne: Heinemann 1971.
De Rullecourt. Hobart: 1842. In *Plays, and Fugitive Pieces in Prose*.

Loreda. Hobart: 1842. In *Plays, and Fugitive Pieces in Prose*.
Our First Lieutenant. Hobart: 1842. In *Plays, and Fugitive Pieces in Prose*.
The Queen's Love. Hobart: 1842. In *Plays, and Fugitive Pieces in Prose*.
Regulus. Hobart: 1842. In *Plays, and Fugitive Pieces in Prose*.
Sydney Delivered—or, The Princely Buccaneer. Sydney: 1845.

further reading
BORCHARDT, D. H. David Burn. *Australian Dictionary of Biography* 1. Melbourne University Press 1966.
MILLER, E. MORRIS. *Pressmen and Governors*. Sydney University Press 1973.

Burst of Summer

Play in three acts by Oriel Gray. **premiere** 20 February 1960 at St Martin's Theatre, Melbourne, by Melbourne Little Theatre Guild. Cast: Morris Brown, Max Bruch, Marcella Burgoyne, Brian Burton, Frank Camm, Eric Colladetti, Margaret Cruikshank, Margaret Flynn, Dennis Jones, Morris Murphy. Designer: John Truscott. Director: Irene Mitchell.

This fine social-realist play, which won a competition sponsored by J. C. Williamson's and the Melbourne Little Theatre Guild in 1959, brought strong dramatic truth to a human-rights issue at a time when racial prejudice was hardly questioned. It was suggested by the promotion of Ngarla Kunoth, an Aboriginal girl who played the title-role in Charles Chauvel's film *Jedda*, and by ORIEL GRAY's experience of life in the 1940s in Lismore (NSW), where her husband, John Hepworth, was a journalist. The play is set in a country milk bar during a three-week summer heat-wave. The town is divided over a new housing development for the Aboriginal population and passions are stirred by press interest in Peggy, an Aboriginal girl who has won brief fame as a film actress; entrenched pastoral interests, represented by the sexual preoccupations of Sally Blake; envy and racism, represented by Mervyn, a failed sporting hero; and perceived Aboriginal fecklessness, represented by the boy Eddy. Mediating between the parties are Don, a saintly black lawyer who has forfeited a brighter future to remain with his people, and Joe, the 'dago' cafe owner. Despite their intercessions the summer heat bursts into violence. ❦*Katharine Brisbane*

reference
The manuscript is in the Campbell Howard Collection, University of New England (Armidale NSW).

Burton's circus

Burton's National Circus, as it was usually billed, was an institution throughout eastern Australia and New Zealand from early 1851 until early 1880. It was founded by Henry Burton, born in 1823, who had been associated with the famous Cooke family circus in England before he sailed for Australia, apparently intending to form his own circus. He and his wife arrived in Adelaide on 23 December 1849 with the Blythe Waterland Minstrels, whom he toured through NSW and Tasmania as in 1850. Late in 1850 Burton opened a riding school at the Sir Joseph Banks Hotel, a pleasure resort on the shores of Botany Bay, and began to train some horses and youths from the Sydney district for circus work.

Burton's troupe gave its first public performance in the hotel gardens on Boxing Day 1850. After engagements at the Royal Australian Equestrian Circus in Sydney, Burton inaugurated his own circus on 1 March 1851, and it began its travels at Parramatta, Windsor and Richmond. It was the first circus to appear on an Australian goldfield. It was appearing in Maitland (NSW) when the discovery of gold in the Turon River valley was announced in June 1851. Finding themselves bereft of an audience, Burton and his company made a difficult journey overland from Maitland to Mudgee and the diggings. The troupe played around the Turon diggings for six months before travelling overland to newly discovered Victorian goldfields in 1852.

In the early 1860s Burton bought a property near Deniliquin (NSW) for breeding and training horses and for winter quarters for his circus. In Adelaide in May 1873 his company defeated Bird and Taylor's Great American Circus in a hippodrome of chariot and other races to establish the premier circus of the colonies. The event was reported at length in the Adelaide press on 24 May 1873.

One of the proprietors of the Great American Circus, Robert Taylor later parted company from Thomas Bird, to join Burton in Burton and Taylor's Grand United Circus. This enlarged circus claimed in the *Queanbeyan Age* on 11 November 1874 to present 'the united efforts of the best clowns, acrobats, lady riders' and an 'unrivalled brass band'. Early in 1878, Taylor left Burton's company to join the new ST LEON'S CIRCUS. Later in the year, Burton took his circus on a tour of New Zealand. A season in Sydney from 30 August 1879 to early 1880 was the last before an insolvent Burton sold the circus to his former business manager, William Woodyear, who promoted the circus under the Burton name for some years.

Burton, the 'king of the ring', spent the rest of his life in obscurity, although he lent his still respectable name to a circus that toured Tasmania for the entrepreneur Frank Clark in 1895. Burton died in the Dramatic Home in Melbourne in March 1900, leaving no descendants. He was not a performer, but he was a pre-eminent showman throughout the colonies during his 30 years' activity. The 'exquisite suavity and pompousness' of his showmanship apparently contrasted sharply with the rougher style of JAMES HENRY ASHTON, who was 'a showman of a distinct and bygone period', according to reminiscences in the Sydney *Bulletin* of 26 December 1891. Burton's was the only early circus to enjoy regular viceregal patronage. Burton was the first Australian circus proprietor to visit both the cities and the bush towns with regularity.

Many famous Australian circus identities were connected with Burton's National Circus. They included the rider George Gilham, the all-round part-Aboriginal performer Billy Jones, the equestrian Mme La Rosiere and the Ridgeway brothers, trapeze artists whom Burton engaged in 1865, shortly after their arrival from London. Descendants of the Ridgeways operate a circus under that name in New Zealand today. ❦*Mark St Leon*

further reading
Henry Burton. *Australian Dictionary of Biography* 3. Melbourne University Press 1978.
SALOMON, MARY A. An old-time circus. *Town and Country Journal* (Sydney) 3 August 1904.
ST LEON, MARK. *The Circus in Australia*. Melbourne: Greenhouse 1983.
The Grand United Circus. *Town and Country Journal* 11 July 1874.

Bush drama

Since early colonial days the bush has been central to Australian drama as myth and as setting, whether refuge or site of action, where resolution is achieved and where character is defined. It has been the main element in defining distinctive national and individual character. The adaptation of MELODRAMA to the Australian theatre usually concerned some decisive action in the bush involving escaped convicts, bushrangers or gold miners. Plays about bushrangers, particularly versions of the Kelly Gang story, were popular until the First World War, although the authorities frowned upon them and newspapers and the *Bulletin*, seeing a threat to social order, derided them. Women played much more physically active roles in many bush melodramas than in their English and American counterparts. The settings ranged widely and the scene painter had high billing. In BLAND HOLT's version of *The Great Rescue*, for instance, the action moves from Charters Towers in north Queensland to the Snowy River in southern NSW to Fern Tree Gully at Katoomba in the Blue Mountains and back to north Queensland at Townsville.

The bush also appeared in PANTOMIME, providing a tableau in a traditional show or the main characters or setting in a distinctively Australian production such as Garnet Walch's AUSTRALIA FELIX or THE BUNYIP.

BERT BAILEY's production in 1912 of Steele Rudd's ON OUR SELECTION heralded the heyday of the homely bush comedy, always advertised as reeking of gum leaves, echoing with kookaburras, and written by Australians for Australians. Numerous bush comedies appeared over the next 25 years, some of the most popular being Kate Howarde's POSSUM PADDOCK in 1919 and *Gum Tree Gully* (1927), Fred White's *Cockatoo Farm* (1923) and *Dingo Flat* (1924), Tal Ordell's *Kangaroo Flat* (1926), and GEORGE SORLIE's *My Pal Ginger* (1928). Other companies attempted to adapt overseas plays to an Australian setting by giving them bush titles, such as the Fowler Company's *Our Homestead*, but these were rarely as successful.

Contemporary with Bailey, LOUIS ESSON and others attempted a literary bush drama inspired by the Irish theatre; and the harsh conditions of the outback became central to the realist drama of writers in the nationalistic amateur theatre like HENRIETTA DRAKE-BROCKMAN, GEORGE LANDEN DANN, Jean Devanny, KATHARINE SUSANNAH PRICHARD, BETTY ROLAND and, later, ORIEL GRAY and RAY MATHEW. Since the Second World War the bush has not been central to the drama. JACK HIBBERD, however, returned to the legendary past in *A STRETCH OF THE IMAGINATION* (1972). His *DIMBOOLA* (1969) a comic dismantling of country wedding conventions, revives with a new satirical attack on stock characters of the old bush comedy. ❦*Barbara Garlick*

The Bush King

Play in four acts by W. J. Lincoln. **premiere** 6 November 1893, Surrey Theatre, London. **Australian premiere** 29 September 1894, Theatre Royal, Melbourne, by Taylor–Carrington Company. Cast: F. C. Appleton, Ella Carrington, J. J. Ennis, N. Griffiths, J. E. Haynes, May Hesford, J. G. Patten, Isabel Vernon. **revived** in five-act revision by Lincoln and Alfred Dampier, 26 January 1901, Criterion Theatre, Sydney.

Like many other young Australian actors and playwrights, William Joseph Lincoln tried his luck on the London stage. In 1893, the Surrey Theatre briefly staged his first play, *The Bush King*. The hero, an Englishman and former army officer, is unjustly accused of the murder of his father and forced to flee to Australia. As Captain Dart, he becomes leader of a gang of bushrangers and 'the terror of half the Antipodes', though he takes no part in the gang's raids. 'In fact he is what may be called the conscience of the brigands, and hence it is not surprising to note that they frequently disagree with him', said the Melbourne *Age* on 1 October 1894. After bank robberies in England and Australia, the death of his jealous girl friend Elsie—who first betrays him and then throws herself in front of police guns to protect him—and a fight and an explosion in an underground mine, Captain Dart's innocence is revealed and he marries a bank manager's daughter.

Lincoln returned to Melbourne in 1894, claiming that his play had been performed at three London theatres. The TAYLOR–CARRINGTON COMPANY saw merit in it, and produced it in Melbourne. The *Age* of 1 October 1894 thought the play, which had a large cast of 'Troopers, Cattle Duffers, Loafers, etc.', was 'a very good creation of its class' but it lasted only a week. Lincoln persisted, however, and in 1897 he secured another short London season, at the Novelty Theatre. There matters might have rested had not the actor-manager ALFRED DAMPIER needed a new play in his repertoire and had he not been growing too old and tubby to play Captain Starlight in ROBBERY UNDER ARMS.

Dampier became coauthor with Lincoln of a new version of *The Bush King*. The hero's name was changed to Captain Midnight, and the minor part of the pubkeeper Ned Harling was expanded to give Dampier a starring role. For five years *The Bush King* toured Australia with great success, undergoing several more rewrites on the way, and in 1911 Dampier's son-in-law ALFRED ROLFE directed and starred in a film version, *Captain Midnight, the Bush King*. LILY DAMPIER was also in the cast of the film, which no longer exists. ❦*Richard Fotheringham*

reference
The 1893 Surrey Theatre version of *The Bush King* is in the British Library (London), add. ms 53534H.

The Bushrangers

Melodrama in three acts by David Burn. **premiere** 8 September 1829, Caledonian Theatre, Edinburgh (Scotland). **Australian premiere** 1971, Leslie Hall, Barker College (Sydney) by students. **published** Melbourne: Heinemann 1971.

DAVID BURN based *The Bushrangers*, the first Australian drama performed on stage, on the exploits of the notorious Tasmanian bushranger Matthew Brady, who was hanged in May 1826. Burn portrayed Brady sympathetically and satirised the colonial governor. This precluded his play from performance in Australia though it was accepted in distant Edinburgh. *The Bushrangers* opens at the Macquarie Harbour penal settlement, with Brady denouncing the brutality of the convict system. He escapes in the name of liberty and further engages the audience's sympathies by rescuing a woman from rape. As in most English melodramas of the time, the hero's nobility is set against corruption in high places—a thinly-veiled portrait of Lieutenant-

Governor George Arthur—but history denies Brady the conventional last-minute reprieve from death. The new-chum Fitzmuggins family provides comic relief. Angelina Fitzmuggins's thwarted ambitions to star at the Surrey Theatre, the London home of sensational melodrama, permit some nice theatrical in-jokes as well as typical bush–city and Australia–England contrasts. ❦Elizabeth Webby

reference
The manuscript of *The Bushrangers*, incorporating some post-1835 modifications, is in the Mitchell Library (Sydney).

The Bushrangers

—*or, Norwood Vale*. Melodrama in three acts by Henry Melville. **premiere** 29 May 1834, Theatre Royal in the Argyle Rooms, Hobart, by J. P. Deane's company. **revived** 24 November 1835, British Hotel, Launceston. **published** Hobart 1834 in *Hobart Town Magazine*.

The first local play performed in Australia was *The Bushrangers* by Henry Melville. He published it in his *Hobart Town Magazine* in April 1834, and J. P. Deane's company performed it in the Theatre Royal in the Argyle Rooms in Hobart on 29 May and 2 June 1834. The play opens in the hut of Norwood, a settler who has fallen from affluence into poverty, for which he wrongly blames Frederick Seymour, his daughter Marion's beloved. The Norwoods' servant Ellen, who sings, and Murrahawa, an Aborigine who performs a corroboree, provide some comic relief. The plot develops with the introduction of three bushrangers, Bill Fellows, Charley Hoodwink and Harry Fawkes, who have some fairly authentic dialogue, especially in contrast to the conventional, stilted speeches of the hero and heroine. In the second act the bushrangers attack, leaving Frederick for dead and carrying off Marion. Fawkes attempts to rape her but she is saved by Frederick and Murrahawa. They return to the hut in time to save Norwood from the bushrangers. The lovers are united with his blessing. Murrahawa has his revenge on Fawkes, who had killed his wife and children. ❦Elizabeth Webby

The Bushwoman

Play in four acts by Jo Smith. **premiere** 28 August 1909, King's Theatre, Melbourne, by William Anderson company. Cast: Bert Bailey, Lillie Bryer, Max Clifton, Edmund Duggan, Laurence Dunbar, Fanny Erriss, Temple Harrison, J. H. Nunn, Roy Redgrave, Daisy Scudamore, Stirling Whyte, Olive Wilton. Directors: Bert Bailey, Edmund Duggan. **revived** 1913, as *The Bush Girl*.

Jo Smith accompanied *The Bushwoman*, his third play and greatest success, with interviews in which he announced his determination to break with traditions of both Australian and English melodrama. 'There is not even the suggestion of a bushranger in it', he said. Instead Smith set the play on the farm of an old selector who has 'worried through floods and droughts, and established himself on a comfortable footing'. A squatter's son is the villain and his crime is the killing of an Aborigine. Sheep stealing by two Indian hawkers complicates matters.

Reviewers of the premiere were so positive about the accurate atmosphere of the production that it is odd to discover that Daisy Scudamore, who played the title-role, was an Englishwoman who had arrived from England only ten days before. Nevertheless she 'acquitted herself well, falling naturally into the fashion of the Australian bush', said *Table Talk* on 2 September 1909. Her husband Roy Redgrave, who had been here longer, was acclaimed as the young selector Jack Dunstan, who has to hide in the bush when wrongly accused of the murder of the 'blackfellow'. In the play's biggest sensation the villain starts a bushfire that traps the hero on the wrong side of a chasm. The Bushwoman sees a partly cut tree left by fleeing timber-getters, finishes it off with a few mighty axe blows 'and the giant tree trembles and falls across the chasm; Jack crawls across it and while the Bushwoman faints the audience rise and cheer to the echo', said *Table Talk*. Further local atmosphere was provided by Sundowner Jim, 'a long colonial', and the comic wooing of a pert schoolmistress and the farmer's son, always interrupted by the arrival of 'cow time'.

The Bushwoman was produced by the William Anderson organisation at a time when Anderson was overseas and Bert Bailey and Edmund Duggan were in charge. Sections of *The Bushwoman* strongly resemble their reworking of Steele Rudd's On Our Selection three years later, and Smith's play might well be thought of as a worthy part-model for that hugely successful work. ❦Richard Fotheringham

reference
A script survives in the Australian Archives (Canberra), CRS A1336/2, item 1166.

Alex Buzo

Dramatist. Born 23 July 1944 in Sydney. Educated at Armidale (NSW) and International School, Geneva (Switzerland). Studied arts, including drama, at University of NSW (Sydney). Emerged with *Norm and Ahmed* 1968. Principal Sydney playwright of late 1960s and 1970s. Writer-in-residence with Melbourne Theatre Company 1972–73. Australian Literature Society's gold medal 1972 (for *Tom* and *Macquarie*).

During the 1970s Alex Buzo established himself as one of Australia's leading dramatists. He was one of the first contemporary Australian playwrights recognised overseas, especially with successes in the USA, with Rooted (1969), *Tom* (1972) and Makassar Reef (1978). He has attempted a dramatic study of individuals' alienation from society and from one another, broader in its reach and more universal in its application than any other Australian stage writer of the 1970s. The subtle moral argument in his plays points to a solution in the 'niceness', or moral charm, that his central characters embody. This simple, old-fashioned humanism, rather than the brittle wit in which he cloaks it, gives Buzo his special quality. Perhaps partly because his wit so successfully hides his underlying humanist interests, Buzo has suffered from a great deal of critical misunderstanding—of himself as a writer and of his characters—in Australia. His books on contemporary language and lifestyles, such as *Tautology* and *Glancing Blows*, made him much sought-after by the daily press as a commentator on fashionable issues. His reputation in the late 1980s unfairly rested more on his journalism than on his plays.

Buzo's second play Norm and Ahmed (1968) was a highlight of the Old Tote Theatre Company's Australian play season in Sydney in 1968 and a test case in battles against censorship. Over the next four years *The Front Room Boys* (1969), Rooted (1969), *Macquarie* (1972), *The Roy Murphy Show* (1970) and *Tom* made Buzo a leader of the 'new wave' of playwrights. CORALIE LANSDOWNE SAYS NO (1974), *Martello Towers* (1976), MAKASSAR REEF and *Big River* (1980) appeared at two-yearly intervals, each a major new achievement. These plays represent stages in Buzo's progression from a witty satirist of Australian social conformism to a mature commentator on more personal human anxieties and striving. The major plays were interspersed with shorter pieces for theatre, radio and film, teleplays of some of his stage works, some satirical journalism and two novels.

Buzo is unique in contemporary Australian drama. His early success was based on his wit and facility in creating comic satirical portraits of distinctive types, such as the nouveau-ocker young office workers and business executives who use new affluence to pursue vulgarly hedonistic lifestyles in his early plays. Along with DAVID WILLIAMSON, and to a lesser extent JACK HIBBERD and JOHN ROMERIL, he popularised the comic exploitation of the Australian urban vernacular on stage. Even in his early plays, however, Buzo went beyond social satire to an interest in a personal search for moral value—at first rather unconscious—in his principal characters. The later plays pursue the search and begin to explore the difficulties of maintaining it in an increasingly chaotic and amoral society.

In *Coralie Lansdowne Says No* and *Martello Towers* the principal characters withdraw from society altogether and rail against it from their retreats, with all of Buzo's satirical wit. Coralie Lansdowne and Edward Martello are bitter commentators who mask sensitivity and need for human warmth beneath cynical, often savage wit. In *Makassar Reef*, one of Buzo's best plays, he uses a romantic adventure in the tropics as a metaphor for the self-protective styles that the characters have adopted. Almost all of them have retreated from society and are struggling to come to terms with their human needs before facing again the outside world. They desperately circle one another as they try to decide whom to love and trust and how to save and preserve what they value.

In Buzo's plays of the 1980s, *Big River* and *The Marginal Farm* (1983), the protective surface has dropped away. The principal characters, Adela in *Big River* and Toby in *The Marginal Farm*, struggle openly to rescue something of worth from decaying old worlds—pre-federation Australia in the first play, and colonial Fiji in the second—as the brash new modern world begins to encroach. In recent plays such as *Shellcove Road* (1988) and *Armadillo*, Buzo's writing is increasingly subtle and understated, and his impact on the repertoire has been almost negligible, but he remains a sophisticated dramatic stylist. ♥*John McCallum*

published plays
Big River (1980). Sydney: Currency Press 1985.
Coralie Lansdowne Says No (1974). Sydney and London: Currency Methuen 1976.
The Front Room Boys (1969). Melbourne: Penguin 1970 in *Three Australian Plays*.
Macquarie (1972). Sydney: Currency Press 1971, revised 1994.
Makassar Reef (1978). Sydney: Currency Press 1979.
The Marginal Farm (1983). Sydney: Currency Press 1985.
Martello Towers (1976). Sydney: Currency Press 1976.
Norm and Ahmed. (1968). Sydney: Currency–Methuen 1973.
Rooted (1969). Sydney and London: Currency–Methuen 1973. Sydney: Currency Press, revised, 1993.
The Roy Murphy Show (1970). Sydney: Currency–Methuen 1973.
Tom (1972). Sydney: Angus and Robertson 1975.

further reading
BRISBANE, KATHARINE. In *Contemporary Dramatists* (ed. K. A. Berney) 5th edn. London: St James Press 1993.
MCCALLUM, JOHN. *Buzo*. Sydney: Methuen 1987.
STURM, TERRY. Introduction. *Rooted* and *Norm and Ahmed* by Alexander Buzo. Sydney: Currency Press 1980.

The Cake Man

Play in three acts by Robert J. Merritt. **premiere** 12 January 1975 at Black Theatre Arts and Culture Centre, Sydney, by Black Theatre. Cast: Dan Adcock, Max Cullen, Zac Martin, Lisa Maza, Teddy Phillips, Justine Saunders, Rob Steele. Designers: Sandy Gray and Nick Hollo. Director: Bob Maza. **revived** 30 April 1977, Bondi Pavilion Theatre, Sydney. Cast: Cullen, Phillips, Saunders, Brian Syron. Director: George Ogilvie. **published** Sydney: Currency Press 1983.

A milestone in Aboriginal theatre, *The Cake Man* was the first black Australian play to be published, to be televised and to tour overseas. It represents one of the most successful debuts by an Australian dramatist but it remains Robert J. Merritt's only play. He has concentrated upon television and film script-writing since he wrote *The Cake Man* as a youth in Bathurst Jail in 1974. He has acknowledged substantial help in its writing from the playwright JIM MCNEIL, then a long-term prisoner. Merritt has stated that he wrote the play to express 'the root causes of Aboriginal despair'.

The main theme of the work, however, is optimistic—that black Australian children can be 'the instrument of hope and change for the future'. The play relates the struggle of an Aboriginal father, mother and son at a mission, or reserve, in Cowra (NSW) in the 1950s. Growth of family pride in the son Pumpkinhead and growth of sensitivity and awareness in a white citizen, Peterson, are the major developments. The main action is bracketed by Aboriginal myths and a less successful, stylised introductory segment.

In 1977 GEORGE OGILVIE directed a six-week season at the Bondi Pavilion Theatre, with JUSTINE SAUNDERS repeating her Ruby and BRIAN SYRON playing Sweet William. All productions of the 1980s starred Saunders and Syron and were directed by the author and Syron. The first was by the Australian Aboriginal Theatre Company in 1982 as a prelude to a two-week season at the World Theatre Festival in Denver (Colorado, USA) later in the year. Richard Coe, senior theatre critic of the *Washington Post*, wrote: 'The Australian Aboriginal Theatre's *The Cake Man* is precisely the sort of production a World Theatre Festival suggests … it has the vitality of truth, imagination and human understanding, which ideally can make the world one'. ♥*Adam Shoemaker*

further reading
MCCALLUM, JOHN. Black Theatre—Robert Merritt's *The Cake Man*. *Meanjin* 36/4 (Melbourne, December 1977).
ROBINSON, PETER. Black drama of a black drama. *Australian Financial Review* (Sydney) 1 June 1982.
WALTON, ALASTAIR. 'This'll get 'em for sure!' *Aboriginal Law Bulletin* December 1985. Interview with Merritt.

Zoë Caldwell OBE

Actor, director. Born 14 September 1933 in Melbourne. First appeared professionally at nine in *Peter Pan*. Union Theatre Repertory Company (Melbourne) 1953. Toured for Australian Elizabethan Theatre Trust 1954–57. Royal Shakespeare Company at

Stratford-upon-Avon 1958–59 and on tour of Russia. Royal Court Theatre (London) 1960. Shakespearean Festival (Stratford, Ontario) 1961. Toured Australia for Trust 1962. Tyrone Guthrie Theatre (Minneapolis, USA) 1963. New York City debut 1965. Married American producer Robert Whitehead 1969. Debut as director at Belasco Theatre (New York City) 1977. OBE 1970.

One of Australia's most distinguished actors, Zoë Caldwell returned in 1962 to star as George Bernard Shaw's Saint Joan at the second ADELAIDE FESTIVAL OF ARTS and on national tour for the AUSTRALIAN ELIZABETHAN THEATRE TRUST. Her visit coincided with the discovery of PATRICK WHITE's plays and she played the Girl in THE HAM FUNERAL for the Union Theatre Repertory Company and created Nola Boyle in THE SEASON AT SARSAPARILLA. 'Miss Caldwell, tawny-headed, a proud slattern, showed us Nola—the childless Nola, the trapped Nola struggling in the throbbing insistent flesh, mother of men and lover of men—in slack shuffle, in taut and ugly stance, in wide, sidelong hooded glance or in blazing candour' wrote H. G. KIPPAX in the Nation. 'By any standard it was a remarkable performance'.

Caldwell was marked for stardom. She showed early signs of acting talent and her mother, a small-part Gilbert and Sullivan singer, encouraged her with elocution lessons. She is remembered in her youth for daring, single-minded concentration upon her craft and restless demands for new challenges. Her early performances on tour for the Trust included Bubba in Ray Lawler's SUMMER OF THE SEVENTEENTH DOLL and a chorus member in Medea, starring Judith Anderson in 1956. Studying with the Royal Shakespeare Company on a three-year scholarship from the Trust, she began to make an impact in England in 1959, as Bianca to Paul Robeson's Othello, Helena in All's Well that Ends Well, and Cordelia to Charles Laughton's Lear.

She is now widely regarded as one of the best actors working in America. Christopher Plummer, with whom she played many roles, once called her 'the perfect chameleon'. On Broadway she won Tony Awards for best dramatic actress for her 1968 performance in the title-role of Muriel Spark's The Prime of Miss Jean Brodie and in 1982 for her Medea. The production of Medea, directed by her husband Robert Whitehead, was reproduced for the grand opening of the Playhouse at the VICTORIAN ARTS CENTRE in Melbourne in May 1984. ❦Katharine Brisbane.

further reading
HERBERT, IAN (ed.). Who's Who in the Theatre 17th edn. Detroit (USA): Gale Research 1987.
KIPPAX, H. G. Razzle-dazzle over dog pack. Contemporary Australian Drama (ed. Peter Holloway). Sydney: Currency Press 1981.

Cordelia Cameron

Actor. Probably born in England. Originally Cordelia Bouchiere. Came to Hobart with husband Samson Cameron 18 September 1833. Acted in first dramatic performance in Hobart, 24 December 1833. In first dramatic season in Launceston, 5 June to 6 December 1834. Hobart from December 1834 to September 1836. At Theatre Royal, Sydney, from 22 October 1836 to January 1837. At Royal Victoria Theatre, Sydney, 1837–39. Acted in Adelaide 1840–41. Retired from theatre 1857.

With her husband SAMSON CAMERON, Cordelia Cameron launched theatre in Tasmania, as Mrs Haller in Friedrich von Kotzebue's The Stranger in Hobart on 24 December 1833. In Hobart and Launceston she was considered a classical actress of the highest order and a respectable mother, but it was in Sydney that she made her mark. The Australian described her on 21 October 1836 as a regularly educated English actress.

She was seen as a realistic performer with little tricks of naturalism such as playing with the hands and props to show emotion. At the Theatre Royal in Sydney in October–November 1836 other actresses picked up Cameron's affectation of catching her breath. Cameron and ELIZA WINSTANLEY were noted as the only actresses in town who would disfigure the countenance with make-up in the name of art. But in the first King Lear at the Theatre Royal on 23 January 1837 her dead Cordelia laughed in the face of CONRAD KNOWLES when he forgot his lines.

Cordelia Cameron's career followed her husband's in most details, except for two temporary separations, probably for financial reasons. In September and October 1834 she managed his theatre at the British Hotel in Launceston while he tried unsuccessfully to arrange a season for them in Sydney. In October 1839, the Sydney Gazette mentioned that Mrs Cameron had a family 'depending on her unaided exertions for support'. Next month she bolted from her creditors by the Augustus Caesar to Hobart. She performed at the Steam Packet Tavern in Launceston in December 1839 and January 1840, then took her two children to join Samson Cameron at his little Royal Victoria Theatre in Adelaide. She arrived on 15 February 1840, to sympathetic reports in the South Australian Register.

Later highlights of her career include acting with FRANCIS NESBITT, Knowles and GUSTAVUS ARABIN at F. B. Watson's Royal Olympic Theatre in Launceston on 24 July 1843, and starring opposite Nesbitt in John Howard Payne's Brutus at the Queen's Theatre Royal in Melbourne on 23 June 1845. Like her husband, she appears to have ended up in provincial theatres. In her extensive provincial career she maintained her reputation as a serious actor of heavy roles, forsaking Cordelia and Nell Gwyn for Lady Macbeth as she aged. She is last heard of as Lady Macbeth opposite MORTON KING in Adelaide in early April 1851. The fate of the Camerons is a mystery. They probably became anachronisms as public taste for their classical pieces waned. ❦Helen Musa

further reading
CAMERON, CORDELIA. Letter. Launceston Advertiser 29 October 1839.

Reginald Cameron OAM

Actor. Born 7 July 1912 at Rockhampton (Qld). Began acting in radio in 1930s. Studio manager in commercial radio. Acted in theatre 1960–88. Also in film and television. Advance Australia Award 1989. Lifetime achievement award from Queensland Theatre Company 1991. OAM 1994.

A distinguished character actor in Brisbane for 50 years, Reginald Cameron is especially remembered as Pizarro in the QUEENSLAND THEATRE COMPANY's inaugural production of Peter Shaffer's The Royal Hunt of the Sun in 1969. He was also notable in William Wycherley's The Country Wife for TWELFTH NIGHT THEATRE, as Shylock for the COLLEGE PLAYERS, and as Gonzalo in The Tempest and Dr Chasuble in Oscar

Wilde's *The Importance of Being Earnest* for the Queensland Theatre Company. Cameron's was one of the best-known voices in ABC radio drama. ❦*Bruce Parr*

Samson Cameron

Actor, manager. Arrived at Hobart with wife Cordelia 18 September 1833. Gave first public dramatic performance in Hobart 24 December 1833. Gave first dramatic season in Launceston, 5 June to 6 December 1834. Acted in Hobart from December 1834 to September 1836. Acted at Theatre Royal, Sydney, 22 October 1836 to January 1837. Opened Theatre Royal, Hobart, 6 March 1837. Acted at Royal Victoria Theatre, Sydney, 1837–39. Opened Victoria Theatre, Adelaide, 27 November 1839. Acted in Adelaide 1840–41. Opened Victoria Theatre, Launceston, April 1842. Insolvent September 1842. Acted at Royal Olympic Theatre, Launceston, from October 1842 and became partner of F. B. Watson. Ran Royal Victoria Theatre, Melbourne, May 1844 to March 1845. Acted at Queen's Theatre Royal, Melbourne, from April 1845. Acted in Geelong from March 1846. Retired from theatre 1857.

Samson Cameron founded professional theatre in Hobart and Launceston and made his mark in NSW, South Australia and Victoria. Hundreds were turned away when he launched professional theatre in Van Diemen's Land in the FREEMASON'S TAVERN in Hobart on 24 December 1833 with Friedrich von Kotzebue's *The Stranger*, starring his wife CORDELIA CAMERON.

The *Hobart Town Courier* praised Cameron on 27 December as an 'intelligent, moral man' and he was seen as the standard-bearer of culture. But next month there were complaints about his high seat prices—four shillings and six shillings—and his heavy repertoire. It was in the heavy pieces, however, that Cameron established his credentials in an era when critics set the formal standards. He was always his wife's artistic inferior, constantly attacked for bad taste in sets and props and for affected pronunciation and he was probably an incompetent manager, but he survived by energetically fighting bitter battles with his rivals and by manipulating the press.

Cameron chose *The Stranger* again when he opened the first theatre in Launceston at the British Hotel in June 1834. He left his wife in charge in September and rushed to Sydney to negotiate the use of a theatre, the *Sydney Herald* reported on 22 September 1834. But he returned empty-handed and extended the season to December, when he went to Hobart. He played at the ARGYLE ROOMS until mid-1835. During a second season at the British Hotel in Launceston, Cameron staged the first performance of Evan Henry Thomas's play THE BANDIT OF THE RHINE. A season at the Freemason's Tavern in Hobart failed in January 1836. The *Colonial Times* of 22 March 1836 accused the Camerons of 'courting the aristocracy' with their prices and star manners. Cameron joined the company of his rival JOHN MEREDITH but seceded in July 1836 and in September he took rooms in the Macquarie Hotel for performances.

In October 1836 the Camerons began a 12-week engagement for JOSEPH WYATT in *The Stranger* at the Theatre Royal in Sydney. Sydney reviews in November 1836 show Samson Cameron as a preachy actor with a weak voice that had not been helped by working in the tiny theatres of Hobart. He was regarded as a realistic actor whose 'cool air' put even CONRAD KNOWLES in the shade, according to the *Sydney Gazette* of 5 January 1837. Cameron acted in the controversial first Australian production of *King Lear*—with the tragic ending—in January 1837. He left the Theatre Royal after a disagreement with Wyatt, reported in the *Australian* on 20 January 1837, and obtained a licence for dramatic entertainments at the Pulteney Hotel.

In Hobart again in March 1837, Cameron opened the New THEATRE ROYAL, in opposition to Meredith. After several weeks Meredith, JAMES BELMORE and Moses joined Cameron in a 'coalition management' until the season closed on 31 July. Cameron's rivalry with Meredith in Hobart led them to mutually request licensing laws, but none was passed until 1 October 1842.

Cameron returned to Sydney and played at the Royal Victoria Theatre until October 1839, when Wyatt reduced salaries and Cameron fled creditors. He went to Adelaide, where in November 1839 he opened the Victoria Theatre in a stringybark building with *The Stranger*, which was attacked for 'German sentimentality'. His wife joined him in a second Adelaide season in 1840. He was in the cast when JOHN LAZAR opened the Queen's Theatre in Adelaide with *Othello* on 11 January 1841.

In Launceston in April 1842 Cameron opened the Royal Victoria Theatre in the Kangaroo Hotel in competition with the Royal Olympic Theatre run by F. B. WATSON. The rivalry ended with Cameron insolvent, and Watson engaged the Camerons as performers at the Olympic.

In May 1844, after the death of Conrad Knowles, Cameron took over the ROYAL VICTORIA THEATRE in Melbourne. In September there were riots when he refused to withdraw *The Jewess* in response to demands from Catholics who were offended by a representation of Passover, believing it to mock the mass. Eventual withdrawal of the play caused losses that led to closure of the theatre. Cameron was imprisoned at Christmas for not handing the theatre over to the receiver.

He later gained a new licence, however, and reopened the Royal Victoria in February 1845. When the QUEEN'S THEATRE ROYAL opened in April 1845, under the management of FRANCIS NESBITT, Cameron joined the company. He joined a theatre company in Geelong in March 1846 and he seems to have remained there, managing a theatre for Hassett. Cameron appeared at the Theatre Royal in Geelong on 28 November 1848 and he is last mentioned, in the *Adelaide Times* of 12 April 1851, as playing Banquo to MORTON KING's Macbeth. ❦*Helen Musa*

Beverley Campbell Jackson

Designer, puppet-maker. Born 16 May 1935 in Melbourne. Trained in graphic arts and teaching. Introduced to puppetry by Peter Scriven in Malaysia 1971. Tutor in Australia Council puppetry trainee scheme 1975–76. Died 9 June 1989 in Sydney.

A talent for developing and improving construction technique made Beverley Campbell Jackson especially valuable in puppetry. In 1981 she helped to found the SPARE PARTS PUPPET THEATRE COMPANY in Fremantle (WA), and designed and made puppets for *Faust*. For the MARIONETTE THEATRE OF AUSTRALIA she designed *Aesop's Fables* and *Bottersnikes and Gumbles* in 1982. She also worked for the TASMANIAN PUPPET THEATRE, the Puppet People in Brisbane and for television puppet series. ❦*Richard Bradshaw*

Canberra

The national capital, Canberra supports a range of performing arts that is astonishing for a city of 300 000 people. The only fully planned city in Australia, it was laid out in a valley in the Southern Highlands, 300 km from Sydney and 600 km from Melbourne. Building began in 1913. The population grew sharply whenever the federal government moved a department to the new capital, but the World Wars and the Great Depression made for slow and sporadic growth before 1950. There was artistic talent among the young university graduates who formed a large proportion of the growing community, but there was no arts activity until a few energetic enthusiasts set about creating their own. In 1925, when the population was about 5500, volunteers built the Causeway Hall. Next year it housed the first theatrical production in Canberra, Douglas Murray's comedy *The Man from Toronto*. staged by A. J. Pate and the Community Players—their only production.

In 1927 the Society for Arts and Literature was set up to encourage music, drama, the visual arts and literature. The leading figures included Sir Robert Garran, Solicitor-General; R. A. Broinowski, later Clerk of the Senate; Harold White, later National Librarian; and Leslie Allen, lecturer in English at Royal Military College, Duntroon. The society comprised a central committee plus subcommittees to organise programs in the visual arts, music and drama—initially talks and play readings.

Within a year the visual arts and music subcommittees had withdrawn and set up separate societies, leaving the parent body with literature and drama. Lewis Nott, a flamboyant amateur actor who came to Canberra as independent member for the Queensland seat of Herbert, took the drama committee from one-act play evenings to popular full-length plays in the large Albert Hall. His productions from 1928 included Sydney Grundy's *Much Married*, Fred Jackson's *The Naughty Wife*, Cyril Harcourt's *A Pair of Silk Stockings* and Clemence Dane's *A Bill of Divorcement*. Nott's choice of plays and his disregard for budgets and the committee's resolutions gave rise to tension. After many rows, Nott walked out in 1932 and formed the CANBERRA REPERTORY SOCIETY. For a year the two societies competed in staging plays at the Albert Hall, draining themselves of funds and energy. The Arts and Literature Society, plagued by debt, was wound up by 1938. Nott was also producer of the Canberra Amateur Operatic Society, which presented an operetta or two a year at the Albert Hall from 1934 to 1939.

Annual subsidy

The Canberra Repertory Society obtained a small annual government grant in 1949. This enabled it to expand its programs and employ a full-time manager–producer and a part-time secretary. The manager-producer in 1961, Allen Harvey, founded Canberra Children's Theatre, in which adults staged plays for children. Canberra Repertory remains an important theatrical presence in the city, as does the CANBERRA PHILHARMONIC SOCIETY, established in 1951. This amateur society relies on its members for its successful seasons of musical theatre but draws upon professionals as required.

Canberra's population was 88 500 and growing rapidly when the CANBERRA THEATRE CENTRE, housing the Canberra Theatre and the Playhouse, opened in 1965. New theatrical groups emerged in the 1960s, including the Theatre Players, founded and directed by Joyce Goodes. Productions she staged in various venues included *Marriages are Made in Heaven*, a musical by the creators of THE SENTIMENTAL BLOKE, Albert Arlen, Nancy Brown and Lloyd Thomson. The group was wound up in 1972 and Goodes invested the remaining funds and arranged for Canberra Repertory to allocate the interest annually to a small scholarship for an ACT tertiary student of performing arts.

In the late 1960s the local playwright Mil Perrin and the directors Warwick Baxter, Rod Charls and Ralph Wilson set up the Australian Theatre Workshop to stage low-budget productions of new scripts and experimental plays. Its productions at Childers Street Hall and at the Australian National University Arts Centre, opened in 1979, included ALEX BUZO's *Rooted*, ROGER PULVERS's *Drop Drill*, Sam Shepard's *Buried Child* and four plays by Samuel Beckett directed by Wilson—*Embers*, *Play*, *Eh Joe* and *Not I*. Another 1960s group was Al Butavicius's short-lived Prompt Theatre, whose productions included works by writers in Papua, New Guinea and Indonesia.

University satirists

Students' theatre flourished at the Australian National University during the 1960s and early 1970s, when satirical revues and plays were staged at Childers Street Hall. A company of graduates and undergraduates, Stage presented offbeat end-of-year pantomimes by Viv Whittaker and annual Victoriana nights during the 1960s. In 1972, a federal election year, Stage played to packed houses with *Misrepresentations—or, No matter who you vote for a politician always gets in*, a political revue written by the journalist Mungo MacCallum and directed by Anne Godfrey-Smith.

Canberra Children's Theatre moved to Reid House in 1972 and was renamed CANBERRA YOUTH THEATRE. Its five actor–tutors also worked as a theatre-in-education troupe formally established in 1974 as the JIGSAW THEATRE COMPANY. The two groups, both directed by Carol Woodrow, comprised Reid House Theatre Workshop. They became separate organisations, each with its own director and performing space, in 1982, after they moved to Gorman House Arts Centre. Two children's theatre companies were formed in the 1970s. Blue Folk Community Theatre, directed by Domenic Mico, staged plays for children, mostly in the open air. It is defunct, but Alpha Children's Theatre, established to provide shows for children on Saturday and Sunday afternoons, still stages an annual production.

Carol Woodrow brought together a project-funded, full-time collective of actors called Fool's Gallery, which created six impressive productions during 1979–83 and toured them extensively. These works were mostly feminist in theme. *Standard Operating Procedure*, on rape, was perhaps the most powerful of them.

In 1980 Joe Woodward, a director, and David Bates, a composer, leased a back bar from the Canberra Rex Hotel and established Pits Theatre. In conjunction with guest directors they produced political revues, melodrama, Shakespeare, colonial plays and original scripts until they lost their lease in 1984.

Canberra gained its first professional theatre company in 1980 when Fortune, a small actor's co-operative for several years, obtained funding. It gave its first production at the newly opened ANU Arts Centre. Then the company—renamed Theatre ACT by its first artistic director, GEORGE WHALEY—gave several poorly attended seasons at the Playhouse. On returning to the ANU Arts Centre it had its first big success with RON ELISHA's *Einstein*. Audiences increased satisfactorily but the company lost support after Whaley and his successor Peter Barclay moved on.

In the early 1980s, when Canberra's population was about 250 000 there were several new ventures. Women on a Shoestring began activity in 1981, directed by Camilla Blunden. She developed the group from Women's Theatre Workshop with the help of the Commonwealth Employment Program. The women devised their own scripts on the basis of a text or a theme; *Old Girls Never Die* and *Did You Say Love?* sent up 1930s schoolgirl stories and Barbara Cartland novels respectively. They also staged little-known plays, such as Grazyna Monvid's powerful *The Enemy Within,* and new works. Among the latter have been Mary Hutchison's *Child of the Hurricane,* about the writer KATHARINE SUSANNAH PRICHARD, and two plays by Merrilee Moss—*Over the Hill,* about menopause myths, and *Empty Suitcases,* a play with songs about historic and present-day female travellers.

Another project-funded group was People Next Door, a partnership of Monica Barone and Boris Laraski (Boris Kelly). In a variety of venues they performed their own scripts, such as *When You Wish,* a musical satire on Australia after the Second World War.

Young people's stories

A Canberra Youth Theatre project for unemployed young people gave rise to Troupe. With the director Gail Kelly, in 1981–85 Troupe staged group-devised and commissioned scripts, including *Treatment,* a moving play about handicapped children in an institution, and *The Wish Palace* by Kate McNamara, about young people exploited by consumer society. Stagecoach Theatre School, set up in 1982, encourages young people to explore stories and themes and develop their own scripts for production. Successive casts of Stagecoach students have presented *Real Kids,* a show about young people in Canberra, to thousands of visiting schoolchildren. *Real Kids* is now entirely produced by the students. Stagecoach was directed by its founder, Chris Rutter, until 1985 and by Joe Woodward from 1985 to 1994.

Aldo Gennaro and Domenic Mico founded a broad-based community theatre group, THROUGH ART, UNITY, in 1983, and in 1984 the Skylark Puppet and Mask Company was formed to perform for children and adults. Now called Skylark Theatre Company, it often deals with contemporary issues, such as drug abuse in *The Inside Story,* a play written for puppets and an actor. It staged a fine production by PETER J. WILSON, *Inside Dry Water,* at the National Festival of Australian Theatre in October 1993.

Joyce McFarlane and others founded Tempo Theatre, an amateur society, in 1975 to stage small-scale, lesser-known musicals at the Playhouse and later at Canberra Repertory's Theatre 3. They included *A Funny Thing Happened on the Way to the Forum*; *Oh, What a Lovely War!*; *Will—Man from Stratford* by the local playwright Don McInnis; and *Overpaid, Oversexed and Over Here,* written and directed by Trevor Findlay. During 1984–86 Tempo, sponsored by the Canberra Theatre Trust, staged three large-scale, semiprofessional productions—*Chicago*; *Hello, Dolly!* and *Sweeney Todd*—at the Canberra Theatre. Tempo now stages straight plays from time to time. In 1993 it began a nine-month finance-restoring tour of NSW clubs, playing Jack Hibberd's DIMBOOLA for the entrepreneur Andrew Laing.

Theatre ACT was revived in 1986 as Fortune Capital Theatre, with a company of ten and DON MAMOUNEY as artistic director. It presented some interesting productions in the Childers Street Hall but audiences stayed away. Financial problems led to withdrawal of funding and Fortune Capital Theatre was wound up. Three companies were interested in succeeding it as the regional professional company—Eureka! Theatre, an actors' co-operative set up by Phillip MacKenzie and Rod Charls in 1986; Black Inc., directed by Paul Corcoran; and Interact, formerly Ensemble Theatre Project, set up by Carol Woodrow and funded by the Commonwealth Employment Program.

All three companies received project grants, but none was offered funding as Canberra's professional company. They all staged productions in various venues—the Playhouse, the ANU Arts Centre, Gorman House Arts Centre, and the Canberra Theatre rehearsal room for lunchtime seasons, which are always popular in Canberra. Eureka! Theatre's productions included Michael Gow's *AWAY*, Louise Page's *Salonika*, HANNIE RAYSON's *Room to Move* and Sam Shepard's *Lie of the Mind*. Black Inc. seasons included the cabaret-revue *Jacques Brel is Alive and Living in Paris*, Henrik Ibsen's *A Doll's House*, Alfred Jarry's *Ubu-roi* and Luigi Pirandello's *Naked*. Interact, directed by Woodrow, presented a mixture of classical and new Australian plays. The latter included *Grandfather is Dying* by Lissa Benyon and *An Ocean at My Window* by ANDREW BOVELL.

The Australian Theatre Workshop developed into Rawil Productions, formed by Ralph Wilson in 1987 to stage low-cost, high-quality productions of contemporary and classic European plays in a theatre at Gorman House Arts Centre that was later called the Ralph Wilson Theatre. Rawil productions included *The Wild Duck* by Henrik Ibsen, *Bring Back Our Heroes* by the local playwright Jane Bradhurst, *Strategy for Two Hams* by Raymond Cousse, *Mother Courage* by Bertholt Brecht and *Happy Days* and *Footfalls* by Beckett.

In 1988 Eureka! Theatre and Interact amalgamated as the Canberra Theatre Company, with Carol Woodrow as director and Rod Charls as associate director. The company gained a grant from the ACT Arts Development Board and a major sponsor offered it $100 000 a year for three years. In 1989 it began a program of plays at the Playhouse and the ANU Arts Centre. The plays included *A Midsummer Night's Dream, Les Liaisons dangereuses* by Christopher Hampton, *Wallflowering* by Peta Murray, *Balancing Act* by Jennifer Paynton, *Hate* by STEPHEN SEWELL and *The Popular Mechanicals* by Keith Robinson and TONY TAYLOR. Charls left Canberra after the second season. In 1990 the company lost its chief sponsor and it was wound up.

Eureka! Theatre co-operative has continued to operate with the help of project grants, staging well-attended lunchtime, twilight and evening seasons of contemporary short plays in the Courtyard Studio, formerly the Canberra Theatre rehearsal room. With Camilla Blunden as director, Eureka! Theatre presented a revue satirising politicians and bureaucrats, *A Night on the PS*, in 1992 and gave it a return season in 1993.

In 1990 the Australian National University set up a drama program with a convenor to lecture in drama and direct plays. The first convenor did not stay long and was succeeded by Pierre Bokor, a Canadian. Using local professional and amateur actors and students from the program, he staged productions under the title of Studio. They included *Jacques and His Master* by Milan Kundera, *The Kiss of the Spiderwoman* by Manuel Puig and *Les Belles-soeurs* by Michel Tremblay. Bokor left in 1992 and was succeeded by Geoffrey Borny, who stages productions under the title Paper Moon. They have included *A Streetcar Named Desire* and *The Glass Menagerie* by Tennessee Williams, *The Cherry Orchard* by Anton Chekhov, *Breaking the Silence* by Stephen Poliakoff and *Julius Caesar*. The Paper Moon productions are managed by the ANU Arts Centre but otherwise rely on box office to cover costs.

The university's Campus Amateur Dramatic Society also stages plays. In 1993 Nicholas Bolonkin directed an imaginative production of Christopher Marlowe's *The Tragical History of Doctor Faustus* in the Courtyard Studio. There is another student group at the University of Canberra, the Canberra University Theatre Society. It staged plays in the Belconnen Community Centre and the Ralph Wilson Theatre until a small theatre was opened on the campus. There are keen drama teachers and students in several secondary schools in Canberra. Peter Wilkins, formerly artistic director of the Jigsaw Theatre Company, runs the drama program at Narrabundah College, which has a graduate company, the Actors Company, attached to it.

Professional companies' problems
Carol Woodrow, Monica Barone and Boris Kelly combined in 1993 to form a new professional company called WBK. Granted funding on an annual basis, it staged its inaugural production, Ariel Dorfman's *Death and the Maiden*, in the Playhouse in May 1994. Funding was later withdrawn. With rising costs and little likelihood of increased government funding, full-time professional companies in a city of Canberra's size face multiplying problems. In late 1994 these companies were Eureka! Theatre, Jigsaw and Skylark Theatre. Out-of-town professional companies visit the Canberra Theatre Centre more frequently nowadays, and the centre has run the National Festival of Australian Theatre in three Octobers between 1990 and 1994. Given these developments, it seems likely that most of Canberra's talented performers will continue to find work with project-funded groups or else, paid or not, with companies like Canberra Repertory or the Canberra Philharmonic Society.

Tango 160 is another project-funded enterprise, in which the playwright Fiona McVilly and the actor–director Renald Navarro explore themes and imagery based on a character. In their widely toured *Solitude, My Mother*, they projected magnificent wilderness slides as the backdrop to Navarro's exploration of the world of the nature photographer Olegas Truchanas. A newcomer, the Company, directed by Eulea Kiraly, impressively presented *Ficky Stingers*, based on a script by Eva Lewis, in 1993 and followed it with Jean Anouilh's *Antigone* at the ANU Arts Centre in July 1994. Fire, street circus, masks and pageant feature largely in the work of Splinters, a controversial and confrontational young collective, which performs locally and in fringe festivals.

Some community-theatre groups have disappeared after a season or two of activity. More established groups include Latin America Live, which is led by the playwright–director Jorge Bagnini and develops opportunities for actors and writers among Latin Americans in Canberra. It staged Bagnini's play *Malleo Man of Salt* in 1993 and Nelly Fernando Tiscornia's *Made in Argentina* in 1994. The Phoenix Players, active in Belconnen for some years, stage mostly musicals. Domenic Mico, now a community arts officer, organises and directs productions for Tuggeranong Playgroup Theatre. A new community theatre, the Street Theatre, was opened in May 1994. It is run by a management group called Stagemaster. ❦*Anne Edgeworth*

Canberra Philharmonic Society

Amateur musical-theatre society founded in 1951 by William Hunt and Bob Wallace. **venues** Albert Hall 1951–65. Canberra Theatre 1965–. **artistic directors** 1977–78 Bill Stephens. 1979 Hec McMillan. 1980–81 Lois Adamson. 1982–83 John Thomson. 1984–86 Moya Hubbard. 1987 Lois Adamson. 1988 Coralie Wood. 1989 Wayne Shepherd. **musical directors** 1951–59 William Hunt. 1960–63 Roland Pogson. 1964–67 William Hunt. 1968–71 Alan Christie. 1972 Gillian Bonham. 1973–78 Don Whitbread. 1979 Myra Law. 1980 Christopher Lyndon-Gee. 1981–85 Colin Fischer. 1986 Wilf Jones. 1987–88 Liz Hemer. 1989 Jim McMullen.

The first amateur society to venture into the large Canberra Theatre at the CANBERRA THEATRE CENTRE was the Canberra Philharmonic Society, which staged *The Yeomen of the Guard* there in 1965. This Gilbert and Sullivan operetta was also the work with which the society made its debut, in a concert performance in the Albert Hall in 1951. The society first presented fully staged works in 1953—*Bless the Bride* in April and *The Arcadians* in October. Both drew full houses for three-night seasons. For the next 12 years the society staged one or two operettas a year, battling limitations of acoustics and stage in the Albert Hall. William Hunt, musical director, and Lois Bellingham, producer, were in charge of most works. Gilbert and Sullivan predominated among English and European operettas until 1965, when the society staged *Oklahoma!*, its first American musical.

At the Canberra Theatre the society staged two or three productions a year. In 1969, Terry Vaughan, general manager of the Canberra Theatre Centre and formerly of the KIWIS, directed a fine production of *La Belle Hélène* as guest producer and conductor. *Annie Get Your Gun*, directed by Bill Stephens, was outstanding in 1976. Stephens directed five more productions, including *Fiddler on the Roof* in 1978, *Mame* in 1983 and *Kismet* in 1986. By the 1980s the orchestra numbered more than 20 players, mostly professionals. This fact, plus the employment of guest directors, designers, choreographers and singers as required, steadily increased production costs. Public and private funding was obtained and since 1989 the society has not appointed a musical director and an artistic director to organise and oversee its productions. The executive committee now appoints directors for each show. Professional input ensures high standards, but the society depends upon its members for its achievements. These include *The Sentimental Bloke*, directed by Lois Adamson, in 1984 and its most ambitious production, *Les Misérables*, with an entirely local cast directed by Colin Anderson in 1994. The latter season, sold out in advance, was a triumph. ❦*Anne Edgeworth*

Canberra Repertory Society

Amateur dramatic company founded in 1932 by Lewis Nott. In recess 1943–44. **venues** 1932–34, 1940–43, 1944–46 Albert Hall. 1947–51 Radio 2CA theatrette. 1952 Albert Hall. 1953–65 Riverside Theatre. 1965–72 Playhouse. 1973– Theatre 3. **directors** 1950–51 Adrian Borzell. 1952–53 Alan Burke. 1954–58 Anne Godfrey-Smith. 1959 Eric Reiman. 1960-63 Allen Harvey. 1964–67 Peter Batey. 1970–71 Allen Harvey. 1972 Sean Surplus. 1973–77 Ross McGregor. 1978–79 Michael Lanchbery. 1980 Ken Boucher. 1981 Pam Rosenberg. **managers** 1982–84 Jesse Shore. 1984–86 Robyn Newton. 1986–93 Evol McLeod. 1994– Stephanie Hayes.

In its first 62 years the Canberra Repertory Society staged 329 mainstage productions plus 20 Old Time Music Halls and many workshop productions and one-act plays. From 1955 to 1959 it organised the drama section of the National Eisteddfod at its Riverside Theatre. In the 1970s it ran seven annual non-competitive festivals of one-act plays, in which many works by local playwrights were staged. In 1980 the society set up a biennial competitive Festival of Australian Drama with large cash prizes donated by local firms. Interest was keen but only two festivals were held, partly because visiting entrants faced rising travel costs.

Canberra Repertory no longer employs a resident director, but has a full-time manager and engages directors as required. It stages four or five seasons a year at Theatre 3, plus its chief source of income, the Old Time Music Hall, directed by Rosemary Hyde, at the Australian National University Arts Centre. During the late 1980s the society's Classical Theatre Ensemble, directed by Ralph Wilson, staged productions of Aristophanes's *Lysistrata*, Nikolai Gogol's *The Government Inspector*, Molière's *Tartuffe* and William Wycherley's *The Country Wife*.

Lack of finance confined the society's activities to members' nights until 1940, when it gave public performances in aid of the war effort. Canberra Repertory was in recess in 1943–44. In 1947, with a growing membership and a lease of the radio 2CA theatrette, the society expanded its program from sporadic shows at the Albert Hall to seven or eight productions a year. In 1949, through the support of the Prime Minister, Ben Chifley, the local Committee for Cultural Development awarded the society an annual government grant of £900—the first to any theatre group in Australia. It was used to pay for a full-time manager–producer and a part-time secretary.

In 1953 the Department of the Interior leased a hut at Riverside, a former workers' hostel, to the society. The architects converted it into a small theatre, which opened with *The Government Inspector*, directed by the manager–producer, Alan Burke. For the next 12 years at the Riverside Theatre the society gave seven or eight seasons over ten months of the year, playing on Friday and Saturday nights; for the first five years it gave Sunday-night play-readings as well. It presented mainly contemporary plays, mostly by Irish, American and European playwrights. It also gave a few premieres of Australian works—Ric Throssell's plays *Devil Wear Black*, *Day before Tomorrow*, *Legend* and *For Valour*, Alan Seymour's *Swamp Creatures*, Albert Arlen's musical *Girl from the Snowy*, and *Ulterior Motifs*, a musical satirising bureaucrats and politicians by Throssell, Anne Godfrey-Smith and Peter Sculthorpe.

In 1965 the society took its major productions to the new Playhouse in the Canberra Theatre Centre. The Riverside Theatre was used for lunchtime performances and workshop productions until it was destroyed by fire in 1967. The Playhouse involved higher costs and fewer and shorter seasons. Peter Batey, then manager–producer, employed professional actors and was keen for Canberra Repertory to become the region's professional company. The membership, however, did not accept his proposal.

In 1973, the society leased the old Canberra High School hall and members converted it to an excellent intimate theatre called Theatre 3, with gantry and a revolving stage. With Ross McGregor as resident director, Theatre 3 housed some exciting productions, especially of contemporary American and Australian works. The society received grants from the Australia Council as well as the ACT Committee for Cultural Development. These organisations also pressed the society to become Canberra's professional regional theatre company, but it elected to remain amateur, with professional input, and as a result lost its Australia Council funding. Funding from local government also began to disappear. The quality of the society's annual programs, however, remains consistently high as does the community's support. ❦*Anne Edgeworth*

further reading
Edgeworth, Anne. *The Cost of Jazz Garters—A history of the Canberra Repertory Society 1932–82*. Canberra Repertory Society 1992.

Canberra Theatre Centre

Performing-arts centre in Civic Square, opened 24 June 1965. Architects: Yuncken Freeman. Comprises multipurpose **Canberra Theatre**, seating 1200 (later 1189), and **Playhouse**, seating 310 Directors: Terry Vaughan MBE 1965–80; Christopher Bedloe 1980–85. General managers: George Whaley 1983–85; Simon Dawkins 1986–89; David Gration 1990–.

The first government-initiated performing-arts centre completed in an Australian capital city was the Canberra Theatre Centre, conceived by the National Capital Development Commission. When it opened, the multipurpose one-level Canberra Theatre—for touring orchestras, opera, ballet and dramatic companies—had the largest stage in the country, 29·5 metres deep with a proscenium adjustable up to 17 metres wide. The smaller Playhouse, for use by local groups, has a shallow eight-metre-deep proscenium stage without fly tower. A covered way linking the theatres was enclosed in the late 1970s to provide additional box-office space and a foyer-cum-art gallery. Behind the main theatre is the Courtyard Theatre, a flexible space used for rehearsals and performances. A general manager runs the complex for the Canberra Theatre Trust, whose members are appointed on three-year contracts by the ACT Minister of the Arts. The centre houses local and touring productions of drama, ballet and opera. Since 1990 the theatre trust has run in October three National Festivals of Australian Theatre, directed by Robyn Archer. In 1994 it initiated a Performing Arts Market to show new work to visiting entrepreneurs. ❦*Ross Thorne*

Canberra Youth Theatre

> Youth-theatre organisation founded in 1961 as Canberra Children's Theatre. Renamed Canberra Youth Theatre 1972. **venues** 1972–81 Reid House. 1982– Gorman House Arts Centre. **directors** 1974–78 Carol Woodrow. 1979 John Oakley. 1980–82 Tim Mackay and Steve Payne. 1983–85 Gail Kelly. 1986–89 Amanda Field. 1990– Roland Manderson.

In 1961 the manager-producer of the CANBERRA REPERTORY SOCIETY, Allen Harvey, encouraged parents to form Canberra Children's Theatre, in which adults staged plays for children. In 1972, after working in various venues, it moved to Reid House, becoming Canberra Youth Theatre and part of the Reid House Theatre Workshop. Its first director, Carol Woodrow changed it to a youth theatre group emphasising workshops. Encouraged by their tutors, the young people have devised many interesting productions, including *The Adventures of the Super Space Pongs*, a commentary on current global issues.

Canberra Youth Theatre has also staged Dylan Thomas's *Under Milk Wood*, Eugène Ionesco's *The Killing Game*, Frank Wedekind's *Spring's Awakening*, and *Spanner in the Works*, written and directed by Fiona McVilly. In 1982, after a move to Gorman House, Canberra Youth Theatre became a separate body. In 1993 it took its play *Shopping—For Boys* to the Aberdeen Festival in Scotland. *Anne Edgeworth*

Capitol Theatre

> Theatre in Campbell Street, opened 3 April 1916 as **Hippodrome**, seating 1846 on three levels. Architects: R. H. Brodrick and G. Merriman. Reopened with rebuilt interior seating 2973 on two levels, as **Capitol Theatre**, 7 April 1928. Architects: John Eberson and Henry E. White. Closed 1983. Rebuilt and restored for reopening in 1995.

Built as a circus-cum-theatre, the Capitol Theatre stands on a site in Haymarket with a long history of entertainment. In 1854 markets for hay, corn and cattle occupied land bounded by Campbell, Elizabeth, Hay and George Streets and intersected by Pitt and Castlereagh Streets. In 1869 a vegetable market was built on the cattle market, between Castlereagh and Pitt Streets, but the hay market, between Pitt and George Streets, remained largely open space, called the Haymarket Reserve. This was used on Saturday nights for 'Paddy's Market' and sideshows. Visiting circuses also pitched their tents there, including Wilson's San Francisco Palace Circus in 1876 and Cooper and Bailey's circus, also from the USA, in 1877. The Wirth brothers set up their first circus there in 1882. In 1892–93 the Sydney City Council built the enclosed Belmore Market on the site. On nearby open space E. I. Cole's BOHEMIAN DRAMATIC COMPANY performed bush melodramas in a tent called the Hippodrome from 1903 to about 1908.

The Belmore Market building quickly outgrew its usefulness and from 1909 the markets were progressively removed. The council then leased the Belmore Market for theatrical purposes. In 1912 WIRTHS' CIRCUS took it for 10 weeks, and then leased half the site for 21 years. On this council built the Hippodrome for the Wirths. It was a theatre with a 12-metre-diameter circus ring in the front stalls. Behind this was a large fly-tower stage for melodrama, which alternated with the touring circus.

The elaborate brick-and-terracotta exterior of the Belmore Market was dismantled and re-erected in the Hippodrome. It remained when the Hippodrome was converted to the Capitol Theatre, an 'atmospheric' picture palace with simulated Florentine garden walls and 'sky' ceiling. The stage was reduced to half its depth and the capacity increased to 2973 on two levels. Film shows included variety performances on stage during the 1930s.

Stage performance returned and the Capitol's acoustic suitability for musical theatre was revealed in August 1970, when the Australian Opera moved in after HER MAJESTY'S THEATRE was destroyed by fire. HARRY M. MILLER leased the Capitol for two years from December 1971 and presented a long season of his spectacular production of the rock musical *Jesus Christ Superstar*. For the remainder of the 1970s the theatre was a venue for rock concerts. Through the 1980s and into the 1990s theatrical entrepreneurs pressed for rehabilitation or rebuilding of the theatre, because Sydney could not house large musical or dance productions. This precluded such shows coming to Sydney and sometimes to Australia. There were also heritage conservation pressures, but the town clerk and the actor NOEL FERRIER advised the Sydney City Council to demolish the building.

In 1985 the Royal Australian Institute of Architects held a competition for ideas for the building. This produced publicity and aroused more interest within the council and the NSW government. The dilapidated theatre was opened for public inspection in 1987. To detractors' surprise, it drew large crowds, and visitors petitioned for its retention. After numerous false starts, caused by changes in the council, developers began rebuilding and restoration in April 1993.

The work included extending the stage across half of Hay Street, and building new dressing rooms, green room, rehearsal room, scene dock, foyer and bars in an adjoining building. The new foyers feed the audience in through the side of the existing foyer. The atmospheric auditorium has been restored, with projected clouds and twinkling stars. Technical elements such as lighting bridges have been designed to be out of sight until the lights are dimmed for performance. The exterior has been cleaned back to the terra cotta and brickwork from the Belmore Market of 1892. The council has leased the theatre for 99 years to the Capitol Theatre Management Company, a joint venture between the developers and Arena Management, which runs the 11 500-seat Sydney Entertainment Centre. The restored Capitol opened in February 1995 as a large house for touring musical-theatre productions. *Ross Thorne*

further reading

THORNE, ROSS. *Capitol Theatre—A case for retention*. University of Sydney 1985.

THORNE, ROSS. *Cinemas of Australia via USA*. University of Sydney 1981.

Carclew Youth Arts Centre

In 1971 the Premier of South Australia, Don Dunstan, announced that Carclew, a mansion in North Adelaide, would become a centre for creative activities by and for young people. He set up the South Australian Performing Arts Centre Inc., with a theatrical focus. HELMUT BAKAITIS was appointed artistic director in 1975. A subsequent government report concluded that Carclew should become the focal point for resources, projects, policy and support for youth performing arts in the state. In 1980 the Minister for the Arts appointed a new Youth Performing Arts Council to oversee this development. It appointed Roger Chapman as director of the new Carclew. Chapman, from the United Kingdom, had directed young people's theatre in the 1976 Adelaide Festival and established the MAGPIE THEATRE COMPANY. Carclew Youth Performing Arts Centre officially opened in February 1982.

By 1988, when Chapman's term ended, Carclew's staffing, programs and facilities had changed, major changes had occurred in the arts generally and youth arts other than performing arts had grown remarkably. The government established a committee of review, which reported in October 1988. It recommended that a new body should assume responsibility for all the Youth Performing Arts Council's activities and all other youth arts. The South Australian Youth Arts Board was set up in 1989 and performing, literary and visual arts have thrived at its renamed Carclew Youth Arts Centre. It has developed and maintained *Lowdown*, a national magazine of youth performing arts; the International Association of Theatre for Children and Young People; and, since 1985, the COME OUT YOUTH ARTS FESTIVAL, Australia's premier youth festival. All have been pivotal in promotion and recognition of youth performing arts. Carclew also manages the Odeon, South Australia's only theatre devoted entirely to performances for or by young people. *Michael FitzGerald*

Moira Carleton

Actor, director. Born 1910 in England. Father and grandfather were actors. Began acting in father's productions at 14. Acted in repertory from 1927. Married Australian actor Alan Matheson. Emigrated to Melbourne with family 1939. Acted and directed for Melbourne Little Theatre Company and Union Theatre Repertory Company. Acted in many radio and television productions. Died 13 June 1978 in Melbourne.

Moira Carleton was an archetype of the well-trained all-round professional who emigrates and becomes a seminal influence in the new land. She came to Melbourne with her husband Alan Matheson, whom she met in the early 1930s after he had graduated from the Royal Academy of Dramatic Art in London. He joined the Australian Army and she quickly established herself in Melbourne radio as a character actor with a brilliant command of accents. She was equally adept at comedy and drama, and on stage she had a commanding presence that made her widely popular. Her favourite role was the mother in Federico García Lorca's *The House of Bernarda Alba* at the ARROW THEATRE in the early 1950s. Later in the 1950s and in the 1960s Carleton divided her stage work, as actor and occasional director, between the Melbourne Little Theatre Company and the Union Theatre Repertory Company. With the latter in 1960 she directed the melodrama *Sweeney Todd* and played Mrs Lovett. *Laurie Landray*

Carmo the Great

Juggler, magician. Born 8 November 1881 in Melbourne. Originally Henry Cameron. Performed in minstrel shows, circus and vaudeville to 1906. Left Australia 1907. Toured with Le Roy, Talma and Bosco 1914. Toured magic shows in England. Died 1 August 1944 in Coventry (England).

A great showman, Carmo entered show business by joining the Premier Nigger Minstrels Troupe, which played in village and town halls. He was a strong man and juggler in J. D. Rowley's Waxworks and Variety Show, and later joined ASHTON'S CIRCUS. He performed head and hand balancing and juggling at the Tivoli Theatre in Melbourne in 1906. Next year he was a great hit in Paris as a juggler. England was next, and by 1910 he had become a headliner. He was a featured artist with the Le Roy, Talma and Bosco magic troupe on a short tour of Australia in 1914.

In England, Carmo had a magic show which became so big that it developed into a magical circus. He used live animals in his effects and he played big theatres such as the London Palladium. Crowds queued for tickets when he opened in London in 1929. But disasters in Birmingham, a snowstorm and then a fire, cost him much of his capital. He returned to a small magic act and played all over Britain. During the war he entertained troops. He was preparing a big new show at the time of his death. *Gerald Taylor*

further reading
FISHER, JOHN. *Paul Daniels and the Story of Magic*. London: Jonathan Cape 1987.

Freddie Carpenter

Choreographer, dancer, director. Born 15 February 1908 in Melbourne. Began professional dancing in Melbourne 1924. Danced in New York 1928. London 1929. Choreographed and directed musicals and pantomimes in England. Directed musicals for J. C. Williamson's in Australia 1964–74. Died 19 January 1989 in London.

As a speciality dancer should be, Freddie Carpenter was dazzlingly handsome when he began attracting attention in the mid-1920s. At 16 he began professional dancing at the Princess Theatre in Melbourne, where HUGH J. WARD was presenting spectacular operettas. In July 1925, in the first Australian production of *No! No! Nanette*, Carpenter was noticed as a 'handsome and dashing' performer of dance specialities with Elma Hardman as his partner. In 1926, he was added to the Sydney production of *Katja, the Dancer*, in which MARIE BURKE played the leading female role. The agile young dancer appeared in a sequence called 'Dance Eccentric', arranged by Minnie Hooper, the leading choreographer for J. C. WILLIAMSON'S. 'Mr Carpenter practises three hours a day', the program boasted.

Carpenter's ambition took him overseas and in 1928 he appeared at the Erlanger Theatre in New York City in the revue *John Murray Anderson's Almanac*. In 1929 he made his London debut as a solo dancer at the Palladium. A career on both sides of the Atlantic followed. As the years went by he spent his time staging pantomimes and musicals in England. As a natural extension, he turned to directing, always with a close eye on the dancing. For a while he was a personal assistant to Noël Coward, around the time of the production of his *Nude with Violin* in 1957.

In 1964 Carpenter began returning to Australia to stage musicals for J. C. Williamson's, starting with *How to Succeed in Business without Really Trying* and *A Funny Thing Happened on the Way to the Forum*. Later came *Charlie Girl* and *No! No! Nanette*. In 1974 he directed a revival of *Irene*, and helped to nurture the young lead JULIE ANTHONY. Two years later she repeated the role in London, again directed by Carpenter. The London producer was the Harold Fielding organisation, for which Carpenter had already worked extensively. ❦*John West*

Kim Carpenter

Designer, dramatist. Born 1 April 1950 in Newcastle (NSW). Studied production at National Institute of Dramatic Art 1968–69. English National Opera Design School 1970. Resident designer in Old Tote Theatre Company (Sydney). Resident designer in Melbourne Theatre Company 1972, 1978. Has designed for Australian Dance Theatre (Adelaide), Australian Opera, Belvoir Street Theatre (Sydney), Marionette Theatre of Australia (Sydney), Nimrod Theatre Company (Sydney), Sydney Dance Company, Theatre of the Deaf and Victoria State Opera. Artist-in-residence at Atelier Artistique Internationale (France) 1976. Loudon Sainthill Scholarship 1981. Churchill Fellowship 1988.

In designing for most major Australian theatre, dance and opera companies through two decades, Kim Carpenter has increasingly gone beyond decoration. He has been influenced by PERFORMANCE ART, the choreographer Pina Bausch, and the slow-motion producer Robert Wilson, with whom he worked in New York during 1982. In recent years Carpenter has adapted, devised or directed major works he has designed through his Theatre of Image company.

He created *Slice* and directed it for the NIMROD THEATRE COMPANY in July 1981 and the MELBOURNE THEATRE COMPANY in April 1983. From poems by DOROTHY HEWETT he devised *Rapunzel in Suburbia*, and RICHARD BRADSHAW directed it for the Marionette Theatre of Australia in 1983. Carpenter designed David Malouf's *An Imaginary Life* for the AUSTRALIAN ELIZABETHAN THEATRE TRUST at the Belvoir Street Theatre in 1986. For World Expo '88 in Brisbane he devised, designed and directed *The Sky Wizard* and directed *The Pathfinder*, a musical work by Darryl Emmerson about the life and poetry of John Shaw Neilson. In 1993 Carpenter designed and directed an adaptation by RICHARD TULLOCH of Oscar Wilde's *The Happy Prince* for the SYDNEY THEATRE COMPANY. ❦*Pamela Zeplin*

further reading
BENNIE, ANGELA. Myth and magic. *Weekend Australian* 12–23 November 1988.

Neva Carr Glyn

Actor. Born 10 May 1911 in Victoria, to theatrical parents. In Fullers' chorus at 13. Toured Australasia in pantomime and revue 1924–29. Toured South Africa in comedies 1929–30. In England 1931–37. ABC radio in Sydney, 1938–41. Married actor John Tate 1940. In commercial radio from 1941. Minerva Theatre (Sydney) 1943 and 1946–49. Toured New Zealand for J. C. Williamson's 1944. Toured Australia in John Alden Company 1951–52. Elizabethan Theatre (Sydney) and Trust Players 1957–60. Died 10 August 1975 in Sydney. Mother of actor Nick Tate.

A star with great vitality and presence, Neva Carr Glyn was experienced in theatre from revue to Shakespeare. She was born when her theatrical parents were touring Victoria with the Fred Niblo company. At four she played Little Willie in *East Lynne*, with her mother in the lead. At a mature 13 she won a place in the chorus-line of a pantomime in Sydney. This led to a Fullers' contract that took her all over Australasia, singing, dancing, and performing in sketches with such people as JIM GERALD, MARIE LA VARRE, ROY RENE and GEORGE WALLACE. In 1929 she went to South Africa with a FRANK NEIL company, and then worked in England for six years, mainly in comedies with the Leslie Henson Company. Back in Australia, she won an Australian Broadcasting Commission contract as a leading actress in 1938 and became one of the great stars of radio drama.

Carr Glyn returned to the stage in 1943. At the MINERVA THEATRE in Sydney in 1946–49 she starred in plays, including Frank Vosper's *Love from a Stranger* and Benn W. Levy's *Clutterbuck*. She also performed in these works with her husband John Tate for Fifi Banvard Productions at the Theatre Royal in Hobart in 1950. She toured with the JOHN ALDEN COMPANY in 1951–52. She played Leila Pratt in the premiere of Richard Beynon's *THE SHIFTING HEART* in 1957. During two years with the TRUST PLAYERS her most memorable role was Oola Maguire the SP bookie in *THE SLAUGHTER OF ST TERESA'S DAY*, which Peter Kenna wrote for her. In the 1970s she appeared in melodrama at the MUSIC HALL THEATRE RESTAURANT in Sydney. ❦*Richard Lane*

further reading
RUTLEDGE, MARTHA. Neva Carr-Glyn. *Australian Dictionary of Biography* 13. Melbourne University Press 1994.

Dan and E. J. Carroll

Dan Carroll. Entrepreneur. Born 28 June 1886 at Redbank Plains (Qld). Joined brother E. J. Carroll as junior partner 1908. Managed Queensland division of film exhibition and theatre management company. Ran family companies 1931–59. Died 11 August 1959 in Sydney.

Edward John Carroll. Entrepreneur. Born 28 June 1868 at Gatton (Qld). Railway clerk 1883. Later fruit merchant, caterer, hotel owner. Film exhibitor from 1907. Built cinemas, theatres and skating rinks in Queensland and NSW. In Sydney from 1913. Managed tours by international concert and theatrical artists. Staged plays in Australia and London. Died 28 July 1931 in Sydney.

E. J. Carroll and his much younger brother Dan shared an unusually high reputation for financial fair dealing and were warmly regarded by Australian artists such as STEELE RUDD for their support for local artistic enterprise. E. J. Carroll made a fortune as caterer to Queensland Government Railways refreshment rooms, and then bought hotels in Brisbane. In 1907 he bought the Queensland exhibition rights to the pioneer feature film *The Story of the Kelly Gang*, and through various partnerships built up a major film exhibition company, known since 1923 as Birch, Carroll and Coyle. Carroll presented many concert artists, including Harry Lauder, Fritz Kreisler and Florence Austral. He organised a lecture tour by the Antarctic explorer Ernest Shackleton, and he staged plays in Australia and England. The Australian and Hollywood film star and director Louise Lovely toured Australia for Carroll in several stage plays in 1927. ❦*Richard Fotheringham*

further reading
BRAND, SIMON. *Picture Palaces and Flea Pits*. Sydney: Dreamweaver 1983.
PIKE, A. F. and MARTHA RUTLEDGE. Edward John and Daniel Joseph Carroll. *Australian Dictionary of Biography* 7. Melbourne University Press 1979.

Garnet H. Carroll

Entrepreneur. Born 4 December 1902 at Singleton (NSW). Began performing in chorus. Formed Gaiety Theatres Ltd with Benjamin Fuller 1941. Formed Carroll–Fuller Theatres Pty Ltd 1946. Managed Princess Theatre, Melbourne. Presented plays and musicals. Died 23 August 1964 in Melbourne.

A 20th-century entrepreneur in the 19th-century mould, Garnet H. Carroll came from behind the footlights to sell entertainment, always aiming to please the widest public. By 1927 he was playing small roles and learning the ropes as assistant stage manager in the company that opened the Empire Theatre in Sydney with the musical comedy *Sunny*. A year later he was Sergeant Joe Wilkins and assistant stage manager for the Fullers' production of *Rio Rita*.

Carroll was a protégé of BENJAMIN FULLER. By 1941 they were joint managing directors of Gaiety Theatres Ltd, which leased the KING'S THEATRE in Melbourne. After five months, however, they subleased the theatre to a film exhibitor. It remained a cinema until 1949, when Carroll made the King's a live theatre again, in partnership with KENN BRODZIAK's company Aztec Services. From 1951 the King's reverted permanently to films. In the meantime Carroll–Fuller Theatres Pty Ltd had bought the PRINCESS THEATRE from Fuller's. In 1947 Carroll returned the Princess to live performance, presenting WHITEHALL THEATRICAL PRODUCTIONS shows from Sydney and visiting companies.

By 1955 Carroll fully controlled the Princess Theatre. He began presenting commercial plays, often with veteran American film stars, including Melvyn Douglas and Richard Arlen, in the leading roles. Carroll then challenged the supremacy of J. C. WILLIAMSON's in musicals. He produced *Kismet* with HAYES GORDON, *Salad Days* with Judy Banks and John Proper, *Bells Are Ringing* with Shani Wallis, *The King and I* with Jeff Warren and *Wildcat* with TONI LAMOND. He also imported the Sadler's Wells Opera Company production of *Orpheus in the Underworld*. Carroll had no circuit upon which to tour any of these productions. He had only the Capitol Theatre in Perth so he had to be co-producer with the AUSTRALIAN ELIZABETHAN THEATRE TRUST or the TIVOLI CIRCUIT to get his pieces out of Melbourne.

Carroll brought the trailblazing American musical *West Side Story* to Melbourne and Sydney in 1960–61. It was a splendid, vigorous and exciting production with a large component of American talent, but it lost Carroll a lot of money. He had a big success, however, with the *The Sound of Music*, which he presented with the Trust. Starring JUNE BRONHILL and Peter Graves, it opened at the Princess Theatre on 20 October 1961 and transferred to the Tivoli Theatre in Sydney on 28 September 1962.

Early in 1963 Carroll allowed Bronhill to return to London—Renée Guerin replaced her—to take the leading role in *Robert and Elizabeth* by the expatriate Australian composer Ron Grainer. Carroll planned to attend the world premiere in October 1964 but on the eve of departure for England he died from a heart attack. Carroll–Fuller, Aztec Productions and the Trust brought the musical to Melbourne in May 1966, with Bronhill and KEITH MICHELL in the leading roles. It transferred to Sydney on 19 November. Initial slow business alarmed the producers and they announced that the show would close on 22 December. Houses then improved but it was too late. ❦*John West*

further reading
MCKINNON, JULIE. Garnet Carroll. *Australian Dictionary of Biography* 13. Melbourne University Press 1994.
SUMNER, JOHN. *Recollections at Play—A life in Australian theatre*. Melbourne: University Press 1993.

Peter Carroll

Actor. Born 1944 in Sydney. In student drama at University of Sydney 1961–64. Postgraduate study at Central School of Speech and Drama (London) 1968–69. Further study at University of NSW (Sydney) 1971–73. Began professional career with Nimrod Theatre Company (Sydney) 1974.

Peter Carroll is a versatile performer with a fine voice that has helped to extend his career beyond the theatre into radio and film and television voice-overs. He created the role in Ron Blair's monodrama THE CHRISTIAN BROTHERS in 1975, and toured Australia, New Zealand and the United Kingdom in it. In musicals he has sung Che Guevara in *Evita* at the Adelaide Festival; in *Jonah Jones*, *Noel and Gertie* and *Summer Rain* for the SYDNEY THEATRE COMPANY; in *Sweeney Todd* for the MELBOURNE THEATRE COMPANY; and in *Les Misérables*. In straight theatre he created roles in two plays by DAVID WILLIAMSON, *The Perfectionist* (1982) and *Money and Friends* (1992). His other significant roles include Stalin in David Pownall's *Master Class* for the Stage Company in Adelaide in 1984, Tesman in Henrik Ibsen's *Hedda Gabler* for the Melbourne Theatre Company in 1989 and the title-part in Anton Chekhov's *Uncle Vanya* for the Sydney Theatre Company in 1992. ❦*Paul McGillick*

W. F. Carver

American manager, sharpshooter. Born in 1840s in Nebraska. Backwoodsman from 1860s to 1877. Began professional rifle-shooting demonstrations 1878. Partner of 'Buffalo Bill' Cody 1883. Toured Canada with own show 1884. Combined with W. W. Cole's show 1886, and with Adam Forepaugh jnr's circus 1887-89. Visited eastern Australia with his Wild America troupe 1890-91. Starred in Dampier Theatre Company's *The Scout* and *The Trapper* 1891. Played *The Scout* throughout USA 1892–93. Died 1927.

While Nate Salsbury was touring Australia with his troubadour company in 1876 he compared Australian riders with American and Mexican cowboys. This, he claimed, gave him the idea of an event that began at the Omaha Fairgrounds on 17 May 1883 as the Wild West Show of his sometime partner 'Buffalo Bill' Cody. In Omaha in 1883 Buffalo Bill's partner was 'Dr' William Francis Carver, who claimed to be the world's champion rifle shot. In 1888 he hit more than 60 000 wooden blocks thrown in the air over six days with only 650 misses.

Carver brought his own cowboy-and-Indian troupe, Wild America, to Australia in 1890. Next year the playwrights ALFRED DAMPIER and GARNET WALCH wrote two spectacular dramas, THE SCOUT and *The Trapper*, to star Carver and his company. Dampier staged them for nine weeks at the Alexandra Theatre in Melbourne. Carver, no actor, generally arrived on horseback with shouts and rifle shots to save the heroine at the end of the act. *The Scout*'s greatest sensation—admired by SARAH BERNHARDT—was when Carver's horse fell from a bridge into a tank of water, leaving him clinging to the broken railing. He also fired over his shoulder, aiming in a mirror, to smash a glass ball. Carver later played *The Scout* throughout the USA, but his plays and shows were never as successful as those of Buffalo Bill—whom he spent the rest of his life vilifying—and even his sharpshooting feats were quickly eclipsed. ❦*Richard Fotheringham*

further reading
RUNELL, DON. *The Lives and Legends of Buffalo Bill*. Norman (Oklahoma, USA): University of Oklahoma Press 1960.

Fanny Cathcart

Actor. Born 1833. Originally Mary Frances Cathcart. Father was provincial theatre manager. Discovered by G. V. Brooke at Liverpool 1853. Played briefly at Theatre Royal, Drury Lane, London, 1854. Australian debut at Queen's Theatre, Melbourne, 26 February 1855. Married actor Robert Heir July 1855. Widowed 1868. Toured with own company. Married George Darrell in London, 20 January 1870. Toured in his plays, 1872–77. Died 3 January 1880 in Melbourne. Sister of actors James and Rowley Cathcart.

The *Sydney Morning Herald* described Fanny Cathcart as 'the first great English actress to be seen on the colonial stage'. She was not an international star but she was the foremost female actor resident in Australia in the mid-19th century, and she supported imported stars, such as JOSEPH JEFFERSON, with whom she appeared at the opening of the Haymarket Theatre in Melbourne in September 1862.

When Cathcart arrived in Melbourne with G. V. BROOKE in 1855, only months after she had joined his company, she was so fresh and attractive that admirers showered her with gifts of jewellery. She made her debut as Desdemona to Brooke's Othello. Her marriage to the youthful actor Robert Heir caused a professional rift with Brooke and a publicised court case in August 1855.

As Mrs Robert Heir she was leading actress in BARRY SULLIVAN's Shakespeare season at the Theatre Royal in Melbourne in 1863. Her brother James Cathcart was in the rival company of CHARLES AND ELLEN KEAN at the Haymarket Theatre. He told Kean that she privately complained of the 'wretched inefficiency' of her Australian colleagues.

After the death of Heir she married GEORGE DARRELL. She returned to the stage as Mrs George Darrell in March 1871, playing Camille to Darrell's Armand Duval at the Prince of Wales Opera House in Sydney. Her return allowed audiences and critics alike to sentimentalise over the palmy days of Brooke. She even encouraged Darrell the melodrama specialist to tread the proper English path of Shakespeare for a time.

As a performer she consistently outshone both her husbands and she set new standards on the Australian stage. As Portia and Lady Teazle she was a revelation to local audiences with her ringing, intelligent delivery, although the Sydney *Empire* complained that she had a 'habit of metallic enunciation.' She maintained a handsome presence and a reputation as grand actress of the old school, although the Melbourne *Argus* found her declamatory as an aging Ophelia in July 1871. In the era of sensation drama she was possibly an anachronism. She matured into a pillar of society, and her respectability was a favourite subject of the critics. She was so respected and loved that there were obituaries throughout Australia and New Zealand after her death in 1880. ❦*Helen Musa*

further reading
NEILD, J. E. Obituary of Fanny Darrell. *Australasian* (Melbourne) 10 January 1880.
VAN DER POORTEN, HELEN. Mary Fanny Cathcart. *Australian Dictionary of Biography* 3. Melbourne University Press 1978.
Argus (Melbourne) 5 January 1880. Obituary.

Lawrence H. Cecil

Actor, director. Born 24 September 1888 in NSW. Trained with Frank Benson's company at Stratford-upon-Avon (England) 1911. Military service in France 1914–18. Acted and directed in USA 1920–32. Married actor Rosalind Kennerdale 1933. Producer for ABC radio 1933–43, Macquarie Broadcasting 1944–53. Production manager for Grace Gibson Productions 1953–63. Died 21 April 1968 in Sydney. Father of radio actor Amber Mae Cecil.

In Australia Lawrence H. Cecil's career was predominantly in radio but as senior drama producer for the Australian Broadcasting Commission he helped to mould successful stage careers for many young actors, notably PETER FINCH. He returned to Australia in 1933 after a decade in the theatre in the USA, acting on Broadway with such great actors as John and Lionel Barrymore, Helen Hayes and Frederic March, and directing, among others, Bette Davis and Humphrey Bogart. In 1950 he produced *Julius Caesar* and Eugene O'Neill's *SS Glencairn* for INDEPENDENT THEATRE in Sydney, using casts of polished professional actors who had developed their skills in radio, largely under the guidance of his experienced hand. ❦*Richard Lane*

The Cedar Tree

Musical comedy. **book** Edmund Barclay. **lyrics** Helene Barclay, with additions by Jack McLeod and Varney Monk. **music** Varney Monk. **premiere** 22 December 1934, Princess Theatre, Melbourne. **cast** Claude Flemming, Gladys Moncrieff, Russell Scott. **director** Claude Flemming.

After the success of the Australian musical comedy COLLITS' INN in Melbourne and Sydney in 1933–34, the entrepreneur F. W. THRING decided on another from almost the same stable. For *The Cedar Tree* VARNEY MONK again provided the melodies, this time to words by Helene Barclay, whose husband Edmund Barclay wrote the book. There are echoes of *Collits' Inn* in *The Cedar Tree*—redcoats, an officer hero, bushrangers and a similar sense of history. It is set in Windsor (NSW) in the early 19th century. Daniella Weston is the strong-minded owner of a small shipyard, and a fine old cedar tree—with a useful cleft where objects essential to plot development can be concealed—dominates the opening and closing scenes.

The comedian ALFRED FRITH, making his first appearance for Thring, played the Flying Pieman, a role based on the historical figure of an eccentric pastry vendor who was renowned for feats of pedestrianism. GLADYS MONCRIEFF again played the heroine, with a new leading man, Russell Scott. CLAUDE FLEMMING again played the second male lead and directed the show. It opened in late December 1934 in Melbourne and played until mid-February. In Sydney it managed only a miserable two weeks from 16 March 1935. Compounded of over-familiar materials, *The Cedar Tree* probably deserved the tepid response. After it, Thring gave up his idea of producing local musicals. ❦*John West*

Censorship

Europeans brought censorship to New South Wales in their invisible luggage in 1788. The early governors, well aware of the Stage Licensing Bill of 1737, considered control of dramatic productions even more important in a convict colony comprising the 'dangerous classes' than in Great Britain. However, political considerations were secondary in colonial censorship until politics and the Irish arrived in New South Wales in 1800. The authorities were more concerned with morality, maintenance of the public peace and the social structure of the colony. The first play, George Farquhar's *The Recruiting Officer*, was performed in Sydney on 4 June 1789 with the permission and support of Governor Arthur Phillip, but there was considerable censorship of the text to remove indecency and bad taste.

Early governors were prepared to countenance convict actors, but not rowdy audiences. Governor John Hunter ordered the closure of SIDAWAY'S THEATRE in 1798. In 1829 Governor Ralph Darling revoked his permission for the Sydney merchant BARNETT LEVEY to hold balls and concerts in his Royal Hotel, 'our prison population being unfit subjects to go to plays'. Dramatic censorship in Australia was random, arbitrary and *ad hoc* until the 1830s.

The system became institutionalised on 22 December 1832, when Governor Richard Bourke licensed Levey to stage plays in his THEATRE ROYAL. Bourke was limited in his liberalism and determined to follow English precedents. He restricted performance to 'such Plays and Entertainments only as has been performed at one of His Majesty's Licensed Theatres in London'. Two years later the governor inserted a proviso in Levey's new licence, prohibiting convicts from appearing on stage. This rule was enforced, not always efficiently, until 1847. Bourke left much of the licensing of plays to the Lord Chamberlain in London. Colonial managers circumvented the system by staging 'occasional sketches' written by local actors such as JOSEPH SIMMONS and CONRAD KNOWLES. During the late 1830s theatre managers consistently and blatantly ignored the rule against local authors, which they realised was not the main aim of colonial censorship.

Preserving morality

During the early 1840s the NSW Colonial Secretary, Edward Deas Thomson, relaxed censorship and created a precedent on 23 April 1842 by licensing *The Mock Catalani in Little Puddleton*, a play by the local author Charles Nagel, as long as 'oaths' were removed. The authorities were concerned about the 'special circumstances of the colony' and discouraged Australian settings, but they followed London in concentrating censorship on challenges to morality, the portrayal of religious and scriptural stories, political drama, and the depiction of the criminal, political or otherwise, as a hero. For example, Deas Thomson refused to license the burletta LIFE IN SYDNEY in 1843, ostensibly because the author was anonymous but in reality because the subject was crime, larrikinism and social conflict.

Sydney managers, desperate for licences, censored themselves. In June 1844 Joseph Simmons assured the Colonial Secretary that his play *The Duellist* was 'perfectly free in dialogue and plot from anything local, political, sectarian or immoral'. It was a description that neatly encapsulated much of the Sydney stage during the rest of the century. Unoriginal comedies set in foreign places or in the past, farces, pantomimes and burlesques dominated the field. The complexities and nuances of colonial life were ignored, either from fear of censorship or because entrepreneurs judged that a population alienated from the new capitalist environment wanted escape rather than reality. Desire for escape may explain the interest in bushranger dramas, although these resembled the Newgate plays in England, which made folk heroes of highwaymen.

Bushranger dramas were first staged in the 1850s in Victoria and Tasmania, where the licensing regulations were far less severe than in NSW. The NSW Colonial Secretary refused to approve *Jackey Jackey* by J. R. McLachlan and Thomas McCombie in 1845, but it appeared at the Theatre Royal in Geelong (Vic.) in 1853 as *Jackey Jackey the NSW Bushranger*. Some four years before, McLachlan's *Arabin—or, The Adventures of a Settler*, an 'entirely colonial production', had been staged in Melbourne, which was replacing Sydney as the theatrical centre of Australia. The separation of Victoria from NSW in 1851, the gold rushes and beginning of provincial performance in the goldfields all contributed to the break-up of censorship by making policing difficult. A relaxation of licensing rules in Sydney during the 1850s owed more to self-censorship than to the victory of liberal principles. Even the bushranger plays are full of myth, legend and bathos; they are free from class conflict, sectarianism and the realities of agrarian capitalism.

The stage was a vehicle for comment and reform only in pantomime, which blossomed in the 1860s because the licensing system fell into disuse. Garnet Walch's AUSTRALIA FELIX in 1873 lampooned the Lord Chamberlain and gently criticised politicians, corruption and land speculation; it was not banned because it did not violate morality and breach the canons of middle-class society. However, censorship was never far away. In January 1880 Marcus Clarke's adaptation of THE HAPPY LAND, an attack on Gladstone and his ministry by Gilbert A'Beckett and W. S. Gilbert, was staged at the Academy of Music in Melbourne. Clarke replaced the English cabinet with the radical Premier of Victoria Graham Berry and his ministers. The Victorian government threatened to withdraw the theatre's licence, effectively censoring the pantomime. As a protest, a performance was given in which the actors replaced excisions with the words 'Ahem! Censored.'

The victory of bourgeois society—with its concentration on respectability—in the 19th century meant that there was no real movement against stage censorship. Colonial liberalism was self-righteous, moral, and philistine. A form of cultural imperialism kept religion, politics and indecency off the stage. Managers and playwrights censored their own productions, leaving the realities of Australian society to others. Censorship helped to produce barren, second-rate local drama that maintained decorum and false consciousness at the cost of originality and intellectual honesty. *T. G. Parsons*

20th century

Since the colonies became states in 1901 their governments have developed laws to control and regulate theatrical production and performance. These laws permit measures ranging from prior censorship of plays by tampering with scripts or banning productions to holding performers liable for offences such as 'obscenity and indecency'. The laws involve wide ministerial discretion and the exercise of police powers. They have been rarely invoked, but the history shows the danger that is in their existence.

There have been essentially two justifications for censoring theatre in this century. The first is that the state must have power to protect itself and the government of the day from unrestrained attacks. This has resulted in political censorship. In England, the Gilbert and Sullivan operetta *The Mikado* was banned out of respect for a visiting Japanese dignitary. In 1936, the NSW Chief Secretary, acting on a complaint by the German consul, advised NEW THEATRE not to perform Clifford Odets's anti-Nazi play *Till the Day I Die* as it was 'unjust to a friendly power'. This was legally justified because Hitler's Germany, no matter how abhorrent, was then a friendly power. New Theatre ignored the hint and the NSW government—on the advice of the federal Attorney-General, Robert Menzies—banned the play under the Theatres and Public Halls Act of 1908 to protect 'good manners and decorum'. Victoria also banned it and a suburban council prevented a performance in Melbourne later in the year by locking out the audience and cast. The bans on the play were lifted in 1941, when Australia had been at war with the friendly power for two years.

Preserving the state

The second and more common justification for censorship is that the state is entitled to protect the minimum standards of conduct essential to its survival. This position is used to support prevention of blasphemy, obscenity, indecency, offensive behaviour or immorality. The power of direct censorship is to be found in legislation concerned primarily with theatre buildings. It allows legislation designed to regulate safety and hygiene—such as fire exits and toilets—to be used to close down theatres for ulterior reasons. Sumner Locke Elliott's RUSTY BUGLES was banned in Sydney under the Theatres and Public Halls Act in 1948 because of words considered blasphemous and indecent. Public outcry followed, the NSW Chief Secretary and INDEPENDENT THEATRE negotiated an agreement to temper the language and the play was allowed to run.

The charge of blasphemy has been brought rarely in this century, but there appears to have been a revival in prosecution that has the potential to restrict free speech in the theatre. Indecency and obscenity have been the major grounds for censoring modern productions and there are many instances of theatres being required to tone down the language of plays and voluntarily amending scripts to avoid prosecution. The most infamous cases of censorship occurred in 1968–70, when plays produced overseas under newly liberalised censorship laws came to Australia.

America Hurrah!, three short plays by Jean-Claude van Itallie, ran for five weeks in Sydney in 1968, until the police acted on a complaint. After viewing a performance, the police warned the actors they would be summoned if they continued to perform the play called *Motel*. It was offensive to public good taste and decorum, the theatre was told, and continued performance could result in repeal of the New Theatre's licence. *Motel* was replaced with *Hotel*, a new production designed as a spoof on censorship laws. But a special public performance of *America Hurrah!* including *Motel*, sponsored by prominent members of the community, was announced. Some 3000 persons turned up for the performance at the Teachers' Federation Theatre. The police and the audience viewed *Motel* in silence. At the end the police were unable to fight through the crowd to arrest the actors. The effect of the ban on *Motel* by the Chief Secretary of NSW was to prevent independent productions in the state, such as one planned in Newcastle. In Perth, the HOLE-IN-THE-WALL THEATRE COMPANY gave private club performances of *America Hurrah!* after the Western Australian police had warned against going ahead in public. In other states *America Hurrah!* was modified.

The Victorian authorities were more concerned with sexual promiscuity than indecency or obscenity. In September 1969 police in Melbourne took action after three weeks of Mart Crowley's *The Boys in the Band*, a play about homosexuals which had run for seven months in Sydney. Three actors were charged with using offensive or obscene language in a public place. On the evidence of police officers who had no experience of serious theatre, convictions were sought against the actors for using words such as 'fuck', 'cunt' and 'arsehole'. The magistrate went to see the play and found the charges proven, but refused to convict the actors because the offences were trifling. The Victorian Supreme Court rejected this reasoning and the actors were convicted and fined. The Victorian Chief Secretary took no action to ban the play, however, and it ran uncut.

In NSW, South Australia, Tasmania and Victoria a minister or specified government official may prohibit any public entertainment whenever they are of the opinion that it is appropriate to do so to preserve good manners and decorum, or, in some states, to preserve public morality. The meanings of good manners, decorum, and morality have not remained constant. In Western Australia and Queensland no general power of censorship is granted to a government official. It is, however, a specific criminal offence in those states to 'publicly exhibit any indecent show or performance'. In addition, each state has laws that penalise indecent or obscene behaviour, speech and publications by means of summary or indictable charges or both.

Charges under criminal law

The most basic criminal law involves charges against individual offenders. For example, in Melbourne in 1970 nine actors performing in *Whatever Happened to Realism?* were convicted of using obscene language. However, standards of obscenity and indecency have not been static. In most legislation the word 'obscene' has been used without further definition, and the current test of obscenity involves a consideration of whether the behaviour in question is acceptable by current community standards.

In 1972, a street-theatre performer at a pop concert who dressed up as a cigarette/condom and sprayed shaving cream through a hole in the top of his costume was convicted of indecent behaviour in a public place. The appeal judge said there 'was no real doubt that, whatever else the appellant was symbolising, he was also symbolising a penis in a state of erection being worked up to ejaculation'. By contrast, in 1988 the World Health Organisation praised an AIDS-awareness program in which three students wandered round the Monash University campus in condom costumes in a 'safe sex' display.

The extent of the allowance to be made for artistic expression is not clear. Judges and magistrates frequently have different views from police on this question. Nudity has caused some problems for Australian authorities. Because of its nude scenes the rock musical *Hair* was the subject of heated debate in 1969 but the production was allowed to run in Sydney, and later in Melbourne. In Western Australia, an actor who appeared nude in Peter Shaffer's play *Equus* was charged with indecent exposure. The magistrate's dismissal of the case was upheld by the Supreme Court in 1977.

When the threat of a charge of breach of the criminal law does not appear to be a sufficient deterrent, the court may grant injunction to prevent the commission of an offence. The Queensland government sought to deal with production of Alex Buzo's play NORM AND AHMED in this way in 1969, seeking an injunction to prevent an actor in the play from using language alleged to violate a provision of the Vagrants Gaming and Other Offences Act 1931. The Supreme Court refused because it was uncertain whether the language actually was unlawful and it considered that the question should not be decided on an application for an injunction. The issue was tested in 1970 and an actor in *Norm and Ahmed* was convicted of using indecent or obscene language, but the Supreme Court overturned the conviction because adequate account had not been taken of the artistic circumstances. The High Court refused leave to appeal against this decision, also refusing to endorse it.

Every possible device available to interfere with the freedom of the theatre, including the granting of an injunction, was used against the nude revue *Oh, Calcutta!* in 1970. The producers even had a problem getting the script into Australia. It was initially classified as a prohibited import but eventually allowed in. In NSW the Chief Secretary prohibited production. One charity performance of *Oh, Calcutta!* was given in that state, and the whole cast was charged with obscene and indecent behaviour. The Victorian Attorney-General was granted an injunction to prevent performance. The South Australian Attorney-General said that the play would be banned if it breached the law of obscenity. When the producers decided to go ahead the 'Moral Action Committee' sought an injunction to prevent the performance. The judge examined the script and granted the injunction, and the Supreme Court upheld his judgment in 1971.

It is clear that in the 1990s the community in general has a much broader liberal view than it did in the 1960s and 1970s. It appears that there is almost complete freedom to perform any play whatever, but the criminal sanctions and the powers of direct censorship remain part of Australian law. Until laws are reformed, theatre operates under the threat of government intervention. ❦*Melinda Jones*

further reading
CAMPBELL, E. and H. WHITMORE. *Freedom in Australia* 2nd edition. Sydney University Press 1973.
DUTTON, GEOFFREY and MAX HARRIS (eds). *Australia's Censorship Crisis*. Melbourne: Sun 1970.
GAZE, B. and M. JONES. *Law, Liberty and Australian Democracy*. Sydney: Law Book 1990.
POLLAK, M. *Sense and Censorship*. Sydney: Sydney: Reed 1990.
STEPHENS, J. R. *The Censorship of English Drama 1824-1901*. Cambridge (England): Cambridge University Press 1980.
TURNER, A. (ed.). *Censorship*. Melbourne: Heinemann 1975.

The Chapel Perilous

—or, the Perilous Adventures of Sally Banner. Play in two acts by Dorothy Hewett. **premiere** 21 January 1971, New Fortune Theatre, Perth. Cast: Margaret Ford, Helen Neeme, Colin Nugent. Director: Aarne Neeme. **revived** 1974, Drama Theatre, Sydney Opera House, by Old Tote Theatre Company. **published** Sydney: Currency Press 1972; revised 1977; in Hewett's *Collected Plays* 1, 1992.

DOROTHY HEWETT's early play *The Chapel Perilous* is still her best-known work. It has been revived many times, and it is widely studied in schools and university courses. Written in Hewett's freewheeling 'epic' style, the play includes an expressionist set dominated by giant totemic 'authority' figures, representing the power of conservatism, who comment upon the rebellious actions of the heroine. There are multiple roles for several young actors, a chorus that refracts into various characters, sudden leaps in setting, style and tone, and moments of song, dance and poetry.

The play also exhibits the qualities that have made Hewett controversial—affirmation of female sexuality, questioning of conventional authority and morality, and a tendency towards anarchy in dramatic structure and social attitudes. The central character, tempestuous Sally Banner, draws on much of Hewett's own experience in her search —analogous to the traditional romantic 'quest'—to express herself fully in provincial Australia from the 1930s to the 1960s. Sally seeks initially fulfilment through her poetic gifts and sexual relationships, and later turns to political activism, but ultimately finds freedom in self-acceptance.

The character of Sally, who is seen from rebellious schooldays to late middle age, has provoked strong reactions, from passionate identification to dismissal as insufferable. Both responses sometimes overlook the play's strong vein of irony, from which Sally herself is not exempt. ❦*Margaret Williams*

Gordon Chater

Actor. Born 1922 in London. Came to Sydney after naval service during Second World War. Began acting in Sydney, December 1947. Acted in plays, revue, radio and television. Dramalogie award (Los Angeles) for best actor 1979. Obie award (New York City) for best actor 1979. Lived mainly in New York until he retired to Gold Coast (Qld) in 1991.

Though Gordon Chater is most widely known as a comic actor his skill has encompassed almost everything an actor may be called upon to do. Quite handsome in his younger days, he later acquired a typical clown's face. After a long tour of New Zealand in J. B. Priestley's *Dangerous Corner* for WHITEHALL THEATRICAL PRODUCTIONS in 1946, Chater began his Sydney career at the Minerva Theatre in the London revue *Sweetest and Lowest*. It was good preparation for his long stint in PHILLIP STREET REVUES from the mid-1950s.

In 1976 Chater gave a dazzling bravura performance in Steve J. Spears's monodrama THE ELOCUTION OF BENJAMIN FRANKLIN in Sydney and on tour. He repeated it in London, Los Angeles and New York, where he settled. On one of his occasional trips back to Australia, in 1981 he played Sir, a character based on Donald Wolfit, in Ronald Harwood's *The Dresser*. In 1986 he played opposite BARRY CREYTON, and later Keith Baxter, in Gerald Moon's two-hander *Corpse!* In 1991 he played the butlers Lane and Merriman in Oscar

Wilde's *The Importance of Being Earnest*, with Ruth Cracknell as Lady Bracknell. He followed this by playing a solo piece, *Lady Bracknell's Confinement* by Paul Doust, at the 1993 Melbourne International Festival. *John West*

Wal Cherry

Director. Born 10 May 1932 at Ballarat (Vic.). Began directing at University of Melbourne. Manager of Union Theatre 1955–57. Director of Union Theatre Repertory Company 1956–58. Co-founded Emerald Hill Theatre Company (Melbourne) 1962. Director 1961–66. Professor of drama at Flinders University (Adelaide) 1967–79, and Temple University (Philadelphia, USA) 1979–86. Died 8 March 1986 in Boston (USA) 1986.

High standards of acting and production and uncompromising programming marked Wal Cherry's regimes in two companies in Melbourne. He came to notice with imaginative productions when he was an undergraduate at Melbourne University. After several guest productions for the Union Theatre Repertory Company, forerunner of the Melbourne Theatre Company, Cherry was offered its directorship in 1956. During his three years with the company he introduced Bertolt Brecht to its audience, with *The Threepenny Opera*. His seasons were strong on contemporary works from England, including John Osborne's *Look Back in Anger*, and from the USA, including plays by William Inge, Arthur Miller and Tennessee Williams. But his tastes were ahead of his audience, and at the beginning of 1959 he resigned to become a freelance director and to set up his own Theatre Workshop and Actor's Studio.

Out of this grew the Emerald Hill Theatre Company, which Cherry founded with the actor and director George Whaley in 1961. In five years, before the era of government subsidy, the company presented 29 major productions, including a handful of Australian plays, but it was unable to pay its way. Cherry was always loath to lower its standards and play safe, so at the end of 1966 the Emerald Hill Theatre closed its doors. Cherry took up the inaugural chair of drama at Flinders University in Adelaide and mixed teaching there with regular bouts of professional directing in the USA. Other directors were envious and resentful of his brilliant introspective imagination and in his latter years in Australia he became an isolated figure. He later moved to the USA and he was working on a production in Boston when he died. *Leonard Radic*

further reading
Sumner, John. *Recollections at Play—A life in Australian theatre.* Melbourne: University Press 1993.

The Cherry Pickers

Play in three acts by Kevin Gilbert. **premiere** August 1971, Nindethana Theatre, Melbourne. Cast: Athol Compton, Lynette Gilbert et al. Director: Kevin McGrath. **published** Canberra: Burrambinga Books, revised 1988.

The first play written by an Aboriginal dramatist and the first performed publicly was *The Cherry Pickers*. Like a later Aboriginal play, Robert Merritt's *The Cake Man*, it was written in prison. Kevin Gilbert wrote the first draft in 1968. It was highly commended in the Captain Cook Bicentenary Competition in 1970. After a workshop performance at the Mews Theatre in Sydney in August 1971 the same all-Aboriginal cast, again directed by Kevin McGrath, performed the play at the Nindethana Theatre in Melbourne. It has never been performed since, although it was substantially revised in 1985 and a new prologue was workshopped in Canberra in 1987 at the First National Black Playwrights' Conference. Because the play has been so rarely performed, critical reaction has been sparse but all commentators note its vibrancy, the passion of its ideas and its significance as a historical and a dramatic document.

Gilbert has stated that it 'is a play of humanity, of the search for justice, of a return to spirituality'. It achieves this by focusing upon a few important days in the lives of black Australian cherry pickers who come together at the same orchard each year to work, celebrate, make love, sing, laugh and reminisce. This year tragedy mars the reunion as the leader of the group dies on the way to the orchard at the same time as the largest cherry tree wilts in sickness. The revised version of the play adds overtly political and polemical material, including an introductory poem in mock-heroic form, a stylised history of the invasion of Australia by Europeans, and a final cameo emphasising the contemporary land rights campaign. *Adam Shoemaker*

further reading
Brisbane, Katharine. Black drama of white laws. *Australian Book Review* (Melbourne) July 1988.
Wright, Judith. Colonialism and criticism. *Overland* (Melbourne) October 1988.

Child companies

Children performed regularly on stage throughout the 19th century. Small family companies often had a resident 'infant phenomenon'. Towards the end of the century companies of children, playing mainly operetta and variety, toured widely throughout Australia, New Zealand, South Africa, Canada the USA and East Asia. The most famous were the Pollard opera companies. Most companies relied for their popularity on the skill with which the children could ape adult performers.

Legal restrictions on child performers were haphazard. On overseas tours the larger companies liked to advertise that a government-supplied teacher gave the children two hours of schooling each weekday. The smaller companies did not always adhere to this official requirement. Children under the employment age—which ranged from 14 to 16 for boys and from 16 to 18 for girls—came under colonial child-welfare acts, but action against exploitation was possible only if the child could be proved to be a 'neglected child'. This catch-all included begging, street trading, residence in a brothel, parents who were habitual drunkards, and public performance 'whereby the life or limb of such child is endangered'. From the 1890s the child-welfare laws were tightened to include mandatory licensing of children who gave public entertainment for profit. Children who were below employable age were not paid. Those of employable age were legally entitled to a wage and had more redress under anti-exploitation laws. They did not always fit under either factories and shops acts or apprenticeship rules, which presumed that training would be given. When there was training it was usually strict, if not harsh.

In the 1920s child companies multiplied as the use of child performers became more economically attractive.

Professional companies like the Aussie Kiddies, the Pantomime Kiddies and the Nine Amazing Johnsons toured the country. Large cities had resident professional companies, like Jean Findlay's Surprise Packets in Brisbane.

Pupils from many dancing schools performed variety items at picture shows, drawing protests from professional adult performers, claims of surfeit and concern about exploitation. In 1926 the National Council of Women lobbied the Home Secretary of Queensland for legislation to be tightened up.

The Young Australian League toured variety throughout Australia, New Zealand and South Africa from the late 1920s until the Second World War. It gave musical and stage training to children whose parents could afford to pay. Its resident stars throughout the period—COLIN CROFT, Bill Kerr, George Nicholls and Charlie Stanton—were never paid. Since the war professional children's companies have become rarities, possibly because ACTORS' EQUITY rigorously oversees conditions and payment. One of these rarities is the FLYING FRUIT FLY CIRCUS. ❦*Barbara Garlick*

Children's Activities Time Society

Children's theatre organisation in Perth, founded in 1965 by Ron Bell, Joan Malden, Margaret Pitt Morison, Brian Pope, Joan Pope and Penny White.

Young audiences were encouraged to take part directly and creatively in theatrical performances presented by the Children's Activities Time Society (CATS). It aimed to stimulate children into discoveries in the arts through their involvement in performances. A non-profit association, CATS grew from a fortnight-long festival for children presented by Joan Pope and other artists and educators in the Perth suburb of Dalkeith in January 1965. It performed at weekends and holiday times, mostly in informal spaces in Perth suburbs, and also toured kindergartens and play groups and regularly visited country towns.

The director RICHARD DAVEY and 14 others, touring as the Round Earth Company under the aegis of CATS, performed in the North West, the Western Desert and Arnhem Land in 1970. To mark the International Year of the Child in 1979, CATS adapted a freight wagon as a play centre and made a two-week rail tour across the Nullarbor Plain, taking performances to communities along the transcontinental railway. CATS annually presented original works such as the Professor Cobalt 'operas' devised by Davey and Jeff Carroll, Living Museum history projects, and 'big' plays such as *Ned Kelly* directed by Sean Grant, *The Great Ballagundi Damper Bake* directed by Colin Nugent, and *Theseus* directed by Christine Mearing. CATS had federal and state funding from 1969 to 1980. When funding ended CATS reduced its activities. ❦*Bill Dunstone, Joan Pope*

Chiltern Theatre

Theatre at corner of Conness and Main Streets, Chiltern (Vic.), opened *c*.1859 as **Star Theatre**. Destroyed by fire. Rebuilt in brick 1866. Renamed **Chiltern Theatre** and used for motion pictures in early 20th century. Now antiques shop.

The barn-like brick theatre at Chiltern is the only remaining hotel hall of the type that was fitted up for theatre in goldfields towns in Victoria in the mid-19th century. During the gold rushes in Queensland in the late 19th century similar halls behind hotels were built in timber. There was a gold rush in the Chiltern district in the second half of the 1850s. In 1859 the *Chiltern Standard* was advertising the Star Theatre attached to the White Star Hotel. Like most early theatres in gold-mining towns in Victoria, it was a hall built of flimsy temporary materials, fitted up with a stage for visiting entertainers. It was a separate building, linked to the hotel in front. There was no box, circle or gallery.

In 1866 the hotel was rebuilt in brick after a fire. The new Star Family and Commercial Hotel had a 'splendid hall adapted for concerts, public meetings and theatrical programmes', according to the *Federal Standard* of 2 January 1867. During the year the hall was described as 'a splendid theatre', but few theatrical entertainments were advertised apart from an occasional solo show, such as Edith Palmerston in *Wanted, a Star*, dioramas and a 'grand moving panorama of a voyage round the world with hosts of novelties in melody'. The theatre doubled as the Star Assembly Rooms for balls. It remained an all-purpose theatre and hall until it became the Chiltern Theatre for films. The hotel is now a museum and tourist information centre and the theatre is an antiques shop. ❦*Ross Thorne*

Simon Chilvers

Actor, director. Permanent member of Melbourne Theatre Company 1962–82; associate director 1973–82. Then mainly in Sydney, acting for Belvoir Street Theatre and Sydney Theatre Company. Green Room award for best supporting actor 1986 (*Master Class* by David Pownall). Many film and television roles.

In his long career Simon Chilvers has played a remarkably wide range of roles—particularly dramatic roles—in classics and modern Australian and overseas plays. Those that stand out include Hathorne in Arthur Miller's *The Crucible* for the MELBOURNE THEATRE COMPANY in 1968, Zhdanov in *Master Class* for the SYDNEY THEATRE COMPANY in 1986 and Pound in *Sixteen Words for Water* by Billie Marshall-Stoneking for the same company in 1991. In his fondly remembered 21 years with the Melbourne Theatre Company he directed plays as diverse as David Williamson's *THE CLUB*, Joseph Kesselring's *Arsenic and Old Lace* and Henrik Ibsen's *Hedda Gabler*. ❦*Geoffrey Milne*

Chinese performers

Large Cantonese opera-style Chinese companies performed in the Victorian goldfields towns and in Melbourne from the 1850s to the 1870s. Their audiences, mainly Chinese men, saw lengthy performances of acrobatics, full Chinese operas or opera highlights, and military plays. Critics in the English-language press had reservations about Chinese music, and the association of sung dialogue with acrobatic mime. They reserved their praise for the costumes, the choreography and the skill of the female impersonators. The managers of the companies included Lee Gee, Leong Chan-Kwong, Po An Toy and Ah Goon.

Restrictions on Chinese entry to Australia from the 1880s coincided with a decline in China's international influence, and subsequent political and social upheavals. The Chinese in Australia kept tradition alive with dragon dances, acrobatics and street performances at festival times, and the

Chinese Youth League, established in 1939, produced Chinese theatre pieces in its concerts. In 1956 Australian audiences saw the Peking Opera Company, led by Hsu Kung-hsiao. It included members of the Song and Dance Company of the Wuhan People's Art Theatre. Again uneducated critics tended to admire spectacle and deride much else. In 1983 Australian entrepreneurs brought the Jiangsu Peking Opera Theatre to Australia to perform opera highlights, including an excerpt from a revolutionary opera, *Shajiabang*. The tour coincided with the first international conference on Chinese theatre in Australia, which increased understanding of the history, conventions and practice of Chinese opera and western-derived Chinese drama. The Peking Opera Troupe of China performed a complete opera, Wu Zuguang's *The Three Beatings of Tao Sanchun*, in Australian capitals in 1988, and the Taijin Municipal Beijing Opera toured four capitals in 1992.

In Melbourne in 1986 Geoff Hooke directed *The Imposter* by Sha Yexin, and the playwright took part in the Melbourne Writers' Festival in 1988. Some plays by the Malaysian–Chinese dramatist John Lee Joo For were produced in Perth and Melbourne in the 1970s. *The Propitious Kidnapping of a Pampered Daughter* included stylistic devices from Chinese opera in a story based on the abduction of the American heiress Patty Hearst.

Chinese acrobats have always attracted large Australian audiences, and since 1980 they have contributed to Australian circus performance, particularly by the FLYING FRUIT FLY CIRCUS and CIRCUS OZ. The Guangzhou Acrobatic Company toured Australia in 1972, 1978 and 1980, the Wushu (Martial Arts) Group of China in 1977, the Nanjing Acrobatic Troupe of China in 1980 and 1986, and the Yunnan Provincial Acrobatic Troupe in 1992. Lu Yi, artistic director of the Nanjing Acrobatic Troupe, greatly increased the skill and professionalism of young Australian performers in training workshops in 1983–85. In 1987-1988 eight young Fruit Flies trained for three months with the Guangzhou Acrobatic Troupe in China. ❦*Alison Broinowski*

further reading
LOVE, HAROLD. Chinese theatre on the Victorian goldfields 1858–70. *Australasian Drama Studies* 3/2 (Brisbane, April 1985).

Robert Chisholm

Actor, singer. Born 18 April 1898 in Melbourne. Educated at University of Melbourne. Studied for stage in London. Engaged by J. C. Williamson's for first Australian production of *The Maid of the Mountains* 1921. Performed in New York and London 1924–33. Returned to Australia for F. W. Thring 1933. Returned to USA 1936. Appeared in many musicals and some films. Died 11 November 1960 in Melbourne.

A well-trained baritone, Robert Chisholm played opposite GLADYS MONCRIEFF in six musical comedies, including *The Beloved Vagabond*, COLLITS' INN, *The Maid of the Mountains* and *Sybil*, between 1921 and 1935. He spent most of his career in the USA, on stage and in some films. He appeared in the New York and London seasons of *My Fair Lady*. After the London season he retired and came home to Melbourne, where he died. ❦*Alwyn Capern*

further reading
Age (Melbourne) 7 November 1960.
Australasian (Melbourne) 29 January 1921.

The Christian Brothers

Monodrama in one act by Ron Blair. **premiere** 1 August 1975, Nimrod Theatre, Sydney. Cast: Peter Carroll. Designer: Laurence Eastwood. Director: John Bell. **published** Sydney and London: Currency Methuen 1975.

RON BLAIR's virtuosic MONODRAMA *The Christian Brothers* takes place in a classroom, and the audience is the class. Only a single vacant chair, which signifies the Brother's most troublesome student, qualifies that impression. The Brother is presented as a type and he seems to warrant the plural in the title. Satire initially contains him fairly comfortably. His speech habits nicely epitomise his period and his role, and appeal to a collective memory of comic classroom tyrants. The humour shifts in focus, though. The Brother's manic persecution of the 'stubborn hound' in the front desk becomes disturbing in its persistence and in its relation to his emotional confusion.

The Brother is progressively humanised and becomes progressively more complex psychologically. The tensions between his faith, which is variously desperate and visionary, and his perfunctory religious observances, become central to the second half of the play. Other tensions relate to his teaching vocation and his attitudes to the boys, to his sexual insecurities, and to his sense of the value of his life and the ways in which that might be judged.

In its latter stages the play shifts in mode as well as tone. As the Brother recites the litany, he gently and rhythmically paints the chair blue. This closing image has a beauty that the parodic style of the opening could not have permitted. Blair's final presentation of the Brother is generous, allowing him dignity and even sentimentalising him a little despite all the evidence of his deficiencies as both teacher and divine. The piece is finally concerned more with understanding than with ridiculing him. ❦*Peter Fitzpatrick*

Church and theatre

Ever since the church spawned the theatre in the Middle Ages their relationship has been uneasy. Theatre was carried out of the church and into the wide world under clerical guidance by those who saw the vivid enactment of moral dilemmas as a source of spiritual illumination. On the other hand, there have always been clerics who see the theatre as deception and actors as disseminators of moral corruption. Nowhere has this dichotomy been more marked than in Australia. Typical of the clergy who opposed the stage root and branch, seeing it as a corrupting influence in a vulnerable new society, was the Rev. Trigg in PERTH. In an attempt to suppress the town's lively amateur theatre in 1839 the *Swan River Gazette* published his diatribes, which quoted classical precedent, at enormous length. Similar reservations in Sydney's convict colony played a part in Governor Ralph Darling's determination to suppress BARNETT LEVEY's attempt to start a professional theatre. And fulmination from the pulpit against the stage has been heard occasionally down to recent times.

Despite the rise of the temperance movement and the moral majority within the rising middle class, knighted actors on the English stage from the end of the 19th century and the social acceptance of such entrepreneurs as J. C. WILLIAMSON did much to weaken clerical hostility to the professional stage in Australia. So did the vogue for elevating and sentimental melodramas like Wilson Barrett's *The Sign of the Cross*, presented by Williamson in 1897. Indeed, Williamson produced one of his rare local scripts to stage one of his most extraordinary and lavish spectacles, the Rev. T. Hilhouse Taylor's edifying PARSIFAL.

The rise of serious amateur theatre often attracted positive clerical support. In 1931 the Anglican Archbishop of Brisbane stoutly championed the BRISBANE REPERTORY THEATRE SOCIETY's choice of George Landen Dann's IN BEAUTY IT IS FINISHED, a play involving miscegenation and prostitution, when many nonconformist clergy vehemently seconded a scandal whipped up by *Smith's Weekly*. But in Sydney in 1968, a Presbyterian minister, William Pollak, was tried and severely disciplined by his peers for defending *America Hurrah!*, Jean-Claude van Itallie's scathing attack on depersonalised and morally decadent Western society, after the NSW government censored the NEW THEATRE production.

Many church-based drama groups have given members opportunities for social activity and production of drama of perceived moral value. Several Roman Catholic societies have made serious contributions to amateur theatre and performed some substantial plays. The Therry Society—named after Father John Joseph Therry, the first official Roman Catholic priest in Australia—formed branches in Melbourne in 1936 and in Adelaide and Perth in 1943. It aimed to improve the moral standards of live theatre. Its repertoire was generally unsurprising, but it tackled controversial subjects such as abortion—in *Why the Innocent*, a one-act play by the Adelaide writers Marie Burton and Leonora Walsh, in 1939. One critic saw it as a provocative work symbolic of 'the Therry Society's courage and enterprise in endeavouring to come to grips with modern problems through the medium of a Catholic drama'. In Melbourne it mounted some huge spectacles—*Credo* with a cast of more than 3000 played to 80 000 people at the Melbourne Cricket Ground in 1939. FRANK BADEN-POWELL, who joined the society in Perth, described it as a form of Catholic action whose aim was to 'fight the serious theatre on its own ground, and to provide good, clean, witty, devoted-to-God entertainment'. The Therry Society survives in Adelaide.

In Brisbane, another Catholic group, the Villanova Players, founded in 1948, has produced Australian plays and encouraged its members, particularly BARBARA STELLMACH, to write for it. The Ignatians, one of the Brisbane's most successful amateur groups, was founded in 1973 by Father Leo Flynn, who had previously established the Loyolans in Melbourne. The most significant group in Sydney has been the Genesians, formed in 1944 at a meeting of the Catholic Youth Organisation and still active. It took its name from St Genesius, the patron saint of actors. The group's first production was Henri Ghéon's *The Comedian* in January 1945 at the Australian Hall (later the Phillip Theatre). A program note said it would 'not only present religious plays but plays of real worth, untainted by the materialism and lewdity of so much Modern Drama'. After ten years, the church provided the group with a permanent home in Kent Street, where it opened on 8 April 1954 with a revival of James Lang's successful 1951 production of T. S. Eliot's *Murder in the Cathedral*. During their heyday in the 1950s and 1960s the Genesians produced a wide variety of classical and contemporary plays. Their record the included no Australian works but they gave practical theatrical experience to future writers. RON BLAIR, NICK ENRIGHT and PETER KENNA all acted or produced with the group, as did the actor PETER CARROLL, who first came to notice with the Genesians. ❦*Philip Parsons*

Church and circus

Some 19th-century circus proprietors in Australia strove to present a public image of respectability, even of extreme moral righteousness. Circus owners often gave benefit performances for local causes such as the building of a church. Ashton's Circus made an outstanding contribution, and many a provincial Catholic church was partly financed by the generosity of JAMES HENRY ASHTON and his family. Many other early circus families were Catholics, including the Perrys, the Wirths, the FitzGeralds and Gus St Leon's family. Apprentice children in FITZGERALD BROTHERS' CIRCUS around 1900 were 'never allowed to neglect their church duties on Sunday', according to the *New Zealand Mail* of 21 March 1901. The Perry children in Eroni Brothers' Circus had to attend a service in a little tent every Sunday. The widow of James Henry Ashton taught them religion.

The proprietors of the huge American circus of Cooper and Bailey, which visited the colonies in 1876–77, would not permit anything to disturb 'the respect due to the Sabbath', according to the Sydney *Town and Country Journal* of 1 December 1877. They presented it as the 'Great Moral Show', the circus patronised by the clergy. Its caravans were decorated with Biblical scenes. ❦*Mark St Leon*

further reading
MORIARTY, BERNARD J. *Fifty years of Therry*. Adelaide: Therry Dramatic Society 1993.
RADBOURNE, JENNIFER. Little theatre—Its development since World War II in Australia, with particular reference to Queensland. University of Queensland MA thesis 1978.

Diane Cilento

Actor. Born 2 April 1934 in Rabaul (New Britain). Daughter of Sir Raphael and Lady Cilento. Trained at American Academy of Dramatic Arts (New York) and Royal Academy of Dramatic Arts (London). Made professional debut in USA 1950. Australian stage debut 1975. Has lived in north Queensland since 1977. Was on board of New Moon Theatre Company. Opened Karnak Playhouse at Miallo (Qld) 1992. Married writer Andre Volpe 1956, actor Sean Connery 1962, playwright Anthony Shaffer 1985. Mother of actor Jason Connery.

An international film star famous for her beauty and smoky voice, Diane Cilento made her first appearance on the stage in Australia in 1975 when she played Katharina in *The Taming of the Shrew* for the QUEENSLAND THEATRE COMPANY. Since then she has given notable performances in John Pielmeir's *Agnes of God* and ROBYN ARCHER's *The Three Legends of Kra* in 1985. She appeared with the company again in 1991, as Mme Ranevsky in Anton Chekhov's *The Cherry Orchard*. She opened the open-air Karnak Playhouse on her property in north Queensland in 1992 by directing *Murderer* by Anthony Shaffer. ❦*Gregory Gesch*

writings
Hybrid. London: Hodder and Stoughton 1970. Novel.
The Manipulator. London: Hodder and Stoughton 1967. Novel.

Circus

In the second half of the 19th century the circus was a major form of entertainment in Australia, in town and bush. The first true circus—a circular arena where artists display physical and comic skills to entertain an audience—in the colonies was the Royal Circus in Launceston (Tas.), which opened on 27 December 1847. Its proprietor was ROBERT RADFORD, owner of the adjoining Horse and Jockey Inn. He presented feats of horsemanship, equestrian burlesque, vaulting, gymnastics, acrobatics, dancing and clowning throughout 1848. The equestrian feats included *The Courier of St Petersburg* and other pantomimes devised by Andrew Ducrow, manager of Astley's Amphitheatre in London at the height of its fame from 1825 to 1842. Ducrow revolutionised circus riding with his equestrian pantomimes and it was a rare equestrian who did not claim to have performed at Astley's under his direction. Rarer still was the circus that did not present at least one of Ducrow's scenes.

Astley's, near the southern end of Westminster Bridge, was opened in 1770 by Philip Astley, who was the first to realise that a horse cantering in a fixed circle generates centrifugal force which can allow a standing rider to balance upon its back. Astley fixed the diameter of his ring at some 12·8 metres, and circus rings throughout the world are still this size. Astley and other trick riders of his day performed such feats as riding with a foot placed in a stirrup of each saddle as two horses cantered side by side, and *voltige* acts, in which the rider leapt on and off a quickly moving horse. Soon after Astley opened his amphitheatre he combined equestrians, acrobats, rope dancers, clowns and other actors into a single entertainment for the first time. He also introduced burlesque and drama in the form of brief equestrian skits and scenes. Circus and theatrical arts became even more closely blended in hippodrama, in which riders engaged in combat as their mounts galloped across a long stage overlooking the conventional circus ring. These equestrian melodramas were produced at Astley's Amphitheatre from 1807. Trick horsemanship did not die away, however, because early travelling circuses could not carry all the paraphernalia for theatrical productions.

Pioneers of circus

In 1848 Radford opened an amphitheatre in Hobart which was described in the *Hobart Town Courier* as 'quite as good a building as any of those erected by Batty, Adams, Cooke and other equestrian managers who have exhibited in English provincial towns'. Nearly all Australian circuses can trace their origins to Radford's pioneering enterprise, chiefly through two performers in his company. John Jones, a dancer and acrobat at Radford's Royal Circus from its beginning, founded ST LEON'S CIRCUS, and James Henry Ashton, an equestrian, founded ASHTON'S CIRCUS. By the late 1870s sons of both men were accomplished equestrians in their respective family circuses.

J. S. Noble opened the OLYMPIC CIRCUS in Sydney on 19 September 1851 with a small troupe, apparently from England. This was the first overseas circus to visit an Australian colony. By the 1850s circus entertainment had been given in many towns in eastern Australia, in the open air or in amphitheatres modelled on Astley's or other contemporary English establishments. George Croft, a ropewalker, opened an amphitheatre in Brisbane in April 1847 but he sold up after a few months. Audiences seem to have fallen away because Aborigines were admitted and improper songs were performed. Brisbane regularly saw circuses only from 1855. Circus does not appear to have been given in Adelaide before the 1850s. The first circus seen in Western Australia was Frank Stebbing's Intercolonial Circus, which entertained more than 800 people under canvas on the Fremantle cricket ground on 27 April 1869. Stebbing, active in the eastern colonies from the late 1850s, may have organised this circus specifically for the tour of the colony. Circus companies from the east did not regularly visit the west until the 1890s, however.

Touring with tents

By the late 1850s tents had replaced cumbersome wood and corrugated-iron amphitheatres that had to be erected and dismantled for transport. The gold rushes in NSW and Victoria and the growth of inland towns and trade routes encouraged early circus proprietors to adopt the tenting system, perhaps as early as 1851. American circuses had performed in calico tents since 1825 and a touring American circus popularised tenting in Europe in the early 1840s. The tents that housed the circus in Australia do not appear to have differed markedly in design from those used by American or European circuses. Circus proprietors long patronised the Sydney tent-making firms Hardie's and Walder's. Large circus tents are now often made of synthetic material, imported from Italy or Germany.

From the earliest days of touring, advance agents were employed to advertise the circus along its route, keeping ahead of the company by perhaps two to four weeks. No Australian circus adhered to a defined itinerary until the 1890s. A circus was obliged to procure a theatrical licence

James Henry Ashton performed an act called The Kaffir's Flight *with his pupil Liliputian Charley at his Royal Amphitheatre in Sydney in 1855. 'But for the fact of knowing what a perfect master of his profession Mr Ashton is, there might be a feeling of fear come over a person, from the great daring displayed', said the* Illustrated Sydney News

in each colony it visited. This usually cost one guinea and it remained valid for 12 months. Illustrated circus posters are known to have been pasted on billboards as early as 1863.

Word of a circus's progress and its reputation quickly spread throughout the colonies by exchanges of news between provincial newspapers. Showmen sent complimentary tickets to newspaper editors along their route, in return for a favourable announcement of the impending visit, but journalistic criticism seem to have been remarkably objective and astute. Journalists' reports and criticisms of circus performances in the second half of the 19th century were usually precise and admirably detailed. In the absence of other records or recollections of colonial circus people, these critiques document the early development of the Australian circus. They usually recorded information such as the name and nature of the acts presented in each performance, the route of a circus through a district, and the names and roles of the people associated with a circus.

Henry Burton was the first to take a circus to a goldfield in Australia. He formed his company in 1851 and toured it until 1880. Burton arrived from England in 1849, bringing the first minstrel troupe to Australia

After the experience with amphitheatres in the 1840s and 1850s, there was no permanent circus building in Australia until 19 October 1901, when FITZGERALD BROTHERS' CIRCUS opened the Olympia in Melbourne on the site now occupied by the VICTORIAN ARTS CENTRE. Later the rival WIRTHS' CIRCUS leased the Olympia. In Sydney the Wirths were instrumental in having the Hippodrome, now called the CAPITOL THEATRE, built in 1916 and they used it on their annual visit to Sydney until the late 1920s. Australian circuses generally continue to perform in tents, largely because of the need to cater for widely dispersed and small populations and the lack of suitable permanent buildings.

Dangerous lighting methods

From the earliest times, colonial circus proprietors struggled to develop a lighting system that was safe, quiet and effective. Until the advent of portable petrol-driven electricity generators in the 1920s, lighting systems were as diverse as jam tins filled with fat, kerosene lanterns and carbide plants. In spite of these dangerous methods no catastrophe during a performance is known. The proprietors of Sole Brothers' Circus were killed, however, when their carbide plant exploded while they were inspecting it before the show opened at Blayney (NSW) in June 1923.

Many proprietors have operated travelling circuses. The best known, at least for the size and consistency of their companies, were James Henry Ashton and his family, Henry Burton, John Jones and his family (later known as the St Leon family), the Wirth brothers, the FitzGerald brothers and the Perry family, a branch of which assumed the pseudonym of Eroni in the early 1890s.

The smaller circuses often went to great lengths to take entertainment to people in the remotest parts of the bush, such as shearers, miners and railway construction gangs. In an age when few people could regularly travel, the circus people were highly valued because they brought with them first-hand knowledge of conditions in other parts of the country. An essay in the magazine *Imperial Review* of July 1884 hints at their breadth of knowledge of the social and economic conditions and regional developments: 'We have talked with the employees of these nomad troupes and their experiences form quite a romance of the gold diggings, bush townships, inns, roads and no roads, forests, streams and mountains …'.

Popularity of equestrianism

The circus made few, if any, intellectual demands upon its audience but it reflected the cultural values of a new society that was already concentrating its attention on athletic achievement. The English writer Richard Twopenny noted the popularity of circuses in the Australian colonies in his *Town Life in Australia* in 1883, remarking '… perhaps in no other part of the world can a circus obtain so critical and appreciative an audience'. Twopenny rightly attributed this to the popularity of horses and horsemanship in colonial Australia. Equestrianism was the principal feature of the circus in Australia until the end of the 19th century at least. In the early decades equestrianism appears to have fallen into three broad categories: the classic repertoire of Ducrow; other established pieces of traditional English circus horsemanship, such as *The Peasant's Frolic*; trick riding, such as posing and posturing on horseback. From the mid-1870s the trend was increasingly towards an acrobatic style, derived from or paralleling similar developments in American and European circuses. Young equestrians began to vault and tumble on horseback as acrobats would on the ground. Visiting American circuses appear to have given impetus to the new style. By the early 1880s the art of Ducrow had all but disappeared from Australian circus.

Fine equestrians prominent during the second half of the 19th century included the sons of James Henry Ashton and John Jones; George Gilham, for many years the star rider of BURTON'S CIRCUS; and Aboriginal riders such as Billy Jones and Ashton's pupils Combo Combo and Mongo Mongo. The star female equestrian of Burton's company during the late 1860s and the 1870s was Mme La Rosiere, the only woman of the day capable of the difficult 'bounding jockey' act. In this act, the lineal descendant of the *voltige* riding at Astley's, the rider moved rapidly onto and off the back of a cantering horse as it circled the ring.

In the later decades of the 19th century, purely human acts challenged the predominance of the horse and horsemanship in European and American circuses. Some of these—such as ACROBATICS, gymnastics, JUGGLING, ROPEWALKING—had been minor circus acts since Astley's time. Others were adapted from theatrical traditions, particularly variety. Among them were mind-readers, high divers, 'talking' horses and performers on the trapeze, which was devised in 1859 by a Frenchman, Jules Léotard. These changes were increasingly evident in Australian circus as the 19th century ended. A decline in appreciation of the equestrian arts began in 1895, when FitzGerald Brothers' Circus, responding to changed audience preferences, began annually importing companies of American, English, European and Japanese artists who concentrated on variety turns. Wirths' Circus adopted this practice too in the early 1900s. To this day many of the major performers in Australian circuses are imported, particularly from Europe.

The rise of animal acts put the feats of horses and riders further into the shade. In 1882, St Leon's circus, following the example of visiting American circuses, acquired its own menagerie. At that time the role of the menagerie, as a travelling zoo, was partly educational and partly entertainment. By 1887 St Leon's circus had a lion tamer on the program. The large FitzGerald Brothers' and Wirths' Circuses in the early 1900s emphasised performances by trained lions, tigers, elephants, seals and polar bears.

Australia still produced fine equestrians, but they usually found showcases for their skills only in the smaller provincial circuses or overseas. MAY WIRTH, an equestrian of world stature, gained only passing recognition in Australia. She left to pursue a career in American circuses, as did contemporaries including Clarence and Vera Bruce, Freddy and Ethel Freeman, and PHILIP ST LEON. Increasing urbanisation and preference for motor vehicles over horse-drawn transport further diminished appreciation of equestrian skills. After May Wirth and Philip St Leon left in 1916, the disappearance of old families from the circus scene, the Great Depression and the Second World War arrested development in equestrianism. By the late 1940s the Five Riding St Leons and a few others were the only Australian riding acts of a high standard. Equestrianism of a high order has all but disappeared from the circus in Australia.

The Australian circus retained an identity quite separate from other forms of entertainment until the early 1900s, when the rise of vaudeville circuits in the cities encouraged more frequent exchanges of artists between the two forms. This was usually confined to acrobats, gymnasts, wire-walkers and jugglers, as Australian vaudeville houses were too small or otherwise inappropriate for full-scale equestrian acts. The First World War—in which many circus performers were killed or injured—and the Great Depression served to accentuate the rise of animal acts, which were less expensive than human acts. The ability of circus artists to adapt to the requirements of vaudeville, which offered greater continuity of employment and better pay, may have contributed to a decline in artistic quality that became increasingly apparent in Australian circus from the 1920s.

Although the Australian circus developed from the British circus it forged its closest links with the American circus. In the second half of the 19th century at least ten American circuses visited the Australian colonies, some of them two or three times. Most came between 1873 and 1892, when competition between large circuses in the USA was at its height. American circuses began to travel by rail during the Civil War of 1861–65. In 1869 railway connection of the eastern and western seaboards permitted the largest railroad circuses to visit California and more American circuses had the chance to tour the Pacific region. The cost of excursions across the Pacific to Australia—as much as $40 000 to transport a modest-size company from San Francisco to Sydney and back in the 1880s—the delay and additional expense in moving from one colony to another caused by the colonies' differing railway gauges, and strict colonial quarantine regulations, all contributed to the end of visits by American circuses. By the early 1900s, after a five-year visit to Europe by the Barnum and Bailey troupe, American circuses had all but ceased overseas touring. In the first two decades of the 20th century the American circus industry was at its height and a company could not remain competitive after a prolonged absence overseas. The principal American companies to visit Australia were:

Chiarini's Royal Italian Circus. The proprietor, Giuseppe Chiarini, was a member of a famous Italian circus family but his circus was substantially American. It visited Australia in 1873, 1880–81 and 1884–85.

Cole's Concorporated Shows. Unscrupulous marketing and organisational methods on its 1880–81 tour made this the only visiting American circus to encounter negative criticism. William Washington Cole, a flamboyant showman, reputedly left a fortune of $5 million when he died in 1915.

Cooke, Zoyara and Wilson's circus. A strong little company, it was organised in San Francisco especially for its Australian tour. It included John Barry, perhaps the first somersault bareback rider seen in the colonies. The com-

Equestrianism and a menagerie of wild animals have equal prominence in an advertisement for Cooper and Bailey's huge circus from the USA in 1876. The circus boasted the presence of 'the peerless and undisputed challenge champion bareback rider of the world', James Robinson. His salary of £200 a week was the largest ever paid to a single artist, it claimed

pany opened in Sydney on 5 March 1866. It became insolvent in December 1867 after returning to Sydney from a tour of Queensland. H. P. Raphael, an Amerindian who came to Australia as 'infant equestrian prodigy' with the North American Circus, became its proprietor early in 1868.

Cooper and Bailey's circus. The largest railroad circus of its day, the forerunner of today's Ringling Brothers and Barnum and Bailey Circus, came in 1876–77 and 1877–78. More than any other American visitor the Cooper and Bailey circus gave fresh impetus to the development and diversification of the Australian circus—with its menagerie of wild animals, its long, flamboyant street parades, its boisterous advertising and its use of the railway.

D. M. Bristol's Great American Cirque and Equescurriculum. It toured in 1897–98.

Flying Jordan Circus Carnival. The last complete American circus to visit Australia, it toured in 1897–1900.

Fryer's Circus. It toured Australia and New Zealand during 1885–86. It was probably the only American circus to visit Western Australia, late in 1885.

North American Circus. The first circus on the Californian goldfields in the 1849 gold rush, it played on the Victorian goldfields and in Melbourne during 1852–54. So successful was this visit that the proprietor, Joseph Andrew Rowe, brought his company back in 1858–59, but to a less enthusiastic reception. The clown William Worrell took control of Rowe's circus in 1859.

San Francisco Palace Circus. This large circus was owned by John Wilson, one of the 1866–67 Cooke, Zoyara and Wilson triumvirate. It toured in 1876 and in 1881–82.

Sells Brothers. This circus from Columbus (Ohio) successfully toured NSW and Victoria in 1891-92. It rivalled the immense Barnum and Bailey organisation in size and in Australia, free from the prospect of legal action, it adopted the Barnum and Bailey boast of 'greatest show on earth'. On its return to the USA, the Sells circus made capital out of its tour by heading its florid advertising 'just returned from Australia'.

Many performers who came to Australia with these circuses remained here. Some joined local companies and others organised their own circuses to tour Australia. The Mathews family, for example, remained after the 1881–82 tour of John Wilson's circus and toured successfully with its own circus from 1883 to 1887.

Australian circuses—Ashton's, Burton's, FitzGerald Brothers', Perry's, St Leon's and Wirths'—did not offer the American visitors direct competition. The American companies were bigger but not always better. Ashton's Circus and BURTON'S CIRCUS of 1875 each probably comprised as many as 40 persons, including performers and their families, bandsmen, grooms and management. Each circus may have needed as many as 80 horses, most of which hauled perhaps a dozen covered and flat-top wagons. A few horses would have been employed in the performance. St Leon's circus claimed in the *Illawarra Mercury* on 7 November 1883 that it comprised 150 men and horses and that its parade through a town stretched for more than half a mile.

Ornate bandwagons headed circus processions as long as the horse-and-wagon era lasted. Some large wagon circuses, such as Eronis', prided themselves upon owning a fleet of richly decorated, custom-built living wagons. The coach-building firm of Dallinger in Albury (NSW), was regarded as the finest manufacturer of circus wagons in the early years of this century. In contrast to the low-wheeled, heavy wagons of the American circus, the Australian circus wagon was a high-wheeled affair which facilitated travel through a wide variety of conditions in the outback.

At least three circuses of British origin came to Australia, but none directly from the United Kingdom, largely because of the greater difficulty and cost of transporting a circus so far by sea. Harmston's Circus, a large company that visited Australia in 1890–91, was organised in San Francisco. It came again in 1897–98, when it was based in southeast Asia. The English circus–menagerie–vaudeville show of Bostock and Wombell played to good business in Australia in 1906, after an indifferent reception in South Africa. The fine South African circus of Frank Fillis was popular in Australia in 1892–94.

Travelling by rail

The Cooper and Bailey circus became the first to use a colonial railway system on 5 May 1877, when it was put aboard a special train of 35 carriages and wagons in Sydney to tour NSW. The first Australian circus to travel by rail was St Leon's circus in Tasmania early in 1881. By the late 1880s FitzGerald Brothers' Circus and Wirths' Circus travelled regularly by rail. Probably inspired by the large visiting American circuses, they also began to travel by ship and adopted standard routes through Australasia in the late 1880s and early 1890s. In 1901, FitzGerald Brothers' Circus required 34 railway carriages and wagons to transport its entire company of 112 persons, and its horses, elephants, wild animals and paraphernalia.

Not all Australian circuses could adopt American methods, however, because the market was too small and the railway systems were fragmented and insufficiently developed. In the 20th century smaller circuses occasionally used trains for particular runs, but only the largest circuses could afford to rely on rail transport.

There was a general transition from horse-drawn to motor transport in the 1920s. All circuses eventually benefited from motor transport, for it enabled a company to cover more territory than hitherto possible and generate greater revenues to cover increasing overheads. The cost of star acts was rising, musicians were becoming increasingly militant and cinemas were proliferating in country districts. The travelling picture show began to reach country districts about 1916, but did not alone affect the viability of the circus. The circus had long competed with other entertainments, such as itinerant buckjumping and variety shows. Even the establishment of permanent cinemas in the larger country towns made no substantial impact.

The circus remained popular in city and country between the wars but during the Second World War all companies' activities were curtailed to varying extents. Even Wirths' Circus had its daily advance limited by petrol rationing. After the war the circus flowered anew. Two circuses enjoyed great success in the prosperous postwar decade—BULLEN BROTHERS' CIRCUS and SILVER'S CIRCUS. The introduction of television in 1956 was the principal cause of the decline of the Australian circus in recent decades. When Wirths' Circus had to cease operations in 1963, after more than 80 years of continuous operation, the management specifically blamed the spread of television.

As early as the 1860s circuses and circus performers of Australian origin could be found in the Americas, the Far East and India. Australian circuses have toured New Zealand since the 1870s. Wirths' Circus toured through southern Africa, South America, England, India and southeast Asia in 1893–1900, an odyssey not paralleled by any other Australian circus. A small FitzGerald circus annually toured east Asia and India in the early 1900s. From the early 1900s many Australian circus performers pursued their careers in the large circuses of the USA, where the pay and possibilities for artistic development were far greater.

The circus brought entertainment to the greatest number of people at the lowest cost, in a country where only the largest towns could support theatres or even tax the capacity of a circus marquee to its limit. Old Australian circus marquees appear to have held no more than 1200 persons. With tickets at one, two and three shillings, takings up to £50 for an evening performance were customary, though as much as £100 could be earned in a large provincial town.

Many of Australia's circus proprietors are known to have amassed personal fortunes. James Henry Ashton and many others were noted for their generosity in donating their takings to local appeals for funds to build a church, school, hospital, masonic hall or other civic buildings. The artists the proprietors employed appear to have been modestly remunerated, however. The entire Walter St Leon family—a circus in itself—worked for one of the FitzGerald brothers' circuses during the 1902–03 season for a wage of £10 a week with board and keep. The entire Sole family of two parents and six children worked for Gus St Leon's circus in 1914–15 for £12 a week.

Individual artists in the early 1900s earned from £1 to £5 a week, depending upon the nature and number of the acts they presented in the ring. A top-class act such as the Winskills, three trapeze performers who toured Western Australia with St Leon's circus about 1929, received £25 a week. The Garcias, an automobile somersault act and a particularly big draw for a circus, apparently received £80 a week plus a share of the gross when touring with the Gus St Leon Circus in 1914. In the larger companies the performer was not expected to fill any other role, but artists in the smaller family circuses often had other responsibilities.

Australian circus performers have worn costumes similar to those worn by their contemporaries overseas. Female performing attire has steadily become briefer since the 1850s, when female equestrians wore long, flowing skirts in the ring. Many costumes appear to have been designed and made by the circus people themselves. The larger and more prosperous circuses could afford to outfit their supernumeraries, such as bandsmen and ring attendants, in specially designed uniforms.

Training of children

The professional life of a circus artist has been known to extend beyond 60 years of age, but the prime of a performer lasts from the late teens until the early thirties, when strength and agility are at their peak. Training usually begins at an early age. Marriages between artists from different circus families produces offspring with the physique necessary for accomplished performance. Through circus families, skills have been handed down from generation to generation, and refined and perfected along the way.

Circus artists have also been drawn from outside the profession. In earlier days this was usually by adoption or apprenticeship of young children to be raised and trained within a circus. These children appear to have come largely from the less privileged sections of society. The oral history of the Australian circus is dotted with mentions of children, often of Aboriginal descent, being given away to travelling circuses by single mothers or parents unable to support them. A few older children have voluntarily taken up circus careers after being trained in a city gymnasium or school of acrobatics. The training of children in the circus was intense and for infants it appears to have been harsh at best. Cruelty has not been unknown.

Circus artists were expected to learn all the circus disciplines by carefully following a regimen of increasingly difficult exercises and acts. No matter what line of performance a child was trained for, dancing was basic as it secured grace. Children practised in every spare moment —in the afternoons before an evening performance, while camped between towns in the bush or during the extended camps in the winter months, when many circuses suspended touring. In the absence of enforced laws against child labour, children appeared in the circus ring as soon as they were able. Some circus people of the colonial era appear to have received a surprisingly good education for their day, but formal education was not of major importance in the training of a circus artist. In providing any formal education circus families appear to have given preference to their own offspring over adopted and appren-

Trained in contortionism and other circus skills as a child, May Wirth graduated to bareback riding. She became one of the greatest equestrians the circus has known, but her excellence was more readily recognised in the USA than in Australia

Wirth's Circus comes to Wingham (NSW) in 1917, challenging the Arcadia picture show. The elephant-hauled wagon indicates that the circus has arrived by rail. Wirth's, the foremost circus in Australia at that time, could afford to travel only by rail. Smaller circuses, such as those on the agricultural-show circuit, went by train occasionally, but generally they travelled in horse-drawn wagons, taking entertainment and news to people in remote places

ticed children. A teacher would be engaged to travel with a circus sometimes, or a circus bandsman would provide tuition. Some children took correspondence courses.

The majority of Australian circus artists appear to have been of European origin, generally English. A surprising number of the prominent early circus families—such as the Ashtons, the Perrys, the Wirths, the FitzGeralds and the Gus St Leon family—were or became Roman Catholic.

There have been a significant number of Aboriginal performers, by virtue of intermarriage or adoption for apprenticeship. When John Jones returned from the Turon River goldfields to appear at Malcom's Royal Australian Circus in Sydney on 19 May 1852, his little company included 'his two Aboriginal boys', according to an advertisement in the *Sydney Morning Herald*. This was the first engagement of Aborigines as circus performers. Since then many people of Aboriginal descent have been acclaimed in circuses in Australia and abroad. Several were riders, including Mongo Mongo, from the Tamworth district of NSW, who appeared in Ashton's Amphitheatre in Sydney in 1855. Combo Combo from the Sydney district and Master Callaghan from Gracemere (Qld) were in ASHTON'S CIRCUS during the 1860s and 1870s. Bob West of Narrabri (NSW) was active in the early 1900s. Harry Cardella, born in 1884, was found on the banks of the Paroo River in Queensland and apprenticed to FitzGeralds' Circus at an early age. Billy Jones was apprenticed to Henry Burton in 1853 and became a capable rider, wirewalker, ringmaster and acrobat. He was associated with nearly every notable Australian circus of his time and, despite increasing age and proportions, he pursued his career until his death in Sydney in July 1906. Late in the 19th century the acrobats Ernie Gilbert and Alex Orlandi—fatally injured while performing in St Leon's Circus in 1896—and the clown George Mackay were prominent in provincial circuses.

Circus proprietors prized the athleticism and adaptability of Aboriginal performers but they employed few Aborigines as performers or workmen. This was because authorities restricted the movements of Aborigines, and because a circus could not afford to alienate its provincial patrons. From the late 1870s it was customary to bill Aboriginal performers as South Americans or other dark-skinned people under Latin-sounding pseudonyms such as Antonio (for Tony Hargreaves), Cardella (for Dunn), and Colleano (for Sullivan). Colleano's All-Star Circus, which was at its peak in 1917–23, billed the family acrobatic troupe as the Royal Hawaiians. Other members of the Colleano family adopted pseudonyms such as Zeneto, Panko and Sanchez. This family, of West Indian and Aboriginal descent, won international renown. Most of the Colleano children formed an acrobatic troupe, the Akabah Arabs, who went to the USA in 1924. Their brother was the great wirewalker CON COLLEANO and their sister Winifred Colleano was a famous trapeze artist.

Aborigines in old Australian circus troupes appear to been treated strictly the same as other members of the company. Aborigines were customarily excluded from circus audiences, however. Matters may have been more relaxed in country towns, such as Ulmarra (NSW), where in 1886 the circus proprietor Mathew St Leon 'admitted our sable brethren to the free list thus performing a kindly action in an unostentatious manner', according to the *Clarence and Richmond Examiner*.

The arrival in Australia of many JAPANESE PERFORMERS— acrobats and jugglers—in the 1870s and 1880s produced another ethnic strand. Artists of other ethnic origins have included Chinese, such as the acrobat Chin Foo Lam Boo, who appeared with Ashton's Circus in 1861; Indians, such as Mahomed Cassim and Abdullah, jugglers with Burton's circus in 1861–62; and the Mauritian gymnast John Edwin Zinga, who had arrived by the late 1880s.

Tradition and alternatives

Recently, the increasing sophistication and diversification of Australian tastes, as well as advances in electronic media, have brought into relief the deterioration in the artistic quality of the traditional circus. With the departure from the scene of old circus families, in which knowledge was handed on from one generation to the next, the refinement and enrichment of skills has significantly diminished. The present-day traditional circus therefore largely relies upon established trained and wild animal acts, and variety acts which give little suggestion of the artistic and performing standards that once characterised the circus. Equestrian feats are nearly unknown in Australian traditional circuses today.

The 'poor cousin' status of the circus in relation to other performing arts has done little to enhance its cause in the face of municipal restrictions, taxation laws and policies for government arts subsidy. Federal and state arts-funding agencies lack comprehensive policies in support of the circus or the circus arts. A position paper on circus developed for the AUSTRALIA COUNCIL in 1985 led eventually to the first national conference of circus people, the Circus Summit, attended by 160 delegates at the Victorian Performing Arts Centre in Melbourne in April 1990. In 1994 the performing arts board of the Australia Council identified circus as an issue for special attention in 1995.

The Australian public can still appreciate high-calibre circus entertainment, as attested by the visits in recent years of the Moscow State Circus and the popularity of televised spectacles of major American and European circuses. In addition, two small 'alternative' circus troupes have won wide acclaim in Australia and overseas. CIRCUS OZ has unified elements of circus, vaudeville, variety and cabaret into an entertainment with a thread of burlesque. The FLYING FRUIT FLY CIRCUS has revived many skills that had been dormant in Australian circus for a generation or more. Neither of these circuses exhibits wild animals. In 1987 at least 25 alternative circus groups were scattered throughout all states and territories of Australia. Many of them owed their initial inspiration to groups such as Circus Oz and the Flying Fruit Fly Circus. Circus skills are promoted in several high schools in Western Australia, and the Victorian and federal governments have jointly funded the Acrobatic Arts Community School at Wodonga (Vic.).

In its promotion of an array of human physical skills in an artistic rather than aggressive or competitive context the circus could still be highly relevant to a young nation that prides itself on athletic achievement. In addition, a properly organised touring circus may still be the best way to introduce the public to the live performing arts throughout a large, sparsely populated country.

Also deserving attention are full documentation of Australia's circus history, provision of adequate venues where various types of circuses may perform, compilation of a national register of people with circus skills, unification of the objectives of the various circus groups, resolution of issues concerning presentation of wild animals, and promotion of the circus to a level of dignity within overall cultural development. These and many other issues were debated at the Circus Summit. ☙*Mark St Leon*

further reading

CROWLEY, W. G. *The Australian Tour of Cooper, Bailey and Co.'s Great International Allied Shows*. Brisbane: Thorne and Greenwell 1877.

DRESSLER, ALBERT (ed.). *California's Pioneer Circus, Joseph Andrew Rowe, Founder*. San Francisco: H. S. Crocker 1926.

FERNANDEZ, NATALIE. *Circus Saga*. Sydney: Ashton's Circus 1971.

GRIEG, A. W. When the circus came to town. *Argus* (Melbourne) 8 June 1930. Visits of Chiarini and Cooper and Bailey circuses.

LORD, FRED A. *Little Big Top*. Adelaide: Rigby 1965.

SHETTELL, JAMES W. Circus without horses. *The White Tops* (USA) 8 September 1940.

ST LEON, MARK. *Spangles and Sawdust*. Melbourne: Greenhouse 1983.

ST LEON, MARK. The circus in the context of Australia's regional, social and cultural history. *Journal of the Royal Australian Historical Society*, December 1986.

ST LEON, MARK. Whither the circus. *Arts National* (Brisbane) July–August 1985.

STOTT, R. TOOLE. *Circus and Allied Arts—A world bibliography* 4 vols. Derby (England): Harpur and Sons 1958.

STURTEVANT, C. G. When the American circus went abroad. *The White Tops* December 1939, January 1940.

VAIL, R. W. G. *Random Notes on the History of the Early American Circus*. Worcester (Massachusetts, USA: American Antiquarian Society 1934.

VAN WYCK, S. R. The origins of Rowe's Original California Circus. *The White Tops* December 1937, January 1938.

WEINER, ALBERT. The short unhappy career of Luigi Dalle Case. *Educational Theatre Journal* 27 (March 1975).

WIRTH, GEORGE. *Round the World with a Circus*. Melbourne: Troedel and Cooper 1925.

WIRTH, PHILIP. *A Lifetime with an Australian Circus*. Melbourne: Troedel and Cooper 1930.

Rope and wirewalking. *This Australia* spring 1985.

Spangles and sawdust. *Theatre Magazine* 2 December 1907 to 1 December 1908.

Le Grand Livre du Cirque 2 vols. Geneva (Switzerland): Bibliothèque des Arts 1977.

Imperial Review July 1884.

Circus Oz

Professional circus ensemble founded in December 1977 at Pram Factory, Melbourne. Awarded inaugural Sidney Myer Award for the Performing Arts in 1984. **first season** Moomba Festival (Melbourne) and Adelaide Festival of Arts in March 1978.

landmark seasons National Gallery of Victoria, Melbourne, November–December 1978. Last Laugh Theatre Restaurant, Melbourne, May–December 1979. Paris Theatre, Sydney, April–June 1980. Perth and Adelaide Festivals on five-state tour January–August 1982. Tour of Aboriginal settlements in central Australia 1985. Melbourne Town Hall 1986. Adelaide and Melbourne International Comedy Festivals, World Expo (Brisbane), tour of Arnhem Land, 1988.

Circus Oz has given CIRCUS in Australia a status it has not had since the days of CON COLLEANO and MAY WIRTH. Blending artistic experiment, entertainment and social comment, it has revised and extended a form that was in danger of withering away. Its 10 to 15 performers present an intimate and unrelentingly energetic spectacle of knockabout physicality, with anti-authoritarian humour, social satire and brash live music. There are usually at least two musicians.

Circus Oz was founded upon ideas that informed new Australian theatre in the late 1960s and early 1970s—development of an Australian voice, ensemble playing and group creativity, heightened and exuberant physicality, exploration of comedy, populism, focus on the performer and stands on political issues. It has supported worker control and women's rights by example, and commented on other issues by overt statement or satire. It expressed its particularly strong anti-nuclear position, for example, in a disastrous plate-spinning routine involving mad scientists and a nuclear meltdown.

Two groups amalgamated to form Circus Oz in December 1977. One was Soapbox Circus, a roadshow set up by the AUSTRALIAN PERFORMING GROUP in 1976. The other was the New Ensemble Circus, a continuation of the New Circus, established in Adelaide in 1974. Together they had performed more than 700 times to a total audience of more than 300 000. None of the 25 original members had a traditional circus background, although some had worked in circuses to learn particular skills. Many had developed their attitudes in 'new wave' performance.

The group chose circus as its medium through a somewhat romantic intellectual process. Theoretically at least, circus was the perfect context in which to develop the sort of performance and—equally important—the sort of life that the members wanted. The company's founding principles were collective ownership and creation; integration of work and living; multiple skills in the personnel; equality of the sexes; aiming for a uniquely Australian signature; being open to the widest range of inspiration; a balance between intimate, accessible performance and a high level of experiment and innovation; and creating a show that exemplified teamwork rather than star turns. These principles have more or less informed the group's work throughout its existence. The concept of a family living permanently on the road has faded and the organisation has become more specialised but the original credo remains.

An impressive range of aerial routines—high wire, trapeze, slack wire, cloud swing, web rope and roof walk are standards—distinguish Circus Oz from other 'alternative' circuses. Critics have made much of the fact that it is a circus without animals, but economics rather than philosophy may have determined its distinctive human focus. Perhaps the most significant change in the performance over the years has been the introduction of hoop-diving, pole balancing and group bicycle—skills learned in training with the Nanjing Acrobatic Troupe in 1983–84 and 1985. Broadening of physical skills has led to ever more daredevilry but the performers appear to be unable to resist sending themselves up and this perhaps is their most endearing—and essentially Australian—quality.

Many see Circus Oz as the only surviving symbol of the 1970s, but it is far more than a living museum. Its continuing vitality may be partly due to its special relationship with the FLYING FRUIT FLY CIRCUS, from which it has drawn more than 20 per cent of its performers in recent years. The two circuses share the use of a 1200-seat big top designed for the Flying Fruit Fly Circus by Tim Coldwell, the longest-serving member of Circus Oz. This tent incorporates contemporary design, construction and staging precepts, while conforming to traditional standards.

Circus Oz has toured every Australian state and territory, mounted numerous international tours, performed at three Adelaide Festivals and three Edinburgh Fringe Festivals and represented Australia at the South Pacific Arts Festival in Port Moresby (Papua New Guinea) in 1980 and the Los Angeles Olympic Arts Festival in 1984. Later overseas tours have included visits to the United Kingdom and Dublin in 1988; New Zealand, the USA and Japan in 1990; South America, the USA, Spain and Thailand in 1992, South America in 1993; and Israel, the Netherlands, Denmark and the USA in 1994.

Circus Oz, which began as a radical experiment in form and structure, has become a cultural standard-bearer. It has not lost its original bite and sparkle in the transformation.
❦*Jon Hawkes*

Jennifer Claire

Actor, dramatist. Born 20 February 1940 in Altrincham (England). Acted in repertory 1957–61. Came to Australia for marriage, 1961. Joined Young Elizabethan Players. Played in more than 50 Melbourne Theatre Company productions over 11 years. Founding member of Paris Theatre Company (Sydney). In major productions by Nimrod, Old Tote and Sydney Theatre Companies in Sydney. Also acted in film and television.

In more than three decades in Australia, Jennifer Claire has written for and acted with many leading theatre companies in Melbourne and Sydney. A critic has described her as 'an actress in the classic vein, who brings a depth of emotional intensity to her work which is totally compelling'. Early in her acting career a pivotal role was Christina in Eugene O'Neill's *Mourning Becomes Electra* for the OLD TOTE THEATRE COMPANY in Sydney. Other landmarks have been Maggie in Harold Brighouse's *Hobson's Choice* for Old Tote; Lucette in John Mortimer's adaptation of Georges Feydeau's *Cat among the Pigeons*, Lady Macbeth, and Vanya in Anton Chekhov's *The Cherry Orchard* for the MELBOURNE THEATRE COMPANY; Hessione Hushabye in George Bernard Shaw's *Heartbreak House* for the SYDNEY THEATRE COMPANY; the title-role in John Webster's *The Duchess of Malfi* for the NIMROD THEATRE COMPANY; and Lillian Hellman in the solo show *Lillian* for the Playhouse in Melbourne in 1987. The Sydney Theatre Company and Melbourne's Playbox Theatre Company performed her play *Butterflies of Kalimantan* in 1972. In 1987 the Sydney Theatre Company produced her *Siestas in a Pink Hotel*. ❦*Janet Greason*

published play
Butterflies of Kalimantan (1972). Sydney: Currency Press 1982.

John Clark AM

Director, teacher. Born 30 October 1932 in Hobart. Educated at University of Tasmania. Trained in theatre at University of Bristol and Bristol Old Vic Theatre School (England) 1956–57. Debut as director for Hobart Repertory Theatre Society 1959. Tutor in theatre history at National Institute of Dramatic Art (Sydney) 1959–68. Director of plays for Old Tote Theatre Company (Sydney) 1963–68. Went to USA on Harkness Fellowship in 1966 and completed MA at University of California (Los Angeles). Director of NIDA 1969–. Director of Jane Street Theatre (Sydney) 1969–81. Chairman of NSW government Cultural Grants Advisory Council 1976–80. Artistic adviser to Sydney Theatre Company 1979. President of Producers and Directors' Guild of Australia 1983–84. On board of Northside Theatre Company 1983–89. Director of NIDA Company 1990-. AM 1981. Husband of Henrietta Clark, television producer.

John Clark has combined a distinguished career as head of the NATIONAL INSTITUTE OF DRAMATIC ART with membership of boards and direction of plays. He directed Max Frisch's *The Fire Raisers* in the first season of the OLD TOTE THEATRE COMPANY in 1963. His powerful production of Edward Albee's *Who's Afraid of Virginia Woolf?*, with JACQUELINE KOTT and ALEXANDER HAY, brought him and the company to national attention. After a season in Sydney it toured nationally and to New Zealand. Clark followed it with a series of arresting productions—Joe Orton's *Entertaining Mr Sloane* and Rolf Hochhuth's *The Representative* in 1965; Harold Pinter's *The Homecoming* in 1967 and Thomas Keneally's allegory about the Vietnam War, *Childermas*, in 1968.

After Clark became director of NIDA his work was rarely seen outside that institution, although his production of David Williamson's *DON'S PARTY* in the 1972 JANE STREET THEATRE season transferred to the Parade Theatre and toured Australia for eight months. In 1979 he directed Bertolt Brecht's *The Caucasian Chalk Circle* as NIDA's contribution to the guest season in the Sydney Opera House that inaugurated the SYDNEY THEATRE COMPANY under Clark's artistic advice. With his administrator Elizabeth Butcher, Clark has made NIDA the country's pre-eminent drama school. He has done this by attracting outstanding students and teachers, by arranging international exchanges and through the establishment in 1990 of the professional NIDA Company, for which he commissioned new plays and musicals from young writers such as Hilary Bell, Timothy Daly, Nicholas Parsons and Steven Vidler. Clark also instigated a vigorous building program, which took NIDA from small weatherboard premises to a substantial complex. ❦*Ron Blair*

further reading
HOWIE, ANN C. (ed.). *Who's Who in Australia 1991* 27th edn. Melbourne: Information Australia.

Anne Clarke

Actor, manager, singer. Born about 1806. Sang in London. Arrived in Hobart as Anne Remans, August 1834. Made debut in J. P. Deane's company 23 August 1834. Married Michael Clarke 1834. Gave birth to daughter 1835. Acted at Royal Victoria Theatre, Sydney, 1837–39. Managed Royal Victoria Theatre, Hobart, 1840. Went to England to recruit performers February 1841. Returned to Hobart February 1842. Gave seasons in Hobart and Launceston (Tas.) 1843–47. Retired from stage 1847.

The first woman to manage an Australian theatre for a significant period was Anne Clarke. She also imported several actors who took leading parts in the development of musical theatre here. Her early life is not known. When she made her first appearance at J. P. DEANE's Theatre Royal in Hobart on 23 August 1834 it was claimed that she had formerly starred at the 'Theatre Royal English Opera House'. This may have been a reference to the Lyceum Theatre in London, which was known as the English Opera House from 1816 to 1830, when it burned down. Certainly, she was recognised from the start as an excellent singer. But her arrival in Hobart as an assisted immigrant suggests that her English career had been far from lucrative.

She made her Australian debut in *The Lord of the Manor*, an opera by John Burgoyne. The *Hobart Town Courier* of 29 August 1834 commented that her talents as a singer were 'highly respectable', while the *Tasmanian* allowed her to be 'accurate in time and tune'. The *Colonial Times* of 26 August also noted her stage experience: '… it is evident that this lady has trod the boards before; she had a good deal of tact and stage attitude, which cannot be obtained but by continued appearances before the public'. On 25 October 1834, Anne Remans married Michael Clarke, a widower and possibly a musician. In November 1834 she joined SAMSON CAMERON's company, and played with it in Hobart and Launceston during 1835. Next year she appeared with JOHN MEREDITH's company in Hobart. Meredith, according to a contemporary reviewer, helped her to extend her acting talents to match her fine singing.

Reviewing her performance of one of her favourite parts, the title-role of the operatic burlesque *Don Giovanni in London*, the *Tasmanian* of 17 February 1837 noted that she 'cannot be excelled, we may perhaps say, cannot be equalled, out of London. She dressed, sang and also acted to the perfect satisfaction of a crowded audience'. There are no physical descriptions of Anne Clarke but she had a fascination for such 'breeches parts'—she also frequently played Captain Macheath in *The Beggar's Opera*—that augurs for an attractive figure at least.

At the Royal Victoria Theatre in Sydney from October 1837 to October 1839 it was again her voice and singing that drew most critical attention, though the *Sydney Herald* on 12 September 1838 commented that she was 'letter-perfect in every part she plays', something said of few others on Australian stages at that time. She was back in Hobart in March 1840 and next month she took over as manager of the Royal Victoria Theatre, later called the THEATRE ROYAL. There were few other women in the company, so she had to play most of the female parts.

The shortage of women may have prompted her to return to England in February 1841 to recruit more performers. She returned in February 1842 with Gerolamo Carandini, FRANK HOWSON and his wife Emma and his brother John, and THEODOSIA STIRLING, all of whom contributed significantly to the development of theatre, especially musical theatre, in Australia. The Royal Victoria was occupied by another company so the Clarke company played briefly at the older Theatre Royal in the ARGYLE ROOMS. Anne Clarke renamed it the Albert Theatre. By July she had resumed control of the Royal Victoria. Her new actors gained excellent reviews. 'Her company is in toto very superior,' the *Cornwall Chronicle* observed on 16 July 1842. The *True Colonist* joined the praise on 7 October: '… the colony is indebted to Mrs Clarke for introducing a better class of performer and a superior style of management'. The latter critic also noted that respectable families were now prepared to attend the Royal Victoria, but Anne

Clarke never seems to have attracted the audiences and the money that her efforts and talents as a manager clearly warranted. During 1843 there were constant newspaper reports of poor houses at the theatre and on 8 March 1844 the *Hobart Town Courier* advised that its pit was to be boarded over so that it could be used for concerts and balls.

In April 1844 Anne Clarke took her company to Launceston and continued to play seasons both there and at the Royal Victoria Theatre in Hobart for the remainder of her period in Van Diemen's Land. Her daughter Anne Theresa began to appear with the company in February 1846, chiefly as a dancer. She was only ten years old, but actors' children took to the stage early at that time. Anne Clarke became estranged from her husband, who was named as a lessee of the Royal Victoria Theatre in Hobart in May 1847. Neither she nor her daughter appears in the playbills after that month. The 'life of great labour and anxiety' observed by a writer in the *Britannia and Trades' Advocate* of 5 March 1846 had clearly become too burdensome. There was a rumour that she had retired to Melbourne but nothing further has yet been discovered about her life.

A report in the *Britannia* on 21 January 1847 summarised Anne Clarke's achievements: 'It is seldom we notice except in general terms, the untiring exertions of Mrs Clarke for the amusement of the public. No praise we could bestow on her would exceed what she is entitled to, as an indefatigable actress of high character. Had Mrs Clarke been upon the English Stage, and, had she had the benefit of its advantages, she would have been a star. Here, although her qualifications are not lost, they are neutralised by distance, time, and circumstances. Untiring in her study, and *therefore* always perfect in her music, and characters, she is on all occasions, *excellent*. … We admire the attempt to make human beings rationally happy, and we care not for the particular method in which it is done, and thus it is that we hail with delight and approval, the manner in which the Hobart Town Theatre is now conducted. It is in every sense excellent.' ❦*Elizabeth Webby*

Doreen Clarke

Dramatist. Born 6 May 1928 in Lancashire (England). Emigrated to Australia 1958. Began writing for theatre 1978. Writer-in-residence with State Theatre Company of South Australia (Adelaide) 1981, City of Elizabeth (SA) 1982, Corrugated Iron Youth Theatre (Darwin) 1985, Junction Theatre Company (Adelaide) 1985, Riverland Youth Theatre (Renmark SA) 1986, Newcastle (NSW) Bicentennial Committee 1988 and Terrapin Puppet Theatre (Hobart) 1988. Lives in Adelaide.

Doreen Clarke weaves strong social commentary into humorous and engaging stories, with skilful use of the vernacular and strong depiction of characters, including women who exhibit humour and tenacity in the face of adversity. Since she began writing for the stage in 1978, after raising four sons, Clarke has worked in COMMUNITY THEATRE and youth theatre in South Australia and with groups in Brisbane, Darwin, Hobart and Melbourne, creating plays and conducting writing workshops. More than 24 of her community-theatre plays have been performed and she has had eight plays performed professionally—*Roses in Due Season* in 1978; *Bleedin' Butterflies*, *Missus Queen* and *Coppin and Company* (with David Allen) in 1980; *Farewell Brisbane Ladies* and *The Sad Song of Annie Sando* in 1981; *A Sort of Chimera* in 1984; and *Cornerstones* in 1990. Her most frequently performed plays are *Farewell Brisbane Ladies* and *Bleedin' Butterflies*. They show the breadth of her range. The first is a bawdy play about 'two old tarts' whereas the second is more serious, examining life in a Depression camp in Western Australia. Both plays explore the human condition with wit and compassion, however. ❦*Carolyn Pickett*

published plays
Bleedin' Butterflies (1980). Sydney: Currency Press 1982.
Farewell Brisbane Ladies (1981). Melbourne: Yackandandah Playscripts 1982.
Roses in Due Season (1978). Sydney: Currency Press 1982.

Marcus Clarke

Dramatist, journalist, novelist. Born 24 April 1846 in London. Arrived in Australia 1863. Wrote songs, sketches, burlesques, comedies, dramas and pantomimes for Melbourne stage from mid–1860s. Married actor Marian Dunn 1869. Sub-librarian of Melbourne Public Library from 1873. Died 2 August 1881 in Melbourne. Father of actor Marian Marcus Clarke.

Best known today for his 1874 novel *His Natural Life*, Marcus Clarke was not primarily a professional dramatist but he wrote intermittently for the Melbourne stage, chiefly to gain income. He married into a family of actors—his wife Marian Dunn and her sister Rose Lewis and brother John Dunn were the children of John Dunn, a popular low comedian. Clarke's interest in theatrical matters is evident in his journalism and satirical writing, including amusing parodies of contemporary theatrical styles and fads published in the magazine *Humbug* in 1869.

Most of Clarke's theatrical work was translations or adaptations of French or English texts. A notable exception was the comedy *Reverses*, which he wrote with ROBERT P. WHITWORTH in 1876 but was not performed until 1979. It delineates the 'coming Australian type' with the satire of colonial snobbery that is also found in his 1874 'Wicked World' journalism in the *Weekly Times*. Clarke wrote for numerous newspapers, notably as 'Atticus' in the *Leader*, with keen interest in cultural and social life and politics. In his first drama, *Foul Play* (1868), Clarke used the novel by Charles Reade and Dion Boucicault. He adapted Victorien Sardou's play *Fernande* for the tragic actor Mary Gladstane and translated Molière's *Le Bourgeois gentilhomme* as *Peacock's Feathers* in 1871, and adapted the novel *Le Vicomte de Bragelonne* by Alexandre Dumas *père* as *Plot!* in 1872. Both royal brothers in *Plot!* were played by Eloise Juno.

In 1879 Clarke adapted Wilkie Collins's novel *The Moonstone*. He wrote comedies, *Baby's Luck* in 1879 and *A Daughter of Eve* and *Forbidden Fruit* in 1880, to ease the financial situation that was leading to his second bankruptcy in 1881. In the last two Marian Dunn returned to the stage, which she had left in 1868. Clarke wrote songs for particular performers, and for HARRY RICKARDS he wrote sketches in 1872. His extravaganza *Alfred the Great*, with music by Henry Keiley, achieved a good run at the Academy of Music in Melbourne in 1878. His cantata *Proi*, set to music by the Italian composer and conductor Paolo Giorza, was performed in 1881. At his death he left an incomplete libretto for a comic opera, *Queen Venus*, which was performed as *A Lesson in Love* in 1882, and in full as

Moustique, with music by Henri Kowalski, a visiting French composer, in Sydney in 1889. With one notorious exception, Clarke found the topical stage more remunerative than the musical theatre. His spectacular pantomimes *Goody Two Shoes and Little Boy Blue* (1870) and *Twinkle, Twinkle Little Star* (1873), for the Theatre Royal in Melbourne, comment on politics with acerbic wit. This talent brought him public disgrace in January 1880, when he localised W. S. Gilbert's burlesque THE HAPPY LAND in the sensitive period before an election in Victoria and the government prohibited performance.

Clarke has made his impact on the theatre, however, through his novel *His Natural Life*, which appeared in serial form 1870–72 and was revised as a book in 1874. It was reprinted in 1882 as FOR THE TERM OF HIS NATURAL LIFE, the title used by ALFRED DAMPIER and THOMAS SOMERS for the most popular of a dozen or more stage adaptations written and performed between 1885 and 1913 in Australasia, the United Kingdom and the USA. The most successful of the other adaptations performed in Australia was the first, *His Natural Life* by the rival actor-manager GEORGE LEITCH. DAN BARRY, E. I. Cole and EDMUND DUGGAN were among the others who adapted the book. It was first filmed in 1908, and in 1927 Norman Dawn made a famous silent version, with the novelist's daughter Marian Marcus Clarke in the cast. Dramatisations of the novel keep Clarke's name before the theatregoing public. ❦*Veronica Kelly*

published stage works
Alfred the Great, extravaganza. Melbourne: Troedel 1879.
A Daughter of Eve—or, A Lesson in Love, play. Melbourne: Monash University 1985.
Goody Two Shoes and Little Boy Blue—or, Sing a Song of Sixpence! Harlequin Heydiddle-diddle'em and the Kingdom of Coins. pantomime. Melbourne: Robert Bell 1870; Monash University 1993 reprinted (ed. Dennis Davison).
The Happy Land, burlesque (as H. E. Walton) after W. S. Gilbert. Melbourne: McKinley 1880.
Reverses, comedy drama with Robert P. Whitworth. Melbourne: Clarson, Massina 1876; Monash University 1981 reprinted (ed. Dennis Davison).
Twinkle, Twinkle Little Star—or, Harlequin Jack Frost, Little Tom Tucker and the Old Woman who Lived in a Shoe, pantomime. Melbourne: Azzopardi Hildreth 1873.

other writings
A Colonial City (ed. L. T. Hergenhan). Brisbane: University of Queensland Press 1972. Selected journalism.
Civilisation Without Delusion. Melbourne: Bailliere 1880.
Four Stories High. Melbourne: Massina 1877.
His Natural Life (ed. Stephen Murray-Smith). London: Penguin 1970. Original long serial version.
Holiday Peak and Other Tales. Melbourne: George Robertson 1873.
Old Tales of a Young Country. Melbourne: Mason, Firth and McCutcheon 1871.
The Future Australian Race. Melbourne: Massina 1877.
The Mystery of Major Molineux and Human Repetends. Melbourne: Massina 1881.

further reading
BURROWS, J. F. *His Natural Life* and the capacities of melodrama. *Southerly* 3 (1974).
CLARK, MANNING. *A History of Australia* 4. Melbourne University Press 1978.
ELLIOTT, BRIAN. Marcus Clarke. *Australian Dictionary of Biography* 3. Melbourne University Press 1969.
ELLIOTT, BRIAN. *Marcus Clarke*. Oxford: Clarendon Press 1958.
GREEN, H. M. *A History of Australian Literature* 2 vols, revised (ed. Dorothy Green). Sydney: Angus and Robertson 1984.
KELLY, VERONICA. The Banning of Marcus Clarke's *The Happy Land*. *Australasian Drama Studies* 2/1 (October 1983).
WILDING, MICHAEL (ed.). *Marcus Clarke*. Brisbane: University of Queensland Press 1976. Includes *For the Term of His Natural Life* in short, revised form as novel.
WILDING, MICHAEL. *Marcus Clarke*. Melbourne: Oxford University Press 1977.

reference
The Mitchell Library (Sydney) has manuscripts of operetta libretti, songs and other unperformed musical pieces by Clarke.

Terence Clarke

Actor, composer, director, teacher. Born 10 February 1935. Began acting 1941. Graduated from University of Sydney 1966. Worked as actor in United Kingdom. Associate director of National Theatre Company (Perth) 1973–75. Founding artistic director of Hunter Valley Theatre Company (Newcastle NSW), 1976–78. Joined committee of Australian National Playwrights' Conference 1978; artistic director of 1980 conference; director of script assessment 1984-88. Head of directing and in charge of playwriting and new work at National Institute of Dramatic Art (Sydney) 1991–93.

Terence Clarke has worked at the grass roots of playwriting since the late 1960s, when he gave up teaching mathematics to share in the early euphoria at the Nimrod Street Theatre in Sydney as actor and pianist. There, in RON BLAIR's *Flash Jim Vaux* in 1971, he first composed for the theatre. He has contributed melodious ballad-style scores, often with an edge of pastiche, to three musicals with libretti by NICK ENRIGHT. THE VENETIAN TWINS was immensely successful in 1979. *Variations* followed in 1981 for the NIMROD THEATRE COMPANY. *Summer Rain*, commissioned by the NATIONAL INSTITUTE OF DRAMATIC ART as a graduation play in 1983, was reworked as a bicentennial project and presented in 1989 by the SYDNEY THEATRE COMPANY. Clarke has also composed and arranged music for plays, including works by DAVID ALLEN, DOROTHY HEWETT and GEORGE HUTCHINSON.

Clarke has directed more than 80 productions. The first major one was David Williamson's *Jugglers Three* for the NATIONAL THEATRE COMPANY in Perth in 1973. Another, Peter Kenna's A HARD GOD with JOAN SYDNEY as Aggie in 1975 is still remembered in Perth. Clarke chose to open the HUNTER VALLEY THEATRE COMPANY's first season with John Romeril's THE FLOATING WORLD, which proved controversial fare. He developed a working partnership with the Newcastle writer JOHN O'DONOGHUE, whose first play, *A Happy and Holy Occasion*, he presented in 1976, and for the Sydney Theatre Company in 1982. Clarke directed O'Donoghue's JONAH twice—in Newcastle and in 1982 at NIDA. He was similarly supportive of the early work of JANIS BALODIS. He directed Balodis's first play, *Backyard*, for Nimrod in 1980, with Bryan Brown and Joan Sydney. He also conducted the early workshop of Balodis's *Too Young for Ghosts* and directed it at NIDA in 1989. ❦*Katharine Brisbane*

Clarke and Meynell

Two immigrants, Clyde Meynell and John Gunn combined in 1906 to present a slambang melodrama called *The Fatal Wedding* at the Theatre Royal in Melbourne. In November 1907 they leased the theatre. Meynell (c.1867-1934), said to have qualified in medicine in Edinburgh, began acting in English stock companies and played small parts in London. He came to Australia in 1903 as stage manager of a company—sent out from London by Herbert Beerbohm Tree—starring JULIUS KNIGHT and Maude Jeffries in stylish melodrama. Gunn (c.1869-1909), born in Ireland, was also an actor and stage manager. He came to Australia in 1890 for the tour of the English comedian John L. Toole.

Two wealthy Melbourne men—Sir Rupert Clarke, an English baronet, and the entrepreneur John Wren—became partners of Meynell and Gunn. The expanded firm intended, the *Sydney Mail* reported on 16 September 1908, 'to extend its operations over the whole of Australia and New Zealand, and where no theatres are available, they will be built'.

With long leases on the THEATRE ROYAL in Melbourne and the CRITERION THEATRE in Sydney, 'Rupert Clarke, John Wren, Meynell and Gunn's Company' presented romantic costume dramas of the type made popular by Julius Knight. Gaston Mervale directed lavishly mounted and popular productions starring Harcourt Beatty and Madge McIntosh. The firm's greatest achievement was to import the Asche–Brayton Shakespeare Company in 1909.

On 20 October 1909 John Gunn died of pneumonia in Sydney. The firm became Clarke and Meynell Pty Ltd. It formed the New English Opera Company, which presented *The Belle of Mayfair*, *The Girl behind the Counter*, *Miss Hook of Holland* and *The Arcadians*. The last, Clarke and Meynell's biggest success, opened on Easter Saturday 1910 at the Theatre Royal in Melbourne with 16 imported players, including Maie Sydney, a young Australian singer who had been studying in London. The comedian Tom Walls stopped the show with his comically dismal 'Jockey Song'. In the novel racecourse scene English showgirls wore lavish dresses and special hats from Paris, and Clarke's Australian Cup winner Dreamland occasionally appeared. *The Arcadians* toured successfully. Clarke and Meynell then presented drama, including Matheson Lang in Jerome K. Jerome's *The Passing of the Third Floor Back* and Lewis Waller in *Henry V* with GEORGE S. TITHERADGE and his Australian-born daughter Madge Titheradge, who played the Chorus and Princess Katherine.

On 1 September 1911 Clarke and Meynell amalgamated with J. C. WILLIAMSON'S. Meynell joined HUGH J. WARD and GEORGE TALLIS as a managing director. Clarke looked after the Firm's business in London until Williamson died in 1913, when control passed to Meynell, Tallis and Ward. In 1923, three years after J. C. Williamson's had merged with J. AND N. TAIT LTD, Meynell resigned and retired to England. He was 'too much of a gentleman for show business', said Tallis, who was noted for his tough infighting with the Taits. ❦*Lynne Murphy, John West*

further reading
GIBBNEY, H. J. and ANNE G. SMITH. *A biographical register 1788–1939*. Canberra: Australian Dictionary of Biography 1987.
SOUTHEY, R. J. *Rupert Clarke. Australian Dictionary of Biography* 8. Melbourne University Press 1981.

Harry Clay

Entrepreneur. Born c.1864 in Newcastle (NSW). Began career as performer and entered vaudeville management in Sydney c.1900. Developed suburban Sydney and country circuits. Built Bridge Theatre, Newtown, 1911. Died 17 February 1925 in Sydney.

Harry Clay managed suburban vaudeville circuits that were training grounds for rising artists such as the teenage ROY RENE. *Theatre* magazine's obituary said Clay was 'a staunch friend of Australian artists with a high name in the profession for his generosity'. He neither smoked nor drank but had a prodigious flow of invective. Clay began management about 1900 at St George's Hall in the inner Sydney district of Newtown. By 1905 he was playing one-night stands in Balmain, Parramatta, Newtown, North Sydney and Petersham and at the Masonic Hall in downtown Castlereagh Street. In 1911, he built the Bridge Theatre in Newtown and this became his base. At various times he also ran the Princess Theatre in Railway Square and the Gaiety Theatre in Oxford Street, near Hyde Park.

Clay also sent shows to NSW country districts. In 1917 his rural circuit included Bathurst, Cowra, Goulburn, Grenfell, Harden, Katoomba, Lithgow, Murrumburrah, Wagga Wagga, Yass and Young. He also had a circuit around Newcastle. ❦*John West*

further reading
GIBBNEY, H. J. and ANNE G. SMITH. *A biographical register 1788–1939*. Canberra: Australian Dictionary of Biography 1987.
MCPHERSON, AILSA. *A Dream of Passion—Theatre activity in North Sydney*. Sydney: Stanton Library 1993.
RENE, ROY with ELIZABETH LAMBERT and MAX HARRIS. *Mo's Memoirs*. Melbourne: Reed and Harris 1945.

Faith Clayton

Actor. Born in Perth. Began acting at University of Western Australia (Perth). Graduated BA 1949. Studied speech and drama with Lily Kavanagh in Perth. Worked as clinical psychologist in London. Professional debut as actor in Perth 1953. Acted in Perth for National Theatre Company 1957, Hole-in-the-Wall Theatre Company from 1974, Interstar 1980, Mason-Miller Theatre Company 1981, Western Australian Theatre Company from 1985. Has also appeared in Adelaide, Alice Springs, Canberra, Darwin, Melbourne and other towns. Acts in radio, television and film. Inaugural Swan Gold Award for best actress 1989.

For more than 40 years Faith Clayton has been a popular and versatile actor in Perth, equally at home in tragedy and comedy, classical and modern drama, and musical plays. Her notable parts have included the title-roles in Bertolt Brecht's *Mother Courage and Her Children*, Sean O'Casey's *Juno and the Paycock*, Elizabeth Jolley's *The Newspaper of Claremont Street* and Nicholas Wright's *Mrs Klein*; and such leading roles as Pearl in Ray Lawler's SUMMER OF THE SEVENTEENTH DOLL, the nurse in *Romeo and Juliet*, Mrs Alving in Henrik Ibsen's *Ghosts*, Mrs Peachum in *The Beggar's Opera*, Miss Prism in Oscar Wilde's *The Importance of Being Earnest*, Enid in Louise Page's *Salonika*, Gunhild in Ibsen's *John Gabriel Borkman* and Bessie Burgess in O'Casey's *The Plough and the Stars*. She played Jocasta in Sophocles's *Oedipus Rex*, which opened the University of Western Australia's Sunken Garden Theatre in 1948; the Duchess of York in *Richard III*, the first FESTIVAL OF PERTH production, in 1953; Lizzie in *The Rainmaker* by N. Richard Nash on the first state tour by the NATIONAL THEATRE COMPANY, in 1957; and Gertrude in *Hamlet*, which opened the NEW FORTUNE THEATRE in 1964. For the Black Swan Theatre Company Clayton created Miss Murphy in Sally Morgan's *Sistergirl*, which toured nationally and was revived in 1994. ❦*Bill Dunstone*

David Clendinning

Actor, designer, director, teacher, translator, singer. Born 23 August 1937 at Townsville (Qld). Educated at University of Queensland (Brisbane) 1964–67 and Sorbonne (Paris) 1968. Acted in College Players. Co-founded Brisbane Actors' Company 1976. Associate artist of Queensland Theatre Company. Matilda Award for contribution to theatre 1990. Also acts in radio, film and television.

One of Queensland's leading performers in drama and operetta, David Clendinning is also a translator of classics. He has translated Pierre Beaumarchais's *The Marriage of Figaro* and Pierre Marivaux's *The Game of Love and Chance* from French and Ivan Turgenev's *A Month in the Country* from Russian for the QUEENSLAND THEATRE COMPANY, and Carlo Goldoni's *La locandiera* from Italian for La Boîte Theatre. To inaugurate the BRISBANE ACTORS' COMPANY in 1976, Clendinning designed and directed a production of Molière's *The Misanthrope* in which he played Alceste, winning *Theatre Australia*'s award for the best actor in Queensland. Other notable performances by Clendinning have been Hamlet for the COLLEGE PLAYERS in 1967; Mr Ortabee in the premiere of DOROTHY HEWETT's *Bon-Bons and Roses for Dolly* in Perth in 1972; Monk in the premiere of JOHN POWERS's *The Last of the Knucklemen* in Melbourne in 1973; Macbeth for the BRISBANE ACTORS' COMPANY in 1979; Daddy Warbucks in the musical *Annie* for the Queensland Theatre Company in 1981; Molière's Tartuffe for TN in 1987; Gaev in Anton Chekhov's *The Cherry Orchard* for the Queensland Theatre Company in 1991; and the title-role in *King Lear* for the ACRONYM Theatre Company in 1993. ❧*Bruce Parr*

Frank D. Clewlow

Actor, director. Born 1887 in Staffordshire (England). Joined Birmingham Repertory Theatre. Came to Australia to join Allan Wilkie Shakespearean Company 1927. Artistic director of Melbourne Repertory Theatre Company1928–30. Producer and studio manager for ABC radio in Melbourne. ABC federal controller of productions 1936–50. Died 13 June 1957 in Tasmania.

Frank D. Clewlow's theatrical importance in Australia lies less in his own work than in the enthusiasm with which he disseminated great theatrical plays to a vast audience through the new medium of radio. He came to Australia in 1927, as leading actor and stage director for the ALLAN WILKIE SHAKESPEAREAN COMPANY, bringing with him a wealth of theatrical knowledge. Clewlow was reading science at Birmingham University when he decided on the theatre. He learnt his trade as actor and stage manager in Shakespeare and melodrama in provincial theatres. This led to his becoming a director with the Gaiety Repertory Theatre in Manchester, touring India as director and stage manager with Shakespeare and modern plays, then going to the Birmingham Repertory Theatre, where he became associate director with the playwright John Drinkwater. He remained there for five years, then held other positions, including director of the Scottish National Theatre. A man of great enthusiasms, Clewlow declared that it was 'passion for living and thirst for further experience' that brought him to Australia. After his engagement with Wilkie, in 1928 he took over the running of the MELBOURNE REPERTORY THEATRE COMPANY from Gregan McMahon. There he recognised the quality of *THE TOUCH OF SILK* by the young Betty Roland, and presented its premiere. Other plays Clewlow directed included George Bernard Shaw's *You Never Can Tell*, in which 17-year-old CORAL BROWNE began her career. Clewlow described her as 'a rare find'. But the society was disintegrating, and Clewlow moved to radio.

By 1930 he was producing great plays at station 3AR in Melbourne for relay to larger audiences than the theatre could command. With the advent of the Australian Broadcasting Commission in 1932 he became its producer and studio manager in Melbourne and in 1936 he moved to Sydney as federal controller of productions. His enthusiasm led him into battle against official opposition time and again. One victory was winning money and program time to broadcast all 37 of Shakespeare's plays. ❧*Richard Lane*

Colleen Clifford

Actor, director, teacher. Born 17 November 1898 in Somerset (England). Married Douglas Leslie Blackford 1933. Studied pianoforte at Brussels Conservatoire. Studied drama with Edith Child. Began theatrical career in London 1919. Began television career 1939. Entertained troops at Hollywood Canteen during Second World War. Widowed 1954. Settled in Perth 1954. Founded Theatre Guild and Drama School. Moved to Sydney 1969. Acted for Old Tote Theatre Company. Glugs award for contribution to theatre 1987. John Campbell Mo Award for services to theatre 1994. Also in film and television.

In the Australian portion of her long life Colleen Clifford has worked tirelessly to promote theatre. In Perth she directed six musicals—*Bitter-Sweet*, *The Boy Friend*, *Annie Get Your Gun*, *The Highwayman*, *Oklahoma!* and *South Pacific*—for the Edgley organisation and refused to use imported performers. She first acted in Australia in 1971, when she began two years as the dotty author in *Move Over, Mrs Markham* by Ray Cooney and John Chapman. She has performed five versions of one solo show. In London she played Salvation Army General Mathilda B. Cartwright in a two-year run of *Guys and Dolls* from 1951. She excels in teaching voice production and coaching for auditions. Her pupils include Paula Duncan, Mark Lee, Andrew McFarlane and Julie McGregor. A spectacular benefit night for Clifford was held at the Ensemble Theatre on 13 November 1994. ❧*Miriam Davis*

further reading
AMADIO, NADINE. *Giants of Time*. Sydney: Sally Milner 1990.
DEVESON, ANNE. *Coming of Age*. Newham (Vic.): Scribe 1994.

Alfred Clint

Scene-painter. Born 28 August 1842 in London. Son of Alfred Clint (1807–83), marine artist. Arrived in Melbourne *c*.1865. Worked in Melbourne and Adelaide. Moved to Sydney 1869. Worked at Prince of Wales, Royal Victoria, Criterion and Her Majesty's Theatres and Opera House. Founding member of Royal Art Society. Newspaper cartoonist in Adelaide 1872–74. Died 20 November 1923 in Sydney.

A fine scenic designer, Alfred Clint ran a scene-painting studio at Camperdown in Sydney with his three sons, Alfred T., George and Sydney. When he came to Australia he worked in Melbourne with John Hennings on pantomimes and other productions at the Theatre Royal. At the Prince of Wales Theatre in Sydney he designed for a famous production of *The Tempest* by WILLIAM HOSKINS.

Clint was also a prolific cartoonist. His drawings appeared in the *Lantern* and *Mirror* in Adelaide *Sydney Punch* and early issues of the *Bulletin*. ❧*Mimi Colligan*

further reading
The Artist 1/2 (25 July 1941).

Clowning

A clown named Holland was in the company of the ROYAL VICTORIA THEATRE in Sydney on 13 August 1841 but, judging by the *Sydney Gazette* of 5 March 1842, he was not the first clown seen in the colonies. In Launceston (Tas.) an advertisement in the *Cornwall Chronicle* of 29 December 1847 for the Royal Circus listed a Mr Axtell as 'clown to the circus'. The old-time circus clowns embellished the performances of other artists in the ring, without diverting attention. When Ashton's Royal Amphitheatre in Launceston presented an equestrian piece, *Yankee Doodle's Come to Town Upon his Little Pony*, in 1851, not only a clown but the pantomime characters Harlequin, Columbine and Pantaloon were involved in the performance.

Among the earliest clowns to tour the colonies were Englishmen who purveyed 'jests, wits and bon mots' to adult audiences. Many were skilled in parody of Shakespeare or the speeches of parliamentarians. Walter Airey, a Shakespearean jester, singer and clown, can be traced as far back as 1861, when his name appeared on the bill of the Star Company, a variety troupe touring northeastern Victoria. Sydney *Town and Country Journal* praised him on 17 June 1871 for his 'high moral and intellectual tone … [and] a style of dress which is rich and handsome in the extreme'. It added that 'his sayings are calculated to tickle the fancy of the masses, while they incur the admiration of the most intelligent audiences'.

By the mid-1870s critics and adult audiences were beginning to weary of long-familiar buffoonery. Charles Bliss, a celebrated English humorist and vocalist engaged by ST LEON'S CIRCUS, perpetuated 'the same old jokes', the *Gundagai Times* noted in October 1879. Clowns began to disappear from the main action and play a secondary role, entertaining the audience between acts. Stale circus clowning appears to have given rise to some desire for improvement. Some folksy clowns diligently developed humour that related directly to the townspeople for whom they performed. ❧*Mark St Leon*

The Club

Play in two acts by David Williamson. Performed in USA as *Players*. **premiere** 24 May 1977, at Russell Street Theatre, Melbourne, by Melbourne Theatre Company. Cast: Terence Donovan, Frank Gallacher, Harold Hopkins, Gerard Maguire, John Walton, Frank Wilson. Designer: Shaun Gurton. Director: Rodney Fisher. **published** Sydney: Currency Press 1978.

The Club has been widely recognised as perhaps the most sustained and controlled piece of comic writing in the contemporary Australian theatre. It has had many productions in Australia and others in the USA, Berlin and London. Its unprecedented success no doubt owes something to its subject—Australian football, which has a special status in Melbourne, where the play has proved particularly popular. For many of its devotees this game is not only a passion but a source of self-definition.

DAVID WILLIAMSON's play sets out to analyse some of the sources of that deep commitment, and some of the needs it meets. But the play also explores institutional politics in general and the subsuming of individual needs within structures of received myth and quest for power. It is astute on these matters, and, above all, funny. *The Club* is a finely crafted moral comedy in the Jonsonian mode, in which the least attractive and most accomplished schemers are hoist on their own petards.

The plot involves a battle between the old-fashioned ethic of club spirit and callous new pragmatism. Both offer the participants in this all-male power-game a rationalisation for asserting or defending individual ego, but the club-spirit party is more congenial if less hilarious, and is set to pull off an improbable victory at the end. The satisfaction of the reversals and moral reprisals in the second act tends to override the logic of the analysis, in which all forms of commitment to the football club are shown—with varying degrees of affectionate indulgence—to be absurd. The satire in *The Club* has Williamson's characteristic blend of relentless exposure and ritual celebration. While the play was critically received in Melbourne as a satire on the growing practice of buying and selling footballers, reviewers in other states and countries quickly claimed it as a metaphor for the power games of sport in general, the corporate world and politics. ❧*Peter Fitzpatrick*

Club entertainment

Many see clubs as the backbone of the entertainment industry. Many of the average performers, production staff, and others who comprise the industry have been kept in work by clubs. Club entertainment was always analogous to private events until 1956, when clubs in NSW were licensed to provide slot-machine gambling. This fuelled an expansion that made club entertainment big business. At its peak in the 1970s the NSW club-entertainment industry employed more people weekly than such entertainment capitals as Las Vegas and London. Licensed clubs, which visitors to the state liken to small casinos, booked more than $70 million worth of entertainment in 1987.

Club entertainment in Sydney had its origins in the Great Depression, when social and sporting clubs booked entertainers at 'POVERTY POINT', a street corner frequented by artists and agents. In the late 1940s and early 1950s returned servicemen's clubs looked to entertainment to augment their Sunday-morning drinking gatherings. Six to eight artists appeared every Sunday morning in prominent clubs like the Leichhardt Returned Services League Club. These mornings were usually for men but women later sought separate nights.

Bill Sadler, who had been stage doorman at the Tivoli Theatre in Sydney, introduced star entertainers to the clubs. He organised some Tivoli performers to work at clubs such as the Leichhardt RSL Club and the Illawarra Leagues Club in Wollongong. At first major stars appeared either without payment or for a minimal fee. Artists in the late 1950s and early 1960s regarded a club engagement as low in prestige. The facilities for artists and patrons were not much better than in municipal halls, but as cash flowed ever-increasingly from the poker machines, clubs became stronger and able to attract the best performers. The Trinidadian pianist Winifred Atwell and other Tivoli headliners provided variety entertainment in clubs. As the TIVOLI CIRCUIT began to use only imported artists the clubs became great supporters of Australian performers. The closure of the Tivoli and touring TENT SHOWS was hastened as patrons became used to more comfortable facilities in the clubs, which offered opulent surroundings and food and beverages at reasonable prices. Pioneers in club entertainment included Richard Gray, Bobby Limb, Jim Macdonald and Jack Neery in addition to Bill Sadler, whose early work has been carried on by the Sadlier Vidette entertainment agency, managed by his son Hugh. Limb and Neery were responsible for Tivoli-style revues at the Kogarah RSL Club in Sydney in the 1960s. Limb was well known for his television shows and he brought many leading television entertainers into the clubs.

Macdonald became the first club-entertainment agent to introduce large-scale production shows. In the 1970s he produced musical shows like *The Sound of Music*, *Jesus Christ Superstar* and *Hair* at the St George's Leagues Club in Sydney. He has moved on to producing shows at Jupiter's Casino in Surfers Paradise (Qld). In recent years club entertainment has been in a lull compared to the lively days before random breath-testing of motorists. Tastes in entertainment in many clubs have also changed away from variety and cabaret to more contemporary forms. Entrepreneurial spirit has weakened as competition has increased and commercial realism has taken charge.

Large clubs like the South Sydney Juniors still spend more than a million dollars a year on entertainment and employ a large full-time entertainment staff but most clubs now heavily subsidise their entertainment as a service to the members. The concept of a club as a profit-sharing association based in the local community has meant that members, visitors and guests have been able to see some of the best in entertainment at reasonable prices. At many clubs the entertainment is free. *Nigel Lampe*

Con Colleano

Wirewalker. Born 24 December 1899 at Lismore (NSW). Originally Cornelius Sullivan. Taught himself wirewalking in outback circuses. Left Australia 1923. Married Winnie Trevail, Australian vaudeville soubrette, in Detroit (USA) 1925. Star of Ringling Brothers and Barnum and Bailey Circus in USA 1925–42. In Australia on Tivoli circuit 1937. Retired 1959. Died 14 November 1973 in Miami (USA). Brother of Bonar, Maurice and Winifred Colleano and other circus artists. Uncle of film actor Bonar Colleano.

While practising in Sydney in 1919 Con Colleano achieved a trick previously thought impossible—a feet-to-feet forward somersault on the wire. In this the performer loses sight of the wire, whereas in the backward somersault the wire is seen a split second before alighting. It took Colleano seven years to perfect the feet-to-feet forward somersault for public exhibition. It helped to bring him admission to the Circus Hall of Fame in Sarasota (Florida)—the supreme honour of the American circus world. His elder sister Winifred Colleano—a solo trapeze artist and an exponent of the difficult heel and toe catch—and the equestrian MAY WIRTH were the only other Australians to receive it. Con and Winifred Colleano came from an obscure family of carnival and boxing-show people. Their father, Cornelius Sullivan, was of Irish descent and their mother was of Aboriginal, West English and English ancestry. About 1907 the family settled for a time at Lightning Ridge (NSW), so that the eldest children could receive some education. They also began to learn circus skills. The Sullivans eventually resumed their outback travels with a carnival and a merry-go-round. Cornelius Sullivan wanted to start his family in the circus business, a hard life but lucrative for a successful family of performers. About 1912 at Collarenabri (NSW) the Sullivans sold their carnival and merry-go-round and joined Rowan Brothers' Circus, a small outback show. They assumed the name of Colleano at this stage, perhaps inspired by the Great Kellino Family, English acrobats who began an Australian tour in Sydney on 24 December 1897.

The Colleano children used their time in the Rowan circus to improve and diversify their skills. Young Con and an older brother, Bonar, learned wirewalking. Winifred performed as a contortionist in the circus and began to learn the trapeze. When the circus appeared at Hillston (NSW) on 14 December 1912, Bonar and Con were already performing some 'of the most dangerous feats ever performed on the elastic rope [including] single and double back somersaults, landing on the rope as they first started'.

In 1913 the Colleano family (then spelling their name Collino), left the Rowan circus to join the James Ashton family circus. Then they joined the King Carnival to tour NSW and Queensland. The King Carnival went broke at Winton (Qld), and the Colleanos were left to fend for themselves. In 1915 or 1916 they set out from Winton with a few wagons as a circus in their own right. They reverted to the name of Sullivan for a time, but by early 1917 the circus was being promoted as Colleano's All-Star Circus. Like other outback circus families, the Colleanos struggled to establish their name and reputation, but by early 1919 the circus had grown so large that it was touring Queensland and northern NSW by special train.

At one stage, young Con Colleano played nine different roles in the family circus, including wirewalker, bareback rider, flying-trapeze artist, balancing-ladder performer, tumbler and trombonist in the band. He concentrated, however, on perfecting his wirewalking and as the circus became solidly established he specialised in that. He practised up to seven hours a day and, with no other wirewalker as a model, taught himself in probably the hardest way possible—on a 'bounding' tight wire without holding a pole for balance. Con, his brothers and his sisters took special names on the bills of the family circus, apparently to mask their part-Aboriginal identity. The acrobats in the family dubbed themselves the Five Royal Hawaiians, while Con was billed as 'Zeneto, Prince of Wirewalkers'.

Con Colleano did not realise that his style and technique were unique until he left Australia late in 1923 to play vaudeville houses in South Africa, England and the USA. In Johannesburg he first wore the Spanish toreador costume that was his trademark for the rest of his career. Colleano's American debut in 1924 at the New York Hippodrome, a large vaudeville house, was so extraordinary that the circus magnate John Ringling, who saw the act, engaged him as a star attraction for the next season. This was the start of his 11 years as a centre-ring attraction of the three-ring

Ringling Brothers and Barnum and Bailey Circus. In winter in the 1920s and 1930s, Colleano played vaudeville houses and indoor circuses in the USA and Europe. His European admirers included Hitler and Mussolini. Like many others, they assumed from his Spanish costume and the music accompanying his act that he was of Spanish ancestry. Colleano remained in the USA for most of his life. He returned to Australia on several occasions, first and most memorably for the Tivoli circuit in 1937. His last engagement was with the E. K. Fernandez circus in Hawaii in 1960, when he was aged 60. ❦*Mark St Leon*

further reading
St Leon, Mark. The great Con Colleano. *This Australia* summer 1986–87.
St Leon, Mark Valentine. Con Colleano. *Australian Dictionary of Biography* 13. Melbourne University Press 1994.
St Leon, Mark. *The Wizard of the Wire*.

College Players

Semiprofessional dramatic company in Brisbane, formed in 1959 as amateur group by students at University of Queensland. **first production** *Patience* by Gilbert and Sullivan, 1959. Shakespearean and musical productions and tours 1965–69. Disbanded 1969.

The College Players went on ambitious old-style barnstorming train tours along the Queensland coast from 1964 to 1969, with a repertoire based on popular musical theatre and Shakespeare. They gave public performances, developed audiences in schools and established a far-flung support group, particularly from Townsville to Cairns in the north. Founded as a student group to produce *Patience*, the College Players, combined energetic young artists with older performers who were working in radio at a time when the Australian Broadcasting Commission was still producing drama and features in Brisbane. The dominant force was Bryan Nason, a director with a passion for Shakespeare and a flair for the grand statement.

The group expanded its activity in 1964 by touring the musical *Salad Days* along the Queensland coast, but in the same year a professional tour of a historical revue, *The Last of Lands*, was unsuccessful. In 1967 Nason staged a groundbreaking *Hamlet*, starring David Clendinning, in a boxing ring in Brisbane's Festival Hall. The other central figure in the College Players, Don Batchelor directed a milestone production of *The Merchant of Venice* in 1969, with Nason as Antonio and Leonie Amiel as Portia. It toured to Canberra.

Under Nason's direction the company mounted Peter Shaffer's *The Royal Hunt of the Sun* as the inaugural production of the new Queensland Theatre Company in October 1969. It could have grown into the fully fledged state company but Nason did not gain the job of artistic director and the College Players closed down. Nason soon founded the Grin and Tonic Theatre Troupe and continued his Shakespearean work throughout Queensland. Other key participants in the College Players have contributed to theatre in Australia as artists, administrators and teachers. Actors who had early experience with the company include Robyn Gurney, Jane Harders, Shane Porteous, Geoffrey Rush and Jack Thompson. ❦*Rod Wissler*

further reading
Batchelor, Don. The College Players—in retrospect. *Makar* 5/4 (Brisbane, December 1969).

Peter Collingwood

Actor, director. Born 6 May 1920 at Farnham (Hampshire, England). Educated at Royal Naval College (Dartmouth) 1933–37; Embassy School of Acting 1938. Stage debut at New Theatre, London, 1939. In Royal Navy during Second World War. Joined Young Vic Company after war. Member of British Communist Party 1948–56. Worked in repertory. Emigrated to Australia 1960. National Theatre Company (Perth) 1961–63. Left Australia and returned 1965. Directed and acted for Q Theatre (Sydney) 1968–69. Artistic director of Community Theatre (Sydney) 1971–73. Artistic director of Australian National Playwrights' Conference 1974. Associate director of Old Tote Theatre Company (Sydney) 1976–79. Also acted in film and television. Married to actor Margery Shaw.

Peter Collingwood's debonair precision kept him in particular demand for roles of colonial governors and judges. He was a memorable Sir Peter Teazle in R. B. Sheridan's *The School for Scandal* for the Old Tote Theatre Company in Sydney in 1967. He played Davis in Harold Pinter's *The Caretaker* for the National Theatre Company in Perth in 1961. As a director Collingwood brought a light touch to English comedy. ❦*Ron Blair*

Collits' Inn

Musical comedy. **book** T. Stuart Gurr. **lyrics and music** Varney Monk. **premiere** December 1932, Savoy Theatre, Sydney. Cast: Norman Barnes (Captain Lake), Robert Keane, Rene Maxwell (Mary Collits), Donald McNiven. Musical director: Howard Carr. **revival** 23 December 1933, Princess Theatre, Melbourne. Cast: Robert Chisholm (Captain Lake), Marshall Crosby, John Dobbie, Claude Flemming, Robert Keane (Dandy Dick), Gladys Moncrieff (Mary Collits), Byrl Walkley, George Wallace. Designers: Rupert Brown, W. R. Coleman, George Kenyon. Director: Claude Flemming. **published** Sydney: Currency Press 1990.

A forgotten triumph of the Australian stage, *Collits' Inn* was the brainchild of the composer Varney Monk. She heard some legends about the real Collits' Inn while on holiday in the Blue Mountains and persuaded T. Stuart Gurr, a newspaper editor who lived next door, to write a script to go with her lyrics and music. Using the stock structure of the stage musical, they devised a stirring story of a landlord's daughter in NSW during the building of a new road across the Blue Mountains in 1829–30.

The dashing soldier John Lake and the bushranger Robert Keane both love Mary Collits. Her father dislikes the military government and has used Keane to help him change the route of the new road to pass his inn. Torn by her love for the handsome redcoat, who leaves for duties elsewhere, her 'duty' to her father, and the bushranger's earnest advances, Mary loses her memory but recovers in time for a happy ending when Lake returns some years later. Gurr and Monk's story won second prize in a Sydney contest for an 'Australian operetta or musical play'. It was given a semiprofessional production, with the soprano Rene Maxwell as Mary Collits, at the Savoy Theatre in December 1932 by Nathalie Rosenwax, the Sydney music teacher who had organised the competition. Through the show's musical director, Howard Carr, Monk approached F. W. Thring, who was seeking an Australian musical to stage and then film. Thring gave the script star treatment. He engaged Gladys Moncrieff as Mary Collits, the great comedian GEORGE WALLACE as a rouseabout at the inn and the matinée idol ROBERT CHISHOLM—who came back from New York for the show—as Captain Lake. The play was reworked and a spectacular revolving stage provided visual splendours such as the red-coated soldiers marching towards the distant Blue Mountains.

The show ran in Melbourne for more than 100 nights, and on 22 June 1934 began a two-month season at the Tivoli Theatre in Sydney. The Melbourne *Argus* said on 26 December: 'Collits' Inn satisfies like no *Rose Marie* or *Lilac Time* can satisfy, the thirst for the symphony of the shaded road or the bushland barbarism of the corroboree'. Gladys Moncrieff was less than complimentary about the show in her memoirs, but she included the song 'Last year' in her concert repertoire, and the duet 'Stay while the stars are shining', which she sang with Robert Chisholm, was a popular hit. ❦*Richard Fotheringham*

Hugh Colman

Designer. Born 10 February 1946. Educated at University of Melbourne. Design assistant with Melbourne Theatre Company 1968; resident designer 1971–73. Resident designer for South Australian Theatre Company 1974, 1978–79. Freelance since 1980. Also designs for ballet and opera.

With a penchant for blues and pastel colours, Hugh Colman designs quietly elegant and understated sets that director and lighting designer can adopt for their own purposes. Frequently a Colman set does not stand on its own as a sculptural structure but comes to life under light. Colman has designed for most major Australian theatre companies. For the MELBOURNE THEATRE COMPANY Oscar Wilde's *An Ideal Husband* in 1972 and Nick Enright's *Daylight Saving* in 1990 were notable. These were touring productions, as was Julianne O'Brien's *The Women There* for the ARENA THEATRE COMPANY in 1987. ❦*Tom Bannerman*

Colonial Experience

Comedy in three acts by Walter Cooper. **premiere** 4 July 1868, Royal Victoria Theatre, Sydney. Cast: William Andrews, Charles Burford, Rosa Cooper, H. H. Davis, H. N. Douglas, J. Hasker, Edmund Holloway, William Hoskins, George Ireland, Stuart O'Brien, Clara Stephensen. **revived** 29 August 1962, Albert Hall, Brisbane, by Twelfth Night Theatre; designer: Quentin Hole; director: Joan Whalley. 1981, New Theatre, Sydney. **published** Sydney: Currency Press 1979.

The *Sydney Morning Herald* on 6 July 1868 acclaimed *Colonial Experience* as 'the most successful colonial play produced on the Sydney boards'. WALTER COOPER's second play, it was notable for local colour and for integrating familiar colonial types into a comedy of Australian manners set in Sydney in the 1860s. Alfred Arkwright, an Englishman newly arrived in the colonies, is the new chum, which undermines the fact he is also the hero, whose adventures give the play its title. The *Sydney Mail* thought Joe Grudge, an amiable if rather boorish young bushman, was 'really the character of the piece' with his colourful slang. The plot centres on the parsimony of Joe's father, Matthew Grudge. He has been trying to hide the fact that Alfred, his nephew, is the heir to the fortunes of his deceased brother John and to arrange financially advantageous marriages for his son and daughter. His plans are complicated by crafty Captain Fluent, a confidence man with his own ideas, and eventually thwarted by Peter Shrivel, his mistreated clerk who remains faithful to his former employer John. The actors who played Joe Grudge, Captain Fluent and Peter Shrivel were the most popular with the audience in the six performances in Sydney. Cooper himself played Joe Grudge in a benefit performance in Melbourne on 24 November 1871. The play has been revived several times since it was published in 1979. ❦*Philip Parsons*

Come Out Youth Arts Festival

Biennial youth arts festival in Adelaide. Founded by youth program committee of 1974 Adelaide Festival of Arts. Incorporated 7 November 1984. **directors** 1985–87 Malcolm Moore (artistic co-ordinator 1985–86). 1989–91 Michael FitzGerald.

The largest community-arts festival in the world, the Come Out Youth Arts Festival began in 1975 as a largely free festival for children, with a limited program of performances and workshops. Now it is among the three foremost youth arts festivals, with events in Lyon and Vancouver. It broadly aims to provide workshops and performances by and for young people aged five to 25. It is in three parts:

1 A central program of professionally produced activities.
2 Community access and outreach run largely through primary and secondary schools.
3 Touring throughout South Australia of the best professional activity from the central program.

The festival originally comprised local activities within the Adelaide Festival, co-ordinated by the Come Out committee and ADELAIDE FESTIVAL CENTRE TRUST staff. In 1981 it presented world premieres of works by Australian artists and companies. By 1983 the festival, having drawn more than 200 000 young people in Adelaide and thousands in other South Australian towns since 1975, was too big to remain within the Adelaide Festival. In 1984 the Come Out Youth Arts Festival became an independent incorporated body and moved to CARCLEW YOUTH ARTS CENTRE. Since 1985 the central Come Out program has comprised Aboriginal arts, dance, music, theatre, visual arts, the Over to Youth school activity program and the Allwrite! literature festival. Overseas visitors have taken part, notably Dong Rang Theatre for Young People from Korea in 1987, Honolulu Theatre for Youth in 1987, Roald Dahl as guest of Allwrite! in 1989 and Japan's Theatre Erumu in 1991. ❦*Rachel Healy*

further reading
BLEBY, ANDREW. Being grown-up about kids' theatre—Adult companies involved in Come Out 81. *Lowdown* 3 (Adelaide 1981).
BRAMWELL, MURRAY. Divining a future—Come Out 91. *Lowdown* 13/3 (June 1991).
BRAMWELL, MURRAY. Interpreting the new dreaming—Come Out 89. *Lowdown* 11/3 (June 1989).
BRAMWELL, MURRAY. The new dreaming—An interview with Come Out 89's director Michael FitzGerald. *Lowdown* 10/5 (October–November 1988).
BROKENSHA, PETER and ANN TONKS. *Culture and Community—Expectations and economics of the arts in South Australia*. Wentworth Falls (NSW): Social Science Press 1986.
EMERY, JOHN. Consulting the passengers: An assessment of Come Out 87. *Lowdown* 9/3 (May 1987).

RICKARDS, HELEN. A restless festival—Come Out 83. *Lowdown* 5/3 (July 1983).
SLUCKI, CHARLES. Coming across to come out. *Lowdown* 3/4 (1981).

The Coming of Stork

Play in nine scenes by David Williamson. **premiere** 25 September 1970, La Mama Theatre, Melbourne. Cast: Peter Cummins, Alan Finney, Shirley-Ann Kear, Martin Phelan, Bruce Spence, Dennis Wilson. Directors: Alan Finney, Martin Phelan. **published** Sydney and London: Currency Methuen 1974 in *Three Plays* by David Williamson. Sydney: Currency Press 1986 in *Collected Plays I*.

DAVID WILLIAMSON's first major play deals with one of his recurring themes—male sexual insecurity. The focus is less on the wry self-mockery with which Williamson's men characteristically handle their inadequacies and more on the naked anxiety and competitiveness that the jokes aim to cover. A household of randy recent graduates vigorously express the cheerfully vulgar humour that dominates the play. Its particular triumph is the neurotic Stork, a bean-pole in shape but Falstaffian in comic resilience. The action contrasts his ineptitude in the sexual stakes with the career of Clive, a most unlikable macho high achiever.

The only comfort for Stork and his scruffy companion West, a loser, is their capacity for ineffectual but gratifying comic reprisal. They take a stand against the concept of failure as well as conformity when, in the final moments of the play, they flush down the toilet the wedding-rings of their flatmates who have 'made it' in every sense. *The Coming of Stork* celebrates the new freedom of the late 1960s to say and do things on stage that could not have been contemplated a few years before. The dramatic impetus is in joyful crudity of language and in a sustained assault on tact and decorum which is illustrated by Stork's party trick—the reflective removal of a smoked oyster from a nostril.

The plot is fragmented into set-pieces that show the influence of university revue, and the female sex-object of the play, the obliging Anna, perfectly fits the males' low expectations of her character and intelligence. But the vitality of the play makes it more than just a period-piece, and it has had seasons in Vancouver in 1981 and Los Angeles in 1984 as well as Australian revivals. Bruce Spence played the title-role in a 1972 film version. ❦*Peter Fitzpatrick*

Community theatre

The term 'community theatre' has been as much a strategic weapon as a generic description in Australia. Various companies and individuals have formed a loose alliance, initially centred on national community-theatre conferences in the mid-1980s. They are linked by a concern to make theatre with and for 'communities'—by some shared methods of generating theatrical material. Some community companies emerged from alternative-theatre groups of the early 1970s, such as the AUSTRALIAN PERFORMING GROUP in Melbourne and the POPULAR THEATRE TROUPE in Queensland, which reintroduced street theatre and workplace performance as part of a political project. Some emerged from a theatre-in-education movement based on British models of the mid-1960s, which has spread through the country since the early 1970s. Others modelled themselves upon British small-scale touring groups of the 1970s. Still others had origins in the counterculture of the late 1960s and early 1970s. Their most direct descendant is the large-scale community festival incorporating a performance piece, which is exemplified in Neil Cameron's work with the WEST THEATRE COMPANY and elsewhere. At the VICTORIAN COLLEGE OF THE ARTS in the late 1970s Peter Oyston encouraged students to form community companies, leading directly to West, the MURRAY RIVER PERFORMING GROUP and THEATREWORKS.

All community theatre has been shaped by the wider community-arts movement of the 1970s, which has in turn been influenced by shifting emphases in SUBSIDY. In the 1970s European theories of 'sociocultural animation' influenced arts-funding initiatives centred on the concept of 'cultural democracy'. These initiatives entailed a retreat from attempts to popularise 'high art', acceptance of culture as something wider than the professional arts, and an emphasis on communities' ability to produce their own culture. A definition of professional artist widened to include facilitator and animator became embodied in the policy of the AUSTRALIA COUNCIL's community arts board and its four incentive schemes—Art and Working Life, Multicultural Arts, Youth Arts and Artist-in-Community. All have been sources of funds for community theatre.

These initiatives, partly responses to a community-arts lobby, have helped to shape community-theatre practice. A community is loosely defined as a social group with common interests and experiences resting on class, sex, ethnicity, work or locality. In community theatre, a piece is tailored to the needs, expectations and cultural experiences of a specific community, which is assumed to have a distinctive culture. As facilitator, the artist or company involves members of the community in generating and sometimes performing a work. In strictly interpreted facilitation a small nucleus of professionals assists a community to generate a performance piece out of its own experiences or interests. Both West and the STREET ARTS THEATRE COMPANY in Brisbane have worked in this way. They have moved between outdoor participatory performances and more conventional indoor theatre pieces involving members of communities. For example, members of the Royal Australian Nurses' Federation performed West's *Vital Signs*, while Street Arts' *Once Upon Inala* (1984) was written by Nick Hughes in consultation with residents of a suburb in Brisbane, who then performed the play.

Other notable examples have been produced by the Murray River Performing Group (particularly PAUL BROWN's *Murray River Story* in 1988 and *Two Cities* in 1990) and by DEATH DEFYING THEATRE (*Site* by P. P. CRANNEY in 1994, *Cafe Hakawati* by Brown in 1991 and *Blood Orange* by Noelle Janaczewska in 1992). Free lances have produced other plays—*The Wonthaggi Celebration* by Ken Harper in Victoria and *The Logan City Story* in Queensland in 1984 and *The Yallourn Story* in Victoria in 1989, both by Cranney. The Sydney branch of the Federation of Italian Migrant Workers and their Families (FILEF) has been particularly influential. It has generated community shows since 1984, when it started with *Nuovo Paese/New Country* by Cranney. The work of Maud Clark with the Fairlea Drama Group—inmates and ex-inmates of Fairlea Women's Prison in Melbourne—has received public attention more recently.

The youth-theatre movement has also been particularly involved with these kinds of participatory shows. Very little documentation of the form exists.

Little better documented is theatre for communities. This rests on a less expansive notion of facilitation but has also been highly productive, particularly with trade unions. In the early 1980s the SIDETRACK PERFORMANCE GROUP performed plays generated with particular communities to working-class and non-anglophone audiences in workplaces, schools and community venues in Sydney. Its work with trade unions is best exemplified by *Loco* (1983), the result of a residency in Chullora Railway Workshop. Similar consultative mechanisms have become standard, and are evident in the work of JUNCTION THEATRE COMPANY in Adelaide in the mid-1980s and MELBOURNE WORKERS' THEATRE in the late 1980s, also with trade unions. Other work has resulted from collaborations with social-welfare agencies, ethnic organisations and residents' groups. Work with ethnic communities, by companies like DOPPIO TEATRO in Adelaide and the Filiki Players in Melbourne, and through organisations like the Multicultural Theatre Alliance in Sydney, has become particular notable.

The characteristic method of generating a performance entails making contact with a recognisable community organisation, which either applies for funding on behalf of a company—or a group of free lances—or underwrites an application. A play is then developed. Consultation and research with the community leads to the drafting of a script, which undergoes further consultation, redrafting and rehearsal. The work is then performed in an appropriate community venue, usually not a theatre—a football oval in Collinsville (Qld) in the case of Death Defying Theatre's *Coal Town* in 1984—and toured to similar venues.

In the 1990s community theatre has become more prominent, broadening audiences through touring to theatres. The DECKCHAIR THEATRE COMPANY did this with *Emma* by Graham Pitts and Melbourne Workers' Theatre with *Daily Grind* by Vicki Reynolds. Some scripts have been produced by mainstream companies—for example, Paul Brown's *Aftershocks*, first produced by the Workers' Cultural Action Committee of Newcastle Trades Hall Council in 1991 and revived at the BELVOIR STREET THEATRE in Sydney in 1993.

There are now community-theatre companies in most major cities and in smaller towns, and there are itinerant individual facilitators. Most receive some subsidy, but it is invariably inadequate in relation to the developmental nature of their work and inequitable in relation to their social reach. Community theatre accounts for less than two per cent of the spending on grants by the performing arts board of the Australia Council. One mainstream company, THEATRE SOUTH in Wollongong (NSW), has acknowledged the form in several plays, but the movement's vitality still lies in the largely undocumented work of small, overworked and underfunded companies. They continue to produce intelligent, engaging theatre of great importance to the social and cultural lives of the diverse communities with which they work, and to contribute, largely unheralded to the theatrical life of the country. ❦*David Watt*

further reading
BINNS, VIVIENNE (ed.). *Community and the arts*. Sydney: Pluto 1991.
BLAYLOCK, MALCOLM. Subsidy, community, and excellence in Australian theatre. *New Theatre Quarterly* 11/5 (Cambridge, England, 1986).
CAMERON, NEIL. *Fire on the water*. Sydney: Currency Press 1993.
FOTHERINGHAM, RICHARD (ed.). *Community Theatre in Australia*. Sydney: Currency Press 1992.
HARPER, KEN. The Wonthaggi Celebration. *Meanjin* 43/1 (1984).
HAWKINS, GAY. *From Nimbin to Mardi Gras—Constructing community arts*. Sydney: Allen & Unwin 1993.
LAURIE, ROBIN. A thousand bloomin' flowers. *Meanjin* 43/1 (1984).
MITCHELL, TONY. Italo-Australian theatre. *Australasian Drama Studies* 11 (Brisbane, October 1987).
MITCHELL, TONY. Nuovo paese—nuovo direzione. *New Theatre Australia* 1 (Sydney 1987).
PERRIER, ROBERT. Finding an audience. *Meanjin* 41/1 (1982).
RICHARDS, ALLISON. We can work it out. *Meanjin* 46/4 (1987).
WATT, DAVID. Community theatre—a progress report. *Australasian Drama Studies* 20 (Brisbane, April 1992).
WATT, DAVID. 'Excellence/access' and 'nation/community'. *Canadian Theatre Review* 74 (1993).

Company of Four

Professional dramatic company in Perth, founded in 1950 by Lily Kavanagh, Dorothy Krantz, Nita Pannell and Sol Sainken. Amalgamated with Repertory Club to form National Theatre Company 1956. **first performance** *The Play's the Thing* by Ferenc Molnar, February 1950, at Somerville Auditorium, University of Western Australia.

Established as the first professional theatre company resident in Western Australia, the Company of Four, through its high standards of presentation, gave crucial impetus to the development of professional theatre in Perth. Its four founders, after whom it was named, began it experimentally with the assistance of the Adult Education Board of the University of Western Australia as a resident company to promote professional production and training, which had not been available in the state.

Employing local amateurs, who might work professionally in Perth should the opportunity arise, the company functioned as a non-profit organisation until it merged into the new NATIONAL THEATRE COMPANY. In association with the board, it regularly produced modern plays for presentation at the FESTIVAL OF PERTH and in Perth, Fremantle and country towns at other times of the year. Perth productions included Somerset Maugham's *Home and Beauty* at His Majesty's Theatre in 1951; Robert Ardrey's *Thunder Rock* in the Somerville Auditorium and Mary Chase's *Harvey* at His Majesty's in 1952; *Richard III* in the Somerville Auditorium, and J. B. Priestley's *When We Are Married* at His Majesty's with the Adult Education Board for the festival in 1953, both directed by the English director Michael Langham; and Jean Anouilh's *Ring Round the Moon* in the university's Sunken Garden Theatre for the 1954 festival. The Company of Four encouraged, among others, the actors Margaret Anktetell, Kevin Caporn, Gina Curtis, Henry Cuthbertson, Margaret Ford, Ken Goodlet, RON GRAHAM and Nancy Lee; the director CORALIE CONDON and the designers Sydney Davis and Neil Hunsley. ❦*Bill Dunstone*

Coralie Condon

Actor, director, writer. Born in Fremantle (WA). Educated at University of Western Australia (Perth). Active in Repertory Club and Therry Society in Perth. On board of National Theatre Company. Co-founder of Old Time Music Hall, Perth. Managing director of Dirty Dick's group of companies 1987–. Sister of actor and director James Condon.

In 1967 Coralie Condon and the present writer devised, wrote and directed the first show at the Old Time Music Hall, Perth's first theatre-restaurant. The Music Hall Company expanded into Australia's largest chain of THEATRE-RESTAURANTS. Upon the writer's retirement in 1987 she became managing director of the parent company. Condon now writes and directs mostly for theatre-restaurants. She formerly specialised in musicals and directed *Bitter-Sweet*, *Florodora* and *The Lilac Domino*. She also wrote a Western Australian musical, *The Good Oil*, and wrote the text and music for three successful musical revues, *On the Beam*, *On the Beam Again* and *On the Beam 1955*, all of which she directed. She also directed plays for the COMPANY OF FOUR in the Festival of Perth. ❦*Frank Baden-Powell*

James Condon

Actor, director, writer. Born 27 September 1923 in Fremantle (WA). Trained as actor in amateur theatre in Perth. Military service 1942–45. Worked in ABC radio drama in Perth 1946–49, 1951–56. Acted in BBC radio and television in England 1949–51. Moved to Sydney 1956. Works in radio, television and theatre. Married to actor Anne Haddy. Brother of Coralie Condon, actor, director, writer.

An all-rounder, reliable in all spheres, James Condon has appeared in many productions. In his early years in Perth he acted for the COMPANY OF FOUR from its first production in 1950 until 1956. Later he acted for the NATIONAL THEATRE COMPANY. In Sydney he has acted for INDEPENDENT THEATRE, the Northside Theatre Company, and the OLD TOTE THEATRE COMPANY, for which he appeared with his wife ANNE HADDY in Thomas Muschamp's *The Brass Hat* in 1976. They also acted together in Garson Kanin's *Born Yesterday* for the SYDNEY THEATRE COMPANY in 1984. Condon has also acted for the MELBOURNE THEATRE COMPANY and numerous commercial managements. ❦*Frank Baden-Powell*

Mike Connors

Variety artist. Born 1892 in New York City. Came to Australia with Freddy Witt for Fullers' vaudeville 1916. Married Queenie Paul and formed new vaudeville act, November 1917. Established Con-Paul Theatres 1931. ABC radio announcer from September 1941. Died 16 January 1949 in Sydney.

With his wife and partner QUEENIE PAUL, Mike Connors revitalised revue in the Great Depression by establishing Con-Paul Theatres, the cornerstone of the second TIVOLI CIRCUIT, in Sydney in 1931. Connors and his first vaudeville partner in Australia, Freddy Witt, arrived from the USA in 1916 for FULLERS' and performed songs at the piano in the style of a famous American duo, Van and Schenk. It was 'a fine little act of its kind', said a reviewer. In November 1917, while on tour in Newcastle (NSW) with a Bert Le Blanc company, Connors married Paul, an Australian soubrette who combined singing with directing dance. Witt, deprived of his partner, later had a long career in Australian radio. The death of a beloved child took Connors and Paul out of revue management in 1934, but they continued to perform. Connors's career took a new turn in September 1941, when he became the Australian Broadcasting Commission's national breakfast announcer. His homespun philosophy brought him many new fans. ❦*John West*

Patricia Conolly

Actor. Born 29 August 1933 at Tabora (Tanganyika), to Australian parents. Acted for Sydney University Dramatic Society. Union Theatre Repertory Company (Melbourne) 1956–58, 1960–61. Trust Players (Sydney) 1959. In England on Australian Elizabethan Theatre Trust scholarship 1961–64. Returned to Australia 1964. Settled in North America 1965. Has been guest director at Juilliard School (New York City) and North Carolina School of the Arts; and taught Shakespeare at Boston University. Returned to Australia 1970, 1979, 1982, 1991. Erik Kuttner Award 1965 (*After the Fall* by Arthur Miller). Widow of Dan Bly, actor, director and production manager in USA.

A chameleon actor with a classical grace and melodious clarity of voice, Patricia Conolly has played characters from Blanche Dubois in Tennessee Williams's *A Streetcar Named Desire* to Madame Arcati in Noël Coward's *Blithe Spirit*. She has a record of apparently effortless employment on stages in three continents. Small and slim with large expressive eyes, she was known for her elfin qualities as an ingenue, and her physique has enabled her to play women of any age throughout her career. GEOFFREY HUTTON has described her as 'one of the most complete technicians I have known'.

JOHN SUMNER saw her when was playing in a SYDNEY UNIVERSITY DRAMATIC SOCIETY production and invited her to join the Union Theatre Repertory Company in Melbourne. She gave her first professional performance in its 1956–57 season as Emily in Thornton Wilder's *Our Town*. Other roles she played during two seasons included Isabelle in Jean Anouilh's *Ring Round the Moon*, Maggie in Tennessee Williams's *Cat on a Hot Tin Roof*, Blanche in *A Streetcar Named Desire* and the title-role in Aristophanes's *Lysistrata*.

A member of the TRUST PLAYERS from the outset, she created the juvenile role of Thelma in Peter Kenna's *THE SLAUGHTER OF ST TERESA'S DAY*. Her other parts included Laura in *The Glass Menagerie* by Tennessee Williams and the young girl in *The Bastard Country* by Anthony Coburn. She returned to the Union Theatre company to play Ann Whitfield in George Bernard Shaw's *Man and Superman*.

In England on a three-year AUSTRALIAN ELIZABETHAN THEATRE TRUST scholarship she joined Laurence Olivier's 1962 Chichester Festival company as an understudy and received high praise as Calantha in John Ford's *The Broken Heart*, replacing Joan Greenwood. Conolly played Jan Castle in the London season of Alan Seymour's *THE ONE DAY OF THE YEAR*. During a brief return to Australia in 1964–65 she played Margaret Pinchwife in William Wycherley's *The Country Wife* and Desdemona in *Othello* for the OLD TOTE THEATRE COMPANY in Sydney, and Maggie in Arthur Miller's *After the Fall* for the Union Theatre company. On her way back to London, she unexpectedly began an American career when she was invited to replace an actor in *You Can't Take it With You* by George S. Kaufman and Moss Hart, which ran six months on Broadway. She settled in North America, acting in the USA and Canada. Conolly has returned to Australia several times. In 1970 she played Helena in Tyrone Guthrie's production of *All's Well that Ends Well* on national tour, and Nora in Henrik Ibsen's *A*

Doll's House and Sister Jeanne in John Whiting's *The Devils* for the MELBOURNE THEATRE COMPANY. In 1979 she played Mary Tyrone in Eugene O'Neill's *Long Day's Journey into Night* for the Sydney and Ensemble Theatre Companies. For the Melbourne Theatre Company she played the title-role in Ibsen's *Hedda Gabler* in 1982 and Judith Bliss in Coward's *Hay Fever* in 1991. ❦*Katharine Brisbane*

William Constable

Designer. Born 8 March 8 1906 at Eaglehawk (Vic.). Abandoned electrical engineering apprenticeship to become commercial artist. Studied at National Art Gallery (Melbourne) and St Martin's School of Art (London). Returned to Australia 1930. Designed for drama, opera and ballet 1933–40. Resident designer of Borovansky Ballet 1941–55. Scenic director of Whitehall Theatrical Productions (Sydney). Designed for J. C. Williamson's. Moved to London 1957. Art director for many films. Settled in Australia 1973.

For more than half a century William Constable's contribution to visual stagecraft and art direction has been internationally acclaimed and he has inspired later generations of Australian scenic artists. He has been quoted as saying: 'If they applaud the set, then something is wrong. The set works hardest in the first minute it is seen. If they are applauding they're not looking.' Constable launched his career with innovative sets for GREGAN MCMAHON's production of James Bridie's *Jonah and the Whale* in 1933, and worked for the New Theatre Club in Melbourne from 1939. Sets and costumes for the MARIE NEY company in 1940 established his reputation as a significant modernist. He was subsequently resident designer for the Borovansky Ballet for 14 years. In Sydney, Constable worked for WHITEHALL THEATRICAL PRODUCTIONS, INDEPENDENT THEATRE and MERCURY THEATRE and designed 15 operas for the NSW State Conservatorium of Music before he moved to London in 1957. There he increasingly integrated poetic expression, movement and 'sculpting in light' and developed a preference for ballet and film work. ❦*Pamela Zeplin*

writings
CONSTABLE, WILLIAM. *Flying Artist*. Sydney: Legend Press 1951.
further reading
HAINAUX, R. *Stage Design Throughout the World Since 1953*. Brussels: Harrap 1964.

Convicts and theatre

Convicts were involved in most early theatrical performances in Australia. A play was given aboard the convict transport *Scarborough* as it neared Sydney on 2 January 1788. On 4 June 1789 convicts honoured the King's Birthday by performing the first play on Australian soil, *The Recruiting Officer*, written by George Farquhar in 1706. Convicts were the actors at the first theatre, which opened in Sydney on 16 January 1796. It was run by an ex-convict, ROBERT SIDAWAY. At the penal settlement on NORFOLK ISLAND convicts performed plays once a month from May 1793 to early 1794 and again from 1838 to 1840. On both occasions, subsequent performances were banned by official decree. The same fate befell the EMU PLAINS CONVICT THEATRE, which flourished west of Sydney between 1825 and 1830. Clergymen and many others saw theatres as dens of iniquity and arguments over their appropriateness for convict colonies helped to slow the development of professional theatre. After the second closure of SIDAWAY'S THEATRE, some time between 1804 and early 1808, there was no theatre in Sydney until 1829, when BARNETT LEVEY first used his THEATRE ROYAL for concerts. Levey struggled until 1832 to obtain a licence for theatrical performances. His first licence, in addition to restricting him to plays already licensed in London and banning performances on Sundays, required only that he maintain good order in the theatre. When renewed in 1833 the licence additionally prohibited the employment of convicts in the theatre. So when the convict EDWARD GEOGHEGAN wrote plays for the Royal Victoria Theatre in Sydney in the 1840s his name did not appear on any bill.

It appears that convicts were also banned from theatres in Van Diemen's Land, although these were not controlled by a licensing system until the 1840s. On 1 July 1834 the *Colonial Times* reported that J. P. DEANE had been charged with 'harbouring a prisoner'—that is, allowing him into the Theatre Royal in the ARGYLE ROOMS. The *Cornwall Chronicle* advised on 25 November 1843 that ticket-of-leave men were permitted to attend the theatre but they were still prohibited from performing. In 1850, the *Launceston Advertiser* reported on 30 January that five ticket-of-leave men had been charged with misconduct in playing at the circus and theatre contrary to regulations. The bench discharged them with a reprimand and a caution not to venture on the stage again. The next day, however, they were back in court, after performing again that evening, and each was sent to the treadmill for two months. By that time transportation to NSW had ceased and was on the point of doing so in Van Diemen's Land. Indeed, the 1850 Easter pantomime in Launceston was entitled *Transportation versus Emigration—or, Harlequin in Launceston*. ❦*Elizabeth Webby*

Coo-ee

—*or, Wild days in the Bush*. Play in prologue and four acts by E. W. O'Sullivan. **premiere** 14 April 1906, Hippodrome, Sydney, by Bohemian Dramatic Company. Cast: W. H. Ayr, Belle Cole, Percy Goodwin, George Linden, Vene Linden, G. McGowan, Amy Sherwood, J. R. Wilson. Director: E. I. Cole.

E. W. O'SULLIVAN, a member of the NSW Legislative Assembly, claimed to have been the first politician to climb to the top of Mt Kosciusko. He remembered the event in his melodrama *Coo-ee*, which he is said to have written in two weeks early in 1906. He set the play in the Braidwood and Monaro districts of NSW. For the prologue, set on top of Mt Kosciusko, the stage in the Hippodrome tent theatre of E. I. Cole's BOHEMIAN DRAMATIC COMPANY included raised mountain ridges, which had to carry real 'naked horses' in a chase after brumbies similar to that immortalised in *The Man from Snowy River*. O'Sullivan peopled the play with bushrangers, squatters, bullock drivers, 'horse-herders', troopers and Aborigines, But in spite of these characters, local scenery and 'coo-ees', the play had many of the stock ingredients of current English melodrama. A blackmailing villain threatens a squatter and his daughter. A gold nugget is found, the heroine is imprisoned in the Jenolan Caves, the hero is rescued from under a wool press by his faithful Aboriginal friend Nardoo, and the squatter is tied to his horse and nearly sent on a fateful ride down the mountainside. The villain is eventually dispatched by his fellow bushrangers, who think he has betrayed them, and all ends happily. A very British new-chum newspaper reporter provided comic relief—the cast yelling 'Rats!' every time he appeared and the audience often joining in. Cole's low prices—sixpence and a shilling—attracted crowds of boys and young men but in spite of this larrikin element 'good order prevailed, and close attention was paid', the Herald reported. ❧Richard Fotheringham

reference
A typescript of *Coo-ee* is in the O'Sullivan papers in the Mitchell Library (Sydney).

Clyde Cook

Comedian. Born 16 December 1891 at Port Macquarie (NSW). Began performing as child. On Tivoli circuit from 1903. In music-hall in England and Ziegfeld Follies in USA. Married Ziegfeld girl Alice Draper. Divorced 1938. In many Hollywood films. Died 13 August 1984 in USA.

At the age of seven Clyde Cook began dancing and performing acrobatics between rounds of boxing matches, and by 12 he was a featured comedian on the TIVOLI CIRCUIT. He went on to play in pantomimes, including *Jack and the Beanstalk* in 1911, and musicals for J. C. WILLIAMSON's, and in music-hall in England. He scored a hit at the Alhambra in London in the revue *Now's the Time* in 1915. After service in the Royal Navy he returned to Australia, where his eccentric dancing was a feature of *His Only Chance*, a lost film. He then moved to the USA and appeared at the New York Hippodrome and in the Ziegfeld Follies. In Hollywood he starred in popular two-reel comedies from 1921. He played smaller roles in sound films—including an Australian in *The Man from Down Under* in 1943—until *Donovan's Reef* in 1963. ❧Frank Van Straten

H. C. Coombs

Administrator. Born 24 February 1906 at Kalamunda (WA). Educated at University of Western Australia (Perth) and London School of Economics. Director-General of Department of Post-War Reconstruction 1943–49. Governor of Commonwealth Bank 1949–60. Chairman of Australian Elizabethan Theatre Trust 1954–68. Governor of Reserve Bank of Australia 1960–68. Chairman of NSW Advisory Committee on Cultural Grants 1966–68. Chairman of Australian Council for the Arts 1968–74.

Herbert Cole ('Nugget') Coombs was central to the development of subsidy for the performing arts in Australia. The process would have taken longer without his persistence and personal conviction that the arts were worthy of national promotion through statutory subsidy agencies. He used his position as a senior commonwealth official to argue his case under seven prime ministers from 1944 to 1974. Overriding pragmatism and patience characterised Coombs, though he fervently believed in the Keynesian argument that economic prosperity was critical in meeting wider social goals. Recognising political realities, he took circuitous routes to his goals. He attracted leading citizens and influential public servants to his cause. The latter, particularly Charles Moses of the Australian Broadcasting Commission, provided the greater practical support.

Coombs's involvement in cultural matters can be traced to a report to the federal government by Eugene Ormandy, conductor of the Philadelphia Orchestra, who toured for the ABC in 1944. Ormandy made recommendations on orchestras and provision of concert halls and theatres and advocated a national theatre. Commonwealth officials suggested a council encompassing performing and visual arts. The Prime Minister, John Curtin, was sympathetic, even enthusiastic, but he delayed consideration until peace time. Coombs wanted cultural plans to be considered only through his Department of Post-War Reconstruction and he manoeuvred to gain the responsibility. Ben Chifley, who succeeded Curtin as Prime Minister in 1945, preferred popular entertainment and remained unconvinced. Coombs spent the next four years salvaging the issue as the proposals were watered down from an all-embracing cultural council to a NATIONAL THEATRE and finally to the export-import plan in the GUTHRIE REPORT.

Coombs made his first significant contribution in 1954, when Robert Menzies was Prime Minister, by creating the AUSTRALIAN ELIZABETHAN THEATRE TRUST, a de facto arts council, subsidised but privately managed. The Arts Council of Great Britain and the plans of the Department of Post-War Reconstruction provided Coombs with the model for a national—but not nationalistic—theatrical organisation. With Moses involved in frustrating negotiations between Menzies and the director JOHN ALDEN, Coombs was privy to the ideas and objections raised. With the support of state premiers, business and the press, Coombs approached Menzies with his plans, which limited government responsibility, and launched a public appeal. Once Menzies supported the trust, which was strategically linked to the monarch, he was committed to its survival.

As chairman of the Trust, working closely with the board and executive directors, Coombs concerned himself primarily with negotiations to gain ever-increasing state and federal subsidy and with general policy and he left selection of repertoire and daily operations to the staff. Coombs encouraged the states to make greater cultural contributions generally and promoted the provision of venues for expanding theatrical production, including the Sydney Opera House and the Victorian Arts Centre.

By 1964 the Trust and Coombs were so influential that concerned and aggrieved individuals mounted vitriolic public attacks against the Trust's artistic policy and monopoly and Coombs's position as 'cultural tsar'. Coombs, characteristically, responded by quietly continuing a review of the Trust's role that had begun before the attacks, and approaching Menzies and his successor Harold Holt when public attacks dissipated. The Trust was now an entrepreneurial body responsible for developing increasingly autonomous opera, ballet and regional drama companies.

Responsibilities for subsidy were handed over to the Australian Council for the Arts, which was announced on 1 November 1967. Coombs became its chairman, resigning from the Trust and the NSW Advisory Committee on Cultural Grants. His circumstances were now entirely different. John Gorton, who became Prime Minister in January 1968, was a populist who had little time for Coombs or high cultural forms. He preferred film, in which he was supported by two members of the council, Peter Coleman and Barry Jones. The council, with delayed establishment, inadequate accommodation, understaffed on a minimal first-year grant, immediately set about assisting a widened range of arts organisations and activities. Coombs, appreciating the delicate situation, cautiously developed policy as circumstances dictated. He used Jones's friendship with Gorton to promote the council's activities and the Trust for administrative support of the council's misnamed special projects funds. As the council settled down and William McMahon replaced Gorton as Prime Minister, Coombs took the council down new pathways in the performing and visual arts. At the same time he tried to ensure that the Trust, until then the leading national arts organisation, stayed within the limits the new circumstances required. Coombs later remarked that it might have been better if he had stayed with the Trust to offset its obstinacy.

Gough Whitlam became Prime Minister and Arts Minister in December 1972 and next month the council was expanded. It now had seven advisory boards, greater funding and a promise of statutory status, which was realised when it became the AUSTRALIA COUNCIL in 1975. Coombs's position at the apex of a subsidy agency was again publicly criticised and there were calls for greater representation of artists. In a perverse way those periods of criticism indirectly recognised Coombs's contribution to subsidy and arts development generally. ❦*John Andrews*

writings
Trial Balance. Melbourne: Macmillan 1981. Autobiography.
further reading
ANDREWS, JOHN. Subsidy for the performing arts in Australia, 1942–1970. Monash University thesis 1988.
BADGER, C. R. Government patronage of the arts in Australia, 1945–73. La Trobe Library MS. 9857.
Ten years of the Trust. *Quadrant* 8/4 (Sydney 1964)
Meanjin 23. (Melbourne, September 1964).
reference
H. C. Coombs papers, M448/1 in Australian Archives (Canberra).

Rosa Cooper

Actor, manager. Born in England. Leading lady in Shakespeare, melodrama and burlesque in Victoria and NSW in 1860s and 1870s. Arrived in Sydney during Duke of Edinburgh's visit 1868; managed Royal Victoria Theatre from December 1868 to April 1869 and Theatre Royal Adelphi in late 1869. Directed Garnet Walch's early burlesques. Toured California and India. Died 1877 in India. Married actor Lionel Harding.

Described as 'intelligent, careful and conscientious', Rosa Cooper was one of the tireless and versatile workers who helped to build a high standard of ensemble work in the colonial theatre. Her alternation between acting and management suggests flexibility, as does her repertoire, which was possibly necessitated by a paucity of professional actors. Though not an outstanding actor, she played the title-role in Augustin Daly's *Leah the Forsaken*, Miami in J. B. Buckstone's *The Green Bushes* and Isobel Vane in *East Lynne*; Douglas Jerrold's *Black-Eyed Susan* and many burlesque roles; Gertrude in *Hamlet*, Emilia in *Othello*, Lady Macbeth and on one occasion Romeo to FANNY CATHCART's Juliet. In sensation drama, she was the earliest Australian performer of Laura Courtland in Augustin Daly's *Under the Gaslight* in Sydney in 1868, Mrs Fairweather in Dion Boucicault's *The Streets of London* in Melbourne in 1864 and the Countess in John Oxenford's *The Two Orphans* in Melbourne in 1875. In 1868 she created the role of Helen in WALTER COOPER's *Colonial Experience*. She was reported in late 1877 to be dying in 'reduced circumstances' in Calcutta. ❦*Veronica Kelly*

further reading
IRVIN, ERIC. Introduction to *Colonial Experience* by Walter Cooper. Sydney: Currency Press 1979.
KELLY, VERONICA. Garnet Walch in Sydney. *Australasian Drama Studies* 9 (Brisbane, October 1986).
Australasian Sketcher (Melbourne) 7 August 1875.
L'Entr'acte (Melbourne) 20 November 1877.

Walter Cooper

Dramatist. Born 6 July 1842 in Sydney. Journalist in Queensland and with *Sydney Morning Herald* and Melbourne *Argus*. Wrote seven plays 1866–80. Member of NSW Parliament 1873–74. Became barrister December 1875. Died 26 July 1880 in Sydney.

The plays of Walter Cooper began a flowering of native drama in the second half of the 19th century. He was the first Australian writer of sensation melodrama in the style of DION BOUCICAULT, and the precursor of ALFRED DAMPIER and GEORGE DARRELL. Cooper used the 'new chum' and 'currency' characters in his plays and the comic character was typically a local lad who spoke rich slang and displayed sharp intelligence. When Cooper acted in his own plays he was often in this role.

His first play was a burlesque, *The History of Kodadad and his Brothers*, first performed in 1867 in New Zealand by the Nathan Juvenile Troupe. It concerned a Persian prince who forsook his kingdom for squatterdom in NSW, and it included operatic airs and contemporary songs. It was followed in 1868 by COLONIAL EXPERIENCE, a three-act comedy. The *Sydney Morning Herald*—on which Cooper was a parliamentary reporter—declared it to be the most successful colonial play yet produced in Sydney. Cooper received two benefit nights, the second of which included his farce *A New Crime*. It owes a large debt to English comedy but incorporates colonial types, including a genial young bushman and a new chum.

Cooper next turned to sensation drama, writing *Sun and Shadow* in 1870; *Foiled*, his most popular play, in 1871; and *Hazard* in 1872. All were well received and had runs of 22–24 nights in Sydney. The first two had Melbourne runs of 13 and 15 nights respectively. *Hazard*, did not go south, however, as during the Victorian country tour of *Foiled* Cooper, in financial trouble, ran out after paying the actors with dud cheques. He went to America with FRANK HUSSEY, the American actor for whom he had written *Hazard*, Mrs Hussey and another actor, J. J. Bartlett.

Cooper fought with Hussey and returned alone in January 1873, but all three sensation plays were seen in the USA, which made Cooper the first Australian dramatist performed abroad. *Foiled*, staged in America as *Magdalen*, was revived in Sydney and Melbourne in 1879, in Sydney again in 1888 and in Sydney and Melbourne in 1896. On return from the USA, Cooper spent a year as a member of the NSW Parliament, until injudicious remarks about land selectors ended his political career. He turned to law and was admitted to the bar in 1875. He was then deeply in debt, his health was bad and his legal career was not a success. But he showed no sign of returning to melodrama. In 1878 he wrote in the *Sydney University Magazine* denouncing the fashion for theatrical spectacle and devices he had used himself: '… we have rushing railway trains, and sharp saws, and heaving oceans. … to convey feebly; sometimes ridiculously; to the eye, what the ancient dramatists conveyed with all the force of genius, to the sense'. Cooper wrote one more play, *Fuss. A Tale of the Exhibition*, a comedy with a tangled plot involving the Sydney International Exhibition of 1879. The *Sydney Morning Herald* said it was 'full of jest and humorous word-twisting' but it had only five performances at the Royal Victoria Theatre in April 1880. Cooper was then in poor health and badly in debt. He died three months later, aged 38. ❦*Victoria Chance*

published plays
Colonial Experience (1868). Sydney: Currency Press 1979.
Hazard—or, Pearce Dyceton's Crime (1872). Sydney: Cunningham 1872. Melbourne: Monash University 1987.
The History of Kodadad and his Brothers (1867). Brisbane: Fairfax 1866.

further reading
NAIRN, BEDE. Walter Cooper. *Australian Dictionary of Biography* 3. Melbourne University Press 1969.

Campbell Copelin

Actor. Born c.1902 in England. Came to Australia 1923. Leading juvenile by late 1920s, then leading actor. Went to England 1938. Returned to Australia 1958.

With an Oxford education, smooth good looks and an attractive, sometimes eccentric personality, Campbell Copelin came to Australia in 1923 with the VANBRUGH–BOUCICAULT COMPANY. He remained to become one of the country's most accomplished actors. As a polished juvenile lead for J. C. WILLIAMSON'S in the later 1920s his most memorable performance was as the dissipated young Tom Prior in a notable production of Sutton Vane's *Outward Bound* in Melbourne. He played a romantic Tyrolean mountaineer in C. L. Anthony's *Autumn Crocus* in 1932 and a breezy young chap in John Drinkwater's *Bird in Hand*, and he was in a season of plays with LEON GORDON in 1928.

In 1931 Copelin first acted with the experienced FRANK HARVEY. They worked together a great deal in the 1930s and tended to dominate the casts of straight plays in the professional theatre. Harvey directed Copelin in 1934 in the highlights of his career—leading roles opposite the great French star Alice Delysia in F. W. THRING's productions of the operetta *Mother of Pearl* and *Her Past*. His polished acting and his sense of comedy won wide acclaim. Copelin returned to London in 1938 and worked successfully in the West End. Back in Australia he acted in ROBERT HELPMANN's production of Noël Coward's *Nude with Violin* in 1958, in the comic role of an English father in Peggy Caine's *Who'll Come A-Waltzing*, and in the American comedy *Never Too Late* by Sumner Arthur Long in 1964. ❦*Richard Lane*

Alec Coppel

Director, dramatist. Born 1910 in Melbourne. Studied medicine at Cambridge University for two years before switching to advertising. Wrote successful plays and film scripts in spare time. Returned to Australia, July 1940. Formed Whitehall Theatrical Productions with Kathleen Robinson 1940. Directed most productions at Minerva Theatre, Sydney, 1941–44. Left Australia 1944. Died 1972 in England.

As a director of WHITEHALL THEATRICAL PRODUCTIONS, Alec Coppel was a perfectionist. He set up a permanent unit of producer, scene designer, set decorator and dress designer, and used the finest actors in Australia, seeking 'a standard which would satisfy the most exacting theatregoer'. He gave WILLIAM CONSTABLE his first professional work as designer, and Whitehall was the first company to sign a standard Actors' Equity contract. Coppel and KATHLEEN ROBINSON formed Whitehall in 1940, soon after he returned to Australia to direct plays starring MARIE NEY for J. C. WILLIAMSON'S. Whitehall opened at the MINERVA THEATRE on 10 May 1941 with *Mr Smart Guy*, a new play by Coppel, who had been a successful playwright in London since his *I Killed the Count* at the Whitehall Theatre in 1938. Coppel directed *Mr Smart Guy* and all but three Whitehall plays over the next three years, working closely with his production team and assisted splendidly by Harry Short, the stage manager. Coppel was invited to direct the inaugural season of 2GB's *Macquarie Radio Theatre* in December 1941. In May 1944 he announced a drama festival at the Minerva, but only George Bernard Shaw's *Pygmalion* was performed. Disagreement with Kathleen Robinson brought their partnership to an abrupt end and by 1945 Coppel was back in England, writing film scripts. ❦*Lynne Murphy*

published play
I Killed the Count (1938). London: Heinemann 1938.

George Coppin

Actor, entrepreneur. Born 8 April 1819 in Steyning (Sussex, England). Son of actor. Performed as actor, fiddle-player and singer in Belfast, Dublin, Glasgow and London from at least 1826. Arrived in Sydney with Maria Augusta Watkins Burroughs, known as Mrs Coppin, 10 March 1843. Acted at Royal Victoria Theatre. Acted in Hobart and formed company in Launceston 1845. Moved to Melbourne, June 1845. To Adelaide, August 1846. Ran theatres and hotels. In Geelong 1852–53. Returned to London 1853–54. Opened Olympic Theatre, Melbourne, 30 July 1855. Married to Harriet Hilsden 1855–59. Ran three theatres, four hotels and amusement park in Melbourne 1856–59. Member of Victorian Legislative Assembly 1858–63, 1874–77, 1883–88, and member of Legislative Council 1889–95. Married Lucy Hilsden 4 June 1861. Opened Haymarket Theatre, Melbourne, 15 September 1862. Managed tour by Charles and Ellen Kean 1863–65. Rebuilt Theatre Royal, Melbourne, 1872. Died 14 March 1906 in Melbourne.

One of the great survivors of the theatrical profession in the second half of the 19th century in Australia was George Coppin. An unquenchable entrepreneur, he imported everything from Sindhi camels and English thrushes to actors. He catered for an audience demand for stars, spectacle and pantomimes, and in 'dressing up' his shows he was a pacesetter. As an actor, Coppin was a comedian who excelled in low-life parts like the title-role in Douglas Jerrold's *Paul Pry* and the off-colour BILLY BARLOW. He played Sir Peter Teazle in R. B. Sheridan's *The School for Scandal*, but the classical mode was not for him. He was initially helped by Maria Coppin, who could act in the 'scientific style' of the day.

On arrival in Sydney in 1843 Coppin joined JOSEPH WYATT at the Royal Victoria Theatre in Sydney, acting in comedy. Then he invested disastrously in the scandalous Clown

Hotel, which the *Sydney Morning Herald* exposed on 17 October 1844. In January 1845 he opened in Hobart as an actor with ANNE CLARKE. She claimed he had stolen her best actors when he left to open a theatre in Launceston. There Coppin demonstrated an eye for advertising and program design which marked his career. His own best publicist, he also opened eyes by personally leading the supernumeraries on stage in the romantic spectacle *Timour the Tartar*.

In June 1845 Coppin moved his company to Melbourne for a season at the Queen's Theatre Royal in opposition to FRANCIS NESBITT. He astonished audiences with his attention to sets and eventually took over Nesbitt's ROYAL VICTORIA THEATRE. In September 1846 Coppin moved to Adelaide, where he turned a billiards room into the New Queen's Theatre, which opened on 2 November 1846. He dabbled in the hotel business, horse-breeding and importation of luxury goods for a time and then joined JOHN LAZAR in turning the Queen's Theatre into the Royal Victoria Theatre. Maria Coppin died in Adelaide on 10 August 1848.

In 1851 insolvency led Coppin to the goldfields, where he presented plays to miners living in tents. From 14 June 1852 he tapped the entertainment business in Geelong by taking over a theatre from HENRY DEERING and in 1853 he fully repaid his creditors at a large function in Adelaide. Then he left for London. There he hired the Haymarket Theatre and played comedy for two weeks as an advertising exercise. He engaged the tragedian G. V. BROOKE for an Australian tour at an initial fee of £10 000. In December 1854 Coppin returned to Melbourne with a £5000 prefabricated iron building which became the OLYMPIC THEATRE. He played favourite comic roles at the Queen's Theatre Royal from 18 December 1854 and Brooke opened there as Othello on 26 February 1855. The Olympic Theatre opened in July 1855, in opposition to John Black's £95 000 THEATRE ROYAL. In the 'Iron Pot' Brooke swept himself and Coppin into financial success.

In August 1855, Coppin married Brooke's sister-in-law Harriet Hilsden, after a love-letter he had written to the actor FANNY CATHCART was read aloud in court in Melbourne, during a case brought by Brooke against Cathcart and her new husband Robert Heir. By June 1856 Coppin was able to buy the Theatre Royal from Black. In September Coppin bought the CREMORNE GARDENS in suburban Richmond and went into partnership with Brooke in this amusement park, Astley's Amphitheatre, the Olympic Theatre, the Theatre Royal and four hotels.

In 1858, after a business trip to England, Coppin was elected to the Richmond Council. He staged one of his many retirements from the theatre and was elected to the Victorian Legislative Council. He split with Brooke in February 1859, retaining only the Cremorne Gardens and the Olympic Theatre, which he converted into Turkish baths. In December 1860 Coppin took over the Theatre Royal after a public reconciliation with Brooke, who left Australia in May 1861. Coppin, a widower since 1859, married his stepdaughter Lucy Hilsden on 4 June 1861. He lost the Theatre Royal in 1861, but he built the HAYMARKET THEATRE and the adjoining Apollo Music Hall and opened them in September 1862. He engaged the American actor JOSEPH JEFFERSON for the opening of the Haymarket in September 1862. On 18 February 1863 Coppin resigned from the Legislative Council after an insolvency case. For a time he acted in various places in Victoria, and in Sydney and Dunedin (New Zealand). He was again able to pay his creditors in full after he brought the English actors CHARLES AND ELLEN KEAN to Australia in 1863–64. He travelled with the Keans to the USA as their agent and actor, and parted from them acrimoniously in Philadelphia in 1865.

Coppin returned to Melbourne in 1866 and, after a political defeat, performed as a comedian at the Haymarket Theatre. He was manager of the Theatre Royal when it burned down in March 1872. Coppin leased the site of the uninsured theatre and raised capital to build a new Theatre Royal. He engaged J. C. WILLIAMSON and MAGGIE MOORE to open it in 1874. Coppin resumed his political career as a member of the Legislative Assembly in 1874. Williamson became sole lessee of the Theatre Royal in 1881. Next year Coppin gave 'retirement' performances for a year, but he retained a stake in the Theatre Royal and set up a lucrative copyright agency which owned performing rights to about 8000 works. The 1880s saw Coppin back in theatre management, lavishly producing pantomimes. With BLAND HOLT he produced *The Babes in the Wood* in 1892, *Aladdin* in 1894 and *The House that Jack Built* in 1895.

As a public figure he was involved in setting up a post office savings bank and St John's Ambulance in Victoria as well as the first skating rink in Australia. Coppin is said to have favoured the establishment of a training school for actors, but he had litle interest in indigenous offerings. He made his mark with his ambitious importations of stars—Brooke perhaps the most loved, the Keans the most respected and Williamson the most successful. Coppin calculated all his theatrical ventures in pounds, shillings and pence, as his documented complaints about the Keans' illnesses show. He was often a shady dealer, and his dodges were a byword for unscrupulousness. Ellen Kean in a letter of 23 February 1864 refers to his reputation as 'dangerous person to deal with.' His background is well recorded in many insolvency and other legal cases that dotted his career. One of his numerous children, Daisy Coppin became custodian of his papers. Another daughter, Georgina, was the second wife of GEORGE RIGNOLD. ❦*Helen Musa*

further reading
DUFF, HELEN. Keans' tour of Australia. University of NSW BA (hons) thesis 1965.
HARDWICK, J. M. D. *Emigrant in Motley*. London: Rockliff 1954.
O'NEILL, SALLY. George Selth Coppin. *Australian Dictionary of Biography* 3. Melbourne University Press 1969.
OPPENHEIM, HELENE. Coppin, how great? *Australian Literary Studies* (Hobart) October 1967.

Copyright

Copyright is the exclusive right of an author or creator of an original work to control the manner in which that work is used. Australian copyright law is closely modelled on that of the United Kingdom, where statutes have recognised copyright since 1709. The Dramatic Copyright Act 1833 and the Literary Copyright Act 1842 were passed in Great Britain, and from 1869 the five mainland Australian colonies passed supplementary legislation and established copyright offices. Dramatic copyright in Australia in the colonial period differed considerably from modern law. The right to make copies of a script—in the form of books, for example—was distinct from the right to perform a script in public. A dramatist who completed a play had to have it staged in public before the performing right could be granted. This led to the practice of giving a 'copyright performance' with actors, sometimes in costume, reading the script in a public hall. The playwright, or the actor-manager who had bought the script, could then apply to register the play with the copyright office in the colony where it had been performed. Registration was not automatic and refusal was sometimes used as CENSORSHIP, as in the famous case of Marcus Clarke's THE HAPPY LAND in 1880.

Performing right was granted only for a colony where a performance had been given. Reg Rede's play *The Kelly Gang*, registered in Victoria in 1896, was plagiarised in 1899 by Arnold Denham in NSW and by J. H. Greene in Queensland and South Australia, and these authors were granted the performing rights for those colonies respectively. Denham demanded payment from any company performing a Kelly Gang play in NSW. Another weakness was that no law prevented plays being made from novels. This led to press complaints in 1886 about several versions of *For the Term of His Natural Life* being staged without benefit to MARCUS CLARKE's impoverished widow and children.

However the major cause of dramatic piracy in Australia was the result of Lord St Leonards's judgment—in a major English case, Jefferys v. Boosey in 1854—that copyright could be sold in its entirety but not divided up amongst licensees in different parts of the British Empire. This prevented an Australian manager from purchasing Australian rights to plays from London and New York. At the same time other actor-managers performed the same plays without restriction as only the authors themselves could sue for breach of performing right—and they were 20 000 km away. In 1879, however, J. C. WILLIAMSON obtained a temporary injunction to prevent the KELLY AND LEON MINSTRELS from continuing to perform *HMS Pinafore*. From then on he proclaimed that he had validated licence agreements in the Australian colonies and aggressively pursued his 'rights'. In fact it appears that he had benefited from a legal error. In 1896 Lord St Leonards's judgment was set aside as irrelevant when the NSW Chief Justice, in Holt v. Woods, drew a distinction between copyright, which continued to be empire-wide, and performing right, which was essentially local and could therefore be divided geographically.

In an 1892 South Australian case, Fishburn Brothers v. Adelaide Cyclorama Company, the work of scene-painters was found to be protected both by British law and by the international agreements formulated at the Berne Convention of 1886. As a result a pirated copy of a German panorama, *Jerusalem and the Crucifixion of Christ*, was withdrawn from exhibition. Two other cases, Broadhurst v. Nicholls in NSW in 1903 and Meynell v. Pearce in Victoria in 1906, finally established a licensee's right to the title of a play. Suburban and provincial managers could no longer offer *The Wrong Mrs Wright* or *The Fatal Wedding Day* after a major company had presented *The Wrong Mr Wright* or *The Fatal Wedding*. The latter case also swept away the dubious claim of some minor entrepreneurs that they were exempt from copyright law because they performed in shire halls and the like and not in licensed theatres.

The rights of the writers themselves were still not adequately covered. It is not until 1907 that there is a known instance of dramatists receiving a royalty for each performance—Bert Bailey and Edmund Duggan for *The Squatter's Daughter*—rather than selling a script outright.

In 1905 the Commonwealth of Australia passed a Copyright Act which led to the establishment of a Commonwealth Copyright Office in 1907. This act was repealed from 1 July 1912, when the Australian Parliament adopted the 1911 United Kingdom Copyright Act, the first codification of the law into a single act. At the same time all earlier laws, including the substantive provisions in laws of the individual states, were repealed.

Novelists had to wait for the 1912 commonwealth legislation to gain legal protection for dramatisations of their stories, although from the 1880s some—notably Rolf Boldrewood for *Robbery Under Arms*—had persuaded 'honourable' managers to pay a small royalty (usually £1 a performance) for stage adaptations. *Richard Fotheringham*

Copyright law since 1968

The 1912 Act was substantially amended by the Copyright Act 1968, which, with its own amendments, contains the present law. To be protected by copyright a work must be 'original' and must exist in a 'material form'. Originality does not require that the work be inventive or novel in ideas, but only that it not be copied. The 'material form' requirement is widely defined, and now includes, for example, storage in computers.

There can be no copyright in a performance, however, unless there is some fixed script. Once the requirements of originality and material form are satisfied protection of copyright is completely automatic. No registration is required, nor is any mark or notice on the work itself needed for protection under Australian law.

Copyright is protected for 50 years, generally from the end of the calendar year in which the author of the work dies. For joint authors it is the year of death of the last survivor. Anonymous works or works published under pseudonyms are protected for 50 years from the end of the year of first publication. Works which at the date of the creator's death have never been performed, published or offered to the public, are protected for 50 years from the year of first publication or performance.

Generally the author or creator of a work owns any copyright in it. The main exceptions are works written by employees generally—in which copyright for the employer's purposes lies with the employer—and commissioned photographs, portraits and engravings, in which the commissioner owns copyright. Joint authors own copyright jointly unless their contributions are distinct. The writers of the lyrics and music of a song, for example, each have a copyright in their own contribution. An author or other copyright owner is free to transfer all or part of the copyright or to bequeath it in their will. Copyright must usually be specifically mentioned in the transfer. Selling a book or manuscript will not generally transfer the copyright.

If copyright is infringed the copyright owner is generally entitled to an injunction to prevent further infringement, damages (the amount of loss suffered), or an account of profits (the amount of unjust gain to the infringer) and to seizure of the infringing copies. Damages are not available, however, if the infringer can show that they were not aware of infringing copyright and had no reasonable grounds for suspecting infringement. Infringing copyright can also be a criminal offence, and in some cases—such as video piracy—very substantial penalties exist.

Australia is a signatory of both the Berne Convention of 1886 and the Universal Copyright Convention. These provide that works protected by copyright in Australia are protected in other member countries and vice versa. The familiar © mark on the work, together with the name of the copyright owner and the year of first publication, is sufficient to satisfy any formal copyright requirements, such as registration and deposit, in other countries.

Works in material form
'Dramatic works' are protected by the Copyright Act 1968. A dramatic work is one that is intended to be performed or presented, rather than read. The act does not fully define the term, but it does specifically include some works, for example 'a choreographic show or some other dumb show' or the script of a film. The requirement that the work be in a material form can raise difficulties. For example, dance is protected only if 'described in writing in the form in which the show is to be presented'. Recording in specialised notation is entirely adequate for this purpose but video-taping is not. Additionally, improvisations and shows (such as some mimes) that vary substantially with each performance are not protected by copyright.

The fact that copyright protects the work itself and not the ideas within it can cause problems in the theatre. For example, scenery, stage directions and costumes are protected only to the extent that they are reduced to writing, unless they are separately protected by copyright as 'artistic works', as is sometimes the case for scenery. There is no copyright in ideas or methods of production and staging.

A dramatic work can infringe the copyright of another literary or dramatic work without copying any of the words, if the incidents and actions sufficiently resemble the earlier work for it to be said that the work itself has been copied and not just the ideas upon which it was based. An example, is Kelly v. Cinema Houses Ltd, decided in 1928, in which the plaintiff complained that a novel had been dramatised without the permission of the author, in spite of the fact that the words themselves had not been copied.

Among the rights protected by copyright is that of 'public performance', which means any performance beyond the home and domestic life of a family and its guests. Thus any public performance of a dramatic work without the copyright owner's permission can constitute an infringement. It is also an infringement to reproduce a dramatic work in a material form. Thus to record a dramatic work either on audio or video equipment is an infringement of copyright, not in the performance, but in the written play or script. Taping an opera or filming a play without proper permission can be an infringement. This was determined in Hawkes v. Paramount Film Services Ltd, decided in 1934. The anomaly here is that bootleg recordings infringe the copyright in the work of dramatists, playwrights or composers, but performers have no such rights under the copyright law. ❦*Peter Banki*

further reading
ATKINSON, ROSLYN and RICHARD FOTHERINGHAM. Dramatic copyright in Australia to 1912. *Australasian Drama Studies* 11 (Brisbane, October 1987).

KELLY, VERONICA. The banning of Marcus Clarke's *The Happy Land*. *Australasian Drama Studies* 2/1 (Brisbane, October 1983).

Coralie Lansdowne Says No

Play in three acts by Alex Buzo. **premiere** 9 March 1974, Theatre 62, Adelaide, by Nimrod Theatre Company. Cast: Donna Akersten, Lloyd Casey, Kevin Howard, Jude Kuring, Berys Marsh, Robert Newman, John Orcsik. Designer: Kevin Brooks. Director: Ken Horler. **published** Sydney and London: Currency Methuen 1976.

One of ALEX BUZO's most successful plays of the mid-1970s, *Coralie Lansdowne Says No* achieved some notoriety because it appeared to show a high-flying, independent woman brought down to earth. Coralie succumbs to the advances of a suitor who is apparently unworthy of her and ends up saying 'yes' to marriage. Now, distanced from the ideological debates of the time, the play emerges as a more intimately personal study of compromise and acceptance in the individual's search for happiness. Coralie, tough, outspoken and witty, retreats from the hollow trendiness and tawdry glamour of the world she has known to a luxurious clifftop hideaway at Palm Beach, Sydney. Her fierce independence and bitchy wit mask a warmer personality. She is pursued into her retreat by her sister and by several selfish men who want different things from her, but mainly reassurance for their fragile egos. The play shows her slowly sifting their demands, and finally realising that the person who asks least and offers most is the 'worm' to whom she had at first said, so loudly, 'no'. ❦*John McCallum*

Peter Corrigan

Designer. Born 1941 in Daylesford (Vic.). Studied architecture at University of Melbourne and Yale University (USA). Worked in New York City as architect and stage designer 1970–74. Has designed many productions in Australia since 1974. Lectures at Royal Melbourne Institute of Technology.

Since Peter Corrigan returned to Australia in 1974 he has designed more than 60 productions for many mainstream and alternative companies throughout Australia. He made many notable contributions to the AUSTRALIAN PERFORMING GROUP, especially for *Crackers at the Savoy*, John Romeril's *THE FLOATING WORLD* and Bertolt Brecht's *The Mother*. His approach has been influenced by Jerzy Grotowski's 'poor theatre', the theories of the painter Marcel Duchamp and, at one stage, 'the annual APG liquidity crisis'.

At Melbourne University in the 1960s Corrigan designed 13 undergraduate productions, ranging from *Hamlet* in a tent to Harold Pinter's *The Birthday Party*. After studying at Yale University in 1969 he worked in Manhattan as an architect and stage designer for off-Broadway companies such as La Mama and the Ridiculous Theatre Company.
❦*Tom Bannerman, Pamela Zeplin*

writings
Australian architecture and the stage, 1979. *Architecture Australia* 68/4 (September 1979).
Carlton designs by Peter Corrigan. *Theatre Australia* (Sydney) August 1977.
Gentlemen only. *Theatre Australia* 3/54 (Sydney, September 1979).
Stage space. *Contemporary Australian Drama* (ed. Peter Holloway). Sydney: Currency Press 1981.

further reading

ANDERSON, MICHAEL A. R. Designing the dybbuk—Peter Corrigan. *Interior* 1/3 and 4 (February 1992).
BORLASE, NANCY. The answer to the Biennale is good. *Sydney Morning Herald* 30 May 1981.
Howie, Ann C. (ed.). *Who's Who in Australia 1991* 27th edn. Melbourne: Information Australia.
PEGRUM, ROGER. A quest for relevance. *Pol* (Sydney) March 1981
PULVERS, ROGER. The evolution of a design. *Theatre Australia* (Sydney) 5/11 (July 1981).
Carlton designs. *Theatre Australia*, August 1977.

Ruth Cracknell AM

Actor. Born 6 July 1925 at Maitland (NSW). Trained in Sydney with Modern Theatre Players and Independent Theatre. Joined John Alden Company 1948. Worked for BBC radio in London 1952–53. In Phillip Street revues in Sydney in 1950s. Leading actor since 1960. On board of Sydney Theatre Company 1980–94. Became patron of Sydney Theatre Company 1994. Green Room Award 1985 (Emma in *The Doll Trilogy* by Ray Lawler). AM for services to theatre 1980. HonDLitt (Sydney). Mother of actor Anna Phillips.

It would be hard to find an actor in contemporary Australian theatre with more varied talents and achievements than Ruth Cracknell. She stands at the top of the profession she entered in the JOHN ALDEN COMPANY in 1948. She played a strikingly evil Goneril to Alden's King Lear in Sydney in 1950. In 1952 she was in August Strindberg's *The Father* for MERCURY THEATRE. In London in 1952–53 she auditioned successfully for the Old Vic Theatre Company but family reasons compelled her to return to Sydney.

The English director Lionel Harris saw Cracknell in Peter Ustinov's *The Love of Four Colonels* at the INDEPENDENT THEATRE in 1955. He cast her in the title-role of R. B. Sheridan's *The Duenna* and changed the direction of her career. For the next four years Cracknell paraded a gallery of comic characters in PHILLIP STREET REVUES, including *A Cup of Tea, a Bex and a Good Lie Down*, *Cross Section* and *… But I Wouldn't Want to Live There*. Much later she appeared at WILLIAM ORR's Music Loft in Manly in *Crackers*, written for her by John McKellar, writer of most of the Phillip Street revues.

At the Adelaide Festival of Arts in 1960 Cracknell began a long professional partnership with RON HADDRICK. It has been perhaps most notable for their performances as Jocasta and Oedipus in Tyrone Guthrie's production of Sophocles's *King Oedipus* for the OLD TOTE THEATRE COMPANY in 1970. They starred in a two-hander, *The Gin Game* by D. L. Coburn, in Sydney in 1979 with great distinction and pathos, and they were memorable parents in DAVID WILLIAMSON's *What If You Died Tomorrow?* in Sydney in 1973 and London in 1974. In 1983 they were teamed as the theatrical Crummleses in David Edgar's *The Life and Adventures of Nicholas Nickleby* for the SYDNEY THEATRE COMPANY. Cracknell appeared in her own solo show, *Just Ruth*, for the South Australian Theatre Company in Adelaide in 1977. She excelled in another solo performance, as the redoubtable Leah Hunt in JOHN UPTON's *Machiavelli, Machiavelli* in Sydney in 1984. Cracknell's creation of the tough, likeable Elaine in David Williamson's EMERALD CITY took her to the West End of London in the play in 1987. In the same year she was praised for a graceful performance as Viv's mother in Michael Hastings's *Tom and Viv*. Cracknell played Lady Bracknell in Oscar Wilde's *The Importance of Being Earnest*, for the MELBOURNE THEATRE COMPANY in 1988. She played Winnie in Samuel Beckett's *Happy Days* in 1991 in Adelaide and Sydney and on tour to critical acclaim. Cracknell was honoured in 1993 at a command performance at the Sydney Opera House to mark its 20th anniversary. In Geoffrey Atherden's comedy *Hotspur*, performed in Melbourne and Sydney in 1994, she created the indomitable Fiona McPherson, another strong woman. ❦*Lynne Murphy*

further reading

HERBERT, IAN (ed.). *Who's Who in the Theatre* 17th edn. Detroit (USA): Gale Research 1981.
Howie, ANN C. (ed.). *Who's Who in Australia* 17th edn. Melbourne: Information Australia 1991.

Rex Cramphorn

Critic, designer, director, translator. Born 10 January 1941 in Brisbane. Originally Rex Cramphorne. Active in student theatre at University of Queensland. Studied production at National Institute of Dramatic Art (Sydney). Formed Performance Syndicate 1969. Sydney theatre critic of *Bulletin* 1969–71, *Sunday Australian* 1971–72, *Theatre Australia* 1976–77. Directed for Old Tote Theatre Company (Sydney) 1976–78. Resident director and artistic co-director of Playbox Theatre Company (Melbourne) 1981–85. Studied at Australian Film, Television and Radio School (Sydney) 1986–89. Died 22 November 1991 in Sydney.

Rex Cramphorn was one of the most innovative directors Australia has produced, but his relationships with established theatre companies were restless and short-lived. When he died an obituary published in the *Sydney Morning Herald* and the Melbourne *Age* said that the Australian theatre had lost one of its most challenging and sensitive talents. 'Those who worked with him … count him as a formative influence,' it said. 'His range of remembered productions was wide. But if he had one quality that stood out it was his capacity to take a play and turn it into an object of contemplation, to penetrate its mystery so that it stayed in the mind long after the image faded.'

In Melbourne he raised the ailing fortunes of the Playbox Theatre Company with a diet of Shakespeare, French classics and aggressive modern works. His notable productions included Sam Shepard's *True West* in 1981; *Antony and Cleopatra* in 1983; and Terry Johnson's *Insignificance* and Athol Fugard's *'Master Harold' … and the Boys*, both of which toured in 1983–84. Playbox launched the biennial Rex Cramphorn Memorial Scholarship for a director, which was first awarded in 1993 by the NSW Arts Ministry.

Cramphorn's early influences included the French avant-garde, the Polish director Jerzy Grotowski, with whom he worked in Australia in 1972, and the English director Peter Brook. He combined these influences with yoga exercises, meditation and Asian performance styles in experiments into style and content. To develop actors' physical and mental skills and to challenge the received view of the theatre, he formed the PERFORMANCE SYNDICATE as an unpaid workshop group in 1969. A small cast undertook multiple roles, performing on a flat floor surrounded by the audience. Cramphorn's most memorable productions for the Performance Syndicate were probably its own adaptation of Hans Andersen's *The Marsh King's Daughter* and *The Tempest* in 1972–73. Both had national tours. By 1975 the Performance Syndicate had dissolved in exhaustion but some actors built on Cramphorn's methods as they moved into more conventional theatre.

In 1976 Cramphorn joined the OLD TOTE THEATRE COMPANY as a director but he resigned in protest at its conservative policy in 1978. He and JIM SHARMAN set up the Paris Theatre Company in Sydney in 1978 with the support of PATRICK WHITE and others to present new Australian work on a major scale but the venture lasted only one season.

Cramphorn's favourite dramatists were Shakespeare, the Jacobeans and Jean Racine (he directed *Berenice* in 1975 and *Britannicus* in 1982). He did experimental productions of French classics in his own translations for the University of Sydney's French department and the Centre for Performance Studies, from Pierre Corneille's *The Theatrical Illusion* in 1979 to Molière's *Don Juan* in 1991.

At the university in 1980 he experimented in Shakespearean performance with A Shakespeare Company, which included RUTH CRACKNELL, RON HADDRICK and JOHN HOWARD. Cramphorn directed the first of his four productions of *Measure for Measure* for this company. The fourth, for the 1990 Adelaide Festival and on tour, was a controversial production in which he sought to draw attention to the play's morality by integrating emblematic film images into the action. Cramphorn designed many of his own productions, and he designed the costumes for *Richard III* in the 1968 Festival of Perth and for the musical *Jesus Christ Superstar* in Sydney in 1972. ❦*Katharine Brisbane*

P. P. Cranney

Dramatist. Born 6 August 1954 in Sydney. Worked as film lighting technician for seven years in 1970s. Began writing for Kirribilli Pub Theatre (Sydney) 1979. Resident writer for Sidetrack Theatre Company (Sydney) 1983. Director of Mainstreet Theatre Company (Naracoorte SA) 1989.

P. P. Cranney has written prolifically for COMMUNITY THEATRE, employing a wide range of styles and methods. He took part in projects that established models in Australia, from the SIDETRACK PERFORMANCE GROUP's social-realist play with songs for trade-union audiences to the play with a large amateur cast that has become standard for youth-theatre and community-theatre groups. His best works have been social-realist collaborations with the director Geoff Crowhurst for the MAINSTREET THEATRE COMPANY and the JUNCTION THEATRE COMPANY in South Australia, particularly those produced with trade unions under the AUSTRALIA COUNCIL's Art and Working Life incentive program.

These plays have usually centred on a few 'typical' characters during a crisis or major change in a union or a community and interlaced their public, political and private lives. They have gripped the intended audience by accurate detail—the result of careful research—and a pervading tone of bitter-sweet comedy. Perhaps because they addressed specific audiences and were performed in untheatrical venues, these plays received little critical attention. Two recent plays for Junction, have received more notice and been seen more widely, *Offshore* (1991) perhaps because it less community-based and *Hello Down There* (1993) as a result of a remount for the Adelaide Festival.

The large-cast, community-generated play is Cranney's major contribution to the stylistic repertoire of community theatre. His most notable plays have been *Nuovo Paese/New Country* for the Federation of Italian Migrant Workers and their Families (FILEF) in Sydney in 1984, *The Logan City Story* for the STREET ARTS THEATRE COMPANY in Brisbane in 1984, *The Yallourn Story* for the Gippsland Trades and Labour Council in 1989, and *Site* for DEATH DEFYING THEATRE in Sydney in 1994. All were written in collaboration with specific communities, and entailed consultation as part of community development designed to impart skills to amateur participants and to ensure a sense of 'ownership' by the groups that took part. Cranney has made coherent and effective theatre from these projects and has trained young writers within them.

He has also been responsible for theatre-in-education plays, most notably *Busted*, a funny and touching piece on runaway children, written for Sidetrack in 1983 and revived several times. He has written occasional pieces for specific political circumstances, like *Professor Quack's Travelling Medicine Show*, written in two days for strikers at a paper mill in Burnie (Tas.) in 1992. It was toured nationally as part of a union campaign. ❦*David Watt*

further reading
STANWELL, John. and Ann JONES. The *Logan City* story. *Community Theatre in Australia* (ed. Richard Fotheringham). Sydney: Currency Press 1992.
WATT, DAVID. Mainstreet—Making theatre in the country. *Meanjin* 50/2–3 (Melbourne 1991).

Letty Craydon

Actor. Born 1899 in Sydney. Daughter of vaudevillian James Craydon. Early roles as child in touring tent shows. In revue and vaudeville. New Tivoli Theatre, Sydney, 1932. Minerva Theatre, Sydney, 1941–42. In United Kingdom 1949–51. Toured revues with husband Ron Shand. Died 2 November 1965 in Sydney.

A chubby blonde with a disarming air of innocence, Letty Craydon projected her delight in performance to her audience with the perfect timing of the true comedian. The third generation of a theatrical family, she spent her early years touring with her parents in TENT SHOWS. She first appeared on stage at six months of age. Her first speaking role was Little Eva in *Uncle Tom's Cabin*. During the 1920s Craydon worked in revue and vaudeville and began writing her own material. She appeared with GEORGE WALLACE among others. When the theatre collapsed in the 1930s, she turned to writing for radio. She also appeared in films.

In the 1940s she returned to the stage in Clare Boothe's *The Women* at the Theatre Royal in Sydney. For WHITEHALL THEATRICAL PRODUCTIONS she acted in two plays by George S. Kaufman and Moss Hart. She played the crazy Harriet Sedley in *The Man Who Came to Dinner* in 1941 and Penelope Sycamore in *You Can't Take it with You* in 1942. She was also one of the genteel murderers in Joseph Kesselring's *Arsenic and Old Lace* in 1942. At the Theatre Royal she played Madam Arcati in Noël Coward's *Blithe Spirit* and then she was in operettas, including *The Dancing Years* and *Gay Rosalinda*.

In 1949 Craydon went to London and appeared in revue at the Hippodrome and touring shows in leading Scottish theatres. On return to Sydney in 1951 she acted with the English stars Evelyn Laye and Frank Lawton, as Mrs Tuckett in Daphne Du Maurier's *September Tide*, and as the gentle head witch in John Van Druten's *Bell, Book and*

Candle. In 1954-1955 she toured with Googie Withers and JOHN MCCALLUM in Terence Rattigan's *The Deep Blue Sea* and Alan Melville's *Simon and Laura*. In 1956 she was Miss Addy in Caroline Green's Broadway comedy *Janus*, which starred Jessie Matthews.

Craydon married RON SHAND in the late 1940s and together they wrote much of their material for sketches in revue and television. They appeared together in comic roles in the musical *Grab Me a Gondola* in Sydney in 1959. Shand used to say that in 20 years of marriage they only spent about ten years together because they were usually touring in different shows, but they were known to be the best pen friends in the business. ❦*Lynne Murphy*

Cremorne Gardens

Outdoor pleasure gardens, or amusement parks, became popular in Europe in the mid-18th century. London had the Vauxhall Gardens, the Surrey Zoological Gardens and the Cremorne Gardens. In 1852 a former manager of the Cremorne Gardens, James Ellis, opened pleasure gardens of the same name beside the Yarra River at Richmond, near prosperous goldrush Melbourne. Like the London establishment they copied, they were mainly a summer venue. They offered the Pantheon, a small theatre where JULIA MATTHEWS starred; a bandstand and rotunda for outdoor dancing; and a three-dimensional panorama. This was modelled in plaster, canvas and timber to a scale of 1 : 48, and painted to represent scenes such as the sieges of Sevastopol or Canton, the eruption of Vesuvius. There was a fireworks show with the panorama, which showed a different historical scene each summer. In 1860 Giuseppe Garibaldi's triumph at Palermo was a topical subject.

Most visitors arrived at the Cremorne Gardens by river on a small paddle-steamer, the *Gondola*. The gardens proved very popular, though some regarded them, like their London counterparts, as a place of immoral assignation and prostitution. The theatrical entrepreneur GEORGE COPPIN took over the management in 1856. By 1863, however, over-commitment in other entertainment ventures forced him to close the gardens. They were converted into a private mental asylum.

Similar pleasure gardens, also called the Cremorne Gardens, opened at Mosman's Bay, on the north shore of Sydney Harbour, at Easter 1856. They were never quite as successful as Melbourne's Cremorne Gardens but people flocked there by harbour ferry until 1865. They were especially popular for their *bals masqués*. Lack of 'respectability' contributed to their closure, long after which the area became known as Cremorne.

The name of Cremorne Gardens also persisted in outdoor entertainment. In Perth in 1895 Mrs Annie Oliver opened the Cremorne Gardens adjacent to the Cremorne Hotel, between Hay and Murray Streets. Well furnished with plants and surrounded by a high wall painted with murals of alpine scenery, 'the Cremorne was a place where in hot weather people [took] their amusements in the open air, while smoking and otherwise refreshing themselves', according to a press report. Around a rotunda were kiosks, each named after a Western Australian goldmining locality, where the public sat to watch 'continental' variety performances by local and visiting artists, including the Harry Rickards Tivoli Company, Pollard's Liliputian Opera Company, the Banvards, Celia Ghiloni, NEVA CARR GLYN, Ettie Williams and Millie Finkelstein. About 1899 the rotunda was moved to the Perth foreshore and replaced by a covered outdoor stage with a proscenium arch, drop curtains, an orchestra pit and dressing rooms. Troops were entertained at the Cremorne Gardens during the First World War. The gardens closed in 1920, when Mrs Oliver transferred the equity of the theatre and the hotel to the Young Men's Christian Association.

At the height of Western Australia's goldrush prosperity Kalgoorlie had a Cremorne Gardens. Photographs from 1907 show an open-air auditorium with rows of seats, a proscenium-arch stage with fly tower and backdrop, and an orchestra pit. The building, since roofed, still stands.

By 1911 outdoor theatres called Cremorne Gardens were presenting seaside Pierrot entertainment in the Melbourne suburb of St Kilda, and in Adelaide and Brisbane. By the 1920s there was an Australia-wide circuit, featuring Edward Branscombe's Dandies, Pat Hanna's DIGGERS COMPANY and similar companies. Many of the Cremorne venues soon became open-air cinemas, while the one in Brisbane was roofed and became the Cremorne Theatre, owned and managed by John N. McCallum, father of the actor JOHN MCCALLUM. The theatre, noted for variety but sometimes used as a cinema, burned down in February 1954. ❦*Mimi Colligan, Bill Dunstone*

further reading
WROTH, WARWICK. *Cremorne and the Later London Gardens*. London: 1907.

William Creswick

English actor 1813–88. Acted in west of England 1839–45. In London from 1846, particularly noted in Shakespeare. Sometime co-manager of Surrey Theatre. In Australia 1877–80.

William Creswick told the Urban Club in London that he had never 'met with due appreciation' until he visited Australia, according to the *Era* of 10 October 1880. He was a veteran tragedian of the 'intellectual' Shakespearean kind who, the *Lone Hand* magazine said, could 'pose with dignity and deliver blank verse in telling style'. His Australian tour was an unexpected triumph. He came without an engagement, but turned a six-week Sydney season into nearly six months. He was then denied a theatre in Melbourne, but when he eventually obtained a booking at the Prince of Wales Opera House, he 'hit them very strongly', according to EMILY SOLDENE. Creswick's greatest part was the title-role in Sheridan Knowles's 1820 tragedy *Virginius* —though unkind critics said he simply copied William Macready—and he was also successful as Hamlet, King Lear and Shylock. ❦*Richard Fotheringham*

Barry Creyton

Actor, composer, director, dramatist. Born 29 December 1939 in Brisbane. Trained in amateur theatre in Brisbane, and with Babette Stephens. Announcer on radio 4BH Brisbane in late 1950s. Moved to Melbourne. Professional acting debut 1960. Wrote for and performed at Music Hall Theatre Restaurant, Sydney, 1961–64. In Phillip Street revues from 1962. In *Mavis Bramston Show* on television 1964–66. Worked mostly in England 1968–77. Performed in his *Double Act* at Ensemble Theatre, Sydney, and on tour 1987–88. Norman Kessell Memorial Award for contribution to Australian theatre as actor, director and playwright 1988. Has lived in USA, writing for television, since 1991.

Barry Creyton has made a successful career as writer, director and composer and he acts with immense skill and charm in comedy and wry pathos in character parts. His beautifully modulated voice brought him work in radio drama before he made his professional stage debut touring for J. C. WILLIAMSON'S in Clifford Odets's *Winter Journey*. Then he appeared with great panache as the villain in *East Lynne*, the opening production of the MUSIC HALL THEATRE RESTAURANT in Sydney in November 1961. During the next two years he was a popular villain in *The Evil Men Do* and *The Face at the Window* at the Music Hall and he wrote two of its most successful shows, an adaptation of Miss Braddon's 1862 melodrama *Lady Audley's Secret* and *How the West Was Lost*. In 1962 he appeared at the Phillip Theatre in the revue *What's New* with Noeline Brown. Subsequently he wrote music for several PHILLIP STREET REVUES and for Frank Strain's Downstairs Revue. Creyton appeared in and wrote the theme song, much other music and sketches for the satirical *Mavis Bramston Show* on ATN–7 television, which brought him wide popularity.

In London from 1968 Creyton worked consistently in West End theatre. He acted in MICHAEL BLAKEMORE's production of David Williamson's *Don's Party* in London in 1975 and wrote a comedy, *Follow That Husband*, which was produced by Ray Cooney. In 1977 the producers of the television series *The Naked Vicar Show* brought Creyton back to Australia to star in a stage version, *Son of the Naked Vicar*, at the Speakeasy Theatre Restaurant in Sydney.

For the next ten years Creyton acted and wrote extensively for television. In 1979 he acted on stage in Alan Ayckbourn's *Bedroom Farce* in Sydney and on tour throughout Australia. Creyton toured Australia again in 1983–84 in Blakemore's production of Michael Frayn's *Noises Off*, which he considers the best comedy ever written. He appeared for the Northside Theatre Company in Sydney in two plays by Ayckbourn, *Season's Greetings* in 1984 and *Absurd Person Singular* in 1986. In the latter he had a leg in plaster after a motorcycle accident.

While in hospital with his broken leg, Creyton wrote *Double Act*, a comedy two-hander for Noeline Brown and himself, inspired by Noël Coward's *Private Lives*. It opened in Sydney on 19 September 1987, directed by Sandra Bates, and broke box-office records for the ENSEMBLE THEATRE COMPANY in its first season and on its return after touring Australia in 1988. 'An examination of a broken marriage, it begins in blaze away style with salvos of almost continuously funny one-liners, and then modulates towards comedy and, eventually, even a kind of acid pathos', wrote H. G. KIPPAX. 'Its craftsmanship as entertainment is first-rate.' *Double Act* has been successfully produced in Belgium, Canada, Germany and New Zealand, and has been translated into Dutch, French, German, Portuguese and Swedish. A production starring Rowena Wallace and Rod Mullinar toured Australia for five months in 1991.

Creyton made his debut as a director with Dan Goggin's musical *Nunsense*, which opened in Sydney in January 1987 and broke box-office records all over Australia. With Goggin's permission, he revised the dialogue for Australian audiences, and for Irish audiences when he directed the Dublin production in June 1988. ☙*Lynne Murphy*

published play
Double Act (1987). Sydney: Currency Press 1987.

Criterion Theatre

Theatre on corner of Park and Pitt Streets, Sydney, opened 27 December 1886. Architect: George Johnson. Partially rebuilt 1892. Architects: Backhouse and Laidley. Closed 13 July 1935 and demolished.

For almost 50 years the Criterion Theatre was Sydney's major intimate playhouse. When it opened in 1886, with the operetta *Falka*, it was noted that the stage curtain was gold-fringed, dark red plush instead of the green baize of Georgian–Regency convention. The *Sydney Morning Herald* said the theatre 'made the spectator feel far nearer to London than usual', the nearest approach being the 'pretty little' BIJOU THEATRE in Melbourne. It was 'a great advance in Sydney theatres'. The NSW Government Architect thought otherwise in 1887, when he inspected it as a postscript to a royal commission on the safety of theatres. He complained that the smell from poorly ventilated dressing rooms and their lavatories was so overpowering as to make him sick. He described a forced ventilation system that seemed to move air from this malodorous basement into the auditorium and expel it into the stalls urinals whence 'it must find its way back to the parts of the theatre from which it was drawn, carrying with it a proportion of the vitiated air from the urinals and closets'.

George Johnson, the architect who designed the theatre for John Solomons, had previously produced a nightmare for officialdom in Melbourne, the Opera House in Bourke Street. The *Sydney Morning Herald* claimed a capacity of 1500–1700 for the Criterion, but the Government Architect calculated seating for only 991 persons on the three levels of the auditorium—stalls, dress circle and a combined family circle and gallery. After only five years another firm of architects was commissioned to redesign the auditorium, push back the proscenium wall, raise the roof by 3·7 metres, build new dressing rooms that could have light and air, and improve the foyer space. The high proscenium was lowered and widened, opening onto a stage 11 metres deep by 17·7 metres wide. The ceiling of the auditorium was raised and a dome with a sliding roof was inserted. Now the interior was in keeping with the solid, deeply modelled Victorian, neo-baroque Renaissance exterior.

This work was undertaken for the BROUGH–BOUCICAULT COMEDY COMPANY, which leased the theatre for a few years. Later, *The Kelly Gang* was performed with sensational stage effects in 1898, and WILLIAM ANDERSON presented Australian melodramas, including GEORGE DARRELL's *The Land of Gold* and Bert Bailey and Edmund Duggan's THE SQUATTER'S DAUGHTER in 1907. Modifications in 1905 increased the seating capacity beyond 1300. FRANK MUSGROVE bought the theatre in 1913 and in 1915 it passed to J. C. WILLIAMSON'S and as the Firm's Sydney outlet for West End comedies from London. The Criterion also housed the Australian premiere of the musical comedy *Irene* in August 1920 and specialists such as Dante the Magician in 1933. It closed in 1935 with *The Patsy* by Barry Connor. ☙*Ross Thorne*

Criticism and journalism

Australia produced reviewers as soon as it had theatres and newspapers. The early writers concerned themselves with standards of performance—mostly making unfavourable comparisons with remembered performances back home—or with encouraging local endeavour. Their uninhibited commentary, in largely improvised and parochial journals, vividly reflects the nature of the society. So do the concerns they gradually established—first to emphasise the civilising nature of drama and music and the quality of performance, and then to deplore the uncivilised behaviour of the growing emancipist audience and the consequent degrading of the repertoire.

Opposing attitudes

Most information about the theatre in Australia from the 1820s to 1850 is to be found in early newspapers and magazines, much of it only in advertisements. Reviews appeared irregularly and varied enormously in quality and length. Most papers would notice the opening night of a new theatre and, later in the period, the appearance of a new star performer, but few reviewed their local theatre consistently throughout a season. Most reviewers pretended to an intimate knowledge of English theatre but few really seem to have had it, and no theatrical critic of any note appeared in Australia before 1850.

Two opposing attitudes are clear in comments on theatre in Sydney and Tasmanian newspapers before professional performances became regular in the 1830s. Some saw theatres as a civilising and refining influence, offering a form of rational entertainment that was seriously lacking, and so especially welcome and necessary, in a land of outcasts. Opponents of theatres saw them as dens of crime and iniquity, haunted by prostitutes and pickpockets, and only too liable to encourage the young of both sexes to fall from virtue. Theatres therefore were totally inappropriate for colonies designed as places of punishment and deterrence.

The same two attitudes lurk behind most reviews of performances and other published comments well after regular professional theatre had begun. Those who believed in the civilising function of theatre were troubled by rising audience demand for farce and melodrama rather than the older comedies and tragedies. Those who opposed theatres on moral grounds also objected to the actors' practice of 'gagging', claiming that much of the improvised material so introduced was obscene. But most were more concerned about audience behaviour and the need to regulate drinking, smoking and, in particular, the presence of prostitutes.

Whichever the attitude, most who wrote about theatre and theatrical performance in early Australia were out of touch with theatrical realities and audience demands. As Helene Oppenheim has observed: 'The critics belonged to a cultural minority in the new country, they adhered to standards as they remembered them, standards which no longer had validity; they were outdated in the mother country and had never gained any degree of reality in the antipodes'. So, the constant complaint that theatre would never succeed in Australia unless patronised by the colonial aristocracy—the governor and higher officials—overlooked the fact that theatre was already the popular entertainment form of the 19th century and was being controlled by audience demand rather than from above.

Most reviewers, however, assumed a superior attitude to local performances, performers and audience reaction, constantly referring back to productions seen in England, sometimes many years before, and to great English actors of the past. The highest praise that they could give was a comparison with the London stage. So, the *Sydney Monitor* of 2 November 1833 commended Angus Mackay's acting as 'worthy of any boards save London; and, even there, would have been held most respectable'. Mackay was specifically praised not only for knowing his part perfectly—a fairly rare virtue in Sydney at that time—but for the realism and truth to nature of his acting. Realism—in costumes and sets as well as in acting style—was increasingly demanded by critics as the century progressed.

When critics were reviewing new Australian plays—and hence were unable to draw on memories of English productions—they generally retained their superior attitudes, disdaining to join in audience approval. So, the reviewer of Edward Geoghegan's ballad opera THE CURRENCY LASS in the *Australian* on 30 May 1844 observed: 'The dialogue is truly Colonial—rather too much so for our taste—although the "Cabbage-tree hats", that crowded the pit and galleries on its first night of representation testified their approbation of its merits, in their estimation, by clamorous applause'. As always, the critic aligned himself with the boxes rather than the pit and galleries. Local dramatists, like other local authors, were also victims of the intense press rivalry common at this period. So, if one paper praised a new work, its opponent damned it as a matter of course, as happened with the production of DAVID BURN's *The Queen's Love* in Sydney in October 1845.

The first attempt to provide an overview of the development of theatre in Australia appears to have been Daniel Deniehy's 'The Rise and Progress of the Drama in Australia', printed in Sydney's *Colonial Literary Journal* on 27 February 1845. Deniehy gives a brief, though fairly accurate description of the development of theatre in Sydney from the 1830s, before joining in the condemnation of the popular taste for melodrama, a form seen as sinning 'against reason and common sense'. *Elizabeth Webby*

Criticism in 19th-century Melbourne

Goldrush immigration made Melbourne a British city in exile, whose wealth allowed it to purchase the best of theatre and to support outstanding journalism. There was a widespread assumption that the *Argus* was second only to the London *Times*. In 1883 the English journalist Richard Twopenny questioned this view but accepted that the *Argus* was 'the best daily paper published out of England'. He also considered that Melbourne was 'decidedly the theatrical centre of Australia' and its audiences were 'more appreciative and critical' than Sydney's. For this it had to thank its critics, who undertook their task with vigour, seriousness and a love of good writing.

The most distinguished tradition of daily notices was that of the *Argus*, whose critics included MARCUS CLARKE, J. E. NEILD and JAMES SMITH. Since notices are unsigned and there was usually more than one contributing critic, attributions need to be made with caution. However, Neild, whose main job was critic for the associated weekly the *Australasian*, can sometimes be spotted when he repeats an opinion in the other paper, and Smith when he recycles text in his several series of stage reminiscences. Both contributed, with intermissions, from the late 1850s to the mid-1880s, and possibly beyond in Smith's case. Clarke wrote regularly between 1867 and his departure for the *Herald* in November 1873. Their approaches differed strongly—Neild the reformer, Clarke the dandy, and Smith the cultured man of the world. Neild and Clarke tended to submerge their highly individual prose styles when writing daily notices, while Smith's style, lacking marked idiosyncrasies, does not always declare itself. Nonetheless, notices of any length will often reveal their author through a combination of language and attitudes. Smith was away from the paper for part of 1858–59, during his tenure of the parliamentary librarianship in 1863–69 and overseas in 1882–83. Neild became principal critic during the first absence but then severed his connection from 1859 to 1865. The *Age* in 1855 enjoyed the services of both Smith and Neild. Both soon departed, although Smith resumed his connection briefly at the end of the decade. The paper's major critic over the next two decades was the splenetic James Williams. At the *Herald* from the mid-1850s until 1870 the principal critic was the playwright W. M. Akhurst, writing with a shrewd understanding of stage practicalities. In 1863–64 notices may also have been contributed by Neild, who was writing leaders for the *Herald* and theatre material for its weekly *Bell's Life in Victoria*. After the *Herald* was taken over by David Syme in 1868 and converted into an evening paper, dissident staff members founded a morning paper, the *Daily Telegraph*, whose critics are so far unidentified.

An intemperate crusader for theatrical realism, J. E. Neild wrote weekly notices in Melbourne for three decades. From 1865 to 1878 he combined the duties of critic for the Australasian, *editor of the* Australian Medical Journal *and lecturer in forensic medicine at the University of Melbourne*

Each of the main dailies also issued a weekly: the *Leader* published by the *Age*, *Bell's Life* by the *Herald*, the *Examiner* and later the *Australasian* by the *Argus*, and the *Weekly Times* (later affiliated with the *Herald*) by the *Daily Telegraph*. The *Australasian* appeared on Thursday in a country edition and on Saturday in a heavily revised town edition which was Australia's leading journal of news and opinion. Neild wrote virtually all the drama notices in this publication between 27 March 1865 and 15 March 1890, whether or not they are signed with a nom-de-plume. He had previously been critic of the *Examiner* and T. L. Bright's *My Note Book*. *Bell's Life* and later the *Australasian* acted as clearing houses for professional information, often printing letters from performers. The *Australasian*'s women's pages describe first-night audiences and the costumes worn by actresses. James Williams was the *Leader*'s 'Autolycus' and Richard Birnie its 'Holofernes'. The illustrated monthlies published by each leading newspaper contain little of critical value, but are valuable sources of theatrical illustrations. The society magazines, the *Tatler* and *Table Talk*, are useful for interviews and contain some critical material.

Some of the issues that concerned the critics were realism versus conventionalism, the propriety or otherwise of 'fallen woman' melodramas, whether the function of the stage was to teach as well as entertain (and if so what), and whether it was proper for performers to acknowledge the presence of the audience. The rights of spectators are also debated, especially with regard to noisy and often disruptive adolescents in the gallery. Criticism was highly politicised, though in ways that are not always immediately apparent. Thus while both Smith and Neild wrote for the 'conservative' *Argus*, Smith was a pre-Disraeli Tory and Neild a Liberal free-trader in the tradition of Bright and Cobden. Neild, consequently, opposed the founding of Williamson, Garner and Musgrove in 1882 because it would diminish competition. Smith emphasised the communal aspect of theatrical performance, seeing the task of the critic as the aristocratic one of guiding and articulating the collective experience of the audience. Neild, as well as incessantly urging performers to break with inherited traditions, seems to have seen the theatrical experience in free-trading terms as an individual transaction between himself and the performer in which the rest of the audience was not concerned.

The 1867 controversy over the merits of James Anderson and Walter Montgomery as Hamlet divided on political lines. Neild supported Montgomery as a kind of free-trade artist who had liberated himself from the incubus of stage tradition, while the *Argus* writers branded Anderson's full-blooded rendering of the time-sanctioned 'points' as a theatrical version of *Age* populism. The *Leader* retaliated by presenting Neild and Clarke as engaged in a plot to destroy Anderson because he was the approved favourite of the people. Smith hovered uneasily on the margin, unwilling to side with the *Age* but equally disturbed by the radical individualism of Montgomery's interpretation. In the end he decided that Anderson's version was truer to the text but that the Hamlet of the text was a savage and a maniac. The ease with which the theatrical passed into the political is shown by the frequent use of scenes from popular plays as the basis for cartoons in *Melbourne Punch*.

George Scott Hough attacked the *Argus* critics and their satellites in a witty Pope-style satire, *Brown the Great—or, Press and Stage* in 1870. The critics became visible as individuals in March 1874 when the actor G. R. Ireland brought a libel case against the *Licensed Victuallers' Gazette*, one of many minor journals with a house critic. Witnesses included the writers of other notices of the performance: Clarke (*Argus*), Neild (*Australasian*), Williams (*Leader*), F. W. Hughan (*Herald*) and two unspecified, John Lynch and Robert P. Whitworth. ❦*Harold Love*

Changing aims and standards

All these men were characterised by a broad liberal education acquired overseas, and broad interests and standing in the affairs of the colony. They worked in a notably lively period of artistic development and their preoccupations were variously the preservation of classical standards, the creation of an Australian theatre and the contest between the old gesturing style of acting and the new realism that was raging simultaneously in Europe. In Sydney the *Sydney Morning Herald* and its weekly companion the *Sydney Mail* covered equally lively theatrical life. Among their writers was Sara Jenny Fischer, known as Mrs Carl Fischer, one of the first female journalists and possibly the first female musical or dramatic critic in Australia. She arrived in Melbourne in 1856 and she wrote for papers there before becoming head of a girls' school in Geelong (Vic.). In 1879 she moved to Sydney, where she wrote musical and dramatic criticism and social notes for the *Herald* and the *Mail* and became a cultural force. One observer described her as 'a vigorous writer of strong and sometimes prejudiced views, influenced by personal likes and dislikes'. Nellie Stewart in her autobiography *My Life Story*, however, looked back with fondness on Mrs Fischer and other critics. She acknowledged help and advice from the press, 'whose critics included the late Mrs Carl Fisher, the late Dr Neild of Melbourne and Mr Gerald Marr Thompson of Sydney. Their criticism was always genuine, and not to be bought. I have to thank them for helping me to correct the restlessness and mannerisms that I showed in the beginning of my career, caused, I fancy, by too much vitality', she wrote. 'Criticism should be honest, and critics should be left to say what they really think, always provided that the critics shall be honest. Adverse criticisms may be expressed kindly, and should always be couched in such direct and simple language as shall prevent misunderstanding of the sum of its purport.'

In the *Sydney Morning Herald*'s first 50 years it had no specialist arts writers, though the journalist F. C. Brewer became a knowledgeable critic over many years and wrote a monograph on local drama for the NSW government to distribute at the Chicago World's Columbia Exposition in 1893. William Curnow, a clergyman who was the third editor of the *Herald*—and 'a discriminating and friendly critic of plays and actors', according to Gavin Souter—appointed a British journalist and reviewer, Austin Brereton, in 1889 as the first dramatic critic. He held the position for two years, and then took work in the USA. He later became general manager to the actor H. B. Irving and wrote a life of his father, the great Henry Irving. Brereton laid the ground for GERALD MARR THOMPSON, who was the most influential critic in Sydney from 1891 to 1924. Conservative in taste but kindly in style, Thompson preferred to confine himself to reportage when the work was not to his taste. He was highly respected by his readers and the profession.

Reviews in journals
This was the era of journals, most of them short-lived. Most serious journals carried theatrical and musical notes and reviews, especially in Sydney and Melbourne, the major theatrical capitals. Among the earliest journals were weeklies—the *Examiner* (1857–64) for which Neild wrote; the Melbourne *Leader* (1856–62) for which Smith and Clarke wrote; and *My Note Book* for which they all wrote. Sydney had the *Sydney Mail* (1870–1938), an illustrated weekly. Among specialist journals were Melbourne's *L'Entra'cte* (1861–74) and Sydney's *Entr'acte* (1868–92), which published programs, news and views on music and theatre. *Melbourne Punch* (1855-1929) with its lively cartoons of performers and accounts of performances set a style for reviewers which was taken up by the Sydney *Bulletin*,

launched in 1880. In the period leading up to federation the *Bulletin*'s reviews of operatic and classical performances and visiting artists did as much as its news pages to debunk the pomposity and shortcomings of the middle class. Most magazine editors combined theatre with literary, social, or sporting interests. *Dead Bird—A journal devoted to sport and the drama* was published in Sydney from 1896 to 1916. Titles sometimes had a hint of desperation, like the *Australian Police News and Music and the Drama*, which lasted a month in 1895.

One of the most useful publications for research is *Lorgnette* (1876–86), which listed casts and first appearances with its commentary. Some theatres also published their own newsletters as promotion, and many of the critics wrote accounts of the forthcoming plays for these. Neild wrote under the pseudonym 'Christopher Sly' for the Theatre Royal's *Green Room* magazine. Most journals of this kind died or became movie magazines with the coming of film. One that did survive as a substantial record was Sydney's *Theatre* (1904–26). The *Lone Hand*, a literary offshoot of the *Bulletin* first published in 1907, took a lively interest in a developing indigenous theatre but died in 1921.

The 20th century brought with it war and depression, which changed the nature of Australia and caused lasting damage to reviewers' sense of humour. The depression of the 1890s and the rising pro-British Australian chauvinism of the federation movement had served to shake the population down to a more stable and homogeneous community with ambitions to be taken seriously as a nation and growing self-consciousness of national immaturity.

Geoffrey Serle sums up the transformation in the first two decades of the 20th century in his cultural history *From Deserts the Prophets Come*: 'The political rulers were now philistine businessmen, farmers and trade union officials— no longer, like Henry Parkes, a determined versifier, or Alfred Deakin, a playwright and literary critic, or Samuel Griffith, a translator of Dante. Australian taste in the arts was now utterly conservative and backward—the product, it seemed, of growing isolation and a wider time-lag of ideas than in the nineteenth century.'

The newspapers—apart from radical, labour-oriented papers—reflected this new hidebound, uncritical imperialism, which persisted, with occasional exceptions, into the 1960s. Newspapers subscribed to the British news agency Reuter, and most of their overseas correspondents were British in outlook. During the second World War the newspapers suffered censorship without complaint. Literary and theatre reviewing became similarly conservative and Eurocentric, and similarly subject to blind impositions. The old humane arguments that marked the optimism of the pre-federation decades died with Neild, Thompson and their colleagues. Cinema and the gramophone also changed the expectations of audiences and began a run of woes for local performing artists. Local performance was now set against international standards on the big screen and at prices with which theatres could not compete.

All these social changes were reflected in the theatre. Entrepreneurs, finding themselves in competition with cinema, at first competed by adapting their shows to the silent screen; and latterly by abandoning the working-class audiences to the movie house and creating more and more middle-class fare. By 1932 all but a handful of theatres had

Theatrical and literary interests were still common among leading journalists in 1922, when Sydney's Home *magazine published two pages of photographs of local newspaper and magazine celebrities. In the centre of this page is C. N. Bayaertz, founding editor of the* Triad *magazine and a ferocious arts critic. Around him, clockwise from top left, are Jack Moses, a* Bulletin *balladeer; E. J. Dempsey of the* Evening News*; the playwright Arthur H. Adams, then on the staff of the* Sun*; William Moore, playwright, critic and arts writer for the* Daily Telegraph*; Gerald Marr Thompson, music and theatre critic of the* Sydney Morning Herald*; Frank Morton, a* Triad *critic; D. D. Braham, editor of the* Daily Telegraph*; J. B. Dalley, novelist and acting editor of the* Bulletin*; Charles Brunsdon Fletcher, editor of the* Sydney Morning Herald*; and Adam McCay, editor of the* Sunday Times *and former press agent for the Tivoli circuit. The other page included the former publicist Claude McKay and W. Farmer Whyte, 'a fervent Shakespearean' who edited the* Daily Telegraph*.*

been closed or converted into cinemas or mini-golf courses. Melodrama and sensation drama were long dead and now replaced by thrillers, drawing-room comedies and the occasional importation of 'classy' stars like MADGE ELLIOTT. At the other end of the scale rose literary and socially-patronised AMATEUR THEATRE, equally middle-class, often with liberal or left-wing leanings, aimed at self-education in 'the world's best plays' and often in the principles of George Bernard Shaw, Maurice Maeterlinck, Konstantin Stanislavsky, the Abbey Theatre and the avant-garde. The only traditional theatre that survived this new division of loyalties was vaudeville, sporting a host of native-born stars like QUEENIE PAUL, ROY RENE and GEORGE WALLACE.

With this new outlook came a generation of editors with a declining interest in the humanities and a rising interest in primary industry; and a generation of Australian-educated literary critics and reporters, who on one level began to concern themselves with questions of national identity and on the other with the theatre as a social occasion. Amateur theatrical performances were noticed in the social columns of most newspapers, often with debutante-style photographs of the juvenile lead, and in magazines like *Home*, which emphasised the social standing of the SYDNEY REPERTORY THEATRE SOCIETY and the ALLAN WILKIE SHAKESPEAREAN COMPANY; and the promotional journals like the *Australia Magazine*, which interviewed celebrities staying at Sydney's Australia Hotel. The theatre was again seen as a civilising social influence. Serious theatrical reviewing, on the other hand, lost its clout almost entirely (while Australia's musical life burgeoned with an influx of artists who had fled from Central Europe).

In fact, radical ideas often circulated in these amateur companies in the 1930s and 1940s. Keith George in Perth and COLIN BALLANTYNE in Adelaide held open-house parties in which ways of changing the world were hotly debated. Curiously, radical thought was not generally equated with radical action in Perth and Adelaide—perhaps because of naivety, perhaps because of middle-class entrenchment. In those cities the class system was so stable that the work of leftist theatre groups was seen largely as intellectual exercise and not political subversion, though the groups themselves saw it as political protest against social injustice and the suffocating escapism of professional theatre and film.

Things were different, however, with NEW THEATRE in Sydney and Melbourne. These groups were committed to socialist political writings and had active Communist members as well as fellow-travellers. They suffered from CENSORSHIP but this arose more from the government line than from examination of the issues debated. New Theatre in Sydney was prosecuted in 1936 on the complaint of the German consul for presenting Clifford Odets's anti-Nazi play *Till the Day I Die*; and the *Sydney Morning Herald* stopped reviewing the group until the late 1960s.

In Perth the conservative press, according to a contemporary, 'far from ignoring the Guild, immediately recognised it for its initiative, innovation and courage. Packed houses and extended seasons demanded that.' The critic PAUL HASLUCK wrote of the Workers' Art Guild production of *Till the Day I Die* which opened on 20 June: 'One came away from the theatre with an excitement of a prize fight in the air. The play greeted by New York critics as one of the most vital to punch America between the eyes, is frankly propagandist … But the propaganda glows with such a fierce fervour and the play has such tremendous energy that one is exhilarated by it.'

Similarly, social standing was often used in an educative way in the amateur theatre. PATRICIA HACKETT, an Adelaide lawyer, was one who did this. Romantic and misunderstood, she was a victim as well as a product of the Adelaide establishment, whose horizons she unsuccessfully attempted to widen with Greek classics and similar significant drama. The *Advertiser*'s review of her opening production in her private theatre in 1934 was typical of the time: 'The Torch Theatre, Miss Patricia Hackett's new theatrical venture, was opened last night with a special performance of Oscar Wilde's banned play, *Salome*, in the presence of his Excellency the Governor and Lady Hore-Ruthven. A "full house" was charmed by the little theatre, which is situated in the basement of Claridge's Arcade, Gawler Place, and the appointments are all that could be desired; but the choice of the play cannot but be regarded as exceedingly unfortunate. Written in 1893, *Salome* ... has been repeatedly banned. Only last year the authorities at Cambridge declined to allow a dramatic society to perform the work there ... the reasons for the unpopularity of the play were evident; many among the audience found them distressingly so. The general verdict probably was that *Salome* is quite an unnecessary work of art, and in any case quite unsuitable for public presentation.'

The play was drawn to the attention of the Chief Secretary, and a member of the State Censorship Board, Mrs A. K. Goode, reported on the performance. She said she 'thoroughly enjoyed it but it would scarcely do for a public show'. The week's season was permitted to continue, however, on the grounds that the audience were subscribers and 'it is a play meant for what are described as the intelligentsia, who obviously know the story before they go. They are simply interested to see how young amateurs will tackle the problem of presentation and I considered that some of the work was exceedingly good for amateurs.'

Hackett's career continued to be controversial. After the journalist Sid Downer reviewed one of her productions in the *Advertiser* on 4 September 1934 Hackett pursued him to the parliamentary press gallery and charged him with prejudice. She threw a bottle of ink at him, splashing his clothes and injuring him above the left eye. She was fined £20 in the Adelaide Police Court for unlawful assault. Later she regretted the incident and 'made an honourable reparation'. 'Ink for ink', was her comment. 'Now we are quits. There let the matter rest.' It did not, however, prevent her from advising the *Advertiser* that its representative would in future be banned from the Torch Theatre.

Downer's review today reads fairly harmlessly: 'Geza Silberer's *Caprice*, a sophisticated problem play, was presented at the Torch Theatre last night. It failed to arouse any great degree of enthusiasm in the crowded audience, due perhaps, as much to weakness in the play itself as to its interpretation. Certainly Miss Patricia Hackett was not happily cast as the leading woman. Against this deficiency may be quoted Mr Frank Johnston's excellent portrayal of the part of the amorous Viennese lawyer....'

Hackett closed the Torch Theatre in 1936 and went abroad. Her search for artistic expression was again thwarted by a critic in 1944, when she directed *Gild the Mask Again*, a one-act play by T. B. Morris about Elizabeth and Essex, for the ADELAIDE UNIVERSITY THEATRE GUILD. Max Harris, a modernist reformist, wrote in the Adelaide University newspaper *On Dit*: 'As a play it was shocking, sentimental, pretentious balderdash. As theatre it was ham.' After demolishing the performance he added: 'For a while let the Theatre Guild forget the panther passions of the Hackett demi-monde ... *The Yellow Book* died with Aubrey Beardsley. The local Theatre Guild is churning out the vestigial relicts of that period's pretentiousness ... More stress on Theatre and less on Art. This shouldn't be an alien message to a genuine theatre.'

In retrospect this seems a fair description of many amateur theatres of the period. But it proved an alien message to Patricia Hackett, who sued for and got a 'sincere and humble' apology for a 'gross and malicious libel', namely the word 'demi-monde'. Harris claimed it had been a typographical conversion of 'beau-monde'. Undeterred, Harris reviewed local theatre in *Mary's Own Paper*, a popular satirical newspaper that he published in the 1950s.

Amateur theatre

Loss of distinction between amateur and professional production muddied the waters for journalists who covered the arts between the 1920s and the 1960s and militated against a clear view of artistic development. In the 1920s and 1930s many frustrated professional performers began to run their own amateur theatres. University dramatic societies sought to fill the yawning gap between commercial light entertainment and the 'real' drama.

Reviewers' moods swung between encouragement of promise and irritation at limitations. As journalists their chief challenge became how to discriminate between the pleasures and purposes of amateur performance and those of professional, between the committed and the social at all levels. A few strong voices made their views known, however. As 'Polygon', dramatic critic of the *West Australian* from 1933 to 1938, Paul Hasluck considerably influenced the development of theatrical taste in Western Australia. A widely read senior journalist and historian, he was probably the last of the influential classical conservatives of the calibre of Thompson and Smith.

Another critic as advocate was LESLIE REES, a West Australian who had been a critic in London and settled in Sydney in 1936. As honorary drama critic of the *Australian Quarterly* for ten years, he provided a unique overview of Sydney theatre in the 1940s. In 1938 he founded the PLAYWRIGHTS' ADVISORY BOARD and became a formidable advocate of Australian playwriting and the movement for a national theatre. In 1949 he led the opposition to the GUTHRIE REPORT to the federal government, which rejected it.

Other journalists became indefatigable supporters of theatre wherever they could find it. Like other theatre critics in the 1930s, Arthur H. Thomas of the Brisbane *Telegraph* was concerned at the wholesale closing of theatres in the Great Depression and the impact upon the theatrical profession. He saw his role as to encourage aspiring artists in the amateur movement and to divert the former audience of the commercial theatre towards them. As many productions were performed only once, Thomas sometimes previewed scripts or rehearsals. The Brisbane playwright GEORGE LANDEN DANN claimed that Thomas never gave a bad review. A Twelfth Night Theatre tribute in 1946 read: 'When Dramatic Critic for the *Telegraph* he was a source of inspiration and help ... His constructive, kindly and frank criticism encouraged many a beginner to further effort.' Dann had reason to be grateful for Thomas's personal support. On 4 July 1931, when his play IN BEAUTY IT IS FINISHED was in rehearsal for its premiere in Brisbane, *Smith's Weekly* previewed the text with the banner headline: 'Brisbane Repertory Society's Extraordinary Decision: £50 prize Awarded to Filthy Play: Sordid Drama of Miscegenation'. It continued: 'The story is a sordid and soiled one of the dubious romance of a self-confessed woman of the streets and a half-caste ... It is now for the Rep. Society to explain how it came to accept this unwholesome story ... For there are terms and expressions in the script that cut across the accepted traditions of the stage, situations that reach new depths in the sordid.'

The article led to lively controversy in the press and the pulpit, culminating in a tense opening night. In the event the play was received with respect by both audience and critics, who voted the subject legitimate for tragedy. And the society received the written approbation of the Anglican Archbishop of Brisbane. But the voice of moral censure continued to be heard in strident outbursts from the Queensland press, particularly in reference to language and sex in the theatre and literature, for the next 60 years.

Changes in newspapers

In 1923 Australia had 26 metropolitan daily newspapers with 21 proprietors. By 1980 there were 15, owned by three corporations. Changes in ownership in the 1920s and a move towards shorter notices, together with the vacuity of the professional theatre and the amateur nature of the thoughtful theatre, tended to debase the standing of theatrical criticism in Australian newspapers up to the 1950s. The quality of the writing continued to depend upon the dedication, taste and background of the reviewers. But a wedge was being driven between popular opinion and middle-class concern with 'world standards' and national status. The papers were losing their literary and artistic roots. For example, the *Brisbane Courier* and the *Daily Mail*, which boasted high-quality weekly literary supplements in the first decades of the 20th century, were forced into amalgamation in 1929 and lost their old grace.

The *Bulletin* was also losing its traditional readership as Australia and its interests became more urbanised. The famous Red Page, however, began to move from popular contributions to setting literary standards, and reached its zenith under the editorship of the critic, dramatist and poet DOUGLAS STEWART from 1940 to 1960. New magazines with serious literary and political intent—quarterlies like *Overland*, *Westerly*, *Southerly* and *Meanjin*—did not follow the example of their antecedents by including theatre reviews. There were occasional assessments, however, particularly in the *Current Affairs Bulletin*, which concerned itself with questions of national identity and growth. The theatre for these magazines was an issue, not a daily reality.

Postwar rise in standards

After the Second World War a boom in theatre and the return of many journalists from overseas brought new life to the theatre columns of many papers. The *Sydney Morning Herald* brought LINDSEY BROWNE back from New York in 1946 when Neville Cardus returned to England after eight years writing on music and cricket. Cardus had revived musical criticism at a time when music reached far beyond other forms of performance in Australia, and Browne began to restore theatrical criticism to the same standard. In Melbourne, Bruce Grant was a perceptive film and theatre critic for the *Age* from 1949 to 1953, when he again became a foreign correspondent. Grant was followed in 1959 by a former war correspondent, GEOFFREY HUTTON. He was leader writer and theatre and dance critic until his retirement in 1974 and remained an elegant and authoritative reviewer until his death in 1985. As reviewers, stylists and leader writers, these men and others with widened horizons contributed to the climate of opinion that created the Australian Council for the Arts in 1968, and to the burgeoning growth and lively debates that followed.

They gave strong competition to some of the indefatigable reporters in the old style who survived into the 1960s, covering every level of theatre. These included H. A. STANDISH on the Melbourne *Herald*, Frank Murphy of the Catholic *Advocate*, Bob Money at *Listener In—TV* and Howard Palmer on the Melbourne *Sun News–Pictorial*. Palmer took the consumer-guide approach, 'a duty to the bloke who spends his 40 cents for the *Sun* in the morning'. He is particularly remembered for his one-line review of *A Cheery Soul* by PATRICK WHITE: '*A Cheery Soul* is a sorry play'. Of the same generation in Sydney were the popular NORMAN KESSELL on the *Sun* and later the *Daily Telegraph*, and Frank Harris of the *Daily Mirror*. Adelaide had the stable figure of Mary Armitage on the staff of the *Advertiser* from 1950 to 1965, reporting on largely amateur theatre.

Short-lived journals

The establishment of the AUSTRALIAN ELIZABETHAN THEATRE TRUST in 1954 and its entrepreneurial promotion of Ray Lawler's SUMMER OF THE SEVENTEENTH DOLL and its theatre, opera and ballet companies gained press attention that encouraged renewed public interest in local development. And the arts critic assumed a position of greater prominence, which remained reasonably stable until technological changes in the 1970s caused further reconstruction of the newspaper industry.

From the ferment of change emerged short-lived journals of review, notably the *Nation*, the *Observer* and specialist magazines like *Theatregoer* and the Perth university newssheet the *Critic*. *Theatregoer*, edited by Frank Harvey, was launched in 1960 in the flurry of activity surrounding the Trust. It survived for three years before dying, like all Australian arts journals, with the founders' resources of energy and money. The *Nation*, with wider interests and greater philosophical and literary merit, survived through the 1960s and gave birth to the thundering expositions of H. G. KIPPAX as 'Brek'. In 1966 Kippax reluctantly deserted the *Nation*'s expansive columns for the discipline of daily reviewing in the *Sydney Morning Herald*, of which he was then literary editor. Until he retired in 1989 he was unrivalled, an uncompromising critic, unswervingly devoted to the classic text and the creation of Australian theatre of international standing. He was a difficult advocate of Australian writing, embracing the early work of Patrick White, but then resisting for a long time the work of the new wave of the late 1960s. His commitment to a view of drama as the dynamic conflict of individual characters in action made him one of the few critics to pursue a visionary aesthetic agenda in his reviewing. In the end it meant that he lost touch with new writing. After 1972 only DAVID WILLIAMSON consistently satisfied his strict criteria of 'good drama'.

Revived interest in the arts resulted in higher status for some contributing reviewers. DONNA SADKA, the *West Australian*'s critic from 1965 to 1986, encouraged theatrical development in the west with quiet generosity. On the *Canberra Times* Hope Hewitt held her position for a similar length of time. An academic, she had been the *Bulletin*'s Canberra critic. Since then other academics have acquired security as contributing critics, providing some of the historical background surrendered by newer journalists and reduced newspaper space. Among them are Murray Bramwell and Michael Morley in Adelaide; Helen Thomson, Melbourne reviewer for the *Australian*; and Paul McGillick of the *Australian Financial Review*.

Covering the nation

The most significant development in arts journalism in the 1960s was the launching of the *Australian*, the country's first national daily, by Rupert Murdoch in 1964. It enlisted a team of commentators who quickly began to concern themselves with national culture, identity, politics and style. The first theatrical critic was Francis Evers, a young Irishman and friend of Samuel Beckett. He endured token payments and primitive transport to visit theatres around Australia. He was the first of a new generation of theatrical critics outside the journalistic hierarchy who began to gain respect from their own energies, with little more than sufferance from their editors.

Evers was succeeded in 1967 by KATHARINE BRISBANE, formerly theatre reviewer of the *West Australian*. Her seven years as national critic coincided with political change and artistic revolution, which she monitored through her columns. A strong critical vision informed her reviews. She was a pioneering advocate of the new 'larrikin' Australian theatre and, as the first influential critic to cover all capitals, she wielded great influence during the crucial years of the new wave of theatrical nationalism. In 1967 the actor-director PETER O'SHAUGHNESSY sued the *Australian* over her review of his *Othello*, which she claimed to be a 'dishonest production'. The *Australian* won the case, which went to appeal and then to the High Court, where a retrial was ordered on the ground that the judge had misdirected the jury on the distinction between fact and opinion. The case was then settled out of court, thus denying reviewers the chance of a legal precedent. A decade later changes in the Privacy Act put further constraints upon the press.

Brisbane resigned in 1974, and thereafter reviewed occasionally for the *Australian* in Sydney and had 12 months of expansive national overview in 1981–82 as a feature writer for the *National Times*. She was succeeded by BARRY OAKLEY as a reviewer with a similar national brief. Brisbane's rival reviewers responded, some more slowly than others, to the stimulus provided by the *Australian* and the proliferation of artistic activity. They began to become industrial commentators and to relate the events on stage to those in the street outside. The long-running SYDNEY OPERA HOUSE row; battles over censorship; divisions over the Australian Council for the Arts; the establishment of the state theatre companies; a new film industry; the destruction of old theatres and the building of new performing-arts centres—all these things contrived to keep the theatre in the news pages during the late 1960s and 1970s. One of the first to respond was LEONARD RADIC, successor to Geoffrey Hutton on the *Age*. His dedication to encouragement of Australian work has been unswerving. His history of contemporary Australian theatre, *The State of Play* is an important work of historical reportage. Another valued recorder of changing events was LAURIE LANDRAY, theatre, ballet and opera critic of *Listener In–TV* from 1963 to 1974, and theatrical critic of the Melbourne *Herald* from 1976 to 1985. The ferment resulted in the broadsheet dailies appointing arts editors in the 1970s, in response partly to the rise of publicists in subsidised arts organisations and partly to a move towards specialist departments within the editorial room. A dedicated space for the arts in the daily paper has been a benefit but distancing of arts commentary from the cut and thrust of the news desk has been a disadvantage in some cases.

The Australian Elizabethan Theatre Trust contributed journals of record. Its first publication was a newsletter in the 1960s, replaced in 1967 by the successful bimonthly *Masque*. This incorporated Trust subscribers' news and was independently published until 1971 by its editor, John Allen. An in-house magazine, the *Elizabethan Trust News* began in 1971 and was superseded in 1976 by *Theatrescope*. This ceased publication in the same year, when a trio of academics at the University of Newcastle launched *Theatre Australia*. Robert Page, his wife Lucy Wagner and—at first—Bruce Knappett sought to restore a national overview with this monthly. It attempted comprehensive national coverage by reviewing everything while also providing substantial investigative articles and interviews. It survived seven argumentative years as a force behind the interests of a newly maturing publicly-funded cottage industry and it contains some of the best theatrical journalism of recent times. But long lead times always placed it between a magazine of topical comment and a journal of record, and its financial dependence upon the AUSTRALIA COUNCIL and a self-absorbed industry so widely diverse in ambitions and ideologies led inevitably to its demise.

In 1987 an attempt was made to revive it as *New Theatre—Australia* with new editorship, including the *National Times* critic James Waites. It had a consciously contemporary critical agenda, although practical constraints limited its actual coverage, and it lasted until 1989. Australia Council backing for *New Theatre—Australia* forced the closure of *Centrestage* (1986–87), a commercial venture, conservative in format, which had operated quite successfully for 12 months. The Australian Theatre Studies Centre at the University of NSW began publishing the *Australian* (later *Australasian*) *Theatre Record* in 1987 and it has survived into the 1990s as the only national theatrical journal of record. It reproduces published newspaper reviews, providing a candid account of reviewing quality around the capitals. In 1994 the editors of the long-established *Opera Australia* in Sydney launched a companion monthly, *Theatre Australia*.

Reviewers from outside

Changes in technology and newspaper ownership in the 1970s again took their toll of arts reviewers. Commentary was increasingly handed over to outside contributors with a more specific brief than in-house reporters received. Promotion was becoming an increasing force in what were now 'arts and entertainment' pages; and critical opinion was being downgraded. Some senior figures had died. By 1980 the only retained senior holders of staff positions were the sensitive BRIAN HOAD on the *Bulletin*; Neil Jillett, the whimsical film and theatre reviewer of the Melbourne *Herald*; H. G. Kippax; Leonard Radic; David Rowbotham, poet, literary editor and gloomy reviewer of the Brisbane *Courier–Mail*; and Peter Ward, Adelaide reviewer for the *Australian*. Rowbotham was a long-standing critic with a strongly ethical bias that reflected the ambivalence of Queenslanders towards public funding of theatre. He caused a stir in 1978 by writing of the Queensland Theatre

Company's production of Kenneth Ross's play *Don't Piddle against the Wind, Mate*: 'It's no good.' This peremptory review, without qualification or even the virtue of an epigram, incited the second-night audience to call for 'three boos' for the critic and provoked a brief but lively correspondence in the editorial pages.

The trend towards piecemeal reportage continued during the 1980s until 1989, when the *Australian* tried to restore its overview by appointing Rosemary Neill as theatre reviewer and arts reporter for the eastern seaboard and Peter Ward to cover Perth as well as Adelaide. But the field proved too wide and the travelling costs too great. The paper quickly returned to state boundaries, retaining Neill as reviewer and arts reporter in Sydney.

In the early 1990s the situation was more stable than it had been since the 1960s. Most major dailies had a dedicated arts page and made some attempt at comprehensive critical reviewing by specialist theatrical writers. Most of the reviewers were again staff members, like Ron Banks, Peta Koch and Tim Lloyd, arts editors of the *West Australian*, the *Courier–Mail* and the *Advertiser* respectively. And some were tenured reviewers like Frank Gauntlett on Sydney's *Daily Telegraph-Mirror* and Bob Evans on the *Sydney Morning Herald* or senior journalists like Peter Ward. But until it becomes financially possible to reinstate national critics, in papers such as the *Australian* or the *Financial Review*, the theatre will continue to be seen as a cottage industry confined within city boundaries.

The influence of the tenured reviewers within each city depends on their individual authority. In the early 1990s this remained a subject of debate. In Sydney in 1989 Bob Evans wrote of Rachel Ward in *Hopping to Byzantium*: 'Such mindless, heartless, skin-deep acting is a travesty of theatre and not to be endured'. Twelve months later he received a glass of red wine in the face from Ward. Her co-star Robert Coleby had begun but abandoned legal proceedings. In 1990 the *Advertiser*'s Peter Goers, who practised the kind of splenetic turn of phrase favoured by South Australian reviewers, received a Molotov cocktail on his front lawn. He had been frequently under attack that year for his coverage of the Adelaide Festival.

There have been other celebrated incidents, such as alleged fisticuffs between playwright and critic outside a Melbourne restaurant after Leonard Radic reviewed David Williamson's *Top Silk* in 1989. The writer–barrister JUSTIN FLEMING and the director RICHARD WHERRETT joined in proceedings against John Carmody of the *Sun–Herald* in 1989 for his review of their *Harold in Italy* at the Sydney Opera House. The matter was settled by debate in the pages of the *Sun–Herald*. In 1992 there was press debate about CARRILLO GANTNER's advice to the *Bulletin* that his Playbox Theatre would exclude its Melbourne reviewer, Alison Croggon, on the grounds of personal discourtesy. The antipathy between the critic and the artist is timeless. Nevertheless, the recent outburst of hostilities does seem to reflect a new level of resentment in the profession at what it perceives as critical incompetence—failure to understand what theatre is about. The London *Guardian*'s theatre critic Michael Billington noted in February 1993 after attending a critics' conference in Perth, that 'the gulf which exists in all societies between the critic and the artist in Australia threatens to widen into a chasm … I have noticed an extraordinary preoccupation, especially in theatre, with the role of the critic. In Britain we are, in Robert Robinson's immortal phrase, "anonymous men (and women) who get the last bus back to Muswell Hill". But in Australia the critic is a hotly contested public figure: a reflection of the fact that in most cities, as in the US, there is a single dominant paper.'

The problem is rooted, however, in editorial attitudes and practice. Theatre criticism in Australia reached a high point of informed debates in the years after the gold rushes when theatre drew a huge and popular audience and fortunes were made and lost. Its decline in the first half of this century was reflected in an editorial loss of interest which reached its nadir when the gardening writer who liked shows volunteered to do the reviews. Things have picked up with the rise of the subsidised state companies; but old editorial attitudes die hard, and the theatre is still far from regaining its lost status as hard news.

The situation has been aggravated by the radical cultural change of the last 20 years towards the aggressively materialist values of monetarism. In Australia this has raised into high visibility an underlying Philistinism that has robbed the arts of any serious editorial weight. Individual protests may have their validity but they are also the expression of a larger malaise—the marginalisation of the arts from the newsmaking process. But social values are making a comeback and the profit motive is no longer the only gauge of the quality of life. There is a fresh public recognition that the arts too have their place. These changes may bring a rise in the standards of theatrical journalism, a move away from the consumer guide and the personal anecdote in favour of serious, informed discussion of matters in the national interest. ❦*Katharine Brisbane and John McCallum*

further reading

ANTHONY, DELYSE. The early history of Twelfth Night Theatre 1936-1946. University of Queensland BA(hons) thesis 1990.
CARMODY, JOHN. Gerald Marr Thompson. *Australian Dictionary of Biography* 12. Melbourne University Press 1990.
CRAIG, TERRY. Radical and conservative theatre in Perth in the 30s. *Western Australia Between the Wars* (ed. Jenny Gregory). Perth: University of Western Australia 1990.
MCCALLUM, JOHN. Some preoccupations in Australian theatre criticism from 1955 to 1978. University of NSW MA thesis 1981.
SERLE, GEOFFREY. *From Deserts the Prophets Come*. Melbourne: Heinemann 1973.
SOUTER, GAVIN. *A Company of Heralds*. Melbourne University Press 1981
STUART, LURLINE. *Nineteenth Century Periodicals—an annotated bibliography*. Sydney: Hale and Iremonger 1979.
A Century of Journalism. Sydney: John Fairfax and Sons 1931.

Colin Croft

Actor, entertainer. Born 21 March 1922 in Sydney. In Australian Army Entertainment Unit in Pacific during Second World War. Died 16 August 1989 in Sydney.

An entertainer from the age of seven, Colin Croft concentrated on straight acting from 1972. In September that year he made a striking appearance in the leading role in Tom Stoppard's *Enter a Free Man* for Sydney's ENSEMBLE THEATRE COMPANY, for which he again acted in later years. He also appeared with the SYDNEY THEATRE COMPANY, the MARIAN STREET THEATRE COMPANY and others. In 1932 the ten-year-old Croft was a tiny drum major in celebrations for the opening of the Sydney Harbour Bridge. Early in the Second World War he began to attract attention in the *Youth Show* on radio. In 1946 Croft and other talents that had emerged from wartime entertainment were in *Clambake*, a Tivoli revue. He toured in operetta for J. C. WILLIAMSON'S—playing roles such as Leopold in *White Horse Inn*, Billy Early in *No! No! Nanette* and Tonio in *The Maid of the Mountains*—and then spent ten years in England. On return to Australia he found television flourishing and leapt joyfully into it.

Years of variety work culminated in a long tour with the comedian ANNA RUSSELL. Croft directed as well as performed and his co-star later wrote that she had learned a great deal from him. Croft received a setback in 1968 when an explosion while filming affected his hearing. Three years later he was awarded $12 000 in damages for his disability. ❦*John West*

further reading
PATE, MICHAEL. *An Entertaining War*. Sydney: Dreamweaver Books 1986.
RUSSELL, ANNA. *I'm Not Making This Up, You Know*. New York City: Continuum 1985.

Don Crosby OAM

Actor. Born 29 October 1924 in Sydney. Son of Marshall Crosby, actor. Worked for J. C. Williamson's and in radio. Served in RAAF 1942–45. Commonwealth scholarship to Royal Academy of Dramatic Art (London) 1946–48. Returned to Sydney 1949. Acted in radio, films, television and theatre. Federal president of Actors' Equity 1976–85. Died 3 December 1985 in Sydney. OAM for services to media and theatre 1980. Father of Michael Crosby, federal secretary of Actors' Equity 1982–91; Matthew Crosby, actor; and Liz Crosby and Marshall Crosby, film directors.

Don Crosby was respected as no other in his profession, as an actor and for his work as the actors' champion. Like his father MARSHALL CROSBY, he was a man of great integrity. He first appeared on stage when he was one year old, with his father and GEORGE WALLACE in *His Royal Highness* at His Majesty's Theatre in Perth in 1925. He interrupted a stage and radio career to join the air force during the Second World War, and he was stationed in England until 1945. He returned in 1946 to study at the Royal Academy of Dramatic Art and after graduating he worked in English repertory theatre for 18 months. In 1950–51 he was in DORIS FITTON'S production of Howard Richardson and William Berney's *Dark of the Moon* in Sydney and Melbourne. This was followed by Christy in J. M. Synge's *The Playboy of the Western World* at the Little Theatre in Melbourne in 1951 and a three-year tour in Hugh Hastings's SEAGULLS OVER SORRENTO for J. C. WILLIAMSON'S in 1951–54.

As Crosby matured he was in great demand for television drama and films, but he still worked on stage. He played Merlin in *Camelot*, with his RADA contemporary Paul Daneman as Arthur, on tour for J. C. Williamson's in 1963–65. In the early 1970s he was with the NIMROD THEATRE COMPANY as the police sergeant in David Williamson's THE REMOVALISTS and in JIM MCNEIL'S *The Old Familiar Juice*. His disillusioned Alf in Alan Seymour's THE ONE DAY OF THE YEAR at the Independent Theatre in 1970 and his dignified Dad in George Whaley's adaptation of Steele Rudd's ON OUR SELECTION at the Jane Street and Nimrod Theatres in 1980 exemplified a description of him by the critic Jeremy O'Brien: '… he brings to a part qualities that are as true as the throbbing of a heartbeat'. ❦*Lynne Murphy*

Marshall Crosby

Actor. Born 1881 in South Australia. Had long career in musicals and plays to 1940s. In vaudeville in 1920s and 1930s. Played character roles in film and radio until 1950s. President of Actors' Equity 1942–45 and 1948–51. Died 1954 in Sydney. Father of Don Crosby, actor, and Pat Crosby, singer.

Among his colleagues Marshall Crosby was highly respected for a varied and solid career and for a strength of character that won him two terms as president of Actors' Equity during its early stormy years. During the 1920s he worked as straight man to his close friend GEORGE WALLACE on the Fuller vaudeville circuit and at HARRY CLAY'S Gaiety Theatre in Oxford Street, Sydney. In 1925 he toured with Wallace in *His Royal Highness*, a burlesque operetta. F. W. THRING made this show into a film of the same name in 1932. Crosby supported Wallace in it and in two more Efftee films in the next two years.

In 1933 Crosby played the landlord Pierce Collits in Thring's production of the musical comedy COLLITS' INN. He had a fine baritone voice and sang in many musicals for J. C. Williamson's in the 1920s and 1930s. He also acted character roles in plays. He continued to play substantial character roles in films during the 1940s and he gained great popularity in leading roles of kindly patriarchs in radio serials. ❦*Lynne Murphy*

further reading
VALE, GILL E. Marshall Crosby. *Australian Dictionary of Biography* 13. Melbourne University Press 1994.

CUB Malthouse Theatre

Theatres in Sturt Street, South Melbourne, converted from a malthouse by John Beckett. **Beckett Theatre**, seating 198, opened March 1990. **Merlyn Theatre**, seating about 400, opened May 1990.

The splendidly equipped and intimate Malthouse theatre complex is the artistic and administrative home of the PLAYBOX THEATRE CENTRE. Outside its annual season, it is also very popular with many hiring companies. The Playbox company itself spent six years in hired venues after its base in Exhibition Street burned down in 1984. Carlton and United Breweries donated a site and buildings in 1986 and the complex—two theatres, rehearsal and function rooms, workshops, gallery and cafe—was completed with donations from the state government, corporate bodies and private citizens. The company's long-serving designer John Beckett planned the conversion and his design brought him the Sidney Myer Performing Arts Award in 1992. Within the original three-storey redbrick malthouse, built in 1892, he created the Beckett Theatre—named after him—and a foyer, gallery, bistro and bar, offices and rehearsal rooms. It opened with TES LYSSIOTIS'S *The Forty Lounge Cafe*. The larger, wider Merlyn Theatre—named after Dame Merlyn Myer, great aunt of the Playbox director CARRILLO GANTNER—is an adjoining new building. It opened with ROBYN ARCHER'S *Cafe Fledermaus*. The theatres are moderately flexible in stage–audience configuration, although upstairs galleries on three sides in both—and on three

Royal Victoria by giving legitimate drama as well as equestrian and gymnastic acts. According to the *Australian* of 5 February 1842, he offered Conrad Knowles and his wife jointly £10 a week—exceptionally high pay for actors in Australia then—to leave the Royal Victoria. Other defectors included Eliza Winstanley and her sister Ann.

The two theatres competed fiercely, often playing the same piece on one night. The balance finally tipped in favour of the Royal Victoria when a new star, Francis Nesbitt, made his debut on 3 March. The Olympic closed on 16 April. Ten days later Dalle Case was declared bankrupt. In June 1842 the Olympic was sold and in October it reopened as a gymnasium.

Dalle Case and his company toured the NSW towns of Maitland, Parramatta and Windsor and returned to Sydney for a farewell benefit at the Royal Victoria on 30 September 1842. On 14 November they opened in Hobart with a variety concert, which included tightrope dancing and athletic exercises, at the Royal Victoria Theatre. An additional attraction, announced for Signorina Anna's benefit on 21 November, was the 'wonder dog Munito', said to be able to translate any word from a list of 350 foreign words, to select and wave any national flag nominated by a spectator, and to play dominoes with gentlemen in the audience.

The company later shifted to the Albert Theatre, where Dalle Case took a farewell benefit on 13 January 1843. Then they travelled to Launceston for three nights at the Royal Olympic Theatre. After a brief country tour Dalle Case and his troupe left for India. They evidently made an impact on Launceston, for the *Examiner* reported on 6 March 1847 that they had returned to Mauritius after eight years' absence. In Asia the company had been augmented by 'some of the inhabitants of the Celestial Empire, remarkable for their talent'—presumably Chinese acrobats—and 'the celebrated Orang-Outang Gertrude who will give lessons in good manners and politeness à la Chesterfield'. Munito and the signorine were claimed to be 'much improved', and reports of Dalle Case's death much exaggerated. ❦*Elizabeth Webby*

further reading
Weiner, Albert. The short unhappy career of Luigi Dalle Case. *Educational Theatre Journal* 27 (Washington DC, March 1975).

Alfred Dampier

Actor, dramatist, manager. Born 28 February 1843, 1845 or 1847 in England. Acted in English provinces *c.*1863–73. Married Katherine Russell, pianist. Leading actor and stage manager at Theatre Royal, Melbourne, for three years from 20 September 1873. Formed company and toured widely in Australasia and elsewhere 1877–85. Seasons in London 1878, 1881. Major seasons in Sydney 1885–88 and Melbourne 1888–92. Bankrupt 1894. Acted in London 1894. Toured eastern Australia from 1895 until retirement through ill-health on 10 November 1905. Died 23 May 1908 in Sydney. Father of actors Alfred Dampier jnr, Lily Dampier and Rose Dampier.

One of the best actors in colonial Australia, Alfred Dampier combined performances of Shakespeare with seasons of popular melodrama. Between 1886 and 1905 he was particularly famous for his productions of *For the Term of His Natural Life* and *Robbery Under Arms*, stage versions of Australian novels. The plays that Dampier jointly wrote were sometimes criticised for their rough-and-ready construction, but as an actor he rarely received an unfavourable review in the colonies. London critics acclaimed him too. He may have modelled his style on Henry Irving, with whom he acted in the English provinces in the 1860s.

Dampier arrived in Melbourne in September 1873 with his wife and infant daughters to begin a three-year contract at the Theatre Royal. He played some seasons of starring roles and stage-managed performances by other actors, including J. C. Williamson and his wife Maggie Moore in *Struck Oil* in 1874. Dampier's own wife, Katherine Russell, also acted professionally but with little success.

Critics disliked Dampier's stage adaptations of Johann von Goethe's *Faust* in 1873 and Victor Hugo's *Les Misérables* in 1875, and from about 1875 he always sought a literary collaborator. He thereby became, deliberately or incidentally, the major supporter and promoter of Australian playwrights in the second half of the 19th century. F. R. C. Hopkins and Garnet Walch responded to Dampier's request for stage vehicles to suit him, his wife, nine-year-old Lily Dampier and seven-year-old Rose Dampier. Hopkins dramatised Eugène Sue's novel *Le Juif errant* as a melodrama called *All for Gold* and Walch adapted a comic novelette, *Helen's Babies*.

In Australia between 1880 and 1885 he staged three other plays by Hopkins and two by 'the Vagabond', a Melbourne journalist who was also known as Julian Thomas but was really John Stanley James. Dampier collaborated in writing most of these plays. The Vagabond's *No Mercy* was successful in Sydney from 4 March 1882, but Dampier's legendary support for Australian drama really began with a long residence in Sydney between 1885 and 1888. In 1886 he co-wrote, directed and starred in a stage adaptation by Thomas Somers of Marcus Clarke's *His Natural Life*. This was not the first play from the famous novel but it was one of the most popular and it held sway on Australian stages for 40 years. Dampier also organised a centennial competition for an Australian play, and staged the winner, John Perry's *The Life and Death of Captain Cook* for a short season from 28 January 1888.

Dampier gave a long series of seasons at the Alexandra Theatre in Melbourne between late 1888 and 1892. He presented Marvellous Melbourne by himself and J. H. Wrangham, his business manager, on 19 January 1889 and followed it on 1 March 1890 with his and Walch's version of Rolf Boldrewood's *Robbery Under Arms*. By then Lily and, less frequently, Rose Dampier were playing adult heroines such as Sylvia in *For the Term of His Natural Life* and Aileen Marston in *Robbery Under Arms*. Katherine Russell had improved her acting and could master supporting roles. She also contributed to regular scriptwriting sessions that Dampier and his collaborators held at his house, and wrote one play herself, a version of the Flying Dutchman legend. This was occasionally staged between 1880 and 1890 with moderate success.

The depression and bank closures of 1891–93 were disastrous for Dampier, who had taken a three-year lease on the Alexandra Theatre when 'marvellous Melbourne' was still in the heady whirl of a speculative land boom. In 1891 and 1892 the company lost money heavily, although audiences still flocked to occasional successes such as four plays in which Dampier collaborated with Walch—*The Miner's Right* (1891), another Boldrewood adaptation; *The* for the opening of the Sydney Harbour Bridge. Early in the Second World War he began to attract attention in the *Youth Show* on radio. In 1946 Croft and other talents that had emerged from wartime entertainment were in *Clambake*, a Tivoli revue. He toured in operetta for J. C. WILLIAMSON's—playing roles such as Leopold in *White Horse Inn*, Billy Early in *No! No! Nanette* and Tonio in *The Maid of the Mountains*—and then spent ten years in England. On return to Australia he found television flourishing and leapt joyfully into it.

Years of variety work culminated in a long tour with the comedian ANNA RUSSELL. Croft directed as well as performed and his co-star later wrote that she had learned a great deal from him. Croft received a setback in 1968 when an explosion while filming affected his hearing. Three years later he was awarded $12 000 in damages for his disability. ❦*John West*

further reading
PATE, MICHAEL. *An Entertaining War*. Sydney: Dreamweaver Books 1986.
RUSSELL, ANNA. *I'm Not Making This Up, You Know*. New York City: Continuum 1985.

Don Crosby OAM

Actor. Born 29 October 1924 in Sydney. Son of Marshall Crosby, actor. Worked for J. C. Williamson's and in radio. Served in RAAF 1942–45. Commonwealth scholarship to Royal Academy of Dramatic Art (London) 1946–48. Returned to Sydney 1949. Acted in radio, films, television and theatre. Federal president of Actors' Equity 1976–85. Died 3 December 1985 in Sydney. OAM for services to media and theatre 1980. Father of Michael Crosby, federal secretary of Actors' Equity 1982–91; Matthew Crosby, actor; and Liz Crosby and Marshall Crosby, film directors.

Don Crosby was respected as no other in his profession, as an actor and for his work as the actors' champion. Like his father MARSHALL CROSBY, he was a man of great integrity. He first appeared on stage when he was one year old, with his father and GEORGE WALLACE in *His Royal Highness* at His Majesty's Theatre in Perth in 1925. He interrupted a stage and radio career to join the air force during the Second World War, and he was stationed in England until 1945. He returned in 1946 to study at the Royal Academy of Dramatic Art and after graduating he worked in English repertory theatre for 18 months. In 1950–51 he was in DORIS FITTON's production of Howard Richardson and William Berney's *Dark of the Moon* in Sydney and Melbourne. This was followed by Christy in J. M. Synge's *The Playboy of the Western World* at the Little Theatre in Melbourne in 1951 and a three-year tour in Hugh Hastings's SEAGULLS OVER SORRENTO for J. C. WILLIAMSON's in 1951–54.

As Crosby matured he was in great demand for television drama and films, but he still worked on stage. He played Merlin in *Camelot*, with his RADA contemporary Paul Daneman as Arthur, on tour for J. C. Williamson's in 1963–65. In the early 1970s he was with the NIMROD THEATRE COMPANY as the police sergeant in David Williamson's THE REMOVALISTS and in JIM MCNEIL's *The Old Familiar Juice*. His disillusioned Alf in Alan Seymour's THE ONE DAY OF THE YEAR at the Independent Theatre in 1970 and his dignified Dad in George Whaley's adaptation of Steele Rudd's ON OUR SELECTION at the Jane Street and Nimrod Theatres in 1980 exemplified a description of him by the critic Jeremy O'Brien: '… he brings to a part qualities that are as true as the throbbing of a heartbeat'. ❦*Lynne Murphy*

Marshall Crosby

Actor. Born 1881 in South Australia. Had long career in musicals and plays to 1940s. In vaudeville in 1920s and 1930s. Played character roles in film and radio until 1950s. President of Actors' Equity 1942–45 and 1948–51. Died 1954 in Sydney. Father of Don Crosby, actor, and Pat Crosby, singer.

Among his colleagues Marshall Crosby was highly respected for a varied and solid career and for a strength of character that won him two terms as president of Actors' Equity during its early stormy years. During the 1920s he worked as straight man to his close friend GEORGE WALLACE on the Fuller vaudeville circuit and at HARRY CLAY's Gaiety Theatre in Oxford Street, Sydney. In 1925 he toured with Wallace in *His Royal Highness*, a burlesque operetta. F. W. THRING made this show into a film of the same title in 1932. Crosby supported Wallace in it and in two more Efftee films in the next two years.

In 1933 Crosby played the landlord Pierce Collits in Thring's production of the musical comedy COLLITS' INN. He had a fine baritone voice and sang in many musicals for J. C. Williamson's in the 1920s and 1930s. He also acted character roles in plays. He continued to play substantial character roles in films during the 1940s and he gained great popularity in leading roles of kindly patriarchs in radio serials. ❦*Lynne Murphy*

further reading
VALE, GILL E. Marshall Crosby. *Australian Dictionary of Biography* 13. Melbourne University Press 1994.

CUB Malthouse Theatre

Theatres in Sturt Street, South Melbourne, converted from a malthouse by John Beckett. **Beckett Theatre**, seating 198, opened March 1990. **Merlyn Theatre**, seating about 400, opened May 1990.

The splendidly equipped and intimate Malthouse theatre complex is the artistic and administrative home of the PLAYBOX THEATRE CENTRE. Outside its annual season, it is also very popular with many hiring companies. The Playbox company itself spent six years in hired venues after its base in Exhibition Street burned down in 1984. Carlton and United Breweries donated a site and buildings in 1986 and the complex—two theatres, rehearsal and function rooms, workshops, gallery and cafe—was completed with donations from the state government, corporate bodies and private citizens. The company's long-serving designer John Beckett planned the conversion and his design brought him the Sidney Myer Performing Arts Award in 1992. Within the original three-storey redbrick malthouse, built in 1892, he created the Beckett Theatre—named after him—and a foyer, gallery, bistro and bar, offices and rehearsal rooms. It opened with TES LYSSIOTIS's *The Forty Lounge Cafe*. The larger, wider Merlyn Theatre—named after Dame Merlyn Myer, great aunt of the Playbox director CARRILLO GANTNER—is an adjoining new building. It opened with ROBYN ARCHER's *Cafe Fledermaus*. The theatres are moderately flexible in stage–audience configuration, although upstairs galleries on three sides in both—and on three levels in the Merlyn—render them highly suitable for thrust-stage performance. ❦*Geoffrey Milne*

Max Cullen

Actor. Born 29 April 1940 in Wellington (NSW). Trained at Ensemble Theatre, Sydney; began professional career there 1963. Nimrod Theatre Company (Sydney) 1970. Many film and television roles.

Max Cullen's idiosyncratic, non-projective style of acting has earned him the title of 'Australia's leading anti-actor'. He has been particularly noted in plays by Patrick White and David Williamson. After seeing Cullen in *The Season at Sarsaparilla* in 1976 White wrote a part in *Big Toys* for him. In 1989 Cullen starred in the Sydney Theatre Company's revival of *The Ham Funeral* by White. During the first five years of his professional acting career Cullen combined acting for the Ensemble Theatre Company with freelance cartooning for the *Bulletin* and painting and sculpture. This phase culminated in a memorable Ensemble production of John Herbert's *Fortune and Men's Eyes* in 1968.

Cullen and Anna Volska were the first actors recruited for the Nimrod Theatre Company in 1970. Cullen acted in the premiere of Robert J. Merritt's *The Cake Man*, which inaugurated Black Theatre in Sydney in 1975. From the late 1970s he concentrated on screen work. In 1985 he revived his stage career as Kevin in Williamson's *Sons of Cain*, on tour of Australia and in London. He had an outstanding year in 1991, appearing for the Melbourne Theatre Company in its revival of *This Old Man Comes Rolling Home* by Dorothy Hewett and for the Sydney Theatre Company in *The Government Inspector* by Nikolai Gogol and in *Racing Demon* by David Hare. He was a notable Polonius in *Hamlet* at the Belvoir Street Theatre in 1994. ❦*Paul McGillick*

Peter Cummins

Actor. Born 2 June 1931 in Melbourne. Taught trades subjects in Victorian technical schools. Joined La Mama Company (Melbourne) 1968. Australian Performing Group (Melbourne) in early 1970s. Lighthouse Company (Adelaide) 1982–83. Melbourne Theatre Company since 1985. Many film and television roles.

Peter Cummins is one of the most enduring and more versatile of the actors who emerged from the Australian Performing Group. He is well remembered for his irascible but lovable octogenarian Monk in Jack Hibberd's *A Stretch of the Imagination*—which he created in 1972 and for many other Australian roles, including the Comic in John Romeril's *The Floating World* in 1974, a splendid Alf in the Melbourne Theatre Company's revival of Alan Seymour's *The One Day of the Year* in 1986 and the original Doug Fitzgerald in Stephen Sewell's *The Blind Giant is Dancing* for Lighthouse in 1983. He also succeeded for Lighthouse as Malvolio in *Twelfth Night* in 1983, and for the Melbourne Theatre Company as Captain Shotover in George Bernard Shaw's *Heartbreak House* in 1986 and as Den in Katherine Thomson's *Diving for Pearls* in 1991. ❦*Geoffrey Milne*

The Currency Lass

—*or, My Native Girl*. Musical play in two acts. **libretto** Edward Geoghegan. **music** composed and traditional song tunes. **premiere** 27 May 1844, Royal Victoria Theatre, Sydney. Cast: Mr Fenton, J. G. Griffiths, Mr James, Mme Louise, Joseph Simmons, Mrs Wallace. **revived** October 1966, Jane Street Theatre, Sydney. Cast: Gaye Anderson, Anne Bannon, Martin Harris, Edward Hepple, Beverley Kirk, Ross Thompson, Anthony Thurbon. Designer: David Copping. Director: Robin Lovejoy. **published** Sydney: Currency Methuen 1976 (ed. Roger Covell).

The first Australian comedy on a local theme, *The Currency Lass* is a charming conventional ballad opera with 14 songs and spoken dialogue by Edward Geoghegan. A patriotic and high-spirited romp, it hinges upon a misunderstanding in which the description of Susan Hearty as a 'native girl' is taken to mean an Aboriginal girl rather than a white girl born in Australia—a currency lass. Geoghegan's dialogue had an original colonial flavour—'rather too much so' for the taste of the *Australian* of 20 May 1844—that appealed to the local 'boys in the cabbage tree hats'. At the time there was growing division between these standard-bearers of the native-born and the immigrant population.

Susan Hearty tricks her fiancé's pompous playwriting uncle Sir Samuel Simile with virtuoso impersonations of three different singing, dancing characters. The father of Australian-born Tilly Jones probably commissioned *The Currency Lass* as a vehicle for her talents. He approached the Colonial Secretary in 1843 about a licence. Before the play was produced, however, the 14-year-old currency lass had married and retired from the stage. Susan was played by Mme Louise, an English dancer, who was not equal to the singing and adoption of disguises. ❦*Helen Musa*

Stephen Curtis

Designer. Born 19 April 1957 at Wangaratta (Vic.) Studied at National Institute of Dramatic Art (Sydney). Resident designer at State Theatre Company of South Australia (Adelaide). Travelled in Europe and Turkey on Loudon Sainthill Scholarship 1990.

Neil Armfield, who has directed many productions designed by Stephen Curtis, regards him as the leading designer of his generation. 'His work is marked by the intelligence of its conception and textual interpretation, the clarity of its line and imagery, and a gorgeous palette in which the blues, greens and ochres of the Australian landscape and the harsh clarity of Australian light are fundamental', writes Armfield. 'More than anything else, however, his designs, both in sets and costumes, are distinguished by a personal sense of humour which is both cheeky and highly theatrical—meticulous in detail yet broad in the sweep of its gestures.'

In the premiere of Stephen Sewell's *The Blind Giant Is Dancing*, directed by Armfield for the Lighthouse Company in Adelaide in 1983, Curtis employed exposed stage machinery which powerfully expressed the play's themes. In the same year he was designer of Armfield's acclaimed production of *Twelfth Night* for the Lighthouse Company, and in 1985 he designed a feature film of this production. Other productions in which Curtis and Armfield have worked together are William Wycherley's *The Country Wife* in 1987, Sewell's *Hate* in 1988 and Nikolai Gogol's *The Government Inspector* in 1991, all for the Sydney Theatre Company. Curtis launched his professional career with this company in 1979, in the world premiere of the musical *The Venetian Twins*. This led to his designing many first productions of Australian plays. He developed a passion for using curtains and exposed scene changes in 1981, with Howard Barker's *No End of Blame*, directed by JOHN GADEN for the STATE THEATRE Company of South Australia. In 1985 he pushed naturalism to its most expressive limit in George Bernard Shaw's *Heartbreak House*, directed by ROBYN NEVIN for the Sydney Theatre Company. ❦*Tom Bannerman*

further reading
Reviews—1988. Sydney: Mead and Beckett 1989.
Sydney Theatre Company 1978–1988. Sydney: Focus Books 1989.
A Year In The Arts. Sydney: Mead and Beckett 1989.

Dymphna Cusack AM

Dramatist. Born 22 September 1902 at Wyalong (NSW). Educated at Sydney University. Schoolteacher in NSW. Married writer Norman Freehill. Won Anzac Festival play competition with *Anniversary* 1935. Won Western Australian Drama Festivals Prize for *Morning Sacrifice* 1942. Retired from teaching because of illness 1944. Became full-time writer. Won Western Australian Drama Festivals prize for *Call Up Your Ghosts* 1945. Won Sydney *Daily Telegraph* novel prize with Florence James for *Come in Spinner* 1948. Lived mainly in Europe 1949–72. AM 1981. Died October 1981.

An eloquent, caustic voice against cultural subservience, Dymphna Cusack wrote plays for stage and radio with little hope of commercial production. Her work bridged the depressing gap in the 1930s and 1940s between the brave attempts of LOUIS ESSON and the bright promise of RAY LAWLER. Writing from strong humanist concerns about justice, peace, racism, she advanced dramatic themes from agrarian motifs to issues that polarised urban society. She believed that struggle against injustice, successful or not, is ennobling and carries the seeds of eventual victory for the ordinary people. These beliefs energise her plays and illuminate her vision of the world. In *Red Sky at Morning* (1935) an Irish political convict faces death rather than submission. Sincere teachers in MORNING SACRIFICE (1943), perhaps her finest play, fight an evil superior who is backed by a corrupt school system. Their defeat raises issues that are still relevant to education. This play received professional production in 1986 and is one of the few mid-century plays in the contemporary repertoire. In *Pacific Paradise* (1955), a small island community stands alone against the world powers. This play became a seminal influence on anti-nuclear drama and protest around the world.

Cusack was an activist for world peace. Her commitment often produced stereotyped characters, excessively idealised or totally evil, but the fault also facilitated conflict and dramatic purpose. Many of her 12 novels were adapted for radio or stage, which points to talent for drama as a basic element in her success as a novelist. ❦*Vic Lloyd*

published plays
Comets Soon Pass (1943). Sydney: Australasian 1950 in *Three Australian Three-Act Plays*.
Exit. In Hungarian as *Halaltusa*. Budapest: International Theatre Institute 1957.
The Golden Girls (1955). London: Deane 1955.
Morning Sacrifice (1942). Sydney: Mulga 1943, Currency Press 1986.
Pacific Paradise (1955). Sydney: *Theatregoer* 2/1 (March 1963).
Red Sky at Morning (1935). Melbourne University Press 1942.
Shallow Cups (1933). Melbourne: Dramatists Club 1934 in *Eight Plays by Australians*.
Shoulder the Sky. Sydney: Australasian 1950 in *Three Australian Three-Act Plays*.

other writings
My unpaid career. *Australian* 24 October 1979.
A Window in the Dark (ed. Debra Adelaide). Canberra: Australian National Library 1991.

further reading
CARROLL, DENNIS. *Australian Contemporary Drama*. Sydney: Currency Press 1995.
FREEHILL, NORMAN and DYMPHNA CUSACK. *Dymphna Cusack*. Melbourne: Nelson 1975.
LLOYD, VIC. Conscience and justice. University of Queensland MA thesis 1986.
Comets Soon Pass published in Russia. *Overland* 18 (August 1960).

reference
Unpublished plays in Cusack papers MS 4621 in National Library of Australia (Canberra). Short plays at University of New England (Armidale NSW) MSS 59–60.

Dags

Comedy for teenagers by Debra Oswald. Awgie award for theatre-in-education or community theatre 1986. **premiere** 9 May 1985, Seymour Centre, Sydney, by Canberra Youth Theatre. Cast: Megan Cameron, Diana Carr, Ben Grieve, Ursla Hawthorne, Mary Stansfield. Designer: Fred Lynn. Director: Gail Kelly. **published** Sydney: Currency Press 1987.

Dags, which capitalises on the awkward, painful and funny journey of the Australian teenager in familiar and excruciating detail, has been performed in every Australian capital city, New Zealand and the United Kingdom and to popular and critical acclaim. Its central figure is 16-year-old Gillian, a consummate 'dag', an anxious adolescent misfit who fails to be beautiful, popular and 'cool'. *Dags* has been lauded for its view of adolescent consciousness, forceful vernacular dialogue and celebratory conclusion. The *Sydney Morning Herald* hailed it as 'a celebration of survival … a paean to self reliance and self respect'. CANBERRA YOUTH THEATRE commissioned the work from Debra Oswald, who had been writing for film, television, radio and theatre since she was a teenager. ❦*Rachel Healy*

Luigi Dalle Case

Italian gymnast, manager. Arrived in Sydney from Mauritius with troupe of gymnasts 1841. Ran Australian Olympic Theatre 26 January 1842 to 16 April 1842. Played in Tasmania 1842–43.

Luigi Dalle Case mounted the first challenge to the ROYAL VICTORIA THEATRE in Sydney. He arrived from Mauritius in August 1841 with his company, which included two young Brazilian girls, Signorine Anna and Emilia, and a clown and dancer, Signor Auguste. Dalle Case initially leased the Royal Victoria for Wednesday nights from 18 August to 1 October. He then decided to build an amphitheatre on the corner of George and Hunter streets 'for the exhibition of feats of horsemanship' and other entertainment, along the lines of Astley's Amphitheatre in London. The proprietors of the Royal Victoria opposed Dalle Case's plan and the authorities were reluctant to approve it but eventually he received a nine-month general theatrical licence. His Australian Olympic Theatre, with decoration and scenery painted by JOHN SKINNER PROUT, opened on 26 January 1842. Dalle Case decided to compete more directly with the

Royal Victoria by giving legitimate drama as well as equestrian and gymnastic acts. According to the *Australian* of 5 February 1842, he offered CONRAD KNOWLES and his wife jointly £10 a week—exceptionally high pay for actors in Australia then—to leave the Royal Victoria. Other defectors included ELIZA WINSTANLEY and her sister Ann.

The two theatres competed fiercely, often playing the same piece on one night. The balance finally tipped in favour of the Royal Victoria when a new star, FRANCIS NESBITT, made his debut on 3 March. The Olympic closed on 16 April. Ten days later Dalle Case was declared bankrupt. In June 1842 the Olympic was sold and in October it reopened as a gymnasium.

Dalle Case and his company toured the NSW towns of Maitland, Parramatta and Windsor and returned to Sydney for a farewell benefit at the Royal Victoria on 30 September 1842. On 14 November they opened in Hobart with a variety concert, which included tightrope dancing and athletic exercises, at the Royal Victoria Theatre. An additional attraction, announced for Signorina Anna's benefit on 21 November, was the 'wonder dog Munito', said to be able to translate any word from a list of 350 foreign words, to select and wave any national flag nominated by a spectator, and to play dominoes with gentlemen in the audience.

The company later shifted to the Albert Theatre, where Dalle Case took a farewell benefit on 13 January 1843. Then they travelled to Launceston for three nights at the Royal Olympic Theatre. After a brief country tour Dalle Case and his troupe left for India. They evidently made an impact on Launceston, for the *Examiner* reported on 6 March 1847 that they had returned to Mauritius after eight years' absence. In Asia the company had been augmented by 'some of the inhabitants of the Celestial Empire, remarkable for their talent'—presumably Chinese acrobats—and 'the celebrated Orang-Outang Gertrude who will give lessons in good manners and politeness à la Chesterfield'. Munito and the signorine were claimed to be 'much improved', and reports of Dalle Case's death much exaggerated. ❦*Elizabeth Webby*

further reading
WEINER, ALBERT. The short unhappy career of Luigi Dalle Case. *Educational Theatre Journal* 27 (Washington DC, March 1975).

Alfred Dampier

Actor, dramatist, manager. Born 28 February 1843, 1845 or 1847 in England. Acted in English provinces *c*.1863–73. Married Katherine Russell, pianist. Leading actor and stage manager at Theatre Royal, Melbourne, for three years from 20 September 1873. Formed company and toured widely in Australasia and elsewhere 1877–85. Seasons in London 1878, 1881. Major seasons in Sydney 1885–88 and Melbourne 1888–92. Bankrupt 1894. Acted in London 1894. Toured eastern Australia from 1895 until retirement through ill-health on 10 November 1905. Died 23 May 1908 in Sydney. Father of actors Alfred Dampier jnr, Lily Dampier and Rose Dampier.

One of the best actors in colonial Australia, Alfred Dampier combined performances of Shakespeare with seasons of popular melodrama. Between 1886 and 1905 he was particularly famous for his productions of FOR THE TERM OF HIS NATURAL LIFE and ROBBERY UNDER ARMS, stage versions of Australian novels. The plays that Dampier jointly wrote were sometimes criticised for their rough-and-ready construction, but as an actor he rarely received an unfavourable review in the colonies. London critics acclaimed him too. He may have modelled his style on Henry Irving, with whom he acted in the English provinces in the 1860s.

Dampier arrived in Melbourne in September 1873 with his wife and infant daughters to begin a three-year contract at the Theatre Royal. He played some seasons of starring roles and stage-managed performances by other actors, including J. C. WILLIAMSON and his wife MAGGIE MOORE in *Struck Oil* in 1874. Dampier's own wife, Katherine Russell, also acted professionally but with little success.

Critics disliked Dampier's stage adaptations of Johann von Goethe's *Faust* in 1873 and Victor Hugo's *Les Misérables* in 1875, and from about 1875 he always sought a literary collaborator. He thereby became, deliberately or incidentally, the major supporter and promoter of Australian playwrights in the second half of the 19th century. F. R. C. HOPKINS and GARNET WALCH responded to Dampier's request for stage vehicles to suit him, his wife, nine-year-old LILY DAMPIER and seven-year-old ROSE DAMPIER. Hopkins dramatised Eugène Sue's novel *Le Juif errant* as a melodrama called ALL FOR GOLD and Walch adapted a comic novelette, HELEN'S BABIES.

In Australia between 1880 and 1885 he staged three other plays by Hopkins and two by 'the Vagabond', a Melbourne journalist who was also known as Julian Thomas but was really John Stanley James. Dampier collaborated in writing most of these plays. The Vagabond's *No Mercy* was successful in Sydney from 4 March 1882, but Dampier's legendary support for Australian drama really began with a long residence in Sydney between 1885 and 1888. In 1886 he co-wrote, directed and starred in a stage adaptation by THOMAS SOMERS of Marcus Clarke's *His Natural Life*. This was not the first play from the famous novel but it was one of the most popular and it held sway on Australian stages for 40 years. Dampier also organised a centennial competition for an Australian play, and staged the winner, John Perry's *The Life and Death of Captain Cook* for a short season from 28 January 1888.

Dampier gave a long series of seasons at the Alexandra Theatre in Melbourne between late 1888 and 1892. He presented MARVELLOUS MELBOURNE by himself and J. H. Wrangham, his business manager, on 19 January 1889 and followed it on 1 March 1890 with his and Walch's version of Rolf Boldrewood's *Robbery Under Arms*. By then Lily and, less frequently, Rose Dampier were playing adult heroines such as Sylvia in *For the Term of His Natural Life* and Aileen Marston in *Robbery Under Arms*. Katherine Russell had improved her acting and could master supporting roles. She also contributed to regular scriptwriting sessions that Dampier and his collaborators held at his house, and wrote one play herself, a version of the Flying Dutchman legend. This was occasionally staged between 1880 and 1890 with moderate success.

The depression and bank closures of 1891–93 were disastrous for Dampier, who had taken a three-year lease on the Alexandra Theatre when 'marvellous Melbourne' was still in the heady whirl of a speculative land boom. In 1891 and 1892 the company lost money heavily, although audiences still flocked to occasional successes such as four plays in which Dampier collaborated with Walch—*The Miner's Right* (1891), another Boldrewood adaptation; THE

Scout (1891) and *The Trapper* (1891), wild-west dramas starring the sharpshooter 'Dr' W. F. CARVER; and *Wilful Murder* (1892) a mystery thriller localised to refer to a notorious Melbourne murderer, Frederick Bayley Deeming. But by mid-1892 Dampier was insolvent and he was forced to declare himself bankrupt after a disastrous New Zealand tour in 1893. He was unconditionally discharged in June 1894 but he found performing in Victoria difficult thereafter. A bad fall during a performance, scandals concerning Lily Dampier's private life and poor economic conditions combined to make the next few years difficult for Dampier.

In spite of all this and health problems suffered by him and his wife from 1897, Dampier clawed his way back to prosperity, principally through highly successful seasons as Captain Starlight in *Robbery Under Arms*. He performed this play in England in 1894, opening at London's Princess Theatre on 22 October to mixed reviews. Critics judged the play a failure but, as always, Dampier's acting was highly praised, even though he was rather too old to play a dashing bushranger. An English company later toured the play throughout England.

On Friday nights Dampier often staged his first love, Shakespeare, particularly *As You Like It*, *Hamlet* and *Romeo and Juliet*. This made him popular with the academic and literary elites of Sydney and Melbourne, just as his belief in Australian writers and stories of Australian life endeared him to colonial playwrights, artists and journalists. A 'courtly gentleman and scholarly actor', he was a sentimental favourite of the Australian stage in his later years. He was, by some accounts, too gentle to be an effective stage or business manager, and he was never a threat to the more prosperous companies of WILLIAM ANDERSON, BLAND HOLT or J. C. WILLIAMSON.

Dampier's company broke up almost immediately after his death in 1908. Lily Dampier and her husband ALFRED ROLFE used his scripts as the basis of several early silent films, and later prominent Australian actors, managers and playwrights such as EDMUND DUGGAN and BERT BAILEY freely acknowledged their debt to him. Katherine Russell died in Pennsylvania (USA) in 1915. Rose Dampier and her brother Alfred Dampier jnr—who was born in Melbourne in 1884 and acted briefly as comedian and trainee business manager in his father's company about 1904–05—were with her and no further details of their lives have been traced. ❧*Richard Fotheringham*

published play
Robbery Under Arms with Garnet Walch. Sydney: Currency Press 1985.
further reading
RICKARD, JOHN. Alfred Dampier. *Australian Dictionary of Biography* 4. Melbourne University Press 1972.
reference
The manuscript of *Saint or Sinner*, adapted from Victor Hugo's *Les Misérables*, is in the British Library (London), add. MS 53250G. The Mitchell Library (Sydney) has manuscripts of *For the Term of His Natural Life* (MSS 2283), *Marvellous Melbourne* (MS B753), *The Scout* (MS B752) and *To the West* (MS B751).

Lily Dampier

Actor. Born probably 11 January 1868 in Newcastle-upon-Tyne (England). Eldest child of actors Alfred Dampier and Katherine Russell. Came to Australia with parents, September 1873. Began acting 1877. Leading actor in father's company 1885–1905. Married 1889, divorced 1892. Married Alfred Rolfe 12 July 1893. Died 6 February 1915 in Melbourne. Sister of actors Alfred Dampier jnr and Rose Dampier.

One of 19th-century Australia's great actors, Lily Dampier was noted equally for Shakespeare, tearfully-innocent wronged heroines in English melodramas, and flamboyant horse-riding, sharpshooting heroines in Australian and Wild West adventure stories. Lily and her younger sister Rose first appeared in 1877 in Dunedin (New Zealand) in children's roles written for them by their father, ALFRED DAMPIER. Describing her Melbourne debut, the critic for the *Australasian Sketcher* said on 7 July 1877: 'I have seen many child actors and actresses, but I have seen none so truly natural as little Lily Dampier. … The audience appeared to be completely taken by surprise, and laughed, cried, and applauded as if they could do nothing else.'

As the two little boys in Garnet Walch's adaptation of the American comic novelette *HELEN'S BABIES* the sisters toured the world. In Sydney in 1885–88 and in Melbourne in 1888–92 Lily played opposite her father as Rosalind, Juliet, Ophelia, Portia, Sylvia Vickers in *FOR THE TERM OF HIS NATURAL LIFE*, Aileen Marston in *ROBBERY UNDER ARMS* and many other adult roles. She was unable to play Aileen during the Dampiers' last season in London in 1894 because of her marriage to the actor ALFRED ROLFE in Sydney and the birth of their only child two months afterwards. She may have played minor roles in London in 1898–99. She toured Australia again in 1899–1905.

After her father died in 1908 Lily Dampier acted with PHILIP LYTTON's tent-theatre company in New Zealand. She acted in silent films of *Robbery Under Arms* and *For the Term of His Natural Life* directed by Rolfe in 1911. In 1914 she possibly became Australia's first female professional non-acting director when she produced *Robbery Under Arms* for the King's Royal Dramatic Company in Brisbane. Her health was always fragile and she died when she was 47. ❧*Richard Fotheringham*

further reading
FOTHERINGHAM, RICHARD. Introduction. *Robbery Under Arms* by Alfred Dampier and Garnet Walch. Sydney: Currency Press/ Australasian Drama Studies 1985.

Rose Dampier

Actor, singer. Born probably 21 October 1870 in Manchester (England). Daughter of actors Alfred Dampier and Katherine Russell. Came to September 1873. Began acting in father's company 1877. Played adult roles 1888–1905. Last heard of in USA 1915. Sister of actors Alfred Dampier jnr and Rose Dampier.

'The Dampiers, both Lily and Rose' were celebrated in song as the stars of the company run by their father ALFRED DAMPIER, but Rose was very much the understudy. She made her debut in *ALL FOR GOLD* in Sydney in March 1877. The sisters were acclaimed as the naughty boys in Garnet Walch's *HELEN'S BABIES*. But when LILY DAMPIER graduated to playing leads opposite her father during his Sydney season from October 1885 to May 1888 Rose was still 'Henri, their son' in Charles Webb's *Belphegor the Mountebank* and a street urchin in Henry Pettitt's *The Black Flag*. As the 'Spirit of Light' in her father's *Faust and Marguerite* she sang 'Walpurgis Night' with the chorus, and her singing career at times took her on tour independently of the company, and guaranteed her principal-boy roles in pantomimes. Lily's hurried marriage and temporary withdrawal from the company in 1893 thrust Rose into leading roles such as Aileen Marston in *Robbery Under Arms*, but she was never as popular as her big sister. ❦*Richard Fotheringham*

George Landen Dann

Dramatist. Born 1 January 1904 at Sandgate (Qld). Worked as Government Survey Office draftsman and later design engineer for Brisbane City Council. Wrote comedies for Sandgate Amateur Dramatic Society. Wrote scripts for army entertainment unit during Second World War. Resigned from council job to write and explore Australia c.1950. Made life member of Brisbane Repertory Theatre Society 1952. Died 6 June 1977 at Noosaville (Qld).

George Landen Dann's career exemplified the solitary life of the Australian playwright from the 1930s to the 1950s, when recognition and remuneration came almost only through PLAYWRITING COMPETITIONS and RADIO. Dann first came to national attention in 1931 when the BRISBANE REPERTORY THEATRE SOCIETY performed his *IN BEAUTY IT IS FINISHED* amid great controversy after it had won a £50 prize. Almost all his subsequent plays were finalists in similar competitions. His works were widely produced on radio but confined to the amateur theatre until Brisbane Repertory successfully revived *In Beauty it is Finished* in March 1977, a few weeks before he died.

Dann's work ranges from country comedy to bleak tragedy, but his reputation is based chiefly upon the recurring themes of isolation, matrimonial and filial duty and racial prejudice in his major plays *In Beauty it is Finished*, *FOUNTAINS BEYOND* (1942), *NO INCENSE RISING* (1937) and a lyrical radio play, *The Orange Grove*. His dramas are influenced by European realist writers and his comedies by the English genres of the time. His work is violent in feeling, but physical violence is notably absent; instead the characters' emotions are driven inwards into a powerful realist energising force. Dann's comedies and dramas both reveal his deep feeling for the effects of the harsh Queensland environment upon the ordinary needs of people, black and white.

A shy man who never married, Dann had an early ambition to be a pastor to the Aborigines but his family could not provide the necessary education. He spent much of his life travelling in remote parts of Australia, where he gained material for his writing and a knowledge of Aboriginal lore. He returned to concern for prejudice against Aborigines in his unperformed last work, *Rainbows Die at Sunset*. It was a finalist in the Newcastle College of Advanced Education national play competition in 1975, in which John Romeril's *THE FLOATING WORLD* and Jennifer Compton's *No Man's Land* shared first place. ❦*Katharine Brisbane*

published plays
Caroline Chisholm (1939). Sydney: Mulga 1943. Dann's most widely produced play, first staged as *A Second Moses*.
Fountains Beyond (1942). Sydney: Australasian c.1944.

further reading
CARROLL, DENNIS. *Australian Contemporary Drama*. Sydney: Currency Press 1995.
FOTHERINGHAM, RICHARD. George Landen Dann. *Australian Dictionary of Biography* 13. Melbourne University Press 1994.
RASMUSSEN, DEBORAH. The plays of George Landen Dann. University of Queensland honours thesis 1976.

The giant. *Telegraph* (Brisbane) 3 September 1932.
reference
George Landen Dann's collected papers are in the Fryer Library, University of Queensland (Brisbane).

Eamon D'Arcy

Designer. Born 14 August 1954 in Belfast (Northern Ireland). Came to Australia 1957. Graduated from National Institute of Dramatic Art (Sydney). Trained at English National Opera (London) 1977–78. Studied fine arts at University of Sydney 1988–. Has worked in Sydney with Death Defying Theatre Company and Nimrod Theatre Company and in London 1977–80 at Royal Court Theatre and with Royal Shakespeare Company.

One of Australia's more radical and intellectual designers, Eamon D'Arcy believes that 'theatre should be developed and produced towards a "moment" that will be different. Theatre is an example of a "designed" environment which is a constructed representation of political, economic and cultural power and values. Designers in the theatre are directly responsible for our cultural "seeing". Design, for me, is a visual construction.' D'Arcy has worked with mainstream and alternative companies; his most significant productions include David Mercer's *Cousin Vladimir* for the Royal Shakespeare Company and STEPHEN SEWELL's *Welcome the Bright World* for the NIMROD THEATRE COMPANY. He has also designed for the writers JANIS BALODIS, Edward Bond, ALMA DE GROEN, David Hare and BOB MAZA; the English director Bill Gaskill and the American composer Phillip Glass. ❦*Pamela Zeplin*

further reading
MCGILLICK, PAUL. Those final moments. *Art and Australia* 23/1 (spring 1985).

George Darrell

Actor, dramatist, manager. Born 11 December 1841 in Bath (England). Originally George Price. Emigrated to Australia c.1860. Went to New Zealand goldfields c.1865. Returned to Australia c.1868. Juvenile lead actor to Walter Montgomery in Shakespeare in Melbourne, September 1869. Joined Mrs Robert Heir's company and toured New Zealand. Married Mrs Heir in London, 20 January 1870, and with her toured Australasia. Wrote first play in USA, 1873–74. Launched Darrell's Dramatic Company 1877. Wife died 3 January 1880. Visited USA again 1880-81. Married actor Christine Peachey in New Zealand, 6 May 1886. Wife died during South African tour devoted to Darrell's plays, 6 November 1892. Committed suicide January 1921. Father of Rupert Darrell, actor.

'Gentleman George' or 'Georgious' Darrell was the most prolific dramatist and the most widely travelled actor-manager in 19th-century Australia. He was also the first successful exporter of Australian melodramas. He equalled his playwriting hero DION BOUCICAULT in volume of output. By 1905 he had written as many as 55 plays, 35 of which were produced. He may have written his first play, *The Trump Card*, in collaboration with Boucicault. It was produced in New York City while Darrell was in the USA in 1873–74 with his first wife, who began her Australian career as FANNY CATHCART.

In 1876 Darrell presented *Transported for Life* in Dunedin (New Zealand). In Sydney next year it packed the Theatre Royal for 24 nights at from 23 June, launching Darrell's

Dramatic Company for the Production of Australian Plays. The company played *Transported for Life*, *The Trump Card* and *Man and Wife* in Sydney, Melbourne and the provinces, and from then Darrell generally staged his own melodramas, which made him famous. He gave *Back from the Grave* spectacular productions in Melbourne and Sydney in 1878.

He had a great success with his British Empire play *The Forlorn Hope*, in which gallant Australians travel to fight in the Franco-Prussian War. But on 3 January 1880, ten days after the play began a five-week run in Melbourne, Fanny Darrell died. A week later the Australian Natives Association gave the widower a benefit for his 'services to patriotic drama'. He went to the USA again that year.

In March 1883 Darrell's play THE SUNNY SOUTH, with ESSIE JENYNS as the Australian heroine Bubs Berkley, opened at the Prince of Wales Opera House in Melbourne and ran for 36 nights. In the same season Darrell made a daring attack on hypocrisy in sexual morality with *The Naked Truth*. The *Argus* attacked him on 28 May 1883 for his 'monotonous uniformity' as an actor. He was constantly criticised for attitudinising and even the kindest descriptions show him to have been an unimaginative actor. He was unaware of the trend towards realism in acting and the *Bulletin*, which ridiculed him mercilessly, noted when he appeared in *The Squatter* in 1885 that he was 'a leetle too beautiful for a squatter'. Darrell was satirised for his boasting, his sartorial whims and the rings on his fingers. He puffed his own productions as being 'hugely grand' and 'stupendously vast'.

The *Bulletin* of 22 December 1883 reported Darrell as saying: 'There are only two plays, so-called, nowadays—*Hamlet* and *The Sunny South*'. In the same month *The Sunny South* began a successful run at the Opera House in Sydney. It opened in London, at the Grand Theatre in Islington on 27 October 1884, with J. C. Williamson in the audience. A successful season was cut short when Darrell was injured by a bowie knife on stage. He then retired for a year.

In New Zealand on 6 May 1886 Darrell married a 21-year-old Australian actor in his company, Christine ('Cissie') Peachey. A son was born in December 1886, while Darrell was suffering from a lengthy bout of typhoid. He was helped to recoup consequent financial losses by a benefit presentation given by GEORGE COPPIN in Melbourne on 23 August 1887 for his services 'to the 'native drama'.

In 1890 Darrell became general manager in Melbourne for the new firm of WILLIAMSON, GARNER AND CO. He also tried the new fashion for American dramas by writing *Mr Potter of Texas*, and in an interview with *Melbourne Punch* of 14 August 1890 he admitted: 'I do not like the stage as a profession'. He travelled to London with his wife in 1892. They had no engagements there but toured South Africa in Darrell's plays. At Johannesburg on 6 November 1892 Christine Darrell died of dysentery.

Darrell returned to Australia and continued to write and produce plays, including a dramatisation of Nat Gould's Melbourne Cup novel *The Double Event*. He toured Australia, New Zealand, the USA and England again. He made a huge impact at the Theatre Royal in Perth from 5 June to 13 August 1897 with *The Sunny South* and *The King of Coolgardie*, a renamed version of *The Queen of Coolgardie*. *The Sunny South* played at the Surrey Theatre in London for 15 nights in September 1898. Darrell lingered on as playwright and manager until the end of the century, seeing his plays give way to more genuinely Australian melodramas like those of ALFRED DAMPIER. His last play, *The Land of Gold*, was produced in 1907 at the Criterion Theatre in Sydney.

In 1916 one of his short stories, *The Belle of The Bush*, was published in Sydney, and in the Shakespeare tercentenary celebrations he declaimed lyrics at the Adelphi Theatre. He was increasingly ill and lonely after his son Rupert emigrated to the USA. His body was washed up on Dee Why Beach, Sydney, on 29 January 1921. A suicide note said he was 'going on a long journey'. J. C. Williamson's paid for his funeral on 31 January.

Anglo-Australian melodramas

Darrell is remembered for his 12 Anglo-Australian melodramas, which usually begin in England and involve emigration to Australia and a triumphant return 'home'. His plays generally put an Australian theme into a conventional melodramatic plot. Darrell enlivened all his productions with spectacular visual sensations, usually stylised into tableau curtain freezes. He presented a gallery of familiar colonial characters—blustering bushrangers, good-hearted diggers, naive 'new chums' and spirited Australian girls. An immigrant himself, he took an expatriate English and anti-Irish stance. In *The Sunny South* some Irishmen are beaten up for not toasting Her Majesty the Queen. The *Sydney Morning Herald* accused *The Sunny South* of having the literary merit of 'a third-rate novel', but in commercial success, wide recognition and reception overseas it has perhaps only been equalled by Bert Bailey's ON OUR SELECTION. Darrell's play has had several modern revivals, notably as the opening piece for the SYDNEY THEATRE COMPANY at the Sydney Opera House in 1980.

Darrell put his personal mark upon the plays although, as *Table Talk* saw it in 1885, he 'seems to lack the true literary faculty'. His more serious concerns are evident in the much-criticised 'debatery' of *The Forlorn Hope*, which covers free trade and the Chinese question while giving insights into colonial life. As a piecer-together of plays rather than a really original writer, Darrell resembles the present-day screenwriter more than the traditional playwright. As a skilful writer of spectacular 'sensation dramas' he anticipated the cinema. In 1914 *The Sunny South* was made into a film. ❦*Helen Musa*

published play
The Sunny South (1883). Sydney: Currency Methuen 1975.
further reading
VAN DER POORTEN, HELEN M. George Darrell. *Australian Dictionary of Biography* 4. Melbourne University Press 1972.

Darwin Theatre Company

Semiprofessional dramatic company in Darwin, formed in 1959 as amateur Darwin Theatre Group. Renamed 1989. **venue** Brown's Mart 1971–. **artistic directors** 1977–78 John Kesl. 1979 Robert Kimber. 1980–84 Ken Conway and Simon Hopkinson. 1985–86 William Gluth. 1987–88. 1989 Mary Hickson, Geoff Hooke. 1990–91 Stephen Clark. 1992 Patrick Mitchell. **first production** *Had We But World Enough* by Oriel Gray.

The Darwin Theatre Company is the only semiprofessional company to receive recurrent funding from the AUSTRALIA COUNCIL. Its strengths over the last two decades have been productions of new Australian works, outdoor performances of Shakespeare during the tropical dry season and the creation of works about the Northern Territory. The most significant of these have been *Buffaloes Can't Fly* by Simon Hopkinson in 1981, *Wet and Dry* by JANIS BALODIS in 1986, *Death at Balibo* by Mary Alice Casimiro, Jose Monteiro and Graeme Pitts in 1988 and *Overcome by Chlorine* by the present writer in 1992.

Opportunities for professional theatre artists are increasing in Darwin but the company still relies substantially on a core of experienced amateur workers. Its semiprofessional structure dates from the opening of Brown's Mart as its permanent home in 1971, when it was called the Darwin Theatre Group. The group led a public campaign to save this historic stone building in the centre of Darwin when it was threatened in 1969. The building was converted to an intimate, versatile 140-seat theatre and the group engaged its first professional director, Bryan Nason, to direct THE LEGEND OF KING O'MALLEY by Michael Boddy and Bob Ellis for the opening. This began a practice of employing visiting directors for particular productions.

The group performed in outdoor venues as well as Brown's Mart, which was severely damaged by Cyclone Tracy in 1974 but reopened in 1976. There was a serious threat to the Darwin Theatre Group's funding when the Northern Territory government created the State [sic] Theatre Company of the Northern Territory in 1988, but this was abandoned after six months and the group's funding stabilised. ❦*Suzanne Spunner*

Richard Davey

Actor, director, dramatist, manager. Born 1938 in Sydney. Began theatrical work at Wayside Theatre (Sydney). Theatre '62 (Adelaide). Director of Hole-in-the-Wall Theatre (Perth) 1968–70. Established Round Earth Company with his wife Kathi Davey 1972. Directed Children's Activities Time Society (Perth) 1975. Settled in Tasmania 1980. Writer with Salamanca Theatre Company (Hobart). Board member, artistic director and executive director of Zootango (Hobart) 1986–92.

Richard Davey has contributed significantly to theatrical life in Hobart. Aiming to reflect the special character of the community in the theatre, he has written 20 plays, including *Annie's Coming Out*, *Filthy Lucre*, *Guarding the Perimeter* and *Hallelujah Lady Jane*. All have been produced by local companies, and several have been performed on the mainland. Theatre to Davey is a vehicle for social comment and a popular means of relating Tasmanian history. He staged one of his historical plays, *The Ship that Never Was*, at the actual location of its action—Sarah Island in Macquarie Harbour. In 1983 The Round Earth Company produced *Broken Dreams*, a trilogy about contact between Aborigines and settlers in 19th-century Tasmania. It toured Tasmania and was performed at the Adelaide Festival and in Melbourne. Richard and Kathi Davey established the Round Earth Company in 1972 as a result of his increasing interest in children's theatre and Aboriginal dance. Their aim was partly to explore theatre arts in isolated communities and during 1973–74 they travelled through outback Western Australia and the Northern Territory, working with Aboriginal communities. From 1976 to 1979 the Daveys travelled in North America, Europe and India, working with children and indigenous peoples. ❦*Gillian Winter*

John Davies

Actor, manager. Born 1813 in London. Transported for fraud and served sentence in NSW 1831–37. Began acting in Melbourne 1842. Settled in Hobart 1850. Managed Theatre Royal, Hobart, from 1853. Died 11 June 1872 in Hobart.

A popular actor in Melbourne and a successful manager in Hobart, John Davies was also a publican, policeman, journalist, newspaper proprietor and politician. He came to Australia as a convict, described in his jail report as 'audacious and impudent'. At the end of his seven-year term in 1837 he moved to Melbourne, where he undertook various jobs before he made his theatrical debut to popular acclaim at the ROYAL VICTORIA THEATRE in 1842. For the next three years he acted frequently, appearing in Hobart in 1844. He unsuccessfully sought Melbourne's second theatrical licence in 1845 and returned to NSW for several years. He settled in Hobart in 1850, becoming a publican. In 1853 he became manager of the THEATRE ROYAL. Next year he founded the *Mercury* newspaper and finally he became a member of the Tasmanian House of Assembly. His son, C. E. Davies, was part-owner of the Theatre Royal from 1889 until 1921. ❦*Gillian Winter*

further reading
GREEN, F. C. John Davies. *Australian Dictionary of Biography* 4. Melbourne University Press 1972.
LEVI, J. S. *Australian Genesis*. Adelaide: Rigby 1974.

Lindy Davies

Actor, director, teacher. Born 1946 in Melbourne. Educated at Monash University. Member of Australian Performing Group 1970–76. Lectured in drama at Melbourne State College 1970–76, and belonged to its Open Stage group 1972–76. Studied overseas 1977–78. Head of acting at Victorian College of the Arts (Melbourne) 1979–82. Dean of drama 1995. Playbox Theatre Company (Melbourne) 1982–85. Has worked widely as freelance teacher and coach since 1983. Also film and television roles. Condor Critics' Award 1985 (Martha in Edward Albee's *Who's Afraid of Virginia Woolf?*). Sidney Myer Special Performing Arts Award 1993 in recognition of her exceptional qualities as actor and teacher.

Lindy Davies played in the premieres of Jack Hibberd's DIMBOOLA and JOHN ROMERIL's *I Don't Know Who to Feel Sorry For* at LA MAMA THEATRE in 1969 and was a key link between the Secondary Teachers' College—as Melbourne State College was then called—and the founding of the AUSTRALIAN PERFORMING GROUP. In the college's Open Stage group she became director of Carshop (Creative Arts Workshop for Children), for which she wrote and directed 20 plays and performed in group-devised work and a variety of avant-garde drama. She acted with the APG from its first production, MARVELLOUS MELBOURNE by Jack Hibberd and John Romeril in 1970. Next year she created Jenny in David Williamson's DON's PARTY. She began directing plays in 1972. While overseas in 1977–78 she spent three months with Kristin Linklater in New York learning the Linklater voice method, three months at Peter Brook's International Centre of Theatre Research in Paris and a month working intensively at Jerzy Grotowski's Actors' Laboratory in Kraków (Poland).

In 1979 she returned to work in Melbourne's alternative theatre. In 1982 she began working with REX CRAMPHORN at the Playbox Theatre in several notable productions. She played Agrippina in Jean Racine's *Britannicus*, Cleopatra in *Antony and Cleopatra* in 1983, Kate in Terry Johnson's *Unsuitable for Adults* in 1984 and Gertrude in *Hamlet* in 1985. She played Martha in *Who's Afraid of Virginia Woolf?* for the HUNTER VALLEY THEATRE COMPANY in 1985 and again in 1987 for the STATE THEATRE Company of South Australia. Her own productions include HANNIE RAYSON's *Room to Move* for the latter company in 1985. ❦*Ron Blair*

Allan Davis

Director, producer. Born 30 August 1913 in London to Australian parents. Educated at University of Sydney. Acted for Sydney University Dramatic Society, Bryant's Playhouse and Independent Theatre. Made professional debut in film *The Squatter's Daughter* 1933. Went to London 1934. Acted in revue at Comedy Theatre, London, and at York Citizens' Repertory Theatre. In army 1939–46. Director of Bexhill Repertory Company 1946. Assistant director of Bristol Old Vic 1947; director 1949–50. Lecture tour of American universities for Rockefeller Foundation 1950. Directed films in Hollywood and United Kingdom from 1951. Director and producer in London West End theatres from 1954. Member of council of English Stage Company at Royal Court Theatre, London.

The only working theatre director to appear in the *Guinness Book of Records* is Allan Davis—for having had his name in lights for 17 years as director of *No Sex Please, We're British* by Anthony Marriott and Alistair Foot, the longest-running comedy in the British theatre with 6761 performances from 1971 to 1987. Davis is probably also the longest-working director and at 80 he was still working in the West End.

Davis's field is romantic comedy, which has gained him a reputation for integrity, inventiveness and seamlessness. He acknowledges that he is indebted for his taste in theatre to the 'outstanding quality' of professional and amateur theatre in Sydney in the late 1920s and early 1930s. The standard of J. C. WILLIAMSON's productions was, he believes in retrospect, equal to any in the world. The storytelling quality of DORIS FITTON's production of J. B. Priestley's *Dangerous Corner* changed the direction of his life and she had a profound influence upon his early career. 'She was one of those people who changed the world through the theatre', he has said. 'My object has not been to change the world but to make it laugh.'

In 1968 Davis directed ANNA RUSSELL in *Breath of Spring* by Peter Coke at Fitton's INDEPENDENT THEATRE in Sydney. He returned to Australia to direct his 1965–68 West End success, Bill Naughton's *Spring and Port Wine*, with Alfred Marks on a tour for J. C. Williamson's. ❦*Katharine Brisbane*

further reading
HERBERT, IAN (ed.). *Who's Who in the Theatre* 17th edn. Detroit (USA): Gale Research 1981.
MATTHEWS, PETER (ed.). *Guinness Book of Records*. London: Guinness Publishing 1993.

Jack Davis AM BEM

Actor, dramatist. Born 11 March 1917 in Perth. Member of Bibbulmun tribe. Spent early years in Yarloop (WA). Stockman and itinerant worker for nearly 30 years. Director of the Aboriginal Centre, Perth, 1967–71. First chairman of Aboriginal Lands Trust in Western Australia 1971. Managing editor of Aboriginal Publications Foundation 1972–77. First full-length play performed 1979. Sidney Myer award 1984. Australian Writers' Guild Awgie award 1986 (*No Sugar*). Ruth Adeney Koori Award 1992 (*No Sugar*). Hon.DLitt University of Western Australia. Hon.DLitt Murdoch University. BEM 1977, AM 1985.

Jack Davis has such a sure eye and ear for the stage that it is difficult to believe that he wrote his first full-length play, *Kullark* (1979) at the age of 61. After a long and distinguished career as a worker for Aboriginal advancement he has become one of the most talented and influential black Australian writers and one of Australia's major dramatists. One key to his success is his lifetime fascination with language. As a child in Yarloop (WA), a small mill town in the southwest, he used to read an English dictionary—his only book—in bed at night. He wrote his first poetry at 14. Davis left school after eight years' primary education and worked briefly at the Moore River Native Settlement, where he began to study the Nyungar language of the Aborigines of the southeast. He developed his knowledge of language and other tribal culture during many years as a stockman and itinerant worker in the northwest. Throughout his varied career in the bush he was known for his habit of pencilling verse on scraps of paper, and he has always had a remarkable ability to remember dialogue verbatim.

Davis has said he is 'Aboriginal and parochial West Australian—in that order' but he never allows polemics to obscure the realism of his plays. Even in *Barungin (Smell the Wind)*, his most overtly political work, he not only criticises white Australian behaviour but also shows traps, such as poverty and alcoholism, into which many black Australians have fallen. *Barungin* shows the trials of the Wallitch family in the context of Aboriginal protests against the bicentenary and a rash of Aboriginal deaths in custody. Its performance at the Fitzroy Town Hall, Melbourne, in May 1988 as part of the *The First-Born* family trilogy—with *No Sugar* (1985) and *The Dreamers* (1982)— was a highlight of Davis's dramatic career.

As an occasional play prompted by repudiation of a white Australian anniversary, *Barungin* resembles *Kullark*, which dissented from official history during Western Australia's sesquicentenary in 1979. Here Davis goes back to the first contact between whites and blacks in the state and shows how initial attempts at peaceful coexistence soon degenerated into near-genocidal violence.

Davis accentuates the contact motif in *Kullark* by paralleling historical episodes with contemporary examples of interracial contact and conflict in Western Australia. Integration of past and present, of the Nyungar language and English, and of young and old characters enable him to achieve far more than an examination of the historical record. He often explores serious themes through comic devices.

The wise humour of the characters is a hallmark of all Davis's plays. Whether it is in a play that focuses upon racial bigotry (such as *In Our Town*), in a pointed monodrama of life on the fringe (like *Wahngin Country*) or in a play that engages the enthusiams and openmindedness of the younger generation (such as *Moorli and the Leprechaun*), Davis is always able to show how generations should be judged—not only by their worst but also by their best examples. As often as not, the children in his works are at least as wise as their parents, especially in *Honey Spot*

(1985), a play directed at multicultural Australian youth. Here a white girl and an Aboriginal boy develop a friendship which their parents distrust and discourage. But as a result of the youngsters' relationship the life of the white father is saved, as is the livelihood of the black father. This optimism and wisdom seems to emanate from the author, who has achieved his stature as a playwright without alienating either the Aboriginal people or others in his audience. ❦*Adam Shoemaker*

published plays
Barungin (1988). Sydney: Currency Press 1989.
The Dreamers (1982). Sydney: Currency Press 1982, revised (1984) in *Plays from Black Australia* 1989.
In Our Town (1990). Sydney: Currency Press 1992.
Kullark (1979). Sydney: Currency Press 1982.
Moorli and the Leprechaun. Sydney: Currency Press 1994.
No Sugar (1985). Sydney: Currency Press 1986; 1989 in *Plays from Black Australia*.

other writings
Aboriginal writing. In *Aboriginal Writing Today* (ed. Jack Davis and Bob Hodge). Canberra: Australian Institute of Aboriginal Studies 1985.

further reading
BRISBANE, KATHARINE. In *Contemporary Dramatists* (ed. K. A. Berney) 5th edn. London: St James Press 1993.
BRISBANE, KATHARINE. Looking out from Australia. *Island Magazine* (Hobart) spring 1984.
CHESSON, KEITH. *Jack Davis*. Melbourne: Dent 1988.
WATEGO, CLIFF. Aboriginal Australian dramatists. In *Community Theatre in Australia* (ed. Richard Fotheringham). Melbourne: Methuen 1987. Sydney: Currency Press 1992.

Judy Davis

Actor. Born 1956 in Perth. Graduated from National Institute of Dramatic Art (Sydney) 1977. Q Theatre Company (Penrith NSW) 1978. Many film roles in Australia and overseas. Married to actor Colin Friels.

An actor of striking emotional intensity, with a quality suggesting danger, Judy Davis has performed only seven roles on stage in Australia. They include the title-roles in *Lulu*, LOUIS NOWRA's adaptation of works by Frank Wedekind, in Adelaide and Sydney in 1981, and Henrik Ibsen's *Hedda Gabler* for the SYDNEY THEATRE COMPANY in 1986; and Cordelia and the Fool in *King Lear* for the NIMROD THEATRE COMPANY in Sydney in 1985. She has also played Marilyn Monroe in Terry Johnson's *Insignificance* at the Royal Court Theatre in London and the title-role in Tom Stoppard's *Hapgood* in Los Angeles. Like MEL GIBSON, Davis quickly became a screen star in Australia and overseas and many Australian actors see her as a career model. ❦*Ken Healey*

further reading
HUBBARD, LINDA S. and OWEN O'DONNELL (eds). *Contemporary Theatre, Film and Television* 7th edn. Detroit (USA): Gale Research 1989.

Gloria Dawn

Actor, comedian, singer. Born 26 February 1929 in Melbourne. Originally Gloria Dawn Evans. Performed in vaudeville with parents from age of three. Toured in child troupe 1939–41. On Tivoli circuit 1941–45. Married juggler Frank Cleary 1945. Performed in musical comedy. Toured in caravan 1949–59. In major musicals from 1959. In revue at Phillip Theatre, Sydney, 1965–67. Dramatic roles from 1972. National Critics' Circle Award 1972 (Oola Maguire in *The Slaughter of St Teresa's Day* by Peter Kenna). Died 2 April 1978 in Sydney. Mother of entertainer Donna Lee.

A dynamic Tivoli soubrette, often likened to Betty Hutton, Gloria Dawn expanded her career to encompass musicals, radio, television and intimate revue and then took an unexpected turn into legitimate theatre. She found herself in the 1970s becoming in the eyes of the younger generation a living symbol of an indigenous theatre that was being rediscovered at the time. She was born into six generations of circus performers on both sides. She was the only child of Zilla Weatherly, a contortionist and singer who performed with her sisters Zaida and Queenie, and Billy Andros, ventriloquist, magician and paper-tearer. They were well established on the Tivoli circuit in 1929 when 14-day-old Gloria first appeared on stage. At three she was singing and dancing in the family act as Baby Dawn.

In 1939 ten-year-old Gloria Dawn joined the Tivoli Gang, gifted children who toured the country playing two shows a day six days a week. Two years later, she joined Actors' Equity and struck out on her own. Her mother, seeing the wartime shortage of overseas talent, restyled Gloria's hair into a blonde pompadour, disguised her with lipstick and powder and launched her—at the age of 12—as an adult soubrette. After four years on the Tivoli circuit, where she appeared opposite JIM GERALD and ROY RENE, Dawn eloped to Brisbane with Frank Cleary, a juggler. In Brisbane she bore the first of her four children and performed in her first musical comedies—*Little Nellie Kelly* and the title-role in *Sunny*, produced by WILL MAHONEY in 1949.

The next ten years saw the growing Cleary family on the road in a caravan, playing in tents, variety theatres, tin huts, even in the open air. The producer GARNET H. CARROLL tracked Dawn to a Victorian country town and offered her the Carol Burnett role in the musical *Once Upon a Mattress*. It opened in Melbourne on 4 December 1959 and her performance led to a featured role in Anthony Kimmins's *The Amorous Prawn* in Melbourne from 1 April 1959, and a lengthy run in the Australian musical THE SENTIMENTAL BLOKE from 4 November 1961. Her performance as Rose in the latter prompted one critic to declare: 'She has no equal in the land as a musical comedienne'.

A move to Sydney and the club circuit resulted in a three-year association with WILLIAM ORR, who fashioned uproarious intimate revues around Dawn's talents, especially *A Cup of Tea, a Bex and a Good Lie Down* at the Phillip Theatre from 18 September 1965. In 1972, after two successful productions of *Annie Get Your Gun*, Dawn's old friend PETER KENNA persuaded her to undertake her first dramatic role, Oola Maguire in his play THE SLAUGHTER OF ST TERESA'S DAY at the Community Theatre in Sydney. Next year Dawn was rather dismayed to find herself playing the title-role in Bertolt Brecht's *Mother Courage and Her Children* for the MELBOURNE THEATRE COMPANY in June, Aggie in Kenna's *A Hard God* for the NIMROD THEATRE COMPANY in Sydney in August, and Mrs Peachum in *The Threepenny Opera*, for the OLD TOTE THEATRE COMPANY in Sydney in October.

Her last great role was Mamma Rose in the musical *Gypsy* in Melbourne from 3 May 1975. During the run she was stricken with cancer and forced to relinquish the part to TONI LAMOND. In March 1977, her illness in remission, Dawn bade a fitting farewell to the stage at the Nimrod

Theatre in Sydney by portraying QUEENIE PAUL in *Young Mo*, a study of Australian vaudeville by Steve J. Spears.

Dawn's entry into the legitimate theatre at the age of 43 after a lifetime as an entertainer brought with it the kind of earthy vitality that the new Australian playwrights were seeking. Her anti-intellectual instinct for theatrical rightness, her ability to follow directions precisely without taking a single note, her vaudevillian habit of never revealing her act until opening night, were all a mystery and a delight to those who were trying to reinvent the theatre.

Particularly memorable was her work for Peter Kenna, whose plays evoked the suburban Catholic family life she knew so well. As Oola Maguire, the blowsy starting-price bookmaker in *The Slaughter of St Teresa's Day*, she drew upon the comic skills she had made memorable at the Phillip Theatre. Into her creation of Aggie, the patient mother in *A Hard God*, she put all the pain, sardonic wit and resilience of a tough life. Though she belonged to a bawdy profession, Dawn was strict about language and behaviour on and off stage. The words and sentiments of the bawdy Mrs Peachum in Jim Sharman's King's Cross adaptation of *The Threepenny Opera* made that role one of her most difficult. Kenna wrote a tribute to Gloria Dawn's life through the character of the actress Doris in his play *Furtive Love* (1978). Though she did not live to play the role, it is the most vivid account of her that remains. ❦*Tony Sheldon*

further reading
BRISBANE, KATHARINE. Goodbye, Gloria. *Australian* 10 July 1980.
HOGAN, SUSAN. Gloria Dawn. *Australian Dictionary of Biography* 13. Melbourne University Press 1994.

Leslie Dayman

Actor, director. Born 19 January 1933 in Adelaide. Played leading roles in Adelaide productions from 1954. Artistic director of South Australian Theatre Company (Adelaide) 1968–70. Melbourne Theatre Company 1970–80. Nimrod Theatre Company (Sydney) 1981. Many television and film roles.

A dedicated and able performer, Leslie Dayman championed postwar American and British drama in Adelaide, playing leading roles in works by John Arden, Arthur Miller, John Osborne and Tennessee Williams. As artistic director of the South Australian Theatre Company he presented works by Joe Orton and Tom Stoppard. He created Digger Mason in Patrick White's *A SEASON AT SARSAPARILLA* in 1962. Dayman also directed productions for the STAGE COMPANY and HARVEST THEATRE COMPANY, and JACK DAVIS's *Honey Spot* for an AUSTRALIAN ELIZABETHAN THEATRE TRUST tour. ❦*Murray Bramwell*

Alma De Groen

Dramatist. Born 1941 in Foxton (New Zealand). Settled in Australia 1964. Lived in Canada with her husband, artist Geoffrey De Groen 1969–72. Began writing for stage 1968. Also writes for television. NSW Premier's award 1988. Victorian Premier's award 1988. Awgie award 1993 for *The Girl Who Saw Everything*.

Alma De Groen is unusual in Australian theatre in seeking dramatic forms specifically appropriate to each play. She identifies strongly as a feminist playwright, but her plays also express concern for artists, eccentrics and others on the margins of society. Her social themes are contained within a concern for a larger metaphysical relationship between human life and the universe, and she feels that her plays evolve towards a 'feminist existentialism'.

De Groen was encouraged to write for the theatre by BRIAN SYRON, who read her first script, *The Sweatproof Boy*, in 1968. In her first performed play, *The Joss Adams Show* (1970), non-realistic, fluid dramaturgy evokes the mental state of a helpless young mother who batters her baby to death. Workshopped at the Shakespeare Theatre in Stratford (Ontario), it received a Canadian national prize. De Groen was still in Canada when *The Sweatproof Boy*, her first full-length play, was produced by Sydney's NIMROD THEATRE COMPANY in 1972. In 1973 De Groen developed this script as the short piece *Perfectly All Right*, in which deceptively realistic dramaturgy shows a woman trapped in domesticity using an obsession with housework to compensate for her loss of reality. Fluid dramaturgy presents eccentric characters sympathetically in *The After-Life of Arthur Cravan* (1973), centred on the life of Oscar Wilde's nephew Fabien Lloyd. and in *Chidley* (1976), about William James Chidley, an Australian health and sex reformer.

In the realistic *Going Home*, focused on Australian expatriate artists living in Canada, De Groen uses the closed set of a snowbound house to represent the entrapped lives of the characters. The homelessness and loss of identity of the housewife Zoe are paralleled by her artist husband's sense of exile and alienation in a society that ignores or commercialises art. The comedy *Vocations* (1982) blurs and merges the stage space and properties of two adjoining flats to reinforce its satirical questioning of gender-determined expectations and roles in marriage and career. Experimenting with a disrupted form to reflect the dislocation felt by women and artists in society, *The Rivers of China* (1987) interweaves the last weeks of the life of Katherine Mansfield at the Gurdjieff Institute at Fontainebleau, with an episode in a hospital set in a feminist dystopia.

A return to semi-realism in *The Girl Who Saw Everything* (1991) allowed De Groen to present a thoughtful study of two generations of women responding to feminism, and the awakening consciousness of a middle-aged couple, Liz and Gaz Ransom, when the death of a girl focuses their attention on the violence to women endemic in society. *Available Light* (1993), commissioned by the ABC as a radio play, comprises monologues by a poet mother and a daughter photographer and returns to the theme of the female artist struggling to retain the integrity of her work. ❦*Elizabeth Perkins*

published plays
Available Light (1993). In *LiNQ* 20/1 (1993).
Chidley (1976). Melbourne: Yackandandah 1993.
The Girl Who Saw Everything. Sydney: Currency Press 1993.
Going Home (1976). Sydney: Currency Press 1977.
The Joss Adams Show (1970). Sydney: Currency Press 1977.
Perfectly All Right (1973). Sydney: Currency Press 1977.
The Rivers of China (1987) Sydney: Currency Press 1988.
Vocations (1981). Sydney: Currency Press 1983.

further reading
GILBERT, HELEN. In *Contemporary Dramatists* (ed. K. A. Berney) 5th edn. London: St James Press 1993.
PALMER, JENNIFER (ed.). *Contemporary Australian Playwrights*. Adelaide University Union Press 1979.
PERKINS, ELIZABETH. *The Plays of Alma De Groen*. Amsterdam: Rodopi 1994.

Alfred Deakin

Dramatist. Born 3 August 1856 in Melbourne. Prime Minister of Australia 1903–04, 1905–08, 1909–10. Died 7 October 1919 in Melbourne.

Australia's second Prime Minister, Alfred Deakin had early and transitory aspirations to become an actor and playwright. In his teens he wrote high-minded moralistic dramas, of which *Quentin Massys*, a surging historical piece in poetic form, is the sole survivor. It was published in 1875. Young Deakin, disappointed in not obtaining a production with himself as the main character, a 16th-century Flemish painter, burned all but a few copies. The Mitchell Library in Sydney has one. ❦*Leslie Rees*

published play
Quentin Massys. Melbourne: J. P. Donaldson 1875.
further reading
NORRIS, R. Alfred Deakin. *Australian Dictionary of Biography* 8. Melbourne University Press 1981.

Dulcie Deamer

Dramatist. Born 13 December 1890 in Christchurch (New Zealand). Won *Lone Hand* story competition 1906. Married Albert Goldie, advance manager for J. C. Williamson's, 1907. Travelled, wrote and acted overseas 1908–22. Separated from husband and lived in Sydney 1922–70 as freelance journalist. Published five novels and two collections of poetry 1913–48. Died 16 August 1972 in Sydney.

Dulcie Deamer, who epitomised the playful Bohemia of Sydney's Kings Cross between the wars, wrote sketches and choreographed for DUNCAN MACDOUGALL's Playbox Art Theatre in the late 1920s and made a noteworthy contribution to Australian symbolist and expressionist drama in the 1930s. On 29 July 1933 the Tom Thumb Theatre presented four short symbolist 'morality plays' in which her characters are personified abstractions and the religious message is patterned on *Everyman*. *Easter* was praised for its dialogue.

Deamer's longer plays reflected international tensions. *The Lucid Interval* (1932), *That by which Men Live* (1936) and *Victory* (1938) are all set in a future militarist dictatorship of Reason, which persecutes a minority of believers in peace and spiritual values. Some of the oppressors are converted —but too late to prevent apocalypse. Expressionism is suggested in heavily typified characters and demanding lighting and scenic effects. *The Messenger*, never performed, exploits interesting directional choral speaking, some of it behind the audience. ❦*Dennis Carroll*

published plays
Easter. Sydney: Angus and Robertson 1937 in *Best Australian One-Act Plays*.
In the Heart of a Woman. Sydney: Australian Theatre Society.
In the Mind of a Child. Sydney: Australian Theatre Society.
In the Soul of a Man. Sydney: Australian Theatre Society.
further reading
RUTLEDGE, MARTHA. Mary Elizabeth Kathleen Dulcie Deamer. *Australian Dictionary of Biography* 4. Melbourne University Press 1972.
reference
The unpublished plays of Dulcie Deamer are in the Campbell Howard Collection of the Dixson Library, University of New England (Armidale). Her autobiography, written in 1965, is MS 3173 in the Mitchell Library (Sydney).

J. P. Deane

Entrepreneur. Born 1 January 1796 in London. Came to Hobart 1822. Taught pianoforte and violin, and played organ. Organised public concerts from 1826. Fitted up Argyle Rooms as Theatre Royal and presented drama 1834. Moved to Sydney in 1836 and concentrated on music. Died 18 December 1849 in Sydney.

John Philip Deane promoted theatrical activity in Hobart between SAMSON CAMERON's 1833–34 season at the FREEMASON'S TAVERN and the opening of the New THEATRE ROYAL in 1837. Deane had organised the first public concert in the Van Diemen's Land in 1826 and with similar enterprise he capitalised upon enthusiasm for theatre engendered by Cameron's season. In February 1834 he leased the ARGYLE ROOMS and presented concerts that ended with short plays. These were so successful that he fitted up a theatre and in May 1834, when Cameron had moved to Launceston, he opened it three nights a week as the Theatre Royal. His first production was *THE BUSHRANGERS*, commissioned by him from Henry Melville. Later in 1834 Deane launched ANNE CLARKE and DINAH MURRAY on colonial acting careers. By remodelling the Argyle Rooms, he gave Hobart a more suitable venue than the Freemason's Tavern, but he seems to have lacked business acumen. Failures in other ventures—he was also bookseller, publican and auctioneer— and perhaps more experienced competitors forced him to abandon his foray into theatrical management within a year. In 1835 he was imprisoned for debt. ❦*Gillian Winter*

further reading
WENTZEL, ANNE K. John Philip Deane. *Australian Dictionary of Biography* 1. Melbourne University Press 1966.

Death Defying Theatre

Professional community-theatre company in Sydney, founded in 1981 as touring street-theatre collective by Paul Brown, Christine Sammers and Kim Spinks. Became community-theatre company 1991. **first production** *Dr Floyd's Fly by Night Medicine Show* 1982.

In its first ten years as Australia's only professional street-theatre company Death Defying Theatre gave free, outdoor performances of what it described as socially responsible entertainment. It employed eye-catching popular theatre skills—such as *commedia dell'arte*-style characters, juggling, sight gags and music—to develop an exuberant, informal style and to create shows that comically criticised the institutions of Australian society. For example, the original performers devised *Dr Floyd's Fly By Night Medicine Show* in 1982 as a critique of health care and took it to festivals, shopping centres, caravan parks, prisons, campuses and community events around the country. Other shows in the early years included *Discipline and Punish*, a radical examination of the prison system; *Living Newspaper*, *The Really Interesting Gypsies* and Paul Brown's *Coal Town*. More recent successful shows include *Blood Orange* by Noëlle Janaczewska, and *Eye of the Law* by Kominos.

During the 1980s Death Defying Theatre established itself on the festival and community-events circuit and it helped to establish outdoor theatre at cultural events. It was never in the mainstream, however, and was often dismissed as children's theatre. Like much COMMUNITY THEATRE, in funding disputes in the 1980s it was accused of lacking innovation and not attaining excellence.

Originally the company comprised five to eight resident performers who devised all its work, although it often hired teachers and designers for projects. From 1984 it employed administrators and later writers and others. From the outset a belief in the social necessity of art led Death Defying Theatre to provide its skills as a communal resource in street-theatre 'residencies', particularly in western Sydney. In 1991 it settled in the western suburb of Auburn and became a community-theatre company. It is no longer an ensemble but has an artistic director, Fiona Winning, and hires personnel as required. ❦*Kim Spinks*

Deckchair Theatre Company

Professional community-theatre company in Fremantle (WA), founded in January 1983 by Brian Peddie and Di Shaw. Incorporated 1984. **artistic directors** 1988–90 Phil Thompson. 1991– Angela Chaplin.

Production of new Australian works is the primary interest of the Deckchair Theatre Company. It initially concentrated on devising plays for high-school students. *Wheezily Distinguished* in 1983 looked at real and imagined disabilities and *A Chord is Struck* in 1984 showed the pressures of school, family and peers upon a young girl. By 1986 the company was focusing on a wider community. The cultural diversity and maritime activity of Fremantle, once a bustling port, have inspired works such as *Fleets of Fortune*, a joyful celebration of the Italian fishing community written in 1987 by Ken Kelso and Phil Thompson. In 1988 Thompson and the actor John Walker wrote *Paddy*, based on the life of a renowned Fremantle trade unionist, Paddy Troy. Deckchair's plays about women include Mary Hutchinson's *Salt, Mustard, Vinegar, Pepper* in 1985, looking at life choices, and her *Birthworks* in 1987, showing childbirth as a metaphor for women's careers and artistic endeavour. KATHERINE THOMSON wrote *Barmaids* for Deckchair during a writer's residency in 1991. It became nationally popular and won the 1992 AUSTRALIAN WRITERS' GUILD award for best play.

The company performs in unusual venues, more by choice than necessity. Wharf sheds, historic buildings and outdoor settings have appealed particularly to new audiences. Since 1987, Deckchair has held the Western Australian licence for Theatresports. In 1988 it was given a Swan Gold Theatre Award for outstanding development in theatre. ❦*David J. Hough*

Henry Deering

Actor, manager. Arrived in Sydney from London 3 January 1843. Acted at Royal Victoria Theatre 1843–46. Managed theatres in Adelaide, Hobart, Geelong (Vic.) and Launceston (Tas.) 1846–52. Abandoned theatre for local politics in Geelong. Wife was actor.

Like most early actor-managers in Australia, Henry Deering had a rather chequered career but he persevered in promoting theatre outside the major centres. Engaged by JOSEPH WYATT in England, he arrived in Sydney with his wife in January 1843 to begin a three-year contract at the Royal Victoria Theatre. Billed as 'from the Queen's Theatre, London', Deering quickly found favour with Sydney audiences. 'A poetical review of Sydney actors' in the *New South Wales Magazine* of March 1843 said of him:

The talent of DEERING decidedly runs,
To nature's own rustic and unpolished sons;
With simplicity, pathos and humour replete,
His countrymen *offer a genuine treat;*
His sailors, *with feeling and nature abound,*
And in these have his efforts with plaudits been crowned;
Then let not ambition provoke him to roam
From the track where success has proclaimed him at home.

After his contract with Wyatt expired, Deering left for Adelaide, where he gave concerts in March 1846. On 22 June he opened the Royal Adelaide Theatre at the Bush Club House. Initially, he was praised for good management. 'Neatness, good order, and a well lighted house are prime requirements, especially in Adelaide', remarked the *Adelaide Observer* on 27 June.

A week later, however, the paper was waxing indignant over the announcement that *Jack Sheppard* was to be performed. J. B. Buckstone's drama, based on Daniel Defoe's novel about a notorious highwayman, had been banned in England by the Lord Chamberlain on the grounds of incitement to crime. 'We are rather surprised that a manager of Mr Deering's reputed discernment should venture to offer such an insult to a community not proverbially inclined to patronise the drama, much less to foster crime by facilitating its introduction amongst them through scenic representations', the paper said. Nevertheless, *Jack Sheppard* was produced on 7 July and several times later.

When the season concluded at the end of October 1846, Deering was engaged for GEORGE COPPIN's New Queen's Theatre. Before long, however, he had quarrelled with Coppin and he reopened the Royal Adelaide Theatre on 22 February 1847. On 3 February 1848 he was listed as stage manager of the New Queen's Theatre, but he left again after JOHN LAZAR took over as manager on 21 February, and on 1 May he reopened the Royal Adelaide.

Towards the end of 1848 Deering left for Geelong, where he worked as stage manager of the new Theatre Royal, which opened on 27 November. He remained at Geelong throughout 1849 but by July 1850 he had appeared in Launceston at the Royal Olympic Theatre. There was considerable praise for Deering's acting, but a successful season ended prematurely when the theatre owner broke his agreement with Deering.

Later Deering and his company performed at the Royal Victoria Theatre in Hobart, where there was again praise for his management. Deering subsequently resumed control of the Theatre Royal at Geelong but on 26 May 1852, after he was elected to the local council, he transferred his licence to Coppin. ❦*Elizabeth Webby*

Olly Deering

Actor. Born 1843 in NSW. Son of actors Henry and Eliza Deering. Acted with many companies all over Australasia. Died November 1906 in Sydney. Married actor Linda Raymond, who survived him.

Versatile Olly Deering probably acted in every important town of Australasia. He was convincing in a wide variety of roles, from comic to villain. One of his earliest was the new chum in Walter Cooper's *Hazard*, and one of his best was Deacon Skinner in *Struck Oil*. After his early appearances he seems to have concentrated on Australian plays.

He acted with numerous companies, including those that performed the plays of GEORGE DARRELL and the operettas of Luscombe Searelle. At his death he was a member of Meynell and Gunn's dramatic company. ♥*Joan Maslen*

further reading
Argus (Melbourne) 21 November 1906.

Dick Diamond

Dramatist. Born 27 July 1906 in England. Came to Australia at 11 with family and settled in Melbourne. Worked as a journalist on minor magazines and in film. Joined Communist Party 1934. Joined Workers' Theatre Group 1936. Secretary of Actors' Equity, Victoria, 1945–55. Lived in Vietnam 1956–57, China 1958–61. Left Communist Party c.1963. Worked in public relations in Sydney from 1966 until retirement in 1972. Died 1989.

Among the politically motivated plays Dick Diamond wrote for production by NEW THEATRE in Melbourne was *Reedy River*, an enormous popular success in 1953. A folk musical based on the shearer's strike of 1891, it dominated New Theatre repertoire for four years, playing to an estimated 450 000 people across Australia. Its incorporation of traditional bush songs contributed to the revival of Australian folk music and the development of the bush band. It has been frequently revived.

Before the Second World War Diamond wrote documentary scenes and agitprop sketches for the Workers' Theatre Group to perform at street meetings, factory gates and union functions. His first full-length play was *Soak the Rich* (1941), a satire in living newspaper style of Arthur Fadden's 'soak the poor' federal budget in 1941. *Jack the Giant Killer* in 1947 was a political pantomime. Diamond's second Australian musical, *Under the Coolibah Tree*, was first produced by the New Theatre Club in Brisbane on 18 March 1955. ♥*Angela O'Brien*

published play
Reedy River, libretto for musical (1953). Melbourne: Heinemann 1970. Sydney: Currency Press 1989.

Barry Dickins

Dramatist. Born 6 November 1949 in Melbourne. Studied fine arts. First play staged at La Mama Theatre, Melbourne, 1975. Writer-in-residence at La Mama 1980. Also cartoonist and occasional actor in film and television.

With wistful humour, and mordant satire sometimes, Barry Dickins has chronicled bygone Melbourne in many plays. They often feature down-and-outs and battlers, portrayed in a broad, cartoon-like style that blends surrealism with elements of the theatre of the absurd. Much of Dickins's subject matter is distinctly local in flavour, which may account for some lessening of appeal outside Melbourne. His whimsical iconoclasm is seen at its best at LA MAMA THEATRE, where he has had numerous plays produced since *Ghosts!* in 1975.

His first professional production was *Fool's Shoe Hotel* at the Pram Factory in 1978. Dickins has developed monodrama to a high degree, especially in his finest play, *Lennie Lower*, a compassionate portrait of the last night in the working life of the eponymous eccentric Sydney humorist, and in *Between Engagements* (1988). The Playbox Theatre Company produced *Lennie Lower* in 1982 and many other plays by Dickins, including *The Death of Minnie* (1980) and *Royboys* (1987). The MELBOURNE THEATRE COMPANY produced *Reservoir by Night* (1985) and *Bedlam Autos* (1989). The STATE THEATRE Company of South Australia produced *Beautland* in Adelaide in 1985 and *The Death of Minnie* was staged at the HOLE-IN-THE-WALL THEATRE in Perth in 1990. ♥*Geoffrey Milne*

published plays
The Banana Bender (1980). Sydney: Currency Press 1981.
Beautland (1985). Sydney: Currency Press 1992.
Bridal Suite (1979). Melbourne: Yackandandah 1985.
The Death of Minnie (1980). Sydney: Currency Press 1981.
A Dickins Christmas (1992). Sydney: Currency Press 1992.
The Golden Goldenbergs (1980). Melbourne: Yackandandah: 1982.
The Horror of the Suburban Nature Strip (1978). Melbourne: Yackandandah: 1982.
Lennie Lower (1982). Melbourne: Yackandandah 1982.
Mag and Bag (1978). Melbourne: Yackandandah 1985.
One Woman Shoe (1981). Melbourne: Yackandandah 1984.
Remember Ronald Ryan (1994). Sydney: Currency Press 1994.
Royboys (1987). Sydney: Currency Press 1987.

Wendy Dickson

Designer. Born in Broken Hill (NSW). Studied painting in Sydney and stage design at Central School of Arts and Crafts (London) and Sydney College of the Arts. Has designed for Australian Elizabethan Theatre Trust, Lighthouse Company (Adelaide), State Theatre Company of South Australia (Adelaide); Union Theatre Repertory Company (Melbourne); Nimrod Theatre Company (Sydney) Old Tote Theatre Company (Sydney), Sydney Theatre Company, and in London for Royal Opera House, Covent Garden, and Old Vic Theatre Company. Also Australian and British films.

Wendy Dickson has worked extensively for the theatre since she returned to Australia from London—where she studied stage design and gained practical experience—to join the Union Theatre Repertory Company design team with Quentin Hole. Her designs have included costumes for *Camille* at the Sydney Opera House and Peter Shaffer's *The Royal Hunt of the Sun* for the 1966 Adelaide Festival and the premieres of Patrick White's THE HAM FUNERAL (1962) and THE SEASON AT SARSAPARILLA (1964). ♥*Pamela Zeplin*

Desmond Digby

Designer. Born 4 January 1933 in Auckland (New Zealand). Studied art at Auckland University College 1949–52, Slade School of Art (London) 1955–57. Settled in Sydney 1959. Designed for Australian Elizabethan Theatre Trust and Old Tote Theatre Company (Sydney). Resident designer with Australian Opera 1967–69. Many operatic commissions. Also illustrates children's books.

In the early 1960s Desmond Digby, now primarily a designer for opera, designed productions of plays in Sydney, Adelaide and Melbourne, including the premieres of Patrick White's THE SEASON AT SARSAPARILLA and *A Cheery Soul*. His costume and set designs for drama were colourful and detailed. His understanding of the text and feeling for style reinforced the richness of the stage picture in classics such as Sophocles's *Oedipus Rex* for the Theatre Project in Sydney in 1960, and *Hamlet* for the OLD TOTE THEATRE COMPANY in 1963 and *Henry V* for the Adelaide Festival of Arts in 1964. ♥*Tom Bannerman, Tom Brown*

Digger companies

After the First World War, digger companies, which had begun as all-male soldier concert parties, toured main centres in Australia and New Zealand, clearly identifying their origins with names like the Gallipoli Strollers, the Hello Mimi Entertainers and the Smart Set Diggers. They were promoted as 'warrior entertainers', and much was made of their war service and appearances before members of the Royal Family. The shows relied on realistic female impersonation and glamorous cross-dressing and minimal sets. The Smart Set Diggers included five female impersonators. Digger companies toured extensively for about a decade after the war, although as early as 1922 there were complaints that they had become too repetitive and 'lost their punch'. The Dinkum Diggers had a short life in 1929, while Pat Hanna's DIGGERS COMPANY survived until about 1933.

Concert parties formed during the Second World War relied more heavily on comic drag, and only the KIWIS REVUE COMPANY from New Zealand stayed together as a distinct troupe for long after the war. They quickly diversified their repertoire, however. ❧*Barbara Garlick*

Diggers Company

Professional touring revue company founded by New Zealand soldiers in Köln (Germany) 1919. Toured New Zealand 1919. Opened as Digger Pierrots, at Theatre Royal, Sydney, 24 April 1920. Playhouse, Melbourne, 17 July 1920. As Famous Diggers and Lady Artists at Arcadia Theatre, St Kilda (Melbourne), November 1920. As Famous Diggers Company at Cremorne Theatre, Brisbane, from November 1923 to 1925. Disbanded *c*.1933.

The longest lasting of the DIGGER COMPANIES that toured Australasia after the First World War was also known as Pat Hanna's Diggers Company. Hanna formed the troupe in Germany after the armistice, from the New Zealand Pierrots, a wartime concert party that had entertained troops in Egypt and France. J. C. WILLIAMSON'S brought his company across the Tasman to Australia in 1920, when J. AND N. TAIT Ltd was promoting the Smart Set Diggers and the All Diggers.

Billed as the Digger Pierrots, the New Zealanders—21 ex-servicemen, including ten musicians—presented songs and comedy routines interspersed with a few dramatic sketches. The Sydney *Bulletin* on 29 April 1920 thought they were only 'best amateur standard'. Among those praised was Hanna, a laconic comedian with a monologue, 'The Gospel According to Monash'. He rewrote this on topical subjects over the years and recorded it in the early 1930s as 'The Gospel According to Cricket', in which 'Pommieland' laments the slaughter of English bowling by Bill Woodfull and Don Bradman.

In November 1920 the 'Famous Diggers … and Lady Artists', based on the Digger Pierrots and organised by Hanna, opened at the Arcadia in St Kilda, where they built up a large repertoire of acts, including many comic scenes about life in uniform. Hanna teamed with another comedian, Joe Valli, and they built two characters who appeared in many of their early scenarios—short, energetic Private Joe Mulga (Valli) and lanky, lazy Private Chic Williams (Hanna). Both were fond of beer and Chic (short for Chicken, a running gag) was romantically inclined. In November 1923 the company moved to the Cremorne Theatre in Brisbane and stayed there for nearly two years. George Moon later took over Joe Mulga while Valli developed a new character, Jock McTavish, an eccentric Scot. The Diggers made three feature films, the last two directed by Hanna. *Diggers* in 1931 and *Diggers in Blighty* in 1933 linked wartime comedy scenarios. *Waltzing Matilda*, also in 1933, was set in the Great Depression and showed Chic as a poor, lonely swagman. Hanna went to the USA in 1934 and Valli went on to other film roles. ❧*Richard Fotheringham*

further reading
COLLIGAN, MIMI. Pat Hanna. *Australian Dictionary of Biography* 9. Melbourne University Press 1983.
PIKE, ANDREW and ROSS COOPER. *Australian Film 1900-1977.* Melbourne: Oxford University Press 1981.

reference
Diggers sketches. Australian Archives (Canberra) CRS A1336/1 item 14215.

Dimboola

Play by Jack Hibberd. **premiere** 6 July 1969, La Mama Theatre, Melbourne. Cast: Australian Performing Group. Director: Graeme Blundell. Music: Lorraine Milne. **published** Melbourne: Penguin 1984, in *A Country Quinella.*

The members of the audience for *Dimboola* are supposed to be guests at a wedding reception in a rural Australian township, like the Victorian one after which the play is named. *Dimboola* owes something to Anton Chekhov's play *The Wedding*, but is much more vulgar, bawdy and violent. Unlike Chekhov, JACK HIBBERD has his audience partake of the wedding banquet and enter into the festivities. He achieves participation without embarrassment because of the familiarity of the wedding reception ritual and, because the audience itself is involved, he excludes condescension from the satire. *Dimboola* is celebration as well as satire. It celebrates order, represented by the wedding. And it celebrates disorder, into which the occasion rapidly and enjoyably disintegrates, as incompatibilities and antagonisms—social, religious, domestic and sexual—come to the surface. *Dimboola* has succeeded in theatre-restaurants in Australia and overseas. In Sydney and Canberra productions ran for two years**.** Lately the play has been performed by country amateur dramatic groups, for which, Hibberd says, it was meant . ❧*J. D. Hainsworth*

Dinks and Onkus

Australia's first pair of knockabout acrobatic comedians, Jack Paterson (Dinks) and GEORGE WALLACE (Onkus) joined forces in 1919 because of the success of STIFFY AND MO. Short, stocky Wallace and tall, lanky Paterson were incongruous partners. As drunks and boxers, they fell about the stage to the delight of their audiences. Wallace had a particular talent for sliding across the stage on his face. Dinks and Onkus only ever appeared in HARRY CLAY's suburban Sydney theatres, where they were popular with audiences and critics alike from 1919 to 1924. No other vaudeville act is so well remembered purely from Clay's theatres. After they split, Paterson formed an act with his wife Trixie and Wallace moved to the FULLERS' circuit, where he soon became a leading comedian. ❧*Victoria Chance*

Directors and directing

Directing—giving theatrical coherence to works of dramatic imagination—became a special activity in the English-speaking theatre in the early 20th century. This was partly a reaction against the STAR SYSTEM, which had been virtually institutionalised under 19th-century actor-managers such as Henry Irving and Herbert Beerbohm Tree in London, EDWIN BOOTH and Richard Mansfield in the USA, and GEORGE COPPIN, BLAND HOLT and J. C. WILLIAMSON in Australia. But it was also bound up with revolutionary changes in playwriting, away from melodrama and romanticising toward more realistic, closely observed studies of character and social conflict. Important influences were coming from Europe, particularly from the Moscow Art Theatre, where Konstantin Stanislavsky and Vladimir Nemirovich-Danchenko were devising new approaches to interpreting text and building new methods of ensemble.

For some decades there was considerable semantic confusion over the words 'director' and 'producer'. In Australia and the United Kingdom, plays were 'produced'. The 'producer' was chief planner and controller in the staging of a play, with wide-ranging authority over the technical, physical and interpretative details of performance. But in the USA these functions were carried out by a 'director', while the entrepreneur, or financial-managerial boss, was the 'producer'. Eventually, in the 1960s, American usage prevailed here and in the United Kingdom. Nevertheless, GREGAN MCMAHON, who might well be considered the father of directing in Australia, was called a 'producer' until his death in 1941.

McMahon established himself as a remarkably skilful director when he ran the MELBOURNE REPERTORY THEATRE COMPANY in 1911–18, although the actors were almost all amateurs. As a professional actor he had worked mostly in conventional farce and melodrama, but he quickly grasped the significance of artistic breakthroughs overseas. He also saw opportunities for himself in bringing new realistic drama to Australia and, as a *régisseur*, exercising full responsibility for its presentation. When he went to Sydney in 1918, J. AND N. TAIT LTD engaged him to direct not only 'literary' plays but standard entertainment. Over the next ten to 15 years, he directed such popular visiting stars as Sara Allgood, MAURICE MOSCOVITCH, EMELIE POLINI and Guy Bates Post. But on the whole he found more scope for his talents with amateur or semiprofessional groups.

That the art of direction should have first taken hold in amateur rather than professional theatre is hardly surprising. Throughout the 1920s and 1930s the star system still predominated professionally. Moreover, Australian entrepreneurs had little interest in high-quality drama beyond proven box-office successes from the West End or Broadway. Even in the United Kingdom and Europe, amateur movements—such as the Stage Society in London, André Antoine's Théâtre Libre in Paris and the Moscow Art Theatre—had been first to recognise the need for some form of conceptual control over production. The real distinction in Australia was not between amateurism and professionalism—for experienced professionals often acted with amateur groups—but between amateurism and commercialism. McMahon was distinguished as a director by his capacity to transform his intelligent understanding of modern drama into theatrical terms that captured the mood, rhythm and intellectual meaning of a play. Technically he was unsurpassed in his command of lighting and every aspect of stage management. Indeed, he was perhaps the only director who made a fully successful transition from the age of gaslight to the age of electricity. His weakness, particularly in later years, was a lack of rapport with all but his finest actors. In his handling of large casts he tended to be either slack or dictatorial.

This weakness in McMahon was the great strength of DOLIA RIBUSH, a Latvian immigrant who leaned heavily on the theories of Stanislavsky and, like McMahon, depended mainly on amateurs. Ribush was rather more careful, thorough and detailed in his preparation than McMahon. According to the literary critic Arthur Phillips, he was also far less inclined to use 'short-cuts'—clichés and traditional 'business'—in the portrayal of character. The calibre of his contribution to theatre in Australia can be illustrated by Manning Clark's comment that one of his sources of inspiration to write *A History of Australia* was seeing the Ribush production of Douglas Stewart's *NED KELLY* in 1944.

In the commercial theatre, direction was a process of reproduction, rarely creation. Productions, whether of operetta, contemporary musicals or straight drama, were usually modelled on or even copied from the original overseas show. At best, direction was concerned with little more than arranging space to suit the histrionic requirements of lead actors from the United Kingdom or the USA. However, in 1948 the touring OLD VIC THEATRE COMPANY, despite its reliance on the star attributes of Laurence Olivier, showed well-disciplined ensemble in which the directorial abilities of John Burrell and Olivier himself were evident—if only rather fitfully. In 1949 John Gielgud's zestful, beautifully composed production of *Much Ado About Nothing*, done by the Shakespeare Memorial Theatre Company from Stratford-upon-Avon, was notable for its choreographic precision and sense of vocal harmony. More important, the postwar years brought some competent directors to the fore in Australia, including COLIN BALLANTYNE, JEANA BRADLEY, RHODA FELGATE, DORIS FITTON (who had trained under McMahon), Keith George, MAY HOLLINWORTH, SYDNEY JOHN KAY, BRETT RANDALL and JOHN SUMNER. Even though the general level of accomplishment was not yet high, audiences and actors alike were gradually recognising that the director's role was important. *Allan Ashbolt*

Since the Second World War

Until the mid-1960's, Australian professional theatre was strongly influenced by foreign interests. For the most part, entrepreneurs imported British or American directors to reproduce West End or Broadway successes. Directing was not a career for Australians to take very seriously.

However, the next 20 years were a period of rapid theatrical expansion, national self-confidence and artistic self-reliance. This was largely due to the work of a few farsighted and multi-talented directors who established fully professional theatre companies, lobbied successfully for federal and state government support and generated entertaining productions of Australian plays, international classics and contemporary works. These few company directors created the conditions in which a profession of directing could emerge and with it a distinctive Australian theatre influenced by, but no longer dependent upon, foreign ideologies. DORIS FITTON was the senior member of this group. In 1930, she founded INDEPENDENT THEATRE and attracted Sydney's best actors to appear in plays by Australian and foreign writers, many of which she directed herself. The Independent's greatest success was Fitton's production of Sumner Locke Elliott's play RUSTY BUGLES, but her most lasting contribution was to develop the careers of Australian actors, playwrights and directors.

In 1954, HUGH HUNT had a brief but profound influence on the development of Australian theatre through his play productions with the AUSTRALIAN ELIZABETHAN THEATRE TRUST. So too did ROBIN LOVEJOY, founder of the TRUST PLAYERS, 1958 to 1961. In the early 1960's, EDGAR METCALFE transformed a Perth semiprofessional company into the fully professional NATIONAL THEATRE COMPANY.

Other prominent pioneers were ALEXANDER ARCHDALE, who founded the Community Theatre and HAYES GORDON, founder of ENSEMBLE THEATRE COMPANY in Sydney, BRETT RANDALL, founder of the ST MARTIN'S THEATRE COMPANY in Melbourne and DOREEN WARBURTON, founder of Q THEATRE in western Sydney.

But two Englishmen trained in mainstream British theatre, ROBERT QUENTIN and JOHN SUMNER, had even more profound effects on the profession of directing in Australia. Sumner set up the Union Theatre Repertory Company, under the patronage of the University of Melbourne, well before there was government support for the performing arts. Over a total of 34 years, he guided the fortunes of the company—which became the MELBOURNE THEATRE COMPANY—with passionate energy and regularly directed its most successful productions. When the company took his production of Ray Lawler's SUMMER OF THE SEVENTEENTH DOLL on a national tour and then to London in 1956 he ushered in a new era for Australian theatre. BRUCE MYLES, GEORGE OGILVIE and many other distinguished directors began their careers with the Union Theatre Repertory Company. Perhaps the most notable was CARRILLO GANTNER, Sumner's general manager from 1973 to 1975. He went on to found the Playbox Theatre Company, the first professional company devoted entirely to the production of Australian plays.

ROBERT QUENTIN set up the NATIONAL INSTITUTE OF DRAMATIC ART (NIDA) in Sydney in 1958 and four years later he launched the OLD TOTE THEATRE COMPANY with a production of *The Cherry Orchard* that helped to establish Anton Chekhov as one of Australia's favourite playwrights. The Old Tote company profoundly affected audience tastes with seasons of classical and contemporary plays. A new generation of actors, directors and designers began their careers working on serious drama, including Australian plays. Many went on to establish their own organisations. JOHN BELL acted with the Old Tote company in 1963 and taught at NIDA in 1970. His production of THE LEGEND OF KING O'MALLEY by Michael Boddy and Bob Ellis in 1970 was one of the first to develop an individual Australian style—a self-conscious larrikinism that Bell has since carried over to Shakespeare. With others Bell founded the NIMROD THEATRE COMPANY in 1971, and in 1992 he founded the Bell Shakespeare Company.

The present writer's Old Tote production of Edward Albee's *Who's Afraid of Virginia Woolf?* in 1964 took the theatre in new directions. The writer became director of NIDA in 1969 and established the tiny JANE STREET THEATRE as a regular venue where new Australian playwrights, actors and directors could develop their skills. His NIDA–Jane Street production of David Williamson's *Don's Party* toured Australia in 1972 and 1973.

ALAN EDWARDS, who came from the United Kingdom to join the NIDA staff in 1964 and worked with the Old Tote company, founded the QUEENSLAND THEATRE COMPANY in 1969. An actor, director, administrator and astute politician, he built up the company over 20 years into the third largest in Australia. JOHN TASKER worked at NIDA in 1965 and went on to found—with COLIN BALLANTYNE—the South Australian Theatre Company. He directed PATRICK WHITE'S first three plays and had a long and controversial career as a freelance director. His productions of Jean-Claude van Itallie's *America Hurrah!* and Mart Crowley's *The Boys in the Band* in 1968 aroused the watchdogs of public morality and debates on CENSORSHIP.

RICHARD WHERRETT, was associate director of the Old Tote company from 1970 to 1972 and joint artistic director of Nimrod from 1974 to 1979, when he took over the SYDNEY THEATRE COMPANY and ran it with great success until 1990.

Drama directors emerge

Largely because of the political and artistic skills of these company directors, by the mid-1970s professional theatre companies had been established in most Australian capital cities. They stimulated the growth of an extensive network of smaller companies and government-sponsored regional PERFORMING-ARTS CENTRES in all states and territories. As the profession of theatre director became a practical reality, skilful drama directors began to emerge.

During the early 1970s, REX CRAMPHORN was one of Australia's most innovative directors. His productions of *The Tempest*, the group-devised *10 000 Miles Away*, and Alan Simpson's two pieces, *Muriel* and *Mariner*, will be remembered as high points in experimental theatre that anticipated many of the techniques developed in Europe by Eugenio Barba, Jerzy Grotowski and Ariane Mnouchkine.

RODNEY FISHER made a reputation for visually striking productions of unusual plays while he shared the direction of the South Australian Theatre Company in the late 1970s and he became one of the most successful directors in Australia. He moves easily between stage and screen.

AUBREY MELLOR served a long apprenticeship at NIDA before he was appointed co-director of Nimrod in 1981. He was artistic director of the Queensland Theatre Company from 1988 until 1993, when he moved to the same position with Playbox. He is a caring and intelligent director, sensitive to the needs of actors and at his best with plays by Chekhov, Shakespeare and Australian authors such as JANIS BALODIS and MICHAEL GOW.

GEORGE OGILVIE came to prominence as John Sumner's associate director in the Melbourne Theatre Company and later as director of the South Australian Theatre Company. Sensitivity, taste and intelligence characterise Ogilvie's productions, which are strongly influenced by French theatre and eastern philosophy. He is popular with actors and excels in stylish comedy and farce.

JIM SHARMAN, influenced by a family background in showgrounds and aware of developments in European and American theatre, stands out for consistent originality. He began his career with NIDA and the Old Tote company and quickly developed a highly personal approach to Shakespeare, contemporary plays and rock musicals. He did his most interesting work for the STATE THEATRE Company of South Australia—which he renamed Lighthouse—and he has created deep respect for the plays of Jean Genet, August Strindberg and Patrick White. JOHN GADEN, Michael Gow, WAYNE HARRISON, RODGER HODGEMAN, Peter Kingston, JOHN KRUMMEL, Jean-Pierre Mignon, ROBYN NEVIN and SIMON PHILLIPS are other directors who have made major contributions to theatre in Australia.

Three young directors of drama and musical theatre stand out. NEIL ARMFIELD has steadily developed a bold and imaginative style in highly successful productions of Ibsen, LOUIS NOWRA, Shakespeare, Patrick White and opera. Baz Luhrmann trained as an actor at NIDA and very rapidly established an international reputation as a director of film and opera. Gale Edwards, who served an apprenticeship with NIDA, established a youth theatre company in Adelaide and became an associate director with John Gaden of the State Theatre Company of South Australia. Her productions of Shakespeare, opera and musical theatre have revealed a major talent that combines energy, sensitivity and intelligence. Her reputation now extends beyond Australia. In 1994 she directed George Bernard Shaw's *Saint Joan* in London. She is the first Australian to be invited to direct a major production for the Royal Shakespeare Company. The success of these three directors suggests that Australian theatre has not only justified its existence in this country, but is now producing artists of international calibre. ❦*John Clark*

Disabled people's theatre

The evolution of disabled people's theatre from therapy to creative work has contributed greatly to the mental welfare of the participants. They cheerfully create theatre for the general public with the aim of entertaining first and educating second. The impetus came from drama therapists who, working in institutions during the 1970s, recognised a vast untapped resource of creativity among the intellectually and physically disabled, sufferers from multiple sclerosis and others. By the 1980s, theatrical groups were being established apart from institutions. In 1983 Annette Innis, a former actor who had worked in creative drama with the disabled, moved from Sydney to Brisbane and helped to establish Access Arts Theatre of the Disabled. Funding came from the community-arts board of the AUSTRALIA COUNCIL and the Queensland Department of Cultural Activities. Access Arts now uses guest directors from Brisbane theatre. Other groups that cater for disabled people who are interested in creative theatre include Artreach in Sydney, Arts in Action in Adelaide, Arts Access in Melbourne and Theatre of the Disabled in Perth. THEATRE OF THE DEAF is a distinct theatrical form, although deaf people are involved with disabled people's theatre. ❦*Nicky Bricknell*

further reading
CUMMINS, CHRIS. Mr Gennaro lifts the curtain on 'theatre of the handicapped'. *Weekend Australian* 3 November 1979.
INNIS, ANNETTE. Theatre of the Disabled. *Community Theatre* (ed. Richard Fotheringham). Sydney: Methuen 1987.

Agnes Dobson

Actor, director, dramatist. Born c.1900. Played child parts for her father, actor-manager Collet Dobson. Acted in Fullers' stock company as teenager, playing Camille at 15. In J. C. Williamson's stock companies. Acted in Adelaide with Ab Intra Studio Theatre, Adelaide Repertory Theatre, Esmond George Players and WEA Little Theatre in 1930s. Directed Independent Repertory Theatre in Adelaide 1936–40. Worked in radio from Second World War. Also acted in film and television. Died February 1987.

An actor and director of more than ordinary ability, Agnes Dobson founded Adelaide's Independent Repertory Theatre and ran it in Stow Hall. She was the only professional director in Adelaide amateur theatre and her productions were usually of a high standard as she invited actors from other groups to take part when necessary. An attractive, red-haired woman, she was impulsive and volatile, with an enormous capacity for work. She was often at one time acting in one show, directing another and rehearsing a third—not necessarily all for the same group. COLIN BALLANTYNE said of her: 'When she directed you, you knew she was right—everything was rhythmical and worked in remarkable ways to the total rhythm of the stage ... A wilful woman. A ferocious woman. I think she brought a new intelligence and direction to the entire theatre in this city ... She taught the secrets of vitality.'

Dobson courageously and skilfully adapted classic plays and books to her tiny stage. 'She shaped the hundreds of pages of Swinburne's trilogy *Chastelard*, *Bothwell* and *Mary Stuart* into a presentable three-act form, then produced it ... a definite triumph for her', said *Progress in Australia* in 1937. In 1938 Dobson produced *Antony and Cleopatra*, portraying the lovers as middle-aged; Cleopatra was a rather staid woman in Greek costume. In the 1936 South Australian centenary play competition Dobson's *Dark Brother* tied for second place. It dealt with Aboriginal life and half-castes, and showed white settlers subconsciously influenced by Aboriginal spirit-places. ❦*Thelma Afford*

The Doll Trilogy

Three three-act plays by Ray Lawler: *Kid Stakes*, *Other Times*, *Summer of the Seventeenth Doll*. **premiere as trilogy** 12 February 1977, Russell Street Theatre, Melbourne, by Melbourne Theatre Company. Cast: Christine Amor, Peter Curtin, David Downer, Sandy Gore, Irene Inescort, Bruce Myles, Carole Skinner. Designer: Anne Fraser. Director: John Sumner. **revived** by Melbourne and Sydney Theatre Companies 1985. **published** Sydney: Currency Press 1978, revised edition 1983.

It is unusual for a play to inspire a sequel but it is stranger still for a play to become a sequel to another that emerges 20 years later. Even more extraordinary is the case of SUMMER OF THE SEVENTEENTH DOLL. RAY LAWLER made his 1955 play into the sequel to two other plays—*Kid Stakes* and *Other Times*, first performed on 2 December 1975 and 14 December 1976 respectively. *Summer of the Seventeenth Doll* tells of Barney and Roo, sugar-cane cutters who have come to Melbourne annually for 16 years to spend the 'layoff' with the barmaids Olive and Nancy. In the 17th summer, however, Pearl replaces Barney's girl Nancy, who has left to be married. Nancy is not seen in the *Doll*, but Lawler gives a strong sense of the vivacity and intelligence that is missing with her in the 17th summer. In *Kid Stakes* and *Other Times* she is at the centre of the action. Both retrospective sequels are marked by the liveliness, and the psychological and period interest that distinguish their predecessor; but neither seems designed to stand alone.

Barney, Roo and Olive are defined in the *Doll* as people who have essentially ceased to grow, and in the earlier summers they are accordingly thoroughly recognisable as the older selves we have met before. In each of the earlier plays, one of the girls is faced with a romantic option. In *Kid Stakes*, in the first summer, Olive has the safe option of Dickie Pouncett, who is studying advertising at night school. He throws into relief the happy days and glamorous nights that Roo seems to offer. At the same time, Nancy is establishing her understanding with the more shop-soiled Barney. In *Other Times*, in the ninth summer, Josef Hultz offers Nancy the world of intellectual sophistication that she presumably seeks in her eventual marriage to 'that book bloke' Harry Allaway. She is still the life of the party in *Other Times*, but more inclined to drink alone, out of a sense of what she missed in her life. Her decision to stick with Barney has none of the air of bobby-sox romance that marks Olive's unswerving and uncomplicated commitment to Roo; it is a weary, self-critical recognition that she cannot have everything, and may not deserve to, anyway.

Kid Stakes and *Other Times* elaborate on things explored or implicit in the *Doll*, and they are necessarily incomplete. Where the *Doll* invoked its own past and hypothetical future in the dramatisation of present conflicts, they rely upon a substantiation that is deferred to the third play. Neither *Kid Stakes* nor *Other Times* matches the *Doll* for richness and concentration, but they offer a distinctive and affectionate revisiting of the values, verbal habits, and bric-a-brac of suburban Australia just before and just after the Second World War. A sense of meeting old friends again is evident in the conservative form, as well as the familiar substance, of *Kid Stakes* and *Other Times*. Logistics mean the three plays are unlikely to be staged together often. But the appearance of the trilogy in 1976 proved a great occasion for celebrating the theatrical creation of images of cultural distinctiveness for Australians. ❧*Peter Fitzpatrick*

further reading
Sumner, John. *Recollections at Play—A life in Australian theatre.* Melbourne: University Press 1993.

Don's Party
Play in two acts by David Williamson. **premiere** 22 July 1971 at Pram Factory, Melbourne, by Australian Performing Group. Cast: Lindy Davies, Kerry Dwyer, Graham Hartley, Ros Horin, Bruce Knappett, Evelyn Krape, Wilfred Last, Yvonne Marini, Rod Moore, John Smythe, Tony Taylor. Director: Bruce Spence. **published** Sydney and London: Currency Methuen 1973; in David Williamson's *Collected Plays* 1, 1986.

In his widely performed *Don's Party* David Williamson is in territory that has become characteristically his—the crises, complacency and self-dramatising of the affluent, educated middle-class. The party, intended to celebrate a Labor election victory after a long spell in the political wilderness, turns sour as that hope—and the energetic flirtations of most of the guests—comes to nothing. The political context is significant for what commitment to Labor politics means to the men and for the way Labor's waning electoral fortunes provide a structural analogy to the progressive disenchantment of all the guests. But the primary focus of the play is on specific kinds of male role-playing, particularly in relation to the rituals of mateship and sexual competitiveness. The men at the party—old mates, except for a misplaced Liberal-voting accountant—set the conversational agenda, in which jokes fail to cover a multitude of insecurities. The richly comic rudeness of the piece is juxtaposed with a mounting impression of the hollowness and desperation of the lives of the characters, especially the young women. The play has been produced in London and Scandinavia. ❧*Peter Fitzpatrick*

Doppio Teatro
Professional dramatic company in Adelaide, founded in 1983 by Christopher Bell and Teresa Crea. Performs in Italian and English.
artistic director Teresa Crea.

Doppio Teatro (Double Theatre) offers some of the best bicultural theatre in Australia. It started performing Italian works such as Luigi Pirandello's *Cece*, but soon began to develop original works reflecting the experiences of Italians in Australia and Australians of Italian descent, such *Il cabaret dell'emigrante* (The emigrant's cabaret) in 1984, *Un pugno di terra* (A fistful of earth) in 1986, *Just Call Me Jo* and *La madonna emigrante* (The emigrant Madonna) in 1987. *Ricordi* (Memories) in 1989, devised by the director Teresa Crea and the performers Josie Composto Eberhard, Lucia Mastrantone and Antonietta Morgillo, epitomised Doppio Teatro's best work. Sparely staged and lit, *Ricordi* comprised vignettes and recollections by Italian women of emigration and their experiences in Australia. Doppio Teatro took it to Melbourne and Sydney in 1989 under the auspices of the Australian Elizabethan Theatre Trust. At the Adelaide Festival the company presented *The Olive Tree* in 1990 and *Una festa di nozze* (A wedding feast), a burlesque on Italian weddings and attitudes to marriage, in 1992. In 1991 it toured *Red Like the Devil*, based on experiences of Italians interned at Loveday (SA) during the Second World War. *Filling the Silence* in 1994 featured Lucia Mastrantone and the musician Linsey Pollak. ❧*Murray Bramwell*

Desmonde Downing
Designer. Born 1920. Became actor and singer after wartime army service. Designer for stage from 1947. Designer for Australian Broadcasting Commission television from 1957. Died 11 July 1975.

An innovative and original designer, Desmonde Downing studied electronics and architectural drawing and based her sets on her own research to ensure period authenticity. In 1956 she designed the sets and costumes for the Australian Elizabethan Theatre Trust's production of Douglas Stewart's *Ned Kelly* in Sydney; Sidney Nolan created the backcloths. In the same year Downing employed large-scale projected imagery for the first time in the Elizabethan Trust Opera Company's production of Mozart's *The Magic Flute*. ❧*Christopher Chapman*

reference
Material on Downing is held by the National Gallery of Australia (Canberra) and the Performing Arts Museum (Melbourne), which has stage and costume designs.

Henrietta Drake-Brockman

Dramatist. Born 27 July 1901 in Perth. Originally Henrietta Jull. Daughter of first Public Service Commissioner and first female medical practitioner in Western Australia. Educated in Perth (WA), Scotland and Mittagong (NSW). Studied painting. Married in 1921 to civil engineer who became commissioner for northwest. Began writing in Broome (WA) 1921–26. Founding member of Western Australia Fellowship of Australian Writers. Published seven novels, short stories and nonfiction. Died 8 March 1968 in Perth.

Henrietta Drake-Brockman was a vocal advocate for Australian drama at a time when such advocacy was rare. Her own major contribution was MEN WITHOUT WIVES, a three-act realist drama of the northwest which won the Commonwealth Sesquicentenary Prize for a play in 1938. Her other full-length play, *Hot Gold*, is a large-cast melodrama about life and crime on the goldfields. *The Blister*, which was published in a worldwide anthology, is a compelling and colourful short piece set in Broome. A young pearler finds a shell with a promising blister, and then must choose between the surety of selling it unopened at a fixed price and gambling on the promise it holds. While he dreams of the wealth that could return him to his upper-class origins, his barmaid lover more realistically grieves for the end of their happiness. Most of Drake-Brockman's inspiration for plays and novels stemmed from her own years at Broome in the 1920s, during which she travelled extensively and began writing under the pseudonym Henry Drake. She was an early member of the REPERTORY CLUB in Perth and a radio writer and broadcaster. ❧*Katharine Brisbane*

published plays
The Blister (1940). London: Gollancz 1940 in *Fifty One-Act Plays*. Sydney: Angus and Robertson 1955 in *Men Without Wives and Other Plays*.
Dampier's Ghost (1933). Sydney: Angus and Robertson 1955 in *Men Without Wives and Other Plays*.
Hot Gold (1940). Sydney: Angus and Robertson 1955 in *Men Without Wives and Other Plays*.
The Lion Tamer. Sydney: Angus and Robertson 1948.
The Man From the Bush (1933). Melbourne: Dramatists' Club 1934 in *Eight Plays by Australians*.
Men Without Wives (1938). Perth: Paterson 1938. Sydney: Angus and Robertson 1955.
Order of the Day (1942). *Southerly* (Sydney) December 1942.

The Dreamers

Play in two acts by Jack Davis. **premiere** 2 February 1982, Dolphin Theatre, Perth, by Swan River Stage Company. Cast: Wayne Byndor, Jack Davis, Luke Fuller, Michael Fuller, Shane McIntyre, Lynette Narkle, Maxine Narkle, Trevor Parfitt. Choreography: Richard Walley. Designer: Keith Edmundson. Director: Andrew Ross. **published** Sydney: Currency Press 1982, revised (1984) in *Plays from Black Australia* 1989.

A strikingly original and deceptively simple play, *The Dreamers* is JACK DAVIS's most performed and probably best-known dramatic work. It forms the second part of his trilogy *The First-Born*. Thematically and chronologically it follows NO SUGAR, which was written later, in 1984–85. The trilogy concludes with *Barungin (Smell the Wind)* of 1988. Most of the action in *The Dreamers* is set in the Wallitch family kitchen, where sons, daughters, cousins, parents and one grandparent face many choices—to rebel or to conform, to fight or to compromise. The humour, endurance and resilience of black Australians stand out during conflict, togetherness, drunkenness and sobriety. Davis draws his dramatic strength from the extended family that he explores so perceptively in *The Dreamers*. The naturalism is most appealing but the play offers much more than realistic observation. Davis's liberal use of the Nyungar language and his framing of scenes with Aboriginal dancing strongly connect the play with tradition. *The Dreamers* was the first Aboriginal play to be taken on a national tour. In 1983 the AUSTRALIAN ELIZABETHAN THEATRE TRUST toured a production by the NATIONAL THEATRE COMPANY, directed by Andrew Ross, with Ernie Dingo as Eli. The climax of the six-month tour was a four-week season in the Playhouse of the Sydney Opera House. Davis has said that these 30 performances 'will always stick in my memory and are a highlight of my career'. All critics agreed that the play also marked a new level of achievement for Aboriginal and Australian drama. Ross again directed it in May 1987, when it was remounted in Portsmouth, the first Aboriginal play performed in the United Kingdom. ❧*Adam Shoemaker*

further reading
DAVIS, JACK. The Dreamers. *Meanjin* 43/1 (Melbourne, March 1984).
SHOEMAKER, ADAM. An interview with Jack Davis. *Westerly* (Perth) December 1982.

Marien Dreyer

Dramatist. Born 1911 at Mornington (Vic.). Left school at 14 to become stenographer. Published first of some 4000 short stories at 16. Became full-time journalist 1942. Won prizes for one-act plays 1959. Joint winner of Australian Elizabethan Theatre Trust–General Motors Holden play award with *Wish No More* 1961. First full-length play staged 1962. Won Sydney Journalists' Club 1963–64 play award with *Bandicoot on a Burnt Ridge*. Banjo Patterson Memorial Award for one-act play 1965. Society of Women Writers' Award 1976. Also wrote radio plays. Died January 1980 in Sydney.

Marien Dreyer was one of many Australian playwrights whose talent never received the encouragement it needed. A childhood ambition to become an actor was frustrated by the loss of a leg at ten. She became a journalist with a realistic understanding of character and an ear for spoken language. Her plays, like her columns in *New Idea* magazine, were based on keen observation, particularly in the Kings Cross district of Sydney, where she spent most of her life. She tied with Lawrence Collinson, John Pinkney and ALAN SEYMOUR for the AUSTRALIAN ELIZABETHAN THEATRE TRUST–General Motors Holden play award, but her *Wish No More* was not produced because it required a large cast and an elaborate wardrobe. Her only play produced professionally was BANDICOOT ON A BURNT RIDGE. After it won the Sydney Journalists' Club award she received a publication offer from a newspaper and contracts from the Trust, an Adelaide company and the Hampstead Theatre Club in London, but all eventually lapsed. Even the Union Theatre Repertory Company production in Melbourne in 1965 was unsatisfying. ❧*Katharine Brisbane*

reference
Dreyer's unpublished plays *Bandicoot on a Burnt Ridge* and *Wish No More* are in the Hanger Collection, Fryer Library, University of Queensland (Brisbane).

The Drovers

Play in one act by Louis Esson. **premiere** 1923, Temperance Hall, Melbourne, by Pioneer Players. Director: George Dawe. **published** London: Henderson 1920. Sydney: Mulga 1944 in *Six One-Act Australian Plays*. Brisbane: University of Queensland Press 1977 in *Five Plays for Stage, Radio and TV*.

The Drovers is the best of the terse one-act dramas of situation at which LOUIS ESSON excelled. It is set on the vast Barkly Tableland. As the play opens there is a stampede of cattle offstage, and Briglow Bill, a casually heroic drover straight out of the bush legend of the 1890s, is carried on injured. The naive protests of a 'new-chum' jackeroo speak for the audience as the play reveals the relentless logic of the stock trails, whereby Briglow Bill must be left to die in the camp while the drovers press on to find water for the restless cattle. His mates make laconic farewells and leave Bill to breathe his last under the stars, as he wants, with only an Aborigine called Pigeon to keep him company and chant a lament over his body. In spite of reliance on the romantic conventions of the bush legend the play has power through its simplicity and concise narrative. The only element that dates it today is Pigeon, a stock figure not far removed from the conventional blackfellows of 19th-century melodrama. *John McCallum*

The Duchess of Coolgardie

Play by Euston Leigh and Cyril Clare. **premiere** 19 September 1896, Theatre Royal, Drury Lane, London. Director: John Coleman. **Australian premiere** 5 November 1898, Criterion Theatre, Sydney. Cast: F. C. Appleton, George Buller, Alfred Dampier, Rose Dampier, Edmund Duggan, John Forde, Katherine Russell, Johnson Weir. Designer: Edward Vaughan. Director: Alfred Dampier.

Augustus Harris, manager of the Theatre Royal, Drury Lane, died suddenly in 1896, leaving the London theatre without its autumn spectacular melodrama. *The Duchess of Coolgardie* was hurriedly devised, with the backing of a Perth millionaire, Herbert Love. It was set on the Western Australian goldfields and Australia was seen romantically through the eyes of the hero, an English barrister turned gold-digger. The play was a long-running success. ALFRED DAMPIER's production in Sydney two years later was closer to reality. The *Sydney Morning Herald* on 7 November 1898 commended Edward Vaughan for a 'not too faithful' depiction of the 'cheerless and the ugly' scenery, but noted that 'the theatre was well filled with people who had been to the West, and as a rule could think of nothing romantic in life as they found it there'. The season lasted two weeks, thanks largely to the villain, 'one of the most picturesque scoundrels imaginable'. *Richard Fotheringham*

Edmund Duggan

Actor, dramatist. Born c.1862 at Lismore (Ireland). Came to Victoria at nine with parents. As youth, with elder brother P. J. Duggan founded the Roscians, amateur Shakespeare society in Melbourne. Toured widely c.1884–1900 with George Titherage, Alfred Dampier, Charles Holloway and own companies. Had plays staged from 1891. Worked as actor and stage director for brother-in-law William Anderson 1900–12, 1917–30. Died 2 August 1938 in Melbourne. Brother of actor Eugenie Duggan.

Edmund Duggan wrote plays that were dour moral tracts and he had his biggest successes in collaboration with BERT BAILEY, whose more humane views and lighter comic touch made their *THE SQUATTER'S DAUGHTER* a great success in 1907. Less popular were *The Man from Outback* in 1909 and *The Native Born* in 1913. Duggan also contributed a little to *ON OUR SELECTION* (1912). He learned his stagecraft as a provincial actor in the 1880s and 1890s, but showed little of it in *The Democrat*, an early attempt to dramatise the Eureka Stockade. A sermon on *noblesse oblige* rather than democracy, it had small success in Sydney in 1891 or in Adelaide in 1897, or—as *The Southern Cross*—in Newcastle (NSW) and Sydney in 1907. *MY MATE* (1911), an early attempt to present male mateship on the stage, was more successful. Duggan's last known play was a satire, *The Killjoys*, in 1926. He specialised in acting Irish and Jewish roles, with an approach which even in his time was sometimes considered racially offensive. About 1910 he described Aborigines in his 'musical extravaganza' *A Spirit of the Bush* as a 'worthless and indolent people'. He played Dad Rudd in *On Our Selection* while Bailey was overseas in 1920, and directed and starred in another STEELE RUDD play, *The Rudd Family*, in 1928. *Richard Fotheringham*

published play
On Our Selection with Bert Bailey, Steele Rudd and Beaumont Smith. Sydney: Currency Press 1984.

further reading
Williams, Margaret. Edmund Duggan. *Australian Dictionary of Biography* 8. Melbourne University Press 1981.

Eugenie Duggan

Actor. Born c.1872. Made professional stage debut as Juliet 1890. Starred in provincial companies of Dan Barry and Charles Holloway. Married entrepreneur William Anderson in Melbourne, 30 November 1898. Leading actress in Anderson's company 1900 until they separated in 1920s. Ran private drama school in Melbourne. Died 2 November 1936 in Melbourne. Younger sister of actor and dramatist Edmund Duggan.

For more than 20 years as the star of WILLIAM ANDERSON's company, Eugenie Duggan played roles ranging from Roxanne in Edmond Rostand's *Cyrano de Bergerac* to the squatter's daughter in *The Winning Ticket* by Anderson and Temple Harrison, and in melodramas such as *The Worst Woman in London*. *Richard Fotheringham*

William Duke

Mechanist, scene-painter. Baptised 16 July 1815 in Cork (Ireland). Arrived in Sydney 16 December 1840. Scene-painter and mechanist at Royal Victoria Theatre. Set up as portrait painter in Auckland (New Zealand). Arrived in Hobart 7 May 1845. Worked as scene-painter and professional artist. Moved to Melbourne about 1851. Died 17 October 1853 in Melbourne.

The versatile William Duke was an outstanding scene-painter, a theatre painter and a decorator of illustrated lectures. He also painted portraits, landscapes and whaling scenes and he created a grand diorama. His scene-painting and artistic sense were well regarded by the Hobart press and his work was compared favourably with that of EDWARD OPIE, with whom he decorated the QUEEN'S THEATRE ROYAL in Melbourne. *Caroline von Oppeln*

further reading
OPPELN, CAROLINE VON. William Duke. *Dictionary of Australian Artists, Photographers and Engravers, 1770–1870* (ed. Joan Kerr). Melbourne: Oxford University Press 1992.
WESLEY, C. A. William Duke. *Art Bulletin of Tasmania* 1983.

Catherine Duncan

Actor, dramatist. Born 17 March 1915 in Launceston (Tas.). Left Melbourne University after 18 months to become professional actor. Acted and wrote for radio 1935–47. Joined Workers' Theatre Group in Melbourne 1936. Member of Australian National Film Board 1945. Has lived in France since 1947.

A prolific radio writer until she turned to writing for documentary film in 1945, Catherine Duncan has also been an innovator in writing and directing in the theatre. She employed stylised settings and cinematic lighting techniques in *Thirteen Dead*, a 'dramatic reportage' on a mine disaster at Wonthaggi (Vic.), which she co-wrote and produced in 1937 for the New Theatre Club in Melbourne. In 1986 she based a surrealist sound-and-light fantasy, *Shadow of Light*, on images made by collage. Duncan won a New Theatre League competition in Sydney in 1938 with *The Sword Sung*, a feminist verse play with a debt to the agit-prop style. There is greater control over the dramatic effectiveness of verse in *Sons of the Morning*, which was written for radio and adapted for the stage and won the 1945 PLAYWRIGHTS' ADVISORY BOARD competition. It is set in a Cretan farmhouse in the during the German invasion and is a romantic depiction of Greek partisans and Australian soldiers. While the message is anti-war, the play's resolution accommodates an optimistic attitude towards the postwar era. ❦*Angela O'Brien*

published plays
Sons of the Morning (1945). Sydney: Mulga Publications 1946.
Thirteen Dead (1937). Melbourne: New Theatre 1993.

Beverley Dunn

Actor. Born in Melbourne. Began acting with Melbourne Little Theatre Company 1952. Then Melbourne Theatre Company and South Australian Theatre Company (Adelaide). Solo shows in Australia and overseas from 1978.

Beverley Dunn has made a successful career as a solo performer in shows she has devised and written. She opened her first, *As We Are*, an anthology of Australian writing, at the 1978 FESTIVAL OF PERTH. Arts Council tours of all states followed, plus two MELBOURNE THEATRE COMPANY seasons—185 performances in all. She performed her second solo show, *To Botany Bay on a Bondi Tram*, celebrating the writer Mary Gilmore, for the Melbourne Theatre Company in 1984 and the Northside Theatre Company in Sydney in 1987. In 1986 the show was part of a cultural exchange with Boston (USA), and in 1988 Dunn presented it in Melbourne, New Zealand, the USA and the United Kingdom. In Melbourne in 1989 she appeared in LINDA ARONSON'S monodrama *Reginka's Lesson*. Dunn's first stage success was in the title-role of Jean Anouilh's *Antigone* with Melbourne Little Theatre in 1952. With this company she was also notable as Kattrin in John Van Druten's *I Remember Mama* and as Joan of Arc in Anouilh's *The Lark* in 1956, a role she has made particularly her own. ❦*Richard Lane*

Wladyslaw Dutkiewicz

Actor, designer, director. Born in 1918 in Lviv (Ukraine). Trained in theatre in Poland and studied painting in Paris. Assistant director, designer and decor artist of Lwów Opera Theatre before Second World War. Emigrated to Australia and settled in Adelaide 1949. Began designing for Adelaide Theatre Group 1950. Formed acting school 1957. Formed Art Studio Players 1958.

Wladyslaw Dutkiewicz kept Adelaide theatregoers in touch with events in contemporary theatre and founded the first amateur group to attempt to bring relevant aspects of the Stanislavsky method of acting to the stage in the city. He is best known as a painter, but the theatre was his first love. He had years of Stanislavskian training in Poland. In Paris on a painting scholarship from 1937, he immersed himself in French avant-garde theatre. After the Second World War he formed Nowy Teatr in the Hohenfels displaced persons' camp in Bavaria, writing his own scripts, and toured the American zone of Europe.

Lack of English prevented Dutkiewicz from acting when he came to Adelaide but he worked in technical aspects of theatre and created outstanding sets, posters and programs. In 1950 he designed the ADELAIDE THEATRE GROUP'S production of *A Man Must Live*. 'No finer sets have been seen on the nonprofessional stage here in the last 20 years', wrote the critic C. B. de Boehme. A serious accident in 1956 left Dutkiewicz with brain damage and memory loss, but he painted sets for Noël Coward's *Fallen Angels* later in the year and for William Inge's *Bus Stop* in 1957, both for Independent Productions.

At the request of leading theatre workers he set up a school for training in the Stanislavsky method in 1957. Next year he formed the Art Studio Players. Their first production was Maxim Gorky's *The Lower Depths*, translated from Russian by Dutkiewicz. He also played Kotylyov. Max Harris described it as 'a freak theatrical tour de force'. The next production was Henrik Ibsen's *Master Builder*, in which Dutkiewicz eschewed period costume.

In 1959 the ADELAIDE UNIVERSITY THEATRE GUILD had its first full-scale practical experience of the method when Dutkiewicz directed and played Antoine in Jean-Jacques Bernard's *The Unquiet Spirit*. It was followed by Arthur Miller's *All My Sons* and Arnold Wesker's *Roots* in 1961, Bernard Kops's *The Dream of Peter Mann* and August Strindberg's *The Father* in 1962. The Art Studio Players disbanded in 1963, when Dutkiewicz had resumed painting. In 1967 he directed Ibsen's *The Wild Duck* at the invitation of the university guild and the *Advertiser* found him beguiling, with 'an unerring eye for form and composition'. Dutkiewicz did his last acting on television. Many of his students became outstanding actors. ❦*Josephine Landsberg*

Edward Dyson

Dramatist. Born 4 March 1865 at Morrison (Vic.). Worked in mines and factories, as hawker and briefly as journalist in Melbourne. Freelance writer c.1887–c.1919. Died 22 August 1931 in Melbourne.

A major short-story writer, a 'Bohemian of the *Bulletin*' and perhaps the most financially successful freelance author of his time, Edward Dyson began writing plays mainly for money. He did token localisations of English melodramas for BLAND HOLT from about 1901 to 1907. One of these became *The Breaking of the Drought*. He adapted *The Golden Shanty*, his famous 1887 story of a bush pub built from gold-bearing clay, and it had a two-week season in Sydney in 1913. So did *Fact'ry 'Ands* in 1916. Dyson set this play in a paper-bag factory and devised a murder mystery plot to link his stories of city slum life. The mystery was tolerated rather than enjoyed, and humorous moments carried the evening. The *Sydney Morning Herald* complained on 28 February 1916 that, although the set aimed at 'sordid realism', there was so much farce and romance in the play that making paper bags was 'pretty well excluded'. ❧*Richard Fotheringham*

further reading
Davison, Graeme. Edward Dyson. *Australian Dictionary of Biography* 8. Melbourne University Press 1981.

Laurence Eastwood

Designer. Born 1 December 1948 in London. Began training in architecture. Studied design and theatre production at E15 Acting School (London) 1969–70. Came to Sydney 1970. Co-founder of Nimrod Theatre Company and production manager 1970–76. Free lance since 1976. Has also designed for ballet, film and television. Married to Debbie Baile, actor and film art director.

As production manager for the Nimrod Theatre Company Laurence Eastwood was responsible for more than 40 productions and was in effect resident designer. 'His role in the huge success of Nimrod at this time should not be underestimated', the director Richard Wherrett has said. Eastwood came to Australia at the invitation of Wherrett, with whom he had worked at the E15 Acting School in London, to join in converting stables that opened in 1970 as the Nimrod Street Theatre. He also contributed to Vivian Fraser's design for the Nimrod Theatre in Surry Hills—the only real use he was able to make at Nimrod of his architectural training. Eastwood's landmark production designs for Nimrod included *The Elocution of Benjamin Franklin* by Steve J. Spears, *The Removalists* by David Williamson, *Summer of the Seventeenth Doll* by Ray Lawler, *The Tooth of Crime* by Sam Shepard, *Hamlet* and *Much Ado About Nothing*. In 1987 he designed the Sydney Theatre Company's production of Williamson's *Emerald City* in the Drama Theatre of the Sydney Opera House. Its large stage gave full scope to his architectural propensities and prevailing post-modernist influences. ❧*Tom Bannerman*

Eric Edgley

Comedian, entrepreneur, producer. Born August 1899 in Birmingham (England). Probably originally Eric Edgley White. Came to Australia 1920. Performed in revue with brothers Clem Dawe, Eric Dawe, Leslie White, Dick White and sister Dorothy White from 1923. Married dancer Phyllis Amery, who died in childbirth 1930. Took revue company to England 1935. Returned to Australia after South African tour with Clem Dawe 1940. Married dancer Edna Luscombe 1940. Became entrepreneur 1952. Imported Soviet companies from 1960. Died 3 February 1967 in Perth. Father of entrepreneur Michael Edgley and actor Phillip Edgley.

Eric Edgley, who brought a stream of Soviet companies to Australia, became an entrepreneur after a successful career in revue as performer and producer. He was one of the five children of an accountant who occasionally played the violoncello in theatre orchestras and his wife, who was a pantomime dancer when she married. All the children went onto the stage. After their father died Eric and his younger brother Clem toured with the Eight Lancashire Lads. When this troupe was disbanded in the First World War they branched out as the Two Lancashire Lads. In 1916 they took the names Edgley and Dawe and played leading variety theatres as comedians and eccentric dancers. Bert Bailey saw them performing in pantomime in Edinburgh in 1919 and persuaded them to come to Australia.

They made their debut in a J. C. Williamson's pantomime in 1920. They decided to stay and, after other members of their family joined them, they created their own topical revue company. They called it Midnight Frolics, after a Florenz Ziegfeld revue in New York, and advertised 'London's brightest and smartest sketches, song scenas and so forth'. The 20-member company successfully toured Australia until 1935, when shortage of theatres prompted Edgley and Dawe to it take to England. The venture was a financial failure. Edgley and Dawe returned to Australia in 1940 and appeared in revues for J. C. Williamson's, including *Funny Side Up* and *Thumbs Up* in Sydney in 1942. In the late 1940s, after four years of radio entertainment, they revived their revues in Hobart.

They settled in Perth and in 1952 leased His Majesty's Theatre, where Edgley and Dawe Attractions began presenting local shows and east-coast successes. Eric Edgley's eldest son, Phillip, appeared on stage with his father and uncle. Clem Dawe died suddenly in 1955, but Eric, Edna and Phillip Edgley continued the business. Losses in the late 1950s—attributed to rising costs and competition from television—prompted Eric Edgley to seek new attractions overseas in 1960. A meeting in London with the Soviet ambassador led to an invitation to Moscow for discussions with the Soviet Ministry of Culture. Over the next seven years, Edgley brought to Australia more than 20 attractions from the Soviet Union, including the Bolshoi Ballet and the Great Moscow Circus and famous regional groups such as the Georgian Dancers. After Eric Edgley's death in 1967 his family continued the company. Phillip Edgley soon bowed out because of ill-health, but Edna and Michael Edgley continued as directors of the company. ❧*Victoria Chance*

Michael Edgley MBE

Entrepreneur. Born 17 December 1943 in Melbourne. Son of entrepreneur Eric Edgley and dancer Edna Edgley. Joined Edgley and Dawe Attractions as assistant accountant at 19. Became director 1967. Managing director of J. C. Williamson's 1971. Principal of Michael Edgley International Pty Ltd and Edgley Ventures Pty Ltd.

The Michael Edgley organisation has introduced a wealth of circus, ballet, theatrical and other performing talent to Australian audiences, chiefly from Russian and Chinese sources. Michael Edgley's father, Eric Edgley, died in 1967 and at the age of 23 he assumed direction of the family company, through which had worked his way since finishing high school at 19. In 1968 he presented his first venture, a tour by the Great Moscow Circus, which attracted 1·2 million people and grossed more than $7 million. This success gave Edgley the capital and confidence to launch his own entrepreneurial career. At 27 he was managing director of J. C. WILLIAMSON'S but the failing firm's partnership with Edgleys lasted only a year. In 1991 Edgley and two partners formed Edgley Ventures Pty Ltd, which presents theatrical spectacles throughout Australasia and in Asia and the United Kingdom. ❦*Mark St Leon*

Marion Edward

Actor. Born 13 March 1935 in Melbourne. Left convent school at 14. Worked as telephonist before training as preschool teacher. Began studying voice with Lorna Forbes. In Melbourne amateur theatre 1955. Joined Union Theatre Repertory Company as assistant stage manager 1959. Has played more than 30 roles for Melbourne Theatre Company. Toured for J. C. Williamson's in *Oliver!* in 1964 and *Hello, Dolly!* in 1965. Many television roles. Sister of actor and stage manager Bryan Edward.

A versatile actor and powerful singer with a strong stage presence, Marion Edward has proven her range in a career encompassing drama, comedy, musical theatre, revue, music-hall, film, radio and television. She learned her craft in amateur theatre and first acted professionally with the Union Theatre Repertory Company in Jean Anouilh's *The Waltz of the Toreadors*. Her early roles included Lady Bracknell in Oscar Wilde's *The Importance of Being Earnest* in 1961 and Mavis Knott in Patrick White's THE SEASON AT SARSAPARILLA in 1962. Her roles for the MELBOURNE THEATRE COMPANY include the slovenly Beatrice in Paul Zindel's *The Effect of Gamma Rays on Man-in-the-Moon Marigolds* in 1970, the childlike Lola in William Inge's *Come Back Little Sheba* in 1970, the Widow in Tyrone Guthrie's production of *All's Well that Ends Well* in 1970–71, Regan in *King Lear* in 1971, and the demanding Giza in the premiere of RON ELISHA's *In Duty Bound* (1979), genteel Irene Harding in John Romeril's THE FLOATING WORLD in 1982, and self-deprecating Helene Hanff in Hugh Whitemore's *84 Charing Cross Road* in 1983–84. For the Playbox Theatre Company she played Robbie and Norah in Dorothy Hewett's *The Golden Oldies* in 1977. For the Victoria State Opera in Melbourne she played the male role of Big Louie in *Guys and Dolls* in 1986 and Mrs Pearce in *My Fair Lady* in 1988. ❦*Katharine Brisbane*

Alan Edwards AM MBE

Actor, administrator, director. Born 17 January 1925 at Chatham (England). Director of Forces Broadcasting Service in Kenya during Second World War. Graduated from Old Vic School 1949. Joined Young Vic Players and the Young Vic Company. Worked in English repertory theatres, including Birmingham Repertory Theatre for two years. Acted in London on stage, radio, television and film 1956–64. Taught at Royal Academy of Dramatic Art, Central School of Speech and Drama and other schools. Tutor in acting at National Institute of Dramatic Art (Sydney) 1964–69. Acted with Old Tote Theatre Company (Sydney), at Theatre Royal, Hobart, and on radio and television. Selected by Yevgeny Yevtushenko to read English translations of his poems with Judith Anderson during Australian tour 1966. Founding director of Queensland Theatre Company (Brisbane) 1969–88. Queensland Performing Arts Trust 1978–88. Theatre board of Australia Council 1978–82. MBE 1983. AM 1990.

Sixty productions and numerous performances for the QUEENSLAND THEATRE COMPANY have made Alan Edwards one of most respected identities of the Australian stage. Many well-known artists owe much to the opportunities and encouragement he has given to young talent. His last production in 19 years with the company, Ray Mathew's *A SPRING SONG*, drew the largest audience of the Australian theatre season in World Expo '88. Other high points were spectacular outdoor annual productions of Shakespeare in Brisbane, especially *Henry V*, *A Midsummer Night's Dream* and *The Tempest*. Also notable were *King Lear* and *Twelfth Night*, *Burke's Company* by BILL REED, *The Perfectionist* by DAVID WILLIAMSON, *Long Day's Journey into Night* by Eugene O'Neill, *The Circle* by Somerset Maugham, *The Ghost Train* by Arnold Ridley, *The National Health* by Peter Nichols and the musicals *Annie*, *Lock Up Your Daughters*, *Oh, What a Lovely War!* and *A Rum Do!* As an actor Edwards has retained an elegant Englishness. His notable performances for the company included Hadrian in Peter Luke's *Hadrian the Seventh*, Professor Higgins in George Bernard Shaw's *Pygmalion*, Dr Dysart in Peter Shaffer's *Equus*, Sydney Bruhl in Ira Levin's *Deathtrap*, Salieri in Shaffer's *Amadeus* and the elderly Cooper in Bob Larbey's *A Month of Sundays*. ❦*Arthur Frame*

further reading
ALLEN, JOHN (ed.). *Entertainment Arts in Australia*. Sydney: Paul Hamlyn 1968.
EDWARDS, ALAN. Introduction to *Tufff* and *The Jade Garden*. Brisbane: Playlab Press 1990.
HEDGE, DOUGLAS. *The Company We Keep—The first 10 years of QTC*. Brisbane: Queensland Theatre Company 1980.
HOWIE, ANN C. (ed.). *Who's Who in Australia* 17th edn. Melbourne: Information Australia 1991.

Ron Elisha

Dramatist. Born 19 December 1951 in Jerusalem. Came to Australia at two. Graduated in medicine from University of Melbourne 1976. Has combined medical practice with playwriting since 1979.

Ron Elisha's strengthening craft and his uncompromising interest in ideas make him one of the most distinctive voices in contemporary Australian theatre and one of those most worth listening to. His work has so far had the most exposure and recognition in Melbourne. He has had a particularly strong relationship with the MELBOURNE THEATRE COMPANY. The Jewish experience of homelessness and atrocity is a recurrent theme and a potent metaphor in much of his writing. It gives particular intensity to the intellectual debate that always distinguishes his plays. The persistence of that reference and the seriousness of the debate take his work far from a theatrical mainstream that has been concerned with mostly comic mythologising of local culture.

The directness of Elisha's moral and intellectual concerns at times produces conceptual abstraction that the dramatic action can barely contain. The three Einsteins whose speculative self-awareness fuels the passionate arguments of *Einstein* represent mental phases rather than constructed selves, and Elisha generalises the humanity of his subject in a way that seems to limit its development. The self-consciously intellectual and cosmopolitan qualities of *Einstein* suggest Elisha's distinctive voice in contemporary Australian theatre. A debate between a faithless rabbi and his pupil in the two-hander *Two* reflects a more assured sense of structural rhythms, but the dramatic climaxes rely on extended narratives of the Holocaust which, though very powerful, are in a sense adjacent to and imposed upon the central interaction. Elisha found less dramatically difficult ways of being genuinely serious in the comparatively conventional interactions of the Jewish family in *In Duty Bound* (1979), his first produced play, and especially in the wild and disturbing comedy of *The Levine Comedy*. Both plays involve the invocation of familiar stereotypes of Jewishness, though in the latter they are cunningly adapted. Levine's compulsive wisecracking is a means of coping in the absence of hope. In the way it directs and defies the audience's expectations it sharpens rather than palliates the pain of being human.

Safe House reflects in a moving, funny and disturbing study of the Russian defector at its centre a similar development in Elisha's reconciliation of farce and emotional force. Despite his attempts to acclimatise after 30 years in Australia, he remains one of Elisha's men on the margin, caught in a conflict of cultures that seems irreconcilable. With its time-jumps and orchestration of voices, *Safe House* also represents an extension of the theatrical daring first glimpsed in *Einstein* and in *Pax Americana* (1985), a suitably clever and glossy pageant of the Kennedy years in the White House. Elisha's determined fascination with the difficult has limited his appeal to both audiences and critics, but he remains a writer committed to the excitement of intellectual debate in the theatre. ❦*Peter Fitzpatrick*

published plays
Choice (1994). Sydney: Currency Press 1994.
Einstein (1981). London: Faber and Faber 1985.
Esterhaz (1990). Sydney: Currency Press 1990.
In Duty Bound (1979). Melbourne: Yackandandah 1983.
Safe House (1989). Sydney: Currency Press 1989.
Two (1982). Sydney: Currency Press 1985.

further reading
McNaughton, Howard. In *Contemporary Dramatists* (ed. K. A. Berney) 5th edn. London: St James Press 1993.

Elizabethan Theatre

Theatre in Newtown, Sydney, opened 2 June 1917 as **Majestic Theatre**, seating 1642. Architect: Henry E. White. Reopened as **Elizabethan Theatre** 27 July 1955. Destroyed by fire 19 January 1980.

The Elizabethan Theatre housed many major productions of drama, opera and ballet before the Sydney Opera House opened. The Australian Elizabethan Theatre Trust reopened the old Majestic Theatre because the two other live theatres in Sydney were tied to prosperous commercial circuits. As the Elizabethan Theatre it saw the Sydney premiere of Ray Lawler's *Summer of the Seventeenth Doll*, touring shows organised by the Trust and Garnet H. Carroll, and such stars as Judith Anderson, Lewis Casson, Ralph Richardson and Sybil Thorndike. It has been claimed that the Majestic, which was built in an inner suburb for Fullers', was a music-hall or a variety house. It was near Harry Clay's Bridge Theatre, a low-class vaudeville house that became the Hub cinema, but Benjamin Fuller's son remembered the Majestic as a stock-company melodrama house with a weekly change of program. Agnes Dobson was the leading lady and Frank Neil was the producer, Benjamin Fuller jnr said, and 'the cast received the play on Friday and had it off by heart by Monday. When audiences flagged *East Lynne* always dragged them back … .'

Fullers' employed Henry E. White, who had renovated the National Amphitheatre in Melbourne for them, to design the Majestic. The stage was adequate, with an 11-metre-wide proscenium and 11·3 metres of useable depth behind a 760 mm apron. The full stage was 18·3 metres deep by 22 metres to the fly floor and there were four floors of dressing rooms immediately behind. For a suburban theatre the Majestic was elaborate. White's auditorium was typical of his Louis XV style, with Baroque moulded panelling, cartouches, flourishes and bellied balcony fronts. The site was tight and the foyer spaces were little more than lobbies because, said Benjamin Fuller jnr, 'women would not go out into the foyers to stand about, smoke, or even go to the lavatory'. Social mores had changed in 1954, when the Trust leased the rundown theatre—a cinema for some 20 years—and it removed seats from the back stalls to provide a promenade space. The theatre was cleaned and stage improved, but the auditorium was left in pastel blue. The Trust moved its operations to city theatres early in 1961, but leased the Elizabethan Theatre again in 1970 after fire destroyed Her Majesty's Theatre. To suit patrons of the Australian Ballet and the Australian Opera the auditorium was transformed into an Edwardian joy in warm white and gold. Every available inch of space was taken to enlarge the original foyers for patrons of the stalls and the dress circle. But those in the gallery had only an unadorned stairway leading directly to the street, as in the more class-conscious era when the theatre was built. ❦*Ross Thorne*

Madge Elliott

Actor, dancer, singer. Born 12 May 1898 in London. Family migrated to Australia and settled in Toowoomba (Qld). Began dancing in musical comedy 1915. First danced with Cyril Ritchard 1919. Went to London 1925. Teamed with Ritchard again 1926. In Australia 1932–36. Married Ritchard in Sydney 1935. Worked with Ritchard in London and New York. Toured Australia 1946, 1951. Died August 1955 in San Francisco.

One of the most graceful and skilful dancers the Australian stage has produced was Madge Elliott. Her dancing and her great charm made her a firm favourite with audiences. Her singing voice was never her strongest point, but her blonde good looks and lithe body were ideal for the roles she played, and her early death robbed the theatre of a skilful actor in revue and romantic comedy.

Elliott showed an early aptitude for dancing. Her mother took her to Sydney for further tuition and she was chosen to dance with the Melba–Williamson Opera Company in 1911. In 1915 she danced solo roles in the operettas *High Jinks*, *So Long Letty* and *Canary Cottage*. She was partnered at first with Jack Hooker, who was much shorter than her. She refused to dance with the taller Cyril Ritchard because he was new to the company, but he became her partner for *Going Up* in 1919, when they introduced the Tickle Toe. They continued in *Kissing Time*, *The Cabaret Girl* and others until 1925, when Elliott went to London as a solo dancer.

She was reunited with Ritchard in 1926 and by the early 1930s they were often criticised for dancing in an unusually acrobatic style. They returned to Australia in 1932 for *Blue Roses* and *Hold My Hand*. Elliott and Ritchard were married in 1935. Their baby died and in 1936 they went back to London and played in revue and Restoration comedy. They returned to Australia in 1946 with some plays by Noël Coward and in his *Private Lives* in 1951. They worked together in London and New York until the early 1950s, when ill-health forced Elliott to retire. ❦*Alwyn Capern*

further reading
BEVAN, IAN. *The Story of the Theatre Royal*. Sydney: Currency Press 1993.
PARKER, JOHN. *Who Was Who in the Theatre 1912–1976*. Detroit (USA): Gale Research.

Sumner Locke Elliott

Actor, dramatist. Born 17 October 1917 in Sydney. Son of writer Sumner Locke, who died after giving birth. Joined Independent Theatre (Sydney) at 15. Had seven full-length plays performed by Independent Theatre 1937–48. Radio actor and scriptwriter 1937–42, 1946–48. In army 1942–46. Acted on Tivoli circuit 1946–48. Emigrated to USA July 1948. Successful television dramatist in New York City. Became US citizen 1955. Patrick White Literary Award 1977. Died 23 June 1991 in New York.

Sumner Locke Elliott's career is a classic example of the loss Australia sustained in the mid-20th century as a result of its cultural domination by England, the USA and the mass media. While awaiting discharge from the army after the Second World War he wrote RUSTY BUGLES, a major achievement of 20th-century Australian drama. But he never saw a production. In 1948 he emigrated to New York.

Elliott had established himself before the war with INDEPENDENT THEATRE in Sydney as a writer, actor and director in the traditions of Noël Coward and the fashionable drama of the 1930s, and as a writer of radio serials and comedy. His early plays are set in England or an international Australia, with well-made plots and sophisticated conversation. *Interval* (1939) is set backstage during performances of a successful West End play. *The Little Sheep Run Fast* (1940) is set in an Australian guesthouse but the *Sydney Morning Herald* said it was 'not in any way typically Australian'. *Goodbye to the Music* (1942) is about a pianist deserted by his wife after he had suffered a brainstorm during a concert. Elliott acted minor parts in these three romantic comedy-dramas. *Your Obedient Servant* (1943) is a symbolic drama about a jealous second wife—representing Nazi totalitarianism—and an Australian family with a French housekeeper and a 'dinkum Aussie' handyman. *Invisible Circus* (1946) is a satiric comedy set in a radio station.

Rusty Bugles, by contrast, is a realist comedy drama based solidly on Elliott's own army experience. A well-observed account of the tensions, boredom and discomfort of life in a tropical outpost expressed in vivid army vernacular, the play was an instant success with audiences. Elliott, who had heard only a reading of the play before his departure, later said he consequently 'had a curious ambiguity towards it; almost as though it were something written by someone else'. Elliott became prominent in American television writing and a successful novelist, but he contributed no more to the Australian theatre. He retired from the theatre altogether after *Buy Me Blue Ribbons* (1951), an unsuccessful Broadway comedy about a previous Broadway debacle. Brooks Atkinson described it in the *New York Times* as 'a stock farce about a vain and repulsive young motion picture star who produces a poetic drama in which he expects to play the leading part'. After Elliott's death it was announced that he had left most of his $US200 000 estate and future royalties to New Dramatists of New York, an organisation for promoting and assisting new playwrights, to which he had belonged since 1950. Some of this legacy is to be used to set up two-way exchange between New Dramatists and the AUSTRALIAN NATIONAL PLAYWRIGHTS' CONFERENCE. ❦*Axel Kruse*

published plays
Buy Me Blue Ribbons (1951). New York: Dramatists Play Service 1952.
Interval (1939). Melbourne University Press 1942, 1947.
Rusty Bugles. Brisbane: University of Queensland Press 1968, in *Khaki, Bush and Bigotry*. Sydney: Currency Press 1980, revised.

further reading
ARNOLD, ROSLYN. Introduction to *Rusty Bugles*. Sydney: Currency Press 1983.
CARROLL, DENNIS. *Australian Contemporary Drama*. Sydney: Currency Press 1995.
PACKER, CLYDE. *No return ticket. Studies in Australian Drama* 4. Sydney: Angus and Robertson 1984.

Bob Ellis

Dramatist. Born 10 May 1942 in Lismore (NSW). Writer and production assistant at ABC. Two Australian Writers' Guild Awgie awards 1971 for *The Legend of King O'Malley*. Owned Stables Theatre, Sydney, 1975–85. Married writer Anne Brooksbank 1977. Writes for film and television and directs films.

The establishment of alternative theatre in Sydney owed much to Bob Ellis. With MICHAEL BODDY he wrote *THE LEGEND OF KING O'MALLEY* (1970), a seminal piece of stagecraft that stimulated a widespread resurgence of interest in 19th-century and early 20th-century burlesque and a wave of productions at the Nimrod Street Theatre in Sydney. The rediscovery of old works was short-lived but it provided the impetus for the NIMROD THEATRE COMPANY's 1971 season and, indirectly, inspired other historical plays such as ALEX BUZO's *Macquarie*. Ellis himself made another foray into history when he collaborated with Dick Hall on *The Duke of Edinburgh Assassinated—or, The Vindication of Henry Parkes* (1971). Ellis has written scathingly satirical theatre reviews in the *Nation*, *Nation Review*, *Sydney Morning Herald* and *National Times*, rejecting 'naturalistic' and 'middle-class' theatre in favour of a more bawdy and polemical style. He celebrated another colourful Sydney writer, Francis James, in a musical, *The James Dossier* (1975). ❦*Rémy Davison*

published plays
Down Under, with Anne Brooksbank (1975). Sydney: Angus and Robertson 1977.
The Legend of King O'Malley, with Michael Boddy (1970). Sydney: Angus and Robertson 1974; Currency Press 1987.

The Elocution of Benjamin Franklin

Comedy-drama in three acts for one actor by Steve J. Spears.
premiere 28 August 1976, Nimrod Theatre Downstairs, Sydney, by Gordon Chater. Designer: Laurence Eastwood. Director: Richard Wherrett. **revived** 1984, York Theatre, Sydney; 1994, Melbourne Theatre Company with Bob Hornery. **published** Sydney: Currency Press 1977, 1989.

The play is set in the living-room—furnished with a piano and a bust of Shakespeare—of an apartment in the Melbourne suburb of Toorak. Here the Man, Robert O'Brien, conducts elocution classes at his Shakespeare Speech and

Drama Academy. During rapid repartee in the first act he reveals his life as a teacher and homosexual transvestite, chatting to his friend Bruce, a heterosexual transvestite and stockbroker; addressing Shakespeare; and conducting classes with a variety of pupils. His life is disturbed by the arrival of Benjamin Franklin, a 12-year-old stutterer who responds to therapy by confessing his sexual exploits. The Man's neighbours discover his fancy for frocks, and stone the apartment. The third act finds him a sad old man confined to a mental hospital by a contrived committal order.

The work is a fairly unstructured vehicle for a versatile actor and GORDON CHATER made the role his own. Its debut was well timed. The life of gays was still exotic to the theatregoer and sympathy was growing, but the establishment and the authorities—represented here by wealthy Toorak—were still demanding that such things be kept under wraps. The play also draws attention to the knowingness of many modern children and the predicament in which they may place the trusting and old-fashioned adult.

The NIMROD THEATRE COMPANY production transferred to the New Arts Theatre in suburban Glebe, and then went on a tour of all states but Queensland—where censorship and moralists had been acting against the theatre—playing to a total of 200 000 people.

While the production was at the Playbox Theatre in Melbourne, Spears received a writ for breach of copyright from a female speech teacher in Toorak, who claimed that he had acquired certain vocal exercises during speech therapy with her. The matter was settled out of court.

The London management James Hammerstein bought world rights and Chater gave 900 performances abroad. In London he played at the Mayfair Theatre for six months in 1978. He won an award for best actor in Los Angeles and in New York City in 1979 the play won three of the five Obie awards for off-Broadway productions: best play, best actor and best direction. Chater settled in New York but returned to Sydney for the 1984 revival. The play has been translated and staged in Canada and several countries in Europe and South America. *Katharine Brisbane*

Elston, Hocking and Woods

Since 1979 Elston, Hocking and Woods has been Melbourne's most dynamic and imaginative theatrical entrepreneur. The group has produced shows in its ATHENAEUM THEATRES since 1986 and in the Universal Theatre in Fitzroy from 1979 to 1991, when it sold the lease to New World Productions. It also runs Park Entertainments for the Melbourne City Council and Performers Management, a large artists' agency. It has presented the German actor Ekkehard Schall and Samuel Beckett's San Quentin Theatre Workshop productions, and produced *Wogs Out of Work* and a host of successful rock 'n' roll nostalgia shows. Greg Hocking and Tim Woods formed the partnership as entrepreneurs to take over the lease of the Universal Theatre, where they opened with a concert by the Bushwackers band in December 1979. Their production manager on tour with Los Trios Ringbarkus, Glenn Elston became a partner in 1986. Since then he has mounted brilliantly successful open-air productions yearly in the Royal Botanic Gardens, including *A Midsummer Night's Dream*, which has been seen elsewhere in Australia. *Geoffrey Milne*

Emerald City

Play in two acts by David Williamson. **premiere** 1 January 1987, Drama Theatre of Sydney Opera House, by Sydney Theatre Company. Cast: John Bell, Ruth Cracknell, Max Cullen, Dennis Grosvenor, Andrea Moor, Robyn Nevin. Designer: Laurence Eastwood. Director: Richard Wherrett. **published** Sydney: Currency Press 1987.

The premise for *Emerald City* is autobiographical. Colin, a playwright and scriptwriter, has moved from Melbourne to Sydney, as DAVID WILLIAMSON himself had done. The play is much concerned with Colin's unresolved mixed feelings about the two cities, and about the moral implications of his move. The vision of Sydney is of startling beauty allied with moral anarchy that almost constitutes a force for evil. The quest for views of the harbour symptomises not only hedonism but a turning away from the emotional realities and responsibilities of a community. Colin wants to write about contemporary life in the suburbs and symbolically significant minor episodes in Australia's past. But pressure to write for export is strong. It wins even untalented Mike a harbour view, and it offers tangible forms of status. Even Colin's wife Kate, a publisher of worthy books that few read, sacrifices principles for first-class travel.

The film industry brings into focus another perception of the city. The hustlers consistently use 'international' as a euphemism for 'American', and this relationship redefines debates for and against parochialism in Australian art and in perceptions of Australia's most cosmopolitan city. The second act has a sense of indeterminacy because of limitations imposed by self-reference, but *Emerald City* is considerably more than the elaboration of personal ambivalence. It explores the mythology of the modern city, and develops the interest in iconography of place that is at the centre of Williamson's TRAVELLING NORTH.

In the successful seasons of *Emerald City* in Australia, critics were inclined to argue about the plot at the expense of the metaphorical structure. It is a nice irony that Melbourne values are asserted by a myth that is itself drawn from American mass-culture. The original Emerald City was in another Oz. When Dorothy chants the magic words 'there's no place like home', which carry her back to Kansas, she chooses the enduring ties of the traditional community. Williamson in *Emerald City* is concerned with the importance and perhaps impossibility of rediscovering them. *Peter Fitzpatrick*

Emerald Hill Theatre Company

Professional dramatic company in Melbourne founded in 1961 by Wal Cherry and George Whaley. Closed 1966. **venue** Emerald Hill Theatre, South Melbourne. **artistic director** Wal Cherry. **first production** *Not with Yours Truly* by Bill Hannan, March 1962.

The Emerald Hill company is remembered in Melbourne as an essential forerunner of the Australian new wave. It was an actors' theatre, dedicated to ensemble performance as the most sympathetic to indigenous drama, and to the methods and philosophies of Bertolt Brecht and Konstantin Stanislavsky in particular. Its acting was vigorous, its staging was simple and bold, and it expressed complex ideas. The company aimed to challenge assumptions and to encourage debate in an accessible and lively public forum.

It was ahead of its time in its rigorous and intelligent pursuit of these objectives in eclectic programing. WAL CHERRY directed remarkable productions of the Sophoclean tragedies *Oedipus Rex* and *Antigone*, the latter played in repertoire with Jean Anouilh's *Antigone*. This was directed by the present writer, who also staged provocative productions of John Antrobus's *You'll Come To Love Your Sperm Test* and Spike Milligan's Australian version of *The Bed-Sitting Room*. Other European works were *Macbeth* and plays by John Arden, Brendan Behan, Max Frisch, Eugène Ionesco, Molière (*The Would-Be Gentleman* rehearsed over nine months), John Osborne and Harold Pinter. Contrary to plans, there was only one Brecht production—the anthology *Brecht on Brecht*. American playwrights were Edward Albee, Lewis John Carlino, Arthur Miller, Murray Schisgal, Thornton Wilder and Tennessee Williams.

The company was less successful in implementing its stated policy of developing and presenting local plays, though it opened its theatre with *Not With Yours Truly* by Bill Hannan, with music by Ivan Hutchinson, after rehearsal over a year. The theatre was a former church converted by the architect Robin Boyd and members of the ensemble from Cherry's Theatre Workshop and Actor's Studio. It had a thrust stage, a revolve and tiered seating for 150. Planned productions of numerous new Australian plays never reached the stage, but there were landmark productions, including *The Last of The Rainbow* by John Hepworth, *When the Gravediggers Come* by Robert Amos and *A Bunch of Ratbags*, a musical. New plays often divided and occasionally confused critical opinion. The company found more general appreciation of its energetic style and coherent objectives when it played in Adelaide, Canberra or Perth.

A close and at times turbulent collaboration between Cherry and the present writer—the regular principal actor—defined the company's work and provided continuity as membership of the ensemble changed. Other actors with the company included Georgina Alcock, John Derum, Terry Donovan, AARNE NEEME, Gerda Nicholson and PETER O'SHAUGHNESSY. The company depended on box office, classes, donations, the dedication of its members and occasional minuscule project funding. It was established at a time when the AUSTRALIAN ELIZABETHAN THEATRE TRUST, the only public funding body, supported only major regional companies. After 31 play productions and programs of dance, folk music, poetry and vaudeville, it closed in 1966 when Cherry was appointed to the chair of drama at Flinders University in Adelaide. Its last show was *A Funny Thing Happened on the Way to The Front*, a revue opposing the Vietnam War and conscription. ❦*George Whaley*

further reading
CHERRY, WAL. The Emerald Hill Theatre, Melbourne. *Komos* 3/1 (Melbourne, 1973).
WORBY, GUTHRIE. Emerald Hill and the ensemble ideal. *Contemporary Australian Drama* (ed. Peter Holloway). Sydney: Currency Press 1987.

Emu Plains convict theatre

The second theatre in Australia and the first outside Sydney was a makeshift building about 56 km to the west at the penal settlement of Emu Plains. Popular plays of the time were performed there, with much ingenious contrivance of properties, lights and costumes, to audiences of local gentry, prison officials and prisoners between 1825 and 1830. In a letter in the *Sydney Gazette* on 21 July 1825 'A Lover of Rational Pleasures' noted that the convicts at Emu Plains 'have erected a theatre, and established dramatic performances, thus providing for themselves a congenial relief from the rigours of compulsory servitude'. A recent performance of W. B. Rhodes's popular 1810 burlesque *Bombastes Furioso* and David Garrick's 1741 comedy *The Lying Valet* had been attended by many of the local gentry, including Sir John Jamison, a wealthy landowner. The acting, the scenery—'painted with great taste'—and the dresses, some supplied by the ladies of the neighbourhood, had all received great applause.

The most detailed account of this theatre comes from *Ralph Rashleigh*, a novel supposedly written in the 1840s by JAMES TUCKER, who had been a prisoner at Emu Plains in 1827. According to Tucker, the theatre was a slab-and-bark building, with the gaps in the walls filled with mud, and whitewashed with pipe clay inside. It was fitted out with conventional pit and boxes. The seating was made from local timber. Canvas for the scenery was scrounged from bags, bedding and clothing, and painted with more pipe clay, other coloured earths and charcoal. Oil lamps and candles donated by prison officials provided light.

The theatre's leading light, whom Tucker calls Jemmy King, was 'at once architect, manager, carpenter, scene-painter, decorator, machinist, mechanician, and to crown all, a very passable comic actor'. He was especially adept at devising properties and costumes. Tucker tells of *Bombastes Furioso*, in which King Artexomines's crown was made from pieces of tinplate and copper garnished with bits of window glass and his wig was contrived from sheepskin powdered with bone ash. All the costumes were similarly made from odds and ends of old clothes and other castoff materials. Tucker says the theatre even had an orchestra, composed of a violin—apparently made by Jemmy King from tinplate—a fife, a tambourine and a huge drum.

Tucker describes a performance attended by Sir John Jamison and other guests. Sir John chose the pieces—Monk Lewis's 1800 melodrama *Raymond and Agnes* and a 1732 ballad opera, *The Devil to Pay*, in abridged form. The program was even more ambitious when Sir John took his guests to the theatre in 1830. As reported by the *Sydney Gazette* on 10 July, it consisted of Isaac Pocock's 1818 *Rob Roy* and George Colman the younger's 1803 comedy *John Bull*. Apparently more than 200 people squeezed into the Emu Plains theatre for this performance.

In 1825 'A Lover of Rational Pleasures' had suggested 'the expediency of giving public notice in future of their performances, as their fraternity do at home'. In 1830 the convicts began to do just that, advertising in the *Sydney Gazette* to attract the theatre-starved public of Sydney. This unfortunately brought the Emu Plains theatre to the notice of Governor Sir Ralph Darling, who was then fighting all attempts to establish a theatre in Sydney on the grounds that such an amusement was inappropriate for a convict settlement. Under this policy, he ordered the closure of the Emu Plains theatre in November 1830. ❦*Elizabeth Webby*

further reading
TUCKER, JAMES. *Ralph Rashleigh*. Sydney: Angus and Robertson 1952.

English influences

London remained the theatrical centre of England throughout the 19th century. Until 1843 the only theatres licensed to open in the capital were the patent theatres—the Theatres Royal at Covent Garden and Drury Lane—during the winter months and the Theatre Royal in the Haymarket in summer. In the early years of the century, however, growth of population led to a spread of theatres in London, not only in the centre, but also in the east and south. In 1843 the Theatres Act brought all theatres in the London area under the control of the Lord Chamberlain's Office, which became responsible for licensing them. Growth of population in provincial cities as a result of the Industrial Revolution led to an increase in theatres outside London too.

Theatre in all the Australian colonies—where the English were the most numerous settlers—followed English practice in everything from architecture to acting style. The format for an evening's entertainment—several plays interspersed with songs, dancing or other novelties—came from England. The early repertoire was almost entirely English, since restrictions were initially placed on indigenous plays, especially in Sydney, where the Colonial Secretary's Office was concerned to control any dramatic output emanating from former convicts and to uphold the Lord Chamberlain's right to veto plays deemed unsuitable for public consumption.

Eighteenth-century plays were popular but by far the most of the plays BARNETT LEVEY's company staged at the Theatre Royal in Sydney in the 1830s were recent London productions, such as Douglas Jerrold's *Black-Eyed Susan*. Most of the plays that Levey presented had been first performed at the patent theatres in London but a substantial number came from Sadler's Wells, the Surrey Theatre or minor theatres with less sophisticated audiences.

By the 1860s the melodramas of DION BOUCICAULT, Shakespearean revivals, the burlesques of H. J. Byron and F. C. Burnand and the more realistic comedies of Tom Robertson were all popular. The visiting London Comedy Company in 1879–80 and the BROUGH-BOUCICAULT COMEDY COMPANY in the 1880s and 1890s helped to perpetuate the English repertoire. Heavily anglicised versions of French *opéras-bouffes* drew crowded houses prior to the arrival of the GILBERT AND SULLIVAN operettas, which were extremely popular from 1879.

Reflections of English provinces

The major cities in the Australian colonies were not large enough to follow exactly the pattern of theatrical life in London. They more closely approximated developments in the larger English provincial cities like Birmingham, Liverpool, Manchester and Newcastle-upon-Tyne. Australian cities, like their English counterparts, played host to visiting stars, and to touring companies as steamships sped up travel between continents. As in England, stock companies gradually gave way to entrepreneurial managements competing for touring companies. As in the English provinces, most of the repertoire originated in London. There was eventually a small local contribution.

The structures of English MELODRAMA and domestic farce were easily adapted to Australian settings. The ballad opera *THE CURRENCY LASS* is strongly influenced by 18th-century sentimental comedy. The English PANTOMIME, with its structure of a lengthy opening followed by a short harlequinade, was also the model for the Australian version. The liberating adaptability to local subject matter of pantomime, melodrama, BURLESQUE and farce enhanced the development of Australian drama.

The 19th century was the age of the actor. Initially, English acting predominated in Australia, but even when Australian actors emerged English influence remained strong. Many actors came from England, although not every actor initially advertised as from a Theatre Royal in London could have proved such an association. The English 'stars' who visited Australia from the middle of the century onwards were generally leaders of the second rank. They were often actors who, taking Edmund Kean or William Macready as their model, had achieved prominence in the English provinces, Ireland, Scotland, North America and in melodrama theatres in the East End of London, but had rarely become West End stars. The most popular were James Anderson, WILLIAM CRESWICK, Charles Dillon, J. B. Howe, WALTER MONTGOMERY, GEORGE RIGNOLD and BARRY SULLIVAN. All had numerous Shakespearean roles in their repertoires. The most distinguished English actors to visit Australia were JANET ACHURCH, interpreting Henrik Ibsen in an English translation by William Archer, CHARLES AND ELLEN KEAN, CHARLES MATHEWS and J. L. TOOLE. Later WILSON BARRETT and JULIUS KNIGHT were successful visitors. The Keans, far past their prime, were considered too restrained for the Australian public in 1863–64. In the 1870s the restraint of Mathews in light comedy was welcomed as a beneficial influence. In 1879-80 the LONDON COMEDY COMPANY demonstrated the value of strong ensemble work. Toole, England's leading low comedian, came in the 1890s with outdated performing style and repertoire. HARRY RICKARDS was amongst those who brought the traditions of English music-hall to Australia.

Charles Kean and his wife Ellen, stars from London, drew crowds in Australia, but colonial audiences preferred the more robust style of actors from the English provinces

Touchstone for critics

England provided a touchstone in many press reviews. The 19th-century Australian press tended to assume that anything English—actor or play—must be better than the local product. Critics like J. E. NEILD and, from the 1880s, the Sydney *Bulletin* and *Melbourne Punch* were useful correctives to this view, but English cultural hegemony fostered a pervasive belief in English cultural superiority. Critics had often experienced English acting before they came to Australia, and many actors had learnt their craft in England. For example, WILLIAM HOSKINS, a popular Sydney actor and light comedian, had acted with Samuel Phelps's company at Sadler's Wells. GEORGE COPPIN, in the role of Paul Pry, modelled himself, even in costume and posture, on its originator, the English comedian John Liston. In the second half of the 19th century English immigrants formed the backbone of the Australian theatrical industry—authors such as W. M. AKHURST and MARCUS CLARKE; actor–managers such as ARTHUR GARNER, GEORGE DARRELL, ALFRED DAMPIER and BLAND HOLT; and scenic designers such as PHILIP W. GOATCHER, WILLIAM PITT SNR and W. J. WILSON.

At its best the English influence strengthened ties between the two countries and enabled the development of a theatre that could grow from no other tradition. At its worst it saw mediocre English efforts welcomed more readily than local products, merely because they were English and because the upper echelons of society and the more conservative newspapers, such as the *Sydney Morning Herald* and the Melbourne *Argus* valued them the more on that account. Moreover, entire English companies of varying quality toured with largely English repertoires later in the 19th century. This, together with the preference of J. C. WILLIAMSON, an American, for non-Australian plays and overseas stars, was detrimental to employment of Australian actors and development of fully Australian drama.

THEATRES in Australia initially followed Georgian architectural tradition, at least in their interiors. The ROYAL VICTORIA THEATRE in Sydney was the first to show more of a Regency influence, especially in the extension of the pit beneath the dress circle. Amphitheatres modelled on Astley's Amphitheatre in London opened in the 1840s and 1850s for equestrian presentations but most eventually reverted to use for drama. The fit-up stage seems to have been more common than in England in the 19th century, perhaps because plays were performed in new and remote settlements. By the 1850s, partly as a result of the goldrush boom, larger theatres, such as the THEATRE ROYAL in Melbourne, were built in emulation of Drury Lane and Covent Garden. As in England, a trend to build large theatres emerged towards the end of the century. Many theatres were rebuilt, not only after fires but also in accordance with the increasingly commercial values of the era. The capacity, social segregation and ornate interior design of Australian theatres also reflected English practice. So did the development of the horseshoe-shaped auditorium, the downstage advance of the proscenium arch and the replacement of the pit by the stalls as the century progressed.

Stage machinery and scenic design also followed English practice. The mania for spectacular sensation scenes in melodrama, gorgeous transformations in pantomime and realistic settings was as common in Australia as in England. Managers often copied elaborate London productions down to the last detail, as GEORGE RIGNOLD apparently did with G. R. Sims's *The Lights of London* at the Princess's Theatre in Melbourne. At Her Majesty's Theatre in Sydney late in the 19th century, Rignold seems to have emulated Henry Irving at the Lyceum Theatre in London with lavish productions of Shakespeare and melodrama.

As in England, drama was subject to censorship. The colonial secretaries initially fulfilled a function similar to that of the Lord Chamberlain's office, rejecting plays that encouraged crime or immorality or were too politically oriented. Just as W. S. Gilbert's THE HAPPY LAND was censored in England for lampooning contemporary politicians, performance of Marcus Clarke's Australian adaptation was stopped in Melbourne in 1880.

English censorship echoed in Melbourne in 1880. Marcus Clarke adapted W. S. Gilbert's 1873 burlesque The Happy Land, *which had been banned in England because it lampooned politicians; it showed party politics creating havoc in fairyland. Clarke's target was Graham Berry, Premier of Victoria. Berry, facing an election, had Clarke's play banned by refusal of copyright registration. Melbourne Punch alluded to the ban when it portrayed Berry in fairy costume. When Berry was defeated the magazine reprinted the cartoon with the caption 'The "Happiest Land" at last'*

In many ways the Australian theatre of the 19th century largely replicated changes in English and American practices. As English theatres moved towards more compact programs and longer runs later in the century, so did Australian theatres. Yet, despite English theatrical traditions, genuine Australian drama began to emerge in the 19th century, to the extent that by Federation, many English dramas were Australianised. In adopting the forms and structures of contemporary English drama, together with its obsession with local detail, the Australian theatre paradoxically found a voice of its own. ❦*Jim Davis*

1900–50

The professional repertoire from 1900 to 1950 was heavily weighted towards MUSICAL THEATRE, with legitimate drama increasingly restricted to Australian productions of West End successes. Australian playwrights generally tended to follow closely the changes in English styles in writing, production and performance. The most influential English playwrights were Noël Coward, John Galsworthy, Harley Granville-Barker, Somerset Maugham, Terence Rattigan, George Bernard Shaw and lesser-known writers of West End plays. Australian playwrights tended to adapt these models to a local context. The diverse styles of LOUIS ESSON and the realism of other Australians' plays performed by the PIONEER PLAYERS and Gregan McMahon's MELBOURNE REPERTORY THEATRE COMPANY and in WILLIAM MOORE'S Annual Drama Nights owed much to the English 'new drama', despite Australian themes, characterisation and idiom. In the 1930s and 1940s the verse plays of W. H. Auden and Christopher Isherwood, T. S. Eliot, Tyrone Guthrie and Stephen Spender influenced verse dramatists, notably CATHERINE DUNCAN, Helen Simpson and DOUGLAS STEWART. MAX AFFORD's popular thrillers for stage and radio followed West End styles with some adaptation.

A steady stream of touring productions from England gave English production and acting styles a dominant influence. These tours countered tendencies towards provincialism and amateurishness and kept Australian theatre abreast of the expanding potential of live theatre. They also curbed development of an Australian tradition by maintaining the overwhelming prestige of the metropolitan culture and of English styles of articulation and acting. The visits of English companies also reminded Australian communities that the dramatic arts had social and cultural significance. In all capital cities and many provincial towns, AMATEUR THEATRE developed, maintaining the English professional repertory companies' tradition of competent performance of translations of Henrik Ibsen and well-made English plays. In its early repertoire and its lasting role in the community, ADELAIDE REPERTORY THEATRE, dating from 1908, exemplified the influence of dozens of amateur groups of varying standards before 1950. Its early productions included plays by Arnold Bennett, Galsworthy, St John Hankin, Ibsen and Shaw, and two plays by writers living in Australia, ARTHUR H. ADAMS and John Le Gay Brereton. In 1947 Adelaide Repertory Theatre had about 2575 members. Touring companies brought them a new impulse which Australian audiences and amateur groups absorbed and necessarily modified. Newspaper reviewers, tending to assume that all English companies represented the highest achievements, promoted their influence. The fact that many professional actors received their first—sometimes only—training in amateur groups reinforced the dominance of English styles in Australian professional theatre.

Irene Vanbrugh came to Australia from London for long tours by the Vanbrugh–Boucicault Company in the 1920s

BLAND HOLT's Australianised English melodramas and the visiting actors Charles Arnold, H. B. Irving, JULIUS KNIGHT, Laura Villiers and Lewis Waller affected performance styles and repertoire early in the 20th century. In 1906 HUGH J. WARD and George Willoughby introduced OLIVE WILTON, whose professional discipline set new expectations for Australian actors, especially when she played serious roles in plays by Eugène Brieux, Ibsen and Shaw under the auspices of J. C. WILLIAMSON's in later years. Another influence on acting and production styles was Geelong-born OSCAR ASCHE, who played in Shakespeare with Ellen Terry in London. In Australian tours in 1909–10 and 1912–13 his Shakespeare repertoire included lesser-known plays like *Measure for Measure* as well as favourites like *The Taming of the Shrew*. The sensuous flamboyance of his Shakespeare performances found even more popular expression in spectaculars like Edward Knoblock's play *Kismet* and the musical comedy *Chu Chin Chow*.

In 1917 Marie Tempest made a lasting impression with her crisp performances in comedy of manners. After 1918 came frequent tours by celebrities like DION BOUCICAULT JNR, Gertrude Elliott (Lady Forbes-Robertson) and Irene Vanbrugh. The VANBRUGH–BOUCICAULT COMPANY presented Angela Baddeley in popular plays by J. M. Barrie, which left their mark on amateur repertoire and local playwriting.

From 1920 to 1930 the English actor-manager ALLAN WILKIE influenced Australian ideas of Shakespearean production, especially in the attention he paid to careful and elaborate costuming. His performances are sometimes remembered for their later mannerisms, but his wife, FREDISWYDE HUNTER-WATTS, had a more natural acting style, which influenced many Australian actors. Wilkie also familiarised a generation of urban Australians with a 19th-century classical repertoire in productions for schools from 1915 and in a series of lectures.

Touring in 1932, during the Great Depression, Sybil Thorndike and her actor–director husband Lewis Casson asserted the social importance of theatre. They challenged the popularity of light comedy and musicals with serious plays like *Macbeth*, Shaw's *Saint Joan*, Ibsen's *Ghosts* and Euripides's *Medea*. The Thorndike–Casson styles of performance and production were memorable for natural delicacy and insight that were unusual at the time. English influence maintained its hold even while social-realist plays of American origin were finding expression in the NEW THEATRE movement. The English-bred sisters EVELYN AND BEATRICE TILDESLEY encouraged the English connection. Evelyn Tildesley founded the Sydney branch of the British Drama League in 1937.

English influence reached a new peak in 1948 with the six-month tour of the OLD VIC THEATRE COMPANY led by Laurence Olivier and Vivien Leigh. Olivier's energy and passion, Leigh's delicacy and precision, and the intellectual acuity that underlay their performances set new goals for Australian actors. Sydney-born Cicely Courtneidge, returning in 1948, represented for many the embodiment and quintessence of 'a famous tradition of English comedy', and her acting was recommended as 'a fascinating study for young players'. In 1949 Tyrone Guthrie, touring as actor and director, maintained Australian enthusiasm for the new English postwar exuberance. He was asked to advise on the possible development of a national theatre. Some interpreted the ensuing GUTHRIE REPORT as patronising, but it directly and indirectly stimulated further advance in indigenous writing and performance.

The Australian play required strong realistic Australian acting to complement its form and characterisation. SUMNER LOCKE ELLIOTT's early training with INDEPENDENT THEATRE in Sydney, for which he wrote comedies and sketches, was in the English tradition. Nevertheless it gave him the stagecraft to write an indigenous work in *Rusty Bugles*, which appeared in 1948. ❧*Elizabeth Perkins*

Since 1951

English influences have become less marked since the 1950s, although English plays still account for almost half of Australia's theatrical output. The professional repertory companies that emerged in the 1950s and 1960s and became state theatre companies from 1968—such as the Union Theatre Repertory Company and the OLD TOTE THEATRE COMPANY—were established almost exclusively by English immigrants and were modelled on English provincial repertory companies. The dominant acting style, which had largely developed in AMATEUR THEATRE, was also English in origin. So was much of the repertoire. It depended heavily upon the London magazine *Plays and Players*, which provided scripts of the latest popular successes in London, and the output of English publishers of drama.

The NATIONAL INSTITUTE OF DRAMATIC ART was established in 1958 on the model of the Royal Academy of Dramatic Art in London, and concentrated initially on perpetuating the accepted English style of acting, which encouraged actors to shed their Australian accents. This tendency lasted more than a decade, until proliferation of Australian writing led to a demand for Australian characters on stage, film and television. A further influence was the competition of the VICTORIAN COLLEGE OF THE ARTS, founded in 1976 by Peter Oyston upon a determination to create community-based regional theatre. The WESTERN AUSTRALIAN ACADEMY OF PERFORMING ARTS, established in 1979 in Perth, where English immigrants' influence is particularly noticeable, still retains a strong component from English theatre schools.

An Englishman, ROBERT QUENTIN, founded the first university drama department in Australia at the University of NSW in Sydney in 1964, and modelled it on the drama department of Bristol University. It was followed in 1967 in Adelaide by the drama department of Flinders University, established by WAL CHERRY, whose major influences were Bertolt Brecht and the new American drama. Since then the grip of English literature upon the academic study of drama has weakened.

In both the professional and amateur theatre of the 1950s and 1960s the plays of George Bernard Shaw and Noël Coward were staples. Coward remains popular, but Shaw and the well-made plays of William Douglas Home, John Galsworthy, J. B. Priestley and Terence Rattigan have almost disappeared from Australian playbills. Since the 1980s commercial theatre has been dominated by large-scale English musicals by Andrew Lloyd Webber and others, and the London entrepreneur Cameron Mackintosh has established a stronghold. State companies' attempts at large-scale work, like the extravagant production of *The Life and Adventures of Nicholas Nickleby* by the SYDNEY THEATRE COMPANY and the Australian Opera in 1982–83, have been thwarted by lengthy residences in the large theatres by Mackintosh and his rivals.

The abrasive social-realist drama that began at the Royal Court Theatre in London in 1956 with John Osborne's *Look Back in Anger* had a considerably diminished effect in Australia. The production of Osborne's first play by the AUSTRALIAN ELIZABETHAN THEATRE TRUST, an organisation initially steeped in traditional English theatrical practice, was a failure. Plays dealing with the injustices of the English class system—by John Arden, Shelagh Delaney, Ann Jellicoe, Arnold Wesker and others—were performed in the 1960s, but struck few chords with audiences. The parallel movement about working-class life in Australia, led by Ray Lawler's SUMMER OF THE SEVENTEENTH DOLL (1955) and Alan Seymour's THE ONE DAY OF THE YEAR (1961), was seen as more relevant. It was nevertheless greatly influenced at the outset by English naturalism, an almost obligatory choice for dramas at the time. It enjoyed more immediate rapport with audiences than PATRICK WHITE's contemporary plays, with their more complex expressionist influences. The *Doll* was first produced for Melbourne's Union Theatre Repertory Company by JOHN SUMNER, an immigrant who, David Williamson has said, 'could present a cold English superiority and yet more than anyone else he encouraged and pushed Australian writing'.

Osborne played the haughty celebrity at the AUSTRALIAN NATIONAL PLAYWRIGHTS' CONFERENCE in 1977. His comment 'If there is a hell, it is somewhere in Australia', did little to boost his popularity here. Another English playwright, Harold Pinter, on the other hand, remains widely performed in Australia. A festival of six of his plays was staged at the Rocks Theatre in Sydney in 1979.

With the rapid expansion of theatre since the 1970s, works by English playwrights with a record of commercial success at home, like Alan Ayckbourn, Alan Bennett, Peter Nichols and Tom Stoppard, have been widely performed in Australia. Ayckbourn's trilogy *The Norman Conquests* was presented by the OLD TOTE THEATRE COMPANY in Sydney in 1974, and his plays continued to dominate playbills throughout the 1980s, most notably those of the ENSEMBLE THEATRE COMPANY and the MARIAN STREET THEATRE COMPANY in Sydney. Stoppard was a guest at the FESTIVAL OF PERTH in 1979 for *Night and Day*, and of the Sydney Theatre Company for *Arcadia* in 1994. Peter Shaffer was a guest at the 1981 Festival of Perth when his *Amadeus* was performed. His *Equus* has been produced in all states. The revival of the outrageous farces of Joe Orton in England in 1986—after the release of his diaries and the film *Prick Up Your Ears*—had echoes in Sydney and elsewhere.

The politically committed English playwrights of the 1970s 'second wave' contributed to the more experimental programs encouraged by the injection of government funding. Their work had some impact upon new thinking, although most have had only isolated productions. Works by Howard Barker, Edward Bond, Howard Brenton, Trevor Griffiths, David Hare and John McGrath have been staged, notably by NEW THEATRE in Melbourne and Sydney. Hare has directed the world premiere of his 'Asian play' *A Map of the World* at the Adelaide Festival in 1982, and Griffiths, Brenton, McGrath and Snoo Wilson have been guests at the AUSTRALIAN NATIONAL PLAYWRIGHTS' CONFERENCE and have influenced left-wing playwrights like STEPHEN SEWELL.

The British women's theatre movement of the late 1970s was influential, most notably at the BELVOIR STREET THEATRE in Sydney. Micheline Wandor and Louise Page have visited Australia, while the plays of Caryl Churchill, especially *Top Girls*, have been widely performed.

The most influential English director to visit Australia in recent years has been Peter Brook, who brought his International Centre of Theatre Research to the Adelaide Festival in 1980 with *Conference of the Birds*, *Ubu-roi* by Alfred Jarry and *The Ik*, and in 1988 with his nine-hour epic *Mahabarata*. Steven Berkoff has numerous Australian advocates, who have been impressed by his wild, coarse and grandiose productions—*East* in Adelaide in 1978, *The Fall of the House of Usher* at the Festival of Sydney in 1982, *Salome* in 1990 and *One Man* in 1994. Lindsay Kemp delighted audiences with his camp extravaganza *Flowers* in the late 1970s. Mike Leigh improvised *Greek Tragedy* with Greek–Australian actors at Belvoir Street in 1989.

The same year saw the Royal Court Theatre Company in repertoire at the Wharf Theatre in Sydney in Max Stafford-Clark's productions of Timberlake Wertenbaker's *Our Country's Good*, an exploration of Australia's convict origins, and George Farquhar's *The Recruiting Officer*, the first play performed in Australia. The season delivered a lesson in how to create incisive, brilliant theatre on a small budget, casting across race and sex. It gave Australian audiences new expectations of English theatre.

The English Shakespeare Company and the Royal Shakespeare Company toured in the 1980s, as did Cheek by Jowl and the more earthbound, popular tent-show Shakespeare of Footsbarn Theatre. All stimulated the foundation of the Bell Shakespeare Company and helped to keep Shakespeare in local repertoires. In the 1990s the work of Théâtre de Complicité has been well received at the Adelaide and Sydney festivals, and the National Theatre's lavish production of J. B. Priestley's *An Inspector Calls* toured nationally in 1995.

The AUSTRALIAN PERFORMING GROUP and the NIMROD THEATRE COMPANY rose in the 1970s in direct response to perceived English domination of Australian theatre, and both made concerted attempts to produce a distinctively Australian style. British influences have become increasingly less evident in Australian drama, although the initial successes of DAVID WILLIAMSON and ALEX BUZO, both of whom had plays performed at the Royal Court in London in the 1970s, could be attributed to the presentation of strikingly local characters and issues within an English-influenced naturalistic framework. In 1988 the bicentenary of European colonisation marked the end of English influence, by acknowledging the primary importance of Aboriginal culture and the multicultural nature of Australia. Since then the Australian theatre has begun to explore more fully the diversity of its own territory and those of its Asian and Pacific neighbours. ❦*Tony Mitchell*

further reading

BOOTH, MICHAEL R. *Prefaces to English Nineteenth Century Theatre*. Manchester University Press 1980.

BULL, JOHN. *New British Political Dramatists*. London: Macmillan 1984.

LAURI, GEORGE. *The Australian Theatre Story*. Sydney: Peerless Press 1968.

LEECH, CLIFFORD and C. W. CRAIK (eds). *The Revels History of Drama in English* 6. London: Methuen 1975.

ROWELL, GEORGE. *The Victorian Theatre* revised. Cambridge: 1978.

TAYLOR, JOHN RUSSELL. *The Second Wave*. London: Eyre Methuen 1978.

TILDESLEY, BEATRICE. Fifty years of the theatre in Australia. *Australian Quarterly* 23 (Sydney, December 1951).

VASEY, RUTH and ELIZABETH WRIGHT. A Calendar of Sydney Theatre Performances 1870-79. Sydney: Australian Theatre Studies Centre 1986.

WANDOR, MICHELENE. *Carry On Understudies*. London: Routledge 1986.

A national theatre? *Current Affairs Bulletin* 13/13 (12 April 1954).

Jon English

Actor, rock singer. Born 26 March 1949 in London. Emigrated to Australia with family as teenager. Began musical career in Sydney.

Jon English graduated from rock bands to the theatre as Judas in HARRY M. MILLER's production of *Jesus Christ Superstar* in 1972. After two years in that show, English often worked as an actor. In the early 1980s he began organising a rock musical titled *Paris*, after the Trojan Wars. A recording of the score was well received but the show still awaits full-scale production. English was a distinctive, dynamic Pirate King in the Victoria State Opera's production of the Broadway version of *The Pirates of Penzance* in 1984. Ten years later he played the role in an even funnier version for Essgee Entertainment. ❦*John West*

Nick Enright

Actor, director, dramatist, translator. Born 22 December 1950 in Newcastle (NSW). Educated at University of Sydney. Began acting in Sydney 1967. Trained at New York University School of the Arts 1975–77. Associate director of South Australian Theatre Company (Adelaide) 1979–81. Taught acting at National Institute of Dramatic Art 1983–84. Acted for Nimrod Theatre Company (Sydney), State Theatre Company of South Australia (Adelaide), Hunter Valley Theatre Company (Newcastle), Griffin Theatre Company (Sydney). NSW Premier's Award for *Variations* 1982. Australian Writers' Guild Awgie award 1990 for *Daylight Saving*, 1993 for *The Property of the Clan*. Also writes for radio, film and television.

In a widely varied career Nick Enright has produced outstanding works for the theatre. Many of his plays, such as his collaborations with the composer TERENCE CLARK—*Summer Rain*, *Variations* and *The Venetian Twins*—show his love of music and proficiency as a writer for musical theatre. Affectionate familiarity with life in small rural communities informs *Summer Rain* and is the topic of 'Back to Jindyworobak', the hit song in *The Venetian Twins*.

Enright shows particular sympathy for the resilience and friendship of isolated or vulnerable women in *First Class Women* and *On the Wallaby*, which address Australian social history—transportation and the Great Depression respectively. He is a prolific translator and adaptor—of Sophocles, Euripides, Carlo Goldoni, Carlo Gozzi, Pierre Beaumarchais and Molière—and strong senses of classical comedy and farce form pervade his own work. They are particularly evident in his acclaimed comedy *Daylight Saving*, which shows the romantic and familial entanglements of a group of articulate jet-setting Sydneysiders, working the generic and sociological territory popularised by DAVID WILLIAMSON. *St James Infirmary* is set in a Jesuit boys' college near Sydney—Enright himself attended St Ignatius's College, Riverview, in Sydney—during the Vietnam War, showing the options of the artist's acquiescence in or rebellion against social and political conformity. Enright's most powerful and complex drama is *Mongrels*, which is informed by the rivalry of two of Australia's leading Irish Catholic playwrights, PETER KENNA and JIM MCNEIL. A script that balances savagery and wit displays the personal and sexual costs borne by inhabitants of the theatrical world and those close to them, and their sometimes outrageous negotiation of the competing claims of love, talent and morality. His 1992 play for Freewheels,

The Property of the Clan, dealing with the rape and murder of a schoolgirl, shows his ability to write sensitively for young people. ❦*Veronica Kelly*

published plays
Daylight Saving (1990). Sydney: Currency Press 1990.
Don Juan (1984) translation of Molière. Sydney: Currency Press 1984.
On the Wallaby (1980) musical play. Sydney: Currency Press 1982.
The Property of the Clan (1992). Sydney: Currency Press 1994.
St James Infirmary (1992). Sydney: Currency Press 1993.

other writings
The Maitland and Morpeth String Quartet. Sydney: David Ell 1980.
Carnival of the Animals. Sydney: ABC 1990.

further reading
BALLET, ARTHUR H. In *Contemporary Dramatists* (ed. K. A. Berney) 5th edn. London: St James Press 1993.
KELLY, VERONICA. A form of music—An interview with Nick Enright. *Australasian Drama Studies* 24 (Brisbane, April 1994).
KELLY VERONICA. Enright's *Mongrels* as intervention in the canon of contemporary Australian playwriting. *Southerly* 54/2 (Sydney, June 1994).

Ensemble Theatre Company

Professional dramatic company in Sydney, founded as Ensemble Company on 11 May 1958 by Hayes Gordon. Renamed 30 August 1958. **artistic directors** 1958–86 Hayes Gordon. 1986– Sandra Bates. **venues** 1958 Cammeray Library. 1958–60 corner Miller and Berry Streets, North Sydney. 1960– Ensemble Theatre, Kirribilli. **landmark productions** *The Man* by Mel Dinelli. *The Drunkard* by William Sedley-Smith. *The Buffalo Skinner* by Lonny Chapman. *Billy Liar* by Willis Hall and Keith Waterhouse. *Garden District* by Tennessee Williams. *The Physicists* by Friedrich Dürrenmatt. *Fortune And Men's Eyes* by John Herbert. *An Enemy of the People* by Henrik Ibsen. *Philadelphia Here I Come* by Brian Friel. *The Night Thoreau Spent In Jail* by Jerome Lawrence and Robert E. Lee. *Comedians* by Trevor Griffiths. *Rain* by John Colton and Clemence Randolph. *The Petition* by Brian Clark.

The oldest professional theatrical company in NSW, the Ensemble Theatre Company has, in the words of the critic H. G. KIPPAX, made a 'distinctive and distinguished contribution to Sydney's theatre culture'. From its beginning as the Ensemble Company, presenting one-act plays by Tennessee Williams in a library in a northern suburb in May 1958, it has been dominated by the vision, teaching, artistic criteria and policies of its founder, HAYES GORDON.

The group was renamed the Ensemble Theatre to present *The Man* by Mel Dinelli and *Orpheus Descending* by Tennessee Williams on 30 August 1958 in a North Sydney venue which was soon declared a firetrap. Ensemble Theatre Pty Ltd, set up in June 1959, bought a tumbledown boatshed on the northern shore of Sydney Harbour, converted it and opened it on 7 January 1960 as Australia's first continuously running theatre-in-the-round.

The company won a unique reputation based on the intimacy of its theatre, the truth of its acting, its emphasis on relevance to contemporary social needs in selection of plays, its meticulous attention to details of production, its co-operative company structure and its concern for comfort and needs of the audience.

'There's a marked difference about a visit to the Ensemble', wrote the reviewer NORMAN KESSELL. 'It's an attitude, a feeling of being at a friend's place for a pleasant evening, almost a family get-together.'

The Ensemble expanded its activities to include readings of Australian poetry by the authors, assisted by actors, in 1964–65; a popular series of programs introducing schoolchildren to theatre in 1970–74; a second venue at the STABLES THEATRE in 1977–80; festivals of Sydney playwrights in 1979–81; subsidiary productions called Sunday Showcase Theatre from 1979; extensive programs of subsidiary productions, films, talks and social gatherings for subscribers; a tour of the United Kingdom and Ireland of its production of *No Room for Dreamers* by GEORGE HUTCHINSON in 1980; and the SIDETRACK THEATRE COMPANY in 1980–81. Sidetrack, whose principals were former Ensemble students, used the Ensemble premises and administrative assistance.

Under Rosemary Jones, general manager from 1965 to 1984, the Ensemble company made many administrative advances, especially in services and the building, which was improved with a restaurant, bar and air-conditioning by 1978. Theatre-in-the-round was abandoned in 1980, primarily to permit more seating. Then a new theatre was designed for the site by the architect Alan Williams. To permit the first stage of building during 1983–84, the Ensemble company leased the cinema at the SYDNEY OPERA HOUSE. It proved that venue suitable for live theatre, which led to its conversion into the Playhouse. In 1984 the Ensemble Theatre returned to its home, which had an updated theatre space and new entrance, foyer, bar and harbourside restaurant. The second stage remains to be built.

Hayes Gordon retired from the Ensemble Theatre in 1986. He had directed more of the company's 145 productions of Australian and overseas plays than any of the other directors who have contributed to a distinctive Ensemble style. These include Sandra Bates, JON EWING, John Macleod, Brian Young and the present writer. Actors associated with the company from early years include Lorraine Bayly, Jon Ewing, Clarissa Kaye, Sophie Krantz, Robin Lawler, REG LIVERMORE, Jerry Luke, Tony Wickert and the writer. ❦*Don Reid*

further reading
GORDON, HAYES. *Acting and Performing*. Sydney: Ensemble Press 1993.
MCPHERSON, AILSA. *A Dream of Passion—Theatre activity in North Sydney*. Sydney: Stanton Library 1993.

Entertainment taxes

To assist the war effort, in 1916 federal GOVERNMENT POLICY imposed an entertainments tax on the price of each ticket at the rates of one halfpenny on the first two shillings and sixpence and another halfpenny on each further sixpence. The tax was not repealed until 1934 and in the late 1920s some states imposed an additional tax. NSW, for example, charged amusement tax on all admissions costing one shilling and sixpence or more.

Cinema tickets usually cost about one shilling but few theatre tickets were less than two and sixpence because the cost of presenting live performance was higher. Theatrical entrepreneurs claimed that the live theatre bore the main weight of the second tax and they found the double taxation a particular burden during the Great Depression. ❦*Annette Bain*

Entr'acte Theatre

Professional movement-theatre company in Sydney, founded in 1979 as Sydney Corporeal–Mime Theatre by Elisabeth Burke and Pierre Thibaudeau. Renamed 1982. **artistic directors** Elisabeth Burke and Pierre Thibaudeau. **first production** *The Shape of Time*, devised and performed by Burke and Thibaudeau, 1980 at Orange Doors, Sydney.

Entr'acte has been the most influential exponent of movement theatre in Australia. Since the late 1980s it has contributed to the growth of the art form in Australia through the complexity, spectacle and movement of its productions. The company is noted for its training classes in corporeal MIME. Entr'acte has evolved its own style of movement training from the teaching of Etienne Decroux, whose influence upon it was at a peak from 1979 to 1983. Elisabeth Burke and Pierre Thibaudeau studied at Decroux's school in Paris and Thibaudeau was his assistant.

Entr'acte was at first connected with the University of Sydney's Theatre Workshop at the SEYMOUR THEATRE CENTRE, where it revived its first production, *The Shape of Time*, in February 1981 and presented *A la Carte* in September. These two shows, combined as *Mime Spectrum*, toured to Melbourne and Adelaide in 1982 and to Sydney schools in 1983. Most Entr'acte productions since 1983 have been first performed at the PERFORMANCE SPACE in Sydney and then reworked for national and international touring.

Refractions, inspired by the Bauhaus design school of Weimar Germany, brought the company national recognition in 1983. Entr'acte toured parts of *Refractions* and *The Shape of Time* to Montreal and Amsterdam in 1983. It took *Refractions* to the Adelaide Festival Fringe, Canberra, Melbourne, Perth, Newcastle (NSW), Sydney and Wollongong (NSW) in 1984; to Tasmania, the United Kingdom, the Netherlands and France in 1985; and to Queensland and to Indonesia for cultural exchange in 1986.

With *Ostraka*, derived from a short story by Marguerite Youcenar on Clytemnestra's trial for the murder of Agamemnon, in 1986 the combination of natural voice with expressive corporeal movement became the basis of the Entr'acte performing style. A company of six, including Nigel Kellaway, performed *Ostraka* with original live music by Colin Offord in a double bill with *On Archeology*, directed by Nicholas Tsoutas, at the Performance Space. The production departed from pure mime with music by including sections of recorded voice-over.

In 1987, the company returned to Indonesia for a seven-week cultural exchange, including performances of *Refractions*. Indonesian movement influenced *The Last Circus* in 1988. The present writer worked with the company in this production and later as dramaturge in a new presentation of *Ostraka* that toured NSW and South Australia and went to London and other cities in the United Kingdom.

In 1989 Thibaudeau directed and designed *The Memory Room*, with music composed by Sarah de Jong. Starting with a large aluminium cube, a cast of five explored the concepts of memory and the senses. A reworked production toured to the 1990 Adelaide Fringe Festival, and to the Toga Festival in Japan.

In 1991 Burke directed *Possessed/Dispossessed* with a live soundscape composed by Paul Charlier and a set design by Thibaudeau. This production represented Australia at the 1991 Prague Quadrennial and a reworked version toured to Indonesia in 1992. ☙*Bruce Keller*

Leon Errol

Comedian. Born 3 July 1881 in Sydney. Began writing, staging and appearing in small revues while studying medicine at University of Sydney. Began performing in vaudeville 1896. Married dancer Stella Chatelaine and went to USA 1906. Played in musical comedy and burlesque. Became American citizen 1923. Died 12 October 1951 in California.

Before he began a long American career Leon Errol toured Australia for a decade in a variety of roles—from operetta to Shakespeare's Romeo. He made his professional debut as a red-nosed comic in vaudeville at the Royal Standard Theatre in Sydney in 1896, and soon perfected a rubber-legged drunk act that was his stand-by throughout his career. In 1906 he married and went with his wife to the USA, where he played in musical comedy and burlesque stock companies. His big break came in 1911 when he starred in the *Ziegfeld Follies*. He made his London debut at the Hippodrome in 1919. In 1920 Errol created the role of Connie in Florenz Ziegfeld's production of *Sally*, and he starred in the film version in 1925. His career was thereafter split between stage and screen. He made widely popular two-reel film comedies until his death. ☙*Frank Van Straten*

further reading
KATZ, EPHRAIM. *The International Film Encyclopedia*. London: Macmillan 1982.
Film Fan Monthly June–July 1970.
Parade (Melbourne, Sydney) February 1961.

Louis Esson

Critic, dramatist. Born in 1879 in Edinburgh (Scotland). Brought to Australia as a child. Grew up with aunts and uncles, including painter John Ford Paterson. Studied at University of Melbourne without taking degree. Went on overseas trip, initially to Paris with Leon Brodsky. Met J. M. Synge and W. B. Yeats 1905. Overseas, mainly in England, 1916–21. Founded Pioneer Players in Melbourne 1922. Melbourne dramatic critic for *New Triad* 1924–27. Died 1943. Married Hilda Bull, medical practitioner and writer.

Under the influence of the Irish dramatists W. B. Yeats and J. M. Synge, Louis Esson turned his back on youthful bohemianism and interest in modernist art and worked to establish a nationalist folk drama in which Australian themes of working-class urban and, especially, bush life, would become the basis for great international artistic achievements. Esson's writing for the stage was concentrated in two bursts, each coming after an overseas trip during which he met and was advised by Yeats, co-founder of the Abbey Theatre in Dublin. On the first trip, in 1905, he also met Synge, the greatest Abbey dramatist. Both Yeats and Synge told Esson, against his own inclination, to stick to Australian subjects. Synge gave him the most famous piece of advice, according to VANCE PALMER: 'You ought to have plenty of material for drama in Australia. All those outback stations with shepherds going mad in lonely huts.'

Back in Australia in 1906, Esson joined the bohemian artistic circle of inner Melbourne and became a foundation member of the Victorian Socialist Party. One of the two great ironies of Esson's life and work was that his tastes and education were for the bohemian, early modernist culture that he found in the artistic café life of Melbourne in his youth and pursued in London, New York, and Paris. Yet he abandoned all that to embrace a bush culture which he came to believe was the proper subject for pioneering Australian drama. The other irony was that this kind of nationalism was itself an international trend in the early 20th century and that the Abbey Theatre of Yeats, Esson's chief mentor, was the great success of nationalist theatre.

Esson met Yeats again on his second overseas trip, which lasted from 1916 to 1921 and included a long stay in England. There he also met Palmer and other Australians. In London during this stay, he wrote THE DROVERS, probably the most successful of the plays for which he wanted to be remembered. On return to Australia Esson founded the PIONEER PLAYERS with his second wife, Hilda Bull, and other friends, including Palmer. This marked the beginning of his most productive period, in which he was inspired not only by the Irish model but by the excitement of having a theatre to write for. The amateur company, influenced by the Abbey Theatre, strove to bring Australian playwrights to the public but the plays were not forthcoming and Esson himself struggled to supply a large part of its repertoire in 1922–23. After a two-year hiatus the company presented its last production, Esson's *The Bride of Gospel Place*, in 1926.

After the failure of the Pioneer Players, Esson tinkered with old plays and wrote a few new ones, but none of his later work was successful. He became increasingly disillusioned about the possibility of establishing any lively artistic culture in a society he saw as arid and philistine.

Esson's plays include an early, Shavian-style political comedy, THE TIME IS NOT YET RIPE, his best-known play today. It is so well written and charming that it is tempting to wish that he had written more plays like it. But he soon turned his back on it, and began the great task he had set himself—to build a folk theatre with simple 'country comedies' and grim little dramas of the hard life of the outback.

Dead Timber, *The Drovers* and *Andeganora* are austere vignettes of the harshness of life in the bush. In *The Drovers* a romantic bushman is injured in a stampede and has to be left to die so that his mates can push on to find water for the restless cattle. *Dead Timber* is an extremely gloomy picture of life on a small selection, with the hostility of the land manifesting itself in the emotional turmoil and defeat felt by an unnamed farmer and his family. Esson explored similar themes at greater length in MOTHER AND SON (1923), a melodramatic story of the clash between a young man yearning for the excitement of city life and his stoically patient mother, struggling to survive on a small apiary in the Gippsland region of Victoria. These three plays, with their interest in the tragedy of the human struggle to survive in a difficult environment, and their portrayal of the conflicting claims of the bush and the modern attractions of the new cities, set the tone for a great deal of the grim outback drama of the 1930s and 1940s.

Parallel with these bush plays are Esson's colourful portraits of low life in inner Melbourne, in *The Woman Tamer*, *The Sacred Place* and the full-length *The Bride of Gospel Place*. These lighter works, perhaps closer to Esson's actual experience, lean towards comedy, although there is a bleakness about the portrayal of the inner-city slums in the last play, which ends in tragedy for the bride and is reminiscent of the ominous power of the landscape in the bush plays. Esson's other works include *The Battler*, or *Diggers' Rest*, a charming and underrated country comedy; *Shipwreck*, a splendidly Gothic sea-melodrama heavily influenced by the early Eugene O'Neill; and *The Southern Cross*, a laborious historical drama about the Eureka Stockade, probably written in the late 1930s. Esson lost the original manuscript of *The Battlers* with other work in a fire and hastily reconstituted it for the Pioneer Players' production.

One of his worst plays is one of his last, *The Quest*, a sad sign of the disillusionment he faced when his audiences and the theatrical world he lived in failed to realise his great dreams. That he was aware of this—that his embarrassment at the Philistinism of his own country seemed to him to be vindicated, in spite of all his struggles for a folk drama—was one of the great sadnesses in his life. He lived as a journalist all his life, in the later years he was supported, emotionally as well as financially, by Hilda Bull. His reputation as Australia's pioneer modern dramatist partly depends on her advocacy, especially her organisation of the publication in 1946 of a volume of his full-length plays, with obituary tributes. *John McCallum*

published plays
Andeganora. Sydney: Angus and Robertson 1937 in *Best Australian One-Act Plays*.
The Bride of Gospel Place (1926). Melbourne: Robertson and Mullens 1946 in *the Southern Cross and Other Plays*.
Dead Timber (1911). Melbourne: Fraser and Jenkinson c.1912 in *Three Short Plays*. London: Henderson 1920 in *Dead Timber and Other Plays*.
The Drovers (1923). London: Henderson 1920 in *Dead Timber and Other Plays*. Sydney: Mulga 1944 in *Six One-Act Australian Plays*. Brisbane: University of Queensland Press 1977 in *Five Plays for Stage, Radio and TV*.
Mother and Son (1923). Melbourne: Robertson and Mullens 1946 in *The Southern Cross and Other Plays*.
The Sacred Place (1912). Melbourne: Fraser and Jenkinson c.1912. London: Henderson 1920 in *Dead Timber and Other Plays*.
Shipwreck. Armidale: University of New England 1986 in *Australian Drama 1920–1955*.
The Southern Cross. Melbourne: Robertson and Mullens 1946 in *The Southern Cross and Other Plays*.
The Time is Not Yet Ripe (1912). Melbourne: Fraser and Jenkinson 1912. Sydney: Currency Press 1973.
Vagabond Camp. Ascot Vale (Vic.): Red Rooster Press 1980 in *Ballades of Old Bohemia*.
The Woman Tamer (1910). Melbourne: Fraser and Jenkinson c.1912 in *Three Short Plays*. London: Henderson 1920 in *Dead Timber and Other Plays* Sydney: Currency Press 1976.

other writings
Ballades of Old Bohemia (ed. Hugh Anderson). Ascot Vale (Vic.): Red Rooster Press 1980. Anthology of verse, short plays and journalism.
Louis Esson and the Australian Theatre (ed. Vance Palmer) Melbourne: Georgian House 1948. A collection of Esson's letters, with a long introduction by Palmer.

further reading
CARROLL, DENNIS. *Australian Contemporary Drama*. Sydney: Currency Press 1995.
MCCALLUM, JOHN. Something with a cow in it. *Overland* 108 (September 1987).
WALKER, D. R. Thomas Louis Buvelot Esson. *Australian Dictionary of Biography* 8. Melbourne University Press 1981.
WALKER, DAVID. *Dream and Disillusion*. Canberra: Australian National University Press 1976.

reference
Unpublished plays by Esson are in the Campbell Howard Collection, University of New England, Armidale (NSW).

European influences

There was a considerable continental European presence in colonial theatre, mostly manifest through French and German plays in English-language versions that had joined the standard Anglo-American repertoire. France particularly attracted British playwrights of the period. The appearance of a new piece in Paris—where authors were paid much better than in London—would often lead to several quite different English versions being written under various titles. So E. L. A. Brisebarre's *Les Pauvres de Paris* of 1856 became *The Poor of New York*, *The Streets of London*, *The Poor of Liverpool*, *The Streets of Melbourne* and so on. For every *Camille* or *Frou Frou* that declared its original authorship there were probably a dozen or more melodramas and comedies that disguised it. In Australia the repertoire depended upon the publications available, and these were mainly classics and English publications of currently popular works. Awareness of continental repertoire in the audience was exemplified by the charge that Charles Nagel had plagiarised his burlesque *The Mock Catalani in Little Puddleton* from *Die falsche Catalani in Krahwinkel* by Adolf Bauerle. Such local adaptations were as common in Australia as in Europe at that time, when copyright in a work lay with the publisher, not the author. Jacob Montefiore, supporting his application for a licence to perform his play *John of Austria* in 1847, admitted that it was adapted from a play of the same title by Casimir Delavigne.

The first play from continental Europe to be seen in Australia was probably Friedrich von Kotzebue's Gothic drama *The Stranger* (*Menschenhass und Reue*) in December 1833 at the FREEMASON'S TAVERN in Hobart. Benjamin Thompson's published translation of 1789 had made this drama of infidelity and forgiveness a huge success in Great Britain. *The Stranger* became one of the most popular plays in the Australian colonies. Maria Coppin played it with great success in Sydney in 1843 and later. NELLIE STEWART made her debut in the play in 1863 at the age of five.

Predominant among German contributions to the repertoire was Friedrich von Schiller's *The Robbers* (*Die Räuber*). Part 1 of Johann von Goethe's *Faust* was seen in a variety of popularisations, including CHARLES AND ELLEN KEAN's *Faust and Marguerite*. The bilingual Daniel Bandmann, who had several successful seasons in Australia between the late 1860s and the early 1880s, included in his repertoire not only Charles Moor in *The Robbers* but Shakespearean interpretations influenced by the German heritage of Emil Devrient. The high artistic calibre of the German contribution reflected the seriousness and intellectual interests of 19th-century immigrants in Australia from German-speaking states. Political tensions attending German unification and Prussian–Austrian rivalry were reflected in the presence of more than one German-language cultural club in most large cities. These clubs supported performances of national dramas in both English and German.

Another bilingual actor, Francesca Janauschek, a Czech and a leading figure on the German stage, toured Australia in 1875. She was primarily an imitator of the Italian star ADELAIDE RISTORI and was unfortunate enough to coincide with a tour by Ristori herself, who was considered to be the greatest actress in the world. Italian spoken drama made its strongest impression when Ristori, touring with a huge company to celebrate the unification of Italy, performed in Sydney, Melbourne, Adelaide and Ballarat for four months in 1875. She acted in Italian to packed houses, although initial response was poor. The Melbourne critic J. E. NEILD pronounced the language no barrier—'the hands, the eyes, the inflection of the voice' communicated 'that kind of eloquence which is so much richer than spoken words'. Audiences in Sydney and Melbourne organised torchlit processions for Ristori, while spectators in Ballarat were said to have thrown gold nuggets at her curtain calls.

Ristori played most of her great roles—Lady Macbeth, Medea, Phèdre, and Paolo Giacometti's Lucrezia Borgia, Marie Antoinette and Pia De Tolomei. Two members of her company, EDUARDO AND GIULIA MAJERONI, remained in Australia and performed their own English-language adaptations of Italian melodramas, which otherwise would hardly have been known in Australia.

Early European visitors

The first touring company to visit Australia comprised six French performers, who arrived in Sydney in 1839 and performed drama, vaudevilles and opera. A French dancer, M. Charrière, and his wife arrived in Sydney from Mauritius in 1841. They teamed up with LUIGI DALLE CASE, an Italian strong man, who also arrived from Mauritius in 1841, with his Foreign Gymnastic Troupe and opened an early hippodrome, the Australian Olympic Theatre. In 1842 Charrière hired the Royal Victoria Theatre for a benefit in which Mme Charrière made her debut. She, CONRAD KNOWLES and Mary Anne Larra, a resident French actor, acted in French. They performed three more French plays that year before the Charrières departed.

Australia received touring performers from all over the world after the discovery of gold in the 1850s, but its sparse population had no substantial pockets of speakers of European languages and European touring companies were rare here, as in Europe. In Germany touring companies had been driven out of existence by subsidised municipal theatres; in France they had to submit to the supremacy of the Paris theatres. Only in Italy did the strolling player survive.

In other fields of theatre and in music, however, European performers were significant. Opera and *opéra bouffe* were the most popular forms of theatre. As in the United Kingdom, the resident companies mostly sang in English, but when visiting artists were on stage it was not uncommon to have two or even three languages at once. Italian opera singers performed frequently in Australia from 1860. German musicians were popular on the goldfields. Johannes Wirth, a Bavarian musician who arrived at the diggings in 1855 with his brothers Jacob and Peter, founded WIRTHS' CIRCUS.

Australian circus received many European immigrants and many more European artists toured Australia. Puppeteers also came from all over the world. In Sydney 1877 an Italian Marionette Company performed in Italian. Distinguished French variety artists seen in Australia included the tightrope walker Blondin, who toured in 1874 and in 1875–76, leaving behind a legacy of 'Australian Blondins'. During one of his sensational displays in Melbourne German pit musicians irreverently struck up 'Der Wacht am Rhein' as a reminder of the Prussian victory over France in 1871.

The wealth that flowed from the goldfields changed Australian social life, and with the rise of the middle class came first satirical PANTOMIME and sensational dramas and then polite comedy. The 19th century was a golden era of scene-painters and stage design and the masters of the craft were from Europe. Among those with long careers were Bremen-born JOHN HENNINGS, Australia's premier scenic artist, and his nearest rival, ALEXANDER HABBE, a Dane.

The plays of Victor Hugo, Alexandre Dumas *fils*, and Victorien Sardou were in the repertoires of companies such as Arthur Garner's LONDON COMEDY COMPANY and the BROUGH–BOUCICAULT COMEDY COMPANY. The former's production of Sardou's *Friends* in 1879 was described by the *Sydney Mail* as 'unquestionably superior to any drama yet presented on the Sydney stage'. In the same year J. C. WILLIAMSON presented a French play, *Au Fond de la mer*, translated and adapted by actor GEORGE LEITCH as *The Pearl Divers*. In 1890 the American actor Cora Brown Potter and Kyrle Bellew, a young English actor, had a notable success with a repertoire of fashionable plays including Sardou's *La Tosca* and Dumas's *Camille*. In the same year Williamson introduced Henrik Ibsen to Australia with the English realist players JANET ACHURCH and Charles Charrington—only weeks after they had caused a scandal in London with William Archer's English translation of *A Doll's House*.

The memory of Ristori was eclipsed by a spectacular east-coast tour by SARAH BERNHARDT with her own company in 1891. Audiences were provided with English texts of the nine plays in her repertoire. The season was so successful that at the final curtain call J. C. Williamson filled the Sydney stage with the stars of the Australian theatre, some of whom had travelled from Melbourne for the occasion.

Musical theatre

The most direct and substantial European influence was through various forms of musical theatre, particularly French grand opera and *opéra-bouffe*, Italian romantic opera, and German romantic opera and operettas. The remarkable popularity of Giacomo Meyerbeer's grand operas *Les Huguenots* and *Le Prophète* in 19th-century Australia parallels that of paintings on Protestant themes such as 'John Bunyan in Prison' and 'The Departure of the Pilgrim Fathers', which were among the earliest acquisitions of the Melbourne art gallery. While Lyster's resident opera and *opéra-bouffe* companies mostly performed in English, his various Italian companies all sang in their own language in presenting versions of Italian opera—and Meyerbeer and Wagner—that were musically and theatrically independent of British tradition. English versions of the *opéras-bouffes* of Jacques Offenbach and Charles Lecocq were extraordinarily popular during the 1870s. The Paris-trained soprano Fannie Simonsen took part in some of these but did not perform in French. The operettas of GILBERT AND SULLIVAN later eclipsed the French works.

In short, 19th-century audiences were eclectic in their tastes and eager for entertainment of all kinds. Performers who could afford it went abroad for training. Education was entirely Eurocentric and a large proportion of the educated classes, including the influential theatre critics who sprang up in the last decades of the century, had been educated abroad. Another subject of influence, though it had little bearing upon performance, was Australian literary drama, or closet drama, of the 19th century. It was probably more influenced by the continental tradition than the British, consisting as it did of romantic tragedy, Gothic sensation and *comédie larmoyante*. An early work to receive publication and a single performance was THE BANDIT OF THE RHINE by Evan Henry Thomas, Charles Harpur's STALWART THE BUSHRANGER was palpably influenced by Schiller's *The Robbers* as much as by Shakespeare. Other works were ALFRED DEAKIN's *Quentin Massys* (1879) and Francis Adams's *Tiberius* (1894). ❦*Katharine Brisbane, Harold Love*

20th century

Federation and the arrival of cinema brought with them social changes that divided and changed the entertainment industry. The movies siphoned off popular entertainment and the professional theatre became the preserve of the middle class, offering largely English or American comedy of manners, the English classics and continental operetta. European vaudeville acts continued to tour the circuits, and Europe was still the centre of musical excellence for Australian audiences.

J. C. Williamson made another notable attempt to capture the changing moods of the middle class by commissioning the Rev. T. Hilhouse Taylor to write a play based on the Parsifal story as a vehicle for MINNIE TITTELL BRUNE, a forceful American actress. Richard Wagner's opera *Parsifal* was restricted to his Bayreuth theatre by his widow, but religious themes were much in vogue, popularised in Australia by the British actors JULIUS KNIGHT and Wilson Barrett. Taylor's PARSIFAL, a four-act blank-verse epic, relied more on spectacular staging than on the text for its impact but it had a record-breaking season in Sydney in 1906.

Serious drama became the preserve of AMATEUR THEATRE and between 1908 and the 1950s the great European movements of naturalism, expressionism, social realism and absurdism could be found reproduced in amateur theatres in most capital cities, directed by dedicated people who were refugees from Europe or had read in translation the work of the leading theorists. While the professional theatre was becoming increasingly vacuous in competition with the cinema, most of the advanced thinking about the purpose of theatre was taking place among amateurs.

The new movements in theatre began in Europe in the 1880s in revolt against the extravagance of the period and the seductions of the new technology. The influential new companies included the Théâtre Libre founded in Paris in 1887, the Freie Bühne in Berlin in 1889 and the Moscow Art Theatre, started by Konstantin Stanislavsky and Vladimir Nemirovich-Damchenko in 1898. The direction of these companies was towards realism, the 'slice of life' studies of the small comedies and tragedies of ordinary people, expressed not by the grand gestures of earlier convention but by revealing the internal life of a character through the pathology of his or her behaviour. The skills that actors had once learnt by experience began to be developed as a new dramaturgy, in some cases a science. Sometimes a play would be rehearsed for months, to achieve this minute realism, and as part of the process the role of the director became more powerful. The age of the director as visionary and educator had been born. Under the influence of the symbolists and the expressionists who followed in the 20th century—figures like Adolphe Appia, Edward Gordon

Craig, Maurice Maeterlinck and Vsevolod Meyerhold—the idea of the *auteur* as creator and the actor as puppet became more and more prominent. These theories suited amateur theatre. They offered intellectual stimulation and exploration; but also the opportunity for the creation, not of stars as in commercial theatre, but of gurus, behind-the-scene directors and theorists. The actors no longer carried the major responsibility. The German-inspired English repertory movement was the earliest amateur movement to reach Australia. It inspired the embryonic ADELAIDE REPERTORY THEATRE in 1908 and a stream of others.

MAURICE MOSCOVITCH, who had acted at the Moscow Art Theatre, expounded its method on a tour of Australia in 1924–25. Gradually the theories of Stanislavsky came to be a dominating influence upon the more advanced amateur theatres. From the 1930s to the 1950s influential figures such as Keith George of the WORKERS' ART GUILD in Perth, COLIN BALLANTYNE in Adelaide and DORIS FITTON in Sydney were disciples of Stanislavsky. The repertory movement was followed in the 1920s by the rise of political theatre and in Australia in the 1930s by the NEW THEATRE movement, whose influences were from Moscow, New York and the theatre of Bertolt Brecht and Erwin Piscator.

An influential advocate for Italian theatre in the 1950s and 1960s was Frederick May, professor of Italian at the University of Sydney, especially with his translations of Luigi Pirandello. Sydney saw its first professional production of Pirandello's *Six Characters in Search of an Author*—in May's translation—only in 1988, however.

Subsidised theatre

Brecht and Anton Chekhov did not enter the repertoire of professional theatre until the 1960s. With the establishment of federal theatre subsidy in 1968 the role of producing 'the world's best plays' began to shift from the amateur to the professional theatre. In the 1960s and 1970s it espoused the methods of Jerzy Grotowski and the works—in English translation—of early avant-garde writers like Antonin Artaud (whose theory was first published in English in 1958) and Alfred Jarry, and of new-wave writers like Eugène Ionesco and the Austrian Peter Handke.

Pre-Brecht German playwrights whose works have had an impact in Australia include Frank Wedekind and Georg Büchner. LOUIS NOWRA translated Wedekind's Lulu plays for the STATE THEATRE Company of South Australia in 1981, and went on to translate Heinrich von Kleist's *The Prince of Homburg* after a revival in Europe following a notable production by the German director Peter Stein. Büchner's *Woyzeck* has been performed in numerous versions.

The British critic and author of *The Theatre of the Absurd*, Martin Esslin visited Australia in 1979 and directed a reading of Günter Grass's critique of Brecht, *The Plebeians Rehearse the Uprising*. Rolf Hochhuth's controversial play about Pope Pius XII and Nazi Germany, *The Representative* was performed at the Old Tote Theatre in Sydney and elsewhere in 1965. Peter Weiss's highly influential combination of Brechtian and Artaudian theatre practice, *The Persecution and Assassination of Marat as Performed by the Inmates of the Asylum of Charenton under the Direction of the Marquis de Sade* has received numerous student productions, while AUSTRALIAN NOUVEAU THEATRE in Melbourne in 1982 did one of the earliest English-language productions of *Hamletmachine* by Heiner Müller. *The Conquest of the South Pole*, by another East German, Manfred Karge, was directed by JIM SHARMAN at the BELVOIR STREET THEATRE in Sydney in 1989, inspired by the 1988 production at the Royal Court Theatre in London.

The plays of controversial German film-maker Rainer Werner Fassbinder were introduced to Australia by the AUSTRALIAN PERFORMING GROUP in 1978 with *The Bitter Tears of Petra von Kant*. This was followed by his *Bremen Coffee*, produced by the BRISBANE REPERTORY THEATRE SOCIETY in 1978 and by the MELBOURNE THEATRE COMPANY in 1980. In 1981 Brisbane Repertory also gave the Australian premiere of *The Enemy Within*, Monvid Graznya's play about four women in Nazi Germany. The plays of the influential Bavarian neo-naturalist Franz Xaver Kroetz have been slow to arrive. *Stallerhof* was produced at the Belvoir Street Theatre and in Melbourne in 1989, while *Request Program* was seen at the Adelaide Festival in 1988 in Nancy Diuguid's British production.

Peter Handke has been well represented in Australia by, among others, *Kaspar*, performed by the NIMROD THEATRE COMPANY in Sydney in 1973 and by TROUPE in Adelaide in 1979; *The Ride Across Lake Constance* by Nimrod in 1975 and by the HOLE-IN-THE-WALL THEATRE COMPANY in Perth in 1976; and *My Foot My Tutor* by the QUEENSLAND THEATRE COMPANY in Brisbane in 1976. The revival he encouraged of 'folk plays' by his fellow Austrian Ödön von Horváth was reflected in productions of the latter's *Tales from the Vienna Woods* by Brisbane Repertory in 1978, the State Theatre Company of South Australia in 1979, and the Nimrod Theatre Company in 1981. Botho Strauss's lugubrious and challenging play *Big and Little* had its Australian premiere in Adelaide in 1985, and received a major but unpopular production for the SYDNEY THEATRE COMPANY in 1988 by two visiting Germans, the director Harald Clemen and the designer Peter Schulz.

The Swiss playwrights Friedrich Dürrenmatt and Max Frisch have been reasonably well represented, with the former's *The Physicists* produced by New Theatre in Sydney in 1970 and the latter's *The Fire Raisers* by the OLD TOTE THEATRE COMPANY in 1963 and *Andorra* by New Theatre in Sydney 1965. Dürrenmatt's *The Visit* had a famous production by INDEPENDENT THEATRE in Sydney in 1963 with DORIS FITTON in the lead. The British Théâtre de Complicité brought its production to the 1990 Adelaide Festival and the Sydney Theatre Company presented it in 1993. The Swiss mime group Mummenschanz performed at World Expo '88 in Brisbane.

The aimlessness and provinciality of Chekhov's characters appeal even more than Shakespeare to Australian audiences. The earliest Chekhov performances were probably *Three Sisters* by Independent Theatre in 1936 and *The Cherry Orchard* by the DOLIA RIBUSH Players in Melbourne in 1938. With subsidy Chekhov had become a regular part of the national repertoire. His major plays have been many times translated in Australia in the last 20 years to increase the bond of sympathy.

Ibsen is probably the second most-produced of the major European dramatists; Molière is seen not infrequently but is less sympathetically received; Pierre Corneille and Jean Racine, Goethe and Schiller are rarely seen. Nikolai Gogol's *The Government Inspector* is frequently revived and has had several adaptations to an Australian setting. Various forms of *commedia dell'arte* have been essayed in Australia—most notably Nick Enright's Australianised versions of Carlo Gozzi and Carlo Goldoni. Nimrod performed the latter's *I gemelli veneziani* as The Venetian Twins, a musical, by Enright and Terence Clarke in 1979. *The Three Cuckolds*, Leon Katz's English version of a medieval work, has been performed by New Theatre in Sydney in 1972 and Brisbane Repertory in 1987. It also was the opening production by the South Australian Theatre Company at the Adelaide Festival Centre in 1974, directed by George Ogilvie.

The most widely performed and successful contemporary Italian playwrights are Dario Fo and his wife Franca Rame, although productions of their plays in Australia are mainly a result of their success in London. Many Australian productions have used British adaptations of the plays—the Melbourne Theatre Company's production of Fo's *Trumpets and Raspberries* in 1985, for instance. A notable exception was Brent McGregor's production of Fo's *Accidental Death of an Anarchist* for Nimrod and Theatre ACT in 1981 and the Melbourne Theatre Company in 1983. It was criticised because topical Australian political references had been inserted—in accord with recommendations by Fo. McGregor also directed the first Australian production of Fo's *We Can't Pay? We Won't Pay!* in Newcastle (NSW) in 1980. New Theatre in Sydney performed it two months later.

Fo and Rame's *Female Parts* was workshopped in Nimrod's Women and Theatre project and performed in 1982. When the Nimrod Theatre became the Belvoir Street Theatre in 1985 Fo and Rame's *Whore in a Madhouse* was a controversial early production. Evelyn Krape has performed Rame roles in Melbourne—in *Female Parts* in 1983, in Fo and Rame's *The Open Couple* in 1985 and *A Day Like Any Other* in 1989. Zootango in Hobart performed Fo's *Tale of a Tiger* in 1987, and Leonard Kovner toured his English-language version of Fo's series of monologues *Mistero buffo* in 1988 and *The Obscene Fables* in 1992. In 1994 Robyn Archer directed her own adaptation of *Accidental Death of an Anarchist* in Adelaide and Sydney.

The feminist playwright Dacia Maraini visited Australia in 1987 and 1988, conducting workshops with Doppio Teatro in Adelaide, and her play *Stravaganza* was read at the Australian National Playwrights' Conference in 1987 and performed by Through Art, Unity in Canberra in 1988 and in Melbourne in 1992. Maraini's *Mary Stuart* was performed in Sydney in 1986, and *Dialogue Between a Prostitute and Her Client* and *Don Juan* in 1988.

In recent times French companies and performers have been seen in Australia in festivals and through the Alliance Française. The Comédie-Française paid a visit in the 1960s and another in 1988, performing Molière. Le Treteau de Paris included Australia and New Zealand in its world tours in the 1960s and 1970s. The puppeteer Philippe Genty and other French performers have appeared regularly in Australia. Thus Australian audiences are also exposed to French theatre by productions in which French departments of universities are catalysts for their own students and the Francophone community in general. In Sydney Théâtre Nouveau and the semiprofessional Sydney French Theatre carry the flag. The semiprofessional Théâtre Française de Melbourne has staged two or three productions a year since its inception in 1977, and it has toured New Caledonia. The trend for these companies is to aim beyond émigré or academic culture with bilingual productions that alternate between French and English, with space and movement unifying the performance.

There remains a strong streak of anti-intellectualism in the Australian theatre, both with audiences and the profession; and plays that can find a bond with audiences without making too great a leap from a foreign context, are probably the most successful. Audiences are generally incurious about what they do not easily understand.

Immigrants' theatre
Nevertheless, Australia is a country of immigrants and has supported many cultural clubs that seek to preserve the language and traditions of their birthplace. Among these have been many theatrical and musical groups, particularly since the Second World War. Atzala, a Lithuanian group in Sydney, was founded in 1955 by the actor Xana Dauguvietis and the director Paulius Rutenis, and has presented more than 40 productions.

The most significant French influence by far has come from Australian Nouveau Theatre in Melbourne, and its director Jean-Pierre Mignon, born and trained in France. This company, active from 1981 to 1994, consistently broadened its repertoire and emphasised ensemble work in the best traditions of that seminal figure of French theatre Jacques Copeau. It staged works by Antonin Artaud, Raymond Cousse, Jean Genet, Bernard-Marie Koltes, Molière and Roland Topor, as well as works by Samuel Beckett, other European playwrights and Australians.

Puppetry in Australia has been deeply influenced by European teachers, and from the 1930s by refugees from Europe. A Polish refugee, Igor Hychka taught Peter Scriven, who came to national attention in the 1950s. In Adelaide and around South Australia a Polish puppet theatre performs children's plays. A Polish group, Theatre Zart, directed by Kristof and Marta Kaczmarek, was formed in Perth in 1985. The Polish director Bogdan Koca, whose Thalia Theatre had a short life in the 1980s, ran the Lookout Theatre in Sydney until 1993 with a mixture of continental European and other modern works, in English, and has written his own works for performance.

The Hellenic Arts Theatre was formed in Sydney in 1984 and has performed classical Greek plays in Greek and English. Tes Lyssiotis, an Australian of Greek descent, founded the Filiki Players in Melbourne in the same year and directed a number of her own plays in English, Greek, Italian, and German, about immigrants' experiences in Australia. She uses Greek, Italian and English in her plays.

Doppio Teatro, led by Teresa Crea and Christopher Bell, performs in Italian and English in Adelaide and tours occasionally. Sydney had two Italian groups—the community theatre of the Federation of Italian Migrant Workers and their Families (FILEF), and the Gruppo Teatrale Napoletano directed by Raffaele Matarese.

Innovative community-theatre companies with a pluralistic policy have also adopted the life of immigrants as themes for study. A notable example is the Sidetrack Theatre Company in Sydney, founded in 1979. The establishment of a community arts board by the Australia Council in 1976 assisted a proliferation of ethnic groups in the 1980s. Ethnic and other cultural festivals have brought foreign-language companies to Australia. Professor Toni Comin of Flinders University was instrumental in a festival of Italian theatre in Adelaide in 1978. He directed Dario Fo's *Mistero buffo* in Italian and a visitor, Edmo Fenoglio, directed the State Theatre Company of South Australia in Goldoni's *Il servo di due padroni* (*The Servant of Two Masters*).

Excerpts from Giorgio Strehler's famous production of *Il servo di due padroni* were included in *Arlecchino e gli altri* (Harlequin and the others), which the famous Arlecchino Ferruccio Soleri and other members of the Piccolo Teatro di Milano performed in Perth, Canberra and Sydney in 1982. The environmental Teatro Settimo from Torino visited the Melbourne Spoleto Festival in 1986 and 1987. The Teatro dell'IRAA (Theatre of the Institute for Research into the Anthropology of the Actor) from Rome, directed by Renato Cuocolo, performed *Atacama* and *Nowhere to Hide* in Sydney and Melbourne in 1985 and 1988, and is now based in Melbourne. Recent festivals have included Georgian, Spanish, Dutch and Lithuanian theatre companies.

Playwriting in European languages

Through community theatre many playwrights have emerged. Osvaldo Maione, who lived in Australia from 1968 to 1988, wrote at least seven plays in Italian which were performed in Melbourne and Adelaide. He also performed in the work of Nino Randazzo, editor of the Italian newspaper *Il Globo* and co-founder of the Italo-Australian Theatre Company in Melbourne in 1980. Seven of Randazzo's plays have been performed in Italian at the Melbourne Italian Arts Festival.

Greek immigrants and their children have been particularly active. Playwrights of the second generation who write in both languages include Vasso Kalmaras and Theodore Patrikareas in addition to Tes Lyssiotis. Blagoja (Bill) Neskovski, who came to Australia at the age of eight, celebrated the Macedonian community in Wollongong (NSW) in three plays in Macedonian in 1964–89.

Some immigrants have chosen to write only in English about the immigrant experience, beginning the move into the mainstream and providing opportunities, hitherto denied, for actors of the same ethnic origin. Rudi Kraussman, a poet and critic from Austria, has written several experiments in dramatic form; and Dasha Blahova, a Czech actor from Prague, has written and performed her own work. In Adelaide, Anne-Marie Mykyta, the Australian wife of a Ukrainian, has written about her experience of the clash of cultures. JANIS BALODIS, an Australian of Latvian parentage, has also written about immigrants.

Translations for Australians

Until the 1970s it had been customary to use the standard translations provided by English literary texts, though there had been occasional translations by classical scholars of the Greek and Latin texts. But as the subsidised theatre companies matured the question of providing dialogue more sympathetic to the Australian ear began to arise. By the 1980s the practice had become established and in some cases controversial, consisting of conflations of existing translations by a theatre practitioner aided by an interpreter, evading the question of copyright ownership. Among the notable translators of recent years are the Norwegian May-Brit Akerholt (Ibsen), DAVID CLENDINNING (Chekhov and Pierre Marivaux), REX CRAMPHORN (French classics), Russian-speaking Robert Dessaix (Chekhov), John Golder (Molière), Tony Mitchell (Fo and Maraini), and Louis Nowra (French and German classics). The director AUBREY MELLOR set the pattern for new translations with his production of Chekhov's *Three Sisters* at the Nimrod Theatre in 1981, and the exercise has been influential in breaking the long domination by British and American plays. ❦*Katharine Brisbane, Tony Mitchell, Anne C. Murch*

further reading
BRISBANE, KATHARINE (ed.). *Entertaining Australia*. Sydney: Currency Press 1991.
CASTAN, CON. Greek-Australian plays. *Australasian Drama Studies* 12-13 (Brisbane 1988). Lists nearly 30 Greek-Australian playwrights.
KRAUSSMAN, RUDI (ed.). *Multicultural Arts Today in Australia*. Sydney: Australia Council 1986. Includes interview with the Turkish poet and playwright Gun Genger and article on Atzala by Jurgis Janavicius.
MITCHELL, TONY. Italo-Australian Theatre. *Australasian Drama Studies* 10 and 11 (Brisbane, April and October 1987).
MITCHELL, TONY. Nuovo paese, nuova direzione. *New Theatre-Australia* 1 (Sydney, September-October 1987).
TAYLOR, T. HILHOUSE. *Parsifal*. Sydney: Angus and Robertson 1906.

Jon Ewing

Actor, director, designer. Born 6 October 1936 in Sydney. Began theatrical work with Mercury Theatre and Independent Theatre in Sydney in early 1950s. Foundation member of Ensemble Theatre Company (Sydney) 1958. Director with St Martin's Theatre Company (Melbourne) 1970–71. Green Room Awards for best actor in a musical 1986 (Albin in *La Cage aux folles*) and supporting actor 1987 (Judge in *Sweeney Todd*). Also in film, radio and television.

In comedy and musicals Jon Ewing is regarded as a personality actor, expert in characters like Pangloss in *Candide* and Monsieur Firmin in *The Phantom of the Opera*. He is also capable of vulnerability and sexual ambiguity in characters like Albin in *La Cage aux folles* and Sylvia in PETER KENNA's *Mates*, of ambiguous evil as the Master of Ceremonies in *Cabaret* and calculated evil as the Judge in *Sweeney Todd*. His capabilities as a comic character actor have overshadowed his beginnings in naturalism. In 1958 he played the title-role in *The Man* by Mel Dinelli, the ENSEMBLE THEATRE COMPANY's first production in its own theatre. In the company's early years Ewing was a leading actor and director, and he designed many productions.

Ewing created Sylvia in *Mates* for the NIMROD THEATRE COMPANY in Sydney in 1975. Other major roles include Mordred in *Camelot* for J. C. WILLIAMSON's in 1964, the Master of Ceremonies in *Cabaret* in Sydney in 1971 and at the Festival of Perth of 1972, Pancrazio in *THE VENETIAN TWINS* for Nimrod in 1979, Voltaire/Pangloss in *Candide* for Nimrod in 1982, various parts in David Edgar's *The Life and Adventures of Nicholas Nickleby* for the SYDNEY THEATRE COMPANY in 1983, Gloucester in *King Lear* for Nimrod in 1984, and Belconnen in the AUSTRALIAN ELIZABETHAN THEATRE TRUST revival of DAVID WILLIAMSON's *Sons of Cain* that toured to London, in 1986 and Monsieur Firmin in Melbourne in 1990–92. Ewing has worked widely as a director, including a term with the ST MARTIN's THEATRE COMPANY in Melbourne during a period of readjustment and achievement after it first received government subvention. ❦*Katharine Brisbane*

Experimental theatre

As elsewhere in the world, experimental theatre continually re-evaluates the character and function of theatre in order to maintain or restore its ritual and aesthetic value in society. Since the 1960s experimental theatre has consciously opposed political and social orthodoxy, commercial and subsidised theatre and the conventions of the theatrical mainstream. It reached its peak between the mid-1960s and the mid-1970s, when opposition to the Vietnam War coincided with rebellion against the programming and production values of mainstream theatre and outrage at the neglect of Australian plays and suppression of the Australian accent on stage.

Experimental theatre can be distinguished from the alternative theatre constituted by COMMUNITY THEATRE, street theatre, the socially conscious NEW THEATRE movement and some plays. It has tended to divide into opposing ideologies—the eclectic and the reductionist. The eclectic tendency sees the conventional definition of theatre as too narrow and aims to be more inclusive, drawing attention to the potential of other elements, such as movement and music, and emphasising *mise en scène* and the semiotics of design while reducing the importance of text. This ideology typically speaks of 'performance' rather than 'theatre' in order to emphasise all-inclusiveness. The reductionist ideology seeks to strip away the extraneous in order to rediscover the uniqueness of theatre—usually the physical reality of the action and the actor's presence.

Experimental theatre did not exist in Australia until the 1960s, although immigrants since the 1930s had brought with them a modern-dance movement inspired by people such as Isadora Duncan, Emile Jaques-Dalcroze, Rudolf von Laban and Mary Wigman. Ida Beeby, Ruth Bergner, Gertud Bodenwieser, Patricia Edie and Sonia Revid were its outstanding exponents. Modern dance was essentially a female art form in Australia. It became a self-sustaining tradition, even though the critical establishment almost totally ignored the movement and regarded it as an exotic novelty—the pastime of macrobiotic loonies and faddists.

Experiment ostracised

The press, the theatrical establishment and funding bodies have consistently marginalised experimental theatre. By choice and definition experimental theatre is marginal, but elsewhere in the world there has been greater readiness to accept experiment as intrinsic to artistic practice. In Australia there has been a notable tendency for the theatre's Young Turks either to make accommodation with the establishment or to be ostracised. This has also been true of theatre companies. For example, the NIMROD THEATRE COMPANY in Sydney lasted 15 years from 1970 but its experimental highlights belonged to its early days, when it presented formally innovative Australian and overseas plays and developed a reputation for fresh interpretations of Shakespeare. Its demise was largely attributable to its failure to develop a coherent and articulated aesthetic to support its otherwise admirable forays into the work of people like Peter Handke, BERTOLT BRECHT and Ödön von Horváth. RICHARD WHERRETT's excellent productions of Handke's *My Foot, My Tutor* and *The Ride Across Lake Constance*, for example, were never positioned within an intellectual or aesthetic context. In this respect, Nimrod reflected a general failure among smaller, more ephemeral and more radical groups to go beyond a reliance on overseas models, together with an apparent inability to absorb the principles of, say, a Jerzy Grotowski or a Richard Schechner into the Australian context. This failure was more serious in Sydney than in Melbourne, where the AUSTRALIAN PERFORMING GROUP, for example, successfully adapted the character of the Bread and Puppet Theatre first into street theatre and then into popular forms epitomised by shows like Jack Hibberd and John Romeril's *MARVELLOUS MELBOURNE* (1970) and *THE HILLS FAMILY SHOW* (1975). Experiment has continued in Melbourne but in Sydney there has been almost no continuity of experiment and the focus remains mainly on new plays by established writers,

A lack of informed critics aggravated the problem. There were exceptions like KATHARINE BRISBANE, in the *Australian* from 1967 to 1974, and REX CRAMPHORN, in the *Bulletin* from 1968 to 1972, but when the avant-garde emerged in the early 1960s it did not receive enough educated feedback and critical pressure to force it to clarify its values and intentions. One result of this general lack of critical rigour was that, until the 1980s at least, the Australian theatrical avant-garde fought not a war on many fronts, but several wars simultaneously—a re-evaluation of the function of theatre in society, a questioning of theatrical conventions, the apparent prejudice against Australian plays and voices, the exploration of new forms of theatre and interdisciplinary experiment. Confusion of purpose also contributed to this state of affairs. As individuals and companies disappeared they were replaced by newcomers largely ignorant of what had gone before. The absence of critical support and documentation and the failure of mainstream theatre to feed on experiment has meant that there has been no continuity of theatrical experiment.

Spaces for experiment

Experimental activity has three elements—individuals, groups and spaces. Often all three coincide—as in the original La Mama Company, disparate individuals who united to work in their own permanent space at the LA MAMA THEATRE in Melbourne. There has been no other long-term space for experimental theatre, although Sydney has had the PERFORMANCE SPACE since 1983. Likewise, long-term experimenters are few. Many important writers, directors and performers have either left the theatre or made an accommodation with commercial and mainstream activity, usually at the expense of their original experimental ideals. In 1970 the successor to the La Mama Company, the Australian Performing Group, published a booklet summarising its first few years and signposting a move into its own Pram Factory, a few blocks from La Mama. It said the very thing that had made La Mama so revolutionary—its idiosyncratic intimacy as a space—was now 'the major limitation as far as the APG was concerned. That La Mama was essentially a space, and there was not much room for process, for developing as a group.'

The La Mama Theatre was inspired by small coffee-shop theatres in New York, but Melbourne had a precedent of its own—the EMERALD HILL THEATRE in South Melbourne run by WAL CHERRY from 1962 to 1966. Emerald Hill fell short of the radicalism of La Mama and it was a very different space, with a thrust stage and seating for 140, but it represented a new seriousness about the making of theatre. Indeed, it articulated an important principle of experimental theatre—that playmaking is as important as playwriting. Taking the Berliner Ensemble and Joan Littlewood as models, Cherry ran regular actors' classes and, through extremely cosmopolitan and adventurous programming, set about exploring the process of making theatre.

Whereas Cherry as artistic director shaped the character of Emerald Hill, Betty Burstall played more a managerial role at La Mama, vetting what went on but not imposing an aesthetic. The result was a mix of the eclectic and the reductionist. There was a lot of experiment with form. With ideas lifted from magazines like the *Tulane Drama Review* and *Cahiers du Cinéma* and from individuals as diverse as Julian Beck, Jerzy Grotowski, Buster Keaton, Jerry Lewis, Judith Malina and Richard Schechner, the La Mama Company tried out all kinds of actor-preparation exercises, confrontations, psychotherapy, encounter-group exercises and what are best described as group-gropes. Typical of this kind of work were the performances of Doug Anders's group Tribe and *The Birth of Space*, a group-devised work in 1969 initiated by CLEM GORMAN from Sydney in collaboration with GRAEME BLUNDELL and Kerry Dwyer. Described by Gorman as being about 'the conquest of ego', it was of the group-grope variety, involving audience participation.

The reductionist tendency was led by the writers, especially JACK HIBBERD, who fed the La Mama Theatre with an enormous amount of material in the first few years. Similarly, the actors were exploring the nature of performance, looking for a more immediate and more honest acting style than those they identified with companies like the MELBOURNE THEATRE COMPANY and the ST MARTIN'S THEATRE COMPANY in Melbourne and the OLD TOTE THEATRE COMPANY in Sydney. The tiny informal space at La Mama helped because it forced intimacy upon actors and audience—whose first encounter with an actor would probably be in buying a ticket at a door. The space did not permit anything false or overblown. Nor did it allow for sophisticated technical effects.

Social and political objectives

By 1969, the La Mama Company was beginning to define its ideas more clearly. It also took on a more overtly political stance in that year with the arrival of politically committed performers and writers from Monash University, such as Bill Garner, Jon Hawkes and JOHN ROMERIL. When the Australian Performing Group moved out of La Mama it declared: 'The APG is a new theatre company dedicated to the exploration of the forms, techniques and materials of today's theatre in a collective workshop … The main thrust of its experimentation is towards the development of a truly indigenous theatre, strongly rooted in the community and dealing with the myths and realities of life in Australia; a theatre built from the fabric—past, present and future—of Australian society itself.'

The manifesto listed objectives such as production of Australian and 'relevant' overseas plays, initiation of 'a theatre of research' and (quoting Konstantin Stanislavsky in support of a proposed 'struggle against prosarch [proscenium arch] naturalism') development of a socio-political and collective theatre. Ten years later the APG dissolved, partly as a result of disintegration—increasingly strident ideology had forced out many of its most talented writers, directors and performers—and partly as a result of financial constraints and the loss of its building. The APG left a legacy that transformed Australian theatre. Writers learned their craft with the APG, the only company—except possibly Nimrod—to consistently develop and perform the work of resident writers. The APG also trained some of Australia's best performers and created the possibility of authentic Australian performance styles such as the rough, vaudevillian and sometimes super-realist style now so commonly associated with Australian writing and performance. The extraordinary CIRCUS OZ was born out of *The Hills Family Show*, a recreation of a vaudeville family.

Sydney has never welcomed rigorous experimentation. Practically the only experimenter working in Sydney in the 1960s was Clem Gorman, who eclectically explored audience participation, multimedia presentations and ritual. His work had a near equivalent in light-shows put on by Ellis D. Fogg and Action Poetry, which combined readings with actions and projections.

ROBERT QUENTIN, director of the Old Tote Theatre Company, which had been criticised for neglecting Australian work, opened a rundown suburban church in 1966 as the JANE STREET THEATRE. It was to be used for the 'development of work in progress, not immediate exploitation' and for the next few years it contributed to the re-evaluation of theatre in Australia. There was never a Jane Street company, but the development of actors' theatre was encouraged there. Jane Street launched many Australian plays, but its main experimental contribution was *THE LEGEND OF KING O'MALLEY* by Michael Boddy and Bob Ellis in 1970. It launched the knockabout musical burlesque style taken up later by the Nimrod company.

After *King O'Malley*, there were two other significant experiments at Jane Street—JIM SHARMAN's *Terror Australis* and *10 000 Miles Away*, a group-devised show directed by Rex Cramphorn. It was strongly influenced by the practice of Jerzy Grotowski, who had become known in Australia through the *Tulane Drama Review* and then his own book *Towards a Poor Theatre*. The Cramphorn show saw the formation of the PERFORMANCE SYNDICATE, which was the most important experimental group in Sydney in 1971–75, though it toured Australia much of the time. The Performance Syndicate drew heavily on the ideas of Grotowski, exploring them in workshops and daily classes. Apart from group-devised works, the Performance Syndicate's output reflected Cramphorn's interest in Jacobean texts and Shakespeare. The group disintegrated because of internal divisions, insufficient funding and lack of a permanent space, and because Sydney's anti-intellectualism and preference for the superficial was inimical to such a serious experimental company.

More closely in tune with the Sydney sensibility was the Nimrod Theatre Company. When it began in 1970 it was not strictly a company, but there were key figures—JOHN BELL, RON BLAIR, MICHAEL BODDY, Ken Horler and Richard Wherrett—and there was at times an articulated philosophy. For example, in the published version of *King O'Malley* Boddy states: 'Remember what Bert Brecht said: "There's a time when a man has to choose between being human, and having good taste". The bourgeois crap concepts, "Good Taste" and "Artistic Sensibility" are dead. Let us dance on their graves.' Nonetheless, Nimrod never represented a clear ideology about anything. Its main contribution was to fashion a new informality in the theatre and to question orthodox theatre spaces at the small Nimrod Street Theatre in Kings Cross and the Nimrod Theatre. The former, now the STABLES THEATRE, remains a venue for marginal theatre, especially as a home for the GRIFFIN THEATRE COMPANY, which produces Australian plays. The latter is now the BELVOIR STREET THEATRE.

Constraints on experiment
Experimental theatre has become enfeebled since the mid-1970s. Experiment is still encouraged at the Performance Space in Sydney and at La Mama in Melbourne, which provided a venue for the early work of Chamber Made Opera and Barrie Kosky. Some might see Kosky as a European epigone, but his work, especially with his own Gilgul Jewish Theatre Company (founded in 1992), has represented the most single-minded assault on theatrical conventions in Australia in the 1990s. Companies like the RED SHED COMPANY in Adelaide and the Sydney Front have worked with limited resources, although the dissolution of the latter in 1994 came out of ideological conviction rather than financial difficulty. Individuals like Kosky and Jenny Kemp in Melbourne (whose work both questions the power of language and pushes it to its apparent limits within the context of a physical theatre), work as best they can. With a few exceptions such as Hibberd, Romeril and DANIEL KEENE, Australian playwrights have thrown out few challenges to theatrical conventions in recent years. An early exception to the poor record was PATRICK WHITE, who first rejected naturalism in favour of expressionistic and symbolic devices, married to highly poetic and frequently turgid language, in his 1947 play THE HAM FUNERAL. Probably because of their inherent contradiction between literariness and theatrical experiment, White's plays seem to have engendered no inheritors. Perhaps the writer who has most consistently and coherently challenged the forms of theatre has been JACK HIBBERD. However he stopped writing for the theatre in the late 1980s out of frustration at what he sees as entrenched naturalism and only began writing for the stage again in 1994.

The two tendencies in experimental theatre survive tenuously in Sydney. The eclectic was represented by the Sydney Front, which focused on highly provocative and abrasive explorations of the nature of performance, mainly at the Performance Space but also touring extensively in Australia and overseas. With the demise of the Sydney Front, only ENTR'ACTE survives—part-time with no significant public funding. An early work like *Refractions*—a free recreation of the work of Oskar Schlemmer at the Bauhaus in Weimar and Dessau—must be regarded as reductionist, although Entr'acte's more recent work has veered in the opposite direction. Apart from Kosky's company, other companies in Melbourne—like THEATREWORKS and MELBOURNE WORKERS' THEATRE—continue to work consistently. AUSTRALIAN NOUVEAU THEATRE under the direction of Jean-Pierre Mignon—which must be regarded as reductionist since it rigorously explored the text, eliminating inessentials—had its funding withdrawn despite its considerable reputation.

Experimental activity appears to have been constrained by rising property values and costs of living in Sydney and Melbourne, an unsympathetic funding policy in the AUSTRALIA COUNCIL, failure by the major subsidised companies to foster experiment as a way of maintaining the vitality of their own work, and the conservative training policy of the NATIONAL INSTITUTE OF DRAMATIC ART. The major sources of hope for renewed activity must lie in the smaller cities and in the training programs of new universities that can offer alternatives to NIDA. ❦*Paul McGillick*

further reading
WILLIAMS, MARGARET. *Drama*. Melbourne: Oxford University Press 1977.

Extravaganza

Like the closely allied BURLESQUE, extravaganza was a spectacular musical form of the 19th century, with fantastic plots and topical interest. Using music from operetta and popular tunes set to new words, extravaganza created idealised, fantastic or grotesque worlds, treated with whimsy and grace rather than the caricature of burlesque. The two forms had many theatrical and generic similarities, and both were closely related to PANTOMIME. By mid-century the terms burlesque and extravaganza were used interchangeably, while a pantomime merely added a harlequinade to the now-conflated form.

J. R. Planché, influenced by the early romantic *féerie*, which dramatised French fairy tales, introduced the fairy extravaganza into England with his *Riquet with the Tuft* in 1836. Classical fable also lent its plots. Planché and George Dance's *Olympic Revels* in 1831 showed the low life of the gods in the manner of Jacques Offenbach's *opéras-bouffes*. Local productions of English extravaganzas fed the colonial appetite for theatrical fantasia.

There was some localisation but little native writing appeared in the form as strictly defined, because by the time of the gold rushes pantomime and burlesque dominated and these met the demand for ideal, comic and fabulous spectacle combined with the homely or local touch. Colonial playwrights, performers and scene-painters were adept creating such material, but they concentrated it in burlesque and pantomime—with their greater scope for local adaptation—and operetta. The spirit of the extravaganza was pervasive, however. It was evident wherever scenes of refined grace, or of the weird and fantastic, provided an uncanny or spiritual leavening to the satirical and topical vigour of the theatrical practice of a highly materialistic age.

A good example of the charm and felicity of fairy extravaganza can be found in the 1874 Adelaide pantomime *Prince Enterprise—or, Harlequin Ogre and the Kangaroo, Cockatoo and Possum-too* by Samuel Lazar and Arthur Diamond. Thorough localisation makes it the more delightful. T. Hilhouse Taylor's ponderous allegory *PARSIFAL* (1906), displays something of the fantastic world of extravaganza, but lacks its light touch. The ability of the cinema to create Gothic worlds has carried forward to the present day at least the grotesque and eerie phases of extravaganza. Its satirical, refined and spectacular elements are dispersed amongst contemporary theatrical practices. ❦*Veronica Kelly*

further reading
BOOTH, MICHAEL (ed.). *English Plays of the Nineteenth Century* 5. Oxford: Clarendon Press 1976.
KOVÁCS, KATHERINE. A history of the féerie in France. *Theatre Quarterly* 8/29 (London, spring 1978).
NICOLL, ALLARDYCE. *A History of English Drama 1660-1900: English drama 1900-1930*. Cambridge University Press 1973.
PLANCHÉ, J. R. *The Recollections and Reflections*, 2 vols. London: Tinsley Brothers 1872.
LEECH, CLIFFORD and C. W. CRAIK (eds). *The Revels History of Drama in English* 6. London: Methuen 1975.

George Fairfax AM

Actor, administrator, director. Born 4 April 1928 in Melbourne. Began acting at University of Melbourne in early 1950s. Union Theatre Repertory Company (Melbourne) 1953–54. Studied production and worked in repertory and with BBC television in United Kingdom 1954–55. Director of Melbourne Little Theatre, later St Martin's Theatre Company, 1956–68. Chairman of Producers and Directors' Guild of Australia 1969–71. Member of council of Victorian College of the Arts 1973–89; theatre board of Australia Council 1973–76. Chief executive officer of Victorian Arts Centre building committee 1972–80. General manager of Victorian Arts Centre Trust 1980–89. Has also worked in film and television. Erik Kuttner Awards for best producer 1965, best actor 1958 (*The Caine Mutiny Court Martial* by Herman Wouk). AM 1984.

In recognition of George Fairfax's enormous contribution to the success of the VICTORIAN ARTS CENTRE its Studio theatre has been named after him. He was appointed technical adviser to the building committee in 1969, he was involved throughout the planning and building of the centre and from 1980 to 1989 he was its general manager. Fairfax has acted and directed in Melbourne since his university days. He played a leading role opposite ZOË CALDWELL in the first production of the Union Theatre Repertory Company, Jean Anouilh's *Colombe* in 1953. While he was a director of the Melbourne Little Theatre and its professional successor the ST MARTIN'S THEATRE Company he directed the musical *Oh, What a Lovely War!* After its season at St Martin's in 1968 J. C. WILLIAMSON's presented it in Sydney and Melbourne.

Fairfax is a fine character actor who can explore compassionately the dilemmas of the outwardly confident but inwardly unsure modern male. He did not appear on stage during the 1970s and 1980s but since leaving the Victorian Arts Centre he has acted with the MELBOURNE THEATRE COMPANY in *The Marriage of Figaro* by Pierre Beaumarchais in 1991. He directed Ron Elisha's *Esterhaz* for the PLAYBOX THEATRE CENTRE in 1991 and *Man of La Mancha* at the State Theatre in Melbourne in 1989 and at the Lyric Theatre in Brisbane in 1990. His direction is reasoned, detailed and committed to the playwright's vision. ❦*Malcolm Robertson*

Arthur Falchon

Irish actor, singer. Flourished 1837–52. In Samson Cameron's company in Hobart 1837. In Sydney from 1838. In Anne Clarke's company in Hobart during 1840–46.

A popular and successful actor in the early years of theatre in Hobart and Sydney, Arthur Falchon excelled in Irish parts. He had 'a brogue richer and more genuine' than fellow actors who attempted similar parts, it was noted. When he was a principal actor in SAMSON CAMERON's company in Hobart in 1837 his singing 'received unbounded applause' and formed a significant part of the entertainment, between the main work and the afterpiece. Falchon went to Sydney in 1838 and gained a reputation for being drunk during performances, especially on Saturday nights. Back in Hobart in mid-1840 he became stage manager as well as a principal actor in ANNE CLARKE's company. While she was in England in 1841 Falchon was stage manager for F. B. WATSON. He returned to Clarke's company in 1842 and remained with it until 1846, but played supporting roles, chiefly because she had recruited talented actors in England and her success attracted some of the best colonial players to her company. ❦*Gillian Winter*

further reading
OPPENHEIM, HELENE. Colonial Theatre. Mitchell Library (Sydney) MS 3266. Microfilm copy in State Library of Tasmania.

Ronald Falk

Actor. Born 23 August 1935 in Geelong (Vic.). Abandoned chemistry training at University of Melbourne. Worked with W. P. Carr at National Theatre (Melbourne). In United Kingdom 1958–68, with Old Vic Theatre Company, Birmingham Repertory, English Stage Company, Royal Shakespeare Company, Traverse Theatre of Edinburgh, Phoenix (Leicester) and Scottish National Theatre. National Theatre Company (Perth) 1968. Community Theatre, Independent Theatre and Old Tote Theatre Company in Sydney. Melbourne Theatre Company. State Theatre Company of South Australia (Adelaide) 1977–78. Green Room Award for supporting actor (*The Life and Adventures of Nicholas Nickleby* by David Edgar) 1985. Sydney Critics' Award for supporting actor (*Rough Crossing* by Tom Stoppard) 1988.

A valued character actor, Ronald Falk enjoys physical and technical challenges. He has the comic's mimetic capacity to be manic, irascible, sinister and tragically vulnerable in turn. 'Our own antipodean Jacques Tati', wrote a reviewer of Falk's performance as the steward Dvornichek in *Rough Crossing* for the STATE THEATRE Company of South Australia and Gary Penny Productions in 1988.

Falk is of the generation of actors who learned their craft in the amateur theatre and repertory companies. His first significant role was the Aboriginal hero in George Landen Dann's FOUNTAINS BEYOND for the Geelong Repertory Company in 1954. In Melbourne, Falk quickly assumed leading roles at the National Theatre—Hamlet, Richard II, Joseph in R. B. Sheridan's *The School for Scandal*, Cleante in Molière's *The Miser* and Bassanio in *The Merchant of Venice*.

After a decade in the United Kingdom and six months in Perth he divided his time between the OLD TOTE THEATRE COMPANY, for which he played Tiresius in Tyrone Guthrie's production of Sophocles's *King Oedipus* in 1970, and the MELBOURNE THEATRE COMPANY. Falk created MacNaughton in ALEX BUZO's *Macquarie* in 1972 and the writer's agent Michael O'Hearn in DAVID WILLIAMSON's *What If You Died Tomorrow?* in 1973. With the State Theatre Company of South Australia he played Uncle in the premiere of RON BLAIR's *Marx* and the title-role in both parts of *Henry IV*. Falk returned to Sydney to play the Baron in Liviu Ciulei's production of Maxim Gorky's *The Lower Depths* in 1977. He played Newman Noggs and other roles for the SYDNEY THEATRE COMPANY in David Edgar's *The Life and Adventures of Nicholas Nickleby* in 1983-84. After this he undertook a two-year art course at Wollongong Technical College; his other occupations are painting and printmaking. He rejoined the SYDNEY THEATRE COMPANY in 1987 and created the role of Kenneth Slessor in KATHERINE THOMSON's *Darlinghurst Nights* in 1988. In 1992 Falk played Father D'Arcy in NICK ENRIGHT's *St James Infirmary* for Q THEATRE at Penrith (NSW); Lloyd Rees in KIM CARPENTER's *Swimming in Light*, which toured to the Caracas Ninth International Festival in Venezuela; and Clive in MICHAEL GOW's *On Top of the World* in Croydon (England). ❦*Katharine Brisbane*

Judi Farr

Actor, director. Born in Cairns (Qld). Began acting as amateur. Played small comedy roles in Phillip Street revues in Sydney in early 1960s. Acted in plays in Sydney from 1974 for Old Tote, Nimrod, Sydney Theatre Company and Marian Street Theatre Companies. Many radio and television roles. Sydney Critics' Circle Award 1992 (*The Women of Troy*).

Slim, fair Judi Farr has played many variations of the soubrette, the spinster and the formidable housewife. She is an accomplished comedian and has spent much of her life in commercial comedy, on stage and screen. At the same time she is a fine dramatic actor with a capacity to convey the painful dilemmas of the female condition. 'Judi Farr gives a cruelly comic performance of a woman we don't know whether to hate or pity', wrote a reviewer when she played Gwen in Michael Gow's *Away* for the SYDNEY THEATRE COMPANY in 1987. This production went to the USA in 1988, together with Ray Lawler's SUMMER OF THE SEVENTEENTH DOLL, in which Farr played Emma.

Farr took a new direction in 1992, when she played Hecuba in Gow's reworking of Euripides's tragedy *The Women of Troy*. One critic called it 'a landmark performance ... the exemplar of nobility in extremity'. Another said: 'In an extraordinary, raw-nerved performance, Judi Farr presents a woman almost totally overwhelmed ... The mourning over the body of her small grandson ... is a scene of pure horror.' In 1993 she played Friedrich Dürrenmatt's vengeful billionaire Claire Zachanassian in *The Visit*. Farr has directed plays, including David Williamson's TRAVELLING NORTH for the MARIAN STREET THEATRE COMPANY in 1984. ❦*Katharine Brisbane*

further reading

NEILL, ROSEMARY. Mum goes murdering. *Weekend Australian* 20–21 November 1993.

George Fawcett

Actor, dramatist, scene-painter. Born 24 July 1832 at Exeter (England). Originally George Curtis Rowe. Son of artist. Began as scene-painter in England. Came to Australia 1853; known as George Fawcett. Variously leased and managed Princess's Theatre, Melbourne, 1859–63. Left for New Zealand 1864. Acted in England and USA as George Fawcett Rowe for rest of life. Married and divorced American actor Kate Girard in 1879. Supposedly married to Adelaide Arthur at death on 29 August 1889 in New York City.

An outstanding impersonator and eccentric actor, George Fawcett dramatised many works of Charles Dickens. He was acting in Bendigo and Geelong soon after his arrival on the Victorian goldfields in 1853, and by 1856 he was acting in Dickens adaptations and burlesques in Melbourne. He soon began writing in both these forms and in 1862 his *David Copperfield* launched his Mr Micawber character, which he played everywhere throughout his career.

During his tenure of the Princess's Theatre Fawcett wrote 15 plays, many of which were adaptations of novels or burlesques displaying his comic and eccentric skills. *The Captain of the Vulture* in 1863 irrelevantly introduced a famous ghost effect, while *The Chamber of Horrors* allowed him to impersonate topically the denizens of Professor Sohier's waxworks.

After a time in New Zealand, Fawcett made his acting debut in New York City in 1866. From then he wrote and performed 40 plays, dividing his career between the USA and the English provinces, where he was managed by CLARANCE HOLT. In Australia in 1880 Holt's son BLAND HOLT produced *The New Babylon*, a sensation melodrama written by Fawcett and Paul Merritt in 1878. It was the forerunner here of dramas dealing with sport and society. Contemporaries describe Rowe as irascible but good company and a tireless raconteur. Despite his industriousness and prodigious dramatic output, he seems to have lacked the acumen to capitalise on his properties. Two comedies with variety acts written in the USA are supposed to have made him money, yet he died impoverished while planning a Canadian tour. Frequent comparisons of Fawcett with Micawber are not inapt. ❦*Mimi Colligan and Veronica Kelly*

further reading

SHERSON, ERROLL. *London's Lost Theatres of the Nineteenth Century*. London: John Lane and Bodley Head 1925.

Michele Fawdon

Actor. Born 15 December 1947 at Harrow (England). Studied ballet, tap dance, modern dance, music and drama. Came to Sydney 1965. Studied singing at NSW State Conservatorium of Music, acting at Ensemble Theatre under Hayes Gordon and dance at Bodenwieser Dance School. Began work at Bull and Bush Theatre Restaurant, Sydney 1967. Melbourne Theatre Company; Tasmanian Theatre Company (Hobart); Old Tote Theatre Company, Marian Street Theatre Company, Jane Street Theatre (Sydney) 1973–79. Nimrod Theatre Company (Sydney) 1980–82. Sydney Theatre Company. Many radio, film and television roles.

Versatile Michele Fawdon is impressive across a wide range. She has deft comic flair; she can be deeply moving; and she is a talented performer in music-theatre and cabaret. She was nationally acclaimed in her first important role, Mary Magdalene in the rock musical *Jesus Christ Superstar* in 1971. Her roles in eight NIMROD THEATRE COMPANY productions included Anna in STEPHEN SEWELL's *Traitors* in 1980 and two parts in his *Welcome the Bright World* in 1982. Since then her appearances have included Robyn Archer's feminist cabaret THE PACK OF WOMEN in 1983, Paula in Nicholas Wright's *Mrs Klein* for the MARIAN STREET THEATRE COMPANY in 1990, and Maria in *Twelfth Night* for Q THEATRE at Penrith (NSW) in 1991. For the SYDNEY THEATRE COMPANY she played Louise Kraus in Sewell's *THE BLIND GIANT IS DANCING* in 1984 and two roles in Michael Gow's *Away*—Coral in 1987 and Vic in 1988. In 1988 *Away* went to the USA together with Ray Lawler's SUMMER OF THE SEVENTEENTH DOLL, in which Fawdon played Olive.

Her career entered a new phase when she was associate director of LOUIS NOWRA's *Così* at the BELVOIR STREET THEATRE in 1992. In May 1993 she became a trainee director with Q Theatre. She directed Bruce Keller's play for young children *Puppy Love* in September 1974. ❧*Pamela Payne*

Rhoda Felgate

Director, speech and drama teacher. Born 1901 in London. Came to Australia at 18 months. Foundation member of Brisbane Repertory Theatre Society 1925. Founding director of Twelfth Night Theatre (Brisbane) 1936–61. Died 14 September 1990 in Brisbane.

From 1936 to 1949 Rhoda Felgate directed most of the plays produced by TWELFTH NIGHT THEATRE. She was also deeply involved in theatrical education as a private teacher, and in courses organised through Twelfth Night, including drama schools for members of amateur theatre groups and Junior Twelfth Night Theatre. She travelled throughout Queensland as senior speech examiner for the Australian Music Examinations Board. ❧*Alrene Sykes*

reference
Tape recordings of Rhoda Felgate's memories of life and theatre in Brisbane, and visits of personalities such as Sybil Thorndike, Lewis Casson, Allan Wilkie and Margaret Wolfit are in the Fryer Library, University of Queensland (Brisbane).

Effie Fellows

Male impersonator. Born 1893 in Melbourne. Moved to Perth with family 1896. Began international stage career in Fullers' vaudeville. Went to USA 1917. Married clown–comedian Piquo and boxing promoter Sammy Chapman. Died 1977 in Perth.

The first international performer from Perth, Effie Fellows sang risqué songs such as 'I've never seen a straight banana' to her own ukelele accompaniment. In her youth in Perth she dressed as a boy to work as a bellboy at the Palace Hotel. The masquerade continued in Melbourne, where she worked in a newsagency until she learned that the law compelled all boys over 14 years of age to join cadets, which involved medical examination. BENJAMIN FULLER launched her on her stage career. In the USA she appeared on the same bill as Al Jolson and Sophie Tucker. She returned several times to Perth's Luxor Theatre. In the 1930s she toured English music halls as Bobby Folson. ❧*Ivan King*

Feminist theatre

Much of the theatre that has been produced by women in Australia since the early 1970s has reflected developments in feminist thought and debate and can be traced back to *Betty Can Jump*, a production by women from the AUSTRALIAN PERFORMING GROUP at the Pram Factory in Melbourne in January 1972. Its impetus came from feminist theory—particularly consciousness-raising—and the frustrations of working in the male-dominated APG. *Betty Can Jump* attracted enthusiastic audiences and aroused positive responses in the APG and the burgeoning women's movement. It provided a model for originating scripts from improvisation based on personal experience or documentary material and it became the prototype for work produced by the Women's Theatre Group at the Pram Factory between 1974 and 1976. This group had a core of APG women but most members were unskilled outsiders. It was an intense, brief conflagration but it fired many writers, performers, directors, designers, technicians, similar groups and landmark productions all over Australia. Among the most significant were the Adelaide Women's Theatre Group and Fool's Gallery in Canberra.

The physical, immediate, performer-oriented theatre of the Women's Theatre Group informed the strong feminist slant of CIRCUS OZ and led to the formation of the Wimmins Circus and its current incarnation the Women's Circus. It also led to women working in the development of cabaret and THEATRE-RESTAURANTS in Melbourne and Sydney. Meanwhile, another strain of women's theatre developed among innovative individuals who gathered at LA MAMA THEATRE in Melbourne under Betty Burstall and Liz Jones and worked alone or in small groups.

Community theatre

In the late 1970s and early 1980s community theatre especially nurtured the development of female writers and directors. The MILL THEATRE COMPANY in Geelong and companies formed by graduates of the VICTORIAN COLLEGE OF THE ARTS—the WEST THEATRE COMPANY, the MURRAY RIVER PERFORMING GROUP and THEATREWORKS—provided opportunities and training, approached theatrical form experimentally and allowed feminist theatre to develop in a non-separatist environment and some fine feminist works were direct results, including *Roma* by West, *Mary* by TheatreWorks and *Ladies of Fortune* by the Mill company. In the 1990s feminism informed the work of the SIDETRACK PERFORMANCE GROUP in Sydney, the RED SHED COMPANY in Adelaide and MELBOURNE WORKERS' THEATRE. The writers Patricia Cornelius and Melissa Reeves and the directors Maude Clarke, Lisa Dombroskis, Meme (Jan) McDonald and Christine Totos have been notable; and the performer–director Robin Lauri remains a key figure in the arena.

In Sydney, the Women and Theatre Project in 1981 and the Women and Arts Festival in 1982 were significant forums initiated by CHRIS WESTWOOD which brought the NIMROD THEATRE COMPANY into a feminist sphere of influence. Playworks was instigated by the director Ros Horin in 1985 to promote female writers through script-development and productions, and it has grown in strength and influence over a decade.

Several important women's theatre groups whose work gained public attention had emerged by the 1980s. The most significant were the Home Cooking Theatre Company, formed in Melbourne in 1981 by Barbara Ciszewska, Andrea Lemon, Meredith Rogers and Suzanne Spunner; and VITALSTATISTIX, formed in Adelaide in 1984 by Roxxy Bent, Ollie Black and Margaret Fischer.

Some other groups and writers defined their work in a lesbian context, including the playwright Sandra Shotlander, the writer–director Lois Ellis and the performer–writer Sara Hardy in Flash Rat in Melbourne. Since 1986 there has been a women's season in the Melbourne Fringe Festival.

In the mainstream theatre LINDA ARONSON, ALMA DE GROEN, Jill Dwyer, DOROTHY HEWETT and Mary Gage have consistently articulated women's concerns in their writing. Elaine Acworth, Hilary Beaton, Hilary Bell, Beatrix Christian, JENNIFER CLAIRE, DOREEN CLARKE, Mary Morris, Verity Laughton, Tobsha Learner, Karin Mainwaring, Peta

Murray, Joanna Murray Smith, Heather Nimmo, THÉRÈSE RADIC and Alana Valentine are other writers who entered mainstream theatre at a receptive moment for work informed by feminism. HANNIE RAYSON and KATHERINE THOMSON are among Australia's foremost playwrights. Directors who have kept women's theatre afloat in the mainstream are Ewa Czajor, Kim Durban, Kerry Dwyer, Gale Edwards, Ros Horin and ROBYN NEVIN in Sydney and Melbourne; Cath McKinnon in Adelaide; Sue Rider in Brisbane; Camilla Blunden and Carol Woodrow in Canberra; and Pippa Williamson in Perth.

Solo performance
The 1970s and the 1980s also saw development of solo performance, which is among the most exciting and significant work produced from the women's theatre movement. It has taken many forms, including revelation of an individual by Cathy Downes in *Katherine Mansfield*, Doody in *Doody—The Progress of a Stripper* and Chris Meering in *About Marie Stopes*. Dina Panozzo in *Varda che bruta ... poretta*, ROBYN ARCHER in *A Star is Torn*, Meredith Rogers in *I Am Whom You Infer*, Helen Noonan in *Recital* and Ningali Lawford in *Ningali* adopted multiple personas. The genre has been refined in *The Serpent's Fall* and *Walking on Sticks* by Sarah Cathcart and Andrea Lemon and in courageous and outrageous shows by SUE INGLETON.

Feminism and the experiences of migration have informed a substantial body of work. Bilingual productions by TES LYSSIOTIS in Melbourne; Teresa Crea and DOPPIO TEATRO in Adelaide, and Mishline Yasmine Jammal and Taqa in Sydney have explored Greek–Australian, Italo-Australian and Arab–Australian identities respectively.

Aboriginal women's theatre had a notable debut with Eva Johnson's *Tjinderella* in 1984 at the first Aboriginal Women's Art Festival. Johnson's work as actor, director and playwright has been significant. Many Aboriginal women have made their mark, including the actors Kylie Belling, Ningali Lawford, Deborah Mailman, Rachel Maza, Lydia Miller, Lynette Narkle and JUSTINE SAUNDERS; the director Kathryn Fisher; and the emerging writers Cathy Craigie and Cherie Imlah.

Theatre-in-education and youth theatre have also nurtured women, in particular the writers Debra Oswald with CANBERRA YOUTH THEATRE and Julianne O'Brien with the ARENA THEATRE COMPANY in Melbourne. Feminists have been at the helm of many companies, including Angela Chaplin at Arena, MAGPIE THEATRE in Adelaide and the DECKCHAIR THEATRE COMPANY in Fremantle (WA); Barbara Ciszewska at Arena; Chris Johnson at Magpie; Gail Kelly at Canberra Youth Theatre; Janet Robertson at Corrugated Iron Youth Theatre in Darwin and BROLGAS in Queensland.

Formal experimentation, particularly in relation to critiques of representational practices and narrative structure, has been evident in much work produced since the mid-1970s. Virginia Baxter, Noelle Janaczewska, Lyndal Jones, Jenny Kemp and Peta Tait have consistently produced significant work that often bridges theatre and performance art. Aesthetic, formal and political concerns have diverged and women's theatre in the 1990s shows signs of accepting the notion of plural 'feminisms' encompassing differences of class, culture and race as well as gender. ❦*Hilary Glow and Suzanne Spunner*

further reading
DOBBIN, CLAIRE and HILARY GLOW. Women's theatre and the APG. *Meanjin* 43 (Melbourne 1984).
FRASER, SUSIE and HILARY GLOW. The myth of the earth goddess—*The Serpent's Fall*. *New Theatre Australia* (Sydney) September-October 1987.
GARNER, HELEN. Article on *Betty Can Jump*. *Dissent* (c.1973).
GLOW, HILARY. Andrea Lemon. *New Theatre Australia* (Sydney) July–August 1988.
GLOW, HILARY. Theatrical practice and critical analysis—A report on the Women's Theatre Forum. *Women's Studies Journal* 1 (May 1985).
HARMER, WENDY. *It's a Joke Joyce*. Melbourne: Pan 1989. Sydney: Currency Press 1994.
MOSS, MERRILEE. Running up a dress—Home Cooking Theatre Company. *New Theatre Australia* (Sydney) March–April 1988.
SPUNNER, SUZANNE. Since Betty jumped—Theatre and feminism in Melbourne. *Meanjin* 38 (Melbourne 1979).
TAIT, PETA. *Converging realities—Feminism in Australian theatre*. Sydney: Currency Press 1994. Melbourne: Artmoves 1994.
TAIT, PETA. *Original Women's Theatre*. Melbourne: Artmoves 1993.
Australasian Drama Studies 21 (Brisbane, October 1992). Women in theatre issue.
Lip 1–7 (Melbourne 1976–84). A magazine about women in the visual and performing arts, containing profiles, interviews and reviews of many groups and individuals.
Meanjin 43/1 (Melbourne, 1988) and 51/1 (1992).
Program of Third International Women Playwrights' Conference, Adelaide 1994. Contained more than 40 biographies of Australian playwrights, directors and performers.

Willie Fennell
Actor. Born 1920 in Sydney. Began as radio comedian 1945. Began stage career in Sydney 1965. Died 9 September 1992 in Sydney.

The timing of a consummate comedian and the pathos of a sad clown made Willie Fennell a first-rate actor on the stage, to which he came after writing, producing and playing the title-role in the radio comedy series *Life With Dexter* for ten years. When variety and drama ceased on commercial radio, he began his new career in David Turner's *Semi-Detached* for the ENSEMBLE THEATRE COMPANY in Sydney in 1965. But he brought much more than mere pathos to emotional roles. When, as Wacka in Alan Seymour's THE ONE DAY OF THE YEAR in 1987, he described the ghastly assault on Gallipoli, the scene left the Ensemble audience and him shattered. He was particularly notable as the derelict old man in PETER KENNA's *Trespassers Will Be Prosecuted* at the Jane Street Theatre in Sydney in 1976. ❦*Richard Lane*

Noel Ferrier
Actor, producer, administrator. Born 20 December 1930 in Melbourne. Worked in advertising and cinemas. Acted on radio and in amateur theatre. Union Theatre Repertory Company (Melbourne). Artistic director of Marian Street Theatre Company (Sydney) 1990–91. Many film and television roles.

A man who has written 'I do not think I am a particularly good actor', Noel Ferrier has made his mark in a wide variety of show business. He was a founding member of the Union Theatre Repertory Company and created the role of Roo in its tryout production of Ray Lawler's SUMMER OF THE SEVENTEENTH DOLL in November 1955. A professional career —often playing second leads to imported 'stars'—for

GARNET H. CARROLL and J. C. WILLIAMSON'S followed. Then came radio, television and films. A jocose and orotund personality, Ferrier defeated an addiction to alcohol with the assistance of Alcoholics Anonymous in the early 1970s.

A devotion to the idea of an Australian musical-theatre company led him into the AUSTRALIAN ELIZABETHAN THEATRE TRUST. The association resulted in a 1983 production of *The Sound of Music*, which Ferrier implies brought less glory to the Trust than to its co-producers. In 1990 the MARIAN STREET THEATRE COMPANY in Sydney appointed Ferrier to its artistic directorship in a triumvirate with RODNEY FISHER and John Rayment. After a year of this clumsy arrangement Ferrier became sole artistic director, with a policy of presenting popular plays. After 18 months, with more failures than successes, Ferrier quit. ❦*John West*

writings
There Goes Whatsisname. Melbourne: Macmillan Australia 1985. Autobiography.
further reading
HERBERT, IAN (ed.). *Who's Who in the Theatre* 17th edn. Detroit (USA): Gale Research 1981.

Festival of Perth

Annual international arts festival in Perth. Founded 1953.
directors 1953–54 Fred Alexander. 1955–76 John Birman. 1976– David Blenkinsop.

The oldest international arts festival in Australia, the Festival of Perth is a highlight of the arts calendar and a significant influence in other Australian cities, southeast Asia and the Pacific. Emeritus Professor Fred Alexander initiated it in 1953 to provide entertainment for students at the University of Western Australia's summer school. It was established under the director of the Adult Education Board, John Birman, and it is a subcommittee of the senate of the university, with its offices on the campus. The opening production was *Richard III* at the Somerville Auditorium, by the English director Michael Langham. JAMES BAILEY played the title-role and other actors were drawn from all the amateur theatres in Perth.

The festival's charter is to offer Western Australians performing and visual arts of the highest standard. Over three weeks and a half in February and March each year it presents extensive programs of theatre, music, dance, film, visual arts, television and outdoor community activities. Its funds come from the state government, the Lotteries Commission, the City of Perth, the university, private sponsors and ticket sales. David Blenkinsop began entrepreneurial initiatives when he became director in 1976 and since then more than 3000 international artists have visited Perth. Many have been exclusive to Perth. For example, in 1993 the ROYAL SHAKESPEARE COMPANY in *The Comedy of Errors* and the Steppenwolf Theatre Company and Ladysmith Black Mambazo in *The Song of Jacob Zulu* were not seen elsewhere in Australia. Other outstanding theatrical companies that have appeared at the festival include Peter Brook's Centre International de Créations Théâtrales, the Grupo Teatro Macunaima from Brazil and the Peking Opera Company. Visiting artists stimulate local artists through performances, master classes at tertiary institutions and workshops. The festival regularly includes local works of high standard. ❦*Penny Young*

Festivals

In large and sparsely populated Australia theatre festivals have had a special significance. With the near-demise of the theatre industry in the Great Depression, major towns inevitably developed their mainly amateur theatrical culture in isolation. For the serious amateur and semiprofessional theatrical groups that proliferated in the vacuum left by the entrepreneurs, opportunities to meet, compare work and exchange ideas in a festival were of enormous value.

Local drama festivals, usually held annually and generally competitive, became major events in the theatrical community. These festivals were organised by such bodies as the British Drama League or the Victorian Drama League or by standing committees set up by various theatre groups in a state capital. The Theatre Council of Western Australia, for example, staged annual drama festivals over 21 years from 1949. Casts travelled many hundreds of kilometres to take part and large Perth audiences saw and compared the work.

Sometimes individual theatre groups ran such festivals. In the 1930s the REPERTORY CLUB in Perth maintained collaborative contacts with country repertory societies and ran its own annual state drama festival. This work survives in such organisations as annual regional competitions in NSW and the state organisation Theatrefest, which holds its annual festival in Sydney.

Opportunities for interstate contact between amateur companies extended to an annual Intervarsity Drama Festival, established in the 1940s, which rotated between state capitals. Over some 20 years these brought together some of the most lively, informed and accomplished performing groups in the country, for performance and extended critical discussion. The Intervarsity Drama Festivals were an important stimulus since the university societies were prominent in the theatrical lives of their respective communities. For example, the climate created at the University of Melbourne's Union Theatre stimulated the establishment of a part-time professional theatre company in 1953. In 1968 it became the MELBOURNE THEATRE COMPANY.

Festivals become international

With the rise of subsidised state companies from 1968 the amateur movement became less influential, and the professional festivals that had begun to grow in the 1950s out of local need, inevitably began to become international. Like the old amateur festivals they have been invaluable in infusing new ideas into theatrical life. The annual FESTIVAL OF PERTH, dating from 1953, grew out of summer schools conducted by the Department of Adult Education at the University of Western Australia. It began as a leisurely five-week affair in the summer heat, bringing together local groups and companies in the spirit of the previous drama festivals, and for some years centred on student and professional performance side by side on the campus.

In contrast, the biennial ADELAIDE FESTIVAL OF ARTS was established in 1960 with the Edinburgh Festival as its model. Increasing collaboration with the Adelaide Festival inevitably changed the direction of the Festival of Perth. Today it is distinguished from its Adelaide counterpart chiefly by a more relaxed style inherited from its past. In both festivals, however, the adventurous spirit of the amateur festivals continues in a lively and well-organised fringe of alternative theatre. Since 1988 the festival fringe in Perth has established itself as the independent ARTRAGE, held in October. The same is more or less true of the later established Melbourne International Festival of the Arts, which has developed an avant-garde fringe. The fringe of the Festival of Sydney has in recent years been subsumed by the Gay and Lesbian Mardi Gras Festival, held in March and now the largest event of its kind in the world. It has provided increasing opportunity for GAY THEATRE, including new writing on homosexual themes, to which both fringe and mainstream theatres contribute. The main event of the Mardi Gras is a spectacular street parade.

The Melbourne festival had its origin in a street parade and seasonal festivity. Moomba—meaning 'get together and have fun'—began in March 1955 as a month of popular entertainment. In 1973 the presence of an international book fair introduced a literary program which has become an annual Writers' Festival. In 1985 a collaboration between the Italian composer Giancarlo Menotti and his Festival of Two Worlds in Spoleto (Italy) transformed Melbourne's celebrations into the Melbourne Spoleto Festival, held in September. In 1988 it became the Melbourne International Festival, on similar lines to the Adelaide Festival, and with a fair amount of challenging intellectual content.

Participants in Queensland's centennial celebrations in 1959 saw the need for a community arts festival in Brisbane, with the result that the first Warana Festival was held in October 1962. Warana (an Aboriginal word meaning 'blue skies') was conceived as a festival of popular entertainment like Moomba. Today it is an eclectic mixture of artistic and community events, including dance, ethnic performances, a diversity of music and children's entertainment. Since the Queensland Festival of Arts Society combined with Warana in 1977 other public events have contributed to its style, including the Commonwealth Games in 1982, to which Warana responded with an international arts festival, and World Expo '88. The 1990s have seen a focus upon the arts of Asian neighbours.

The Festival of Sydney in January had its origins in the Waratah Spring Festival and it retains much party atmosphere. The first Sydney festival was held in January 1977 and traditionally has begun with an open-air concert and fireworks on New Year's Eve. Its events extend to venues throughout Sydney, with a high concentration of theatrical and musical performances. Carnivale, Sydney's folk festival celebrating the work of immigrants, moved from September to join the summer festival in 1993. ❦*Philip Parsons*

Buster Fidess

Actor, comedian. Originally Leslie Anderson. Began as acrobat in circus in Victoria. Worked on stage and in radio and television in comedy and drama. Died 14 January 1972 in Sydney.

A comedian with a beat-up face, squashed nose and soft voice, Buster Fidess barely had to open his mouth to provoke laughter. On the TIVOLI CIRCUIT at one time he shared the stage with his dog Jake, which would bark appropriately in his song 'Little Sir Echo'. Fidess loved pantomime and he was playing an ugly sister in *Cinderella* at the time of his death. He was then thought to be well into his sixties, though his age was his best-kept secret. ❦*Victoria Chance*

La Fille du tambour-major

Opéra-bouffe. **music** Jacques Offenbach. **libretto** Henri Chivot and Alfred Duru. English translation by H. B. Farnie. **world premiere** 13 December 1879, Théâtre des Folies-Dramatiques, Paris. **Australian premiere** 27 December 1880, Prince of Wales Opera House, Melbourne. **cast**: Albert Brennir, Jessie Grey, Minnie Hope, Pattie Laverne, Fred Mervin. **designer** Alexander Habbe.

GEORGE MUSGROVE's production of *La Fille du tambour-major* was the culmination of a long series of Offenbach productions mounted by his uncle, W. S. LYSTER, and a landmark. It ran for 101 nights, a new record for the Australian colonies, and proved that theatregoers would go several times to a superlatively presented show. It also marked a decisive break with stock-company practice. Musgrove assembled cast, showgirls, costumes and props in England. This rejection of local performing traditions and performers was an unhappy innovation for the Australian profession but it resulted in a considerable rise in production standards. It paved the way for the even more spectacular commercial success of GILBERT AND SULLIVAN operettas and other lavishly mounted touring musical shows, which became the mainstay of WILLIAMSON, GARNER AND MUSGROVE. The *La Fille du tambour-major* company, which also had a great success with Offenbach's *Madame Favart*, toured to Adelaide and Sydney and returned to Melbourne. Then the original contracts expired and *La Fille* became a repertory piece for the Musgrove comic opera company on tour. ❦*Harold Love*.

further reading
LOVE, HAROLD. *The Golden Age of Australian Opera*. Sydney: Currency Press 1981.

Peter Finch

Actor. Born 28 September 1916 in England. Brought to Australia 1926. In vaudeville in Sydney 1934–35. Toured Queensland in tent theatre 1936. Radio actor from 1936. Joined army 1941. Artistic director of Australian Army Amenities Services theatre section 1945. Co-founded Mercury Theatre in Sydney 1946. Left for London 1948. Distinguished international career. Died 14 January 1977 in Hollywood (USA).

Peter Finch was Australia's finest actor of the 1940s, perhaps of all time. His theatrical career here was brief, but his influence was enormous through his impact as an actor and his power to communicate his passion for the theatre. Rejected by his parents in infancy, he was brought to his father's native Australia by Theosophists when he was ten. He was never taught acting, but—fearing illegitimacy, not knowing where he belonged—he found himself acting in every second of his life from earliest childhood, as self-protection. Lively intelligence, generous enthusiasm and a charming mercurial personality made him a natural actor.

His first stage roles were tiny parts for Doris Fitton's INDEPENDENT THEATRE in 1934, but he gained tougher experience in vaudeville with the comedians Bert Le Blanc and Joe Coady around inner Sydney in 1935. He learned eagerly from all his experiences—a Queensland country tour with GEORGE SORLIE in six plays presented in a huge tent; acting with radio veterans like LOU VERNON for BSA Players; being taught stage technique by the American actor Robert Capron in the ERNEST C. ROLLS production *So This is Hollywood*; maturing and extending his range by acting in world theatre classics on radio under contract to the Australian Broadcasting Commission in 1939–41.

When he was in the army in Tel Aviv he was fascinated by the Jewish actors of the Habima Theatre, and their work stirred his enthusiasm for the teachings of Konstantin Stanislavsky. In 1943 he married Tamara Tchinarova, a Russian ballerina, who not only provided the stabilising influence his life so desperately needed but led him to a passionate love of European, especially French and Russian, dramatic literature. He read voraciously on theatre, philosophy and comparative religion. In 1944, on leave from the army, Finch played leads in Ayn Rand's *The Night of January 16th* and Terence Rattigan's *While the Sun Shines* at the MINERVA THEATRE in Sydney and co-starred in the film *Rats of Tobruk* for Charles Chauvel. In 1946 and 1947 he gave performances in Macquarie Radio Theatre that established him beyond any doubt as Australia's finest actor. His great passion was to develop in Australia a theatre that represented all the best in European theatre and acting. He set about doing this in 1946—as actor, director and teacher—with MERCURY THEATRE. But ambitious for an international career, he left for London late in 1948. He won outstanding fame in films. ❧*Richard Lane*

further reading
DUNDY, ELAINE. *Finch, Bloody Finch*. London: Michael Joseph 1980.
FAULKNER, TRADER. *Peter Finch*. London: Angus and Robertson 1979.
reference
Peter Finch papers, MS 7003 in National Library of Australia (Canberra).

Don Finley

Designer. Born 29 March 1902 in Melbourne. Trained in Melbourne at National Art Gallery and Swinburne Technical College. Became commercial artist. Designed for amateur theatre in Melbourne and Sydney. Founder-member of Pioneer Players (Melbourne) 1922; Playbox Art Theatre (Sydney) 1925. Burdekin House Little Theatre (Sydney). Founded Turret Theatre (Sydney) 1928. Independent Theatre (Sydney) 1930. Founded Junior Theatre League (Sydney) with Faye Hornby. Went to England 1935. Designed for Shakespeare Memorial Theatre, Stratford-Upon-Avon, and in Nottingham and London. Organised and designed Australian and British art and theatre exhibitions. Published and illustrated articles and books on art and theatre. Died 6 January 1982 in Ireland.

Don Finley designed for amateur groups for 14 years, and wrote and lectured on contemporary theatrical theory. Edward Gordon Craig's writings, German expressionism and theories of constructivism were influences on Finley, as his designs for Capek's *The Makropoulos Secret* and Aristophanes's *Lysistrata* showed. The resources of the amateur movement, however, constricted the horizon of his vision for radical reform of Australian stagecraft and in 1935 he left the country. After travelling throughout Europe and the Soviet Union he settled in England, where major repertory companies and playwrights, including Karel Capek and George Bernard Shaw, acknowledged his talents for more than three decades. ❧*Pamela Zeplin*

further reading
ZEPLIN-WAITE, PAMELA. Three shillings for a bolt of hessian. *Australasian Drama Studies* 2/1 (Brisbane, October 1983).

Rodney Fisher AM

Director. Born 11 May 1939 on Darling Downs (Qld). Early theatrical experience at University of Queensland in 1960s. Worked as bookseller in United Kingdom and Melbourne. Began working for Melbourne Theatre Company 1969. Literary adviser and associate director of South Australian Theatre Company (Adelaide) 1973–76. Member of Belvoir Street Theatre (Sydney) board 1983. Joint artistic director of Marian Street Theatre Company (Sydney) 1990–91. Sydney Theatre Critics' major award for an outstanding contribution to theatre 1982. John Tasker Memorial Award for freelance director 1989. Green Room Award for direction in musical theatre 1989. AM 1988.

Probably the first director to grasp opportunities offered by subsidised theatre since 1968 and carry the industry to a new level of excellence was Rodney Fisher. By the 1980s he was the leading exponent of the ideal of the director's authorial vision. Sometimes he was criticised for making the text too much his own, but his work is informed by careful understanding of text and theatrical style. He owns a large library and at his best he demonstrates the fruits of careful research and design, and the choice of actors capable of physical as well as vocal expression. He devotes the appropriate resources to each production, from the classics to popular entertainment, from the gritty realism of Ronald Harwood's *The Dresser* and the public-service manners of DAVID WILLIAMSON'S *The Department* to romantic period recreations of Noël Coward's *Hay Fever* and Robert David Macdonald's *Chinchilla*.

Fisher's early work was full of reforming zeal. With GEORGE OGILVIE in the MELBOURNE THEATRE COMPANY in 1969 he wrote and directed *A Long View*, an innovative attempt to reconsider the original inhabitants' view of European settlement in Australia. When Ogilvie became director of the South Australian Theatre Company in 1972, Fisher joined him as literary adviser and associate director. Under Ogilvie, Fisher and HELMUT BAKAITIS, the director of youth activities, the company was avowedly socialist and committed to expressing the 'social workshop' that the Labor Premier, Don Dunstan, was promoting in the state. Fisher's first production in Adelaide was Trevor Griffiths's political drama *Occupations* in 1973. His notable productions included Eugene O'Neill's *Long Day's Journey into Night* in 1973, the first professional production of LOUIS ESSON'S *The Bride of Gospel Place* for the 1974 Adelaide Festival, and the premiere of *The Department* in 1974. *The Department*, which toured to Melbourne and in 1975 to Sydney, brought Fisher to national attention and he became Williamson's preferred director. He directed Williamson's next play, *A Handful of Friends*, in Adelaide in 1976, and the premieres of THE CLUB (1977), *The Perfectionist* (1982) and *Top Silk* (1989).

The early years of the SYDNEY THEATRE COMPANY, when the cream of Australian talent was drawn to the Drama Theatre at the Sydney Opera House, allowed Fisher to reach a new degree of stylistic excellence. In 1980 he made an impact with his first production, Simon Gray's *Close of Play*. *Chinchilla* and Dorothy Hewett's THE MAN FROM MUKINUPIN were successes in 1981. Fisher directed the premiere of Hewett's *The Fields of Heaven* at the Festival of Perth in 1982 and revived it next year in Sydney.

He has devised entertainments based on community history and popular figures. Particularly successful was

The Bastard from the Bush (1977), a realisation of Henry Lawson, written with Robin Ramsay. Fisher also collaborated with the singer Robyn Archer and they devised her character study of female vocalists *A Star is Torn* (1979). These ventures attracted commercial managements to Fisher. For Helen Montagu he directed *The Dresser*, with Gordon Chater and Warren Mitchell, in 1981 in Sydney and on tour from Melbourne to North Queensland. For the Davis Morley organisation he directed a highly successful production of Nell Dunn's *Steaming* in Sydney and on tour in 1982, Claire Luckham's *Trafford Tanzi* in Sydney in 1983, and Richard Harris's *Stepping Out* on national tour from Adelaide in 1985. For the 1984 Adelaide Festival Fisher directed a much-praised production of David Pownall's *Master Class*, which was revived in Sydney in 1985 and in Melbourne in 1986. He directed *My Fair Lady* for a national tour by the Victoria State Opera in 1987. He works steadily for the state theatre companies. ❦*Katharine Brisbane*

Doris Fitton DBE

Actor, director, producer. Born 1897 in Manila (Philippines) of English and Australian parentage. Arrived in Australia 1903. Studied with Gregan McMahon. Acted with Melbourne Repertory Theatre Company. Moved to Sydney and married 1922. Acted with Sydney Repertory Theatre Society and J. C. Williamson's to 1927. Turret Theatre (Sydney) 1928–30. Founded Independent Theatre (Sydney) 1930; artistic director 1930–1977. Jointly founded Playwrights' Advisory Board 1938. Died 2 April 1985 in Sydney. OBE 1953, CBE 1975, DBE 1982.

Doris Fitton earned accolades by devoting much of her life to the advancement of theatre. Ambition, determination and forceful personality gained her respect as she fought for nearly 50 years to keep the Independent Theatre open to inform and entertain the Sydney public with plays from Australia and other parts of the world. As a director she had a flair for casting and a reputation as a formidable disciplinarian. Exceptional presence masked a certain indecisiveness in her acting, probably caused by her renowned difficulty in remembering her lines and a tendency to giggle at inopportune moments.

In 1914 Fitton became a student of Gregan McMahon and worked with his Melbourne Repertory Theatre Company. Next year she rejected her first professional offer because her mother thought that at 18 she was too young to tour and McMahon considered her too inexperienced. A few months later she accepted another offer, from J. C. Williamson's. When she moved to Sydney she joined the Sydney Repertory Theatre Society, which was directed by McMahon. Through him she played in Williamson productions, including a season with Muriel Starr.

After the society closed in 1928 Don Finley invited Fitton to be an actor and secretary at the Turret Theatre at Milsons Point. There she studied theatre administration and the history of English repertory theatre, the Theatre Guild of New York and the Moscow Art Theatre, and found inspiration in Konstantin Stanislavsky's book *My Life in Art*. Turret Theatre closed in 1930, and in May that year Fitton formed her own Independent Theatre.

She directed her first play, A. A. Milne's *Michael and Mary*, in June 1931 and thereafter she concentrated on directing and only acted occasionally. She was memorable in Robert Quentin's marathon production of Eugene O'Neill's *Mourning Becomes Electra* in 1945, in *Maria Stuart* directed by Raoul Cardamatis, in Lillian Hellman's *The Little Foxes* directed by Quentin and in Jean Anouilh's *Antigone* directed by William Rees. She played the Nurse to Judith Anderson's Medea for the Australian Elizabethan Theatre Trust in 1955. In 1974 Fitton took over a role in the J. C. Williamson's production of *A Little Night Music*.

Fitton joined Rex Rienits and Leslie Rees in initiating the Playwrights' Advisory Board in 1938 and she was its secretary for a time. She went to England to observe theatre in 1949, and while there she directed an Australian play, *The Earth Remains* by Bill Gates, for Q Theatre in suburban London. On a second overseas trip in 1965 she studied American and French theatre and saw Anton Chekhov's *Three Sisters* at the Moscow Art Theatre.

When Independent Theatre was in financial difficulties in the 1970s Fitton concentrated on the Independent School of Dramatic Art. She was the legally registered proprietor of the school, which ran continuously from 1931 to 1977 as an adjunct of Independent Theatre. Its notable students include Maggie Dence, Stuart Littlemore, Reg Livermore, Jackie Weaver and Barbara Wyndon. In May 1977 Fitton directed Independent Theatre's last major production—*Our Town* by Thornton Wilder. A little later she wrote her memoirs, *Not Without Dust and Heat*. The title is part of a quotation from John Milton in *Michael and Mary*—the first play she produced. ❦*Benita Brebach and Jessica Noad*

writings
Not Without Dust and Heat. Sydney: Harper and Row 1981.
further reading
Bevan, Ian. *The Story of the Theatre Royal*. Sydney: Currency Press 1993.
Harvey Brebach, Benita. Sydney's little theatres. With particular reference to the Independent Theatre—1930–1939. University of Technology (Sydney) masters thesis 1991.

FitzGerald Brothers' Circus

At its peak, FitzGerald Brothers' Circus far exceeded in size and scope of operation any circus hitherto seen in Australia, except the large visiting American circuses of 1873–92. It toured Australasia, India and southeast Asia in the 1890s and 1900s. The proprietors were Daniel and Thomas FitzGerald, sons of a schoolteacher who died when Dan was 11 years old. Dan was born in New Zealand in 1859 and his family brought him to Australia at an early age. They settled at Shellharbour (NSW), where Tom was born in 1861. A third brother, John D. FitzGerald (1863–1921) had a career as barrister, writer and NSW Labor parliamentarian. Men of some education, the FitzGerald brothers approached the circus as entrepreneurs, not as performers in the tradition of the old Australian circus families.

When Dan FitzGerald was about 15, after a brief period as a school pupil-teacher, he became an apprentice saddler in Bathurst (NSW). Then asthma obliged him to seek an outdoor life and, beguiled by the sawdust ring, in 1878 he became a groom in the small circus of Hayes and Benhamo. These partners split and Dan accompanied Hayes to Tasmania and Western Australia. Then he joined Benhamo to tour outback towns in NSW and Queensland. He was billed as 'Australia's Greatest Jester' with Benhamo's English

Circus at Roma (Qld) in 1883. Soon afterwards, he became a part-owner of the circus in settlement of an outstanding debt, and went into partnership with Tommy and Andrew Herbert, brothers who were renowned trapeze artists and equestrians. The partners toured New Zealand with their Great United Three-in-One Circus late in 1886.

In 1888 the circus went broke at Charleville (Qld) and the firm was dissolved. Dan FitzGerald wrote to Tom, who had become a professional singer in Brisbane, asking him to join in a fresh circus venture. They began with only £32, a rider named Billy Duckworth, six horses, a van wagon and a highly trained pony that was the foundation of eventual success. The FitzGeralds battled through the backblocks, far into western NSW and Queensland. Sometimes, if things went badly, one brother would stay with the circus while the other pressed wool in shearing sheds.

FitzGerald Brothers' Circus was large and well organised by 1889, when it toured widely in NSW. On 16 April 1892, it opened in Melbourne, the 'boss show town' of Australia. So enthusiastically was the circus received that the projected short season became a stay of 14 weeks, during which 118 performances were given; and a suburban tour followed. The FitzGeralds, departing from the prevailing philosophy in Australian circus, proudly advertised their company as 'an Australian speculation, worked with Australian money, Australian brains and Australian artists'. The Melbourne success was repeated in Sydney, where the company, enlarged by additional performers and a menagerie of wild animals, played for 14 weeks, from 22 May to 19 August 1893.

During the winter of 1895 the FitzGerald brothers visited the USA, England and Europe, procuring the best artists available in circuses and music halls. Their first fully imported collection of artists, the New London Company toured Australia and New Zealand with the circus during the 1895–96 season. Chief among them were a Romanian trapeze artist, Adeline Antonio, who had been at the London Aquarium for more than a year after a triumph in Paris; Charles O. Peart, a sensational high diver who died in the FitzGeralds' service during the opening performance in Sydney in May 1896; and Ellsworth Probasco, an American horse trainer with a 'talking' horse named Mahomet. Thereafter the FitzGerald brothers annually imported a company from the principal circuses of the USA, England and Europe, a practice later followed by their successors, the Wirth brothers.

The circus year
By the mid-1890s, the FitzGeralds toured Australia and New Zealand by special trains and ships on fairly standard routes. High points of the year were a visit to Melbourne in October and November to coincide with the Melbourne Cup festivities, and a Sydney visit at Easter to coincide with the Royal Agricultural Show. The FitzGerald company lacked a serious Australian rival at that time. Its only challenger was Harmston's Circus from southeast Asia in 1897–98. Late in 1897 the two companies struck an agreement reminiscent of the 'territory' deals by which large American circuses of that era informally regulated their activities for mutual benefit. It allowed the FitzGerald Brothers' Circus to have the undivided attention of Sydney while Harmston's Circus played Melbourne for the Cup season. Like previous tented circuses, Harmston's Circus pitched its tent upon waste land in St Kilda Road, on the south bank of the Yarra River. FitzGeralds' Circus opened its 1901 Melbourne season on 19 October on the same site, in an octagonal building of galvanised iron called the Olympia. The Melbourne City Council leased the land to the FitzGeralds but refused them permission to retain the building as their own, though they were allowed permissive occupancy until 1905. Thereafter the building was occupied by Wirths' Circus. Today the site is occupied by the Victorian Arts Centre.

The FitzGeralds did not neglect employment of Australian artists and many early stalwarts of their circus remained with it into the 20th century. Gus St Leon and his family were listed on the bill during 1899–1901. Other Australian artists, such as Jack Heller, Ernest 'Daisy' Shand, Katie Montgomery and Bob West appeared with FitzGerald Brothers' Circus during the early 1900s. Star performers from other countries on the FitzGerald bill in the same era included the American rider Billy Ware; the Dunbars, trapeze artists from Barnum and Bailey; the Moultons, a troupe of American gymnasts; the Flying Meteors, a trapeze troupe from the Ringling circus; and Oscar Pagel, a German strong man who later established his own successful circus in South Africa.

By 1902 the FitzGeralds' company had grown so large that it was divided into two, with one brother taking the lesser circus—containing the more stereotyped acts—on a tour of Southeast Asia and India each year. In Australian circus folklore, this policy was the rock upon which they perished, as few Australians wanted to see what they thought was only half of the old FitzGerald circus. In contrast, the rival Wirths' Circus, which returned to Australia late in 1900 after an epic seven-year overseas tour, rose upon the ticket of 'We Never Divide'. The ascendancy of the Wirths was complete when Dan and Tom FitzGerald died in 1906—Dan in Melbourne in February and Tom two months later, while on tour in India with the second company. Tom's widow brought the circus back from India in May 1907 and valiantly attempted to resurrect the FitzGerald name, but by 1909 she was forced to liquidate her enterprise. ❦*Mark St Leon*

further reading
A morning in a circus tent. *Sydney Mail* 26 April 1905.
FitzGerald brothers' monster Australian circus and menagerie. *Bulletin* (Sydney) 20 May 1893.
Some elephants and FitzGeralds' Circus. *Bulletin* 20 April 1905.
Australasian Stage Annual 1900 and 1901.
Bulletin 26 November 1892.
Bulletin 27 May 1893.
Sunday Times (Perth) 10 November 1895.

Kate Fitzpatrick

Actor, writer. Born 1 October 1947 in Perth. Graduated from National Institute of Dramatic Art (Sydney) 1967. Professional stage debut in *The Legend of King O'Malley* 1970. Worked in Europe 1986–90. Many films and television roles.

A strikingly beautiful woman, Kate Fitzpatrick has a charismatic stage presence which she has transformed by degrees from voluptuousness to aristocratic elegance. As Hamlet in the Nimrod Theatre Company's pantomime

HAMLET ON ICE in 1972 and as Magenta in the *Rocky Horror Show* in 1974 she demonstrated comic skills to notable effect, but she has most often been required to represent cool sophistication and indolent luxury. Her outstanding performance as the sensual Nola Boyle in Patrick White's THE SEASON AT SARSAPARILLA for the OLD TOTE THEATRE COMPANY in 1976 led the author to write the part of Mag in BIG TOYS for her. After her performance as Marilyn Monroe in his *Insignificance* in 1983-84 Terry Johnson wrote the stripper Tish in *Unsuitable for Adults* with Fitzpatrick in mind.

Her other major roles include Kate Mason in Harry M. Miller's production of David Williamson's THE REMOVALISTS in 1973; Jenny Diver in BERTOLT BRECHT's *The Threepenny Opera* for the Old Tote in 1973 and Madame Lynch in LOUIS NOWRA's *Visions* for the Paris Theatre Company in 1978, both directed by her longtime associate JIM SHARMAN; Celimène in Molière's *The Misanthrope* for the Old Tote in 1978, the title-role in *The Lady of the Camellias* by Alexandre Dumas *fils* for the MARIAN STREET THEATRE COMPANY in 1979, Junie in Jean Racine's *Britannicus* for the SYDNEY THEATRE COMPANY in 1982, and Margaret in Ray Mathew's *A Spring Song* for the PLAYBOX THEATRE Company in Melbourne in 1985, all REX CRAMPHORN productions. ❦*Katharine Brisbane*

Neil Fitzpatrick

Actor. Born in Melbourne. Acted in Therry Society, Melbourne Little Theatre and other amateur groups. Trust Players 1959–60. Union Theatre Repertory Company (Melbourne) 1961–62. Old Tote Theatre Company (Sydney) 1963. Went to England on Australian Elizabethan Theatre Trust scholarship 1964. National Theatre (London) 1964–69. Melbourne Theatre Company 1970–71. Acted for state theatre companies in 1970s. At American Contemporary Theatre in Seattle (USA) on exchange 1980. Acted in eastern capitals in 1980s. Erik Kuttner Award (title-role in Dennis Potter's *Son of Man*) 1970. Green Room Award (Gaev in Anton Chekhov's *The Cherry Orchard*) 1988.

Neil Fitzpatrick's career has spanned the radical changes that have affected the life of the actor in Australia. He began in the commercial theatre in 1956 as the boy Tom Lee in GARNET H. CARROLL's production of Robert Anderson's *Tea and Sympathy* in Melbourne and Sydney, and later toured in *Not in the Book* by Arthur Wakyn for J. C. WILLIAMSON's. He was a pioneer in the first nationally sponsored theatre company, the TRUST PLAYERS. His classical training at the National Theatre in London contributed greatly to the early work of the state theatre companies.

'Come back and have a go with the rest of us', wrote ROBIN LOVEJOY, inviting Fitzpatrick to play Rosencrantz in Tom Stoppard's *Rosencrantz and Guildenstern are Dead* and three other roles for the OLD TOTE THEATRE COMPANY in 1969. He came back and during the 1970s moved among the state companies. Fitzpatrick was in the original cast of the musical LOLA MONTEZ in 1958 and he has created numerous roles in Australian plays, including Robbie in DAVID WILLIAMSON's *The Department* (1975), Marx in RON BLAIR's *Marx* (1978), Barra in CLEM GORMAN's *A Manual of Trench Warfare* (1978), Rodney in DONALD MACDONALD's *Caravan* (1983) and Tom in NICK ENRIGHT's *Daylight Saving* (1989). He played the Brother in Ron Blair's THE CHRISTIAN BROTHERS for the ENSEMBLE THEATRE COMPANY in Sydney and Q THEATRE at Penrith (NSW) in 1991. ❦*Katharine Brisbane*

Justin Fleming

Dramatist. Born 3 January 1953 in Sydney. Educated at University of Sydney and University of London. Admitted as barrister in NSW. Trained at Ensemble Acting School, Sydney. On board of directors of Australian National Playwrights' Conference 1988–90. Has also written for television and film.

Justin Fleming's dramas bear a concentration of poetically expressed intellectual ideas filtered through intense theatricality. His structural and narrative vision tends towards the ambitiously surreal rather than 'well-made' naturalism and he owes more to DOUGLAS STEWART than to RAY LAWLER. Fleming's works are diverse, ranging from his first success, *Hammer* (1981), which dealt with a boy's killing of his parents, to *Harold in Italy* (1989), an environmental-conservationist fantasy dance–drama set to the Berlioz score of the same title. Fleming has given legal assistance to the arts, including the drafting of the constitution of the AUSTRALIAN NATIONAL PLAYWRIGHTS' CONFERENCE and the stage agreement for the AUSTRALIAN WRITERS' GUILD. ❦*Brett Sheehy*

published plays
The Cobra (1983). Sydney: Sydney Theatre Company 1983.
Hammer (1981). Stockwell.
further reading
CULLEN, ANNE. Vision and dream—The plays of Justin Fleming. University of New England MA thesis.

Claude Flemming

Actor, director, bass-baritone singer. Born 22 February 1884 at Camden (NSW). Acted in George Rignold's company 1903–05 and with Nellie Stewart in Australia. In Herbert Beerbohm Tree's company in London 1907. Sang in opera and operetta in London and New York to 1917. In musical comedy and revue in Australia. Turned to directing and film-making in mid-1930s. Returned to stage during Second World War. Died 23 March 1952 in Sydney.

Claude Flemming was tall and well built—advantages in the early 20th century, when most leading men were stocky—and equally proficient in operetta and drama, though he had no formal training for the stage. He learned enough by experience in GEORGE RIGNOLD's company and with NELLIE STEWART in Paul Kester's *Sweet Nell of Old Drury* to go to the USA with Stewart in 1906 and to be accepted by Herbert Beerbohm Tree in London. After some vocal training, Flemming sang opera and operetta in London and on tour, with successes in *The Chocolate Soldier* and *The Night Birds*. He also played in the latter operetta in New York in 1913, when it was called *The Merry Countess*. From then until 1917 he alternated between London and New York. In 1914 in Hollywood he began a sporadic film career, which included four Australian films between 1918 and 1938.

In Australia, he sang in operetta and revue for HUGH D. MCINTOSH and had engagements with J. C. WILLIAMSON's from 1921 to 1926 and F. W. THRING from 1932 to 1935. By the 1920s he was best suited to dramatic, or 'heavy', roles. Between 1923 and 1937 he partnered GLADYS MONCRIEFF in operettas, including *A Southern Maid*, *Sybil*, *The Lady of the Rose*, COLLITS' INN and THE CEDAR TREE. He directed the last two works for Thring. Flemming moved away from musical performance and into production and films, particularly documentary and travel films, until 1944, when the comedy *Kiss and Tell* by F. Hugh Herbert brought him back to acting on the stage. His greatest latter-day success, it ran for three years. A three-year run as Buffalo Bill in *Annie Get Your Gun*, ended his career. ❦*Alwyn Capern*

further reading
PARKER, JOHN (ed.). *Who's Who in the Theatre*. London: Pitman 1914.

Herbert Flemming

Actor, director. Born *c*.1855 in England. Acted as amateur in London. Professional actor in William Hoskins's company in Christchurch (New Zealand) *c*.1875. Came to Australia as juvenile lead for Mrs Scott-Siddons 1876. Acted for George Darrell; Williamson, Garner and Musgrove; Dion Boucicault; Brough-Boucicault Comedy Company; Janet Achurch. Went to England *c*.1891 and acted in London. In South Africa as actor and manager 1895–1903. Returned to Australia as manager of Mel B. Spurr 1903. Went to London. Formed Brough-Flemming Company with Robert Brough 1905. Managed own company 1906–08. Died 23 October 1908 in Melbourne.

In the 1880s Herbert Flemming was a consistent but seldom acclaimed actor and between 1903 and his death in 1908 he was a significant minor theatrical manager. From about 1876 many major local and visiting actor-managers eagerly employed him as second or third lead. 'Never a conspicuously clever actor, he was always effective, and when his personal appearance got a fair chance the girls thought him lovely indeed', the *Bulletin* observed after his death. In London in the 1890s he played Nils Krogstad in Henrik Ibsen's *A Doll's House* and Dick Marston in Alfred Dampier and Garnet Walch's ROBBERY UNDER ARMS.

In South Africa, where he acted for eight years and began to manage other performers, he met the humorous storyteller Mel B. Spurr. He returned to Australia late in 1903 as co-manager of Spurr's tour, a lucrative enterprise that ended when Spurr died from diabetes in Melbourne on 25 September 1904. Flemming returned to London, where he persuaded ROBERT BROUGH and his wife to join him in touring Australia with a new troupe modelled on the famous BROUGH-BOUCICAULT COMEDY COMPANY. After a promising start, Brough died in April 1906. Flemming was also in poor health. He formed his own company and played leading roles opposite the English actor Beatrice Day, but he died in 1908. He had lost nearly all his money on his ill-fated ventures. ❦*Richard Fotheringham*

further reading
GIBBNEY, H. J. and ANNE G. SMITH. *A biographical register 1788–1939*. Canberra: Australian Dictionary of Biography 1987.
SPURR, HARRY B. *Mel B. Spurr*. London: Brown and Sons 1906.

The Floating World

Play in 20 scenes by John Romeril. **premiere** 6 August 1974, Pram Factory, Melbourne. Cast: Jane Clifton, Peter Cummins, Wilfred Last, Rob Meldrum, Carol Porter, Bruce Spence, Eddie van Roosendael. Designer: Peter Corrigan. Director: Lindzee Smith. **revived** 1982, Melbourne Theatre Company with Marion Edward and Frederick Parslow. 1986, Sydney Theatre Company with Ron Haddrick and Melissa Jaffer. **published** Sydney: Currency Press 1975, revised 1982.

The Floating World became a 'classic' in the 1980s and is now found in many high-school and university courses as a major modern Australian play. In the 1970s, however, its subject matter and profane language made it a controversial piece, staged only by alternative companies. Its relentless sexual limericks place it very much in the 1970s, when attacks on lingering CENSORSHIP laws had a precise liberating purpose, but *The Floating World* has survived critically better than many plays of that time. Particularly admired has been JOHN ROMERIL's attempt to use short scenes, vaudeville routines, fragmented and stream-of-consciousness speeches and jokes to make the structure of the play itself mirror the growing mental instability of Les Harding. He is a former prisoner of war with bitter memories of the brutality of Japanese guards and the deaths of many of his mates on the Burma–Thailand Railway.

Les and his wife Irene are given a package tour to Japan as an anniversary present. The voyage brings Les into contact with Herbert Robinson, a pompous British former vice-admiral; a Malaysian waiter; an unlimited supply of beer; and revived memories of his past suffering. Tormented by the ghost of McLeod, a fellow prisoner who died on the railway, Les breaks down and on arrival in Yokohama goes berserk with a knife. The play ends with a long speech by a straitjacketed Les, in which he justifies his action by relating some of his war experiences in disturbed and disturbing detail. The play switches uneasily between satirising Les's xenophobic attitudes to Asia, recounting the war legacy, and querying Japanese postwar economic imperialism. ❦*Richard Fotheringham*

further reading
DAVIDSON, JIM. Interview with John Romeril. *Meanjin* 37/3 (Melbourne 1978).
GRIFFITHS, GARETH. Experiments with form in recent Australian drama. *Kunapipi* 2/1 (Århus, Denmark, 1980).
KERR, DAVID. Language and metaphor in *The Floating World*. *Viewpoints 85 HSC English Literature* (ed. Joanne Lee Dow). Melbourne: Longman 1984.
MERCER, LEAH. A fairly hybrid talent—an interview with John Romeril. *Australasian Drama Studies* 17 (Brisbane, October 1990).
WEBBY, ELIZABETH. The Floating World. *Modern Australian Plays*. Sydney University Press 1990.

Cedric Flower

Designer. Born 22 August 1920 in Sydney. Studied at Dattilo Rubbo's Art School. Designed many productions for New Theatre (Sydney) from 1943. Has exhibited widely as painter. First wife was Pat Flower, dramatist.

Between 1943 and 1950 Cedric Flower designed settings and costumes for more than 25 NEW THEATRE productions in Sydney. He joined New Theatre largely because of his interest in its secretary, Patricia Bullen, whom he married in 1950. In 1949 they largely devised and acted in a revue called *Pot of Message*. His first work for the company was the set and costumes for ORIEL GRAY's play *Lawson* in 1943. Between 1944 and 1950 he was virtually resident stage designer and he served as adviser on choice of plays as well as on ways of staging them on the awkwardly wide and shallow stage in New Theatre's Castlereagh Street premises. In later years Flower has worked less frequently for New Theatre. In 1982 he redesigned Ben Jonson's *The Alchemist* in Jerome Levy's production to celebrate the company's 50th anniversary. His work for other companies includes sets and costumes for the J. C. Williamson's production of the musical THE SENTIMENTAL BLOKE in 1961. ❦*Paul Herlinger*

reference
The Mitchell Library (Sydney) has a collection of Flower's stage designs and posters.

Jennifer Flowers

Actor, director, teacher. Born 16 October 1946 at Gympie (Qld). Graduated as teacher 1966. Acted for Grin and Tonic Theatre Company, Brisbane Actors' Company, La Boîte Theatre. Full-time actor from 1984. Director from 1991. Matilda Award for contribution to theatre 1988 (acting), 1992 (directing). Also film and radio roles.

Jennifer Flowers is noted for her ability to play a vast range of roles and styles. Her first professional role, Célimène in Molière's *The Misanthrope* for the BRISBANE ACTORS' COMPANY in 1983, brought her critical acclaim. After Flowers directed Brian Friel's *Dancing at Lughnasa* for the QUEENSLAND THEATRE COMPANY in 1994 Sue Gough described her in the *Bulletin* as Queensland's most accomplished actor 'who may also be the state's most accomplished director'. Flowers is especially remembered as Amanda in Noël Coward's *Private Lives* in 1984 and Henrik Ibsen's Hedda Gabler in 1988 for the TN Theatre Company, and as Mrs Alving in Ibsen's *Ghosts* in 1989 and Elizabeth Proctor in Arthur Miller's *The Crucible* in 1991 for the Queensland Theatre Company. ❦*Bruce Parr*

Flying Fruit Fly Circus

Children's circus company in Albury (NSW) and Wodonga (Vic.), founded in 1979 as part of Murray River Performing Group. Separate entity 1987. **artistic directors** 1984–87 Robert Perrier. 1987–90 guests. 1990– Charles Parkinson.

A company of school-age performers, the Flying Fruit Fly Circus has an impressive reputation at home and abroad. Its name is particularly relevant in the twin cities of Albury (NSW) and Wodonga (Vic.), where interstate travellers must surrender fruit at the border to impede the spread of fruit fly. The circus developed out of a project for the Year of the Child in 1979, generated by Robert Perrier, artistic director of the MURRAY RIVER PERFORMING GROUP. By 1984 the circus was so active that Perrier became its full-time artistic director. He remained until 1987, when the circus and the Murray River group became separate legal entities. They share a complex in Albury, where the circus has its training, rehearsal, wardrobe and administrative facilities.

Most of the performers attend the Acrobatic Arts Community School, an annex of the Wodonga High School established by the Victorian and federal governments in 1987. It caters for pupils from years three to ten. The timetable accommodates regular circus training sessions, for which the performers go to Albury. The Victorian Ministry for Education designates circus tours during the school term as excursions and a teacher accompanies the performers to minimise disruption of their studies. Staff and international guests train the pupils. In 1987 Jane Mullett was appointed full-time training co-ordinator and Lu Guang Rong was appointed master trainer. Lu had worked with the circus in 1984 and 1985, when he came from China in the Nanjing Acrobatic Troupe, which conducted intensive training. Eight young Fruit Fly performers lived and trained for three months with the Guangzhou Acrobatic Company in China in 1987. The Flying Fruit Fly Circus has toured widely in Australia, and visited Canada in 1981 and 1984, and Great Britain in 1988. In 1990 the Flying Fruit Fly 'tower of chairs' and 'web' acts were included in the Veneto Festival in Italy, and Flying Fruit Fly aerialists performed with the Great Moscow Circus during its Australian tour. The circus receives funds from the Victorian and NSW arts ministries, the AUSTRALIA COUNCIL and the federal Department of Employment, Education and Training. It also derives income from private, corporate and community sponsorship, membership fees, commissioned shows, box office and hire of its 1200-seat tent. ❦*Pamela Payne*

For the Term of His Natural Life

Play by Alfred Dampier and Thomas Somers, adapted from *His Natural Life*, novel by Marcus Clarke. **premiere** 5 June 1886, Royal Standard Theatre, Sydney. Cast: Walter E. Baker, Alfred Boothman, Lily Dampier, Harry Leston.

While MARCUS CLARKE's impoverished widow Marian struggled to raise their large family during the 1880s, dramatists in Australia, New Zealand, England and the USA, helped by lax copyright laws, freely adapted his great novel *His Natural Life* to the stage. These plays were particularly popular in Sydney and in the English provinces. They told of Richard Devine, alias Rufus Dawes, transported for a crime he did not commit; his suffering at Macquarie Harbour, Port Arthur and Norfolk Island at the hands of the sadistic Maurice Frere; and his love for Sylvia Vickers, an officer's daughter. Actors eagerly sought these roles and those of the cannibalistic convict Gabbett, the true criminal John Rex, and the kind but powerless Reverend North, who drinks to blot out the horror.

The most successful and enduring adaptation was written in 1886 by the actor-manager ALFRED DAMPIER and THOMAS SOMERS. It was the first of Dampier's productions of Australian plays to take the public's imagination. Many were turned away from the small Royal Standard Theatre in Sydney on opening night and the play ran for 43 performances over seven weeks. 'It would have been hardly possible for a skeleton to introduce himself sideways into any part of the house' said the *Bulletin* on 19 June. Like many another big success in Sydney, it failed in Melbourne, where it lasted six performances two years later. Elsewhere it remained popular for many decades.

Like some other dramatisers, Dampier and Somers opted for a happy ending—after a prologue and six long acts—with Sylvia recovering her memory just in time to save the condemned Rufus Dawes from the gallows. The *Sydney Morning Herald* on 7 June 1886 found it 'as satisfactory an adaptation as could be desired'. It also commented on the 'bright and sparkling' language 'in the humorous portions', which suggests that some liberties had been taken with Clarke's story. On 16 June the paper said the comedian Harry Leston was 'intensely funny' as the Rev. Meekin and Alfred Boothman—who in 1908 toured as narrator of the first film version—was able to 'entirely enlist the sympathy of the audience' as Dawes. LILY DAMPIER was Sylvia and Walter E. Baker, later leading man in the BLAND HOLT company, was the brutal Frere. Alfred Dampier was a good friend of the Clarke family, and always voluntarily paid Marian Clarke a royalty of £1 or one guinea a performance. Dampier and Somers (under his real name of Walker) revised the play in 1895, and in 1905 the Rev. North was the last role Dampier played on stage. The play was then sold to WILLIAM ANDERSON, whose company performed it in Melbourne in 1909.

Clarke's daughter Marian Marcus Clarke reclaimed the copyright about 1912 and she acted as agent for all future productions. Consequently Dampier's was almost certainly the version that was still being performed in the 1920s, and it was a starting point for the famous 1927 silent film. ❦Richard Fotheringham

reference
The manuscript is in the Mitchell Library (Sydney), MSS 2283.

Lorna Forbes

Actor, director. Born 1 February 1890 in Melbourne. Daughter of actor–producer Wilson Forbes and actor Ada Lawrence. Granddaughter of actor Carrie George. On stage at five in parents' company. Professional debut 1901. Toured in melodrama for Meynell and Gunn. Married Frederick Chapman, musician, 1906. In Allan Wilkie Shakespearean Company 1919–30, except when teaching elocution and drama in Melbourne 1924. Formed touring Metropolitan Artists 1930. Acted for J. C. Williamson's in plays and musicals. Established Lorna Forbes Repertory Players 1941. Founded Melbourne Repertory Theatre 1944. Last stage appearance 1962. Also worked in radio and television. Died 26 May 1976 in Melbourne. Mother of Russell Chapman, actor.

With a deep, richly expressive voice and hypnotic violet eyes, Lorna Forbes was foremost as an actor, most prominent as a member of the ALLAN WILKIE SHAKESPEAREAN COMPANY. Her favourite roles included Cleopatra in *Antony and Cleopatra*, Gertrude in *Hamlet* and Mistress Page in *The Merry Wives of Windsor*. She turned her hand to all theatrical styles and created her own companies when work was scarce. RAY LAWLER, one of her pupils at the MELBOURNE REPERTORY THEATRE, recalled that she taught and directed intuitively, emphasising diction, audibility, respect for a classical text and awareness of an audience. She also gave importance to the building of entrances and exits and the art of taking a successful bow—which she herself used to brilliant effect. She passed on almost unknowingly a rich and practical store of theatrical traditions—preserved only by actors' word of mouth—that illuminated stage business and acting styles. ❦Victoria Chance

Margaret Ford MBE

Actor. Born at Boksburg (South Africa). Trained as speech teacher. Went to England to study acting in 1939. Returned to South Africa when Second World War began and became military nurse. Married Frederich James Ford in Perth 1947. Acted as amateur with Patch Theatre, Repertory Club and Independent Players 1949–50. Professional debut with Company of Four 1951. Also acted in Perth with National Theatre Company and Hole-in-the-Wall Theatre Company. Works in film, radio and television. MBE 1978.

A leading performer in Perth professional theatre since the 1950s, Margaret Ford is an accomplished comic actor with a highly distinctive stage presence and a stylistic range that extends from 18th-century ballad opera to the darker contemporary plays of Arthur Miller, Edward Albee and DOROTHY HEWETT. After her first professional appearance in Emlyn Williams's *The Corn is Green* Ford acted in nine more COMPANY OF FOUR productions, including Noël Coward's *Hay Fever* in 1951, Mary Chase's *Harvey* in 1952, *Richard III* in 1953 and Jean Anouilh's *Ring Round the Moon* in 1954.

She had a long association with the NATIONAL THEATRE COMPANY, appearing regularly at the Playhouse in EDGAR METCALFE's revues until the late 1960s and in many plays, including Clare Boothe's *The Women* in 1958, Alan Seymour's THE ONE DAY OF THE YEAR in 1961, Edward Albee's *A Delicate Balance* in 1969, Alan Ayckbourn's *Absurd Person Singular* in 1974, Anton Chekhov's *Three Sisters* in 1979 and George Bernard Shaw's *Pygmalion* in 1981. Her appearances in musicals included *Salad Days* in 1965 and *And So to Bed* in 1967. She toured to the northwest of Western Australia and Darwin with Richard Todd in the 1975 National Theatre production of Peter Shaffer's *Equus*.

Ford has appeared in the premieres of several of Dorothy Hewett's plays. She was the Mother and the Headmistress in THE CHAPEL PERILOUS at the New Fortune Theatre in 1970, Ollie Pullett in *Bon-Bons and Roses for Dolly* (a bravura performance in a production which caused loud public debate) in 1972, and Miss Clarry Hummer and the Widow Tuesday in THE MAN FROM MUKINUPIN in 1979. She played several roles in Hewett's rock opera *Catspaw* in 1979.

In the commercial theatre Ford's work has included a tour of New Zealand with Arthur Lowe in the farce *Beyond a Joke* in 1980, and appearances in Perth in Alan Bennett's *Habeus Corpus*, Philip King's *See How They Run* and the musical comedy *Irene*. ❦Bill Dunstone, Maurice Jones

Florrie Forde

Comedian, singer. Born 14 August 1876 in Melbourne. Originally Florence Flanagan. Debut 1 February 1893. Performed in pantomime and vaudeville in Melbourne. Debut in London 1897. Became star of British music-hall. Died 18 April 1940 in England.

The contagious style of her delivery made Florrie Forde popular wherever she sang 'Down at the Old Bull and Bush' and other catchy chorus songs. She began her career with a song-and-dance routine in Melbourne in 1893. In the same year she joined a Billee Barlow production in Sydney, playing dramatic roles in *The Enemy's Camp* and *The Work Girl*. She returned to vaudeville at the Alhambra in Melbourne. She played her first pantomime role in GEORGE RIGNOLD's *The House that Jack Built* in 1894. She was acclaimed as 'the Australian Marie Lloyd' in 1896, when the touring English comedian G. H. Chirgwin 'discovered' her. He offered her a contract to work in Great Britain for three years but she decided to tour under her own management. Rignold organised a benefit concert, which brought her £260. She made her London debut in 1897 and by 1904 she was recognised as a music-hall star. ❦Jeff Brownrigg

further reading
MANDER, RAYMOND and JOE MITCHENSON. *British Music Hall*. London: Studio Vista 1965.
RUST, BRIAN. *British Music Hall*. Harrow (England): Gramophone Publications 1979.
VAN STRATEN, FRANK. Fabulous Florrie Forde. *Victorian Arts Centre magazine*, 1986.

Drew Forsythe

Actor. Born 23 August 1949 in Sydney. Graduated from National Institute of Dramatic Art 1969. Old Tote Theatre Company (Sydney) 1970–73. Nimrod Theatre Company (Sydney) from 1970. Variety Heart Award for work in musical theatre 1990. Many film, radio and television roles.

A bravura performer with immaculate comic timing, Drew Forsythe has built a reputation as one of the finest comic actors in the country. His work is astutely observed and technically highly polished, and it owes something to a tradition of knockabout comedy in Australian revue. Forsythe is, however, most versatile. After graduation he rapidly developed his career by playing a variety of classical, comic and contemporary roles in four years with the OLD TOTE THEATRE COMPANY, including Bernard in Arthur Miller's *Death of a Salesman* in 1970, Grumio in *The Taming of the Shrew* in and Octavius in *Julius Caesar* in 1972, Mortimer in Joseph Kesselring's *Arsenic and Old Lace* in 1973, and Gunter in DAVID WILLIAMSON's *What If You Died Tomorrow?* in London in 1974. He also worked with the NIMROD THEATRE COMPANY from its opening production in 1970, *Biggles*, in which he played Ginger. Among his most notable roles have been Dogberry in *Much Ado About Nothing* in 1975, Truffaldino in Carlo Goldoni's *The Servant of Two Masters* in 1983, and the dual title-role written for him in the musical THE VENETIAN TWINS—all with the Nimrod company.

His extensive work with other companies has included Mozart in Peter Shaffer's *Amadeus* in 1982, Witwoud in William Congreve's *The Way of the World* in 1983 and Tesman in Henrik Ibsen's *Hedda Gabler* in 1986 for the SYDNEY THEATRE COMPANY; King in *Big River* in 1988–89; and both twins in *The Venetian Twins* for the QUEENSLAND THEATRE COMPANY in 1990–91. In 1990 Forsythe, Phillip Scott and Jonathan Biggins wrote a comic cabaret, *Three Men and a Baby Grand*, and performed it in four seasons at Sydney's Tilbury Hotel, in other states and in two London seasons separated by performances on the 1992 Edinburgh Festival fringe. A new show written and performed by the trio, *Three Men and a Baby Grand Too!* opened at the Tilbury in August 1994 and next month a comedy series, *Three Men on a Baby Grand*, began on television. ❦*Pamela Payne*

Fountains Beyond

Drama in three acts by George Landen Dann. **premiere** 28 January 1942, Sydney, by New Theatre League. **published** Sydney: Australasian 1944.

This realist drama by GEORGE LANDEN DANN concerns Vic Filmer, a community leader of an Aboriginal settlement on the fringe of a town. An English travel writer, Miss Harnett, and a councillor who is about to stand for mayor, Mr Watson, visit Vic and ask him to organise a corroboree for her benefit. He refuses but his larrikin friend Wally seizes the chance to make money. The corroboree is the expected travesty and accelerates the push to have the settlement removed. Miss Harnett takes up the Aboriginal cause with Vic but without success. Vic's wife is seduced by Wally and the play ends in tragedy mixed with hope.

Dann acknowledged that the play had its origins in three months he spent among timber workers on Fraser Island (Qld) in the 1930s. The character of Vic had origins in Fred Ross, an Aboriginal logger who made a deep impression on Dann and opened his eyes to Aboriginal lore and social conditions. He followed this interest for the rest of his life. Dann's style of presenting Aboriginal dialogue on the page has dated but the play's argument is as contemporary as ever. The characters are vividly observed and the issues of land ownership, loss of heritage and inhumane living conditions demonstrate an understanding of black people rare among white Australians in 1942.

The NEW THEATRE League did not print the names of the cast or director in the program for the premiere, possibly because some were in, or being called up for, the armed forces. Dann adapted the play for radio and it was first broadcast on 2 November 1942 by the ABC. In 1950 the play came first in a drama eisteddfod in Llandridod Wells in Wales, and an experimental theatre in London produced it in the same year. ❦*Katharine Brisbane*

J. Beresford Fowler

Actor, director, producer. Born *c.*1893 in Sydney. Father was musician; mother was actor in Brough–Boucicault Comedy Company. Grew up in Melbourne. Acted with Melbourne Repertory Theatre Company 1911–14 and in professional touring companies. Performed in army concert parties in United Kingdom and France during First World War. Acted in Allan Wilkie Shakespearean Company. Founded Art Theatre Players Company at Queen's Hall, Collins Street, Melbourne, 1925. Died 17 July 1972.

From 1925 until the 1950s J. Beresford Fowler staged ambitious productions with the amateurs and drama students of his Art Theatre Players Company in Melbourne. He gave the Australian premieres of August Strindberg's *Miss Julie* in 1928 and *Richard II* in 1936, and he produced plays by Anton Chekhov, Noël Coward, John Galsworthy, Henrik Ibsen, Arthur Wing Pinero and George Bernard Shaw, and dramatisations of novels by Charles Dickens. Fowler's *Richard II* gave a generation of Victorian schoolchildren an unforgettable, but not always favourable introduction to Shakespeare. In later years he played John of Gaunt. From time to time Fowler also directed country groups, such as the Ballarat Players, for whom he directed Coward's *Easy Virtue* and *Fallen Angels*. Stories of Fowler's improvised productions became legendary—most were true. PETER O'SHAUGHNESSY, one of Fowler's actors, has written that he put Dickens's Vincent Crummles in the shade but 'people tend to forget just what an oasis The Art Theatre Players was in Melbourne's cultural desert'.

Fowler was a superb Bottom in *A Midsummer Night's Dream*, says O'Shaughnessy, for 'in his innocence, egotism and penchant for playing all the parts he had much in common' with Shakespeare's character. Fowler's actors also included Sylvia Archer, Dulcie Bland, Wilfred Blunden, June Clyne, Douglas Kelly, LLOYD LAMBLE, RAY LAWLER, Mona Pepyat, Wyn Roberts and Bambi Smith. Fowler's mother also acted frequently with the Art Theatre Players. Widowed in 1893, she took the family to Melbourne in 1896. She took in boarders and sometimes acted under the name of Mrs Fanny Fowler or Ethel Adele. Fowler, educated at state schools, became an omnivorous reader, an avid follower of cricket and football and a theatregoer. He began work as a messenger boy and was later unsuccessful as a dentist's apprentice. Despite signs of deafness, which became acute, he acted in plays by Ibsen and George Bernard Shaw in Gregan McMahon's amateur MELBOURNE REPERTORY THEATRE COMPANY. He toured with a J. C. Williamson company in *Joseph and his Brethren*, with NELLIE STEWART as an assistant stage manager, and with the Bailey and Grant Company as Billy Bearup in ON OUR SELECTION. After military service in Europe, he rejoined Bailey and Grant in 1919, and then directed an amateur revival of Ibsen's *John Gabriel Borkman*, in which he played the title-role. He worked with the ALLAN WILKIE SHAKESPEAREAN COMPANY for nearly three years, until he was sacked.

Fowler had everything against him: deafness, a harsh voice that lacked any modulation, a slight speech impediment and a determination to promote plays that professional companies would not touch. Despite deafness, isolation and poverty, he never seemed to despair, although he was bitter that Melbourne newspapers ceased to review his productions. He never married, although he harboured a passion for some of his leading ladies.

Fowler wrote several plays. He had an impressive collection of autographed letters, documents and photographs which he hoped to auction to raise capital for a permanent theatre. It was dispersed. ❦*Barry O. Jones*

writings
The Green-eyed Monster. Ilfracombe (England): Arthur H. Stockwell 1968. Autobiography.
Stars in my Backyard—A survey of the Australian stage. Ilfracombe (England): Arthur H. Stockwell 1962.

Franquin

Hypnotist. Born Frank H. Quinn in Christchurch (New Zealand) Opened first stage show 1949. Came to Australia 1950. Gave final performance 1968. Retired to Gold Coast (Qld).

The most successful stage hypnotist ever to perform in Australia, Franquin played long seasons in Melbourne and Sydney in the 1950s in a solo show that included demonstrations of memory and lightning calculations as well as hypnotism. It was fast, hilarious, wholesome and educational. Grandparents could take grandchildren and everyone left delighted. Franquin showed hypnotic abilities at an early age. In New Zealand after the Second World War he worked in showgrounds to finance a stage show, which he opened in Wellington in 1949. He had no model as a stage hypnotist and the show was not very successful. He persevered, however, and when he reached Auckland some months later he played to immense audiences. He came to Australia and opened at Her Majesty's Theatre in Brisbane in 1950 with great success. Then he played for months at the Empire Theatre in Sydney and did capacity business for more than a year at the Princess Theatre in Melbourne. He played return seasons in Australia and New Zealand and performed in Honolulu. ❦*Gerald Taylor*

writings
The Eyes Have It. Sydney: Angus and Robertson 1957.
Open Your Mind. Sydney: Robyn Publications 1950.

Anne Fraser

Designer. Born 1 August 1928 in Auckland (New Zealand). Brought to Australia at early age. Trained in advertising at Royal Melbourne Institute of Technology, 1946–50. Designed for National Theatre Movement (Melbourne) 1948–55. Resident designer with Union Theatre Repertory Company (Melbourne) 1955. Head of design with Old Tote Theatre Company (Sydney) 1971–77. Freelance designer for Australian Elizabethan Theatre Trust, J. C. Williamson's, Melbourne Theatre Company, Playbox Theatre Company (Melbourne), South Australian Theatre Company (Adelaide), St Martin's Theatre Company (Melbourne), ballet and opera companies and television.

When prospects were often bleak for Australian designers, especially women, Anne Fraser consistently championed their potential and demonstrated it in accomplished decor, distinguished by sophistication, wit and versatility. She began designing for the stage with the encouragement of RAY LAWLER in 1946, when she was an aspiring actor working as an advertising artist. Her career took a historic turn when she was appointed the first resident designer of the Union Theatre Repertory Company in 1955. She was, says GEOFFREY HUTTON, 'the first of a line who have talent, training and time to work out their decors instead of improvising them from whatever odds and ends were available'.

Historic too were her designs for the company's production of Lawler's SUMMER OF THE SEVENTEENTH DOLL in the same year. In 1956 the ST MARTIN'S THEATRE COMPANY, formerly the Melbourne Little Theatre Company, engaged Fraser for its first play under its new name, *Tiger at the Gates* by Jean Giraudoux. Since then her career has included major residencies with the OLD TOTE THEATRE COMPANY and the MELBOURNE THEATRE COMPANY and a wide range of freelance work. ❦*Pamela Zeplin*

writings
Thirty years of design—A photo essay. *Australian Theatre Design* (ed. Kim Spinks). Sydney: Australian Production Designers Association NSW 1992.

further reading
PRERAUER, MARIA. Design of the times. *Australian* 20 June 1977.
SUMNER, JOHN. *Recollections at Play—A life in Australian theatre*. Melbourne: University Press 1993.

Vivian Fraser

Architect. Born 21 March 1936. Trained at Sydney Technical College. Converted Nimrod Theatre (Sydney) 1974. Designed Grant Street Theatre (Melbourne) for Victorian College of the Arts 1983. Converted Wharf Theatre (Sydney) 1984, 1986.

Vivian Fraser believes that 'what makes a good theatre building is what makes good theatre ... an element of [visual] drama needs to be put into the building right from where the public steps off the street'. He began his architectural practice in Sydney when he was converting a food factory into the Nimrod Theatre, now the BELVOIR STREET THEATRE. The conversion brought him a merit award from the Royal Australian Institute of Architects. His Grant Street Theatre for the VICTORIAN COLLEGE OF THE ARTS is a flexible 300-seat teaching and working theatre. His conversion of the upper level of an Edwardian timber wharf and warehouse on Sydney Harbour into the WHARF THEATRE for the Sydney Theatre Company brought him the Sir John Sulman Medal from the NSW chapter of the RAIA in 1985 and the RAIA President's Medal for the best recycled building in Australia in 1984–85. His conversion of the lower level for the Sydney Dance Company in 1986 won him a merit award from the RAIA in 1987. ❦*Ross Thorne*

writings
Designing theatres for 'found' spaces. *Australian Theatre Design* (ed. Kim Spinks). Sydney: Australian Production Designers Association NSW 1992.

further reading
Architecture Australia. December 1978–January 1979.
Architecture Australia. December 1985.
Builder NSW. September 1979.
Builder NSW. May 1986.

Kristian Fredrickson

Designer. Born 12 October 1940 in Wellington (New Zealand). Trained as journalist. Studied design at Wellington Technical College. Began designing for opera and ballet 1962. Commissions from Australian Ballet in 1963, J. C. Williamson's and Emerald Hill Theatre (Melbourne). Resident designer with Melbourne Theatre Company 1966–73. Five Irene Mitchell Awards for best set design. Studied in United Kingdom and Germany and taught in London during 1970s. Also designs for dance, opera, film and television.

Kristian Fredrickson's designs are layered, chunky and bold in their attack on the eye. Landmarks in his career have been commissions for big occasions with energetic directors, such as Anton Chekhov's *Three Sisters* directed by GEORGE OGILVIE for the MELBOURNE THEATRE COMPANY in 1967. In this Fredrickson expressed disillusion by restricting his palette to black, white and greys. He worked with Ogilvie again in a monolithic, economic production of Arthur Miller's *Death of a Salesman* in 1982. *Pericles* for the SYDNEY THEATRE COMPANY in 1987 was another notable Fredrickson design. ❦*Tom Bannerman*

Colin Free

Dramatist. Born 1 September 1925 in Sydney. Wrote stage plays in 1960s. Prolific writer for radio and television.

A highly original writer for radio and television, Colin Free also wrote stage plays that were produced in Sydney in the 1960s. Witty, offbeat dialogue marked *Where Did Vortex Go?* and *Cannonade of Bells*, both directed by ALEXANDER ARCHDALE for Community Theatre in 1965. Free wrote two one-act plays, *Striptease* and *A Walk Among the Wheeneys*, for Q THEATRE, which presented them at lunch time in the AMP Theatrette. *A Walk Among the Wheeneys*, a comedy about two bucolic brothers with a grapefruit orchard, was the precursor of Free's television series *Nice 'n' Juicy*. Free also wrote *Ice Palais* for the TASMANIAN PUPPET THEATRE in Hobart in the 1960s. ❦*Richard Lane*

published plays
Nightmares of the Old Obscenity Master (1973). Sydney: Currency Methuen 1975 in *Five Plays for Radio* (ed. Alrene Sykes).
A Walk Among the Wheeneys (1966). Sydney: Currency Methuen 1975 in *Five Plays for Radio* (ed. Alrene Sykes).

Freemason's Tavern

Theatre on corner of Harrington and Davey Streets, Hobart, opened 24 December 1833. Used until 1835.

SAMSON CAMERON fitted up a large room in the Freemason's Tavern, where the Freemason's Hotel now stands, to stage the first professional theatrical production in Tasmania. The theatre had a gallery, pit seats on a rake, a proscenium, and a dais 450–600 mm high for a small stage which, it was said, 'admits two or three good scenes'. The *Colonial Times* said 'a more respectable assembly was never collected in Hobart Town' for the opening. The theatre held an audience of 150 but the first-comers spread themselves on the benches because of the heat of the night and some ticket holders were among the hundreds who failed to gain admission to see *The Stranger* by August von Kotzebue. Cameron's season ran until May 1834, with twice-weekly productions, and he returned to the theatre for another season in December 1835. ❦*Gillian Winter*

Anna French

Designer. Born 19 May 1950 in Melbourne. Both parents were artists and mother was member of Borovansky Ballet. Studied fashion design at Prahran Technical College (Melbourne) 1972–73. Resident designer for South Australian Theatre Company (Adelaide) 1975–76. Resident designer for National Theatre Company (Perth) 1977. National Theatre Critics' Award for best designer in Western Australia 1977. Went to study in Europe on inaugural Loudon Sainthill Scholarship 1977. Free lance since 1978, working for major Australian theatre companies, ballet and films.

A minimalist, Anna French, provides extraordinary detail in small set designs and wearable clothing. GEORGE OGILVIE, a director with whom she has often collaborated, says: 'She is one of the most serving designers we have—one of the few concerned not with design itself but with serving the play, which may account for her relative anonymity. Actors love working with her and wearing her clothes; she attends rehearsals and often redesigns garments to assist the actors' work. She is also capable of creating with very little money.' Ogilvie productions designed by French include *Major Barbara* by George Bernard Shaw, *No Names … No Pack Drill* by BOB HERBERT and *You Can't Take It With You* by George S. Kaufman and Moss Hart. Her finest work also includes productions of JOHN POWERS's *The Last of the Knucklemen*, Eugene O'Neill's *Not About Heroes* and *Long Day's Journey Into Night*, and costumes for Tennessee Williams's *Kingdom of Earth* for the South Australian Theatre Company. ❦*Tom Bannerman*

Jan Friedl

Actor, singer. Born 14 September 1948 in Melbourne. Worked with Melbourne Youth Theatre while studying at University of Melbourne. Married composer Martin Friedel 1971. Joined La Mama Company and Australian Performing Group 1971. Joined Melbourne Theatre Company 1973. Studied singing on Australia Council scholarship at Komische Oper, Berlin (East Germany), 1989. Founded Seduction Opera Company in Melbourne with Friedel 1991. Appears frequently in film and television.

Jan Friedl is an intense performer who has been at the forefront of new developments and has rarely refused a challenge. She is a dramatic actor and soprano singer and an accomplished comedian. Blackly comic roles are her favourites—'Good comedy always has a layer of chill or bitter pill underneath', she has said. Her early work with the AUSTRALIAN PERFORMING GROUP included leading roles in Jack Hibberd's *DIMBOOLA* and *Peggy Sue* and Max Richards's *Cripple Play*. She has since performed a wide variety of parts with MELBOURNE THEATRE COMPANY and the PLAYBOX THEATRE CENTRE, including leading roles in plays by Alan

Ayckbourn, Samuel Beckett, John Guare, Henrik Ibsen, Tennessee Williams and Restoration dramatists. In the Australian repertoire she played Francesca in ALEX BUZO's *Martello Towers* in 1976 and created the title-roles in BARRY DICKINS's *The Death of Minnie* (1980) and Margot Hilton's *Potiphar's Wife* (1980) for Playbox; Joy in ALMA DE GROEN's *Vocations* (1982) and Marge in KATHERINE THOMSON's *Diving for Pearls* (1991). Friedl has sung in *Sweeney Todd* and other musicals, opera, cabaret, concerts and recitals. She has a particular affinity with the music of Kurt Weill and contemporary composers, including her husband. She performed several roles in the premiere of his opera *Sin*, for which JACK HIBBERD wrote the libretto. With Friedel she wrote the libretto of his short opera *Seduction of a General*. ❧Katharine Brisbane

Colin Friels

Actor. Born 15 September 1952 in Scotland. Emigrated to Australia 1965. Graduated from National Institute of Dramatic Art 1976. South Australian Theatre Company 1977–81. Numerous film roles. Married to actor Judy Davis.

Colin Friels is most widely known as a film actor but the athletic and engaging personality he conveys on screen has also assisted an impressive stage career. Though his stage presence is handsome and commanding, he offers, among his distinctive qualities, a compelling country-boy simplicity, apparent in Hamlet, Orestes in *The Oresteia* and Barrie Moon in Clem Gorman's *A Manual of Trench Warfare*. He created Barrie Moon in 1977, when he was in the South Australian Theatre Company.

After a season of *Trench Warfare* in Sydney in 1979 Friels settled there and played the Soldier in BERTOLT BRECHT's *The Caucasian Chalk Circle* for the SYDNEY THEATRE COMPANY. He played several major roles for the NIMROD THEATRE COMPANY in 1980, including Rubin in STEPHEN SEWELL's *Traitors*, Orestes, and Bert in LOUIS NOWRA's *Inside the Island*. In 1981 he returned to the Sydney Theatre Company to play Harry and Jack in Dorothy Hewett's THE MAN FROM MUKINUPIN, Hamlet, Macduff in *Macbeth*, and Pete in the premiere of JENNIFER CLAIRE's *Butterflies of Kalimantan* (1982).

Friels appeared in Sydney with JUDY DAVIS in Anton Chekhov's *The Bear* in 1983 and as Loevborg in Henrik Ibsen's *Hedda Gabler* in 1985. In 1988 he played Treat in Lyle Kessler's *Orphans* on national tour. For the QUEENSLAND THEATRE COMPANY he played Lopakhin in Chekhov's *The Cherry Orchard* in 1991 and Viktor Sager in JIM SHARMAN's *Shadow and Splendour* at the 1992 Adelaide Festival. ❧Katharine Brisbane

further reading
O'Donnell, Owen. *Contemporary Theatre, Film and Television* 8th edn. Detroit (USA): Gale 1990.

Alfred Frith

Actor, comedian, singer. Born *c*.1885 in London. Served in British Army in South African War and in India. Resigned from army and toured Asian countries in musical comedy and drama. Came to Australia 1914. Toured South Africa for J. C. Williamson's. Made Australian debut 1915. Had success in New York 1927. Returned to Australia for musical-comedy roles for Williamson's and F. W. Thring. Retired in late 1930s. Died 28 May 1941.

Alfred Frith exploited his big mouth and teeth to become a popular character comedian in musical comedy from his first star role in Australia, in *High Jinks* in 1915. In the mid-1920s he went to New York and won a role in the Broadway production of Hamilton Deare's dramatic adaptation of Bram Stoker's novel *Dracula*, which was a huge success in 1927. Tired of depending upon his appearance, Frith had his teeth extracted, but Australian audiences found him less amusing. His last popular role, in THE CEDAR TREE in 1935, did not compare with former triumphs. He was playing in radio revues at the time of his death. ❧Alwyn Capern

Benjamin Fuller Kt

Entrepreneur. Born 20 March 1875 in London. Joined family in New Zealand 1894. Presented vaudeville in Sydney 1901. Moved to Sydney 1912. Knighted 1921. Staged operetta with Hugh J. Ward 1922–26. Formed Gaiety Theatres Ltd with Garnet H. Carroll 1941. Governing director of Carroll–Fuller Theatres Pty Ltd from 1946. Died 10 March 1952 in London.

Ben Fuller was a complete showman. At the peak of his career he had 40 separate companies operating in Australasia. He presented first-class vaudeville, revue, pantomime, melodrama, operetta, opera and film. As a nine-year-old boy chorister he was a juvenile in a Gilbert and Sullivan production at the Savoy Theatre in London and he preserved a love of singing and opera all his life. It made him—and at least once lost him—a lot of money.

The second of seven Fuller children, Ben emerged as the dominant personality of John Fuller and Sons, an entertainment business begun by his father in New Zealand in the 1890s. He was its general manager by 1901 and he remained the effective head of various FULLERS' organisations for the rest of his life. He came to Sydney and took over the BRENNAN VAUDEVILLE CIRCUIT for Fullers' in 1912. In 1915 he joined forces with GEORGE MARLOW in running the Adelphi Theatre in Sydney. During the First World War Fuller was generous to the University of Sydney and to war widows and patriotic funds. He was rewarded in 1921 with the first knighthood given to a member of the theatrical profession in Australia.

Ben Fuller and his brother John split Fullers' Theatres Ltd in 1934. Ben kept most of the assets. In the same year he celebrated the centenary of Victoria by painting the Palace Theatre in Melbourne, giving it 'the biggest Neon light in Australia as a beacon', renaming it the Apollo Theatre and presenting Sir Benjamin Fuller's Royal Grand Opera Company. This gave seasons of opera in English with Australian and British stars in Melbourne, Sydney and Newcastle (NSW) and cost Fuller so much money—£30 000, cynics said—that he did not seriously return to stage production until after the Second World War.

In 1941, when a J. C. Williamson's lease expired, Fuller took the King's Theatre in Melbourne in partnership with an old colleague, GARNET H. CARROLL, as Gaiety Theatres Ltd. After the war they formed Carroll–Fuller Theatres Pty Ltd and combined with KENN BRODZIAK's Aztec Services to bring shows to the King's and Princess Theatres in Melbourne and the Palace Theatre in Sydney. The Palace was rescued from films when Noël Coward's *Present Laughter* opened there on 27 May 1949, after a good run in Melbourne. Other Carroll–Fuller attractions were farces with Clifford Mollison, melodrama with Sonia Dresdel, and a fey performance by Elisabeth Bergner in *The Two Mrs Carrolls* by Martin Vale.

In 1951 Fuller combined with J. C. WILLIAMSON'S to bring the international stars CYRIL RITCHARD and MADGE ELLIOTT back to Australia to perform Noël Coward's *Private Lives*. They combined again later in 1951 to stage F. Hugh Herbert's mildly racy Broadway comedy *The Moon is Blue*. This was Fuller's last offering on the Australian stage. He died while in London looking for material. ❦*John West*

further reading
RUTLEDGE, MARTHA. Sir Benjamin and John Fuller. *Australian Dictionary of Biography* 8. Melbourne University Press 1981.

Fullers'

The brothers BENJAMIN FULLER and John Fuller jnr (1879–1959), members of an extensive family that was successful in New Zealand entertainment, were outstanding impresarios in Australia from 1912. Their vaudeville circuit competed vigorously with the first of the TIVOLI CIRCUITS for 20 years. The Tivoli was the premier home of vaudeville but it relied strongly on overseas stars as headliners while the Fuller circuit placed more emphasis on home-grown talent.

The head of the family was John Fuller snr, a printer. Late in life he discovered that he had a silvery tenor voice and became a professional singer. Legend says he rescued a singing teacher from a canal in London and the grateful man offered him free singing lessons. Fuller came to Australia in the London Pavilion Theatre Company in 1889, playing in St George's Hall in Melbourne in August and a couple of months later at the Opera House in Sydney. The venues place the company below the first rank.

Fuller's family joined him, and in 1894 they settled in Auckland (New Zealand). The Fullers built up a theatrical circuit with such success that they advertised themselves in the 1901 *Stage Annual* as 'the pioneers of permanent vaudeville in New Zealand'. They were sole proprietors of the Alhambra Theatre in Dunedin, the Oddfellows Hall in Christchurch (managed by Walter Fuller), the Choral Hall in Wellington (managed by Lydia Fuller) and the Agricultural Hall in Auckland (managed by John Fuller snr). John Fuller jnr managed their touring company and Ben Fuller was general manager of the circuit.

Early in 1901 John Fuller and Sons leased one of Sydney's lesser theatres, the ROYAL STANDARD THEATRE. Ben Fuller renamed it the Empire and on 16 March 1901 Mr John Fuller's Empire Minstrel and Variety Company presented its first weekly-change program. On the opening bill John Fuller snr sang; Lennon, Hyman and Lennon tumbled; and Will Watkins and May Marlow entertained. Orchestra stalls cost two shillings. Stalls behind them cost one shilling, and sixpence bought admission to the small, uncomfortable gallery.

'Hilarity without vulgarity' was the Fullers' motto, and it carried them for almost a year. Then they withdrew to New Zealand and consolidated and expanded their circuit. In Auckland and Christchurch they had an Opera House, in Dunedin the Alhambra and Princess Theatres and in Wellington His Majesty's Theatre and the Theatre Royal, the head office. The Fullers made another foray across the Tasman Sea in 1912. They took over the BRENNAN VAUDEVILLE CIRCUIT and rapidly enlarged it. In 1913 the *Illustrated Tasmanian Mail* listed the Fullers' Australian theatres:

Adelaide King's Theatre.
Brisbane Empire Theatre.
Broken Hill (NSW) Crystal Theatre.
Fremantle (WA) Princess Theatre.
Perth Melrose Theatre.
Port Pirie (SA) Empire Theatre.
Melbourne Bijou Theatre, Gaiety Theatre, National Amphitheatre.
Sydney Fullers' National Theatre, the base.

In 1914 Ben and John Fuller became joint governing directors of John Fuller and Sons. Next year Ben joined forces with GEORGE MARLOW in running the Adelphi Theatre in Sydney. John joined Ben in Sydney in 1916, leaving Walter in charge of the business in New Zealand. Ben indulged his love of opera by managing a tour by the Gonsalez Opera Company from Italy, which lasted from June 1916 to August 1917 and prompted him to rename the Adelphi the Grand Opera House. A star tenor, Bettino Capelli, stayed after the tour as a headliner in Fullers' vaudeville, billed as Tino Capelli. Their supreme attraction in vaudeville, however, was probably the comedy team of STIFFY AND MO. They were the stars of the all-Australian pantomime *THE BUNYIP*, which Fullers' produced at the Grand Opera House for Christmas 1916, with huge success. It later toured the Fuller circuit, which programs in 1922 listed as:

Adelaide King's Theatre, Majestic Theatre, Prince of Wales Theatre.
Brisbane Empire Theatre.
Melbourne Bijou Theatre, Gaiety Theatre, Lyric Theatre (St Kilda), Palace Theatre, Princess Theatre.
Newcastle (NSW) Victoria Theatre.
Perth His Majesty's Theatre, Theatre Royal.
Sydney Fullers' National Theatre, Grand Opera House, Majestic Theatre (Newtown).

The Fullers leased the two Perth theatres but owned almost all the others and six more in New Zealand. They always tried to ensure business solidity by owning theatres and their sites. Some of their theatres, like the Palace in Melbourne and the Majestic in Sydney, now played comedies and dramas all year round, except for an annual pantomime. Eclectic in their choice of entertainment, the Fullers did not scorn moving pictures if money was to be made from them. By 1922 the Theatre Royal in Perth had long been filled with movies. His Majesty's in Perth was usually filled with J. C. Williamson's shows or J. AND N. TAIT LTD concerts. In Brisbane, the Empire seldom had Fullers' attractions, but a succession of short leases. In Adelaide the Fullers played vaudeville at either the King's or the Majestic, while the Prince of Wales was devoted to drama, played by a local company run by the producer Collett Dobson. In Melbourne, Fullers' vaudeville was seen at the Bijou and the Gaiety, sometimes with Stiffy and Mo heading the bill. At the Palace—the National Amphitheatre renamed—the fare included a season by ADA REEVE, some classics from the ALLAN WILKIE SHAKESPEAREAN COMPANY, and some films filling the gaps. The Fullers Dramatic Players played at the Princess until the Fullers closed it in August 1922 for an overdue renovation. In Sydney in 1922,

JIM GERALD and his revue company played for a solid ten weeks at the National, the headquarters of Fullers' variety. The 1921 Christmas pantomime, starring Stiffy and Mo, ran on into 1922, playing for more than 100 performances at the Grand Opera House.

The Fullers joined HUGH J. WARD, who had sold his shares in J. C. Williamson's, in forming a new production company in 1922. Hugh J. Ward Theatres Pty Ltd proclaimed its capital as £500 000 and listed its governing directors as 'Sir Benjamin Fuller, Mr Hugh J. Ward, Mr John Fuller'. The positions of the three men in photographs seem to confirm this peck order. The stylish Ward would add some higher-class fare to the Fullers' usual melodrama and vaudeville. In Sydney the venue would be the Grand Opera House, until Fullers' new St James Theatre opened. In Melbourne, Ward productions would play in the Palace Theatre and the Princess Theatre. The latter, its auditorium rebuilt by HENRY E. WHITE, reopened on 26 December 1922 with a recent American musical comedy, *The O'Brien Girl*. This had been been run in for three months in Sydney and it ran for 202 performances in Melbourne.

Ward's emphasis was on operetta, interspersed with some high-class drama and comedy. His 1925 Melbourne production of the musical comedy *No! No! Nanette*, starring Elsie Prince, a cute import from London, opened the Fullers' St James Theatre in Sydney with gala nights on 26 and 27 March 1926. But all was not well between the partners and, for reasons not satisfactorily explained, Ward retired in October 1926. *Everyone's* magazine said the Fuller brothers, on their own again, would revert to staging vaudeville and the yearly pantomime, leasing the more important theatres, like the St James and the Princess, to other managements. This is substantially what happened, although the Fullers did present their backlog of operettas in Sydney. They achieved a big hit in 1928, when they brought GLADYS MONCRIEFF back from London to star in *Rio Rita*.

From 1929 the Great Depression severely curtailed the operations of Fullers' Theatres Ltd and wedded the brothers to film exhibition. Films did not ask for more money or complain about their billing and they could be played four or more times a day. Fullers' revue companies, headed by Fred Forbes, JIM GERALD, Frank O'Brien or GEORGE WALLACE, continued, but the Fuller theatres became cinemas, often with a change of name. Live entertainment could occasionally be slotted into a converted theatre without difficulty. The Fullers often rented theatres to companies directed by FRANK NEIL, whose impact on the live theatre was increasing. In 1934 the Fuller brothers split their assets. John took the St James Theatre and later profitably sold it to Metro–Goldwyn–Mayer before retreating into real-estate investment. Ben, now sole governing director of Fullers' Theatres Ltd, kept the other assets. ❦*John West*

Fullers' National Theatre

Theatre in Castlereagh Street, Sydney. Built as **National Sporting Club** 1902. Converted to theatre and opened as **National Amphitheatre** 26 December 1906, seating 1410 on one level. Renamed **Fullers' National Theatre** 1912. Converted to two-level theatre 1919, seating 1382. Architect: Henry E. White. Renamed **Roxy Theatre** cinema 28 February 1930. Renamed **Mayfair Theatre** 1932. Closed 1980. Demolished 1984.

The National Sporting Club, with a large hall seating 2000 persons for boxing and other athletic entertainments, was built on the western side of Castlereagh Street, a little south of King Street, in 1902. In 1906 James Brennan converted the hall to a one-level theatre for variety performances and called it the National Amphitheatre. FULLERS' took control of the BRENNAN VAUDEVILLE CIRCUIT in 1912 and renamed the house Fullers' National Theatre. The licensing authorities noted it as 'antiquated and dangerous' in June 1912 but rebuilding was not approved until September 1918.

The architect HENRY E. WHITE converted the amphitheatre into a two-level theatre with twin stage boxes at each side on both levels. It had a shallow fly-tower stage. In the 1920s it was a popular vaudeville theatre. FRED BLUETT, MIKE CONNORS and QUEENIE PAUL, Edgley and Dawe, STIFFY AND MO, and GEORGE WALLACE performed there. But on 24 February 1930 the *Sydney Morning Herald* announced the end of Fullers' vaudeville and closure of the 'Nash'. Quickly redecorated, it reopened four days later as the Roxy Theatre, showing a film, *Hollywood Revue*. In February 1932 the Roxy briefly returned to live variety under FRANK NEIL, who was touring ADA REEVE. But at the end of the year Fullers' Theatres Ltd decided to show British films. The theatre, its auditorium refurbished in Art Deco style, was renamed the Mayfair. Later Hoyts Theatres bought the Mayfair and from the mid-1950s it showed major widescreen films. In 1977–78 there were live shows, including a revival of the rock musical *Godspell*, Q THEATRE's rock show *St Marys Kid*, and PETER WILLIAMS's production of *Crown Matrimonial*, starring JUNE SALTER and John Hamblin. After this rediscovery of its potential there were protests when demolition threatened the theatre and the NSW government indicated that efforts would be made to retain it. As usual, the protesters were lulled into false security. In 1980 the foyers and dress-circle stairs were converted into shops and in 1984 the building was demolished. ❦*Ross Thorne*

Ben Gabriel

Actor. Born 25 February 1918 in England. Son of actor Ethel Gabriel. Brought up in Australia. Began acting 1947. Member of Young Elizabethan Players 1960–63. With wife Doreen Warburton co-founded Q Theatre, Penrith (NSW), 1979. Resident actor at Q Theatre 1979–89.

A supreme performer of classic Australian roles, Ben Gabriel played Barney in Ray Lawler's *SUMMER OF THE SEVENTEENTH DOLL* on an Arts Council tour in 1958–59, on a tour of the Northern Territory in 1960, and in a production by Q THEATRE in Sydney. In 1961 he went on an Arts Council tour as Wacka in Alan Seymour's *THE ONE DAY OF THE YEAR*. In 1964 he played a lead role in the revival of Sumner Locke Elliott's *RUSTY BUGLES* for INDEPENDENT THEATRE in Sydney. In 1966 he again played Wacka in a production in Tokyo of *The One Day of the Year*. For Q Theatre at Penrith he played Dad in *ON OUR SELECTION* in 1981. Gabriel also did fine work for the OLD TOTE THEATRE COMPANY, especially as Willy Loman in ROBIN LOVEJOY's 1970 production of Arthur Miller's *Death of a Salesman*. After Gabriel's performance as the innocent priest in Edward Albee's *Tiny Alice* in 1966 Robin Lovejoy said he was an actor of 'innate goodness'. In 1984 the NSW government gave Gabriel and his wife DOREEN WARBURTON a scholarship to study in the USA and

England, in recognition of their work in establishing Q Theatre on Sydney's western outskirts. ❦*Richard Lane*

Ethel Gabriel

Actor. Born 31 October 1888 in London. Came to Australia as war bride 1919. Died May 1967 in Sydney. Mother of actor Ben Gabriel.

Ethel Gabriel's name will always be associated with SUMMER OF THE SEVENTEENTH DOLL. She played Emma Leech in all the AUSTRALIAN ELIZABETHAN THEATRE TRUST tours of Ray Lawler's play. A suffragette in her youth—she claimed to have been the first female conductor on a British tram during the First World War—she carried a lusty forthrightness within a slight frame and brought a great comic spirit to the part she made her own. She played it in London and New York and she was the only member of any stage cast to appear in the 1959 film. In 1958–59, under the supervision of JOHN SUMNER, she reproduced his original production with a new cast and took it on tour over most of Australia, sponsored by J. C. WILLIAMSON'S, the Trust, and the ARTS COUNCIL OF AUSTRALIA. She played Emma.

Before *The Doll*, her great success in a long career as a character actor was Abby Brewster in ALEC COPPEL'S 1942 Minerva Theatre production of Joseph Kesselring's *Arsenic and Old Lace*. With tours, she played this classic comedy for two years. In 1930 she played the cleaning woman in LESLIE HAYLEN'S *Two Minutes' Silence* at the tiny Community Theatre in Sydney, and in 1934 she appeared in the McDonagh sisters' film version. In 1934 she also acted with the French star Alice Delysia in the operetta *Mother of Pearl*, presented by F. W. THRING at the New Tivoli Theatre in Sydney. She appeared with MARIE NEY in *Ladies in Retirement* by Edward Percy and Reginald Denham in 1940 and with MARIE BURKE in *Robert's Wife* by St John Ervine in 1941. An excellent seamstress and costumier, she made costumes for Sydney's INDEPENDENT THEATRE for many years and dressed all the kewpie dolls—which were smashed nightly—in her performances of *Summer of the Seventeenth Doll*. ❦*Richard Lane*

John Gaden AM

Actor, director. Born 13 November 1941 in Sydney. Studied arts and law at University of Sydney 1959–66. Performed in Adelaide with Theatre '62 and South Australian Theatre Company 1967–68. Australian Theatre for Young People (Sydney) 1969. Octagon Theatre Company (Perth) 1970. Old Tote Theatre Company (Sydney) 1972–73. South Australian Theatre Company and Nimrod Theatre Company (Sydney) 1974–77. Visited USA on study grant 1977. Associate director of Sydney Theatre Company 1980–83. Artistic director of State Theatre Company of South Australia (Adelaide) 1986–89. Freelance since 1990. Also television. Sydney Critics' Circle Awards 1975 (*Travesties* by Tom Stoppard), 1978 (*Kold Komfort Kaffee* by Robyn Archer), 1992 (*Death and the Maiden* by Ariel Dorfman). AM 1986.

An intelligent and genial actor of considerable range, John Gaden has established specialities over 30 years. He has the precision and theatricality required for BERTOLT BRECHT and the urbanity and pace for Tom Stoppard. A Shakespearean of distinction, he played the title-role in the OLD TOTE THEATRE COMPANY production of *Richard II* that opened the Sydney Opera House Drama Theatre in 1973. He was memorable as Leontes in *The Winter's Tale* in Adelaide in 1973 and as Menenius in *Coriolanus* in Sydney 1993. In the 1970s Gaden was a leading man for the NIMROD THEATRE COMPANY and made notable contributions in a wide variety of works, from Stoppard's witty *Travesties* in 1975–76 and *Jumpers* in 1979 to David Rudkin's gruelling study of infertility, *Ashes*, in 1977 and Brecht's *Galileo* in 1979. He created the title-role in RON BLAIR'S ballad opera *Flash Jim Vaux* for Nimrod in 1972, and played Russell in DAVID WILLIAMSON'S *A Handful of Friends* in Adelaide in 1976 and Peter in his *Money and Friends* on national tour in 1991–92.

Becoming artistic director of the STATE THEATRE Company of South Australia when it was in some disarray, Gaden pragmatically attracted subscribers with a repertoire suited to mainstream tastes. He led from the front with performances of Platonov in Michael Frayn's *Wild Honey*, the Lawyer in August Strindberg's *A Dream Play* and Simon Wilson in STEPHEN SEWELL'S *Dreams in an Empty City*. He directed David Hare's *Pravda*, Christopher Hampton's *Les Liaisons dangereuses*, and *The Tempest*, and with Gale Edwards he co-directed *Much Ado About Nothing* and Stoppard's *The Real Thing*. He co-directed the SYDNEY THEATRE COMPANY'S production of David Edgar's *The Life and Adventures of Nicholas Nickleby* in 1984. ❦*Murray Bramwell*

Gaiety Theatre companies

Many British immigrants who came to Australia in the last 30 years of the 19th century had memories of glamour and fun at the Gaiety Theatre in London. This theatre, created by John Hollingshead in 1868, became famous in the 1870s for burlesques. Hollingshead retired in 1886 and George Edwardes took over the management. In 1888 WILLIAMSON, GARNER AND MUSGROVE reinforced the potency of the Gaiety as a symbol of home by bringing a complete Gaiety company to Australia as a centennial gift.

The London Gaiety Burlesque Company was headed by Nellie Farren, a specialist in cheeky Cockneys and other boy roles, and Fred Leslie, a perfect foil to her, according to the theatrical historian W. Macqueen Pope. The touring company was also strong in dancers, particularly Sylvia Grey and Letty Lind, whose 'alluring grace' and 'subtle witchery' NELLIE STEWART mentions in her autobiography. Writing in 1923, she also remarks pensively that touring companies containing as many stars as this Gaiety company would be 'impossible in these days of high salaries'. The company was hugely successful, despite a 50 per cent increased in admission prices for its seasons. The repertoire included burlesques, for which the Gaiety Theatre was famous—*Monte Cristo Junior* and *Miss Esmeralda*.

GEORGE MUSGROVE, no longer in partnership with J. C. WILLIAMSON, imported a second Gaiety company in 1892. It was headed by Addie Conyers, Marion Hood, Alice Leamar and E. J. Lonnen and the fare included *Faust Up To Date*, *Carmen Up To Date*, *Joan of Arc* and *Miss Esmeralda*. The old magic did not work so well, and Nellie Stewart bluntly calls this Gaiety tour a failure.

In 1895, when WILLIAMSON AND MUSGROVE were partners again, they brought a third Gaiety company here. This time Australia saw a new form of MUSICAL THEATRE that had burst upon London only three years before with *In Town* at the Gaiety Theatre—musical comedy. *In Town* was among the company's offerings, together with *A Gaiety Girl* (1893) and

The Shop Girl (1894). The leading artists included Fred Kaye, Harry Monkhouse, Decima Moore and GRACE PALOTTA. The economy was depressed, so admission prices were only slightly increased to six, four and two shillings. The tour opened at the Princess Theatre in Melbourne, where the company was described as 'the most popular theatrical company that the colony has ever seen'. *A Gaiety Girl* and *In Town* each ran for three weeks and *The Shop Girl* filled the last week of the season. At the Lyceum Theatre in Sydney, from June to September the season comprised three weeks of *A Gaiety Girl*, four weeks of *In Town*, three weeks of *The Shop Girl*, two weeks of *Gentleman Joe* (1895) and another week each of *A Gaiety Girl* and *In Town*. The company returned to Melbourne in September and played a week each of *The Shop Girl*, *A Gaiety Girl* and *In Town*.

J. C. Williamson imported yet another Gaiety company, headed by G. P. Huntley, in 1904. It brought with it *The Girl from Kay's* (1902), *Kitty Grey* (1900) and *Three Little Maids* (1902). ❦*John West*

further reading
HARTNOLL, PHYLLIS (ed.). *Oxford Companion to the Theatre*, 3rd edn. London: Oxford University Press. 1972.

Frank Gallacher

Actor. Born 7 April 1943 in Scotland. Came to Australia 1963. Regular actor with Melbourne Theatre Company since 1984. Also with Queensland Theatre Company (Brisbane), Playbox Theatre Company (Melbourne), State Theatre Company of South Australia (Adelaide), Marian Street Theatre Company (Sydney) and Nimrod Theatre Company (Sydney). Numerous television roles.

Frank Gallacher has played leading roles with the MELBOURNE THEATRE COMPANY but is also very effective in smaller roles. Noted mainly as a dramatic actor, he showed his versatility in numerous minor roles in Caryl Churchill's *Serious Money* in 1988 and STEPHEN SEWELL's *Dreams in an Empty City* in 1989. The latter alternated in repertory with *Macbeth*, in which Gallacher played the title-role. In 1991 his ebullient John Proctor in Arthur Miller's *The Crucible* contrasted effectively with his restrained Astrov in Anton Chekhov's *Uncle Vanya*. Gallacher has occasionally directed productions for the Melbourne Theatre Company, including the premiere of Bill Garner's *Sunday Lunch* in 1991. ❦*Geoffrey Milne*

Keith Gallasch

Director, performer, writer. Born 13 October 1945 in Adelaide. Educated at Adelaide University 1963–68 and University of Essex (England) 1974–75. Taught at Salisbury College of Advanced Education (SA) 1970–79. Founding member of Troupe (Adelaide) 1976–81. Artistic director of State Theatre Company of South Australia (Adelaide) 1984–86. Formed Open City (Sydney) with Virginia Baxter 1987. Founded performance journal *Real Time* 1993. Also writes and performs for radio.

In his writing and performing Keith Gallasch blends the anecdotal, biographical and imaginative with critical and theoretical concerns, while developing a 'non-theatrical' style of performance and presentation by incorporating various other media, by using unconventional performance spaces such as galleries and office buildings, and particularly by utilising the conventions of events such as the interview, the talk show, the guided tour or the dinner-party conversation. He has developed his work in collaboration with various other artists, including musicians, dancers, film-makers and other visual artists. He has integrated photographs into works such as *Photoplay* (1988).

In Adelaide he wrote and directed *Gents* in 1978 and *Suburban Mysteries* in 1981, both for the alternative-theatre company TROUPE. Since leaving Troupe, Gallasch has frequently returned to writing for performance without significant dialogue, exploring gesture, non-verbal utterance and image. The results have included *Black Rainbow* for Canberra Youth Theatre in 1983, *Just Walk* in collaboration with Virginia Baxter in 1983, and two works for the Legs on the Wall company—*Off the Wall* (1989) and *Hurt* (1992).

Gallasch's artistic directorship of the STATE THEATRE Company of South Australia was distinguished by a commitment to new Australian writing and an attempt to include emerging forms of theatrical practice. In Sydney from 1986, Gallasch and Baxter have collaborated in writing and performances by their Open City company at the PERFORMANCE SPACE. In the 1990s Gallasch and Open City have become more involved in exploring the performance possibilities of multiple media. ❦*Tony MacGregor*

Carrillo Gantner

Actor, administrator, director. Born 17 June 1944 in USA. Educated at University of Melbourne, Stanford University (USA), Harvard University (USA). Diploma in arts administration from Harvard. Assistant administrator of Adelaide Festival 1969–70. Drama officer for Australian Council for the Arts 1970–73. General manager of Melbourne Theatre Company 1973–75. Co-founder of Hoopla Productions (Melbourne), later Playbox Theatre Centre, 1976; director, sometimes with others, 1976–84, 1988–93. Cultural counsellor at Australian Embassy in Beijing 1985–88. Chairman of Sidney Myer Performing Arts Award 1989–. Chairman of performing-arts board of Australia Council 1990–94.

Carrillo Gantner worked tirelessly to establish the Playbox Theatre Company as Melbourne's second largest company and to gain it a splendid home in the CUB MALTHOUSE in 1990. It became the PLAYBOX THEATRE CENTRE of Monash University in the same year. Gantner's success in winning large-scale corporate and government support for an almost entirely Australian artistic program is remarkable.

Gantner has long had contacts with Asian cultural organisations. As a result Playbox brought the Fujian and Hunan Puppet Theatres from China to Australia in 1979 and 1983. At Australia's Embassy in Beijing Gantner was responsible for a wide range of cultural, scientific, sporting and educational programs. He directed a remarkable production of Jack Hibberd's *A STRETCH OF THE IMAGINATION* with a Chinese actor in Shanghai in 1987 and Beijing in 1988. As an actor, Gantner made a mark as Albert Einstein in Terry Johnson's *Insignificance* for Playbox in 1984. In 1992 he acted in the Playbox production of Tadashi Suzuki's *The Chronicle of Macbeth*. He celebrated his departure from Playbox in 1993 by undertaking the title-role in *King Lear*. He has also acted for other companies and directed several Playbox productions. ❦*Geoffrey Milne*

further reading
HOWIE, ANN C. (ed.). *Who's Who in Australia* 17th edn. Melbourne: Information Australia 1991.

Arthur Garner

Actor, entrepreneur. Born 1851 in Bath (England). Acted in England. Leading member of stock company at Theatre Royal, Melbourne 1873–76. Returned to England. Brought London Comedy Company to Australia in partnership with W. S. Lyster 1879. Opened Garner's Theatre, Adelaide, 1880. Partner in Williamson, Garner and Musgrove 1882–90. Partner in Williamson, Garner and Co. 1890–91. Married to actor Blanche Stammers.

The least publicised member of the WILLIAMSON, GARNER AND MUSGROVE triumvirate, Garner did well out of his association with J. C. Williamson and George Musgrove. In evidence in court in 1897, he said nine years had yielded £40 000 as his share of the gross profits. Garner came to Australia as an actor with his wife Blanche Stammers, and first appeared on 23 June 1873 in Melbourne. He had some trouble with the 'pitch' of the Theatre Royal, and the gallery urged him: 'Speak slowly! Speak up!' But he won them over before long. One critic found him quiet, self-possessed and not ungraceful. Garner stayed at the Theatre Royal for three years before returning to England.

In 1879 he came back to Australia, leading the LONDON COMEDY COMPANY, which played popular successes in splendid seasons in Melbourne and Sydney. During the tour Garner leased White's Rooms in Adelaide and had the assembly room enlarged and remodelled. It reopened as Garner's Theatre in May 1880, presenting a company headed by the actor–manager WYBERT REEVE.

When Garner and Williamson became partners in the triumvirate in 1882, GEORGE COPPIN wrote in a letter: 'The only difficulty I see is the improbability of their agreeeing very long together—both Williamson and Garner are very self-opinionated with bad tempers …'. According to George Musgrove's brother Harry, writing in the magazine *Table Talk* in 1926, 'Garner was the financial pillar of the firm, J. C. handled the acting end of it, and G. M. the productions'. Details of Garner's life remain to be discovered, but in March 1913 a correspondent of the *Bulletin* noted that an Arthur Garner of Streatham had written to the London *Referee*, discussing changes in pantomime presentation over the years. *John West*

further reading
BEVAN, IAN. *The Story of the Theatre Royal*. Sydney: Currency Press 1993.

Garrick Theatre

Amateur theatre company in Perth. Began with readings in private homes in Guildford 1932. Began public performance 1933.
venues 1933 Guildford Mechanics' Institute. 1934– Commissariat Building, Guildford.

Perth's oldest amateur theatre represents nonprofessional theatre at its most attractive. It presents several works annually to season-ticket subscribers and others in its 100-seat theatre in outer-suburban Guildford. Its range covers classic and modern plays, operetta and revue. Garrick Theatre's standards are consistently high, especially in acting and direction, and it has won numerous awards in Western Australian drama festivals. The group receives no subsidy but the Swan Shire Council gives help in kind. In 1960 Garrick Theatre presented the first televised play in the state, *Colour Bar* by Joe Corrie. *Maurice Jones*

Gay theatre

Organised gay theatre in Australia dates from the formation of the Gay Theatre Company in April 1979 and its presentation of *As Time Goes By* at the Filmmakers Cinema in Sydney. The company grew out of Gay Men's Rap, a group that met to explore gay liberation. It sought to produce plays with 'gay relevance' and between 1979 and 1982 it mounted six productions, some with assistance from the theatre board of the AUSTRALIA COUNCIL. Directors included Ian Tasker, JOHN TASKER, the television producer John Barningham and Richard Turner, who had directed the first gay film produced in Australasia. In 1982, with a theatre board grant, the company presented its only season of new Australian plays: *Hormones* by James Mellon and *Writer's Cramp* by Barry Lowe. The company folded shortly afterwards, but Lowe continued to write plays, chiefly comedies exploring aspects of modern gay life. He generally produced them under the banner of his own company, Hullabaloo Productions. He has since had plays with gay and other themes produced in Melbourne and Brisbane.

Gay festivals in Sydney and Melbourne have both fostered theatre. Richard Turner, who directed Lowe's first two gay plays, staged gay cabarets between 1985 and 1987 as part of the annual Gay Mardi Gras Festival in Sydney. Alex Harding, an early member of Gay Sweatshop in London, appeared in all four of Lowe's plays. His *Only Heaven Knows*, a musical about gay life in Sydney in the 1940s and 1950s was produced by the GRIFFIN THEATRE COMPANY in Sydney in May 1988 and by the Playbox Theatre Company in Melbourne in February 1989. The Sydney Gay and Lesbian Mardi Gras Festival in February 1990 included his play *Blood and Honour*, which deals with racism, AIDS and sexual honesty. It won the Human Rights and Equal Opportunity Commission's award for drama in 1980.

Melbourne's Midsumma Festival in January 1990 included the Software season of gay theatre. In late 1990, Arthur Dicks, Gai Diller-Anderson and Paul Booth set up In the Pink, a new gay and lesbian theatre company, which mounted readings of new gay and lesbian plays in the following three years. It staged its first production, Peter Anthony Ryan's *Nothing Personal*, during the 1993 Mardi Gras Festival. In 1994 Sydney Gay and Lesbian Mardi Gras adopted a new approach to planning the annual festival, which included funding for development of new work.

Drag has long been popular entertainment in gay life, and periodically attracts wider interest. In the early 1960s several drag venues opened around Sydney. One was the Purple Onion, which doubled as a theatrical hangout and a 'camp' venue. It began a tradition of lavish shows, which continued during the 1970s and early 1980s at Capriccio's in Oxford Street. In Melbourne, Pokey's a popular Sunday-night gay venue, also established a strong theatrical drag tradition. There are regular drag performances in gay pubs and discos. *Larry Galbraith*

Edward Geoghegan

Dramatist. Born c.1812. Studied medicine in Dublin. Sentenced to transportation in Dublin, 6 June 1839. Served seven-year sentence in Sydney. Wrote plays performed at Royal Victoria Theatre, Sydney, 1844–45. Last heard of in Melbourne 1852.

While Edward Geoghegan was a convict on Cockatoo Island in Sydney Harbour he wrote Australia's first local comedy, THE CURRENCY LASS, and possibly its first tragedy, THE HIBERNIAN FATHER. Geoghegan, transported for obtaining papers under false pretences, had 'special employment' status as a medical dispenser on the island. On his weekly leave he met actors at the Royal Victoria Theatre. One of them was FRANCIS NESBITT, a friend and one-time landlord. He championed Geoghegan at the theatre and unsuccessfully recommended him for a ticket-of-leave in 1843.

Eight plays written by Geoghegan were presented at the theatre in 1844–45, either anonymously or under pseudonyms, because he was a convict. They yielded the prolific author only £3. Accusations of plagiarism plagued his short career. Doubts hang over *The Hibernian Father*, but *The Currency Lass* undoubtedly shows local invention and Geoghegan's appreciation of his new country. In a letter to the Colonial Secretary on 16 September 1846 he clearly distinguished adaptations from original scripts. Geoghegan was of his time as a writer but his plays have vigour and theatricality. After his release he sought work at the Royal Victoria Theatre. He is last heard of in 1852, writing from Melbourne to the NSW Colonial Secretary for a copy of his unperformed play *The Jew of Dresden*. ❦*Helen Musa*

published play
The Currency Lass, musical play (1844). Sydney: Currency Methuen 1976.

further reading
OPPENHEIM, HELENE. The author of *The Hibernian Father*. *Australian Literary Studies* 2/4 (December 1966).

Rob George

Dramatist. Born 2 April 1950 at Mannum (SA). Graduated in psychology from University of Adelaide. Began writing undergraduate revues in collaboration with Steve J. Spears. Formed Circle Company in Adelaide with his wife Maureen Sherlock and Malcolm Blaylock. Wrote for Stage Company (Adelaide) 1977–86, then moved to writing for film and television.

Rob George's best-known play is *Percy and Rose* (1982), about the Australian pianist–composer Percy Grainger and his mother. It toured widely and became a vehicle for its performers, Daphne Grey and DENNIS OLSEN. It was one of George's two most successful works for the STAGE COMPANY. The other was *Sandy Lee Live at Nui Dat*, which examines Australian attitudes to the Vietnam War from the viewpoints of a participant, a protester and a country-music entertainer. Amateur groups regularly perform George's *Prompt* (1973), written while he was teaching at Burra (SA). ❦*Murray Bramwell*

published play
Sandy Lee Live at Nui Dat (1981). Sydney: Currency Press 1983.

Jim Gerald

Comedian. Born 2 January 1891 in Sydney. Originally James Fitzgerald. Professional tumbler at seven. Toured world with Oscar Pagel's circus for ten years. Started in vaudeville for Harry Clay. Moved to Fullers as revue comedian and pantomime dame. On Tivoli circuit in 1930s. Headed army entertainment during Second World War. Returned to Tivoli and worked in farce and musical comedy after war. Died 2 March 1971 in Melbourne. Married to comedian Essie Jennings. Brother of actor Max Clifton, comedian Cliff Stevens and actor Lance Vane.

One of Australia's foremost comedians in 20th-century variety and its favourite pantomime dame during the 1920s was Jim Gerald. His trademarks were an improbable wig and incredibly baggy pants, and in his work as a droll comedian he retained the style of the circus, where he had started his professional life as a tumbler. In contrast to the Australianness of his rivals, the larrikin ROY RENE and the rustic GEORGE WALLACE, Gerald was unashamedly international in his work. He and his wife Essie Jennings travelled abroad in search of new material. His revues frequently had overseas settings and much of his humour depended on spoofing foreign names—he once played 'Admiral Pitchitoffski' of the Ruritanian navy. But, like other revue comedians, he lampooned horse racing and domestic situations. In 1931 he starred in *The Digger Duke* in vaudeville at the Theatre Royal in Sydney. A Gerald song about the suburbs prompted the *Bulletin* of 10 February 1932 to claim that if he 'turned himself to Australian themes he would start a local renaissance'. It was then a common critical attitude that Australian artists should concentrate on Australian themes and promote a national culture. Rene and Wallace were praised for this aspect of their work. Gerald won acclaim mostly for his 'wholesomeness', proving, according to critics, that vulgarity was not a prerequisite for popularity. His fans were known as the Geraldines.

Gerald did not write his own scripts, but was meticulous in preparing his shows, demanding the best technicians and fellow performers available. His major success was in Australia. He ventured abroad in the late 1920s, and made two-reel films in the USA, but returned to Australia prematurely when he was panned by critics in a London stage season. He appeared in *Ladies' Night in a Turkish Bath* in 1951 and made his last stage appearance in *Many Happy Returns* for Harry Wren in 1959. ❦*Victoria Chance*

further reading
BRIDGES, NANCYE and FRANK CROOK. *Curtain Call*. Sydney: Cassell 1980.

Mel Gibson

Actor. Born 3 January 1956 in Peeksville (New York, USA). Came to Australia at 12. Graduated from National Institute of Dramatic Art (Sydney) 1977. Has acted in numerous films in Australia and Hollywood since 1979.

Those who recalled the lyricism of Mel Gibson's Romeo for the NIMROD THEATRE COMPANY in 1978 were not surprised by his success as Hamlet in Franco Zeffirelli's 1991 film. *Romeo and Juliet* was one of only ten stage productions in which Gibson has appeared in Australia. His principal role in an Australian work was Rebel the American deserter in BOB HERBERT's *No Names … No Pack Drill* for the SYDNEY THEATRE COMPANY in 1980. His last stage role was Biff opposite WARREN MITCHELL's Willie in Arthur Miller's *Death of a Salesman* for the Nimrod company in 1982. Gibson's teachers at the NATIONAL INSTITUTE OF DRAMATIC ART acclaimed him as a gifted comic actor. His only professional opportunity to demonstrate this gift has been as Estragon opposite Geoffrey Rush's Vladimir in Samuel Beckett's *Waiting for Godot* in Sydney in 1979. ❦*Ken Healey*

further reading
HUBBARD, LINDA S. and O'DONNELL, OWEN (eds). *Contemporary Theatre, Film and Television* 6th edn. Detroit (USA): Gale Research.

Gilbert and Sullivan

The operettas of W. S. Gilbert and Arthur Sullivan have enjoyed a special place in MUSICAL THEATRE performance in Australia, because of the rare polish of the libretti and music, and because the texts are in English and ridicule many English institutions. The first of the works performed here was the one-act *Trial by Jury*, given by W. S. LYSTER's opera company as an afterpiece to Jacques Offenbach's *La Belle Hélène* in Melbourne on 26 June 1876, barely a year after its premiere in London. Many companies gave unauthorised performances of *HMS Pinafore* and *The Sorcerer* until, under an agreement signed in San Francisco on 2 May 1879, J. C. WILLIAMSON secured the COPYRIGHT of *HMS Pinafore* for the Australasian colonies for one year at a cost of £300. He extracted compensation from companies that were currently contravening his rights, reputedly gaining more than he had paid. As a result of these endeavours, Gilbert persuaded Rupert D'Oyly Carte to sub-license the Australasian rights to all Gilbert and Sullivan operettas to Williamson for a total of £300 a year. This became the basis of Williamson's fortune and his theatre chain. He brought a new professionalism to operetta production through Gilbert and Sullivan, making extraordinary efforts to match the quality of the London productions, particularly in costumes and sets, many of which he imported.

The 1880s saw frequent performances in the main cities. *The Pirates of Penzance* in 1881, *Patience* in 1882, *Iolanthe* in 1885, *The Mikado* in 1886 and *The Gondoliers* in 1890 were immediate favourites. Williamson himself performed throughout Australasia in early productions. He brought many members of the D'Oyly Carte company to Australia. Alfred Cellier, the senior conductor in the London company after Sullivan himself, led *The Mikado* in Melbourne in 1886. Famous singers who toured Australia included the contraltos Alice Barnett and Evelyn Gardiner, the soprano Leonora Braham, the tenor Courtice Pounds and the comedians Charles Workman and IVAN MENZIES. Many Australians have sung extensively in Gilbert and Sullivan, including GLADYS MONCRIEFF, MAX OLDAKER, DENNIS OLSEN, NELLIE STEWART and HOWARD VERNON.

J. C. Williamson's Comic Company was formed in 1886 to present the pieces in repertoire. Various touring companies followed over the years. While J. C. WILLIAMSON's controlled the rights, the operettas were generally performed in a conservative style, similar to that of the D'Oyly Carte Opera Company. Since the works entered the public domain in 1960, however, many professional and amateur groups have staged them. In recent years the Australian Opera has performed *The Gondoliers*, *The Mikado*, *Patience* and *Trial by Jury* and Gilbert and Sullivan operettas are important in the repertoires of state opera companies. Recent productions of *HMS Pinafore*, starring the English actor Paul Eddington, and *The Pirates of Penzance*, in Broadway style with JON ENGLISH and JUNE BRONHILL, have confirmed their box-office appeal. Equally important is the huge popularity of the works with amateur performers and their audiences. In most Australian cities there are societies dedicated solely to performing a work or two a year from the Gilbert and Sullivan canon of 13 operettas. For example, the Gilbert and Sullivan Society of Western Australia, has presented innovative and increasingly polished productions in Perth for more than 40 years. The society was founded in 1951 by Bernard Manning, who had played principal bass roles for J. C. Williamson's in Gilbert and Sullivan seasons in the 1940s. It performs at His Majesty's Theatre, in rented premises in suburban Leederville and on tour in Western Australia. Professional designers, directors and singers and other musicians have contributed to its success, which is especially remarkable as only about half of the Gilbert and Sullivan repertoire appeals strongly to Perth audiences. ❦*Phillip Lawton, Maurice Jones*

further reading
BEVAN, IAN. *The Story of the Theatre Royal*. Sydney: Currency Press 1993.
DE LOITTE, VINIA. *Gilbert and Sullivan in Australia*. Sydney: privately published 1933.
LOVE, HAROLD. *The Golden Age of Australian Opera*. Sydney: Currency Press 1981.
OSBORNE, CHARLES. *Max Oldaker*. London: Michael O'Mara 1988.

Max Gillies

Actor. Born 16 November 1941 in Melbourne. Educated at Monash University. Lectured in drama at Secondary Teachers' College (Melbourne) 1966–70. Joined Australian Performing Group 1970. Began performing satirical revues 1981. Also television. Melbourne Critics' Award 1976.

A journalist once described Max Gillies as 'the thinking man's satirist', summing up his double role as a serious comic actor who has long specialised in impersonating living public figures on the stage and on television. Gillies's awesome talent for mimicry and impersonation was originally fostered within the AUSTRALIAN PERFORMING GROUP in Melbourne. He co-directed and acted in its inaugural production at the Pram Factory, MARVELLOUS MELBOURNE by Jack Hibberd and John Romeril. Subsequently he established his flair as a character actor with acute powers of observation and attention to physical and vocal detail in plays by BARRY OAKLEY, including *The Feet of Daniel Mannix*, *Beware of Imitations* and *Bedfellows*, in group works such as *The Hills Family Show* and in Hibberd's monodrama *A Stretch of the Imagination*. Gillies created two principal roles in Stephen Sewell's early plays—Kolya in *Traitors* at the Pram Factory in 1979 and the physicist Max Lewin in *Welcome the Bright World* for the NIMROD THEATRE COMPANY in Sydney in 1982. He played Kolya for Nimrod in 1980.

Gillies opened his first satirical revue, *Squirts*, in 1981 in in Adelaide. By the time it reached Melbourne, under the title *A Night with the Right*, Gillies was playing 17 characters, including the prime ministers Malcolm Fraser and Sir Robert Menzies and the former governor-general Sir John Kerr. In his next solo show, *A Night of National Reconciliation* in 1983 he extended the range to include two more prime ministers, Bob Hawke and Sir William McMahon, and the Queen. Out of this show came *The Gillies Report*, a series of satirical shows on ABC television in 1984, and its successor *The Gillies Republic*. In 1985 in Sydney Gillies returned to the stage, launching another topical revue, The

Gillies Summit. It extended his range of caricatures to include Ronald Reagan, the Pope and Sir Johannes Bjelke-Petersen. All told, his portrait gallery runs to more than 70 individuals, most of them right-wing or authoritarian figures, and calculated to make the models wince with embarrassment. The main scriptwriters for all these shows, from *Squirts* onward, were the cartoonist Patrick Cook and Don Watson, a historian who has become a political speechwriter. Gillies returned to the legitimate stage with the MELBOURNE THEATRE COMPANY in Alan Ayckbourn's *A Chorus of Disapproval*, acted in a popular revival of DAVID WILLIAMSON's *The Department* and played Tevye in the Australian Opera's 1988 production of *Fiddler on the Roof*. ❧Leonard Radic

further reading
HOWIE, ANN C. (ed.). *Who's Who in Australia* 27th edn. Melbourne: Information Australia 1991.

The Girl of the Never Never

Play by Jo Smith. **premiere** 26 December 1912, King's Theatre, Melbourne, by William Anderson company. Cast: Lillie Bryer, Edwin Campbell, Max Clifton, Eugenie Duggan, Fanny Erris, Helen Fergus, Cyril Mackay, Frank Mills, J. H. Nunn, Olive Wilton.

After JO SMITH had introduced audiences to life on an Australian farm in *THE BUSHWOMAN* he turned to the Northern Territory as a location for even more spectacular outback adventures. *The Girl of the Never Never* has a cattle king, a mine manager, a Port Essington pearler, a British Victoria Cross winner, an American geologist, a Japanese pearl diver, a Chinese cook, a comic boat captain, Aborigines, stockmen and a heroine with the improbable name of Pearl Grey. To current widespread anxiety about invasion of the great empty north Smith added 'moralisings on the prospect of a white Australia', which the Melbourne *Argus* 27 December 1912 found the only low note of a beautifully staged play. A gold strike, a flooded river and the blowing-up of a motor launch were among the visual sensations.

The central story was strangely old-fashioned and domestic. Pearl's mother, who deserted her as an infant, arrives unexpectedly and unrecognised by nearly all the characters, who subsequently try to keep mother and daughter apart. This also causes difficulties between Pearl and her lover (played by EUGENIE DUGGAN and Cyril Mackay), as do attempts to rob the hero of his gold, but as the *Age* noted: 'The story is admirably worked out, and, of course, ends to the sound of marriage-bells'. The play ran for a solid 20 performances but was not revived. ❧Richard Fotheringham

reference
A script survives in the Australian Archives (Canberra), CRS A1336/2, item 2689.

Philip W. Goatcher

Designer, scene-painter, theatre decorator. Born 1851 in London. Taught scene-painting as teenager by John Hennings in Ballarat (Vic.). Painted in New Zealand, West Indies, USA, France and United Kingdom from *c*.1866. Worked in major New York City theatres 1875–85. Returned to Australia for J. C. Williamson 1891. Decorated and leased Palace Theatre, Sydney, 1896. Went to Western Australia for health reasons in late 1890s. Painted murals for His Majesty's Theatre, Perth, 1904. Died 8 October 1931 in Perth.

J. C. WILLIAMSON made Philip W. Goatcher the world's highest-paid theatrical designer when he brought him back to Australia at 1000 guineas a year in 1891. Goatcher was arguably one of the world's finest designers of the late-Victorian style of theatrical decor. Overseas he worked for companies led by David Belasco, EDWIN BOOTH, DION BOUCICAULT, Lillie Langtry and Ellen Terry. He sometimes 'painted-up' others' designs, including almost certainly some of Hawes Craven's designs for the original productions of Gilbert and Sullivan operettas.

Goatcher has probably never been equalled in Australia as a *trompe l'oeil* painter. His act drops were virtuosic displays of his skill, especially in representing velvet, satin and carpet. He painted 40 act drops for American theatres. Goatcher decorated the interior of the PALACE THEATRE in Sydney in Asian patterns. His murals in HIS MAJESTY'S THEATRE in Perth were painted over in 1948 but the theatre has one of his drop-curtain designs. Elsewhere in Western Australia, there are a superb drop curtain by Goatcher in the town hall at Boulder and murals by him in churches at New Norcia and Collie. ❧Maurice Jones

further reading
HAIGH, DAVID. Remembrance of scenes past. *Bulletin* (Sydney) 15 October 1991.

The Golden Age

Play in two acts by Louis Nowra. **premiere** 8 February 1985 at Studio Theatre of Victorian Arts Centre, Melbourne, by Playbox Theatre Company. Cast: Maggie Blinco, Robin Cuming, Melita Jurisic, Robert Morgan, Terry O'Brien. Director: Rex Cramphorn. **published** Sydney: Currency Press 1985.

The Golden Age deals with problems of culture and civilisation, and Australians' relationships to European and Australian history. LOUIS NOWRA loosely based it on a factual incident, the discovery in 1939 in the forests of southwest Tasmania of an isolated family descended from runaway convicts and goldseekers. They were incarcerated by the authorities lest their physical degeneration be used by the Nazis as racist propaganda. The play narrates the meeting of these 'old' Australians and their 1939 contemporaries, the tribe's gradual extinction in the asylum, and the love of the young soldier Francis for Bethsheb, culminating in their reunion on his return from the war. The story of the lost people reflects upon experiences of immigrants and refugees and particularly upon Aboriginal history.

A highly theatrical play, *The Golden Age* uses classical drama—Shakespeare and Euripides—as framing or embedded texts. It requires physical energy and vocal expertise. GEOFFREY HUTTON described it in the *Australian* on 12 February 1985 as 'a play of power and purpose'. In Sydney, NEIL ARMFIELD directed *The Golden Age*, with additional material, for the NATIONAL INSTITUTE OF DRAMATIC ART in 1986 and the NIMROD THEATRE COMPANY produced it with Melita Jurisic as Bethsheb in 1987.

H. G. KIPPAX described it in the *Sydney Morning Herald* on 7 August 1987 as 'anti-war, anti-American, anti-science propaganda'. Brian Hoad, in the *Bulletin* on 25 August 1987, said it was 'a big, brave, defiant play which is looking for some sort of guiding spirit in a wasteland of crass materialism'. It has had numerous productions in Australia and abroad. ❧Veronica Kelly

Goldfields

Discoveries of gold in NSW and Victoria in the 1850s gave the colonies wealth and an immense influx of people. Before long theatres prospered on the goldfields and in the cities. In Melbourne, for example, six new theatres opened between 1855 and 1862. But at first the rush to the goldfields depopulated cities and many theatres closed. In 1851 the exodus from Adelaide damaged GEORGE COPPIN's theatrical interests and pushed him into insolvency. Coppin restored his fortunes from June 1852 by entertaining diggers in Geelong (Vic.). He imported many prominent actors, including G. V. BROOKE and CHARLES AND ELLEN KEAN.

The early gold rushes were mainly in Victoria. Publicans on the goldfields offered the itinerant, largely male audience an early form of music hall, known as concert hall. The balladeer Charles Thatcher, unsuccessful as a digger, became popular with colourful local songs. The Victorian gold towns, which were close together and linked to one another and Melbourne by roads, formed a touring circuit for a wide range of performers, from BROOKE to the scandalous Irish dancer Lola Montez. Ballarat had three theatres in 1854, within a year of the first diggers pitching their tents. Theatres also sprang up in Bendigo, Castlemaine and other Victorian towns. Both theatres and performances were rough and ready at first, and audiences were uninhibited, noted for throwing gold nuggets to favourite performers. Stock companies emerged in most towns, in spite of unlikely buildings, inadequate facilities and fluctuating populations. CHINESE PERFORMERS entertained their compatriots with Cantonese opera. ♥*Victoria Chance*

Gulgong NSW

Gold was discovered at Gulgong on 14 April 1870. Twenty thousand goldseekers flocked there from all over the world and theatrical enterprises were soon on the scene. Three theatres stood within 100 metres of one narrow, winding street. An Englishman, John Cogdon (the Iron-Clad Minstrel) first opened Cogdon's Assembly Room, a barn-like bark theatre; it was rebuilt as the Prince of Wales Opera House in December 1871. The superior Theatre Royal, a slab building at the rear of an Irishman's Turf Hotel, seated 600. Between these two stood the Music Hall and Star Theatre, attached to German-born William Binder's Star Hotel. These theatres presented such notable performers as FANNY CATHCART, MORTON TAVARES, aging CHARLES YOUNG, and the Duvalli Sisters, dancers of the scandalous cancan.

In 1871–72 Gulgong had a stock company, the Star Dramatic Company, managed by the 'world renowned artiste' JOEY GOUGENHEIM. On 6 October 1871 the novelists Rolf Boldrewood and Anthony Trollope saw the company perform Dion Boucicault's *The Colleen Bawn* at the Theatre Royal. Pantomimes included *Lalla Rookh*, the most lavish pantomime ever seen outside a city. The diggers of the 1870s had encountered good theatre elsewhere and were a discriminating audience. When the actor MAGGIE OLIVER arrived to join the Star company diggers met her coach, released the horses and drew it into town in triumph. The idolised Oliver spent at least five months acting with Gougenheim, though the latter was always the star. The theatrical feast ended when the gold dwindled. Only the Prince of Wales Opera House remains. Its owner, the Gulgong Musical and Dramatic Society performs old-fashioned melodramas. ♥*Roma Wallis*

Western Australia

Discoveries of gold in central southern Western Australia in 1887 began a rush to Coolgardie and Kalgoorlie. The first entertainment of the thousands of fortune-seekers who rode horses and camels or walked to the goldfields was songs around the campfire, accompanied by fiddle, mouth-organ or other portable instruments. Soon primitive outdoor theatres were built and given pretentious names, such as Theatre Royal and Royal CREMORNE GARDENS. When a railway was built, big theatrical companies visited the goldfields, giving scaled-down presentations of their city successes. The first was WILLIAMSON AND MUSGROVE's Royal Comic Opera Company in 1898. 'It beats most playgoers how the Williamson-Musgrove Company is going to stage its pieces in the Goldsfields', the Perth *Western Mail* remarked. 'At Coolgardie, Kalgoorlie and Kanowna efforts have been made to provide for visiting companies but in making such provisions the proprietors of halls and theatres never contemplated a visit from the Firm! From Princess's Theatre in Melbourne to So-and So's hall in the very far west is an extreme transition.'

As demand for entertainment increased, more ambitious venues were built. In 1908 Kalgoorlie and Boulder erected imposing town halls, which still stand. Other venues have long gone, except a Coolgardie goldrush hall whose pressed-metal interior has been moved to Merredin, where it forms part of the Cummins Theatre. ♥*Ivan King*

further reading
KIRBY-SMITH, VIRGINIA. The development of Australian theatre and drama—1788–1964. Duke University (Durham, North Carolina), PhD thesis, 1969.
ROBERTS, SUSAN. Some aspects of 'rough' and 'refined' theatre on the Victorian goldfields in the 1850s. University of NSW hons thesis 1978.
TROLLOPE, ANTHONY. *Anthony Trollope's Australia*. Brisbane: University of Queensland Press 1967.
WALLIS, ROMA. *Gulgong in the Roaring Days—The history of the Prince of Wales Opera House*. Dubbo (NSW): Macquarie Publications 1982.

Goldfields Repertory Club

Amateur theatrical group in Kalgoorlie (WA), founded in 1931 by Charles Gordon as Goldfields Players. In recess during Second World War. Reactivated as Goldfields Repertory Club 1946.
venues 1931–50 Kalgoorlie Town Hall, Boulder Town Hall, Returned Services League halls, Wesley Hall. 1950–72, 1976– Theatre in Brookman Street, Kalgoorlie.

At a time when talking pictures and the Great Depression had curtailed professional theatre in provincial towns, Charles Gordon, a speech teacher, founded the Goldfields Players. Among those who joined this club were Seddon and Frieda Vincent, who settled in Kalgoorlie in 1937. He was a barrister—and later a senator—and she was an actor and speech and drama teacher. The club ran classes, held regular evenings, published newsletters, and encouraged youth participation until the Second World War. After the war the Vincents revived the club under its present name. It was given low-rental use of various halls until it opened its own 230-seat theatre in 1950. In 1951 Frieda Vincent's production of *Ladies in Retirement* by Edward Percy and Reginald Denham represented Western Australia in the Commonwealth Jubilee Amateur Theatrical Group Competition in Hobart and was highly commended. Lively years followed, with up to five public productions annually—Australian plays, English repertory and West End plays, Broadway fare, classics, Victorian melodrama, musicals and Christmas pantomimes. In 1959 the Vincents produced *A Midsummer Night's Dream* in Victoria Park, Kalgoorlie, and in the 1960 Festival of Perth the production was presented in the Sunken Garden. Seddon Vincent was chairman of a Senate committee on the encouragement of Australian productions for television in 1963. The VINCENT REPORT was published shortly before he died in that year.

The club bought its theatre in 1968 and improved it. But in April 1972 fire destroyed the theatre and sets, costumes, properties and scripts. Productions returned to the Boulder and Kalgoorlie Town Halls until April 1976, when the club opened a new theatre in a disused railway building moved to the site. Since the early 1970s the club has been helped financially or professionally in occasional projects by bodies such as the ARTS COUNCIL OF AUSTRALIA, the Western Australian Arts Advisory Board, and Acting Out, the touring arm of the Western Australian Theatre Company. The latter commissioned a musical play, *A Touch of Midas*, from a club member, Heather Nimmo of Kalgoorlie, in 1985. Members of Acting Out lived in Kalgoorlie for seven weeks and intensive teaching and rehearsal preceded a fortnight of public performances. ❧*Bill Dunstone*

George Gordon

Scene-painter. Born 12 June 1839 in Edinburgh. Son of scene-painter William Gordon (1801–74). From 14 worked for Charles Kean at Princess Theatre, London, under scenic artists Thomas Grieve and William Telbin. Leading scene-painter at Theatre Royal, Bristol, 1857–65. Came to Australia 1879. Died 12 June 1899 in Melbourne. Father of scene-painter John Gordon (1872–1911).

Like many 19th-century scene-painters, George Gordon was noted for architectural scenes. He learned his craft by working with his father from an early age. ARTHUR GARNER brought Gordon to Australia in 1879 for the LONDON COMEDY COMPANY's tour. He worked in Adelaide, Melbourne and Sydney with the scene-painters JOHN BRUNTON, ALFRED CLINT and JOHN HENNINGS. In Adelaide in 1880 he painted the act drop and designed interiors for Garner's Theatre. WILLIAMSON, GARNER AND MUSGROVE employed Gordon in 1882, and in 1886 he designed decorations and painted the original act drop for the triumvirate's new PRINCESS THEATRE in Melbourne. Later he worked for J. C. WILLIAMSON. He passed his knowledge to his son John, who assisted him. Gordon died from injuries sustained in a fall from a Melbourne tram. ❧*Mimi Colligan*

further reading
GORDON, JOHN. Scene Painting in Australia. *Lone Hand* (Sydney) 2 November 1908. Illustrated with three photographs of stage settings by John Gordon and another, 'A Venice Scene', which is most likely by George Gordon.
Directory of Victorian Scene Painters. *Theatrephile* (London, March 1984).
Argus (Melbourne) 13 June 1889.
Table Talk (Melbourne) 22 March 1889.

Hayes Gordon OBE

Actor, director, drama teacher, singer. Born 25 February 1920 in Boston (USA). Began acting 1936. Became registered pharmacist 1941. Studied with director Bob de Lany in Boston. Acted and sang in summer stock company. In original Broadway production of *Oklahoma!* 1942. Studied with Lee Strasberg and Sandy Meisner. In US Air Force. In *Winged Victory* propaganda show. Musicals and cabaret and television shows 1945–51. Acted in Australia 1952–84. Principal of Ensemble Studios (Sydney) since 1954. Governing and artistic director of Ensemble Theatre Company (Sydney) 1958-86. Returned to stage in *Fiddler on the Roof* 1967. Directed musicals at Menzies Hotel, Sydney, 1966–68. Life member of Producers and Directors' Guild of Australia.

A commanding presence, powerful acting and a rich baritone voice brought Hayes Gordon critical acclaim for leading roles in musicals from 1952 until 1984. He founded the ENSEMBLE THEATRE COMPANY in 1958 and he directed 59 of its productions before he retired in 1986. As a director he primarily aimed at productions that provided entertainment and at the same time argued some worthwhile polemic. These aims and, especially, the freshness of Gordon's Method approach, resulted in productions that quickly gathered audiences and built the Ensemble's reputation. Among the Gordon productions that stirred audiences, won admiring reviews and had box-office successes were Mel Dinnelli's *The Man*, William Sedley-Smith's *The Drunkard*, Lonny Chapman's *The Buffalo Skinner*, Friedrich Dürrenmatt's *The Physicists*, Henrik Ibsen's *An Enemy of the People*, Trevor Griffiths's *Comedians* and Neil Simon's *The Prisoner of Second Avenue*.

Gordon came to Australia in 1952 to play the lead in the J. C. WILLIAMSON's production of *Kiss Me, Kate*. During the season he began giving backstage classes in acting. He stayed for revivals of *Annie Get Your Gun* and *Oklahoma!* and settled here. In 1954 he founded the Ensemble Studios, offering comprehensive training.

Gordon is a most influential teacher and has published many articles and a book on acting. He bases his teaching on objective analysis and combining content with its formal expression, and derives his tenets from Konstantin Stanislavsky and American teachers of the Method—Harold Clurman, Elia Kazan, Robert Lewis, Sandy Meisner and Lee Strasberg.

Gordon played the lead in GARNET H. CARROLL's production of the musical *Kismet* in 1956 and worked in radio and early television. From 1966 to 1968 at the Menzies Hotel theatre-restaurant in Sydney he directed a resident company in musicals—*Brigadoon, Can-Can, Kiss Me, Kate, Oklahoma!, Out Of This World* and *South Pacific*. After a long absence from the stage he returned in 1967 as Tevye in *Fiddler On the Roof*, giving a bravura performance that showed he had lost none of his skill as a musical-theatre star. He repeated the role for the Australian Opera in 1983–84. ❧*Don Reid*

writings
Acting and Performing. Sydney: Ensemble Press 1993.
further reading
HERBERT, IAN (ed.). *Who's Who in the Theatre* 17th edn. Detroit (USA): Gale Research 1987.
HOWIE, ANN C. (ed.). *Who's Who in Australia* 27th edn. Melbourne: Information Australia 1991.

Leon Gordon

> English actor, dramatist, 1884–1960. Acted at Booth Theatre, New York City, 1918. Wrote *White Cargo*, a hit in London 1923. Successful as actor and playwright in Australia 1926–30.

Leon Gordon's steamy play *White Cargo*, based upon Ida Vera Simonton's novel *Hell's Playground*, brought him huge success in Australia. J. C. WILLIAMSON's imported Gordon to present it with an English cast in Sydney in 1926. He portrayed a cynical young rubber planter and Helen Stransky played Tondelayo, a beautiful native temptess who brings him down. *White Cargo* was revived in Sydney in 1928 and 1930. Gordon appeared with JUDITH ANDERSON on her 1927 tour in Margery Vosper's *Tea For Three* and Michael Arlen's *The Green Hat*. Other plays in which he acted for the Firm included his own *The Man Upstairs* in 1928, and two Edgar Wallace thrillers directed by GREGAN McMAHON in Melbourne and Sydney in 1929, *The Flying Squad* and *The Squeaker*. In 1930 Gordon went to the USA, where he wrote the screenplay for a film of *White Cargo*. ❦*Lynne Murphy*

published play
White Cargo. Boston (USA): Four Seas 1925.

Gordon Frost Organisation

> Entrepreneurial organisation founded by Ashley Gordon and John Frost in Sydney in April 1983 as sales and marketing consultancy to entertainment industry. Opened Footbridge Theatre, Sydney, 1984.

Two young show-business consultants, Ashley Gordon, born in 1959, and John Frost, born in 1952, leased a students' theatre in the grounds of the University of Sydney in 1984 and renamed it the Footbridge Theatre after a nearby footbridge spanning busy Parramatta Road. The Footbridge is a long rectangle with a restricted stage space, which had defeated many directors, but Gordon and Frost began presenting shows. One of their first was EDGAR METCALFE's production of Marsha Norman's *'Night, Mother* from the NATIONAL THEATRE COMPANY in Perth. JILL PERRYMAN and JUNE SALTER gave luminous performances.

Gordon Frost's first big success, however, was in August 1987 with *Jerry's Girls*, in which a cast of ten women pay tribute to the female (and some male) stars of the musicals of Jerry Herman. It toured round Australia, as did the musical *Big River* two years later. This was too big for the Footbridge and it opened in Sydney at Her Majesty's Theatre on 7 January 1989. It was a deserved success.

Ashley Gordon died suddenly in Sydney on 16 September 1989, but the Gordon Frost Organisation has continued to grow and has extended to other venues. In June 1991 a sumptuous production of the musical *The King and I* began a national tour in Adelaide, with the English actor Hayley Mills playing Anna in most capitals. Big musicals and export to Asia marked John Frost's aims in the 1990s.

Both founders of Gordon Frost entered the theatre in their teens. In late 1968 John Frost took a backstage job in the J. C. WILLIAMSON's production of the musical *Mame* in Adelaide and travelled with show to Perth, Brisbane and Sydney. He worked for the Firm again and for other entertainment organisations before he became general manager of the MARIAN STREET THEATRE in Sydney in early 1982. When Ashley Gordon was 17 he began working as a publicist in Melbourne for the entrepreneur KENN BRODZIAK. Later he came to Sydney and publicised the MARIONETTE THEATRE OF AUSTRALIA. ❦*John West*

Sandy Gore

> Actor. Graduated from National Institute of Dramatic Art (Sydney) 1966. Professional debut at St Martin's Theatre, Melbourne, 1968. Advanced NIDA course 1969. Acted regularly with Melbourne Theatre Company during 1970s. National Theatre Critics' Award 1977 (Nancy in *The Doll Trilogy* by Ray Lawler). Many film and television roles.

Sandy Gore is a stylish actor known for her glowing vitality on stage and her expressive, throaty voice. She has created roles in several Australian plays, including three by ALEX BUZO. In 1969 she played Diane in the Sydney premiere of *ROOTED*—there was another in Canberra on the same night. With the MELBOURNE THEATRE COMPANY she created Beth in *MAKASSAR REEF* (1978) and Adela in *Big River* (1980). For the same company Gore also created the role of Elizabeth in DAVID WILLIAMSON's *Jugglers Three* in 1972, and vividly brought to life the adventurous, worldly Nancy in Ray Lawler's *THE DOLL TRILOGY* in 1976 and 1977. This character, absent from *SUMMER OF THE SEVENTEENTH DOLL*, the play that began the trilogy in 1955, realised a myth of dramatic literature. In Sydney Gore made an impact in the premiere of NICK ENRIGHT's popular comedy *Daylight Saving* with the ENSEMBLE THEATRE COMPANY in 1989. ❦*Katharine Brisbane*

Clem Gorman

> Dramatist. Born 18 October 1942 in Perth. Moved to Sydney 1960. Studied at Ensemble Theatre 1962–63. Involved with Sydney University Dramatic Society while at university 1963–65. Pioneer of alternative theatre in Sydney in late 1960s with Human Body, Paddington Arts Lab and his own Australian Free Theatre Troupe. Studied arts administration in London. Stage manager and arts administrator in Australia and England 1970–78. Had first play produced 1978. Won prize in Western Australian government's 150th anniversary play competition in 1979 with *The Making of the Documentary D'Arcy Conran*. Australia Council writer's fellowships 1980, 1982. Nephew of dramatist Alan Seymour.

In the late 1960s Clem Gorman was a leader in a brief, colourful movement of hippy-inspired HAPPENINGS and theatrical ceremonies in Sydney. Then he went to London and expanded his interests into multimedia events, particularly at the Round House in Camden Town, where he was a community arts officer and deputy administrator.

Gorman began writing plays with *A Manual of Trench Warfare*, an examination of the emotions aroused by the extremes of front-line fighting. Colin George, artistic director of the STATE THEATRE Company of South Australia, took up the play and encouraged Gorman to return to Australia for a writer's residency. When it was performed in Sydney, where it brought COLIN FRIELS to attention in the leading role, the play was accused of alleging homosexual behaviour in the armed forces.

A Manual of Trench Warfare remains the most lasting of Gorman's eight professionally produced plays. Major companies have performed *A Night in the Arms of Raeleen* and *A Fortunate Life*. Gorman, an experienced dramaturge, also teaches dramatic writing. ❦*Katharine Brisbane*

published plays
A Manual of Trench Warfare (1978). Sydney: Currency Press 1980.
A Night in the Arms of Raeleen (1981). Sydney: Currency Press 1983.
A Fortunate Life (1984). Sydney: Currency Press 1987.
The Harding Women (1981). Sydney: Currency Press 1983.
The Motivators (1981). Melbourne: Yackandandah 1983.

other writings
The Book of Ceremony. London: Whole Earth Tools 1972. An alternative theatre handbook.
National Survey of Dramaturgy. Wollongong (NSW): Scarp Press 1992.

Joey Gougenheim

Actor, dancer. Born in Dublin (Ireland) c.1843. Originally Josephine Gougenheim. Made debut with sister Adelaide at Olympic Theatre, London, 1850. Successful with sister in New York and California from 1850. Australian debut at Princess's Theatre, Melbourne, May 1857. Co-managed Princess's Theatre, 1858. Went to USA 1859. Returned to Australia 1861. Married Marmaduke Constable 8 July 1865. Starred and managed theatrical company at Gulgong (NSW) 1871–72. Retired from stage and opened boarding house in Sydney. Died 13 September 1900 in Sydney.

The attractive, young, spirited sisters Adelaide and Joey Gougenheim could act, sing, dance, perform burlesque and play the violoncello. They had a wealth of international experience when they made their Australian debuts under George Coppin's banner. Patronage was poor, however, and the sisters were so annoyed that they refused to perform again unless they were given half the proceeds. Two months elapsed before they reappeared. Eventual release from their contract cost them £400.

When they left Australia Joey continued her career in the USA and London but Adelaide married and later lived in London. Joey returned to Victoria in 1861. In September 1871 she arrived at the Gulgong goldfields in NSW with a solo show of 16 characterisations called *Joey at Home*. She then went to Sydney, formed the Star Dramatic Company and returned to Gulgong to give the goldfields a theatrical feast at the Theatre Royal. In December 1871 Gougenheim leased a new theatre at Gulgong and grandiosely called it the Prince of Wales Opera House. She managed her company there for nine months until she retired. ❦*Roma Wallis*

further reading
Brown, T. Allston. *History of the American Stage*. New York: Dick and FitzGerald 1870, reissued Benjamin Blom 1969.
O'Dell, George C. D. *Annals of the New York Stage* 6 and 7. New York: Columbia Press 1936.
Wallis, Roma. *Gulgong in the Roaring Days*. Dubbo (NSW): Macquarie Publications 1982.

William Buelow Gould

Scene-painter. Born 8 November 1803 in Liverpool (England). Original surname Holland. Worked for lithographer and studied painting. Convicted of theft in January 1827. Arrived in Van Diemen's Land as convict December 1827. Freed in 1835. Worked as scene-painter 1835–37. Died 11 December 1853 in Hobart.

A major colonial easel painter, William Buelow Gould had a brief theatrical career. After penal servitude he was working for a coachbuilder in Launceston when he was engaged to paint his first backdrop—for John Meredith's production of Henry Melville's *The Bushrangers*. Gould also painted some scenery for Meredith at the Theatre Royal in the Argyle Rooms in Hobart early in 1837, when it was in competition with the New Theatre Royal. ❦*Gillian Winter*

further reading
Allport, Harry. William Buelow Gould. *Australian Dictionary of Biography* 1. Melbourne University Press 1966.
Darby G. *William Buelow Gould*. Sydney: Copperfield Press 1981.
Kerr, Joan (ed.). *Dictionary of Australian Artists, Photographers and Engravers, 1770–1870*. Melbourne: Oxford University Press 1992.
Miller, E. M. *Pressmen and Governors*. Sydney University Press 1973.

Government policy

Colonial governments' views on law and order frustrated early attempts to have professional theatre licensed. Only in 1831, when Major-General Sir Richard Bourke was Governor of NSW, was the first licence for a theatre building granted to Barnett Levey. Nevertheless, strict censorship prevailed for works of local origin, with particular attention to blasphemy and sedition. Many subsequent colonial governors became regular patrons of the arts. The first official encouragement came in 1908, when the Prime Minister, Alfred Deakin, established the Commonwealth Literary Fund for authors in penury.

When the film industry became established state governments quickly took advantage of a new source of revenue, Tasmania and South Australia leading the way in the introduction of entertainments tax. The federal government doubled the impost by introducing its own tax in 1916. The Great Depression forced its removal in 1933 but it was reintroduced from 1942 to 1952. While the intention was to achieve extra revenue from importation of film, these taxes imposed heavy handicaps upon performing arts at a time when they were particularly vulnerable to competition from film. The last entertainment tax, on film alone, was abolished in Tasmania in 1976.

James Scullin, Labor Prime Minister from 1929 to 1931, reformed the Commonwealth Literary Fund to foster new writing. The fund benefited playwrights in the 1940s and 1950s, including Richard Beynon, David Ireland, Betty Roland and Alan Seymour. In 1932 the new United Australia Party government, adopting a Labor initiative, set up the Australian Broadcasting Commission. Drama on ABC radio gave vital training and employment to actors, directors and writers, especially in the 1940s and 1950s, decades when there was little opportunity to perform Australian works in the live theatre.

In 1944 Eugene Ormandy, conductor of the Philadelphia Orchestra, was touring for the ABC when the Labor federal government asked him to report on Australia's cultural needs. Among Ormandy's recommendations was a national theatre. The Prime Minister, John Curtin, was sympathetic but set the matter aside until peace came. Curtin died before the Second World War ended.

His successor, Ben Chifley, established a Committee for Cultural Development in Canberra and in 1949 part of its annual grant was allotted to the Canberra Repertory Society for a director and a part-time secretary. This was the first government grant to any theatrical group in Australia Chifley was also interested in establishing a national theatre and in 1949 the English theatre director Tyrone Guthrie was invited to advise him. The GUTHRIE REPORT won Cabinet approval but Labor lost office and the new Liberal government of Robert Menzies rejected the report.

However, the governor of the Reserve Bank, H. C. COOMBS, gained government support to raise funds for a private patron of the performing arts, the AUSTRALIAN ELIZABETHAN THEATRE TRUST, which was founded in 1954. Private donation initially raised £89 509, to which the federal government added £29 836 6s 8d—one pound for every three. Tax deductibility for donors was granted as part of the Trust's charter—which later made the Trust a significant banker for the arts community. No further concession of this kind was made to the arts until the Trust's finances collapsed in 1991.

Until the 1950s state governments had rarely done much to support the arts. They granted free railway transport to the Allan Wilkie Shakespearean Company in the 1920s. The Arts Council movement in the 1940s attracted sporadic state government funding but never enough to sustain continuous professional theatre. In the year in which the Trust was founded, however, the NSW government decided to build the SYDNEY OPERA HOUSE and next year the Victorian government began to implement a long-delayed scheme for an arts centre in Melbourne.

In 1963 a select committee of the Senate, chaired by Senator Seddon Vincent, reported on encouragement of Australian productions for television. To provide a foundation for locally produced television drama the VINCENT REPORT recommended government support for live theatre. It probably influenced those whose urging of a direct government role in policy-making and support led the Prime Minister, Harold Holt, to decide in November 1967 to set up an arts council.

Australian Council for the Arts
Holt's accidental death in January 1968 left implementation of the decision to his successor, John Gorton. He transferred policy and support from the privately-run Trust to a federal government agency, the Australian Council for the Arts. Coombs was again founding chairman and Jean Battersby was his executive officer. A board of nine members was appointed, with responsibility for dispensing funds to applicants in drama, opera, ballet and film, and for liaison with other government bodies such as the Australian Broadcasting Commission, the Commonwealth Literary Fund and the Commonwealth Art Advisory Board.

The council's first budget was $1·8 million. Annual allocations were made to selected individuals and organisations. A recipient group was required to be a non-profit organisation administered by a board of directors; commercial enterprise was excluded. The establishment of the council began a revolutionary restructuring of the arts according to its guidelines. Official state theatre companies were established. Some amateur theatre groups became fully professional. Others were unable to do so and died.

The formation of the Australian Council for the Arts spurred most state governments to follow suit. Queensland led in 1968, setting up a Directorate of Cultural Activities within the Education Department. By the mid-1970s every state had an arts agency that, among other activities, oversaw government spending on theatre. South Australia's Labor government was particularly active in the 1970s. It supported the ADELAIDE FESTIVAL OF ARTS, established the CARCLEW YOUTH ARTS CENTRE and related organisations and promoted the performing arts beyond greater Adelaide by establishing five cultural trusts in SOUTH AUSTRALIAN PROVINCIAL TOWNS, each with a modern theatre modelled on the Playhouse at the ADELAIDE FESTIVAL CENTRE.

Gough Whitlam's Labor government enlarged the scope of Gorton's council in 1973. Next year it legislated to create the AUSTRALIA COUNCIL as a statutory body and in two successive budgets it greatly increased its allocation.

The government also established the Industries Assistance Commission in 1973 to inquire publicly into and report on the needs for financial and other government assistance to develop Australian industry. The Australian Council for the Arts believed that the commercial theatre might warrant some government assistance and recommended an inquiry. In October 1974 Whitlam asked the commission to investigate 'whether assistance should be accorded the performing arts in Australia and, if so, what should be the nature and extent of such a system'.

The terms of reference lacked the word 'commercial', however, and the commission, headed by Richard Boyer, scrutinised all performing-arts subsidy with an economic focus. Unmoved by arguments of 'social benefit' or 'community good' arising from public subvention, the commissioners challenged the Australia Council's subsidies for theatre, opera and ballet and the Australian Broadcasting Commission's maintenance of its orchestras. They proposed a five-year phase-out of direct assistance and its replacement by federally funded educational programs and electronic dissemination to broaden the appeal of the arts involved and make them self-sufficient. Malcolm Fraser's Liberal–Country government, which received the report in April 1977, formally rejected its findings on 14 September 1977 and confirmed that direct federal support for performing-arts companies would continue.

Inquiries have continued, seeking ever-better and more cost-effective ways of delivering government support to the arts. An inquiry into the government's proposed reconstruction of the Australia Council by the House of Representatives' Standing Committee on Expenditure produced the McLeay report in 1986. This led to amalgamation of the Australia Council's music and theatre boards. The report also urged a move towards democratising the arts, devolving small grants to other organisations and establishing a major organisations unit to grant allocations. It also recommended a review of the tax laws relating to the arts.

Since the late 1970s the focus of policy-making has inexorably shifted to the Arts Department—now called the Australian Cultural Development Office—in Canberra. This directly funds all public cultural institutions, including the Australia Council, the NATIONAL INSTITUTE OF DRAMATIC ART and the Australian Film, Television and Radio School. The collapse of the Trust delivered approval of tax deductibility for arts companies—a key power in times of increased reliance on the corporate dollar—into the hands of the Arts Department.

The building of the Sydney Opera House and the resulting praise inspired other state governments to follow suit during the 1960s and 1970s. The first government-initiated performing-arts centre to be completed in a capital city, however, was the Canberra Theatre Centre in 1965. It was a project of the National Capital Development Commission. Major investment in constructing performing-arts centres to house federally-funded companies has brought state and federal bodies into conflict in the battle to support the programming of such centres and other smaller arts properties. Since 1985 the commonwealth and the states have striven in the Cultural Ministers' Council—a meeting of all state and federal arts ministers and the permanent heads of their departments—to map out spheres of interest and reduce overlap in support and supervision.

Under Bob Hawke's Labor government from 1983 to 1992 the arts were not a priority, although the Treasurer, Paul Keating, in 1989 introduced the annual Australian Artists' Creative Fellowships. Keating's personal interest in the arts made for rapid changes when he became Prime Minister. One of his first acts was to combine the ministries of arts and communications, bringing them closer to an industrial base than the Australia Council, with its non-profit brief, had been able to achieve alone.

In 1994 Keating rewarded the arts community for its support in the 1993 election by making the federal government's first major cultural policy statement, which gave an undertaking to deliver $252 million in grants over four years and to 'end cultural insecurity'. This 'Creative Nation' statement adopted some of the recommendations of the McLeay report, including the establishment of a major organisations board to engage in forward planning, with triennial funding for the leading theatre and music organisations, funding for more television drama and feature films, and founding of new national training institutions. ❦*Katharine Brisbane*

Michael Gow

Actor, director, dramatist. Born 14 February 1955 in Sydney. Began work with Australian Theatre for Young People 1970. Acted and directed in Sydney University Dramatic Society as student 1973–76. Lived in London 1977–78. Acted professionally for Nimrod, Thalia and Sydney Theatre Companies. Directed for Griffin and Sydney Theatre Companies. Associate director of Sydney Theatre Company 1991–94. Green Room Award 1986, NSW Premier's Award 1986, Sydney Theatre Critics' Circle Award 1986, Australian Writers' Guild Awgie award 1987 for *Away*. Sydney Theatre Critics' Circle Award 1992 for *Furious*. Has also written for television.

Michael Gow is generally regarded as the leading playwright to emerge in the 1980s. His plays have been popular with audiences and critics. He writes in a lucid, visualised and allusive style, sharpened by his knowledge of stagecraft—gained from acting—and his directorial awareness of the techniques of non-naturalistic theatricality. Much of Gow's drama acutely analyses the lower middle-class family since the Second World War, whether showing its equivocal resilience in *Away* and *On Top of the World* or its fracturing and dispersal in *The Kid* and *Furious*. A son and a daughter attempt to celebrate their father's birthday in *On Top of the World*, which characteristically mixes farce with pain. It anatomises the encroaching death of a patriarch, the trauma of a lost mother and the children's despair, and the family's tenuous reconstitution around a surrogate mother, the proletarian survivor Baby. A more pervasive motif is physical illness, spiritual damage or even death of young people, as exemplified by Tom in *Away*. The causes are social, including alienation and social deprivation in *The Kid* and affluence and the boredom of suburbia in *On Top*. Gow's interest in writing for the young and about their problems is evident in *All Stops Out*, which deals with the social and personal pressures imposed by the NSW matriculation examination. It was written for AUSTRALIAN THEATRE FOR YOUNG PEOPLE.

Most of Gow's plays chart conflict between generations, when parents formed by economic hardships of the Great Depression and the Second World War become remote from the difficulties of their socially mobile children. These postwar offspring are more secure financially but beset by sexual ambivalence, which is impossible to communicate. They are also alienated by a media-dominated suburban culture that is seemingly divorced from metropolitan meaning. In Gow's more recent writing, characters like Dean in *The Kid* or Chris in *Furious* openly express their homosexuality, suggesting an alternative to the endemic stresses of the nuclear family.

The historical drama *1841* savagely dramatises post-colonial cultural and political alienation. It was widely condemned by critics who sought a repetition of what they saw as the consoling harmonies of *Away*. In contrast, the two-hander *Europe* comically plays out a version of the Australian ambivalence towards metropolitan high culture in a stop-start love relationship between an European actress and a stage-struck young Australian man. *Furious* takes up the themes of spiritual chaos in artistic creation and the unfinished business of a family past with which the artist must come to terms.

European high culture is distinctively interwoven into Gow's dramaturgy. Music from Wagner's *The Nibelungs' Ring* comments ironically on the urban dislocation of the young people in *The Kid* and suggests an apocalyptic dimension to their predicament. *King Lear* and *A Midsummer Night's Dream* frame the family rituals of *Away* and the Trojan cycle those of *On Top of the World*, while the fate of Hedda Gabler shadows Barbara in *Europe*. ❦*Veronica Kelly*

published plays
1841 (1988). Sydney: Currency Press 1988.
All Stops Out (1989). Sydney: Currency Press 1991.
Away (1986). Sydney: Currency Press 1986, revised 1989.
Europe (1987). Sydney: Currency Press 1987.
Furious (1991). Sydney: Currency Press 1994.
The Kid (1983). Sydney: Currency Press 1983.
On Top of the World (1986). Sydney: Currency Press 1987.
Sweet Phoebe (1994). Sydney: Currency Press 1995.

further reading
AKERHOLT, MAY-BRIT. Michael Gow talks to May-Brit Akerholt. *Australasian Drama Studies* 12–13 (Brisbane 1988).
GILBERT, HELEN. Monumental moments—Michael Gow's *1841*, Stephen Sewell's *Hate*, Louis Nowra's *Capricornia* and Australia's bicentenary. *Australasian Drama Studies* 24 (Brisbane, April 1994).
KELLY, VERONICA. Apocalypse and after—Historical visions in some recent Australian drama. *Kunapipi* 9/3 (Århus, Denmark, 1987).
KELLY, VERONICA. The melodrama of defeat—Political patterns in some colonial and contemporary Australian plays. *Southerly* 50/2 (Sydney 1990).
KELLY, VERONICA. In *Contemporary Dramatists* (ed. K. A. Berney) 5th edn. London: St James Press 1993.

MITCHELL, TONY. Great white hope or great white hype? The critical construction (and demolition) of Michael Gow. *Spectator Burns* 3 (Sydney1989).
SIMON, LUKE. *Michael Gow's Plays*. Sydney: Currency Press 1991.

Ron Graham

Actor. Born 1926 at Aldershot (England). Performed as catcher in circus flying act. Took acting course while in army. Emigrated to Australia 1949. Took evening classes at Mina Shelley School of Theatre (Sydney). Worked in radio. Toured Australia playing Shakespeare in John Alden Company. Joined National Theatre Company (Perth) 1954.

An enormously versatile actor who has worked all over Australia, Ron Graham represents one of the few remaining links to Australian theatre in the years immediately after the Second World War. He established his reputation with the NATIONAL THEATRE COMPANY during the 1950s and 1960s and in the 1970s he played an important part in the revival of Australian drama. In seven years in Perth he played 80 parts, including leading roles in a wide range of plays. He made memorable appearances in two Adelaide Festivals—with Robert Speaight in T. S. Eliot's *Murder in the Cathedral* in 1964 and as Pizarro in Peter Shaffer's *The Royal Hunt of the Sun* in 1966. In Sydney he worked mostly with the OLD TOTE THEATRE COMPANY, for which his performances included the title-role in *King Lear*, and the NIMROD THEATRE COMPANY. For the latter he appeared in the 1980 production of David Williamson's THE CLUB, which toured to the United Kingdom, and in five classics during the company's last two years. He has acted in several notable SYDNEY THEATRE COMPANY productions, including THE BLIND GIANT IS DANCING by Stephen Sewell in 1985 and *Coriolanus* in 1993. ❦*Paul McGillick*

Oriel Gray

Dramatist. Born 26 March 1920 in Sydney. Originally Oriel Bennett. Joined New Theatre League (Sydney) 1937. Member of Communist Party 1942–50. Playwright-in-residence for New Theatre League 1942. Shared first prize in Playwrights' Advisory Board play competition with *The Torrents* 1955. Won play competition conducted by J. C. Williamson's and Little Theatre Guild with *Burst of Summer* 1959. Has written for television since 1960s. Married to actor John Gray 1940–45, and later to journalist John Hepworth. Lives in Melbourne.

Oriel Gray is one of the socialist writers brought up during the Great Depression of the 1930s who sought to extend the imagination and raise social issues through the theatre. Her father—a public servant and Labor Party activist—the Depression and the Spanish Civil War helped her to commit herself to socialism, which she has said was her form of Christianity. Her first theatrical influence was Kursaal Theatre, an avant-garde amateur group in Sydney. At 17 she joined the socialist NEW THEATRE League, performed agitprop plays on the back of a truck and in workplaces, and became an accomplished comedian. Her early writing included 14 five-minute radio dramas for a trade-union education program, which developed into personal dramas deeply influenced by the American radio innovator Norman Corwin and his Columbia Broadcasting workshop. These brought her appointment in 1942 as the New Theatre League's playwright-in-residence at £2 10s a week. She was possibly the first salaried stage playwright in Australia. She had two revues performed in 1942: *Marx of Time* and *Let's Be Offensive*. Much of Gray's writing had political content during the 1940s. She was influenced by Will Lee, an actor with the reformist Group Theatre of New York City, who was stationed in Sydney as an army corporal during the Second World War. He introduced New Theatre to social realism and expressionism and American writers like Maxwell Anderson, Lillian Hellman, Eugene O'Neill and Robert Sherwood. Gray's first stage play, *Lawson*, was performed in 1943. An adaptation from Henry Lawson's works, it has been performed many times. *Milestones*, a short socialist history of Australia, followed. Then came *Sur le pont*; *Western Limit*, a drama about the plight of the poor farmer; *My Life is My Affair*; and *Had We But World Enough*, a three-act drama about love and racial injustice in a country town. In 1950, the year Gray left the Communist Party, New Theatre performed her *Sky Without Birds*, a three-act drama dealing with isolation and prejudice against postwar immigrants on a Nullarbor Plain railway siding. It was the first play Gray wrote in rebuttal of her party beliefs and it gave primacy to individual morality. Nevertheless, all her plays share her concern for the underprivileged—and her actor's dramatic drive.

A three-act Shavian comedy set in a country newspaper office, *The Torrents* shared first prize in the 1955 PLAYWRIGHTS' ADVISORY BOARD competition with Ray Lawler's SUMMER OF THE SEVENTEENTH DOLL. It was first produced by Adelaide New Theatre in 1956. In 1984 Ray Kolle and Peter Pinne adapted it as a musical, *A Bit o' Petticoat*. *Drive a Hard Bargain*, a bush comedy with a Faustian theme, won a Royal South Street Society competition in Ballarat (Vic.), in 1957 and was performed there. Gray's best-known play, BURST OF SUMMER was produced in 1960 by the St Martin's Theatre Company in Melbourne. She published several one-act plays for schools in 1965–71. ❦*Katharine Brisbane*

published plays
Belle and the Bushranger. Adelaide: Rigby 1971.
Drive a Hard Bargain (1957). Sydney: Australian Drama League 1958.
The Ghost of Dog-Leg Creek. Melbourne: Nelson 1969.
Lawson (1943). Adelaide: Rigby 1968. Melbourne: Yackandandah Playscripts 1989.
The Three Good Witches and the Bad Bad Prince. Adelaide: Rigby 1970.
The Torrents (1956). Melbourne: Penguin 1988 in *Australian Women's Writing*.

other writings
Exit Left, Memoirs of a Scarlet Woman. Melbourne: Penguin 1985. Autobiography of her early years.
The Golden Touch. Melbourne: Nelson 1965. Radio play.

further reading
KOLLE, RAY and PETER PINNE. *A Bit o' Petticoat*. Melbourne: Yackandandah 1990.

The Great Levante

Magician. Born 5 March 1892 in Sydney. Originally Leslie Cole. Began professional career 1912. Toured New Zealand, Pacific Islands and some Asian countries 1927. Performed in Japan, China, Malaya, India and northwest Asia 1929–33. Went to England 1933 and built large show. Returned to Australia 1940. On Tivoli circuit 1942–44. Died 20 January 1978 in Sydney.

Les Levante performed in Australian country towns and city theatres for 15 years before he began touring overseas with an illusion show that he gradually enlarged until it ranked among the largest in the world. Spectacular scenery and Levante's dignified bearing and charm made it lavish and entertaining. He did a season at the Kingsway Theatre in London in 1940 and then he returned to Australia because of the Second World War. Levante opened his magical revue *How's Tricks* at the King's Theatre in Melbourne on Boxing Day 1940 and played to capacity business until 1 March 1941. A tour of New Zealand followed, then a season in Brisbane. From 1942 to 1944 he supplied half the show for the TIVOLI CIRCUIT for five weeks in Sydney and Melbourne. After two tours of England Levante retired in Sydney, but he performed club shows until his death. ❦*Gerald Taylor*

further reading
RITCHIE, JOHN. Leslie Cole. *Australian Dictionary of Biography* 13. Melbourne University Press 1994.
People (Sydney) 24 February 1954.
Sydney Morning Herald 24 January 1978.
reference
The Performing Arts Museum (Melbourne) has a tape recording of an interview with Levante.

Gregan McMahon Players

Semiprofessional dramatic company in Melbourne founded in 1929 by Gregan McMahon. Presented short seasons until 1941.
first production *Bird in Hand* by John Drinkwater, 26 November 1929, Palace Theatre, Melbourne. **repertoire** included many plays by George Bernard Shaw and works by John Galsworthy, Jean Giraudoux, Henrik Ibsen, Somerset Maugham, Sean O'Casey and Oscar Wilde.

For 12 years the Gregan McMahon Players presented short semiprofessional seasons of drama in Melbourne. For many years after GREGAN MCMAHON's death in 1941 supporters claimed that his company alone had kept good non-commercial theatre alive in Melbourne in the 1930s. The truth is more complex. Live theatre was struggling against talking films in late 1929, when McMahon, as a first step towards setting up his own semiprofessional company, staged John Drinkwater's *Bird in Hand*. This had been one of the more popular lightweight pieces he produced for the MELBOURNE REPERTORY THEATRE COMPANY and the SYDNEY REPERTORY THEATRE SOCIETY.

McMahon began the company while he was producing plays for J. C. WILLIAMSON's in 1929. By the late 1930s, when subscription and ticket prices were competitive with the cinema, the McMahon Players had more than 2000 subscribers. They were less nationalistic in repertoire than amateur companies, whose acting was of generally lower standard. McMahon attracted the best young players from among the amateurs. Newspapers said he had a 'Svengali-like' ability to get professional standards from them. The most notable was CORAL BROWNE, who played leading roles for McMahon before leaving for London and international fame in mid-1934.

Old professionals also appeared occasionally with McMahon's company. After a successful run in 1933 of Christie Winsloe's *Children in Uniform*—a tragedy about education in Prussia, with Hitlerian resonance—McMahon revived it in 1934 for F. W. THRING's Efftee Players, with ADA REEVE as the dancing mistress.

From mid-1935 until his death in 1941, J. C. Williamson's employed MCMAHON to direct popular shows, and gave him credit and cheap hire of otherwise dark theatres for his own company. The Players annually performed eight plays for Williamson's. Most of them had been staged professionally in London but were not, in the Firm's view, viable in Australia. McMahon's productions were constrained by limited funds and poor publicity—they were often advertised in small type below large illustrations of Williamson revivals like *Rio Rita*. McMahon's melodramatic style of acting and directing was by now beginning to be reviewed less favourably.

His repertoire, heavily dependent on George Bernard Shaw, seemed less radical than it had in the 1910s and 1920s. Much has been made of Shaw allowing the Gregan McMahon Players to stage the 'world premiere' production of *The Millionairess* in Melbourne on 7 March 1936. The play had been performed once in Vienna two months before, however, and rejected elsewhere. The *Age*, which generally applauded McMahon's work, noted sympathetically that he 'did a difficult job well with this rickety play'. Luigi Pirandello's *Henri IV* in 1937, Jean Giraudoux's *Amphytrion 38* in 1941, Thornton Wilder's *Our Town*, André Obey's *Noah* and *The Ascent of F6* by W. H. Auden and Christopher Isherwood showed McMahon's preference for the metaphysical and the poetic.

He did not encourage local writers, in spite of his tirade in an interview in *Table Talk* of 2 May 1935 that 'the snob audience cannot (will not) believe that anything Australian can be good'. The few Australian plays he staged were aberrations like Ambrose Pratt's philosophical study of old and new China, *Point in Time*. In this one actor's lines 'were not memorised', according to the *Age* on 31 March 1941, which suggests the decline in standards that Allan Ashbolt has noted in McMahon's last years. Nevertheless, as the *Table Talk* interviewer argued, McMahon 'made actors out of the most unpromising material', and his company presented 'plays that would never have, otherwise, come our way'. ❦*Richard Fotheringham*

further reading
ASHBOLT, ALLAN. Courage, contradictions and compromise—Gregan McMahon 1874-1941. *Meanjin* 37/3 (1978).
DOUGLAS, DENNIS and MARJORY M. MORGAN. Gregan McMahon and the Australian theatre. *Komos* 2/2 (1969), 2/4, 3/1-4 (1973).

Daphne Grey

Actor. Born in Essex (England). Studied at Central School of Speech and Drama (London). Worked in theatre, radio and television. Settled in Adelaide 1963. Foundation member of South Australian Theatre Company (Adelaide)1965. Regular appearances for Melbourne, Nimrod (Sydney), and Sydney Theatre Companies and State Theatre Company of South Australia (Adelaide). Green Room Award 1982 (*Percy and Rose* by Rob George).

An actor with a vibrant stage presence, Daphne Grey has a distinguished list of credits in classic works by Anton Chekhov, Henrik Ibsen, Molière, Shakespeare and August Strindberg. Her Shakespearean roles include Gertrude in *Hamlet*, Lady Macbeth and Volumnia in *Coriolanus*. In 1989 she brought shrewd assured comedy to the role of Marion Brewster-Wright in Gale Edwards's production of Alan Ayckbourn's *Absurd Person Singular*, teamed with EDWIN HODGEMAN, and in 1993 she played Mrs Pugh to his poisoner Pugh in Dylan Thomas's *Under Milk Wood*. She gave her award-winning performance in *Percy and Rose* for the STAGE COMPANY in Adelaide. ❦*Murray Bramwell*

Griffin Theatre Company

Professional dramatic company in Sydney founded in 1979. **venue** Stables Theatre 1980–. **artistic directors** 1985–88 Peter Kingston. 1988–90 Ian Watson. 1992– Ros Horin.

The Griffin Theatre Company has maintained the dedication to new Australian plays upon which the NIMROD THEATRE COMPANY was founded. Since 1981 it has performed only Australian plays, giving both world and Sydney premieres. The most significant have been by MICHAEL GOW, whose *Away* (1986) and *Europe* (1987), written with the encouragement of Griffin's artistic director Peter Kingston, enjoyed success and have entered the repertoire. New writers presented by Griffin included Richard Barrett, Grant Fraser, Noel Hodda, Karin Mainwaring and Jennifer Paynter. Fraser's *Love and the Single Teenager* (1981), the most popular of his four plays for Griffin, was revived in 1984. Group-devised pieces also marked the company's work in the 1980s. One was *Soft Targets* (1986), the first Australian play to deal with AIDS.

The Griffin company began in 1979, when a group of NATIONAL INSTITUTE OF DRAMATIC ART graduates—including Peter Carmody, Penny Cook, Noel Hodda, Rosemarie Lenzo and ROBERT MENZIES—produced *The Ginger Man* by J. P. Donleavy in a gallery in Surry Hills. The enterprise took its name from nearby Griffin Street, where its first general manager, Jenny Laing-Peach, lived. The play made a small profit, which funded further productions. In April 1980 the company moved to the STABLES THEATRE and in 1985 the co-operative changed its structure by appointing Kingston as artistic director.

Penny Cook, a popular television actor, contributed substantially to Griffin's reputation in the 1980s with personal and financial sponsorship. The Seaborn, Broughton and Walford Foundation, which bought the Stables Theatre in 1985, has been a generous patron. It has provided a theatre and offices at minimal cost and gave further support when debt and the withdrawal of subsidy kept the company out of business for periods in 1990–91. Ros Horin continues the all-Australian policy, determined that Griffin, as custodian of the Stables Theatre, should 'become truly Sydney's writers' theatre'. Her highly successful 1993 production of Timothy Daly's *Kafka Dances* transferred to the Wharf Theatre in the following year. ❦*Ron Blair*

J. G. Griffiths

Actor, manager. Born August 1810 in Shropshire (England). Trained in Scottish theatres. Arrived in Sydney with family 3 January 1843. Actor and often manager at Royal Victoria Theatre, Sydney, 1843–55. Died 4 March 1857 in Sydney. Father of actor Annie Griffiths and dancers Emily and Fanny Griffiths.

Among early actors, John Gordon Griffiths was unusual in that he had a career in one city and virtually one theatre. He was a mainstay of the ROYAL VICTORIA THEATRE in Sydney, usually playing second leads. Griffiths went onto the stage immediately after leaving school, joining the troupe of the Scottish actor Charles McKay. He later worked in Glasgow and Edinburgh and he gained an intimate knowledge of Lowlands manners and language that made him successful in Scots dialect parts. He also managed the Shrewsbury theatre circuit before moving to London, where JOSEPH WYATT saw him in 1842 and contracted him to the Royal Victoria for three years as actor and manager.

Griffiths made his debut on 23 January 1843 with a resounding failure as Hamlet. One of the kinder reviews, in the *Sydney Morning Herald* on 25 January, concluded that 'in characters of less importance he may be found useful; but in tragedy he will never succeed'. Griffiths redeemed himself with the critics and the public, however, partly through a success as Shakespeare's Coriolanus. Second leads were his forte, though. In February 1846, for example, he played Iago to Francis Nesbitt's Othello and Wellborn to his Sir Giles Overreach in Philip Massinger's *A New Way to Pay Old Debts*. He appeared in the premieres of two Australian works in 1844—as Harry Hearty in Edward Geoghegan's ballad opera THE CURRENCY LASS and as Macbeth in SHAKESPERICONGLOMOROFUNNIDOGAMMONIAE, a burlesque by Charles Nagel.

Griffiths was replaced as manager of the Royal Victoria by JOHN LAZAR in mid-1843. He resumed the management in 1846 and retained it until 1854. He also managed Wyatt's new PRINCE OF WALES THEATRE in Sydney before he retired from the stage in 1855. He became a publican, buying the Pier Hotel at Manly, where he died. ❦*Elizabeth Webby*

further reading
HEATON, J. H. *Australian Dictionary of Dates and Men of the Time*. Melbourne: George Robertson 1879.

Robert Grubb

Actor. Born 31 January 1950 in Hobart. Graduated from National Institute of Dramatic Art (Sydney) 1978. State Theatre Company of South Australia and Lighthouse Company (Adelaide). In numerous productions by Melbourne Theatre Company. Also film and television roles.

A versatile and accomplished actor, Robert Grubb was a mainstay of the South Australian Theatre Company from its inception. He appeared in *Hamlet*, in George Bernard Shaw's *Arms and the Man* as Nicola, in RON BLAIR's *Last Day in Woolloomooloo* and in the Wakefield mystery plays. He was Sir Toby Belch in NICK ENRIGHT's production of *Twelfth Night* and he appeared in Enright's production of his own musical *On the Wallaby*. With JIM SHARMAN's Lighthouse Company Grubb appeared in ten productions, including Stephen Sewell's THE BLIND GIANT IS DANCING, Federico García Lorca's *Blood Wedding*, PATRICK WHITE's *Netherwood* (as Sergeant Bell) and in the musical *Pal Joey* (as Joey). He left Adelaide in 1983 and returned in 1987 to appear in Michael Frayn's *Wild Honey*.

After a long and popular stint on television as Dr Geoffrey Standish in *The Flying Doctors*, Grubb returned to the stage for the 1992 tour of Neil Simon's *Lost in Yonkers*. In 1994 he created the role of the aggressive television reporter Bob King in David Williamson's *Sanctuary* for the PLAYBOX THEATRE CENTRE in Melbourne. ❦*Murray Bramwell*

Michael Gurr

Actor, director, dramatist. Born 29 October 1961 in Melbourne. National Theatre Drama School workshops 1972–76. Writer-in-residence with Melbourne Theatre Company 1982. Australia Council young writer's grants 1983, 1984. Began directing 1988.

In his plays Michael Gurr has been preoccupied with Australia's political, cultural and trade relations with the rest of the world, with its moral responsibilities towards the crimes of others and, in particular, with its relationship to Asia. *A Pair of Claws* (1982) deals with the effects of a diplomatic scandal upon a family, and *Dead to the World* (1986) with a diplomat's family faced with political crimes in Central America. *The Hundred Year Ambush* (1990) is about Australian-Japanese property deals. In his major work, *Sex Diary of an Infidel* (1992) Gurr uses Australian men's sex tours in the Philippines and investigative journalism as tools in examining and questioning today's moral certainties. *Underwear, Perfume and Crash Helmet* (1994) again relates politics, sex and moral philosophy.

Gurr wrote his first play when he was 18 years old, and he had his first professional production at 21, when the MELBOURNE THEATRE COMPANY staged his short play *Magnetic North*. He had early encouragement from RAY LAWLER, associate director of this company, and he was its playwright-in-residence in 1982. Gurr directed Lawler's SUMMER OF THE SEVENTEENTH DOLL at the Victorian Arts Centre in 1991. He has acted in his own plays on stage and in radio adaptations. *A Pair of Claws* and *Worlds Apart* (1987) have been adapted for film, the former as *Departure*. ❦Katharine Brisbane

published plays
Dead to the World (1986). Melbourne: Yackandandah 1986.
Magnetic North (1982). Melbourne: Yackandandah 1983
A Pair of Claws (1982). Melbourne: Yackandandah 1983.
Sex Diary of an Infidel (1992). Sydney: Currency Press 1992.
Underwear, Perfume and Crash Helmet (1994). Sydney: Currency Press 1994.

Shaun Gurton

Designer. Born 4 July 1948 at Loughton (England). Studied art at Swinburne College (Melbourne). Acted with Young Elizabethan Players 1967 and Melbourne Theatre Company 1968–70. Returned to Europe to study theatre 1970. Australia Council director's grant 1971. With South Australian Theatre Company (Adelaide) as trainee director 1972–73, actor and designer 1973–75, resident designer 1975–78. Assistant designer with Timothy O'Brien in London 1978–80. Freelance designer in Australia 1980–89. Associate director and designer with State Theatre Company of South Australia (Adelaide) since 1990. Worked with Shanghai People's Art Theatre 1991.

One of the few designers to be involved in the direction of a major theatre company, Shaun Gurton prefers an epic approach to theatrical interpretation. He designed the premiere productions of five of DAVID WILLIAMSON's plays—*The Club* (1977), *A Handful of Friends* (1976), *The Perfectionist* (1982), *Sons of Cain* (1985) and *Top Silk* (1989). For World Expo '88 in Brisbane he designed the Rainbow Serpent Theatre, a performance of an Aboriginal legend devised by Mike Browning, which utilised film overlays and broke new ground in performance technology. ❦Tom Bannerman

writings
Walls in the empty space. *Australian Theatre Design* (ed. Kim Spinks). Sydney: Australian Production Designers Association NSW 1992.

Guthrie report

Excitement aroused by the OLD VIC THEATRE COMPANY's 1948 tour helped to stimulate the Department of Postwar Reconstruction, headed by H. C. COOMBS, to ask the British Council to send someone to advise the Prime Minister, Ben Chifley, on establishing a national theatre. Tyrone Guthrie, a progressive English theatre director, spent two weeks in Australia in April 1949 as a guest of the British Council. He wrote in *A Life in the Theatre* that he 'visited the six principal cities … attended endless receptions and cocktail parties, met the federal Premier and the Prime Minister of each state [sic], and saw a great many amateur theatrical performances of widely varying quality … I can remember nothing which struck me as distinctively Australian … I knew that many talented young Australians were knocking on the theatrical doors in London and New York, to say nothing of slightly older people like Judith Anderson, Coral Browne, Cyril Ritchard and Robert Helpmann, who have gained honourable admittance. It was no surprise to find Australia an extraordinary mine of talent. There was at that time no satisfactory organisation for its expression, no considerable public appreciation to develop it and little enlightened criticism to lead the public.'

In his report Guthrie addressed first the question 'Why is a National Theatre desirable?' and argued:

> It was a means of using leisure creatively. 'With the forty-hour week and a great deal of spending money available, this wise use of leisure is a dominant national problem—the statistics of liquor consumption and betting alone are evidence of this.'
>
> 'Australia, Canada and the United States alone among the important civilised communities … leave the provision of dramatic entertainment to Private Enterprise—with the result that it is treated not as an Art but as a Business … For so influential a means of expression this hardly seems a wise criterion by political, social or moral standards ….'
>
> It was a matter of national prestige. '… Until recently Australia has been dominantly a primary producing appendage of Great Britain; now, growing national consciousness and national self-respect demand further means of expression ….'

Private enterprise, Guthrie wrote, was not 'doing a job'. 'The standard of performance, whether professional or amateur, has nowhere begun even to approach what I consider best world-standard. The reasons for this (largely a matter of Australia's geographical isolation and the smallness of population in relation to area) do no discredit to the community. But it is a fact that standards are very low both of performances and, more importantly, of appreciation—the public, with no standards of comparison, does not know what to expect of theatrical performance, nor how to discriminate between gold and dross. A sad consequence of this is that the best local actors … leave Australia ….' Guthrie recommended education of the audience and development of the best local talent on a long-term plan that would enable it to be useful at home. For the audience, he suggested the importation over three years of nine to 12 first-class British and continental productions, to improve the quality of appreciation. For experienced but underdeveloped theatre workers he recommended two-year scholarships based on London, as 'a means of helping them to teach themselves, by the application of cosmopolitan, not provincial standards'.

He envisaged about two-thirds of the students returning to Australia, where their experience would boost the standards of amateur theatre. This had 'done a creditable and persistent job against odds', he wrote, 'and any National Theatre scheme should take account of this and ensure that such groups participate directly in its advantages'. He recommended that the remaining third—the most promising actors—should be formed in London into an acting ensemble and train under Australian directors. This company's repertoire should be the English classics, 'since the basis of any artistic training must be classical', Guthrie said, but its aim should be to present the classics and ultimately the work of indigenous writers with a distinctively Australian style. 'The actors should not waste their time learning to speak with an English accent', he added. 'One of their functions should be to set a standard of Australian speech ... I believe a theatrical company, speaking well but in a recognisably and consistently Australian lingo, could succeed in England; and that this success of dialect would be an important element in the resolution of a complex that is seriously detrimental to Australian national self-confidence.' Guthrie believed that an Australian national company would gain the glamour needed to make it saleable at home only if it made its debut overseas. The report ended with recommendations for finance and administration.

Guthrie's recommendations polarised opinion. The critic LESLIE REES in *Australian Quarterly* applauded the idea of regular visits by overseas companies, saying 'no one except Actors' Equity in its more bellicose moods would quarrel with such a plan'. But overall he found the report 'compounded of truisms and visionary notions out of touch with practical Australian realities'. He attacked the notion of an Australian company abroad. 'Give us as much help from abroad as possible', Rees concluded, 'but if the theatre of our dreams is not to muddle itself into a wishy-washy eclecticism, let it grow out of Australian soil and ripen in Australian sunshine.'

Advocates of subsidy within the Department of Post War Reconstruction were disappointed with the recommendations but reluctantly accepted them when it was clear that the government was receptive. State co-operation was gained in principle at the Premiers' Conference in August and Cabinet approved the scheme in October. But in December 1949 the Labor government fell and the new Prime Minister, Robert Menzies, rejected the report. The issue of subsidy was held over until the formation of the AUSTRALIAN ELIZABETHAN THEATRE TRUST in 1954. Several promising actors received scholarships from the Trust or the British Council in the following years, notably JOHN BELL, ZOË CALDWELL, PATRICIA CONOLLY and NEIL FITZPATRICK.

The Trust sought Guthrie as executive director to replace Hugh Hunt in 1961 and again in 1965 and 1970. As a pioneer of the non-naturalistic thrust-stage theatre, he was asked by the University of Western Australia for advice on the design of its OCTAGON THEATRE, and he recommended against a multipurpose hall in favour of a drama theatre. He directed notable productions of Sophocles's *Oedipus Rex* and *All's Well that Ends Well* for the OLD TOTE THEATRE COMPANY in Sydney and the MELBOURNE THEATRE COMPANY in 1970. He died shortly after his return to his home in Ireland. ❦*John Andrews, Katharine Brisbane*

further reading
ANDREWS, JOHN. Subsidy for the performing arts in Australia, 1942-1970. Monash University PhD thesis 1988.
COOMBS, H. C. *Trial Balance*. Melbourne: Macmillan 1981.
GUTHRIE, TYRONE. *A Life in the Theatre*. London: Hamish Hamilton 1961.
GUTHRIE, TYRONE. Report on Australian Theatre. *Australian Quarterly* (Sydney) June 1949.
REES, LESLIE. Develop the national theatre on home ground. *Australian Quarterly* June 1949.

reference
Report on Australian Theatre by Tyrone Guthrie, 2 May 1949, Australian Archives, Department of the Treasury [1] CRS A571, Correspondence Files, Annual Single Number Series, 1010-1976, Item 44/1171, Part l: 'National Theatre Policy File, 1944-49'.

Alexander Habbe

Scene-painter. Born 1829 in Copenhagen (Denmark). Arrived at Victorian diggings 1855. Painted scenery for goldfields theatres. Worked at Theatre Royal, Melbourne, 1858. Went to Sydney c.1859. Decorated theatres and painted scenery in partnership with W. J. Wilson from 1863. Returned to Melbourne c.1871. Worked at Theatre Royal and Prince of Wales Opera House to 1890. Died 14 April 1896 in Melbourne.

Alexander Habbe claimed to have been self-taught in painting, although he may have learned from his brother Nicholas Habbe, an artist who died in Sydney in 1889. Like many scenic artists, Alexander Habbe worked for W. S. LYSTER's opera companies, his scenery for Friedrich von Flotow's *Martha* being much admired. Habbe was also praised for his pantomime work. His painting for GARNET WALCH's *Trookulentos, the Tempter* in Sydney in 1871 was described as 'remarkably brilliant'. His designs for George Musgrove's production of *LA FILLE DU TAMBOUR-MAJOR* in 1880 were also admired. *AUSTRALIA FELIX* in 1888 was another pantomime success. He did his last work for NELLIE STEWART's production of the operetta *Paul Jones* at the Prince of Wales Opera House in 1890. ❦*Mimi Colligan*

reference
Habbe's watercolour study for the Battle of Trafalgar moving panorama that he painted in 1879 for *Harlequin Robinson Crusoe* at the Prince of Wales Opera House, Melbourne, is in the Performing Arts Museum in Melbourne.

Patricia Hackett

Actor, designer, director. Born 1908 in Western Australia. Daughter of Sir Winthrop Hackett, journalist, lawyer and politician. Educated in Adelaide and London. Barrister of Inner Temple (London). Practised law in Adelaide and Solomon Islands. Acted in Adelaide Repertory Theatre productions from 1930 to late 1940s. Founded and ran amateur Torch Theatre (Adelaide) 1934–35, 1952–55. Worked regularly with Adelaide University Theatre Guild in 1940s. Died August 1963 in Adelaide.

The first woman to own and direct a theatre in Adelaide, Patricia Hackett had imagination and driving energy. She was also egocentric and unpredictable, and controversy lingers about her name. Adverse CRITICISM sometimes provoked her to litigation. In a converted basement in Claridge Arcade, she courageously opened her first Torch Theatre, with Oscar Wilde's *Salome*. It shocked some in the audience, but discerning critics praised Hackett. She later produced such plays as Euripides's *Medea*, Geza Silberer's *Caprice* and the Chinese classic *The Circle of Chalk*, and dramatised pieces including Cardinal Newman's poem *The Dream of Gerontius*. A dramatisation of *Song of Solomon* aroused disapproval in 1935, though many acknowledged the spell of the words, sets and costumes. On a tiny stage she created 'a feeling of oriental splendour and beauty—a necessarily pagan sensuousness', said Gerald O'Hagen in *Progress in Australia* in June 1935.

In 1952 Hackett opened her second Torch Theatre in the basement of the house she and Mildred Mocatta owned in the suburb of St Peters. One of her productions there was *Legends*, based on a collection of her poems. She revived it as a fringe item for the first ADELAIDE FESTIVAL OF ARTS in 1960. ❧*Thelma Afford*

further reading
KIFFIN-THOMAS, K. Patricia Hackett as I knew her. *Westerly* (Perth) May 1965.
MOCATTA, MILDRED. Canticle for Patricia. *Westerly* May 1965.

Ron Haddrick MBE

Actor. Born 9 April 1929 in Adelaide. Studied voice production at Elder Conservatorium (Adelaide). Stage debut at Tivoli Theatre, Adelaide, 1946. Acted with Adelaide Repertory Theatre and in semiprofessional theatre and radio from 1947. Played Sheffield Shield cricket for South Australia 1952. In Shakespeare Memorial Theatre Company (Stratford-upon-Avon, England) 1953–58. Joined Trust Players (Sydney) 1959. Foundation member of Old Tote Theatre Company (Sydney) 1963. On theatre board of Australian Council for the Arts 1973–74. Sydney Critics' Circle Award 1987 (James Tyrone in *Long Day's Journey into Night* by Eugene O'Neill and Nat in *I'm Not Rappaport* by Herb Gardner). Many radio and television roles. MBE 1974. Father of actor Lynette Haddrick.

Ron Haddrick's eminent career has spanned the most significant developments in Australian theatre over 40 years. Like most actors of his generation, he came out of amateur theatre and had classical training in England. He chose, however, to make his career at home and he has been a force in raising standards. His choice of roles is eclectic and he has retained resilience and independence of spirit in widely diverse productions and working conditions. An athletic actor with a recognisably Australian style, he has a loyal following in Sydney. He can give great spiritual dimension to rare roles like Oedipus, Les Harding in John Romeril's THE FLOATING WORLD, James Tyrone and King Lear, and inject robust comedy into such parts as Alf Cook in Alan Seymour's THE ONE DAY OF THE YEAR, Houses O'Halloran in JOHN O'DONOGHUE's *A Happy and Holy Occasion*, Jock in DAVID WILLIAMSON's THE CLUB, Cooper in Bob Larbey's *A Month of Sundays* and the dying Clive in MICHAEL GOW's *On Top of the World*.

In 1953 Haddrick joined the Shakespeare Memorial Theatre Company, then touring Australia, at the invitation of Anthony Quayle. He remained with the company for five seasons, including a tour of Russia in three productions in 1958. He returned to Australia in 1959 to join the TRUST PLAYERS. In 1961 he played Alf Cook in their production of *The One Day of the Year*, which transferred to London. Back in Australia in 1962, he toured as Dunois to ZOË CALDWELL's Saint Joan. Next year he appeared as Gaev in Anton Chekhov's *The Cherry Orchard*, the inaugural production of the OLD TOTE THEATRE COMPANY. He remained a regular player in almost 40 of this company's productions, including its early Australian play seasons. In 1970 he played Oedipus in Tyrone Guthrie's production of Sophocles's *Oedipus the King*.

For the MELBOURNE THEATRE COMPANY in 1971 Haddrick played the title-role in ALEX BUZO's *Macquarie*. In 1974 he played Ken Collins in the Old Tote production of David Williamson's *What If You Died Tomorrow?*, which transferred to Melbourne and then to London. Haddrick was back in London in 1977-78 as Jock in the NIMROD THEATRE COMPANY's production of *The Club*.

In 1980 he worked with REX CRAMPHORN in Shakespeare. In 1981 he played Chebutykin in Chekhov's *Three Sisters* for Nimrod, and Eek and Zeek Perkins in Dorothy Hewett's THE MAN FROM MUKINUPIN for the Sydney Theatre Company. He worked largely for the latter company until 1985. In 1988–89 he had a lengthy success in Sydney as Cooper in the Northside Theatre Company's production of *A Month of Sundays*, which toured to Adelaide and Brisbane. In 1991 he played Danforth in the SYDNEY THEATRE COMPANY's production of *The Crucible* by Arthur Miller. In 1993 he created the expatriate paterfamilias Max in STEPHEN SEWELL's *The Garden of Granddaughters*; it played in Melbourne and Sydney. ❧*Katharine Brisbane*

further reading
HERBERT, IAN (ed.). *Who's Who in the Theatre* 17th edn. Detroit (USA): Gale Research 1981.

Anne Haddy

Actor. Born at Quorn (SA) in 1930. Early training with Adelaide Repertory Theatre and Adelaide University Theatre Guild. Spent some years in England. Theatre and radio in Perth 1955–60. Moved to Sydney and acted for Independent Theatre, Q Theatre, Community Theatre, and Old Tote Theatre Company. Has acted only for television since 1985. Married to actor James Condon.

An actor of cool poise, great style and elusive gamin beauty, Anne Haddy was a leading player for Community Theatre during its first years and for the OLD TOTE THEATRE COMPANY in the late 1960s and early 1970s. She came to Sydney from Perth, where she had worked mainly in radio, although she played the title-role in Sophocles's *Antigone* in ROBIN LOVEJOY's production at the Festival of Perth in 1957.

In Sydney she acted in radio and television until 1962, when she played in Frederick Knott's *Write Me a Murder* at the Palace Theatre. This was followed by roles for INDEPENDENT THEATRE in 1966. She acted opposite Ray Milland in *Hostile Witness* by Jack Roffey in 1967. For Q THEATRE she scored a great success in Harold Pinter's enigmatic *The Lover* with Max Meldrum, both showing deftness in sophisticated comedy. During the first two years of Community Theatre's repertory season in 1968–69 she played 17 leading roles under contract. In 1971, contracted to the Old Tote company, she played Natalya in Ivan Turgenev's *A Month in the Country* and acted in Peter Nichols's *The National Health* and two Restoration plays. Haddy and Meldrum teamed successfully again in Michael Frayn's *The Two of Us* in 1972, and in Terence Rattigan's *In Praise of Love* in 1974 for the MARIAN STREET THEATRE COMPANY. In 1984 Haddy appeared for the SYDNEY THEATRE COMPANY in Garson Kanin's *Born Yesterday*, with her husband JAMES CONDON for the first time since Thomas Muschamp's *The Brass Hat* for the Old Tote in 1969. ❦*Lynne Murphy*

Jennifer Hagan

Actor. Born 5 October 1943 in Perth. Graduated from National Institute of Dramatic Art (Sydney) 1963. Toured in Shakespeare with Young Elizabethan Players 1964–65. Old Tote Theatre Company (Sydney) 1967. National Theatre Company (Perth) 1968–69. Community Theatre (Sydney) 1971–72. Melbourne Theatre Company 1973–79. Returned to Sydney 1980. Began to teach acting at NIDA 1989. Married to playwright Ron Blair.

From the moment she strode onto the small stage of the Old Tote Theatre in Sydney in the title-role of Henrik Ibsen's *Hedda Gabler* in 1967, dark and febrile with flashing eyes, Jennifer Hagan showed that she was a classical actor *par excellence*. She has strong presence and a lithe, stalking gait, pervaded by a sense of danger at her best. She also excels in comedy. Her parts with the NATIONAL THEATRE COMPANY in Perth ranged widely, from Gwendolen in Oscar Wilde's *The Importance of Being Earnest* to Regina in Ibsen's *Ghosts* and Stella in Tennessee Williams's *A Streetcar Named Desire*. At the Community Theatre after a year overseas she acted in period pieces—T. W. Robertson's *Caste* and Frederick Lonsdale's *On Approval*.

Under contract to the MELBOURNE THEATRE COMPANY she appeared as Yvette in Bertolt Brecht's *Mother Courage and Her Children* in 1973, Dionyza in *Pericles* and Jennifer Dubedat in George Bernard Shaw's *The Doctor's Dilemma* in 1974, Beatrice in *Much Ado About Nothing* and Valma in JOHN POWERS's outback comedy *Shindig* in 1975, and the title-role in Sophocles' *Electra* in 1977.

In Sydney Hagan created the part of Helen in David Williamson's *TRAVELLING NORTH* for the NIMROD THEATRE COMPANY in 1979. In 1980 she joined the small band of classical actors in REX CRAMPHORN's Limited Life Shakespeare Company. She returned to Melbourne to play the title-role in Eduardo De Filippo's *Filumena* in 1981. In the same year she did her first work for a commercial management as Madge in Ronald Harwood's *The Dresser* for Helen Montagu in Sydney. Playing the Unknown Woman in *As You Desire Me* for the SYDNEY THEATRE COMPANY in 1982 drew her to Luigi Pirandello, and in 1988 she played the Mother in his *Six Characters in Search of an Author*. In 1987 she played the Marquise de Merteuil in Christopher Hampton's *Les Liaisons dangereuses* for the STATE THEATRE Company of South Australia in Adelaide. At the NATIONAL INSTITUTE OF DRAMATIC ART she began directing plays as well as teaching. She also played a notable, obsessive Agrippina in Jean Racine's *Britannicus* for the NIDA Company in 1992. ❦*Katharine Brisbane*

further reading
PAYNE, PAMELA. Command performance. *Sydney Morning Herald* 22 April 1992.

The Ham Funeral

Play in two acts by Patrick White. Written in 1947. **premiere** 15 November 1961, Union Theatre, Adelaide, by Adelaide University Theatre Guild. Cast: John Adams, Brian Bergin, Joan Bruce, Hedley Cullen, Anne Dibden, Tony Georgeson, Pat Griffith, Dan Porter, Kathleen Steele-Scott. Designer: Stanislaus Ostoja-Kotkowski. Director: John Tasker. **published** London: Eyre and Spottiswoode 1965. New York: Viking Press 1966. Melbourne: Sun 1967. Sydney: Currency Press 1985 in *Collected Plays* 1.

PATRICK WHITE mounted the first serious challenge to naturalistic theatre with *The Ham Funeral*, an expressionistic play whose characters are complex individuals who symbolise ideas. The ADELAIDE FESTIVAL OF ARTS board of governors rejected it for the 1962 festival 'because it is an abstract play which the general public will find difficult and impossible to understand'. The ADELAIDE UNIVERSITY THEATRE GUILD then gave the first production and critics and audiences acclaimed the play. The AUSTRALIAN ELIZABETHAN THEATRE TRUST transferred it to Sydney.

Inspired by William Dobell's painting *The Dead Landlord*, *The Ham Funeral* dramatises the struggle for artistic expression through the spiritual journey of the Young Man from an inert and introspective artist-in-embryo to a poet ready to embrace the world, even its landladies. The locked-in intellect of the Young Man and his evanescent spiritual guide, the Girl-Anima, are Upstairs. Downstairs, battered by the experiences of life, are the Lustys with their imprisoned passions. White manipulates audience response through a mixture of seriousness and laughter, the grotesque and the poetic. Two tattered music-hall figures feast on garbage in the street, and inside raucous, wisecracking funeral celebrations explore aspects of death, pain and guilt. The *Ham Funeral* draws on a variety of traditions and conventions. As in Greek tragedy, the hero is his own antagonist, acting out inner conflicts but finally discovering his soul through the intervention of other characters. But the play defies categorisation. Its achievement lies in the way White imposes his own ideas and style on a wealth of literary and dramatic traditions to create a unique theatrical experience. ❦*May-Brit Akerholt*

further reading
CANTRELL, LEON (ed.). *Bard, Bohemians and Bookmen*. Brisbane: University of Queensland Press 1976.

Julie Hamilton

Actor. Grew up in Adelaide. Began acting with Therry Society and other amateur groups. South Australian Theatre Company 1969–76. Major roles with Melbourne, Nimrod (Sydney), and Sydney Theatre Companies. Film and television roles from 1974. Lives in Sydney. Variety Club of Australia award 1988 and Sydney Critics' Circle award 1989 (both for *Shirley Valentine* by Willy Russell).

Julie Hamilton's wide range included Shakespeare's heroines in her early career in Adelaide—Helena in *A Midsummer Night's Dream* in 1972, Isabella in *Measure for Measure* in 1973 and Rosalind in *As You Like It* in 1975. She has also played Portia in *The Merchant of Venice*, for the MELBOURNE THEATRE COMPANY in 1977, and acted in plays by Bertolt Brecht, Anton Chekhov, Oliver Goldsmith, Henrik Ibsen, Plautus and J. M. Synge. She created the timid Wendy in DAVID WILLIAMSON's *A Handful of Friends* in Adelaide in 1976 and the ebullient good-time girl Joycie in BOB HERBERT's *No Names ... No Pack Drill* in Sydney in 1980. In 1991 she was a notable Aggie in Peter Kenna's A HARD GOD for the ENSEMBLE THEATRE COMPANY in Sydney. Hamilton showed her sense of humane comedy in the everyday at its best as Hilda Bloggs in Peter Nichols's nuclear-bomb play *When the Wind Blows* in Sydney and Melbourne in 1985 and as the rebellious housewife Shirley Valentine. ❤*F. H. Mares*

Hamlet on Ice

Pantomime. **book** Ron Blair, Michael Boddy, Marcus Cooney and cast. **lyrics and music** Grahame Bond and Rory O'Donoghue. **premiere** 14 December 1971, Nimrod Street Theatre, Sydney. **cast** Grahame Bond, John Derum, Kate Fitzpatrick, Bob Hornery, Rory O'Donoghue, John Wood. **director** Aarne Neeme.

The most frequently produced Australian musical of the 1970s, *Hamlet on Ice* has been a moneyspinner wherever it has played. It is a good night of bawdy fun which originated as the NIMROD THEATRE COMPANY's 1971 Christmas attraction. The show was to have been a hard-edged political revue but the completed scripts were deemed either too risky or too unfunny and MICHAEL BODDY suggested that the cast instead create a pantomime based on *Hamlet*.

Within the traditional form of the English pantomime, the plot concerns the plight of Hamlet, back home in Denmark after undergoing a sex-change operation in Wittenburg because he has fallen in love with his muscle-bound, bone-headed friend Horatio. Hamlet is portrayed by a beautiful woman in principal-boy guise: doublet, fishnet hose and high heels. Buttons, the court jester, is instantly smitten by the new-look Hamlet, but he must fight off the unwanted attentions of Queen Gertrude, played by a male comedian as the traditional dame. After much cross-dressing, all true identities are revealed. The pantomime element saves *Hamlet on Ice* from becoming ludicrous. Audience participation in community singing is encouraged throughout the evening. ❤*Tony Sheldon*

Handspan Theatre Company

Professional company, blending puppetry with other forms, in Melbourne, founded in 1977 by Ken Evans, Andrew Hansen, Helen Rickards, Maeve Vella, Peter J. Wilson and Christine Woodcock. **artistic director** Ken Evans.

Handspan Theatre was formed to develop new directions in puppetry. An aversion to puppets imitating actors led the company away from dialogue-based scripts towards an emphasis on visual imagery and action, and an exploration of puppetry as a medium for metaphor, parody, fantasy and spectacle. Handspan has designed material for adults, adolescents and children and for theatres, cabarets, schools and outdoor events.

Early productions like *The Mouth Show* in 1978 combined booth staging with *bunraku* and mask. Later Handspan placed the puppet and puppeteer on the open stage with other performers. It has often challenged distinctions between puppets, sets, props and costumes, particularly in NIGEL TRIFFIT's *Secrets*, which was produced in 1982 and played on several overseas tours. Handspan's production of Pablo Picasso's play *Four Little Girls*, adapted and directed by ARIETTE TAYLOR, won a UNESCO arts award at the Ibero–American Theatre Festival in Bogota (Colombia) in 1994. The company tours regularly in Australia. It maintains a full-time administration and its 31 members determine the policy to be implemented by the artistic director. ❤*Maeve Vella*

further reading
VELLA, MAEVE and HELEN RICKARDS. *Theatre of the Impossible—Puppet theatre in Australia*. Sydney: Craftsman House 1989.
The workings of Handspan. *Manipulation* May 1984.
Handspan turns 10. *Manipulation* November 1987.

Eunice Hanger

Actor, director, dramatist. Born 1911. Lecturer in drama at University of Queensland (Brisbane) 1955–72. Formed Hanger Collection of Australian playscripts. Died October 1972 in Brisbane.

Disturbed by Australian dramatists' ignorance of playwriting other than the gritty three-act realism popularised by Ray Lawler's SUMMER OF THE SEVENTEENTH DOLL, Eunice Hanger began to collect manuscripts of Australian plays in 1958, and used the collection to teach undergraduates the history of Australian theatre. The Hanger Collection in the Fryer Library at the University of Queensland now contains some 2000 unpublished playscripts—the largest collection in the country.

Hanger's own plays were popular amongst amateur groups in the 1950s and 1960s. Her verse drama *The Flood*, set in a tropical veranda-fringed bungalow during 'the wet', won a special award in the 1955 PLAYWRIGHTS' ADVISORY BOARD competition. Brisbane's TWELFTH NIGHT THEATRE—with which she had a long association — performed it on 19 October 1955. Hanger edited several anthologies of Australian drama and championed David Ireland, RAY MATHEW and PATRICK WHITE before their plays were produced or published. ❤*Richard Fotheringham*

published plays
2D and Other Plays. Brisbane: University of Queensland Press 1978. Includes *The Flood*.

other writing
Australian drama. *The Literature of Australia* (ed. Geoffrey Dutton). Melbourne: Penguin 1964.

Happenings

An anarchic spirit, long since dead, produced joyous, celebratory and ephemeral happenings between 1967 and the early 1970s. They left at best an insubstantial legacy for the fringe theatre. They had no roots here but sprang from a characteristically Australian impulse to import Americana, although attempts were made to explore Aboriginal ceremonies. In the late 1960s, Judith Gemes, Johnny Allen and the present writer staged several large events, using projections, sounds and performance, in Sydney venues such as the Cell Block Theatre and the Roundhouse. They essentially created an ambience within which people could dance, make love, or simply 'groove' on the 'total environment'. Little was rehearsed, and the loosely structured nonverbal performances staged by the Human Body—later known as the Australian Free Theatre Troupe—often went unnoticed by many in the audience.

There were other events elsewhere, often associated with theatre of the absurd. In Perth in 1967 John Aitken illegally closed a street before the opening of David Halliwell's stage play *Little Malcolm and His Struggle Against the Eunuchs* and the arriving audience was confronted with evening-suited men dancing with store dummies on the pavement to a chamber orchestra.

In 1969 performance happenings flowered briefly at 10 Cunningham Street, a Sydney experimental arts centre which was soon closed by the fire authorities. In the early 1970s in Sydney, at the Central Street Gallery and later the Power Institute of Fine Art, Paul McGillick, Mike Parr, Noel Sheridan and Albie Thoms staged free-form art actions—partly structured, participatory, thematic 'art–life' events designed to focus attention upon the event itself. Ubu Films and Ellis D. Fogg Lights staged some happening-type rock events in Melbourne and Sydney during this period, as did Tribe in Brisbane. *Clem Gorman*

The Happy Land

Burlesque in two acts adapted by Marcus Clarke from Gilbert A'Beckett and W. S. Gilbert. **premiere** 17 January 1880, Academy of Music, Melbourne. Cast: Olly Deering, John Dunn, Tilly Earle, Marie Gordon, Henry Walton. **published** Melbourne: McKinley 1880.

The Premier of Victoria, Graham Berry, facing a crucial election in 1880 over constitutional reform, banned MARCUS CLARKE's burlesque *The Happy Land* for its allegedly anti-government stance. Clarke had adapted to Victorian politics an 1873 London burlesque of the same title, which satirised William Gladstone's ministry and provoked the Lord Chamberlain into an attempt to ban it. In it three 'Popular Statesmen' create havoc in peaceful fairyland by introducing the bored fairies to party politics. Their pupils learn all too readily and discord reigns. Finally the statesmen decamp hastily back to earth.

In Melbourne the Academy of Music gave two performances in spite of the ban, which was imposed by refusal of COPYRIGHT registration. Actors inserted the word 'censored' in place of offending passages. The ensuing public controversy over the legality of the ban aired the question of theatrical CENSORSHIP more widely than ever before. In the same month the KELLY AND LEON MINSTRELS produced *The Happy Land* at the Opera House in Sydney. The *Evening News* observed that 'with equal force the same satire could be directed, by simply substituting names, against any colonial legislature or statesmen'. It was localised to New Zealand politics and produced in Wellington twice and in Dunedin, all in 1880. *Veronica Kelly*

A Hard God

Play in two acts by Peter Kenna. **premiere** 17 August 1973, Nimrod Street Theatre, Sydney. Cast: Gloria Dawn, Gerry Duggan, Kay Eklund, Frank Gallacher, Graham Rouse, Andrew Sharp, Tony Sheldon. Designer: Laurence Eastwood. Director: John Bell. **published** Sydney and London: Currency Methuen 1974, revised 1982.

One of the best-loved Australian plays, *A Hard God* is PETER KENNA's finest achievement. It is a richly comic and moving account of the struggles of a working-class Irish-Australian Catholic family trying to understand their God, as they stumble on blindly through life 'with his mercy raining down on us like thunderbolts'. Parallel stories run through the play—that of the older generation, which is centred on Aggie and Dan Cassidy and includes Dan's brothers Martin and Paddy; and that of Aggie and Dan's teenage boy Joe and his friend Jack. The older Cassidys accept disasters with stoic faith, not understanding why their God should do this to them but believing in the ultimate power of his love. Joe is discovering a more earthly love for his friend. The two stories join at the end of the play, as Joe is rejected by Jack, and Aggie has to face Dan's inevitable death from cancer. From their separate worlds mother and son find that they need each other's comfort.

The play values these people's love for one another; their sense of humour in the face of tragedy; and the power of their traditions, especially religion, in helping them face loss, the transience of earthly happiness and the uncertainty of any other happiness. The first production was notable for GLORIA DAWN's Aggie, one of the great acting performances of the 1970s. *John McCallum*

Jane Harders

Actor. Born in Toowoomba (Qld). Trained as classical dancer. Began acting with University of Queensland Dramatic Society. Later acted with College Players (Brisbane). Gained experience in music-hall and television revue. Professional debut with Old Tote Theatre Company (Sydney) 1970. Performed in opening season of Nimrod Theatre Company (Sydney) 1970. Worked mainly in Sydney in 1970s and 1980s. Many radio and television roles.

Jane Harders is a graceful, fine-boned actor with great elegance and a distinctive throaty voice that makes her shine in aristocratic classical roles like Mme Ranevskaya in Anton Chekhov's *The Cherry Orchard*. She is equally at home in musicals and broad comedy. In 1973 she toured New Zealand and Fiji in Michael Boddy and Bob Ellis's burlesque THE LEGEND OF KING O'MALLEY. She played Janet in the HARRY M. MILLER production of *The Rocky Horror Show* in Sydney in 1974. At the 1974 Adelaide Festival she created the role of Lil in the first professional production of LOUIS ESSON's 1926 play, *The Bride of Gospel Place*.

For the SYDNEY THEATRE COMPANY she played Miss Clarry in Dorothy Hewett's THE MAN FROM MUKINUPIN and Tamara in Robert David Macdonald's *Chinchilla* in 1981, Essie in George S. Kaufman and Moss Hart's *You Can't Take it with You* in 1982 and Mme Ranevskaya in 1983. She played Coral in Michael Gow's AWAY for the company in 1988 and Pearl in Ray Lawler's SUMMER OF THE SEVENTEENTH DOLL. Both productions toured to the USA. Harders's later roles include Aline Solness in Henrik Ibsen's *Master Builder* at the BELVOIR STREET THEATRE in 1991, and Clara in the musical JONAH and Raymonde in Georges Feydeau's *A Flea in her Ear* for the STATE THEATRE Company of South Australia in 1991. *Katharine Brisbane*

Frank Hardy

Dramatist. Born 1 March 1917 at Southern Cross (Vic.). Grew up in large Catholic family at Bacchus Marsh (Vic.). Joined Communist Party 1940. Enlisted 1942. Employed as artist on army journal *Salt* 1944. Joined Realist Writers' Group in Melbourne after discharge from army. Worked as a freelance writer. Began writing plays 1950. Died 28 January 1994. Brother of actor Mary Hardy.

Frank Hardy's novels and short-stories overshadowed his plays, and his outspokenness and politics made it difficult for him to achieve production other than through the leftist NEW THEATRE. Hardy's early dramatic works are social-realist in style. While awaiting trial for criminal libel over his novel *Power Without Glory* in 1950—he was acquitted—he wrote his first stage play, the one-act *Nail on the Wall*. It is about the Communist Party Dissolution Act 1950, which was invalidated by the High Court. New Theatre Melbourne performed it in 1951. It is informed by Hardy's understanding of the labour movement, characterised by clear depiction of a variety of unionist types, precise rendering of Australian idiom and a good sense of its comic possibilities—as are two later plays performed by New Theatre Sydney. *Black Diamonds* (1958) is a dramatisation of a coal-miners' sit-in strike, and *The Ringbolter* (1967) is the story of a stowaway whose discovery is a catalyst in exposing division among the ship's crew.

Hardy's most significant theatrical work, *Faces in the Street* (1988), explores the life of Henry Lawson in a drama interspersed with 13 songs composed by Martin Friedel. It was performed in Sydney, with ROBIN RAMSAY as Lawson. Also musical theatre, employing Brechtian techniques to deliver political commentary, is an unperformed adaptation of Hardy's 1971 comic novel *Outcasts of Foolgarah*. *Mary Lives!*, performed by the PLAYBOX THEATRE CENTRE in Melbourne in 1992, is about his sister Mary, a Melbourne comedian and television personality, who committed suicide in 1985. ❦*Angela O'Brien*

published play
Mary Lives! (1992). Sydney: Currency Press 1992.

Jonathan Hardy

Actor, director, singing teacher. Born 20 September 1940 in Wellington (New Zealand). Educated at Victoria University College (Wellington). Trained at New Zealand Players Drama School and London Academy of Music and Dramatic Art. Made professional debut for New Zealand Players. In England 1962–66. Toured New Zealand in Royal Shakespeare Company 1966. Worked in England and Majorca (Spain) 1967–72. Came to Australia 1972. Joined Melbourne Theatre Company 1973. Directed Mercury Theatre (Auckland) 1980–85. Member of Queensland Arts Advisory Committee 1991–92. Acts in and writes for radio and television.

Jonathan Hardy is a strong actor, noted largely for his comedy roles. He came to Sydney in 1972, after acting in ALEX BUZO's *The Front Room Boys* in London in 1971, and played the title-role in the second season of RON BLAIR's *Flash Jim Vaux*. Next year in the MELBOURNE THEATRE COMPANY he created Mad Dog in JOHN POWERS's *The Last of the Knucklemen*. He brought classical training, considerable comic skills and frenetic energy to the Australian theatre in the 1970s at a time of rapid development.

These qualities, together with his substantial build and expressive dark, bushy eyebrows have made Hardy a familiar figure on television and natural casting for roles like Tony Hancock in Heathcote Williams's *Hancock's Last Half-Hour*, Propitchkin in an adaptation of Nikolai Gogol's *Diary of a Madman* and Toby Belch in *Twelfth Night*. A critic described his Dromio of Syracuse in *The Comedy of Errors* as 'an idiot of extraordinary latent intelligence'. In addition to acting, teaching, and directing plays, operas and films Hardy is a prolific and successful writer for film and television. His remarkable output led to a breakdown in his health in 1986, and in 1988 he received a heart transplant. But this barely slowed the pace. He continued to write for the screen and in 1991 he returned to the stage as Danforth in Arthur Miller's *The Crucible* for the QUEENSLAND THEATRE COMPANY. As a director, his first love is opera and he has directed many works for Victoria State Opera and the New Zealand Opera Company. As a teacher he has been generous in supporting and training young talent in Australia and New Zealand. ❦*Katharine Brisbane*

Alan Harkness

Actor, director. Born 1908 in Western Australia. Studied art at Perth Technical College and National Gallery School (Melbourne). Acted with Allan Wilkie Shakespearean Company until 1930. Co-founded Ab Intra Studio Theatre (Adelaide) 1931. Began studying with Michael Chekhov in England 1935. Went to USA with Chekhov's company 1939. Married Swiss actress Mechthild Johannsen 1946. Died 2 March 1952 in car–train accident at Ojai (California).

For Alan Harkness true theatre consisted of mime, movement, pattern, colour and light—endless dialogue was merely literature adapted to the stage. He also believed that portrayal of character must be inspired within the actor, and that there was unlimited scope for creating the inner content of a play orally, mentally, emotionally and atmospherically. He put these theories into practice from 1931 to 1935 in AB INTRA STUDIO THEATRE, which he and KESTER BARUCH founded in Adelaide.

In England in 1935 Harkness met Michael Chekhov, who had worked with Konstantin Stanislavsky and held theories that accorded with Harkness's own less developed views. Chekhov gave Harkness a scholarship to his Chekhov Studio Theatre at Dartington Hall in Devon. At the outbreak of the Second World War the company moved to the USA and Harkness became Chekhov's assistant director. When the USA entered the war Chekhov disbanded the company.

Harkness and other members moved to southern California. After the war they formed High Valley Theatre at Santa Barbara with Harkness as director and playwright. He was travelling to a rehearsal when he was killed in a level-crossing smash in 1952. In 1969 his widow and their son came to Sydney. She worked as voice coach for the OLD TOTE THEATRE COMPANY until 1974 and later set up a school of speech, eurhythmics, improvisation and drama. She died in Sydney in 1986. ❦*Thelma Afford*

Harlequin in Australia Felix

—*or, Geelong in an Uproar*. Pantomime. **premiere** 21 January 1845, Albert Theatre, Geelong (Vic.).

Apparently the first wholly Australian PANTOMIME, *Harlequin in Australia Felix* is known only from an advertisement in the *Geelong Advertiser* of 18 January 1845. Its unknown author departed from the usual 19th-century pantomime by setting its opening scenes not in some fantasy land but in Geelong. The hero, later to be transformed into Harlequin, was 'Luckless Looseall, (a Tax-Ridden Settler in Search of a Wife)'. The heroine, later to become Columbine, was Flora, daughter of Araminta Shortweight 'widow of a wealthy Storekeeper, fond of the ready'. This was a dame part, played by the male actor who was to be transformed into Pantaloon. The other mortal character in the opening scenes, who was to become Clown in the harlequinade, was another clearly recognisable local type, 'Gregory Graball, (a Wealthy Speculator, just arrived)'. The harlequinade included several local scenes, which had become customary in pantomime in Australia, as well as some of the traditional clowning with fishes and meat pies. Another local touch was that staple of the 19th-century Australian stage, the bushranger. As usual, all ended happily, with the characters retransformed and the lovers united by the Queen of the Stars. ♥*Elizabeth Webby*

Charles Harpur

Dramatist. Born 23 January 1813 at Windsor (NSW). Acted at Theatre Royal, Sydney, October 1833. Died 10 June 1868 at Eurobodalla (NSW).

The first Australian-born playwright was Charles Harpur. The child of convicts, he became convinced early in life of his role as Australia's first notable poet—a vision endorsed by posterity but shared by few of his contemporaries. He was employed as an actor at the Theatre Royal in Sydney but his lack of stage experience and training soon became apparent and BARNETT LEVEY sacked him. Harpur sued unsuccessfully for unpaid salary.

His experiences at the theatre left their mark on his first attempt to write for the stage, but his reading of Shakespeare was a stronger influence. Harpur showed his play *The Tragedy of Donohoe* to Edward Smith Hall, editor of the *Sydney Monitor*. On 10 May 1834 Hall published an article on Harpur and his play. He felt that Harpur should abandon his attempt at blank verse, that the bushranger Donohoe was too vulgar to be a tragic hero and that Shakespearean ghosts and witches were inappropriate in an Australian play, but he praised *The Tragedy of Donohoe* as 'superior to half the stuff' being performed at the Theatre Royal. Hall recognised the strong appeal of a local subject for local audiences and predicted that, if performed, the play would be a success.

A production was impossible in mid-1830s Sydney, however, given Harpur's falling-out with Levey and the colonial authorities' reluctance to license plays dealing with such local issues as bushranging. Hall's article suggested that the play was entirely in blank verse but when he published extracts on 7–28 February 1835, some scenes were in prose, so Harpur may have rewritten it. He did rewrite it later and it was published in Sydney in 1853 as the centrepiece of his *Bushrangers, a play in five acts, and other poems*. Further rewriting resulted in yet another version, STALWART THE BUSHRANGER, completed in 1867. Harpur noted in a postscript that the 1853 version had been condemned on the grounds of its subject matter rather than properly considered on its merits as a play, and that this discouragement had turned him against writing for the stage. What 'a happy time was Shakespeare's, when the only critic was a lively audience', he concluded. ♥*Elizabeth Webby*

published plays
Stalwart the Bushranger with *The Tragedy of Donohoe*. Sydney: Currency Press 1987 (ed. Elizabeth Perkins).

further reading
NORMINGTON, RAWLING J. *Charles Harpur, an Australian*. Sydney: Angus and Robertson 1962.
NORMINGTON, RAWLING J. Charles Harpur. *Australian Dictionary of Biography* 1. Melbourne University Press 1966.

Martin Harris

Actor. Born c.1944. Early training at New Theatre, Sydney. Worked as a labourer, signwriter and storeman. Studied at National Institute of Dramatic Art (Sydney) 1964–65. Toured with Young Elizabethan Players. Acted at Jane Street Theatre, Sydney, from 1966. Nimrod Theatre Company (Sydney).

The early career of Martin Harris, an outstanding, wiry actor, coincided with the rise of aggressive Australian theatre and his work became synonymous with the muscular new style. While he also appeared comfortably in plays like Somerset Maugham's *Home and Beauty*, his forte was the role that celebrated the Australian character in its variety. In the first season of Australian plays at the JANE STREET THEATRE in 1966 Harris created Colin in James Searle's *The Lucky Streak* and Penthouse in RODNEY MILGATE's *A Refined Look at Existence*. In 1968 he played Snowy Baker in DOROTHY HEWETT's *This Old Man Comes Rolling Home* at the Old Tote Theatre. He played Tosser in the premiere of JIM MCNEIL's *The Chocolate Frog* in 1971.

At Jane Street in 1972 Harris created Father Lawrence Henry in THOMAS KENEALLY's *An Awful Rose* and played the title-role in JOHN CLARK's landmark production of David Williamson's *Don's Party*. In 1972 he also played Kenny in the NIMROD THEATRE COMPANY's production of Williamson's THE REMOVALISTS. He played the same role in the 1975 film version. In 1974 he created Mick in McNeil's *How Does Your Garden Grow*. He continued to work at intervals in theatre, film and television until he succumbed to drug and alcohol addiction dating from the 1970s. In 1980 he created Hugh Burton in THOMAS KENEALLY's *Bullie's House*. He last acted on stage as Michael Webb in Stephen Sewell's THE BLIND GIANT IS DANCING in Canberra in 1984. ♥*Katharine Brisbane*

Wayne Harrison

Actor, director, dramaturge. Born 7 March 1953 in Melbourne. Mother was soubrette in variety and musical theatre. Began singing and dancing lessons at three. Professional debut at seven in pantomime. Regular child performer in musicals and on television. Educated at Universities of Melbourne and NSW. Worked as arts journalist and in other jobs. Dramaturge and resident director with Sydney Theatre Company 1981–87. Assistant director of Northside Theatre Company (Sydney) 1987–89. Director of Dramaturgical Services Inc. 1987–90. On secondment to Royal National Theatre of Great Britain 1990. Director of Sydney Theatre Company 1990–.

By choosing Wayne Harrison as its director in 1990 the SYDNEY THEATRE COMPANY gave new status to dramaturgy. He was the first dramaturge appointed to the staff of a state theatre company and he has considerably influenced the development of some playwrights. His historical knowledge and his grassroots experience of commercial theatre —he was in *A Little Night Music, Gypsy, Man of La Mancha* and other J. C. WILLIAMSON's musicals—were appropriate to the changing needs of theatre and to the widening responsibilities of the director of a company. Harrison's first production for the company was Pamela van Amstel's *Late Arrivals* in 1985. Other Australian works followed—DAVID HOLMAN's *No Worries* and Tim Gooding's *King of Country* in 1986 and John Romeril's THE FLOATING WORLD in 1987.

As dramaturge and director (with RICHARD WHERRETT) of *The Floating World* Harrison was the first to address the task of transforming a major work from the contemporary alternative theatre for the mainstage. After this he worked on developing text with writers like ALEX BUZO, MICHAEL GOW, FRANK HARDY and DAVID WILLIAMSON. In 1989 he directed Larry Kramer's American drama *The Normal Heart*. His productions for this company also include Lanford Wilson's *Burn This* in 1990, the musicals *A Little Night Music* in 1991 and *Into the Woods* in 1993, *Much Ado About Nothing* in 1992 and Mary Morris's popular children's play *Two Weeks with the Queen* several times in 1992–94. A need to empower the actor and to bridge the gap between audience and actor has characterised his productions.

To this end he has involved the Sydney Theatre Company in daylight performance of Elizabethan plays and in studio reassessment of the European and American repertoires. Harrison and PHILIP PARSONS initiated experiments into Elizabethan production methods in 1986, presenting Christopher Marlowe's *Doctor Faustus* under daylight conditions. At the Sydney Theatre Company Harrison encouraged further experiment by giving Michael Gow studio facilities to work as a director and writer; and in 1992 he invited JOHN HOWARD to form a multicultural troupe of actors to create works and tour country districts.

For the Northside Theatre Company Harrison directed Hugh Whitemore's *Breaking the Code* and Alex Buzo's *Shellcove Road*. He also adapted Bob Larbey's popular *A Month of Sundays* to an Australian setting, and developed and directed Frank Hardy's Henry Lawson play *Faces in the Street* for the 1988 Festival of Sydney. In 1992 Harrison directed Gow's *On Top of the World* at Croydon in England. ❦*Katharine Brisbane*

writings
Entertainment as Australian history—the late 19th century example. University of NSW BA(hons) thesis 1979.

further reading
BRISBANE, KATHARINE. Stage presence. *Good Weekend* (Sydney) 31 December 1994.
HOWIE, ANN C. (ed.). *Who's Who in Australia* 27th edn. Melbourne: Information Australia 1991.

Harvest Theatre Company

Touring dramatic company in South Australia, formed in 1982 by Eyre Peninsula Regional Cultural Centre Trust at Port Lincoln. Closed June 1991. **artistic directors** 1982 Nick Hughes. 1983–84 Mike McLaren. 1985–87 Brian Debnam. 1988–91 Garry Fry. **first production** *Get Big or Get Out* 1982. Director: Nick Hughes.

A unique initiative of the Eyre Peninsula Regional Cultural Centre Trust, the Harvest Theatre Company began in 1982 with a community work about farming issues. Next year it shifted its focus from COMMUNITY THEATRE to become a touring company serving the towns of Mount Gambier, Port Augusta, Port Lincoln, Port Pirie, Renmark and Whyalla. It began receiving South Australian government funding in 1985. This was withdrawn in 1991 and the company disbanded. Its productions had included *A Streetcar Named Desire* by Tennessee Williams, directed by LESLIE DAYMAN and starring HELEN MORSE, *Middle Age Spread* by Roger Hall, *Songs from Sideshow Alley* by ROBYN ARCHER, and *Down an Alley Filled with Cats* by Warwick Moss. ❦*Murray Bramwell*

Frank Harvey

Actor, director, dramatist. Born 22 December 1885 in Jersey (Channel Islands). Son of French actor-manager and playwright who worked in England as Frank Harvey. Acted in London. Played leading roles for J. C. Williamson's in Australia 1914–26. Returned from England 1931. Acted on ABC radio, Sydney, from 1935. Wrote screenplays for Cinesound 1935–39. Produced and acted at Minerva Theatre, Sydney, 1939. ABC radio drama producer 1942–50. Died 10 October 1965 in Sydney.

For more than two decades Frank Harvey was the most renowned leading man in Australian professional theatre. He came to Australia in 1914 for J. C. WILLIAMSON's to play in *Joseph and His Brethren* by Louis N. Parker and remained for 12 years, working continuously for the Firm. He was Marie Tempest's leading man in 1916. In 1921 he acted with Maude Hanaford in *Scandal* by Cosmo Hamilton and *Adam and Eva* by Guy Bolton and George Middleton. His most notable association was with EMELIE POLINI, particularly in Edward Knoblock's *My Lady's Dress*, in the nine scenes of which he played seven different roles. As MURIEL STARR's leading man in 1924, he excelled as Monsieur Beaucaire and in *Seventh Heaven* by Austin Strong.

After a 'farewell to Australia' in *The Silver King* by Henry Arthur Jones and Henry Herman, he returned to England in 1926. He was back in Australia in 1931, playing a gangster in Edgar Wallace's *On the Spot*. Wallace's *The Calendar* followed. Then, with the English actor Iris Darbyshire, he repeated his success in *My Lady's Dress*. One critic wrote: 'Each character is as separate and individual as if he had been the only one Harvey created in the night. He completes, in one evening, seven different lives.' Harvey followed this by directing and acting in his own *Cape Forlorn*. From 1935 he performed in some of the films he wrote for Cinesound and acted on ABC radio. By 1943 he was the ABC's chief drama producer, esteemed as a great influence on younger actors. ❦*Richard Lane*

Henry Richard Harwood

Actor, manager. Born in London 19 October 1830. Began work as builder and contractor. Came to Australia 1852. Began acting at Royal Victoria Theatre, Sydney, 1855. Co-manager of Theatre Royal, Melbourne, 1867–77. Resumed acting in 1890s. Died in Melbourne 16 April, 1898. Second wife was actor Docie Stewart.

Opinions vary on the acting of Henry Richard Harwood, who played many roles, especially comic parts. He was often praised for his great versatility, but his sister-in-law NELLIE STEWART described him as 'ponderously unctuous' and out-of-date. He began acting as Flavius Corunna in John Howard Payne's *Brutus* during G. V. BROOKE's first engagement at the Royal Victoria Theatre in Sydney in 1855. After playing several utility parts he was engaged as prompter and gained experience in stage management.

After a visit to New Zealand he played Blueskin in J. B. Buckstone's *Jack Sheppard* at Ballarat, then went to Geelong, where he specialised in equestrian parts for G. B. Lewis, including Mazeppa, whom he played without a double. In 1867 he embarked on theatrical management in partnership with Messrs Lambert, Vincent, Bellair and John Hennings at the Theatre Royal in Melbourne. This firm later became Harwood, Stewart, Hennings and Coppin. Harwood lost money in the banking crisis of 1893 and was forced to resume his stage career. ❦*Joan Maslen*

further reading
Australasian (Melbourne) 23 April 1898.
Leader (Melbourne) 23 April 1898.
Men of the Time in Australia—Victorian Series. Melbourne: McCarron Bird 1878.
Tatler (Melbourne) 30 April 1898.

Paul Hasluck KG GCMG GCVO

Critic. Born 1 April 1905 in Fremantle (WA). Educated at University of Western Australia. Amateur actor with University Dramatic Society and Repertory Club (Perth) in 1930s. Drama critic of *West Australian* as 'Polygon' 1933–38. Active member of Canberra Repertory Society from 1941; president 1943. Liberal MHR for Curtin 1949–69. Cabinet minister in various portfolios 1956–69. Governor-General of Australia 1969–74. GCMG 1969, GCVO 1970, KG 1979. Died 9 January 1993.

A forceful advocate for Australian writers, Paul Hasluck made a deeper impact as dramatic critic for Western Australia's daily newspaper than his short period of service suggests. Terry Craig writes: '"Polygon" wrote with a clarity and depth of dramatic criticism unmatched before or since. His reviews, or perhaps more appropriately his essays of Shavian proportion, revealed a highly intellectual mind and thorough understanding of the arts. His precise and articulate reporting reached the height of journalistic excellence which he later attributed to his historical research skills and university studies. In his autobiography he says, far too modestly: "I think we can claim that the two of us [the other was the music critic A. H. Kornweibel] gave our paper a sound reputation for well-informed and perceptive discussion of music and the stage and did something to advance the practice and raise the standards of appreciation of both in Western Australia".'

In 1937 Hasluck initiated the annual Western Australian Drama Festivals, in which country and metropolitan clubs competed at His Majesty's Theatre. They were sponsored by West Australian Newspapers and the REPERTORY CLUB and Hasluck was an adjudicator of the first two. He directed the first Australian productions of T. S. Eliot's *Murder in the Cathedral* and Dorothy Sayers's *The Zeal of Thine House* for St George's College at the University of Western Australia in 1938 and 1939 respectively. While at university in the 1920s he wrote a one-act play, *A Game of Billiards*. The university magazine published it and WILLIAM MOORE produced it in Sydney. ❦*Katharine Brisbane*

published play
A game of billiards. In *The Black Swan* (Perth) September 1931.
other writings
Mucking About. Melbourne University Press 1977.
further reading
Craig, Terry. Radical and conservative theatre in Perth in the 1930s. *Western Australia Between the Wars* (ed. Jenny Gregory). Perth: University of Western Australia 1990.
Who's Who in Australia 1991. Melbourne: Information Australia.

Alexander Hay

Actor, director, teacher. Born 31 December 1919 in London. Originally John Alexander Lindsay. Studied at Royal Academy of Dramatic Art after audition for Violet Vanbrugh and George Bernard Shaw. Acted in Donald Wolfit's company. Founded small theatre in St Andrews (Scotland). Abandoned theatre and emigrated to South Australia c.1954. Returned to acting and directing after fire devastated his Adelaide Hills property. Toured Central Australia in solo show. Head of acting at National Institute of Dramatic Art (Sydney) 1971–76. Artistic director of Australian National Playwrights' Conference 1975. Died c.22 July 1987 in Sydney.

Alexander Hay had an enormous influence on an important generation of acting students at the NATIONAL INSTITUTE OF DRAMATIC ART. He left them with a touch of his style and consistently instilled into an unbelieving generation his 'rule of poverty', the 'right to fail', and the notion of acting as a sacred profession. A fastidious professional with a reputation as a traditional artist, Hay acted others off the stage in classical parts such as Holofernes in William Gaskill's 1977 production of *Love's Labour's Lost*. Sydney theatregoers were attracted to the OLD TOTE THEATRE COMPANY's productions of Edward Albee's *Who's Afraid of Virginia Woolf?* in 1964 Rolf Hochhuth's *The Representative* in 1965 as much by Hay's interpretations of George and the Pope respectively as by the plays.

Hay's eccentric, mannered style and his saturnine looks divided the theatrical world. They also made him less employable as he aged and local theatre directors looked for more naturalistic 'Australian' types in their casting. In his fading years he became at once the old man of the theatre and an experimenter outrageously ahead of his time. His ventures into anti-naturalism brought him roles in KIM CARPENTER's *Slice* in 1981 and many campus contracts. His skill as a raconteur provided the basis for his solo show *The Pale Sergeant* in Sydney from July 1981, and his macabre storytelling inspired Thomas Keneally's novel *The Survivor*.

Hay was first noted in Sydney in *The Devil's Advocate*, adapted from Morris West's novel by Dore Schary, for INDEPENDENT THEATRE in 1967. He directed Keneally's play *Halloran's Little Boat* in the Old Tote Theatre Company's first JANE STREET THEATRE season in 1966. His more unusual productions included DOROTHY HEWETT's *The Tatty Hollow Story* in 1976, Jean Genet's *The Maids* with himself as Madame in Sydney in 1977 and *A Midsummer Night's Dream* in Indonesian *wayang-kulit* style at the University of Western Australia in 1982. Hay's last role was in *An Imaginary Life*, an adaptation of David Malouf's novel by KIM CARPENTER, in Sydney in 1986. Failing voice and amputation of a leg in 1987 led him to retire. He died after cutting short a trip to Java. ❦*Helen Musa*

Evie Hayes

Actor, singer. Born 1911 in Seattle (Washington, USA). Made debut at six, touring USA in children's speciality act. Spent several years in Hollywood. Had radio program in New York City. Came to Australia with husband, vaudeville star Will Mahoney 1938. Presented variety shows for troops at Cremorne Theatre, Brisbane, during Second World War. Extraordinarily successful in *Annie Get Your Gun* in 1947 and *Call Me Madam* in 1954. Popular early television performer. Died 26 December 1988 in Melbourne.

The career of Evie Hayes took a turn in 1947, when J. C. WILLIAMSON'S gave her the title-role in *Annie Get Your Gun* after JENNY HOWARD had been announced for it. Hayes played Annie Oakley more than 3500 times and became so identified with the role that managements offered her virtually every other part created on Broadway by Ethel Merman. In 1947 Hayes was already a seasoned performer. In Hollywood she had appeared in musical shorts for Warner Brothers, moved to Metro–Goldwyn–Mayer, where Cecil B. DeMille cast her in his 1930 extravaganza *Madam Satan*, and been a contract player with Fox Films. She had her own radio program in New York, and made frequent guest appearances on Rudy Vallee's radio show.

From 1933 Hayes appeared with the vaudeville star WILL MAHONEY. They had a Palladium season in London in 1935 and in 1938 they came to Australia on their honeymoon. They became well known in revue and variety. During the Second World War they toured extensively and presented variety shows for the troops at the Cremorne Theatre in Brisbane. Hayes was much sought after as principal boy in pantomimes for the TIVOLI CIRCUIT.

After Annie Oakley, Hayes's next great success was in another Merman role, Mrs Sally Adams in *Call Me Madam* in 1954, again for J. C. Williamson's. In between these roles, audiences in Perth and Adelaide saw her teamed with HAYES GORDON in *Kiss Me, Kate*, a revival of *Annie Get Your Gun* and *Oklahoma!*, in which she played Ado Annie.

When television arrived in 1956, Hayes became a popular personality, appearing in her own tonight-show. She returned to the musical stage in 1966 to play Mrs Brice in *Funny Girl* for J. C. Williamson's. Will Mahoney, also in the cast as Mr Keeny, died during the show's run. In later years, Hayes devoted her energies to training and encouraging child performers, and she was a permanent judge on the television program *Young Talent Time*. Stricken with multiple sclerosis in 1974, she retired to write her autobiography, which was completed after her death by her friend John Compton. Five weeks before she died she made her last stage appearance, in the Nancye Bridges Vaudeville Show at World Expo '88 in Brisbane. ❦*Tony Sheldon*

further reading
BEVAN, IAN. *The Story of the Theatre Royal*. Sydney: Currency Press 1993.
CROMPTON, JOHN. *And I Loves Ya Back—Evie Hayes*. 1992.

Nancye Hayes OAM

Actor, dancer. Born 1944 in Sydney. Studied dance with Hazel Meldrum. Performed in amateur musicals. In J. C. Williamson choruses from 1960. First title-role, in *Sweet Charity*, 1967. OAM for services to performing arts 1981.

Vivacious, blonde Nancy Hayes rose from chorus lines to stardom in musicals and drama during the late 1960s. At 16 she won a place in the chorus of the long-running J. C. WILLIAMSON'S production of *My Fair Lady*. Two years later she auditioned for *Bye Bye Birdie*, but was told she looked too old to play a teenager. She was rewarded, however, with a place in the Williamson chorus for *How to Succeed in Business Without Really Trying*. She was moved up to understudy the role of Hedy La Rue after reading one line with a Bronx accent, and she took over the role when the American star Betty McGuire returned home after a year. In 1965 FRED HEBERT cast Hayes as Mrs Rose in the J. C. Williamson's production of *Hello, Dolly!* but she was called as an emergency understudy to JILL PERRYMAN as Irene Molloy when Perryman replaced the ailing star, Carole Cook, within the first week. Hayes left *Hello, Dolly!* to take the comic role of Luce in the Firm's production of *The Boys from Syracuse*. Then she moved to the theatre-restaurant at the Menzies Hotel in Sydney, where HAYES GORDON was directing potted musicals, and played Lois in *Kiss Me, Kate* and Meg in *Brigadoon*. In 1967 J. C. Williamson's failed to obtain Betty Grable for the title-role in *Sweet Charity*. With Gordon's encouragement, Hayes auditioned for the part. She won it and gave a luminous performance that instantly elevated her to stardom.

JON EWING brought her back to the Menzies Hotel for the starring roles in *Annie Get Your Gun* and *Little Me*. In 1969 she starred in HARRY M. MILLER'S production of *Dames at Sea* and she has since appeared in numerous musicals and plays. Hayes scored successes as Roxie in the SYDNEY THEATRE COMPANY'S production of *Chicago* in 1981, as Adelaide in *Guys and Dolls* in 1986 and as Dorothy Brock in *42nd Street* in 1990–03. In 1987 she played Mrs Lovett in *Sweeney Todd* as a guest artist with the State Opera of South Australia. In 1993 she played Stella Deems in *Follies in Concert* for the Melbourne Festival of Arts. In 1994 she appeared in *Legends* at the Sydney Opera House and choreographed *Falsettos* for the Sydney Theatre Company. ❦*Tony Sheldon*

Leslie Haylen

Dramatist. Born 23 September 1899 near Canberra. In army 1917–19. Journalist 1920–43. Labor MHR for Parkes 1943–64. Published two plays, seven novels, two books of memoirs, articles, short stories and verse 1933–69. Died 11 September 1977 in Sydney.

Leslie Haylen's play *Two Minutes' Silence* ran to full houses for 24 nights over six months from 15 July 1930 at CARRIE TENNANT'S Community Playhouse in Sydney, where the average run was nine or ten nights. The *Sydney Morning Herald* rightly praised Haylen's structure as ingenious. In the first scene, a general in Europe presides over his servants and employees in observance of two minutes' silence on the anniversary of the 1918 armistice. Each underling is then the main figure in a 'flashback' that reveals how the war had blighted their life and how the general had perpetrated an unsuccessful 'surprise attack'. The antiwar theme is effectively understated, for the general meets no retribution and the others' lives are not transformed. A film version released in February 1934 met mixed critical reaction; it no longer exists. Haylen's unproduced plays include *Blood on the Wattle*, a lively but unfocused treatment of the Eureka Stockade episode of 1854. ❦*Dennis Carroll*

published plays
Blood on the Wattle. Sydney: Angus and Robertson 1948.
Two Minutes' Silence (1930). Sydney: Macquarie Head Press 1933.

further reading
SHIRLEY, GRAHAM and BRIAN ADAMS. *Australian Cinema* revised. Sydney: Currency Press 1989.
Sydney Morning Herald 13 September 1977.

reference
Three unproduced and unpublished plays by Haylen—*Change of Policy*, *Freedom has a Beard* and *The Stormy Blast Vietnam*—are in his papers in the National Library of Australia (Canberra).

Haymarket Theatre

Theatre in Bourke Street, Melbourne, opened 15 September 1862, seating 2500. Destroyed by fire 22 September 1871.

The Haymarket Theatre, said GEORGE COPPIN proudly when it opened in 1862, 'is the fifth theatre I have built at my own expense'. He had built it because he was forced out of his preferred playhouse, the THEATRE ROYAL, farther west in Bourke Street. The Haymarket housed some remarkable talents. It opened with the American actor JOSEPH JEFFERSON, one of Coppin's celebrities. CHARLES and ELLEN KEAN, imported for the Haymarket in 1863, faced stiff competition from BARRY SULLIVAN at the Theatre Royal. Later performers were less starry and no-one seemed to regret the Haymarket's demise in 1871. 'It was the ugliest and most cheerless place of amusement in the colonies', said the *Australasian* after the fire. There was a long walk from the street through an unroofed vestibule to the theatre proper. Dress-circle patrons went 'up steps and along a dreary corridor'. On the plus side, 'there was more space to sit in and to stretch one's legs than at the Royal, it was better ventilated and … there was a much better view of the stage than in the latter house. To be sure, the eye rested on ugly beams, angles, iron rods, gaunt pillars, and a good deal of blank wall.' ❦*John West*

Chris Haywood

Actor. Born 24 July 1948 in Billericay (Essex, England). Trained at E15 Acting School (London). Worked with Barn Theatre, Loughton (Essex). Came to Australia 1970. Nimrod Theatre Company (Sydney). Artistic director of Ormond School workshops 1974–75. Artistic director of Pros and Cons Playhouse at Parramatta Jail (NSW) 1979–91. In many films and television productions.

Chris Haywood is better known for his work on the screen than in the theatre, but in the early 1970s he was a leading actor at the Nimrod Street Theatre in Sydney. He joined the NIMROD THEATRE COMPANY as a volunteer labourer, through its technical director, LAURENCE EASTWOOD, with whom he had worked in the English theatre. Haywood's eventual parts included the removalist in David Williamson's THE REMOVALISTS in 1971, Crow in Sam Shepard's *The Tooth of Crime* in 1973—which he considers his best theatre role—and Jim in ALMA DE GROEN's *Going Home* in 1977. He also appeared in OLD TOTE THEATRE COMPANY productions, including *The Resistible Rise of Arturo Ui* by Bertolt Brecht and *The Government Inspector* by Nikolai Gogol. Haywood takes the view that theatre should be for the disadvantaged. In many ways he considers his work with prisoners at Parramatta Jail and with youth at Ormond School, a welfare home, to be far more important than his time at Nimrod Street. ❦*Janet Greason*

Noni Hazlehurst AM

Actor. Born 17 August 1953 in Melbourne. Originally Leonie Elva Hazlehurst. Descended from four generations of British variety performers on both sides of family. Educated at Flinders University (Adelaide). BA 1973. Privately studied ballet, singing, piano, speech and drama. Began acting at Theatre '62 (Adelaide) 1972. Has worked mainly with Sydney Theatre Company. Member of Company B at Belvoir Street Theatre (Sydney) 1984–85; chair 1985. Has directed productions for National Institute of Dramatic Art, (Sydney) and for 1982 Women and Arts Festival in NSW. Numerous film and television roles. Australian Artists' Creative Fellowship 1990–92. AM 1995.

An actor of considerable talent, Noni Hazlehurst first performed as a singer with a jazz band in Adelaide. The first major production in which she acted was GEORGE WHALEY's adaptation of *ON OUR SELECTION* in Sydney in 1978. Next year she created Polly and Lily in the premiere of Dorothy Hewett's musical play THE MAN FROM MUKINUPIN in Perth. She played the dual role again for the SYDNEY THEATRE COMPANY in 1981. With the same company in 1980 she played Dai-Yu in the Australian premiere of LOUIS NOWRA's *The Precious Woman* (1980) and Kathy in the Sydney premiere of BOB HERBERT's *No Names … No Pack Drill*. In 1980 she also played Anita and Ekatarina in the Sydney premiere of Stephen Sewell's TRAITORS. She is most widely known for her performances in films and children's television. ❦*Janet Greason*

Fred Hebert

American director, c.1912–72. Directed musicals and plays in Australia for J. C. Williamson's from 1957.

One of the successes of the J. C. WILLIAMSON's policy of importing Americans to direct productions of Broadway musicals was Fred Hebert. Many who came to Australia after the Second World War did their job and disappeared but Hebert made his mark and returned again and again, directing almost a dozen productions, plays as well as musicals. Like many of the other imports, Hebert was a production stage manager from New York. With the experience of overseeing a long Broadway run, these men were well trained to provide copycat productions in Australia with American talent—often minor—in the lead roles. This was what their Australian producers expected.

Hebert came to Australia in 1957 to direct *The Pajama Game* after two and a half years' involvement in the Broadway production. There were no imports in the Australian cast. TONI LAMOND was Babe, William Newman was Sid, Keith Petersen was the comedy lead Hines, Tikki Taylor had the sure-fire comic role of Gladys, and JILL PERRYMAN acted against her usual style as Mabel. Betty Pounder restaged the choreography, which she had been sent to New York to absorb.

The program notes said of Hebert: 'He has staged a perfect replica of the New York show here, and assures our audiences that what they see stands in most favourable comparison with the New York and London presentations of this difficult production'.

Hebert returned in 1965 to begin a long series of directing jobs, beginning with the musical *Hello, Dolly!* and Samuel Taylor's play *Beekman Place*, starring Googie Withers and Richard Wordsworth. In 1966 he presided over the production of *Funny Girl* that confirmed JILL PERRYMAN as a star. A year later he directed *Sweet Charity*, which did the same for NANCYE HAYES, and *Fiddler on the Roof*, which brought HAYES GORDON back to the commercial musical. In 1969 Hebert directed the two-hander musical *I Do, I Do* with Stephen Douglass, an American import, and Jill Perryman, who to some sounded more fun than Mary Martin on the Broadway cast recording. ❦*John West*

O. P. Heggie

Actor. Born 17 September 1879 at Angaston (SA). Made professional debut in *Stolen Kisses* at Theatre Royal, Adelaide, 1899. London debut 1906. Toured USA with Ellen Terry 1907. Acted in London and New York. Acted in some 30 Hollywood films 1927–36. Died 7 February 1936 in Hollywood (California, USA).

One of the gifts of Otto Peter Heggie was the ability to project an illusion of old age. He developed his talent for character acting from 1899 to 1905, playing many small but significant roles in W. F. Hawtrey's touring company in Australia. Before he made his professional debut he had attended the Elder Conservatorium in Adelaide with the idea of becoming a singer and worked in a bank while appearing with amateur companies. ❦*Charles Grahame*

further reading
JONES, K. D. and A. S. MCCLURE and A. E. TOOMEY. *Character People—The stalwarts of the cinema*. New York: A. S. Barnes.
PARISH, JAMES ROBERT. *Hollywood Character Actors*. New Rochelle (New York, USA): Arlington House 1978.
Who's Who in the Theatre 8th edn. London: Pitman and Sons 1936.

Helen's Babies

Play by Garnet Walch, from novella by John Habberton. **premiere** 20 July 1877, Theatre Royal, Melbourne. Cast: Alfred Dampier, Lily Dampier, Rose Dampier, Maggie Stewart, Nellie Stewart. Director: Alfred Dampier.

ALFRED DAMPIER had great success with his production of *Helen's Babies*, a vehicle for himself and his small daughters LILY and ROSE. GARNET WALCH based the comedy on a popular American novella about a confirmed bachelor uncle who unwittingly agrees to look after his sister's children while she takes a holiday. Farce about his ineptitude in the face of two mischievous young devils becomes romance as this trial fatherhood breaks down his resistance to marriage and impresses Helen's friend Alice. Young NELLIE STEWART played Alice in Dampier's production. Dampier also presented *Helen's Babies* on a long tour of the USA, including a successful New York engagement from 14 February 1878. The author of the novella, John Habberton saw the play and is supposed to have been delighted. *Helen's Babies* was also performed in London in 1878. It was only ever a curtainraiser, as it ran less than an hour. Another version of the story, *The Imps* by ARCHIBALD MURRAY, had a season in Sydney in November 1880. ❦*Richard Fotheringham*

reference
A script is held in the British Library (London), add. ms 53205K.

Robert Helpmann KBE

Actor, choreographer, dancer. Born 9 April 1909 at Mount Gambier (SA). Professional debut, dancing as Bobbie Helpman, in Adelaide 1923. Changed surname while dancing in Anna Pavlova's company 1926. Involved in Ab Intra Studio Theatre (Adelaide). Joined Vic–Wells Ballet in London 1933. Left Royal Ballet to work as actor and director 1950. Toured Australia in Old Vic Theatre Company 1955, 1961. Also film and television roles. Died 28 September 1986 in Sydney. KBE 1968. Swedish and Lebanese knighthoods. Brother of actors Max and Sheila Helpmann.

A dancer and choreographer of exceptional talent, Robert Helpmann was also a notable actor. In London in 1937 he was assessed as 'eerie and impressive' when he appeared as Oberon, with Vivien Leigh as Titania, in an Old Vic production of *A Midsummer Night's Dream*. Later he played the title-role in *Hamlet* and Shylock in *The Merchant of Venice*. He was seen in a Shakespearean season with Katharine Hepburn in Australia in 1955. His Shylock was suitably odious and his fine comprehension of menace stood him in good stead in *Measure for Measure*. As Petruchio in *The Taming of the Shrew* he was overmatched by Hepburn's lithe and bouncy Kate. Three years later he seemed ill at ease in Noël Coward's *Nude with Violin*, in which he had already appeared in London.

In the SYDNEY THEATRE COMPANY's 1983 production of Justin Fleming's play *The Cobra* Helpmann was superb as an old and embittered Lord Alfred Douglas, mentally raking over the ashes of his infamous affair with Oscar Wilde. An image of Douglas, terrified, peering through the back of a rocking chair during the Blitz, was unforgettable. ❦*John West*

further reading
HELPMAN, MARY. *The Helpman Family Story 1796–1964*. Adelaide: Rigby 1967.
HERBERT, IAN (ed.). *Who's Who in the Theatre* 16th edn. London: Pitman 1977.

John Hennings

Scene-painter. Born 6 July 1835 in free city of Bremen. Apprenticed at 14 to house decorator in Düsseldorf (Prussia). Studied art at Düsseldorf Academy and in Vienna. Arrived in Melbourne 6 July 1855. Became leading scene-painter at Theatre Royal. Married Ellen Targett, ballet dancer, in late 1850s. Died 12 October 1896 in Melbourne. Father of scene-painter John Henry Hennings.

Attracted to Australia by the gold rushes, John Hennings arrived in Melbourne on his 20th birthday and stayed to dominate stage design at the THEATRE ROYAL for 30 years. He was engaged first by GEORGE COPPIN for his Olympic Theatre. In 1857 he had his first success for the Theatre Royal—Lord Byron's *Sardanapalus*, which he based on recently discovered ruins of Nineveh, capital of the Assyrian Empire.

From the 1860s—a time when the scenic artist shared top billing with the performers—Hennings was so valued as a designer that he was included in the management of the Theatre Royal. He was particularly appreciated for his moving panorama of current events in the annual pantomime. J. E. NEILD, JAMES SMITH and other critics admired his architectural accuracy, sky effects, and poetic imagination. In 1889 the newly arrived Scottish scene-painter GEORGE GORDON compared him favourably with London artists. Hennings also painted at the BIJOU THEATRE in the 1880s.

Eye trouble began to limit his work in the 1880s but in 1892 at the Exhibition Building he painted a cyclorama of early Melbourne; it is now owned by the State Library of Victoria. He was prominent in the German community. ❦*Mimi Colligan*

further reading
CALLAWAY, ANITA. John Hennings. *Dictionary of Australian Artists, Photographers and Engravers 1770–1870* (ed. Joan Kerr). Melbourne: Oxford University Press 1992.

Her Majesty's Theatre Adelaide

Theatre in Grote Street, opened as **Rickards Tivoli Theatre**, 6 September 1913, seating 2160. Architects: Williams and Good. Renamed **Prince of Wales Theatre** 1920. Renamed **Tivoli Theatre** 1930. Remodelled to seat 1200 and reopened as **Her Majesty's Theatre** 1962. Remodelled and reopened as **Opera Theatre**, March 1979. Renamed **Her Majesty's Theatre** 1988.

After the death of HARRY RICKARDS in 1911, HUGH D. MCINTOSH bought his Tivoli vaudeville circuit and formed Harry Rickards Tivoli Theatres Ltd to lease an unfinished theatre in Adelaide. The owners intended to call it the Princess Theatre but when McIntosh leased the building in 1913 he decided to name it Rickards Tivoli Theatre. It had a 25·9-metre-wide four-storey frontage and a stage that was 24·3 metres wide, 18·9 metres deep and 15·9 metres high to the grid. The original proscenium was narrow at 9 metres. The auditorium—equipped with an early example of mechanical ventilation—seated 622 in the stalls, 238 in the dress circle and 1300 in a deep gallery.

From 1920, when the building was renamed the Prince of Wales Theatre, various entrepreneurs used it, presenting mostly plays. It was in the FULLERS' circuit until 1929. The theatre returned to variety as the Tivoli in 1930. From 1940 ADELAIDE REPERTORY THEATRE leased the Tivoli for 14 years, staging its own productions and letting it to commercial entrepreneurs. Then the owners leased it to a sporting club.

J. C. WILLIAMSON'S bought the rather derelict Tivoli before closing its own Theatre Royal in 1959. The Firm had the interior remodelled in the nondescript functional style of the time to produce a two-level auditorium. The theatre reopened as Her Majesty's Theatre. Upon the demise of J. C. Williamson's in 1976, Her Majesty's came under threat of redevelopment, although it was the city's only medium-capacity theatre and it was needed for the ADELAIDE FESTIVAL OF ARTS. The South Australian government bought the theatre and remodelled the interior to be reminiscent of Scandinavian modern style in its combination of simplicity and adequate richness. It reopened in March 1979 as the Opera Theatre and housed the State Opera of South Australia until 1988. ❦*Ross Thorne*

Her Majesty's Theatre Ballarat

Theatre, opened 7 June 1875 as **Academy of Music**. Architect: George Browne. Altered and renamed **Her Majesty's Theatre** 1898. Architect: William Pitt jnr. Leased as cinema from 1938. Bought by Royal South Street Society in 1965 and renamed **South Street Memorial Theatre** 1966. Given to City of Ballarat and restored. Reopened 7 November 1990 as **Her Majesty's Theatre**, seating 931. Architects: Clive Lucas, Stapleton and Partners.

One of the finest Australian theatres is Her Majesty's in Ballarat (Vic.). No other has as many extant 19th-century architectural elements in the auditorium and stage. The theatre belongs to the second generation of the gold town's development. Within five years of the initial Victorian gold rush three significant theatres were built in Ballarat—the Charles Napier Theatre in 1854, the Victoria Theatre in 1856 and the Montezuma Theatre in 1856. All were associated with hotels and the Academy of Music in 1875 was exceptional in not having bars or a hotel in front. A patron, Sir William J. Clarke, built the theatre and for its first ten years it was run by community leaders, mostly lawyers interested in promoting the performing arts. The opening program included W. S. LYSTER's opera company.

The building was a substantial brick structure on a steeply sloping site which allowed for future expansion into the basement space. There were shops in front of the auditorium, which was a lofty two-level hall. The circle was partly supported by four cast-iron posts but largely hung by iron rods from the roof trusses. The roof continued over the raked stage. About 10·5 metres above the stage the grid was fixed to the bottom of the trusses. The stage itself was generous at 18 metres wide by more than 15 metres deep. The hall was 18 metres wide by 22 metres long by 12·3 metres high. Within this height, in 1898, the architect WILLIAM PITT JNR managed to rebuild the existing circle and add another above it, utilising the same balcony-front design. He cut a large hole in the old coffered ceiling and inserted an opening dome to provide ventilation through a new sliding segment in the roof.

The brick wall between stage and auditorium was extended to the roof line as a fire wall, and a new grid was inserted about 1·5 metres above the bottom of the truss line. As a result, full-height scenery could be flown between the roof trusses. The stage was cleared of dressing rooms and the paint frame. New dressing rooms and a scene dock were housed in an extension at the side of the building. Pitt also raked the stalls floor. Renamed Her Majesty's, the theatre now rivalled some in the capital cities. At first it was under the direction of WILLIAMSON AND MUSGROVE, who toured major productions and personalities. In 1911 the Plimmer–Denniston Company was so popular that the crowd blocked the street and women were knocked down in the rush for tickets. Touring companies played in the theatre until the 1930s but it was mostly used as a Hoyts cinema from the Great Depression until the Royal South Street Society, which had held competitions in performance in the theatre since 1896, bought it in 1965.

Alterations in 1906, 1912, 1927 and 1943 resulted in minor changes to the auditorium and undistinguished lobby and foyer accommodation, which left nothing of the original front of house. In the 1980s restoration the entrance was given a quasi-Victorian canopy and front doors. A new lobby replaces all the original shops and offices on the second floor have been sympathetically converted to the foyer–bar. Pitt's large dome has been reinstated in the auditorium, which has been restored close to the 1898 version. The stage has been re-equipped with mechanised fly lines. The theatre now presents local and touring productions with entrepreneurial flair. ❦*Ross Thorne*

Her Majesty's Theatre Brisbane

Theatre in Queen Street, opened 2 April 1888 as **Her Imperial Majesty's Opera House**, seating 2200. Architect: Stombucco and Son. Originally owned by G. Byrne and leased by C. H. Holmes. Leased by Harold Ashton and reopened as **His Majesty's Theatre** 23 March 1901. Rebuilt and reopened 30 March 1929, seating 1387. Architect: Cedric Ballantyne or George McLeish. Later renamed **Her Majesty's**. Demolished 1983.

Until the QUEENSLAND PERFORMING ARTS COMPLEX was built the only Brisbane theatre with a stage that could take the scenery of productions toured from Melbourne or Sydney by subsidised companies was Her Majesty's Theatre. When it was built as Her Imperial Majesty's Opera House, with a hotel in front, it looked grand indeed. It rose high above all other buildings in Queen Street, palatial, almost voluptuous, encrusted with more heavily modelled decoration in the Victorian Italianate style than any of them. The theatre was designed to seat 1200 persons on the ground floor—500 in the stalls and 700 in the pit. Closely spaced, substantial cast-iron posts supported the 400-seat dress circle and above it the 600-seat 'family circle', which was not initially called a gallery. The daughter of W. H. Wallace, who managed the theatre from 1901 to 1928, remembered 'packers' being employed to squeeze patrons into this uppermost balcony. A good packer could squeeze in an extra 50.

The stage measured 18 metres by 19 metres. The proscenium was decorated with gold-painted Corinthian columns, but the auditorium was otherwise almost devoid of decorative plasterwork. The theatre opened with the new style of maroon velvet house curtain instead of the traditional scenic act-drop and green baize curtain. The auditorium lighting was originally gas but converted to electricity about two years later. Earthenware pipes and windows provided ventilation until 1901, when the architect WILLIAM PITT was commissioned to undertake minor alterations, including a sliding roof.

In 1929 His Majesty's Theatre reopened after major rebuilding of the auditorium and foyers. Reports are not clear on who was the architect responsible for the design, which provided a more comfortable theatre, in many ways more like a picture palace than a traditional theatre. There was now a single deep balcony, unsupported by posts in the stalls below. Two decorative but rather useless boxes were cantilevered from the side walls near the proscenium. All was decorated in a deeply modelled Renaissance–rococo style. The Brisbane *Courier* said the theatre presented a 'charming spectacle'. It quickly became the venue for major lyric and dramatic performances, especially those toured by the large entrepreneurs. The AMP Society bought the site from Byrne Hart and his sons in 1973, promising that it would build a new theatre when it developed this and adjacent sites. But in 1980 AMP sold the theatre to another developer, who demolished it in 1983. At that time there was criticism of the seating rake and backstage conditions. ❦*Ross Thorne*

Her Majesty's Theatre Melbourne

Theatre in Exhibition Street, opened as **Alexandra Theatre** 1 October 1886, seating 2500. Architect: Nahum Barnet. Renamed **Queen's Theatre** 1897. Altered and reopened as **Her Majesty's Theatre** 19 May 1900. Architect: William Pitt. Renamed **His Majesty's Theatre** 29 March 1924. Auditorium gutted by fire 1929. Rebuilt and reopened 1934. Architect: Walkeley and Hollinshed.

Melbourne's principal light musical theatre in the 20th century, as Her Majesty's or His Majesty's Theatre, was its principal melodrama house in the late 19th century as the Alexandra Theatre. Nahum Barnet designed it as an ambitious scheme for a building to cover a large site. On the long, three-storey elevation to Exhibition Street he used a late Victorian style with French Renaissance overtones, the main entrance being marked by a central pavilion surmounted by a steeply pitched roof.

This street frontage was highly decorative but the interior finish was austere because of lack of funds, which also caused delays in building. The three-tier auditorium was 26 metres wide by long 23 metres long, with a 10-metre-wide proscenium and a flat floor on the pit–stalls level. A forest of posts supported the tiers above the stalls. All this made for poor viewing for many of the 2500 or more persons it was designed to hold. The stage was adequate at 15 metres in depth, and had an early example of a fly tower—rising 16 metres to the grid. Within a year of the opening alterations were announced to 'suitably decorate' the walls of the dress-circle level and fit a new ceiling dome. Only four years later, in 1891, the building was in such disrepair that a writer in the *Australian Builder and Contractor News* said redecoration by the architect Philip Kennedy was required to bring about 'a nearer approach to a theatre than hitherto'. The theatre was used mainly for melodrama, particularly by Alfred Dampier and William Anderson. J. C. Williamson reopened it, principally for operetta, in May 1900. It was now Her Majesty's Theatre, after alterations directed by William Pitt. These included raking the stalls floor, lowering the stage, adding dressing rooms, installing a fire curtain in the proscenium opening, and general redecoration. The forest of posts remained until a fire gutted the auditorium in 1929.

His Majesty's lay semi-derelict during the early years of the Great Depression. F. W. Thring briefly used it as a film studio. When the Theatre Royal was demolished in 1934, J. C. Williamson's employed Pitt's successors, Walkeley and Hollinshed, to rebuild the auditorium of His Majesty's Theatre and refit other damaged parts. The architects dispensed with theatrical tradition and redesigned the interior as the first live theatre in Art Deco style in Australia. They also worked with the pioneer acoustic consultant H. Vivian Taylor to evolve an acoustically functional decorative scheme for the auditorium. It retained the proscenium and traditional stalls, dress circle and gallery. The theatre continues to house long-run musicals. ❦*Ross Thorne*

Her Majesty's Theatre Sydney 1887–1933

Theatre in Pitt Street, opened 10 September 1887, seating 1650 on four levels. Architects: Morell and Kemp. Interior burnt out 23 March 1902. Rebuilt on three levels and reopened 1 August 1903. Architect: William Pitt. Closed 10 June 1933. Converted to variety store and offices 1934. Finally closed 2 March 1970 and demolished to make way for Centrepoint.

The most elaborate and best-equipped theatre in Sydney before the Sydney Opera House was Her Majesty's Theatre. It was the first theatre built in strict conformity with regulations that resulted from the NSW Royal Commission on Theatres in the early 1880s. Fire-resistant iron doors protected connections between the auditorium and the public spaces of the theatre, which were in a hotel in front. A thick brick firewall, a 'fireproof' asbestos drop curtain at the proscenium opening and iron doors in other openings all separated the auditorium from the stage. Every effort was made to use fire-resistant materials, and any inflammable materials were coated with fire-retardant liquids.

The auditorium and stage were lit by both electricity and gas. Scene-changing was by the continental European system of flat wings moved along slots in the stage floor on wheeled carriages at the mezzanine level of the stage basement. The *Builder and Contractor's News* of 22 October 1887 gave the width of the stage as 25·6 metres and the depth as 15·2 metres, but published dimensions varied. The proscenium opening was 11·6 metres square. Iron trusses spanned the width of the stage, supporting a grid for flying scenery, 33·2 metres above the basement. The building was 31 metres in front, 38 metres wide at the rear, and 51 metres deep. The façade was elaborately modelled in a baroque–Renaissance style with applied Corinthian columns, surmounted by a carved pediment and a roof pavilion in French Renaissance style. The building was designed for the Grand Opera Company, which leased the site from the William McQuade estate. The theatre was near completion when financial difficulties saw the site owner take it over. GEORGE RIGNOLD then leased the theatre until 21 September 1895 and opened it, some four months late, playing Henry V in his famous production. He interspersed spectacular Shakespeare productions with comedies.

Her Majesty's housed many productions that offered spectacle or famous overseas performers, including SARAH BERNHARDT in 1891. WILLIAMSON AND MUSGROVE presented JULIUS KNIGHT in Wilson Barrett's *The Sign of the Cross*, Anthony Hope's *The Prisoner of Zenda* and W. G. Wills's *A Royal Divorce*. PATTIE BROWNE's return in J. M. Barrie's *The Little Minister* was the feature of 1898. The comedian Harry Connor appeared with his American company in Charles H. Hoyt's *A Trip to Chinatown* in 1899. J. C. WILLIAMSON's production of *Florodora*, with GEORGE LAURI, CARRIE MOORE, GRACE PALOTTA and HUGH J. WARD, ran for 96 performances in 1901. Next year Williamson staged W. Young's dramatisation of General Lew Wallace's novel *Ben Hur*, with live horses and chariots racing on electric treadmills in front of moving backdrops. On a Sunday during the season, fire broke out at the rear of the stage. The asbestos fire curtain did not drop automatically and the theatre was destroyed.

The owner, Cecily McQuade, had WILLIAM PITT design a new auditorium in Edwardian style. It had two tiers—supported by posts—above the stalls instead of three. The public spaces and stairways were improved in size and finish. Williamson leased the new theatre and opened it as his Sydney flagship. It housed his most notable attractions, including H. B. Irving as Hamlet in 1911. J. C. WILLIAMSON's bought the building in 1922 but sold it during the Great Depression, after complaining of council taxes on the site and ENTERTAINMENTS TAX on gross receipts. ❦*Ross Thorne*

Her Majesty's Theatre Sydney 1960–

Theatre in Quay Street, opened 28 February 1927 as **Empire Theatre**, seating 2515. Architects: Kaberry and Chard. Closed mid-1929. Reopened 7 December 1929 as talkies cinema. Used for live theatre from 27 December 1948. Bought by J. C. Williamson's 1949. Closed for major alterations 1954. Reopened 10 June 1954, seating 1728. Renamed **Her Majesty's Theatre** 21 May 1960. Destroyed by fire 31 July 1970. New **Her Majesty's Theatre** opened 30 November 1973, seating 1492. Architects: John W. Roberts and S. A. Baggs.

The Empire Theatre—the third of that name in Sydney—enriched the city after the Second World War by its very existence, though it was a mean house for performers and audience. The theatre had been built in 1926–27, with optimal capacity and minimal facilities, by Empire Theatres Ltd, whose governing director was Rufe Naylor. The building was designed on a diagonal axis across the site. The proscenium stage, with fly tower, was tucked into the southwest corner, and a wide two-level auditorium fanned out to the opposite corner. There was a minimal entrance lobby but no foyer. Press reports claimed that the Empire housed 3000 persons, but it was licensed for 2515. It opened with the musical comedy *Sunny*. Marlow–Rolls Theatres Ltd took over the Empire in December 1928 but after six months of stage shows it was closed. At the end of 1929 it reopened as a talkies cinema. The lessees, Empire Talkies Ltd, bought the building in 1934 and dedicated it to B-pictures and second runs.

After the Second World War there was a resurgence of theatre but a lack of venues. Most live theatres had been closed, demolished or converted to cinemas since 1929. To allow J. C. WILLIAMSON's to present an opera company at the Tivoli Theatre, the TIVOLI CIRCUIT went to the capacious Empire, then a poorly attended cinema, in December 1948 to stage its Christmas shows. These were *Take a Bow*, a twice-nightly revue starring Two-Ton Tessie O'Shea, and *Babes in the Wood*, a twice-daily pantomime with Rex Dawe and JENNY HOWARD. In 1949 J. C. Williamson's bought the Empire and opened it with a 53-week season by the KIWIS Revue Company. The hypnotist FRANQUIN, *Hellzapoppin*, *Oklahoma!*, *Ice Parade* and a Gilbert and Sullivan season followed. The theatre was much altered in 1954. New side walls were installed to narrow the extremities of the auditorium, reducing the capacity. The proscenium was modified and traditional boxes were installed. A portion of the back stalls was walled off to become a stalls foyer.

Shows after the alterations included the musicals *Can-Can*, *Kismet*, *The Land of Smiles*, *Paint Your Wagon* and *The Pajama Game*. A change of name to Her Majesty's Theatre and more improvements in 1960 heralded the arrival of *My Fair Lady*. During the next decade the theatre also housed *Camelot*, *Hello Dolly!*, *Fiddler on the Roof* and *Funny Girl*. During an opera season in 1970 fire destroyed the theatre.

The architects John W. Roberts and S. A. Baggs cleverly designed a new theatre on the tight site. They shifted the axis of the auditorium to run down the middle of the lot from front to back. To provide foyer space of modern standard they reduced the capacity of the stalls to 660, less than that of the 832-seat dress circle. They enlarged the stage, however, to some 26 metres wide by 14·3 metres deep, with a 12·2 metre-wide proscenium placed almost centrally. The new theatre opened with the musical *A Little Night Music*, with Taina Elg, JILL PERRYMAN and ANNA RUSSELL. It had a slight downturn after J. C. Williamson's faded away and sold its properties, but it has remained a major commercial theatres, mostly presenting musicals. ❦*Ross Thorne*

further reading
Builder NSW. December 1974.

Bob Herbert

Dramatist. Born 6 April 1923 at Yea (Vic.). In army and air force during Second World War. Studied at School of Theatre Arts (Melbourne) 1949. Toured Victoria as actor with Anew McMaster Shakespearean Company 1950. Actor, stage manager and stage director for J. C. Williamson's. Also in pantomime, revue and film.

Married Lorraine Baker, dancer and ballet mistress, 1964. Had six works produced at University of New England while theatre manager there from 1971. Uncle of playwright Louis Nowra.

Bob Herbert's lifelong experience in the commercial theatre has taught him the craft of theatrical storytelling. His best-known play, *No Names … No Pack Drill* is a dramatic thriller set in wartime Sydney. An American marine deserts and hides in the Kings Cross apartment of an unwilling army wife. Part of the play's success was its nostalgic evocation of good-hearted black marketers and good-time girls. It jointly won the Western Australian 150th anniversary play-writing competition in 1979 and was produced professionally at the University of New England prior to a season at the Sydney Opera House with NONI HAZLEHURST and MEL GIBSON in 1980. Herbert adapted the play for radio and jointly wrote the script for its film version, *Rebel*.

Laurence Olivier's OLD VIC THEATRE COMPANY production of R. B. Sheridan's *The School for Scandal* in 1948 inspired Herbert to write his first play, since destroyed. He had no play produced until 1971, when *An Isolated Case of Heterochromia* was staged in Sydney. Herbert reworked it as *The Girl with Odd-coloured Eyes*. He has provided libretti for two musicals, *Sex and Violets* with music by Sharon Raschke and *The Last Wake at She-oak Creek* (1986) with music by Allan McFadden. Both began as plays workshopped at the AUSTRALIAN NATIONAL PLAYWRIGHTS' CONFERENCE, in 1981 and 1982 respectively. ❦*Katharine Brisbane*

published works
The Adventures of Brer Rabbit, children's play with songs (1986). Sydney: Currency Press 1989.
The Last Wake at She-oak Creek, libretto for musical (1986). Sydney: Currency Press 1986.
A Man of Respect (1975). Armidale: New England Theatre Texts 1979.
No Names … No Pack Drill (1979): Sydney: Currency Press 1980.

Norman Hetherington OAM

Puppeteer. Born 29 May 1921 in Sydney. Studied art at East Sydney Technical College 1937–38. Worked in advertising. Lightning sketch artist in 1st Australian Army Entertainment Unit in Pacific 1942–46. Cartoonist ('Heth') for *Bulletin* 1946–61. Began experimenting with marionettes with Clovelly Puppet Theatre (Sydney) 1952. Presented puppets on television from 1956. Performed marionette shows in puppetry festivals in Melbourne (*St George and the Dragon*) 1975 and Hobart (*Aladdin*) 1979. Resident designer of characters for Marionette Theatre of Australia (Sydney) 1986–89. Creates puppets for television with wife Margaret.

Norman Hetherington's brightly coloured puppets, usually marionettes, reflect the dancing, almost lyrical, line of his drawings and support his belief that puppetry is at best a personal statement. He is best known for television puppets, including the marionette Mr Squiggle, who draws with his nose and has appeared regularly on ABC children's television since 1959. Hetherington designed and constructed puppets for the University of Sydney Theatre Workshop, and for the MARIONETTE THEATRE OF AUSTRALIA he designed *The Mysterious Potamus* in 1979, *The Wind in the Willows* in 1986 and *Pinocchio* in 1987. ❦*Richard Bradshaw*

writings (with Margaret Hetherington)
Hand Shadows—Easy shapes and exciting action plays. Sydney: Angus and Robertson 1988.

Mr Squiggle and the Great Moon Robbery. Sydney: ABC 1980.
Mr Squiggle and the Preposterous Purple Crocodile. Sydney: ABC 1992.
Puppets of Australia. Sydney: Australian Council for the Arts. 1974.

Dorothy Hewett AO

Dramatist. Born 21 May 1923 in Perth. Educated at University of Western Australia (Perth). Began publishing poetry in teens. Won ABC national poetry competition at 22. Factory worker and Communist Party activist in Sydney 1949–59. Tutor in English at University of Western Australia from 1959. Early plays staged at New Fortune Theatre (Perth). Left Communist Party 1968. Received Australia Council literary grant and settled in Sydney 1974. Writer-in-residence with universities, theatre companies and student groups. Australian Artists Creative Fellowship 1993. AO 1986. HonDLitt (University of Western Australia) 1995.

Best known for her early semi-autobiographical play THE CHAPEL PERILOUS (1971) and the musical play THE MAN FROM MUKINUPIN (1979), Dorothy Hewett is generally regarded as standing among the foremost Australian playwrights, despite some critical dismissiveness, even hostility. Initially a poet and fiction writer, she turned late to the theatre. Her first play, *This Old Man Comes Rolling Home* (1966) is a fairly realistic drama of working-class family life in inner-suburban Sydney. Her subsequent work falls into two groups—intensely personal and partly autobiographical plays of sexual and family relationships up to the late 1970s, and from the mid-1970s less directly personal plays that assert the need for imaginative cherishing of the Australian landscape and cultural heritage.

Hewett's plays range widely in style but all exploit the imaginative possibilities of language, music and overt, sometimes brash, theatrical effects. *The Chapel Perilous*, with its chorus, totemic settings, broad comedy and caricature, song and dance, and sudden shifts in place and time as well as style and tone, epitomises the 'epic' theatricality for which she is best known. Other plays in this style include *Mrs Porter and the Angel* (1969), which sets the tormented intimate lives of a group of academic households against the second-hand passions of literature; *Bon-Bons and Roses for Dolly* (1972), a musical set in a 1930s picture palace, through which the heroine Dolly succumbs to the seductiveness and destructiveness of escapist fantasy; *Joan* (1975), a musical pageant version of the Joan of Arc story, set in a lunatic asylum with Joan refracted into four personae; and *The Rising of Pete Marsh* (1988), set in Great Britain during the Roman occupation and the year 2000.

The plays that focus on more intimate sexual and family relationships are much more tightly written and less flamboyant, though they incorporate poetry and song. An unperformed melodrama, *The Beautiful Mrs Portland,* shows a beautiful middle-aged woman destroyed by the male double standard, while *The Tatty Hollow Story* (1974), more surreal, portrays its central female figure through the fantasies of her male lovers, who destroy the image they have created. *The Golden Oldies* (1967), for two female actors, explores three generations of mother-daughter-sister relationships dominated by the memory of unconforming, sexually liberated but unseen Becca. Mixing styles from the lyrical to the grotesque, and referring explicitly to such taboo female subjects as menstruation, abortion and menopause, these early plays provoked some critical and audience hostility. The theatre foyer was vandalised at the Perth premiere of *Bon-Bons and Roses for Dolly*.

Hewett's later plays, from the mid-1970s assert the power of the creative imagination to resist the threat to the Australian landscape and cultural heritage posed by materialistic 'progress'. The rock operas *Catspaw* (1974) and *Pandora's Cross* (1978) both create a wonderful gallery of Bohemians and eccentric old-timers, while exemplifying the combination of 'high' and 'popular' culture characteristic of Hewett's work. *Catspaw* places the 'alternative' culture of the 1970s in the context of Australia's pioneering tradition and literary-theatrical heritage, and *Pandora's Cross* is set in Kings Cross in Sydney. The 1981 radio play *Susannah's Dreaming* and the children's plays *Golden Valley* (1981) and *Song of the Seals* (1983) develop the theme of humans' relationship to the natural world through a recurrent Hewett device, dual or multiple personalities to show the endless imaginative possibilities of the self. Two full-length 'pastoral plays' are set in the West Australian countryside Hewett knew as a child. THE MAN FROM MUKINUPIN portrays the daily life and dark underside of a typical country town and *The Fields of Heaven* (1982) chronicles the relentless destruction of a once-beautiful property through deforestation and commercial exploitation.

Although established as a playwright, Hewett retains some of her early maverick image and an ability to polarise audiences and critics. Her explicitness about female sexuality is less shocking than in the 1970s, but her freewheeling style—with its leaps in time, logic and tone, and its rejection of conventional linear structures and clearly-defined characterisation in favour of more layered and fluctuating dramatic forms—is still 'radical' for the mainstream theatres in which she is increasingly performed. RODNEY FISHER and AARNE NEEME have often directed her works. ❦*Margaret Williams*

published plays

The Beautiful Mrs Portland (1976). In *Theatre Australia* (Sydney) November–December 1976.
Bon-Bons and Roses for Dolly (1972). Sydney: Currency–Methuen 1976.
The Chapel Perilous (1971). Sydney: Currency Press 1972.
The Golden Oldies (1967). Sydney: Currency Press 1981.
Golden Valley (1981). Sydney: Currency Press 1985.
Joan musical (1975). Melbourne: Yackandandah 1984.
The Man From Mukinupin musical (1979) Sydney: Currency Press 1985.
Pandora's Cross rock opera (1978). In *Theatre Australia* September–October 1978.
Song of the Seals children's play (1983). Sydney: Currency Press 1985.
Susannah's Dreaming (1980). Sydney: Currency Press 1981. Radio play.
The Tatty Hollow Story (1974). Sydney: Currency–Methuen 1976.
This Old Man Comes Rolling Home (1966). Sydney: Currency Press.

other writings

Bobbin Up. 1959. London: Virago 1985. Novel based on her Redfern experiences.
Wild Card. London: Virago 1990. Melbourne: McPhee Gribble 1990. Autobiography.

further reading

AKERHOLT, MAY-BRIT. Female figures in the plays of Dorothy Hewett and Patrick White. *Westerly* 29/1 (Perth 1984).
BRISBANE, KATHARINE. In *Contemporary Dramatists* (ed. K. A. Berney) 5th edn. London: St James Press 1993.
FERRIER, CAROLE. Dorothy Hewett. *Contemporary Australian Drama* (ed. Peter Holloway) revised. Sydney: Currency Press 1987.
GOSTAND, REBA. Quest or question? *Bards, Bohemians and Bookmen* (ed. Leon Cantrell). Brisbane: University of Queensland Press 1976.
HOPKINS, LEKKIE. Language, culture and landscape in *The Man From Mukinupin*. *Australasian Drama Studies* 10 (Brisbane April 1987).
KIERNAN, BRIAN. Seeing her own mischance. *Contemporary Australian Drama* (ed. Peter Holloway) revised. Sydney: Currency Press 1987.
WHITEHEAD, JEAN. Ordeal by freedom. *Westerly* 1 (Perth, 1971).
WILLIAMS, MARGARET. A debt repaid. *Contemporary Australian Drama* (ed. Peter Holloway) revised. Sydney: Currency Press 1987.
WILLIAMS, MARGARET. *Dorothy Hewett—The feminine as subversive*. Sydney: Currency Press 1992.

Robert Hewett

Actor, dramatist. Born 9 May 1949 in Melbourne. Studied drama under Wal Cherry at Flinders University (Adelaide) 1971. Began acting with Melbourne Theatre Company theatre-in-education 1972. Green Room Award for best new play for *Gulls* 1983.

After acting throughout the 1970s with Hoopla Productions in Melbourne and the Melbourne, Nimrod (Sydney) and Tasmanian Theatre Companies, Robert Hewett wrote his first play, *Just … One Last Dance*. Its premiere was at the Mercury Theatre in Auckland (New Zealand) on 31 October 1980 and the first Australian production, by the MELBOURNE THEATRE COMPANY, opened on 12 December 1980. In 1983 the latter company gave the first production of Hewett's second play, *Gulls*, a compassionate work about a brain-damaged man and his faithful sister. It makes use of a puppetmaster and the device of allowing the man to rage to the audience with sardonic wit, while remaining imprisoned in a childlike body to those about him. It has been widely performed around Australia and in the United Kingdom, the USA, New Zealand and South Africa. Hewett's third play, *The Adman*, is a satirical comedy of the advertising world. The PLAYBOX THEATRE CENTRE produced it in Melbourne in 1991. ❦*Katharine Brisbane*

published plays

Gulls (1983) Sydney: Currency Press 1984.
The Adman (1991) Sydney: Currency Press 1991.

Jack Hibberd

Dramatist. Born 12 April 1940 at Warracknabeal (Vic.). Abandoned medical career to concentrate on writing plays 1967. Involved in formation of La Mama Company and Australian Performing Group. National Critics' Circle Award 1976 for original contributions to Australian theatre. National Professional Theatre Award 1976 (*A Toast to Melba*). Married to actor Evelyn Krape.

Jack Hibberd is the most innovative Australian playwright of his generation—and one of the most productive. His best work seems likely to endure. He gave up a career in medicine at the end of 1967, when he was a hospital registrar, to concentrate on writing plays. Next year a program of his short plays called *Brainrot* was performed at the University of Melbourne and led to the formation of the La Mama Company, which became the AUSTRALIAN PERFORMING

Group. A senior writer's fellowship from the literature board of the Australia Council in 1973 enabled Hibberd to write full time. He was a member of the Australian Performing Group until 1977 and its chairman in 1974. The rough vigour of the group's acting style suited his plays and he enlarged his understanding of dramatic performance through working with actors. He left the group when he felt the relationship was no longer fruitful and he wanted his work to develop in new ways. In 1983 he became first president of Melbourne Writers' Theatre, which aims for a theatre dedicated to Australian plays. He now writes prose and verse instead of drama, and in 1986 he resumed part-time medical practice.

Hibberd's early short plays exhibit traits significant in some of his later drama, in particular, a preoccupation with distinctively Australian attitudes and behaviour—which can be satirical or appreciative or both at once—and an exuberant theatricality drawing on revue. Both traits are seen in *One of Nature's Gentlemen* (1968), which deals with violence in the relationship of two bar-room mates. Other early short plays are *Three Old Friends* (1967), *This Great Gap of Time* (1967), *Just Before the Honeymoon* (1967), *O* (1968), *Who?* (1968) and *No Time Like the Present* (1968). More recent are *Glycerine Tears* (1982), a brilliant two-hander, and the burlesque *Death of a Traveller* (1985).

Ideas determine dramatic form in *White With Wire Wheels* (1967), the first full-length play Hibberd had performed. One actor, with no attempt at disguise, represents four different women, thus satirising the obliviousness of the play's three young men to all that is unique and personal about each woman. Another striking departure from conventional realism is a dream-like scene in which the men in turn visit one of the women, each bearing a motor-car part, and make identical versified confessions of confusion and fear. Later Hibberd plays—*Commitment* (1968), *Customs and Excise* (1970), *Klag* (1970), *Aorta* (1971), *Captain Midnight VC* (1972), *Peggy Sue* (1974)—also provoke thought on the behaviour of Australian men towards women and on other Australian social issues, including conformism, intolerance and racial discrimination.

Several of Hibberd's plays aim at attracting those unaccustomed to theatregoing. Dimboola (1969), *Goodbye Ted* (a collaboration with John Timlin, 1970) and *Liquid Amber* (1982) all involve the audience in a celebratory meal. Marvellous Melbourne (1970), a collaboration with John Romeril, looks at Melbourne between 1888 and 1902. *The Les Darcy Show* (1974) and *A Toast to Melba* (1976) celebrate famous Australians of the past, not without irony.

Hibberd has written several plays for a solo actor. A Stretch of the Imagination (1972) is the best known. Later monodramas—*Memoirs of a Carlton Bohemian* (1977), *A Man of Many Parts* (1980), *Mothballs* (1981), *Lavender Bags* (written in 1982 but not performed), *Malarky Barks* (written in 1983, unperformed) and *Death Warmed Up* (1984)—differ from it in important respects. For their protagonists, isolation is not, as for Monk O'Neill in *A Stretch of the Imagination*, a deliberate choice, but inescapable and painful. Their compulsive monologue seems a desperate effort to combat loneliness and their compulsive playing of roles and games, including games with words, a frantic attempt to create pattern and meaning. Monk O'Neill's reminiscences often provoke incredulity, but with the protagonists of *A Man of Many Parts* and subsequent monodramas, fantasy seems involved even in their perception of the present. This creates a tantalising uncertainty, as if the dramatist were playing his own game with the audience.

Hibberd has increasingly distanced himself from realism as his art has developed. Whereas, in his early plays, the stage usually represents for the audience a defined locale, in later plays, most notably *A Man of Many Parts*, it remains primarily a stage. Characters like Les Darcy and Nellie Melba, consistently observed from the outside, illustrate Hibberd's declared lack of interest in psychological realism. In the monodramas, where there is direct access to the protagonist's consciousness, the psychological interest, though not eliminated, is never dominant. In his language, Hibberd allows himself a scope not available to the realistic playwright. It ranges from the vulgar, violent and bawdy to the ludicrously sesquipedalian. Sophisticated wit, puns and comic lyricism enrich the later monodramas.

Hibberd's use of music and song, often without realistic justification, owes something to Brecht, but he is an innovator in his own right. His musical range is considerable. Popular songs of the 1950s and 1960s help to structure *Peggy Sue*. *A Toast to Melba*—one of the many Hibberd plays in which his wife Evelyn Krape has performed—draws on classical music. George Dreyfus, Martin Friedel and Lorraine Milne have composed music for other plays. Music in Hibberd's plays is never merely illustrative: it is often ironic and always helps to articulate meaning.

Hibberd has also written two operetta libretti, *Jack Juan* (1968) and *Sin* (1978); a satire on musicals, *Smash Hit* (1981); and adapted three foreign plays, *Women!* (1972) from Aristophanes in collaboration with James McCaughey, *The Overcoat* (1976) from Nikolai Gogol and *Odyssey of a Prostitute* (1984) from Guy de Maupassant. Even when his subject matter is Australian, Hibberd writes with an awareness of drama as an international endeavour. As local a play as *One of Nature's Gentlemen* takes its title from a remark about an Australian in Oscar Wilde's *Lady Windermere's Fan*. Hibberd's internationalism is less a matter of indebtedness to particular writers than of informed awareness of what is happening in world theatre and a sensitivity to what is possible and appropriate here and now. *J. D. Hainsworth*

published plays
Captain Midnight VC (1973). Melbourne: Yackandandah 1984.
Dimboola (1969). Melbourne: Penguin 1984 in *A Country Quinella*.
Glycerine Tears (1982). In *Meanjin* 41/4 (Melbourne 1982).
Goodbye Ted with John Timlin (1970). Melbourne: Yackandandah 1983.
Lavender Bags (unperformed). In *Aspect* 25 (Sydney 1982).
The Les Darcy Show (1974). Melbourne: Outback Press 1976 in *Three Popular Plays*.
Liquid Amber (1978). Melbourne: Penguin 1984 in *A Country Quinella*.
Marvellous Melbourne, with John Romeril (1970). In *Theatre Australia* 2/4 and 2/5 (Sydney, August and September/October 1977).
Memoirs of a Carlton Bohemian (1977). In *Meanjin* 36/3 (Melbourne 1977).
Mothballs (1981). In *Meanjin* 39/4 (Melbourne 1980).
One of Nature's Gentlemen (1968). Melbourne: Outback Press 1976 in *Three Popular Plays*.
The Overcoat (1976) from Nikolai Gogol. Sydney: Currency Press 1981.
Peggy Sue (1974). Melbourne: Yackandandah 1982.

Sin, libretto for operetta by Martin Friedel (1978). Sydney: Currency Press 1981.
Squibs, 16 short plays (some performed 1967–73). Brisbane : Phoenix Publications 1984.
A Stretch of the Imagination (1972). Sydney: Currency Press 1973, 1977.
A Toast to Melba (1976). Melbourne: Outback Press 1976 in *Three Popular Plays*
White With Wire Wheels (1967). Melbourne: Penguin 1973 in *Four Australian Plays*.
Who? (1968). Melbourne: Penguin 1973 in *Four Australian Plays*.

further reading
CARROLL, DENNIS. *Australian Contemporary Drama*. Sydney: Currency Press 1995.
HAINSWORTH, J. D. *Hibberd*. Melbourne: Methuen 1987.
HOLLOWAY, PETER (ed.). *Contemporary Australian Drama* revised. Sydney: Currency Press 1987.
MCGILLICK, PAUL. *Jack Hibberd*. Amsterdam (Netherlands): Rodopi 1988.

The Hibernian Father

—or, *The Warden of Galway*. Blank-verse tragedy in five acts by Edward Geoghegan. **premiere** 6 May 1844, Royal Victoria Theatre, Sydney. Cast: Francis Nesbitt (the Warden).

After the Royal Victoria Theatre in Sydney produced this strongly melodramatic play letters in the *Sydney Morning Herald* accused its unidentified author of plagiarism. It was alleged that the playwright—who was the convict EDWARD GEOGHEGAN—had stolen from *The Warden of Galway*, a play by the Rev. Edward Groves, which had been performed in Dublin. The subject of both plays is an Irish judge, who condemns his own son to death for murder. When officers of the law refuse to execute the sentence he does so himself. A. B. Weiner and Helene Oppenheim both compared the Geoghegan and Groves texts and drew different conclusions on Geoghegan's originality. The scandal surrounding its staging gives useful insights into the status of free adaptations. *The Hibernian Father* was revived seven times in its first two months—theatres needed a high turnover of 'strong' plays at that time—and occasionally until 1871. A journalist who wrote in the *Colonial Literary Journal* in February 1845 that 'a real tragedy, and one of considerable merit into the bargain' had been performed in Sydney was undoubtedly referring to this play. ❦*Helen Musa*

further reading
OPPENHEIM, HELENE. The Hibernian Father—Mysteries solves and unsolved. *Australian Literary Studies* 3/1 (1967).
WEINER A. B. The Hibernian Father. *Meanjin* 25/4 (Melbourne 1966).

reference
The manuscript of *The Hibernian Father* is in the State Archives of NSW.

Charles B. Hicks

Manager, minstrel. Born probably in Baltimore (Maryland), USA. Toured Australia with Georgia Minstrels 1877–80 and Hicks–Sawyer Minstrels 1888–90 as manager and performer. Died 1902 in Surabaya (Dutch East Indies).

Charles B. Hicks was probably the father of African-American show business and he also helped to shape the Australian popular stage. Blacks were not allowed to perform on the American professional stage until after the Civil War, when they were allowed to become professional MINSTRELS. In 1865 Hicks organised the first financially successful African-American minstrel troupe, the Brooker and Clayton Georgia Minstrels. He managed the company and performed as interlocutor and singer. But black minstrels found it extremely difficult to survive in American show business. They experienced discrimination wherever they travelled. The Georgia Minstrels, for example, often had to sleep in theatres because hotelkeepers refused them lodging. At the same time, theatre managers and rival white minstrel managers were envious and intolerant of the success of the Georgia Minstrels. In 1866, 1872 and 1877 white managers stole Hicks's companies away from him. On the last occasion Hicks, who had a deserved reputation for ruthless cunning, retrieved his troupe and sailed with it for Australia to avoid blacklisting or another takeover.

Led by Hicks, the Georgia Minstrels on their 1877–80 tour were perhaps the most popular and successful minstrels ever to visit the colonies. They played to overflowing audiences in the capitals, on the goldfields and throughout pastoral districts. In mid-1878 the troupe joined forces with the L. M. Bayless Dramatic Company to stage *Uncle Tom's Cabin*. This was a box-office triumph, running for 78 nights in Melbourne and then having a remarkable success in Sydney. Hosea Eastern took the role of Uncle Tom and the other Georgia Minstrels played spiritual-singing field hands. In 1879 the troupe was drawing smaller audiences and late in the year it disbanded after Hicks had abandoned it to join the New Princess's Uncle Tom's Cabin Company and Lewis's Georgia Jubilee Singers. This company also did badly at the box office and in 1880 Hicks, plagued with debts, fled back to the USA.

In the next eight years Hicks moved from one minstrel company to another. He undertook a short stint as advance agent for the white-owned Callender Minstrels and in 1881 he toured Great Britain with Haverly's Colossal Coloured Carnival. He also tried to manage his own black companies. He briefly fielded Hicks's Original Georgia Minstrels and then formed a partnership with a famous black minstrel, Billy Kersands, to organise the Kersands Coloured Minstrels. Finally, he joined forces with another black entrepreneur, A. D. Sawyer, to produce the Hicks-Sawyer Minstrels. However, white theatre-owners remained prejudiced against black-run troupes and bookings were hard to secure. In 1888 Hicks again sought refuge in Australia.

The Georgia Minstrels in 1877–80 sang genuine African-American music in the form of spirituals and performed plantation sketches that focused on the alleged eccentricities or stupidities of slaves. By 1888 slavery and the plantation were passé and African-Americans were nominally free and increasingly urban. The repertoire of the Hicks-Sawyer Minstrels had a core of 'coon' songs and sketches that concentrated on the alleged character and culture of urban northern blacks after the Civil War. The Hicks-Sawyer Minstrels were never as successful as the Georgia Minstrels but they did well enough to make a tidy profit for Frank Hiscocks, the entrepreneur who sponsored their tour of the colonies from 1888 to 1890, when the troupe broke up. Its star comedians, IRVING SAYLES and CHARLES POPE, later joined Harry Rickards's vaudeville as permanent endmen. Hicks became the advance agent for Harmston's Circus and spent the remainder of his life travelling with the show through Australia, India, Singapore, Japan and the Dutch East Indies, where he died of cholera. ❦*Richard Waterhouse*

further reading
TOLL, ROBERT C. *Blacking Up*. New York: Oxford University Press 1977.

George Highland

Director. Born *c*.1870 in London. Produced Henry Irving's last American tour, 1898. Moved into production of musical comedy. Directed musical comedies and plays for J. C. Williamson's from 1916. Finally retired 1939. Died 16 April 1954 in Melbourne.

Initially engaged by J. C. WILLIAMSON'S to produce *A Little Bit of Fluff*, a farce by Walter W. Ellis, in South Africa and Australia in 1916–17, George Highland became the Firm's principal producer of musical works. He also presented many successful plays. He went overseas to check plays bought by Williamson's and he insisted that an Australian production replicate the original. Highland was a martinet. He loathed the Australian accent and refused to allow it in plays. But he also said: 'I insist … that this everlasting rage for imported players is damnable and absurd. I find invariably that when I want anything from Australia, Australia has it.' He trained some of Australia's best-known artists for stardom, including JOSIE MELVILLE, GLADYS MONCRIEFF and CYRIL RITCHARD. Highland retired several times but he came back to work with Moncrieff on her returns to the Firm in 1930, 1932 and 1933. His last production was a revival of *Wildflower* with MARIE BURKE in 1939. ❦*Alwyn Capern*

further reading
KINGSTON, CLAUDE. *It Don't Seem a Day Too Much*. Adelaide: Rigby 1971.

The Highwayman

Musical comedy. **book, lyrics and music** Edmond Samuels. **Australian premiere** 17 November 1950, King's Theatre, Melbourne. **cast** Shirley Bushelle, Earl Covert, Ann Donald, Charles Norman, Beryl Seton. **director** Carl Randall.

Eddie Samuels, a well-known Sydney character, was a pharmacist by profession but preferred to think of himself as an author, playwright, composer, poet and philosopher. In 1935 he wrote *The Highwayman*, set in the Bendigo goldfields in the 1860s, and took it to London. A management agreed to mount it with Alice Delysia in the lead, but it opened, much altered, as *At the Silver Swan*. Samuels was credited as part-author and one of the composers.

In the late 1940s Samuels, disgusted by the lack of Australian musicals, decided to revive his original version of *The Highwayman*. His friend Carl Randall, an American actor, dancer and director, was willing to direct the project, so Samuels offered his show to J. C. WILLIAMSON'S. The Firm expressed interest but stalled so long about opening dates and limited seasons that Samuels and Randall decided to produce it themselves as Australian Musical Productions. They hired the recently unemployed chorus of *Annie Get Your Gun*—which Randall had directed—as well as that show's male lead, the American baritone Earl Covert, the English soprano Beryl Seton and the popular Australian comedian CHARLES NORMAN for the principal roles.

The plot, echoing COLLITS' INN, revolves around Mary Brown of the Eagle Hawk Inn and her infatuation with a dashing masked highwayman who relieves her of a locket on the Melbourne stagecoach. Pursuing Mary is villainous Mervyn Smith, in reality a notorious bushranger known as the Phantom. True love conquers all when Mary's highwayman turns out to be the captain of the guard, disguised in order to capture the Phantom. *The Highwayman* received almost unanimous praise from the Melbourne critics in spite of—or perhaps because of—its naive, old-fashioned qualities. The first-act finale, an Aboriginal corroboree, brought the house down. On 9 March 1951, the show transferred to the Palace Theatre in Sydney with a new leading man, Tod Hilton. Frederick Parslow played the title-role in Perth. EMI recorded excerpts on 78 r.p.m. discs and thought enough of the score to release an LP of the songs almost a decade later. ❦*Tony Sheldon*

further reading
BEVAN, IAN. *The Story of the Theatre Royal*. Sydney: Currency Press 1993.

Alfred Hill CMG OBE

Composer, dramatist. Born 16 November 1870 in Melbourne. Grew up in New Zealand. Studied music in Leipzig (Germany) 1887–91. Lived in Sydney 1897–1902, conducting orchestral and choral concerts. Moved to Sydney from New Zealand 1910. Composed operettas and wrote plays. Founded Sydney Repertory Theatre Society 1913. Died 30 October 1960 in Sydney. Coronation Medal 1937. OBE 1953. CMG 1960.

The most widely recognised Australian composer before the First World War was Alfred Hill. His compositions for the theatre span the larger part of his professional creative years in Australia and New Zealand from 1892 to 1923. In his operettas he favoured spoken dialogue with interpolated songs, duets and, sometimes, dances and choruses. The style recalls Arthur Sullivan and Edward German, and occasionally Jacques Offenbach or Albert Lortzing. His literary collaborators provided him with libretti of four types. *The Whipping Boy* (1893), *Lady Dolly* (1898) and *Don Quixote in La Mancha* (1904) are social comedy. ARTHUR H. ADAMS's *Tapu* (1902) has a Maori theme and *A Moorish Maid* (1905) an 'oriental' theme. *The Ship of Heaven* (1933) is a literary fantasy by HUGH MCCRAE.

Hill occasionally provided compositions or arrangements of his own music to serve the legitimate theatre. Under the Maori pseudonym Arapeta Hira, he also wrote several small plays, which were produced by the first Sydney Repertory Theatre Society. ❦*Andrew D. McCredie*

further reading
MCCREDIE, ANDREW D. *Alfred Hill 1870–1960*. *Miscellanea Musicologica* 3 (Adelaide 1968).

Ross Hill

Puppeteer, puppet-maker. Born 7 November 1954 at Mildura (Vic.). Worked with Tasmanian Puppet Theatre (Hobart) 1973–77. Principal puppet-maker for Marionette Theatre of Australia (Sydney) 1977–83. Worked on film for Jim Henson in London 1984–85. Died 6 January 1991 in Sydney.

An exceptionally talented puppet-maker, Ross Hill was invaluable to the MARIONETTE THEATRE OF AUSTRALIA in its exploration of new forms of puppetry. He often worked from sketches by cartoonists, notably Patrick Cook. In 1980

Hill presented a solo adult cabaret, *Balls*. Interested in puppets from the age of six, and helped and encouraged by a mother with an enthusiasm for puppetry, he was influenced by THE TINTOOKIES in his teens. He made and presented marionettes on Mildura television while still a student. With the TASMANIAN PUPPET THEATRE he produced and directed a 13-part television series and worked on 14 theatrical productions. ❦*Richard Bradshaw*

Samuel Prout Hill

Actor, theatre decorator. Born 1821 at Devonport (England). Emigrated to Sydney 1841. Moved to Hobart 1849. Died 23 October 1861 in Hobart. Cousin of artist John Skinner Prout.

During his 20 years in the colonies Samuel Prout Hill's involvement in cultural activities was pervasive and continuous. He was employed as an accountant when he came to Sydney in 1841 but he spent his leisure time at the Mechanics' School of Arts as lecturer, secretary and librarian, and in painting and writing, including a poetic drama, *Tarquin the Proud*. In Hobart Hill became a draughtsman and then a public service clerk. He also lectured at the Mechanics' Institute on drama and other subjects. He exhibited dioramic views of Victoria at the School of Arts in October 1852. In 1853 he was employed in the redecoration of the THEATRE ROYAL and in May he acted there. One reviewer noted that 'if he minds his p's and q's [cues] he will no doubt make a very creditable actor'. His decorations were admired. Hill later turned to politics; he won him a seat in the Tasmanian House of Assembly in 1861, but died before he could take it. ❦*Gillian Winter*

further reading
BUCKIE, HARRY. *Samuel Prout Hill. Australian Dictionary of Biography* 1. Melbourne University Press 1966.
KERR, JOAN (ed.). *Dictionary of Australian Artists, Photographers and Engravers, 1770–1870*. Melbourne: Oxford University Press 1992.

The Hills Family Show

Musical revue written by Bill Hannan, John Romeril and cast. **premiere** June 1975, Pram Factory, Melbourne, by Australian Performing Group. Cast: Bill Garner, Max Gillies, Sue Ingleton, Evelyn Krape, Fay Mokotow, Rob Meldrum, Tony Taylor.

Sometimes sentimental, frequently crass and always anarchic, *The Hills Family Show* is a tribute to the era of travelling TENT SHOWS. In early 1975, a core group of actors in the AUSTRALIAN PERFORMING GROUP gave themselves ten weeks to write and stage a piece exploring the nature of comedy. It was a feminist credo of the time that variety exploited women, so the group decided to create a non-sexist, non-exploitative play about a performing family that revives its travelling vaudeville show in an attempt to wean audiences away from television.

Calling themselves the Hills family, the actors developed acts and personae that appealed to their own sense of comedy. MAX GILLIES created a drunken ventriloquist, Fay Mokotow and Rob Meldrum formed an elegant ballroom dancing team, Bill Garner became a pompous mind-reader and TONY TAYLOR, whose fantasy was to be Vic Damone, invented the anguished crooner Winston Hills. Perhaps the most ingenious character was Granny Hills, an octogenarian contortionist, equestrian and whipcracker. As portrayed by EVELYN KRAPE she bore a marked resemblance to GLORIA DAWN's mother Zilla Weatherly. Romeril provided a one-act melodrama for the family, *The Accidental Poke*. All the tickets for the six-week season sold out in one day, and the 'Hills' were surprised to find themselves playing two return engagements in Melbourne, with several changes of cast, and a Victorian country tour encompassing 17 cities in four weeks in 1976. Country audiences were particularly responsive as they frequently mistook the itinerant players for a real family. A successful Sydney season followed.

The *Hills Family Show* invigorated the Australian Performing Group and directed it away from the writer to the performer. It drew national attention particularly to Max Gillies, SUE INGLETON, Evelyn Krape and Tony Taylor, who have since helped to create a popular new style of socially critical comedy. With slapstick comedy in *The Hills Family Show* the APG furthered the experiment of its audience-participation play DIMBOOLA. The show also began a series of experiments in circus and vaudeville tradition centred on the APG. These spawned the Captain Matchbox Circus and CIRCUS OZ, and made Melbourne in the 1970s a platform for original cabaret comedy, which has expanded into television and the annual Comedy Festival. ❦*Tony Sheldon*

further reading
ROMERIL, JOHN. *The Accidental Poke*. Sydney: Currency Press 1985 in *Popular Short Plays* 1.

Frank Hinder

Designer. Born 26 June 1906 in Sydney. Trained at East Sydney Technical College 1925–27, and in USA at Art Institute of Chicago, New York School of Fine Art, and Master Institute at Roerich Museum (New York) 1927–34. Married Margel Ina Harris, sculptor, 1930. Taught costume design at Child-Walker School of Fine Arts (Boston) 1931, 1932–34. Returned to Sydney 1934. Designed for May Hollinworth's Leonardo Group 1935. Taught at National Art School (Sydney) until 1958. Member of National Institute of Dramatic Art board of studies 1958. Head of art department, Sydney Teachers' College 1958–64. Irene Mitchell Award for theatrical design 1958. Represented Australia at Prague Quadrennial of Theatre Design and Architecture 1967.

At a crucial time in the development of Australian theatre, after the success of Ray Lawler's SUMMER OF THE SEVENTEENTH DOLL, Frank Hinder, one of Sydney's 'artist' designers, designed several significant first productions. He designed the sets for Richard Beynon's THE SHIFTING HEART for the AUSTRALIAN ELIZABETHAN THEATRE TRUST in 1957. He designed Anthony Coburn's *The Bastard Country* for the TRUST PLAYERS in 1959, T. S. Eliot's *Murder in the Cathedral* for the first ADELAIDE FESTIVAL OF ARTS in 1960 and Anton Chekhov's *The Cherry Orchard*, the first production of the OLD TOTE THEATRE COMPANY, in 1963. ❦*Tom Bannerman*

writings
Designing for the stage. *Hemisphere* 6/11 (Sydney, November 1962).
Stage design. *Art Gallery of New South Wales Quarterly* 7/2 Sydney, January 1966).

further reading
BLOOMFIELD, LIN. *Aspects of Frank Hinder*. Sydney: Bloomfield Galleries 1988.
Hinder Retrospective. Sydney: Art Gallery of NSW 1980.

His Majesty's Theatre

Theatre at corner of Hay and King Streets, Perth, opened 24 December 1904, seating 2584. Architect: William Wolf. Closed 1976. Bought by Western Australian government 1977. Restored and reopened as general-purpose lyric–drama theatre, 28 May 1980.

An Edwardian delight, carefully modified to meet 1980s requirements in function, comfort and sense of occasion, His Majesty's Theatre is testimony to the Perth theatre architect, PETER PARKINSON, who restored it. Thomas Molloy, a land speculator built the original theatre, combined with a four-storey hotel, near his THEATRE ROYAL in Hay Street on a quarter-hectare site. The architect of the new theatre was William Wolf, a German-trained American who emigrated to Australia in 1877 and began to practise in Perth in the mid-1890s. In His Majesty's he followed the current English model but, perhaps showing European influence, gave it a fly-tower stage, which at 20 by 23 metres was larger than tradition suggested. The three-level auditorium had two waterfalls to help to cool the air and a sliding dome and roof for ventilation.

The theatre opened with *The Forty Thieves*. Later lessees —WILLIAM ANDERSON, FULLERS', J. C. WILLIAMSON'S, Edgley and Dawe and MICHAEL EDGLEY successively—presented many major productions from the eastern states, from NELLIE STEWART in Paul Kester's *Sweet Nell of Old Drury* to *My Fair Lady*. Other famous performers who appeared in the theatre included H. B. Irving, Sybil Thorndike and Vivien Leigh. When Michael Edgley's lease ended in 1976 His Majesty's closed. Its owner, Norman B. Rydge, chairman of the film-exhibiting Greater Union Organisation, asked $2 million for the theatre, which he had bought from Edgley in 1973 for $825 000. The theatre was threatened with redevelopment until the Western Australian government bought it for $1·9 million in 1977 with the intention of restoring the auditorium and refitting the stage.

Parkinson made structural modifications to reposition posts supporting the two balconies to give the audience a better view and hide new air-conditioning ducts. The old hotel with its ground-floor bars and shops, first-floor public rooms and dining-room, and 48 bedrooms and bathrooms on the upper floors was converted to provide the theatre with comfortable foyers and bars, new toilets, administrative offices, rehearsal space, and improved dressing rooms and orchestra rooms. The complex houses the West Australian Opera and Ballet Companies and the Theatre Collection. ❦*Ross Thorne*

further reading
CAMPBELL, R. McK. His Majesty's Theatre—A report. *Architecture Australia* 68/4 (Melbourne, September 1979).
His Majesty's Theatre. Perth Theatre Trust *c.*1980.

Brian Hoad

Critic. Born 29 April 1938 in London. Graduated from University of London in chemistry 1959. Worked as chemist. Joined *Chemical Age* as science and industry reporter 1962. Reporter on London *Times* 1966. Came to Sydney and joined *Bulletin* 1967. Theatre, opera and dance critic of *Bulletin* 1970–.

One of the few arts journalists in Australia trained in news reporting, Brian Hoad is assured in his background, passionate in his responses and rounded in his outlook. He arouses conflicting emotions in readers of the *Bulletin* and has often clashed with theatre companies. For some years he had running battles with the SYDNEY THEATRE COMPANY under Richard Wherrett, the Australian Ballet administration and Barry Cohen when he was Arts Minister. Hoad's vintage period was the 1970s and 1980s, when he was free to range widely and express himself trenchantly. He retains his visceral, poetic style, which vividly evokes theatrical experience. Regular travel to other centres of theatre has given him assurance in defining new directions at home, and enthusiasm for much new work, from *THE LEGEND OF KING O'MALLEY* (1970) by Michael Boddy and Bob Ellis and *A HARD GOD* (1973) by Peter Kenna to *The Rain Dancers* by Karin Mainwaring in 1992. *King O'Malley* was the first play Hoad reviewed for the *Bulletin* and he regards it as one of his greatest evenings in Australian theatre.

Hoad was a dedicated theatregoer when he came to Sydney but on the *Bulletin* at first he specialised in business reporting, particularly of the mining boom. In 1969 the editor, Donald Horne, invited him to 'look after the arts'. He remained arts editor until 1989, gradually taking over reviewing of performances in Sydney as contributors retired. Editorial changes have diminished the *Bulletin*'s emphasis on the arts but Hoad retains his hold. His outlook on reviewing recalls the penultimate lines of *King Lear*:

> *The weight of this sad time we must obey;*
> *Speak what we feel, not what we ought to say.*

❦*Katharine Brisbane*

Maie Hoban

Teacher of speech and drama. War widow with four children. Moved from Ballarat (Vic.) to Melbourne and founded Modern School of Speech and Drama in 1930s. Eminent for three decades.

A woman of dynamic personality, great enthusiasm, and rich teaching ability, Maie Hoban pursued a vigorous policy of nurturing actors that was unique at the time. In the mid-1930s her Melbourne studio was in Allan's music store in Collins Street. She then moved to a large studio on the first floor of the Garrick Theatre. There she received critical acclaim for the first production in Melbourne of *Richard of Bordeaux* by Gordon Daviot, cast from her pupils. They were called the Garrick Players. After two years she moved to a building attached to St Peter's Church, near the Houses of Parliament. Her studio stage was in constant use for play readings and recitals. Her student productions were mostly performed in the nearby National Theatre. She coined the title Un-named Players for the performing arm of her school, which provided aspirants to a theatrical career with practical experience and exposure to audiences. Because of Hoban's emphasis on voice many of her pupils moved easily into the burgeoning radio drama. Her pupils included CORAL BROWNE, Keith Hudson, FREDERICK PARSLOW and the present writer. ❦*Patricia Kennedy*

Hobart

In its early years Hobart was central to the professional touring circuit, but after the 1850s slow growth in wealth and population increasingly distanced the town from the mainstream of theatrical activity and led to dependence upon amateur groups. Hobart has remained a small city (population 218 000), and although it is the capital of Tasmania, it has all the problems of a provincial centre in financing high-quality theatre. Government grants only partially solve them.

Theatre began in Hobart on 24 December 1833, when SAMSON CAMERON staged August von Kotzebue's *The Stranger* in a fit-up theatre at the FREEMASON'S TAVERN. His season was so successful that it lasted until May 1834 and as early as January 1834 stimulated a proposal to build a proper theatre. While it was being built plays were staged at the Theatre Royal in the ARGYLE ROOMS, which J. P. DEANE opened with *THE BUSHRANGERS* by Henry Melville of Hobart on 29 May 1834. Another local play, *THE BANDIT OF THE RHINE* was also performed there. Samson Cameron and JOHN MEREDITH later gave seasons there. The New Theatre Royal opened on 6 March 1837. The simple Georgian structure has been remodelled several times but it still stands—now called the THEATRE ROYAL—as a monument to unbroken theatrical activity.

Hobart's theatrical life was unrestricted, except for an embargo on convicts taking part in or attending performances, whereas in Sydney official opposition to theatre was expressed through rigorous licensing of buildings and plays. Theatrical companies plied between Hobart and Sydney, also giving seasons in Launceston and, later, Adelaide, Melbourne and Geelong. Melodrama, farce and some opera and ballet were the staple fare. The gymnast LUIGI DALLE CASE, and his company provided variety and novelty in 1842–43. ROBERT RADFORD presented equestrian dramas at his Royal Circus in 1848. Child performers included a six-year-old acting prodigy, Anna Marie Quinn. Men played female roles and vice versa—Mrs Mereton, for example, played Richard III on her own benefit night. Mr Newland illuminated the Royal Victoria Theatre by gas for the first time in January 1849 for *The Flying Dutchman* by Edward Fitzball. Another theatrical venue was the Music Hall, later the Royal Pantheon Theatre. Standards of production waxed and waned but it became clear that the small theatregoing public could sustain only one company.

ANNE CLARKE, a singer and actor, emerged as a theatrical manager in late 1840. She brought a company of talented performers from England in 1842, under contract so that they could not immediately defect to form a rival company. She ran the Royal Victoria Theatre—the New Theatre Royal renamed—well, emphasising drama and opera rather than vulgar farce. This countered distaste for theatre expressed by some influential members of the public and the press. During the 1840s local works emerged—the drama *SOUTH POLAR EXPEDITION* and the pantomime *Transportation and the Demon Discord*.

Ouside the mainstream

In the 1850s the goldmining and pastoral wealth of Victoria and NSW outstripped Tasmania's early economic strength, and small population and isolation placed the colony increasingly beyond the mainstream of theatrical activity. Resident companies playing long seasons gave way to Australian and European touring companies in the 1850s, when theatres in Adelaide, Melbourne and Geelong were added to the Sydney–Hobart–Launceston circuit. JOHN DAVIES remodelled the Theatre Royal in 1856 in an attempt to attract visiting stars. The actors G. V. BROOKE, MARY SCOTT-SIDDONS and Sir William and Lady Don, and W. J. HOLLOWAY's dramatic company and W. S. LYSTER's opera company all appeared at the Theatre Royal in the 1860s and 1870s. The Amateur Dramatic Club staged occasional successful performances for benevolent purposes, and the talented Louisa Anne Meredith produced masques under viceregal patronage for a select audience at Government House. The Temperance Hall, the Mechanic's Institute, the Masonic Hall, Del Sarte's Rooms, the Town Hall and later the City Hall were all venues for visiting artists.

GEORGE DARRELL, ESSIE JENYNS, GEORGE RIGNOLD, J. C. WILLIAMSON and many other performers provided virtually every type of dramatic entertainment in the 1880s. The Theatre Royal was remodelled again in 1890 and continued to accommodate popular companies from England, the USA and other Australian colonies. HARRY RICKARDS brought his vaudeville troupe to Hobart. The 1890s were also notable for the activities of the Hobart Operatic Company, an amateur group directed by Lucy Benson; the Gaiety Amateur Dramatic Company; the Derwent Dramatic Company and the Idler's Dramatic Company. Other amateur performances sprang from particular circumstances. For example, in 1894 the Earl of Yarmouth, a keen amateur actor, visiting Hobart during his world travels, hired the Theatre Royal to head the bill in a charity music-hall performance under viceregal patronage.

Before the First World War films became increasingly popular and met the need that had been filled by touring theatrical companies. The Temperance Hall was converted into the Avalon cinema. The King's Hall (later the King's Theatre) in Bathurst Street, the Grand Empire Theatre (opened on 31 December 1910) and His Majesty's Theatre (opened on 23 January 1911), later the Prince of Wales Theatre, all began as live theatres but were soon converted for films. Films were screened regularly at the Theatre Royal from 1912. The Strand (later Odeon) Theatre, built as a cinema, opened in 1916.

After the First World War a change in shipping routes made Tasmania even more inaccessible to touring companies. The ALLAN WILKIE SHAKESPEAREAN COMPANY was a notable exception, paying annual visits in the 1920s. Local amateur theatre to some extent filled the vacuum left by touring companies. The HOBART REPERTORY THEATRE SOCIETY was founded under OLIVE WILTON in 1926 and has staged classical and contemporary plays ever since. A glamorous season by the OLD VIC THEATRE COMPANY in 1948 did much to awaken public interest in live theatre, and the enthusiasm of Laurence Olivier for the Theatre Royal revived interest in the shabby building. FIFI BANVARD managed a resident theatre company at the Theatre Royal from 1949 to 1952. The NATIONAL THEATRE AND FINE ARTS SOCIETY, owner of the Theatre Royal, fostered a youth theatre workshop and, with the AUSTRALIAN ELIZABETHAN THEATRE TRUST, ensured that drama was seen in Hobart.

During the 1970s and 1980s the cost of importing large productions and the popularity of competing entertainments led to the staging at the Theatre Royal of plays with small casts, often with stars from television or film. The Tasmanian Theatre Company was established in 1971 with federal funds but by 1977, without further increases in funds, it had to suspend local productions. It continued to act as an entrepreneurial body, for opera and ballet as well as drama, after 1980. In the 1980s Hobart had a diversity of theatrical venues: Backspace, the Convention Centre at the Wrest Point Casino, the Derwent Entertainment Centre, the Mt Nelson Theatre, the Peacock Theatre and the University Studio Theatre. Polygon, a semiprofessional dramatic company, flourished until lack of government funding undermined its viability in 1983. ZOOTANGO under Richard Davey, Mainstage, a dramatic company, and a vigorous Gilbert and Sullivan society were all prominent in the early 1990s. High-quality performing-arts bodies for youth perhaps provided the greatest reason for optimism. Apprentice Theatre, which trained young people in classical theatre for 25 years, had ceased operation but the youth theatre company Theatre Now, the SALAMANCA THEATRE COMPANY and TERRAPIN PUPPET THEATRE stimulated the next generation of theatregoers. *Gillian Winter*

further reading
WINTER, GILLIAN. A colonial theatrical experience—The Royal Victoria Theatre, Hobart, 1837-1857. Tasmanian Historical Research Association *Papers and Proceedings* 32/4 (December 1985).

Hobart Repertory Theatre Society

Amateur dramatic company founded 21 July 1926 by Olive Wilton and others. **venues** 1926–38 Theatre Royal. 1938– Playhouse. **first production** *Mice and Men* by Madeleine Lucette Ryley, 1926, at Theatre Royal.

For more than 60 years the respected and popular Hobart Repertory Theatre Society has provided opportunities for gifted amateurs and pleasure for audiences. A moving force in its foundation was the English actor and director OLIVE WILTON, who staged productions at the Hobart Town Hall in the early 1920s. Their success and her strong personality enabled her to enlist influential Hobart people to form an organisation that would permanently alleviate the financial risk and managerial burden of a solo entrepreneur. The society was established, under the patronage of Governor Sir James O'Grady, as a limited liability company whose profits furthered its work. Its 256 members enjoyed free seats, preferential booking rights and the opportunity to perform in or assist with productions. The society aimed to produce four plays annually. Wilton was resident director until she retired in 1933, and thereafter guest director and patron.

The society staged its early productions at the Theatre Royal but after ten years its success enabled it to buy a cinema that had been built in 1863 as a Romanesque-revival chapel. It added a stage and dressing rooms and opened the 350-seat Playhouse on 26 November 1938 with *The Taming of the Shrew*. In this fine theatre with excellent acoustics the society—the first amateur group in Australia to own its theatre—has regularly presented the popular and the best in dramatic writing from classics to modern works. During its first 50 years it staged 400 productions, including plays by CATHERINE SHEPHERD and other members. Other notable members include the producer Olive Burn and Sir Stanley Burbury, Chief Justice of Tasmania and Governor from 1973 to 1982. For the society he was actor, pianist, director, administrator and Wilton's successor as patron. His efforts ensured the exemption of amateur theatre from federal ENTERTAINMENTS TAX. Recently the society has striven to improve the facilities and restore the exterior of the Playhouse, which is on the register of the National Estate. *Gillian Winter*

Clifford Hocking AM

Entrepreneur. Born 9 February 1932 in Melbourne, into musical family. Began as ABC messenger 1949. Opened record store with Kevin McBeath 1956. Became entrepreneur 1961. Director of Hocking, Vigo and Gerrand. Directed Melbourne Summer Music Festival 1988. Directed Adelaide Festival 1990. Inaugural Kenneth Myer Medallion for service to performing arts 1991. AM 1991.

The most influential theatrical entrepreneur in Melbourne is Clifford Hocking. In a career spanning three decades, he has demonstrated showmanship and an unparalleled eye for star quality. His organisation has staged hundreds of dramatic, dance and musical shows. Hocking has introduced audiences to a remarkably eclectic range of performers, including a young satirist named BARRY HUMPHRIES, whom he persuaded to tour Australia in 1962 in his first solo show, *A Nice Night's Entertainment*. With his partner David Vigo, Hocking has also been at the forefront of Melbourne's development as a cultural capital. Believing in the need to nourish live performance, he has worked hard at widening public appreciation of the arts. He divides his time between Melbourne and New York. *Simon Plant*

Edwin Hodgeman

Actor. Born 26 June 1935 at Alberton (SA). Acted in amateur theatre in Adelaide from 1951. Trained at National Institute of Dramatic Art (Sydney) 1959–60. Toured NSW and Queensland with Young Elizabethan Players 1961. Played title-role in Ben Jonson's *Volpone* at 1962 Adelaide Festival. Three years with Stratford (Ontario, Canada) Festival Company. Has worked since 1973 for South Australian Theatre Company (Adelaide), Nimrod Theatre Company (Sydney) and Melbourne Theatre Company. National Critics' Award for best actor in South Australia 1976. Also films and numerous television roles.

Edwin Hodgeman has a distinguished record as an actor, particularly in Adelaide and Melbourne. Slightly built and understated, he brings good judgment and often unexpected intensity to the stage. He is as fluent with new writing as with the classical repertoire and he is a conscientious performer—stylish in Alan Ayckbourn, staunch in Henrik Ibsen and saturnine as Prospero. In 1992 he played Bonaventura in John Ford's *'Tis a Pity she's a Whore* and Max in Michael Gurr's *Sex Diary of an Infidel*. He also brought his eccentric comedy to the role of Mrs Gavin in Louis Nowra's *Crow* in 1994. *Murray Bramwell*

Roger Hodgman

Director. Born 1 December 1943 in Hobart. Educated at University of Tasmania. ABC television director 1965–70. Taught acting and directed in London 1971–77. Director of Vancouver (Canada) Playhouse Acting School 1977–78. Director of Vancouver Playhouse 1978–81. Dean of drama at Victorian College of the Arts (Melbourne) 1982–86. Married actor Pamela Rabe 1984. Associate director of Melbourne Theatre Company 1984–87; artistic director 1987–.

An accomplished and versatile director of a wide variety of plays, Roger Hodgman has had success with Shakespeare, Henrik Ibsen and George Bernard Shaw. He has a particular affinity with contemporary American dramatists, such as Tennessee Williams and Arthur Miller. He has also directed plays by modern British writers, notably Caryl Churchill and Timberlake Wertenbaker, and Australian drama, especially works by JANIS BALODIS, his associate director with the MELBOURNE THEATRE COMPANY. Hodgman's artistic direction of this company has been distinguished by well-balanced and sometimes innovative programming—notably a repertory season of *Macbeth* and STEPHEN SEWELL's *Dreams in an Empty City* in 1989. At the VICTORIAN COLLEGE OF THE ARTS he made the training of actors and directors more orthodox than it had been under his predecessor Peter Oyston. ❧*Geoffrey Milne*

further reading
HOWIE, ANN C. (ed.). *Who's Who in Australia* 27th edn. Melbourne: Information Australia 1991.

Hole-in-the-Wall Theatre Company

Professional dramatic company in Perth, founded in 1965 by Frank Baden-Powell and John Gill. Amalgamated with Western Australian Theatre Company as State Theatre Company of Western Australia 1991. **venues** 1965– Braille Hall. 1967–68 Hole in the Roof. 1968–84 Southport Street Theatre, Leederville. 1984–91 Subiaco Theatre Centre. **artistic directors** 1965–67 Frank Baden-Powell and John Gill. 1968–70 Richard Davey. 1970–73 Ronald Denson. 1974–78 John Milson. 1978–79 Colin McColl. 1980–81 Edgar Metcalfe. 1981–89 Raymond Omodei. 1990–91 Aarne Neeme.

The Hole-in-the-Wall Theatre Company, named after the ramshackle building in which it first performed, was Perth's first experiment in intimate theatre-in-the-round. It presented contemporary experimental work from other countries and fostered Australian playwrights and actors, especially Western Australians. It developed a distinctive naturalistic house style and a close relationship with its audience in the confines of its early theatres. FRANK BADEN-POWELL, who had been artistic director of the NATIONAL THEATRE COMPANY, and John Gill founded the privately owned company to provide fresh theatrical experience at a time when other managements were presenting the British repertoire and conventional fare in Perth.

The Hole-in-the-Wall Theatre Company converted the Braille Hall into a 142-seat theatre-in-the-round. The company and its theatre owed their names to the last-minute penetration of an interior wall to provide access between the auditorium and the bar and foyer. The company used all its profits to pay artists or for improvements to the building. The company's experimental brief extended to improvisatory theatre, jazz sessions and readings of plays and poetry. In 1967 the last four plays of the season were by Western Australian playwrights. Then at Christmas Baden-Powell reopened the theatre as the Old Time Music Hole, for melodrama and music-hall.

The Hole-in-the-Wall Theatre Company moved across the road to what it called the Hole in the Roof—virtually an open backyard. It lost these premises at the end of 1968, when its production of David Halliwell's *Little Malcolm and His Struggle Against the Eunuchs* offended by lese-majesty and by spilling onto the street. The Public Health Department closed the Hole in the Roof on the grounds that it had insufficient exits. When the company moved to Leederville in 1968 it was reconstituted as an incorporated company with a committee of management.

Friends of the company helped it to secure freehold of the land and the new theatre, which had a small peninsular stage and an auditorium seating 156. It opened on 1 August 1968. Despite a vigorous program, the company was near financial collapse by April 1969. A ten-month season of *There's a Girl in My Soup* by Terence Frisby stabilised its finances but it had to rebuild its audience when it reverted to presenting adventurous new works. The artistic director, Ronald Denson, elected to mix new and unusual plays with proven successes. In 1970 the company began to receive subsidies from the Western Australian Arts Council and the Australian Council for the Arts.

John Milson introduced an artistic policy more akin to the founders' intentions in 1974. With Sydney's NIMROD THEATRE COMPANY as a model, he instituted a challenging program of new plays, revues, musicals and a peppering of classics, and developed a band of vibrant young actors. The company developed an entertaining, popular style, providing new directions in Perth theatre.

After 1978 the company lost creative impetus and audiences, but Edgar Metcalfe, appointed artistic director in 1980, restored its artistic vitality and confidence and stabilised its finances with carefully balanced programs and an insistence on high standards. Under Raymond Omodei's direction from 1981 to 1989, the company continued to offer new Australian works, alongside innovative versions of Greek drama, Shakespeare and more recent classics by Henrik Ibsen, Anton Chekhov, Eugene O'Neill and Irish playwrights. Omodei introduced subscriptions, and instituted a repertory system in 1983. The Southport Street Theatre was too small to pay, so in August 1984 the company moved to a new 300-seat thrust-stage Hole-in-the-Wall Theatre in the Subiaco Theatre Centre. It opened with *A Midsummer Night's Dream*.

In 1991 the Hole-in-the-Wall company agreed, after much discussion and some dissension, to amalgamate with the Western Australian Theatre Company to form the STATE THEATRE COMPANY OF WESTERN AUSTRALIA. The Hole-in-the-Wall Theatre Company, however, remained a legal entity, though without public funding. It had members at $10 a year, an unpaid artistic director—initially Jenny McNae—and an elected board of directors, as before.

After the demise of the the State Theatre Company in early 1993, the government's policy became to support a variety of separate small companies by providing occasional funding —which many saw as a retrograde step. Under this new system the Hole-in-the-Wall company managed to secure subsidy from the state Department of the Arts for two productions at the Subiaco Theatre Centre. These were Rona Munro's *Bold Girls*, directed by Jenny McNae, in November 1993, and Elizabeth Coleman's *It's My Party (and I'll Die If I Want To)*, directed by Catherine Hill in April 1994. ❧*Maurice Jones*

further reading
NEWBY, JAKE (ed.). *By a Railway Line*. Perth: Hole-in-the-Wall Theatre Company 1983.
NEWBY, JAKE (ed.). *Theatre Moves*. Perth: Hole-in-the-Wall Theatre Company 1984.

Jane Holland

Actor. Born 1921 in Sydney. Trained at Bryant's Playhouse (Sydney). First worked professionally in radio drama. Went to England 1946. Married actor Leo McKern 1946. Toured Australasia with Shakespeare Memorial Theatre Company 1953. Retired from theatre after birth of first child, actor Abigail McKern. Also mother of film director Harriet McKern.

During the early 1940s Jane Holland was the most promising young classical actor in Sydney and she was the first young Australian actor to go overseas after the Second World War. Her performances, particularly in tragic roles, were memorable for strong emotional power, clarity of focus and a haunting, fragile grace. She won the Harry Tighe Cup for best acting in the British Drama League's Australia Festival with her performance in Arthur Symon's poetic drama *The Harvesters* at BRYANT'S PLAYHOUSE in 1942. For INDEPENDENT THEATRE she was an exquisite Ophelia in *Hamlet* in 1943. She was a spirited, elfin Peter Pan in J. M. Barrie's play at the Minerva Theatre. For Metropolitan Theatre she was outstanding as Christina in CATHERINE DUNCAN's *Sons of the Morning* and as Emily in Thornton Wilder's *Our Town* in 1945. Early in 1946 the director Eric Reiman engaged Holland and LEO MCKERN for the Will Mahoney Company at the Theatre Royal in Brisbane. After the season of plays Holland, aiming to work in England, sailed on the first available passenger ship. She returned to Australia with the Shakespeare Memorial Theatre Company in 1953, playing Bianca in *Othello*, in which McKern, now her husband, was Iago. ❦*Lynne Murphy*

May Hollinworth

Director, producer. Born May 1895 in Sydney. Daughter of actor–manager W. H. Hollinworth. Studied chemistry and worked in pharmacology department at University of Sydney. Began directing plays for Sydney University Dramatic Society 1926; producer 1929–43. Member of Playwrights' Advisory Board 1938–63. Founded Metropolitan Theatre (Sydney) 1943. Retired because of illness 1950. Directed for Independent Theatre (Sydney) 1955–57. Died November 1968 in Sydney.

'For the best part of three decades May Hollinworth was one of the outstanding champions of an indigenous theatre and drama in Sydney', wrote H. G. KIPPAX, an early member of her METROPOLITAN THEATRE, in an obituary. She aimed to reveal the playwright's intention on a level deeper than words. Hollinworth created memorable stage pictures by using lighting and by grouping her actors. She gave them no direction other than where to move, but required them to think their own way through the play, to develop self-reliance and flexibility. DORIS FITTON, once a rival director, paid Hollinworth a tribute in her autobiography: 'May was an extraordinary director; she never seemed to do much with her actors, but the results were always superb.'

Hollinworth began directing plays for the SYDNEY UNIVERSITY DRAMATIC SOCIETY in 1926 and won the prize for best production in a competition run by GREGAN MCMAHON in 1927. She raised the society to a high level and many of its actors became leading professionals. She mounted many beautiful productions in the Savoy Theatre, the NSW State Conservatorium of Music and the Great Hall of the university. Poetic drama and Restoration comedy were her forte.

When the society acquired a small experimental theatre in 1938 Hollinworth extended her repertoire to intimate theatre to great effect. She also gave memorable productions of contemporary plays, including DYMPHNA CUSACK's *Shallow Cups*. This was one of many Australian plays Hollinworth directed for the society and for Metropolitan Theatre, which she founded in 1943, aiming to create a professional repertory company. She trained another company of talented young players but illness forced her to retire in 1950, her dream unrealised after 120 productions in 24 years.

In 1955 Doris Fitton invited Hollinworth to direct for INDEPENDENT THEATRE. Her production of Peter Ustinov's *The Love of Four Colonels* 'showed that Sydney's Little Theatres cannot afford the retirement of highly self-critical and inventive artists like Miss Hollinworth', wrote LINDSEY BROWNE in the *Sydney Morning Herald* on 14 May 1955. Her crowning achievement was in directing Richard Beynon's THE SHIFTING HEART for the AUSTRALIAN ELIZABETHAN THEATRE TRUST in 1957, with some of her original players in leading roles. ❦*Lynne Murphy*

Charles Holloway

Actor, manager. Born in London c.1848. Brought to Australia 1856, mother dying on voyage. Began acting c.1874. Managed family company with brother W. J. Holloway 1880–c.1888. Married actor Alice Deorwyn. Ran own company, mainly in provincial Victoria c.1894–99. Died c.1900. Father of actor Beatrice Holloway.

Charles Holloway formed his own company by 1894 and in partnership with WILLIAM ANDERSON he performed popular melodramas throughout the eastern colonies until ill-health forced his retirement in December 1899. He began acting about 1874, when he joined his brother W. J. HOLLOWAY in GEORGE COPPIN's company. The brothers formed their own company in 1880, but Charles had left it by 1887. In Sydney in November 1887 he was playing with distinction in GEORGE RIGNOLD's season of William Gillette's *Held by the Enemy* at the Theatre Royal while the W. J. Holloway company was giving *Twelfth Night* at the Criterion Theatre. Around this time Charles Holloway married Alice Deorwyn. They acted in DAN BARRY's company in the early 1890s. Their daughter Beatrice Holloway also became a star, touring for MEYNELL AND GUNN in J. A. Campbell's *The Little Breadwinner* in 1908. ❦*Richard Fotheringham*

W. J. Holloway

Actor, manager. Born 4 February 1843 in London. Brought to Australia 1856. Mother died on voyage. Apprentice engineer in Sydney. Amateur theatricals led to professional engagements in Brisbane, Adelaide, Melbourne c.1868–80. Married widowed actor Kate Arden 30 June 1871. Formed first company at Ballarat (Vic.) 1880. Gave Shakespeare seasons in Sydney, Melbourne and other towns 1885–88. Acted in London from 1889. Took own companies on South African tours. Died February 1913. Daughters Cecil Arden and Juliet Sydney, son W. E. Holloway and stepdaughter Essie Jenyns all acted in his companies.

William John Holloway, his wife Kate Arden and his look-alike brother CHARLES HOLLOWAY, actors in stock companies in the 1870s, formed a company in Ballarat in 1880 at his wife's insistence. She was business manager, wardrobe mistress, advance agent, and occasional actor. Their first success was *The Comedy of Errors* with W. J. and Charles Holloway as the two Antipholuses. A series of brilliant Shakespearean productions followed between 1885 and 1888, starring Arden's daughter ESSIE JENYNS. The couple's own children all appeared in the productions too.

W. J. Holloway returned to England with his family. He appeared as Kent in Henry Irving's production of *King Lear* at the Lyceum in London in November 1892. Next January Irving became ill and Holloway learned the role of Lear in five hours and performed it to acclaim for a week until Irving recovered. The great actor-manager invited him to alternate in the role for the rest of the season. The Holloways' daughter Juliet Sydney (named after her birthplace) was their leading lady on successful tours of SOUTH AFRICA. Only their son W. E. Holloway performed again in Australia, about 1898. ❧*Richard Fotheringham*

further reading
HOLLOWAY, DAVID. *Playing the Empire*. London: Harrap 1979.

David Holman

Dramatist. Born 4 March 1942 in England. Educated at University of Sussex. Taught at University of Ontario (Canada) 1964–66, London Film School 1966–67. Film writer in London 1967–69. Secondary school teacher 1966–70. Joined Belgrade Theatre (Coventry) 1970. Wrote more than 20 theatre-in-education programs and theatre shows 1970–73. Writer-in-residence at Joan Littlewood's Theatre Royal (London) 1978. Emigrated to Australia 1986. Australian Writers' Guild Awgie award 1993 for best feature film script for his adaptation of his play *No Worries*.

David Holman's accounts of social adjustment—from country to town, for refugee children or across ethnic divides—are perceptive and endearing. They combine keen observation with narrative craft. *The Small Poppies*, about four children on their first day at primary school, is already a classic. It stands amongst Holman's best work, along with *No Worries*, which he wrote for performance by the MAGPIE THEATRE COMPANY at the Adelaide Festival in 1986, after he had been in Australia for only seven weeks.

Holman came to live in Australia after he had written more than 70 plays on politically progressive themes in the United Kingdom. By his own admission the move gave his writing renewed spirit and purpose. After a successful collaboration with the Magpie directors Chris Johnson and GEOFFREY RUSH, Holman returned to London in 1988 for further successes with the Young Vic. He now works alternately in Australia and England. His adaptation of Nikolai Gogol's *Diary of a Madman* was a hit at the BELVOIR STREET THEATRE in Sydney in 1990 and toured extensively. *No Worries* was made into a film in 1992. ❧*Murray Bramwell*

published plays
Beauty and the Beast (1988). Sydney: Currency Press 1989.
No Worries (1986). Sydney: Currency Press 1989.
The Small Poppies (1986). Sydney: Currency Press 1989.

Bland Holt

Actor, manager. Born 24 March 1851 in England. Originally Joseph Thomas Holt. Son of actor-manager Clarance Holt. Educated in Melbourne, New Zealand and England. Acted in father's productions c.1863–c.1870. Manager at Queen's Theatre, Dublin, 1872. In USA as clown and writer and director of pantomimes 1873–75. Came to Australia as clown and comic actor 1876. Established own company in Sydney 1880. Managed Surrey Theatre, London, and with father organised provincial tours of Drury Lane melodramas. Returned to Melbourne for Williamson, Garner and Musgrove 1887. Married actor Florence Anderson 1887. Formed own company. Retired from stage 1909. Died 28 June 1942.

Probably the most successful actor-manager on the Australian stage between 1880 and his retirement in 1909, Bland Holt spent much of his childhood in Australia and New Zealand. His father CLARANCE HOLT, twice visited the colonies between 1854 and 1864, acting on tour and managing theatres in Melbourne and Dunedin (New Zealand). Bland Holt returned to Australia in 1876 as a brilliant young comedian, appearing first in F. C. Burnand's *Ixion* in Sydney on 28 October and in roles ranging from pantomime clown to the First Gravedigger in *Hamlet*.

Father and son corresponded extensively, and Clarance Holt was able to secure for his son the Australasian rights to many of the most successful plays of the London stage. Clarance Holt had his greatest success with *The New Babylon*, a melodrama by Paul Merritt and George Fawcett Rowe. It presented a multitude of stage sensations, including a mid-Atlantic collision between two steamships, a horse race, and scenes displaying the delights and moral dangers of the 'wicked city' of London. Bland Holt staged this play in Sydney on 24 April 1880 and Melbourne on 12 June 1880. His production, meticulously based on extensive details sent from London by his father, lifted him quickly into the first rank of Australian theatrical managers, despite some bitter opposition.

Bland Holt's first wife died in 1883 and then he returned to England and stayed there for almost four years. His father was the provincial agent for Sir Augustus Harris, manager of the Theatre Royal, Drury Lane, and he toured Harris's sensational melodramas throughout the United Kingdom. Bland Holt leased the Surrey Theatre in Lambeth, south London, and from this base, in association with his father, he sent productions on tour. Bland Holt also formed friendships and good business relationships with many of the major playwrights and entrepreneurs of the popular London stage.

In 1884 J. C. WILLIAMSON, after seeing all the London pantomimes, wrote to Holt that there was 'no clown that can in any way compare with you', and in 1887 Holt returned to Australia for WILLIAMSON, GARNER AND MUSGROVE. He brought with him rights to the latest London successes and opened in a Drury Lane horse-racing drama, *A Run of Luck* by Henry Pettitt and Augustus Harris. Florence Anderson, an actor he had employed in England, followed him to Adelaide and they were married. 'The Bland Holts' became Australia's favourite stage comedians for the next 20 years.

Bland Holt formed his own company but he maintained a working relationship with WILLIAMSON AND MUSGROVE until about 1894. Holt's near-monopoly on the rights to the most successful and sensational comedy-melodramas from Drury Lane and the Adelphi Theatre in London, combined with his meticulous, opulent and spectacular staging, made him the most consistently successful actor-manager of his time. He staged the English Derby with real horses crossing and recrossing the stage, fox hunts in snowy English country settings, and other pastimes such as test cricket at Lord's and pheasant shooting on the moors. All these were designed to evoke in Australian audiences nostalgia and admiration for the 'home' country. This identification extended to several intensely imperialistic South African War dramas, in which Holt staged battles using hundreds of actors. Other sensations in Holt's productions included a car chase, a collapsing dam, and an 'underwater' fight to the death between two deep-sea divers. His major productions included Pettitt and Harris's *Taken from Life* in 1890, *The Prodigal Daughter* in 1892 and *A Million of Money* in 1893; Cecil Raleigh and Henry Hamilton's *The Derby Winner* in 1896 and *The White Heather* in 1898; and Arthur Shirley and Benjamin Landeck's *Woman and Wine* in 1899.

Holt was friendly with J. F. Archibald of the *Bulletin*, Henry Lawson and 'Banjo' Paterson, but in spite of these contacts with literary nationalists he was reluctant to follow the trend towards Australian stories, such as those successfully presented by ALFRED DAMPIER. In 1899 he tentatively localised to Sydney a play about a bank robbery, Sutton Vane's *The War of Wealth*, and was surprised by its warm reception. Holt failed to interest Lawson in localising plays, but the short-story writers EDWARD DYSON and, later, Henry Fletcher, worked on six subsequent scripts. The first, *Riding to Win* in 1901, showed a bicycle race at the Melbourne exhibition grounds and presented Holt as an Australian soldier returned from South Africa who lit a barbecue on the stage and cooked steaks using his bayonet as a skewer.

Other English and American melodramas localised by Dyson and Fletcher for Holt included *A Desperate Game* in 1903, *The Betting Book* in 1905, *Besieged at Port Arthur* in 1905, *A Path of Thorns* in 1905, and *The Great Rescue* in 1907. The most famous of all was THE BREAKING OF THE DROUGHT in 1902. It had real crows picking at the carcasses of cattle, a display of diving into a tank of water, risqué dancing at a gentleman's club, a spectacular bushfire and, of course, rain in the final scene. The play was made into a film by Franklyn Barrett in 1920.

Early Australian silent-film makers reused plots of many of the plays in Holt's repertoire, and their most exciting incidents in particular. Holt in turn used a motion-picture background for a car chase down Sydney's George Street. Other Australian scenes in his plays were John Wren's Collingwood tote and a car–train race from Charters Towers to Townsville in north Queensland. In 1906 the English playwright Arthur Shirley reported that Australian actors in London thought Bland Holt excelled Drury Lane in the production of spectacular and sensational melodramas. Even if Holt's 'Australian' plays were dubiously indigenous, his stars were Australians, notably Walter E. Baker and Frances Ross.

Health problems struck both Holts in 1907. They retired two years later, after the death of the scene-painter, JOHN BRUNTON. Bland Holt said he could not find a replacement. The Holts lived on in luxury in Melbourne for more than 30 years. Florence Holt died in 1946, four years after her husband. ❦*Richard Fotheringham*

further reading
FOWLER, J. BERESFORD. *Stars in My Backyard*. Ilfracombe (England): A. H. Stockwell c.1960.
SHOESMITH, DENNIS. Joseph Thomas Holt. *Australian Dictionary of Biography* 4. Melbourne University Press 1979.

Clarance Holt

Actor, manager. Born 12 January 1826. Originally Joseph Frederick Holt. Debut in London 1843. Married actor Marie Browne 1848. Performed in Australia and New Zealand 1854–56 and 1859–64. Subsequently major actor-manager in English provinces and London. Second marriage 1883. Father of actor-manager Bland Holt and producer and writer May Holt. Died 1904 in London.

According to Clarance Holt, Captain Cook had been simply his advance agent, particularly in New Zealand, where in 1862 Holt was avowedly 'the Pioneer of the English Drama'. Holt was already a formidable 'heavy' actor when he and his wife decided to seek their fortunes by entertaining miners on the Australian goldfields. He was a 'rough and ready actor of the ranting school' with 'the unenviable reputation of being the most foul-mouthed member of his profession', according to Errol Sherson. 'When he spoke no dog dared to bark', wrote George Arliss in a funny account of his first audition for Clarance Holt, who 'was not over-generous in his ideas of salary, so no aspiring actor stayed with him very long'.

Holt had a setback in Geelong (Vic.) with *The Elephant of Siam and the Fire Fiend*, attributed to Thomas Dibdin. His partner HENRY DEERING hired a real elephant for spectacle. The stage door and ramps had to be rebuilt and the stage strengthened to support the animal. Deering paraded it through the streets daily to publicise the show but townspeople saw no need to pay to see the elephant again at night. The partners lost £1100 before they dissolved their partnership. Nevertheless, Holt was one of the few to compete successfully with GEORGE COPPIN. There was no question of a partnership—Coppin's father had been merely Holt's prompter in Norwich—but Holt did agree to play with Coppin's star G. V. BROOKE in *Othello* in 1859. This was during Holt's second tour of the colonies, 'travelling with my own company of twenty-two artistes and a repertoire of forty legitimate plays, staying a month in each town and changing the program nightly'. Holt leased theatres in Ballarat (Vic.) in 1860, Melbourne in 1861 and Dunedin (New Zealand) in 1862–64, but then returned to England.

He managed the Duke's Theatre in London from 1878 to 1880 and produced one outstanding hit, Paul Merritt and George Fawcett Rowe's *The New Babylon*. The colonial rights to this melodrama gave his son BLAND HOLT his start as an entrepreneur. Clarance Holt lost the Duke's Theatre in a fire, but he became the major provincial manager of the 1880s by touring the sensational melodramas staged at the Theatre Royal, Drury Lane. Holt played old Ben Marston the ex-convict in Alfred Dampier's London season of ROBBERY UNDER ARMS in 1894. He acted as Drury Lane stage manager and provincial manager for another Australian story, THE DUCHESS OF COOLGARDIE, in 1896. He died widely remembered as an old tyrant. ❦*Richard Fotheringham*

writings
Twice round the world. Ms. in National Library of Australia (Canberra). A major source for the Australian stage in 1850s and English theatre from 1840s to 1900.

further reading
ARLISS, GEORGE. *Up the Years from Bloomsbury*. New York: Blue Ribbon Books 1927.
SHERSON, ERROL. *London's Lost Theatres of the Nineteenth Century*. London: John Lane 1925.

W. R. Honey

Amateur actor, dramatist. Flourished in Hobart 1865–79. Probably William Richard Honey, born 1 June 1829, died 5 May 1920 in Launceston (Tas.).

W. R. Honey, who wrote at least three plays and had two published, is believed to have been William Richard Honey, a clerk in the Audit Office in Hobart from 1859 to 1892. Honey was also a reciter and took leading parts in amateur theatrical productions. *Rosano* was staged as a benefit for him in 1879. A reviewer, noting that the play had been performed in Hobart several times, said an 'immense audience' saw 'one of the most brilliant amateur gâla [sic] ever seen in Hobart Town'. Descendants of Honey, notably Cecil Honey, have been active in Launceston theatre. ❧*Gillian Winter*

published plays
Glaucus. Hobart: Tasmanian Times 1870.
Madeline Clifton—or, Woman's Revenge (1869). Hobart: Tasmanian Times 1869.

The Honeys

An acrobatic troupe, the Honeys were three sons and three daughters of an American gymnast and a granddaughter of John Jones, the founder of ST LEON'S CIRCUS. Daisy St Leon, the eldest daughter of Gus St Leon, was a young bareback rider in Probasco's and FitzGerald Brothers' circuses in 1899–1901, before she went with her family to the USA, where she rode in the Ringling Brothers' circus in 1902–03. In Mexico in 1904 she married Alfred Honey, a gymnast in a large Mexican circus. He formed a gymnastic act with Frank Cherry.

Late in 1908 Gus St Leon's children returned to Australia and the Honeys and Cherry came with them. Honey and Cherry appeared in vaudeville with the Five St Leons acrobatic troupe in January 1909 at the Opera House in Melbourne and at Brennan's National Amphitheatre in Sydney. Then the St Leons and the Honeys formed Gus St Leon's Great United Circus.

The first of the Honey children to appear in the circus ring was Golda, the oldest. She performed as a wirewalker at Hay (NSW) in August 1917. Her performance was distinguished by a slack-wire routine learned from her father. 'A specially pleasing turn was an exhibition of wire rope walking and running by Mademoiselle Golda unassisted by the usual parasol', said the *New Zealand Herald*, reviewing the St Leon circus on 26 December 1920. By that time Golda's acrobatic brothers and sisters were also performing as the Honeys.

In the 1925–26 season the Honeys appeared with WIRTHS' CIRCUS. Then they went to the USA, where they played vaudeville houses and indoor circuses during the late 1920s and the 1930s with an act that combined music, comedy and teeterboard acrobatics. They appeared with the St Leon European Circus, part-owned with PHILIP ST LEON, which toured New England states in 1931. Members of the Honey family were active in American show business until the early 1960s. ❧*Mark St Leon*

further reading
ST LEON, MARK. *Spangles and Sawdust*. Melbourne: Greenhouse 1983.

Alan Hopgood

Actor, dramatist. Born 29 September 1934 in Launceston (Tas.). Educated at University of Melbourne. Acted in 31 Union Theatre Repertory Company productions 1956–69. In England 1970–71. Also writes for film and television.

One of the first Australian playwrights promoted by the Union Theatre Repertory Company (now the MELBOURNE THEATRE COMPANY) was Alan Hopgood, who began professional acting in the company in 1956. His first play, *Marcus*, had a student production at the University of Melbourne in 1959. In a week in 1963, while acting in George S. Kaufman and Moss Hart's *The Man Who Came to Dinner*, Hopgood wrote his comedy, *And the Big Men Fly*, about a barefoot country football player who becomes a star. He played J. J. Forbes, president of an Australian football club, when the play opened five weeks later. It was an immediate popular success and was later performed in other states. The play helped Australian playwrights to gain public acceptance and almost 200 000 copies of it have been sold. The Melbourne Theatre Company revived it in 1988, Hopgood again playing Forbes.

The company staged two more of Hopgood's plays, *The Golden Legion of Cleaning Women*, a comedy at the expense of business practice, and *Private Yuk Objects* (1966), which explored Australia's participation in the Vietnam War. In 1970 Hopgood left for England. On returning late in 1971 he turned to film and television writing. He has also acted in long-running television series. He returned to the stage with libretti for *Little Redinka* (1991), a children's opera, and *Petrov* (1992), a musical based on the 1950s spy scandal; and two musical biographies, *Callas—The Woman*, first performed at the Port Fairy (Vic.) Spring Music Festival in 1992, and *The Mario Lanza Story* (1994). ❧*Leonard Radic*

published plays
And Here Comes Bucknuckle (1968). Melbourne: Heinemann 1980.
And the Big Men Fly (1963). Melbourne: Heinemann 1969.
The Golden Legion of Cleaning Women (1964). Melbourne: Heinemann 1979.

other writings
From the Battlements. Melbourne: Bay Street 1987.
Neighbours. Melbourne: Heinemann 1990.
The Twin Book. Melbourne: Heinemann 1986.

further reading
SUMNER, JOHN. *Recollections at Play—A life in Australian theatre*. Melbourne: University Press 1993.

F. R. C. Hopkins

Dramatist. Born 1849 near Bombay (India). Son of naval officer. Educated in England. Became journalist but emigrated to Australia c.1865. Managed and owned grazing properties in Victoria and NSW. Wrote plays 1875–82 and 1909. Also wrote essays, poetry, short stories and edited annuals. Died 20 July 1916 near Carcoar (NSW) after accident.

One of Australia's few squatter–playwrights, Francis Hopkins had the good fortune to be in Victoria in 1875–77 when the actor–manager ALFRED DAMPIER was looking for someone to adapt European novels for his stage company. Much of Hopkins's playwriting was this kind of hack work —such as ALL FOR GOLD in 1877, *Only a Fool* in 1880 and *Michael Strogoff* in 1882—but in 1882 he also attempted a comedy set in Sydney, *L.S.D.* It failed in spite of the character of Major Chilley Chutney, 'an adventurer from India'; possibly a self-parody. Later Hopkins, inspired by *An Englishman's Home*, a 1909 London success which warned that England had gone soft and could easily be invaded, wrote a similar jingoistic drama, *Reaping the Whirlwind*. It attacked strikes, sport and political corruption for diverting Australians' attention from defence. As the final curtain falls an invading 'Asiatic Fleet' is sighted off Townsville (Qld). Hopkins published the play anonymously, but it was not performed. ❦*Richard Fotheringham*

published play
Reaping the Whirlwind. Sydney: Websdale, Shoosmith 1909.

further reading
RICKARD, JOHN. Francis Rawdon Chesney Hopkins. *Australian Dictionary of Biography* 4. Melbourne University Press 1972.

reference
A script of *All for Gold* is held in the British Library (London), Add. ms 53205J.

William Hoskins

Actor, manager. Born 1816 in Derbyshire (England). Briefly studied law at Cambridge University. Began acting in provincial companies 1834. Pupil of Samuel Phelps at Sadler's Wells Theatre, London. Acted at Olympic Theatre, London, under William Farren's management, and taught Henry Irving elocution. Married singer Julia Harland 1850. Arrived in Australia 1856. Manager of Theatre Royal, Ballarat (Vic.), 1860. Manager of Theatre Royal, Melbourne, 1863. At Haymarket Theatre, Melbourne, in late 1860s. Married actor Florence Colville 1874. Moved to New Zealand 1875. Returned to Melbourne after wife's death, 1881. Married Maude Bowman 1882. Retired from stage 1884. Died 28 September 1886 in Melbourne.

William Hoskins was noted for his teaching ability, his interpretation of Shakespeare, and especially for his acting of light comedy. He played many supporting Shakespearean roles, notably Mercutio and Lucio, and brought to Australia the Shakespearean traditions of the Sadler's Wells Theatre under the tragedian Samuel Phelps. Hoskins himself influenced notable actors, including Marie St Denis and his second wife Florence Colville. Like many actor-managers, he lost and won several fortunes. He arrived in Melbourne with his first wife, Julia Harland, daughter of the American actor Henry Wallack, in 1856 and played at the Queen's Theatre. After touring the colonies he became manager of the Theatre Royal at Ballarat. There he had many successes. including an elaborate production of *The Tempest*, in which he played Prospero. In 1868 he reopened the Royal Victoria Theatre in Sydney as actor–manager and played Captain Versatile Fluent in the premiere of Walter Cooper's COLONIAL EXPERIENCE. Hoskins and his second wife based themselves in Christchurch (New Zealand) and toured widely from 1875 until she died in 1881. An American tour was not a success. Hoskins married again on return to Melbourne. After playing Dr Pangloss in *Candide* he retired from the stage in 1884 and taught elocution until he died from cirrhosis of the liver. ❦*Mimi Colligan*

further reading
IRVIN, ERIC. Introduction. *Colonial Experience* by Walter Cooper. Sydney: Currency Press 1979.
Argus (Melbourne) 29 September 1886.
Town and Country Journal (Sydney) 2 October 1886.

Jenny Howard

Comedian, singer. Born c.1904 in London. Gained experience in provincial variety. Performed in Melbourne and Sydney with husband Percy King, 1929. Returned to Australia 1940. Performed in revue and pantomime until 1970s. Retired 1984.

The most durable of Australia's pantomime stars, Jenny Howard was probably the best-known principal boy in the last 50 years. She came to Australia in 1929 with her husband Percy King to play the TIVOLI CIRCUIT after an engagement at the London Palladium. Their first season in Melbourne was so successful that the star, ADA REEVE, insisted they be taken out of the show. They were sent to Sydney's Tivoli Theatre and after 10 weeks there they returned to London. Howard came back to Australia for the Tivoli circuit in 1940, with King now her manager. She starred in *The Crazy Show* with GEORGE WALLACE, BOB DYER and the young GLORIA DAWN, beginning 30 years as an institution in revue and pantomime, especially *Aladdin*. She toured for HARRY WREN in *Thanks for the Memory* in 1955 and *Many Happy Returns* in 1959, and made her operetta debut in *Pippin* in 1974. She had been on the stage for almost 60 years when she retired to Queensland's Gold Coast after the death of her husband. ❦*Alwyn Capern*

reference
The Performing Arts Museum (Melbourne) has a tape recording of an interview with Howard.

John Howard

Actor, director. Born 22 October 1952 in Corowa (NSW). Moved to Sydney with family at six. Studied medicine for one year and law for two years at University of NSW in 1970–72. Worked in public service and finance. Studied at National Institute of Dramatic Art (Sydney) 1976–78. Has since played principal roles for all state theatre companies, Nimrod Theatre Company (Sydney) and Belvoir Street Theatre (Sydney). Married actor Elizabeth Maywald 1991. Associate director of Sydney Theatre Company 1993. Variety Club of Australia award for stage actor of year 1992. Sydney Theatre Critics' Circle award 1992 (John Proctor in *The Crucible* by Arthur Miller and Edmund Burke in *Mongrels* by Nick Enright).Regular appearances in films and television drama.

John Howard is one of Australia's most dynamic stage actors. A man with a powerful figure and an inquiring mind, he has throughout his career taken every opportunity to extend his understanding of his craft. He has worked with the AUSTRALIAN NATIONAL PLAYWRIGHTS' CONFERENCE and REX CRAMPHORN's experimental Shakespeare Company and taken part in the experiments of the Performing Arts Centre at the University of Sydney and Dramaturgical Services Inc. He made his professional debut in 1978 as Aubrey in Lindsay Anderson's production of Ben Travers's farce *The Bed Before Yesterday* in Sydney. He followed this role with Clifford Anderson in Ira Levin's thriller *Deathtrap* on national tour, and Sandy Taylor in GEORGE WHALEY's adaptation of Steele Rudd's *On Our Selection* for the NIMROD THEATRE COMPANY in 1979. In 1980 he played Orin in Eugene O'Neill's *Mourning Becomes Electra* for the MELBOURNE THEATRE COMPANY before spending six months in Cramphorn's company in Sydney.

Howard's first role for the SYDNEY THEATRE COMPANY, Lopakhin in Anton Chekhov's *The Cherry Orchard* in 1983, led to his being cast in the title-role of the epic nine-hour production of David Edgar's *The Life and Adventures of Nicholas Nickleby*. This brought Howard national acclaim. In Sydney 1984 he played Kent to JOHN BELL's King Lear in Sydney and in 1986 Lucio in the Sydney Theatre Company's *Measure for Measure* and Mike in Philip Barry's *The Philadelphia Story*. In 1986 Howard also learned the title-role of Christopher Marlowe's *The Tragical History of Doctor Faustus* in five days for a public experiment by Dramaturgical Services Inc. in the working capacities and conditions of Elizabethan actors.

In 1987 he created the aggressive cattle station owner Horse in Gordon Francis's *God's Best Country* for the Western Australian Theatre Company at the Festival of Perth and on tour in northern Australia. In the same year he adapted and directed a program of Kenneth Slessor's poetry as *Out of Time* in Sydney and created the Man in ALMA DE GROEN's play about Katherine Mansfield, *The Rivers of China*. In 1989 Howard played Iago in *Othello*, Edmund in *King Lear*, Trigorin in Anton Chekhov's *The Seagull*, Torvald in Henrik Ibsen's *A Doll's House* at the BELVOIR STREET THEATRE, and the title-role in Gale Edwards's landmark revival of Aphra Behn's *The Rover* for the STATE THEATRE COMPANY of South Australia. He created Tony Turner in David Williamson's *Top Silk* in 1989 and next year he played the title-role for the QUEENSLAND THEATRE COMPANY.

Howard's notable roles since then have included John Proctor in Arthur Miller's *The Crucible* in 1991 and 1992, Benedick in *Much Ado About Nothing* and *Coriolanus* in 1993, both for the Sydney Theatre Company. Of his John Proctor Ken Healey wrote in the Sydney *Sun-Herald*: 'For 15 years or more Howard has been the outstanding actor of his generation in Australian theatre. Nothing he has done, not even his unforgettable Nicholas Nickleby for the STC, has been bigger, more daring, or more affecting than this portrayal of a strong man too conscious of his weakness.' In 1992 the Sydney Theatre Company appointed Howard an associate director to establish a company of actors from a variety of cultures to develop a style of popular theatre with a poetic base, and to tour country and suburban centres. The group has been called the Australian People's Theatre. ❦*Katharine Brisbane*

Kate Howarde

Actor, director, dramatist, entrepreneur. Born 1869 in Southwick (Sussex, England). Originally Catherine Clarissa Jones. Emigrated to New Zealand with family before 1878. Began professional writing at nine. Came to Australia. Toured with Kate Howarde Company c.1886–c.1900. Worked in USA as journalist and scriptwriter c.1906–11. Ran National Theatre in Balmain, Sydney. Married William De Saxe, comedian (died c.1899) and Elton Black, vaudevillian. Died 20 February 1939 in Sydney. Mother of Lesley Adrien, actress.

In 1929 the *Australian Woman's Mirror* could ask: 'Is there anyone who doesn't know Kate Howarde?' A unique personality of the Australian stage, Howarde was a serious dramatist who worked within professional constraints and a woman who displayed philosophy, ambition and driving force remarkable for her time. She was unique as an outstanding actor-manager, touring her company through outback Australia, New Zealand and South Africa. She was praised for her service to country people, who often saw theatre for the first time when the Kate Howarde Company performed in their local hall or in a tent. The plays she wrote for her own company are remarkable for their sheer theatrical vitality. She is particularly remembered for a remarkable outback comedy drama, *POSSUM PADDOCK*.

Howarde began writing as a child in Wellington (New Zealand) and by the age of nine she had received her first payment for her work. She was encouraged to write by the editor of the Wellington *Evening Post*, who published her reports on school events. She arrived in Sydney, carrying her first serious drama, *When the Tide Rises*, written when she was 16. It was later performed by her own company.

At the age of 17 she founded her first company—an achievement unmatched by any theatrical entrepreneur of her time. The Kate Howarde Company primarily produced musical comedy and pantomime, genres to which Howarde returned throughout her career. Many well-known Australian performers began their careers with the Kate Howarde Company, including the actors George Cross, Horace Denton, Collet Dobson, S. A. Fitzgerald and Charles Villiers. Her first comedian was BERT BAILEY.

While still in her teens Howarde sailed for the USA, where she spent five years writing sketches, vaudeville acts and songs, and worked as a journalist, covering Broadway productions for the New York press. She also travelled to London. Returning to Sydney, Howarde established a theatrical company at the National Theatre in Balmain, a working-class harbourside suburb. She staged pantomime, musical comedy and drama, changing weekly along the lines of the old stock companies. An evening at the National involved sketches, musical interludes, burlesque acts as well as the advertised drama.

During her time there Howarde wrote several successful dramas. *The White Slave Traffic* (1914) was set in Manly and centred on xenophobic fears of traffic in white Australian women to 'gratify the vile passions of an Asiatic monster'. *Why Girls Leave Home* (1914) concerned the plight and vulnerability of single women and the social pressure for them to rely on men. These were typical melodramas of the time, with colourful villains and heroes who paled in the light of Australian heroines who personified the 'squatter's daughter' tradition.

While she was at the National Theatre Howarde also wrote *Possum Paddock*, which opened at the Theatre Royal in Sydney on 7 September 1919. She directed and starred in this simple, homespun, earthy outback tale. It ran for six weeks, making a net profit of £5000. Howarde gained further artistic recognition and financial reward when she toured the play to Adelaide, Brisbane, Melbourne, Western Australia and New Zealand. In 1920 she produced, directed and starred in a film version, which is preserved by the National Film and Sound Archive in Canberra.

Possum Paddock had numerous revivals as late as 1932 but *Gum Tree Gully* (1924) was less popular. *The Limit* (1923) and *Common Humanity* (1927) were influenced by the trend toward realism in structure and characters. They were in three acts rather than four, and rigidly prescribed, two-dimensional melodramatic types gave way to emotionally dense, realistic characters defined by their relationships to one another. Stage directions became increasingly detailed to create atmosphere and mood and included directions on emotion rather than simply action. Finally, the predictable melodramatic plot was redirected to a more sophisticated interpretation of characters and relationships. Writing for the professional stage, Howarde was obliged to provide popular rather than experimental drama. She utilised what would work theatrically, and discarded what would not. Her plays display subtle responses to the desires and expectations of the popular audience. ♥*Michelle Ballard*

further reading
HILL, FRANK. Kate Howarde. *Truth* 8 June 8 1958.
HILL, R. R. Actress, authoress and manageress. *Australasian Picture Magazine* 1 November 1920.
WRIGHT, ANDRÉE. *Brilliant Careers*. Sydney: Pan 1986.
Kate Howarde. *Australian Woman's Mirror*, 15 January 1929.

reference
Six unpublished playscripts by Kate Howarde are in the Australian Archives (Canberra) A1336/2.

Lydia Howarde

Actor, manager, singer. Born in Australia. Began career as concert singer. Formed *opéra-bouffe* and burlesque companies that toured widely in Australasia 1875–81.

A concert singer who became a foremost exponent of comic MUSICAL THEATRE, Lydia Howarde formed companies that toured *opéra-bouffe*, burlesque and pantomime with considerable success. She came to these genres through works by GARNET WALCH—his extravaganza *Trookulentos, the Tempter* in Sydney in 1871 and his pantomime AUSTRALIA FELIX. in Melbourne in 1873. In February 1875 she sang in *Chilperic, King of the Gauls*, an *opéra-bouffe* by Hervé, in Sydney. Shortly afterwards she formed her own company and took it to Brisbane later in 1875. Until 1881 her companies, under various names, toured Australia and spent two lengthy spells in New Zealand. Their repertoires included *Chilperic, Fatinitza, Trial by Jury* and *HMS Pinafore*, burlesques of operas such as *Il trovatore* and *Lucia di Lammermoor*, and pantomimes, including *Pygmalion and his Gal (a Dear!)*, specially written for Howarde by Garnet Walch. In his works and in Gilbert and Sullivan operettas Howarde played female roles, but she appears to have taken breeches parts in other works. ♥*Joan Maslen*

reference
Lydia Howarde scrapbook, box 95615 in Australian manuscripts collection of La Trobe Library (Melbourne).

Edward Howell

Actor, director. Born 15 July 1902 at Bromley (Kent, England). Son of theatrical couple, Edward Gilbert Howell and Madeleine Anne Howell. Made debut on tour in Australia 1912. Returned to Australia 1915. Spent five years in Suva (Fiji) and with father helped to form Suva Drama Guild. Returned to Sydney and joined Playbox Society 1924. Married actor Therese Desmond, May 1927. Ran Royal Academy of Dramatic Art (Sydney) 1927–32. Acted for J. C. Williamson's and at Minerva and Independent Theatres in Sydney. Formed Radio Players (Sydney) 1947. Also worked in film, radio, television. Retired 1985. Died 20 August 1986 in Sydney. Brother of actor Lewis Howell. Father of actor Madeleine Howell.

Edward Howell was prominent in many aspects of entertainment during a 73-year career. He is probably best remembered as writer, producer, director and co-star with his wife Therese Desmond of the radio comedy series *Fred and Maggie Everybody*, which ran from 1932 to 1963. The stage was his first love, however, and he worked in major theatres in every capital city for many years. He came to Australia as a child to act with his father and brother Lewis in a production of Maurice Maeterlinck's *The Blue Bird*, which was stage-managed for J. C. WILLIAMSON's by Claude Rains. After leaving school, Howell did clerical work for the Colonial Sugar Refining Company in Suva until 1924. Then he returned to Sydney and joined DUNCAN MACDOUGALL's Playbox Society, with which he spent four years. Howell formed the Royal Academy of Dramatic Art in 1927, and the Governor of NSW, Admiral Sir Dudley de Chair, summoned him to Government House to demur at the unauthorised suggestion of royal patronage.

In the early 1930s Howell worked as a radio announcer in Brisbane after contracting tuberculosis. His heart was still with acting, however, and he returned to Sydney to resume his theatrical career in 1935. In the 1930s he was a staunch and vocal supporter of the little theatre movement, which, although amateur, was led mainly by professionals. Howell, who particularly supported Doris Fitton's INDEPENDENT THEATRE, felt that the movement should remain essentially professional and wrote several articles deploring an influx of unskilled amateurs into its domain.

In 1947 Howell, his wife, their daughter Madeleine and three other radio actors formed the Radio Players, who presented several plays at BRYANT'S PLAYHOUSE in Phillip Street. Authority intervened on the grounds of inadequate fire safety and the project was abandoned, despite strong support from the press and the public. Howell made his last theatrical appearance at the Marian Street Theatre in Sydney in J. B. Priestley's *I Have Been Here Before* in October 1971. At the same theatre in 1985 the industry honoured him at a special performance of Christopher Hampton's *The Philanthropist*. ♥*Bronwyn Coy, Walter Sullivan*

writings
The little theatre movement—what impedes it? *Harmony* (Sydney) 17 February 1934.
Union is strength. *Little Theatre Magazine* 1/2 (Sydney).

further reading
CARRUTHERS, VIRGINIA. The development of Australian theatre and drama 1788–1964. Duke University (Durham, North Carolina, USA) PhD thesis 1969.
COY, BRONWYN. The significance of the little theatre movement in Australia in the 1930s with particular reference to the Independent Theatre. University of NSW BA (hons) thesis 1990.

Frank Howson

Actor, singer. Born 1817, probably in London. Son of Francis Howson, music teacher in London. Showed early musical talent. Initial career in army. Fought in Spain 1834–40. Married Emma Richardson, dancer and actor. Came to Hobart for Anne Clarke 1842. Moved to Sydney 1845. Left for USA 1866. Died 16 September 1869 in USA. Brother of Emma Albertazzi and John Howson, singers, and Henry Howson, violinist. Father of Frank A. Howson, musician; John Jerome Howson, actor and violinist; and Emma Howson, soprano singer.

As a singer Frank Howson played a large part in the development of operatic performance in Australia, but he was recognised first as an actor with ANNE CLARKE's company in Hobart. Later, he became well known for his comic roles, the *Sydney Morning Herald* observing on 2 December 1855 that 'the broadest of broad farce is his element, and in that there are few that come near him'. He signed a three-year contract with Anne Clarke, who recruited him and his brothers John and Henry during a visit to England in 1841. When they arrived in Hobart early in 1842 the Royal Victoria Theatre was occupied by F. B. WATSON's company and Frank Howson's first appearance was delayed until 11 July. Then, as the *Cornwall Chronicle* noted on 16 July, his performance as Pedrigo Potts in Daniel Auber's opera *John of Paris* 'elicited great applause'. He retained his initial popularity, and the *Hobart Town Courier* of 30 September 1842 said of his first benefit night: 'We believe, if he could obtain the extent of Covent Garden for the night, it would be completely filled'.

As well as starring in operas and taking major roles in legitimate dramas such as *Hamlet*, *Macbeth* and Edward Bulwer-Lytton's *The Lady of Lyons*, Howson was Anne Clarke's stage manager for seasons in Hobart and Launceston from May 1843 until his contract expired. In March 1845 he moved to Sydney, where he made his first appearance on 26 May as Broomy Swash in *The Aldgate Pump*, a farce by J. S. Faucit, at the Royal Victoria Theatre. Howson appeared in many non-singing roles as well as operatic parts. In 1855, after the retirement of J. G. GRIFFITHS, he managed the Prince of Wales Theatre in Sydney. Howson left Sydney for San Francisco in 1866 together with his daughter and his sons. There he formed Howson's English and Italian Opera Troupe and toured in the USA until he died from cancer three years later. ❦*Elizabeth Webby*

further reading

BREWER, F. C. *The Drama and Music of New South Wales*. Sydney: NSW Government Printer 1892.

IRVIN, ERIC. *Dictionary of the Australian Theatre 1788-1914*. Sydney: Hale and Iremonger 1985.

Jean Hugard

Magician, writer. Born 30 December 1872 at Toowoomba (Qld). Originally John Gerard Boyce. Toured Australia as magician. Went to USA 1915. Died 4 August 1959 in New York City.

A prolific writer on magic, Jean Hugard wrote many classic text books for magicians. He became interested in magic at 10 years of age when he saw a touring show by one Louis Haselmayer. He went into banking at his father's wish but after a time he deserted the bank to perform as a travelling magician. Hugard toured Australia, perfecting his show, which featured billiard-ball manipulation, catching a bullet, and an elaborate act in which he played a Chinese magician. He was in Melbourne at the Gaiety Theatre in 1908 and at the Athenaeum Hall in 1912. Hugard went to the USA in 1915. He ran a Theatre of Magic at Coney Island, New York, for many years and published *Hugard's Magic Monthly* for 17 years. At his death he was revered by American magicians and almost blind. ❦*Gerald Taylor*

writings

Card Manipulations. New York City: Dover.
Encyclopedia of Card Tricks. New York City: Dover.
Expert Card Technique. New York City: Dover.
Handkerchief Magic. USA: New York City: Dover.
Modern Magic Manual. USA: Harper. London: Faber and Faber.
More Card Manipulations. New York City: Dover.

Barry Humphries AO

Actor. Born 17 February 1934 in Melbourne. Educated at University of Melbourne 1952–53. Acted in Union Theatre Repertory Company 1953–54. In Phillip Street Theatre revues, Sydney, 1956. Acted and performed revue in Melbourne 1957–58. Settled in London 1959. Solo shows in England and Australia since 1962. London West End Managements' Award for comedy performance of year in *A Night with Dame Edna* 1979. AO 1982. HonDLitt (Griffith University) 1994.

After ROY RENE, Barry Humphries is probably the most popular stage comedian Australia has produced, and he is undoubtedly the best known overseas. Since the 1960s he has shuttled between the United Kingdom and Australia with his one-man shows, with his material becoming ever more international. While Rene's place in the affections of Australians has been unassailable, Humphries's style was shocking from the start and his popularity remains strongly coloured with disapproval. His satire has its origins in a deeply ambivalent attitude to his native land and in particular to his origins in the middle-class Melbourne suburbs of Camberwell and Hawthorn.

During his childhood the family lived in houses built as speculations by his father, through whom he learned about popular styles, sandblasted glass, Axminster carpet, and the central role of the bathroom and hygiene in Australian life. From his mother he gathered the culture of the *Australian Women's Weekly*. Looking back at the age of 50, Humphries wrote: '[All through] my childhood, in the midst of—at the very heart of—niceness and decency and cleanliness and comfort, I perceived the little dramas of Australian suburban life; the war against stains, and creepy-crawlies and the mysterious Outback; the knowledge that we didn't really live in Bournemouth or Wimbledon, but on the ghostly periphery of Asia, with no traditions or even ghost stories to palliate our fear.'

Humphries's years at the University of Melbourne were chiefly notable for two Dada exhibitions at the union and a revue, *Call Me Madman*, in which the audience was pelted with vegetables. He mounted elaborate practical jokes such as 'kidnapping' his wife, planted at a bus stop in school uniform; having his breakfast progressively supplied to his railway carriage by waiters at the stations; and raiding rubbish bins for paper bags of what appeared to be vomit. Such behaviour was redolent of fierce revenge as well as malevolent satirical wit.

During a country tour with the UNION THEATRE REPERTORY COMPANY—playing Orsino in *Twelfth Night*—Humphries invented his most famous character, Edna Everage. From that moment he became a monologist and began to realise his acting skills to present his individualist view of the world. Edna first appeared in an end-of-season revue, *Return Fare*, in 1955. Next year she was heard on Humphries's first record, *Wild Life in Suburbia*. On the other side of this 45 r.p.m. disc Sandy Stone made his debut with accounts of his week between the shopping and the RSL, and evenings of 'nice night's entertainment'. The two monologues revealed Australian suburbia as materialist, sentimental, self-satisfied, cosily racist, and lacking in any understanding of the legacy of civilisation that mattered so much to the young Humphries—the intellectual life of art, languages, literature and the theatre. Sandy Stone first appeared on stage in 1958 in *Rock and Reel*, a revue presented in Melbourne by Humphries and the actor PETER O'SHAUGHNESSY. They had become partners in 1957 to perform revue and Samuel Beckett's *Waiting for Godot*. In 1959, Humphries made his London debut, in *The Demon Barber* at the Lyric Theatre, Hammersmith. Next year he played the undertaker Sowerberry in *Oliver!* and later took over the role of Fagin. Encouraged by the entrepreneur CLIFFORD HOCKING, he developed his first solo show and returned to Australia in 1962 for a national tour. In this show, *A NICE NIGHT'S ENTERTAINMENT*, and its successor, *Excuse I*, the characters—Edna and Sandy, the Minister for National Identity, the beatnik Morrie Tate and Neil Singleton the failed trendy—all demonstrated a keen understanding of the implications of language and manners, and the Australian image abroad. By 1968, when Humphries was at the height of his powers, Edna had taken the limelight from Sandy, his favourite character. He did away with Sandy in 1971 but the loss proved too great and from 1974 Sandy revisited his old surroundings as a ghost.

In the 1960s Humphries became involved in the anti-establishment movement in London. In Peter Cook's satirical magazine *Private Eye* he created a comic strip—drawn by Nicholas Garland, a cartoonist from New Zealand—about Barry McKenzie, an innocent Australian tourist. Mckenzie became the hero of two films, *The Adventures of Barry McKenzie* in 1972 and *Barry McKenzie Holds His Own* in 1974. Humphries played Edna in both, and in the second she was dubbed a dame, Now Dame Edna Everage is a citizen of the world and a friend of princes and prime ministers. As Edna rose from housewife to superstar her wardrobe moved from department store to boutique and designer's fantasy; and her character from homely caricature to Gargantuan prejudice. Her conspiracy of seduction and abuse includes cross-examination of spectators, holding up to public ridicule their name, clothing, address and other personal items.

The rapid social change that culminated in the election of Gough Whitlam's Labor government in 1972 provided the strongly right-wing Humphries with material for characters like Brett Grantworthy the grant manipulator, Lance Boyle the corrupt and hedonistic trade-union secretary and Sir Les Patterson, the extremely vulgar Australian cultural attache to the Court of St James in London. Les was invented for a Hong Kong cabaret in 1974 and introduced to theatre audiences in *Housewife-Superstar* in 1976.

Humphries's antipathy to suburban values has warmed into affection, evidenced in the lists of Australian place and brand names that his characters are given to reciting, but a hypnotic spider-fly relationship with his audience remains essential to his performance. Humphries was possibly the first comedian to break the territorial contract by which the actor invades only the private emotions of the audience.

He has appeared on Australian and British television many times, most notably as Edna Everage. Since the late 1970s he has ceased to write all his own material and his work in the mass media has taken him away from the grass roots of local content. The extreme aggression of Edna Everage and Les Patterson and their satirical self-styled roles as 'ambassadors' for Australia have caused some unease among Australians, who see Humphries as exploiting his native land for the delectation of its former colonialists. His lasting contribution to Australian theatre and life has been his examination and celebration of the minutiae of language and manners by which Australians have discarded false values of conformity, bred from lack of assurance. It was no coincidence that Edna Everage emerged in the same year and from the same environment as Ray Lawler's *SUMMER OF THE SEVENTEENTH DOLL*, the landmark from which modern indigenous Australian drama is measured, or that Lawler, then director of the Union Theatre Repertory Company, was Humphries's mentor in preparing Edna for the stage. In retrospect Humphries's work has been as significant as Lawler's in freeing the Australian comic spirit from the burden of being British. From the 1950s to the 1970s Humphries's work was in the forefront of a movement to lash Australians into a recognition of their real identity. If he has in the process exploited his discoveries, then that is his privilege. ❦*Katharine Brisbane*

published scripts
A Nice Night's Entertainment. Sydney: Currency Press 1981.
The Life and Death of Sandy Stone. Melbourne: Pan Macmillan 1990.
ALLEN, JOHN (ed.). The *Humour of Barry Humphries*. Sydney: Currency Press 1984.

other writings
The Barry Humphries Book of Innocent Austral Verse. Melbourne: Sun 1968.
Barry Humphries' Treasury of Australian Kitsch. Melbourne: Macmillan 1980.
More Please. London: Viking Penguin 1992.

further reading
COLEMAN, PETER. *The Real Barry Humphries*. London Robson 1990.
HOWIE, ANN C. (ed.). *Who's Who in Australia* 27th edn. Melbourne: Information Australia 1991.
LAHR, JOHN. *Dame Edna Everage and the Rise of Western Civilization*. London: Nick Hern 1990.
O'DONNELL, OWEN. *Contemporary Theatre, Film and Television* 8th edn. Detroit (USA): Gale 1990.

Hugh Hunt CBE

Director. Born 25 September 1911 in England. Began directing in Oxford University Dramatic Society. Director of Abbey Theatre, Dublin, 1935–38. Director of Bristol Old Vic Company 1945–48. Director of Old Vic Company, London, 1949–53. Foundation executive director of Australian Elizabethan Theatre Trust 1955–60. Established Trust Players and Elizabethan Trust Opera Company. Left Australia 1960. Professor of drama at Manchester University 1961–73. Artistic director of Abbey Theatre 1969–71. CBE 1977. Chairman of Welsh Arts Council 1979–85. Died 22 April 1993 at Criccieth (Wales).

Hugh Hunt widened the audience for the theatre, and he extended the possibilities for theatrical artists and writers to train and work in Australia. He arrived in 1955, with high professional credentials and high ideals, to develop a national theatre that would stimulate audiences with classical and indigenous plays and educate future audiences. When he left in 1960 he had laid the groundwork for subsidised theatre, established a company of actors and a school to train actors, and run seasons of Australian plays, with some notable successes.

When Hunt was appointed first executive director of the AUSTRALIAN ELIZABETHAN THEATRE TRUST he had been a professional director for 22 years, accustomed to the best conditions and highest standards. At the Abbey Theatre in

Dublin from the age of 24 he had directed more than 30 original Irish plays. He was handed his opportunity to encourage Australian indigenous theatre with Ray Lawler's script of SUMMER OF THE SEVENTEENTH DOLL. His belief in the quality of the play led him to appoint JOHN SUMNER to direct a production by the Union Theatre Repertory Company in Melbourne in November 1955, and to make arrangements with Laurence Olivier that resulted in a seven-month season in London from April 1957.

The first play Hunt directed in Australia was Euripides's *Medea* in a new translation by Robinson Jeffers, starring the expatriate JUDITH ANDERSON. *Medea* opened in Canberra in October 1955, launching the Australian Drama Company, which toured nationally for six months. Other productions by Hunt included *Hamlet* and *Twelfth Night* with the English actor Paul Rogers and T. S. Eliot's *Murder in the Cathedral* with Robert Speaight as Thomas à Becket, the role he had created in 1935. *Murder in the Cathedral* was a highlight of the 1960 Adelaide Festival.

The success of *The Doll* encouraged Hunt to press ahead with another prizewinning play, Richard Beynon's THE SHIFTING HEART in October 1957. MAY HOLLINWORTH of Sydney's amateur Metropolitan Theatre directed a production so successful that Hunt again arranged a London season in partnership with Olivier. The play did not strike the same response there as *The Doll*, however.

In 1958 Hunt decided to form a fully professional permanent company based in Sydney. ROBIN LOVEJOY formed the TRUST PLAYERS for him, and directed the first play, Peter Kenna's THE SLAUGHTER OF ST TERESA'S DAY, in March 1959. The establishment of a national school of dramatic art was high on Hunt's agenda. He approached the Universities of Sydney and Melbourne in vain before coming to an agreement with the University of NSW for the NATIONAL INSTITUTE OF DRAMATIC ART to be set up on its campus. It opened in 1959, with ROBERT QUENTIN as its director. A recurrent charge of brushing aside semiprofessional and amateur organisations that had kept theatre alive in the hard times led Hunt to resign in 1960. There is no doubt that he felt safer in giving the more responsible jobs to people who had worked or trained in England, but Sumner, Lovejoy and Quentin justified their appointments by their outstanding achievements. Hunt retained a strong affection for Australia and twice returned to direct productions for the OLD TOTE THEATRE COMPANY—Henrik Ibsen's *Peer Gynt* in 1974 and Sean O'Casey's *The Plough and the Stars* in 1977. ❦*Lynne Murphy*

writings
The Making of Australian Theatre. Melbourne: Cheshire 1960.
  Collection of lectures given by Hunt at University of Sydney.
further reading
HERBERT, IAN (ed.). *Who's Who in the Theatre* 16th edn. London: Pitman 1977.

Hunter Valley Theatre Company

Professional dramatic company in Newcastle (NSW) formed in 1975. **venue** Civic Playhouse 1979–. **artistic directors** 1976–78 Terence Clarke. 1978–79 Ross McGregor. 1980–82 Aarne Neeme. 1983–92 Brent McGregor. 1992–94 Kingston Anderson. **first production** *The Floating World* by John Romeril, 12 March 1976, Arts–Drama Theatre, University of Newcastle.

The Hunter Valley Theatre Company has brought Australian playwriting to the attention of NEWCASTLE—a city based on coal, steel and heavy industry—and stimulated the emergence of vigorous local writing to mirror the region's diversity of concerns and backgrounds. Its landmark productions have included plays by the Newcastle dramatist JOHN O'DONOGHUE, particularly *A Happy and Holy Occasion*, directed by TERENCE CLARKE in 1976, and *Essington Lewis: I am Work*, directed by AARNE NEEME in 1981.

Initiatives by the Arts Council of NSW and the Joint Coal Board led to the company being formed to provide a theatrical focus for the Hunter region, which stretches from Newcastle to Gosford in the south, Taree in the north and Merriwa in the west. It was the first provincial theatre company funded by the AUSTRALIA COUNCIL. It performed in various venues around Newcastle until it gained a permanent home in the Civic Playhouse. Constructed within the Wintergarden of the Civic Theatre, the Playhouse seats 191 in a fan-shaped auditorium which partly encloses a shallow stage. It opened on 23 March 1979 with the musical *Cabaret*, directed by Ross McGregor.

The company's history remained chequered until 1982 because of insufficient funding and a haphazard policy on the function of a professional company in a community which had been dominated by a long amateur tradition. Brent McGregor, artistic director from 1983, put the company on a firm financial basis with a mixture of plays from the standard repertoire and Australian plays ranging from Ray Lawler's THE DOLL TRILOGY to new works—sometimes commissioned —including DAVID ALLEN's *Once a Bold Collier* and Stephen Abbott's *Headbutt*.

A notable event in 1991 was the presentation by the workers' cultural action committee of Newcastle Trades Hall Council of a production of *Aftershocks*, a community work written by PAUL BROWN, about the after-effects of the 1989 Newcastle earthquake. ❦*Victor Emeljanow*

further reading
BRISBANE, KATHARINE. The theatre goes bush. *National Times* (Sydney) 4–10 October 1981.
EMELJANOW, VICTOR. *A Survey of Audiences Attending the 1987 Season of the Hunter Valley Theatre Company*. University of Newcastle 1988.
TRENCH, T. The Hunter Valley Theatre Company—How and why. *Theatre Australia* 2/5 (Sydney, September-October 1977).

Frediswyde Hunter-Watts

English actor. Born 1887. Played Shakespeare and Shaw in Allan Wilkie's touring company 1906–14. Married Wilkie 1908. Played Shakespeare, Sheridan, Goldsmith and popular melodrama throughout Australia and New Zealand 1914–31. Left Australia 1931. Toured New Zealand, Canada, USA and Great Britain with Wilkie in scenes from Shakespeare for rest of career. Died 1951.

Between 1916 and 1930 Frediswyde Hunter-Watts played leading roles in 27 of Shakespeare's plays in Australia, including Portia, Rosalind, Viola, Juliet and Lady Macbeth. She was generally agreed to be a graceful performer, with charm and artistry, strongest in light or comedy roles. As leading lady of the ALLAN WILKIE SHAKESPEAREAN COMPANY from 1920 to 1930 she also assisted with management and costume design. ❦*Lisa Warrington*

Frank Hussey

Comedian. Probably English in origin. Partner of Frank Weston in Hussey and Weston's Minstrels in Melbourne and Adelaide, 1869–70. Formed Hussey, Kelly and Holly's Minstrels in Sydney. Went to England. Toured South Africa 1883. Returned to Australia. Formed Hussey and Lawton's Minstrels in Melbourne.

The audience at Weston's Opera House in Melbourne in May 1869 shrieked with laughter when Frank Hussey made his Australian debut in a comic routine titled *Jobias and Biancas*. Hussey and Weston's Minstrels performed in Melbourne until January 1870, and then gave a season in Adelaide, where the partnership broke up. FRANK WESTON returned to Melbourne and Hussey went to Sydney. He formed Hussey, Kelly and Holly's Minstrels, which opened at the Prince of Wales Theatre and later shared the bill with Rogers's California Troupe at the School of Arts.

Hussey later went to England and in 1883 he toured South Africa with a minstrel troupe which failed financially. Hussey returned to Australia, and joined the Federal Minstrels. In 1885 he teamed up with his old partner Weston, who became manager of Hussey and Lawton's Minstrels. This troupe adopted the Nugget Theatre, formerly the Hall of Science, in Melbourne as its home base. ❦*Richard Waterhouse*

George Hutchinson

Dramatist. Born 26 March 1930 in Sydney. Educated at University of Sydney and became high-school teacher. Participated in 1972 playwrights' studio at the National Institute of Dramatic Art. First full-length play produced 1974.

George Hutchinson, who took up playwriting in his forties, has added to the variety of theatrical style and outlook with a *faux-naïf* yet critical celebration of Australian idealism in his 'Dreamers' trilogy. The subjects—William Chidley, an eccentric sex-reformer; William Lane, who founded a utopian 'New Australia' in Paraguay; and Louisa Lawson, a formidable suffragist and mother of Henry Lawson—are drawn from the last decades of the 19th century, when, as Hutchinson describes it, 'in the days of our innocence, many Australians believed that Australia was destined to lead the world into a golden age'.

Hutchinson uses ballad verse and traditional melodies in the trilogy, which began with his best-known play, *No Room for Dreamers*. This was workshopped in 1978 at the AUSTRALIAN NATIONAL PLAYWRIGHTS' CONFERENCE and first performed by the STAGE COMPANY in Adelaide in 1979. Seasons in every capital followed. The Sydney production, by the ENSEMBLE THEATRE COMPANY, had four seasons before it went to the Edinburgh and Dublin Festivals under the aegis of the World Theatre Exchange Program. The London *Sunday Telegraph* voted it the best play of the 1980 Edinburgh Festival Fringe. *The Ballad of Billy Lane* had its premiere at the Ensemble Theatre in 1982. The Oz Theatre Company, formed in London for the purpose, took it to the Edinburgh Festival Fringe and later in 1982 it had a season in London. The third 'Dreamers' play, *Henry and Peter and Henry and Me*, has music by TERENCE CLARKE. It was workshopped as the Australian contribution to the 1984 American International Playwrights' Conference in Waterford (Connecticut, USA) and first produced by the Tasmanian Theatre Trust in Hobart in 1985. Hutchinson's first full-length play was *My Shadow and Me*, produced in the 1974 JANE STREET THEATRE season in Sydney. Later in the year it was followed by *Island on the Rocks* for the Salamanca Theatre Company in Hobart. The Ensemble Theatre Company presented *Fair and Tender Ladies* at during the 1984 Festival of Sydney. In 1985 residents of Helensburgh (NSW) celebrated the centenary of their mining town by performing Hutchinson's *Back to the Burgh*, a community play tracing its history. ❦*Katharine Brisbane*

published plays

No Room for Dreamers (1979). Sydney: Currency Press 1981.
Henry and Peter and Henry and Me (1985). Sydney: Currency Press 1985.

Geoffrey Hutton

Critic. Born 18 October 1909 in England. Came to Australia at 14. Educated at University of Melbourne. Joined Melbourne *Argus*. War correspondent in New Guinea and Europe during Second World War. Moved to *Age* 1954. Drama and dance critic from 1959 until retirement in 1974. Dance and theatre critic for *Australian* 1974–85. Died 1 December 1985 in Melbourne.

Geoffrey Hutton assumed a dual position as leader writer and drama and dance critic of the *Age* on his return to Australia in 1959 after two years as the newspaper's London correspondent. He was a perceptive and generous critic. He worked at a time when morning newspaper critics were expected to file overnight, so his *Age* reviews tended to be brief by today's standards. But they were always elegantly phrased and, in the words of Creighton Burns, editor of the *Age*, they combined authority and passion. ❦*Leonard Radic*

writings

It Won't Last a Week! Melbourne: Sun 1975. History of first 21 years of Melbourne Theatre Company.

Ric Hutton

Actor. Born 8 March 1926 in Sydney. Acted in radio in Sydney and London 1942–59. Military service 1944–47. First worked in theatre 1960. Combined radio and television work with theatrical career in musicals, dramas and comedies over next 30 years. In London, working mainly in television, 1963–67.

Ric Hutton has achieved most success in musicals, although he claims he cannot sing. His tall, elegant presence and fine, resonant voice have suited him well to roles in drama, and his timing and style have helped him to excel in light comedy. His first musical was *The Boy Friend* in Sydney and Melbourne in 1968. His later appearances have included John Hancock in *1776* for J. C. WILLIAMSON'S in 1971 and President Franklin Delano Roosevelt in *Annie*.

Hutton first acted on stage as Peter Cochon in George Bernard Shaw's *Saint Joan* at the 1960 Adelaide Festival, then in Sydney in 1961. Next year he played Ford in *The Merry Wives of Windsor* in Perth. Hutton showed Sydney his skill in performing the work of Noël Coward in the revue *Cowardy Custard* at the Marian Street Theatre in 1969, and in the roles Coward wrote for himself in *A Suite In Three Keys*, for INDEPENDENT THEATRE in 1970. Hutton acted with Ralph Richardson in *Lloyd George Knew My Father* by William Douglas Home in Melbourne, Sydney and Adelaide in 1976. In 1986 in Melbourne, he won critical praise as the Marquis of Queensberry in JUSTIN FLEMING's play about Oscar Wilde, *The Cobra*. For the SYDNEY THEATRE COMPANY he was a roguish Uncle Willie in Philip Barry's *The Philadelphia Story* in 1986, and gave a fine performance as Viv's father in Michael Hastings's *Tom and Viv* in 1987. *Lynne Murphy*

Igor Hychka

Puppet master. Born 20 March 1914 in Poland, to Russian parents. Originally Ygor Hyczka. Mother wrote and produced plays for children's theatre. Uncle and two cousins were opera singers. Studied art and ballet in Warsaw. Worked for four years with Teatro dei Piccoli of Vittorio Podrecca, mainly in Argentina. Helped to establish a puppet theatre in Belo Horizonte (Brazil). Arrived in Australia 1954. Puppet master for Peter Scriven. Property-maker for Australian Opera. Retired in Sydney.

The expertise Igor Hychka gained with Vittorio Podrecca's famous Italian marionette company had a profound influence on marionette work in Australia, beginning with PETER SCRIVEN's *The Tintookies* and *Little Fella Bindi* and continuing in Phillip Edmiston's Queensland Marionette Theatre and Bruce Rowland's Newcastle Marionette Theatre. Under Hychka's gentle but insistent influence Australian marionettists developed stronger performing skills. He created theatrically effective puppets and he was an outstanding manipulator of marionettes. *Richard Bradshaw*

Agnes Hyland

Circus equestrian. Originally Agnes Roberts. Born 1878 in Queensland. Died 1939 in Western Australia.

A member of a large family that ran the only circus based in Western Australia, Agnes Hyland was an internationally acclaimed equestrian and a skilled trainer of horses. 'Educated ponies', performing complex manoeuvres under her direction, were a feature of Hyland's Circus during the early 1900s. In 1911 she was invited to present an equestrian exhibition in London to celebrate the coronation of King George V. Before returning to Australia, she appeared with Schumann's Circus in Berlin and with the Hagenbeck and Wallace circus in the USA.

Agnes was eldest of 12 children who developed into fine riders, acrobats, wirewalkers and clowns, despite congenital blindness in some of them. Their father, originally named John Thomas Roberts, developed Hyland's Circus after giving public exhibitions of horsemanship in outback Queensland during the 1880s. Hyland, a show-business pseudonym, eventually became the accepted family name. The circus appears to have begun touring in Victoria in 1888 and it did not regularly appear in NSW and Queensland until after 1895. It visited Western Australia in 1905 and stayed there. It was particularly popular in mining communities. During the First World War the circus gave benefits for the Red Cross and military hospitals, and special performances for troops about to embark. Hylands' Circus disbanded in 1920. *Mark St Leon*

further reading
MANERA, BRAD. The Hyland's Circus and its relevance to mining communities in Australia from the 1890s to the Great War. In Australian circus sources, ms. by Mark St Leon 1985. Copies in major public and university libraries throughout Australia.

In Beauty it is Finished

Drama in three acts by George Landen Dann. **premiere** 16 July 1931, His Majesty's Theatre, Brisbane, by Brisbane Repertory Theatre Society. Cast: Cecil R. Carson, Hilda Hastie, Royston Morris, Edith Rowett, Dulcie Scott, Mrs P. J. Symes. Director: Barbara Sisley.

One of GEORGE LANDEN DANN's most powerful critical studies of the harsher side of Queensland life was *In Beauty it is Finished*, his first significant work. A strong realist drama, it introduces the themes that came to dominate Dann's work —isolation, familial entrapment and prejudice. Its setting is a lighthouse on a remote island—inspired by the Moreton Island lighthouse, where Dann had stayed frequently—and it examines the dilemma of the lighthouse-keeper's two daughters. Trapped by the overbearing character of their father and their mother's hopelessness, they have made a pact to escape by turns for three years to the mainland. As the play opens Marion is due home and Joyce is eagerly awaiting a return to her lover in Brisbane. But the island has prepared neither woman for the society of men. Marion has become a prostitute. She makes friends with Tom, a fisherman, who offers to marry her. She rejects him when she discovers he is half-Aboriginal. The play asks: is it more degrading to be a whore or a half-caste?

The play won the £50 first prize in a BRISBANE REPERTORY THEATRE SOCIETY national play competition in May 1931. *Smith's Weekly* obtained a copy of the script, quoted lines out of context and accused it of being a filthy play about miscegenation. Nonconformist churches took up the cry and by the time the play reached the stage it was a public scandal, causing the 25-year-old author considerable trauma. 'My sister and I used to go to church on Sunday evenings and listen to the sermons preaching hellfire against me', he wrote. After the play was performed the scandal—engineered to boost flagging sales of the newspaper, it has been claimed—quickly died and Dann received many letters of support from clergy, doctors and other writers. *Katharine Brisbane*

further reading
REES, LESLIE. *A History of Australian Drama* 2 vols. Sydney: Angus and Robertson 1987.

Independent Theatre

Dramatic company in Sydney founded in May 1930 by Doris Fitton. Amateur 1930–55; semiprofessional 1955–67; professional repertory company 1967–68; semiprofessional 1969–77. Established Independent Theatre for Children 1951. Closed May 1977 with *Our Town* by Thornton Wilder. **venues** 1930 St James Hall. 1931–37. Savoy Theatre. 1937–39 NSW State Conservatorium of Music. 1939–77 Independent Theatre, North Sydney. **artistic director** Doris Fitton 1933–1977. **first production** *By Candlelight* by Siegfried Geyer at St James Hall, August 1930. Director: Harry Tighe.

During 47 years of continuous production Independent Theatre in Sydney was a bridge between amateur and professional theatre, providing a training ground for actors, directors, technicians, designers, playwrights and audiences. DORIS FITTON founded the company to present plays not usually attempted by professional managements—Shakespeare and other classics, new plays from Europe and the USA and Australian works. She named it after J. T.

Grein's Independent Theatre Club, which performed plays by Henrik Ibsen and George Bernard Shaw in London in the 1890s. The Sydney group was formed with 20 actors, each of whom subscribed ten shillings to defray expenses. GREGAN MCMAHON declined Fitton's invitation to become resident producer but her experiences with his SYDNEY REPERTORY THEATRE SOCIETY and with Turret Theatre influenced the structure of her venture. The group secured club rooms in King Street, where rehearsals, acting classes and social events were held, and began a drive for members. The first production, *By Candlelight*, was a considerable success.

After three productions at St James Hall the company transferred to the nearby Savoy Theatre, where it played for almost seven years. Fitton directed her first production, *Michael and Mary* by A. A. Milne, there in January 1931. Later in the year the first of many Independent Theatre productions was taken up by a commercial management when J. C. WILLIAMSON'S transferred *The Constant Nymph* by Margaret Kennedy and Basil Dean to the Palace Theatre. Independent Theatre now seemed firmly established. Its status as the major Sydney company was such that while Sybil Thorndike was playing in Sydney in 1932 she asked to meet Fitton and the company performed a special matinée of *The Constant Nymph* for the visitors. Membership was growing and houses were constant. Independent Theatre Ltd was formed in 1933 with a board of directors to control financial matters and a memorandum of association that clearly stated: 'Doris Fitton shall have free and unfettered artistic control of all productions'.

In 1937 the Savoy Theatre became a cinema, and Independent Theatre moved to the NSW State Conservatorium of Music. The company was now presenting a wide variety of plays, including classics and popular plays by modern authors of high literary value. The conservatorium was available only on two Saturdays each month so the more intimate plays were presented at the club rooms, where the Independent School of Dramatic Art was established. There were also regular readings of plays, many by young or new Australian playwrights, and some went into full production. During a rehearsal of Dodie Smith's *Call it a Day* at the conservatorium, fire destroyed the club rooms but the play opened on time. New rooms were found in Pitt Street, and *You Can't Take It With You* by Moss Hart and George S. Kaufman was presented there.

Theatre at North Sydney

In 1939 HARALD BOWDEN, general manager of J. C. Williamson's, made it possible for Independent Theatre Ltd to take over the tenancy of the Coliseum, an old vaudeville theatre in North Sydney. Terence Rattigan's *French Without Tears* opened it on 2 September 1939, and war broke out next day. The first great success at North Sydney was Thornton Wilder's *Our Town* in 1940. Plays by MAX AFFORD, SUMNER LOCKE ELLIOTT and GWEN MEREDITH and many other Australian writers were staged in this theatre. It was threatened with conversion into a furniture warehouse but a public meeting in late 1947 gave rise to holding company, Theatre Freeholds Ltd, which raised £10 000 from public subscriptions to buy the building for the use of Independent Theatre.

In December 1945 Fitton gave a memorable performance in ROBERT QUENTIN's production of Eugene O'Neill's *Mourning Becomes Electra*, which lasted five hours with a dinner interval. The production was so successful that it was transferred to Melbourne. Fitton retained a steady, friendly relationship with J. C. Williamson's and from time to time she supplied productions to the Firm's theatres when a show folded unexpectedly. In 1948 Sumner Locke Elliott's *Rusty Bugles* was censored and the theatre closed. When the furore ceased the play had an excellent season and was bought by KENN BRODZIAK and GARNET H. CARROLL for an extensive Australian tour.

After Fitton visited England in 1949 she expressed a wish for Independent Theatre to turn professional, and in 1955 the company became semiprofessional. Actors' Equity agreed to up to four of its members taking part in a performance for minimum rates, waiving the 'closed shop' rule if the actors' names were not used in paid advertising. Peter Summerton joined the company in 1959 as associate director and worked closely with Fitton. After 12 months with the Royal Shakespeare Company, he rejoined as associate director and in 1963 he directed Friedrich Dürrenmatt's *The Visit* in a most successful season with outstanding performances by Fitton and ALEXANDER ARCHDALE. Summerton died suddenly in 1969.

Professional repertory company

The company had minimal funding from the AUSTRALIAN ELIZABETHAN THEATRE TRUST and from 1962 a state government grant of £1000 a year for three years, but the financial problems were ever-present. Independent Theatre had rivals at various times during the 1960s—the better-funded OLD TOTE THEATRE COMPANY south of the harbour and Community Theatre and the ENSEMBLE THEATRE COMPANY in the north. In 1967 Independent Theatre became a professional repertory company as a bid to become the state theatre company. There was a push for formation of an arts council and Fitton thought she could prepare for subsidised theatre by hiring a company to play in round repertoire. In six months the eight actors were worn out and Independent Theatre was irrecoverably in debt when the professional venture was disbanded in late 1968. The company reverted to semi-professionalism in 1969. Professional actors organised fund-raising evenings but from 1976 the financial difficulties were great and Independent Theatre closed in 1977. It had given early encouragement to many in the profession, including AILEEN BRITTON, ALLAN DAVIS, PETER FINCH, REG LIVERMORE, Sumner Locke Elliott and GWEN MEREDITH. The Independent Theatre building survived precariously until 1993, when it was bought by the Seaborn, Broughton and Walford Foundation, with plans for restoration and revival as a live theatre. ♥*Benita Brebach, Jessica Noad*

further reading

COY, BRONWYN. The significance of the little theatre movement in Australia in the 1930s with particular reference to the Independent Theatre. University of NSW honours thesis 1990.

FITTON, DORIS. *Not Without Dust and Heat*. Sydney: Harper and Row 1981.

HARVEY BREBACH, BENITA. Sydney's little theatres. With particular reference to the Independent Theatre—1930–1939. University of Technology (Sydney) masters thesis 1991.

MCPHERSON, AILSA. *A Dream of Passion—Theatre activity in North Sydney*. Sydney: Stanton Library 1993.

Industrial relations

Theatrical employees first went on strike in Australia at the Prince of Wales Theatre in Sydney in October 1859. Charles Poole, lessee of the theatre, appealed to his company to grant him the proceeds of a week's business to settle his debts. The employees, who included some of Poole's creditors, agreed to this and added two benefit performances. Instead of paying his debts Poole used the earnings to create a monopoly for himself by buying the leases of the Royal Victoria and Lyceum Theatres from Samuel Colville for £600. To add to the insult he demanded that all his employees accept a 25 per cent reduction in salary until Christmas. They refused and when at the end of the week no salaries were paid they walked off the job.

Colville took over the Prince of Wales but no actor would work for him either. His reputation was no better than Poole's because he had exploited actors by failing to honour employment agreements during three previous seasons at the Royal Victoria. Colville attempted to ingratiate himself by advertising a Saturday benefit for unemployed actors. This was rejected as unfair recompense and a performance by a 'Theatrical Union' was announced at the Royal Victoria on 26 November. Colville remained as manager of the Prince of Wales and there were intermittent performances but the actors in the dispute did not work there or at the Royal Victoria. The dispute was resolved only on 3 October 1860, when the Prince of Wales burned down and Joseph Raynor took over the lease of the Royal Victoria. Poole left Sydney.

Litigation and bankruptcy

In the 1850s and until well into the 20th century actors had to negotiate individual contracts for salary and working conditions or appoint an agent or manager to do so. The civil court was the only resort available to an injured party and 19th-century theatre history is littered with incidents of litigation. The only resource for actors in distress was the benefit performance, either for the individual or for a benevolent fund. Bankruptcies were legion.

The actor's place in society was not elevated. In NSW the Public Entertainments Act of 1897 still deemed 'any person performing in an unlicensed hall' to be 'a rogue and vagabond, and shall be liable and subject to all such penalties and punishments as are inflicted on or are appointed for the punishment of rogues and vagabonds'. However, in the first national census of 1911 the occupation of 'actor, actress, circus performer' was grouped with 'those ministering to Religion, Charity, Health, Education, Art and Science'. This census indicates that among 1797 listed as performers there were some 100 Australian artists, of whom 15 per cent were out of work at any one time.

The first craft association established in the theatre was the Sydney Stage Employees' Association, which was registered in 1905. It united performers of all kinds and backstage crew. Similar associations sprang up in other states and in 1909 they amalgamated to form the Federated Stage Employees' Association.

An Australian Vaudeville Artists' Association was formed in Sydney in 1907, after an industrial dispute in England in December 1906 and January 1907. The English Variety Artists' Federation had challenged the right of managers to make artists perform at more than one theatre on the same night. This resulted in strikes and pickets, and blacklisting of performers. While it was generally agreed that Australian managements were fair, the formation of an association was regarded as a precaution. It leased club rooms in the Queen's Hall in Pitt Street, diagonally opposite POVERTY POINT, the corner where unemployed performers gathered and were sometimes hired. Senior members of the association hoped the club rooms would remove the need for this degrading institution. The journal *Stageland* reported that Sam Gale 'hoped that the existence of the club … would do away with the humiliating spectacle of managers seeking talent at Poverty Point now, for performers out of collar could meet and discuss the wheat market at the rooms instead of at a street corner, where they attracted the finger of derision and the scowls of the unregenerate. No member would be allowed to engage at a less fee than 10s. a night and the disgraceful system that had become common of civil servants and others in regular employment taking on stage work at night at "scab" wages, would be done away with.'

Another concern of the Vaudeville Artists' Association was the COPYRIGHT of performers' original material. Songs, jokes and business were commonly stolen. Fred Allen, an American vaudevillian who toured Australia in 1915, noted in his autobiography that 'on his small salary the Australian actor could not afford to have original material written, and if he did have money there were no writers who could create songs, jokes or scenes for him. To survive in their profession most Australian performers had to resort to plagiarism.'

The Vaudeville Artists' Association did not register as a union with the Commonwealth Conciliation and Arbitration Court and it had collapsed under the weight of its own inactivity by 1910. In that year there was another unsuccessful attempt at unionisation. On 17 November 1910 an application was published for registration of an Australian Theatrical Choristers' Association for 'male and female members of the chorus and ladies of the ballet'. The formation of the Federated Stage Employees' Association in 1909 and rumours of impending disbandment of two of the four choruses employed by J. C. WILLIAMSON'S may have stimulated the application.

The Firm opposed registration of the Australian Theatrical Choristers' Association on technical grounds. It claimed that choristers were not legally an industry. The case went to appeal, when it was argued that 'had it been suggested that these provisions were likely to be applied to the ladies of the ballet the framers of the Constitution would have been very much surprised. These young ladies might be unusually industrious with their feet but that does not convert them into an industry within the Act.' The judge rejected that argument. 'To my mind it is obviously an industry … catering to the public for reward by theatrical entertainments', he said. But he found fault with the association's rules of membership and cancelled its registration.

In 1911 an informal log of claims for wages and conditions that had existed since the start of the century became the basis of the Federated Stage Employees' Association's theatrical award by agreement with J. C. Williamson's and its vaudeville award with HARRY RICKARDS. The Musicians' Union of Australia was registered in the same year. The musicians' award proved complex and contentious and was not agreed nationally until 1917.

The J. C. Williamson's monopoly and the new taste for middle-class comedy led to the establishment of the Australian Actors' Union at a meeting of more than 50 actors in Sydney on 19 November 1911. They claimed that importing of whole English and American companies took jobs from local performers. The group sought immediate affiliation with the NSW Trades and Labour Council and the Political Labour League. It also sought to create a Federal Council of Theatrical Industry Associations, uniting representatives of the Actors' Union, the Federated Stage Employees' Association, the Musicians' Union, the remnants of the Vaudeville Artists' Association, supernumeraries and bill-posters.

The union's application for registration with the Conciliation and Arbitration Court was published on 16 December 1911. Theatre managements attempted a coordinated defence for the first time. WILLIAM ANDERSON, GEORGE MARLOW, GEORGE TALLIS and HUGH J. WARD were among the managers who attended a meeting in Sydney in January 1912. It resolved to oppose registration of the Actors' Union and to offer work to nonunion actors. The union responded by charging that its members were being victimised and calling on the support of the entire trade union movement.

Imported and amateur competitors

Supporting the union, 'Australian Actor' wrote to the Melbourne *Age*: 'At the present moment the Melbourne theatres the Royal, Her Majesty's and the Princess are exclusively devoted to the performances of imported English companies … we are promised half a dozen more English companies in the next twelve months. The King's Theatre is the only house in Melbourne at present where the native-born has a chance … The rank and file of the imported companies are almost invariably paid such small salaries that the expense of their importation, which is so much advertised, is saved in a few weeks, and surely no theatregoer has the hardihood to suggest that these importations are invariably superior to the native artist? …

'But the question of the imported artist is by no means the only trouble of the Australian actor. For instance, it is required of him to perform at matinée performances absolutely without fee or payment of any kind. Again, I have often been engaged for several weeks rehearsing, without payment, for a play which ran one inglorious week only. Another grievance is the 'talented amateur', who, for a few shillings a week is ready to play small parts, and who is eagerly employed by the managers … to the utter exclusion of the professional actor who depends on art for his bread and butter', the writer said.

In another response in January 1912, a meeting was called to form an Actors' Association of Australia to oppose the idea of an actors' union. The meeting tabled its 'desire to utterly dissociate ourselves from the body of persons styling themselves the Actors' Union. So far as business relations with our respective managers are concerned, we are perfectly satisfied with the present system.' The president of the Actors' Association was the actor GEORGE S. TITHERADGE. Addressing the Commonwealth Club a few months later, he said he approved of the principle of an actors' union but objected to its association with Trades Hall. 'If its demands are acceded to through the medium of that body it means the stagnation and ultimate deterioration of dramatic art in this country …', he said. 'This union … is controlled by a few men who have attained a certain prominence as stage failures. Their demands are such that no theatrical manager, save one, would be able to exist ….' The Actors' Association naturally received the united support of theatrical employers.

The Actors' Union advanced some positive proposals, including agitation for a state-supported theatre. It planned to lease the Hippodrome in Sydney as a union house but the plans came to nothing. The Actors' Union was registered in January 1912. By error, registration took place one day before the required 30 days' notice had elapsed. The employers, who had raised no objection, saw their chance and had the registration cancelled. The judge summed up apologetically: 'I am compelled to do a stupid piece of injustice by the Act. No one has been hurt by the mistake, and all the material objections would be dealt with, if this objection were not taken.'

A new application was published. The employers asked the full bench of the High Court for an order to prohibit the registrar from hearing an application for registration from any association of actors, on the ground that the theatre was not an industry within the meaning of the federal Arbitration Act. The applicants for the order were William Anderson, Brennan's Amphitheatres Ltd, George Marlow Ltd, the trustees of Harry Rickards's estate and J. C. Williamson Ltd. The other parties were the Actors' Association, arguing that the theatre was not an industry, but a profession with contracts for service; the Actors' Union, arguing that an industrial dispute was a collective dispute between employer and employees and actors were employees; and the Deputy Industrial Registrar. The court chose to ignore the industry argument but found that the managements' application would place a major restriction on the registrar's power to carry out his duty.

Actors' right established

The managements lost the battle but won the war. The Actors' Union applied again for registration but was refused on the grounds that insufficient members were financial and that proper minutes and accounts had not been kept. Nevertheless the right of actors to constitute an association under the Arbitration Act had been established.

During preparations for the court case, the tension between the two actors' unions was heightened when the Actors' Association organised matinées in Sydney and Melbourne to raise funds to set up an actors' benevolent fund and a general theatrical pension fund. The Actors' Union saw this plan as an attack on trade union principles and boycotted the events, preventing members of the Musicians' Union and front-of-house staff from participating. Prominent performers undertook their tasks, adding to the publicity value of the occasion.

In 1913 a resurgent group established the Australian Vaudeville Artists' Federation. It was registered with the state and commonwealth arbitration courts in 1914, after minor industrial action against small picture-show proprietors who refused to employ its members as interval performers. It died by 1916. In 1915 the Actors' Association began negotiations with the major employers for an actor's standard contract. Protracted discussions led to renewed agitation for a union. On 3 December 1915 Walter E. Baker called a meeting to propose the formation of an Actor's Union of Australasia. However, before application was made the Actors' Association reached an agreement for a contract with the Bailey, Duggan and Grant management, George Marlow and J. C. Williamson's. It recognised the Actors' Association as the official representative of the theatrical profession, agreed to make all contracts in writing, defined a week's work as six nights and two matinées, and set terms for length of contract and rehearsals. There was a clause giving preference to unionists, which was a major setback for employers.

In 1917 the Federated Stage Employees' Association, now called the Australian Theatrical and Amusement Employees' Association, argued in court for a new log of claims. A new award provided for improved wages and conditions and a form of preference for union members. Together with the federal ENTERTAINMENTS TAX imposed in 1917, the award stimulated employers to form their own body. The Theatrical Producers and Managers' Association of Australia sought registration in August 1917.

New actors' union

Disruptions of the First World War and internal disputes led to the Actors' Association becoming seen as incompetent, and theatre workers suffered badly from the closure of theatres and halls in 1919 during the influenza epidemic. In 1919 a new union, the Actors' Federation of Australia, sought registration in Melbourne. Its first president was Eardley Turner, its secretary was Charles Dunn and the committee included CLAUDE FLEMMING, FRANK HARVEY, GREGAN MCMAHON and the visiting stars Sara Allgood and Barry Lupino. A spur to action was a major but unsuccessful strike by Actors' Equity in New York in August 1919.

The battle for registration was bitter and protracted. The Producers and Managers' Association succeeded twice in overturning registration on technical grounds, despite the registrar's view that 'the merits of the case are all with the applicants'. Meanwhile, a dispute arose within the Actors' Federation over a proposal to move its office from Melbourne to Sydney, where 80 per cent of the profession lived. It was resolved in December 1919 when Eardley Turner resigned and the head of the Sydney branch, Walter E. Baker, replaced him. The third application for registration in January 1920 succeeded after the federation received a letter from E. J. Tait of J. AND N. TAIT LTD, stating that the Producers' and Managers' Association would no longer oppose registration.

Upon the registration of the federation the Actors' Association was voluntarily wound up; and the registration of the Australian Vaudeville Artists' Federation—by then defunct—was cancelled by the Arbitration Court. The federation became the sole organisation representing 'persons employed or usually employed as actors, actresses, dancers, singers, vaudeville artists and public entertainers in or in connection with the industry of entertaining the public'. One of the first issues the new union addressed was the importation of whole companies of actors. It sought affiliation with the American, British and French unions in the hope of exchange agreements, and at home with the NSW Trades and Labour Council, the Musicians'

Union and the Theatrical Employees' Association. Its principal work in the first year, however, was a log of claims. It applied to the Conciliation and Arbitration Court for a compulsory conference, to which were called representatives of the Producers' and Managers' Association, J. C. Williamson's, FULLERS', J. and N. Tait Ltd, ALLAN WILKIE and the Federated Picture Showmen's Association.

Standard industrial award

Australian performers received their first standard industrial award on 20 December 1920. Because it was done hastily to cover the high employment over Christmas its duration was only six months. Nevertheless it became the basis for a standard agreement. It set wages for chorus and ballet (£5 for men and £4 for women), actors (£5 5s and £4 15s), juveniles (£4 10s and £3 10s) and supernumeraries (5s a call). It also set hours of work, times and payment for rehearsals, and required the employer to keep a time book. Performers were required to provide their own make-up and contemporary clothes. Strong clauses dealing with discrimination and victimisation on the part of either the employer or the union, attested to hostility on both sides. The Actors' Federation sought to have the award extended to all other employers and by the end of 1921 its provisions bound 75 employers.

The Actors' Federation remained effective until theatres closed in the Great Depression. Then it became inactive and accepted support from the employers in return for not recruiting new members. In 1939 a dancer, Hal Alexander, organised a group to take control of the union, which was reorganised as the Actors' and Announcers' Equity Association of Australia. Under the Arbitration Court rules a union had to prove it represented 85 per cent of the industry, and ACTORS' EQUITY acted to improve its membership before the employers moved to have it deregulated.

A dispute with J. C. Williamson's over its employment of non-union performers resulted in a major strike in 1944. The matter came to a head when two speciality dancers, Karinska and Vardi, employed by the Firm in the operetta *Viktoria and Her Hussar*, resigned from the union and the cast went on strike. Frank Tait claimed that the principals, who were being paid over-award rates, were outside the scope of the award. The strike spread and the case went to the Arbitration Court. Non-unionists, including many radio performers, rallied to fill theatres with variety shows. In Melbourne the Comedy Theatre presented the Lorna Forbes Players in Ivor Novello's *Comedienne* and spectators crammed Exhibition Street to watch picket lines led by DON NICOL, the Firm's principal comedian. Police protected the 'scabs' as they travelled between the stage doors of the Comedy and His Majesty's Theatres. Coins were thrown at GLADYS MONCRIEFF. At the Theatre Royal in Sydney, two-thirds of the cast in *Lilac Time* walked off and Lloyd Berrell presented MAX OLDAKER, the leading man, with a bunch of lilies. A strike began and actors put on fund-raising shows in suburban theatres around the country.

The strike lasted nearly three weeks. The federal Minister for Labour and Social Services, E. J. Holloway, became arbitrator and found in favour of the actors, thus establishing the principle of 100 per cent union membership. Karinska and Vardi rejoined the union, and immediately precipitated a further crisis by resigning. Gladys Moncrieff was the go-between this time and the dancers withdrew their resignations. Viola Tait, in her account, concluded: 'It must be said the strike led to a better understanding between managements and artists. The Taits realised the value of a strong union, and that the discipline it exacted helped make Australian theatre among the most responsible in the world.' Since the 1944 strike Actors' Equity has achieved nearly 100 per cent membership in the entertainment industry. ❦*Katharine Brisbane and Richard Hunter*

further reading
ALLEN, FRED. *Much Ado About Me*. Boston (USA): Atlantic Monthly Press and Little, Brown 1956.

Irene Inescort

Actor. Born 26 April 1928 in Kent (England). Began as stage manager at Playhouse, Newcastle-upon-Tyne, 1949. In repertory in 1950s. National Theatre (London) 1964. Came to Australia 1968. Acted with National Theatre Company (Perth). Joined Melbourne Theatre Company 1972. Erik Kuttner Award 1972 (Mom in *Sticks and Bones* by Dave Rabe). Died 1992 in Melbourne.

Irene Inescort was a consummate player of leading and character roles. In Perth she played Phoebe in *The Entertainer* by John Osborne in 1968 and Blanche in *A Streetcar Named Desire* by Tennessee Williams in 1969. In the MELBOURNE THEATRE COMPANY in 1972 she played Mom in David Rabe's *Sticks and Bones*, a play of protest against the Vietnam War. In 1973 she was Bessie Burgess in Sean O'Casey's *The Plough and the Stars*. She played Emma in Ray Lawler's *Kid Stakes* in 1976 and the same character in the premiere of the DOLL TRILOGY in 1977. Her later roles for the company included Helen in Athol Fugard's *The Road to Mecca* and the title-role in Nicholas Wright's *Mrs Klein* in 1990, and the Headmistress in Dymphna Cusack's *Morning Sacrifice* in 1991. ❦*Robert Hewett*

Sue Ingleton

Actor, director, writer. Born 20 July 1944 in Melbourne. Graduated in architecture from University of Melbourne 1966. Went to London 1967. Married actor Graeme Brady and had two children. Returned to Melbourne and joined Australian Performing Group 1971. Founding member of APG women's theatre project 1974–75. Formed Stasis 1976. Sidney Myer Performing Arts Award 1990.

Sue Ingleton built a national profile with acerbic cabaret performances as a stand-up comic during the 1980s. These grew out of *Love Slick Blooze*, a cabaret she performed with Rick Ludbrook in the Netherlands and the United Kingdom in 1980. They had a child in 1981, which inspired Ingleton's renowned character Bill Rawlings the pregnant man and shows such as *A Chip of the Old Cock*, *Strip Jack Naked*, *Mother's Courage* and *The Blood and Milk Show*. Ingleton enlarged her reputation as a writer and actor with *Near Ms's* in Sydney in 1989. This show later had seasons at the 1989 Spoleto Fringe Festival and the 1990 Adelaide Festival, and it brought Ingleton the Sidney Myer Award for her contribution to comedy. She made her debut as a director on a CIRCUS OZ tour of Cairns (Qld) and the Northern Territory in 1988–89. Then she directed shows featuring Sue Ann Post and Gerry Connolly for the 1991 and 1992 Melbourne Comedy Festivals respectively. Ingleton has acted in several notable Australian premieres, including *Traitors* by Stephen Sewell in 1979, Jenny Kemp's adaptation of *The White Hotel* by D. M. Thomas in 1984, *Whore in a Madhouse* by Dario Fo and Franca Rame in 1985, *Siestas in a Pink Hotel* by Jennifer Claire in 1988 and *Pennies Before the Holidays* by Lissa Benyon in 1988. ❦*Bob Evans*

writings
Contribution to *Memories of Melbourne University*. Melbourne: Hutchinson 1983.
Sue Ingleton's Almanaic. Sydney: Allen and Unwin 1990.

Irish influences

The First Fleet in 1788 and the Second Fleet in 1790 brought Irish people to Australia as convicts, crew, officers and guards. By the time transportation to the eastern colonies ended in 1853 just on 40 000 convicts had been sent directly from Ireland, a quarter of them women. A Dublin medical student, EDWARD GEOGHEGAN, transported in 1839 at the age of 27, was a convict when he met FRANCIS NESBITT, a star of the Royal Victoria Theatre in Sydney. This led to his becoming the first playwright to produce a body of work in Australia. One of the earliest free settlers to write for the theatre was an Irishman, Evan Henry Thomas of Launceston. His THE BANDIT OF THE RHINE (1836) was one of the first plays written, performed and published in Australia.

Irish immigrants were drawn to Australia first by land hunger and then by gold. It was after the discovery of gold that Irish Australia became established. When CHARLES and ELLEN KEAN and their English company performed in Melbourne in 1863, the Dublin-born actor BARRY SULLIVAN, fresh from American successes, would brook no rivalry. 'The Irish party here are very strong and they are dead against us', Mrs Kean wrote home. As Irish immigrants settled into Australia they became attracted to professions that depended upon verbal dexterity—politics, journalism and the law. This produced a disputatious, litigious society which, combined with a passion for horses and a fondness for liquor, has a peculiarly Irish stamp upon it. All these ingredients found expression in exuberant 19th-century theatre given over to melodrama, farce and operetta.

The most popular tragedian ever to act in Australia was G. V. BROOKE, a Dubliner, like Sullivan. He stayed from 1855 to 1861, wisely interspersing his Shakespearean productions with Irish comedy, and is said to have made and lost £50 000. Another Dubliner, DION BOUCICAULT, an actor and author of 190 plays, popularised the stereotypical Irish characters that had been the stock of the English stage for well over a century—the quick-witted serving girl, the quarrelsome soldier and the charming, lovable stage Irishman. His plays were widely popular in the colonies. In 1871 Anthony Trollope saw *The Colleen Bawn* played 'with a great deal of spirit and a considerable amount of histrionic talent' in a local production in Gulgong (NSW). Boucicault himself arrived in Melbourne in 1885 with a company of six on a ten-week tour for J. C. WILLIAMSON. It was a triumph and grossed more than £15 000.

In 1905 LOUIS ESSON saw performances at the Abbey Theatre in Dublin and met J. M. Synge and W. B. Yeats, who encouraged him to return to Australia and write country comedies. This strand of literary folk theatre, though never realised, remained central to intellectual ambitions for a national theatre movement until the 1960s. HUGH

HUNT, the first director of the Australian Elizabethan Theatre Trust, in his farewell lecture in 1960 blamed Australians for being inarticulate and urged them to look to the Irish.

The Irish Players, a company from the Abbey Theatre, toured Australia in 1922 with Synge's *The Shadow of the Glen* in its repertoire. The critical reception was respectful but the box-office was disappointing. The Abbey Theatre toured in 1990 with Sean O'Casey's *The Shadow of a Gunman* at the Adelaide Festival and in 1993 with Brian Friel's *Dancing at Lughnasa* at the Festival of Sydney.

The folk theatre, a success in Ireland, failed in Australia. The Australian-Irish experience became increasingly incubated in urban sectarianism, which found early expression through the Australian Labor Party. In the capital cities there were Catholic-controlled amateur theatres largely run by and for those of Irish descent—the Cardignians in Melbourne, the Genesians in Sydney, the Therry Dramatic Society in Adelaide and a Therry society in Perth. A member of the Genesians was PETER KENNA, an actor who later became the first major playwright to evoke the lives of Irish immigrants and their hardships. Other writers in recent years to be influenced by the same traditions of storytelling, grim humour and exuberant fantasy are NICK ENRIGHT, JACK HIBBERD, JIM MCNEIL, JOHN O'DONOGHUE, BARRY OAKLEY, John Summons and the present writer. ❦*Ron Blair*

further reading
FAWKES, RICHARD. *Dion Boucicault*. London: Quartet 1979.
MCCALLUM, JOHN. Irish memories and Australian hopes. *Westerly* 2 (June 1989).
O'FARRELL, PATRICK. *The Irish in Australia*. Sydney: NSW University Press 1986.

Eric Irvin

Theatre historian. Born 30 November 1908 in Sydney. Left school at 15 and worked in various jobs and as free-lance journalist. Served in AIF 1940–45. Sub-editor on *Sydney Morning Herald* 1962–73. Wrote four books on 19th and early 20th-century Australian theatre, many articles and poems. Moved to Brisbane 1989. University of Queensland HonDLitt for services to Australian theatre 1989. Died 1 July 1993 in Brisbane.

Journalists have been more significant than academics as scholars of Australian theatrical history, and Eric Irvin was one of the most respected. He was introduced to the theatre by a pair of theatre-mad aunts but he only occasionally went to see a play. His interest lay less in performance than in the lives of actors, the mechanics of production and the architecture of old theatres. He was a painstaking researcher, sceptical of secondary sources. His style is lively and engaging, reflecting his journalistic fascination with anecdotal evidence. His books have become essential reference for workers in the field. ❦*Katharine Brisbane*

writings
Australian Melodrama. Sydney: Hale and Iremonger 1981. A history of the golden age of 19th-century theatre.
Dictionary of the Australian Theatre 1788-1914. Sydney: Hale and Iremonger 1985. An eclectic collection of research.
Gentleman George. University of Queensland Press 1980. A biography of George Darrell.
Theatre Comes to Australia. University of Queensland Press 1971. An account of Barnett Levey's exploits.
Critical introduction in Cooper, Walter, *Colonial Experience*. Sydney: Currency Press 1979.

J. and N. Tait Ltd

From 1920 until 1965 J. and N. Tait Ltd controlled J. C. WILLIAMSON'S, perhaps the largest theatrical circuit in the world. The corporate designation obscured the presence of the TAIT BROTHERS—Charles, E. J., Frank, John and Nevin Tait. In 1903, Charles Tait, an executive at Allan's Music Warehouse in Melbourne, created a firm that his brothers ran, presenting concerts in a small way. It soon expanded into film exhibition and production. Registered in 1908 as J. and N. Tait Ltd, concert directors, in its early years it managed such stars as the singers Clara Butt and Emma Calvé and the comedian Harry Lauder.

J. C. Williamson's Melbourne manager, GEORGE TALLIS, had met E. J. Tait at Allan's in 1900 and made him assistant to the treasurer, RICHARD STEWART. However, by degrees Tallis, who became dominant in J. C. Williamson's after its founder died in 1913, began to think that E. J. Tait's loyalties were divided between 'the Firm' and his brothers, whose activities were expanding. Matters came to a head when the Taits entered theatrical production by beating Williamson's for the right to produce J. Hartley Manners's sentimental comedy *Peg o' My Heart*. It opened on 15 April 1916 in Sydney, with the title-role played by Sara Allgood, who later created Juno in Sean O'Casey's *Juno and the Paycock* in Dublin. E. J. Tait resigned from Williamson's to join his brothers and the two managements joined battle.

The PALACE THEATRE in Sydney and the KING'S THEATRE in Melbourne were the Taits' main outlets. In the next four years the Taits had theatrical successes and their concert ventures flourished. They imported the English pantomime star Barry Lupino in 1917 to play in the musical comedy *Very Good Eddie*, Guy Bates Post in 1918 to play in American melodrama and EMELIE POLINI in the same year to act in various plays. Tallis, a pragmatist, saw the writing on the wall, and on 3 July 1920, after considerable negotiations, J. C. Williamson's and J. and N. Tait Ltd merged. Tallis headed the theatrical side, with E. J. Tait, HUGH J. WARD and Clyde Meynell. The other Taits ran J. and N. Tait Ltd, which presented concerts and some theatre. Ward, disgruntled, soon left J. C. Williamson's to join FULLERS'. The Tait brothers were now the most powerful people in the Australian theatre.

J. and N. Tait Ltd tried to help the cause of worthwhile drama with GREGAN MCMAHON as its resident director. When he was directing Polini in Edward Clark's *De Luxe Annie* for the Taits in Sydney in 1918, he also directed J. and N. Tait's New Repertory Company 'for the production of literary drama', which gave Thursday matinées of plays of the calibre of George Bernard Shaw's *The Doctor's Dilemma* and John Galsworthy's *The Pigeon*. In 1919 the company's offering in Melbourne and Sydney was Henrik Ibsen's *John Gabriel Borkman*, with McMahon acting as well as directing, but sets were apparently skimped. Sparse audiences were put down to the great postwar influenza epidemic rather than to popular dislike of serious theatre. J. and N. Tait Ltd entered into further ventures with McMahon through the SYDNEY REPERTORY THEATRE SOCIETY in 1920 and the MELBOURNE REPERTORY THEATRE COMPANY in 1927. ❦*John West*

further reading
BEVAN, IAN. *The Story of the Theatre Royal*. Sydney: Currency Press 1993.

J. C. Williamson's

J. C. WILLIAMSON resumed his career as a solo entrepreneur after WILLIAMSON AND MUSGROVE was dissolved in December 1899. In Sydney, the 54-year-old Williamson put the pantomime *Red Riding Hood* into HER MAJESTY'S THEATRE, with CARRIE MOORE as principal boy and Dorothy Vane as principal girl. Nearby at the Theatre Royal he had Paul Potter's *Trilby* as the major attraction of a company that included Edith Crane and Tyrone Power, father of the Hollywood idol. A few weeks later Williamson presented the American actor Nance O'Neil for the first time in Australia. Her range was wide, encompassing Peg Woffington in *Masks and Faces* by Charles Reade and Tom Taylor, Lady Teazle in *The School for Scandal* by R. B. Sheridan, Nancy in a version of *Oliver Twist*, and the title-role in *Hedda Gabler* by Henrik Ibsen. In February 1900 Williamson moved *Red Riding Hood* to the Princess Theatre in Melbourne. He tried to lease the theatre but his former partner GEORGE MUSGROVE thwarted him. The prospect of being shut out of Melbourne galvanised Williamson into leasing the Alexandra Theatre, a 'cold, inhospitable place, where the Ghost rarely walked with vigour', according to the *Bulletin*. Williamson redecorated the melodrama house and reopened it as HER MAJESTY'S THEATRE on 19 May 1900 with a revival of *HMS Pinafore*. News of the relief of Mafeking had just reached Australia, so there was an extra reason for celebration. Publicity spelt out the new peck order: 'Under the Direction of Mr J. C. Williamson. Business Manager Mr George Tallis. Treasurer Mr Richard Stewart'. GEORGE TALLIS had joined WILLIAMSON, GARNER AND MUSGROVE as Williamson's private secretary in 1886. RICHARD STEWART was assisted by E. J. Tait, one of the five TAIT BROTHERS who went into show business. Stewart died in 1902 and Tait succeeded him.

Edith Crane, one of J. C. Williamson's stars of 1900, as Trilby

By October 1900 Her Majesty's had been more substantially altered and improved. There was a new entrance to the dress circle with crush rooms, or foyers, retiring rooms and open-air balconies. At street level a row of little shops—'wine shops and dealers in the succulent trotter', the *Bulletin* said—was swept away in favour of entrances and stairways. The renovated theatre had its first spectacular success on 15 December 1900, when the Williamson Comic Opera Company—the Royal Comic Opera Company of WILLIAMSON, GARNER AND MUSGROVE days temporarily renamed—presented the Australian premiere of *Florodora*, the biggest musical-comedy hit in years.

Australia entered into federation and the 20th century simultaneously on 1 January 1901 and Williamson marked the new era with suitably starry theatrical attractions. They included the great English melodrama actor and dramatist Wilson Barrett; a specially formed Italian opera company, which lost £8000; musical comedies like *The Toreador*, *A Country Girl*, and *San Toy* with CARRIE MOORE, FLORENCE YOUNG and GEORGE LAURI; Cuyler Hastings as Sherlock Holmes; JULIUS KNIGHT as Monsieur Beaucaire and other heroes; and the American tragedian MINNIE TITTELL BRUNE.

Outshining all these was W. Young's *Ben Hur*, starring a dashing young American actor, Conway Tearle. He was a half-brother to the younger and subsequently more famous British actor Godfrey Tearle. Williamson spent without restraint on scenic and technical effects in *Ben Hur*, which opened on 8 February 1902 at Her Majesty's Theatre in Sydney. Choristers from the recently disbanded opera company were transformed into singing extras. The chariot race with its charging horses and the spectacular crash of Messala caused a furore. But it was an unlucky show. Bubonic plague had broken out in Sydney and a case was diagnosed in the block that held Her Majesty's Theatre. The authorities closed *Ben Hur* for a week while the theatre was fumigated. The play reopened on 22 February and quickly regained its large and appreciative audiences. But on 23 March the theatre burned to the bare walls in about an hour. Williamson was reported to have lost £14 000.

The owner of Her Majesty's, Cecily McQuade gamely built a new theatre, designed by WILLIAM PITT JNR, and Williamson leased it as his Sydney flagship. He opened it on 1 August 1903, the 29th anniversary of his Australian debut, and celebrated by acting for the first time in years. For the first week Ethel Knight Mollison played the title-role in David Belasco's *Madame Butterfly*, and Williamson followed in two of his favourite short pieces, *Cousin Joe* and Dion Boucicault's *Kerry*. Then he gave Sydneysiders a week of that old favourite *Rip Van Winkle*. On opening night, after the viceregal party was seated, Williamson made a speech of welcome. He remarked that 18 months before he had been contemplating retirement but on that very evening, with his companies playing in Sydney, Melbourne, Perth, Adelaide, and Dunedin (New Zealand), he might be fairly described as being up to his neck in the 'troubled waters of theatrical management'. Williamson was nevertheless feeling the strain of solo management. To ease it, on 30 June 1904 he took on his old friends GUSTAVE RAMACIOTTI—an astute speculator who was his legal adviser—and George Tallis as partners. They each had a quarter share in Williamson, Tallis and Ramaciotti.

In 1911 Williamson marked the 50th anniversary of his entry into professional theatre with suitable éclat by presenting H. B. Irving and the first Melba–Williamson Opera Company. Irving, eldest son of Henry Irving, made his Australian debut at Her Majesty's Theatre in Sydney on 24 June 1911 as Hamlet, with his wife Dorothea Baird as Ophelia. He then did his father's famous roles: in Sydney in *The Lyons Mail* and Dion Boucicault's *Louis XI* and in Melbourne in Leopold Lewis's *The Bells*. In mid-1911 Ramaciotti retired and J. C. Williamson Ltd replaced Williamson, Tallis and Ramaciotti. HUGH J. WARD became a director of the new company, which took over CLARKE AND MEYNELL on 1 September 1911. Williamson remained governing director, mainly as a consultant, while the other directors, Clyde Meynell, Tallis and Ward, ran the business in Melbourne. E. J. Tait was general manager, unhappy at having been bypassed for Ward and Meynell.

Sydney society, led by the Governor of NSW, Sir Harry Rawson (in the upper box) turned out in force for opening night at the rebuilt Her Majesty's Theatre in 1903. The theatre was the Sydney flagship of J. C. Williamson's until 1933

Williamson died in Paris on 6 July 1913. Australian theatres went dark for a night after the news was received. He left nearly £200 000 in his NSW estate and more than £60 000 in Victoria. His death caused further upheaval in the board room of J. C. Williamson Ltd. Viola Tait says Tallis bought Williamson's shares and sold some to his close friend Arthur W. Allen, a lawyer. Their combined holdings were large. Ward, Sir Samuel Hordern and Anthony Hordern also bought some shares. E. J. Tait, not offered any shares, was sent to run the business in Sydney. The years to 1920 were not without difficulties, but there were also theatrical delights, including the emergence in 1913 of a new sort of entertainment called REVUE. There were also standard musical comedies and other operettas, pantomimes and plays that met Williamson's criterion of engaging both heart and head. And there was a rising crop of young stars, among them DOROTHY BRUNTON and GLADYS MONCRIEFF. Meanwhile, another upstart theatrical management was asserting itself. The brothers of E. J. Tait had gone into concert promotion as J. AND N. TAIT LTD. Their financial success with a tour by Harry Lauder in 1914 disturbed J. C. Williamson's but the Firm, as it was known, found them supportable as long as they stuck to concert promotion. In 1916 the Taits entered theatrical production. The Firm thought it had secured the rights to J. Hartley Manners's sentimental comedy *Peg o' My Heart* from an agent in England, but his authority covered only a provincial tour in Great Britain. Meanwhile, Nevin Tait was in New York, dealing with the author himself. Tait made a higher offer, which was accepted. The Firm offered the Taits a co-production but they refused and mounted a successful tour of the play, starring Sara Allgood from the Abbey Theatre in Dublin.

The scarecrow dance was a speciality of the comedian Hugh J. Ward until he gave up performing in 1911 to become a director of J. C. Williamson's. He left the Firm in 1920 and later went into partnership with Benjamin Fuller

E. J. Tait, doubtless finding his position impossible, resigned after 15 years with the Firm and joined his brothers. Competition grew until the pragmatic Tallis, over Ward's opposition, offered the Taits amalgamation. After July 1920 the board of J. C. Williamson Ltd consisted of Tallis as chairman, with E. J. Tait, Ward and Meynell in Sydney, John and Frank Tait in Melbourne, and Nevin Tait in London. Concert attractions would continue to be presented under the J. and N. Tait banner.

For a decade to come there were theatrical productions to be proud of—Gladys Moncrieff's enormous success in *The Maid of the Mountains*; the return of OSCAR ASCHE; JOSIE MELVILLE in *Sally*; Harriet Bennet and Reginald Dandy in *Rose-Marie*, which ran for 317 performances in Sydney alone; the VANBRUGH–BOUCICAULT COMPANY in society drama. Added to this impressive list were a flirtation with vaudeville on the TIVOLI CIRCUIT from 1924; substantial film exhibition interests in New Zealand; and radio in Australia. But if the 1920s were the most impressive period in the history of J. C. Williamson Ltd for production, management had its traumas. Tallis, the Tait brothers and Ward were not a harmonious team. Ward resigned in 1922 and went off to produce operetta in collaboration with FULLERS'. Lady Tait says he sold his shares to Tallis's ally Arthur W. Allen for £120 000. Meynell retired in 1924.

The Firm began buying up the freehold of its theatres as opportunity offered and late in the 1920s it essayed some productions in London, the English provinces and the USA. Tallis flirted with the idea of building a theatre in London but the Taits were dubious. At His Majesty's

Theatre in Melbourne, 1929 was a year of operetta, apart from a month of ballet with Anna Pavlova. In August *Show Boat* rapidly failed and a revival of *Rose-Marie* was rushed on. Then, on 25 October—four days before the Wall Street stock market crashed—fire destroyed the auditorium.

The Great Depression arrived just as the advent of talking pictures and the federal entertainments tax complicated an already difficult time for show business. J. C. Williamson's decided to get out of vaudeville. It was reported in 1929 to have cancelled £20 000 worth of overseas artists' contracts. Profit figures help to explain the Firm's caution. *Everyone's* magazine reported on 8 January 1930 that J. C. Williamson Ltd had made a profit of £50 000 in 1928–29. That was £34 000 less than in 1927–28. The Melba–Williamson Opera Company in 1928 had lost £35 000.

Early in 1930 Tallis announced severe economies— reconstruction of His Majesty's to be abandoned, the THEATRE ROYAL in Melbourne to be sold, moving pictures for Her Majesty's Theatre in Sydney and general activities to be reduced by half. The firm lost £18 000 in 1929-30. The degradation of Her Majesty's by films was averted, however, and in 1930 it housed musical shows. These were mostly revivals, including three with Gladys Moncrieff. The Theatre Royal in Melbourne pursued a parallel course. The pattern was repeated in 1931, though Gilbert and Sullivan came to the rescue with long seasons, by Depression standards, in Sydney and Melbourne. These revivals introduced the contralto Evelyn Gardiner and the comedian IVAN MENZIES, who both remained favourites for years to come. MADGE ELLIOTT and CYRIL RITCHARD returned after successes in London. In 1932 a company headed by Sybil Thorndike and Lewis Casson toured with *Macbeth*, George Bernard Shaw's *Saint Joan*, Henrik Ibsen's *Ghosts* and other challenges. A profit of £3000 was recorded in 1932–33.

Her Majesty's Theatre in Sydney closed on 10 June 1933 with a performance of *The Maid of the Mountains*. Sydney was reduced to the THEATRE ROYAL for operetta and the CRITERION THEATRE for plays. In Melbourne, where it was centred, the Firm closed the Theatre Royal in November 1933, again with Gladys Moncrieff in *The Maid of the Mountains*. It put operettas into the KING'S THEATRE, which it had leased since mid-1931, and plays into the Comedy Theatre, opened in 1928. In July 1934 it reopened His Majesty's. In

Formally dressed theatregoers in the foyer of Sydney's Criterion Theatre in 1927. In the 1920s the intimate Criterion was the principal Sydney theatre for the Firm's productions of West End comedies

1935 the Criterion in Sydney was demolished for widening of Park Street, and its loss made running a circuit between Melbourne and Sydney difficult.

Among the J. C. Williamson's attractions in the second half of the 1930s were visits from the American monologist Ruth Draper, and Fay Compton and her company in Laurence Housman's *Victoria Regina*. Meanwhile J. and N. Tait Ltd presented concerts by overseas stars. Tait had been the only name on the masthead of J. C. Williamson programs since Tallis retired at the end of 1931, ending a career in management that was longer than J. C. Williamson's own. He retained his shares and seat on the board. E. J. Tait proposed building a replacement for Her Majesty's Theatre in Sydney on a site owned by the Firm in Castlereagh Street, but he could not persuade the board. This was partly because the Taits were not the dominant shareholders in J. C. Williamson Ltd. Tallis and Arthur W. Allen had 46 per cent between them, the Taits had 40 per cent and 14 per cent was shared among outsiders. Tallis and Allen would not sell separately and the Taits could not obtain the backing to acquire the joint holding.

But in 1937 John McKenzie, a Victorian who ran a prosperous chain of variety stores in New Zealand, bought the shares of Tallis and Allen. They apparently did not give the Taits a chance to match the offer. Viola Tait suggests that the mastermind of the takeover was ERNEST C. ROLLS, an extravagant, publicity-seeking producer who seems to have been admired more for his production skills and flair than his business acumen or ethics. McKenzie wrought some profound changes in the Firm when he gained control in mid-1938. J. C. Williamson Ltd, the parent company, became the property and investment arm. Production was to be the responsibility of a new company named Australian and New Zealand Theatres Ltd and Rolls was to be a managing director and principal producer. Some of the Taits remained on the boards of the parent company and the production company, but Rolls was in effective control. He immediately went overseas to secure talent and shows. He proclaimed in the J. C. Williamson program magazine of 12 November 1938: 'Australia will become the greatest show centre of the world. My travels, which covered 60 000

Elaborate production and Sigmund Romberg's rousing tunes placed The Desert Song *among the many successful operettas presented by J. C. Williamson's in the 1920s*

miles, embracing Europe, England and America, revealed eloquently that everywhere the importance of this country's entertainment was recognised, and in New York alone I interviewed over one thousand stage personalities, all of whom sought engagements in Australia.' The shows that Rolls actually brought to Australia included the musical *I Married an Angel*, which did not take; a London Casino revue; the operetta *A Waltz Dream*; and a play called *Yes My Darling Daughter*, which ran in Melbourne for less than two weeks. Rolls's best import was Clare Boothe's bitchy comedy *The Women*. It did well in Melbourne, but in Sydney a newspaper dubbed it 'moronic—distasteful and unashamedly vulgar' and suggested that it be banned. Scandal helped the show but it was not enough to save Rolls. In one year Australian and New Zealand Theatres Ltd ran up a loss of more than £60 000. Rolls resigned for 'health' reasons and returned to England. In September 1939 the managing directors were E. J. Tait, Frank Tait, John Tait and, in London, Nevin Tait. The production company was renamed J. C. Williamson Theatres Ltd. Financial control remained in New Zealand but theatrical control was essentially vested in Australia.

During the Second World War, running theatres was particularly difficult in Australia, so far from the principal sources of shows and artists. Fortunately a GILBERT AND SULLIVAN company with first-rate stars had arrived just in time, and the Firm had the Australasian performing rights for every Gilbert and Sullivan operetta. Among the singers were the old favourites IVAN MENZIES and Evelyn Gardiner, John Fullard, Bernard Manning, MAX OLDAKER, Gregory Stroud, Richard Watson and Viola Wilson, a young Scottish soprano, who married Frank Tait in August 1941. The company opened at the Theatre Royal in Sydney on 16 March 1940 and during the war years a new generation of theatregoers was introduced to the 'Savoy operas', and older generations had memories revived.

The Firm also had storehouses full of material from past musical successes and well-loved artists to revive them. Some expatriate performers had decided to come home and there were a few newcomers to promote. Williamson's educated the new theatregoers of the 1940s in the hit shows of the 1920s and 1930s. MARIE BREMNER again became the captive of the Red Shadow in *The Desert Song*. Max Oldaker made the latter role his own. Gladys Moncrieff, recovered from a serious car accident, returned to the Mountains, and Strella Wilson again ran the White Horse Inn. In Sydney, where theatres were scarce, the Firm experimented at the Theatre Royal by presenting plays at 5.30 p.m. and musicals at 8 p.m. During the war, Williamson's gave local performers leading roles much more quickly than it would have done if imports had been readily available.

In 1944 members of Actors' Equity went on strike against nonunion labour in Williamson productions. The contracted principals kept shows going without chorus members or small-part players and there were sharp exchanges. The federal Minister for Labour and Social Services, E. J. Holloway, was accepted as arbitrator. He gave the strikers what they wanted, the principle of a closed shop was established in the theatre and accepted even by the Taits.

After the war, a shortage of foreign currency made it hard to secure new shows and taxation was a constant worry, but conditions began to return slowly to normal. In

The Empire Theatre loomed large on the Sydney horizon of J. C. Williamson's after the Second World War. The Firm began renting the theatre, then a cinema, in 1949 to present the Kiwis revue company, bought it and renamed it Her Majesty's Theatre in 1960 and lost it to fire in 1970

1945–46 Williamson's staged a fine production of Noël Coward's *Blithe Spirit* with resident performers—Edwin Styles as Charles, AILEEN BRITTON as Ruth, BETTINA WELCH as Elvira and LETTY CRAYDON as Madame Arcati. Soon afterwards MADGE ELLIOTT and CYRIL RITCHARD flew out to tour Australia in a selection of one-act plays from Coward's *Tonight at 8.30*. The flight from London took 63 hours.

E. J. Tait organised the Australian production of *Annie Get Your Gun*, the first of the big 'new' American musicals to come here. The strain of long overseas trips told on him at the age of 69 and he died two days before the Australian premiere at His Majesty's Theatre in Melbourne on 14 July 1947. The director, Carl Randall, and the male star, Webb Tilton, were imported and Annie was played by EVIE HAYES, an American who had performed in variety here throughout the war. She had an enormous success in *Annie Get Your Gun* and other star roles followed.

The death of E. J. Tait caused a rearrangement of J. C. Williamson Theatres Ltd. Frank Tait, the youngest brother, stepped up to senior managing director, John Tait's name followed his, and Nevin Tait remained the London managing director. HARALD BOWDEN, long a Williamson executive, was made general manager. Nevin Tait was responsible for assembling the J. C. Williamson Italian Opera Company in 1948. Its tour spurred the Firm to do something about the Melbourne–Sydney imbalance of its theatres. In Melbourne it had His Majesty's Theatre and the Comedy Theatre, but in Sydney only the Theatre Royal. When a large theatre was needed in Sydney in December, complicated arrangements had to be made with the TIVOLI CIRCUIT, which temporarily moved its revues to the Empire Theatre, displacing films. In 1949 Williamson's needed a Sydney home for the KIWIS REVUE COMPANY, an all-male former New Zealand army entertainment unit, which had played for two years at the Comedy Theatre in Melbourne. The Theatre Royal was occupied by *Annie Get Your Gun*, so Williamson's leased the Empire. The Kiwis played there for 54 weeks.

Postwar Williamson successes included Robert Morley in *Edward, My Son*, the play he wrote with Noel Langley, in 1949. There was also the musical *Oklahoma!*, for which numerous American principals were imported in 1949. As its long tour proceeded, the Americans gradually went home and were replaced by Australians, with no detriment to the production. In Mary Chase's comedy *Harvey* in 1950 Joe E. Brown, mouth agape, played the amiable drunk with a huge invisible rabbit for a friend. At the final curtain he did a monologue routine that was better than much of the play. In 1952 *Kiss Me, Kate* had an American leading man, HAYES GORDON, who stayed to contribute significantly to Australian theatre.

John Tait died on 23 September 1955. Frank and Nevin Tait remained the managing directors, with Harald Bowden as general manager. The Firm needed new blood. At that time Anthony Quayle of the Shakespeare Memorial Theatre Company had been involved in a proposal for the Firm to merge with the H. M. Tennent organisation in London. At home, a merger with the Tivoli circuit or the GARNET H. CARROLL organisation was a possibility, but nothing eventuated.

Frank Tait asked the expatriate Australian actor JOHN MCCALLUM to join the Firm as assistant managing director. McCallum was touring Australasia with his wife Googie Withers in Alan Melville's comedy *Simon and Laura* and Terence Rattigan's tragedy *The Deep Blue Sea*. The couple returned to England after the 18-month tour and in mid-1957 McCallum, with his wife's concurrence, accepted the job. While still acting in London, he began to get the feel of the management of the Firm through Nevin Tait's vast experience. One of his first tasks was to select talent for the Australian production of *My Fair Lady*. McCallum was in Melbourne on 24 January 1959 when *My Fair Lady* opened in Her Majesty's Theatre on a hot night—43° C, by his account. He announced the next day that the theatre would be air-conditioned. Frank Tait asked: 'Do you realise that you have just spent £30 000?' But he agreed that the innovation was overdue.

My Fair Lady was a glorious success. By the time it had been running a year in Melbourne with no sign of slackening, the Firm's New Zealand connections were said to be wondering if they would ever see it. The Firm put a whole new second company into Her Majesty's in Melbourne and brought the original troupe to the Empire Theatre in Sydney, which was renamed HER MAJESTY'S THEATRE for the opening on 21 May 1960. These two companies then leapfrogged around Australia, plus New Zealand and South Africa. The firm bought the Empire Theatre for a reported £150 000 in 1960. Nevin Tait died on 7 March 1961, and Frank Tait, knighted in 1956, was the only brother left. John McCallum became joint managing director.

More than five years of planning came to fruition at Her Majesty's Theatre in Melbourne on 10 July 1965, when

J. C. Williamson founded his entrepreneurial success on a monopoly on the Gilbert and Sullivan operettas and they remained a mainstay of the firm that bore his name until the copyright on the works expired. This production of The Mikado *was mounted in the 1950s, when the end of the copyright term was drawing near*

Frank Tait presented the first night of the Sutherland–Williamson International Grand Opera Company. The tour was a cultural triumph and a financial loss for the Firm. Nobody, least of all Tait, had expected a profit, but for a while it seemed that the loss might bankrupt the Firm. Joan Sutherland's three performances a week filled the house but it was distressingly empty at other performances. The AUSTRALIAN ELIZABETHAN THEATRE TRUST agreed to a late appeal to share the expenses, and in the event, the loss was only about £12 000.

On 23 August 1965, nine days after the opera season in Melbourne ended, Frank Tait died. He had been chairman of both the parent company and its production subsidiary, but in the reconstruction that followed, John McCallum, now the sole managing director of the production company, was not on the parent board. This bred dissension. McCallum bought some good things in England and the USA but some prior productions were not so good at the box office and there was an alarming loss. A return to profit was not long delayed, but McCallum was not here to enjoy it. The parent company had appointed John McFarlane, a Melbourne businessman with some amateur theatrical experience, to 'help' McCallum as an executive director of the production company. McCallum resigned and went back to his career as actor, director and maker of television films. McFarlane himself resigned a few weeks later, citing differences on managerial policy as the reason. No new managing director was appointed.

The Firm had successes with the musicals *Fiddler on the Roof* and *Man of La Mancha* in 1967 and 1968 respectively. There was another shift of power in 1969, when the big Herald and Weekly Times newspaper group bought one-third of the organisation. In July 1970 Her Majesty's Theatre in Sydney burned down. In September 1971 J. C. Williamson Ltd formed a subsidiary, Williamson-Edgley Theatres, with MICHAEL EDGLEY as managing director. He had 40 per cent of the shares and Williamson's 60 per cent.

By January 1973 this venture had ended. J. C. Williamson's opened a new and better Her Majesty's Theatre in Sydney later in 1973. Next year was the centenary of the founder's arrival in Australia and the Firm made an appropriate gesture by awarding the title-role in a big revival of the 1919 musical comedy *Irene* to an Australian, young JULIE ANTHONY.

Meanwhile, the managing director of the production arm, Alastair Mitchell (a grandson of John Tait), told the Industries Assistance Commission that production costs were skyrocketing, competition from subsidised theatre companies was growing vigorously and importing artists was costly. The commission did not accept the proposal of some form of subsidy for the commercial theatre. In 1976 J. C. Williamson Ltd gave up, sold its theatres and realised its other assets. It was largely a victim of its own inadequate response to changes in taste, plus ever-rising costs. KENN BRODZIAK of Aztec Services secured the right to call the offerings of his company J. C. Williamson Productions, and later the name passed into other hands. *John West*

further reading
BEVAN, IAN. *The Story of the Theatre Royal*. Sydney: Currency Press 1993.
GREEN, STANLEY. *Encyclopedia of the Musical*. London: Cassell 1976.

Melissa Jaffer

Actor. Born 1 December 1936 at Gladstone (SA). Trained as dancer at Borovansky Ballet School (Melbourne). Member of National Theatre Drama Company 1954–56. Professional debut 1955. Toured for J. C. Williamson's from 1958. Old Tote Theatre Company (Sydney) from 1971. Lighthouse Company (Adelaide) 1982.

Slight, fair-haired Melissa Jaffer is an actor with a wide range, from revue and commercial comedy to Tennessee Williams. A trained classical dancer, she has excelled in roles that require physical deftness, like Shente and Shuita of Bertolt Brecht's *The Good Woman of Setzuan*, which she played in 1972. She is also outstanding at portraying the complexities of febrile, immature or anxiously dominating women. These include Olive in Ray Lawler's SUMMER OF THE SEVENTEENTH DOLL, which Jaffer played in a landmark revival by the NIMROD THEATRE COMPANY in 1973; Irene Harding in John Romeril's THE FLOATING WORLD, which she played in the first mainstage revival, by the SYDNEY THEATRE COMPANY in 1986; and Amanda Wingfield in Tennessee Williams's *The Glass Menagerie*, which she played for the STATE THEATRE Company of South Australia in 1988 and for the MARIAN STREET THEATRE COMPANY in 1989.

Roles Jaffer has created include Smeraldina in *How Could You Believe Me?*, an adaptation of Carlo Goldoni's *I gemelli veneziani* (*The Venetian Twins*) by the cast with music by Sandra McKenzie for the OLD TOTE THEATRE COMPANY in Sydney in 1972, Ivy in PATRICK WHITE's *Signal Driver* in 1982 and Helen in LOUIS NOWRA's *Spellbound* in 1982, both with the Lighthouse Company in Adelaide. Her other roles with this controversial company included Puck in *A Midsummer Night's Dream* in modern dress, Baron Golz in Heinrich von Kleist's *The Prince of Homburg*; and Irina in Bill Harding's *Silver Lining*. Of her Ivy, Patrick White wrote: 'Melissa Jaffer would be regarded as a great actress anywhere else'.

Jaffer settled in Sydney after the Phillip Street Theatre's national tour of Ray Cooney's *Not Now, Darling* in 1969 and worked regularly for the Old Tote company from 1971. Her roles included Yelena in Anton Chekhov's *Uncle Vanya*, Avonia Bunn in Arthur Wing Pinero's *Trelawney of the Wells* and in 1973 the title-role in Aristophanes's *Lysistrata*. In the premiere of Ned Manning's *Kenny's Coming Home* (1992) she played Aunt Dorothy. *Katharine Brisbane*

June Jago

Actor. Born in Melbourne. Trained by W. P. Carr of National Theatre Movement and others. Joined Union Theatre Repertory Company 1955. In United Kingdom from 1957, acting with Bristol Old Vic, Citizens' Theatre in Glasgow and Royal Shakespeare Company, and at Chichester Festival Theatre, Oxford Playhouse and Royal Court Theatre, London. Returned to Australia with Chichester Festival company 1978. In Melbourne Theatre Company 1979–80. Retired

In Melbourne in 1955 June Jago created Olive in Ray Lawler's SUMMER OF THE SEVENTEENTH DOLL. Geoffrey Hutton wrote in the *Age* that she gave 'a truthful and moving portrait, genuinely and sincerely in character'. She later played the part in Sydney, London and New York. A distinguished career in leading British companies followed, during which Jago's dramatic horizons were widened by workshopping Peter Weiss's *The Persecution and Assassina-*

tion of Jean-Paul Marat as Performed by the Inmates of the Asylum of Charenton under the Direction of the Marquis de Sade and Jean Genet's *The Screens* with Peter Brook in London. Jago returned to Australia in 1978 with KEITH MICHELL's Chichester Festival Company, playing Emilia in *Othello* and the Postmistress in George Bernard Shaw's *The Apple Cart*. After playing Mrs Malaprop in R. B. Sheridan's *The Rivals*, Maggie in Harold Brighouse's *Hobson's Choice* and Gertrude in *Hamlet* in MELBOURNE THEATRE COMPANY seasons in 1979–80 she joined the VICTORIAN COLLEGE OF THE ARTS, where she lectures in classical drama. ❦*Laurie Landray*

Brian James

Actor. Born in 1918 in Maryborough (Vic.). Schoolteacher 1937–41. In navy 1941–47. Then theatre in Australia. Studied at Central School of Drama (London) 1950. Returned to Australian theatre. Leading radio actor in Melbourne and Sydney by mid-1950s. Has worked consistently in most state theatre companies. Outstanding television actor. Erik Kuttner Award for best actor 1964 (*Who's Afraid of Virginia Woolf?* by Edward Albee).

Brian James has worked constantly in the theatre at the highest levels for more than 40 years. He began his career in an 18-month season of Noël Coward's *Present Laughter* for GARNET H. CARROLL, before he studied in London. He returned to Australia to appear for J. C. WILLIAMSON's in long runs of three armed-forces comedies, *SEAGULLS OVER SORRENTO* by Hugh Hastings in 1952, *Reluctant Heroes* by Colin Morris and *Worm's Eye View* by R. F. Delderfield. Later he appeared for the Firm with Googie Withers in Clifford Odets's *Winter Journey* and Somerset Maugham's *The Constant Wife*. With the Union Theatre Repertory Company in Melbourne in 1964 he gave an award-winning performance in *Who's Afraid of Virginia Woolf?*

In Sydney in 1967 he was a member of the INDEPENDENT THEATRE repertory company; two of his outstanding performances were as Harry in Charles Dyer's *Staircase* and as the bishop in George Bernard Shaw's *Getting Married*. He was the only Australian actor to be cast in both of Tyrone Guthrie's productions in 1970, *All's Well that Ends Well* and Sophocles's *King Oedipus*.

In 1988 James gave a deeply moving performance as the mentally-troubled septuagenarian Aylott in Bob Larbey's *A Month of Sundays* for the Northside Theatre Company. ❦*Richard Lane*

Jane Street Theatre

Theatre in Jane Street, Randwick, Sydney. Built as chapel of St Jude's mission hall 1887. Opened as theatre seating fewer than 100, 1 October 1966. Closed 1981.

The Jane Street Theatre was intended as a place where the OLD TOTE THEATRE COMPANY could 'have another theatre, no matter how modest, in which new Australian plays can be produced, simply but professionally', according to one of its program notes in 1966. An initiative of ROBERT QUENTIN with funding from the University of NSW Drama Foundation and the Calouste Gulbenkian Foundation of Lisbon, it was a joint enterprise of the Old Tote company, the NATIONAL INSTITUTE OF DRAMATIC ART and the university's School of Drama. The university leased a former chapel, adjacent to the campus, and converted it into a theatre. The opening night included two new Australian plays—*I've Come about the Assassination* by Tony Morphett and *The Pier* by Michael Thomas—and a revival of Edward Geoghegan's 1844 *THE CURRENCY LASS*. ROBIN LOVEJOY directed all three.

In 1969 NIDA assumed the management of Jane Street as a part of its advanced course. Under the direction of JOHN CLARK a season of two or three plays, often specially commissioned, became an annual event. The outstanding premiere was of the burlesque *THE LEGEND OF KING O'MALLEY* by Michael Boddy and Robert Ellis in 1970. Its success encouraged its director, JOHN BELL, and others to establish the NIMROD THEATRE COMPANY. The most successful production at Jane Street was *DON'S PARTY* by David Williamson, directed by Clark, in 1972. Between 1966 and 1981, some 28 Australian plays were produced, including early works by ALEX BUZO, GEORGE HUTCHINSON, THOMAS KENEALLY and RODNEY MILGATE. GEORGE WHALEY's popular adaptation of Steele Rudd's *ON OUR SELECTION* was produced in 1979 and LOUIS ESSON's *The Bride of Gospel Place* was revived in 1980.

In 1978 the policy changed and classics relating to the school syllabus were performed at Jane Street. Money raised from tours and transfers was invested and went towards funding the NIDA Company, which began in 1990. ❦*Ron Blair*

further reading
SOUTH, JOSEPHINE and HARRY SCOTT. *Ten on the Tote*. Sydney: Old Tote Theatre 1973.

Japanese performers

When it ceased to be a capital offence for Japanese subjects to go abroad—in 1866—the first passports were issued to troupes of acrobats and jugglers and these performed in North America and Europe in January and February 1867. Later in that year two similar groups reached Australia. The Tannaker troupe was here from November 1867 to October 1968 and Lenton and Smith's Great Dragon troupe from December 1867 to January 1869. They were followed on December 1870 by the Satsuma troupe, which remained until May 1871.

The repertoires of such troupes usually included rope-walking and other balancing acts, tumbling, juggling and top-spinning. In a typical 'pedal-balancing' act the adult performer balanced on his feet a five-metre-high ladder topped by a shorter horizontal ladder on which his juvenile partner did contortions. Acrobatics would sometimes be varied with a sword-fighting scene from a famous *kabuki* drama. The Great Dragon troupe, for example, performed a 30-minute adaptation of a scene from *Yoshitsune Sembon Zakura*. In juggling, the 'butterfly trick' held pride of place. The performer deftly formed two paper butterflies and then, by means of by air currents from a fan in each hand, launched and maintained them in prolonged and intricate flights—in and out of bottles, on and off perches and so on. The Sakuragawa troupe arrived in in 1873 and toured Australasia until 1877, when its members dispersed among local circuses. Its leader, the shoulder-balancer Decenoski, had married his juvenile partner, an Australian called Ewar, in 1875 and they performed in Queensland towns until his death in 1884. Ewar married an Australian acrobat in 1892 and, with children from both her marriages, they operated an itinerant show out of Quilpie (Qld) until 1917.

The tumbler and ropewalker Cooma Kitchie was a working partner in WIRTHS' CIRCUS at its inauguration in 1882 and was joined in 1883 by Bungaro the pedal-balancer and his juvenile partner Itchi. This pair performed in vaudeville and at country shows until shortly before Bungaro died at Grantham (Qld) in 1903. Cooma Kitchie's son, born at St George (Qld) in 1887, was adopted as a young child by Perry's Circus and spent his life with it and Soles' Circus, first as clown and acrobat and later as advance agent.

Later Japanese groups to play in Australia included the Tetsuwari–Tachibana troupe. It formed part of the Japanese Village, an exhibition of Japanese traditional craftsmen at work engaged by the Australian actor and impresario Pemberton Willard. It toured Australia from April 1886 to July 1887. The Godayou family arrived in 1891 and performed in vaudeville and with Wirths' Circus and FITZGERALD BROTHERS' CIRCUS until Godayou died in Melbourne in 1900. Two Japanese equilibrists, the Kodamas, arrived with Woodlochs' American Circus in 1895. They settled in NSW, appearing with ASHTON'S CIRCUS in 1907–12 and Eroni Brothers' Circus in 1914–17 and later as Kodamas' United Circus. The Lukashima troupe toured Australia with Bostock and Wombell's English circus in 1906, and in 1913 the Taiichi troupe was on the Brennan–Fuller vaudeville circuit. Wirths' Circus brought the Riogoku troupe to Australia in 1917 and the Royal Uyeno troupe in 1920 and later years. The Royal Uyenos were performing here when war against Japan was declared in 1941. ❦D. C. S. Sissons

Classical and avant-garde performers

At the 1978 ADELAIDE FESTIVAL OF ARTS Australian audiences saw *kabuki* performed for the first time. Classical *noh* and *kyogen* (comic interludes) followed when the Kanze troupe toured in 1986. Min Tanaka brought his form of *butoh* (performance art originated in the 1930s by Mijikata and Ono Kazuo) here in 1982. Sankai Juku in 1988, Dai Rakuda Kan, Byakkusha and other groups followed him in the late 1980s, performing to growing audiences at capital-city festivals. The avant-garde drama company Tenkei Gekijo performed in Perth and Adelaide in 1984. In 1992 Tadashi Suzuki, who had toured his *The Trojan Women* in Australia in 1989, trained Australians in his technique for performances of *The Chronicle of Macbeth*. The Asian-focused 1994 Adelaide Festival included Daisan Erotica's interpretation of *Macbeth*, the *butoh* group Tomoe Shizune and Hakutobo, and the technological performance group Dumb Type. Bunraku Theatre from Osaka performed traditional puppetry. The Falstaff story was adapted to the populist *kyogen* tradition by Yasunari Takahashi. ❦Alison Broinowski

Joseph Jefferson

American actor, 1829–1905. Toured Australia from November 1861 to April 1865.

Perhaps the greatest overseas actor to devote a significant part of his mature career to the Australian stage was Joseph Jefferson. He was also a major influence in the movement to replace the iconic conventions of early 19th-century acting with the new principles of complete absorption in the role and refusal to acknowledge the presence of the audience. His other main principle was 'never anticipate a strong effect'. His performances were characterised by a Chaplinesque mixture of comedy and pathos, the latter most famously in the last act of *Rip Van Winkle* when Rip returns from his 20-year sleep to find his world changed and his wife and friends dead. He played Rip Van Winkle in Australia, but not in the version of the play that gave him a 170-night London season in 1865–66 and made him a major star of English and American stages. His 1903 recordings of extracts from *Rip Van Winkle* show highly expressive changes of pitch and register.

Jefferson came to Australia after achieving success on Broadway in comedy roles from 1856. He later widened his range to include character parts and some melodrama leads, but during his Australian years he played a wider range of parts than he ever essayed again. Local reviews are consequently an important source for the study of Jefferson's art. He himself particularly admired those of JAMES SMITH in the Melbourne *Argus*, and later described them as 'models in style and strength'. However, these same reviews led to an accusation by the rival critic J. E. NEILD, that Smith had taken a £100 bribe to puff Jefferson's performances. Only spite between the two critics can have been reason for the allegation as it is unlikely to have been true, and Neild was himself a great admirer of Jefferson's powers. Apart from this episode, and an unnerving performance of *The Ticket-of-Leave Man* by Tom Taylor before a Hobart audience largely composed of ex-convicts, Jefferson greatly enjoyed his Australian stay. His autobiography—a classic of its genre—includes an account of a chance meeting in a park in Melbourne, between himself, CHARLES KEAN and an Aboriginal family. He also gives an invaluably detailed description of a visit to a Chinese opera company—probably that of Lee Gee or Leong Chan Kwong—at Daylesford (Vic.). ❦Harold Love

writings
Rip Van Winkle. London: Reinhardt and Evans 1949. Autobiography.

further reading
COLE, TOBY and HELEN K. CHINOY. *Actors on Acting*. New York: Crown 1965.

Jemmy Green in Australia

Farce in three acts by James Tucker. **premiere** 10 March 1966, Union Hall, Adelaide, by Adelaide University Theatre Guild. Cast: June Bell, Max Height, Margery Irving, Khail Jureidini, Norene Lower, Mark McManus, Peter Meredith, Harold Minear, Mick Rodger. Design: Barry Warren. Director: Peter O'Shaughnessy. **published** Sydney: Angus and Robertson 1955, ed. Colin Roderick.

Supposedly written by the convict JAMES TUCKER for performance at the Port Macquarie (NSW) penal settlement in 1845, this farcical comedy is set in Sydney in the 1840s. Jemmy Green was a character in William Moncrieff's 1821 play *Tom and Jerry—or, Life in London*, which was popular on the Australian stage. A local version of *Tom and Jerry*, LIFE IN SYDNEY, remained unperformed because it was refused a licence, so Tucker presumably took the name from Moncrieff's play. In all three plays the gullibility implied by his name leads Jemmy Green into unwise bidding at a land auction. As a foolish new chum, Jemmy Green is also strongly linked to the ballad 'BILLY BARLOW in Australia', which was first performed in amateur theatricals at Maitland (NSW) in August 1843. The plot of *Jemmy*

Green closely follows the ballad. Jemmy is sold sheep and cattle at exorbitant prices and building blocks in non-existent townships. On the way to his station he is attacked by bushrangers and then mistaken for an escaped convict. When he reaches the station, he finds his sheep diseased, his buildings burnt by Aborigines, his employees lazy and dishonest. Beset by creditors, he returns to Sydney to take advantage of the new Insolvency Act. And, since *Jemmy Green* is a comedy, he is just in time to prevent his wealthy fiancée from marrying one of the villains. The play was first performed in a radio adaptation by Colin Roderick, on ABC radio on 8 December 1952. ❦*Elizabeth Webby*

Essie Jenyns

Actor. Born October 1866, probably near Gympie (Qld). Originally Essie Jennings. Daughter of actor Kate Arden. Stage debut *c.*1882 in Hobart. In England 1884–85. Acted in Shakespeare 1885–88. Married John R. Wood in Sydney, 1 December 1888, and retired from stage. Died 1920.

Essie Jenyns's story was Australia's Cinderella legend. She is supposed to have been born to a penniless deserted mother in a single-roomed log cabin outside Gympie and to have endured a miserable childhood. She found sudden fame as an actor, had three years of brilliant stage successes and was successfully wooed by the young heir to a vast fortune. She spent her married life touring the world in a steam yacht her husband had built for her or living in a grand mansion in London and dabbling in charity work. Much of this was true. Her mother, after a disastrous marriage and poverty in Queensland and Sydney, became a successful actor and married her colleague W. J. HOLLOWAY in 1871. Jenyns was brought up 'on the road'. She first appeared in Hobart in the early 1880s as the page in Edward Bulwer-Lytton's *Richelieu* in WILLIAM CRESWICK's company, and came to prominence in 1883 as the heroine in George Darrell's melodrama THE SUNNY SOUTH. In 1884 the Holloway family visited England, where Jenyns is supposed to have studied to good effect the acting of the great Sarah Bernhardt and the American star Mary Anderson. She collected a stunning wardrobe in Paris.

Back in Australia, the Holloway company was devastated in May 1886 when its costumes and sets were lost in a shipping disaster, but Jenyns rescued their fortunes by setting theatres and reviewers alight with some remarkable performances, mostly in Shakespeare. The Bard was fading fast as a crowd-puller, but Jenyns became the toast of lovers of fine theatre as Juliet and most of Shakespeare's other heroines. The besotted *Bulletin* critic noted on 5 November 1887: 'Twelfth Night has been doing another season and another success at Sydney Criterion. We did not go to see it this time, because when last we attended we went home in a rowdy and clamorous condition from over-excitement, and went to sleep under the shower-bath, with our best hat held in both hands against our chest and a sweet smile on our features. But we will be on hand to witness *Cymbeline* next Saturday, and our voice will be heard hollering in the dress circle, provided the inflated pirate at the door will let us in. As far as we can recollect, Essie Jenyns disguises herself as a boy in this drama, and lives with three bears in a cave, and we wouldn't miss that for anything.' As this commentator hints, the attraction of Jenyns's performances was partly her ability to exude an 'unconscious' sexuality, enhanced by Shakespeare's tendency to ask his heroines to appear in male attire.

In October 1887 Jenyns came of age and decided that there were other things in the world besides rehearsals every day and working every night. She took a few days off after a final performance in Melbourne on 20 October 1888, on the eve of departure for London, where Holloway wanted to launch her international career. She went to Sydney and wrote to her parents, saying she was leaving the stage to marry an extremely rich young man. The *Bulletin* on 1 December 1888 congratulated her on her good sense:

> O! prudent lady, wise as clever,
> Fame is but a bubble fair...
> How many Essies sigh in vain,
> And wish they'd not appeared again.

The Holloway family biographer claims she soon regretted her missed career opportunities and her life of enforced idleness. ❦*Richard Fotheringham*

further reading
HOLLOWAY, DAVID. *Playing the Empire*. London: Harrap 1979.

Jigsaw Theatre Company

Professional community-theatre company in Canberra, founded 1974. **venues** 1974–81 Reid House. 1981– Gorman House. **directors** 1974–78 Carol Woodrow. 1979 Peter Wilkins. 1980 Joe Woodward. 1981 Graeme Brosnan. 1982–85 Peter Wilkins. 1986–89 Rod Wilson. 1990– Stephen Champion.

Founded as a theatre-in-education company, Jigsaw initially concentrated on presenting plays for schools, from pre-school to year 12. It devised some scripts, commissioned some and acquired some from other companies, such as *The White Man's Mission* from the POPULAR THEATRE TROUPE, for senior secondary students. Peter Wilkins extended the company's range to community theatre for adults. Its productions have included *The Dream Circle* by Ron Evans, about Walter and Marion Burley Griffin, the designers of Canberra; *Just a Bloke from Murwillumbah* by Simon Hopkinson, at the Australian War Memorial, *Shadows*, devised by the company, about the plight of refugees; and *Spitting Chips* by Peta Murray. ❦*Anne Edgeworth*.

Alan John

Composer. Born 14 September 1958 in Sydney. Studied piano from five. Studied at NSW State Conservatorium of Music and University of Sydney. Part-time dramaturge and composer with Nimrod Theatre Company (Sydney) 1981. Composer and performer in Lighthouse Company (Adelaide) 1982. Musical director of State Theatre Company of South Australia (Adelaide) 1984.

A distinctive, often uncompromising composer, Alan John has enhanced productions of STEPHEN SEWELL's plays with spacious, energetic music. He composed scores for the State Theatre Company of South Australia's premiere productions of Sewell's *The Blind Giant is Dancing* (1983) and *Dreams in an Empty City* (1986). Perhaps his finest score is *Frankie*, an opera for young performers commissioned by the COME OUT YOUTH ARTS FESTIVAL in Adelaide in 1987. John created this minor masterpiece in collaboration with DAVID

HOLMAN, the librettist, and NEIL ARMFIELD, the director. He also wrote scores for Holman's *Beauty and the Beast* (1988) and his adaptation of Nikolai Gogol's *Diary of a Madman*, which Armfield directed at the BELVOIR STREET THEATRE in Sydney in 1990. John wrote music for Armfield's production of *The Tempest* at Belvoir Street in the same year.

The SYDNEY THEATRE COMPANY commissioned John to write the music for *Jonah Jones*, a musical with a libretto by John Romeril, which was staged in 1985. A revised version, JONAH, was presented in Adelaide in 1991, directed by Armfield. ❦*Murray Bramwell*

John Alden Company

Professional dramatic company in Sydney, formed in 1950 by John Alden. **first production** *King Lear*, 25 August 1950, St James Hall, Sydney. **leading actors** John Alden, Neva Carr Glyn, Ruth Cracknell, John Meillon, Peter O'Shaughnessy, Max Oldaker, Diana Perryman, Dinah Shearing, Nancye Stewart, Owen Weingott.

JOHN ALDEN's company presented the first Australian professional productions of Shakespeare since the ALLAN WILKIE SHAKESPEAREAN COMPANY in 1930, and it provided some training in classical theatre, which Australian actors had lacked. Its intermittent existence and limited repertoire do not bear comparison with ALLAN WILKIE's achievement but the company was similarly hailed as a possible national theatre. When Elsie Beyer, who had managed the Australian tour of the Old Vic Theatre Company in 1948, became business manager, the company sought federal subsidy to ensure its permanence. Alden was reluctant to cede his personal control, however.

Although Alden's interpretation of Shakespeare drew upon his experiences in England with Donald Wolfit and the Old Vic, it was modified by his own theatrical sense and the need to communicate with Australian audiences. He was technical rather than intellectual as a director, but he attracted some leading actors to his company. His choice of plays such as *Measure for Measure*, *The Winter's Tale* and *King Lear* was adventurous, but when his company went on professional tour *The Merchant of Venice* and *A Midsummer Night's Dream* came to the fore. In leading roles his commanding stage presence and technical skills were increasingly overshadowed by his mannerisms, a tendency heightened by his reluctance to be directed by others.

Alden first assembled a company to play Shakespeare in 1948, at the Independent Theatre in Sydney. It was an amateur company, though some professionals acted without pay. The company became professional after Alden's production of *King Lear* was successful in Sydney in 1950. In 1951 *King Lear* played for five months in Sydney, attracting a total audience of 17 000. J. C. WILLIAMSON's took the company to mainland capital cities in 1951–52, billing it as 'A Jubilee Shakespeare Season'. ❦*John Rickard*

further reading

RICKARD, JOHN. *John Alden. Australian Dictionary of Biography* 13. Melbourne University Press 1993.

Jonah

Musical. **book and lyrics** John Romeril, from the novel by Louis Stone. **music** Alan John. **premiere as** *Jonah Jones* 25 October 1985, Wharf Theatre, by Sydney Theatre Company. Cast: Valerie Bader, Simon Burke, Peter Carroll, Michele Fawdon, Alan David Lee, Geraldine Turner. Designer: Roger Kirk. Director: Richard Wherrett. **premiere as** *Jonah* 31 August 1991, Space Theatre, Adelaide, by State Theatre Company of South Australia. Cast: Maurice Annese, Paul Blackwell, Heather Bolton, Eileen Darley, Ian Dixon, David Field, Jane Harders, Nancye Hayes, Carmel McGlone, John Wood. Designer: Mary Moore. Director: Neil Armfield.

Louis Stone's 1911 novel charts the financial rise of Jonah Jones, a hunchbacked Sydney larrikin who starts as a cobbler and finishes as a major footwear retailer. JOHN ROMERIL's script sharpens the symbolism. The violent 'Jonah the Boot' kicks his slum opponents when they are down, and the upwardly mobile Mr Jones prospers in the cutthroat world of capitalism. The end of the play moves forward to 1914, when Jonah is contracting to supply boots to the Australian Army, which is preparing for the First World War. Some lightness is provided by the play's best role, the larger-than-life washerwoman, Mrs Yabsley, who gives Jonah £20 to start his first shop and whose daughter marries him only to develop a fondness for the bottle.

Jonah's romantic intrigue with a piano teacher, Clara Grimes, and a subplot romance between two cheerful young battlers, Chook and Pinkey, also enrich the storyline. But when Romeril and ALAN JOHN's musical first appeared as *Jonah Jones* in 1985 David Malouf, in the *Australian* on 28 October, described the Sydney Theatre Company production as 'depressing', and 'as dark a piece as anything devised by Brecht and Weill'. An Adelaide season was hastily cancelled. In Adelaide six years later a much-revised version called *Jonah* was more favourably received. The director NEIL ARMFIELD and the designer Mary Moore solved the problem of what critics saw as cold cynicism by staging the play in promenade style, with the audience standing and moving from set to set while the actors performed between and around them. 'This may not be the Great Australian Musical', observed John Edge in the *Bulletin* on 17 September, but 'it was certainly one of the Great Nights at the Theatre'. ❦*Richard Fotheringham*

Charles Jones

Actor, agent, manager. Born *c*.1812, probably in England. Jeweller in Birmingham. Convicted of theft and transported for seven years, 1832. Arrived in Hobart February 1833. Freed 1839 and began acting. Married actor Mary Christina Thomson 1841. Acted in Sydney and Hobart to 1850. Settled in Sydney 1858. Committed suicide 14 June 1864 in Sydney.

For more than 20 years in a turbulent period Charles Jones demonstrated ability, versatility and durability as an actor, manager and agent in Hobart and Sydney. His earliest known theatrical activity was in 1840, the year after he completed his sentence and resumed his craft as a jeweller and silversmith. He was given a benefit in July 1840. Next year he married Mary Christina Thomson, sister of MRS CHARLES YOUNG. Their own daughter Rebecca appeared with W. S. LYSTER's opera company. After their marriage Jones and his wife moved between the Sydney and Hobart theatres. He acted in a variety of roles, including an equestrian performance in a Hobart circus in 1848. From 1850 he concentrated on management and in 1858 the Jones family settled in Sydney, where they were well known, respected and popular. Jones was a theatrical agent as well as manager until his suicide, which was precipitated by personal and business worries. ❦*Gillian Winter*

further reading
O'Driscoll, B. Y. Charles Jones, convict silversmith of Van Diemen's Land. *Art Bulletin of Tasmania* 1986.
O'Driscoll, S. Charles Jones gives an encore. *Australiana* 9/4 (November 1987).

Doris Egerton Jones

Dramatist. Born 23 December 1889 in Adelaide. Graduated from University of Adelaide 1911. Abandoned legal studies for health reasons. Published five novels 1913–18. Went to London in 1918. Married Australian soldier. Returned to Sydney 1922. Two plays professionally produced 1923–30. Returned to writing after raising family but found no publisher. Died 30 September 1973 in Sydney.

The two professionally produced plays of Doris Egerton Jones aroused some excitement, particularly because of their local origin. The *Sydney Morning Herald* thought *The Flaw*, a conventional detective drama, 'might have been written anywhere' but it had been skilfully done with 'unquestionable interest, apt dialogue, fine characterisation, occasional thrill and an atmosphere of mystery'. Jones wrote *The Flaw* with the touring actor Emelie Polini and J. C. Williamson's produced it in Sydney on 27 January 1923, starring Polini and Frank Harvey. Others in the cast were young Sheila Helpmann, Raymond Lawrence, Mayne Lynton, Gerald Kay Souper and Nancye Stewart. Jones made a bigger impact with *Governor Bligh*, a three-act play based on the arrest of William Bligh in Sydney in 1808. Allan Wilkie played the title-role at the Grand Opera House in Sydney on 2 August 1930. Jones's sympathetic portrayal of Bligh and her villainous John Macarthur provoked controversy in the *Sydney Morning Herald*, but made successful drama. 'It has been left to an Australian writer with an Australian play to make the legitimate stage in Sydney sit up and look rejuvenated', declared the *Bulletin*. Melbourne, however, was indifferent to the play when the Wilkie company took it there. ❦*Victoria Chance*

further reading
Edgar, Suzanne. Doris Egerton Jones. *Australian Dictionary of Biography* 9. Melbourne University Press 1983.

reference
Manuscripts of *The Flaw* are held at the Fryer Library of the University of Queensland in Brisbane, the University of New England in Armidale (NSW) and the National Library of Australia (MS 718/175, 176) in Canberra. *Governor Bligh* is at the University of New England and the National Library of Australia (MS 718/173, 174, 174A).

Gillian Jones

Actor, dramatist. Born 19 April 1947 in Newcastle (NSW). Brought up in Sydney. Trained in ballet until 17. Graduated from National Institute of Dramatic Art (Sydney) 1968; advanced course 1970. In original Australian cast of *Hair*. Member of Performance Syndicate (Sydney) 1970–74. Lighthouse Company (Adelaide) 1982–83. Returned to Sydney 1984. Won Prix Future in Berlin in 1981 for radio play *The Flight*.

Gillian Jones brings originality, restless insight, passion and control to classical and contemporary roles. She is able to transform character into intense poetic imagery, and she moves with a vivid elegance that is a legacy of her early ballet training. She has been associated with many leading directors, particularly three with faith in the actor—Neil Armfield, Rex Cramphorn and Jim Sharman. She was a founder member of Cramphorn's Performance Syndicate. Sharman invited her to join the Lighthouse ensemble of the State Theatre Company of South Australia. She epitomised sleazy glamour as Titania–Hippolyta in its memorable modern-dress *A Midsummer Night's Dream* and poignant charm as Viola in *Twelfth Night*. In Pierre Beaumarchais's *The Marriage of Figaro* she had a rare comic role as the Countess. She created the charismatic Rose Draper in Stephen Sewell's *The Blind Giant is Dancing* for Lighthouse in 1983. Jones had a notable success in Michael Gow's *Europe* in Sydney in 1987. She created Celia in Sewell's *Hate* in Melbourne and Sydney in 1988.

For a Women in Theatre project at the Nimrod Theatre in Sydney, Jones wrote and performed two monodramas, *Passengers in Overcoats* and *Anorexia Sometimes*; the latter went to the 1980 Adelaide Festival. In 1986–87 she was awarded a literary grant from the Australia Council for a novel, *Peers and Powerful People*. ❦*Guy Sherborne*

Harriet Jones

Actor, singer. Born c.1804. Arrived in Sydney on *Mountaineer*, November 1825. Performed mainly in Sydney, 1826–43. Went to London with Conrad Knowles 1837. Returned to Sydney, calling herself Mrs Knowles, October 1838. Performed mainly in Melbourne 1844–45.

The first female professional performer in Australia, Harriet Jones is said to have excelled in comic parts, but she played a wide range of characters, particularly in the early days of Barnett Levey's company at the Theatre Royal in Sydney. Little is known of her early or later life. She arrived in Sydney with two children in November 1825; she may have been married to a convict. She sang at Levey's concerts on 9 and 16 August 1826, and the *Sydney Monitor* praised her 'great simplicity and sweetness of style'.

As Mrs Love she was leading lady of Levey's first company, playing the name-part in Douglas Jerrold's *Black-Eyed Susan* on the opening night of his theatre in the saloon of the Royal Hotel on 26 December 1832. Also in the company was Conrad Knowles, with whom she left for London in May 1837. Unable to obtain theatrical engagements there, they returned to Sydney in October 1838. Conrad and Harriet Knowles—as she was now known—joined the Royal Victoria Theatre company. They defected to Luigi Dalle Case's Australian Olympic Theatre in February 1842 but after it closed they returned to the Royal Victoria. In 1843 they joined another rival company, at Joseph Simmons's Royal City Theatre. When that also closed after a brief season they performed in Hobart and Launceston and then went to Melbourne. After Conrad died in May 1844 Harriet remained in Melbourne, appearing with Samson Cameron's and Francis Nesbitt's companies in 1844 and 1845.

Of small stature and apparently slim even in middle age, she often appeared in breeches roles, such as the title-role in *Don Giovanni in London*, which she played for her benefit at the Royal Victoria Theatre on 6 December 1842. The *Sydney Herald* of that date said: 'She has always been a general favourite. During a considerable portion of this season she was the only actress capable of undertaking serious characters, and there has scarcely been a piece played in which she has not taken a prominent part'. ❦Elizabeth Webby

Tilly Jones

Actor, dancer, singer. Born 3 October 1829 at Port Macquarie (NSW). Originally Matilda Jones. Made debut as dancer in *Bombastes Furioso* at Theatre Royal, Sydney, 1834. Retired from stage to marry 1843.

Edward Geoghegan wrote THE CURRENCY LASS to display the talents of Tilly Jones, the first notable actor of Australian birth. Before the premiere in Sydney, however, she retired from the stage to marry and Mme Louise, an English dancer and occasional singer, played the title-role instead. The *Australian* on 30 May 1844 mourned the loss of the 'real Currency Lass', and castigated the Royal Victoria Theatre for its 'cockney imports'. Early in April 1845 Tilly Jones returned to the Royal Victoria as Mrs Crane to sing 'Australia, land of my birth' at a benefit. Thereafter nothing is heard of her. She began performing in BARNETT LEVEY's child troupe at the Theatre Royal, together with her sister Emma, her brother Stephen 'the Australian Roscius', and another brother identified only as Master C. Jones. She played the young prince York in *Richard III* in 1836 and Fleance in *Macbeth* in June 1841. As she matured her versatility caught the attention of the chauvinist Australian-born 'cabbage-tree hat boys', and at 12 she gave a benefit under their patronage on 15 June 1841. In that year the litigious and envious sisters Ann and ELIZA WINSTANLEY seceded from the Royal Victoria Theatre when Jones sang 'Rory O'More', a song Ann Winstanley had sung. ❦Helen Musa

further reading
GEOGHEGAN, EDWARD. *The Currency Lass* (ed. Roger Covell). Sydney: Currency–Methuen 1976.
OPPENHEIM, HELENE. The author of *The Hibernian Father*. *Australian Literary Studies* 2/4 (Hobart, December 1966).

Juggling

The ancient art of juggling, which entered the circus ring from the fairground in England in the late 18th century, appears in early Australian circus programs only in the late 1850s. One of the first jugglers in the colonies was James Klaer, in BURTON'S CIRCUS in 1857. Robert Taylor (1833–1917), an Australian-born apprentice of the circus proprietor JAMES HENRY ASHTON, won renown as a juggler later in his career. '… nobody could beat Taylor in his juggling act on the running globe', a correspondent wrote in the *Bulletin* of 20 September 1917. The renowned German juggler Paul Cinquevalli and the American comic juggler W. C. Fields, later famous as a film comedian, toured Australian vaudeville circuits in the early 1900s. ❦Mark St Leon

Junction Theatre Company

Professional community-theatre company in Adelaide, founded in 1983 by Malcolm Blaylock. **artistic directors** 1983–90 Malcolm Blaylock. 1990– Geoff Crowhurst. **venues** 1987–90 Falcon Avenue, Mile End. 1990– George Street, Thebarton. **first performance** *This Year's Model* by Allen Lyne in 1984 at automobile plant, Woodville.

Since its establishment by the Association of Community Theatres as a full-time COMMUNITY-THEATRE company for the northern and western suburbs of Adelaide the Junction Theatre Company has made theatre about the lives and concerns of working people. It maintains close links with trade unions and work sites and devises theatre for working people, based on their industrial experiences. It began production in 1984 with performances of *This Year's Model*, involving the director Malcolm Blaylock and the writer–performers Irene Tunis and Mark Reedman, under the AUSTRALIA COUNCIL's Art and Working Life incentive program. DOREEN CLARKE's *Checkout* followed in 1985, and the occupational health and safety cabaret *Oops!* in 1986. Other productions include Mij Tanith's *Just Write* (1987) on adult literacy; *Wild About Work* by Anne Brookman (1989); *This Dying Business* (1990), a play by Peta Murray on palliative care; *Florence Who?* by Roxxy Bent (1991); and *Offshore* by P. P. CRANNEY (1991). Cranney and the artistic director Geoff Crowhurst have continued an Art and Working Life collaboration that they began in the MAINSTREET THEATRE COMPANY at Millicent (SA). ❦Murray Bramwell

Paul Kathner

Designer, scenic artist. Born 17 July 1935 in Sydney. Studied painting and drawing at East Sydney Technical College 1952-55, while assisting William Constable in scene painting and design for Borovansky Ballet. Began designing for Independent Theatre (Sydney) 1954–58. Later worked for Australian Elizabethan Theatre Trust and John Alden Company. Resident designer of St Martin's Theatre Company (Melbourne) 1962–73. Scenic artist for J. C. Williamson's 1973–76. Formed Scenic Studies Pty Ltd 1976. Irene Mitchell Award 1969 (*Eden House* by Hal Porter). Green Room Award 1989 for outstanding technical achievement.

Paul Kathner's talents have often brought other designers' concepts to life. His work as a scenic artist probably overshadows his own design work. He is a product of the 1950s and 1960s, when box sets, sky and garden cloths dominated stage design, and he is one of the few scenic artists who can still use 'hot' paint, mixed and boiled with glue-size and treacle. Kathner's ability to blend colours into the canvas stamps his work with a glowing depth and gives it richness. He painted for many J. C. WILLIAMSON's productions and, with Ross Turner, designed John McCallum's *As It's Played Today*. Kathner and Turner formed Scenic Studies Pty Ltd after the Firm's demise, employing its scenic staff. This commercial scene studio has become the largest in Australia, painting for a wide range of productions including musicals, opera and ballet. Kathner designed the scenery and costumes for the MELBOURNE THEATRE COMPANY's productions of *Privates on Parade* by Peter Nichols in 1980, *The Suicide* by Nicholas Erdmann in 1981 and *A Man for All Seasons* by Robert Bolt in 1981. ❦

Lily Kavanagh MBE

Actor, speech teacher. Born 1897 in Kalgoorlie (WA). Studied violin. Taught speech privately and in schools in Perth. Founding member of Company of Four (Perth). Died January 1988 in Perth. MBE 1976.

Under Lily's Kavanagh's guidance the COMPANY OF FOUR set high standards in speech and deportment. She was an occasional and rather reluctant performer on the stage, but those who saw her were struck by the clarity and beauty of her voice and by her timing, especially in modern English comedies such as those of Ben Travers.

With no formal qualification in speech, she was a noted teacher for more than 60 years. She taught many leaders in business and the professions and well-known actors, including FAITH CLAYTON, JAMES CONDON, JUDY DAVIS, NITA PANNELL, Patricia Skevington, Leith Taylor, NEVILLE TEEDE and Mary Ward. In 1982 a group of her friends set up the Lily P. Kavanagh Awards, a trust fund for seminars, classes and awards for students. ❦*David J. Hough*

Sydney John Kay

Director, producer, musician. Born c.1904 in Germany of Jewish and Peruvian extraction. Original surname Kaiser. Came to Australia in German jazz group 1939. Ran Theatre for Children in Sydney 1944–45. Managing director of Mercury Theatre Pty Ltd and producer–director of Mercury Mobile Players 1946–49. Revived Mercury Theatre 1952–53. Worked in London as composer-arranger from 1954 until death in 1969.

Through MERCURY THEATRE, Sydney John Kay widened artistic horizons for actors and audiences. His energy, ingenuity and vast technical knowledge enabled the Mercury Mobile Players to take classic comedy, usually in shortened versions, to audiences in factories, schools, hospitals and public halls in Sydney. His best-known production, Molière's *The Imaginary Invalid* with PETER FINCH in the title-role, was much praised by Laurence Olivier and Vivien Leigh in 1948.

In 1952 Kay set up Mercury Theatre again, in St James's Hall, and introduced the European repertory system to Australia. By rotating productions regularly, sometimes changing them nightly, he attempted to break away from the commercial long-run system, which he saw as trapping actors in routine. Despite an impressive range of plays and high standards of performance, financial problems forced him to close down in late 1953.

In the 1920s and 1930s Kay played in the Weintraubs, a leading German jazz group, with which he appeared in the film *The Blue Angel*. The Weintraubs were touring Australia when the Second World War broke out and all were interned as enemy aliens. Kay was released in 1942. He settled in Sydney, changed his name by deed poll, became musical arranger for the Colgate-Palmolive radio unit and wrote musical scores for documentary and feature films. His Theatre for Children in 1944–45 was innovative but he suffered heavy financial loss because of a poliomyelitis epidemic. ❦*Allan Ashbolt*

Charles and Ellen Kean

English actors, husband and wife. Toured Australia 1863–64.
Charles Kean 1811–68. Son of tragedian Edmund Kean. Stage debut at Theatre Royal, Drury Lane, London, 10 October 1827. Director of Queen Victoria's private theatricals at Windsor Castle 1848-58. Manager and star of Princess's Theatre, London, 1850-59.
Ellen Kean 1806–80. Originally Ellen Tree.

'I daresay we shall revolutionize their taste', wrote Charles Kean's wife Ellen of their impending descent on the barbarous colonies in 1863. The couple sailed for Australia in July 1863 with their niece Patty Chapman and the actors James Cathcart and George Everett, under contract to GEORGE COPPIN. They opened in Edward Moore's 1753 play *The Gamester* at Coppin's HAYMARKET THEATRE in Melbourne on 10 October 1863. Critics, especially in the *Argus* and the *Age*, rhapsodised about experiencing such great actors, but there was no revolution in taste. Local audiences preferred the 'superhuman' acting of BARRY SULLIVAN at the Theatre Royal to the Keans' more subdued style. But the Keans' sheer status placed them ahead of other theatrical tourists and their ostentatious respectability allowed fashionable upper-middle class patronage and high prices to flourish for a short time in the colonies.

In Sydney, where the Keans opened with G. W. Lovell's *The Wife's Secret* on 2 December, they found their keenest fans were 'dead sticks'. Charles suffered from an illness which brought false reports of his death on 18 January 1864. Next month the Keans were pleasantly surprised by intelligent audiences in Ballarat (Vic.) and they made huge profits there from 23 February 1864. Back in Melbourne, Coppin and Charles Kean took over the Haymarket Theatre after its lessee, James Simmonds, became insolvent. Bailiffs seized their costumes but all was resolved when Kean loaned Simmonds £100. After performing in Bendigo and Geelong in May 1864, the Keans gave their last Sydney performances in late June and early July 1864.

They left Sydney for California on 9 July and Ellen remarked: 'I never left any place with so little regret'. Coppin, who was able to pay his creditors in full after the tour, went with the Keans to the USA as their agent. On their return to England the Keans continued to play their favourite roles. When Charles died in 1868 the widowed Queen Victoria wrote to Ellen, expressing a commonality of grief for the loss of a loved husband. ❦*Helen Musa*

further reading
DUFF, HELEN. Charles and Ellen Kean in Australia 1863–64. University of NSW BA(hons) thesis 1965.
VAN DER POORTEN, HELEN. Charles Kean. *Australian Dictionary of Biography* 5. Melbourne University Press 1974.

Daniel Keene

Director, dramatist. Born 21 December 1955 in Melbourne. Began acting 1979. First play, *Skelta*, performed at La Mama Theatre, Melbourne, March 1981.

Eight of the 12 plays Daniel Keene has written and had performed since 1981 have had multiple productions in Australia and six have been produced overseas, particularly in New York City. Keene himself considers *Cho Cho San* and *The Hour Before My Brother Dies* to be landmarks. *Cho Cho San*, based on the same theme as David Belasco's *Madame Butterfly*, was first produced by the HANDSPAN THEATRE COMPANY, employing live performers and puppets, in Melbourne in December 1984. Three years later the play toured five capital cities and towns in Western Australia, the Northern Territory and South Australia. In October 1988 it toured Beijing, Nanjing and Shanghai in China. In July 1991 it was performed in Brisbane. *The Hour Before My Brother Dies* was first produced in July 1985 in Melbourne. Since then there have been five new productions, in New York and Melbourne in 1986, Sydney and Edinburgh in 1990 and Lodz (Poland) in 1991. Keene's *Isle of Swans*, *The Fighter* and *Silent Partner* have also been produced overseas. ❦*Janet Greason*

published plays
All Souls. Sydney: Currency Press 1995.
Cho Cho San (1984). Sydney: Currency Press 1987.
Echoes of Ruby Dark. In Exiles in Paradise. Melbourne: Fringe Network 1981.

Laura Keene

English actor, c.1826–1873. Acted in England and USA. Visited Australia with Edwin Booth and D. J. Anderson 1854. Opened Laura Keene's Varieties, New York City, 1855. Managed Laura Keene's Theatre, New York City, 1856–63. Edited *Five Arts* magazine, wrote and lectured.

A red-haired, pallid beauty, 'Red Laura' Keene gave dignity to comedy in the USA, but made little impact in Australia. She was billed as the star but was overshadowed by EDWIN BOOTH, whom she struggled to keep out of the bars. On the way home Keene parted from Booth in Honolulu. She was playing at Ford's Theatre in Washington DC on 14 April 1865, when Abraham Lincoln was shot by Booth's brother John Wilkes Booth. ❦*Helen Musa*

further reading
CREAHAN, JOHN. *The Life of Laura Keene*. 1897.
RUGGLES, E. *Prince of Players*. London: Peter Davies 1953.
Dictionary of American Biography. New York 1927.
Who Was Who in American Theatre, 1607–1896 revised. Chicago: 1967.

Cecil Kellaway

Actor Born 27 August 1890 in Cape Town (Cape of Good Hope Colony) to English parents. Educated in southern Africa and England. Worked as engineer in South Africa before joining theatre. Came to Australia 1921. Acted in nearly 80 American films from 1939. Died 28 February 1973 in Los Angeles (USA). Brother of actor Alec Kellaway and dancer Leon Kellaway.

For 15 years Cecil Kellaway played leading comedy roles for J. C. Williamson's in operettas, including *Betty*, *Hold Everything*, *Leave It to Jane*, *Mary* and *Primrose*. He first appeared in Australia in January 1922, at the Theatre Royal in Melbourne with MADGE ELLIOTT, MAUDE FANE, ALFRED FRITH and CYRIL RITCHARD in *A Night Out*, a farce by Georges Feydeau with added music. About that time a Melbourne critic aptly referred to Kellaway's 'urbanity and ease'. In 1933 Kellaway entered films. He wrote the story for Cinesound's *It Isn't Done* in 1937 and played the lead with charm and skill that took him to Hollywood. ❦*John West*

Annette Kellermann

Vaudevillian. Born 6 July 1886 in Sydney. Daughter of pianist Alice Charbonnet-Kellermann and violinist Frederick William Kellermann. Began swimming as child. Won NSW championship 1902. Moved to England with father 1904. First woman to attempt to swim English Channel. Performed spectacular tank act on Keith vaudeville circuit in USA. Acted in Hollywood films 1914–24. Triumphant tour of Australasia in vaudeville 1921–1922. Admitted to International Swimming Hall of Fame 1975. Died 6 November 1975 at Anglers Paradise (Qld).

Annette Kellermann spent little of her professional life in Australia but she made a big impression here in her Hollywood films and particularly during her 18-month vaudeville tour in 1921-22. Her French mother, originally Alice Charbonnet, was a leading pianist and teacher and her home was one of Sydney's most admired salons until the 1890s depression left the family in financial difficulties. This was instrumental in Kellermann's decision to become a professional swimmer.

Swimming led her to the stage in THE BREAKING OF THE DROUGHT, and she developed an extravagant vaudeville tank act which she took to London and New York as a variety turn. Billed as 'Australia's Mermaid', she wore a brilliant red one-piece diving suit, stretching from head to toe, and a steel-spangled mermaid tail that reflected coloured lights shining through the tank. Diving and underwater ballet were the focus of the act, in which Kellermann stayed under water for up to three and a half minutes. She continually expanded and improved her act on American vaudeville circuits, denying charges that she owed her popularity to novelty and it would be brief. She incorporated a ballet act, wirewalking, male impersonations and gave a light-hearted lecture on physical culture.

Artistry was very important to Kellermann. She had early hopes of transferring her career from swimming to dancing, and while at the Hippodrome in New York she studied with Luigi Albertieri, ballet master at the Metropolitan Opera House. She danced in a gala concert at the Metropolitan in 1917 and treasured the memory all her life. Ballet brought grace to her underwater work. Kellermann's mother abhorred her career. In an account of her life written as a background for the 1952 film *Million Dollar Mermaid*, in which she was played by Esther Williams, Kellermann recalls wanting her mother to see her first film, *Neptune's Daughter*, in which she felt she brought swimming to the level of art. The tension between Kellermann's upbringing and her career was a creative force. It forged her industry and her aesthetics, both of which were essential to her success. ❦*Victoria Chance*

further reading
WALSH, G. P. Annette Kellermann. *Australian Dictionary of Biography* 9. Melbourne University Press 1983.
reference
A collection in the Dennis Wolanski Library (Sydney) includes the autobiography written for *Million Dollar Mermaid* and a biography written by Kellermann's sister B. Wooster, both unpublished, and official documents and letters.

Kelly and Leon Minstrels

American minstrel troupe. Founded by Edwin Kelly and Francis Leon in 1860s. Came to Australia in 1878. Disbanded 1880.

Edwin Kelly, a minstrel, and Francis Leon, America's most famous female impersonator, joined forces in the early 1860s to form their own minstrel troupe. Kelly filled the roles of interlocutor, balladeer and manager, while Leon was the *prima donna* or *danseuse*, performing sketches that parodied leading female opera singers. Leon, whose real name was Patrick Glassey, was born on 21 November 1840, probably in the USA, and began his professional career at Wood's Marble Hall of Minstrelsy in New York City. Kelly, born in Ireland in 1835, made his first stage appearances with Ordway's Aeolian Minstrels. The Kelly and Leon Minstrels were based first in Chicago, then Cincinatti and from 1866 in New York City.

In 1878 the Kelly and Leon Minstrels opened at the Queen's Theatre in Sydney and later visited Melbourne and Adelaide. Their programs emphasised vocal music and light comedy and sketches involving caricatures of contemporary operas and operettas, in which 'the only Leon' was prominent. They staged the first Australian performance of Gilbert and Sullivan's operetta *HMS Pinafore*, with Leon as Josephine. In early 1880 the duo opened Kelly and Leon's Opera House in Sydney, with programs consisting of comic opera, opera burlesques, and even Marcus Clarke's burlesque THE HAPPY LAND. In late 1880 the partnership was dissolved, with Kelly forming his own Comedy Opera Company and Leon organising a Mastodon Minstrel Party.

By 1883 Leon had returned to the USA and joined forces with Frank Cushman to form the Leon and Cushman Minstrels. This company toured Australia in 1885. Cushman later enjoyed a successful career in vaudeville but Leon adhered tenaciously to the minstrel business. His revived Kelly and Leon Minstrels failed in Chicago in 1900 and he went into retirement. He was last recorded living in the USA in 1913. Kelly never returned to the USA but joined forces with J. C. WILLIAMSON and became a regular performer in his Gilbert and Sullivan productions. He was particularly acclaimed as Sir Joseph Porter in *HMS Pinafore* and he also appeared in *The Mikado*, *Patience* and *The Pirates of Penzance*. After Kelly's death from heart failure in Adelaide Hospital on 1 January 1900 Williamson had a monument erected over his grave. ❦*Richard Waterhouse*

further reading
RICE, EDWARD LEROY. *Monarchs of Minstrelsy*. New York 1911.
TOLL, ROBERT C. *Blacking Up*. New York: Oxford 1977.

Myra Kemble

Actor. Born 17 November 1857 in Sligo (Ireland). Originally Maria Gill. Made stage debut in Melbourne 1874. Married bookmaker James Whitehead, 10 December 1878. Won popular actress competition in *Illustrated Sydney News* 10 June 1893. Died 2 October 1906 in Melbourne.

A specialist in light comic roles, Myra Kemble was popular in Sydney in the late 19th century. The *Bulletin* called her 'unquestionably one of the finest actresses the Australian stage has produced' and a national institution. After her debut in the pantomime *Twinkle, Twinkle Little Star* in Melbourne in 1874 she worked in Bendigo (Vic.) in 1874 and joined SAMUEL LAZAR's company at the new Theatre Royal in Sydney in 1875. As a soubrette at John Bennett's Royal Victoria Theatre in Sydney until 1878 she played Biddy in GEORGE DARRELL's *Transported for Life*, Mary Meredith in Tom Taylor's *Our American Cousin* and the Fool in *King Lear*. She appeared in BLAND HOLT's first production in Australia, *The New Babylon* by Paul Merritt and George Fawcett Rowe, in 1880. She went to London in 1889 and, according to the *Bulletin*, had many successes. Her role in *Man and the Woman*, written for her by Robert Buchanan, was not one of them. She was so well received on her return to Sydney that she toured Australasian cities. ❦*Delyse Anthony*

further reading
GITTINS, JEAN. Myra Kemble. *Australian Dictionary of Biography* 5. Melbourne University Press 1974.
Bulletin (Sydney)1 November 1906.

Thomas Keneally AO

Dramatist. Born 7 October 1935 in Sydney. Grew up on north coast of NSW. Studied in Catholic seminary 1952–60 but not ordained. Worked as schoolteacher and clerk. Published first novel 1964, and then another almost every year. Commonwealth Literary Fund fellowships 1966, 1968. Lectured in drama at the University of New England (Armidale NSW) 1968–69. Has also written for film and television. AO 1983.

The novels of the prolific Thomas Keneally have a large popular following, are widely read overseas and have won major awards, including the 1982 Booker McConnell Prize in the United Kingdom—for *Schindler's Ark*. His plays have not had similar success. The most widely performed has been *Halloran's Little Boat*, first produced in 1966 at the JANE STREET THEATRE in Sydney. It is the love story of a soldier and a convict girl, innocents in a world of imported corruption, and it explores the mystical in a way characteristic of Keneally's novels. Like his 1967 novel *Bring Larks and Heroes*, it draws on the writings of Watkin Tench, an officer in the marine corps with the First Fleet. Keneally returned to that period in his 1987 novel *The Playmaker*, upon which the British dramatist Timberlake Wertenbaker drew for her successful play *Our Country's Good*.

Childermas (1968) is an allegorical account of the Nativity which Keneally and his director at the Old Tote Theatre in Sydney assembled from work by a committee of writers concerned with the children of the Vietnam War. *An Awful Rose* (1972) is a complex account of a Catholic priest's relationship with his dying father. *Ned Kelly and the City of Bees* (1978) is a children's fantasy based on a 1968 story. *Bullie's House* (1980), set on an Aboriginal mission station, critically examines tribal, anthropological and missionary approaches to life. *Gossip from the Forest* (1983) is an account of the First World War peace negotiations, adapted from the novel of the same title. ❦*Katharine Brisbane*

published plays
Bullie's House (1980). Sydney: Currency Press 1981.
Gossip from the Forest (1983). Sydney: NSW Building Society and Sydney Theatre Company 1983.
Halloran's Little Boat (1966). London and Melbourne: Penguin 1975.

further reading
CARROLL, DENNIS. *Australian Contemporary Drama*. Sydney: Currency Press 1993.
Who's Who in Australia 1991. Melbourne: Information Australia.
Who's Who of Australian Writers. Melbourne: D. W. Thorpe and National Centre for Australian Studies 1991.

Peter Kenna

Actor, dramatist. Born 18 March 1930 in Sydney. Left school at 14. Joined amateur theatre groups. Became professional radio actor in early 1950s. Stage actor from mid-1950s. Won General Motors Holden playwriting competition with *The Slaughter of St Teresa's Day* 1959. Worked in London 1959–71, with brief return to Sydney in 1966. Died 29 November 1987 in Sydney.

Peter Kenna contributed to Australian drama a unique combination of earthy larrikin Irishness and spirituality in a quest for intimacy. This quest is expressed in his plays in the ambivalence, and paradox, of the earthiness with which his characters seek out their God, and the spirituality with which they approach sex. Kenna's best writing is in his energetic studies of working-class Irish Catholic family life, especially *An Eager Hope*, *A Hard God* and *The Slaughter of St Teresa's Day*. He was born into a large Irish Catholic family in working-class Balmain. While still at his Christian Brothers school during the Second World War he was in a concert party that entertained troops around Sydney. He left school at 14 and worked in various jobs and joined amateur theatre groups. In the early 1950s he became a professional actor, and performed in the radio serials *Portia Faces Life* and *Life Can Be Beautiful*. In the mid-1950s he became a stage actor.

Like Ray Lawler, Kenna wrote many plays throughout the 1940s and early 1950s, but few were produced. Then in 1959 *The Slaughter of St Teresa's Day* won a playwriting competition and was taken up by the Trust Players in the general enthusiasm of the time. Like Lawler, Kenna went to London. He worked there until the mid-1960s, when he directed his own play *Muriel's Virtues* at the Independent Theatre in Sydney. Then he returned to London, suffering from kidney failure, which required prolonged treatment. Both these events are treated in his play *An Eager Hope*.

Kenna returned to Sydney in 1971 and embarked on a new career as a playwright, the highlight of which was the production of his finest play, *A Hard God*, at the Nimrod Street Theatre in 1973. At that time Kenna was the only playwright who straddled the dramatic renascences of the 1950s and the 1970s. His talent was slightly obscured by energetic young writers such as Alex Buzo, Jack Hibberd, John Romeril and David Williamson. Kenna's extension of *A Hard God* into a trilogy, *The Cassidy Album*, was in turn overshadowed by Ray Lawler's *The Doll Trilogy*, but he continued to write throughout the 1970s and 1980s. His last major work was the screenplay for *The Umbrella Woman*, a feature film released in 1987.

The central concern that runs through all his plays is the difficulty of achieving intimacy between people and the effects of its loss. In different plays he explores this failure of human intimacy in families and in sexual partnerships. These two come together in the dual action of *A Hard God*. In *Mates* and *Trespassers Will Be Prosecuted* the issue is explored in tight little encounters between people who do not know each other but are forced together. In *The Slaughter of St Teresa's Day* the central character, Oola McGuire, has spent her entire life trying to conduct human relationships along almost commercial lines. As she tries to come to terms with this in advancing middle age she realises that it has not been enough.

Between this play and *A Hard God*, Kenna produced variations on the theme of intimacy in plays of different styles and emotional tones. *Talk to the Moon* is a realistic drama that explores the shifting relationships within a particularly quarrelsome family, with a pervasive mood of the sadness of transience, failed communication and loss. It was first produced at the Hampstead Theatre Club in London in 1963, and its Australian premiere was at St Martin's Theatre in Melbourne in 1972.

Trespassers Will Be Prosecuted is a savage study of an encounter between an old derelict and a disturbed young boy who seek refuge under a railway bridge. They spar and bicker, and have one climactic moment of true contact that only reveals the barriers each has set up to exclude other people. *Listen Closely*, produced at the Independent Theatre in Sydney in 1972, is a lively farce which shows the strained marriage of respectability and larrikinism in Australian suburban life. Many of the strands of these early plays are gathered into *A Hard God*. Richly realised working-class Irishness in the parents Aggie and Dan and tentative reaching for closeness by young boys together evoke one of the most enduring images in Australian drama of the difficult struggle for warm enduring intimacy in a harsh world. In *Mates* and in the two plays that complete *The Cassidy Album*—*Furtive Love* and *An Eager Hope*—Kenna began to explore themes of homosexual love that he had first suggested in *A Hard God*. In *Furtive Love* the autobiographical character Joe rejects his parents' God and embraces the earthly attractions of homosexual love. Joe, now an actor, decides to have an affair with a fellow actor, Tom, not only challenging his God but also compromising his friendship with Tom's lover George.

In the third play, *An Eager Hope*, Joe has become a playwright. He faces illness and a crisis in his career. He comes back to his family, survives the crisis, and reaches some sort of weary reconciliation between the claims of his sexuality and the demands of his hard God. This ambivalence is most powerful in *A Hard God*. Part of the appeal of *An Eager Hope* is that it reintroduces Aggie, over 70 and still battling on. *The Cassidy Album* is a bold and interesting experiment but as a unit it is less successful than Lawler's trilogy, perhaps because in the two later plays Kenna was too close to his subject to create independent characters to embody it. *John McCallum*

published plays
Furtive Love (1978). Sydney: Currency Press 1980.
A Hard God (1973). Sydney and London: Currency–Methuen 1974, revised 1982.
Listen Closely (1972). Sydney: Currency Press 1977.
Mates (1975). Sydney: Currency Press 1977 in *Drag Show*.
The Slaughter of St Teresa's Day (1959). Sydney: Currency Press 1972.
Talk to the Moon (1963) Sydney: Currency Press 1977.
Trespassers Will Be Prosecuted (1976). Sydney: Currency Press 1977.

further reading
Brisbane, Katharine. In *Contemporary Dramatists* (ed. D. L. Kirkpatrick) 4th edn. London; St James Press 1988.
Carroll, Dennis. *Australian Contemporary Drama*. Sydney: Currency Press 1995.
McCallum, John. Peter Kenna and the search for intimacy. *Contemporary Australian Drama* revised (ed. Peter Holloway). Sydney: Currency Press 1987.

Patricia Kennedy OBE

Actor. Born 17 March 1917 at Queenscliff (Vic.). Trained as kindergarten and primary teacher in Melbourne. Attended Maie Hoban's Modern School of Drama 1934–38. Stage debut in Melbourne 1935. Foundation member of Union Theatre Repertory Company (Melbourne) 1953–56, 1959–60, 1967–68. Acted in United Kingdom at Citizens' Theatre, Glasgow, and Bristol Old Vic 1969–70. Drama consultant to Australian Council for the Arts 1972–73. Erik Kuttner Award (Miss Madrigal in *The Chalk Garden* by Enid Bagnold) 1957. OBE 1982.

A distinguished leading actor in classical and contemporary roles, Patricia Kennedy made a breakthrough for Australian actors when she was cast as Miss Madrigal in *The Chalk Garden* opposite Sybil Thorndike and Lewis Casson on their Australasian tour for J. C. Williamson's in 1957. Until then Australians had been relegated to minor supporting roles in the professional theatre since the 1940s. Kennedy became widely known in radio drama during the late 1930s and gave notable stage performances in Melbourne as Portia in *The Merchant of Venice* in 1947 and in the title-role of George Bernard Shaw's *Candida*, directed by Ray Lawler for the National Theatre Movement in 1955.

In the Union Theatre Repertory Company's initial season in 1953 she played Lady Starcross in Diana Morgan's *After My Fashion* and the Countess in Christopher Fry's *The Light is Dark Enough*. After 18 months in the United Kingdom, she played the Countess in Tyrone Guthrie's MELBOURNE THEATRE COMPANY production of *All's Well that Ends Well* in 1971. Her later notable performances included Mary Tyrone in Eugene O'Neill's *Long Day's Journey into Night* in Adelaide and Melbourne in 1973; the Aunt opposite Deborah Kerr in *The Day After the Fair* in Melbourne in 1979; and the Nurse in Euripides's *Medea*, which opened the Playhouse in Melbourne in 1984. In 1991 she was acclaimed in Melbourne as Weekly in the stage adaptation of Elizabeth Jolley's *The Newspaper of Claremont Street* at the Beckett Theatre. *Robert Hewett*

Norman Kessell OAM

Journalist, theatre writer. Born 31 August 1903 in London. Emigrated to Australia 1926. Became share farmer in Singleton (NSW). Founded Singleton Musical Society. Moved to Sydney 1930. Active in Northbridge Musical Society, Neutral Bay Players' Club, Mosman Players and Mosman Musical Society. Married Marguerite Clinch, amateur actor and singer 1931. Joined Sydney *Daily Telegraph* 1937. Began writing reviews 1944. Editor of Sydney *Daily Mirror* 1954. Features editor and chief subeditor of Sydney *Sun* 1957–69. Editor of *Retail World* 1969. Wrote reviews for *Daily Telegraph* and *Sunday Telegraph* 1969–78. Stringer for New York *Variety* 1971 until death. Chairman of Australian National Playwrights' Conference 1974–75. Occasional columnist for *Theatre Australia*. Died 12 January 1986 in Sydney. OAM 1980.

Norman Kessell preferred the word 'reviewer' to 'critic' and called himself 'an ideal audience' with eclectic taste, equally happy with serious drama and revue, eager to be entertained and with total recall of the wide variety of performances that came his way. In the popular newspapers for which he wrote, he said, 'the most one can do is tell the readers where the show is, what it's about, who is in it, whether they are likely to enjoy it'. He did that and in the process conveyed, briefly and succinctly, a sense of the excitement he had felt as part of the occasion. His influence upon audiences was steady and much larger than the space allocated to his columns suggested. His show-business news column in the *Sun* became a valuable reference guide to theatre performance in Australia and overseas.

Kessell's parents were avid theatregoers and in London between 1920 and 1926 he saw every show that opened. In Australia he became quickly involved in amateur theatre. He began writing occasional film and theatre reviews for the *Daily Telegraph* in 1944 and a radio column in 1947. From 1955 he wrote the 'Sydney Man' column for the *Daily Mirror*, emphasising local show business, and a radio and television column in 1964. He started an influential show-business column in the *Sun* in 1959 and a television column in 1964.

In 1962 he began full-time reviewing for the *Sun*. When he retired from the *Sun* in 1969 the *Daily Telegraph* invited him to bring his show-business column to it and he soon became a full-time reviewer. The column was transferred to the *Sunday Telegraph*, dropped in 1974, and then revived as theatre reviews.

In 1968 Kessell founded the Glugs, a weekly lunch club for theatre-lovers. He presided over it until his death. Upon retirement in 1978 he was made the first honorary life member of the OLD TOTE THEATRE COMPANY and he received a long-service medallion from the Sydney Critics' Circle. *Katharine Brisbane*

reference
Interview with Norman Kessell by Hazel de Berg, 27 February 1981, on tape no. 1221 in National Library of Australia (Canberra).

Morton King

Actor. Born 1809. Originally Mark Last. Apprenticed to silk trade in London. Arrived in Sydney 1838. Acted in Sydney, Hobart, Launceston, Melbourne and Adelaide. Became auctioneer in Melbourne in 1850s. Elected to Victorian Parliament 1859. Became silk merchant. Died 1879.

Morton King and FRANCIS NESBITT were both styled 'the Charles Kean of the Southern Hemisphere' by the South Australian press during GEORGE COPPIN's management in Adelaide. King never achieved the skill of Nesbitt but like him established a reputation as a tragedian as the circuit of Sydney, Hobart, Launceston, Melbourne and Adelaide emerged before the gold rushes.

He was well received in those towns, though the *Port Phillip Patriot* on 1 March 1848 acknowledged King as an adequate Richard III but considered him a conventional actor, lacking in spirit and tending to rant. *Hamlet*, *Othello*, *Macbeth*, *The Merchant of Venice* and *Romeo and Juliet* were also in King's Shakespearean repertoire and he appeared in R. B. Sheridan's *The School for Scandal*, Isaac Pocock's *Rob Roy*, Sheridan Knowles's *William Tell*, Philip Massinger's *A New Way to Pay Old Debts* and Edward Bulwer-Lytton's *The Lady of Lyons*. He often performed selections from favourite plays in one program.

King appears to have had some theatrical experience before he arrived in Sydney. His publicity in Tasmania in the 1840s suggested he had come from Theatres Royal in London as well as Sydney. Strong competition from overseas performers in the goldrush 1850s ended King's career and he became an auctioneer in Melbourne. After his election to the Victorian Parliament in October 1859 he returned to the silk trade. *Paul Richardson*

King's Theatre Fremantle

Theatre in South Terrace, opened 27 September 1904 as **Dalkeith Opera House**. Architect: F. W. Burwell. Soon renamed **King's Theatre**.

Designed as a lyric theatre, and briefly designated as an opera house, the King's Theatre appears to have functioned as a multipurpose venue until it closed in 1920. It opened with Maude Jeffries, JULIUS KNIGHT and a London company in four plays presented by J. C. WILLIAMSON. The theatre, built adjacent to the Freemason's Hotel for James Gallop, had a 27-metre Renaissance-style frontage which included five shop fronts at street level. An upstairs supper room gave onto a full-length gaslit balcony above the pavement. The stalls and circle seated about 1200 people, and there was room for more in the gallery.

In hot weather the auditorium could be cooled by opening a sliding panel in the roof and numerous decorative ventilators. In response to adverse reports on the safety of the THEATRE ROYAL in Perth, numerous safety measures were incorporated in the King's Theatre, including sprinklers over the stage and 13 fire-escape doors. The provision of backup electricity and gas systems suggests that the King's Theatre was technically well-equipped. The stage measured 18·29 by 12·19 metres, with fly galleries at 7·92 metres and a grid at 15·85 metres above the floor. When the theatre closed part of the building was converted to a panel-beating workshop. Another part was temporarily converted to an ice rink in 1978, and part of this is now a night club. ❦*Bill Dunstone*

King's Theatre Melbourne

Theatre in Russell Street, opened 11 November 1908, seating 2200. Architect: William Pitt jnr. Reopened 11 March 1959 as **Barclay** cinema. Demolished for construction of multiplex cinema 1977.

The 'essentially Australian and patriotic' entrepreneur WILLIAM ANDERSON staged melodrama at the King's Theatre in Melbourne. It was built for him in 1908, when he was operating two dramatic companies and had been unable to lease the large THEATRE ROYAL. The King's had a fly-tower stage 19·2 metres wide by 15·2 metres deep and the first production, a revival of the melodrama *Man to Man*, demonstrated its capacity for spectacle by showing a prison escape and a railway collision with burning carriages and injured passengers. Anderson's repertoire largely comprised bush dramas.

The King's Theatre, described by *Table Talk* of 16 July 1908 as the most beautifully decorated theatre in Melbourne, had a three-level auditorium in gold, cobalt blue and royal blue. To the western side of Russell Street it presented an imposing asymmetrical three-storey façade in Edwardian style with a French Renaissance flavour. It comprised a pavilion at the Bourke Street end and five equal bays. The three central bays opened into the usual small vestibule, in which there were stairs to the dress circle and entrances to the stalls. There was no vestibule for gallery patrons, who climbed stairs to their seats from lanes on each side of the building.

After Anderson other managements, including J. AND N. TAIT LTD and J. C. WILLIAMSON'S used the theatre for drama, pantomime and variety. When a Williamson lease expired the Gaiety Theatres company of GARNET H. CARROLL and BENJAMIN FULLER leased the King's and in 1942 installed movie projection equipment. Warner Brothers screened films there until Carroll, in partnership with Aztec Services, reconverted the theatre to stage presentation in 1949 for the variety entrepreneur HARRY WREN as sub-lessee. In 1951 the King's reverted permanently to films, and in 1959 it was renamed the Barclay cinema, after remodelling of the interior and façade for Norman B. Rydge, who now owned the freehold. ❦*Ross Thorne*

Kinsela's Cabaret Theatre

Theatre-restaurant in Darlinghurst, Sydney, opened 4 September 1982, seating 240. Built as three-storey draper's shop and offices 1910. Remodelled as funeral parlour 1933. Architect: Bruce Dellit. Converted to restaurant and theatre restaurant 1982. Architects: Michael Davis and Glen Murcutt.

Comedy revue returned to Sydney for about four years in the 1980s at Kinsela's, a theatre-restaurant named after an undertaker. Charles Kinsela leased the 'Mansion House' building in 1932 and had the architect Bruce Dellit remodel the ground floor in angular art-deco style. In 1981 Kinsela sold the building. In a clever and sympathetic conversion, the ground floor became a restaurant, with the lofty chapel, a superb example of Art Deco, preserved as required by a heritage order. A stair rose to bar, dressing rooms and toilets on the first floor, and the theatre-restaurant on the second. The audience sat at tables stepped up slightly toward the rear of an almost square room, facing a narrow open stage stretching the length of one wall.

The Sydney Theatre Company prepared the first cabarets, which began with *The Stripper*, and other revues or variety in late-night second shows. On 23 November 1982 *Four Lady Bowlers in a Golden Holden* brought back John McKellar and Lance Mulcahy, the writer and the composer of many PHILLIP STREET REVUES some 25 years before. MAX GILLIES was among the performers in the new wave of revue. The restaurant licence, requiring food to be consumed with alcoholic drink, created problems and after four years the proprietors closed Kinsela's and sold the property. The new owners changed to a hotel licence, converted the chapel into a bar and reopened in 1988, with mainly musical shows. There was a major production, *Forbidden Broadway*, in mid-1991. ❦*Ross Thorne*

H. G. Kippax AO

Critic, journalist. Born 6 October 1920 in Sydney. Joined *Sydney Morning Herald* as a cadet journalist 1938. Abandoned studies at University of Sydney and joined army 1941. War correspondent 1945. News editor of *Sydney Morning Herald* 1950–54; foreign correspondent 1954–57; leader writer 1957–83; literary editor 1965–68; theatre reviewer 1966–89; associate editor 1971–79. Began writing on theatre as 'Brek' in *Nation* 1958. On Commonwealth Literary Fund board 1971–73. Critic-in-residence at University of NSW School of Theatre Studies 1985. AO 1988.

H. G. Kippax is one of the most authoritative theatre critics Australia has produced. His wide experience of the classic theatre of many countries, and his own literary interests made him uncompromising in his belief in theatre and fair in his assessment of what Australian theatre could achieve. A fine stylist and a good journalist, he understood the impact of his argument upon reader and performer and presented it with sound evidence and consideration.

His first love is Shakespeare and he was at his best on productions of classic texts. But his first concern from early days was the declining force of the theatre as an indigenous art form and the failure of all but a few Australian plays to match the achievements of Australian poets, novelists and painters. He summed up his concern in influential essays in *Meanjin* and the sociological book *Australian Society*. His first response to the new wave of playwrights was cautious but he 'surrendered', as he put it, when he reviewed his first David Williamson play, DON'S PARTY in 1972: 'I have no doubt that Mr Williamson is the best playwright working in Australia and one of the best in the world.' He was also forthright in seeking out early signs of stardom. Of JOHN BELL's first professional appearance at the Old Tote Theatre in Sydney in 1963, he wrote: 'Mr Bell suggests to me that here we may have—in the raw—the finest acting talent Sydney has produced since Peter Finch and Leo McKern'. Kippax saw himself as a propagandist for good theatre and as critic, journalist and leader writer, he oversaw the changes in the arts in the 1960s and 1970s. As the voice of the *Sydney Morning Herald* in its editorials he wielded crucial influence for good upon government and public opinion during a heady period.

As a 'bookish' child he gained an early love of the theatre from reading Shakespeare's plays and later acted in school plays and with MAY HOLLINWORTH, a close friend. He assisted her in forming her Metropolitan Theatre in 1945–46. In London he formed a lifetime habit of attending theatre and concerts. He established himself as a writer on theatre in the independent fortnightly *Nation* with a major article on Peter Kenna's THE SLAUGHTER OF ST TERESA'S DAY in 1959. In 1962–64 he wrote long adulatory articles on PATRICK WHITE's early plays. White's biographer David Marr described Kippax as the 'evangelist' for White as dramatist, but his advocacy ended abruptly with *Netherwood* in 1983.

In 1966 Kippax reluctantly complied with the *Sydney Morning Herald*'s decree that he take over theatre reviewing after Roger Covell relinquished drama criticism to take up an academic post. He quickly established himself with a large readership as a critic with a wide literary and musical background and wielded formidable power at the box-office. ❦*Katharine Brisbane*

writings
Australian drama since *Summer of the Seventeenth Doll*. In *Contemporary Australian Drama* (ed. Peter Holloway) revised. Sydney: Currency Press 1987.
Drama. *Australian Society* (ed. A. Davies and S. Encel) revised. Melbourne: Cheshire 1970.

reference
H. G. Kippax interviewed by Hazel de Berg, 23 June 1972, on tape no. 608, National Library of Australia (Canberra).

Roger Kirk

Designer. Born 31 July 1948 in Sydney. Joined ATN–7 television in Sydney. Apprentice in design department of National Theatre (London) 1975–76. Joined ABC television in Sydney as set and costume designer 1977. Has designed for major theatre companies since 1981. Established his own couture label in 1980s. Green Room Award for best costume design 1989 (*Anything Goes*).

In the 1980s Roger Kirk contributed hugely to theatre design. His output was immense and ranged widely in period and style. His reputation as a costume designer is high and he has formed close working partnerships with set designers, particularly BRIAN THOMSON. He learned set designing in the ABC television studios and he can solve difficult problems. His design for Tom Stoppard's *The Real Thing* on the narrow stage of the Drama Theatre at the Sydney Opera House in 1985, said RICHARD WHERRETT, 'ingeniously created on a single revolve a variety of rooms as well as a train carriage, which at the same time hid the mechanics of the set and enhanced the play's central idea of the fusion and confusion of reality and illusion'.

Kirk's first major stage work was with the SYDNEY THEATRE COMPANY in 1981, when he designed costumes for Wherrett's outstandingly popular production of the musical *Chicago*. This and the production of Edmond Rostand's *Cyrano de Bergerac* in the previous year set the standard for the strongly visual style of the company over the 1980s. In partnership with Wherrett, he designed costumes for *Macbeth* in 1982, JUSTIN FLEMING's *The Cobra* in 1983 and the musical *Jonah Jones* in 1985.

Other Sydney Theatre Company productions designed by Kirk include *Chinchilla* by Robert David McDonald in 1981, *As You Desire Me* by Luigi Pirandello in 1982, *Born Yesterday* by Garson Kanin in 1984, *Woman in Mind* by Alan Ayckbourn in 1987, *Six Characters in Search of an Author* by Pirandello in 1988, the musical *Summer Rain* in 1989, *Once in a Lifetime* by George S. Kaufman and Moss Hart in 1990 and the musical *Lost in Yonkers* in 1992. The last show toured Australia, as did Robyn Archer's THE PACK OF WOMEN, for which Kirk designed sets and costumes in 1983.

In Adelaide he has designed for the STATE THEATRE Company of South Australia in Noël Coward's *Private Lives* and Joe Orton's *Entertaining Mr Sloane* in 1984, Christopher Hampton's *Les Liaisons dangereuses* in 1987, and Jean Anouilh's *Ring Round the Moon*. In 1991 he designed the Adelaide Festival Centre Trust's production of *The King and I*, which toured nationally.

Other musicals designed by Kirk include *Anything Goes* for Hayden Productions in Sydney, *The Wizard of Oz* for the Victorian Arts Centre in Melbourne, *South Pacific* for the GORDON FROST ORGANISATION and *Aspects of Love* for the Really Useful Company in Sydney and Birmingham (England) in 1992–93. Birmingham also saw his designs for Victoria State Opera's long-running *The Pirates of Penzance*, which transferred to the D'Oyly Carte Opera there. ❦*Katharine Brisbane*

Maggie Kirkpatrick

Actor. Born 29 January 1941 at Albury (NSW). Grew up in Newcastle (NSW). Trained with Enid Rowthorn in Newcastle and at Independent Theatre School (Sydney). Professional debut with John Alden Company 1961. New Theatre Sydney 1963–68. Jane Street Theatre seasons in Sydney 1971, 1977. Numerous television roles.

A strong, generous actor, Maggie Kirkpatrick ranges from song-and-dance to realist drama and is committed to the grass roots of Australian theatre. In the mid-1960s she appeared frequently with NEW THEATRE in Sydney, notably as Meg in Brendan Behan's *The Hostage* in 1964, Sabina in Thornton Wilder's *The Skin of Our Teeth* in 1968, and in JOHN TASKER's historic production of Jean-Claude van Itallie's *America Hurrah!* in 1968. Much of her best work has been with Tasker, who also came from Newcastle, particularly her compelling creation of the mother Aggie Cassidy in all three plays in PETER KENNA's *The Cassidy Album* in 1978. She also created Winnie in DOREEN CLARKE's *Farewell Brisbane Ladies* (1981) for the State Theatre Company of South Australia and Hilda in David Malouf's *Blood Relations* (1987) for the SYDNEY THEATRE COMPANY.

European and American plays in which Kirkpatrick has appeared include John Mortimer's *A Voyage Round My Father*, with Michael Redgrave in 1973; Maxim Gorky's *The Lower Depths* for the OLD TOTE THEATRE COMPANY in Sydney in 1977; Ira Levin's *Deathtrap* for J. C. WILLIAMSON'S in 1977; Hugh Leonard's *Da* (as Mother) and Tennessee Williams's *The Night of the Iguana* (as Maxine) for the Old Tote in 1978; Alan Ayckbourn's *Absurd Person Singular* (as Marion) for the Sydney Theatre Company in 1986; *Sailor Beware* by Philip King and Falkland L. Cary and *Love Letters* by A. R. Gurney for the MARIAN STREET THEATRE COMPANY in Sydney in 1991. Musicals in which Kirkpatrick has performed include *Flash Jim Vaux* for the NIMROD THEATRE COMPANY in Sydney in 1972, *Irene* for J. C. Williamson's in 1974 and *Anything Goes* (as Mrs Evangeline Harcourt) for Hayden Attractions and the Victoria State Opera, which toured in 1989–90. ✻*Katharine Brisbane*

Kiwis revue company

Professional revue company of New Zealand ex-servicemen. Toured Australia and New Zealand for J. C. Williamson's 1946–54. **director** Terry Vaughan MBE (Milit.). **first performance** 1 May 1941 in Egypt. **last performance** 16 January 1954, His Majesty's Theatre, Auckland (New Zealand).

An all-male, ex-army troupe, the Kiwis packed theatres in Australia and New Zealand over eight record-breaking years. It originated in Egypt in early 1941, when the commander of the New Zealand Division, General Bernard Freyberg ordered an entertainment unit to be formed from available talent within the division, preferably men who had seen action. The Kiwi Concert Party, infantry-trained and armed, was unique in the Allied forces. Its primary function was to play to the division in the field, moving to other forces nearby when appropriate, so it was fully mobile, with its own portable stage, tents, cookhouse and trucks. The unit often worked close to the front line, and five members were captured by the Germans in Crete. In Italy, the first trumpet player was killed while playing.

Throughout its existence the company presented a fast, smooth mixture of music and comedy, ranging from sophistication to foolery. Dressing and decor were slick and stylish. The music, apart from specially written numbers, was familiar but not hackneyed. The humour was never more than occasionally risqué.

The company comprised about 14 singer–actors and a 12-piece orchestra, which appeared on stage. Two men played all the female roles in the army unit—Wally Prictor, whose unusual full soprano voice made big romantic scenas possible, and Phil Jay, a deft 'comedienne'. Bill Bain replaced Jay for the Italian campaign, and Ralph Dyer and John Hunter were later recruits to the show. During the postwar tour of Australasia there were three performers of female roles at any one time—Hunter, Prictor and either Bain, Dyer or Jay.

These performers' ability to convince audiences in a wide range of female characters—glamorous, dramatic or knockabout—was a style of impersonation not seen before and one of the show's great strengths. Although the company was a co-operative with a firm 'no-star' system, certain players stood out. John Hunter was, on stage, virtually a charming young actress who could sing and dance—on point if necessary. His balcony scene from Noël Coward's *Private Lives*, playing the voices of both Amanda and Elliot, was a *tour de force*.

Other popular principals were the singers Tony Rex, Taffy Owen and James Lavery; the comedians Stan Wineera, John Reidy and Ernie Fish; the vocal impressionist Red Moore, the magician Ces Morris and the 'demented' white-haired conductor and pianist Leopold Popoffsky, played by Terry Vaughan. After studying at the Royal Academy of Music in London , Vaughan joined up as a gunner in 1939 and was transferred to the Entertainment Unit for its first performance. He became the driving force of the troupe: deviser, director, conductor and company manager.

In Brisbane on 13 April 1946, the Kiwis began a three-month tour of Queensland for J. C. WILLIAMSON'S. It became an eight-year tour, twice round the major cities of Australia and New Zealand. A fill-in season at the 1000-seat Comedy Theatre in Melbourne was extended by public demand to 857 performances, from 21 December 1946 until 6 January 1949. This record run was followed by a comparable 53 weeks in the 2500-seat Empire Theatre in Sydney from 2 February 1949.

Almost half the men who had played the first show in Egypt were still in the company when it closed. Bill Bain, John Hunter, Phil Jay and Reg Moore continued acting in Australia. Terry Vaughan spent three years with the New Zealand Broadcasting Service and then later joined J. C. Williamson's, first as personal assistant to Frank Tait and then as director of music for Australasia and casting director. In 1965 he opened the CANBERRA THEATRE CENTRE as its first director. ✻*Alwyn Capern*

Julius Knight

English actor, 1863–1941. Debut 1884. Visited Australia with Laura Villiers Company 1890. Played leading roles in Henry Irving's company 1894–97. Made highly successful Australian tours 1894–97, 1898–99, 1902–06, 1907–11 and 1913–16. Acted in England until retirement in 1919.

The most popular actor in romantic costume drama to visit Australia, Julius Knight was a complete man of the theatre. Audiences—particularly women—loved his handsome, magnetic presence, splendid voice, virility and grace with sword and cloak, but his success also depended upon his expert direction of plays, meticulous attention to detail, and flair for selecting costumes and settings.

He first became popular here in *The Dancing Girl* by Henry Arthur Jones and *A Royal Divorce* by W. G. Wills during an unsuccessful tour by the Laura Villiers Company in 1890. In 1894 he began a three-year engagement with Henry Irving's company in London. Roles such as Valentine in Johann von Goethe's *Faust* and Sir Lavaine in Comyns Carr's *King Arthur* prepared him for the enormous success in costume drama that began with his 1898–99 tour of Australia and New Zealand for J. C. WILLIAMSON. On this tour Knight played in Wilson Barrett's *The Sign of the Cross* as Marcus Superbus, Anthony Hope's *The Prisoner of Zenda* and Edward Bulwer-Lytton's *The Lady of Lyons*. There was also G. R. Sims's *Harbour Lights*, a contemporary play set on a battleship, with sensational effects. It opened at Her Majesty's Theatre in Sydney on 26 November 1898 and drew large audiences. Back in England Knight played Praed in the premiere of George Bernard Shaw's *Mrs Warren's Profession* in 1902, and toured with Lillie Langtry.

For Knight's Australasian tour in 1902–06 Herbert Beerbohm Tree chose casts for *Monsieur Beaucaire* by Booth Tarkington, *Pygmalion and Galatea* by W. S. Gilbert, *Redemption* by Lev Tolstoy, *A Royal Divorce*, a dramatisation of Baroness Orczy's novel *The Scarlet Pimpernel*, and *The Silver King* by Henry Herman and Henry Arthur Jones. Knight played the leads in all these plays, opposite Maude Jeffries. His performance as Prince Nehludoff in *Redemption* was a highlight of the tour.

Knight began his extensive 1907–11 tour with his favourite role in *Monsieur Beaucaire*, and added to the repertoire of old favourites *The Corsican Brothers* by Dion Boucicault, *The Third Degree* by Charles Klein, *Henry of Navarre* by William Devereux and *The Duke's Motto* by J. H. McCarthy. There were phenomenal bookings for *The Lion and the Mouse* by Charles Klein, with Knight and Katherine Grey, said *Theatre* magazine on 1 February 1910. 'Quite unlike the usual dramatic pieces it is a stinging commentary on wealth', it added. In 1911 GREGAN MCMAHON directed Knight and his company in Shaw's *Arms and the Man*.

Knight spent 1912 in England, acting in Manchester and London and finding new plays for his repertoire. On return to Australia in 1913 he appeared as John Rhead in *Milestones* by Arnold Bennett and Edward Knoblock, and Dr Myer Isaacson in *Bella Donna* by J. B. Fagan, then played the standbys *Monsieur Beaucaire*, *The Lifeguardsman* by Walter Howard and *The Scarlet Pimpernel*. He ended the tour with an early triumph, *The Silver King*, in Sydney in 1916. In this season Knight used many local actors, including Lizette Parkes, in leading roles. ❦*Lynne Murphy*

further reading
FOWLER, J. BERESFORD. *Stars in My Backyard*. Ilfracombe (England): A. H. Stockwell c.1960.
MARLOWE, MARY. *That Fragile Hour*. Sydney: Angus and Robertson 1990.

Conrad Knowles

Actor, dancer, manager. Born c.1810. Came to Swan River Colony from England. Arrived in Hobart 1830. Began acting in Sydney, December 1832. Acting manager at Theatre Royal. Returned to legal career in England 1837. Back in Sydney by late 1838. Stage manager at Royal Victoria Theatre 1840. Joined Australian Olympic Theatre, Sydney, February 1842. Returned to Royal Victoria. Seceded to Royal City Theatre 1843. Went to Hobart. Managed Royal Victoria Theatre, Melbourne, from November 1843 to death on 19 May 1844. Married, probably de facto, to actor Harriet Jones.

The most talented and only educated actor in early Sydney theatre, Conrad Knowles was a self-taught star. Gentlemanly and refined, with some French, which he used on stage in mannered comedy parts, he was Sydney's notion of an ideal actor until FRANCIS NESBITT arrived. Knowles was Australia's first Hamlet and King Lear, and Sydney's first Romeo, Othello and Shylock. No-one else played Hamlet in Australia while he was alive. Tragedy appears to have suited his deep, resonant voice best, but he lived by comedy parts and dancing too.

The son of a Wesleyan clergyman, he called himself Cooper when he wrote and performed the opening prologue at BARNETT LEVEY's fit-up theatre in the Royal Hotel in Sydney on 26 December 1832. From the next season he performed under his own name.

Knowles was also Levey's notion of an ideal manager, and his talents were shamelessly exploited. He rarely received the proceeds of benefit nights at Levey's THEATRE ROYAL. Acrimonious correspondence in the *Australian* in March 1834 revealed that Knowles had to learn up to five roles a week, play two or three roles a night, call the cues as acting manager and operate the curtain at times. On one occasion a critic felt Knowles should apologise to the audience for his lack of study because he knew less than half of Falstaff. He was constantly attacked by critics for his poor lines and his habits of over-gesticulating and speaking directly to the audience. He would have been ill-suited to the incoming mood of theatrical realism.

The *Sydney Monitor* on 19 January 1838 assessed Knowles as a candle lit at both ends and the *Sydney Gazette* praised him in October 1840 as one who has at heart 'a feeling to further the dramatic interests in Australia'. He dramatised Edward Bulwer-Lytton's novel *Leila* as *Salathiel*, a tediously conventional three-act play, which was first performed on 4 August 1842 at the Royal Victoria Theatre in Sydney. Knowles was warmly welcomed at the ROYAL VICTORIA THEATRE in Melbourne, where he obtained a temporary licence with difficulty in November 1843, but he was then obliged to permit bawdy songs to hold audiences. ❦*Helen Musa*

published play
Salathiel—or, The Jewish Chieftain (1842). Sydney: T. Trood 1842.

further reading
OPPENHEIM, HELENE. Conrad Knowles. *Australian Dictionary of Biography* 5. Melbourne University Press 1974.
WINSTANLEY, ELIZA. *Shifting Scenes in Theatrical Life*. London: 1859.
Herald (Melbourne) 2 May 1844. Obituary.
Sydney Morning Herald 31 May 1844. Obituary.
Weekly Courier (Melbourne) 2 May 1844. Obituary.

Nellie Kolle

Comedian. Born 1891 in United Kingdom. Came to Australia with touring concert party 1914. Died 5 July 1971 in Adelaide.

Nellie Kolle's stylish male impersonations were extremely popular on the FULLERS' vaudeville circuit, and she also appeared frequently as principal boy in Fullers' pantomimes. She wrote much of her own material, and several of her songs were published. She worked on the TIVOLI CIRCUIT in the 1940s. She settled in Adelaide, and appeared regularly at the Olde King's Music Hall theatre-restaurant until shortly before her death at 80. ❦*Frank Van Straten*

Jacqueline Kott

Actor. Born in Perth. Studied at University of Western Australia. Moved to Sydney in late 1940s. Acted in repertory in United Kingdom 1950–55. Returned to tour Australia and New Zealand with Ralph Richardson and Sybil Thorndike 1955. Member of Independent Theatre repertory company (Sydney) 1967–68. Vice-president of Peter Summerton Foundation 1969–.

The vocal power, ferocity and emotional breakdown of Jacqueline Kott's Martha in Edward Albee's *Who's Afraid of Virginia Woolf* for the OLD TOTE THEATRE COMPANY in 1964 will long be remembered. She played the role in three seasons in Sydney and two in Canberra, in Adelaide, in Brisbane, in New Zealand and on tour in NSW for the ARTS COUNCIL. It was the landmark performance by this statuesque actress during the 1960s, when she hit her peak. She had given notice of her dramatic strength when she played the arrogant fading beauty 'Princess' in Tennessee Williams's *Sweet Bird of Youth* for INDEPENDENT THEATRE in Sydney in 1963. In 1965 she toured for the Old Tote company in another powerful drama, Eugene O'Neill's *Moon for the Misbegotten*. In James Goldman's *The Lion in Winter* for the Independent Theatre repertory company, in 1967 she again demonstrated power and stage presence that few of her contemporaries possessed. ❦*Richard Lane*

Dorothy Krantz

Actor. Born 30 August 1912 in Perth. Originally Dorothy Powell. Trained from three years as dancer, and studied elocution with Lionel Logue and Sister Mary Coleman. Child performer 1915–18. Acted with Repertory Club (Perth) 1929–52. Professional debut with Arthur Maxwell Comedy Company in Perth c.1930. Acted for ABC radio 1935–37. Appeared in Perth with Garrick Theatre and Workers' Art Guild, Company of Four 1950–55, National Theatre Company 1956–62. Died 6 December 1994 in Perth. Married to Harold Krantz, architect of Playhouse, Perth.

By performing in productions of some 80 contemporary mainstream plays, Dorothy Krantz greatly helped to develop high standards of amateur acting in Perth in the 1930s and 1940s. She was crucial in the transition to fully professional theatre in the city as a founding member and a leading actor of the COMPANY OF FOUR, with which she played Blanche in Tennessee Williams's *A Streetcar Named Desire*. When the Company of Four and the REPERTORY CLUB merged in 1956 Krantz joined the resultant professional NATIONAL THEATRE COMPANY as an actor and board member. She acted in experimental productions for Frank Baden-Powell in 1961, and made her last appearance in his production of Williams's *Cat on a Hot Tin Roof* in 1962, ending a career begun in 1912.

As a child she specialised in popular cowboy and bushranger recitations. She performed regularly at White City, with the Eight Bouncing Busters at the Shaftesbury Theatre, at His Majesty's Theatre, and competitions and camp concerts for troops. At SOL SAINKEN's invitation, Krantz joined the Repertory Club to play Amanda in Noël Coward's *Private Lives* in 1929. She became a professional on the Arthur Maxwell Comedy Company's tour of Perth and nearby towns. Alan Cuthbertson wrote a leading role for her in a murder mystery that was first performed by the Repertory Club in 1938. ❦*Bill Dunstone*

Evelyn Krape

Actor, singer. Born 2 August 1949 in Melbourne. Studied singing at Melbourne Conservatorium of Music. Studied drama at Melbourne State College 1966–70. Founding member of Australian Performing Group. Married dramatist Jack Hibberd 1978. Performed with Melbourne Theatre Company, Playbox Theatre Company, TheatreWorks. Critics' best actor award 1976 (Melba in *A Toast to Melba* by Jack Hibberd). Green Room Award for best female performer in musical 1992 (*Ginger*).

Evelyn Krape's performing skill and her Jewish-Australian ironic humour combine to make her a great performer. She aims at an intrinsically Australian style of acting, and her work draws upon her early days as a member of the AUSTRALIAN PERFORMING GROUP at the Pram Factory in Melbourne. She appeared in *Don's Party* by David Williamson; *DIMBOOLA*, *One of Nature's Gentlemen* (1968) and *A Toast to Melba* (1976) by JACK HIBBERD; *MARVELLOUS MELBOURNE* by Hibberd and John Romeril; and *THE HILLS FAMILY SHOW*. She co-devised and appeared in the revues *Back to Bourke Street*, *Betty Can Jump* and *Sonia's Knee and Thigh Show*. In 1978 she directed *Add a Grated Laugh or Two* for International Women's Year. In 1982 Krape and the director Lois Ellis collaborated in several plays by Dario Fo and Franca Rame for the Hocking and Woods management. With Ellis, Tomi Kalinski and Lorraine Milne she devised *Ginger* for the PLAYBOX THEATRE CENTRE in 1992. ❦*Sara Hardy*

John Krummel

Actor, director, producer. Born 20 August 1944 in Broken Hill (NSW). Educated at University of NSW. Graduated from National Institute of Dramatic Art (Sydney) 1964. Toured with Young Elizabethan Players. Acted with Old Tote Theatre Company (Sydney) in 1960s. Acted in Sydney for Community Theatre, Green Room Society at University of NSW and Nimrod Theatre Company in 1970s. Also Melbourne Theatre Company and Queensland Theatre Company (Brisbane). Resident director at Queensland Theatre Company 1978–80. Director of Northside Theatre Company (Sydney) 1982–89. Sydney Critics' Circle Award and Variety Club Award (Alan Turing in Hugh Whitemore's *Breaking the Code*) 1988.

During the Melbourne season of HARRY M. MILLER's production of Mart Crowley's *The Boys in the Band* in 1969, John Krummel, playing an acid-tongued homosexual, was arrested on a charge of using obscene language in a public place. Krummel's resultant trial and conviction—a nominal fine was imposed upon him—caused a public uproar and placed him and the production at the forefront in the battle to liberate Australian theatres and society from the stultifying conservatism of the Menzies era.

Krummel's roles for the OLD TOTE THEATRE COMPANY in the 1960s included a memorable Tesman in Henrik Ibsen's *Hedda Gabler*, Teddy in Harold Pinter's *The Homecoming* and Young in THOMAS KENEALLY's *Childermas*. With the NIMROD THEATRE COMPANY in the 1970s Krummel's roles included the title-role of *President Wilson in Paris* (1973), which RON BLAIR wrote for him.

In 1978 he made his directorial debut with Anton Chekhov's *The Cherry Orchard* for the QUEENSLAND THEATRE COMPANY. As director of the Northside Theatre Company Krummel directed and acted in many of its hits, raising it to national importance. ❦*Wayne Harrison*

La Mama Theatre

Theatre in former shirt factory in Carlton, Melbourne, opened by Betty Burstall, 30 July 1967.

The new Australian drama of the late 1960s and the 1970s was first nurtured and developed in a pocket playhouse in Melbourne. La Mama Theatre, like its namesake in New York City, was essentially a resource centre, open to groups that could persuade the management they had a worthwhile project. Poets, film-makers, folk singers and other musicians were also encouraged to read, show or perform their works there. It was the first home of the influential AUSTRALIAN PERFORMING GROUP before its members turned professional and moved to the larger Pram Factory.

La Mama was the brainchild of Betty Burstall, a former high school teacher. She was living in New York in the mid-1960s, when the coffee-house theatres in Greenwich Village were staging the works of the new generation of American playwrights, including Sam Shepard, Megan Terry and Jean-Claude Van Itallie. She was impressed by the new and informal audience-actor relationship made possible by these venues, which also allowed new ideas and new modes of expression to be tried out. On return to Melbourne, Burstall leased a shabby two-storey brick building in inner-city Carlton and officially opened it as La Mama Theatre with a production of JACK HIBBERD's brief three-hander *Three Old Friends*. This was followed by BARRY OAKLEY's *Witzenhausen, Where Are You?* and by another Hibberd double bill.

Creative vitality and energy distinguished the early years at La Mama. It brimmed with talent. The main occupants were the La Mama Company, which later became the Australian Performing Group; Tribe, an experimental and improvisational group run by Doug Anders; and a group under the leadership of Syd Clayton which specialised in 'happenings' involving music and drama. Since the Australian Performing Group moved out in 1970 La Mama Theatre has never had its own resident company.

In the first two years some 25 plays by Australian writers were presented there, as well as seven events or 'happenings' and eight plays from abroad. Seven of the 25 local plays were by Hibberd, five by the English-born poet Kris Hemensley, four by Frank Bren and two by JOHN ROMERIL. Plays in the early years included Hibberd's *DIMBOOLA* and *White with Wire Wheels*; David Williamson's *THE COMING OF STORK* and *THE REMOVALISTS*; Romeril's *Chicago, Chicago* and *I Don't Know Who to Feel Sorry For*; and Alex Buzo's *NORM AND AHMED* and *The Front Room Boys*. The playwrights most frequently represented at La Mama have been Buzo, Hibberd, Romeril and, in more recent times, BARRY DICKINS, Lloyd Jones, Peter Mathers, Phil Motherwell, ROGER PULVERS, Max Richards and Colin Ryan.

In a tenth anniversary season in 1977 La Mama repeated some of the best plays and productions from the early years, including *The Removalists* with its original cast. In 1986 it won a Sidney Myer Performing Arts award for sustained achievement. By its 25th anniversary in 1992 it had played host to 675 productions, as much as three-quarters of them Australian in origin. La Mama's importance lies chiefly in its nurturing of writers and other creative people and its provision of a sympathetic environment in which their work can be staged free from box-office pressures. In its early years La Mama used to stage 15–20 productions a year, but in recent times its annual output has risen to 40 or more. On many nights there are two shows. Audiences have increased too, reflecting the vitality of Melbourne theatre and the keen interest in new and experimental works. ❦*Leonard Radic*

further reading
JONES, LIZ with BETTY BURSTALL and HELEN GARNER. *La Mama*. Melbourne: McPhee Gribble/Penguin 1988.

Marie la Varre

Actor, singer. Born c.1890 in England, to French and English parents. Performed in wartime revues in London. In Australia 1917–35. Returned to Australia 1938. Retired 1953. Died in 1970s.

Marie la Varre first won notice in popular revues in London during the First World War. In 1917 HUGH D. MCINTOSH gave her a six-month contract to star in similar revues at Sydney's Tivoli Theatre, and she proved popular in such shows as *The Officers' Mess* and *My Lady Frayle*. She remained after her contract ended and found her greatest success with J. C. WILLIAMSON's in operettas such as *The New Moon* in 1930, *Roberta* in 1934 and *Yes, Madam?* in 1935. She returned to London but she was back in Australia in 1938 for revivals of *No! No! Nanette* and *Wildflower*, and she remained for the rest of her life. La Varre's last star role was Dolly Tait in the first Australian season of *Annie Get Your Gun*. After the three-year run, she ended a career of more than 40 years with a small role in a revival of *White Horse Inn* in Sydney in 1953. ❦*Alwyn Capern*

Lady in Danger

Play in three acts by Max Afford. **premiere** 28 February 1942, Independent Theatre, Sydney. Cast: Kenneth Fowles, Gwen Plumb, James Pratt. Director: Doris Fitton. **revived** 1944, Theatre Royal, Sydney. Cast: Aileen Britton, Arundel Nixon, John O'Malley. Director: John Alden. **published** Sydney: Mulga Press 1944.

A wholly entertaining comedy thriller with witty dialogue and splendidly realised characters, MAX AFFORD's *Lady in Danger* was one of the rare Australian plays presented by an Australian professional management in the 1940s. It was also produced at the Broadhurst Theatre in New York City in 1945 by the Allan and Fisher management, with Helen Claire, James Gannon and Alexander Kirkland heading the cast. It was the first Australian play to reach Broadway in the 20th century. ❦*Richard Lane*

Lloyd Lamble

Actor. Born 1914 in Melbourne. Radio announcer from 1932. Began acting with Lee Murray Radio Players. First stage performance 1934. Minerva Theatre, Sydney, 1939–40. Leading radio actor 1939–50. President of Actors' Equity 1942–48. Went to England 1950. Married to actor Lesley Jackson.

Lloyd Lamble was a leading man of considerable power and authority during the 1940s. Early radio acting in Melbourne led to his stage debut, for J. C. WILLIAMSON's in Ivor Novello's *Fresh Fields* in 1934. A brilliant performance as Danny, a murderous Welsh pageboy, in the Firm's 1936 production of Emlyn Williams's 1935 play *Night Must Fall* stamped him as potentially Australia's finest young stage actor. At the MINERVA THEATRE in Sydney in 1939–40 he appeared in a succession of plays as disparate as Noël Coward's *Design for Living* and John Steinbeck's *Of Mice and Men*, in which his performance as Lennie was highly praised. During this period Lamble also established himself as a strong leading man in drama on commercial radio.

In 1944 he was director and leading man opposite NEVA CARR GLYN in a J. C. Williamson's company that toured New Zealand with six plays. In Australia later in the 1940s he played in companies with Robert Morley and Cicely

Courtneidge. In 1950, at the Theatre Royal in Hobart, he co-starred with his wife Lesley Jackson in George Bernard Shaw's *Pygmalion* and Aldous Huxley's *The Gioconda Smile* for FIFI BANVARD Productions. Shortly afterwards the couple left for London, where Lamble has had a successful career on stage and in television and film. ❦*Richard Lane*

Stella Lamond

Comedian. Born 12 March 1909 in Sydney. Married comedian Joe Lawman 1931; divorced 1939. Married comedian Max Reddy 1940. Died 5 July 1973 in Melbourne. Mother of actor Toni Lamond and singer Helen Reddy. Grandmother of actor Tony Sheldon.

Stella Lamond made her stage debut as a baby, carried on in *Uncle Tom's Cabin* by her mother, Stella Coffey, a supporting actor in stock drama. Stella and her sister Lyle studied at Chrissie Royal's dancing school in Sydney. At four, Stella appeared in *Babes in the Wood* at the Grand Opera House in Sydney. By 20 she was on the Tivoli circuit as 'the Cutie with the Uke'. Lamond and her second husband Max Reddy became popular as 'the Nitwits of Radio'. After the war, they ran a touring variety company called The Follies for 15 years. When television arrived, Lamond turned to drama, and was in *Bellbird* at the time of her death. ❦*Frank Van Straten*

further reading
LAMOND, TONI. *First Half*. Sydney: Pan Books 1990.
The fabulous Lamonds. *TV Times* (Sydney) 28 April 1973.

Toni Lamond

Dancer, singer Born 29 March 1932 in Sydney. Originally Patricia Lamond Lawman. Daughter of soubrette Stella Lamond and comedian Joe Lawman. Married dancer Frank Sheldon (Frank Smith) May 1954. Worked in USA 1976–88. Returned to Australia 1989. Stepdaughter of comedian Max Reddy. Half-sister of singer Helen Reddy. Mother of actor Tony Sheldon.

A consummate entertainer, Toni Lamond comes from a show-business family. After the Second World War her stepfather Max Reddy emerged from service in ARMY ENTERTAINMENT UNITS and teamed up again with her mother STELLA LAMOND. A spell in variety in Perth for the family and a long bout of pernicious anaemia removed Toni from the schoolroom and set her on her life as a full-time entertainer. She played feed to the British comedian Tommy Trinder on his second tour on the Tivoli circuit in 1952 and attracted favourable attention.

In 1955, she took leave from performing in variety with her husband Frank Sheldon at the Theatre Royal in Brisbane for the birth of their son Tony. In the first year of television, 1956, Toni Lamond appeared on TCN–9 in Sydney, and later she became prominent in television variety in Melbourne. Her husband retreated behind the cameras into production. She also moved into musical theatre in 1957 with Babe, the female lead in *The Pajama Game*. In 1963 she played the lead in *Wildcat* for GARNET H. CARROLL. In 1966 she played Nancy in a revival of *Oliver!* Her success put severe strains on the marriage and it ended in 1966. Frank Sheldon took his own life on 18 September that year.

Toni Lamond moved to Sydney and took up club engagements again. There followed years of overwork and illness, including dependence on prescription drugs. Her treatment included two experiences of deep sleep in Sydney's Chelmsford Hospital, later notorious for the deaths of patients who underwent that therapy. Later she went overseas to work, but by 1969 she was back on the treadmill in Australia. Her mother and her stepfather both died in 1973 and on Christmas Eve she attempted suicide. A long period of treatment and convalescence followed.

In 1976, at the suggestion of her half-sister Helen Reddy, a recording star in the USA, Lamond went to live in Los Angeles, where she worked for the next 14 years. She returned to Australia in 1989 to play a major supporting role in the musical *42nd Street*, which she did with her expected style and attack. After a long season, the production was scheduled to move intact to East Berlin. The unification of East and West Germany sank that plan, but the production did play in Perth in June 1992, with Lamond in the cast. The musical *Better Known as Bee*, staged by Q Theatre at Penrith (NSW) in 1992, was written for her. ❦*John West*

writings
First Half. Sydney: Pan Books 1990. Autobiography.

Laurie Landray

Critic, journalist. Born 8 October 1927 in London. Reporter in London 1948–52. Subeditor and arts writer on *Geelong Advertiser* 1953-55. Subeditor and music writer on *Evening Argus*, Brighton (England). *Geelong Advertiser* 1957-1959. *Sun News-Pictorial* (Melbourne) 1959. Subeditor of *Listener In–TV* 1959–74; theatre, ballet and opera critic 1963–74. Subeditor and show-business feature writer on *Australasian Post* 1974–88. Theatre and ballet critic of Melbourne *Herald* 1976–85.

At a time of radical growth and change Laurie Landray was largely responsible for maintaining a profile for new theatre in journals published by the *Herald–Sun* group. An enthusiastic and knowledgeable reviewer, he understood better than some of his contemporaries in the 1960s the intentions of the new wave of British playwrights. He was also one of the first to recognise the experimental work at LA MAMA THEATRE in Melbourne and to appreciate its iconoclasm and physicality. His *Listener In–TV* columns remain a meticulous record of the early work of this new wave, and his unassuming views were sensitive, balanced and couched in popular journalistic style. ❦*Katharine Brisbane*

Diana Large AO

Actor, administrator, director. Born 28 June 1923 in Chester (England). Trained at Royal Academy of Dancing (London) and London Academy of Music and Dramatic Art. Professional debut at 15. Became dance and drama teacher and broadcaster. Arrived in Tasmania 1965. Worked with Theatre Royal Workshop in Hobart. Artistic director of Apprentice Theatre 1972–90. Taught at University of Tasmania in 1970s. Died 29 August 1991. AO 1992.

As a director, an entrepreneur for visiting companies and individuals, a member of performing-arts committees, an adjudicator at drama festivals and a university tutor in verse and drama, Diana Large enriched and stimulated Hobart's theatrical life. She constantly aimed to offer the public the classics of European theatre in good local or imported productions. Her most ambitious achievement was a production of the Wakefield mystery plays in 1972, the first performance of a full cycle of medieval mystery plays outside England. Among her former pupils in Apprentice Theatre are Anthony Ackroyd, Genevieve Picot and Michael Siberry. ❦*Gillian Winter*

George Lauri

Actor, dancer, singer. Son of ballet master at Alhambra Theatre, London. Made stage debut at nine in New York. Briefly apprenticed to architect in London. Returned to theatre as dancer and then as actor in comedies. Toured USA with Marie Tempest in *Dorothy* in 1890. Brought to Australia by J. C. Williamson. Committed suicide 4 January 1909 in Sydney.

From 1890 to 1907 George Lauri was considered the best comic actor on the Australian musical-comedy stage and he was a remarkably agile dancer, although he was short and stout. He was a success as Fluellen to GEORGE RIGNOLD's Henry V, but broad comedy in musical works was his forte and his best role was Tweedlepunch in *Florodora* in 1901 with CARRIE MOORE. Some of his interpretations were criticised and his attempt at an Irish accent in *My Lady Molly* in 1903 was disastrous. *The Orchid* in 1904 was a success for Lauri but his last years were ruined by ill health, mainly caused by his belief that he was becoming insane. He retired late in 1905 but returned to the stage in 1907 for *The Girls of Gottenberg* and *The Dairymaids*. Three testimonial performances raised a large sum of money, which would have ensured a worry-free retirement, but he cut his throat at his home in Manly. ❦*Alwyn Capern*

further reading
DeWarre, T. M. *Through Opera Glasses*. Sydney: Deaton and Spencer 1908.
Fowler, J. Beresford. *Stars in My Backyard*. Ilfracombe (England): Arthur H. Stockwell 1962.

Ray Lawler OBE

Actor, director, dramatist. Born in 1921 in Melbourne. Left school at 13 and worked in factories. Began writing plays at 19. Actor and director with Melbourne Repertory Theatre, National Theatre Movement and other Melbourne companies. Joined Union Theatre Repertory Company (Melbourne) 1954. Great success with *Summer of the Seventeenth Doll* 1955–57. Wrote for stage and television in England, Denmark and Ireland 1957–75. With Melbourne Theatre Company as literary adviser, script assessor and associate director 1975–87. OBE 1980. Retired 1987. Emeritus award from literature board of Australia Council 1993. Married actor Jacqueline Kelleher.

Ray Lawler's great contribution to Australian theatre, after more than 40 years' work in different capacities, remains SUMMER OF THE SEVENTEENTH DOLL, the ninth of his 16 plays. The legend of the *Doll* overshadows his acting, his directing at the MELBOURNE THEATRE COMPANY and his development with Carmel Powers of its script-assessment program. He has expressed surprise and bewilderment at the enormous impact of the *Doll*, claiming to have written the play simply as a 'night's entertainment in the theatre', and even as a vehicle for a short actor, such as himself, in the role of the sugar-cane cutter Barney. Lawler played the part in the original production by the Union Theatre Repertory Company. He travelled to London with the production of the *Doll* in 1957 and did not return to Australia until 1971, when the Melbourne Theatre Company gave the first production of his play *The Man Who Shot the Albatross*. With the encouragement of his friend JOHN SUMNER, who had directed *The Doll*, he wrote this play as a vehicle for LEO McKERN. It toured nationally but was not a success. In 1975 Lawler returned to Melbourne for good and, with a commission from Sumner, began work on *Kid Stakes* and *Other Times*, the plays that complete *The Doll Trilogy*.

When Lawler turned to other subjects he seemed to be on less firm ground. The *Doll* aroused great enthusiasm in London in the 1950s for its 'Australianness'. The failure of *The Piccadilly Bushman* (1961), which reflected the lives of the Anglophile Australian middle-class theatregoing public much more directly, perhaps shows that the appeal of the *Doll* had lain as much in the exotic colour of its story as in its revaluation—critically acclaimed at the time—of the 1890s bush-inspired mythology of 'Australianness'. *The Piccadilly Bushman* also failed partly because of awkwardness in reconciling dramas of ideas and character.

The Man Who Shot the Albatross is a historical drama about Governor William Bligh and his conflict with John Macarthur, culminating in the rebellion of the New South Corps. *Godsend* (1982) uses the imagined discovery of St Thomas à Becket's tomb in a country church in Kent to explore the nature of Christian belief and how individual believers create their own faith. Both are interesting and sometimes powerful plays, but they have not been revived. From 1975 to 1987 Lawler worked as a director and dramaturge for the Melbourne Theatre Company, the direct descendant of the Union Theatre Repertory Company, which gave him his first break as a writer. ❦*John McCallum*

published plays
Kid Stakes). Sydney: Currency Press 1978.
Other Times (1976). Sydney: Currency Press 1978.
Summer of the Seventeenth Doll (1955). Sydney: Currency Press 1978.

further reading
Carroll, Dennis. *Australian Contemporary Drama*. Sydney: Currency Press 1995.
McCallum, John. In *Contemporary Dramatists* (ed. K. A. Berney) 5th edn. London: St James Press 1993.
McCallum, John. The Doll and the legend. *Australian Literary Studies* 3/2 (Brisbane 1985).
Sumner, John. *Recollections at Play—A life in Australian theatre*. Melbourne: University Press 1993.

John Lazar

Actor, manager. Also known as John Lazarus. Born 1 December 1801 in Edinburgh. Arrived in Sydney 26 February 1837. Made debut at Theatre Royal 18 May 1837. Managed Theatre Royal, December 1837 to March 1838. Managed Royal Victoria Theatre, Sydney, March 1838 to November 1840. Acted at and managed Queen's Theatre, Adelaide, January 1841 to November 1842. Managed Royal Victoria Theatre, Sydney, May 1843 to September 1844 and December 1845 to 1846. Managed New Queen's Theatre, Adelaide, 1848–50. Co-proprietor and manager of Royal Victoria Theatre, Adelaide, from December 1850. Left theatre for jewellery business. Mayor of Adelaide 1855-1858. Emigrated to New Zealand 1863 and became town clerk in Dunedin and Hokitika. Died 8 June 1879 in New Zealand. Father of dancer Rachel Lazar and manager Samuel Lazar.

The name of John Lazar, a hard-working, resourceful manager and an acceptable low comedian, was a byword for competence in Sydney and in Adelaide. He was the first manager to undertake a sustained theatrical enterprise in Adelaide. In Sydney he laid the groundwork for opera performances. He also took a keen interest in derivative works that he called 'local drama'. In two days in 1840 he staged four new Australian plays.

Lazar's claim to have come to Australia from 'The Theatres Royal Drury Lane and Covent Garden' was ridiculed. He had probably been a tailor and supernumerary in English theatres. He arrived at Sydney aboard the 'fever ship' *Lady McNaughton*, upon which 56 passengers had died, including three of his own children. While he was still officially in quarantine he may have been the anonymous actor who played King Lear at Barnett Levey's Theatre Royal on 10 April 1837. He made his official debut as Shylock in *The Merchant of Venice* on 18 May 1837 and led in tragic parts for the season. As the star of the theatre Lazar left much to be desired. The *Sydney Herald* noted on 15 June that he retained Shylock's Jewish accent as Othello.

Lazar managed the Theatre Royal from December 1837 until it closed in March 1838. Then he moved to Joseph Wyatt's new Royal Victoria Theatre as manager. In a good working relationship with Wyatt, Lazar's managerial skill flourished. He was publicly noted for tact and firmness in his dealing with the temperamental Eliza Winstanley in September–October 1840 and in his suppression of offensive behaviour. Lazar became almost indispensable to Wyatt but after a dispute over salaries in November 1840 he moved to Adelaide. On 11 January 1841 he opened as Othello at the Queen's Theatre in Adelaide. He also took on the management until November 1842.

In May 1843 he was back in Sydney as manager of the Royal Victoria, but anti-Semitic outbursts by Wyatt's partner Joseph Knight forced him to withdraw in September 1844. He returned in December 1845, when Knight pulled out, and left again a year later when Knight bought a proprietary interest in the theatre. Lazar returned to Adelaide, where he went into partnership with George Coppin at the New Queen's Theatre in 1848. He managed this little theatre until it was closed in 1850, and then the former Queen's Theatre, which partners enlarged and reopened as the Royal Victoria Theatre. He was often criticised in staid Adelaide for permitting racy entertainment. *Helen Musa*

further reading
Fischer, G. L. John Lazar. *Australian Dictionary of Biography* 2. Melbourne University Press 1967.

Samuel Lazar

Manager, theatre-owner. Born c.1838 in Sydney. Son of actor-manager John Lazar. Stage debut at Royal Victoria Theatre, Sydney, c.1843. Went to Adelaide with father 1840. Left stage for stock-and-station agency. Joined others in building Theatre Royal, Adelaide, 1868, and managed it for several years. Leased and managed Queen's Theatre, Sydney, 1875. Built Theatre Royal in Sydney, 1875. Brother of dancer Rachel Lazar.

Samuel Lazar controlled Sydney theatres for much longer than his father John Lazar ever did but he shines less brightly in history because he operated behind the scenes in a more complex era beset with stars. He remodelled the Queen's Theatre for the Sydney debut of J. C. Williamson and Maggie Moore in *Struck Oil*. He built the Theatre Royal on the site of the Prince of Wales Theatre in Castlereagh Street and opened it on 11 December 1875. Lazar became a considerable producer of pantomimes, which were published in Adelaide in 1874 and Sydney in 1875, 1877 and 1878. It has been claimed that he died in 1883, but he was lessee of the Theatre Royal for Dion Boucicault's season in 1885. Lazar warrants further research. *Helen Musa*

Bobby Le Brun OAM

Comedian, dancer. Born 25 February 1910 in Sydney. Originally Eric Stanley Marshall. Studied at Lew Dunn's Dancing Academy in Sydney. Began dancing in revue 1927. Danced on Clay vaudeville circuit 1928. Tivoli Theatre, Sydney, 1929. Acted in Kate Howarde's Dramatic Players in Queensland 1930–31. Solo comedian in Sorlie's Revue Company 1933–37. Married Grace Boyd, dancer, 1941. In Barton's Follies 1941–45. On Tivoli circuit 1946–47. Toured Australia and New Zealand 1948–49. Proprietor and principal comedian of Sorlie's Revue Company 1949–61. Floor shows and television at Brisbane, Coolangatta (Qld) and Newcastle (NSW) 1961–74. Retired 1975. Died September 1985 in Newcastle. 'Mo' Fellowship 1977. OAM 1981.

Bobby Le Brun spent the most significant part of his career as a revue comedian, touring in tent shows up to 48 weeks a year. He toured from about 1930 to 1961, when few companies took entertainment to country districts. He was an engaging personality on stage, bawdy by the standards of the day but never offensive. He was equally accomplished in sketches, in stand-up comedy, in drag—as in *Bessie the Belle of the Bowling Green*—and as a pantomime dame.

He billed himself as 'Bobby Le Brun ... Just for Fun' to emphasise the anglicised pronunciation of his French surname. He took it from the Australian Le Bruns, a skating act of his dancing teacher Lew Dunn. Bob was a schoolboy tag. He teamed with Harry Portlock as the Le Brun Brothers, Simultaneous Steppers, a dance act on Harry Clay's vaudeville circuit; appeared with the female impersonator Tikki Carpenter in Mo's Merry Monarchs; then toured with Kate Howarde, acting in her melodramas *Possum Paddock* and *Gum Tree Gully*. Later he danced with George Chanti.

During the Great Depression Le Brun worked in cinemas and ballrooms until 1933. Then he was engaged by George Sorlie, a great entertainer who had changed his tent show from stock company to revue because of the talkies. From then Le Brun concentrated on comedy and took Sorlie's advice to work essentially in rural Australia. He spent the years 1941–45 mostly in Newcastle (NSW) in another tent show, Barton's Follies, and did much voluntary work for the war effort. He then toured with the magician Great Levante, and appeared in city theatres with performers such as Jenny Howard and Gladys Moncrieff. He returned to Newcastle in Diamond's Marquee and Theatre.

From 1949 to 1961 Le Brun was owner and principal comedian of Sorlie's Revue Company. Sorlie's tent show began its year in Newcastle at Christmas with a children's pantomime matinee and weekly-change vaudeville at night for six weeks. The company consisted of variety acts hired in Sydney, a ballet and band. The best running order would be established for the tour, and the show was then on the road for up to 48 weeks, through New England to the Darling Downs in Queensland; through Gympie, Townsville, Rockhampton and Mackay to Mossman; back again to western NSW and Riverina cities like Wagga Wagga, usually playing a week at each stop. During the annual layoff Le Brun would recruit new acts for the next year's show. His wife of 43 years, Grace, an accomplished dancer, was ballet mistress. They had no children, but they were like parents to the people in their companies. Le Brun spent his last dozen years as a comic, mostly in hotels and cabarets. The variety profession honoured him as the first recipient of its 'Mo' Fellowship. ❦*Charles Grahame*

further reading
RISNEY, KEVIN P. *The Curtain's Up*. Newcastle: 1944.

Anita Le Tessier OAM

Actor, entrepreneur, speech and drama teacher. Born 18 April 1891 in Sydney. Originally Anita FitzGerald. Moved to Perth with family at seven. Stage debut in *Little Lord Fauntleroy* at His Majesty's Theatre, Perth, 1911. Studied piano and singing at NSW State Conservatorium of Music. In Allan Wilkie Shakespearean Company. Staged productions in Perth. Married John Le Tessier 20 December 1927. Studied voice production with Elsie Fogarty in London. Founded Shakespeare Club (Perth) 1930. Died July 1986.

Perth's first female theatrical entrepreneur, Anita Le Tessier produced light commercial plays at His Majesty's Theatre and the Theatre Royal, after acting in the ALLAN WILKIE SHAKESPEAREAN COMPANY in Sydney. She was the first West Australian to study at the NSW State Conservatorium of Music and she performed in its first concert. The Repertory Club in Perth employed her on a percentage of gross to direct Clemence Dane's *A Bill of Divorcement* in 1922 and Gertrude Jennings's *A Young Person in Pink* in 1923. ❦*Ivan King, Marie Simmons*

J. H. S. Lee

Actor, manager. Began career in Hobart 1834. Later worked in Adelaide, Geelong, Launceston, Melbourne and Sydney.

A noted utility man and comedian, John Lee achieved many firsts in the Australian theatre but he drank to excess and never achieved the full success he deserved. He was the first to work regularly with performing dogs and one of first to sing blackface minstrel songs. Lee made his debut with J. P. DEANE's company at the ARGYLE ROOMS in Hobart on 29 May 1834, playing Harry Fawkes, a bushranger, in the premiere of Henry Melville's THE BUSHRANGERS.

Initial reports of Lee's acting were less than complimentary. The *Colonial Times* of 29 July 1834 said of his performance as Malvoglio in *A Tale of Mystery* by Thomas Holcroft: '… he is all attitude, he looks like the dancing harlequins children play with, which by pulling a thread, set both arms and legs in queer and unnatural positions'. Lee was evidently of small and irregular physique. When he appeared in the current fad of 'living statues' the *Sydney Gazette* on 20 January 1842 called him 'no more than a Hercules in miniature, and then, very out of proportion'.

In Launceston in 1835 Lee appeared in the premiere of another Australian melodrama—Evan Henry Thomas's THE BANDIT OF THE RHINE. He took a benefit on 28 November 'in consequence of the premature death of Mrs Lee, occasioned by a brutal assault from some unknown ruffians'. On 1 January 1836 Lee made his debut at the Theatre Royal in Sydney. In its final days, Lee was drunk and disrupted performances on 15 March 1838, but the manager, JOHN LAZAR, engaged him for the new ROYAL VICTORIA THEATRE.

Lee was among runaway actors who left debts in Sydney in late 1839 but—after a brief season with CORDELIA CAMERON in Launceston in December—he returned to the Royal Victoria in early 1840 and stayed until early 1843. In March and April 1843 Lee played a short season with his dogs at the Royal Victoria Theatre in Hobart and introduced 'Jumping Jim Crow', a blackface minstrel act, to the city. In May Lee joined JOSEPH SIMMONS's short-lived Royal City Theatre in Sydney and late in the year he appeared with F. B. WATSON's company in Tasmania.

In late 1844 Lee went to Melbourne and played with Cordelia and SAMSON CAMERON at the Royal Victoria Theatre and the new Queen's Theatre Royal. In 1846 he was in Tasmania as ANNE CLARKE's acting manager, devising some remarkable productions on the small Launceston stage. In May 1847 he moved to Adelaide to join the New Queen's Theatre, where he was billed as a celebrated Irish comedian. His performing dogs and his daughter Clara, a child prodigy, also appeared there. By June 1848 he was with Samson Cameron's company in Geelong, and in 1849 he returned to Launceston to manage the Royal Amphitheatre, Australia's first CIRCUS. In June the Royal Olympic Theatre opened one night a week under Lee's management. He missed Mrs Moore's benefit on 26 July and was said to have been seen 'rolling drunk'. He lost the management of the Royal Amphitheatre and the stage management of the Royal Olympic to J. R. Kenney but remained acting manager at the theatre. By January 1851 Lee was appearing at the Theatre Royal in Geelong to universally favourable notices. ❦*Elizabeth Webby*

Margo Lee

Actor. Born 1923 at Camden (NSW). Originally Margaret Hogg. Studied piano at NSW State Conservatorium of Music (Sydney). Regular performer on radio 2GB–Macquarie *Youth Show* in 1940s. Starred in Phillip Street revues in Sydney in 1950s. Green Room Award for best supporting actress (*Stepping Out* by Richard Harris) 1985. Died October 1987 in Sydney.

Throughout career on radio, television and stage Margo Lee retained glamorous blonde good looks and the sobriquet 'golden girl', with which she was tagged when she began on radio. In 1982 she was 'still gorgeous and superlatively stylish', said 'Dionysius' in the Sydney *Jewish Times*. Lee developed her craft in radio plays, as she declined to make long tours away from the family. She won a trip to perform in Hollywood in *Lux Video Theatre* in 1956, but returned promptly to Sydney television. For WILLIAM ORR she appeared in early PHILLIP STREET REVUES and at his Music Loft in Manly in the 1980s. Her versatility on stage and her timing brought her a wide range of roles. She tap-danced with Anna Neagle in the musical *Charlie Girl* in Melbourne in the 1970s and played the Queen of Hearts in *Alice in Wonderland* in Sydney in 1976. By contrast she was Queen Gertrude in *Hamlet* for the NIMROD THEATRE COMPANY in 1973 and she played Christine Mannon in Eugene O'Neill's *Mourning Becomes Electra* for the QUEENSLAND

THEATRE COMPANY. Her performance in *Sister Mary Ignatius Explains It All for You* by Christopher Durang at the Phillip Street Theatre in 1983 was a *tour de force*. ❦Susan Hogan

The Legend of King O'Malley

—*or, Never Say Die Until a Dead Horse Kicks You*. Musical burlesque in two acts. **libretto** Michael Boddy and Bob Ellis. **music** hymns and standards. **premiere** 11 June 1970, Jane Street Theatre, Sydney. Cast: David Cameron, Rex Cramphorn, Kate Fitzpatrick, Gillian Jones, Nicos Lathouris, Robyn Nevin, Terry O'Brien, John Paramor (King O'Malley), William Yang. Choreography: Keith Bain. Design: Janet Dawson with Sue Lloyd. Director: John Bell. **published** Sydney: Angus and Robertson 1974, Currency Press 1987.

Contemporary Australian theatre took its direction from *The Legend of King O'Malley*. This landmark is based on the life, factual and apocryphal, of an American who became an Australian politician and claimed to have founded Canberra and the Commonwealth Bank. Born in Texas in 1854, King O'Malley became a banker, real-estate agent, insurance salesman and leader of his own revivalist Waterlily Rockbound Church. Told he was dying of consumption, O'Malley sailed to Australia in 1893. He was shipwrecked on the Queensland coast. Then, selling insurance as he went, he walked some 5000 km from Rockhampton by way of Hobart to Adelaide, where he set up a real-estate business. O'Malley was member for Encounter Bay in the South Australian House of Assembly from 1896 to 1899. In the first Australian House of Representatives in 1901 he was member for the Tasmanian seat of Darwin and he held it until 1917, when he was defeated over the conscription issue and retired from politics. As Minister for Home Affairs he was in the forefront of labour reform and social legislation. He died in Melbourne in 1953.

The Legend of King O'Malley begins with a prairie revival meeting in which the audience joins. It then takes a journey of adventure and hardship, culminating in a satirical view of federal Parliament as a bunch of clowns. Beyond the outrageous irreverence Australian myths can be glimpsed in the portrait of the lonely outsider, the farseeing idealist in conflict with the conservative pragmatists, the fatalism, the failure, the Irish sensibility.

JOHN BELL's production was successfully transferred to the Parade Theatre in August 1970, under the aegis of the OLD TOTE THEATRE COMPANY, in an enlarged and slightly revised version, with musical arrangements by Richard Connolly and backcloths designed by Janet Dawson. Under the banner of the AUSTRALIAN ELIZABETHAN THEATRE TRUST, a touring version of this production then played all capitals and a return season in Sydney in 1971, presented by Dudley Goldman Pty Ltd at the Phillip Theatre. The Queensland Theatre Company toured its own production to Canberra, rural NSW, Brisbane and Queensland in 1971–72, and new productions were taken to the Northern Territory, and to New Zealand and the Pan-Pacific Arts Festival in Fiji. In 1973, J. C. Williamson's and Dudley Goldman revived the play for a season at the Richbrooke Theatre in Sydney. There have been other professional productions in the United Kingdom, the USA and West Germany, and *The Legend of King O'Malley* is still produced by amateur groups, schools, and colleges throughout Australia. In retrospect the play's popular success lay in its definition and celebration of Australia as a working-class nation at a time of middle-class domination. The employment it offered led John Bell and others to establish the NIMROD THEATRE COMPANY, whose iconoclastic early work was greatly influenced by the O'Malley experience. It also led to further rethinking of the classics by the PERFORMANCE SYNDICATE. All the original cast except John Paramor were or soon became members of this group. ❦Katharine Brisbane

George Leitch

Actor, dramatist, manager. Born 1842 in London. Originally George Goodyear. Also known as George Leitch Walker, George Ralph Walker. Came to Australia as low comedian for J. C. Williamson 1883. Remained until 1897. Died 1907 in England.

Leitch is chiefly remembered for his sensation melodrama *The Land of the Moa*, the most successful New Zealand play of the 19th century. From 1894 it toured the four major New Zealand cities and then to Sydney, Brisbane and Melbourne. Leitch was also the first person in Australia to adapt Marcus Clarke's novel *His Natural Life* for the stage. It opened in Brisbane on 26 April 1886 and competed against FOR THE TERM OF HIS NATURAL LIFE by Alfred Dampier and Thomas Somers for some years. ❦Adrian Kiernander

published play
The Land of the Moa (1894) ed. Adrian Kiernander. Wellington (New Zealand): Victoria University Press 1990.
reference
A large collection of Leitch's personal papers is in the Mitchell Library (Sydney).

Fred Leslie

Choreographer, dancer, producer. Born *c*.1882 in Melbourne. Originally Frederick Stoneham. Began performing in variety with father and uncle at early age. Performed character roles, danced and choreographed for J. C. Williamson's 1901–14. Married dancer Nellie Borthwick *c*.1903. Worked in England as Fred A. Leslie, mainly as choreographer and producer, from 1914. Returned to Australia in retirement in 1949. Date of death unknown.

Fred Leslie's dance routines, particularly with Ivy Schilling, who succeeded Tilly Woodlock as his main partner in 1911, consistently attracted critical and popular acclaim. They were 'the very essence of fun' and his dancing could 'lighten up dull dialogue with clever eccentricities', said critics. Leslie carefully prepared his routines in front of mirrors, then simplified them to achieve the maximum effect for the minimum action. The newspaper columnist Bill Rodie, recalling the versatility, speed, grace, ingenuity, and 'satanic sustainment' of Fred Leslie's performances for J. C. WILLIAMSON'S, concluded in 1950 that he was the most gifted Australian-born light comedian and dancer in musical-comedy history.

Productions in which Leslie appeared included *The Casino Girl* in 1901; *The Messenger Boy* and *A Runaway Girl* in 1902; *A Country Girl* in 1903; *The Orchid* and *The Girl from Kay's* in 1904; *The Cingalee* in 1905; *The Little Michus* and *The Spring Chicken* in 1906; *The Dairymaids*, *The Girls of Gottenberg* and *San Toy* in 1907; *The Red Mill* in 1908; *Our Miss Gibbs* in 1910; and *The Quaker Girl* in 1912.

Leslie was the grandson of William Stoneham, bandmaster of the first volunteer band organised in Australia and a musician with circuses and Simonsen opera companies. As a child he began performing small song-and-dance parts with his father and uncle, Fred and Will, successful variety entertainers known as the Leslie Brothers in Australia, the United Kingdom and USA. His wife Nellie Borthwick was a dancer in Pollard's Opera Company and for J. C. Williamson's.

In England he called himself Fred A. Leslie, presumably to avoid confusion with the English actor Fred Leslie, whose father, also named Fred Leslie, had toured Australia with GAIETY THEATRE COMPANIES in 1888 and 1891. Leslie and Ivy Schilling performed with considerable success in England. Schilling came back to Australia but Leslie remained in England, performing occasionally but mainly working as choreographer and producer of more than 100 revues, musicals, pantomime and other shows until the 1940s. ❦*Paul Bentley*

reference
Fred Leslie and Nellie Borthwick collection, Dennis Wolanski Library, Sydney Opera House.

Barnett Levey

Entrepreneur. Born c.1798. Arrived in Sydney December 1821. Married Sarah Emma Wilson 1825. Presented and performed in concerts 1826. Built theatre and Royal Hotel 1829. Presented plays in Royal Hotel from 26 December 1832. Opened Theatre Royal 5 October 1833. Managed Theatre Royal alone or in partnership until April 1835. Proprietor of Theatre Royal from April 1837. Died 1 October 1837 in Sydney.

The founder of professional theatre in Australia, Barnett Levey was also the first male Jewish free settler. He came to Sydney to join his brother Solomon Levey, an emancipated convict who had become a successful businessman. From 1825 Barnett Levey was an auctioneer, general merchant, currency dealer, builder, banker and publican. He was also a keen freemason. In 1827 he founded a company to build a theatre but he became involved in a dispute with the Governor of NSW, Lieutenant-General Ralph Darling, which made it difficult for him to obtain a theatrical licence.

Levey built a theatre in a warehouse and a dwelling which was partly opened as the Royal Hotel in March 1829. In June 1829 this was licensed for concerts and balls. Levey gave formal concerts and later established eating-and-drinking 'at-homes', which were more popular. The at-homes were stopped in January 1830 as unsuitable for the 'prison populace' of the town and Levey, insolvent, sold the buildings in December 1830. In 1832 he was permitted to stage four at-homes in the Royal Hotel to finance his theatre and on 26 December, after Governor Sir Richard Bourke granted him a licence, he opened a playhouse in the hotel saloon. Douglas Jerrold's *Black-Eyed Susan* and the farce *Monsieur Tonson* played to a packed house of at least 600. Levey ensured crowds by offering half-price tickets at 9 p.m. The season lasted until May 1833.

Many land and property investments supported Levey's theatrical habit. In 1833 he completed the theatre in the warehouse and opened it under licence as the THEATRE ROYAL on 5 October 1833. After an opening address read by CONRAD KNOWLES, a melodrama, *The Miller and His Men* by Isaac Pocock, and a farce, *The Irishman in London*, were performed. The *Sydney Gazette* soon found fault with the management and the actors' lines but the *Sydney Herald* and other newspapers took up the cudgels for Levey. In December 1833 he lowered actors' salaries. In 1834 he refused benefits in an effort to discipline his actors and was himself punished when they performed in a salon of the Pulteney Hotel for a short time. In February 1834 JOSEPH SIMMONS joined Levey as partner and became acting-manager.

Levey gradually lost control of the theatre to Simmons and other lessees, who took over the management after a farewell benefit for Levey in April 1835. This was quite ignored by the newspapers, but his return in a spirited if drunken manner in April 1836 heralded unremitting ridicule in the press. Levey was promised the manager's position for £30 a week, in succession to Simmons, who had been in sole charge since November 1835. He then lost a court case to Knowles over payment for the 1833 address and libelled Simmons, who later received only one farthing in damages. The lessees withdrew their offer to Levey, but he became manager and proprietor in April 1837.

There followed a period of theatrical politics, secession by actors and vitriolic press attacks, especially by the *Sydney Gazette*'s critic William Kerr. He was thrown out of the theatre by Levey and a brave ticket man, whom Kerr later unsuccessfully sued for assault. Ridicule in the press culminated in June 1837 in heated correspondence in the *Sydney Gazette* and elsewhere as to whether all the local failures in drama could be laid at Levey's feet. He was accused of purging his theatre of all its talent with the departure of 'stars' like Knowles and JOHN MEREDITH.

On 23 September 1837 Levey's stage manager, Thomas Simes, banned him from going backstage because of his disruptive influence. Driven to despair by litigation and debt and enslaved by drink, Levey died on 1 October 1837, leaving his widow and four children £500. Sarah Levey managed the Theatre Royal until March 1838, when Joseph Wyatt opened the Royal Victoria Theatre.

An obituary in the *Sydney Times* on 21 October 1837 condemned Levey's addiction to drink but recognised that 'to his spirit and perseverance are the public indebted for the introduction of theatricals in New South Wales'. On the same day in the *Sydney Gazette* William Kerr congratulated himself on having helped Australian theatre by hurrying Levey to an early demise. The editor reluctantly apologised for this article five days later. The *Sydney Monitor* on 29 October 1838 commented on the 'laborious' attempts of Levey to found a theatre, no matter how rough.

The press had constantly attacked Levey for his lack of knowledge of theatrical practice and regularly ridiculed him as 'the patriarch of the drama in New South Wales'. Some external comments, such as a most favourable report on a trip to Levey's temporary theatre in 1833 by the visiting surgeon George Bennett, suggest that some of the ridicule arose from prejudice against the theatrical profession. This was shown in constant attacks over employment of emancipated convicts and charges of indecency in wit and looseness backstage. Levey remained enthusiastic in spite of the attacks, his own inexperience, rebellious actors and the rival management of Wyatt. His enthusiasm led him to refurbish his theatre with tinsel ribbon, a mirror stage curtain and paintings of marine victories, but to neglect to repair the upholstery. While Levey's amateurism led the *Sydney Gazette* to charge that he was not fit to be a manager, his ignorance of backstage precedent in England also meant a rare period of originality in local theatre. He was often ahead of his time, as in his employment—criticised by the press as immoral—of a company of juvenile actors. He understood the 'rougher' mass theatrical tastes and habits, but he also fostered the first professional performance of Shakespeare in Australia—*Richard III* in Colley Cibber's version on 26 December 1833. *Othello* followed in July 1834 and *Hamlet* with the popular Knowles in August 1834. In September 1837, shortly before his death, Levey was supporting Shakespeare with a classical season by SAMSON and CORDELIA CAMERON. ♥*Helen Musa*

further reading
BERGMAN, GEORGE F. J. Barnett Levey. *Australian Dictionary of Biography* 2. Melbourne University Press 1967.
BEVAN, IAN. *The Story of the Theatre Royal*. Sydney: Currency Press 1993.

Nigel Levings

Lighting designer. Born 29 September 1949 in Manchester (England). Brought to Melbourne 1951. Studied arts–law at Monash University (Melbourne) 1967–69. Head electrician and lighting designer for Melbourne Theatre Company 1971–73. Studied lighting design in United Kingdom and USA on Australia Council travel grant 1974-75. Began long association with South Australian Theatre Company (Adelaide) 1975 and State Theatre Company of South Australia 1979. Lighting designer for many musicals.

Since the mid-1980s major theatre companies have regularly commissioned Nigel Levings to design the lighting of their productions. He is noted for enhancing the director's interpretation. His work, originally poetic and highly impressionistic, has become more powerful and economical. Landmarks in his career include Ben Jonson's *Volpone* at the Nimrod Theatre in Sydney in 1980; *Lulu*, Louis Nowra's conflation of plays by Frank Wedekind, for the State Theatre Company of South Australia in 1981; DOROTHY HEWETT's *The Man From Mukinupin* for the SYDNEY THEATRE COMPANY in 1981; August Strindberg's *A Dream Play* for the STATE THEATRE Company of South Australia in 1988; Patrick White's THE HAM FUNERAL for the Sydney Theatre Company in 1989; and Henrik Ibsen's *Master Builder* at the BELVOIR STREET THEATRE in 1991. ♥*Tom Bannerman, Aubrey Mellor*

Life in Sydney

—*or, The Ran Dan Club*. Burletta in two acts, written in Sydney in 1843. **premiere** 29 March 1978, Downstairs Theatre, Seymour Centre, Sydney, by Cartwheel Theatre. Cast: David Brown, Paul Brown, Melisande Clark, Richard Healy, Bruce Keller, Aldo King, Jeremy Lovelock, Peta Murray, Lindy Piggin, Tony Piggin, Sue Roberts, Gerry Robinson, Christine Sammers, Kim Spinks. Designer: Melody Cooper. Director: Rex Cramphorn.

The NSW Colonial Secretary refused to license *Life in Sydney* for performance at the Royal Victoria Theatre in Sydney in 1843 because 'it contained matters of a libellous character, independently of other objections'. The letter requesting a licence referred to the play as a 'parody of Tom and Jerry', indicating its close resemblance to William Moncrieff's *Tom and Jerry—or, Life in London*, a very popular extravaganza based on Pierce Egan's novel *Life in London*. Like the English originals, which both came out in 1821, *Life in Sydney* used three young men out on a spree, Tom, Jerry and Bob, as a means of displaying local scenes, manners and entertainments—Macquarie Place, the Royal Hotel, the Shakespeare Tavern, a low pub in the Rocks and Sam Lyons's Auction Mart. It also offered plenty of opportunities for local humour and satire, and song and dance. The libel appears to have been chiefly upon Sam Lyons, a well-known auctioneer, who is shown fleecing ignorant new chums. Henry O'Flaherty, husband of the actor ELIZA WINSTANLEY, may have written the play. ♥*Elizabeth Webby*

reference
The manuscript is in the Colonial Secretary's Papers in the Archives Office of NSW.

Lighting design

The responsibility of the lighting designer is to realise the director's and designer's vision in light. Increasingly the lighting designer is seen as major contributor to the concept of a production, working with the director and designers before designs or casting are completed. This role has developed since the mid-1980s. Until the late 1970s the theatre technician or head electrician organised the lighting of a production, occasionally guided by a director with a particular interest in lighting. Some of the first directors to realise the potential of lighting to contribute to the style of a production were COLIN BALLANTYNE, Stefan Haag, ROBIN LOVEJOY, IRENE MITCHELL and JOHN SUMNER. They encouraged technicians who showed a flair for design. Technicians were enabled to develop lighting design to its present high standard by the advent of the state drama companies and other permanent performing companies. As PERFORMING-ARTS CENTRES and new theatres burgeoned, lighting-control technology became highly specialised.

Most Australian lighting designers in the 1960s and early 1970s closely followed the techniques of British designers, particularly Richard Pilbrow. In the era of manual control, after the disappearance of footlights, the standard practice was warm light from one side and cool from the other—'straw' and 'steel'. With better equipment, more lamp functions and computerised systems, designers were able to 'paint' in light more accurately. Naturalism, the dominant style on Australian stages, led to rich, pretty and sometimes subtle evocations of natural light and time of day.

The Australian plays that emerged in the late 1960s were supported by imaginative direction and much bolder use of space in design. New theatres such as the Nimrod Street Theatre and the Ensemble Theatre in Sydney freed the design elements from the proscenium and lighting was often predominant among them. Exposed lighting rigs, revealing the source of the light, became common. With the development of more open scenic design in the late 1970s, lighting designers were able to help to create dynamic stage pictures by using stronger back and side lighting and relying less upon the traditional 45-degree lighting angle. Luminaires from rock-music shows—higher powered and cheaper than traditional theatrical equipment—permitted high light levels and saturated colours for the first time. John Rayment in particular explored high-contrast white lighting with great style. The 1980s saw the first use of automated fixtures that permitted the light beams to move.

This lighting has been used mainly in commercial musical theatre, where budgets permit it and high sound levels mask the noise of the fittings.

Lighting design must be planned with great skill and in most theatres time for realisation is insufficient because of inadequate facilities and economic pressures. Lights are usually rigged, focused and plotted within two or three days. The lighting designer NIGEL LEVINGS has calculated that in order to light a show in the given time it is necessary to focus each lantern in 2·5–3 minutes, and that plotting rates of ten cues an hour must be achieved—improved from three to five cues an hour with manual systems. A mainstream drama production would use 150–250 luminaires, while a musical could employ more than 500.

Another hindrance to the development of lighting design is lack of appreciation of what a lighting designer can contribute to the development and presentation of a production. A third is low fees. To make a living a lighting designer must undertake more than three times as many productions as a set or costume designer or a director. Lighting designers normally end up being paid lower hourly rates than the stage electricians whose work they direct. With the notable exceptions of Jamieson Lewis of the MELBOURNE THEATRE COMPANY, John Beckett of the PLAYBOX THEATRE CENTRE and David Walters of the QUEENSLAND THEATRE COMPANY, most lighting designers are freelances.

Since the early 1980s lighting for most productions in all states has been designed by members of a core that includes Roger Barratt, Donn Byrnes, John Comeadow, Nigel Levings, David Murray, John Rayment, Ken Raynor and Tony Youlden. All the senior designers work in drama, musicals, opera and ballet. Some have been prolific in commercial theatre. Sue Nattrass, now general manager of the Victorian Arts Centre, designed many shows for J. C. WILLIAMSON's. Duncan Ord, who was responsible for most of the lighting designs in Perth during the 1980s, also turned to administration. Notable young lighting designers are Ben Cobham, Jeff Cobham, Rory Demster, John Hoenig, Mark Howett, Nick Schlieper, Mark Shelton and Effie Soropos. ❦*Aubrey Mellor, Tony Youlden*

Vane Lindesay
Designer. Born 2 October 1920 in Sydney. Designed sets, costumes and graphics for New Theatre Melbourne in 1940s and 1950s. Worked with directors Alfie Bass and Will Stampe at Unity Theatre, London, in 1950s.

Working as an amateur with the radical, political NEW THEATRE, Vane Lindesay contributed substantially to a modernist sensibility of wit and brevity in Australian theatrical design. Despite economic and physical restrictions imposed by the small New Theatre, his design solutions were striking, dynamic statements that reinforced the mood and content of productions covering satirical cabaret such as *Soak the Rich* and a wide range of drama. In 1947 Lindesay's designs for *Call Up Your Ghosts* by Miles Franklin and DYMPHNA CUSACK and *A Physician in Spite of Himself* by Molière were selected by for an exhibition of Australian theatre decor at the Art Gallery of NSW. He has contributed illustrations, cartoons and articles to various publications, including *New Theatre Review*, for more than 40 years. ❦*Pamela Zeplin*

further reading
ZEPLIN-WAITE, PAMELA. Three shillings for a bolt of hessian. *Australasian Drama Studies* 2/1 (October 1983).

Little Theatre
Professional dramatic company in Sydney, founded in 1913 by Hugh Buckler and Violet Paget. Closed 1915. **venue** Little Theatre. **first production** *The Man on the Box* by Grace Lavangstone Furneff, 22 March 1913, Little Theatre.

Little Theatre filled a theatrical niche—vacant since the demise of the Brough Comedy Company in 1908—by producing serious contemporary plays and high-class comedies that were generally not seen in Sydney's big theatres. The main force behind it was Hugh Buckler, who had managed the National Theatre in Cape Town and acted in the companies of Oscar Asche and Herbert Beerbohm Tree in London. He came to Australia in 1910 with *The Night of the Party* by Weedon Grossmith. Buckler and his wife Violet Paget, who came to Australia with him, refurbished the ROYAL STANDARD THEATRE to create an intimate atmosphere and renamed it the Little Theatre. They instituted post-matinee afternoon teas on stage for the cast and holders of orchestra stalls tickets. A writer in *Theatre* magazine in May 1913 denounced these events as cheap and tawdry advertising that destroyed the audience's illusion.

As the lead in Little Theatre productions, Buckler was once described as the closest to Sydney's 'beau ideal' for the matinée girl. Critics regularly admired his acting, though *Theatre* complained that his modern style was totally unsuited to R. B. Sheridan's *The School for Scandal* in 1914. His wife was less popular. A typical review in 1914 praised Buckler for acting 'from within' in Arthur Wing Pinero's *His House in Order* but said Paget, though 'clever and refined', acted 'from without'.

The company toured to Melbourne in August 1913, New Zealand in 1914 and Brisbane in 1914–15. Buckler enlisted in the army while the company was in Brisbane and it returned to Sydney and struggled without him. R. C. Carton's *Liberty Hall* opened in April 1915 and was followed by Tom Robertson's *Caste*, possibly the company's last production, despite plans for several more. Buckler resumed his career on the London stage in March 1918. He died on 30 October 1936, aged 66.

Other members of the Little Theatre company included its general manager, Reynolds Denniston, a New Zealand actor who had been invited to Australia by JULIUS KNIGHT; Dorothy Sydney, brought to Australia in 1908 by J. C. WILLIAMSON's; Gerald Kay Souper, who took over Buckler's roles when he enlisted; Victor Fitzherbert; Arthur Cornell and Lillian Lloyd. Buckler also recruited amateurs. Other Little Theatre productions included *The Gay Lord Quex* and *Sweet Lavender* by Pinero in 1914, *Fanny's First Play* and *Man and Superman* by George Bernard Shaw in 1913 and 1914 respectively, and *The Master of Angerstroon* by an unidentified Australian. ❦*Victoria Chance*

Reg Livermore
Actor, director, writer. Born 1938 in Sydney. Began theatrical training with John Alden and Independent Theatre School (Sydney). Professional debut at Phillip Street Theatre, Sydney, 1957.

Studied with Hayes Gordon, founder-member of Ensemble Theatre Company (Sydney). Union Theatre Repertory Company (Melbourne) 1961–63. Acted with major companies in Melbourne, Adelaide and Sydney. In revue at Phillip Theatre, Sydney. Began appearing in rock musicals 1969. Presented first solo show 1975. Australian Artist Creative Fellowship 1994–95.

A classically trained actor, Reg Livermore changed direction in mid-career by creating innovative and controversial solo shows that brought him a huge cult following. He began his career in PHILLIP STREET REVUES and then became a founder-member of the ENSEMBLE THEATRE COMPANY. With the Union Theatre Repertory Company he acted roles ranging in time from Malcolm in *Macbeth* to Roy in Patrick White's THE SEASON AT SARSAPARILLA, directed Richard Beynon's THE SHIFTING HEART and wrote and appeared in his own musical, *Good Ship Walter Raleigh*. He returned to Sydney and was acclaimed for performances in Arthur Kopit's *Oh Dad, Poor Dad, Mama's Hung You in the Closet and I'm Feelin' So Sad* for INDEPENDENT THEATRE and Oscar Wilde's *The Importance of Being Earnest* for the OLD TOTE THEATRE COMPANY. At the Ensemble Theatre he devised and produced a play, *The Canterville Ghost*. With the South Australian Theatre Company in Adelaide he directed his own musical, *West of the Black Stump*. In Sydney in 1965, he began a long run in the Phillip Theatre's smash-hit intimate revue *A Cup of Tea, a Bex and a Good Lie Down*.

In 1969 Livermore brought new life to the role of Berger in the rock musical *Hair*. He stayed with the show for two years. He made further excursions into rock musicals in the 1970s as Herod in *Jesus Christ Superstar* and as Frank'n Furter in *The Rocky Horror Show*—a landmark portrayal. During this period he also wrote the libretto for and appeared in the musical *Lasseter* for the Old Tote company. In 1975 Livermore, with PETER BATEY, put together his first solo show, THE BETTY BLOKK BUSTER FOLLIES. It toured for 15 months. Bizarre female impersonations and barbed social comment continued in another solo show, *Wonder Woman*.

After a break to direct his own musical *Ned Kelly* for the ADELAIDE FESTIVAL OF ARTS in 1978, Livermore returned to solo performance with *Sacred Cow* in 1979 and *Son of Betty* in 1980. In 1982, he appeared in the title-role of *Barnum*, a musical that he publicly deplored. Next year he presented another solo show, *Firing Squad*. After a revival of *The Rocky Horror Show* in 1984 he retired to the Blue Mountains to devote himself to painting and cultivating an enormous garden, which he opened to the public.

Livermore returned to the stage in his own musical *Big Sister* at Parramatta in 1989, and presented a new solo show, *Wish You Were Here*, at the Melbourne Festival of Arts in 1990. He played Major-General Stanley in *The Pirates of Penzance* for the Victoria State Opera in 1992 and Buddy in *Follies in Concert* at the 1993 Melbourne Festival. He gave the premieres of two solo shows, *Mother Goose* (1993) and *Red Riding Hood* (1994), at the Clarendon Hotel in the Blue Mountains. ❦*Tony Sheldon*

Johnny Lockwood

Actor, entertainer. Born 7 December 1920 in London. Orphaned young, entered show business as dancer. Became impressionist and comedian. Contracted to Jack Hylton 1939. In Royal Variety Command Performance 1949. Came to Australia for Tivoli circuit 1957.

An all-round entertainer, Johnny Lockwood first starred in Australia in a Tivoli revue, *Say It With Stars*, in 1957. In 1961 he gave a memorable performance as Fagin in the musical *Oliver!*, touring for J. C. WILLIAMSON'S. Then he returned to London to follow Ron Moody and John Bluthal as Fagin. Back in Australia from 1963 he played in cabaret, in clubs, on television and in the theatre in musicals. These included *The Canterbury Tales* for KENN BRODZIAK and an adaptation of J. B. Priestley's farce *When We Are Married* for Phillip Productions. ❦*John West*

Lola Montez

Musical play. **libretto and additional lyrics** Alan Burke. **lyrics** Peter Benjamin. **music** Peter Stannard. **premiere** 19 February 1958, Union Theatre, Melbourne. Cast: Patricia Conolly, Neil Fitzpatrick, Frank Gatliff, Alan Hopgood, Monica Maughan, George Ogilvie, Robin Ramsay, Justine Rettick. Director: John Sumner.
revised version 1 October 1958, Her Majesty's Theatre, Brisbane. Cast: Mary Preston (Lola Montez), Frank Wilson, Eric Thornton, Jane Martin. Director: George Carden.

John Sumner's production of *Lola Montez*, an ambitious attempt at a Broadway-style Australian musical for the Union Theatre Repertory Company, caught the attention of the AUSTRALIAN ELIZABETHAN THEATRE TRUST, which mounted an expanded version directed and choreographed by George Carden, with a chorus of 24. The story is based on the visit of the dancer Lola Montez to the Ballarat goldfields in the 1850s. She is portrayed as ageing and destitute, reduced to performing her torrid Spider Dance for the miners. When the editor of the *Ballaarat Times* writes an insulting criticism of the dance, Lola publicly horsewhips him. A subplot involves Daniel, a young miner smitten with Lola, and the virtuous Jane, who is determined to save him from a fate worse than death.

In Sumner's staging, the title-role was played by Justine Rettick, an operetta comedian who correctly conveyed an air of glamour going to seed. Unfortunately, the revised version starred a young English dancer Mary Preston, who had neither the maturity or vocal technique to carry the show. It garnered middling reviews and closed to a loss of £31 581. A Columbia recording with the Brisbane cast made the song 'Saturday Girl' something of a popular hit. The musical was revived with minor revisions in Canberra for the bicentenary in 1988. ❦*Tony Sheldon*

further reading
SUMNER, JOHN. *Recollections at Play—A life in Australian theatre*. Melbourne University Press 1993.

London Comedy Company

English professional company. Toured Australia 1879–80. Opened 21 June 1879 at Prince of Wales Opera House, Melbourne. Closed November 1880 at Gaiety Theatre, Sydney. **actor–managers** Arthur Garner, Blanche Stammers.

The London Comedy Company signalled the end for the system of star and stock company and it set standards for the 1880s, probably the most prosperous decade of the colonial stage. It also encouraged the colonial cringe in Australian high society, and began the tendency for entrepreneurs to import 'the entire London cast', denying work to resident actors. For the next 80 years Anglophile critics and audiences would look eagerly on every new London import as evidence of not just better acting styles and stories, but also of how to dress, live and behave.

Every reviewer noted the care and lavishness with which the company's sets and costumes were created. The designer GEORGE GORDON came to Australia with the company. J. E. NEILD of the *Australasian* thought his boudoir set for *Friends* was good enough to 'make one review one's own house, and think whether it is not possible to introduce some such element of art-furnishing at home'. The repertoire was not spectacular: *Friends*—Victorien Sardou's *Nos intimes* with a boudoir scene cleaned up to suit English sensibilities—and old London successes such as Edward Bulwer-Lytton's *Money*, W. S. Gilbert's *Pygmalion and Galatea* and Tom Taylor's *New Men and Old Acres*.

Little was known in Sydney or Melbourne about the actors that ARTHUR GARNER and his wife Blanche Stammers recruited in London for the tour, but Garner and the stage director George Wade drilled them into ensemble playing of a kind previously unknown in Australia. The company had several genuine stars and added another in GEORGE S. TITHERADGE. In *Friends*, the *Sydney Mail* thought Blanche Stammers's portrayal of a young wife who almost succumbs to the advances of her husband's best friend had 'nothing to offend the most fastidious. She is a beautiful fragile creature, a gay moth who has been so near the fire of danger ... but there is no taint or sullied spot on her dainty wings'. Every entrance of the comedian Fred Marshall occasioned applause.

When Marshall left to join the troupe at Sydney's new Gaiety Theatre in November 1880 Garner wisely closed the company. It had played for 75 weeks in the eastern states, including 20 weeks in Melbourne from 21 June 1879 and 38 weeks in Sydney from 15 March 1880. The Australian stage could never be the same again, and the Garners were £10 000 richer. ❦*Richard Fotheringham*

Minnie Love

Actor, singer. Born c.1890 in United Kingdom. Trained as child actor by aunt Lily Ernest. Made debut at Middlesex Music-Hall, London. Child actor in drama then principal boy in pantomime. Star of musical theatre in Australia 1914–20. Returned to Australia in 1930s. Acted until late 1950s. Died 3 August 1967.

Minnie Love played everything from principal boys in pantomime to the classics. Tall, slim and blonde with a piquant gamine face, she had a wicked sense of comedy and could move her audience to tears with a sad song or a dramatic scene. She was immensely popular with Australian audiences during the First World War. She was playing principal boy in South Africa when J. C. WILLIAMSON'S took her up for a boy's part in the operetta *The Girl on the Film*. The Firm then brought her to Australia to play Dandini in *Cinderella* in Sydney in 1914. This gorgeously mounted and costumed pantomime was popular with adult audiences and when it was revived in 1915 Love played the Prince and toured New Zealand and South Africa with it.

The Firm's Royal Comic Opera Company cast her in a leading role in *The Cinema Star* in 1916 and in the title-role in *The Pink Lady* in 1917, both in Sydney. She sang special songs for soldiers, and once they pulled her cab from the theatre to her hotel. In Sydney in 1917 Love starred with Jack Cannot and Leslie Holland in a spectacular revue, *The Bing Boys Are Here*, and in 1918 with GUS BLUETT in *Hello Everybody*. In 1920 she starred in revues and had a leading role in the musical comedy *His Little Widows* in Sydney.

During the 1920s and 1930s Love spent several years in England. On her return to Australia she worked mainly in radio. In 1949 she delighted country audiences by playing Mrs Malaprop in R. B. Sheridan's *The Rivals* with great verve and comic invention on a six-week tour by METROPOLITAN THEATRE. She played Lady Brockhurst in the musical comedy *The Boy Friend* in Sydney and on tour in 1956. In Melbourne and Sydney in 1958 she acted with ROBERT HELPMANN in Noël Coward's *Nude with Violin*. She played a vague, sweet character 'just like Billie Burke', she said, perhaps recalling the early years of the century when both were pin-up girls on postcards. ❦*Lynne Murphy*

Robin Lovejoy OBE

Actor, designer, director. Born 17 December 1923 in Fiji. Director of Metropolitan Theatre (Sydney) 1950-51. Directed Arrow Theatre (Melbourne) 1952. Studied in Europe on International Theatre Institute travelling scholarship 1953–55. Produced drama and opera for Australian Elizabethan Theatre Trust 1956–74. Artistic director of Trust Players 1958–61. Studied in USA on Harkness Fellowship of Commonwealth Fund of New York 1961–63. In charge of developing Australian plays for Elizabethan Trust 1963–65. Co-director of Old Tote Theatre Company (Sydney) 1965–68; artistic director 1968–74. On board of studies of National Institute of Dramatic Art (Sydney) 1969–81. On board of directors of Elizabethan Trust 1977–81. Freelance director of drama and opera 1974–1982. Head of design and directing courses at NIDA 1982–85. Died 14 December 1985 in Sydney. OBE 1974.

The first to sustain a long and distinguished career as a professional director of classical and modern plays and opera in Australia was Robin Lovejoy. He began acting and directing with METROPOLITAN THEATRE in Sydney after his return from the Second World War. During five years he designed or directed 26 productions in Sydney and Melbourne. He joined HUGH HUNT's Australian Drama Company in 1956 and directed and designed operas and plays for the AUSTRALIAN ELIZABETHAN THEATRE TRUST. In 1959 he founded the TRUST PLAYERS and directed all but two of their first 14 productions, beginning with Peter Kenna's THE SLAUGHTER OF ST TERESA'S DAY. In 1961 Lovejoy directed Alan Seymour's THE ONE DAY OF THE YEAR before leaving to study theatre in the USA. He returned in 1963 and in 1965 became co-director with TOM BROWN of the OLD TOTE THEATRE COMPANY in Sydney. As sole director from 1969 he guided the company into the Drama Theatre of the SYDNEY OPERA HOUSE, which opened in 1973 with his production of *Richard II*. Lovejoy is remembered for the elegance and structural discipline of his work. He survived a palace revolution by his associate directors and resigned in 1974 to work as a free lance in Australia and overseas. ❦*John Clark*

further reading
DRAPER, W. J. (ed.). *Who's Who in Australia* 25th edn. Melbourne: Herald and Weekly Times 1985.
HERBERT, IAN (ed.). *Who's Who in the Theatre* 16th. London: Pitman 1977.
SUMNER, JOHN. *Recollections at Play—A life in Australian theatre*. Melbourne: University Press 1993.

Barry Lovett

Actor. Born 11 October 1935 in Newcastle (NSW). Trained at Independent Theatre (Sydney). Professional debut with J. C. Williamson Shakespeare Company 1959–60. Music Hall Theatre Restaurant (Sydney) from 1961. Studied theatre in Europe 1966–68. Acted for major theatre companies from 1968. Died 21 June 1988 in Sydney.

Barry Lovett delighted a generation of audiences at the MUSIC HALL THEATRE RESTAURANT with inspired clowning and a splendid gallery of monsters. In contrast he gave impressive performances in classical and contemporary plays from 1968 until his untimely death. He began his professional career in Shakespeare, under the direction of JOHN ALDEN in the J. C. Williamson Shakespeare Company on tour in 1959–60, and in 1960 he played Feste in *Twelfth Night* on an Arts Council tour.

At the Music Hall Lovett learned how to deal with audiences who were encouraged to hiss the villain and cheer the heroine, and he revelled in the immediate response. He played comedy roles and pathetic monsters, including the clown–murderer in *The Worst Woman in London*, the title-role in *The Mollusc*, and Jack the hunchback in *The Spring-Heeled Terror of Stepney Green*. In an interview in 1982 Lovett said his favourite roles were monsters: 'The monster mask appeals to me very much. I like the feeling of a hideous outside and a glorious soul shining through.'

After a study tour in Europe, he played Brazen in George Farquhar's *The Recruiting Officer* at the 1968 Adelaide Festival, and the Fool in *King Lear* for the OLD TOTE THEATRE COMPANY in Sydney. In 1969 he played Bob Acres in R. B. Sheridan's *The Rivals*, the sinister Player in Tom Stoppard's *Rosencrantz and Guildenstern are Dead*, Polonius in *Hamlet* and a succession of zany characters in Jules Feiffer's *Little Murders*. In 1970 Lovett played Charlie in Arthur Miller's *Death of a Salesman*, the bizarre general in Georges Feydeau's *Cat Among the Pigeons* and the Priest in Tyrone Guthrie's production of Sophocles's *King Oedipus*. He acted in some of the NIMROD THEATRE COMPANY's successes, including JOHN WOOD's *On Yer Marx*, Stoppard's *Jumpers*, and Ted in David Williamson's THE CLUB, on tour in Australia in 1977 and in London in 1987.

In 1981–82 Lovett played in *The Tempest*, Somerset Maugham's *The Circle* and Ben Hecht's *The Front Page* for the QUEENSLAND THEATRE COMPANY. In Sydney in 1983 he drew praise for one of his most satisfying roles, the bookseller in Warwick Moss's *Down an Alley Filled with Cats*. H. G. KIPPAX wrote: 'Mr Lovett gives us benevolence with hooded eyes and a brand of untrustworthy candour that grows more and more chilling. Rich acting.' Lovett continued to work in a wide range of character roles, notably for Nimrod. His last role was one of four clergymen in Philip King's farce *See How They Run* for the MARIAN STREET THEATRE COMPANY in 1987. ♥*Lynne Murphy*

Betty Lucas

Actor. Born 31 May 1926 in Sydney. Began acting for Metropolitan Theatre (Sydney) 1945. Acted in theatre and television in England 1950 to mid-1960s. Has acted with leading companies in Adelaide, Melbourne and Sydney. Married to dramatist Ralph Peterson. Mother of cinematographer Joel Peterson.

An actor of luminous truthfulness and distinction, Betty Lucas has a deft light touch in comedy and emotional strength in drama. Early in her career the petite, blonde Lucas played leading roles for METROPOLITAN THEATRE in Restoration plays, Shakespeare and new Australian works. Of her Margery Pinchwife in William Wycherley's *The Country Wife*, DOUGLAS STEWART wrote in the *Bulletin*: 'She was pretty, she was alive, she was the play'. In England she was engaged by the Nottingham Playhouse for 18 months, toured for the Arts Council and acted in television drama.

On return to Australia, she played a witch in *Macbeth* and the Nurse in Euripides's *Medea* with JUDITH ANDERSON at the 1966 Adelaide Festival. She acted for the South Australian Theatre Company in 1967 in John Osborne's *Inadmissible Evidence* and Edward Albee's *A Delicate Balance*. In 1968, on returning to Sydney, Lucas began a run of impressive performances for the OLD TOTE THEATRE COMPANY, playing the disillusioned, bottle-loving Laurie in DOROTHY HEWETT's *This Old Man Comes Rolling Home* and the Mother in RODNEY MILGATE's *A Refined Look at Existence*. In 1970 she played Linda in Arthur Miller's *Death of a Salesman*; in 1971 Elizabeth in Miller's *The Crucible*; in 1973 the Mother in Henrik Ibsen's *Peer Gynt*, directed by HUGH HUNT; in 1977 Mrs Grogan in Sean O'Casey's *The Plough and the Stars*, again directed by Hunt; and Anna in Liviu Ciulei's production of Maxim Gorky's *The Lower Depths*.

In 1969 Lucas created Mrs Shadow in Hewett's *Mrs Porter and the Angel* at PACT Theatre and for INDEPENDENT THEATRE gave a performance as Mary in Clare Boothe's *The Women* that brought her the accolade of best actress of the year. With the MELBOURNE THEATRE COMPANY in 1972 she played opposite LEO MCKERN in Marcel Achard's *Patate*. In 1973 she toured Australia with Ralph Richardson in William Douglas Home's *Lloyd George Knew My Father* and played the distraught wife in RALPH PETERSON's *The Third Secretary*. Lucas has drawn praise in widely contrasting leading roles—Frances in David Williamson's TRAVELLING NORTH for the Stage Company in Adelaide in 1983; Joan in Gordon Dryland's *Paddington Red* for Q THEATRE at Penrith (NSW) in 1985; Peggy in HANNIE RAYSON's *Room to Move* for the GRIFFIN THEATRE COMPANY in Sydney in 1986; Lady Elizabeth Milne in Brian Clark's *The Petition* for the ENSEMBLE THEATRE COMPANY in Sydney in 1988; and Maud in Jennifer Johnston's one-act play *The Porch* at the Crossroads Theatre in Sydney in 1992. In 1991–94 Lucas appeared as the frail but indomitable Rebecca Nurse in RICHARD WHERRETT's acclaimed production of *The Crucible* for the SYDNEY THEATRE COMPANY. ♥*Lynne Murphy*

Mayne Lynton

Actor. Born 4 May 1885 in England. Trained with Frank Benson. Acted in USA from 1912. Married actor Nancye Stewart 1921. Brought to Australia by J. C. Williamson's 1922. Radio actor and producer in Sydney and Melbourne 1929–47. Acted in films in Australia. Worked in stage, television and film in England 1949–55. Died 20 May 1965 in Sydney.

From 1922 to 1929 Mayne Lynton, a strong, good-looking man, acted in main supporting roles with Gertrude Elliott, Pauline Frederick, EMELIE POLINI, MURIEL STARR and other visiting stars for J. C. WILLIAMSON's. In the 1930s and 1940s he was a heavy. He came to Australia from the USA, where he had acted on the stage with George Arliss and Douglas Fairbanks and served with the British military mission during the First World War. Lynton produced matinee seasons of Shakespeare in association with J. C. Williamson's in 1947–49. ❦*Richard Lane*

Tes Lyssiotis

Dramatist. Born at Horsham (Vic.), of Greek immigrant parents. Trained as schoolteacher. Began writing plays for her pupils. Writer-in-residence at La Mama Theatre (Melbourne) 1984. Founded Filiki Players 1984.

Tes Lyssiotis has portrayed the problems of immigrant women with warm humour, great linguistic skill and a strong sense of realism in several plays. The first produced professionally was *I'll Go to Australia and Wear a Hat*, based on her mother's experiences as a mail-order bride, at LA MAMA THEATRE in 1982. The AUSTRALIAN ELIZABETHAN THEATRE TRUST toured a trilogy of her early multilingual plays, *The Journey*, in NSW and to Brisbane in 1987. The basis of *The Journey* was *On the Line*, a play in English, Greek, Italian and German about immigrant workers at the Ford factory. In addition to *The Journey*, Lyssiotis's best plays are the monodrama *A White Sports Coat* (1988) and *The Forty Lounge Cafe* (1990), first produced by THE PLAYBOX THEATRE CENTRE in Melbourne. ❦*Geoffrey Milne*

published play
The Forty Lounge Cafe (1990). Sydney: Currency Press 1990.

further reading
MITCHELL, TONY. In *Contemporary Dramatists* (ed. K. A. Berney) 5th edn. London: St James Press 1993.

W. S. Lyster

Entrepreneur. Born 21 March 1827 in Dublin (Ireland). Visited Australia during health cruise 1842. Was soldier of fortune before becoming operatic manager in USA. Toured with opera company in Australia and New Zealand 1861–68. Leased Prince of Wales Opera House, Sydney, 1863–66. Disbanded company in California 1869. Leased Princess's Theatre, Melbourne, 1870–73. Presented musical theatre, drama and variety at Prince of Wales Opera House, Melbourne, 1873–80. Assisted in management by wife Georgina Hodson, contralto singer. Partner of Arthur Garner in London Comedy Company 1879–80. Died 27 November 1880 in Melbourne. Uncle of entrepreneur George Musgrove.

William Lyster's great achievement was in his developing a tradition of opera performance but he was also an influential intercolonial manager. He pioneered many of the methods employed from 1882 by WILLIAMSON, GARNER AND MUSGROVE and its successors. During the 1860s he toured the major theatres of the eastern colonies with a large company at a time when most stage activity was organised around the stock companies of individual houses. During the 1870s Lyster, while retaining permanent control of the Prince of Wales Opera House in Melbourne, expanded his touring to include a company for Italian opera and another for English opera and *opéra-bouffe*, concert artists, drama companies and variety performers. In the 1880s the systems he had devised became dominant with the advent of the touring production and his associates GEORGE MUSGROVE and ARTHUR GARNER drew on his experience. Lyster also pioneered the more elaborate dressing of productions that accompanied the shift from the rotation of a large repertoire by a stock company to the long run. He devised striking effects for a season with Lytton Sothern in 1877, and provided sets and costumes of consistently high standard for the LONDON COMEDY COMPANY. He would finance such extravagances by skimping on revivals of *opéras-bouffes*, relying on their high spirits and happy improvisations by performers to compensate for makeshift sets, costumes and sometimes orchestras. ❦*Harold Love*

further reading
LOVE, HAROLD. *The Golden Age of Australian Opera*. Sydney: Currency Press 1981.
LOVE, HAROLD. Drama and music in colonial Melbourne. *Victoria's Heritage* (ed. A. G. L. Shaw). Melbourne: Allen and Unwin 1986.

Philip Lytton

Actor, dramatist, entrepreneur, teacher. Originally Charles Ernest Phillips. Married actor Madge Hope. Began theatrical career c.1900. Ran tent-theatre companies 1907–23.

The leading touring tent-theatre entrepreneur before the First World War was Philip Lytton. He was perhaps the first to take 'legitimate' tent theatre to the country, though E. I. Cole's BOHEMIAN DRAMATIC COMPANY had played in tents in Sydney from 1903 and Melbourne from 1907. Lytton, reputedly inspired by SARAH BERNHARDT's American tour 20 years before, bought a large tent in 1907, laid out about £1000 and started a company that could follow the show circuit without having to compete for bookings at the few theatres and halls. For a decade Lytton had up to three companies on the road. West Australia (too far away) and New Zealand (poor weather for tents, he said) got only one tour apiece and Victoria seemed indifferent to his offerings. In New South Wales and Queensland the weather and audiences were warmer, and Lytton was a rich man when he sold out of tents to GEORGE SORLIE in 1923.

Lytton is first heard of about 1900, making a living in Sydney and Melbourne by teaching stagecraft to would-be actors—for which his qualifications are unknown—and staging productions to give them stage experience. J. C. WILLIAMSON referred hopefuls to him and allowed him amateur rights to old plays. About this time Lytton also co-founded a theatrical journal, the *Playgoer*, which was incorporated into *Theatre* in 1904–05.

In his first tent seasons Lytton starred opposite his wife Madge Hope, who was famous for her height, beauty, musical voice and expensive wardrobe. Later he toured guest stars like LILY DAMPIER, Lottie Lyell, ROY REDGRAVE and ALFRED ROLFE. He also began to dramatise stories himself—*The Cup Winner* in 1907, *The Man They Could Not Hang* and *The Girl from Outback* in 1912 and *The Waybacks at Home and in Town* in 1915. He filmed the first two with success, and *The Waybacks* became both a long-running stage show and a popular film, made in 1918 and re-released in 1925. Lytton, who was always based in Sydney, registered copyright on a play, *The Singing Gold Diggers*, in 1933. He is last recorded in a small role in the 1936 film *The Flying Doctor*, but much of his career is unknown. ❦*Richard Fotheringham*

further reading
LYTTON, PHILIP. The drama under canvas. *Theatre* (Sydney) 1 December 1915.

Keith Macartney

Amateur actor, producer. Born 18 July 1903 in Melbourne. Studied at Universities of Melbourne and Cambridge. Acted in George Rylands's early productions at Cambridge. Returned to University of Melbourne as lecturer in English 1936. Associate professor of drama and English for many years. Co-founded Tin Alley Players 1939. Formed Barnstormers revue group. Died 21 March 1971 in Melbourne.

In the 20 years straddling the Second World War Keith Macartney was a dominating figure in amateur theatre in Melbourne. After the death of GREGAN MCMAHON in 1941, he kept the works of Maxwell Anderson, Anton Chekhov, Sean O'Casey, Clifford Odets, Eugene O'Neill, J. B. Priestley, George Bernard Shaw and others alive for Melbourne audiences. His notable productions with the TIN ALLEY PLAYERS in the Union Theatre at the University of Melbourne included *Macbeth* in 1947 with GEORGE FAIRFAX in the title-role. Macartney himself gave memorable performances as Puck in *A Midsummer Night's Dream* in 1942, Joxer in O'Casey's *Juno and the Paycock* in 1944 and Firs in Chekhov's *The Cherry Orchard* in 1962. In many ways he prepared the ground for the foundation in 1953 of the Union Theatre Repertory Company, which became the MELBOURNE THEATRE COMPANY. He also formed a group called the Barnstormers, unique in Melbourne for their sophistication, who played revue sketches for charity.

Macartney was gifted at teaching people to speak verse meaningfully and musically. With the help of professional figures such as DOLIA RIBUSH and IRENE MITCHELL, he trained several generations of student actors. Many of them went straight into the professional theatre, including Charles Colville, Robin Cuming, GEORGE FAIRFAX, Anne Harvey, Alan Money and Gerda Nicholson. Macartney, an expert musician, was at his piano when he died. ❦*David Bradley*

Andrew MacCunn

Composer, conductor. Born 1883 at Greenock (Scotland). Trained as a concert pianist. Came to Australia with London Gaiety Company 1904 and stayed until 1907. Returned 1910. Musical director for J. C. Williamson's 1910–61. Died 1966 in Melbourne. Younger brother of composer Hamish MacCunn.

Andrew MacCunn conducted—always without a score—most of the big musical-comedy hits between 1910, when he returned to Australia to conduct *Our Miss Gibbs* for J. C. Williamson's, and 1961, when he retired. He was a brilliant musician and a strict disciplinarian in all things musical on stage. As a young pianist he accompanied the famous contralto Louise Kirkby Lunn in a recital for Queen Victoria. During his first stay in Australia, in 1906 he wrote a play without words, *The Gardener's Dream*, with the actor GEORGE LAURI. From 1911 to 1920, MacCunn wrote songs, incidental music, ballets and marches for pantomimes and revues. His ballet music for *Puss In Boots* in 1912 incorporated music from current stage successes such as *The Quaker Girl* and *Nightbirds*. Other shows for which he wrote music included *Sinbad the Sailor* in 1911, *The Forty Thieves* in 1913, *Goody Two Shoes* in 1918 and *The Passing Show* in 1920. MacCunn also wrote songs with Claude McKay, including 'Keep me in your heart' and 'God send you back to me' for DOROTHY BRUNTON in 1917. ❦*Alwyn Capern*

Donald Macdonald

Actor, dramatist. Born in Sydney. Acted at Independent Theatre and Music Hall Theatre Restaurant, and in Phillip Street revues in Sydney. Acted in London in 1970s. Returned to Australia 1974.

Donald Macdonald was well known as a stylish comic actor when the ENSEMBLE THEATRE COMPANY gave the premiere of his play *Caravan* in Sydney on 13 August 1983. It was an unfailingly amusing situation comedy, set in a caravan big enough for two fortyish married couples and their almost-40 friend, who has a new romance with a 22-year-old. Age-gap complications, a little adultery and verbal interplay rapidly made *Caravan* one of the most successful local comedies. It was produced throughout Australia, in New Zealand and, in 1991, on an English provincial tour. Macdonald did not repeat its success with *Bathroom*, a farce which he directed for the MARIAN STREET THEATRE COMPANY in November 1985. Since then Macdonald has continued acting. He drew praise as Gareth the confused husband in Alma de Groen's *The Girl Who Saw Everything* for the SYDNEY THEATRE COMPANY in 1992. ❦*John West*

published play
Caravan (1983). Sydney: Currency Press 1983.

Fred MacDonald

Actor. Sometimes Macdonald. Born 1895. Acted on stage and in films *c.*1910–*c.*1940. Died 5 October 1968 in Sydney.

Fred MacDonald created Dave in the stage adaptation of Steele Rudd's *ON OUR SELECTION* on 4 May 1912 and played the role for most of the next 30 years. His monotonously drawling Dave, rolling along with knees and elbows turned out, was the quintessential slow-witted country bumpkin, though the character sometimes demonstrated shrewd bush common sense. MacDonald played thinly disguised variants on the role in other bush comedies. On the screen he played Dave in four sound films based on Rudd's characters and the remarkably similar Jim Hayseed in three silent films for Beaumont Smith. He acted with the Kate Howarde Company and spent some time with the ALLAN WILKIE SHAKESPEAREAN COMPANY, playing Snug in *A Midsummer Night's Dream* in 1921. An obituary described the unmarried MacDonald as the 'life associate of Richard Sydney Handel'. ❦*Delyse Anthony, Richard Fotheringham*

further reading
PIKE, ANDREW and ROSS COOPER. *Australian Film 1900-1977*. Melbourne: Oxford University Press 1980.

Duncan MacDougall

Actor, director, manager. Born 1878 in Scotland. Came to Sydney with family 1887. Taught elocution and worked as bookseller. Went to England 1905. Worked in repertory theatre in England. Worked as producer and manager in USA for seven years, associated with Provincetown Players and Eugene O'Neill. Returned to Australia 1920. Formed professional company which toured northern NSW before disbanding in Brisbane 1922. Founded Playbox Society (Sydney) 1923. Ran Playbox Art Theatre at various premises in Sydney, 1925–31. Died 1953.

In the 1920s Duncan MacDougall produced important avant-garde plays in Sydney, often within months of their first season overseas. The first was Eugene O'Neill's 1922 play *The Hairy Ape* at the St James Hall on 12 November 1923, with MacDougall as director and leading actor for the Playbox Society. Reviews were generally encouraging but few critics understood the expressionist style and the play's content and 'coarse' dialogue shocked most people. In August 1924 a NSW politician accused the Playbox Society of 'assisting the communistic movement' by producing Ernst Toller's *Masses and Man*. He thereby increased audiences for the play. Critics were outraged because MacDougall played the leading female role. He typically played leading parts although he was unsuited to most of them. Reviewers' opinions on his acting varied, but he was always praised in character roles.

MacDougall formed the Playbox Society for production of Australian as well as European expressionist drama and he campaigned unceasingly for an Australian national theatre, to be developed from his group, where 'national drama' would be fostered and 'the best of foreign material' staged. As early as 1925 he canvassed government ministers, spoke in public and wrote articles for newspapers, but Sydney was not ready.

In 1925 the society moved its productions to 11 Rowe Street, where MacDougall had already opened a studio theatre and rehearsal rooms, and changed its name to the Playbox Theatre Circle. It proposed one performance a week for two months and a monthly evening of readings, lectures or discussion. MacDougall gave his most praised productions at the 80-seat Playbox Art Theatre in Rowe Street. They included *The Insect Play* by Josef and Karel Capek and *The Emperor Jones* by O'Neill in 1925, *Juno and the Paycock* by Sean O'Casey and *Spring's Awakening* by Frank Wedekind in 1927. The *Bulletin* thought O'Casey's play was a drama of 'muck and muddle' but 'the whole production was a genuine theatre sensation'.

In 1929 Playbox moved to Crown Street, near Oxford Street. The premises were larger, seating about 200, but the location was less salubrious and MacDougall lost followers. In 1930 several of his 11 productions were safe repertory fare and four were revivals of previous successes. Playbox moved again in 1931, to 150-seat premises at Young Street, near Circular Quay, previously occupied by JOAN AND BETTY RAYNER's Theatre of Youth. Its last major production was Marc Connelly's *Green Pastures*, in which MacDougall, dressed in a top hat and frock coat, played God. The *Sydney Morning Herald* condemned his costume and his performance, saying he has 'failed totally to capture the symbolism, the mystic beauty and the spiritual exaltation of the script except in one small scene'. According to the actor EDWARD HOWELL, this production began the disintegration of Playbox. It gave its last performance in November 1931. MacDougall conducted public play readings—mainly farce and comedy—at 39 Rowe Street from May 1933. By mid-August he had moved to the Tom Thumb Theatre at 117 King Street, where he read old favourites such as *The Hairy Ape* and *Juno and the Paycock*. His theatrical activity seems to have ended in October 1933, when he read 'a fearless comedy' called *The Man they Buried*. ❦*Bronwyn Coy, Elizabeth Wright*

further reading
WRIGHT, ELIZABETH. Duncan MacDougall—A man of theatre. University of NSW honours thesis 1981.

Frances Mackay

Actor. Member of Barnett Levey's first Sydney company as Mrs Weston. Lived with actor Angus Mackay and called herself Mrs Mackay from August 1833. Acted in Tasmania 1834. Sydney 1835. Hobart 1836–38. Married actor Gustavus Arabin. Acted as Mrs Arabin in Sydney 1838–40, Adelaide 1841, Launceston 1842. Ran away with actor Thomas Spencer Boyd 1842. Acted in Melbourne 1842–46.

Under various names, Frances Mackay performed in nearly all the major Australian theatres between 1832 and 1846, but the rest of her life is obscure. She played Dolly Mayflower in Douglas Jerrold's *Black-Eyed Susan* on the opening night of BARNETT LEVEY's theatre in the Royal Hotel in Sydney on 26 December 1832, as 'Mrs Weston', although she was married to Edward Laverty. He died in July 1833 and Levey offered her a special benefit. The couple appear to have been living apart, however, and by August the widow was calling herself Mrs Mackay in acknowledgment of her association with her colleague Angus Mackay. After disagreements with Levey, Frances Mackay left the company in November 1833.

The couple went to Hobart, where they joined SAMSON CAMERON's company in January 1834. The Mackays quarrelled with Cameron over playing on benefit nights and they were dismissed. They joined J. P. DEANE's rival Hobart company on 2 May 1834. In September the Mackays were in fights with others at a benefit night at Launceston. They set up their own company and played in Launceston and Hobart before returning to the Theatre Royal in Sydney at the end of the year.

Angus Mackay remained at the Theatre Royal but Frances did not appear there after May 1835. By October 1836 she was back in Hobart with JOHN MEREDITH's company. There she met GUSTAVUS ARABIN, recently arrived from London, and as Mrs Arabin she returned to Sydney to join the company at the new ROYAL VICTORIA THEATRE. She played Emilia to her husband's Othello on opening night in 1838. The Arabins left Sydney in November 1840 to join JOHN LAZAR's company in Adelaide. After it failed they joined F. B. WATSON's company in Launceston in June 1842.

In October 1842 Frances Arabin eloped to Melbourne with another actor, Thomas Spencer Boyd. She appeared at the Royal Victoria Theatre and the Queen's Theatre Royal in Melbourne from 1842 until 1845, and played a season at Geelong in 1844–45. In July 1845 Boyd was committed to an asylum after he had stabbed another actor on stage when his property pistol misfired. Frances worked hard to secure his release in May 1846. On 15 October 1846 she made what seems to have been her final appearance, at the Queen's Theatre for Boyd's benefit. ❦*Elizabeth Webby*

MacMahon Brothers

In the late 1880s MacMahon Brothers rivalled WILLIAMSON, GARNER AND MUSGROVE as the leading theatrical organisation in Australia. The principals were three brothers, James (c.1858–1915), Charles (c.1861–1917) and Joseph (c.1863–1918), all born in Bendigo (Vic.), sons of a contractor. James MacMahon began a theatrical agency in Bendigo in 1875 and ran it until 1877, when he went overseas, leaving his brothers in charge. He returned in 1884, after managing star actors like MARY SCOTT-SIDDONS and Henry Irving, and resumed his place as senior partner. The brothers toured many major stars and companies throughout eastern Australia and New Zealand.

In 1890 the MacMahons presented a Professor Douglas Archibald, who was demonstrating Thomas A. Edison's new phonograph, and James MacMahon decided to visit the USA. He returned in 1891 with contracts for tours by three spectacular and extremely expensive shows—the Evangeline Burlesque Company; a melodrama, *The County Fair*, with real horses racing on treadmills in front of a moving cyclorama; and an Irish sporting melodrama, *Honest Hearts and Willing Hands*, starring the world heavyweight boxing champion, JOHN L. SULLIVAN. These tours coincided with a disastrous financial depression, and the MacMahon company almost foundered. But James had made contact with Edison and he began to import and exhibit his inventions, including the Kinetoscope, a peepshow device that provided the first commercial form of motion pictures. MacMahon imported five of these in November 1894.

Late in 1896 James MacMahon opened a film show in Sydney. The *Bulletin* on 23 January 1897 was greatly impressed by the 'pictorial glitter' of 'a gorgeous coloured view of the great fountains at Versailles'. From then onwards the MacMahons progressively abandoned live theatre, except in New Zealand, where they were still touring plays like *The Kelly Gang* in 1907. They had their own cinemas in the major cities and they set up a film distribution agency. Charles MacMahon, who gradually became senior partner, also directed two early and successful feature films—*Robbery Under Arms* in 1907 and *For the Term of His Natural Life* in 1908. Their business later went into decline. ❦*Richard Fotheringham*

further reading
KINGSTON, CLAUDE. *It Don't Seem a Day Too Much*. Adelaide: Rigby 1971.
PIKE, ANDREW and ROSS COOPER. *Australian Film 1900–1977*. Melbourne: Oxford University Press 1980.
WILLIAMS, MARGARET. James and Charles MacMahon. *Australian Dictionary of Biography* 10. Melbourne University Press 1986.

Magic shows

Magicians began appearing in Australia during the first gold rushes. Many were itinerants who performed in small halls, but in 1855 GEORGE COPPIN brought the famous Wizard Jacobs from England to open his OLYMPIC THEATRE in Melbourne. The wizard's drawing power was so great that his seasons in Melbourne and other cities helped to launch Coppin on his long entrepreneurial career.

From then on the list of magicians who performed here reads like a review of London and New York theatres. It includes Robert Heller; vaudeville performers, such as Carl Hertz in 1892 and 1896 and Charles Morritt in 1897; drawing-room performers, such as Charles Bertram in 1901 and Max Malini in 1914; and comedy performers such as the sensational Le Roy, Talma and Bosco in 1905 and Carlton in 1907. Maskelyne and Devant, proprietors of the Egyptian Hall in London, sent out a touring company in 1908, with the society entertainer Owen Clark as the featured magician. Chung Ling Soo, whose real name was William Elsworth Robinson, amazed the public in 1909 with a spectacular Oriental show, unlike any seen here previously. In 1910 HARRY RICKARDS brought out Harry Houdini, the most famous magician of the day, to perform feats of escapology. In Melbourne 20 000 people watched Houdini jump manacled into the Yarra River and escape. Apart from the famous, many other magicians played in Australia so successfully that the money they made enabled them to establish themselves at the top overseas. Examples are Harry Kellar, here in 1876, and Howard Thurston, who triumphed in 1905. Cardini, later the world's most famous card manipulator, played the Tivoli circuit in 1923.

In contrast to close-up performers who present effects with small items such as cards, coins, thimbles, illusionists present large effects such as Sawing in Half or the Vanishing Lady. Horace Goldin, the Royal Illusionist, presented the first fast-moving illusion show in 1916. A host of big names followed until the 1960s, including John Calvert, Carter the Great, Chang, Chefalo, Dante, the GREAT LEVANTE, MAURICE ROOKLYN, Sorcar and Virgil. All presented elaborate productions with colourful scenery and many assistants and ballet girls.

Because Australian magicians saw the world's best perform here, they were able to aspire to great heights themselves. Some who established themselves in Australia were also tremendously successful overseas. The Great Levante, the billiard-ball manipulator Rooklyn, the mental telepathists Arthur and Helen Buckley, the escapologist MURRAY and the illusionists CARMO—who used live animals—and JEAN HUGARD all became 'greats' in the profession overseas. On the other hand, CHARLES WALLER, author of original magical effects, never left Australia but was known around the world for his writings.

When variety theatres closed in the 1960s, magicians changed their style and adapted to television, and performed in clubs and cabaret shows. Magicians who succeed in entertaining audiences today must call upon acting ability, humour and pace. ❦*Gerald Taylor*

Magpie Theatre Company

Theatre-in-education branch of State Theatre (Adelaide), founded in 1978. **artistic directors** 1978 Roger Chapman. 1979–83 Malcolm Moore. 1984–85 Geoffrey Rush. 1986–88 Chris Johnson. 1989–90 Angela Chaplin. 1991–93 Steven Gration. 1994– Neill Gladwin. **first production** *Dunno's Journey* by the company, 1978. Director: Marilyn Allen.

A conscientious and often innovative company, Magpie has represented the best in theatre-in-education, maintaining strenuous performing schedules and high production standards. It has formed relationships with the playwrights DOROTHY HEWETT, RICHARD TULLOCH and, especially, DAVID HOLMAN that have produced memorable works. Magpie grew out of youth activities run by the South Australian Theatre Company for ten years until 1977. In that year the company employed Roger Chapman to carry out a reorganisation and early in 1978 it launched Magpie with Chapman as artistic director.

His successor, Malcolm Moore directed Hewett's *Golden Valley* in 1981, and Magpie performed its first play by Holman, *The Disappeared*, in 1982. Hewett's *Song of the Seals* and *Year 9 Are Animals*, written and directed by Tulloch, followed in 1983. *No Worries*, written by Holman and directed by Chris Johnson, was a hit in the 1984 Adelaide Festival and remains one of Magpie's finest works.

The Small Poppies in 1986, researched and written by Holman while playwright-in-residence, was among many lively productions during Geoffrey Rush's term as artistic director. Johnson continued the association with Holman and directed *Solomon and the Big Cat* in 1986 and *Beauty and the Beast* in 1988, as well as *A Sporting Chance* by Katherine Thomson in 1987. Robert Draffin directed Tulloch's adaptation of *Hating Alison Ashley* in 1988 and Angela Chaplin's term as artistic director included *Couple of Kids* by Julianne O'Brien, *Mimini's Voices* by Eva Johnson and *The Arbor* by Andrea Dunbar in 1990 and *White Paper Flowers* by Mary Hickson in 1991. Steven Gration's production of *Funerals and Circuses*, written by Roger Bennett with music by Paul Kelly, was among the most admired shows in the 1992 Adelaide Festival. ❦*Murray Bramwell*

Will Mahoney

Comedian, manager. Born 5 February 1894 at Helena (Montana, USA). Made debut as eight-year-old dancer at Spokane (Washington). Became vaudeville star, appearing in major revues and variety in New York and London. Came to Australia in 1938 with wife, singer Evie Hayes, 1938. Managed Cremorne Theatre, Brisbane, in late 1940s. Died 8 February 1967 in Melbourne.

When Will Mahoney came to Australia in 1938 he had made himself one of the best-known performers in American vaudeville with a unique act that combined comedy, song and eccentric dancing. It included a speciality in which he danced on the keys of a xylophone, tapping out a tune. Mahoney appeared in major revues and variety in New York and London during the 1920s and 1930s, after working briefly with his brother Frank in a double act. He teamed with the singer Evie Hayes in 1933, and they appeared at the London Palladium in 1935. Three years later they married and came to Australia on their honeymoon. They performed on the Tivoli circuit, and in 1942 they leased the Cremorne Theatre in Brisbane with Bob Geraghty. Mahoney starred in the 1939 Cinesound film *Come Up Smiling*, retitled *Ants in his Pants*. He appeared on stage in *Finian's Rainbow* and *The Man Who Never Died* in New York in 1955 and 1958 respectively. In Australia he was in the musicals *A Funny Thing Happened on the Way to the Forum* in 1964 and *Funny Girl* in 1966. He died during the run of *Funny Girl*. ❦*Frank Van Straten*

further reading
Crampton, John. *And I Loves Ya Back Evie Hayes*. Sydney: Collins Angus and Robertson 1992.

Mainstreet Theatre Company

Professional community theatre company in Naracoorte (SA), founded in 1983 in Millicent (SA) by South East Performing Arts Collective. Incorporated as professional company 1985. Moved to Naracoorte 1987. **directors** 1985 Ronald Branscombe. 1985–89 Geoff Crowhurst. 1989–90 P. P. Cranney. 1990–91 Catherine Fitzgerald. 1992– Mary McMenamin. **first production** *087* by P. P. Cranney.

Mainstreet has commissioned works that have had lives outside the company—such as Richard Tulloch's *Talking to Grandma While the World Goes By* and Bob Maza's *The Keepers*—and it has instigated less widely known but interesting community theatre. One of the basic forms this has taken is small-cast touring shows. These include collaborations between the writer P. P. Cranney and the director Geoff Crowhurst produced under the Australia Council's Art and Working Life incentive program with trade unionists—timber workers in *Run of the Mill* in 1985, school teachers in *Chalkie* in 1986, meatworkers in *Mixed Kill* in 1988, and municipal workers in *All Those in Favour* in 1989.

The other basic form has been large-scale facilitated plays for amateur casts ranging from schools (*087* in 1985, *Catch that Dove* in 1987, *Taken for Granted* in 1989) to community groups (*The Black Sheep* with the Naracoorte Drama Club in 1988). The program has been filled out with small shows designed for schools or community audiences, such as *Talking to Grandma*, *The Keepers* and Cranney's *Busted*, *Handmade* and *Nonno's Luck*. All but large-cast community shows were toured throughout southeast South Australia, and in some cases far beyond. Mainstreet consistently took its youth shows to the Come Out Youth Arts Festival in Adelaide, where they were generally highly regarded.

The Cranney–Crowhurst collaboration especially distinguished the company. Both men became skilled in constructing social-realist plays through careful community consultation, particularly with trade unionists and young people. Catherine Fitzgerald maintained Art and Working Life plays with productions of Anne Brookman's *Wild about Work*, and Elizabeth Mansutti's *Tipping the Scales*, which is about teachers. Mainstreet has always attempted to offer resources to the community and Fitzgerald expanded this through skills workshops and facilitatory work. This resulted in a shift towards residencies and large-scale community shows, such as *Seasprite it's Dynamite*, by the writer Nick Hughes and young people in Kingston South East in 1991, and *Ladies Bring a Plate*, written and directed by Fitzgerald with women in Naracoorte in 1992. Mary McMenamin has extended this work.

Mainstreet has always struggled under the combined pressures of poverty and the exigencies of project funding by the performing arts board of the Australia Council. This has resulted in a high turnover in membership, and difficulties in the long-term planning and development essential to community theatre. Additionally, Mainstreet, unlike companies in big cities, has never been able to count upon a politically sympathetic audience. This has produced both problems and side-benefits. In particular, Cranney and Crowhurst, in their work with trade unionists, were forced to develop theatrical forms that could play to general audiences which were out of sympathy with their own political leanings. This led them to develop styles that extend beyond the agitprop-based work of some of their big-city colleagues and to become cautious and efficient in community consultation. ❦*David Watt*

further reading
Watt, David. Mainstreet—Making theatre in the country. *Meanjin* 50/2-3 (Melbourne 1991).

Eduardo and Giulia Majeroni

Italian actors. Married c.1868. Came to Australia with Adelaide Ristori's company 1875. Stayed and acted in English from 1876. Parents of Mario and Giorgio Majeroni, actors and managers.

Eduardo Majeroni. Born 1840 in Bergamo (Austria). Civil engineer. Fought in Italian wars of independence 1859–66. Joined Ristori company c.1867. Managed theatres in Australia from 1876. Died 20 October 1891 in Sydney.

Giulia Tessero Majeroni. Born c.1848. Father was Ristori's brother. Trained in Ristori company. Died 8 August 1903 in Melbourne.

Trained in the restrained Italian classical tradition that required extensive historical and biographical research into each character, Eduardo and Giulia Majeroni came to Australia in 1875 as leading actors in ADELAIDE RISTORI's company. They stayed to give acclaimed renditions of many great roles translated from the Italian, German, and French repertoires. The doyen of Melbourne critics, J. E. NEILD, thought their work was 'an example of the best kind of truthful stage-representation'. He greatly admired Giulia's 'emphasised repose' in *A Living Statue* and credited her with the most realistic death scene he had ever witnessed. She based a novel of the same title on *A Living Statue*.

Eduardo Majeroni spoke English on stage for the first time on 24 April 1876 at the Theatre Royal in Sydney, in the title-role of *The Old Corporal* by Enrico Bellotti. The *Sydney Morning Herald* thought his acting vivid, graphic, and 'painfully realistic', but found his pronunciation 'faulty'. It modified this to 'continental' when Giulia joined him at the Royal Victoria Theatre for her English-speaking debut on 21 July. The Majeronis insisted on high standards in all aspects of their presentations. For the season at the Royal Victoria they replaced the stalls benches with chairs and decorated the proscenium with potted palms. Here and later their sets were considered 'pretty' and their orchestral accompaniments 'refined'. On several occasions local Italians used their performances as occasions for affirming patriotic fervour, presenting them with bouquets and streamers in the Italian national colours, but their admirers also included the governors of NSW and Victoria, and reports of crowded houses were common.

The Majeronis' lives were not happy, however. Both suffered from ill-health, Eduardo possibly as a result of his brief but supposedly gallant service in Garibaldi's army. He moved unsuccessfully into the business side of the profession, managing the Bijou Theatre and then the Theatre Royal in Melbourne and finally the Opera House in Sydney. When he died from tuberculosis in 1891 Giulia was herself too ill from chronic influenza to attend his funeral. She did not act again. In a bitter interview published in *Table Talk* on 3 April 1902, she lamented the devaluing of artists who stayed in the colonies, and the consequent lack of opportunities for her sons Mario and Giorgio on the local stage. Mario briefly joined the Brough Comedy Company, and at the time of their mother's death both sons were managing their own small troupe in New Zealand. ❦*Richard Fotheringham, Harold Love*

Majestic Theatre

Theatre in King William Street, Adelaide, opened in 1856 as **White's Rooms**. Architect: George Kingston. Altered to form **Garner's Theatre**, seating 1326, 1880. Renamed **Hudson's Bijou Theatre** 1892. Altered and reopened as **Tivoli Theatre** 20 June 1900. Architects: Backhouse and Backhouse, in association with English and Soward. Renamed **Rickards's New Tivoli Theatre** 1901. Renamed **Star Theatre** for films in 1913. Rebuilt and returned to live shows as **Majestic Theatre** 1916. Architects: Williams and Good. Became **Celebrity Theatre Restaurant** 1967–69. Returned to films as **Warner Theatre** 1969. Demolished 1981.

In 1856 an Adelaide architect designed a development consisting of two shops, offices and a large assembly room for concerts and balls. The front part of the building became the Shades Hotel and Restaurant. The entrepreneur ARTHUR GARNER took over the hall in 1880, added a dress circle with rear amphitheatre and generally remodelled the interior to produce Garner's Theatre. Thomas Hudson renamed it Hudson's Bijou Theatre in 1892 for his vaudeville acts, which within a few years included moving pictures. HARRY RICKARDS leased the theatre in June 1900 and the architects Backhouse and Backhouse remodelled the theatre for him, adding a sliding roof. After Rickards's death, the theatre was renamed the Star Theatre for films in 1913.

FULLERS' leased the theatre for vaudeville and instigated a major rebuilding in 1916. A fourth storey was added to the hotel and both the theatre and the hotel were widened and renamed Majestic. Only fragments of the original walling of White's Rooms were retained. The new auditorium was typical of small intimate theatres of the time. Two banks of private boxes, two boxes high, were adjacent to the proscenium at each end of the orchestra pit. The single tier above the stalls extended between the boxes on each side in a tight horseshoe. In 1928 Fullers' bought the theatre together with the hotel and other buildings in the block between Grenfell and Pirie Streets.

During the 1930s Greater Union showed films at the Majestic. Films and live shows alternated after 1942, when Fullers' again took over the theatre. After a period as the Celebrity Theatre Restaurant in the late 1960s it became a cinema again in 1969 as the Warner Theatre. The historic theatre building, only slightly modified since 1916 and in good condition, was demolished for a multistorey office block in spite of efforts in 1980 to save it. ❦*Ross Thorne*

Makassar Reef

Play in two acts by Alex Buzo. **premiere** 23 March 1978, Russell Street Theatre, Melbourne, by Melbourne Theatre Company. Cast: Max Cullen, Liddy Clark, Sandy Gore, Gerard Maguire, Monica Maughan, Monroe Reimers, Saviour Sammut, Rod Williams. Designer: Tony Tripp. Director: Aarne Neeme. **published** Sydney: Currency Press 1979.

One of ALEX BUZO's best plays, *Makassar Reef* is superficially a romantic tale of westerners adrift in the tropics, with a subplot of drug smuggling and political intrigue. Beneath the surface is a haunting study of people who have fled the dissatisfaction of their past lives and are trying to take stock of themselves in a steamy tropical retreat, before working up the courage to make the compromises necessary to go on. The central action revolves around Weeks Brown and Beth Fleetwood who, after years of living together and working successfully in Australia, have decided to have a honeymoon and then get married. In Makassar they meet two self-protective independent travellers—Wendy, bringing her daughter Camilla 'home' to Australia after many years away, and Perry, a lone sailor fleeing from some undefined past there. Weeks and Beth have their 'last flicker out of bounds' with these two, but the play ends with a rather grim reaffirmation of their commitment to each other. The subplot involves a gloriously rascally Dutch smuggler, a corrupt Indonesian official and a young radical journalist who has designs on Camilla. The play is haunted by powerful images of strength and vulnerability, and contains some beautiful scenes of loving human contact and loss. Unfortunately, it has been rather neglected by major companies since its original production. David Hill, later managing director of the Australian Broadcasting Corporation, saw himself in the character of Weeks Brown and began litigation for defamation. As a result an edition of *Pol* magazine containing the play in 1978 was pulped. The matter was settled out of court. ❦*John McCallum*

Billy Maloney

Comedian, producer. Born 1895 in Melbourne. Turned to theatre after six years as professional jockey in New Zealand. Produced and starred in musical comedy, pantomime, variety and revue in Australia in 1920s. Went to United Kingdom in 1930s. Died 7 July 1957 in Arbroath (Scotland).

When Billy Maloney appeared at a state banquet for the Prince of Wales in Sydney in 1920 the prince presented him with a silver stick. From then Maloney was billed as 'the man with the silver stick'. He appeared frequently on the TIVOLI CIRCUIT and he was especially popular at the Cremorne Theatre in Brisbane in the early 1920s. In association with Lou Handman, a visiting American composer, he wrote the song 'Smithy' in 1928 to celebrate Charles Kingsford Smith's trans-Pacific flight. Maloney's career waned in the 1930s. He went to the United Kingdom, where he appeared on television in 1939 and toured in variety. Then he made his home in Edinburgh, where he produced small revues. ❦*Frank Van Straten*

Don Mamouney

Director. Born 1945 in Bendigo (Vic.). Trained at Ensemble Theatre School (Sydney) and Mountview Theatre School (United Kingdom). Co-founded Sidetrack Theatre Company (Sydney) 1979; artistic director 1979–86, 1990–. Artistic director of Fortune Capital Theatre (Canberra), 1986–87.

Don Mamouney, a founder of COMMUNITY THEATRE in Australia, was the first Australian theatrical artist to found a company that practised multiculturalism in subject matter, casting and choice of audience. He did his pioneering work especially with youth and adult working-class audiences in the western suburbs of Sydney and he now builds on this to address everyday experience in contemporary ways. The sources of Mamouney's creative work include political and cultural analysis and theory, and a commitment to basing the development of theatrical form on the performer rather than the text. Mamouney makes his theatrical works in collaboration with ethnically diverse casts, often employing languages beside English, and using group research and ensemble improvisation. They involve music and sonic technology, and in recent years the composer and sound designer Peter Wells has been a key collaborator with Mamouney.

In his earlier works Mamouney emphasised issues of ethnicity, culture and power, usually employing a form of narrative, moving towards 'magic realism'. Examples are *Down Under the Thumb*, *Out from Under*, *Loco*, *The Number One Thing*, *The Serpent's Contract*, *Just for the Buzz of It* and *Adios Cha-Cha*. Since 1986 he has been an iconoclastic explorer of theatrical form, informed by contemporary theory, especially concerning representation, subjectivity and desire, and drawing on postcolonial and feminist criticism in depicting subjection and power. He also experiments with new formal relationships with the audience in his works, which are generally non-narrative, poetically organised collages of action sequences and physical imagery. They include *The Drunken Boat* (with Guillaume Brugman), *Heaven, Idol* (with Nigel Kellaway), *Manichino*, *The Refugee*, *Sweet Laughter* and *Whispers in the Heart*. Mamouney has also directed plays from texts by authors including Assad Abdi, P. P. CRANNEY, DAVID HOLMAN and Graham Pitts. He directed Anton Chekhov's *The Cherry Orchard* and Molière's *Tartuffe* for Fortune Capital Theatre in Canberra. ❦*Tom Burvill*

further reading
Decentring the theatre—Don Mamouney interviewed by David Watt and Jenny Lee. *Meanjin* 50/2–3 (Melbourne 1991).

The Man From Mukinupin

Musical play in two acts. **libretto** Dorothy Hewett. **music** Jim Cotter. **premiere** 31 August 1979, Playhouse, Perth, by National Theatre Company. Cast: Margaret Ford, Noni Hazlehurst, Richard Tulloch. Director: Stephen Barry. **published** Sydney: Currency Press 1985.

Often said to be DOROTHY HEWETT's finest play, *The Man From Mukinupin* is certainly her biggest box-office success. Since its premiere by the NATIONAL THEATRE COMPANY, which commissioned it for the Western Australian sesquicentennial celebrations in 1979, it has been staged by state companies in Adelaide, Melbourne and Sydney and revived by smaller companies. It shows the lives of residents and transients in a mythical Western Australian country town between 1912 and 1920, years in which the outside world impinged on Australia through the First World War. The life of Mukinupin is seen by day and night, each of the principal daytime characters having its equivalent at night. The daytime sequences portray the world of everyday commerce and courtship with the lightheartedness of musical comedy, but the night-time scenes create a surreal dream-world which links the town's inner life to much older rites and psychic forces and exposes layers of suppressed sexuality and guilt, especially over the crime of a massacre of Aborigines by Mukinupin's most respected citizens. The dominant style is that of musical comedy, with the main characters each having their own number, but the superficial simplicity is combined with evocations of Shakespeare—through quotation and burlesqued performance—Biblical language, old-time melodrama, and old English pastoral rituals. The fusing of high and popular cultural traditions is characteristic of Hewett's work. ❦*Margaret Williams*

Management

Theatrical management can hardly be said to have begun in Australia until the 1830s. Next to nothing is known about the way ROBERT SIDAWAY ran his theatre in Sydney from 1796, but he certainly had an actor-manager, John

Sparrow, to run the enterprise from day to day. Once BARNETT LEVEY had installed an acting company in the THEATRE ROYAL in October 1833 he seems to have relied on his acting manager, CONRAD KNOWLES, to keep things going. After Levey's death in October 1837 his widow Sarah tried her hand at management, but she closed the little theatre just before JOSEPH WYATT opened his big new ROYAL VICTORIA THEATRE opened on 26 March 1838 with a performance of *Othello*. GUSTAVUS ARABIN played the title-role and a Sydney favourite, ELIZA WINSTANLEY played Desdemona. These two actors, Mrs Arabin (formerly FRANCES MACKAY) and JOHN LAZAR headed the stock company of the Royal Victoria for some years. The actors in a stock company were designated according to the kinds of parts in which they specialised. For example, the tragedian played roles such as Hamlet, but also appeared in comedy; the old man played Sir Peter Teazle in R. B. Sheridan's *The School for Scandal*; the old woman played Juliet's nurse, the heavy father played tyrants and melodrama villains; the heavy woman played Lady Macbeth; the juvenile leads played young lovers and young heroes and heroines; the juvenile tragedian played Macduff in *Macbeth*; the low comedian played the Gravedigger in *Hamlet*, clowns and minor roles in tragedy; the walking lady and walking gentlemen played secondary leads in comedy; the general utility played minor roles in anything; and the supernumerary was a walk-on with no lines, and often no pay.

The pool of acting talent was small and actors were prone to disagreements and feuds, which sometimes led them to split off and take other premises, suitable or not, to stage rival attractions. Theatre proprietors like Wyatt in Sydney and ANNE CLARKE in Hobart had to make the long return voyage to England to engage new talent. Some who arrived as performers became managers, such as GEORGE COPPIN. He arrived in Sydney with his companion Maria Watkins Burroughs, known as Mrs Coppin, on 10 March 1843 and that night they met Wyatt at the Royal Victoria. Wyatt rejected a flat salary as too high. Coppin proposed a profit-sharing arrangement for one month. Wyatt agreed and the Coppins were in. Maria's acting and George's comic genius brought them great success.

This sort of arrangement—visiting stars appearing with a theatre's stock company—became regular in the Australian colonies as they lost the taint of penal settlement. Actors of greater stature began to arrive, not just losers, no-hopers and those with some reason to work in a far-off land. A theatre could stage its own productions with its own substantial stock company until a visiting star blew in. Sydney, Melbourne, Hobart and Adelaide were the major show towns, and in provincial centres between them there were nice pickings for travelling actors. Once the gold rushes began in the 1850s thespians from Great Britain and North America came to seek gold, but not by digging.

Coppin based himself in Melbourne and sent out touring companies. He liked to buy talent himself, but over the years he established agencies to engage artists for Australia. His man in San Francisco in September 1875 engaged two local stars, J. C. WILLIAMSON and his wife MAGGIE MOORE, and asserted that they would be 'the most profitable engagement ever made for you by me'. The couple's tour in 1874-75 made fortunes for them and Coppin. In 1879 Williamson was back in Australia as an entrepreneur rather than visiting star. Other managerial talents were also emerging—ARTHUR GARNER with his first-class London Comedy Company, and GEORGE MUSGROVE, unsurpassed in his feeling for musical theatre. These three men were the most powerful in Australian theatre by 1882 and from that year until 1890 they combined in WILLIAMSON, GARNER AND MUSGROVE. They controlled theatres in Adelaide, Brisbane, Melbourne, Sydney and had entrée into Perth and cities in New Zealand. They achieved a kind of theatrical federation of the Australasian colonies at a time when politicians were just beginning to talk about their version. Smaller managements were intimidated by the dominance of the triumvirate, but they became monopolists too if they became powerful enough. HARRY RICKARDS's rise to predominance in vaudeville in the 1890s was typical.

Theatrical 'federation' thus replaced the old stock-company system. Big Brother had taken over the best of the Australian theatres and a central organisation now sent complete companies on tour to the principal moneymaking centres. On the whole this worked for the general benefit of the profession—fewer bands of thespians were stranded far from home by fly-by-night managers—and it gave the public higher standards of performance.

The men of the triumvirate ended their partnership and formed new ones, and others arose to supplant them. J. AND N. TAIT LTD, dominant in the concert hall, became a power in the theatre. From 1918 the TAIT BROTHERS experimented with allowing GREGAN MCMAHON, who directed their professional successes, to present occasional matinée performances of the offbeat works that were his real love, sometimes with professionals. The experiment lasted for about ten years and gave some legitimacy to the efforts of the usually unrewarded amateur tillers of the theatrical field. The Taits became hugely powerful by merging with J. C. WILLIAMSON's in 1920, even though competing managements of varying strength, such as FULLERS', tempered their power. Not content with dominance in Australasia, the Firm, as J. C. Williamson's was known, toured its companies to SOUTH AFRICA and even took on London. The Great Depression put a stop to such expansion. The professional theatre pursued a policy of 'steady as she goes', the entertainment became blander and exposition of the new and challenging was more and more left in the sometimes shaky hands of AMATEUR THEATRE. *John West*

Since the Second World War

After the Second World War the federal government gave financial and moral support to generating an increase in interest in the arts. Ben Chifley, Prime Minister from 1945 to 1949, removed the ENTERTAINMENTS TAX from admission charges; established an Education Department committee to examine proposals for a national theatre; supported the British Council's policies of touring lecturers, exhibitions, orchestras and performers; and recognised the establishment of the Council for the Encouragement of Music and the Arts, forerunner of the ARTS COUNCIL OF AUSTRALIA.

Alongside this government support were the entrepreneurial managements—Aztec Services, Carroll-Fuller, the TIVOLI CIRCUIT, J. C. WILLIAMSON's, HARRY WREN. Imported musicals, in which Australians performed only supporting roles, predominated among their tours from 1948 to 1955. A company headed by BENJAMIN FULLER toured the OLD VIC

Theatre Company from London in 1948, and in 1949 and 1953 J. C. Williamsons' presented the Shakespeare Memorial Theatre Company from Stratford-upon-Avon. Since 1965 the entrepreneur MICHAEL EDGLEY has regularly toured the Moscow Circus and other overseas companies throughout Australia.

The AUSTRALIAN ELIZABETHAN THEATRE TRUST was formed in 1956 to develop national drama, opera and ballet companies. It co-ordinated funding from federal, state and local governments, private donations and subscriptions, and it co-operated with entrepreneurs and theatre managers by providing venues and co-producing tours such as those of the Sutherland-Williamson International Grand Opera Company in 1965 and the Athens Drama Company's production of Aristophanes's *Lysistrata* in 1966. The Trust nurtured development by subsidising theatrical performance under the charter of professionalism for actors, directors, writers and designers. It directly formed the TRUST PLAYERS in 1959 and the OLD TOTE THEATRE COMPANY in 1963 and established the South Australian Theatre Company in 1965. It also acted as catalyst in the foundation of other state drama companies.

The Trust lost its subsidising role when the Australian Council for the Arts was founded in 1968 to provide opportunities for development of artistic talent, professional employment of Australian artists, community appreciation through higher artistic standards, and administrative and training arrangements to ensure the development of the arts. In 1975 the council and advisory bodies covering visual arts, literature, composers, film and television were amalgamated to form the AUSTRALIA COUNCIL, a statutory body that advises the federal government on development of the arts. A company subsidised by the Australia Council must have a board of elected or appointed directors, which makes policy and is accountable for subsidy. The general manager and artistic director are responsible for managing operations and artistic planning and production.

Other professional companies, semiprofessional companies and co-operatives have existed concurrently with the major subsidised companies. The JOHN ALDEN COMPANY presented Shakespeare and other classics between 1952 and 1961. The Playgoer's Co-operative Ltd produced the PHILLIP STREET REVUES in Sydney from 1954 to 1963. The ENSEMBLE THEATRE COMPANY in Sydney has been professional since 1958. The La Mama Company in Melbourne made collective decisions from 1967 to 1969, when it became the AUSTRALIAN PERFORMING GROUP. Members of the GRIN AND TONIC THEATRE TROUPE under Bryan Nason lived in commune style as they toured Shakespeare and classics to schools in Queensland.

From the early 1980s boards and managers in non-profit theatre have been required to run theatre companies as businesses with artistic goals. Contemporary theatre managements must compete with commercial entrepreneurs such as Cameron Mackintosh, whose huge budgets and marketing attract audiences by the planeload to shows such as *Cats* and *The Phantom of the Opera*. Future development depends on successful management without substantial government patronage. ❦*Jennifer Radbourne*

further reading
CARGHER, JOHN. *Opera and Ballet in Australia*. Sydney: Cassell 1977.
FITTON, DORIS. *Not Without Dust and Heat*. Sydney: Harper and Row 1981.
PARSONS, PHILIP (ed.). *Shooting the Pianist—The role of government in the arts*. Sydney: Currency Press 1987.
RADBOURNE, JENNIFER. Commonwealth arts administration—an historical perspective 1945–1990. University of Queensland PhD thesis 1992.
ROWSE, TIM. *Arguing the Arts*. Melbourne: Penguin 1985.

Marian Street Theatre Company

Professional dramatic company in Killara, Sydney, founded in 1965 by Alexander Archdale as Community Theatre. Renamed Marian Street Theatre in January 1974, Northside Theatre Company 1984, Marian Street Theatre Company 1990. **venues** 1965–66 St Alban's Church hall, Lindfield. 1966– Marian Street Theatre. **artistic directors** 1965–70 Alexander Archdale. 1971–73 Peter Collingwood. 1973–80 Alastair Duncan. 1981–82 John Milson. 1982–89 John Krummel. 1990–91 Rodney Fisher, Noel Ferrier and John Rayment. 1991–92 Noel Ferrier. 1994–Rodney Fisher, Noel Ferrier and John Rayment. 1995 John Krummel. **first productions** *A Phoenix Too Frequent* by Christopher Fry and *Krapp's Last Tape* by Samuel Beckett, October 1965, St Alban's Church hall.

The subscription-based Marian Street Theatre Company was one of the most stable and financially self-sufficient theatrical companies in Australia in the 1980s, but its fortunes have been mixed in the 1990s. It presents contemporary commercial plays and an occasional affectionately revived classic. It has operated on the North Shore of Sydney as a non-profit company limited by guarantee since 1965, when the English actor ALEXANDER ARCHDALE and subscribers formed it as Community Theatre. The company began production at St Alban's Church hall in Lindfield in October 1965. It moved to adjacent Killara to stage *Romeo and Juliet* on 14 September 1966 in the Soldier's Memorial Hall in Marian Street.

This building, erected in 1906 as a community hall, suited the company and, with a secured bank loan and 500 paid-up members, it took a lease. The Ku-ring-gai Municipal Council provided funds to fit out the hall as a theatre and the NSW government gave $9500 to subsidise the first full season. The company opened on 27 March 1968 with John Osborne's *The Entertainer*, starring Archdale, JOAN BRUCE, ANNE HADDY and Max Meldrum. Early seasons included works by William Congreve, Noël Coward, Shakespeare and George Bernard Shaw, and some Australian works, including Colin Free's historical drama *Cannonade of Bells* in September 1968 and Anne Brooksbank's children's piece *Curtains for Cocky* in August 1969. *Oh Killara!* a topical revue in November 1969, had contributions by PETER BATEY, REG LIVERMORE and WILLIAM ORR.

Archdale retired in 1970. His successor as artistic director, PETER COLLINGWOOD had successes with *Caste* by Tom Robertson and *Mrs Warren's Profession* by Shaw. In 1972 AARNE NEEME revived Peter Kenna's THE SLAUGHTER OF ST TERESA'S DAY, giving GLORIA DAWN her first legitimate role as Oola Maguire. Alastair Duncan in 1973–80 gave the company a reputation for producing potted musicals. The auditorium was refurbished in December 1979, then completely reraked in 1982, with assistance from the local council and private donors. This gave it a capacity of 308.

JOHN KRUMMEL, who became artistic director in late 1982, changed the operating name to Northside Theatre Company. He took the company from financial precariousness to stability with successes including *84 Charing Cross Road* by Hugh Whitemore in 1983, Alan Ayckbourn's *Season's Greetings* in 1984, Eugene O'Neill's *Long Day's Journey into Night* in 1987, Whitemore's *Breaking the Code* in 1988 and Rudolf Besier's *The Barretts of Wimpole Street* in 1989. From 1990 to 1994 the company had a succession of artistic directors—and an artistic counsel—before it ceased trading. John Krummel was reappointed artistic director for a reopening in 1995.

The company began operating a theatre school in February 1968 but it did not achieve substantial success until Audrey Blaxland was appointed director in 1974. It evolved into the Marian Street Children's Theatre and Drama School and these institutions survive under the direction of Helen Martin. ❦*Wayne Harrison*

Marionette Theatre of Australia

Professional puppet-theatre company in Sydney, founded in 1965 by Peter Scriven with Arts Council of Australia as division of Australian Elizabethan Theatre Trust. Autonomous January 1979. Ceased performance 1988. **artistic directors** 1965–70, 1974–75 Peter Scriven. 1976–84 Richard Bradshaw. 1984–85 Terry O'Connell. 1986–88 Michael Creighton.

In its heyday the Marionette Theatre of Australia stood alongside the opera and ballet companies of the AUSTRALIAN ELIZABETHAN THEATRE TRUST, with the distinction that it performed Australian works. PETER SCRIVEN formed the company with the Trust and the ARTS COUNCIL OF AUSTRALIA in 1965 with the idea of establishing a national puppet theatre. Its first project was a national tour of the musical play THE TINTOOKIES, directed by Scriven. Then Scriven revived his production of the play *Little Fella Bindi* for a tour of 14 Asian countries from October 1966 to May 1967, followed by an Australian tour. Another Scriven production, *The Explorers*, toured Australia in 1968–69, thereby escaping a fire that destroyed the company's other sets of puppets in 1969. In 1970 Scriven's *Tintookies 2000*, which departed from the marionette tradition by using large rod-puppets, was performed with a version of Norman Lindsay's story *The Magic Pudding* at World Expo '70 in Osaka (Japan) and on a short Asian tour.

Charles Dlask directed *Young Person's Guide to the Orchestra* and *Peter and the Wolf* in 1971, using ultra-violet lighting. For the first half of 1972 Jan Bussell, from the Hogarth Puppets in England, was artistic adviser to the Marionette Theatre of Australia. He directed *The Water Babies*. In 1973 Joanne Priest directed the first puppet show in the new Sydney Opera House, *Tales From Noonameena*, based on Aboriginal legends. It was written by Hal Saunders, who had written the lyrics for *The Tintookies*. Scriven returned in 1974 to direct *The Tintookies* with new puppets. The first half used the original soundtrack, but the second half was entirely new. The show opened at the Princess Theatre in Melbourne in January 1975 and after touring Australia toured Asia for three months in 1976.

With the present writer as artistic director and ROSS HILL as puppet-maker, the Marionette Theatre moved from marionettes to rod-puppets. Large rod-puppets worked from below were used in 1979 in *The Mysterious Potamus*, based on a Russian puppet-play, and smaller rod-puppets for *The Magic Pudding* in 1980. Shows for adult audiences began with *Captain Lazar and His Earthbound Circus* at the Adelaide Festival in 1980. The play and the character designs were by the cartoonist Patrick Cook and the music and songs were by ROBYN ARCHER. The puppeteers provided the voices and there was a live band. Puppeteers who were themselves part of the play worked almost life-size puppets from behind in *Smiles Away*, a kind of outback fairy tale at the Sydney Opera House in 1981. In the same year a Marionette Theatre show, *General Macarthur in Australia* by ROGER PULVERS, was slotted into a subscription series of the Playbox Theatre Company in Melbourne.

In late 1980 the Marionette Theatre moved into the former Sailors' Home in the Rocks in central Sydney. A new theatre opened in the renovated building in July 1983. A highlight of the opening season was *Rapunzel in Suburbia*, a show for adults created by KIM CARPENTER and based on poems by DOROTHY HEWETT. With Terry O'Connell as artistic director in 1984–85, the Marionette Theatre widened its scope to incorporate plays with marginal puppet content. The theatre became known as the Rocks Theatre, and Michael Creighton, who became artistic director in 1986, concentrated on shows for children. As well as such classics as *The Wind in the Willows* in 1986, *Pinocchio* in 1987 and *The Magic Pudding* in 1988, he presented *Kakadu*, based on the writings of the traditional landowner Bill Neidjie, and *Sydney Coves*, both in 1988. At the end of 1988 funding problems caused the Marionette Theatre to cease performing. Finally, in December 1990 the administrator arranged an auction of nearly all the puppets and vacated the Rocks Theatre. ❦*Richard Bradshaw*

George Marlow

Entrepreneur. Born 24 September 1876 in Birmingham (England). Originally Joseph Lewis Marks. Brought to Sydney in 1882. Began acting in melodrama *c.*1892. Married actor Ethel Buckley 1903. Variously leased and sub-leased Sydney theatre known as Adelphi Theatre, Grand Opera House and Tivoli Theatre, alone or with others 1911–13, 1914–39. Died 21 May 1939 in Sydney.

An old-time showman, George Marlow boasted when the Adelphi Theatre opened in Sydney in 1911: 'I am now the lessee of the two largest theatres in Australia'. The other was the PRINCESS THEATRE in Melbourne, and the boast was largely justified. Marlow's rise to this eminence began at 15 when, after a couple of office-boy jobs, he appeared at the Opera House in Sydney in *The White Slaves*, starring Jennie Lee. He adopted George Marlow as his stage name—and later took it legally—and played small parts in touring companies. Moving up in the world, Marlow played with GEORGE RIGNOLD and then in melodramas staged by CHARLES HOLLOWAY and WILLIAM ANDERSON. He essayed running his own melodrama company in the suburbs, but this was not financially rewarding so he went back to Anderson on the managerial side. Early in 1903 the budding entrepreneur gained a ready-made leading lady when he married Ethel Buckley, a teenager whose acting had been attracting attention. Marlow also became the Sydney agent for FULLERS', the New Zealand theatrical firm.

Marlow leased the Princess Theatre in late 1910 and next year he sub-leased the large new theatre in Sydney that was to be named the Adelphi Theatre, probably in honour of the famous London melodrama house. The opening attraction was *The Bad Girl of the Family*, a melodrama by Frederick Melville, which Marlow modestly advertised as 'the latest and most outstanding drama that has ever been introduced in Australia, which ran for over 600 nights in London and was attended by Royalty, All Society and the Masses'. The Adelphi was off on a career of rapid-change melodrama. Less than a year later Marlow promoted himself to governing director of George Marlow Ltd, and George Willoughby, an experienced actor-manager, was made managing director.

Friction arose between Marlow and the other directors and in August 1913 Marlow was bought out and the company became George Willoughby Ltd. In 1914 BENJAMIN FULLER became a director of this company, and in May he bought out Willoughby and the other directors. Marlow then bought a half-interest in Fuller's purchase, but Fuller dominated the running of the Adelphi Theatre. He had it modernised in 1915 and renamed the Grand Opera House in August 1916 to mark the import of the Gonsalez Opera Company, a big success. The theatre soon settled into a routine of nine months of the Fuller Dramatic Players, followed by a Christmas pantomime—often with STIFFY AND MO as stars—which usually ran until Easter.

In 1923 Marlow secured the lease of the Grand Opera House from Thomas Rofe, and from then billed himself as 'sole proprietor', although George Monte became joint lessee in April 1924. Hugh J. Ward Theatres Ltd subleased the theatre and presented musical comedies and superior action dramas until the St James Theatre opened in 1926. Marlow's subsequent sublessees were varied, including Frank Neil's Comedians in *Charley's Aunt*, *Getting Gertie's Garter* and *Not Tonight Dearie*; Nellie Bramley's company in popular plays such as J. Hartley Manners's *Peg o' My Heart* and *Uncle Tom's Cabin*, the Allan Wilkie Shakespearean Company, vaudeville companies and even, for seven weeks in 1930, Wirths' Circus. During the Great Depression the popular-priced vaudeville shows of MIKE CONNORS and QUEENIE PAUL in 1932 helped the Grand Opera House back onto an even keel, as the New Tivoli Theatre. Marlow slipped into the background in connection with the theatre, which became the city's third TIVOLI THEATRE, although he maintained his interest in the lease until his death. He was well-known in Sydney racing circles. ❦*John West*

Mary Marlowe

Actor, journalist, novelist. Born 18 February 1884 in Melbourne. Originally Margaret Mary Shanahan. Granddaughter of John O'Shanassy, Premier of Victoria. Toured Australasia with Julius Knight. Acted in London 1910–12. Toured Australia for Bailey and Grant 1912. Acted in North America 1913–16. Returned to Australia 1919. Worked as journalist and radio interviewer in Sydney. Died on 19 February 1962 at Rooty Hill (NSW).

Mary Marlowe played leading roles on three continents in a short theatrical career. Reviews suggest that she was a wholesome and graceful soubrette whose youth and good looks were a great part of her appeal. She was pretty and plump, with a dimple and a 'haunting melodious voice', and an incurable romantic. She was also a devout Catholic whose struggle against the vamp image imposed upon actors of her time finally led her to abandon the stage.

When she was 16 her aunt Blanche O'Shanassy, an actor and a niece of G. V. BROOKE, persuaded NELLIE STEWART to give the stage-struck girl a walk-on part in Paul Kester's *Sweet Nell of Old Drury*. This was followed by walk-on roles on tour in the 1902–06 JULIUS KNIGHT company. She soon made an impression by learning 18 roles in the repertoire and by her singing and dancing. Her first speaking part was the Governess in *A Royal Divorce* by W. G. Wills. In 1904 she won the soubrette part of Sally Jellibrand in a dramatic adaptation of Baroness Orczy's novel *The Scarlet Pimpernel*, and this was followed by the Widow Melnotte in Edward Bulwer-Lytton's *The Lady of Lyons*. In 1907 the Melbourne *Argus* published her first journalism, an article about seeking work as a stage extra.

In 1910 Marlowe left for London with a letter to DION BOUCICAULT JNR. He did not employ her but in 1911 she won her first leading role, in Hall Caine's drama *The Christian*, which she played for many months on tour and in London. She also played in *The Manxman* by Caine and Wilson Barrett and in *The Man from Mexico* by H. A. du Souchet.

In 1912 the Bailey and Grant company advertised in London for a leading lady to play Violet Enderby, the title-role in THE SQUATTER'S DAUGHTER by Bert Bailey and Edmund Duggan. Marlowe returned to Australia to play that role, Kate Rudd in Steele Rudd's *On Our Selection* and roles in four other plays on national tour. The facts that she had been a leading lady in London and was prepared to sail for Australia in less than a week were more germane to her engagement than the coincidence that she was Australian.

She returned to London in 1912 and the next year signed a six-month contract to play in Canada. In 1914 she went to the USA, where her first substantial roles were Adriana in *The Comedy of Errors* on tour with the Ben Greet Players, and Katherine to Greet's Petruchio in *The Taming of the Shrew*. Between roles she wrote her first novel, *Kangaroos in King's Land* and began to earn a living as a short-story writer. In 1916 she returned to London became a Red Cross nursing aide. The Red Cross shipped her to Australia in 1919 and she joined GREGAN MCMAHON on tour with *The Luck of the Navy* by Mrs Clifford Mills, starring MARIE NEY and FRANK HARVEY. She then retired from the stage and joined the Sydney *Sun* as a feature writer.

From 1921 she wrote a weekly theatre column for the *Sunday Sun* under the pseudonym 'Puck'. She also wrote theatre notices and book reviews, and became a ghostwriter for Anna Pavlova and other visiting stars. In 1923 she published *Gypsy Royal, Adventuress*, a semi-autobiographical novel about an actress, and in 1927 *An Unofficial Rose*, based upon the birth of an illegitimate child to a chorus girl she had witnessed when on tour with Julius Knight. In 1934 Marlowe joined radio 2UE Sydney with 'A Woman's View of the News', a program in which she interviewed many stage personalities. She retired in 1946 but from the 1930s to 1957 she wrote the Dorothy Dix replies to letters from the lovelorn in the *Sun*. She never married, remaining faithful to a lost lover, and she consistently destroyed evidence of her family and past. As a journalist she could be acerbic and intrusive. As a broadcaster she promoted women's domestic virtues and the romantic images of the famous. She conducted a robust debate with the formidable feminist and union leader Muriel Heagney on 2UE in 1937. ❦*Katharine Brisbane*

writings
Gypsy Royal, Adventuress. London: Collins 1923. Novel.
Kangaroos in King's Land. London: Simpkin 1911. Novel.
That Fragile Hour. Sydney: Angus and Robertson 1990. Autobiography.
An Unofficial Rose. London: Collins 1927. Novel.
'SILVER ARROW'. Extra ladies. *Argus* (Melbourne) 16 March 1907.
further reading
CAMPBELL, DEBORAH. From theatre to radio—The popular career of Mary Marlowe. *Australian Popular Culture* (ed. Peter Spearitt and David Walker). Sydney: Allen and Unwin 1979.
RUTLEDGE, MARTHA. Margaret Mary Marlowe. *Australian Dictionary of Biography* 10. Melbourne University Press 1986.
reference
Mary Marlowe papers in Mitchell Library, SS 735/1. Personal papers, theatre writings, transcripts of radio interviews, literary work, unpublished plays and a film script, *I Am Caesar*.

Jean Marshall AM

Actor, director, teacher. Born 31 March 1917 in Glasgow (Scotland). Came to Australia 1927. Studied speech with James Anderson at Elder Conservatorium (Adelaide) 1933 and drama with Agnes Dobson. Married Desmond White, actor and theatre technician, 1942. Acted for Adelaide University Theatre Guild, Adelaide Repertory Theatre, WEA Little Theatre and J. C. Williamson's, 1933–65. Artistic director of Adelaide Theatre Group 1963–70. Honorary adviser for Jimmy Zoole Productions 1989. Performing Arts Collection advisory committee from 1989. AM 1987.

A passionate champion of Australian playwrights, Jean Marshall has been tireless as actor, director and teacher of great influence in amateur, community and semiprofessional theatre in Adelaide. One of the city's most versatile and spirited actresses, between 1933 and 1965 she essayed a wide range of roles in plays by Eugene O'Neill, Luigi Pirandello, Shakespeare, J. M. Synge, Tennessee Williams and Australian writers. By the 1950s she was a leading director. She directed the Australian premiere of Arthur Miller's *Death of a Salesman* in 1956. In 1960 she directed the world premiere of Alan Seymour's THE ONE DAY OF THE YEAR for the ADELAIDE THEATRE GROUP. She was chosen to direct excerpts from *Macbeth* and Sophocles's *Medea* starring JUDITH ANDERSON in the 1966 ADELAIDE FESTIVAL OF ARTS. After her husband died in 1970 Marshall turned almost entirely to directing and teaching. She directed for the AUSTRALIAN NATIONAL PLAYWRIGHTS' CONFERENCE in Canberra in 1975. She has directed plays by COLIN BALLANTYNE, RICHARD BRADSHAW, ALEX BUZO, John Hepworth, Audrey Hewlett, Patricia Hooker, RALPH PETERSON, HAL PORTER, Betty Quin, DOUGLAS STEWART and DAVID WILLIAMSON. The legion of actors and directors she has trained includes Di Chamberlain, Chris Connelly, LESLIE DAYMAN, John Derum, Peter Goers, KEITH MICHELL and Terry Stapleton. ❦*Jo Peoples*

David N. Martin

Entrepreneur. Born 15 August 1898 in Perth. Worked in advertising. Became publicity manager for motion picture companies. Controlled cinemas in Sydney. Opened Minerva Theatre, Sydney, 1938. Controlled Tivoli circuit 1944–58. Died 2 March 1958 in San Francisco (USA). Father of Lloyd Martin, general manager of Sydney Opera House Trust.

On the eve of the Second World War David N. Martin gave Sydney a new theatre, and after the war he set the TIVOLI CIRCUIT in a new direction. Martin came to the theatre from the film industry. He was managing director of Imperial Theatres Ltd, which in 1934 rebuilt a cinema in Pitt Street, Sydney, as the Liberty Theatre. Designed by C. Bruce Dellit, an architect who specialised in the Art-Deco style, it was luxurious and seated only 650, foreshadowing the vogue for smaller cinemas.

In 1937 Martin employed Dellit to design the MINERVA THEATRE in Kings Cross. This modern, elegant house, designed as both cinema and live theatre, opened on 18 May 1939. It was a wonderful cinema, but the back of the dress circle was a long way from the stage and it was hard to make money in a 1000-seat live theatre on the fringe of city. David N. Martin Pty Ltd was mainly responsible for the management until WHITEHALL THEATRICAL PRODUCTIONS took over the lease in May 1941. In 1944 a group headed by Martin gained control of Tivoli Theatres Ltd. Martin began extensive importation of stars for the TIVOLI CIRCUIT in 1946, displacing the Australian performers who had come to the fore during the war. Martin was seeking new talents to face the challenge of television when he died suddenly in San Francisco. ❦*John West*

Florence Martin

Designer. Born 1908 in Ballarat (Vic.). Studied painting in Melbourne. Designed sets and costumes with sister Kathleen in Melbourne to 1942. Designed *Lutte Eternelle* for Original Ballet Russe 1940. Went to USA 1942. Studied theatre design with Serge Soudeikine in New York City 1945–46. Designed costumes and decor for Grant Mouradoff Ballet Company (New York) and Teatro Municipale Ballet (Rio de Janeiro).

Florence Martin and her sister Kathleen collaborated on costumes and sets for two major productions by DOLIA RIBUSH in Melbourne—Maxim Gorky's *The Lower Depths* in 1936 and Anton Chekhov's *The Cherry Orchard* in 1938. In 1940 they designed T. S. Eliot's *Murder in the Cathedral* at the University of Melbourne Conservatorium of Music and the Russian dancer and choreographer Igor Schwezoff, touring Australia with the Original Ballet Russe in 1940, discovered their work.

Later in the year they were commissioned to design Schwezoff's ballet *Lutte Eternelle* for its world premiere in Sydney—the first Australians to create scenery and costumes for a new Russian ballet. After this success they contributed innovative sets and costumes to KEITH MACARTNEY's production of *A Midsummer Night's Dream* at the University of Melbourne in 1941. Next year Florence Martin went alone to New York. In 1952 she abandoned theatre design, for health reasons, to be a full-time painter in London. ❦*Pamela Zeplin*

Lloyd Martin

Manager. Born 30 April 1934 in Sydney. Son of entrepreneur David N. Martin. Executive director of Tivoli circuit 1960–66. Chairman and general manager of NLT Productions television and film company. Deputy general manager of Sydney Opera House Trust 1973–79; executive director and general manager since 1 March 1979. Chairman of Confederation of Australasian Performing Arts Presenters. Director of Sydney Convention and Visitors Bureau. On board of National Institute of Dramatic Art 1979–92.

There was little doubt that Lloyd Martin was destined for the managerial side of show business. His father was DAVID N. MARTIN, a showman in film and theatre and from 1944 managing director of the TIVOLI CIRCUIT of variety theatres. After school and university, Lloyd Martin worked his way up the Tivoli hierarchy. About 18 months after his father's death in 1958 he became executive director, and subsequently, joint managing director with Gordon Cooper. He held the post until the company went out of business in 1966. As deputy general manager of the Sydney Opera House, he assisted Frank Barnes to see in the first productions when performances began in September 1973. Poor health forced Barnes to retire as general manager in October 1978 and Martin succeeded him in 1979. *John West*

Marvellous Melbourne 1889

Play in five acts by Alfred Dampier and J. H. Wrangham, from Thomas Walker's play *Voices of the Night* (1886). **premiere** 19 January 1889, Alexandra Theatre, Melbourne. Cast: Alfred Boothman, Walter E. Baker, Alfred Dampier, Lily Dampier, Edmund Holloway, Katherine Russell. Designer: 'Alta' (Alfred Tischbauer). Director: Alfred Dampier.

One of the few visiting British writers to express openly enthusiasm for life in the colonies, George Augusta Sala popularised the phrase 'marvellous Melbourne' in 1885. ALFRED DAMPIER and his then business manager J. H. Wrangham cemented it more strongly into Australian history with this popular play early in 1889. More than one reviewer remarked that the story was a hotchpotch of any number of earlier melodramas and could have been set in any city in the world, but as the *Argus* noted sniffily on 21 January 1889: 'Every attempt has ... been made to create fun by local allusion fit only for burlesque'. The story opens at Spencer Street Railway Station, moves over to the Burke and Wills memorial, and out to Fairholme House, from which Melbourne can be viewed in the distance—and all this was only in the first act. After journeying around Melbourne and into a Chinese opium den the play ends happily when the heroine's horse wins the Melbourne Cup.

Dampier played five roles, including Charles Harold Vane Somers Golightly, a silly English 'new chum' complete with monocle, 'skipping gait' and lisp. Another comic indulgence was Dick Ledger, a 'revolutionary' who spoke on behalf of 'the down-trod wukkin' man, wot is a slave every day o' the week and ain't erlowed to git 's beer on a Sunday!' In 1893 the play was retitled *Slaves of Sydney* for a season in that city but it was far less popular. In 1970 the AUSTRALIAN PERFORMING GROUP included the opium-den scene from *Marvellous Melbourne* and several of the Dampier family as characters, in its own play of the same title. *Richard Fotheringham*

reference
The script of *Marvellous Melbourne*, much annotated and as localised for the Sydney season, is in the Mitchell Library (Sydney), MS B753.

Marvellous Melbourne 1970

Play in two acts by Jack Hibberd and John Romeril. **premiere** 11 December 1970, Pram Factory, Melbourne, by Australian Performing Group. Cast: Graeme Blundell, Ros Brown, Michael Christie, Meg Clancy, Damien Coleridge, Lindy Davies, Claire Dobbin, Kerry Dwyer, Bill Garner, Max Gillies, Evelyn Krape, Wilfred Last, Yvonne Marini, Rod Moore, Tony Taylor. Designers: Chris Berkman, Jock Campbell, Garth Brown. Directors: Graeme Blundell, Max Gillies. Music: Lorraine Milne.

published *Theatre Australia* 2/4 and 2/5 (Sydney, August and September/October 1977).

JACK HIBBERD and JOHN ROMERIL's satirical extravaganza marked the AUSTRALIAN PERFORMING GROUP's move from the tiny LA MAMA THEATRE in Carlton to the more spacious Pram Factory. The title was suitably celebratory, not only in its triumphant parochialism but in its invocation of ALFRED DAMPIER's melodrama of the same title and the rich tradition of late 19th-century popular theatre to which it belonged. The subject is Melbourne from 1888 to 1902, though land-grabbing scandals in government, the Anglophile establishment and passionate debates about the need for truly indigenous theatre are all shrewdly contemporary in their reference. Melbourne is a panorama of splendid depravity, from the crooks and hypocrites who run the place to the wide boys and girls who scrabble for what they can at the bottom of the heap. The cry of the oppressed is there, particularly in the songs that often frame the sequences. But the primary impulse is revelry in all that diversity, expressed particularly in idioms ranging from the pious claptrap of city fathers to the lively vernacular of larrikins and racecourse touts. Even the prodigious grossness of Sir Wallace Pork becomes another element in a richly vulgar pageant rather than a means to expose routine oppression.

The satire has the quintessential APG balance of political radicalism and rumbustious myth-making, which could be almost affectionate as well as devastating. *Marvellous Melbourne* is closer to carnival than to agitprop, and anticipates the way in which the APG's delight in language so often complicated and sometimes qualified its political purpose. The production proclaimed the APG's commitment to collaboration, both in the combination of its coauthors' different talents and in the indebtedness of its picaresque routines to group improvisation. *Peter Fitzpatrick*

Ray Mathew

Dramatist. Born 14 April 1929 in Sydney. Educated at Sydney Teachers' College. Taught in NSW country towns 1949–51, acting with drama groups in Forbes and Orange. Freelance journalist 1951–52. Worked for Commonwealth Scientific and Industrial Research Organisation 1952–54. Tutorial department of University of Sydney 1955–60. Commonwealth Literary Fund fellowship 1958. Received Arts Council of Great Britain bursary and settled in London 1960. Moved to New York 1968. Senior editor and art critic for *Art/World* from 1981. Has published a novel, two collections of short stories and three volumes of poetry.

In the 1950s Ray Mathew was a prolific writer of plays, poetry and criticism, a journalist and lecturer on the arts in Australia, and a thoughtful observer of the rhythms and character of Australian life, particularly rural life. As a playwright he awaits the critical attention he deserves. His work is distinguished by a keen ear for the music of Australian language and a dramatist's grasp of character and emotional interaction, often expressed in poetic self-revelation. Most of Mathew's plays received only amateur production. His plays were not among those in the brief burst of playwriting that captured the imagination of managements and audiences, but in retrospect his was the most innovative mind. His work also foreshadowed the more indigenous new forms that emerged in the 1960s. Like Sumner Locke Elliott's RUSTY BUGLES, and the sympathetic work of PATRICK WHITE and PETER KENNA, his plays are concerned with the interrelationship between human beings and nature, and particularly with loneliness.

Mathew drew his earlier work from the rural life he saw as a young schoolteacher. His first play, *Church Sunday*, written in 1950 but not performed, is a gem of a one-act bush comedy in which the domestic relationships of two couples are played out over the bodies of two thieves who have suffered summary justice at the opening. It was followed by another short play, *Lonely without You*; then *Sing for St Ned*, which attempts to define an Australian embattled kind of hero, and in many ways anticipates the 1960s larrikin plays like RON BLAIR's *Flash Jim Vaux* and Michael Boddy and Bob Ellis's THE LEGEND OF KING O'MALLEY. Mathew has described it as being influenced by 'Hellzapoppin, *Our Town*, *The Maid of the Mountains*, *Ned Kelly*, *Punch and Judy* ... and a number of others'.

A repeated theme of Mathew's plays is arbitrary and unnecessary death. *Sing for St Ned* argues that arbitrariness. '[Ned's father] was a bad lot—and Irish, you can imagine what that means ... He might have been a farmer who planted and grew things, or a carpenter who built and made things, or a penpusher who wrote things or a counterjumper who sold things but he happened to be a Kelly who took things. It wasn't a matter of choice.' *Sing for St Ned*, written in 1951, was first performed in 1960, by a student group at the University of Queensland.

We Find the Bunyip was first presented in 1955, by INDEPENDENT THEATRE in Sydney, directed by Geoffrey Thomas. It is a warm, humorous study of a group of boarders in a country pub who catch a moment of poetry one moonlit night and have their lives touched by it. *The Life of the Party* was a finalist in the 1957 London *Observer* competition along with plays by ALAN SEYMOUR and RICHARD BEYNON and had a short season in London. The most difficult of Mathew's plays, it is a bitter comedy based on his experience of bohemian life among the writers and artists of Sydney's Kings Cross. It is a multiple portrait of febrile artistic energy, immature and frustrated by a parochial society and, like the characters in *Summer of the Seventeenth Doll*, unwilling to come to terms with the responsibilities and restrictions of adulthood. Mathew's best-known play, *A SPRING SONG*, was first performed by the TWELFTH NIGHT THEATRE COMPANY in Brisbane. It is a Chekhovian piece, set in a homestead where a young teacher is billeted. Over a season he watches the interaction of three young sisters: one, Juliet-like, is having a forbidden love affair; another has come home to die. ❦*Katharine Brisbane*

published plays
The Bones of My Toe (1957). Adelaide: Rigby 1970 in *Australian One-Act Plays* 1 (ed. Greg Branson).
A Spring Song (1958). Sydney: Currency Press 1985.
We Find the Bunyip (1955). Brisbane: University of Queensland Press 1968 in *Khaki, Bush and Bigotry—Three Australian plays*.

other writings
Australian drama and theatre. *Current Affairs Bulletin* 28 July 1958.

further reading
HANGER, EUNICE. The lonely playwrights. *Contemporary Australian Drama* (ed. Peter Holloway) 2nd edn. Sydney: Currency Press 1987.
JENNINGS, KATE. Uncountable within our hearts. *Voices* (Canberra) spring 1993. Interview with Ray Mathew.

Charles Mathews

English actor, 1803–78. Son of actor and entertainer Charles Mathews. Made stage debut at Olympic Theatre, London. Married to actor Mme Vestris 1838–56. Married actor Lizzie Davenport. Toured Australia 1870–71.

The outstanding light comedian of the 19th-century English stage, Charles Mathews visited Australia in 1870–71, with his second wife. The Australian press praised his acting for diversity of characterisation, self-abnegation, natural gesture and detailed, truthful observation of life. He was frequently cited as a model for young Australian actors. 'We shall now be able to appreciate the true art of natural representation', said the *Town and Country Journal*. Mathews's repertoire comprised largely comedies and farces, usually featuring roles he had created. His itinerary included Melbourne, Ballarat, Sydney and Adelaide, with returns to Melbourne and Sydney. In Melbourne initially the public did not support him wholeheartedly at the Theatre Royal because of raised prices. Mathews pointed out that they were lucky to have such a commodity as himself among them and must be prepared to pay a realistic price for their good fortune. On his return to Melbourne, however, normal prices were restored. ❦*Jim Davis*

further reading
BOOTH, MICHAEL R. The acting of Charles Mathews. *English Plays of the Nineteenth Century* 4. Oxford University Press 1973.
DAVIS, JIM. Colonial experience—English comedians in Australia in the nineteenth century. *Nineteenth Century Theatre* 16/1 (Amherst, Massachusetts, 1988).
DICKENS, CHARLES THE YOUNGER (ed.). *The Life of Charles James Mathews*. London: Macmillan 1879.

Monica Maughan

Actor, director. Born 15 September 1938 at Nuku'alofa (Tonga) to Australian parents. Educated at University of Melbourne. Joined Union Theatre Repertory Company (Melbourne) 1957. Acted in British repertory theatre 1963–66. Erik Kuttner Award 1968 (title-role in *The Prime of Miss Jean Brodie* by Muriel Spark), 1971 (Anna Bowers in *Three Months Gone* by Donald Howarth). Green Room Awards for best supporting actress 1983 (Mollie in *Gulls* by Robert Hewett), 1987 (Madame Arcati in *Blithe Spirit* by Noël Coward), 1990 (Miss Prism in *The Importance of Being Earnest* by Oscar Wilde). Also in film and television.

Monica Maughan, described by the critic Phillip Adams as 'one of the unsung heroes of Australia's thespians', has given strong character performances, especially in Australian works. She created Emma in RAY LAWLER's *Kid Stakes* and the Mother in ALEX BUZO's *Martello Towers* in 1975 and Wendy in Buzo's MAKASSAR REEF in 1978—all for the MELBOURNE THEATRE COMPANY. She played Aggie in Peter Kenna's *A HARD GOD* for the State Theatre Company of South Australia in 1981, and the following year created the roles of Percy and Rose in THÉRÈSE RADIC's *A Whip Round for*

Percy Grainger for the Playbox Theatre Company. In 1986 she directed the premiere of *The Celebrated* by Stephen Guard, and Terry Stapleton's *Some Night at Julia Creek*, both for the Melbourne Theatre Company. She has won all her awards in this company's productions. ❦*Robert Hewett*

Bob Maza AM

Actor, director, dramatist. Born 25 November 1939 on Palm Island (Qld). Began acting in Melbourne 1969. Founding member of National Black Theatre (Sydney) 1972. Continuously involved in stage, television and film productions since then. Father of actor Rachel Maza. AM 1993.

A quiet but tireless campaigner for reconciliation and better understanding between blacks and whites, Bob Maza has been a central force in Aboriginal theatre. As performer, director, author, educator and organiser he has done much to give black Australians confidence and pride in their own abilities. He came late to the stage and had little formal training as an actor. After he completed his schooling in Cairns (Qld) he spent some years as a manual labourer and then took an office job in Darwin. He became involved in theatre in Melbourne in 1969, when his Koori compatriot Jack Charles encouraged him to take part in revues, such as *Jack Charles is Up and Fighting* in 1970 and *Basically Black* in Sydney in 1971. As a result, Maza became a founding member of National Black Theatre in Redfern, Sydney, in 1972. He directed his first play, the premiere of Robert J. Merritt's THE CAKE MAN there in 1975.

Major plays in which he has acted include Thomas Keneally's *Bullie's House* in 1980, Eric Bentley's *Are You Now, or Have You Ever Been?* in 1976 and Michael Frayn's *Clouds* in 1980—all at the Nimrod Theatre in Sydney. Maza's own plays include *Tiddalik*, *Rain For Christmas*, *Mereki* and *The Keepers*. The last had its premiere at Naracoorte (SA) in February 1988 and was also presented as part of the 1988 Adelaide Festival Fringe. In 1989 Maza directed Roger Bennett's *Up the Ladder Again* in Adelaide. He has become heavily involved in producing and directing radio and television drama. ❦*Adam Shoemaker*

published play
The Keepers (1988). Sydney: Currency Press 1989 in *Plays From Black Australia*.

other writings
Isn't it a true story? In *Bullie's House* by Thomas Keneally. Sydney: Currency Press 1981.

further reading
THOMPSON, LIZ (ed.). Bob Maza. *Aboriginal Voices—Contemporary Aboriginal artists, writers and performers*. Sydney: Simon and Schuster 1990.

Orpheus McAdoo

Entrepreneur. Born in USA. Came to Australia with Fisk Jubilee Singers 1886. Imported Georgia Minstrels and Alabama Cakewalkers 1899. Died July 1900 in Sydney.

The original Fisk Jubilee Singers were the undergraduate choir of Fisk University in Nashville (Tennessee). From 1871 they toured the USA and Europe to raise money for their institution, which was founded for freed black slaves in 1865. This choir popularised black spirituals among whites in the USA and England. It is unlikely that Orpheus McAdoo or any of the other nine Fisk Jubilee Singers who arrived in Australia in 1886 had ever sung in the Fisk University choir. Their Australian concerts were sometimes advertised as 'for the benefit of Fisk University', but they were a private organisation, raising money only for themselves. Between 1886 and 1889 the troupe toured the colonial capitals and made long journeys to bush towns, as far north as Charters Towers (Qld) in search of audiences. It also visited India and South Africa during this period. The singers performed programs of spirituals in church halls to religious-minded audiences—although Henry Bishop's 'Home, sweet home' was always in the repertoire.

In 1899 McAdoo returned to the USA to recruit performers for a new troupe, the Georgia Minstrels and Alabama Cakewalkers, who opened in Sydney in June 1899. Their repertoire consisted of 'coon songs' and cakewalk dancing, with ragtime accompaniment. McAdoo's minstrels and Curtis's Afro-American Minstrels—who toured Australia at the same time, featuring the notorious 'coon song' author and performer Ernest Hogan—were the first entertainers to introduce full-blown ragtime music to Australian audiences. The Georgia Minstrels enjoyed a successful season at the Palace Theatre in Sydney but proved less popular later at St George's Hall in Melbourne. They returned to the Palace in 1900 to stage a revival of *Uncle Tom's Cabin*.

McAdoo also continued to operate his Jubilee Singers, whose repertoire now included excerpts from opera, 'coon' numbers and juggling and balancing acts as well as the religious songs. McAdoo died in 1900—and was buried in Sydney's Waverley Cemetery—but his company continued to perform in church halls around Australia. One of its last Australian appearances was in Fullers' vaudeville in Sydney in 1916. ❦*Richard Waterhouse*

further reading
MARSH, J. T. B. *The Story of the Jubilee Singers*. London 1887.

John McCallum AO CBE

Actor, director, entrepreneur. Born 14 March 1918 in Brisbane. Son of John N. McCallum, theatre manager. Educated in England and Australia. Acted in Brisbane, in *Henry VIII* at Cremorne Theatre 1934, and in *Hamlet* and *Richard II* at Scala Theatre. Trained at Royal Academy of Dramatic Art (London). Professional debut in repertory. Shakespeare Memorial Theatre Company (Stratford-upon-Avon) and Old Vic (London) 1939. In Australian Army in New Guinea during Second World War. Directed a play and performed in two operettas for J. C. Williamson's in Sydney 1944–45. Returned to London after war and entered films. Married actor Googie Withers 1948. Assistant managing director of J. C. Williamson's 1958–61; joint managing director 1961–65; managing director 1965–66. President of Producers and Directors' Guild 1969–71. Founder president of Australian Film Council 1970–71. Father of actor Joanna McCallum. CBE 1971, AO 1992.

John McCallum and his wife Googie Withers toured Australasia in 1955–56 in Alan Melville's comedy *Simon and Laura* and Terence Rattigan's drama *The Deep Blue Sea*. At the end of the tour, Frank Tait, one of the TAIT BROTHERS who had run J. C. WILLIAMSON'S since 1920, offered McCallum the job of assistant managing director of the Firm. McCallum accepted and joined Tait in 1958. Seven years later Tait died and McCallum became sole managing director. His tenure was short. Commercial theatre was languishing and the Williamson's board was difficult to work with. McCallum resigned in 1966 and took to television production. Later still, McCallum and his wife acted together in England and Australia. Withers, a dancer who became an actor, has always been a fine dramatic performer but excels in comedy, which she plays with great style and individuality. As they grew older the couple became a splendidly integrated comedy team. ❦*John West*

writings
Life with Googie. London: Heinemann 1979. Autobiography.

further reading
BEVAN, IAN. *The Story of the Theatre Royal*. Sydney: Currency Press 1993.
HERBERT, IAN (ed.). *Who's Who in the Theatre* 17th edn. Detroit (USA): Gale Research 1987.
HOWIE, ANN C. (ed.). *Who's Who in Australia 1994*. Melbourne: Information Australia.

Hugh McCrae

Dramatist. Born 4 October 1876 in Melbourne. Published seven volumes of poetry, four of prose, one play, articles and reviews 1909–58. Acted in small roles in New York and Australia 1914–20. Died 17 February 1958 in Sydney.

The poet Hugh McCrae's one play, *The Ship of Heaven* had an important non-realist production at the Savoy Theatre in Sydney in 1933. This musical fantasy is distinguished by its stream of scenic images, not its verse or plot. Grounded in Victorian music-hall and pantomime and works by J. M. Barrie and John Houseman, it exemplifies dreamlike juxtapositions of surrealism and the darker, erotic side of the Pierrot–Columbine tradition. Although completed by 1920 and set to music by ALFRED HILL in 1923, it was not staged in full until DORIS FITTON directed it for INDEPENDENT THEATRE in 1933. The designer DON FINLEY had limited resources but a snow-machine on a painted drop gave an illusion of the Ship of Heaven sailing for the Milky Way. A student orchestra from the NSW State Conservatorium of Music played Hill's music under his baton. ❦*Dennis Carroll*

published play
The Ship of Heaven (1933). Sydney: Angus and Robertson 1951.

further reading
CARROLL, DENNIS. *Australian Contemporary Drama*. Sydney: Currency Press 1995.
COWPER, NORMAN and MARTHA RUTLEDGE. Hugh Raymond McCrae. *Australian Dictionary of Biography* 10. Melbourne University Press 1986.

Garry McDonald

Actor. Born 30 October 1948 in Sydney. Graduated from National Institute of Dramatic Art (Sydney). Began playing small parts 1968. Went into film and television. Married to actor Diane Craig.

After winning great popularity as a bogus television personality named Norman Gunston, Garry McDonald appeared at the Nimrod Theatre in Sydney in January 1977 in *Young Mo*, a play by STEVE J. SPEARS. It was an amazing recreation of the comic genius ROY RENE—the voice, the make-up, almost the style. Martin Sharp's poster of McDonald as Mo became the NIMROD THEATRE COMPANY's trademark. In 1986 McDonald played Rene again in *Sugar Babies*, the AUSTRALIAN ELIZABETHAN THEATRE TRUST's variety show about American burlesque. The 1980s also saw him play the transplanted Melbourne writer in the cast of David Williamson's *EMERALD CITY* that toured to London, Fagin in *Oliver!* and roles in David Mamet's *Glengarry Glen Ross* and *Speed the Plow*. He created for cabaret performance an overblown lair called Phil Stine and introduced him into the character of the ship entertainer in the SYDNEY THEATRE COMPANY's revival of John Romeril's *THE FLOATING WORLD* in 1986. In this company's 1992 production of *Much Ado About Nothing* McDonald was a popular Dogberry. ❦*John West*

Hugh D. McIntosh

Entrepreneur. Born 10 September 1876 in Sydney. Became caterer, then sporting entrepreneur. Controlled Tivoli vaudeville circuit 1912–21. NSW Legislative Councillor 1917–23. Lived mainly in England 1921–30. Returned unsuccessfully to theatre in Australia 1930. Died 2 February 1942 in England.

During the nine years when he controlled the TIVOLI CIRCUIT, the colourful, bustling Hugh D. McIntosh was undoubtedly the best-known showman in Australia. He regarded himself as the Australian counterpart of his English idol Charles B. Cochran. He developed his entrepreneurial skill first in professional cycling and then in boxing. He built the Sydney Stadium in 1908 for a world championship fight between Tommy Burns and Bill Squires. On Boxing Day 1908 he staged a sensational world championship bout between Burns and Jack Johnson and he later presented a film of the fight throughout the world. He also controlled the Sydney *Sunday Times* newspaper group.

In 1912 McIntosh sold the Stadium and bought control of the Tivoli circuit from the heirs of HARRY RICKARDS. He abolished the first-half revue of the Rickards format in favour of a full vaudeville program of unrelated acts. He imported stars, including the expressive dancer Maud Allan; Gene Greene, the 'Emperor of Ragtime'; the comedian ADA REEVE; and the ventriloquist Fred Russell. When the First World War made importation of big acts almost impossible, McIntosh switched to musicals and revues. The *Tivoli Follies*, a revue starring Vera Pearce, opened in Sydney in November 1914 and played around Australia and New Zealand for two years and a half.

After the war, the new policy of revues, musicals—and occasional plays—continued. The most notable productions were *Chu Chin Chow*, *The Lilac Domino* and an Australian musical comedy, *F.F.F.*, which was presented in Adelaide, Melbourne and Perth in 1920. With characteristic extravagance, McIntosh brought camels from central Australia to Melbourne for his production of *Chu Chin Chow*. It opened on Boxing Day in 1920, when Melbourne was crippled by a transport strike. McIntosh unsuccessfully tried to deliver patrons to the theatre privately by bus. Financial difficulties forced him to sell the production to J. C. WILLIAMSON'S. The Firm moved it to the Grand Opera House in Sydney, where it opened on 26 March 1921. McIntosh sold his Tivoli interests to HARRY G. MUSGROVE and until the end of the decade he lived flamboyantly, mainly in England. An attempt to revive his theatrical fortunes in Australia in 1930 ended in financial disaster. He returned to England, failed with a chain of Australian-style milk bars and died in poverty. ❦*Frank Van Straten*

further reading
CUNEEN, CHRIS. *Hugh D. McIntosh. Australian Dictionary of Biography* 10. Melbourne University Press 1986.

Claude McKay

Publicist. Born 1878 at Kilmore (Vic.). Journalist on country newspapers and in Melbourne. Became J. C. Williamson's secretary 1908. Remained with Williamson firm until 1918. Founded *Smith's Weekly* 1919. Retired 1950. Died 15 February 1972 at Bowral (NSW).

Claude McKay, a genius with publicity, had no theatrical experience until he became J. C. WILLIAMSON's secretary in 1908. He handled public relations for NELLIE STEWART on her tour of outback towns in 1911 and later in the year had his first big success publicising the Melba–Williamson Opera Company. Then he publicised OSCAR ASCHE's 1912–13 tour. He helped to raise £1 000 000 for war loans in 1917–18. With others he started *Smith's Weekly* in 1919. He sold his interest in 1927 but returned as editor in 1939 and stayed until the newspaper folded in 1950. ❦*Alwyn Capern*

writings
This is the Life. Sydney: Angus and Robertson 1961.
further reading
JULIUS, HARRY. *Theatrical Caricatures*. Sydney: NSW Bookstall Co. 1912. With 'marginal anecdotes' by McKay.

Leo McKern

Actor. Born 1920 in Sydney. In army during Second World War. Debut at Metropolitan Theatre, Sydney, 1944. Distinguished career in England from 1949. Returned to Australia in Shakespeare Memorial Theatre Company 1953 and many other times. Many film and television appearances. Married actor Jane Holland 1946. Father of actor Abigail McKern and film director Harriet McKern.

Highly regarded for the diversity of his work, Leo McKern brings rare insight into his characters with generosity of spirit. He draws his audience in to share this illumination—to delight in the quirky gallantry of his Boswell, be chilled by the bluff callousness of his Iago, or be moved by the frayed dignity of his Horace Rumpole on television. McKern developed skill in characterisation with METROPOLITAN THEATRE in Sydney in 1944. After a season of professional work, in 1946 he left for London, hard on the heels of his future wife, the actor JANE HOLLAND. Success came in 1949, when he played many leading roles with distinction in the OLD VIC THEATRE COMPANY.

McKern returned to Australia with the Shakespeare Memorial Theatre Company in 1953. He played a memorable Iago in *Othello*, a hauntingly splendid Glendower in *Henry IV—part 1* and a thistledown-light Touchstone in *As You Like It*. Back in England McKern had a return season at Stratford-upon-Avon and successes in the West End. In 1956 he came to Australia to play the title-role in Douglas Stewart's NED KELLY for the AUSTRALIAN ELIZABETHAN THEATRE TRUST. He also directed and acted in N. Richard Nash's *The Rainmaker* in Sydney. McKern rejoined the Old Vic company in 1962–63.

In 1970–72 he was back in Australia again, with his family. For the MELBOURNE THEATRE COMPANY he played in Michel Achard's *Patate*, which toured to the Adelaide Festival, and Governor Bligh in RAY LAWLER's *The Man Who Shot the Albatross*, which toured to Sydney in 1971.

McKern's greatest popular success in Australia has come from the solo role of Boswell in *Boswell for the Defence*, written by Patrick Edgeworth, an Australian. Performances were sold out in Melbourne in 1988, Perth in 1989, and Sydney in 1990. McKern toured Canberra, Adelaide, Brisbane and provincial Queensland in 1991. ❦*Lynne Murphy*

writings
Just Resting. London: Methuen 1983.

Marjorie McLeod BEM

Actor, director, dramatist, teacher. Born 27 February 1893 at Dimboola (Vic.). Originally Marjorie Young. Married 1913. Taught speech and drama in Melbourne. Won Australian Literature Society's Awards for best one-act play with *A Shillingsworth* 1931, *Moonshine* 1932 and *Travail* 1934. Associated with Gertrude Johnson in establishing National Theatre Movement, Victoria. Acted and wrote plays for ABC radio for six years. Also wrote poetry. Moved to Swan Hill (Vic.) c.1942. Directed Swan Hill National Theatre 1946–65. Retired and returned to Melbourne 1965. Died 6 August 1988 in Melbourne. BEM 1977.

Amateur theatre flourishes in the northern Victorian town of Swan Hill as a direct result of the vision and drive of Marjorie McLeod, who introduced thousands of people to classical and modern plays. A church presentation in 1942 led to her forming a group to raise patriotic funds and entertain personnel at a nearby air force base. This group staged productions in the district until 1946, when McLeod formed the permanent Swan Hill National Theatre under the banner of the NATIONAL THEATRE MOVEMENT.

She had a deep love of Shakespeare. She staged scenes and songs from his works in 1946 and in April 1947 she launched a festival to celebrate his birthday with a full-length production of *Romeo and Juliet*. In a town of some 5000 people, the Swan Hill Shakespeare Festival became an annual five-day event, with a Shakespearean production, debates on theatre, a street procession, an Elizabethan fair and pageants. From 1947 to 1976, 30 Shakespearean plays and 83 others were produced. McLeod's contacts ensured that the festival continually attracted eminent guest actors.

Between festivals the Swan Hill National Theatre toured plays around Victoria, entered and won awards in the Victorian Drama League and National Theatre Movement drama competitions, presented regular play and poetry readings and conducted a weekly half-hour radio program. During the 1940s and 1950s McLeod's work was a model for several other Victorian theatre groups. Her Swan Hill National Theatre is now the Swan Hill Theatre Group, with its own theatre—unusual amongst amateur groups—and an unbroken record of 47 years of quality productions.

McLeod wrote plays on early Australian history and on the social concerns and human relationships of her day—the Great Depression, patriotism, immigration and family. Her most successful play, *Within These Walls*, about an Australian colonial dynasty, had professional and amateur productions in Melbourne and provincial Victoria over 15 years. A successful example of her poetic writing was a fantasy verse play, *The Enchanted Tryst*. ❦*Pauline Thomas*

published plays
The Enchanted Tryst. Swan Hill (Vic.): Swan Hill National Theatre 1946 in *Verses from Swan Hill*.

Horizons (1952). Swan Hill (Vic.): author 1958 in *Four Period Plays*.
Mine A Sad One (1956). Swan Hill (Vic.): author 1958 in *Four Period Plays*.
Moonshine (1932). Melbourne: Dramatists' Club of Australia 1936 in *Five Plays by Australians*.
Travail (1934). Melbourne: Dramatists' Club of Australia 1934 in *Eight Plays by Australians*.
Within These Walls (1936). Swan Hill (Vic.): author 1958 in *Four Period Plays*.
A Shillingsworth (1931). Swan Hill (Vic.): author 1958 in *Four Period Plays*.

other writings
All The World's A Stage. Barn Publishing 1980. History of Swan Hill National Theatre 1943–68 and Swan Hill Shakespeare Festival.

Gregan McMahon CBE

Actor, director. Born 2 March 1874 in Sydney. Acted in Sydney University Dramatic Society while studying arts. Articled to law firm after graduating in 1896. Joined Brough Comedy Company as actor 1900. Established Melbourne Repertory Theatre Company in 1911 and directed it until 1918. Returned to professional theatre. Established Sydney Repertory Theatre Society in 1920 and directed it until 1928. Formed Gregan McMahon Play Company 1928. Formed Gregan McMahon Players 1929 and directed them for various managements until his death. Died 30 August 1941 in Melbourne. Married to Mary Hungerford, amateur actor. CBE 1938.

Gregan McMahon pioneered literary theatre in Australia and secured professional backing in the era when serious theatre was mostly left to amateurs. Following the leads of John Vedrenne and Harley Granville-Barker at the Royal Court Theatre in London in 1904–07 and the growing English repertory movement, McMahon produced works by leading dramatists of his day. Among them were Anton Chekhov, Henrik Ibsen, Sean O'Casey, Eugene O'Neill, Luigi Pirandello and George Bernard Shaw.

McMahon scored his first big success as Horace Parker in Richard Ganthony's *A Message from Mars*—a role he eventually played more than 700 times—with William Hawtrey's company. He joined this company in 1901, on return from touring Australia, India and China with the BROUGH COMEDY COMPANY, and stayed with it until it disbanded in 1906. Then he worked with various companies until he formed the MELBOURNE REPERTORY THEATRE COMPANY in 1911. As its director, between 1912 and 1917 McMahon averaged nine plays in three seasons annually. He relied on subscriptions for funds and most of his productions were new. To educate theatrical tastes, he established a club room, a library and several lecture series for subscribers.

McMahon began to direct occasional professional productions for J. and N. TAIT Ltd, through which the TAIT BROTHERS were challenging J. C. WILLIAMSON'S. In 1918 he moved to Sydney, where he directed the EMELIE POLINI Company in Edward Clark's *De Luxe Annie* for the Taits. Drawing from the Polini company, he also produced his first professional repertory theatre in special matinées, beginning with Shaw's *The Doctor's Dilemma*. The matinées were not successful and lasted only until the great influenza epidemic closed theatres early in 1919.

In 1920 McMahon agreed with the Tait brothers—who now controlled J. C. Williamson's—to establish the SYDNEY REPERTORY THEATRE SOCIETY. McMahon, as its director, would have artistic control and the Taits, if at least 700 subscriptions were collected, would provide a theatre and take financial responsibility for the society's production costs and club rooms. For seven years the society concentrated on the new British drama but members, suspicious of the Taits' intentions, became uneasy about the McMahon-Tait relationship. There were rumours that the Taits made undue profits from the society.

The tension snapped in 1928 when the Taits proposed that the society support a full-time professional repertory company directed by McMahon. It would produce six plays a season, including an Australian work, and tour these around Australia, putting repertory theatre on a surer commercial footing. McMahon had been reinstated as director of the Melbourne Repertory Theatre Company two years before, and the Taits intended to use Sydney and Melbourne subscriptions. Both societies rejected this. After a stormy meeting in Sydney, McMahon told journalists: 'Repertory is dead, it has been killed by the amateurs who thought that repertory only existed for themselves and their friends. During the last seven years Messrs J. and N. Tait have lost £5000 in entertaining 700 people.' The Sydney society, constitutionally linked with the Taits, folded and the Melbourne company found a new director.

The Taits' plan went ahead with McMahon forming the Gregan McMahon Play Company. It opened at the King's Theatre in Melbourne on 12 May 1928, with Shaw's *Getting Married*. A note in the program, headed 'Amateurs Goodbye', proclaimed the dream of instituting professional repertory in Australia. *Getting Married* was followed by J. M. Barrie's *Dear Brutus* with McMahon as Lob, Eugene O'Neill's *Anna Christie*, John Drinkwater's *Bird in Hand*, Louis Stone's *Lap of the Gods*, John Galsworthy's *The Pigeon* and Githa Sowerby's *Rutherford and Son*, each playing two weeks. The company then moved to Sydney, opening with *Dear Brutus* on 3 September 1928. Each play again ran for two weeks, except *Lap of the Gods*, which was taken off after a week and replaced by a revival of *Bird In Hand*.

Critics in Sydney and Melbourne praised the plays and performances and reported large, enthusiastic first-night audiences. However, audiences fell away sharply after the opening, LOUIS ESSON observed. He described the company as a 'mixture of duds and derelicts'. The Taits apparently saw the enterprise as a training ground for commercial productions and poached McMahon's actors, to the detriment of the new company. And when it was not a box-office success, J. C. Williamson's quickly began to use McMahon for commercial productions. He did not renew his contract but joined FULLERS', reviving *A Message from Mars* in 1929 at the Bijou Theatre in Melbourne and later at the Palace. He also established a semiprofessional company, the GREGAN McMAHON PLAYERS in 1929. He stayed with Fullers' until mid-1931 and then returned briefly to J. C. Williamson's, drawing crowds with his production of Galsworthy's *Loyalties*, starring FRANK HARVEY. The Gregan McMahon Players also appeared in the Firm's theatres.

In 1933 McMahon moved to the Garrick Theatre in Melbourne, directing F. W. THRING's Efftee Players in Christie Winsloe's *Children in Uniform*. The Gregan McMahon Players also appeared there. Next Thring and McMahon jointly established the New Comedy Company, which announced a three-month season from Boxing Day 1933. This was McMahon's last fully professional repertory company. In

April 1934 the Gregan McMahon Players were back at the Garrick. From mid-1935 until his death in 1941, McMahon was again with J. C. Williamson's, for which the Players performed eight plays a year.

McMahon was criticised for his repertoire and patronage. LOUIS ESSON, striving to establish a national theatre, looked to the poetic drama of the Abbey Theatre in Dublin rather than the 'so-called intellectual drama' associated with the Royal Court in London. 'What did McMahon create?' he cried, advocating the production of local plays. McMahon did produce Australian plays. The Melbourne Repertory Theatre Company staged 13 in six years from 1911. In 1916, a magazine produced by the company, the *Repertorian*, offered to aid budding dramatists through a play-reading service. After 1917 McMahon produced less Australian material, but perhaps because of a shortage of plays. The *Repertorian* argued that many plays it received showed 'an entire lack of knowledge of dramatic technique and of the requirements of either a Repertory or a Commercial Theatre'. Esson, for all his enthusiasm, encountered the same problem with the PIONEER PLAYERS.

The quality of the play was of central importance to McMahon and he argued that it was a service to Australian writers to let them see excellent foreign plays. His propensity for producing British plays also reflected the mood of the times, particularly in the 1920s. McMahon had the trappings of the professional middle-class. His dramatic preferences, nurtured at the University of Sydney, attracted support from leading academics, lawyers and doctors. His seasons were certainly fashionable but audiences and critics alike appreciated his productions, for both technical excellence and the overall quality of performance.

Through his remarkable talents as a judge of drama, a character actor, a director and a trainer of acting talent he created a theatre that excited people of a similar background. It was neither the folk theatre of Esson's dreams nor a sterile intellectual theatre—indeed McMahon's theatricality led others to chastise him for a tendency towards melodrama. It was a literary theatre open to the best on the international stage. For 30 years he championed his personal theatrical vision and for much of that time was subsidised by a professional management known for its shrewdness. Such combinations are rare.

McMahon's career depended greatly upon his own energy. He considered himself a moulder of talent and he was suspicious of the flexibility of performers spawned by the professional theatre. He wrote in a draft letter in 1938: 'My organisation occasionally employs a professional actor'. In parentheses, but crossed out, is added: 'tho' a competent one is difficult to find'. Many of the amateurs McMahon trained only remained in the theatre for recreation. Those who turned professional, such as CORAL BROWNE, typically went abroad. The Gregan McMahon Players died with him, as there was no-one to take his place. ❦*Victoria Chance*

further reading
ASHBOLT, ALLAN. Gregan McMahon. *Australian Dictionary of Biography* 10. Melbourne University Press 1986.
ASHBOLT, ALLAN. Gregan McMahon. *Focus* 2/12 (February 1948) and 3/1 (March 1948).
ASHBOLT, ALLAN. Courage, contradiction and compromise. *Meanjin* 37/3 (Melbourne 1978).

DOUGLAS, DENNIS and MARGERY MORGAN. Gregan McMahon and the Australian theatre. *Komos* (Melbourne) 2/2, 2/4, 3/1–4.
Triad 10/3 (Sydney, 1 January 1925).
reference
Gregan McMahon papers are in the Mitchell Library (Sydney).

Anew McMaster
> Irish actor-manager 1891–1962. Made stage debut in London under Fred Terry 1911. Toured Australia with Oscar Asche 1922–24. Formed touring company 1925. Toured Australia in association with Carroll–Fuller management 1949. Formed local company in Perth. Returned to Ireland 1950.

Anew McMaster first toured Australia playing Iago to the Othello of OSCAR ASCHE. After successful career on the London stage he formed his own company in 1925 and devoted most of the next 30 years to playing Shakespeare in the cities and small towns of Ireland. He believed that the Irish were closest to the Elizabethans in language and iconography. Allied to this belief was an ill-defined nationalist support for the recently independent Irish Free State.

In 1949 McMaster toured Melbourne, Adelaide and Perth with a company mainly recruited in England and augmented by Australian actors. PETER O'SHAUGHNESSY played major supporting roles in Melbourne and Adelaide. After the tour McMaster stayed in Perth and formed a company of local actors. He produced *Macbeth*, Oliver Goldsmith's *She Stoops to Conquer*, and a dramatisation of Charles Dickens's *Oliver Twist* in which 12-year-old Margaret Anketell played the title-role. She later trained and made a career in England. She was asked to play Desdemona to McMaster's Othello in Dublin in 1962, but he died during rehearsals. A stalwart of Perth theatre since 1970, Anketell attributes her career to his encouragement.

McMaster had a boundless sense of fun and a great dramatic talent that was frequently marred by his lack of discipline and stage eccentricities. Too often it was his relationship with his audience rather than his talent that determined the quality of his performance. Harold Pinter, who joined the McMaster Company in the early 1950s, describes, with affection and humour, McMaster's personality and eccentricities in his book *Mac*. ❦*Colm O'Doherty*

further reading
FITZ-SIMON, CHRISTOPHER. *The Boys*. London Nick Hern 1994.
MACLIAMMÓIR, MICHEÁL. *All for Hecuba*. London: Methuen 1946.
PINTER, HAROLD. *Mac*. London: Pendragon Press 1968

Jim McNeil
> Dramatist. Born 23 January 1935 in Melbourne. Spent 14 years in prison during 1956–74. Began writing plays 1970. First plays produced 1972. Australian Writers' Guild Awgie award 1975 for *How Does Your Garden Grow*. Married to actor Robyn Nevin 1975–77. Died 16 May 1982 in Sydney.

Jim McNeil holds an unassailable place among prisoners who have written plays. His playwriting career was the brief flowering of an extraordinary instinctive talent. He was a product of a singular evolutionary moment when everything Australian was of absorbing interest and the rough convict origins of NSW—previously a matter of shame in polite society—were being openly aired for the first time. McNeil was the youngest child of a Scots-Irish family. His father died when he was small and he had a desultory formal education in Catholic schools until he was 13. During the Second World War he joined gangs of children who tried the patience of American soldiers and their girls in the St Kilda district of Melbourne. He soon learned small confidence tricks to earn pocket money for himself and cigarettes for his mother. As a teenager he graduated into the underworld of brothels and racing gangs and soon claimed to be a familiar of famous criminals. In 1956 he was married and received his first conviction, for receiving stolen goods, after an escapade with his elder brother Patrick. He spent all but four years in jail until 1974, when he was released after serving seven years of a 17-year sentence for armed robbery and the shooting of a policeman. McNeil and his wife had six children—'one for each release'.

He began writing seriously in the prison at Parramatta, where he was a member of an exclusive group of intellectual prisoners who debated teams from outside. His first work was *The Chocolate Frog* in 1970. *The Last Cuppa*, later retitled *The Old Familiar Juice*, followed in 1972. After they were performed in prison, both plays were introduced into the professional theatre in Sydney in the same year. Perhaps as a result of the press attention they received, McNeil was moved to the jail at Bathurst (NSW), where he wrote his major work, *How Does Your Garden Grow*.

His growing reputation as a playwright led to a campaign in support of his parole, and on 12 October 1974 he was released with the premiere of *How Does Your Garden Grow* in rehearsal at the Nimrod Theatre in Sydney and a grant from the literature board of the Australia Council. In the same year his wife divorced him and in 1975 he married the actor Robyn Nevin. This stormy union lasted two years. McNeil completed his last play, *Jack*, in 1977. After the years of institutional life he found it impossible to adapt to self-reliance and the strange world of the writer in which he found himself. He began to drink heavily and he spent his last years on the charity of friends and in homes for alcoholics in Melbourne and Sydney.

Though he was almost devoid of formal education, McNeil was a voracious secret reader from childhood, and his brother Patrick, a seaman and knockabout who filled the place of his father, introduced him to philosophy and the classics. The gloomy prophets Friedrich Nietzsche and Arthur Schopenhauer, Omar Khayyam and Oscar Wilde were among Jim McNeil's favourite writers, and references can be found in his work. He was quite ignorant of the theatre, but he found it an ideal platform. His prison education contributed to this. The economy of his dialogue, the rhythms of time too slowly passing, the word-games played by characters fearful of being overheard or understood; and the rich subtext of unspoken truths, are evidence of a writer to whom privacy was all important. He had a real need to communicate to the outside world his simple statement that prisoners are ordinary people trapped by an outdated social system, and have the same domestic needs as people outside.

Though the fervour of the early 1970s made possible the discovery of McNeil's talents, he was not a seminal influence upon the prison system. What appears at first surprising about the plays he wrote in jail is the emphasis, not on violence but on the ways in which the inmates improvise, create hierarchies and deceive the warders; and the ways they find to make a private space in an institution where privacy is systematically invaded. McNeil's last play, *Jack*, contains a first half that was conceived, and possibly written, in the Bathurst jail, and stands on its own as a statement of the extremes to which a man deprived of love may go. The second half, written after three years of 'freedom', is the work of a mind angered by disappointment, who sees prison as irredeemably cruel and destructive. The unrelenting viciousness of the warder and the repetitious expletives with which the protagonist expresses his blind frustration, are evidence of freedom for the first time from prison censorship and from the constraints of an institution whose ordered life had been fundamental to the creation of a playwright. ❦*Katharine Brisbane*

published plays
The Chocolate Frog. (1971). Sydney: Currency Press 1973, 1986.
The Old Familiar Juice (1972). Sydney: Currency Press 1973, 1986.
How Does Your Garden Grow (1974). Sydney: Currency Methuen 1974.
Jack (1977). Sydney: Currency Press 1987 in *Collected Plays by Jim McNeil*.

further reading
TRIBE, PAUL and BRUCE HOGG. *Jim McNeil's 'The Chocolate Frog' and 'The Old Familiar Juice'*. Sydney: Currency Press 1987. Resource material.

John Meillon OBE

Actor. Born 1934 in Sydney. Stage debut 1946. Professional debut 1948. Toured in John Alden Company 1951. In England 1959–64. Many film and television roles. Married to actor June Salter 1958–71 and to actor Bunny Gibson from 1971. Died 11 August 1989 in Sydney. OBE 1979. Father of actor John Meillon jnr.

John Meillon's career lay chiefly in film and television but his early training was in the theatre, where he developed delicate accuracy of timing and the finesse of holding a moment of stillness. He used these qualities most effectively throughout his career. It began with INDEPENDENT THEATRE in Sydney when he was 12. In 1948, his fourteenth year, he acted in the premiere of DOROTHY BLEWETT's *The First Joanna*, played Puck in *A Midsummer Night's Dream* for METROPOLITAN THEATRE, and gave a telling performance in the title-role of Terence Rattigan's *The Winslow Boy* at the Minerva Theatre. This was his professional stage debut, although he had been acting professionally on radio.

His training had continued in the classic tradition when he toured in Shakespeare with the JOHN ALDEN COMPANY in 1951. At the Independent in 1953 he played Biff in Arthur Miller's *Death of a Salesman* and in 1955 the young director in Clifford Odets's *Winter Journey*. He toured with Ursula Jeans and Roger Livesey in William Douglas Home's *The Reluctant Debutante* in 1956–57. He had great success in the Phillip Street revue *Cross Section* in 1958 and at the end of the season he married his co-star JUNE SALTER.

Film work took Meillon to England for six years. He returned to star with Salter in Charles Dyer's *Rattle of a Simple Man* in Sydney in 1964. Later his prestige in film and television grew and his forays into the theatre became rare. One was to play Jock, the bullying club manager, in David Williamson's THE CLUB for the HUNTER VALLEY THEATRE COMPANY in Newcastle (NSW) in 1978–79. ❦*Lynne Murphy*

Melbourne

A temperate climate supplies Melbourne with the exposure to cold that is essential to a serious theatrical culture indoors. A gently undulating site, uninterrupted by watery incursions, permitted a grid of wide streets, giving easy access to a theatreland-cum-red-light district. This centred on eastern Bourke Street from the mid-1850s, when large-scale professional theatre came to Melbourne after a few years' meagre pioneering at the ROYAL PAVILION SALOON and the Queen's Theatre, at the other end of town. In the 1850s sizeable parcels of inner-city land could still be bought cheaply, and three of these are still occupied by theatres.

The expansion was a consequence of the enormous immigration brought about by the gold rushes. Big new theatres were meeting places for a population that was young and for a time predominantly male, well educated and surprisingly sophisticated in its tastes. As these tastes had generally been formed by the travelling tragedians of the British provinces, Melbourne entrepreneurs were soon offering these same stars—including James Anderson, G. V. BROOKE, Charles Dillon and BARRY SULLIVAN—enormous inducements to undertake tours. Several of them also had periods in management. The timing was lucky. A decade earlier the provincial stage had been of much lower calibre, while the recovery of London theatre only dated from the late 1840s. It was also new for theatregoers to be avid readers of newspapers. In Melbourne the press set standards for the rest of the continent and made theatre the focus of furious disputes between ideologically committed critics.

The spacious, ornate theatres of the gold-boom and land-boom years, 1854–88, the Princess's Theatre, the THEATRE ROYAL, the Haymarket Theatre, the Prince of Wales Opera House and the Alexandra Theatre, were not successful speculations for their builders. In the best traditions of unbridled *laissez-faire*, fortunes were made and lost by undercapitalised lessee managements for whom the unearthing of a hit play or a new star was often the only shield against bankruptcy. Amid this entrepreneurial chaos, two promoters, GEORGE COPPIN and the opera king W. S. LYSTER, succeeded in staying afloat while working in patient rivalry towards the ideal of an intercolonial touring chain based in Melbourne.

To fulfil this aim, each had to adapt to a drastic change in public tastes from 1870 onward, as the older gold-boom generation, with its preferences formed in Great Britain, was supplanted by its colonial-born children. Juveniles also made their way on stage in large numbers, especially in pantomime and comic opera. The leading male players were still mostly imports, but the first Australian superstar, NELLIE STEWART, and several other locally trained female stars began their careers in the 1870s. Since the decade also brought fewer overseas stars, local performers had to exercise greater creativity in working up scripts for which professional memories carried no blueprint. What HATTIE SHEPPARDE and Eleanor Carey made of Tom Robertson's *School* in 1872 was reportedly very charming, but can have owed little to Squire and Marie Bancroft, who presented it in London. The lengthening of runs resulted in diminished versatility but allowed roles to be done with greater polish.

The 1880s, the climax of the land boom, saw the general audiences that had supported the huge multi-tier houses breaking down into separate working-class, *petit-bourgeois* and wealthy constituencies. The working class followed low melodrama at the Princess's and Alexandra Theatres, while the *petits bourgeois* favoured operetta and expensively mounted sensation plays at the Theatre Royal, and the wealthy supported the more intimate Bijou Theatre, the home of West End light comedy and the occasional 'problem play'. The Prince of Wales Opera House began the decade as a 'high-class' venue but eventually evolved into the Melbourne home of vaudeville.

The working-class audience was the most hospitable of the three to locally written plays on Australian themes. These patterns suffered some disruption at the hands of the aspiring monopolists WILLIAMSON, GARNER AND MUSGROVE. But during the triumvirate's early years its control was intermittent, sometimes extending over three theatres and at other times shrinking to one. Its initial base was Melbourne, which then had a larger population than Sydney, but it was often cheaper to open the tour of a new show in free-trade NSW than in protectionist Victoria.

The depression of the 1890s changed this, as it did the very soul of Melbourne, which became a stuffy, rather puritanical place. The theatre did not suffer as severely as other aspects of the Victorian economy, but it did become a target for moralistic politicians. Theatres had always relied heavily on bars and prostitution, the former for direct profit and the latter for ticket sales. An outcry was raised against these supports of the industry, and the final blow came in 1916 with the introduction of 6 p.m. closing of bars.

The years leading up to the First World War saw opulence and variety return to the Melbourne stage, but by then much of its individual character had gone, the victim of the touring production and domination by national chains. The pro-imperial attitudes of the period meant that the higher-priced circuits were dominated by British names and products. The conductor Alfred Cellier had already imposed Savoyard orthodoxy on Gilbert and Sullivan productions and the theatres in Bourke and Exhibition Streets were increasingly presenting the previous year's West End successes with the West End names of the previous or the next decade.

The exceptions to this rule were mostly due to the Sydney resident J. C. WILLIAMSON, a relic of an earlier period when there had been close ties between the Melbourne and

Opened in 1855, when Melbourne was only 20 years old, the Theatre Royal boasted an auditorium and stage to rival the largest London theatre. Its first owner went bankrupt within a year and from then until its destruction by fire in 1872 it was rarely profitable for any management

San Francisco stages. AMERICAN INFLUENCES remained strong in vaudeville, preparing the ground for the coming celluloid invasion from Los Angeles. The war years strengthened this tendency but also encouraged new heights of imperialist ardour. The bright point in a theatrical scene which was rapidly losing its regional identity was the brave work from 1911 of the MELBOURNE REPERTORY THEATRE COMPANY, but even this drew its inspiration from London. Meanwhile, ON OUR SELECTION had its premiere in Sydney. ❦*Harold Love*

20th century

The distinction between Sydney's mixture of energetic sophistication and bright superficiality, and Melbourne's combination of intellectual seriousness with parochial propriety does not do justice to the cultural life of either of Australia's largest cities. But Melbourne's primary place in the development of an Australian tradition of repertory theatre does give the cliché some substance. Despite the long and vigorous life of J. C. WILLIAMSON'S, the initiatives of risk-takers like KENN BRODZIAK, GARNET H. CARROLL and DAVID N. MARTIN, and the survival of the Comedy Theatre, HER MAJESTY'S THEATRE and the PRINCESS THEATRE through several recessions and refurbishments, it is in the growth of mostly small but tenacious 'alternatives' that Melbourne's theatrical life seems most distinctive in the 20th century. The movement began with all the requisite earnestness of purpose. In 1904 LEON BRODZKY set up the Australian Theatre Society with the dual aim of producing important plays from overseas and Australian plays reflecting 'the national life of the country'. Ominously, the society's plans for performance were never realised. The conflict between the promotion of indigenous writing and the reflection of the best that was being seen and heard overseas has continued in Australian repertory theatre, from its amateur beginnings to its expensively professional present.

The first Melbourne initiative in repertory performance, the Annual Drama Nights run by WILLIAM MOORE from 1909 to 1912, was wholly committed to the production of short plays by local playwrights—including LOUIS ESSON and Moore himself—in a style of presentation very suggestive of a club for the cognoscenti. If profits were occasionally made they were likely to be dissipated by the free coffee and cigarettes that accompanied long discussions at interval. The more prominent MELBOURNE REPERTORY THEATRE COMPANY, which GREGAN MCMAHON ran from 1911 to 1918, offered three plays a season and three seasons a year. But it increasingly focused on dedicated productions of plays by Anton Chekhov, Henrik Ibsen, George Bernard Shaw and August Strindberg, and found little room for local work. In 1912 Esson's full-length play *The Time is Not Yet Ripe*—a political comedy of manners that the playwright later disowned—was performed.

McMahon's approach brought into relief another of the perennial crises of choice faced by amateur theatre—the uneven performance standards of his amateur company coexisted uncomfortably with high ambitions for social acceptance. McMahon was proud of the viceregal support he enjoyed, and his company perhaps anticipated the dilemma of subsidised theatre later in the century in trying to reconcile creative vitality with sufficient respectability to avoid offending the taxpayer or the tourist.

The playful injunction 'Citizens in evening dress not admitted' on Moore's programs is more representative of the ideology of Melbourne repertory theatre in its 'alternative' manifestations. It implies a defiance of proprieties that suggests theatrical innovation, and might equate rough performance and poor attendance with integrity of purpose. The conventional view of Melbourne as high-minded in matters of principle and stable in commerce might suggest a dominant conservatism, but this is belied by the strength and influence of anti-establishment movements and debate on social issues in the city's cultural life.

The two most significant initiatives between the wars, the PIONEER PLAYERS and NEW THEATRE set themselves squarely against the status quo. The Pioneers' one-night-a-week repertoire was exclusively Australian, and sought to dramatise distinctive inner-urban and, especially, outback myths, but its founders' radical political attitudes were not particularly evident in the plays themselves. The left-wing New Theatre Melbourne, on the other hand, had a primary commitment to social change which consistently influenced its choice of plays, local in origin or not. It has existed since 1935 whereas other Melbourne alternative groups have been ephemeral. Its durability is probably a product largely of its appeal to an extra-theatrical interest group with a strong sense of common political purpose.

In the lean years after the Second World War strong groups based on the fringes of the city centre, like the amateur Melbourne Little Theatre Company in South Yarra and the radical EMERALD HILL THEATRE in South Melbourne, juggled commitments to works from overseas and scripts by Australian writers. But the most significant force in the city's theatrical life emerged from the University of Melbourne. The Union Theatre Repertory Company, under the direction of JOHN SUMNER, a man with broad experience in English repertory, began at the university's Union Theatre in 1953. Later, as the heavily subscribed and richly subsidised MELBOURNE THEATRE COMPANY, it moved to multiple premises in the centre of the city. With the opening of the VICTORIAN ARTS CENTRE the company became established in the Playhouse as the city's theatrical showcase.

This company has enjoyed a consistency of box-office success unparalleled by any other state company. Its detractors have seen in it a mixture of social conservatism and theatrical imperialism, and a tendency to conform to the English repertory model at the expense of challenging forms of theatre from other cultures and of local writing in particular. Its record is still impressive. It has established a

A new theatrical era began in Melbourne in 1955 when the Union Theatre Repertory Company performed Ray Lawler's Summer of the Seventeenth Doll. *In 1975 Lawler told the story of the summer of the first doll in* Kid Stakes. *In 1976* Other Times *told of the ninth summer. All three plays were performed in 1977 as the* Doll Trilogy *with (left) Sandy Gore as Olive and Bruce Myles as Roo*

A seedbed of Australian drama in the 1970s was the Pram Factory (left). Here the Australian Performing Group acted new plays and in a new style. The audience enjoyed close proximity to the action, as indicated by the spectators behind the bottles in this scene from the first production of David Williamson's Don's Party. *The central actor is Rod Moore*

near-monopoly of Melbourne actors and of audiences in productions of classics and of recent overseas triumphs, and it is certainly better than any other state company at promoting Australian plays—at least those that have come to be defined as the mainstream. It earned a place in history as the company that mounted the first performance of Ray Lawler's *Summer of the Seventeenth Doll* and successfully played it in London's West End. It has faithfully offered the plays of the spectacularly popular DAVID WILLIAMSON. Despite the unmistakably establishment aura that surrounds the company, it has been sufficiently pre-emptive in repertoire to make competition difficult. In the highly centralised Melbourne theatrical scene, there have often seemed to be few openings.

The tradition of defiantly anti-establishment little theatre in Melbourne and the solid existence of the Melbourne Theatre Company contributed to the new wave of 'rough theatre' that shaped Australian drama in the heady late 1960s and the 1970s. This was fuelled on the campuses of Latrobe, Melbourne and Monash Universities and the Secondary Teachers' College in Carlton. The confines of the tiny LA MAMA THEATRE in Carlton encouraged a close-up stylisation that suited the dominant political satire. By 1970, when the AUSTRALIAN PERFORMING GROUP moved from La Mama around the corner to the Pram Factory the man-

ner of the stage cartoon had virtually pre-empted the Grotowskian and other flirtations of the La Mama period. The APG survived for a decade, and established itself as by far the most significant single force in a revolution in Australian theatre. To the mainstream theatre and to critical recognition it bequeathed the work of JACK HIBBERD, BARRY OAKLEY, JOHN ROMERIL and Williamson and to the performing arts such original minds as GRAEME BLUNDELL, PETER CUMMINS, LINDY DAVIES, MAX GILLIES and TONY TAYLOR. The authentic voice of the new drama was heard in their accents. That influence was consolidated with the establishment of the VICTORIAN COLLEGE OF THE ARTS, which gave Melbourne a professional training institution to rival the NATIONAL INSTITUTE OF DRAMATIC ART in Sydney.

By the 1980s that movement had lost some impetus. At the Anthill Theatre in South Melbourne and later at the Gasworks in Albert Park the AUSTRALIAN NOUVEAU THEATRE offered a determinedly non-parochial alternative in its programs of the contemporary European avant garde. At its best Anthill could be very exciting, but its pride in being counter-cultural involved repudiation of the dream of a genuinely popular indigenous theatre, which the APG had striven—with very little success—to realise. John Ellis's Church Theatre struggled to stay open as a venue for mostly new Australian writing, but found that its suburban location in Hawthorn exacerbated the problems that had bedevilled the Pioneer Players.

The PLAYBOX THEATRE CENTRE, which began life in 1976, has passed through several crises in its efforts to establish an identity and a home beyond the MELBOURNE THEATRE COMPANY's long shadow. After perilous if often exciting trial and error, its move to the CUB MALTHOUSE in 1990 and its accompanying commitment wholly to new Australian writing promised to strengthen its position as Melbourne's other leading professional company. But Playbox is hardly an alternative in the radical sense, though it continues to take risks on untried plays and on experiments with acting styles such as Tadashi Suzuki's *The Chronicle of Macbeth* in 1992, and the Suzuki-inspired *King Lear* in 1993.

The most enduring forms of alternative theatre in Melbourne in the late 20th century, however, are perhaps to be found outside the little theatres that have devoted much of their energies to bending society to a particularly ideology. THEATRE-RESTAURANTS might be seen as the form that, at its best, could most effectively relate a perception of real life to models created in performance. There were few of the full-scale satirical revues that proved so successful in Sydney theatre. The Melbourne form of theatre-restaurant began with music-hall and fruity melodrama but it evolved into a kind of cabaret based largely on STAND-UP COMEDY, which could move easily between the outrageously zany and the politically confronting. ♥*Peter Fitzpatrick*

further reading
DAVIDSON, GRAEME. *The Rise and Fall of Marvellous Melbourne*. Melbourne University Press 1978.
DAVIDSON, JIM (ed.). *The Sydney-Melbourne Book*. Melbourne: Allen and Unwin 1986.
DOUGLAS, DENNIS and MARGERY MORGAN. Gregan McMahon and the Australian Theatre. *Komos* 2/2 (November 1969), 2/4, 3/1-4 (March 1973).
LOVE, HAROLD. *The Golden Age of Australian Opera*. Sydney: Currency Press 1981.
O'BRIEN, ANGELA. The road not taken—Melbourne New Theatre 1935 to 1960. Monash University PhD thesis 1990.
SUMNER, JOHN. *Recollections at Play—A life in Australian theatre*. Melbourne: University Press 1993.

Melbourne International Festival of the Arts

Melbourne's international festival has seen controversy and undergone several metamorphoses since it began in 1986, but its growth has reflected the increasing awareness of Melbourne's ethnic diversity. There were some initial misgivings about the diversion of arts subsidy when the Victorian government, lobbied by the Italian community, began the festival in 1986 as the Spoleto Melbourne Festival of Three Worlds. The artistic director of the first two festivals was the American composer Giancarlo Menotti, who linked it to his original Festival of Two Worlds in Spoleto (Italy) and his Spoleto festival in Charleston (South Carolina, USA). The Melbourne festival was renamed in 1990. Opera and music-drama are the dominant interests but drama contributes substantially.

The first festival presented world premieres of four Australian plays and one French play, all by Melbourne companies, and the Colla Family Marionettes from Milano. The highlight was Darryl Emmerson's music-drama, *The Pathfinder*. Menotti's second festival commissioned NIGEL TRIFFITT's multimedia spectacle *The Fall of Singapore* and JOHN ROMERIL's adaptation for the Playbox Theatre Company of a Chinese play, *The Imposter* by Sha Yexin, but imported its other productions. Asian connections have featured in most subsequent festivals.

The highlight of the mainly international 1988 Spoleto Festival was the touring English Shakespeare Company's *Wars of the Roses* cycle. JOHN TRUSCOTT replaced the largely absent Menotti as director for the 1989 festival. He brought a more festive atmosphere to this and the next two festivals, especially by introducing free street theatre outside the Victorian Arts Centre, which became the principal venue. Truscott offered short seasons of few drama productions, mixing imported attractions, such as the Moscow Art Theatre in *The Seagull* by Anton Chekhov in 1991, and local commissions, such as Nigel Triffitt's lavish *Moby Dick* in 1990.

Richard Wherrett directed the 1922 and 1993 festivals. He brought a largely Spanish and Latin-American flavour to the former, with productions of Pedro Calderón's *Life is a Dream* by AUSTRALIAN NOUVEAU THEATRE and Lope de Vega Carpio's *Fuente Ovejuna* by the QUEENSLAND THEATRE COMPANY. The 1993 festival was broadly international. Highlights included the Romanian National Theatre of Craiova in *Titus Andronicus* and a production of Roger Bennett's *Funerals and Circuses* by Adelaide's Magpie Theatre Company. Leo Schofield became artistic director in 1994.

An independent but enterprising and highly stimulating Fringe Festival accompanies the Melbourne International Festival, and predates it by several years. There was also a short-lived parallel multicultural festival, Piccolo Spoleto. ♥*Geoffrey Milne*

Melbourne Repertory Theatre

Amateur dramatic society in Melbourne, founded in 1944 by Lorna Forbes and Sydney Turnbull. Closed 1949. **venue** refurbished cinema in Middle Park. **first production** *The School for Scandal* by R. B. Sheridan, 9 June 1945. Director Lorna Forbes.

A noted Shakespearean actor, LORNA FORBES, and an amateur director, Sydney Turnbull, founded Melbourne Repertory Theatre. Turnbull manufactured stage machinery in his engineering business and as a hobby he produced musical and dramatic shows to give young people a chance to develop their talents. In Middle Park, an inner suburb, Turnbull leased a cinema and converted it for stage productions. It held only 200 but the stage area was large. Young performers were offered tuition in a theatre workshop, separately at first and later in association with the Melbourne Repertory Theatre.

Forbes, who undertook to direct eight plays, played Mrs Candour in her opening production of *The School for Scandal*. The cast also included RAY LAWLER, a 24-year-old engineering student, whose first play, *Hal's Belles*, a three-act comedy, opened at the theatre on 29 September 1945. It featured FRANK THRING as Henry VIII. The group appears to have presented at least one Australian musical, *Alaya* in 1947. When the lease expired in 1949 the Turnbulls did not renew it, because his health was poor, and the company folded. Thring took over the theatre and reopened it as the ARROW THEATRE in 1951. ♥*Sally Dawes, Joan Maslen*

reference
Melbourne Repertory Theatre papers, MS 9758 in Australian manuscripts collection, La Trobe Library (Melbourne).

Melbourne Repertory Theatre Company

Amateur dramatic society in Melbourne, founded in 1911 by Gregan McMahon. Moved to Playhouse Theatre c.1916. Closed August 1918. Revived 1924-30. **first production** Act 2 of *The Critic* by R. B. Sheridan and *The Two Mr Wetherbys* by St John Hankin, 26 June 1911, at Turnverein Hall, Melbourne. **artistic directors** 1911-18, 1926-28 Gregan McMahon. 1928-30 Frank D. Clewlow.

The actor and director GREGAN MCMAHON established the Melbourne Repertory Theatre Company to present modern literary drama on the model of Annie Horniman's professional Repertory Theatre Company in Manchester (England). The stock companies in which McMahon had learned his craft no longer existed and he aimed to replace them with a repertory school in which the play was the primary consideration. He was not interested in grooming actors to be popular stars on the professional circuits. McMahon's company offered intellectual drama by modern writers as an alternative to the melodrama and musical comedy favoured by the professional managements. The company's first productions, Act 2 of *The Critic* and *The Two Mr Wetherbys*, alternating with Henrik Ibsen's *John Gabriel Borkman*, drew full houses and favourable reviews, especially the Ibsen.

From 1911 to 1916 the Melbourne Repertory Theatre Company staged three seasons a year, each comprising two new plays and one revival. McMahon was a staunch admirer of George Bernard Shaw, whose plays the company punctuated with works by Arnold Bennett, Anton Chekhov, John Galsworthy and Ibsen. A club with 400 subscription-paying members supported the company. McMahon was sympathetic to plays by Australian writers, and 13 of the more than 65 plays he presented between 1911 and 1918 were Australian, including LOUIS ESSON's *Dead Timber* in 1911 and THE TIME IS NOT YET RIPE in 1912.

In 1916 McMahon managed to secure a permanent residence for his company at the Snowden Picture Theatre, on a site now occupied by the VICTORIAN ARTS CENTRE. It was lavishly remodelled as the Playhouse Theatre. Nellie Melba attended the opening production, Shaw's *Man and Superman*, on 24 June 1916. By 1918 the First World War had deprived the repertory company of actors and adequate financial returns, and McMahon was forced to close the company and go to Sydney for a professional engagement with J. AND N. TAIT LTD.

The Melbourne Repertory Theatre Company re-emerged in 1924 from a University of Melbourne amateur group, the Mermaid Players. A former member of the original company, Helton Daniell, led the revival and directed the first production, Galsworthy's *Loyalties* at the Playhouse Theatre in December 1924. Without McMahon, the company tended to present entertainments staged and attended by figures from the social pages of *Table Talk*.

In 1926 J. and N. Tait Ltd, which now controlled J. C. WILLIAMSON's, proposed to build a drama theatre—the Comedy Theatre in Exhibition Street—that a repertory company directed by McMahon could occupy for three months of the year. In anticipation, the Melbourne Repertory Theatre Company reappointed McMahon as director and in 1927 J. and N. Tait Ltd presented six Melbourne Repertory productions, including Shaw's *Androcles and the Lion* and Anatole France's *The Man Who Married a Dumb Wife* at the Theatre Royal in February. In 1928 the Taits offered to finance a professional touring repertory company by enlisting the support and subscriptions of the SYDNEY REPERTORY THEATRE SOCIETY as well as the Melbourne company. Both declined the offer, however, electing to maintain independence and amateur status. McMahon, disappointed, departed from the Melbourne company to establish the Gregan McMahon Play Company for J. C. Williamson's. In March 1928 the Melbourne Repertory Theatre Company imported FRANK D. CLEWLOW from England to direct its productions. He resigned in 1930 and the company folded. McMahon's hopes of a repertory school were not completely without results. Two of his students, CORAL BROWNE and DORIS FITTON, went on to establish professional careers. So did the designer Loudon Sainthill, who began his training with McMahon. *Sally Dawes*

further reading

ASHBOLT, ALLAN. Courage, contradiction and compromise—Gregan McMahon 1874-1941. *Meanjin* 37/3 (Melbourne 1978).

DOUGLAS, DENNIS and MARGERY MORGAN. Gregan McMahon and the Australian Theatre. *Komos* (Melbourne) 2/2 (November 1969), 2/4, 3/1-4 (March 1973).

Melbourne Theatre Company

Professional dramatic company, founded in 1953 by John Sumner and University of Melbourne as Union Theatre Repertory Company. Renamed Melbourne Theatre Company 1968. **venues** 1953-66 Union Theatre, University of Melbourne. 1966-94 Russell Street Theatre. 1973 St Martin's Theatre. 1977-84 Athenaeum Theatre. 1984- Playhouse at Victorian Arts Centre. 1994– George Fairfax Studio at Arts Centre. **artistic directors** 1953-55 John Sumner. 1955 Ray Lawler. 1956-59 Wal Cherry. 1959-87 John Sumner. 1987- Roger Hodgman. **first production** *Colombe* by Jean Anouilh, 31 August 1953 at Union Theatre. Cast: Zoë Caldwell, George Fairfax. Director: John Sumner.

Australia's oldest extant professional theatre company, the Melbourne Theatre Company has had a reputation over the years for solid conservatism with occasional patches of excellence. Among its many strong and memorable productions must be counted *Who's Afraid of Virginia Woolf?* by Edward Albee in 1964, *The Homecoming* by Harold Pinter in 1965, *Moby Dick Rehearsed* by Orson Welles in 1967, *The Cherry Orchard* by Anton Chekhov in 1968 and *Henry IV—part 1*, staged outdoors at the National Gallery of Victoria in 1969, with FRANK THRING as Falstaff and ROBIN RAMSAY as Prince Hal. Notable Australian plays include Richard Beynon's THE SHIFTING HEART in 1962 and 1986, DAVID WILLIAMSON's *Jugglers Three* in 1972, JOHN POWERS's *The Last of the Knucklemen* in 1973, Ray Lawler's THE DOLL TRILOGY in 1976, JACK DAVIS's *The First-Born* trilogy at the Fitzroy Town Hall in 1988 and the musical THE VENETIAN TWINS in 1990.

The company has introduced audiences to most of the important contemporary writers from the USA, England, Ireland and, to a lesser extent, other European countries. It has also produced or done workshop productions of some 200 Australian plays. Nearly every Australian playwright of note has been on the company's lists at some time, and DAVID WILLIAMSON and ALEX BUZO have been produced most frequently. The company has also played host over the years to many of the country's leading actors, directors and designers. Its audiences have grown steadily, and by 1987, when ROGER HODGMAN took over as director, it was regularly playing to about 350 000 people. Since then total audiences, split between the RUSSELL STREET THEATRE and the Playhouse at the VICTORIAN ARTS CENTRE, have fallen back to about 300 000—a consequence in part of the recession, which hit Melbourne early and hard.

In many ways the Melbourne Theatre Company has reflected the tastes and background of its creator, JOHN SUMNER. He arrived from England in 1952 to manage the University of Melbourne's refurbished Union Theatre. Next year he persuaded the university to join him in founding a non-profit professional theatre company, which would operate from the Union Theatre between September and April, when it was not being used by students, and tour Victorian country towns for the remainder of the year. The university provided a £1500 guarantee against loss for the first season of the Union Theatre Repertory Company, as it was originally known. In the event the season made a profit of £895, playing to 38 507 paying customers. The second season, which played to 42 223, broke even financially and it was not until the tenth season, when the company incurred a loss of £13 507 that the university was actually called upon to contribute to the company's upkeep.

The Union Theatre Repertory Company was constructed on British repertory lines. Productions were changed every fortnight initially, but as the company grew in popularity, the normal production run was extended to three weeks. The company's stated objectives, set out in a brochure and repeated in programs, originally included:

Presentation of theatrical works which were not provided by commercial managements and which sought both to educate and to entertain.
Encouragement of Australian playwrights.
Presentation of Australian playwrights' works 'whenever practicable'.

The brochure was drawn up by David Derham, professor of law and later a member of the company's board. It expressed the hope that out of the enterprise would grow 'a truly professional Australian theatre, one which will be an expression of the drama and of the life of the people of this country and whose impact will be felt the world over'. The objectives remained company policy until 1992, when Hodgman introduced his own 14-point 'mission statement', which placed a new emphasis on widening public access through touring, while reinforcing the original commitments to new Australian writing and to first-class theatre with classic works from the past and the best of current overseas writing for the stage.

The company opened with Jean Anouilh's *Colombe*. Other playwrights in the first season included Christopher Fry, Terence Rattigan, George Bernard Shaw and Oscar Wilde. Notable early members of the company included ZOË CALDWELL, PATRICIA CONOLLY, NOEL FERRIER, Frank Gatliff, BARRY HUMPHRIES, MONICA MAUGHAN, FREDERICK PARSLOW, Alex Scott and FRANK THRING. The early seasons also included Carmel Dunn, who later became play-reader for the company and gave strong support to Australian playwrights. Sumner left the company in 1955 to manage the ELIZABETHAN THEATRE in Sydney. RAY LAWLER, who had joined the company the previous year, replaced him.

In November 1955 the company performed its first Australian play, Lawler's SUMMER OF THE SEVENTEENTH DOLL, with immediate success. The director was Sumner. Lawler, who played a role, stayed with the production on its subsequent Australian tour and went to London and New York with it.

WAL CHERRY, who had done several well-received guest productions, replaced Lawler as director of the company and ran it for the next three years. His term was marked by adventurous programming, high production standards, and financial problems. Cherry's repertoire included plays by Aristophanes, Ugo Betti, Bertolt Brecht, Federico García Lorca and Eugène Ionesco and strong representation from the USA. His tastes were a little in advance of the audience's, and patronage fell off.

Sumner returned as administrator-director of the company at the beginning of 1959 and held the position until he retired at the end of 1987. Under him, the company grew and prospered. In 1960 it began using the downtown Russell Street Theatre for occasional productions and then for short seasons, including an Australian-play season. This season lost money but one of the four plays, *The Shifting Heart*, proved a popular talking point. When the Union Theatre became unavailable in 1966, the company moved to Russell Street and operated there all year round. Over 39 weeks in 1966 the company played to 39 853 people, or 75·5 per cent of capacity. Sumner persuaded GEORGE OGILVIE, who had been with the company in its early days at the Union Theatre, to rejoin as associate director. Between them, they shared most of the directing load. The next few years were one of the company's best periods, with a high standard of production. The production policy, as defined by Sumner, now consisted of one-third classical writing, one-third new Australian writing and one-third writing from overseas. Mainstream companies in other states later followed this broad policy.

In 1968 the company improved the Russell Street Theatre and changed its name to the Melbourne Theatre Company. The company's close association with the university was not affected, however. At Russell Street, Sumner created a company of 20 actors who played throughout 1968, supplemented by another 24 who came and went. Malcolm Robertson was in charge of youth activities, and under him the company had an active program of touring to schools.

In 1971 Sumner greeted Ray Lawler's return to Australia, after a long sojourn in England and Ireland, by leasing the PRINCESS THEATRE for a season of Lawler's play on Governor Bligh, *The Man Who Shot the Albatross*, and Marcel Achard's *Patate*. The lead actor in both plays was LEO MCKERN, briefly returning to Australia. The company expanded its operations to the ST MARTIN'S THEATRE in 1973, in preparation for the eventual move into the VICTORIAN ARTS CENTRE, and later to the 884-seat ATHENAEUM THEATRE, where it also had the use of the 100-seat experimental Athenaeum 2.

Sumner systematically set about building up the audience in preparation for the Arts Centre. He was also concerned to improve standards. One way was to run each play at Russell Street and St Martin's for six weeks, with an option of a two-week extension. This meant that for the preparation of each new play eight weeks were available, four of them being devoted to rehearsals. In 1976, when total audiences exceeded 250 000 for the first time, nine-week seasons for each new play were introduced.

Sumner had used St Martin's as a stopgap, hoping that by 1977, when the lease would run out, the Arts Centre would be ready. Frustrated by the long delays, he leased the Athenaeum Theatre. It was designated for classical plays and revivals, and Russell Street, which the company owned, for contemporary works. There were accusations of empire-building in 1982 when two productions were switched to the Universal Theatre in Fitzroy while Athenaeum 2 was temporarily closed on fire department orders. The company opened at the Playhouse in the Arts Centre in May 1984 with Euripides's *Medea*. ZOË CALDWELL returned from the USA to play the title-role. It confined its operations to the Playhouse, where it has occupancy rights for 40 weeks a year, and the Russell Street Theatre until late 1994. Then it announced that it would leave the Russell Street Theatre—which was rundown and unpopular with audiences—for the George Fairfax Studio (since renamed the Fairfax) at the Arts Centre on the South Bank.

Roger Hodgman's period as director, which coincided with a drop in federal funding, has seen greater emphasis on touring and on co-productions with other mainstream companies. While pursuing a safe and more commercial-minded course, he has taken risks with productions such as Jack Davis's *The First Born* trilogy and ALMA DE GROEN's *The Rivers of China* in 1988, and JANIS BALODIS's *Heart for the Future*—the company's 500th production—and STEPHEN SEWELL's *Dreams in an Empty City* in 1989, The company also staged de Groen's *The Girl Who Saw Everything* in 1991 and Balodis's *No Going Back* in 1992, reflecting Hodgman's confidence in both playwrights. While its audiences have fallen from their record levels, the company still enjoys wide public and corporate support. ❦*Leonard Radic*

further reading

SUMNER, JOHN. *Recollections at Play—A life in Australian theatre*. Melbourne University Press 1993.

Melbourne Workers' Theatre

Professional collective of performers and writers, formed in 1987 by Michael White, Stephen Payne and Patricia Cornelius. **first production** *State of Defence* by Andrew Bovell. Cast: Payne, White and Cornelius. Director: Russell Walsh. Music: Irene Vela.

Melbourne Workers' Theatre was formed to produce plays with and for trade unionists, through the AUSTRALIA COUNCIL's Art and Working Life incentive program, and until 1994 was based in the Jolimont Railway Workshop. The company retains its union connections and it has widened its constituency to include work with communities ranging from Aborigines in Archie Weller's *Nidjera* in 1990 to sex workers in Reynolds's *Daily Grind* in 1992. It has consistently produced distinctive and high-quality multi-lingual music-theatre.

The company's first project, which gave rise to *State of Defence*, established a model for its work with unions, both in the relationships it consolidated and the methods it established for generating theatrical material. For each project a committee is formed to advise on issues, suggest avenues of research and act as sounding-board for scripts as they develop. Research, conducted by the writer and the performers, usually consists of informal interviews with people in the community at the centre of the project. The writer bases the script on the results of interviews, and checks it in open workshops, rehearsals and readings for the advisory committee, interviewees and interested members of the particular community. In this way plays are built out of the experiences and stories of members of a community with their direct assistance, and then performed in appropriate venues. Problems of access to workplaces have led to a shift towards performance in theatres, which has given the company's work greater prominence.

The centrality of research in the company's processes has grounded all its performances in social realism, although it has moved between conventional narrative drama and cabaret, both rendered distinctive by the contribution of the composer Irene Vela. ANDREW BOVELL established the former style in *State of Defence* and—with JOHN ROMERIL as dramaturge—in *The Ballad of Lois Ryan* in 1989. This style is represented at its most sophisticated in Romeril's *Black Cargo*, a powerful and inventive adaptation of a short story by John Morrison, with music by Vela, at the Anthill Theatre in 1991. This was the company's first show in a theatre.

Patricia Cornelius has been responsible for the development of the more cabaret-based style, in her *Dusting Our Knees* in 1988 and *The Aftermath* in 1990. Both mix monologue and song with social-realist storytelling and move easily between the private and personal and the more conventionally political. Cornelius and Vicki Reynolds extended the style in *Taxi*, which is more directly based on cabaret, in 1990. ❦*David Watt*

further reading

WATT, DAVID. Art and Working Life—Australian trade unions and the theatre. *New Theatre Quarterly*, 6/22 (Cambridge, England, May 1990).

WATT, DAVID. The trade union movement, Art and Working Life and Melbourne Workers' Theatre. *Australasian Drama Studies*, 14 (Brisbane, April 1989).

Aubrey Mellor OAM

Director, teacher, translator. Born 7 November 1947 at Gayndah (Qld) to Hec and Heather Mellor, magicians. Performed as child with two brothers in parents' act on Queensland and NSW variety circuits. Graduated from National Institute of Dramatic Art (Sydney) 1969. Churchill Fellowship to study Asian theatre 1972. Visited China 1973, 1979. Acting tutor at NIDA 1973-80. Artistic director of Jane Street Theatre (Sydney) seasons 1978-79. Joint artistic director of Nimrod Theatre Company (Sydney) 1981-83. Deputy director of NIDA 1986-87. Artistic director of Queensland Theatre Company 1988-93. Artistic director of Playbox Theatre Centre (Melbourne) 1993-. Has directed in every state. Guest director and teacher in United Kingdom, USA and Asian countries. OAM 1992.

Aubrey Mellor's career has been much influenced by political and social change within and without Australia. A popular acting teacher, he joined the NIMROD THEATRE COMPANY as joint artistic director at a time when it had lost direction after the advent of the SYDNEY THEATRE COMPANY, and he gave it a new impetus. He achieved prominence as a director of Anton Chekhov with *Three Sisters* in 1981 and *Uncle Vanya* in 1983. He has carried his care for detail in actors' work over into his directing career, and it has shone in his Chekhov productions. Nevertheless, he has evinced a taste for the bizarre and a love of the diverse European styles of theatre that address the larger issues.

He led Nimrod's adoption of a program of politically aware European theatre, including works by Dario Fo, Vaclav Havel, Ödön von Horváth and Caryl Churchill. He introduced a policy of making translations of European work specifically for Australian audiences—a policy now widely followed by other companies. He also experimented with group-devised work in *Burn Victim* in 1982; and directed MICHAEL GOW's first play *The Kid* in 1983. With JOHN BELL he oversaw Nimrod company's transfer to the SEYMOUR THEATRE CENTRE in 1984.

As artistic director of the QUEENSLAND THEATRE COMPANY Mellor devoted his energies to building performance standards and audiences, and to negotiations for a company home, together with a new Drama Theatre as stage 5 of the QUEENSLAND PERFORMING ARTS COMPLEX. He greatly increased the youth arm of the company, introduced a young people's playwriting competition, initiated a 'new writing' scheme of commissions and workshops and the George Landen Dann Award for a Queensland playwright. Among Mellor's productions for the Queensland Theatre Company were Henrik Ibsen's *Ghosts* in 1989, Dorothy Hewett's *The Man From Mukinupin* in 1989, Tennessee Williams's *The Glass Menagerie* in 1990, Chekhov's *The Cherry Orchard* and ERROL O'NEILL's *On the Whipping Side* in 1991, and two DAVID WILLIAMSON plays which toured nationally as a joint venture of the state theatre companies—*Money and Friends* (1991) and *Brilliant Lies* (1993). A notable production was the premiere of HANNIE RAYSON's *Hotel Sorrento* (1990) for the PLAYBOX THEATRE CENTRE in Melbourne and subsequently the Sydney Theatre Company.

Translations Mellor has co-written have included most of Chekhov's plays, August Strindberg's *Miss Julie* and Nicholas Erdman's *The Suicide* for Nimrod, Ibsen's *The Lady from the Sea* for the SOUTH AUSTRALIAN THEATRE COMPANY and Bertolt Brecht's *Mother Courage and her Children* for the JANE STREET THEATRE. ❦*Katharine Brisbane*

further reading
BRISBANE, KATHARINE. Nimrod faces renewal task. *National Times* 10-16 January 1982.
RICKETSON, MATTHEW. As they like it. *Australian Magazine* 5–6 March 1994.

Melodrama

Jean-Jacques Rousseau used the term melodrama in 1763 to refer to dialogue spoken to a musical accompaniment, but melodrama became a specific genre of spoken drama 30 years later in plays staged first in Paris after the French Revolution. René de Pixérécourt is credited with writing the first *mélodrames*—*Victor* in 1798 and *Coelina* in 1800. Thomas Hobcroft adapted the latter for the London stage in 1802 as *A Tale of Mystery*. *The Times* thought it had 'natural' dialogue where 'the words appear to be suggested by the circumstances'.

This story already had many of the characteristics of early melodrama as it is often parodied today—an orphaned heroine, a stern father and a villain with a guilty conscience. It used music to suggest the mood of scenes and the emotions of the characters, and finished with a visual and dramatic climax set in wild mountains, where the villain is smitten with remorse and refuses to kill the defenceless hero:

> No! Too much of your blood is upon my head! Be justly revenged: take mine!

When the hero in turn refuses to shoot him, the villain runs to a high bridge linking two mountain peaks, fights with his pursuers, and falls; he is injured but remains alive to hear his victims plead for his life to be spared.

Melodrama borrowed heavily from the Gothic novel, with its haunted castles, graveyards, and macabre stories, and quickly became ideally suited to examining the psychology of the individual and of a society under stress. Wish-fulfilment, nightmares, tricks of memory, telepathy, guilt and revenge, chivalry, infatuation, private thoughts and public postures, and the effects of the environment on the individual, were all popular subjects for dramatic treatment. So in J. S. Jones's 1839 *Captain Kyd* virtue and the devil fight for the pirate's soul, while he sees himself in competing visions as captain of a majestic three-masted ship and as a skeleton hanging from a gibbet. Cross-class marriages were frequent, villains were often unscrupulous capitalists, heroes and heroines were often poor and worthy, and pointed contrasts were made between scenes of wealth and luxury and scenes of poverty and suffering. 'Stonyheart the landlord' now appears only in mock, or 'cod', melodrama, but in the early 19th century melodrama gave powerful and sometimes radical expression to the anxieties of a society rent by the Industrial Revolution.

Another influence on melodrama was the fact that in both Great Britain and France 'legitimate' drama—in which dialogue was spoken—was allowed only in a few theatres licensed for the purpose. Other theatres circumvented this law by dialogue with music and other strategies, often accompanied by mime, pantomime, musical interludes, dance, visual spectacles, and trained animal acts. At Astley's Amphitheatre in London the story of the highwayman Dick Turpin was told, with his noble mare Black Bess carrying him safely beyond the reach of his enemies before falling down and raising her head to give him a dying nuzzle. Dogs would rescue heroes and heroines from drowning, and then, when the villain in turn fell into the (sometimes real) water, stand and bark at him.

In the second half of the 19th century the legitimate theatre transformed melodrama into a more politically conservative entertainment. The actor CHARLES KEAN, who toured Australia in 1863-64, was associated with the development of 'gentleman' melodrama in plays such as *The Corsican Brothers* and *Louis XI*, which the Irish playwright DION BOUCICAULT adapted for him from French originals in 1852 and 1855 respectively. Boucicault also pioneered 'sensation' melodrama, which increasingly relied on machinery and technical effects to create a thrilling climax to a scene. In his earliest, *The Poor of New York* of 1857, real fire engines extinguished a 'real' fire in an apartment building—the precursor of *Towering Inferno* movies. A decade later Augustin Daly, an American, invented sensation scenes which, with variations, are also still copied—the hero tied to the railway tracks in *Under the Gaslight* in 1867 and tied to a log that is cut in half by a timber saw in *The Red Scarf* in 1868.

When professional theatre established itself in Australia between 1830 and 1850 melodrama had already become the major form of British drama. By the 1860s GEORGE COPPIN, promoting Kean's tour of the colonies, noted that plays like *Louis XI* were proving more popular with Australian audiences than the lavish Shakespearean productions for which the actor was famous. A stage version of Harriet Beecher Stowe's novel *Uncle Tom's Cabin* arrived in

Australia in 1853, an adaptation of Mrs Henry Wood's *East Lynne* in 1867, and most of Boucicault's and Daly's plays within a year or two of their New York or London premieres. These kinds of plays were enduringly popular in the colonies. As late as 1907-09 the Brisbane theatrical calendar still contained many hoary old mid-century melodramas like *Camille* by Alexandre Dumas *fils*, *The Colleen Bawn* by Boucicault, *The Lady of Lyons* by Edward Bulwer-Lytton, *Ten Nights in a Bar-Room* by W. W. Pratt, *The Ticket of Leave Man* by Tom Taylor, *Lady Audley's Secret*, *Uncle Tom's Cabin* and *East Lynne*.

Fascination with the evils of the sinful city was a perennial theme, as in *Her Luck in London*, *How London Lives*, *Lost in London*, *Lured to London*, *Saturday Night in London*, *When London Sleeps* and *The Worst Woman in London*. Turf drama, started by Boucicault's *Flying Scud* in 1866, was followed in Australia in 1907 by PHILIP LYTTON's tent-theatre production of *The Cup Winner*, in which the canvas sides were lifted to allow horses to gallop past a finishing line set up between the orchestra and the audience.

Hybrid Anglo-Australian stories such as *No Wedding Bells for Her* began in 'The real Australian Bush ... Where the Kookaburras Laugh' before moving home to England and the development of the murky domestic plot. Australian melodramas were only ever a novelty item, but sometimes a very popular one. As early as 1834 Henry Melville's THE BUSHRANGERS was published and performed in Hobart. Even earlier J. Amherst's *Michael Howe, the Terror of Van Diemen's Land* and David Burn's THE BUSHRANGERS had appeared in Great Britain—the former in London in 1821, the latter in Edinburgh in 1829.

In 1870 WALTER COOPER, a Sydney journalist, showed that expensively-mounted Australian sensation melodramas could be financially successful when his *Sun and Shadow* ran for 22 nights in Sydney. It was followed within months by Archibald Murray's *Fleeced*. In 1871, after a visit to New York where doubtless he saw *The Red Scarf*, Cooper again succeeded in Sydney with *Foiled*, which 'borrowed' the log-saw sensation from Daly's play. Encouraged by this success, other Australian writers like F. R. C. HOPKINS and Julian Thomas ('The Vagabond') had moderate successes in the 1870s with similar plays.

Bushrangers in melodrama
From the 1880s onwards a few Australian stories could be found in the repertoires of some of the most prominent actor-managers, notably GEORGE DARRELL, ALFRED DAMPIER and DAN BARRY. There were convict dramas (three versions of FOR THE TERM OF HIS NATURAL LIFE appeared in 1886); goldrush dramas (Darrell's THE SUNNY SOUTH was a hit in 1884 and reached London in 1885 and, more successfully, in 1898); and evil-doings-in-the-big-city dramas (Dampier and Garnet Walch's MARVELLOUS MELBOURNE in 1889). But the most popular melodramas were based on the lives and deaths of the Kelly gang of bushrangers. The earliest was staged in Melbourne only weeks after the Stringybark Creek massacre in November 1878. Called *Fleeced*, it was a hasty rewrite of Murray's play. E. C. Martin's *Ostracised* was presented in 1881, the year after Ned Kelly was hanged. It ran for 29 performances in Melbourne but staging in Sydney was stopped by the police in 1882. Dampier and Walch tinkered with Rolf Boldrewood's novel to give a Kelly Gang flavour to ROBBERY UNDER ARMS in 1890. Reg Rede's *The Kelly Gang* in 1896 tinkered with Dampier and Walch and was a great success for Dan Barry's company during the next decade. At least seven other versions of the story, mostly plagiarised from Rede, appeared on Australian professional stages before the First World War. Other Australian melodramas with bushranging themes included Bert Bailey and Alfred Duggan's THE SQUATTER'S DAUGHTER, which was set in the days of Ben Hall and his gang, and ran for a near-record 12 weeks in Sydney in 1907. Australian melodrama had two twists of characterisation that were considered 'local' in nature. One was a heroine who could ride, shoot, swim, did not faint, and was seldom in danger of 'a fate worse than death'. Dorothy Deane in *Marvellous Melbourne* dives into the Yarra to save another girl from drowning. Violet Enderby in *The Squatter's Daughter* rejects an unworthy lover with scorn:

> You forget, Dudley, that I am an Australian girl. I've been accustomed to station life from childhood, and when I am thrown upon my own resources you will find me quite capable of managing my own affairs without your assistance.

The other twist was an Aboriginal companion, faithful to the hero unto death. Aborigines—always played by blacked-up whites, as far as is known—appeared as early as Burn's 1829 *The Bushrangers*, in which they were seen as colonists' enemies. The Aboriginal companion became popular after *Uncle Tom's Cabin* and Boucicault's *The Octoroon* of 1859 portrayed black Americans more sympathetically. The best-known stage Aborigine was Warrigal in *Robbery Under Arms*—not the treacherous half-caste of the novel but a resourceful, energetic, comic figure who smuggles the injured Captain Starlight away from the final shootout and nurses him back to health. These characters appear almost unchanged in present-day Australian films. Sybilla in Miles Franklin's 1901 novel *My Brilliant Career* is a typical squatter's daughter character and the 1979 film celebrates her independent spirit. In the *Crocodile Dundee* films of the 1980s David Gulpilil plays an Aborigine who has the same function as stage Aborigines a century ago.

Stage melodrama went into decline after the First World War. Greater realism and mass appeal made film and, later, television the natural entertainment forms which could continue to offer melodramatic stories without invoking derision from audiences. Comic send-up melodrama had a vogue in THEATRE-RESTAURANTS in the 1970s and 1980s but this had little in common with the most successful and enduring form of dramatic entertainment ever devised.
♥*Richard Fotheringham*

James Melville

Circus equestrian. Born 15 October 1837 in Scotland. Original family name Munro. Debut at Malcom's Royal Australian Circus, Sydney, in January 1852. Emigrated to USA. Toured USA with Melville's Australian Circus in 1860s. Died 1908 in USA. Father of equestrian Frank Melville.

A program for Malcom's Royal Australian Circus in the *Sydney Morning Herald* on 10 May 1852 described 'Master Melville' as 'the Australian Star Rider, whose acknowledged talent as an equestrian stands unrivalled'. He would 'exhibit his extraordinary performance on his favourite bareback steed, leaping bars, canvases and through a balloon!' it said. A son, Frank James Melville, was born to the young equestrian and his wife in Sydney on 16 September 1854, and some time after this the family left for the USA, never to return. An article in the American circus magazine *White Tops* in June 1932 recalled that in Washington in 1857 James Melville, 'the Australian champion', had been defeated by the American rider James Robinson in a contest to establish 'the greatest trick bareback rider in the world'. By 1861 Melville was touring with his own circus. It was billed as Melville's Australian Circus at St Louis (Missouri) in July 1861. In 1870 T. Allston Brown wrote that Melville was regarded as one of the best equestrians in the USA. Melville's obituary in the New York *Clipper* in 1908 said: 'He was recognised as being among the greatest bareback riders in the annals of the circus, and for years did an equestrian act which was in great demand'. This apparently involved somersaulting from the ground onto the bare back of a galloping horse. ❦*Mark St Leon*

further reading
BROWN, T. ALLSTON. *History of the American Stage*. New York: Dick and FitzGerald 1870.

Josie Melville

Actor, dancer, singer. Born c.1905 in Adelaide. Musical-comedy star in 1920s. Died c.1970 in Sydney.

Teenage Josie Melville became an overnight star in Jerome Kern's musical comedy *Sally*. The title-role of a little foundling who becomes a great dancer requires qualities that the musical-comedy director GEORGE HIGHLAND could not find in current stars in 1922. Highland believed in casting Australian actors and singers in leading roles and with the support of J. C. WILLIAMSON's he set out to find a fresh talent. In Adelaide he saw Melville in a revue, *The Peep Show*, and her brilliant dancing, remarkable personality and intelligence made her an immediate choice. He did not know if she had ever acted or could sing, but he was sure that he could help her to be right for *Sally*.

Sally opened in Sydney on 6 January 1923 and within two months it had broken all Williamson box-office records on the way to a total run of more than 500 performances. Critics raved about Melville's charm and her dancing. 'On the musical stage of Australia Miss Josie Melville is the most notable event since Miss Nellie Stewart was the one golden girl', declared the *Triad* of 10 February 1923. Melville became the darling of the gallery girls, her photographs were sold for charity, and Highland went to New York especially to secure Kern's new *Good Morning Dearie* for her. It opened in Sydney on 5 July 1924 and ran well but broke no records. In 1929 Melville appeared with Claude Hulbert and Stanley Holloway in a revue staged by J. C. Williamson's in London. She returned to Adelaide in the early 1930s and married John Glover. When the marriage failed she moved to Sydney. ❦*Lynne Murphy*

Men Without Wives

Play in three acts by Henrietta Drake-Brockman. **premiere** 30 April 1938, St James Hall, Sydney, by Sydney Players' Club. Cast: Valerie Ball, John Bishop, Edward Cavill, James Flanagan, Claude Fleeting, Eila Langton, Molly Ramsay, Valerie Scanlon, William Smith, William State, Doris Williams, Leslie Williams, William Wines, Walter Wright. Director: S. R. Irving. **published** Perth: Paterson 1938. Sydney: Angus and Robertson 1955.

A realist drama of station life in northwest Western Australia, *Men Without Wives* won HENRIETTA DRAKE-BROCKMAN the 1938 Commonwealth Sesquicentenary Prize for a play. She was in distinguished company—the novel prize went to Xavier Herbert for *Capricornia* and the poetry prize to R. D. Fitzgerald for *Essay in Memory*. 'In Ma Bates Mrs Drake-Brockman has created a character who will live long and deservedly in the affection of all Australians', wrote the competition's chief judge, S. Elliott Napier. The play has a variety of colourful characters, including hard-boiled stockmen, house-gins, a caddish jackeroo and restless young people but the most enduring personality is Ma Bates, 'a hard-bitten Northerner'. In the opening scene she has ridden bareback a hundred miles to seek quinine for a feverish fossicker. John Abbott, a station owner, arrives from Perth with his society bride, Kit. Life is picturesque at first but Kit's excitement soon turns to depression as she discovers the harshness and loneliness of the outback and the men's solace with black women. Her city-bred manners disturb the Bates family and their neighbours. The crisis comes when Ma's concealed pain is diagnosed as cancer and she is forced to travel south for treatment. But a rising flood bars her and the escaping Kit Abbott. For Ma it is an act of God, allowing her to die on her beloved land. For Kit it is a chance to reassess her values.

In November 1938 the REPERTORY CLUB produced the play in Perth and PAUL HASLUCK in the *West Australian* admired the colour and realism of its characters, social setting and plot. '"Ma" Bates steps at once to a front place among the memorable figures of Australian literature—a real "character" in the popular sense of the term, a woman as individual as any local identity in out city', he wrote. He had reservations about the structure, which built the conflict around Kit, who is well not so drawn. ❦*Katharine Brisbane*

Ivan Menzies

English actor, singer, 1896-1985. Trained as pianist and singer. Made professional debut in chorus of D'Oyly Carte Opera Company, March 1921. Principal in New D'Oyly Carte Opera Company 1922. Toured Australia and New Zealand for J. C. Williamson Gilbert and Sullivan Opera Company 1930, 1935-37, 1940-45 and 1950-51. Married to Elsie Griffin, operetta singer.

On four tours during more than two decades Ivan Menzies delighted Australasian audiences with his energy, movement and clear diction in the major comic baritone roles in GILBERT AND SULLIVAN operettas. He had been the understudy of Henry Lytton, the leading exponent in the 1890s of such roles as the Lord Chancellor in *Iolanthe*, the Duke of Plaza Toro in *The Gondoliers*, Ko-Ko in *The Mikado* and Jack Point in *The Yeomen of the Guard*. Menzies also performed in musical comedy and in 1943 he and BERYL BRYANT produced *Battle for Australia*, a wartime revue performed before both houses of the federal Parliament. He often visited community groups and schools, exploiting his fame to promote not only the J. C. Williamson Gilbert and Sullivan company but Moral Rearmament. This often caused conflict. After his last tour he devoted himself mainly to producing and performing plays and musicals consistent with the teach-

ings of Moral Rearmament, which he had joined in the early 1930s when it was known as the Oxford Movement.
❦*Phillip Lawton*

further reading
BEVAN, IAN. *The Story of the Theatre Royal*. Sydney: Currency Press 1993.
DE LOITTE, VINIA. *Gilbert and Sullivan Opera in Australia*. Sydney: privately published 1931.
MAGOR, CLIFF and EDNA MAGOR. *The Song of the Merryman*. London: Grosvenor 1976.
Canberra Times 24 April 1985.
Courier Mail (Brisbane) 19 June 1985.

Robert Menzies

Actor. Born 4 November 1955 in Melbourne. Grandson of Prime Minister Robert Menzies. Graduated from National Institute of Dramatic Art (Sydney) 1977. Professional debut at Jane Street Theatre, Sydney 1978. Artistic counsel to Belvoir Street Theatre (Sydney) 1988; Company B board 1988-89. Many film and television roles. Green Room Award for supporting actor 1982 (Limpy in musical *The Selection*).

The directors REX CRAMPHORN, JEAN-PIERRE MIGNON and JIM SHARMAN, all leaders in the search for an approach to the classics, have particularly influenced the career of Robert Menzies. His lean figure and rather haunted look, combined with a capacity to convey internalised emotion, quickly won him a reputation in classic outsiders' roles. He is equally skilled as a loose-limbed comic in roles like Cranky Jack in George Whaley's adaptation of ON OUR SELECTION, and Kiri Kuki in Mikhail Bulgakov's *The Crimson Island*, which he played at the 1992 Adelaide Festival.

Menzies played Lucky in Samuel Beckett's *Waiting for Godot* and Cranky Jack when he was in the JANE STREET THEATRE company in 1979. In 1980 he played the title-role in Jean Racine's *Britannicus* for Cramphorn at the University of Sydney and was selected for A Shakespeare Company, the director's investigation into acting style. In 1983 Menzies played Caesar in Cramphorn's landmark production of *Antony and Cleopatra* for the Playbox Theatre Company in Melbourne, followed by Angelo in *Measure for Measure* and Hamlet in 1985.

Between these roles he joined Sharman's Lighthouse Company in Adelaide, and played Lysander in *A Midsummer Night's Dream*, Warren in LOUIS NOWRA's *Spellbound*, the Recruiting Sergeant in Bertolt Brecht's *Mother Courage and Her Children* and the title-role in Nowra's adaptation of Heinrich von Kleist's *The Prince of Homburg*. Menzies first worked with Mignon in 1986, as Konstantin in *The Seagull* by Anton Chekhov for the SYDNEY THEATRE COMPANY and as Macbeth for AUSTRALIAN NOUVEAU THEATRE in Melbourne.

Other notable performances include Sydney Manus in Brian Friel's *Translations* in 1983, Edgar in *King Lear* for the NIMROD THEATRE COMPANY in 1984 and Oswald in Ibsen's *Ghosts* in 1988. Menzies played Hamlet and the title-role in *Henry IV—part 1* for Dramaturgical Services Inc. in Sydney in 1987. His roles for the MELBOURNE THEATRE COMPANY include the Man in ALMA DE GROEN's *The Rivers of China* in 1988, Wisehammer-Collins in Timberlake Wertenbaker's *Our Country's Good* and Plume in George Farquhar's *The Recruiting Officer* in 1989, Peter in Wendy Wasserstein's *The Heidi Chronicles* and the Rev. John Hale in Arthur Miller's *The Crucible*. ❦*Katharine Brisbane*

Mercury Theatre

Professional dramatic company in Sydney founded in 1946 by Allan Ashbolt, Peter Finch, Sydney John Kay, Colin Scrimgeour and John Wiltshire. **first production** *Diamond Cuts Diamond* by Nikolai Gogol, *The Pastrybaker* by Lope de Vega Carpio and *The Broken Pitcher* by Heinrich von Kleist, 16 July 1946, at NSW State Conservatorium of Music. **last production** *Ring Round the Moon* by Jean Anouilh, December 1953, St James Hall, Sydney.

Strong dissatisfaction with the state of Australian theatre felt by servicemen and many civilian theatre-lovers towards the end of the Second World War led to the formation of Mercury Theatre in Sydney in 1946. The catalyst for its formation was SYDNEY JOHN KAY, a German musician and theatre zealot. He and the actor PETER FINCH formed Mercury Theatres Pty Ltd with Allan Ashbolt, a drama critic and theatre historian who had worked with Finch in the Army Theatre Company; John Wiltshire, a former serviceman and a radio producer; and Colin Scrimgeour, a commercial radio manager who had come to Sydney after a stormy career as a radio preacher and head of commercial broadcasting in New Zealand. They aimed to form a professional repertory company, 'beginning where Continental and Russian traditions have now arrived', Kay said. He was the driving force and Finch was Mercury's director, its star and the charismatic personality who gave it prestige.

Mercury Theatre presented three classic European one-act plays to critical acclaim at the NSW State Conservatorium of Music on 16 and 17 July 1946. Kay directed Nikolai Gogol's *Diamond Cuts Diamond* with a cast including Peter Bathurst, Finch, Dennis Glenny and June Wimble, secretary of the company. Finch directed Lope de Vega's *The Pastrybaker* with a cast including Jerome Levy and Alan Poolman. Wiltshire directed Heinrich von Kleist's *The Broken Pitcher* with a cast including Finch, Tom Lake and Wimble. WILLIAM CONSTABLE designed the costumes and sets, Margaret Olley painted the sets and Kurt Herweg conducted the orchestra in music written by Kay.

A Mercury Club and a Mercury Theatre School were formed and student productions were given in tiny leased premises in Phillip Street, near Circular Quay. Ashbolt lectured students on theatre history and Finch taught them acting, taking his theories from Konstantin Stanislavsky and Louis Jouvet. Finch, the passionate theatrical idealist and mercurial communicator, made fanatical disciples of his pupils. He inspired many dedicated young actors with a passion for fine acting, including his special protégés Alan White and Trader Faulkner.

No suitable premises could be found to house Mercury Theatre so in 1947 the Mercury Mobile Players came into being, to take the plays to the people. Kay designed a folding stage and proscenium to fit on the truck that carried props to their venues. Finch directed Lajos Biro's *Midsummer Night* and Arthur Schnitzler's *Anatole's Wedding*. Kay produced Molière's *The Imaginary Invalid*, which catapulted Finch towards international fame when he played Argan at O'Brien's Glass Factory in 1948, with Laurence Olivier and Vivien Leigh in the audience. Finch departed for London.

In February 1952 Kay, the sole remaining director, leased ST JAMES HALL, and there, in less than two years, Mercury Theatre staged 29 plays and gave 505 performances. The plays ranged from Plautus, Shakespeare and August

Strindberg through George Bernard Shaw and John Masefield to such moderns as Maxwell Anderson, Jean Anouilh, Christopher Fry, Sidney Howard, John van Druten and Terence Rattigan. The theatre was run as a co-operative, performers receiving a percentage of box-office. The first 20 or more plays were presented in repertory. Sometimes a different play could be seen every night of the week. Leading radio actors appeared in the Mercury plays and gained valuable stage experience. They included Barrie Cookson, RUTH CRACKNELL, Diana Davidson, Bruce Stewart and Rod Taylor. Lloyd Berrell and Kenneth Warren, both of whom went on to play Roo in Ray Lawler's SUMMER OF THE SEVENTEENTH DOLL, were other Mercury actors. ROBIN LOVEJOY directed and designed some of his early productions there. ALEXANDER ARCHDALE acted and directed at the Mercury soon after his arrival in Australia. Kay was forced to close the Mercury late in 1953. His energy remained, but his finances were exhausted. He had given Sydney good theatre, but his dream of a professional repertory company remained unfulfilled. ❦*Richard Lane*

Gwen Meredith

Dramatist. Born 18 November 1907 at Orange (NSW). Ran dramatic club in Sydney 1932-39. On staff of Independent Theatre (Sydney). Wrote long-running serials for ABC radio.

In the 1930s Gwen Meredith ran a book club in Sydney with an attached dramatic club for which she, Kathleen Carroll and others began to write plays. Meredith's *Wives Have Their Uses*, a comedy of divorce with Maughamesque wit, was described as breaking new ground in Australia. For INDEPENDENT THEATRE in Sydney, where she was on the staff, Meredith wrote lightweight plays. *Ask No Questions*, with an all-female cast, was about hospital patients. In 1955, her 'sombre drama of family entanglement' *Cornerstone* was a runner-up to Ray Lawler's SUMMER OF THE SEVENTEENTH DOLL in a PLAYWRIGHTS' ADVISORY BOARD competition. It was produced by Independent Theatre. Meredith is chiefly famous, however, for writing two ABC radio serials —*The Lawsons* and its successor *Blue Hills*—that totalled 5795 episodes over 33 years until 1976. J. C. Williamson's toured a stage adaptation of *The Lawsons* in country districts in the 1950s. ❦*Leslie Rees*

published play
Wives Have Their Uses. Sydney: Mulga 1944.

John Meredith

Actor, manager. Publican who began acting in Sydney 1832. Ran theatres in Hobart 1835-38. Reappeared in Sydney 1838. Sporadical theatrical appearances after 1839. Wife acted as Mrs Meredith.

John Meredith was a popular actor, especially in comic roles, and competent in most other aspects of theatre, but he had a particularly chequered career. This appears to have been partly because he was temperamentally averse to working under others. The *Australian* on 27 July 1832 listed Meredith among Sydney's publicans. On 1 October 1832 he made his first theatrical appearance in Sydney, playing *The Stage Struck Tailor* in one of BARNETT LEVEY's 'at homes'. His parody of Hamlet was particularly well received. Meredith became stage manager for Levey's fit-up theatre in the Royal Hotel and on opening night, 26 December, he played the leading role of William in Douglas Jerrold's *Black-Eyed Susan*.

Meredith was granted a six-week licence for a theatre at nearby Parramatta. He opened in the Woolpack Inn on 20 July 1833 but closed after four weeks because of poor audiences. Levey did not initially re-engage Meredith for the first season at the Theatre Royal, from 5 October 1833. The *Sydney Herald* reported on 23 September that Meredith had rejected Levey's offer of £3 3s a week as insufficient. Meredith wrote to the newspaper on 30 September, pointing out that at the Royal Hotel he had been paid £5 a week and given a free benefit. In return he had lent Levey his collection of theatrical wigs and playbooks, and contributed greatly to running the theatre. 'No performer was engaged —no dress designed—no piece contemplated—no theatrical character cast to any performance, and nothing done without consulting Meredith', he claimed.

Audiences resented Meredith's absence. Shouts of 'Meredith! Meredith!' resounded when another actor played Job Thornbury in *John Bull* by George Colman the younger, the *Sydney Herald* reported on 21 October. Meredith rejoined the company at the end of October and took over as stage manager. Levey allowed no benefits at the end of the season on 4 April 1834, much to the consternation of Meredith and others. Meredith sought a theatrical licence but was licensed only for concerts at the Pulteney Hotel. He was not at the Theatre Royal when it reopened on 18 April, but he was back with Levey by May 1834.

In May 1835 the Theatre Royal did not engage Meredith or his wife. They went to Launceston and from July to November they acted in SAMSON CAMERON's company. Meredith was also stage manager. He took over the Theatre Royal in the ARGYLE ROOMS in Hobart after J. P. DEANE was declared bankrupt in December 1835. Competing with the Camerons at the Freemason's Tavern, he won the support of public and critics. The *Colonial Times* on 19 January 1836 praised his management and the *Tasmanian* on 25 January commended him as 'perfectly master of all the tact of the London stage—walks well, dances well, and speaks well'. The Camerons gave up and left for Sydney.

On 5 April 1836 the *Colonial Times* praised improvements to the theatre, adding: 'We understand Meredith himself was the principal workman and chief manager of the whole of the improvement.' The *Tasmanian* on 3 March 1837 noted that for his wife's benefit Meredith had manufactured not only fireworks but stage machinery that allowed a descent from the roof in *The Fairy of the Lake*. He must be engaged for the New THEATRE ROYAL, it said. But the new theatre was leased to Samson Cameron, who opened it on 6 March 1837.

Meredith and Cameron competed until the end of March. On 7 April the *Hobart Town Courier* announced that Meredith, Cameron, JAMES BELMORE and J. Moses would be cotenants of the new theatre. By 21 April Meredith's inability to work in partnership was causing trouble. The Camerons went to Sydney, and the second season at the New Theatre Royal opened on 25 September with D. P. Grove and Meredith as managers. Meredith also became licensee of the Shakespeare Tavern in the basement. Audiences remained poor and in January 1838 it was announced that Meredith would manage the new ROYAL VICTORIA THEATRE in Sydney at a joint salary of £6 6s for himself and his wife. But on 5 March he was still in Hobart, taking a farewell benefit. The *Sydney Gazette* said on 17 March that Meredith had also 'taken the benefit of the Insolvent Act, he may therefore be expected in Sydney as soon as practicable'. Before the bankrup Meredith reached Sydney, however, JOSEPH WYATT engaged JOHN LAZAR to manage the new theatre in his stead. Wyatt offered 100 guineas (£105) to cancel their agreement but Meredith refused. In July he was engaged at £6 a week for acting only. 'On his entrance, Meredith was rapturously applauded; he proceeded to his business with the same easy confidence for which he was ever remarkable above his competitors', the *Sydney Gazette* reported on 19 July.

On 18 December 1838, however, Meredith was dismissed for refusing to play minor roles and he later became a publican again. He sued Wyatt for breach of contract and in July 1839 he was awarded £382 in compensation for lost salary and benefits. Meredith was at the Royal Victoria Theatre in June 1840. In September he was insolvent again, despite his large damages from Wyatt. He appeared at the Albert Theatre in Hobart for ARTHUR FALCHON's benefit in February 1843 and he was in JOSEPH SIMMONS's short-lived Royal City Theatre company in Sydney from 20 May to 23 June 1843. An advertisement in the *Sydney Morning Herald* on 3 June 1846 announced that Meredith had hired the Royal City to take a benefit that evening. The rest is silence. ❦*Elizabeth Webby*

Henry Beaufoy Merlin

Actor, manager, showman, theatre-builder. Born *c*.1830. Arrived in Sydney 8 December 1848. Opened Royal Marionette Theatre in Sydney, 11 April 1853. Built Queen's Theatre, Maitland (NSW), 1856. Active in theatre in Newcastle (NSW) 1856-57. Acted at Our Lyceum Theatre, Sydney, July 1857. Died 27 September 1873 in Sydney.

Principally remembered as the photographer responsible for the Holtermann collection of photographs in the Mitchell Library in Sydney, Henry Beaufoy Merlin lives on in theatrical history as the presenter of a puppet theatre that was possibly the first in Australia. He was almost certainly responsible for a one-night display of scenes animated with mechanical figures in the Royal Hotel in Sydney on 14 September 1852 under the name of the Royal Marionette Theatre. He opened a Royal Marionette Theatre with 'Mr Albany Brown' in *The Manager's Room* and the burlesque *Bombastes Furioso* in the Olympic Circus on 11 April 1853. In this he followed a company that opened in London on 12 January 1852, but he differed in having items by live performers and 'panoramic scenes' animated with many small mechanical figures. He claimed his company to be the London company, but he had arrived in Sydney in 1848 with his widowed mother, Mrs Murlin. Henry spelt his own surname Murlin at the time.

After a fire—deliberately lit—the theatre reopened on 2 May 1853 with the program enlarged by a marionette version of *Tom Thumb*. The Royal Marionette Theatre performed in Parramatta (NSW) on 14 May and on 24 May opened at Maitland (NSW), where Henry changed his surname from Murlin to Muriel. The company played elsewhere in the Hunter Valley and gave its last known performances in Newcastle (NSW) in late June and early July. Henry was still calling himself Muriel in late 1855, when he seems to have returned to Maitland with a display of Crimean War scenes. He built a live theatre, the Queen's Theatre, which opened on 4 June 1856 but burned down a week later. A public subscription helped him to build a replacement, which opened on 21 August 1856. He appears to have left Maitland a few weeks later after public criticism of his acting. On 27 and 28 November 1856 he presented *Othello* and *Bombastes Furioso*, using local actors, in the Old Stockade at Newcastle. This led to the building of the town's first theatre, behind Croft's hotel on the corner of Watt and Hunter Streets. Joseph Croft funded the project and Henry supervised it. The Newcastle Theatre opened on 5 February 1857, but in May Henry was exhibiting MOVING PANORAMAS in Sydney and in July he was acting at Our Lyceum Theatre. He reverted to his original surname—but spelt it Merlin—and went to London, where he was married in 1863. On his return to Australia he established himself as a photographer. In 1872-73 he also contributed articles to the *Town and Country Journal*. ❦*Richard Bradshaw*

further reading
BRADSHAW, RICHARD. The Merlin of the south. *Australasian Drama Studies* 7 (Brisbane, October 1985).

Edgar Metcalfe AM

Actor, director, dramatist. Born 18 September 1933 in Blackpool (England). Early training with Blackpool Repertory Company as actor and assistant stage manager. Artistic director of National Theatre Company (Perth) 1963-67 and 1970-72. Associate director of Melbourne Theatre Company 1968-70. Free lance in United Kingdom and Australia in 1970s. Artistic director of Hole-in-the-Wall Theatre (Perth) 1980-85. Moved to Sydney 1985 and worked in theatre, radio and film. Returned to Perth 1989. Erik Kuttner Award 1970. Green Room Award for direction 1970 (*What the Butler Saw* by Joe Orton and *The Devils* by John Whiting). AM 1978.

As director and actor Edgar Metcalfe is noted for versatility and craftsmanship, particularly in English comedy. He is a character actor of great precision and range. In Perth, he was the second director of the NATIONAL THEATRE COMPANY. Three versatile British actors, James Beattie, Frederic Lees and Judy Wilson, joined Metcalfe as assisted immigrants. They brought new energy and skills to the small local pool of actors and together they created for the first time a secure standard of three-weekly repertory on the English model, with a loyal audience. The repertoire ranged from classical and European contemporary drama to musicals and farce. The company also introduced the Christmas pantomime, with Metcalfe himself playing the dame, Wilson returned home at the end of her contract, Lees remained for some years and Beattie settled in Perth.

Metcalfe's productions included national tours of Jean-Paul Sartre's *Altona* in 1966 and Marsha Norman's '*Night Mother* in 1984 with JILL PERRYMAN and JUNE SALTER. His major performances include Salieri in Peter Shaffer's *Amadeus* for the 1981 Festival of Perth. His plays *Garden Party* (1980), *Vinegar and Brown Paper* (1981) and *After Sunday* (1986) all had their premieres at the Hole-in-the-Wall Theatre. ❦*Katharine Brisbane*

published play
Garden Party (1980). Perth: Artlook 1980.

Metropolitan Theatre

Amateur dramatic company in Sydney, formed in 1943 as Metropolitan Players by May Hollinworth. Became Metropolitan Theatre, March 1946. Closed 1956. **venues** 1946-48 Northcote House, Reiby Place. 1949-56 Christ Church St. Laurence Hall.

Metropolitan Theatre developed from the Metropolitan Players, formed in 1943 by MAY HOLLINWORTH. Her aim was a professional repertory company but her immediate purpose was to take good dramatic entertainment to troops in military camps and hospitals within 160 km of Sydney. In 1944 and 1945 she toured 11 plays, ranging from the thriller *Suspect* to Thornton Wilder's *Our Town* and *Sons of the Morning*, a verse play by CATHERINE DUNCAN. The players, who also performed in outer suburban halls, included Kevin Brennan, John Dease, JANE HOLLAND, ENID LORIMER, LEO MCKERN, Jack Needham and Alathea Siddons.

Metropolitan Theatre was established in March 1946 in Northcote House with a boxing ring for a stage and 72 old cinema seats on platforms in the auditorium. The company had 500 subscribers, each paying £1 1s to see six plays. Its opening production, *Othello*, was 'far and away the finest performance of a Shakespeare in Sydney for many years', said LINDSEY BROWNE in the *Sydney Morning Herald* on 1 April 1946. The *Herald* critic wrote on 3 June that in the second play, Maxwell Anderson's *Winterset*, Hollinworth had 'produced a clear decisive statement in admirable fashion'. Of the fourth play, Ferenc Molnar's *Liliom*, the *Bulletin* said on 9 October: 'It is really staggering to see a play of this quality in a tiny hall while the big professional theatres show only trivial and meaningless potboilers'.

The company had a policy of presenting at least one new Australian play a year. Douglas Stewart's *NED KELLY* opened the 1947 season and DOROTHY BLEWETT's *The First Joanna* the 1948 season. Subscribers had by then reached 1200, and the company had expanded its activities. It presented open-air Shakespeare in city parks, and sent three plays on a professionally-mounted tour of northern NSW and Queensland. The time seemed ripe to set up the professional repertory company. Though not commercially viable, pro-tem premises seating 200 were found at Christ Church St Laurence Hall, near Central Railway. The English director Tyrone Guthrie, in Australia to study the feasibility of a national theatre, opened the 1949 season, which began with *Romeo and Juliet* and a new play by DOUGLAS STEWART, *Shipwreck*. The new theatre did not work. The stage was too high and the seating could not be raised. The vaulted ceiling echoed. Subscribers who had complained of claustrophobia at the Reiby Place theatre now yearned for its intimacy.

In 1950 serious illness forced Hollinworth to leave Metropolitan Theatre, her vision unrealised. Afterwards ROBIN LOVEJOY directed some fine productions and Alan Burke, Lesley Lindsay, Nigel Lovell and David Nettheim also provided good work. WILLIAM ORR produced his first revue at the Metropolitan before he moved to the Philip Street Theatre. But without Hollinworth the company lacked centre, guide and collective ambition. By the early 1950s most of the original members had left, and Metropolitan closed in 1956. Among its actors had been LYNDALL BARBOUR, Kevin Brennan, John Bushelle, Nigel Lovell, BETTY LUCAS and DINAH SHEARING. The designers included WILLIAM CONSTABLE and Lovejoy. In its heyday Metropolitan Theatre developed a unique bond between actors and audience and strengthened it with the *Metropolitan* magazine, which invited comment and letters from subscribers and gave out news of the personalities and policies of the theatre. One issue contained an outline plan, drawn up by the committee, for a national theatre. ♥*Lynne Murphy*

Keith Michell

Actor, director, designer. Born 1 December 1928 in Adelaide. Grew up in Warnertown (SA). Educated at South Australian School of Arts and Crafts. Taught art in Adelaide schools. Began designing sets in amateur theatre. Debut as actor at Playbox Theatre (Adelaide) 1945. Trained at Old Vic Theatre School (London). Young Vic Theatre Company 1950-51. London debut 1951. Toured Australasia in Shakespeare Memorial Theatre Company 1952-53. Toured New Zealand with New Zealand Players 1954-55. Married actor Jeanette Sterke 1957. First appeared in USA 1960. Artistic director of Chichester Festival (England) 1974-77. Many film and television roles. Has exhibited paintings in London, New York and Australia. Father of actor Helena Michell. Green Room Award 1993 (Scrooge in *A Christmas Carol*).

Keith Michell is a versatile actor whose good looks, drive and athletic bearing rapidly launched him on a career as a juvenile lead in British classical theatre at a time when physicality was an uncommon quality among actors. He acquired an admired elegance in England but the Australian dynamism remains and it has enabled him to play roles as diverse as Antony, King Henry VIII and King Magnus in *The Apple Cart* by George Bernard Shaw. These qualities and a pleasant baritone voice have gained him equal success as Georges in *La Cage aux Folles* and other musicals, though he remains at his best in the classical repertoire.

He entered amateur theatre as a designer and his early performances were in productions for which he had designed the sets—as Roger in *Lover's Leap* by Philip Johnston at LLOYD PRIDER's Playbox Theatre in 1945, in the operetta *Mercenary Mary* and in *Lightning Strikes Twice* by Rex Rienits. During 1946-48 he designed the musical *Girls Please* for Playbox at the Tivoli Theatre and *Othello*, directed by COLIN BALLANTYNE at the Tivoli for the Workers' Educational Association. He appeared with Adelaide Repertory Theatre as Darcy in an adaptation of Jane Austen's *Pride and Prejudice* and for Playbox in Patrick Hamilton's *Rope*. In 1948 Michell auditioned in Melbourne and gained one of two places reserved for Australians at the Old Vic Theatre School in London. After training there he joined the Young Vic Company to play Bassanio in *The Merchant of Venice* in 1950-51. He made his first London appearance as Charles II in the musical comedy *And So to Bed* in 1951. On the Shakespeare Memorial Theatre Company's Australasian tour in 1952-53 Michell played Orlando in *As You Like It* and Hotspur in *Henry IV—part 1*. He acted with the company at Stratford-upon-Avon in 1953 and 1955.

At the Comedy Theatre in Melbourne in 1964 Michell and Googie Withers began an Australian tour in *The First Four Hundred Years*, a celebration of Shakespeare's quatercentenary. Later in the year in London Michell created Robert Browning in the musical *Robert and Elizabeth* opposite JUNE BRONHILL. Michell toured Australia in the role in 1966. He toured Australia again in 1978 as Othello and as

King Magnus in the 1977 Chichester Festival production of *The Apple Cart*. In 1981 Michell was a guest at the Festival of Perth in a solo concert performance of songs from his musicals and *Captain Beaky*, poems for children by Jeremy Lloyd which Michell had illustrated for a book. Two television shows and a popular LP recording by Michell were based upon these poems and drawings. In 1981 Michell wrote an Australian adaptation of Ibsen's *Peer Gynt*, titled *Pete McGynty and the Dreamtime*, in which he played the title-role for the Melbourne Theatre Company. Later, with the composer Timothy Sexton, he wrote a concert musical version that was performed at the Westminster School in Adelaide in 1989 and at the Victorian Arts Centre in 1990. In 1985-86 Michell was in Sydney and Melbourne to play Georges in a production of *La Cage aux folles* that also had seasons in San Francisco and New York. He returned to Melbourne in 1993 to play Scrooge in the Princess Theatre's *A Christmas Carol*. ❦*Katharine Brisbane*

writings
Practically Macrobiotic. London: Thorsons 1987. Philosophy and favourite foods.

illustrations
LLOYD, JEREMY. *Captain Beaky*. London: Warner Chappell 1981.
Shakespeare's Sonnets. London: Curwen Press 1975. Melbourne: Lansdowne Press 1980. Limited edition of lithographs

further reading
HERBERT, Ian (ed.). *Who's Who in the Theatre*. 17th edn. Detroit (USA): Gale Research 1987.
The making of Michell. *Age* (Melbourne) 25 April 1988.
Keith Michell. *Australian* 16 February 1985.
Michell lowers the mask. *Advertiser* (Adelaide) 13 February 1981.

Rodney Milgate

Actor, dramatist. Born 30 June 1934 at Kyogle (NSW). Parents were musicians. Qualified as art teacher. Trained with Doris Fitton and John Alden at Independent Theatre (Sydney) 1957-58. In Trust Players 1959. Phillip Street revues 1960. Also acted in radio and television. Married actor Dinah Shearing 1960. Harkness Fellowship 1968. In New York for two years. Associate professor of art at University of NSW 1990. Many solo exhibitions and several awards as painter. Has written poetry, two novels, for film and television, and on visual arts. Father of Adam Milgate, magician and writer.

Rodney Milgate's early experimental plays contained strong messages for suburban Australia, which he saw as existing in unseeing materialism. They were not fully successful but they followed the path into imaginative territory blazed by PATRICK WHITE and opened the way for a new larrikin kind of theatre in Sydney. Milgate's first plays were *A Refined Look at Existence*, produced at the JANE STREET THEATRE in 1966, and *At Least You Get Something Out of That*, produced in the OLD TOTE THEATRE COMPANY's Australian season in 1968. Both plays transposed Greek legend into an Australian setting, burst the boundaries of naturalism and the proscenium arch, and experimented with popular language and song. Milgate's plays are informed by his painter's outlook. Others include *A Golden Pathway through Europe* (1980), *Triage or the Fortunates* (1979) and *Archibald Prize* (1984). ❦*Katharine Brisbane*

published play
A Refined Look at Existence (1966). London: Methuen 1968.

Mill Theatre Company

Professional community-theatre in Geelong (Vic.), founded in 1978 by James McCaughey. Closed 1987. **venue** Mill Theatre. **artistic directors** 1978–84 James McCaughey. 1985-87 Richard Murphet. **first production** *The Wool Game*, 1978. Director: James McCaughey. Design: Barbara Ciszewska. Cast: Tom Considine, William Henderson, Robyn Hewitt, Ian Scott. **landmark productions** *The Caucasian Chalk Circle* by Bertolt Brecht, 1979. *Clyde Company Station* by Phil Gardner, Ernie Gray, William Henderson and David Porter, 1980. *The Dolphin Play* by Gavin Daws, 1984. *William Buckley and the Wathaurong Tribe* by Barry Hill, 1986. **final production** *A Stretch of the Imagination* by Jack Hibberd, 1987.

The Mill Theatre Company was known for strong physicality, imaginative transformation of careful research and a lively rapport with its audience. It was among the earliest of the COMMUNITY-THEATRE companies established throughout Victoria in the late 1970s and early 1980s. James McCaughey originally developed the company as a theatre laboratory to complement his course in theatrical performance at Deakin University, but it rapidly became autonomous and professional, although it always maintained links with the university.

The company's policy of developing theatre for and with the local community resulted in shows about aspects of Geelong history, such as *The Clyde Company Station*; shows about contemporary issues; evenings of theatre-making in which the company would join forces with interested members of the public; improvisation in response to suggestions from the audience; and contemporary versions of classical plays. Amongst those who worked with the company were Sarah Cathcart, Angela Chaplin, Barbara Ciszewska, Robert Draffin and Ernie Gray. A successful youth theatre company, the Woolly Jumpers, began as a branch of Mill Theatre. ❦*Richard Murphet*

Maggie Millar

Actor. Born 6 January 1941 in Sydney. Took evening classes in acting at private theatre school in Sydney. Toured with Trust Players 1958-60. Played small roles on Old Vic Theatre Company's tour of Australasia 1961-62. Went to London 1963. Trained at Royal Academy of Dramatic Art. Joined Union Theatre Repertory Company (Melbourne) 1965. Joined Hoopla (Melbourne) 1977. Erik Kuttner Award 1967 (title-role in *The Heiress* by Ruth and Augustus Goetz). Extensive film, radio and television work.

Maggie Millar is a graceful actor who has seldom been seen on stage beyond Melbourne. She has specialised in accents and is noted for the warmth and psychological truth of her performances. She won the Gertrude Lawrence Award for the best performance of her graduation year at the Royal Academy of Dramatic Art and in 1965 she appeared at the academy's Vanbrugh Theatre in Anton Chekhov's *Ivanov*. Then she returned to Australia and joined the Union Theatre Repertory Company, where her roles included Princess Maria in *War and Peace* and Madame Xenia in Frank Marcus's *The Killing of Sister George* in 1966; Beatrice in Carlo Goldoni's *The Servant of Two Masters* and the title-role in *The Heiress* in 1967; Masha in GEORGE OGILVIE's landmark production of Chekhov's *Three Sisters* and Elizabeth Proctor in Arthur Miller's *The Crucible* in 1968. A critic wrote of Millar's outstanding Masha in 1969: 'the stillness broken only by an occasional sudden movement, is a distillation more of the spirit than the flesh'.

An illness led to her collapse during a performance of Arthur Miller's *The Prince* in 1969 and caused a petition to the management by Melbourne actors, and action by their union, over working conditions. The dispute was resolved but resulted in Millar being denied work in the theatre for some years, during which she married and lived in Germany for 18 months. When a second company—Hoopla, later the PLAYBOX THEATRE CENTRE—was formed in Melbourne she returned to the stage to create Esme and Ellie in the premiere of DOROTHY HEWETT's *The Golden Oldies* (1977). For Playbox she also played roles in two plays by August Strindberg—Kristin in *Miss Julie* and Alice in *The Dance of Death* and leading roles in two Sam Shepard plays at the 1982 Adelaide Festival, all directed by ROGER PULVERS. She returned briefly to the Union Theatre Repertory Company, renamed the MELBOURNE THEATRE COMPANY, to create Fania in RON ELISHA's *In Duty Bound* and to play Olivia in the premiere of ALEX BUZO's *Big River* at the 1980 ADELAIDE FESTIVAL OF ARTS. Millar's roles in Melbourne Theatre Company productions since 1988 include Pauline in STEPHEN SEWELL's *Dreams in an Empty City* and Rosa in JOHN ROMERIL's *Top End* in 1989; Stephanie in NICK ENRIGHT's long-running *Daylight Saving* in 1990-91; and Lydia in the premiere of JANIS BALODIS's *No Going Back* in 1992. ❦*Katharine Brisbane*

Harry M. Miller

Entrepreneur. Born 6 January 1934 in Auckland (New Zealand). Entered show business 1953. Moved to Sydney 1963. Opened Playbox Theatres in Sydney and Melbourne. Produced rock musicals *Hair*, *Jesus Christ Superstar* and *The Rocky Horror Show* with great success 1969-74. Imprisoned for financial offences in connection with failure of Computicket agency 1982. Has concentrated on personal management since 1983.

Harry M. Miller cut his show-business teeth in his native New Zealand. He managed restaurants, sold appliances, promoted concerts, ran a record company, did public relations work and managed the New Zealand segments of Australasian tours by visiting stars. He formed an association with the entrepreneur Lee Gordon in Australia. In 1961 he toured the Kingston Trio in Australia, without success. Miller settled in Sydney in 1963 and soon afterwards imported Louis Armstrong. In 1964 he presented Judy Garland in headline-strewn concerts in Sydney and Melbourne. Later in the 1960s he advised the AUSTRALIAN ELIZABETHAN THEATRE TRUST, the Australian Ballet, and the MELBOURNE THEATRE COMPANY on promotion. By 1968 Miller had moved into the legitimate theatre. He turned the auditorium of Sydney radio station 2GB into the small but satisfactory PLAYBOX THEATRE. Another Playbox Theatre he opened in Melbourne later was less satisfactorily adapted. Miller's second production at the Playbox in Sydney, in October 1968, was *The Boys in the Band*, a play by Mart Crowley about New York homosexuals. This was bracing stuff for a country that was just learning to cope with 'the love that dare not speak its name' shrilly shouting its preference from the rooftops. Sydney survived the shock easily enough, but in Melbourne, where JOHN TASKER's excellent production ran for eight months, three members of the cast were hauled into court on obscene-language charges. The magistrates imposed no fine because 'the offences are so trifling' but a superior court later ruled that fines should be imposed. Nevertheless, it was a significant victory in the liberation of community standards from wowserism. In June 1969 Miller, with KENN BRODZIAK of Aztec Services as co-producer, staged the rock musical *Hair*, in Sydney's old MINERVA THEATRE. It was the first of many successes for Miller in theatre, entertainment promotion and personal management of artists.

In 1978 he established an agency which was to use the most modern electronic equipment to sell entertainment tickets as widely as possible. The company collapsed in 1979 and Miller was later charged with financial offences. The jury could not agree in his first trial but in a retrial in April 1982 Miller was found guilty on five charges of aiding and abetting fraudulent misappropriation and sentenced to three years in prison. Release on parole in March 1983, after serving ten months, Miller continued to provide personal management for prominent persons, and he ran a speakers' bureau.

He re-entered show business through television production, and in 1992 he returned to *Jesus Christ Superstar*, in association with the International Management Group and Garry van Egmond. Miller mounted a spectacular concert version of the show, using the largest venues available and the best pop singers—John Farnham as Jesus, Jon Stevens as Judas and Kate Ceberano as Mary Magdalene. A gross of $40 million was reported at the end of a 78-performance, 17-week tour. In 1994 Miller returned to the stage with the show, opening a tour in Newcastle (NSW). With the Melbourne Theatre Company, in 1993 he co-produced David Henry Hwang's Broadway success *M. Butterfly*. Directed by Gale Edwards this sensational play—based on the real-life liaison of a Beijing Opera singer and a French diplomat—succeeded in Melbourne but at the Seymour Theatre Centre in Sydney it had trouble drawing houses. The rest of the tour was cancelled. ❦*John West*

writings
My Story. Melbourne: Macmillan 1983.

Mime

Modern mime, strictly defined as mute dramatic presentation beyond dance and drama, has its origins in the *commedia dell'arte* of Italy in the 16th and 17th centuries, and the earlier theatre of Greece and Rome. Traditionally a popular art form strongly linked to comedy, it was most popular in the 18th century as PANTOMIME. Its influence in the 20th century can be seen in vaudeville and variety theatre as evinced in the film work of Charlie Chaplin, Stan Laurel and others. Etienne Decroux, 'the father of modern mime', revived mime as a serious stage art form in France in the 1930s. His pupils Jean-Louis Barrault and Marcel Marceau have popularised mime, Barrault through his portrayal of a 19th-century mime artist in the film *Les Enfants du paradis* and Marceau through his stage career, which included several visits to Australia. Contemporary European companies, such as Henryk Tomaszewski's Polish Mime Theatre, have also developed mime from speciality acts and comedy to a revival in street theatre and skills theatre, and as a means of expression in movement theatre.

The development of mime in Australia has followed the same pattern. The major influences have been Decroux, with an analytical emphasis on corporeal mime and training the body to express itself in more abstract forms, and another Parisian, Jacques Lecoq, with a basis of *commedia dell'arte*, traditional pantomime and creation of external images. There have also been influential teachers in Australia, including Zora Semberova in Adelaide, A. E. Gibson and Annie Mangin in Perth and Ton Witzel in Adelaide, Canberra and Sydney, whose pupils include Michael Freeland and the solo mime John Paul Bell.

Interest in mime began to revive in the late 1960s. In the 1970s Freeland founded the Modern Mime Theatre in Sydney, and groups in NSW such as PIPI STORM CHILDREN'S CIRCUS and the White Company presented outdoor work that acknowledged its surroundings. B'Spell, whose members included the solo mime Paul Voermans and the mime storyteller Carl Presser, applied mime to theatrical presentation in Melbourne in the 1970s, and Victorian groups such as Chris Dickins's Artisan did the same in the early 1980s. In the mid-1980s Chrome emerged in Adelaide and performed widely, led by Tony Strachan, Michael Pearce, Paul Adolphus and others. Groups such as Red Weather, Et Cetera and Antebodies further blurred the line between street and theatrical performance. Groups such as Teatro dell'IRAA (Theatre of the Institute for Research into the Anthropology of the Actor) from Rome also use mime and influences from many cultures in their exploration of movement and expression.

The mime Joe Bolza, a pupil of Decroux, and the dancer Bob Thorneycroft presented the *Bob and Joe Show* at the Pram Factory in Melbourne in 1971–72. Most individual mimes began to perform in theatres, cabaret and schools in the 1980s. They included Bob Burton with his short-lived Monkey-based Theatre, Marc Furneaux, Jenny Hope, Nola Rae, Heather Robb and Ira Seidenstein. GEOFFREY RUSH, trained by Lecoq, went into mainstream theatre as a performer and director, and Isabelle Anderson explored the possibilities of mime in dramatic and dance performances.

Mime has manifested itself in Australian theatre principally through the Sydney company ENTR'ACTE. It spent years presenting work inspired by the Decroux style and in the mid-1980s the company expanded its horizons and began training in breath and voice. It produced *Ostraka* to great acclaim in Australia and the United Kingdom in 1987, and *The Memory Room* in Sydney in 1989 and in Adelaide and at the Toga Festival in Japan in 1990. Another development was psychotherapy. Trained mime artists went into self-development and psychiatry and used their skills for practical and therapeutic goals in institutions. A variation on this approach is the use of mime in the THEATRE OF THE DEAF. In the late 1980s mime was an important influence in the cross-fertilisation of art forms within fringe and avant-garde performance. The word 'mime' became too stale for many of the participants, who preferred to speak of 'movement theatre', 'gestural theatre', 'corporeal theatre' or 'physically based theatre'. Especially in Sydney, performances began to merge mime with other styles. JAPANESE PERFORMERS seemed to be the major influence for this trend. Min Tanaka introduced *butoh* in 1982 and a member of his company, Tess de Quincy, promoted his work on teaching and performing visits. The Sankai Juku company toured in 1988. Tadashi Suzuki toured his company in 1989, visited Australia as a teacher in 1991, and devised an Australian-cast production, titled *The Chronicle of Macbeth* for the 1992 Adelaide Festival. ❦*Bruce Keller*

Minerva Theatre

Theatre in Orwell Street, Kings Cross, opened 18 May 1939, seating 1016 on two levels. Architects: Guy Crick and Bruce Furse; Bruce Ward. Became cinema as **Metro Theatre** 29 April 1950. Returned to live theatre 5 June 1969. Converted to shopping market 1979. Now film studio.

Possibly the finest modern theatre built in Australia in the 1930s, the Minerva Theatre was intended to have a companion but this was never built. Minerva Centre Ltd aimed to build two theatres on facing sites at Kings Cross, according to the *Sydney Morning Herald* on 27 August 1937. The company's managing director was DAVID N. MARTIN, formerly managing director of Imperial Theatres Ltd, which owned the Liberty Theatre, designed in 1934 by C. Bruce Dellit, an exponent of the fashionable Art Deco style. A share prospectus published on 7 September 1937 showed Dellit's design for the Minerva Theatre. It would be erected in Orwell Street opposite the rather monumental Paradise Theatre Building, which would face Macleay Street and include a dance hall and a restaurant as well as a theatre.

Other architects, Guy Crick and Bruce Furse, prepared the Minerva Theatre drawings that were submitted to the Sydney City Council and the licensing authority, but the two designs showed similarities of style. Crick's Moderne interior demonstrated his interest in German expressionist theatre design. The resulting theatre was very comfortable, with lounge chairs throughout a cocoon of sweeping, wide plaster troughs washed with indirect lighting. The foremost lighting trough curved down to the stage floor on each side of a striated proscenium frame. The stage apron extended to a rarely used small side stage on each side.

The theatre, grandly opened with Robert E. Sherwood's play *Idiot's Delight* on 18 May 1939, brought the number of professional theatres in Sydney to three—the others were the THEATRE ROYAL and the TIVOLI THEATRE. It was initially managed by David N. Martin Pty Ltd in association with J. C. WILLIAMSON'S. Then there were several changes of management until Martin's company resumed control. Some 25 plays were performed, including Shakespeare at matinées, until 1 May 1941, when WHITEHALL THEATRICAL PRODUCTIONS took over the lease. Under this management the Minerva became the only commercial playhouse in Sydney producing comedies, thrillers and mysteries, usually starring actors who were well known on radio, such as LYNDALL BARBOUR, NEVA CARR GLYN and LLOYD LAMBLE.

Metro–Goldwyn–Mayer bought the building and used it as the Metro cinema from 29 April 1950 and later sold it to the Greater Union Organisation. It was not a success as a cinema and on 5 June 1969 HARRY M. MILLER reopened the Metro as a live theatre with the rock musical *Hair*. It had a long run but the theatre generally would have been unprofitable for large-cast shows. In 1979 Greater Union flattened the floor of the stalls and converted the space to a shopping market. This was also unsuccessful and the Kennedy-Miller organisation finally took over the building as a film studio. ❦*Ross Thorne*

Minstrels

In the 19th century minstrels began to draw Australia into the orbit of American culture, which has strongly influenced Australian society in the 20th century through cinema, radio, television and popular music. Minstrelsy's origins are the USA in the 1820s and 1830s, when white men performed blackface entertainments in circuses and between plays at theatres. In Boston in 1843 four white men who called themselves the Virginia Minstrels gave the first full evening of 'a combination of Negro stuff'. It was intended as a novelty for one night only but it became an institution. Other companies, inspired by the success of the Virginia Minstrels, soon sprang up all over the country.

The early minstrel performances included most of the elements that characterised the show when it developed its classic form. The subject matter of the songs, sketches and jokes was the 'character' and 'culture' of African-Americans, both slave and free. The performers blacked their faces, dressed in exaggerated costumes, 'imitated' Negro manners and dialect and delivered stump speeches—comic speeches parodying the styles and values of politicians, preachers and reformers. E. P. Christy's troupe, the Christy Minstrels, in 1846 organised the classic three-part program. In the first part the singers sang comic and sentimental songs. They sat in a semicircle, with the interlocutor, or compere, in the centre. At either end were Tambo, who played the tambourine, and Bones, who played bones. These endmen exchanged jokes exchanged with the interlocutor, who played straight man. The second part, or olio, comprised variety acts and the third part was burlesque, or 'Ethiopian opera'.

Crude, gritty humour was the hallmark of early minstrel performances but in the 1850s sentimentality invaded the repertoire. The words of Stephen Foster's minstrel songs proclaimed carefully crafted nostalgia as slaves lamented the death of 'massa' and the loss of old plantations. After the Civil War the minstrel-show repertoire increasingly moved away from 'the nigger business' as the performers ignored the plantation and emphasised the pathetic. Now their songs were about lost lovers and dead mothers. The minstrel show remained the most popular form of stage entertainment in the USA until the late 1870s, when vaudeville, comprising nine unrelated acts, replaced it.

The minstrel show quickly became a British institution. The original Virginia Minstrels toured Great Britain in 1843 and they were soon followed by other American companies. By the 1860s more than 100 parties of 'Negro delineators' were performing in Great Britain. Minstrelsy in the USA, with its emphasis on raucous and bawdy humour, was part of working-class culture together with prize fighting and the saloon. In England minstrelsy was much more middle-class and the programs emphasised music and played down wit. In London, the More and Burgess Christys, acknowledged as the premier English troupe, ran from 1859 to 1904 at St James's Hall in Piccadilly.

Minstrels in Australia

In Australia, strolling blackface minstrels performed at fairs and race-meetings in the 1820s and 1830s. The first recorded stage performance of this kind was a 'Jim Crow' routine—an imitation of African-American dance devised by 'Daddy' Rice in the USA. It was performed at the Royal Victoria Theatre in Sydney in 1838, probably by J. H. S. Lee. The Blythe Waterland Minstrels performed Australia's first structured minstrel show at the Royal Hotel in Sydney in 1850. This company, like the Howard Serenaders, which also performed here in 1850, was English in origin.

The discovery of gold attracted minstrels as well as miners from California. They included the New York Serenaders in 1851, Rainer's Ethiopian Serenaders in 1852, and the Backus Minstrels in 1855. The long voyage from San Francisco was hazardous in the 1850s and travel difficulties experienced by the visitors, combined with economic difficulties encountered by Australian theatrical managers, discouraged immediate further tours from the USA. Most of the minstrel troupes that visited Australia in the 1860s were English Christy parties, which accentuated music more than humour and drew audiences of the 'best' citizens. English minstrels' programs were of high quality, often including excerpts from operas. Critics sometimes noted the incongruity of singers dressed as 'niggers' rendering choruses from Vincenzo Bellini's *La sonnambula*.

The completion of the American transcontinental railroad in 1869 and the establishment of a regular steamship service to Australia in 1871 allowed American minstrels to reclaim the Australian popular stage. They emphasised humour rather than music and drew audiences of the 'common sort'. In the next 30 years some of the most famous stars of the American minstrel stage performed here, including Billy Emerson, regarded as the most talented minstrel of all, and the Kelly and Leon Minstrels. Perhaps the most successful touring companies were two black troupes organised by a remarkable African-American, Charles B. Hicks—the Georgia Minstrels in 1877-80 and the Hicks-Sawyer Minstrels.

Minstrelsy and vaudeville

In the 1880s the Australian minstrel show evolved towards vaudeville. Theatres combining minstrelsy and vaudeville were established in Melbourne and Sydney, such as the Alhambra in Sydney. This program structure continued on the Tivoli circuit and the Brennan vaudeville circuit. Each theatre on a circuit had its own endmen and interlocutor who appeared in the first half of the program to perform minstrel songs and sketches. Roy Rene began his career dressed as a 'coon' singing 'My Creole Belle' at the Tivoli Theatre in Adelaide.

In 1901 the Tivoli management introduced revue into the minstrel first half under titles such as *Hiawatha* and *Happy Holland*. Tambo, Bones and interlocutor may have seemed out of place but so much did the patrons 'like a dash of minstrelism out here'—as an anonymous correspondent wrote to the *New York Clipper*—that they remained an integral part of the program until Hugh D. McIntosh introduced straight vaudeville to the Tivoli circuit in 1912.

The minstrel show was a popular amateur as well as professional entertainment in Australia. Fund-raising charity concerts performed by church, sporting and fraternal organisations usually took the form of a minstrel show. The C and G Minstrels still had their own radio show in Melbourne in the 1940s. Even in the 1980s schoolchildren are still taught such classic minstrel songs as 'Jim Crow', 'Shoo Fly' and 'Ole Dan Tucker'. Minstrelsy appealed to the public because it was good entertainment, comprehensively combining songs and sentimentality, banter and burlesque. Moreover the minstrel-show Negro was not a specifically American creation but was derived from and reminiscent of Harlequin, Punchinello and Clown, pantomime characters familiar to Australian audiences. The minstrel show was adapted to strike specific local chords. The Howard Serenaders satirised the Bathurst Market Commissioners, the Christy's repertoire included such songs as 'Hurrah for Sydney' and 'Manly Beach is the place, boys'. Kelly and Leon lampooned the Victorian Premier and his ministers in *The Happy Land*. Comedians anticipated MAX GILLIES with their stump speeches filled 'with local allusions'. But in most programs both the songs and sketches consisted of American material. ❦*Richard Waterhouse*

further reading
BRATTON, J. S. English Ethiopians—British audiences and blackface acts, 1835-1865. *Yearbook of British Studies* 2 (1981).
TOLL, ROBERT C. *Blacking Up*. New York: Oxford 1977. American minstrel shows in the 19th century.
WATERHOUSE, RICHARD. Antipodean odyssey—Charles B. Hicks and the New Georgia Minstrels in Australia, 1877-1880. *Journal of the Royal Australian Historical Society* 72 (June 1986).

Irene Mitchell MBE

Actor, director, producer. Born in Melbourne. Trained at Louise Dunne School of Drama (Melbourne). Studied Stanislavsky method of acting and direction with Dolia Ribush in Melbourne. Acted on radio throughout 1930s. Taught at Irene Mitchell Academy of Dramatic Art 1938-56. Associate director of Melbourne Little Theatre Company 1942-56; artistic director 1956-62. Artistic director of St Martin's Theatre Company, Melbourne 1962-73; director 1962-77. Governor of Australian Elizabethan Theatre Trust (Victoria) 1975-87. MBE 1975.

A talented director, Irene Mitchell was artistic director of the Melbourne Little Theatre Company and its professional successor, the ST MARTIN'S THEATRE COMPANY, from 1956 until 1973. Mitchell began professional acting in 1932 as a supernumerary in George Bernard Shaw's *Saint Joan* and Sybil Thorndike's performance in the title-role inspired her for the rest of her long career. During the 1930s she acted and sang on radio, and performed with the DOLIA RIBUSH Players and the GREGAN MCMAHON PLAYERS in Melbourne. She began acting with the Melbourne Little Theatre Company in Georg Kaiser's *From Morning to Midnight* in 1934.

During the Second World War Mitchell became stage manager at the Little Theatre and directed many productions, notably Clare Boothe's *The Women* in 1945. In October 1946 she directed the world premiere of *Enduring as the Camphor Tree* by an Australian playwright, RUSSELL OAKES. The play 'unfolded in a legendary atmosphere which owed much of its success to the poetic apprehension of the producer Irene Mitchell', said the Melbourne *Herald*. At the Princess Theatre in 1951 she produced and directed *Out of the Dark*, a presentation of music and dance by the Australian Aborigines' League to celebrate the jubilee of federation. She also notably directed Sophocles's *Antigone* and Anton Chekhov's *The Bear* at the Union Theatre in 1952, Eugène Ionesco's *The Chairs* in 1960 and the Australian premiere of Harold Pinter's *The Caretaker* at the Russell Street Theatre in 1961. She remains connected with the theatre as an honorary archivist at the Performing Arts Museum of the Victorian Arts Centre. ❦*Sally Dawes*

Warren Mitchell

Actor. Born 14 January 1926 in London. Trained at Royal Academy of Dramatic Art, London. Acted with National Theatre and Royal Shakespeare Company. Became famous in *Till Death Us Do Part* on BBC television 1964. First acted in Australia 1969.

A journeyman actor in the United Kingdom for years, Warren Mitchell suddenly became famous on television as Alf Garnett, a rabidly prejudiced Cockney, in *Till Death Us Do Part*. A stage and cabaret spin-off, *The Thoughts of Chairman Alf*, brought him to Australia in 1969 and he has been back many times since. The character of Alf has sometimes hung heavily around Mitchell's neck, obscuring his splendid serious acting skills. He has revealed these in Australia as King Lear for the Queensland Theatre Company in 1978, as the mincing backstage character in Ronald Harwood's *The Dresser* for the Helen Montagu management at the Theatre Royal in Sydney in 1981, as Willy Loman in Arthur Miller's *Death of a Salesman* at the Nimrod Theatre in Sydney in 1982, as Alfred Doolittle in *My Fair Lady* for the Victoria State Opera in 1987 and in the leading role in Lyle Kessler's *Orphans*, which he played with his son Danny and COLIN FRIELS on national tour in 1988. Mitchell made an impact in the leading role in Harold Pinter's *The Homecoming* for the SYDNEY THEATRE COMPANY in 1992. ❦*John West*

further reading
O'DONNELL, MONICA M. (ed.). *Contemporary Theatre, Film, Television* 2nd edn. Detroit (USA): Gale Research 1986.

Gladys Moncrieff OBE

Singer. Born 13 April 1892 at Bundaberg (Qld). Taught singing teacher by mother, who guided her early career. Studied singing with Grace Miller in Sydney under contract to J. C. Williamson's from 1911. Starred in *Katinka* 1918, *The Maid of the Mountains* 1921. Married dancer Tom Moore in Sydney 20 May 1924. Sang in London 1926-27. Returned to Australia 1928. Toured in *Rio Rita* for Fullers' 1928-30. J. C. Williamson's 1930-33. F. W. Thring productions 1933-35. Severely injured in car accident 1938. Returned to stage 1942. Retired 1962. Died 8 February 1976. OBE 1952.

'Australia's Queen of Song', Gladys Moncrieff came from a musical family. Her mother was a soprano who had sung professionally as Ada Lambell. Her father, among other activities, tuned and repaired organs and pianos. He was also an early motion-picture exhibitor in outback north Queensland and Gladys sang at his film presentations as a teenager. He accompanied her when she made her first public appearance, at the age of six, in a charity concert in Bundaberg. She sang a song titled 'The merriest girl that's out", and won an encore, and a shilling from her father for her efforts. She became a professional performer when DAN BARRY's touring company needed a local child for the role of Little Willie in *East Lynne*. She earned an unwanted laugh when she moved convulsively as Lady Isobel declared 'and he never called me mother' and collapsed in tears across the bed of her dead child.

The family moved to Townsville, where Gladys played leads in school productions of Gilbert and Sullivan operettas, and later earned money singing to lantern slides in a local skating rink. She was also soprano soloist in Handel's *Messiah* with the Townsville Choral Society. A benefit concert in April 1909 raised money to send Gladys, with her mother, to Sydney for vocal training. They broke their journey in Brisbane, where Gladys won a six-week contract at Holland and St John's Empire Theatre, at £7 10s a week. This company had a reciprocal agreement with J. C. BAIN's vaudeville circuit in Sydney, so when Gladys arrived in Sydney with her mother early in 1910 she joined the vaudeville company to sing and to act in skits.

Her mother arranged an audition with J. C. WILLIAMSON's in 1911. The managing director, HUGH J. WARD, heard her and in her third audition Nellie Melba—in Australia with the Melba-Williamson Opera Company—joined her on stage. The great soprano took the girl through scales until she reached E in alt, of which Gladys had thought herself incapable. 'It was the greatest morning of my life', she said 60 years later. The Firm gave Gladys a three-year contract —£3 a week in the first year, £4 in the second, £6 in the third, and free singing tuition from Grace Miller, Ward's wife. After 18 months' training Gladys was allowed to stand in the back row of the chorus on the last night of *Nightbirds* at the Criterion Theatre in Sydney. Then it was back to study, now with stage movement and acting.

Moncrieff began to take small roles and understudies, and attracted critical notice when she replaced Pearl Ladd as Josephine in *HMS Pinafore* in Sydney for a week in 1914. After this she took over other leading soprano roles in Gilbert and Sullivan operettas on tour. Steady progress brought her a tour of South Africa in 1916, heading a company of English and Australian artists. Now earning £12 a week, she played the lead in *The Arcadians*, *Betty*, *The Merry Widow*, *The Quaker Girl* and *Tonight's the Night*. Her first star role, however, was the lead in *Katinka*, which she first played in Wellington (New Zealand) and repeated in Melbourne in June 1918. The second lead was FLORENCE YOUNG, the former queen of operetta, whose career was ending.

The Maid of the Mountains

Moncrieff starred in *Maytime*, *Oh! Oh! Delphine* and other shows until late 1920, when the director GEORGE HIGHLAND told her that she was to play the lead in *The Maid of the Mountains*. The Firm had held the rights to this musical play since 1918 but had been looking for an opera singer. *The Maid of the Mountains* opened in Melbourne on 22 January 1921 and from then Moncrieff was a star. Pressed to remember that night 50 years later, Moncrieff, not always articulate in interviews, recalled masses of flowers after the final curtain. 'I was all ethereal, I think. I wasn't there, yet I was', she said. The initial season lasted for two years, but the role was not Moncrieff's favourite. She preferred the title-role in *The Merry Widow*—called Sonia in the English version then played in Australia. *The Maid of the Mountains* is unusual in that the leading man does not sing, and Moncrieff had 18 of them in the next 30 years. She recalled the Shakespearean ANEW MCMASTER as 'perhaps the best'.

Near the end of a run of *The Merry Widow* in Sydney in 1924 she married Tom Moore. They left on a six-month overseas honeymoon, a gift from the Firm. However, when Moncrieff's salary was up for review at the end of 1925 the Firm reneged on the option of £180 a week. She refused to sign a new contract and, with her husband as manager, sailed for London. Moncrieff made her London debut in *Riki-Tiki* in 1926. A newspaper declared that she had 'a beautiful, clear and sympathetic voice, which she used with great skill', but the operetta ran only two weeks. She was offered other roles but waited until early 1927, when she was asked to replace a singer whose English was incomprehensible as the lead in Lehár's *The Blue Mazurka*. Moncrieff learned the role in two weeks and was a huge success, but the operetta closed after four months because the owner of Daly's Theatre committed suicide.

J. C. Williamson's had asked Moncrieff to come home for *The Desert Song* and *The Vagabond King*, but she accepted FULLER's offer of *Rio Rita*, after insisting that she go to New York to see the show before signing a contract. BENJAMIN FULLER sent a perspicacious message: 'Tell her she will lose nothing in prestige and honour by joining us', so she returned home at a salary of £250 a week, plus a percentage. *Rio Rita* opened at the beautiful new St James Theatre in Sydney on 28 April 1928. It was a smash hit and a two-year tour of Australia and New Zealand followed.

By its end Australia was in the Great Depression. Live theatres closed everywhere. The Moore–Moncrieff Theatre Company failed in 1929, after an American play bought by Tom Moore flopped and the couple lost everything. Moncrieff and her husband separated because of this and his affairs with other women. He returned to his family's hotel business. Moncrieff sang on stage in cinemas and on radio, and in 1930 she returned to the Firm for revivals and a successful season of *The Chocolate Soldier*. In 1933 she sang in *The Maid of the Mountains* for the last performance in HER MAJESTY'S THEATRE in Sydney on 10 June and to close Melbourne's THEATRE ROYAL on 17 November. Moncrieff then signed with F. W. THRING for the new Australian musical comedy COLLITS' INN. It had a successful run in Melbourne and at Christmas 1935 Moncrieff sang in another work by the composer Varney Monk, THE CEDAR TREE. Neither work repeated its Melbourne success in Sydney.

After more work for the Firm and a concert tour for the Australian Broadcasting Commission, Moncrieff was asked to go to Melbourne to discuss a radio performance of Puccini's opera *Tosca*. Her manager drove her from Adelaide. Near Geelong (Vic.) the car developed steering trouble and crashed into a lamppost. Moncrieff received severe injuries, including a punctured diaphragm, which kept her in hospital for six months. A long convalescence and vocal training in New Zealand allowed her to make a concert tour for New Zealand National Broadcasting Service. She did not regain her former vocal quality, however, until she had further tuition from Grace Miller in Sydney.

The accident left Moncrieff with one leg 40 mm shorter than the other, and she wore special shoes for the rest of her life. Thinking that her musical-theatre career was over, she concentrated on concerts and radio work and during the war sang for the troops. She managed to return to the stage in October 1942 and she played various operettas around Australia and New Zealand for four years.

In 1944 she was involved in an INDUSTRIAL RELATIONS dispute. She refused to take part in a strike against J. C. Williamson's by ACTORS' EQUITY because she was a principal. After the principle of a closed shop was established Moncrieff helped to resolve a further dispute, and she joined the union. After the Second World War she had a long holiday in the USA and England, and then sang for the troops in Korea and Japan. After five years in her own radio shows, she joined Harry Wren for her farewell tour of Australia and New Zealand in a variety show called *Many Happy Returns*, which opened at the Empire Theatre in Sydney on 28 January 1959 and closed in Hamilton (New Zealand) in 1961. She later did two television shows in Brisbane for George Wallace jnr, but her health was failing. She sold her Sydney home and, with her faithful secretary and companion Elsie Wilson, moved to a canalside bungalow on the Gold Coast. She would appear daily to wave to tourists on a pleasure cruiser. She died after suffering from cancer for many months. Her husband, who lived nearby, attended her funeral. ❦*Alwyn Capern, John West*

writings
My Life of Song. Adelaide: Rigby 1971.

Varney Monk

Composer. Born 18 January 1892 at Bacchus Marsh (Vic.). Originally Varney Peterson. Went to Tasmania with family as infant. Wrote prizewinning musical comedy *Collits' Inn* 1932. Died 7 February 1967 in Sydney. Wife of violinist Cyril Monk.

A composer with a gift for melody, Varney Monk had her Collits' Inn, an Australian historical musical comedy, successfully produced in Melbourne and Sydney in 1933-34. For reasons not connected with its worth—in which she never ceased to believe—it did not become the forerunner of a vigorous stream of Australian musicals, although F. W. Thring gave it a first-rate production. Thring produced a second Monk musical comedy, The Cedar Tree, a year later but it was less successful. ❦*John West*

Monodrama

Some Australian dramatists have developed monodramas —complete works in which one actor portrays one or more characters in dramatic situations—to a high degree since the early 1970s. Jack Hibberd's A Stretch of the Imagination (1972), Ron Blair's The Christian Brothers (1975) and Steve J. Spears's The Elocution of Benjamin Franklin (1976) were early landmarks in the genre. All portray larger-than-life central characters at crucial moments in their lives with down-to-earth realism, rich humour and great linguistic dexterity. Many other characters are evoked or actually portrayed, especially in the Hibberd play, where the single actor brings them fleetingly to life in the dialogue and action of the central character's reminiscences. Barry Dickins has adopted similar strategies in many monodramas since the 1980s, notably in his finest play, *Lennie Lower* (1982).

Most of the men in these plays are seen at a point of decay and usually death. Male monodrama of the 1970s and 1980s typically portrayed one man struggling against a vast, hostile environment—physical or cultural—in negative or even absurdist terms. The same description applies to women's monodramas by men, such as Dickins's *Bridal Suite* (1979) and *The Death of Minnie* (1980) and John Upton's *Machiavelli, Machiavelli* (1984). More recent monodramas by women, however, have examined multifaceted characters in the act of fulfilling or enriching their lives. Richly peopled monodramas with highly optimistic affirmations of contemporary female life are *A White Sports Coat* (1988) by Tes Lyssiotis, and *The Serpent's Fall* (1987) and *Walking on Sticks*, both written by the dynamic performer Sarah Cathcart with Andrea Lemon. *The Serpent's Fall* portrays with great wit and energy five highly differentiated Australian women in search of spiritual fulfilment, while *Walking on Sticks* examines the lives of four women in relation to their experiences of war in Nicaragua. Tobsha Lerner, with *Witch Play* (1987) and *Mistress* (1990) and Beverley Dunn, with *To Botany Bay on a Bondi Tram* (1984), are other women to have essayed different kinds of monodrama with success.

Solo shows doubtless have a purely economic appeal for theatre managements. But there are more important influences behind the remarkable number and frequent success of contemporary Australian monodramas. The form also enables the disempowered or dissenting voice—of writer and performer alike—to find an audience outside commercial theatre and, above all, it seems to represent a deeply satisfying expression of individual humanity against the homogenisation of contemporary life. ❦*Geoffrey Milne*

Walter Montgomery

Actor. Born 1827 in USA. Originally Richard Tomlinson. Grew up in England. Acted in provinces and became favourite in Nottingham. London debut 1863. Acted at Theatre Royal, Drury Lane. Toured Australia 1867-69. Died 1871 in England.

Long remembered by many as the finest Hamlet on the 19th-century Australian stage, Walter Montgomery was influenced by Charles Fechter's concept of the role. He began his tour of Australia at the Theatre Royal in Melbourne on 21 July 1867 as a Hamlet who sported flowing light brown locks and, more contentiously, a perfectly sane disposition. Montgomery toured at the same time as James Anderson, who performed a similar repertoire and the contrast could not have been greater. Anderson played a conventional Hamlet in black garments and wig, with an 'elongated expression of countenance', according to the Melbourne *Argus* on 15 July 1867. In what became known as the 'Hamlet controversy', Melbourne's literary men, including the critics J. E. Neild and James Smith, debated Hamlet's sanity and the accuracy of Montgomery's reading in the correspondence columns of newspapers.

Montgomery travelled to every colony with a Shakespearean repertoire that also included *Henry IV*, *King John*, *Macbeth*, *The Merchant of Venice*, *Much Ado About Nothing*, *Richard III* in Colley Cibber's version and *Romeo and Juliet*. He also acted in Dion Boucicault's *Louis XI* and Tom Taylor's *Still Waters Run Deep*, a comedy made popular in Melbourne by G. V. Brooke. Hamlet was Montgomery's best and most sensational role. His Othello and Mark Antony were less contentious and less successful. Montgomery was an exceptionally fine reader and in Melbourne he performed 42 dramatic recitals, including royal recitals during the 1888 visit of the Duke of Edinburgh, Queen Victoria's theatre-loving son. Montgomery's advertising, sometimes eccentric and exaggerated, reached new heights as he shamelessly exploited the duke's support.

Montgomery shot himself in London in 1871, just two days after his marriage. Next year the new Theatre Royal in Melbourne testified to his impact on the city's theatrical and cultural life. In the central dome, along with scenes of London and Melbourne, there were busts of Montgomery and Brooke. ❦*Paul Richardson*

further reading
The Hamlet Controversy. Melbourne: 1867.

Ray Mooney

Director, dramatist. Born 29 January 1945.

Ray Mooney, who is best known for 'issue' plays, had his first play, *A Blue Freckle*, performed in Pentridge Prison, Melbourne, when he was a prisoner in 1975. He defies categorisation as a prison dramatist, however. Although some of his plays, like *Every Night, Every Night* (1978) deal explicitly with prison, Mooney's dramatic range is wide and his output encompasses a variety of subjects. The most distinctive theme in his work is social injustice in various forms, including police corruption in *A Blue Freckle* and white injustice towards Aborigines in *Black Rabbit* (1988). Mooney has been one of the most prolific and most performed playwrights of Melbourne Writers' Theatre, which has continued the radical tradition fostered at the LA MAMA THEATRE in the late 1960s and early 1970s. ❦*Rémy Davison*

published plays
Black Rabbit (1988). Sydney: Currency Press 1988.
A Blue Freckle (1975). Melbourne: Yackandandah 1985; Melbourne Writers' Theatre 1990.
Every Night, Every Night (1978). Melbourne: Yackandandah 1985, Melbourne Writers' Theatre 1991.
St Joey's Local Club. Melbourne: Theatre for Australian Playwrights 1981.

other writing
A Green Light. Melbourne: Penguin 1988. Novel based on his prison experiences.

Carrie Moore

Actor, singer. Born 20 July 1882, in Geelong (Vic.). In pantomime from 1895. Went to London in 1903 and achieved theatrical success. Returned to Australia for first production of *The Merry Widow* 1908. Died 5 September 1956 in Sydney.

As the first Australian performer of the title-role in *The Merry Widow* Carrie Moore achieved her greatest success. She was cast in the part by J. C. WILLIAMSON, who had discovered her as a child performer. When she was 12 an uncle in Melbourne took her for an audition with his friend the impresario. She sang a sad little song and when it ended she saw the great man crying. The song had touched a raw spot. It was Lizzie's Farewell from *Struck Oil*, once sung by Williamson's estranged wife MAGGIE MOORE. The audition was a success, however, and Carrie Moore spent the years until she was 21 in Williamson's employ.

She came to prominence in the 1895-96 Christmas pantomime *Djin Djin the Japanese Bogie Man*, written by Williamson and Bert Royle. In this 'fairy tale of Old Japan' the Djin-Djin was a bogeyman who had turned the son of the ruling shogun of Japan into a baboon. Moore played the baboon and Flora Graupner and FLORENCE YOUNG played the more conventional lovers, as principal girl and principal boy. It was exotic, enchanting and a big financial success for WILLIAMSON AND MUSGROVE. Moore became something of a pantomime specialist, working her way up to principal boy. Pantomime seasons could be extensive because a successful Christmas show would run well into the next year and then switch cities at Easter. Moore also expanded into operetta, notably as Dolores in *Florodora* in 1900-01, *San Toy* in 1901-02 and Gilbert and Sullivan. In 1903 she went to London and during the next five years—according to her memories late in life—she created leading roles in five musical comedies. In 1907, J. C. Williamson, in England seeking a star for the Australian production of *The Merry Widow*, decided to bring Moore home for the part. The operetta, created in Vienna in 1905, was a huge hit in London in June 1907. It created fashions in hats, gowns and corsets. It began a long run in Melbourne on 16 May 1908. After a run in Adelaide *The Merry Widow* played for 100 nights in Sydney—a record for the city. After *The Merry Widow* life held for Moore an advantageous marriage and more pantomime and other light-hearted theatrical entertainment. Asked in old age whether she thought a woman could combine marriage with a career, she replied stoutly: 'Of course I do! If you have a gift, you must work hard to develop it—and always have faith in yourself.' ❦*John West*

further reading
PARKER, JOHN (ed.). *Who's Who in the Theatre.* London: Pitman 1926.
RUTLEDGE, MARTHA. Carrie Moore. *Australian Dictionary of Biography* 10. Melbourne University Press 1986.

Maggie Moore

Actor, dancer, singer. Born 10 July 1851 in San Francisco (USA). Originally Margaret Virginia Sullivan. Stage debut at Olympic Theatre, San Francisco, 1859. Played engagements at Alhambra, Metropolitan and Californian Theatres in San Francisco, 1871-74. Married J. C. Williamson in San Francisco, 2 February 1873. Co-starred with Williamson on Australian tour 1874-75, and in England and USA 1876-79. Returned to Australia and played comedy and operetta with Williamson 1879-87. Produced and appeared in her own productions after separation from Williamson 1891. Divorced from Williamson 29 May 1899. Married actor Harry Roberts in New York, 2 April 1902. Final Australian stage appearance in Sydney, 1 August 1924. Died 15 March 1926 in USA. Sister of actor James E. Moore.

In partnership with J. C. WILLIAMSON and later on her own, Maggie Moore brought to Australian theatre a vivacity, a sense of fun and an ability to tug the heartstrings that won her a depth of popular affection enjoyed by only the rarest performers. She was a versatile character actor, dancer and singer, equally adept at comedy, operetta and pantomime.

In San Francisco—where she was born to Irish parents who had settled in Australia before the gold rush drew them to California—Maggie made her stage debut at the age of eight. She took the same stage surname as an elder sister who was already in vaudeville. From child roles at six dollars a week she graduated to soubrette roles. Williamson, the leading comedian at the Californian Theatre, saw her playing a seriocomic role and spotted that she had the comic talents he needed in a stage partner. He persuaded the Californian to engage her and she first appeared there on 28 October 1872. The stage partnership led rapidly to marriage on 2 February 1873.

In the same year Williamson acquired the rights to a one-act melodrama called *Struck Oil* and had it revised and expanded by Clay M. Greene. The work, which provided the couple with leading roles ideally suited to their talents for comic dialect and characterisation, had its premiere in Salt Lake City in February 1874. In April they embarked on an Australian tour with *Struck Oil* and other plays, taking Maggie's brother James with them. Under the management of GEORGE COPPIN, they opened with *Struck Oil* at the Theatre Royal in Melbourne on 1 August 1874.

'Their merit is of so high an order that ... there can hardly be a difference of opinion concerning them', the *Argus* declared. 'The lady is especially remarkable in that she is able to sustain eccentric parts of a kind not commonly affected by actresses.' Applauding the season, the *Australasian Sketcher* said: 'Mrs Williamson has seized upon the public favour with a firmness of which we have no previous parallel'. It emphasised her talent for mingling comedy with pathos: 'The audience laughs and cries at the same moment, because she laughs and cries with them'. *Struck Oil* broke records in Melbourne with 43 capacity performances, and Moore had a racehorse named after her.

With *Struck Oil* and other established favourites—Dion Boucicault's *Arrah-na-Pogue* and *The Colleen Bawn*, and *Little Nell and the Marchioness*, a dramatic adaptation of Charles Dickens's *The Old Curiosity Shop* in which Moore played both title-roles—the Williamsons repeated their Melbourne success in Sydney, Castlemaine, Geelong, Bendigo and Adelaide. In October 1875 they sailed for London, where *Struck Oil* played for 100 nights at the Adelphi Theatre, followed by performances of *Arrah-na-Pogue* and *The Colleen Bawn*. Engagements elsewhere in the United Kingdom concluded a three-year world tour and 605 performances. The couple spent the next two years touring the USA with *Struck Oil*, which proved so popular that it ran to three revivals in New York.

They returned to Australia in July 1879 with Gilbert and Sullivan's *HMS Pinafore*, to which Williamson had acquired Australasian rights. Moore surprised and delighted theatregoers as the elegant, aristocratic Josephine, a sharp contrast to her much-loved knockabout antics in *Struck Oil*. There was a successful revival of *Struck Oil* in 1887. In 1890 Moore scored great hits as Meg in *Meg and the Castaway* with Frank Clark's Irish American Comedy Company, and later as principal boy in the pantomime *Dick Whittington*. By then her relationship with Williamson had begun to deteriorate. They separated in 1891 and in 1894 Moore revived *Struck Oil* with her own company, to the great annoyance of Williamson, who claimed exclusive rights. Lengthy litigation resulted in a victory for Moore. Her continuing production of the play estranged her from Williamson for the rest of his life. They were divorced in 1899, and in 1902 Moore married Harry Roberts, the actor who had played Williamson's role in *Struck Oil* in 1894.

Moore's career continued with major hits, including the operettas *The Mikado*, *Patience*, *The Pirates of Penzance* and *La Mascotte*; *The Child of the Regiment* by J. B. Buckstone; *The Danites* by Joaquin Miller; *The Colleen Bawn* and numerous revivals of *Struck Oil*. Moore and Roberts acted in a film of *Struck Oil* in 1919 but no copy of it has been found. She made her final stage appearance at Her Majesty's Theatre in Sydney on 1 August 1924, in the role she had played on her Australian debut exactly 50 years before—Lizzie Stofel in *Struck Oil*. The audience wept. ❦*Ian Dicker*

further reading
BEVAN, IAN. *The Story of the Theatre Royal*. Sydney: Currency Press 1993.
FANTASIA, JOSIE. Considering gender in nineteenth century Australia theatre—The case of Maggie Moore. *Australasian Drama Studies* 21 (Brisbane, October 1992).
WALCH, GARNET. *The Williamsons*. Melbourne: William Marshall 1885.

William Moore

Dramatist. Born 11 June 1868 at Bendigo (Vic.). Became journalist and art historian. Organised William Moore's Annual Drama Nights in Melbourne 1909-12. Went to England in 1912 and joined Harley Granville-Barker's theatrical company. Served in France during First World War. Returned to Sydney 1919. Married New Zealand dramatist and poet Dora Wilcox 1923. Died 6 November 1937 in Sydney.

William Moore claimed in 1930 that the four annual drama nights he organised in Melbourne in 1909–12 had been 'the first in which the sole object was the production of local plays with a literary as well as a dramatic quality'. In fact several groups in different states were simultaneously imitating the English repertory movement. Moore's first night, at the Oddfellows' Hall on 30 March 1909, consisted of four dramatic sketches of his own. The next, at the Turnverein Hall on 5 October 1910, included KATHARINE SUSANNAH PRICHARD's *The Burglar* and LOUIS ESSON's *The Woman Tamer*, the first work by each writer to be performed. Esson's *Dead Timber* was presented in 1911 and *The Sacred Place* in 1912. Moore, whose own plays were slight short pieces, organised the last of his evenings in conjunction with Gregan McMahon's MELBOURNE REPERTORY THEATRE COMPANY. In the early 1930s in Sydney Moore supported CARRIE TENNANT's Community Playhouse, where one of his wife's plays was produced. ❦*Richard Fotheringham*

writings
Introduction. *Best One-Act Australian Plays* (ed. William Moore and T. Inglis Moore). Sydney: Angus and Robertson 1937.
A manager for a night. *Community Magazine* (Sydney) 1930.
further reading
HOLDEN, ROBERT. William Moore. *Australian Dictionary of Biography* 10. Melbourne University Press 1986.

Wilton Morley

Entrepreneur. Born 27 August 1951 in London. Son of actor Robert Morley. Came to Australia 1973. Worked for J. C. Williamson's. Formed Parachute Productions. Filed for bankruptcy 1989.

After fragmentary schooling and some English experience in stage management, Wilton Morley came to Australia in 1973, when his father toured in Alan Ayckbourn's *How the Other Half Loves*. As an entrepreneur, he presented Bernard Slade's comedy *Same Time, Next Year*, stylishly acted by NANCYE HAYES and Lewis Fiander, in Australia, with J. C. WILLIAMSON's in 1976. Morley also co-produced shows with other organisations, including the AUSTRALIAN ELIZABETHAN THEATRE TRUST, the MELBOURNE THEATRE COMPANY and the THEATRE ROYAL in Sydney. His co-productions included Pam Gems's *Dusa, Fish, Stas and Vi*, Mary O'Malley's *Once a Catholic*, Ronald Harwood's *The Dresser*, Nell Dunn's *Steaming*, and *The Rocky Horror Show*. Late in 1989 Morley filed for bankruptcy and left for England. ❦*John West*

Morning Sacrifice

Play by Dymphna Cusack. **premiere** 8 October 1942, Repertory Theatre, Perth. Cast: Coralie Condon, Joan Evans, Nancy Hill, Doris Jefferson, Dorothy Krantz, Ella Munyard, Sheila O'Halloran, Ruth Rowell, Rose Stace. Director: Joyce Mortlock. **revived** 3 June 1986, Stables Theatre, Sydney, by Griffin Theatre Company. Cast: Alisa Carpenter, Karyn Greig, Sher Guhl, Tracey Higginson, Jean Korchman, Susan Leith, Helen McDonald, Barbara Phillips, Pat Thomson. Designer: Jack Ritchie. Director: Ian Watson. **published** Sydney: Australasian 1950; revised, Currency Press 1986.

Dymphna Cusack's second play, written while she was teaching at Sydney Girls' High School, is a protest at what she saw as the stifling of individuality and promise by the conventions and power games of the education system. The play has a cast of nine women and is set in the staff room of a girls' high school during the Second World War. Sheila Ray has returned to teach at her old school. The deputy headmistress, Portia Kingsbury is jealous of Sheila's brilliant university record. She also resents Sheila's replacing her in the affections of a pupil, Mary Grey. When Mary is caught kissing a boy at a school dance, Miss Kingsbury threatens expulsion. She accuses Sheila of having an immoral influence over the girl. The last act reveals that Miss Kingsbury has prevented a last meeting between Sheila and her departing soldier lover, and that Sheila has thrown herself under a bus. Miss Kingsbury will be promoted to headmistress. *Morning Sacrifice* has entered the repertoire since its first professional performance in 1986, 44 years after it won the Theatre Council of Western Australia Drama Festivals Prize in 1942. ❦*Ron Blair*

further reading
LLOYD, VIC. *Dymphna Cusack's Morning Sacrifice*. *Australasian Drama Studies* 10 (Brisbane, April 1987).

Helen Morse

Actor. Born at Harrow-on-the-Hill (England). Graduated from National Institute of Dramatic Art, Sydney, 1965. Has appeared in nearly 60 stage productions. Also in 25 film or television productions until 1984.

An actor whose fragile beauty is immediately compelling, Helen Morse seems to have turned her back on the money and fame associated with film and television to become Melbourne's leading female stage actor. She recommitted herself to the stage in 1986, playing Blanche Dubois in Tennessee Williams's *A Streetcar Named Desire* for the HARVEST THEATRE COMPANY in South Australia. In classical roles, from the Countess in Pierre Beaumarchais's *The Marriage of Figaro* to Blanche Dubois, she is outstanding, bringing to them profound patrician serenity under threat from more superficial emotional brittleness. She has been equally memorable in ALMA DE GROEN's *The Rivers of China* and Michael Gow's *Europe* and *Away*.

Morse was originally based in Sydney, where she played Celia in *As You Like It*, Portia and other Shakespearean roles for the OLD TOTE THEATRE COMPANY. She played Roxanne in Edmond Rostand's *Cyrano de Bergerac* for the SYDNEY THEATRE COMPANY in 1980, and Tom Kempinski's *Duet for One* on a national tour for the MARIAN STREET THEATRE COMPANY in 1982. Since 1987 she has played 15 major roles for the MELBOURNE THEATRE COMPANY, whose artistic director, ROGER HODGMAN, has recognised and nurtured her star quality on stage. She showed undiminished idealism for theatre with serious concerns when she acted in Ariel Dorfman's *Death and the Maiden* for the SYDNEY THEATRE COMPANY and on national tour in 1992–93. ❦*Ken Healey*

Maurice Moscovitch

Russian actor, 1871-1940. Acted with Moscow Arts Theatre. Played in Europe, North America and England in Russian, German, Yiddish and English. Highly successful Australian tours for J. C. Williamson's 1924-25 and 1926-29. In Hollywood films in 1930s.

A brilliant exponent of the Moscow Arts Theatre method, Maurice Moscovitch arrived on the Australian stage 1924 like a fresh wind. He believed that actors should live their parts and his dictum was 'an actor shall not act'. After seeing his vital Shylock in *The Merchant of Venice* at the Theatre Royal in Melbourne, Louis Esson wrote in the *Triad* of 1 January 1925: 'Moscovitch's portrayal of the Elizabethan Jew, though modern in method and technique, would have been a great artistic creation in any age or country'. Portia to his Shylock and leading lady on this tour was Jean Robertson, a beautiful and talented Australian who had acted extensively in New York and London. Audiences in Melbourne, Sydney and Adelaide were thrilled equally by Moscovitch's powerful characterisation of the charlatan Ragatzy in *The Outsider* by Dorothy Brandon and his appealing, dynamic Jean Paurel in *The Great Lover* by Leo Ditrichstein and Frederick and Fanny Hatton.

Moscovitch began his second tour on 9 October 1926 in Sydney, directing and playing the lead in Sidney Howard's *They Knew What They Wanted*, which had had a good run in New York City in 1924. In Australia it was criticised as 'crude' and the public greatly preferred Moscovitch's magnificent Svengali in Paul Potter's *Trilby*. Ellen Pollock was the female lead in these two plays. Mary McGregor, a young Australian, acted in two Edgar Wallace thrillers, *The Ringer* and *The Terror*. These and possibly George Bernard Shaw's *Arms and the Man* were directed by GREGAN MCMAHON. George D. Parker directed *Trilby*, Frederick Lonsdale's comedy *The Fake* and *The Silent House* by John G. Brandon and George Pickett.

J. C. WILLIAMSON's was so impressed by Moscovitch's success that in 1930 it went into partnership with New York promoters to star him in the London success *Jew Süss*, by Ashley Dukes from the novel by Lion Feuchtwanger. It opened brilliantly in Newark (New Jersey) but failed after a few weeks in New York City. ❦*Lynne Murphy*

further reading
Who's Who in the Theatre 9th edn. London: Pitman 1939.

Mother and Son

Play in three acts by Louis Esson. **premiere** June 1923, Temperance Hall, Russell Street, Melbourne. Director: George Dawes. **published** Melbourne: Robertson and Mullens 1946 in *The Southern Cross and other plays*.

The best of LOUIS ESSON's longer bush dramas, *Mother and Son* was a prototype for the genre that dominated Australian playwriting throughout the 1930s and 1940s. Set in a lonely apiary in Victoria, the play presents the conflict between Mrs Lind, a battling bushwoman of the type that Henry Lawson wrote about first—and familiar in later drama—and her tearaway son Harry. The young man is dissatisfied with the harshness of bush life and yearns, especially under the influence of the worldly Emma, for the attractions of the city. Harry has a gift for the violin. He plays it at shearers' dances, but would like to play in concerts in the city. His artistic sensibilities are, however, just one side of his wild nature, which leads him deeper and deeper into trouble and eventually to a wild ride through the bush in which he falls from his horse and is killed. The play is evocative, sometimes rather self-consciously, of life in the bush on the fringes of settlement. The style is melodramatic and heavily influenced by such writers as Eugene O'Neill and J. M. Synge, but the play has a power that ensures it a minor place in the repertoire. *John McCallum

Moving panoramas

Moving panoramas were 19th-century picture shows in which a great painted canvas, up to 90 metres long, was rolled from one side of a stage to the other while a lecturer commented on the scenes of foreign travel or historic battles depicted. A special kind called a moving diorama had transparent sections where lighting effects gave an illusion of enhanced movement. Entrepreneurs, who usually delivered the lectures, took moving panoramas around the Australian goldfields from the 1850s to the 1880s. In the cities they showed them in small halls rather than in large theatres. From the 1860s moving panoramas contributed to the spectacle in the big pantomimes in Melbourne and Sydney. The paintings were usually the work of theatrical scene-painters, including ALEXANDER HABBE, JOHN HENNINGS, WILLIAM PITT SNR and W. J. WILSON. In 1861 Pitt and John Fry painted a moving diorama of the Burke and Wills expedition within three months of the news of the loss of the explorers. In 1858 the puppet-theatre pioneer HENRY BEAUFOY MERLIN managed a panorama of the Indian Mutiny, one of many current or recent events overseas treated by moving panoramas until the cinematograph eclipsed them soon after its arrival in Australia in 1896. *Mimi Colligan

further reading
ALTICK, RICHARD. *The Shows of London*. Cambridge (Mass.), USA: Belknap Press of Harvard University Press 1978.
COLLIGAN, MIMI. Canvas and wax. Monash University PhD thesis 1987.
OPPENHEIM, HELENE. Early Australian scene painters. *Masque* 1/1 (Sydney, September-October 1967).

Mrs Pretty and the Premier

Play in three acts by Arthur H. Adams. **premiere** 26 September 1914, Athenaeum Hall, Melbourne. Cast: F. B. Reeve, Allie Robson. Director: Gregan McMahon. **published** Sydney: Brooks 1914, in *Three Plays for the Australian Stage*.

ARTHUR H. ADAMS's most successful play, *Mrs Pretty and the Premier* is a stylish but inconsequential romantic intrigue based upon the premise—found improbable by both Australian and English reviewers—that a bachelor prime minister would have to resign after the press saw him at 2 a.m. escorting a 'respectable' lady from his office. Helen Pretty owns a large sheep property that is about to be broken up by legislation, and is engaged to the Leader of the Opposition; Premier Bill Power has three days to woo and marry her before the 'scandal' breaks. Reviewers found the central roles lively and witty, though Helen's uninhibited use of 'feminine wiles' might not find favour today. Adams wrote the play for the commercial stage. After amateur seasons in Melbourne and Sydney in 1914 and a production as *The Division Bell* in Birmingham in 1915, it had a major production at Herbert Beerbohm Tree's Her Majesty's Theatre in London in 1916. The *Times* remarked: 'Aren't they just darlings, these Antipodeans?' but the play managed 36 performances. *Richard Fotheringham

J. W. B. Murphy

Musician, manager. Born c.1865. Arrived in Melbourne from New Zealand 1881. Moved to Hobart c.1896. Managed Theatre Royal, Hobart, for more than 45 years. Died 1958 in Hobart.

A singer and trombonist, J. W. B. Murphy conducted a stage band in Melbourne until he moved to Hobart, where he was initially employed at the *Mercury* newspaper. Its owner, C. E. Davies, also owned the THEATRE ROYAL and he appointed Murphy its manager. He remained there for more than 45 years, which included periods as Tasmanian representative of J. C. Williamson's and manager of the Prince of Wales Theatre in Hobart. He amassed memorabilia which a descendant deposited in the Tasmaniana Library, State Library of Tasmania, in 1984. The Murphy Collection, invaluable to performing-arts historians, comprises 364 theatre and cinema posters from 1896 to 1920 and 385 theatre programs for productions between 1860 and 1960, chiefly at the Theatre Royal. *Gillian Winter

Lynne Murphy

Actor. Born 6 May 1923 in Melbourne. Trained at Bryant's Playhouse (Sydney) from 1940. Metropolitan Theatre (Sydney) 1945-50. Radio from 1945. Television from 1959. Professional theatre 1947-50 and since 1964. Married to radio and television dramatist Richard Lane.

Early in her career Lynne Murphy brought sensitivity and tall, willowy beauty to classic and contemporary roles. Later she invested character parts with comic energy and lent quiet maturity to her playing of sophisticated women. Her love of theatre was stirred at BRYANT'S PLAYHOUSE, where she played Fanny in *Fanny's First Play* by George Bernard Shaw, but her talent was developed by MAY HOLLINWORTH when the Metropolitan Players toured plays to army camps and suburban halls. She alternated with Wendy Gibb as Desdemona in *Othello* in METROPOLITAN THEATRE's first production in its Reiby Place theatre in 1946. In 1947 Murphy's playing of Lady Windermere in Oscar Wilde's *Lady Windermere's Fan* won her her first professional role, the outraged young schoolteacher Judith Drave in Joan Temple's *No Room at the Inn*, at the MINERVA THEATRE in Sydney. Other parts at the Minerva followed quickly.

In 1949 Murphy, with the veteran MINNIE LOVE, led a Metropolitan Theatre company of 12 on a six-week tour of northern NSW and southern Queensland. Later in the year she was chosen to appear with Robert Morley in his play *Edward, My Son* in Sydney, Melbourne and New Zealand.

For Metropolitan in 1950 she scored a success in the first production for nearly a century of Edward Reeve's RAYMOND, LORD OF MILAN.

Murphy left the stage to bring up her family but kept on working in radio and television. She returned in the mid-1960s in lunchtime theatre, particularly for Q THEATRE in Sydney. Roles for the OLD TOTE THEATRE COMPANY followed, including Voynitskaya in Anton Chekhov's *Uncle Vanya*, Edna Shaft in Simon Gray's *Butley* in 1973 and Miss Fellowes in Tennessee Williams's *The Night of the Iguana* in 1978. In 1982 at Sydney's Marian Street Theatre she played one of four gently grotesque sisters in *Morning's at Seven*, Paul Osborn's affectionate backward glance at the Middle America of 1922. Later appearances have included SYDNEY THEATRE COMPANY productions of Friedrich Dürrenmatt's *The Visit*, Howard Jackson's *Just Bent*, Arthur Miller's *The Crucible* and Jean Racine's *Phedra*. ❦*Richard Lane*

Murray

Magician. Born 11 November 1901 in Melbourne. Originally Murray Carrington Walters. Travelled widely in youth. Returned to Australia 1921. Performed in England from 1920s. Toured Australia on Tivoli circuit 1928. Toured Australia 1947. Retired from stage 1953. Died 22 January 1988 in Blackpool (England).

A magician with a flair for publicity, Murray began to perform escapology to draw attention to his show while touring the eastern states of Australia after his return from world travels in 1921. From then he concentrated on escape feats. He was inspired to become a magician as a small boy, when he saw Howard Thurston perform in Melbourne in 1905. In his teens Murray left for Canada as a ship's boy. He worked his way across America from Seattle, Washington, always performing magic. During travels that took him to Singapore, Bombay, Buenos Aires and other cities he constantly improved his act. With his escape act, Murray left Australia again and went to England by way of India and Egypt. He was a feature act at the London Coliseum in 1926. Then came a tour of Britain and a return to Australia for the Tivoli circuit in 1928. Back in Europe his sensational feats of escapology took him to the top of the bill. He was playing at the Wintergarden in Berlin with a full illusion show when war was declared in 1939. He had to abandon all his apparatus and leave within hours of hearing the news. He went to India, then back to England for the duration of the war. He toured Australia again in 1947. At the height of his success, performing in England with a full illusion show in 1953, Murray was stricken with a nervous disorder that forced him off the stage. He ran a magic shop in Blackpool until he died. ❦*Gerald Taylor*

Archibald Murray

Scottish actor, dramatist. Active in Scottish and Australian journalism, notably for *Sydney Punch*. Acted in Hobart 1853. Wrote or adapted five dramas, a pantomime and two burlesques while in Sydney 1860-82.

Archibald Murray pioneered the introduction of colonial incidents and types into sensation melodrama. His melodrama *Captain Hayes* (1869), capitalising on the topical notoriety of the American blackbirder Bully Hayes, was referred to as 'the greatest bosh that human being ever penned' when it was revised in 1871 as *The Fatal Gap*. His sensational bushranger drama *Fleeced* (1870) with bushfires and multiple gun battles, was accused of promoting subversive sympathies when it was revived in Melbourne in November 1878, a few days after the Kelly Gang killed three policemen. ❦*Veronica Kelly*

published works
Captain Hayes (1869). Revised as *The Fatal Gap* 1871. Sydney: Beard and Holmes 1873 (as *Forged*).
Harlequin Blue Beard, the Great Bashaw—or, The Good Fairy Triumphant over the Demon of Discord, pantomime (1872). Sydney: Lenthall Brothers 1872.

further reading
KELLY, VERONICA. Garnet Walch in Sydney. *Australasian Drama Studies* 9 (Brisbane, October 1986).

Dinah Murray

Actor, manager. Born c.1816. Originally Dinah Rudelhoff. Arrived in Hobart August 1834. Debut in J. P. Deane's company in Hobart 23 August 1834. Married James Pulteney Murray, December 1836. Manager of Geelong Theatre 1845.

One of the earliest theatrical managers in Australia, Dinah Murray was also considered by Hobart critics to be a 'capital' actress, particularly adept at light comedy. She came to Hobart as Dinah Rudelhoff on the female immigrant ship *Strathfieldsay* with ANNE CLARKE. Described as 'from the Theatre Royal English Opera House', they made successful debuts at the Argyle Rooms for J. P. DEANE. After marriage and a trip to England, Dinah Rudelhoff resumed her acting career as Mrs Murray, despite her husband's objections. In March 1838 she went to Sydney for the opening of the ROYAL VICTORIA THEATRE; her acting was judged coarse. In 1845 she was acting in and managing the Geelong Theatre. She and Anne Clarke were the only female managers of their time. ❦*Gillian Winter*

Edith Murray BEM

Puppeteer, teacher. Born 26 February 1897 in Sydney. Founding member of Puppetry Guild of NSW 1948. Founding secretary of Australian section of L'Union Internationale de la Marionnette (UNIMA) 1968. Member of honour of UNIMA 1980. Died 30 January 1988 in Sydney. BEM 1979.

A driving force in Australian puppetry, Edith Murray inspired, encouraged and helped amateur and professional puppeteers throughout Australia and established lines of communication. Her special interest was in the value of puppetry in creative leisure. As a teacher in the 1930s, she used puppets in teaching disturbed children. She used puppetry in Creative Leisure Movement centres (formerly the Children's Library and Crafts Movement) and on 28 May 1949 she opened the Clovelly Puppet Theatre, which she directed for nearly 30 years. In 1965 she worked 'black light' puppets in pantomime in Glasgow (Scotland). She was invited to Japan as honoured guest of the PUK Puppet Theatre in 1976. ❦*Richard Bradshaw*

Murray River Performing Group

Professional community-theatre company in Albury (NSW) and Wodonga (Vic.) founded by Robert Perrier, Mark Sherrifs and Lloyd Suttor on 12 January 1979. **artistic directors** 1979-87 Robert

Perrier. 1979-81 Mark Sherrifs. 1982-83 Richard Meredith. 1984-86 Phil Thompson. 1987 Richard Collins. 1988-91 Louise Permezel. 1992- Susan McClements. **first production** *A Big Hand for the Limbs*, Wodonga Theatrette, February 1979. Written and designed by cast: Boris Conley, Bettina Eijsma, Ian Mortimer, Robert Perrier, Mark Sherrifs, Lloyd Suttor, Lucy Taphouse. Director: Robert Perrier.

One of the few companies that has survived changes in perceptions of COMMUNITY THEATRE, the Murray River Performing Group still creates theatre about and for the place where it operates. It responds to the life and spirit of Albury–Wodonga in particular. The group began operations with a year's funding from the Victorian Ministry for the Arts, the NSW Ministry of the Arts, the Australia Council and the Albury-Wodonga Development Corporation. The first production, *A Big Hand for the Limbs*, opened in February 1979, ran all year in regional venues and concluded with a tent season at the Festival of Sydney in 1980.

The founders, strongly influenced by their training at the VICTORIAN COLLEGE OF THE ARTS when it was oriented towards community theatre, employed nonstandard theatrical techniques to reach an audience that was largely unfamiliar with theatre. The company produced shows that could easily be adapted to various venues and it frequently took to the streets to maintain its prominence. In the early days Robert Perrier shared the direction with Mark Sherrifs, who directed a clown ensemble from 1980 to 1981. Perrier, with the company from 1979 to 1986, had much to do with its divergent operations and the phenomenal growth of the FLYING FRUIT FLY CIRCUS. This emerged from an eight-week circus workshop run by the Murray River group for 90 children in 1979 and became legally separate in 1987.

The company attracted a new audience with its first theatre-restaurant show, *The Riverboat Show*, in 1980. *Crystal Dewdrops* in 1981 established the combination of music and comedy, and the Spangles, founded in 1985, made it so popular that they eventually operated autonomously. Galah Bar Shows, established in 1982, attracted a younger audience to the company and opened up entrepreneurial possibilities. *Murray River Story* in 1988 established the large community-participation shows for which the company has become known. *Louise Permezel*

George Musgrove

Entrepreneur. Born 21 January 1854 at Surbiton (England). Mother was actor and singer Fanny Hodson. Came to Victoria at 12. Trained in theatrical management by uncle W. S. Lyster. Left Lyster and imported record-breaking production of *La Fille du tambour-major* 1880. Partner in Williamson, Garner and Musgrove 1882-90. Partner in Williamson and Musgrove 1892-99. Organised Williamson and Musgrove Italian Opera Company 1893. Toured Musgrove's Grand Opera Company 1900-01. Unsuccessful US tour 1906. Toured Musgrove's Royal Grand Opera 1907. Retired 1914. Died 21 January 1916 in Sydney. Companion of actor Nellie Stewart. Father of actors Rose Musgrove and Nancye Stewart.

One of the premier impresarios in the late 19th and early 20th centuries, George Musgrove came from a theatrical family. His mother had acted at Drury Lane and his aunt Georgina Hodson was an opera singer and the wife of W. S. LYSTER. After Musgrove finished his schooling his uncle gave him a job on the managerial side of the business. A month after Lyster died in November 1880, his 26-year-old nephew, by then independent, had one of the successes of his life with Jacques Offenbach's *LA FILLE DU TAMBOUR-MAJOR*, performed in Melbourne by a largely imported company. It was so popular that it ran for a record 101 nights.

During preparations to move the show to Adelaide in April 1881, the original Griolet left and 23-year-old NELLIE STEWART auditioned for the part. In her autobiography she says that she sang badly but Musgrove engaged her anyway. She became his most valuable star and a major asset to the firm of WILLIAMSON, GARNER AND MUSGROVE, formed in 1882. She also became the love of Musgrove's life, but never his wife. He had married in 1874 and was never divorced. Nevertheless Stewart and Musgrove were parted only by death. A daughter was born to them in 1893 and became a successful actor as NANCYE STEWART.

Musgrove withdrew from Williamson, Garner and Musgrove in 1890, and presented operettas starring Nellie Stewart. The first was *Paul Jones*, which had been a big success for the triumvirate at the Prince of Wales Opera House in Melbourne from 27 March 1890. Musgrove opened it in Sydney at the Theatre Royal, which he controlled, on 12 July. Later came *Boccaccio* and *La Fille de Mme Angot*, which were toured to other colonies. The second of the GAIETY THEATRE COMPANIES to come to Australia was a failure for Musgrove in 1892, when he was going through a lean period, and later in the year he rejoined forces with J. C. Williamson as WILLIAMSON AND MUSGROVE.

During a long stay in England at the time of Queen Victoria's diamond jubilee in 1897, Musgrove leased the Shaftesbury Theatre in London under Williamson and Musgrove banner. The first show was a failure. Then he imported a complete company from New York City in *The Belle of New York*. It had not been a success there but in London the lilting melodies of Gustave Kerker, the speed and efficiency of the production and the charms of the diminutive 18-year-old star, Edna May, made it a huge success. Williamson feared that the Australian firm might be sucked into Musgrove's grandiose schemes. Musgrove's reassurances that he was definitely not liable for the London debts did not appease Williamson. He grumbled that Musgrove was spending too much time on his own ventures and not enough on the firm's business. Musgrove sent a company to Australia to perform *The Belle of New York*, opening on 1 April 1899 at the Princess Theatre in Melbourne. It was insufficiently starry for Williamson and his charges against Musgrove led to the dissolution of their partnership at the end of the year.

Nellie Stewart, of course, went with Musgrove. His only total success in London since 1897 had been *The Belle of New York*. He returned to Australia in 1900 to present drama and a large opera company. His trump card was his lease of the Princess Theatre in Melbourne, where in 1902 Stewart essayed her first dramatic role in Paul Kester's *Sweet Nell of Old Drury* with great success. Nellie Melba's first concert tour of Australia in 1902 was another financial success for Musgrove. In 1906 he took Stewart and a large company on an ambitious tour of the USA. It was not successful and Musgrove barely escaped with his life in the San Francisco earthquake. After a week in which Stewart and the company heard nothing from him, he rejoined them in Colorado. He was 'unshaven, ragged and battered',

Stewart said. The last 10 years of Musgrove's life were plagued by financial worries and ill health. Soon after an eight-month tour of *Sweet Nell* in New Zealand and the Australian backblocks in 1910-11 Stewart's own money began to disappear in grandiose plans in which Musgrove became involved. He was 'the victim of designing schemers', she said. Musgrove spent the morning of 21 January 1916, his 62nd birthday, in their garden in Sydney. When he did not answer the lunch bell, Stewart went to fetch him and found him dead on the porch. ❦*John West*

further reading
Bevan, Ian. *The Story of the Theatre Royal*. Sydney: Currency Press 1993.
Gittins, Jean. George Musgrove. *Australian Dictionary of Biography* 5. Melbourne University Press 1984.

Harry G. Musgrove

Entrepreneur, manager. Born 2 August 1884 in Melbourne. Son of Harry Musgrove, theatrical manager. Nephew of entrepreneur George Musgrove. Worked in film exhibition with T. J. West, Union Theatres and Australasian Films 1906-20. Formed Carroll-Musgrove Theatres with E. J. and Dan Carroll 1920. Formed First National Exhibitors of Australia 1921. Formed Musgrove Theatres 1921. Operated Tivoli Theatres in Melbourne and Sydney 1921-24. Bankrupt 1924. Represented United Artists Films in Shanghai (China) *c*.1926-30. Died 27 April 1951 in Sydney.

Harry G. Musgrove—as Henry George Musgrove was popularly known to distinguish him from his father Harry—was active mainly in film exhibition but he made a foray into vaudeville in the 1920s. He spent his youth largely in the offices of his uncle GEORGE MUSGROVE at the Princess Theatre in Melbourne. In 1906 he joined the pioneer film exhibitor T. J. West, who was screening motion pictures in Sydney and Melbourne. West's Pictures became part of Union Theatres and Australasian Films, and Harry G. Musgrove was a director of both companies.

In 1920 Musgrove resigned from the combine to join DAN AND E. J. CARROLL in forming Carroll-Musgrove Theatres. Musgrove gained the Australian rights to First National films and to facilitate their exhibition he formed Musgrove Theatres. In 1921 this company took over the Tivoli Theatres in Sydney and Melbourne from Hugh D. McIntosh and converted them to cinemas. The venture was not successful and Musgrove soon switched the theatres back to vaudeville. He operated them until 1924, with the help of his cousin JACK MUSGROVE, presenting international artists, including Wilkie Bard, Claude Dampier, ANNETTE KELLERMANN, ELLA SHIELDS, Lee White and Clay Smith, and Wee Georgie Wood.

Musgrove successfully produced the pantomime *The Babes in the Wood* at the Cremorne Theatre in Brisbane for Christmas 1922. Next Christmas a disastrous production of *The Forty Thieves* at the Hippodrome in Sydney led him into bankruptcy and he was forced to sell his Tivoli interests to J. C. Williamson's. He worked for a while as United Artists' representative in Shanghai, but his fortunes never recovered. Once a dapper, good-looking, charming man of ideas, he died in penniless obscurity, aged 66. ❦*Frank Van Straten*

further reading
GIBBNEY, H. J. and ANNE G. SMITH. *A biographical register 1788-1939*. Canberra: Australian Dictionary of Biography 1987.

Jack Musgrove

Entrepreneur, manager. Born 9 October 1893 in Sydney. Worked for Fullers' in Sydney and Melbourne. Controlled Fullers' vaudeville in Victoria from 1918. Managed National Theatre, Sydney. Controlled Tivoli presentations as general manager of Musgrove Theatres 1921-24 and general manager of J. C. Williamson's Tivoli Vaudeville 1924-29. Managed cinemas 1929-36. Managed Trocadero dance hall, Sydney, 1936-56. Died 8 May 1956 in Sydney.

Jack Musgrove helped his cousin HARRY G. MUSGROVE to manage the TIVOLI CIRCUIT after its return to vaudeville in 1921 and then he managed J. C. WILLIAMSON's vaudeville interests. He was the son of Arthur Musgrove, treasurer of Her Majesty's Theatre in Sydney, and his middle names were William Lyster, after his illustrious great-uncle W. S. LYSTER. He had his theatrical grounding with FULLERS' vaudeville, first at the National Theatre in Sydney and then at the Bijou Theatre in Melbourne. By 25, he controlled all Fullers' Victorian vaudeville activities.

Jack Musgrove turned to cinema management in Melbourne and then joined his cousin's Musgrove Theatres. He managed first the Theatre Royal in Perth, and then the Tivoli Theatre in Sydney until Musgrove Theatres collapsed in 1924, Then he joined J. C. Williamson's as manager of their new vaudeville interests, which were based on the Theatres Royal in Sydney and Melbourne. He toured the USA, the United Kingdom and South Africa, booking acts for J. C. Williamson's Vaudeville.

J. C. Williamson's then bought out Musgrove Theatres, and concentrated its vaudeville operations on the Tivoli Theatres under Jack Musgrove's management. He maintained a high standard, presenting such international stars as MARIE BURKE, Sonny Clay, EDGLEY AND DAWE, Will Fyffe, Will Hay, Little Tich, Arthur Lucan ('Old Mother Riley') and Kitty McShane, Olsen and Johnson, ADA REEVE, Nellie Wallace, ALBERT WHELAN, Lee White and Clay Smith, and Bransby Williams. Musgrove also promoted Australian talent, and it was he who first presented ROY RENE on the Tivoli circuit—in 1926, in a double act with FRED BLUETT.

After J. C. Williamson's Tivoli Vaudeville collapsed in 1929, Musgrove supervised the conversion of the Theatre Royal in Sydney to talking pictures. He gave up managing cinemas for Hoyts in 1936 to become manager of the new Trocadero dance hall. Its owner, Ezra Norton, also entrusted him with the management of the lucrative amusement advertising columns of his *Daily Mirror* newspaper. ❦*Frank Van Straten*

Music Hall Theatre Restaurant

Theatre-restaurant in Neutral Bay Junction, Sydney, opened on 8 November 1961 by George and Lorna Miller. Closed 6 September 1980. **first production** *East Lynne*. Cast included Barry Creyton. Director: Bette Bailey Stainton. **last production** *East Lynne*.

At a time when serious theatre was renewing itself in smaller and smaller venues, the Music Hall Theatre Restaurant offered actors a rare opportunity to battle with an audience from the footlights on an almost Shakespearean scale. In its heyday the Music Hall was a red plush affair with stalls and a gallery seating 500 at tables covered with red-checked cloths, and a foyer crammed with Victorian bric-a-brac. Moustachioed waiters in Edwardian waistcoats would serve the hearty patrons while the genial George and Lorna Miller, moved among them, playing violin and accordion. At 8.30 p.m. the musical director, Don Harvie, would begin the overture at the piano and the velvet curtain would rise upon an extravagant setting and an absurdly complicated plot. The audience might choose to attend to it or not. It was a challenge for any actor.

The Millers opened the Music Hall in 1961 with the melodrama *East Lynne*, which they had produced successfully at the Bowl Music Hall in Melbourne. The new Sydney production starred BARRY CREYTON. The early shows were rough affairs. The villain had to learn to duck not only bread rolls but spoons and other missiles. But it was secure work and as the Music Hall's reputation grew and seasons extended to a year or more, many well-known performers learned new skills there. DAVID ATKINS, Pat Bishop, NEVA CARR GLYN, Beryl Cheers, Linda Cropper, RON HADDRICK, ALEXANDER HAY, Sheila Kennelly, Frank Lloyd and JOHN UNICOMB were among them.

BARRY LOVETT, a versatile actor, was the much-loved master clown; he spent ten years with the company. Alton Harvey was the longest-running villain. The designs, created by opera designers like Tom Lingwood, became more extravagant year by year.

The mood gradually changed after John Faassen, an actor and singer, took over as director in 1966 and began writing his own shows. The plays became more sophisticated burlesques of musical and dramatic genres, particularly opera. By 1968 nationalism was making its mark. *Her Only Mistake* was the first show set in colonial Australia. Stanley Walsh replaced Faassen in 1970 and his first show, *The Trials of Hilary Pouncefortt*, tapped the new preoccupation with Australian history. It was a melodrama, critical of military authority, set in colonial Sydney in 1850. Walsh in turn was succeeded by MICHAEL BODDY as director and resident playwright. He mounted two successful shows in 1977-78 but when he retired in 1979 the Music Hall returned to revivals. It had run out of energy by 1980, when, despite protests by loyal supporters, it closed after a two-year battle with the local council and the state government over fire safety. ❧*Katharine Brisbane*

further reading
MCPHERSON, AILSA. *A Dream of Passion—Theatre activity in North Sydney*. Sydney: Stanton Library 1993.

Music halls

The passage of the Beer Act in England in 1830 encouraged a proliferation of beer shops and English publicans found themselves facing stiff competition. They countered this by opening 'free-and-easies', or 'singing saloons', in their public houses or in adjacent premises and offering their patrons entertainment as well as alcohol. These places thrived from the outset. In 1843 some Sydney publicans began to advertise free-and-easies in their hotels on certain nights. One of them was GEORGE COPPIN, who used the profits from a successful stint at the Royal Victoria Theatre to purchase the Clown Tavern in Pitt Street. But free-and-easies did not flourish in Sydney, and Coppin lost his investment and retreated to Hobart to re-establish his stage career.

The most famous English music halls were in London. Canterbury Hall, opened in 1851, and the Oxford Music Hall, opened in 1861, both presented mainly classical music and ballads in their early years. Programs in the small music halls attached to hotels included traditional songs, dances and tricks from travelling troupes, as well as music borrowed from MINSTRELS. The entertainment was bawdy and derisive of authority. A chairman acted as master of ceremonies, announcing the series of unrelated turns. In most halls the customers sat at tables and waiters circulated among them, selling food and drink.

In Australia the gold rushes of the 1850s brought single men into Melbourne and they sought entertainment different from that at the city's theatres. This stimulated the establishment of music halls. The authorities quickly closed the first hall to open, the Royal Music Hall, on the grounds that performances there were marked more by 'scurrility than by wit'. In 1857 a concert room was opened in Tilkes's City Hotel and its success prompted imitations. Soon Melbourne boasted a host of halls, including Tilkes's, the Apollo, O'Halloran's, the Canterbury, the Surrey, and later, Ellis's London Music Hall and the Varieties.

From the late 1860s music halls were increasingly replaced by minstrel and variety theatres. These featured fixed rows of seating and patrons had to adjourn to the adjoining hotel for a drink. Sydney's most famous music hall, the Scandinavian Hall, opened in Castlereagh Street in 1868 but by 1870 it was renamed the St James Hall and it had metamorphosed into a variety theatre. There was a charge for admission and fixed rows of seats had replaced the tables and chairs because food and drink were no longer served in the body of the hall.

The programs performed in Australian music halls differed little from those offered in their English counterparts. Topical songs containing contemporary and controversial allusions were often sung; variety acts and blackface 'turns' were prominent. It is also clear that the entertainment tended to be more irreverent and 'vulgar' than that offered in theatres. The cancan was first danced to Australian audiences on the stage of the Scandinavian Hall in Sydney. Music-hall entertainers were reputed to lack refinement on stage and this often hampered them in gaining work in minstrel or variety theatres. Men and women from all classes went to variety theatres, whereas music halls had been patronised mostly by working-class men.

HARRY RICKARDS came to Australia from London music halls and established a national vaudeville circuit. Many of his songs were about costermongers, and the repertoire of English music-hall remained prominent in Australian variety. In the period up to 1914, some of the greatest English music-hall stars, including Lottie Collins, Marie Lloyd, and Little Tich toured Australia for Rickards. Appropriately, his TIVOLI THEATRE in Sydney stood on the site of the Scandinavian Hall. ❧*Richard Waterhouse*

further reading
BAILEY, PETER. *Leisure and Class in Victorian England*. London: Routledge and Kegan Paul 1978.
STEDMAN JONES, GARETH. Working class culture and working class politics in London, 1870-1900. *Journal of Social History* 7 (summer 1974).
SUMMERFIELD, PENNY. Patriotism and empire. *Imperialism and Popular Culture* (ed. John McKenzie). Manchester University Press 1986.
Bulletin (Sydney) 2 October 1929. Account of the Scandinavian Hall.

Musical theatre

Music has enlivened theatrical performance in Australia since 23 July 1796, when William Shield's one-act comic opera *The Poor Soldier* was performed in SIDAWAY'S THEATRE in Sydney. The oldest surviving playbill of the theatre, for Saturday 8 March 1800, announces 'the comedy of the Recruiting Officer. To which will be added A Musical Entertainment called The Virgin Unmasked'. This was *An Old Man Taught Wisdom—or, The Virgin Unmasked*, a ballad opera by Henry Fielding. Another ballad opera by Fielding, *The Mock Doctor*, opened the EMU PLAINS CONVICT THEATRE, west of Sydney, in 1825.

Sydney's second theatre proprietor, BARNETT LEVEY was 'a good mimic and also a fair comic and patriotic vocalist', according to the theatre historian C. H. Bertie. He had this from F. C. Brewer, who had met some artists associated with Levey. In his Royal Hotel towards the end of 1829 Levey was giving monthly vocal and instrumental concerts called 'Barnett Levey's "at Home" (à la Mathews)'. This was a reference to Charles Mathews, an English entertainer renowned for his 'at homes'—solo performances of comic songs and stories about amusing and eccentric characters. When Levey presented Douglas Jerrold's nautical melodrama *Black-Eyed Susan* and the farce *Monsieur Tonson* in his hotel on Boxing Night 1832 it was advertised that the performances would 'be supplemented by the band of His Majesty's 17th Regiment kindly allowed by Colonel Despard and conducted by Mr Lewis'.

In 1838 Joseph Wyatt engaged an orchestra for his new ROYAL VICTORIA THEATRE in Sydney. It consisted of four violins, two violas, a violoncello, a double bass, two clarinets, two flutes, two horns, a trumpet, a bassoon, a serpent—a bass wind instrument of wood and leather which looked like an undulating snake—and a drum. Theatre orchestras played for opera and ballet, provided overtures and entr'actes, met Shakespeare's demands for music and often increased the effectiveness of scenes in melodrama.

In the 1860s managers, following the lead of the English theatre, swelled their profits by presenting light musical shows called burlesques and extravaganzas. A BURLESQUE was usually an amusing parody of a well-known contemporary drama, while an EXTRAVAGANZA contained less satire and more pure entertainment and its plots often came from a fairy tale or mythology.

PANTOMIME also utilised music, borrowed from anywhere, and when W. S. LYSTER introduced the *opéras-bouffes* of Jacques Offenbach to Australia in 1871 many of the tunes were already familiar. *The Grand Duchess of Gerolstein* was the first of Offenbach's *opéras-bouffes*, in which farcical libretti set up classical mythology and other institutions, to be performed here. *Opéras-bouffes* by Offenbach's rival Hervé and operettas by other French composers—Edmond Audran, Charles Lecocq and Robert Planquette—also found favour with Australian audiences. They were performed in English adaptations made for London theatres, often by H. B. Farnie. The London star of *opéra-bouffe* was EMILY SOLDENE, and in 1877 she brought her troupe of girls, the Emily Soldene Opéra-Bouffe Company, from London to Australia in 1877 to play pieces by Offenbach and others. Soldene slipped a four-year-old American popular song, 'Silver threads among the gold', into the score of Offenbach's *Geneviève de Brabant*. Nightly high-kicking contests between Florence Slater and Mlle Sara also gave the show a lift. Slater delighted the young men in the gods by kicking her slipper into their gallery, which was nearer to the stage in those days.

Lyster gave the first Melbourne season of Offenbach's *La Belle Hélène* in June 1876 at one performance he included the one-act GILBERT AND SULLIVAN operetta *Trial by Jury* as an afterpiece. Gilbert and Sullivan produced their first full-length operetta, *HMS Pinafore*, in London in 1878 and within a year it had unauthorised performances in Australia. Later in 1879 J. C. WILLIAMSON returned to Australia claiming exclusive rights to perform the work.

On Boxing Night 1880, a month after Lyster's death, his nephew GEORGE MUSGROVE presented his first major theatrical offering at his uncle's theatre, the Prince of Wales Opera House in Melbourne. It was an entire London company performing Offenbach's *LA FILLE DU TAMBOUR-MAJOR*. The London favourites Albert Brennir, Pattie Laverne and Fred Mervin and the charm of eight imported showgirls, including Consuelo—'nearly six feet of blazing loveliness', according to Nellie Stewart—helped the show to an unprecedented run of 101 consecutive performances. This set Musgrove on the path to becoming one of the three leading impresarios in the country. Williamson and Arthur Garner were the others. These three men, who came to be known as the 'triumvirate', formed Williamson, Garner and Musgrove in July 1882. Their first production in Melbourne, *Patience* at the Theatre Royal, began a boom in Gilbert and Sullivan. Smaller companies also helped to spread the popularity of operettas. One was the Wallace–Dunning Troupe, whose prima donna was often Emily Melville. At the Prince of Wales Opera House in Melbourne on 2 September 1882 it gave the first Australian production of Franz von Suppé's *Boccaccio*, with Kate Chard in the title-role. This is said to have been the first Viennese operetta to become popular in Australia.

Griolet the drummer-boy in La Fille du tambour-major *was initially played in George Musgrove's production by Jessie Grey. When she left the cast Nellie Stewart replaced her, beginning a great career in operetta*

WILLIAMSON, GARNER AND MUSGROVE soon vigorously operated a policy of importing stars. From the Savoy Theatre in London came creators of Gilbert and Sullivan roles—Alice Barnett (Ruth in *The Pirates of Penzance*, Lady Jane in *Patience* and Queen of the Fairies in *Iolanthe*) in 1886, Henry Bracy (Hilarion in *Princess Ida*) and Leonora Braham (Phyllis in *Iolanthe*, Princess Ida, Yum-Yum in *The Mikado* and Rose Maybud in *Ruddigore*) in 1887. Australia was also producing its own favourite performers in Gilbert and Sullivan, such as NELLIE STEWART—in *Patience* 1881, *Iolanthe* in 1885 and *The Yeomen of the Guard* in 1889. Among the

A scene from Williamson and Musgrove's production of The Mikado *at the Lyceum Theatre in Sydney in 1895.*

men, Howard Vernon played many principal comic roles; John Forde and W. H. Woodfield were also prominent. After the triumvirate broke up, in 1890 Musgrove's association with Nellie Stewart brought him success with Robert Planquette's *Paul Jones*.

New works appeared on Australian stages with little delay, though musical comedy, the offspring of English 19th-century burlesque and operetta, took two years to arrive. The first show specifically called a musical comedy was *A Gaiety Girl*, presented by George Edwardes at the Prince of Wales Theatre in London in October 1893. In November 1894 Edwardes replaced burlesque at his Gaiety Theatre with a musical comedy, *The Shop Girl* and the Gaiety became the home of a long line of musical comedies, often with the titillating word 'girl' in the title.

In 1895 the third of the GAIETY THEATRE COMPANIES to visit Australia presented for WILLIAMSON AND MUSGROVE *A Gaiety Girl*, *The Shop Girl* and *In Town*, a musical farce first staged at the Prince of Wales in 1892, which is sometimes seen as having initiated musical comedy. Later popular musical comedies included *The Geisha* in 1898, *Florodora* in 1900, *The Girl from Kay's* in 1904, *The Girl Behind the Counter* in 1909, *Our Miss Gibbs* in 1910 and *The Sunshine Girl* in 1913. Other hits, described by their authors as musical plays, in Australia were *The Toreador* in 1902, *A Country Girl* in 1903, *The Orchid* in 1904 and *Miss Hook of Holland* in 1908.

Musical comedy did not displace its forerunners. They all existed side by side, because audiences expected revivals of familiar shows in every season by J. C. Williamson's Royal Comic Opera Company, even if it began with something new. In 1903 George Musgrove introduced the American operettas of the German-trained Irish composer Victor Herbert. In 1908 Williamson had a huge success with *The Merry Widow*, composed in Vienna by Ferencz Lehár, whose forename was then invariably rendered in the German form Franz—and often still is. From 1908 until the First World War, the leading entrepreneurs presented a string of operettas from Vienna composed by Lehár and the Austrians Leo Fall and Oscar Straus and from Budapest by the Hungarian Imre Kálmán. They all reached Australia by way of London, where translation, adaptation and interpolation had left them resembling English musical comedies. Fall's *Der geschiedene Frau* emerged in Australia in 1911 as *The Girl on the Train*. The first two decades of the 20th century produced a line of star singing actors in musical theatre. Some, like GRACE PALOTTA, were visitors who adopted Australia. Others, like CARRIE MOORE and FLORENCE YOUNG, were native Australians.

The postwar years saw little change in Australia. The great wartime London successes, *Chu Chin Chow* and *The Maid of the Mountains*, were not performed in Australia until 1920 and 1921 respectively. In the USA a Viennese-trained Hungarian composer, Sigmund Romberg and a Czech, Rudolf Friml, adapted the Viennese operetta style. Friml's *Rose-Marie* and Romberg's *The Desert Song* had their Australian premieres in 1926 and 1929 respectively. They are still revived today, as are *No! No! Nanette*, first performed in Australia in 1925, and *Rio Rita* of 1928.

In the American theatre of the 1920s musical comedy was a light-hearted entertainment with a beautiful and (ideally) talented leading lady, a handsome leading man and silly-ass comedians. The all-important comedians in Australian productions included GUS BLUETT, ALFRED FRITH, George Gee, CECIL KELLAWAY and DON NICOL. New Australian female stars during the First World War and the early 1920s were DOROTHY BRUNTON, Maude Fane, MINNIE LOVE and GLADYS MONCRIEFF. Later came MARIE BREMNER, MADGE ELLIOTT and STRELLA WILSON. Visiting stars in the 1920s and 1930s included Jennie Benson, MARIE BURKE, Robert Coote, Annie Croft, Beppi de Vries, Oskar Denes, Robert Halliday (Broadway's original Red Shadow in *The Desert Song*), Elsie Prince and Sylvia Welling.

The mindlessness of musical comedy hastened its demise as more intelligent writers began to create more sophisticated songs and stories and artless fooling was turned into humour emerging more directly from characters who were naturally comical. *Show Boat* by Oscar Hammerstein II and Jerome Kern is given the honour of having changed the course of the American musical theatre in New York in 1927, by bringing more realism into its plot and music. But when this seminal musical play arrived at His Majesty's Theatre in Melbourne in August 1929 its importance was not truly discerned. It played for only ten weeks in Melbourne and seven weeks in Sydney, where locals replaced imported stars.

Disaster struck J. C. WILLIAMSON'S on 25 October 1929. The auditorium of His Majesty's Theatre in Melbourne was burned out. Next month the Wall Street stock market crashed and in the ensuing Great Depression the firm found it necessary to sell Her Majesty's Theatre in Sydney and the Theatre Royal in Melbourne. Both were closed and demolished. Theatres belonging to FULLERS' and other managements were also demolished, or turned into cinemas for the new talking pictures.

There was a flicker of interest in local works when F. W. THRING took the Princess Theatre in Melbourne in 1933 with the avowed intention of staging Australian material when possible. He found a musical comedy, COLLITS' INN, gave it a strong cast headed by Gladys Moncrieff and put it on for Christmas 1933. It was a success and played for three months. Thring, lacking an interstate circuit, was forced to transfer it to a less suitable theatre in Sydney, and there it halted. He tried again with less success with THE CEDAR TREE for Christmas 1934. Again Varney Monk was the composer, Moncrieff was the heroine. Thring muttered about enmity from J. C. Williamson's and went back to imports. The Firm thought it might try the 'Australian-made' gimmick and in 1934 it staged BLUE MOUNTAIN MELODY, WITH a libretto by J. C. Bancks, music by Charles Zwar and a strong cast. It ran a reasonable six weeks in both Sydney and Melbourne and slipped out of sight.

In 1934 J. C. Williamson's brought Strella Wilson back from London to sing the leading role in *White Horse Inn*, which reopened His Majesty's Theatre in Melbourne in July. The depression was ending when the Second World War brought further disruption. Morale-boosting entertainment became a priority, but it was impossible to stage new shows, especially American shows because financial regulations blocked overseas payments. Travel difficulties drastically reduced the importation of stars. This was a bonus for local performers and for some expatriates who quickly realised the attractions of home when Europe began to go up in flames.

Williamson's settled into a comfortable round of revivals of old favourites. An excellent Gilbert and Sullivan company opened at the Theatre Royal in Sydney on 16 March 1940. IVAN MENZIES played the principal comic roles and the other singers included John Fullard, Evelyn Gardiner, MAX OLDAKER, Gregory Stroud, and Viola Wilson. Gilbert and Sullivan operettas alternated with other old musical shows. After 1942 Gladys Moncrieff introduced a new generation of theatregoers to her performances in *The Maid of the Mountains*, *Rio Rita* and *The Merry Widow*. Marie Bremner and Strella Wilson found new audiences, and many young performers rose quickly to stardom. One was Dot Rankin, who succeeded JOSIE MELVILLE as the lead in *Sally*. Others were John Howard and Leonora Laye in *The Student Prince*, Daphne Lowe in *Kissing Time* and Joy Beattie and MAX OLDAKER in *The Desert Song*. Don Nicol was the principal comedian in most of the revivals.

New American musicals

After the war the musical theatre slowly began to edge back toward normality. *The Dancing Years* made a belated appearance in 1946, with Tara Barry, Max Oldaker and the BOROVANSKY BALLET, but Australian taxation policies made it too difficult to bring the big new American musicals here. In July 1947 *Annie Get Your Gun* had its Australian premiere, with EVIE HAYES, an American who had settled here, in the title-role. Audiences were so hungry for something new to them, recently created and famous, that it played for a year in Melbourne and then another year in Sydney. Evie Hayes's achievement gave her enough box-office power to be selected for a similar Ethel Merman success, *Call Me Madam*, in 1954, but then it was 12 more years before J. C. Williamson's presented a major American musical with Australian stars.

The success of *Annie Get Your Gun* paved the way for *Oklahoma!* which in New York in 1943 had finally laid the old-fashioned musical comedy to rest. In *Oklahoma!* the dance component became complicated, dazzling and balletic and unified with the action of the story. The favourite kind of operetta was now simply termed a 'musical'. Early in 1949 *Oklahoma!* arrived in Melbourne, with ten American principals. This was perhaps partly because the original American promoters were reluctant to entrust valuable property to Australian talents unknown to them, but there was also an Australian distrust of domestic talent, mixed with an easy acceptance of second-rate Americans. Australians began to replace the Americans as a long tour around the Firm's circuit ground on.

Australian musicals

In 1950 Edmund Samuels, a Sydney chemist, staged his own musical THE HIGHWAYMAN in Melbourne. Gold mining around Bendigo in 1860 was the theme and there were some resemblances to *Collits' Inn*. Ballarat in goldrush days was the setting for LOLA MONTEZ, which was seen in Melbourne, Brisbane and Sydney in 1958. In 1961 J. C. Williamson's took up THE SENTIMENTAL BLOKE, a musical comedy first produced by amateurs in Canberra, and staged it with a local cast and heartwarming success at the Comedy Theatre in Melbourne. All these and other postwar Australian experiments in musicals conformed strongly to established forms, but venturesome and experimental Australian writing has occasionally appeared, with varying success. From the 1950s larky 'cod' melodramas with music enlivened most capital cities, most consistently

MUSICAL THEATRE

During the Great Depression, J. C. Williamson's spent lavishly on mounting White Horse Inn, *modelling its production on Oswald Stoll's 1931 London staging of the 1930 Berlin success. As at the Coliseum in London, there was a revolving stage. The lighting, the* Sydney Mail *said, 'was on new lines and a very lavish scale, and combined with the bewildering colour of the costumes and the number of their wearers to make an extraordinarily brilliant spectacle'. The cast included yodellers and dancers brought from Tyrol, although the historic inn is in the Salzkammergut region of Austria. Strella Wilson returned from London to play the landlady and Charles Norman made a hit as the head waiter with the popular 'Goodbye' song, added to the score in London. The production opened in Sydney in March 1934. After playing in the capital cities the show toured country towns, the cast travelling by special train*

at the Music Hall Theatre Restaurant in Sydney. Phillip Street revues in Sydney in the mid-1950s were the descendants of 19th-century burlesque and extravaganza—satire on current events, singing, dancing and audience laughter.

There were Australian stars in the musical *The Pajama Game*—Toni Lamond as Babe, Bill Newman as Sid and Keith Petersen as Hines—which arrived in 1957. The Broadway blockbuster *My Fair Lady* opened at Her Majesty's Theatre in Melbourne in 1959 and settled in so comfortably that 16 months later the cast was transferred to Sydney, which had been waiting impatiently, and a new cast continued the run in Melbourne.

West Side Story arrived in Australia in 1960, three years after its Broadway premiere, with a mostly imported cast. The dancing, acting and singing American performers were a revelation for their zip, attack and integration into a seamless production but *West Side Story* was not a great success for its principal sponsor, Garnet H. Carroll. The lyricist of *West Side Story*, Stephen Sondheim also displayed his talents as a composer, first in *A Funny Thing Happened on the Way to the Forum*, which came here in 1964. In Sydney in 1966 J. C. Williamson's, under its new managing director John McCallum, presented an Australian company in a major American musical, *Funny Girl*. The only American involved was the director Fred Hebert. Jill Perryman portrayed Fanny Brice exceptionally well, with comedy, charm and pathos. She has been a star ever since. Her success eased the way to the top for Nancye Hayes, a talent of similar magnitude, who had also worked her way up through chorus, small parts and understudying. She has been a star since she played the leading role in *Sweet Charity*, which opened on 21 January 1967 in Sydney.

In 1970 the National Institute of Dramatic Art launched The Legend of King O'Malley, a glorious political and musical romp, and had it snapped up by the commercial theatre. Next year the Nimrod Theatre Company in Sydney mounted its first version of Flash Jim Vaux, a ballad opera celebrating a petty criminal whose main claim to fame is that he was transported to Australia on three occasions.

In Sydney in June 1969 Harry M. Miller opened the American rock musical *Hair* at the Metro Theatre (once the Minerva). Its celebration of youth in all its charm and gaucherie made it a smash hit from the first night. Every night at the end of the show members of the audience danced on stage with the cast. Theatrical purists who denied that unrelenting rock music was a proper foundation for a theatrical score found unexpected allies in the writers of rock musicals themselves. Well aware of the need for musical contrast, the creators of *Hair* significantly included a tender ballad like 'Frank Mills' among the roars of 'Gimme a head with hair' or 'Let the sunshine in'. After running for almost two years in Sydney *Hair* moved to the Metro Theatre (once the Palace) in Melbourne in May 1971. It closed in February 1972 and the company set out for New Zealand. The whole tour closed in April 1973 in Launceston (Tas.). Miller had an even bigger rock hit in 1972 with *Jesus Christ*

The Sound of Music *was one of the shows with which Garnet H. Carroll challenged the supremacy of J. C. Williamson's in musical theatre. He had a huge success. Starring June Bronhill and Peter Graves, it opened in Melbourne in October 1961 and ran there for 11 months before moving to Sydney. In 1963 Bronhill had to return to London and Renée Guerin, seen here, replaced her as Maria von Trapp*

Superstar. It had an open-air concert performance at the ADELAIDE FESTIVAL OF ARTS and began its stage life in Sydney in May. A softer rival, *Godspell* had opened in Sydney a month before and had its own success, but spectacular staging, strong performances and vibrant melodies gave *Jesus Christ Superstar* an Australia-wide run lasting at least four years. It also established the 'religious rock musical'. Many saw resemblances to its approach in *The Jesus Christ Revolution* by Peggy and Enzo Toppano and Lorrae Desmond, which had its premiere in Adelaide in 1971 and played in Sydney a year later under the title *Man of Sorrows*. *The Rocky Horror Show* added decadence to rock-musical recipe in Sydney in April 1974. It had a long run and has been repeatedly revived into the 1990s.

Two years after its opening on Broadway, the backstage musical *A Chorus Line* reached Australia in 1977. This searingly accurate portrayal of life for the dancing 'gypsies' of Broadway musicals, confronted some audiences with its lack of glamour—until the top-hat-and-tails finale. Baayork Lee, a member of the original company, definitively reproduced Michael Bennett's original New York production. She has since made a career as a disciple of Bennett, touring the world faithfully reproducing his production, as she did again in Australia in 1994.

In the 1980s, as at the beginning of the century, the top international musicals again came out of England. This time the favoured composer was Andrew Lloyd Webber, whose writing tended more towards the operatic concept. Exceptional tunes are rationed, the orchestral writing is florid and compelling, and each new production is brilliantly supported by publicity. Most of them, including some revivals from the 1970s, came to Australia—*Cats*, *Evita*, *Jesus Christ Superstar*, *Joseph and his Amazing Technicolour Dreamcoat*, *Song and Dance*, *Starlight Express*. *Evita* blended a rock feeling with the beat of Latin America. It arrived in April 1980 in Adelaide with an all-Australian cast under the famous New York director Hal Prince. The first to sing the punishing title-role was Jennifer Murphy, previously known principally as a club singer. When she withdrew a year later in Sydney, the original New York star Patti LuPone performed the role for three months and made an indelible impression. In 1983 *Song and Dance*, a double bill by Don Black and Lloyd Webber, fused a show with songs to a set of violoncello variations celebrating modern dance. The dancer John Meehan returned from the USA to star in the dance half and Gay MacFarlane sang the songs of a difficult love affair in the first part of the evening.

Lloyd Webber's setting of T. S. Eliot, *Cats* opened in Sydney in 1985 and, helped by exceptional promotion, ran for two years. Its blockbuster success was matched in other capital cities after the Sydney season. Some audiences were puzzled by the show's format of loosely connected scenas. In 1988 the spectacular *Starlight Express*, in which roller skaters linked together to become trains, dazzled the eye with a huge, clever set and brilliant costumes. The words and tunes bemused the ear but the plot was gauche—engine meets engine, engine loses engine, engine gets engine. A leaky tent in a wet January made the premiere season in Sydney difficult. *Starlight Express* met better weather in other cities but no great success.

Since the demise of J. C. Williamson's co-productions have helped to spread the risk in producing music. The ADELAIDE FESTIVAL CENTRE TRUST, the Queensland Performing Arts Trust and Harry M. Miller have been among those involved. *John West*

Works performed in Australia

The following musical-theatre works are mentioned in the main text of articles in this book:

Alaya. Musical (1947 Melbourne). Libretto: Edith Harrhy and Richard Lomas. Music: Edith Harrhy.

And So to Bed. Musical comedy (1951 London). Libretto: J. B. Fagan. Music: Vivian Ellis.

Annie Get Your Gun. Musical comedy (1946 New York City). Libretto: Herbert and Dorothy Fields. Music: Irving Berlin.

Annie. Musical (1977 New York City). Book: Thomas Meehan. Lyrics: Martin Charnin. Music: Charles Strouse.

Anything Goes. Musical comedy (1934 New York City). Libretto: Guy Bolton and P. G. Wodehouse. Music: Cole Porter.

Arcadians, The. Musical play (1909 London). Book: Mark Ambient and Alexander M. Thompson. Lyrics: Arthur Wimperis. Music: Lionel Monckton and Howard Talbot.

Balalaika. Musical play (1936 London). Libretto: Eric Maschwitz. Music: Bernard Grun and George Posford.

Ballad of Angel's Alley, The. Musical (1958 Melbourne). Libretto: Jeff Underhill. Music: Bruce George.

Barbe-bleue. Opéra-bouffe (1866 Paris). Libretto: Henri Meilhac and Ludovic Halévy. Music: Jacques Offenbach.

Barnum. Musical (1980 New York City). Book: Mark Bramble. Lyrics: Michael Stewart. Music: Cy Coleman.

Beach Blanket Tempest. Rock musical (1984 Townsville). Libretto: Dennis Watkins after *The Tempest*. Music: Chris Harriot.

Beauty Spot, The. Musical comedy (1917). Libretto: Arthur Anderson, from the French. Music: James W. Tate.

Belle Hélène, La. Opéra-bouffe (1864 Paris, 1866 London). Libretto: translated from French of Henri Meilhac and Ludovic Halévy. Music: Jacques Offenbach.

Belle of Mayfair, The. Musical comedy (1906 London). Book: Charles H. E. Brookfield and Cosmo Hamilton. Lyrics: George Arthurs. Music: Leslie Stuart.

Belle of New York, The. Musical comedy (1897 New York City). Libretto: Charles Morton. Music: Gustave Kerker.

Beloved Vagabond, The. Musical comedy. Libretto: Adrian Ross from the novel by W. J. Locke. Music: Dudley Glass.

Better Known as Bee. Musical (1984 Penrith NSW). Libretto: Ian Dickson, David Mitchell and Peter Thorburn. Music: Tony Rees.

Betty. Operetta (1915 London). Libretto: Percy Greenbank. Music: Paul Rubens.

Big River. Musical (1985 New York City). Libretto: William Hauptmann after Mark Twain's *Huckleberry Finn*. Music: Roger Miller.

Bit o' Petticoat, A. Libretto: Ray Kolle and Peter Pinne from *The Torrents*, play by Oriel Gray. Music: Peter Pinne.

Bitter-Sweet. Operetta (1929 London). Libretto and music: Noël Coward.

Blue Mazurka, The. Operetta (1927 London). Libretto: from *Die blaue Mazur* (1920 Vienna) by Bela Jenbach and Leo Stein. Music: Ferencz Lehár.

Blue Mountain Melody. Musical comedy (1934 Sydney). Libretto: J. C. Bancks. Music: Charles Zwar.

Blue Roses. Musical comedy (1931 London). Libretto: Desmond Carter and Caswell Garth. Music: Vivian Ellis.

Bluebell in Fairyland. Musical play (1901 London). Libretto: Seymour Hicks. Music: Walter Slaughter et al.

Bobadil. Operetta (1884 Sydney). Libretto: Walter Parke. Music: Luscombe Searelle.

Bon Bons and Roses for Dolly. Musical play (1972 Perth). Libretto: Dorothy Hewett. Music: John Williamson.

Boy Friend, The. Musical comedy (1953 London). Libretto and music: Sandy Wilson.

Boys from Syracuse, The. Musical (1938 New York City). Libretto: George Abbott after *The Comedy of Errors*. Lyrics: Lorenz Hart. Music: Richard Rodgers.

Boys' Own McBeth. Comic musical play (1979 Sydney). Libretto: Grahame Bond and Jim Burnett. Music: Grahame Bond and Rory O'Donoghue.

Bran Nue Dae. Musical (1990 Perth). Libretto: Jimmy Chi. Music: Jimmy Chi and Kuckles band.

Brigadoon. Musical (1947 New York City). Libretto: Alan Jay Lerner. Music: Frederick Loewe.

Brunswick—The musical. (1982 Melbourne). Book: John Lonie. Lyrics and music: Geoffrey O'Connell.

Buckley's! Musical (1981 Adelaide). Book: David Allen and Ariette Taylor. Lyrics: Nick Enright. Music: Glenn Henrich.

Bunch Of Ratbags, A. Musical (1966 Melbourne). Book: Don Battye after the novel by William Dick. Lyrics and music: Peter Pinne.

Bunyip and the Satellite, The. Musical play for children (c.1958 Melbourne). Libretto: Peter O'Shaughnessy and Jeff Underhill.

Bye Bye Birdie. Musical (1960 New York City). Book: Michael Stewart. Lyrics: Lee Adams. Music: Charles Strouse.

Cabaret Girl, The. Musical comedy (1922 London). Music: Jerome Kern.

Cabaret. Musical play (1966 New York City). Libretto: Joe Masteroff. Lyrics: Fred Ebb. Music: John Kander.

Cage aux folles, La. Musical (1983 New York City). Libretto: Harvey Fierstein. Music: Jerry Herman.

Cairo. Musical comedy (1921 London). Libretto: Oscar Asche. Music: Percy E. Fletcher.

Call Me Madam. Musical (1950 New York City). Book: Howard Lindsay and Russel Crouse. Lyrics and music: Irving Berlin.

Camelot. Musical (1960 New York City). Libretto: Alan Jay Lerner after T. H. White's *The Once and Future King*. Music: Frederick Loewe.

Can-Can. Musical (1953 New York City). Book: Abe Burrows. Lyrics and music: Cole Porter.

Canary Cottage. (1917 New York City). Book: Oliver Morosco and Elmer Harris. Lyrics and music: Earl Carroll.

Candide. Musical (1956 New York City). Libretto: Lillian Hellman. Music: Leonard Bernstein.

Canterbury Tales. Musical (1968 London). Libretto: Neville Coghill and Martin Starkie. Music: John Hawkins and Richard Hill.

Carnival. Musical (1961 New York City). Book: Michael Stewart. Lyrics and music: Bob Merrill.

Carousel. Musical (1945 New York City). Libretto: Oscar Hammerstein II from play by Benjamin F. Glazer after Ferenc Molnár's *Liliom*. Music: Richard Rodgers.

Cash! (1972 Hobart). Musical. Libretto: Michael Boddy and Marcus Cooney. Music: traditional.

Casino Girl, The. Operetta (1900 New York). Libretto: Harry B. Smith. Music: Ludwig Englander.

Cats. Musical (1981 London). Libretto: T. S. Eliot's *Old Possum's Book of Practical Cats*. Music: Andrew Lloyd Webber.

Cedar Tree, The. Musical comedy (1934 Melbourne). Book: Edmund Barclay. Lyrics Helene Barclay, with additions by Jack McLeod and Varney Monk. Music: Varney Monk.

Charlie Girl. Musical (1965 London). Libretto: Hugh and Margaret Williams. Music: David Heneker and John Taylor.

Chicago. Musical (1975 New York City). Libretto: Fred Ebb and Bob Fosse. Music: John Kander.

Chilperic, King of the Gauls. Opéra-bouffe (1870 London). Libretto: H. B. Farnie from *Chilpéric* (1868 Paris) by Hervé. Music: Hervé.

Chocolate Soldier, The. Operetta (1909 New York City). Libretto from *Der tapfere Soldat* (1908 Vienna) by Rudolf Bernauer and Leopold Jacobson after George Bernard Shaw's *Arms and the Man*. Music: Oscar Straus.

Chorus Line, A. Musical (1975 New York City). Book: James Kirkwood and Nicholas Dantel. Lyrics: Edward Kelban. Music: Marvin Hamlisch.

Chu Chin Chow. Musical comedy (1916 London). Libretto: Oscar Asche. Music: Frederic Norton.

Cinema Star, The. Operetta (1914 London). Libretto: from *Die Kinokönigin* (1913 Berlin). Music: Jean Gilbert.

Cingalee, The. Musical play (1904 London). Book: James T. Tanner. Lyrics: Adrian Ross and Percy Greenbank. Music: Lionel Monckton, with additions by Paul Rubens and Howard Talbot.

Collits' Inn. Musical comedy (1932 Sydney). Libretto: T. Stuart Gurr. Lyrics and music: Varney Monk.

Come Hell or High Water. Rock musical (1988 Alice Springs). Libretto: Barney Foran. Music: Bob Sharp.

Company. Musical (1970 New York City). Libretto: Stephen Sondheim from plays by George Furth. Music: Stephen Sondheim.

Country Girl, A. Musical play (1902 London). Book: James T. Tanner. Lyrics: Adrian Ross and Percy Greenbank. Music: Lionel Monckton.

Cousin From Nowhere, The. Operetta (1923 London). Libretto: from *Der Vetter aus Dingsda* (1921 Berlin). Music: Eduard Künneke.

Currency Lass, The. Ballad opera (1844 Sydney). Libretto: Edward Geoghegan. Music: various.

Dairymaids, The. Musical comedy (1906 London). Libretto: Arthur Wimperis and Robert Courtneidge. Music: Paul Rubens and Frank E. Tours.

Dames at Sea. Musical (1968 New York City). Libretto: George Haimsohn and Robin Miller. Music: Jim Wise.

Dancing Years, The. Musical play (1939 London). Book and music: Ivor Novello. Lyrics: Christopher Hassall.

Dearest Enemy. Musical play (1925 New York City). Libretto: Lorenz Hart. Music: Richard Rodgers.

Desert Song, The. Operetta (1926 New York City). Libretto: Otto Harbach, Oscar Hammerstein II and Frank Mandel. Music: Sigmund Romberg.

Dorothy. Operetta (1886 London). Libretto: B. C. Stephenson. Music: Alfred Cellier.

Dubarry, The. Operetta (1932 London). Libretto: from *Die Dubarry* (1931 Berlin) by Paul Knepler and Welleminsky after *Gräfin Dubarry* (1879 Vienna) by F. Zell and Richard Genée. Music: Karl Millöcker arranged by Theo Mackeben.

Estrella. Operetta (1883 London). Libretto: Walter Parke. Music: Luscombe Searelle.

Evita. Musical (1978 London). Libretto: Tim Rice. Music: Andrew Lloyd Webber.

MUSICAL THEATRE

F.F.F. Musical comedy (1920 Adelaide, Melbourne, Perth). Libretto: Jack De Garis. Music: Reginald Stoneham.

Falka. Operetta (1883 London). Libretto: H. B. Farnie from French of Eugène Leterrier and Albert Vanloo. Music: F. Chassaigne.

Fantasticks, The. Musical (1960 New York City). Libretto: Tom Jones after *Les Romanesques* by Edmond Rostand. Music: Harvey Schmidt.

Fatinitza. Operetta (1876 Vienna, 1878 London). Libretto: from German of Richard Genée and F. Zell after Eugène Scribe's *La Circassienne*. Music: Franz von Suppé.

Fiddler on the Roof. Musical play (1964 New York City). Book: Joseph Stein after Sholom Aleichem. Lyrics: Sheldon Harnick. Music: Jerry Bock.

Fille de Madame Angot, La. Operetta (1872 Brussels). Libretto: Jules Clairville, Konig, Siraudin. Music: Charles Lecocq.

Fille du tambour-major, La. Opéra-bouffe (1880 London). Libretto: H. B. Farnie from French of Henri Chivot and Alfred Duru (1879 Paris). Music: Jacques Offenbach.

Finian's Rainbow. Music (1947 New York City). Libretto: E. Y. Harburg and Fred Sady. Music: Burton Lane.

Flash Jim Vaux. Ballad opera (1971 Sydney). Libretto: Ron Blair. Music: various.

Fledermaus, Die. Operetta (1874 Vienna, 1876 London). Libretto: from German of Richard Genée and Karl Haffner after *La Réveillon*, vaudeville by Ludovic Halévy and Henri Meilhac. Music: Johann Strauss II.

Florodora. Musical comedy (1899 London). Book: Owen Hall. Lyrics: Ernest Boyd-Jones and Paul Rubens. Music: Leslie Stuart.

Follies. Musical (1971 New York City). Book: James Goldman. Music: Stephen Sondheim.

42nd Street. Musical (1980 New York City). Libretto: Al Dubin. Music: Harry Warren.

Frasquita. Operetta (1922 Vienna, London 1925). Libretto: from German of Heinz Reichert and A. M. Willner after *La Femme et le pantin*, novel by Pierre Louys. Music: Ferencz Lehár.

French Maid, The. Musical comedy (1896 Bath, England). Libretto: Basil Hood. Music: Walter Slaughter.

Funny Face. Musical comedy (1927 New York City). Book: Fred Thompson and Paul Gerard Smith. Lyrics: Ira Gershwin. Music: George Gershwin.

Funny Girl. Musical (1964 New York City). Book: Isobel Lennart. Lyrics: Bob Merrill. Music: Jule Styne.

Funny Thing Happened on the Way to the Forum, A. Musical comedy (1962 New York City). Book: Burt Shevelove and Larry Gelbart based on Plautus. Lyrics: Stephen Sondheim. Music: Stephen Sondheim.

Gaiety Girl, A. Musical comedy (1893 London). Book: Owen Hall. Lyrics: Harry Greenbank. Music: Sidney Jones.

Gay Divorce. Musical comedy (1932 New York City). Book: Dwight Taylor. Lyrics and music: Cole Porter.

Gay Parisienne, The. Musical comedy (1894 Northampton). Libretto: George Dance. Music: Ivan Caryll.

Gay Rosalinda. Musical comedy (1874 Vienna, 1945 London). Libretto: from German of Richard Genée and Karl Haffner after *La Réveillon*, vaudeville by Ludovic Halévy and Henri Meilhac. Music: Johann Strauss II.

Geisha, The. Musical comedy (1896 London). Book: Owen Hall. Lyrics: Harry Greenbank. Music: Sidney Jones.

Geneviève de Brabant. Opéra-bouffe (1859 Paris). Libretto: Hector Crémieux and Etienne Tréfue. Music: Jacques Offenbach.

Gentleman Joe. Musical farce (1895 London). Libretto: Basil Hood. Music: Walter A. Slaughter.

Girl Behind the Counter, The. Musical comedy (1906 London). Libretto: Leedham Bantock and A. Anderson. Music: Howard Talbot.

Girl Friend, The. Musical comedy (1926 New York City). Libretto: Lorenz Hart. Music: Richard Rodgers.

Girl from Kay's, The. Musical comedy (1902 London). Libretto: Owen Hall. Music: Ivan Caryll.

Musical theatre has been a staple of amateur groups as well as professional managements. This chorus line appeared in Our Miss Gibbs, *produced by the local operatic society in Kempsey (NSW) in 1928*

Girl from Snowy River. Musical (1960 Canberra). Libretto: Lloyd Thomson. Music: Albert Arlen and Nancy Brown.

Girl in the Taxi, The. Musical comedy (1912 London). Libretto: F. Fenn and Arthur Wimperis from *Die keusche Susanne* (1910 Magdeburg) by Georg Okonkowski. Music: Jean Gilbert.

Girl on the Film, The. Musical comedy (1913 London). Book: James T. Tanner from *Filmzauber* (1912 Berlin). Lyrics: Adrian Ross. Music: Walter Kollo.

Girl on the Train, The. Operetta (1910 London). Libretto: from *Die geschiedene Frau* (1908 Vienna) by Victor Léon. Music: Leo Fall.

Girls of Gottenberg, The. Musical comedy (1907 London). Libretto: George Grossmith jnr and L. Berman. Music: Ivan Caryll and Lionel Monckton.

Giroflé-Girofla. Operetta (1874 Brussels). Libretto: Eugène Leterrier and Albert Vanloo. Music: Charles Lecocq.

Godspell. Rock musical (1971 New York City). Book: John-Michael Tebelak. Music and lyrics: Stephen Schwartz.

Going Up. Musical play (1917 New York City). Libretto: Otto Harbach. Music: Louis Hirsch.

Gondoliers, The. Operetta (1889 London). Libretto: W. S. Gilbert. Music: Arthur Sullivan.

Good Morning Dearie. Musical comedy (1921 New York City). Libretto: Anne Caldwell. Music: Jerome Kern.

Good Oil, The. Musical (1958 Perth). Libretto and music: Coralie Condon.

Good Ship Walter Raleigh. Musical (1962 Melbourne). Book: Reg Livermore. Lyrics and Music: Paul Eddey.

Grand Duchess of Gerolstein, The. Opéra-bouffe (1867 Paris). Libretto: from *La Grande-Duchesse de Gerolstein* by Henri Meilhac and Ludovic Halévy. Music: Jacques Offenbach.

Guys and Dolls. Musical comedy (1950 New York City). Libretto: Abe Burrows. Lyrics and music: Frank Loesser.

Gypsy Love. Operetta (1912 London). Libretto: Basil Hood from *Zigeunerliebe* (1910 Vienna) by Robert Bodanzky and A. M. Willner. Music: Ferencz Lehár.

Gypsy. Musical (1959 New York City). Book: Arthur Laurents. Lyrics: Stephen Sondheim. Music: Jule Styne.

Hair. Rock musical (1967 New York City). Libretto: Gerome Ragni and James Rado. Music: Galt MacDermot.

Half a Sixpence. Musical (1963 London). Book: Beverley Cross after *Kipps* by H. G. Wells. Lyrics and music: David Heneker.

Hamlet on Ice. Pantomime (1971 Sydney). Book: Ron Blair, Michael Boddy, Marcus Cooney and original cast. Lyrics and music: Grahame Bond and Rory O'Donoghue.

Handsome Ransom, The (1894 Perth). Operetta. Libretto: Francis Hart. Music: William Robinson.

Happily Never After. Musical (1982 Darwin). Libretto: Janis Balodis after Grimms' fairy tales. Music: Frank Millward.

Hello, Dolly! Musical (1964 New York City). Book: Michael Stewart after Thornton Wilder's play *Matchmaker*. Lyrics and music: Jerry Herman.

Her Soldier Boy (1916 New York City). Musical comedy. Libretto: Rida Johnson and Edgar Wallace from *Gold gab ich für Eisen* (1914 Vienna). Music: Imre Kálmán with additions by Sigmund Romberg and Frederick Chappelle.

High Jinks. Operetta (1913 New York City). Book: Otto Harbach and Leo Dietrichstein. Lyrics: Otto Harbach: Music: Rudolf Friml.

High Society. Musical. Libretto: Richard Eyre from *The Philadelphia Story*, play by Philip Barry. Music: Cole Porter.

Highwayman, The. Musical comedy (1950 Melbourne). Libretto and music: Edmond Samuels.

His Little Widows. Musical comedy. Libretto: Rida Johnson Young and William Carey Duncan (English version by F. F. Shepherd). Music: William Schroeder.

HMS Pinafore. Operetta (1878 London). Libretto: W. S. Gilbert. Music: Arthur Sullivan.

Hold Everything. Musical comedy (1928 New York City). Libretto: B. G. DeSylva and Lew Brown. Music: Ray Henderson.

Hold My Hand. Musical comedy (1931 London). Libretto: Stanley Lupino. Music: Noel Gay.

Horrortorio. Musical (1992 Brisbane). Book: Ailsa Piper, Tony Taylor and Denise Wharmby. Lyrics: Tony Taylor. Music: Denise Wharmby.

How to Succeed in Business without Really Trying. Musical (1961 New York City). Book: Abe Burrows. Music and lyrics: Frank Loesser.

I Do, I Do. Musical (1966 New York City). Libretto: Tom Jones after Jan de Hartog's play *The Fourposter*.

I Married an Angel. Musical comedy (1938 New York City). Libretto: Lorenz Hart. Music: Richard Rodgers.

I'd Rather Be Right. Musical (1937 New York City). Libretto: Lorenz Hart and George S. Kaufman. Music: Richard Rodgers.

In Town. Musical farce (1892 London). Libretto: Adrian Ross and James T. Tanner. Music: Osmond Carr.

Into the Woods. Musical (1986 SanDiego). Libretto and music: Stephen Sondheim.

Iolanthe. Operetta (1882 London). Libretto: W. S. Gilbert. Music: Arthur Sullivan.

Irene. Musical comedy (1919 New York City). Libretto: James Montgomery. Lyrics: Joseph McCarthy. Music: Harry Tierney.

Isidora. Operetta (1885 Melbourne). Libretto and music: Luscombe Searelle.

Isle of Bong Bong, The. Musical comedy (1905 Chicago). Libretto: Frank R. Adams. Music: Joe Howard.

Jack Juan. Operetta (1968 Melbourne). Libretto: Jack Hibberd. Music: Stuart Challender.

James Dossier, The. Musical (1975 Canberra). Libretto: Bob Ellis. Music: Patrick Flynn.

Jesus Christ Revolution, The. Rock musical (1971 Adelaide). Peggy and Enzo Toppano and Lorrae Desmond.

Jesus Christ Superstar. Rock musical (1971 New York City). Book: Tom O'Horgan. Lyrics: Tim Rice. Music: Andrew Lloyd Webber.

Joan. Musical play (1975 Canberra). Libretto: Dorothy Hewett. Music: Patrick Flynn.

Jolly Roger. Operetta (1933 London). Libretto: Scobie McKenzie and V. C. Clinton-Baddeley. Music: Walter Leigh.

Jonah Jones. Musical (1985 Sydney). Libretto: John Romeril, after the novel by Louis Stone. Music: Alan John.

Jonah. Musical (1991 Adelaide). Libretto: John Romeril from *Jonah Jones*. Music: Alan John.

Katinka. Operetta (1915 New York City). Book: Otto Harbach. Music: Rudolf Friml.

Katja, the Dancer. Operetta (1925 London). Libretto: Frederick Lonsdale from *Katja, die Tänzerin* (1923 Berlin) by Jacobson and Oesterreicher. Music: Jean Gilbert.

Kenny's Coming Home. Musical (1992 Penrith NSW). Book: Ned Manning. Lyrics and music: Shane McNamara.

King and I, The. Musical play (1951 New York City). Libretto: Oscar Hammerstein II after Margaret Landon's book *Anna and the King of Siam*. Music: Richard Rodgers.

Kismet. Musical (1953 New York City). Libretto: Charles Lederer and Luther Davis after play by Edward Knoblock. Music: Alexander Borodin arranged by Robert Wright and George Forrest.

Kiss Me, Kate. Musical (1948 New York City). Libretto: Bella and Samuel Spewack after *The Taming of the Shrew*. Music: Cole Porter.

Kissing Time. Musical comedy (1919 London). Libretto: Irving Caesar. Music: Ivan Caryll.

Kitty Grey. Musical comedy (1900 London). Libretto: J. S. Pigott from *Les Fêtards* by Mars and Hennequin. Music: Lionel Monckton and Howard Talbot.

Lady of the Rose, The. Operetta (1921 London). Libretto: from *Die Frau im Hermelin* (1919 Berlin). Music: Jean Gilbert.

Land of Smiles, The. Operetta (1932 London). Music: Ferencz Lehár. Libretto: from *Das Land des Lächelns* (1929 Berlin) by Ludwig Herzer and Fritz Löhner-Beda.

Lasseter. Musical (1971 Sydney). Libretto: Reg Livermore. Music: Sandra McKenzie and Patrick Flynn.

Last Wake at She-oak Creek, The (1986 Sydney). Libretto: Bob Herbert. Music: Allan McFadden.

Leave It to Jane. Musical comedy (1917 New York City). Libretto: Guy Bolton and P. G. Wodehouse. Music: Jerome Kern.

Legend of King O'Malley, The. Musical burlesque (1970 Sydney). Libretto: Michael Boddy and Bob Ellis. Music: various.

Let's Face It! Musical comedy (1941 New York City). Book: Herbert and Dorothy Fields. Libretto and music: Cole Porter.

Life and Adventures of Nicholas Nickleby, The. Musical play (1980 London). Book: David Edgar after the novel by Charles Dickens. Lyrics and music: Stephen Oliver.

Lilac Domino, The. Operetta (1914 New York City). Libretto: from *Der lila Domino* (1911 Leipzig). Music: Charles Cuvillier.

Lilac Time. Operetta (1922 London). Libretto: Adrian Ross from operetta *Dreimädlerhaus* (1916 Vienna). Music: Franz Schubert arr. Heinrich Berté and G. H. Clutsam.

Little Me. Musical comedy (1962 New York City). Book: Neil Simon after the book by Patrick Dennis. Lyrics: Carolyn Leigh. Music: Cy Coleman.

Little Michus, The. Musical comedy (1905 London). Libretto: from *Les P'tites Michu* (1897 Paris) by Albert Vanloo and C. Duval. Music: André Messager.

Little Nellie Kelly. Musical play (1922 New York City). Libretto and music: George M. Cohan.

Little Night Music, A. Musical (1973 New York City). Book: Hugh Wheeler after Ingmar Bergman's film *Smiles on a Summer Night*. Lyrics and music: Stephen Sondheim.

Lock Up Your Daughters. Musical (1959 London). Libretto: Bernard Miles after *Rape upon Rape* by Henry Fielding. Music: Laurie Johnson.

Lola Montez. Musical play (1958 Melbourne). Libretto and additional lyrics: Alan Burke. Lyrics: Peter Benjamin. Music: Peter Stannard.

Love's Awakening. Operetta (1922 London). Libretto: from *Wenn Liebe erwacht* (1920 Berlin). Music: Eduard Künneke.

Madame Favart. Opéra-bouffe (1878 Paris). Libretto: Henri Chivot and Alfred Duru. Music: Jacques Offenbach.

Maid of the Mountains, The. Musical play (1916 Manchester). Book: Frederick Lonsdale. Lyrics: Harry Graham, Clifford Harris and 'Valentine'. Music: Harold Fraser-Simson.

Mame. Musical (1966 New York City). Libretto: Jerome Lawrence and Robert E. Lee after Patrick Denis's novel and play *Aunty Mame*. Music: Jerry Herman.

Man From Mukinupin, The. Musical play (1979 Perth). Libretto: Dorothy Hewett. Music: Jim Cotter.

Man of La Mancha. Musical (1965 New York City). Libretto: Dale Wasserman. Lyrics: Joe Darion. Music: Mitch Leigh.

MUSICAL THEATRE

Man of Sorrows. Rock musical (1972 Sydney). Originally *The Jesus Christ Revolution* by Peggy and Enzo Toppano and Lorrae Desmond.
Mandrake. Musical (1969 Bristol, England). Libretto: Michael Alfreds. Music: Anthony Bowles.
Manning Clark's History of Australia. Musical (1988 Melbourne). Libretto: Tim Robertson, John Romeril and Don Watson. Music: Martin Armiger, George Dreyfus and David King.
Mary. Musical comedy (1920 New York City). Libretto: Otto Harbach. Music: Louis Hirsch.
Mascotte, La. Operetta (1881 London). Libretto: H. B. Farnie from French of Henri Chivot and Alfred Duru (1880 Paris). Music: Edmond Audran.
Matilda Mine. Musical (1986 Mt Gambier SA). Libretto: Jeremy James Taylor. Music: David Neild.
Maytime. Operetta (1917 New York). Libretto: Rida Johnson Young from *Wie einst im Mai* (1913 Berlin) by Rudolf Bernauer and Rudolf Schanzer. Music: Sigmund Romberg.
Me and My Girl. Musical comedy (1937 London). Libretto: L. Arthur Rose and Douglas Furber. Music: Noel Gay.
Mercenary Mary. Operetta (1925 London). Libretto: Isobel Leighton and William B. Friedlander. Additional lyrics: Irving Caesar. Music: Con Conrad, William B. Friedlander.
Merrie England. Operetta (1901 London). Libretto: Basil Hood. Music: Edward German.
Merry Widow, The. Operetta (1907 London). Book: Basil Hood from *Die lustige Witwe* (1905 Vienna) by Victor Léon and Leo Stein after Henri Meilhac's *L'Attaché*. Lyrics: Adrian Ross. Music: Ferencz Lehár.
Messenger Boy, The. Musical comedy (1900 London). Libretto: Percy Greenbank and Adrian Ross. Music: Ivan Caryll and Lionel Monckton.
Mikado, The—or, The Town of Titipu. Operetta (1885 London). Libretto: W. S. Gilbert. Music: Arthur Sullivan.
Misérables, Les. Musical (1980 Paris, 1985 London). Libretto: from the French of Alain Boublil after the novel by Victor Hugo. Lyrics: Herbert Kretzmer. Music: Claude Michel Schönberg.
Miss Hook of Holland. Musical play (1907 London). Libretto: Paul Rubens and Austen Hurgon. Music: Paul Rubens.
Mock Doctor, The. Ballad opera (1732 London). Libretto: Henry Fielding. Music: popular airs.
Mother of Pearl. Operetta (1933 London). Libretto: A. P. Herbert from *Eine Frau, die wiess was sie will* (Berlin 1932) by Alfred Grünwald. Music: Oscar Straus.
Music Man, The. Musical comedy (1957 New York City). Libretto and music: Meredith Willson.
My Fair Lady. Musical play (1956 New York City). Libretto: Alan Jay Lerner after George Bernard Shaw's play *Pygmalion*. Music: Frederick Loewe.
My Lady Frayle. Musical play. Libretto: Arthur Wimperis and Max Pemberton. Music: Howard Talbot and Herman Finck.
Ned Kelly. Musical (1978 Adelaide). Libretto: Reg Livermore. Music: Patrick Flynn.
New Moon, The. Musical comedy (1928 New York City). Libretto: Oscar Hammerstein II, Frank Mandel and Laurence Schwab. Music: Sigmund Romberg.
Nice Goings On. Musical (1933 London). Book Douglas Furber. Lyrics: Douglas Furber and Frank Eyton. Music: Arthur Schwartz.
Nightbirds. Musical comedy (1911 London). Libretto: G. Unger from *Die Fledermaus* (1874 Vienna) by Richard Genée and Karl Haffner. Music: Johann Strauss II.
No! No! Nanette. Musical comedy (1924 Detroit). Book: Otto Harbach and Frank Mandel after comedy *His Lady Friends*. Lyrics: Otto Harbach and Irving Caesar. Music: Vincent Youmans.
Not with Yours Truly. Musical (1962 Melbourne). Libretto: Bill Hannan. Music: Ivan Hutchinson.
Nunsense. Musical (1985 New York City). Libretto and music: Dan Goggin.

O'Brien Girl, The. Musical comedy (1921 New York City). Libretto Otto Harbach and Frank Mandel. Music: Louis Hirsch.
Oh! Oh! Delphine. Musical comedy (1912 New York City). Libretto: G. McLellan. Music: Ivan Caryll.
Oh, Lady! Lady!! Musical comedy (1918 New York City). Book: P. G. Wodehouse and Guy Bolton. Lyrics: P. G. Wodehouse. Music: Jerome Kern.
Oh, What a Lovely War! Musical (1963 London). Libretto: various. Music: various.
Oklahoma! Musical (1943 New York City). Libretto: Oscar Hammerstein II. Music: Richard Rodgers.
Old Man Taught Wisdom, An—or, The Virgin Unmasked. Ballad opera (1735 London). Libretto: Henry Fielding. Music: various.
Oliver! Musical (1960 London). Music and libretto: Lionel Bart.
Olivette. Operetta (1880 London). Libretto: H. B. Farnie from *Les Noces de Olivette* by Henri Chivot and Alfred Duru (1879 Paris). Music: Edmond Audran.
On Stage Vietnam. Musical (1967 Sydney). Libretto: Mona Brand and Pat Barnett. Music: various.
On the Wallaby. Musical play (1983 Sydney). Libretto: Nick Enright. Music: traditional.
Once upon a Mattress. Musical (1959 New York City). Libretto: George Abbott. Music: Mary Rodgers.
Orchid, The. Musical play (1903 London). Libretto: James T. Tanner. Music: Ivan Caryll and Lionel Monckton with additions by Paul Rubens.
Orpheus in the Underworld. Opéra-bouffe (1865 London). Libretto: J. R. Planché from *Orphée aux enfers* (1858 Paris) by Hector Crémieux and Ludovic Halévy. Music: Jacques Offenbach.
Our Miss Gibbs. Musical comedy (1909 London). Book: 'Cryptos' and James T. Tanner. Lyrics: Adrian Ross and Percy Greenbank. Music: Ivan Caryll and Lionel Monckton.
Out of This World. Musical (1950 Philadelphia). Libretto and music: Cole Porter.
Pacific Overtures. Musical (1976 New York City). Book: John Weidman. Lyrics and music: Stephen Sondheim.
Paint Your Wagon. Musical comedy (1951 New York City). Libretto: Alan Jay Lerner. Music: Frederick Loewe.
Pajama Game, The. Musical (1954 New York City). Book: George Abbott and Richard Bissell after Bissell's novel *Seven-and-a-half Cents*. Music and lyrics: Richard Adler and Jerry Ross.
Pal Joey. Musical comedy (1940 New York City). Book: John O'Hara. Lyrics: Lorenz Hart. Music Richard Rodgers.
Patience. Operetta (1881 London). Libretto: W. S. Gilbert. Music: Arthur Sullivan.
Paul Jones. Operetta (1887 Paris). Book: H. B. Farnie from Henri Chivot and Alfred Duru's *Surcouf*. Music: Robert Planquette.
Périchole, La. Opéra-bouffe (1868 Paris). Libretto: Henri Meilhac and Ludovic Halévy after Prosper Merimée's *La Carosse du Saint Sacrement*. Music: Jacques Offenbach.
Peter Pan. Musical play (1954 New York City). Book: after the play by J. M. Barrie. Music: Jule Styne.
Petrov. Musical (1992 Melbourne concert). Libretto: Alan Hopgood. Music: Michael Easton.
Phantom of the Opera, The. Musical play (1986 London). Book: Andrew Lloyd Webber and Richard Stilgoe after the novel by Gaston Leroux. Lyrics: Charles Hart. Music: Andrew Lloyd Webber.
Pink Lady, The. Operetta (1911 New York City). Libretto: Harry Morton. Music: Ivan Caryll.
Pippin. Musical (1972 New York City). Book: Roger O. Hirson. Lyrics and music: Stephen Schwartz.
Pirates of Penzance, The. Operetta (1879 Paignton, England). Libretto: W. S. Gilbert. Music: Arthur Sullivan.
Poor Soldier, The. Opera (1783 London). Libretto: J. O'Keefe. Music: William Shield.
Primrose. Musical comedy (1924 New York City). Book: George Grossmith and Guy Bolton. Lyrics: Desmond Carter and Ira Gershwin. Music: George Gershwin.

Princess Charming. Operetta (1926 London). Libretto: Arthur Wimperis and Laurie Wylie, after Alexandra. Music: Albert Szirmai.

Promises, Promises. Musical comedy (1968 New York City). Book: Neil Simon after Billy Wilder and I. A. L. Diamond's film *The Apartment*. Lyrics: Hal David. Music: Burt Bacharach.

Quaker Girl, The. Musical comedy (1910 London). Book: James T. Tanner. Lyrics: Adrian Ross and Percy Greenbank. Music: Lionel Monckton.

Red Mill, The. Operetta (1906 New York City). Libretto: Henry Blossom. Music: Victor Herbert.

Reedy River. Musical (1953 Melbourne). Libretto: Dick Diamond. Music: various.

Riff Raff. Rock musical (1979 Melbourne). Libretto: Jan McDonald and Phil Sumner. Music: Men at Work band.

Riki-Tiki. Operetta (1926 London). Libretto: Leslie Stiles. Music: Eduard Künneke.

Rip Van Winkle. Operetta (1882 London). Libretto: H. B. Farnie. Music: Robert Planquette.

Rio Rita. Musical comedy (1927 New York City). Book: Guy Bolton and Fred Thompson. Lyrics: Joe McCarthy. Music: Harry Tierney.

Roar of the Greasepaint, the Smell of the Crowd, The. Musical (1965 New York City). Libretto: Anthony Newley. Music: Leslie Bricusse.

Robert and Elizabeth. Musical (1964 London). Libretto: Ronald Millar after Rudolf Besier's play *The Barretts of Wimpole Street*. Music: Ron Grainer.

Roberta. Operetta (1933 New York City). Libretto: Otto Harbach from *Gowns by Roberta*, novel by Alice Duer Miller. Music: Jerome Kern.

Rocky Horror Show, The. Rock musical (1973 London). Libretto and music: Richard O'Brien.

Rose-Marie. Operetta (1924 New York City). Book: Otto Harbach and Oscar Hammerstein II. Music: Rudolf Friml with additions by Herbert Stothart.

Rum Do!, A. Musical (1970 Brisbane). Libretto: Rob Inglis. Music: Robin Wood.

Runaway Girl, A. Musical play (1898 London). Book: Seymour Hicks and Harry Nicholls. Lyrics: Aubrey Hopwood and Harry Greenbank. Music: Ivan Caryll and Lionel Monckton.

Salad Days. Musical comedy (1954 London). Libretto: Dorothy Reynolds and Julian Slade. Music: Julian Slade.

Sally. Musical play (1920 New York City). Book: Guy Bolton. Lyrics: Clifford Grey et al. Music: Jerome Kern.

San Toy. Musical play (1899 London). Book: Edward Morton. Lyrics: Percy Greenbank and Adrian Ross. Music: Sidney Jones.

Sentimental Bloke, The. Musical (1985 Melbourne). Libretto: Graeme Blundell. Music: George Dreyfus.

Sentimental Bloke, The. Musical comedy (1961 Canberra). Libretto: Lloyd Thomson after poems of C. J. Dennis. Music: Albert Arlen and Nancy Brown.

1776. Musical play (1969 New York City). Book: Peter Stone. Lyrics and music: Sherman Edwards.

Shanghai. Operetta (1918 London). Libretto W. Carey Duncan and Lauri Wylie. Music: Isidor Widmark.

Shop Girl, The. Musical comedy (1894 London). Libretto: Adrian Ross. Music: Ivan Caryll, Lionel Monckton.

Show Boat. Musical (1927 New York City). Book: Oscar Hammerstein II after the novel by Edna Ferber. Music: Jerome Kern.

Side by Side by Sondheim. Compilation by Ned Sherrin from libretti and music of Stephen Sondheim (1975 London).

Sin. Operetta (1978 Melbourne). Libretto: Jack Hibberd. Music: Martin Friedel.

So Long Letty. (1916 New York City). Libretto: Earl Carroll. Music: Alfred Francis and Alfred Robyn.

Song and Dance. Concert for the theatre (1982 London), comprising *Tell Me on Sunday* and ballet *Variations*. Libretto: Don Black. Music: Andrew Lloyd Webber.

Sorcerer, The. Operetta (1877 London). Libretto: W. S. Gilbert. Music: Arthur Sullivan.

Sound of Music, The. Musical play (1959 New York City). Book: Howard Lindsay and Russel Crouse after Maria von Trapp's *The Trapp Family Singers*. Lyrics: Oscar Hammerstein II. Music: Richard Rodgers.

South Pacific. Musical play (1949 New York City). Book: Oscar Hammerstein II and Joshua Logan after James Michener's *Tales of the South Pacific*. Lyrics: Oscar Hammerstein II. Music: Richard Rodgers.

Southern Maid, A. Musical play (1920 London). Book: Dion Clayton Calthrop and Harry Graham. Lyrics: Douglas Ferber, Adrian Ross and Harry Graham. Music: Harold Fraser-Simson.

Spirit of the Bush, A—or, the Birth of Australia. Musical extravaganza (c.1910 Melbourne). Libretto: Edmund Duggan.

Spring Chicken, The. Musical comedy (1905 London). Libretto: George Grossmith jnr after *Coquin de Printemps* by C. Duval and Adolphe Jaime. Music: Ivan Caryll and Lionel Monckton.

Starlight Express. Musical (1984 London). Libretto: Richard Stilgoe. Music: Andrew Lloyd Webber.

Student Prince, The. Operetta (1924 New York City). Libretto: Dorothy Donelly. Music: Sigmund Romberg.

Sugar. Musical (1972 New York City). Libretto: Bob Merrill. Music: Jule Styne.

Summer Rain. Musical (1983 Sydney). Libretto: Nick Enright. Music: Terence Clarke.

Summerland. Musical (1984 Brisbane). Libretto: Janis Balodis after Grimms' fairy tales. Music: John Rush.

Sunny. Musical comedy (1925 New York City). Libretto: Otto Harbach and Oscar Hammerstein II. Music: Jerome Kern.

Sunshine Girl, The. Musical comedy (1912 London). Book: C. Raleigh. Music: Paul Rubens.

Sweeney Todd. Musical (1979 New York City). Book: Hugh Wheeler after the play by Chris Bond. Lyrics and music: Stephen Sondheim.

Sweet Charity. Musical (1966 New York City). Book: Neil Simon after Federico Fellini's film *Nights of Cabiria*. Lyrics: Dorothy Field. Music: Cy Coleman.

Sybil. Operetta (1916 New York City). Libretto: Harry B. Smith and Harry Graham. Music: Victor Jacobi.

Tapu. Operetta (1903 Wellington, New Zealand). Libretto: Arthur H. Adams. Music: Alfred Hill.

They're Playing Our Song. Musical (1979 New York City). Book: Neil Simon. Lyrics: Carol Bayer Sager. Music: Marvin Hamlisch.

Three Little Maids. Musical comedy (1902 London). Libretto and music: Paul Rubens.

Threepenny Opera, The. Musical play (1953 New York City). Libretto: translated from *Die Dreigroschenoper* (1928 Berlin) by Bertolt Brecht. Music: Kurt Weill arranged by Marc Blitzstein.

Tintookies, The. Musical play for marionettes (1956 Sydney). Libretto: Hal Saunders. Music: Kurt Herweg.

Tip-Toes. Musical comedy (1925 New York City). Book: Guy Bolton and Fred Thompson. Lyrics: Ira Gershwin. Music: George Gershwin.

Tommy. Rock musical (1969 London). Libretto and music: The Who.

Toreador, The. Musical play (1901 London). Lyrics: Adrian Ross and Percy Greenbank. Music: Ivan Caryll and Lionel Monckton.

Trial by Jury. Operetta (1875 London). Book: W. S. Gilbert. Music: Arthur Sullivan.

Ulterior Motifs. Musical (1957 Canberra). Libretto: Anne Godfrey-Smith and Ric Throssell. Music: Peter Sculthorpe.

Under the Coolibah Tree. Musical (1955 Brisbane). Libretto: Dick Diamond. Music: various.

Vagabond King, The. Musical play (1925 New York City). Libretto: Brian Hooker, Russell Janney and W. H. Post after J. H. McCarthy's novel *If I Were King*. Music: Rudolf Friml.

Variations. Musical (1981 Sydney). Libretto: Nick Enright. Music: Terence Clarke.

Venetian Twins, The. Musical comedy (1979 Sydney). Libretto: Nick Enright after *I gemelli veneziani*, play by Carlo Goldoni. Music: Terence Clarke.

Very Good Eddie. Musical (1915 New York City). Book: Philip Bartholomew and Guy Bolton. Lyrics: Schuyler Green and Herbert Reynolds. Music: Jerome Kern.

Waltz Dream, A. Operetta (1908 London). Music: Oscar Straus. Libretto: translated from *Ein Waltzertraum* (1907 Vienna) by Felix Dörman and Leopold Jacobson.

Waltzes of Vienna. Operetta (1931 Paris). Libretto: from *Valses de Vienne* by Max Eddy, Jean Marietti and Mouëzy-Eon after *Walzer aus Wien* (1931 Vienna). Music: Strauss family, arr. Julius Bittner, Erich Wolfgang Korngold and Eugène Cools.

West of the Black Stump. Musical (1965 Adelaide). Libretto: Reg Livermore. Music: Sandra Mckenzie.

West Side Story. Musical play (1957 New York City). Book: Arthur Laurents. Lyrics: Stephen Sondheim. Music: Leonard Bernstein.

White Horse Inn. Operetta (1931 London). Libretto: Harry Graham from *Im weissen Rössl* (1930 Berlin) by Erik Charell and Hans Müller after *Zum weissen Rössl*, farce by Kadelburg and Blumenthal. Music: Ralph Benatzky with additions by Robert Stolz, Bruno Granichstädten, Robert Gilbert and Eduard Künneke.

Wildcat. Musical (1960 New York City). Libretto: Carolyn Leigh. Music: Cy Coleman.

Wildflower. Musical comedy. (1923 New York City). Libretto: Otto Harbach. Music: Herbert Stothart and Vincent Youmans.

Wrong Side of the Door, The. Opéra-bouffe (1868 Melbourne). Libretto: W. M. Akhurst from *Un Mari à la porte* (1859 Paris). Music: Jacques Offenbach.

Yeomen of the Guard, The. Operetta (1888 London). Libretto: W. S. Gilbert. Music: Arthur Sullivan.

Yes, Madam? Operetta (1934 London). Libretto K. R. G. Browne, Bert Lee and R. P. Weston. Music: Joseph Tunbridge and Jack Waller.

Yes, Uncle! (1917 London). Libretto: Clifford Grey. Music: Nat D. Ayer.

Zilch. Rock musical. (1985 Penrith NSW). Martin Sharman and cast.

further reading

BEVAN, IAN. *The Story of the Theatre Royal.* Sydney: Currency Press 1993.

GAMMOND, PETER. *The Oxford Companion to Popular Music.* Oxford University Press 1991.

GREEN, STANLEY. *Encyclopedia of the Musical.* London: Cassell 1976.

HARTNOLL, PHYLLIS (ed.). *Oxford Companion to the Theatre*, 3rd edn. London: Oxford University Press. 1972.

MILLER, HARRY M. *My Story.* Melbourne: Macmillan 1983.

TRAUBNER, RICHARD. *Operetta.* Oxford University Press 1989.

My Mate

—or, *A Bush Love Story*. Play by Edmund Duggan. **premiere** 4 February 1911, King's Theatre, Melbourne. Cast: Bert Bailey, Rutland Beckett, Nellie Bramley, Lillie Bryer, Edwin Campbell, Max Clifton, Edmund Duggan, Eugenie Duggan, Temple Harrison, J. H. Nunn, Roy Redgrave, Harry Sweeney, Olive Wilton. Designer: Rege Robins. Director: J. H. Nunn.

EDMUND DUGGAN's best play, *My Mate* is chiefly memorable for the first explicit representation on the Australian stage of mateship—'an affection passing the love of women', according to *Melbourne Punch*. The mateship of two young selector farmers survives the fact that they both love the same girl, the daughter of a prosperous farmer who was once a struggling selector. The villains are a lecherous squatter who tries to rape the heroine, a money-grubbing storekeeper who tries to bankrupt her father, and a vindictive police officer. Beautiful stage scenes of a bush track, the farmer's house, and the selectors' hut were much admired by *Table Talk*. It thought a garden 'with the arbour overrun with sweet briar and clematis, would inevitably turn the thoughts of any young people to sentiment', and that it was convincingly 'realistic' that 'the folks arrive on horseback, in buggy or by bicycle, but not on foot, for it is proverbial people outback do not walk unless under dire compulsion'. *My Mate* appeared just after several other plays, notably those of JO SMITH, had begun to see to the squatter–selector struggle from the selector's point of view, and just before Australian rural drama moved on to the broader comedy of ON OUR SELECTION. It ran a creditable four weeks in Melbourne and in 1915 it was staged in Sydney and taken on a country tour. ❦*Richard Fotheringham*

reference

A typescript of *My Mate* is in the Edmund Duggan papers, MS 6304, in the National Library of Australia (Canberra).

Bruce Myles

Actor, director. Born 29 November 1940 in Sydney. Trained at Independent Theatre (Sydney). Joined John Alden Company 1960. Worked in USA 1963–65. Worked in United Kingdom 1965–72, including repertory at Bristol Old Vic and Nottingham Playhouse. Associate director of Melbourne Theatre Company 1979–86. Green Room Award for direction (*Sex Diary of An Infidel* by Michael Gurr) 1992.

Bruce Myles has been particularly associated with the MELBOURNE THEATRE COMPANY at the Russell Street Theatre. There he played Tom in JOHN POWERS's *The Last of the Knucklemen* in 1973 and Barney in the premiere of Ray Lawler's THE DOLL TRILOGY, and directed the world premiere of RON ELISHA's *Einstein* in 1981 and the present writer's *Gulls* in 1983. As a director of new Australian plays he is known for working closely with writers from first draft to staging. In 1992 he directed the world premiere of MICHAEL GURR's *Sex Diary of an Infidel*, which resulted in five Green Room Awards. ❦*Robert Hewett*

Valantyne Napier

Balancer, contortionist. Born at Chelsea (Vic). Daughter of contortionist Hector Napier and dancer Dorothy Yvonne. Trained in classical ballet and contortion. Made solo debut as child in Melbourne, 1930. Abandoned study of pharmacy to go on stage, entertaining troops during Second World War. Studied ballet with Edouard Borovansky 1945. Master classes with Espinosa in London. Toured Japan 1947. Performed with Ted Weeks as Vine and Valantyne in United Kingdom 1948–51. Thereafter performed solo as Human Spider. Married Jeffrey Jones, English stage manager. Returned to Australia 1961.

Valantyne Napier renewed the Human Spider act on the professional stage. Her father, Hector Napier, created it in Chicago 1912, exploiting his extraordinary flexibility by performing 'sextuple' dislocations on a huge rope web.

Born Arthur Reid in Berwick (Scotland) in 1891, he made his professional debut in variety in London in 1901. Before 1912 he visited Australia, performing with WIRTHS' CIRCUS and on the Brennan–Fuller and Tivoli vaudeville circuits. He was here at the outbreak of the First World War and enlisted in the Australian Imperial Force. He was wounded at Gallipoli and repatriated to Australia in 1916.

Back in vaudeville, he formed a double act with Blanche Smith, a Melbourne dancer. Initially called Napier and Cartledge, they became 'Hector Napier and Dorothy Yvonne, the Spider and the Butterfly'. A critic described their act: 'Yvonne, the butterfly, pirouettes and poses gracefully until she finally falls a victim to the great evil-looking black spider which had been twisting itself into inconceivable shapes'. The couple married in 1916 and toured Australasian and world vaudeville circuits until 1933. All their children performed the Human Spider act from an early age. Valantyne Napier, who was on the stage at one year, first performed it as a child in 1935. From 1951 she performed it alone in variety, revue and pantomime, notably in the pantomime *Little Miss Muffet*. After returning to Australia she organised charity shows, and last performed the Human Spider act in 1970. ❦*Victoria Chance*

writings
Act as Known. Melbourne: Globe Press 1986. About Australian speciality acts on international variety circuits.
reference
The National Film and Sound Archive (Canberra) has a film of the abbreviated act of Napier and Yvonne, made in 1916.

National Institute of Dramatic Art

The first school in Australia to offer full-time theatrical training was the National Institute of Dramatic Art. It has been the largest single contributor of professional actors, designers, theatre technicians, and directors to the Australian theatrical industry. In its first 32 years it produced more than 850 graduates, of whom 57 per cent were actors, 23 per cent were stage managers and technicians, 10 per cent were designers and 10 per cent were directors. NIDA is best known for its acting graduates, including Penny Cook, JUDY DAVIS, COLIN FRIELS, MEL GIBSON, KATE FITZPATRICK, GARRY MCDONALD, HELEN MORSE and ROBYN NEVIN.

HUGH HUNT, executive director of the AUSTRALIAN ELIZABETHAN THEATRE TRUST, and ROBERT QUENTIN, both English, were the prime movers in the establishment of NIDA in 1958. They envisioned a theatre school, modelled on English schools like the Royal Academy of Dramatic Art, that would prepare Australian actors trained in the classics for the Australian stage. The University of NSW offered housing—huts and former racecourse buildings—on its campus. The university, the Trust and the other main sponsor, the Australian Broadcasting Commission, were represented on the board when NIDA was founded as an independent institution.

Quentin was the founding director. TOM BROWN worked closely with him as deputy director from 1961 to 1963 and succeeded him when he became head of the School of Drama in the university in 1964. Clement McCallin, an English actor who had toured Australia for J. C. WILLIAMSON's, was appointed at the first teacher of acting. Quentin remained influential at NIDA. Until 1965 he was director of the OLD TOTE THEATRE COMPANY, which NIDA founded in 1962 and ran until 1969. In 1966 he was instrumental in the opening of the JANE STREET THEATRE for new Australian plays. NIDA managed it from 1969 as part of its advanced course.

In 1969 JOHN CLARK, a teacher at NIDA since 1959, was appointed director. He has maintained NIDA's mission and interpreted Quentin's vision in changing times. Elizabeth Butcher was appointed administrator in 1969, and remains, working with Clark. In 1969 ALAN EDWARDS, acting teacher since 1964, and Joe MacColum, head of speech since 1963, both left to found the QUEENSLAND THEATRE COMPANY and there were changes in courses. These included extension of the acting and production (renamed technical production) courses from two years to three.

After Edwards with his English repertory background, JOHN BELL brought an exuberant project-based Australian orientation to the acting course in 1970–71. ALEXANDER HAY in 1972–75 influenced the direction of the course with his long experience in classical theatre. GEORGE WHALEY brought to the course a Brechtian concern for ideas in 1976–81. NICK ENRIGHT from 1982 to 1984 demonstrated an overriding care for the development of each student actor as an individual. As heads of acting came and went during the 1970s and 1980s there were accompanying changes of direction in the acting course. These kept students in touch with current professional issues and attitudes, but the effects of discontinuity upon the students produced regular vocal protests. As a result, in 1985 AUBREY MELLOR was commissioned to review aspects of the course and its operation. An experiment with associate heads of acting—Dean Carey, Tony Knight and TONY TAYLOR—in 1989 suggested uncertainty over the purpose of the position. Knight was appointed head of acting in 1990 and continuity in the 1990s reflects a more mature phase of NIDA's development. Staff who have had long-term influence in the acting course include Margaret Barr and Keith Bain (movement) and Mellor (acting). Other leading teachers include Peter Cooke (design), ROBIN LOVEJOY (directing and design) and John Saltzer (technical). The design course and a one-year directing course, which has contributed greatly to the professional infrastructure of the theatre, were introduced in 1972.

In 1988 NIDA moved from the temporary buildings it had occupied since 1962 to purpose-built facilities adjacent to the Parade Theatre at the university. This facilitated developments including the operation of the Performance Centre, which supports new writing, in 1983; the NIDA Company, a professional group recruited from outside to revive the Jane Street operation in 1990; further specialist courses in theatre crafts, voice and movement; and the development of short courses. ❦*Peter Lavery*

National theatre

The great distances separating Australia's capital cities and the rivalries that would inevitably confront any plan for a single nationally-endowed theatre complex on a single site have meant that it has seldom been envisaged. But arguments and proposals for a publicly funded theatre enterprise with outlets in all capitals, and maybe provincial cities, have manifested themselves over many years. As silent films, radio, talkies and television successively stole audiences from the theatre, concern grew among the culturally minded that its basic cultural activities needed and were entitled to have public organisation and assistance. Governments in Australia were not prone to agree but campaigners persisted. Their concept usually embraced high professional aims in production and acting, and presentation of plays that did not reliably come within the scope of entrepreneurs—including revivable classics, the better current works from overseas and plays that reflected Australian values and aspirations and, in the words of David Bradley, 'images of what it means to be human in our particular society'.

Just before the First World War some Melburnians persuaded the Victorian government to consider providing a theatre building, but the war killed the proposal. A decade later DUNCAN MACDOUGALL, who ran the tiny Playbox Theatre in Sydney, developed a detailed plan for state-endowed theatrical companies. He wanted to begin in Sydney or Melbourne or both. Companies were to exchange venues and visit country towns. There would be a studio for experiment. Australian works would be included.

The Great Depression and the Second World War doused such dreams. The only interest some states took in theatre was to tax it. However, the provision of travelling companies to entertain troops in camp was a wartime benefit for the theatre. Towards the end of the war many thought such support of the performing arts should continue into peacetime, on the lines of the Council of the Encouragement of Music and the Arts in the United Kingdom and of state-supported radio. Professor L. F. Giblin, chairman of a prime ministerial advisory committee, had ideas on a national theatre and he is said to have been on the point of achieving federal government backing when the Prime Minister, John Curtin, died.

With a general postwar freshening of interest in theatre, helped by the visits of the OLD VIC THEATRE COMPANY and the Shakespeare Memorial Theatre Company, leaders of amateur theatre held conferences that sent resolutions to the federal government. Writers such as George Farwell, LESLIE HAYLEN, Rex Rienits, L. L. Woolacott and the present writer wrote campaign articles. In Melbourne Gertrude Johnson ran the NATIONAL THEATRE MOVEMENT to stage drama, opera and ballet. Under various pressures, the new Prime Minister, Ben Chifley, agreed to consider proposals for a national theatre and to set up a governmental committee. In 1949 he invited the English director Tyrone Guthrie to report on Australian theatre reform. The GUTHRIE REPORT was an export-import plan for taking the best Australian actors to England, bonding them into a high-grade company and sending them back. The press and theatre people cold-shouldered this as imperialist, colonialist or impractical. The federal government now declared that its support for theatre organisations was to be dependent upon co-operation from the state governments. These, except the Victorian government, vacillated or refused. Enthusiasts' hopes faded.

In 1954, after many informal discussions with friends such as Professor Giblin and the present writer, who was chairman of the PLAYWRIGHTS' ADVISORY BOARD, H. C. COOMBS announced on behalf of an influential committee that a theatre trust would be formed. Funds were to be raised with the ultimate aims of helping existing organisations, stimulating native drama, opera and ballet and giving professional employment to Australian actors, singers and dancers. Appeals to business houses and the public raised £90 000 and the federal government added £30 000 —£1 for every £3 raised. State governments and some city councils were persuaded to assist. And so the AUSTRALIAN ELIZABETHAN THEATRE TRUST was established, to be followed by the formation of the AUSTRALIAN COUNCIL FOR THE ARTS and general growth of federal and state subsidy for the performing arts. As a result of this development regional interests and distinctions have grown into prominence and the idea of a national centre has faded. Recent moves have focused on touring as a way of gathering strength and have involved ventures such as the Bell Shakespeare Company, founded in 1990, and the now annual agreements made among the state theatre companies for co-operative touring productions. ❦*Leslie Rees*

further reading
ALOMES, STEPHEN. The search for a national theatre. *Voices* (Canberra) spring 1993.
PALMER, VANCE. A national theatre. *Meanjin Papers* 4/2 (Melbourne 1945).
PHILLIPS, ARTHUR. A principle and a policy. *Meanjin Papers* 4/2 (Melbourne 1945).
STARGAZER. Australian notes. *Lone Hand* (Sydney) May 1908.

reference
National Theatre papers, A431, A432, A 461, A571, A1361, CP286/2 in Australian Archives (Canberra).

National Theatre and Fine Arts Society

In a period when no professional group existed in Hobart, the National Theatre and Fine Arts Society (NATFAS) ensured that audiences there and in Launceston enjoyed a varied theatrical program. It was a semiprofessional theatrical management, production and entrepreneurial body incorporated under an act of the Tasmanian Parliament in 1949. The Tasmanian government provided funds for it to buy the old THEATRE ROYAL in Hobart in 1950. Vigorous fund-raising enabled NATFAS to renovate the theatre substantially in early 1952, but repaying a government debt incurred for the renovation, and the cost of providing modern facilities remained constant distractions from presenting a theatrical program.

At first NATFAS acted as landlord to FIFI BANVARD's company and then to the Theatre Royal Company, but in 1955 it sponsored the establishment of the Theatre Royal Opera Company to undertake local productions. This successful venture was enhanced by visits from AUSTRALIAN ELIZABETHAN THEATRE TRUST companies from that time. A formal agreement between NATFAS, the Trust and the Tasmanian government in 1962 ensured that NATFAS received financial assistance, a professional manager–director and tours of Trust productions. Recognising that training facilities were required for local productions and would assist in developing a discerning audience, NATFAS set up the Theatre Royal Ballet School in 1959, the Theatre Royal Workshop in 1961 and a chorus training group. It also encouraged local theatrical activity by sponsoring a Theatre Royal Musical Comedy Company in 1961 and a Theatre Royal Light Opera Company in 1968. The Tasmanian Theatre Company took over the production and entrepreneurial functions of NATFAS in 1971. Separation of production from maintenance and management of the theatre was formally recognised in 1974 with the establishment of the Theatre Royal Management Board and the winding-up of NATFAS. ❦*Gillian Winter*

National Theatre Company

Professional dramatic company in Perth, founded in 1956 as semiprofessional company. Fully professional 1960. Closed 1984. **venue** Playhouse. **artistic directors** 1956–60 Frank Baden-Powell. 1960–62 Raymond Westwell. 1963–67 Edgar Metcalfe. 1964–70 Barry J. Gordon. 1970–72 Edgar Metcalfe. 1973–77 Aarne Neeme. 1978–81 Stephen Barry. 1982–85 Edgar Metcalfe. **first production** *The Teahouse of the August Moon* by John Patrick, August 1956, in Playhouse, Perth. Cast: Michael Cole, James Condon, Garry Meadows. Director: Nita Pannell.

For 28 years the National Theatre Company was the vanguard in Western Australia. It evolved from the REPERTORY CLUB, a leader in Perth's strong amateur movement, and the COMPANY OF FOUR. These groups raised funds, augmented by a small state government loan, to build the Playhouse, which the new company opened with *The Teahouse of the August Moon* in August 1956. As the company strengthened its professionalism in its early years JAMES BAILEY, JOAN BRUCE, MARGARET FORD, RON GRAHAM, DOROTHY KRANTZ and Nancy (Lee) Nunn appeared in the standard repertoire of the era under the guidance of FRANK BADEN-POWELL, Peter Summerton and other directors. An early highlight was Richard Beynon's THE SHIFTING HEART, directed by ROBIN LOVEJOY as a guest.

RAYMOND WESTWELL, an Englishman, was appointed artistic director in 1960. When he left in 1962 PETER BATEY took over the administration until EDGAR METCALFE arrived from England in 1963 for the first of three terms, accompanied by James Beattie, Frederic Lees and Judy Wilson. They acted in Metcalfe's controversial production of *The Devils* by John Whiting in the 1964 FESTIVAL OF PERTH. Lees won immediate popularity with his superb character work. He and Wilson returned to London but Beattie remained to become a mainstay of Perth theatre. In 1966 Beattie appeared with Rosemary Barr and Eileen Colocott in Jean-Paul Sartre's *Altona* on the company's first interstate tour. Barry J. Gordon was notable as artistic director for presenting Lila Kedrova, whose performance in *Zorba the Greek* won her the 1964 Academy Award for best supporting actress, in Ferenc Molnár's *The Guardsman* in the 1970 Festival of Perth. When Metcalfe returned to the Playhouse in 1971 he recruited NATIONAL INSTITUTE OF DRAMATIC ART graduates, including Pamela Stephenson, on six-month contracts to present the best of the flinty new plays coming out of England, as well as the occasional worthy new Australian works. RAYMOND OMODEI was guest director during Metcalfe's second term and in 1972 he staged *Bon Bons and Roses for Dolly*, DOROTHY HEWETT's first play for the National Theatre. It met fierce rejection and Omodei discovered production photographs, taken from showcases in the foyer, stuffed down toilets.

AARNE NEEME, at the helm from 1973 to 1977, was a link with the new wave of writing coming from the NIMROD THEATRE COMPANY in Sydney and LA MAMA THEATRE in Melbourne. He converted rehearsal space into a tiny Greenroom Theatre for experimental productions. Conservative Playhouse audiences resisted, even rejected, ALEX BUZO and DAVID WILLIAMSON, however. Traditional theatregoers were more comfortable with stage portrayals of the distant problems of England and the USA, and English influence remained distinctly stronger in Western Australia than elsewhere. Neeme struggled to find a new audience. For the 1975 Festival of Perth he directed the British film star Richard Todd in Peter Shaffer's *Equus*. A tour of Western Australia followed and Robert van Macklenberg won national notoriety when the nude scene had him arrested for indecency in Geraldton.

Stephen Barry began his directorship with Alan Ayckbourn's trilogy *The Norman Conquests* for the 1978 Festival of Perth. He then presented JUDY DAVIS in Pam Gems's *Piaf* and WARREN MITCHELL as Willy Loman in Arthur Miller's *Death of a Salesman*. For the sesquicentenary of Western Australia in 1979 National Theatre commissioned THE MAN FROM MUKINUPIN from Dorothy Hewett. It was considered a return to the fold for Hewett after a period of 'artistic alienation' in the eastern states. Barry's final task for the company before he returned to England was to direct JILL PERRYMAN in the full-scale musical *Annie* at His Majesty's Theatre in 1981. Metcalfe returned to the directorship in 1982 but, in spite of some artistic successes, the company was flagging. The opening of a new studio theatre did little to halt the decline and the company went into liquidation in 1984. It was replaced soon afterwards by the Western Australian Theatre Company. ❦*Ivan King*

National Theatre Movement

The foundation of the National Theatre Movement, Victoria on 5 December 1935 seemed a timely response to an ailing professional theatre. It began as an amateur production company with semiprofessional training programs and later formed professional drama, opera and ballet companies. It aimed to develop theatrical arts in Melbourne as the basis of a national organisation but its aspirations remained largely unrealised because the necessary management and financial skills were lacking. Its significance rests with its roles in the genesis of subsidy in Victoria and as a bridge between amateur and subsidised theatre. Ray Lawler's career as a playwright began with the National Theatre, as did the careers of many Melbourne actors, dancers and singers in the 1940s and 1950s. Opera was the major interest of its founder, Gertrude Johnson. She became honorary director of the National Theatre Movement after returning to Melbourne from England, where she had had a career as a soprano in opera. A headstrong woman of independent means, she obtained the support of leading citizens, including Sir Robert Knox and Sir Arthur Smithers, who was the movement's director of finance from 1937 to 1959. Neither Johnson nor the executive and production staff was capable of sustaining a fully professional operation. They planned for the short term and refused to co-operate with other organisations, including the AUSTRALIAN ELIZABETHAN THEATRE TRUST.

The first production was *Joyous Pageant of the Holy Nativity* at the Princess Theatre on 12 December 1936. The organisation gained a permanent home in St Peter's Hall at Eastern Hill on 1 May 1938. Next year it began producing opera. It was renamed the National Theatre Movement of Australia on 10 April 1940. Sir Robert Knox, president of the movement from 1944 to 1964, helped Johnson to gain subsidy from the Victorian Cultural Development Fund, established in August 1948. In 1949 the National Theatre Ballet gave its first performance. The movement formed a subsidiary company, Australian National Memorial Theatre Ltd, in 1953, and in the mid-1950s it reverted to amateur status. In December 1961 it moved to the Village Theatre in Toorak. This was destroyed by fire on 18 April 1962 and in June the organisation moved into the David Hamilton Academy at 316 Toorak Road. In continual financial difficulties, the National Theatre Movement increasingly lacked the repertoire to extend its performers and to attract audiences. They preferred the ST MARTIN'S THEATRE COMPANY, the Union Theatre Repertory Company, the Elizabethan Trust Opera Company and the Australian Ballet.

In 1969 the movement ceased production to concentrate upon training and theatre hire under John Cargher, general manager from December 1969 to January 1989. From 1969 it was known as the Victorian National Theatre Movement Ltd. Johnson remained honorary director until her death in 1973. The company was based at the Empress Theatre in Prahran from 5 March 1970 to July 1971 and at the Victory Theatre at St Kilda, from 7 September 1974.

Drama was the least developed branch of the movement and all its dramatic productions were amateur except from 1951 to the mid-1950s. As a state-subsidised organisation the National Theatre Movement professed to widen the drama repertoire, but its unadventurous policy brought criticism from Melbourne's amateur groups. From mid-1937 until mid-1976 drama was mainly the province of William P. Carr, although there were other directors during the 1950s, including BUNNEY BROOKE, Ray Lawler and Malcolm Phillips. As opportunities arose, people such as Brooke, Lewis Fiander, Reg Gillam, PATRICIA KENNEDY, Lawler and JOHN TRUSCOTT left to establish careers elsewhere. The movement relied heavily upon Shakespeare and British and American works from the commercial theatre, although Phillips marginally widened the range of plays to include Henrik Ibsen's *The Lady from the Sea* and T. S. Eliot's *Murder in the Cathedral*. Incomplete records document 16 Australian works, including *Hal's Belles*, *Stars in the Home* and *Cradle of Thunder* by Lawler; *Quiet Night* by DOROTHY BLEWETT; *Red Sky at Morning* by DYMPHNA CUSACK; *Within These Walls* by MARJORIE McLEOD and *Daybreak* by CATHERINE SHEPHERD. ❦*John Andrews*

further reading
ALOMES, STEPHEN. The search for a national theatre. *Voices* (Canberra) spring 1993.

Ned Kelly

Play in three acts by Douglas Stewart. **premiere** 14 October 1942, Sydney, by Sydney University Dramatic Society. Cast included Bruce Beeby, Kevin Brennan, Wanda Herbert, Guy Manton, Ian Maxwell, David Saxby, Molly Shackleton, Maurice Travers. Director: May Hollinworth. **revived** 3 October 1956, Elizabethan Theatre, Sydney, by Australian Elizabethan Theatre Trust. Cast: Douglas Bladon, Bunney Brooke, Paul Cohen, Peter Cohen, Lloyd Cunningham, Benita Harvey, Patricia Hill, Collins Hilton, Robert Levis, Frank Lloyd, Charles McCallum, Leo McKern, Kevin Miles, Des Rolfe, Ron Shand, Edward Smith, Nancye Stewart, Neville Teede, Frank Waters. Designers: Desmonde Downing, Sidney Nolan. Director: John Sumner. **published** Sydney: Angus and Robertson 1943. Melbourne: Penguin 1963, *3 Australian Plays*.

DOUGLAS STEWART wrote *Ned Kelly* in verse and prose. The triumph of the verse lies in its combination of eloquence and the easy rhythmic speech of country men. Passages describing the landscape contain some of Stewart's finest writing. The play has many thrilling passages and some excellent humour, but its cast of 23 characters and lack of dramatic development have made it more often read than performed. Written for the stage in 1941, it was first performed—abridged for radio—under the direction of LAWRENCE H. CECIL on the ABC on 21 June 1942. It opens in 1879 when the Kelly gang is at the height of its career and Ned and Joe Byrne rob the Jerilderie bank. Next year they are on the run with a price on their heads. When Byrne discovers that a friend has informed on them, he kills him. The police arrive next day at the Glenrowan hotel and Ned strides out in full armour to face the gunfire. ❦*Ron Blair*

further reading
SUMNER, JOHN. *Recollections at Play—A life in Australian theatre*. Melbourne: University Press 1993.

Aarne Neeme

Director. Born 19 February 1945 at Gera (Germany) of Estonian parentage. Arrived in Australia 1949. Trained in classical and modern dance 1955–65. Danced with National Theatre Ballet and Victorian Ballet Guild. Joined Emerald Hill Theatre Company (Melbourne) 1963–65. Majored in drama at University of NSW 1966–69. President of DramSoc 1967–69. Resident director at University of Western Australia 1969–71. Resident director with Nimrod Theatre Company (Sydney) 1971–72. Artistic director of National Theatre Company (Perth) 1973–77. Churchill Fellowship 1978. Worked with National Playwrights' Conference 1979, 1982, 1983. Artistic director of Hunter Valley Theatre Company (Newcastle NSW) 1980–82. Trans-Tasman Fellowship 1983. Head of theatre department of Western Australian Academy of Performing Arts (Perth) 1985–89. Artistic director of Hole-in-the-Wall Theatre Company (Perth) 1990–91. Sydney Critics' Circle Award 1985.

Aarne Neeme is one of the most respected directors and teachers of theatre in Australia. He has worked extensively in cities on both the eastern and western seaboards, championing Australian plays and playwrights, and covering the classical and contemporary repertoires. He has had long-term collaborations with several playwrights and he has been associated with most of the major theatre companies, acting schools and university drama departments in Australia and New Zealand.

While still at university he assisted PHILIP PARSONS in directing *Richard III* for the Festival of Perth in 1968 and the premiere of DOROTHY HEWETT's *Mrs Porter and the Angel* in Sydney in 1969. His collaboration with Hewett extended to directing the premieres of her *The Chapel Perilous* (1971), *Catspaw* (1974), *Christina's World* (1983) and *The Rising of Pete Marsh* (1988). As resident director at the University of Western Australia he directed memorable productions of Edward Bond's *The Pope's Wedding* and *Narrow Road to the Deep North*. As artistic director of the NATIONAL THEATRE COMPANY he directed 58 plays. Neeme directed the premieres of *HAMLET ON ICE* (1971) and seven other Australian works for the NIMROD THEATRE COMPANY. He directed premieres of three works by ALEX BUZO—*MAKASSAR REEF* (1978), *The Marginal Farm* (1983) and *Stingray* (1987). He directed the premiere of JOHN O'DONOGHUE's *Essington Lewis: I Am Work* for the HUNTER VALLEY THEATRE COMPANY in 1981, and then productions in Sydney in 1985, Adelaide in 1986, Perth in 1987 and Brisbane in 1991. ❦*David J. Hough*

Frank Neil

Comedian, director, manager. Born 21 December 1886 in Corindhap (Vic.). Acted in melodrama, pantomime and farce. Established Frank Neil Comedy Company 1925 and staged farces. Began staging revues 1931. Took over Tivoli circuit 1934. Died 1 January 1940 in Melbourne.

Energetic, enterprising Frank Neil presented the most popular forms of theatre to audiences around Australia. He established a formula of topical revues with imported stars on the TIVOLI CIRCUIT, and he gave opportunity and encouragement to countless young hopefuls. Neil himself began as actor and property man with E. I. Cole's BOHEMIAN DRAMATIC COMPANY. He later wrote and produced pantomimes for FULLERS' and HUGH J. WARD. In 1924 he played Rosenthal in Seymour Hicks's production of his own play *The Man in Dress Clothes*. Next year he formed his Frank Neil Comedy Company. He often acted in its popular farces, and he claimed to have played Lord Fancourt Babberley in Brandon Thomas's *Charley's Aunt* more than 2000 times.

In 1929 he bought the faltering ERNEST C. ROLLS productions of *Whoopee* and *Clowns in Clover*, a revue, but he could not make them pay. After financial reverses, Neil took a farce company to South Africa in 1930, saying on departure that it was impossible for an entrepreneur to survive in Australia and blaming the Great Depression and the 'ridiculous' arbitration system for regulating wages. He toured for almost a year. In late 1931 he staged his first revue, *Hullo Paris*, at the Roxy Theatre in Sydney. He presented the great male impersonator ELLA SHIELDS in revue in 1932. In 1935 he engaged WALLACE PARNELL as producer for the Tivoli circuit. Parnell took control when Neil died from injuries received in a car accident. ❦*Frank Van Straten*

J. E. Neild

Critic. Born 6 July 1824 in England. Methodist family. Studied medicine in Sheffield and London and practised in Lancashire. Came to Australia as gold-seeker 1853. Joined Melbourne *Age* reporting staff 1855. Wrote reviews for *My Note Book* from 6 December 1856. Critic of *Examiner* 24 October 1857 to 20 August 1859. Editor of *Australian Medical Journal* 1862–78. Leader writer for *Herald* and reviewer for weekly *Bell's Life* 1863–64. Critic of *Australasian* 27 March 1865 to 15 March 1890. Also contributed to *Argus*. Lecturer in forensic medicine at University of Melbourne 1865-1903. Active in many cultural and scientific bodies. Died 17 August 1906 in Melbourne.

James Edward Neild's three decades of weekly notices constitute the most substantial and best body of theatrical criticism written in Melbourne. A dark, Swiftian humorist and remorseless crusader against the otiose traditions of the Regency stage, he could be intemperate both in his dislikes and his enthusiasms, but he is redeemed for modern readers by the intensity of his love for theatre and for language. Demanding realism and insisting that actors should remain 'within the picture' in an era when both performers and audiences were attuned to a high degree of conventionalism, Neild stood for everything that Bertolt Brecht later loathed, but he was a no less doughty reformer of the stage as he found it. He found his ideals fulfilled in the acting of JANET ACHURCH, G. V. BROOKE, WALTER MONTGOMERY, ADELAIDE RISTORI, G. H. ROGERS and NELLIE STEWART and had little sympathy for other, perhaps equally talented artists, such as MRS SCOTT-SIDDONS and BARRY SULLIVAN, who directed the audience's attention to the performer at the expense of the role. In 1858 opera performers, whose art represented the extreme violation of Neild's ideals, responded to his stinging notices by denouncing him in posters. Later in the year, a touring English magician, 'Wizard' Anderson, reacted to similar treatment by haranguing Neild from the stage, after which a colleague pelted him with apples.

While condemning egotism in performers, and conceptualising the artistic experience as an escape from self, Neild was himself the supreme critical egoist. It is what he thinks about the performance, not the physical actuality, that is conveyed to the reader of his notices. While using his celebrated pseudonyms of 'Christopher Sly', 'Jaques' and 'Tahite' he becomes a kind of actor in print, polishing a role which Ken Stewart has described as that of 'a candid, sometimes wittily extravagant or malicious, often cantankerous or condescending, play-going individual'. His critical individualism, which he absorbed from the English free-trade advocate John Bright, finds expression in his admiration for Montgomery, who rejected the received public language of the stage in order to instil his performances with a mould-breaking subjectivity.

Though often a stern critic of actors, Neild was nonetheless a personal friend to many and he served for decades as an unpaid medical consultant to the profession. As editor of the *Australian Medical Journal* he successfully opposed public health policies of Victorian governments in the 1870s. His private life, like his writings, was marked by imprudent excesses. His relations with HATTIE SHEPPARDE, Marie Saint Denis and Cecilia Padmore Hill all led to public scandal. The last-named made him the villain of her scurrilous *roman à clef Checkmated* in 1878. ❦*Harold Love*

further reading
LOVE, HAROLD. James Edward Neild. *Australian Dictionary of Biography* 5. Melbourne University Press 1984.
LOVE, HAROLD. *James Edward Neild, Victoria Virtuoso*. Melbourne University Press 1989.

Francis Nesbitt

Actor. Born 1809 or 1810 in England or Ireland. Probably originally Francis McCrone or McCron. Reported to have studied medicine in Ireland. Acted in Edinburgh, Glasgow and Liverpool. Arrived in Sydney 7 January 1842. Debut at Royal Victoria Theatre 3 March 1842. Acted 1843–45 at Royal City Theatre, Sydney; Royal Olympic Theatre, Launceston; Royal Victoria Theatre, Hobart; Royal Victoria Theatre and Queen's Theatre, Melbourne. In California 1849 to 1851 or 1852. Died 29 March 1853 in Geelong (Vic.).

A powerful declamatory actor in a traditional provincial style, Frances Nesbitt took Sydney by storm in 1842. Women fell at his feet and audiences queued to see a real professional actor who, according to the critics, understood his business. An actor of strong secondary parts on the Edinburgh–Glasgow–Liverpool circuit, Nesbitt was described in the *Glasgow Courier* of 21 July 1838 as 'not much removed above respectable mediocrity'. After a frustrating stint as first gentleman in Walter Scott adaptations under the Glasgow manager J. H. Alexander, he came to Sydney with 'Mrs McCrone'. His debut at the Royal Victoria Theatre as R. B. Sheridan's Pizarro brought him immediate acceptance as the finest tragedian in Australia.

When Nesbitt played Richard III in Colley Cibber's version of Shakespeare's play in March 1842, the audience gave him four rounds of applause for his rendering of 'Off with his head; So much for Buckingham' and he became the first actor to be called before the curtain in Sydney. His Sir Giles Overreach in Philip Massinger's *A New Way to Pay Old Debts* was another vigorous interpretation and his tragic Shylock was a novelty in Sydney. His style suited tragic roles like Pizarro, the Walter Scott villains, and the leading role in *The Hibernian Father*, written for him by his friend EDWARD GEOGHEGAN. The convict playwright probably also wrote Nesbitt's 1843 tragedy *Ravenswood*, after Scott. Nesbitt was later accused of monotony. Even as the public packed in to see him in *Coriolanus* in October 1844 critics tired of his 'unimpassioned recitation' and 'rant of assumed rage'.

Playing Nesbitt the great actor took its toll, and in August 1842, only five months after his debut, he retreated from the theatre—suffering from a nervous breakdown, in the view of Helene Oppenheim. Alcoholic indisposition sometimes prevented Nesbitt from performing. His drunkenness sabotaged CONRAD KNOWLES's tragedy *Salathiel* in 1842, leading to barbed comments in the *Australian* thereafter. Nesbitt joined JOSEPH SIMMONS's Royal City Theatre in 1843, then went to F. B. WATSON's Royal Olympic Theatre in Launceston and ANNE CLARKE's Royal Victoria Theatre in Hobart. He abused a brick-throwing audience in Hobart, earning a stern reprimand from the *Colonial Times*, and in 1844 Mrs Clarke dismissed him for drunkenness.

Nesbitt's gambling was as habitual as his drunkenness and in August 1847, during one of his cancellations, he was spotted at the races by a friend of the *Australian*'s critic. This brought a public accusation that Nesbitt had nothing but 'contempt of the public by whom he lives'. Nesbitt's increasing distance from critics is explained by his lack of theatrical scholarship in an age newly obsessed with historical accuracy and realism in the serious theatre. This also partly accounts for his never playing Hamlet. But audiences mourned the loss when he died in 1853, after collapsing on stage in Sheridan Knowles's *William Tell* in Geelong (Vic.). His death certificate said he was aged 42. His friend and former colleague G. V. BROOKE paid to erect a gravestone to 'the genius of a brother tragedian'. ❦*Helen Musa*

further reading
OPPENHEIM, HELENE. Francis Nesbitt McCron. *Australian Dictionary of Biography* 2. Melbourne University Press 1967.

Robyn Nevin AM

Actor, director. Born 25 September 1942 in Melbourne. Graduated from National Institute of Dramatic Art (Sydney) 1960. Trust Players 1961. Announcer and interviewer on ABC television in Hobart 1963–67. Went to England 1968; worked at Kenton Theatre, Henley-on-Thames, for two years. Jane Street Theatre season (Sydney) 1970. Nimrod Theatre Company (Sydney) from 1970. Old Tote Theatre Company (Sydney) from 1970. Has directed plays for most state theatre companies. Married to playwright Jim McNeil 1975–77. AM 1981. Australian Artist Creative Fellowship 1992–94.

One of Australia's few star stage actors, Robyn Nevin has been a leading actor in Sydney since the early 1970s, when she played Lady Macduff in *Macbeth* for the NIMROD THEATRE COMPANY, and Imogen Parott in Arthur Wing Pinero's *Trelawney of the Wells* and Mrs Shin in Bertolt Brecht's *The Good Woman of Setzuan* for the OLD TOTE THEATRE COMPANY. She established herself particularly in 1975 as Blanche in Tennessee Williams's *A Streetcar Named Desire* and Lavinia in Eugene O'Neill's *Mourning Becomes Electra*, both for the Old Tote. She consolidated her reputation in three successful plays that DAVID WILLIAMSON wrote for the SYDNEY THEATRE COMPANY with her in mind—*The Perfectionist* (1982), *Emerald City* (1987) and *Money and Friends* (1992). 'She is a virtuoso and acts a text like a great musician plays a score', says Williamson. 'The shadings, the emphases and the rhythms are awesomely precise and enormously effective.'

Nevin has considerable comedic gifts as well as a great capacity for big dramatic roles that call for toughness and flinty fury, like Lady Macbeth, which she played for the Sydney Theatre Company in 1982, and Hedda Gabler, for the STATE THEATRE Company of South Australia in 1990. She has excelled in plays that required her to demonstrate mental instability, such as Michael Hastings's *Tom and Viv* and Alan Ayckbourn's *Woman in Mind*, and she is seen at her best playing strong, unhappy, driven women. She was outstanding at the BELVOIR STREET THEATRE in 1991 as Barbara in *Diving for Pearls*, KATHERINE THOMSON's play about a woman struggling to escape her working-class origins. The first play she directed was Mil Perrin's *Is This Where We Came In?* for the Sydney Theatre Company in 1981. ❦*Ron Blair*

further reading
BLAIR, RON. Robyn Nevin—Actress at the front of the bus. *National Times* (Sydney) 25-30 April 1977.
HOWIE, ANN C. (ed.). *Who's Who in Australia 1991* 27th edn. Melbourne: Information Australia.

New England Theatre Centre

Professional touring dramatic company based in Armidale (NSW). Founded in 1962 by Brian D. Barnes. Closed 1965. **artistic director** Brian D. Barnes. **first production** *Game of Love and Chance* by Pierre Marivaux, translated by Barnes.

The first provincial professional company in Australia, the New England Theatre Centre mounted 15 tours of the New England region for up to ten weeks. Each consisted of a production for adults and one for children. Its school shows, sponsored by the NSW Education Department, included the Chinese classic *The Circle of Chalk*; an adaptation of *Wuthering Heights* by Harold Bennet, the centre's administrator; *History of the Theatre*; and *The King and the Fly*, devised for primary children. The centre also held weekend workshops and summer schools for children.

It was modelled on French provincial companies known as Centres Dramatiques, where its founder, Brian D. Barnes, had trained and worked. Barnes, born in 1931, trained as a sound technician with the ABC and worked with METROPOLITAN THEATRE in Sydney as an actor and stage manager before leaving for England in 1953. In 1956–57 he trained with Michel St Denis in Strasbourg and he was stage manager for La Comédie du St Etienne until 1958. He had begun touring one-man shows when the Arts Council invited him to Australia for eight months in 1961. He was appointed artistic director of the Sydney Union Repertory Theatre, which was funded by the AUSTRALIAN ELIZABETHAN THEATRE TRUST. The company foundered after only six weeks and Barnes moved to Armidale, the centre of a region that was then proposed as a new state. He envisaged the New England Theatre Centre as a place where amateur groups could drop in for information and participate in workshops. It was run as a co-operative by Barnes and Bennet, the only full-time staff. Actors were employed for individual productions, although some stayed for long periods. Carole Skinner worked with the company for two years. Financial difficulties forced its closure in 1965. ❦*Victoria Chance*

New Fortune Theatre

Theatre at University of Western Australia, Perth, opened 29 January 1964. Architect: Marshall Clifton.

The first attempt in modern times to reproduce the dimensions of the stage and auditorium of a public theatre of the time of Queen Elizabetha I of England was the New Fortune Theatre. It is a square quadrangle with a thrust stage, pit and three galleries inside the arts faculty building at the University of Western Australia. It conforms in general to the layout of the surrounding galleries and tiring house, or dressing room, of the Fortune Theatre that Edward Alleyn built in London in 1600. It does not replicate a 17th-century London theatre but simply provides the same actor-audience relationship as a theatre of Shakespeare's time.

Allen Edwards, professor of English at the University of Western Australia, promoted the idea of following the Fortune dimensions when the architect was designing the arts faculty building. He saw it as a tribute to Harley Granville-Barker, who had advocated a replica of Shakespeare's Globe Theatre as essential to any university department of English that specialised in performance studies. Members of the English department, including JEANA BRADLEY, PHILIP PARSONS and NEVILLE TEEDE, supported Edwards,

The dimensions of the Globe Theatre do not exist but the basic measurements of the Fortune are on record. The stage platform, 13·1 metres wide by 8·4 metres deep, projects into the yard, which is 21 metres deep by 19·8 metres wide, including the depth of the 'galleries'. These are verandahs, which in the New Fortune conform to the three levels of the arts faculty building rather than to the heights of the galleries in the original theatre. Cutting across the quadrangle to provide access from one side of the building to the other is a three-level walkway, which has been modified to supply the principal theatrical requirements of a tiring house. The university banned rehearsal and performance during the academic year because tutorial rooms overlooked the quadrangle. The actor–audience relationship has nevertheless led to significant research, particularly by Parsons and Collin O'Brien, into Shakespeare's use of the stage.

The New Fortune opened with *Hamlet* during the FESTIVAL OF PERTH in 1964, the quadricentenary of Shakespeare's birth. John Gielgud, who was visiting Perth, recorded Ben Jonson's tribute to Shakespeare as a prologue. It has been regularly used during the festival and in February 1968 there was a memorable production by AARNE NEEME and Parsons of *Richard III*, with Martin Redpath in the title-role. DOROTHY HEWETT wrote her early plays *This Old Man Comes Rolling Home* (1966), *The Chapel Perilous* (1971) and *Catspaw* (1974) for the New Fortune. On the university campus the New Fortune Theatre complements the proscenium-stage Dolphin Theatre, the thrust-stage OCTAGON THEATRE and the open-air Sunken Gardens Theatre. ❦*Ross Thorne*

further reading
PARSONS, PHILIP. The New Fortune and Shakespeare studies. *Westerly* 4 (Perth, 1963).
PARSONS, PHILIP. Unique Elizabethan theatre in a university setting. *Airways* 32/1 (Sydney, January 1966).
Australian 12 February 1968.
Sydney Morning Herald 8 February 1964.
West Australian (Perth) 25 January 1964.
West Australian (Perth) 13 November 1994.

New Moon Theatre Company

Professional theatrical company in Townsville (Qld) 1982–88, 1990–91. Founded by Townsville City Council as New Moon Central and Northern Theatre Company. **venue** Civic Theatre, Townsville. Also gave annual seasons in Cairns, Mackay and Rockhampton. **artistic directors** 1982–83 Terry O'Connell. 1984–86 Helmut Bakaitis. 1987 Ian Tasker. 1990 Rod Wissler. 1991 David Fenton. **administrative director** 1988–89 Ruth Berenson.

Serving audiences in northern and central Queensland, the New Moon Theatre Company played in Civic Theatres in Cairns, Mackay, Rockhampton and Townsville, with state and federal funding and contributions from local councils. The Townsville City Council founded the company, adopting a proposal by Sheila Keeffe and John Lamb, director of the city's Civic Theatre. Initially the company mounted seasons every six months with an ensemble comprising an artistic director, six to eight actors, and theatre personnel. The repertoire, determined by the interests of the ensemble and the assumed interests of the audience, included musicals, modern comedies, thrillers and popular classic and Australian works.

In 1984 the company devised *Beach Blanket Tempest*, a rock musical based on *The Tempest*. It toured northern centres and beyond Queensland. Other musicals the company performed include *Guys and Dolls*, *Tommy*, David Bowie's *Life on Mars* and REG LIVERMORE's *Ned Kelly*. JOHN WATERS devised and performed *Imagine*, a play about the life of John Lennon. Other Australian works were Michael Gow's *AWAY*, LOUIS NOWRA's *Royal Show*, TONY SHELDON's *Return Engagement* and David Williamson's *DON'S PARTY*. DIANE CILENTO starred in John Pielmeir's *Agnes of God*. The company presented modern versions of *A Midsummer Night's Dream* and *Macbeth*, and Maxwell Anderson's *Key Largo*.

New Moon supported La Luna Theatre, a largely self-financed youth group in Townsville. It also co-operated with amateur and professional organisations, and Queensland state and private schools. It fostered local talent and critical audiences. It emphasised works relevant to tropical Queensland and was sensitive to local conditions, including isolation, a multiracial population and the need for flexible productions for varied venues. Long racked by financial difficulties, it closed in 1991. ❦*Elizabeth Perkins*

New Theatre

Established in 1932 and still active in Sydney and Melbourne, New Theatre claims to be Australia's oldest radical theatre movement. From the start, it has maintained clear objectives—to promote national drama, educate workers and present 'plays with a purpose'. It has been a training ground for performers and writers, and when commercial theatres would not sponsor unknown plays by unknown writers it was one of the few outlets available. New Theatres ran play competitions, conducted regular classes and summer schools in all aspects of theatrical craft. New plays were 'hammered out under the criticism of producers, actors and New Theatre members', the dramatist CATHERINE DUNCAN has said.

In the 1930s Australian New Theatre groups belonged to a loose international movement of workers' theatres. These originated in the United Kingdom and the USA in the 1920s, inspired by Soviet agitprop groups, and after 1929 the worldwide Great Depression and the growth of fascism sharpened their political focus. In the USA, the League of Workers' Theatres was formed in 1932. It became affiliated with the Soviet-led International Workers' Dramatic Union and in 1935 it was renamed the New Theatre League, with the slogan 'art is a weapon'. A similar movement, Unity Theatre, developed throughout the United Kingdom.

Radical theatre groups sprang up in Australian capital cities, often initiated by left-wing artists who had been to the Soviet Union. The Workers' Art Club, founded in Sydney in 1932, included a theatre group. The Left Book Club Theatre Group in Adelaide, Student Theatre in Brisbane, the Workers' Theatre Group in Melbourne and the WORKERS' ART GUILD in Perth all began in 1936. At first they performed short propagandist pieces in union halls and at street meetings, including plays like *Roar, China!* by the Soviet dramatist Sergey Tretyakov and local pieces such as Nellie Rickie's *The Emissary* in Sydney in 1933 and BETTY ROLAND's *Wedding Bells* in Melbourne in 1935.

New Theatre plays were often unashamedly didactic, and concerned with the fight against war and fascism, labour problems, support for the Spanish republic, advocacy of the Soviet way of life and satirical attacks on capitalism. In 1935 the American New Theatre League produced Clifford Odets's *Waiting for Lefty* at a benefit night for striking New York taxi drivers. Compellingly realistic language, revolutionary spirit and actors planted in the audience for a final rousing cry to strike made the play an immediate success. Workers' theatre groups around the world enthusiastically adopted it. In Melbourne in 1936 it was the first play performed in public by the Workers' Theatre Group. In Sydney the Workers' Art Club, renamed the New Theatre League, won the one-act play contest in the 1936 City of Sydney Eisteddfod with it.

A companion piece by Odets, *Till the Day I Die*, brought the groups into conflict with CENSORSHIP in 1936. This anti-Nazi play was banned in NSW and Victoria on the advice of the Australian Attorney-General, Robert Menzies. After a complaint from the German consulate, police interrupted a performance in Sydney on 9 June. In Melbourne, thousands arrived for a private performance in the Collingwood Town Hall on 18 November and found that they and the actors had been locked out. In Perth, Nazi sympathisers in the audience protested against the attack on Hitler.

The Communist Third International declared a popular front in 1935, calling for liberal-to-left elements of all classes to unite in the fight against fascism. By the late 1930s the members of New Theatre groups included trade unionists, intellectuals, students, artists, journalists, theatre workers, Communists and unemployed people. Groups proclaimed their international links with new names—New Theatre League in Sydney in 1936, New Theatre Club in Melbourne and Unity Theatre in Brisbane in 1937.

Moscow initially condemned the Second World War as 'a phoney war' and the Communist Party was banned in Australia in 1940. Germany attacked the Soviet Union in June 1941, but the ban remained until 1942. New Theatres in Brisbane, Perth and Adelaide closed but the Sydney and Melbourne groups survived 'underground', by often omitting names from programs and by obscuring Communist affiliations. Non-Communists took leading positions in Melbourne, and in Sydney, where the rooms were raided, documents were held privately. When the ban on the Communist Party was lifted, its membership swelled and New Theatre flourished.

Women particularly assumed responsibility in direction and artistic leadership during the war. Notable were Hilda Esson in Melbourne and KATHARINE SUSANNAH PRICHARD in Perth. New Theatre groups were outlets for female writers. Up to 1945, New Theatre mounted the first productions of Catherine Duncan's *The Sword Sung* in 1938 and *Sons of the Morning* in 1945, BETTY ROLAND's *War on the Waterfront* in 1939, ORIEL GRAY's *Let's Be Offensive* in 1943 and *Lawson* in 1944, and Miles Franklin and DYMPHNA CUSACK's *Call Up Your Ghosts* in 1945. For a time New Theatre in Sydney employed Gray as resident writer, working on scripts and a weekly program on radio 2KY.

Writers' groups developed, often working co-operatively on political revues, which became characteristic of the repertoire, or providing agitprop sketches for 'contact' or 'mobile' groups. These operated in each state, performing on the back of a truck at factory gates or at street meetings. As early as 1942, New Theatre in Sydney explored the theme of injustice to Aborigines, in George Landen Dann's *FOUNTAINS BEYOND*. In the Melbourne revue *Coming Our Way* in 1946 actors from New Theatre and the Aborigines' League performed in *White Justice*, a dance drama based on the strike by Aboriginal workers in northwest Australia. These performers were also involved in *Fountains Beyond* in 1946 and other productions in Melbourne.

New Theatre also provided space for scenic artists who introduced Australian audiences to constructivist, expressionist and stylised stage settings. They included Harald Vike and Herbert McClintock in Perth, WILLIAM CONSTABLE and VANE LINDESAY in Melbourne and CEDRIC FLOWER and Les Tanner in Sydney. Perhaps the most influential director in the early years was Victor Arnold of the New Theatre League in Sydney. He spent periods in Perth and Melbourne as professional artistic director.

Apart from Australian plays, New Theatre performed plays imported from affiliates. Among them were *Where's That Bomb?* and *Love on the Dole* from Unity Theatre, Albert Maltz's *Rehearsal* and Irwin Shaw's antiwar *Bury the Dead* from the American New Theatre League, and Soviet plays like Valentin Katayev's comedy *Squaring the Circle*.

After the war, Adelaide New Theatre and Unity Theatre in Brisbane reopened in 1947 and the New Theatre League in Perth in 1948. The Sydney group convened a meeting of progressive amateur groups from all states in 1948 in an effort to form a common policy for fostering a 'people's theatre'. This meeting led to establishment of New Theatre Australia, which linked the state groups and maintained a national executive. Conferences were held each Easter to establish policy and to exchange plays and information. From Christmas to New Year each year a state group held a national drama school.

New Theatre suffered from the Cold War in the 1950s. Some members were investigated by security services, actors used stage names, membership and audiences dwindled. In some places the newspapers refused to take New Theatre advertising or review productions. Despite this, a dedicated nucleus remained in each state and Newcastle New Theatre opened in 1957.

A new generation of radical writers provided scripts for production after the war. There was strong political commentary on contemporary issues—the effect of weapon testing at Woomera on local Aborigines in Jim Crawford's *Rocket Range* in 1947, small-town prejudice against an Aboriginal child in Oriel Gray's *Had We But World Enough* in 1950, the Korean War in Nance MacMillan's *Christmas Bridge* in 1951, British colonialism in Malaya in MONA BRAND's *Strangers in the Land* in 1952, the horrors of atomic-bomb testing in the Pacific in Dymphna Cusack's *Pacific Paradise* in 1955. These and similar plays were performed in most states. Ralph de Boissiere, Len Dowdle, FRANK HARDY, John Hepworth, David Martin and RALPH PETERSON also contributed plays. New Theatre gained enormous popular support with Dick Diamond's folk musical REEDY RIVER. It dominated New Theatre's repertoire for four years from 1953, playing to an estimated 450 000 people, and assuring the movement's financial survival.

Disintegration in the labour and left movements resulted in splits in the Australian Labor Party and the Communist Party in the 1950s and disrupted New Theatre. By the end of the 1960s, the national organisation had disbanded, and the groups in Brisbane, Adelaide and Perth had closed, followed eventually by Newcastle. But in Melbourne and Sydney there was consolidation. Mona Brand's *On Stage Vietnam* had extended seasons in both cities. In 1968 CENSORSHIP of productions of *America Hurrah!*, Jean-Claude van Itallie's satire on capitalism, caused sensations comparable with *Till the Day I Die* 32 years before. The media lifted their bans, and memberships and audiences developed broader social and political bases. Since 1970, many radical groups in Melbourne and Sydney have competed with New Theatre in attracting performers, playwrights and audiences. It has survived where others have not, however, and it provides a committed alternative. *Angela O'Brien*

Adelaide

During February 1937 John Simms Baker, a telegraphist and communist sympathiser, established a nameless workers' theatre ensemble in Adelaide. Little is known of this group, but articles Baker wrote for the *Workers' Weekly Herald* in 1937–38 clearly show that it had national and international links with the New Theatre movement. Baker's group was replaced in November 1938 by the Left Book Club Theatre, which changed its name to New Theatre League in February 1939. It concentrated on producing agitprop until it was driven out of existence late in 1939 because it supported the Communist Party's backing of the Hitler–Stalin nonaggression pact.

Early in 1941 Victor Arnold from Sydney re-established the New Theatre movement in Adelaide by forming Labor Youth Theatre. Its major productions in 1941 included *Squaring the Circle* in June, and *Waiting for Lefty* and Catherine Duncan's living newspaper *Soak the Rich* in September. Labor Youth Theatre disbanded midway through 1942 because of military demands on its members and the Communist Party's commitment to the war effort. It also produced agitprop, including *Federal Budget, No Conscription, The People's Movement, Thoughts About the War, Three Wives, Union Label* and *War on the Western Front*.

In 1947 two union activists and theatre enthusiasts, Mary Warren (later Miller) and Rosemary Smith (later Porter), started an agitprop ensemble. This group began larger-scale activity by staging *Waiting for Lefty* and calling itself Adelaide New Theatre. By 1950 it had an extensive membership, links with the national New Theatre network and an impressive list of productions, including Aristophanes' *Lysistrata*, W. H. Auden and Christopher Isherwood's *The Ascent of F6* and Arthur Miller's *All My Sons*. It reached its highest level of achievement, however, between 1952 and 1957, when it presented local premieres of new Australian plays. These included Joan Clark's *Home Brew* in December 1954; Dymphna Cusack's *Pacific Paradise* in 1955; DICK DIAMOND's *Under the Coolibah Tree* in 1955; Len Dowdle's *Song of '54* in 1955; Oriel Gray's *Had We But World Enough* in August 1953, *Lawson* in June 1954, *Sky Without Birds* in September 1952 and *The Torrents* in August 1957; Nance McMillan's *Land of Morning Calm* in April 1952; and RIC THROSSELL's *The Day Before Tomorrow* in November 1957.

An Australian Security Intelligence Organisation agent worked within Adelaide New Theatre between 1952 and 1960, when it finally disbanded because of increasing political pressure on its diminishing membership. The stigma of involvement in an organisation known for Communist sympathies had compelled some members to use stage names in programs. *Peter Douglas*

Brisbane

The New Theatre group in Brisbane was associated with the Communist Party and it maintained a clearer political focus than its Melbourne or Sydney counterparts. It began as the radical left-wing Student Theatre with a production of *Squaring the Circle* on 19 November 1936. Next it performed *Waiting for Lefty*. The group took the name Unity Theatre in 1937. It folded in 1942 and reopened in November 1947 with a production of George Farwell's *Sons of the South*. Syd Davis, an original member of Student Theatre, became the company's leading director. The group had no permanent theatre and it staged productions in the Princess Theatre or the All Saint's Hall. It also maintained rooms and a theatrette in Fortitude Valley, and it offered their use to a radical artists' group, Miya Studio, in return for assistance with sets. In 1949 Unity Theatre became the New Theatre Club, and Miya became its artists' group.

The New Theatre Club, which subsequently affiliated with New Theatre Australia, notably produced the plays of two radical Queensland writers, Jim Crawford and Nance McMillan, who now writes as Nance Wills. Crawford, a controversial left-wing journalist, wrote as a committed revolutionary and his plays are propagandist but he was a competent stylist. He was prolific too, and the New Theatre Club performed nine of his plays, including *Billets and Badges*, *The Governor's Stables*, *Miner's Right*, *Welcome Home* and *Rocket Range*, which was thrown out of a Sydney drama festival in 1948 as politically subversive. New Theatres throughout Australia performed McMillan's *Christmas Bridge* and in 1961 the Brisbane group performed her *The Painter*, based on the life of Albert Namatjira. A production of *Reedy River* gave the New Theatre Club publicity and financial impetus in 1954, but by the late 1950s its membership was dwindling and increasingly divided politically by Cold War pressures. It closed in 1962. ❧*Angela O'Brien*

Melbourne

Frank Huelin and Betty Roland founded the Workers' Theatre Group, under the auspices of Friends of the Soviet Union, in 1935. Initially it performed agitprop sketches and short plays in union halls and at street meetings, including Roland's satire on marriage, *Wedding Bells*, and Huelin's play about the Depression, *To Mildura by Rattler*. Its first public performance on stage was *Waiting for Lefty* at the Central Hall on 11 August 1936.

The group became the New Theatre Club early in 1937 and before and during the war it established a reputation for innovation. By performing 'plays with a purpose' it attracted radical professional artists, many of whom could find no other serious vehicle for their skills. They included the popular radio actor and playwright Catherine Duncan, the actor Eric Reiman, the journalists Dick Diamond and Lillian Diamond, and the scenic artists Jeb Bucklow, William Constable, Eve Harris and Vane Lindesay. In the 1940s the New Theatre Singers and the Unity Dance Group were established. With support from members and trade unions, the club established successive New Theatres—in Flanigan Lane 1937, in Queen Street in 1939 and in Flinders Street from 1942 to 1949. New Theatre worked as a touring company from 1959 to 1963, performed at Centre 63 from 1963 to 1970 and at the Pram Factory and other theatres for the next five years. Since 1976 it has been at the Organ Factory, an arts centre in Clifton Hill.

New Theatre obtained scripts from left-wing groups in the USA, the United Kingdom, the Soviet Union and in other states. These scripts were often crudely didactic but New Theatre Melbourne was more concerned than groups in other cities to find a balance between art and politics, largely because Hilda Esson, its director from 1940 to 1947, argued for classics and quality plays of social significance. She developed an artistic policy based on the Stanislavsky method. Dot Thompson, director from 1955 to 1990, maintained and extended this policy. In 1970 she directed the Aboriginal actor Jack Charles in Athol Fugard's *The Blood Knot*, and later she developed an independent ensemble of black actors called Nindethana Theatre. Thompson joined New Theatre in 1940 and is still involved with it.

New Theatre Melbourne has encouraged Australian writers through play competitions, classes and co-operatively written political revues. In all, 85 Australian works by 26 writers have been performed. The group has always been committed to education. It published the bimonthly *New Theatre Review* from 1943 to 1948, and it has held annual summer schools, and for most of its existence maintained a 'contact' or 'mobile' group. Dot Thompson developed a professional theatre-in-education team, New Theatre Daytime, in the 1970s.

The group's record was inconsistent during the 1980s, a period of theatrical pluralism. The role of radical alternative was increasingly difficult to sustain and New Theatre Melbourne can no longer be identified as the artistic vehicle of a unified left. Yet it can still respond to contemporary political issues—as it did in 1985 with *Sandinista*, a history of the Nicaraguan revolution, and in 1986 with *The Sun on Our Backs*, the story of the British miners' strike—with the theatrical energy and reformist passion that have characterised it in the past. ❧*Angela O'Brien*

Newcastle

Newcastle New Theatre created and built audiences in the Hunter Valley for classical and contemporary drama by European, American and Australian playwrights. Its founders included Dawn and John Allen and Phyllis and John Robson, who had met when they were students at the University of Sydney and enthusiastic supporters of New Theatre. They were strongly committed to presenting works with artistic merit and social relevance. Brendan Behan, Max Frisch, Oriel Gray, THOMAS KENEALLY, Arthur Miller, Molière, Shakespeare and Dylan Thomas were among the dramatists whose works Newcastle New Theatre produced. Its first production was *Reedy River*, directed by Dawn Allen, at the Roxy Theatre, Newcastle, in 1957.

From the outset Newcastle New Theatre had strong ties with a supportive Trades Hall Council. For example, it shared the profits or losses of its May productions with the May-Day Committee. It was linked to New Theatre Australia and participated in national conferences and courses.

In the early 1960s Newcastle New Theatre established a rough but comfortable intimate theatre-space, the Dungeon, in beer cellars below the Newcastle Workers' Club. The club reclaimed the Dungeon in 1973. The last production there was *The Feet of Daniel Mannix* by BARRY OAKLEY in 1972. Occasionally combining with other groups such as Newcastle University Student Players, Newcastle New Theatre continued to operate until 1977. It paved the way for the HUNTER VALLEY THEATRE COMPANY. ❧*Marjorie Biggins*

Perth

Joan Broomhall, Harold Leighton, Katharine Susannah Prichard and Robert Smith formed the New Theatre League on 12 July 1948 in a bold attempt to break out of the conservative 'West End' theatrical mould in postwar Perth. Like the prewar WORKERS' ART GUILD, the league aimed to present plays with left-wing sociopolitical content, but most of its members were only moderately leftist in ideology. Some supported the Australia–Russia Friendship Society, and a few were members of the Communist Party. The latter formed an agitprop wing to take songs and satires to factory gates during strikes and political protests. The league never built up a large following nor produced any landmarks but it did encourage Western Australian playwrights and it provided a vehicle for their unconventional and expressionist plays. The league's centre was the

Modern Women's Club, where it gave its first performance, *Call Up Your Ghosts* by Dymphna Cusack and Miles Franklin, directed by Robert Smith on a makeshift stage, on 10 August 1948. It also played at the Fremantle Trades Hall and the Perth Repertory Theatre. In 1956 the club closed and the league, without premises, disbanded after producing Dick Diamond's *Under the Coolibah Tree* at Fremantle Trades Hall in 1956. ☙*Terry Craig*

Sydney

New Theatre in Sydney claims the longest history of continuous play production in Australia. It began in 1932 as the drama section of the Workers' Art Club, proclaiming its radical attitude with the slogans 'art is a weapon' and 'plays with a purpose'. Its first production was *The Ragged-Trousered Philanthropists* on 15 April 1933. Harry Broderick adapted the play from Robert Tressell's proletarian novel and directed the production. Other works performed in 1933 included Sergey Tretyakov's *Roar, China!*, Vsevolod Ivanov's *The Armoured Train*, and an adaptation of Upton Sinclair's novel *The Spy*. followed by anticapitalist plays from London's Unity Theatre, and the famous Depression play *Love on the Dole* in 1935.

The Workers' Art Club became the New Theatre League in 1936 and produced *Waiting for Lefty*. Its guiding ideals from 1936 to 1940 were commitment to peace, opposition to fascism, condemnation of capitalism, belief in socialism and support for the Republican cause in the Spanish Civil War. Betty Box's *Angels of War* and Irwin Shaw's *Bury the Dead* opposed war. Vladimir Bill-Belotserkovsky's *Life is Calling* asserted belief in socialism and *Señora Carrar's Rifles*, the first play by Bertolt Brecht performed in Australia, supported the Spanish republic.

When war broke out in 1939, the New Theatre League maintained its pacifist stance. In 1940 a production of Rupert Lockwood's *No Conscription* involved the league in a censorship case with the federal government. Federal and state police later confiscated files and some scripts. The league entered the field of political revue with *I'd Rather be Left* in 1941, and by 1988 it had staged 16 more revues. Particularly memorable were *Let's Be Offensive* in 1943, *Pot of Message* in 1951, *You've Never Had It So Good* in 1965 and *At Last the 1984 Show* in 1984.

After the German invasion of the Soviet Union in June 1941, there was a change in the New Theatre League's attitude to war, marked by plays such as Ted Willis's *Sabotage*, Janet and Philip Stevenson's *Counter Attack* and Maxwell Anderson's *The Eve of St Mark*. The league presented programs of sketches and songs in military camps and hospitals around Sydney. In 1943 it moved into Castlereagh Street premises where there was space to develop actors and directors through classes and workshops. In 1945 the league was renamed New Theatre and Jerome Levy produced its first classic, Molière's *A Physician in Spite of Himself*, followed by a Molière season which included *Le Tartuffe* and *Le Bourgeois gentilhomme*. Since then New Theatre has produced plays by Aristophanes, Anton Chekhov, Nikolai Gogol, Henrik Ibsen, Ben Jonson, Shakespeare and Lope de Vega Carpio with varying success. After the war, uncertainty of direction appeared in the choice of plays for 1946, which included *Where's That Bomb?*, a prewar anticapitalist farce; *Mooney's Kid Don't Cry*, the first Tennessee Williams play produced in Australia; and John Steinbeck's *Of Mice and Men* in a memorable production by Lloyd Lamble. For the next ten years a legal injunction prevented the New Theatre from producing contemporary American plays. From 1948 to 1961 another severe handicap was the refusal of the *Sydney Morning Herald* to publish New Theatre's advertisements or review its productions.

The Sydney production of Reedy River in December 1953 won back audiences and enabled New Theatre to survive the loss of its Castlereagh Street premises in 1954. New Theatre has revived this folk musical eight times in Sydney. Between 1954 and 1962 New Theatre managed to stage a surprising number and variety of productions in the Waterside Workers' Federation hall, including an increasing number of Australian plays. From 1963 to 1973 New Theatre again had its own premises, in St Peter's Lane in inner-city Darlinghurst. In keeping with a changing world, it became less party-aligned in its choice of plays but maintained its radical stance. The overseas contribution began to include voices as various as Edward Albee, Howard Barker, Brendan Behan, Howard Brenton, Jules Feiffer, Dario Fo, Brian Friel, Max Frisch, John McGrath, Georges Michel, Arthur Miller, Sean O'Casey, Dennis Potter, William Saroyan, Jean-Paul Sartre, George Sklar, Tom Stoppard, David Storey, Jean-Claude van Itallie, Kurt Vonnegut, Dale Wasserman, John Whiting, Tennessee Williams and Carl Zuckmayer.

Between 1953 and 1976, Mona Brand, almost a house playwright, provided scripts for revues, musicals, political plays, domestic comedies, dramas and children's plays. Other Australians who have had their plays performed by New Theatre include Dymphna Cusack, Sumner Locke Elliott, Nick Enright, George Farwell, Joan Gibson, Oriel Gray, Frank Hardy, R. C. Herbert, Kevin McGrath, Kevin Barry Morgan, Barry Oakley, Ralph Peterson, Alan Seymour, John Upton and Eleanor Witcombe.

New Theatre has been fortunate with its designers. Cedric Flower was the mainstay for nearly seven years, providing sets and costumes for plays and revues. Les Tanner followed him and provided memorable settings for J. B. Priestley's *An Inspector Calls*, Sean O'Casey's *The Star Turns Red*, Oriel Gray's *Sky without Birds* and Lope de Vega Carpio's *Spanish Village*. David Milliss became the group's main designer in 1957 and has provided setting for a considerable variety of plays including Dymphna Cusack's *Pacific Paradise*. Yvonne Francart's decorative skill has enlivened productions including Molière's *Les Précieuses ridicules*, *Othello* and The Ballad of Angel's Alley. Roderick Shaw has long provided brilliant set and costume designs for plays and contributed to graphic design.

In 1968 there was a censorship scandal when van Itallie's *America Hurrah!*, a play protesting at the dehumanising of American life, was alleged to be obscene. The NSW Chief Secretary, acting upon a complaint made to the police by a member of the public, threatened to close the theatre under the regulations of the Theatres and Public Halls Act. An anti-censorship action group was formed, calling itself Friends of America Hurrah!, and arranged a free protest performance in the Teachers' Federation Theatre in the city. The occasion attracted some 2500 sympathisers, only 500 of whom were permitted to enter. This caused a near riot. At the end of the performance plain-clothes police confiscated scenery upon which graffiti had been drawn and attempted to arrest the actors, who escaped into the crowd. In the face of a large sympathetic audience the police dropped threats of prosecution and have not attempted to intervene in a public performance since.

Since 1973 New Theatre has had its own premises, with a 160-seat auditorium, in the inner-western suburb of Newtown. It has stated its determination 'to continue its role as a socially relevant and committed theatre' but the kind of committed plays it alone presented have become the norm for theatres everywhere. The group says, however: 'It is a source of satisfaction to New Theatre members that the pioneering role of their theatre has helped to open the way for a wider general acceptance of socially relevant drama'. It has become more difficult for New Theatre to be seen as radical and it seems to be producing the repertoire available to most amateur groups. Recent successful productions include DAVID WILLIAMSON's *Sons of Cain*, Robert Bolt's *A Man for all Seasons*, Mart Crowley's *The Boys in the Band*, Arthur Miller's *After the Fall* and a remarkable *King Lear*.
❧Paul Herlinger

further reading
BRAND, MONA. New Theatre movement. *Theatre Australia*, October–November 1978.
DOUGLAS, PETER. Origins—A history of the Adelaide New Theatre movement 1937 to 1960. Flinders University of South Australia thesis.
GODDARD, H. and L. LAYMAN. *Organise*. Perth: Trades and Labour Council 1988.
GRAY, ORIEL. *Exit Left*. Melbourne: Penguin 1985.
HERLINGER, PAUL. A new direction for the New? *Australian Drama Studies* 8 (Brisbane, April 1986).
Herlinger, Paul. The history of Sydney New Theatre 1939–53. University of Sydney MA (hons) thesis 1989.
HILLEL, ANGELA. *Against the Stream—New Theatre Melbourne 1936–1986*. Melbourne: New Theatre 1986.
O'BRIEN, ANGELA. The road not taken—Performance and political ideologies, Melbourne New Theatre, 1935–1960. Monash University PhD thesis 1989.
THOMPSON, DOROTHY. *From My Direction—Stanislavski in practice*. Melbourne: New Theatre 1991.
10 Years of New Theatre. Melbourne: New Theatre 1948.
50 New Years 1932–1982. Sydney: New Theatre 1982.
New Theatre Review (Melbourne) 1943–1948.
Notes on the History of New Theatre, Australia. New Theatre Australia 1959.

New Zealand theatre in Australia

Theatrical trade between New Zealand and Australia has been two-way since the later 19th century, and for a long time it ran in Australia's favour. Australia has imported talent in the form of actors, directors and other stage personnel, and occasionally playwrights, and exported finished products like playscripts and touring productions. In the 19th and early 20th centuries New Zealanders increasingly found that to develop a professional theatrical career they had to be where companies were signed up—Melbourne and Sydney. Some dependable actors, such as HERBERT FLEMMING, began their stage careers in New Zealand.

New Zealand's literary awakening of the 1890s was less substantial than Australia's and produced very few plays. Two melodramas by Australian writers who were in New Zealand opened in Wellington and were brought back to Australia. Both exploited local colour. GEORGE DARRELL's *The Pakeha* (1890), later renamed *Life for Life*, had a gold coach stuck up in a narrow gorge amidst Southern Alps scenery painted from photographs. GEORGE LEITCH's *The Land of the Moa* (1895) provided scope for display of Maoris, geothermal activity and a volcanic eruption accompanied by an earthquake. The production toured Sydney, Brisbane and Melbourne, but with ever-decreasing success. The only playwright of any note from New Zealand at that time was ARTHUR H. ADAMS. He wrote the libretto for ALFRED HILL's operetta *Tapu*, which was successful in Sydney in 1904—Maori poi dancers and haka performers were a feature, not for the first time in Australia.

During the first half of the 20th century, London was increasingly the theatrical mecca of New Zealanders. In Australia New Zealand's theatrical presence was at its lowest, apart from some entrepreneurial activity. FULLERS' extended its vaudeville empire to Australia. Later, in 1937 John McKenzie, an Australian businessman in New Zealand, bought a controlling share in J. C. WILLIAMSON's. Later still, HARRY M. MILLER, a concert entrepreneur, crossed the Tasman Sea to develop an Australian career.

From 1895 until 1930, hardly any New Zealand play reached even the New Zealand stage. After 1930, for several decades, writing for the stage meant one-act plays for amateurs. A very early example from the one-act repertoire is Alan Mulgan's *For Love of Appin* (c.1920), which was given a performance in Sydney, but with a local Australian setting. Lack of Australian interest in New Zealand experience apparently persisted as late as the 1970s, when Roger Hall's *Glide Time* (1976) was localised as *Flexitime*. At that time Australian plays were relished in New Zealand for their distinctive trans-Tasman tang, but were still commonly localised as they moved from state to state at home. A playwright of earlier years who settled in Australia was DOUGLAS STEWART. His verse play *The Golden Lover* is a love comedy ostensibly set in a Maori village, but it takes no real note of Maori custom, language or imagery.

Small professional theatre companies established in the main cities in New Zealand in the 1960s and 1970s provided venues between 1975 and the early 1980s for sudden successes by Roger Hall, Greg McGee, Joseph Musaphia and other playwrights. Most of these successes have been tried in Australia, but have not generally taken, at least not in subsidised theatres. Musaphia's *Mothers and Fathers* (1975) had a successful season with the failing OLD TOTE THEATRE COMPANY in Sydney in 1977 and went on to the Adelaide Festival. There was an amateur production of Hall's *Glide Time* (*Flexitime*) in Canberra and his *Middle Age Spread* had a production in Adelaide. *Flexitime*'s first professional production, also in Adelaide, was followed by an extensive tour. The musical *Footrot Flats*, with a book by Hall and A. K. Grant, did particularly well in Western Australia in 1984 and topped 250 performances altogether.

Traffic in fully-mounted productions has not been only one-way. In the late 1940s Ngaio Marsh took students from Canterbury University College to Sydney, Melbourne and Canberra, and her productions of *Othello* and Luigi Pirandello's *Six Characters in Search of an Author* were enthusiastically reviewed. More popular New Zealand shows, usually of a revue character, have done better under commercial auspices. Probably the greatest New Zealand successes ever to come to Australia were two wartime concert parties. After the First World War the DIGGERS COMPANY toured Australia for more than 12 years. The KIWIS REVUE COMPANY, with only three distinct shows, played from 1946 to 1954. More recently, Stephen Sinclair and Anthony McCarten's comedy *Ladies' Night* and the revue group Front Lawn have been successful.

The Trans-Tasman Theatre Exchange scheme, was established in 1981 to encourage a regular flow of personnel and productions across the Tasman. It did not achieve this but it did in particular enable AARNE NEEME to stage at the Stables Theatre in Sydney, to considerable critical acclaim, a three-month season of McGee's *Foreskin's Lament*, Hall's *Middle Age Spread* and Robert Lord's *Bert and Maisie*. Grant Tilly, a leading New Zealand actor, was invited to take part. Under the scheme, McGee and Renée attended the AUSTRALIAN NATIONAL PLAYWRIGHTS' CONFERENCE, at which Lord had had a play workshopped. The scheme has also helped to establish the monthly *Australian and New Zealand Theatre Record*.

New Zealand's theatrical presence in Australia now is very much as it was a century ago. The occasional playwright like ALMA DE GROEN and Jennifer Compton have settled here, while others like Hilary Beaton have spent time here. Many New Zealand actors and stage personnel have worked in Australia. Richard Campion is an example. In the 1960s, as resident producer for J. C. Williamson's in Melbourne, he directed two new Australian plays, including Marien Dreyer's BANDICOOT ON A BURNT RIDGE; productions at the Adelaide Festival, one of them designed by the Wellington designer Raymond Boyce; and at the Old Tote Theatre the musical *Sydney Rocks* and the first Australian production of Bertolt Brecht's *The Caucasian Chalk Circle*.

JOHN SUMNER, director of the Melbourne Theatre Company, said in 1985 that his key designers had nearly always been New Zealanders. It has been argued that smaller, usually unconventional theatre spaces and rapid turnover of productions have given New Zealand theatrical personnel an edge in their experience of production work. But given the physical and cultural closeness of the two countries, it is surprising how little each knows of the other's drama. While few Australian productions now cross the Tasman, some scripts do, and there are marginally more opportunities to see Australian plays performed in New Zealand than New Zealand plays in Australia. *John Thomson*

Newcastle

The theatrical history of Newcastle and the Hunter Valley is representative of provincial theatre in New South Wales, which combines regional identity and insularity, isolation, and physical and political domination by the metropolis. Performances were given in the Court House and halls in Newcastle until a publican, James Croft, opened the Newcastle Theatre behind his hotel on the busy corner of Hunter and Watt Streets in February 1857. It was designed by HENRY BEAUFOY MERLIN, actor and puppeteer. Fire destroyed it in 1859. It was followed by the Theatre Royal and in 1876 by the Victoria Theatre in Perkins Street. The proprietor of the latter was John Bennett of Sydney.

The Victoria was the first theatre in Newcastle that was built for the purpose and adequate in size. Regular touring companies soon appeared, alternating with lectures and local performances for charity. Newcastle's audience of merchants in the circle and miners and seamen in the stalls, all willing to be entertained, gave it the reputation of being 'a good show town'. A local company bought the Victoria Theatre in 1887 and rebuilt it in 1890–91, when the population of Newcastle—then 12 municipalities—numbered 50 000. The result was rightly described by the lessee, James MacMahon of MACMAHON BROTHERS, as 'the first grand theatre in Newcastle'.

In 1897 ALFRED DAMPIER and his company came to the Victoria Theatre, not for the first time, to celebrate the centenary of the European discoveries of the Hunter River estuary and of coal by giving a week of nightly changes. The plays included *Hamlet*, *East Lynne*, ROBBERY UNDER ARMS by Dampier and Garnet Walch and *A Transvaal Heroine* by Dampier and J. H. Wrangham. There were major renovations in 1905 and again in 1921, to remove the hotel and modify the theatre for moving pictures. FULLERS' leased the Victoria Theatre from 1922 to 1948, and alternated films with operettas and vaudeville in the 1920s and 1930s. There was an opera season in 1957 and an operetta in 1963, before the theatre closed its doors in 1966.

The comedian GEORGE SORLIE first took his tent show to the Hunter coalfields in 1918 and later began his tours in Newcastle. From 1948 to 1961 his successor, BOBBY LE BRUN, also mounted new Sorlies' shows in Newcastle for touring.

The council-owned Civic Theatre, designed by HENRY E. WHITE, opened in December 1929 and was immediately leased for films. In 1974 it was converted and managed for live presentations, as the only major, fully-used theatre between Sydney and Brisbane. After a comprehensive $10 million refurbishment, in which its Spanish decor and its 1660 seats were retained, it reopened in November 1993 and it can now present almost any production. The building includes the HUNTER VALLEY THEATRE COMPANY's Playhouse, which seats fewer than 200 and has an awkward sunken stage. The company, formed in 1975, was an initiative of the ARTS COUNCIL and the director JOHN TASKER. Its early years were fraught with difficulties. It lacked a theatre and adequate grants, despite the support of the Joint Coal Board, until local support was assured. In the company's first season the Newcastle playwright JOHN O'DONOGHUE attracted attention with *A Happy and Holy Occasion*, set in Mayfield near the steelworks. He has continued to make Newcastle life the subject of his plays.

Freewheels, a permanent theatre-in-education company operating since 1976, moved to a converted hall at Boolaroo in 1988 and has identified itself with the outer suburbs in the City of Lake Macquarie.

The most durable amateur groups include the Newcastle Dramatic Art Club, established by Colin Chapman in 1938, soon after he became a full-time music and drama teacher. He operated at the Roxy, a former cinema in suburban Hamilton, from 1955 until it was closed for demolition in 1971. Then he moved to a converted hall in the same street.

The Gilbert and Sullivan Society, founded in 1951, presents annual productions. The Newcastle Repertory Theatre, established in 1957, bought and converted a suburban hall in Lambton in 1968. Its founder, the still-active Peter Bloomfield, began in eisteddfods—introduced to the Hunter Valley by Welsh miners and conducted annually by the Abermain Society since 1917—and the Workers'

Educational Association Drama Club. Newcastle Repertory is perhaps most typical of a provincial town in its economical and practical approach, relying on a large membership and mailing list and heeding audience taste.

The University of Newcastle's drama department, headed by Professor Victor Emeljanow, combines performance and teaching. It aims to serve the local community and eventually to expand into a faculty of performing arts.

Newcastle provides a large market, a rich tradition of activity and a body of research stimulated by the university and the presence of durable records in the *Maitland Mercury*, established in 1843, and the *Newcastle Herald*, a daily since 1876. In 1979, for the jubilee of the Civic Theatre and the Town Hall, the Newcastle City Council began presenting its annual CONDA awards in several categories from drama critics' nominations. ❦*L. E. Fredman*

further reading
Bradshaw, Richard. The Merlin of the south. *Australasian Drama Studies* 7 (Brisbane, October 1985).
Fredman, L. E. Down Memory Lane—The Victoria, Newcastle's first grand theatre. *Journal of Hunter Valley History* 11/2 (Newcastle 1988).
Goold, W. J. Amusements of Newcastle. *Journal of Newcastle and Hunter District Historical Society* 9 (Newcastle, June 1955).
Singleton, Sharon. Australian regional theatre—A pioneering and exemplary case. University of Newcastle hons thesis 1982.
Wallis, Roma. *Gulgong in the Roaring Days*. Dubbo: Macquarie Publications 1982.

Marie Ney

Actor. Born 18 July 1895 in London. Trained as musical-comedy singer with Tom Pollard in Wellington (New Zealand). Joined George Marlow Grand Shakespearean Company 1916. Acted for J. and N. Tait Ltd and J. C. Williamson's 1919–22. Successful in England. Toured Australia tour 1940–41. Toured South Africa and Middle East. Returned to London 1945. Last noted performance at Salisbury Playhouse 1960.

A superb actor in Shakespearean and contemporary drama, Marie Ney first appeared on stage as the Widow in *The Taming of the Shrew* with the George Marlow Grand Shakespearean Company, headed by Allan Wilkie, at the Princess Theatre in Melbourne in 1916. Later she played Nerissa, Phoebe and the Player Queen. In 1919–20 she toured in J. and N. Tait Ltd's production of J. Hartley Manners's *Peg o' My Heart*. Ney was engaged to play Dinah in A. A. Milne's *Mr Pim Passes By* on Marie Tempest's tour in 1921. Next year she was with the Emelie Polini company, playing Liza and Mrs Collinson in *My Lady's Dress* by Edward Knoblock and Lucy Shale in *The Lie* by Henry Arthur Jones. Encouraged by Marie Tempest, Ney then went to London. Great success in Shakespeare with the Old Vic Theatre Company launched her on a distinguished career. In 1940 Ney returned to Australia for J. C. Williamson's to star in *Ladies in Retirement* by Edward Percy and Reginald Denham, *No Time for Comedy* by S. N. Behrman and *Private Lives* by Noël Coward in Melbourne and Sydney. She also presented a solo show, *Shakespeare's Women*, for Australian war funds. ❦*Lynne Murphy*

further reading
Gaye, Freda (ed.). *Who's Who in the Theatre*. London: Pitman 1967.

A Nice Night's Entertainment

Solo show comprising nine monologues and songs written, composed and directed by Barry Humphries. Toured 1962.

The solo shows that have made Barry Humphries internationally known began with *A Nice Night's Entertainment*, his first national tour. It opened and closed with Edna Everage, included Sandy Stone's first live appearance, and introduced characters including Morrie Tate, beatnik moulded in the image of 'hip'; the Minister for National Identity scheming for a nation of clones; and a small-minded literary critic traducing successful expatriates who were his 'personal friends'. Audiences relished Humphries's startling ability to convert his aversion to conformity into maliciously witty monologues. In the Melbourne *Age* on 31 July 1962 Geoffrey Hutton welcomed him as a long-needed satirist: 'Nobody, surely, has ever made a more complete collection of Australian clichés, nor fired them off with more artful menace'. ❦*Victoria Chance*

further reading
Humphries, Barry. *A Nice Night's Entertainment—Sketches and monologues 1956–1981*. Sydney: Currency Press 1981.

Don Nicol

Comedian. Born 10 October 1906 in Melbourne. Originally Daniel Robert McNicol. Began as caricaturist. Married Oda Larsen, performer. Star comedian for J. C. Williamson's 1936–47. Died 18 February 1949 in Melbourne. Brother of performer Beth Nicol.

After Gus Bluett died in 1936 Don Nicol replaced him as star comedian in musical shows for J. C. Williamson's. His early tours as a performer owed as much to his ability to draw posters as to his usefulness on stage. He began drawing caricatures for the *Circle*, a Melbourne sporting newspaper, as a teenager and he later sold his sketches in hotels to make his fare home when he was stranded twice in Queensland and twice in Tasmania. Things improved when he joined a Pierrot company in seaside St Kilda, Melbourne. By 1926 he was touring with Williamson no. 2 companies. By the 1930s he had graduated to small comedy roles in capital cities. In 1937 he made his mark in the musical play *Balalaika* and never looked back. But after the American musical *Follow the Girls* in 1947 tuberculosis, which had been diagnosed when he tried to enlist during the Second World War, confined him to a Melbourne sanatorium. After two years there he died. ❦*John West*

W. D. Nicol

Puppeteer, teacher. Born 28 April 1907 in Scotland. Arrived in Australia 1922. Served apprenticeship in wood-machining. Studied at Melbourne Teachers' College; became lecturer in art and craft there 1939. Formed Teachers' College Marionette Guild 1942. Instrumental in founding Puppet Guild of Australia in Melbourne. Started Littlest Theatre, Melbourne, 1945. Died 13 June 1978 at Phillip Island (Vic.).

Working with finely crafted puppets, Bill Nicol was an important pioneer of Australian puppetry. His work often had adult appeal and included dramatised Aboriginal legends. He provided valuable training for puppeteers, including Peter Scriven. In 1945, with the National Fitness Association, he started the Littlest Theatre in a basement where members of the Puppet Guild of Australia gave weekly performances until the lease expired about 1950. At the 1964 Adelaide Festival Nicol directed his students in shadow-puppet plays for a week. At Kormilda (NT) in 1968–69 his Aboriginal students in an art course performed legends with shadow puppets. ❧*Richard Bradshaw*

writings
Puppetry. Melbourne: Oxford University Press 1962.

Nimrod Theatre Company

Professional dramatic company in Sydney, founded in 1970 by John Bell and Ken Horler. Closed 1987. **first production** *Biggles* by Ron Blair, Michael Boddy and Marcus Cooney. **artistic directors** 1970–74 John Bell and Ken Horler. 1974–79 John Bell, Ken Horler and Richard Wherrett. 1980 John Bell and Ken Horler. 1980–81 Neil Armfield, John Bell and Kim Carpenter. 1981–82 Neil Armfield, John Bell and Aubrey Mellor.1982–85 John Bell and Aubrey Mellor. 1985–87 Richard Cottrell. **venues** 1970–74 Nimrod Street Theatre. 1974–84 Nimrod Theatre. 1984–87 Seymour Theatre Centre. **last production** *Kiss of the Spider Woman* by Manuel Puig.

The key companies in establishing and promoting the new wave of Australian theatre of the early 1970s were the NIMROD THEATRE COMPANY in Sydney and the AUSTRALIAN PERFORMING GROUP in Melbourne. They did much of the work in decolonising Australian theatre and they are now often associated with the larrikin masculinity of the new wave. But during the 1970s each pursued an open radical agenda that, for example, allowed for early stirring of FEMINIST THEATRE and Aboriginal theatre as well as the new middle-class nationalism for which they are best known.

Many commentators see Nimrod as a model of the alternative joining the establishment as it grew up and moved to increasingly larger theatres over 17 years. Yet, throughout its career it thrived on eclecticism and often-controversial new moves and new directions. At first it was self-consciously 'alternative', reacting against the dominance of the OLD TOTE THEATRE COMPANY, which 'alternative' theatre workers saw as Anglophilic and culturally conservative. A triumvirate of the classical actor JOHN BELL, Ken Horler, and the director RICHARD WHERRETT ruled Nimrod for most of its early days. They gathered writers, actors, designers and musicians who became well known in the 'cultural renascence'. Particularly important in the early years were the designer LAURENCE EASTWOOD and the writer RON BLAIR. Horler found a tiny building in Kings Cross which was renovated with donated money (much of it from him) and volunteer labour (much of it by Eastwood) as the Nimrod Street Theatre, now the STABLES THEATRE.

From 1970 to 1976, Nimrod established a powerful presence as a radical young company with a clearly expressed manifesto, realised with remarkable popular and critical success, of doing new Australian work and finding new Australian ways of doing classics, especially Shakespeare, whose plays the company embraced with irreverent enthusiasm. Of its first 18 productions 15 were of new Australian plays, nine of them written specifically for the Nimrod Street Theatre. Given that it was playing to an average 75 per cent capacity, this was a record rarely equalled before or since. It introduced an impressive list of writers, directors and performers, and established the Sydney version of the aggressively nationalistic style that was the feature of the New Wave. Among the writers whose work Nimrod promoted were ALEX BUZO, ALMA DE GROEN, NICK ENRIGHT, PETER KENNA, JIM MCNEIL, DAVID WILLIAMSON and, towards the end of the 1970s, LOUIS NOWRA and STEPHEN SEWELL.

In 1974 the company moved to the Nimrod Theatre—now the BELVOIR STREET THEATRE—in Surry Hills amid much criticism that it was 'selling out'. Its work there at first confounded doubting critics by remaining, on the whole, provocative and innovative—especially in what came to be known as the company's 'Marxist feminist' period in the early 1980s. At that time the founders more or less handed the company over to a new radical team. Like the Australian Performing Group's similar attempt to salvage its original radical aims in 1980, this finally led Nimrod into a dead end, for box-office reasons, but not before some interesting new works had been produced.

Wherrett left the company in 1979 to become artistic director of the SYDNEY THEATRE COMPANY. Horler left suddenly after a palace coup in 1980 and returned to the legal profession. His work as a political and economic mover and shaker makes him an unsung hero of the early Nimrod. Bell stayed until 1985, presiding increasingly distantly over Nimrod's later successes amid the different radicalism of the late 1970s and early 1980s. Influential figures in the company in the early 1980s included the directors NEIL ARMFIELD and AUBREY MELLOR, the designer KIM CARPENTER and the administrator CHRIS WESTWOOD. By the mid-1980s Nimrod was feeling the tensions of being an alternative company grown so large that it was seen as mainstream. After financial disasters and last-minute salvage operations the company moved in 1984 to the soulless SEYMOUR THEATRE CENTRE, where it closed in 1987. The last works produced under the Nimrod name, during the artistic directorship of Richard Cottrell, ironically recapitulated the repertoire of the Old Tote company, against which the early Nimrod had rebelled so effectively. Some of the old Nimrod spirit continued to be felt in the work of the GRIFFIN THEATRE COMPANY at the Stables and Company B at Belvoir Street in the late 1980s and early 1990s. ❧*John McCallum*

reference
The Nimrod Theatre Company's records are held in the Dennis Wolanski Library of the Performing Arts (Sydney).

No Incense Rising

Drama in three acts by George Landen Dann. **premiere** 24 November 1937, NSW State Conservatorium of Music, Sydney, by Independent Theatre. Cast: Arnold Barker, Valentina Diakoff, Betty McConnell, Margaret Ruthven, Edna Todd, Pat Tuohill, Dorothy Whiteley. Director: Doris Fitton.

GEORGE LANDEN DANN centres this play on Ada, one of three children of Mrs Bergmann, a widow in a remote Queensland fishing village. Her husband and son have died at sea; the other daughter has escaped into a wealthy marriage. Ada is torn between her love for the fisherman Carl Nilssen and the ties of her possessive mother. The claustrophobic atmosphere slowly gathers to a Strindbergian end when the mother commits suicide and Ada, at last free, finds herself trapped by her own emotions. The characters' Norwegian and Irish names betray influence by the Scandinavian and Irish realists, but stronger than this is the oppressive power of climate and circumstance that occupied much Australian writing at the time. The play won first prizes in an INDEPENDENT THEATRE national play competition in October 1937 and in the Dramatists' Club of Australia competition, judged by a committee in London, in February 1938. It was produced in Melbourne in April and by the BRISBANE REPERTORY THEATRE Society in May. ❦*Katharine Brisbane*

reference
The manuscript is in the George Landen Dann collection in the Fryer Library, University of Queensland (Brisbane).

No Sugar

> Play in four acts by Jack Davis. **premiere** 18 February 1985 at Maltings, Perth, by Western Australian Theatre Company. Cast: Charmaine Cole, Jedda Cole, Dorothy Collard, Ernie Dingo, Morton Hansen, Jim Holland, Colin Kickett, Dibbs Mather, Bill McCluskey, Shane McNamara, Brooke Michael, Lynette Narkle, Annie O'Shannessy, John Pell, Kelton Pell, Sally Sander, Richard Walley. Designer: Steve Nolan. Director: Andrew Ross. Choreography and music: Richard Walley. **published** Sydney: Currency Press 1986.

JACK DAVIS set *No Sugar* in Western Australia but his insights are not restricted to that state or even to Australia. The naturalistic plot revolves around the infamous forced removal of 90 Aborigines from the town of Northam to the Moore River Native Settlement during the Great Depression. Davis focuses upon the trials of members of the Millimurra family, mistreated by the police, patronised by the Chief Protector of Aborigines and exploited by the superintendent of the Moore River settlement. The overall theme is Aboriginal vitality and endurance and the play is neither heavy-handed nor two-dimensional. There is an 'Uncle Tom' character and there are sympathetic whites.

Davis has reached overseas audiences in an unprecedented fashion with *No Sugar*. Andrew Ross directed the premiere of a revised version on 15 May 1986 at the West End Community Centre in Vancouver (Canada) in conjunction with the World Theatre Festival of Expo '86. This production, with Ernie Dingo as Jimmy and Davis as Billy, was later performed at the National Arts Centre in Ottawa. Ross directed another revival, by the Marli Biyol Company, at the Riverside Studios in London on 16 June 1988. There were favourable reviews. ❦*Adam Shoemaker*

further reading
BRITTON, DAVID. The making of an Aboriginal theatre. *Fremantle Arts Review* July 1986.
HOAD, BRIAN. Taking an epic journey to Canada. *Bulletin* (Sydney) 22 April 1986.
LANGSAM, DAVID. Jack Davis and Marli Biyol in London. *Australian Society* (Melbourne) August 1988.

Jessica Noad

> Actor. Born 23 October 1920 in Sydney. Early training in music with Julie Scully, dance with Frances Scully and speech with Monica Scully. Independent Theatre (Sydney) from 1937. Acted for Whitehall Productions at Minerva Theatre, Sydney, 1945–48. In Will Mahoney Company at Theatre Royal, Brisbane, 1946. Toured for J. C. Williamson's and other managements from 1952.

The career of Jessica Noad spanned three decades of work almost wholly within the commercial theatre, from fresh, bright-faced juvenile leads to the charming dignity of her character roles. Her first professional work was in radio drama. As a child she had acted on radio 2BL's children's session, and in shows devised by the Scully sisters at the Palace and Philip Street Theatres in Sydney. As a teenager she acted with Independent Theatre in plays by Australian writers, including SUMNER LOCKE ELLIOTT's *Little Sheep Run Fast*, Lynn Foster's *There is no Armour* and GWEN MEREDITH's *Shout at the Thunder*. Noad began professional theatre in June 1944 with a tour of army camps and theatres in NSW and Queensland for Hayward Scott Productions. In 1945 she began acting for Whitehall Productions at the Minerva Theatre in *Yes and No* by Kenneth Horne.

After three years in England, Noad returned to Australia in 1952 to tour with Jessie Matthews in *Larger than Life* for KENN BRODZIAK and GARNET H. CARROLL. After tours of Victoria for the Council for Adult Education and running an actors' co-operative with LETTY CRAYDON, John Edmund and NOEL FERRIER at the Arrow Theatre in Melbourne, Noad began touring for J. C. WILLIAMSON's in 1956 in Alan Melville's *Simon and Laura* with JOHN MCCALLUM and Googie Withers. She played supporting roles for the Firm on tours with Ursula Jeans and Roger Livesey in William Douglas Home's *The Reluctant Debutante* in 1956; with Lewis Casson and Sybil Thorndike in Enid Bagnold's *The Chalk Garden* in 1957–58; with Edwin Styles in Arthur Watkyn's *Not in the Book* in 1959; with CYRIL RITCHARD and Cornelia Otis Skinner in *The Pleasure of His Company* in 1960; and with McCallum and Withers in Somerset Maugham's *The Constant Wife* in 1961. Noad also toured in 1959 with the J. C. Williamson's Shakespeare Company directed by JOHN ALDEN, playing Goneril in *King Lear*, Paulina in *The Winter's Tale* and Hippolyta in *A Midsummer Night's Dream*. She crowned her career by playing opposite Michael Redgrave in John Mortimer's *A Voyage Round My Father* which opened on 14 March 1973 in Melbourne and toured to Adelaide and Sydney. Later she worked mainly in television until she retired in 1990. ❦*Lynne Murphy*

Norfolk Island

Convicts gave theatrical performances at penal stations on Norfolk Island in 1793–94 and again in 1840. A party of convicts and soldiers was sent to the island to found a settlement in February 1788, shortly after the establishment of the first English colony in Australia at Sydney. The British government saw Norfolk Island as strategically important because it was thought that the indigenous pine trees would be excellent timber for ships' masts and the local flax would supply linen for sails. Neither the timber nor the flax proved suitable for these purposes, but in 1790 a much larger group of marines and convicts was sent to Norfolk Island to relieve pressure on food supplies in Sydney. By 1792 the island had more than 1100 inhabitants. In May 1793 Lieutenant-Governor Philip Gidley King permitted free men and convicts to open a playhouse. Plays were given once a month and on public holidays but by March 1794 King had ordered closure of the theatre because of disturbances caused by soldiers.

The Norfolk Island settlement was abandoned in 1814, but in 1825 it was re-established as a place of secondary punishment. It became the most notorious in the Australian convict system but Captain Alexander Maconochie, who believed in rehabilitation rather than punishment and terror, was appointed superintendent in 1840. He declared a holiday in honour of Queen Victoria's birthday, and it was celebrated with the issue of special rations, fireworks and a theatrical performance. A hut was transformed into the 'Royal Victoria Theatre' and on 25 May 1840 convict performers, all men, presented two acts of Samuel Arnold's 1782 comic opera *The Castle of Andalusia*, followed by 'A Musical Melange', 'The Tent Scene' from *Richard III*, a naval hornpipe and a Tyrolean waltz. Another musical drama, William Reeve's 1794 *The Purse*, was followed by the songs 'Paddy Carey' (performed in character) and 'Banner of War'. 'God Save the Queen' concluded the evening, for which a handwritten playbill survives in the Public Record Office in London. The performance was extensively reported in Sydney and Hobart newspapers later in 1840. The Governor of NSW, Sir George Gipps, was not pleased and he ordered that there be no further theatrical performances at the penal station. ❦*Elizabeth Webby*

Norm and Ahmed

Play by Alex Buzo. **premiere** 9 April 1968, Old Tote Theatre, Sydney, by Old Tote Theatre Company. Cast: Ron Graham, Edwin Hodgeman. Designer: Allan Lees. Director: Jim Sharman. **published** Melbourne: in *Komos* 1969. Sydney and London: Currency Methuen 1973.

One of the best-known 'new wave' plays of the late 1960s, *Norm and Ahmed* was a success in the OLD TOTE THEATRE COMPANY's first Australian play season in Sydney in 1968. ALEX BUZO shows an old working-class Australian called Norm engineering a late-night encounter with Ahmed, a young Pakistani studen. It gradually becomes clear that the complacent ocker feels just as alienated from the society of which he speaks so proudly as does the polite and circumspect Ahmed. Their relationship swings between tension and uneasy camaraderie. Just as the audience is beginning to think that a tentative friendship has been reached, Norm reveals the insecurity beneath his self-confidence in a sudden outburst of savagery. He bashes Ahmed, shouting 'Fuckin' boong'. This final line made the play the subject of a controversial CENSORSHIP debate and prosecutions or threats of prosecution on obscenity charges arose from at least three productions. It was 'fuckin'', rather than 'boong' or the accompanying bashing that was considered obscene. The play became well-known for its funny use of the Australian vernacular, juxtaposed with Ahmed's stilted formal English. It is regularly produced, especially in universities and colleges. ❦*John McCallum*

Charles Norman

Comedian. Born in United Kingdom. Came to Australia with parents as a boy. Began performing in vaudeville in Melbourne suburbs. Later on Clay vaudeville circuit in Sydney. Performed in operetta and revue in United Kingdom and Australia from late 1920s until 1939. Played in farces, musicals and pantomimes in Australia. Entertained troops in Japan and Korea 1952.

Charles Norman appeared as a light comedian in many musical shows, including the first Australian productions of *White Horse Inn* in 1934 and *Anything Goes* in 1936. He formed a double act with Chick Arnold, and performed song-and-dance routines in suburban vaudeville theatres. Norman became a solo act and moved into revue and musical comedy for FULLERS' in the 1920s. In the late 1920s he teamed with Arnold again to play in variety in the United Kingdom. After performing in the London Hippodrome revue *Black and Blue* in 1939 he returned to Australia to star in *Charley's Aunt* by Brandon Thomas in Melbourne. He subsequently played this and other farces on national and country tours. He worked in pantomime and revue on the TIVOLI CIRCUIT. In Melbourne, he created the part of Wilton Chute in the musical THE HIGHWAYMAN in 1950, and appeared in the musical *Salad Days* at the St Martin's Theatre in 1950, in George Miller's presentation of *Uncle Tom's Cabin* at the Bowl Music Hall in 1962, and in *Waltzes of Vienna* at the Palais Theatre in 1968. ❦*Frank Van Straten*

writings
When Vaudeville Was King. Melbourne: Spectrum Publications 1984.

Northern Territory

Theatre generally developed along traditional lines in the Northern Territory until the 1970s, when it began to be influenced by the environment and cultural diversity of the territory and the use of unconventional venues. The first recorded theatrical event in the territory was in 1839, when European settlers at Port Essington, on the Cobourg Peninsula, staged a farce, *Cheap Living*, in a tin shed they dubbed the Victoria Theatre. The first in Darwin was in 1869 when the surveyors who had been sent from Adelaide to survey the town performed *Trial of Bardell and Pickwick* and J. M. Morton's *Box and Cox* in a prefabricated iron house. The main organiser of entertainment in early Darwin—settled as Palmerston in 1870—was the Palmerston Dramatic and Musical Society which performed regular mixed shows in the Town Hall from 1883 until early in the 20th century. The local entertainers were sometimes joined by visitors such as the Carandini Opera Company in 1881 and various POLLARD OPERA COMPANIES. The Town Hall site is now called 'the ruins', as a memorial to the damage done to Darwin by Cyclone Tracy in 1974, and in the dry season is used for outdoor productions, particularly of Shakespeare.

In the 1920s and 1930s entertainment focused on dance and musical revue rather than drama. After the Second World War amateur theatrical groups emerged in Alice Springs, Darwin, Katherine, Tennant Creek and other towns. More recently groups have sprung up in smaller places such as Nhulunbuy and Alyangula. Totem Theatre in Alice Springs and the Darwin Amateur Musical Comedy Society built 'tin shed' theatres, designed to suit the climate. The society, formed in 1950, gradually switched to drama and changed its name to Cavenagh Theatre Group.

The Darwin Theatre Group, established in 1959 to study and promote dramatic art, began with a production of ORIEL GRAY's play *Had We But World Enough*. It performed mainly at the Darwin Town Hall, the old Cavenagh Theatre and outdoors. In 1969 the Darwin Theatre Group saved Brown's Mart, a sandstone auction market built in 1885, from the bulldozer. By 1971 it had been converted to an intimate theatre. Now the permanent home of the group, it is one of the most versatile open-style theatres in Australia.

In 1970 ARTS COUNCIL funding enabled the Darwin Theatre Group to engage Bryan Nason to direct THE LEGEND OF KING O'MALLEY in the Cavenagh Theatre and a policy of short-term engagement of visiting directors was instituted. Nason returned in 1972 to direct the first production in Brown's Mart, condensed versions of *The Taming of the Shrew* and Aristophanes's *Lysistrata*.

Cyclone Tracy substantially damaged Brown's Mart and the Darwin Theatre Group, again homeless, performed wherever possible for 18 months. In 1977 the group appointed John Kesl from the NATIONAL INSTITUTE OF DRAMATIC ART as its first artistic director and administrator. By 1989 the group had become the Darwin Theatre Company with funding enabling it to maintain a full-time staff of four, including administrative and artistic directors, and to engage professional actors and other guest artists. Funding had been threatened in 1988 when the Northern Territory government established the State Theatre Company but this was disbanded after six months, and the Darwin Theatre Company resumed its place as the major semiprofessional adult theatre group in the territory. Since 1970 it has aimed to tour and serve the entire Northern Territory. It has transported equipment and performers by light aircraft to remote areas.

Corrugated Iron Youth Theatre, for Territorians aged from eight to 25 years, deals almost exclusively in original works, some commissioned. It also give priority to touring. In 1984 the Brown's Mart community-arts group in Darwin appointed Christine Bolt as the first full-time director of Corrugated Iron Youth Theatre. It also employs an administrator and engages visiting writers, tutors and choreographers. Brown's Mart has also promoted drama and dance amongst youngsters by initiating TIE/DIE (theatre-in-education/drama-in-education) in 1975 and the Kid's Convoy, a troupe of local and visiting performers which toured remote areas from 1979 to 1986, when both groups were disbanded. Jack Hibberd's *DIMBOOLA* was performed in Katherine in the early 1980s after participants (mostly from surrounding pastoral properties) had rehearsed over the School of the Air radio for weeks. They first met as a group only two days before the sellout performance. In 1978 the Darwin Community College Theatre Group was formed for performances by students. It became the Territory North Theatre Company, serving the Northern Territory University and the community for several years.

Specially-written Darwin Theatre Company productions have included Simon Hopkinson's *Occupied*, based on experiences in Cyclone Tracy, and his award-winning *Buffaloes Can't Fly*; and *Death at Balibo*, a moving play by Maria Alice Casimiro, Jose Monteiro and Graham Pitts about the killing of Australian television journalists in East Timor, written and presented in 1988 in association with the Timorese Association of the Northern Territory. In the same year, a group from Alice Springs toured the Northern Territory with performances of a locally written and produced rock opera, *Come Hell or High Water* by Barney Foran and Bob Sharp. In 1985 Anne Dunn directed a diverse group of nearly 100 women in writing and staging an original production, *Women's Own Work*, in Brown's Mart to mark the end of the Decade for Women.

Since the 1980s there has been a growth in productions by freelance artists based in the Northern Territory, including Bronwyn Calcutt's solo show *Disenchantment*; Gary Lee's *Keep Him My Country*, a Philippine–Larrakia love story; and Suzanne Spunner's *Overcome by Chlorine*, *Ingkata's Wife* and *Dragged Screaming to Paradise*. The last was staged as the opening production in the Darwin Performing Arts Centre's new Studio Theatre in 1994.

The influence of COMMUNITY THEATRE has resulted in original creations, including Neil Cameron's *Fire on the Water*, *Macbeth* in the Katherine Gorge and performances on the dry bed of the Todd River at Alice Springs. Representatives of the Aboriginal, Torres Strait Islands, Papua New Guinea and Philippine communities took part in *Diablo* in 1992. Since the late 1980s the people of Lajamanu, in the desert about 600 km southwest of Katherine, have conducted community theatre in association with Brown's Mart.

The Darwin Theatre Company began the year 1994 by touring Graham Pitts's *Emma* to Katherine, Tennant Creek and Alice Springs and ended it by celebrating 35 years of existence with a series of theatrical events staged in Darwin over two weeks. ❧*Barbara James*

Louis Nowra

Dramatist. Born 12 December 1950 in Melbourne. Began playwriting at La Mama Theatre, Melbourne, 1973. Resident playwright of Sydney Theatre Company 1979–80. Associate director of Lighthouse Company (Adelaide) 1982–83. Has written 23 plays and five translations of European classics, plus novels, radio and television plays, films and opera libretti. Nephew of dramatist Bob Herbert.

Louis Nowra came to prominence, after experimental work at LA MAMA THEATRE, with *Inner Voices* at the Nimrod Theatre in Sydney in 1977. It revealed an original dramatic style and an outlook that has been called international. It has been extensively produced in Australia and overseas. Plays by Nowra have been performed throughout Australia and in Europe, the USA and New Zealand.

Responses to his plays have sometimes been sharply divided. They explore the interior world of dream, vision and nightmare, and its interaction with the public faces of societies in conflict. His style is non-naturalistic, using an epic scenic structure with rapid alternations between tragedy and farce, usually with significant musical content. Poetically treated fables, cultural colonialism, outsiders and the persistence of the past in the present make Nowra's theatre particularly expressive of Australia.

His early plays from *Inner Voices* to *The Precious Woman* (1980) are historical fantasies set in other countries, although they deal with issues relevant to Australia. His works from *Inside the Island* (1980) are set here, dealing either obliquely or directly with contemporary predicaments, especially the continuing effects of historical trauma —colonisation of Aboriginal land, class oppression, fascism, Gallipoli, Vietnam and the radioactive desert left at Maralinga (SA) by British nuclear tests in the 1950s. *The Golden Age* (1985) is a striking culmination of these concerns, juxtaposing the Aboriginal and convict past with Australian experiences in Europe in the Second World War. *The Summer of the Aliens* (1992) and *Così* (1992) are semi-autobiographical comedies in which a bewildered young Lewis learns about life and theatre. *Radiance* (1993) and *Crow* (1994) continue the development of Aboriginal stories begun in *Capricornia* (1988), adapted from Xavier Herbert's 1938 novel. His satiric farce *The Temple* (1993) charts the career of a 1980s entrepreneur.

Nowra worked closely with REX CRAMPHORN, who directed *Visions* in Sydney in 1978 and *The Golden Age* in Melbourne in 1985; they collaborated in writing. RICHARD WHERRETT directed *The Precious Woman* and Nowra's translation of Edmond Rostand's *Cyrano de Bergerac* for the SYDNEY THEATRE COMPANY in 1980. NEIL ARMFIELD directed *Inside the Island* for the Nimrod Theatre Company in 1980, *Spellbound* for the Lighthouse Company in Adelaide in 1983 and *The Golden Age* at the NATIONAL INSTITUTE OF DRAMATIC ART in 1986, and was an associate director with Nowra in Lighthouse. The artistic director of Lighthouse, JIM SHARMAN, directed the premieres of *Lulu*—Nowra's adaptation of plays by Frank Wedekind—in 1981, *Royal Show* in 1982 and *Sunrise* in 1983. Directors of recent premieres include Kingston Anderson, Rosalba Clemente, Adam Cook, Egil Kipste, BRUCE MYLES and Nadia Tass.

Nowra likes to integrate musical content into his plays and Sarah de Jong has written extensively for his plays. He adapted *Inner Voices* as an opera with the composer Brian Howard and wrote the libretto of Howard's *Whitsunday*. Nowra has frequently written for specific interpreters, including Kylie Belling, JUDY DAVIS, Melita Jurisic, KATE FITZPATRICK, LYDIA MILLER, ROBYN NEVIN, JUSTINE SAUNDERS and DINAH SHEARING. Male actors who have created major Nowra roles include JOHN BELL, Laurence Clifford, JOHN GADEN, TONY SHELDON and JOHN WOOD. ❦*Veronica Kelly*

published plays
Albert Names Edward. Sydney: Currency Press 1983.
Capricornia (1988). Sydney: Currency Press 1988, revised 1992.
Così (1992). Sydney: Currency Press 1992, revised 1994.
Crow (1994). Sydney: Currency Press 1994.
The Golden Age (1985). Sydney: Currency Press 1985.
Inner Voices (1977). Sydney: Currency Press 1983.
Inside the Island (1980). Sydney: Currency Press 1981.
The Precious Woman (1980). Sydney: Currency Press 1981.
Radiance (1993). Sydney: Currency Press 1993.
The Song Room (1980). Sydney: Currency Press 1983.
The Summer of the Aliens (1992). Currency Press 1994.
Sunrise (1983). Sydney: Currency Press/State Theatre Company of South Australia 1983.
The Temple (1993). Sydney: Currency Press 1993.
Visions (1978). Sydney: Currency Press 1979.

other writings
At the crossroads. *Australasian Drama Studies* 2/2 (Brisbane 1984).
The shrinking vision. *Island Magazine* 39 (Hobart 1989).
Translating for the Australian stage. *Australian Literary Studies* 10/3 (1982).

further reading
CARROLL, DENNIS. *Australian Contemporary Drama*. Sydney: Currency Press 1995.
GILBERT, HELEN. Post-colonial grotesques—Re-membering the body in Louis Nowra's *Visions* and *The Golden Age*. *SPAN* 36/2 (Perth 1993).
KELLY, VERONICA. In *Contemporary Dramatists* (ed. K. A. Berney) 5th edn. London: St James Press 1993.
KELLY, VERONICA. 'Nowt more outcasting'—Utopian myth in Louis Nowra's *The Golden Age*. *A Sense of Exile* (ed. Bruce Bennett). Perth: Centre for Studies in Australian Literature 1988.
LITSON, JO. A newer Nowra. *24 Hours* (September 1993). Interview.
MAKEHAM, PAUL. The black hole of our history. *Canadian Theatre Review* 74 (Guelph, Ontario, 1993). Interview.

RIDGMAN, JEREMY. Interview—Louis Nowra, Stephen Sewell and Neil Armfield talk to Jeremy Ridgman. *Australasian Drama Studies* 1/2 (Brisbane 1983).
TURCOTTE, GERRY. 'The circle is burst'—eschatological discourse in Louis Nowra's *Sunrise* and *The Golden Age*. *Australasian Drama Studies* 11 (Brisbane, October 1987).

Russell Oakes

Dramatist. Born 1910. Officer in the Australian Army. Served in New Guinea in Second World War. Wrote stage and radio plays, short stories and verse. Died 15 June 1952 in Sydney.

Russell Oakes is most likely to be remembered for *Enduring as the Camphor Tree*, which has been described as a Chinese play written and produced through Western eyes. After the premiere by the Melbourne Little Theatre Company on 12 October 1946 the Melbourne *Sun News–Pictorial* said Oakes had 'introduced humour and pathos delicately into the quaint formal speech of his characters, yet manages to keep the dialogue well within the reach of audiences unused to Chinese drama'. The play toured Victorian country centres, and was performed in Adelaide in 1947 and Perth in 1950. It has since been performed particularly by school groups. Oakes's other published play, *Judgement*, is a one-act work intended for use in schools. It draws on his wartime experiences. At the outbreak of war in 1939 he was a soldier stationed in Western Australia. After serving as an instructor he was sent to New Guinea, where he contracted a disease that was to end his life. ❦*Joan Maslen*

published plays
Enduring as the Camphor Tree. Melbourne University Press 1967.
Judgement. Sydney: Fenton and Oakes c.1950.

Barry Oakley

Critic, dramatist. Born 24 February 1931 in Melbourne. Educated at University of Melbourne. Taught in secondary schools in Victoria 1955–62 and at Royal Melbourne Institute of Technology 1963. Two years in advertising. Successes as short-story writer and novelist. Prominent as playwright in Melbourne in 1970s. Journalist for Department of Trade in Melbourne 1966–73 and London 1974–75. Arts Council of Australia fellowship 1974. Moved to Sydney 1976. Australia Council Fellowship 1977–80. Headed writing workshop at Australian Film, Radio and Television School (Sydney) 1982. Canada–Australia Literary Award 1982. National theatre critic for *National Times* and *Times on Sunday* 1986–88. Literary editor of *Australian* 1988–.

Barry Oakley's early plays for the AUSTRALIAN PERFORMING GROUP at the Pram Factory in Melbourne, along with those of JACK HIBBERD, JOHN ROMERIL and DAVID WILLIAMSON, helped to create an audience for indigenous theatre. The first plays Oakley had performed were two short comedies, *Witzenhausen, Where Are You?* at the LA MAMA THEATRE shortly after its opening in mid-1967, and *At the Desk of Eugene Flockhart*. In its early years La Mama staged other short plays by Oakley, including *A Lesson in English* and *It's a Chocolate World*. Oakley's first full-length play was *The Feet of Daniel Mannix*, a hit with audiences at the Pram Factory in 1971. It is a richly inventive comedy, with parodic and revue elements, about Daniel Mannix, the long-lived Irish-born Archbishop of Melbourne, who played a dominant part in Australia for more than half a century. This was followed in 1973 by *Beware of Imitations*, another biographical play with a strong parodic vein. Its thinly disguised hero was the long-serving Liberal prime minister, Robert Menzies.

The third of Oakley's plays to have its premiere at the Pram Factory was *Bedfellows* in 1975. It is a sharp-edged marital comedy and, like *The Feet of Daniel Mannix* and *Beware of Imitations*, it featured the gifted comic actor, MAX GILLIES. He was also the star of Oakley's fourth and last play for the Pram Factory, *The Ship's Whistle* in 1978. In dealing with Mannix and Menzies, Oakley had taken giants of the Australian political scene and wittily cut them down to size, but this time he took a nonentity from the goldrush period—Richard 'Orion' Horne, a failed playwright, rotten poet and low-wattage literary luminary—and built him into an extravagant man of action in the romantic mould.

Marsupials, a three-character domestic comedy, was first produced by the MELBOURNE THEATRE COMPANY in 1979, while *Scanlan*, a short, witty monologue by a boozy English lecturer, had its premiere in 1980 at the Nimrod Theatre in Sydney before going on a highly successful national tour. This was Oakley's last play of significance. ❦*Leonard Radic*

published plays
Bedfellows (1975). Sydney: Currency–Methuen 1975.
Beware of Imitations (1973). Melbourne: Yackandandah 1985.
The Feet of Daniel Mannix (1971). Sydney: Angus and Robertson 1975.
The Great God Mogadon (broadcast 1987). Brisbane: University of Queensland Press 1980.
A Lesson in English (1969). Sydney: Currency Methuen 1976.
Marsupials (1979). Brisbane: University of Queensland Press 1981.
Politics (1979). Brisbane: University of Queensland Press 1981.
The Ship's Whistle (1978). Melbourne: Yackandandah 1985.
Witzenhausen, Where Are You? (1967). Brisbane: University of Queensland Press 1970 in *Six One-Act Plays*.

other writings
Scribbling in the Dark. Brisbane: University of Queensland 1985. Critical writings and journalism.

Octagon Theatre

Theatre at University of Western Australia, Perth, opened 1 February 1969, seating 600. Architect: Peter Parkinson.

The name of the Octagon Theatre describes its form within and without. Five blocks of seating fan around a thrust stage—the first in Australia—which has a proscenium arch behind it. Part or all of the stage can be removed to uncover an orchestra pit. One of Perth's most frequently used venues, the theatre succeeds for a wide range of drama, opera, dance, chamber and orchestral music because of its versatile performing space, its excellent sightlines and acoustics, and its sound and lighting equipment.

The theatre is also a large and acoustically fine lecture hall. This was a primary purpose, because of requirements for federal government funding, when the University of Western Australia decided to build a multi-use theatre. Allen Edwards, professor of English, had promoted the NEW FORTUNE THEATRE at the university and he pressed for the new theatre. PHILIP PARSONS, a member of his department, and KATHARINE BRISBANE, theatre critic of the *West Australian*, advocated PETER PARKINSON of Perth as architect. The university announced his appointment on 25 March 1965. The theatre committee was divided over his brief, so a consultant was sought. At Parsons's suggestion, the English director Tyrone Guthrie came to Perth in July 1965 for consultation with Parkinson and the university's own architect. As a result, Parkinson developed the Octagon. It opened with the MELBOURNE THEATRE COMPANY's production of *Henry IV—part 1*.

In 1969 AARNE NEEME was appointed director of a loosely formed company with three professional actors—Arthur Dignam, JOHN GADEN and Michael Rolfe—and various experienced amateurs. Its first productions were *Mandragola* by Niccolò Machiavelli, *Rosencrantz and Guildenstern are Dead* by Tom Stoppard and *The Man of Mode* by George Etherege. Later offerings included Neeme's production of *Othello* in repertoire with *Twelfth Night* directed by JEANA BRADLEY.

The Festival of Perth has been a frequent client of the Octagon ever since its opening. Successes at the Octagon include ROBYN ARCHER in her *A Star is Torn*, Steve Berkoff in his adaption of Edgar Allan Poe's *Fall of the House of Usher*, and Roy Dotrice in John Evelyn's *Brief Lives*. The Old Tote Theatre Company from Sydney appeared in Tyrone Guthrie's productions of *All's Well that Ends Well* and Sophocles's *Oedipus Rex* in 1973.

Perth's National Theatre Company gave the world premiere of Elizabeth Backhouse's *Mirage* under Raymond Omodei's direction at the Octagon in 1972. Omodei also directed Oscar Wilde's *The Importance of Being Earnest* in 1980 and *King Lear* and *As You Like It* in 1981 for the Mason–Miller Theatre Company. Andrew Ross presented Jack Davis's *The Dreamers* for the National Theatre Company in 1983, the musical *Bran Nue Dae* for the Western Australian Theatre Company in 1990 and *Twelfth Night* for the Black Swan Theatre Company in 1991. ❦*Maurice Jones*

further reading
The Architectural Work of Peter Parkinson. Perth: His Majesty's Theatre 1975.
The Octagon Theatre, University of Western Australia. *The Architect* (Perth) June 1969.

John O'Donoghue

Dramatist. Born 5 August 1929 in Newcastle (NSW). Educated at Balmain Teacher's College and University of Newcastle. Taught English and mathematics in schools. At Newcastle College of Advanced Education as lecturer in English from 1972, director of community programs from 1982. Sydney Critics' Circle Award for most significant contribution to theatre 1985.

Newcastle's finest and best-loved playwright, John O'Donoghue deserves a wider audience. He fashions plays from the preoccupations that have shaped the history of Newcastle, documenting the minutiae of life to reveal the universal drives behind people's behaviour. His finest and most successful play, *Essington Lewis: I Am Work* is a dynamic epic drama. It tells about a leading force in the development of the Newcastle steelworks, whose motto was 'I am work'. O'Donoghue sets Essington Lewis against a backdrop of the industrial history of Australia in the first half of this century, and uses the techniques developed by Joan Littlewood and Bertolt Brecht to create a powerful piece of total theatre. Since its premiere in Newcastle in 1981 it has been performed in all capital cities except Hobart, and in England at Leeds University in 1984. A production at the Stables Theatre in Sydney in 1985 won O'Donoghue the Sydney Critics' Circle Award.

O'Donoghue's first major play was *A Happy and Holy Occasion*, a domestic drama with fatalistic overtones, in which he worked out preoccupations with his Irish Catholic upbringing. Set on the eve of 12-year-old Christy's admission to a seminary, the play explores sexual repression and domestic violence through one night in the life of a working-class Newcastle family. *A Happy and Holy Occasion* has been produced in Adelaide, Melbourne, Perth and Sydney since the premiere by the HUNTER VALLEY THEATRE COMPANY in 1976. It returned to Newcastle in 1986 in a production starring HELEN MORSE.

Apart from his Irish ancestry, O'Donoghue's other obsession is the writer Louis Stone. His play *Jonah* is an adaptation of Stone's 1911 novel of the same title and his latest work, *Abbie and Lou, Norman and Rose* is about interrelationships between Stone and Norman Lindsay and their wives. The major works of O'Donoghue, which have been championed by the directors TERENCE CLARKE and AARNE NEEME, also include *In the Field Where They Buried Peter Pan* (1982). ❧Felicity Biggins

published plays
Abbie and Lou, Norman and Rose. Sydney: Currency Press 1993.
Essington Lewis: I Am Work (1981). Sydney: Currency Press 1987.
A Happy and Holy Occasion (1982). Sydney: Currency Press 1987.
other writing
Essington Lewis. Sydney: Currency Press 1992. Resource material for teachers and students.
further reading
Brady, Veronica. *Playing Catholic*. Sydney: Currency Press 1991.

George Ogilvie

Actor, director. Born 5 March 1933 at Goulburn (NSW). Brought up in Canberra. Worked with Canberra Repertory Society from childhood. Acted in touring repertory in United Kingdom 1953–56. Returned to Australia 1956. Trust Players. Union Theatre Repertory Company (Melbourne). Studied mime with Jacques Lecoq in Paris from 1960. Formed Les Comédiens-Mimes de Paris and toured Europe; performed at Edinburgh Festival. Taught at Central School of Drama (London). Held actors' workshops at Stratford-upon-Avon for Royal Shakespeare Company. Returned to Australia as associate director of Union Theatre Repertory Company 1965. Artistic director of South Australian Theatre Company (Adelaide) 1972-1976. Freelance director of drama, opera, ballet, television and film since 1976. Melbourne critics' award for best director 1966 (*The Knack* by Ann Jellicoe), 1967 (*The Royal Hunt of the Sun* by Peter Shaffer), 1968 (*A Flea in Her Ear* by Georges Feydeau). Australian Artist Creative Fellowship 1994–96.

George Ogilvie's career has embraced most of the performing arts and his ability to elicit sub-textual references from varied and difficult works has established him as one of Australia's foremost directors. He introduced new interpretations of classics and his training as a mime artist and a teacher contributed immensely to the development of the Union Theatre Repertory Company (later the MELBOURNE THEATRE COMPANY) and the South Australian Theatre Company (later STATE THEATRE). His directing of 23 plays in six years for the former company and his work with every other major Australian company have impacted greatly upon two generations of playwrights, directors and actors. Ogilvie is rare among Australian directors in having been able to work with a permanent company on a series of plays. The results of his training with the Melbourne Theatre Company were quickly evident in his landmark productions of Arthur Wing Pinero's *The Magistrate* and Anton Chekhov's *Three Sisters*—the company's first Chekhov—in 1969. His developmental priorities made his stay in South Australia an uneasy period. He spent months exercising his ensemble behind closed doors, which caused anxiety to those eager to see the company on stage. He presented some fine work, however, notably *The Comedy of Errors* in 1973 and Oliver Goldsmith's *She Stoops to Conquer* in 1974, and he was a major influence upon his dramaturgical assistant RODNEY FISHER as a director. Ogilvie has been described as an 'actor's director' and this is illustrated by his fast-moving, flowing style, which to some extent anticipated trends to 'cinematic' play construction. He moved into television in 1982 and began directing feature films in 1984, but he has continued to work in theatre. In 1987 he directed *Pericles* for the SYDNEY THEATRE COMPANY and in 1991 *Twelfth Night* for Q THEATRE at Penrith (NSW). ❧Rémy Davison.

further reading
HERBERT, IAN (ed.). *Who's Who in the Theatre* 17th edn. Detroit (USA): Gale Research 1981.
SUMNER, JOHN. *Recollections at Play—A life in Australian theatre*. Melbourne: University Press 1993.

Old Tote Theatre Company

Professional theatre company in Sydney, founded in 1962 by National Institute of Dramatic Art. Independent 1969. Closed 1978. **venues** 1962-69 Old Tote Theatre. 1969-73 Parade Theatre (University of NSW). 1973-78 Sydney Opera House. 1974-78 Seymour Theatre Centre. **artistic directors** 1962-65 Robert Quentin. 1965-68 Robin Lovejoy and Tom Brown. 1969-74 Robin Lovejoy. 1975-78 Bill Redmond. 1978 Robert Helpmann. **first production** *The Cherry Orchard* by Anton Chekhov, 1963, Old Tote Theatre. Cast: John Bell, Sophie Stewart. Director: Robert Quentin. **landmark productions** *Who's Afraid of Virginia Woolf?* by Edward Albee 1964, *King Oedipus* by Sophocles 1970, *The Resistible Rise of Arturo Ui* by Bertolt Brecht 1971.

During a life of 16 years the Old Tote Theatre Company became the leading professional company in NSW and one of the foremost in Australia. It was the first fully professional company to present the classics, as well as Australian plays and innovative work. It developed the careers of a generation of young actors, directors and designers. The NATIONAL INSTITUTE OF DRAMATIC ART set it up in 1962 as a professional company to produce classical plays and modern writing from Australia and overseas, and to provide an arena for young artists. The company staged plays in a converted army recreation hall, which became the Old Tote Theatre, on the campus of the University of NSW. Other facilities were in buildings that had once been part of the Kensington racecourse, including the old totalisator. Roger Covell, writing in the *Sydney Morning Herald*, suggested the name Old Tote in 1962 on the ground that it would remind people that all theatre was a gamble.

NIDA ran the Old Tote until 1969. NIDA staff directed most plays and students undertook backstage and front-of-house duties as part of their training. The first season comprised plays by Anton Chekhov, Eugène Ionesco, Max Frisch, Shakespeare and J. M. Synge. The project enlisted Sydney's best actors, including JOHN BELL, GORDON CHATER, RON HADDRICK, BRIAN JAMES, NEIL FITZPATRICK, REG LIVERMORE, GWEN PLUMB, Sophie Stewart and ANNA VOLSKA. Audience demand exceeded seating capacity. The seasons were initially underwritten by the AUSTRALIAN ELIZABETHAN THEATRE TRUST and later subsidised by the Australian Council for the Arts and the NSW government.

In 1963, the Old Tote embarked on a policy of steady expansion that resulted in some of the most exciting developments in Australian theatre but eventually brought about the company's downfall. In 1963, it inaugurated Sydney's first lunchtime theatre at the PALACE THEATRE in the city, where in three weeks 7000 people saw the present writer's production of *The American Dream* by Edward Albee. Next year his production of Albee's *Who's Afraid of Virginia Woolf?* was transferred to the Palace Theatre and began an Australasian tour that extended over two years. Touring became a regular activity of the company.

In 1966, the company converted an old suburban church in adjacent Randwick into the JANE STREET THEATRE, where new writers would be encouraged and experimental theatre by Australian and foreign playwrights would be presented. In 1969, the Old Tote company separated from NIDA. It moved from the 'old tin shed' into the larger Parade Theatre at the University of NSW and was asked to assume the responsibilities of a state theatre company by the Australian Council for the Arts. There was further expansion in 1973, when the NSW government invited the Old Tote company to become the major producer for the Drama Theatre at the new SYDNEY OPERA HOUSE, in addition to giving a yearly season at the Parade Theatre and making regular tours to country towns and other states. The following year saw the York Theatre in the Seymour Theatre Centre at the University of Sydney become the company's third major production venue. At this high point the Old Tote's fortunes began to decline. By 1978, it was all over. Three theatres overstretched the company's financial and artistic resources, and there was uncertainty in its direction. Neither state nor federal subsidiser was prepared to support the company through a crisis and it went into liquidation. It had created a wealth of talent, experience and theatrical knowledge that was passed on and put to good use by the SYDNEY THEATRE COMPANY when it arose from the ashes of the Old Tote in 1979. *John Clark*

further reading
SOUTH, JOSEPHINE and HARRY SCOTT. *Ten on the Tote*. Sydney: Old Tote Theatre 1973.

Old Vic Theatre Company

English professional dramatic company. Toured Australia 1948, 1955 and 1961.

In 1948 the Old Vic Theatre Company from London, led by Laurence Olivier and his wife Vivien Leigh, burst upon Australian audiences with the force of revelation and gave impetus to the rising demand for a NATIONAL THEATRE. Classical and serious modern drama of such quality had not been seen in Australia since Sybil Thorndike toured her famous Saint Joan and a large classical and modern repertoire with Lewis Casson in 1932. The Old Vic Theatre was famous from 1914 for its Shakespeare seasons under the management of Lilian Baylis. It became the acknowledged centre of classical excellence in the English theatre during the 1930s, when it was supported by a generation of such brilliant rising talents as Peggy Ashcroft, John Gielgud and Laurence Olivier. War damage closed the theatre in 1940 but the Old Vic Theatre Company carried on the policies, high standards and name of the theatre, performing in various West End theatres and on tour.

The 40-strong Old Vic company opened its first Australian tour to immediate and huge acclaim in Perth on 20 March 1948 at the Capitol Theatre—a cavernous cinema requiring formidable projection—with the premiere performance of a new production by Olivier of R. B. Sheridan's *The School for Scandal*. Leigh played Lady Teazle to Olivier's Sir Peter. Others in the cast included Peter Cushing and Terence Morgan as Joseph and Charles Surface and Mercia Swinburne as Lady Sneerwell. In the larger eastern capitals Olivier also performed his electrifying Richard III, first seen in London in 1944, and revived his 1945 production of Thornton Wilder's *The Skin of Our Teeth*. In the latter Leigh repeated her delectable performance as Sabina the maid, this time to Olivier's Antrobus.

Extraordinary popular enthusiasm greeted the company throughout its entire tour. The Oliviers were accorded the status of visiting royalty, expected to attend endless official and unofficial receptions, and even invited to review the troops. Over seven gruelling months they gave 179 performances in Australia and New Zealand to a total audience of more than 300 000, grossing £226 318 at the box office, and astonishing the British Council, their backer, with return of £42 000—remarkable sums at the time. A prime aim of the tour had been to counter the manifest decline throughout the war of British prestige in Australia and New Zealand, Olivier, Leigh and the Old Vic among them more than fulfilled every hope. The tour was managed by D. D. O'Connor Pty Ltd, a company of which BENJAMIN FULLER was chairman.

The astonishing popular success of the tour was not, of course, generated entirely by enthusiasm for classical theatre. As the company immediately noticed at the Perth premiere, the audience consisted largely of people who appeared never to have gone to theatre before. Some of these were doing their middle-class duty by official culture at its most prestigious. Many of those who queued patiently round several blocks for tickets and all those who crowded the streets wherever the Oliviers went, had come to see in the flesh two famous film stars. All were certainly drawn by the sheer glamour of sumptuously mounted star theatre after the austere war years. But beyond all such explanations was a huge groundswell of response by a theatre-starved public to the English-speaking world's finest theatre company led by a man already hailed by some as the greatest actor of his day and now at the height of his powers. In a community acutely aware of cultural isolation and too often subjected to second-rate 'star' imports in third-rate commercial pieces, it was a nice change.

The significance of the tour for the Australian theatre lay not so much in any immediate impact on the industry as in a heightened cultural awareness. The industry—effectively J. C. WILLIAMSON'S—was concerned with little beyond musicals and similar lightweight entertainment and, although the unexpected box-office success of the Old Vic encouraged Williamson's to venture into quality drama, with tours by the Shakespeare Memorial Theatre Company from Stratford-upon-Avon in 1949 and 1953, the future of the Australian theatre lay elsewhere. More important was the influence of the Old Vic's dazzling style and standards on rising young talents in the serious amateur and semi-professional theatre, such as ROBIN LOVEJOY, who were soon to pioneer around the country a new professional theatre. But most important of all was the effect of the Old Vic on the opinion-makers—it changed expectations of what Australian theatre should be.

Change had long been on the way, perhaps even since the rise of the amateur repertory movement and the work of GREGAN MCMAHON. But the embattled war years had brought to Australia, as to the United Kingdom, a heightened awareness of cultural values. In Britain the Old Vic had in its way been a spearhead of national purpose and national pride. In Australia it was left to the TIVOLI CIRCUIT to become in its way a rallying point for national sentiment as the dearth of imports at last gave Australian stars their proper role. But the Old Vic's kind of drama was to be found only in the dedicated little theatres, where the country's finest talent—'brilliant performance in as expert a production as could be imagined', noted Olivier of PETER FINCH in the Mercury Mobile Players' production of Molière's *The Imaginary Invalid*—was often to be found but sheer achievement must always be restricted by limited resources. Just how limited those resources had been was now painfully revealed by such delights as Cecil Beaton's superb evocation of the 18th-century theatre, in a series of huge line engravings of Georgian houses flown in as the brilliantly stylish figures of *The School for Scandal* moved to music of Handel. Amateur theatre, however gifted, was not enough. The rising demand from the increasingly influential amateur movement for a national theatre of international standard was powerfully endorsed.

Homeward bound, Olivier told his companions 'We are the first National Theatre company', and in the current British debate about a national theatre the Old Vic offered an obvious model, though it was another 15 years before its theatre became the first home of the National Theatre. The Old Vic company's influence in shaping Australian aspirations was more equivocal. Inevitably the program it implied was classical and international as seen through English rather than Australian eyes, and middle-class deference to the British as cultural arbiters could only be reinforced. It followed all too naturally that in the year after the tour an English director, Tyrone Guthrie, would arrive at the invitation of the federal government to report on the case for an Australian national theatre, that subsequently Englishmen should head the AUSTRALIAN ELIZABETHAN THEATRE TRUST and the NATIONAL INSTITUTE OF DRAMATIC ART and that state theatre companies in Melbourne, Sydney, Perth and Brisbane should all have English founding directors. Today, however, when the pendulum has swung so far in the opposite direction, the Old Vic tour 1948 is worthy of recall as a reminder of the richness of the Australian theatre's British classical heritage and the need for new assessment and appreciation in a post-colonial world.

Ironically, during Olivier's absence from London to carry the banner of British classical theatre to Australasia he was removed from the directorate of the Old Vic, which reopened in 1950. The great days were over. In 1955 ROBERT HELPMANN returned home with an Old Vic company to give Australians a rare and curious opportunity to see the great dancer playing his role as star actor opposite Katharine Hepburn in a Shakespeare repertoire. And in 1961 the Old Vic, making its final appearance in Australia, brought back Vivien Leigh with an indifferent company to star in *Twelfth Night* and two plays translated from French, *The Lady of the Camellias* by Alexandre Dumas *fils* and *Duel of Angels* by Jean Giraudoux, all directed by Helpmann. Sadly, neither company could revive the glories of 1948. ❦*Philip Parsons*

further reading
HOLDEN, ANTHONY. *Olivier*. London: Weidenfeld and Nicholson 1988.
ROBERTS, PETER. *The Old Vic Story*. London: Allen 1976.
WILLIAMS, HARCOURT. *The Old Vic Saga*. London: Winchester 1949.

Max Oldaker

Actor, singer. Born 17 December 1907 near Launceston (Tas.). Toured Australia and Far East as tenor with Westminster Glee Singers from 1930. Went to London April 1931. Toured England in Gilbert and Sullivan with D'Oyly Carte Opera Company 1932. Studied at Royal Academy of Music 1935–36. Returned to Australia 1939. Contracted to J. C. Williamson's 1940–47, singing leads in operetta. Shakespearean tour with John Alden Company 1951–52. Philip Street revues in Sydney 1955–56. Understudied Rex Harrison in *My Fair Lady* at Theatre Royal, Drury Lane (London) 1958–59. Stage, radio and television work in Sydney, Melbourne and Tasmania. Died February 1972 in Launceston.

Charm, good looks, a spirited tenor voice and stylish ease of acting won Max Oldaker tremendous popularity in J. C. WILLIAMSON'S productions during the 1940s and the title of 'the last of the matinee idols'. The quality of his voice was recognised when he sang the leading role of Walther in Richard Wagner's *Die Meistersinger von Nürnberg*, conducted by John Barbirolli, for the Royal Academy of Music in London in 1935. Next year he won a prize awarded annually to the academy's finest pianist-singer by Arnold Bax, the Master of the King's Music, to encourage musicianship in singers. The London representative of J. C. Williamson's, Nevin Tait showed interest in Oldaker's skills, especially when Noël Coward wrote the juvenile singing lead in *Operette* for him in 1938. At the onset of the Second World War, Oldaker returned to Australia and began playing leading roles in Gilbert and Sullivan operettas for the Firm. In 1942 he sang the leading role of Eisenstein in *Die Fledermaus*, and next year he played opposite GLADYS MONCRIEFF in the non-singing role of the bandit chieftain Baldasarre in *The Maid of the Mountains*. Moncrieff and Oldaker were an immensely successful combination and *The Merry Widow* was revived for them in 1943.

Oldaker's enormous following reached its peak when he played the Red Shadow in *The Desert Song* in 1945, opposite Joy Beattie. They resumed their partnership in *Rose-Marie* in 1946. Next year Oldaker played the lead in *Gay Rosalinda*, a new English adaptation of *Die Fledermaus*. *The Dancing Years* followed. Then in mid-1947 J. C. Williamson's had nothing to offer the star who had filled its theatres around Australia and New Zealand for more than seven years.

Oldaker toured Australia with the JOHN ALDEN COMPANY in 1951–52. His Bassanio in *The Merchant of Venice* and a stylish Oberon were notable. In satirical PHILLIP STREET REVUES in Sydney he sent himself up as the Red Shadow. An overwhelming ambition to play Professor Higgins when J. C. Williamson's presented *My Fair Lady* in Australia took him to London when casting for the Drury Lane production was due. He auditioned so successfully for the librettist Alan Jay Lerner and the director Moss Hart that he was made understudy to Rex Harrison and given the role of Zoltan Karpathy. He played the lead to critical acclaim several times when Harrison was ill. Despite this, he was passed over for the Australian production in favour of Robin Bailey, an English import. Oldaker was told he had been associated with too many old-fashioned musicals.

He played for Williamson's again as a flamboyant old actor in *Half a Sixpence* in Melbourne in 1967. By then he lived mainly in Tasmania, writing musical criticism for the *Launceston Examiner*, coaching young singers, and appearing on radio and television. ❦*Richard Lane*

further reading
BEVAN, IAN. *The Story of the Theatre Royal*. Sydney: Currency Press 1993.
OSBORNE, CHARLES. *Max Oldaker*. London: Michael O'Mara 1988.

Maggie Oliver

Actor. Born 14 December 1844 in Sydney. Joined Redfern Dramatic Society 1862. Turned professional c.1866. Acted in NSW country towns. Returned to Sydney 1868. Married John Edward King 21 March 1869. Later divorced. Won little notice after 1888. Died of liver cirrhosis 21 May 1892 in Sydney.

A comic actor, Maggie Oliver played character roles of all kinds. Critics pointed to her ability to breathe life into even the most wooden of farcical parts. From her earliest work at the Redfern Dramatic Society, which claimed to stage plays 'of a high-class character', she was known for excellence in Irish comic parts and she impressed audiences with her lively sense of comedy. Her favourite part was Paddy Miles in *The Limerick Boy*, a popular comedy.

Touring helped her to develop a rapport with audiences that characterised her work. A fellow player in amateur theatricals, W. J. HOLLOWAY suggested that she and others should form a professional company to tour the goldfields and country towns. What happened next is unclear but in 1866 Oliver was engaged as principal comedienne by the Princess Theatres of Forbes and Grenfell (NSW). By 1868 she was performing at the Royal Victoria Theatre in Sydney and she became well established as a character actor, known for her extraordinary ability to change her voice and appearance. She also played principal boys in pantomime in Melbourne and performed extensively in Queensland after meeting the actor–manager MORTON TAVARES in 1871. She acted at the opening of his Queensland Theatre in Brisbane on 21 April 1874.

Oliver received the most consistent critical acclaim in Sydney. She moved from the Theatre Royal, which was dominated by visiting stars, to the Theatre Royal Adelphi, which specialised in contemporary sensation dramas. She became celebrated in the title-role of Dion Boucicault's *Arrah-na-Pogue*. She was associated with the playwright WALTER COOPER and the actors Charles and Clarrie Burford.

In later years she played low comedy roles, supporting GEORGE DARRELL and others. ❦*Helen Musa*

further reading
VAN DER POORTEN, HELEN. Maggie Oliver. *Australian Dictionary of Biography* 5. Melbourne University Press 1974.

Dennis Olsen AO

Actor, director, singer. Born 28 February 1938 in Adelaide. Trained as pianist. Joint winner of ABC National Concerto Competition 1959. Acted in premiere of Patrick White's *The Ham Funeral* 1961. Graduated from National Institute of Dramatic Art (Sydney) 1962. Leading actor with Melbourne Theatre Company 1967–69, Old Tote Theatre Company (Sydney), State Theatre Company of South Australia (Adelaide) and Sydney Theatre Company. Erik Kuttner Award 1972 (*The Cherry Orchard* by Anton Chekhov). AO 1987.

A connoisseur of, and specialist in, musical theatre and a fine general actor, Olsen has a technical command and lightness of touch that have made him a leading stage presence in this country. Slim of build, Dennis Olsen has a demeanour of great economy and elegance of gesture. He has done much to continue the popularity of Noël Coward, Terence Rattigan and other luminaries of Shaftesbury Avenue. He has also contributed to the revival of interest in European operetta, particularly the works of Imre Kálmán, whose *Countess Maritza* and *The Czardas Princess* he has directed for the State Opera of South Australia.

His early work for the MELBOURNE THEATRE COMPANY was chiefly dramatic but showed the promise of his developing style in roles like the 89-year-old Solomon in Arthur Miller's *The Price*. 'He takes the script whizzing to its limits and beyond with a character of high, fragile wit, confident, unexpected, which engages the affections of the audience from the first skip of his shaky gait', said the *Australian*. Olsen is an exemplary and widely loved performer of GILBERT AND SULLIVAN. After performing the patter roles in *HMS Pinafore*, *Iolanthe* and *Pirates of Penzance* for the Australian Opera in 1969 he was invited to join the D'Oyly Carte Opera Company in England. On return to Australia he performed in *Patience* and *The Gondoliers* for the Australian Opera. He has directed productions of *HMS Pinafore* and *The Gondoliers*. In 1990 he toured his solo show *A Song to Sing O*, based on the D'Oyly Carte singer John Reed.

Olsen has starred and toured in the musicals *Big River* and THE VENETIAN TWINS and he played the MC in *Cabaret* for the STATE THEATRE Company of South Australia in 1991. On the legitimate stage, he toured with Googie Withers in *The Cherry Orchard* and Oscar Wilde's *An Ideal Husband*. His style and his pianistic gifts made him ideal for performances as Percy Grainger in ROB GEORGE's *Percy and Rose* and as Sergey Prokofiev in David Pownall's *Master Class*. His performances in the former around Australia for the STAGE COMPANY of Adelaide and in the latter for the 1984 Adelaide Festival, were widely admired. ❦*Murray Bramwell*

Olympic Theatre

Theatre at corner of Lonsdale and Exhibition Streets, Melbourne, opened 30 July 1855, seating 1150. Architect: C. F. Ohlfsen Bagge. Prefabricated in cast and corrugated sheet iron by E. and T. Bellhouse, Manchester. Became dance hall 1857, theatre during 1859, Turkish baths 1860 and finally warehouse. Demolished 1894.

In England in 1854 GEORGE COPPIN signed the tragedian G. V. BROOKE to give a 20-week season in Melbourne for £10 000. Knowing that the young town had few theatres, he bought one from a Manchester ironworking company known for prefabricated buildings, including a theatre and ballroom for Prince Albert at Balmoral Castle. Brooke laid the foundation stone on 18 April 1855 and in six weeks the theatre was erected.

Possibly the largest prefabricated iron building assembled in Australia until then, it seated 700 in the pit and stalls and 450 more in a rectangular dress circle, which had boxes in the side legs and rear of the auditorium and seats immediately facing the stage. Six gilded, fluted Corinthian columns supported a 10-metre-wide proscenium arch. WILLIAM PITT SNR decorated the interior, which was fitted out in timber. It had a pitched roof of corrugated iron, painted blue on the inside and dotted with gold stars. A couple of reviewers thought the theatre resembled a chapel. The iron roof made the building hot in summer, cold in winter and noisy in rain. Its two off-street sides were also covered in corrugated iron. The two street frontages, consisting of shops and entrances to the theatre, were framed in decorative cast iron, filled in with large sheets of glass—a precursor of the curtain walls that have been popular with architects since the 1950s. ❧Ross Thorne

Raymond Omodei

Director. Born 11 April 1936 in Wiluna (WA). Trained as schoolteacher in Perth 1955–56. Taught in schools in Western Australia 1957–67. Acted and directed with Goldfields Repertory Club (Kalgoorlie WA), 1953–62; then university and amateur companies in Perth until 1968. Founder member, actor and dramaturge at Triple Action Theatre Company (London) 1968–1971. Associate director of National Theatre Company (Perth) 1971–73. Resident director with Old Tote Theatre Company (Sydney) and artistic director of Australian Theatre for Young People 1973–76. Artistic director of Old Tote's inaugural Armidale (NSW) project 1977–78. Directed national multi-arts project in Western Australia for Curriculum Research and Development Centre (Canberra) 1978–80. Artistic director of Mason–Miller Theatre Company (Perth) 1981–82; Hole-in-the-Wall Theatre Company (Perth) 1982–89; State Theatre Company of Western Australia (Perth) 1991–93.

As an educator and as artistic director of the HOLE-IN-THE-WALL THEATRE COMPANY and the State Theatre Company of Western Australia, Raymond Omodei has contributed substantially to the development of mainstream professional theatre in Western Australia. He maintained a repertory system at the Hole-in-the-Wall Theatre from 1982 to 1984, and oversaw the company's move from its Leederville premises to the Subiaco Theatre Centre. As a director Omodei works closely with actors to achieve freshly nuanced psychological readings, especially in classical plays. He prefers modernist open stagings, with strong non-realist visual effects built around the actors.

Omodei directed the first productions of Elizabeth Backhouse's *Mirage* (1972), DOROTHY HEWETT's *Bon Bons and Roses for Dolly* (1972), JACK HIBBERD's *A Man of Many Parts* (1980) and RON ELISHA's *Pax Americana* (1984). He also directed the Australian premieres of Willy Russell's *Educating Rita* in 1984 and *Shirley Valentine* in 1989. Omodei has a keen interest in ancient and modern classics. He directed, in association with the Mucky Duck Bush Band, experimental productions of Sophocles's *Oedipus the King* in 1983 and *Antigone* in 1986, and *A Midsummer Night's Dream* in 1984. He directed the first Australian professional productions of Anton Chekhov's *Ivanov* in 1975 and Paul Claudel's *Partage de midi* in 1989 in a commissioned translation by Lisette Nigot. ❧Bill Dunstone

On Our Selection

Play by Steele Rudd, Beaumont Smith, Bert Bailey and Edmund Duggan. **premiere** 4 May 1912, Palace Theatre, Sydney. Cast: Lilias Adeson, Bert Bailey, Arthur Bertram, Alfreda Bevan, Willie Driscoll, Edmund Duggan, Sam Ellerton, Alfred Harford, Guy Hastings, Arthur Joyce, George Kensington, Jack P. Lennon, Fred MacDonald, Mary Marlowe, Laura Roberts, Queenie Sefton, George Treloar. Designer: Robert Vaughan. Director: Bert Bailey.
published Sydney: Currency Press 1984.

More than one million people in Australia and New Zealand saw *On Our Selection* between 1912 and 1916. It was not 'the greatest play ever written', as it was sometimes advertised, but it was unquestionably the most successful Australian play of its time and probably—relative to population—of all time. The melodramatic plot—which links episodes in the life of Dad, Mum, Dave, Joe and Sarah Rudd and their neighbours—has been thought ridiculous by audiences and critics since 1912, but individual sketches such as the parson and the scone, bush dentistry, and Dave's conversation-lolly courtship of Lily White, are among the great comic routines of the Australian stage. The *Bulletin*, reviewing the original production, said it had 'more humour to the square inch … than to the fathom of many allegedly humorous plays imported from London or Noo York'. In the original production and the film, FRED MACDONALD's laconic Dave and BERT BAILEY's noble if irascible Dad were the outstanding characterisations.

The basis of the appeal of Dad's character was the play's great claptrap, a speech at the end of the first act. In this Dad, a selector bankrupted by a squatter, declares he will 'start again'. This allowed Bailey to emphasise the nobility of Dad's character as the archetypal battler and representative of the ordinary Australian. The Rudds' progression from near-bankruptcy to prosperity supported the myth of the independent yeoman farmer. There were many other bush comedies after *On Our Selection* but it alone suggested that success could be achieved by hard work and self-help, without striking gold or inheriting a fortune.

Who actually adapted STEELE RUDD's stories for the stage is in dispute. Rudd himself, assisted by the journalist BEAUMONT SMITH, completed a version in 1907. Smith suggested the plot, probably influenced by an American play, *In Mizzoura* by Augustus Thomas, which toured Australia in 1903. In both plays the plot concerns the romantic entanglement of a daughter named Kate. J. C. WILLIAMSON took an option to produce this version but allowed it to lapse. In 1908 Smith tried to stage a rehearsed reading to claim the copyright but was prevented by Rudd, with whom he had quarrelled. Nevertheless Smith later received 50 per cent of the profits from Bailey's production and for a time he was credited as coauthor.

Rudd independently continued work on another version—also rejected by Williamson—and alluded to it in a prose story published in 1910, *The Play's the Thing*. Like the play as staged by Bailey two years later, it adds Kate, Uncle, and an Irish neighbour to the characters in the stories. It also includes a draft of the 'I can start again' speech. Bailey, with some assistance from EDMUND DUGGAN, revised and expanded the Rudd–Smith script. He apparently did not see Rudd's own later version, so either he had read *The Play's the Thing* or this material was already in the play when he began work on it.

Probably Rudd's vindictive desire—displayed in several subsequent interviews—to downgrade Smith's contribution also diminished his own. Helen Musa, editor of the published script, attributes the dramatisation almost exclusively to Bailey. It made his fortune. Rudd, who had been dudded by first Smith and then Bailey through an exploitative contract, had little reward from a play that he had coauthored and largely comprised dialogue and situations from his many stories.

Bert Bailey took *On Our Selection* to London in 1920. His Dad Rudd was acclaimed but the play was not. While he was away Duggan played Dad in Australia. During the 1920s, when *On Our Selection* was played intermittently, Bailey sometimes directed other actors as Dad. In 1932 he came out of retirement to codirect and star in a wildly successful sound film. Rudd fared better under the contract for this film. It was the first of four in which Bailey capitalised on the character of Dad during the Great Depression.

GEORGE WHALEY adapted the play, adding new scenes and songs, and directed a modern staging in 1979. Today *On Our Selection* is the most popular of the Rudd plays and is regularly revived by professional and amateur companies throughout the land. ❦*Richard Fotheringham*

further reading
IRVIN, ERIC. The great Australian play. *Quadrant* (Sydney) January 1976.
Steele Rudd—His books, and his play. *Theatre Magazine* (Sydney) 1 June 1912.

The One Day of the Year

Comedy-drama in three acts by Alan Seymour. **premiere** 20 July 1960, Willard Hall, Adelaide, by Adelaide Theatre Group. Cast: Francis Flanagan, Patsy Flanagan, Georgina Mackie, Tony Ogier and Terry Stapleton. Director: Jean Marshall. **revived** 26 April 1961, Palace Theatre, Sydney, with Judith Arthy, Ron Haddrick, Lew Luton, Reginald Lye and Nita Pannell; designed by Anne Fraser; directed by Robin Lovejoy. 25 October 1961, Theatre Royal, Stratford East, London, with Patricia Conolly, Lewis Fiander, Haddrick, Lye and Pannell, directed by Raymond Menmuir. **published** Sydney: Angus and Robertson 1962. Melbourne: Penguin 1985, revised, in *Three Australian Plays*.

The One Day of the Year was a turning point in the postwar movement away from British gentility towards examination of the knotty working-class roots of Australian life. It anticipated by a decade the confrontational theatre of the AUSTRALIAN PERFORMING GROUP and it suffered from the same early censorship problems. The play deals with the Cook family and their friend Wacka, a Gallipoli veteran. Alf Cook, a lift-driver and returned serviceman, lives in a cramped inner-city cottage with his wife Dot and their son Hughie, a university student. Alf is angry and frustrated, and he expresses his frustration in bold expletives against everything that challenges his conservative outlook. Since his discharge from the forces after the Second World War he has been disappointed. Only on 'the one day of the year'—25 April, Anzac Day, Australia's day of remembrance of war—can he feel a man again.

Hughie and his upper-crust girl friend Jan Castle have resolved to document Anzac Day for the university paper. Conflict arises when Hughie for the first time refuses to attend the dawn service with his father. With great skill ALAN SEYMOUR builds up both sides of the argument. To the young it is a day when Sydney's streets are littered with drunken men in medal-laden suits vomiting in the gutter. To the old ex-servicemen it is a day of grieving they can share only with one another. The mutual rage reaches a quiet resolution as Wacka, the real Anzac, pays his tribute to the past and Alf and Hughie learn an uneasy acceptance of the other's life experience and the widening gap that education is wedging between them.

In 1959 a panel of judges recommended *The One Day of the Year* for performance at the first ADELAIDE FESTIVAL OF ARTS in 1960. The festival's governors rejected it on the grounds that it might offend the powerful and conservative Returned Services League. The decision caused a public controversy and in response the amateur ADELAIDE THEATRE GROUP gave the play a season, with some assistance from the AUSTRALIAN ELIZABETHAN THEATRE TRUST. After the successful tryout the Trust presented the play in Sydney, opening appropriately on 26 April. While the street observances of Anzac Day were giving colour to the final rehearsals, a bomb threat was received. Police searched the Palace Theatre for 24 hours, but no bomb was found and the performance went forward without incident. The Sydney season was followed by a tour for the Arts Council of NSW, a Melbourne production and tour of country centres for the Victorian Arts Council by the UNION THEATRE REPERTORY COMPANY, and productions in other capitals. In London a production in the East End ran for four weeks and the play was respectfully received by the press. *The One Day of the Year* has since been performed in virtually all west European countries and Japan, and it has been adapted for Australian, British and German television.

There have been many Australian stage revivals. Seymour came to Australia for the 1980 Adelaide production, which also toured Tasmania. While here he substantially revised the role of Jan, which had been repeatedly criticised for being less credible than the other characters. The new lines give her a family context and a process of self-discovery that were not in the original play.

With the years the play has come to be seen in its proper light, not as an assault on national values but as a study of a family limited in emotional expression, for whom their son's education is suddenly no longer compensation for their own upbringing but a cause of estrangement and social embarrassment. Like other plays of its period it presents the archetypal Australian—Anglo-Celtic, physically powerful but unworldly, the battler who in earlier decades fought fire and flood with unflagging spirit. Deprived of a cause, confined to an urban backyard and no longer his own master, Alf awaits the revolution of Hughie's generation who, with new confidence, will challenge the conventions and find a new vocabulary of emotion. ❦*Katharine Brisbane*

further reading

HARRIS, MAX. Seymour's Anzac play. *Nation* (Sydney) April 1961.
RICHARDS, KEITH and ALRENE SYKES. Another look at the old warhorse. *Australasian Drama Studies* 2/2 (Brisbane, April 1984).
SEYMOUR, ALAN. *The One Day of the Year*. London: Souvenir Press 1967. Novel.
SUMNER, JOHN. *Recollections at Play—A life in Australian theatre*. Melbourne: University Press 1993.

Errol O'Neill

Actor, director, dramatist. Born 8 March 1945 in Brisbane. Studied philosophy and theology in Rome and arts at University of Queensland. Worked for Popular Theatre Troupe 1977–83.

One of the few theatrical workers in Queensland who has striven to bridge the gap between community theatre and mainstream theatre is Errol O'Neill. He became simultaneously interested in politics, social criticism and theatre at the University of Queensland and he refined his skills in social comment and political satire while working for the POPULAR THEATRE TROUPE. He wrote six plays—all about social and historical issues—for this company.

Since it disbanded in 1983 his plays have generally been about the need for individuals to assess the movements to which they belong; many of his characters must choose between being true to a group or to their own sense of what is right. O'Neill employs satire and naturalism in varying proportions to promote his political message and vibrant humour and warmth give Brechtian vitality to his plays. His trilogy on significant moments in the Queensland labour movement—*Faces in the Street*, *Popular Front* and *On the Whipping Side*—has been well received by critics and audiences in the state and in Melbourne. O'Neill has given many performances for the QUEENSLAND THEATRE COMPANY. ❦*Patsy McCarthy*

published plays
Faces in the Street (1983). Brisbane: Playlab Press 1993.
On the Whipping Side (1991). Brisbane: Playlab Press 1991.
Popular Front (1986). Brisbane: Playlab Press 1988.

reference
The Fryer Library, University of Queensland (Brisbane), holds the manuscripts of *Faces in the Street* (1983), *It's M.A.D.* (1981), *Popular Theatre Troupe's Australia* (1979), *Says Who?* (1979).

Edward Opie

Actor, scene-painter, theatre-decorator. Born in Devonshire (England) 1809. Arrived in Adelaide 1839. First stage appearance November 1839. Worked in Tasmania and Melbourne. Died 31 October 1879.

A popular comic actor, Edward Opie was also one of the best theatrical scene-painters in Australia before the gold rushes. He also decorated theatre auditoria in several cities. Nothing in Opie's career in England suggests any association with the theatre. He was the son of a painter and nephew of John Opie, a celebrated portraitist. He appears to have joined SAMSON CAMERON's company in Adelaide in 1839 because of limited demand for paintings. There was much praise for new scenery he prepared for *Rob Roy* by Isaac Pocock and *Isabelle*, in which he also played a Savoyard boy, but in March 1840 he was replaced as Cameron's scene painter by a man named Langeake.

In May 1840 GEORGE BUCKINGHAM engaged Opie for his short-lived Argyle Rooms. On 2 June 1840 Opie advertised in the *South Australian Register* that he was ready to paint portraits, clean and repair oil paintings, and teach drawing. Before long, however, he had designed and executed the decorations for the new QUEEN'S THEATRE, which opened on 11 January 1841. Opie was engaged as scene-painter and he continued to act. After the Queen's closed in late 1842, he moved to Tasmania. He made his first appearance in Launceston for F. B. WATSON's benefit on 19 September 1842 and, despite announcements of impending departure, he stayed in Launceston until mid-1844, when the company transferred to ANNE CLARKE's management. Opie returned to Hobart with Mrs Clarke and was responsible for redecorating the Royal Victoria Theatre in Louis XIV style.

When GEORGE COPPIN took over the Clarke company in 1845 Opie accompanied him to Launceston and then to Melbourne, where he painted a new act drop for the opening of the QUEEN'S THEATRE ROYAL. Later in 1845 Opie completed a portrait of Coppin as BILLY BARLOW and for a while he attempted a career as a painter outside the theatre. In May 1847, however, he left Melbourne to rejoin Coppin's company at the New Queen's Theatre in Adelaide, and made his debut there on 4 June. He also arranged new *tableaux vivants*, redecorated the theatre in 'the Parisian style' between seasons, and painted new scenery, a new act drop and a grand panorama of local scenery for benefit nights.

In 1848, when JOHN LAZAR replaced Coppin as manager of the New Queen's, Opie transferred to HENRY DEERING's Royal Adelaide Theatre. He redecorated its auditorium and proscenium and painted a new drop scene for its reopening on 1 May 1848. He occasionally appeared at the New Queen's on benefit nights, however, and he began regular appearances when Coppin returned to the stage in May 1849. 'Mr Opie is a capital low comedian, and his appearance from behind the scenes was always a prelude to roars of laughter', said the *Adelaide Times* on 14 May.

Opie excelled himself for the 1849 Christmas pantomime at the New Queen's, painting American as well as local scenes. The scenery, said the *Adelaide Times*, 'was a chef d'oeuvre of its kind, and in some parts, particularly the "Bee Hive" front window, with its sprinkled, dangling drapery, the illusion was perfect. San Francisco, Sacramento and Port Adelaide were equally happy.' Opie played at the New Queen's throughout 1850 and also redecorated the old Queen's Theatre, which Coppin reopened as the Royal Victoria Theatre on 23 December. When Coppin became bankrupt and his theatre closed at the end of 1851, Opie and others left for Melbourne.

Opie redecorated the Theatre Royal at Geelong for its opening by Coppin on 14 June 1852. He was still there in July 1853, when he appeared in a local ballet, *Squatters and Gold Diggers*. In 1856 Opie was responsible for a major redecoration of the Royal Victoria Theatre in Hobart. The fronts of the private boxes, dress circle and gallery were painted with classical figures and the interior of the dome with illustrations of Shakespeare's seven ages of man and a portrait of the 'immortal bard' himself. ❦*Elizabeth Webby*

further reading
CANDY, J. G. Edward Andrew Opie. *Dictionary of Australian Artists, Photographers and Engravers, 1770–1870* (ed. Joan Kerr). Melbourne: Oxford University Press 1992.

William Orr

Director, manager. Born 12 July 1924 in Glasgow (Scotland). Stage manager with Old Vic Theatre Company (London). Came to Australia 1950. Began directing revue at Metropolitan Theatre, Sydney, 1952. Produced revue at Phillip Street Theatre 1954–61, Phillip Theatre 1961–71. Produced revues at Doncaster Theatre Restaurant, Sydney, 1965–71. Ran Music Loft, Manly, 1972–83.

When William Orr was allowed to direct a production of his choice at the Metropolitan Theatre in Sydney in 1952, he decided to introduce intimate revue to the city. He had experienced small-scale satirical revue in London and he had seen University of Sydney revues and noted the talents of the writers John McKellar and Gerry Donovan. He engaged them and the composer Lance Mulcahy to write a new show, called *Merry-Go-Round*. Its success encouraged Orr to believe that Sydney could support a theatre devoted to intimate revue and in May 1954 he opened the PHILLIP STREET THEATRE with *Top of the Bill*. Many of the performers, including GORDON CHATER, MARGO LEE and Lyle O'Hara, became favourites in a long series of PHILLIP STREET REVUES. The Phillip Street Theatre was closed in 1961 and Phillip Productions continued revues at the Phillip Theatre in Elizabeth Street. It interspersed them with special guests and branched out into play production. Expansion eventually overextended the company and in the 1971 the theatre became the Richbrooke Theatre, run by Dudley Goldman.

From 1965 to 1971 Orr also produced grander revues on the Las Vegas pattern at the suburban Doncaster Theatre Restaurant. Sheila Bradley, Ron Frazer, Kamahl and REG LIVERMORE were among the stars. Intimate revue in the Orr style surfaced again in 1972 in the Music Loft, run by Orr and his partner Eric Duckworth in seaside Manly. It was largely the mixture as before plus dining and liquor. There were some worthwhile shows until ill health forced Orr's retirement in September 1983. Duckworth went with him, leaving the Music Loft to be run by others. ❦*John West*

Peter O'Shaughnessy

Actor, director, writer. Born 1924 in Melbourne. Started in amateur theatre at 17. Professional training in England. Joined Union Theatre Repertory Company (Melbourne) 1954. Formed own company 1954 and presented productions. Collaborated with Barry Humphries 1955–58. Worked in England 1959–65. Acted and directed for Independent Theatre and Q Theatre (Sydney) from 1965. Has lived abroad since early 1970s returning to Australia several times with solo shows. Married to actor Shirley Smith.

Keen intelligence and power as actor and director made Peter O'Shaughnessy prominent during the late 1950s in Melbourne and the late 1960s in Sydney. His greatest recognition probably came from brilliant one-man shows that he wrote or devised. In his early productions he showed particular affinity for Shakespeare and Irish playwrights, especially George Bernard Shaw. He was widely praised for his portrayals of Hamlet in 1954 and King Lear in 1957. He produced plays at University of Melbourne colleges and at Nicholas Hall, where *Love's Labour's Lost* in 1955 had sets designed by Arthur Boyd. In this production he cast BARRY HUMPHRIES as Holofernes, beginning a fruitful collaboration. Humphries starred in Molière's *Le Malade imaginaire*, with which O'Shaughnessy pioneered lunchtime theatre in Melbourne in February 1955. In another lunchtime show, O'Shaughnessy played the Sentimental Bloke in a dramatisation of C. J. Dennis's verses. 'His monologues from *The Sentimental Bloke* have reopened a closed chapter in Australian humour, and one which is as racy today as it was when Dennis's Fitzroy slang was really topical', wrote GEOFFREY HUTTON.

In September 1957 O'Shaughnessy staged the Australian premiere of Samuel Beckett's *Waiting for Godot*, with Humphries as Estragon and himself as Vladimir. It attracted wide interest and in May 1958 toured to the Independent Theatre in Sydney, along with *The Bunyip and the Satellite*, a musical play for children by O'Shaughnessy and Jeff Underhill. It starred Humphries as the Bunyip. O'Shaughnessy's wife Shirley Smith also played in many of his productions. She was Eliza Doolittle to his Higgins in Shaw's *Pygmalion* at the National Theatre in January 1958. In July 1958, O'Shaughnessy and Humphries wrote and performed a lunchtime revue in Melbourne with such success that they expanded it into *Rock and Reel* at the New Theatre. It included 'Sponsor a Migrant', a sketch between Edna Everage and her mother, played by O'Shaughnessy, and in the second half Sandy Stone had his stage premiere in 'Wildlife in Suburbia'. A testimonial performance of their work together was presented at the Assembly Hall in February 1959, before Humphries left for London.

O'Shaughnessy began a season with the J. C. Williamson Shakespeare Company at the Comedy Theatre in June 1959, alternating with JOHN ALDEN as Shylock in *The Merchant of Venice*, Leontes in *The Winter's Tale* and Bottom in *A Midsummer Night's Dream*. Then he went to England. He worked at the Old Vic in London and Bristol, and presented two solo shows at the Dublin Theatre Festival. In 1965 he brought his solo adaptation of Nikolai Gogol's *Diary of a Madman* to Australia for the Festival of Perth and a tour. He settled in Sydney, where he played the troubled antihero in John Osborne's *Inadmissible Evidence* for the OLD TOTE THEATRE COMPANY in 1965. For Q THEATRE he gave an electrifying performance in Eugène Ionesco's *The Lesson*, played popular solo shows on Shaw and Henry Lawson, and directed John Arden's *The Business of Good Government*.

In 1967 O'Shaughnessy directed and played in *Othello* at the NSW State Conservatorium of Music. A review of the production by KATHARINE BRISBANE in the *Australian* resulted in a defamation action against the newspaper. It won the first case and an appeal but when the High Court ordered a retrial the matter was settled out of court. For INDEPENDENT THEATRE in 1969 O'Shaughnessy directed *Waiting for Godot*, again playing Vladimir, and Edward Bond's *Narrow Road to the Deep North*. He now lives in Ireland. He has returned to Australia several times with solo shows, notably in 1984 as part of an international tour with *All for the Love of a Lady*, his adaptation of Neville Coghill's translation of Chaucer's *Troilus and Criseyde*. The critic Ken Healey commented that 'it would be hard to imagine a better way to encounter this great tale'. ❦*Lynne Murphy*

Stanislaus Ostoja-Kotkowski

Designer. Born 28 December 1922 in Golub (Poland). Studied at Golub and Kunst Akademie, Düsseldorf (West Germany) 1946–49. Came to Australia 1949. National Gallery School (Melbourne) 1950–

51. Worked as commercial artist in Melbourne. Settled in Adelaide. Designer for drama, ballet and opera companies. Also works as sculptor, painter, photographer, film-maker and graphic designer.

In Adelaide during the 1950s and 1960s Stanislaus Ostoja-Kotkowski produced many innovative décors, exploiting light through sophisticated projection techniques. His notable designs included *The Prisoner* by Bridget Boland in 1956, Samuel Beckett's *Waiting for Godot*, the world premiere of Patrick White's THE HAM FUNERAL in 1961, *Macbeth* for the AUSTRALIAN ELIZABETHAN THEATRE TRUST in 1964 and *The Unknown Soldier and His Wife* by Peter Ustinov for the CANBERRA REPERTORY SOCIETY in 1971. From 1964 Ostoja's quest for a 'total work of environmental expression' led him to present spectacular sound and image productions in which music, visuals, dance—and on one occasion a science-fiction play—were wedded to electronics. He was using lasers on stage by 1968 and he used them outdoors in *Chromasonic Towers* at the Adelaide Festival of Arts in 1970 and in Canberra in 1972. He continues to experiment in combining electronics, sound and light. ❦*Pamela Zeplin*

further reading
MCCULLOCH, A. Letter from Australia. *Art International* 14/6 (summer 1970).

Ostracised

—or, *Every Man's Hand Against Them*. Play by E. C. Martin.
premiere 6 August 1881, Princess's Theatre, Melbourne. Cast: G. Atkins, W. G. Carey, W. Carle, G. A. Coleman, Mrs Ford, Ada Grantleigh, May Vivian. Director: W. G. Carey.

The best-known early staging of the Kelly Gang story, *Ostracised* became a great popular success but most Melbourne newspapers attacked it as a scurrilous incitement to disorder. Edward Castilidine Martin had written an anti-hanging play, *What May Happen to a Man in Victoria*, and he considered himself a serious dramatist. But *Ostracised*, said the *Age* on 8 August 1881, was 'a curious mixture, evidencing a conflict between the desire of the author to be didactically moral, and the determination of the stage manager, at all hazards, to be funny'. In vain did advance notices insist: 'The motive of the play is … to show that when men outrage the laws of the country, society, as a matter of self-protection, must rise against them'.

There was praise only for W. G. Carey as Ned Kelly, who showed 'proper remorse' for his 'cruel and wanton slaughter' of Sergeant Kennedy. The sergeant, wounded and dying, asks to be spared long enough to see his wife and children again. Kelly is sympathetic but is outvoted by his fellow bushrangers. He assumes his 'duty' as leader and shoots the man. With G. Atkins as a comical and musical Steve Hart, *Ostracised* ran for four weeks and was quickly brought back after a brief season of another bushranging drama. After a New Zealand tour, *Ostracised* arrived in Sydney on Easter Saturday 1882 with a new cast and a new, even more moral subtitle, *The Downfall of Crime*. This failed to impress the authorities and the play was banned on Easter Monday. ❦*Richard Fotheringham and Veronica Kelly*

E. W. O'Sullivan

Dramatist. Born 17 March 1846 in Launceston (Tas.). Newspaper reporter and editor in Hobart and Sydney. NSW parliamentarian 1885–1910. Had four plays performed 1898–1908. Died 25 April 1910 in Sydney.

One of several politician-playwrights in colonial and early federal Australia, Edward William O'Sullivan wrote plays full of propaganda for his nationalist and protectionist views. In the production of *The Eureka Rebellion*, 'male and female O'Sullivans talk yards upon yards of O'Sullivanese to each other in the form of stump speeches', said the *Worker* on 16 April 1898. O'Sullivan started work on this play, his first, as early as the 1870s, but it was not performed until seven years after EDMUND DUGGAN's *The Democrat*, the first Eureka Stockade melodrama to be publicly performed. Both plays were later revised and revived, O'Sullivan's in 1907. It was performed by E. I. Cole's BOHEMIAN DRAMATIC COMPANY at the Haymarket Hippodrome tent theatre in Sydney.

Cole also staged two of O'Sullivan's later plays in rip-roaring circus style. There were real horses in a brumby hunt in *COO-EE* in 1906 and in the Sydney Cup in *Keane of Kalgoorlie* in 1908. Both plays were huge successes. *Coo-ee* attracted 2800 people on opening night but the premiere of *Keane of Kalgoorlie* was a disaster. Heavy rain 'poured through roof leaks', the actors forgot their lines, and 'the scenes in which boxing and two-up were presented were by no means convincing', according to the *Sydney Morning Herald* on 20 April 1908. O'Sullivan's only other play, the one-act comedy *A Quiet Little Dinner*, had a single amateur performance. ❦*Richard Fotheringham*

further reading
MANSFIELD, BRUCE. *Australian Democrat*. Sydney: 1965.
MANSFIELD, BRUCE. Edward William O'Sullivan. *Australian Dictionary of Biography* 11. Melbourne University Press 1988.
reference
E. W. O'Sullivan Papers in Mitchell Library (Sydney).

Barry Otto

Actor. Born in Brisbane. Educated at Brisbane Technical College. Began acting as amateur. Worked regularly for Brisbane Repertory Theatre Society, Queensland Theatre Company and Twelfth Night Theatre in 1970s. Moved to Sydney 1975. Worked steadily for Nimrod and Old Tote Theatre Companies in Sydney from 1976. Sydney Theatre Company from 1980s. Australia Day Award for outstanding achievement in entertainment 1987. Green Room Award 1991 (Figaro in *The Marriage of Figaro* by Pierre Beaumarchais). Many film and television roles in 1980s. Married to former theatre manager Sue Hill. Father of actor Miranda Otto.

Barry Otto has brought variety and daring to performances in Sydney, particularly in giving a larger, non-naturalistic dimension to modern roles. He became an important actor for the NIMROD THEATRE COMPANY in its search for new forms and dynamic statements in the 1970s, particularly in his work with the directors AUBREY MELLOR and NEIL ARMFIELD, with whom he has had steady and fruitful associations. His first Nimrod role was Lenin in Tom Stoppard's *Travesties* in 1976. He played Orsino in JOHN BELL's notable production of *Twelfth Night* in 1977 and D. H. Lawrence in DAVID ALLEN's *Upside Down at the Bottom of the World* in 1978.

With Nimrod in 1979 Otto showed a capacity for strenuous political roles when he played three parts in *Protest*, an extraordinary evening of short plays by Vaclav Havel. Then came the torturer Krasin in STEPHEN SEWELL's *Traitors* in 1980 and Sebastian in the premiere of Sewell's *Welcome the Bright World* in 1982; and several roles in Caryl Churchill's challenging cross-dressing play *Cloud Nine*. Other landmark performances were in Chekhov— Kulyshin in *Three Sisters* in 1981 and Uncle Vanya in 1982. Otto joined the SYDNEY THEATRE COMPANY for roles including Adolf Hitler in Christopher Hampton's *The Portage to San Cristobal of A. H.* in 1986, T. S. Eliot in Michael Hastings's *Tom and Viv* in 1987 and Figaro in Pierre Beaumarchais's *The Marriage of Figaro* in 1990. In 1992 he created the role of Mozart-loving, schizophrenic Roy in Louis Nowra's *Così*.

Otto made his first impact with the BRISBANE REPERTORY THEATRE COMPANY in 1970 as Bri in Peter Nichols's *A Day in the Death of Joe Egg*. He played a wide variety of demanding roles in Brisbane, including the title-role in Nikolai Gogol's *The Government Inspector*, Horner in William Wycherley's *The Country Wife*, Cooley in David Williamson's DON'S PARTY, Monk O'Neill in Jack Hibberd's A STRETCH OF THE IMAGINATION, Torvald in Ibsen's *A Doll's House*, Gerald in Ben Travers's *Rookery Nook* and Mick in JIM MCNEIL's *How Does Your Garden Grow*. ❦*Katharine Brisbane*

Harrison Owen

Critic, dramatist. Born 24 June 1890 in Geelong (Vic.). Began in journalism on Sydney *Bulletin* 1912. Later on newspapers in Melbourne; drama critic for *Herald*. In London 1919–40. Died 1966.

While Harrison Owen was a freelance journalist in London he wrote three plays that were all performed in the West End. *The Gentleman in Waiting* (1925) was generally found amusing if over-literary, but *The Happy Husband* (1927), with Charles Laughton and Madge Titheradge, was a popular success. It later played in New York, Paris and Vienna, and it was filmed as *Uneasy Virtue* in 1931. *Doctor Pygmalion* (1932), with Ronald Squire and Gladys Cooper, enjoyed a similar response, and seasons in Melbourne, Sydney and Amsterdam. Owen broke no new ground, but showed an assured sense of the playwright's craft. He was eminently qualified to produce the book on writing for the theatre that he published in 1940. In that year he returned to Melbourne and ceased theatrical activity. That may have been a reflection of his unassuming personality or a product of the still more modest opportunities he found in the city. Owen developed his interest in the theatre in personal contacts with men like LOUIS ESSON and VANCE PALMER, with whom he founded the nationalist Australian Authors' and Writers' Guild. ❦*Peter Fitzpatrick*

writings
The Playwright's Craft. 1940.

The Pack of Women

Cabaret devised by Robyn Archer. **premiere** 1981, Drill Hall, London. Performers: Robyn Archer, Margo Random, Jane Wood. Director: Pam Brighton. Musical director: Andrew Bell. Producers: Diana Manson and Diane Robson for Diehard Productions. Rewritten version. **premiere** 1983, Downstairs Theatre, Seymour Theatre Centre, Sydney. Designer: Roger Kirk. Director: Robyn Archer. Musical director: Andrew Bell. Performers: Jane Clifton, Judy Connelli, Michele Fawdon. Producers: Sue Hill and Chris Westwood for Understudies Pty Ltd.

In *The Pack of Women* ROBYN ARCHER, employing song, prose, poetry and dance, set out to shock audiences into examining the role of women in western society. The title is a metaphor for a game of life played according to rules in which sexual politics were critical, and its exploration of feminist thinking resulted in exceptionally successful seasons in London and Sydney. ❦*Michelle Potter*

further reading
ARCHER, ROBYN and DIANA MANSON, HELEN MILLS, DEBORAH PARRY and ROBYN STACEY. *The Pack of Women*. Sydney: Hessian 1986.

PACT Youth Theatre

Youth-theatre company in Sydney, founded in 1964 by Robert Allnut as Producers, Authors, Composers and Talent. Became PACT Youth Theatre 1974. **artistic director** Jack Mannix 1970–89.

In PACT Youth Theatre young people aged from six to 25 years work with a full-time artistic co-ordinator and part-time professional tutors and directors on productions of works that include self-devised pieces, creations of a resident playwright and established scripts. They present their productions to audiences of family and friends or to the general public. PACT aims to promote confidence and self-esteem, to enhance the ability to communicate, to stimulate creativity, to encourage initiative, to raise community awareness, and to offer these benefits of theatrical activity to young people who otherwise would not have access to them. It is a non-profit organisation funded by the AUSTRALIA COUNCIL, the NSW Ministry for the Arts and the South Sydney City Council. There are no membership fees.

PACT was originally a tryout company for new Australian work. It also gave experience to performers and directors. Among those who worked with PACT in its early years were the actors Gordon Glenright, LEONARD TEALE and Jack Thompson, the comedian Grahame Bond, the stage director Ian Tasker, the film director Peter Weir, the playwrights ALEX BUZO and DOROTHY HEWETT, and the folksinger Margaret Roadknight. The first board included Jack Mannix, Patrick Milligan and Leonard Teale.

By the end of 1973 the needs of local playwrights, performers and directors had altered. New Australian works were being produced at places such as the JANE STREET THEATRE. There was a quota for Australian content on television and the AUSTRALIAN NATIONAL PLAYWRIGHTS' CONFERENCE was newly formed. PACT changed direction and in 1974 PACT Youth Theatre began operations. Until the end of 1987 all PACT's workshops, meetings and performances were in central Sydney at the old Corn Exchange, except plays at the Pilgrim Theatre from 1970 to 1973. Since January 1988 PACT has been at the Sydney Street Theatre Space in suburban Erskineville. ❦*Pamela Payne*

Palace Theatre Melbourne

Theatre in Bourke Street, opened 6 April 1912 as **Brennan's Amphitheatre**, seating c.2000. Renamed **National Amphitheatre** 1912. Redesigned by Henry E. White and reopened 4 November 1916 as **Palace Theatre**, seating 1700. Interior redecorated by White 1923. Became cinema as **Apollo Theatre** c.1929. Redecorated and renamed ST JAMES THEATRE, November 1940. Renamed **Metro Theatre**. Returned to live musical theatre in early 1970s. Renamed **Palace Theatre** 1973. Became church. Metro Nightclub in late 1980s.

When Brennan's Amphitheatre opened on Easter Saturday 1912 the auditorium was a plain white room with a single rake of seating with a 'balcony' at the rear. The theatre 'could seat 2000 people any night they care to pay the price of admission', said the *Bulletin* on 2 May. 'The cost of the land and the building is set down at £32 000 and none of the money was wasted on interior decoration.' Fullers' obtained a controlling interest in the BRENNAN VAUDEVILLE CIRCUIT shortly after the theatre opened and renamed it the National Amphitheatre. In 1916 Fullers' employed their architect, HENRY E. WHITE, to redesign the interior as a three-level auditorium, similar to theatres he had designed or redesigned for them in Sydney (the Adelphi), Brisbane (the Tivoli) and Wellington, New Zealand. Renamed the Palace Theatre, it opened for vaudeville, revue and musicals but became the home of Fullers' melodrama companies. In 1923 Fullers' commissioned White to redesign the plaster decoration of the auditorium in the more elegant Adam style he had just used in the nearby PRINCESS THEATRE.

With the onset of the Great Depression Fullers' turned their theatres over to talking pictures. The Palace became the Apollo Theatre. Snider and Dean showed films there from March 1936 until 1940, when Fullers' Theatres renamed it the St James Theatre. Then Metro–Goldwyn–Mayer bought the theatre and renamed it the Metro. Under this name it briefly returned to live performance with the rock musical *Hair*. A new owner renamed it the Palace Theatre in 1973. In 1978 it was bought by a revivalist Christian organisation, which moved out in 1986. Then it was turned into a technologically elaborate disco nightclub, still with White's 1923 interior decor. ❦*Ross Thorne*

Palace Theatre Sydney

Theatre in Pitt Street, opened 19 December 1896, seating 1000. Architect: Clarence Backhouse. Remodelled to seat 872, 1923. Architects: Ballantyre and Hare. Closed late 1969. Demolished 1970.

The small Palace Theatre was truly theatrical in its architecture. The brick-and-plaster exterior was an eclectic mixture of baroque arches and cornices with a French-style roof pavilion topped by an Indian-style cupola. Heavily modelled baroque was the style for the lobby, toilets and a small dress-circle foyer, which had a ceiling painting of diaphanously attired young women floating in a misty sky. The original auditorium was unique in Australia. Eight posts rose from the stalls floor to support the fronts of two circles above and then the roof by way of vaults in 'Hindoo Gothic' style. This amalgam of Mogul and Hindu detail continued in an ogee-arched proscenium and side boxes in the form of cupolas with onion-dome 'roofs'. Most of the auditorium was ornamented in sheet steel embossed in elaborate patterns designed and painted by PHILIP W. GOATCHER, one of the last scene-painters to follow the custom of designing the interior decoration of a theatre. Many of the decorative elements he used in the Palace Theatre appear to have come from the Broadway Theatre built in Denver (Colorado, USA) in 1890.

Goatcher was also the first lessee and director of the Palace Theatre. Its owner was George Adams, who built it as part of his Tattersall's Hotel complex. He intended it to be a palace of varieties—as close to an English music hall as NSW laws would allow. Until 6 p.m. closing of bars was introduced in 1916, patrons could leave the theatre by side exits, cross a narrow private alley and enter the hotel by side doors almost opposite. This satisfied regulations that theatres and hotels had to be on separate sites. The Palace had many later lessees, mainly minor entrepreneurs finding a short-term home or major managements needing an overflow theatre, and it housed entertainment of all kinds. Redesign of the auditorium in 1923 removed most of the posts and converted the decor to a more sedate European Renaissance style. The Palace became a full-time cinema during the Great Depression. After the Second World War it fluctuated between film and live theatre until its demise. The AUSTRALIAN ELIZABETHAN THEATRE TRUST and GARNET H. CARROLL sub-leased it from Hoyts Theatres in 1960–61 and 1964. ❦*Ross Thorne*

Palais Theatre

Theatre in St Kilda, Melbourne, opened 11 November 1927 as cinema seating 2968. Architect: Henry E. White. Converted in 1960 to opera theatre seating 2854.

For nearly a quarter of a century from 1960 Melbourne's venue for large-scale musical theatre and dance was the 2854-seat Palais Theatre in suburban St Kilda. Since the opening of the VICTORIAN ARTS CENTRE the Palais has been more used for concerts but it remains the largest-capacity theatre in Australia. HENRY E. WHITE designed it for Harold, Leon and Hermann Phillips as a palatial suburban cinema, in a composite French and Oriental style, to replace the New Palais Pictures, opened in 1922 and destroyed by fire in 1926. The new cinema originally seated 1630 in the stalls and 1338 in the dress circle and it had a large stage and orchestra pit suitable for the variety acts that supplemented de luxe film presentations in the 1920s, but it was devoid of dressing rooms for performers. It showed films until 1960, when it was used for an opera season. The pit was enlarged to take the orchestra, reducing the stalls seating to 1516. Dressing rooms were built in 1962. The Palais housed the Melbourne season of *Jesus Christ Superstar*. ❦*Ross Thorne*

Vance Palmer

Dramatist. Born 28 August 1895 at Bundaberg (Qld). Married Nettie Higgins, poet and critic, in London, 23 May 1914. Opposed conscription but joined army 1918. Helped to found Pioneer Players in Melbourne 1922. Freelance writer most of his life. Closely associated with *Meanjin*. Died 15 July 1958 in Melbourne.

Best known for fiction and literary journalism, Vance Palmer became interested in theatrical writing through a friendship with LOUIS ESSON, whose Irish-inspired vision of a national theatre appealed to his strong nationalism. Palmer formed the social ideal of a genuinely national theatre—as opposed to the professional theatre—that would perform plays by local authors and help to create an 'Australia of the spirit'. This, rather than creative expression, led Palmer to write such plays as *The Black Horse* (1924) and *Hail Tomorrow*, an unperformed four-act study of the radical leader William Lane. Palmer's most ambitious play, *Hail Tomorrow* affirms his commitment to the democratic values of the 1890s. His plays are competent exercises in realism, aiming to evoke characteristic Australian settings and types. They reflect his belief that a national literature should focus on 'the bush' as the source of Australianness. He underlined his identification with the Henry Lawson tradition by dramatising a Lawson story as *Telling Mrs Baker*. It was published with three other one-act plays. Among them *The Black Horse* stands out through the conflict of a husband and wife on an outback station, a conflict that leads to the death of their only son. As early as 1905 Palmer had defined the aim of Australian writing as revealing 'the various undertones of our national life'. This simple, unpretentious drama does so better than anything else he wrote for the stage. Like Esson's THE DROVERS, it offers unsentimental insight into the masculine ethos of the bush and suggests authentically Australian moral issues. Palmer, however, lacked Esson's command of dramatic speech and his instinct for the theatrical.

The Black Horse reflects the stimulus of the PIONEER PLAYERS upon the young Palmer and indicates a potential that might have been more fully realised if that venture had succeeded. It was Palmer's only foray into the theatre itself, though he remained interested in writing plays all his life. He had completed his first, *A Happy Family*, by 1915, and he was working on a full-length play, *Prisoner's Country*, at the time of his death. The Union Theatre Repertory Company in Melbourne produced it in 1960. ❦*John Barnes*

published plays
The Black Horse (1924). Sydney: Angus and Robertson 1963 in *Mask and Microphone*.
Hail Tomorrow. Sydney: Angus and Robertson 1947.
Telling Mrs Baker (1922). Sydney: Angus and Robertson 1963 in *Mask and Microphone*.
The Prisoner (1919). Sydney: Angus and Robertson 1963 in *Mask and Microphone*.
Travellers (1923). Sydney: Angus and Robertson 1963 in *Mask and Microphone*.

further reading
CARLOLL, DENNIS. *Australian Contemporary Drama*. Sydney: Currency Press 1995.
SERLE, GEOFFREY. Vance Palmer. *Australian Dictionary of Biography* 11. Melbourne University Press 1988.
SMITH, VIVIAN. *Vance and Nettie Palmer*. Boston (USA): Twayne 1975.
WALKER, DAVID. *Dream and Disillusion*. Canberra: Australian National University Press 1976.

Grace Palotta

Actor, singer. Born *c*.1870 in Vienna. Studied singing at Royal Academy of Music (London). Became popular in pantomime and operetta in London and USA. In Australia 1895, 1897–1901, 1906, 1908, 1912–18. Details of death unknown.

On her five tours of Australia between 1895 and 1915 Grace Palotta was one of the best performers of musical comedy and fashionable drama. She came first with the London Gaiety Company in 1895 and returned in 1897 for the WILLIAMSON AND MUSGROVE production of *A Runaway Girl*. Her biggest success came in 1900 as Lady Holyrood in *Florodora*, her best role. Palotta was equally able in drama. She toured in popular dramas and operettas for George Willoughby and HUGH J. WARD in 1906 and in Ward's company in 1908. She returned for J. C. WILLIAMSON's in 1912, and stayed until the end of the First World War, though she left the stage in 1915 and opened a hat shop in Melbourne. She returned to Europe after the war and lived in comfortable retirement into her eighties. She last appeared in public in 1949, at the launching of W. MacQueen Pope's book on the Gaiety Theatre. ❦*Alwyn Capern*

further reading
MACQUEEN POPE, W. *Gaiety, Theatre of Enchantment*. London: W. H. Allen 1949.

Nita Pannell OBE

Actor, director. Born in 1904 in southwest Western Australia. Acted with amateur group at Goomalling (WA) in 1930s. Studied speech with Lily Kavanagh in Perth. Patch Theatre (Perth) 1944. Member of Repertory Club. Co-founded Company of Four 1950. National Theatre Company 1956. OBE 1977. University of Western Australia HonDLitt 1990. Died 29 December 1994.

A force in the shift from amateur to professional theatre in Perth, Nita Pannell helped to found the COMPANY OF FOUR and directed the NATIONAL THEATRE COMPANY's inaugural production, *The Teahouse of the August Moon* by John Patrick, in 1956. There in the next year she played Mamma Bianchi in Richard Beynon's THE SHIFTING HEART and toured with it through NSW, Victoria and outback Queensland. In Sydney in 1961 she played Dot Cook in the TRUST PLAYERS' production of Alan Seymour's THE ONE DAY OF THE YEAR, and repeated the role in London later in the year. In 1963 in Melbourne she created the title-role in PATRICK WHITE's *A Cheery Soul*, which he adapted for her from his short story.

The greater part of her career, however, was in Perth, where she was a leading actor and director. Her later work in Perth included an all-female production of Samuel Beckett's *Waiting for Godot*, in which she played Estragon to JOAN SYDNEY's Vladimir. Pannell played the pioneer Eliza Shaw in *Swan River Saga*, a solo show on which she collaborated with the writer Mary Durack. It had its premiere was at the Hole-in-the-Wall in the 1972 FESTIVAL OF PERTH and a national tour in 1973. She acted with the HOLE-IN-THE-WALL THEATRE COMPANY until well into her eighties. ❦*Ivan King*

Pantomime

Pantomime, usually children's entertainment nowadays, deliberately appealed to the broadest audience in its colonial heyday—to old and young, highbrow and lowbrow, urban and rural. Many country people made their only annual excursion to town for the pantomime at Christmas. Pantomime combined political satire written by journalists and other highly-educated men with gross knockabout comedy, breathtaking spectacles, music borrowed from every source, massed female beauty and child actors. It gave free rein to the 19th-century love of pastoral fantasylands and exquisite dreams of perfection, tinged with the grotesque edge peculiar to the age.

At its inception in the 18th century, English pantomime consisted of alternating scripted and mimed scenes. The mimed scenes used characters from the Italian *commedia dell'arte*—Harlequin, Columbine, Pantaloon and Clown—while the scripted plots used material from literature and legend. The genius of 'Joey' Grimaldi ensured that the main features of the Regency period were the Clown character and the harlequinade, the second part of the performance. By mid-19th century the acrobatic harlequinade had shrunk under the influence of kindred forms of spectacle, BURLESQUE and EXTRAVAGANZA, and the 'opening' had stretched to as long as three hours. Burlesque actors—and music-hall stars later—more expert in comedy and vocal specialities than in demanding acrobatics, took over the opening. The harlequinade diminished to a token slapstick routine, and by the end of the century was all but forgotten. The longer opening advanced the writer, who supplied plots—originally from any branch of literature but by the 1880s consisting of half a dozen familiar fairy tales—atrocious puns and the crucial local allusions. The writer was complemented by the scene-painter, the music-arranger, the choreographer, the costumier, mechanists, scene-shifters and performers. A spectacular pantomime at the end of the 19th century could employ a production team and cast of some hundreds, though the vigorous colonial shows of 1860–80 made their impact with less spectacle and greater immediate relevance. Pantomimes used many children as animals, fairies or in the 'juvenile harlequinade', and lots of glamorous ballet dancers for the 'March of the Amazons'.

The scene-painter, providing glittering and sumptuous scenes, was possibly the strongest drawcard. GEORGE GORDON, ALEXANDER HABBE, JOHN HENNINGS and W. J. WILSON were notable scene-painters. MOVING PANORAMAS incorporated in the spectacle showed topographical scenes and historical or current world events. Scenery depicted not only jewelled caverns or the temple of Venus, but increasingly showed audiences their own environment—Bourke Street, Manly Beach or Fern Tree Gully. The pantomime culminated in a transformation scene, a 'dream of joy' where scenery, music and female beauty interacted in a sequence of set changes ending in a tableau, usually allegorical.

Pantomime demanded considerable topicality, so it was the first theatrical form to undergo much Australian localisation. This was initially confined to a few local scenes and allusions, but by the mid-1840s wholly Australian pantomimes such as HARLEQUIN IN AUSTRALIA FELIX were being performed. More pantomime libretti have survived than any other form of locally written colonial theatre. They are extraordinary documents, not only for recording traces of performance of vibrant theatricality, but for their social and cultural evidence. A pantomime libretto surveyed the events of the year and all the topical jokes. Little of the passing scene escaped the librettist's eye, and in these scripts one can discern colonial history as seen by the average citizen. Gold fever, constitutional reform, parish-pump or international politics, education acts, the Woman Question, wars and depressions all provided material for comment on the comic stage. Pantomime also recorded the daily preoccupations of the urban colonists—polluted harbours, uncertain gas or water supplies, chignons and bustles, new modes of transport. It also reflected theatre itself, burlesquing popular operas, sensation dramas, famous performers or whatever was the fashion.

The writers chiefly associated with the Australianising of pantomime were W. M. AKHURST, with at least 14 scripts, and GARNET WALCH with at least 17. Other writers included the cartoonist Thomas Carrington, MARCUS CLARKE, James Eville, W. B. Gill, G. S. Hough, SAMUEL LAZAR, ARCHIBALD MURRAY and Bert Royle. There were countless more, usually anonymous and mostly journalists. A journalist as writer guaranteed the up-to-date political allusions that were vital in adapting English libretti to Australian realities. The writers and the performers provided colonial audiences—too often reduced to consuming imperial literary ideologies—with jokes and fresh images of their own environment. Pantomime could demonstrate imperial moods, but it pioneered Australian mass imagery, it was produced locally, and it aimed to please audience tastes. Localisation was sometimes merely introduction of random jibes or caricatures, though no less appreciated by audiences for that. But by the 1860s there was a reasonable tradition of writing in which complete fantasies were elaborated upon local themes—sometimes acutely partisan—using pantomime's structural conventions.

Little is known of an anonymous Geelong pantomime *Harlequin Separation—or, the Demon of Sydney and the Fairy of Victoria*, but its 1851 date is explanatory. The title of the 1866 Sydney show *Harlequin Tu-mut-chu, Prince of Wivinghoe—or, Chow-cow-pa, Skidmalink and Jeema-ma-ten* is opaque until one recognises in its cast-list such personalities as Charles Cowper, James Martin, Geoffrey Eagar and David Buchanan disguised in Arabian-Nights costumes. Marcus Clarke's Melbourne pantomimes *Goody Two Shoes* (1870) and *Twinkle, Twinkle Little Star* (1873) read today like a hybrid of vaudeville and an *Age* editorial, so pungent are their political attacks. W. B. Gill's *Harlequin Man in the Moon* (1873, Sydney) has the fairy Luna thus rebuke the demon Larrikinos for his parliamentary procedures:

> *If manners such as these disgrace our seats*
> *No wonder larrikins infest our streets.*

Besides the perennial targets of public life, some pantomimes developed into original allegories, revealing for the construction of 'Australian' mythologies. Among the most charming and clever is Samuel Lazar and Arthur Diamond's 1874 *Prince Enterprise—or, Harlequin Ogre and the Kangaroo, Cockatoo and Possum-too*. In it Prince Enterprise defeats the Ogre Absentee, who has transformed the inhabitants of 'Farinacea' (South Australia) into a kangaroo, etc. The reformed Ogre resolves to reside in Farinacea and 'never spend his cash in other states'. Akhurst's *Tom Tom, the Piper's Son*, produced in Melbourne in 1867, shows his persistent interest in the benefits of education, and the log-cabin-to-Lord-Mayor-of-Melbourne plot culminates in a patriotic procession of English monarchs, in deference to the Duke of Edinburgh's 1867 visit. Akhurst's *Harlequin Robinson Crusoe* (1868) burlesques this patriotic theme in a parade of British literary worthies.

The theme of 'young Australia' growing to meet adult challenges is explored humorously in Akhurst's *The House that Jack Built* (1869, Melbourne) and Walch's *Trookulentos, the Tempter* (1871, Sydney). Most appealing is Walch's 1873 AUSTRALIA FELIX—or, *Harlequin Laughing Jackass and the Magic Bat*, where the tradition of helpful wallabies, Aborigines or cockatoos culminates in a kookaburra character that is, along with Mirth, instrumental in ridding Victoria of English gloom.

At the end of the 19th century pantomime expanded to gigantic proportions, full of imported stars, spectacle and variety acts. J. C. WILLIAMSON and other managers toured huge 'Christmas' shows around Australasia for months. One show had to serve many regions, and pantomime eventually lost its traditional local material and local appeal. Even so, Williamson was saved from the 1890s depression by vigorous pantomimes he wrote with Royle, *Djin Djin the Japanese Bogie Man* (1892) and *Matsa, Queen of Fire* (1896). The 1900 federation pantomime *Australis—or, the City of Zero*, set in Sydney in 2001; Ella Airlie's THE BUNYIP (1916) and NAT PHILLIPS's *Cinderella* (1920) with STIFFY AND MO as the comic talent, were in the tradition of popular local spectacle.

After the First World War, pantomime decayed, its functions replaced by newsreel, musical comedy and REVUE. Its diverse theatrical components, opportunistically syncretised through its two centuries of practice, dispersed. The revue of the 1920s and 1930s, with ROY RENE and others, was its immediate comic heir. However, the elements of colonial pantomime persist in various contemporary forms —cabaret, musicals, political revue, puppetry, circus, ballet, mime and, of course, children's panto replete with dame, principal boy and routines as old as *commedia dell'arte*. So pantomime has not really died, but merely mutated once again. ❦*Veronica Kelly*

further reading
BOOTH, MICHAEL (ed.). *English Plays of the Nineteenth Century* 5. Oxford: Clarendon Press 1976.
BOOTH, MICHAEL (ed.). *Victorian Spectacular Theatre 1850–1900*. London: Routledge and Kegan Paul 1981.
FANTASIA, JOSEPHINE. J. C. Williamson's vision for Australia— *Australis: or, The City of Zero* (1900). *Australasian Drama Studies* 23 (Brisbane 1993).
KELLY, VERONICA. Melodrama, an Australian pantomime, and the theatrical constructions of colonial history. *Journal of Australian Studies* 38 (Melbourne 1993).
MAYER, DAVID. *Harlequin in his Element—The English pantomime 1806–1836*. Cambridge, Mass., USA: Harvard University Press 1969.
RICHARDSON, PAUL. Garnet Walch's *Australia Felix*: a reconstruction. *Australasian Drama Studies* 1/2 (Brisbane, April 1983).
RICHARDSON, PAUL. Harlequin in the Antipodes. *Southerly* 42/2 (June 1982): 212–20.
WALCH, GARNET. *Australia Felix—or, Harlequin Laughing Jackass and the Magic Bat* (ed. Veronica Kelly). Brisbane: University of Queensland Press 1988.

Peter Parkinson MBE
Architect. Born 15 November 1925 in London. Came to Australia March 1952. Designed Octagon Theatre at University of Western Australia (Perth) 1969. Restored His Majesty's Theatre, Perth, 1980.

Peter Parkinson's restoration of the 1904 HIS MAJESTY'S THEATRE in Perth earned him the gratitude of many theatregoers. Commissioned to convert it to a modern theatre, Parkinson persuaded his client, the Western Australian government, to restore the old auditorium instead of gutting it and building a new one. The restoration was done with seemingly slight but difficult alterations to satisfy present-day requirements for audience facilities, sightlines and air-conditioning. This extraordinarily handsome building brought Parkinson an MBE for services to architecture and the theatre and the West Australian chapter of the Royal Australian Institute of Architects gave him its architecture award in 1980 and its bronze medal in 1984.

Parkinson was encouraged to enjoy theatre by his father in England, who taught engineering and directed musical productions. His interest in theatre was reinforced when he was at the Architectural Association School in 1947–50 by a project to design a theatre school building for the Old Vic Theatre Company. In 1952 Parkinson emigrated to Perth, where he obtained a position with an architectural firm. In 1954 he designed the Subiaco City Hall, but otherwise he worked on commercial buildings and houses until the firm was dissolved in 1964. Next year he formed the practice of Hill and Parkinson, which lasted until 1981.

Theatre had become a passion for Parkinson. He designed sets for plays, set up the Shiralee Theatre in a coffee shop in Perth with his partner Lex Hill, and then a compact Restoration-style theatre in his own backyard. He was commissioned to design a new multipurpose theatre for the University of Western Australia and the British director TYRONE GUTHRIE was invited to Perth in 1965 to advise on the design brief. Out of the meeting of Parkinson and Guthrie grew the Octagon Theatre, the first thrust-stage theatre in Australia. When it opened in 1969 it was claimed to be the most exciting new building in Australia. It won the West Australian RAIA bronze medal for 1969.

In 1973 the university decided to replace the Dolphin Theatre, in a temporary asbestos-cement building, with a new end-stage, fly-tower theatre designed by Parkinson. In 1978 he renovated the Hayman Hall of the School of Arts and Design in the former Churchlands College of Advanced Education to produce a flexible theatre space. During the restoration of His Majesty's Theatre, Parkinson contributed to his firm's design for the regional performing-arts centre at Geraldton (WA), the Queen's Park Theatre. In 1981 he resigned from the partnership and established himself as a theatre consultant and architect, still occasionally designing sets. ❦*Ross Thorne*

Wallace Parnell
Producer. Born 14 October 1894 in London. Son of famous ventriloquist Fred Russell (originally Thomas Frederick Parnell). One of five brothers who made careers in entertainment. Worked in advertising and promotion in USA in early 1920s. Produced revues in United Kingdom in 1930s. Came to Australia as producer for Tivoli circuit 1935. General manager of Tivoli circuit 1940–44. Died 19 May 1954 in Los Angeles (USA).

Wallace Parnell's most productive and successful years were the nine he spent in Australia with the TIVOLI CIRCUIT. He created and produced a new revue every four to six weeks for the entire period, fostered the circuit's considerable contribution to the war effort, and encouraged many local artists, designers and musicians. When FRANK NEIL engaged him as producer in 1935 Parnell was known in the United Kingdom as a producer of first-class touring variety revues. A London production, *West End Scandals* in 1934 fell foul of the Lord Chamberlain for alleged indecency. Parnell became general manager of the Tivoli circuit on Neil's death, and ran it until DAVID N. MARTIN bought it in 1944. Parnell then went to Los Angeles. Attempts to establish himself as a theatrical producer and as a promoter of new products ended in failure and in 1954 he killed his secretary and committed suicide. ❦*Frank Van Straten*

Richard Parry
Actor, director. Born 1897 in Wales. Came to Australia 1923. Acted with Independent Theatre (Sydney) and J. C. Williamson's 1930–35. In England 1935–39. In Marie Ney Company in Australia 1940.

Joined Whitehall Theatrical Productions (Sydney) as actor and director 1941; director of company 1947–50. Leading radio actor in 1940s. Directed children's radio plays for ABC from 1942 until retirement in late 1960s. Died 1973 at Bowral (NSW).

At the MINERVA THEATRE in Sydney Richard Parry acted in and directed many successful shows for WHITEHALL THEATRICAL PRODUCTIONS. He directed *The Corn is Green* by Emlyn Williams and played leading roles in *The Wind of Heaven* also by Williams, *The Winslow Boy* and *Love in Idleness* by Terence Rattigan and *The Guinea Pig* by W. Chetham Strode. In 1946 Whitehall toured Australia and New Zealand under Parry's direction.

Parry was DORIS FITTON's leading man in the first production by INDEPENDENT THEATRE, *By Candlelight* by Siegfried Geyer, in 1930. Many successful roles for Independent followed, notably Lewis Dodd in *The Constant Nymph* by Margaret Kennedy and Basil Dean in 1931. After this Parry had leading roles in plays for J. C. WILLIAMSON's. He was Louis XV in the operetta *The Dubarry* in 1934 and after more musical roles for the Firm he went to England. He had a season at the Birmingham Repertory Theatre, played in *Pygmalion* and *Saint Joan* under the watchful eye of George Bernard Shaw at the Malvern Festival and played in the West End. Back in Australia, he joined the MARIE NEY company in 1940, in S. N. Behrman's *No Time for Comedy* and Noël Coward's *Private Lives*. ❦*Jessica Noad*

Parsifal

—or, *The Redemption of Kundry*. Play in four acts by T. Hilhouse Taylor. **premiere** 22 December 1906, Her Majesty's Theatre, Sydney. Cast: Minnie Tittell Brune, Vivian Edwards, Thomas Kingston, Gaston Mervale. Composer and conductor: Christian Hellemann. Designers: John Gordon, W. R. Coleman, W. Little. Director: J. C. Williamson. **published** Sydney: Angus and Robertson 1906.

One of J. C. WILLIAMSON's rare acts of faith in an Australian author was *Parsifal*. It was a 'colossal spectacular', said the *Sydney Morning Herald* on 24 December 1906. 'Colossal is the word', echoed the *Sydney Mail* a week later. *Parsifal* had 180 stagehands, ten scenes of mythological splendour, a huge cast of Knights of the Holy Grail—'stalwart warriors in chain-mail with gigantic cross-handled swords at their sides'—'Priestesses of Satanas', 'Siren Vampires', and the American actress MINNIE TITTELL BRUNE as Kundry 'the cursed one'. She was a singing and dancing medieval temptress who sought goodness, love and marriage with the White Knight Amfortas (Vivian Edwards) but was bound to obey every wish of the evil sorcerer Klingsor (Gaston Mervale). The theatre had to be closed for a day to prepare for the opening. The lighting was considered a triumph in itself. The moral wrath of God culminated in the destruction of Klingsor's castle by an earthquake at the end of the fourth act 'when pillars and towers and temples toppled right and left with a noise like thunder, and all the sky was lurid with a panorama of direful, swiftly moving clouds'.

The 'Reverend' Thomas Hilhouse Taylor—as he was advertised—was one of several Australian authors who dramatised religious and Biblical stories after the long-standing official disapproval of such subjects was lifted in 1896 with the production in London of Wilson Barrett's *The Sign of the Cross*. Taylor made Kundry the central role and her 'redemption' the central theme. Christian Hellemann's score included the prelude to Richard Wagner's opera *Parsifal*. After publishing the script Taylor added a short speech for Tittell Brune to make from the stage at the end of the play, asking 'the audience to take home with them the spirit of the mystery-play, instead of remembering only its superficial splendours'. On opening night this caused wild enthusiasm. Williamson made a speech of gratitude 'for the success of a purely Australian production, and for the magnificent work of scene painters and stage staff in one of the most exacting pieces he had ever attempted to put on during his career'. The show ran in Sydney for 51 packed performances, transferred for five weeks at Her Majesty's Theatre in Melbourne from 23 March 1907 and six performances at the Theatre Royal in Adelaide from 1 June. Taylor was also coauthor of successful non-religious plays as 'Toso' Taylor. ❦*Richard Fotheringham and Veronica Kelly*

Frederick Parslow

Actor. Born 14 August 1932 at Shepparton (Vic.) Worked in bank and trained for theatre with Maie Hoban and Katherine Wiellaert in Melbourne. Joined Union Theatre Repertory Company (Melbourne) 1955. Erik Kuttner Award 1959. Married to Joan Harris, actor and director of National Theatre Drama School.

A leading actor closely associated with the Union Theatre Repertory Company and its successor the MELBOURNE THEATRE COMPANY for more than 30 years, Frederick Parslow estimates he has acted in more than 250 plays in his career. He gave his first professional performance as Fortinbras in *Hamlet* for Peter O'Shaughnessy's lunch-hour theatre in Melbourne. JOHN SUMNER saw him and asked him to join the new Union Theatre Repertory Company to play juvenile leads and be assistant stage manager in a season of fortnightly repertory. In 1955 he was promoted to stage manager for the first production of Ray Lawler's *Summer of the Seventeenth Doll*. His roles as he matured included Jimmy Porter in John Osborne's *Look Back in Anger* in 1957, Heracles in Benn W. Levy's *The Rape of the Belt* in 1959 and Richard II. He played the Priest in *The Devils* by John Whiting in 1970 and the Cook in Joachim Tenschert's production of Bertolt Brecht's *Mother Courage* in 1974. In 1981–82 he created the role of old Einstein in RON ELISHA's *Einstein*. He played Dad in the enormously popular *On Our Selection* in 1982–83 and the old Bert Facey in *A Fortunate Life* in 1984. In the mid-1960s he was seen on television for four years in revue and condensed plays on *In Melbourne Tonight*. ❦*Robert Hewett*

Fred Parsons

Scriptwriter. Born 1 April 1908 in Harrogate (Yorkshire, England). Emigrated to Australia with parents while young. Joined Melbourne *Herald* as copy boy and worked there for 11 years. Began writing for stage as hobby in mid-1930s. Scriptwriter and stage director at Tivoli Theatre 1937–43. Wrote for radio from 1940. Also wrote for television. Died 20 August 1987 in Melbourne.

Fred Parsons wrote scripts for the major revue comedians of his day, including SYD BECK, Dick Bentley, JIM GERALD, CHARLES NORMAN, CYRIL RITCHARD, ROY RENE and GEORGE WALLACE. He also wrote for the American vocal group the Mills Brothers and the English comedian Arthur Askey. He began writing sketches for the first Australian *Crazy Show* at the Princess Theatre in Melbourne in 1934, and in 1935-36 he wrote for Rene, who was then with the Connors–Paul revue company. He became particularly associated with Rene and wrote his biography. WALLACE PARNELL employed Parsons as a sketch writer and stage director on the Tivoli circuit in 1937–43. Full-time employment as a scriptwriter was unusual in the theatre, but not in radio, for which Parsons began working full-time in 1943 with the Colgate-Palmolive production unit. ❦*Victoria Chance*

writings
A Man Called Mo—A biography of Roy Rene. Melbourne: Heinemann 1973.

Philip Parsons AM

Academic, critic, director, dramaturge, publisher. Born 27 January 1926 in Adelaide. Grew up in Perth. Graduated from University of Western Australia 1950. Harkness Fellowship to Cambridge University 1951. Lecturer in English literature, University of Western Australia 1959–64. Married critic and writer Katharine Brisbane 1960. Joined University of NSW drama department 1965; retired as senior lecturer in School of Theatre and Film Studies 1987. Founded Currency Press with wife 1971; chairman until death. Died 20 June 1993 in Sydney. Sydney Critics' Circle Major Award for services to Australian theatre, with Katharine Brisbane, 1992. AM 1993. Father of Nicholas Parsons, dramatist and director.

The most enduring influence of Philip Parsons has been as teacher and mentor to many of the students, scholars, actors, directors and playwrights associated with the new wave of Australian drama in the 1970s. At the University of Western Australia and the University of NSW in the 1960s Parsons pioneered an approach to the study of theatre that incorporated practical work into the predominant study of play texts in literature departments. He thereby laid the groundwork for the rise of departments of theatre and performance studies.

Fascinated by theatre from childhood, Parsons became a leading actor in undergraduate productions, with a penchant for playing villains. At Cambridge University his thesis on Restoration tragedy was a radical reappraisal from the viewpoint of performance, and he found a special milieu among students who later became influential in the development of British theatre. One of these was John Barton, later a director for the ROYAL SHAKESPEARE COMPANY. His tutor at King's College was George Rylands, an influential background figure. Through these men Parsons gained the insight that later earned him the nickname 'Dr Colon' among actors—a sobriquet that referred to his dramaturgy, in which he claimed that punctuation in the first folio edition of Shakespeare was there to assist the actor's phrasing, not the reader's understanding.

He pursued this in early experiments in Elizabethan performance practice at the University of Western Australia. In 1964 he was involved in the design of the university's NEW FORTUNE THEATRE, where he directed *Richard III* for the 1968 Festival of Perth, with Martin Redpath in the title-role. Designed by REX CRAMPHORN, the production simulated Elizabethan daylight conditions.

With his wife KATHARINE BRISBANE, he founded Currency Press to publish Australian play texts. In its National Theatre Series, to which he devoted special attention, he attempted to establish an Australian classic repertoire, rediscovering dramatists such as LOUIS ESSON, KATHARINE SUSANNAH PRICHARD and BETTY ROLAND. He resumed his experiments in Elizabethan performance in Sydney in 1986 and in retirement from academic life he continued to work on his lifetime project of forging links between the academy and the theatrical profession. With WAYNE HARRISON he founded Dramaturgical Services Inc.—a tongue-in-cheek name—and embarked on a practical and popular research program of productions of Shakespeare in daylight with minimal props. These productions, which were aimed at renewing the power of the poetry by enlarging the audience's imagination, culminated in the annual 'Shakespier' series at the Sydney Theatre Company's WHARF THEATRE. The last was *Antony and Cleopatra* in 1992. Shortly before he died he was made a member of the Order of Australia for the work of Currency Press, and later in 1993 the NSW Ministry for the Arts instituted an annual Philip Parsons memorial lecture on the performing arts. His widow gave first on 1 December 1993 at the Wharf. ❦*John McCallum*

further reading
BRISBANE, KATHARINE. Investing in authors—A history of Currency Press. *Voices* (Canberra, spring 1993).

Patch Theatre

Amateur theatre company in Perth, founded in September 1939 by Edward (Bill) and Ida Beeby as speech, drama and dance studio.
venues Bon Marché Arcade, Barrack Street. Munster House, Murray Street. William Street. Colin Street, West Perth. Albany Highway, Victoria Park. Burswood Road, Victoria Park.

From 1939 to 1949 Patch Theatre offered the only organised drama instruction in Perth. Bill and Ida Beeby's immersion of their students in movement, music, speech, song and dance was unique in Australia until government-funded academies were set up. Patch Theatre trained many teachers and provided the professional theatre with many performers, including Ray Angel, MARGARET FORD, NITA PANNELL and Alan Trevor. Competing with the long-established REPERTORY CLUB, Patch had a reputation for daring in its productions, although most of the plays were standard fare. Bill Beeby's lighting was especially notable. Sidney Davis, a gifted designer, contributed outstanding settings and Flo Barnard's costumes were significant.

Patch Theatre gave plays on two and later three nights a week for up to 14 weeks. Besides standard classics and West End and Broadway plays, works by local playwrights such as Raymond Bowers appeared. The 120-seat auditorium in the proscenium theatre at Munster House was well patronised. Patch made no charge for seats until the late 1940s, but asked patrons to give a silver coin after the performance. This avoided entertainments tax and reduced royalty payments. Bill Beeby became well known as a political commentator on radio during the war. Patch gave much to patriotic funds and took productions to armed forces establishments during the Second World War. The production standard was high despite a shortage of male performers and wartime restrictions.

The company took its name from a patchwork front curtain when it graduated from music lectures to the presentation of Stephen Phillips's *Paolo and Francesca* in 1939. Patch was as much a dance and music theatre as a dramatic establishment. By 1947, 500 students attended classes in drama, speech, singing or dancing every week, and plays ran five nights a week for 11 months of the year. A highlight of Patch's career was a teaching visit by the American dancer Ted Shawn at Ida Beeby's invitation in 1948.

Thereafter dance became less important in the curriculum. The Beebys' 15-year marriage proved to be by common law and ended in 1949 when Ida married Morris Hertz, a dance student 40 years younger than herself. They settled in Sydney and she died in a car accident in 1957. Mary Senior and Jean Rule took over the school and theatre and from 1959 COLLEEN CLIFFORD was a principal teacher and director. David Crann has been its actor-manager since 1965. He has instituted a wide range of theatrical activity in Perth and extended schools tours to the remote parts of Western Australia and even to South Australia, providing professional work for many young actors. ❦*Peter Mann*

further reading
THOMPSON, PATRICIA. *Accidental Chords*. Melbourne: Penguin 1988. Autobiography of Ida Beeby's daughter.

Patch Theatre Company

Professional youth-theatre company in Adelaide, founded in 1972 by Morna Jones as Little Patch Company. **artistic directors** 1972–81 Morna Jones. 1981 Tony Strutton. 1982–83 Peter Townsend. 1984 Des James. 1985 Jacqy Phillips. 1986–91 Christine Anketel. 1992– Dave Brown.

The energetic, creative Patch Theatre Company has developed from a privately operated company, specialising in mime and puppetry for young audiences, into a subsidised young people's theatre. Under Christine Anketel it presented mainstage productions such as Mem Fox's *Wilfred Gordon McDonald Partridge* in 1987, Margaret Mahy's *The Man Whose Mother was a Pirate* in 1988 and adaptations of Gillian Rubinstein's *Space Demons* in 1989 and *Beyond the Labyrinth* in 1991. Productions in 1992 included *Paula* by Gillian Rubinstein, *Birds of the Moon* by Anna O'Connor and *Once Upon a Ruby Red* by Carolyn Burns, who also adapted Victor Kelleher's *The Red King*. This was produced in 1993, as was *Pigs Might Fly*, adapted by Dave Brown and Lisa Philip-Harbutt from Emily Rodda's novel. Brown, Robert Crompton, Pilawuk and Simone Tur wrote *Rak Awin*, performed in 1994. ❦*Murray Bramwell*

Queenie Paul

Entrepreneur, producer, singer. Born 1894 in NSW. Originally Eveline Paul. On stage at 16 as singer. Formed Fullers' vaudeville act and produced revues with husband Mike Connors. Formed Con-Paul Theatres to revive variety 1931. Sold out to Frank Neil 1934. Coproducer with Connors until he died in 1949. Began producing revues with veteran performers 1953. Died 1 August 1982 in Sydney.

For nearly 70 years Queenie Paul produced and performed in variety throughout Australasia, and in venues from Tivoli theatres to licensed clubs she never failed to find an audience. She was also principal boy in many pantomimes, including THE BUNYIP in 1916. From the start of her career as a singer for FULLERS' during the First World War, Paul had a sentimental streak. With her husband MIKE CONNORS, an American brought to Australia by Fullers', she sang love duets notable for their syrupy lyrics. Later, on the club circuits, she exploited nostalgia with songs like 'Chattanooga Choo Choo'. More significant was her work as a producer in the early 1930s. The major vaudeville circuits, Tivoli and Fullers', had collapsed at the end of the 1920s, when theatres everywhere were closing. Other individual producers had foundered when Connors and Paul found financial backing and opened at the Haymarket Theatre in Sydney in March 1931. Offering any seat in the house for one shilling at matinées and a maximum evening price of three shillings, they quickly built up a regular audience.

Six months later they moved into the Theatre Royal in Sydney and the Tivoli Theatre in Melbourne. In July 1932 they moved into the Grand Opera House in Sydney and renamed it the New Tivoli Theatre. ROY RENE and JIM GERALD revue companies spearheaded the couple's success in reviving the TIVOLI CIRCUIT. The famous ballet lines, the Con-Paul Boys and the Exquisite Eight, were choreographed and costumed by Paul. She also introduced the hugely successful Beef Trust ballet, a line of eight women who weighed more than 127 kg apiece.

The pair sold their interest in the circuit to FRANK NEIL in 1934, and worked together until Connors died in 1949. Paul then became a solo performer. She was touring Asia with a nightclub act when HARRY WREN asked her to produce a revue with veteran performers, *Thanks for the Memory*, in 1953. She also produced *The Good Old Days* in 1956 and *Many Happy Returns* in 1959 for Wren, and she toured clubs with her own Queenie Paul Show. RON SHAND, who worked for Connors and Paul in the 1930s, remembered Paul as the driving force, a hard boss with brains, untold energy and a flair for costume. Others recall her as larger than life, playing the star with alacrity. She was incredibly tough. She ignored severe chest pains to perform at the Newtown Leagues Club in Sydney on the night before she died from a heart attack. ❦*Victoria Chance*

Vera Pearce

Actor, singer. Born 1895 in Australia. Began acting in pantomime at four. Sprang to musical-comedy fame in Sydney 1911. Toured England in musical comedies 1912–13. Star of Tivoli circuit 1914–20. In two Australian films 1914, 1916. In musicals and plays overseas from 1922. Died 18 January 1966.

Vitality, versatility and resilience carried Vera Pearce through 50 years as a star of musical comedies, revues, plays and films. At 16 she was a typical postcard beauty, voted the most beautiful girl in NSW by adoring admirers of her performance as Lady Muriel in *Our Miss Gibbs*, J. C. WILLIAMSON's huge musical-comedy success of 1910–11. Pearce was already a veteran performer, having worked in Williamson pantomimes since she was four. From 1914 she worked for Hugh D. McIntosh's TIVOLI CIRCUIT. She starred in the *Tivoli Follies* revue throughout its two-and-a-half-year tour from November 1914, *The Beauty Shop* in 1917; *My Lady Frayle* and *The Officers' Mess* in 1919; and *His Little Widows* in 1920. In *Chu Chin Chow* at the Tivoli Theatre in Melbourne in 1920 Pearce starred as Zahrat-al-Kulub with Charles Workman. By 1922 she was in London, starring in *Love's Awakening*. In the 1930s Pearce, now statuesque, gained great popularity in musical comedies at the Hippodrome in London. Her last noted performance was in

Georges Feydeau's farce *Hotel Paradiso* in New York City in 1957. ❦*Lynne Murphy*

George Peck
Manager, violinist. Carver and gilder by trade. Arrived in Hobart 1833. Managed Theatre Royal in Argyle Rooms 1834.

During Hobart's first theatrical season, at the Freemason's Tavern from December 1833 to May 1834, George Peck led the orchestra. He also gave concerts and late in 1834 he became manager of the Theatre Royal in the ARGYLE ROOMS. Essentially an entrepreneur, Peck was not hampered by modesty. He advertised for an apprentice at the beginning of 1834: 'None but a youth of genius and the most respectable parentage and education need apply'. From 1835 Peck diversified into other forms of entertainment, such as panoramas. In 1837 he held an art exhibition and in 1839 he exhibited a scale model of Hobart Town. He continued to play in theatre orchestras. ❦*Gillian Winter*

further reading
Kerr, Joan (ed.). Dictionary of Australian Artists, Photographers and Engravers, 1770–1870. Melbourne: Oxford University Press 1992.

Meta Pelham
Actor. Born c.1850 in Ireland. Perhaps originally Meta Vanston. Emigrated as child to Victoria. Married actor named Poole c.1866. Acted as Meta Pelham c.1876–c.1928. Details of death unknown.

For more than 50 years Meta Pelham supported the stars of major companies, from J. C. WILLIAMSON's in the 1880s to the ALLAN WILKIE SHAKESPEAREAN COMPANY in the 1920s. She was never a star, according to Hal Porter, but 'one of an army of performers whose painstaking craftsmanship provides the solid support and muted background to those more volcanic and flashy stars whose careers burnt down, often, as quickly as they flared up'. She began in 1876 in MRS SCOTT-SIDDONS's Company. In 1878 the critic J. E. NEILD did not like her in Ouida's *Puck* in Melbourne. Brief fame came in Sydney in 1898, when she began to play leads with the Frank Thornton Company, with which she also acted in London in 1899. In 1928, aged 78, she was in *Paddy the Next Best Thing* and in 1934 the Old Players' and Playgoers' Association in Melbourne claimed her as 'the oldest living actress in the British Empire'. ❦*Richard Fotheringham*

W. S. Percy
Actor, singer. Born 23 December 1872 in Melbourne. Played in children's productions of Gilbert and Sullivan operettas in 1887. Joined J. C. Williamson's Royal Comic Opera Company 1890. Toured in Pollard opera companies. Leading comedian for J. C. Williamson's. Left Australia 1914. Played more than 200 roles in operetta and pantomime in Australia and overseas. Retired 1937. Died 19 June 1946 in London.

William Stratford Percy had an ideal comic style for Edwardian operetta. After touring in POLLARD OPERA COMPANIES and being trained by J. C. WILLIAMSON, he played Nisch in the first Australian season of *The Merry Widow* in 1908. After many similar comic roles, Percy played in New York and London. He retired in 1937 after starring in the last operetta presented at Daly's Theatre in London. He made a short comedy film in Australia in 1912 and another in Hollywood in 1914. ❦*Alwyn Capern*

further reading
PARKER, JOHN (ed.). *Who's Who in the Theatre*. London: Pitman 1939.

Performance art
About 1973 'performance art' displaced 'HAPPENINGS' as the preferred name for ephemeral performances devised by sculptors, painters or, sometimes, poets. They were usually the performers, but actors, dancers or machinery occasionally gave the performance. Usually small audiences saw the performances, in adventurous dealer's galleries, artists' collectives, subsidised experimental art spaces or art museums. But sometimes only photographers or reporters saw the performance, and some performances took place in the street or countryside. Occasionally in galleries or museums, performances lasted all day, every day for weeks or months. In 1973 Gilbert & George, imported from Europe, shuffle-danced on a tabletop to a recorded music-hall song, *Underneath the Arches*, all day every day for a week in the Art Gallery of NSW in Sydney. Their hands and faces were made up as bronze and they tried to insist that they were 'living sculptures'.

Performance art is neither an art form nor an art movement. It is best perceived as technique within the art form of sculpture. It is not taught as a separate course in art schools but it breaks out in sculpture departments if teachers have a personal interest. It had been fused with ephemeral installation-sculpture since the 1960s.

It is often against art (and for real experience of real life); it is also anti-theatre, especially mainstream theatre. Its special role as an art technique is its unmediated immediacy. At its best, whether in pure abstract minimalism or, more often, in the emotional extremes of expressionism, it brings the work of art closer to its viewer than any painting, sculpture or theatrical performance. Physical closeness helps the full shock of recognition of meaning, by heart and mind. Performance art always hopes (vainly) to offer direct experience without cultural conditioning. It is deeply suspicious of illusion. It rushes forward from the distancing caused by picture frames, gallery spaces and proscenia.

Performance art had a particular strength in Australia in the 1970s but it already had an interesting history and it continues vigorously in the 1990s. Since 1969–70 Stelarc has produced extraordinary technological work in Melbourne, Japan and elsewhere. Devices have destroyed the audience's normal vision, have created sound, light and moving images from Stelarc's internal bodily impulses, and have become robotic additional limbs. The most sensational, however, are low-tech events in which his own body is suspended face down, and sometimes swung, from hooks inserted into the flesh on his back.

At Inhibodress, an artists' co-operative in Sydney, attention was first focused on hard, abstract or highly challenging performance art in 1970-72. Peter Kennedy, Mike Parr and Tim Johnson presented performances that would generally have been perceived as conceptual art, the newest shift within the New York avant-garde in 1969. Kennedy's and Parr's most characteristic piece was *Idea Demonstrations*. One of the many masochistic 'ideas' was *hold your finger in a candle flame for as long as possible.* Some were performed for audiences at Inhibodress in 1972 or at the 1974 Adelaide Festival fringe, including Parr's *Tackline*—drawing pins stuck into his calf. In another, shirt buttons were sewn onto his chest, a shirt was attached and then used to rip them out of his flesh.

The impulse shifted in the 1970s into community arts, codifying and awakening a community's experiences and concerns. In the 1980s at Wattamolla Beach in the Royal National Park near Sydney, composers, dancers and film artists devised environmental-awareness events, with underwater swimming by divers from science research agencies, holograms, lasers and projections on cliff faces. The 'soft' participatory performance of community arts is seldom included in accounts of performance art. It is often very beautiful, not raw; usually devised by theatre professionals; and is above all intended to empower the marginalised and inarticulate in society, not to subvert the powerful in art institutions or in politics. A rare example of a disturbing community-arts event was the 1985 Invasion of Orange, a remarkably progressive provincial city in NSW. Mike Mullins's head-bandaged General No-One gradually proliferated over a week into 130 silent, yellow-uniformed child No-Ones, who were known to be debating nuclear weapons and subsidies for private education. They provoked abuse and attack by citizens.

At the PERFORMANCE SPACE, established in 1983 in Sydney by Mike Mullins, performance art became more theatrical. His own *New Blood* of 1980, re-worked as *Long Long Time Ago* in 1983, was more like theatre than performance art. It was the inspiration for the fictional Sand Pit theatre in PATRICK WHITE's last novel, *The Memoirs of Many in One.* Avant-garde companies, the SIDETRACK PERFORMANCE GROUP and the Sydney Front, have aligned themselves with or performed at the Performance Space. In Melbourne, Kevin Mortensen's *Why People Go to Traffic Accidents* in 1987 was a play with a five-week season presented by THEATREWORKS, and Lyndal Jones in 1992 used the resources of a professional theatre in the Victorian Arts Centre during the Melbourne International Festival, whereas in 1982 she had performed alone in a bare university room in Canberra. In 1992 Anne Marsh, the principal theorist of performance art in Australia, noted that, although still found in contemporary art spaces, performance art had moved into Melbourne cabarets, dance clubs, bars and sex clubs.

From the 1980s major performing-arts festivals like the Adelaide Festival and Melbourne International Festival and their fringes often presented the crossovers from performance to performing arts, or the near-performance performing arts—Australian works by Lyndal Jones or the Sydney Front's *Don Juan*, more often imports like the American singer Laurie Anderson, Pina Bausch's and Jan Fabre's European dance groups, the Japanese groups Enkei Gejiko, Sankai Juku and Dumb Type or, in 1992, the highly sculptural American 'opera', Robert Wilson's *Einstein on the Beach*. An early import was the 1976 Adelaide Festival's Merce Cunningham Dance Company.

The comparable 'festivals' for new visual art have always accommodated performance art—the Sculpture Triennials at Mildura (Vic.), especially from 1973; the international Biennales of Sydney from 1976; the Australian Perspectas in Sydney from 1981; ANZART in Christchurch (New Zealand) in 1981 and Hobart in 1983 and their ARX successors in Perth. The Museum of Contemporary Art in Sydney, opened in 1991, includes performance art in its exhibitions. There have been specialist performance-art festivals: Act 1, Act 2, and Act 3, organised by Ingo Kleinert of the Canberra School of Art in 1978, 1980 and 1982 respectively; the Experimental Art Foundation's Performance Week organised by Noel Sheridan for the 1980 Adelaide Festival fringe; Woop Woop, organised in Adelaide by Pamela Zeplin and Casey van Sebille in 1987; and Anne Marsh's performance week at Monash University in 1989.

Major European, American and Japanese performance artists have been brought to these exhibitions, notably Stuart Brisley to the Biennale of Sydney in 1976, Min Tanaka in 1982, and Marina & Ulay in 1979. The last returned for the 1981 Australian Perspecta to perform a work with central Australian content—a gold-leaf boomerang and a live snake. The stars Gilbert & George in 1973, and Charlotte Moorman, performing works by Nam June Paik, Joseph Beuys, Takehisha Kosugi and others in 1976, were brought to Australia as John Kaldor Art Projects.

Eight capital-city, publicly supported contemporary art spaces now provide year-round opportunities for performance art. This institutional network began in 1974 with the Experimental Art Foundation in Adelaide, whose first director was the performance artist Noel Sheridan. It was completed in 1990 with 24 Hour Art, Darwin. In the early 1990s three spaces had directors who were performance artists—Sheridan in Perth, Nicholas Tsoutas in Brisbane, Richard Grayson in Adelaide. ❧*Daniel Thomas*

further reading

BRITTON, STEPHANIE (ed.). *A Decade of the Experimental Art Foundation 1974–84*. Adelaide: Experimental Art Foundation 1984.

BROMFIELD, DAVID. *Identities—A critical study of the work of Mike Parr 1970–1990*. Perth: University of Western Australia Press 1991.

BRONSON, A. A. and PEGGY GALE (eds). *Performance by Artists*. Toronto (Canada): Art Metropole 1979.

CRAMER, SUE. *Inhibodress 1970–72*. Brisbane: Institute of Modern Art: 1989.

GOLDBERG, ROSE LEE. *Performance Art—From Futurism to the present*. London: Thames and Hudson 1988.

HUMPHRIES, BARRY. *More Please*. London: Viking 1992.

MARSH, ANNE and JANE KENT. *Live Art*. Adelaide: private 1984.

MARSH, ANNE. *Body and Self—Performance art in Australia 1969–92*. Melbourne: Oxford University Press 1993.

MARSH, ANNE. Technobodies: spectacles, dreams and desires. *Binocular—Focusing, time lapses* (ed. E. McDonald and J. Engberg). Sydney: Moët et Chandon 1992.

MENDELSSOHN, JOANNA. *The Yellow House 1970–72*. Sydney: Art Gallery of NSW 1990.

PAFFRATH, JAMES D. with STELARC. *Obsolete Body/Suspension/Stelarc*. Davis (California, USA): JP Publications 1984.

STURGEON, GRAEME. *The Development of Australian Sculpture 1788–1975*. London: Thames and Hudson 1978.

THOMAS, DANIEL (ed.). *An Australian Accent—Three artists, Mike Parr, Imants Tillers, Ken Unsworth*. Sydney: John Kaldor 1984.

Performance Space

Theatre in Cleveland Street, Redfern, Sydney, opened 1983.

Mike Mullins set up the Performance Space for experimental theatre and dance in an old railway workers' union hall that had been occasionally used for performances since his

New Blood in 1980. His ambition was to provide a professional venue for what he called 'new form'. Many individuals and the University of Sydney's Theatre Workshop helped to turn the hall into a theatre and it officially opened in 1983 with Mullins's *Long Long Time Ago*. Its uses have gradually encompassed the visual arts—particularly with a performance, temporal or installation aspect—theory and criticism. In mid-1983 the present writer joined Mullins as co-ordinator and brought ENTR'ACTE THEATRE to the Performance Space as resident company. Nicholas Tsoutas followed with his All Out Ensemble. ❦*Christopher Allen*

Performance Syndicate

Experimental-theatre company in Sydney founded in 1969 by Rex Cramphorn. Dissolved 1975. **first production** *Orestes* by Euripides adapted by William Yang, 16 August 1971 at Arts Factory, Sydney. Cast: David Cameron, Gillian Jones, Nicos Lathouris, Terry O'Brien, William Yang. Director: Rex Cramphorn.

Many of the productions of the Performance Syndicate have become legendary for their rigorous form, concentration upon storytelling and contemplative—in some cases Oriental—visual impact. No group in Australia, outside the modern-dance companies, has since attempted to impose such rigorous disciplines upon its members with the aim of creating total performers. The director REX CRAMPHORN founded the group to develop a team of actors capable of extreme concentration and to re-examine the purpose and meaning of the theatrical process.

Like alternative-theatre companies performing in unconventional spaces overseas, the syndicate sought to challenge the direction of mainstream theatre, which then largely flowed from London and New York. It began as an informal group that used the rehearsal space at the NATIONAL INSTITUTE OF DRAMATIC ART in Sydney for experiment and membership was by association. Most of the actors were, like Cramphorn, recent graduates of NIDA. They included initially David Cameron, GILLIAN JONES, Nicos Lathouris, Terry O'Brien and William Yang, and later KATE FITZPATRICK, ROBYN NEVIN, Bjarne Ohlin, John Paramor and Andrew Siman.

Cramphorn had a strong academic background in the texts of European classics and he set about revising and rethinking performance of the classics in a climate of student revolution, protest against censorship and the ferment of recently achieved government support for the arts. He was impressed by Jerzy Grotowski's account of his Polish Laboratory Theatre in *Towards a Poor Theatre*, and by other theatrical communes. The group set up as a commune to live and work towards a common goal of simply expressed, concentrated performance achieved through the daily discipline of yoga and martial arts, musicianship and vocal training. Their early discipline was probably seen at its most extreme in *10 000 Miles Away*, a surreal work by William Yang. It made connections between the voyages of Captain Cook, the bicentenary of whose landing in Australia had just been celebrated, and the space travellers who had landed on the moon in 1969. The cast ran without pause for nearly an hour during the first half.

Of more lasting memory were productions of *The Tempest* and *Pericles*, played with a handful of props and a cast of eight or so telling the story simply in a flat space surrounded by audience. In *The Tempest* the cast when not acting sat at the side of the stage, providing music and sound effects and occasionally dialogue, as in the case of the spirit Ariel, who was evoked in imagination by ribbons floating from Prospero's magical staff. The Shakespeare productions were admired but the syndicate's work generally was little understood by a theatrical hierarchy bent upon establishing new mainstream standards in the early years of subsidy. The concept of a company of actors living and working together—creating performance as a way of life—was mostly greeted with hostility. The imperatives of earning subsistence as best they could, the use of drugs by some members, and tensions between a desire to perform only when ready and management's need to prepare for an opening night, told on the members.

In 1973 the ST MARTIN'S THEATRE COMPANY in Melbourne invited the syndicate to be the resident company in its theatre for six months, but the parties—a conservative, once-amateur company with a list of aging subscribers and a young anti-establishment group challenging the boundaries of experience—proved incompatible. In 1974 the syndicate spent a $7500 special-project grant from the Australian Council for the Arts—which allowed $60 a week for each member's wages—on mounting a complex rendering of the Sanskrit classic *Shakuntala* but flagging energies led to a mortal split during the Adelaide season. A nucleus stayed with Cramphorn for his production of Alan Simpson's *Muriel*, a study of a schizophrenic committed to an institution, but during 1975 the syndicate dissolved.

The principal productions—many in co-operation with other organisations—undertaken by Cramphorn and members were: *The Revenger's Tragedy* by Cyril Tourneur in Hobart, in 1970; THE LEGEND OF KING O'MALLEY directed by John Bell in 1970; *Ten Thousand Miles Away* in Sydney in 1970; the so-called 'black' *Macbeth* with Nicos Lathouris, directed by Bell at the Nimrod Street Theatre, *Orestes*, adapted from Euripides and *Pericles* in Sydney in 1971; *The Tempest* in Sydney and on three Arts Council of NSW tours in 1972–73; *The Marsh King's Daughter*, adapted from Hans Andersen by the company in Sydney in 1973; *Shakuntala* at the Adelaide Festival in 1974; *Muriel* in Sydney in 1974; Racine's *Berenice* and Molière's *Scapin* translated by Cramphorn, in Sydney in 1975. ❦*Katharine Brisbane*

Performing-arts centres

The construction of performing-arts centres has been a phenomenon in English-speaking countries, in western Europe and in some countries elsewhere since the Second World War, arising from a growing sense of cultural responsibility among public authorities. In this, as in other areas, Australia has followed suit. The construction of so many public buildings for the performing arts in capital cities and country towns is related to events going back to the eclipse of the touring theatre by films in the 1920s and the Great Depression in the 1930s. During and after the Second World War organisations were set up to revise the situation. The Arts Council of Great Britain, established in 1946, provided an impetus for a renascence of theatre-building from about 1950. West Germany gave a priority to replacing its destroyed theatres and opera houses quickly after the war, inducing in English-speaking countries an awareness of the significance of the performing arts in European countries.

By that time civic leaders in some Australian cities were beginning to feel that Australia was artistically backward. The ARTS COUNCIL OF AUSTRALIA, the British Drama League and various adult-education organisations were providing encouragement at grassroots level. The inauguration of the AUSTRALIAN ELIZABETHAN THEATRE TRUST and moves for a cultural centre in Melbourne, an opera house in Sydney and an arts festival in Perth all seemed to coalesce in 1953–55. At the same time civic leaders in New York City in sympathy with the new mood began considering the need for a major performing-arts centre. The building committee for the future Lincoln Center visited the new Royal Festival Hall in London and new German opera houses. These buildings were also on the itineraries of Australian politicians and architects, including those who in 1956 formulated the design brief for the competition for Australia's first major performing-arts centre, the SYDNEY OPERA HOUSE.

In 1960 the first ADELAIDE FESTIVAL OF ARTS was held, along the lines of the Edinburgh Festival. It was soon realised that Adelaide desperately needed a major theatre and concert hall and from this grew the ADELAIDE FESTIVAL CENTRE. In 1968 the federal government, which had been increasingly funding 'excellence' in performance through the Trust since 1955, set up the Australian Council for the Arts, following British, Canadian and American examples. The resulting burst of activity placed a new demand upon existing performing venues and soon produced a demand for better facilities. It was also discovered that audiences were attracted not only by good performances but also by an exciting venue like the Sydney Opera House, and that new methods of publicity and subscription could markedly increase audiences.

State governments set in motion plans for a performing-arts centre—the Sydney Opera House, the VICTORIAN ARTS CENTRE in Melbourne, the ADELAIDE FESTIVAL CENTRE and the QUEENSLAND CULTURAL CENTRE in Brisbane. In Perth HIS MAJESTY'S THEATRE would be restored as a state-owned lyric theatre. Under sometimes difficult circumstances—the Sydney Opera House, for example—theatre consultants and architects collaborated to produce solutions ranging from the effective to the inspired. Some early attempts by local governments to produce venues for the performing arts were less successful. Councillors and other civic leaders believed in flat-floored halls—like 19th-century schools of arts, literary and mechanics' institutes and town halls. With improved stage facilities, these would satisfy 20th-century needs for touring and local performing arts and the town's social needs as well, it was thought. Civic Theatres opened at Wagga Wagga (NSW) in 1963 and Albury (NSW) in 1964 were among the few exceptions. Two studies of towns in NSW published in 1972 and 1973 indicated the paucity of available facilities. One town had 35 flat-floored halls—the last one built in 1965—but not one was suitable for performing arts.

In 1978 the AUSTRALIA COUNCIL, formerly the Australian Council for the Arts, concerned about the quality of existing spaces for its community-arts program, commissioned a case-study of some well-designed and traditional venues. Its aim was to make local government aware of the problem of mixing performance and social uses of halls, as at Mount Isa (Qld), Broken Hill (NSW) and Willoughby and Bankstown in suburban Sydney.

State government subsidies for performing-arts centres helped to persuade local councils to build more appropriate structures. Before funds were granted the state arts ministry would review the application and the final design. The result has seen as marked improvement in country towns' amenities. Since 1974 Queensland has gradually built a chain of local-government theatre centres along the east coast at Cairns, Townsville, Rockhampton, Gympie, Ayr, Mackay and finally the Gold Coast in 1988. Victoria produced a greater variety of designs for its centres, perhaps reflecting the differing needs of cities of different sizes. The Paramount Arts Centre at Echuca includes a small end-stage theatre. The imposing old town hall at Ararat was remodelled into a handsome art centre with a hall which has a movable temporary proscenium, movable stage and a huge bank of pull-out bleacher seats—one of the few successful attempts to solve the problem of dual function. Warrnambool converted its town hall into a single-rake auditorium attached to a new fly-tower stage. Geelong did the same for its old School of Arts hall-cum-cinema, but added a small studio-type theatre.

The centre at Warragul (Vic.) conforms to a format that appeared in 1976 at the Civic Theatre in Orange (NSW) and has become a kind of standard. It has continued in some of the Queensland centres, and in South Australia at Mount Gambier, Port Pirie, Renmark and Whyalla. Others of the same format are the Araluen Arts Centre at Alice Springs (NT), the Illawarra Performing Arts Centre at Wollongong (NSW) and the centre at Griffith (NSW). All these centres have proscenium stages, most with a single-raked auditorium, seating about 500 but occasionally as many as 1000. There is usually a restaurant as these centres, like the Sydney Opera House, have discovered that catering can make an important contribution to income. Some centres also have a studio theatre, a space for a gallery or a bar. The development of this format has given country towns their version of a commercial city theatre, pragmatically meeting local expectations and the requirements of touring shows.

The Mount Gambier, Port Pirie, Whyalla, Alice Springs and Wollongong centres were all designed by Hassell Pty Ltd, the Adelaide architectural firm that designed the Adelaide Festival Centre. In South Australia, Hassell had not only to design theatre complexes but to understand the problems of managing them and enticing audiences. The firm knows the need for a suitable design brief, particularly when the client is a local council whose members have little knowledge of the technical, administrative and audience needs of a performing-arts centre. It therefore insists on working on the design brief with the client, usually involving the theatre consultants TOM BROWN and Dennis Irving.

There are many other centres. Well before provincial centres proliferated the CANBERRA THEATRE CENTRE was built, simply because the national capital had no theatre. Mildura (Vic.) like Wagga Wagga and Albury, saw the need for a true theatre and built its own in 1966. Hobart has the historic THEATRE ROYAL as its state theatre and the former Odeon cinema as its concert hall. The Launceston City Council bought the Princess Theatre as its performing-arts centre. Leeton (NSW) has the Roxy, an Art Deco cinema, and Perth has its spectacular His Majesty's Theatre.

Town halls have been converted to theatres in Toowoomba (Qld), and Albany (WA). In Western Australia, theatres have been built at Esperance and at Geraldton. The Geraldton theatre is a two-tiered modern version of a traditional theatre. This style of theatre design epitomises the philosophy of the English theatre director Peter Hall—to paper the wall with audience. It recurs successfully at Parramatta, the city at the geographical centre of Sydney, where the principal theatre of the Riverside Theatres complex is a fine design. Like the Darwin Centre in the Northern Territory, the SEYMOUR THEATRE CENTRE in Sydney and others, the Riverside complex is a creation of civic authorities who desire the prestige of a facility but are unwilling to face the interconnected issues of subsidy and entrepreneurial management. ❦Ross Thorne

further reading
THORNE, ROSS. *Housing the Arts*. Sydney: Australia Council 1979.
THORNE, ROSS. Performing arts centres—The phenomenon and what has influenced their being. *Australian Theatre Design* (ed. Kim Spinks). Sydney: Australian Production Designers Association NSW 1992.
THORNE, ROSS and P. FRAME. *Country Theatre—aspects of audience, financial support and the buildings used with particular reference to NSW*. University of Sydney 1972.
UREN, T. and APRU. *Performing Arts in Country Towns, Case Study*. University of Sydney 1973.

Perry family circuses

The Perry family has probably been associated with Australian circus since ROBERT RADFORD operated amphitheatres in Hobart and Launceston in 1847–50. George Perry, a violinist, landed in Van Diemen's Land on 2 March 1835, transported for seven years. After receiving his ticket of leave, he married Mary Heifferman, a convict from Ireland, at Launceston in January 1843. She received her own ticket of leave two years later. The Perrys were living in Launceston in the late 1840s and there is every possibility that George provided some musical accompaniment to performances in Radford's Royal Circus, which opened in the town on 27 December 1847.

George and Mary Perry had 13 children. Nine of them, all sons, were outlived by their father, who died in 1878. The surviving children at that time were the sons William George and Charles Henry Perry and the daughters Mealia and Bridget Perry. Charles Henry performed as a child with ASHTON'S CIRCUS in 1855 in Sydney and again in 1863. This suggests that the entire Perry family worked in Ashton's Circus at these times. It is also probable that during the early 1860s the family toured outback goldmining centres with a small variety show. C. H. Perry is mentioned as a trapeze artist in Ashton's Circus in 1875. He was manager of Ridge's Royal Tycoon Circus, when it gave its inaugural season in Sydney in April 1877. He remained with Ridge for some years, and was billed as 'the champion rider of the colonies', when the circus appeared in Cowra (NSW) in March 1880. He was probably the proprietor of the small United States Circus, which appeared in Young (NSW) on 26 January 1884. By 1891 C. H. Perry's circus, billed as Perry's Jubilee Circus, was large enough to combine its talents with WIRTHS' CIRCUS for a performance at Grafton (NSW) on 21 April. William George Perry, born in Hobart about 1846, played the violin. When he was 19 he married Mary Ann Ahearn at Ballarat (Vic.). She is supposed to have been a dancer and the couple appear to have worked as itinerant entertainers before they bought a hotel near the Northampton Downs station in Queensland, between Tambo and Blackall, in 1885. In June 1889, W. G. Perry and his family sold the hotel and apparently bought the circus of a showman named Hayes. They began their travels as Perry's Young Queensland Circus, giving their first performance at Tambo. The circus toured central Queensland for about two years before entering NSW. When it visited Roma (Qld) on 29 November 1890 the local *Western Star* praised the brass band. This was headed by four brothers from Eidsvold (Qld)—Bill, Edward, Harry and Jim Sole. They appear to have joined the circus during 1890. Bill Sole married W. G. Perry's eldest daughter Eliza at Thargomindah (Qld) on 1 May 1891, Their first child was the versatile circus artist MARY SOLE.

In 1893 the W. G. Perry family called its circus Eroni Brothers' Great International Circus in order to avoid confusion with Perry's Jubilee Circus or with another, unrelated, Perry circus. The origins of the new name appear to lie with a brother of Mrs W. G. Perry, Johnny Ahearn, who had used the same pseudonym when appearing in circuses in the 1860s. On a bill for Risley's Circus in Shanghai in 1863 a Master Eroni is described as 'the wonderful daring Australian rider'. The Mr Erone (sic) who performed with the International Circus at Our Lyceum Theatre in Sydney between 26 December 1866 and 26 January 1867 was probably the same youth.

About 1897, C. H. Perry was killed in a wagon accident. His widow Bridget became proprietor of the Jubilee Circus and ran it until August 1899, when it was amalgamated with the Eroni Brothers' Circus. Bridget Perry died in November 1899. She and her husband left no offspring.

At the end of the 19th century, the Eroni Brothers' Circus was supreme in Australia as a wagon show and second only to FITZGERALD BROTHERS' CIRCUS, which travelled by train. The Eroni circus largely toured the backblocks of the eastern states, although it visited Melbourne at least twice early in the 20th century. The first visit began on 6 April 1901 when the company pitched its tents opposite Her Majesty's Theatre at the corner of Lonsdale and Exhibition Streets, the site occupied by J. A. Rowe's North American Circus in 1854. Recalling the Eroni circus's first Melbourne season, the *Bulletin* said in July 1914 that the company had played to big business but then 'left a lot of money behind by closing the season suddenly. "Too much noise here", said old Bill Perry …'.

In the early 1900s, as the FitzGeralds' and Wirths' circuses fought for supremacy in the cities, the Eroni circus toured the backblocks unchallenged. The widow of James Henry Ashton was tutor of the circus children, who were marched to a small tent each day to receive instruction in reading, writing, arithmetic and, on Sundays, religion. The Eroni circus toured Tasmania in 1908.

The Sole family left the Eroni circus in 1909 and joined Gus St Leon's newly formed Great United Circus, an engagement that lasted at least two years. During this period W. G. Perry relinquished the management of his circus to his eldest son, Charles. The latter was the proprietor when, in 1912, the Sole family left Gus St Leon and rejoined the Eroni circus for a short time. Eroni and Sole's Circus opened at Broken Hill (NSW) on 22 June 1912. One of its attractions was a Japanese clown, Cooma Kitchie, who had been in Australia since the 1870s.

By early 1914, the Perry family had fragmented into three separate concerns. The main one, Eroni Brothers' Circus continued in strength, but the Soles had rejoined Gus St Leon, on a salary of £12 a week. Late in 1913 the younger son of W. G. Perry, Jim Perry had formed his own small circus under the name of Perry Brothers' Circus and this became the major Perry circus during the 1920s and 1930s.

The Sole family left the Gus St Leon circus for the last time during 1915, acquired a menagerie of wild animals and, by early 1916, entered into partnership with Ashton's Circus. By 1917, the Sole family was established in its own Sole Brothers' Circus, which still exists. The Eroni, Perry and Sole circuses often combined with one another if playing the same town but otherwise conducted their businesses separately. The Eroni circus ceased operations in 1922 and much of its equipment and many of its performers were taken over by Sole Brothers' Circus. Bill Sole and his brother-in-law Charles Eroni were killed instantly by an explosion of acetylene gas when Sole Brothers' Circus was at Blayney (NSW) in 1923. The accident was reported at length in the *Sydney Morning Herald* on 4 June 1923. During 1926–29 Sole Brothers' Circus made a highly profitable tour of South Africa and on its return travelled throughout Australia and New Zealand. Between the wars Perry Brothers' Circus, operated by the four sons of W. G. Perry's son James—Albert, Henry ('Dummy'), Edward ('Teddy') and James ('Jim')—was at times the largest in Australia, although it appears never to have surpassed Wirths' Circus in quality. Perry Brothers' Circus survives, run by descendants of James Perry. ❦*Mark St Leon*

Diana Perryman MBE

Actor. Born 19 November 1925 in Melbourne. Parents toured in J. C. Williamson companies. Early training at Independent Theatre (Sydney). Erik Kuttner Award 1960 (Gittell in *Two for the Seesaw* by William Gibson). Prominent television career in late 1950s and 1960s. Died 10 January 1979. Sister of actor Jill Perryman. Posthumous MBE 1979.

Diana Perryman was 'one of the finest actresses to come out of the Independent Theatre in its heyday under Doris Fitton', said the critic FRANK HARRIS. 'If you saw Diana Perryman listed on a program you could bank on the performance—it would be keen, sensitive and often powerful playing.' Perryman's stage persona seemed to be split into three—the vulnerable young girl, the powerful temptress and the warm dependable woman. As a young actor with INDEPENDENT THEATRE in Sydney she played Shakespeare—Jessica in *The Merchant of Venice* in 1945 and Viola in *Twelfth Night* in 1946. In 1947 she went from kind Linda Manners in Max Afford's AWAKE MY LOVE to the abrasive Stepdaughter in Luigi Pirandello's *Six Characters in Search of an Author*.

In 1948 her splendid playing of the late-blossoming seductress Lavinia in ROBERT QUENTIN's second production of Eugene O'Neill's *Mourning Becomes Electra* brought her temptress roles—in which her striking dark good looks were seen to advantage—and the praise of Laurence Olivier. He spoke in London of Diana Perryman and PETER FINCH as the strongest talents he had seen in Australia.

Perryman's lighter, warmer mode was set in 1955 as Beauty in Peter Ustinov's *The Love of Four Colonels*, and as Georgie, the good wife, in Clifford Odets's *Winter Journey*. One of her finest roles was Gittell in William Gibson's *Two for the Seesaw* for J. C. Williamson's in Sydney in 1960 and later in Melbourne. Perryman retired for several years to bring up her family. She returned to the stage for the OLD TOTE THEATRE COMPANY in Peter Shaffer's *Equus* in 1976 and August Strindberg's *The Father* in 1977. ❦*Lynne Murphy*

Jill Perryman AM MBE

Actor, singer. Born 30 May 1933 in Melbourne. Daughter of actors William Perryman and Dorothy Duval. Played small parts and second leads in J. C. Williamson's musicals 1953–66. Title-role in *Funny Girl* 1966; other leading roles followed. Married Kevan Johnston, actor, dancer and choreographer. Mother of musician Tod Johnston and drama teacher Trudy Johnston. Sister of actor Diana Perryman. Erik Kuttner Award 1966 (*Funny Girl*), 1972 (*No! No! Nanette*). MBE 1979. AM 1992.

Jill Perryman's performance as Fanny Brice in *Funny Girl* in 1966 lifted her to stardom and ended the era of second-rate imports in musicals. Since then she has become better and better. She is a powerful actor, a stylish singer and a skilful mover rather than a dancer. She occupies a special place in show business and has contributed richly to cultural life in Perth, where she has lived for much of her career.

She began attracting attention when she was 20, in the J. C. WILLIAMSON'S production of *Call Me Madam*. She headed the female singing ensemble and understudied the star, EVIE HAYES, who missed only one performance. Roles in *South Pacific*, *Paint Your Wagon* and *Can-Can* followed. As Mabel, the middle-aged secretary in *The Pajama Game*, her comic talents blossomed. She then appeared in nine PHILLIP STREET REVUES in Sydney before playing the Incomparable Rosie in the musical *Carnival* for J. C. Williamson's.

After marrying and having two children, Perryman returned to the stage as the second female lead in *Hello, Dolly!* in 1965. She played the title-role many times when the American star Carole Cook was indisposed. Perryman was ready for real stardom when Williamson's and its director FRED HEBERT chose her to play Fanny Brice. More musicals followed—*I Do, I Do* in 1969, *No! No! Nanette* in 1972, *A Little Night Music* in 1973 and *Annie* in 1981.

She realised her powers as a straight actor when she played the frumpish, suicidal daughter in Marsha Norman's *'Night Mother* for the 1984 Festival of Perth. Then came national tours of Michael Frayn's *Noises Off* and Neil Simon's *Brighton Beach Memoirs*. In 1987 she sang the role of Anna in the West Australian Ballet Company's production of Bertolt Brecht's *The Seven Deadly Sins*. For the Hole-in-the-Wall Theatre Company in Perth she appeared in *Side by Side by Sondheim* and Ray Lawler's SUMMER OF THE SEVENTEENTH DOLL and in the 1990 Festival of Perth Perryman and Kevan Johnston were acclaimed in *Wallflowering*, Peta Murray's two-hander about a couple of aging champion ballroom dancers. In 1995 she triumphantly starred in a revival of *Hello Dolly!* ❦*Ivan King, John West*

further reading
O'DONNELL, MONICA HUBBARD and OWEN O'DONNELL (eds). *Contemporary Theatre, Film and Television* 5th edn. Detroit (USA): Gale Research 1988.

Perth

Isolation on the western seaboard, about 2000 km from the nearest Australian city—Adelaide—has produced self-reliance and a sense of local identity in Perth theatre. These characteristics were especially manifested in AMATEUR THEATRE, from 1839 until 1892, when the discovery of gold at Coolgardie stimulated an influx of touring companies, and from the 1920s until the mid-1950s. Isolation and a small population, mainly British in derivation, combined until recently to make Perth a theatrical client of larger cities in Australia and overseas. In particular, theatre in colonial Perth tended to reproduce the class characteristics of 19th-century English amateur theatricals, and to sanction the English distinction between 'legitimate' and 'non-legitimate' stages. Strong demands for overseas modern and classical plays developed later, particularly from the 1930s, coinciding with a conscious nurturing of specifically Western Australian playwriting and 'house' styles. In the 1990s Perth's theatrical community is driven by quests for identity and distinctive artistic policy in a fast-changing city.

The earliest public performance recorded in the Swan River Colony—founded in 1829—was a corroboree given by Aborigines in Purkis's yard on 16 March 1833. It was attended, 'at the solicitation of Yagan', by the Lieutenant-Governor and 'nearly the whole of the respectable inhabitants of Perth, including several ladies'. The *Perth Gazette* praised Yagan, but dismissed the corroboree as a 'novelty' that had failed to sustain the settlers' interest.

The local press accorded the honour of 'the first theatrical representation in this colony' to a private performance by 'a few gentlemen and ladies' of Major Hort's brief musical farce, *Love à la Militaire*, at Leeder's Hotel in St George's Terrace on 16 July 1839. *Love à la Militaire* was probably a garrison play, because it had its British premiere in Edinburgh two years later.

Morality and class

The socially elite group that gave the Perth performance became known as the Amateur Theatricals and produced two private seasons of short comedies and musical farces at Leeder's Hotel in September and October of 1839. A nonconformist lay preacher named Trigg wrote to the press in October 1839 inveighing against the immorality of actors and the moral danger to young persons. This opened a controversy that was nominally based on religion and morals but was really about class. Defenders responded on behalf of the pastime of 'a few respectable families' but the debate continued until 1842, when males took the female roles in the farces *Raising the Wind* by J. Kenney and *The Queer Subject* by Joseph Coyne and the travesty *Bombastes Furioso* by W. B. Rhodes. The women withdrew gracefully, declaring *Bombastes Furioso* to be vulgar. The Amateur Theatricals gave three programs at Hodge's Hotel in St George's Terrace between August 1842 and April 1843. The 'operative classes' were admitted to dress rehearsals for a fee. The Amateur Theatricals evoked the domestic ethos of the Home Counties in their performances and drew their repertoire almost exclusively from the stock comedies, farces and burlettas of Covent Garden and Drury Lane.

A group of 'tradesmen and mechanics of the town' seized the theatrical high ground and produced Edward Fitzball's *The Inchcape Bell—or, The Dumb Sailor Boy* and *The Innkeeper of Abbeville* at Hodge's Hotel on 22 December 1842 and 26 April 1843 respectively. The press welcomed the plays as the first melodramas produced in Western Australia but the establishment *Perth Gazette* placed them 'beyond the pale of legitimate criticism'.

After 1843, according to Edmund Clifton, 'theatricals languished'. The Swan River Colony itself developed slowly and there was much economic hardship among the settlers, who numbered only 6000 by 1850. Importation of convict labour from 1850 until 1868 brought a gradual return to prosperity, at least for big landowners, merchants and shopkeepers. With prosperity came a modest revival of amateur theatre in Perth. The Amateur Theatricals gave two further seasons, including an abridged version of Isaac Pocock's *The Miller and His Men*, at the Old Court House in the Supreme Court Gardens in July and September 1854. The Perth Dramatic Club began life with a customary season of short comedies in April 1863, and the Amateur Dramatic Corps offered similar fare when it opened in nearby Fremantle in August 1865.

The chief legacy of convict labour to colonial theatre was the completion of the Perth Town Hall in 1870. This was ill equipped as a theatre and vilified as a 'great barn … a trying place for the voice, and cheerless, bleak and uncomfortable to sit in', but for more than two decades it was a major venue for dramatic, variety and minstrel companies, along with ST GEORGE'S HALL and the Mechanics' Hall. The first electric stage lighting in Western Australia was installed in the Town Hall in 1886.

Government House theatricals

While Sir William Robinson was Governor of Western Australia in 1875–77, 1880–83 and 1890–95 he gathered an establishment coterie to present amateur theatricals and musical recitals at Government House in Perth. His protégés included Francis Hart, a poet and librettist, and HENRY PRINSEP, a writer and designer who designed a drop-curtain and a portico for St George's Hall. Its owners, Messrs Burt and Stone, also belonged to the governor's circle. In 1894 St George's Hall was the venue for the premiere of *The Handsome Ransom*, the first operetta written in the colony. Its libretto was by Hart and its music by the governor. Touring companies played at St George's Hall into the early 1890s. Despite the stages there and in the Town Hall, Hart wrote in 1891 that 'Perth has not its theatre, though the erection of one is contemplated'.

An outdoor theatre, the CREMORNE GARDENS opened in 1895 and offered variety concerts for respectable audiences until it declined as a venue for troop entertainments during the First World War. It closed in 1920. Contemporaneous with the Cremorne, but shorter lived and less respectable, Ye Olde English Fayre presented acrobats, illusionists and variety entertainment in the open air in Hay Street, where HIS MAJESTY'S THEATRE now stands. The Fayre had a Fremantle branch. The first pantomime written in Western Australia, E. Hyacinth Tottenham's *The Golden West*, opened there for a lucrative season in January 1898, and transferred to Perth with equal success. During the 1890s gold rushes ALFRED DAMPIER's company, the TAYLOR-CARRINGTON COMPANY, the Wilkinson Dramatic Company, and two local groups, the Ettie Williams Happy Hours

His Majesty's Theatre shortly before it opened in 1904. Now restored, it remains Perth's principal theatre

Vaudeville Company and the amateur Thespians, played in the Town Hall.

The theatre contemplated in 1891 became a reality on 19 April 1897, when the THEATRE ROYAL opened in Hay Street with C. R. STANFORD in *The Silver King* by Henry Arthur Jones and Henry Herman. It was the first purpose-built, technically up-to-date theatre in Perth but its financial viability was not assured at first. In the event it was overshadowed in 1904 by the opening of the KING'S THEATRE in South Terrace, Fremantle, on 27 September and HIS MAJESTY'S THEATRE in Perth on 24 December. Both were larger than the Theatre Royal and among the most comfortable, best-equipped theatres to have been built in Australia. Their designs reflected the new affluence and incorporated extensive safety measures, and in His Majesty's the most advanced construction materials and techniques were utilised. The Theatre Royal, and to a lesser extent the King's Theatre, housed distinguished touring companies and each was used for variety, but neither theatre survived economic downturn and the advent of cinema. The King's closed in 1920, and the Theatre Royal was converted in 1936 to show only films.

His Majesty's Theatre opened with Pollard's Adult Opera Company in *The Forty Thieves*, an extravaganza by ARTHUR H. ADAMS. The theatre was used from its earliest days for plays, variety, pantomime, ballet, opera, musical comedy and occasionally films. The adjoining His Majesty's Hotel made it attractive to touring companies from the outset. In the heyday of His Majesty's Theatre, the departure of the Trans-Australia Express to Adelaide was often delayed on closing nights to suit touring companies. His Majesty's was the preferred Perth venue for J. C. WILLIAMSON's, and was the home of Edgley and Dawe Attractions in the 1950s and 1960s. It was also a significant venue for local amateur performers until the mid-1950s. His Majesty's Theatre was renovated, redecorated in Edwardian style and extended backstage in 1980. It is now Perth's principal venue for ballet, opera and musical theatre and is home to the PERTH THEATRE TRUST.

With the decline of commercial theatre in Perth during the Great Depression, the Marlowe Club, the Pleiades, the Therry Society, the Shakespeare Club and many other amateur groups emerged. Until the end of the Second World War serious theatre was sustained principally by the REPERTORY CLUB and, for more limited periods by 'little theatres', such as the Playbox, PATCH THEATRE and the WORKERS' ART GUILD. In the three decades after the Repertory Club opened in 1919 there was a huge expansion in local amateur production and playwriting, and amateurs regularly produced modernistic plays from overseas. By 1933 the Repertory Club was one of the leading amateur producers in Australia. It had plays constantly in rehearsal and performance, a metropolitan membership of 600 subscribers and affiliations with 18 provincial amateur groups. It gave the community a stake in its own theatre, introduced important modern plays and provided training for amateur actors, directors and designers in Perth. From 1936 to 1940 the WORKERS' ART GUILD presented several agitprop pieces and a full-length play, *Solidarity—or, The Penalty Clause*, by KATHARINE SUSANNAH PRICHARD.

Vigorous amateur theatre in the decade after the Second World War gave impetus to a resolute movement to establish a professional theatre company in Western Australia. The THEATRE COUNCIL OF WESTERN AUSTRALIA was formed, on the initiative of the UNIVERSITY DRAMATIC SOCIETY, as a loose federation of 15 amateur groups in 1948. It promoted and co-ordinated amateur theatre, but also pressed for establishment of state and national theatres in Western Australia. From 1949 until its liquidation in 1970, the council staged important annual drama festivals under the direction of Dorothy Lyall. These festivals were revived for a time from 1971 by the new Cultural Development Council of Western Australia, with assistance from the AUSTRALIAN ELIZABETHAN THEATRE TRUST. The Theatre Council was frustrated in its long-term aim of securing government support for amateur theatre, but it promoted new Australian plays in its festivals, and provided a framework within which such diverse groups as Q Theatre, the Independent Players, the Mercury Players, the New Theatre League, the GARRICK CLUB, Patch Theatre and university and college groups could operate.

Steps towards the establishment of professional theatre were the appointment of David Lopian as director of the Repertory Club in 1949 and the engagement of Michael Langham by the Adult Education Board of the University of Western Australia to direct *Richard III* for the inaugural FESTIVAL OF PERTH in 1953 and to be a tutor for several months. The COMPANY OF FOUR, formed in 1950 to test the viability of permanent professional theatre, operated until 1955 on a share basis under the direction of the Adult

The auditorium of the Playhouse Theatre, Perth, in 1956, when the National Theatre Company opened it with The Teahouse of the August Moon

Education Board. Working to professional standards under local directors, the Company of Four successfully staged 15 seasons of contemporary European, American and British plays, undertook country tours for the Adult Education Board and appeared annually at the Festival of Perth.

The Adult Education Board advanced postwar developments in both amateur and professional theatre. It offered regular training at its annual summer school and throughout the year in the city, and sponsored tutors' visits to amateur groups in the country. The Festival of Perth, founded by the university and administered through the Adult Education Board, provided an annual showcase for metropolitan and provincial companies and amateur groups until the early 1970s. Since then the festival has consolidated its international entrepreneurial activities and local theatrical participation has declined.

Having proved its point, the Company of Four merged with the Repertory Club in 1956 to establish the city's first permanent professional stage company, the NATIONAL THEATRE COMPANY at the new Playhouse Theatre in Pier Street. NITA PANNELL directed *The Teahouse of the August Moon* by John Patrick to mark the occasion. Since then professional companies have proliferated, each attempting to differentiate itself in artistic policy, market sector and theatre form. This has been productive but has made Perth theatre fluid. By 1965 the Hole-in-the-Wall Theatre Company had emerged as an alternative to the mainstream National Theatre. Both relied substantially on American, British and European plays but promoted local playwrights. The Hole-in-the-Wall company staged 12 new local plays, six of them written by John Gill, between 1970 and 1976. The National Theatre Company presented its first local musical, CORALIE CONDON's *The Good Oil*, in 1958, occasionally produced local plays in the 1960s, and had a sustained development program for mainstage and studio plays from 1972 to 1979. The major playwright to emerge in the 1970s was DOROTHY HEWETT.

With disputes over their shifting artistic policies, the National Theatre and Hole-in-the-Wall companies dominated Perth theatre until the National Theatre collapsed financially in 1983. To replace it the Western Australian Theatre Company was formed in 1985. The new company was given a broad charter, but it concentrated on developing Aboriginal theatre, especially plays by JACK DAVIS and Richard Walley, and other original work. The Hole-in-the-Wall company shifted to larger premises at Subiaco in 1984, and increasingly occupied the artistic middle ground. Its major success and financial bonanza was Willy Russell's *Shirley Valentine* in 1988. By 1989 it was clear that, despite internal reconstruction of the Western Australian Theatre Company, the two companies were competing for similar audiences in venues of similar size. To resolve a financial crisis in the Western Australian Theatre Company, and to settle its artistic relations with the Hole-in-the-Wall, the two companies were merged to form the STATE THEATRE COMPANY OF WESTERN AUSTRALIA in 1991. A section of the industry charged that the State Theatre Company's charter to produce established and new plays was too conservative. In March 1993 the State Theatre Company closed after a dispute over funding with the state Department for the Arts. Questions of artistic policy, ideology and funding continue to beset Perth's professional theatre.

Dorothy Hewett's musical play, The Man From Mukinupin, *performed by the National Theatre Company for the Western Australian sesquicentennial celebrations in 1979, shows daily life in a mythical country town in 1912–20. All is sunny by day but at night sombre forces emerge, as in this encounter between Touch of the Tar (played by Noni Hazlehurst) and Harry Tuesday (Richard Tulloch)*

Smaller, newer and more specialised professional companies in Perth have undertaken vigorous development programs with strong community or regional flavour. The SPARE PARTS PUPPET THEATRE COMPANY, formed in 1981, explores multiple puppetry forms in Fremantle. The PERTH THEATRE COMPANY, identified with experimental work since 1983, commissions new works and adaptations by local writers over a wide variety of non-realist styles. The DECKCHAIR THEATRE COMPANY, founded in Fremantle in 1984, has moved from theatre-in-education to community theatre. The Black Swan Theatre Company, formed in 1991 to develop distinctive regional theatre with links to Indian Ocean littoral cultures, has made a strong bid to produce recognisably Western Australian theatre.

Each of the Perth companies has had to mark out a distinctive style, find its audience, adjust to the presence of productive and diverse local playwrights and respond to the cultural policies of governments and statutory funding bodies. All Perth's professional theatre companies depend to some degree upon government and corporate subvention. Western Australian governments have funded theatre since 1973, when the Arts Council of Western Australia was established. In 1986, responsibility for state funding of theatre, now substantial, was transferred to the Minister for the Arts, through the Department for the Arts.

Vocational training for professional theatre at the WESTERN AUSTRALIAN ACADEMY OF PERFORMING ARTS since 1979 and theatre studies programs at Perth's four universities since the 1980s have greatly enhanced local participation in Perth's professional theatre. These influences have also been evident in the proliferation and quality of local alternative performances presented each year since 1988 at the city's ARTRAGE festival. *Bill Dunstone*

further reading
CLIFTON, E. Music and theatre in the early days. *Western Australian Historical Society Journal and Proceedings* 1/8 and 9 (Perth, 1930).

CRAIG, TERRY. Radical and conservative theatre in Perth in the 30s. *Western Australian Between the Wars* (ed. Jenny Gregory). Perth: University of Western Australia Centre of WA History 1990.

DUNSTONE, BILL. Imperialist discourses—Amateur theatrical performances in Perth to 1854. *Australasian Drama Studies* (Brisbane) October 1993.

DUNSTONE, BILL. Drama. *The Literature of Western Australia* (ed. Bruce Bennett). Perth: University of Western Australia Press 1979.

Perth Theatre Company

Youth-theatre company in Perth, founded as Swy Theatre Company in 1983 by Penny Why and graduates from special theatre and dance courses at John Curtin Senior High School. Renamed 1994. **venue** 65 Murray Street, Perth. **artistic director** Alan Becher 1991–.

Talented young actors from training institutions, especially the WESTERN AUSTRALIAN ACADEMY OF PERFORMING ARTS, have found ready employment in vigorous and exciting productions by the Swy Theatre Company. It uses a minimum of scenery and props and concentrates on developing a strong ensemble. Developing new productions with young actors has always been its first consideration.

Gambling with risky theatre was part of the fledgling company's philosophy, so it called itself Swy after the alternative name for two-up—from German *zwei*, 'two'. In 1984, Swy performed John Catlin's *Children of War* in Perth, Adelaide and Melbourne. In 1985, Ross Coli directed the first Australian production of *Greek* by Steven Berkoff, with Brandon Burke as guest actor, at the Maltings in inner Perth. In 1986, Alan Becher from Sydney was engaged to direct *Boomeroo!*, an adaptation of Paul Radley's novel of adolescence, *My Blue-Checker, Corker, and Me*. Pamela van Amstel's *Are You Lonesome Tonight?* in 1986 was followed in 1987 by productions of an adaptation of Tom Collins's novel *Such is Life*, George Hutchinson's *No Room for Dreamers* and David Allen's *Cheapside* and *Zen and Now*, mostly directed by Becher as a guest.

In 1987 funding from the Western Australian Department for the Arts enabled Swy to acquire its own 142-seat theatre in Murray Street for a peppercorn rental. By 1989 the company had created a keen following for its excellent productions of unusual plays. *Teachers*, *It's a Girl* and *Separation*, for example, attracted large young audiences. Swy conducts the annual Western Australian Young Playwrights' Workshop. Swan Gold Theatre Awards for outstanding theatre development went to the company in 1991 and 1992, with an individual award to Becher in the latter year. ♥*David J. Hough*

Perth Theatre Trust

When the Western Australian government bought HIS MAJESTY'S THEATRE in Perth it initially decided to place its management with television station TVW–7, which managed the large government-owned Perth Entertainment Centre. This was unpopular so it was proposed to vest the management of the historic theatre in an independent body that could also manage the Perth Concert Hall. The City of Perth, which was managing the concert hall, and the government decided to form the Perth Theatre Trust. As established by act of parliament in 1979, the trust comprised three trustees nominated by the Perth City Council and four, including the chair, by the government.

The trust expanded rapidly in 1984. After the demise of the NATIONAL THEATRE COMPANY it took over the lease of the Playhouse Theatre on behalf of the government; it devolved day-to-day management of the building to the West Australian Theatre Company. The trust also negotiated the conversion of the Subiaco Theatre Centre into a new home for the HOLE-IN-THE-WALL THEATRE COMPANY, which opened in August. The demise of the National Theatre Company also meant that the trust took over the lease of the Performing Arts Workshop in Belmont. It subsequently bought this building with the aid of a $300 000 grant from a lottery.

By the end of 1986 the trust managed His Majesty's Theatre, belonging to the state government; the Playhouse Theatre on land leased from the Anglican Church; the Subiaco Theatre Centre, under lease from the Subiaco City Council; the Perth Concert Hall and the outdoor Quarry Amphitheatre in City Beach—which has housed music, dance and drama every summer since November 1986—under lease from the City of Perth. The trust acted for the government on the Perth Entertainment Centre, which was leased to TVW–7 to operate. In addition the trust managed the BOCS computer ticketing system—which it introduced in September 1985. This system was subsequently sold to users in Sydney and Melbourne. It owned the Performing Arts Workshop, which housed production facilities for the Western Australian Theatre, Ballet and Opera Companies; the trust sold this building for a substantial profit in June 1990. The state government was by far the major source of funds and in 1987 the Perth Theatre Trust Act was amended to add the Director of the Department for the Arts to the trustees.

A gradual reduction in the number of theatrical entrepreneurs operating in Australia meant that occupancy rates for His Majesty's Theatre started to fall towards the end of the 1980s. As a consequence the trust was obliged to increase its own entrepreneurial activities and in March 1988 it established its own programming unit. The trust negotiated Perth seasons of Cameron Mackintosh's productions of the musicals *Cats* and *Les Misérables* in 1989 and 1990 respectively. Together they attracted more than 200 000 people to the theatre in 22 weeks of performances and grossed $8·5 million at the box office. These successes overturned the commonly held view that His Majesty's Theatre was too small for commercial musical theatre and Perth has rejoined the national touring circuit for major musicals. ♥*Will Quekett*

Peter Summerton Foundation

The Peter Summerton Foundation has encouraged the professional development of directors and actors by sponsoring international figures in a wide range of workshops. This was the aim of Peter Summerton, who died suddenly at the age of 40 in 1969, when he was an associate director of INDEPENDENT THEATRE in Sydney. On 27 October 1969 the actor Jone Winchester and relatives, friends and professional peers of Summerton formed the foundation to raise sufficient capital to fund a biennial directors' workshop with the interest. The foundation campaigned for theatregoers to become 'dollar donors' and persuaded theatre companies to donate performances. The OLD TOTE THEATRE COMPANY led with Tyrone Guthrie's production of Sophocles's *Oedipus Rex* in Sydney in 1970. Although never richly endowed, the foundation has managed to fulfil the initial aims. William Ball, from the American Conservatory Theatre in San Francisco, held the first workshop in Sydney in 1971. It lasted for two weeks and involved 23 directors from around Australia. Since then, workshops have been held by the Prospect Theatre Company in 1972, the New York teacher Stella Adler in 1973, the English director William Gaskill in 1975, the expatriate Australian director MICHAEL BLAKEMORE in 1976, the New York director and Samuel Beckett specialist Alan Schneider in 1977, the emigré Russian director Yevgeny Lanskoy in 1982 and 1983, the New York speech teacher Rowena Balos in 1984 and 1985, and the Royal Shakespeare Company director Bill Alexander in 1988–89. It supported productions at the Stables Theatre in Sydney in 1993 and 1995.

In 1988 the committee awarded a grant to a young director, Katerina Ivak, and in 1990 it assisted a workshop in Japanese *butoh* technique by Yoko Ashikawa. The workshops have been held in Sydney and sometimes in Melbourne too, at little cost to the participants, who have come from all over the country. Jone Winchester has been president of the foundation since its inception. ❦*Jacqueline Kott*

Ralph Peterson

Actor, dramatist. Born 21 February 1921 in Adelaide. Began acting as child. Began writing for radio and film after army service in Second World War. Married actor Betty Lucas. Wrote stage plays 1951–65. Wrote and produced *My Name's McGooley, What's Yours?* for television 1966–69.

Comedy has always been the forte of Ralph Peterson, who has written successfully for stage, television, radio, and film. He learned much about comedy from Rex 'Wacka' Dawe, writer and producer of the comedy series *Yes What?* on radio 5AD Adelaide from 1937. Peterson began playing a raucous schoolboy in the series at 16, after acting on the professional stage in Adelaide as a child.

In Sydney, Peterson joined the Metropolitan Players in 1945, and played Keghead in INDEPENDENT THEATRE's premiere production of Sumner Locke Elliott's *RUSTY BUGLES* in 1948. In 1951, while working for the British Broadcasting Corporation in London, he developed a radio serial he had written for the ABC into his first stage play, *The Square Ring*. A story of a boxer's tragic attempt to make a comeback, it was performed in London and Melbourne in the same year and later made into a film by Ealing Studios.

Peterson's second play, *The Night of the Ding-Dong* (1954) played in Britain and the USA, and toured Australia in 1966 in a South Australian Theatre Company production directed by JOHN TASKER. It was a comedy set in Adelaide at the time of the Crimean War, when the locals feared a Russian invasion. Peterson's other stage plays are *The Third Secretary* (1958) about the human and political implications of defection; *The Mating of Ulrich Dooley* (1965) a sad comedy about a lonely man; and *The Big Boat* (1965) a humorous parallel to the Noah's ark story set on Sydney Harbour, which won a playwriting competition sponsored by the *Australian*. ❦*Richard Lane*

published plays
The Square Ring (1951). London: Arthur Barker 1954.
The Third Secretary (1958). Sydney: Currency Press 1972.
other writing
Greater the Truth. London: Arthur Barker 1956.

Phillip Street revues

In Australia intimate revue had a short career, largely in Sydney. The form emerged in the London theatre just before the Second World War. It had no big scena, no lavish ballet, but a small group of performers working with slick, sophisticated material that had a strong sardonic sheen and presupposed a knowing appreciation of people, places and current events by metropolitan audiences. The most famous revue, *Sweet and Low*, opened in 1943, and its two follow-up editions ran for years. In December 1947 the MINERVA THEATRE in Sydney staged *Sweetest and Lowest* with a company of sharp talents like FIFI BANVARD, MINNIE LOVE, MAX OLDAKER, the English comic Wee Georgie Wood and his partner and stage mother Dolly Harmer, and GORDON CHATER, a young Englishman.

To a dedicated Sydney theatregoer of a certain age, however, intimate revue is synonymous with long-running revues at the PHILLIP STREET THEATRE from 1954 to 1961. These were inspired by WILLIAM ORR. In revues at Sydney University, he observed the talents of two clever writers, John McKellar and Gerry Donovan, and a gifted composer, Lance Mulcahy. This trio devised for Orr a revue that became known as *Metropolitan Merry-Go-Round*, partly because it was at the Metropolitan Theatre. It had enough success to encourage Orr and his partner Eric Duckworth to conjecture that Sydney could support a full-time intimate-revue theatre. They launched the Phillip Street revues in May 1954 with *Top of the Bill*. It included many performers who became mainstays of future revues, in particular Chater, an entertainer of insouciant charm who would do anything for a laugh. Others associated with these revues, which were mostly written by McKellar, included MARGO LEE, Lyle O'Hara, MAX OLDAKER and JILL PERRYMAN.

Typical Phillip Street revues featured small but strong casts, minimal sets, little dancing, much mockery and songs with a sting in the tail. Occasionally there were special guests, beginning with Joyce Grenfell in her solo show in 1959. The Phillip Street Theatre was closed for demolition in 1961 and the company moved to the slightly larger Australian Hall in Elizabeth Street, near Liverpool Street. Redecorated and renamed the Phillip Theatre, it housed the best of all the Phillip Street revues, *A Cup of Tea, a Bex and a Good Lie Down*. The show ran for a year in 1965–66 and the phrase passed into the language. McKellar devised and wrote it, Sybil Graham and Jim Wallett composed the music and Orr directed a superlative cast headed by RUTH CRACKNELL as a dour English landlady ('I've never known a *moment* free of pain'), the irreplaceable GLORIA DAWN at her peak, REG LIVERMORE and Barbara Wyndon.

Intimate revue was a Sydney phenomenon, though attempts were made in other capital cities. It faltered and largely disappeared because television took over much of its style and attack. The Phillip Street sort of intimate revue is unlikely to come again, but its best shows have left a comforting and lingering afterglow. ❦*John West*

Phillip Street Theatre

Theatre in Phillip Street, Sydney, opened as **St James Hall** seating 650, 17 December 1903. Architect: Burcham Clamp. Seating reduced to 447 by new stage and proscenium 1916. Called **Mercury Theatre** 28 February 1952 to 19 December 1953. Redecorated and reopened 7 May 1954 as **Phillip Street Theatre**, seating 368. Closed 14 January 1961. Demolished and replaced in late 1963 by 15-storey building, including new 300-seat **St James Hall**, sometimes known as Phillip Street Theatre. Architects: Peddle Thorp and Walker. Closed for renovation of building, 7 October 1989.

The theatre where WILLIAM ORR presented the acclaimed PHILLIP STREET REVUES for nearly seven years was originally the St James Hall, built by Church of England on a site it has owned since the nearby St James Church was built in 1820–24. The three-storey brick building was erected in 1903. Above a semi-basement for church offices were a concert hall and, on the third level, a school. The church hoped to repay large borrowings for the building by frequent letting of the hall, which was praised for good acoustics, harmonious proportion, central location and lack of noise from trams. The gallery, which had an intricate cast-iron balustrade, extended along the side walls. The original bare platform was replaced with a miniature stage in 1912, when the Sydney Stage Society produced *Prunella*. In 1916 the stage was rebuilt and enlarged, though a new proscenium reduced the seating capacity. The hall then became a popular venue for amateur, semiprofessional and professional theatrical groups, including the Modern Theatre Players and the New Sydney Repertory Society.

On 25 August 1950 the JOHN ALDEN COMPANY began a professional season of *The Merchant of Venice* and *Measure for Measure*. MERCURY THEATRE opened its first repertory season of plays in early 1952 and despite financial difficulties continued to the end of 1953. Then the hall was redecorated, reseated and renamed for the Phillip Street Theatre Company. Its fast, saucy, topical intimate revues won a great reputation and 14 were presented in the theatre until the building was closed in 1961. The new building contained a one-level raked hall which lacked the atmosphere of the old St James Hall, with its deep horseshoe balcony crowding the audience around the stage. It seated only 300, yet for seven years during the 1980s PETER WILLIAMS conducted a commercial enterprise there, including performances for schoolchildren and an acting school. ❦*Ross Thorne*

further reading
KABLE, K. J. St James Hall. *Church of England Historical Society Journal* 8/2 (June 1963).
Church hall in this Sydney office building. *Architecture Today* 6/2–3 (December 1963–January 1964).

Mrs Alfred Phillips

Actor, dramatist. Born 1822 in London. Originally Elizabeth Elsbee. Married Alfred Phillips, low comedian, at Dover 1842. Successful in supporting roles at Olympic Theatre, London, in early 1850s. Also wrote and produced plays and gave 'lecture entertainments'. Came to Australia 1855. Acted with husband and son Hans Phillips. Died 12 August 1876 in Melbourne.

While Elizabeth and Alfred Phillips were acting at the Olympic Theatre in London during the early 1850s, she also wrote and produced six plays, including a hit with a goldrush theme, *Life in Australia*, in 1853. In 1855 she came to Australia with her infant son Hans, to join her husband, who had arrived in the previous year to set up a hotel in Bendigo (Vic.). *Life in Australia* was a flop in Melbourne in November 1855. Elizabeth Phillips specialised in 'old women'. Mrs Malaprop in R. B. Sheridan's *The Rivals* and the Hostess in *Henry IV* were among her notable roles. Her 'lecture entertainment', a mixture of music and 'character delineations', was claimed to be the first one-woman show in London. Her husband, who was also described as a journalist, became a publican in later years. Their Melbourne-educated son Hans acted in their entertainments from his teens. Critics admired his painstaking work, resonant voice and natural manner as Henry Corkett in GEORGE S. TITHERADGE's production of *The Silver King* by Henry Arthur Jones and Henry Herman. He married Fanny, a daughter of the scenic artist JOHN HENNINGS, in 1878 and died in Melbourne on 23 December 1917. ❦*Mimi Colligan*

further reading
Argus (Melbourne) 14 August 1876.
Australasian Sketcher (Melbourne) 2 September 1876.

Nat Phillips

Vaudeville comedian. Born about 1883 at Brewarrina (NSW). On stage at 10 years. At 20 went abroad for 12 years. In partnership with Roy Rene (Mo) as Stiffy and Mo 1916–25 and 1927–28. Died 21 June 1932 in Sydney. Married to Daisy Merritt, comedian.

As partner of ROY RENE in the STIFFY AND MO vaudeville act Nat Phillips achieved his greatest fame. Phillips suggested a partnership when Rene was a young 'Hebrew' comedian in the Beletso Revue Company, which Phillips produced for FULLERS'. After a knockout season in Sydney, the pair opened in Fullers' all-Australian pantomime THE BUNYIP at Christmas 1916. They went on to half-bill revues, which packed theatres for months on end. Phillips was the producer, wrote scripts for many of the early revues and as Stiffy, wearing a football guernsey and outsize boots, he fed the comedian with accomplished ease. In 1919 Phillips told *Theatre* that before he brought Stiffy to life as a Sydney larrikin Australian low-life characters had been played as costermongers, a result of imported comic material. Stiffy and Mo split in 1925, when Rene was sacked for vulgarity, and in 1928, when Phillips thought they were tiring. When not with Rene, Phillips teamed with other comedians, including SYD BECK and Joe Lawman (as Stiffy and Joe), performing in Sydney, Melbourne and Adelaide, but he never achieved the same popularity. Nevertheless long seasons at the Grand Opera House in Sydney during the Depression earned him praise for lack of the vulgarity that critics always deplored in Stiffy and Mo. ❦*Victoria Chance*

Simon Phillips

Director. Born 4 April 1958 in Penang (Federation of Malaya). Educated at University of Auckland (New Zealand). Directed plays and musicals at Mercury Theatre (Auckland). Moved to Australia in mid-1980s. Resident director at Western Australian Academy of Performing Arts (Perth) 1984–86. Directed for Western Australian Theatre Company. Associate director of Melbourne Theatre Company 1987–89. Artistic director of State Theatre Company of South Australia (Adelaide) 1990–93.

A young, accomplished director, Simon Phillips has been regarded as something of a *Wunderkind* on both sides of the Tasman. His flair and fearlessness have produced memorable mainstage productions noted for their striking design and confident use of space. For the MELBOURNE THEATRE COMPANY, with the designer TONY TRIPP, he directed a production of Oscar Wilde's *The Importance of Being Earnest* influenced by Aubrey Beardsley. With the designer SHAUN GURTON and the musical director Ian McDonald he directed a production of *The Comedy of Errors* after the Belgian painter René Magritte in 1990 and a high-tech *Julius Caesar* in 1991, both for the STATE THEATRE Company of South Australia. He has staged plays by STEPHEN SEWELL in Melbourne and Adelaide, and with the writer Carolyn Burns he has adapted and restaged the musical *High Society*. Phillips received an AUSTRALIAN ELIZABETHAN THEATRE TRUST travel fellowship during the 1980s to direct comedy with the farce writer and director Ray Cooney in London. In Melbourne in 1987 he directed the premiere of JILL SHEARER's *Shimada* in Melbourne, which attracted a Broadway producer. As a free lance since 1994 he has produced distinguished works for the Melbourne Theatre Company, the Sydney Theatre Company and State Theatre. ❦*Murray Bramwell*

John Pinder

Entrepreneur. Born in Timaru (New Zealand) 6 January 1945. Came to Australia 1966. Began promoting rock shows in inner Melbourne suburbs in late 1960s. Operated Flying Trapeze Cafe 1972–75, Last Laugh Theatre Restaurant and Zoo 1975–88, Le Joke 1979–88, all in Melbourne. Works in Sydney as consultant and producer in many fields of entertainment.

Modern Australian STAND-UP COMEDY owes much to John Pinder. He first presented comedy in the late 1960s, when he invited then-unknown local performers such as MAX GILLIES and BRUCE SPENCE to perform short sketches during bands' setting up in his suburban rock shows. In 1972 he returned to Melbourne from Europe and found the lack of coffee shops and cafes frustrating. He opened the Flying Trapeze Cafe in Fitzroy, more to satisfy his own need for somewhere to go than to present new cabaret acts. Its tiny stage was just deep enough to accommodate an upright piano and the legal seating capacity was 24.

Word of the 'Flytrap' spread quickly and the crowd was far beyond the limit nightly. Pinder soon discovered that a good atmosphere induced performers to appear, and his experiment became the springboard for the alternative cabaret boom of the 1970s. Pinder and most of the performers were working for fun, but ACTORS' EQUITY, unhappy with what amounted to indoor busking, compelled payment. The room was financially unworkable but it was clear that something important was happening.

Pinder sold the Flying Trapeze and with Roger Evans established the Last Laugh Theatre Restaurant and Zoo in Collingwood in 1975. This was a bold business decision. The Last Laugh, seating more than 200, enabled Pinder to stage large-scale shows that could run for months. Upstairs he opened Le Joke, where many well-known comics cut their teeth. Pinder sold the premises in 1988.

In 1987 Pinder was instrumental in establishing the first official Melbourne International Comedy Festival, similar to an event he had staged in the early 1980s. He remained involved with the festival for a couple of years. Pinder took the comedians Los Trios Ringbarkus to the Edinburgh Festival in 1983, and as a bicentennial project in 1988 he took a huge collection of Australian acts to Edinburgh under the banner of Oznost. It firmly established Australian comedy in the United Kingdom. ❦*David Taranto*

Pioneer Players

Amateur dramatic company in Melbourne founded in May 1922 by Louis Esson, Vance Palmer and Stewart Macky. Closed in 1926.
director George Dawe.

The Pioneer Players have had an influence entirely disproportionate to their theatrical achievements but exactly in proportion to their aspirations for Australian drama. The founders, inspired by Dublin's Abbey Theatre, aimed to promote Australian plays and provide a public outlet for the writers whom LOUIS ESSON and VANCE PALMER imagined were waiting for just such an opportunity. The plays did not arrive and Esson ended by supplying a large part of the company's repertoire. He wrote some of his best plays for the Pioneer Players and by prompting him to this work the company may be said to have partly achieved its goal.

The company's production standards appear to have been poor. It was amateur theatre, and surviving accounts of the productions give an alarming impression of dilettante standards. A professional, George Dawe, was brought in to oversee the productions but he seems to have had little understanding of the aims of the company. 'An actor of the old school', according to Palmer, he presumably observed the popular conventions of 19th-century ACTING. The company's seasons nevertheless had some impact, which suggests that there was a small audience for its work. Reviews were kind, even when they imply that things went wrong in the performance.

Esson and Palmer, in their nationalistic fervour, were anxious to break down the social restrictions of the established theatre. They advertised that gentlemen in evening dress would not be admitted and Esson, in one of his several anticipations of Bertolt Brecht, wanted people to feel free to smoke in the theatre. The Pioneer Players struggled to make up their seasons. They produced three full-length plays in 1922—Esson's *The Battler*, Stewart Macky's *John Blake* and Palmer's *A Happy Family*. In 1923 the only full length-play was Esson's MOTHER AND SON. The rest of the repertoire was made up of bills of one-act plays.

After the last 1923 season and the death of George Dawe, there was a gap of two years and in 1926 the Pioneer Players returned with a one-night final performance of Esson's *The Bride of Gospel Place*. Esson never really fully recovered from his disappointment at the failure of the company. After *The Bride of Gospel Place* he produced no plays of real worth and the tone of his other writing became more bitter. Palmer went on to develop his career as a novelist, critic and later broadcaster, but Esson, all of his energies tied up in a theatre that no longer existed, declined into silence. The aspirations of the Pioneer Players were high and in different times their achievements perhaps would have matched them. In a later period of theatrical nationalism, the late 1960s and early 1970s, the AUSTRALIAN PERFORMING GROUP started work in Melbourne and referred back to the Pioneer Players as a model. ❦*John McCallum*

further reading

PARSONS, PHILIP. Introduction to Louis Esson. *The Time is Not Yet Ripe by Louis Esson.* Sydney: Currency Press 1973.

WALKER, DAVID. *Dream and Disillusion.* Canberra: Australian National University Press 1976.

Pipi Storm Children's Circus

Professional touring company founded as co-operative in 1975 by Russell Cheek, Margaret Fischer, Brian Joyce, Linsey Pollack, Murray Oliver and Bronwyn Vaughn. Became Pipi Storm Ltd in 1978. Closed 1986.

Pipi Storm Children's Circus used and taught circus skills, music and folk dance to enhance children's self-image through physical activity. It also worked with young offenders, prisoners, Aborigines, the isolated and the dislocated. Initially an outdoor company performing in the round, it toured extensively, establishing circuits and going where no-one had toured such theatre before— Broome (WA), Groote Eylandt (NT), Tibooburra (NSW), Arnhem Land, along the Murray River.

Pipi Storm generated productions and made artistic and administrative decisions collectively although it eventually appointed directors and administrators. It coined its name for the Australia '75 Festival in Canberra. Its production was *Children's Circus*, followed by workshops and folk dancing. In 1979, after 14 months' continuous touring, Pipi Storm expanded from six to upwards of 21 members. In addition to its parks program of games, circus skills, music and dance, Pipi Storm developed models of collectivity and creativity that were influenced by community arts and influenced theatre-in-education and COMMUNITY THEATRE. It gave theatre-in-education shows on issues from drugs to peer pressure, and its work took it to children at Bondi Beach, prisoners in Long Bay Jail, Aborigines in Wilcannia (NSW) and isolated housing estates in southwest Sydney. In 1986 the company was hiring by the project and seeking to incorporate visual arts into its community-development programs in western Sydney. Applications for grants for projects in 1987 failed and Pipi Storm ended. ♣*Bill Blaikie*

William Pitt jnr

Architect. Born 4 September 1855 in Melbourne. Son of theatrical artist William Pitt snr. Apprenticed as architect. Began practice 1879. Designed and altered theatres in Adelaide, Ballarat (Vic.), Hobart, Melbourne, Sydney and New Zealand. Member of Victorian Legislative Council for 18 years. Died 25 May 1918 in Melbourne.

William Pitt jnr is best remembered for the PRINCESS THEATRE in Melbourne but from 1898 until 1915 he designed or rebuilt at least ten theatres. He received his first theatrical commission in the early 1880s, when he was engaged to alter the old Colosseum in Melbourne and erect the Victoria Hall behind it. He had previously designed and supervised the erection of the multistorey Melbourne Coffee Palace in Bourke Street, and won design competitions for the Falls Bridge over the Yarra River and the head office of the Premier Permanent Building Society. After the Colosseum project Pitt was called to Sydney to prepare plans for a New Queen's Theatre in York Street and for extensive alterations to the Opera House. Neither project seems to have gone ahead. Nor was an 1883 design for a Comedy Theatre in Russell Street, Melbourne, carried out.

In Melbourne in 1884 Pitt designed, for the entrepreneur GEORGE COPPIN, the Improved Lodging-houses and Dwellings, which accommodated 300 beds. Then the 500-room, nine-storey Federal Coffee Palace was constructed to Pitt's design. Shortly afterwards he was commissioned to design the Princess Theatre. It opened in 1886 and established Pitt as a theatre architect, but over the next few years he designed some huge warehouses, the Rialto and Olderfleet buildings in Collins Street, and the Stock Exchange edifice, which contemporaries considered his masterwork. The depression of the 1890s hit Pitt almost as much as any of his banker friends, but he fully paid all his creditors.

He began a rash of theatre work in 1898 with considerable alterations to the Academy of Music in Ballarat. It was renamed HER MAJESTY'S THEATRE. So was the Alexandra Theatre in Melbourne, the auditorium of which Pitt rebuilt in 1900. In the same year he built a completely new Opera House in Melbourne for HARRY RICKARDS. He went to Sydney in 1902 to rebuild the auditorium and stage of HER MAJESTY'S THEATRE after a fire. In the same year he completed his design for His Majesty's Theatre in Auckland (New Zealand). In 1904 he reconstructed the auditorium and stage of the THEATRE ROYAL in Melbourne and in 1907 he produced his designs for the new KING'S THEATRE in Russell Street. In 1911 the historic THEATRE ROYAL in Hobart reopened with a completely new and larger auditorium and additional audience facilities, all designed by Pitt.

Until this time Pitt's designs had followed a pattern but there was a considerable change in his next three designs— the Opera House in Wellington (New Zealand) in 1912–14, the rebuilt auditorium of the THEATRE ROYAL in Adelaide in 1914 and an unrealised scheme for a J. C. WILLIAMSON's theatre in Bathurst Street, Sydney, in 1914. In all three the proscenium, and its side boxes, was splayed with a deeply arched and angled sounding board over the orchestra and a portion of the front stalls. By 1915 the designs from Pitt's office were quite Edwardian in externals, but the interior of the Hoyts De Luxe cinema in Bourke Street, Melbourne, was still rich and deeply modelled with a ceiling little different from that of the foyer of the Princess Theatre, designed by Pitt almost 30 years before. ♣*Ross Thorne*

William Pitt snr

Scene-painter. Born *c.*1820 in Sunderland (England). Arrived in Melbourne 1853. Died 1879 in Melbourne. Father of theatre architect William Pitt jnr.

A successful publican as well as a scene-painter, William Pitt was associated with GEORGE COPPIN in both capacities. In 1856 he was manager of the Olympian Hotel attached to Coppin's Olympic Theatre in Melbourne and at Coppin's CREMORNE GARDENS amusement park he worked with F. Arrigoni, JOHN HENNINGS and W. J. WILSON on a modelled fireworks panorama of Vesuvius and in the Pantheon Theatre. In Melbourne he also painted scenery for G. V. BROOKE at the Theatre Royal; his sets for *The Winter's Tale* were well received. In February 1859 Pitt worked with another scene-painter, Thomas Tannett, on *Once Upon a Time there were Two Kings*, a burlesque, at the Royal Victoria Theatre in Sydney. Pitt was the first treasurer of the

Victorian Academy of Art, founded in 1870, and he exhibited paintings in its shows. At his death he was licensee of the Café de Paris at the Theatre Royal. ❧*Mimi Colligan*

reference
Biographical notes in La Trobe Collection, State Library of Victoria (Melbourne).

Playbox Theatre Sydney

Theatre in Phillip Street, opened as **Macquarie Auditorium** 1941, seating 306. Became **Playbox Theatre** 1968. Demolished 1973.

Radio 2GB in Sydney fitted out new studios, including a theatrette on the ground floor, in late 1941. The raked auditorium, with well-upholstered seats, was lined with sound-absorbing soft fibreboard, the geometrically cut edges of overlapping sheets providing late Art Deco decoration. The radio shows it housed gradually disappeared after television came to Sydney in 1956, and in 1968 HARRY M. MILLER began live theatrical presentations in the little theatre. For the second stage production—Mart Crowley's *The Boys in the Band*, produced by Miller and Phillip Productions—the small stage was converted to a fixed two-level apartment set. The Playbox proved to be popular for well-proven overseas plays not taken up by larger commercial managements and, under Miller, it remained a live theatre almost until it was demolished in 1973. ❧*Ross Thorne*

Playbox Theatre Centre

Professional dramatic company in Melbourne, founded in 1976 as Hoopla Productions by Graeme Blundell, Carrillo Gantner and Garrie Hutchinson. Called Playbox Theatre Company 1978–89. Renamed Playbox Theatre Centre of Monash University 1990. **venues** 1977–84 Playbox Theatre. 1978–84 Upstairs theatre. 1984– St Martin's Theatre. 1984– Studio Theatre. 1990– CUB Malthouse Theatre. **artistic directors** 1976–79 Blundell and Hutchinson. 1979–81 Hutchinson. 1981–83 Rex Cramphorn and James McCaughey. 1984–85 Cramphorn, James McCaughey, Jill Smith. 1986 McCaughey and Peter Oyston. 1987–88 Oyston and Gantner. 1989–93 Gantner. 1993–Aubrey Mellor. **first production** *Chidley* by Alma de Groen at Grant Street Theatre, December 1976. Designer: Peter Corrigan. Director: Garrie Hutchinson.

Melbourne's second major theatre company, the Playbox Theatre Centre was founded, as Hoopla, to answer the perceived need at the time for an alternative to the powerful MELBOURNE THEATRE COMPANY. Two of the founders, GRAEME BLUNDELL and Garrie Hutchinson, had been members of the AUSTRALIAN PERFORMING GROUP and the initiative was seen as taking the fight for innovation into mainstream theatre. As one of Hoopla's brochures put it, 'we wanted a theatre that was contemporary, important, alive, Australian and fun'. From the outset it strongly emphasised new Australian writing, but it also presented interesting, innovative overseas works at the Playbox Theatre, which it took over with the help of the Victorian Ministry for the Arts. It began with ALMA DE GROEN's *Chidley* late in 1976 and DOROTHY HEWETT's *The Golden Oldies*, directed by Blundell, early in the New Year. Then Steve J. Spears's *THE ELOCUTION OF BENJAMIN FRANKLIN* ran for six months in a production originated by the NIMROD THEATRE COMPANY in Sydney. In 1978 Playbox opened the tiny Upstairs theatre. Many of its best productions were staged there, including DAVID ALLEN's *Upside Down at the Bottom of the World*, Michel Tremblay's *Hosanna*, BARRY DICKINS's *The Golden Goldenbergs* and Peter Handke's *My Foot, My Tutor*. When REX CRAMPHORN was resident director he made innovations, including the Actors' Development Stream, which concentrated chiefly on classic texts. They included Jean Racine's *Britannicus*, Molière's *Scapin*, a cut-down *Antony and Cleopatra*, *Hamlet* and *Measure for Measure*. Cramphorn also directed plays by Australians, including THÉRÈSE RADIC's *A Whip Round for Percy Grainger*, Dickins's *A Couple of Broken Hearts*, Louis Nowra's *THE GOLDEN AGE* and Ray Mathew's *A SPRING SONG*. A member of the company at that time was ROGER PULVERS, whose puppet play *General Macarthur in Australia*, with puppets by Patrick Cook, was included in the 1981 Downstairs season. Pulvers's *Bertolt Brecht Leaves Los Angeles*, with music by Felix Werder, was staged in the Upstairs theatre in 1979.

On 7 February 1984 fire destroyed its two city theatres. Productions had to be transferred to the St Martin's Theatre and later shared between it and the Studio Theatre at the Victorian Arts Centre. The company also began regular transfers of productions to the Alexandra Theatre at Monash University; and in 1990 the university's partnership was cemented in a new company title.

The Playbox company was also involved in initiating visits to Australia by theatre companies from China and Japan, and in developing two-way theatrical connections. The last of the founding directors, CARRILLO GANTNER left the company at the end of 1984 to become cultural counsellor at the Australian Embassy in Beijing. There followed a period in which the company was run by Cramphorn as artistic director and Jill Smith and James McCaughey as joint executive directors. This triumvirate, a compromise arrangement, soon ran into difficulties. Cramphorn left first, and then McCaughey, who had wanted to make Playbox a development company rather than a production company. But the board decided that the company should maximise its audience in anticipation of the move to bigger and permanent premises. Carlton and United Breweries had given the company a disused malthouse in South Melbourne to develop a new theatre. Gantner rejoined the company in 1987 and shared the artistic direction with Peter Oyston, formerly dean of drama at the VICTORIAN COLLEGE OF THE ARTS. Oyston resigned in 1988, leaving Gantner as artistic director. After a season at the Victorian Arts Centre the company moved into the handsome CUB MALTHOUSE THEATRE in 1990. After six years the company again had a permanent home, this time with two theatres as well as rehearsal space and new amenities.

Gantner's first two seasons at the Malthouse were entirely Australian in content. Five of the eight plays in the opening season were by women—ROBYN ARCHER, TES LYSSIOTIS, Joanna Murray-Smith, Thérèse Radic and HANNIE RAYSON. Since then the company's faith in the drawing power of Australian playwrights has remained unshaken. The only non-Australian work in the 1992 season was a co-production with the Japanese director Tadashi Suzuki, *The Chronicle of Macbeth*, which was first performed at the Adelaide Festival and later taken to the Mito Festival in Japan. The company's 1993 production of *King Lear* also toured to Japan, and to South Korea and the Festival of Perth. AUBREY MELLOR's first season as artistic director in 1994 continued the Australian policy. ❧*Leonard Radic*

further reading
GANTNER, CARRILLO and JOHN BECKETT. The Malthouse, South Melbourne. *Australian Theatre Design* (ed. Kim Spinks). Sydney: Australian Production Designers Association NSW 1992.

Playwrights' Advisory Board

In 1938, when professional playwrights' AGENTS were non-existent and Australian plays were neglected, the Playwrights' Advisory Board was formed in Sydney to secure more prominence, profit and honour for playwrights in the Australian theatre. The board comprised at any time about a dozen organisers of theatrical groups, playwrights and critics, working in an honorary capacity. For a small fee it offered to read scripts, give written criticisms, circulate worthwhile works among groups all over Australia, negotiate productions and collect royalties for authors without deduction. More than 260 productions were arranged and in only two cases were royalties not obtained. A second aim was to organise publication of the best plays in book form and about 17, mostly in three acts, went into print.

The board also arranged PLAYWRITING COMPETITIONS from 1944. In 1950–51, the federal government invited the board to assist in judging its play competition for the jubilee of federation. The board's most notable success came in 1954–55 when Ray Lawler's SUMMER OF THE SEVENTEENTH DOLL AND ORIEL GRAY's *The Torrents* shared first prize in its own competition. The board was prominent in negotiating the initial production of the *Doll*, which was by no means automatic. The board was later invited to judge competitions with large prizes promoted by the Journalists' Club in Sydney. The board remained in existence for 25 years, during which most stage playwrights accepted help. O. D. Bisset, MAY HOLLINWORTH, BEATRICE TILDESLEY and the present writer all stayed the quarter-century course. Many noted theatrical figures also gave long service. ❦*Leslie Rees*

Playwrights and the screen

Film and television have been seminal influences on the sensibilities of modern writers. Australian playwrights as diverse as DOROTHY HEWETT, PETER KENNA and STEPHEN SEWELL have acknowledged the potent effect of films on their imaginations. In the 1950s and 1960s, however, Australia offered playwrights little opportunity to write for film or television. RICHARD BEYNON, RAY LAWLER, SUMNER LOCKE ELLIOTT, RAY MATHEW and ALAN SEYMOUR are in an impressive list of people who sought to live as writers overseas and turned to television, the novel or other forms. None made an international name as a playwright. An expatriate playwright is an oxymoron.

With the new wave of playwrights in the late 1960s and early 1970s came an explosion of theatrical styles that were far from the visual dreams of movies and the naturalism of television. It is not surprising that ALEX BUZO's high-wire walk between naturalism and irony is too subtle for media that do not deal in irony. Nor is it a surprise that JACK HIBBERD's baroque verbosity and JOHN ROMERIL's cornucopias of words and images are too theatrical to sit comfortably in either medium, as is attested by their respective screenplays for the films *Dimboola* (1979) and *The Great Macarthy* (1975). By contrast, it is a common observation that Stephen Sewell, a later playwright whose work is profoundly rooted in the paranoia of the *film noir* thriller, writes not so much plays as substitute film scripts. It is a mistake, however, to regard Sewell's short, concise scenes as filmic. As his 1985 telefeature *A Long Way Home* showed, his language is so visceral, so strident that it is completely theatrical and lacks the 'transparency' of film language. His screenplay for *Isabelle Eberhardt* in 1992, however, showed that he was quickly coming to grips with the form.

In the late 1970s and during the 1980s playwrights were willingly seduced by the money to be made in television and a huge list of playwrights who dipped their toes into or fully immersed themselves in the medium—among them DAVID ALLEN, LINDA ARONSON, JANIS BALODIS, RON BLAIR, Anne Brooksbank, ALMA DE GROEN, ROB GEORGE, Tim Gooding, MICHAEL GURR, ALAN HOPGOOD, Joanna Murray-Smith, Billy Marshall-Stoneking, STEVE J. SPEARS and DAVID WILLIAMSON. For some of these playwrights television has been an insidious influence in its deployment of language that should be natural and never call attention to itself.

Williamson's career provides a potent example. His original screenplays, such as *Gallipoli*, and adaptations of his own plays, such as TRAVELLING NORTH, have shown his neat touch with film structure, just as he understood the form of the television mini-series in *A Dangerous Life* in 1988. His astonishing run as a screenwriter has benefited his work for both film and stage. In plays like *Travelling North* he has expertly used the short, intense scenes of screenplays to great effect, and there is no doubt that his increasing use of asides to the audience is a theatrical equivalent of the close-up. But there are signs that this cross-pollination can have a detrimental effect. In his 1988 play *Top Silk* it was noticeable how he was touching the bases of story points and ideas rather than exploring them, as if the play needed a movie camera to zoom in on the emotional core of the scenes. This intrusion of film writing became evident in Williamson's next play, *Siren* in 1990, where his dialogue, usually taut and sharp, had a flatness that caused some critics, including BRIAN HOAD of the *Bulletin*, to speculate that his screenwriting was beginning to undermine his work for the stage. Williamson's 1994 play *Sanctuary*, however, was a return to a much more theatrical technique, sacrificing an impressionistic, filmic narrative for the gradual revelation of story through character development. ❦*Louis Nowra*

further reading
BUZO, ALEX. *Young Person's Guide to the Theatre and Almost Everything Else*. Melbourne: Penguin 1989.
MCFARLANE, BRIAN. *Australian Cinema 1970–1985*. Melbourne: Heinemann 1987.
O'REGAN, TOM. The historical relations between theatre and film. *Australian Journal of the Media* 1/1 (Melbourne 1987).
REID, DON and FRANK BLADWELL. *Close Up—Scripts for television's second decade*. Melbourne: MacMillan 1970.
RICE, CECILIA. David Williamson—Plays into films. *Cinema Papers* 32 (May–June 1981).
SPEAR, PETA. *Get the Picture—Essential data on Australian film, television and video*. Sydney: Australian Film Commission 1989.
SYKES, ALRENE (ed.). *Five Plays for Stage, Radio and Television*. Brisbane: University of Queensland Press 1977.
WHITE, PATRICK. *The Night, The Prowler—The screenplay*. Melbourne: Penguin 1978.
WILLIAMSON, DAVID. *Gallipoli—The screenplay*. Melbourne: Penguin 1981.

Playwriting

Australia was settled in the last years of the Age of Enlightenment. Literature, painting and the performing arts were regarded as refining influences then, so even in hard conditions people sought to lighten the burden with music, dance and theatricals. Amateur performances flourished in the early days in the officers' barracks and convict settlements at Parramatta, EMU PLAINS and even NORFOLK ISLAND.

Published plays existed only in private libraries so enterprising performers soon resorted to improvisation. Convicts who turned their hand to acting and theatregoers with vivid memories all shared nostalgia for the world they had abruptly left behind. No record has been found of original writing performed in SIDAWAY'S THEATRE, which opened in Sydney in 1796–98 or in barracks theatricals. The first locally written material known to have been performed was a short piece by BARNETT LEVEY, *The Stage-Struck Tailor and the Trickish Youth*. He performed it himself in 1832 in the Royal Hotel in a fund-raising 'at home' for his newly licensed THEATRE ROYAL. The *Currency Lad* indulgently promoted it as 'one of the most ludicrous compositions we ever read'.

More serious work was afoot in Hobart. Henry Melville published his play THE BUSHRANGERS—or, *Norwood Vale* in his *Hobart Town Magazine* of April 1834, and on 29 May 1834 it opened the Theatre Royal in the Argyle Rooms. It is believed to be the first dramatic work published in Australia. The second was THE BANDIT OF THE RHINE by Evan Henry Thomas, published and performed in Launceston in 1835. The first to write a play in Hobart, however, was David Burn, a Scottish journalist. Also called THE BUSHRANGERS, it was inspired by the execution of the Tasmanian bushranger Matthew Brady in 1826, which Burn is believed to have witnessed as a reporter. It may also have owed inspiration to the popular 1825 play *Jack Sheppard* by J. B. Buckstone, which was banned in London as an 'incitement to crime'. Burn's play is essentially a romantic drama in a local setting, but it has gritty realism and it is sufficiently unsympathetic in portraying Lieutenant-Governor George Arthur and his administration to account for its failure to be performed in Hobart. The Byronic concepts of liberty and the championing of the oppressed held particular significance and popularity in Australia, and Burn's outlaw hero was probably the first in an Australian line.

More orthodox is *The Bushrangers* by Melville, an entertainment in an English genre, about a country gentleman who has settled in Australia seeking (ironically) greater security and social justice than Great Britain offered. A bushranger lays claim to his property and his daughter but is foiled by the girl's lover and a resourceful Aborigine. The dramatic work of most significant literary merit on the bushranger theme was an unperformed piece by the poet CHARLES HARPUR. He was a minor member of the cast at the opening of the THEATRE ROYAL in Sydney in 1833 but was dismissed because he 'understood as much of theatricals as the candle snuffer's apprentice'. Next year the editor of the *Sydney Monitor* received a visit from the youth with 'the first blank verse tragedy composed on this side of the equator, which we ever heard of'. It was called *The Tragedy of Donohoe*. It was published in 1835 but did not receive a production, and Harpur revised it over the next 30 years, eventually titling it STALWART THE BUSHRANGER. The revisions changed the character of the bushranger from an adventurer to one possessed by the warring demons of social conscience and guilt. The play has obvious debts to Shakespeare, particularly the Forest of Arden and Gadshill; and the soaring repentance of the final scenes carries overtones of Christopher Marlowe's *Doctor Faustus*.

The first locally written play licensed for performance in Sydney was Charles Nagel's *The Mock Catalani in Little Puddleton*, in which JOSEPH SIMMONS impersonated an Italian diva with great success at the Royal Victoria Theatre in 1842. *The Mock Catalani* was also probably the first local work charged with plagiarism. A German correspondent of the *Australian* claimed that it was a rewrite of *Die falsche Catalani in Krahwinkel*, a piece seen in Vienna in 1818. Skill in plagiarising was the first, and probably chief, attribute of the early colonial playwright. To copy and, it was hoped, improve upon admired models, was standard neoclassical practice but here it was prized for its reminders of home.

Compensating for shortage of scripts

The English Copyright Act of 1833 gave all performance rights to the publisher. According to the scholar Helene Oppenheim, publishers were reluctant to supply orders at great distance, and there was a serious shortage of acting texts in Australia by the 1840s. Plays recycled under new titles, localised overseas plays, local works and sketches— mostly written by managers and actors—began to be substituted. Afterpieces with local reference began to appear. Regulation by licensing, however, amounted to CENSORSHIP —an inevitability in a society with no reason to love authority. Unbridled free speech from the stage, particularly by emancipists, was a sensitive matter. Even works already licensed in England were scrutinised lest they appear 'locally objectionable'.

Such regulation discouraged use of local context and restricted a theatre industry that was still finding its way, but it had a benefit for posterity. Copies of plays performed in Sydney and Melbourne during the 1840s and 1850s were lodged with the Colonial Secretary, and many have survived in the NSW Archives. The objects of censorship, besides commentary on colonial identities, appear to have been swear words, depiction of religious figures and representation of criminal as hero, even in a historical context. After the discovery of gold and the separation of Victoria from NSW this control gradually dissipated, though issues of moral righteousness survived into the 20th century.

The NSW Archives collection, uncovered by Oppenheim in the 1960s, consists largely of comedy sketches, burlesques and historical dramas. Two pieces that received licences were the farce BILLY BARLOW and its sequel *The Barlow Family* by Charles Alexander Dibdin, who had several plays staged in Sydney in the 1840s. Another was Charles Nagel's pantomime *Shakespericonglomorofunnidogammoniae*, 'an original, laughable, comical, operatical, tragical, melo-drammatical Burletta', first performed at the Royal Victoria on 1 July 1844. This Shakespearean burlesque, full of allusions to the poor economic state of NSW, was an early example of a genre that gained wide popularity. A more realistic account of contemporary life, LIFE IN SYDNEY—or, *the Ran Dan Club*, submitted anonymously, was refused a licence. The play was an adaptation of William Moncrieff's

Tom and Jerry—or, Life in London, in which an innocent lad is initiated into the pleasures of city low life.

Despite censorship, there was sufficient liveliness for a journalist to write in the *Colonial Literary Journal* on 27 February 1845: 'Our Sydney theatres have not been altogether barren in the production of the original drama: from time to time various morceaux of Australian manufacture have been enacted, and very lately a tragedy—yes, a real tragedy, and one of considerable merit into the bargain—has been submitted to the judgement of an Australian audience'. The tragedy in question was undoubtedly *The Hibernian Father* by EDWARD GEOGHEGAN, an Irish convict who wrote plays for the Royal Victoria Theatre—anonymously, because convicts were banned from theatres. Geoghegan was accused of plagiarism after *The Hibernian Father* was performed in 1844. The accusers compared it to an Irish drama, *The Warden of Galway*. Margaret Williams finds Geoghegan's play the more substantial.

Nine surviving plays, mostly verse tragedies, are attributed to 'the author of *The Hibernian Father*' and two others have been lost. Two comedies, *True Love—or, The Interlude Interrupted* and THE CURRENCY LASS, have local settings. In the latter the central conceit is a misreading of the word 'native' but apart from this naive racism the play is charming. It has been performed many times since the manuscript was published in 1976.

Aborigines were treated more sympathetically in early plays than even in the novels of the period. This may be because the novelist's largely overseas readership had different expectations from the playwright's immediate audience at home. In Burn's *The Bushrangers* the Aborigines are primitive but moral. In Melville's *The Bushrangers* an Aborigine whose family has been murdered receives the sympathetic ear of the heroine, and demonstrates compassion and nobility. One of the most vivid accounts of colonial life to survive, *Arabin—or, The Adventures of a Settler* (1849) by J. R. McLachlan has an amiable Aboriginal character called Warren Warren who discourses upon the pleasures of nomadic life and makes fun of the innocent new chum. McLachlan's unperformed *Jackey Jackey—or, The Australian Bushranger*, in the NSW Archives, has an Aboriginal hero. This sympathetic view is repeated in later melodramas. The Aborigines are again instruments of good in THE AUSTRALIAN BUNYIPS by Monsieur Richard, a 'great Australian drama' staged at Malcom's Amphitheatre in Sydney on 24 January 1857. It had genuine Aborigines providing 'the corroberies, war dances &c which occur in the bush scenes of this powerful drama'. In later melodramas like E. W. O'Sullivan's COO-EE and Edmund Duggan's MY MATE friendly Aborigines have evolved into stock characters alongside squatters and convicts. The *Australasian* said of King Charley in Julian Thomas's play *No Mercy* (1882), as played by Sam Poole for the Dampier company: 'It is the best representation of a blackfellow we have ever had upon the Melbourne stage ... he carries neither spear, waddy nor boomerang but he is a real native for all that, and for all that he has undergone the process of civilisation, and wears a trooper's dress and swears like any white man'.

New chums were favourite stock characters in early local pieces. One example is JEMMY GREEN IN AUSTRALIA, assumed to be the work of a convict, James Tucker, and believed to have had a private performance at Port Macquarie in 1845. Jemmy Green is the engaging innocent in Moncrieff's *Tom and Jerry*. In Tucker's play he learns the hard way about rural and urban life in the colony. The author also exploits the popularity of the BILLY BARLOW ballads.

When Victoria separated from NSW in 1852 it broke the censorship pattern. Plays refused licences in NSW began to be performed in the booming Victorian goldfields towns, and Melbourne, a new financial centre with a freespending population, drew actors and producers away from Sydney. For the next 20 years Melbourne was the theatrical centre and it developed vigorous colonial pantomime and burlesque. Into these leading writers—W. M. AKHURST, GARNET WALCH and MARCUS CLARKE—increasingly injected social and political satire, including much commentary upon Victoria's sudden prosperity and upon its rivalry with the parent colony. The first colonial pantomime was probably *Transportation and the Demon Discord—or, Harlequin in Van Diemen's Land* by G. H. ROGERS and CHARLES YOUNG, performed at the Royal Victoria Theatre in Sydney in 1847. Young's *The Goblin of the Gold Coast—or, Harlequin and the Melbournites in California*, first performed in Melbourne in 1850, anticipated Australia's own gold rush by less than a year. Melbourne's first real theatre, the QUEEN'S THEATRE ROYAL opened in 1845 and became a patron of colonial playwrights. It produced its first colonial piece, *The Heir of the Sept—or, Ireland in the Eleventh Century*, a historical tragedy by 'a native', in 1845 and works by David Burn and FRANCIS BELFIELD and McLachlan's *Arabin* followed.

With the rise of the middle classes arose middle-class comedy—much of it adaptation—and trifling, sometimes extravagant, entertainments loosely based on topical issues and events. Characters like Billy Barlow became regular commentators from the stage and gold became an almost universal theme. Akhurst was Melbourne's most prolific playwright from the 1850s to the 1870s, writing comedies, burlesques, musical pieces and journalism. Among his most popular works were the comedy *Colonial Experience* (1854) and the burletta *The Rights of Women* (1854). Along with gold and the middle class came the temperance movement. The theme appears on stage as early as 1852 in Geelong with *The Spirit of the Goldfields—or, Avarice, Intemperance, and Ruin*, a fantasy in 14 tableaux, showing the Spirit of Avarice and the Spirit of Temperance watching over the fortunes of a prospector.

From the 1850s to the 1870s was the high period of PANTOMIME, offering vigorous social and political comment of the broadest kind. Some manuscripts survive but their topicality and whimsicality unfortunately make revival unlikely today. Typical are Akhurst's immensely popular parody of the new affluence, *The House that Jack Built—or, Harlequin Progress and the Loves, Laughs, Laments and Labours of Jack Melbourne and Little Victoria* (1869), and Walch's engaging celebration of cricket, AUSTRALIA FELIX (1873).

WALTER COOPER, who has a claim to be the first noteworthy Australian-born playwright, began his career writing pantomime. The first work he had performed was *The History of Kodadad and His Brothers* in 1867, an Arabian nights extravaganza about the power of Queensland squattocracy. It was followed by a romantic comedy, COLONIAL EXPERIENCE (1868), and Australia's first sensation drama, *Sun and Shadow* (1870), which introduced new mechanical devices to the stage of the Royal Victoria Theatre. *Foiled*

(1871) borrowed the log-saw sensation from a contemporary American play and used steam on stage for the first time. These and his 'murderously sensational' *Hazard* (1872) were perhaps the first Australian plays to have extended tours in the USA.

Prosperity brought such a demand for ever more spectacular entertainment that the rising new producers could hardly supply it. The playwright's status was lowly. This was the golden age of the actor-manager and the scene-painter. From the late 1860s theatres were built with boxes eliminated, and a proscenium to frame visual sensations. Gas lighting gave way to electric lighting, which brought with it the opportunity to darken the auditorium completely and create a cabinet of illusions within the stage.

The great majority of the writers, like their audience, had been born and educated outside Australia. Waves of immigration meant that not until the 1880s did native-born white Australians outnumber immigrants and the concept of nationhood become addressed seriously. Meanwhile the theatre was a small world reflecting the larger, exploiting, celebrating and satirising the local scene for the enjoyment of audiences who were secure in the knowledge that their roots were elsewhere. Australian irony as a weapon for dealing with tragedy and failure may have had its origins in the exploitative nature of the early colonies and the tough sceptical outlook it produced. But Margaret Williams perspicaciously comments that melodrama reached its height in Australia when the beginnings of realism pushed it into satire. Certainly, Australian melodrama reflected a tough, anti-authoritarian outlook in which virtue and social order were arbitrary affairs. In the theatrical portrait of Australia winning was a matter of gambler's luck from the start, unlike the American dream of progress.

Australia did have comedies that examined contemporary society more seriously, but they seem few compared with the proliferation of works built around athletics, horses, aquatic feats and scenic effects. Examples of these comedies are Grosvenor Bunster's *Class* (1878), the story of an ironfounder and a squatter's daughter which argues the case for egalitarianism, and Samuel Stevens's *A Girl's Frolic and What Came of It*, a delightful account of two girls' unchaperoned day in the city. And Cooper's *Colonial Experience*, though essentially an English genre piece, has some rich comments upon larrikin aspects of a post-convict society. Bunster, Stevens and Cooper were all journalists, as were some of the more literary playwrights who used the theatre as a platform for social commentary. But on the whole political, patriotic or domestic themes were chosen for topicality, not debate.

Some of the leading actor-managers wrote or adapted their own sensation melodramas. GEORGE DARRELL, a handsome Englishman, wrote some 16 melodramas, chiefly to star himself and either his first wife FANNY CATHCART or his second wife Christine Peachey. The common theme was the adventures of an English emigrant, punctuated with visual sensations in which fortunes were lost and won. In 1880 his play *The Forlorn Hope*—which anticipated by five years the dispatch of 734 NSW soldiers to assist Great Britain in Sudan—reflected in lively debate the growing nationalism that led to federation and the imperial sentiment that bound Australia to the mother country. One of Darrell's few surviving melodramas, and reputedly his best, is THE SUNNY SOUTH (1883), which conveys all the optimism of a new country unlimited in resources and bursting with energy and self-reliance. Darrell's later plays were mostly set in the USA or New Zealand.

His dominance faded in the 1890s before ALFRED DAMPIER, who came to Australia as a leading man and soon formed his own company. Dampier became the patron of another Englishman, F. R. C. HOPKINS, whose first play with an all-Australian setting was a comedy-drama, *L.S.D.*, presented in Sydney in 1882. The *Sydney Morning Herald* described the characters as 'for the most part such as might be met with

Alfred Dampier's production of Robbery Under Arms, *evocative of bush life, enjoyed great popularity. Dampier adapted Rolf Boldrewood's novel with Garnet Walch*

any day'. They included a philosopher-philanthropist and member of the Legislative Assembly, a male 'Sydney exquisite', a woman 'not altogether in society' and Major Chilley Chutney, an adventurer from India. Dampier himself was a prolific author. In Sydney in 1877 he had a notable success with an adaptation of *Les Misérables*, which he probably wrote before coming to Australia. His spectacle was for a time unsurpassed, and involved the use of water, fire, horses and bush scenery.

Dampier was a genuine enthusiast for Australian national drama in the years that led up to federation and in Melbourne from 1888 to 1892 he was successful as lessee of the Alexandra Theatre, which he subtitled the Australian Theatre. He collaborated with a variety of writers and his years at the Alexandra became a landmark in the history of Australian playwriting. The Sydney *Bulletin* was fanning nationalism and Dampier documented a heady time of political change. No doubt commercially motivated, he rode the wave of nationalism skilfully. For example, he could not let pass unchallenged the actor GEORGE LEITCH's announcement of his adaptation of Marcus Clarke's novel *His Natural Life*. Leitch opened in Brisbane in April 1886 and by June Dampier had *For the Term of His Natural Life* by himself and THOMAS SOMERS on stage, pre-empting Leitch's announced tour to Melbourne and Sydney. Both versions represented convicts as comic relief and introduced a happy ending to the tragic events of the novel. The Dampier–Somers version proved the more enduring.

Dampier's greatest success at the Alexandra was ROBBERY UNDER ARMS, his adaptation with Garnet Walch of Rolf Boldrewood's novel, in 1890. Again the morality of the novel was distorted to make the outlaws romantic and to provide a happy ending. Nevertheless, in a period of growing nationalist euphoria its audience recognised it as a genuine evocation of bush life and a milestone for Australian drama. A *Bulletin* critic wrote on 22 November 1890: '… a vast multitude rocked the cradle of Australian national drama with their feet and the native gallery-boy whistled and howled like the wind among the gums'. Margaret Williams says *Robbery Under Arms* 'was the first truly national, as distinct from colonial or parochial, play that the Australian theatre had seen'.

In 1890 a contributor to the *Lorgnette* of 1 March took issue with Austin Brereton, theatre critic of the *Sydney Morning Herald*, who had claimed in the London magazine *Theatre* that 'there is no native dramatist. If there were, he might make a fortune in a few months.' The writer hotly rebutted both claims: 'In the first place we can assure him that there is a native dramatist, and a fairly numerous one at that, as any playgoer who has been many years in the colonies well knows … And now for the statement, "If there were, he (native dramatist) might make a fortune in a few months." Certainly he *might*, but then again, he *mightn't* … Is he not aware that there is almost insuperable objection on the part of nearly all managers to producing anything, no matter how good, that has not what they term "the London Hall Mark" impressed on it. Truly that same London Hall Mark is impressed on some very pinchbeck goods, if we may judge by many of the "great London successes" they have given us out here.'

Nathaniel Barrett, giving advice to visiting performers in the London *Dramatic Yearbook* of 1892, exclaimed: 'There is perhaps no country in the world where the drama has made such rapid strides and attained such a high standard in so short a period as Australasia'. But he also said that Australian dramatic authors 'are in still worse case, for owing to prejudice on the part of most managers, the stage portal is utterly barred against them … the parrot cry, "the London Hall Mark" effectively shuts them out'.

An Australian writer who did make a name in London at that time was Haddon Chambers. In 1888 he pursued Herbert Beerbohm Tree into a Turkish bath and, holding him thus captive, read him all of his melodrama *Captain Swift*. Tree had enough equanimity to recognise talent, even under trying circumstances. Chambers made his career in England and wrote 21 plays between 1886 and 1913.

In 1940 Morris Miller, in his *Australian Literature*, proclaimed Chambers to be Australia's major playwright on the grounds of his being 'the only Australian who has gained a niche in English drama'. And, as proof of Australia's poor output, he added: 'Though he occupies the supreme place as yet among Australian playwrights, his standing among contemporary English dramatists is not comparable with his position here'. The judgment testifies to the huge change that was about to overtake Australian drama. The viewpoint, notably more colonial than half a century before, is that of a literary man for whom Australian drama is almost entirely confined to published texts. His book lists few plays with Australian content until the period of Esson and Palmer. He mentions the old popular theatre only through its literary connections, while giving attention to many unperformed verse tragedies, of which Francis Adams's *Tiberius* is typical. Clearly, Australia by 1940 had become much more self-conscious place than in the 1880s, when Darrell remarked: 'There are only two plays, so-called, nowadays—*Hamlet* and *The Sunny South*'.

Bush melodrama

A popular theatre based on action and effects was inevitably obsessed with bushranging, prospecting, horse racing, and other colourful aspects of Australian life. The apotheosis of nationalist sensation drama was DAN BARRY, a barnstormer who toured country towns from the 1890s to the 1920s. He also created a version of *His Natural Life*, for which he loudly advertised the horrors awaiting the ticket buyer. His company's season at the Alexandra Theatre in 1896 made his name synonymous with melodrama that overflowed into the ridiculous. His most successful creation was *The Kelly Gang*, which opened at the Alexandra in 1898 with Barry in the title-role. The work bore a close resemblance to *Robbery Under Arms* and was performed in a variety of forms under a variety of attributions (principally Arthur Denham) as late as 1929.

Barry's true successor was E. I. Cole, whose BOHEMIAN DRAMATIC COMPANY played in a tent in country towns from about 1899 and in Sydney in 1903–06. It performed bushranging plays with equestrian feats—some shows were nearer to circus than drama—based on local stories probably written by Cole. Usually no author was named but Cole staged three plays by E. W. O'SULLIVAN, a journalist and parliamentarian. The best known was *COO-EE* (1906). On a higher plane, BLAND HOLT specialised in localised English plays and spectacular Australian scenery. From 1903 he introduced actuality film into his stage design,

The two men seated among the original cast of On Our Selection, *Fred MacDonald (left) and Bert Bailey built careers on their respective roles of Dave and Dad Rudd. Bailey also had a hand in writing the play, which gave rise to a flood of bush comedies, including Kate Howarde's* Possum Paddock *in 1919*

replacing the old MOVING PANORAMAS. His most famous production, THE BREAKING OF THE DROUGHT, adapted from an English play, depicted the drought of 1902 so graphically that fears were expressed about its effect on the wool market. It was particularly noted for its contemporary setting, and its prodigal-son plot is one of the best-defined examples of the opposition between bush and city, which was then growing, and being exploited by *Bulletin* writers.

The rise of realism

City-country antagonism was the first new theme to emerge with realism and character drama, a new form that had been evident in Europe since the 1870s. The country became synonymous with homely virtues and the city—education, business, politics, the police or 'foreigners'—with sophisticated vice. Later the conflicts were with more remote, invincible forces—the inhospitable land, European wars, the bureaucracy, the 'system'. Winning continued to be seen as a matter of luck, not achievement; but with the new century optimism began to die and luck ran out.

In the *Sydney Morning Herald* on 16 December 1905 GERALD MARR THOMPSON mused upon dissatisfaction behind NELLIE STEWART'S departure for San Francisco: 'She may give as a further reason that there are no Australian plays. The best plays, or rather the best comedies are a reflection of life of the period. If the characters are slightly more brilliant than the people we are accustomed to meet, their actions and speeches are, at all events, formed and controlled by the same influences as our own. Such a comedy demands a society of men and women who understand and are prepared to be amused at each other's foibles. It cannot be produced where the life is an imperfect reproduction of a life lived more fully elsewhere. ... While we are in the imitative stage, while our imagination is fostered almost exclusively on English novels and English magazines, there is unlikely to be a demand for a comedy of our own.' Three years later LEON BRODZKY was complaining in the *Lone Hand*: 'Many of us are almost in despair when we see how little relation the theatre in Australia has to the national life of the country'. They were right. In all the activity of the previous decades there had been little that might be called the beginnings of national drama. Emulating Bland Holt, the entrepreneur WILLIAM ANDERSON localised an overseas play in 1905 and had such success that he became a patron of local drama. Two years later, two actors in his company, BERT BAILEY and EDMUND DUGGAN, under the pseudonym Albert Edmunds, wrote an enormously successful bush drama, THE SQUATTER'S DAUGHTER, the story of a spirited and independent countrywoman. It was quickly followed by the adventures of an even more independent young woman in *The Man from Outback* (1908). Though their roots in the conventions of melodrama are distinct today, these plays, along with *Robbery Under Arms*, mark the passage from colonial taste to bush realism. They extol the virtues and hardships of rural Australian life, and depend less on exploitation of other characters than on ingenuity and yarn-telling.

'Build your drama with a concrete, damp-proof foundation of human interest', Bailey wrote in 1918. 'Place on it a two-foot wall of characterisation. Strengthen it with girders of bright comedy, floor it with incident and roof it with good ends of acts. Papering the walls with the dialogue is easy. If you are a literary man you can put a dado in the drawing-room. It won't make any difference to the strength of the building.' When Bailey wrote this advice his bush comedies and dramas had been seen by a million people. The 1910 adaptation of STEELE RUDD's best-selling *Bulletin* stories, ON OUR SELECTION held the stage to 1929, and spawned other stage works and a series of films. The authorship of this and other Rudd plays is still the subject of controversy, but Bailey made a career of playing Dad Rudd, whose character in *On Our Selection* affirms the independence of the new nation, though the play's basis is slapstick comedy about yokels.

A more serious playwright of briefer career was JO SMITH, whose plays *The Miner's Trust* (1908) and *The Bushwoman* (1909) took realistic detail a step further. *Table Talk* said of *The Bushwoman* on 2 September 1909: 'The plot is not involved, the characters life-like ... and the heroics are neither strained nor too liberally introduced. In those rare instances where the emotions are tense and the situation calls for a burst of passionate sentiment, the effect is judiciously subdued and never descends to bathos.' Smith's last play, *The Girl of the Never Never* examined the need to defend Australia's northern shores and expressed racial prejudices and preoccupations current in 1910.

Bush comedy—and a lesser city equivalent—had a popular vogue for 20 years until it was ousted by film. One of the best-known exponents was KATE HOWARDE, whose POSSUM PADDOCK (1919) followed all the conventions of the Rudd model and enjoyed success in the country into the 1930s. Among the distinguishing characteristics of Australian melodrama and bush comedy were:

The independent woman. There was almost no equivalent of the dependent heroine of English melodrama, though the character was familiar in imported plays and the convention was strong enough for J. C. Williamson to press JANET ACHURCH to change Henrik Ibsen's ending to *A Doll's House*.

A pragmatic kind of class system. Most playwrights adopted an anti-authoritarian stance from the start. The hero was usually without means, and the heroine of independent means. The villains were on the whole upper-class English, squatters or convicts, but bushrangers often adopted the Robin Hood mantle and became more gentlemanly as living memories faded.

A developing Australian accent. Hero and heroine spoke with standard English accents while the comic and homely characters developed a 'natural' Australian language and outlook.

There was much incongruity between the 'naturalness' of some characters and stage conventions that required, for example, the villain to wear a frock coat and top hat and the Aborigine a loincloth. Naturalness was largely an illusion arising from contrast with the melodramatic and satirical conventions of other characters. Stage cloths were commonly reused and authors often had to put up with their play being housed in a recognisably northern-hemisphere setting, but in later years this practice was abandoned and accurate portrayal of familiar landscapes and monuments became a major attraction. The melodrama conventions finally foundered on the improbability of plots from foreign parts set in recognisable home territory.

Australia settled down in the 20th century to become a more homogenous, less travelled, less educated, less cosmopolitan society than the immigrants of the 19th century had created. In the theatre the old impresarios retired one by one and were superseded by the J. C. WILLIAMSON's conglomerate. With the break-up of partnerships between actors and writers, dependence upon overseas texts became dominant. The overwhelming demand was for British or Irish comedies and imported operetta. Among the outriders were a handful of historical dramas offered by J. C. Williamson's in the 1920s. EMELIE POLINI and FRANK HARVEY popularised DORIS EGERTON JONES's detective thriller *The Flaw* in 1923, and ALLAN WILKIE presented her historical drama *Governor Bligh* in 1930. In 1931 J. C. Williamson's produced Harvey's *Cape Forlorn*. In 1933 F. W. THRING took up COLLITS' INN, a musical comedy by Stuart Gurr and Varney Monk, with notable success. It was one of the last works to spin out the bushranger theme, but this time the British officer was favoured. Australia's outlook had changed radically since federation.

Intellectual theatre

Melbourne was Australia's centre of Fabian intellectual debate and in the new federation it soon threw up groups like LEON BRODZKY's Australian Theatre Society in 1904. The critic WILLIAM MOORE's Annual Drama Nights replaced it between 1909 and 1912. Moore presented the early plays of LOUIS ESSON, a socialist journalist with a claim to be the first genuine Australian dramatist, in the sense of providing dramatic texts that delved into the character of Australian life. Esson was one of a literary set in Melbourne who attempted to create a grounding for an indigenous literature. His wife Hilda Bull, Stuart Macky, Furnley Maurice, HUGH MCCRAE, William Moore, Nettie and VANCE PALMER, KATHARINE SUSANNAH PRICHARD and others created a climate of debate—through mutual support, readings, performances and contributions to literary journals—which lasted until the 1920s, when their dramatic ambitions were revived in the PIONEER PLAYERS.

When GREGAN MCMAHON presented Esson's short play *Dead Timber* in 1911 *Table Talk* commented on 21 December: 'If Mr Esson could only have his play produced in London with the same truthful setting, realism and fidelity to nature, and the same simplicity, he would probably find himself famous in a night'. But it was not to be. Esson's finest comedy, THE TIME IS NOT YET RIPE (1912) is just the kind of comedy of middle-class manners and foibles whose lack Gerald Marr Thompson had mourned seven years before. While other playwrights of the time allowed improbable plots to dictate the behaviour of characters from a jumble of conventions, Esson had written a coherently styled comedy of class and politics in Toorak. Perhaps the shock of recognition blocked its path to the professional theatre.

Esson followed *The Time is Not Yet Ripe* in 1921 with *The Battler*, which owes much to the Duggan–Bailey style of bush comedy. After this he experimented in various ways with comedy and tragedy in low-life Melbourne and the outback, under the spell of W. B. Yeats, who had inspired him with the idea of an Australian folk drama on the model of the Abbey Theatre in Dublin. One regrets the loss of a comic genius that could have flourished in another period, but Esson was the first to create a drama out of the rhythms of Australian life. The best known of his later plays is the 1920 short tragedy THE DROVERS, in which the mates of an injured rider must leave him to die on the track. None of Esson's plays reached the professional stage in his lifetime.

The other major playwright to emerge from the Melbourne socialists was KATHARINE SUSANNAH PRICHARD, who settled in Perth. In 1927 she won the *Triad* magazine's playwriting prize with BRUMBY INNES, which was published but never performed in her lifetime, because of its uncomfortable realism. A remarkable study of a rough station owner, it gives probably the first realistic representation of open sexuality in Australian drama—an astonishing jump from the stock characters of Bailey and Duggan in one generation. But the time was not yet ripe.

The sharp division between the new indigenous amateur theatre and the professional theatre—which suffered successively from the First World War, the cinema, the Great Depression, taxation and the Second World War—had at least the advantage of concentrating the new nationalists' minds upon the interpretive purpose of drama, free from the constraints of popular entertainment.

The questioning minority's need for artistic growth and a worldwide reaction against the emptiness of professional offerings produced a remarkable rise in AMATEUR THEATRE in the first half of the 20th century. Along with its examination of world theatre it provided a nursery for a new generation of playwrights, and latterly for actors and directors who peopled a new kind of theatre that emerged in the 1960s. One of the playwrights was GEORGE LANDEN DANN, whose IN BEAUTY IT IS FINISHED won a playwriting competition in 1931, earning itself an amateur season in Brisbane. But before opening night a newspaper exposed alleged 'sordid miscegenation' and aroused the kind of furore that might have struck *Brumby Innes* had it been produced. The play was one of several by Dann in which he sympathetically examined the life of Queensland Aborigines.

HENRIETTA DRAKE-BROCKMAN in Perth also wrote about black–white relations and the outback settler's attachment to the land in MEN WITHOUT WIVES, which was performed by amateurs in 1938. In *Open Spaces* HARRY TIGHE created a provocative sexual triangle between a farmer, his city-bred ex-wife, and his laconic, 'animal-like', implicitly Aboriginal mistress. It had a short amateur season in London in 1927. In the 1940s BETTY ROLAND wrote *Granite Peak* after visiting the Northern Territory. Its theme again is black and white ownership of land, and the catalyst is a station black caught between the two cultures. *Granite Peak* was performed on British television in 1951 but it has not been staged.

Revolutionary intentions
Exploitation of the Aborigines was part of white Australians' relationship with the land, which became the single most important theme of the new socially-conscious drama. Freed from popular convention and isolated from the imperialist search for novel local variations on familiar themes, the new playwrights began to see their work as revolutionary. They began consciously to define and interpret the life they knew, in pursuit of heroes in some cases, of political change in others.

The new middle class was industrial, increasingly urban and dependent upon the United Kingdom as its major trading partner and arbiter of opinion and taste. With the growth of film and the gramophone had come the mass media and American influences that increasingly threatened this fragile sense of cultural identity. In the face of such commodity thinking, the potential for new interpretive theatre was unpromising.

A succession of writers bemoaned the lack of Australian drama. As early as 1908 ARTHUR H. ADAMS, an old-guard dramatist who wrote three middle-class comedy-dramas in the manner of Arthur Wing Pinero and Henry Arthur Jones, had written in *Lone Hand*: 'Our only hope is to write plays that no Australian can refuse; and to learn our trade we must have our plays produced. Meantime we must hope for a manager patriotic enough to do as the London managers do—put up a play from an untried Australian author that has a chance of success'. He further suggested that Dante's line 'All ye who enter here abandon hope' be hung above the door of every theatre manager. His amusing but conventional comedy MRS PRETTY AND THE PREMIER did manage a London season. But the new guard was moving in a different direction.

Esson and Palmer in Melbourne were for discarding the old ways in favour of a new concept of theatre based upon national identity—a folk theatre, as Esson called it, that would not be confined to the little theatres. It did happen, but not in their lifetimes. Meanwhile, in Sydney proliferating little theatres were seeking to encourage young playwrights. Among the significant writers who emerged in the 1930s were MAX AFFORD, DYMPHNA CUSACK, ORIEL GRAY and SYDNEY TOMHOLT. These four fairly represent the schools of thought that prevailed until the 1950s.

Afford, a consummate craftsman with a prodigious output, became a highly successful writer of radio serials. For the stage he wrote a historical drama, AWAKE MY LOVE (1936), and three popular comedy-thrillers aimed at the West End stage—LADY IN DANGER (1942), *Mischief in the Air* (1944) and *Dark Enchantment* (1945). The first made it to Broadway under American management and the last had an extensive British tour. Australians who made it to the West End were Archie Menzies, a cousin of Robert Menzies the prime minister, and Hugh Hastings. Menzies became a man-about-town in London in the 1920s and 1930s and wrote a string of light comedies and farces for performers like Cicely Courtneidge and Jack Hulbert. Hastings went to England as an actor in 1939 and had five years' wartime service in the Royal Navy. Out of the experience he wrote the long-running SEAGULLS OVER SORRENTO, which played nearly three years in London before being seen in Australia. He followed it with eight further comedies, including a musical, *Scapa!* in 1962, which he also composed.

Dymphna Cusack, like Prichard, was a Communist and in due course abandoned the theatre for the novel. Her plays include *Red Sky at Morning* (1942) MORNING SACRIFICE (1942), and *Pacific Paradise* (1954), the first anti-atomic-bomb play, which added to her international reputation as a novelist. Her works debate individual choice, injustice, exploitation and, in particular, the arbitrariness of wartime conditions and the stresses they imposed on women. Cusack was one of a diverse group of women who used drama on stage and on radio as a medium of expression. Another was DOROTHY BLEWETT, whose hospital comedy *Quiet Night* was published in 1942 and thereafter almost continuously performed by amateurs at home and in the United Kingdom for many years. Her more lasting work, however, was *The First Joanna*, performed by amateurs in Sydney in 1948. This play, about a young wife, rebelling against the restrictions of the South Australian establishment, and discovering the characterful past of the family matriarch, is an early plea for public acknowledgment of Australian convict origins.

Oriel Gray became a principal writer for the socialist NEW THEATRE in the 1940s. She wrote a number of political revues and realist dramas on social issues. *Sky Without Birds* (1950), set on the Nullarbor Plain, deals with the postwar European immigrant, and both *Had We But World*

Radio and the new drama

Radio broadcasting, which began in Australia in 1923, gave work and encouragement to the dramatic form. While a writer's earnings from stage performance from the 1920s to the 1950s were negligible, radio provided an opportunity to develop a craft. The key figure was LESLIE REES, ABC federal drama editor from 1936 to 1966. Rees, FRANK D. CLEWLOW and other radio producers encouraged the writing of plays while the rising commercial radio provided a local market for serials. This was accelerated with the outbreak of the Second World War, which brought about a freeze on the overseas transfer of funds and encouraged American companies like Lux and Colgate–Palmolive to sponsor a lively radio drama industry in Australia.

Many hard-working playwrights made a comfortable living by writing popular entertainment from the 1930s until television usurped radio's hold on the imagination. The radio writer of most seriousness was the New Zealand poet DOUGLAS STEWART, who explored the poetic power of the language farther than any Australian dramatist since Charles Harpur. His major stage works are Shipwreck (1947) and NED KELLY (1943). The critic H. G. KIPPAX wrote that the latter put an end to the realist ambition of previous decades and pointed in a different direction. 'It succeeded well enough to expose the much more serious weaknesses of a generation of playwriting. After it, the Australian drama could never be quite the same.'

Australia at the time was back on European battlefields and looking for heroes. Stewart's work was preoccupied with an indigenous expression of heroism. Stewart opened the way out of the backyard for the Australian playwright, but his stage plays required a greater understanding of dramatic structure and resources than was available to him at that low point in the country's stage history. His radio plays remain major works of their kind.

The rising amateur theatre with its sense of cultural responsibility provided further modest sources of income for the promising playwright. Competitions and awards burgeoned. Almost all of George Landen Dann's plays, for example, won some financial reward from competitions, though they never made it to the professional theatre. In 1938 Leslie Rees, Rex Rienits and colleagues founded the PLAYWRIGHTS' ADVISORY BOARD, which helped writers for 25 years. In 1942 it persuaded the Commonwealth Literary Fund to guarantee against loss the publication of six plays. Melbourne University Press, the Australasian Publishing Company, Angus and Robertson and the short-lived Mulga Publications produced some 20 titles from 1942.

Naturally enough, the models for all these writers were overseas genres: the American left-wing theatre, Maurice Maeterlinck and the expressionists, Henrik Ibsen, Maxwell Anderson, Noel Coward, Terence Rattigan and Ben Travers. The problems of creating a folk theatre, 'simple, free from middle-class pretensions and drawing-room ethics', as Esson had written to Palmer, and of breaking through the barricades of ready-made plays to the professional stage, were still nagging in 1947. And the Irish model, which had so influenced them, was still alive when KEITH MACARTNEY argued in Meanjin: 'What is to be done about Australian drama? Are we ever to achieve a national theatre along the lines of the Irish Abbey Theatre? Is there any hope of a native playwright of the stature of, say, Sean

Leo McKern played the title-role when the Australian Elizabethan Theatre Trust gave the first professional stage production of Ned Kelly *in 1956. Douglas Stewart wrote the play for the stage in 1941 and it was produced on radio before amateurs gave the stage premiere in 1943*

Enough (1950) and BURST OF SUMMER (1960) deal with racism against Aboriginals in a country town. New Theatre was a significant patron of Australian writing. Kathleen Carroll, DICK DIAMOND, George Farwell, FRANK HARDY, David Martin, LESLIE REES, BETTY ROLAND and ELEANOR WITCOMBE are among New Theatre's authors. One of its most loyal was MONA BRAND, a socialist who wrote eight plays and revues for New Theatre in Sydney. Her major work, Here Under Heaven (1948) tackles the dilemma faced by a Chinese war bride in Australia. It has been translated and performed in China and Eastern Europe.

Sydney Tomholt fought in the First World War and in 1936 he published a collection of plays driven by a need to express the mixed emotions the experience aroused. The plays are written at white heat in various realist and symbolist styles. Only two are set in Australia: Bleak Dawn, which painfully examines the emotions of a divorced woman visited by her former husband, and Anoli—the Blind, about a vendetta among Italians in Queensland.

Other writers of the period were DULCIE DEAMER, who wrote symbolist plays; CATHERINE DUNCAN, from Hobart, whose wartime love story Sons of the Morning (1944), set in Greece, had some success; GWEN MEREDITH, today remembered for a distinguished career in radio; RUSSELL OAKES, whose Chinese willow-pattern romance Enduring as the Camphor Tree was successfully presented by Melbourne Little Theatre in 1946; and CATHERINE SHEPHERD, who wrote several biographical plays about international literary figures and a historical drama, Daybreak (1942), set in Hobart.

O'Casey and Eugene O'Neill ... we still lack a truly national voice in the theatre, the most social of the arts ....'

Within a year a playwright proved that the Irish signpost pointed the wrong way. SUMNER LOCKE ELLIOTT, who had written satirical revues and English-style comedies for Independent Theatre in Sydney before the war, produced a comedy based on his army life which had instant success and made the big leap to a professional production. Its unsentimental account of mindless routines, expressed in robust army vernacular, made it the first play to burst out of the amateur theatre with a 'truly national voice'. It was also one of the few plays since Esson to display a natural gift for relating the rhythms of Australian life to the dramatic medium. The modern, genuinely indigenous Australian theatre can be most accurately dated from *Rusty Bugles* in 1948. Its author, however, left Australia without seeing his play performed and made a successful career in New York.

By 1953 Leslie Rees, in *Towards an Australian Drama*, was blaming the playwright's isolation from mainstream theatrical practice for the poverty of Australia's record and was pressing ambitiously for new training grounds: '... what we want is a producer who will treat the new and unknown author as though he were Shakespeare. Such a tryout theatre, aided by the best theatre men, could give new Australian plays the chance they need; help them, after trimming and grooming, recasting and resetting, towards full-scale success in the larger theatre. It would also train audiences to widen their scope of likes and appreciate the themes nearest to their own community living.'

Next year the establishment of the AUSTRALIAN ELIZABETHAN THEATRE TRUST took the first steps in that direction. This unexpected encouragement produced in quick succession Ray Lawler's SUMMER OF THE SEVENTEENTH DOLL and RAY MATHEW's *We Find the Bunyip* in 1955; Ru Pullen's *Curley on the Rack* and Richard Beynon's THE SHIFTING HEART in 1957; Alan Burke's musical LOLA MONTEZ, Mary Durack and James Penberthy's opera *Dalgerie*, Anthony Coburn's *The Bastard Country* and Peter Kenna's THE SLAUGHTER OF ST TERESA'S DAY in 1959; Alan Seymour's THE ONE DAY OF THE YEAR in 1960 and Patrick White's THE HAM FUNERAL in 1961. The plays had varied success in the new Trust-led professional theatre. The leader was the *Doll*, which rocketed to success both nationally and in London.

Euphoria and hope were short-lived. There was no proper development, as Ray Mathew argued in the *Current Affairs Bulletin* in 1958. Actors and audiences were conditioned by overseas theatre. Local works suffered from lack of dramaturgy and, ironically, lack of an Australian acting style. Most of the playwrights quickly retired or left for London—Lawler for the West End with his Melbourne cast and others for the British Broadcasting Corporation. PATRICK WHITE stayed and was inspired to write three more plays in quick succession before disillusion set in and he returned to the novel. A few other writers emerged briefly, notably Canberra's RIC THROSSELL, for his anti-nuclear-war play *The Day Before Tomorrow* (1956) and post-First-World-War *For Valour* (1960); and MARIEN DREYER, whose Kings Cross drama BANDICOOT ON A BURNT RIDGE won a Sydney Journalists' Club competition in 1963. But despite this brief summer of playwriting the time was still not ripe.

HUGH HUNT, who became disillusioned with his limited resources as the first director of the Trust and departed, saw Australian playwrights as falling short of the Irish benchmark. 'When realism descends to the inhabitants of the backyard, conflict has to be couched in monosyllables and emotions have to take the form of physical violence. It is difficult to think of any Australian play which does not end up with a 'blue'. Passionate expression almost inevitably takes the form of fists and boots in a drama which cannot make full use of language. The great virtue of the Irish drama was that it could ...', he wrote in *The Making of Australian Theatre*. And yet the Trust had supported the work of such poetic writers as Peter Kenna, Ray Mathew, Douglas Stewart and Patrick White.

The rising generation

Help was soon forthcoming. The 'tryout theatres' advocated by Leslie Rees took the form of makeshift venues in back streets and on university campuses, adopted by the baby-boom students who led the revolution of the 1960s. The first to be established, under the influence of tough new worldwide movements, was Wal Cherry's EMERALD HILL THEATRE in Melbourne from 1961 to 1966. No major writing talent was discovered there, but it prepared the way for the experimental LA MAMA THEATRE, which opened in 1967. La Mama provided freedom to experiment with form and content and gave a platform to JACK HIBBERD, JOHN ROMERIL, DAVID WILLIAMSON and others. With its offshoot, the AUSTRALIAN PERFORMING GROUP at the Pram Factory, it gave support to agitprop, left-wing and early FEMINIST THEATRE. La Mama maintains its brief today.

The Removalists by David Williamson helped to take Australian playwriting into the mainstream, especially after John Bell directed an award-winning production for the Nimrod Theatre Company in 1971. Don Crosby, Jacki Weaver (centre) and Carole Skinner were among the cast

The reminiscences of reclusive Monk O'Neill, the sole character in Jack Hibberd's A Stretch of the Imagination, *have provided opportunities for many actors since Peter Cummins (above) created the role at the Pram Factory in 1972*

In Sydney the principal experimental venues were PACT Theatre (founded in 1964) the JANE STREET THEATRE (1966), the NIMROD STREET THEATRE (1970), the Mews Playhouse (1970) and the Nimrod Theatre (1974). Later came the PERFORMANCE SPACE and the Black Theatre. In Canberra Prompt Theatre opened in 1969. In Brisbane the University of Queensland was the centre of experiment, encouraged by the residency of the British agitprop creator Albert Hunt, and by the transformation of the Trades Hall into a venue for happenings. A ferment of protest theatre at the University of Adelaide and the growing Adelaide Festival Fringe produced the playwrights STEVE J. SPEARS and ROB GEORGE.

Aided by funding from the new Australian Council for the Arts, the Australian playwright 'arrived' with startling rapidity. David Williamson's THE REMOVALISTS and Jack Hibberd's DIMBOOLA quickly became national successes and by 1973 the new playwright had a firm foothold on the mainstage. Now it was possible for authors to think of earning a living in Australia. In the years since, many writers have not only done this but have made a principle of it. Williamson, who has described himself as 'storyteller to the tribe' has argued, rightly, that Australia needs its own stories if it is to justify its existence as a nation. With Williamson and his generation the wheel has come full circle: no longer is the playwright exploiting the aspects of Australia that seem colourful from a viewpoint in the metropolitan theatre. Today the drama is genuinely local; the play's language, rhythm, character and content (regardless of form or setting) are unselfconsciously Australian.

The first new wave of playwrights was largely occupied with ridiculing and celebrating the broader aspects of Australian life, its history and manners, and then with more closely examining contemporary domestic life and values. Key plays documented the major concerns of the time. The frustrations of the artist in the kind of inarticulate community that Hugh Hunt described were seen in the early work of RODNEY MILGATE and CLEM GORMAN. They received lasting record in Dorothy Hewett's THE CHAPEL PERILOUS (1969), an epic, poetic, satirical account of the lot of the female artist growing up in Australia. Its heroine, Sally Banner, became a symbol for a generation of women.

Satire and melodrama on the history and politics of Australia briefly burgeoned in the style of the late 19th century at the MUSIC HALL THEATRE RESTAURANT in Sydney and more significantly in THE LEGEND OF KING O'MALLEY (1970) by Michael Boddy and Bob Ellis. This vaudevillian account of an early parliamentarian summed up the iconoclasm and optimism of the 1960s and had much in sympathy with the fantasies of Marcus Clarke and Garnet Walch. In similar but deeper vein was Jack Hibberd's A STRETCH OF THE IMAGINATION (1971), which distantly echoes a story told by Alfred Dampier in 1905 of a recluse on the banks of the Murray River who had 'resolutely shut up his life's history in a sealed book' and was later found dead on a tree stump 'with his beloved Homer lying on his breast'. Hibberd's Monk O'Neill, former classics scholar and libertine, plays out the legends of Australia as he awaits a welcome death. Related in form is John Romeril's THE FLOATING WORLD (1974), a mixture of poetry and vaudeville that meditates on Australia's growing trade relations with Japan against the shadow of the Pacific War and the atrocities of the Burma-Thailand Railway.

Meanwhile on the domestic front, David Williamson was charting the rapid political and social changes of the 1970s, in a string of hits that included DON'S PARTY (1971) and *What If You Died Tomorrow?* (1973), about the climate for change within the postwar generation; and *The Club* (1976), about the rise of the manager, a dominant phenomenon in the 1980s. ALEX BUZO emerged as a master satirist. Taking up and extending themes popularised by BARRY HUMPHRIES, he wrote bristly plays about Australia's preoccupation with losers and winners, and documented them with extravagant vernacular. His short play NORM AND AHMED (1968) was one of the first contemporary works to point the finger at Australia's suppressed xenophobia; and ROOTED (1969) is a black comedy about the cruel penalties of conformity. One of the noticeable aspects of this social charting was the Irish Catholic background—the mores, the poetic temperament, the humour and the guilt—from which many writers drew, and continue to draw. Ron Blair's small classic THE CHRISTIAN BROTHERS (1976) is one example. Another is the work of a writer who sprang fully-grown but briefly into the mainstream, JIM MCNEIL, a recidivist inmate of NSW jails who found the dramatic form a way of communicating with the changing world outside. An expert raconteur, widely read and skilled in game-playing, he produced a small output of enduring quality. Sadly, the capacity did not survive his release. A number of writers' groups for prisoners, and ex-prisoners, flourished in the 1970s amid social change. RAY MOONEY in Melbourne was the most prolific of these playwrights.

Peter Kenna returned to Australia and in 1973 produced his masterpiece, *A HARD GOD*, an adventurous study of an Irish-Australian family. It more than met Hugh Hunt's criteria of dramatic language, and formed a family trilogy with two later plays. Another to return was RAY LAWLER. Encouraged by the MELBOURNE THEATRE COMPANY, he wrote two more plays about the characters of *Summer of the Seventeenth Doll*. The three became known as *The Doll Trilogy*. The third mature writer who gave substance to the joyous activity of the 1970s was Dorothy Hewett, enabled by the

Peter Carroll created the role of the lonely, ageing teacher in Ron Blair's The Christian Brothers *for the Nimrod Theatre Company in 1976. Blair, who drew upon his own education in this monodrama, is one of many playwrights who have emerged from Irish Catholic culture, especially in Sydney*

new writers' grants to move from Perth to Sydney in mid-decade. Her sensibilities combine poetry, music, satire and conscious references to the works of Australian, British and American writers which, like the earlier plays of Patrick White, gave new breadth to the contemporary dramatic imagination. White himself rejoined the theatre in 1977 with BIG TOYS and three more plays in quick succession.

Establishment of state theatre companies and proliferation of secondary theatres—encouraged by federal and state subsidy—led to extraordinary growth in performance of new writing. Much of it was polemical and ephemeral, but it created a compost from which professional writers have grown in increasing numbers. Concurrent with the rise of the new theatres were a revival of employment of writers in the theatre industry and growth in the television industry. These industries have been prey to constraints of commerce, ownership and varying tax incentives and equity rulings, but Australian films and television serials now have an accepted prime place in Australian programming and a recognised profile in the worldwide industry.

Another contributor to the compost was the annual AUSTRALIAN NATIONAL PLAYWRIGHTS' CONFERENCE, established in 1973 in Canberra as a workshop for new writers. Many have taken advantage of its selection process and its national forum; as many have since become scriptwriters as have made their name on stage. In 1986 the conference established in Sydney a full-time advisory centre for playwrights. Its work supplements that of the older AUSTRALIAN WRITERS' GUILD, a strong-minded industrial association for scriptwriters. PUBLISHING of plays also developed. Currency Press began modestly in 1971, advertised as 'the playwright's publisher', and in due course became a major publishing company and established texts for the study of Australian drama in schools and universities. It was followed by Playlab Press in 1978 and Yackandandah Playscripts in 1982.

In the 1970s the black civil rights movement encouraged the use of the stage as a platform. Robert Merritt's play *The Cake Man* (1975) quickly moved from the Black Theatre in Redfern to the mainstream professional theatre. A black activist in Perth, JACK DAVIS emerged as a major writer with a series of plays, notably *The Dreamers* (1983) and *No Sugar* (1985). A new consciousness assisted black artists to gain attention, and the development of Aboriginal actors, particularly by the Myoli and Black Swan companies in Western Australia, has in turn assisted writers to achieve their voice. Their plays so far have been largely concerned in theme with the unhappy history of blacks under white law, but in form they increasingly reflect humour, daily rituals and values distinct from those of white Australia and characteristically use dance as a medium of expression. All these aspects are combined in the most striking work so far, *Bran Nue Dae* (1990) by Jimmy Chi and the Kuckles band. This heartening musical from the old pearling port of Broome (WA) combines all the musical and cultural influences that have made up its multiracial history, and confirms black pride by humorously demonstrating that everyone in the world is related.

With the 1980s the disputants about backyard realism finally declared an armistice. Playwrights had emerged writing in every kind of style. JANIS BALODIS, of Latvian parentage, was producing epic plays in shifting time zones, examining the history behind an immigrant society and its responsibilities for the future. In his best-known work, TOO YOUNG FOR GHOSTS (1985), a group of postwar immigrants share their territory with the German explorer Ludwig Leichhardt's expedition a century before. MICHAEL GOW, from an English tradition, examines the unequal burden of European history upon a young country. RON ELISHA, born in Jerusalem, has charted the Jewish inheritance from the Second World War in both comedy and dramatic argument; STEPHEN SEWELL, Marxist and Catholic in his background, has sought passionately to shake complacency in a disintegrating world of war, politics and finance. LOUIS NOWRA, like Sewell, began creating myths of international turmoil but has by degrees brought that chaotic world to his own doorstep; while JOHN O'DONOGHUE, chronicler of Newcastle's steel-working history, has found the world without ever leaving his doorstep. BARRY DICKINS, a nostalgic comic writer and cartoonist, takes a childlike joy in memories of life in the bleak Housing Commission suburbs of Melbourne; while NICK ENRIGHT's urban world is largely middle class and intellectual. ALMA DE GROEN, who has argued the feminist perception of history in the theatre over 20 years, has repeatedly used the artist as her model and is a major re-interpreter of the female character on stage. More recently such contributors have included HANNIE RAYSON, KATHERINE THOMSON and TES LYSSIOTIS. The last, of Greek parentage, was one of the first playwrights to weave a second language into her dialogue. Writing for children and teenagers has also produced some significant authors, notably Debra Oswald and the prolific commuting Englishman DAVID HOLMAN. All this work is marked by spontaneous use of the resources to hand in the theatre; and by unselfconsciously regional accent and rhythm.

In the 1990s there are some 150 performed playwrights achieving a living in Australia. They have available to them a group of state theatre companies, smaller mainstream subsidised companies, alternative theatres and a variety of experimental spaces. There are writer's grants and residencies allocated by the literature board of the Australia

Council, substantial prizes offered annually for writers by state governments and residential writers' centres. For the exceptional senior artist there is a federal creative fellowship, worth $51 000 a year for three to five years. (Jack Davis, Dorothy Hewett and John Romeril have been among the recipients.) A season in a major venue can earn a playwright between $30 000 and $80 000. Despite this, and largely because Australia's population is only 17 million and the failure so far of this genuinely parochial drama to break into the theatre abroad, only a handful of playwrights earn a secure living. For the others the annual income from all sources is likely to be little more than the basic wage. ❦*Katharine Brisbane*

further reading

ADAMS, FRANCIS. *Tiberius*. London: Unwin 1894.
CARROLL, DENNIS. *Australian Contemporary Drama*. Sydney: Currency Press 1995.
FOTHERINGHAM, RICHARD. Introduction. *Robbery Under Arms* by Alfred Dampier and Garnet Walch. Sydney: Currency Press/Australasian Drama Studies 1985.
HUNT, HUGH. *The Making of Australian Theatre*. Melbourne: Cheshire 1960.
MACARTNEY, KEITH. Louis Esson and the Australian Drama. *Meanjin* 6/2 (Melbourne 1947).
MATHEW, RAY. Australian drama and theatre. *Current Affairs Bulletin* 28 July 1958.
MILLER, E. MORRIS. *Australian Literature from its Beginnings to 1935* 2 vols. Melbourne University Press 1940.
MUSA, HELEN. Introduction and notes. *On Our Selection* by Bert Bailey and Edmund Duggan. Sydney: Currency Press 1984.
NAGEL CHARLES. *Shakespericonglomorofunnidogammoniae*. Sydney: W. A. Duncan 1843.
THIERSCH, M. L. An investigation of patronage in the development of Australian playwriting from 1870 to the present day. University of NSW PhD thesis 1974.
The drama in Australia. *Lorgnette* (Melbourne) 1 March 1890.
Australian Playscripts—A checklist of unpublished scripts in the Hanger Collection, Fryer Library, University of Queensland. Brisbane: University of Queensland 1987.

Playwriting competitions

Although they originated in ancient Greece, playwriting competitions seem to have been essentially a 20th-century phenomenon, usually in countries like Australia, where the tradition and rewards of writing plays were uncertain and playwrights needed encouragement. The best competitions have often galvanised writers into action to meet a deadline, and at times they have certainly uncovered new talent or confirmed emergent writers. Repertory and literary societies all over the country have run play competitions, but the professional theatre less often. Absence of a stage production for a competition-winning play has often precluded the possibility of its author achieving fame or lasting critical regard, though matters are improved today.

In 1927 KATHARINE SUSANNAH PRICHARD won a *Triad* magazine contest with *BRUMBY INNES*, a play famous as a literary work but rarely performed. When CARRIE TENNANT ran the tiny Community Playhouse in Sydney during the Great Depression, her competitions brought forth plays by LESLIE HAYLEN and young Rex Rienits, who was later successful in radio and television drama in Sydney and London.

In Perth in the 1930s the THEATRE COUNCIL OF WESTERN AUSTRALIA, representing amateur groups, organised an annual play competition. The prize play was staged at the large HIS MAJESTY'S THEATRE, not the best place for intimate pieces. From these contests emerged works such as BETTY ROLAND's *Are You Ready, Comrade?*, ALEXANDER TURNER's *Royal Mail*, Kathleen Carroll's *Saturday*, DOROTHY BLEWETT's *Quiet Night* (subsequently performed hundreds of times by groups in England as well as Australia) and two plays by DYMPHNA CUSACK, *Comets Soon Pass* and *MORNING SACRIFICE*.

The Adelaide *Advertiser*'s South Australian centennial play competition in 1936 was won by MAX AFFORD with his *Colonel Light—The Founder*. In Sydney, INDEPENDENT THEATRE's competition in 1937 brought GEORGE LANDEN DANN into fuller public consciousness with *No INCENSE RISING*. CATHERINE SHEPHERD won a Melbourne group's competition with *Daybreak*. New Theatre Melbourne's competition fell to the present writer's historical *Lalor of Eureka*. DOUGLAS STEWART won an ABC radio play competition with *NED KELLY*, a play written for stage production.

From 1944 the PLAYWRIGHTS' ADVISORY BOARD conducted annual competitions for a full-length play. Winners of the first three were CATHERINE DUNCAN with *Sons of the Morning*; Lynn Foster and GEORGE LANDEN DANN with *And the Moon Will Shine* and *Ha Ha Among the Trumpets* respectively; and DOROTHY BLEWETT with *The First Joanna*. In 1951 first prize in the federal government's jubilee competition went to Kylie Tennant for her play about Alfred Deakin, *Tether a Dragon*. George Farwell's *The House that Jack Built*, about John Macarthur and Governor Bligh, came second.

The 1954–55 Playwrights' Advisory Board competition had 130 full-length entries and the most spectacular results. The prize of £200 was equally divided between ORIEL GRAY for *The Torrents*, a story of the 'new woman', and RAY LAWLER for a turbulent drama about canecutters in Melbourne with their girls in the layoff season, *SUMMER OF THE SEVENTEENTH DOLL*. *The Torrents* was judged to be the more finished play. The *Doll*, the more captivating on paper, needed revision, as the author acknowledged.

The *Doll* had great international success. This led to further contests; prize-money, once so hard to find, became readily available in ever larger amounts. In 1959 Oriel Gray won a competition run by the Little Theatre Guild of Melbourne and J. C. WILLIAMSON's—which now saw commercial possibilities in Australian plays—with her *BURST OF SUMMER*, a drama about an Aboriginal girl film-star. The same year brought the playwright PETER KENNA to national attention when his comedy-drama *THE SLAUGHTER OF ST TERESA'S DAY* won a General Motors Holden competition and the play was presented by the TRUST PLAYERS. John Hepworth won a $2000 Manifold competition with his allegorical *The End of the Rainbow*.

The Journalists' Club in Sydney, under the presidency of the poet Kenneth Slessor, promoted playwriting contests, mostly judged by the Playwrights's Advisory Board. RICHARD BEYNON won the first competition with *THE SHIFTING HEART* in 1956. In an *Observer* newspaper competition in London this play was placed equal third with two others from nearly 2000 entries. Four of the 25 finalists in this competition were Australians. Robert Amos with *When the Gravediggers Come* and HAL PORTER with *The Tower* shared honours in the next Journalists' Club contest. MARIEN DREYER won the third with *BANDICOOT ON A BURNT RIDGE*.

In later years many play competitions have been organised in country centres or by cultural clubs, with token prizes. There have also been healthy-sized rewards. Amateur theatres have run contests to celebrate jubilees—NEW THEATRE in Sydney, ADELAIDE REPERTORY THEATRE and BRISBANE ARTS THEATRE, for example. The AUSTRALIAN WRITERS' GUILD instituted the Awgies competition for script writers in 1968, and included stage plays from 1971.

Western Australia ran a state competition in 1979 to celebrate its sesquicentenary, the winners being Mary Gage and BOB HERBERT. Plays are now eligible for entry in various state literary awards, the Miles Franklin Award and other cash prizes. The annual NSW State Literary Awards, established in 1979 as the Premier's Literary Awards and renamed in 1988, include a $10 000 award for drama. The Victorian Premier's annual literary awards include the $7500 Louis Esson Prize for Drama, for a theatre or radio script. It was established in 1988. The Jill Blewett Playwrights' Award of $16 000, established in 1992, is a biennial award, coinciding with the Adelaide Festival of Arts. The annual $5000 George Landen Dann Award for Playwrights was also established in 1992. It is given to Queensland writers by the QUEENSLAND THEATRE COMPANY and the Brisbane Courier–Mail. All the other awards are open to writers throughout Australia. ❦*Leslie Rees*

Gwen Plumb AM

Actor. Born 1912 in Sydney. Began acting as amateur 1939. Independent Theatre (Sydney) in 1940s. Professional stage debut at Minerva Theatre, Sydney, 1948. Old Tote Theatre Company (Sydney) 1963–64. Also radio and television. AM 1993 for services to entertainment and community as charity fund-raiser.

During an energetic career in theatre, radio and television over more than 50 years Gwen Plumb's pert looks and humour have made her a great favourite as a personality, but her first big stage success came only in the 1980s with Nell Dunn's *Steaming*. She toured Australia for three years as Mrs Meadows in this play, including four seasons in Sydney and four in Melbourne.

With INDEPENDENT THEATRE in Sydney during the 1940s Plumb created leading roles in three Australian plays: GWEN MEREDITH's *Ask No Questions*, Max Afford's *LADY IN DANGER* and SUMNER LOCKE ELLIOTT's *Goodbye to the Music*. She played several roles for the OLD TOTE THEATRE COMPANY, including the middle-aged nymphomaniac in Joe Orton's *Entertaining Mr Sloane* in 1964. In 1983 she played Madame Arcati in Noël Coward's *Blithe Spirit* for the MARIAN STREET THEATRE COMPANY, and for the NIMROD THEATRE COMPANY in 1984 she and JUDI FARR, as her daughter, made a memorable duo in Louise Page's *Salonika*. In 1991 she co-starred with JUNE BRONHILL in Joseph Kesselring's comedy *Arsenic and Old Lace* in Sydney. A record-breaking season was followed by a successful repeat season and a tour to Adelaide, Melbourne, Gosford (NSW) and Brisbane. ❦*Richard Lane*

Pocket Playhouse

Amateur dramatic group in Sydney, formed by Norman McVicker on 4 December 1947 as St Peters Community Players. Renamed 1957. Formed Pocket Children's Theatre 1961. Closed 17 November 1973. **venue** Pocket Playhouse, Sydenham 1949–73. **first production** *The Ghost Train* by Arnold Ridley, 1948, in church hall in St Peters. **landmark productions** *The Importance of Being Earnest* by Oscar Wilde, 1960; *The Sleeping Prince* by Terence Rattigan, 1961; *The Teahouse of the August Moon* by John Patrick, 1964; *No Room at the Inn* by Joan Temple, 1968; *Spoon River* by Edgar Lee Masters, 1969; *The Limelighters* by McVicker, 1970; *Banjo* by McVicker, 1972. **last production** *Damper and Tea* by McVicker.

In postwar Sydney, before theatre was subsidised, young actors and writers found training at the Pocket Playhouse. It aimed to introduce new works, performers and directors to its audience, and NORMAN KESSELL wrote in the *Daily Telegraph* on 2 September 1970 that it 'achieved an artistic integrity few nonprofessional groups—as distinct from amateur—could match'.

The group's energetic founder, Norman McVicker, directed the vast majority of its productions. Always interested in Australian works, he directed *A SPRING SONG* by Ray Mathew in 1958, three short plays by MARIEN DREYER collectively titled *Marian Dreyer's World* in 1959, *Image in the Clay* by David Ireland in 1960, *The Torrents* by ORIEL GRAY and *The Beast in View* by John Hepworth in 1962, and plays by SUMNER LOCKE ELLIOTT and DOROTHY BLEWETT. The associate director, Brendan Dunne, trained the stage crew, designed sets, shared the administrative burden, and acted many character roles. The St Peters Community Players rented a hall in working-class Sydenham in 1949. It had no stage or lighting equipment but the group gradually improved it while averaging four productions a year. In 1956 the group renovated the hall and renamed it and itself the Pocket Playhouse when it reopened with *I Remember Mama* by John van Druten on 1 February 1957. In 1960 the group bought the 66-seat hall and rebuilt it. Next year McVicker formed the Pocket Children's Theatre after a trip to the USA. *The Wizard of Oz* in 1962 was a notable children's production.

In September 1970 McVicker announced that the group would be forced to close, largely because the Australian Council for the Arts and other funding bodies refused to subsidise nonprofessional theatres. He argued bitterly that amateur groups were underrated as training grounds for the professional theatre. 'Friends of the Pocket' rallied and saved the theatre, but it closed through lack of funds three years later. Many professionals began there, including the actor Noeline Brown, the singer Lionel Long, the lighting designer Roger Barratt, the costume designer Dorothy Duncombe and Robert Findlay, later stage manager at the Mermaid Theatre in London. ❦*Victoria Chance*

Emelie Polini

English actor. Acted in Australia 1918–24. Died 1927 in USA.

An actor with a 'voice of velvet and gold', according to a local magazine, Emelie Polini came to Australia for J. AND N. TAIT LTD when that firm was expanding its theatrical interests during the First World War. She made her debut in Sydney on 27 April 1918 in Edward Clark's comedy thriller *De Luxe Annie*, a play that she regularly revived. Other plays in this season, which was directed by GREGAN McMAHON, were *The Invisible Foe* by Walter Hackett and *Eyes of Youth* by Max Marcin and Charles Guernon. At the end of June the company transferred to Melbourne, and again opened with *De Luxe Annie*. During the run, on 16 July 1918, Polini married a Sydney-born soldier who was on furlough from the British Army.

In late 1920 she withdrew into private life and in October 1921, while living on a farm near Bathurst (NSW), she gave birth to a daughter. Within six months Polini was back on stage in Sydney, in *My Lady's Dress* by Edward Knoblock, another success. When she appeared in *The Lie* by Henry Arthur Jones in 1922, the *Triad* said it was abundantly clear that she was 'an admirable actress in heavy emotional work only' and had been wasted when J. C. WILLIAMSON'S employed her in 'social comedy and the lighter stuff'. With DORIS EGERTON JONES she wrote *The Flaw*, and starred when the Firm produced it in Sydney on 27 January 1923. She was busy, usually with FRANK HARVEY as co-star, until early 1924, when she made farewell appearances before going to New York to act on Broadway.

Polini and her husband had become estranged and fought over custody of the child, whom Polini wanted to take with her. She lost a custody suit because NSW law gave the father prior rights over the children of a marriage, and in the USA mother and child would have been beyond the jurisdiction of the NSW courts. Feminists campaigned vigorously for the law to be changed. Polini was ill in New York with a 'nervous collapse' in June 1927. By August she was dead. Her will asked that her daughter be handed over to her sister Marie and her husband, Owen Nares, a popular English romantic actor. This was invalidated, but in November 1934 the NSW Parliament enacted the Guardianship of Infants Bill, which gave neither parent an automatic superior claim to custody and specified that the welfare of the child was to be paramount. ❦*John West*

Polish influences

News of Polish theatrical experimentation, seminal for contemporary theatre, was slow to reach Australia, perhaps as much because of the language barrier and distance as of low interest in innovation. Since the 1960s, however, with the wave of the absurdist theatre spilling into Australia, names such as Slawomir Mrozek, Tadeusz Rózewicz, Wladyslaw Ignacy Witkiewicz and Witold Gombrowicz have become known here as well as in Europe.

If the poetic plays of Rózewicz remain confined to university drama courses, without professional production, the scintillating satirist Mrozek attracts considerable attention. His best-known play, *Tango*, was taken up by student groups and in Sydney by INDEPENDENT THEATRE and Q THEATRE in 1968 and 1985 respectively. Thalia Theatre Company, founded in Sydney in 1983 by Bogdan Koca, performed *The Emigrants* in 1984 and *The Ambassador* in 1986. Koca exemplified the creative initiative of young Polish artists and intellectuals who arrived in Australia in the 1980s, in the wake of suppression of Solidarity in Poland.

Witkiewicz—painter, playwright, philosopher, novelist and precursor of the European absurdist movement—visited Australia in 1914 with the anthropologist Bronislaw Malinowski. He commemorated the experience in *The Metaphysics of the Two-Headed Calf—Tropico-Australian Play in Three Acts* in 1921. It was translated in Australia by ROGER PULVERS, and given experimental productions in the 1970s before Pulvers himself staged it in Melbourne in 1981. During the 1970s Pulvers produced some of Witkiewicz's plays in Canberra, and Nicholas Tsoutas directed *The Madman and the Nun* in Melbourne in 1981. Gombrowicz, who was 'discovered' in Europe in the 1960s and performed in many languages, is becoming known in Australia too. Pulvers made him a subject of his play *Witold Gombrowicz in Buenos Aires*, which he directed in Melbourne in 1980. A wider public had the opportunity to see Thalia perform Gombrowicz's masterpiece *The Marriage* at the 1986 ADELAIDE FESTIVAL and in Sydney. Koca rehearsed it concurrently with *Hamlet*, using the same cast, and produced the plays on alternate nights to reveal their thematic link. The event demonstrated some characteristically Polish avant-garde theatre techniques, which have also been evident in Koca's other productions of Polish, European and Australian drama.

The most influential events in the Polish–Australian theatrical relationship have been tours by Jerzy Grotowski's Theatre Laboratory in 1974 and Tadeusz Kantor's *The Dead Class* at the 1978 Adelaide Festival and in Sydney. For many people the experience of seeing these groups was a revelation of the creative nature of theatre. The work of Kantor, the inimitable 'total artist' in the tradition of Richard Wagner and Gordon Craig, portrays the uniqueness and complexity of Polish culture in such a way as to illuminate the essential features of modern culture. Theatre Laboratory sent shock waves through the theatrical profession and audiences in Sydney when, in *Apocalypsis cum Figuris*, its group improvisation on the theme of the Gospels, it demonstrated Grotowski's radical revaluation of the actor's art and training and of theatre itself.

In preparation for this event, conducted at the invitation of the ARTS COUNCIL OF AUSTRALIA, Grotowski came to Australia alone and gave public talks in Sydney and Melbourne on 9 and 11 August 1973 respectively. The entire group arrived in Sydney on 26 March 1974 for a stay of three months, during which it gave 32 performances of *Apocalypsis cum Figuris* in the chapterhouse of St Mary's Cathedral, followed by workshops in Sydney and Armidale (NSW). Some of these workshops were Grotowski's first try-out of post-theatrical work that he began in Poland in the next year.

Many actors reacted defensively to the spectacle of the 'holy actor', finding a theatre that draws on the actors' own substance and private responses to their own history, culture and belief system too demanding. On the other hand, the NIMROD THEATRE COMPANY, the NATIONAL INSTITUTE OF DRAMATIC ART and other companies and schools included the Theatre Laboratory's exercises in their own training. Grotowski's influence had preceded his 1974 visit, notably in the work of the PERFORMANCE SYNDICATE. Groups formed after the visit were usually short-lived, except the Theatre Research Group, begun in Armidale in 1975 by Igor Persan. It has settled in Paris under the name Le Théâtre en Spirale.

Other Polish theatrical groups in Australia are the Adelaide puppet theatre Carouselle, which performs children's plays around South Australia, and Theatre Zart, formed in Perth in 1985. It is directed by Kristof and Marta Kaczmarek, and its productions include *Goodbye Judas* by Ireneusz Iredynski in 1988. ❦*Maria Kreisler*

further reading
BARBOUR, J. Apotheosised in mob upheaval. *Nation Review* (Sydney) 19 April 1974.
BRISBANE, KATHARINE. The gospel according to Grotowski. *Australian* 8 April 1974.

HOAD, BRIAN. Grotowski's gospel. *Bulletin* (Sydney) 20 April 1974.
KIPPAX, H. G. Where words become flesh. *Sydney Morning Herald* 10 April 1974.

Pollard opera companies

The best known of many professional CHILD COMPANIES in the late 19th and early 20th centuries began in Launceston (Tas.) in 1880 when 47-year-old James Joseph Pollard formed Pollard's Liliputian [sic] Opera Company, mainly from children in his own large family. Its first performance was *HMS Pinafore* on 17 May. The company toured the Australasian colonies, the East Indies and India, performing this and other operettas. The leading singers included May Pollard, who starred in many operettas produced by J. C. WILLIAMSON when she grew up.

J. J. Pollard died in 1884 and control of the company passed to his son Charles and his son-in-law Tom Pollard, stage manager of the company, who was really O'Sullivan but called himself Pollard for professional uniformity. In 1886 they disbanded the company, as the youngsters were growing up. Tom Pollard formed a new juvenile troupe in 1891, in conjunction with Williamson. The latter withdrew in 1892 and Pollard changed the company's name from Williamson Juvenile Comic Opera Company to Pollard's Liliputian Opera Company. It toured throughout Australasia and became a considerable attraction. Its leading performers were May and Maud Beatty, Marion Mitchell and the comedian W. S. PERCY, who had played in child productions of Gilbert and Sullivan operettas since 1887.

Charles Pollard and his sister Nellie Pollard Chester established their own separate Pollard Liliputian Opera Company in 1896. It performed in South Africa during the war of 1899–1902 and later made frequent tours of East and South Asia, the USA, Canada, and occasionally Australia. Among the child performers were three sisters of Carrie Moore—Lily, Eva and Olive. After appearances in India all the children were returned to Australia in May 1910, when the company was ended. Meanwhile, Tom Pollard, acknowledging that his teenage performers were no longer children, had renamed his troupe the Pollard Opera Company in 1896. He entered into an arrangement with Williamson which gave him the right to present the latest musical comedies in New Zealand.

In Wellington in 1903 Pollard produced ALFRED HILL's operetta *Tapu*, after the librettist ARTHUR H. ADAMS had reworked it under Williamson's supervision. W. S. Percy starred as 'George Wright', a thinly disguised portrait of George Reid, who became Prime Minister of Australia later in the year. Williamson saw the Pollard production in Hobart and later staged his own grandiose production in Sydney. Hill preferred Pollard's.

Tom Pollard's company toured South Africa in 1903–04 as the Royal Australian Comic Opera Company but a theatre fire in Durban destroyed many of its costumes and properties. In Australia in 1904 the company embarked on another national tour. It was disbanded towards the end of 1905. Percy became a leading comedian for Williamson until he left Australia in 1914. He retired in 1937, after having played more than 200 roles in operetta and pantomime in Australia, the USA and the United Kingdom. May Beatty also starred in musical comedies for Williamson and worked successfully on the musical stage and in variety in the United Kingdom for many years. She moved to Hollywood in the early 1930s and appeared in several films. In 1907 Tom Pollard put together his third juvenile troupe, the Pollard Juvenile Opera Company. It toured successfully throughout Australasia until it was overcome by rising costs and heavy competition from vaudeville and moving pictures. It closed in April 1910.

Another brother, Henry Pollard operated a music business in Brisbane from 1882 and occasionally formed amateur groups of local children to perform operetta in the district under the Pollard name. *Peter Downes, Richard Fotheringham*

further reading
DOWNES, PETER. The perennial Pollards. *Opera in New Zealand:* (ed. A. Simpson). Wellington (NZ): Witham Press 1990.
DOWNES, PETER. *Shadows on the Stage—Theatre in New Zealand 1840-1910.* Dunedin (NZ): John McIndoe 1975.
PERCY, W. S. The story of the Pollard Opera Company. Ms in Alexander Turnbull Library, Wellington (New Zealand)
THOMSON, J. M. *A Distant Music.* Melbourne: Oxford University Press 1980.

Charles Pope

American comedian. Joined Hicks–Sawyer Minstrels in Saratoga (New York, USA) 1887. Came to Australia with company 1888. Joined Alhambra Minstrel Company 1891. In Tivoli vaudeville 1892–1902. Acted in Sandford's American Players. In vaudeville on Brennan and Fullers' circuits 1906–18.

Charles Pope, a black American, became so familiar to Australian audiences that the description of his act in James Brennan's vaudeville programs simply read 'Nuf Sed'. He came to Australia in 1888 with the Hicks–Sawyer Minstrels, in which he acted as Bones while IRVING SAYLES occupied the other 'end' as Tambo. This company broke up in Brisbane in 1891 and the comedy duo joined Frank Smith's Alhambra Minstrel Company and then, in late 1892, began a decade-long association with HARRY RICKARDS's Tivoli organisation. On the TIVOLI CIRCUIT Pope and Sayles occupied the Bones 'end' together and performed the material that had proven so successful in the Hicks–Sawyer Minstrel programs. In the first half of the performance each sang a comic song—'All coons look alike to me' and 'Two little ragged urchins'—while in the second they combined in a comic speciality act, 'Coons on the warpath'.

Beginning in 1901, the Tivoli theatres dropped the minstrel first half in favour of a 'revue', which did not always include Tambo and Bones. Sayles remained with Rickards but apparently there was no place for Pope in the new program structure. Instead he joined Sandford's American Players, starring in such productions as *Uncle Tom's Cabin* and Dion Boucicault's *After Dark*. The opening of James Brennan's National Amphitheatre in Sydney in late 1906 gave him an opportunity to resume his vaudeville career—the Brennan programs featured a minstrel first part. Pope remained with the Brennan, later Fullers', circuit for some 14 years, although gout increasingly restricted his stage appearances. His last recorded engagement was in 1918, when he produced and starred in a 'minstrel cabaret' at the Bijou Theatre in Melbourne. *Richard Waterhouse*

Popular entertainments

Before 1850 Australian theatres presented diverse programs to audiences that represented a microcosm of colonial society. At the Theatre Royal in Sydney in the 1830s the bill of fare often included three plays, with songs and dances during the intervals. In the 1840s the programs at the Royal Victoria Theatre in Sydney usually comprised two plays, one serious, one comic, while dances, songs, tightrope walking and other circus and travelling-show acts were still included in the entertainment. Sometimes popular songs were even inserted into the main production.

A colonial version of English music-hall came to Sydney in 1843, when publicans began to hold 'free and easies' in their hotels. A tradition of a special Christmas PANTOMIME season emerged in the 1840s, although pantomime performances had sometimes shared the bill with plays at the Theatre Royal in Sydney in the 1830s. Pantomime appealed to a broad cross-section of the population in the 19th century, although it was particularly designed to attract what the bills called 'the juvenile portion of the community'. It was a measure of its popularity that in 1858 all three of Sydney's theatres staged Christmas pantomimes. From the late 1870s MELODRAMA increasingly replaced pantomime as the main vehicle for Australian themes and settings. Pantomime remained a Christmas tradition but now the emphasis was on spectacular scenery and the productions often starred overseas performers.

CIRCUS appeared in Launceston, Hobart, Melbourne and Sydney between 1847 and 1850. This was the traditional English circus that emphasised equestrian acts, although juggling, tightrope and gymnastic acts were also presented. J. S. Noble brought the first visiting circus to Australia in 1851. In the last quarter of the 19th century no fewer than six American circuses visited Australia—some more than once. They staged their performances on a much larger scale than English-style circuses. The Cooper and Bailey circus that landed here in 1871 had a menagerie of lions, tigers, hippopotamuses, elephants, giraffes, zebras, orang-utans, leopards and jaguars. It announced its arrival with a grand street parade consisting of chariots, decorated cages and performers in Greek and Roman costumes. The entertainment included equestrian acts, trapeze acts, balancing, juggling and tumbling and animal acts.

In contrast to the spectacular shows staged by visitors, local troupes, such as ST LEON'S CIRCUS and Eroni Brothers' Circus, produced modest programs, mostly for small-town audiences. In 1895 FITZGERALD BROTHERS' CIRCUS copied American methods, importing talent from all over the globe and staging mammoth, spectacular programs. It toured the capitals and other major towns by rail.

Perhaps the most common form of popular stage entertainment in Australia in the second half of the 19th century was the minstrel show. Most of the MINSTRELS performing in Australia between 1850 and 1870 were from the British Isles and performed English-style programs, which accentuated music rather than humour. In the 1870s minstrel troupes arrived from the USA and American-style minstrelsy, which emphasised humour, became predominant. The Americans' style of wit was in keeping with long popular traditions of defying authority and celebrating sexual promiscuity, gambling and drinking. American-style programs included sketches that mocked religion (*The Coon Salvation Army*), laughed at authority (*The Toff's Banquet*) and challenged the right of do-gooders to regulate the habits and recreations of ordinary people.

In the late 1880s the Australian minstrel show began to evolve recognisably towards VAUDEVILLE. From 1892 to 1901 programs in HARRY RICKARDS's Tivoli vaudeville theatres consisted of a minstrel first part and a pure variety second part. In the 1890s and early 1900s vaudeville became the predominant popular entertainment. Stars from English music halls and American vaudeville stages presented the latest acts from London and New York. There were few attempts to provide songs and sketches with Australian flavours and settings. Australian audiences had so little taste for the local product that at least one songwriter published his work under the names of British and American authors. The few songs written by Australian composers were in overseas genres. For example, patriotic songs extolling the Australian colonies' contribution to the British Empire—popular during the South African War—were copied from English music-hall songs, which also emphasised the colonial contribution to imperial security. Songs evoking nostalgia for 'an old bush town' were copied from American 'carry-me-back' songs. Songs celebrating the glamour and excitement of life in Sydney and Melbourne were inspired by city-life songs from New York's Tin Pan Alley. From 1901 to 1912 Tivoli programs featured revues, which consisted of a series of turns linked by a theme. In 1912 HUGH D. MCINTOSH, who succeeded Rickards at the Tivoli helm, abolished revues and introduced American-style vaudeville programs—simply a series of acts.

During the First World War vaudeville entrepreneurs found it difficult to recruit overseas talent so they reverted to revue-style programs, often featuring indigenous talent. It was during the war years that ROY RENE and NAT PHILLIPS first popularised the STIFFY AND MO revues, for example. After the war the TIVOLI CIRCUIT reverted to vaudeville bills featuring imported stars, but the rival organisation FULLERS' continued to employ local performers. In 1925 BENJAMIN FULLER claimed that 85 per cent of the entertainers in his theatres were Australians.

By the late 1920s vaudeville had ceded dominance to film. In 1927 Fullers' abandoned vaudeville and concentrated on revue and musical comedy. Tivoli programs still consisted of vaudeville turns, although a 1929 bill ominously included one of the new talking pictures. The Tivoli Theatre and Fullers' Theatre in Sydney closed in 1929 but the Tivoli in Melbourne carried on. A new Tivoli circuit was formed in the 1930s and, under various managements, it presented revue until 1966. Vaudeville survived, although diminished in importance, in CLUB ENTERTAINMENT in NSW. From 1954 clubs presented vaudeville programs, minstrel entertainments and revues. ♥*Richard Waterhouse*

Popular Theatre Troupe

Professional touring political-theatre company, founded in Brisbane 1974. Toured 1975–82. Disbanded 1983.

From 1974 to 1982 the Popular Theatre Troupe performed widely throughout eastern Australia, mainly at minimum-security prisons, industrial work sites, community-group meetings and at universities and colleges of advanced education. It was a professional touring company that specialised in short, portable political entertainments with strong musical and comic elements. Its members also organised large-scale participation games for local festivals, including the 1976 ADELAIDE FESTIVAL OF ARTS.

The troupe was often controversial and was several times banned from venues controlled by the Queensland government. It spent relatively little time in its home city of Brisbane. Its founding administrator, Peter Sutherland, focused it on month-long community projects—involving performances, workshops, games events, and community-support activities—in Dubbo (NSW) and Queensland towns, including Moranbah and Townsville.

The company emerged from a semiprofessional group set up as the 'fringe' component of the 1974 Queensland Festival of the Arts. It took a half-hour farce *Startrick*—based on *Star Trek* and dealing with the 1974 federal elections—to shopping centres, old-age homes, hospitals, pensioners' clubs and leagues clubs. On this and two subsequent projects the Popular Theatre Troupe was joined by the English alternative-theatre director Albert Hunt. He was the principal writer of one of the troupe's best-known plays. *The White Man's Mission*, a musical documentary on race relations in Australia. Written in 1975 and occasionally revived, this bitterly comic story of massacres of Aborigines, the Kanaka slave trade, and modern liberal tokenism, resulted in the troupe being asked to be part of the official program at the 1976 Adelaide Festival. A London season followed in 1978.

Between 1976 and 1981 the company devised seven more shows, including *Fallout* and *Follow Me* on uranium mining, *Ladies' Day* on women in the work force and *Crook Shop* on police corruption. The group's longest-serving actor, Roslyn Atkinson took over as administrator and won financial and organisational support from several trade unions, most significantly the Amalgamated Metal Workers' Union, which sponsored a two-week tour of Sydney work sites in 1977. The group was reorganised in 1979–80 with ERROL O'NEILL as principal writer and director. His scripts *The Australia Show* (on economics) and *Says Who* (on media ownership and control) were particularly popular in secondary schools. This new target audience marked a shift in the company's work during these years. AUSTRALIA COUNCIL funding, which had aided the group's survival from 1976, was withdrawn at the end of 1982.

Many of the troupe's performers and organisers were prominent in COMMUNITY-THEATRE companies in the 1980s. They include Nick Hughes, artistic director of the HARVEST THEATRE COMPANY in 1982–83; Jo Caust, acting director of the theatre board of the Australia Council in 1984 and artistic director of the Sidetrack Theatre Company in 1988–89; Jan Oates, administrator of the WEST THEATRE COMPANY; the writer Allen Lyne, and the community arts officer Lynne Samson. Janet Fielding went on to international television fame as Tegan in *Dr Who*. ❧*Richard Fotheringham*

Hal Porter AM

Dramatist. Born 1911 in Melbourne. Wrote four plays, short stories, novels, poetry and autobiography. Died 1984. AM 1982.

Three of Hal Porter's four plays received professional stage productions in London but none was taken up by a mainstream theatre company in Australia, although they were produced on stage, radio and television. His most successful play, *The Tower*, a costume drama set in colonial Hobart, had its first production at the Hampstead Theatre Club in London in 1964. *The Professor*, first produced in Adelaide in 1965 as *Toda-San*, was produced in London in 1966. *Eden House*, first performed at St Martin's Theatre in Melbourne in 1969, was renamed *Home on a Pig's Back* for a production at the Royal Court Theatre in London in 1972. They are well-crafted, one-set, satirical melodramas with crisp and witty dialogue, but stereotypical characters and sensational plot elements. Their assumption of the old-fashioned proscenium arch made them seem curiously dated even in their own time. They are indisputably period pieces now. A fourth play, *Parker*, received an amateur production in Ballarat in 1976. ❧*Mary Lord*

published plays
Eden House (1969). Sydney: Angus and Robertson 1970.
The Professor (1965). London: Faber and Faber 1966.
The Tower (1964). Melbourne: Penguin 1963 in *Three Australian Plays*.

other writings
Stars of Australian Stage and Screen. Adelaide: Rigby 1965.

further reading
CARROLL, DENNIS. *Australian Contemporary Drama*. Sydney: Currency Press 1995.

Possum Paddock

Play in four acts by Kate Howarde. **premiere** 6 September 1919, Theatre Royal, Sydney. Cast: Neill Alexander, John Cosgrove, Jessie Dale, Kate Howarde, Jack Kirby, Vivian Langley, Fred MacDonald, Louis McHilton, Rose Rooney, Jack Soutar, Alice Walton, Cora Warner, Johnson Weir, Leslie Woods. Design: Harry Whaite. Director: Kate Howarde.

KATE HOWARDE, one of Australia's most remarkable female actor-managers and playwrights, reached her peak of popularity in 1919 with *Possum Paddock*. It continued the tradition of homely bush comedies established by STEELE RUDD, BERT BAILEY and others. More romance than bush realism, *Possum Paddock* reduced its account of pioneering struggle to its first act, in which the 50-acre paddock has to be sold to pay the debt on the farm of the old cocky Andrew McQuade. His wife's city cousin and wealthy widow Nella Carsley (played by Howarde at the premiere) arrives for a visit, just in time to bid at the auction and stop Possum Paddock falling into the hands of a cantankerous neighbour, Dan Martin. Later it is revealed that the building of a railway will increase the value of the paddock and restore the McQuades' fortunes.

The rest of the play develops romantic possibilities and problems. Billy and Bobby McQuade successfully court the two Martin girls in spite of their father's opposition, and when his spinster sister is forced to spend time at the McQuades' after a riding accident she too finds happiness in the arms of her rescuer, old Shad the rouseabout. The McQuades' daughter Nancy, back from education in the city at her Uncle Jim's expense, is wooed by Fred Deiring, an unscrupulous stock inspector. Nella, jilted by Fred years before, interrupts their planned elopement. In the climax to the third act she tricks Fred, in Nancy's hearing, into admitting that he only wants Nancy for money Uncle Jim has left her. In the last act the railway is opened with much rejoicing. The grieving Nancy is successfully wooed by an honourable, refined new chum. She turns matchmaker herself and pairs Nella with Hughie Bracken, a tubby, good-hearted young selector with prospects and a motor car.

Possum Paddock was immensely successful. On opening night, said the *Sydney Morning Herald* on 8 September 1919, the Theatre Royal 'was uproariously rushed, eager holidaymakers tumbling over one another to get in and after the curtain had been drawn up their paroxysms of laughter would have put a circus crowd on the edge of the Never-Never to the blush! The little tea party at which the two bashful young freaks from Dan Martin's were entertained by their shy boys at the 'Possum homestead, threw the audience into a convulsion of mirth. Enjoyment reached a climax when Bobby McQuade's sausage stuck out of his mouth until the united efforts of his brother and the girls tore it from his throat just as suffocation-point was reached! Then did the Theatre Royal stalls wave like a cornfield in the wind! It was a strange, weird spectacle.' *Possum Paddock* was beautifully staged. Harry Whaite's settings included real kookaburras, kangaroo and possum skins nailed up on the doors to dry, and a 'vista of gum trees with their golden autumn tints on graceful massed foliage'. *Possum Paddock* was revived at regular intervals for the next decade, and it was filmed in 1920. As Louis Esson pointed out in the *Triad* in April 1927, in Kate Howarde's work the focus changed from the earlier bush comedies. 'The old bush school has gone, and the Waybacks are interested now only in motor cars and the movies,' he said. Although most critics found Howarde's work plotless, artless and a dilution of earlier genres, *Possum Paddock* is immensely energetic and entertaining to read and is still stageable. ❦*Richard Fotheringham*

reference
A script is in the Australian Archives (Canberra).

Poverty Point

Acknowledged meeting-places for out-of-work performers were called Poverty Point. In Melbourne it was at the junction of Swanston and Bourke Streets. In Sydney, according to Isadore Brodsky, Poverty Point had various sites—at King and York Streets, near the Opera House, in the 1890s; at King and Castlereagh Streets near the THEATRE ROYAL; and opposite the CRITERION THEATRE at the northeast corner of Pitt and Park Streets. For many years a plaque identified this last site as Poverty Point: 'Within easy reach of several theatres, it was a meeting place for performing artists, particularly those temporarily "resting". It was a place where theatrical news and gossip was exchanged and where representatives of managements sometimes engaged actors and vaudeville artists usually for small parts or for work in suburban and travelling companies.' ROY RENE remembered this corner as Poverty Point before the First World War. Another comedian, BOBBY LE BRUN recalled: 'Any impresario taking out a show on the road would come there to find comics, actors, scenic artists, clowns, geese for the pantomime'. Bert Howard, the 'Lord Mayor of Poverty Point', booked acts on the footpath for his suburban shows. 'His office was a doorway and he would leave messages in chalk on the pavement.' ❦*Charles Grahame*

John Powers

Dramatist. Born 12 January 1935 in Melbourne. Lecturer in professional writing at Deakin University (Geelong, Vic.) since 1976. Scholar-in-residence at Yale University Drama School (USA) 1980. Wal Cherry Award for *The Second Story* 1990. Has also written television dramas and documentaries.

John Powers's major work, *The Last of the Knucklemen*, helped in the 1970s to steer drama away from middle-class urban situations to a realistic depiction of wider Australian themes. It is set in a northern mining camp where a mixed bunch of escapers from the city reassess their beliefs and lives. The play was first staged by the MELBOURNE THEATRE COMPANY in 1973. There were overseas productions in Edinburgh in 1976, Auckland in 1977, and New York City in 1983. In 1979 it appeared as a novel and as a film directed by Tim Burstall. Other plays by Powers are *The Hot Centre of the World* (1970), *Shindig* (1975), *The Reluctant Rebel* (1977) and *The Second Story* (1990). ❦*Dennis Davison*

published play
The Last of the Knucklemen (1973). With *Dimboola*. Melbourne: Penguin 1974.

other writings
The Last of the Knucklemen (1973). Melbourne: Sun 1979. Novel.

Katharine Susannah Prichard

Dramatist. Born 4 December 1883 in Levuka (Fiji). Father was editor of *Fiji Times*. Brought up mainly in Melbourne. Had short stories published in local papers as teenager. Became journalist after two years as governess. Went to London for Melbourne *Herald* 1908. Wrote first novel *The Wild Oats of Han* 1908. Won Hodder and Stoughton All-Empire Novel Competition with *The Pioneers* 1915. Returned to Australia 1916. Married Captain Hugo Throssell VC, 1919. Joined Communist Party of Australia 1920. Published 13 novels, five collections of short stories and numerous other writings; translated into 15 languages. Died 2 October 1969 at Greenmount (WA). Mother of playwright Ric Throssell.

The theatre attracted Katharine Susannah Prichard from childhood but her playwriting career was confined to occasional performance and became overshadowed by her reputation as a novelist and political writer. Her plays were often a working of material she later used in her novels. She liked the dramatic economy of stage writing and was able to confront the emotional and social issues of her characters more directly in this form than was possible in writing fiction at the time. Commitment to and concern for working people informed all her work. She joined the Communist Party when it was founded in 1920 and remained a member all her life. Most of her short plays are agitprop pieces and realist drama dealing starkly with women's rights, industrial conditions and women's suffering in war.

An early example of her political questioning was her first play, *The Burglar*, first presented in WILLIAM MOORE's Annual Drama Night in Melbourne in 1910. A one-act comedy, *The Burglar* is an entertaining encounter between a girl with socialist pretensions and an upwardly mobile young man who is financing his university studies by theft. Her next plays, *Her Place* (1913) and the lost *For Instance* (1914) were first produced in London, by the Actresses' Franchise League. *The Great Man*, a three-act comedy about a baby, was produced by the PIONEER PLAYERS in Melbourne in 1923. *Bid Me to Love*, a charming comedy about the pitfalls of open marriage, was first performed on 10 March 1973, by the CANBERRA REPERTORY SOCIETY, directed by Prichard's son RIC THROSSELL. It is a light-hearted counterpoint to the unbridled sexuality expressed by the three-act drama *BRUMBY INNES*, Prichard's most significant play. She wrote these plays concurrently and entered them in the *Triad* magazine's play competition in 1927. *Brumby Innes* won the prize but was not performed until 1972. In Perth, the WORKERS' ART GUILD gave first performances of her one-act plays *Women of Spain* (1935) and *Forward One* (1937) and the three-act *Penalty Clause* (1940), later titled *Solidarity*, and the New Theatre League produced her one-act sketch *Good Morning* in 1955. ❦*Katharine Brisbane*

published plays
Bid Me to Love (1973). Sydney: Currency Methuen 1974; Currency Press 1983.
Brumby Innes (1972). Perth: Paterson 1940. Sydney and London: Currency Methuen 1974. Sydney: Currency Press 1983.
The Pioneers (1937). Sydney: Angus and Robertson 1937, in *Best Australian One-Act Plays* (ed. William Moore and T. Inglis Moore). Reprinted in *Drama and the School* 34 (1967).

further reading
CARROLL, DENNIS. *Australian Contemporary Drama*. Sydney: Currency Press 1995.
FERRIER, CAROL (ed.). *As Good as a Yarn With You*. Melbourne: C.U. Press 1992. Correspondence between Prichard and other female writers.
HAY, JOHN. Katharine Susannah Prichard. *Australian Dictionary of Biography* 11. Melbourne University Press 1988.
THROSSELL, RIC. *Wild Weeds and Windflowers*. Sydney: Angus and Robertson 1976. Biography of Prichard
WILLIAMS, MARGARET. Natural sexuality: Katharine Prichard's *Brumby Innes*. *Meanjin* 32/1 (Melbourne 1973).

reference
Manuscripts of most of Prichard's plays are in the Campbell Howard Collection, University of New England.

Lloyd Prider

Actor, designer, director. Born 1907 at Kalangadoo (SA). Founded Playbox Theatre (Adelaide) 1932. Went to London 1947. Died 1960 in London.

For 15 years Lloyd Prider produced a yearly program of seven plays for his Playbox Theatre in Adelaide, always including at least one musical created entirely by local talent. He was the sole director. His brother Jack and sister Joy played active parts. Lloyd Prider also acted frequently in other amateur companies' productions. A perfectionist, he excelled in producing costume plays. He designed costumes and sets that reflected his concern with visual presentation, colour and light.

His aim was primarily popular entertainment but he was not averse to experiment within the theatre's policy. The five or six plays he produced each year were works of quality and audience appeal such as Lionel Hale's *She Passed through Lorraine* and Oliver Goldsmith's *She Stoops to Conquer*. Also notable were *I'll Leave it to You* by Noël Coward, *Lightning Strikes Twice* by Rex Rienits, *The Winter's Tale* and two musical works, *The O'Brien Girl* and *Tropical Trouble*. At times Prider would adapt a modern or period play into a musical by interweaving songs and music provided by local musicians and adding chorus and ballet. In this there was a certain anticipation of today's musicals for some of his productions evolved from unlikely social or political plays and carried a cast of up to a hundred. These productions were popular successes. Prider died while watching a play in a West End theatre. ❦*Thelma Afford*

Prince of Wales Theatre

Theatre in Castlereagh Street, Sydney, opened 12 March 1855, seating 3250. Architect: Henry Robertson. Burned down 3 October 1860. New theatre opened 23 May 1863. Architect: J. F. Hilly. Burned down 6 January 1872.

JOSEPH WYATT sold his ROYAL VICTORIA THEATRE and leased it back in 1849. In 1854 he could not renew the lease so he commissioned the theatre's architect, Henry Robertson, to design another. The result was the Prince of Wales Theatre, a large and well fitted-out house by contemporary standards. The auditorium was 21·3 metres to the orchestra by 18·3 metres across and had four tiers—a pit holding 1500 persons, a dress circle for 500, upper boxes for 750 and a gallery for 500. The fronts of the tiers were in the old style of flat wooden panelling. The ceiling, with a 4·6-metre-diameter dome, was 17·7 metres above the pit floor and painted to represent a bright Italian sky. The proscenium opening was 11 metres wide and the stage was 18·3 metres wide by 26·5 metres deep from the gas footlights. Beneath it were the male actors' dressing-rooms, with neither natural light nor ventilation. At first Wyatt leased the theatre to Andrew Torning, who was also lessee of the Royal Victoria. He concentrated on shows there to the neglect of the Prince of Wales, which Wyatt sold in 1858. In 1859–60 the theatre saw a yearlong dispute between Samuel Colville and Charles Poole, who had interlocking leases of Sydney's two theatres, and the actors, who went on strike for a time over pay and conditions.

In 1860 fire broke out in a bakery in King Street and wind sent the flames into the pine-framed roof of the theatre. Three Sydney insurance companies' fire brigades and two volunteer fire companies arrived, but their efforts, even in heavy rain, could not prevent two deaths, several injuries and almost total destruction of the theatre. R. Fitzgerald bought the site and commissioned the architect J. F. Hilly to design a second Prince of Wales Theatre. Hilly is little known today but in his time he was considered a better architect than the famous Edmund Blacket. Hilly reused the front wall of the first Prince of Wales in the new theatre, which opened in 1863. Like its predecessors, it accommodated the audience on four levels. The auditorium was three metres shallower than in the previous building but the stage was now 30.5 metres deep, framed by a proscenium opening only 9.1 metres wide. The stage equipment was possibly the most up-to-date in Australia. Wing and back flats and borders in grooves were operated by shafts and purchase wheels, drums, winches and pulleys to provide maximum flexibility and simultaneous changing of all flats from scene to scene. There was a mezzanine floor beneath the stage for the operation of traps and a stage cellar below that. The second theatre opened under a firmer arrangement than the first, with W. S. Lyster taking a three-year lease and alternating seasons of opera and drama. Fire destroyed the second Prince of Wales Theatre on 6 January 1872. The front wall survived again. A new THEATRE ROYAL opened on the site in December 1875. ❦*Ross Thorne*

Princess Theatre Bendigo

Theatre at corner of McKenzie and View Streets, opened 1874, seating 2000. Architect: George R. Johnson, superintended by Vahland and Getzschman. Also called **New Sandhurst Theatre** or **Royal Princess's Theatre**. Altered to form cinema and theatre 1936. Architects: Cowper, Murphy and Appleford. Demolished 1963.

Soon after the first gold rush in 1851 a few theatres were built in Bendigo, then called Sandhurst. The first was the Royal Theatre in 1854. The Royal Victoria followed in the same year and soon closed. The Criterion Theatre, reported to seat only 350, opened in 1856. All were associated with hotels. In 1874 it was reported that there was no regular theatre in the town but a new one would remedy that.

The new Princess Theatre was behind deep shops, and long corridors reached to the various parts of the house. The axis of the auditorium and stage ran parallel to the street. The auditorium was 24 metres wide by 18 metres deep and the stage, contrary to published dimensions, was only about 18 metres wide by less than 15 metres deep, with a nine-metre-wide proscenium opening flanked by banks of three private boxes. The floor of the pit and stalls appears to have been flat, with 11 posts supporting the dress circle and the gallery above it. Six posts at the edge of the circles continued to support the domed ceiling. During its first 50 years the theatre saw touring companies of entrepreneurs such as WILLIAM ANDERSON, WYBERT REEVE and J. C. WILLIAMSON, as well as local performers and oddities like the Egyptian War Diorama in January 1885. In 1936 major alterations to produce an Art Deco cinema and theatre reduced the auditorium to two levels but extended the theatre into a former warehouse behind. ❧*Ross Thorne*

further reading
Australasian Sketcher (Melbourne) 11 July 1874.

Princess Theatre Melbourne

Theatre in Spring Street, opened as **Astley's Amphitheatre** 11 September 1854. Redecorated and renamed **Royal Amphitheatre** February 1856. Renovated and reopened as **Princess's Theatre and Opera House** 22 April 1857. Further modified 1861. Closed 1863. Reopened after major alterations 2 December 1865. Demolished 1886. Replaced by **Princess Theatre**, opened 18 December 1886. Architect: William Pitt jnr. Auditorium rebuilt and theatre reopened 26 December 1922. Architect: Henry E. White. Theatre reopened 1990 after stage rebuilt and building restored and refurbished.

This century-old theatre, restored as a lyric theatre for commercial productions of major musicals, stands on a site that has been occupied by a theatre since Thomas Mooney opened Astley's Amphitheatre there in 1854, under the direction of George Lewis. Astley's Amphitheatre, named after a famous CIRCUS in London, was designed for both stage and equestrian events. In September 1855 a newspaper complained of the transformation of *Richard III* into 'a monopolylogue' on horseback. By the next month the competition from two new theatres, the OLYMPIC THEATRE and the THEATRE ROYAL, caused loss of patronage in the 2000-seat Astley's, and it was auctioned off.

GEORGE COPPIN leased Astley's in February 1856, lit it with gas, remodelled it slightly and renamed it the Royal Amphitheatre, but after eight weeks it closed for lack of support. John Black took over the building to reconstruct the interior for presentation of lyric drama and reopened it after minor alterations as the Princess's Theatre in April 1857 with Anna Bishop in the title-role of Bellini's opera *Norma*. After two further leases the Princess's Theatre again fell on bad times. James Simmonds took it over from Achilles King, who then supervised reconstruction for the new lessee, transforming the inelegant and disproportionate auditorium into a 'perfect gem of a house'.

The *Illustrated Melbourne Post* of 25 November 1865 shows substantial timber posts continuing up to a deep cornice supporting a slightly domed ceiling, painted with nymphs floating in a cloudy sky. The proscenium was 2.4 metres deep and contained doors giving onto an apron of the same depth. The proscenium opening was 9.9 metres wide, the stage being 17.4 metres deep by 23.7 metres wide. The gross dimensions of the auditorium were 23.7 metres wide, 23.1 metres deep by 9.6 metres high. It was lit by gas and decorated in white, blue and gold. The fronting building, which housed a hotel, the theatre entrances and shops, was substantially built in masonry, but the auditorium appears to have been externally clad in weatherboards.

By 1886 the theatre was neglected, and WILLIAMSON, GARNER AND MUSGROVE commissioned WILLIAM PITT JNR to design a new one for the site. The substantial Princess Theatre was built in less than eight months. It was favourably compared to major European theatres. The three-level auditorium was lit by electricity and there was ventilation through a central sliding section of the ceiling dome, which opened to a 7.2 metre diameter tube (still in existence) rising to a sliding segment of the roof. The exterior is still almost as it was built, in an Italian Renaissance style with French overtones, although the open terraces were enclosed in 1901 to form a coloured glass wintergarden.

After buying the theatre in 1915 BENJAMIN FULLER and his brother John entered into partnership with HUGH J. WARD in 1922 to rebuild the auditorium to eliminate the forest of cast-iron columns supporting the two tiers above. HENRY E. WHITE designed a new auditorium in Adam style which is not out of place with the remainder of the building. It opened on Boxing Day with an American musical comedy, *The O'Brien Girl*. Ward left the partnership but FULLERS' maintained the theatre until 1929, when they leased it to Union Theatres for talkies. The lease then passed to F. W. THRING, who presented musical comedies and Efftee films.

After the Second World War the Princess returned to live theatre under Carroll–Fuller Theatres Pty Ltd. GARNET H. CARROLL took over full control of the freehold and entrepreneurial activity in 1951. He leased the theatre for short terms until he died in 1964, when his son John took control through Carroll Freeholds Pty Ltd.

From 1969 to 1985 the AUSTRALIAN ELIZABETHAN THEATRE TRUST leased the theatre. David and Elaine Marriner bought Carroll Freeholds in 1986 and renamed the company Princess Theatre Holdings Pty Ltd on 3 May 1990. After a conservation study, the company had the stage rebuilt to suit the requirements of the entrepreneur Cameron Mackintosh and the remainder of the theatre restored and refurbished. Leased to the Mackintosh organisation, it reopened with the musical *Les Misérables* in 1990. ❧*Robyn Riddett, Ross Thorne*

Richard Prins

Designer. Born 12 November 1938 in Christchurch (New Zealand). Studied art in New Zealand. Came to Australia c.1956. Worked for Australian Elizabethan Theatre Trust. Studied at East Sydney Technical College. Joined Union Theatre Repertory Company (Melbourne) 1961. Irene Mitchell Award for set design 1965, 1970.

Richard Prins sculptured on stage with the shapes and textures of wood and metal and the actors moved in and out of his settings. He liked the twisted forms of junk and his stage always exuded power. He frequently added aura and sometimes bravura with hints of symbolism but never destroyed his focus on the heart of a play. As resident designer of the MELBOURNE THEATRE COMPANY he designed the set for Tyrone Guthrie's production of *All's Well that Ends Well* at the Princess Theatre in 1970 and productions of Arthur Miller's *Incident at Vichy* in 1967, Peter Ustinov's *The Unknown Soldier and his Wife* in 1969, Bertolt Brecht's *The Caucasian Chalk Circle* at the Russell Street Theatre in 1970, Ray Lawler's *The Man Who Shot the Albatross* at the Princess Theatre in 1971, and *Henry IV—part 1* in the courtyard of the National Gallery of Victoria.

Henry Prinsep

Amateur actor, designer, dramatist, scene-painter, singer. Born 1844 in Calcutta (India). Educated in United Kingdom. Taught painting by G. F. Watts. Moved in literary and artistic circles. Came to Western Australia to visit family estates 1865. Married Josephine Bussel 1868. Moved to Perth 1874. Worked as government draughtsman. Retired to Busselton (WA) 1909. Mayor for some years. Died 1922 at Busselton.

Henry Prinsep was a leader in Western Australian cultural life. He sang at social gatherings, took part in Governor Sir William Robertson's amateur theatricals, wrote comedies that were performed, and designed and painted scenery. He also painted act drops—large stretched canvases that filled the proscenium opening during scene changes—for ST GEORGE'S HALL and the Mechanics' Institute in Perth and the Mechanics' Institute at Geraldton. Near-naked classical figures in act drops brought him criticism. *Maurice Jones*

further reading
STAPLES, A. C. Henry Charles Prinsep. *Early Days* 5. Perth 1953.
reference
The Royal Western Australian Historical Society has prologues, epilogues and scale drawings of stage sets by Prinsep.

Prisoners' theatre

Convicts acted the first play in Australia, *The Recruiting Officer* by George Farquhar, in 1789, and performed in most early colonial theatre. Convicts such as EDWARD GEOGHEGAN and JAMES TUCKER, have written plays but drama as a creative process was not formally established in Australian prisons until the late 1950s, when Ian Grindlay, governor of Bendigo Prison in Victoria, allowed prisoners to perform plays for invited audiences.

It is difficult to consider prison drama with a sense of continuity because its existence depends upon the goodwill of state prison departments, but today there are drama groups in most male and female prisons and some juvenile detention centres. Since the 1960s groups such as the Hole in the Wall at Fremantle Prison (WA), the Resurgents at Parramatta Prison (NSW) and the Mess Hall Players at Pentridge Prison in Melbourne have staged quality productions and works by prisoner playwrights such as Michael Byrnes, JIM MCNEIL, Robin Thurston and the present writer have been performed in major theatres.

Initially these groups presented 'safe' plays like *Stalag 17* by Ronald Bevan and Edmund Trzinski, *The Caine Mutiny Court Martial* by Herman Wouk and *The Hasty Heart* by John Patrick. These were carefully vetted by prison authorities, who saw the productions as showcases for rehabilitation. But as radical attitudes swept the western world in the 1960s and 1970s prisoners saw theatre as a way to focus attention on their situation.

Assisted by theatrical people outside—such as Ken Horler and MALCOLM ROBERTSON with the Resurgents, and Rex Callaghan and Max Tomkins with the Mess Hall Players—they began to write and direct their own works to raise public awareness of their unique world, dealing specifically with rehabilitation, punishment, violence and drugs in prison, homosexuality and the role of prison in society. They created a prison-theatre genre.

Thus Jim McNeil dealt with prison in *The Last Cuppa* (1970), *The Chocolate Frog* (1972) and *The Old Familiar Juice* (1972), a revision of *The Last Cuppa*, all written as a member of the Resurgents; *How Does Your Garden Grow*, written at Bathurst Prison; and *Jack* (1977), written upon his release. Other writers wrote on similar themes: Robin Thurston and Maurice Hurt's *Record of Interview* (1975), Robert Golding's *Brylcreme and Maggot Pies* (1976) and Bernie Matthews's *The Other Side is Greener*.

Upon release Thurston wrote *Sisters*, about female prisoners. Similarly, *Seventy Times Seven* (1973) by Rod Smith, from Woorooloo Prison Training Centre (WA), is about prison life. Upon release from Boggo Road Prison in Brisbane Michael Byrnes wrote about alcoholics in *The River Jordan* (1976).

Writers with the Mess Hall Players avoided writing about prisons though their themes dealt with varying forms of oppression. The present writer's *A Blue Freckle* (1975) was about police corruption, Stan Taylor's *Victor Hara, Companero* (1977) was about the death of a Chilean folk hero and Peter Brennan's *Conspiracy* invalidated charities. The works of Taylor, the present writer and others were produced for three years by a theatre company called Governor's Pleasure, formed in 1978 by ex-prisoners from the Mess Hall Players. They disbanded because of lack of funding. Both the Resurgents and the Mess Hall Players were disbanded in the early 1980s, mainly because of pressure from prison officers' unions. Parramatta Prison was reclassified as maximum security, and a member of a Mess Hall Players cast departed from Pentridge with the invited audience. *Ray Mooney*

John Skinner Prout

Scene-painter, theatre decorator. Born 19 December 1805 at Plymouth (England). Came to Sydney 1840. Painted scenery and interior decorations for Australian Olympic Theatre, Sydney, 1842. Moved to Hobart 1844. Returned to England 1848. Died 29 August 1876 in London. Nephew of painter Samuel Prout. Cousin of theatre decorator Samuel Prout Hill.

A colonial artist whose Australian landscapes, remarkable portraits of Aborigines and invaluable pictorial record of colonial life in the 1840s gave him considerable stature, John Skinner Prout made one foray into theatrical painting. In January 1842 LUIGI DALLE CASE employed him to paint vignettes on the front of the boxes at the new Australian Olympic Theatre in Sydney. He also painted scenes for Thomas Otway's *Venice Preserv'd*, basing them on a volume of lithographs by his uncle, the distinguished watercolour painter Samuel Prout. After opening night it was stated that theatregoers would be attracted 'not more by the entertainment than by the magical effects of the artist's pencil'. His scenery set new standards and was alone well worth the price of admission, it was claimed. Unfortunately after six months, Dalle Case was declared insolvent. His largest debt was Prout's salary but when his effects, including Prout's scenery, were sold, a technicality prevented the painter from claiming on the proceeds.

Prout had published four volumes of lithographs and exhibited with the New Society of Painters in Water Colours in London before he came to Sydney. He taught, lectured, undertook painting trips in NSW and published lithographs. In Hobart he established an influential amateur sketching club and organised the first major Australian art exhibition in 1845. ❦*Tony Brown and Gillian Winter*

further reading
HODGMAN, V. W. John Skinner Prout. *Australian Dictionary of Biography* 2. Melbourne University Press 1967.
BROWN, TONY. John Skinner Prout. *Art and Australia* 22/4 (Sydney 1985).

Publishing

Playscripts have rarely been best-selling books, and in earlier times many only appeared in print if the author paid for publication. Some 19th-century playwrights such as John Finamore and F. R. C. HOPKINS saw themselves as men of letters, offering verse tragedies and social problem dramas for the education of their fellow colonists. Several politicians, including ALFRED DEAKIN and William Forster, joined them in this vanity publishing of mostly unperformed (and sometimes unperformable) moral tracts.

Newspaper editors occasionally gave an aspiring Australian playwright the chance to be read, and it is thanks to them that a few very early plays survive. Henry Melville's *THE BUSHRANGERS—or, Norwood Vale* was published minus one scene in the *Hobart Town Magazine* in 1834 and extracts from CHARLES HARPUR's *The Tragedy of Donohoe* appeared in the *Sydney Monitor* in 1835. Authors and copyright-holding managements often consciously avoided publication of major Australian comedies and melodramas, however, since it invited plagiarism. Such major successes as George Darrell's *THE SUNNY SOUTH* (1883), and the dramatisation of Steele Rudd's *ON OUR SELECTION* (1912), were not published until modern critical editions, based on surviving manuscripts, appeared in Currency Press's National Theatre series. Exceptions to this tendency were pantomime libretti, which until the mid-1890s were printed for the first performance and sold as programs. Copies of many have survived, including scripts by W. M. AKHURST, MARCUS CLARKE, and GARNET WALCH. Walch's *AUSTRALIA FELIX* (1873), has been republished by the University of Queensland Press in a meticulous reconstruction by Veronica Kelly. The 'literary' plays and playwrights of the 20th century up to 1971 fared better, although print runs—and sales—were often minuscule and some major authors were not published. Several of LOUIS ESSON's plays were published. Most of Louis Stone's were not. Betty Roland's *THE TOUCH OF SILK* appeared belatedly in 1942, 14 years after its premiere. Paterson's Printing Press in Perth supported prize-winning Western Australian authors such as HENRIETTA DRAKE-BROCKMAN and KATHARINE SUSANNAH PRICHARD and the Australasian Publishing Company in Sydney printed Dymphna Cusack's *MORNING SACRIFICE* in 1950, but these are rare books today.

The first major publisher to build up a substantial drama list was Angus and Robertson in Sydney. Early examples of its involvement with Australian drama were SYDNEY TOMHOLT's *Bleak Dawn and Other Plays* in 1936 and *Best One-Act Australian Plays* edited by WILLIAM MOORE and T. Inglis Moore in 1937. Angus and Robertson's successes included the verse plays of DOUGLAS STEWART, whose *The Fire on the Snow* was reprinted 21 times between 1944 and 1972, and Ray Lawler's *SUMMER OF THE SEVENTEENTH DOLL*, which entered its list in 1957 and was marketed internationally in paperback by Collins Fontana two years later. As universities and schools began to set Australian plays as texts for study Angus and Robertson was the first publisher to achieve large sales. Then it seemed to lose interest and the international publisher Penguin Books dominated the schools' market with *Three Australian Plays* from 1963. This volume was chiefly successful because of Alan Seymour's *THE ONE DAY OF THE YEAR*; it also included Douglas Stewart's *NED KELLY*, and HAL PORTER's *The Tower*. Penguin tried again, less lucratively, in 1970 with *Four Australian Plays*, early works by ALEX BUZO, JACK HIBBERD, and JOHN ROMERIL.

In 1967 the vigorous but short-lived Sun Books in Melbourne secured the paperback rights to *Four Plays by Patrick White*, published in a hardcover edition in London in 1965 by Eyre and Spottiswoode, and made it available to university students in Australian drama courses. The only academic press to attempt more than an occasional volume of drama was the University of Queensland Press; poor sales of mostly second-ranking plays led it to withdraw from regular drama publishing about 1980.

Important Australian plays began to appear in print with certainty and regularity only after KATHARINE BRISBANE and PHILIP PARSONS established Currency Press in 1971, during the dramatic renascence. It built its initial success on the works of DAVID WILLIAMSON, the most successful playwright of the 1970s. Currency has sought to identify interesting new writers and it has devised several schemes for marketing their works. The most innovative has been the Current Theatre series in which a saddle-stitched volume of the play is published in association with the company producing it and sold as a program. The only drawback has been that such a published script often lacks rewriting done during rehearsals. However, when a play has been successful on stage and in the schoolroom—Louis Nowra's *THE GOLDEN AGE* (1985) and Michael Gow's *AWAY* (1986) are examples—Currency has subsequently replaced the Current Theatre script with a more substantial revised edition.

From the 1960s small grants from the Commonwealth Literary Fund, and later from the literature board of the

Australia Council, began to permit publication of plays of specialised interest. The development of computer 'desktop publishing' techniques has accelerated this trend toward diversity, but the problem of achieving mass distribution and readership remains. The authors and readers of some publishers—such as Yackandandah Playscripts in Melbourne and Playlab in Brisbane—are mostly associated with their own states. Tantrum Press in Adelaide has produced several volumes of South Australian women's plays. During the 1980s the enthusiasm for multiculturalism saw small, often one-off companies begin to publish plays by writers of non-Anglophone origin—in European languages or original or translated English. From 1988 onwards a few of the many plays produced by the burgeoning COMMUNITY THEATRE movement appeared in the journal *Australasian Drama Studies*.

The only company apart from Currency to build up a substantial list and sales to schools has been Heinemann Educational. Its diverse but lightweight Australian Theatre Workshop series, begun in the 1960s, contains several of ALAN HOPGOOD's popular comedies, particularly *And the Big Men Fly*, theatre-in-education plays, some television scripts, a few plays from earlier periods and others mainly suitable for teaching Australian history at secondary level. ❦*Richard Fotheringham*

further reading
BRISBANE, KATHARINE. Investing in authors—A history of Currency Press. *Voices* (Canberra) spring 1993.

Roger Pulvers

Director, dramatist. Born 4 May 1944 in New York City. Educated at University of California (Los Angeles), Harvard University (USA) and Warsaw University (Poland). Lived in Japan 1967–72 and began translating Japanese, Polish and Russian literature. Came to Australia as lecturer in Japanese language and literature at Australian National University (Canberra) 1972. Director and writer-in-residence with Hoopla Productions (Melbourne) 1979. Resettled in Japan with family in 1982 and worked as writer, broadcaster, film director. Returned to Australia 1992. Has published short stories, novels and essays in English and Japanese. Has worked in film as assistant director and scriptwriter.

The first immigrant writer in the early 1970s to begin interpreting Australia in the perspective of a wider world was Roger Pulvers, who speaks some seven languages. His earlier plays were informed by a cosmopolitan outlook and an awareness of the damaging consequences of American foreign policy in some regions, particularly Asia. His style has been influenced by the writers of the American protest movement of the 1960s and modern European movements, including Brecht and the absurdists. Like others before him he found such work not readily understood in Australia in a decade preoccupied with domestic reassessment.

He returned to Australia in 1992 to a new climate. The first of his plays performed in Australia was *Bones* in December 1973 at the LA MAMA THEATRE in Melbourne. Subsequent plays were performed chiefly at La Mama and by Hoopla Productions in Melbourne and the Australian Theatre Workshop in Canberra. They include *Australia Majestic* (1980); *Bertolt Brecht Leaves Los Angeles* (1979); *Cedoona* (1978); *The Covenant of the Rainbow* (1974); *Dreamtime*, a Japanese–Australian children's play (1984); *Drop Drill* (1976); *Fair Go*, later renamed *Joe* (1975); *The Fat Lady* (1973); *Ice* (1974); *General Macarthur in Australia* (1981); *The Senator from California* (1974); *Witold Gombrowicz in Buenos Aires* (1978); and *Yamashita* (1977). Pulvers has directed 15 plays in Australia and Japan, including his own translations of August Strindberg's *The Dance of Death* and *Miss Julie* in Melbourne for the Playbox Theatre Company. ❦*Katharine Brisbane*

published plays
Bertolt Brecht Leaves Los Angeles (1979). Melbourne: Yackandandah 1982.
Dreamtime children's play (1984). Tokyo: Labo Kyoiku Centre Press 1984 in English and Japanese.
Yamashita (1977). Sydney: Currency Press 1981.

Puppetry

In recent years puppetry in Australia has broken through traditional barriers as playwrights, composers, designers, performance artists, dancers and actors have explored the medium. Something resembling traditional puppetry will no doubt continue, mainly for children's audiences, but the term 'puppet theatre' no longer seems apt for the theatrical forms that are developing. Significant puppet theatre in Australia seems to have begun in the mid-19th century, and for a century the field was dominated by Punch and Judy and visiting marionette companies.

A Royal Marionette Theatre opened in Sydney on 11 April 1853 in the former Olympic Circus. It was claimed to be the 1852 London company of that name but it was run by HENRY BEAUFOY MERLIN, who had emigrated to Australia in 1848. Marionettes provided only part of the program—*Bombastes Furioso* and, later, *Tom Thumb*. A Punch and Judy show was given in Government House in Sydney about 2 December 1855 by a performer recently arrived from England. Early in the 20th century there were at least three Punch 'professors' in Sydney—Freeman, Blair and Beckford. DAVID ALLEN wrote his play *The Professor* around Joe Gladwin's 1987 version of Punch and Judy.

The first full-length marionette show seen in Australia seems to have been the Royal Marionettes of McDonough and Earnshaw from the USA, which toured for more than eight months in 1875–76. It was in three parts—a minstrel show, traditional *fantoccini*, or variety acts, and an elaborate pantomime of *Little Red Riding Hood* and sometimes *The Babes in the Wood* too—and it was a virtual copy of Bullock's Royal Marionettes in England. Two members of the company, Charles and Mrs Webb, had worked with Bullock. They left the tour and, joined later by a Mr Trotter, the trio built a similar but smaller show which toured Australia for a few years. In March 1877 the Webbs' season in Sydney coincided with an Italian marionette company performing a pantomime in Italian. Later in 1877 the Webbs played at the Theatre Royal in Ballarat (Vic.), where in April rioters provoked by Levity's Royal Marionettes had thrown fruit, vegetables and a dead possum on stage. The Webbs returned from England in 1884 with a new pantomime, *Beauty and the Beast*, and toured from Adelaide to Townsville (Qld) until at least early 1886.

D'Arc's Marionettes, from Dublin and England, came in 1892 with a full-length program, including the pantomime *Bluebeard*. There was a marionette theatre at WILLIAM

Anderson's Wonderland City, which opened at Tamarama, Sydney, on 1 December 1906. A related D'Arc's company came in 1912, but as part of a variety bill, in keeping with a trend overseas and here. It was in variety that Australian audiences saw some leading marionette performers from overseas—Fred Davys in 1888–90, the Barnards in 1906 and 1908, Deave's Manikins in 1909, Jewell's Marionettes in 1918, Mantell's Marionettes in 1927, Salici's Marionettes in 1939 and Walton and O'Rourke from the USA in 1953.

Away from the variety theatre, a local interest in marionettes developed, and on 29 November 1932, with puppets less than 25 cm high, the Sydney Marionettes of Eleonore Lange and Edith Lanser presented *Joseph and His Brethren*. Then in 1936 Alan and Kay Lewis created a marionette show, *All Aboard for Happiness*, which toured schools in NSW. The leading characters were an elderly Australian couple on a world tour.

In Melbourne, W. D. Nicol, a teachers' college lecturer, directed the 100-seat Littlest Theatre on Saturday afternoons from 1945 to 1950. *The Insect Play* by Josef and Karel Capek was an early production at the theatre, which provided experience for Robert Akins, Peter Scriven and other puppeteers. In Sydney, the Clovelly Puppet Theatre, directed by Edith Murray, borrowed marionettes from Nicol and began Saturday-afternoon shows for children in 1949. This amateur group of children and adults presented shows for many years, with glove-puppets as well as marionettes, and the theatre is still occasionally used.

Growing interest in puppetry, especially among amateurs and educators, was stimulated in the 1950s by three Australian tours, from 1952, by the Hogarth Puppets—Jan Bussell and his wife Ann Hogarth—from England. They tailored their marionette programs to suit different audiences—scenes from *Macbeth* for teenage audiences and Oscar Wilde's *The Happy Prince*, with shadow puppets by Lotte Reiniger, for older audiences. Subsequent exploration of shadow puppetry by local puppeteers led to the work of the present writer.

Local puppeteers usually appeared in small venues. In Sydney, Raeburn and Freda Griffiths from Auckland (New Zealand) presented a marionette program in the radio 2KY auditorium in 1949, and Norman Hetherington's marionettes appeared at the Mercury Theatre in 1953. But in 1953–54, young Peter Scriven boldly and successfully presented his marionettes in the Theatre Royal. No puppeteer has had greater impact in Australia than Scriven. The biggest event in Australian puppetry was at the Elizabethan Theatre in Sydney on 12 June 1956, when he opened The Tintookies, an extravagantly mounted, large-scale marionette musical with an Australian bush setting. Scriven's puppet-master, Russian-born Igor Hychka, had toured Argentina with the celebrated Italian marionette company of Vittorio Podrecca, whose indirect influence on marionettes in Australia continues notably in the work of Phillip Edmiston of Queensland Marionette Theatre.

The Tintookies toured extensively, and Scriven followed it with *Little Fella Bindi* in 1958 and *The Magic Pudding* in 1959. The success of these productions led the Australian Elizabethan Theatre Trust to form the Marionette Theatre of Australia in Sydney to create and tour such productions. A national tour of *The Tintookies* in 1965 was followed by a new show, *The Explorers* and in 1966–67, with government support the Marionette Theatre of Australia, toured 14 southeast Asian countries with *Little Fella Bindi*. Scriven's public success led to puppetry becoming accepted as worthy of financial support from governments.

Visible puppeteers

In Hobart L. Peter Wilson and Peter Oldham formed Tasmanian Puppet Theatre in 1969. Under Wilson the company gradually made a break—made in Europe many years before—with the marionette tradition. Nigel Triffitt was invited to work on a project initiated by Wilson and in 1976 he created *Momma's Little Horror Show*. There was no obvious story line as puppeteers dressed in black manipulated, often visibly, a variety of figures and objects, some quite large, to create evocative and haunting images to a background of music. The show appealed to adult theatregoers and had a great success in 1978 at the Last Laugh in Melbourne, where patrons normally expected comedy. It toured Europe in 1982 and was revived for the Festival of Sydney in 1988–89.

The Marionette Theatre of Australia also broke with its marionette tradition. Under the present writer, who became artistic director in 1976, the company explored rod-puppets and other puppet-theatre forms, and the relationship between puppeteer and puppet. In the 'outback fairy tale' *Smiles Away* in 1981 the puppeteers were on stage with their almost life-size puppets, as 'extras'.

In Melbourne, Handspan Theatre, formed by young puppeteers in 1977, has gradually departed from conventional puppetry to something it describes as 'visual theatre'. For Handspan's adult audiences Nigel Triffitt devised, designed and directed *Secrets*, which opened in Melbourne in 1982 and toured in Europe and the USA in 1984–85. One of the original Handspan puppeteers, Peter J. Wilson notably exemplified the trend for puppeteers to be seen, and their individual performing skills to be recognised, in 1984 in *Cho Cho San*, a musical play, based on the Madame Butterfly story. The title role is played by an actress and also by a puppet representing her youth and innocence.

In the small touring puppet shows the performers, often soloists or husband-and-wife teams, usually make their own puppets but specialist designers and puppet-makers have emerged with the growth of larger companies. Ross Hill, from Mildura (Vic.), was puppet-maker for Tasmanian Puppet Theatre and the Marionette Theatre of Australia and worked in London in 1984–85 on Jim Henson's film *Labyrinth*. Beverley Campbell Jackson worked on new puppets for the 1975 revival of *The Tintookies* and later worked as a designer and puppet-maker with companies around Australia. L. Peter Wilson moved to Perth in 1980 and, with Campbell-Jackson and the writer Cathryn Robertson, established the Spare Parts Puppet Theatre Company, which moved to its own theatre in Fremantle in 1986.

Puppeteers characteristically tour widely but there have been several attempts to establish permanent puppet theatres. In 1975 Robert and Nancy Akins built the Pilgrim Puppet Theatre in a church in the Melbourne suburb of Hawthorn and opened it with a marionette version of Kenneth Grahame's story *The Wind in the Willows*. Costs proved prohibitive and the theatre ceased in 1980. Polyglot Puppet Theatre of Melbourne, founded by Naomi Tippett in 1978, has presented regular school-holiday shows in its own theatre in South Yarra since 1992, in addition to touring schools. The PATCH THEATRE COMPANY in Adelaide is a permanent children's theatre that uses puppetry. The Marionette Theatre of Australia initially tried to cater to adults as well as children in its own theatre in the Rocks in Sydney, in 1983–89. Since 1992 local puppeteers have presented free shows at weekends and on school holidays in the small Puppet Cottage in the Rocks.

Puppeteers in Australia have been united by local puppetry guilds, the magazine *Manipulation*, started by Maeve Vella, and the Australian section of L'Union Internationale de la Marionnette, the international association of puppeteers. Puppet festivals have brought puppeteers together and enabled them to see the work of visitors from Germany in Melbourne in 1975, from China and Japan in Hobart in 1979 and from China, Czechoslovakia, France, India, Indonesia and the USA in Adelaide in 1983. Australia now has puppeteers from Egypt, Japan, the USA and several European countries. At the same time, NEVILLE TRANTER, from Toowoomba (Qld), is based in Amsterdam as a leading solo puppeteer in Europe. Perth-born Roger-Daniel Bensky of Georgetown University in the USA is a leading authority on puppet-theatre theory whose works in French have been published in Paris.

Puppeteers have usually been trained on the job, but in 1975–76 a puppetry panel set up by the theatre board of the AUSTRALIA COUNCIL funded training for three who attended courses at the NATIONAL INSTITUTE OF DRAMATIC ART, studied with local puppet companies and acting tutors and toured with the visiting Coad Canada Puppets in 1975. Others have sought overseas training. L. Peter Wilson has arranged for puppeteers from Czechoslovakia, England, Japan, China and the USA to work with his teams here.

Visiting companies

Some outstanding overseas companies have appeared at the Adelaide Festival, including the Salzburg Marionettes in 1954, Bunraku Puppet Theatre in 1972 and 1994, Bread and Puppet Theatre from the USA in 1978, Philippe Genty's Company from France in 1978 and Triangel from the Netherlands in 1992. Genty was such a success that his company returned for several extensive tours. The work of Genty and the Coads and the visits of Black Theatre of Prague stimulated an interest in 'black theatre' techniques.

Puppets have also appeared in film and on television. In 1947, Alan and Kay Lewis made a marionette film of *Cinderella*. Tasmanian Puppet Theatre produced *Big Nose* when the Japanese puppeteer Takeshi Hoshino worked with them in 1976 and Michael Creighton of the Marionette Theatre of Australia was responsible for the prizewinning films *A Puppet Pudding* (1980) and *Rubbish* (1982). Norman Hetherington's *Mr Squiggle* has been appearing on ABC television for more than 25 years and the ABC's series of *Blinky Bill*, *Lift Off* and *The Ferals* used the talents of several local puppeteers. ❦*Richard Bradshaw*

further reading

BRADSHAW, RICHARD. Webb's Royal Marionettes (1876–1886). *Australasian Drama Studies* 19 (Brisbane October 1991).
HARTLAND, PETER. *Life Among the Little People*. Perth: Pembroke 1997.
HETHERINGTON, NORMAN. *Puppets of Australia*. Australian Council for the Arts 1974.
MCPHARLIN, PAUL. *The Puppet Theatre in America*. New York: Harper 1949.
SPEAIGHT, GEORGE. *The History of the English Puppet Theatre*. London: Harrap 1955.
VAN STRATEN, FRANK. *Discovering Puppets*. Performing Arts Museum (Melbourne) information sheet 1981.
VELLA, MAEVE and HELEN RICKARDS. *Theatre of the Impossible—Puppet theatre in Australia*. Sydney: Craftsman House 1989.
WALLER, CHARLES. *Magical Nights at the Theatre*. Melbourne: Gerald Taylor 1980.

Q Theatre

Amateur theatrical company in Adelaide, founded in 1970 by Betty and Don Quin. Closed 1984. **venue** Q Theatre, Halifax Street. **first production** *The Dinkum Bambino* by Betty Quin, 29 April 1970. **final production** *East Lynne*.

Betty Quin, an Adelaide actor, director and writer, and her husband Don rented a historic bluestone building and converted it to a 150-seat theatre, primarily to promote Australian plays. From 1970 they annually presented eight to ten productions by Australian writers, including RAY LAWLER, REG LIVERMORE, RALPH PETERSON, HAL PORTER, Betty Quin, ALAN SEYMOUR and BARBARA STELLMACH. Workshops were held to develop skills in acting, writing, directing and backstage work. Aspiring local writers—Vivienne Causby, Ethel Shippen and Carlene Tilbrook—had plays produced. In 1972 Q Theatre presented Bernard Hesling's *My Life with an Interval for Aspirin* on the Adelaide Festival fringe, and introduced lunchtime theatre.

The Quins bought the building in 1973 and, unable to survive with a purely Australian repertoire, introduced light comedies and two musicals a year. Plays by Noël Coward, John Mortimer, Terence Rattigan, Neil Simon and Brandon Thomas were popular and two musicals devised by Betty Quin—*Our Glad* in 1976 and *The Golden Years* in 1977—were among the most successful productions.

Betty Quin left Adelaide in 1977 to become a television scriptwriter. The theatre continued successfully under the administration of Anne O'Day until 1984, when Betty Quin sold the building. When it went to auction the Adelaide *Advertiser* said in an editorial that the theatre 'had been a model of its kind' and with no government subsidy 'had retained a solid and dedicated audience for its unpretentious amateur productions. The Q is the type of theatre people give their hearts to.' The director John Edmund leased the building and operated it as the John Edmund Theatre in 1989–90. The city council closed the theatre in 1994 after complaints that new lessees were showing pornographic movies ❦*Jo Peoples*

Q Theatre Company

Professional dramatic company at Penrith (NSW), founded in Sydney in 1963 as Amp-i-theatre by Ben Gabriel, Edward Hepple, Robert McDarra, Terry McDermott, Walter Sullivan and Doreen Warburton. Renamed Q Theatre for second production. **venues** 1963–77 AMP Theatrette, Sydney. 1977– Q Theatre, Penrith. **artistic directors** 1963–89 Doreen Warburton. 1989 Egil Kipste. 1989– Helmut Bakaitis. **first production** *The Dumb Waiter* by Harold Pinter, 2 December 1963, AMP Theatrette.

Q Theatre has been adventurous and remarkably successful in winning an audience outside the metropolitan centre.

Critics have applauded its enterprise and, particularly after its westward move to Penrith, its unpretentious style and energetic ensemble playing. In Sydney it began modestly, performing at lunch time in the 250-seat AMP Theatrette at Circular Quay. Early critical acclaim helped to build audiences. While presenting classical and contemporary works, Q Theatre fostered Australian writing from the start. Its first full-length play was Ray Lawler's SUMMER OF THE SEVENTEENTH DOLL, an evening production in 1966, directed by John Gray, with ETHEL GABRIEL recreating Emma and BEN GABRIEL as Barney. Other Australian works at the AMP Theatrette included plays by LEILA BLAKE, Michael Cove, CEDRIC FLOWER, Pat Flower, COLIN FREE, Mary Gage, Pat Hooker and Harry Martin and solo shows by BEVERLEY DUNN in 1972 and COLLEEN CLIFFORD in 1974.

Dependent on voluntary labour in its early years, Q Theatre gained subsidy in 1968. From 1970 it took theatre to workplaces. It gave the premiere of JIM MCNEIL's *The Chocolate Frog* at the AMP Theatrette on 13 July 1971 and played it to workers at the Sydney Opera House construction site in November. Q Theatre began visiting western suburbs in 1972 and giving regular shows at the Bankstown Civic Centre in 1974. It soon established theatre workshops and toured productions around 12 western suburbs. Increasing difficulty in finding good new plays of 40–50 minutes' duration and a rent increase in 1975 influenced DOREEN WARBURTON to move the company to Penrith with five professional actors. With the aid of the Penrith City Council the company converted a Railway Institute building into a 130-seat thrust-stage theatre. It opened on 30 March 1977 with the musical *Lock Up Your Daughters*.

Warburton, trained in the communal principles of Joan Littlewood's Theatre Workshop in London in the 1940s, insisted that the permanent members of the company live in the Penrith district. Through community activities, a low-price policy and energetic productions Q Theatre established itself firmly, achieving 75 per cent capacity in 1977 and 94 per cent in 1980. Q Theatre developed a vigorous house style.

In the interim season of the SYDNEY THEATRE COMPANY at the Sydney Opera House in 1979 Q Theatre performed George Bernard Shaw's *The Devil's Disciple* under Warburton's direction. The production won the Sydney Critics' Circle Award and Warburton believed that its success helped Q Theatre's credibility in Penrith. To accommodate the expanding audience the company built a new 286-seat theatre on its site and opened it on 17 November 1982 with *Charley's Aunt* by Brandon Thomas.

The company describes its repertoire as 'hard-hitting entertainment'. Comedy and music have been important and works by Alan Ayckbourn, Joe Orton, Sam Shepard and DAVID WILLIAMSON are familiar. Musicals are a speciality and two rock musicals written locally by Kevin Bennett, David Mason-Cox and Max Iffland—*St Marys Kid* (1978) and *Paradise Regained* (1979)—have been cast largely from local talent under the company's policy of community participation. A commitment to Australian writing has led to occasional revivals such as *ON OUR SELECTION* in 1981, *THE CURRENCY LASS* by Edward Geoghegan in 1989 and the 1950s musical *THE SENTIMENTAL BLOKE* in 1983 and 1988.

Productions by HELMUT BAKAITIS, who is experienced in young people's theatre, have included the premiere of the football musical *Kenny's Coming Home* in 1992. Other successful Australian musicals at the Q Theatre have been *On the Wallaby* in 1983, *St James Infirmary* in 1992, and *Better Known as Bee*, based on the life of the Sydney eccentric Bee Miles, in 1984 and 1992.

Key figures in Q Theatre have included Ron Ferrier, a frequent director in 1968–74; the designer Arthur Dicks; and the director and workshop coordinator Richard Brooks, who settled in Penrith. New talent has been encouraged. JIM SHARMAN and REX CRAMPHORN both directed for Q Theatre in Sydney early in their careers and JUDY DAVIS spent 1978, her first year out of the NATIONAL INSTITUTE OF DRAMATIC ART, acting at Penrith. ♥*Victoria Chance*

further reading
BRISBANE, KATHARINE. Far out shows. *Australian* 21 June 1978.
CARPENTER, A. The Q comes of age and is still growing. *Sydney Morning Herald* 22 October 1989.
Q Theatre 84—1963–1964. Penrith: Q Theatre 1984.

Queen's Theatre

Theatre in Gilles Arcade, Adelaide, opened 11 January 1841, seating c.1000. Closed 28 November 1842. Restored, enlarged and reopened as **Royal Victoria Theatre** 23 December 1850. Closed 10 November 1851. Reopened 1859. Closed 1868. Proclaimed heritage site 15 April 1994.

The remnants of the Queen's Theatre, the first building to house continuous theatre in Adelaide, have yielded more architectural elements and artefacts than any other mid-19th-century theatre–tavern site in Australia. The theatre held a pit for 700 persons, a dress circle of boxes and an upper circle. Its layout was advanced for the time, with the pit penetrating beneath the dress circle, in a similar way to the then recent Royal Victoria Theatre in Sydney. The brothers Vaiben and EMANUEL SOLOMON spent £10 000 in 1841 to build the Queen's Theatre, the Shakespeare Tavern—which opened into the auditorium—and five large houses. The theatre was run in a respectable manner by JOHN LAZAR but he was forced to close it in November 1842, during an economic depression in South Australia. In 1843 the theatre was converted to a courthouse.

When GEORGE COPPIN arrived in Adelaide in 1846 he found no theatre available, so he arranged with Emanuel Solomon to convert a billiards saloon adjacent to the Shakespeare Tavern into a temporary two-level theatre to house some 900 persons. This New Queen's Theatre operated until the end of 1850. Edward Snell visited it on 21 November 1850 and noted in his diary that it was 'a wretched place, only pit and boxes in it and the stage illuminated by 5 foot lights and 2 side lights only. The actors were a set of dull dogs, the scenery was damnable, and the audience a mixture of prostitutes and pickpockets.'

While performing at the New Queen's Theatre, Coppin and Lazar restored, enlarged and improved the old theatre, after the Supreme Court had moved out. It reopened on 23 December 1850 as the Royal Victoria Theatre. It had a new, more imposing front, with applied columns, entablature and pediment, constructed almost 4·2 metres in front of the central portion of the older Georgian-style façade. Architectural fragments of the original Queen's Theatre still exist—window openings of the first façade and structural timber members cut off at the wall surface, which indicate the dress-circle and gallery levels. Exits from the dress circle to the saloon and tavern bar respectively are discernible. In addition, excavations in 1989–90 revealed walls of the Queen's Theatre stage and dressing room, the adjoining tavern and the stage and auditorium of the New Queen's Theatre. Also found were two bases for posts that supported the dress circle and the gallery of the Queen's, and some 2000 artefacts related to the theatre and the tavern. Excavation of the dressing room, stage and orchestra pit revealed grease paint, sequins, military buttons, a Tudor jester's shoe, candlestick holders, clay pipes, glass bottles and stoneware bottles and shards of crockery.

A plan of the Queen's Theatre before it was converted to a courthouse shows the auditorium as 16·2 metres long, possibly including the orchestra pit, the stage as 9·1 metres deep, and the whole as 9·8 metres wide. It shows the pit and gallery entrances from Weymouth Street to the front of the auditorium, with rooms behind and along one side of the stage and the Shakespeare Tavern along the other side. The press reported that up to 400 persons could pack into the gallery, making the total capacity about 1200.

The gold rush in Victoria in 1851 denuded Adelaide of men and whole families. Deprived of an audience, Coppin became bankrupt and the Royal Victoria Theatre closed in November. It was occasionally used by touring companies until Alex Henderson reopened it permanently in 1859 after minor alterations. It was closed in 1868, just before the new THEATRE ROYAL opened in Hindley Street. The old theatre became successively an extension to the tavern, premises for the City Mission and a horse bazaar. Buyers sat in the dress circle and gallery to study horses paraded in the pit, which was paved in bricks. In 1900 the circle and gallery and above-ground stage walls were removed, leaving the building as it is today. The South Australian government has undertaken to preserve it as a state and national heritage item. *Ross Thorne*

further reading
FISCHER, G. L. The Queen's Theatre, Adelaide, 1841–1842. Pioneers Association of South Australia paper 30/57.
GRIFFITHS, T. (ED.). THE *Life and Adventures of Edward Snell*. Sydney: Angus and Robertson 1988.
THORNE, ROSS. Theatre buildings as one indicator of the social history of Australia. *Architecture Australia* 68/4 (September 1979).

reference
The ground plan of the Queen's Theatre in 1843 is in the State Library of South Australia (Adelaide).

Queen's Theatre Royal

Theatre in Queen and Little Bourke Streets, Melbourne, opened 21 April 1845, seating about 1000. Became carriage factory in 1860s.

Melbourne's second theatre, the Queen's Theatre Royal opened with a benefit performance in which the manager, FRANCIS NESBITT, was principal actor. The official first season, also starring Nesbitt, began on 1 May. John Thomas Smith, a town councillor who went on to be seven times mayor of Melbourne, built the theatre, which the *Port Phillip Patriot* said was 'a plain, substantial, brick, shingle roof building with no attempt at architectural ornamentation'. GEORGE COPPIN brought his company from Van Diemen's Land into the new theatre in June 1845 and played there for a year off and on. The Queen's Theatre saw the first performance in Australia by G. V. BROOKE—as Othello—on 26 February 1855, but its days were numbered with the advent of Coppin's OLYMPIC THEATRE and the THEATRE ROYAL. *John West*

Queensland Performing Arts Complex

Performing-arts centre in Brisbane, opened 20 April 1985 as part of Queensland Cultural Centre. **Concert Hall** seats 2000. **Cremorne Theatre** seats up to 315. **Lyric Theatre** seats 1000, 1500 or 2000 people on three levels. Architect: Robin Gibson. Managed by Queensland Performing Arts Trust.

The last mainland state capital to complete a performing-arts complex, Brisbane benefited from the others' experience and obtained good value for the $66 million spent between 1979 and early 1985. The origins of the Queensland Performing Arts Complex date back to 1969, when the state government set up a committee to assess the needs of a new art gallery. In 1973 the architect Robin Gibson won a two-stage limited competition for that building. On 8 November 1974 the government announced that it would establish a cultural centre with a performing-arts complex as its major element. On 16 June 1975 Gibson was appointed to produce a conceptual design for an integrated complex, including the Performing Arts Complex, Queensland Art Gallery, Queensland Museum and State Library. Gibson, the theatre consultant TOM BROWN and others produced the planning brief for the Performing Arts Complex in January 1978, and a building contract was let in 1979.

The Art Gallery, which opened first, set the pattern by winning an award from the Royal Australian Institute of Architects. Its interior spaces were not lavish, but provided the public with a great feeling of comfort. The foyers, the Concert Hall and the Lyric Theatre continue in this vein, providing a quiet richness more appropriate to a theatrical occasion, yet without architectural gimmicks or postmodern references to past styles.

The Lyric Theatre was designed for current styles of performing opera, ballet and musicals, with a proscenium width of 14·7 metres and depth from house curtain to last flying line of 15·5 metres. The total width of the stage behind the proscenium is 40·5 metres. The almost rectangular auditorium has two balconies of almost equal size, each seating about 500 persons. The rake of each balcony extends in a leg down each side of the auditorium as a modern equivalent of the horseshoe balcony. The colours of Queensland walnut wall panelling and deep rose carpet and upholstery are graded from back to front of the theatre to direct the eye towards the proscenium arch. Opera and dance companies and musical-theatre companies toured by commercial entrepreneurs perform in this theatre.

The Queensland Theatre Company has used the Cremorne Theatre since it opened. It is a studio theatre which can be arranged into any of five modes—cabaret, in-the-round, thrust stage, flat-floor concert and single-rake cinema. Its name commemorates an old vaudeville theatre that stood on part of the site from 1911 to 1954.

The two-level Concert Hall is used for events ranging from symphony-orchestra concerts to rock concerts and solo shows by popular entertainers. The whole complex also caters for convivial social occasions through the bar service, a cafe and two restaurants. *Ross Thorne*

Queensland provincial towns

Professional theatre had begun in several Queensland provincial towns by the 1860s. In 1861 Rockhampton had Grant's Music Hall, sometimes advertised less boastfully as 'Grant's large room'. A Theatre Royal was operating at the end of the decade. Townsville also had a Theatre Royal, run by Thomas Fawcett, and the Exchange Assembly Rooms. All were modest structures in or attached to hotels. Publicans were the earliest entrepreneurs. In Stanthorpe in 1873 a theatre of 'bark, canvas, and wood' behind Sheahan's Hotel was grandly titled the Prince of Wales.

The first entertainments in these early venues were variety evenings. At Grant's in Rockhampton in September 1862 J. M. Foans, 'late of Rayner's Serenaders', gave 'drawing room entertainments', accompanied by George B. Mason, who was prominent in Brisbane music and theatre. On 26 November 1862 Grant's had a 'grand concert' with Madame Haimberger and others giving instrumental and vocal pieces. There were numerous circuses, with ASHTON'S CIRCUS, Barlow's Circus and ST LEON'S CIRCUS among the larger and better known troupes.

At the same time as these professional initiatives amateurs were starting theatrical, operatic and musical societies all over the colony. In 1864 the Rockhampton Dramatic Society—'for gentlemen only'—did a comedietta, *Nine Points of the Law*, starring Robert L. Dibdin, who also painted the backdrop. Men played the female roles, and women did not appear until many years later, presumably because their participation was thought unladylike. Other amateur groups are known to have existed in Beenleigh by 1886, in Gladstone by 1885, in Maryborough by 1890, in Stanthorpe by 1875 and in Townsville by 1879.

Curiosities of unknown quality abounded. In Childers an original comic opera, *Southward Bound—or, The Polar Ice Cap* by Arthur Childs Dubourg Collins, was staged on 5 November 1908. A year later in Charters Towers the Amateur Dramatic Society presented Thomas Fisher's original drama *The Face of Crime* at the Show Grounds Hall. A more typical evening's fare would have been an English comedy followed by a 'screaming farce'. A local orchestra nearly always provided music for the plays and supplemented the program. Around 1910 many of these instrumentalists began to find professional work accompanying silent films. This and the First World War caused some theatrical and musical groups to disband. A remarkable survivor was STEELE RUDD's Dramatic Company in Toowoomba, which presented the world premieres of Rudd's *Duncan McClure* in 1915 and his *On Grubb's Selection* in 1924. A Repertory Theatre Society, initially modelled on the BRISBANE REPERTORY THEATRE SOCIETY, was formed in Toowoomba in 1930.

Difficulties of touring

The major obstacles to professional drama in provincial Queensland were difficult transport and lack of suitable performance spaces. In the 1860s Beenleigh, Ipswich, Sandgate and other nearby towns rivalled Brisbane in importance, and travel from one to another by coach was feasible for small groups. Companies also travelled by ship up the coast to Cooktown, Maryborough, Normanton, Rockhampton, Townsville and other ports, from which they ventured inland to mining towns such as Charters Towers, Croydon, Gympie and Mount Morgan and to the Palmer River goldfields. They took with them only the actors' costumes and essential props. In *A Millionaire in Memories* Frank Gerald chronicled the adventures of the Gerald and Duff Company in miners' tent cities in the 1880s: 'There was no hall, but they would build one. In two days it was there. A wooden framework, roofed with sheets of corrugated iron, a raised platform at one end, a door at the other, two tents for dressing rooms, kerosene lamps inside, candles for footlights. Tree stumps, packing-cases and planks for seats … We played four nights a week for six weeks.'

Misadventures were common, on and off stage. In 1892 all but two of the 16 performers of Harris's Circus deserted when the troupe left the coast, and while playing in Barcaldine the troupe's tent collapsed onto the audience when a 'waltzing' horse broke the mainstay. The band—the two had not deserted plus members of the local Oddfellows lodge—struck up 'Summer flowers' to calm the trapped spectators while repairs were made.

Travelling by train

Railways made it possible for organisations to tour with large sets and equipment. From 1888, when the Brisbane–Sydney line was completed, southern companies travelling to or from Brisbane often played in Ipswich, Stanthorpe, Toowoomba and Warwick on the way. The Townsville–Hughenden line opened in 1887, Brisbane–Charleville in 1888 and Rockhampton–Longreach in 1892. The northern line from Brisbane to Cairns was not completed until 1924, however, and companies had to continue travelling by sea between ports. WIRTHS' CIRCUS and Cole's Players both hired special trains. Lytton's Moving Theatre was involved in a fatal accident west of Toowoomba in July 1909. A wagon laden with 15–16 tonnes of theatrical equipment was blamed for the derailment. The company erected its tent beside the line and tended the injured passengers, and the actresses were 'eulogised for their good work'.

The availability of theatres and halls was a particular problem because most companies followed the show circuit. After long periods of inactivity a town would have several companies arriving at the same time for the annual show and the accompanying horse races. PHILIP LYTTON claimed to have pioneered touring TENT THEATRE in Australia in 1907 as a solution. He preferred Queensland and NSW because of favourable climate. Even so, the life of a tent was only eight months, and Lytton kept a spare in Rockhampton. His tents were oblong and could have extra central sections added to give a seating capacity varying from 750 to 2000, though some reviews claim 3000. Lytton's idea was widely imitated. In 1927 the Rockhampton Show attracted GEORGE SORLIE's Musical and Dramatic Company, Jack Macdonald's World's Wonder Show and Newton Carroll's Dramatic Company—all performing under canvas. In 1929 Cole's Players performed *The Unwanted Child* and *Spooks* in their 'huge waterproof marquee' in Barcaldine. In 1935 Sorlie's, the Cameos Musical Revue Company, Val Mack's, and Barton's Follies were all on the show circuit. For many years this jostle of tent shows was known in one town as the annual 'Battle of Bundaberg'. Tales of sabotage were rife but have not been substantiated.

For the amateurs and smaller professional groups Oddfellows' and Foresters' lodge halls, schools of arts, and other halls were constructed throughout the second half of the 19th century, followed by more substantial purpose-built theatres and town halls in the 1880s and 1890s. Longreach Public Hall advertised in 1892—the year the railway arrived—that 'the building has lately been supplied with Scenery, and being well lighted, and having a roomy stage, offers every facility to theatrical companies visiting the Western districts'. Even so, few actors regularly ventured west. A major exception was MAGGIE MOORE. She played *Struck Oil* in Richmond during the 1891 shearers' strike, returned to rural Queensland with her second husband Harry Roberts in 1904—and doubtless many other times— and in 1910 was still touring 'the play that will never die'. Another husband-and-wife team was W. J. Coulter and Ada Clare, who were in Robert Henry's Company doing *Charley's Aunt* by Brandon Thomas in 1901. Their own Coulter Dramatic Company toured the western districts early in 1910, and they were back in Edwin Geach's troupe later the same year, performing *East Lynne*, *Little Lord Fauntleroy* and Bret Harte's *The Luck of Roaring Camp*. The actresses' hats were 'lovely dreams of the millinery art', said the *Western Champion* on 3 September.

The major coastal cities fared better. They saw theatre regularly from the mid-1880s, when James MacMahon began promoting tours by major artists such as GEORGE LEITCH. The craze for Ned Kelly plays began in Queensland at Charters Towers on 6 May 1899 with W. J. HOLLOWAY and WILLIAM ANDERSON's production of J. H. Greene's version of *The Kelly Gang*. Anderson restaged it in a tent in 1909 for another Queensland tour. The 1920s saw J. C. WILLIAMSON's touring plays and musicals as far north as Rockhampton, and ALLAN WILKIE gave an annual Shakespeare Week.

The Great Depression ended nearly all tours of legitimate drama, but in Townsville and other cities annual pantomimes were performed on cinema stages by professional leads and local children until television arrived. Variety shows kept rolling through each year at least until 1961, when Sorlie's, run by BOBBY LE BRUN, came off the road. This kind of entertainment moved into pubs and clubs and Le Brun subsequently spent five and a half years at the Hotel Coolangatta. The coming of casinos and poker machines in the 1990s has given variety theatre a major boost, and spectacular commercial shows have been imported from the USA, like *Hollywood Legends* at Jupiter's Casino on the Gold Coast in 1989.

Amateur groups flourish

After the Second World War the void in provincial theatre was quickly filled by the little theatre movement. Probably more than 100 amateur groups were founded in towns including Buderim in 1958, Cairns in 1954, Gatton in 1951, Ipswich in 1946, Mackay in 1947, Maryborough in 1949 (two groups combined), Mount Morgan in 1962, Rockhampton in 1945, Wynnum in 1949 and Yeppoon in 1969. Annual one-act drama festivals were established at Barcaldine in 1965, Cairns in 1957, Gatton in 1959, Goondiwindi in 1961 and Ipswich in 1955.

Most groups attempted to promote local writers and to produce occasional Australian plays, but the bulk of their repertoire was English society drama and comedy. Some transcended their limitations. Rockhampton gave premieres of several of EUNICE HANGER's plays, and Buderim was one of the first to present Alan Seymour's revised version of *THE ONE DAY OF THE YEAR* in 1983. Ipswich Little Theatre gained a remarkable theatre in 1969 when members converted the old city incinerator, designed by Walter Burley Griffin, into an intimate performing space.

Subsidised touring professional theatre began in the mid-1960s largely through the efforts of the Queensland Arts Council and the AUSTRALIAN ELIZABETHAN THEATRE TRUST. The high costs of touring have always tended to favour one-actor and one-set productions. In 1965 PETER O'SHAUGHNESSY starred in his own dramatisation of Nikolai Gogol's *Diary of a Madman*. The Young Elizabethan Players toured in 1967–70 and were subsequently incorporated into the QUEENSLAND THEATRE COMPANY as its plays-for-schools group. The Arts Council has also sponsored tours by the Queensland Theatre Company of some of its main-house Brisbane offerings each year from 1970, as well as productions by the TWELFTH NIGHT THEATRE COMPANY and other Brisbane groups. Other notable tours were the ROYAL SHAKESPEARE COMPANY's *The Hollow Crown* in 1976 and John Derum's *More Than a Sentimental Bloke* in 1980.

Professional community-theatre companies have made occasional forays to isolated communities. The POPULAR THEATRE TROUPE was the pioneer, visiting central and north Queensland mining towns in 1975–77. Recent examples of this kind of work have been the remarkable *The Logan City Story*, devised by the STREET ARTS THEATRE COMPANY in association with schools and community groups and performed in a shopping centre at Logan City in 1984, and DEATH DEFYING THEATRE's *Coal Town* in Collinsville in 1986.

Civic theatres and halls

Some provincial city councils have responded to renewed interest in theatre by building large civic theatres with assistance from the state government, including: Cairns (669 seats, 1974), Charleville (600 seats, 1988), Cunnamulla (800 seats, 1981), Gold Coast (1200 seats, 1986), Gladstone (700 seats, 1981), Mackay (1090 seats, 1988), Mount Isa (1006 seats, 1974), Rockhampton (about 900 seats, 1979) and Townsville (1066 seats, 1978). Toowoomba rebuilt its 486-seat Town Hall Theatre in 1973. Other communities have built multipurpose halls with flat floors and raised end stages, such as Longreach in 1961 and Roma in 1986. Logan City has a small 206-seat 'Butter Box' in its Kingston Butter Factory Community Arts Centre (1988).

Most of the shows presented at the larger venues have been touring productions by commercial organisations or the Arts Council. In Toowoomba a semiprofessional company has evolved from the actor-training course at the University of Southern Queensland, using the university's own theatre, which was completed in 1977.

Townsville, which already had a small professional, not purely commercial theatre-restaurant, the Stage Door, from the late 1960s, took a major step in 1982 when its city council established the fully professional NEW MOON THEATRE COMPANY. With assistance from the councils in Cairns, Mackay and Rockhampton, this company presented seasons of plays in each of the four cities every year. Under Terry O'Connell, artistic director in 1982–83, and his successors, the primary emphasis was on rock-music theatre for young audiences. DIANE CILENTO, now resident in North Queensland, acted in several New Moon productions, and in 1992 opened her own 300-seat playhouse near Port Douglas. ♣*Richard Fotheringham*

Rockhampton Little Theatre

In Rockhampton the Pilbeam Theatre presents a high proportion of touring professional shows. Rockhampton Little Theatre receives a smaller share of local spending on theatre, and in recent years this amateur group has concentrated upon smaller, more intimate seasons in its clubrooms, built in 1964 by the city council. Rockhampton Little Theatre staged its first production, *Full House* by Ivor Novello, in the School of Arts Theatre—then the only live theatre in the town—in October 1945. Over the years the group has presented plays in Biloela, Emerald, Mackay and Toowoomba. The Twelfth Night Theatre Company invited Graham Macdonald to present the Little Theatre's production of Mary Haley Bell's *Duet for Two Hands* in Brisbane in place of a scheduled production in April 1950. In 1961 Rockhampton Little Theatre was host to the first Central Drama Festival, which by the mid-1960s was recognised as the most important in Queensland. ♣*Tom Bencke*

further reading
GERALD, FRANK. *A Millionaire in Memories*. London: Routledge 1936.
GIBSON-WILDE, DOROTHY. *Gateway to a Golden Land—Townsville to 1884*. Townsville: James Cook University 1984.
GOULD, NAT. *Town and Bush* 1896. Melbourne Penguin 1974.
HARSLETT, JEAN and MERVYN ROYLE. *They Came to a Plateau—The Stanthorpe saga*. Stanthorpe: Girraween 1972.
LYTTON, PHILIP. The drama under canvas. *Theatre* (Sydney) 1 December 1915.
McDONALD, LORNA. *Rockhampton*. Brisbane: University of Queensland Press 1981.
Gladstone. Gladstone: Boolarong 1988.

Queensland Theatre Company

Professional dramatic company in Brisbane. Established by statute on 8 April 1970 as Queensland Theatre Company. Styled Royal Queensland Theatre Company 1984–93. **venues** 1970–93 SGIO Theatre. 1993– Queensland Performing Arts Centre. **artistic directors** 1969–88 Alan Edwards. 1988–93 Aubrey Mellor. 1993– Chris Johnston. **first production** *The Royal Hunt of the Sun* by Peter Shaffer, directed by Bryan Nason, 1 October 1969 at SGIO Theatre.

For much of the first 20 years of its life the Queensland Theatre Company promoted itself as a training and touring company. For the next five years it emphasised the importation of actors and directors from other states, the lifting of its own national profile and the development of Queensland playwrights. The company's origin lay in a decision by the Queensland government on 11 February 1969 to appoint a board to establish it. The government supervened when no agreement could be reached to develop an amateur group as the state company after the Australian Council for the Arts decided to fund a company in each state. The company, granted statutory recognition in 1970, was the first federally funded professional theatre in Queensland. It took up residence in the government's new 611-seat SGIO Theatre—renamed the Suncorp Theatre in 1986—near the central business district of Brisbane. The founding artistic director was ALAN EDWARDS, an English actor. His regular performances were a feature of the company while he was artistic director. The first production he directed for it was the musical *A Rum Do!* It opened on 10 April 1970 and three days later Queen Elizabeth II, the Duke of Edinburgh and Princess Anne attended the second act. The next production—Brian Friel's *Philadelphia, Here I Come*—became the centre of public debate over blasphemy and bookings were cancelled. As the company strove to build a regular audience over the next few years it suffered similar public attacks when the language or content of works offended certain conservative tastes.

There was also antagonism for some years because of a feeling that the company—and Edwards—had been imposed upon Brisbane at a time when AMATEUR THEATRE was particularly thriving. Few local actors were employed at the start but Edwards gave young, mainly Queensland actors opportunities to develop in a resident company. BILLE BROWN, Carol Burns, FRANK GALLACHER, Peter Kowitz, GEOFFREY RUSH, GERALDINE TURNER and Shane Withington are some actors who have achieved wider prominence after working with the company during its first decade. Joe MacColum, appointed speech and drama coach in 1971, was associate director from 1973 to 1978. Cliff Simcox designed 23 of the company's first 26 productions.

According to the company history, *Oh What a Lovely War!* was the first big hit and *Juno and the Paycock* by Sean O'Casey in 1978 was the first 'serious' play to draw big box office. For the first five years the company, sensing popular demand, began each season with a musical. In its first 25 year seven of its best-attended productions were musicals. *Godspell* in 1974 remained its greatest box-office success. As the company settled into the community the audience grew. In 1975 *The Taming of the Shrew*, starring DIANE CILENTO, played to full houses, and Peter Shaffer's *Equus* enjoyed a return season and tour of rural NSW. Oscar Wilde's *The Importance of Being Earnest*, David Williamson's THE REMOVALISTS and Dale Wasserman's *One Flew Over the Cuckoo's Nest* were critical and popular successes.

Touring for young audiences

In its first 12 years the Queensland Theatre Company toured more widely than any other state company. Until 1981, when tours were curtailed because of funding cuts and increased costs, it toured one to three productions annually throughout Queensland and regularly to rural NSW. It also toured four theatre-in-education programs over prodigious distances in Queensland each year. The company set up training opportunities for young people through its Theatre Experience Week, Theatre Techniques Week and Queensland Youth Theatre. Special activities for young people peaked in 1977 with Project Spearhead, which emphasised workshops rather than performances, and Darling Downs Youth Theatre, a performance event for young people from country towns. The theatre-in-education team, called Roadwork since 1981, was renamed BROLGAS in 1988 and a policy of touring plays for young people by established playwrights was introduced.

In 1978 the English actor WARREN MITCHELL played the title-role in the company's production of *King Lear*. Many considered this casting an enormous gamble, but it won the company great acclaim in Brisbane and Sydney. In the same year the company produced its first mainhouse play by a Queensland resident, Beverley Mahoney's *Flight Path*. It had won a Queensland playwrights' competition sponsored by the company in 1977. By 1985 the inclusion of three Australian plays in a total of nine mainhouse shows was no longer matter for comment.

At the end of the company's first ten years, artistic and financial pressures caused changes, notably from a policy of maintaining a resident company of actors to one of hiring according to need. Economising saw production budgets reduced, salaries reviewed and staff dismissed. Demand for tickets continued to rise, however. Subscriptions introduced in 1973, built up rapidly in the early 1980s as audiences rushed to shows such as the musical *Annie*, Anton Chekhov's *The Seagull*, David Pownall's adaptation of Jane Austen's *Pride and Prejudice*, and David Williamson's *Sons of Cain*. In 1981 the company played to an average audience of more than 96 per cent and in 1983 subscriptions peaked at 8708.

Innovations included Shakespeare in Albert Park. The first production, *A Midsummer Night's Dream* in 1983, involved the Queensland Ballet, the Australian Youth Ballet Company, the Queensland Opera Company and a recording of Felix Mendelssohn's incidental music by the Queensland Theatre Orchestra. In 1984 *The Tempest* broke box-office records for the Queensland Theatre Company by playing to nearly 19 000 people. Shakespeare in the Park drew larger audiences than any regular production over the next few years. These outdoor productions ended in 1988, after changes to the Albert Park site.

Royal charter

Responding to criticism of conservatism, the Queensland Theatre Company formed QTC Tangent Productions in 1981 to mount new, more experimental or predictably less popular work in a converted downtown office building. In 1985 the company opened the new Cremorne Theatre in the QUEENSLAND PERFORMING ARTS COMPLEX with *Cheapside* by DAVID ALLEN. In preparation for this event, and perhaps as an insurance of permanence in an uncertain climate of political patronage, the company sought and received a royal charter, the only one in Australia's theatrical history. But the mood changed and the company reverted to its original public title when its administration moved to the Queensland Performing Arts Complex in 1993.

After the mid-1980s, subscriptions began to fall. The introduction of ceiling funding by the theatre board of the AUSTRALIA COUNCIL in 1986 curtailed current and planned activities. The company suffered a decrease in income in 1988 because it staged fewer productions in the face of competition from World Expo '88 in Brisbane. Competition also came from commercial producers, who were increasingly attracted to the arts centre.

Alan Edwards retired in 1988 and Brisbane-born AUBREY MELLOR was appointed artistic director. Anne McNeill was appointed to the new position of general manager. In an attempt to enhance its national reputation, the company adopted a policy of bringing the best actors and the finest directors in Australia to work together. In addition it decided that at least half the works in each season would be Australian. The annual production of a play by a Queensland writer and the introduction of the George Landen Dann Award promoted the state's dramatists. Interstate touring and exchanges of productions with companies in other states culminated in national tour of two new plays by DAVID WILLIAMSON, *Money and Friends* (1992) and *Brilliant Lies* (1993), both directed by Mellor. In 1993, Mellor's last year as artistic director, *Brilliant Lies*, the musical *High Society* and *Romeo and Juliet* achieved attendances among the company's ten best. ❦*Greg McCart*

further reading
HEDGE, DOUGLAS. *The Company We Keep—The first ten years of the Queensland Theatre Company*. Brisbane: Ken Kennett 1979.

Robert Quentin

Administrator, director, educator. Born 3 August 1917 in England. Educated at Oxford University. Visited Sydney during wartime naval service and directed for Independent Theatre. Returned to Sydney upon discharge. Stage director for J. C. Williamson's 1946–47. Stage director for Old Vic Theatre Company in Bristol 1947–49 and London 1950–51. Producer and manager of London Old Vic company 1952–53. Settled in Sydney 1955. General manager of Australian Elizabethan Trust Opera Company 1955–59. Married actor June Collis 1956. Founding director of National Institute of Dramatic Art 1958–63. Associate professor of drama at University of NSW 1959. Founding director of Old Tote Theatre Company 1962–65. Founding head of department of drama at University of NSW 1964. Director of drama for Elizabethan Trust 1964–65; later adviser. Established Jane Street Theatre 1966. Member of UNESCO committee on theatre and drama. Co-founder of Australian branch of International Theatre Institute. Retired 1977. Died 7 July 1979 at Robertson (NSW).

Robert Quentin greatly influenced Australian theatre after the Second World War and the direction taken by subsidised theatre, particularly in Sydney. He was highly influential in setting up structures at the University of NSW that supported the first state theatre company, although he had no concept of an indigenous theatrical culture.

He first came to Sydney during the war, in the intelligence division of the Royal Navy, and worked occasionally in amateur theatre. While on leave in 1945 he directed a notable production of Eugene O'Neill's *Mourning Becomes Electra* for INDEPENDENT THEATRE, starring Doris Fitton. He returned to Sydney upon discharge and worked for J. C. WILLIAMSON'S before going to the Bristol Old Vic. This was directed by HUGH HUNT, who became executive director of the AUSTRALIAN ELIZABETHAN THEATRE TRUST and in 1955 appointed Quentin to manage the Trust's opera company. While he held this post Quentin persuaded the new University of NSW that Australia needed a performing-arts academy, and he was appointed to establish the NATIONAL INSTITUTE OF DRAMATIC ART on the campus. He was also invited to establish an academic drama discipline and appointed associate professor of drama, attached to the English department. He later established his own department—the first of its kind in Australia—which is now the School of Theatre and Film Studies.

To give his NIDA graduates a platform, Quentin began employing actors for productions in a small theatre on the campus. This led to the formation of the OLD TOTE THEATRE COMPANY. Quentin opened the Old Tote Theatre in February 1963 with a notable production of Anton Chekhov's *The Cherry Orchard*, with a cast including Sophie Stewart as Madame Ranevsky and the young JOHN BELL as Trofimov. At the downtown PALACE THEATRE Quentin began lunchtime theatre in Sydney, three months before Q THEATRE was founded for that purpose. He made various attempts to establish companies to tour NSW. In 1966 he achieved a Gulbenkian Foundation grant to convert a small church hall in Randwick into the JANE STREET THEATRE for experimental use. In 1967–68 he lobbied successfully for the Old Tote company to be selected by the Australian Council for the Arts as its NSW state theatre company. He remained active in its administration until the mid-1970s.

As a director Quentin was admired chiefly for Chekhov productions, the major one being *Three Sisters* in 1966. His last production was Alan Ayckbourn's *The Norman Conquests* for Old Tote at Christmas 1977. This was his attempt to rescue the finances of the company, but the problems were too great and it went into liquidation in the next year. Those close to Quentin believed that his sudden death from a heart attack in 1979 was not unrelated to the demise of the company he had founded. ❦*Katharine Brisbane*

further reading

SOUTH, JOSEPHINE (ed.). *Ten on the Tote—An illustrated history of the Old Tote Theatre Company to celebrate its tenth anniversary, 1963–1973*. Sydney: Old Tote Theatre Company 1973.
Who's Who in Australia, 1971.

Robert Radford

Entrepreneur. Born c.1817 in Devonshire (England). Arrived at Adelaide 1841. Presented circus in Launceston (Tas.) 1847–50 and Hobart 1848. Left Launceston for Adelaide on *Queenstown* 29 August 1850. Died 30 March 1865 near Kapunda (SA).

Nearly every notable Australian circus can trace its origins to the enterprise of Robert Radford, who opened the first circus in the colonies on 27 December 1847 in Launceston. An expert horseman, Radford described himself as a veterinary surgeon who had worked in the principal studs of England and France. He moved to Launceston within a year or two of his arrival in Adelaide in 1841 and ran a racetrack and a livery stable. In September 1845 he applied for a licence for the Horse and Jockey Inn in York Street.

Launceston had numerous public houses and regular race meetings but saw only intermittent and usually unsuccessful theatrical entertainment in the 1840s. The town had about 7500 people, including a significant proportion of ex-convicts and a transient military population. Radford must have realised that theatrical entertainment based on equestrianism could appeal to both the horse-loving common people and the more 'respectable'. In 1847 he received the Colonial Secretary's permission to build 'Astley's Amphitheatre on a limited scale', and began building the Royal Circus adjacent his inn. It was erected in a few weeks so it was probably a simple structure of canvas and timber palings spread over a timber frame. It appears to have had a circus ring in front of a stage, in the style of Astley's in London, and seating divided into pit, gallery and boxes.

Radford recruited a little company of equestrians, acrobats, actors and singers and began two years of entertaining audiences up to three evenings a week with items from the repertoires of British circus, popular theatre and music hall. He moved his company overland to Hobart after attempted arson at the Royal Circus in March 1848. He opened an arena behind the Bath Arms, a public house in Murray Street, on 24 May 1848. The building was known as the Amphitheatre until its demolition in February 1859.

The horseman JAMES HENRY ASHTON made his colonial debut for Radford in Hobart on 7 December 1848. After that month Radford based his company in Launceston. By then most of its early circus performers had departed. Some fresh circus talent was engaged to replace them, but more and more of the company were actors. During 1849 Radford presented *Mazeppa*, *The Battle of Austerlitz* and many other hippodramas long popular with the audiences of London amphitheatres. A local melodramatic spectacle, *Trial by Battle* by W. Barrymore, was adapted for representation under the direction of J. H. S. LEE, who became manager of the Royal Amphitheatre in 1849.

A dedicated corps of actors, equestrians and singers, an attractive and diverse program and occasional reductions in prices could not save the Royal Amphitheatre, however. Neither could special attractions in the ring, ranging from a grand balloon ascent to an exhibition by a celebrated pugilist who was about to seek the championship of England. The company gave its presumed last performance on 29 January 1850. Radford, his resources at an end and in debt, was unable to resurrect either his theatrical or racecourse enterprises. He left Launceston, intending to start afresh in Adelaide. There he may have been instrumental in the opening of E. H. Taylor's Circus Royal in Currie Street in October 1850, as several members of the company had been in his Tasmanian troupe. ❦*Mark St Leon*

further reading

SAXON, A. H. *The Life and Art of Andrew Ducrow and the Romantic Age of English Circus*. Hamden (Connecticut, USA): Archon Books 1978.
SPEAIGHT, GEORGE. *A History of the Circus*. London: Tantivy Press 1980.
ST LEON, MARK. Robert Avis Radford—The Tasmanian Astley. *Australian Drama Studies* 24 (Brisbane, April 1994).

Leonard Radic

Critic, dramatist. Born 6 March 1935 in Melbourne. Educated at University of Melbourne. Journalist on Melbourne *Age*; deputy theatre critic 1968–74; theatre critic 1974–94. Australia Council literature board fellowship 1974. Married dramatist and musicologist Thérèse Radic 1957. Father of Stephen Radic, writer and film-maker. As critic has travelled at invitation of governments of Canada, China, Hong Kong, Japan, New Zealand, Singapore, United Kingdom, USA and Yugoslavia.

As reviewer and commentator Leonard Radic can be relied on to be constructive and to set his work in the context of long experience. A journalist with a broad theatrical background, he was one of the earliest newspaper writers to seek out and recognise the developments in Melbourne in the 1960s, and his loyalty to the concept of indigenous drama has been unswerving. In 1991 he published *State of Play*, a history of the drama he had documented over 30 years. In the process his own career as a playwright has suffered from the ambivalent relationship between the theatrical profession and the critic.

Radic's involvement with theatre began at Puckapunyal army camp in Victoria in 1954, when he was coauthor of a 'futuristic' opera presented by the 15th National Service Training Battalion. The sets and costumes were by BARRY HUMPHRIES and the cast included ALAN HOPGOOD and the composer Colin Brumby. His plays are mostly predicated

on the gap between belief and reality, and his style varies from the realistic to the absurd. He often uses the device of presenting the abstract as concrete, as in the short *Ground Rules*, in which a middle-aged man is building a brick monument to his life. In *Cody Versus Cody* a judge and his wife examine their marriage in the manner of a court case. Radic's most substantial play is probably *Sideshow*, an iconoclastic documentary that looks at the political and personal responsibilities of those involved in the Gallipoli campaign and intersperses the action with diggers' songs.
❦*Katharine Brisbane*

published plays
Clean Sweep (1979). Melbourne: Yackandandah 1984.
Cody Versus Cody (1975). Brisbane: Playlab Press 1980.
The General (1965). Melbourne: Yackandandah 1974.
Ground Rules (1979). Melbourne: Yackandandah 1984.
The Particular (1965). Melbourne: Yackandandah 1974.
Sideshow (1971). Melbourne: Yackandandah 1987.
Some of My Best Friends are Women with Thérèse Radic (1976). Melbourne: Yackandandah 1983

other writings
'Call the shots as you see them and stay till the end'. *Age* (Melbourne) 5 November 1994.
State of Play—The revolution in the Australian theatre since the 1960s. Melbourne: Penguin 1991.

Thérèse Radic

Dramatist. Born 7 September 1935 in Melbourne. Originally Maureen Thérèse O'Halloran. Studied music at University of Melbourne. Married critic and dramatist Leonard Radic 1957. Work as musicologist includes several biographies of musicians.

Thérèse Radic's provocative plays mostly deal with relationships between women and power. In *Madame Mao*, for example, the power conferred on Jiang Qing by marriage is seen in relation to the revolution itself. Radic's style is non-naturalistic, visual and highly theatrical. *Madame Mao* explores personal and political status via Chinese acrobatics; it was coproduced by CIRCUS OZ and the PLAYBOX THEATRE CENTRE, with which she has a strong relationship. *Madame Mao* was also presented by the Liverpool Playhouse in England in 1980, with Tsai Chin in the title-role. Radic's other most frequently performed play, *Peach Melba*, explores personality, with two Nellie Melbas questioning each other's motives. ❦*Geoffrey Milne*

published plays
The Emperor Regrets (1992). Sydney: Currency Press 1992.
Madame Mao (1986). Sydney: Currency Press 1986.
Peach Melba (1990). Sydney: Currency Press 1989.
Some of My Best Friends are Women, with Leonard Radic (1976). Melbourne: Yackandandah 1983.
A Whip Round for Percy Grainger (1982). Melbourne: Yackandandah 1984.

other writings
Extracts from a half-breed's diary. *Sweet Mothers, Sweet Maidens—Journeys from Catholic childhoods* (ed. K. Nelson and D. Nelson). Melbourne: Penguin 1986. Autobiographical.
Still life with mirrors. *The Half Open Door* (ed. P. Grimshaw and L. Strachan). Sydney: Hale and Iremonger 1982. Autobiographical.

further reading
HOLT, FIONA AND MAURICE RINALDI. *Australian Women*. Melbourne: Macmillan 1985.
JEFFREYS, ELAINE. Jiang Qing—Under western eyes. University of Adelaide honours thesis 1991.

Radio and theatre

The first radio station in Australia, 2BL Sydney, opened in November 1923. The second, 2FC Sydney, opened in January 1924 with a broadcast from Her Majesty's Theatre of the entire performance of the musical comedy *A Southern Maid* with GLADYS MONCRIEFF. Probably the first play of any consequence written for radio was one that won a competition in 1928 for John Pickard, a student and actor in the SYDNEY UNIVERSITY DRAMATIC SOCIETY. He was later the leading radio actor in Australia until he went to the USA in 1936.

No actor was skilled in radio method in the 1920s so the whole cast of an amateur presentation might be invited to a studio to speak their lines into a microphone exactly as on stage. This was a novelty, but by later standards the performance was stilted and too long for listeners. One actor of the old school actually insisted on wearing flowing period costume to the studio and pacing at varying distances from the microphone as he declaimed. But more flexible actors soon mastered the intimacy of the microphone, the art of addressing the audience as individuals in separate homes.

Non-advertising 'A-class' stations dispensed mixed programs supplied by the Australian Broadcasting Company, a private consortium formed by FULLERS', the cinema chain Greater Union Theatres and the music publisher J. Albert and Sons. In 1932 the federal government metamorphosed this service into the Australian Broadcasting Commission, which was charged with the responsibility of taking all means 'conducive to the full development of suitable broadcasting programs', including drama. ABC production units operated autonomously in the states, mostly presenting stage plays. In 1933 the ABC engaged LAWRENCE H. CECIL, an experienced stage actor and director, as head of drama production and Edmund Barclay as a writer. They collaborated on many plays and serials.

In 1936 the ABC adopted a federal policy, co-ordinating drama programs in Sydney for the whole commonwealth and widening the choice from the world's drama. It tried to nourish a type of play that explored the radio medium and it invited Australians to write it. FRANK D. CLEWLOW, who had been the ABC's producer in Melbourne, became federal controller of productions. The present writer, back from six years as a drama critic in London, was appointed federal play editor, to handle scripts and programming. He had seen nearly 1000 plays, many of which appeared suitable to broadcast, and he was keen to develop indigenous talent. The commission's chairman, W. J. Cleary, expressed the hope that some of Australia's more serious authors—who had until then doubted or scorned the new medium—would be encouraged to write original plays for radio.

The ABC began stimulating writers by buying the radio rights to the few published stage plays of such approved authors as LOUIS ESSON, VANCE PALMER and SYDNEY TOMHOLT. MAX AFFORD, who had won an ABC competition and the South Australian centenary stage-play competition, was engaged as a staff playwright. At that time he specialised in thriller plays and serials. The other staff writer, Barclay worked on *As Ye Sow*, a serial that dramatised the spread of Australian history for the first time in any medium. Following one family's involvement in actual events through six generations from 1788, the serial ran for nine months and won a nationwide following.

Scripts flowed in from freelance writers. The fees were not lavish, though perhaps superior to any that the theatre offered local playwrights. Writers were offered the maximum practical freedom in duration, subject matter and prose or verse style. Advice was given on building promising scripts and friendly criticism accompanied rejections. Experiment was given its head in a special weekly program. There was a play every night in an Australian drama week. A new contest attracted numerous entries. George Farwell won it with *Portrait of a Gentleman*, concerning T. G. Wainewright, forger and supposed murderer. 'M. Barnard Eldershaw' (the pseudonym of two historians) took second prize with *Watch on the Headland*, about an episode in early Sydney. In these ways radio drama was energised and enlivened as entertainment and art.

Prolific writers included Shan Benson, CATHERINE DUNCAN, Maxwell Dunn, SUMNER LOCKE ELLIOTT, Richard Lane, Coral Lansbury, Eugene Lumbers, GWEN MEREDITH, D'Arcy Niland, Ruth Park, Charles Porter, Rex Rienits, BETTY ROLAND, CATHERINE SHEPHERD, ALEXANDER TURNER, BARBARA VERNON and ELEANOR WITCOMBE. Some had already tried their hand at a stage play. Other writers contributed an occasional radio play over the years, including Jessica Anderson, Jon Cleary, DYMPHNA CUSACK, GEORGE LANDEN DANN, Mary Durack, ORIEL GRAY, DOROTHY HEWETT, Ernestine Hill, PETER KENNA, Seaforth Mackenzie, HAL PORTER, DOUGLAS STEWART and Colin Thiele. Stewart's *The Fire on the Snow* soon became famous and was repeated several times. It gave recognition to the play written specifically for radio, and stimulated poetic drama. The ABC held a competition for plays in verse. It was won by Stewart with *The Golden Lover* and it yielded works of value by CATHERINE DUNCAN and T. Inglis Moore.

Classics of the stage

Some authors also sold their radio plays overseas. Australian recorded productions of other plays were accepted in English-speaking countries. At the same time the value for radio listeners of stage drama from other countries and ages was explored. Works that relied on the magic of words rather than on physical action were adapted by Joy Hollyer, Richard Lane, David Nettheim and others who were skilled at reducing a play to 90, 75 or 60 minutes without damaging essential theme, motive, conflict or characterisation. Listeners in town and country from time to time had the rare experience of hearing such classics as *Oedipus Rex* and *Alcestis* from ancient Greece, the medieval morality play *Everyman*, the entire canon of Shakespeare, the comedies of Molière, Christopher Marlowe's *Doctor Faustus*, John Dryden's *All for Love*, Percy Bysshe Shelley's *The Cenci*, R. B. Sheridan's *The School for Scandal* and the dramas of Henrik Ibsen.

From a later repertoire were drawn John Galsworthy's *Strife*, J. M. Synge's *The Playboy of the Western World*, the engaging whimsies of J. M. Barrie, and six works in a George Bernard Shaw festival. A weekly program often presented adaptations of Australian or foreign contemporary comedies and dramas.

ABC producers in earlier days largely came from the professional theatre. Chances there were thin and professionals happily accepted opportunities for radio work. Lawrence H. Cecil had had American stage experience. John Cairns in Melbourne had performed with ALLAN WILKIE. Others emerged from amateur ranks, including Paul O'Loughlin in Melbourne and ALEXANDER TURNER in Perth. Most national broadcasts came from Sydney or Melbourne, where the pools of freelance actors were larger, but all other capitals contributed. Radio acting reached a high level of expertise, judged by the standards of other countries. Among those who achieved star quality and reputation during radio drama's golden period were Queenie Ashton, LYNDALL BARBOUR, Robert Burnard, John Bushelle, JAMES CONDON, Alastair Duncan, Catherine Duncan, BEVERLEY DUNN, PETER FINCH, NEVA CARR GLYN, ANNE HADDY, PATRICIA KENNEDY, LLOYD LAMBLE, Nigel Lovell, FREDERICK PARSLOW and THELMA SCOTT.

Drama in hundreds of episodes

A major success among the ABC's many serials was *Blue Hills*, GWEN MEREDITH's perennial documentation of the humours of country life. It ran, following the related story of *The Lawsons*, until 1976 in 5795 12-minute episodes, basically from Meredith's hand alone. She was judged to have written 14·5 million words—the equivalent of 250 novels. Serials were also a major attraction on the commercial stations. Max Afford, Lynn Foster, Maurice Francis and other hard-working writers ingeniously sustained adventures or domestic entanglements for years, building hundreds of episodes around a few central characters. Regular appearances of homely characters sustained perennials such as *Fred and Maggie Everybody* from 1936, *Dad and Dave* from 1937 and *Mrs 'Obbs* from 1940.

When national commercial networks were expanding, commercial stations took up the challenge of producing individual plays, some years after the ABC. A wartime shortage of newsprint boosted radio advertising, which supported dramatic presentations on an American model, such as the Sunday-night *Lux Radio Theatre*. The content was mostly lighter theatre plays or Hollywood film scripts reduced to essentials in 49 minutes and the production style was new to Australia. The ABC announced and introduced a play in a few words within a closed studio and let the story speak for itself either in a live broadcast or, later, in a recording on disc or tape. The producer of *Lux Radio Theatre*, Harry Dearth, invited an audience of a few hundred to a theatrette, usually in Sydney, to see the actors in evening dress address microphones on a stage, while he directed them. Audiences appreciated this personality show. The precisely timed hour, advertisements and all, was broadcast live and recorded for future use.

Other sponsors backed similar shows in succession—*Macquarie Theatre*, *Caltex Theatre* and *General Motors Hour*. Annual Macquarie Awards for the best acting performances in *Macquarie Theatre* productions were presented before an audience with show-business glitter. There was such enthusiasm for plays on air during the 1940s that about half the population of Australia was estimated to listen on Sunday nights, choosing from one ABC and two commercial productions. Popular actors had to reconcile radio and stage work. A character played by an actor who took a full-time stage engagement might have to be 'written out' of a serial; so too through holiday, accident or even death.

As soon as television began in 1956, radio drama started to weaken. All commercial programs were soon at an end.

The ABC staunchly continued to encourage radio playwrights and to present theatre plays from all over the world, produced by John Croyston, Henry Cuthbertson, Stafford Dyson, Neil Hutchison, Eric John, Ray Menmuir, Frank Zeppel, the present writer and others. Eventually drama had fewer spots in programs and less funding, but the medium was used by such esteemed writers as Jessica Anderson, ALEX BUZO, Elizabeth Jolley, COLIN FREE, LOUIS NOWRA, BARRY OAKLEY, RALPH PETERSON, Noel Robinson, STEPHEN SEWELL and Thomas Shapcott.

Over all, the theatre provided many and diverse helping hands for radio but radio plays have not often directly fed the theatre. Max Afford built one of his radio thrillers into the stage play *Dark Enchantment*, which was presented at the Minerva Theatre in Sydney in 1945 and taken on a long tour in England. Sumner Locke Elliott wrote a satire on the making of commercial radio serials, *Invisible Circus* (1946). Douglas Stewart's *The Fire on the Snow* was thrice adapted to the stage in Sydney and had professional seasons, one highly successful. Catherine Duncan, who wrote radio shows for John Hickling's *Living Theatre* in Melbourne during the war, adapted one of them into the stage play, *Sons of the Morning*, which won a PLAYWRIGHTS' ADVISORY BOARD competition and had several productions. Lynn Foster's *The Lost Generation* came from a radio play she wrote for a war loan campaign, and had a season at the Minerva Theatre. Ralph Peterson's boxing play *The Square Ring* (1951) was based on his ABC radio serial *Come Out Fighting*.

Indirectly, radio aided the theatre by maintaining a corps of actors ready for stage opportunity. The fluidity of radio has helped, along with cinema and television, to free the writing of stage drama from rigid conventions of construction or development. But more significantly it contributed by providing Australian audiences with the best of the world's classics, together with adventure and romance during a grey period of Australian history made barren by economic depression, war and too little public encouragement of the creative imagination. ❦*Leslie Rees*

further reading
AFFORD, MAX. *Mischief in the Air*. Brisbane: University of Queensland Press 1974.
KENT, JACQUELINE. *Out of the Bakelite Box*. Sydney: Angus and Robertson 1983.
LANE, RICHARD. *The Golden Age of Australian Radio*. Melbourne University Press 1994.
MOORE, T. INGLIS. *We're Going Through*. Sydney: Angus and Robertson (1945.
MOORE, WILLIAM and T. INGLIS MOORE (eds). *Best One-Act Australian Plays*. Sydney: Angus and Robertson 1937.
MORELL, MUSETTE. *Three Radio Plays*. Sydney: Australasian Publishing 1948.
REES, LESLIE (ed.). *Australian Radio Plays*. Sydney: Angus and Robertson 1946.
REES, LESLIE. *Hold Fast to Dreams—50 years of theatre, radio, TV and books*. Sydney: Alternative Publishing Co-operative 1982.
REES, LESLIE. *A History of Australian Drama* 2 vols. Sydney: Angus and Robertson 1987.
STEWART, DOUGLAS. *The Fire on the Snow and The Golden Lover*. Sydney: Angus and Robertson 1944.
SYKES, ALRENE, (ed.). *Five Plays for Radio*. Sydney: Currency Press 1975.
TURNER, ALEXANDER. *Hester Siding and Other Plays*. Perth: Paterson 1937.
TURNER, ALEXANDER. *Royal Mail and Other Plays*. Perth: Paterson 1944.

Gustave Ramaciotti

Manager. Born 13 March 1861 in Livorno (Italy). Emigrated to Australia in teens. Naturalised 1880. Defence Force volunteer, law clerk in Sydney, theatrical manager *c*.1897–1911. Partner in Williamson, Tallis and Ramaciotti 1904–11. Military commander to 1920. Died 6 December 1927 in Melbourne.

A self-made Italian immigrant, Gustave Ramaciotti became the partner of J. C. WILLIAMSON and GEORGE TALLIS. He was financially involved with the THEATRE ROYAL in Sydney from about 1897 and in 1911 he bought it and a nearby hotel. His daughter Vera sold the theatre to a developer in 1969 for $7·25 million. Ramaciotti became a major-general and commandant of the military forces in NSW during the First World War. His chatty letters to BLAND HOLT are full of information about Sydney theatre, its personalities, standards, successes and failures. ❦*Richard Fotheringham*

further reading
NEUMANN, C. Gustave Mario Ramaciotti. *Australian Dictionary of Biography* 11. Melbourne University Press 1988.
reference
Bland Holt papers, National Library of Australia (Canberra).

Robin Ramsay

Actor. Born 31 May 1939 in Melbourne. Graduated from Royal Academy of Dramatic Art (London) 1958. Went to USA 1960. Worked with Tyrone Guthrie, American National Repertory Theatre and Theatre Company of Boston 1962–63. Played Fagin in Broadway production of *Oliver!* 1965-66. Returned to Australia 1967 and acted for Old Tote Theatre Company (Sydney) and Melbourne Theatre Company. Toured Australia and performed in London as Henry Lawson in *The Bastard from the Bush* 1979. In many television dramas and films. National Critics' Awards 1970 (title-role in *Henry IV—part 1*), 1974 (title-role in *Pericles*). Father of actor Tamasin Ramsay.

One of Australia's most complete character actors, Robin Ramsay is noted for the precision and economy of his performances and their sense of reserved power. He ranges widely, from larrikin comedy to the spiritual dimensions of classic tragedy, and he has a stillness rare in Australian acting. His choice of roles has reflected the work available as much as his own capacities, but he energises each one.

Ramsay won two National Critics' Awards for performances in Shakespeare with the MELBOURNE THEATRE COMPANY, and a forum of international critics named him best actor in the opening season of the Sydney Opera House in 1973 for his performance as Macheath in Bertolt Brecht's *The Threepenny Opera*. In 1979 he won the Australian Arts Award for his popular solo performance as Henry Lawson in *The Bastard from the Bush*, which he wrote with RODNEY FISHER. He toured it nationally and had a successful London season. Other notable performances given by Ramsay include Bri in Peter Nichols's *A Day in the Death of Joe Egg* and Horner in William Wycherley's *The Country Wife*, both in 1968; Bertram in Tyrone Guthrie's production of *All's Well that Ends Well* for the Melbourne Theatre Company in 1971; a memorably aristocratic Pontius Pilate in *Jesus Christ Superstar* in 1973–74; five roles in Ferenc Molnár's *The Wolf* in 1975; Shylock for the Melbourne Theatre Company in 1977 and the Comte de Guiche in Edmond Rostand's *Cyrano de Bergerac* for the SYDNEY THEATRE COMPANY in 1980.

In the USA, Ramsay shared the bill with the Beatles in the Ed Sullivan Show on television in 1964, singing a song from Lionel Bart's *Oliver!* Next year he began playing Fagin in the first Broadway production of *Oliver!* He toured in the role throughout the USA and played it in a revival in London and in Tokyo in 1968–69.

Since 1984 Ramsay has been on the faculty of the Brahma Kumaris World Spiritual University, a non-governmental organisation that serves the United Nations through its Economic and Social Council and its children's fund, UNICEF. He toured more than 70 countries in solo performance of works by Henry Lawson and Rabindranath Tagore in 1989–90. In Helsinki (Finland) in 1989 his monodrama about Tagore, *Borderland* was the theme production of the International Theatre Institute's world congress on theatre as a cultural bridge. ❦*Katharine Brisbane*

Brett Randall

English actor, director, producer. Born 15 September 1884. Originally William Herbert Ralland. Father was D'Oyly Carte Opera Company tenor and theatre manager. Stepmother was character actor Henrietta Cavendish. Toured fairgrounds in England 1900–08. Managed Holloway Empire (London) 1908–14. Married actor Eve Dawnay 1910. Managed touring operetta companies. Australian stage debut 1926. Playscript agent from 1926. Co-founded Melbourne Little Theatre Company 1931; director 1931–56. Director of St Martin's Theatre Company (Melbourne) 1956–63. Died 3 July 1963 in Melbourne. Father of actor, director and administrator Peter Randall.

Brett Randall was the driving force behind the ST MARTIN'S THEATRE COMPANY, which he and Hal Percy, another actor, founded as the Little Theatre Laboratory of Dramatic Art in 1931. Randall expounded his aims in the Melbourne *Herald* on 9 January 1932: 'Ever since I have been in Australia I have wondered why repertory has not been exploited in a professional way ... There are, in Melbourne, several amateur companies that one might term Little Theatre movements, but their activities are at the best irregular and spasmodic ... My idea is to build up the Little Theatre movement that would be part amateur and part professional ... There is no doubt that the players are available. The job is to find an outlet for their ability.' In 32 years he oversaw more than 300 plays staged by the company and directed many of them. He dedicated his life to uniting artists and audience and fostered a generation of professionals by encouraging actors, writers, directors, designers and stage managers to develop their talents in the company.

Randall himself first appeared on stage at eight with his father in Gilbert and Sullivan on tour with the D'Oyly Carte Opera Company in 1892. He learned the theatrical trade with travelling fit-up shows in English fairgrounds. In 1908 he moved into management at the Holloway Empire music hall in London. After serving in the army during the First World War and managing touring companies in the provinces, he came to Australia in 1925. Next year he appeared with the Joseph Cunningham New English Comedy Company in Sydney and Melbourne. He toured New Zealand with NELLIE BRAMLEY's company and in Sydney in 1930 he directed MURIEL STARR in *In the Next Room* by Eleanor Robson and Harriet Ford and *The Enemy* by Channing Pollock. ❦*Sally Dawes*

Peter Randall

Director. Born 27 September 1915 in London. Came to Australia with parents, actor-manager Brett Randall and actress Eve Dawnay, 1925. Foundation member of Melbourne Little Theatre 1931. In army 1939–44. Married actor Trixie Gray 1943. Associate director of Melbourne Little Theatre Company 1945. Managed touring Everyman's Theatre. Director of Melbourne Little Theatre Guild 1951. Program manager of HSV-7 television (Melbourne) 1958–62. Director of St Martin's Theatre Company (Melbourne) 1962–66. Died 15 June 1971 in Melbourne.

Peter Randall began a life dedicated to theatre in 1931, when his father BRETT RANDALL made him a foundation member of the Little Theatre Laboratory of Dramatic Art, which became the Melbourne Little Theatre Company. He quickly absorbed every aspect of administration. In 1944 he began publishing the company's monthly magazine, *Foyer*, edited by Allan Aldous. In 1948 Randall became responsible for managing Everyman's Theatre, which toured 48 country towns in Victoria, for the company. After the Melbourne Little Theatre Guild was formed in 1951 he was largely involved in planning a new building and the issue of debentures, but he directed the company at the National Theatre while the present writer directed its activities at the Arrow Theatre in Middle Park. When the new Little Theatre opened in 1956 he returned to full-time production. In 1958 his production of *The Caine Mutiny Court Martial* by Herman Wouk was the first stage production transferred successfully to commercial television. ❦*Irene Mitchell*

Raymond, Lord of Milan

Tragedy in three acts by Edward Reeve. **premiere** 14 September 1863, Royal Victoria Theatre, Sydney. Cast: Mr Appleton, Mr Burford, Mr Musgrove, Mrs Charles Poole, Mr Selwyn, Mr Walsh, Mr West. **revived** 1950, Metropolitan Theatre, Sydney. Cast: John Dease, Nigel Lovell, Richard Meikle, Lynne Murphy. Designer: Alick McKenzie. Director: May Hollinworth. **published** Sydney: Hawksley and Cunninghame 1851.

A typical blank-verse closet drama—a play intended only for reading—of the time, this tragedy was published in Sydney in 1851. It was heavily cut for the 1863 production, which was said to have been an 'unqualified success', attracting large audiences. Reviewers said little about the play itself but praised the new scenery, 'historically correct' costumes and 'admirable tableaux'. Set in 13th-century Italy, the play deals with various plots to overthrow Raymond, while revealing his own far from pure past. There are a few fine speeches, such as Raymond's denunciation of the corrupt church in Act 2, but the play lacks direction and dramatic tension. ❦*Elizabeth Webby*

Joan and Betty Rayner

Betty Rayner. Actor, director, dramatist. Born 1907 in Wellington (New Zealand). Died November 1981 in Melbourne. AM 1978.

Joan Rayner. Actor, director, dramatist. Born November 1900 in Dunedin (New Zealand). AM 1978.

Daughters of Fred Rayner, cartoonist. Arrived in Sydney c.1920. Studied art of 'strolling players' with Constance Smedley of

Greenleaf Theatre in London. Further studies in Paris and Berlin. Worked together throughout professional life. Directed Theatre of Youth (Sydney) 1929–31. Toured in Australia, North America and Europe as 'strolling players' performing folksongs and folk-plays 1932–48. Founded Australian Children's Theatre (Melbourne) 1948. Published books of story-songs in 1964 and short plays 1968–70. Sisters of film actor Molly Raynor (sic).

Pioneers in children's theatre in Australia, Joan and Betty Rayner took simple theatre of high quality to children in cities and country towns. With the unsubsidised, non-profit Australian Children's Theatre they toured their own shows and guest performers through Australia and New Zealand until the late 1970s. Always thorough in their approach, they inspired and encouraged other performers and groups. They often performed for adult audiences, such as British forces during the Second World War. ❦Richard Bradshaw

further reading
CLARKE, MAVIS THORPE. *Strolling Players*. Melbourne: Lansdowne Press 1972.

Hannie Rayson

Dramatist. Born 31 March 1959 in Melbourne. Studied acting at Victorian College of the Arts (Melbourne). Founding member of TheatreWorks (Melbourne) 1980. Writer-in-residence at Mill Theatre Company (Geelong) 1984, and in Melbourne at Playbox Theatre Company 1985, La Trobe University 1987, Monash University 1990 and Victorian College of the Arts 1990. Australia Council literature board fellowship 1989. Australian Writers' Guild Awgie award 1986 for *Room to Move*. Green Room Award 1990 and NSW Premier's Award 1991 for *Hotel Sorrento*. Works as film editor and writer.

Hannie Rayson's strong, biting comedies have wide appeal and have been performed by mainstream theatre companies all round Australia. Her work has developed from specialised community-theatre scripts for THEATREWORKS into broad-based works with universal application. Her plays explore social situations and relationships and incorporate strong feminist views. *Room to Move* explores the effects of feminism on the lives of an adult family. *Mary* examines the home lives of two girls of different ethnic origins; *Hotel Sorrento* the familial rivalries of three sisters; and *Falling from Grace* the friendship between three women who are struggling with ethical decisions that conflict with professional and personal relationships. As Rayson's subject matter has widened her characters and structure have become harder-edged. ❦Carolyn Pickett

published plays
Hotel Sorrento (1990). Sydney: Currency Press 1990.
Mary (1982). Melbourne: Yackandandah 1985.
Room to Move (1985). Melbourne: Yackandandah 1985.

further reading
FITZPATRICK, PETER. In *Contemporary Dramatists* (ed. K. A. Berney) 5th edn. London: St James Press 1993.

Red Shed Company

Alternative-theatre collective in Adelaide, founded in 1986 by students at Flinders University Drama Centre. **venue** Red Shed, Cardwell Street. **first production** *Bazaar and Rummage* by Sue Townsend.

Working in the round, often in promenade and frequently using comedy and music, the Red Shed Company has won over Adelaide audiences with engaging, accomplished theatre since it was set up by enterprising final-year students at Flinders University Drama Centre. These actors, directors and writers lacked opportunity and were facing the prospect of emigration to equal uncertainty in other cities. Encouraged by the centre's director, Julie Holledge, they leased the Red Shed, an inner-city venue that had housed TROUPE five years before. The Red Shed Company revived some of its campus work for public performances and continued with productions of its own devising. It has always decided on repertoire and policy by consensus.

Highlights in Red Shed seasons include *Immaculate Deceptions*, a play by Cath McKinnon, in 1988; *In Cahoots*, a comic play by Melissa Reeves about the Brownie movement, in 1989; David Carlin's *Frankenstein's Children*, a play about medical ethics, at the 1990 Adelaide Festival. Carlin also wrote *Dog Eat Dog* for the 1992 festival. McKinnon's *A Rose By Any Other Name* used expressionist techniques to examine domestic violence and the law and Reeves's fine play *Sweetown* in 1991 explored the vexed history of Aboriginal massacres. With such productions, and vigorous staging of new works from the United Kingdom, such as Jim Cartwright's *Road* and Frank McGuinness's *The Carthaginians*, the Red Shed Company has established a strong young audience that is responsive to its frankly political, theatrically direct techniques. ❦Murray Bramwell

Roy Redgrave

Actor, dramatist. Born 1872 in England. Originally George Ellsworthy Redgrave. Married Daisy Scudamore, actor. First performed in English provincial theatre and at age 22 at London's East End. Arrived in Australia 1904 under contract to J. C. Williamson. Joined William Anderson's company 1909. Acted in many Australian silent films. Died May 1922 in Sydney. Father of actor Michael Redgrave. Grandfather of actors Corin, Lynn and Vanessa Redgrave.

Redgrave usually played the romantic lead in melodramas. When he arrived in Sydney he played the character role of Flambeau in J. C. Williamson's 1904 production of Edmond Rostand's *L'Aiglon*, which toured Australia and New Zealand for more than 12 months. Once back in Sydney he appeared in *Camille* by Alexandre Dumas *fils*. By 1908 he had returned to London to perform in *Robbery Under Arms* by Alfred Dampier and Garnet Walch.

In May 1909 Redgrave was again in Australia, to play Dave Goulburn, the hero of *The Man from Outback* by BERT BAILEY and EDMUND DUGGAN with William Anderson's company in Melbourne. Later in the year he played Jack, the hero in Jo Smith's *The Bushwoman*, opposite his wife Daisy Scudamore in the title-role. Redgrave also appeared with Anderson's company as Jack Dunstan in *The Miner's Trust* by Jo Smith in 1908, the young engineer in *White Australia* by RANDOLPH BEDFORD in 1909, the French villain in *The Winning Ticket* by Anderson and Temple Harrison in 1910, Jack Melton in *My Mate* by Duggan in 1911 and Robert Shannon in *England's Hope* by Bernard Espinasse in 1911. Redgrave wrote a stage version of Marie Corelli's novel *The Sorrows of Satan*, which Anderson's company performed in October 1911. ❦Delyse Anthony

further reading
PIKE, ANDREW and ROSS COOPER. *Australian Film 1900-1977.* Melbourne: Oxford University Press 1980.

Bill Reed

Dramatist. Born 18 July 1942 in Perth. Educated at University of Adelaide. Worked as writer with Royal Court Theatre, London, during 1960s. Returned to Australia soon after first English production 1966. Also novelist and publisher.

Bill Reed's contribution to the Australian theatrical renascence in the 1970s is not as well known as those of his contemporaries, but in his plays he shares many of their concerns. His first two plays examined the concept of human conscience in different ways, through two events that have become national myths. *Burke's Company*, first produced by the Union Theatre Repertory Company in Melbourne in 1967, was about the ill-fated Burke and Wills expedition, and *Truganinni* (1971) was about the white settlers' genocide against the Tasmanian Aborigines. Much of Reed's other work has been along similar lines, taking an Australian view of universal themes. Reed wrote one play, *Paddlesteamer* in 1975, under the pseudonym Barvar Adele. ❤*Janet Greason*

published plays
Burke's Company (1967). Melbourne: Heinemann 1969.
Truganinni (1971). Melbourne: Heinemann 1977.
I Don't Know What To Do With You. Melbourne: Heinemann 1980.
Mr Siggie Morrison with his Comb and Paper (1972). Melbourne: Heinemann 1972.
further reading
CARROLL, DENNIS. *Australian Contemporary Drama.* Sydney: Currency Press 1993.

Reedy River

Musical. **libretto** Dick Diamond. **music** traditional, Miles Maxwell. Director: John Gray. **premiere** 11 March 1953, at 92 Flinders Street, Melbourne, by New Theatre Melbourne. Choreographer: Peggy Campbell. Conductor: Miles Maxwell. Dancers: Unity Dance Group. **revivals** 5 December 1953, New Theatre, Sydney. 4 September 1954, New Theatre, Brisbane. October 1954, New Theatre, Adelaide. 22 October 1954, New Theatre, Perth.

Australia's first folk musical, *Reedy River* won enormous popular and critical success by its affirmation of Australian popular culture. It was variously described as: 'uniquely Australian and comradely entertainment … a homegrown ambling casually charming musical play based on Australian songs'; 'a landmark in our theatrical history'; and 'good theatre, and as unmistakably Australian as a blue gum or a kangaroo … the stage counterpart of a Sidney Nolan painting'. NEW THEATRE archives indicated that 3000 saw the first season in Melbourne and 100 000 saw the Sydney production when it played throughout NSW.

The impetus for the musical came from a growing interest in traditional Australian ballads and bush songs and their collection and restoration by George Farwell, John Gray (Eric Grayson), John Meredith, VANCE PALMER and Margaret Sutherland. Gray chose about ten songs, sufficiently linked in content and atmosphere to provide the basis for a play. DICK DIAMOND developed a script based on the shearers' strike of 1891. The play is resolved by a victory for unionism and reconciliation for the worker-hero, Joe Collins, and his estranged wife, Mary Campbell.

The folk songs included 'Ballad of '91' and 'Eumeralla Shore'. Diamond wrote two new songs for the musical and Miles Maxwell set them to music. Maxwell conducted a small orchestra in the first Melbourne production, but in the first Sydney production the orchestra was replaced by the Bushwackers Band, which played guitar, harmonica, and accordion and introduced audiences to the lagerphone and bush bass. *Reedy River* has been toured widely and had numerous revivals in most states. In Melbourne, it was revived in July 1955 and toured until 1956, and subsequently in 1966 and 1980. Revivals were mounted in Sydney in 1960, 1963, 1969, 1980, and 1988. ❤*Angela O'Brien*

Leslie Rees AM

Critic, dramatist, historian. Born 28 December 1905 in Perth. Drama critic in London 1930–35. Returned to Australia 1936. With Australian Broadcasting Commission until 1966, mainly as federal drama editor. Chairman of Playwrights' Advisory Board 1938–63. Dramatic critic of *Australian Quarterly* 1939–49. AM 1981.

Leslie Rees's great service to Australian theatre has been in encouraging playwrights, developing their works and seeking production for them. He founded the PLAYWRIGHTS' ADVISORY BOARD in 1938 and was its chairman throughout its 25-year existence. In this capacity he was influential in securing the initial production of Ray Lawler's SUMMER OF THE SEVENTEENTH DOLL in 1955.

His own output as a playwright has been small, but over 30 years he compiled and wrote three volumes that still comprise the most comprehensive history of Australian drama, and are the most frequently consulted. His one-act play *Sub-Editor's Room* was performed by NEW THEATRE in Sydney in the 1930s. It was the first Australian play performed on television, directed by Rees for the ABC in 1956. In 1939 he won a competition organised by MELBOURNE NEW THEATRE with *Lalor of Eureka*, a historical drama, and he combined with Ruth Park to adapt her novel *Harp in the South* into a stage play, which was first produced by INDEPENDENT THEATRE in Sydney in 1949. His greatest discovery as the ABC's federal drama editor was DOUGLAS STEWART's radio play *The Fire on the Snow*, which has had numerous theatrical presentations. After his retirement from the ABC in 1966 Rees devoted his time to research and writing. ❤*Richard Lane*

writings
A History of Australian Drama 1—The Making of Australian Drama, revised. Sydney: Angus and Robertson 1987.
A History of Australian Drama 2—Australian Drama 1970–1985, revised. Sydney: Angus and Robertson 1987.
Hold Fast to Dreams: 50 Years of theatre, radio, TV and books. Sydney: Alternative Publishing Co-operative 1982. Autobiography.
Towards an Australian Drama. Sydney: Angus and Robertson 1953.

William Rees

Actor, director. Born c.1905 in Newcastle (NSW). Acted with Independent Theatre (Sydney). Worked in USA as actor and director in theatre and films 1937–46. Returned to Australia 1946. Worked mainly as director. Died c.1961.

Few his generation in Australia knew more about the theatre than William Rees. Before he went to the USA he acted with INDEPENDENT THEATRE at the Savoy Theatre in Sydney. When he returned after the war he acted for J. C. WILLIAMSON'S and at the MINERVA THEATRE, but he had developed primarily as a director. He directed some outstanding productions for Independent Theatre, especially Arthur Miller's *Death of a Salesman* in 1953. 'Such [a] controlled and sensitive account of a modern "heavy" play has not been seen in Sydney for a good many years', wrote LINDSEY BROWN in the *Sydney Morning Herald*. After acting with Googie Withers and JOHN MCCALLUM on a 20-month tour of Alan Melville's *Simon and Laura* and Terence Rattigan's *The Deep Blue Sea* for J. C. Williamson's, Rees became established as the Firm's permanent director. His outstanding production for J. C. Williamson's was William Gibson's comedy-drama *Two for the Seesaw*. ❦Richard Lane

Ada Reeve

Comedian, singer. Born 3 March 1876 in London. Originally Adelaide Reeves. Child singer and dancer. Star of Gaiety Theatre, London, 1894–1900. Toured Australia 1897–98, 1914, 1917–18, 1922. Married comedian Bert Gilbert 1895; divorced 1900; remarried 1902. Lived in Melbourne c.1924–35 except for 1928–31 in Sydney. Returned to London 1935. Performed in drama, film and television. Died 1964 in London. Mother of actor Goodie Reeve.

Pert, tiny, with huge bright eyes, Ada Reeve was a favourite of the Australia public in musical comedy, pantomime, vaudeville and revue for more than 30 years, during a career that began in childhood—singing and dancing in east London and busking on the Isle of Wight with her musician father—and stretched to television. She became a music-hall star in the early 1890s, with 'What do I care?', a song during which she did cartwheels in skirts while the audience sang 'Over, Ada!'. She then moved to musical comedy at the Gaiety Theatre in the title-role of *The Shop Girl* and as Julie Bon Bon in *The Gay Parisienne*.

She played these roles, which she later described as 'frivolous, vivacious, and exquisitely attired', in Australia in 1897–98 for J. C. WILLIAMSON'S. She toured with her first husband Bert Gilbert, a comedian, playwright and composer of popular songs, whose infidelities with several gallery girls were greatly enjoyed by the Australian comic papers. A pantomime season and a short vaudeville tour for Harry Rickards's TIVOLI CIRCUIT confirmed Ada Reeve's popularity with the Australian public, although she did not return until 1914. By then she had created Lady Holyrood in *Florodora*—a role played in Australia by another Gaiety girl, GRACE PALOTTA—gone into management with her second husband, and toured the English-speaking world several times. George Bernard Shaw modelled Cleopatra in his *Caesar and Cleopatra* on her after he saw her in a burlesque version of the story.

Rickards's successor, HUGH D. MCINTOSH brought Ada Reeve back to the Tivoli circuit just before the First World War to counter the touring Scottish comedian Harry Lauder. McIntosh paid her the record salary of £350 a week. She was a huge success as singer and actor and she made several subsequent tours. She also used her seaside mansion in England as a convalescent home for wounded Australian soldiers and raised funds for their London Buffet. They responded by buying seats at her London performances and calling her 'Anzac Ada'.

While Ada Reeve and her first husband toured the world their daughter Goodie Reeve, born in 1897, was brought up by a nanny in London. She attended the Guildhall School of Music and then played in the comedy *The Better 'Ole*, a major success with Australian diggers in London during the First World War. McIntosh brought the show to Australia in 1919. Goodie Reeve arrived before the rest of the cast and scored an immediate success in the Tivoli revue *Everybody's Doing It*. About 1921 she left the stage and married a Melbourne doctor. Widowed about 1923, she raised their child and in the 1930s had a successful career as 'Miss Radio' on 2GB Sydney.

During the 1920s Ada Reeve also lived in Australia, touring in musical comedy, pantomime, revue and drama, and having an affair with Tom Holt, whose son Harold became prime minister. Holt was general manager of Efftee Films, for which Reeve filmed one of her later songs, 'I never forget I'm a lady', in 1932. Unfortunately she was past her prime, and it is difficult to see the great talent she must have been. Many Australians remembered Reeve long after her return to England in 1935 and ABC radio played a recorded message from her on her 80th birthday in 1954. Compton Mackenzie's foreword to her gossipy, generous, but sanitised autobiography suggested that 'her art … had a French perfection which no actress of the British stage in musical comedy has rivalled'. ❦Richard Fotheringham

writings
Take It for a Fact. London: Heinemann 1954. Autobiography.
further reading
BARTON, BART. Bert Gilbert passes on. *Radio Pictorial of Australia* 1 November 1937.
MISS RADIO (Goodie Reeve). I remember when. *Radio Pictorial of Australia* 1 October 1938.
PARKER, JOHN (ed.). *Who's Who in the Theatre*. London: Pitman 1926.

Wybert Reeve

Actor, dramatist, manager. Born c.1831 in London. Officer in 5th Dragoon Guards, supposedly in Australia during gold rushes c.1852. Provincial theatrical manager, actor and prolific playwright in England c.1859–79. In Australia 1879-1900. Ran theatres in Adelaide. Died November 1906 in England.

Wybert Reeve, an experienced actor and manager, was unlucky to arrive in Melbourne in 1879, when the better-known ALFRED DAMPIER, ARTHUR GARNER, BLAND HOLT, GEORGE MUSGROVE and J. C. WILLIAMSON were all moving into management. Reeve wisely withdrew from the unequal competition to Adelaide, where for the next 20 years he became a major figure in South Australian society. He wrote and produced his own plays, adapted other works, including Rosa Praed's novel *Policy and Passion*, and wrote short stories for the Melbourne *Australasian*. He managed and leased theatres, and became vice-president of the South Australian University Shakespearean Society. His health failed in 1900 and after a farewell dinner he went 'home' to England.

Reeve is supposed to have been in Sydney as a young man, possibly during his early army career, and to have had a farce, *An Australian Hoax*, performed there in 1852. His later Australian career came after many years of moderate success as actor, manager and playwright, particularly in Bristol, Bath, Cardiff and Swansea. He learned his trade in small provincial companies. On the Isle of Wight, he claimed, he once found himself 'cast for Ross, Banquo, and the First Murderer, which necessitated my murdering myself, and reporting to Macbeth I had done so'. He wrote numerous plays in England, including *Won at Last* in 1869 and *Pyke O'Callaghan*, which had its premiere in London in 1870. ❧*Richard Fotheringham*

further reading
REEVE, WYBERT. *From Life*. Adelaide: George Robertson 1891.

The Removalists

Play in two acts by David Williamson. **premiere** 22 July 1971, La Mama Theatre, Melbourne. Cast: Fay Byrne, Peter Cummins, Kristin Green, Paul Hampton, Bruce Spence, David Williamson. Director: Bruce Spence. **published** Sydney: Currency Press 1972.

The Removalists made a transition from 'alternative' to 'establishment' theatre with spectacular success, despite its disturbing material. The action deals with police brutality that gets out of hand, but Williamson has justly claimed that his play is concerned with authoritarian behaviour on a wider scale. It probes the defensive anonymity of men whose identities are subsumed by the job or the uniform, and it explores the nexus between the propensity for violence and male sexual attitudes. For each of the men the capacity to deal out or withstand violence is a 'test of a man' related quite directly to sexual performance. The play originated in a tale told to DAVID WILLIAMSON by a removalist and of all his plays it has the least relationship to his own experience. Detachment makes the inexorable logic of the plot even more chilling.

The Removalists shows considerable assurance in structural control. Early in the play it seems that only egos are at stake, as a couple of policemen offer their services in protecting a young wife and her sister from a troublesome husband in the hope of some sexual rewards. When Kenny Carter the husband comes home, the situation sours, and culminates in brutality that makes it clear that much more than ego is on the line. Humour and horror coexist in ways that place the reactions of the audience under constant scrutiny, especially in relation to Carter's seeming death, joky recovery and real death.

The Removalists has been played widely and been professionally revived in Australia, and it has had several productions in Europe and the USA. The NIMROD THEATRE COMPANY's production in Sydney in 1972 transferred to Melbourne, toured for five months and was joint winner of the George Devine Award in London. After a production in London in 1973 the *Evening Standard* named Williamson the most promising playwright of the year. A film version appeared in 1975. The play is also a key work in the study of Australian drama. ❧*Peter Fitzpatrick*

Roy Rene

Revue comedian. Born 15 February 1891 in Adelaide. Originally Henry Vande Sluice in birth registration, but Harry van der Sluice according to him. Began performing as boy soprano. Corner man in suburban Melbourne minstrel shows. Moved to Sydney at 19. Called himself Roy Rene during 18-month New Zealand tour for Fullers'. In partnership with Nat Phillips as Stiffy and Mo 1916–25 and 1927–28. On Tivoli circuit with Fred Bluett 1926. Formed Mo's Merry Monarchs company 1928. Married performer Dot Davis in 1917; later divorced. Married vaudevillian Sadie Gale 1929. Joined Mike Connors and Queenie Paul at the New Tivoli Theatre, Sydney, 1931. On Tivoli circuit 1936–45, with one break. Full-time radio from 1946 until ill-health forced retirement. Last stage appearance in Harry Wren's *McCackie Moments* 1949. Died 22 November 1954 in Sydney.

Roy Rene was unsurpassed in his ability to pack vaudeville theatres for months on end. Made up in the white face and black beard of the stage Jew as Mo, he played Queen Elizabeth ('the Virgin Queen'), Henry VIII and a variety of henpecked husbands and low-life characters. He spluttered and lisped Jewish-accented Australian colloquialisms in high tones to the delight of audiences around the country. Even without his famous voice and language Rene could hold the audience in the palm of his hand with his immaculate timing, ridiculous costumes and leering elastic face. When Arthur Prince, a ventriloquist with a life-size dummy, was at the Tivoli Theatre in Melbourne during the Great Depression, Rene made the audience at the Bijou Theatre laugh by playing the dummy in a spoof of the act.

Roy Rene began performing in his native Adelaide as 'Little Roy the boy soprano'. He left school at 13 when his family moved to Melbourne, and continued singing until his voice broke. Afterwards he became 'Boy Roy', an endman in suburban minstrel shows with a speciality act as a comic singer and dancer. When not performing he studied the stars at HARRY RICKARDS's Opera House where, he said, he learnt the importance of 'polish, finesse and finish'. He played a jockey and stablehand in a play, *The Whip*, for J. C. WILLIAMSON's and at 19 he went with the production to Sydney. Later he went on J. C. BAIN's suburban vaudeville circuit as a corner man. BENJAMIN FULLER saw his blackface Hebrew act and contracted him to tour New Zealand. During the tour he adopted the name Rene, apparently after a famous French clown named René, and his characteristic make-up. Back in Sydney he worked in a Fullers' revue company run by NAT PHILLIPS who suggested a partnership. STIFFY AND MO made their debut in July 1916 and were an immediate success in revues filling half the bill, the perfect vehicle for Rene's larrikin style of comedy.

Rene split from Phillips in 1925 and acted in his only straight play, *Give and Take*, with Harry Green, an American. Rene stole the show, and when Green restaged the play in the USA he took Rene's part himself. In 1926 Rene teamed up with FRED BLUETT in an act on the TIVOLI CIRCUIT until Fuller persuaded him to reunite with Phillips in Brisbane. In Sydney, Sadie Gale joined the show. The daughter of Sam and Myra Gale, both performers, she had been on stage since she was two years old and had worked in musical comedy and vaudeville. She also joined Mo's Merry Monarchs, a company formed by Rene after he and Phillips split finally in New Zealand in 1928. The Sydney *Bulletin* likened an early Merry Monarchs show to *Hamlet* without the Prince of Denmark. The new company played in Sydney and Melbourne for Fullers' and toured north Queensland for HARRY CLAY after Rene and Gale married in July 1929. In late 1929 they were playing in *Clowns in Clover* in Melbourne for FRANK NEIL—who convinced Rene to work without make-up—when Rene collapsed with peritonitis. Complications kept him off the stage for six months. He returned for Hugh D. McIntosh in *Pot Luck* at the Tivoli Theatre in Melbourne in mid-1930, but business was bad and he joined a J. C. Williamson's pantomime.

Rene was touring New Zealand when he received a telegram asking him to join Mike Connors and Queenie Paul who were reviving vaudeville in Sydney. He was instrumental in their success at the New Tivoli Theatre. Rene stayed on the Tivoli circuit after Connors and Paul sold out to Frank Neil in 1933, but he was soon playing in other productions. His only film, *Strike Me Lucky*, was unsuccessful in 1934. In Ernest C. Rolls's *Rhapsodies* in 1935 he again performed without his make-up. In 1935–36 he was in partnership with Connors and Paul in the Connors–Paul Revue Company until he signed with the Tivoli circuit. Frank Neil did not renew Rene's contract in 1939, but Wallace Parnell brought him back after Neil died in January 1940. Rene stayed on the Tivoli circuit until 1945, when he rejected a substantial salary cut proposed by a new proprietor, David N. Martin. He then joined the Colgate-Palmolive Radio Unit and soon became famous as Mo McCackie.

On stage as Mo, Rene was the quintessential Australian clown, playing the part of the underdog with lashings of sentimentality or the society toff with flippant derision. His characters often made those in authority look foolish. As a toff he made an idiot of himself by pretending to understand something that he did not comprehend. As an ingratiating underling he made the powerful look ridiculous. While an army captain barked out a rigorous order for the day, Private Mo stood motionless and then asked in dulcet tones: 'In my spare time could I scrub the battlefield?'

Mo's liberal use of colloquialisms brought him much popularity and expressions such as 'Strike me lucky' became his own. Rene insisted that he picked up his language in city streets. He said of his expressions: 'They are just ordinary Australian sayings—they are household words. I use those expressions in my sketches because they are Australian and so am I.' Australians, however, credited him with invention rather than imaginative reproduction. Although he never wrote his own scripts, he transformed those that were written for him. He was famous for his ad-libbing, which often broke up colleagues on stage.

Contemporary critics had mixed reactions to Rene. Most recognised his comic genius but many deplored his vulgarity. 'A comedian of the standard of Rene', declared the *Sydney Morning Herald* of 6 November 1933, 'should be able to gain applause without resorting to crudity'. In Rene's heyday vaudeville managers, keen to appeal to middle-class audiences, tried to keep their performers in line, but it was an uphill battle with Rene. He could make a perfectly clean line suggestive, so censoring his material was never enough. Once he was on stage there was little a manager could do, although one in Adelaide sacked him when he came off. Benjamin Fuller instructed a theatre manager to record Rene's use of three banned words. In the middle of a sketch, Rene noticed the manager and, excusing himself to Phillips, walked over to his box and pronounced: 'God, god, god; damn, damn, damn; hell, hell, hell. Have you got those down George?'

Many critics tried to explain what they saw as a contradiction between Mo's vulgarity and his success. 'He is Art', decided a *Bulletin* writer, comparing Rene with Chaplin and Beethoven. 'He founds his appeal on the fundamental elements in human nature'. Explaining this, the writer pondered: 'Why does the spectacle of this Semite, with his death's head, his paralytic walk and his unspeakable clothes, cuckolding a good-looking husband fill the audience with delight when it ought to fill it with moral indignation? Obviously because Mo's example inspires it with the feeling that ... it could go and do likewise despite its pitiful inadequacies.'

Mo always complemented his comedy with unashamed sentimentality, which he called his 'lovely pathos'. A reviewer in the *Sydney Morning Herald* of 4 December 1933 commented on *Brothers in Distress*: 'Though he appeared with his usual white masklike face, it was a mock pathetic number. The audience which up to that moment had been laughing at him uproariously, was sobered by his first words and listened to his maudlin sentimental speeches in respectful silence.' Yet his sentimental work was often as ridiculous as his comedy. Fred Parsons recalled *The Harassed Comedian*, in which Mo tried to tell jokes that 'plants' in the audience found offensive. After several false starts he eventually gave up and rather sorrowfully said:

> *Life's a very funny proposition, after all*
> *Imagination, hypocrisy and gall—*
> *Three meals a day, but you're always in the way*
> *Life's a very funny proposition after all.*

The audience was invariably moved by Rene's soulful rendition of these meaningless lines. He was proud of this ability, often to the amusement of those around him. Yet just as his pathos was infused by a sense of the ridiculous, in his comedy he was always vulnerable. Mo never won as a super-hero, but only with his inadequacies intact. Because Rene's sentimentality reinforced his comedy he was able to tap both laughter and tears. Rene was a comic genius but his popularity has often been explained in terms of his 'Australianness'. Commentators note his extensive use of 'slanguage' and Mo's 'typical' Australian traits of championing the underdog, mocking sacred cows and comical vulgarity. Many of the most Australian aspects of Mo's comedy, however, come straight from English music-hall. This genre was ideal for Australian popular sentiment because it was malleable in form and embodied the right values. Rene certainly made it his own. Throughout his career there were rumours that he had refused English contracts. For example, the *Bulletin* reported on 25 November 1931 that he had rejected Sir Oswald Stoll's offer of £110, three times his current fee, because he 'might be out of his element in the Strand'.

Mo has not been forgotten. In the mid-1970s Steve J. Spears wrote a tribute in the form of a play known as *Young Mo*, though he called it *The Resuscitation of the Little Prince Who Couldn't Laugh as Performed by Young Mo at the Height of the Great Depression of 1929*. Since 1975 the annual Mo Awards for variety performers have honoured the memory of the great comedian. ❧*Victoria Chance*

further reading
McDermott, Celestine. Roy Rene. *Australian Dictionary of Biography* 11. Melbourne University Press 1988.
Rene, Roy with Elizabeth Lambert and Max Harris. *Mo's Memoirs*. Melbourne: Reed and Harris 1945.

Repertoire

Before 1850 the plays that were performed in the Australian colonies—cultural outposts of Great Britain—were predominantly by English dramatists. There were also translations of plays by French and German dramatists and, in the 1840s in particular, new plays by local authors. Traditional comedies and tragedies were common in the earlier decades but by the 1840s melodrama and farce dominated the repertoire—plus pantomimes at Christmas —as in England and the USA. Opera and ballet were increasingly prominent. Shakespearean and other standard plays were held in the repertoire for star performers.

The availability of acting copies inevitably determined the first plays that were performed in Australia. Someone in the First Fleet apparently had a taste for George Farquhar, which enabled his *The Recruiting Officer* to be performed in Sydney on 4 June 1789. Other entertainments on that occasion appear to have been confined to a specially written prologue and epilogue, but the standard double bill of the period appeared on 16 January 1796, when ROBERT SIDAWAY opened his theatre in Sydney with Edward Young's 1721 tragedy *The Revenge* and T. Vaughan's 1776 farce *The Hotel*. Other plays performed in SIDAWAY'S THEATRE included *Henry IV*, Nicholas Rowe's 1703 tragedy *The Fair Penitent*, David Garrick's 1772 comedy *The Irish Widow* and, in 1800, *The Recruiting Officer*.

BARNETT LEVEY'S first dramatic production, in the saloon of his Royal Hotel on 26 December 1832, was a popular melodrama recently performed in London—Douglas Jerrold's 1829 *Black-Eyed Susan*—but he took most of his repertoire during the first season in his THEATRE ROYAL in 1833 from collections of early plays, particularly *The London Stage*. Besides *Black-Eyed Susan*, only two of the 23 plays presented were written in the 1820s. When Levey's company made its first attempt at tragedy with *Richard III* on 26 December 1833 the results did not encourage a repetition. 'It was a complete failure ... The pit and galleries hissed incessantly, and the boxes laughed incessantly, joining ever and anon in the hissing', said the *Sydney Monitor* on 28 December 1833.

In contrast, professional theatre in Tasmania began with August von Kotzebue's celebrated German drama *Menschenhass und Reue* in English translation as *The Stranger*. The leading female role, Mrs Haller, long remained a favourite of CORDELIA CAMERON, who played it in the Hobart premiere, and many of her contemporaries. Her husband SAMSON CAMERON based his initial repertoire in Tasmania on such legitimate pieces. He was said to have failed by playing too much to the 'aristocracy'—neglecting popular taste. So, the *Tasmanian* noted on 2 January 1835, 'if instead of those well-established five-act "stock-pieces" which Mr Cameron has produced with so much pain and expense, he had brought forward little light entertainments, of less weight and more lively character, he would have rendered his theatre more attractive'. Cameron appears to have learned from the experience for he advised on opening his Victoria Theatre in ADELAIDE in 1841 that the repertoire would consist of 'Domestic Drama, Burletta, Interlude, and Farce which, from experience, the Manager contemplates will best please the Patrons of the Drama'. By the 1840s this menu of melodrama, farce and other light pieces, interspersed with pantomime at Christmas and Shakespeare for visiting stars, was very much the Australian standard. When GEORGE COPPIN opened the New Queen's Theatre in Adelaide in 1846, he concentrated on farces and other light comic pieces, often playing three or four each evening. Then he added melodrama and towards the end of the year he tried 'fashionable nights', presenting such legitimate drama as *The Stranger* and Edward Bulwer-Lytton's *The Lady of Lyons*. But, as the Adelaide *Observer* remarked on 12 December, even in Adelaide the 'leaders of fashion' were not prone to patronise the theatre.

Thereafter, in Adelaide as elsewhere, tragedies and older standard pieces tended to appear only as vehicles for visiting stars. The tragedian MORTON KING, for example, visited Adelaide in 1847 with a repertoire comprising *Hamlet*, *Macbeth*, *The Merchant of Venice*, *Othello*, *Richard III* and *Romeo and Juliet*—virtually the only Shakespeare plays performed in Australia then—plus *The Stranger*, *The Lady of Lyons*, Sheridan Knowles's *The Hunchback* and Philip Massinger's *A New Way to Pay Old Debts*. The same plays were in the repertoire of the other leading tragedian of the 1840s, FRANCIS NESBITT, but were rarely played otherwise.

While the older plays were still seen as the true test of an actor's ability, and may have been preferred by most who wrote theatrical criticism, Australian audiences greatly favoured more spectacular new forms: melodrama, pantomime and romantic opera. Michael Balfe's 1843 *The Bohemian Girl* and Vincent Wallace's 1845 *Maritana* and other operas were extremely popular in Sydney by the late 1840s, though the Christmas PANTOMIME still achieved the longest runs. As a staple of the 19th-century repertoire, pantomime, with its demand for local and topical references, was the first English theatrical form to undergo much Australianisation. This usually consisted mainly of local scenery and jokes in the harlequinade, though a new local pantomime, HARLEQUIN IN AUSTRALIA FELIX—or, *Geelong in an Uproar*, had been played in Geelong as early as 1845.

Some local melodramas, including Henry Melville's THE BUSHRANGERS were produced in Tasmania in the 1830s, but most plays written in Australia before 1850 were either romantic tragedies that were published but never performed or comic interludes, farces and pantomimes that were performed but never published. It was customary for actors to offer, whenever possible, new plays for their benefit nights and for a few years in the first half of the 1840s, notably 1844 and 1845, a comparatively large number of new Australian plays were produced at the ROYAL VICTORIA THEATRE in Sydney. They were usually performed only once or twice before vanishing from the repertoire. Helene Oppenheim attributed their appearance to a local shortage of new English plays, because of British COPYRIGHT legislation. Apart from the localised pantomimes, Australian plays did not become a regular feature of the repertoire of the Australian stage until much later in the century.
❦*Elizabeth Webby*

1850–80

In the 1850s and 1860s Australian theatres maintained a repertoire virtually identical to those of the British and American stages. This fact encouraged and was consolidated by regular movement of performers between the three countries. Under the prevailing stock-company system, actors were expected to know all the parts pertaining to their 'line' in the current repertoire and to be able to perform them at a few hours' notice. Touring stars would rarely go beyond the stock pieces, in which they were assured of receiving competent support from company to company. New pieces entered the stock repertoire as old ones were discarded, but it was a gradual process. In order to avoid monotony, a play was seldom run for more than a few days, the idea being to rotate a large repertoire in small bursts. In a benefit week it was standard practice to offer a new play every night.

The policies of individual theatres also determined repertoire. From the mid-1850s to the early 1870s the leading theatre in each major centre would assume special responsibility for what was called high-class drama, leaving more popular pieces—and prices—to lesser houses. High class meant drama that could be played without loss of dignity by a tragedian. Stars of this elevated kind, such as G. V. BROOKE and BARRY SULLIVAN, sustained a repertoire built on heavily-cut acting versions of Shakespeare. John Spring's list of performances in Melbourne in 1860–69 identifies the best-liked Shakespearean plays as, in descending order of popularity: *Hamlet*, *Richard III*, *Othello* (Brooke's speciality), *Macbeth*, *Much Ado About Nothing*, *The Taming of the Shrew*, *Romeo and Juliet*, *The Merchant of Venice*, *The Comedy of Errors*, *Henry IV—part 1*, *King John* and *Twelfth Night*. *Hamlet*, with 95 performances, was also the most popular play of the decade. The only other Elizabethan play regularly acted was Massinger's *A New Way to Pay Old Debts*.

The Shakespearean core was supplemented by modern dramas by Bulwer-Lytton (*The Lady of Lyons*, *Money*, *Richelieu*) and Sheridan Knowles (*The Hunchback*, *Virginius*, *The Love Chase*); adaptations of German romantic drama (Kotzebue's *The Stranger* and *Die Spanier in Peru* adapted by R. B. Sheridan as *Pizarro*, E. von Münch-Bellinghausen's *Der Sohn der Wildnis* adapted by Mrs G. W. Lovell as *Ingomar the Barbarian*, and Friedrich von Schiller's *The Robbers*); and time-sanctioned comedies by Sheridan (*The Critic*, *The Rivals*, *The School for Scandal*), Oliver Goldsmith (*She Stoops to Conquer*) and George Colman father and son. Charles Reade and Tom Taylor's *Masks and Faces* and DION BOUCICAULT's early *London Assurance* were also in this exclusive company.

Among other stock-company pieces that a tragedian might essay were four French costume-dramas, each of which existed in a variety of English versions—*Belphegor* by Philippe d'Ennery and Fourmier, *The Corsican Brothers* by Alexandre Dumas *fils*, *Don César de Bazan* by d'Ennery and Pinel Dumanoir and *Louis XI* by Mély-Janin. In addition, most stars had parts that they regarded as their own. Brooke had a sideline in Irish farces, normally played as afterpieces. Charles and Ellen Kean were so associated with G. W. Lovell's *The Wife's Secret* that they were outraged when Sullivan threatened to mount a rival production in Melbourne, though there was then no dramatic copyright to stop him. WALTER MONTGOMERY liked to appear in drag as Meg Merrilies in a version of Walter Scott's novel *Guy Mannering*. James Anderson, WILLIAM CRESWICK, Daniel Bandmann, Montgomery and MORTON TAVARES all carried the tragedian's repertoire into the 1870s. Tragedians did not essay the second repertoire of the 1850s and 1860s. It comprised 'shocking' melodramas by J. B. Buckstone (*Green Bushes*, *The Flowers of the Forest*), Edward Falconer (*Peep o' Day*), and Tom Taylor (*The Ticket-of-leave Man*), together with BURLESQUES of varying degrees of subtlety and Boucicault's Irish dramas (*Arrah-na-Pogue*, *The Colleen Bawn*, *The Shaughraun*). In the early 1860s the American JOSEPH JEFFERSON acted with great success in Boucicault's sensation drama *The Octoroon*, Taylor's comedy *Our American Cousin*, and the phenomenal *Rip Van Winkle*, which he later had rewritten by Boucicault. Like all stars in the popular tradition, Jefferson often appeared in Dickens adaptations. 'High-class' performers usually drew the line at Walter Scott. At both levels the main repertoire piece was likely to be followed by a farce, burlesque or comedietta. These were often kept on when the main program was changed and they counted among the most performed scripts of the era.

Advent of the long run

The 1870s brought a change in theatrical economics that saw the 'high-class' theatres, become, in effect, pantomime and melodrama houses. A sense of this decline was recorded as early as 1872, when J. E. NEILD compared the destruction by fire of the THEATRE ROYAL in Melbourne to 'the melancholy end of a man who has closed a tolerably virtuous life by taking to evil courses'. The last play performed there had been Boucicault's *The Streets of New York*. Stock-company rotation of programs now began to give way to the long run, in Melbourne first and later in Sydney. An early landmark was the 1867 seasons of Boucicault's racing drama *Flying Scud*—an initial run of 27 nights followed by frequent revivals. In token of this change, the rebuilt Theatre Royal had its greatest hit of the 1870s when J. C. WILLIAMSON and MAGGIE MOORE played *Struck Oil*, a comico-pathetic Yankee drama, very much in the Jefferson tradition. In Sydney they played at an avowed melodrama house, the Queen's Theatre.

Shakespeare in a major theatre was now likely to be a single play, elaborately mounted, on the model of the Lyceum Theatre in London. By 1880 Boucicault was yielding primacy to the scenically spectacular but dramatically simple-minded English melodramas of the Paul Merritt (*The New Babylon*) school. Lesser melodrama houses were sustained by a predominantly American repertoire centring on well-tried tearjerkers such as *Uncle Tom's Cabin* and W. W. Pratt's *Ten Nights in a Bar-Room*, and action pieces such as *Kit*, which Neild characterised as 'a story of bigamy, bullets, bowie-knives, bar-drinking, blowings-up, blood-shedding, and final blessedness'.

In 1872, a new style of drama, written for performance in relatively intimate theatres to a middle-class audience, began to arrive from London. This included the new 'natural' comedy of Tom Robertson (*Caste*, *Home*, *Ours*, *School*, *Society*), the early satirical dramas of W. S. Gilbert (*Engaged*, *The Palace of Truth*, *Pygmalion and Galatea*) and the mature dramas of H. J. Byron (*Cyril's Success*, *Daisy Farm*, *Our Boys*). At first, however, only Melbourne, with St George's Hall and later the Academy of Music, had the kind of theatre, and perhaps audience, that the plays demanded. A successful tour of *Les Danicheff*, a Franco-Russian drama of ideas by Corvin and Dumas *fils*, in 1877–78 showed the beginnings of an interest in more intellectually challenging fare, but it was symptomatic of the 1870s that this should be

Pantomime contributed fantasy and scenic splendour to the theatre in the 19th century. Satire became an element in the 1870s but by the 1890s, when George Rignold mounted this production of Jack the Giant Killer, *its presence was minimal*

presented not by one of the legitimate managers but by the operatic organisation of W. S. LYSTER. Throughout the period, opera troupes often presented operas based on familiar plays (Vincent Wallace's *Maritana* from *Don César de Bazan*, Giuseppe Verdi's *La traviata* from *La Dame aux camélias* by Dumas *fils* and Julius Benedict's *The Lily of Killarney* from *The Colleen Bawn* by Boucicault).

The other important innovation of the 1870s was the consolidation of a repertoire for 'high-class' female stars. This combined a selection of Shakespearean roles (Rosalind, Juliet, Lady Macbeth, Queen Katherine in *Henry VIII* and often a *travestito* Hamlet) with European dramas created for Rachel (Ernest Legouvé's *Medea*) and ADELAIDE RISTORI (Paolo Giacometti's *Marie Antoinette* and *Elizabeth, Queen of England*) and a group of highly popular fallen-woman or woman-as-revenger dramas. This last category included three long-established imports from continental Europe (*The Lady of the Camellias*, or *Camille*, by Dumas *fils*, *The Stranger* by Kotzebue, *Leah the Forsaken* by Augustin Daly from a German drama) a more recent French contribution in *Frou Frou* by Henri Meilhac and Ludovic Halévy and sensationally popular adaptations of three novels—Mrs Henry Wood's *East Lynne*, Miss Braddon's *Lady Audley's Secret* and Wilkie Collins's *The New Magdalen*. Stars who specialised in this repertoire were Louisa Cleveland, Augusta Dargon, Mary Gladstane and MARY SCOTT-SIDDONS. The Ristori vehicles gained fresh lustre when the star herself visited Australia in 1875. Her company included GIULIA and EDUARDO MAJERONI, who remained and performed a personal repertoire of modern Italian dramas in translation (*A Living Statue*, *The Old Corporal*).

In all this the resident dramatists were largely restricted to following overseas formulas. They did their best work not for the legitimate stage but in pantomime and burlesque, in which reliance on local topicality at least left some room for originality. ❦*Harold Love*

1880–1949

The early 1880s saw the arrival of a new generation of actor–entrepreneurs, and their attempts at product differentiation led to particular managers being strongly associated with different 'lines' of business. In 1880 GEORGE MUSGROVE's production of Jacques Offenbach's LA FILLE DU TAMBOUR-MAJOR, and its record run of 102 performances at the Prince of Wales Opera House in Melbourne, led the way into a new emphasis on *opéra-bouffe*. J. C. WILLIAMSON had already bullied his way to the Australasian rights to the Gilbert and Sullivan operettas. *HMS Pinafore* in 1879, *The Pirates of Penzance* in 1881, *Patience* in 1882, and *The Mikado* and *Iolanthe* in 1885 were followed by hundreds of other operettas—a form of entertainment that dominated the Australian professional stage for near a century.

There was often only a fine generic line between musical comedies, and comedies with music, though in the latter male actors were more likely to have top billing, like John F. Sheridan in the drag role of the Widow O'Brien in his *Fun on the Bristol* in 1884. Brandon Thomas's *Charley's Aunt* continued this tradition when it arrived in 1893. The stock-in-trade of companies appealing to the higher-priced end of the market was comedy-dramas like Paul Kester's *Sweet Nell of Old Drury* (starring Nellie Stewart in 1902), comedies like Mrs Hodgson Burnett's *Little Lord Fauntleroy* from 1889 and J. M. Barrie's *The Admirable Crichton* from 1904, and outright farces such as those of George M. Cohan, which Fred Niblo brought from New York in 1912. Fantasy, especially oriental fantasy, and science-fiction gravitated towards the same managers and theatres, with Richard Ganthony's *A Message from Mars* in 1900, J. M. Barrie's *Peter Pan* in 1908, Edward Knoblock's *Kismet* and Maurice Maeterlinck's *The Blue Bird* in 1912. While the banner of J. C. WILLIAMSON's flew high over many of these shows, HUGH D. MCINTOSH challenged the Firm in 1921 with Oscar Asche's musical fantasy *Chu Chin Chow*.

The annual Christmas pantomime was another source of fantasy throughout the period, although the topical original works of the 1870s were more often reduced to localised scenes and satire within orthodox narratives like

Among the operettas that dominated the professional stage for decades was HMS Pinafore. *All kinds of troupes performed it, before and after J. C. Williamson gained control of Gilbert and Sullivan's works in 1879. These children, who performed under vice-regal patronage at Gawler (SA) in 1880, were amateurs but professional child companies also did the work. The most famous of these was Pollard's Liliputian Opera Company, which made its debut with* HMS Pinafore *in Launceston (Tas.) in May 1880*

Aladdin, Bluebeard, Humpty Dumpty and *Sinbad*. Only Ella Airlie's THE BUNYIP (1916) stands out as a major local contribution to the form, although Nat Phillips's scripts for FULLERS' between 1917 and the late 1920s went far from the stories suggested by titles like *Mother Goose* and *Cinderella*.

At the 'quality' end of the market Shakespeare was offered by GEORGE RIGNOLD, especially as Henry V; by ESSIE JENYNS in a short career as interpreter of the Bard's heroines, by ALFRED DAMPIER'S company with *Hamlet, Romeo and Juliet* and other plays. The BROUGH-BOUCICAULT COMEDY COMPANY offered an acclaimed *Much Ado About Nothing* in 1891, and OSCAR ASCHE and Lily Brayton presented five Shakespeare plays in 1909–10 and *A Midsummer Night's Dream* in 1912–13. Most of these seasons were staged as spectacular melodrama. In 1920, however, ALLAN WILKIE formed a more educational Shakespeare company, which lasted until 1930, with a repertoire of more than 27 plays.

'Modern' playwrights such as Barrie, Henry Arthur Jones, Arthur Wing Pinero and Oscar Wilde found their way to Australia through the various companies of ROBERT BROUGH and his wife Florence between 1886 and 1908. Hugh Buckler and Violet Paget continued this line of business—with *The School for Scandal* and *She Stoops to Conquer* as well—at the LITTLE THEATRE in Sydney until about 1916. Anton Chekhov, John Galsworthy, Eugene O'Neill, George Bernard Shaw and August Strindberg, however, had to wait for the repertory theatre movement to establish itself in the 1910s before any of their plays were seen. JANET ACHURCH's seasons of *A Doll's House* in 1889–91 and Nance O'Neill's of *Hedda Gabler* in 1900 were professional offerings, but later Ibsen too was abandoned to the amateur stage. Greek classic drama was the preserve of university societies, which also attempted other works from dramatic literature. A performance of *Everyman* sponsored by J. C. Williamson in Melbourne in 1905 was a rare exception.

BLAND HOLT dominated the popular sensation melodrama. His production of Paul Merritt's *The New Babylon* in 1880 began a long string of Adelphi Theatre and Drury Lane melodramas from London presented by him and others until the First World War. George Rignold offered one of the first Drury Lane 'autumn' dramas, *Youth* by Merritt and Augustus Harris, in 1882. Holt presented *A Run of Luck* by Henry Pettitt and Harris in 1887, and followed it with more than 20 other stories of horse-racing, shipwreck, car-chases and the like. Alfred Dampier in 1898 brought home THE DUCHESS OF COOLGARDIE, an Australian story offered in curious circumstances at Drury Lane two years before. WILLIAM ANDERSON joined the field with plays such as Walter Melville's *The Worst Woman in London* in 1901–02, Williamson with W. Young's *Ben Hur* in 1902 and Cecil Raleigh and Henry Hamilton's *The Whip* in 1910, and MEYNELL AND GUNN with Thomas Kremer's *The Fatal Wedding* in 1906. Expensively-staged melodrama declined during the 1910s, but provincial companies still regularly offered stock melodramas, particularly 'women's plays' such as *East Lynne* and *Camille*, and GEORGE SORLIE had a musical version of *Uncle Tom's Cabin* as late as 1931.

Genres of drama enjoyed significant success, including spy, mystery and detective dramas, Christian plays and westerns. *The Irish Detective* in 1880 and William Gillette's *Held by the Enemy* in 1887 and *The Secret Service* in 1899 were followed by Gillette's *Sherlock Holmes* and E. W. Hornung and Eugene Presbrey's *Raffles—The Amateur Cracksman* in the new century, although Tom Taylor's 1860s detective story *The Ticket-of-Leave Man* was still popular. An Australian, DORIS EGERTON JONES, collaborated with the visiting star EMELIE POLINI in writing *The Flaw*, a 1923 success set at 'The Manor' with a butler, a French maid, and 'Detective Steel of Scotland Yard'. Plays by Arnold Ridley and Edgar Wallace later dominated the spy, murder, and mystery field.

Stories from the Bible

Wilson Barrett's *The Sign of the Cross* did not reach Australia until 1897, when news of its success in legitimising quasi-religious stories from the Old Testament and elsewhere had already inspired *Joseph of Canaan* by a local writer, George Walters, in 1895. Another local offering, T. Hilhouse Taylor's PARSIFAL was a huge success in Sydney for J. C. Williamson in 1906. Buffalo Bill, Deadwood Dick, and other western stories were particularly popular in circus and hippodrama venues, with E. I. Cole's BOHEMIAN DRAMATIC COMPANY continuing this kind of repertoire until the 1920s. THE SCOUT by Alfred Dampier and Garnet Walch was a long-running success. More substantial American dramas—such as Augustus Thomas's *Arizona* and *In Mizzoura* in 1903, David Belasco's *The Girl of the Golden West* in 1908, and *At Cripple Creek* in 1913—were of interest to Australian playwrights who were trying to break away from English formulas.

The 1880s saw occasional and growing professional success by Australian playwrights. Bushranging and goldmining were combined in George Darrell's THE SUNNY SOUTH in 1883 and Dampier and Walch's ROBBERY UNDER ARMS in 1890, but the most significant popular success came for plays about the Kelly Gang. A contemporary flurry of interest in 1879–81 was revived in 1896 by DAN BARRY'S staging of Reg Rede's play *The Kelly Gang*. Numerous plagiarisations and imitations followed, and this genre was still alive in the touring theatres after the First World War. E. W. O'Sullivan's COO-EE in 1906 and Bert Bailey and

Edmund Duggan's THE SQUATTER'S DAUGHTER in 1907 were squatting dramas with similar preoccupations. Randolph Bedford's WHITE AUSTRALIA in 1909 was the most successful of several militaristic and racist plays that anticipated an Asian invasion of Australia, imitating the German invasion of Great Britain shown in the controversial presentation of Guy Du Maurier's *An Englishman's Home* in the same year.

The 1912 staging by Bert Bailey of a dramatisation of STEELE RUDD's *On Our Selection* stories led to a brief golden age of Australian commercial playwriting. In Brisbane in 1918 alone audiences could see ON OUR SELECTION, the most successful of all Australian plays; a thinly-disguised imitation called *The Heart of Australia—or, Dad Dalton's Selection*; two other Steele Rudd plays; *Keane of Kalgoorlie* by O'Sullivan and Arthur Wright; and *The Bunyip*.

BEAUMONT SMITH's dramatisations of Ethel Turner's *Seven Little Australians* in 1914 and Henry Lawson's *While the Billy Boils* in 1916, EDWARD DYSON's *The Golden Shanty* in 1913 and *Fact'ry 'Ands* in 1916, Con Drew and Oswald Anderson's *Jinker, the Grafter's Mate* in 1917 and RANDOLPH BEDFORD's *The Boss Cocky* in 1920 were other successes in various genres. Later C. J. Dennis's dramatisation of his *The Sentimental Bloke* (1921) and Rudd's *The Rudd Family* (1928) also appealed to the cheaper and more nationalistic end of the market. NELLIE BRAMLEY, E. I. COLE, KATE HOWARDE, PHILIP LYTTON, Tal Ordell, GEORGE SORLIE and others offered popular bush comedies in the same period, but the Great Depression ended their reign at the box office.

Literary drama

The amateur theatre had in the meantime begun to promote both overseas 'literary drama' and non-commercial Australian playwriting. Louis Esson's city comedy THE TIME IS NOT YET RIPE in 1912 was an early milestone, although Esson later repudiated it in favour of harsher bush tragedies like THE DROVERS, written in 1919 and performed in 1923, and slum dramas like *The Bride of Gospel Place* in 1924. Works by VANCE PALMER, KATHARINE SUSANNAH PRICHARD, Louis Stone and others had brief seasons through the work of the PIONEER PLAYERS in Melbourne. The repertory theatres were beginning to offer both literary drama from Britain and elsewhere, and serious Australian plays like LESLIE HAYLEN's antiwar drama *Two Minutes' Silence* in Sydney in 1930 and George Landen Dann's study of interracial marriage IN BEAUTY IT IS FINISHED in Brisbane in 1931. Betty Roland's THE TOUCH OF SILK, staged in Melbourne in 1928 and then in most other capital cities, and Esson's *The Time is Not Yet Ripe* are the only plays that have survived to reappear in the present-day Australian theatre.

The Great Depression, the introduction of talking films, a duplicated ENTERTAINMENTS TAX, and the suburbanisation of Australian cities caused a sudden collapse of the professional stage. In downtown Sydney venues for legitimate theatre declined from seven in 1929 to one by 1935. In Brisbane the number of plays presented declined by 60 per cent—from about 100 to 40—in just two years, 1929 to 1931. J. C. WILLIAMSON's fell back on seasons of Gilbert and Sullivan and revivals of musical comedies such as *The Maid of the Mountains* and *Rio Rita*.

Professional staging of classics was rare. In 1932 a tour by Sybil Thorndike and Lewis Casson included *Macbeth*, Euripides's *Medea* and Shaw's *Saint Joan*, but it was only after the Second World War that regular tours by major English companies and artists revived interest and audiences. Laurence Olivier and Vivien Leigh and the OLD VIC THEATRE COMPANY came in 1948 with *Richard III*, *The School for Scandal* and Thornton Wilder's *The Skin of Our Teeth*. The Shakespeare Memorial Theatre Company (now the ROYAL SHAKESPEARE COMPANY) followed in 1949 and 1953.

Amongst local professionals only JOHN ALDEN's companies gave regular tours of Shakespeare's plays, mostly for schools and sometimes backed by J. C. Williamson's, from 1951 onwards. Stylish comedy had a revival from 1946 when CYRIL RITCHARD and MADGE ELLIOTT toured with Noël Coward's *Tonight at 8.30*. Other British comedies followed —Coward's *Present Laughter* and Robert Morley in his own *Edward, My Son* in 1949—and there were occasional American comedies such as Mary Chase's *Harvey* with Joe E. Brown in 1950. Serious drama included Clare Boothe's *The Women* in 1938, Terence Rattigan's *The Winslow Boy* in 1948 and Tennessee Williams's *A Streetcar Named Desire* in 1950. Few Australian authors made any headway professionally, though some mystery and comedy genre pieces had short seasons—ALEC COPPEL's *I Killed the Count* in 1939 and *Mr Smart Guy* in 1941, and MAX AFFORD's *Lady in Danger* and *Laughter in the Dark* in 1944.

The most interesting and occasionally enduring work was done by the amateur theatres, although their contemporary impact was minimal. The works of Chekhov, Jacques Copeau, O'Neill, Luigi Pirandello, Strindberg, Wilder and, most often, Shaw were presented by AB INTRA STUDIO THEATRE in Adelaide, the GREGAN McMAHON PLAYERS and the MELBOURNE LITTLE THEATRE COMPANY in Melbourne, INDEPENDENT THEATRE and the Playbox Society in Sydney, and NEW THEATRE and other amateur companies in most capital cities. Plays by DOROTHY BLEWETT, MONA BRAND, DYMPHNA CUSACK, DULCIE DEAMER, ORIEL GRAY, GWEN MEREDITH, Ruth Park, BETTY ROLAND and Kylie Tennant were also performed. Cusack's 1942 MORNING SACRIFICE is one play of the period that has attracted recent interest and revival. The major success and a true Australian classic was Sumner Locke Elliott's RUSTY BUGLES in 1948, a semidocumentary account of his wartime experiences in a Northern Territory weapons-storage depot. ❧*Richard Fotheringham*

Since 1950

In the postwar years the repertoire offered to theatregoers was essentially limited to imported light comedies, dramas or musicals presented by professional managements and the work of amateur companies. One company that sought to offer audiences something more substantial was the COMPANY OF FOUR, founded in Perth in 1950. The first major break came in 1953 when the English director JOHN SUMNER created the Union Theatre Repertory Company, the first year-round professional theatre company in Australia. Later renamed the MELBOURNE THEATRE COMPANY, it operated initially at the Union Theatre at the University of Melbourne for seven months of the year and toured for the other months. Its objectives included encouragement of Australian playwrights and presentation of their work 'wherever practicable'. It opened with Jean Anouilh's *Colombe* and its early seasons included such playwrights as Christopher Fry, Rattigan, Shakespeare and Shaw. Later the repertoire was widened to included Aristophanes,

Bertolt Brecht, Federico García Lorca and the leading representatives of the contemporary American school—William Inge, Arthur Miller, William Saroyan and Williams. John Osborne's *Look Back in Anger* and *The Entertainer* and Arnold Wesker's *Roots* were all staged soon after their London premieres.

The triumph of Ray Lawler's SUMMER OF THE SEVENTEENTH DOLL in 1955 gave a fillip to Australian playwriting. It was taken up by the AUSTRALIAN ELIZABETHAN THEATRE TRUST and presented in Sydney with huge success. The production then went on national tour, and on to London and then New York with its Australian cast. Thereafter every season saw one or more works by Australian writers. In 1989, when the Melbourne Theatre Company celebrated its 500th production, it could boast that in 36 years it had presented almost 200 Australian plays.

WAL CHERRY, who had succeeded Sumner and Lawler as director of the Union Theatre Repertory Company in 1956, left it three years later to found the EMERALD HILL THEATRE COMPANY with the actor–director GEORGE WHALEY. The 140-seat Emerald Hill Theatre in South Melbourne opened in March 1962 with a large-scale Australian musical, *Not with Yours Truly*. In the next four years it did 29 major productions, with strong emphasis on new American and European writing. They included a compilation program *Brecht on Brecht*, Jean Anouilh's *Antigone*, Brendan Behan's *The Quare Fellow*, Spike Milligan's *The Bed Sitting Room*, Osborne's *Luther* and Sophocles's *Antigone*.

In 1962 there were three fully professional companies in Melbourne, the third being the ST MARTIN'S THEATRE COMPANY in South Yarra. It presented light West End comedies or thrillers balanced with more serious-minded contemporary plays and the occasional new Australia play. Until it ran down in the mid-1970s under competition from the Melbourne Theatre Company, St Martin's provided work for many leading actors, including GEORGE FAIRFAX, Norman Kaye and FRANK THRING. INDEPENDENT THEATRE and the PHILLIP STREET REVUES did the same for actors in Sydney. The TRUST PLAYERS were also based in Sydney. This company, founded by the AUSTRALIAN ELIZABETHAN THEATRE TRUST in 1959, toured productions including *Twelfth Night* and Sheridan's *The Rivals*, to other states until 1962. Another play taken up by the Trust and widely and successfully toured was THE SHIFTING HEART (1957), Richard Beynon's tragi-comedy on the theme of xenophobia.

The commercial theatre was vigorous at that time, with J. C. Williamson's and entrepreneurs such as GARNET H. CARROLL, KENN BRODZIAK and later young MICHAEL EDGLEY offering a wide, if traditional, variety of West End and Broadway entertainments. REVUE gradually succumbed to competition from television, on the TIVOLI CIRCUIT in 1966 and at the Phillip Theatre in 1971.

One by one the other capitals followed Melbourne's lead and created their own full-time professional companies. In Perth in 1960, RAYMOND WESTWELL was appointed the first artistic director of the NATIONAL THEATRE COMPANY and began a standard repertoire of popular classics, comedies, dramas and thrillers at the Playhouse. When EDGAR METCALFE took over in 1963 the company was fully professional. Perth also had the radical HOLE-IN-THE-WALL THEATRE COMPANY, which presented modern American, British and local plays. The OLD TOTE THEATRE COMPANY in Sydney opened its doors in 1963. The South Australian Theatre Company in Adelaide followed in 1965 and major companies in Brisbane and Hobart thereafter. The Old Tote company's professed aim was to present 'the best drama, whether classical or modern'. Its repertoire for the first few years included plays by Edward Albee, Brecht, Max Frisch, Eugène Ionesco and Joe Orton as well as Shaw, R. B. Sheridan, Wilde and William Wycherley. In 1966 it gave an experimental season of six Australian plays at the tiny JANE STREET THEATRE. Two years later the company presented a season of six Australian plays at its own theatre.

The Australian Council for the Arts, created in 1968, did much to underwrite the emergent Australian theatre and put it on a secure professional footing. Initially the council concentrated on establishing a mainstream theatre company in each state capital. But in the early 1970s it widened its policy to include funding for second-line and alternative companies, which were springing up in most states. The most influential were the AUSTRALIAN PERFORMING GROUP in Melbourne and the NIMROD THEATRE COMPANY in Sydney. Both opened their doors early in December 1970—the APG at the Pram Factory in Carlton and Nimrod at a one-time stables in Darlinghurst. The APG, which had grown out of laboratory-style experiments at the LA MAMA THEATRE, opened with MARVELLOUS MELBOURNE, a large-cast satirical work by Jack Hibberd and John Romeril which offered a cartoon view of early Melbourne. Nimrod opened with *Biggles*, a spoof on military-style fanaticism as well as a lighthearted send-up of Boy's Own literature. Together with THE LEGEND OF KING O'MALLEY by Michael Boddy and Bob Ellis, first performed at JANE STREET THEATRE in Sydney earlier in 1970, they marked the beginning of a long line of plays with maverick or larrikin heroes.

Commitment to Australian plays

From different starting-points Nimrod and the APG developed a fast-paced, strongly physical and mostly comic acting style, with a basis in revue, pantomime and vaudeville traditions. Between them, they revolutionised Australian playwriting. Two of their leading playwrights, ALEX BUZO and DAVID WILLIAMSON entered the mainstream repertoire in the early 1970s. Nimrod developed a keen interest in the classics, particularly Shakespeare, which the more radical APG did not share. They were both impatient with current theatre, which they claimed was derivative, secondhand and of little relevance to Australian audiences. Other alternative-theatre companies shared this view—particularly the Playbox Theatre Company in Melbourne, TROUPE and the Australian Stage Company in Adelaide, the HOLE-IN-THE-WALL THEATRE COMPANY in Perth and the BRISBANE REPERTORY THEATRE SOCIETY. All were strongly committed to the local product.

Playbox had begun at the end of 1976 as an alternative-theatre company with a strong commitment to new Australian writing and to 'theatre with an edge'. Playbox also declared itself to favour theatre that was 'contemporary, important, alive, Australian and fun'. This was a sideswipe at the Melbourne Theatre Company, whose work, the Playbox management believed, was far from being lively and never fun. The commitment to new Australian writing has been studiously maintained. At the company's original home in Exhibition Street, new Australian plays predominated. But there was also a strong emphasis on contemporary writing from England and the USA, especially Sam Shepard. During Rex Cramphorn's five years with the company, some classics were also in the repertoire, including three Shakespeare plays, Jean Racine's *Britannicus* and Molière's *Scapin*. The company—now the Playbox Theatre Centre of Monash University—has maintained its faith in the drawing power of the Australian playwright. In 1990 it moved to the CUB Malthouse Theatre, where Australian plays made up the entire repertoire in the first two years, with a preponderance of works by women.

The 1970s were a boom period for Australian writers. For example, an Australia Council survey showed that in the five years between 1975 and 1980, the general-grant companies—which excluded the Australian Stage Company, La Mama, Playbox and Troupe—gave professional productions of 277 plays by 169 Australian playwrights. Australian plays then formed more than 30 per cent of the repertoire of the general-grant companies. The figure has risen beyond 40 per cent, though individual companies like the Playbox far exceed that figure. When La Mama celebrated its 25th anniversary in 1992 it had hosted 675 productions, of which between two-thirds and three-quarters were Australian in origin.

While the volume of Australian work has increased sharply, so has the range. The early to middle 1970s were marked by preoccupation with Australian identity, behaviour and character. The outstanding example of this was Williamson, whose plays microscopically examining the behaviour patterns and power play of the Australian middle classes set audience records wherever they were played. Buzo was popular with audiences too, while Hibberd achieved critical success with his play for a solo actor, *A Stretch of the Imagination*, and wide popularity at home and abroad with his comedy of nuptial manners, *Dimboola*. As well as plays in a naturalistic or seminaturalistic vein, the decade also saw a rash of plays examining social issues such as police corruption and life in prison. The biographical play, exploring in none-too-reverential terms the lives of Australia's mythic or semi-mythic heroes and heroines, also proved a fertile field.

In the 1980s the ground occupied by the new Australian drama began to shift, the early obsession with Australia's roots and origins and with heroic figures giving way to new interests and concerns. Williamson continued to dominate the scene. But with *Sons of Cain* (1985) the social satirist gave way to the moralist interested in such topics as power-seeking, criminality and corruption. Louis Nowra and Stephen Sewell emerged as important playwrights too. Both set their plays abroad, earning for themselves the label of 'internationalists'. But progressively they turned their spotlight onto Australian society, with Sewell taking as his target the capitalist system with all its abuses in his panoramic parable play *Dreams in an Empty City* (1986). The 1980s also saw a renewed interest in Patrick White's work.

In 1982 Jim Sharman became artistic director of the State Theatre Company of South Australia and renamed it the Lighthouse Company. His statement of artistic policy included the active promotion and development of the work of Australia's 'finest playwrights—past, present and future'. It also included a commitment to broaden his audience's cultural and theatrical perspective by 'interpreting theatre from other times, traditions and cultures'. In practice, this meant shunning the British repertory tradition of Shaw, Wilde, Coward and Chekhov laced with contemporary comedies and proven farces. In two years in Adelaide, Sharman gave his audience Brecht, Heinrich von Kleist, Pierre Beaumarchais, Shakespeare, three plays by Nowra—*Spellbound*, *Royal Show* and *Sunrise*—and two by White, *Signal Driver* and *Netherwood*. The second year included Sewell's *The Blind Giant is Dancing*, another hard-hitting parable of Australian business and political life.

For a decade and more the community theatre movement was an important development. It began as a reaction against the work of the mainstream companies which were seen in some quarters to be highbrow, esoteric, and remote from the day-to-day interests and concerns of particular communities. Theatre, it was argued, had to be made more 'relevant'. So companies were created that set out consciously to create a grassroots form of theatre connected with the felt life of a particular community, town or district. Some of the most important of these groups were the Brisbane-based Popular Theatre Troupe, the Sidetrack Theatre Company in Sydney's western suburbs, the Deckchair Theatre Company in Fremantle (WA), and the Murray River Performing Group, based in Albury (NSW) and Wodonga (Vic.) and serving communities on both sides of the border. Many of the works created by these companies were group-devised. In general, those works were actor-based rather than text-oriented, focusing strongly on local identities, local experiences and local history. Sometimes the companies performed in traditional venues; at other times they created shows that could be performed in pubs, parks, historic homes, circus tents, factories or non-theatre settings. TheatreWorks performed its *Storming Mont Albert by Tram* on a Melbourne tram.

The community-theatre movement was the creature of its time and its heyday has passed, although vestiges can still be found in the work of such companies as the Arena Theatre Company in Melbourne and the Magpie Theatre Company in Adelaide. The interest of audiences, and of the funding bodies, has shifted to other fields, in particular black, multicultural and feminist writing and visual and performance theatre. Performance theatre is at its strongest in Sydney. Black theatre has found a fertile seedbed in Perth. Melbourne, which has long had a tradition of intelligent, thought-provoking theatre, has spawned companies whose work crosses stylistic barriers or geographical and cultural boundaries. They include Barrie Kosky's Gilgul Theatre Company, the first professional Jewish theatre company in Australia; Handspan Theatre, a visual theatre and puppetry company whose national and international successes include *Secrets* and Pablo Picasso's *Four Little Girls*; and Chamber Made Opera. The last company's works are primarily musical, but it has sought to extend the boundaries of conventional opera in highly theatrical works such as *The Cars That Ate Paris* and the internationally acclaimed *Recital*. Melbourne's popular Comedy Festival provides a showcase for comedians and cabaret artists.

Black theatre began modestly with the creation by Bob Maza of the National Black Theatre in Sydney. The first show, *Basically Black*, proved popular with both black and white audiences, as did Robert J. Merritt's *The Cake Man* (1975). But Jack Davis's *Kullark* shifted the centre of black writing to Perth, for whose sesquicentennial celebrations it was written. *Kullark* was followed at three-year intervals by the three plays that made up Davis's *The Firstborn* trilogy—No SUGAR, THE DREAMERS and *Barungin*. All three were first produced in conjunction with the Festival of Perth, which also commissioned Sally Morgan's *Sistergirl*, and were later performed together in Melbourne under Melbourne Theatre Company auspices. Another Aboriginal play of note to originate from Perth is Richard Walley's *Munjong*. Black theatre received a huge fillip with the production, first in Broome, then at the 1990 Festival of Perth, of the engaging upbeat Aboriginal musical BRAN NUE DAE, created by Jimmy Chi and the Kuckles band. It has since played to large audiences and critical acclaim around Australia.

In the commercial theatre the most remarkable change has been a move away from imported stars towards Australians, particularly for musicals. The advent of bustling, successful entrepreneurs such as HARRY M. MILLER hastened the demise of J. C. Williamson's, which had become fixed in its ways and its tastes, in 1976. Even so, commercial managements have not always found the going easy, and fortunes have been lost as well as made. Huge audiences still turn out for the big imported and heavily-promoted musicals such as *Les Misérables* and *Cats*. In Melbourne, *The Phantom of the Opera*, a carbon copy of the London production but with a strong Australian cast, played to capacity audiences for 1048 performances at the refurbished Princess Theatre, eclipsing the previous record for a musical held by *My Fair Lady*. The production also took $82 million at the box-office and injected an estimated $500 million into the Victorian economy before moving to Sydney. Commercial theatre has become big business, intensifying the calls (especially in Sydney) for venues big enough to stage the new blockbuster musicals such as *The Phantom of the Opera* and *Miss Saigon*.

The SYDNEY OPERA HOUSE, with its Drama Theatre, and even better equipped and more versatile PERFORMING-ARTS CENTRES in Adelaide, Melbourne and Brisbane have made theatregoing more comfortable for patrons. Initially, they also meant that companies could embark on large-scale productions that had been beyond their reach—for example, the Melbourne Theatre Company's productions at the Playhouse of *A Fortunate Life* by CLEM GORMAN in 1984 and *Our Country's Good* by Timberlake Wertenbaker in 1989. But in recent years such productions have become rarer. Companies, hard hit by the recession and by the steady decline in government funding, have had to pull in their horns. High rentals at the theatre complexes have proved an added financial burden. As a result, the mainstream companies have had to play cautiously and for the most part to eschew risks. They have also taken to sharing productions, which reduces rehearsal and production costs but also reduces the opportunities for actors, designers and directors. Already the West Australian Theatre Company, has gone into liquidation. If other capital-city companies are not to go the same way, the question of public funding —which determines repertoire to a marked degree—will have to be addressed. ❦*Leonard Radic*

further reading
HECKENBERG, PAMELA. The Australian playwright in the commercial theatre: 1914-1939. *Australian Drama 1920-1955*. Armidale: University of New England 1986.

NICOLL, ALLARDYCE. *A History of English Drama* 4–6. Cambridge University Press 1955–59.
VASEY, RUTH and ELIZABETH WRIGHT. A calendar of Sydney theatre performances 1870-79. Australian Theatre Studies Centre 1986.

Repertory Club

Amateur dramatic group in Perth, formed in December 1919. Incorporated 1922. Closed 1956. **first production** *Lady Windermere's Fan* by Oscar Wilde in His Majesty's Theatre. **venues** 1921–33 St Andrew's Hall (later Assembly Hall), Pier Street. 1933–56 West Australian Chambers, St George's Terrace.

For 37 years the Repertory Club was a dynamic force in Perth, where isolation gave amateur theatre a strength and importance not exceeded elsewhere in Australia. The club was formed soon after a successful amateur production of *Lady Windermere's Fan* under the leadership of Mrs G. L. Burgoyne at HIS MAJESTY'S THEATRE to raise funds for charity. Initially it was a small group with closed membership which interspersed performances in St Andrew's Hall with social events. In 1933 the club created its own theatre in premises in St George's Terrace.

The first season included HENRIETTA DRAKE-BROCKMAN's *Dampier's Ghost*. With the local manager for the ABC, Basil Kirke, the club formed a broadcasting subcommittee and made its first attempt at radio drama with *Dampier's Ghost*. The Repertory Club balanced local and other plays. Between 1932 and 1942 it gave first performances of some 30 new Australian plays, among them works by DYMPHNA CUSACK, Drake-Brockman, RUSSELL OAKES and ALEXANDER TURNER. From 1936, the club offered prizes for new Australian plays as part of its annual State Drama Festival.

In 1938 the club appointed Jerold Wells, from Sydney's NEW THEATRE League, honorary director. He brought a left-wing flavour to the club's staid audiences, in which there were few who had sampled the stark realism of Keith George's productions for the WORKERS' ART GUILD in Perth. Wells's first job was to stage Drake-Brockman's MEN WITHOUT WIVES. One of the club's principal actors in the 1930s was Alan Cuthbertson, who later built a career on caddish roles in British films.

Wartime travel restrictions intensified Perth's isolation by preventing visits by companies from eastern states so the Repertory Club almost alone provided the city's entertainment. In 1942 the club opened its seasons to non-members. Its shows raised many thousands of pounds for wartime charities. After the war splinter groups such as the COMPANY OF FOUR reached toward professionalism. In 1952 David Lopian, an Englishman, was appointed director of drama. In the inaugural Festival of Perth in 1953 he directed *Dark of the Moon* by Howard Richardson and William Berney. Its theme of voodoo and marital infidelity in American backwoods aroused huge controversy and calls for a ban. Lopian, distressed by the controversy and the underlying insularity, resigned in 1954. The club did not appoint another professional director but concentrated on raising funds which, aided by a small government loan, enabled it to build the Playhouse Theatre in Pier Street. With the opening of this new theatre in August 1956, the NATIONAL THEATRE COMPANY was inaugurated and the Repertory Club folded. ❦*Ivan King, Marie Simmons*

Research and scholarship

Until the 1960s most historical research into theatre in Australia was done by working or retired journalists, often using newspaper files as sources, and by memoir-writing old actors who seldom let truth spoil a good story—even when failing memory did not betray them. Perhaps the first attempt at documentation and analysis was in 'The rise and progress of drama in Australia', an article in the *Colonial Literary Journal* in 1845; it has been attributed to Daniel Deniehy. Listings of opening nights for historically significant or major plays and performers start to appear in encyclopaedias, yearbooks and annuals later in the 19th century. J. H. Heaton's 1879 *Australian Dictionary of Dates* has several pages on 'the drama', included the incorrect claim that the famous 'Barrington Prologue' was spoken at the opening of the SIDAWAY'S THEATRE in 1796.

In 1892 F. C. Brewer wrote an account of Sydney theatre for the 1893 World Exposition in Chicago. Another partial account is C. H. Bertie's history of the Theatre Royal in Sydney. A major early chronicler, principally of the Melbourne stage, was the journalist and playwright ROBERT P. WHITWORTH, who edited the theatrical journal *Lorgnette* in 1889-98. He wrote numerous biographical and historical articles for this magazine—which is a major source—and when popular plays were revived he often included details of previous Australian performances. Unfortunately, what he described as 'the theatre profession's archives' for the Colony of Victoria were lost in the Bijou Theatre fire in April 1890, and thereafter his accounts are less accurate. The earliest known surveys of some other cities are Gerald Fischer's 'The professional theatre in Adelaide 1838–1922', Michael Roe's booklet on the Theatre Royal in Hobart, E. Clifton's 'Music and the stage in the early days' in Perth, and anonymous articles on Brisbane in the *Queenslander* of 7 August 1900 and the *Brisbane Courier* of 28 July 1924.

Between 1890 and the beginnings of substantial scholarly work in the 1960s, many short contemporary and historical surveys, of varying scope, subject matter and quality, appeared in Australian and English publications. They include Austin Brereton's 'The drama in Australia' in *Theatre*, Nathaniel Barrett's 'The theatre and drama in Australia', several articles by Morgan McMahon in the *Lone Hand* in 1909-10; W. Farmer Whyte's 'The Australian stage—A glimpse of the past' and George Esmond's 'Theatre cavalcade'. A series of letters to the editor of the Melbourne *Age* in 1934, prompted by the closing of the THEATRE ROYAL, led to the formation of an Old Players' and Playgoers' Association. It had more than 200 members, who formed a large collection of photographs, playbills, programs and other memorabilia. A major exhibition was mounted in 1935, but the fate of this collection is unknown.

This kind of approach, drawing principally on newspaper reviews and personal and library collections of photographs and programs, culminated in the first book-length attempt to consider Australian theatre in several states across a substantial period, *The Australian Theatre* by Paul McGuire, Betty Arnott and Frances McGuire in 1948. It was followed by LESLIE REES's *Towards an Australian Drama* in 1953, and several booklets by John Kardoss in 1955 and 1960. John West's *Theatre in Australia*, like its forerunners, is directed to theatre-lovers rather than theatre historians, but it is more substantial, accurate, determinedly national in coverage and international in repertoire. With its overview of management and entrepreneurs it places theatre firmly in its commercial context. Its show-business focus, however, almost entirely excludes non-commercial theatre, which presented much of the most important Australian dramatic writing before 1970.

In modern reference works, chapters on drama like those by EUNICE HANGER and KATHARINE BRISBANE in various editions of Geoffrey Dutton's *The Literature of Australia* and entries on dramatists in the *Oxford Companion to Australian Literature* are substantial and significant. Terry Sturm's chapter in the *Oxford History of Australian Literature* has been particularly admired for its charting of strands of development and attempt at a historical overview. The literary emphasis in such accounts, however, gives little space to the economics of the performing arts. Edmund Fisher's 'The business side of drama' in 1909 is a rare early comment. Theatre scholars have tended to leave questions of finance and cultural policy-making to economists and government agencies. C. D. Throsby and G. A. Withers's *The Economics of the Performing Arts*, Tim Rowse's *Arguing the Arts* and Justin Macdonnell's *Arts, Minister* are sources for these matters. Ross Thorne's two-volume *Theatre Buildings in Australia to 1905* is the major product of scholarly research into theatrical architecture.

Writers and critics

In the 1920s and 1930s major Australian writers and critics such as Flora Eldershaw, Miles Franklin, John Le Gay Brereton and Nettie Palmer lectured on or published short accounts of Australian drama. Most were polemical and directed towards building an appreciation of the amateur movement. Like Allan Aldous's short *Theatre in Australia*, they disregarded the art form as industry or entertainment.

VANCE PALMER's *Louis Esson and the Australian Theatre*, an annotated collection of letters, shows the value of published documentation. It is by no means certain that LOUIS ESSON would be so central to accounts of literary–national drama in Australia between the world wars if material concerning other claimants had been readily available. Dramatic nationalism culminates in Leslie Rees's *Towards an Australian Drama*, which includes radio drama. Revised and expanded into two volumes as *A History of Australian Drama* in 1978, Rees's work is the most comprehensive in the entire field and has been deservedly acclaimed, although its aesthetic evaluations of plays are highly personal, and its occasional historical inaccuracies and deficiencies in its scholarly apparatus sometimes drive the reader back to primary sources. The second volume has been supplanted by more recent accounts of contemporary playwrights. LEONARD RADIC's *The State of Play* is similarly valuable and opinionated, a professional newspaper critic's survey of the Australian theatre since the late 1960s.

Personal memoirs have been major theatre documentation for hundreds of years, but they are notoriously unreliable in a profession that has depended so much on beating up publicity. Perhaps the most outrageous is Frank Gerald's *A Millionaire in Memories*, which manages to provide a fascinating glimpse of touring theatre in outback Queensland and other colonies and to be unbelievable in almost every other respect. Rather better are the letters of

Charles and Ellen Kean and the memoirs of John McCallum, Billy Moloney, Gladys Moncrieff, Ada Reeve, Emily Soldene and Nellie Stewart, to name but a few.

There are also uncritical biographies of celebrated theatrical personalities, performers and companies, such as Alec Bagot on George Coppin, Ian Dicker on J. C. Williamson, Trader Faulkner on Peter Finch, Geoffrey Hutton on the Melbourne Theatre Company, Eric Irvin on George Darrell, Fred Parsons on Roy Rene, Marjory Skill on Nellie Stewart, Josephine South on the Old Tote Theatre Company, Harry Spurr on his brother Mel B. Spurr, and Peter Ward on the State Theatre Company of South Australia. Virtually the only analytical works that provide a social context for their subject are Harold Love's *James Edward Neild* and Brian Kiernan's *David Williamson*.

Quality varies greatly, from Eric Irvin's meticulously accurate books, particularly his definitive *Theatre Comes to Australia*, to discursive, memory-based accounts such as Isidore Brodsky's *Sydney Takes the Stage*, and Hal Porter's *Stars of Australian Stage and Screen*. Viola Tait's history of J. C. Williamson's, *A Family of Brothers*, is a work of piety rather than of scholarship, but is useful as the only coverage of an important and neglected subject. David Holloway's *Playing the Empire* is valuable, although the chapters on the Holloway Company in Australia are the least documented. By far the most useful attempt at a historical overview is *The Australian Stage* edited by Harold Love. It reproduces a remarkably wide range of written and visual source material, with an explanatory introduction to each section, to offer an accurate and balanced survey of the nearly 200 years of live theatre in Australia.

Sources of colonial playscripts

One limitation shared by the above accounts (except Rees's and Radic's books) of individuals, companies, industry, architecture and occasionally society is that they do not analyse the stories told on stage. It was long assumed that most colonial playscripts were lost, and Irvin's *Australian Melodrama* draws principally on plot synopses in contemporary reviews. However many early scripts are now known to exist in the William Anderson, Bert Bailey, Bland Holt, and J. C. Williamson papers, the Australian Archives and elsewhere. Currency Press has published some of them with historical introductions in its 'National Theatre' series. Margaret Williams's *Australia on the Popular Stage 1829–1929* is the only book based on close reading of many early manuscripts. The result is a detailed interpretation of colonial stage and society, although Irvin's work is more accurate in empirical matters. Later work in this field includes the present writer's *Sport in Australian Drama*.

Research is in progress for the 20th century up to about 1968, but little has been published. *Australian Drama 1920–1955* is an unedited, poorly proofread volume based on papers given at a conference in Armidale in 1984. Alrene Sykes's 'Theatrical events 1950-1965' in *The Australian Stage* is by far the best account of the period, in which she had unique expertise. Her early death in 1990, like those of Helene Oppenheim in 1969 and Eunice Hanger in 1972, robbed Australia of a major theatrical scholar. Hanger was the first to draw international scholarly attention to modern Australian playwrights, and Oppenheim was the pioneer in archival research into the early Sydney stage.

Circus and vaudeville have produced a mixture of personal and scholarly accounts. Geoff Greaves's *The Circus Comes to Town* is slight. Mark St Leon's *The Circus in Australia* is the best researched account of the period to about 1870, while his biography of Mervyn King is excellent for the period from about 1912 onwards. Nancye Bridges's *Curtain Call*, Franquin's *The Eyes Have It*, Charles Norman's *When Vaudeville Was King* and Valantyne Napier's *Act as Known* are personal accounts of vaudeville life; the last is a major collection of documents and useful information. Richard Waterhouse's *From Minstrel Show to Vaudeville* is the first substantial work of scholarship and interpretation in an area of growing interest.

Occasional attempts have been made to produce calendars of Australian stage performances, beginning with short-lived series such as the *Australian Stage Annual* from 1901, various Australian Elizabethan Theatre Trust Yearbooks from 1956, and *Performing Arts Yearbooks* (1976–81), which collect performance records for those years.

The Australian Drama Bibliography Project based at the University of Queensland, begun principally by Alrene Sykes and carried on by Veronica Kelly, produced a microfiche of *Australian Drama Productions 1950–1969* in 1984 and a printed edition of plays for 1850–1869 has been announced. In 1986 the School of Theatre Studies at the University of New South Wales produced *A Calendar of Sydney Theatrical Performances 1870–1879*. A corresponding work by John Spring covers performances advertised in the Melbourne *Argus* in 1860–69. Eric Irvin's *Dictionary of the Australian Theatre 1788–1914* is an essential general guide to the colonial period, although it is less comprehensive for the years after about 1890. Several of Irvin's other books contain calendar appendices to their subjects, as does Liz Jones's 1988 commemorative volume on the La Mama Theatre in Melbourne.

Contemporary dramatists

Much present-day research is intended to inform study of the plays of contemporary dramatists. Peter Fitzpatrick's *After 'The Doll'* is a significant survey and analysis. In 1987 Methuen began a series of full-length studies on individual authors such as Alex Buzo, Jack Hibberd and David Williamson and published a collection of essays on community theatre. Peter Fitzpatrick's study of Stephen Sewell and Margaret Williams's study of Dorothy Hewett in the same series were published under the Currency imprint. About the same time Rodopi began producing 'Australian Playwrights', an innovative series of collections of essays or monographs edited by Ortrun Zuber-Skerritt on—and sometimes video interviews with—Hibberd, Louis Nowra, Stephen Sewell, Patrick White and Williamson.

Aboriginal playwrights have yet to be given extended analysis, except in more general works like Jack Davis and Bob Hodge's *Aboriginal Writing Today* and Adam Shoemaker's *Black Words, White Page* and *Swimming in the Mainstream*. The same is true of multicultural theatre, for which *Community Theatre in Australia* offers a guide to specialised research and documentation.

Articles on all the above can be found in journals such as *Komos* (1968–73) and *Australasian Drama Studies* (1982–) and magazines such as *Masque* (1968–71), *Theatre Australia* (1976–1982) and *New Theatre—Australia* (1987–89), while particular issues of other journals, such as *Meanjin* (1964/3 and 1984/1), *Aspect* 32–33 (1985), and the British *Theatre Quarterly* 26 (1977) and *New Theatre Quarterly* (1986) have focused on many aspects of theatre in Australia. Articles from such sources have been collected by Peter Holloway in *Contemporary Australian Drama*. ❦*Richard Fotheringham*

Collections

There are collections of books, periodicals, manuscripts, press cuttings, programs, pictures, posters, sound recordings, films, artefacts and other material related to Australian theatrical history in the National Library of Australia, state libraries, performing-arts centres and other institutions. All carry out acquisition, cataloguing, documentation, conservation, reference and exhibition functions but the attention each gives to a particular one varies considerably, depending upon funding, staffing, accommodation and the services available in other institutions in its city.

Adelaide

Colin and Gwynneth Ballantyne Performing Arts Collection of South Australia. Established in 1979 by the state government under the aegis of the State Theatre Company of South Australia, this collection was moved in 1985 from a church hall at Norwood to the Adelaide Festival Centre; in December 1986 it became the administrative responsibility of the ADELAIDE FESTIVAL CENTRE TRUST. Its named collections include the COLIN BALLANTYNE collection of theatre photographs 1936–72; the AGNES DOBSON collection; the Adelaide Q THEATRE collection; Tanya Moiseiwitsch's *Oedipus* costumes, masks and shoes; and the Wally Speed magic collection.

University of Adelaide. On 15 April 1993 the university opened its Performing Arts Library, a facility for its new performing-arts faculty, which was created through the university's amalgamation with the South Australian College of Advanced Education and incorporates the Elder Conservatorium.

Armidale NSW

University of New England. The Dixson Library holds the Campbell Howard Collection of unpublished Australian plays performed between 1920 and 1955.

Brisbane

University of Queensland. The Fryer Library holds the Hanger Collection of Australian stage and radio plays, and an extensive index to Australian literature.

Queensland Performing Arts Centre. The Gladys Moncrieff Library was opened in June 1988, with a gift of GLADYS MONCRIEFF memorabilia and theatrical material from Elsie Wilson.

State Library of Queensland. The John Oxley Library has theatre programs.

Canberra

Australian Archives. The repository for the records of federal government departments and agencies, such as the Australian Broadcasting Corporation. Patent and copyright records from the 1870s to 1969 include 100 metres of theatrical, film and radio scripts, sheet music, photographs, posters and other material. The collection of 85 000 items includes plays and other scripts by WILLIAM ANDERSON, BERT BAILEY, MARCUS CLARKE, EDMUND DUGGAN, EDWARD DYSON, KATE HOWARDE, WILLIAM MOORE, BETTY ROLAND, STEELE RUDD, Louis Stone and GEORGE WALLACE, and manuscript copies of historic plays and operettas, such as *Struck Oil* and *COLLITS' INN*.

National Film and Sound Archive. Officially established in 1984, this archive grew out of the National Library of Australia. It is responsible for collecting, preserving and making available material from the recorded-sound and moving-image industries. Since many great theatrical careers have embraced sound recording, film, radio and television, the archive is an invaluable source for theatrical history. The collection includes material relating to the careers of QUEENIE ASHTON, GRAEME BLUNDELL, PETER FINCH, FLORRIE FORDE, GLADYS MONCRIEFF, JUNE SALTER, LEONARD TEALE and BILLY WILLIAMS.

National Library of Australia. In addition to the national legal deposit collection of monographs and serials, the National Library holds records of J. C. WILLIAMSON'S from 1874 to 1973; national bodies such as the ARTS COUNCIL OF AUSTRALIA, the AUSTRALIAN ELIZABETHAN THEATRE TRUST and the AUSTRALIAN NATIONAL PLAYWRIGHTS' CONFERENCE 1973–75; and organisations based in the Australian Capital Territory, such as the ACT Council of Cultural Societies, the CANBERRA PHILHARMONIC SOCIETY and the CANBERRA REPERTORY SOCIETY. Individuals whose papers and manuscript collections are in the library include ROBYN ARCHER, Albert Arlen, BERT BAILEY, ALEX BUZO, EDMUND DUGGAN, LOUIS ESSON, ROBERT HELPMANN, DOROTHY HEWETT, JACK HIBBERD, BLAND HOLT, RAY MATHEW, RODNEY MILGATE, HARRY M. MILLER, GLADYS MONCRIEFF, VANCE PALMER, BETTY ROLAND, Geoffrey Rothwell, DINAH SHEARING, DOUGLAS STEWART, NELLIE STEWART, SYDNEY TOMHOLT and DAVID WILLIAMSON. There are oral-history interviews with many actors, critics, designers, directors and writers, including THELMA AFFORD, JOHN BELL, RICHARD BEYNON, RON BLAIR, Malcolm Blaylock, MONA BRAND, KATHARINE BRISBANE, JUNE BRONHILL, Nancy Brown, Alan Burke, Betty Burstall, ALEX BUZO, ZOË CALDWELL, COLLEEN CLIFFORD, RUTH CRACKNELL, REX CRAMPHORN, JACK DAVIS, GLORIA DAWN, John Derum, CATHERINE DUNCAN, DORIS FITTON, MAX GILLIES, HAYES GORDON, DOROTHY HELMRICH, ROBERT HELPMANN, JACK HIBBERD, Ken Horler, JENNY HOWARD, EDWARD HOWELL, BARRY HUMPHRIES, HUGH HUNT, PETER KENNA, NORMAN KESSELL, H. G. KIPPAX, TONI LAMOND, Ethel Lang, RAY LAWLER, BOBBY LE BRUN, Grace Le Brun, SUMNER LOCKE ELLIOTT, ROBIN LOVEJOY, GARRY MCDONALD, Amy McGrath, JIM MCNEIL, Robert J. Merritt, KEITH MICHELL, George Miller, HELEN MORSE, LOUIS NOWRA, BARRY OAKLEY, GEORGE OGILVIE, DENNIS OLSEN, PHILIP PARSONS, Michael Pate, JILL PERRYMAN, ROBERT QUENTIN, CYRIL RITCHARD, ALAN SEYMOUR, JIM SHARMAN, TONY SHELDON, BARBARA STELLMACH, Peter Summerton, JOHN SUMNER, BRIAN SYRON, BRIAN THOMSON, RIC THROSSELL, John Timlin, KERRY WALKER, RICHARD WHERRETT, DAVID WILLIAMSON, Jone Winchester, ELEANOR WITCOMBE. The pictorial collection contains original artwork, posters and photographs, including images of actors brought to Australia by GEORGE COPPIN. The collection of programs and ephemera is large.

Hobart
State Library of Tasmania. Includes J. W. B. Murphy collection of Tasmanian theatre posters 1896–1920.

Melbourne
Monash University Library. Sara Jenny Fischer's scrapbooks of her writings on theatre in Sydney 1879–82.

Victorian Arts Centre. The Performing Arts Museum, established in 1979, maintains a vigorous program of exhibitions on all aspects of the performing arts from 19th-century theatre to rock videos. Its innovative work includes touring exhibitions, a weekly radio program, a video lending library, annual awards and competitions, and educational programs. Its administrative, research and storage facilities were housed in several temporary locations between 1979 and 1988 before finding a permanent home beneath the Concert Hall of the arts centre. The museum has collections on ASHTON'S CIRCUS, the AUSTRALIAN PERFORMING GROUP, the EMERALD HILL THEATRE, the Melbourne Little Theatre Company and ST MARTIN'S THEATRE, and the NATIONAL THEATRE MOVEMENT and the Melbourne archives of J. C. WILLIAMSON'S. Other named collections include the Almost Managing Company collection, the Barbara Angell collection, the Holden circus collection, the BARRY HUMPHRIES collection, the Harry Jay photographic collection, the Les (GREAT) LEVANTE collection of stage illusions, the Bonnie McCallum photographic collection, the George Upward collection of Australian scenic design and the Angus Winneke collection of costume designs.

State Library of Victoria. The La Trobe collection is large and varied and is supplemented by the art, music and performing-arts collections. Holdings include the WILLIAM ANDERSON collection of Australian playscripts; the original papers of GEORGE COPPIN and BLAND HOLT, comprising more than 1000 playbills, printed plays, set and costume designs, letters and other material from 1819 to 1910; the papers of IRENE MITCHELL and DOLIA RIBUSH; original material performed by the goldfields balladeer Charles Thatcher; and the autobiography of ALLAN WILKIE. The library has the records of the Australian Children's Theatre, the AUSTRALIAN PERFORMING GROUP at the Pram Factory, the MELBOURNE REPERTORY THEATRE records and the Melbourne TIVOLI THEATRE. There are outstanding collections of posters relating to BARRY SULLIVAN in 1865 and posters printed by Troedel and Co. from 1870 to 1910. The library also holds a large collection of programs covering all the performing arts in Victoria from the 19th century to the present, the J. R. McEwen collection of lists of theatre performances advertised in Melbourne 1845–1970, and an outstanding collection of printed playscripts, such as *Cumberland's British Theatre*.

Perth
University of Western Australia. The Reid Library has scripts from the Playhouse.

State Library Service of Western Australia. The J. S. Battye Library of West Australian History has oral-history tapes on theatre.

Theatre Collection. The actor Ivan King began gathering material during the restoration of HIS MAJESTY'S THEATRE in Perth in 1977–80. The collection was established at His Majesty's in 1980 as the archive of the Perth Theatre Trust. It is responsible for collecting memorabilia relating to the performing arts in Western Australia and for presenting foyer displays at His Majesty's and other Perth theatres. Its major collections include records of His Majesty's, the NATIONAL THEATRE COMPANY from 1956 to 1984, the PERTH THEATRE TRUST and the REPERTORY CLUB from 1919 to 1956. The oldest item in the collection is a silk program from an 1856 amateur performance.

Sydney
Dennis Wolanski Library of the Performing Arts. The primary responsibility of the library is the preservation of archival material on the history of the architecture, construction and performance of the SYDNEY OPERA HOUSE, where it was established in 1973. It was named after a Sydney businessman and sculptor in recognition of his financial support. The library has named collections relating to the Actors Company, the ARTS COUNCIL OF NSW, the INDEPENDENT THEATRE COMPANY, the NATIONAL INSTITUTE OF DRAMATIC ART, NEW THEATRE SYDNEY, the NIMROD THEATRE COMPANY, THE OLD TOTE THEATRE COMPANY, the Paris Theatre Company, the Pipi Storm Children's Circus, the Professional Drama Council and the TIVOLI THEATRE. People represented by named collections include: MADGE ELLIOTT and CYRIL RITCHARD, NICK ENRIGHT, WILLIE FENNELL, ROBERT HELPMANN, ANNETTE KELLERMANN, FRED LESLIE and NELLIE STEWART. The library also has the Mark St Leon circus collection, the Frank Harris collection of theatre, music and dance reviews from 1953 to 1984 and an extensive press clippings file that holds information on the performing arts in Australia since 1843. The library's collection of scrapbooks includes volumes on theatre in Australia 1853–1911, variety theatre in Australia 1911–1927 and 1921–34, modern dance in Australia 1930–50, the Independent Theatre production of *Rusty Bugles* in 1948 and the NSW country tour of *Summer of the Seventeenth Doll* in 1958. The library's pictorial collection includes the Royce Rees collection of Australian theatre negatives 1946–64 and original portraits of DORIS FITTON, ROY RENE and NELLIE STEWART and other notable figures. Stage design is represented by collections of original works by WILLIAM CONSTABLE, DESMONDE DOWNING, FRANK HINDER, Tom Lingwood and LOUDON SAINTHILL. Changes to the collection were initiated in 1994 to accommodate TheatreWorks, a performing-arts museum, due to open in 1997.

State Library of NSW. The Mitchell Library holds the earliest documents relating to theatre in Australia. These include a playbill for *The Recruiting Officer* in 1800 and a playbill for *Black-Eyed Susan* in 1832. The major theatrical collection is from the Sydney office of J. C. WILLIAMSON'S from about 1895 to 1970. Other collections include the JOHN ALDEN papers from about 1943 to about 1951; the WILLIAM ANDERSON collection of Australian playscripts from about 1894 to 1921; Drama League of Australia records; DORIS FITTON papers 1933–1942; Lazar theatrical papers 1849–1880; the DUNCAN MACDOUGALL collection; records of the MARIONETTE THEATRE OF AUSTRALIA; MARY MARLOWE papers 1875–1958; records of the Phillip Theatre in Sydney; records of the POCKET PLAYHOUSE

1957–76; HAL PORTER papers 1924–83; JAMES SMITH papers; Turret Theatre Ltd papers 1928–29. There are particularly useful handwritten compilations relating to the period 1789–1857: a chronological list of plays, lectures and concerts in Sydney compiled from newspapers 1826–57; Drama in NSW—a collection of comments from the contemporary press 1789–1830; Early Performances of Plays in Sydney—a list in chronological order, 1789–1855; lists of performers in amateur and public concerts at the Theatre Royal, 1826–1837. The Shakespeare Tercentenary Memorial Library is one of the world's major Shakespearean collections, and includes the only First Folio in Australia.

University of Sydney. The Fisher Library holds theatre programs from 1930 to the present, mainly from Sydney theatres. 🍃*Paul Bentley*

sources for reference

AKERHOLT, MAY-BRIT. *Patrick White*. Amsterdam (Netherlands): Rodopi 1988.

ALDOUS, ALLAN. *Theatre in Australia*. 1947. Melbourne: Cheshire 1947.

BAGOT, ALEC. *Coppin the Great*. Melbourne University Press 1965.

BARRETT, NATHANIEL. *The Dramatic Year Book for the year ending Dec. 31st 1891 The theatre and drama in Australia*. London: 1892.

BEDSON, JACK and JULIAN CROFT (eds). *The Campbell Howard Annotated Index of Australian Plays 1920–1955*. Armidale (NSW): University of New England 1993.

BERTIE, CHARLES H. *The Story of the Royal Hotel and the Theatre Royal Sydney*. Sydney: Kralco Printing 1966.

BRERETON, AUSTIN. Australian theatre. *Theatre* (London) January 1890.

BREWER, FRANCIS C. *The Drama and Music in New South Wales*. Sydney: NSW Government Printer 1892.

BRIDGES, NANCY and FRANK CROOK. *Curtain Call*. Sydney: Cassell 1980.

BRISBANE, KATHARINE. Australian drama. *The Literature of Australia* (ed. Geoffrey Dutton) revised. Melbourne: Penguin 1976.

BRODSKY, ISIDORE. *Sydney Takes the Stage*. Sydney: Old Sydney Free Press 1963.

CARROLL, DENNIS. *Australian Contemporary Drama*. Sydney: Currency Press 1995.

CLIFTON, E. Music and the stage in the early days. *Western Australian Historical Society Journal* (Perth) 1930.

DAVIS, JACK and BOB HODGE (eds). *Aboriginal Writing Today*. Canberra: Australian Institute for Aboriginal Studies 1985.

DICKER, IAN G. *J.C.W.—A short biography of James Cassius Williamson*. Sydney: Elizabeth Tudor Press 1974.

DYCE, J. R. *Patrick White as Playwright*. Brisbane: University of Queensland Press 1974.

ESMOND, GEORGE. Theatre cavalcade. *South Australian Homes and Gardens* (Adelaide) 1 June 1936.

FARMER WHYTE, W. The Australian Stage—A glimpse of the past. *Journal of the Australian Historical Society* (Sydney) 1917.

FAULKNER, TRADER. *Peter Finch*. London: Angus and Robertson 1979.

FISCHER, GERALD. The professional theatre in Adelaide 1838–1922. *Australian Letters* 2/4 (Adelaide, 1960).

FISHER, EDMUND. The business side of the drama. *Lone Hand* (Sydney) 1 July 1909.

FITZPATRICK, PETER. *After 'The Doll'—Australian drama since 1955*. Melbourne: Edward Arnold 1979.

FITZPATRICK, PETER. *Stephen Sewell—The playwright as revolutionary*. Sydney: Currency Press 1991.

FITZPATRICK, PETER. *Williamson*. Sydney: Methuen 1987.

FOTHERINGHAM, RICHARD (ed.). *Community Theatre in Australia*. Sydney: Currency Press 1992.

FOTHERINGHAM, RICHARD. *Sport in Australian Drama*. Melbourne: Cambridge University Press 1992.

FRANQUIN. *The Eyes Have It*. Sydney: Angus and Robertson 1957.

GERALD, FRANK. *A Millionaire in Memories*. London: Hutchinson 1936.

GREAVES, GEOFF. *The Circus Comes to Town*. Sydney: Reed 1980.

HAINSWORTH, J. D. *Hibberd*. Melbourne: Methuen 1987.

HEATON, J. H. *Australian Dictionary of Dates and Men of the Time*. Melbourne: George Robertson 1879.

HOLLOWAY, DAVID. *Playing the Empire*. London: Harrap 1979.

HOLLOWAY, PETER (ed.). *Contemporary Australian Drama* revised. Sydney: Currency Press 1987.

HUTTON, GEOFFREY. *It Won't Last a Week*. Melbourne: Sun 1975.

IRVIN, ERIC. *Australian Melodrama*. Sydney: Hale and Iremonger 1981.

IRVIN, ERIC. *Dictionary of the Australian Theatre 1788–1914*. Sydney: Hale and Iremonger 1985.

IRVIN, ERIC. *Gentleman George, King of Melodrama*. Brisbane: University of Queensland Press 1980.

IRVIN, ERIC. *Theatre Comes to Australia*. Brisbane: University of Queensland Press 1971.

JONES, LIZ with BETTY BURSTALL and HELEN GARNER. *La Mama*. Melbourne: McPhee Gribble/Penguin 1988.

KEAN, CHARLES and ELLEN. *Emigrant in Motley* (ed. J. M. D. Hardwick). London: Rockliffe 1954.

KELLY, VERONICA (ed.). *Louis Nowra*. Amsterdam (Netherlands): Rodopi 1987.

LOVE, HAROLD (ed.). *The Australian Stage*. Sydney: University of NSW Press 1984.

LOVE, HAROLD. *James Edward Neild*. Melbourne University Press 1989.

MACDONNELL, JUSTIN. *Arts, Minister?* Sydney: Currency Press 1992.

MOLONEY, BILLY. *Memoirs of an Abominable Showman*. Adelaide: Rigby 1968.

MCCALLUM, JOHN. *Buzo*. Melbourne: Methuen 1987.

MCCALLUM, JOHN. *Life with Googie*. London: Heinemann 1979.

MCCALLUM, JOHN. Studying Australian drama. *Australasian Drama Studies* 12–13 (Brisbane, 1988).

MCGILLICK, PAUL. *Jack Hibberd*. Amsterdam (Netherlands): Rodopi 1988.

MCGUIRE, PAUL with BETTY ARNOTT and FRANCES MARGARET MCGUIRE. *The Australian Theatre*. London: Oxford University Press 1948.

MONCRIEFF, GLADYS. *My Life of Song (Our Glad)*. Adelaide: Rigby 1971.

NAPIER, VALANTYNE. *Act as Known*. Melbourne: Globe Press 1986.

NORMAN, CHARLES. *When Vaudeville Was King*. Melbourne: Spectrum Publications 1984.

OPPENHEIM, HELENE. Colonial theatre. Mitchell Library MS. 3266. Microfilm copy in State Library of Tasmania.

PALMER, VANCE. *Louis Esson and the Australian Theatre*. Melbourne: Georgian House 1948.

PARSONS, FRED. *A Man Called Mo*. Melbourne: Heinemann 1973.

PFISTERER-SMITH, SUSAN. Playing with the past—Towards a feminist deconstruction of Australian theatre historiography. *Australasian Drama Studies* (Brisbane) October 1993.

PORTER, HAL. *Stars of Australian Stage and Screen*. Adelaide: Rigby 1965.

POTTER, MICHELLE. *A Full House—The Esso guide to the performing arts collections of the National Library of Australia*. Canberra: National Library of Australia 1991.

RADIC, LEONARD. *The State of Play*. Melbourne: Penguin 1991.

REES, LESLIE. *A History of Australian Drama* 2 vols. Sydney: Angus and Robertson 1987.

REES, LESLIE. *Towards an Australian Drama*. Sydney: Angus and Robertson 1953.

REEVE, ADA. *Take It for a Fact*. London: William Heinemann 1954.

ROE, MICHAEL. *A History of the Theatre Royal, Hobart, from 1834* revised (ed. Gillian Winter). Hobart: Law Society of Tasmania 1965.
SHOEMAKER, ADAM. *Black Words, White Page*. Brisbane: University of Queensland Press 1989.
SHOEMAKER, ADAM. *Swimming in the Mainstream*. London: University of London 1990.
SKILL, MARJORIE. *Sweet Nell of Old Sydney*. Sydney: Urania 1974.
SOLDENE, EMILY. *My Theatrical and Musical Recollections*. London: Downey and Co. 1897.
SOUTH, JOSEPHINE (ed.). *Ten on the Tote—An illustrated history of the Old Tote Theatre Company to celebrate its tenth anniversary, 1963–1973*. Sydney: Old Tote Theatre Company 1973.
SPRING, JOHN. *A Frequency List of Dramatic Performances Advertised in the Melbourne Argus between January 1860 and December 1869—English department bibliographical checklist no. 5*. Melbourne: Monash University 1977.
SPURR, HARRY B. *Mel B. Spurr*. London: Brown and Sons 1906.
ST LEON, MARK. *Spangles and Sawdust*. Melbourne: Greenhouse 1983.
ST LEON, MARK. *Australian Circus Reminiscences*. Ms. 1984. Copies in major public and university libraries throughout Australia, national libraries of United Kingdom, Wales, Scotland and New Zealand, and in several libraries in USA.
ST LEON, MARK. *Australian circus sources*. Ms. 1985. Copies in major public and university libraries throughout Australia, national libraries of United Kingdom, Wales, Scotland and New Zealand, and in several libraries in USA.
ST LEON, MARK. *The circus in Australia 1842–1921*. Ms. 1981. Copies in major public and university libraries throughout Australia, national libraries of United Kingdom, Wales, Scotland and New Zealand, and in several libraries in USA.
STEWART, NELLIE. *My Life's Story*. Sydney: John Sands 1923.
STURM, TERRY. Drama. *Oxford History of Australian Literature* (ed. Leonie Kramer). Melbourne: Oxford University Press 1981.
TAIT, VIOLA. *A Family of Brothers*. Melbourne: Heinemann 1971.
THORNE, ROSS. *Theatre Buildings in Australia to 1905*. University of Sydney 1971.
THORNE, ROSS. *Theatres in Australia*. University of Sydney 1977.
THROSBY, C. D. and G. A. WITHERS. *The Economics of the Performing Arts*. Melbourne: Edward Arnold 1979.
VELLA, MAEVE and HELEN RICKARDS. *Theatre of the Impossible—Puppet theatre in Australia*. Sydney: Craftsman House 1989.
WARD, PETER. *A Singular Act—Twenty-five years of the State Theatre Company of South Australia*. Adelaide: Wakefield Press 1992.
WATERHOUSE, RICHARD. *From Minstrel Show to Vaudeville*. Sydney: NSW University Press 1990.
WEST, JOHN. *Theatre in Australia*. Sydney: Cassell 1978.
WHITE, OLGA and ANN-MARIE SCHWIRTLICH and JENNIFER NASH. *Our Heritage—A directory of archives and manuscript repositories in Australia*. Canberra: Australian Society of Archivists 1983.
WILDE, WILLIAM and JOY HOOTON and BARRY ANDREWS. *The Oxford Companion to Australian Literature*. Melbourne: Oxford University Press 1983.
WILLIAMS, MARGARET. *Australia on the Popular Stage 1829–1929*. Melbourne: Oxford University Press 1983.
WILLIAMS, MARGARET. *Dorothy Hewett—The feminine as subversion*. Sydney: Currency Press 1992.
ZUBER-SKERRETT, ORTRUN (ed.). *David Williamson*. Amsterdam (Netherlands): Rodopi 1988.
Australian Drama 1920–55. Armidale (NSW): University of New England 1986.
Calendar of Sydney Theatrical Performances 1870-1879, A. Sydney: University of NSW 1986.
Directory of Arts Libraries and Resource Collections in Australia. Sydney: Australia Council 1983.
Directory of Special Collections in Australiana. Sydney: Library Association of Australia, Acquisition Section, NSW Group 1988.
Guide to Collections of Manuscripts Relating to Australia. Canberra: National Library of Australia 1965.

Revue

Revue, which went from France to London in the late 19th century, is traditionally a mixture of satire, songs and sketches, and usually looks with a jaundiced eye at the events and personalities of the day. A successful revue should be substantially incomprehensible to audiences of the next generation. Revue has a company of performers working together, a strong comic presence, a backing chorus, plenty of music and a structure of sketches and songs. Vaudeville on the other hand was composed of 'slick variety bills of eight to ten acts, one after another without pause', says VALANTYNE NAPIER, a vaudevillian. 'There were no comperes … Neither were there any "openings" or scenas or finale with all the performers on stage together. Nor was there a producer!'

Twentieth-century revue is an adjunct of the jazz age, and its first success in London was *Hullo, Ragtime* in 1912. A revue called *Come Over Here* was the Christmas attraction of J. C. WILLIAMSON's at Her Majesty's Theatre in Sydney in 1913. During the First World War the two major vaudeville managements, FULLERS' and the TIVOLI CIRCUIT, adopted revue and often made it half of the bill, with vaudeville in the other half. By the 1930s revue had ousted true vaudeville completely.

A variation, intimate revue, emerged in London before the Second World War. WILLIAM ORR made this form of entertainment immensely popular with his PHILLIP STREET REVUES in Sydney from 1953. ♥*John West*

Dolia Ribush

Director. Born 13 June 1896 in Russia, of Jewish parents. Studied medicine but did not graduate. Trained for theatre in early 1920s. Worked as actor and confectioner in Soviet Union and Germany. Married Rosa Revid, Latvian language teacher, 1927. Settled in Melbourne and established confectionery company 1928. Formed amateur Dolia Ribush Players. Died 5 October 1947 in Melbourne.

Dolia Ribush extracted excellent performances from amateur and inexperienced actors through exacting and lengthy rehearsals over six to eight months. In productions in the tradition of the Moscow Art Theatre, he used techniques derived from Konstantin Stanislavsky and developed through his own experiences and experiments. Ribush advocated detailed analysis of the text, and an evolutionary rather than prescriptive approach to directing. He demanded that an actor 'become' the character, avoiding imitative stock gesture and accent.

He formed the amateur Dolia Ribush Players after producing some short plays for the Russian Club in 1931–32. Productions of Maxim Gorky's *The Lower Depths* in 1936 and Anton Chekhov's *The Cherry Orchard* in 1938 established him as Melbourne's most innovative director. In 1942 Ribush was invited to direct a contemporary Soviet play, *Distant Point* by Alexander Afinogenov, for the New Theatre Club.

Ribush turned his attention to new Australian plays with Douglas Stewart's NED KELLY at the Melbourne University Union Theatre in 1944. He was working on *Hail Tomorrow* by VANCE PALMER when he suddenly died of heart disease. Ribush and his widow are commemorated by AWARDS. ♥*Angela O'Brien*

further reading
PHILLIPS, A. A. *Dolia Ribush. Australian Dictionary of Biography* 11. Melbourne University Press 1988.
reference
Ribush papers in La Trobe Library (Melbourne).

Wendy Richardson

Dramatist. Born 21 December 1933 at Singleton (NSW). Educated at Newcastle Teachers' College. Taught in schools to 1977. Community worker in Wollongong to 1983. Studied drama at University of Wollongong. Began writing 1986.

A professional community playwright, Wendy Richardson draws her subjects from the Illawarra region of NSW, where she has lived for 25 years. She began writing plays in 1986, when Wollongong's THEATRE SOUTH commissioned *Windy Gully*, which deals with a mine disaster at nearby Mt Kembla in 1902. Her plays present a virtual social history of the region. The text, derived from detailed research, especially oral history, emerges as 'folk history', portraying events and issues of local import and celebrating the spirit of people in times of stress and crisis. Richardson employs familiar practices of Australian popular theatre—'docu-drama', music and 'Oz larrikinism'—with a leavening of poetic naturalism. The plays work well on stage and have been well received by audiences in the region and beyond, when toured by Theatre South. This suggests that they go beyond their parochial subjects to tap into shared experience. ❦*Maurie Scott*

published play
Windy Gully (1987). Sydney: Currency Press 1987.

Harry Rickards

Comedian, entrepreneur. Born 4 December 1843 in London. Originally Benjamin Harry Leete. Made professional debut at Theatre Royal, Runcorn, in *Rob Roy*. Appeared as Harry Rickards in suburban London music halls for John Wilton. Toured Australasia with Enderby Jackson and small company 1871–74, and USA 1874–75. Toured Australasia with own companies 1885–87 and 1888–91. Settled in Australia 1892. Opened Tivoli Theatre, Sydney, 18 February 1893. Expanded operations to Melbourne 1895 and Adelaide 1900. Died 13 October 1911 in England.

The style and character of the golden era of vaudeville in Australia, from 1895 until the early 1930s, stemmed from Harry Rickards, who imported many top overseas acts and encouraged emerging local artists. Australia's vaudeville king was born, the son of a printer, in the slums of Stratford in the East End of London. As a youth he was apprenticed to an engineer but he preferred to sing for pennies in local pubs. His natural voice and easy manner led to regular professional engagements—as Harry Rickards—in the smaller music halls that peppered the London suburbs.

Rickards's break came in 1863 with a rollicking song 'Captain Jinks of the Horse Marines'. Five years later, still in his mid-twenties, he was commanding £20 a week and appearing at the best halls in London as a *lion comique*—the toff, with moustache and cane, singing of champagne and the high life. He tried his hand at management and took control of the Swiss Cottage, a small music hall. This enterprise ended in bankruptcy, and in 1871, he attempted to recoup his fortunes by touring the colonies in partnership with the manager Enderby Jackson, with a small company, which included his first wife, Carrie Tudor.

Rickards made his Australian debut on 2 December 1871 in a benefit performance at the Princess's Theatre in Melbourne. The company then appeared with great success for many weeks at St George's Hall. The tour continued through Australia and New Zealand, covering small towns as well as big cities. In 1874 the company sailed for San Francisco. It toured across the USA, appearing in New York City at the Theatre Comique from 15 February 1875. Rickards returned to London, where he starred at the important London Pavilion music hall. In 1876 he toured South Africa with a small company. Back in England, he leased St James' Hall in Plymouth, and managed it with the help of his second wife, a Melbourne-born dancer named Kate Roscoe or Roscow. In 1885 he organised another company for a tour of Australia and New Zealand. It opened at the Academy of Music in Adelaide on 6 June 1885. This company played the 'smalls', such as Wagga Wagga (NSW) and Gympie (Qld), as well as the cities. It returned to England in 1887.

Rickards set out for Australia again in 1888, accompanied by his wife, their three children, and a supporting company of eight. This tour, which started on 28 April 1888 at the Theatre Royal in Adelaide, was a mixed success. For a while Rickards was reduced to singing aboard pleasure boats on Sydney Harbour. He decided to make Australia his home, and returned to England in 1891 to settle his affairs, book artists and pick up some new songs. Rickards returned by way of South Africa, where he and his brother Jack Leete, now his business manager, had organised a six-month tour. He found Australia vastly changed. The economic boom had collapsed and theatre attendances had dwindled. Courageously Rickards leased the Opera House in Sydney for his New Tivoli Minstrel and Grand Specialty Company of Forty Great Artistes, and opened there on 10 December 1892. Success encouraged him to take a long-term lease of the Garrick Theatre. Rickards refurbished the house, renamed it the TIVOLI THEATRE, and rang up the curtain on 18 February 1893. He operated it on traditional English music-hall lines

Entrepreneurial success encouraged Rickards to limit his stage appearances and to extend his operations to the PRINCE OF WALES OPERA HOUSE in Melbourne, which he leased in 1895. Later that year he returned to Britain to book acts for his theatres. His early star imports included a fellow *lion comique*, Charles Godfrey; the comedian G. H. Chirgwin, 'the White-Eyed Kaffir'; the great juggler Paul Cinquevalli; and the American illusionist Carl Hertz, who screened the first motion pictures in Australia at the Opera House on 22 August 1896. In 1897 Rickards failed with two musical comedies, *A Bunch of Keys* and *Binks, the Photographer* but fared better with a lavish pantomime, *Jack the Giant-Killer*, at Christmas. In 1898 PATTIE BROWNE appeared under his management in pieces such as *Sweet Nancy* and J. M. Barrie's *The Little Minister*.

In March 1899, Rickards bought the freehold of the Tivoli Theatre in Sydney. Less than six months later fire destroyed the theatre. Rickards rebuilt it and opened his new Tivoli Theatre on 12 April 1900. In June 1900 he leased Hudson's Bijou Theatre in Adelaide, and renamed it the

Tivoli Theatre. On 18 May 1901 he opened the New Opera House in Melbourne, built on the site of the old Prince of Wales Opera House.

Rickards continued to import the world's finest vaudeville stars. The magician Carter the Great, the mysterious Chung Ling Soo, the young comic juggler W. C. Fields, the enigmatic American entertainer George Fuller Golden, the escapologist Harry Houdini, Walter C. Kelly 'the Virginian Judge', the diminutive comic Little Tich, the cheeky comedian Marie Lloyd, Julian Rose (whose 'Hebrew' act inspired young ROY RENE), the ventriloquist Fred Russell, Sandow the strong man, the rumbustious Harry Tate, the Australian comic singer BILLY WILLIAMS—and dozens more. Many Australian stars, including MARSHALL CROSBY, FLORRIE FORDE, Essie Jennings, Charlie Vaude and ALBERT WHELAN got their start on Rickards's bills.

Rickards, astute and benevolent, reigned as Australia's vaudeville king for 16 years. His empire was his consuming passion and he was on a talent-buying trip when he died in England in 1911. His body was returned to Sydney for burial at Waverley Cemetery. He was survived by his wife and two daughters, his son having died at the age of eight. Rickards left a fortune of £135 000, and the first TIVOLI CIRCUIT, one of the most successful and important vaudeville circuits in the world. HUGH D. MCINTOSH paid £100 000 for the control of it in 1912. ❦*Frank Van Straten*

further reading
FOWLER, J. BERESFORD. *Stars in My Backyard*. Ilfracombe (England): A. H. Stockwell *c*.1960.
RUTLEDGE, MARTHA. Harry Rickards. *Australian Dictionary of Biography* 11. Melbourne University Press 1988.

Grattan Riggs

Actor. Born 1835 in Buffalo (New York, USA). Began career in Buffalo. Established himself in New York City at National Theatre, American Theatre, New Bowery and Bowery Opera House. Arrived in Australia in 1880 under contract to George Coppin. Later played in companies of J. C. Williamson, George Musgrove and MacMahon Brothers, appearing in all Australian colonies. Died 15 June 1899 at Strahan (Tas).

One of the best-known and most genial theatrical figures of his time, Grattan Riggs was most appreciated in comic Irish parts. He was particularly identified with *The Shaughraun* by DION BOUCICAULT, *Shin Fane* and *The Irish Detective*, in which he played five different characters. Despite age, ill-health and changes in metropolitan taste Riggs undertook country tours and, according to the *Tasmanian Mail*, he retained 'a wonderful hold upon his public' until his death. ❦*Gillian Winter*

further reading
Age (Melbourne) 16 June 1899.
Mercury (Hobart) 16 June 1899.
Tasmanian Mail (Hobart) 24 June 1899.

George Rignold

Actor, manager. Born *c*.1834 in England to actor parents. Originally George Richard Rignall. Began professional career at Theatre Royal, Bristol, and other theatres in west of England. Acted in London in early 1870s. In *Henry V* at Manchester 1872. Took over title-role for tour of USA, Australia (1876) and New Zealand. Unsuccessful London season 1879. Settled in Australia 1884. Leased Her Majesty's Theatre, Sydney, 10 September 1887 to 21 September 1895. Visited London 1901. Died in Sydney 1912. Second wife was Georgina Coppin, daughter of entrepreneur George Coppin.

George Rignold came to Australia in 1876 to play the role by which he was to be known and remembered all his life—Shakespeare's Henry V. He arrived in Sydney from San Francisco with a small group of players and engaged more than 30 local actors for minor roles and a huge number of extras. 'Wanted Immediately: 100 Smart Young Men', said advertisements in the *Sydney Morning Herald*. Some reports claimed that more than 400 persons were on stage in the great battle scenes of *Henry V*, which opened at the Theatre Royal on 28 August 1876.

Rignold staged Shakespeare in tableau fashion, editing and rearranging the text to provide continuous action in one location and a sequence of vast three-dimensional pictures of famous events and places. These included 'the Throne Room in the Palace at Westminster', 'the Siege of Harfleur', 'the Battle of Agincourt', 'Reception of King Henry V in London' and—a scene not in Shakespeare's play—'Interior of the Cathedral at Troyne', where King Henry and Princess Katherine of Valois were married. The crowds of citizens and soldiers were carefully posed on the stage so as to blend in perspective with hundreds more figures painted on the backcloth, so that at Agincourt 'the entire breadth and depth of the stage is one mass of fighting figures extending … as far as the eye can reach', said the *Sydney Morning Herald* on 30 August 1876. 'In the front King Henry and a French nobleman, on horseback, are engaged in hand-to-hand conflict'. The curtain fell on this spectacle, but on opening night had to be raised again several times 'in response to the general acclamations'. Enormous houses were reported, as loyal British subjects hurried to this splendid example of what the *Herald* called 'poetical patriotism'. When Rignold revived his production in 1887 the anti-British Sydney *Bulletin* on 17 September grudgingly allowed that 'George Rignold who represented this inhuman compound of doggy meanness, managed to make him look every inch a king—the sort of miserable king they had in those days who wore petticoats'.

'Gorgeous George', 'that hunky kid' as the *Bulletin* also called him, always sought to encourage the Anglophilic tendencies of white colonists. His first season was under the patronage of the Governor of NSW, Sir Hercules Robinson, and Lady Robinson, and the powerful and the respectable were always to be seen on opening nights. He organised a 'tribute matinee' to Henry Parkes, Premier of NSW, in 1887. A benefit performance for Rignold in 1895 was attended by the acting governor, 'the Ministry, both Houses of Parliament, the City Council of Sydney, the Speaker, the President of the Fossilised Chamber, Major-General Hutton, Parkes … and a fashionable audience', the *Bulletin* reported, though it may have been exaggerating. There was another political connection when young Billy Hughes appeared as a soldier in *Henry V*. He recounted in later years how the 102-kilogram Rignold, in complete armour, walked on the future Prime Minister of Australia before the battle of Harfleur.

After failing to conquer London, Rignold made his home in Sydney during the 1880s and he was long remembered there for helping to build Her Majesty's Theatre. He opened it on 10 September 1887 with *Henry V* and played there continuously for eight years. He presented more of his tableau revisions of Shakespeare, including *Julius Caesar*, *Macbeth*, *The Merry Wives of Windsor* and *A Midsummer Night's Dream*. As late as 1899 he added *Othello* to his repertoire. Perhaps wanting to offset the impression that he was a one-role actor, he thought it was 'the strongest thing I have done'. But in spite of his affection for the Bard, the economics of popular theatre meant that most of Rignold's seasons consisted of the latest English melodramas. One of these, *In the Ranks* by G. R. Sims and Henry Pettitt, played for 83 performances from December 1887 to 6 April 1888. This 14-week season set a record for a non-musical play in a large commercial theatre in Sydney.

Rignold played villains like Mephistopheles in Goethe's *Faust* and the 'subtle Italian' Paolo Macari in *Called Back* by Hugh Conway and J. Comyns Carr, heroes like Frank Darlington in *Youth* by Paul Merritt and Augustus Harris, the pathetic Colonel Challis in *Alone* by J. P. Simpson and H. C. Merivale and the American miner Joe Saunders in *My Partner* by B. Campbell. He appeared infrequently outside Sydney, and he took little interest in Australian stories or writers. Consequently he is less well remembered in theatrical history than his contemporaries Alfred Dampier, George Darrell, Bland Holt and J. C. Williamson.

He did, however, have a spectacular success with *Joseph of Canaan*, a play written by the Rev. George Walters of Sydney, a Progressive Unitarian minister. It retold the Biblical story and was the last play Rignold presented at the end of his eight-year stay at Her Majesty's. It was not expected to be a major success but, as the *Bulletin* noted on 31 August 1895, it was staged with 'glittering magnificence' and 'people who have been choked-off Joseph by a fear of a flapdoodle combination of stage and Sunday-school are … certain to find out their mistake'.

Rignold's corpulence and full-blown melodramatic acting always brought out the best in the *Bulletin*'s acid critic, who observed that he played Joseph as 'a substantial middle-aged person with a sleek humility of demeanour which strongly suggests the possibility that the original Mrs Potiphar's story was correct after all'. A week later the same critic noted that the play was indeed proving a success with the public, the audiences primarily consisting of 'murky females in black frock ... and men with monkey beards and those badly-fitting clothes which are a sign of grace within. The whole establishment, in fact, bears the appearance of a vast prayer-meeting.'

Rignold was known as a tyrannical and exacting director. He appears to have suffered some kind of collapse around 1897, and his last years were a sad anticlimax. He became semi-dependent on his former rival Bland Holt, to whom he wrote begging for the rights to any old plays Holt no longer wanted, and asking whether Holt would allow his contracted scenic designer John Brunton to help to prepare Rignold's new productions. In 1899 a mutual friend wrote to Holt, describing Rignold's decline: 'His brain is giving way and he loses himself even in his old parts.' He performed only occasionally from then and last appeared in August 1907, when he took a minor role in Holt's production of *The Bondman* at the Theatre Royal in Melbourne. He retired to a house on Sydney's Middle Harbour.
♣*Richard Fotheringham*

further reading
Mercer, Leah. 'A worthy scaffold'—George Rignold's rewriting and staging of *Henry V*. *Australasian Drama Studies* (Brisbane) October 1993.
Norman, Campbell. Great figures of our stage—George Rignold. *Life Magazine* (Sydney) 1 September 1938.
reference
Bland Holt Papers. National Library of Australia MS 2244.

Adelaide Ristori
Italian actor, 1822–1906. Performed in Ballarat, Melbourne and Sydney with large Italian company 1875.

The successor to Rachel as the world's best-known tragedienne, Adelaide Ristori came to Australia for four months in 1875 as part of an ambitious world tour. This was a celebration both of her art and of the unification of Italy, which had been completed only in 1870 with the incorporation of Rome. She travelled with the full range of sets and costumes required for her company's opulent productions of the historical dramas of Ernest Legouvé and Paolo Giacometti. She performed in Italian, except in gala performances, when she did excerpts in English and French. She played initially to thin houses but by the time she left each of the major cities she had won over the public. The critics were unanimous in their praise. J. E. Neild extolled her acting as 'one of those truths concerning which, like gravitation or the science of numbers, there is no doubt'. Her ability to blend grandeur with intimacy was praised. Characters such as Medea and Marie Antoinette became softened and appealing in her hands without any sacrifice of majesty. Language was not seen as a barrier by Neild, since 'the hands, the eyes, the inflection of the voice' communicated 'that kind of eloquence which is so much richer than spoken words'. Another Melbourne critic, James Smith spoke of her 'absolute grace of mute appealing'.

An unanticipated consequence of Ristori's tour was the banishing of prostitutes from the stalls of the major Australian theatres, where they had previously solicited without hindrance. Ristori, a woman of unimpeachable virtue, insisted that they should be refused entrance to her performances. After her departure from Melbourne, where she had appeared at W. S. Lyster's Prince of Wales Opera House, the reform was reversed, but public opinion forced its restoration. The previously disreputable stalls now became a favourite area for middle-class families and were extended backwards at the expense of the low-price pit. Two members of the company, Eduardo and Giulia Majeroni remained in Australia. ♣*Harold Love*

further reading
Knepler, Henry. *The Gilded Stage*. New York: William Morrow 1968.

Cyril Ritchard
Actor, dancer. Born 1 December 1898 in Sydney. Began as dancer in musical comedy 1917. In New York 1924. In London 1925–32. In Australia 1932–36. Married actor Madge Elliott 1935. Toured Australia 1946, 1951, 1960. Directed opera from 1950s. Died 18 December 1977 in Chicago (USA).

From the end of the First World War until after the Second World War, Cyril Ritchard formed a popular romantic team in musical comedy with Madge Elliott. They made their careers—which placed them in the second rank of theatrical stars—largely overseas, but they returned to Australia several times and Ritchard remained a confirmed Australophile, even to having the Southern Cross inlaid in the entrance hall of his New York apartment.

Australian theatregoers spoke of them as Cyril and Madge and they were much loved in the years of their early successes. She was blonde and beautiful and he was elegant, with a plangent and individual voice. His family meant him to be a doctor and when he decided on a stage career his mother was shocked. He won her over, however, and by 1917 he was dancing in musical comedy for J. C. WILLIAMSON'S. Reminiscing during an ABC radio interview in 1974, Ritchard recalled that as a reluctant and hopelessly stage-struck medical student at Sydney University he had, against parental opposition, approached the Firm and the dance teacher Minnie Hooper. Even though he was tall and good-looking, it is surprising to find him dancing in the back row of the chorus within a couple of weeks. He was a good dancer in the ballroom but he had had no real dance training. A few weeks later he was featured, dancing with Maie Baird. Hooper suggested to Elliott that Ritchard—who worshipped Elliott from afar—might make a suitable partner. Elliott's reply was chilling: 'I don't dance with beginners'. 'So I didn't go to New Zealand with the company', Ritchard recalled, 'and I didn't see her again for two years'. By then he was no longer a beginner and, because they were tall, they were teamed as dancers and their lifelong partnership began. They drew immediate attention, especially in the aeroplane musical *Going Up* in 1919.

Ritchard tried his luck in New York and a year later appeared in London for the first time. He was joined by Elliott and the pair were, in his words, 'an instantaneous success'. They returned to Australia as overseas stars in 1932 in *Blue Roses*. Over the next four years in Australia they played in other musical comedies, including *Gay Divorce*, *Roberta* and a local work, *Blue Mountain Melody*. They were married in 1935 in a spectacular public ceremony at St Mary's Cathedral in Sydney.

The couple returned to England in 1936. They spent the war years largely in revue and in a big revival of *The Merry Widow*, which they later played for troops in Egypt and Europe. Ritchard's career as a serious actor also developed during the war. He played Algernon Moncrieff opposite John Gielgud in Oscar Wilde's *The Importance of Being Earnest* in 1942. Ritchard and Elliott returned to Australia in 1946 in Noël Coward's *Tonight at 8.30* and were exceptionally well received. The expatriate stars had a similar welcome when they returned in Coward's *Private Lives* in1951.

The death of Elliott in 1955, after two years' illness, left a large gap in Ritchard's life. In 1960 he toured Australia with Cornelia Otis Skinner in *The Pleasure of His Company* by Skinner and Samuel Taylor. Late in life he had success as a director of opera at the Metropolitan Opera House in New York and elsewhere. He co-starred with Anthony Newley on Broadway in the musical *The Roar of the Greasepaint, the Smell of the Crowd* in 1965, and with Robert Morse in *Sugar* in 1972. While touring in 1977 he had a heart attack and died in hospital three weeks later. ❦*John West*

further reading
BEVAN, IAN. *The Story of the Theatre Royal*. Sydney: Currency Press 1993.

GUINNESS, DAPHNE. Cyril goes against the mob. *Bulletin* (Sydney) 2 March 1974.
Who's Who in the Theatre 15th edition. London: Pitman 1972.

Riverina Theatre Company

Professional dramatic company in Wagga Wagga (NSW) founded in 1976 as Riverina Trucking Company by Terry O'Connell. Renamed 1983. **venue** Riverina Playhouse 1986–. **artistic directors** 1976–78 Terry O'Connell. 1979 Damien Jameson. 1908–81 Peter Barclay. 1982–83 Colin Schumacher. 1984–86 Margaret Davis, 1987–88 Scott Alderdyce. 1989–90 Des James. 1991– John Saunders.

One of the oldest provincial companies, the Riverina Theatre Company has struck a happy balance between meeting demands for a fully professional company in the region and the needs of many to participate. It supplements its fully professional subscription program of four plays with touring, co-productions with other provincial companies, full-scale community productions, play readings, workshops for new writers and others, and specialised classes.

Terry O'Connell founded the Riverina Trucking Company after seeing the potential for a professional company in Wagga Wagga during two visits in the 1970s to direct for the amateur School of Arts players. Its long-term objectives were: to provide the Riverina with a professional theatre company; to provide drama that would not otherwise be available to Riverina audiences (with an emphasis on contemporary Australian scripts); to inaugurate the region's first annual subscription season; and to maintain a regional touring program. A provincial company faces heavy demands upon its resources and heavier costs and a smaller audience base than capital-city companies, and the early years were exciting and precarious. Devised productions and large-scale rock musicals dominated the repertoire, together with emblems of the new Australian drama such as HAMLET ON ICE, David Williamson's THE REMOVALISTS and THE CLUB, and JACK HIBBERD's *A Toast to Melba*.

The company survives because the public recognises the high quality of its productions and through the energy and talent of its staff and local supporters, federal and state subsidies, and the support of Charles Sturt University and other local sponsors. The company and the university have owned and shared the purpose-built, 250-seat, thrust-stage Riverina Playhouse since 1986. Recently the company has turned financial adversity to advantage by co-production with other provincial companies. ❦*Ray Goodlass*

Robbery Under Arms

Play in five acts by Alfred Dampier and Garnet Walch from the novel by Rolf Boldrewood. **premiere** 1 March 1890, Alexandra Theatre, Melbourne. Cast: Walter E. Baker, Alfred Boothman, J. Caesar, Alfred Dampier, Lily Dampier, Edmund Holloway, J. H. Martin, Reg Rede, Alfred Rolfe, Katherine Russell, Watkin Wynne. Designer: 'Alta' (Alfred Tischbauer). Director: Alfred Dampier. **published** Sydney: Currency Press 1985.

Until about 1915 this stage version of *Robbery Under Arms* was possibly better known than Rolf Boldrewood's novel itself. It was a huge success for the Alfred Dampier Company throughout Australia, although it made no impression in London in 1894. The stage version, made with Boldrewood's permission, was a free adaptation, with a much more vigorous Aileen Marston (the heroine), a friendlier Warrigal (Captain Starlight's Aboriginal friend) and a climax that saw Starlight survive the final shootout, be pardoned for his crimes, and marry Aileen.

The play was many times rewritten. It started life with a much larger cast than the Dampiers could afford to pay after the bank crashes in the 1890s. It was also originally a quasi-Ned Kelly story with an episode in which a policeman tries to ravish Aileen and is attacked by Starlight and her brothers: 'You are a disgrace to your uniform. It's scoundrels like you that make honest men turn rogues'. This portrayal of the constabulary, which certainly had no antecedents in Boldrewood's work, was retained, but later versions offset it by emphasising the valour of a 'good' policeman, Sir Ferdinand Morringer.

Alfred Dampier played Starlight hundreds of times between 1890 and his retirement 15 years later. In his last season in 1905 the *Theatre* still noted packed houses and an enthusiastic reception. The play was later staged by other companies and filmed in 1911 with Dampier's son-in-law ALFRED ROLFE as Starlight. LILY DAMPIER produced the play in Brisbane in 1914, but her death the next year ended the saga of a great popular success. ❦*Richard Fotheringham*

Malcolm Robertson

Actor, director, producer. Born 16 March 1933 in Sydney. Associate director of Melbourne Theatre Company 1972–75. Artistic director of St Martin's Youth Arts Centre (Melbourne) 1984. Literary manager of Playbox Theatre Company (Melbourne) 1989–. Works as drama tutor and adjudicator at drama festivals. Also works in film and television.

One of Australia's most experienced theatrical all-rounders, Malcolm Robertson has had long associations with the MELBOURNE THEATRE COMPANY and the PLAYBOX THEATRE CENTRE, Melbourne's major companies. He has also been involved with smaller organisations, particularly the LA MAMA THEATRE since its inception in 1967. He directed three plays in its first year, and he still does occasional guest productions and remains on its board. In 1970 he conducted drama workshops at Parramatta Jail in Sydney, where JIM MCNEIL was an inmate. Next year Robertson directed the first professional production of McNeil's play *The Chocolate Frog* for Q THEATRE in Sydney. He left the Melbourne Theatre Company to join the newly-formed Hoopla (later Playbox) company early in 1977. He freelanced from 1981 to 1985, when he returned to Playbox as literary manager, also acting and directing.

Robertson began his acting career with the JOHN ALDEN COMPANY in Sydney, and later on national tour. Works in which he has given notable performances include *Judgement* and Anton Chekhov's *The Cherry Orchard* for Playbox, *Twelfth Night* (as Sir Toby Belch) and David Williamson's *Jugglers Three* for the Melbourne Theatre Company, the last also for HARRY M. MILLER. He took his solo production *St Mark's Gospel* on a national tour in 1985–87. ❦*Leonard Radic*

Tim Robertson

Actor, director, dramatist. Born 1944 at Braintree (England). Emigrated to Australia in 1952 with his mother. Educated at University of Western Australia. Taught drama at Flinders University 1967–72. Joined Australian Performing Group in Melbourne as actor, director and writer 1972. Has also acted with Nimrod Theatre Company (Sydney), Playbox Theatre Company (Melbourne) and State Theatre Company of South Australia (Adelaide) and in film and television.

Tim Robertson, a highly imaginative playwright, explores the more bizarre edges of human behaviour. Academic and practical experience has given him a universal knowledge of theatrical form that enables him to move easily through drama, pantomime, comedy, rock opera and musicals. His work is pyrotechnic with explosions of mirth, sudden transformations, characters appearing from unlikely contexts, and scenes redolent of Dante's *Inferno* or the Marx Brothers. His *Mary Shelley and the Monsters* (1975) and his adaptation of Laurence Sterne's *Tristram Shandy* (1981) show great inspiration creatively mixed with a depth of scholarship unusual in Australian theatre.

Nearly all Robertson's work demonstrates his brilliance as a lyricist and with JOHN ROMERIL and Don Watson in *Manning Clark's History of Australia—The Musical* (1988) he wrote some of the best song lyrics in the Australian theatrical lexicon. He has also collaborated with Romeril in writing a rock opera libretto, *Bummerz* (1973), and a pantomime, *Waltzing Matilda* (1974).

As an actor Robertson prefers comic roles. He directed the AUSTRALIAN PERFORMING GROUP in the premieres of Michael Byrnes's *The River Jordan*—named production of 1975 by the Melbourne *Herald*—and JACK HIBBERD's adaptation of Nikolai Gogol's *The Overcoat* in 1976. In Ottawa in 1978 Robertson directed Romeril's THE FLOATING WORLD for the National Theatre Company with BRUCE SPENCE leading an otherwise Canadian cast. ❦*John Timlin*

published works
Mary Shelley and the Monsters, play (1975). Melbourne: Yackandandah 1983.
Tristram Shandy, play (1981). Melbourne: Yackandandah 1985.
Waltzing Matilda, pantomime with John Romeril (1974). Melbourne: Yackandandah 1984.

Kathleen Robinson

Actor, director. Born 1901. Grew up on station near Bourke (NSW) and went to boarding school. Went to London 1925. Studied at Royal Academy of Dramatic Art 1930–31. Toured Australia and New Zealand with Sybil Thorndike and Lewis Casson 1931. Returned to London. At Westminster Theatre 1932–35. Toured Scandinavia and Baltic states with own company 1937–38. Visited Australia 1939. Returned to settle 1940. Codirector of Whitehall Theatrical Productions 1940–50. Died 28 December 1983 in Sydney.

A rich woman, Kathleen Robinson poured money into WHITEHALL THEATRICAL PRODUCTIONS, which gave Sydney high-quality professional entertainment at the MINERVA THEATRE from 1941 until 1950. The company emerged as a result of Robinson meeting ALEC COPPEL at the Theatre Royal in Sydney in 1940 on the first night of *Ladies in Retirement* by Edward Percy and Reginald Denham, starring MARIE NEY. He was director of the Marie Ney Company and, like Robinson, had returned to Australia after success overseas. They founded Whitehall and Robinson shared in directing the company—and acted in and directed many of its productions—until 1950. Just before Metro–Goldwyn–Mayer took over the Minerva, an accident left her an invalid and she retired to her home at Bowral (NSW), where she transcribed books into Braille for the Royal Blind Society. Her interest in theatre never waned and the annual Kathleen Robinson lectures in drama at the University of Sydney perpetuate her name. ❦*Jessica Noad*

G. H. Rogers

Actor. Born 11 July 1820 at St Albans (England). Arrived in Hobart as soldier 1839. Acted in amateur theatricals. Discharged from army 1842. Became professional actor. Married Emma Young, actor and singer, 1844. Died 12 February 1872 in Melbourne.

George Herbert Rogers was widely regarded as one of the most competent actors on the Australian stage in the 1840s and 1850s. He was particularly famous for playing old men, although his repertoire also included the Widow Twankey in *Aladdin*, Fagin in *Oliver Twist*, Sir Peter Teazle in R. B. Sheridan's *The School for Scandal* and Falstaff. Rogers arrived in Tasmania as a private soldier in the 51st Foot Regiment in 1839 and appears to have acted for the first time while he was still in the army in Hobart. He acted in the companies of F. B. WATSON and ARTHUR FALCHON at the Royal Victoria Theatre in 1841, taking a benefit on 22 July. Rogers was discharged as a sergeant in 1842 and from then until 1845 he played in Hobart and Launceston with Watson's and, later, ANNE CLARKE's companies. 'Either as an old or young man [he] is truly an acquisition to the stage', said the *Colonial Times* on 9 May 1843. Evidently Rogers, not yet 23, was already skilled at playing old men. In 1844 he married Emma Young, an actor and singer in the Clarke company and sister of the actor CHARLES YOUNG.

When GEORGE COPPIN took over the company in 1845, Rogers was among those who accompanied him to Melbourne, where they appeared at the QUEEN'S THEATRE ROYAL in June. By July 1846, after Coppin's departure for Adelaide, Rogers and his wife had returned to Tasmania. He was Anne Clarke's stage manager in Hobart and later at Launceston but he left her company in March 1847 after a disagreement over salaries. In May 1847, Rogers, Charles Young and Anne Clarke's estranged husband Michael were named as joint lessees of the Royal Victoria Theatre in Hobart. Rogers was also acting manager.

Later in 1847 he was offered £4 a week plus benefits to join the Royal Victoria Theatre in Sydney. Rogers was well received by Sydney audiences. 'The histrionic abilities of Mr and Mrs Rogers continue to draw excellent houses, and the gentleman especially is an invaluable acquisition to the Victoria', noted *Bell's Life in Sydney* on 22 January 1848. Rogers remained in Sydney until 1854, when he moved to the Queen's Theatre Royal in Melbourne. Later he went to the Theatre Royal, where he became a great favourite of the leading Melbourne critic J. E. NEILD. On 13 March 1858 Neild called Rogers 'the best actor in the whole of these colonies'. In 1863 Rogers was a member of W. S. LYSTER's company, appearing at the Prince of Wales Theatre in Sydney. There he met his old friend George Coppin. After a brief season at the School of Arts, they toured together to Newcastle and Maitland (NSW) and New Zealand, though Rogers was frequently laid up with gout. They also played together at the Theatre Royal in Adelaide in 1868. Rogers died penniless in 1872, and Coppin organised a benefit for his destitute widow and children. ❦*Elizabeth Webby*

Betty Roland

Dramatist. Born 22 July 1903 at Kaniva (Vic.). Originally Mary Isobel Maclean. Journalist in Melbourne for *Table Talk* and *Sun News-Pictorial*. Married Ellis Davies 1923. Ran away to Russia with Guido Baracchi and changed name to Betty Roland, 1933. Returned to Sydney 1935. Separated from Baracchi 1942. Wrote radio plays. In London 1952–61. Lived at Montsalvat artists' colony, near Melbourne, 1961–83. Lives in retirement in Sydney. Mother of film producer Gilda Baracchi.

A versatile writer, Betty Roland has been influenced by the works of Henrik Ibsen and Eugene O'Neill, the rules of the well-made play and the myths of ancient Greece. She draws her material from strong, challenging situations that have at their base the morality of survival. She began writing plays while at school, and her first adult work reveals a childlike delight in storytelling that she retained all her life. As Betty Davies she wrote a contemporary comedy based on the Pygmalion and Galatea legend, *Feet of Clay*, in 1924, and her first major work, THE TOUCH OF SILK IN 1928. She wrote a libretto for a spectacular musical comedy, *The Lotus Flower* in 1929 in the hope of attracting professional production, but it was not taken up. In 1931 a short melodramatic radio play, *The Spur of the Moment* provided the story for one of the first sound films made in Australia. BRETT RANDALL produced Roland's *Morning*, a short play with a tough message of outback survival in the goldrush period, at the Kiosk Theatre in Fawkner Park, Melbourne, in 1932.

Next year she ran away to Russia with Guido Baracchi, a prominent communist, and changed her name to Betty Roland, using her father's forename in quasi-Russian style. In 1935 they returned to Sydney, where she joined the Communist Party and wrote polemical and agitprop plays for the NEW THEATRE League. *Are You Ready, Comrade?*, a full-length play with a strong left bias, won a West Australian Theatre Council competition in 1938 and leftist groups in Perth and Sydney produced it. The manuscript has been lost. Disillusioned with communism after Stalin's trials in 1936–38, she left the Communist Party in 1939. She parted from Baracchi in 1942 and devoted herself to writing plays and serials for ABC and commercial radio. One serial, *A Woman Scorned* became the basis of the popular television serial *Return to Eden* in 1983. In 1946 at DORIS FITTON's request she adapted Gustave Flaubert's *Madame Bovary* for the stage. Fitton played the title-role for INDEPENDENT THEATRE in Sydney. In 1952 Roland went to London with her young daughter Gilda and, after two years of struggle, established herself as a writer of children's fiction.

Early in her career Roland rejected the popular middle-class theatre in favour of the reality of human conflict. Sadly, there was no place for such work in the professional theatre of the time. Neither in Australia nor abroad could she find a sympathetic climate for her stage work. Even *The Touch of Silk*, probably the most widely produced play in amateur theatre and many times broadcast on radio, had no professional season until 1976. Her other major work, *Granite Peak*, about loneliness and racial prejudice in the outback, was televised in 1957 by Associated-Rediffusion in the United Kingdom but it has never been performed on stage. In his introduction to the published text PHILIP PARSONS writes: '*Granite Peak* has the simplicity of romance but romance was born of those unfashionable qualities—

human aspiration and hope. Here its simplicity is deeply felt and says something permanent about Australians and human nature itself.' ❧*Katharine Brisbane*

published plays
Granite Peak. Sydney: Currency Press 1988.
Morning (1932). Sydney: Angus and Robertson 1937 in *Best Australian One-Act Plays*.
The Touch of Silk (1928). Melbourne University Press 1942. Sydney: Currency–Methuen 1974, Currency Press 1986. Sydney: Currency Press 1988 (1955 revision).

autobiography
Caviar for Breakfast, Melbourne: Quartet 1979.
The Eye of the Beholder, Sydney: Angus and Robertson 1984.
An Improbable Life. Sydney: Imprint 1990.
The Devious Being. Sydney: Imprint 1990.

Alfred Rolfe

Actor. Born 1862 in Melbourne. Originally Alfred Roker. Acted as Alfred Rolfe with Alfred Dampier Company 1888–1905. Married Lily Dampier 12 July 1893. Acted in London 1898. Directed films 1911–18. Died 9 September 1943 in Sydney.

After ALFRED DAMPIER retired in 1905 Alfred Rolfe took over his role of Captain Starlight in ROBBERY UNDER ARMS, having already established himself as another dashing bushranger, Captain Moonlight in THE BUSH KING. His wife LILY DAMPIER was the leading actress of the Dampier company, which did not survive long. By 1910 the couple were touring New Zealand for PHILIP LYTTON.

Rolfe first acted with Dampier's company in Melbourne late in 1888. Presumably he had amateur or minor professional experience as he played major roles in *Robbery Under Arms*, FOR THE TERM OF HIS NATURAL LIFE and other Australian plays in Dampier's seasons at the Alexandra Theatre until he went on tour with the Dampiers to New Zealand in 1892 and to Sydney in 1893. In 1897 Rolfe and his wife went to England, where he worked at the Theatre Royal, Drury Lane, in London. They returned to Australia in March 1899.

In 1911 Rolfe and his wife began making films from their stage scripts. He became the most prolific early Australian silent-film director, but he encountered censorship difficulties with his bushranger films. Lily Dampier died in 1915 and Rolfe is not known to have made films after 1918. In retirement he devoted himself to organising amateur athletics. ❧*Richard Fotheringham*

Ernest C. Rolls

Producer. Born *c.*1890 in London. Originally Rolls Darewski. Specialised in production. Bankrupt 1920. Worked in Australia with Rufe Naylor and Fullers' 1927–29. Married Jenny Benson, revue artist. Leased International Attractions Ltd theatres in New Zealand. Head of production for J. C. Williamson's 1938–39. Died 20 January 1964 in England. Brother of British composers and conductors Herman and Max Darewski.

Ernest C. Rolls had a flair for producing lavish revues and revue-style musical comedies but he when he had charge of production for J. C. WILLIAMSON'S he almost destroyed the firm. In his early years in Australia he helped FULLERS' to score a huge success with a lavish production of *Rio Rita* in 1928. In the early 1930s Rolls and his wife Jenny Benson presented spectacular and successful revues for J. C. Williamson's with stars such as GUS BLUETT, ELLA SHIELDS and GEORGE WALLACE, but his musical comedies after *Rio Rita* flopped and lost heavily. Rolls managed to lease a chain of theatres in New Zealand. John McKenzie, an Australian chain-store magnate in that country, gained control of J. C. Williamson's in 1938 and insisted that Rolls be a managing director and chief producer of a new production subsidiary called Australian and New Zealand Theatres Ltd. Lavish but unsuccessful shows followed, culminating in a disastrous musical, *I Married an Angel*. Australia and New Zealand Theatres lost heavily and moved out of theatrical production. By the end of 1939 Rolls had quietly returned to London. He spent his last years presenting variety shows at English seaside resorts. ❧*Alwyn Capern*

further reading
BEVAN, IAN. *The Story of the Theatre Royal*. Sydney: Currency Press 1993.

John Romeril

Dramatist, dramaturge. Born 26 October 1945 in Melbourne. Studied at Monash University (Melbourne). Founding member of Australian Performing Group and house writer 1970–80. Australian Artist Creative Fellowship 1993. Has written for film and television.

After two decades of concentrated work and commitment, John Romeril endures as one of Australia's most successful political playwrights. He is probably the writer who has responded most widely and flexibly to the range of possibilities in contemporary Australian theatre. He wrote the first of his more than 40 plays as an undergraduate. In 1968 he joined what became the AUSTRALIAN PERFORMING GROUP. In this collective the writer was seen as the inspirational and articulating force behind the 'collective imagination', co-ordinating, shaping, and augmenting the ideas of all the theatrical workers involved in the creative process. Plays such as *I Don't Know Who to Feel Sorry For* (1969) and *The Man From Chicago* (1969, revised as *Chicago, Chicago* 1970) reflected libertarian socialism, passionate commitment to the 'home-made' Australian play and opposition to the impact of multinational corporate capital.

As house writer with the APG from 1970 to 1980 Romeril amassed 26 writing credits. His best-known play from those years, and the only one to enter major companies' repertoires, is THE FLOATING WORLD (1974). It deals with Australian–Japanese relations and it began Romeril's continuing interest in Japan and its theatre. His other works for the APG include *Bastardy* (1972), *Carboni* (1980), *Dudders* (1976) with John Timlin, *The Earth, Air, Fire and Water Show* (1973), a revue with JACK HIBBERD, MARVELLOUS MELBOURNE (1970) with Hibberd, *Mickey's Moomba* (1978), *Mrs Thally F* (1971) and *Waltzing Matilda* (1974) with TIM ROBERTSON.

Romeril and DAVID WILLIAMSON are the only writers with the APG, which disbanded in 1981, who are still actively shaping Australian theatre. Romeril has remained a firm believer in collaboration. He was an important influence in COMMUNITY THEATRE, working in Canberra with the JIGSAW THEATRE COMPANY in 1980, in Adelaide with TROUPE in 1981 and 1984 and with MAGPIE THEATRE in 1985, in Melbourne with the VICTORIAN COLLEGE OF THE ARTS in 1985 and in Hobart with the SALAMANCA THEATRE COMPANY in 1987. His ground-breaking work with Troupe resulted in *The Kelly Dance* (1984) a bush-dance piece about Ned Kelly. At the Victorian College of the Arts he wrote *Legends* (1985), with

Chris Anatassiades and Jennifer Hill. He wrote the musical *Jonah Jones* (1985) with the composer Alan John. In 1988 he worked on another musical, *Manning Clark's History of Australia*, with Tim Robertson and Don Watson.

Romeril's singular vision is more apparent in his later works fashioned for major state theatre companies, including *Lost Weekend*, produced by the State Theatre Company of South Australia in Adelaide, and *Top End*, produced by the Melbourne Theatre Company, both in 1989. The content of these later plays suggests a palatable mellowing, but all retain Romeril's humane political essence. He has worked as a dramaturge, particularly for the Victorian College of the Arts, the Australian National Playwrights' Conference and Melbourne Workers' Theatre. For the last he worked in 1987–88 on Andrew Bovell's *The Ballad of Lois Ryan*, which was performed in workplaces. In 1991 he wrote *Working Out* for secondary students as part of the Victorian Arts Centre's ArtEd program; *Reading Boy*, a puppet play for Handspan Theatre; and *Black Cargo* for Melbourne Workers' Theatre. *Bring Down the House* was produced by the Arena Theatre Company in Melbourne in 1992. ❦*Wayne Harrison*

published plays
The Accidental Poke in *The Hills Family Show* (1975). Sydney: Currency Press 1985 in *Popular Short Plays* 1.
Bastardy (1972). Melbourne: Yackandandah 1982.
Brudder Humphrey (1971). Monash University Press in *Two Plays*.
Chicago, Chicago (1970). Melbourne: Penguin 1970.
Definitely Not the Last—A Rock 'n' Roll Fable (1989). Melbourne: Yackandandah.
The Floating World (1974). Sydney: Currency–Methuen 1975, revised 1982.
I Don't Know Who to Feel Sorry For (1969). Sydney: Currency–Methuen 1973.
The Kelly Dance (1984). Melbourne: Yackandandah 1986.
The Kitchen Table (1971). Melbourne: Monash University Press in *Two Plays*.
Legends. Melbourne: Cambridge University Press 1986.
Marvellous Melbourne, with Jack Hibberd (1970). In *Theatre Australia* 2/4 and 2/5 (Sydney, August and September–October 1977).
Mrs Thally F (1971). Sydney: Currency Press 1983.
Waltzing Matilda, pantomime with Tim Robertson (1974). Melbourne: Yackandandah 1984.

further reading
Griffiths, Gareth (ed.). *John Romeril* Amsterdam (Netherlands): Rodopi 1993.

Maurice Rooklyn

Magician. Born 6 March 1905 in England. Came to Australia at five. Began performing in tent show at 15. Toured England 1936–40. Returned to Australia and played Tivoli circuit 1940. Began touring with illusion show in mid-1940s. Toured New Zealand, Pacific Islands and Japan 1947. Toured New Zealand again 1949. Ceased touring 1954. Died 22 July 1992 in Sydney.

The winner of many overseas awards, including 'World's Greatest Manipulator', Maurice Rooklyn built a large illusion show and began touring Australia with it in the mid-1940s. He became interested in magic at the age of seven. At 15 he was on the road with a tent show and in his twenties he opened a magic department in Anthony Horden's department store in Sydney. At the Tivoli Theatre in Sydney in 1934 Rooklyn was shot on stage while performing a bullet-catching act. He abandoned that act and began billiard-ball manipulation. He became so skilled that in 1936 he and his wife Ettie left for England, where he toured with great success, and came to be regarded as the foremost billiard-ball manipulator of the time. ❦*Gerald Taylor*

Rooted

Play in three acts by Alex Buzo. **Canberra premiere** 14 August 1969, Childers Street Hall, by Stage. Cast: Peta Adams, Karin Altmann, Clive Scollay, Philip Wheeler, Bruce Widdop. Designer: Jon Stephens. Director: Allan Mawer. **Sydney premiere** 14 August 1969, Jane Street Theatre. Cast: Pat Bishop, Sandy Gore, Jeff Kevin, Garry McDonald, Gregory Ross. Designer: Kevin Carpenter. Director: Rick Billinghurst. **revived** Hartford (Connecticut, USA) by Hartford Stage Company 7 January 1972. **published** Sydney and London: Currency Methuen 1973. Sydney: Currency Press, revised, 1993.

Alex Buzo's first full-length play, *Rooted* was instrumental in establishing his early reputation by its wit and its tough portrayal of the materialistic 'lifestyle' culture of Sydney society at the time. It is a blackly comic absurdist allegory of the alienation of nice people in an amoral world. The central character, Bentley, grins amiably and tries to be pleasant as he is systematically stripped of everything he has worked for. An ominous, all-powerful character who never appears on stage, Simmo, takes over Bentley's apartment and his wife, finally driving him out of society altogether. Bentley is a willing victim, caught up in the sun-and-surf culture of his mindless mates, but his simple humanity survives intact and this makes his destruction possible. The play is a strong indictment of the society that lets this happen. The dialogue is sharp, witty and formal, satirising both the jargon of the newly affluent but vulgar ocker world that Bentley inhabits and the public-service language with which he habitually masks his true feelings.

Buzo caused comment by granting the amateur rights for a premiere in Canberra on the same night as the professional premiere in Sydney and then attending the Canberra performance. The American production gained a sympathetic notice in *Time* and was generally well reviewed. This success might have attracted more attention in the Australian media in a time of nationalistic self-assertion had not David Williamson at that time been establishing himself as Australia's 'first' internationally noticed new-wave dramatist. ❦*John McCallum*

Ropewalking

The portable and inexpensive art of ropewalking lends itself to open-air spectacle, so its traditions in Australia are to be found beyond the circus and the theatre. An exhibition of tightrope-dancing by George Croft at the Theatre Royal in Sydney on 16 December 1833 was probably the first professional display of any circus art in the Australian colonies. Croft remained active in the colonies as a ropewalker until 1851 at least. His pupil John Quinn, was licensed to perform as a ropewalker in NSW in 1838. The strong man Luigi Dalle Case and his tightrope dancers, acrobats, tumblers and clowns performed in Sydney in 1841–42. Quinn danced on the tightrope with his feet tied in baskets in the Royal Amphitheatre in Hobart on 17 May 1848. In

November 1848 he walked along the forestay to the main topmast of a sailing ship anchored in Hobart. At Port Phillip in 1850 an estimated 5000 people watched spellbound as Quinn walked a rope across the Yarra River.

In the circus it was customary for a ropewalker to entertain a crowd outside the tent in the afternoon to attract an audience to the evening's performance. Usually the ropewalker, with only the aid of a balancing pole, would walk up a long rope stretched from the ground to the top of the centre pole protruding from the tent. Among the fine ropewalkers attached to Australian circuses from the 1850s to the 1870s were Billy Banham, a British black ropewalker who called himself Pablo Fanque after his famous uncle; Billy Jones, an all-round Aboriginal performer; and James Brame, who was with BURTON'S CIRCUS in 1879.

The French acrobat and ropewalker Blondin became famous by walking a 335-metre rope stretched above the Niagara Falls in 1859. Billing himself 'the Australian Blondin', Vertelli walked a wire across a waterfall at Mt Lofty (SA) in August 1865. The wire was apparently 30 metres long and strung some 12 metres above jagged rocks at the base of the waterfall. This was the first known Australian use of wire in preference to rope. Wire appears to have won general acceptance by the early 1880s.

Blondin himself came to Australia in 1874. In Sydney he performed in a huge tent in the Domain, and in Melbourne near the present site of the Victorian Arts Centre. He was so successful that he returned in 1875–76. Another 'Australian Blondin', Harry L'Estrange walked a rope stretched across Sydney's Middle Harbour on 18 April 1877, and is supposed to have earned £10 000 for the feat. Thereafter no open-air high ropewalking or wirewalking in Australia is known until the Frenchman Philip Petit walked a tightrope stretched between the northern pylons of the Sydney Harbour Bridge in 1970.

In the Australian circus a tradition of ropewalkers and wirewalkers continued to develop in the second half of the 19th century and the early years of the 20th. James and Annie Ashton, children of James Henry Ashton, were accomplished tightrope-walkers in ASHTON'S CIRCUS in 1875. A daughter of James Ashton, Ethel, was an expert tight-wire artist in 1912. Golda Honey, a granddaughter of Gus St Leon, was in demand in American vaudeville in the 1930s for the wire act she had developed in the family circus, until a serious fall during a performance ended her career. The Perry circus family also produced wirewalkers in the early 1900s, including George Eroni, Albert Perry and MARY SOLE. Australian wirewalking reached its zenith in CON COLLEANO, possibly the first person to achieve the feet-to-feet forward somersault, although Albert Perry claimed to have done so as well. Albert Perry's son Robert and Mervyn Ashton have been well-known wirewalkers since the Second World War. ❦*Mark St Leon*

Andrew Ross

Director. Born 15 October 1947 in Melbourne. Took part in student and fringe productions in Melbourne in 1960s and 1970s. Founding director of Theatre-in-Education and Green Room, National Theatre Company (Perth) 1976–79. Study tours to United Kingdom, East Germany and India 1979 and 1980. Founding artistic director of Swan River Stage Company (Perth) 1982. Artistic director of Brisbane Repertory Theatre Society 1983–84. Director of theatre department, University of Melbourne, 1986–90. Directed numerous productions for Western Australian Theatre Company 1983–90. Foundation artistic director of Black Swan Theatre Company (Perth) 1991. Member of theatre board of Australia Council 1983–86. Board of Australian Ballet 1987–90.

The artistic policies of Andrew Ross have extended the agenda of Western Australian theatre. As founder of three stage companies in Perth, he has successively developed an advocacy for theatres that cross cultural boundaries and intersect with regional literature and journals. Ross has become especially associated with theatre generated by Aboriginal playwrights, actors, designers and directors. He directed the first productions of JACK DAVIS's *Kullark* (1979), *THE DREAMERS* (1982), *NO SUGAR* (1985), *Barungin (Smell the Wind)* in 1988 and *The First-Born* trilogy (1988); Jimmy Chi's *BRAN NUE DAE* (1990); and Sally Morgan's *Sistergirl* (1992). He directed adaptations of Albert Facey's autobiography *A Fortunate Life* (1985) and Randolph Stow's novels *Midnite* (1986) and *Tourmaline* (1993). In 1993 he also directed Lois Achimovich's *Meekatharra*, and in 1994 EDGAR METCALFE's *Alleycat Alice and Friends*. ❦*Bill Dunstone*

Kenneth Rowell

Designer. Born 1920 in Melbourne. Studied at Melbourne Technical College 1942–43. Danced with Borovansky Ballet. Began designing for Ballet Rambert in Australia 1948. Has designed décor for more than 70 productions in Australia, England and Europe since 1950.

A successful international career designing for drama, ballet and opera began for Kenneth Rowell when he was commissioned to design a new ballet by Walter Gore, *Winter Night*, for the touring Ballet Rambert in 1948. When Gore discovered him in Melbourne, Rowell was an aspiring dancer with the Borovansky Ballet, an emergent painter and a designer influenced by the Original Ballet Russe. Rowell designed productions by the Melbourne Little Theatre Company and the University of Melbourne Marlowe Society before he left to study in England on a British Council scholarship in 1950. He soon established himself in London as a leading stage designer with memorable neo-romantic sets and costumes for productions including *Macbeth* at the Shakespeare Memorial Theatre, Stratford-upon-Avon. He also designed for the Old Vic Theatre Company, the AUSTRALIAN ELIZABETHAN THEATRE TRUST and J. C. WILLIAMSON's. Rowell has exhibited regularly as a painter for more than 40 years in Australia, London and New York and his stage design is integral with his painting. He has settled in Australia. ❦*Pamela Zeplin*

Royal Olympic Theatre

Theatre at corner of Cameron and St John Streets, Launceston (Tas.), opened 1834. Attached to London Inn. Also known as **Olympic Theatre**. Closed 1874.

Soon after the London Inn was licensed in 1834 its attached theatre became Launceston's established theatrical venue. It superseded the assembly rooms of the British Hotel, where SAMSON CAMERON opened the town's first theatrical season in June 1834. The licensee of the London Inn from 1838 to 1843, an emancipist named B. Hyrons, improved the theatre in 1842. He added a new stage, dressing rooms and an elevated tier of boxes with a private entrance and cloakrooms, ensuring 'a season with every comfort which good arrangements can secure'. F. B. WATSON was the first lessee of the improved theatre. He transferred the Olympic name from the room in the Steam Packet Tavern where his company had been playing. Cameron opened the Royal Victoria Theatre in competition and bankrupted himself in a few months of rivalry. Watson continued until 1844. GEORGE COPPIN gave a notable season at the Royal Olympic in 1845 and ANNE CLARKE used it later in the 1840s. The building was altered again in 1853, but its popularity waned after the Lyceum and Clarence Theatres and the Theatre Royal were built in the 1850s. ❧*Gillian Winter*

further reading
CRAIG, C. *Notes on Tasmaniana*. Launceston: Foot and Playsted 1986.
Cyclopedia of Tasmania 2. Hobart: Maitland and Krone 1900.

Royal Shakespeare Company

English professional dramatic company. Toured Australia as Shakespeare Memorial Theatre Company 1949, 1953. As Royal Shakespeare Company 1970, 1973, 1975, 1976.

The Royal Shakespeare Company has been influential by example in Australia. It first came here when it was called the Shakespeare Memorial Theatre Company, after the theatre that opened in Stratford-upon-Avon in England in 1879 with its first annual summer festival of Shakespeare performance. BARRY SULLIVAN returned from a long stay in Australia to play Benedick to Helen Faucit's Beatrice in *Much Ado About Nothing*, the opening work. He was the star of the first two festivals.

In 1949 J. C. WILLIAMSON'S, bitterly regretting its rejection of the OLD VIC THEATRE COMPANY in 1948, hastened to import the Shakespeare Memorial Theatre Company for a brief tour. The company was headed by its artistic director, Anthony Quayle, and Diana Wynyard. Quayle returned in 1953, with British Council support, on a 37-week tour of Australia and New Zealand with *As You Like It*, *Henry IV—part 1* and *Othello*. The company included two young Australians who had quickly made names in English classical theatre—LEO MCKERN, who played Glendower, Iago, Northumberland and Touchstone, and KEITH MICHELL, who played Hotspur and Orlando.

During the second tour, Quayle was influential backstage in setting the directions of both the old professional theatre and the new. J. C. Williamson's, concerned about successors to the aging TAIT BROTHERS and the coming of television, had begun talks with Stratford principals about a merger. Professional theatre was still on a global metropolitan circuit and Frank Tait could write to his directors: '… it must be remembered that the London and New York offices are the fountainheads from where our theatrical supplies must come'. During the 1953 tour Quayle spoke to the directors of J. C. Williamson's in New Zealand but the parties failed to agree on who should head the new structure. The Stratford tour was successful but the Tait brothers were in two minds about the English classical repertoire. 'We cannot overlook the fact that the Australian public is really not so keen on the higher drama', Nevin Tait wrote in 1953. Quayle was also an advocate to the Prime Minister, Robert Menzies, in support of H. C. COOMBS's plan for a national theatre. The AUSTRALIAN ELIZABETHAN THEATRE TRUST was established in the following year.

In 1961 the Stratford company was renamed the Royal Shakespeare Company, with Peter Hall as director, a second theatre in London and a permanent company of actors. In 1970 the Royal Shakespeare Company, headed by Judi Dench, Richard Pascoe and Michael Williams, was the star of the Adelaide Festival. It presented *The Winter's Tale*, startlingly dressed in 1960s Carnaby Street mode in Trevor Nunn's production, in which King Leontes makes a painful journey from a nursery playground to the realities of adult responsibility; and *Twelfth Night*, an elegy by the director John Barton to winter, middle age and disappointment. These vintage productions eloquently demonstrated radical changes wrought by Nunn, appointed artistic director in 1968 at the age of 28, and by the impact of social change upon reinterpretation of Shakespeare, particularly in relation to hierarchical English society.

Peter Brook's revolutionary 1970 production of *A Midsummer Night's Dream*, in which the actors appeared as circus performers, arrived in Australia in 1973 after many changes of cast and a tour of the world. The production re-examined the 1960s playway of life. The company disbanded in Sydney and several members remained for a period, notably Philip Sayer, who contributed to experimental work at the Nimrod Street Theatre, and Ralph Cotterell and Hugh Keays-Byrne, who joined the PERFORMANCE SYNDICATE and became Australian residents.

In 1975 the Royal Shakespeare Company toured Australia with Henrik Ibsen's *Hedda Gabler*, with Glenda Jackson in the title-role and Timothy West as Judge Brack. The tour preceded the British season, suggesting the commercial ambitions that the company increasingly revealed in the 1980s. Jackson drew large crowds but Nunn's production rather bemused the critics and the public, revealing a gap between middle-class theatre in Britain, where classic roles were continually redefined, and Australia, where few in the audience had seen *Hedda Gabler* before.

In 1975 the Trust and a British consortium brought out Brenda Bruce, Paul Hardwick, Derek Jacobi and Michael Redgrave on an Australasian tour of two Shakespearean recitals—*The Hollow Crown*, a selection on the theme of royalty, and *Pleasure and Repentance*, on love. In 1976 a second company, led by Charles Kay and Edward Petherbridge, toured widely in NSW and Queensland with *The Hollow Crown* for the Arts Councils of those states. They were worthy projects but made little lasting impact.

With the assistance of the British Council, the Royal Shakespeare Company toured Adrian Noble's acclaimed production of *Richard III* in 1986. Boasting a dangerous performance as a grotesquely crippled 'bottled spider' by the South-African-born actor Antony Sher, the production received mixed reviews. Critics praised Sher but accused the company of short-changing the audience with second-string actors in other roles. BRIAN HOAD in the *Bulletin* on 8 May 1986 and H. G. KIPPAX in the *Sydney Morning Herald* on 10 May both pointed out that Queen Margaret had been omitted from the play, apparently for reasons of economy. The debate showed Australian audiences with an ambivalent attitude to their English heritage—appreciation of the pre-eminence of British interpreters and vigilance against hints of colonialist patronage.

In the 1980s the commercial activities of Trevor Nunn were of more lasting consequence in Australia than the Royal Shakespeare Company's performances of the classics. As subsidy and patronage dwindled, the company launched into the commercial world with David Edgar's epic adaptation of Dickens's *Nicholas Nickleby* in 1980, and the development of the musicals *Cats* (1981), *Starlight Express* (1984) and *Les Misérables* (1985). The SYDNEY THEATRE COMPANY and the Australian Opera successfully mounted *The Life and Adventures of Nicholas Nickleby* on national tour in 1983. Nunn directed the Australian productions of *Cats* in 1985 and *Les Misérables* in 1987 for the Royal Shakespeare Company's entrepreneurial partner Cameron Mackintosh. ❦Katharine Brisbane

further reading
SHER, ANTONY. *The Year of the King*. London: Methuen 1986.

Royal Standard Theatre

Theatre in Castlereagh Street, Sydney, opened 29 April 1886 as **Royal Foresters' Hall**, seating 906. Architects: Ellis and Slatyer. Renamed **Royal Standard Theatre** 8 May 1886. Renamed **Empire Theatre** 16 March 1901; **Standard Theatre** 24 November 1906; **Little Theatre**, 22 March 1913; **Playhouse** 1917. Demolished *c*.1923.

After nearly 30 years of melodrama, vaudeville, boxing, seances and two-up games, this modest hall-cum-theatre became significant in 1913, when Hugh Buckler and his wife Violet Paget made it the home of their LITTLE THEATRE. This company was the first in Sydney to specialise in literary drama, following the lead of the Royal Court Theatre in London and the Birmingham Repertory Theatre.

The theatre began as a hall in a building on the western side of Castlereagh Street, south of Bathurst Street. It was erected by the Ancient Order of Foresters, a lodge and friendly society. There was a lodge room behind the dress circle and there were more rooms above the auditorium. According to the NSW Government Architect, the hall was 29·2 metres long by 11 metres wide. The stage was the same width but only 7·6 metres feet deep with a 6·1 metre-wide proscenium opening. The original lessee, Frank Smith, had a slight slope built into the floor. He also had 308 iron tip-up chairs, upholstered in crimson velvet, put into the front stalls and 220 into the dress circle. The rear stalls, occupying less than half of the floor, were 442 hard tip-up seats.

Nine days after the hall opened it was renamed the Royal Standard Theatre for the first stage performance— ALFRED DAMPIER's production of *The Phantom Ship,* based on the legend of Vanderdecken, the Flying Dutchman. The premiere of FOR THE TERM OF HIS NATURAL LIFE by Dampier and Thomas Somers followed on 5 June 1886.

In 1901 FULLERS' from New Zealand leased the theatre, renovated it and reopened it as the Empire Theatre. Their Empire Minstrel and Variety Company played there for nearly a year. From November 1906 it was called the Standard Theatre and occupied by HARRY CLAY's Vaudeville Company. In 1913 the theatre, renovated, redecorated and reseated, reopened as the Little Theatre, 'the Home of High-Class Comedy'. Gone was the 'mouldy, mediocre unloveliness' of the auditorium, said the management, which had installed a tea and coffee lounge beneath the stage so that patrons could exchange ideas after matinée performances. A photograph of the Little Theatre in 1913 corresponds to a description published in 1886—a three-storey building surmounted by the largest carved stone pediment in Sydney. This displayed rich foliage and the arms of the Foresters' lodge.

During the First World War the lease passed from Hugh Buckler to Sid James, who again renovated the theatre and reopened it as the Playhouse on 29 September 1917, with *The New Sin*, a play by Basil Macdonald Hastings. Later J. and N. TAIT LTD took over the Playhouse. It seems to have ended its days with the final performance of the Aussie Smart Set Diggers on 15 January 1921. ❦*Ross Thorne*

Royal Victoria Theatre Melbourne

Theatre in Bourke Street, opened 12 April 1841 as **Royal Pavilion Saloon**. Called **Theatre Royal** in 1842. Closed and reopened August 1842 as **Royal Victoria Theatre**. Closed 24 April 1845. Reopened as Canterbury Hall but soon demolished.

Only four years after Melbourne was officially named and planned, Thomas Hodge, or Hodges, built the first theatre. Hodge, whose interest in theatre had arisen from some menial contact with the English actor-manager CHARLES KEAN, was apparently a barman. His employer at the Eagle Inn, J. Jamieson, put up adjoining land and most of the finance for construction of a shed-like timber building measuring 22·5 by 10·5 metres. The Colonial Secretary in Sydney refused Hodge a licence for theatrical performances but the local police magistrate gave permission for musical concerts and the Royal Pavilion Saloon, generally known as the Pavilion, opened on 12 April 1841. The musical performance was 'spiced with low buffoonery, ribaldry and interludes of riot and confusion' and Hodge was imprisoned for infringing a law introduced in the 1820s.

GEORGE BUCKINGHAM offered to organise and direct a company of local players but this was initially unacceptable to the authorities. In December 1841 six leaders of the community formed themselves into a board of stewards to set up an Amateur Theatrical Association to obtain a temporary licence for performances for the benefit of a projected hospital. The Colonial Secretary issued a licence for one month from 24 January 1842. Buckingham prepared the theatre and stage decorations and doubtless rehearsed the casts for amateur performances of *Rob Roy* and *The Widow's Victim* in aid of the hospital fund on 21 February. The theatre was then called the Theatre Royal. It was given a continuous 12-month licence on 8 July and in August it reopened as the Royal Victoria Theatre, sometimes called the Victoria Theatre.

According to vague descriptions, the dress boxes were so low that occupants could bend and touch people in the pit, so the floor of the dress circle must have been at stage level, in Georgian style. An unstable ladder-like stair led to an upper circle of small pens graced with the name of boxes. The partitions between them were soon removed to form a more conventional gallery. The theatre leaked and it was so unstable that it swayed in a wind. Inebriated 'swells' once attempted to capsize it by applying brute force beneath the floor. Successive managers, Buckingham, CONRAD KNOWLES and SAMSON CAMERON were all criticised for poorly prepared actors and riotous behaviour in the audience. Three days after the opening of the more substantial QUEEN's THEATRE ROYAL the Royal Victoria was closed. ❦*Ross Thorne*

further reading
Garryowen. *The Chronicles of Early Melbourne 1835 to 1852*. Melbourne: 1888.

Royal Victoria Theatre Sydney

Theatre in Pitt Street, opened 26 March 1838, seating 1900 in four tiers. Architect: Henry Robertson. Auditorium rebuilt in three tiers for reopening on 2 December 1865. Destroyed by fire 22 July 1880.

For most of its existence the Royal Victoria Theatre was Sydney's largest and most important theatre. JOSEPH WYATT decided to build it in mid-1836, shortly after he became sole lessee of Barnett Levey's THEATRE ROYAL and on 7 September the foundation stone was laid, on the western side of Pitt Street, between King and Market Streets. The architect, Henry Robertson designed a building in the Regency colonial style—a restrained, three-storey façade with pilasters above the ground floor topped by an entablature and modest cornice. His early sketches of the elevation, published prior to construction, have been misinterpreted as representing the Theatre Royal.

The front section of the Royal Victoria housed a hotel and a shop. Entry to the more expensive seats was between the hotel bar and the shop, while patrons reached the cheaper seats from a side alleyway. The interior broke with Georgian tradition and heralded the Regency style of theatre design. The Royal Victoria was the first theatre in Australia to have the ground-floor pit extend beneath a dress circle raised above stage level. Above the dress circle were a family circle and a gallery—four tiers in all. There was a splayed-arch proscenium but Georgian proscenium doors for actors' entry to the stage were retained until 1854, when they gave way to proscenium boxes. The Georgian scene-changing system of wing flats and shutters sliding in grooves was also installed.

Drawings in the Mitchell Library (Sydney) show the auditorium to have been 16·75 metres long by 15 metres wide by 11·38 metres high. The stage apron was 3·05 metres deep and the depth from the curtain line to the rear stage wall was 12·42 metres. In 1840, for Edward Fitzball's play *The Flying Dutchman*, an opening 4·72 metres wide was made in the rear stage wall to allow scenic vistas for a further 15·24 metres in depth. At first the theatre was lit by Argand oil lamps but in 1841 gas lighting, fed by a private gas generator on site, was installed in the auditorium.

The Royal Victoria opened on 26 March 1838 with *Othello* followed by the farce *The Middy Ashore*. Complaints that Wyatt had a monopoly subsided when GEORGE COPPIN took over the theatre for a season in 1843. Wyatt and his wife Rachael sold the land on which the theatre stood on 5 November 1847 and then leased back the building on 4 January 1849. On 31 December 1851 they sub-leased the hotel part to ANDREW TORNING. In 1854 Wyatt was unable to renew the lease on favourable terms and Torning became lessee at the start of September. Wyatt decided to build the PRINCE OF WALES THEATRE, which gave the Royal Victoria its first real opposition. Later lessees of the Royal Victoria included Samuel Colville from 1 October 1859, R. Tolano from 2 December 1865 and Coppin for six months in 1867. In 1865 the auditorium was gutted and rebuilt with only three tiers, which reduced the capacity from the original 1900 or more persons and improved comfort and safety. Until its destruction in 1880 the Royal Victoria continued to be upgraded and redecorated—20 times in all—and to house leading performers. In the 1850s CLARANCE HOLT and his wife, RICHARD STEWART and the Australian tragedian H. N. Warner performed there. The 1860s included two seasons by CHARLES AND ELLEN KEAN, and the 1870s saw WILLIAM CRESWICK, ALFRED DAMPIER, GEORGE DARRELL in his own *Transported for Life* and other works, BLAND HOLT and ADELAIDE RISTORI at the Royal Victoria. ❦*Ross Thorne*

reference
A six-part video from the University of Sydney Television Service, *A Colonial Theatre—The Royal Victoria, Sydney*, illustrates through reconstruction and acting the architecture, lighting and staging of the theatre, the nature of the audience and part of the murder scene of *Othello*.

Deidre Rubenstein

Actor, singer. Born 28 February 1948 in Melbourne. Graduated from National Institute of Dramatic Art, (Sydney) 1967. Melbourne Theatre Company 1970–72. Travelled overseas. Returned to Australia 1979. Has worked for every major theatre company.

A powerful actor and singer, Deidre Rubenstein performs extensively in self-devised cabaret. She won plaudits for her debut, as Hortense in the musical comedy *The Boy Friend* at the Phillip Theatre in Sydney in 1968. She performed in 16 plays with the MELBOURNE THEATRE COMPANY, including RAY LAWLER's *The Man Who Shot the Albatross* in 1970, before she went overseas. In 1980 she began a long and fruitful association with the NIMROD THEATRE COMPANY in Sydney when she helped to devise and starred in *You and the Night and the Housewine*. Subsequent roles included Natasha in Anton Chekhov's *Three Sisters* and Edward and Betty in Caryl Churchill's *Cloud Nine* in 1981, the Old Lady in the musical *Candide* in 1982, Celia in *As You Like It* in 1983, Anna Petrovna in Michael Frayn's *Wild Honey* in 1986, and Mme de Tourvel in Christopher Hampton's *Les Liaisons dangereuses* in 1987. She returned to Melbourne in 1991 and appeared in several plays for the PLAYBOX THEATRE CENTRE and the Melbourne Theatre Company before she devised two successful solo shows, *What's a Girl to Do?* and *As Dorothy Parker Once Said*, which she toured nationally in 1994. ❦*Tony Sheldon*

Steele Rudd

Dramatist. Born 14 November 1868 in Drayton (Qld). Real name Arthur Hoey Davis. Had *Selection* stories published in *Bulletin* from 1895. Wrote and revised plays 1907–32. Also wrote novels, short stories and screenplays. Died 11 October 1935 in Brisbane.

Until the advent of DAVID WILLIAMSON 40 years later, Steele Rudd was Australia's most successful playwright. Four of his plays were professionally produced and all were triumphs. Two sound films were made from his plays and he co-wrote scenarios for three silent films. One million people in Australia and New Zealand saw Rudd's first play, *ON OUR SELECTION*, between 1912 and 1916. It was followed by *Duncan McClure and the Poor Parson* in 1915 and *Gran'dad Rudd* in 1917. Rudd's last play, first staged by amateurs in 1924, became another national success as *The Rudd Family* in 1928. A fifth play, *In Australia* was not staged in Rudd's lifetime but it has been professionally adapted twice since 1987. In 1907 the journalist BEAUMONT SMITH persuaded Rudd to collaborate in making *On Our Selection* from his earliest stories of life on a small 'selected' farm. After several vicissitudes, and some double dealing by Smith, this play was rewritten by the actor-manager BERT BAILEY, with some input from his partner EDMUND DUGGAN. Bailey staged it in 1912, with spectacular success. The most memorable roles were those of Dad, Mum and Dave, who were broader than Rudd's original characters.

Rudd, who had been excluded from work on the final draft of *On Our Selection*—and from most of the profits—extensively rewrote his version under its original title, *In Australia*, but could not find a producer. He moved away from pioneering to the prosperous but still tightfisted farmers of the early 20th century in his next play, a 'Scottish–Australian comedy'. He wrote it only months after the landing at Gallipoli and staged it as *Duncan McClure* with an amateur company in Toowoomba (Qld) in August 1915 during a day of fund-raising for the war effort. In this version a wounded Alex McClure, the eldest son, returns at the end of the play to eulogise on his fallen Anzac comrades. Rudd revised the play for Bailey's professional production as *Duncan McClure and the Poor Parson* in 1916. The revised script minimised references to the war, which had become a less popular theme, and approached knockabout farce. Alex McClure's departure to take horses to South America is much less moving than his harrowing farewell to his parents to enlist as a soldier in the 1915 version. The ebullience of the big-hearted Duncan McClure, Bailey's own role, drives the action of every scene, though the most memorable character is Bill Eaglefoot, a lazy farm-hand, played in Bailey's production by FRED MACDONALD. Rudd provides an unusual and sympathetic portrayal of a Presbyterian minister, Mr McCulloch, who lives in stoic poverty in a small farming community.

In *Gran'dad Rudd* the Rudd family has advanced a generation. Dad is now Gran'dad and Dave and Joe are middle-aged family men. Again Rudd does not just repeat a successful formula, nor does he simply dramatise his *Grandpa's Selection* stories. A young farmer and inventor, Tom Dalley, has the plans for his successful potato harvester stolen, and the plotting is predictable though at times spirited. 'Ain't it wonderful 'ow you city blokes always takes us bushmen for mugs', comments Dave as he and Dan Rudd confront the thief and execute joyful revenge. Dan is Gran'dad's eldest son, who had quarrelled with his father and left home many years before. His return and his wooing of the 'guiding star' of the local temperance movement, Amelia Banks, form the major comic element.

Dubious claims to the authorship of *Gran'dad Rudd* abound. Bert Bailey has been credited with writing the play 'from the stories by Steele Rudd' but this is unfounded. Rudd's own surviving drafts are close to the play as performed, and Bailey's company was not the only one to stage it professionally.

The play was revised, however, by two employees of Cinesound, Victor Roberts and George D. Parker, for a film version starring Bailey in 1935. In the play Gran'dad opposes the marriage of the young lovers Nell Rudd and Tom Dalley, and becomes a much less attractive figure. The film has him support Tom against the odious Henry Cook, whose sophisticated attentions at first flatter an older, independent-minded Nell. Cook's true character is revealed at the altar.

Rudd's last play, many times rewritten and known by several titles, is a curious work, partly fresh and interesting, partly old-fashioned melodrama with an intense, brooding villain. It is probably an otherwise lost play, *On Sibley Settlement*, that Rudd submitted unsuccessfully to J. C. WILLIAMSON'S in 1921. It reached the stage in 1924 as *On Grubb's Selection* in amateur charity performances in Toowoomba and Brisbane, with characters loosely based on stories that had appeared in *Steele Rudd's Annual* in 1922–23. This version, marginally rewritten and retitled *The Rudd Family*, was a commercial success throughout Australia in 1928, with Edmund Duggan as director and star. The characters were all named Dickson—perhaps because Bailey held the rights to the names of the Rudd family—but the title and the character types were intended to suggest that the play was a sequel to *On Our Selection*. The 1928 version marked a significant change in Rudd's attitude to the characters, most clearly in a new comedy sequence where the 'bushies' try to comprehend newspaper items about current city topics.

The financial crash in 1929 cut short the Duggan tour, but Rudd made a shorter script that may have toured country towns as late as mid-1932. He omitted the villain from this version, leaving a plotless flow of comic and epic sequences. Finally Rudd was unable to resist the drive by actors, managers and the public to create figures of fun. Revue sketches, cartoons, jokes, and a long-running radio serial later gave rise to the idea of 'Dad and Dave' as a comedy duo—to be laughed at rather than with—only tenuously linked to even the stage plays. ❦*Richard Fotheringham*

published plays
In Australia—or, The Old Selection (1987). Brisbane: University of Queensland Press 1987 (ed. Richard Fotheringham).
On Our Selection (1912). Sydney: Currency Press 1984 (ed. Helen Musa).

further reading
DAVIS, ERIC. *The Life and Times of Steele Rudd*. Melbourne: Lansdowne Press 1976.
IKIN, VAN. Arthur Hoey Davis. *Australian Dictionary of Biography* 8. Melbourne University Press 1981.

Geoffrey Rush

Actor, director. Born in Toowoomba (Qld). Acted with College Players before 1971. Queensland Theatre Company productions 1971–74. Trained at Lecoq school in Paris. British Theatre Association director's course in London. Returned to Queensland Theatre Company 1978. Moved to Sydney 1978. Member of Lighthouse Company (Adelaide) 1982–83. Artistic director of Magpie Theatre Company (Adelaide) 1984–85. Married to actor Jane Menelaus.

Geoffrey Rush is a stylish and sometimes stylised performer. His acute physical control is as remarkable as his imaginative characterisation. His Parisian training is obvious. He works in ensemble and experimental productions as well as on the mainstage. Before he went to Paris he acted in 17 QUEENSLAND THEATRE COMPANY productions, including *Twelfth Night*, Sean O'Casey's *Juno and the Paycock*, Molière's *The Imaginary Invalid*, Noël Coward's *Present Laughter* and the musical *Godspell*. He returned to the company for *King Lear* in 1978. As a member of the

Lighthouse ensemble in Adelaide he acted in 13 plays and directed six productions, including David Holman's *Small Poppies*. He played Proposhkin in NEIL ARMFIELD's production of Holman's adaptation of Nikolai Gogol's *Diary of a Madman* at the BELVOIR STREET THEATRE in Sydney in 1990, on tour in Russia and Georgia in 1991, at the Adelaide Festival in 1992 and at Belvoir Street again in 1992. For the MELBOURNE THEATRE COMPANY he played Jack Worthing in Oscar Wilde's *The Importance of Being Earnest* in 1991–92 and for the SYDNEY THEATRE COMPANY he played Astrov in Anton Chekhov's *Uncle Vanya* in 1992 and John in *Oleanna* in 1993. At Belvoir Street in 1994 he played Horatio as the still centre of *Hamlet*. Rush is best known as a director for the production of *Popular Mechanicals* at Belvoir Street in 1987 and its sequel *Pop Mex 2* in 1992. He collaborated with Keith Robinson and TONY TAYLOR in the writing of *Popular Mechanicals*, which is based on characters from *A Midsummer Night's Dream*. ❧*Ken Healey*

Anna Russell

Actor, comedian. Born 27 December 1911 in London. Originally Anna Claudia Russell-Brown. Studied piano and singing at Royal College of Music (London). Broadcast on British and Canadian radio. Began international career as comedian in New York City 1948. Performed in Australia from 1955. Lived in Sydney 1968–76. Retired in Canada.

During an eight-year stay in Australia Anna Russell acted in the theatre and performed on radio. She gave a luminous performance as the aged courtesan Mme Armfeldt in the musical *A Little Night Music* for J. C. WILLIAMSON's in 1973–74. She also played the lead in Peter Coke's comedy *Breath of Spring* at the Independent Theatre in Sydney in 1968, directed by ALLAN DAVIS. The ebullient and gregarious Russell settled in Australia after years of touring the world as a comedian specialising in comic commentary on music. During her irresistible recounting of the plot of Richard Wagner's *Der Ring des Nibelungen* she would exclaim: 'I'm not making this up, you know!' ❧*John West*

autobiography
I'm Not Making This Up, You Know. New York City: Continuum 1985.

Russell Street Theatre

Theatre in Russell Street, Melbourne. Converted from church and opened as theatre seating 374, 1944. First used by Union Theatre Repertory Company 20 July 1960. Altered to seat 416—later reduced to 394—and reopened by Melbourne Theatre Company 12 February 1968. Architect: Robin Boyd.

Australia's oldest existing professional theatre company, the MELBOURNE THEATRE COMPANY made the Russell Street Theatre its home during a period of consolidation and development in the 1960s and has remained there ever since. The building in downtown Russell Street was a church until the Victorian Council for Adult Education took it over in 1944 and converted it for amateur theatrical performances. In the late 1950s audiences for amateurs were falling away and the Union Theatre Repertory Company was seeking premises off the University of Melbourne campus. It presented a revue at Russell Street for a month in 1960 and next year it began a six-month season there. The company left the university at the end of 1965 and moved to Russell Street full time in 1966. Between the 1967 and 1968 seasons the architect Robin Boyd remodelled the converted church into a delightfully intimate theatre. The capacity was increased by the addition of two boxes, each seating 15 persons, at the rear of the raked stalls and a small central balcony—virtually another box—seating about 12 and filling one-third of the auditorium width. The proscenium stage, lacking a fly tower, was cleverly designed to minimise separation of the audience from the action. A wall-covering pattern reproducing the company's new symbol in a variety of sizes enriched the red-toned auditorium. The company reopened the theatre with *The Crucible* by Arthur Miller—its first performance as the Melbourne Theatre Company. The company intended to use the theatre only until the larger Playhouse at the VICTORIAN ARTS CENTRE was available in the mid-1970s, but it had to wait until 1984 for that theatre. Since then it has retained the Russell Street Theatre as its second venue. The theatre was redecorated in greys in 1989. ❧*Ross Thorne*

further reading
SUMNER, JOHN. *Recollections at Play—A life in Australian theatre*. Melbourne: University Press 1993.

Russian influences

Interest in Konstantin Stanislavsky's theory of acting and his philosophy of theatre gained momentum in the early 1930s as amateur groups reacted against the attitudes of the professional theatre. DORIS FITTON, who founded INDEPENDENT THEATRE in Sydney in 1931, acknowledged inspiration by the guiding principles of the Moscow Art Theatre as formulated in Stanislavsky's *My Life in Art*. DOLIA RIBUSH, a Stanislavsky-influenced immigrant from Russia, founded the amateur Dolia Ribush Players in Melbourne in 1931 to produce high-quality theatre with extensive rehearsal. Enthusiastic disciples of Stanislavsky in amateur theatre in the 1940s included the directors Keith George in Perth and COLIN BALLANTYNE and his wife Gwenneth in Adelaide.

Later, Stanislavsky's theory often reached Australia through English and American channels, especially pupils of Lee Strasberg. The most remarkable of the Strasberg pupils who brought his 'method' here is HAYES GORDON, who founded the Ensemble Theatre Company in 1958. Stanislavsky's ideas were evident in the MELBOURNE THEATRE COMPANY, founded in 1953, and the OLD TOTE THEATRE COMPANY, founded in Sydney in 1963, and in teaching at the NATIONAL INSTITUTE OF DRAMATIC ART in Sydney. By the 1960s a Stanislavsky or quasi-Stanislavsky approach to acting dominated non-commercial theatre. It has been challenged in the last two decades but it is holding its ground.

An offshoot of the interest in Stanislavsky in the 1930s was the introduction of plays by Anton Chekhov. In 1936 Independent Theatre produced *Three Sisters*, and the Art Theatre Players in Melbourne staged *The Seagull*. In 1938 Ribush directed *The Cherry Orchard* in Melbourne with seven months' meticulous rehearsal. Independent Theatre followed with *The Seagull* in 1943 and *The Cherry Orchard* in 1945. Interest in Chekhov rose in the 1960s, no doubt stimulated by his works' success in England. The Old Tote company opened with *The Cherry Orchard*, and *Three Sisters* followed in 1966. Independent Theatre staged *The Seagull* in 1965 and *Uncle Vanya* in 1968. The Melbourne Theatre Company offered *Three Sisters* in 1968. The number of productions grew through the 1970s and 1980s. Notable were:

The Cherry Orchard by the Melbourne Theatre Company, with Googie Withers in 1972; the South Australian Theatre Company in 1977, with an emphasis on comedy; the Queensland Theatre Company in 1978; the SYDNEY THEATRE COMPANY in 1983, with stunning symbolic sets but naturalistic acting; AUSTRALIAN NOUVEAU THEATRE directed by Jean-Pierre Mignon in Melbourne in 1987.

The Seagull, by the NIMROD THEATRE COMPANY in 1974, contesting Stanislavsky's lyrical pace with a farcical treatment; directed in a post-modern style by Mignon for the Sydney Theatre Company in 1986.

Three Sisters by Nimrod in 1981; Australian Nouveau Theatre directed by Mignon in 1987.

Uncle Vanya by Old Tote in 1972; by Nimrod in 1983; Australian Nouveau Theatre directed by Mignon in 1987.

Chekhov's vaudevilles reached Australia when Ribush produced *A Jubilee* in Russian in 1931; they remain popular with professional companies. Nimrod scored a hit in 1983 with JUDY DAVIS and COLIN FRIELS in *The Bear*. Chekhov's earlier plays arrived quite recently—*Ivanov* produced by Old Tote in 1975; *Platonov*, adapted by Michael Frayn as *Wild Honey*, by Nimrod in 1986; and *The Wood Demon* by Theatre East in Canberra in 1987.

Of other Russian classics the best-known here is Nikolai Gogol's *The Government Inspector*. It has been produced by Independent Theatre in 1947, NEW THEATRE Melbourne in 1953, and Old Tote in 1971. John Cousins adapted the play to an Australian country town for the HARVEST THEATRE COMPANY, which successfully toured several parts of South Australia in 1987, and Graeme Brosnan made another such adaptation which Q THEATRE at Penrith (NSW) performed in 1990. In 1991 there was a major revival of the play in Sydney. Gogol's *The Marriage* was staged in 1963 by New Theatre in Sydney. In 1976 the AUSTRALIAN PERFORMING GROUP staged JACK HIBBERD's adaptation of Gogol's *The Overcoat*, and the Melbourne Theatre Company presented his *Diary of a Madman*. In Sydney the latter was staged by NEIL ARMFIELD for the BELVOIR STREET THEATRE in 1989 with GEOFFREY RUSH in the title-role. This production met with acclaim on a tour of Russia and Georgia in October 1991.

Maxim Gorky's name occurs on theatre posters almost as often as Gogol's. *The Lower Depths* had remarkable productions by Ribush in Melbourne in 1936 and by the Rumanian director Liviu Ciulei, assisted by REX CRAMPHORN, with the Old Tote company in Sydney in 1977. It was also staged by New Theatre Melbourne in 1981 and by the Rocks Players in Sydney in 1985. New Theatre in Sydney performed Gorky's *The Enemies* in 1946 and 1978, and his *Vassa Zheleznova* in 1976. Ivan Turgenev's classic *A Month in the Country* is rarely performed, though Sydney had an opportunity to see it at the Old Tote Theatre in 1971.

Contemporary Soviet socialist-realist plays were performed remarkably frequently in the 1930s and 1940s, corresponding to the rise of the New Theatre movement and the formation of groups such as the WORKERS' ART GUILD, Independent Theatre and the Melbourne Little Theatre Company. In the 1950s Soviet plays virtually disappeared. Since then there has been sporadic interest in playwrights such as Aleksey Arbuzov, whose humanist and compassionate concern with the struggles and feelings of ordinary people made him one of the most popular authors of the post-Stalinist 'thaw' era of Soviet theatre. Independent Theatre performed his *The Promise* in 1968 and the Ensemble his *Old World* in 1982. Recently there has been interest in the new wave of *glasnost* plays. New Theatre Melbourne included Vladimir Gubarev's *Sarcophagus*, on the subject of the Chernobyl nuclear disaster, in its 1989 plan. There is also growing awareness of non-naturalistic Russian theatre, especially Vladimir Mayakovsky's work. For example, in 1987 his *Vladimir Mayakovsky, a Tragedy* was performed at the Spoleto Festival in Melbourne, and a Mayakovsky exhibition was held at the Art Gallery of NSW. Australian Nouveau Theatre produced Mikhail Bulgakov's *Molière* in 1988 and his *The Crimson Island* at the Adelaide Festival in 1992. *Maria Kreisler*

Rusty Bugles

Play in two acts by Sumner Locke Elliott. **premiere** 21 October 1948, Independent Theatre, Sydney. Cast: Michael Barnes, Lloyd Berrell, Ivor Bromley-Smith, Sidney Chambers, Kenneth Colbert, Robert Crome, Frank Curtain, Ronald Frazer, John Kingsmill, Kevin Healy, Frank O'Donnell, Ralph Peterson, Alastair Roberts, John Unicomb. Designer: Steve Hodgkinson. Director: Doris Fitton. **revived** 16 April 1949, King's Theatre, Melbourne. **published** Brisbane: University of Queensland Press 1968, in *Khaki, Bush and Bigotry*. Sydney: Currency Press 1980, revised.

The first Australian play to reach the professional theatre after the Second World War, *Rusty Bugles* was a pioneer of the movement towards abandoning European form in favour of a structure more reflective of Australian life. It was also the centre of a public controversy about the use of realistic Australian language. The play is a comedy-drama set in an ordnance depot near Katherine in the Northern Territory, where 16 Australian soldiers are frustrated by separation from their loved ones and from active service. They watch the seasons come and go in rough camaraderie and ineffective quarrelling.

The play is memorable for the dry wit of the dialogue, varied and vivid characters inspired by SUMNER LOCKE ELLIOTT's own army service—which included six months at Mataranka ordnance depot in the Northern Territory in 1944—and for its loose, circular, Chekhovian structure. The play became a *succès de scandale* when two police officers who had attended the opening night reported to the NSW Chief Secretary, J. M. Baddeley, that it contained blasphemous and indecent words—language common in the armed forces, as most of the audience recognised. The play was banned under the Theatres and Public Halls Act 1908. This brought a storm of protest. A compromise was reached when the play's director, DORIS FITTON, agreed to delete a proportion of the offending words. These were gradually restored in succeeding performances.

The entrepreneurs KENN BRODZIAK and GARNET H. CARROLL then bought the play and opened it in Melbourne in 1949 with four members of the original cast, one of them now named simply Ivor Bromley. It played there for six months and then toured for two years. In 1952 another production was taken to New Zealand. In 1955 the success of Ray Lawler's *SUMMER OF THE SEVENTEENTH DOLL* displaced

Rusty Bugles from its pre-eminence and it was forgotten. INDEPENDENT THEATRE revived it in 1964 and JOHN TASKER directed a fine semiprofessional production for New Theatre in 1979, but there has been no major production. Elliott never saw his play performed. By the time it reached the stage he had emigrated to the USA. The play was adapted for ABC television in 1965 and 1981. ✽*Katharine Brisbane*

Donna Sadka

Critic. Born 14 May 1926 in Perth. Daughter of musical critic A. H. Kornweibel. Studied at Melbourne University Conservatorium 1946–47. Trained in drama with Des Connor, Keith Macartney and Joy Youlden in productions at Melbourne University Union Theatre. Singapore Repertory Theatre 1950–51. Married Frederick Sadka 1952. Settled in Perth with family 1963. Contributing theatrical critic of *West Australian* 1965–86.

A generous supporter of local actors and the development of theatre in Western Australia, Donna Sadka was a popular, knowledgeable, conservative critic with a taste for the well-made play and the classic text. She was unassuming in her views and though not attracted by the new wave of indigenous theatre in the 1970s or by the avant-garde she reported on them faithfully and fairly. ✽*Katharine Brisbane*

Sol Sainken

Actor, administrator, director. Born 12 September 1907 in Jerusalem. Came to Australia at 18 months. Joined Repertory Club (Perth) 1927. Co-founder of Company of Four 1950. On board of National Theatre Company 1956–73.

Western Australia's flourishing theatre owes much to the enthusiasm of Sol Sainken, who pushed to achieve professional presentation of high quality. He was a co-founder of the professional COMPANY OF FOUR, which raised standards until it amalgamated with the amateur REPERTORY CLUB in 1956 as the initially semiprofessional NATIONAL THEATRE COMPANY. Sainken directed conventional but intelligent and polished productions for these and other companies, including bodies associated with the University of Western Australia. He brought administrative expertise to the National Theatre board. ✽*Maurice Jones*

Salamanca Theatre Company

Professional theatre-in-education company in Tasmania, founded in 1972 as Tasmanian Theatre in Education. Renamed 1976.
directors 1972–84 Barbara Manning. 1985–90 David Young. 1991–93 Mary Hickson. 1993– Christine Best.

Since its inception the Salamanca Theatre Company has toured Tasmania, presenting high-quality theatre to school audiences ranging from infants to upper secondary pupils. It bases plays on aspects of society immediately relevant to pupils' and teachers' lives, and employs traditional and experimental skills. The company has commissioned several successful plays, including Anne Harvey's *I Must Have One of My Own* and Ken Kelso's *The Whale, the Biggest Thing that Ever Died*, both of which went into other companies' repertoires. In 1976 it toured the USA for 14 weeks, funded by the Australian government and American bodies in a cultural exchange. In 1989 it performed *Thirst*, a play of its own devising, to critical acclaim in the United Kingdom, and it won the $25 000 Sidney Myer Performing Arts prize. The company was founded under the Tasmanian Theatre Company and based at the Theatre Royal in Hobart, but in 1976 it moved to Salamanca Place and changed its name. The company has grown steadily, employing up to six full-time actors. Its members are able to debate openly its structure and working conditions. It receives federal funding from the AUSTRALIA COUNCIL and state assistance from the Tasmanian Arts Advisory Board. Since 1993 it has looked to including productions for adult audiences in its programs, a development favoured by ROGER HODGMAN's 1993 report into adult theatre in Tasmania. The Salamanca Script Resource Centre, established in 1980, is now a separate national organisation, the Australian Script Centre, containing more than 2000 scripts of all kinds, not only those suitable for young people's theatre. ✽*Gillian Winter*

Salathiel

—or, *The Jewish Chieftain*. Drama in three acts by Conrad Knowles.
premiere 4 August 1842, Royal Victoria Theatre, Sydney. Cast: Harriet Jones, Conrad Knowles, Joseph Simmons, Eliza Winstanley.

CONRAD KNOWLES adapted this historical drama from Edward Bulwer-Lytton's 1838 novel *Leila*. Where the author was followed by Knowles, 'and it was easy to see where he was not', the language 'was polished and appropriate', commented the *Sydney Morning Herald* on 6 August 1842 after the premiere, a benefit for Knowles's wife Harriet Jones. In the play, Salathiel, disguised as a magician, plots to avenge Jewish suffering under Moorish rule by betraying Granada to the besieging Christians in return for civil liberties for his people. King Ferdinand of Aragón and Castile, however, has no intention of honouring his promise. Salathiel's daughter Salome loves the Moorish champion Agib Muza, but her father gives her to Ferdinand as a hostage. In the Christian camp she is befriended and converted by Queen Isabella. Salathiel kills her as she is about to take the veil, and the last Moorish king is expelled from Granada. ✽*Veronica Kelly*

June Salter AM

Actor. Born 22 June 1932 in Sydney. Began acting on radio 1952. First stage appearances in Phillip Street revues in Sydney. In England 1959–64. Many television roles. Married to actor John Meillon 1958–71. Mother of John Meillon jnr. Glugs Awards 1978 (Queen Mary in *Crown Matrimonial* by Royce Ryton). AM 1982.

June Salter's wide range is shown by her appearances in such contrasting plays as Alan Ayckbourn's *Relatively Speaking* and *Bedroom Farce*, Noël Coward's *Blithe Spirit*, Marsha Norman's *'Night, Mother*, Peter Shaffer's *Lettice and Lovage* as Lotte Schoen and Daphne Du Maurier's *Rebecca* as the lowering Mrs Danvers. After appearing in PHILLIP STREET REVUES, such as *Around the Loop* in 1956 and *Cross Section* in 1957, Salter and her husband JOHN MEILLON worked in England for six years. They returned in 1964 to star together in Charles Dyer's *Rattle of a Simple Man*, first in Sydney and then on tour. Years of television work followed for Salter. She began a long run on stage in 1978 in PETER WILLIAMS's production of *Crown Matrimonial*. By contrast, in 1980 she played the lead in the musical *Gypsy* for the Queensland Theatre Company. ✽*John West*

Clive Sansom

Dramatist. Born 21 June 1910 in London. Studied speech and drama at London Academy of Music and Dramatic Art. Became LAMDA examiner and lecturer. Prolific writer of educational works, verse drama and poetry. Sansom and his Tasmanian-born wife Ruth, poet and educationist, were both appointed to Speech Centre of Tasmanian Department of Education in Hobart, 1950. MBE 1972. Died 29 March 1981 in Hobart.

Clive Sansom's English origins and Quaker faith were central to his work. A memorial noted 'his genius for creating characters in his verse-plays—his generous and humane view of our world—his sharp eye and keen wit in expressing ideas in the finest language'. His verse drama *The Cathedral*, written in 1958, was performed to mark the centenary of St David's Cathedral in Hobart in 1968. A lover of the English countryside, Sansom became a vocal conservationist in Tasmania. ❦*Gillian Winter*

further reading
Clive Sansom—by Forty Friends. Hobart: Specialty Press 1990.

Justine Saunders

Actor. Born at Dirranbandi (Qld). Moved to Sydney 1972. Has worked for every major theatre company in Australia. Assistant artistic director of first National Black Playwrights' Conference 1987. Member of board of Aboriginal National Theatre Trust 1988–89. Chair of Aboriginal performing arts committee of Aboriginal Arts Unit 1989–90. Member of performing arts board of Australia Council. On National Institute of Dramatic Art board of studies. Also in film and television.

One of the most prominent Aboriginal actors, Justine Saunders was one of the first to break the barriers of race and sex, by being cast in such roles as Samuel Simile in Edward Geoghegan's *The Currency Lass* for Q THEATRE and as Tituba in the SYDNEY THEATRE COMPANY production of *The Crucible* by Arthur Miller in 1991–92. She came to the fore as Ruby in Black Theatre's premiere of THE CAKE MAN in Sydney in 1975. She repeated this lead role in other productions of Robert J. Merritt's play, including one by the Australian Aboriginal Theatre Company, which won standing ovations at the World Theatre Festival in Denver (Colorado, USA) in 1982. Saunders also acted in the USA in Thomas Keneally's *Bullie's House*, in New Haven (Connecticut) in 1986. In Australia she acted in Richard Walley's *Coordah* in 1987, LOUIS NOWRA's *Capricornia* in 1988 and *Byzantine Flowers* in 1990 and JACK DAVIS's *No Sugar* in 1990. She toured the United Kingdom as the Mother in Davis's *Honey Spot* in 1991. ❦*Lydia Miller*

Irving Sayles

Comedian. Born 1872 in Illinois (USA). Came to Australia with Hicks–Sawyer Minstrels 1888. Partner of Charles Pope to 1902. In Frank Clark Variety Company 1893. On Tivoli circuit 1893–14. Died 9 February 1914 in Christchurch (New Zealand).

A black American, Irving Sayles became an acknowledged Australian theatrical institution. He began his professional career in the USA as a 'piccaninny' in Haverly's black minstrel company, appearing in a singing, dancing and tumbling turn, the Four Hottentots. In 1888 he came to Australia with another black company, the Hicks–Sawyer Minstrels, led by CHARLES B. HICKS, the most successful black American minstrel manager in show business. Sayles was the troupe's star endman and comedian, specialising in the performance of 'coon' songs. The 'coon' was a new image of the American black, who had traditionally been presented as ludicrous, no threat to white supremacy. The 'coon' showed him as not only foolish and stupid but dangerous and aggressive, for he slashed with his razor and had a prodigious sexual appetite.

In 1893, after a brief stint with the Frank Clark Variety Company, Sayles and CHARLES POPE, a fellow refugee from the Hicks–Sawyer Minstrels, joined the TIVOLI CIRCUIT as a comedy duo specialising in minstrel-style sketches such as *The Dark 'Uns* and *The Two Charcoals*. The partnership lasted 15 years until Pope left for the rival BRENNAN VAUDEVILLE CIRCUIT. Sayles, the 'boss' endman, became the longest-serving entertainer on the Tivoli circuit. His singing of 'All coons look alike to me', 'Father of a little black coon' and 'Hot time in the old town tonight' helped to make 'coon' songs widely known here. He was a key figure in the introduction of Afro-American syncopation to Australia.

When the Tivoli circuit introduced first-half revues to its programs in the early 20th century, Sayles featured in many of them, often performing modern vaudeville songs instead of blackface material. He was touring New Zealand with a Tivoli troupe when he died in Christchurch in 1914. Few mourners attended his funeral, but one observer noted had the burial taken place in Sydney or Melbourne 'what a difference there would have been'. ❦*Richard Waterhouse*

further reading
WATERHOUSE, RICHARD. Minstrel show and vaudeville house. *Australian Historical Studies* 23 (Melbourne, October 1989).

Thelma Scott

Actor. Born 1913 in Melbourne. Much stage work with Gregan McMahon 1931–34; Worked almost exclusively in radio in Sydney 1935–51. In England 1951–57. Further stage roles in Australia.

Thelma Scott began acting at 18 in Melbourne, as Ilano Szabo in Ferenc Molnár's *The Play's the Thing*, directed by GREGAN MCMAHON. She then acted in many plays directed by McMahon. In 1934 a success in Margaret Kennedy and Basil Dean's *The Constant Nymph* led to Scott playing opposite the English import George Thirlwell in Anthony Asquith's hit thriller *Ten Minute Alibi* for J. C. WILLIAMSON'S. It opened in Sydney. Scott moved there in 1935, took up a radio contract and virtually abandoned the stage to be a great radio actor until she went to London in 1951. She returned to Sydney in 1957 for the start of television. In 1967 at the Tivoli Theatre she played the female lead in Jack Roffey's *Hostile Witness*, opposite the Hollywood star Ray Milland; and in 1968 she played opposite the English actor Alfred Marks in Bill Naughton's *Spring and Port Wine* for J. C. Williamson's. ❦*Richard Lane*

Mary Scott-Siddons

English actor. Notable appearances in London and New York in 1867–68. In Australia and New Zealand 1876–78.

Always advertised as a descendant of the famous 18th-century actress Mrs Siddons, 'Mrs' Mary Frances Scott-Siddons achieved temporary fame in Australia, especially in Hobart, where she had huge success at the Theatre Royal in 1878. She was praised for her acting but not her interpretation, and she paled in comparison to other visiting stars like ADELAIDE RISTORI. In 1876 she appeared at the Theatre Royal in Sydney in May and moved to the Theatre Royal in Melbourne in July. In January 1877 she played Juliet to GEORGE DARRELL's Romeo in Dunedin (New Zealand). Back in Sydney in mid-1877, she played Rosalind in *As You Like It* at the Theatre Royal. Mrs Scott-Siddons complained about the prevalent popularity of burlesque and melodrama rather than Shakespeare, but when the melodrama writer ARCHIBALD MURRAY made a stage adaptation of Nathaniel Hawthorne's *The Scarlet Letter* for her in 1878 it played for only two nights. ❦*Helen Musa*

The Scout

Play in three acts by Alfred Dampier and Garnet Walch. **premiere** 9 May 1891, Alexandra Theatre, Melbourne. Cast: F. C. Appleton, 'Dr' W. F. Carver, Lily Dampier, Edmund Holloway, Julia Merton, Australian Dramatic Company and W. F. Carver's Wild America troupe. Designer: 'Alta' (Alfred Tischbauer). Director: Alfred Dampier.

In May 1891 the Melbourne *Lorgnette* noted: 'A great novelty will be introduced at the Alexandra Theatre next Saturday, when Dr Carver with his Indians, cowboys &c, will appear in conjunction with Alfred Dampier's dramatic company in a drama, founded on border life, entitled *The Scout*. Great alterations have been made to the Alexandra stage, including the erection of a water tank the full width of the theatre 12 ft [4 metres] wide, and 9 ft [3 metres] in depth, in which the Indians will "paddle their own canoes".' Not only that, but real ducks swam on the 'lake', horsemen chased wild Sioux Indians through it, and in another scene it changed into a rushing river and the bridge over it collapsed, leaving 'Dr' W. F. CARVER hanging 'tooth and nail' while his horse fell 'snorting and screaming' into the torrent below. Small wonder that the *Argus* reported on 11 May that on opening night the audience 'applauded and whistled and yelled for nearly ten minutes in a vain attempt to obtain an encore'.

The American Wild West was already well known to readers of 'yellowback literature' when the actor-manager ALFRED DAMPIER and the journalist GARNET WALCH hit upon the idea of putting the talents of Carver's Wild America troupe into a dramatic story. The sharpshooting Carver and buckjumping riders, lassoers and Amerindian dancers had been performing in Australia for some time but, according to the *Argus*, everything they had previously done paled in comparison with their feats on the stage. With the kidnapping of a settler's daughter by 'savages', the massacre of Indians 'in the most approved fashion', and Carver's ability to wrestle the villain, pick him up bodily, and throw him into the overused tank to drown, the play was a huge success. The theatre seated 2500, but up to 300 more squeezed in on some nights during the first fortnight of its six-week run.

When Carver returned to the USA he played *The Scout* everywhere he could, from San Francisco to New York, where he gave no fewer than ten seasons in different theatres in 1892–93. Strangely, he failed to mention that this 'realistic' portrayal of his 'real-life' exploits had been devised by two Australians whose only experience of the Wild West was Ned Buntline's Buffalo Bill 'dime novels'. *The Scout* was revived several times in Australia, most successfully in Sydney in 1895 as *The Prairie King*, with Walch credited as the sole author. ❦*Richard Fotheringham*

reference
The manuscript of *The Scout* is in the Mitchell Library (Sydney), MS B752.

Peter Scriven MBE

Puppeteer. Born 28 September 1930 in Melbourne. Built glove-puppet show at 14. Gained early experience with marionettes with W. D. Nicol. Toured with solo marionette act at 18. Visited puppet companies in Europe and toured with puppet master Waldo Lanchester in England. Formed Peter Scriven Puppets 1953. Began large-scale marionette productions with *The Tintookies*, Sydney 1956. Founded Marionette Theatre of Australia 1965. Lost early puppets in warehouse fire 1969. Lived in Singapore and Malaysia. Returned to Sydney as puppetry consultant to Australian Council for the Arts 1973-74. Moved to Sri Lanka. Toured Australian schools 1976–77. Left Australia to live in Philippines. MBE 1970.

The most prominent figure in Australian PUPPETRY, Peter Scriven dominated the scene for some 20 years until he left Australia to live in Asia. After he left two of his dreams were realised—the MARIONETTE THEATRE OF AUSTRALIA, which he had founded, became an autonomous company and then gained its own theatre. A thorough professional who chose his colleagues well, Scriven presented shows that were of exceptionally large scale in the western world of the 1950s and 1960s. They were reminiscent of the large 19th-century puppet troupes. These took their own musicians and voices on tour, but Scriven used tape recordings by leading actors and a full orchestra. The scale, the style and the volume of sound suited the shows to large theatres. The puppeteers worked from a 'bridge' 1·8 metres or so above the marionette stage. It supported six or more manipulators who could operate puppets on both upstage and downstage sides. The technique owed much to Scriven's puppet master, IGOR HYCHKA, who had worked with a large Italian marionette troupe of an earlier era. Scriven felt that the bold Italian style of acting with puppets was ideal for Australian puppeteers.

When Scriven was 18 he began touring as a solo act with six 900 mm marionettes in a travelling variety show in NSW and Queensland, working with a magician, the GREAT LEVANTE. As early as 1952 his plans for an Australian puppet theatre impressed the visiting English puppeteer Jan Bussell. Next year Scriven formed Peter Scriven Puppets, a company which gave its first performance in Melbourne on 2 June 1953 and then toured in Victoria and NSW. This company gave school-holiday seasons at the Theatre Royal in Sydney in the summers of 1953–54 and 1954–55. The second season included *Hansel and Gretel* and an original story, *Sammy at Sea*.

Then Scriven devised and directed his first large-scale marionette production, THE TINTOOKIES, which opened in Sydney in 1956 and toured Australia. Next came *Little Fella Bindi*, a moving story about a little Aboriginal boy's friendship with native animals, in 1958, and in 1960 a marionette version by Scriven of Norman Lindsay's story *The Magic Pudding*. For the new Marionette Theatre of Australia

Scriven took *Little Fella Bindi*, his favourite production, on an Asian tour and created *The Explorers*. The puppets for *The Tintookies* and *Little Fella Bindi* and other early Scriven puppets were destroyed in a fire in 1969. Scriven used large rod-puppets for *Tintookies 2000*, part of the Marionette Theatre's program at World Expo '70 in Osaka.

After periods living in southeast Asia and in Sydney as puppetry consultant to the Australian Council for the Arts, Scriven directed a new production of *The Tintookies*, with an additional act, at the Princess Theatre in Melbourne in 1975. Then he moved to Sri Lanka, where he engaged local puppet-makers to create marionettes for a small open-stage show called *The Tintookie Man*, with which he independently toured Australian schools in 1976–77. The show was taken over by Graeme Mathieson, a former head puppeteer of the Marionette Theatre of Australia when Scriven left to live in the Philippines. ❦*Richard Bradshaw*

further reading

VELLA, MAEVE and HELEN RICKARDS. *Theatre of the Impossible—Puppet theatre in Australia*. Sydney: Craftsman House 1989.

Seagulls over Sorrento

Comedy drama in three acts by Hugh Hastings. **premiere** 23 October 1949, London. Cast: Richard Beynon, Denis Quilley. **revived** 14 June 1950, Apollo Theatre, London. Cast: John Gregson, Nigel Stock, Bernard Lee, Ronald Shiner, William Hartnell, Peter Gray, Robert Desmond, Gerald Anderson, David Langton. Director: Wallace Douglas. **Australian premiere** 5 April 1952, Comedy Theatre, Melbourne. Cast: Michael Anderson, Gordon Chater, Don Crosby, Kenneth Firth, William Hodge, Brian James, Kevin Miles, Frank Taylor, Kenneth Thornett. Director: John Casson. **published** London: Samuel French 1951.

A run of 1551 performances at London's Apollo Theatre in 1950–52 gave *Seagulls Over Sorrento* the record as the longest-running West End play for a time. Its author, born Hugh Williamson in Sydney in 1917, left Australia in 1936 and worked in the United Kingdom as a film extra, cabaret performer and repertory actor. He joined the Royal Navy at the outbreak of the Second World War. Five and a half years later he returned to acting and toured with the wartime comedies *Worm's Eye View* and *Fly Away Peter* before graduating to the West End. While employed as an understudy wrote *Seagulls Over Sorrento* and it was given a Sunday-night performance in 1949. It was immediately taken up and opened at the Apollo Theatre next year. In 1952–53 it was performed 600 times on a J. C. WILLIAMSON's tour of Australia and New Zealand.

The play is set on the mess deck of an experimental naval base at Scapa Flow (Scotland). A disparate group of able seamen is sent there for a secret purpose which proves to be underwater trials of an experimental torpedo warhead for use in a new midget submarine. Varied temperaments, discomforts, private worries and a martinet petty officer make the crew restless, and danger is added when the scientist in charge is blown up. The seamen draw lots for the suicide spot for the first trial and Lofty makes a noble sacrifice; but the trial is successful and the crew departs on leave in a mood of camaraderie. Though less comic and more dramatic, the play has much in common with Sumner Locke Elliott's RUSTY BUGLES. Hastings later wrote and composed a musical *Scapa!* (1962). ❦*Katharine Brisbane*

The Season at Sarsaparilla

Play in two acts by Patrick White. **premiere** 14 September 1962 at Union Theatre, Adelaide, by Adelaide University Theatre Guild. Cast: Zoë Caldwell, Morna Jones, Carmel Millhouse, Terry Stapleton. Designer: Desmond Digby. Director: John Tasker. **revived** Old Tote Theatre Company, 3 November 1976, in Sydney Opera House Drama Theatre, with Michele Fawdon, Kate Fitzpatrick, Robyn Nevin and Andrew Sharp, directed by Jim Sharman. State Theatre Company of South Australia, 24 November 1984, in Playhouse, Adelaide, with Madeleine Blackwell, Maggie Dence, Jacqy Phillips and Igor Sas, directed by Neil Armfield. **published** London: Eyre and Spottiswoode 1965 in *Four Plays by Patrick White*. Sydney: Currency Press 1985 in *Patrick White—Collected Plays 1*.

The Season at Sarsaparilla, subtitled 'A charade of suburbia', is generally regarded as PATRICK WHITE's most accessible play. A poetic satire, it examines, indicts and celebrates the cycle of birth, copulation and death, demonstrating in the families of a businessman, a salesman and a sanitary man how demands of the blood defeat the civilising forces of art and education. The satire explores society's automatic acceptance of conventions, embrace of mediocrity and celebration of conformity. The 16 characters represent a cross-section of suburbia, with a poet as chorus observing and taking part in the action. Rapid shifts between realistic and stylised dialogue reveal the characters' inner longings and dreams, and dramatise the monotony of their endless routines as their actions and impulses follow the round of the seasons. The characters' dilemma is reflected in the setting—three adjoining houses, near-identical suburban boxes that offer no escape. ❦*May-Brit Akerholt*

further reading

SUMNER, JOHN. *Recollections at Play—A life in Australian theatre*. Melbourne: University Press 1993.

The Sentimental Bloke

Musical comedy. **libretto** Lloyd Thomson, after poems of C. J. Dennis. **music** Albert Arlen and Nancy Brown. **premiere** 7 March 1961, Albert Hall, Canberra, by Canberra Repertory Society. **professional premiere** 4 November 1961, Comedy Theatre, Melbourne. Cast: Rosemary Butler, Gloria Dawn, Alton Harvey, Edwin Ride, Frank Ward. Director: John Young.

Australia's most popular homegrown musical, *The Bloke* combines the ageless appeal of C. J. Dennis's 1915 poems with charming melodies by Albert Arlen. The simple story revolves around the rocky romance of Bill, a pickle-factory worker, and his 'sheila', the beauteous Doreen, played against the innocence of Melbourne before the First World War. The stormier courtship of Rose and Ginger Mick provides comic contrast.

In 1950 Arlen and his wife, the British musical star Nancy Brown, interested the novelist George Johnston in the idea of a C. J. Dennis musical. Arlen and Brown began work on the score, but Johnston had to bow out and Lloyd Thomson, a Canberra diplomat, took over the libretto. Almost eight years later, after an elaborately staged audition, J. C. WILLIAMSON's took a two-year option on the project but they allowed it to lapse, claiming similarities with their impending blockbuster *My Fair Lady*. After two years of fruitless auditioning in London, the Arlens returned home, deciding to shelve the show. Their next collaboration, *Girl From Snowy River* opened in Canberra on 30 April 1960 and broke house records for the CANBERRA REPERTORY SOCIETY. This inspired the Arlens to mount *The Sentimental Bloke* in Canberra for a week. Then a production planned by J. C. Williamson's fell through and the Firm booked *The Sentimental Bloke* as a six-week fill-in at the Comedy Theatre in Melbourne. The show had an immediate success and a 14-month national tour. It is regularly revived, has spawned two cast recordings, and was televised by the ABC in 1976 with GRAEME BLUNDELL, NANCYE HAYES and GERALDINE TURNER. Blundell wrote the libretto for another version of *The Sentimental Bloke*, with music by George Dreyfus, which the MELBOURNE THEATRE COMPANY produced on 12 December 1985. *Tony Sheldon*

Seven Ashtons

Six brothers and a sister, the Seven Ashtons acrobatic troupe won fame throughout the USA and Europe during the late 1940s and early 1950s. They were the children of Dorothy Ashton, a grandchild of JAMES HENRY ASHTON, and a trumpeter in the Ashton's Circus band. The troupe's speciality was a Risley act, in which one or more performers, lying on the back, juggled smaller partners with the feet. The act sported as many as three 'trinkas', small cradles in which the heavier acrobats lay in order to propel the lighter ones back and forth in a fast and exciting routine. One flier would somersault over another in midair. The troupe toured the USA with Sonja Henie's Ice Show, appeared in a command performance before King George VI in the London Coliseum, and demonstrated its versatility with the American actor Red Skelton in the 1957 film *Public Pigeon No. 1*. Most of the troupe settled in the USA but some returned to Australia, including Dougie Ashton, a featured clown with Sole Brothers' Circus in 1987. *Mark St Leon*

further reading
FERNANDEZ, NATALIE. *Circus Saga*. Sydney: Ashton's Circus 1971.
HIPPISLEY COXE, ANTONY. *A Seat at the Circus*. London: Macmillan 1980.

Stephen Sewell

Dramatist. Born 1953 in Sydney. Graduated from University of Sydney in physics in 1974 and worked in fringe theatre in Sydney. Moved to Brisbane. First play produced in Brisbane 1978. Writer-in-residence with Nimrod Theatre Company (Sydney) 1981–82. Australian Writers' Guild Awgie award 1982 for *Welcome the Bright World*. NSW Premier's Award 1985 for *The Blind Giant is Dancing*. Has also written film and television screenplays.

In a country that is traditionally suspicious of seriousness, Stephen Sewell has won a place as the conscience of Australian theatre. He is one of the younger writers who emerged in the late 1970s to challenge the 'new wave' nationalists of the late 1960s and early 1970s. His work is characterised by seriousness of purpose and an uncompromisingly wide-ranging interest in the social, economic and political contexts in which his characters act and struggle. He is particularly interested in the interaction between their inner emotional life, especially their fear and self-doubt, and the outer violent world that both produces and reflects these feelings. This seriousness made Sewell one of the writers most respected by critics in the 1980s but one of the most problematic in the theatre. His plays have been labelled 'too difficult' or 'too uncommercial' by reviewers and theatre directors. This is a pity, because he brings to his work a sense of humour and a sympathetic interest in the humanity of his characters that ought to make his analysis appealing even to the most narrow-minded artistic director. Sewell once complained that everybody in the theatre approved of his being there but no-one did his plays. There is a sad possibility that the pressures of the theatrical marketplace will eventually crush his spirit, as socioeconomic pressures do for his characters.

The three most important early influences in Sewell's work are the Catholicism of his working-class family background, the Marxism that he embraced in reaction to that background, and the rational, scientific view of the world that he found at university. He has always looked for answers and been unafraid of the work involved in the search. His first play, *The Father We Loved on a Beach by the Sea*, examines working-class conservatism in Australia in the 1950s and, by juxtaposing that world with a future fascist Australia, seeks out the origins of such conservatism in individuals' feelings of insecurity and the economic conditions that cause them.

In 1979 the AUSTRALIAN PERFORMING GROUP in Melbourne commissioned Sewell to complete a play on the early years of Stalin. The result was *TRAITORS*, his most-produced play. Through the eyes of idealistic young Anna—one of the best female characterisations in the male-dominated Australian drama of the 1970s—it examines the Stalinist betrayal of the communist ideal in Russia during the late 1920s. The play has the most straightforward narrative of all Sewell's plays but it is still a complex study of the relationships between individuals and the sociopolitical processes that mould them and they in turn help to mould.

Welcome the Bright World, one of Sewell's best plays, develops this. Set in modern Germany it examines personal responsibility for public political events, as the scientist Max Lewin struggles to maintain his belief in his distance from events he is helping to create, which are destroying his family and intimate life. Sewell wrote this play when he was writer-in-residence with the NIMROD THEATRE COMPANY. He also worked with this company on a group-devised play, *Burn Victim* (1982). The Lighthouse Company in Adelaide commissioned his next play, *The Blind Giant is Dancing*. In it Sewell turned his dramatic analysis on Australia, particularly corruption in the linked worlds of business, politics and crime, which became an important public issue in the 1980s.

Sewell's most ambitious play is *Dreams in an Empty City*. One of his most passionate and warmly human works, it is a powerful parable of the decline of individual and social morality in what it presents as the last days, indeed the last hours of capitalism. The parable is based on the passion of Christ, and represents the beginning of a new search for some secular faith in humanity that might replace the failed gods of Christianity and communism. It was first produced by the STATE THEATRE Company of South Australia. After *Dreams* Sewell turned—with some apparent bitterness at the fact that Australian companies were prepared to produce classics with large casts but not Australian plays—to smaller-scale works such as *Hate* and

Sisters. *Hate* is a closed-house family drama, more or less observing the Aristotelian unities, in which a rich and powerful dynasty of Australian public life turns destructively upon itself. The epic scale of Sewell's early life is cramped in *Hate* but there is still some attempt to reflect broad public concerns in the private interactions of a particularly bitter and anxious group of characters. In *Sisters* Sewell focuses even more specifically on the personal interactions between two long estranged sisters, as in a weekend together they struggle to work out the consequences of a lifetime of distance and of unresolved conflicting reactions to a bitter family past. In these plays the broad political focus of Sewell's earlier writing has become increasingly narrowed onto the politics of family and personal interactions. *John McCallum*

published plays
The Blind Giant is Dancing (1983). Sydney: Currency Press 1983.
Dreams in an Empty City (1986). Sydney: Currency Press 1986.
The Father We Loved on a Beach by the Sea (1977). Brisbane: University of Queensland Press 1980 in *Political Plays*.
The Garden of Granddaughters (1993). Sydney: Currency Press 1993.
Hate (1988). Sydney: Currency Press 1988.
Sisters (1991). Sydney: Currency Press 1991.
Traitors (1979). Sydney: Alternative Publishing Co-operative 1983.
Welcome the Bright World (1982). Sydney: Alternative Publishing Co-operative 1983.

further reading
CARROLL, DENNIS. *Australian Contemporary Drama from 1909* 2nd edn. Sydney: Currency Press 1993.
FITZPATRICK, PETER. *Stephen Sewell—The playwright as revolutionary*. Sydney: Currency Press 1991.

Alan Seymour

Dramatist. Born 6 June 1927 in Perth. Became freelance writer on leaving school in Perth and moved to Sydney. Worked as film and theatre critic and educational writer for ABC radio. Became theatrical director and directed operas for Sydney Opera Group 1953–57. Finalist in London *Observer* play competition 1957. Left for London in 1961 after success of *The One Day of the Year*. Became successful television writer, producer and editor with BBC. Theatre critic of *London Magazine* 1963–65. Wrote novels, stage plays and magazine articles in Turkey 1966–71. Visited Australia 1980. Has written many radio and television plays.

Though he has written many plays, Alan Seymour remains known in Australia for THE ONE DAY OF THE YEAR, one of the two most celebrated works in Australian drama. A realist domestic drama, it is uncharacteristic of Seymour's work, which began with a Gothic thriller, *Swamp Creatures*. This was a finalist in the London *Observer* play competition in 1957 and was first performed by the CANBERRA REPERTORY SOCIETY that year. Seymour moved on to sociopolitical themes of widening internationalism, expressed in a variety of non-naturalistic forms. He returned to the roots of working-class Australian life only in *A Break in the Music* (1966), a play about a young writer whose attempts to give his novel an epic sweep are hindered by intruding memories which demand that he find a pattern and meaning in his life. Two themes, however, do recur in Seymour's work —entrapment of the present by the past, and personal barriers to the expression of love. Controversy surrounding the premiere of *The One Day of the Year* left a deep impression upon Seymour; and he has retained an ambivalent relationship with Australia. Some of his work has been seen in Australia, but he has not had a further stage success here. *Katharine Brisbane*

published play
The One Day of the Year (1960). Sydney: Angus and Robertson 1962. Melbourne: Penguin 1985 revised in *Three Australian Plays*.

further reading
CARROLL, DENNIS. *Australian Contemporary Drama from 1909* 2nd edn. Sydney: Currency Press 1994.
SYKES, ALRENE. In *Contemporary Dramatists* (ed. K. A. Berney) 5th edn. London: St James Press 1993.
VINSON, JAMES (ed.) *Contemporary Dramatists*. London: St James Press 1973.

Seymour Theatre Centre

Performing-arts centre on Darlington campus of University of Sydney, opened September 1975. Architects: Allen, Jack and Cottier. Contains thrust-stage **York Theatre**, seating 788; end-stage **Everest Theatre** for music and dance, seating 600; **Downstairs** studio theatre, seating up to 200.

Metropolitan theatres derive their image from the type of shows performed in them, their district or the sense of occasion they engender but none such distinction serves the Seymour Theatre Centre. It houses a wide range of shows and it is a kilometre from the central business district. In many ways it is like a performing-arts centre in a large country town, but without the local status.

The centre commemorates Everest York Seymour, who developed a chain of shops, bred cattle and took an interest in the arts. When he died in 1966, aged 60, he left the Sydney City Council $4 million for the 'purchase or construction of a building as a centre for the cultivation, education and performance of the musical and dramatic arts befitting the City of Sydney'. No money was provided for maintenance or performances. Building costs virtually meant that the recipient of the bequest would have to provide the land for a new building. The University of Sydney, apparently the only organisation within the city able and willing to provide the land and infrastructure, obtained the funds.

The Seymour Centre was designed to supplement the city's theatres with a fully-equipped thrust-stage theatre, a medium-capacity concert hall-theatre with good acoustics, and an adaptable studio theatre. Its success has varied, in the case of the York Theatre partly because of the dull brick and concrete architectural style and the black interior, so loved by directors, and partly because of the lack of a permanent vibrant company. From 1984 to 1987 the NIMROD THEATRE COMPANY was resident in the York. The seating capacity made viable such productions as Arthur Miller's *Death of a Salesman* with WARREN MITCHELL and MEL GIBSON, but the style of acting contrasted unfavourably with the informal style with which the company had been identified in the smaller Nimrod Theatre. Some actors have found the actor–audience relationship demanding and alienating, but on occasion it could not be bettered, as with the commercial productions of Nell Dunn's *Steaming* and Claire Luckham's *Trafford Tanzi*. The York is mostly used for touring productions of drama, comedy, musicals and dance. The Everest Theatre has been modified for dance and musical theatre as well as concerts. *Ross Thorne*

Shakespeare

The works of William Shakespeare were part of the cultural heritage the British brought with them when they colonised Australia. The subsequent history of Shakespeare in Australian theatre and culture reflects the unfolding of a complex colonial relationship and changing perceptions of 'the Bard' in Great Britain and Australia.

F. C. Brewer began his history of *The Drama and Music in New South Wales* in 1892 with the declaration that 'the British people have an intense love of the drama'. In support of this he cites the self-evident superiority of 'Shakespeare acted' over 'Shakespeare read'. Brewer tells of a convict 'bush performance' of the judgment scene from *The Merchant of Venice* in which Shylock was played by a convict who lacked a 'nasal organ' and wore a false nose made of silver. It fell off at a particularly dramatic moment, much to the merriment of other actors and the audience. However apocryphal this tale, such a courtroom scene would have had a certain piquancy in a convict community. The currency of Shakespeare in colonial parlance is reflected in the habit of referring to a white woman who became involved with a black as 'Madame Desdemona'.

It is claimed that a Shakespeare play was first performed in Australia at ROBERT SIDAWAY's primitive theatre in Sydney on 8 April 1800. The management did not feel it necessary to specify that *Henry IV* was by Shakespeare—the playbill in the Mitchell Library simply refers to 'the favorite play'—or to indicate which part was being played, though the cast list suggests that it was probably a reduced version of part 1.

It was not until Barnett Levey's THEATRE ROYAL opened in 1833 that Shakespeare received something resembling professional performance. On 26 December 1833 Levey staged Colley Cibber's version of *Richard III* with JOHN MEREDITH in the title-role. The performance was marred by the kind of disruption not uncommon in theatres of the time. Indeed, so unruly was the pit that some members of the audience were forced to take refuge on the stage: but the performance, which included a pantomime, was completed.

Levey's company of amateurs turned professional, of whom CONRAD KNOWLES was probably the most proficient, went on to perform *Hamlet*, *Henry IV—part 1*, *Henry VIII*; *King Lear*, *Macbeth*, *The Merchant of Venice*, *Othello* and *Romeo and Juliet* as well as *Catherine and Petruchio*, David Garrick's version of *The Taming of the Shrew*. To some extent these productions were intended to proclaim the respectability of the theatre, but Shakespeare was popular, in the truncated adaptations common in the 19th century.

The gold rushes ushered in an era in which leading English, Irish and American actors and actor-managers toured the colonies, playing Shakespeare in repertoires of popular classics and melodrama. It was not unknown for two tragedians to be playing Shakespeare in opposition. For example, the publicity-conscious BARRY SULLIVAN sought to upstage the more genteel CHARLES AND ELLEN KEAN in 1863, and in 1887 the Hamlets of James Anderson and WALTER MONTGOMERY could be compared. But G. V. BROOKE, who played the colonies in 1855–61, perhaps made the greatest impression, overwhelming audiences with his emotionally charged Othello. The entrepreneur GEORGE COPPIN credited him with civilising colonial taste.

Victorian theatre, with its penchant for spectacle and melodrama, encouraged full-blooded and declamatory renditions of Shakespeare, and plays that were more susceptible to such treatment, such as *Macbeth*, *Othello*, *Richard III* and the now discarded *Henry VIII*, were popular. There was, however, always a delicate balance between an audience's perception of truthful performance and mere rant. Brooke, considered an actor of the old school, could be praised by J. E. NEILD for his 'quiet naturalness'; and Barry Sullivan, although declamatory in style, was commended for his careful and intelligent interpretations. Moreover, changes in taste in England filtered through to the colonies. The Keans thought Australian audiences, having had 'nothing but raving and extravagance', were nonplussed by their 'acting tragedy like ladies and gentlemen'. They seem also to have tried to elevate themselves by charging higher prices than Sullivan. More startling perhaps was Montgomery's introspective and understated Hamlet, which was influenced by Charles Fechter's celebrated London performance of 1861. The contrast between Montgomery and Anderson, a more traditional prince, provoked a public controversy in Melbourne over the reality or otherwise of Hamlet's madness. Yet the success enjoyed by Brooke and Sullivan, both of whom were more

The playbill for Robert Sidaway's theatre in Sydney on 8 April 1800 promised Shakespeare, though it did not say so. Whether the play was performed is not known. Little is known about the theatre, though the prices indicate four divisions in seating

Othello, played by G. V. Brooke, intervenes in the fight between Cassio and Montano at the Royal Victoria Theatre in Sydney in June 1855. Brooke set a standard for Othello that endured long after he had left the colonies

acclaimed in the provinces than in London, suggests that colonial audiences remained more attuned to the grander style inherited from William Macready.

George Coppin claimed that he 'always lost money by Shakespeare without a first-class Star'. Yet Shakespeare, basic to any serious actor's repertoire, was a pillar of mid-Victorian theatre, and it has even been calculated that *Hamlet* was the most-performed play in Melbourne in the 1860s. Later in the century Shakespeare was performed less frequently, though there were still memorable productions, such as GEORGE RIGNOLD's *Henry V*, first presented in 1876 and often repeated. ALFRED DAMPIER's successful Australian melodramas helped to subsidise his Shakespeare productions, which usually played on Friday nights. It became possible for a star such as NELLIE STEWART to have a long career with little experience in Shakespeare.

As the colonies acquired the trappings of cultural life, there was a tendency to emphasise the literary and moral virtues of Shakespeare, rather than his plays' capacity to entertain. As early as 1864, the *Sydney Morning Herald* observed on the occasion of the Shakespeare tercentenary: 'It is not the playgoing portion of the population who are his chief readers. The people at large, if we may judge from their entertainments, prefer dramas of a different cast. We suspect that Shakespere has maintained a hold on the higher intellect of the country rather than pleased the masses of spectators.' Shakespeare societies sprang up in many cities. Their members met to hear readings and papers that explained and interpreted the texts.

With the rising tide of imperial sentiment Shakespeare was increasingly promoted as 'the Great Poet of our race'. So in 1929 R. S. Wallace, vice-chancellor of the University of Sydney, could justify the study of Shakespeare because 'as he taught his countrymen to think nobly of their own country, he has also taught us to think nobly and to feel nobly about those virtues on which the British Empire depends'. In 1914 Henry Gullet presented Sydney with its Shakespeare Memorial and the State Library of NSW acquired a Shakespeare collection (including a First Folio). This was originally intended to be kept in a specially built Shakespeare Room, which boasts a copy of the Tudor ceiling in Cardinal Wolsey's closet at Hampton Court Palace. Shakespeare was integrated into the school syllabus, particularly with the development of state secondary education in the early 20th century. Frank Tate, Victoria's director of education from 1902 to 1928, was a particular enthusiast.

Nevertheless, popular appreciation of Shakespeare persisted. OSCAR ASCHE had particular success on his 1909–10 and 1912–13 tours with his spectacular productions of *The Taming of the Shrew*, *A Midsummer Night's Dream* and the rarely performed *Antony and Cleopatra*. C. J. Dennis humorously juxtaposes popular and respectable appreciations in his account of a visit to the theatre in *The Sentimental Bloke*:

The Drarmer's writ be Shakespeare, years ago,
About a barmy goat called Romeo.

The newer appreciation of Shakespeare was reflected in the foundation of the ALLAN WILKIE SHAKESPEAREAN COMPANY in 1920. It survived for a decade, during which Wilkie staged 27 of the plays, touring capital cities and country towns throughout Australia and New Zealand. Wilkie, who inherited the 19th-century tradition of the English provincial actor-manager, was at heart a romantic but, influenced by the 'Shakespearean revolution', he was sensitive to the modern emphasis on the purity of the text, and he appreciated simple staging that permitted more fluid production, closer to the Elizabethan style. Wilkie flouted theatrical superstition by opening with an impressive *Macbeth*, which he played with only one eight-minute interval. His company soon gathered the support of Shakespearean societies, state education departments and the viceregal set. Wilkie demonstrated his own commitment by founding the *Shakespearean Quarterly*, published in Sydney in 1922–24. The Prime Minister, S. M. Bruce, hailed the company as 'performing a duty of a national character'. Wilkie capitalised on such accolades by promoting his company as the basis of a national theatre, deserving government funding, but he gained only free rail travel. The Great Depression

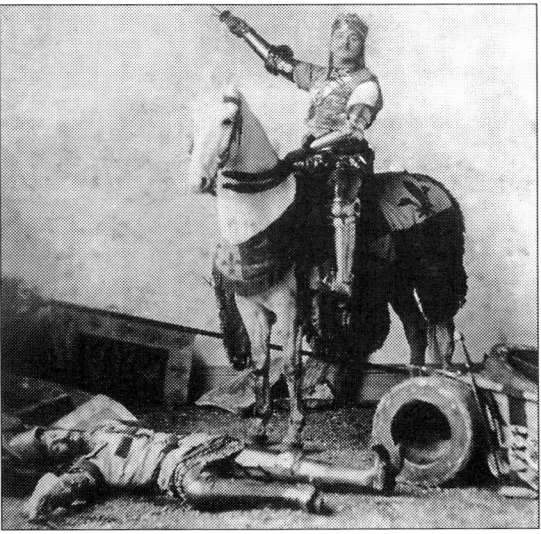

George Rignold staged Shakespeare as a sequence of spectacular tableaux. In his famous production of Henry V, *in which he played the title-role, he even included a scene that Shakespeare had not bothered to provide*

and talking pictures killed Wilkie's company. During the 1930s and 1940s the only professional Shakespeare of note came from England: Lewis Casson and Sybil Thorndike in *Macbeth* in 1932, the legendary 1948 tour of the OLD VIC THEATRE COMPANY with Laurence Olivier as Richard III, and the Shakespeare Memorial Theatre Company from Stratford-upon-Avon in 1949. Tours such as these may have reactivated interest in Shakespeare but they also served to reinforce the English context. Only the unlikely pairing of ROBERT HELPMANN and Katharine Hepburn by the Old Vic in 1955, with *The Taming of the Shrew* as the main drawcard, broke the imperial mould.

Burly Allan Wilkie as Bottom in A Midsummer Night's Dream, *one of his best parts*

JOHN ALDEN attracted attention with a stylish production of *Measure for Measure* at the Independent Theatre in Sydney in 1948. He had been grounded in Shakespeare in England in 1937–40 and the Old Vic was his model in style and repertoire. Alden's powerful production of *King Lear* in 1950 led to a national tour in 1951–52 which received some public and private sponsorship as a federation jubilee event. His repertoire was smaller than Wilkie's and he was handicapped by his mannerisms, but Australian audiences could understand his productions. Alden promoted his company as a potential national theatre but negotiations for an annual federal grant collapsed, largely because he was reluctant to give up his personal control of the company. His powers were flagging when he toured for J. C. WILLIAMSON's in 1959—alternating with the Scottish actor John Laurie as Lear and Shylock—and when he staged a Shakespearean festival in Sydney in 1961.

The AUSTRALIAN ELIZABETHAN THEATRE TRUST, which introduced subsidy in 1956, acknowledged Shakespeare as part of the classical repertoire necessary for the development of theatre. In 1957 it imported Paul Rogers to star in *Hamlet*. The TRUST PLAYERS and the emerging regional companies dutifully paid their respects to Shakespeare with a production from time to time. The Young Elizabethan Players, initiated in 1958, packaged Shakespeare for schools.

For the quadricentenary of Shakespeare's birth in 1964 the University of Western Australia opened its NEW FORTUNE THEATRE, based on dimensions in the builder's contract for the Fortune Theatre of Shakespeare's day. It is still the only theatre that replicates Elizabethan dimensions in both the stage and the auditorium. It has assisted research into Elizabethan acting style and influenced the work of modern playwrights, notably DOROTHY HEWETT. Perhaps the most innovative productions of the 1970s emanated from the NIMROD THEATRE COMPANY, founded in 1970 by JOHN BELL and Ken Horler. Bell had trained at the Bristol Old Vic School and worked with the ROYAL SHAKESPEARE COMPANY in England. Playing Hamlet in the intimate Nimrod Street Theatre, Bell realised that the actors had unwittingly spoken Shakespeare without adopting stage English accents, hitherto *de rigeur*. Productions exploiting the company's boisterous house style at its new and larger Nimrod Theatre included *Much Ado About Nothing* (in which the accent was fruit-shop Italian), *Twelfth Night* with a male Viola, *The Comedy of Errors* and *Romeo and Juliet*. Shakespeare was also being approached experimentally elsewhere. A mesmeric production of *The Tempest* by REX CRAMPHORN, which toured in 1972, for his Performance Syndicate, was very much a product of the counterculture.

Experiments at the New Fortune Theatre in performance under Elizabethan daylight conditions led in 1986 to the first of PHILIP PARSONS's experimental Shakespeare productions with the Sydney Theatre Company. The enlarged acting style and direct address to the audience has in turn impressed itself upon the company's style in the 1990s. Open-air performances of Shakespeare have been popular in capital cities since the 1950s. Provincial companies have increasingly adapted Shakespeare to the local environment and English companies continue to tour. In 1990 the Bell Shakespeare Company was launched, reviving the Wilkie–Alden aspiration to permanence. The association of John Bell's name with the company—which was not his idea—even suggested a reappearance of the actor-manager, and the venture takes its place as part of Sam Wanamaker's international Globe Trust. The company has been funded primarily from private sources but, like its predecessors, it takes Shakespeare to schools.

The process, therefore, of detaching Shakespeare from the culture of the imperial relationship has been slow and halting. Allan Wilkie was the last of the English actor-managers who brought Shakespeare to Australia, though, like some of his 19th-century predecessors, he did seek to integrate himself into the local scene. But Alden and Bell also looked inevitably to the English Shakespearean tradition for training and inspiration, though in Bell's case this has been channelled through the energising experimentalism of the Nimrod years. What has been noticeable for most of the 20th century has been the lack of a developing local tradition. Wilkie, Alden and Bell have all had to start anew—Alden had not worked with Wilkie, nor Bell with Alden. The emergence of modern Australian drama has been necessary before the task of integrating Shakespeare into Australian cultural consciousness could be undertaken. *John Rickard*

The Elizabethan-style New Fortune Theatre in Perth has given rise to experiments in performing Shakespeare under conditions approximating to those of the playwright's time

further reading
BLAKE, L. J. Oscar Asche. *Australian Dictionary of Biography* 7. Melbourne University Press. 1979
GITTINS, JEAN. Barry Sullivan. *Australian Dictionary of Biography* 6. Melbourne University Press 1976.
HARDWICK, J. M. D. (ed.). *Emigrant in Motley*. London: Rockliff 1954.
MERCER, LEAH. 'A worthy scaffold'—George Rignold's rewriting and staging of Henry V. *Australasian Drama Studies* (Brisbane) October 1993.
OPPENHEIM, HELENE. G. V. Brooke. *Australian Dictionary of Biography* 3. Melbourne University Press 1978.
RICKARD, JOHN. Alfred Dampier. *Australian Dictionary of Biography* 4. Melbourne University Press 1979.
RICKARD, JOHN. Allan Wilkie. *Australian Dictionary of Biography* 12. Melbourne University Press 1990.
RICKARD, JOHN. The bloke and the bard—Shakespeare, Empire and cultural hierarchy. *Shakespeare's Books*. University of Melbourne 1993.

Shakespericonglomorofunnidogammoniae

Burlesque by Charles Nagel. **premiere** 1 July 1844, Royal Victoria Theatre, Sydney. **published** Sydney: W. A. Duncan 1843.

As the first half of its title indicates, this burlesque took its characters from some of Shakespeare's best-known plays: *Hamlet*, *Macbeth*, *The Merchant of Venice*, *The Merry Wives of Windsor*, *Othello* and *Richard III*. But, as the second half—meaning a funny, nonsensical conglomeration—suggests, its subject was a comic exposé of life in contemporary NSW, and the financial effects of the 1843 depression in particular. Reviewers easily identified the originals behind the Shakespearean masks and appreciated the local wit and allusions. *Shakespericonglomorofunnidogammoniae*, as usual for works of this type, was written in verse and included many comic songs on popular tunes. ❦*Elizabeth Webby*

Theo Shall

Actor, director. Born in Alsace of French mother and German father. Brought up in Vienna. Acted in films for UFA in Berlin, including European version of *Anna Christie* with Greta Garbo. Came to Australia for J. C. Williamson's 1932. Formed own company in Melbourne. Produced Goethe's *Faust* for Adelaide Repertory Theatre at Australia Hall, 17 March 1934. Returned to Germany later in 1934.

In his spectacular production of *Faust* for ADELAIDE REPERTORY THEATRE Theo Shall used light to achieve a sense of vast space, in a manner almost unknown on the Australian professional stage. One critic described it as 'a brilliant experiment, the most important the Australian theatre has made in 25 years'. Shall came here to play the Tyrolean innkeeper in C. L. Anthony's *Autumn Crocus* for J. C. Williamson's, with the English actor Dorothy Peters and a strong Australian supporting cast. He had spoken English for only three years and he acted before an Anglophone audience for the first time when the play opened in Melbourne in September 1932. The show was successful there but in Sydney it closed after a couple of weeks when Peters suddenly returned to England. Rumour said that Shall had wanted his Viennese wife, Maria von Weihl, to play the lead. The ebullient, egocentric Shall obtained finance to form his own company in Melbourne. The couple stayed there for about 18 months before sailing for Europe, their passages arranged—after a long dispute—by the Firm. At Adelaide, however, the Shalls were met by amateur-theatre enthusiasts and they left the ship to work there. Shall could not find finance to start a company, but he directed and designed *Faust* and played Mephistopheles. The production ran for some six weeks. ❦*Thelma Afford*

Ron Shand

Actor, comedian, dancer, entrepreneur. Born 3 February 1906 in Melbourne. Mother was equestrian dancer and father was circus clown. Trained as dancer. Worked throughout Australia in vaudeville and tent shows. Toured revue company to troops in Japan, Europe and Middle East after Second World War. John Alden Company 1951–52. Performed vaudeville act in clubs until 1986. Married actor Letty Craydon. Brother of Iris Shand, actor and revue entrepreneur. Died 8 August 1993.

Ron Shand was a popular entertainer for more than 60 years. He was, as he said, never a big star but a very adaptable performer. As a child he rarely saw his parents because they were usually touring with a circus. They wanted him to have a good education and a different career, but when he was 14 they relented and allowed him to join his father in a clown act during the school holidays. Later he trained as a dancer and began work in a revue in Perth. He made his mark in vaudeville as an eccentric dancer and worked up a comedy act by exchanging quips with the audience while he caught his breath between dances. In 1931 he replaced Joe Lawman as partner to NAT PHILLIPS (Stiffy) in their *Bright and Breezy, Clean and Wholesome Vaudeville and Revue* in Sydney.

Shand married LETTY CRAYDON in the late 1940s. They wrote and performed their own material in revues. Shand occasionally took a small role in a straight play, but he was nonplussed when JOHN ALDEN asked him to play comic roles in his Shakespearean company. Alden assured him he would perform perfectly at home, and indeed he enjoyed the tour, playing Flute in *A Midsummer Night's Dream*, Slender in *The Merry Wives of Windsor*, Old Gobbo in *The Merchant of Venice* and the Old Man in *King Lear*.

Shand was a dancer in his first musical, *No! No! Nanette* in 1928, and in *The Sentimental Bloke*, an adaptation of C. J. Dennis's poems, in Melbourne in 1932. Over the years he became a featured comedian as well as a dancer in many J. C. WILLIAMSON's shows, including *Can-Can* in 1955, *Grab Me a Gondola* in 1959 and as Sir Jasper Tring in *Me and My Girl* in 1986. ❦*Lynne Murphy*

further reading
LAMOND, TONI. *First Half*. Sydney: Pan Books 1990.

Jim Sharman

Director. Born 12 March 1945 in Sydney. Grew up in sideshow boxing family. Active in amateur musicals. Graduated from National Institute of Dramatic Art (Sydney) 1965. Directed *Hair* in Sydney 1969, Melbourne 1971, Tokyo, Boston. Directed *Jesus Christ Superstar* in Sydney and London 1972. Directed *The Rocky Horror Show* in London 1973, Sydney 1974, New York, Los Angeles. Returned to Australia 1975. Director of Adelaide Festival 1982. Artistic director of South Australian Theatre Company (Adelaide) 1983–84.

One of Australia's leading directors, Jim Sharman has carved out a bold non-naturalistic style in directing dozens of productions. Among them have been new Australian plays by ALEX BUZO, DOROTHY HEWETT, David Malouf, LOUIS NOWRA and PATRICK WHITE and works of classic and contemporary writers, including Bertolt Brecht, Jean Genet, Federico García Lorca, Harold Pinter, Shakespeare, Sam Shepard, August Strindberg and Frank Wedekind. He has been influenced by a colourful background in show business. His father and grandfather, both named Jimmy Sharman, ran a famous boxing troupe which travelled the eastern states with circuses and sideshows from 1911 to 1971. Sharman's own first professional experience was with fellow graduates of the NATIONAL INSTITUTE OF DRAMATIC ART in the late 1960s on works including two group-devised shows in 1966, *On Stage Oz*, a revue based on the satirical magazine *Oz*, and *Terror Australis*, in which the audience was made to enter the JANE STREET THEATRE through sheep railings. *Terror Australis* was defended in the press by PATRICK WHITE, with whom Sharman later had a fruitful association.

In 1967 a controversial production of Mozart's *Don Giovanni* by Sharman for the Elizabethan Trust Opera Company attracted the attention of the entrepreneur HARRY M. MILLER. In 1969 Miller offered the 22-year-old Sharman the production of the rock musical *Hair*. The resulting production, designed by BRIAN THOMSON and directed by Sharman, was seen by 1·3 million people in Sydney alone. The success of *Hair* and Sharman's production of another rock musical, *Jesus Christ Superstar*, in Sydney in 1972, also designed by Thomson, led to their going to London to create *Superstar* there. While they were in London in 1973 they directed and designed David Williamson's THE REMOVALISTS at the Royal Court Theatre, and *The Rocky Horror Show* in a tiny theatre upstairs.

In 1976 Sharman directed a revival of Patrick White's THE SEASON AT SARSAPARILLA. The encouragement it gave to White led him to write BIG TOYS for Sharman and two of the cast. Sharman's relationship with the playwright extended to several new plays, including *A Cheery Soul* with a neo-Brechtian design by Thomson in 1979, and a film.

During the 1980s Sharman worked in various forms, tirelessly encouraging greater sophistication in Australian theatre, presenting new Australian works and personal interpretations of classics. The best of the latter included August Strindberg's *The Dance of Death* for the SYDNEY THEATRE COMPANY in 1985 and Sam Shepard's *A Lie of the Mind* at the BELVOIR STREET THEATRE in 1987. After directing the 1982 ADELAIDE FESTIVAL OF ARTS he became artistic director of the South Australian Theatre Company, which he renamed the Lighthouse Company and operated as an ensemble. He commissioned plays from LOUIS NOWRA and STEPHEN SEWELL, and promoted NEIL ARMFIELD as a director.

In 1990 Sharman returned to Tokyo for the first time in 20 years. Japanese ritual appealed to Sharman and after the best part of two years there he emerged with a play, *Shadow and Splendour*, which he directed for the QUEENSLAND THEATRE COMPANY and the State Theatre Company of South Australia in 1992. ❦*James Waites*

further reading
HOWIE, ANN C. (ed.). *Who's Who in Australia 1994*. Melbourne: Information Australia.

Lionel Shave

Dramatist. Born 1888 in Melbourne. Wrote numerous stage and radio plays during career as advertising executive. Died 11 April 1954 in Sydney.

Lionel Shave's plays were widely popular with amateur groups. Their content, in the manner of the lightweight commercial playwriting of the day, was unremarkable but their adept, strong craftsmanship testifies to a real flair for the theatre. ❦*Philip Parsons*.

published plays
Red and Gold. Sydney: Australasian 1948 in *Five Proven One-Act Plays*.
The Resignation of Mr Bagsworth. Sydney: Australasian 1948 in *Five Proven One-Act Plays*.
A Sirius Cove. Sydney: Australasian 1948 in *Five Proven One-Act Plays*.
That's Murder. Sydney: Mulga 1944 in *Six Australian One-Act Plays*; Australasian 1948 in *Five Proven One-Act Plays*.
Twelve Moons Cold. Sydney: Australasian 1948 in *Five Proven One-Act Plays*.

Jill Shearer

Dramatist. Born 14 April 1936 in Melbourne. Has lived mainly in Queensland. Secretary for British and Japanese Consulates in Brisbane. Began writing seriously 1971. Plays won prizes in local competitions. Arts Queensland Fellowship 1993.

Jill Shearer had written more than 20 plays, mostly produced by amateur or semiprofessional groups in Queensland, when her *Shimada* brought her wider recognition in 1987. The MELBOURNE THEATRE COMPANY gave the premiere production, directed by SIMON PHILLIPS. In 1992 the play had 24 performances on Broadway in New York with a cast including Ben Gazzara, Ellen Burstyn and Estelle Parsons. *Shimada* shows influences of Japanese theatrical forms such as *noh* and *kabuki*. Shearer generally strives towards heightened expression through spare dialogue and dramatic use of the *mise-en-scène*. Her work exhibits passionate concern with social issues and tackles such topics as industrial work practices, abortion, conservation, race relations, and foreign economic influence in Australia. These broader issues are most often played out in Queensland settings through representations of ordinary people and families. Shearer pursues no obvious feminist agenda but she consistently creates strong female characters and her one historical play, *Catherine* (1977), argues for reconsideration of the role of women in Australia's past and present. ❦*Helen Gilbert*

published plays
The Boat. Brisbane: University of Queensland Press 1978 in *Can't You Hear me Talking to You*.
Catherine (1977). Melbourne: Yackandandah 1985.
Echoes (1980). In *Echoes and Other Plays*. Brisbane: Playlab Press 1980.
The Kite (1977). In *Echoes and Other Plays*.
Nocturne (1977). In *Echoes and Other Plays*.
Stephen (1980). In *Echoes and Other Plays*.
The Foreman (1977). Sydney: Currency Press 1978.
Shimada (1987). Sydney: Currency Press 1989.

further reading
DALE, LEIGH and HELEN GILBERT. Dis-guising desire—Gender and imperialism in Jill Shearer's *Shimada*. *Myths, Heroes and Anti-heroes* (ed. Bruce Bennett and Dennis Haskell.) Perth: Centre for Studies in Australian Literature 1992.

GILBERT, HELEN. 'Telling it in Multiple Layers'—An interview with Jill Shearer. *Australasian Drama Studies* 21 (Brisbane 1992).

KELLY, VERONICA. *Shimada*. *Australasian Drama Studies* 17 (Brisbane 1990).

Dinah Shearing AM

Actor. Born 12 February 1928 in Sydney. Studied painting at East Sydney Technical School and singing at NSW State Conservatorium of Music. Began acting at Metropolitan Theatre (Sydney) 1946. Independent Theatre (Sydney) 1950. John Alden Company 1952. Mercury Theatre (Sydney) 1952. Australian Elizabethan Theatre Trust 1956–57. Joined Trust Players 1959. Later acted with Old Tote Theatre Company (Sydney), Sydney Theatre Company and others. Much radio and television work. Sydney Theatre Critics' Circle Award 1993 for best performance in supporting role (Volumnia in *Coriolanus*). AM 1993.

A graceful, intelligent actor with a gift of stillness on stage and a melodious voice, Dinah Shearing turned from singing to acting as a result of a teacher's interest in the quality of her speaking voice. The teacher entered her for the 1945 British Drama League Award, and she shared first place with JANE HOLLAND. In 1946 MAY HOLLINWORTH induced Shearing to join METROPOLITAN THEATRE and she scored a notable success as Viola in *Twelfth Night*. Other plays for the company followed and at the same time she rapidly established herself as a leading radio actor.

In 1952 Shearing was Regan in JOHN ALDEN's celebrated production of *King Lear* and Dynamene in Christopher Fry's *A Phoenix Too Frequent* in a MERCURY THEATRE production. Her acting was particularly attuned to Fry's work and she played Dynamene again on television and several times on radio. She played Viola again and Lydia Languish in *The Rivals* by R. B. Sheridan on an Australian tour for the AUSTRALIAN ELIZABETHAN THEATRE TRUST in 1956. Next year she gave a performance of fire and power as the young Italian girl Maria in Richard Beynon's *THE SHIFTING HEART*. She joined the TRUST PLAYERS in 1959. Her outstanding achievement was the tortured Mary Tyrone in Eugene O'Neill's *Long Day's Journey into Night*. She repeated this moving and distinguished performance for the MARIAN STREET THEATRE Company in Sydney in 1987.

In 1960, at the first Adelaide Festival, Shearing played in T. S. Eliot's *Murder in the Cathedral*. Through the 1960s she worked with the OLD TOTE THEATRE COMPANY. In 1973 she played the Duchess of York in *Richard II* and Carmel Scott in David Williamson's *What If You Died Tomorrow?* In 1974 she played Lady Macbeth for the Old Tote company. She created Lillian in Louis Nowra's *Inside the Island* for the NIMROD THEATRE COMPANY in 1980. She gave an award-winning performance as Volumnia in *Coriolanus* for the SYDNEY THEATRE COMPANY in 1993. ♥*Richard Lane*

Tony Sheldon

Actor, writer. Born in Brisbane, 12 September 1955. Son of singer and dancer Toni Lamond and dancer Frank Sheldon. Grandson of variety performers Stella Lamond and Joe Lawman. Nephew of singer Helen Reddy. Stage debut 1966. National Critics' Circle Award for best actor in NSW 1977 (Ivan in *Inner Voices* by Louis Nowra). Has also worked in television and as comedy writer.

Tony Sheldon's career has been divided by his varied skills as an entertainer, acquired in the world in which he grew up, and a considerable dramatic talent in the legitimate theatre for roles expressing constrained emotions and vulnerability. The intensity of his dramatic strength was summed up by a critic for the *Australian*, writing of the Tyrone brothers in Eugene O'Neill's *Long Day's Journey into Night* in 1987: '[David] Downer and Sheldon succeed in filling their characters with the tortured souls of young men thrust into an unfair world'. In comedy Sheldon dares to be foolish and his antics have been described as 'hilarious', 'endearing' and 'virtuosic'.

He spent his early life in hotels and backstage as his parents worked on the Tivoli circuit, in nightclubs or in musicals. He showed precocious talent as singer and mimic and in 1966 he made his stage debut as one of Fagin's gang in the musical *Oliver!* In Sydney in 1972 he played Birdboot in Tom Stoppard's *The Real Inspector Hound* at the St James Playhouse and Matt in a musical, *The Fantasticks*, at the Intimate Theatre. *The Fantasticks* gained attention and Sheldon was soon working in musicals and pantomimes. In 1973 he made an impact with his first dramatic role, Joe Cassidy in the premiere of Peter Kenna's *A HARD GOD*.

As an inaugural member of the Hunter Valley Theatre Company, in 1976 he was notable as the Comic in John Romeril's *THE FLOATING WORLD*, Tom in Tennessee Williams's *The Glass Menagerie* and the boy Alan in Peter Shaffer's *Equus*. In 1977 he played Sebastian in *Twelfth Night* and Claudio in *Much Ado About Nothing* and created Ivan in LOUIS NOWRA's *Inner Voices* for the NIMROD THEATRE COMPANY. In the MARIAN STREET THEATRE Company's production of *A Funny Thing Happened on the Way to the Forum* in 1978 Sheldon played Hero. In the next year he played Clifford Anderson in Ira Levin's *Deathtrap* for the QUEENSLAND THEATRE COMPANY and created Florindo in the popular musical *THE VENETIAN TWINS* for Nimrod. For the same company he co-wrote, directed and acted in his first variety entertainment, *You and the Night and the Housewine*, in 1980 and played David in Errol Bray's *The Choir* in 1981.

In Sydney and Melbourne in 1984 Sheldon had personal triumphs in his most challenging role until then, the transvestite Arnold in Harvey Fierstein's *Torch Song Trilogy*. In 1985 he wrote and directed a semi-autobiographical entertainment for his mother and himself, *Madonna and Child*.

His later roles include Edmund in Eugene O'Neill's *Long Day's Journey into Night* for the Northside Theatre Company in 1987, the despondent writer in George S. Kaufman and Moss Hart's *Once in a Lifetime* for the SYDNEY THEATRE COMPANY in 1990 and the American Joshua Makepeace in NICK ENRIGHT's *Daylight Saving* for the MELBOURNE THEATRE COMPANY and on tour in 1991. Sheldon was memorably moving as the Baker in the musical *Into the Woods* for the Sydney Theatre Company in 1993. ♥*Katharine Brisbane*

further reading

LAMOND, TONI. *First Half*. Sydney: Pan Macmillan 1990.

Catherine Shepherd

Dramatist. Born 1912 in Rhodesia. Educated in United Kingdom. Came to Australia in 1920s. Lived all working life in Tasmania, writing for theatre and ABC radio. Died 18 February 1976.

Catherine Shepherd made a sustained and important though never spectacular contribution to stage and radio drama. She wrote with probing thoughtfulness and sad eloquence of the aching need of troubled beings to come to terms with their self, to find their own truth. Beyond this was a strongly affirmative cry for human freedom in a wide social sense. Shepherd was among the founders of the HOBART REPERTORY THEATRE SOCIETY, which gave the first production of her play *Daybreak*, winner of a competition in Melbourne. OLIVE WILTON directed the production at the Theatre Royal in 1938, with James Pratt as a young idealist in reckless rebellion against 'the system' in early Hobart, and Junee Cornell as a middle-class girl co-operating spiritedly with him until a tragic outcome. Critics approved of the play's period colour, compassionate feeling and rejection of smug authority. *Jane My Love*, staged in Tasmania in 1951, perhaps lacked intensity yet gave a faithful picture of the years when Sir John Franklin was Lieutenant-Governor of Van Diemen's Land. ❦*Leslie Rees*

published plays
Daybreak. Melbourne University Press 1946.
Delphiniums. Sydney: Mulga 1944, in *Six Australian One-Act Plays*.

Hattie Shepparde

Actor. Born 1846 in Launceston (Tas.), into theatrical family. Performed from mid-teens. Melbourne's leading comedienne 1871–73. Married Henry Hallam 8 November 1873. Toured in rural NSW and New Zealand. Died 22 September 1874 in Melbourne.

Hattie Shepparde's brief career became legendary not simply because of her tragic death from peritonitis after childbirth but through an irresistible personal charm that illuminated both her stage performances and private friendships. MARCUS CLARKE and J. E. NEILD were devoted admirers, the latter adopting the anagrammatic pen-name 'Tahite' in her honour for his reviews in the *Australasian*.

She had particular success in comedies by Tom Robertson, in which she was paired with Eleanor Carey. Her greatest successes were as Bella in Robertson's *School* and Cynisca in W. S. Gilbert's *Pygmalion and Galatea* with the Theatre Royal company during the period after the fire of 1872 when it performed in the more intimate St George's Hall. The *Australasian Sketcher* described her on 27 December 1873 as 'a thoroughly Australian dramatic artist', who 'might very fittingly be selected to represent our stage in the old country; for it is not alone that she possesses great personal attractions, but that her intelligence, her ease, the grace of her manner, and her thorough devotion to her art single her out'. At Shepparde's funeral on 24 September 1874 a riot broke out as hundreds of female fans fought to obtain a glimpse of the coffin. ❦*Harold Love*

Ella Shields

American comedian, singer 1879–1952. Played blackface minstrel in USA from 1898. Went to London in 1904 and became male impersonator. Married English music-hall composer William Hargreaves. Visited Australia 1921, 1925. Worked in USA 1929–47. Returned to Australia 1947. Worked in England from 1948.

A famous male impersonator, Ella Shields is best remembered for the song, 'Burlington Bertie from Bow', which her husband, William Hargreaves wrote for her in 1914. She first visited Australia for the TIVOLI CIRCUIT, and toured widely with a tent show on her return in 1925. She again starred on the Tivoli circuit on her last visit, when she was 70 years old. The playwright HARRY TIGHE wrote of Shields in his memoirs: 'She radiates happiness of the most attractive kind: the kind that has a tear folded into it. A tear, not a sob, is in her voice. … there was not one feature that did not tell of the sensitive artist.' ❦*Frank Van Straten*

further reading
TIGHE, HARRY. *As I Saw It*. London: Stockwell 1937.

The Shifting Heart

Play in three acts by Richard Beynon. **premiere** Elizabethan Theatre, Sydney, 4 October 1957. Cast: Lyndall Barbour, Richard Beynon, Neva Carr Glyn, Tom Farley, Dinah Shearing, Frank Waters. Director: May Hollinworth. **published** Sydney: Angus and Robertson 1960.

RICHARD BEYNON won the first Sydney Journalists' Club playwriting competition in 1956 with *The Shifting Heart*. The play then appeared under the auspices of the AUSTRALIAN ELIZABETHAN THEATRE TRUST and toured with great success amid controversy over its treatment of Australian xenophobia. In retrospect that theme seems a little off-centre, partly perhaps because its violent culmination occurs offstage. A good deal of the play's energy is in the charm and humour of its colourful stereotypes of Italianness, which throw into relief the painful inability of the Australian Clarry to articulate or understand his own feelings. Clarry has married into the lovable Bianchi family, and the implicit tensions snap on Christmas Eve. The problems particularly concern the younger Bianchis—Clarry's very pregnant wife Maria and Gino, who fights at dances where Italians are not liked. Gino is beaten up and dies, but the family tragedy forces a new emotional commitment from Clarry. The shifting of his heart and the birth of his son, little Gino, provide an ending that is symbolically affirmative even in the context of a social conflict too large to be directly dramatised.

The Shifting Heart came equal third with two other plays from nearly 2000 entries in an *Observer* newspaper competition in London in 1956. One of the judges, Alec Guinness, thought *The Shifting Heart* worthy of first prize. Laurence Olivier bought the rights and the play was performed in London at the Duke of York's Theatre in September 1959, with LEO McKERN directing an Australian cast. That production met a disappointing response but the play has had several revivals in Australia. ❦*Peter Fitzpatrick*

Shopfront Theatre for Young People

Co-operative youth-theatre group in Sydney, established in 1975 by Errol Bray and Garry Fry. Initiated National Young Playwrights' Weekend 1977. Began overseas touring 1984. **artistic directors** 1975–77 Errol Bray, 1977 Garry Fry, 1977–84 Errol Bray, 1985–86 Cathy Henkel, 1987 Faye Westwood, 1988–92 John du Feu, 1992–94 Michael McLaughlin.

Each year Shopfront works with 300 young people, producing more than 20 shows, mainly by group-creation. Its extensive use of group-creation has helped youth theatre, which is usually strongly presentational in style, to be accepted as a theatrical form. Shopfront was established in the St George district of Sydney to give young people a voice through the arts. It has been a registered co-operative since 1977 and children are the main shareholders. In 1979 it bought a 300-seat theatre, two shops and a house. Funding has come from a wide range of government bodies but Shopfront has always mainly been financed by its own fund-raising projects. This and its ownership of its premises have ensured its security and greatly helped it to survive and succeed. Shopfront has made numerous overseas tours, giving well-received performances in Canada, Czechoslovakia, France, Hong Kong, Japan, South Korea, Thailand, the United Kingdom and the USA. Many exchanges with overseas youth theatres have resulted. ❦*Errol Bray and John du Feu*

further reading
BRAY, ERROL. *Are We Heroes … ?* Sydney: NSW University Press 1976.
BRAY, ERROL. *Playbuilding*. Sydney: Currency Press 1991. Includes descriptions and photographs of many Shopfront productions.
Roles. Youth arts magazine published by Shopfront Theatre since 1976.
Shopfront Documents. Working papers on youth theatre published by Shopfront Theatre.

Robert Sidaway

Theatre proprietor. Born c.1757 in London. Sentenced to transportation for life 1782. Arrived in Sydney with First Fleet January 1788. Conditionally pardoned 1792. Absolute pardon 1794. Opened Australia's first public theatre, 16 January 1796. Died 13 October 1809 in Sydney.

Australia's first theatre proprietor, Robert Sidaway seems to have had nothing to do with the theatre before he came to Australia. His motive in opening the first theatre in 1796 seems to have been purely business speculation and not management. Little is known of his career before he was convicted of housebreaking and sentenced to transportation for life in 1782, though he was a watchcase maker by trade. Ralph Clark's journal describes him as a 'daring and villainous fellow'. He was put in irons for misbehaviour on the voyage of the First Fleet but his Australian career was marked by ever-increasing prosperity and respectability. He received a conditional pardon in 1792, and it was made absolute in 1794. By then he had become a baker, supplying bread to the garrison.

SIDAWAY'S THEATRE, unlike most of its successors, did not pretend to 'royal' status but was known simply as the Theatre. It opened with Edward Young's tragedy *The Revenge* and an entertainment by T. Vaughan, *The Hotel*, first performed at the Theatre Royal, Drury Lane, in 1721 and 1776 respectively. In 1801 verses on convict performers were published in London and claimed to have been spoken at the opening of Sidaway's theatre by the notorious pickpocket George Barrington. The so-called 'Barrington prologue' was actually written by Henry Carter, who never visited Australia.

According to David Collins, Judge-Advocate of the colony, the house 'was fitted up with more theatrical propriety than could have been expected' and the convicts' performance was 'far above contempt'. Most of the costumes were made by the cast, but some of the best were 'veteran articles' from the theatre at York in England. The usual segregated audience accommodation was sold at prices that remained standard in Australia for many years—five shillings for boxes, three shillings and sixpence for side boxes, two shillings and sixpence for the pit, and one shilling for the gallery. In 1796 Sidaway allowed payment in flour, meat or spirits instead of currency, which was in short supply in Sydney. Next year, according to *Saunders's News-Letter* of 12 September 1797, Sidaway was also running 'the best house of public entertainment' in Sydney. The obvious link between supplying customers with food and drink and supplying them with entertainment was to be replicated many times in the building of Australian theatres. Though his theatre closed some time between 1804 and early 1808, Sidaway himself continued to prosper, running his farm and his public house until his death, when he was about 52 years old. ❦*Elizabeth Webby*

further reading
PARSONS, VIVIENNE. Robert Sidaway. *Australian Dictionary of Biography* 2. Melbourne University Press 1967.
reference
Ralph Clark's journal and letter-book in Mitchell Library (Sydney).

Sidaway's theatre

Theatre in Sydney, in premises of Robert Sidaway, managed by John Sparrow. Opened 16 January 1796.

The evidence is scanty, but it is known that the first theatre building in Australia, known simply as the Theatre, existed somewhere in little Sydney Town at the end of the 18th century. The prices show that it had four divisions in its auditorium—pit, front boxes and gallery. Other descriptions published since the mid-19th century have been based on circumstantial evidence or conjecture. The facts revealed by research so far come from a description by David Collins, Judge-Advocate of NSW, at the time of the first performance in the Theatre; reports printed in a couple of contemporary British journals; and a few playbills in the Mitchell Library in Sydney.

For a century writers have argued whether Sidaway's theatre was near the bakery where he made the colony's bread—somewhere east of Bell Row, now Bligh Street—or near his home off High Street (now George Street), near present-day Jamison Street. Some have assumed that he built the theatre for the cost of £100 cited in one report, yet Collins's words were: '… some of the more decent class of prisoners … obtained permission to prepare a play-house … [and] they had fitted up the house with more theatrical propriety than could have been expected'. Given the costs of the time, £100 would not have been enough to build a theatre from scratch. Furthermore, 'prepare' does not generally indicate 'erect' or 'construct' a whole building. It is likely that the theatre was in existing premises.

Collins wrote of a benefit for widow Eades and her family: 'The house was full, and it was said that she got upwards of twelve pounds by the night'. Paul McGuire, in his book *The Australian Theatre*, assumed that this meant the takings for the night were £12 and, calculating loosely from the seat prices, he deduced that the theatre held 120 persons. A beneficiary, however, generally gained the takings less expenses, so £12 would have been yielded by a performance before many more than 120 persons. The design of the interior, with its four divisions, is also uncertain. It may have been laid out in typical Georgian style on two levels, rough-hewn like the theatre shown in J. Wright's 1788 engraving of W. R. Pyne's painting *Macbeth in a Barn* rather than a typical English provincial theatre. Or it may have been on one raked level, like the fit-ups in barns in which English touring companies played where there was no dedicated theatre; GEORGE COPPIN describes these temporary theatres in his autobiography. If Sidaway's theatre was of the latter type, this would account for its having been 'dismantled' in 1798, on the orders of Governor John Hunter, and its having existed again in 1799 and 1800.

The Theatre's existence was chequered largely because there was a shortage of money in the colony and goods-in-kind were accepted in place of the one to five shillings charged for admission. A contemporary report claims that while the people of Sydney—mostly convicts and emancipists—were at the theatre, other convicts ransacked their houses. ❦*Ross Thorne*

Sidetrack Performance Group

Performance group in Sydney, founded as Sidetrack Theatre Company in July 1979 by Don Mamouney and Graham Pitts. **venue** Addison Road Community Centre, Marrickville, 1979–. **artistic directors** 1979–86 Don Mamouney. 1986–88 collective direction. 1988–89 Jo Caust. 1990– Don Mamouney. **first production** *Drink the Mercury* by David Holman, 1979. Director: Don Mamouney. **landmark productions** *Drink the Mercury*; *Mesh* and *Memo* by Graham Pitts. *Busted* by P. P. Cranney. *Kin* and *Skitsobumski* by company. *Down Under the Thumb*; *Loco*; *Out From Under*; *The Bang*; *Day to Day* and *Adios Cha-Cha* by company and Mamouney before 1988. *Whispers in the Heart* by company and Mamouney 1988 and 1989. *The Serpent's Contract*; *No Condom, No Start*; *Sweet Laughter*; *The Refugee*, *The Measure*; *We Were Going to Make a Movie* and *The Plant* by company and Mamouney. *Idol* by company with Nigel Kellaway and John Baylis. *The Drunken Boat* by company with Guillaume Brugman and Mamouney. *Heaven* by company with Derek Kreckler. **leading actors** Raymond Blanco, Zoe Carides, Allan Chapple, Regina Heilman, Dallas Lewis, Christian Manon, Jai McHenry, Michelle Milner, Stefo Nantsou, Silvio Ofria, Fiona Press, Rolando Ramos, Kathy Thompson, Mémé Thorne, Gino Tomasich, Anne-Marie Wiles.

Australia's leading permanent contemporary-performance group, Sidetrack creates vivid stage images with surreal, subversive humour. It employs sound and music, uses space innovatively and experiments with performer–audience relationships in a continuing exploration of theatrical form. A core ensemble of four performers and a director, with administrative and technical support, is supplemented by guest performers and other collaborators, including musicians, film and video artists and directors.

The company has been strongly influenced by the artistic development of DON MAMOUNEY, who co-founded Sidetrack as a COMMUNITY-THEATRE company to invent new theatrical forms to explore the many cultures of Australia. It first made a reputation in the 1980s by devising works that articulated experiences of immigrants and working-class people. It performed them in a dynamic physical style, involving non-naturalist forms and minimal sets, in workplaces, schools, halls, streets and theatres throughout Sydney, elsewhere in NSW and in other states. As the Sidetrack Performance Group it regularly performs at Addison Road and in 'alternative' venues such as the PERFORMANCE SPACE. Since 1991 Sidetrack has annually held Contemporary Performance Week, a festival of performance-making and training workshops, forums and new performance. Sidetrack's conjunction of ensemble training and collaborative creation is unique in Australia. ❦*Tom Burvill*

further reading
BURVILL, T. M. Discovering the theatricality of community. *New Theatre Quarterly* 11/5 (Cambridge, England, 1986).
BURVILL, T. M. Resistance/deconstruction/nausea—Towards a viable contemporary political theatre. *Spectator Burns* 3 (Sydney 1989).
BURVILL, T. M. Sidetrack's *Kin*—Intervening in multiculturalism. *Australasian Drama Studies* 12–13 (Brisbane 1988).

Silver's Circus

The largest road show in the early 1950s was Silver's Circus, founded in 1946 on the premise that the tastes of the Australian public had 'not been adequately considered by most circus proprietors during recent years'. Its founders were Mervyn King, who began a colourful circus career in 1915 as a seven-year-old apprentice acrobat with Gus St Leon's Great United Circus, and the Hardie family of tent makers in Sydney. During the Second World War, when circus was fettered by restrictions, King worked for the Hardies, making canvas goods for the war effort.

King's circus expertise and the Hardie family's financial and technical support were a winning combination in Silver's Circus, which opened at Rockdale in Sydney. Within five years it consisted of 51 performers and their families, 30 horses, 14 motor trucks, 12 caravans and four cages of animals. It toured every mainland state. At the peak of its success disagreement within the management led to dissolution of the company in 1953. Later circuses have revived its name. ❦*Mark St Leon*

further reading
KING, MERVYN. *The Silver Road—The life of Mervyn King, circus man, as told to Mark St Leon*. Springwood (NSW): Butterfly Books 1990.

Thomas Simes

Actor, costume designer, manager. Born *c.*1803. Employed at Theatre Royal, Sydney, 1832–37. Royal Victoria Theatre, Sydney, 1838–46. Died 1846 in Sydney.

As a low-comedy and utility actor, Thomas Simes was a mainstay but never a star of theatre in Sydney from its professional beginnings in 1832 until his death, partly from overwork, in 1846. At BARNETT LEVEY's Theatre Royal, where he played numerous roles, he also took over responsibility for costumes and properties, becoming the first Australian costume designer. In 1836 newspapers praised his splendid oriental costumes for *Blue Beard*. Simes became acting manager of the Theatre Royal in 1837 and, after Levey's death in October, took over the management until he was replaced by JOHN LAZAR.

In March 1838 Simes was in the opening company at the new ROYAL VICTORIA THEATRE. He was also, with his wife, responsible for costumes and properties. On 17 March 1840 he helped to save the Royal Victoria from the fire that destroyed the adjacent old Theatre Royal. He became acting manager of the Royal Victoria in November 1840 and by September 1842 he was stage manager as well. Little wonder that on 12 October 1846, shortly before his death, the *Sydney Herald* commented: 'Mr Simes has injured his health by the exertions made by him in his multifarious occupations of manager, wardrobe-keeper, etc. etc'. ❧*Elizabeth Webby*

Joseph Simmons

Actor, manager. Born *c*.1810. Claimed early theatrical experience. Came to Sydney May 1830. Performed in Hobart as Joseph Ray, November 1832. Became co-owner, manager and actor at Theatre Royal, Sydney, February 1834 Later co-lessee and manager. Sole lessee November 1835 to May 1836. Engaged for Royal Victoria Theatre, Sydney, July 1838. Manager and actor at Royal Victoria 1842. Opened Royal City Theatre, Sydney, May 1843. Died 1893.

The advent of Joseph Simmons to Barnett Levey's company marked a turn towards professionalism and a widening of the repertoire at the Theatre Royal in Sydney. Like so many of his contemporaries, Simmons played the jack of all trades, moving between acting, management and business with bewildering frequency. He claimed to have worked from the age of 12 in English provincial theatres and minor London theatres. He arrived as a free settler, became an auctioneer, and probably sang in Levey's early concerts. In 1832 he went to England by way of Hobart, where he sang under the name of Joseph Ray and boasted that he would return to the colonies with a theatrical company.

When Simmons did return to Sydney, he opened a bazaar in George Street in January 1834. Next month he joined Levey as joint proprietor, manager and actor in the Theatre Royal. He was also the Theatre Royal's first Macbeth, and a successful Mercutio and Iago. The *Sydney Herald* originally criticised him for 'too much rant and too little feeling', but he excelled in comic acting and was especially praised for his stage Irishmen.

Simmons was unpopular with his colleagues. His unpopularity, exacerbated by anti-Semitism in the profession, reached its nadir when Simmons accused Maria Taylor of felony after she took three costumes with her when she seceded from his company in April 1834. His litigious nature took him to court on many occasions and ended his partnership with Levey in early 1835. By April Simmons had become a co-lessee and manager of the Theatre Royal, and he was solely in charge from November. In May 1836 he went to Hobart and Launceston after a row with Levey.

In July 1838 Joseph Wyatt engaged Simmons for the Royal Victoria Theatre. He acted there while running a public house. In April 1842, when he was manager and performer at the Royal Victoria, he had a success in *The Mock Catalani in Little Puddleton*, a musical burletta by Charles Nagel. Simmons attempted to open his own theatre in 1841–42 but was not granted a licence. In September 1842 he left the Royal Victoria to plan the conversion of a shop into the tiny Royal City Theatre, with the machinist James Belmore as his partner. This opened in May 1843 and closed after a few weeks of competition with the Royal Victoria, to which Simmons returned as an actor. He was immensely popular with the public. He created the character of Lanty O'Liffey in Edward Geoghegan's *The Currency Lass*. His appearances became less frequent and on 3 April 1845, after Wyatt attempted to pocket the proceeds of a benefit, he wrote to the *Sydney Morning Herald*: 'My theatrical career in NSW is ended'. He appears to have retired finally to his publican's business in April 1846 after another row with Wyatt. *Heads of the People* on 6 November 1847 depicted Simmons as a country storekeeper in a town 80 km from Sydney. He is next heard of in June 1879, when he was given a grand complimentary benefit in Sydney's second Theatre Royal. He played Benjamin Bowbell in *The Illustrious Stranger*.

Simmons wrote a play, *The Duellist*, which he claimed to be 'the first truly original drama ever produced in this colony'. When he applied for a licence to perform it in June 1844 he promised that it contained 'nothing local, political, sectarian or immoral'. ❧*Helen Musa*

further reading
Oppenheim, Helene. Joseph Simmons. *Australian Dictionary of Biography* 2. Melbourne University Press 1967.

Barbara Sisley

Actor, director, speech and drama teacher. Born in Surrey (England) 1885. Came to Australia at 11. Father taught elocution in Melbourne. Toured with George Rignold Company and Brough Comedy Company. Began teaching in Brisbane 1916. Formed Barbara Sisley Players during First World War. Studied in England 1923. Formed Brisbane Repertory Theatre Society 1925. Died November 1945, struck by a car in Brisbane.

The first professionally trained teacher of speech and drama in Brisbane, Barbara Sisley contributed greatly to the city's cultural life. Stranded there when a touring theatrical company was disbanded, she began teaching drama at the Young Women's Christian Association and formed the Barbara Sisley Players from her pupils. She produced *Othello* in 1918 and directed several other Shakespeare plays before she formed the Brisbane Repertory Theatre Society. As its chief producer from 1925 until her sudden death in 1945, she directed 57 of the 125 plays it performed.

Imposing in figure and voice, Sisley demanded a professional standard of performance from members and was meticulous about stagecraft, props and settings. Her productions were well received by the *Brisbane Courier*. She was keenly interested in Australian drama and she encouraged George Landen Dann and other writers, and directed their plays. She was also interested in American theatre and she corresponded with writers and directors in the USA. ❧*Joan Massey Cook*

The Slaughter of St Teresa's Day

Play in three acts by Peter Kenna. **premiere** 11 March 1959, Elizabethan Theatre, Sydney, by Trust Players. Cast: Philippa Baker, Neva Carr Glyn, Patricia Conolly, Mary Mackay, Rodney Milgate, Des Rolfe, Dinah Shearing, Grant Taylor, Frank Waters, Dorothy Whiteley. Designer: Phillip Hickey. Director: Robin Lovejoy. **published** Sydney: Currency Press 1972.

When this play first appeared in 1959 it seemed to fit neatly into the 'slum realist' school associated with Ray Lawler's *Summer of the Seventeenth Doll* and its successors. It is in fact much more radical in form and more colourful in content than others of the school, and it might have had a different reputation in a theatrical context less concerned to establish a realistic 'school' of nationalist Australian playwriting. Its comic jocular Irishness, its loosely structured, almost episodic narrative and its reference to the conventions of Hollywood gangster pictures, were seen as weaknesses by some early reviewers but now look like the strengths of a play ahead of its time.

Oola Maguire, a queen of the underworld, holds her annual St Teresa's Day party to celebrate her miraculous recovery from a bullet wound eight years previously. Her convent-educated daughter, Thelma, has turned 16 and has come home for the party. This is at the centre of the play, celebrating in a series of set pieces the colourful Irish larrikinism that underlies the criminal world Oola is struggling to control. The party ends in a violent gun battle. In its aftermath Oola and Thelma, together with members of Oola's household and extended family, have to take stock of themselves and of what they have put into life that will have enduring value.

The play won the General Motors–Holden national playwriting competition a week before the TRUST PLAYERS, of whom Kenna was one, gave the premiere. It has since been widely staged, and produced on radio and television in Australia and the United Kingdom. ❧*John McCallum*

Beaumont Smith

Dramatist, entrepreneur. Born c.1862 in Adelaide. Freelance journalist in Adelaide, Sydney and New Zealand. Co-founded *Gadfly* with C. J. Dennis and A. E. Martin, 1906. Adapted works by C. J. Dennis, Henry Lawson, 'Banjo' Paterson, Steele Rudd and Ethel Turner for stage and screen, 1907–24. Theatrical entrepreneur, and producer, director and distributor of films 1911–34. Died 2 January 1950 in Sydney.

Beaumont Smith began his theatrical career by collaborating with STEELE RUDD on a stage version of ON OUR SELECTION in 1907. Rudd refused to endorse Smith's contribution but, further revised by BERT BAILEY and EDMUND DUGGAN, the result was a major stage success for Bailey between 1912 and 1929. It is a measure of Smith's business methods that from 1917 he simultaneously received half the profits from this production and plagiarised Rudd's stories for film comedies about the Hayseed family.

Smith also collaborated with EDWARD DYSON on several plays, and staged his own dramatisations of Ethel Turner's children's story *Seven Little Australians* in 1914 and Henry Lawson's *While the Billy Boils* in 1916. Smith's support for Australian authors was substantial, if flawed. *Seven Little Australians* enjoyed long matinée seasons throughout eastern Australia in 1914–15 and Smith's Lawson drama, although unified by a conventional melodramatic plot, provided an 'enjoyable evening of sentiment and humour', according to the *Sydney Morning Herald* on 2 October 1916. Two of the four acts were set outside the Railway Hotel, where 'the residents of Redclay … present themselves on the stage of the Theatre Royal as a leisurely class, carrying on in their courtships, wager, gossip, quarrels, and reconciliations in the open air'.

Smith, a major theatrical entrepreneur, toured these and other shows throughout Australia and New Zealand. He made a fortune by importing a troupe of Austrian midgets and presenting them as Tiny Town in a stage show that toured Australasia in 1911 and then Africa and Canada. He invested the profits in film, and by the 1920s he was primarily involved in film production and distribution, including joint ventures with J. C. WILLIAMSON'S. ❧*Richard Fotheringham*

reference
The Australian Archives (Canberra) holds scripts of some of Smith's adaptations, including *While the Billy Boils*, CRSA 1336/1, item 10278.

James Smith

Dramatic critic, dramatist. Born 1820. Editor of provincial newspaper in England. Emigrated to Melbourne in 1854. Critic for *Age* and *Argus*. Died 19 March 1910.

A frequent theatregoer from an early age, James Smith was strongly influenced by the mid-Victorian concept of the morality of art and letters, as propagated by William Hazlitt and John Ruskin among others. While always appreciative of technical ability, he judged the success of a performance by the manner in which the actor conveyed the moral and ethical inferences to be drawn from the playwright's work. Within these confines he was a perceptive critic, and many of his reviews demonstrate his ability to respond to the great passions of the drama when properly portrayed. Smith's critical reputation was established by the first season of the visiting actor G. V. BROOKE in 1855, which he reviewed as a dramatic critic for the *Age*, though he wrote most of his criticism for the *Argus*. During the next two decades he reviewed all the important seasons, including those of JOSEPH JEFFERSON, W. S. LYSTER's opera companies and ADELAIDE RISTORI, but his authority declined in later years because conservatism prevented him from accepting new modes of interpretation. He occasionally wrote under pseudonyms, including 'Touchstone' and 'An Old Playgoer'. His theatrical reminiscences are valuable records of the Melbourne stage, for which he wrote two plays and two translations. ❧*Lurline Stuart*

further reading
JORDENS, ANN-MARI. James Smith. *Australian Dictionary of Biography* 6. Melbourne University Press 1976.
STUART, LURLINE. *James Smith—The making of a colonial culture*. Sydney: Allen and Unwin 1989.

Jo Smith

Dramatist. Born c.1870 in Melbourne. Originally Joseph Smith. Professional actor in 1890s. Became businessman. Prolific playwright c.1904–1917. Details of death unknown.

Jo Smith was a leading playwright at the beginning of the 20th century and he carried on until about 1918, trying to adjust his style to new fashions. After amateur acting with Melbourne's Dragonet Club—where he wrote and staged his one-act play *A Tangled Skein* about 1890—he had a brief professional career. This included working with JANET ACHURCH in Henrik Ibsen's *A Doll's House* during the last year of her 1889–91 Australian tour. Smith's first play to reach the professional stage may have been *A Lease of Life*, which J. C. WILLIAMSON'S bought in 1904. His first success was *The Miner's Trust*, a melodrama of the old type, in which a dying miner persuades his best friend to impersonate him and marry his blind sweetheart back in England—she apparently does not notice the difference. Complications set in when the friend inherits a large fortune but cannot claim it. The play's main virtue seems to have been that it was well written. It opened at the Palace Theatre in Sydney on 31 October 1907 and next year there was another production in Melbourne.

Smith broke away from English formulas in his best-known play, THE BUSHWOMAN (1909). Set on an Australian farm, it anticipated many of the character types that Bert Bailey and Edmund Duggan used in adapting Steele Rudd's ON OUR SELECTION. Bailey and Duggan staged The Bushwoman, which was one of Smith's two major successes for WILLIAM ANDERSON. The other, THE GIRL OF THE NEVER NEVER (1912) went even farther outback, to the station of a cattle king in the Northern Territory.

After a revival of The Bushwoman as The Bush Girl in 1913 Smith seems to have lost contact with the professional theatre. During the First World War he wrote two plays and produced them himself with scratch amateur companies. Before the Dawn was staged in suburban Melbourne in October 1915 in aid of the Wounded Soldier's Fund, and The Reveille was toured for the war effort in 1917. The latter play concerns a farmer whose son has died at Gallipoli, and who blackmails his nephew to keep him on the farm and prevent him from enlisting. Needless to say, when the threat is removed the nephew goes off to do his duty at the front. Neither acting nor production was good, but reviewers felt obliged to praise the author's patriotic fervour.
❦Richard Fotheringham

reference
Scripts of Smith's plays are in the National Library of Australia (Canberra).

Emily Soldene

English actor, director, singer, writer. 1840–1912. Trained as opera singer. Debut in concert at Theatre Royal, Drury Lane, 1865. Became *opéra-bouffe* star in London 1871. Toured USA 1874, 1876. Toured Australia and New Zealand 1877–78. Unsuccessful on return visit 1892. Worked as journalist in Sydney until 1897.

London's leading exponent of French *opéra-bouffe* in the 1870s, Emily Soldene triumphed in Australasia. After sensationally successful tours of the USA in 1874 and 1876 the Soldene Opéra Bouffe Company set out for Australia and New Zealand with a repertoire of ten operettas. The company of 35 included an Australian baritone, Edward Farley. It arrived in Sydney in September 1877, opened at the Theatre Royal with Jacques Offenbach's *Geneviève de Brabant* and *Barbe-bleue*, and played to packed houses for six weeks. The female chorus was the rage of Sydney and blonde, statuesque Soldene caused a furore by singing the interpolated popular songs 'Silver threads among the gold' and 'Wedding Bells'. The triumphs continued in Melbourne at the Prince of Wales Opera House, where Offenbach's *La Périchole* joined the repertoire. In 1878, after a tour of New Zealand, Soldene opened the rebuilt THEATRE ROYAL in Adelaide with a nervously spoken inaugural ode and a dazzling performance of Charles Lecocq's *Giroflé-Girofla*. On a return season in Melbourne she received a farewell presentation from GEORGE COPPIN.

Soldene was trained as a singer and initially earned her living in London by singing at the Canterbury Music Hall and later the Oxford Music Hall under the name of Miss FitzHenry. From 1870 she was star performer and director in condensed *opéras-bouffes*, beginning with Hervé's *Chilperic, the King of the Gauls* at the Lyceum Geneviève de Brabant made her famous at the Philharmonic in Islington in 1871. The Prince of Wales became a devoted admirer. In her productions Soldene used her talent, humour and sparkling intelligence to great effect, along with worldly shrewdness and courage as an innovator. 'From the first moment of going into management—recognising the attractive force of female beauty—I surrounded myself with the best-looking and best set up girls that could possibly be found', she wrote. She introduced 'The Parisian Quadrille' with a quartet of high-kicking girls who became the toast of every city where they performed, especially Florence Slater, who could kick her slipper into the gallery.

Slater was the leading high-kicker in Soldene's company when she returned to Australia in 1892. By then Gilbert and Sullivan operetta had displaced *opéra-bouffe* in popularity and NELLIE STEWART was the reigning star. Soldene turned to journalism in Sydney, although, at Stewart's request, she appeared in one of her former triumphs, Lecocq's *La Fille de Madame Angot* at the Lyceum Theatre in 1895. Soldene wrote her exuberant, humorous and keenly observant memoirs in Sydney. On their publication in 1897 she returned to London, where a new edition was printed in 1898. Her novel *Young Mrs Staples* was also published, and until her death she was London representative of the Sydney *Evening News*. ❦Lynne Murphy

writings
My Theatrical and Musical Recollections, new edition with press opinions. London: Downey 1898.

further reading
BEVAN, IAN. *The Story of the Theatre Royal*. Sydney: Currency Press 1993.
PARKER, JOHN. *The Green Room Book*. London: T. Sealey Clark 1909.
Variety Obituaries 1905–86. New York: Garland 1988.

Mary Sole

Circus proprietor, equestrian, trapeze artist, wirewalker. Born February 1892 at Wentworth (NSW). Eldest child of Bill Sole, circus bandsman, and his wife Eliza, daughter of circus proprietor W. G. Perry. Died 1975.

Mary Sole was born in a 'six-be-eight tent' and trained from an early age for a career in the circus, like her younger brothers and sisters. An early reference to her appeared in the *Wagga Wagga Express* on 25 August 1904 in a review of Eroni Brothers' Circus, one of the PERRY FAMILY CIRCUSES. It mentioned her 'splendid exhibition on the wire rope which aroused frequent cheers' and reported a 'furore of applause for her great feats on the trapeze'. In 1909 the Sole family joined the Gus St Leon family in a successful partnership known as Gus St Leon's Great United Circus. Mary Sole displayed prowess in equestrian and other acts, particularly a 'balancing trapeze' act which, according to the Lismore *Northern Star* of 9 March 1915, 'embodied some of the most difficult acts conceivable'. She maintained, however, that her best act was a wirewalking act she learned in the Great United Circus from Gus St Leon's son Cassimer. By 1917 Mary and her parents, brothers and sisters had established the Sole family's own circus, which is still in existence. During 1921–23 Mary Sole toured British vaudeville houses with her solo trapeze act, billed as La Belle Marie. ❦*Mark St Leon*

Emanuel Solomon

> Theatre proprietor. Born 1800 in London. Came to Sydney as convict 1 May 1818. Became financier, merchant, philanthropist. Financed theatre buildings in Adelaide. Member of South Australian House of Assembly 1862–65 and Legislative Council 1867–71. Died 29 August 1880 in Adelaide.

Emanuel Solomon, a former convict, financed the first purpose-built theatre in Adelaide, the QUEEN'S THEATRE, and many other buildings. Solomon and his brother Vaiben, described as pencil makers, were transported to Sydney in 1818, the former charged with housebreaking and the latter with larceny. When their sentences expired they established themselves in business, and in 1838 Emanuel moved to Adelaide. He opened the Queen's Theatre in January 1841 but a sudden downturn in the economy made it a liability and he leased it to the government for use as a law court. Solomon played some part in economic recovery by promoting copper mines at Burra (SA).

The actor-manager GEORGE COPPIN arrived in Adelaide and 1846 and found no suitable place for performance. He persuaded Solomon to convert a billiards room adjacent to the former Queen's Theatre into the New Queen's Theatre, and gave the first performance there on 2 November 1846. When the government's lease of the first theatre expired, Solomon had it renovated it at a cost of £2000 and opened it in late 1850 as the Royal Victoria Theatre. Shortly afterwards the gold rushes in Victoria attracted audiences and performers away from Adelaide and the theatre became unprofitable. With its closure Solomon's involvement in theatre ceased. He was mourned after his death in 1873 as a generous philanthropist. ❦*Meg Abbie-Denton*

further reading
LOYAU, G. E. *The Representative Men of South Australia*. Adelaide: George Howell 1883.
MUNZ, Hirsch. *Jews in South Australia 1836–1936*. Adelaide: Thornquest Press 1936.
RICHARDS, ERIC. Emanuel Solomon. *Australian Dictionary of Biography* 6. Melbourne University Press 1976.

Thomas Somers

> Dramatist. Born 5 February 1858 in Preston (Lancashire, England). Really Thomas Walker. Child preacher in Canada 1874. Spiritualist lecturer in USA 1876. In Australia 1877–79. Married Andretta Somers in South Africa 1881. Returned to Australia, abandoned spiritualism. Member of NSW Parliament 1887–94. Temperance lecturer (after conviction for drunkenness) in New Zealand and Western Australia. Newspaper editor and Labor member of Western Australian Parliament 1905–32. Admitted to bar 1911. Attorney-General 1911–1916. Died 1932 in Perth.

An extraordinary, brilliant politician and an eccentric, Thomas Walker used his wife's surname Somers for two brief but successful forays into playwriting. With ALFRED DAMPIER he made a play from Marcus Clarke's great convict novel *His Natural Life*. Dampier's company staged FOR THE TERM OF HIS NATURAL LIFE at the Royal Standard Theatre in Sydney for 43 packed performances in 1886. Encouraged, Dampier staged Somers's own play *Voices of the Night*. The *Sydney Morning Herald* on 26 July 1886 thought the Sydney scenery, which included Redfern railway station and the tram line to Coogee, 'was worthy of a better play'. Nevertheless, *Voices in the Night* ran for 17 nights, only a week less than *Uncle Tom's Cabin*. In July 1893, Dampier staged Somers's ambitious five-act verse tragedy *Marmondelle the Moor*. The *Sydney Morning Herald* on 24 July liked it as drama and literature but the economic depression helped to kill it after a week. Dampier and Somers, under his real name of Walker, revised *For the Term of His Natural Life* in 1895 and it became the most enduring of many stage versions of Clarke's saga. ❦*Richard Fotheringham*

further reading
SMITH, F. B. Thomas Walker (Somers). *Australian Dictionary of Biography* 6. Melbourne University Press 1976.

George Sorlie

> Comedian, entrepreneur. Born 7 February 1885 in Liverpool (England) of West Indian ancestry. Grew up in Melbourne, Perth and Kalgoorlie (WA). Won many singing competitions as boy. Began stage career at 14. Played Clay's and Tivoli vaudeville circuits. Associated with Irving Sayles and Charles Pope on Tivoli circuit. Married actor Grace Stewart 1915. Joined Phillip Lytton's touring tent show 1917. Bought show and renamed it Sorlie's 1923. Toured NSW and Queensland, performing mostly melodrama. Switched show to variety 1931. Retired to Sydney 1945. Died 19 June 1948 in Sydney.

The black comedian George Sorlie took the best-known and longest-lived of Australia's TENT SHOWS to the larger country towns of NSW and Queensland annually from 1917 to 1945, except for a break during the Second World War. When Sorlie, the 'J. C. Williamson of the road', drove into town in his latest car—loudly painted, like all the company's cars, in black-and-white or gold-and-white stripes—he and his tent show were the focus of attention. It was said that women in the country, where travelling shows provided most of the live entertainment between the wars, bought two dresses a year—one for the agricultural show and one for Sorlie's.

Sorlie's opened its year on Boxing Day in Newcastle (NSW), where it played pantomime by day and gave a show at night throughout January. In early February it headed for New England, following the agricultural show circuit. At Easter, when country towns were dead because of the Royal Easter Show in Sydney, the company rested in Sydney. After Easter, it headed for western NSW and travelled through Gunnedah, Moree, Goondiwindi and Ipswich (Qld). After spending the winter in northern Queensland it went to the Riverina region of NSW in spring. Touring companies competed in the big Queensland towns during show week. In the 'battle of Bundaberg', for example, all the major companies would set up in competition on the river bank, touting for business with megaphones. Sorlie swamped his competitors with the first amplified public-address system.

Sorlie started with a melodrama repertoire that included *East Lynne*, *The Man they Could Not Hang*, *Uncle Tom's Cabin* and his own *My Pal Ginger*. Sorlie's wife Grace began her career as the Reverend Mother in *The Forbidden Marriage*, but gradually relinquished acting for front-of-house duties. Wearing a lizard brooch with diamond eyes, she collected money, organised seats, settled any disturbances and chatted with patrons she saw once a year. BOBBY LE BRUN said she was 'the fastest usherette in show business', able to seat 1000 children in 15 minutes. She also knew many parts by heart and could always be pulled in to act at short notice.

By 1931 the company had switched to variety in the face of film competition. The first road company included Tiny Douglas and his band, the acrobatic Cleveres and the comedian Sam Stern, and it was a great success. Sorlie himself was master of every known trick with a top hat and walking stick and he sang coon songs and romantic ballads in a fine voice. He recorded his most popular songs, including 'You may not be an angel'.

Le Brun, who was in the troupe from 1933 to 1937, was struck by Sorlie's ability to manufacture several variety acts out of a few. Engaged as part of a double act, Le Brun found himself involved in four acts. Other members of the company included KITTY BLUETT and Hal Lashwood, later ROY RENE's offsider on radio.

Sorlie retired to Sydney in 1945 and went broke as managing director of Sorlie's Construction Company, which aimed to produce modern housing, especially for ex-servicemen in Sorlie Village in Frenchs Forest. After his death June 1948 his widow and Le Brun took his tent show on the road again from 1949 to 1961. ❧*Victoria Chance*

further reading
SPEARRITT, PETER. George Sorlie. *Australian Dictionary of Biography* 12. Melbourne University Press 1990.
People (Sydney) 3/11 (12 March 1952).
Sydney Morning Herald 21 June 1948.

South Africa

Australia and South Africa share much theatrical history. The mail ships bound from England for Australia stopped at Cape Town and other South African ports, so England exported productions and personnel to the South African and Australasian colonies. The traffic was not all one way and in the 19th century pioneers from Australia were conspicuous in all branches of show business in South Africa. By the 1910s J. C. WILLIAMSON's organisation was one of three influential managements in South Africa, and entire Australian productions customarily toured the South African circuit as recently as *My Fair Lady* in the 1960s.

The first troupe from Australia known to have visited South Africa was an Australian Variety Company, which opened in Cape Town in 1875. It included General Tom Thumb, the American midget Charles Sherwood Stratton, who came to Australia in 1872. Luscombe Searelle's operetta company from New Zealand and Australia, opened in Cape Town in 1887 with his *Isidora*, first performed on 7 July 1885 in Melbourne, and followed it with his *Estrella* and *Bobadil*. Searelle and his wife established the first shanty theatre at Johannesburg, which was founded in 1886 after the discovery of gold on the Witwatersrand.

South African material reached Australia as early as 3 March 1888, when *Jess*, an adaptation by ALFRED DAMPIER and J. H. Wrangham of H. Rider Haggard's romance of Transvaal life, opened in Sydney. When the Jameson Raid was the news in 1896, Dampier rejigged the show as *A Transvaal Heroine*. The actor–manager GEORGE DARRELL disembarked at Port Elizabeth on his return from the United Kingdom in September 1892, and began a tour with six plays, including his own *The Nightmare*. His actor wife, Christine Peachey, died in Johannesburg in November.

There was an exchange of circuses in the 1890s. While Frank Fillis's circus from South Africa was touring Australia in 1892–94, WIRTHS' CIRCUS began a seven-year world tour in 1893 at the Opera House in Cape Town. The company of 80 performers and 50 horses was billed as the Australian Circus. The circus connection continued with Oscar Pagel, a German strong man and lion-tamer whose circus was on the road in South Africa through the first half of the 20th century. He made his reputation as a youth in fairgrounds in Tasmania and Queensland and later performed in FITZGERALDS' CIRCUS. In South Africa, where he changed his forename to William after the First World War, he frequently employed Australians, like Kiddo and other members of the Balcombe family and the Warrens, and he imported acts like the Seven Martinettis, the Pedrinis, the Locanas, and Carlisle and Mundy. Sole Brothers' Circus visited in South Africa during an African tour in 1926–29.

W. J. HOLLOWAY and his son W. E. Holloway, who began their careers in Sydney, visited South Africa intermittently with their touring company between 1896 and 1922, in business arrangements with Ben and Frank Wheeler, American managers who had also started in Australia.

The South African War broke out in October 1899 and *A Tale of the Transvaal* by Edwin Lewis Scott opened in Sydney on 23 December. Alfred Dampier resurrected *Jess* as *Briton and Boer* in Melbourne on 1 January 1900. After the war, when the lights went up in His Majesty's Theatre, Johannesburg, on 11 July 1903, it was to *Djin Djin the Japanese Bogie Man*, a spectacular pantomime by Bert Royle and J. C. Williamson, performed by the Royal Australian Opera Company. This was a name adopted for the tour by the Pollard Opera Company, which had toured South Africa during the war in its original form as Pollard's Liliputian Opera Company, the most famous of Australia's CHILD COMPANIES. The Royal Australian Opera Company was followed a few months later by Hall's Australian Juveniles with the operetta *Rip Van Winkle*. In 1912 'thirty little people' arrived from Australia in the form of BEAUMONT SMITH's Tiny Town—a midget circus, including diminutive horses. On their heels came the Payne Steel Bellringers. This Australian troupe left behind Dorothy Gard'ner, who became an influential speech teacher and founded Children's Theatre in English.

Among innumerable Australian visitors to the South African stage were the rising operetta stars MARIE BREMNER and GLADYS MONCRIEFF, in J. C. Williamson's companies. An Australian millionaire impresario, Rufe Naylor bought out the Firm in South Africa and with I. W. Schlesinger founded the African Theatres entertainment monopoly by 1920. During that year African Theatres' social magazine, *LSD*, was edited by Stephen Black, the first South African-born actor–manager and playwright. His issues of *LSD* show that Australian theatrical news was well syndicated and familiar. One of Black's collaborators in the theatre was CECIL KELLAWAY, who emigrated to Australia in 1918 and became a stage star before moving to Hollywood. In 1935 the Young Australian League presented *Around the World* throughout the country and returned to Johannesburg with a revue called *Us Fellers*. The persistence of such child companies seems to indicate that they were well received and financially successful.

When Ray Lawler's SUMMER OF THE SEVENTEENTH DOLL became an international hit, it was presented in Cape Town by a local cast, Leonard Schach's Cockpit Players. This production contributed directly to the development of a local style. From the 1970s, however, entrenchment of apartheid in South Africa and an ensuing cultural boycott resulted in severance of most Australian–South African theatrical links. The dramatist Athol Fugard always seemed to be exempt from boycott in Australia, probably because of his stand against apartheid. As KATHARINE BRISBANE, commenting on his *Hello and Goodbye*, wrote in the *Australian* on 8 February 1974, Fugard's work does 'reverberate as all fine writing does', despite local specificities.

Perhaps the most influential of all Fugard's works have been *Sizwe Bansi is Dead* and *The Island*. Fugard's own productions, performed by John Kani and Winston Ntshona, who created the plays with him in 1973, were seen in Australia from March to May 1976 and won the Melbourne Critics' Award that year. Other Fugard plays produced in Australia have been: *The Blood Knot* (1961) with the Aboriginal actor Jack Charles in Melbourne in October 1970; *Boesman and Lena* (1969) in March 1976; *Statements after an Arrest under the Immorality Act* (1972) in July 1979; and *A Lesson from Aloes* (1978) in July 1981; '*Master Harold*' ... *and the Boys* (1982) in November 1982; and *The Road to Mecca* (1984) in 1990. Several of these productions were originated by the expatriates Olive Bodill and Anthony Wheeler.

South African exiles in New York devised and performed a musical dealing with the Soweto uprising, *Poppie Nongena*. In 1983 the original cast toured Australia successfully in the show, which had been developed by Market Theatre in Johannesburg. The company has since exported similar productions. The satirist Pieter-Dirk Uys presented his solo show *Skating on Thin Uys* in the Festival of Sydney in 1987. He launched some 20 characters from his alternative cabaret, figures that shamed and provoked South Africa during the darkest days of the old regime.

In 1987 venues were desegregated and an Australian play again appeared on the South African stage—ROBERT HEWETT's *Gulls*. It achieved a record run throughout the country, but Kenneth Ross's play *Breaker Morant* was not well received when it was produced in Durban in September 1987. It was regarded as Australian xenophobia for the British and the Boers, and the Bushveld Carbineers were seen as serial killers rather than wronged heroes. South Africans have become familiar with Australian feature films and television programs, but stage shows are nearly unknown. No David Williamson play has yet been staged in South Africa. Doors are opening, however. The Black Swan Theatre Company of Perth has been negotiating a reciprocal deal in South Africa, and other Australian companies are expected to follow. *Stephen Gray*

further reading
BIRKBY, CAREL. *The Pagel Story*. Cape Town (South Africa): Hodder and Stoughton 1948.

MUNRO, MARGARET. The fertility of despair—Fugard's bitter aloes. *Meanjin* 40/4 (December 1981, Melbourne).
RACSTER, OLGA. *Curtain Up!—The story of Cape Theatre*. Cape Town: Juta 1951.
WALKER, SHIRLEY. A man never knows his luck in South Africa. *English in Africa* 12/2 (Grahamstown, October 1985).

South Australian provincial towns

In South Australia more than a million people—half the population—live outside Adelaide. They contribute to the 3·5 million annual attendances at arts events. as 'importers' of culture, as exponents of the arts, and as participants in celebrations like the Copper, Cornish, Bushing, Schützenfest Barossa Music and Tunarama Festivals, which sustain a sense of place and community. The demography, culture and economy of South Australia have been shaped by mining, fishing, agriculture, viticulture, railway and river settlements and major decentralised industrial regions in the southeast and mid-north. Copper was discovered in the mid-north in 1843, and mining towns grew until Burra was briefly more populous than ADELAIDE. Like the GOLDFIELDS in Victoria a decade later, the copper towns attracted travelling players. By the late 1840s Adelaide entrepreneurs like GEORGE COPPIN and JOHN LAZAR were staging farces, melodrama, potted Shakespeare and opera in Burra and other mid-north towns. Settlers strove to augment or outshine the occasional offerings of itinerants and city managements. In the southeast town of Naracoorte, for example, the concert and dramatic club gave its first performance in 1841. It was 'far above the mediocrity of most of our entertainments', a local report said.

Opening of railways at the end of the 19th century allowed Adelaide's leading amateurs, as well as professionals, to make whistle-stop tours as far afield as Broken Hill (NSW). Country people welcomed their visits but seasonal work often made made it difficult for an audience to gather. A mixture of topical song and story, and classical and popular plays was appreciated.

In the last half-century at least five major attempts have been made to alleviate cultural isolation in South Australian provincial communities. The first came with the establishment of the Arts Council of South Australia in 1948. Groups of volunteers endeavoured to secure touring entertainments of quality and to encourage local communities to attend concerts, performances and exhibitions. The state was divided into zones and more than 40 branches were established to facilitate or support the flow of arts—usually from city to country. The council received state and federal government assistance, gained a professional administrative wing, and disbursed over $7 million to the arts over 30 years. In that time it managed visiting-artist and artist-in-residence schemes and established a local presenters' fund in response to a falling demand for small-scale touring in the 1980s. From 1986 this scheme has proved to be the most effective form of subsidy to regional arts. In essence communities take entrepreneurial responsibility for productions of their choice—a change from reactive or passive association and service to partnership. A $40 000 fund guaranteed these ventures against loss of up to $1000, but many branches and groups have learned to assess their market and avoid both loss and debt. In 1987 the council ceased to function as a professional administration but it remains a residual grassroots organisation. The advent of the Arts Council coincided with growth in the AMATEUR THEATRE movement, reflecting the cultural habits and aspirations of settler families and of postwar British and European immigrants who came to work in the mills, foundries and fisheries. In some areas, notably southern Eyre Peninsula, the northern 'iron triangle' and the southeastern 'green triangle', companies of note and strength were established, such as Port Lincoln Players in 1952, the Whyalla Players in 1957 and the Mount Gambier Theatre Group in 1953. Most small towns have at some time boasted a company. Their fare has been situation comedy, melodrama, musical revue, a smattering of classics and, in recent times, popular Australian plays. Many have participated in play competitions and festivals in provincial centres and across the border in Broken Hill.

Yet amateur theatre has been accessible to only some of the people. Organisations have often been closed by nature or circumstance and their halls and auditoria have not been welcoming in appointments or amenities. So between 1977 and 1987 the state government established five cultural trusts—in the southeast in 1977, on Eyre Peninsula in 1978, for the northern region in 1978, in the Riverland in 1980 and in the central region, beyond greater Adelaide, in 1987.

With each trust came a modern theatre, established under the 1976 Theatres Act and modelled on the Playhouse at the ADELAIDE FESTIVAL CENTRE. The facilities for a major touring circuit therefore exist at Mount Gambier, Whyalla, Port Pirie, Renmark and in the southern Adelaide suburb of Noarlunga. In 1988 the government formed the South Australian Regional Cultural Council to coordinate the activities of the trusts and promote the arts throughout the state. Each centre has a professional staff of administrators, technicians and arts development officers. The aim was to encourage local, state and international companies to tour regularly and easily.

Touring by such companies had virtually ceased by 1983, but these new arrangements, along with Foundation South Australia and private support and an infusion of state government touring subsidy in 1990 saw productions from the State Theatre Company of South Australia, the Australian Dance Theatre, the State Opera and the ADELAIDE FESTIVAL OF ARTS visit provincial centres. In early 1993 the 'streamlined' South Australian Country Arts Trust replaced the Regional Cultural Council by the promotional objectives remained the same. Each trust is encouraged and subsidised through the Country Arts and Entertainment Touring Scheme to have some voice in the volume, timing, cost and coordination of programming. This, it is hoped, will encourage local entrepreneurial activity and a move toward self-sufficiency. Ticket prices in excess of $20, film screenings and hiring charges have already generated development funds for some centres.

Two provincial professional theatre companies have served country districts to the north and west and south and east of Adelaide. The HARVEST THEATRE COMPANY began in 1980 as multi-skilled community-theatre company in Port Lincoln and then moved to Whyalla. Through its policy of blending classic productions and 'star' performers with access programs and professional–amateur activity, it extended its reputation across five states. It closed in 1991

and has not been replaced. The MAINSTREET THEATRE COMPANY, formed in 1985, has retained community status and work practices. It produces original work based on issues pertinent but not exclusive to the people of the southeast. Mainstreet is available to a wide range of groups in its region. Its home base is Naracoorte but it tours throughout the state, occasionally visiting Adelaide, and into Victoria.

Regional identity and mobility are key concepts. This is evident in youth theatre. The Riverland Youth Theatre, formed in 1985 at Renmark, has a professional director. It provides the provinces with another model for development and complements the work of Adelaide companies like UNLEY YOUTH THEATRE, Cirkidz and the MAGPIE THEATRE COMPANY, which travels annually to remote settlements and missions like Cook and Ernabella. *Gus Worby*

further reading
MCCREDIE, ANDREW D. (ed.). *From Colonel Light into the Footlights—The performing arts in South Australia from 1836 to the present.* Adelaide: Pagel 1988.

South Polar Expedition
—or, *The Discoveries of Captains Ross and Crozier*. Melodrama in two acts. **premiere** 3 May 1841, Royal Victoria Theatre, Hobart.

In the first half of the 19th century, when plays—particularly with local themes—were rarely written in Australia, *South Polar Expedition* was perhaps unique in its topicality. A lessee of the Royal Victoria Theatre in Hobart wrote it to capitalise on current interest in the Antarctic, according to newspapers. It was being rehearsed within one week of the warmly welcomed return to Hobart of the British Antarctic expedition of Captain James Ross and Commander Francis Crozier, which had discovered the Ross Ice Shelf. Its members had become popular when they spent three months in the town setting up the Rossbank Magnetic Observatory in 1840. Advertisements for the production emphasised authenticity of the Antarctic scenery, which was based on sketches made by officers of the expedition.

The play began with the departure of the expedition from Hobart and Governor Sir John Franklin and Lady Franklin bidding farewell to their close friend Captain Ross at Government House. The expedition stopped at Auckland (New Zealand), where Corporal Prim, the antihero, had several adventures. Act 2, set in the Antarctic, related the men's experiences and closed with Science, Fame and Britannia paying tribute to Ross's success in an allegorical tableau. The play opened to a full and responsive audience of all classes. Critical comment agreed that the captains and the Franklins had been portrayed with suitable dignity, but controversy raged around a fictitious character. It was claimed that Corporal Prim brought the navy into disrepute. A second performance two days later completed the life of the play, no copy of which is known to exist. Sir John Franklin died on an Arctic expedition in search of the Northwest Passage in 1845. *Gillian Winter*

further reading
MILLER, E. MORRIS. *Pressmen and Governors*. Sydney University Press 1973.
WINTER, GILLIAN. 'Tasmania hails you as her favour'd guest'— The British Antarctic expedition in Hobart 1840–41. Tasmanian Historical Research Association *Papers and Proceedings* 38 (1991).

F. M. Soutten

Dramatist. Born c.1834. Worked as journalist in Melbourne. Wrote for stage 1852–54. Died 4 January 1856, drowned in Murray River on journey to Sydney.

One of Melbourne's earliest stage writers, Frank Soutten made a promising start by providing eight farces and vaudevilles, or musical sketches, mostly for Sydney Nelson's family. He also wrote a topical farce, *The Battle of Melbourne*, in collaboration with W. M. AKHURST. His accidental death may have cut short a prolific career. He came of a theatrical family. The playwright Morris Barnett, author of the popular farce *The Serious Family*, was his uncle. ❦*Veronica Kelly*

Spare Parts Puppet Theatre Company

Professional puppet theatre company in Fremantle (WA), founded in January 1981 by Beverley Campbell Jackson, Cathryn Robinson and L. Peter Wilson. **first production** *Faust by Cathryn Robinson 1981. Designer: Beverley Campbell Jackson. Director: L. Peter Wilson.* **venue** *1988– former Fremantle Art Gallery.*

Spare Parts Puppet Theatre has become a leading subsidised company, with a permanent home in Fremantle. Most of its shows are for children and tour widely in Western Australia. Its style is often reminiscent of eastern European ensembles, with puppeteers as visible performers. It has forged strong links with some overseas puppeteers. Spare Parts aims to create an average of three new shows a year as well as remounting productions. In its first project, *Faust* for the 1981 FESTIVAL OF PERTH the company used students of the West Australian Institute of Technology as puppeteers and had two guest puppeteers from Japan, Takeshi Hoshino and Noriko Nishimoto. The latter returned in 1982 and she has become an associate director of the company, writing, directing, performing, and conducting workshops in the eastern states.

Early productions include *Il mondo marionetta* (1981), which was played at the international festival of puppetry in Adelaide in 1983; *Kullener—The Story of the Tasmanian Tiger* (1983) by John Lonie, which became *Wanted—Dead or Alive* in 1985. In 1985 the company devised and L. PETER WILSON directed *Play a Tune For Me*, in which puppets audition for a puppeteer. Wilson's production of *The Pied Piper* toured successfully in the eastern states in 1987 and played in children's festivals in North America in 1988. In the latter year the company opened its Fremantle theatre in March and hosted the Oz Puppet Festival in April. Guest directors have included Josef Krofta of the Drak puppet theatre of Hradec Králové (Czech Republic), who came with the designer Petr Matasek to mount *Kalevala* in 1985, and Eric Bass from the USA in 1988. In 1991 Matasek designed *Carmen*, one of three shows devised and directed by Noriko Nishimoto for the Festival of Perth. The others were *Eros*, which explored erotic themes in 1986, and *Kaguyahime*, based on a Japanese creation myth, in 1988.

In 1989 Wilson and Nishimoto visited Drak Theatre to co-direct a version of Hans Christian Andersen's *The Emperor's Nightingale* that Drak wanted set in Japan. Later in the year they recreated the show for Spare Parts, using carved wooden puppet heads from Drak and designs by Matasek. Also in 1989, with the help of a puppet master and a puppetmaker from China, the company created *The Monkey King*. This was bigger than the company's usual shows and has been performed only in the Spare Parts Theatre. Takeshi Hoshino returned in 1991 to design *Sing a Rainbow*, written and directed by Nishimoto. This production went to China in 1992 and toured Japan in 1993. Spare Parts has also involved artists from outside puppetry. In 1990, for example, the dancer Chrissie Parrott directed JACK DAVIS's *Rainmaker* for a puppeteer and four other performers. The Ghana-born actor Dorinda Hafner appeared in *Africa—Tales from a drum* and manipulated some of the puppets, which had been made by Jan Novak, a Czech artist-in-residence. ❦*Richard Bradshaw*

further reading
VELLA, MAEVE and HELEN RICKARDS. *Theatre of the Impossible—Puppet theatre in Australia*. Sydney: Craftsman House 1989.

Steve J. Spears

Actor, dramatist, musician. Born 21 January 1951 in Adelaide. Early experience at University of Adelaide in Footlights and Law Revues. Had first professional production 1973. National Critics' Award and two Awgie awards 1977 for The Elocution of Benjamin Franklin. *New York off-Broadway Obie award for year's best play 1979 for* The Elocution of Benjamin Franklin. *Has written for television and acted in films.*

Steve Spears achieved remarkably early success in 1976 with his one-man play THE ELOCUTION OF BENJAMIN FRANKLIN at the Nimrod Theatre in Sydney. It was the first contemporary play to have its Australian production achieve international success. The Nimrod production came only three years after Spears had his first professional production, *Stud*, which he wrote and directed in Adelaide. His plays are larrikin, largely nostalgic; and demonstrate his concern with the outlook of society's eccentrics and outsiders. ❦*Katharine Brisbane*

published plays
Africa—A savage musical (1974). Melbourne: Outback Press 1978 in *Early Works*.
The Elocution of Benjamin Franklin (1976). Sydney: Currency Press 1977, 1989.
Glory (1987). Melbourne: Yackandandah 1989.
King Richard (1978). Brisbane: University of Queensland Press 1980 as *Richard* in *Three Political Plays*.
Mad Jean (1978). Melbourne: Outback Press 1978 in *Early Works*.
People Keep Giving Me Things (1978). Melbourne: Outback Press 1978 in *Early Works*.
When They Send Me Three and Fourpence (1983). Sydney: Currency Press 1989.
Young Mo (1976). In *Theatre Australia* (Sydney) February and April 1977.

other writings
In Search of the Bodgie. Sydney: Collins 1989. Collection of memoirs.

Bruce Spence

Actor. Born 17 September 1945 in Auckland (New Zealand). Came to Australia 1966. Studied at National Gallery Art School (Melbourne). Member of La Mama Company and Australian Performing Group 1969–80. Since acted with Melbourne Theatre Company and many others. Many film and television roles.

Much of Bruce Spence's distinguished acting career has been in contemporary Australian comedy, partly because of his exceptional height and laconic wit. At the La Mama

Theatre in Melbourne he created the roles of the gormless bridegroom in Jack Hibberd's DIMBOOLA (1969) and the hypochondriac Stork in David Williamson's THE COMING OF STORK (1970), which he played again in the film *Stork*. One of his principal early roles for the Australian Performing Group was Les Harding in the premiere of John Romeril's THE FLOATING WORLD (1974). He repeated this haunting and compelling performance at the National Arts Centre in Ottawa (Canada) in 1979. Other notable roles—all for the MELBOURNE THEATRE COMPANY—have been Puck in *A Midsummer Night's Dream* in 1984, the title-role in Carlo Goldoni's *A Servant of Two Masters* in 1986 and Wally, the gatecrashing pal from the past in Bill Garner's *Sunday Lunch* in 1991. ❦*Geoffrey Milne*

Albert Spencer

Actor. Born 1811. Trained as sailor. Arrived in Launceston and joined Samson Cameron's company 1834. Moved to Sydney June 1836. Performed at Theatre Royal and Royal Victoria Theatre. Left for England as sailor 1838. Returned to Sydney February 1840. In India 1844–46. Acted at Royal Victoria Theatre, Sydney, 1846–54. Died 1854 in Sydney.

Albert Spencer was one of the first to perform many leading Shakespearean roles in Australia. Receptions of his acting ranged from adulation to castigation. According to F. C. Brewer, 'Spencer somewhat resembled Edmund Kean in person' and 'imitated, but at a considerable distance' his Richard III. He was probably a useful actor who had aspirations beyond his capabilities, for he apparently had no formal theatrical training. He sometimes gave way to drunkenness, a prevailing vice of early Australian actors.

He arrived in Launceston as a sailor and joined SAMSON CAMERON's company. Like many actors of the time, he probably benefited from acting with CORDELIA CAMERON. His early roles included Bassanio in *The Merchant of Venice* and the Baron in Friedrich von Kotzebue's *The Stranger*. The *Launceston Advertiser* of 12 June 1834 praised his Baron but thought 'he somewhat overacted for the size of the theatre'. His Othello, however, caused the *Independent* of 23 July 1834 to 'despair of being able to do anything like adequate justice to the merits of this young man. His "Othello" will never be surpassed in this island.' In October 1834 Spencer appeared in Hobart, and played the lead in *The Stranger* for his benefit on 5 November.

In the Theatre Royal company in Sydney Spencer mainly played second leads to CONRAD KNOWLES. His benefit roles show his aspirations—Richard III on 20 March 1837 and Hamlet on 18 September 1837. He played Iago to Gustavus Arabin's Othello at the opening of the ROYAL VICTORIA THEATRE on 26 March 1838 and King Lear for his benefit on 28 August. During 1838 the *Sydney Gazette* frequently complained about Spencer being drunk on stage, but the *Sydney Herald* of 21 June was complimentary about his lead role in *The Peregrinations of Pickwick*.

Towards the end of 1838 Spencer left for England, returning to his former occupation as a sailor, but he came back to Sydney in February 1840. In 1844 he sailed for India in charge of a cargo of horses and while at Calcutta played Shylock at the Sans Souci Theatre. By February 1846 he was back in Sydney, playing Hamlet at the Royal Victoria Theatre. ❦*Elizabeth Webby*

A Spring Song

Drama in six scenes by Ray Mathew. **premiere** March 1958, Brisbane, by Twelfth Night Theatre. Cast: Carmen Caesar, Win Colvin, Gordon Davies, Ron Finney, Shirley Head, Rodney Jenkins, Wendy Sanders. **revived** 21 April 1983, by Griffin Theatre Company (Sydney) with Michael Bate, Terry Brady, Robyn Gurney, Ron Hackett, Liz Horne, Christine James and Barbara Phillips; designed by Anny Evanson; directed by Peter Kingston. **published** Brisbane: University of Queensland Press 1961. Sydney: Currency Press 1985.

In a production note RAY MATHEW warns of the danger of playing *A Spring Song* as soap opera. It is a delicate piece, only superficially naturalistic, about moments caught between the burgeoning of spring and young love, and the onset of summer with death at the end of it. Peter, a poet and schoolteacher boards with the Dennisons, a farming family. He meets all three daughters and falls in love with Margaret, who is dying. When Dennison tries to prevent his youngest daughter, Kerry, from going out with the local squatter's son she tells him of Margaret's fatal illness and he collapses with a heart attack. Peter decides to resign from teaching and stay on in the house to write.

A Spring Song received a production at the Edinburgh Festival in 1964 and in London at the Mermaid Theatre, directed by Michael Rudman. ❦*Ron Blair*

The Squatter's Daughter

—or, *The Land of the Wattle*. Play in four acts by Bert Bailey and Edmund Duggan. **premiere** 9 February 1907, Theatre Royal, Melbourne. Cast: Bert Bailey, Lillie Bryer, George Cross, Eugenie Duggan, Laurence Dunbar, Ada Guildford, Lena Langridge, L. Lawrence, George McKenzie, J. H. Nunn.

BERT BAILEY and EDMUND DUGGAN's 1907 smash hit was a 'really first class' piece 'crammed with local colour', according to the Melbourne *Age* on 11 February but 'a preposterous piece of fiction … a typical modern English bellowdrama Australianised' in the view of the Sydney *Bulletin* on 14 February. All critics agreed, however, that WILLIAM ANDERSON had staged the melodrama with lavish expense and several realistic sensations. The Melbourne premiere was followed by a near-record Sydney season and *The Squatter's Daughter* became the longest-running Australian play of its day.

It is full of aggressive Australian nationalism. It has one of the earliest 'whingeing Poms' in Miss Virginia Spriggins, governess and chaperone to Violet Enderby, the squatter's daughter. 'Oh why did I ever come to Australia' is Miss Spriggins's catch-phrase. She objects to 'that horrible Australian slang' and to 'mosquitos, flies, kangaroos, and wild sheep'. A more welcome immigrant is a Scottish new chum, Archie McPherson. Set against these characters are a family of aristocratic squatters, a shearing match between the champions of NSW and Victoria, an Aboriginal wedding, a whip-cracking exhibition, villainous bushrangers who tie the hero to a balancing rock and attempt to pack-rape the heroine. Anderson provided all the sound effects and symbols of rural Australia that money could buy, including real kookaburras and a waterfall and lake.

The play celebrates young Australia. Violet, who was played by EUGENIE DUGGAN, is a spirited heroine who chases kangaroos on horseback. She rebukes the complaining Miss Spriggins: 'You're like a good many more, you leave your own country, to try and better yourself and then spend your time in running down the country that keeps you. If it wasn't for Australia, such people as you would be working for five bob a week in "dear old England" …'.

Violet's lover, Tom Bathurst, is discovered at the end of the play to be the long-lost son of the old squatter James Harrington, but long before this his nobility and Australian sense of fair play have shone through his poverty. He prevents the villain from beating an Aboriginal stockman and, when captured by the bushranger Ben Hall, he invites him to 'Fight me like a man with your bare hands … You d—— bushrangers are all alike. Armed to the teeth and travel in mobs like dingoes. You rob and terrorise defenceless men and women, but none of you are game enough to travel single handed or tackle a man with nature's weapons.'

In spite of its popular appeal *The Squatter's Daughter* is full of middle-class moralising, as when Harrington insists on paying his shearers in cash: 'I consider it a disgrace to civilisation that these men are tempted to hand their cheques over a bar counter and are plundered and fleeced of their hard-earned wages by a gang of unprincipled shanty keepers'. Later a shearer leaves the hotel after 'only a drink or two', declaring: 'I've got a wife and kids waiting for my money'. There is also a 'fallen woman', Sarah Lynch, who warns Tom that Violet has been kidnapped by the bushrangers and further redeems herself by knocking down the double-dealing publican Skerritt with a hefty punch. She is told at the end of the play: 'Don't go. You have brought us happiness and we'll endeavour to make your future life as happy as our own.'

The secret of the play's success seems to have been a combination of Anderson's lavish staging, brash appeals to nationalist sentiment in newly federated Australia, and Bailey's ability to lighten Duggan's sermons with comic and spectacular scenes and sensations. In 1908 a fight with a boxing kangaroo was added, and other bush eccentricities kept the script fresh enough to allow frequent revivals until about 1914, when the First World War and Bailey's success with ON OUR SELECTION eased it out of the repertoire. Anderson produced a film of the play in 1910, with Bailey (Archie McPherson), Bryer (Virginia Spriggs), Cross (Tom Bathurst) and Nunn (James Harrington) in their original roles and Edmund Duggan as Ben Hall. Bailey directed the film, which no longer exists. ❦*Richard Fotheringham*

reference
Scripts of *The Squatter's Daughter* are held in Canberra in the Australian Archives (CRS A1336/1, item 22) and in the Bert and Tim Bailey Collection (MS6141) at the National Library.

St George's Hall

Theatre in Hay Street, Perth, opened 4 December 1879.

Establishment amateur performers, writers and designers who had produced operettas and short comedies in the ballroom at Government House under the patronage of the Governor of Western Australia, Sir William Robinson, found a new multipurpose venue in St George's Hall. It opened under viceregal patronage with a local production of Dion Boucicault's *The Colleen Bawn*. HENRY PRINSEP, an English painter, amateur performer and writer of polite comedies, painted the sets and the hall's drop-curtain. His title for the latter 'Come unto these yellow sands', recalls Richard Dadd's painting of the same title from *The Tempest*, and may have been a reference to the Perth terrain. Prinsep also designed six iron Corinthian columns for the Howick Street—as Hay Street was then called—gallery of St George's Hall, after the façade of the Lyceum Theatre in London. They were probably the first cast in Western Australia. Touring companies also appeared at St George's Hall, which was built for Messrs Burt and Stone on land they owned. Its façade, including Prinsep's columns, is retained in the present building on the site. ❦*Bill Dunstone*

Alfred St Leon

Circus equestrian. Born 1859 at Beechworth (Vic.). Originally Alfred Jones. Son of John Jones, founder of St Leon's circus. Joined father and brothers Gus and Walter as St Leon Troupe of gymnasts, early 1865. Trained as equestrian in Burton and Taylor's Grand United Circus Company. Married equestrian Vernon Ida Cousins (c.1863–1935) in Melbourne 22 October 1881. Joined father and brothers in St Leon's Royal Victorian Circus 1875. Thereafter toured in Australia, Asia, the Pacific and USA with his own family. Died 24 February 1909, at Rutland (Massachusetts, USA). Father of circus artists Elsie St Leon (1884–1976), George St Leon (c.1890–1955) and Ida St Leon (1894–1961).

Equestrianism became increasingly acrobatic in Australian circus in the 1870s, and Alfred St Leon was one of the first exponents of the somersault style in the colonies. During the late 1870s and early 1880s, an era when fine horses and horsemanship were readily appreciated, Alfred St Leon and his elder brothers Gus and Walter were the star circus equestrians in the colonies. They were often billed as 'Australia's Favourites' in St Leon's Royal Victorian Circus.

In 1881 Alfred St Leon married Vernon Ida Cousins, who rode regularly in BURTON'S CIRCUS as early as 1873. She was the daughter of a clown known professionally as Reuben Cousins and his wife, a superlative equestrian who called herself Mme La Rosiere. Alfred and Ida St Leon had six children who survived infancy and they were trained in the circus arts. After travels with Perry's Jubilee Circus in 1893–94 and a brief engagement with Abell and Klaer's circus in 1894, the family left Australia with Harry Wirth's Pacific Circus to tour Asia and the Pacific in 1895–96. Wirth died aboard ship in July 1896 and the company broke up. Many of its members, including the Alfred St Leon family, found employment with Harmston's Circus, which was well known throughout India and east Asia.

The St Leons also toured the same regions with Willison's Great World Circus during 1897–98 and, subsequently visited Honolulu and Vancouver. They arrived in the USA by 1898 and were billed as 'the Australian Wonders' when they made their first American appearance, as an acrobatic troupe. The St Leons were accomplished acrobats, wirewalkers and gymnasts, but principally equestrians. Equestrianism was still highly prized in American circus, though it had lost popularity in Australia. Alfred St Leon and his family enjoyed considerable success in major American circuses until 1914. Their engagements included seasons with the Sells-Forepaugh circus in 1902, 1903 and 1907, the William P. Hall circus in 1905, the Great Wallace Shows in 1906 and the Barnum and Bailey circus in 1914.

The family toured Cuba with the large Pubillones Circus during the winters of 1905–06 and 1906–07. ❦*Mark St Leon*

Philip St Leon

Circus equestrian. Born 1889 in Melbourne. Fifth son of Gus St Leon and grandson of John Jones, founder of St Leon's circus. Travelled with family in Eroni Brothers', Probasco's and FitzGerald Brothers' circuses 1898–1901. Went with family to USA 1901. Ringling Circus 1902–03. Returned to Australia. Wirths' Circus 1905–08. Joined family in Gus St Leon's Great United Circus 1908. Returned to USA in May Wirth's troupe 1917. Changed professional name to Wirth. Jointly ran St Leon Brothers' European Circus in USA 1931. Died 1958 at Meriden (Connecticut, USA).

In Australia Philip St Leon was most renowned for a spectacular equestrian act in which he dressed in wig and feminine costume as 'the Spanish Equestrienne, Senorita Philipina'. The impersonation was so perfectly presented that few suspected the disguise. A correspondent wrote in the Hobart *Mercury* on 28 January 1908 that Philipina 'in the hurricane hurdle act and somersault act marked herself as a rider of exceptional grace and perfect skill'. Philip St Leon presumably began his equestrian training when he travelled with his family in the Eroni Brothers', Probasco's and FitzGerald Brothers' Circuses in 1898–1901. Gus St Leon took Philip and his older brothers Cassimer, Sylvester and Reginald and sister Daisy to the USA in 1901. The family appeared as musical clowns, riders and acrobats in the 1902 and 1903 seasons of the Ringling Circus. In late 1904 or early 1905 Philip St Leon and his father alone returned to Australia. They were engaged for the Sydney Easter season of WIRTHS' CIRCUS in 1905 and they toured Australia and New Zealand with this large circus in 1906–08. During this period, Philip developed his equestrian ability in earnest under his father's tutelage and gained renown as Philipina. After the Wirth engagement, Philip and his father toured Western Australia and the south coast of NSW with Walter St Leon's circus for a short time. Then they rejoined the rest of their family, who had returned from the USA late in 1908, in Gus St Leon's Great United Circus. In this new circus Philip displayed his equestrian talents especially as Senorita Philipina.

In 1915–16 MAY WIRTH and her troupe of riders toured Australia and New Zealand. Philip St Leon was asked to join the troupe for its return to the USA on the Ringling Circus program in the 1917 season. He was presented as a comedy rider with the troupe, apparently to parallel the riding of 'Poodles' Hanneford, who appeared with his troupe in the same season for the Barnum and Bailey Circus, the major Ringling company. Philip St Leon assumed the name of Wirth for professional purposes. In New York City in December 1917 he married Stella, a daughter of Marizles Wirth Martin, adoptive mother of May Wirth and a sister of the founders of WIRTHS' CIRCUS.

Philip St Leon made his career largely in the USA, although he returned briefly to Australia several times during the 1920s and 1930s. From 1919, he received equal billing with May Wirth in her troupe's publicity, usually as 'Philo'. The two remained professionally associated until late 1937. With May Wirth's husband, Frank White Wirth, Philip St Leon was instrumental in operating the St Leon Brothers' European Circus in the New England states in 1931. A one-ring circus in the classic European format, this was the only circus conducted under the St Leon name in the USA. During the 1930s Philip St Leon was in the booking-agency business. From 1945 until his death in 1958 he was equestrian director of Hunt Brothers' Circus and his wife played the organ in the circus band. ❦*Mark St Leon*

further reading
ST LEON, MARK. *Spangles and Sawdust*. Melbourne: Greenhouse 1983.

St Leon family circuses

In the 1870s and 1880s the famous St Leon circus paraded through outback townships, the cavalcade of wagons headed by a glittering band carriage. Its tours in the eastern colonies of Australia often took it far beyond the reach of the railway and it journeyed across the seas to Tasmania, New Zealand and possibly New Caledonia.

The name St Leon emerged on 27 January 1865, when four gymnasts billed as the St Leon Troupe opened in their 'celebrated drawing room entertainment' at the Theatre Royal in Melbourne for the actor-manager BARRY SULLIVAN. It was probably at his suggestion that the quartet—John Jones and his three sons—took the pseudonym of St Leon. They and several succeeding generations carried that name —which eventually became accepted as the family name— to circuses, theatres and vaudeville stages on several continents during the next 100 years.

John Jones himself became known as Mathew St Leon. He was an English circus artist whose Australian career began in Robert Radford's Royal Circus in Launceston (Tas.) late in 1847. He appears to have been born in London about 1827 and he died on 14 April 1903 in Melbourne. Orphaned at an early age, he was apparently raised by an elder brother and sister in the Westminster district, within walking distance of Astley's Amphitheatre, where modern circus began. When he was convicted for petty theft in 1842, Jones gave his occupation as 'tumbler' at a place of amusement called the Westminster Theatre. No such theatre is known to have existed at that time, but Jones could been referring loosely to Astley's Amphitheatre, which was in Westminster Bridge Road. A Mr J. Jones appeared at Astley's as principal dancer on the evening of 20 June 1841, and it was as a dancer that John Jones made his appearances at Radford's Royal Circus late in 1847 and early in 1848. It is feasible that they were the same man, especially as dancing is a foundation discipline of the circus arts, particularly equestrianism.

Robert Radford was an expert horseman and Jones began serious riding practice under his guidance. On 23 August 1848 he made his first appearance as an equestrian in Radford's company in *The Arab*. He made his Sydney debut in a traditional equestrian piece, *The Peasant's Frolic*, at the Royal Australian Equestrian Circus on 13 October 1850, claiming to be 'late of the celebrated Ducrow's Royal Amphitheatre, London. Astley's Amphitheatre was known as Ducrow's while the celebrated equestrian Andrew Ducrow was its lessee, from late 1824 until June 1841. After these appearances in Launceston and Sydney, Jones—now an accomplished equestrian, acrobat and tightrope walker —formed his own circus. The *Sydney Morning Herald* on 24 November 1851 reported from the Turon River goldfields in NSW that 'Mr Jones, the equestrian, is building a circus on the flat opposite the junction at Oakey Creek ... The locality is well chosen and the speculation is likely to prove remunerative'. In June 1856 Jones toured the Illawarra district of NSW with JAMES HENRY ASHTON's circus. Jones was active as a showman under his own name on the goldfields and elsewhere in NSW and Victoria until at least 1863, when he took his British-American Circus to Tasmania. His troupe included Billy Banham, a British black tightrope walker who toured the colonies under the name of his more famous uncle Pablo Fanque, in 1858; the Wirth family of musicians in 1858; J. H. Flexmore, a celebrated clown, in 1863.

In the late 1860s Jones toured Australia with his three sons as the St Leon Troupe, presenting entertainments in theatres in cities and large country towns and in hotels and public halls in bush townships. These sons were among eight children born to Jones and an Irishwoman he married in Hobart in December 1848. Augustus (c.1851–1923), known as Gus, Walter (c.1856–1943) and Alfred (1859–1909) all later pursued careers in the circus. In the little St Leon Troupe they became accomplished in gymnastics, trapeze, rolling globe, dancing, singing comic songs, blackface comedy, and ropewalking. Sometimes the St Leons were complemented by other performers such as George Loyal, a gymnast; Robert Taylor, a juggler and rolling-globe performer; and Flexmore the clown. As with another itinerant company active at the time, the Foley Troupe, the juvenile portion of the entertainment was the best received.

Several years' travelling and performing in the St Leon Troupe sharpened the sons' performing abilities in all but the essential circus art of equestrianism. All three therefore took apprenticeships with leading circuses during the early 1870s. Gus had joined Bird and Taylor's Great American Circus by late 1872. During 1873–75 all three brothers appeared in Burton and Taylor's Grand United Circus.

In late April 1875 Alfred and Walter St Leon left Burton and Taylor's circus on the road at Kyneton (Vic.) and joined their father to form St Leon's Royal Victoria Circus. Their brother Gus joined them later. To establish its reputation the new circus toured extensively through Victoria, NSW and Queensland during 1875–76. By 1878 the St Leon circus rivalled BURTON'S CIRCUS in popularity and it became Australia's leading circus. By 1885, the St Leon circus had grown so large that it was reorganised into two separate troupes. The larger, which included a menagerie, began a yearlong tour of New Zealand in Auckland in October 1885. The family came together again in a single circus in 1891 but it was not the large company of earlier years.

The family circus gradually broke up during the 1890s. Gus St Leon and his family, after a period at Tamworth (NSW) in 1896–98, had engagements with the circuses of the Eroni Brothers, the American showman Ellsworth Probasco and the FitzGerald Brothers in 1898–1901. Then Gus St Leon and his daughter Daisy and sons Cassimer, Sylvester, Reginald and Philip left Australia for the USA, where they spent the 1902 and 1903 seasons with the large Ringling Brothers circus as musical clowns, riders and acrobats. In late 1904 or early 1905, Gus and PHILIP ST LEON alone returned to Australia. They toured Australia and New Zealand with WIRTHS' CIRCUS in 1906–08. Walter St Leon and his family toured New Zealand, NSW and Victoria with Probasco's popular circus during 1896–99 before settling at Bega (NSW) for several years to allow the children some education. ALFRED ST LEON and his family left Australia in 1895, arrived in the USA by 1898 and appeared with many major American circuses until 1914.

The Walter St Leon family resumed circus activities in 1902 in FITZGERALD BROTHERS' CIRCUS, toured Queensland with its own circus in 1904–05 and partnered the James Ashton family in a combined circus in 1906–07. In its own circus again in September and October 1912, the Walter St Leon family made an eventful tour along the Darling River, during which the steamer conveying the properties sank. The family then settled at Wentworth (NSW), although several members continued to travel with other circuses.

By late 1908 the rest of the Gus St Leon family had returned from the USA, and in May 1909 Gus St Leon's Great United Circus was formed. This company achieved an excellent standard of production, with some distinguished performers, including Philip St Leon, the Five St Leons as acrobats, the gymnasts Honey and Cherry and a fine brass band that at times comprised as many as 14 musicians. After the circus toured New Zealand in 1920–21, there was a partial break-up of the family. Some carried on with a circus under the St Leon name until 1941, but its size and status suffered particularly severely from the Great Depression.

Gus St Leon's daughter Daisy married the American gymnast Alfred Honey and they produced another family of fine circus artists known as THE HONEYS. After the Second World War, the Five Riding St Leons, grandchildren of Gus St Leon, were a star equestrian act with Wirths' Circus. In 1959 some of the troupe tried without success to revive a circus under the family name. Dimpi St Leon, another granddaughter of Gus St Leon, was a spectacular trapeze artist with Sole Brothers' Circus in the postwar years. The last member of the family in Australian circus life was Norman, a son of Walter St Leon, who retired as advance manager of BULLEN BROTHERS' CIRCUS shortly before his death in Sydney in 1963.

Norman's younger brother, Clyde St Leon, who went to the USA with the Honeys, formed a teeterboard act called the St Leon Troupe with his two sons and several other artists in 1945. It held the important centre ring for Ringling Brothers and Barnum and Bailey's Combined Circus in 1960. *Mark St Leon*

further reading
ST LEON, MARK. *Spangles and Sawdust*. Melbourne: Greenhouse 1983.
Australia's premier circus family. *Theatre* (Sydney) 1 February 1909.

St Martin's Theatre Company

Professional dramatic company in Melbourne, founded in 1931 as semiprofessional Little Theatre Laboratory of Dramatic Art by Hal Percy and Brett Randall. Renamed Melbourne Little Theatre Company 1934. Fully professional as St Martin's Theatre Company 1962. **venues** 1932–34 Kiosk Theatre, Fawkner Park. 1934 St Chad's Church, South Yarra. 1956–73 Little Theatre (renamed St Martin's Theatre 1962). **artistic director** Irene Mitchell 1956–73. **first production** *The Fanatics* by Miles Malleson, 2 December 1931, Central Hall, Melbourne. **last production** *Cowardy Custard* 1973.

Countless actors, directors, playwrights and designers left the Melbourne Little Theatre Company, the forerunner of the St Martin's Theatre Company, with the experience to make successful careers overseas and in Australia. In the postwar Melbourne there was nowhere else for people such as the actor ZOË CALDWELL and the designer JOHN TRUSCOTT to learn their craft. BRETT RANDALL and Hal Percy, both actors, established the Little Theatre Laboratory of Dramatic Art to revive theatrical activity in 1931, when the Great Depression was forcing theatres to close. They promised to devote their time and energy to the little-theatre movement and to present entertaining plays of literary value cast from the best amateur and professional talent available. They would also encourage production of Australian plays. After the opening of The Fanatics on 2 December 1931 the Melbourne Age said: 'If their first production at the Central Hall last evening is a foretaste of things to come the semiprofessional enterprise of the Melbourne Little Theatre Company should be a very interesting addition to those organisations earnestly striving to revive stage drama in this community'.

In early 1932 the company set up a temporary stage in a kiosk in Fawkner Park, South Yarra. Beginning with The Rescue Party by Phyllis Morris, it staged a production every month for three nights and introduced play readings every Sunday. The annual subscription was five shillings and admission to all performances cost two shillings and sixpence. After six months, the company had given six Australian premieres and produced four plays by Australian writers. A season of one-act Australian plays in June 1932 drew an enthusiastic response. The Age hoped 'the public will give a full measure of support to this experiment of the Little Theatre, and so give encouragement to the undoubted playwriting talent we have in our midst'.

The Melbourne Little Theatre School of the Stage was also launched in early 1932, under the direction of Randall, his wife Eve Dawnay, and Percy. In 1933 the school and the Sunday readings were conducted in the foyer of the fire-damaged His Majesty's Theatre. Percy, finding the income insufficient to support his family, sold out and took up radio work in 1933. The company, needing larger premises, converted the disused St Chad's Church in South Yarra into the 115-seat Little Theatre. It opened in early 1934 with Georg Kaiser's expressionist drama From Morning to Midnight, which had 25 performers and seven scene changes on a stage measuring only 4.6 by 3.6 metres. There was neither space to fly scenery nor backstage facilities. Yet the company staged nearly 200 productions there in the next 20 years. It produced three-week seasons of eight plays a year and subscribers increased from 300 to 1500, with a waiting list of more than 1000.

Randall directed most of the productions during the 1930s and in 1936 the company's popularity brought him an invitation to stage a season at the Garrick Theatre. J. M. Barrie's Mary Rose was the great success. The year ended with a season at the Princess Theatre which included Clifford Odets's Paradise Lost, Ivor Novello's Full House, Lillian Hellman's The Children's Hour and Zoë Akins's The Greeks Had a Word for It. Debate ensued in the letters pages of newspapers and the Argus observed in February 1937: 'In a season of modern plays ... it would appear that Mr Brett Randall, the producer, is endeavouring to stir Melbourne playgoers with rather too much severity ... But Mr Randall can be criticised for his choice of plays alone: it is not easy to find fault with his production'.

During the Second World War, when the blackout discouraged theatregoing, Brett Randall worked hard to build up a constituency for Melbourne Little Theatre. He is claimed to have had the only legitimate theatre in continuous production in Australia during the war. Of particular note was the 1945 production of Clare Boothe's The Women by IRENE MITCHELL, an actor who had been in the cast of the company's first play. During the war she became stage manager and quickly proved her talent as a director. PETER RANDALL joined the company as associate director with his father and Mitchell in 1945. Peter Randall managed Everyman's Theatre, a subsidiary established in 1948 to tour Victoria for eight months of the year, presenting three plays in every town. The Little Theatre Company was then concentrating on producing contemporary plays that had succeeded in the West End and on Broadway, but it also introduced several Australian works to its audiences.

Backstage and front-of-house constraints at St Chad's led to plans for a new theatre on the site. In 1951 members of the company and the public formed the Melbourne Little Theatre Guild, which employed the management to stage ten productions annually for a fixed salary. In 1954 the public was invited to subscribe for the new theatre through a £25 000 debenture issue. The Little Theatre, opened on 24 August 1956, is typical of the austere, unattractive modernism of its time. The 414-seat one-level auditorium is well raked and fan-shaped near the stage, which is 8.5 metres deep by 16.5 metres wide with a 7-metre-wide proscenium.

The opening production, Jean Giraudoux's Tiger at the Gates, was beautifully set by ANNE FRASER, lovingly produced by Irene Mitchell and strongly cast, according to GEOFFREY HUTTON in the Age. At his suggestion the Melbourne City Council changed Martin Street to St Martin's Lane, after a street of theatres in Brett Randall's native London. In 1958 the London Stage said in a special feature on Australian theatre: 'This magnificent theatre presents current West End plays and also produces plays by local authors equal to commercial productions'.

On 2 August 1962 the building was renamed the St Martin's Theatre and the company, now with 4000 subscribers, became fully professional as the St Martin's Theatre Company. Brett Randall died in 1963, leaving George Fairfax, Irene Mitchell and Peter Randall as directors of the company. With Mitchell as the moving force, the unsubsidised company was presenting 13 plays a year in three-week seasons by 1966. 'Despite a permanent staff of 16, including a full-time stage designer and running costs (apart from actors' salaries) of $1500 a week, it keeps in the black', said the Bulletin. But in the late 1960s St Martin's found changed audience expectations difficult to meet. Its faithful subscribers were a diminishing generation. The city also had the subsidised, professional MELBOURNE THEATRE COMPANY and alternative companies were emerging at LA MAMA THEATRE. St Martin's received its first government grant in 1969 but it was not enough to recover the financial losses of recent years. At the end of 1972 Christopher Muir and REX CRAMPHORN were employed to give the theatre a new image but a year later the St Martin's Theatre Company staged its last show, Cowardy Custard, a tribute to

Noël Coward. The Melbourne Theatre Company rented the building until 1977 as a second venue. Then the Victorian government bought the theatre and remodelled it as ST MARTIN'S YOUTH ARTS CENTRE. ❦*Sally Dawes, Ross Thorne*

further reading
DENNING, M. Drama in Melbourne. *Australian Quarterly* 25/4 (Sydney, December 1953).
RADBOURNE, JENNIFER. Little Theatre—its development since World War II in Australia, with particular reference to Queensland. University of Queensland MA thesis 1978.
SUMNER, JOHN. *Recollections at Play*. Melbourne: University Press 1993.
Melbourne in lights. *Centrestage* 1/5 (Sydney, March 1987).

St Martin's Youth Arts Centre

Youth-theatre group in Melbourne, founded in 1978 by Victorian government. **venues** St Martin's Theatre; remodelled as St Martin's Youth Arts Centre 1982. **artistic directors** 1978–84 Helmut Bakaitis. 1984 Malcolm Robertson. 1985 John Preston. 1986–87 Peter Charlton. 1990– Chris Thompson. **first production** *The Sensational South Yarra Show* 1978.

Melbourne's principal youth theatre, the St Martin's Youth Centre has been an important training ground for aspiring young theatrical artists since 1978 despite frequent changes of artistic direction, especially from 1984 to 1989. Different directors have pursued differing paths towards the objective of giving workshop training and performance and production experience to 600 young people between 12 and 25 years of age. The centre has staged large-scale, specially written shows like *Cosme* by Peter Charlton in 1987, revivals like *The Legend of King O'Malley* in 1989 and smaller works created by young members of the company under the direction of professionals. Notable successes include a 1985 adaptation of Claire Luckham's *Trafford Tanzi* and the 1991 premiere of *Vincent*, a superb unaccompanied opera by Anthony Crowley and Luke Devenish.

The Victorian government bought the St Martin's Theatre in South Yarra in late 1977 for development as the centre, which HELMUT BAKAITIS and Michael Mitchener operated from 1978. It reopened under its present name in 1982 after refurbishment and the addition of St Martin's Two, a flexible space seating about 100 persons. The first production, in May, was Geoffrey O'Connell's *Brunswick—The musical*, directed by Bakaitis and designed by Shaun Gurton. Numerous companies, especially the PLAYBOX THEATRE CENTRE, have hired the centre's two well-equipped theatres for productions. ❦*Geoffrey Milne*

Stables Theatre

Theatre in Nimrod Street, Darlinghurst, Sydney. Opened 2 December 1970 as **Nimrod Street Theatre**, seating 140. Renamed **The Loft** 1974, **Stables Theatre** 1975.

Since 1970 this little theatre has seen the most innovative and exciting productions in Sydney, especially of Australian plays. It was founded by the actor JOHN BELL and Ken Horler and his wife Lilian, who became business manager. Ken Horler, a lawyer, had been passionately interested in theatre since he and Bell were both in the Sydney University Players. The small, austere building, more than 100 years old, had been a stables for delivery and cab horses, a garage for taxis and a gymnasium. With some money from Horler, members of the proposed company worked unpaid to convert the building into a small, primitive theatre. Double coach-house doors opened into a brick-paved, barn-like foyer. A stair led to a triangular loft, two sides of which contained raked hard wooden benches. The remaining side, which formed the acting area, had a post dead-centre, supporting the low roof. Despite, or even because of these restrictions, the NIMROD THEATRE COMPANY mounted extraordinary productions in the theatre. It opened with *Biggles*, a satire on Returned Services League clubs by RON BLAIR, MICHAEL BODDY and Marcus Cooney, and it developed works by Blair, ALEX BUZO and others in rough, larrikin style. Two high points were David Williamson's *THE REMOVALISTS*, which left members of the audience as emotionally wrung out as if they had experienced police arrogance and brutality at first hand, and the memorable premiere of Peter Kenna's *A HARD GOD*.

After only three years the company decided it needed double the audience capacity of 140, and in May 1974 moved to a new theatre, now called the BELVOIR STREET THEATRE, in Surry Hills. The old theatre was renamed the Loft for a short period during which it was rented to alternative-theatre groups. The dramatist BOB ELLIS bought the theatre in late 1975 and renamed it the Stables Theatre. The GRIFFIN THEATRE COMPANY took up permanent residence in 1980. It was still there when Ellis put the theatre up for sale in 1985. The theatre was threatened with destruction. In 1987, however, a theatrical philanthropist, Dr Rodney Seaborn, established a family foundation, the Seaborn, Broughton and Walford Foundation, to buy and improve the building. In 1988 the roof was raised—enabling patrons in the back seats to stand up straight when the performance ended—and supported with trusses to eliminate the centre-stage post. Air-conditioning was installed and the seating was made more comfortable. The early works of Grant Fraser, MICHAEL GOW, GORDON GRAHAM and HANNIE RAYSON were performed at the Stables. ❦*Ross Thorne*

further reading
BRISBANE, KATHARINE. Preserving the disreputable. *Hemisphere* (Canberra) March 1971.

Stage Company

Professional dramatic company in Adelaide, formed in 1977 by Don Barker, Brian Debnam, John Noble, Ken Ross, Nan Smith and others. Closed 1986. **venues** Price Theatre; Sheridan Theatre; Space at Adelaide Festival Centre; Union Hall; Theatre 62. **artistic director** John Noble.

For the best part of ten years the Stage Company offered opportunities for Australian playwrights and Adelaide actors. It aimed to be an alternative to the State Theatre Company of South Australia and to concentrate on performing Australian plays. The best of the Stage Company's work—including ROB GEORGE's *Sandy Lee Live at Nui Dat* in 1981 and *Percy and Rose* in 1982, DAVID ALLEN's *Cheapside* in 1985 and JANIS BALODIS's *Too Young for Ghosts* in 1985—more than fulfilled its commitment to new writing. The energies of Ken Ross, Brian Debnam and especially John Noble, who performed in many productions, sustained the company against the vagaries of the box office and mixed critical response until it ceased when federal funding was withdrawn. ❦*Murray Bramwell*

Stage design and effects

The penal nature of the colony compelled improvisation in early theatre in Sydney. Watkin Tench's account of the first performance—George Farquhar's *The Recruiting Officer* in 1789—praised the effect achieved by 'the proper distribution of three or four yards of stained paper and a dozen farthing candles stuck around the mud walls of a convict hut' and such ingenuity was common to such entertainments until professional scene painters arrived. Of a convict performance at Emu Plains, a contributor to the *Sydney Gazette* wrote in 1825 that the scenery was painted 'with great taste' and the dresses were 'furnished by some of the ladies in the neighbourhood'. The whole performance 'won the admiration and excited the joyful exclamations of the delighted spectators'. The 'director' of the EMU PLAINS CONVICT THEATRE may have been Australia's first scenic artist. *Ralph Rashleigh, or the Life of an Exile*, a fictionalised account of convict life, describes him as 'a most eccentric genius … at once architect, manager, carpenter, scene-painter, decorator, machinist, mechanician and to crown it all, a very passable comic actor. The author, supposedly James Tucker, risibly describes extravagant costumes contrived for the burlesque *Bombastes Furioso*, from materials including old tins and the skins of sheep and native mammals.

The first Australian theatres were rough-and-ready fit-ups, colonial versions of those put together by itinerant companies in assembly rooms, hotel rooms or barns in Georgian rural England. The first permanent theatre, the THEATRE ROYAL in Sydney, was opened by BARNETT LEVEY in 1833 with amenities and decor reflecting his sparse resources, it was a modest version of the small Georgian theatres of the English provinces, or the minor theatres of London. In a sense Georgian audiences saw stage scenery from the moment they entered the theatre. Throughout the 19th century theatre auditoria were designed as elegantly and even lavishly decorated social venues for actors and audience to meet and create the theatrical occasion. It is in the light of this important function that the very real pathos of Tench's description of that first Australian performance emerges: 'That every opportunity of escape from the dreariness and dejection of our situation should be eagerly embraced will not be wondered at. The exhilarating effect of a splendid theatre is well known …'. The few yards of coloured paper and candles he described 'failed not to diffuse general complacency on the countenances of 60 persons, of various descriptions who were assembled to applaud the occasion'.

In the theatre of the earlier 19th century, tiers of boxes were fronted by painted canvas representations of elaborate wreaths and gilded scrollwork, while the sumptuously decorated wall surrounding the proscenium arch and the arch itself were, again, painted canvas. When a theatre opened such decoration was invariably the subject of extended newspaper comment, culminating in minutely detailed descriptions of the scenic glories of the drop curtain that confronted the audience on arrival. The total experience was pure theatre, manipulated by the scenic artist, who then proceeded to offer on stage the delights of three dimensional illusion, painted in perspective.

With the auditorium lit by candles or oil lamps, actors and audience remained fully visible to one another throughout the performance, which actually took place in the auditorium space, on the large apron stage within and in front of the proscenium arch. Behind the actors the stage was raked up towards the back, so that the scenery, framed by the proscenium arch, offered appropriate pictorial support in a cunning illusion of deep perspective.

Scenery slid on and off from either side in symmetrically-placed sets of wooden grooves on the stage and overhead. Each scene was painted on a pair of huge shutters, which would part like sliding doors to reveal the next in a series of scenes. These were painted in diminishing perspective and finally came the painted backdrop. Masking the outer edges of the shutters from the audience were a series of framing wings which also moved in grooves and, like the shutters, could be withdrawn to reveal the wings appropriate to the following scene—again, presented in diminishing perspective.

A well-managed scene change (which took place in front of the audience with the curtain up) was synchronised by the prompter's whistle, so that shutters and wings changed in the twinkling of an eye and a new scene seemed to be conjured up by magic. In prosaic fact, however, only the grandest metropolitan theatres could afford new scenery for every new play; the rest held in stock their chamber scene, their forest scene, their cave scene, and so forth, so that audiences became all too familiar with them. Sloppy scene-changing was common in minor theatres such as Sydney's first Theatre Royal, so that, for example, half an interior scene could inadvertently be mismatched with half a battle scene. But critics were alert to stage decor. It was noted in 1842 that 'to fine scenery is owing a very material proportion of the pleasure we derive from theatrical presentations'. Another complained in 1843 that 'a street in London, with a flaming gaslight' did not give 'precisely the idea of "Almighty Rome"' in the classical play *Brutus*.

Amateur scene-painters

Before professional scene-painters arrived from Europe, theatre managers regularly employed talented amateurs, such as the actor ANDREW TORNING, or commercial artists, such as William Winstanley, who contributed to Barnett Levey's ambitious productions at the Theatre Royal. The easel painters WILLIAM BUELOW GOULD, JOHN SKINNER PROUT and Augustus Earle were also called upon for scenery and theatre decoration. Immigrant professional scene-painters readily found employment in Adelaide, Launceston, Hobart, Melbourne and Sydney during the 1830s and 1840s. They included the famous English machinist JAMES BELMORE, Edward Orr, Edward Shribbs, and a man named Keough, who claimed links with the eminent English scenic artist William Clarkson Stanfield and died in 1838.

The stage and auditorium were lit by oil lamps and candles in chandeliers, lamps placed behind the proscenium and scenery flats and floats or footlights, which could be raised or lowered mechanically from beneath the stage. Stage lighting was improved with the use of the Argand oil-lamp, which had a glass chimney, was smokeless and gave steadier light than previous oil lamps. The introduction of gas lighting at the ROYAL VICTORIA THEATRE in Sydney in 1841 brought new possibilities for dimming stage and auditorium lighting. By 1875, according to Ross Thorne, the stage arrangements at the new THEATRE ROYAL reported

John Brunton, a master of stage realism, designed and painted the sets for George Rignold's production of Joseph of Canaan *by George Walters in Sydney in 1895. Brunton also created extravagant spectacles, sometimes basing his work on photographs, for Bland Holt's melodrama productions. Holt retired after Brunton died in 1909, declaring him irreplaceable*

by the *Sydney Morning Herald* had been fairly generally adopted. A 'cylinder or dial containing a mass of handles for working the pipes from which the illuminating material is supplied to the various parts of the house' was situated at the prompt entrance to the stage. The newspaper also commented on an innovation in the auditorium: a pilot jet had been attached to the gas chandelier. It was now possible to extinguish the main house lights altogether. This was almost certainly reserved for special effects, however. The custom of illuminating the auditorium was to die hard and did not finally disappear until the ascendancy of naturalism at the end of the century made it unacceptable.

A second wave of English and European scenic artists arrived in Australia in the middle of the 19th century. The most notable were Francis Fearn, John Fry, ALEXANDER HABBE, JOHN HENNINGS, Henry Holmes, WILLIAM PITT SNR and W. J. WILSON. Thus virtuoso scenic art assumed a crucial 'performative' role in its own right, elevating the aspect of visuality and spectacle above sound and sense. The public expected each new production to supply a gallery of new stage pictures. As in Europe, scene-painters' gargantuan canvases afforded most people their only opportunity to experience painting at first hand at a time before the advent of public art galleries. Nineteenth-century audiences regularly applauded when the rising front curtain revealed the act drop, and eminent scene-painters were often called before the curtain.

Scene-painters were required to satisfy a growing public demand for representational verisimilitude, whereas earlier in the century they had suggested locales in a stylised manner. Victorian audiences expected an illusion of three dimensions in a two-dimensional stage picture. As scenery became more naturalistic, stage action gradually moved upstage; so that by the end of the 19th century, the forestage was eliminated and all action was contained within the proscenium. The stage had, in effect, become a picture.

From mid-century audiences expected of the classic stage not only spectacle but topographical and historical accuracy. In sumptuous seasons of Shakespeare in London in the 1850s, CHARLES KEAN, Eton-educated son of the famous Edmund Kean, had resorted to archaeology and the British Museum in the quest for historical accuracy. In Australia John Hennings provided extravagant settings for drama, opera, pantomime and melodrama. His designs for *Antony and Cleopatra* in 1867 were considered to be 'the work of a great artist and a thorough scholar'. The versatile 'Great Dane' Alexander Habbe also distinguished himself over four decades. W. J. Wilson, a direct link with the English tradition, maintained a dual career as scene-painter and exhibiting easel-painter for half a century.

Late in the 19th century the scene-painter's position was consolidated by the Scot JOHN BRUNTON, the Hennings pupil PHILIP W. GOATCHER, and the English scenic artists Alfred Clint, W. R. Coleman, GEORGE GORDON and W. B. Spong. The most ambitious was Brunton, who staged melodramas for BLAND HOLT with audacious hyper-realism and left audiences gasping at three-dimensional scenery and exciting action which included floods, bushfires, a bicycle race and a balloon ascent.

Enterprising managers found that local colour, arousing Australian nationalistic sentiment, guaranteed novelty and full houses. The Australian landscape and occasional city scenes provided motifs for Garnet Walch's *AUSTRALIA FELIX* in 1873, George Darrell's *THE SUNNY SOUTH* in 1883, Alfred Dampier's *FOR THE TERM OF HIS NATURAL LIFE* in 1890, J. C. WILLIAMSON's *Australis* in 1900, and Holt's production of

THE BREAKING OF THE DROUGHT in 1902. Bushfires, floods, gold mines, events such as the Melbourne Cup and city landmarks lent immediacy to WALTER COOPER's *Sun and Shadow* in 1870 and *Foiled* in 1871 and Dampier and J. H. Wrangham's MARVELLOUS MELBOURNE in 1889.

An increasing elaboration of stage effects in the late 19th century was facilitated by developments in THEATRES themselves. In 1875 the stage house of the Theatre Royal in Sydney was made high enough to enable scenery to be flown—hauled up by pulleys. The new theatre also retained the old groove system, but with further progress towards the fully developed fly tower the groove system disappeared. Complete sets could now be flown and stored more efficiently. New opportunities for rapid and spectacular effects were complemented by mechanical developments below the stage. Even in the PRINCE OF WALES THEATRE, which preceded the Theatre Royal on the site, there had been two floors beneath the stage for machines, 'one being a telescopic trap which could be pushed up to the level of the flies', according to Ross Thorne.

Stage magic, generally following the English model, reached its apogee in effects such as phantasmagorical illusions and dissolving views. The scenic artist and the machinist headed a large backstage team who realised these effects with MOVING PANORAMAS and transformation scenes. Vast panoramas depicting famous events or foreign places moved across the stage, presaging the cinema to some extent. In the transformation scene, a feature of PANTOMIME, there was a breathtaking illusion of scenes subtly dissolving into one another, usually ending in a brilliant tableau. One popular transformation took the form of a dark grotto emerging as a light-filled heavenly bower where performers wearing gorgeous costumes appeared to float skyward. Such enchantment was achieved with complex technology beneath, above and behind the stage, chemical fires, coloured lighting, limelight and split-second timing. Gaslight was favoured for its softer effects well into the 1880s, after the introduction of electric light.

Costume was traditionally separate from the scene-painter's sphere and Australian productions in the late 19th and early 20th centuries exploited the prestige of wardrobes imported from English costumiers like Percy Anderson, Attilio Comelli and Charles Wilhelm. Later in the 20th century managements reduced costs and opportunities for local design by importing English and American productions, including set designs and costumes. Firms further reduced costs and scenic artists' work by recycling and hiring out accumulated backcloths and accessories.

The public's passion for spectacle at the end of the 19th century and into the 20th sharpened competition among scene-painters. As late as 1928, an accomplished scenic artist was still considered by a writer in *Table Talk* to be 'an aristocrat of his craft, a jewel to be won away from rivals by any means'. In advertisements, playbills and reviews, scenery was commonly described in terms such as 'gorgeous', 'magnificent' and 'stupendous'. But in fact the scene-painter's status had begun to decline early in the 20th century. An apprenticeship of seven to nine years, involving gruelling conditions, minimal pay and exhausting hours upon a backstage paint-frame, became less and less

Pantomime offered 19th-century scenic artists opportunities to devise fantastic spectacle and illusion in collaboration with machinist. The culmination of a pantomime was the transformation scene, in which music and female beauty interacted with a sequence of scenes dissolving from one to another. It ended in a tableau, of which this is an example

attractive. Talented scenic artists such as Dres Hardingham and George Upward perpetuated skills learned from Coleman, Brunton and others, but the visual magic of the cinema gradually usurped their position of distinction. In the scenic artist's heyday a synopsis of scenery had been prominent on the playbill; but in the 20th century the scene-painter was no longer consistently acknowledged and contributing scene-painters sometimes shared a general attribution. The works themselves were doomed to oblivion by scraping and repainting for the next production and a reputation was only as good as the scene-painter's last set of scenes. 'It seems a pity to ignore the poor scene-painter', observed a theatrical journalist in 1928. 'Yet, important as he is, we never spare him a posy. The public knows little of the scene-painter unfortunately.'

Naturalistic drama also threatened the scene-painter's prestige. By the end of the 19th century naturalistic plays required three-dimensional settings and box sets consisting of freestanding flats instead of illusionist backcloths. A new demand for stage credibility rendered the actors' plastic dimensions ludicrously at odds with flat painted scenery, particularly in the harsh glare and shadows thrown by new incandescent electric lighting.

In Europe in the early 20th century there was a radical shift in the concept of the function of scenery. By the end of the First World War this shift was becoming apparent in Australia. A new kind of scenic artist, the stage designer, was replacing the 'splodger' who used chamber pots as a palette and brooms for brushes. Scene-painters remained in demand for conventional professional theatre and to a lesser extent, for amateur productions, but their glorious era had passed. Progressive amateur theatres rather than the professional theatre, trained theatre artists over the next four decades. Painters, sculptors and architects, influenced by the reformist theories of Edward Gordon Craig and developments in modernist art, were attracted to the new intimate theatres and more complex collaboration between visual and theatrical arts developed there. All aspects of production were increasingly unified, and the designer was frequently involved in all the decisions.

Rather than merely illustrating a play, opera or ballet or providing an arbitrary visual spectacle, modernist stage design began to interpret the mood or theme. The emphasis was changed to a radically simplified style and, just as modern painters had abandoned illustration or narration, the stage designer took the inherent formal properties of the setting—colour, space, shape, massing, light—as raw materials. Sculptural units, not necessarily referring directly to the world beyond the stage, replaced illusionist backcloths of specific time and place. Electric lighting's potential was recognised and exploited with imagination and the designer's brief was broadened to encompass some of the skills of architect, mathematician, painter, sculptor, carpenter and dressmaker. In the more intimate new theatres, audiences were invited to contemplate internal relationships between text, action and visual symbols instead of passively absorbing visual information. Among the enlightened individuals who encouraged new design in Australia between the two world wars were GREGAN MCMAHON, MARIE NEY, DOLIA RIBUSH and ALLAN WILKIE. Ballet and drama companies on tour offered new insights into modern stagecraft from the 1920s. Anna Pavlova's ballet company in 1926 and 1929 introduced new notions of simplified design. In *Autumn Leaves* light filtered through descending leaves. The dramatic company headed by Sybil Thorndike and Lewis Casson in 1932 brought out sets and costumes by Charles Ricketts and Cecil Beaton.

Demonstrations of theories, methods and materials of progressive stagecraft by visiting companies were crucial in the education of Australian artists during the 1930s and 1940s. Apart from imported literature on the arts and the occasional exhibition of contemporary European art during the 1930s, ambitious Australian artists who could not travel abroad saw little of experimental styles. The most overwhelming effect came from Colonel de Basil's ballet companies. They dazzled Australian artists with backcloths by two generations of designers for Sergey Diaghilev's Ballets Russes—the flamboyant Russians Leon Bakst, Alexandre Benois, Natalia Gontcharova and Mikhail Larionov and the modernist painters of the school of Paris, Christian Bérard, André Derain, Giorgio De Chirico, André Masson, Jean Miró, Pablo Picasso and Georges Rouault. These huge stage canvases combined with co-ordinated costumes, lighting, music and daring choreography to propose theatre as a total sensory experience. For the first time, Australian audiences were able to witness modern art in action, a kinetic art gallery on stage.

The Old Vic Theatre Company in 1948 enchanted grey, postwar Australia with designs by Cecil Beaton and Oliver Messel. Particularly daring was a return to the flown cloths of the 19th century—huge evocations of line engravings of Georgian architecture raised and lowered in full view of the audience. Art galleries gave further impetus to stage design in the 1940s by mounting major exhibitions by Australian and British theatre artists, including the Theatre Decor exhibition at the Art Gallery of NSW in 1948.

Designers in the amateur little-theatre movement had minimal technical and economic resources, and they drew upon ingenuity as much as innovation, fashion and skill. They worked voluntarily or they were employed *ad hoc* or they went overseas. Artists who began in amateur theatre and became successful designers overseas include WILLIAM

The 19th-century desire for realism led to the box set, in which flats complete with working doors and windows form three of the four walls of a room and a cloth provides a ceiling. J. C. Williamson's production of L'Aiglon *by Edmond Rostand in Sydney in 1904 employed this elaborate box set*

Anne Fraser's set for the Australian Elizabethan Theatre Trust production of Ray Lawler's Summer of the Seventeenth Doll *at the Elizabethan Theatre in Sydney in 1956 showed sections through a house at varying distances from the missing fourth wall. Australian Nouveau Theatre, directed by Jean-Pierre Mignon, took a different view of the play in Melbourne in 1983. The characters, from left, are Pearl, played by Gillian Seamer, Olive (Julie Forsyth), Barney (Neil Melville), Roo (Bruce Keller) and Emma (Lynne Ellis)*

Constable, Don Finley, Kathleen and Florence Martin, Kenneth Rowell, Loudon Sainthill and John Truscott. Talented designers who, for various reasons, did not further their careers abroad included Warwick Armstrong of Arrow Theatre in Melbourne, Des Connor of the Union Theatre Repertory Company in Melbourne, Cedric Flower of New Theatre in Sydney, Elaine Haxton of Adelaide and Vane Lindesay of New Theatre Melbourne. Painters were drawn to the vitality of the theatre and although most made a single contribution it added to the status and quality of Australian stage art. They included Dorritt Black, Arthur Boyd, Noel Counihan, Wladislaw Dutkiewicz, Jacqueline Hick, Donald Friend, Norman Lindsay, Sidney Nolan and Blamire Young. Australian design was also assisted by the foundation of the Union Theatre Repertory Company in 1953 and the establishment of the Australian Elizabethan Theatre Trust in 1954. The Union Theatre company, which continues as the Melbourne Theatre Company, offered a wide range of drama and in 1955 it appointed Anne Fraser as its first full-time designer. This not only made a career in Australia a serious proposition but opened the field to women. The Union Theatre company allowed young designers such as Hugh Colman, Wendy Dickson, Richard Prins and Kristian Fredrickson to develop limited careers in Australia before gaining experience abroad. From 1961 onwards the Irene Mitchell Award for set design further encouraged the company's designers.

The establishment of other permanent companies in the 1960s benefited other designers, including Desmond Digby, Allan Lees, Stan Ostoja-Kotkowski, Ron Reid and Yoshi Tosa. Designers with permanent theatres as bases had continuous access to advances in construction methods and new materials like fibreglass and plastics. Permanent sets, revolving scenery, simultaneous settings and innovations in lighting and projection equipment and the availability of specialised wardrobes also expanded the designer's expertise. Designers needed to become extremely versatile to execute commissions covering drama, opera, ballet, musical comedy, variety and film. The annual Loudon Sainthill scholarship, which enables young designers to study

The Nimrod Theatre in Sydney, with its stage thrust into the audience from a corner of the auditorium, was one of the new kinds of theatres in which designers faced new problems and devised ingenious solutions in the 1970s. They were assisted by innovations and improvements in materials, construction methods and equipment

overseas, was instituted in 1967 but there was no formal full-time theatre-design course in Australia until the NATIONAL INSTITUTE OF DRAMATIC ART established one in 1974.

Subsidised companies like the Union Theatre Repertory Company were being challenged by more experimental groups in the 1960s and 1970s. In addition to radical university theatre, were companies such as WAL CHERRY's Emerald Hill Theatre, the La Mama Company and the AUSTRALIAN PERFORMING GROUP in Melbourne; the NIMROD THEATRE COMPANY in Sydney; TROUPE in Adelaide and the HOLE-IN-THE-WALL THEATRE Company in Perth. Rough political theatre, anarchic, vernacular and often absurd in style, became identified with a renascence in Australian theatre, in which the basic premises of contemporary theatre and its relations with society were questioned. In particular, relationships between audience, architectural space and stage were being radically re-examined, with profound implications for the designer. Stages were being thrust into space and surrounded by audiences. This set new problems for the designer, who was becoming less a versatile specialist and more an member of a vigorous ensemble.

By the mid-1960s television was a serious rival to live theatre throughout Australia. It presented a variety of design opportunities, in the form of simplified modernist sets for variety and news programs, and the more enduring naturalistic style for drama—a threat to its stage counterpart. During the 1970s production design for an expanding film industry continued to provide opportunities for design work, mainly in a traditional realist style. Luciana Arrighi and BRIAN THOMSON are among the designers who have successfully worked in both film and theatre.

Today designers in Australia tend to be free lances employed for individual productions or for seasons by major dance, drama and opera companies. Large companies still tend to display a preference for successful expatriates over resident local designers, so a long-term partnership with one company is rarely an option. Designers therefore need to be flexible. Not only are they required to move between opera, dance, musicals and drama—and often film, pop concerts and television—but they are expected to be conversant with and skilled in a wide range of artistic styles and theories.

The more enlightened, visually perceptive directors are increasingly realising the advantages of collaboration with designers. Rather than the designer being hired merely to deal with the background, a working partnership between designer and director informs the production so that entirely new visual solutions may be achieved. This is evident, for instance, in the work of EAMON D'ARCY, Mary Moore, Michael Pearce and Brian Thomson, where design provides more than a foundation for the production.

In experimental theatre since the late 1970s there has been a move beyond text to a theatre of images. AUSTRALIAN NOUVEAU THEATRE, Nigel TRIFFITT's puppet theatre, KIM CARPENTER's Theatre of Image and Carol Woodrow's Fool's Gallery are a few examples that have recently expanded the forms of theatre, opening up opportunities for interdisciplinary practice. They have been largely influenced by PERFORMANCE ART, ritualistic and conceptual art of the 1960s and 1970s. Australian designers have also long sought inspiration from the vibrancy and immediacy of Asian and cross-cultural art forms. Stage design has become so complex, flexible and sophisticated that a designer can create theatre from almost any architectural setting. LIGHTING DESIGN has become a distinct practice.

Increasingly since the 1980s designers have been influenced by cultural theories such as feminism, semiotics, postcolonialism and postmodernism. A heightened political awareness of the designer's role continues to be fostered by such organisations as the Australian Production Designers' Association. ❦*Pamela Zeplin*

Stalwart the Bushranger

Verse drama in five acts by Charles Harpur. Completed 1867; never performed. **published** Sydney: Currency Press/Australasian Drama Studies 1987.

Stalwart the Bushranger began life about 1834 as a blank-verse drama, *The Tragedy of Donohoe*. Extracts printed in the *Sydney Monitor* in February 1835 suggest that CHARLES HARPUR had already begun a long process of revision that was to occupy him on and off for almost the rest of his life. In the version published in 1853 as *The Bushrangers*, the historical bushranger John Donohoe (1806–30) has been replaced as hero by the more allegorical Captain Stalwart, whose name was given to the final version of the play. Like Matthew Brady, hero of David Burn's THE BUSHRANGERS (1829), Stalwart blames the brutalities and injustices of the convict system for his becoming a bushranger.

Like Burn, too, Harpur provides satirical exposés of local authorities, including the Justices of the Peace Roger Tunbelly and Wealthiman Woolsack and the cowardly constables Cant and Bomebard. Stalwart is, however, a much more complex and tormented hero than Brady. Stalwart attempts to rape the heroine, rather than save her from rape as Brady does, and then murders her rescuer. Like Macbeth, Stalwart ends defeated as much by his own guilty conscience as by his enemies, proudly proclaiming: 'I do not plead Not Guilty! Guilty, I say!' Harpur's revisions progressively moved the play away from melodrama and towards romantic tragedy, lessening the more spectacular and topical aspects of the earliest version in favour of a more poetic and universal examination of the question of evil in the individual and in society. ❦*Elizabeth Webby*

further reading
ACKLAND, MICHAEL. Plot and counterplot in Charles Harpur's *The Bushrangers*. *Australasian Drama Studies* (Brisbane, April 1986).
KELLY, VERONICA. The melodrama of defeat—Political patterns in some colonial and contemporary Australian plays. *Southerly* (Sydney) June 1990.
PERKINS, ELIZABETH. Introduction. *Stalwart the Bushranger* with *The Tragedy of Donohoe* by Charles Harpur. Sydney: Currency Press/Australasian Drama Studies 1987.

Stand-up comedy

The most popular form of live comedy in Australia since the early 1980s has been stand-up comedy, particularly in Melbourne and Sydney. Alternative cabaret boomed in the 1970s, largely in Melbourne. Groups emerged from university revues and found exposure in new venues such as JOHN PINDER's Flying Trapeze Cafe. Before long performers developed solo acts. By the beginning of the 1980s there were many new comedy venues, such as the Last Laugh and the Comedy Cafe in Melbourne and the Comedy Store in Sydney, and cabaret was making way for stand-up comedy. Rod Quantock was probably the first fully fledged new-wave stand-up comic. Mark Little was another to make a name early. Like many other stand-up comedians of the period, Little claims that videos of American stand-up comedians such as Richard Pryor provided his greatest influence and motivation.

The essence of stand-up comedy is to point out the absurdity of the everyday, so Australian stand-up comedy soon developed its own flavour. Quantock, Little, Wendy Harmer, Rodney Rude and many other comics who emerged in the early 1980s all dealt in Australian ways with issues affecting local audiences. They were larrikin and laconic rather than wisecracking American in style. Australian stand-up comedy can share the English use of irony and subtlety, but it is quite without the English class-consciousness. By the end of the 1980s many Australian comics had performed overseas at events such as the Edinburgh Festival to the point where the billing 'from Australia' sold tickets. Television discovered stand-up comedy in the late 1980s, but the live form remained strong and popular in the 1990s. ❦*David Taranto*

H. A. Standish

Critic. Born 7 July 1906 in northern Queensland. Began writing in Rockhampton (Qld). Journalist and theatre critic for Melbourne *Herald* 1949–70. Helped to establish and maintain Green Room Awards. Died 7 January 1988.

H. A. Standish was widely respected within the theatrical profession. He was regarded as an extremely conscientious critic who saw himself as helping the cause of theatre. His views and tastes appear to have been greatly influenced by his experiences of British theatre in the 1920s and by a European theatre tour in the early 1960s. He was guarded with contemporary theatre, especially when confronted with the kitchen sink. 'Pinter's gone too far', he wrote of *The Homecoming*. He dismissed John Osborne's *Inadmissible Evidence* with 'It's not a play'. ❦*John Preston*

C. R. Stanford

Actor. Probably born in Sydney and taken to USA at early age. Acted in Australia 1886–1919. Married actor Ida Gresham.

C. R. Stanford acted for numerous managements and with his own companies, especially in Western Australia, playing parts ranging from pantomime to Shakespeare. He played the title-role in *The Silver King* by Henry Arthur Jones and Henry Herman, which opened the THEATRE ROYAL in Perth on 17 April 1897. After recovering from illness Stanford returned to the eastern colonies. He later produced and appeared in *The Fatal Wedding* throughout Australia. He appeared in CHARLES HOLLOWAY's company in 1901 with his wife Ida Gresham. The theatrical profession gave Stanford a complimentary matinée at His Majesty's Theatre in Perth on 29 October 1919. ❦*Joan Maslen*

further reading
The Footlight Star 7 (November–December 1917).

John Stanton

Actor. Born 28 October 1944 in Brisbane. Trained as primary school teacher. Involved in amateur theatre in Brisbane. Played first lead role at Independent Theatre, Sydney, 1970. Married actor Jill Forster 1974. Sydney Critics' Award and the Variety Heart Award 1990 (Captain Ahab in *Moby Dick Rehearsed* by Orson Welles). Many film and television roles.

John Stanton is a strong, muscular actor whose forte is the 'heavy' dramatic role and the expression of suppressed or inarticulate emotion. He has been much in demand for such roles on television but on stage he is a classical actor whose voice has been compared with Richard Burton's. When he played the title-role in Henrik Ibsen's *Master Builder*, one of his finest parts, at the BELVOIR STREET THEATRE in 1991, Frank Gauntlett found Stanton breathtaking in 'his bearing, his priceless voice, his compass of yearning and beguiling warmth and frigid, inexorable, terrible isolation'.

Stanton's other major roles include Uncle Ralph in David Edgar's *The Life and Adventures of Nicholas Nickleby* for the SYDNEY THEATRE COMPANY in 1982–83, George in Edward Albee's *Who's Afraid of Virginia Woolf?* for the State Theatre Company of South Australia in 1987, Valmont in Christopher Hampton's *Les Liaisons dangereuses* for the MELBOURNE THEATRE COMPANY in 1988, Undershaft in George Bernard Shaw's *Major Barbara* for the QUEENSLAND THEATRE COMPANY in 1989, Captain Ahab in *Moby Dick Rehearsed* for the MARIAN STREET THEATRE COMPANY in 1990, Antony in *Antony and Cleopatra* for the Sydney Theatre Company and Dramaturgical Services Inc. in 1992 and King Lear for the Sydney Theatre Company in 1994.

Between 1977 and 1979 Stanton worked extensively with the Melbourne Theatre Company, playing Torvald in Ibsen's *A Doll's House* and roles in *Macbeth*, *Richard III*, Dylan Thomas's *Under Milk Wood*, Joseph Kesselring's *Arsenic and Old Lace*, Harold Pinter's *Betrayal* and R. B. Sheridan's *The Rivals*.

His early work included parts in HARRY M. MILLER's production of Mart Crowley's *The Boys in the Band* in Melbourne in 1969–70 and Shaw's *Caesar and Cleopatra* for the ST MARTIN'S THEATRE COMPANY in Melbourne in 1972. ❦*Katharine Brisbane*

Star system

Distance from the European, especially British, culture that spawned Australian theatre has given the star system peculiar significance. From the gold rushes Australia became an increasingly attractive stop on the international touring circuit. Stars of the magnitude of SARAH BERNHARDT paid prolonged and lucrative visits. At the same time, however, managements paraded stars of rather less distinction across Australian stages, to the exclusion, it is often alleged, of Australian artists of superior ability. This claim is contested by KATHARINE BRISBANE in the historical survey *Entertaining Australia*. She finds that Australian audiences have always had international tastes. She detects no reluctance by them to create and acknowledge their own Australian stars—only a reluctance by producers in the latter period of the J. C. WILLIAMSON's monopoly to invest in the future while ready-made overseas product was to hand. It is a question involving wide cultural issues and not easily resolved; but there can be no doubt of the star system's central importance in the history of the Australian theatre.
❧Philip Parsons

Australia's first stars

Before the 1850s the Australian theatre had no stars who would have been accepted elsewhere at that valuation. Only FRANCIS NESBITT in tragedy and GEORGE COPPIN and G. H. ROGERS in comedy were of anything like star calibre, while the talent of Jane Thomson, later MRS CHARLES YOUNG, was still in embryo. But once reliable stock companies existed in the major cities it was only a matter of time before they attracted the new breed of travelling stars who were using railways and steamships to follow the ever-expanding touring circuits of the Anglophone stage. The gold rushes of the early 1850s accelerated the process by providing a large body of theatre-loving immigrants who were eager to re-encounter old favourites.

In Great Britain at the time an ambitious young performer faced a choice: build a career in London on low wages with the expectation of eventually moving into management or perform in short provincial seasons for much higher returns, ideally taking a percentage. The decision was artistically as well as financially crucial because a provincial career demanded a more assertive acting style—unkindly referred to as 'the bow-wow school'—and a repertoire restricted to what local stock companies could get up at 24 hours' notice. It was essential that the star should appear in as many roles as possible.

Provincial stars who came to Australia included the tragedians G. V. BROOKE in 1855, BARRY SULLIVAN in 1862, James Anderson in 1867, WALTER MONTGOMERY in 1867 and WILLIAM CRESWICK in 1877. All had a strong following outside London, in Ireland and in some cases in the USA, but were regarded by the metropolis as rather behind the times. Montgomery's introduction of the revolutionary 'quiet' Hamlet to Australia indicates only that this version was now acceptable to British provincial audiences. In any case he seems to have modernised his style considerably on the voyage out. Because it took several months both to reach and to return from Australia, most of these visitors remained for at least a year. Brooke and Sullivan each had lengthy periods in management at the Theatre Royal in Melbourne. All had their regular leading ladies but these were not regarded as co-stars. Female performers such as Louisa Cleveland, Augusta Dargon, Mary Gladstane, ESSIE JENYNS, Louise Pomeroy, MARY SCOTT-SIDDONS and Genevieve Ward secured top billing in tragic roles, but they were never as peripatetic or as energetically publicised as the male stars.

In England G. V. Brooke was a provincial actor but in Australia he was such a star that he was immortalised in marble

Brooke's arrival was the result of a daring gamble by GEORGE COPPIN, who offered terms of a generosity that was never repeated. During the 1860s Coppin's inducements were still sufficient to attract and enrich performers who were not regular touring stars but London veterans in search of a retirement fund—CÉLINE CÉLESTE, and CHARLES AND ELLEN KEAN. However, Montgomery and Creswick, arriving without firm contracts, had to deal with a cabal of managers who were determined to get their services as cheaply as possible. Montgomery wrote furious letters to the British press denouncing them, and Creswick was in Melbourne many weeks before he could secure an engagement. This monopoly—along with improved communications within the USA, which made the long sea-voyage to Australia less attractive—led to a dearth of major overseas stars between the visit of CHARLES MATHEWS in 1870 and that of DION BOUCICAULT in 1885, though Australia did see ADELAIDE RISTORI with her Italian company in 1875. When the older pattern resumed with tours by JANET ACHURCH and Charles Charrington in 1889 and SARAH BERNHARDT in 1891, it was because J. C. WILLIAMSON and his partners had

In Geelong in 1853 George Coppin presented Francis Nesbitt as a star. Stardom took a toll, however. Nesbitt collapsed on stage in Sheridan Knowles's William Tell *and later died*

formed a national theatre chain with which terms for an entire visit could be negotiated.

Great Britain was always the main source of stars, but until the completion of the transcontinental railway in the USA in 1869, Sydney and Melbourne functioned as extensions of the Californian circuit. The first performers to achieve genuine star billing in Sydney were James and Sarah Stark in 1853, visitors from San Francisco. So in later years were EDWIN BOOTH, LAURA KEENE, Adelaide and JOEY GOUGENHEIM, Marie Provost, McKean Buchanan, JOSEPH JEFFERSON, J. C. Williamson and MAGGIE MOORE. American performers were welcomed in American dialect farces and melodramas and in variety for the rest of the century, although a British accent was normally insisted on for appearances in 'high-class' drama. The American actor Joseph Emmett with Charles Gayler's dialect comedy *Fritz Our Cousin German* in 1876 and the Irish female impersonator John F. Sheridan with his romp *Fun on the Bristol* in 1884 got round this problem by appearing mostly in a single piece tailored to their particular abilities. The English star Jennie Lee adopted the same practice in 1883 with *Jo*, adapted from Charles Dickens's novel *Bleak House*. It was a sign of steadily lengthening runs, and of a new habit of attendance that would bring theatregoers back for several visits to a well-mounted show with a sufficiently charismatic star and a script that left some room for variation.

Meanwhile, Australia was beginning to possess permanently resident stars. At first these were visitors who chose to stay, such as FANNY CATHCART, who had arrived as Brooke's leading lady, and the 1870s newcomers ALFRED DAMPIER, GEORGE DARRELL, BLAND HOLT, Maggie Moore, GEORGE RIGNOLD and J. C. Williamson. Dampier and Darrell were versatile stock-company leads rather than real stars, but they enlarged their prominence by also being playwrights and managers. Holt, Rignold, Moore and Williamson were real international talents who chose Australia as a good place to move into management. Hard on their heels came a native-born generation headed by NELLIE STEWART in operetta and ESSIE JENYNS in Shakespeare. The early death of HATTIE SHEPPARDE cut short a career of at least equal promise. There can be no doubt concerning Stewart's primacy as the superstar of the Australian theatre from 1880 to 1900, but the hegemony of Williamson's various firms was increasingly premised on deference to imported reputation. Leading roles in operetta usually went to imports and meanwhile a generation of singers headed overseas, led by Nellie Melba. The talent flowing out was incontestably higher than the talent flowing in.

In operetta first and then in straight plays, Nellie Stewart was a star for half a century

The 1890s brought a new function for the star system. In the early days, visiting stars had been necessary to give variety to stock companies' performances of a large but tradition-bound repertoire. The theatregoer's aim was to see the star in as many familiar roles as possible and, since it was the star who was the centre of attention, it was not a matter for complaint if the rest of the performance was grossly under-rehearsed. After the establishment of WILLIAMSON, GARNER AND MUSGROVE in 1883 a single production might tour for several months in the firm's theatres and much more careful preparation was possible. Moreover, the fashionable well-made plays of the Henry Arthur Jones school were designed for performance by a balanced ensemble of actors—such as Australia had from 1885 in the BROUGH–BOUCICAULT COMEDY COMPANY—and did not require stars in order to be effective. The star's primary purpose now was to lure audiences into theatres. Once this was conceded, outstanding talent was no longer a requirement. Cora Brown Potter, who made a starring tour of Australia in 1890, was a socialite who had only recently turned to the stage. She acted amateurishly, but her name could sell tickets and that was enough. ❦*Harold Love*

Bland Holt, here with Flora Anstead (left) and his wife in The Fatal Card, *was a comic star who moved into management*

20th century

Control by actor-managers such as J. C. Williamson declined in the 20th century and entrepreneurs such as J. AND N. TAIT LTD arose, but there was no lessening of managers' reliance on star actors, if only because it seemed by long-established custom to be the surest way of attracting audiences. The star system to some extent reflected the economic imperatives of managements, particularly the driving need to find, groom and publicise actors whose galvanising abilities could pull in big houses. It functioned more or less in conjunction with the long-run system.

Today stardom is still partly the measure of an actor's capacity to keep houses full or almost full over a long run. But there is no necessary connection between stardom and artistic excellence. Stardom may be conferred on an actor simply by assiduous promotion and publicity. It may be achieved for a season only, or for the run of one very successful play. It may be maintained for years because an actor's individual talents and idiosyncrasies appeal to some public mood, ethos or expectation. Sometimes a star in one city may not be acknowledged as a star in another city, because of cultural differences between those cities.

Until at least the 1940s, theatre in Australia was umbilically tied to the United Kingdom and the USA, specifically to London and New York as the metropolitan centres of the English-speaking culture. Nearly all Australia's early actor-managers were British or American by birth or background. As a result of this inheritance, Australia's star system came to depend upon imported stars. They would sometimes bring an entire company in support, sometimes scratch together a company here.

There were occasional visiting stars of authentic magnitude, like Sara Allgood, Lewis Casson, Fay Compton, Vivien Leigh, Robert Morley, Laurence Olivier and Sybil Thorndike. There were a few stars of Australian origin, like JUDITH ANDERSON, OSCAR ASCHE, MADGE ELLIOTT and CYRIL RITCHARD, who returned for limited periods after success abroad. Broadly speaking, however, the colonial tour of Australia was undertaken by ageing, financially straitened or less-than-luminous stars who were in the twilight of careers in the West End or on Broadway. Yet managements persistently regarded them as box-office draws, mainly because they brought certain superficial aspects of metropolitan culture to a remote country that was still conscious of its colonial and derivative culture. For example, Edwin Styles, a popular English performer of the 1940s, brought to Australia the sophisticated speech mannerisms of English drawing-room comedy. Under these circumstances, it is hardly surprising that genuine homegrown stars flourished mainly in musicals and vaudeville, where the weight of the ruling culture was less overbearing than in straight drama. GLADYS MONCRIEFF remained a singing star for more than three decades with a repertoire that consisted basically of *The Maid of the Mountains*, *The Merry Widow*, *Rio Rita* and *Viktoria and Her Hussar*. JIM GERALD, ROY RENE and GEORGE WALLACE, constant stars of vaudeville and revue from the 1920s to the 1940s, all developed a distinctively Australian style of knockabout humour. BERT BAILEY—who made virtually a lifetime's work out of playing Dad in *ON OUR SELECTION*—was undoubtedly a star for rural audiences.

When the Great Depression compelled many playhouses to shut down or to become cinemas, actors turned to radio for their main employment. On radio the star system existed only in attenuated form. There was less scope than in the theatre to impress the actor's personality on audiences, because it was projected over the air by voice alone. Furthermore, an accomplished actor might have a monthly workload of daily or weekly serials, plus one or two 60-minute plays. For such an actor there would be some starring and some subsidiary roles. Vocal versatility was much in demand and actors were not encouraged to put the mark of a unique, easily recognisable personality on every character. George Edwards, for instance, could assume a dozen different voices in a single-half hour production. He was admired for his technique and he was a central figure of early radio, but he was more a gifted impersonator than a star. Radio actors of his prominence became known not as stars, but rather as characters in a serial or multi-voiced performers, or simply as household names involved in providing entertainment. Perhaps only PETER FINCH could have

The backdrop for Gladys Moncrieff on her farewell tour suggested that she drew upon a vast repertoire, but in reality a handful of operettas had sustained her stellar status

been considered a star actor on radio. Oddly enough, he was unable to transfer this star status to the stage, not through any deficiency in himself—he was extremely good in the theatre—but through lack of sensitivity in the public to theatrical quality, and gross lack of artistic vision in managements. In 1949 he was hailed as a star in London, yet during the previous five years he had appeared in only two roles on Australia's commercial stage—the district attorney in Ayn Rand's *The Night of January 16* and the Earl of Harpenden in Terence Rattigan's *While the Sun Shines*, both at the MINERVA THEATRE in Sydney. Between 1946 and 1948 Finch played four roles over short runs for MERCURY THEATRE but received no commercial offer that he thought worth taking. He worked chiefly in radio. His predicament clearly demonstrates that management and audiences alike were culturally resistant or at least unresponsive to recognising potential Australian stars. Finch had to go to London to attain stardom, because Australia adjudged only London opinion to be capable of deciding who was a star.

Ultimately, the star system, derived from British and American practice, did not transplant in Australia. At best it had simply been a system of containing Australian actors in colonial activity and it never took root in a significant way. Instead, the growth of indigenous acting styles, eclectic yet grounded in national experience, became closely linked to the growth of indigenous playwriting. It was this creative collaboration of dramatists and actors that eventually lifted Australian theatre out of colonial subservience and dependence upon overseas models and standards. There were still stars—actors of high talent, magnetism and drawing power. But the star system, which had aimed at making one actor the centre and *raison d'être* of theatrical performance—and often encouraged exhibitionism rather than interpretive depth and complexity—was no longer a dominant force. ❦*Allan Ashbolt*

Muriel Starr

Actor. Born 20 February 1888 in Montreal (Canada). Originally Muriel McIver. Acted in melodrama and musical comedy before joining Laurette Taylor's company 1904. Later went to New York City. Starred in *Bird of Paradise* in Chicago and San Francisco for Oliver Morosco. Came to Australia for J. C. Williamson's in 1913 and remained for three years. Later divided her time between Australia, New York and South Africa. Returned permanently to USA 1930. Died 19 April 1950 in New York.

Muriel Starr brought a new natural type of acting to Australia in *Within the Law* by Bayard Veiller in 1913 and her performances did much to rid Australian stages of Victorian melodramatics. She was also noted for her particularly musical voice, and she played long seasons in the title-role of *Madame X*, a French play adapted by John N. Raphael, and similar roles that were not really suited to her looks and style. Her repertoire managed to fill theatres until 1930, when she returned to the USA. For the rest of her career she played on Broadway in a variety of roles. Her last, in Rosemary Casey's *The Velvet Glove*, was a success but she died backstage during the second act. ❦*Alwyn Capern*

further reading
PARKER, JOHN (ed.). *Who's Who in the Theatre*. London: Pitman 1947.
Variety (New York City) 26 April 1950. Obituaries.

State Theatre

Professional dramatic company in Adelaide, founded as South Australian Theatre Company by Australian Elizabethan Theatre Trust 1965. Became statutory body 1972. Renamed State Theatre Company of South Australia in July 1979, Lighthouse Company 1982, State Theatre Company 1984, State Theatre 1994. **venues** 1965–71 Scott Theatre. 1972–73 Sheridan Theatre. 1974– Playhouse at Adelaide Festival Centre. 1980–81 Theatre 62. **artistic directors** 1965–67 John Tasker. 1968–70 Leslie Dayman. 1970–72 Peter Batey. 1972–76 George Ogilvie. 1977–80 Colin George. 1980–82 Nick Enright and Kevin Palmer. 1982–84 Jim Sharman. 1984–86 Keith Gallasch. 1986–89 John Gaden. 1990–93 Simon Phillips. **executive producer** 1994– Chris Westwood. **first production** *Andorra* by Max Frisch at Theatre 62, Adelaide. Director: John Tasker. Cast: Judy Dick, Tom Georgeson, Reg Livermore, Carmel Millhouse. **landmark productions** *The Royal Hunt of the Sun* by Peter Shaffer, 1966 Adelaide Festival. *The Three Cuckolds*, 1974. *Oedipus* and *Oedipus at Colonus* by Sophocles, 1978. *A Midsummer Night's Dream*, 1982. *Signal Driver* by Patrick White, 1982. *A Dream Play* by August Strindberg, 1988. *The Comedy of Errors*, 1990.

South Australia's dramatic company, under various names, has become vital to artistic life in the state. As the South Australian Theatre Company, it struggled hard in its early years. 'It drifted from hired theatre to hired theatre', wrote COLIN BALLANTYNE, a dominant force in Adelaide theatrical life. 'Lack of a permanent home for production and administration has a demoralising effect on all concerned.' The first artistic director, JOHN TASKER, chose *The Royal Hunt of the Sun* by Peter Shaffer for the company's first appearance at the ADELAIDE FESTIVAL OF ARTS, at Bonython Hall in 1966. In 1967 Tasker, who had hoped for enough funds to support a company of contracted players, quarrelled with the board. The Melbourne director WAL CHERRY, who had moved to Adelaide, engineered his dismissal. A South Australian actor and director, LESLIE DAYMAN, succeeded Tasker in 1968; his first production was *Burke's Company* by BILL REED. Ballantyne directed August Strindberg's *The Father* in 1968. This was his only production for the company, to his disappointment.

In 1970 PETER BATEY from Sydney became artistic director. He had a contracted company of actors, gave a steady output of quality plays and toured national occasionally. The confidence of the company grew, along with subsidies and box-office receipts. PETER COLLINGWOOD directed Anton Chekhov's *The Seagull* for the 1970 Adelaide Festival.

Don Dunstan became Premier of South Australia in 1970. He was a supporter of Tasker and a witness to the squabbles within the state company. He wanted to put it on a secure footing financially and to secure the authority of the artistic director. In 1972 his government established the company as a statutory body and appointed Ballantyne chairman. At the end of the year GEORGE OGILVIE was appointed artistic director, with his general pre-eminence and autonomy in production matters entrenched by contract. His associates were RODNEY FISHER and, as director of youth activities, HELMUT BAKAITIS. Ogilvie, according to Peter Ward, brought to the company 'dedication, a romantic commitment to style, passion and the large gesture'. He embarked on daily training for his ensemble of actors and it was months before the public saw the company. A notable production in 1973 was DAVID WILLIAMSON's *Jugglers Three*.

The company had two productions in the 1974 Adelaide Festival—*The Comedy of Errors* and the first professional production OF LOUIS ESSON's *The Bride of Gospel Place*, directed by Fisher. In 1974 the company took up residence at the Playhouse in the ADELAIDE FESTIVAL CENTRE, where it opened with *The Three Cuckolds*, an exercise in *commedia dell'arte*. Ogilvie directed the company in *Coriolanus* at the 1976 Adelaide Festival, when it also presented Tennessee Williams's *Kingdom of the Earth*, directed by Fisher. Ogilvie made a farewell appearance in Ken Campbell's *Old King Cole*, directed by Roger Chapman, an Englishman who was the company's new theatre-in-education director. While Ogilvie was artistic director the company had developed into an integrated ensemble and reached a standard of design and style in its productions that was unusual in Australia at that time.

The new artistic director was Colin George, an Englishman who had been lecturing in drama at the University of New England. He opened the 1977 season with his production of R. B. Sheridan's *The School for Scandal*. A protégé of Tyrone Guthrie, George gave the company new energy, stability and professional focus. NICK ENRIGHT was appointed associate director and Malcolm Moore director of the theatre-in-education MAGPIE THEATRE Company. George favoured bold and lavish productions such as his spectacular Sophocles's *Oedipus* and *Oedipus at Colonus*, designed by Tanya Moiseiwitsch, in the 1978 festival.

George ended his term—during which the company had scheduled more new Australian plays than any other state theatre company—playing Vershinin in his own production of Chekhov's *Three Sisters* in mid–1980. Enright and Kevin Palmer were appointed joint artistic directors. They maintained the policy on new Australian plays, introducing DAVID ALLEN's *Upside Down at the Bottom of the World*, DOREEN CLARKE's *Farewell Brisbane Ladies*, Dorothy Hewett's *THE MAN FROM MUKINUPIN* and ALAN SEYMOUR's *The Float*.

In 1982 JIM SHARMAN directed the Adelaide Festival and was also appointed artistic director of the State Theatre Company. He thought its statutory name felt institutional and instigated a change to Lighthouse Company. He related this to a statue of Colonel William Light, the founder of Adelaide, which appears to be pointing to the Playhouse. The public became confused. WITH NEIL ARMFIELD and LOUIS NOWRA as his associate directors, Sharman established a permanent ensemble of 12 actors and three musicians. He particularly wanted to give audiences new approaches to Shakespeare. One of his triumphs was his production of *A Midsummer Night's Dream*, which became 'a dream within a dream, a play encased in a fantastical twentieth century limbo', according to Peter Ward.

Sharman presented many new Australian plays, including PATRICK WHITE's *Netherwood* and *Signal Driver* and Nowra's *Spellbound* and *Royal Show*. DAVID WILLIAMSON criticised Sharman in 1982 for not taking up his current hit *The Perfectionist*. Sharman replied that the Lighthouse Company was 'not suited to social documentary style. We are not looking for proven box-office smashes—we are looking to create our own'. He was keen to pursue 'a theatricality similar to that of Elizabethan theatre. Domestic comedy is not our forte.'

Another of Sharman's initiatives was Days with Lighthouse, which allowed school parties to spend a day in the company's production department, later attend a performance, and afterwards question the director and cast. This is still practised. KEITH GALLASCH, one of the founders of the Adelaide alternative company TROUPE, joined Lighthouse as an actor and assistant director in November 1982 and succeeded Sharman at the end of 1983, The time had come for a local artistic director, it was thought. The company's name reverted to State Theatre Company of South Australia in 1984. Gallasch's 1984 season included a promenade production of Molière's *Don Juan* for the Adelaide Festival, directed by Jean-Pierre Mignon and superbly designed by SHAUN GURTON, with WILLIAM ZAPPA excellent in the title-role. The associate director of the company, NEIL ARMFIELD impressively directed Patrick White's *THE SEASON AT SARSAPARILLA*. This revival restated the commitment to White's plays instigated by Sharman.

By 1986 subscriptions had dwindled and the shadow minister for the arts complained about the company's policy of producing Australian plays. JOHN GADEN, appointed artistic director in 1986, faced the task of improving the company's prestige and finances. In the 1986 Adelaide Festival he acted in Armfield's production of *Dreams in an Empty City* by STEPHEN SEWELL. Gale Edwards, associate director of the company, joined Gaden to direct Tom Stoppard's play *The Real Thing*. This was a winner at the box office. In 1987 Gaden brought in several SYDNEY THEATRE COMPANY productions, including *EMERALD CITY* by David Williamson, in which an all-star cast led by JOHN BELL, RUTH CRACKNELL, DREW FORSYTHE and ROBYN NEVIN played to 96 per cent capacity. Bell was also a guest director, as were LINDY DAVIES, RODNEY FISHER, Ian Watson and JOHN WOOD.

When Gaden left the company in 1989 its subscriptions and finances had improved dramatically despite severe reductions in funding. The new artistic director was 31-year-old SIMON PHILLIPS. Shaun Gurton became associate director and resident designer and Ian MacDonald became the company's musical director. A talented ensemble of actors included Dennis Coard, Bob Hornery, Carmel McGlone, Jane Menelaus, Richard Piper and GEOFFREY RUSH. In 1994 the government's economic problems, arising from the collapse of the State Bank, led to the chief executives being replaced by an executive producer to generate productions outside the company. ❦*Jo Peoples*

further reading
BRISBANE, KATHARINE. Art needs business. *Australian* (Sydney) 16 December 1967.
BRISBANE, KATHARINE. Bring us a Diaghilev. *Australian* (Sydney) 9 December 1967.
WARD, PETER. *A Singular Act—Twenty-five years of the State Theatre Company of South Australia*. Adelaide: Wakefield Press 1992.

State Theatre Company of Western Australia

Professional dramatic company in Perth, founded 1 January 1992, amalgamating Hole-in-the-Wall and Western Australian Theatre Companies. Closed 1993. **artistic director** Raymond Omodei. **venue** Subiaco Theatre Centre.

Before 1981 the HOLE-IN-THE-WALL THEATRE COMPANY and the NATIONAL THEATRE COMPANY informally discussed artistic and financial issues—especially subsidy—and the viability of two such companies in a city as small as Perth. Neither was able to mount full-scale productions with large casts in either the classical or modern repertoires. In 1990 Hole-in-the-Wall floated the idea of a state company by amalgamating its funding with that of the Western Australian Theatre Company, which had replaced the National Theatre Company. By the second half of 1991 a steering committee appointed by the state Labor government had established the State Theatre Company of Western Australia as a working title. Hole-in-the-Wall presented major productions under its aegis until the State Theatre Company was fully incorporated on the first day of 1992.

The company expected combined funding from state and federal sources to total about $1·2 million, but in the event it received $600 000, from the state only. Nevertheless it played a striking repertoire to more than 55 000 patrons and employed an average of 12 actors a week during 1992. The plays were *Antony and Cleopatra*, William Wycherley's *The Country Wife*, Tennessee Williams's *Orpheus Descending*, Patrick White's THE SEASON AT SARSAPARILLA, Michael Gow's *Away* and Heather Nimmo's *One Small Step*. The last was a world premiere, as were two productions by the company for the 1993 Festival of Perth—*Tell Tales*, monologues by six Western Australian writers, and John Aitken's *Daisy Bates and the Dancer*.

Plans for 1993 were well ahead when the company asked the Department for the Arts for an advance on its funding. The minister for the arts in the new Liberal government, however, announced the withdrawal of all state funding for the company. It has ceased to operate, leaving Western Australia as the only mainland state without its own major theatre company. ❦*Maurice Jones*

Anthony Steel

Administrator. Born 28 October 1932 in England. Educated at Oxford University. In family steel business in Sheffield for five years. General manager of London Mozart Players. Assistant general secretary of London Symphony Orchestra. Worked at South Bank concert halls in London. General manager of Adelaide Festival Centre. Director of Adelaide Festival of Arts 1974, 1976, 1978, 1984, 1986. General manager of Los Angeles Philharmonic Orchestra. Artistic director of Brisbane Biennial 1991, 1993. Appointed artistic director of Festival of Sydney 1994.

In the early 1970s the South Australian government looked in London for a general manager for the ADELAIDE FESTIVAL CENTRE TRUST and a director for the ADELAIDE FESTIVAL OF ARTS. Anthony Steel came to Adelaide to observe the 1972 festival. He then proposed that he take on both jobs, at an appropriate remuneration. Steel oversaw three Adelaide Festivals. They were distinguished in the theatre by Peter Williams's production of Athol Fugard's *Hello and Goodbye* and Poland's Cricot 2 company in Tadeusz Kantor's *The Dead Class*. Steel's artistic manifesto was uncompromising. In an interview in the *National Times* of 13–18 February 1978 he said: 'The Festival of Arts must pursue excellence … or else why bother to have a festival at all?' He was equally uncompromising on his own role: 'There has to be a front man. Someone whose name is synonymously linked with the festival. He should have total artistic responsibility and take both the praise and the blame. He cannot operate without power. Denied, he becomes a rubber stamp for the board of governors, a strutting puppet mouthing borrowed opinions.' Steel's relations with the board were not always placid and he resigned after the 1978 festival to go to Los Angeles. Two years later his love of Australia drew him back, first as advisor to the Cladan Cultural Exchange in Sydney. In May 1981 he became artistic director of the entrepreneurial division of the AUSTRALIAN ELIZABETHAN THEATRE TRUST. He oversaw two more Adelaide Festivals and he has been artistic consultant to international events, including World Expo '88 in Brisbane. ❦*John West*

Barbara Stellmach

Dramatist. Born 23 June 1930 in Warwick (Qld). Brought up in country towns. Studied speech and drama on scholarship at Trinity College (London). Taught speech and drama. Began acting, directing and writing for Villanova Players (Brisbane) after marriage in 1954. Founding president of Playlab 1972–74.

Perhaps the most performed playwright in Australian amateur theatre is Barbara Stellmach, who has been called the 'playwright of the little theatres'. Recognising the needs of amateur companies, she has written some 26 plays. Her second play, *Dust is the Heart* won a drama festival competition in 1961, *Hang Your Clothes on Yonder Bush* won a national competition in 1969 and *From the Fourteenth Floor You Can See the Harbour Bridge* was joint winner of the Society of Women Writers competition in 1976. ❦*Rod Lumer*

published plays
Dark Heritage (1964). Brisbane: University of Queensland Press 1973 in *Four Australian Plays*.
Dust is the Heart (1961). Brisbane: University of Queensland Press 1973 in *Four Australian Plays*.
From the Fourteenth Floor You Can See the Harbour Bridge (1980). Brisbane: Playlab Press 1980.
Hang Your Clothes on Yonder Bush (1969). Brisbane: University of Queensland Press 1973 in *Four Australian Plays*.
Legend of the Losers (1971). Brisbane: University of Queensland Press 1973 in *Four Australian Plays*.
Not Even a Mouse (1974). Brisbane: Playlab Press 1978.

Babette Stephens MBE

Actor, director. Born 1910 in England. Originally Babette Fergusson. Emigrated to Townsville (Qld). Member of Townsville Repertory Group 1928. Joined Brisbane Repertory Theatre Society 1930. Married Tom Stephens 1935. Founding member of Twelfth Night Theatre (Brisbane) 1936. Honorary artistic director of La Boîte Theatre, Brisbane, 1960–68. Turned professional in 1960s and worked in radio, television, film and theatre. Foundation member of board of QUEENSLAND THEATRE COMPANY 1969. QTC Lifetime Achievement Award 1993. MBE 1974.

A pioneer of theatre in Brisbane, Babette Stephens has been associated with the BRISBANE REPERTORY THEATRE SOCIETY for more than 60 years as actor, director, president and artistic director. She joined the society in 1930 and appeared in its 65th anniversary celebrations in July 1990. Her first production for the society was Githa Sowerby's *Rutherford and Son* in 1930. Brisbane Repertory developed its semiprofessional status while Stephens was artistic director of its La Boîte Theatre. After her resignation in 1968 she directed occasional productions for the society. Stephens and her husband were founder members of the TWELFTH NIGHT THEATRE COMPANY in 1936, and she acted and directed for the new company. The QUEENSLAND THEATRE COMPANY made her an associate artist in recognition of her contribution to theatre. She appeared for the company in Oscar Wilde's *The Importance of Being Earnest* in 1975, Ivan Turgenev's *A Month in the Country* in 1990, Arthur Miller's *The Crucible* in 1991 and Martin Buzzacott's *Carnival in Kingaroy* in 1992. ❦*Delyse Anthony*

further reading
ANTHONY, DELYSE. The early history of Twelfth Night Theatre, 1936–1946. University of Queensland honours thesis 1990.

Douglas Stewart

Dramatist. Born 30 December 1915 at Eltham (New Zealand). Came to Australia 1933. Literary editor of *Bulletin* 1940–60. Wrote poetry, criticism and five verse plays 1941–60. Died 14 February 1985 in Sydney.

The foremost verse dramatist in Australia, Douglas Stewart believed, like his American counterpart Maxwell Anderson, that plays should create 'the myths by which the people live' and depict the heroic, legendary figures that help to shape national identity. Stewart's plays, typical of poetic drama of the period—except the lighter folk-play *Fisher's Ghost* (1960)—concern heroism and leadership. They have been seen to contrast the 'Ulyssean' life, with its urge for adventure, with the 'Telemachean' urge for settled, civilised security. NED KELLY shows the bushranger as a romantic but flawed hero, challenging the timidity of townspeople and defeated by the irresistible force of social order. *The Fire on the Snow*, a radio play which has had several stage productions, emphasises human endurance and the role of Captain Robert Scott as leader of a heroic expedition to the South Pole in 1912. *Shipwreck* dramatises the mutiny after the Dutch ship *Batavia* foundered off the northwest Australian coast in 1629. It shows the anarchic mutineers Cornelius, Huyssen and Seevanck with some sympathy. Their defeat by Heynorich, a conscientious butler, and the return of Captain Pelsart subtly question the obligations of authority. *Shipwreck* is, as he believed, Stewart's finest, most complex play. ❦*Elizabeth Perkins*

published plays
The Fire on the Snow (1941 as radio play). Sydney: Angus and Robertson 1944, 1964.
The Golden Lover (1943 as radio play, staged 1953). Sydney: Angus and Robertson 1944, 1962. Brisbane: University of Queensland Press 1977.
Ned Kelly (1942). Sydney: Angus and Robertson 1943. Melbourne: Penguin 1963, in *Three Australian Plays*.
Shipwreck (1951). Sydney: Shepherd Press 1947; Angus and Robertson 1958, in *Four Plays*.

further reading
BURROWS, J. F. An approach to the plays of Douglas Stewart. *Southerly* 23/2 (Sydney 1963).
CARROLL, DENNIS. *Australian Contemporary Drama*. Sydney: Currency Press 1995.
OLIVER, HAROLD J. Douglas Stewart and the art of the radio play. *Texas Quarterly* summer 1962.
PHILLIPS, A. A. *The Australian Tradition*. Melbourne: Cheshire 1958.
SEMMLER, CLEMENT. *Douglas Stewart*. New York: Twayne 1974.

Nancye Stewart

Actor. Born 19 June 1893 at Chingford (Essex, England). Daughter of Nellie Stewart and George Musgrove. Acting debut in Sydney 1914. In plays for J. C. Williamson's and J. and N. Tait Ltd 1915–18. Acted in USA 1919–22. Married actor Mayne Lynton. Acted for J. C. Williamson's 1922–29. Acted on radio in Sydney and Melbourne 1930–49. Toured with John Alden Shakespeare Company 1951–52. Old Vic Theatre Company (London) 1953–54. Shakespeare Memorial Theatre Company (Stratford-upon-Avon) 1954–55. Australian Elizabethan Theatre Trust (Sydney) 1957–58. Television and radio in Sydney in 1960s. Died 8 August 1973 in Sydney.

Nancye Stewart excelled in Shakespeare and character parts. 'It's as a character actress that Nancye excels', said her mother, NELLIE STEWART. 'Our mode of acting is entirely different. In fact, our characters are different. My girlie is more like her father.' GEORGE MUSGROVE, her father, counted the Kembles and Sarah Siddons among his ancestors, and her mother was also descended from notable English actors. Nancye Stewart had a thorough musical and theatrical training, and in 1911 she conducted the orchestra on her mother's six-month outback tour.

She made her acting debut in *Joseph and His Brethren* by Louis N. Parker for J. C. WILLIAMSON'S in Sydney in 1914 and then toured Australasia with her mother's company, playing several parts in David Belasco's *Du Barry* and Kester's *When Knighthood was in Flower*. Her work with J. C. Williamson's to 1918 included understudying and playing with the famous English actor Marie Tempest. After George Musgrove's death in 1916 she appeared with her mother in *Sweet Nell* at the Tivoli Theatres in Sydney and Melbourne, presenting one act a week on vaudeville programs. Later she played Juliet to her mother's Romeo in charity performances of the balcony scene. In the USA in 1919 she played in New York and Boston and in 1920 she toured with George M. Cohan in his *Genius and the Crowd*. She married the English actor MAYNE LYNTON and they came to Australia in 1922. Both worked continuously for J. C. Williamson's until 1929. During the theatrical drought of the 1930s Stewart was a leading dramatic actor on radio.

On stage with the JOHN ALDEN COMPANY in 1951–52 she played Goneril in *King Lear*, Mistress Page in *The Merry Wives of Windsor* and Hippolyta in *A Midsummer Night's Dream*. In England in 1953–55 she played Gertrude with the Old Vic Theatre Company in London and at Stratford-upon-Avon she was in Peter Brook's productions of *Macbeth* and *Titus Andronicus*. Back in Australia, she toured with Margaret Rutherford in John Dighton's *The Happiest Days of Your Life* in 1957–58, then spent most of her remaining years in radio and television. ❦*Richard Lane*

Nellie Stewart

Actor, singer. Born 20 November 1858 in Sydney. Daughter of actors Richard Stewart and Theodosia Stirling. Made stage debut at five. Unrivalled prima donna of Australian musical stage 1882–90. Married Richard Goldsbrough Row 26 January 1884; divorced 1901. Played non-singing roles from 1902. Companion of entrepreneur George Musgrove. Mother of actor Nancye Stewart. Half-sister of actors Maggie and Docie Stewart. Died 20 June 1931 in Sydney.

Vivacity and charm in operetta, pantomime and straight plays, magnetism that reached out to audiences and embraced them, and charity work over many years all brought Nellie Stewart the titles 'Australia's idol' and 'the darling of the Australian stage'. She was born into a theatrical family. Her mother, THEODOSIA STIRLING, had theatrical antecedents stretching back to the mid-18th century, and her father, RICHARD STEWART, had taken up acting in GEORGE COPPIN's company. Stewart took his family to Melbourne in the year after Nellie's birth to join their theatrical friends, especially Coppin and W. S. LYSTER. Nellie made her stage debut at the age of five in Friedrich von Kotzebue's melodrama *The Stranger* with the visiting star Charles Kean at the Haymarket Theatre in Melbourne. Her strict but adoring parents sedulously trained her in all aspects of theatrical arts. As a young girl she appeared occasionally in minor roles in productions by her father and his friends, often with her half-sisters Maggie and Docie, but her father strictly controlled her performances. In 1875, when she was 16, she attracted favourable attention in an important role in a pantomime. In 1877 she and Docie played leading roles in GEORGE DARRELL's melodrama *Transported for Life*.

By this time the various talents of the Stewart family had attracted the attention of the dramatist GARNET WALCH, and he devised for them an entertainment called *Rainbow Revels*, in which they sang, danced and impersonated widely differing characters. Richard Stewart and his three talented daughters toured Australasia with the show, so successfully that Walch set about writing another for them in 1878. While he was doing so Richard Stewart produced *HMS Pinafore* in Melbourne, with Nellie as Ralph Rackstraw.

Walch's new entertainment for the Stewarts was *If*, advertised as 'a meal of mirth, music and mimicry'. Melbourne greeted it enthusiastically in May 1879 and Nellie caught the critics' attention with her naturalness and charm. Stewart and his daughters took *If* overseas, playing in Calcutta and Bombay, and then London. The critics were always enthusiastic and as time went on Nellie increasingly won the highest praise. Back in Melbourne, Coppin was well aware of what was happening. When the family reached New York there was a cable from him, asking them to return home to appear in Walch's pantomime *Sinbad the Sailor*, with Nellie as principal boy.

Return they did, and it was a turning-point in Nellie's life. *Sinbad* opened on 27 December 1880, the same night as GEORGE MUSGROVE's production of Jacques Offenbach's opéra-bouffe LA FILLE DU TAMBOUR-MAJOR. By the end of *Sinbad*'s 14-week run it was obvious that Nellie Stewart was a star. A photograph of her, a delight in ostrich plumes and spangled tights, was in every barber's shop and every postcard album. Her success and beauty were not lost on Musgrove, and when the singer playing the drummer boy Griolet dropped out, he offered the role to Stewart. Her saucy performance was a major contribution to the record-breaking production's continued box-office success.

Stewart was a valuable asset for Musgrove to contribute in 1882, when he entered the partnership of WILLIAMSON, GARNER AND MUSGROVE, known as 'the triumvirate'. As the star of the partners' Royal Comic Opera Company, Stewart was busy in 1882–83. She had important roles in *Les Cloches de Corneville*, *La Mascotte* and *Olivette* as well as *La Fille du tambour-major*. In December 1883 she played the title-role in *Patience* and on Boxing Night opened at the Theatre Royal in Sydney as principal boy in a lavish pantomime, *Jack and the Beanstalk*. All found her bewitching, none more than Richard Goldsbrough Row, scion of a wealthy Melbourne family, who visited the theatre night after night. Finally she succumbed to his ardour, and the two were secretly married on 26 January 1884. But when the Royal Comic Opera Company sailed for New Zealand less than a fortnight later Stewart went without her husband. She never returned to him. Years later, in her book *My Life's Story*, she described her marriage as 'a girl's mad act'. It was also probably a defensive act, for the truth was that she and Musgrove were now deeply in love, but Musgrove was married with children. His marriage—begun when he was only 20—was unhappy but his wife refused to grant him a divorce.

Touring for Williamson, Garner and Musgrove from 1883 to 1887, Stewart sang more than 20 leading roles in operettas, including many by Gilbert and Sullivan, crowned by an impishly individual Yum-Yum in *The Mikado*. After a particularly strenuous season of Gilbert and Sullivan she announced a temporary retirement from the stage and early in 1887 left for London with Musgrove, his mother and his aunt. Musgrove had hoped to launch Stewart's career in London, but she made no professional appearance on that visit. By making the trip, however, she did publicly declare her domestic status. From that time Stewart and Musgrove lived only for each other. Her career and happiness superseded all else in his life. To Stewart he was her 'great and good man'.

They returned to Melbourne at the end of 1887, at a time when the triumvirate had experienced a rare failure, with *Dorothy*. Stewart had seen Marie Tempest acclaimed in the operetta in London and she begged to do it. A revival was quickly mounted at the Princess Theatre, conducted by the work's composer, Alfred Cellier. Stewart scored an enormous success, particularly with the whip-cracking song 'Tallyho!' Cellier was so moved that he persuaded Nellie to sing Marguerite in *Faust*. The triumvirate seemed to treat Gounod's opera as yet another operetta and had Stewart singing Marguerite six nights a week for 22 consecutive performances. 'Miss Stewart sang to the end with unflagging spirit and fine vocal power', wrote the *Argus* critic. But it was a foolhardy feat and her voice was severely strained.

In 1890 Stewart announced that she was going into management herself with a production of a new operetta, *Paul Jones*. She co-starred with Marion Burton, a contralto from the concert platform. Musgrove withdrew from the triumvirate soon after *Paul Jones* opened in Melbourne and consequently the Sydney season of the Nellie Stewart Opera Company was presented by him. That season also included *Boccaccio* and *Chilpéric*, in which Stewart performed vigorously and compounded the damage to her voice.

Stewart made several more visits to London before the end of the century, accompanying Musgrove—who was in an uneasy partnership with J. C. WILLIAMSON from 1892—on business trips. In 1892 she made her London stage debut in *Blue-eyed Susan*, an operetta by G. R. Sims and Osmond Carr. Later in the year she took over the lead in Charles Lecocq's *Incognita* at the Lyric Theatre for what turned out to be a brief engagement. She was disappointed with her work in these two operettas, but she reached a peak of happiness in June 1893 when she gave birth to her daughter Nancye, fathered by Musgrove. Nellie Stewart had her great theatrical success in 26 December 1898, when she appeared at the Royal Theatre, Drury Lane, as principal boy in *The Forty Thieves*, a pantomime written by Arthur Collins and Arthur Sturgess. 'Nellie Stewart was the best principal boy Drury Lane ever had', wrote Collins, who also managed the theatre and produced the pantomime.

On 15 February 1902 Musgrove, who had separately from Williamson since 1900, presented Stewart in her first non-singing role—as Nell Gwyn, the actress who became the favourite of King Charles II, in Paul Kester's play *Sweet Nell of Old Drury*. Musgrove had bought the play after its success in London in 1900. He doubted whether Stewart's speaking voice was strong enough to carry the role, but her singing voice had practically gone, and he had to take the chance. She too was full of pessimism, but after the opening night at the Princess Theatre the *Argus* critic wrote: 'This performance places her among the very best of the comedy actresses who have been seen in Australia'. The play became synonymous with Stewart's name, and she performed the role for the rest of her life.

In 1904, at the Lyceum Theatre in Sydney, she followed her triumph in *Sweet Nell* with *Pretty Peggy*, a comedy-drama about another Drury Lane actress, Peg Woffington. Reviewing this play, the *Sydney Morning Herald* critic said Stewart 'had reigned for more than a decade as the representative and unrivalled comic opera prima donna of the Australian stage and must be recognised as our finest comedy actress'.

On Christmas Day 1905 Musgrove and Stewart, with a full dramatic company, stagehands and a great quantity of scenery, costumes and props, sailed for San Francisco. Musgrove had arranged an American tour presenting Stewart in a lavish production of *Sweet Nell*. They opened in San Francisco and reviewers praised the beauty and magnetism of the star and the grand scale of the production. But an earthquake, followed by fire, devastated the city on 17 April 1906. All the *Sweet Nell* costumes and scenery were destroyed and the tour had to be abandoned.

This was a financial disaster from which Musgrove never really recovered. He travelled to England to sell property he owned there and remitted funds to Stewart in the USA so that the company could be sent back to Australia. Stewart sold every piece of her jewellery so that she and Nancye could join Musgrove in England, where he was attempting to recoup their fortunes by forming an opera company. He returned to Australia, leaving Stewart to try to secure rights to a suitable play for herself. She bought *Sweet Kitty Bellairs* by David Belasco, engaged principals and bought costumes, but when she arrived back in Melbourne she discovered that Musgrove was very ill.

Stewart returned to the Melbourne stage in the Princess Theatre at Easter 1909 with an enormous success in *Sweet Kitty Bellairs*. She was greeted with wild enthusiasm after her long absence, especially by the 'gallery girls', with whom she had a particular bond. She played long exhausting seasons through 1909 and 1910, embracing Melbourne, Sydney and New Zealand, alternating *Kitty Bellairs* with J. M. Barrie's *What Every Woman Knows*, Kester's *When Knighthood was in Flower*, Paul Potter's *Trilby*, Belasco's *Zaza* and, of course, *Sweet Nell*.

During this time Stewart gave a matinée to raise money for radium equipment for Sydney Hospital. It was widely advertised also that she would be selling donated gifts and lavender at David Jones' store in the hour before the performance. All Sydney seemed to turn out to buy from her. The matinée was also a personal triumph. Such was Stewart's popularity that large anonymous donations were made to the fund, which realised £3000. She worked to help such causes for the rest of her life. She was made a life governor of Sydney Hospital and a children's ward was named after her. Later in 1910 Stewart headed Musgrove's company on a two-month tour of New Zealand, playing 32 towns. They were back in Sydney on 27 January 1911. Musgrove gave his company a week's paid holiday before they returned to the road, in Tasmania. Then they played *Sweet Nell* for six months of one-night stands in outback towns on the mainland, ending at Maryborough (Qld). Nellie Stewart was then 53. CLAUDE MCKAY, who toured with her as public relations man, said her vitality never flagged and she never missed a performance. He described her as having a gift of enthusiasm, enduring charm and infectious gaiety. Others have said that she had the secret of perennial youth.

She also had courage. Musgrove in his will stated that Nellie Stewart 'by years of hard work without payment greatly advanced my interests which without her aid I would probably have no estate whatever'. During his lingering illness, Stewart cared for him with the help of Docie, managed his theatrical interests, and appeared on stage continually, notably in Musgrove's last production, Belasco's *Du Barry*. For this Nellie Stewart herself made the costumes, so parlous were their finances. Musgrove died at their Sydney home 'Den o' Gwynne' on 21 January 1916. Stewart mourned for him for the rest of her life.

In these years she played *Sweet Nell* many times and continued her charity work, especially for Sydney Hospital and cancer patients. She had never forgotten her feelings when her much-loved father died from cancer in 1902. In 1930 she studied a new play, *Romance* by Edward Sheldon, and appeared in it in Melbourne. HAL PORTER wrote that although she was 72 her age was not apparent from the auditorium, as she moved with the litheness of a young woman and her voice, with the merest tinge of huskiness, gave the touch of truth to the somewhat trite words of the play. In her 73rd year she played Nell Gwyn for the last time. She died a month later, after a bout of pleurisy, with daughter Nancye at her bedside. ❦*Richard Lane*

writings
My Life's Story. Sydney: John Sands 1923. Autobiography.

further reading
BEVAN, IAN. *The Story of the Theatre Royal*. Sydney. Currency Press 1993.
COOPER, ROSS. Eleanor Towzey Stewart. *Australian Dictionary of Biography* 12. Melbourne University Press 1990.
SKILL, MARJORIE. *Sweet Nell of Old Drury*. Sydney: Urania 1973.

Richard Stewart

Actor, director. Originally Richard Towzey. Born c.1826 in England. Came to Australia 1853. Became actor and changed surname to Stewart. Married Theodosia Stirling in Sydney 1857. Acted and directed plays and pantomimes in Melbourne from 1857. Toured India, London and New York with daughter and stepdaughters 1879–80. Later J. C. Williamson's treasurer in Melbourne. Died 1902 in Melbourne. Father of Nellie Stewart, actor and singer, and Richard Stewart. Stepfather of Docie and Maggie Stewart, actors.

Richard Towzey came to Australia to try his luck on the goldfields but he soon turned up in Sydney, changed his surname to Stewart and became an actor and stage manager in GEORGE COPPIN's company. In 1857 he married THEODOSIA STIRLING, who was then the widowed Mrs

Guerin. They had a daughter, NELLIE STEWART, in 1858 and in the next year, soon after the family settled in Melbourne, their son Richard was born. The elder Richard Stewart was a light comedian and soft-shoe dancer and a well-regarded producer. In his early days in Melbourne he collaborated on productions with Coppin and W. S. LYSTER, often acting in them with some or all of his daughters. Among such productions were *Bluebeard* and *Orpheus in the Underworld*, *opéras-bouffes* by Jacques Offenbach. The theatrical talents of the Stewart family attracted the attention of the writer GARNET WALCH, and he devised *Rainbow Revels*, a program of songs, dances and sketches, for them. Stewart produced it and performed in it with his daughters, and his son looked after front of house. They toured Australia and New Zealand with great success, returning to Melbourne in 1878. Stewart then presented his family in *HMS Pinafore* while Walch devised a new entertainment for them. This was *If*, described in the *Argus* as 'a meal of mirth, music and mimicry'. Stewart and his daughters played *If* with great success in Calcutta and Bombay—and took it on to London and New York. Then a cable from Coppin asked the family to return to Melbourne to play in his pantomime *Sinbad*.

This opened on Boxing Day 1880 with Nellie as principal boy and her stardom began. She owed much to the training in stagecraft she had been given by her father. 'He was a good actor and singer, a master of stagecraft, with a keen dramatic sense, a genuine and cordial sense of humour and a love of music', she wrote in her autobiography. After *Sinbad* Richard Stewart gradually withdrew from performing, and acted nominally as her manager and worked as treasurer for J. C. WILLIAMSON. ❦*Richard Lane*

Stiffy and Mo

In the 1920s Stiffy and Mo were synonymous with Australian VARIETY. In an era when popular artists would change theatres every five weeks, NAT PHILLIPS and ROY RENE, as Stiffy and Mo, would pack one theatre for six months at a time with their revues, which filled half the bill. They met shortly after Phillips returned to Australia from 12 years in Europe and took charge of a FULLERS' revue company. Phillips, already known as Stiffy, suggested a partnership to the young 'Hebrew' comedian. Rene proposed to call himself Ikey, but the agent Bill Sadler came up with Mo and it stuck. After opening in Sydney in June 1916, Stiffy and Mo never looked back. They starred in Fullers' all-Australian pantomime THE BUNYIP at the end of 1916 and their low comedy packed theatres wherever they played.

Many of Stiffy and Mo's early scripts were written in London by Vic Roberts, an Englishman hired by BENJAMIN FULLER. That the pair, using scripts written by an unknown Englishman who had not seen them perform, could be regarded as typically Australian demonstrates the closeness of English and Australian variety at the time. The more experienced Phillips later wrote and produced many of the half-bill revues. Rene's comic genius brought them alive and quickly made him one of Australia's biggest stars. The typical Stiffy and Mo revue was thin in plot and generous in ad-libbing. Mo was the underdog, whom the straight man Stiffy would attempt to berate into submission. Despite Stiffy's authority, Mo generally won, often through his obsequiousness. The pair picked an identity or a venue—they were lords, waiters and wharf lumpers and visited the navy, the races, or a beauty parlour—and worked gags around it. If a gag worked, its relevance to the central motif was unimportant. Stiffy and Mo brought city slang to the stage and popularised it. Rene thrived on the double entendre and an ability to make a perfectly clean line suggestive. This brought the pair some critical disapproval, especially early in their career. Many lines that even Rene could not have said on stage did the rounds in Stiffy and Mo anecdotes. Rene was sacked for vulgarity in Adelaide in 1925, and the pair split. They reunited in Brisbane 18 months later. Their reunion 'almost overshadowed the Royal visit' of the Duke and Duchess of York, said *Just It* on 2 June 1927. 'We are proud of these Prime Ministers of mirth', it declared. At the end of 1928, while on tour in New Zealand, Phillips decided the act was becoming tired and the pair split irrevocably. Phillips worked on the stage until his death in 1932. Rene went on to success on radio as well as in the theatre. ❦*Victoria Chance*

further reading
RENE, ROY with ELIZABETH LAMBERT and MAX HARRIS. *Mo's Memoirs*. Melbourne: Reed and Harris 1945.

Theodosia Stirling

Actor, singer. Born 1815 in Ireland. Originally Theodosia Yates. Great-granddaughter of actors Richard and Mary Anne Yates. Sang contralto roles in opera at Theatre Royal, Drury Lane, in London. Came to Hobart for Anne Clarke. Performed at first as Mrs Stirling and then, after marrying musician James Guerin, as Mrs Guerin. Moved to Sydney with family 1845. Widowed 1856. Married actor Richard Stewart 1857. Settled in Melbourne with family 1859. Retired from stage 1877. Died 19 July 1904 in Melbourne. Mother of actors Docie, Maggie and Nellie Stewart.

Recruited by ANNE CLARKE when she was singing at Drury Lane in 1841, Theodosia Yates went to Hobart and, billed as Mrs Stirling, became a leading theatrical attraction in the colony as both singer and actor. She married James Guerin, leader of the orchestra of the Royal Victoria Theatre in Hobart, and they had two daughters, Maggie and Docie. When Mrs Guerin moved to Sydney in 1845 audiences at the Royal Victoria Theatre there acclaimed her versatility and brilliance. She sang in the first Australian performances of two highly popular Irish operas, *The Bohemian Girl* by Michael Balfe in 1846, and *Maritana* by Vincent Wallace in 1849. She enlarged her range of acting in 1855, when she appeared in GEORGE COPPIN's *Ben Bolt*, which he described as 'a new drama founded on the celebrated song'.

With her second husband, RICHARD STEWART, she settled in Melbourne in 1859 and continued her career particularly in opera. She devoted much time to training her daughters in every aspect of the theatrical arts and by 1877, when the family began touring in GARNET WALCH's *Rainbow Revels*, she had retired from the stage at Stewart's request,

Her daughter NELLIE STEWART described her as having 'lustrous black hair, liquid blue eyes, and a perfect Grecian nose'. She was the great-granddaughter of Mary Anne Yates, who sang in opera at Covent Garden and played Lady Macbeth and other leading roles at Drury Lane with David Garrick, and Richard Yates, whom Garrick chose to play Sir Oliver Surface in the first production of R. B. Sheridan's *The School for Scandal* in 1777. ❦*Richard Lane*

Tony Strachan

Actor, dramatist. Born 9 May 1948 in Sydney. Grew up in Papua, where he was involved in amateur theatre. Attended Julian Ashton Art School (Sydney) 1969–70. Trained at London School of Contemporary Dance 1972–74 and at Merce Cunningham Studio (New York City) 1974. Dancer and choreographer with Australian Dance Theatre (Adelaide) 1975–76. First play, *Food*, produced in Adelaide 1976. Won Adelaide *Advertiser* play-of-the-year award with *The Harlequin Shuffle* 1985.

Tony Strachan's plays have been influenced in one direction by a stand against racism—a legacy of his upbringing in Papua—and in another by his growing interest in fusion of performance forms. His first experiment in fusion was *Slice*, a fantasy of images devised with KIM CARPENTER for the NIMROD THEATRE COMPANY in Sydney in 1981. It set new challenges for visual theatre. Under the title *Chrome*, Strachan created four pieces that fuse words, dance, design and music to rework social rituals centring on particular groups, such as Bondi Beach sun-and-sand worshippers and devotees of the microchip. *Chrome* was performed through the 1980s at festivals in Australia, North America, and Europe. Strachan's favourite acting role has been Truffaldino in Carlo Goldoni's *The Servant of Two Masters*, for the South Australian Theatre Company in 1978. ❦*Katharine Brisbane*.

published plays
The Eyes of the Whites (1981). Sydney: Alternative Publishing Cooperative 1983.
The Harlequin Shuffle (1985). Sydney: Currency Press 1985.
State of Shock (1986). Sydney: Currency Press 1986.

Street Arts Theatre Company

Professional community-theatre collective in Brisbane, founded in October 1982 by Dennis Peel, Pauline Peel and Steve Capelin.

During the 1980s Street Arts performed plays, circus and festival events at the Paint Factory in West End, in outer suburbs of Brisbane, in satellite cities, and on tour throughout Queensland. It began as a group primarily interested in festivals and community events—through the interests of the administrator Pauline Peel and the musician Denis Peel—but quickly moved towards more formal performances. Notable was *The Logan City Story*, devised by P. P. CRANNEY with the students of two high schools and presented in a shopping centre in 1984. In the same year *Once Upon Inala*, directed by Therese Collie, was staged in a park. Two groups evolved from Street Arts as a result of such projects—Rock 'n' Roll Circus in 1986 and Icy Tea (named from the initials of Inala Community Theatre). In collaboration with the Miscellaneous Worker's Union in 1986 Street Arts created *Sweeping Statements* under the Australia Council's Art and Working Life scheme. A successful season at the Paint Factory was followed by a Queensland tour in 1987. A similar project in 1988–89, *The ReUnion Show*, involved 17 unions. Other group-devised shows have explored Australian sporting culture (*Sparring Partners* in 1987) and the dance crazes of the 1940s (*Quick Quick Slow* in 1989). The latter was sponsored by the Brisbane City Council for a tour of suburban community halls. An impressive production of ANDREW BOVELL's *The Ballad of Lois Ryan* at the Paint Factory in 1989 showed both Street Arts's desire to do more sophisticated work and the difficulty of attracting community audiences to formal seasons. Therese Collie's *Out of the Blue* in 1991 examined the lives of female prisoners. A period of inactivity in 1992–93 was followed by the appointment of Brent McGregor as director and a new program of work at the Sitting Duck Cafe in Brisbane's West End, and in the nearby South's Leagues Club. ❦*Richard Fotheringham*

further reading
TUTTLE, DEAN. Street Arts—counting the community. *Australasian Drama Studies* 20 (Brisbane,1992).

A Stretch of the Imagination

Monodrama in one act by Jack Hibberd. **first performance** 8 March 1972, Pram Factory, Melbourne, by Peter Cummins for Australian Performing Group. Director: Jack Hibberd. Songs: Martin Friedel. **published** Sydney and London: Currency Methuen 1973. Sydney: Currency Press 1977.

A Stretch of the Imagination is the first and best-known monodrama by JACK HIBBERD. It concerns elderly Monk O'Neill, who has abandoned civilisation to live in primitive isolation. He fills his time with comic but life-sustaining routine activities, and with enacting real or imaginary events from his past. These enactments people the stage in the audience's imagination and enlarge its understanding of Monk. In some respects, *A Stretch of the Imagination* resembles a morality play, with Monk as a representative figure. He is first a representative Australian, whose conversation is full of reminders of Australia's past and whose situation recalls that of an outback pioneer. He can also be seen as representative of western civilisation and of universal humanity. In all these capacities his response to his circumstances is individual and thought-provoking. As an Australian, for instance, he rejects the grandiose visions of his country's future shared by many of his generation. As a representative of western civilisation he deplores its destructiveness and he has cut himself off from its amenities. As a representative human being he has come to terms with old age and death. To see Monk as an Everyman figure is to do less than justice to the play's complexity, however. He is also an idiosyncratic individual with a strong physical presence, resilient if sardonic humour, a delight in language and a wide-ranging, if sometimes faulty, command of it. The vivid images glimpsed in the distorting glass of his memory are funny but disturbing. His shifting viewpoints complicate and enrich the play.

A Stretch of the Imagination has had many revivals by MAX GILLIES, BRUCE SPENCE and other actors. It has been performed in Europe and, in a Chinese translation, in Shanghai. ❦*J. D. Hainsworth*

Subsidy and patronage

Subsidy has profoundly influenced theatre in Australia since the Second World War and remains a principal source of financial support. The major drama companies could not have developed to international standards without subsidy. The careers of many Australian playwrights, actors, directors and designers have been nurtured in the subsidised theatre. In recent years the spread of subsidy to many smaller drama groups has prompted innovation and a widening of scope that spills over to the whole performing-arts industry and beyond.

Government support for theatre in Australia can be traced back at least to the 1920s, when the ALLAN WILKIE SHAKESPEAREAN COMPANY was granted free transport on all Australian railways, apparently on the grounds that it served an educational purpose. Similarly, an educational rationale lay behind a grant of £600 by the NSW government in 1946 to set up the NSW division of the ARTS COUNCIL OF AUSTRALIA. The federal government did not become involved in subsidy to theatre until the AUSTRALIAN ELIZABETHAN THEATRE TRUST was established in 1954 with the help of a commonwealth grant of £30 000. The Trust promoted drama, ballet and opera in a variety of ways. It was also responsible for founding the main regional drama companies, the Australian Ballet, the Australian Opera, and its own orchestras. By 1967 commonwealth funding of the Trust had grown to just under $1 million.

In November 1967 the first Australian Council for the Arts was established, with responsibility for distributing grants and advising the government on cultural matters. It began operating in July 1968 with a budget for fiscal 1968–69 of $1·5 million—small by the international standards of the day but a considerable increase on previous levels of support. At that time the Trust had major stakes in opera and ballet, and the Australian Broadcasting Commission almost monopolised the musical scene, so the new council saw its main responsibility to the performing arts lying in drama. Its chairman, H. C. COOMBS believed strongly in the 'few but roses' philosophy of giving priority to excellence in arts expenditure and the council accordingly decided that grants should be mainly directed at ensuring high standards among a few 'centres of excellence', located of necessity in the larger capital cities. This laid the foundations of the principal state drama companies—the so-called 'flagships'—which continue to enjoy the highest public funding among Australian drama companies.

By 1971–72 the commonwealth's total expenditure on the arts was around $5 million and the major share was being directed to the performing arts. In the campaign for the federal election that took the Australian Labor Party to power in late 1972 assistance to the arts was no longer an insignificant issue. Artists publicly expressed support for Labor, which was proclaiming a newly-awakened national consciousness. The idea of an Australian cultural renascence was very much consistent with this. In line with election promises, the Labor government of Gough Whitlam moved promptly to reconstitute the Australian Council for the Arts. A disparate collection of federal agencies that had previously had some interest in artistic matters became incorporated into the new council, which was made up of seven boards covering Aboriginal arts, crafts, film and television, literature, music, theatre (including opera and ballet) and visual arts. The first Labor budget in 1973 allocated the council about $15 million, roughly twice total federal spending on all the arts in the previous year.

In 1974, federal legislation re-established the council as a statutory arts-funding authority to be called the AUSTRALIA COUNCIL. This began operation early in 1975 under a charter that included the objectives of promoting excellence, widening access, and fostering a sense of national identity through the arts. At the start the mood was euphoric but the Australia Council has had a turbulent history. It has been criticised in the media and in reports and enquiries, including the Industries Assistance Commission Report on the Performing Arts in 1977 and the Government Expenditure Committee's McLeay report in 1986, for being extravagant, elitist and inefficient. In response the council has reviewed and reorganised its operations several times. By the early 1990s its total annual budget had grown to just under $60 million, of which about $52 million was distributed in grants. Drama remained the largest single art form supported by the Australia Council. In 1992–93 grants to drama (companies and individuals) through the council's performing arts board totalled $8·3 million, with a further $3·2 million going to young people's theatre and puppetry.

The federal government has by no means been the only source of subsidy to theatre. All state governments now have their own arts ministries or cultural agencies, providing funds to support companies and individuals and to assist in the construction and operation of arts centres. The states and territories are now the tier of government that provides the largest share of public funds for cultural facilities and services. Although precise data are lacking on the amounts going specifically to theatre, it appears that by 1990 state governments were providing well in excess of $20 million for drama, with a further amount of around $90 million being spent by state and local governments on performing-arts venues and arts centres, many of which contain facilities used for drama.

In addition there has been some patronage of theatre by private individuals and business corporations through sponsorship, cash grants, donations and support in kind. In 1993 the corporate sector spent about $57 million in support for the arts, not including acquisition of art works. The lion's share—$23 million—of this went to music and opera. Just over $8 million was provided in support of live theatre. Corporate support appears to be less attracted to live theatre principally because drama companies cannot offer sponsors national exposure, and they do not play in repertoire like opera and dance companies, which can revive a sponsored production over the years.

Overall, the significance of subsidy in the theatre is indicated by the fact that, of the roughly 200 theatre companies —including drama, community-theatre, puppet, mime and youth organisations—operating in Australia in 1991, two-thirds received some form of government grant. In that year subsidised theatre organisations played to audiences totalling about 2·5 million, about 70 per cent of all paid attendances at professional legitimate theatre. Government grants provided about one-third of the total revenue of all commercial and non-commercial theatre companies, other than opera, dance and music-theatre in 1991. Controversy over subsidy will continue, of course, and there will never be enough money to go round. But there is no doubt that it will be impossible for a flourishing and truly Australian theatre to grow without continuation of enlightened government support. *David Throsby*

further reading
GULDBERG, HANS. *Cultural Funding in Australia 1988–89*. Sydney: Australia Council 1991.
PARSONS, PHILIP (ed.). *Shooting the Pianist*. Sydney: Currency Press 1987.
ROWSE, TIM. *Arguing the Arts*. Melbourne: Penguin 1985.

Barry Sullivan

Irish actor, manager, 1821–88. Formed touring company 1838. Began playing leading roles in northern England and Scotland 1844. Made reputation as Othello to William Macready's Iago in Liverpool 1850. Played Hamlet in London 1852. In Australia 1862–66. Leased and managed Theatre Royal in Melbourne. In USA 1858. Managed Holborn Theatre, London, 1867–69. Thirteen-week season at Theatre Royal, Drury Lane, 1876–77. In inaugural performance at Shakespeare Memorial Theatre, Stratford-upon-Avon, 1879.

The admiration of George Bernard Shaw, who called him 'the last of the superhuman actors', has ensured Barry Sullivan a place in theatrical history. Many others saw him as a provincial actor. In the Australian colonies he was regarded as intelligent but not great. Like the adored G. V. BROOKE, he was a 'strong actor' and at the height of the gold rush he satisfied the simple taste of Melbourne, where he made his Australian debut as Hamlet on 25 July 1862. He claimed to have performed there 1200 times. Sullivan leased the Theatre Royal for 10 months, opening in R. B. Sheridan's *The School for Scandal* on 7 March 1863. He presented first-rate actors and lavish sets, instituted low prices in the pit and attracted Irish immigrants to Shakespeare in droves. In Sydney, where he opened on 29 September 1863, his reviews were uneven, and Melbourne remained his base until he returned to England after a public testimonial banquet in February 1866.

Sullivan was known for businesslike application to his profession and for 'force of character'. He was a vicious opponent of CHARLES AND ELLEN KEAN when they were in Melbourne in 1863. Charles Kean suffered from a persistent cold—brought on, he said, by the Melbourne weather. Sullivan wired to Ballarat: 'Keans a failure; Kean's hoarseness a sham'. The Keans' company at the Haymarket Theatre included James Cathcart, whose sister FANNY CATHCART was acting in Sullivan's company at the Theatre Royal. Sullivan used his Cathcart connection to learn the Keans' repertoire. He anticipated their Shakespeare productions, but Kean by threatening legal action forced him to withdraw G. W. Lovell's *The Wife's Secret*, of which the Keans had given the premiere in London. The episode set off fireworks in the pro-Kean *Argus* and the pro-Irish and pro-Sullivan *Melbourne Punch*. ❦*Helen Musa*

further reading
DUFF, HELEN. Charles and Ellen Kean in Australia 1863–64. University of NSW BA(hons) thesis 1965.
GITTINS, JEAN. Barry Sullivan. *Australian Dictionary of Biography* 6. Melbourne University Press 1976.
HARDWICK, J. M. D. (ed.). *Emigrant in Motley*. London: Rockliff 1954.
SHAW, GEORGE BERNARD. *Our Theatres in the Nineties* 1. London: 1932.
SILLARD, R. M. *Barry Sullivan and His Contemporaries*.
Argus (Melbourne) 5 May 1891. Obituary.

John L. Sullivan

American actor, 1858–1918. Became professional prizefighter 1878. World heavyweight champion 1882–92. Toured Australia as actor 1891. Continued stage performances to *c*.1900.

The rising power of the American popular press made John L. Sullivan, heavyweight boxing champion of the world, into the first international sporting hero. From 1889 he fought only exhibition bouts and made theatrical appearances as boxer and as actor. The *Police Gazette* and other papers smeared him for 'drinking and womanising'. In August 1890, unfit and unpopular, he tried to capitalise on his fame by acting at Niblo's Theatre in New York City in an Irish melodrama, *Honest Hearts and Willing Hands*. He played a humble village blacksmith who chopped wood on stage and fought a three-round contest against a villainous opponent. Next year Sullivan toured Australia in the play, while two Australian challengers for his crown, Slavin and Jackson, were overseas. In Sydney sports fans objected to his refusal to fight the Australians and theatregoers scoffed at his poor acting and the contrast between his role and his diamond-studded lifestyle. He fared better in Melbourne and on a country tour, but the *Lorgnette*, noting that Sarah Bernhardt had also been in Australia, observed in November 1891: 'Bernhardt has the satisfaction of knowing that in Australia she hit harder than John L. Sullivan'. Next year Sullivan lost his title to James J. Corbett in the first gloved fight under Queensberry rules. ❦*Richard Fotheringham*

further reading
RADER, BENJAMIN G. *American Sports*. Englewood Cliffs (New Jersey, USA): Prentice Hall 1983.

Summer of the Seventeenth Doll

Play in three acts by Ray Lawler. **premiere** 28 November 1955, Union Theatre, University of Melbourne, by Union Theatre Repertory Company. Cast: Malcolm Billings, Carmel Dunn, Noel Ferrier, June Jago, Roma Johnston, Ray Lawler, Fenella Maguire. Designer Anne Fraser. Director: John Sumner. **revived** 11 January 1956, Elizabethan Theatre, Sydney, with Lloyd Berrell, Ethel Gabriel, Jago, Lawler, John Llewellyn, Madge Ryan. 30 April 1957, New Theatre, London, with Gabriel, Jago, Lawler, Fenella Maguire, Richard Pratt, Ryan, Kenneth Warren. **published** Sydney: Angus and Robertson 1957; Currency Press 1978.

The most famous Australian play and one of the best loved, *Summer of the Seventeenth Doll* is a tragicomic story of Roo and Barney, two Queensland sugar-cane cutters who go to Melbourne every year during the 'layoff' to live it up with their barmaid girl friends. The title refers to kewpie dolls, tawdry fairground souvenirs, that they bring as gifts and come, in some readings of the play, to represent adolescent dreams in which the characters seem to be permanently trapped. The play tells the story in traditional well-made, realistic form, with effective curtains and an obligatory scene. Its principal appeal—and that of two later plays with which it forms THE DOLL TRILOGY—is the freshness and emotional warmth, even sentimentality, with which it deals with the simple virtues of innocence and youthful energy that lie at the heart of the Australian bush legend.

RAY LAWLER's play confronts that legend with the harsh new reality of modern urban Australia. The 17th year of the canecutters' arrangement is different. There has been a fight on the canefields and Roo, the tough, heroic bushman, has arrived with his ego battered and without money. Barney's girl friend Nancy has left to get married and is replaced by Pearl, who is suspicious of the whole set-up and hopes to trap Barney into marriage. The play charts the inevitable failure of the dream of the layoff, the end of the men's supremacy as bush heroes and, most poignantly, the betrayal of the idealistic self-sacrifice made by Roo's girl friend Olive—the most interesting character—to keep the whole thing going. The city emerges victorious, but the emotional tone of the play vindicates the fallen bushmen.

Joint winner of a national play competition conducted by the PLAYWRIGHTS' ADVISORY BOARD in 1955, *The Doll* was first produced by the Union Theatre Repertory Company with the backing of the board and the newly formed AUSTRALIAN ELIZABETHAN THEATRE TRUST. After its first season it was taken up and widely promoted as the first sign of a renascence of Australian drama. It was taken as a model for a new school that would represent Australians to themselves and help to define the national character and it was a vehicle for new professional aspirations. The play was also a huge popular success and it single-handedly financed the early seasons of overseas plays promoted by the Trust. It was reported that people drove hundreds of kilometres and a man swam a flooded river to see it in the Northern Territory in 1960. Several companies toured concurrently.

The Doll then went to London, where it won the *Evening Standard* Award for the best play of 1957. The Australian press excitedly reported the London success but was disappointed when it was not repeated in New York. A film version in 1959, with Ernest Borgnine and John Mills as the tough Australian heroes, was set in Sydney so that shots of the Harbour Bridge could be included. It was greeted in Australia with a mixture of cynicism and anxiety that it would not be a good tourist advertisement for the country, the subject being rather improper.

The Doll has been widely translated, is revived regularly, and is studied widely in schools and universities throughout Australia. It is a fine play in its own right but in the 1950s its complex reflection of the nation's confused image of itself made it a central document in Australian culture. As the play ages the simple appeal of the individual struggle between its characters will perhaps become more and more important. In recent years there has been a critical revaluation of the play's own revaluation of the male legend on which it is based. Since the 1980s Olive and Pearl have come to be seen as more interesting characters than Roo and Barney. ❦*John McCallum*

John Sumner AO, CBE

Director. Born 27 May 1924. In merchant navy during Second World War. Entered theatre as assistant stage manager in Dundee (Scotland). Stage director in H. M. Tennent Ltd 1947–52. Manager of Union Theatre at University of Melbourne 1952. Founded Union Theatre Repertory Company 1953. Manager of Elizabethan Theatre (Sydney) 1954. Victorian manager of Australian Elizabethan Theatre Trust 1956–59. Administrator of Union Theatre Repertory Company 1959–62; director 1962–87 (Melbourne Theatre Company from 1968). CBE 1971. AO 1985.

John Sumner towered in the theatrical landscape. He founded Australia's first fully professional repertory company, the MELBOURNE THEATRE COMPANY, and ran it for more than 30 years, systematically building it up until it regularly played to about 350 000 people a year. He established it, in co-operation with the University of Melbourne, as the Union Theatre Repertory Company in 1953. After two years, he left to work for the AUSTRALIAN ELIZABETHAN THEATRE TRUST in Sydney and later in Melbourne. Sumner rejoined the Union Theatre Repertory Company in 1959, first as administrator and from 1962 as director, a position he held until his retirement at the end of 1987. His last year saw audiences at an all-time high. While other companies came and went, the Melbourne Theatre Company grew and prospered under his shrewd, careful management. Even his many critics had to concede his doggedness and energy. He was a hard taskmaster, unforgiving of those who fell below the high standards he set. But he could be warm and generous too, and many a playwright or actor can vouch for his supportiveness. Much of the criticism of the company centred on its perceived conservatism. In many ways it was Sumner's company, reflecting his tastes and his origins in English repertory.

As a director, he was always thorough and reliable and his productions—more than 100 for the company—were never less than workmanlike. They included the premieres of RAY LAWLER's *Summer of the Seventeenth Doll* and *The Doll Trilogy* and plays by ALEX BUZO and DAVID WILLIAMSON. Sumner was supportive of local writing, encouraging Lawler with *The Doll Trilogy* and taking up Buzo and Williamson early in their careers. ❦*Leonard Radic*

writings
Recollections at Play—A life in Australian theatre. Melbourne: University Press 1993.

further reading
HOWIE, ANN C. (ed.). *Who's Who in Australia 1991* 27th edn. Melbourne: Information Australia.
HUBBARD, LINDA S. and O'DONNELL, OWEN (ed.). *Contemporary Theatre, Film and Television* 6th edn. Detroit (USA): Gale Research.

The Sunny South

Melodrama in five acts by George Darrell. **premiere** 31 March 1883 at Prince of Wales Opera House, Melbourne. Cast included George Darrell, Essie Jenyns. **revived** 27 October 1884, Grand Theatre, Islington, London. 5 September 1898, Surrey Theatre, London. January 1980, Drama Theatre, Sydney Opera House. **published** Sydney: Currency-Methuen 1975.

In *The Sunny South* GEORGE DARRELL wrote the Anglo-Australian melodrama par excellence. The hero, Matt Morley returns from the colonies to claim his rightful inheritance. In spite of his manners he is still English at heart. His frank girl friend Bubs Berkeley accompanies him, and by exposure to English villains and snobbish servants they show the sterling qualities they have learnt 'out here'. In Australia again, the hero is rewarded with the discovery of a £7000 gold nugget. This inevitably invites Duggan the bushranger, who holds up a bank, abducts Bubs and stakes out a train. Triumphant at last, Morley and his bride prepare to return to the Old Country. Audiences loved the colour and variety of *The Sunny South*. Darrell cashed in on the capture of Ned Kelly and solved plot problems with anachronistic use of the telegraph. Visual sensations like the train hold-up were captured in eight 'grand tableaux'. Dramatically, the character of Bubs, horsewhipping her way through the play, was an original invention. Matt Morley has been praised as an example of Australian integrity and pragmatism, and *The Sunny South* as unpretentious, schoolboyish and good-humoured. ❦*Helen Musa*

reference
The manuscript of *The Sunny South* is in the British Library (London) MS ADD. 53326.

Sydney

Professional theatre became established in Sydney in 1832. There had previously been sporadic performances by convicts, soldiers and sailors. Convicts celebrated King George III's birthday on 4 June 1789 by performing the first play in Australia, *The Recruiting Officer* by George Farquhar, written in 1706. There may have been other occasional performances later but the next recorded theatrical event is the opening of Australia's first theatre by ROBERT SIDAWAY on 16 January 1796. His theatre operated sporadically into the 1800s, with a repertoire that surviving playbills show to have included *The Recruiting Officer* and *Henry IV*.

Subsequently, colonial governors were not persuaded of the value of theatre to a convict settlement. In 1829 BARNETT LEVEY included a theatre in a new building he erected in George Street but he was allowed to use it only for balls and concerts. In 1832 he received a licence to present plays and he opened a fit-up theatre in the saloon of his Royal Hotel on 26 December with Douglas Jerrold's popular 1829 melodrama *Black-Eyed Susan*. On 5 October 1833 he opened his original THEATRE ROYAL with a melodrama, *The Miller and His Men* by Isaac Pocock, and a farce, *The Irishman in London*. Contemporary melodramas, varied with some older comedies and tragedies (especially by Shakespeare) and followed by farcical afterpieces, formed the staple fare of Sydney audiences for the next 50 years or so. Programs changed nightly and it was rare for a play to receive more than four or five performances in a season. The exception was the Christmas PANTOMIME, which by the 1840s was running for up to three weeks continuously and featuring local scenery and topical comment on current events.

Levey's theatre was succeeded by JOSEPH WYATT's new ROYAL VICTORIA THEATRE. It opened on 26 March 1838 with *Othello* and remained Sydney's premier theatre until it was destroyed by fire in 1880. Some rival venues were attempted in the 1840s—the Australian Olympic Theatre in 1842 and the Royal City Theatre in 1843—but Sydney's population remained too small to support more than one company properly and both soon closed.

Discoveries of gold in the 1850s brought a rapid influx of population, visits by stars from the United Kingdom and North America, and the building of new theatres. A circus amphitheatre opened in 1850 and became the Lyceum Theatre on 23 October 1854, but it soon returned to equestrian acts. On 14 July 1856 it was reopened as Our Lyceum with a Shakespeare season starring the popular Irish actor G. V. BROOKE. After another name change, its high point came as the Queen's Theatre in 1875 with the first Sydney performance of MAGGIE MOORE and J. C. WILLIAMSON in *Struck Oil*. This ran from 3 March to 30 April, the longest run of any play in Sydney until then. About that time, theatres were beginning to present one play in an evening instead of two or more, and stock companies attached to theatres were beginning to give way to touring companies.

In 1855 Joseph Wyatt opened the large PRINCE OF WALES THEATRE. It burned down five years later. A rebuilt Prince of Wales opened in 1863 with a season by W. S. LYSTER's Royal English and Italian Opera Company; nine years later it burned down too. In 1875 a third theatre opened on the Castlereagh Street site. This theatre, called the THEATRE ROYAL, survived, with various minor transformations, for almost a century, and seems to have been the first in Australia to fly its scenery and the first to light the stage by electricity. Such innovations helped to strengthen the spectacle that was the hallmark of staging in the last quarter of the 19th century. It was seen in popular sensation melodramas by DION BOUCICAULT, J. B. Buckstone and Tom Taylor and by the local actor-managers GEORGE DARRELL and ALFRED DAMPIER, in scenically splendid Christmas pantomimes and in lavish productions of Shakespeare and Italian opera.

The next burst of theatre building in Sydney came in the prosperous 1880s. Most of the new theatres were smaller than their predecessors, which suggests that the mass audience was beginning to fragment. Many were now frequenting music halls and variety shows instead of the legitimate theatre. HER MAJESTY'S THEATRE, which opened on 10 September 1887, was the largest and best-equipped theatre of its day, however. From its opening until the end of the century, it often housed GEORGE RIGNOLD's spectacular productions of Shakespeare, especially *Henry V*, and melodrama. The 1880s also saw the establishment of WILLIAMSON, GARNER AND MUSGROVE, which began to standardise professional theatre throughout Australia.

The 1890s brought a great variety of works and performers to Sydney, with seasons of opera, operetta, Dampier's highly successful adaptations of the Australian novels *ROBBERY UNDER ARMS* and *FOR THE TERM OF HIS NATURAL LIFE*, plays by Shakespeare and Henrik Ibsen's *A Doll's House* with JANET ACHURCH as Nora. SARAH BERNHARDT opened her Sydney season on 8 July 1891 in *Camille* by Alexandre Dumas *fils* at Her Majesty's Theatre. The decade also saw VAUDEVILLE flourish, particularly at the Tivoli Theatre under HARRY RICKARDS. He brought out many of the great stars of English music-hall, including G. H. Chirgwin, and promoted local talents such as FRED BLUETT and Tom Dawson.

In addition to the Tivoli, six major theatres were operating in Sydney in 1900—the CRITERION THEATRE, the Lyceum Theatre, the PALACE THEATRE, the ROYAL STANDARD THEATRE, the Theatre Royal and Her Majesty's Theatre. The last two were under the control of J. C. Williamson. From 1900 his firm dominated professional theatre and its large companies toured from city to city.

Sydney city's second large theatre, the Prince of Wales, burned down on 3 October 1860. The Castlereagh Street façade—to the right of the corner building—survived and was incorporated in a new theatre. In the 20th century development replaced fire as the destroyer of downtown theatres

In the early 20th century the professional repertoire remained predominantly a mixture of spectacular melodrama, operetta and society comedy. At Her Majesty's in 1900, for example, Williamson presented a pantomime, *Little Red Riding Hood*, in January and February, melodramas performed by a company led by the American Nance O'Neill from March to May, a season of opera in the winter, and then O'Neill's company again from September to December. Meanwhile, for much of the year there were also the BROUGH COMEDY COMPANY in society drama at the Theatre Royal, George Marlow's company in melodrama at the Royal Standard Theatre and Alfred Dampier giving Australian and English melodrama, with Shakespeare once a week, at the Criterion.

The live theatre was already facing competition from film. The theatre audience declined, the number of venues decreased and the repertoire narrowed. Local melodrama remained popular, reaching its height in 1912 with BERT BAILEY's adaptation of Steele Rudd's *ON OUR SELECTION*. But the bigger theatres were increasingly given over to touring productions of large-scale operettas and the latest English and American hit plays, such as Paul Kester's enormously successful *Sweet Nell of Old Drury*, starring NELLIE STEWART. The direction of serious theatre in the next decades was signalled in 1918, when J. AND N. TAIT LTD engaged the director GREGAN MCMAHON for its New Repertory Company 'for the production of literary drama'. At the Palace Theatre during 1918 he presented George Bernard Shaw's *The Doctor's Dilemma* and *How He Lied to Her Husband*, John Galsworthy's *The Pigeon* and Ibsen's *John Gabriel Borkman*. The season was not a financial success. ❦Elizabeth Webby

1919–45

By 1921 more people were going to motion pictures than to all forms of live theatre combined, yet the 1920s were prosperous for the professional theatre in Sydney. Two newly-built theatres were opened, the St James in 1926 and the Empire in February 1927. There were ten live theatres in downtown Sydney until 1928, when the Hippodrome was converted to the CAPITOL THEATRE, an atmospheric cinema. In spite of competition from the movies, vaudeville and revue underwent a revival in the 1920s, in the downtown venues at least. There was straight vaudeville at the Tivoli Theatre from 1921 to 1929, while at Fullers' National Theatre vaudeville and revue shared the bill. FULLERS' was concentrating on revue and musical comedy by 1927.

In the 1920s Fullers' and other managements presented popular melodramas, thrillers and comedies, changing the program weekly, in city theatres and suburban houses such as the Majestic Theatre in Newtown and the National Theatre in Balmain. Serious drama, however, was infrequently presented on the professional stage and usually only by celebrated companies from overseas, such as those headed by OSCAR ASCHE in 1922 or DION BOUCICAULT JNR and Irene Vanbrugh in 1923 and 1928. Imports were the fashion, and it was often the visiting company's fame rather than its repertoire that attracted the audiences.

The AMATEUR THEATRE movement flourished, although terms such as 'amateur theatre society' were pointedly avoided. Several societies adopted the title of 'art theatre', suggesting a rare dedication to idealism and experimentation, but the only undisputed art theatre of the period was DUNCAN MACDOUGALL's Playbox Society, formed in 1923. Most groups in the 1920s styled themselves 'repertory society', inspired by the English repertory system, which presented plays that were of proven worth but not profitable for professional managements.

In 1920, after J. and N. Tait Ltd had amalgamated with J. C. Williamson's, Gregan McMahon approached the TAIT BROTHERS with a plan that led them to support the formation of the SYDNEY REPERTORY THEATRE SOCIETY. Underwritten by the Taits, McMahon and the society produced about 70 plays—always worthily, according to BEATRICE TILDESLEY—with an emphasis on works by George Bernard Shaw and John Galsworthy. The Taits, however, lost so much money on the venture that they proposed to alter the agreement. Trouble arose within the society, McMahon returned to Melbourne and in 1928 the society closed.

Professional live theatre was assailed by ENTERTAINMENT TAXES and competitors—the portable gramophone, the radio from 1923 and talking pictures from 1928. In 1929 it began to succumb. The Empire Theatre closed in mid-year and reopened in December as a talkies cinema. The Tivoli closed in September, a month before the Wall Street crash signalled the onset of the Great Depression, and was rebuilt as a cinema. Fullers' soon gave up live theatre at the Grand Opera House, the St James Theatre and Fullers' National Theatre. As the depression deepened in 1931 the Palace Theatre became a cinema too, Her Majesty's Theatre closed in June 1933. and the Criterion Theatre was closed in 1935 to permit road-widening.

At the end of 1935 only two live theatres remained. One was the Grand Opera House, renamed the New Tivoli Theatre by MIKE CONNORS and QUEENIE PAUL when they moved there in 1932 after reviving variety in a cinema. The other was the Theatre Royal, which J. C. Williamson's devoted primarily to revivals of imported operettas. After an extremely successful tour by Sybil Thorndike and Lewis Casson in 1932, Sydney saw no major touring company presenting serious drama for almost 15 years.

In the early 1930s AMERICAN INFLUENCES prevailed and dozens of 'little theatres' emerged in Sydney within a few years. Only a handful survived for any length of time and even these often led a precarious existence in draughty halls and basements. There was naturally a great diversity in the quality of the little theatres' productions, but they were not simply 'amateur' ventures. Several little theatres were founded and directed by trained professionals with stated policies. Among them were BRYANT'S PLAYHOUSE, CARRIE TENNANT's Community Theatre, DON FINLEY's Turret Theatre, Doris Fitton's INDEPENDENT THEATRE and May Hollinworth's METROPOLITAN THEATRE. The better little theatres were conscious of their role in a worldwide movement and united in aiming to further Australian drama. They promoted works by new Australian writers through production, play readings, competitions and drama festivals. The Workers' Art Club, founded in 1932, presented 'plays with a purpose'; it became the NEW THEATRE League in 1936.

Independent Theatre gradually assumed the role of Sydney's leading company. Other little theatres became considerably less active and were usually offering diversions by 1939, when DAVID N. MARTIN opened the professional MINERVA THEATRE. Many little theatres disappeared during the Second World War, when audiences shrank and there was a shortage of male actors. The Minerva, Bryant's Playhouse, Independent Theatre and the SYDNEY UNIVERSITY DRAMATIC SOCIETY remained and, despite the difficulties, largely kept drama alive in Sydney throughout the war. The Tivoli Theatre sustained variety. ❦*Bronwyn Coy*

Since 1945

In 1945 the major employer of theatrical artists in Sydney was J. C. Williamson's at the Theatre Royal, with a policy of producing successful shows from overseas with imported leads—but not invariably in musicals. The Minerva Theatre, run on more modern lines by WHITEHALL THEATRICAL PRODUCTIONS, offered more scope for designers and more opportunities for actors, but became a cinema in 1950. The Tivoli Theatre ran revue, and because of its 1900-seat capacity, intermittently housed visiting troupes such as the OLD VIC THEATRE COMPANY in 1948, and the Shakespeare Memorial Theatre Company in 1949 and 1953. These companies inspired young actors who earned their living in radio drama, trained in the amateur little theatres, and dreamed of going to the real theatrical world in London. Many did.

Theatregoers who liked classical plays, contemporary European drama or Australian plays went to the little theatres—Independent Theatre, Metropolitan Theatre, Bryant's Playhouse or, for the politically inclined, New Theatre. An influx of displaced persons from war-ravaged Europe swelled the numbers and refined the tastes of Sydney theatre patrons during the 1940s. SYDNEY JOHN KAY, a German director and musician stranded here by the war, founded MERCURY THEATRE in 1946 with the brilliant actor PETER FINCH and others. The JOHN ALDEN COMPANY became professional after a successful Shakespeare season in 1950. In the early 1950s WILLIAM ORR from London brought satirical intimate revue to Sydney and it became the rage at the PHILLIP STREET THEATRE. Orr moved in 1961 to the larger Phillip Theatre, where the style changed to broader entertainment. HAYES GORDON founded the influential ENSEMBLE THEATRE COMPANY on the northern shore of Sydney Harbour in 1958. Identified with American method acting at first, the company has since settled into the mainstream niche and has provided professional productions without benefit of federal subsidy since the 1980s.

The idea of a NATIONAL THEATRE, mooted as long ago as the 1890s, nourished by writers like LOUIS ESSON and directors such as Gregan McMahon, hovered like a vision of the Holy Grail before ambitious directors of little theatres in the late 1940s. The AUSTRALIAN ELIZABETHAN THEATRE TRUST, set up in 1954 with headquarters in Sydney, aimed to establish indigenous theatre by giving financial support to existing organisations. Although its first artistic director, HUGH HUNT, was an Englishman, his support for Ray Lawler's play SUMMER OF THE SEVENTEENTH DOLL led to a landmark production that changed attitudes to Australian plays. An Australian with London experience, ROBIN LOVEJOY was appointed to form the TRUST PLAYERS, a touring company fully funded by the Trust and based at its ELIZABETHAN THEATRE in Newtown. Lovejoy directed 12 of the players' 14 productions, from the first, THE SLAUGHTER OF ST TERESA'S DAY by Peter Kenna in March 1959, to the last, Alan Seymour's controversial THE ONE DAY OF THE YEAR at the Palace Theatre in April 1961. In three years of operation the Trust Players built up a good public following, but were

Two stars of satirical Phillip Street revues in the 1950s and 1960s had great successes in drama in the 1970s. At the Nimrod Theatre in 1976 Gordon Chater played the transvestite elocution teacher in Steve J. Spears's monodrama The Elocution of Benjamin Franklin *(left) and went on to 900 performances overseas. Gloria Dawn played her first straight role in Peter Kenna's* The Slaughter of St Teresa's Day *(right) at the Community Theatre in 1972. With her are Marion Johns (at left) and Carole Skinner (centre)*

disbanded because of losses on national tours. Thereafter each state developed its own company and the Trust became an entrepreneur. In Sydney it presented Patrick White's THE HAM FUNERAL at the Palace Theatre in 1962.

An officer of the Trust, ROBERT QUENTIN became the first director of the NATIONAL INSTITUTE OF DRAMATIC ART, which was founded under the auspices of the University of NSW in suburban Kensington in 1958. A need to provide its graduates with professional work and supply the public with classical drama led NIDA to found the OLD TOTE THEATRE COMPANY, funded by the Trust. TOM BROWN supervised the conversion of an old storehouse on the campus into a 180-seat theatre. Quentin directed the opening play, Anton Chekhov's *The Cherry Orchard*, in February 1963, using professional actors, graduates in supporting roles and students as theatre staff. The Old Tote company began lunchtime performances at the downtown Palace Theatre in September 1963, with Edward Albee's *The American Dream* directed by JOHN CLARK. He also directed the Old Tote's hit of 1964, Albee's *Who's Afraid of Virginia Woolf?*, which toured Australia and New Zealand for two years, managed by the Trust and J. C. Williamson's. Another lunchtime venture began when Q THEATRE was launched as an actors' co-operative in a theatre at Circular Quay in 1963.

AUSTRALIAN THEATRE FOR YOUNG PEOPLE began under the Old Tote's aegis in 1963 and has contributed greatly to children's theatre ever since. The expanding Old Tote company had to grapple with planning the year's program, arranging country and interstate tours at the behest of the Trust, and meeting the expectations of a subscription audience. These demands led to a more mainstream repertoire and a departure from the company's original objectives. NIDA graduates toured country districts in Shakespeare productions for the Young Tote, and Quentin moved to provide them with a suburban venue in Sydney and to keep faith with Australian playwrights. He instigated the opening of the 80-seat JANE STREET THEATRE in nearby

Randwick in 1966. It soon became an exciting experimental venue for writers, directors and actors. THOMAS KENEALLY, RODNEY MILGATE and Tony Morphett tried out new forms. In 1970 a high-energy musical satire, THE LEGEND OF KING O'MALLEY by Bob Ellis and Michael Boddy, signalled the birth of a confident Australian style. DAVID WILLIAMSON's huge popularity with Sydney audiences began at Jane Street, where DON'S PARTY was a riotous success in 1972 before it moved to sold-out seasons at the Parade Theatre on the University of NSW campus and a two-year tour.

The proliferation of subsidised theatre threatened J. C. Williamson's, which also faced competition from smaller entrepreneurs during the late 1960s and early 1970s. HARRY M. MILLER transformed a radio auditorium into the PLAYBOX THEATRE and ran the latest overseas hit plays and the odd local success. He also rescued the MINERVA THEATRE and the CAPITOL THEATRE from films to present dazzling productions of rock musicals directed by JIM SHARMAN.

Across the harbour at Neutral Bay Junction, melodrama flourished in burlesque form from 1961 until 1980 at the MUSIC HALL THEATRE RESTAURANT, delighting audiences and providing continuous work for actors. Farther north in Killara, ALEXANDER ARCHDALE started Community Theatre in 1965. As the MARIAN STREET THEATRE COMPANY, it presented good professional theatre into the 1990s.

Traditional popular entertainment declined in the face of the onslaught of television and after the TIVOLI THEATRE closed in 1966 variety performers found work in licensed clubs. From 1970 at the intimate Nimrod Street Theatre in inner-city Darlinghurst audience and actors were drawn closely together in a new kind of knockabout theatre. The cast and director developed *Biggles* and *HAMLET ON ICE* as much as the writers, who included RON BLAIR, MICHAEL BODDY and Marcus Cooney. Audiences also went to Nimrod Street to see works by new-wave playwrights such as ALEX BUZO and Williamson, whose *THE REMOVALISTS* was given a frighteningly compelling production. Another landmark production was the satirical revue *Basically Black*, presented with National Black Theatre in 1972.

New theatre for Nimrod

The NIMROD THEATRE COMPANY moved in 1974 to the new Nimrod Theatre in Surry Hills. This had a triangular acting space like the old theatre, but some intimacy was lost in the 320-seat auditorium. A 110-seat experimental theatre was created downstairs. Everything from cabaret to monodrama was tried out there, and *THE ELOCUTION OF BENJAMIN FRANKLIN* by Steve J. Spears was a runaway success.

In 1975 BOB MAZA directed *THE CAKE MAN* by Robert J. Merritt in an open-space theatre and cultural centre in Redfern, an inner suburb with numerous Aboriginal residents. This was the forerunner of the Eora Centre, a community and cultural centre for Aborigines and Torres Strait Islanders administered by the NSW Technical and Further Education Commission. It started a three-year diploma course in visual and performing arts, with state funding, in 1984.

J. C. Williamson's finally appealed for government subsidy and, when it was denied, went out of business in 1976. Since then the big musicals have been presented by overseas entrepreneurs, the SYDNEY THEATRE COMPANY or by smaller firms such as the GORDON FROST ORGANISATION. Light comedy and commercial drama have been taken over by

Sydney was the setting of David Williamson's Emerald City, *a huge success for the Sydney Theatre Company in 1987. John Bell (left) played a high-minded dramatist, newly arrived from Melbourne, and Max Cullen played an unprincipled Sydneysider who writes film scripts for export*

Gary Penny and PETER WILLIAMS. The Old Tote Theatre Company, honouring obligations to two universities and the state government, presented plays in three venues—the Parade Theatre, the SEYMOUR THEATRE CENTRE in the grounds of Sydney University, and the Drama Theatre at the SYDNEY OPERA HOUSE. It was deeply in debt from the injudicious purchase of an impractical property for its headquarters, and when further funding was denied at the end of 1978, the company went into liquidation. The SYDNEY THEATRE COMPANY rose from its ashes on the initiative of the Premier of NSW, Neville Wran, with the support of the AUSTRALIA COUNCIL, which appointed a special board to manage the 1979 interim season under the direction of John Clark. RICHARD WHERRETT was appointed artistic and executive director. A balance of classics and the best contemporary plays, including at least two Australian plays annually, built up a solid audience.

The Sydney Theatre Company's popularity was enhanced by the opening of its second venue and headquarters in a converted wharf building at Walsh Bay, a superlatively beautiful setting west of the Harbour Bridge. The WHARF THEATRE complex, a gift from the NSW government in 1984, includes Wharf 1, seating 350, Wharf 2, seating 140, and Wharf 3, seating 400. The Sydney Theatre Company is a major beneficiary of the NSW Ministry for the Arts, established in 1988. In Sydney the ministry also funds a wide range of theatre-in-education and young people's theatre, and the Festival of Sydney. This January festival includes Carnivale, which was begun as a separate showcase for the diversity of the city's cosmopolitan population.

In 1980 the Nimrod Street Theatre, renamed the Stables Theatre, became home to the GRIFFIN THEATRE COMPANY, which has performed valuable service in presenting new Australian plays and timely revivals of other works. As the Sydney Theatre Company's popularity grew the Nimrod Theatre Company's fortunes declined. It put its theatre up for sale and moved to the less hospitable Seymour Theatre Centre in 1984. Despite fine work by John Bell, AUBREY MELLOR and Richard Cottrell and many actors over two years, the Nimrod company folded in 1987 when federal and state subsidies were withdrawn. A syndicate of 600 theatre workers, determined to save a valuable theatre, bought the Nimrod Theatre in 1984, renamed it the BELVOIR STREET THEATRE, and set up a management company.

The establishment of many different theatre companies resulted in reconstruction of the AUSTRALIA COUNCIL's theatrical funding. Some old-established companies had their funding restricted and others were dropped in favour of a wider spread of special grants and annual project funding for companies such as Theatre of the Deaf; TOE TRUCK THEATRE, specialising in performance for children; the experimental PERFORMANCE SPACE and Performing Lines. Companies receiving smaller slices of the subsidy pie sought sponsorship. Most of the companies functioning in Sydney receive sponsorship as contra-deals or cash. The Bell Shakespeare Company, set up in 1990 by John Bell, has been funded by donors, sponsors and a federal government grant since the collapse of the Australian Elizabethan Theatre Trust, of which it was originally a subsidiary. It is a permanent touring company based in Sydney. Its educational program, which takes it to schools in the metropolitan area as far as the Blue Mountains is funded by the NSW government. Another government-funded initiative is the Australian National Playwrights' Centre, which provides assessment and dramaturgical services in Sydney and organises the annual AUSTRALIAN NATIONAL PLAYWRIGHTS' CONFERENCE in Canberra. Three community-theatre companies funded by the Ministry for the Arts, DEATH DEFYING THEATRE, Legs on the Wall and the SIDETRACK PERFORMANCE GROUP have operated in the western suburbs.

Q Theatre has built up strong local support and an admirable record of production at Penrith, on the western fringe of greater Sydney, where it moved in 1977. At the geographical centre of the Sydney conurbation, Parramatta has the impressive Riverside Theatres, a complex of auditoria with seating capacities ranging from 90 to 700. It can house touring plays and it serves a large population for local productions. Irreverence for tradition and the high price of real estate have cost Sydney its 19th-century theatres. Many were used as cinemas by the 1930s and all were torn down by the 1970s. A new Theatre Royal, however, was incorporated in the building erected on the site of the old one. In the 1980s and 1990s long-running musical theatre exacerbated the scarcity of venues. The Theatre Royal and Her Majesty's Theatre were continually booked and even the State Theatre, a magnificent cinema with an inadequate stage, was housing musicals. But on 24 January 1995 the CAPITOL THEATRE, restored to its atmospheric-cinema splendour and enlarged into a 2100-seat lyric theatre, opened with the Philippe de Coufflé Dance Company, bringing new life to an old theatre district. *Lynne Murphy*

further reading
COY, BRONWYN. The significance of the little theatre movement in Sydney in the 1930s, with particular reference to the Independent Theatre. University of NSW BA(hons) thesis 1990.

Joan Sydney
Actor. Born 5 September 1936 in London. Grew up in Wales. Joined Rhyl Children's Theatre Club at nine. Acted in BBC radio productions. Joined Aberystwyth Repertory Company 1954. Three years in weekly repertory in Oldham (England). Married and temporarily retired from stage. Emigrated to Western Australia with husband and three children 1965. Acted for ABC radio. Returned to stage for National Theatre Company (Perth) 1967. Silver Swan Award 1975 (*Hello, Dolly!*). Silver Swan and National Critics' Awards 1976 (Martha in Edward Albee's *Who's Afraid of Virginia Woolf?*). Sister of actor Maggie King.

Joan Sydney is a remarkable actor with a wide command of technical skills, ranging from music-hall to classic tragedy. She shines at roles that exploit her range and she can make her own. More than one critic has commented that her performance outdistanced her material. She is particularly comfortable with the earthy characters of popular entertainment and with the psychology of exploited and frustrated women. Mardy Amos commented in the *Australian* on her performance in the premiere of DOREEN CLARKE's *Roses in Due Season* (1980) for the HOLE-IN-THE-WALL THEATRE COMPANY in Perth: 'It is difficult to think of another actress who could have played both the tired and loving Lil and the drunken, randy Sal with the empathy that Joan Sydney brought to both roles'.

Sydney quickly became a leading player in Perth after she returned to the stage in 1967 as Maggie Hobson in Harold Brighouse's *Hobson's Choice*. For the NATIONAL THEATRE COMPANY she also played Nancy in the musical *Oliver!* and Leona in Tennessee Williams's *Small Craft Warnings* in 1973. She spent 12 months as Good Queen Bess at Dirty Dick's Theatre Restaurant and in 1975 she played a memorable Aggie in Peter Kenna's *A HARD GOD* and the title-role in *Hello, Dolly!*, both for National Theatre. Her roles for this company in 1976 included Oola Maguire in Kenna's *THE SLAUGHTER OF ST TERESA'S DAY* and Martha in *Who's Afraid of Virginia Woolf?*.

In 1978 she was Vladimir in an all-female production of Samuel Beckett's *Waiting for Godot* for Hole-in-the-Wall. For National Theatre she played Meg in Brendan Behan's *The Hostage*, Madame Arkadina in Anton Chekhov's *The Seagull*, the Big One in *No! No! Nanette* and in 1979 Lady Wishfort in William Congreve's *The Way of the World*. In 1980 she played Lil Birtles in DAVID ALLEN's *Joseph Conrad Goes Ashore* and went to Sydney for the NIMROD THEATRE COMPANY to create Sandshoeboots, the eccentric Nemesis in JANIS BALODIS's first play, *Backyard*. She had a notable success in 1982 in Nell Dunn's *Steaming* in Sydney and Melbourne. In that year she also played the Reverend Mother in the musical *Nunsense* and created the earthbound Ruth Cole in DOROTHY HEWETT's *The Fields of Heaven* for the National Theatre Company.

Work in a television series largely kept Joan Sydney from the stage from 1982 to 1989, although she played Bloody Mary in *South Pacific* in Perth in 1984. She is widely known as Matron Sloane in the long-running television serial *A Country Practice*. In 1990 she played the title-role in Nicholas Wright's *Mrs Klein* for the MARIAN STREET THEATRE COMPANY. She played Susan in Alan Ayckbourn's *Woman in Mind* for the MELBOURNE THEATRE COMPANY in 1991, and in the next year she became a regular member of the company, playing Ilse in Balodis's *No Going Back*, Beatrice in Arthur Miller's *A View from the Bridge* and Lilian in Paul Rudrick's *I Hate Hamlet*. *Katharine Brisbane*

writings
Some few small truths. In *Roses in Due Season*, *Bleedin' Butterflies* by Doreen Clarke. Sydney: Currency Press 1982.

Sydney Opera House

Performing-arts centre on Bennelong Point, opened 28 September 1973. Architects: Joern Utzon, stages 1 and 2, 1957–66; Peter Hall, Lionel Todd and David Littlemore in association with NSW Government Architect, E. H. Farmer, stage 3, 1966–73. Originally comprised **Concert Hall** seating 2690, **Opera Theatre** seating 1550, **Drama Theatre** seating 544, **Music Room** seating 419 and **Recording Hal**l seating 300. Recording Hall became **Broadwalk Studio** April 1986. Music Room became **Playhouse** November 1983.

Whatever the problems of design, cost and function before and after its completion, the Sydney Opera House is a major architectural achievement. Its unique site and exterior design have made it the sight tourists most wish to see in Australia. It has become a symbol and a centre for civic events in Sydney. It gave patrons of the performing arts facilities that remain far superior to any others in Sydney, and this has helped to generate a considerable increase in audiences, especially for drama and opera. It has been the principal venue for the SYDNEY THEATRE COMPANY and its predecessor, the OLD TOTE THEATRE COMPANY.

The Sydney Opera House was the most complex structure proposed for Sydney, perhaps anywhere in Australia, since the Harbour Bridge was built in 1927–32. In 1954, after several years' discussion about a venue for concerts and opera, the NSW government resolved to build a music centre on Bennelong Point. It was to comprise a large concert hall, seating about 3000 persons, that could be converted for performances of opera, and a small multi-purpose theatre for chamber opera and drama, to seat 1200.

Sir Eugene Goossens has been credited with promoting the idea when he was director of the NSW State Conservatorium of Music and conductor of the Sydney Symphony Orchestra, but students at the University of Sydney School of Architecture had a project to design an opera house on Bennelong Point in 1947 and another in 1951, which was exhibited in a department store.

An international architectural competition was held in 1956, judged by Professor H. Ingham Ashworth of Sydney, Professor Leslie Martin of Cambridge (England), the American architect Eero Saarinen and the NSW Government Architect, Cobden Parkes. From 222 entries they chose a design by a 38-year-old Dane, Joern Utzon. It was so sketchy that a perspective drawing had to be made by a local architect before it could be exhibited and a local quantity surveyor had to make a rough estimate of cost. As with many competitions, imagination mattered more than strict conformation to specifications. It is usually argued that because competition designs are hardly more than architectural ideas, it is less important to select a design than to select a designer who will produce a superior building.

In the event there was probably more controversy during the construction of the Sydney Opera House than any other building in Australia. A change of government from Labor to Liberal, changes in the design brief, the lack of a theatre consultant, rising costs, the forced resignation of the architect in 1966, and the appointment of a consortium of architects to complete the design, mostly the interior, all contributed to a first-rate public scandal. The architect, the government and the committee set up to act on its behalf all have been criticised for their actions and their organisation of the job. The government produced a poor design brief for the building and insisted on the work beginning before the design had been satisfactorily developed or proper costing done. The Public Works Department's procedures of calling for public tender were incompatible with Utzon's need to work with manufacturers on the mass production of revolutionary components. A new government in 1966 reviewed and changed the design brief, causing considerable redesign of the interiors to produce the present spaces.

The space originally intended to house the auditorium and fly-tower stage of the main theatre was converted to a concert hall. The space beneath the stage, originally to be occupied by machinery for moving scenery, was converted to the Recording Hall. The original space for chamber opera and drama had to be 'stretched' to become the Opera Theatre—in which 98 seats have poor views of the stage. A space allocated for an 'experimental' theatre became the Drama Theatre. For years designers and directors had difficulty in filling its wide low-proscenium stage with setting and action. The Music Room quickly became a cinema for art films, and when the ENSEMBLE THEATRE COMPANY found a home there during rebuilding of its premises, it became the Playhouse, now used by entrepreneurs. Apart from these five auditoria there is the Reception Hall, which accommodates 200 persons.

The Sydney Opera House was Sydney's first theatre in the 20th century to provide bars serving alcoholic drinks in the foyer. The management has fostered catering as well as performance. Soon after the opening of a restaurant and a harbourside cafeteria, it converted part of the box-office lobby into a cafe. Alterations to the forecourt in 1986–88 added a third restaurant as well as shops and a new pedestrian concourse. The management also hires out the harbourside foyers of the concert hall and the opera theatre for luncheons and other functions. All this and the bar trade provide more income than the box office. ❦Ross Thorne

further reading
DUEK-COHEN, E. *Utzon and the Sydney Opera House*. Sydney: Morgan 1967.
SMITH, MICHAEL POMEROY. *Sydney Opera House*. Sydney: Collins 1984.
YEOMANS, JOHN. *The Other Taj Mahal*. London: Longmans 1968.
Architecture in Australia (Melbourne) October–December 1955, January–March 1957, July–September 1957, September 1961, December 1962, December 1965, April 1968, June 1968, August 1968, October 1968, September 1969, April 1970, August 1972, June 1975.

Sydney Repertory Theatre Society

Semiprofessional dramatic company in Sydney, founded in 1920 by agreement between Gregan McMahon and J. and N. Tait. Disbanded February 1928. **artistic director** Gregan McMahon. **first production** *The Voysey Inheritance* by Harley Granville-Barker, April 1921 at Sydney Playhouse.

A curious example of professional patronage of amateur theatre, the second Sydney Repertory Theatre Society brought the new drama to the Sydney stage. It was directed by GREGAN MCMAHON, who had worked for J. AND N. TAIT LTD before it amalgamated with J. C. WILLIAMSON'S IN JULY 1920. The TAIT BROTHERS consented to McMahon forming an amateur repertory society. They would provide a theatre and club rooms and meet production costs if the society collected at least 700 subscriptions. McMahon, lent to the society by the Taits, would have total artistic control, while they would receive any profit from a season or make up any loss. The Taits probably never thought the society would be unduly profitable. They may have intended to test support for serious theatre and to monopolise the services of McMahon, but there is an equal possibility that they were genuinely interested in supporting a literary theatre of the kind that had a mark in London. The latter proposition is borne out by the Taits' activities such as the financially disastrous tour of the Irish Players from the Abbey Theatre under the banner of J. and N. Tait Ltd in 1922 and their continued support for McMahon without intervention in his work.

The society began with two preliminary productions at the Repertory Theatre in November and December 1920—St John Hankin's *The Two Mr Wetherbys* with Gertrude Robin's *Makeshifts*, followed by George Bernard Shaw's *Getting Married*. Then it opened properly at the Sydney Playhouse in April 1921 with Harley Granville-Barker's *The Voysey Inheritance*. From 1924, plays opened at the NSW State Conservatorium of Music and moved to the Palace Theatre if they were popular. It was very much a director's theatre. McMahon's authority was absolute and the standard of production was good. Casting of principal roles was restricted to actors on the J. C. Williamson payroll who were not busy in professional productions. Unpaid society members took the other roles, though only members who showed real talent could expect to act.

Tensions arose because the amateur members distrusted the Taits and McMahon's dealings with them. Such fears must have seemed justified in February 1928, when the Taits proposed to put the society on a surer financial footing. McMahon was given artistic control of a professional touring company that would spend 16 weeks each in Sydney and Melbourne, and the rest of the year in other cities. The Taits wanted the subscriptions of the Sydney society and the MELBOURNE REPERTORY THEATRE COMPANY to help the finances. The Taits no longer undertook to maintain club facilities, but instead to return 15 per cent of the subscriptions, 'from time to time', for their upkeep. It was a vain hope, for the new professionalism threatened amateur histrionic ambitions. The Melbourne organisation—in which the members did expect to act—politely but firmly rejected the idea. In Sydney there was an explosion of bitterness. The society rejected the proposal, effectively voting itself out of existence as its constitution linked it to the Taits. McMahon left to form a professional company in Melbourne. A former member of the Sydney society, DORIS FITTON vainly attempted to lure McMahon back to Sydney in 1930 by establishing INDEPENDENT THEATRE.

The society produced roughly 70 plays during its seven-year life. An overwhelming majority were British, in tune with the times. Shaw, with 10 plays, and John Galsworthy, with eight, were the favourites, alongside J. M. Barrie, John Drinkwater, Granville-Barker, St John Ervine and Elizabeth Baker, whose *Alf's Girl* was given its world premiere by the society in the early 1920s. The society also performed three plays by Henrik Ibsen. It produced three works by Australians—*The Second Round* by Halcott Glover, *Secondary Considerations* by Marguerite Dale and *The Good Losers* by G. H. Soutar—and *The Flaw* by DORIS EGERTON JONES and the visiting actor EMELIE POLINI and *For Love of Appin* by the New Zealand writer Alan Mulgan. McMahon claimed that he would lose his audience were he to produce more Australian material. ❧*Victoria Chance*

further reading
ASHBOLT, ALLAN. Courage, contradiction and compromise: Gregan McMahon 1874-1941. *Meanjin* 37/3 (Melbourne 1978).
DOUGLAS, DENNIS and MARGERY MORGAN. Gregan McMahon and the Australian Theatre. *Komos* (Melbourne) 2/2 (November 1969), 2/4, and 3/1–4 (March 1973).
NAPIER, S. ELLIOT. *The Sydney Repertory Theatre Society*. Sydney: private 1925.

Sydney Theatre Company

Professional dramatic company, founded in January 1979 by NSW government. **venues** 1980– Drama Theatre in Sydney Opera House. 1984– Wharf Theatre. **artistic directors** 1979–90 Richard Wherrett. 1990– Wayne Harrison. **first production** *The Sunny South* by George Darrell, January 1980, Drama Theatre.

Under RICHARD WHERRETT the Sydney Theatre Company became what he aimed for—grand, vulgar, intelligent, challenging and fun. It has been accused of catering to exclusive taste and of being middle-class and sponsorship-oriented, but it has created a support system which has placed its leading actors and directors on a level of authority hitherto rare in a country whose commercial theatre has for a hundred years regarded stars as by definition coming from outside Australia. It has developed and given new standing to actors like JOHN BELL, PETER CARROLL, RUTH CRACKNELL, JUDI FARR, COLIN FRIELS, JOHN GADEN, RON HADDRICK, NANCYE HAYES, NONI HAZLEHURST, JOHN HOWARD, Heather Mitchell, ROBYN NEVIN, John O'May, GERALDINE TURNER and JACKI WEAVER. It has promoted film stars like JUDY DAVIS, MEL GIBSON, HELEN MORSE and John Hargreaves. Directors who have brought their skills to new levels with its resources have included NEIL ARMFIELD, RODNEY FISHER, MICHAEL GOW, WAYNE HARRISON, Jean-Pierre Mignon and ROBYN NEVIN. Others who did not succeed the first time have not received a second chance.

The company was established as the NSW state theatre company after the previous state company, the OLD TOTE THEATRE COMPANY, disbanded upon withdrawal of funds by the AUSTRALIA COUNCIL and the Premier's Department. There was a swift initiative by the state government to start afresh with a company burdened with fewer administrative costs. Elizabeth Butcher and JOHN CLARK, administrator and director respectively of the NATIONAL INSTITUTE OF DRAMATIC ART, were appointed administrator and artistic director of the Sydney Theatre Company for the initial year, to administer a program of guest productions.

This season helped to lessen tension in the theatrical profession about the sudden demise of the state company, and gave its former rivals chances to show their talents in a major venue. The first production was a revival of PATRICK WHITE's *A Cheery Soul*, directed by JIM SHARMAN for the short-lived Paris Theatre Company. Robyn Nevin reached a new height with a *tour de force* in the title-role. Next came Alexandre Dumas's KATE FITZPATRICK in *The Lady of the Camellias*, directed by REX CRAMPHORN for the MARIAN STREET THEATRE COMPANY; George Bernard Shaw's *The Devil's Disciple* directed by DOREEN WARBURTON for Q THEATRE from

Penrith; Bertolt Brecht's *The Caucasian Chalk Circle* directed by John Clark for NIDA; Eugene O'Neill's *Long Day's Journey into Night* directed for the ENSEMBLE THEATRE COMPANY by Robert Lewis, an American, with the expatriate actor PATRICIA CONOLLY returning for the occasion. The last production was a revival of the NIMROD THEATRE COMPANY's musical THE VENETIAN TWINS, directed by John Bell.

Upon taking office as director, Richard Wherrett, who had been one of Nimrod's triumvirate of artistic directors, reflected the current aspirations of Sydney theatre in a policy statement for the new company. It aimed: 'To provide first-class theatrical entertainment for the people of Sydney —theatre that is grand, vulgar, intelligent, challenging and fun. That entertainment should reflect the society in which we live, thus providing a point of focus, a frame of reference, by which we come to understand our place in the world as individuals, as a community and a nation.'

The company's first year was an outstanding success. Two plays—*Close of Play* by Simon Gray, with Ruth Cracknell and FRANK THRING, and *No Names ... No Pack Drill* by BOB HERBERT, with Noni Hazlehurst and Mel Gibson—transferred to the Theatre Royal for short seasons. A spectacular production of Edmond Rostand's *Cyrano de Bergerac* broke the box-office record for the Drama Theatre. It was Wherrett's homage to his former Nimrod colleague, John Bell, who played the title-role. It was revived in the next year, which was more experimental and slightly less successful and reduced the accumulated surplus from $146 000 to $76 533. It included Dorothy Hewett's THE MAN FROM MUKINUPIN, with Ruth Cracknell, John Gaden and Noni Hazlehurst; *Lulu*, adapted from Frank Wedekind by LOUIS NOWRA, starring Judy Davis; and *Chinchilla*, an exquisite contemplation of Sergey Diaghilev's life created by the director Rodney Fisher from Robert David Macdonald's play. But the hit of the year was Wherrett's production of the musical *Chicago* with NANCYE HAYES and Geraldine Turner. It transferred to the Theatre Royal and to Melbourne and Adelaide. Next year it returned to Sydney and it had a season at the Hong Kong Arts Festival.

Company for actors

The 1981 annual report declared a shift away from new plays to classics. 'This emphasis is implicitly an emphasis on an acting company', it said. 'The theatre which is primarily concerned with new writing must primarily be concerned with writers.' The statement reflected the growing pressure of diverse public responsibilities and too little work space. In 1982 the company ran up a deficit of $66 000 despite an average attendance of 80 per cent. At the end of 1983 the turnover increased from $3 million to $4·4 million and the loss to $290 000. Plays in this period included a joint premiere production at the 1982 Adelaide Festival of *A Map of the World* by the English playwright David Hare; Peter Shaffer's *Amadeus* with John Gaden; *Macbeth* with John Bell and Robyn Nevin; David Williamson's *The Perfectionist* with the same pair, and *The Cobra*, written by JUSTIN FLEMING for ROBERT HELPMANN. *The Perfectionist* went to the American Spoleto Festival in Charleston, West Virginia. The 1983 season pointed the way to the company competing with the commercial theatre, and creating large theatrical events that could attract sponsorship. Creative support of Wherrett by the company's general manager, Donald McDonald, helped to gain the backing of private industry and to publicise the company. McDonald resigned in 1987 to become general manager of the Australian Opera.

Elizabeth Butcher's legacy to the Sydney Theatre Company was a permanent home. She persuaded the NSW government to put $1·8 million into a decaying finger wharf in Walsh Bay. VIVIAN FRASER converted the store to house an open-stage theatre, an open-space studio, a restaurant overlooking the water, rehearsal rooms, workshops and administrative offices. The opening of the WHARF THEATRE in 1984 eased the pressure. Turnover increased from $2·8 million in 1984 to $5·8 million in 1985. With a smaller, more informal venue, the company was able to reconsider its responsibility to new writing, and in 1985 its Australian content was 50 per cent.

At the end of 1984 the company reached a high point, a $1·8 million season with the Australian Opera of David Edgar's nine-hour adaptation of Charles Dickens's *Nicholas Nickleby*. The production at the Theatre Royal, which made $1 million profit, was directed by Wherrett and John Gaden, with John Howard as Nicholas and TONY TAYLOR as Smike heading a large cast. It was later staged in Melbourne and elsewhere. It put the company on a new financial base and was largely responsible for reducing the rising deficit to $29 000.

Other notable productions of this period included Henrik Ibsen's *Hedda Gabler* with Judy Davis in 1985, Ray Lawler's THE DOLL TRILOGY in Sydney and Melbourne in 1985 for the 30th anniversary of *Summer of the Seventeenth Doll*, with Steve Bisley, Ruth Cracknell as Emma, Celia de Burgh, Harold Hopkins and Heather Mitchell; *Jonah Jones*, a musical developed by the company, with Simon Burke in 1986; the musical *Company* with John O'May in 1986. The latter year left the company with a deficit of $606 224. Remarkably, this was turned in 1987 into a surplus of $724 454, principally by David Williamson's comedy EMERALD CITY, starring John Bell and Robyn Nevin. The production played also in Adelaide and Canberra and returned in November with GARRY MCDONALD replacing Bell. It was later presented in London by Helen Montagu.

Other productions in a vintage year included Robyn Nevin in *Woman in Mind* by Alan Ayckbourn, an outrageous and controversial staging by NEIL ARMFIELD of William Wycherley's *The Country Wife* with the comic DAVID ARGUE in his first legitimate theatre role as Sparkish, Helen Morse in ALMA DE GROEN's demanding feminist dialogue *The Rivers of China*, and a popular production of Michael Gow's *Away*. The last, along with a production of *Summer of the Seventeenth Doll*, went to the USA as a guest at the Pepsico Summerfare Festival in Purchase (New York) in 1988 as part of the Australian bicentennial celebrations.

With this new security Wherrett could write in his annual report: 'Our brief is I believe primarily to help develop a repertoire of Australian dramatic works, some of which will survive into the future, and to reproduce the great works from the past that make up the classic repertoire'. The company consolidated its 1987 success in 1988 with a surplus and 'the most successful year' in its history. The season included KATHERINE THOMSON's *Darlinghurst Nights*, a tribute to the poet Kenneth Slessor; Luigi Pirandello's *Six Characters in Search of an Author*; a season of cut-price lesser-known classics; LINDA ARONSON's *Dinkum Assorted* and Caryl Churchill's *Serious Money*.

Wherrett retired in 1990 and was replaced by WAYNE HARRISON, a former dramaturge of the company who was seen at the time as an outside runner. Harrison changed the tone of the company's work, reducing design costs and increasing output. With more plays on offer, subscriptions grew by 84 per cent over two years to 17 100 in 1992. The transition year of 1991 included a notable production by Wherrett of Arthur Miller's *The Crucible*, with John Howard, which was revived to sellout seasons in 1992 and 1993; and Harrison's productions of the musical *A Little Night Music* and William Nicholson's biographical *Shadowlands*, with John Bell as C. S. Lewis and Jacki Weaver as Joy Davidman. The offerings in 1993, a vintage year, included Harold Pinter's *The Homecoming* with Heather Mitchell, WARREN MITCHELL and Richard Roxburgh, directed by Rodney Fisher; and Anton Chekhov's *Uncle Vanya*, with PETER CARROLL and GEOFFREY RUSH, directed by Neil Armfield. Among notable new works were Karin Mainwaring's *The Rain Dancers* with Bryan Brown, and *Two Weeks with the Queen*, a children's play adapted by Mary Morris from Morris Gleitzman's novel.

Experiment at the Wharf

In 1991 Harrison introduced New Stages, an experimental venue at the Wharf under the direction of Michael Gow, and the Australian People's Theatre, a troupe of actors with English as a second language, under the direction of John Howard. New Stages has presented tough new American and Australian works and reinterpretations of the classics. The purpose of the Australian People's Theatre was to reflect the diversity of Australia and its people. It was also an attempt to develop the actor-audience relationship and poetic breadth that had been achieved in experiments with Shakespeare. The troupe toured western NSW for several months, performing in open spaces *The Loaded Ute*, its own adaptation of the Sanskrit comedy *The Little Toy Cart*. The rough-theatre style proved popular in the country, less so at the Wharf. Extending the company's brief remains one of Harrison's policies and it is to be seen in large-scale ventures like Stephen Sondheim's *Into the Woods* and the seven-hour epic *Angels in America* by Tony Kushner, both in the 1993 season; in co-operative interstate tours of major productions like Ariel Dorfman's *Death and the Maiden* and recent David Williamson plays; in the small-scale cutting-edge ventures; and in explorations to festivals in Asia and America. The company maintains profitability to subsidise such ventures. In 1992 it received 87 per cent of its income from the box office, nine per cent from the state government and four per cent from the AUSTRALIA COUNCIL. And, as Harrison stated in the annual report: 'For 14 years the Company has consistently played to approximately 80 per cent capacity.' ❦*Katharine Brisbane*

further reading
FRASER, VIVIAN. Designing theatres for 'found' spaces. *Australian Theatre Design* (ed. Kim Spinks). Sydney: Australian Production Design Association NSW 1992.
WILLSTEED, THERESA and BRET SHEEHY (eds). *Sydney Theatre Company 1978-1988*. Sydney: Focus 1989.
Walking on Water—Sydney Theatre Company at the Wharf. Sydney: Currency Press 1995.

Sydney University Dramatic Society

Amateur dramatic society, founded in 1889. **first production** *The Rivals* by R. B. Sheridan, 1889.

The oldest surviving theatrical group in Australia, the Sydney University Dramatic Society has earned a reputation for producing the classics and innovative work by overseas and local playwrights. In 1989, its centennial year, its membership of 350 made it one of the largest organisations on the campus. From its inception until the 1930s the society played in various venues throughout Sydney, including ST JAMES'S HALL, the Savoy Theatre and the ROYAL STANDARD THEATRE. The records of this period are dim but it is known that after the First World War the society presented notable productions of William Congreve's *The Way of the World* and Francis Beaumont's *The Knight of the Burning Pestle*. A production of Henrik Ibsen's *An Enemy of the People* in 1900 is said to have attracted the attention of the press. MAY HOLLINWORTH began directing for the society in 1927. Her early productions included a controversial modern-dress *As You Like It*, in which Jaques smoked a cigarette in the 'Ages of Man' speech.

During the 1930s the society had its own club rooms in George Street and, under Hollinworth's direction it became one of Sydney's leading AMATEUR THEATRE groups. Many of the actors became leading professionals, including LYNDALL BARBOUR, John Bushelle, Marion Johns, Nigel Lovell, Jack Needham, Peter Osborn, Ken Pawley and Judith Halse Rogers. In 1933 the society produced Edmond Rostand's *L'Aiglon*, a play mainly in verse and with more than six acts and 30 speaking parts. This was an ambitious project for amateurs but it was successful.

The society seems to have been quiescent during the Second World War but epic productions by Sam Hughes brought it back to prominence by the late 1940s. His production of James Elroy Flecker's *Hassan* had music by John Antill and sets by James Cook, Margaret Olley, LOUDON SAINTHILL and other leading artists.

In the late 1950s, with Pamela Trethowan as its artistic director, the society had its greatest revival. It introduced to Australia avant-garde plays such as Samuel Beckett's *All that Fall* and *Endgame*, Eugène Ionesco's *The Bald Prima Donna* and Harold Pinter's *The Birthday Party*. After Trethowan's departure the society continued to promote the theatre of the absurd and proclaimed itself as the 'champion of the avant garde in Australia'. Its productions in the 1960s included Alfred Jarry's *Ubu-roi* and Harold Pinter's *The Dumb Waiter* and *A Slight Ache*. During this period the society also presented the Australian premieres of Fernando Arrabal's *Fando and Lis* and Jean Genet's *Death Watch* and *The Maids*. *A Revue Of The Absurd*, which included work by most of the major dramatists of the absurd plus contributions by Jacques Prévert and Edward Albee, was a great success in 1963 and broke box-office records at the Union Theatre.

Before the NATIONAL INSTITUTE OF DRAMATIC ART existed the society provided a theatrical training ground, and even afterwards it gave valuable experience to many talented actors and directors. The actors JOHN BELL, Arthur Dignam and JOHN GADEN, the directors NEIL ARMFIELD and RICHARD WHERRETT, AND the dramatist BOB ELLIS are former members. ❦*Bronwyn Coy*

Brian Syron

Actor, director, teacher. Born 19 November 1940 in Sydney. Grew up partly with Aboriginal grandmother at Forster (NSW) and partly in institutions. Attended acting classes at Ensemble Theatre, Sydney. Went to study with Stella Adler and Olympia Dukakis in New York City 1961. Became tutor at Adler's acting studio in New York. Worked as actor on and off Broadway. Started own theatre company in Saratoga Springs (New York) and began teaching. Returned to Australia 1968. Associate director of Old Tote Theatre Company (Sydney) 1971–72. Consultant to Aboriginal arts board of Australian Council for the Arts 1973. Co-founder Australian National Playwrights' Conference 1973. Foundation member of Black Theatre Arts and Cultural Centre (Sydney) 1975. Co-founder of Bondi Pavilion Theatre (Sydney) 1975. Received Aboriginal grant to study television direction at BBC in London, 1979. Opened City Acting Studio in Sydney 1980. A principal of First National Black Playwrights' Conference 1987. National Critics' Circle award for best director 1969 (*Fortune and Men's Eyes* by John Herbert). Harold Blair Award for lifetime of achievement in performing arts 1987. Died 14 October 1993.

Brian Syron was a unique talent in Australia who achieved much against overwhelming odds. Acting provided an escape from a childhood that he said was 'like a Kafka nightmare'—before he was 17 he had been in three government boys' homes and Tamworth maximum security prison for boys. His studies and work in the USA gave him an escape. The revolutionary new theatre of the late 1960s in the USA and Australia gave him an outlet and produced memorable productions attacking social abuses.

When Syron returned to Australia he joined the emerging artists who were seeking to create a wholly Australian style of theatre. His Ensemble Theatre production of *Fortune and Men's Eyes*, a Canadian play about life in prison, gained national attention and began a new debate on prison reform. It earned Syron a National Critics' Circle Award and a Polish government scholarship to work with Jerzy Grotowski in Wroclaw—from which he withdrew because of the language problem. He became an associate director of the OLD TOTE THEATRE COMPANY and directed *The Merchant of Venice*, Peter Nichols's *A Day in the Death of Joe Egg* and John Hopkins's *This Story of Yours*.

He also assisted new playwrights, particularly ALMA DE GROEN and ALEX BUZO, and initiated the AUSTRALIAN NATIONAL PLAYWRIGHTS' CONFERENCE in 1973, basing it on his experience of the existing American conference. Full of reforming zeal, Syron made the newly-established subsidised theatre companies uneasy and he was excluded from the mainstream of theatre. He became an activist in the developing black theatre and an interpreter of Aboriginality to white Australians, particularly in the performing arts. In 1975 he directed the musical *The Fantasticks* to open the Bondi Pavilion Theatre; he brought Stella Adler to Sydney for PETER SUMMERTON FOUNDATION master classes; and he helped to realise the first production of Robert J. Merritt's *THE CAKE MAN*. In 1978 he played Sweet William in a landmark production of the play at the Bondi Pavilion. In the same year he played the Actor in Liviu Ciulei's production of Maxim Gorky's *The Lower Depths* at the Sydney Opera House. Syron repeated the role of Sweet William in 1982 when—through his American connections—*The Cake Man* was invited to the World Theatre Festival in Denver (Colorado, USA). Syron received offers to remain but he chose to return to Australia.

At his acting school Syron helped to develop the disciplines of Aboriginal actors and those from other ethnic minorities and in breaking down the traditional dominance of Anglo-Saxon actors in Australian theatre, film and television. He made lasting contributions to the theatre in the courage and discipline he gave to his students and fellow artists. Black and white actors paid special tribute to Syron at the 1993 National Playwrights' Conference, shortly before he died from leukaemia. ❤*Katharine Brisbane*

further reading
BACETIC, CLAUDIA. Brian Syron plays a leading role. *Sydney Morning Herald Good Weekend* 5 September 1987.
LAWLOR, ROBERT. *Voices of the First Day*. Rochester (Vermont, USA): Inner Traditions 1991.
THOMPSON, LIZ. *Aboriginal Voices*. Sydney: Simon and Schuster 1990.
THROSBY, MARGARET. *Sydney People and Places*. Sydney: ABC 1992.

Henri Szeps

Actor. Born 2 October 1943 in Lausanne (Switzerland) to Polish parents. Arrived in Australia December 1951. Studied at University of Sydney 1961–65, graduating in science and electrical engineering. Trained with Hayes Gordon at Ensemble Theatre, Sydney, 1962–66. Began acting on television and working as stand-up comic in clubs. Quit engineering to tour NSW, playing three small roles in *Paint Your Wagon*, for NSW Arts Council. Went to England 1971. Toured Mediterranean with Prospect Theatre Company 1973. Returned to Australia 1974. Created Saul in David Williamson's *Travelling North* (1979). Married to actor Mary Ann Severne.

Henri Szeps is a classic comedy actor, capable of ranging from the inwardness of the small screen to the vaudevillian's outwardness and broad energy. He has a particular bent for fast-talking scripts that engage the audience in direct relationship, like David Mamet's *Glengarry Glen Ross*, and Patrick Süsskind's monodrama *The Double Bass*, which he translated with Timothy Daly and toured nationally after its opening season at the Ensemble Theatre in Sydney in 1990. Szeps is also capable of moving an audience in a dramatic role like *Sky* (1992), another solo show, written for him by John Misto. His roles tend towards the disillusioned—beginning with the suicidal Jewish Harold in Mart Crowley's *The Boys in the Band*, which brought him to national attention in HARRY M. MILLER's production in 1968–70—and the awful, but he always engages the audience's sympathy for his viewpoint. ❤*Katharine Brisbane*

further reading
BARROWCLOUGH, NIKKI. Regarding Henri. *Sydney Morning Herald Good Weekend* 20 November 1993.

Tait brothers

Entrepreneurs, managers. Five sons of Scots father and English mother who lived in Castlemaine (Vic.). Sixth brother, William, was postal official, lay preacher and father of Arthur Tait, who was associated with his uncles' theatrical ventures. Tait brothers had three sisters.

Charles Tait. Born March 1869 at Castlemaine. Joined Allan's Music Warehouse (Melbourne) as office boy 1884. Founded Tait's Concert Bureau 1903. Died 27 June 1933 in Melbourne.

E. J. Tait. Born 21 August 1878 at Castlemaine. Worked for J. C. Williamson's 1900–16. Joined J. and N. Tait Ltd 1916. Director of J. C. Williamson Ltd 1920. Managing director of J. C. Williamson Theatres Ltd 1939–47. Died 12 July 1947 in Sydney.

Frank Tait. Born 12 November 1883 in Melbourne. Worked with brothers in J. and N. Tait Ltd and J. C. Williamson's. Managing director of J. C. Williamson Theatres Ltd 1939–65. Married singer Viola Wilson, August 1941. Knighted 1956. Died 23 August 1965 in Melbourne.

John Tait. Born 10 November 1871 at Castlemaine. Promoted concerts and showed films in Melbourne with brother Nevin. Founded J. and N. Tait Ltd 1908. Managing director of J. C. Williamson Theatres Ltd 1939–55. Died 23 September 1955 in Melbourne.

Nevin Tait. Born 21 February 1876 at Castlemaine. Promoted concerts and exhibited films in Melbourne with brother John. Founded J. and N. Tait Ltd 1908. Director and London representative of J. C. Williamson's 1920–61. Managing director of J. C. Williamson Theatres Ltd 1939–61. Died 7 March 1961 in London.

Five of the six boys in the Tait family were partners in J. AND N. TAIT LTD, which was a major and sometimes dominant force in theatre in Australia over six decades. The eldest boy, William, born in 1863, made his career in the Post Office, though his son Arthur was later associated with the theatrical ventures of the other brothers. Charles Tait left school at the age of 11 and became an office boy at Allan's Music Warehouse. At 26 he was an executive of the firm. He found ways to employ his brothers as ushers and front-of-house assistants at concerts and saved their money, which helped to found Tait's Concert Bureau in 1903. It led to the registration in 1908 of J. and N. Tait Ltd, which amalgamated with J. C. WILLIAMSON LTD in 1920. Charles Tait remained with Allan's, though he advised his brothers.

E. J. (Ted) Tait, a hard, strong man, was devoted to the theatre. He fought all the way for the ventures of J. and N. Tait Ltd and J. C. Williamson's. He entered the latter firm in 1900 when he met its manager, GEORGE TALLIS, at Allan's Music Warehouse. Tallis gave him a job as assistant to the treasurer, RICHARD STEWART. Tait became general manager in 1911 and in 1913 he was sent to run the Sydney branch of the firm. He left to join his brothers in J. and N. Tait in 1916. When the Taits joined with Williamson's in 1920 E. J. Tait moved to the forefront as a director. The latter part of his life was poisoned by acrimony, which changed his personality and ruined his health.

The youngest brother and the last to be a managing director of J. C. Williamson's, Frank Tait was a hard businessman and dedicated to the theatre. With his brothers he developed Australian stars in productions that equalled or surpassed the overseas originals. In 1941, two years after the death of his first wife, he married Viola Wilson, a Scottish singer, almost 30 years his junior, who had come to Australia in 1940 as a star of the J. C. Williamson Gilbert and Sullivan Company.

John Tait, like his brother Charles, moved into the concert field. George Musgrove engaged him to manage Nellie Melba's 1902–03 concert tour. Charles, working for Allan's, had little time to help John so Nevin joined his concert agency and they formed J. and N. Tait Ltd. John Tait always kept a sharp eye on the business but maintained a distance from his staff. Nevin Tait worked with his brothers in early film and theatrical enterprises and when J. C. Williamson's acquired their company in 1920 he became the London representative. Though he remained at his London post until his death, he was a managing director of the Firm for many years. He was primarily interested in opera and concert-giving. ❦*Alywn Capern*

further reading
BEVAN, IAN. *The Story of the Theatre Royal*. Sydney: Currency Press 1993.
KINGSTON, CLAUDE. *It Don't Seem a Day Too Much*. Adelaide: Rigby 1971.
OSBORNE, CHARLES. *Max Oldaker—Last of the matinee idols*. London: Michael O'Mara Books 1988.
VAN STRATEN, FRANK. Tait brothers. *Australian Dictionary of Biography* 12. Melbourne University Press 1990.

George Tallis Kt

Manager. Born 28 October 1869 in Callan (County Kilkenny, Ireland). Emigrated to Australia and joined Williamson, Garner and Musgrove as J. C. Williamson's secretary 1886. Treasurer for Williamson. Married actress Amelia Young, sister of operetta star Florence Young, 1898. Director of Williamson, Tallis and Ramaciotti 1904–11. Director of J. C. Williamson Ltd 1911. Chairman 1913–31. Died 15 August 1948 in Wagga Wagga (NSW). Knighted 1922.

George Tallis led J. C. WILLIAMSON'S for 18 years after the death of its founder in 1913. He continued in the tradition of J. C. WILLIAMSON himself. He had an exceptional flair for business and an understanding of theatre that ensured tight management and productions of high quality. He travelled widely in search of talent and productions, and in 1928–29 he briefly extended the Firm's activities to London, where he produced several plays with some success. He saw the potential of film and radio as entertainment media and involved the Firm in their early development in Australia. He maintained that diversification into these fields and modern business thinking would enable J. C. Williamson's to survive.

Tallis learned the theatrical business as he worked his way from Williamson's private secretary in WILLIAMSON, GARNER AND MUSGROVE through treasurer of the Princess Theatre and the Theatre Royal in Melbourne to chairman of J. C. Williamson's. He brought E. J. TAIT into the company as assistant treasurer in 1900. Tait later left to work with four of his brothers in J. AND N. TAIT LTD. In 1920 Tallis invited the Tait brothers to sell their company to J. C. Williamson Ltd. The amalgamation created the largest theatrical organisation in the world. Tallis was knighted in 1922 for contributions to Australian theatre and charity work during the First World War. He retired as chairman of J. C. Williamson Ltd in 1931 but remained on the board until 1937, when he and Arthur W. Allen sold a controlling parcel of shares to John McKenzie, an Australian who had become a chain-store tycoon in New Zealand.

Bert Levy wrote in the *Stage* in April 1920 that Tallis had worthily upheld the traditions of J. C. Williamson and inherited some of the aloofness of his later years. 'Tallis is a silent man, undemonstrative and … has always kept the actor at a respectful though not unfriendly distance—while attending strictly to business', said Levy. 'It is this characteristic which has earned him the respect of everyone in theatrical Australia.' ❦*Alwyn Capern, G. M. Tallis*

further reading
BEVAN, IAN. *The Story of the Theatre Royal*. Sydney: Currency Press 1993.

Colligan, Mimi. George Tallis. *Australian Dictionary of Biography* 12. Melbourne University Press 1990.

Parker, John (ed.). *Who's Who in the Theatre*. London: Pitman 1922.

Tallis, Joan and Michael Tallis and Sue Knight. *In Search of the Sun—The first 100 years of the Tallis family in Australia*. Adelaide: Lutheran Publishing 1988.

John Tasker

Director. Born 25 May 1933 in Newcastle (NSW). Studied drama through Workers' Educational Association in Newcastle. Went to London in 1952 and studied at Central School of Speech and Drama. Later studied and worked in theatres in Germany and Austria. Returned to Sydney 1959. Began directing plays with amateur actors. Founding artistic director of South Australian Theatre Company (Adelaide) 1965–67. Free lance for rest of career. Resident director of Ensemble Theatre (Sydney) 1983. Artistic director of festival of new Australian plays in 1984 Festival of Sydney. Directed many operas. Died 18 June 1988 in Sydney.

The success of John Tasker's productions is legendary. Above all, his work had integrity, courage and excitement. He had a fine eye for design, casting, audience mood and budding talent. He helped actors to discover their capacities and drew lasting loyalty from them. His best productions were of the demanding drama of the 1960s and 1970s. They were seldom without controversy, aroused by the choice of play, his innovations or his demands. Tasker was ahead of the times, and this made for success with audiences and confrontation with managements. He was outside the territorial imperatives defined for the building of subsidised theatre companies. H. G. Kippax wrote in an obituary in the *Sydney Morning Herald*: 'His inspirational qualities balanced the more challenging traits, compulsions and high principles that made him controversial'.

Kester Baruch, tutor for the Workers' Educational Association in Newcastle, encouraged Tasker in his early theatrical studies. Tasker's production of Sophocles's *Oedipus Rex* in Sydney in 1960 attracted the attention of critics and of Patrick White, who nominated him to direct The Ham Funeral. Tasker's production for the Adelaide University Theatre Guild in 1961 launched his career. He directed two later plays by White, *The Season at Sarsaparilla* (1962) and *Night on Bald Mountain* (1964).

As founding artistic director of the South Australian Theatre Company, Tasker created work of a high order, despite having no company theatre, no company of actors and few funds. He directed ten productions, including Rolf Hochhuth's *The Representative*, John Osborne's *Inadmissible Evidence*, Harold Pinter's *The Homecoming*, Peter Shaffer's *The Royal Hunt of the Sun* and Ralph Peterson's comedy *The Night of the Ding Dong*. Critics praised Tasker's work, but he and his board were at loggerheads from the beginning and after nine months of failing to agree on a program he resigned and returned to Sydney.

There he regained attention with two controversial plays in 1968: Jean-Claude van Itallie's satirical *America Hurrah!* for New Theatre and Mart Crowley's *The Boys in the Band* for Harry M. Miller. The latter, the first contemporary gay play to reach the commercial theatre, was Tasker's biggest commercial success.

In 1972 he led a campaign to save the Theatre Royal in Sydney, enlisting the help of the Builders' Labourers Federation. When the cause was lost he negotiated for a replacement theatre, which was completed in 1976.

Tasker's productions as a free lance included a national tour of Leonard Gershe's *Butterflies are Free* for Harry M. Miller in 1971 and the first professional production of Betty Roland's 1928 drama The Touch of Silk, for Independent Theatre in Sydney in 1975. He directed the premiere of Peter Kenna's *The Cassidy Album* at the Adelaide Festival and in Sydney in 1978. He returned to the South Australian Theatre Company to direct Martin Sherman's *Bent* in 1980. He directed *As You Like It* for the Queensland Theatre Company in 1981 and *The Beggar's Opera* with an international cast for the 1982 Singapore Arts Festival. His production of Tom Kempinski's *Duet for One* with Helen Morse and Don Reid in 1982–83 went on national tour from the Marian Street Theatre in Sydney. At the Ensemble Theatre in 1983 he directed Lanford Wilson's *Tally's Folly*, the premiere of Donald Macdonald's *Caravan* and Brian Friel's *Translations*. After Tasker's death the Sydney Critics' Circle established an annual award in his name, sponsored by Philip Parsons, for a freelance director. ♥*Katharine Brisbane*

writings
Censorship in the theatre. *Australia's Censorship Crisis* (ed. Geoffrey Dutton and Max Harris). Melbourne: Sun 1970.

further reading
Bevan, Ian. *The Story of the Theatre Royal*. Sydney: Currency Press 1993.

Tasmanian provincial towns

After Samson Cameron succeeded with the first public dramatic season in Hobart he investigated theatrical opportunities in Launceston, the second largest town in Van Diemen's Land, as Tasmania was known until 1856. He gave the first performances there in a converted room of the British Hotel on 5 June 1834. Friedrich von Kotzebue's *The Stranger* was again the opening piece. From then visiting companies and artists such as G. V. Brooke and Sir William and Lady Don gave seasons in Hobart and Launceston and single performances at places between them, such as Campbell Town. In Launceston they played at the Royal Olympic Theatre, opened in 1834, and the Royal Clarence Theatre, built in 1853.

The newspapers of the 1840s and early 1850s testify to interest in theatre and a lively theatrical circuit. After the Victorian gold rushes began in 1851, however, Van Diemen's Land became poorer and less important than other colonies and this, coupled with its isolation, reduced professional theatre. Visiting companies became more frequent, however, after mining boomed in the west and northeast of the colony in the 1870s and the northwest coast and the Huon Valley district in the south were opened up for agricultural settlement. All this resulted in more settlements where a travelling company could perform. For example, a company would customarily give brief seasons on the northwest coastal route, one on the outward journey and another when it returned about a month later.

There seems to have been a hierarchy of municipal facilities for recreation in the 1870s: a lending library and reading room were provided first, then a venue for sport, usually cricket, and last a hall for music and theatricals. Many municipalities, however, were like Bothwell, a town of 1300 which in 1874 claimed 'handsome and commodious assembly rooms' where 'public entertainments take place frequently'. In 1884 the western mining town of Waratah (population 2500) and the remote agricultural port of Stanley (4762) each had a hall holding 300 persons.

In Launceston only the circus and minstrels were profitable, according to a contemporary commentator. The lack of adequate facilities deterred actors. The THEATRE ROYAL, built in 1857, was a 'tumbledown shanty'. Moral objections to theatres still prevailed. 'New Chum' wrote in 1879 that at the Mechanics' Institute, built in 1871, the can-can would be allowable but Hamlet at the theatre would be 'a thing to be prayed against and condemned!' The Muffs Dramatic Club, established in 1889, performed under the talented Oscar Balfe at the Academy of Music, built in 1886. The Albert Hall (1890–91) also provided facilities.

Amateur theatricals were buoyant in the 1890s and 1900s. Deloraine, with 4969 people in 1901, had a dramatic club whose productions were touring northwest coastal towns in 1905. By the First World War theatres were being converted to cinemas, and amateur and professional live theatre barely existed—except, perhaps, for variety. Nevertheless, in 1924 Queenstown, a mining town of some 3200 persons, could boast a Shakespeare Club, a Bijou Comedy Company and three musical groups. The Launceston Players was founded in 1927 by Margaret Edgeworth McIntyre and W. P. Holman.

Since the middle of 20th century professional live theatre has been scarce in Tasmania. It has had to contend with isolation, costs, a small theatregoing population, and the competition of cinema, television and video. AMATEUR THEATRE flourishes quietly. Each northwest coastal town has a dramatic group, and those of Burnie and Devonport are noteworthy. The towns of the northeast and east coasts and the Huon and Derwent Valleys also have dramatic groups. In Launceston, the University of Tasmania's drama department and the Launceston Players do outstanding work. Audiences are now more mobile and artists with television reputations can be assured that short seasons in Hobart and Launceston will be profitable. The Silverdome, built near Launceston in 1984 as a velodrome, seats enough people to attract star entertainers to Tasmania. The Princess Theatre in Launceston, seating about 1100, can accommodate smaller productions, and an adjoining performing-arts complex, the Earl Arts Centre, opened on 16 October 1993. ❦*Gillian Winter*

further reading
Cyclopedia of Tasmania 2. Hobart: Maitland and Krone 1900.
DAVIS, G. R. *From Tilly to Zip.* Deloraine (Tas.): Deloraine Dramatic Society 1981.
FITZGERALD, J. *Memoirs of a Citizen.* Launceston: Examiner 1929.
'NEW CHUM'. *A Ramble in Launceston.* Launceston: Cornwall Chronicle 1879.
REYNOLDS, J. *Launceston.* Melbourne: Macmillan 1969.

Tasmanian Puppet Theatre

Professional puppet-theatre company in Hobart, founded in 1970 by L. Peter Wilson and Peter Oldham. Closed 1980. **artistic director** L. Peter Wilson.

The show for which the Tasmanian Puppet Theatre is most often remembered was *Momma's Little Horror Show*, in which black-clad puppeteers created stunning images—a huge mouth, a human form worked by three people, gigantic old people—to an accompaniment of recorded music. L. PETER WILSON initiated this landmark production in 1975, with designs by English-trained Jennifer Davidson. The director NIGEL TRIFFITT was later invited to supervise the project. He created a new version, which opened in July 1976 to an enthusiastic public in Hobart. Triffitt returned in 1977 to direct the show again and add a second act. There was also a successful season at the Last Laugh Theatre Restaurant in Melbourne.

Momma's Little Horror Show was for adults but most of the shows the Tasmanian Puppet Theatre produced during its decade of existence were for children. It presented public shows and toured to schools. Its regular touring extended to include Victoria and Canberra and there were seasons in other states, and eventually the Tasmanian Puppet Theatre became a major company comparable in its funding to the MARIONETTE THEATRE OF AUSTRALIA. The company graduated from traditional puppetry to new forms which often put the performers in view. In 1976 the company moved to new premises in historic Salamanca Place in Hobart. In January 1979 the Tasmanian Puppet Theatre was host to a festival of puppetry with performances by puppeteers from Australia, China and Japan. It took *Kidstuff*, a black theatre show created and directed by L. Peter Wilson, to the Asian-Pacific Puppetry Festival in Tokyo in September 1979.

Financial complications arising from conversion of the Salamanca Place premises to create a theatre brought the Tasmanian Puppet Theatre to an end in 1980. Next year Jennifer Davidson founded TERRAPIN PUPPET THEATRE in Hobart and L. Peter Wilson founded the SPARE PARTS PUPPET THEATRE Company in Fremantle (WA).

Several of the puppeteers joined a company that toured Europe with Triffitt's show, now simply titled *Momma's*. Peter Oldham, who had founded the company with L. Peter Wilson, later set up the Performing Puppet Company. Others who worked with the Tasmanian Puppet Theatre include the composer Don Kay; the designers Silver Harris, Patricia Mullins and Jenny Tate; the puppet designer and puppet maker BEVERLEY CAMPBELL JACKSON; the puppeteer and puppet maker ROSS HILL; and the puppeteer Frank Italiano. ❦*Richard Bradshaw*

Morton Tavares

Actor, manager. Born 1 December 1823, in Kingston (Jamaica). Originally Aaron Tavares. Acted as A. T. Morton in USA from 1850s. Intermittently attempted semiprofessional theatre in Jamaica 1857–68. Successful as Morton Tavares in London 1869–71. Toured Australia, New Zealand, South Africa 1871–82. Died 15 June 1900 in Kingston. Wife acted as Miss Surtees.

In his native Jamaica Morton Tavares was acclaimed as a great international actor but in Australia he was less warmly remembered for doubtful productions and management ventures in the 1870s. Tavares came to Australia for GEORGE COPPIN in 1871, when he was nearly 50 and had just gained minor fame in London in the title-role of Edward Bulwer-Lytton's *Richelieu* and as Shylock, Hamlet and Iago. He and his wife were not liked in Melbourne and the contract lapsed. Tavares teamed in Sydney with GEORGE

DARRELL and FANNY CATHCART, but moved on after a few weeks to play in other colonies.

He was in Brisbane in 1873 and returned the next year. On 11 March 1874 his name appears as proprietor of the Royal Victoria Theatre. He refurbished and reopened it on 21 April as the Queensland Theatre with W. S. Gilbert's *Palace of Truth*. 'A Macadamised Pathway (Lighted) has been made to Side Entrance', he announced. He banned smoking in the gallery and asked the public 'to acquaint the Manager of any incivilities by the door-keepers'. The public disliked the repertoire, which included *Hamlet* and *The Merchant of Venice*, and the *Brisbane Courier* advised Tavares on 11 July 1874 that 'with the present company it would be far more profitable to forgo Shakespeare. … even *Hamlet* cannot shine when almost totally unsupported'. By 1875 Tavares was subletting the theatre to a visiting opera company and his last venture was 'Madame Cora, the only female magician in the world' in May.

Tavares acted infrequently from that time. He was associated with a dubious venture at the PRINCESS'S THEATRE in Melbourne in 1878 and was attacked by J. E. NEILD as a 'bogus manager'. Tavares was Jewish and it is not clear whether racist attitudes contributed to the generally poor reputation he endured. Some personal scandal, discreetly hinted at in personal memoirs, also seems to have precipitated his departure from Australia in the early 1880s.
❦*Richard Fotheringham*

further reading
HILL, ERROL. Morton Tavares: Jamaican and international actor. *Theatre Research International* (Oxford, England) 15/3.

Ariette Taylor

Director. Born 26 August 1938 in Amsterdam (Netherlands). Originally Ariette van Rosen. Studied dance with Karel Poons 1954–56. Married choreographer and dancer Jonathan Taylor 1961. In Amsterdam Ballet (Dutch National Ballet) 1957–61. Soloist of Ballet Rambert (London) 1961–68. Taught in London 1972–76. Freelance choreographer and director in Adelaide and Melbourne from 1977. Artistic director of Jolt, 1984–85.

Ariette Taylor has been influential in youth theatre as teacher, director and member of boards such as that of UNLEY YOUTH THEATRE in Adelaide. She believes that children using their own material on stage are to be heard, respected and enjoyed as much as adults. She began directing soon after arriving in Adelaide, with *Me and Me Mum and Dad* in the COME OUT FESTIVAL in 1977. She directed the musical *Buckley's!* in 1981. She incorporated puppetry by HANDSPAN THEATRE in her production of Pablo Picasso's *Four Little Girls*, which was performed in the 1988 Adelaide Festival of Arts. Taylor choreographed for PATRICK WHITE's play *Signal Driver* and *A Midsummer Night's Dream* in 1982 and the musical *Matilda Mine* in 1986. ❦*Alan Brissenden*

Maria Taylor

Actor, singer. Born c.1813 in London. Originally Maria Hill. Father was singer. Arrived in Hobart in October 1833. Became known as singer. First stage appearance in Hobart, 26 December 1833. Moved to Sydney in February 1834 and acted at Theatre Royal. At Royal Victoria Theatre, Sydney, 1839. Left for India 11 August 1840. Died 13 May 1841 in Calcutta (India).

Maria Taylor became the first female star of the Sydney theatre, although she had apparently never appeared on stage before she played Charlotte in Friedrich von Kotzebue's *The Stranger* with SAMSON CAMERON's company in Hobart in 1833. She had the advantage of the 'enchanting voice of a professional singer', the *Colonial Times* said on 29 October 1833, and she seems to have been a rapid learner. The *Hobart Town Courier* of 27 December commended the 'skill and tact' of her debut performance, and the *Tasmanian* of the same date noted that 'she looked remarkably pleasing'. Although other female performers of the period may have equalled Maria Taylor in natural talent and acquired skills, none seems to have possessed these in combination with quite such good looks.

By February 1834 Maria Taylor had outgrown Hobart. She and her husband John left for Sydney and an engagement at the THEATRE ROYAL. 'The attraction of the evening was Mrs Taylor of Hobart Town, who in addition to a lively and genteel style of acting, possess a voice of great richness', recorded the *Sydney Herald* on 20 March. 'She sang "The harp that once through Tara's halls" with great feeling and was rapturously encored. The upper notes are, however, defective and appear to be produced with some degree of difficulty.' But audiences cared little and Taylor was soon an established Sydney favourite. By April 1835 she was demanding £1 a night from BARNETT LEVEY, insisting that she be allowed to play Mrs Haller in *The Stranger*, and even then refusing to perform.

Tasmanian papers reported that Maria Taylor was to return. Her husband did so in May 1835, but she remained at the Theatre Royal, which was then managed by her friend JOSEPH SIMMONS. She was the star of his 1835 season, playing so many leading roles that by the end of the year she had 'exhausted her constitution' and was 'compelled to withdraw from the stage', according to the *Tasmanian* on 6 November 1835.

In Sydney they knew better. Maria Taylor was carrying on a fairly public liaison with John Thomas Wilson, a well-known businessman, who was soundly condemned in the Rev. John Dunmore Lang's *Colonist* during March and April 1836. By the end of 1836, Wilson had left Sydney, numerous creditors and Mrs Taylor behind.

By May 1837, she was sufficiently recovered to appear regularly again at the Theatre Royal and in April 1838 Joseph Wyatt engaged her for his new ROYAL VICTORIA THEATRE. After she appeared as Miranda in *The Tempest*, the *Sydney Herald* of 17 July 1839 noted: 'As an actress both of genteel and low comedy, Mrs Taylor takes precedence of every performer that ever trod the Sydney stage; and would she but dispense with that disagreeable habit of affectation which she has acquired lately, there would be few who could rival her in the higher walks of tragedy. As a talented and industrious, and consequently a deserving actress, Mrs Taylor is inferior to none, and superior to most of her competitors.'

But Maria Taylor clearly did not wish to spend her life on the boards. She formed a new liaison with a French ship's captain, Pierre Lurgetaux, and left for Calcutta with him in August 1840. By August 1841 both were dead. The *Sydney Gazette* of 28 September said in an epitaph: 'As an actress this lady was more successful than any other that ever took the Sydney boards'. ❦*Elizabeth Webby*

Tony Taylor

Actor, dramatist, singer. Born 15 May 1947 at Morecambe (England). Came to Australia with family 1959. Trained as drama teacher at Melbourne Secondary Teachers College 1966–68. Member of Australian Performing Group (Melbourne) 1970–78. Associate head of acting at National Institute of Dramatic Art (Sydney) 1989–90. Green Room Award 1983 (Smike in David Edgar's *The Life and Adventures of Nicholas Nickleby*).

Tony Taylor scored his greatest success as Smike in the SYDNEY THEATRE COMPANY's production of *Nicholas Nickleby* in 1983. During eight years as a member of the AUSTRALIAN PERFORMING GROUP in Melbourne he acted in the world premieres of Jack Hibberd and John Romeril's MARVELLOUS MELBOURNE (1970), David Williamson's DON'S PARTY (1971), THE HILLS FAMILY SHOW (1975), Hibberd's *A Toast to Melba* (1976) and the group-devised *Back to Bourke Street* (1978).

In 1979 Taylor joined the NIMROD THEATRE COMPANY in Sydney to play Lelio in the musical THE VENETIAN TWINS. He helped to devised the cabaret *You and the Night and the Housewine* at the Nimrod Theatre in 1980. Taylor and Keith Robinson devised *The Popular Mechanicals*, basing it on characters from *A Midsummer Night's Dream*. It has played in every major Australian city since its premiere at the BELVOIR STREET THEATRE in Sydney in 1987, and it spawned a sequel, *Pop Mex 2*, at Belvoir Street in 1992. In that year a musical *Horrortorio*, for which Taylor wrote the book and lyrics and Denise Wharmby the music, was performed at La Boîte in Brisbane. ❦*Tony Sheldon*

published work
The Popular Mechanicals with Keith Robinson (1987). Sydney: Currency Press 1992.

Taylor–Carrington Company

The second-ranking but thoroughly professional Taylor-Carrington Company toured extensively around Australasia and South and East Asia from about 1880 to about 1907. In 1880–81 it was known as the Stray Leaves Opera and Theatre Company. It employed Australian-resident artists from the start and its repertoire was partly Australian because of the playwriting ability of the actor-manager Charles Taylor (1851–1919). His best-liked drama was *Unjustly Sentenced* (later *Unjustly Condemned*), which offered a burning cave, 'a struggle for life in the bushrangers' lair', 'the Australian girl's rescue by the convict' and, in its 1894 Melbourne season, 'an exhibition of Australian rough riding'.

In 1892, with *Melbourne's Mystery Murder*, Taylor attempted to cash in on the topical case of Frederick Bayley Deeming, a multiple murderer who was hanged on 23 May. The *Brisbane Courier* dismissed it as trash. Taylor also dramatised Fergus Hume's *The Mystery of a Hansom Cab*, and the Taylor–Carrington Company presented an early version of W. J. Lincoln's THE BUSH KING. When the company was last heard of—in New Zealand in 1907—it had slipped to minor provincial status and was offering stock pieces like *Uncle Tom's Cabin* and *Rip Van Winkle*.

Taylor, an Englishman, later worked for other managements. He was an all-round 'useful' actor and in 1916–19 he was stage director and business manager for FULLERS'. Ella Carrington, an actor and singer from England, was the acclaimed star of the company throughout its existence. She is last noted in February 1916, playing the Fat Girl in EDWARD DYSON's *Fact'ry 'Ands* at the Palace Theatre in Sydney. ❦*Richard Fotheringham*

Leonard Teale AO

Actor. Born 1922 in Brisbane. Originally Leonard Thiele. Radio announcer in Brisbane and Lismore (NSW) 1939–41. RAAF pilot overseas 1941–45. Sydney radio from 1946. Worked with Independent Theatre (Sydney) from 1949. Elizabethan Players 1956. Trust Players 1956. Television 1960–75. Then largely theatre, including solo shows. AO 1992. Died 14 May 1994 in Sydney.

Leonard Teale took his solo and duo performances, mostly celebrating his love of Australia and the Australian character, to many parts of the country. He developed his skills in the theatre, and established himself as a leading radio actor, in Sydney after the Second World War. In 1949 he played minor roles in Shakespeare under JOHN ALDEN's direction for INDEPENDENT THEATRE in Sydney. In 1950 he played the young Swedish seaman Smitty in LAWRENCE H. CECIL's Independent Theatre production of *SS Glencairn* by Eugene O'Neill, and then the lead in Arthur Laurent's *Home of the Brave*. He toured with the TRUST PLAYERS in *The Rivals* and in *Twelfth Night* as Orsino. In 1957 he was Macbeth in Owen Weingott's production for Independent Theatre. For Independent in 1963 Teale, an admirer of fine language in dramatic literature, was the Narrator in DOUGLAS STEWART's splendid verse play *The Fire on the Snow* and co-star in ROBIN LOVEJOY's production of Archibald MacLeish's verse drama *J. B.*

After playing in *Homicide* from 1965 to 1972 and other television Teale returned to the stage as a solo performer. For four years he toured *While the Billy Boils*, based on the life and works of Henry Lawson. This was followed by *The Quiet Achievers*, dealing with Australian independence and humour, and *The Men Who Made Australia* in 1988. Other notable performances by Teale in the 1980s were in Hugh Whitemore's *84 Charing Cross Road* at the MARIAN STREET THEATRE in Sydney and later in Perth and Tasmania, *The Gin Game* for the QUEENSLAND THEATRE COMPANY and a Queensland Arts Council tour, Tom Kempinski's *Duet for One* for the New England Theatre Company and leads in two plays by RON ELISHA—*Einstein* for the Queensland Theatre Company and *In Duty Bound* at Marian Street. ❦*Richard Lane*

Neville Teede

Actor. Born 10 January 1924 at Bunbury (WA). In air force 1942–45. Began acting at University of Western Australia (Perth) after war. Western Australian Drama Council Award for best actor (Scandal in William Congreve's *Love for Love*) 1949. Trained at Bristol Old Vic Theatre School in England. Acted in repertory. Returned to Australia 1956. Contracted to National Theatre Company (Perth) 1957. Died 10 November 1992.

For years after he returned to Perth in 1957, Neville Teede was the only Western Australian actor working professionally in local theatre. He performed in straight plays and Gilbert and Sullivan operetta, and gave poetry readings. In early years he was best known in high comedy, though he became a strong dramatic actor, playing leading roles in innumerable productions of classics and contemporary drama in professional venues and on the University of Western Australia campus. He later combined performing with teaching at the university, where he had become involved in theatre when was studying and teaching in the English department after the Second World War. In the early 1950s Teede went to the Bristol Old Vic and subsequently appeared with the Old Vic Theatre Company in a Shakespeare season.

After five years in English repertory theatre he returned to Australia in 1956 to play in the AUSTRALIAN ELIZABETHAN THEATRE TRUST production of Douglas Stewart's NED KELLY in Sydney. He was a founding member of the University of Western Australia's Bankside Theatre Productions in the 1960s. In 1979 he took Jack Hibberd's monodrama *A Stretch of the Imagination* to universities in Denmark, Italy and France to demonstrate modern Australian drama. In 1988 he had a success playing the title-role of Henrik Ibsen's *John Gabriel Borkman* for the HOLE-IN-THE-WALL THEATRE COMPANY. ❦*Donna Sadka*

Carrie Tennant

Actor, director, dramatist. Born 1907 in Manchester (England). Originally Caroline Emelie Tennant Watson. Emigrated to Australia. Studied elocution with Barbara Sisley in Brisbane 1925–26. In *Snapshots of 1926*, vaudeville show at Cremorne Theatre, Brisbane, 1927. Moved to Sydney 1927. Founded Community Theatre, December 1929. Formed Play Society to publish and produce local plays 1931. Became social anthropologist after postgraduate studies at University of Sydney and studied Aboriginal problems 1937–47. Died 1 September 1989 at Kyogle (NSW).

Carrie Tennant founded the first Sydney company devoted to Australian plays, Community Theatre. She was already a noted figure in Sydney amateur theatre in July 1928, when she produced her own play *Outback* and acted the leading role in a program of five one-act plays she organised in a theatre fitted up in a ballroom at Burdekin House, a graceful Georgian building in Macquarie Street where artists lived. She wrote and produced two more one-acters, *The Reprieve* and *Secrecy*, at the Aeolian Hall in July 1929.

The playwright WILLIAM MOORE encouraged her to start Community Theatre. It opened in the basement of St Peter's church hall in Darlinghurst in 1929 with *Echoes* by Adrian Consett Stephens. Two years later 73 one-act plays and five full-length plays had been produced there. The most successful was LESLIE HAYLEN's antiwar play *Two Minutes' Silence*. Community Theatre organised play competitions, including a series which offered the writers the incentive of seeing their plays produced and judged before an audience. 'There is no better workshop for the playwright than a little theatre wherein he can take part in all the complicated phases of play production and thereby learn much of vital importance in matters of construction and technique', Tennant told the Australian English Association on 15 October 1931.

Late in 1931 she moved to the Aeolian Hall, where she set up the Play Society to publish and produce local plays. She compiled a list of published and manuscript plays, with playwrights' addresses, so that theatres could acquire production rights. This valuable work foreshadowed the PLAYWRIGHTS' ADVISORY BOARD.

Tennant published most of her anthropological work as Caroline Kelly after she married F. T. A. Kelly on 27 January 1927. They spent their honeymoon walking from Sydney to Brisbane, and on their first wedding anniversary they repeated the walk in order to write a book about it. ❦*Lynne Murphy, Delyse Anthony*

published plays
Outback (1928). Sydney: Skewes and Bowman 1930 in *Three Plays for Little Theatres*. Adelaide: Rigby 1962 in *Australian One Act Plays* 1.
The Reprieve (1929). Sydney: Skewes and Bowman in *Three Plays for Little Theatres*.
Secrecy (1929). Sydney: Skewes and Bowman in *Three Plays for Little Theatres*.

Tent shows

Tent theatre took high-quality shows to country towns and nurtured young performers. PETER FINCH and GLORIA DAWN were among the many artists who had their grounding in tent shows. Performances under canvas in Australia date from 8 January 1830, when officers from HMS *Crocodile* and HMS *Zebra* performed *Agnes—or, the Bleeding Nun* and *The Miller and His Men* in a tent at Fort Macquarie, where the Sydney Opera House now stands. From the 1850s tents housed CIRCUS in eastern Australia and some strolling players performed in tents on the goldfields and in a few small country towns in the second half of the 19th century.

In the 1880s Australian versions of American Wild West shows, glorifying bushrangers and folk heroes, toured the outback under canvas. One was E. I. Cole's BOHEMIAN DRAMATIC COMPANY, which at the start of the 20th century presented a succession of melodramas such as *Hands Up!* for the family audiences on the road and in Sydney. Tent shows were operated principally by performer-managers who took melodrama, vaudeville, musical comedy and Wild West shows on the road. They toured towns from Melbourne to Cairns on the east coast, and went as far afield as Tasmania, Western Australia and New Zealand.

Tent shows usually followed the agricultural shows. Country roads were bad and farmers would stay in town for show week and see four or five tent shows at night. According to old performers, acoustics in tents were excellent, especially if the canvas were tightened by a little dampness. In most places tents were pitched on sites dispersed throughout the town, but in Bundaberg (Qld), there was a stretch of Crown land on the Burnett River where tents were pitched peg to peg. Spruikers competed in 'the battle of Bundaberg'. The comedian BOBBY LE BRUN recalled as many as seven canvas theatres, each holding around 1000 persons, alongside one another, plus a circus. Rivalry sometimes led proprietors into unseemly dealings, and one tent was mysteriously burned down.

In the 1920s and 1930s, the heyday of the tents, the troupes stayed in theatrical pubs and 'digs', but in later years caravans were their lodgings. At first the companies travelled by horse-drawn wagon. Then trains were used extensively but by the 1920s motor transport had mostly taken over. Some showmen's cars were their trademarks; GEORGE SORLIE was known in the 1920s and 1930s for his zebra-striped vehicles. Sorlie's was the last big tent show; the popularity of television and the advent of poker machines in NSW clubs led to its demise in 1961 and virtually ended tent theatre. Other tent shows included Barton's Follies, Cole's Varieties, Coleman's Pantomime Company, KATE HOWARDE's Dramatic Players, Lionel Walsh's Musical Comedy Company, Mack's Players, Maurie Diamond's Marquee Theatre and Pat Hanna's DIGGERS. Humphrey Bishop, the illusionist the GREAT LEVANTE, Stanley McKay, D. B. O'Connor and Les Shipp were other tent-show proprietors. *Charles Grahame*

further reading
CARROLL, BRIAN. *Australian Stage Album*. Melbourne: Macmillan 1975.
LORD, FRED A. *Little Big Top*. Adelaide: Rigby 1965.
Australian Encyclopaedia. Sydney: Grolier 1963.

Terrapin Puppet Theatre

Professional puppet company in Hobart, founded in 1981 by Jennifer Davidson. **artistic directors** 1981–91 Jennifer Davidson. 1991– Annette Downs.

In its first decade Terrapin Puppet Theatre presented works of high artistic merit and won a national reputation. The English stage designer Jennifer Davidson, a member of the TASMANIAN PUPPET THEATRE until it closed in 1980, founded Terrapin in 1981 with a Tasmanian government grant of $10 000 and $14 000 from the Australia Council. She worked as artistic director, administrator and publicist, and employed three puppeteers and a set engineer. The part-time company began touring primary schools and in its first two years of operation it made 280 school visits, comprising 450 performances to audiences totalling 50 000 children. It became a full-time company and expanded its activities to encompass workshops for children and productions for community groups. The Terrapin company engages guest artists and visiting experts to broaden the training of its members. *Gillian Winter*

Theatre of the deaf

Theatre allows deaf persons to express themselves artistically through a medium that makes the handicap of deafness an asset because of the beauty of sign language and the natural ability of the deaf to communicate without words. Theatre of the deaf began in 1973, when deaf societies in NSW and Queensland coincidentally looked to forming drama groups as vehicles for development of self-confidence and self-expression in deaf adults. Nick Neary approached the drama department of the University of NSW, and one of its lecturers, Oliver Fiala, directed the first production. Leslie Abnett's plans in Queensland came to fruition only in 1974, when a visit to Brisbane by the American Theatre of the Deaf generated such interest and excitement that theatre workshops were soon in full swing.

By the mid-1970s, the NSW Theatre of the Deaf and the Queensland Theatre of the Deaf were both receiving government funding. The NSW company was under the administrative umbrella of the AUSTRALIAN ELIZABETHAN THEATRE TRUST and, with a professional director, was heading towards professional status. The Queensland group, funded only for specific purposes such as administration costs, was growing in stature within Brisbane's powerful amateur-theatrical movement. The Victorian Theatre of the Deaf was established in 1978 with assistance from the Drama Resource Centre in Melbourne. At the end of 1982 the theatre affiliated with a theatre-in-education team, QED, and this combined group then affiliated with a disabled-theatre group, Breaking Through, under the name of Drama Education And Fun. In Adelaide, a group called Gestures, specialising in street theatre and cabaret, was formed in 1986.

During the early years, the major difference between the NSW and Queensland theatres was style. While Adam Salzer, the first artistic director, established a strong non-verbal visual base, Queensland espoused the 'visual-vernacular' and sign-language tradition of the American National Theatre of the Deaf. Victoria also chose sign language and the influence of subsequent directors led the NSW theatre to use sign language too. Critics, festival adjudicators and the public have acclaimed the unique style of performance of theatre of the deaf—a lyrical combination of gesture, mime, sign language and speech. Its main influence, however, has been in schools, where children have the opportunity to meet deaf people. *Nicky Bricknell*

further reading
BRICKNELL, NICKY. Let's see the applause. University of Queensland MLitStud. thesis 1984.

Theatre Royal Adelaide

Theatre in Hindley Street, opened 13 April 1868, seating 894. Architect: Thomas English. Enlarged to seat 3000 and reopened 25 March 1878. Architect: George Johnson. Remodelled, reopened 11 April 1914. Architect: William Pitt jnr. Closed 1959. Demolished 1962.

From the 1880s until its closure in 1959 the first Theatre Royal was the Adelaide showplace of J. C. WILLIAMSON's and its forerunners. When it opened in 1868 SAMUEL LAZAR, J. T. Sagar and J. M. Wendt owned it and GEORGE COPPIN leased and directed it. The new theatre was an improvement on others in Adelaide, although its auditorium was quite small—15·3 metres long by 13·8 metres wide by 10·8 metres high. Into this were squeezed the pit and stalls, holding 614 persons, a dress circle seating 200, and a gallery seating 480. The stage was 13·8 metres wide by 16·2 metres deep and fully equipped with traps. The scenery was the traditional system of sliding wings and shutters, with borders that could be raised out of sight, all worked by pulleys and drums. One bar served pit and stalls patrons, and dress-circle patrons had exclusive use of a second bar and a billiards room, adjoining a large saloon. At the foot of the gallery stairs there was a third bar, reached by passing through a restaurant from a separate entrance.

When the theatre was rebuilt in 1878 some of the original façade may have been retained but two-thirds of it was a new and far more imposing neoclassical section. This was symmetrical in itself, with a tripartite first-floor façade of pilasters, pedimented windows, entablature, and a deep cornice, over which was a large central pediment in front of a balustraded parapet wall. The interior was among the earliest in Australia to conform to the new Victorian style. The auditorium, enlarged to 21·9 metres wide by 21 metres deep, housed 3000 people on three levels. The stage was increased in size and the proscenium, widened from 7·5 to 9 metres, was designed like a picture frame. Gas lighting was installed, with the new pilot-light system which permitted lights to be turned off during performances. Separate entries to the various parts of the house still enforced the separation of social classes, to the gratification of a reviewer in *South Australian Register* who referred to pit and gallery patrons as the 'great unwashed' with 'playful eccentricities'. The 1878 auditorium, as in the original building, had three boxes, one above the other in a narrow band directly in front of the proscenium. When WILLIAM PITT JNR altered the auditorium in 1914 he designed a very deep proscenium with a splayed-arch sounding board and four private boxes on each side in two banks of two, all decorated in heavily modelled French rococo. Unfortunately the elderly Pitt had not kept his engineering skills up to date, so the tiers were still supported by six posts. By the mid-20th century, audiences resented these as unnecessary obstructions. In 1959 J. C. Williamson's found it a better proposition to buy and remodel the Tivoli Theatre, now HER MAJESTY'S THEATRE, than to modernise the Theatre Royal. ❦*Ross Thorne*

Theatre Royal Brisbane

Theatre in Elizabeth Street, opened January 1865 as **Mason's Concert Hall**. Architect: W. Coote. Name later alternated between **Victoria Concert Hall** and **Victoria Theatre**. Renovated, reopened on 21 April 1874 as **Queensland Theatre**. Rebuilt and reopened on 18 April 1881 as **Theatre Royal**, seating 1350. Improved with electric lighting and redecoration 1911. Closed 19 December 1959 and converted to cabaret and orchestral rehearsal room.

The first true theatre in Brisbane began as a one-level hall behind the Victoria Hotel. A photograph of the old hotel shows 'Theatre Royal Est'd 1863' in plasterwork above the cornice, but the publican George B. Mason did not open the simple concert hall that became the theatre until early 1865. There were dress seats, stalls and pit on the flat floor, but there was neither gallery nor boxes. The stage appeared 'to be well adapted for theatrical representation', said a correspondent in the *Brisbane Courier*. The theatre was first advertised as the Victoria Theatre on 30 September 1865, but patronage seems to have been mediocre.

After the theatre reopened as the Queensland Theatre on 21 April 1874, the *Brisbane Courier* said the formerly 'dingy and cellar-like' house had been considerably improved. It had a raked floor, a new proscenium, a new gas sunlight, lighter colours and generally increased comfort. The newspapers still did not consider it a good theatre, however. The whole building appears to have been rebuilt from the street backwards in 1881, parts of the hotel becoming integral with the theatre as refreshment and smoking rooms. Both hotel and theatre were named Royal. The theatre housed 350 in the dress circle, 250 in the stalls and 750 in the pit. The newspapers rated it suitable for a city of nearly 30 000 inhabitants. It was rather austere, with numerous closely spaced posts supporting the circle. From 1900 until the Second World War its uses fluctuated between vaudeville and popular light drama. It was in the BRENNAN VAUDEVILLE CIRCUIT for a period after the 1911 refurbishment. During the Second World War it was a theatre for the American armed forces. It returned to vaudeville in 1948 under the direction of George Wallace jnr, but his weekly-change shows lost popularity after television began in Brisbane and it soon closed. ❦*Ross Thorne*

Theatre Royal Castlemaine VIC

Theatre opened *c.*1852. Front portion rebuilt as hotel 1856. Destroyed by fire and immediately rebuilt 1857. Gutted by fire and rebuilt as two-level theatre in 1887. Remodelled as cinema in 1930s.

For more than 130 years there has almost continuously been a place of entertainment on the site of the Theatre Royal in the old gold town of Castlemaine. The first building was made of timber and canvas, but some fragments of masonry walls of the 1857 and 1887 rebuildings remain in the present theatre. A photograph of the interior after the 1887 rebuilding shows a deep horseshoe balcony with a Regency-style deep proscenium, in which there are traditional stage doors and small boxes above. This interior disappeared when the theatre was redecorated in Art Deco style inside and outside in the 1930s. It is used for cinema, live theatre and disco. ❦*Ross Thorne*

further reading
WYLDBORE, J. Castlemaine's unique Theatre Royal. *Kino* 26 (December 1988).

Theatre Royal Hobart

Theatre in Campbell Street, opened as **New Theatre Royal** or **New Theatre**, 6 March 1837. Designed by Peter Degraves. Seated 500–600 on two levels. Later called **Royal Victoria Theatre** for a time. Auditorium rebuilt as three tiers seating about 800, 1856. Architects: W. Coote and E. B. Andrews. Renamed **Theatre Royal**. Major alterations in 1890. Interior rebuilt to design of William Pitt jnr 1911–12. Damaged by fire 18 June 1984. Reopened 6 March 1987 with auditorium restored to 1911 design.

The Theatre Royal in Hobart stands on the oldest theatre site in Australia. A theatre has stood there since 1837 and the present structure contains fragments of the original theatre. This grew out of enthusiasm for the first public theatrical season in Hobart, presented by SAMSON CAMERON in December 1833. Next month Henry Degraves sought shareholders to build a theatre designed by his father Peter Degraves, a brewer and entrepreneur. Building was slow after the foundation stone was laid on 4 November 1834, because of tardiness in paying for completed work. The exterior of the theatre measured about 30 metres long by 15 metres wide. The width has not changed over 150 years, although the length has. The two-storeyed exterior looked almost like a house, with three bays of Georgian multi-paned windows defined by modest pilasters. The auditorium was on two levels, possibly similar to a small Georgian theatre in the English provinces.

The New Theatre Royal was temporarily fitted up on 17 January 1837 for a farewell to the Administrator of Van Diemen's Land. On 6 March it was still not quite finished but Cameron presented Thomas Morton's comedy *Speed the Plough* and *The Spoiled Child*. Cameron was a poor manager and JAMES BELMORE, JOHN MEREDITH and J. Moses came in to share the management until the first season closed on 31 July 1837. Meredith and D. P. Grove were the managers from 25 September 1837 to March 1838. From April 1840 to February 1841 the theatre, then known as the Royal Victoria Theatre, was controlled largely by ANNE CLARKE. She returned from England in February 1842 with actors, dancers and singers and by July 1842 she had resumed control of the theatre. Anne Clarke and her husband held the lease until 1846, after which various companies leased the theatre from Degraves. He died in 1853 and the theatre was sold to Richard Lewis, a local merchant, who leased it to JOHN DAVIES and F. B. WATSON from 1853 to 1856. In 1856 a new three-tier auditorium was squeezed into the old envelope, and some public space was added in a lower extension to the front. The improvements also included gas lighting. The building was now called the Theatre Royal and Davies was the sole lessee. The tragedian G. V. BROOKE was a notable performer in the 1850s, when stock companies had generally given way to touring companies playing a limited repertoire for a short period.

Some minor changes to entrances and removal of boxes at the rear of the pit increased the capacity in 1862. In 1882 the stage was extended rearwards by 4·6 metres to produce a total depth of 16·8 metres. C. J. and David Barclay and C. E. Davies, son of John Davies, bought the Theatre Royal in 1889 and carried out major alterations in 1890. The stage was fitted with a new floor and traps, and with a new roof to produce a fly tower. The auditorium was modified to improve sight lines and comfort. The Theatre Royal housed many public events, including political rallies, religious gatherings, boxing matches, film screenings and the first Hobart demonstration of Edison's phonograph in November 1890. It has been a popular venue for amateur theatre since the 1890s, when the Hobart Operatic Society regularly performed there.

The last major alteration to the auditorium and front of house was made in 1911–12. The architect WILLIAM PITT JNR gutted the interior, raised the walls and spanned them with a new roof, and constructed a new Edwardian-style, three-tier auditorium complete with dome. The renovations also included electric lighting and decoration in Louis XV style picked out in gold and silver. There was no substantial financial benefit, however, because of the First World War and a change in shipping routes that excluded Tasmania from the Australasian theatrical circuit. Nevertheless, the theatre thereafter saw notable artists, including Noël Coward, Harry Lauder and ALLAN WILKIE. It also provided an initial base for the HOBART REPERTORY THEATRE SOCIETY.

C. E. Davies owned the theatre until his death in 1921. It had a private owner until the Theatre Royal Company, formed by a few local shareholders, bought it in 1923. This company still owned the theatre in 1948, when Laurence Olivier and Vivien Leigh, heading the OLD VIC THEATRE COMPANY, performed in it. With their support the theatre was saved from demolition for road works and a car park. The state government set up the NATIONAL THEATRE AND FINE ARTS SOCIETY to buy and control the theatre in 1949, and gave it financial help to redecorate the dilapidated building extensively for a proposed royal tour in 1952.

The Tasmanian Theatre Company was established as a resident in 1971 but by 1977 it functioned as entrepreneur rather than producer. Declining financial success resulted in a government inquiry which set up the Tasmanian Theatre Trust in 1984. The trust's initial problems were compounded on 18 June 1984, when fire destroyed the stage, except for its 1837 stone side walls, and heat, smoke and water damaged the auditorium. The Tasmanian government decided that the theatre was an important inheritance and rebuilt the stage to present-day standards and restored the auditorium to the 1911 design. The Theatre Royal was officially reopened on 6 March 1987, 150 years to the day after its original opening, and *Speed the Plough*, the inaugural play, was performed again. That year the trust was replaced by the Theatre Royal Management Board under the direction of JOHN UNICOMB. There are more modern venues in Hobart but the Theatre Royal has strong sentimental appeal for audiences. The development of Backstage, at the rear of the main theatre, for intimate and alternative theatrical fare has introduced the Theatre Royal to yet another generation of theatregoers. *Ross Thorne, Gillian Winter*

further reading
WINTER, GILLIAN. A colonial theatrical experience—The Royal Victoria Theatre, 1837–1857. *Tasmanian Historical Research Association Papers and Proceedings* 32/4 (Hobart, December 1985).

Theatre Royal Launceston

Theatre in St John Street, opened 1857, seating 800. Architect: W. H. Clayton. Partly rebuilt in 1878 and thereafter known variously as **Gaiety Theatre**, **Empire Theatre** and **Lyceum Theatre**. Now **Lyceum Hall**, used as craft shop.

Possibly the oldest little-altered theatrical structure in Australia is the two-storey Lyceum Hall in Launceston (Tas.). It was built in 1856 by the Manchester Unity Independent Order of Odd Fellows as members' rooms and offices, with a hall in the upper storey. Like many such halls, it would have been fitted up with a temporary or semipermanent stage and dressing rooms in front of the rear windows. The ground floor has been gutted for modern shops but the second-storey front and rear façades retain the windows that originally illuminated the simple, high-ceilinged rectangular hall. A straight stair from a rear lane enters one side of the hall. The original stair came from the main entrance on the ground floor and turned.

As the Theatre Royal from 1857 to 1878 the hall saw major touring performers such as G. V. BROOKE, Sir William and Lady Don, Charles Poole's dramatic company and W. S. LYSTER's Royal Italian and English Opera Company. The building became the property of the Bank of Tasmania in 1872 and was partly rebuilt in 1878. After this it seems to have housed mainly variety. From about 1892 to 1910 the hall was one of four in Launceston that were fitted up for theatrical performances. The others were the Academy of Music, the Albert Hall and the Mechanics' Institute. The Theatre Royal was the home of Todd's (Lyceum) Pictures from early in the 20th century until 1921, when it became the Lyceum Billiard Saloon. *Ross Thorne*

Theatre Royal Melbourne

Theatre in Bourke Street, opened 16 July 1855. Architect: J. R. Burns. Seated 3300 persons in four levels. Destroyed by fire March 20 1872. Rebuilt and reopened 6 November 1872. Architect: George Browne. Seated nearly 4000. Redesigned by William Pitt jnr as three-level auditorium 1904. Closed 17 November 1933 and demolished to make way for department store.

Built in 1854–55, only two decades after the first settlement of Melbourne, this large, substantial theatre rivalled the Theatres Royal at Covent Garden and Drury Lane in London in the sizes of its auditorium and stage. The auditorium was 19·2 metres wide by 22·8 metres from the rear to the stage curtain line. The stage was 26.4 metres from the same curtain line to its rear wall, with a 3.6-metre apron projecting into the auditorium. The stalls–pit floor extended to the boundary walls of the auditorium, with posts supporting three balconies, all rather cramped in height. In front of the theatre was a lofty two-storey hotel in a heavy early-Victorian neoclassical style. The theatre, owned by John Black, was largely an optimistic extravagance for the young town, even with the influx of residents and itinerants brought by the Victorian gold rushes. A year after Black opened the Theatre Royal with R. B. Sheridan's *The School for Scandal*, he went bankrupt and was forced to sell it for £21 000, about one-quarter of the cost of building it. The actor G. V. BROOKE and the actor-manager GEORGE COPPIN bought the theatre, but it was rarely profitable to them or various lessees. In 1861 the theatre came under the control of Ambrose Kyte and then returned to Coppin.

After fire destroyed the building in 1872 Coppin rebuilt the theatre with a high three-storey hotel in front, designed in rococo Victorian style and surmounted by a huge royal coat of arms. The architect George Browne increased the depth and height of the auditorium to 25.5 metres and 18 metres respectively and increased the capacity to nearly 4000 people. The stage was deepened to 36 metres. There was a huge gas chandelier in a 12.6-metre-diameter dome, painted with scenes of Melbourne and London. In 1880 the proscenium was brought forward to eliminate the stage apron. Yet even with these improvements DION BOUCICAULT in 1885 found the theatre to be large, dusty and primitive, with poor audience accommodation and wretched backstage arrangements for the actors.

Coppin operated the theatre in partnership with HENRY HARWOOD, JOHN HENNINGS and RICHARD STEWART until it was taken over by WILLIAMSON, GARNER AND MUSGROVE. This firm and its successors ran until the Great Depression, when it was sold as a redevelopment site. In 1904 J. C. WILLIAMSON had the auditorium gutted and redesigned by WILLIAM PITT JNR with only three levels, but still with a forest of posts. As the Williamson company's premier theatre in Melbourne, the Theatre Royal mainly housed major overseas companies and opera and operetta productions. ❦*Ross Thorne*

Theatre Royal Perth

Theatre in Hay Street, opened 19 April 1897. Seated 1200. Architect: George R. Johnson. Converted to cinema 1936.

The first fully-equipped, purpose-built theatre in Western Australia, the Theatre Royal was the first of several theatres of advanced design built in Western Australia during the gold boom of the 1890s. It was modelled on the BIJOU THEATRE in Melbourne, with a proscenium stage and a three-tier auditorium. Like Melbourne's PRINCESS THEATRE, it had a sliding roof to ventilate the auditorium on hot nights. The Theatre Royal was built for Thomas Molloy and Alexander Forrest and managed by George Jones and George Lawrence, who were known as the Firm of Western Australia. They opened with *The Silver King* by Henry Arthur Jones and Henry Herman, with C. R. STANFORD in the leading role. Jones and Lawrence lost heavily on *The Silver King*. GEORGE DARRELL, on tour with *The Sunny South* and *The Queen of Coolgardie* (a version of THE DUCHESS OF COOLGARDIE), took over from Stanford and a partner named Barnes on 5 June 1897, in time to save the theatre from closure. Darrell's season was profitable, but by 1898 the management was bankrupt. By 1902 the theatre had housed the English Comedy Company, the Hannibal and Williams Company from New York and MAGGIE MOORE in *Struck Oil*. The theatre functioned for short alternating periods as a cinema and variety hall from 1916 to 1936, when the auditorium was extended into the stage area. The building remains in use as a cinema, the former dress circle incorporated into an adjoining building. ❦*Bill Dunstone*

Theatre Royal Sydney 1833–38

Theatre in George Street, opened 5 October 1833. Seated about 900. Closed September 1838. Destroyed by fire 17–18 March 1840.

The first continuously licensed permanent theatre in Australia, the Theatre Royal was the brainchild of BARNETT LEVEY, an amateur singer of comic songs. In April 1826 he began a building spree on the eastern side of George Street, between King and Market Streets. The first structure was to be the Colchester Warehouse, which would include a two-tier theatre, with one floor of grain storage beneath it and two above. During 1827 Levey was preoccupied with building a windmill atop the warehouse and commencing a new building between the warehouse and George Street. This building, which was attached to the warehouse, was at first noted as being a dwelling, purportedly designed by the architect Francis Greenway. By mid-1828 the 'dwelling house' was being roofed and the theatre was being prepared. It then emerged that Levey did not possess title to the land on which the warehouse was built.

Part of the 'dwelling house' was opened as the Royal Hotel in March 1829 and Levey obtained a licence to hold balls, dances and concerts at the hotel, but he appears to have transferred the concerts to the theatre in the warehouse, which was first used on 24 August 1829. Then he went further and performed dramatic sketches at an 'at-home'. This riled Governor Ralph Darling and he further restricted Levey's licence for balls and concerts when it was renewed on 1 January 1830. Unable to use the theatre for theatrical performances, Levey advertised the concerts that he held there as being in the Royal Assembly Rooms.

On 18 December 1830 the hotel and warehouse, including the theatre, were sold by order of the mortgagee. The purchaser transferred the title to the former mortgagee, Daniel Cooper. He employed John Verge, architect and builder, to refit the theatre and enlarge it by adding a third tier in place of a storage floor above. The hotel in front was to be completed and include an 'orchestra surmounted by the royal arms' in the saloon, for concerts. George Sippe, the new licensee, reopened the hotel in September 1831.

Levey leased the theatre and the saloon of the hotel and obtained a licence under a new governor to hold at-homes, including theatrical sketches, in the saloon until work on the theatre was completed. Newspaper reports of the time are confusing as to whether Levey held his at-homes in the saloon or the theatre, but it is clear that the saloon was fitted up with a 'tasty stage' and 'a tier of boxes' for a performance of Douglas Jerrold's *Black-Eyed Susan* on 26 December 1832. Regular performances were given in this temporary abode until the beginning of June 1833. Finally the new three-tier theatre within the warehouse was completed. It opened on 5 October 1833 with a melodrama, *The Miller and His Men*, followed by a farce, *The Irishman in London*. With the exception of an additional tier of audience accommodation, in dimensions and style the theatre was similar to the Georgian Theatre at Richmond in Yorkshire —two tiers of narrow boxes, the lower at the level of the stage, and one tier of gallery, including side slips over the boxes. These, together with the stage, were arranged in a rectangle enclosing a raked pit. The pit and the three tiers above it were contained within a height of 8·8 metres. The theatre was 26 metres long, including the stage, and about 9·7 metres wide. The space for each person at that time was about half today's allowance, so the capacity would have been about 900 persons.

Management fluctuated between Levey and JOSEPH SIMMONS until June 1836, when CONRAD KNOWLES took control as actor-manager until early February 1837. There were consistent complaints of imperfect preparation of plays even after Levey reopened in April 1837. Thomas Simes became manager in May. Levey died on 2 October 1837. His wife Sarah took over the management, with the stage under JOHN LAZAR's control, but closed the theatre without notice just before JOSEPH WYATT opened the Royal Victoria Theatre on 26 March 1838. She continued to occupy the building, and its owner, Daniel Cooper, sued her in September 1838. He won an action for ejection, leaving him free to lease or sell the building to someone else. Wyatt bought all the buildings on 2 January 1839. ❦*Ross Thorne*

further reading
BEVAN, IAN. *The Story of the Theatre Royal*. Sydney: Currency Press 1993.

Theatre Royal Sydney 1875–1972, 1976–

Theatre in Castlereagh Street, opened 11 December 1875. Architect: J. F. Hilly. Auditorium damaged by fire 17 June 1892. Reopened 2 January 1893. Closed 29 April 1972 and demolished. Replaced by new Theatre Royal in King Street, opened 23 January 1976. Architect: Harry Seidler.

After fire destroyed the second PRINCE OF WALES THEATRE in January 1872 its architect, J. F. Hilly, was commissioned to design the third theatre on the site, the Theatre Royal. He reused the Castlereagh Street front of the Prince of Wales Theatre. The stage was reduced to 20·1 metres in depth and the auditorium was slightly increased to 21·3 metres by 18·3 metres. It seated only about 1500 people in comfort, in three levels instead of four. The groove system of scene-changing remained. The outer walls were brick and the posts and basic framing were cast-iron but the interior was still lined in timber with canvas affixed as the base for painted and modelled decoration. The theatre opened under the lesseeship of SAMUEL LAZAR, who offered fairly eclectic fare, ranging from classical drama with MARY SCOTT-SIDDONS and later GEORGE RIGNOLD, through ALFRED DAMPIER's dramas to the LONDON COMEDY COMPANY and the EMILY SOLDENE Opéra-Bouffe Company.

The theatre was refurbished in 1882, when WILLIAMSON, GARNER AND MUSGROVE took it over. In 1883 electricity was installed. This allowed the auditorium to be plunged into darkness, producing a 'peepshow stage', which quickly became the new tradition for proscenium-stage theatres. Fire damaged the auditorium on 17 June 1892, leaving the canvas hanging in shreds. The theatre reopened on 2 January 1893 with the stage-house raised to provide full-height flying facilities. About 1897 the freehold came into the hands of GUSTAVE RAMACIOTTI. Stars who appeared at the Theatre Royal in the late 19th and early 20th centuries included SARAH BERNHARDT, DION BOUCICAULT and NELLIE STEWART. The theatre housed vaudeville in the 1920s. In 1921 the architect HENRY E. WHITE redesigned the façade in an Edwardian style, foyers in classical style and an auditorium, again on three levels, in classical Adam style. There was now only one post in the stalls instead of 13. Lewis Casson and Sybil Thorndike acted there in 1932 but the Theatre Royal was largely given over to musicals during the Great Depression. By the end of 1935 it and the TIVOLI THEATRE were the only live theatres in Sydney.

The Ramaciotti family sold the theatre to developers in 1969 and closure became imminent in 1972. JOHN TASKER tried to save the theatre by organising a small committee of interested citizens, including Jack Mundey, president of the Builders' Labourers Federation. After public meetings, protests and a building workers' ban on demolition, the developer signed an undertaking on behalf of the owners of the site that the MLC Centre would incorporate a new fully professional theatre, seating no fewer than 1000 persons—the old theatre then held 1292 persons. It was agreed to retain items from the old theatre for 'possible inclusion in the new theatre'. These items are not in the new Theatre Royal and no-one knows where they are. The last performance before the old theatre was demolished ended a Shakespeare season by the Prospect Theatre Company from England. The new Theatre Royal, turned 90 degrees to face King Street, seats its audience on two levels, facing an unadorned proscenium. The musicals *Cats* and *Les Misérables* had long runs at the theatre. ❦*Ross Thorne*

further reading
BEVAN, IAN. *The Story of the Theatre Royal*. Sydney: Currency Press 1993.

Theatre '62

Semiprofessional theatre company in Adelaide, founded in 1962 by John Edmund and Donald Gray. Closed 1975. **first production** *Great Expectations* by John Edmund, 31 May 1962 at Theatre '62, Hilton, Adelaide. **landmark productions** *Othello* with Alexander Hay, 1963. Aleksey Arbuzov's *The Promise*, starring Julie Hamilton and Russell Starke and directed by Jean Marshall, 1969. *The Mating of Ulrich Dooley* by Ralph Peterson, 1972.

The first professional theatre company in South Australia in the 20th century, Theatre '62 provided a progressive repertoire of modern overseas plays plus classical dramas, farces, musicals and new Australian plays under John Edmund until 1974. It provided work for experienced professional actors and it trained young actors. Some of them have become well known, including Paul Cronin, Patrick Frost, JOHN GADEN, Tom Georgeson and NONI HAZLEHURST. Edmund, an English actor and director with repertory and West End experience in plays and musicals, came to Australia in 1950 under contract to BENJAMIN FULLER and GARNET H. CARROLL. After touring Australia and New Zealand for J. C. WILLIAMSON's in 1958 he settled in Adelaide, where he set up the John Edmund Academy, taught, acted and produced plays for amateur groups. Donald Gray, a schoolteacher, joined Edmund as a partner, and they converted an old cinema into a theatre-in-the-round and renamed it Theatre '62. It opened with Edmund's adaptation of Charles Dickens's *Great Expectations*, in which John Bannon, later Premier of South Australia, played Herbert.

Edmund established Theatre '62 with his own money, but after a year the company was struggling. An approach to Sir Lloyd Dumas, chairman of the *Advertiser*, brought it a grant for 1963–64. The company received a subsidy from the state government in 1967 and later a small grant from the Australian Council for the Arts. A building next door was converted into an experimental theatre, the Chapel, to stage youth workshops and Australian plays in 1972. BUNNEY BROOKE joined as creative director and helped to revitalise the struggling Theatre '62. The South Australian Theatre Company was now a statutory body and Theatre '62 was forced to redefine its policy. In 1973 it saw itself as non-establishment, eager to try out obscure plays and Australian works. Theatre '62, the HOLE-IN-THE-WALL THEATRE COMPANY of Perth and the ENSEMBLE THEATRE COMPANY of Sydney exchanged their best productions in 1974.

Edmund returned from an overseas trip in 1975 to be told that state subsidy would cease unless he left the company. Its board backed him but he was locked out of the theatre. Shortly afterwards the company folded and the theatre was abandoned for impending road widening. Edmund became a lecturer at the Sturt campus of the South Australia College of Advanced Education and directed for the drama department. The road was not widened and from January 1980 to March 1986 the Youth Performing Arts Council revived the theatre as a venue. The State Theatre Company presented plays there in 1980–81. In 1987 the West Torrens Council improved the building and Theatre '62 Pty Ltd, then directed by ROB GEORGE and Barbara Messenger, took over the lease and fitted out the theatre. Theatre '62 and the Chapel are now run as a commercial venue and rented to groups. ❦*Jo Peoples*

Theatre South

Semiprofessional dramatic company in Wollongong (NSW), founded in 1980 by Des Davis and Faye Montgomery. **venue** 1985– Bridge Theatre, Coniston. **artistic director** Des Davis. **first production** *The Con Man* by Maurice Scott, Wollongong Technical College Theatre, 1980. Cast: John Clayton, Laurie Cruickshank, Geoff Morrell, Faye Montgomery, Anthony Warlow, John Warnock. Designer: Bill Pritchard. Director: Des Davis. **landmark productions** *The Playboy of the Western World* by J. M. Synge, 1981. *The Man From Mukinupin* by Dorothy Hewett, 1984. *Tonight We Anchor in Twofold Bay* by Katherine Thomson, 1985. *Windy Gully* by Wendy Richardson, 1987. *Five Times Dizzy* by Des Davis and Wheatley, 1990.

With experience of provincial theatres in Canada in the 1970s, Des Davis and Faye Montgomery founded Theatre South to give Wollongong regular professional theatre, with particular regard for the character and needs of the city and the Illawarra region. The company has earned a reputation for quality, and on presentation of new or recent Australian drama with an emphasis on development of regional material and talent. In an average season of six plays at least four have been Australian and at least one of these has been an original work, developed or first produced by the company. Outstanding figures who have emerged from the company include the actor Geoff Morrell, the late actor and writer Bill Neskovski, the writer Wendy Richardson, the actor and playwright KATHERINE THOMSON and the actor and singer Anthony Warlow. Neskovski, who was of Macedonian parentage, wrote several plays about Macedonians in Wollongong, and Richardson and Thomson have also drawn on the life of the community for their plays.

In the company's early years modest support from the University of Wollongong was crucial, but gradually increased funding from the NSW Ministry for the Arts, the AUSTRALIA COUNCIL and business had allowed consolidation. It has maintained mutually beneficial relationship with the university by providing staff and students at the School of Creative Arts with experience in professional productions. The company established Seagull Theatre for theatre-in-education and children's theatre in 1980. It tours to NSW country centres and beyond. ❦*Maurice Scott*

Theatre-restaurants

During the 1960s and 1970s theatre-restaurants made a brief appearance that had important consequences. At a time when middle-class 'polite' theatre was only occasionally disturbed by works like Patrick White's THE HAM FUNERAL in 1961 and Edward Albee's *Who's Afraid of Virginia Woolf?* in 1964, theatre-restaurants offered rumbustious, deeply impolite theatrical entertainment that caused a vast uncorsetting of audiences. It filled the gap between the dying forms of musical comedy and Tivoli revue and the theatrical revolution of the 1970s; and it introduced a new audience, which booked in parties, to the pleasure of theatrical entertainment.

The original and most famous theatre-restaurant—in the true sense of providing a three-course dinner and a fully-mounted play—was the MUSIC HALL THEATRE RESTAURANT, which opened in Neutral Bay Junction, on Sydney's lower north shore, in 1961 and ran successfully for almost 20 years. Its origins were in Melbourne, at the Bowl Restaurant under the Capitol Theatre, where the musicians George and Lorna Miller presented their first melodrama, an adaptation of Mrs Henry Wood's novel *East Lynne*, directed by the veteran actor Philip Stainton. The Bowl Music Hall ran for three years, but Victoria's liquor-licensing laws in the 1960s were not sympathetic to late-night carousing. The Millers extended their business to Sydney. Their first production there was again *East Lynne*, directed by Bette Bailey Stainton, widow of Philip Stainton, who had died suddenly. It gave star status to BARRY CREYTON, then an actor in PHILLIP STREET revues. Others whose careers benefited from the Music Hall's yearlong runs, included the actors Terry Bader, NEVA CARR GLYN, Beryl Cheers, Linda Cropper, Alton Harvey, BARRY LOVETT and JOHN UNICOMB, the dancer David Atkins and the singer Sheila Kennelly. The musical director was Don Harvey and the extravagant designs and stage effects gave early opportunity to designers like Tom Lingwood.

The early Music Hall shows were revivals of popular melodramas like *Lady Audley's Secret* and *The Worst Woman in London*. In 1966 John Faassen, an actor and opera singer, took over as director and began writing his own shows, burlesques of musical and dramatic genres, particularly opera. Stanley Walsh, who succeeded Faassen in 1970, tapped the new preoccupation with Australia's history with his first show, *The Trials of Hilary Pouncefortt*, set in Sydney in 1850. By the mid-1970s other theatre-restaurants had entered the field and the vogue was waning. The local council declared the building a fire hazard and the Music Hall closed in 1980.

Theatre-restaurants continued to open in Sydney in the late 1960s with varying success. The veteran actors WILLIE FENNELL and John Ewart performed old radio comedy at the Comedy Theatre Restaurant, but the place was burned out soon after opening. The Menzies Hotel presented mini-musicals with stars like GLORIA DAWN and NANCYE HAYES. From 1965 to 1971 Doncaster Theatre Restaurant offered a luxurious setting and revues directed by WILLIAM ORR. In 1972 he opened the Music Loft in Manly, which lasted until the late 1980s. The Bull 'n' Bush in East Sydney for 20 years offered a singalong with a jovial host and costumed songstresses. It lost popularity after the sudden death of its longtime host Noel Brophy in 1983 and soon closed.

In Brisbane, the actor Russell Jarrett and his partner Frank Mesh established the Mark Twain in 1964 and Mesh founded the larger Living Room in 1967. These inner-city premises, furnished with gilt chairs and red plush fabrics, for a time provided the only secure employment for actors in Queensland. Among the many well-known performers who received early training were the television stars Brian Blain and Shane Porteous, the actors Carol Burns and JANE HARDERS, and the opera singer Beryl Shean. At the Mark Twain the repertoire included classic English comedies like William Wycherley's *The Country Wife*, John Vanbrugh's *The Relapse* and Brandon Thomas's *Charley's Aunt*. At the Living Room audiences enjoyed genuine Victorian melodramas like *The Drunkard* by W. H. Smith and *Lady Audley's Secret* as well as parodies, sometimes written by the comedian Ken Lord and laced with songs from Hollywood films. The Living Room burned down twice and by the time of the second fire in 1981 the pattern of theatre in Brisbane had radically altered. In 1976 Jarrett briefly opened a second Mark Twain in Hurstville, Sydney.

In Adelaide in the late 1960s, Barry Eggington opened the Olde King's Music Hall in the King's Ballroom, built as the King's Theatre in 1911. The decor was Victorian bric-a-brac and the shows were roughly based on Victorian plots, to which were added, with no great sense of style, songs of the 1940s and 1950s. The building burned down in 1975.

Melbourne's lasting success—and the longest-running in Australia—is Tikki and John's, a coffee house in Exhibition Street, adjacent to Her Majesty's Theatre. It was opened in 1965 by Tikki Taylor and her husband John Newman, musical-theatre performers, to provide after-theatre suppers for patrons. It provided variety entertainment, which extended to dinner and holiday entertainment for children. Like the Millers' business, the Newmans' was a family affair. When Tikki and John retired in 1987 their son Paul Newman took over. He changed the name to Tikki and John's Crazyhouse and the entertainment to modern burlesque. The family also owns Dracula's Theatre Restaurant in Melbourne, and two theatre-restaurants on the Queensland Gold Coast—another Dracula's and a cabaret offering nostalgia, which opened in 1993. In Perth, a music-hall season was successful at the Hole-in-the-Wall Theatre Club in East Perth. Its founders, FRANK BADEN-POWELL, CORALIE CONDON and John Gill, transferred the club to Leederville and opened the Music Hole in the old experimental theatre space in 1967. In 1968 they leased the Fremantle Trades Hall, a stone's throw from the wharves and fish markets, and named it the Olde Time Music Hall. They provided fish and chips wrapped in 'colonial' newspaper and an earthy serving of old-style variety. The careers of the actor JOAN SYDNEY and others blossomed from these ventures, which also led to the Diamond Lil theatre-restaurant chain and Dirty Dick's Bawdy Banquets. The first two opened in Perth in 1970. Dirty Dick spread to Sydney and Brisbane in 1972, Melbourne in 1974 and Los Angeles in 1975. CORALIE CONDON has managed the chain since 1985.

In the 1960s theatre-restaurants were virtually the only indigenous form of popular theatre. But by 1971 the style had spread to the new wave and the theatre-restaurants' influence waned. By the late 1970s, however, a new kind of entertainment was flourishing in Melbourne. A form of STAND-UP COMEDY and aggressive social satire had emerged, directly related to the protest theatre of the AUSTRALIAN PERFORMING GROUP. Seminal was a production by the group of Jack Hibberd's farce *DIMBOOLA*. It had first been seen on a small scale at the La Mama Theatre in 1969 but the expanded production by DAVID WILLIAMSON at the Pram Factory in 1973 drew a whole new audience. Its success led to new versions being performed in theatre-restaurants around Australia and in Europe and North America, not always with acknowledgment to the author.

In 1972 JOHN PINDER converted a fish shop into the Flying Trapeze Cafe. It held few people but it offered a stage to performers of all kinds and all qualities—tap-dancers, magicians, comedians and satirists. In 1975 Pinder sold the Flying Trapeze and with Roger Evans opened a larger venue called the Last Laugh Theatre Restaurant and Zoo. It was decorated with circus posters, merry-go-round horses and a collection of humanised aircraft suspended from the foyer ceiling. It was a place of surprises, where patrons were likely to be insulted by the waiters, who might well be the performers. Performers from the Australian Performing Group had a close association with the Pinder venues as they developed comedy and circus techniques. CIRCUS OZ performed at the Last Laugh most of 1979. The Last Laugh also opened a cabaret upstairs, Le Joke. Pinder sold the building in 1988. These places gave rise to such outstanding comic teams as the Busby Berkleys and Los Trios Ringbarkus, and in the 1980s the style developed into television shows like *Australia, You're Standing In It* and *The D-Generation*. A leader the field is the stand-up comic Rod Quantock, who opened the Comedy Cafe in Fitzroy in 1979 as an outlet for comedians, and ran it until the mid-1980s. It changed hands several times and closed in 1992.

By the 1980s the cabaret style had given way to a boom in STAND-UP COMEDY, which found outlets in a variety of venues, notably the Prince Patrick Hotel in Collingwood, Melbourne. Pubs, festivals and cabarets have proliferated particularly in suburbs. Theatre-restaurants in most state capitals now offer burlesque, all-male revues, vaudeville, nostalgia and farce. These provide employment for artists but their influence upon the style of legitimate theatre is significant only occasionally. ❦*Katharine Brisbane*

Theatres

There were theatrical performers among the convicts who arrived at Sydney Cove on the First Fleet in 1788 and on later transports. They mostly came from touring stock companies that played in small two-tier theatres, such as those at Ipswich in Suffolk or Richmond in Yorkshire, and less frequently in three-tier theatres in larger English towns. The theatre in Georgian England epitomised society in its distinctions between the upper, middle and lower classes. 'Dress' boxes for the upper class extended around the perimeter of the auditorium at stage level. Above them was the gallery, sometimes divided into a part for lower-class patrons opposite the stage and boxes for middle-class families along the sides of the auditorium. In a three-tier theatre middle-class families sat in the middle tier. On the floor of the well between the tiers of boxes and in front of the small orchestra pit were benches for the lower middle-class or middle-class men who went to the theatre without their families. This was the pit, precursor of today's stalls.

The proscenium was virtually an extension of the tiers of boxes. It was simple and deep, with a door on each side through which actors entered the stage on a deep apron projecting into the auditorium. Most of the action took place on this part of the stage. Behind it was the scenic machinery. The scenery comprised rolled backdrops or sliding shutters and wing flats, and borders. One set of wing flats was slid aside—usually in two sets of grooves, one on the floor and one hung from the flies—while another was slid into view, transforming the scene.

Candles and oil lamps illuminated the stage and the auditorium throughout the performance, though those on the stage could be shielded to dim their light. In an illuminated auditorium there was much to talk about, including the quality of the performance on the stage. Food and drink and sometimes prostitutes were available. Attendance at a Georgian theatre was a social occasion, and activities and sounds in the auditorium competed with those on the stage, where broad, stylised acting established a contrast between actors and audience.

The proscenium theatre of Georgian England was the only style of theatre the first settlers in Australia knew. But they also brought with them, particularly from the English and Irish provinces, strong traditions of the 'fit-ups' and booth theatres of the annual fairs. In English villages, a small hall, a barn or the saloon of an inn would be fitted up as a temporary theatre, with the auditorium divided into the pit and, around it or behind it, the boxes. The fit-up theatre flourished in Australia, particularly in country pubs, but also in bakeries, warehouses, factories and even suburban houses. Virtually any space could be and was converted into a temporary theatre, which sometimes became permanent. The booth-theatre tradition produced the tent theatre, ideal for touring the vast outback by train.

Performances in fit-ups

On 4 June 1789, in embryonic Sydney, a convict hut was fitted up for a performance of George Farquhar's *The Recruiting Officer* before an audience of 60 persons. The hut had walls of saplings and brush plastered with mud. It may have been similar to a bark-roofed, timber-slab hut used as the EMU PLAINS CONVICT THEATRE west of Sydney in the 1820s. The cracks between the timbers were perhaps plastered with mud and whitewashed. At Emu Plains, according to James Tucker, 'boxes were erected for the comfort of the quality who had signified their intention to be present at the performance'. These and the boxes in SIDAWAY'S THEATRE—the first acknowledged theatre in Sydney—may have been behind the pit benches. An unauthenticated drawing shows Sidaway's theatre, which also had a gallery, as a high, windowless timber shed.

Another theatre was reported to have existed in Sydney around the end of the second decade of the 19th century, but the only evidence for it seems to be 75-year-old Obed West's memories of the town when he was about 13. In 1882 he described the properties in the main streets around 1820, and named their occupiers. Going south from Bathurst Street, along the western side of George Street, West described a clay-pipe manufactory, a large block of land with a cottage and fruit trees, and then 'a painter's named Noble. At the back of his place was a large bakehouse and granary which served two purposes, being both used in connection with baking and as a theatre. Many were the blood and thunder tragedies enacted there …' The fare it provided and its possible illegality suggest that the theatre was a fit-up similar to penny-gaffs in London.

Farther north along George Street, on the opposite side, BARNETT LEVEY began building a theatre in a granary warehouse in 1826. Before he could open his THEATRE ROYAL he gave performances in a fit-up in the saloon of his hotel in 1832. Fit-ups have continued side by side with purpose-built theatres, on the goldfields in the 19th century and as venues for alternative and amateur theatre to this day.

Georgian design

The Theatre Royal and other early purpose-built theatres in Sydney, Melbourne and perhaps Hobart followed Georgian tradition, with some modification of detail to cater for the taste of the Regency times in which they were built. Whether the plan of the auditorium was rectangular or had some relationship to a circle or horseshoe shape, the proscenium incorporated doors giving onto the stage apron, which provided an acting area thrust about two metres into the auditorium. The lowest row of boxes was level with the stage, enclosing the pit, which was raked to provide adequate sight lines to the stage.

Access to the pit was generally by a passage beneath the boxes through a door adjacent to the stage. Every part of the house—pit, dress circle, family circle if there was one, and gallery—had a separate entrance, some from the front of the building, others from side alleyways. This distinction by design attempted to maintain English class distinctions by separating the patrons of the parts of the house. It was first removed between the dress and family circles, and then, as the pit became the more expensive stalls, its entrance was combined with that of the dress circle. But until 1920 the gallery patrons had a separate entrance, without lobby or foyer. A mean stair with cheerless finishes led directly to their bare benches.

The first innovation in design came with the opening of the ROYAL VICTORIA THEATRE in Sydney in 1838. At a time when many major theatres in the USA and the United Kingdom still had pits enclosed by the low dress circle of boxes, the architect Henry Robertson designed the Royal

Victoria with the dress circle lifted so high that the pit could pass beneath it to the side and rear walls of the auditorium.

Other theatres, such as the QUEEN'S THEATRE ROYAL in Melbourne, retained the traditional low dress circle until the mid-1850s, but the QUEEN'S THEATRE in Adelaide, built in 1841, followed the example of Sydney's Royal Victoria. So did the THEATRE ROYAL in Melbourne in 1855. This theatre, like the Royal Victoria in Sydney and the other major theatres, began life as a four-level theatre with pit, dress circle, family circle and gallery. Illustrations show almost impossible conditions for many gallery patrons. Most of these theatres were rebuilt by the end of the 19th century with only three levels, which provided patrons at the rear of the gallery with at least enough headroom to stand up. Such inconveniences as lack of headroom and poor sight lines to the stage—often through a forest of posts supporting the circles, gallery and roof—were exacerbated not only by managers crowding in too many people but by poor safety procedures, flimsy construction, inflammable decorations and unsatisfactory ventilation. Benjamin Backhouse complained in 1882 that he had designed the Opera House in Sydney in 1879 with adequate facilities, sightlines and exits but the client had then altered the design and built the theatre with day labour and without expert supervision. The result was a failure.

Australian theatre architects were not up-to-date in structural design at the end of the 19th century. Slim cast-iron columns replaced heavy timber posts but many posts still supported the tiers above the pit. When Her Majesty's Theatre was built in London in 1897 the use of a semi-cantilever system eliminated most of the usual posts, but the major Australian theatre architect of that era, WILLIAM PITT JNR, did not change his style of structural design after the mid-1880s. When he rebuilt the auditorium of the small THEATRE ROYAL in Hobart in 1911 he supported the two tiers above the stalls with ten posts. Meanwhile, a theatre was being built in Wellington (New Zealand) with more than twice the Theatre Royal's audience capacity and only three posts supporting its much larger circle and gallery. This was Her Majesty's Theatre (now the St James), designed for the Fuller family by HENRY E. WHITE.

About this same time White and FULLERS' both crossed the Tasman Sea to expand their respective interests. Soon after White designed theatres for HUGH D. MCINTOSH in Adelaide Fullers' invited him to modify theatres such as the National Amphitheatres in Sydney and Melbourne and also to build new theatres, such as the Majestic Theatre in Sydney. By 1926, White had managed to reduce the supporting posts to two in Fullers' St James Theatre in Sydney. He eliminated posts two years later, when he designed two cinemas in Sydney for Union Theatres—the 3000-seat two-level CAPITOL THEATRE and the almost equally large three-level State Theatre. After 1929 there was little theatre construction until civic centres and PERFORMING-ARTS CENTRES began to be built in the 1960s. Many were or incorporated proscenium theatres.

Other buildings that housed theatrical performances were town halls and the halls of literary and mechanics' institutes and schools of arts. A spate of these buildings were constructed in suburbs and country towns in NSW in 1882, when the Liquor Act banned professional performances in assembly rooms of hotels. Similar developments

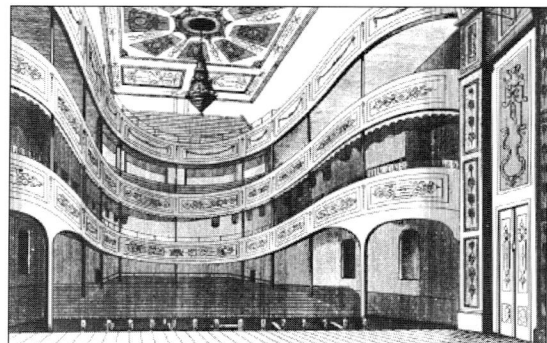

Sydney's Royal Victoria Theatre had its dress circle lifted above the pit in the new Victorian style. Actors still made their entrances and exits through doors in the proscenium

took place in other colonies, and in Western Australia the councils of Boulder and Kalgoorlie built town halls with fly-tower stages in 1908 and 1909 respectively with the intention that they would be civic theatres. The Kalgoorlie hall was built with a partially raised stalls floor and a dress circle and annually housed a three-week season by a touring J. C. WILLIAMSON's company. These town halls were early forerunners of the civic theatres built since the 1960s.

Changing the scenery
From the first theatres to the 1880s Australian stages used the English system of changing scenery, in which wing flats and shuttered back scenes were slid back and forth between grooves. There was no fly tower for lifting full-height scenery out of sight but borders were lifted above the head of the proscenium. There was little space there because the same roof enveloped the stage and the auditorium, usually without fire-resistant separation. In Levey's Theatre Royal in Sydney the continuous ceiling was the floor of a warehouse.

In the 1890s it became the rule to provide full flying space—more than twice the height of the proscenium opening. The managements of some theatres—the Theatres Royal at Broken Hill (NSW) and Hobart, for example—constructed high, lumpy mansard roofs off existing stage walls to provide the required height. At the Academy of Music in Ballarat (Vic.), however, enough height was gained by flying between old roof trusses above the stage. In the first half of the 20th century the fly tower usually appeared externally as a blocky fire-resistant appendage to the auditorium, as in the Prince of Wales Theatre in Hobart, the Princess Theatre in Launceston (Tas.), the Tivoli Theatre in Adelaide, HIS MAJESTY'S THEATRE in Perth and the Kalgoorlie Town Hall. Since the 1970s architects have tried to integrate fly towers within an overall form, as at the ADELAIDE FESTIVAL CENTRE, the Araluen Arts Centre in Alice Springs (NT) and the SYDNEY OPERA HOUSE.

The fly tower of the 1880s eliminated wings and shutters from the stage floor by simply allowing them to be flown out of the way as legs and drops. This clearing of the stage space made it convenient to introduce a new form of setting that was more applicable to the realism of the new literary drama and to the spectacle of melodrama from the

1890s to the 1920s. This was the box-set, composed of flats lashed together and propped up from behind to form naturalistic three-dimensional objects, such as buildings in streets, or interior spaces of rooms. Parts of the box-set might be constructed on low wheeled platforms—trucks—and brought in from the wings to form a complete box-set.

Naturalistic representations of buildings, ships, trains and landscapes were constructed in three-dimensions and could, if necessary, be designed to break apart to simulate spectacular catastrophes—crumbling buildings, conflagrations, shipwrecks, train crashes and so on. Some of these effects were enhanced by large stage lifts—driven by hydraulic and then electric power—and revolving stages. All these mechanical developments of the late 19th and early 20th centuries are still used in proscenium theatres today, but on complex, computerised stages, as in the State Theatre of the VICTORIAN ARTS CENTRE.

Decoration and style

Over more than 150 years, the interior decoration of theatres in Australia has changed considerably. The large apron stage of Georgian and Regency theatres, with the deep proscenium and its doors, lasted in one way and another from 1833 until at least the mid-1870s. The newly designed Academy of Music in Ballarat had proscenium doors in 1875. Some theatres substituted private boxes for the doors, as at the ROYAL VICTORIA THEATRE in Sydney in 1854. As a result the audience extended right round the auditorium from one side of the stage apron to the other. The first Theatre Royal in Melbourne, built in 1855, had four levels of boxes on each side of its 3·5-metre-deep apron stage. This extension of the acting area into the auditorium existed in most major theatres until at least the mid-1870s, though not all had a deep proscenium of private boxes to define the stage. The THEATRE ROYAL in Hobart, as rebuilt in 1856, had an apron projecting from a simple picture-frame proscenium, for example.

By the end of the century the stage was flush with a picture-frame proscenium in most theatres. Even in many of these theatres the concept of a deep proscenium filled with private boxes persisted, but the boxes now flanked the orchestra pit and front stalls seats rather than the stage apron. The architects Pitt and White both used this feature in their designs or alterations during the first two decades of the 20th century—for example, in the THEATRE ROYAL in Adelaide, the TIVOLI THEATRE in Brisbane and the Majestic Theatre in Sydney. These deeply splayed, usually highly decorative elements—often containing two columns of boxes—tended to separate the performer from the audience psychologically.

This separation was not perceived at the time the theatres were built, and indeed, White continued to design in the same way but in a different decorative style through the 1920s. From about 1911 to 1918 he decorated his designs in a heavily modelled version of Louis XV style, which he called 'Louis Seize'. Then, in auditoria constructed from 1921 to 1926 he used a neoclassical style of embellishment. It was based on the interior designs of Robert Adam in 18th-century Britain and it may have been influenced by the American theatre architect Thomas Lamb. White used this style in Melbourne in the PALACE THEATRE and the PRINCESS THEATRE in 1923 and the ATHENAEUM THEATRE in 1924, and in Sydney in the THEATRE ROYAL in 1921 and the St James Theatre in 1926. Rather than recess two or three levels of boxes into a deep, splayed outer proscenium, as he had previously done, he now projected one box or two side by side from the wall at the dress circle level. Both the wall and the boxes were integrated with the frame of the stage at the curtain line.

Some American theatre architects argued that the richer the surrounding decoration, the more the eye would be drawn to the proscenium opening. But followers of the 'functional' Modern movement of architecture from the late 1920s, argued that there should be no decoration. It distracted the eye, they claimed. Their argument prevailed, but not until the end of the 1950s.

This reaction to what seemed to be extraneous elements that weakened performance–audience interaction was not simply architectural. Theatre itself had changed and the modification was one of a series of incremental changes in the design of the proscenium theatre that had perhaps started at the time of the restoration of the monarchy in England in the 17th century or the construction of the first European opera theatre.

When gas lighting became advanced all lights, including those in the auditorium, could be dimmed, though not extinguished. Complete darkening of the auditorium was made possible by electric lighting. This was used first in the Prince of Wales Opera House in Melbourne in 1882, and in the Theatre Royal in Sydney next year, but it was not used on the stage at that time. Actors had less competition from the audience in the darkened auditorium and a more natural style of acting gradually developed.

The Theatre Royal in Melbourne, rebuilt in 1872 after a fire, had boxes on each side of an apron stage, like the first theatre. Later the proscenium was brought forward to eliminate the apron. The theatre, here depicted during a religious service, could seat an audience of nearly 4000

After the first decade of the 20th century film replaced theatre as the mass entertainment of the middle and lower classes. After 1929 talking pictures reduced the audience for live theatre to those who were willing to pay considerably higher seat prices than at the cinema.

Reaction against the highly decorated auditoria built from the 1880s to the 1920s, with their picture-frame proscenia, came after the Second World War in two ways. First, some directors and actors led by the English director Tyrone Guthrie complained that the proscenium theatre was old-fashioned. They promoted other designs in which the actor was partially or wholly surrounded by the audience. Second, other directors and entrepreneurs discovered after reflection that some existing proscenium theatres, such as the Theatre Royal in Hobart, did have an intimacy that permitted strong interaction between the performer and the audience.

From the end of the 1950s it was found that architectural distraction could be minimised by painting black the physical framing of the stage—as in the Opera Theatre of the Sydney Opera House—or by simply stopping the undecorated side walls and ceiling of the auditorium at the stage opening, as in the 1973 HER MAJESTY'S THEATRE in Sydney. In some theatres, particularly those used for opera, there have been attempts to compromise and still provide a rather rich auditorium in the tradition of European opera houses. This was done in the Opera Theatre in Adelaide in 1979 and the State Theatre in the VICTORIAN ARTS CENTRE in 1984. Auditoria in two restored early 20th-century theatres, the Theatre Royal in Hobart and His Majesty's Theatre in Perth show that judicious use of rich dark colours on the large wall and ceiling surfaces with the modelled decoration picked out in lighter colours and gold, can produce a delightful environment.

Theatres designed in the 1960s and 1970s were rather devoid of decoration, following architectural functionalism on the one hand and theatre directors' desire to concentrate attention on the stage on the other. This visual austerity is perhaps epitomised in the Sydney Opera House, where the interiors rely largely on structural and acoustic forms in bare concrete and veneered timber for decorative impact.

Painted decoration

Designers of theatres in the 1830s and 1840s were limited to timber structural forms, which they possibly left showing, but the scene-painters designed and painted decoration on timber panelling. The Royal City Theatre opened in Sydney in 1843 with the fronts of its boxes and proscenium rendered as marble with *trompe l'oeil* mouldings and reliefs painted on the flat surfaces. The interior boarding often had canvas glued to it to provide the scene-painter's usual base. A little three-dimensional applied plasterwork would be combined with the painted surface. Photographs taken after a fire in the Theatre Royal in Sydney in 1892 show strips of canvas hanging off the timber base—the style of decoration employed when the theatre was rebuilt in 1875.

By the end of the century decoration became three-dimensional in reality rather than appearance. It was built up in plaster, sometimes as cast elements affixed to timber or masonry backing. By this time the architect had assumed responsibility for designing the decoration and the offices of William Pitt jnr and Henry E. White turned out hundreds of sheets of detail drawings for the plasterers who worked on their theatres.

Theatres and hotels

Most early theatricals in the cities were held in a room in a hotel. These rooms were variously called long room, saloon or assembly room—an English term indicating a type of private hall within a hotel. They served for the most part as community halls before the advent of publicly funded halls such as schools of arts. Frequently carpenters fitted them up temporarily to provide a stage, pit or stalls for the lower classes and a row or circle of boxes for the upper classes. Equally often, the space would be temporarily graced with the name of 'theatre', prefixed by the name of the town or some appellation honouring royalty—Prince of Wales, Queen's Theatre or Victoria—or suffixed by 'royal'. These temporary names have confused researchers about many buildings that housed theatres, especially as old local newspapers and other documents rarely exist.

One of the earliest temporary names, the Parramatta Theatre, was given to the long room at the Woolpack Inn at Parramatta (NSW) in 1833. In Hobart drama began in the ballroom of the FREEMASON'S TAVERN in 1833. In 1834 the assembly rooms of the Argyle Hotel in Hobart were being referred to as the Theatre Royal, ARGYLE ROOMS. Similarly, early theatres were fitted up in hotels in Launceston (Tas.), in Adelaide and in country towns in most colonies. One such building still exists, the CHILTERN THEATRE, formerly the Star Theatre of the White Star Hotel at Chiltern (Vic.).

When theatres with two, three or four tiers of seating and large, well-equipped stages were built the theatre often became the largest part of the building, situated behind a residential public house, a tavern or bars on the street frontage. Barnett Levey built a hotel in front of his Theatre Royal in the Colchester Warehouse in Sydney in 1828. Joseph Wyatt's Victoria Hotel in the front part of his ROYAL VICTORIA THEATRE in Sydney 1838, seems to have been little more than a tavern and rooms for public use in the two floors above. Levey's hotel displayed to the street the elegant Georgian colonial architecture usually associated with John Verge and Francis Greenway. The Royal Victoria, built at the start of Queen Victoria's reign, retained much of the simplicity of the Georgian style but pilasters, entablature and an overhanging cornice crowning the three-storey structure gave it a more substantial appearance.

The first theatre in Melbourne, the ROYAL PAVILION SALOON, was built next to the Eagle Tavern in 1842, but the 1855 THEATRE ROYAL was fronted by a substantial and ponderous two-storey hotel. This was rebuilt after a fire as a lofty three-storey Victorian extravagance in 1872.

The old Adelphi Hotel in York street in Sydney had an amphitheatre added in the yard behind in 1850, and in 1856 a vaudeville theatre. The Imperial Opera House built in Sydney in 1879 was on the first floor of a warehouse-type building with access through a hotel decorated in Queen Anne style. The first HER MAJESTY'S THEATRE in Pitt street, Sydney, was fronted by a richly modelled five-storey hotel in 1887. Others of this genre were the THEATRE ROYAL in Brisbane in 1881, the Royal Victoria Theatre in Newcastle (NSW) in 1891, the Theatre Royal and the first Tivoli Theatre in Adelaide, the CRITERION THEATRE in Sydney in 1886, the Lyceum Theatre in Sydney in 1892, the Theatre Royal in

Ballarat in 1859, the Theatre Royal in Broken Hill in 1888 and the Gaiety Theatre in Zeehan (Tas.), built behind the Grand Hotel at the end of the century. The most celebrated hotel-theatre combination is His Majesty's Theatre in Perth, built in 1904. The hotel and the theatre existed in the same building until the theatre was rehabilitated in 1980 as the major performance venue for the city. Theatres shared sites with hotels in all the Australian colonies at some time. The bars and saloons of hotels attached to theatres were settings for socialising and conviviality by the audience before a show and at intervals. But towards the end of the 19th century the temperance movement grew stronger and curbs on the sale of alcohol ever tighter. Up to 1882 in NSW and later in some other colonies there was direct connection between the theatre and the hotel bars.

Patrons of George Rignold's production of The Lights of London *in 1882 entered the stalls of Sydney's Theatre Royal through bars in King Street. Other parts of the theatre were reached from the main entrance, in a hotel around the corner in Castlereagh Street*

This was generally eliminated by the end of the century and theatre patrons then had to go out to the street to reach a bar by a separate entrance. NSW legislated in 1912 that a hotel and a theatre could not coexist on a site and then theatre patrons had to go to a nearby hotel. But by 1917 evening theatregoers in all states went dry because bars had to close by 6 p.m.

In the 19th century, when audiences adjourned to the bars of the associated hotels during intervals, theatre foyers were hardly more than lobbies or minimum crush space, and the lower-class patrons of the pit and gallery had none. After hotels were dissociated from theatres the foyers remained just as minuscule, and theatregoers had to sit in their seats during interval and buy ice-creams, soft drinks or sweets from boys who walked up and down the aisles with trays slung from their necks. When hotels were eliminated nothing took their place in the theatre, either for refreshment or socialising.

It was not until some old theatres had part of the back stalls converted into foyer space, as at the Empire Theatre in Sydney, and new theatres were built in the 1960s and 1970s—the Civic Theatre in Albury (NSW), the Pilbeam Theatre in Rockhampton (Qld) and the Theatre Royal in Sydney—that foyers became larger. Bars have become an integral part of them since the relaxation of liquor laws in the 1970s. Nearly all major theatres in cities and country towns now have bars with direct access to the auditorium, and many have restaurants.

The concept of the social centre has returned to the theatre, and the bar and catering trade frequently subsidises the entertainment. The theatre building has become larger, more complex and more expensive than when it was little more than an auditorium, lavatories and a stage and its ancillaries. Generally, such new theatres have helped to generate larger audiences.

Some critics have remarked that major theatres nowadays are not as capacious as the major theatres of England, Europe and even Australia in the first half of the 19th century. They cite audiences of 3000 and more in the Theatre Royal, Drury Lane, in London and the Theatre Royal in Melbourne. Such people have even questioned the acoustic quality of modern theatres, assuming that one could hear every word in old theatres. These critics do not realise that a theatre that held 3000 people in 1855, the Theatre Royal in Melbourne, was smaller in floor area and volume than a modern theatre housing fewer than 1500 people, such as the Opera Theatre in the Sydney Opera House.

Capacities of theatres, as calculated from receipts, stated in newspapers and measured according to the spacing of seats and benches in architects' plans, show that as late as 1875 the average space per person in the Academy of Music in Ballarat was less that half that of today. Patrons in the pit and gallery would have been pressed against neighbours on all sides—knees, back, hips and shoulders.

Not only were expectations of comfort obviously lower than in the 20th century, but people washed less frequently and relied on perfume to cover body odours. The odours and heat generated by the mass of people were not particularly well dispelled by ventilation. Early theatres such as the Royal Victoria in Sydney and the Theatre Royal in Hobart relied upon ordinary multi-pane double-hung sash windows in the side walls.

By the 1880s consideration of climate had entered the design. The pitched roofs of some auditoria had panels that were manually slid apart to allow vitiated air to be exhausted. His Majesty's Theatre in Perth, the Princess Theatre in Melbourne and the Theatre Royal in Sydney were examples. The dome in the ceiling also had large sliding panels, and from this a large cylindrical duct of sheet iron or canvas led up to the roof. Parts of this structure are still evident in the roofs of the Her Majesty's Theatre in Ballarat and the Princess Theatre in Melbourne. In the latter the aperture in the dome and the duct above it are six metres in diameter. In the hotter, often very humid northern climates greater reliance was placed upon lightweight construction, which cooled quickly at night, and large areas of louvred wall, which allowed modest breezes to produce cross-ventilation.

Although summers are warm in mainland Australia, the weather can be disconcertingly inclement at times. In the southern regions the sliding roofs could be quickly winched shut when rain started. Open-air theatres have been built but used irregularly at St Kilda in Melbourne, Castlecrag in Sydney and Leura in the Blue Mountains (NSW). Perth, with a more even climate, has seen seasons of open-air performances during the Perth Festival, at the Sunken Garden Theatre and the NEW FORTUNE THEATRE, both at the University of Western Australia.

Electromechanical ventilation was not installed in theatres as a matter of course when the electric fan was invented. All theatres relied on natural ventilation and remained stuffy in summer until 1939, when the MINERVA THEATRE in Sydney became the first to provide the relief of full air-conditioning. Now this is almost mandatory.

As community standards rose there were also changes in entry and egress. In early theatres it was considered sufficient to have one entrance to each separate part of the house. For example, the Theatre Royal in Hobart, as altered in 1856, had an enclosed spiral stair, with a tread less than one metre wide, rising unbroken from the basement entrance through three storeys to the gallery, which held more than 300 persons. Around the end of the century fear of fire in theatres caused colonial governments to stipulate more effective systems of egress and construction.

Fires were frequent in theatres in the 19th century. In Sydney the first Theatre Royal was destroyed by fire in 1840, the Prince of Wales Theatre in 1862 and 1872 and the Royal Victoria Theatre in 1880. In Melbourne fire destroyed the Duke of Edinburgh Theatre in 1871, the Theatre Royal in 1872, and the Bijou Theatre in 1889. As early as 1 March 1860 a long letter in the *Sydney Morning Herald* described the fire hazards of theatres and warned the authorities to act. But it was not until 1882 that the NSW government established a royal commission to inquire into the construction of theatres, halls and other public places. The commission sat, with changing membership, until 1886 and in 1887 it issued a report that made recommendations for the health and safety of users of these buildings.

The report documents theatres in Sydney in particular. It includes transcripts of evidence from 12 witnesses, including theatre architects, police, J. C. WILLIAMSON and other theatre proprietors, a longtime theatre mechanist and the Superintendent of Sydney Fire Brigades. The evidence provides insights into attitudes to safety, full descriptions of the theatres in Sydney in 1884 and in 1887 and comments on their design. Plans were printed with one of the progress reports. A table of 106 places of public amusement, meeting or resort in the Metropolitan District of Sydney was appended to the final report, stating the purpose of each, the material of which it was built, its dimensions, means of egress and capacity.

In the final report the Colonial Architect, James Barnet, made recommendations for designing safe and healthy theatres and for full inspection before licensing to ensure:
A masonry proscenium wall with fire curtain;
Good accessibility to all parts;
Staircases, ingress and egress ways, landings, passages, doors and gangways of satisfactory width and unobstructed;
Limited seating and seats fixed to the floor;
Satisfactory dressing and retiring rooms, and sanitary arrangements;
Satisfactory ventilation and water service and supply;
Satisfactory lighting;
Communication with the fire station.

Most of the recommendations of the commission were taken into account when HER MAJESTY'S THEATRE was built in Sydney in 1887 and when the Theatre Royal was rebuilt in 1892 after a fire, but it was only in 1909 that licensing was enforced by the NSW Theatres and Public Halls Act, supported by detailed legal standards for space, egress and ventilation. The other states developed similar regulations.

Licensing authorities' files show great concern about lack of safety, overcrowding and poor ventilation in some theatres but, without tight building regulations, and legal space standards for seating and egress, inspectors' recommendations for closure or withholding of licences were mostly ignored. Patrons were often endangered by breaches of regulations committed after the theatre had been licensed. Often the fire curtain was defective or properties and scenery had been stored in emergency exits. As late as 1932 the Tivoli Theatre in Perth had a nailed-up door beneath an exit notice, and vibration from dancing had weakened the brick supports of the stage. Such breaches have prompted tighter regulations, with requirements such as automatic sprinkler systems throughout.

Amateur and alternative theatre

The tradition of setting up a theatre in a space not designed for the purpose—the fit-up theatre—became a way of providing performance space for the experimental wing of the serious amateur and 'alternative' movements in the mid-20th century. Once the experimental mode had been accepted, as with the thrust stage, it became an integral part of purpose-built theatres such as the OCTAGON THEATRE in Perth in 1969 and the York Theatre in the SEYMOUR THEATRE CENTRE in Sydney in 1975.

Serious amateur theatre began in Australia in much the same way as in England. There were a few professional enthusiasts and intellectual theatregoers, headed by BRYCESON TREHARNE in Adelaide and GREGAN McMAHON in Melbourne. Hugh Buckler and his wife Violet Paget leased the hall-like ROYAL STANDARD THEATRE in Sydney in 1913 and renamed it the Little Theatre, for the performance of Arthur Wing Pinero, Shakespeare, George Bernard Shaw and Oscar Wilde. About the same time the undistinguished Snowden Picture Theatre, on the site of the present Victorian Arts Centre in Melbourne, was remodelled for the MELBOURNE REPERTORY THEATRE COMPANY.

From the 1910s to the 1930s amateur groups usually performed in hired halls until a home could be acquired. The first to own its own theatre was the HOBART REPERTORY THEATRE SOCIETY, which converted a cinema that had been built as a church into the Playhouse in 1938. Many hired halls which had proscenium stages but their auditoria were generally too large for the small audiences that attended and they had flat floors, which made it hard to see the action on stage.

In the 1970s and 1980s provincial city councils realised that old-style halls were unsuitable for local amateur groups and visiting professionals and a spate of country PERFORMING-ARTS CENTRES were built.

Some well-established amateur groups had already built their own little theatres, usually austere, one-level raked proscenium theatres such as the Arts Theatres in Adelaide in 1963 and Brisbane in 1961. Even more austere is the Playhouse at Bundaberg (Qld), built in 1975. Once amateurs build their own theatre the running of the group seldom remains purely voluntary, even if the performers remain amateur. One successful group that seemed to balance paid management and basically amateur production was the BRISBANE REPERTORY THEATRE SOCIETY, which turned professional in 1993. In 1972 it built La Boîte, an attractive, practical in-the-round box auditorium in purple brick and concrete, with full ancillaries.

Other amateur groups, finding the arts centres too large and expensive to hire, still search for alternative premises. Amateur groups have generally sought a space that could be converted to a proscenium theatre, but semiprofessional groups, reacting against the limitations of the proscenium stage on the physical relationship between action and audience, have become eclectic since 1960. A church at Emerald Hill in Melbourne was converted to the thrust-stage Emerald Hill Theatre. A boatshed on Sydney harbour became Australia's first permanent theatre-in-the-round, the Ensemble Theatre. At the STABLES THEATRE in Sydney, originally the Nimrod Street Theatre, a loft over a 19th-century stable was converted to a triangular acting area with raked seating on two sides. A courthouse at Scone (NSW) and a horticultural pavilion in a showground at Castle Hill, Sydney, were converted to proscenium theatres for amateur groups.

At Carlton in Melbourne a small two-storey shirt factory became the experimental LA MAMA THEATRE, a flexible open space seating 60 persons. It spawned the AUSTRALIAN PERFORMING GROUP, which moved to a warehouse in the same suburb and made a semi-thrust-stage theatre known as the Pram Factory. The two floors of a salt factory in Sydney were converted into the Nimrod Theatre—now the BELVOIR STREET THEATRE—a flexible open-space theatre and a corner-thrust-stage theatre. At KINSELA'S CABARET THEATRE in Sydney offices above a funeral parlour were converted into a theatre-restaurant. In Darwin a 19th-century mining-exchange building has become Brown's Mart, a flexible open-space theatre for amateur groups.

These are a few examples of people seeing spaces that could be converted to provide a theatre. Possibly the most ambitious project was VIVIAN FRASER's conversion of a long, lofty, two-storey storage shed on a finger wharf projecting into Sydney Harbour. Retaining its large-scale, rough quality, he turned it into the WHARF THEATRE, a complex of thrust-stage theatre, studio theatre, restaurant, administrative offices, rehearsal rooms and workshops. This, like 'space theatres' in recent performing-arts centres—the Adelaide Festival Centre, the Seymour Theatre Centre, the QUEENSLAND PERFORMING ARTS COMPLEX and the Victorian Arts Centre—has taken the flexible space of experimental theatre into the establishment. ❦*Ross Thorne*

further reading
NSW Votes and Proceedings of the Legislative Assembly 1887—Report of Royal Commission of Inquiry into the Construction of Theatres, Public Halls and Other Places of Public Amusement and Concourse.

TheatreWorks

Professional dramatic company in Melbourne, founded as collective in 1980 by Susie Fraser, Carolyn (later Caz) Howard, Hannie Rayson and others. **artistic director** Robert Draffin 1991–. **first production** *Please Return to Sender* by Hannie Rayson, in eastern suburbs of Melbourne from May 1980.

The claim to originality of TheatreWorks lies in its locational or environmental works, mostly written by Paul Davies, who joined the company in 1981. It acted out the first locational play, *Storming Mont Albert by Tram*, in 1982 on board a tram travelling from the Mont Albert terminus to the city. This play was scheduled to run for a fortnight, but it lasted four months until cold weather put an end to its premiere season. It enjoyed several equally successful return seasons as *Storming St Kilda by Tram*. A variation on the theme was *Breaking Up in Balwyn*, set on board a Yarra riverboat, in 1983. Davies also devised two plays that took their audiences around three rooms of a one-time grand mansion in suburban St Kilda: *Living Rooms* in 1986 and *Full House—No Vacancies* in 1989.

TheatreWorks grew out of the VICTORIAN COLLEGE OF THE ARTS and originally had a strong community-theatre orientation. For four years it operated in church halls, schools and other venues in Melbourne's eastern suburbs. Late in 1985 it began operating from a parish hall in St Kilda. For the next five years its works were preoccupied with local community issues. Landmarks included *Herstory* in 1983, based on the lives of three generations of Australian women, and two plays by HANNIE RAYSON—*Mary* in 1982, and the award-winning *Room to Move*, presented in association with the Playbox Theatre Company in 1985. Mainstream companies in other states picked up the latter play. TheatreWorks boldly set out on a new path in 1991, when Robert Draffin promised a strong emphasis on storytelling, as well as new Australian writing. ❦*Leonard Radic*

Al Thomas

Actor, comedian. Came to Australia from Scotland as singer and impersonator of film stars in touring variety company. Settled in Sydney 1934. Performed in revue, drama, film, television and many radio serials. Died 19 December 1984 in Sydney.

Stocky, ebullient Al Thomas was best known in variety but he also played many straight roles, particularly in later life. He was proud of his versatility, but he admitted ad-libbing when he could not remember the lines as joint lead with John Ewart in *The Comedy of Errors*. During the Second World War he was in Tivoli shows, and he achieved instant success on Jack Davey's comedy radio show. Plays in which he appeared in Sydney included *The Time is Not Yet Ripe* by Louis Esson for the OLD TOTE THEATRE COMPANY in 1977, and *No Names … No Pack Drill* by Bob Herbert and *You Can't Take it with You* by George S. Kaufman and Moss Hart for the SYDNEY THEATRE COMPANY in 1980 and 1981 respectively. ❦*Victoria Chance*

Gerald Marr Thompson

Critic, journalist. Born 11 September 1856 in London. Became a bank clerk. Joined two brothers in Adelaide 1881. Worked for bank and wrote musical and dramatic reviews for *Advertiser*. Arts critic for Sydney *Daily Telegraph* 1883. Arts critic of *Sydney Morning Herald* 1891–1924. Died 28 February 1938 in Sydney.

During his working life Gerald Marr Thompson was unrivalled in Sydney as a musical and theatrical critic. While the standard of musical life challenged him more than theatre in the later years, he demonstrated an eclectic taste and commented constructively on work of every level. 'No theatrical first night, no concert that claims to be a concert, is complete without the presence of this veteran dramatic and musical critic of the *Sydney Morning Herald*' said *Home* magazine in June 1922. No other man in Australia can as well tell the truth with a minimum of pain. To read between Thompson's lines is to read the facts.'

Thompson joined the *Sydney Morning Herald* in 1891, working as reviewer, general reporter and 'Music and Drama' columnist. His first task was to cover SARAH BERNHARDT's Sydney season. He wrote some 3000 words a day, reporting on her public appearances and reviewing her repertoire, which changed daily, with some mastery of the French texts. Thompson had grown up in a family atmosphere of music and literature, and he was widely read in European drama and French literature.

Like his contemporaries, he saw Sydney as a metropolitan theatre centre and he reported on the activities of entrepreneurs in Australia and abroad without apparent boundaries. In a career spanning the decline of theatre from its high point in the 1880s to the onslaught of cinema and the rise of social theatricals, Thompson had a wide brief and his expectations were not unrealistic. When tact demanded it he chose to confine his coverage to reportage and courteous comment. His review of the operetta *Autumn Manoeuvres*, starring DOROTHY BRUNTON and William Lockhart, was typical: 'Before the second performance, however, Mr Wybert Stamford, the skilful "producer" for the J. C. Williamson Comic Opera Company, will doubtless make some expert "cuts"'. He was wise and philosophic about Nellie Stewart's departure for San Francisco in 1905, recognising her frustrations and using them to sum up the reasons behind the imitative nature of Australia's theatre.

His 1910 review of OSCAR ASCHE's Shylock defines the new realism: 'Old playgoers fairly gasped at it; but the artist knew what he was about ... there sits Shylock in shabby sordid gait, on the cushioned recess of the windowsill, in oriental fashion, cross-legged, conning his tablets and his ledgers on his knee, a red-haired, stout Colossus with black eyebrows gleaming white teeth and a sulky smile suggesting a strong and savage animalism. Could any figure less resemble the idea which playgoers have learned to admire in Irving, Bellew, Dampier and many others?'

After Thompson retired in 1924 he visited London on full pay and wrote on music in Australia in the London *Daily Telegraph*. Back in Sydney he contributed to the *Sydney Morning Herald* until his death. He copublished some works on music in Sydney and published two travel books of collected journalism, *Through Summer Seas* and *From Old Worlds to New*. ❦*Katharine Brisbane*

further reading
CARMODY, JOHN. Gerald Marr Thompson. *Australian Dictionary of Biography* 12. Melbourne University Press 1990.
SOUTER, GAVIN. *A Company of Heralds*. Melbourne University Press 1981.
A Century of Journalism. Sydney: John Fairfax 1931.
Sydney Morning Herald 1–3 March 1938.
reference
Gerald Marr Thompson newspaper cuttings 1886–1935, Mitchell Library (Sydney) Q780.9901.

Brian Thomson

Designer, director. Born 5 January 1946 in Perth. Studied at Perth Technical College and University of NSW (Sydney). Designed major Australian and international musicals. Numerous productions for Sydney Theatre Company, State Theatre Company of South Australia (Adelaide), Belvoir Street Theatre (Sydney) and Royal Court Theatre (London). Has designed for film and opera.

Generally regarded as the *enfant terrible* of Australian stage, video and film design, Brian Thomson has the widest international reputation of any Australian designer and his work is known for its audacity. 'I have never done anything naturalistic, never have, never will', he once claimed. He abandoned a career in architecture as 'boring' after JIM SHARMAN introduced him to stage design. They have collaborated on numerous productions since the rock musical *Hair*, which established Thomson's national reputation in 1969. His designs for Sharman's production of *Jesus Christ Superstar* in Sydney in 1972, catapulted him to recognition in London. The lyricist Tim Rice and the composer Andrew Lloyd Webber preferred the production to the one in New York City and invited Thomson and Sharman to direct and design the London season. *The Rocky Horror Show*, a high-camp frolic devised by the New Zealand actor Richard O'Brien, Sharman and Thomson in London in 1973, confirmed Thomson as a designer of flamboyant, even bizarre imagination. It brought him acclaim in London, Los Angeles, New York, Oslo, Tokyo, southeast Asia and at home. He also designed the film version in 1981. Thomson and Sharman also collaborated on a cheeky, pop-art *As You Like It* in 1970 and plays by PATRICK WHITE—the premieres of *BIG TOYS* (1977), *A Cheery Soul* (1979) and *Shepherd on the Rocks* (1987) and a revival of *THE HAM FUNERAL* in 1989.

In striving to 'sensationalise theatre' Thomson has ranged in style from radical minimalism for Robert David Macdonald's play *Chinchilla* in 1981 to surrealist devices. He has cross-fertilised film and stage conventions, frequently using images from contemporary vernacular culture—pop art, graffiti, cartoons and advertising. For the SYDNEY THEATRE COMPANY he directed cabaret shows at KINSELA'S CABARET THEATRE—*The Shadow Knows* in 1981 and *The Stripper* in 1982 respectively. ❦*Pamela Zeplin*

writings
I wanted to be a pop artist. *Australian Theatre Design* (ed. Kim Spinks). Sydney: Australian Production Designers Association NSW 1992.

Katherine Thomson

Actor, dramatist. Born 27 July 1955 in Sydney. Educated at Macquarie University (Sydney). Trained at Ensemble Studios (Sydney). Began acting with Australian Theatre for Young People

(Sydney) 1969. Professional actor since mid-1970s. Founding member of Theatre South (Wollongong NSW) 1980–84. Married Bob Evans, theatre critic, 1991. Australian Writers' Guild Awgie award 1992 for *Barmaids*. Victorian Premier's Literary Award for *Diving for Pearls* 1992. Has also written for television.

Ability to capture the ethos of a community through deft evocation of ordinary people's lives distinguishes the playwriting of Katherine Thomson. She is interested in communities in flux, in the everyday struggles of working people who are adjusting to radical change. Her work is implicitly political through its consistent focus on the working class, yet its surface is intensely individual. Character is always in the foreground. Accumulation of many small details, incidents and anecdotes creates the larger picture. Thomson has an ear for idiom and dialogue as sharp as any contemporary satirist or social commentator. Mordant wit always counterpoints buoyant, earthy humour in her work.

In 1982, she wrote *A Change in the Weather*, a two-woman show about women at work in Wollongong, for herself and Faye Montgomery, associate director of THEATRE SOUTH. This was performed as part of the 1982 Women in Arts Festival. *Tonight We Anchor in Twofold Bay*, also for Theatre South, followed closely. It was researched, written and first performed in Eden (NSW), on Twofold Bay. It toured the south coast of NSW and then had a season at the Wharf Studio in Sydney at the invitation of the SYDNEY THEATRE COMPANY. In 1988 this company produced Thomson's *Darlinghurst Nights*, a music-theatre piece based on the light verse of Kenneth Slessor. The DECKCHAIR THEATRE COMPANY in Fremantle (WA) commissioned *Barmaids*, and the MAGPIE THEATRE COMPANY in Adelaide a theatre-in-education show about young people and sport, *A Sporting Chance* (1987). Her major work to date is *Diving for Pearls* (1991), a humane drama about the unfulfilled hopes of an unemployed couple. ❧*Ros Horin*

published plays
Barmaids (1991). Sydney: Currency Press 1992.
Diving for Pearls (1991). Sydney: Currency Press 1992.

F. W. Thring

Entrepreneur. Born *c*.1883 at Wentworth (NSW). Began theatrical career as conjurer. Became film exhibitor. Managing director of Hoyts Theatres 1924–30. Established Efftee Films 1931. Founded Efftee Players 1933. Founded radio 3XY Melbourne, 1935. Died 1 July 1936 in Melbourne. Father of actor Frank Thring.

An entrepreneur with theatrical flair, Frank Thring snr had the courage during the Depression to invest his money in the film and theatre industries, believing they could flourish in Australia. His ultimate aim was to encourage the production of Australian plays which he could later make into films. He campaigned vigorously for the government to protect Australian film production.

Thring abandoned his trade of bootmaker to become a conjurer in variety shows in NSW, and he extended his repertoire by exhibiting films in travelling shows. His fascination with films led him to become managing director of J. C. Williamson Films in 1918 and managing director of the Hoyts chain of cinemas. He was responsible for building Hoyts' palatial Regent Theatres in seven eastern cities. In 1931 Thring sold his Hoyts interests to an American company, Fox Film Corporation, to establish his own film production company, Efftee Films. He installed the latest imported sound equipment, in the fire-damaged His Majesty's Theatre in Melbourne, which became Efftee's studios. Over the next four years Efftee produced seven feature films, three of them starring the revue comic GEORGE WALLACE, and shorter films, including performances by vaudeville stars.

In 1933 Thring established the Efftee Players at the Garrick Theatre in Melbourne, with the policy of presenting 'the best available modern comedies and dramas', and launched a competition for the best Australian play. In the same year, at the Princess Theatre in Melbourne, he produced the first successful Australian musical comedy, *Collits' Inn*, starring GLADYS MONCRIEFF and Wallace. It ran at the Princess Theatre from Christmas 1933 to April 1934, and was followed by *The Beloved Vagabond*, an English musical with a score by the Australian composer Dudley Glass. A revival of *Collits' Inn* was followed by the same company in *Jolly Roger*, an English operetta. At Christmas 1934 Thring presented another musical comedy with a score by Varney Monk, *The Cedar Tree*. It ran until February 1935. ❧*Sally Dawes*

Frank Thring

Actor, critic. Born 11 May 1926 in Melbourne. Son of entrepreneur F. W. Thring. Trained at Irene Mitchell Academy of Dramatic Art (Melbourne). Became radio actor. Performed with Melbourne Little Theatre. Director of Arrow Theatre (Melbourne) 1951–54. Member of Shakespeare Memorial Theatre Company (Stratford-upon-Avon, England) 1955. Seasons with Melbourne Theatre Company since 1959. Also in films. Died 29 December 1994 in Melbourne.

A flamboyant and idiosyncratic personality, Frank Thring acted in a grandiose style that made him particularly popular as Sheridan Whiteside in *The Man Who Came to Dinner* by George S. Kaufman and Moss Hart. He began his career as a sound-effects man at radio 3XY, owned by his father, F. W. THRING. He became an actor and made his debut as Henry VIII in RAY LAWLER's *Hal's Belles* for MELBOURNE REPERTORY THEATRE in 1945. In December 1946 the *Age* said he gave a very fine performance as J. B. the managing director in SUMNER LOCKE ELLIOTT's satire *Invisible Circus* at the Melbourne Little Theatre.

Thring founded ARROW THEATRE and opened with Oscar Wilde's *Salome* in 1951. He ran this amateur group in Melbourne Repertory's old theatre until 1954, when he went to London. He restaged *Salome* at the Q Theatre, Kew Bridge, and it transferred to the West End. Thring then joined the Shakespeare Memorial Theatre Company and played Saturninus in Peter Brook's production of *Titus Andronicus* with Laurence Olivier and Vivien Leigh. In 1959 Thring joined the Union Theatre Repertory Company, later the MELBOURNE THEATRE COMPANY. He was acclaimed as Captain Ahab in Orson Welles's *Moby Dick Rehearsed* in 1967, and in the title-roles in *Henry IV—part 1* in 1969 and Bertolt Brecht's *Galileo* in 1971. In 1981 he staged a solo show called *Frankly Thring* for the Melbourne Theatre Company. He was a forthright drama critic for the *Argus* and *TV Week*. In the words of another critic, GEOFFREY HUTTON, Thring was 'a theatre man of strong opinions and few inhibitions in expressing them'. ❧*Sally Dawes*

writings
The Actor Who Laughed. With Roland Rocchecccioli. Melbourne: Hutchinson 1985.
further reading
SUMNER, JOHN. *Recollections at Play—A life in Australian theatre*. Melbourne: University Press 1993.

Ric Throssell

Dramatist. Born 10 May 1922 at Greenmount (WA). Son of writer Katharine Susannah Prichard. Military service in New Guinea 1942. Worked in Foreign Affairs Department 1943–83. At Australian legations in Moscow (1945–46) and Rio de Janeiro (1949–52). Commonwealth Literary Fund Fellowship 1958. Director of Commonwealth Foundation (London) 1980–83. Lives in Canberra.

A leading advocate and activist for Australian theatre from 1945 to 1966, especially through the CANBERRA REPERTORY SOCIETY, Ric Throssell wrote 26 plays. They were widely performed, especially *The Day Before Tomorrow*, about a family of survivors after a nuclear war, When the London Playgoers' Company produced it on the fringe of the Edinburgh Festival in 1960 the *Scotsman* said it 'erects a small cairn to the indestructibility of the human spirit'. In the same year Throssell accepted high commendation from the judges of the Dame Mary Gilmore Award for his play *For Valour*. Manning Clark describes the subject as 'the failure of a man to make the difficult transition from war to peace'. In this it reflects something of the life and death of the playwright's father, Hugo Throssell VC.

Throssell's plays range from grave dramas to zany satires, exposing the effects of war, the wilder absurdities of modernism, the unhinged mentality of undercover agents, the follies of bureaucracy and the Americanisation of Australian culture. From 1941 Special Bureau files listed his association with the WORKERS' ART GUILD, of which his mother, KATHARINE SUSANNAH PRICHARD, a Communist, had been a founding member.

Later, the Australian Security Intelligence Organisation became alarmed that Throssell should ever have been 'responsible for codes and ciphers at the Australian Embassy in Moscow'. The Petrov inquiry in 1955 cleared him, but his subsequent diplomatic career was prejudiced.

He made several well-received radio adaptations of his plays and one television adaptation. He was a successful amateur actor and director. ❦*Don Batchelor*

published plays
The Day Before Tomorrow (1956). Sydney: Angus and Robertson 1969.
Devil Wear Black (1954). Melbourne: Australasian Book Society 1955.
For Valour (1960). Sydney: Currency Press 1976.
Sailor's Girl (1946). Melbourne: *New Theatre Review* 1945.
South Sea Gold Bay (1965). Adelaide: Rigby 1970 in *Plays for Young Players*.
Suburban Requiem (1955). Adelaide: Rigby 1961, in *Australian One-Act Plays*.
Valley of the Shadows (1948). Perth: Paterson 1949.
other writings
My Father's Son. Melbourne: Heinemann 1989.
Wild Weeds and Windflowers. Sydney: Angus and Robertson 1975. Biography of his mother.
reference
Papers of Ric Throssell 1937–89 are in the manuscript section of the Australian National Library (Canberra).

Through Art, Unity

Community-theatre company in Canberra, founded in 1983 by Aldo Gennaro and Domenic Mico. Renamed Upfront Theatre 1991. Closed 1992. **directors** 1983–84 Aldo Gennaro and Domenic Mico. 1984–87 Domenic Mico. 1987–89 Domenic Mico and Tina van Raay. 1989–91 Tina van Raay.

The directors Aldo Gennaro and Domenic Mico—also a playwright—founded Through Art, Unity to specialise in theatre for and by people with disabilities. It became a broad-based community-theatre company, presenting seasons in a converted vehicle-testing station. It presented visiting companies, staged plays for children—Mico's *The Grey Faced Bandits* and *The Bunyip and the Alien*—in the holidays, ran acting workshops and set up an over-50s group, Mixed Grill, which presented an original play, *The Story So Far*. Regular mainstage productions included Vladimir Mayakovsky's *The Bath House*, Mico's *The Other Side of the Moon*, a fine play about an immigrant coming to terms with his new country, and Kate McNamara's play about domestic violence, *In the Secret Room*.

Through Art, Unity received annual funding from the ACT Cultural Development Committee. In 1986 it established the ACT Playwrights' Festival. The four best entries from local playwrights were staged at TAU Theatre. The play voted best by audience and critics was given a mainstage production at TAU in the next year. In 1989 Mico resigned to run the Backstage Cafe and his co-director, Tina van Raay, continued alone.

In 1990 the theatre burned down, and this created major financial problems. Through Art, Unity moved its activities, including the playwrights' festival, first to the Belconnen Community Centre and then to the Ralph Wilson Theatre at Gorman House. It was renamed Upfront Theatre. Van Raay resigned after directing one play for Upfront. After Upfront ceased activity in 1992, the playwrights' festival ran for another year, organised by Joan McGillivray and Boyd Salter, two of the playwrights involved. As ACTEST it still stages new plays from time to time. ❦*Anne Edgeworth*

Harry Tighe

Dramatist. Born 16 June 1877 near Newcastle (NSW). Lived mainly in England from 17. Active with People's National Theatre run by Nancy Price in London. Amateur theatre in Sydney 1930–35. Wrote four plays and published 15 novels. Died 1946.

Harry Tighe set the most considerable of his four plays, *Open Spaces*, in Australia. It is a four-act bush drama in which a pampered city woman and a battered bushwoman battle for possession of their man on an isolated selection. It was performed in London, first on 3 January 1927, at the Q Theatre, with Jeanne de Casalis, Malcom Keen and Nancy Price, and revived as *Bush Fire* on 27 April 1931 at the Fortune Theatre. Tighe's first published play, *Jean* is a moral melodrama set in a monastery in the Rhône Valley. *Old Mrs Wiley* was performed on 26 September 1907 at the Q Theatre in London with Nancy Price in the title-role. It is a family drama in which an old woman dominates the household of her daughter Fanny, whose husband has been jailed for poisoning his mistress. *The Atonement* was performed at St Paul's Church, Covent Garden, in 1929. In

1930 Tighe directed the first play produced by INDEPENDENT THEATRE in Sydney. He was chairman of the judging committee of the Junior Theatre League's annual drama festival in Sydney in the early 1930s.

A man of private means, he was a friend of such stars as Madge Kendal and Sybil Thorndike. He recorded his association with theatres and actors in *By the Wayside*, one of his two semi-fictional autobiographies. The other, *As I Saw It* is about Australia. He bequeathed the copyright in his work to the British Drama League in Sydney. ❦*Katharine Brisbane*

published plays
The Atonement with Cecil Rose (1929). London: Drane 1929.
Jean. London: Elliot Stock 1901.

other writings
As I Saw It. London: Stockwell 1937.
By the Wayside. London: Heath Cranton 1939.

reference
The manuscript of *Old Mrs Wiley* is in the Mitchell Library, Sydney, QA 822 T. The manuscript of *Open Spaces* is in the Campbell Howard Collection, University of New England, (Armidale NSW).

Beatrice and Evelyn Tildesley

Patrons, teachers. Born at Willenhall (Staffordshire, England). Educated at Girton College, Cambridge. Members of Sydney Repertory Theatre Society 1920–28. Members of Turret Theatre (Sydney) 1929–30. Founding supporters of Australian Elizabethan Theatre Trust.

Beatrice Tildesley. Born 27 September 1886. Arrived in Sydney 1915. Member of Playwrights' Advisory Board. Honorary secretary of Good Film League of NSW. Died 26 January 1977 in Sydney.

Evelyn Tildesley. Born on 8 March 1882. Arrived in Sydney 1913. Co-founder, honorary secretary and a director (1937–67) of British Drama League. Died 6 June 1976 in Sydney.

Women of private means, the Tildesley sisters were widely read and active in a variety of cultural organisations. They both loved theatre and believed drama to be an important part of education. They befriended and encouraged artists and were famous hostesses. They were also expert fencers who gave displays. Beatrice Tildesley acted with Gregan McMahon's SYDNEY REPERTORY THEATRE SOCIETY, appearing as Margaret Orme in John Galsworthy's *Loyalties* in 1922. She aided Doris Fitton in founding INDEPENDENT THEATRE, for which in 1964 she took a leading role in an adaptation of Henry James's novel *The Aspern Papers*. She appeared in plays into her eighties.

In 1930 Beatrice Tildesley gave a paper at the Pan Pacific Women's Conference in Honolulu, in which she expressed concern at the American vulgarisation of Australia through film. The sisters became active in encouraging British taste in the arts. Evelyn was a founder of the British Drama League, which provided a drama library and information bureau for Australia's little theatres, and she contributed regularly to its journal, *Drama*. ❦*Katharine Brisbane*

writings
TILDESLEY, BEATRICE. Cinema in Australia. *Proceedings of Pan-Pacific Women's Conference no. 2* 1930.
TILDESLEY, BEATRICE. Fifty years of the theatre in Australia. *Australian Quarterly* 23 (Sydney, December 1951).
TILDESLEY, BEATRICE. The little theatre movement in Sydney. *Manuscripts* February 1933.
TILDESLEY, EVELYN M. The Australian Elizabethan Theatre Trust. *Australian Quarterly* 27 (Sydney, March 1955).

further reading
BADGER, C. *In Memoriam Beatrice Tildesley 1886-1977*. Sydney: private 1977.
NAPIER, S. E. *Sydney Repertory Theatre Society—Its history and significance*. Sydney: 1925.
RUTLEDGE, MARTHA. Evelyn Mary and Beatrice Maude Tildesley. *Australian Dictionary of Biography* 12. Melbourne University Press 1990.
WYNDHAM, H. *Miss Evelyn Tildesley*. Sydney: private 1976.

The Time is Not Yet Ripe

Play in four acts by Louis Esson. **premiere** 23 July 1912, Athenaeum Hall, Melbourne. Cast: Donald Alsop, Anthony Brook, Mr R. Earle, Leonard Egerton, Mr J. B. Fowler, Lea Halinbourg, Isabella Handly, A. S. Haybittel, Dorothy Hiscock, Mr G. Kirk, Mr C. Nowell, Rose Seaton, Mr T. Skewes, Mr R. Withers. Director: Gregan McMahon. **revived** 20 June 1972, University of Melbourne, by students of Trinity College and Janet Clarke Hall, directed by John Smythe. 8 November 1973, Comedy Theatre, Melbourne, with Elspeth Ballantyne, Andrew Carr, Sydney Conabere, Michele Fawdon, Peter Flett, William Gluth, Sandy Gore, Hamish Hughes, Tony Llewellyn-Jones, Lew Luton, Frederick Parslow, Malcolm Phillips, Valma Pratt, David Ravenswood. **published** Melbourne: Fraser and Jenkinson 1912. Sydney: Currency Press 1973, revised.

An eccentric satirical comedy of political life and manners, *The Time is Not Yet Ripe* is in a style with which LOUIS ESSON obviously felt at home but later rejected in his pursuit of an Australian folk-drama of the bush. It is the eve of a federal election and Doris Quiverton, the daughter of the conservative Prime Minister, finds herself dragooned into standing for the seat of Wombat as the 'Good Woman' candidate on behalf of the Women's Anti-Socialist League. Her beloved fiancé, Sydney Barrett, is a red-ragger with an Oxford degree, contesting the same seat for the Socialist Party. Barrett is a highly idiosyncratic socialist, more interested in enlivening the spiritual and artistic life of his compatriots than in liberating them from capitalism—rather like Esson himself. Doris is presented as having too much good common sense to be seriously interested in politics. She wins the seat but hands it over to a better Good Woman and goes off happily with the defeated but still beloved Sydney. The play ends with the victorious Prime Minister complacently concluding that the time is not yet ripe for socialism.

More than anything else the play reveals the extent to which Esson's socialism was more aesthetic than political, but it has wit and charm, and retains some relevance in revealing, if inadvertently, an alarming lack of serious idealism in Australian political life—a lack only intermittently filled since the play was written.

A rediscovery of *The Time is Not Yet Ripe* by the director John Smythe, who mounted a student production at the University of Melbourne in 1972, inspired the Melbourne Theatre Company to present a lavish production next year. Since then it has been revived several times. It remains one of the very few successful Wildean comedies of social manners in the repertoire and, incidentally, a fine document of Melbourne high-society manners at a time when the city was the seat of the federal government and manners mattered. ❦*John McCallum*

Tin Alley Players

Amateur dramatic group founded at University of Melbourne in November 1939 by Keith Macartney and Maurice Belz. **first production** *Judgement Day* by Elmer Rice, 1940, Union Theatre, University of Melbourne. **landmark productions** *They Came to a City* by J. B. Priestley, 1944. *Daphne Laureola* by James Bridie, 1949. *The Indecent Exposure of Anthony East* by David Williamson, 1968.

The Tin Alley Players, founded in 1939, are believed to be Victoria's oldest continuously operating amateur theatrical group. They took their name from a lane running between the main buildings and the colleges at the University of Melbourne. KEITH MACARTNEY, then an associate professor of drama, saw the group as a way for graduates to maintain an association with the campus, but as it developed its membership widened beyond the university. When undergraduate theatrical activities were almost at a standstill during the Second World War, the Tin Alley Players revived seldom-seen plays from Europe and the USA, and mounted premiere performances of contemporary works like J. B. Priestley's *They Came to a City*. They even spawned a travelling revue troupe known as the Barnstormers.

In the 1950s Tin Alley competed with JOHN SUMNER's fledgling Union Theatre Repertory Company for limited university resources but still managed productions of high quality. Some, like Lillian Hellman's *The Children's Hour*, aroused controversy through their sensitive subject matter. Tin Alley earned a reputation for original Christmas revues from the 1960s.

In the 1960s the group also expanded into school productions, tailored to attract students of English literature, and Australian plays, including *The Indecent Exposure of Anthony East* by DAVID WILLIAMSON, the production of which was the first of any Williamson play. These trends continued into the 1970s. ❦*Simon Plant*

The Tintookies

Musical play in one act for marionettes. **lyrics** Hal Saunders. **music** Kurt Herweg. **premiere** Elizabethan Theatre, Sydney, 1956. Director: Peter Scriven. Puppeteers: Dagmar Dawson, Igor Hychka, Walter Jaeger, Dick Rowse, Paul Rutenas. **revival** 1975, Princess Theatre, Melbourne. Two-act version with added second act (lyrics by Scriven and music by James Cotter) new puppets and set. Director: Scriven.

An extravagantly mounted, large-scale marionette musical with an Australian bush setting, *The Tintookies* caught the imagination of the public so firmly that it replaced Punch and Judy as the first association with puppets. A national tour—and Kurt Herweg's *Tintookie* March on radio—made the 1956 production so well known that 'Tintookies', a word PETER SCRIVEN coined to mean 'the little people who live in the sandhills', came to refer to any of his puppet productions, to the puppets themselves and to the MARIONETTE THEATRE OF AUSTRALIA, which he founded. The story of the play concerns Panjee Possum, Wilpy Wombat and Krumpy Koala, whose wishes are granted through the intervention of the people of Tintookie Town. The original puppets were lost in a fire in 1969. ❦*Richard Bradshaw*

further reading
VELLA, MAEVE and HELEN RICKARDS. *Theatre of the Impossible—Puppet theatre in Australia*. Sydney: Craftsman House 1989.

George S. Titheradge

Actor. Born 1848 in England. Acted in Australia 1879–83, c.1887–1900 and 1908–16. Died January 1916 in Sydney. Father of actors Madge and Dion Titheradge.

For many years George Titheradge was the leading man in the legendary BROUGH-BOUCICAULT COMEDY COMPANY, which set new standards in acting and production in Australia between 1886 and 1906. Noted for his dramatic use of the pause, he was 'the first actor in Australia to introduce the seeming natural method in acting', according to *Theatre* magazine. Titheradge and MRS ROBERT BROUGH were renowned for their subtle, sophisticated encounters in the leading roles of society dramas by writers like Arthur Wing Pinero and J. M. Barrie. His favourite part, however, was the title-role in Sydney Grundy's *A Village Priest*. He opened his first Australian tour in *Clancarty* by Tom Taylor in Sydney on 14 June 1879. A few years later he played the title-role in *The Silver King* by Henry Arthur Jones and Henry Herman, one of the most popular plays of the 1880s.

Between 1900 or 1901 and 1908 Titheradge travelled overseas. He played the husband in Pinero's *The Second Mrs Tanqueray* in London with the author's warm approval, appeared in Richard Ganthony's *A Message From Mars* with Charles Hawtrey, and toured the USA in Mrs Patrick Campbell's company. After joining an American tour by the American star Margaret Anglin he returned to Australia with her in 1908, and remained here. He was for many years president of the anti-union Actors' Association of Australia. Shortly before his death in 1916 he wrote for *Theatre* a series of entertaining reminiscences of his long career. ❦*Richard Fotheringham*

writings
Theatre (Sydney) 2 August 1915. Reminiscences.
further reading
Theatre (Sydney) 1 February 1916. Obituary.

Minnie Tittell Brune

American actor. Born c.1883. Originally Minnie Tittell. Broadway star as child with sister Essie 1891. Married c.1904, probably to Clarence M. Brune, actor. In Australia 1904–09. In London 1910–16.

Among the passengers rescued after the liner *Australia* ran aground at the entrance to Port Phillip Bay at 2 a.m. on 20 June 1904 were a Mr and Mrs Brune, who were travelling from London to Sydney. They were not famous enough to be interviewed, but on 6 August 1904 'Miss' Tittell Brune, 'the celebrated American actress' who 'came from the United States under contract to Mr [J. C.] Williamson', was a huge hit in the title-role of *Sunday* in Melbourne.

For the next five years she kept her husband out of sight while she became the darling of the Australian stage in the title-roles of *Diana of Dobson's* by C. Hamilton and *Merely Mary Ann* by Israel Zangwill and as Juliet, Peter Pan, and Kundry the 'cursed temptress' in a non-Wagnerian *PARSIFAL* by T. Hilhouse Taylor. After a last tour in 1909 with David Belasco's play *The Girl of the Golden West*—which old theatregoers remembered as her best role—Minnie Tittell Brune went to London as an Australian actor. Her career there included the title-role in *Nell Gwynne* by Arthur Shirley and Benjamin Landeck in a long season in 1913. ❦*Richard Fotheringham*

Tivoli circuit

There were two distinct Tivoli circuits of variety theatres. The first lasted from 1893 to 1929 and the second from 1932 to 1966. The first was the creation of the English comedian and entrepreneur HARRY RICKARDS. His New Tivoli Minstrel and Grand Specialty Company of Forty Great Artistes opened on 10 December 1892 in the Opera House in Sydney. The MINSTRELS ran at the Opera House until the following February. Emboldened by this success and urged on by his wife Kate, on 18 February 1893 Rickards took a long lease on the larger but languishing Garrick Theatre in Castlereagh Street. This was busier part of town and there had been entertainment on the site since the OLYMPIC CIRCUS opened there in 1851. The *Bulletin* sniffed: 'The Sydney Garrick is next Saturday to be rechristened the Tivoli and Harry Rickards establishes himself there as a permanent institution. The *Bulletin* wishes him every success and at the same time it begs to state that it regards the new name as stupid, meaningless and sufficiently hackneyed to bring ill luck to any theatre …'. The magazine was half right—Rickards was to be a permanent institution.

Two years after Rickards took over the Tivoli Theatre he saw a chance of securing a foothold in Melbourne. The Prince of Wales Opera House had been reduced to a palace of varieties as the Alhambra Theatre during the depression of the early 1890s. Rickards moved in on 9 February 1895, with a lease for one year and an option for five more. The same year also saw Rickards make his first yearly overseas trip to secure long-term talent for Australia. G. H. Chirgwin, called 'the White-eyed Kaffir' because his blackface make-up had a white lozenge around one eye, came in 1896. Chirgwin would pipe his way through 'The Blind Boy' and 'My fiddle is my sweetheart' to the accompaniment of banjo or one-stringed fiddle. Rickards also introduced a cuckoo into the nest in 1896 by presenting the American magician Carl Hertz, whose act incorporated the latest novelty—moving pictures.

In the years that followed Rickards confirmed his style of presentation. Big overseas stars—usually from London—headed the bill, with Australian acts in support. Rickards gave Australian audiences such famous entertainers as Little Tich with his big boots; the magician Chung Ling Soo; the juggler Paul Cinquevalli, catching a cannonball on the back of his neck; Charles Godfrey singing 'After the ball is over'; ADA REEVE and many others.

The Cockney comedian Harry Rickards—here dressed in the pearly suit of a costermonger—renamed the Garrick Theatre in Sydney the Tivoli when he opened there with his variety troupe in 1893. The old name was still on the building three years later when the magician Carl Hertz topped the Rickards bill. Hertz—advertised on the veranda of the adjoining Imperial Arcade—included in his act a presentation of moving pictures, the medium that eventually helped to destroy the variety circuit begun at the Garrick by Rickards

Rickards was overseas on 12 September 1899, when fire destroyed the Tivoli Theatre in Sydney. His general manager and brother, Jack Leete, showed his mettle and the next night Tivoli performances, improvised to some extent, went on at the PALACE THEATRE. The Tivoli company stayed there until January 1900 and then moved to the nearby CRITERION THEATRE for three months until the new Tivoli Theatre was completed on the old site. It looked much like the old theatre. The undamaged street facade remained and the improvements inside were subtle, though significant. The auditorium was slightly longer, the stage slightly deeper. The dress circle and the gallery were each closer to the stage, increasing the capacity. The Rickards organisation closed at the Criterion on 11 April 1900 and the new Tivoli opened with a matinée next day.

In Melbourne meanwhile, Rickards's interests had been flourishing, although the Opera House was becoming increasingly rickety and the authorities increasingly testy. On 3 February 1899 a Rickards company played there for the last time. Next day the company moved a few metres up Bourke Street to the BIJOU THEATRE. A new Opera House was to arise on the old site. The noted Melbourne architect WILLIAM PITT JNR created a theatre that reminded many of the Princess Theatre he had designed in 1886.

The opening night of the new Opera House on 18 May 1901 was distinguished by the first Melbourne appearance of Marie Lloyd, hailed by the Age as 'one of the finest artists of the English vaudeville stage'. The paper's theatre critic, however, declared that her songs 'were for the most part irredeemably vulgar and sung by anyone else would have been ill received'. Lloyd sang her popular song 'I'm one of the ruins that Cromwell knocked about a bit'. Rickards and his daughters Noni and Madge performed, and his wife designed the costumes.

The Tivoli circuit was now substantial. In addition to the Sydney and Melbourne theatres there was a Tivoli Theatre in Adelaide, and Rickards's companies played in the Theatres Royal in Brisbane and Perth. Tivoli shows toured New Zealand. Rickards bought the freehold of the Sydney Tivoli in 1901. He died in 1911 while on a talent-scouting trip in England. Eleven months after his death a syndicate headed by the boxing promoter HUGH D. MCINTOSH leased the Sydney Tivoli—sale was not permitted by Rickards's will—and bought the remainder of the circuit. He changed the name of the Opera House in Melbourne to the TIVOLI THEATRE. The Tivoli in Adelaide became a cinema, renamed the Star Theatre, in 1913, but in the same year McIntosh leased a new theatre and opened it as Rickards Tivoli Theatre. In 1915 he built a TIVOLI THEATRE in Brisbane.

The minstrel days were done, variety was in and ragtime was the new musical craze. The ragtime vocalist Gene Greene came to Australia for the Tivoli circuit in 1913. Then the First World War shook the country. The Tivoli went into revue and staged a popular series of Tivoli Follies shows. In 1921 McIntosh overreached himself in other theatrical ventures and control of the Tivoli circuit passed to a company headed by HARRY G. MUSGROVE. He put moving pictures into the Sydney and Melbourne Tivolis, but they were not built for showing them and he soon returned them to live variety under his cousin JACK MUSGROVE.

In 1924 J. C. WILLIAMSON'S bought the Tivoli circuit to present 'celebrity vaudeville'. It was an overblown title but high-class artists continued to appear on the Tivoli circuit —the magician Long Tack Sam, the diminutive English comedian Wee Georgie Wood, ELLA SHIELDS, the English comedian and singer Nellie Wallace, and the singer Lee White and her pianist partner Clay Smith. The Rickards philosophy of imported stars and local supports still prevailed. In 1928, after the death of Rickards's younger daughter, McIntosh bought the Sydney Tivoli.

The Great Depression struck in 1929. By the end of year J. C. Williamson's had given up the struggle to keep international variety alive in Australia. Williamson's ceased all importing, cancelling £20 000 worth of overseas acts. The Sydney Tivoli was no longer safe enough to be licensed and McIntosh sold it to a London syndicate, which wanted to build a cinema. In the last performance at the Tivoli, on 28 September 1929, there was a star bill of veteran Australian performers, including James Craydon, who had played on the same site when the Scandinavian Hall, the Academy of Music and the Garrick Theatre were there. Big salaries and small audiences compounded the problem. The large vaudeville circuit run by FULLERS' also collapsed but vaudeville did not totally disappear. Ad hoc companies would band together, try to get themselves an Australian with a big name—SYD BECK, NAT PHILLIPS, GEORGE WALLACE—to be the headliner and book themselves in wherever they could. Cinemas were just beginning to convert to sound, and some still had live entertainment. Fledgling radio also employed vaudeville talent.

Two performers with managerial skills, MIKE CONNORS and his wife QUEENIE PAUL spent a year producing vaudeville at the Cremorne Theatre in Brisbane and then saw an opportunity in Sydney. They gathered a company and chose an imposing but second-rank cinema named the Haymarket as their theatre. Its stage, used for live enter-

The great comedian Roy Rene began his career as a boy soprano at Harry Rickards's Tivoli Theatre in Adelaide. In his act as Mo (above) he was instrumental in the initial success of the second Tivoli circuit. Faced with a pay cut in 1945, he left the Tivoli circuit and became a radio star

Queenie Paul and her husband Mike Connors began the second Tivoli circuit in a Sydney cinema in 1931

tainment with silent films, had been enlarged in 1927 but its backstage facilities were inadequate for anything approaching spectacle. On Easter Saturday 1931 Connors and Paul were in business. They employed first-rate talent and they had success. By August 1931 they had moved into the BIJOU THEATRE in Melbourne, braving the competition of Tivoli Celebrity Vaudeville Pty Ltd at the Tivoli Theatre almost next door. By early September a merger was arranged between the rival companies and Connors and Paul went into the Tivoli. Con-Paul Theatres was announced to be capitalised at £75 000, the subscribers being Connors and Paul and their partner Bert Boland, a behind-the-scenes entrepreneur. Then Connors and Paul returned to Sydney at a much better venue, the Theatre Royal. They opened with their first weekly-change program on 12 November with a strong company. Connors and Paul did their double act, and there were also ROY RENE and his wife SADIE GALE, Syd Beck, James Craydon's daughter LETTY CRAYDON and Ronnie Hay. The season ran until March 1932. Con-Paul Theatres, needed a permanent Sydney home and took over the Grand Opera House, which had been mostly playing host to scratch companies of vaudeville performers. They called it the New Tivoli Theatre, in tribute to Harry Rickards's famous old house, and opened on 23 July 1932.

The partners had a simple philosophy. In the depths of the Depression prices at the Tivoli ranged from three shillings to one shilling in the gallery for evening performances, and a shilling anywhere in the house at matinées. Almost everybody could afford a shilling to forget their problems for two or three hours. The gamble paid off well. JIM GERALD was in the first pantomime. Other early headliners were Syd Beck, Roy Rene and Sadie Gale, Joe Marks, FRANK NEIL and Ella Shields. Neil was also a confident and experienced producer. After 18 months the six-year-old younger daughter of Connors and Paul died and the distressed parents retired from production. There may have also been some backstage financial revolution. Con-Paul Theatres and Frank Neil merged in May 1934 and Tivoli Theatres Ltd was created. The new company's managing director was Wesley Ince and the other directors were Frank Neil and George Dickenson of Melbourne. Neil was general manager of Musgrove Theatres of Melbourne, which was again involved in Tivoli matters. The Tivolis in Melbourne and Sydney were the basis of the new venture.

By late 1935 the company had become Tivoli Circuit Australia Pty Ltd, with Neil as managing director. He leaned towards big overseas talent to bolster up the local performers and made many trips overseas. The foreign invasion increased as times improved. WALLACE PARNELL, brother of the famous Val Parnell of the London Palladium, was brought out to supervise productions. In the late 1930s the Tivoli circuit was displaying such talents as Larry Adler the harmonica virtuoso; Adriana Caselotti, the voice of Snow White in Walt Disney's animated film; Billy Costello, the voice of Popeye the Sailor in countless animated shorts; Anna May Wong from Hollywood; Ada Browne, a singer from Harlem; EVIE HAYES and her husband WILL MAHONEY; the Mills Brothers; and George Robey, 'the Prime Minister of Mirth'.

Frank Neil died on 1 January 1940 and Wallace Parnell took complete control of productions. Overseas talent continued to arrive during the first year of the Second World War. Edwin Styles from the United Kingdom spent much of the war here and moved easily between variety and the legitimate stage. MARIE BURKE came from the USA. GLADYS MONCRIEFF, at last recovered from a serious car accident in 1938, made a welcome return to the stage. JENNY HOWARD played Dandini in *Cinderella* in 1940, on the way to becoming a fixture in pantomime. As the flood of overseas performers dried up, local artists found more work. A wartime pattern of performance emerged. A company would play

Nellie Kolle, a comedian in Australia for 57 years, impersonated men on the Tivoli circuit in the 1940s

five weeks in Melbourne, five in Sydney, three each in Brisbane and Adelaide and then go back to Melbourne to launch a new revue. The recurrent stars were BOB DYER, EDGLEY AND DAWE, Jim Gerald, Jenny Howard, Roy Rene and George Wallace. And there were some newer names— Dick Bentley, BUSTER FIDESS, Peggy Mortimer, Joy Nichols and her brother George, and AL THOMAS.

The Tivoli Circuit began its last phase in 1944 when it was bought by a group headed by DAVID N. MARTIN. Parnell lost his right to hire and fire and resentfully stamped off to the USA. Martin imported stars after the war. In October 1946 he put his first big import into the Melbourne Tivoli— the cheery British comic Tommy Trinder. He was such a hit that audiences tended to laugh right from his entrance. The importations continued—Chaz Chase and Chico Marx from the USA, George Formby and Wee Georgie Wood from England. In Sydney, Tivoli revues moved to the Empire Theatre on 27 December 1948, with Two-Ton Tessie O'Shea heading the bill, and the Tivoli Theatre housed seasons of opera, ballet, musical comedy and Shakespeare because of its size and the lack of other suitable venues. The Folies-Bergère Company toured very successfully for the Tivoli Circuit in 1952–53, with a rumpus over partial nudity.

Variety was doomed as a year-round theatrical enterprise when television came to Australia in 1956. David N. Martin died suddenly in 1958. His business associate Neil Maver took over a large measure of control with Gordon Cooper, the managing director in Melbourne. Cooper and Martin's son LLOYD MARTIN guided the last years of the Tivoli Circuit. The stars included the busty British blonde Sabrina, and the singers Tommy Steele, Sophie Tucker and David Whitfield and occasional musical or operatic visitors from other managements. The biggest hit of the final years was the Black and White Minstrel Company, advertised as 'the £50 000 extravaganza based on the popular BBC Television Series'. The Tivoli Circuit gave up producing revues in 1966. The last show, *One Dam' Thing After Another*, starring Gwen Plumb from television, closed in March. The audience included Roy Rene's widow Sadie Gale, Queenie Paul, and Amy Rochelle, a veteran Tivoli singer. In Melbourne Jim Gerald was in the audience on the last night of a four-week season by Jimmy Edwards of BBC Radio's *Take It From Here*. The Tivoli Theatre then showed films until, a year later, it was practically destroyed by fire. It was replaced by an office block which contains a Tivoli Arcade. In Sydney other managements hired the Tivoli Theatre occasionally, when they could obtain nothing better, but by mid-1969 it was under demolition. The office block that replaced it contains a Stage Door Bar. ❦*John West*

Tivoli Theatre Brisbane

Two theatres in Albert Square, Brisbane, opened 15 May 1915. Comprised three-level proscenium theatre seating 1800 and **Roof-Garden Theatre** seating 1200. Architect: Henry E. White. Reconstructed as two-level cinema 1927. Architects: Kaberry and Chard. Closed 17 June 1965 and demolished.

In 1914 HENRY E. WHITE was reported to be designing 'more theatres than all the other architects in Australasia'. One was the Tivoli Theatre in Brisbane for HUGH D. MCINTOSH's Rickards Tivoli Theatres Ltd. The exterior was in a style variously referred to as Art Nouveau and Spanish. The interior was in White's 'Louis Seize' style, very similar to Her Majesty's Theatre in Wellington (New Zealand), which he had designed in 1911. The main auditorium, 19·2 metres square, was on three levels, each containing two private boxes within a deep proscenium. The stage was 19·2 metres wide by 11·4 metres deep, with a skimpy fly tower. There was a minuscule vestibule—no foyer—to the street. Above this was the one-level Roof-Garden Theatre with a shallow stage—4·5 metres deep—with no fly tower. The auditorium had a latticed ceiling and wide side-wall shutters that could be raised to expose potted plants and creepers and the subtropical night.

The Roof-Garden Theatre remained largely unaltered when Union Theatres had the main vaudeville theatre reconstructed as a two-level cinema. The stage depth was halved to 4·8 metres, the old proscenium firewall was removed and the two tiers above the stalls were removed and replaced by a circle extending back to the front wall of the building over the circle foyer. Every wall and ceiling surface was decorated in a semi-classical picture-palace style with false window-backed balconies along the side walls, and dropped-dome and chandelier on the ceiling. The exterior remained unchanged until the theatre, bought by the City of Brisbane in 1963, was closed in 1965 and demolished to make way for a city square. ❦*Ross Thorne*

Tivoli Theatre Melbourne

Theatre in Bourke Street, opened as Prince of Wales Theatre 24 August 1872. Architect: George Johnson. Became known as **Prince of Wales Opera House**. Renamed **Her Majesty's Opera House** September 1884. Renamed **Alhambra Theatre** 1893. Lost licence 1899. Rebuilt as **Opera House**, opened 18 May 1901, seating 1539. Architect: William Pitt jnr. Renamed **Tivoli Theatre** 1912. Auditorium rebuilt 1956. Architect: Dudley Ward. Closed 2 April 1966. Interior destroyed by fire April 1967. Theatre sold as redevelopment site in 1969.

The *laissez-faire* attitude to safety in theatre design adopted by entrepreneurs and licensing authorities alike in the late 19th century was strikingly exemplified in the Prince of Wales Theatre in Melbourne. It stood on a site that was initially occupied by the Australia Hall, built above a stable in 1866. By the end of the year it was referred to as the Varieties. Singers, instrumentalists and comedians performed on a rough platform at one end of an 'unprepossessing chamber' furnished with tables and chairs and served by two bars in the style of an English music hall. The hall, renamed the Opera Comique in 1869, was destroyed in a fire on 5 July 1870.

On 27 December 1871 the architect George Johnson submitted plans for a theatre on the site to the Victorian Board of Health, the licensing authority. Johnson estimated a capacity of 3000 persons. Each would have had little more than a quarter of a square metre, and the board's inspector believed that 2200 would be more appropriate. In building the Prince of Wales Theatre, it seems, the old rubble stone outer walls of previous buildings on the site were reused to a height of three metres, then brick was added to the height of gallery, which was protected from elements by a timber wall to the roof. The architect chose wooden posts to support the three balconies above the pit and stalls, although cast-iron posts were readily available. Patrons of the top gallery had to negotiate gangway exits that were 560 mm wide with only 1·4 metres' headroom. The entrance to the theatre, reached through the ground floor of the hotel, stood 7·6 metres from the rear of the hotel and it was suspected that contaminated air from the hotel's stable and kitchen yards entered the ventilation intake. Another official observation was that a fire in the hotel would cut off most egress from the theatre.

The new theatre opened on 24 August 1872 with Dion Boucicault's comedy *London Assurance*, starring Mary Gladstane, whose husband, L. M. Bayless, was lessee of the theatre. W. S. LYSTER took over the theatre for his opera companies in March 1873 and it became known as the Prince of Wales Opera House. After Lyster's death in 1880, the theatre housed productions by his nephew GEORGE MUSGROVE. It was lit by electricity in 1882. From September 1884, the theatre was under new management as Her Majesty's Opera House, and from 1886 it was the Melbourne base of the BROUGH–BOUCICAULT COMEDY COMPANY. About that time, only 14 years after the opening, inspectors referred to the theatre as 'this dilapidated makeshift sort of building', though illustrations show a handsome interior and descriptions praise its white-and-gold decoration.

By 1893 the theatre had become a vaudeville house. Despite some slight modifications it limped well behind the ever-rising standards of safety and construction of theatres. The Board of Health's files indicate the social irresponsibility of theatre owners and entrepreneurs and of officials who continued to license the theatre in disregard of inspectors' advice that it breached the board's recommendation. It was finally refused a licence in 1899.

HARRY RICKARDS, lessee since 1895, oversaw the building of a new theatre designed by WILLIAM PITT JNR. A newspaper article described it as French Renaissance but it more closely approached an 'Alhambra style' that was popular for variety theatres at the time. The new Opera House had three levels, including the stalls, and seated only 1539 persons. Although English engineering developments over the previous decade had eliminated most of the need for balcony-supporting posts, Pitt supported the dress circle and the gallery with 14 posts in the stalls. These remained until Dudley Ward redesigned the auditorium in 1956. The stage was commodious, measuring 18·3 by 19·5 metres and it had a fly tower. Rickard's successor, HUGH D. MCINTOSH, changed the name to Tivoli Theatre in 1912 and this remained until the theatre closed in 1966. ❦*Ross Thorne*

Tivoli Theatre Perth

Theatre in Beaufort Street, opened as **Shaftesbury Theatre** 1904. Later known as **Luxor Theatre**, **Ritz Theatre**, **Hollywood Theatre**. Became **Tivoli Theatre** under management of Bruce Carroll 1946. Closed 1949.

Thomas Shafto celebrated his surname and his English home town in 1904 by building a theatre and a hotel and naming each of the neighbouring buildings the Shaftesbury. The theatre, never known for luxurious appointments, was Perth's home of variety from the start, and leading variety artists such as JENNY HOWARD, QUEENIE PAUL and ROY RENE later worked there. It sent shows to Fremantle and the goldfields, and also housed drama, pantomime, boxing, wrestling and silent films. After it closed as the Tivoli Theatre it was converted to a skating rink, and later the Canterbury Court Ballroom. The building was demolished in 1990. ❦*Ivan King*

Tivoli Theatre Sydney 1890–1929

Theatre in Castlereagh Street, opened 22 December 1890 as **Garrick Theatre**, seating about 1000. Architect: E. Weltzel. Renamed **Tivoli Theatre** 18 February 1893. Destroyed by fire 1899. Rebuilt and opened 12 April 1899, seating 1181. Architect: Backhouse and Backhouse. Closed 28 September 1929. Rebuilt as **Embassy** cinema. Closed 1977. Demolished in mid-1980s.

The first Tivoli Theatre in Sydney stood on land where there was entertainment for most of 126 years. In September 1851 an American named J. S. Noble established the Olympic Circus behind the Painters' Arms Hotel on the western side of Castlereagh Street, midway between King and Market Streets. For about 40 years thereafter a large yard behind the street-facing buildings was called Circus Court. The circus was converted to a theatre in May 1852. In July 1854 the theatre and the hotel in front were both called the Royal Albert. Both had gone by 1860.

In 1866 the Scandinavian Hotel was built with the Scandinavian Hall, which was used in the style of a British MUSIC HALL, with tables and chairs and free admission. In December 1869 it saw an Australian burlesque, *Formosa* by W. Read. In 1870 the hall was renamed the St James Hall, with fixed seating and an entrance charge, and the hotel in front was eliminated. By 1872 it was called the Scandinavian Music Hall, with a Columbia Hotel next door. It was an athletic hall by 1875, and a billiards saloon from 1877 to 1880. About 1881 both hall and hotel were renamed Victoria. In December 1881 an Australian extravaganza, *Aladdin and Company Limited*, was performed on the hall's small stage—about 8·5 metres feet wide and 9·4 metres deep with a 6·4-metre-wide proscenium. Dion Boucicault's *The Shaughraun* was also played there. After renovation, the hall was renamed the Academy of Music on 23 September 1882. Its small auditorium—8·5 metres wide by 24 metres long—officially seated 750 on two levels.

The Colonial Architect criticised the hall as old and dilapidated only a few years later and at the end of the 1880s it and an adjacent boarding house facing into Circus Court were demolished to provide a wider frontage for the new Garrick Theatre, again behind a hotel. The Garrick had a three-level auditorium, 13·7 by 16·8 metres. The stage was 13·8 by 15·2 metres. After a short period of drama, HARRY RICKARDS renamed the theatre Tivoli and devoted it to vaudeville. He redecorated it in gold and crimson plush in 1897, but in 1899 fire destroyed the auditorium and stage. Rickards built a slightly larger theatre behind the original façade. He died in 1911 and HUGH D. MCINTOSH acquired control of the Tivoli circuit, but the Rickards estate retained the Sydney Tivoli. It sold the site in September 1928 and the Tivoli closed a year later. ❦*Ross Thorne*

Tivoli Theatre Sydney 1911–66

Theatre in Castlereagh Street, opened 5 April 1911 as **Adelphi Theatre**, seating 2400. Architects: Eaton and Bates. Major alterations reduced seating to 2100 in 1915. Architect: Henry E.

White. Renamed **Grand Opera House** 28 August 1916. Renamed **New Tivoli Theatre** 1932. Closed March 1966. Demolished 1969.

In 1910 the Sydney City Council split its Old Belmore Markets site—bounded by Campbell, Castlereagh, Hay and Pitt Streets—into two lots of about 0·2 hectares each and auctioned off 50-year leases. Both successful bidders claimed they would build theatres, but only Thomas Rofe did. His Adelphi Theatre, designed for the entrepreneur GEORGE MARLOW, had a 18·3-metre square stage behind a 9·1-metre-wide proscenium. Marlow began with Frederick Melville's *The Bad Girl of the Family*, starring Nellie Ferguson and Robert Inman. George Willoughby managed the theatre from 1912 until 1915, when Marlow resumed management. He reopened a renovated Adelphi on 26 June 1915 with his wife Ethel Buckley heading a 'new and brilliant dramatic company' in *Mary Latimer—Nun*.

On 23 October 1915 the theatre closed for major alterations. HENRY E. WHITE redesigned the auditorium, lowering the lofty circle and gallery to improve sight lines and reducing capacity to 2100. The Adelphi reopened on 21 December 1915 with *Dick Whittington and His Cat*, starring CARRIE MOORE as principal boy. In 1916 Marlow's partner BENJAMIN FULLER took over the stage direction, for vaudeville at first. Then he renamed the theatre the Grand Opera House for a season by the Gonsalez Grand Opera Company from Italy. In the early 1920s Fuller combined with HUGH J. WARD to present musical comedy and drama at the Grand Opera House, but at the end of the decade FULLERS' gave up live theatre.

The theatre had a chequered existence until 1932, when MIKE CONNORS and QUEENIE PAUL took it for revue and renamed it the New Tivoli Theatre. In 1934 it became part of the second TIVOLI CIRCUIT. From 1948 until the theatre's closure in 1966 revue was interspersed with drama, musicals and opera, performed by local and touring companies. The OLD VIC THEATRE COMPANY and the Shakespeare Memorial Theatre Company from England performed there. During renovation in 1954 White's rich decoration was removed or painted in a single colour, leaving a bland interior. But the Tivoli remained an asset to Sydney. Its capacious auditorium—1933 seats at the time of closure—and large stage and scenery store made it particularly suitable for touring shows. For a quarter of a century since its demolition in 1969 until the CAPITOL THEATRE was rehabilitated these characteristics were combined in no Sydney theatre. The new developers promised to build a 1300-seat theatre but the part of the site dedicated for this purpose has remained vacant ever since the demise of the Tivoli. ❧*Ross Thorne*

To the West

Play in five acts by Alfred Dampier and Kenneth Mackay. **premiere** 8 February 1896, Her Majesty's Theatre, Sydney. Cast: Alfred Dampier, Lily Dampier, Mrs Harry Marshall, Alfred Rolfe, Alfred Woods. Design: Kinchela and Ricketts.

To the West is a sensation melodrama depicting life in Western Australia. The stage effects in ALFRED DAMPIER's production were sensational. The most celebrated scenes were formation of a human ladder by convicts during an escape from jail and an explosion in a gold mine. The villain, Henry Blackmore uses hypnosis to ensnare the unsuspecting Waratah Lorrimer. Her lover, Loris Zuroff, confronts Blackmore and, losing his temper, knocks him down. Fearing Blackmore is mortally wounded, Zuroff races for a doctor. Meanwhile another victim of Blackmore's hypnotism appears and viciously stabs the villain. Zuroff is arrested for attempted murder, but Dick Stewart, 'a friend worth having', takes the blame. Later Stewart escapes from jail. While almost dying in the bush near Coolgardie, he discovers gold. On several occasions Blackmore hypnotises Curr to kill Zuroff, but Stewart rescues him every time. Blackmore is more successful with Waratah's father, whom he almost ruins by fixing card games.

The *Sydney Morning Herald* said the first performance 'opened well, and as the first act closed upon a strong situation, it appeared likely that Mr Mackay, who has already made successes as a novelist, had hit the mark in his first essay at playwriting'. It was the only play by Kenneth Mackay (1859–1935). He became better known for a military career that took him to the rank of major-general, and as a NSW parliamentarian from 1895 to 1904. He published three volumes of poetry and two novels. ❧*Delyse Anthony*

reference
The manuscript of *To the West* is no. 1038 in the Hanger Collection, Fryer Library, University of Queensland (Brisbane).

Toe Truck Theatre Company

Young people's theatre company in Sydney founded in 1976 by Robert Love and Louise Sanders. Closed 1993. **first production** *Man Friday* by Adrian Mitchell, 1978. **artistic directors** 1977–80 Robert Love. 1981–83 Richard Tulloch. 1984 David Young. 1985–87 Nici Wood. 1987–89 Alison Summers. 1990–91 Russell Thomson. 1992–93 Katerina Ivak.

The longest-established subsidised professional young people's theatre company in Sydney until it closed in 1993 because of loss of funding and financial difficulties, Toe Truck took its name from 'theatre of education'. It followed the English theatre-in-education model, but it seldom performed for small audiences. The performers were usually adult actors, although young people took part in projects such as *The Servants of Vaucluse* by RICHARD DAVEY in 1983–84 and *Here We Are!* in 1991. Most Toe Truck productions toured Sydney schools, but the company made its reputation in theatres during the 1980s with plays such as Debra Oswald's *Dags* (1986) and the present writer's adaptation of Robin Klein's novel *Hating Alison Ashley* (1987).

Toe Truck developed new plays based on issues important to young people or on stories about young people. It first produced new Australian works in 1978, with NIGEL TRIFFITT's *Juke—A milk bar romance* and *Outpost* by Robert Love and students of the NATIONAL INSTITUTE OF DRAMATIC ART. Other companies have since produced plays commissioned by Toe Truck, including *Skin Free* (1986) by Morris Gleitzman; *Monkey See, Monkey Do* (1989) by Bruce Keller; *Spitting Chips* (1989) by Peta Murray; *Year 9 Are Animals* (1981), *If Only We Had a Cat* (1983) and *Could Do Better* (1989) by the present writer; and *Wasting Away* (1984) by DAVID YOUNG. Toe Truck developed the popular *Two Weeks with the Queen*, adapted by Mary Morris from Gleitzman's novel, for the 1992 Festival of Sydney. In 1983 Toe Truck performed *Year 9 Are Animals* and *Kaspajack* in the Rencontres Internationales Théâtre, Enfance, Jeunesse festival in

Lyon (France). It also performed at the 1983 and 1985 Come Out Youth Arts Festivals in Adelaide. ❦*Richard Tulloch*

Sydney Tomholt

Critic, dramatist. Born 6 January 1884 in Melbourne. In business 1911–15. Military service 1915–18. Studied drama at London University 1919. Editor and businessman in China and southeast Asia 1922–32. Radio scriptwriter, Sydney 1933–37. Film, music and drama critic for *Sydney Morning Herald* 1937–44. Later ran literary agency. Died 23 April 1974 in Sydney.

The 11 short plays of Sydney Tomholt include the most substantial contribution to symbolist and expressionist drama in Australia before the 1960s. Some of them elicited the encouragement of George Bernard Shaw and John Drinkwater. Four incorporate 'visions' of the inspired, possessed or dying. *The Crucified* is an expressionist vision of a mortally wounded soldier. *Searchlights* concerns an overwrought woman who is 'visited' by her dead soldier lover at the Shrine of Remembrance in Sydney. *Life and the Idiot* depicts a senile woman and her retarded grandson on an isolated Nordic farm, and includes repetitive and elliptical dialogue. *The Coming*, set on Italian lakes, uses a symbolist scenic archetype. Three more stylistically conventional plays dramatise sexual passion in conflict with better judgement. In *Bleak Dawn*, an Australian city wife fights down a longing to return to her brutal divorced husband. Tomholt's directions are unusually extensive, less to explain the subtext than to clarify exactly what he wanted in performance. *The Woman Mary* is a study of Mary Magdalene's struggle to renounce her Roman lover for Christ. *Anoli—the Blind* is a passionate triangle set amongst Italians in the outback and raises the moral issue of the difference between unpremeditated and deliberate violence.

The amateur little theatres did not stage Tomholt's most stylistically adventurous plays, and rarely staged the others. *Anoli—the Blind* was given a poorly-lit and inaudible production by INDEPENDENT THEATRE in Sydney on 6 February 1937. *Leading Lady* and *Dimmed Lights*, two slight pieces, were also performed in Sydney in the early 1940s. MAY HOLLINWORTH's production of *The Woman Mary* for the Sydney University Dramatic Society on 1 June 1940 was possibly the best a Tomholt play received. It was revived in December and won first prize in a British Drama League competition. ❦*Dennis Carroll*

published plays
Anoli: the Blind (1937). Sydney: Angus and Robertson 1936 in *Bleak Dawn and Other Plays*.
Bleak Dawn. Sydney: Angus and Robertson 1936 in *Bleak Dawn and Other Plays*.
The Coming. Sydney: Angus and Robertson 1936 in *Bleak Dawn and Other Plays*.
The Crucified. Sydney: Angus and Robertson 1936 in *Bleak Dawn and Other Plays*.
Dimmed Lights. Sydney: Angus and Robertson 1936 in *Bleak Dawn and Other Plays*.
Leading Lady. Sydney: Angus and Robertson 1936 in *Bleak Dawn and Other Plays*.
Life and the Idiot. Sydney: Angus and Robertson 1936 in *Bleak Dawn and Other Plays*.
Searchlights. Sydney: Angus and Robertson 1937 in *Best Australian One-Act Plays*.
The Woman Mary (1940). Sydney: Angus and Robertson 1936 in *Bleak Dawn and Other Plays*.

further reading
CARROLL, DENNIS. *Australian Contemporary Drama*. Sydney: Currency Press 1995.
GREEN, H. M. *A History of Australian Literature* 2, revised (ed. Dorothy Green). Sydney: Angus and Robertson 1984.
KEESING, NANCY. *Riding the Elephant*. Sydney: Allen and Unwin 1988.
KEESING, NANCY. Sydney John Tomholt. *Australian Dictionary of Biography* 12. Melbourne University Press 1986.

Too Young for Ghosts

Play in 15 scenes by Janis Balodis. **premiere** 9 July 1985, Studio, Victorian Arts Centre, Melbourne, by Melbourne Theatre Company. Cast: Robynne Bourne, Brandon Burke, Denis Moore, John O'May, Pamela Rabe, Mary Sitarenos. Designer: Eamon D'Arcy. Director: Roger Hodgman. **published** Sydney: Currency Press 1985.

A major initiative in writing about immigrants in English for the mainstage theatre, *Too Young for Ghosts* is in subject and theme one of the notable plays of the 1980s. With its epic style and focus on landscape and time-shifts, it can be compared with the mythic dramas of DOROTHY HEWETT, David Malouf, LOUIS NOWRA and PATRICK WHITE. It deals with postwar displaced persons from Latvia and their encounters with the land and the people in the north Queensland canefields in the late 1940s. These scenes are intercut with scenes in a refugee camp in Germany in 1947 and scenes of Ludwig Leichhardt's 1845 expedition to Port Essington in the far north and his encounter with the Aborigines. The fates of various 'ghosts' inhabiting the land are juxtaposed. In the conflicts of love and the negotiation of past and future, some characters are destroyed.

Murray Bramwell described the play in the *National Times* of 23–29 August 1985 as a 'metaphor for the necessity to settle the grudge with the past before the future can begin'. BRIAN HOAD in the *Bulletin* of 1 October 1985 said: 'It is exploring displacement by displacement'. David Malouf, in the *Australian* on 17 September 1985, found the production by the SYDNEY THEATRE COMPANY visually unforgettable. This company commissioned the play, but the first to produce it was the MELBOURNE THEATRE COMPANY in July 1985. There was a production by the STAGE COMPANY in Adelaide next month. ❦*Veronica Kelly*

J. L. Toole

English comedian 1830–1906. Toured Australasia for Williamson, Garner and Co. April 1890 to March 1891.

England's leading low comedian during the later years of the 19th century, John L. Toole brought to Australia a company that included Irene Vanbrugh and John Billington and had a rather old-fashioned repertoire of comedies and farces. His departure from England was heralded by a succession of benefit performances and banquets, at one of which Henry Irving described him as 'a British institution'. In Australia so many receptions were held in his honour that he was compared to 'a suburban Lord Mayor'. The establishment press praised Toole lavishly, but other journals attacked him severely. The *Bulletin* dubbed him 'Johnny, the Prince of Wales's pal' and suggested that Toole's establishment associations, rather than any discernible talent, attracted audiences. Toole visited Australia towards the end of his career, when his powers were waning, but this hostile reaction emphasised the fact that an English actor of considerable renown need not be taken on trust, since the Australian public was quite capable of exercising its own critical muscle. Toole's tour began in Melbourne in April 1890. Visits to Sydney, Brisbane, Newcastle, Adelaide and New Zealand lasted until December, and he then played return engagements in Sydney, Melbourne and Adelaide, whence he departed in March 1891. ❦*Jim Davis*

further reading
BEVAN, IAN. *The Story of the Theatre Royal*. Sydney: Currency Press 1993.
DAVIS, JIM. Colonial experience—English comedians in Australia in the nineteenth century. *Nineteenth Century Theatre* 16/1 (Amherst, Massachusetts, 1988).
HATTON, JOSEPH (ed.). *Reminiscences of J. L. Toole*. London: George Routledge and Sons 1889.

Andrew Torning

Actor, choreographer, dancer, entrepreneur, pantomimist, scene-painter, theatre decorator. Born 26 September 1814 in London. Son of Danish sea captain. At 18 married Eliza Crew and became actor. Engaged for Royal Victoria Theatre. Arrived in Sydney 21 October 1842 with Louise Torning, dancer, as Mr and Mrs Andrews. Choreographed dances and pantomimes. Redecorated Royal Victoria Theatre 1843, 1854, 1872. Leased Royal Victoria Theatre 1854–55. Leased Prince of Wales Theatre 1855. Worked as painter and fireman in USA 1858–67. Redecorated Queen's Theatre, Sydney, 1875. Died 1900 in Sydney.

An all-round man of the theatre, Andrew Torning arranged the pantomimes at the Royal Victoria Theatre in Sydney for more than ten years and painted much of its scenery. His acting debut, in *The Wreck Ashore* on 31 October 1842, was not well received. The *Sydney Morning Herald* remarked on 2 November that 'it is a pity the Londoners were deprived of his services'. He won praise, however, for his dancing and gymnastic skills, for comic roles, and particularly, as the *New South Wales Magazine* observed in 1843, for 'playing the devil' and the clown in the Christmas pantomime. He was one of the first to choreograph elaborate ballets and pantomimes in Sydney. In 1848 he withdrew from performing for a year and established a painting and decorating firm and an 'Evening Drawing Academy' in Sydney. He became proprietor of the Royal Hotel in 1851 and leased the Royal Victoria Theatre in 1854-1855 and the Prince of Wales Theatre concurrently in 1855. During this period he turned the fire brigade of the Royal Victoria Theatre into the first organised volunteer fire brigade in Australia. ❦*Elizabeth Webby*

further reading
FAGAN, JULIAN and JANE LENNON. Andrew Torning. *Dictionary of Australian Artists, Photographers and Engravers, 1770–1870* (ed. Joan Kerr). Melbourne: Oxford University Press 1992.

Yoshi Tosa

Designer. Born in Choshi City (Japan). Originally Yoshihisa Tosa. Studied design at Sydney Technical College. Began designing for Independent Theatre (Sydney) 1966. Resident designer with Old Tote Theatre Company (Sydney) 1975–77. Free lance 1978–82.

In the late 1960s and early 1970s Yoshi Tosa contributed bold imagery to productions by the OLD TOTE THEATRE COMPANY. His animal-skin designs for *King Lear* in 1968 and his monumental masked costumes and sculptured columns for Tyrone Guthrie's production of Sophocles's *Oedipus Rex* in 1970 were notable. So were his designs for Eugene O'Neill's *Long Day's Journey into Night* for Sydney's ENSEMBLE THEATRE COMPANY, for which he designed many productions in 1978–82. ❦*Tom Bannerman*

further reading
ALLEN, JOHN (ed.). *Entertainment Arts in Australia*. Sydney: Paul Hamlyn 1968.
FORSYTH, JAMES. *Tyrone Guthrie*. London: Hamish Hamilton 1976.

The Touch of Silk

Drama in three acts by Betty Roland. **premiere** 3 November 1928, Playhouse Theatre, Melbourne, by Melbourne Repertory Theatre Company. Cast: Lucy Ahon, George Faulkner, Jack O'Keefe, Betty Rae. Director: Frank D. Clewlow. **revived** 1976, Independent Theatre, Sydney. Cast: Betty Cheal, Kevin Howard, Fay Kelton, Sean Scully. Director: John Tasker. **published** Melbourne University Press 1942. Sydney: Currency–Methuen 1974, Currency Press 1986. Sydney: Currency Press 1988 (1955 revision).

'The first Australian play written by a real dramatist', proclaimed the Melbourne *Herald*'s critic after the first performance of BETTY ROLAND's *The Touch of Silk*. The Sydney *Bulletin* announced the 'birth of poor old Australian drama'. The principal role offers a major opportunity for an actress and in the next two years the play had the first of many amateur productions, in Adelaide, Brisbane and Sydney. Since 1975 there have been mainstage productions in most states. The first of 16 radio broadcasts was in 1938.

The Touch of Silk is an early study of the alienation of the immigrant and of the symbiotic relationship between Australians and the land. The plot is melodrama of its time, but there is notable realism in the drawing of the characters of a French war bride, Jeanne, and her mother-in-law. Jeanne's husband Jim is a sheep farmer in the mallee country of Victoria. The district is drought-stricken, Jeanne is homesick. Jim is suffering the psychological effects of the war, his mother is unfriendly and suspicious of Jeanne and the townspeople react variously to her foreign ways. A salesman who knows Paris befriends Jeanne, and in a moment of despair she buys from him some silk lingerie that reminds her of home. Her impulse provokes tragedy. Cliff is killed in a brawl, and Jim is charged with murder.

In the hope of attracting a professional management, Betty Roland revised the play in 1955, updating some of the dialogue and adding a scene. The original version was published in 1947, an edited version of the original in 1974, and the 1955 revision in 1988. PHILIP PARSONS writes in his introduction to the published 1955 text: 'There can be little doubt that the rewritten text is a more sophisticated piece of dramatic writing and probably more actable on the modern stage. But with the passing of the years the crudities which prompted Betty Roland to revise the original play are looking more and more like an authentic style, demanding realisation in a sympathetic period production. In either version, *The Touch of Silk* speaks clearly to an Australia still exploring its response to a multicultural world.' ❦*Katharine Brisbane*

Touring

The great age of touring theatre in Australia was from the late 1880s to the 1920s. Most actors then had been on the road at some time in their careers and touring companies helped to foster the idea of nationhood and minimise isolation. Entertainers began regularly to travel away from the main towns during the gold rushes in the mid-19th century. They went by coach or, rarely, by river boat for quicker access to outback towns. In the large gold towns, such as Ballarat (Vic.), theatres worthy of the cities were soon built. In camps entertainers performed in the open, in primitive halls or in tents. Companies and solo entertainers on the gold-diggings sold their performances and spruiked in direct competition with travelling salesmen, dentists and doctors. They sometimes sent bill-posters ahead, but often the actors had to employ a bellman or do their own advertising when they arrived. The repertoire was Shakespeare —often in excerpts—standard English melodrama and farces, and, increasingly, adaptations that offered local flavour in the form of convicts, gold-diggers, and bushranger characters and plots. A night's program would usually consist of several different items.

The last 30 years of the 19th century saw a wider range of touring entertainment, including Wild West shows, circus, pantomime, opera, operetta and variety. The large managements developed specialised circuits, concentrating on sizeable towns. These usually were on a main railway line because it was not unusual for up to 400 tonnes of scenery to be moved. A company might tour from Sydney to Cairns, hopping from steamer to rail, or from Melbourne to Sydney through the established provincial cities without any significant travel hazards. Companies visited Adelaide regularly, but Perth and Hobart less frequently. The economics of travelling were closely watched, and if receipts did not keep pace with expenses the tour ended. A company travelled under the name of either its management— WILLIAM ANDERSON, W. S. LYSTER, J. C. WILLIAMSON and others—or its star performer. The practice of naming a touring company after the star—such as NELLIE STEWART— rather than the management increased as the 19th century neared its end and continued until the Second World War.

Numerous small, old-style actor-manager companies still toured the country towns in the last three decades of the 19th century, taking city news, ideas, and entertainment to distant audiences. They pragmatically attuned their repertoires to their audiences' responses, particularly

One of the opulently furnished cars that E. I. Cole, proprietor of the Bohemian Dramatic Company, and his actor wife, Vene Linden, took on tour during the first two decades of the 20th century. The company toured eastern states and performed in a 3000-seat tent. Its cars were designed to be carried on flat-bed rail trucks and offloaded on horse-drawn chassis for travelling beyond the railway

Philip Lytton, a pioneer of touring tent shows, had three companies on the road in eastern states from 1907 to about 1923, when he sold out to the black comedian George Sorlie. This Lytton troupe travelled by charabanc

in the smaller towns. It was not uncommon for such a company to have more than 20 items that it could offer over several nights if need be. There was some pride in being able to play 16 or more different pieces in a single program. Topical references in their acts, patriotic and union banner-waving, and collections for South African War funds generated local enthusiasm. These small companies often played in primitive conditions that were little better than those on the gold-diggings, and they experienced considerable hardship and danger as they travelled through the outback by coach, train or boat. They usually travelled on more restricted circuits than the larger companies, such as the western districts or northern rivers of NSW, or the far north of Queensland. Economics forced them to leave the main lines. They always arranged their tours according to the seasons—north in winter, south in summer.

The more successful actor-manager companies travelled in greater style. E. I. Cole's BOHEMIAN DRAMATIC COMPANY took advantage of increasingly extensive railways by having its own luxuriously appointed caravans, which could be carried on flat-bed rail wagons and then offloaded onto horse-drawn chassis in order to travel farther afield. The company carried its own performance space in the form of a large circus tent, living quarters, and mechanical equipment. TENT SHOWS became a regular sight in the cities and in the country. Tents housed drama and revue until the Second World War. Circus and carnival entertainment are now almost their only uses, but there have been recent attempts to revive tent theatre, by the Bell Shakespeare Company in particular.

Small touring companies were most active, paradoxically, when they were most under threat, in the early decades of the 20th century. The threat came from film. Picture-show men travelled the country, often in their own cars, exploiting the films that poured from the studios of Australia, Europe and the USA. The arrival of film resulted in theatres existing even in small settlements, usually with a stage to accommodate live performance. Vaudeville acts frequently supplemented films, and between picture shows travelling live theatre companies used the theatres. People became accustomed to going out for entertainment.

Touring companies also began to travel by car, extending their circuits. Trade journals frequently reported the hazards of travelling on barely delineated tracks. Melodramas were still popular, partly because they had become the staple plots of the new films. Bushranging epics had given way to homely bush comedies. The actor-manager KATE HOWARDE toured her own film of POSSUM PADDOCK in conjunction with the stage version. There were usually vaudeville items between acts of a play, and in the 1920s the wireless concert was an added attraction.

In addition to the usual economic hazards of drought, floods, strikes and elections, there was fierce competition between the small companies that followed the show circuits. One popular program could mean a rapid move on to the next town for other companies. The struggle was exacerbated by some councils that imposed strict billposting regulations and even their own performance taxes. Small companies were tainted by the poor reputation of carnival workers. A tour would frequently take many months, the company only returning to its base town to repair costumes, collect mail or hire new actors.

Large city companies continued to tour the major provincial centres, although Hobart was increasingly seen as a theatrical graveyard. The balance sheet still dictated the length of the tour. Overseas stars guaranteed special attention, such as a civic reception upon arrival in town. On the grounds of its contributions to culture, the ALLAN WILKIE SHAKESPEAREAN COMPANY was given free railway travel in Queensland from 1923, and later in other states. GEORGE SORLIE's company was also given special treatment on railways, according to Bobby Le Brun.

Australian companies large and small regularly toured overseas. J. C. Williamson's companies regularly visited New Zealand, where he had long leases on theatres, even though profits were often small. Small companies travelled to the more isolated settlements—the 'smalls'—in New Zealand as in Australia. SOUTH AFRICA was a favourite destination. It was similar to Australia in its colonial society and climate and it had an efficient national theatre organisation that made all travelling and booking arrangements. Australian companies and individual entertainers regularly visited India, China, Japan, the Philippines and Java. In India they performed mainly in military camps and to British colonial audiences. In Japan the indigenous population together with expatriate British and American business people comprised the audiences. Elsewhere in East Asia audiences were composed almost solely of British and other European colonial bureaucrats. In all these regions, as in Australia, performance conditions improved as new theatres were built for picture shows. Trade journals regularly printed reports from entertainers travelling in Asian countries, telling where good audiences could be expected and warning of hazards. For instance, female impersonators were not welcome in Java, which was regularly visited by Australian performers.

The Great Depression and the Second World War considerably altered touring theatre in Australia. Many small companies could no longer compete with film. From the 1950s television was another competitor. Sorlie's continued to tour tent vaudeville until 1961. The large companies increasingly confined themselves to major centres, now alternating the big star with the big West End or Broadway production or a version of one.

Since the 1960s some low-budget ethnic, political or other special-interest companies have concentrated on taking theatre to larger country centres, and theatre-in-education groups, usually associated with professional companies in capital cities, regularly travel to schools that

Among the many small companies that toured the outback in the first decade of the 20th century was this comedy troupe, posing in costume at Clermont, in inland tropical Queensland

Touring companies pitched their tents side by side along the Burnett River and their spruikers fought the 'battle of Bundaberg' during show week in the Queensland town

would otherwise never see live theatre. A non-establishment venture like the musical BRAN NUE DAE needed to be refinanced for each new city in which it was performed. Overseas touring, except to New Zealand, is now an isolated rather than regular feature of Australian theatre. 🌿*Barbara Garlick*

The circus on tour

Touring has characterised the circus in Australia, although it performed in amphitheatres in Tasmania, Sydney and Melbourne in the 1840s and 1850s and in longer-lived permanent establishments in this century. Touring circuses have encountered a combination of problems from which their European counterparts were largely free, including formidable extremes of distance and climate, and the necessity to learn about touring conditions largely by trial and error. In the absence of a large population in easily accessible concentrations it was difficult to establish circuses of the size customary in the USA and Europe. Conditions in Europe were approximated only in provincial Victoria, where the towns were close together and a good road system was quickly developed.

American circuses performed in calico tents as far back as 1825 and popularised them among English circuses in the 1840s. Australian circuses appear to have first used tents in 1851, when they had to follow the population to the goldfields. The dispersal of the population to the interior, the development of inland trade routes and, probably, the waning novelty of permanent circuses in the large towns, encouraged the Australian circus to become largely a touring affair. JAMES HENRY ASHTON, Henry Burton, John Jones and other proprietors found that a tented circus—rolling from town to town unencumbered by heavy wood and iron structures that had to be erected and dismantled—was economical and effective in a country where most provincial towns lacked suitable permanent theatres.

Circuses developed routes for touring scattered communities. The first major route, linking townships lying between Sydney and Melbourne, appears to have been travelled from early 1852. As settlement spread in the wake of the gold rushes other routes developed, such as one along the coast of NSW from Bega to the Northern Rivers district; the so-called 'western run' through the townships of mid-western central NSW, and a route from Adelaide through central Victoria to Albury (NSW). The movements of a circus could be affected, however, by expectations of weather, financial considerations, the quality of roads, the accessibility of a region and the availability of grazing for the horses. The practice of 'wintering up' in the colder months was less common among Australian circuses than among their European and American counterparts, as tours of Queensland, northern NSW and, later, Western Australia, were still possible during the winter months.

Circus routes became more or less standardised by the early 20th century. Proprietors then had accumulated knowledge of climatic, financial and travelling conditions, and they had the large visiting AMERICAN CIRCUSES of the 1870s and 1880s as organisational models. The first Australian circus to follow the American example of travelling by rail was ST LEON'S CIRCUS in Tasmania early in 1881. By the late 1880s FITZGERALD BROTHERS' CIRCUS and WIRTHS' CIRCUS regularly toured on the colonies' spreading railway systems to entertain growing populations. The FitzGeralds began to standardise their route through Australasia in the 1890s. Only the largest circuses could afford to rely on rail transport in this century, but smaller circuses occasionally used trains for particular runs. The smaller circuses often travelled on the agricultural-show circuit, which developed from the 1890s. Like provincial race weeks, with which the circus became associated as far back as the 1870s, agricultural shows could be relied upon to bring many country people into town.

Motor transport greatly enhanced the mobility and touring possibilities of provincial circuses during the 1920s and 1930s. Traditional circuses still rely upon motor transport. Touring has also been simplified by sealed roads and the availability of road maps, weather forecasts and other information. Yet traditional circuses face problems unknown in the 19th century, including restrictive municipal councils and opposition from animal-liberationists.

Most major Australian circuses have toured overseas and Australian circuses have been seen on most continents. The first known overseas visit by a circus of Australian origin was an abortive tour of Southeast Asia by the Oriental Circus of 'the celebrated English clown' Reuben Cousins in 1857. Burton's Great Australian Circus visited New Zealand in 1878 but Australian circuses may have previously crossed the Tasman Sea. By the late 1880s, when St Leon's and Wirths' circuses went to New Zealand and New Caledonia, Australian circuses appear to have toured abroad regularly. Harry Wirth's Pacific Circus, organised in 1895 from the remnants of Abell and Klaer's circus, visited East Asia during 1895–96. In 1893 Wirths' Circus left Adelaide for South Africa, beginning a seven-year tour of four continents. During the early 1900s the FitzGerald brothers operated a second company which they sent on tour through India and Southeast Asia each year. Sole Brothers' Circus made a successful tour through South Africa, Rhodesia and the Belgian Congo in 1926–29. ASHTON'S CIRCUS made the first known visit by an Australian circus to Papua in 1975. It was brief and financially unsuccessful. CIRCUS OZ and the FLYING FRUIT FLY CIRCUS have made numerous overseas tours. ❦*Mark St Leon*

further reading
FISHER, EDMUND. The business side of the drama. *Lone Hand* (Sydney) 1 July 1909.
GOULD, NAT. Up-country theatricals. *Town and Bush*. London: Penguin 1974. Reprint of 1896 publication.
LYTTON, PHILIP. The drama under canvas—A successful Australian innovation. *Theatre* 13/12 (Sydney 1 December 1915).
WARD, FREDERICK. Country touring in New South Wales. *Everyones* 5/355 (Sydney 15 December 1926).

Traitors

Play in three acts by Stephen Sewell. **premiere** 26 April 1979, Pram Factory, Melbourne, by Australian Performing Group. Cast: Jan Cornall, Max Gillies, Sue Ingleton, Wilfred Last, Judy McHenry, Mark Michinton. Designer: Dave May. Director: Kerry Dwyer. **published** Sydney: Alternative Publishing Co-operative 1983.

One of the influential plays of the new 'internationalist' movement in Australian playwriting in the late 1970s and early 1980s, *Traitors* remained for a long time STEPHEN SEWELL's best known and most studied play, partly because its relatively simple narrative was more accessible than the epic complexities of his later work up until *Hate*.

Traitors follows Anna, an idealistic Trotskyite struggling to maintain revolutionary principles in the face of Stalin's rise in Russia in the late 1920s. Her private and public lives intermingle when she has an affair with urbane Giorgi Krasin. Unknown to her, he is an officer of the Cheka, the secret police, which is involved in a purge of the Oppositionists, of whom Anna is one. Anna also forms a friendship with her innocent country cousin Ekaterina and starts to educate her in revolutionary theory and practice. As the Stalinists emerge victorious Krasin commits suicide rather than arrest Anna. Warned by Krasin, Anna and Ekaterina flee to the country. Scenes set during the Nazi invasion of Russia, which frame the play, reveal that Ekaterina becomes a 'good communist' in the Stalinist sense.

The play shows with great force the contradictions created for the characters by the conflict between their personal and political lives and how these affect one another. *Traitors* has been produced throughout Australia and in London and New York City. ❦*John McCallum*

Neville Tranter

Puppeteer. Born 5 September 1955 at Warwick (Qld). Studied drama at Darling Downs Institute of Advanced Education (Toowoomba, Qld). Trained in traditional puppetry with Billbar Puppet Theatre (Toowoomba). Based in Amstelveen (Netherlands) since 1978. Tours as solo puppeteer. Performed at Australian International Puppet Festival 1983 and Adelaide Festival 1992.

A leading solo puppeteer in Europe, Neville Tranter performs only for adults and tours widely. In 1977, after working with Pilgrim Puppet Theatre in Melbourne, he formed Stuffed Puppet Theatre with Bert Cooper and Alf Klimek and presented cabaret sketches for adults in Melbourne. After the group attended the Festival of Fools in Amsterdam in 1978 Tranter remained in the Netherlands. He began solo performance with *Studies in Fantasy* for adults in 1981 and won critical acclaim at the International Puppet Theatre Festival in France in 1982. *The Seven Deadly Sins* followed in 1984 and *Underdog* in 1985. In *The Seven Deadly Sins* Tranter acts a central masked Mephisto to life-sized puppets representing sins. In *Underdog*, placed first in a German puppet festival, he acts a central traumatised boy confronted by characters from his past. Tranter works with a technical assistant and a manager. ❦*Richard Bradshaw*

Travelling North

Play in two acts by David Williamson. **premiere** 22 August 1979, Nimrod Theatre, Sydney. Cast: Jennifer Hagan, Julie Hamilton, Graham Rouse, Carol Raye, Henri Szeps, Frank Wilson. Director: John Bell. **published** Sydney: Currency Press 1980.

Critics saw *Travelling North*, DAVID WILLIAMSON's gentlest comedy, as marking a new maturity in his art and as one of the finest Australian plays of the 1970s. It deals with the hard realities of aging and death. Frank, a widower in his seventies, and Frances, a widow in her fifties, travel north together, very much against the wishes of Frances's married daughters, who cloak their dependence upon her in protectiveness. Frank's sharp-witted cussedness gives the play most of its comic energy, while Frances's ambivalent feelings as he becomes more and more her patient come to occupy its emotional centre. The journey north is an ending for Frank, but for Frances it marks the belated beginning of a quest for self-realisation.

The play has been described as Chekhovian in its acceptance of human frailties and failures, and the analogy also holds in the way astringent humour counteracts sentimentality. Music weaves through and enriches the interactions of the generations as the plot moves toward reconciliation. Among the polarities reconciled in *Travelling North* is a fundamental Australian mythic opposition of north and south. Not since SUMMER OF THE SEVENTEENTH DOLL have the metaphorical associations of distant places and contrasting climates been so effectively and richly addressed. *Travelling North* has been played extensively in all states, and in London in 1980. A film, starring Julia Blake and LEO MCKERN, was released in 1987. ❦*Peter Fitzpatrick*

Bryceson Treharne

Welsh composer, director. Born 30 May 1879 in Merthyr Tydfil (Wales). Graduated from Royal College of Music (London) 1899. Taught at University College of Wales (Aberystwyth). Taught piano at Elder Conservatorium (Adelaide) 1901–11. Founded and directed Adelaide Literary Theatre 1908–11. Returned to Europe 1911. Died 1948 in New York State (USA).

Adelaide Literary Theatre, which produced plays by contemporary European dramatists in the first decade of the 20th century, grew out of play readings by Bryceson Treharne and his students at the Elder Conservatorium. The group was known as Bryceson Treharne's Class until 1910. Treharne influenced its repertoire, directed productions and wrote incidental music for many of them, notably

W. B. Yeats's *Deirdre*. His theatrical background is not known but a tribute by Adelaide Repertory Theatre says he was a disciple of George Bernard Shaw, perhaps belonged to the Fabian Society and kept in close touch with many prominent playwrights. Those whose works his group performed included Arnold Bennett, Anton Chekhov, John Galsworthy, John Masefield, Shaw and August Strindberg.

From its inception the group periodically performed Australian scripts. 'It is vital that the country should create its own literature, its own art, and its own music, and it is up to the public to support and sustain those who seek an outlet and a hearing in any of those directions', Treharne said in a letter. The group gave the first performance of *The Wasters* by Arthur H. Adams in 1910 and later performed his *Pierrot in Australia* and *Doctor Death*.

When Treharne left Adelaide the group changed its name to Adelaide Repertory Theatre and its programming changed direction. Treharne wrote: 'If my rather unswerving policy has been changed, or modified, that is no reflection on your efforts and perhaps in the early days I was a little uncompromising. After all, the imposition of one's own tastes on others smacks a little of selfishness, as in any community there is bound to be diversity, not only of interest, but of ideals. And in adopting a less rigorous attitude, you have appealed to larger sections of the community, and by so doing have ensured their support.' He was right—Adelaide Repertory Theatre still performs. ❦*Rose Wilson*

Nigel Triffitt

Designer, director. Born 1949 in Hobart. Ejected from National Institute of Dramatic Art directing course after one year. Worked as dresser at Mermaid Theatre, London. Studied at Drama Centre until expelled. Returned to Australia 1971. Director-in-residence for St Martin's Theatre Company (Melbourne) for 18 months. Formed Yellow Brick Roadshow alternative performing group at Monash University (Melbourne) 1974, and toured Australia until 1976. Has worked as freelance in dance, puppetry, cabaret, opera, sculpture, film, rock music, and theatre-in-education.

Nigel Triffitt is a controversial, eclectic and innovative creator of intensely visual, flamboyant and diverse theatrical and multimedia works. He is probably most renowned as a designer, but for years he was regarded as the *Wunderkind* of alternative theatre, mounting shows to shock, challenge and enrapture, and combining genres. For example, *Momma's Little Horror Show*, his first big hit, utilised mime, music, magic, puppetry, and Japanese *kabuki* and *bunraku* theatre. He devised, directed and designed it for the Tasmanian Puppet Theatre in 1976.

For many years Triffitt found it easier to work with puppets than live performers. He prefers to have total control of his projects and it is not unusual for him to devise, direct, design and cast a work and make the sound track for it. His later shows included *Wild Stars* for Australian Dance Theatre in 1979, *Secrets* in 1983, *The Fall of Singapore* in 1987 and *Moby Dick* in 1990. In 1992 he moved into commercial waters with a revival of the rock musical *Hair* and *The New Rocky Horror Show*. Triffitt's shows have toured to more than 20 countries, usually to acclaim, though *Illustrated History of Rock 'n' Roll* failed spectacularly in the Netherlands in 1982. ❦*Fiona Scott-Norman*

Tony Tripp

Designer. Born 15 May 1940 in Newcastle (NSW). Studied art at Newcastle Technical College. First commissions for Octagon Theatre Company (Perth) 1970. In Europe 1971–72. Resident designer for National Theatre Company (Perth) 1973–75, 1979–81. Resident designer for Melbourne Theatre Company 1976–78, senior designer-in-residence 1982–92. Green Room Award 1992 (*The Crucible* by Arthur Miller). Married to actor Helen Tripp.

Tony Tripp, shy and seldom drawn into the limelight, is a master craftsman. His settings provide detail for the observant but invariably point the eye at the heart of the action. He has worked closely with the lighting designer Jamieson Lewis in evolving stages washed with coloured light to create mood, within which Tripp's detail and symbolism define period and class. Tripp has also developed important collaborations with the directors Gale Edwards, Rodney Fisher, Roger Hodgman and Simon Phillips. He has spent most of his career with the Melbourne Theatre Company, for which he has designed 60 productions, including premieres of Australian plays. Other significant productions include Oscar Wilde's *The Importance of Being Earnest* for national tour in 1991–92 and *The Crucible*. In Tripp's superb set for *The Crucible* long rising lines, black on black, built a forest of intrigue and mystery around the action, though his vertical lines can sometimes overwhelm the actors inside the picture. ❦*Tom Bannerman*

Troupe

Professional alternative-theatre company in Adelaide, formed in 1976 as collective by David Allen, Keith Gallasch and Des James. Reformed 1984. Disbanded 1987. **venues** 1976–81 Red Shed, Cardwell Street. 1981–87 Old Unley Town Hall. **landmark productions** *Serjeant Musgrave's Dance* by John Arden, 1976. *A Stretch of the Imagination* by Jack Hibberd, 1976. *Crunchy* by David Allen, Keith Gallasch and Des James, 1976. *Henry V* adapted by Allen, 1977. *If I Ever Get Back Home Again I'll Stay* by Allen, 1977. *Chidley* by Alma de Groen, 1977. *Gone with Hardy* by Allen, 1977. *Gents* by Gallasch, 1979. *Roses in Due Season* and *Missus Queen* by Doreen Clarke, 1979. *Mrs Thally F* by John Romeril, 1979. *Meat* and *Coppin and Company* by Allen, 1980. *Bleedin' Butterflies* by Clarke, 1980.

One of Adelaide's most inventive alternative companies, Troupe gave opportunities to local writers and actors and staged new works from the La Mama Theatre and the Australian Performing Group in Melbourne. When it operated as a collective Troupe illuminated the talents of the three writer-directors who founded it—David Allen, Keith Gallasch and Des James. At the beginning of 1981 the company moved from the Red Shed—a warehouse behind a left-wing bookshop—to the Old Unley Town Hall, which it preferred. Gallasch left in July. Troupe continued to perform new works but fewer were written by its members.

In 1984 the director Julie Holledge, the designer Mary Moore and the dramaturge Barry Plews generated a new membership, which led to distinctive productions such as *The Kelly Dance*, devised by John Romeril and Holledge with students from the Flinders University Drama Centre. *The Centenary Dance*, a group-devised work, followed. Troupe also presented new works from England—*Tibetan Inroads* by Stephen Lowe and *Salonika* by Louise Page. In

1985 Gavan Strawhan's *The Floating Palais* continued the promenade, music-based formula initiated by *The Kelly Dance*, and *Rundle Rita*, a reworking of Claire Luckham's *Trafford Tanzi*, epitomised Troupe's vitality—bold design by Mary Moore, vigorous performances, and crisp direction by Holledge. By 1986 Holledge and Moore had left the company and Venetia Gillot joined; she directed Strawhan's *The Last Drive-In On Earth* and *Bah Humbug!* and Caryl Churchill's *Top Girls* and *Fen*. Troupe lost funding and disbanded after presenting *Soft Targets*, a group-devised play about AIDS from Sydney's Griffin Theatre Company. A core of the Troupe actors joined the RED SHED COMPANY. ❦*Murray Bramwell*

True Love
—*or, The Interlude Interrupted*. Farce in two acts. **premiere** 23 June 1845, Royal Victoria Theatre, Sydney.

An entertaining and highly theatrical farce that received several performances in Sydney in 1845, *True Love* has been attributed without firm evidence to EDWARD GEOGHEGAN. Several of the scenes represent a play within the play. The leading characters are Mr Brown, 'a respectable master tailor in Sydney, very much opposed to dramatic performances', and his wife, who is 'fond of theatricals, especially "Hamateurs"'. While Mr Brown is away attending to business Mrs Brown is visited by Mrs Gibbs, a member of the ROYAL VICTORIA THEATRE's company, and asked to play the lead in that evening's performance of the interlude *True Love*. Mr Brown returns home early, discovers his wife has gone to the theatre and finds to his horror that she is on stage of the Royal Victoria embracing a stranger. He angrily interrupts the performance but all ends happily, with Mr Brown repenting his previous ignorant condemnation of actors and the theatre. The initial production included many in-jokes, with the real Mrs Gibbs playing Mrs Gibbs and THOMAS SIMES, the Royal Victoria's manager, the theatre-hating Mr Brown. ❦*Elizabeth Webby*

reference
Manuscript copy in the Colonial Secretary's papers in the NSW Archives.

Jean Trundle
Actor, director, speech and drama teacher. Born c.1907. Studied speech with Barbara Sisley. Founded Jean Trundle Players. Married Vic Hardgreaves 1935. Founded Brisbane Arts Theatre with Hardgreaves 1936. Chief producer until death in July 1965.

As chief producer of the BRISBANE ARTS THEATRE for 29 years and as an actor until 1951, Jean Trundle took part in hundreds of productions. Her interests ranged widely but she is perhaps best remembered for her productions and performances of Shakespeare. Many of her pupils became actors of note. A small band of her pupils, the Jean Trundle Players, was the basis for the Brisbane Amateur Theatres, which she founded with her husband Vic Hardgreaves in 1936. The couple had become frustrated by lack of opportunity as members of the BRISBANE REPERTORY THEATRE SOCIETY, which was dominated by its chief producer, BARBARA SISLEY. The new group, which was intended to be a focus for Brisbane's many amateur companies, was renamed the Brisbane Arts Theatre in 1947. ❦*Deslye Kruck*

further reading
RADBOURNE, JENNIFER. Little Theatre—its development since World War II in Australia, with particular reference to Queensland. University of Queensland MA thesis 1978.

John Truscott AO
Designer. Born 23 February 1936 in Melbourne. Studied at Caulfield Technical College (Melbourne). Designed for National Theatre Movement (Melbourne) 1956–57; St Martin's Theatre Company (Melbourne) 1957–64. Worked for London Festival Ballet and English National Opera Company (London) 1964–65. Worked in USA 1966–79. Designed sets and costumes for major theatre and opera companies and films in Australia, England and USA. Interior design consultant to Victorian Arts Centre (Melbourne). Creative director of World Expo '88 in Brisbane. Artistic director of Spoleto Melbourne Festival 1989–91. Artist in residence at Victorian Arts Centre until death. Died 5 September 1993 in Melbourne. AO 1985.

As creative director of World Expo '88 and artistic director of the Spoleto Melbourne Festival, John Truscott greatly influenced the development of Australian design. He began his career with the NATIONAL THEATRE MOVEMENT in Melbourne, as an actor as well as a designer of innovative sets and costumes for *A Midsummer Night's Dream* and other works. Then he became resident designer for the ST MARTIN'S THEATRE COMPANY produced more than 80 sets for productions including Dylan Thomas's *Under Milk Wood* and Jean Anouilh's *Beckett*. He also designed musicals for J. C. WILLIAMSON'S, including *West Side Story* in 1960, *The King and I* in 1962 and *Camelot* in 1963. The St Martin's director IRENE MITCHELL fostered his talent and encouraged him to work in England, where he gained valuable experience in 1964–65. Truscott then went to the USA and within two years he had won Academy Awards for costume and production design for the film *Camelot*. Upon his death Sue Nattrass, general manager of the VICTORIAN ARTS CENTRE, told the *Age*: 'He has more creative ideas in a day than most of us have in a lifetime. But he also had the rare gift of taking people with him … and inspiring them to achieve more than they ever believed they could'. ❦*Pamela Zeplin*

Trust Players
Professional dramatic company founded in Sydney in 1959 by Robin Lovejoy and Hugh Hunt for Australian Elizabethan Theatre Trust. Ceased operating as ensemble company 1961. Mounted productions until late 1962. **first production** *The Slaughter of St Teresa's Day* by Peter Kenna, 11 March 1959, Elizabethan Theatre, Newtown. **actors** Neva Carr Glyn, Patricia Connolly, Neil Fitzpatrick, Ron Haddrick, Rodney Milgate, Des Rolfe, Dinah Shearing, Grant Taylor, Frank Waters. **designers** Wilfred Asplin, Wendy Dixson, Anne Fraser, Phillip Hickey, Frank Hinder. **directors** Hugh Hunt, Robin Lovejoy, Raymond Menmuir.

The Trust Players company gave new distinction and direction to Australian theatre during its short existence, John Moses has written. It was formed because HUGH HUNT, artistic director of the AUSTRALIAN ELIZABETHAN THEATRE TRUST, and ROBIN LOVEJOY decided that the trust needed a new initiative in drama. They felt that continuing to mount productions, play in Sydney and then tour the other state capitals would not help the progress of drama. 'It was trying to spread too little too far', Lovejoy said. It was intended that the Trust Players in Sydney and the Union Theatre Repertory Company in Melbourne should be pilots for similar companies in other capitals. Five plays were to be produced in the ELIZABETHAN THEATRE in Sydney in 1959. Lovejoy had sole responsibility for all artistic and many managerial decisions. One of his aims was to build a faithful audience for a professional company in a season of distinguished classical or modern plays and new Australian plays. Another was to provide constant professional employment for a company that would develop into a truly Australian ensemble. Nine actors were offered long-term contracts for 1959 and others were engaged for plays with large casts. Each play was rehearsed for three and a half weeks and once the first production had opened the actors worked every night too.

Lovejoy directed the first four productions, starting with Peter Kenna's THE SLAUGHTER OF ST TERESA'S DAY, because he wanted to open with an Australian play. George Bernard Shaw's *Man and Superman* and another Australian play, *The Bastard Country* by Anthony Coburn, followed in turn. The actors were rehearsing another play when a cable from New York said that Eugene O'Neill's widow permitted Hunt, with stringent provisos, to produce *Long Day's Journey into Night*. O'Neill's play had then had only two or three productions anywhere. Production began immediately, with two weeks and a half to opening night. The result was one of Lovejoy's greatest achievements as director and the ensemble work of the cast was acclaimed. DINAH SHEARING was outstanding. Hunt directed the last of the five productions, *Julius Caesar*, with costumes from the Old Vic Theatre in London. NATIONAL INSTITUTE OF DRAMATIC ART students understudied roles, and appeared in a professional production for the first time as walk-ons.

Almost immediately after *Julius Caesar* the company began a 17-week tour to all capital cities except Melbourne and a few other towns with *Man and Superman*, *The Bastard Country* (renamed *Fire on the Wind* in mid-tour because of public objections to the title) and *Long Day's Journey into Night*. After a Christmas production of ELEANOR WITCOMBE's *Smugglers, Beware!* in 1960 there were changes in the permanent company of actors. The biggest success of the season was Brendan Behan's *The Hostage*. It had an extended season in Sydney and repeated its success in Melbourne. Hunt resigned and returned to England in late 1960.

Next year the company departed from the original concept. It left the 1500-seat Elizabethan Theatre, which had been too big for most plays and made audiences averaging about 800 a performance seem small. Lovejoy wanted the MINERVA THEATRE in Kings Cross but in the event a season was mounted at the PALACE THEATRE in the city centre. Different casts were engaged for each of three plays—Shelagh Delaney's *A Taste of Honey*, Tennessee Williams's *The Glass Menagerie* and Alan Seymour's THE ONE DAY OF THE YEAR. After directing Seymour's very successful play Lovejoy, who had accepted the offer of a Harkness Fellowship, left for the USA. This really ended the Trust Players, although there were productions in 1962—a financially unsuccessful season of three Australian plays in Sydney and Shaw's *Saint Joan* with ZOË CALDWELL at the second Adelaide Festival. After *St Joan* toured the eastern states the Trust did not embark upon drama production for many years. Reasons for the demise of the company included the lack of a suitable home base and the drain on the finances of touring, which had to be undertaken because all the states were contributing to the Trust. ❧*Ron Haddrick*

James Tucker

Dramatist. Born 1807 in Bristol (England). Sentenced to life transportation at Essex Assizes on 3 March 1826 for sending a threatening letter. Sent to Emu Plains penal settlement, March 1827. Worked in Colonial Architect's Office, Sydney, in 1830s. Received ticket of leave September 1840. Convicted of forgery 1844. Sent to Port Macquarie penal settlement. Died c.1888 in Sydney.

As a convict James Tucker saw and may have taken part in performances at the EMU PLAINS CONVICT THEATRE. He is the supposed author of *Ralph Rashleigh*, a novel that provides the most detailed description of the theatrical activities at Emu Plains in 1825–30. *Ralph Rashleigh* was written about 1845, when Tucker, after a few years on a ticket of leave in the Maitland district, was at the Port Macquarie penal settlement. He apparently also wrote plays which were performed there. A local farce, JEMMY GREEN IN AUSTRALIA, and a historical drama, *The Grahame's Vengeance*, survive in manuscript. Other local comedies have not survived, including *Makin' Money*, which satirised the rum regime in NSW, and *Who Built That Cosy Cottage?*, about the activities of a local magistrate, Major Innes. ❧*Elizabeth Webby*

published play
Jemmy Green in Australia (1966). Sydney: Angus and Robertson 1955.

further reading
TUCKER, JAMES. *Ralph Rashleigh*. Sydney: Angus and Robertson 1973.
SCOTT, PETER. James Tucker. *Australian Dictionary of Biography* 2. Melbourne University Press 1967.

Richard Tulloch

Director, dramatist. Born 1 September 1949 in Melbourne. Involved in student theatre at University of Melbourne. First professional engagement with Magic Mushroom Mime Troupe (Melbourne) 1975. Associate director of National Theatre Company (Perth) 1979–80. Artistic director of Toe Truck Theatre Company (Sydney) 1981–83. Awgie awards 1988 (*Hating Alison Ashley* and *Talking to Grandma While the World Goes By*). Lives in Sydney as free lance.

Richard Tulloch is best known as a specialist in issue-based plays for young people. Every major company presenting theatre for young people in Australia has professionally produced his plays since 1977. Many of his works have been produced overseas. Tulloch's accessible language and humour have gained him enormous popularity in schools. His use of the idiosyncrasies and vernacular of children's language, and strong commitment to social-justice themes also distinguish his work. ❧*Rachel Healy*

published plays
The Cocky of Bungaree (1978). Sydney: Currency Press 1990 (1982 revision).
Could Do Better (1989). Sydney: Currency Press (1992).
Face to Face. Sydney: Cambridge University Press 1987.
Hating Alison Ashley (1987). Melbourne: Penguin 1988.
If Only We Had a Cat. Sydney: Currency Press 1985 in *Learning From Life* (ed. John Lonie).
Space Demons (1989). Sydney: Currency Press 1993.
Year 9 Are Animals (1981). Melbourne: Heinemann 1983.

further reading
PAYNE HECKENBERG, PAMELA. Song and dance and the enemy outside—Richard Tulloch on the festival circuit. *Lowdown* 10/4 (Adelaide, August–September 1988).
SHORNE, PRISCILLA. Richard Tulloch in Britain—Boycotts broken, *Year Nine* sold. *Lowdown* 8/4 (September 1986).

Alexander Turner

Director, dramatist. Born 7 August 1906 in England. Came to Western Australia in 1925. Worked in banks in Geraldton, Meekatharra, Pingelly and Carnamah. Wrote poetry and plays, acted and directed in amateur theatre. Won West Australian Theatre Council contest with *Royal Mail* 1939. Began writing radio plays. Drama supervisor and Perth producer for ABC, 1946 to 1970s. Wrote script for Western Australian sesquicentennial *son et lumière* 1979. Died 12 April 1993.

After a dozen years working in country banks, Alexander Turner, a young Englishman, became 'more Westralian than the Westralians', not so much in loyalty to Western Australia as in imaginative observation of experience. He began writing in the west with verses which, according to the critic PAUL HASLUCK, 'caught the sleepy beauty of our dreaming hills, the romance of the white coast … the sort of wistfulness that is in the blue spring days.' The poet in Turner persisted when he began to write plays. In the small towns where he lived he either worked with an existing repertory group or started one. His three-act *Royal Mail*, which was presented in the huge HIS MAJESTY'S THEATRE in Perth in 1939, is a series of tableaux of life in a Murchison goldmining centre. It is keenly observed with humour of character and scene, strong atmosphere and effective vernacular but its story is less than compulsive. A shorter goldfields play, *The Golden Journey* is about passengers meeting at the Mullewa railway station. Train journeys always fascinated Turner. ❦Leslie Rees

published plays
Centurion. Perth: Paterson 1937 in *Hester Siding and Other Plays*.
The Golden Journey. Perth: Paterson 1944 in *Royal Mail and Other Plays*.
Not the Six Hundred. Perth: Paterson 1937 in *Hester Siding and Other Plays*.
The Old Allegiance. Perth: Paterson 1937 in *Hester Siding and Other Plays*.
One Hundred Guineas. Melbourne: Dramatists' Club of Australia 1936 in *Five Plays by Australians*. Perth: Paterson 1937 in *Hester Siding and Other Plays*.
Royal Mail (1939). Perth: Paterson 1944.

Geraldine Turner AM

Actor, dancer, singer. Born 23 June 1950 in Brisbane. Studied ballet with Phyllis Danaher. Made debut at nine in pantomime. Danced with Borovansky Ballet and Ballet Theatre of Queensland as child. Studied singing at Queensland Conservatorium. Has also performed in film, television and supper clubs. Green Room Award 1984 (Nancy in *Oliver!*). AM 1988.

Beauty and varied talents have enabled the clarion-voiced Geraldine Turner to encompass a wide range of performance. Her first adult successes came in musicals for the QUEENSLAND THEATRE COMPANY—*Oh, What a Lovely War!*, *THE LEGEND OF KING O'MALLEY*, *A Rum Do* and *Lock Up Your Daughters*, in which she scored a hit as Mrs Squeezum. In 1971 Turner first appeared for J. C. WILLIAMSON'S, as Betty Brown in *No! No! Nanette* with Cyd Charisse and Yvonne De Carlo. Since then she has performed in many musicals and sung with the Victoria State Opera in the operettas *La Belle Hélène* and *HMS Pinafore*. On the legitimate stage she has played Gertrude Lawrence in *Noël and Gertie*, and leading roles in George Darrell's *THE SUNNY SOUTH*, Dorothy Hewett's *Pandora's Cross*, JACK HIBBERD's *A Toast to Melba*, David Williamson's *DON'S PARTY*, Bernard Pomerance's *The Elephant Man*, Tom Stoppard's *Jumpers*, David Rudkin's *Ashes* and Noël Coward's *Present Laughter*. ❦Tony Sheldon

Twelfth Night Theatre Company

Professional dramatic company in Brisbane, founded by Rhoda Felgate as amateur society in January 1936. Professional from 1971. Began trading as TN Theatre Company 1979. Closed 1991. **venues** 1936–40 Empire Chambers and Princess Theatre. 1941–66 Albert Hall. 1956–69 Gowrie Hall. 1971–82 Twelfth Night Complex, Bowen Hills. 1982–85 former church at 112 Brookes Street, Fortitude Valley. 1986–91 Princess Theatre. **directors** 1936–61 Rhoda Felgate. 1962–77 Joan Whalley. 1978 Bill Redmond. 1979–80 John Milson. 1981–82 Bryan Nason. 1982–87 Rod Wissler. 1988–91 Rick Billinghurst. **first production** *Touch Wood* by C. L. Anthony, 12 March 1936, Empire Chambers. Director: Rhoda Felgate. Cast: Elsa Brooks, Ludovick Gordon, Tom McMinn, Babette Stephens. **landmark productions** *A House is Built* by Eunice Hanger, 10 November 1949. *The Ham Funeral* by Patrick White, 1962. *Norm and Ahmed* by Alex Buzo, April 1969. **last production** *After Dinner* by Andrew Bovell, 1991.

Twelfth Night trained actors and carried out a consistent development policy over more than 50 years, during which it made an effective transition from amateur to professional status. The founders were performers who were keen to develop their craft, including actors from the BRISBANE REPERTORY THEATRE SOCIETY. The new company gained a name and a mnemonic performance date when the inaugural meeting adopted a suggestion by Tom Stephens that it perform on the twelfth night of each month. The aims and objectives of Twelfth Night were not formal until 1945, when the first constitution of the company was accepted. This document noted the ideals that Twelfth Night had held since its earliest days. It wanted to provide an avenue for a small group of people to study and train in theatrical practice. Membership was restricted to maximise the opportunities for each actor to perform, though it grew from 40 to 60 in the first decade. A group of speech teachers was invited to form a speech and drama school, each with her own paying pupils. In 1938 Elsie Brooks was appointed as Felgate's assistant producer and teacher. From 1948 the studio and club rooms were in a large converted house at 51 Wickham Terrace.

The first play, largely cast from members of Brisbane Repertory, was presented at the Empire Chambers. 'When some more convenient and settled place of abode is found', wrote the *Telegraph* reviewer, 'great things may be expected on the 12th evening of each month'. Most of Twelfth Night's early productions were presented in the building that housed RHODA FELGATE's Speech and Drama studio. Many were English drawing-room comedies like Noël Coward's *Hay Fever* or classics such as *Twelfth Night*. The group's 1937 production of *Twelfth Night* at the Princess

Theatre, with LORNA FORBES playing Olivia, was notable. A photograph of Felgate's protégé Stanley Hildebrandt as Feste in this performance became the company's logotype. Hildebrandt later joined the Old Vic company in London.

From 1950, Brisbane audiences 'began to form a taste for outrageous theatregoing', Roger Covell observed in 1957. By 1954 Twelfth Night was able to announce that its two most successful productions of the season had been verse plays: Fry's *The Lady's Not for Burning* and T. S. Eliot's *The Cocktail Party*. Covell particularly admired the Fry and Eliot plays and Sean O'Casey's *Juno and the Paycock* when he declared in the *Sunday Mail* that Twelfth Night had 'established its right to be considered the most enterprising of the three larger groups [in Brisbane] with as a fine selection of plays as one could desire'.

Joan Whalley, a young teacher from Charters Towers (Qld) joined Twelfth Night as a speech teacher and drama student in 1951. Two years later Twelfth Night set up Brisbane's first comprehensive drama school, covering directing and design as well as acting in a one-week course. Twelfth Night was more committed to ideas than design, possibly because it had close links with the University of Queensland throughout the 1950s and 1960s. In 1956 the group acquired Gowrie Hall at 39 Wickham Terrace, which became a theatre seating 112, and Whalley returned from 15 months' study overseas to add fresh skills to the work and taste for the tough new British drama. Felgate retired and Whalley, after two years' teaching at the NATIONAL INSTITUTE OF DRAMATIC ART in Sydney, returned as director. She received an honorarium but, like Felgate, supported herself by teaching and examining. In 1965 Whalley, while remaining in the group of private teachers, established fee-paying classes in theatrecraft for young people. Income from this School of Speech and Drama helped to defray the costs of operating the group in its building.

Subsidies from state
The group conducted a full annual program of classics and modern work and encouraged a variety of directors. It expanded beyond Gowrie Hall and in 1966 it announced plans for a new theatre. Whalley and her supporters gained the first subsidy in Queensland—a state government dollar-for-dollar grant up to $100 000, and tax deductibility for donors. Twelfth Night was able to claim the whole $100 000 by dint of a bank guarantee from a brewing company, which was interested in supplying a licensed club to the new Twelfth Night Complex. This building opened at a cost of $350 000, and the group had a debt of $186 000.

Furthermore, to gain access to federal government funds—newly available through the Australian Council for the Arts—for its artistic program the group became professional in 1971. Volunteer labour and community support then became less forthcoming, while capital debts and operating costs mounted. The federal and Queensland governments devised a rescue and the Twelfth Night Complex was handed over to a state-appointed trust in 1977. The group, as principal tenant, was still saddled with an operating deficit of $70 000. Joan Whalley, burnt out, had resigned, and it was decided to pay out the remaining members of the company and go black for six months.

In 1978 Bill Redmond, charged with restoring profitability, began presenting boulevard plays to attract larger audiences. Late in the year a stormy meeting of members pushed for a more adventurous artistic policy and the incoming board entrusted this to John Milson in 1979. Relations with the building trust became strained meanwhile and the company sought less expensive venues. To assert an identity deriving from Milson's more 'alternative' productions and separate from the Twelfth Night Theatre Complex, it began trading as TN Theatre Company.

The company gradually entered an arrangement with the drama program at the Brisbane College of Advanced Education, which gave it access to campus offices and facilities, including a performance space at 112 Brookes Street, Fortitude Valley. Students at the college gained practical experience with the company. Under Bryan Nason's careful economic management and audience-oriented production style, even with classics, the company became more financially secure and artistically confident. Rod Wissler built on this foundation with a five-year plan of development that concentrated on local actors, designers, technicians, staff and, to a lesser extent, playwrights. TN exhibited 'an exuberance that everyone should have a taste of', wrote Verity Masters in the *Australian* in 1983.

The company maintained involvement in training by formalising its relationship with the college, now the Queensland University of Technology, and by operating a group of young professional apprentices called TN2. This, like the parent company, began touring widely beyond Brisbane. The Fortitude Valley premises, leased by TN, were becoming unsuitable and after the building was sold to a developer the company moved to the old Princess Theatre in 1986. This entailed financial burdens but the initial signs were good. In 1988, when Rick Billinghurst became artistic director, Brisbane was the site of World Expo. This drained patrons from TN and dragged it into deficit—and permanently transformed the Brisbane scene. TN was forced into cost-cutting—production outlays sank from $579 000 in 1988 to $277 000 in 1989—that constrained artistic achievement. Critics and public began to think that TN had lost its spark. At the same time an arts bureaucracy appointed by a new Labor state government was developing new systems and policies. There was a prevailing belief that under the old National Party regime the performing arts, and mainstream theatre companies in particular, had been privileged for many years. TN fought a losing battle to retain the subsidies that were essential to its survival.

Plays produced in the company's last decade included *The Choir* by Errol Bray in 1981, *Cloud Nine* by Caryl Churchill in 1982, *Accidental Death of an Anarchist* by Dario Fo in 1984, *The Dining Room* by A. R. Gurney jnr in 1985, *Summer* by Edward Bond in 1986, *Tartuffe* by Molière in 1987, *Hedda Gabler* by Henrik Ibsen in 1988, *Speed the Plow* by David Mamet in 1990 and *Cho Cho San* by Daniel Keene in 1991. Directors, in addition to the artistic directors, included Robert Arthur and Sean Mee. Designers included David Bell, Maria Cleary, Bill Haycock and James Maclean. Among the actors were Robert Arthur, Jennifer Blocksidge, Jennifer Flowers, Eugene Gilfedder, Sean Mee, Anthony Phelan, Kaye Stephenson and Rod Wissler. Many people who worked with Twelfth Night Theatre in earlier years have become well-known in professional theatre and in film and television, including Carol Burns, Michael Caton, RODNEY FISHER, Shane Porteous, BABETTE STEPHENS, Jack

Thompson, Sigrid Thornton and Rowena Wallace. ❖*Don Batchelor and Delyse Anthony*

further reading
ANTHONY, DELYSE. The early history of Twelfth Night Theatre, 1936–1946. University of Queensland honours thesis 1990.
BATCHELOR, DON (ed.) *Twelfth Night—The morning after.* Brisbane: Boolarong 1986.
RADBOURNE, JENNIFER. Little Theatre—Its development since World War II in Australia, with particular reference to Queensland. University of Queensland masters thesis 1978.

reference
The Fryer Library of the University of Queensland has 34 volumes of memorabilia collected by Rhoda Felgate, Gwen Harris and Gwen Wheeler 1936–70.

2 Till 5 Youth Theatre

Youth-theatre co-operative in Newcastle (NSW), founded in 1976 by Mike Foster and Barney Langford. **artistic director** Barney Langford 1989–.

Two primary-school teachers, Mike Foster and Barney Langford, founded this vigorous youth-theatre company as a weekly extracurricular drama group that met from '2 till 5' on Saturday afternoons. Langford, full-time artistic director and administrator from 1989, says creating theatre 'gives young people the opportunity to work through and express their thoughts and ideas. The company exists to facilitate this progress.' The usual method of work is to develop a text collectively in workshops and perform it for an audience. The company also presents new plays by young playwrights. Ninety or so participants, aged eight to 25 years, attend weekly theatre workshops, led by either Langford or part-time professional tutors.

The company is a registered co-operative and all members are required to become shareholders in it. Most of the shareholders are young people. There are no auditions. The company receives funds from the performing-arts board of the AUSTRALIA COUNCIL and the NSW Ministry for the Arts. It relies for additional income on workshop fees (waived for needy families), box office and consultancy services to schools and community groups. ❖*Pamela Payne*

John Unicomb

Actor, director, manager. Born 4 July 1928 in NSW. Began acting as child on ABC radio. Acted in England 1951–58. Acted for Old Tote Theatre Company and Music Hall Theatre Restaurant in Sydney 1958–70. Stage, film, radio, television work on return to Australia. Business manager of Theatre Royal, Hobart, 1970. Executive director of Tasmanian Theatre Company 1971–84. Artistic director of Theatre Royal Management Board 1987–94. National Critics' Circle Award for Tasmania 1976.

Since 1970 John Unicomb has been associated with the THEATRE ROYAL in Hobart, except during the administration of the short-lived Tasmanian Theatre Trust. He oversaw the creation of the Tasmanian Theatre Company, which was initially the resident company at the Theatre Royal but became largely an entrepreneur. He has been closely linked with the maintenance of the historic theatre and the development of its modern facilities, including the Backstage Theatre. His use of mime, sound and lighting in directing a production of Peter Shaffer's *Equus* in 1975 brought him the National Critics' Circle Award. ❖*Gillian Winter*

Universities

Students' amateur dramatic groups—such as the SYDNEY UNIVERSITY DRAMATIC SOCIETY, founded in 1889—were the first significant contribution of Australia's universities to the theatre. Rapid turnover of membership made these groups subject to frequent shifts of policy and unreliable standards, but by the early 20th century many of them were showing the influence of the art-theatre movement. However fitfully, they were becoming bastions of classical and contemporary 'serious' drama. They were a significant wing of the amateur theatre movement, which was virtually the only source of high-culture theatre Australians had from the 1930s until the 1950s, since the professional stage was almost entirely given over to boulevard entertainment.

The student societies were frequently guided—and sometimes uncomfortably dominated—by staff members, who brought experience and continuity to them. Examples are MAY HOLLINWORTH at the University of Sydney, Gerry Stables at the University of Queensland, and JEANA BRADLEY at the University of Western Australia. In addition to students' groups, some tertiary institutions spawned loosely associated societies made up of students, ex-students, staff and 'friends', which often pursued art-theatre policies. The classic example is ADELAIDE REPERTORY THEATRE, which was the most influential company in South Australia up to the 1920s. When launched by BRYCESON TREHARNE at the Elder Conservatorium and the University of Adelaide it was remarkably adventurous, but it gradually became more cautious and severed its tenuous links with the university. In 1938 the ADELAIDE UNIVERSITY THEATRE GUILD emerged in similar style, gaining not only access to university venues but also financial support from the university. The guild achieved national prominence in the 1960s by producing plays by PATRICK WHITE. Similar in style, though without the same influence, were the TIN ALLEY PLAYERS, co-founded by KEITH MACARTNEY at the University of Melbourne.

Hopes of state support

When subsidised professional theatre emerged in state capitals in the 1960s some university-linked groups hoped to become the basis for a state company. The Adelaide University Theatre Guild received funding from the AUSTRALIAN ELIZABETHAN THEATRE TRUST for several productions but was bypassed when the South Australian Theatre Company was founded in 1965. In Brisbane, the COLLEGE PLAYERS, a University of Queensland offshoot, were given the privilege of inaugurating the new SGIO Theatre but saw themselves ignored in the setting up of the QUEENSLAND THEATRE COMPANY, which made the SGIO its home.

Individual graduates were initially no luckier than the university-related groups. The new companies recruited mainly from existing commercial and semiprofessional theatres. The proportion of former students was low, though several, including the young BARRY HUMPHRIES, made early appearances with the Union Theatre Repertory Company in Melbourne. Moreover, approaches to the University of Melbourne and then the University of Sydney to house a national training school for the theatre arts met with chilly responses, apparently on the grounds that such studies were not sufficiently academic. It was left to the parvenu University of NSW to take up the project and become the home of the NATIONAL INSTITUTE OF DRAMATIC ART in 1958. But although it was on the campus, and received support from the university, NIDA remained a separate institution, awarding its own diplomas.

The universities proved willing patrons of theatre, however. Many of them had underused theatres, or halls that could be converted to theatres. In addition, the more adventurous universities offered cash grants, as well as substantial support in kind. The University of Melbourne provided the earliest and most spectacularly successful example. In 1953 it set up the Union Theatre Repertory Company, which in 1968 became the MELBOURNE THEATRE COMPANY. This remains affiliated with the university even though it no longer performs on the campus.

In Sydney, after several abortive experiments, the Trust persuaded the University of NSW to convert an old tin shed into a home for the OLD TOTE THEATRE COMPANY. This was launched in 1963 and became Sydney's leading company for more than a decade. It later moved to another theatre provided by the university on the campus, the Parade Theatre. The university also helped with financial grants and general assistance in the establishment of the JANE STREET THEATRE for Australian plays.

University patronage has continued in various forms. The University of Wollongong has appointed the director of THEATRE SOUTH to its staff, thus freeing the company from the need to provide the director's salary. The RIVERINA THEATRE COMPANY has established a warm relationship with the Wagga Wagga (NSW) campus of Charles Sturt University. A tangible sign of this is the new Playhouse in the city centre, built partly with university funds and used by the company and by students.

The campus of the University of Western Australia holds perhaps the most splendid and varied collection of theatres in Australia. These are little used by the university itself but have become a focus for activities during the FESTIVAL OF PERTH, which was founded in 1953 under the university's Adult Education Board for students at its annual summer school. It also arose from the UNIVERSITY DRAMATIC SOCIETY'S tradition since 1948 of giving an open-air summer season in the university's Sunken Garden Theatre, and the creation of the Somerville Auditorium, a memorial 'cathedral of pines', for concerts and films. The NEW FORTUNE THEATRE, a reconstruction of an Elizabethan theatre, was opened in 1964 for Shakespeare's quadricentenary. It has housed innovative Shakespearean productions and the premiere of Dorothy Hewett's THE CHAPEL PERILOUS (1971).

The first phase of university support for subsidised theatre largely comprised one institution giving financial and administrative assistance to another, ignoring to some extent the ideas, talents and hopes of the staff and students. On the whole the new professional companies pursued artistically cautious and Anglocentric policies, but by the late 1960s pressure for stylistic innovation and Australian content was building. The American alternative-theatre movement and off-off-Broadway provided a model, and fringe companies emerged across Australia. Many of them sprang out of undergraduate societies or were largely staffed by students and former students. The University of Melbourne and later Monash University contributed substantially to the flowering at the LA MAMA THEATRE and the development of the AUSTRALIAN PERFORMING GROUP. Former members of the Sydney University Dramatic Society established the NIMROD THEATRE COMPANY. In Adelaide, TROUPE was founded largely by products of Salisbury Teachers' College, and in Brisbane activists from the University of Queensland created the POPULAR THEATRE TROUPE.

Training at universities

This wave of innovation was receding by the late 1970s but many of its leading figures had joined the theatrical establishment. Among those who moved from university through the fringe to the mainstream, were such actors, directors and writers as JOHN BELL, ALEX BUZO, JOHN GADEN, MAX GILLIES, DOROTHY HEWETT, JACK HIBBERD, AARNE NEEME and DAVID WILLIAMSON. The universities have continued to feed graduates into the mainstream—often through an apprenticeship in the somewhat attenuated fringe, as names such as NEIL ARMFIELD, REX CRAMPHORN, MICHAEL GOW, BRIAN THOMSON, CHRIS WESTWOOD and RICHARD WHERRETT attest. But as NIDA, the VICTORIAN COLLEGE OF THE ARTS and the WESTERN AUSTRALIAN ACADEMY OF PERFORMING ARTS have become more firmly established, an increasing percentage of matriculants with a passion for theatre have gone directly to those institutions, bypassing the traditional universities.

If the universities were nervous about accepting a training school on campus they were similarly uneasy about setting up drama studies as an academic discipline. Again the University of NSW led the way. When ROBERT QUENTIN was appointed foundation head of NIDA, the university concurrently appointed him senior lecturer in the school of English. Then he was made associate professor, heading an independent department of drama and finally, in 1964, professor at the head of a fully fledged school of drama. Partly for academic respectability and partly to avoid confusion with NIDA, Quentin virtually excluded practical work from his courses, and gave prominence to study of the dramatic literatures of many cultures.

In 1967 another new university, Flinders University in Adelaide, established a drama discipline under WAL CHERRY, a young Australian director, who was able to push a different line. From the beginning he insisted on the importance of practical work and focused his theoretical teaching on a few areas of special interest, such as Brechtian theatre. By the late 1970s the University of NSW had modified its position and was providing an increasing amount of practical work as well as a rich diversity of theoretical subjects. But by that time Flinders had taken its experiments a stage further. In 1973 it set up a professional training school, the Drama Centre, alongside its liberal arts course. Resulting whispers about erosion of academic standards were one of the causes of a university investigation of drama at Flinders in 1981, but the discipline was vindicated and continued on its path.

In the meantime new departments had been established at the University of Newcastle (NSW), the University of New England in Armidale (NSW), Deakin University in Geelong (Vic.), and Murdoch University in Perth. All adopted positions between the two existing institutions, mixing practical and theoretical work, but did not claim to be providing professional theatre training. Other models emerged, embodying a mixture of theory and practice. There were drama sections within the English departments at Macquarie University in Sydney and the University of Queensland in Brisbane. At the Universities of Adelaide and Melbourne theatre professionals collaborated with academics from music and language departments in free-floating interdisciplinary drama subjects.

At the University of Sydney in the 1980s the designer Derek Nicholson ran the Theatre Workshop in the SEYMOUR THEATRE CENTRE as a service unit for staff and students in arts, music and architecture. Before the PERFORMANCE SPACE opened in 1983 the workshop provided a space for experimental groups and gave many, such as ENTR'ACTE, their first chance to perform in a professional venue. It has been transformed into a research-based academic unit, the Performance Studies Centre. At the Australian National University in CANBERRA the drama program—a liberal arts degree course covering theatre history, theory and practice—set up a drama company in 1990. Now called Paper Moon, it produces three or four plays a year, performed by professional and student actors, cast by open audition.

University drama departments have been strongly influenced by language and literature departments, notably English. In colleges of advanced education the initiative for drama and theatre studies often came from education departments, which introduced drama as a general teaching method or trained drama teachers for schools. The general brief of the colleges—to be more practical and vocational than the universities—enabled them to avoid much of the suspicion that attached to drama studies in the universities. It also enabled an increasing number, such as the Nepean and Kelvin Grove Colleges of Advanced Education, to move towards offering professional or semi-professional training for the theatre. Given the rampant unemployment among Australian actors, this proliferation of training courses could have been a matter of concern, though the Botsman Report of 1985, which addressed the issue, seemed undisturbed.

In 1988 conversion of colleges and institutes into universities, or their absorption into existing universities, became federal government policy. In consequence, the university system now contains a plethora of professional training programs as well as liberal arts courses. Whether professional training sits comfortably in university structures and funding patterns, is a moot point, but some units, such as the WESTERN AUSTRALIAN ACADEMY OF PERFORMING ARTS, at Edith Cowan University, have had impressive results. NIDA escaped the amalgamation fever and remains autonomous, funded by a one-line entry in the federal budget, but in the new climate even it has had to contemplate raising its diplomas to degree status. ❦*Rob Jordan*

University Dramatic Society
Amateur dramatic society in Perth, founded in 1917.

Students in Perth, conscious of their cultural responsibility in Australia's most isolated capital, have over substantial periods set standards of taste and professionalism in theatrical activity. The University Dramatic Society began to provide a generally intelligent and eclectic repertoire of recreational drama six years after the University of Western Australia was founded. The society performed its first play on 5 October 1917, when it had 22 members and Edward Shann, professor of history and economics, as its mentor, director and stage manager. Activities expanded after the First World War. There were frequent play-readings and a production or two a year at the Perth Town Hall, the Assembly Hall in Pier Street and the Hibernian Hall in Murray Street. The choice of dramatists—J. M. Barrie, A. A. Milne, George Bernard Shaw and Oscar Wilde—caused the drama critic of the university magazine, *The Black Swan*, to urge Eugene O'Neill, August Strindberg and Shakespeare. In the late 1920s there was a clash of opinion—whether to concentrate on classic plays probably never before seen in Perth, or to avoid pretentiousness and go after light successes of the day. Compromise resulted in a staging of the morality play *Everyman* and Shaw's one-act *The Dark Lady of the Sonnets*. In another vein, LESLIE REES directed an evening of Lady Gregory, J. M. Synge and W. B. Yeats.

By the late 1930s the society had gone into decline and it no longer existed when DOROTHY HEWETT arrived at the university in 1941. She promptly organised a student production of her own first play, *Time Flits Away, Lady* and with others resuscitated the society in the following year. Alan Trevor, a respected professional, was invited to direct Sutton Vane's *Outward Bound*, and 1943 saw a remarkably eclectic repertoire, including William Saroyan's fantasy *Across the Board on Tomorrow Morning*, Clifford Odets's *Waiting for Lefty*, Wilde's *Salome* with a sensational performance by JACQUELINE KOTT, and commercial fare such as the Hollywood satire *Boy Meets Girl*, which toured local military camps. Activity increased after 1945, largely because of exservicepeople studying at the university, who brought a new maturity to student theatre. The university's campus had been at suburban Nedlands since 1932 but most productions were still given in city venues. There was a breakthrough in 1948, when Jeana Tweedie (later JEANA BRADLEY) of the university's English department directed a revelatory production of Sophocles's *Oedipus Rex* in the Sunken Garden. It enraptured audiences and drew approbation from Laurence Olivier and Vivien Leigh, who were visiting Perth with the OLD VIC THEATRE COMPANY.

Tweedie was a mainstay of university drama for many years, directing an extraordinary repertoire that extended from Shakespeare through such rarities as John Webster's *The Duchess of Malfi* (1614) and Thomas Middleton and William Rowley's *The Changeling* (1622) to Henrik Ibsen and Bertolt Brecht. Many outstanding actors appeared at the university—FAITH CLAYTON, Patricia Skevington and NEVILLE TEEDE are but three.

As interstate travel again became possible after 1945, Intervarsity Drama Festivals enabled student groups to see each other's work and the society often distinguished itself. More organisations became involved in dramatic activity at the university after the war—foreign-language clubs, the Graduate Dramatic Society, Bankside, Swan Players, the Octagon Theatre Company and the long-established St George's College Dramatic Society, latterly in collaboration with the newly-founded St Catherine's College. The popularity of the annual summer classics in the Sunken Garden Theatre from 1948 contributed to the initiative that began the FESTIVAL OF PERTH and university productions were included from the start. ❦*Maurice Jones*

further reading
ALEXANDER, FRED. *Campus at Crawley*. Melbourne: Cheshire 1963.

Unley Youth Theatre

Youth-theatre company in Adelaide, founded in 1981 by Unley City Council. **artistic director** Kim Hanna.

With 140 members aged between six and 25, Unley Youth Theatre operates ten workshops a week, stages public productions and administers a young playwrights' season, which was instituted by TROUPE. The Unley City Council provides premises for a peppercorn rental. The company began as a pilot project of the council's community services department, overseen by the South Australian Youth Performing Arts Council. ❦*Murray Bramwell*

John Upton

Playwright. Born 23 August 1939 in Sydney. First play *The Mad Scene* workshopped at Australian National Playwrights' Conference 1974. Studied writing at Australian Film and Television School (Sydney) 1978. Joint winner of New Theatre's 50th anniversary play competition with *Waiting for Rupert Murdoch* 1982. Awgie for best new play for *Machiavelli, Machiavelli* 1985. Won Australian Elizabethan Theatre Trust bicentennial play competition with *Hordes from the South* 1988. Won Australian Writers' Theatre play competition with *Breach of Trust* 1992.

John Upton is a former country-town journalist with skills that soon took him to a career in television and an interest in grassroots politics that has emerged strongly in his themes. His most frequently performed stage work is *The Warhorse*, a comedy about Labor Party pre-selection branch politics. It was first performed by the King O'Malley Theatre Company at the Stables Theatre in Sydney with WILLIE FENNELL in the title-role. In Upton's award-winning monodrama *Machiavelli, Machiavelli* RUTH CRACKNELL created the role of a female mayor who, forced out of office after 30 years, finds another route to power. *Hordes from the South*, which sees in Australian men's notorious sex tours of the Philippines a reversal of the historical fear of Asian invasion, remains unperformed. Upton's other plays include *The Pirates of Pal Mal* (1977), a satirical revue that he wrote with MONA BRAND for NEW THEATRE. ❦*Katharine Brisbane*

published plays
Machiavelli, Machiavelli (1984). Melbourne: Yackandandah 1986.
The Warhorse (1980). Melbourne: Yackandandah 1987.

Vanbrugh–Boucicault Company

In 1901 Irene Vanbrugh, one of the most talented and charming actors on the London stage, and the actor and director DION BOUCICAULT JNR married and formed a professional partnership as well. They had first met in Australia, when Vanbrugh was touring with JOHN L. TOOLE in 1890–91 and Boucicault was staging fine productions of contemporary plays in the BROUGH–BOUCICAULT COMEDY COMPANY. From 1901 to 1915 the Vanbrugh–Boucicault Company succeeded in London at the Duke of York's Theatre. Vanbrugh was leading lady and Boucicault directed and acted. In 1916 he took over management of the New Theatre, where they continued production.

After a temporary retirement caused by illness, in 1923 Boucicault formed a touring company with Vanbrugh, under the aegis of J. C. WILLIAMSON'S, and set off for Australia via South Africa with plays by London's leading popular playwrights. The couple opened in Melbourne in November 1923 with A. A. Milne's *The Truth About Blayds* and followed it with Arthur Wing Pinero's *Trelawney of the Wells*, *The Second Mrs Tanqueray* and *His House in Order*, and Frederick Lonsdale's *Aren't We All?* with J. M. Barrie's *The Will* and *Half an Hour* alternating as curtainraiser. They drew large houses and praise for their grace and skill in light comedy. These triumphs were repeated in Sydney in 1924 and the tour extended well into 1925. It was January 1926 before the company returned to London.

In January 1928 it reappeared in Australia for Williamson's. Somerset Maugham's *The Letter* opened the tour in Melbourne, followed by Charles Openshaw's *All the King's Horses* and Lonsdale's delicious comedy *On Approval*. Boucicault, directing and sharing the male leads with Norman McKinnel, and Vanbrugh were more popular than ever. 'They could lift the most mediocre play out of the doldrums by their brilliance', said Johnny Farrell, long-time advance manager for J. C. Williamson's. LOUIS ESSON, drama critic of the *Triad* magazine, praised Vanbrugh's versatility and her playing in *Belinda* in Sydney in May. Boucicault died soon after returning to London in 1929. Vanbrugh continued her distinguished career. She was created a dame in 1941 and died in 1949. ❦*Lynne Murphy*

Olga Varona

Aerialist. Born 18 June 1920 at Roma (Qld). Made stage debut at Theatre Royal, Brisbane, 13 July 1934. Went to London with husband Archie Collins, comedian, 1946. Appeared at the Palladium in November 1947. Retired in Australia after 30 years on stage.

Billed as 'Australia's Queen of the Air', Olga Varona played leading variety theatres in an aerial act, first with her two sisters and later with her comedian husband as Olga Varona and Partner. Varona's 'routines on the trapeze and rope were akin to classical ballet performances synchronised to the delightful Strauss waltzes', VALANTYNE NAPIER writes. 'The timing, dress and setting for her act illustrated the difference between the sophisticated presentation required in Variety and the usual circus act'. ❦*Victoria Chance*

The Venetian Twins

Musical comedy. **book and lyrics** Nick Enright, from *I due gemelli veneziani*, play by Carlo Goldoni. **music** Terence Clarke. **premiere** 26 October 1979, Sydney Opera House, by Nimrod Theatre Company. **cast** Valerie Bader, Annie Byron, Jon Ewing, Drew Forsythe, John Frawley, Barry Lovett, Jennifer McGregor, John McTernan, Tony Sheldon, Tony Taylor. **designer** Stephen Curtis. **director** John Bell.

The Venetian Twins, produced in most large Australian cities, is a knockabout, irreverent musical adaptation of Carlo Goldoni's *commedia dell'arte*, in which one actor plays identical twins. When NICK ENRIGHT suggested a translation of the Italian classic to JOHN BELL, artistic director of the Nimrod Theatre Company, it seemed an ideal vehicle for the comic talents of DREW FORSYTHE. At first TERENCE CLARKE considered composing a few scattered songs influenced by 19th-century opera as 'divertissements', but the show soon evolved into a fully fledged musical, encompassing styles from soft-shoe to Kurt Weill pastiche. The setting is Verona but the style is unmistakably Australian. The twins Zanetto and Tonino, separated since childhood, arrive in Verona at the same time. Zanetto, a slow-witted bumpkin, has come to marry the judge's daughter. Tonino, dashing and brave, is in search of his beloved Beatrice. Mistaken identity and interventions by unscrupulous rivals ensure that chaos reigns until the final curtain, when Zanetto is poisoned, the judge's daughter is revealed as the twins' long-lost sister, and Tonino and Beatrice are reunited. Witty designs, canny direction and a talented zany cast brought the romp irresistibly to life. An extensive national tour in 1981 followed the Sydney season. ❦*Tony Sheldon*

Barbara Vernon

Dramatist. Born 25 July 1916 at Inverell (NSW). Served in Women's Auxiliary Air Force. Studied arts at University of Queensland. Became announcer at radio 2NZ Inverell. Joined ABC radio in Sydney as play reader 1960. Became ABC television scriptwriter after five years. Died 1978.

While Barbara Vernon was a radio announcer in Inverell she staged plays in the town hall, including her own *The Passionate Pianist*, *The Naked Possum* and *The Multi-Coloured Umbrella*. The last came second to Richard Beynon's THE SHIFTING HEART in a play competition held by the Journalists' Club in Sydney in 1956. *The Multi-Coloured Umbrella* is part of the saga of the Donnellys, the family of a selfmade bookmaker, previously shown in *The Passionate Pianist*. In the later play tensions erupt violently when there is conflict over ethics, family loyalty and social status. The play is significant in the origins of Australian realist drama. Identifiable Australian types, mostly working class, are presented as worthy of attention and dignity, and their actions, though not always condoned, are treated with respect. Vernon's concern with plot and action, combined with vigorously egalitarian characters, contributed to the success of *Bellbird*, a long-running serial of country-town life that she originated on ABC television. ❦*Susan Hogan*

published play
The Multi-Coloured Umbrella (1957). In *Theatregoer* (Sydney) February–April 1961.

further reading
QUIRK, S. Barbara Vernon. *200 Australian Women* (ed. Heather Radi) Sydney: Women's Redress Press 1988.
Australian 18 April 1978
Sydney Morning Herald 18 April 1978

Howard Vernon

Actor, manager, singer. Born 1845 in Melbourne. Began career as professional concert singer. Sang in opera and operetta. Acted in plays. Founded companies which toured extensively both in Australia and Asia. Married Vinia de Loitte, singer. Retired 1914. Died 27 July 1921 in Melbourne.

During a long career on the stage Howard Vernon became one of Australia's most popular performers, particularly from 1880 to 1906. His popularity soared during the 1880s, when he played leading roles in the first Australian productions of four GILBERT AND SULLIVAN operettas—Ko-Ko in *The Mikado* in 1885, Bunthorne in *Patience* in 1885, Shadbolt in *The Yeomen of the Guard* in 1889 and the Grand Inquisitor in *The Gondoliers* in 1890. He was particularly highly regarded as Ko-Ko and as the Lord Chancellor in *Iolanthe*. He also performed baritone roles in other productions and revivals. He set standards for Gilbert and Sullivan productions which were acclaimed by fellow performers, many of whom, including the conductor Alfred Cellier, had worked in the original London productions. Vernon's popularity was based on his extraordinary range of abilities which ranged from singing in opera through virtually all other vocal styles to straight and comic acting. As an actor Vernon became famous for his work in light comedies as well as many Shakespeare plays. ❦*Philip Lawton*

further reading
DE LOITTE, VINIA. *Gilbert and Sullivan in Australia*. Sydney: privately published 1933.
MASLEN, JOAN. Howard Vernon. *Australian Dictionary of Biography* 12. Melbourne University Press 1990.
Bulletin 4 August 1921.
Sydney Morning Herald 27 July 1921.

Lou Vernon

Actor. Born 1888, in Brisbane. Played many roles in drama, comedy and musicals for J. C. Williamson's before and during 1920s. Thereafter primarily radio actor, but at Minerva Theatre (Sydney) in 1940s. John Alden Company 1951. Died December 1971 in Sydney.

One of the best-loved actors of his time, Lou Vernon inspired such respect that many young actors, including PETER FINCH, turned to him for guidance. By the 1920s Vernon was already a veteran of drama, comedy, operetta and vaudeville. In 1926 and 1928 he played Emile La Flamme in the J. C. WILLIAMSON'S production of the operetta *Rose-Marie*. Parts in *Show Boat* and *Princess Charming* followed. From 1935 Vernon was primarily a leading radio actor, first with the BSA Players and the ABC. He was a fine character actor on radio and as he aged he grew in stature as a stage actor. During the 1940s he made numerous appearances in plays at the MINERVA THEATRE. His leading roles in Eugene O'Neill's *Ah, Wilderness!* and J. B. Priestley's *An Inspector Calls* were outstanding.

Perhaps his most memorable stage role was the old sea captain Chris Christopherson in O'Neill's *Anna Christie*, for the JOHN ALDEN COMPANY in 1951. A Sydney newspaper critic, Tom Breen wrote of this production: 'The realism of this sad savage story of the New York waterfront requires a special quality of truthful acting. The players etched this quality with indelible skill. ... Lou Vernon's Chris will live long in the memory as a piece of consummate acting.' ❦*Richard Lane*

Leslie Victor

English actor *c*.1880–*c*.1953. Toured Australia in *The Liars* by Henry Arthur Jones 1898; Julius Knight Company 1902, 1907–11, 1913–16; with Marie Tempest 1917; Vanbrugh–Boucicault Company 1926.

Leslie Victor was a beloved supporting player of unique excellence. In drama his naturalness was never less than elegant and incisive, and in comedy his timing was perfection. Though frequently cast as servants or parsons, he never gave a stock performance. Each character was an individual study built up with fine detail and subtlety. He settled in Australia after his 1902 tour with JULIUS KNIGHT and appeared as a featured player on Knight's 1907–11 and

1913–16 tours. The *Triad* warmly praised Victor's performances with Basil Radford in three Ben Travers farces in 1928. In the 1940s he had such a solid run at the Minerva Theatre in Sydney that WHITEHALL THEATRICAL PRODUCTIONS began to note in the programs that it felt unable to put on a play without him.

A high spot of Victor's later career was in Noël Coward's *Family Album*, starring MADGE ELLIOTT and CYRIL RITCHARD in Sydney in 1946. Abandoning the frosty calm of the perfect family retainer, he capered tipsily on a table as the curtain fell. ❦*Lynne Murphy*

Victorian Arts Centre

Performing-arts centre in St Kilda Road, Melbourne. Architect: Roy Grounds. **Melbourne Concert Hall**, opened 6 November 1982. Theatres complex includes **State Theatre** opened 12 May 1984, seating 2000; **Playhouse** opened 8 May 1984, seating 809; and **George Fairfax Studio** opened 4 May 1984, seating 250–400.

The largest and most comprehensive arts centre in Australia, the Victorian Arts Centre stands on a site that has been a centre of entertainment since circuses began to perform there in tents in 1870. From 1901 to 1953 circuses performed in permanent buildings, including the Olympia, which was leased as Melbourne's largest cinema in 1911. A dance hall, an ice rink and the MELBOURNE REPERTORY THEATRE COMPANY's Playhouse Theatre were also on this 4·5 hectare site and its surroundings, across the Yarra River from the Flinders Street railway station. In 1943 a committee of architects appointed by the Victorian government proposed that the site be reserved for a new art gallery, including an auditorium to hold 1000 persons, to be built after the Second World War. In 1945 the government passed an act to reserve the site but political turbulence in Victoria delayed its proclamation until 1955.

The two-stage building project began in 1959 with the appointment of Roy Grounds, a notable Victorian architect. He was then much admired in architectural circles for designing houses within simple plan forms such as a triangle or a circle, within which he skilfully manipulated all the functional requirements. His preoccupation with wrapping simple external form around complex internal function also manifested itself in his overall design for the arts centre. His scheme was for two buildings—a strong rectangular form for the National Gallery of Victoria and an elongated teepee-shaped copper-sheathed spire above the theatres and concert hall, which would be underground.

The gallery, built on a foundation of basalt rock, opened in 1968. After it was built it was discovered that the foundation material on the adjacent site was not basalt as expected but silt from Port Phillip Bay and fill dumped there during the 19th century. On such a site, so close to the bay and the Yarra, it would have been enormously difficult and prohibitively expensive to construct a building more below the water table than above it. It was decided to raise the theatre complex partially out of the ground and build the concert hall on a different site. The Melbourne City Council assigned the small triangular Snowden Gardens to the government for the concert hall. It was separated from the remainder of the complex by a busy road but the foundation was basalt, which allowed two-fifths of the building's height to be below ground.

The concert hall was finished two years before the theatres building, which had to be completely redesigned. This fills every corner of its awkwardly shaped site with accommodation below ground, but above two hemicylinders linked by parallel straight sides are to be seen, surmounted by a mast of lacy steelwork. The concert hall appears above ground as a simple cylindrical form but below ground it is a pear shape. Thus, Roy Grounds in his final major work repeated his strong predilection for simple external forms irrespective of the internal function. This approach is more successful visually in the Sydney Opera House.

When the interior finishes and furnishings of the concert hall and theatre buildings were being decided, the current architectural style was off-form, pre-cast or bush-hammered concrete and natural timbers of various types with fabrics and carpets of muted colours. There were already bush-hammered columns in the foyers and prismatic concrete diffusers all over the interior of the concert hall as part of the architect's concept for the interior. Late in the project, the Victorian Arts Centre building committee decided to employ the designer JOHN TRUSCOTT to obtain a more traditional quality in a contemporary manner. He was forced to decorate rather than influence the architectural form. He covered walls and ceilings and foyers with leather, mirrors, brass and glossy surfaces to reflect sparkle from carefully placed electric lighting and make subterranean spaces with rather low ceilings seem spacious. The major revision of the interiors in the theatres building occurred in the principal public spaces as timber panelling had been determined for the State Theatre auditorium at the acoustic design stage.

The State Theatre is in traditional opera-house form, with a large proscenium stage and a three-level auditorium with side boxes. The acoustics are good and a mellow orchestral sound emanates from the pit. The stage is the best in Australia, with 1067 square metres of space, a fly tower incorporating 111 lines and facilities for trucking in complete settings from each side and the rear. It opened with the Australian Opera's production of *Fiddler on the Roof*. The Playhouse is the major performing space for the MELBOURNE THEATRE COMPANY, which opened it with a production of Euripides's *Medea*. It has a modified thrust in front of a proscenium stage of 321 square metres, with fly tower. The seating, on two levels, fans out close to the stage, giving an impression of intimacy, but behind this the auditorium is more narrowly rectilinear.

The George Fairfax Studio opened with the Playbox Theatre Company's production of Jack Hibberd's *A STRETCH OF THE IMAGINATION*. It is fairly typical of the flat-floored, box-type spaces that have become popular as experimental theatres, or studio theatres for professionals, amateurs and students. Comfortable pull-out 'bleachers' seat 250–400, depending on which of the six staging modes is chosen—theatre-in-the-round, corner stage, thrust stage, centre stage, end stage or proscenium stage. There is an access walkway halfway up and all round the walls. The theatres building also houses restaurants and gallery space, and the concert hall building houses the temporary exhibitions of the Performing Arts Museum. ❦*Ross Thorne*

further reading
SUMNER, JOHN. *Recollections at Play—A life in Australian theatre*. Melbourne: University Press 1993.

Victorian College of the Arts

Some of the most influential theatre companies of the 1980s emerged from training at the Victorian College of the Arts in Melbourne. It is noted for the innovative thinking that went into its establishment. The original members of the MURRAY RIVER PERFORMING GROUP, TheatreWORKS and the WEST THEATRE COMPANY graduated from the School of Drama. Other graduates joined the burgeoning comedy and fringe circuits in Melbourne. The School of Drama is a vocational training school for actors, directors, writers, animateurs, stage managers and technicians. It is one of the six training schools that constitute the college, which was founded in 1976. The others are the Schools of Art, Music, Dance, Studies in Creative Arts, and Film and Television. The founding dean of the School of Drama, Peter Oyston, was determined to develop a course directed to the creation of leaders for a new Australian theatre, not one based upon European or American models. Instead of grooming actors to fit into the existing theatre hierarchy the school trained students as theatre-makers in their own right. To this end, over the three-year course each year's intake of students was formed into a small theatre company, able to exist autonomously and to create new theatre in response to issues in the community. Upon graduation many groups established themselves in country towns as community theatre companies.

Oyston was succeeded by Roger Hodgman (1983–86), David Latham (1987–94) and Lindy Davies (1995–). Since the mid-1980s the purposes of the school have been consolidated. The acting and production streams now combine a more traditional training with the making of new performance. The school also provides full-time three-year training for directors and writers. Student animateurs are trained in creating new work in a variety of circumstances. This course retains some of the original vision of the school while acknowledging the increased flexibility needed by theatrical workers in the 1990s. ❦*Richard Murphet*

Vincent Report

A report on the Encouragement of Australian Productions for Television by a select committee of the Senate chaired by Senator Seddon Vincent was a progenitor of many of the enormous developments in the performing arts in the last 30 years. Published on 29 October 1963, the Vincent Report brought together the thoughts of many people involved in or interested in the performing arts and it vigorously asserted sound recommendations for television drama. The report saw television and film as interdependent and dependent on the live theatre for a supply of competent directors and actors. It said qualitative standards in television were merely a reflection of the standard of the live theatre, 'the real home of the actor and the producer'. Some of its recommendations bore directly on the live theatre:

- That Australian theatre productions be shown on television. The report listed 12 recent productions by J. C. WILLIAMSON'S that could have been on television.
- That actors' pay and conditions be improved. This was seen as a matter for conference between the Australian Broadcasting Commission, the Australian Broadcasting Control Board, commercial television, the professional theatre and ACTORS' EQUITY.
- That young actors and producers of high promise and ability be given scholarships for overseas training 'of the most experienced type', subject to conditions on return to Australia.
- That a comprehensive policy be adopted on assistance to reputable and competent theatrical groups. The committee suggested assistance to cover reasonable losses on productions of high-quality or experimental drama; for establishment and maintenance of drama schools; and to offset the high cost of travel of theatrical groups within and between states.

Some of the measures recommended were already in operation. For example, the NATIONAL INSTITUTE OF DRAMATIC ART had been operating since 1958, and the Churchill Fellowship and the AUSTRALIAN ELIZABETHAN THEATRE TRUST had programs for performers and directors.

Seddon Vincent, a lawyer until he entered parliament, was an active member of the GOLDFIELDS REPERTORY CLUB in Kalgoorlie (WA). ❦*Bill Dunstone and Maurice Jones*

further reading
Select Committee on the Encouragement of Australian Productions for Television—part 1, Report; part 2, Minutes of evidence. *Commonwealth Parliamentary Papers* 1962–63 vol. 4.

Vitalstatistix

Professional women's theatre company in Adelaide, founded in 1984 by Roxxy Bent, Ollie Black and Margaret Fischer. **artistic directors** 1984–91 Bent, Black and Fischer. 1991– Bent and Fischer.

The only professional full-time women's theatre company in Australia, Vitalstatistix creates and performs new works by women. The first was *The Dieters' Dilemma*, a lighthearted look at dieting and body image written by the founders, Roxxy Bent, Ollie Black and Margaret Fischer. They performed it in shopping centres and malls around Adelaide in 1985. Vitalstatistix also performs in its home in the historic Waterside Workers' Hall in Port Adelaide, in theatres, jails and community centres. In 1988 the company performed *The Fabulous Apron Parade*, a cabaret by the founders and Anne Brookman, in the lounge cars of trains on a tour to Perth and Sydney.

The artistic directors of Vitalstatistix make collective decisions and they work variously as writers, performers, directors, producers and community consultants. Every project provides paid entrepreneurial, production or workshop opportunities for other women. Black left Vitalstatistix to pursue independent theatrical interests in December 1991 and then Bent and Fischer redefined the collective structure in order 'to generate challenging, successful, visionary feminist theatre, workshops and entertainment within a well-managed, financially viable organisation'. ❦*Phyllis Jane Rose*

further reading
BRAMWELL, MURRAY. *Wanted for Questioning—Interviews with comic artists*. Melbourne: Allen and Unwin 1992. Includes interview with Roxxy Bent and Margaret Fischer.
BENT, ROXXY, ET AL. *Around the Edge—Women's plays*. Adelaide: Tantrum Press 1992.

Murphy, Catherine. Home sweet home. *Artwork Magazine* 6 (Adelaide, March 1990).
Phyland, Joan. Tasty morsel. *Advertiser Arts Magazine* (Adelaide) September 1985.
Tait, Peta. Subverting forms—Women's theatre groups. *Converging Realities—Feminism in Australian theatre*. Sydney: Currency Press 1994.
Tobin, Andrew. Theatre. *Performing Arts News* 1988.

Anna Volska

Actor. Born 1 December 1944 in Milanowek (Poland). Originally Hanna Maria Jadwiga Dobrowolska. Studied at National Institute of Dramatic Art (Sydney) 1961–62. Stage debut for Old Tote Theatre Company (Sydney) 1963. In England 1964–69. Two seasons with Royal Shakespeare Company. Nimrod Theatre Company (Sydney) 1970–85. Bell Shakespeare Company 1991–. Married to actor John Bell. Mother of playwright Hilary Bell and actor Lucy Bell.

Anna Volska's work is precise and intense. With the Nimrod Theatre Company she was at her best in Peter Handke's *The Ride Across Lake Constance* in 1974, as Beatrice in *Much Ado About Nothing* in 1975 and 1977 and as Olga in Anton Chekhov's *Three Sisters* in 1980. She also has a gift for acting light comedy, in which she has not been seen enough. One of her rare comic roles, which she played with panache, was Jill in Patricia Johnson's *Gladbags* for Q Theatre at Penrith (NSW) in 1984. *Ron Blair*

Garnet Walch

Dramatist. Born 10 October 1843 in Broadmarsh (Tas.). Began localising burlesques and pantomimes in Sydney 1869. Became secretary to Melbourne Athenaeum 1872. Wrote burlesques, comedies, dramas, musical sketches, *opéras-bouffes* and pantomimes during 1870s. Bankrupt 1880. Founded *Town Talk* newspaper with John Conway and Robert P. Whitworth 1881. Founded *Melbourne Mirror* newspaper with Nat J. Barnet 1888. Collaborated with Alfred Dampier in melodrama season at Alexandra Theatre, Melbourne, from 1890. Retired 1893. Died 3 January 1913 in Melbourne. Wrote or edited 15 books including poetry, light fiction, biography, almanacs and Christmas annuals.

The most prolific Australian-born theatre writer of the 19th century, Garnet Walch is believed to have produced 57 stage pieces from 1869 to 1894. He wrote in nearly every contemporary genre, but his main achievement was in helping to create an indigenous theatrical tradition by Australianising forms like pantomime and melodrama. Like his contemporaries W. M. Akhurst, Marcus Clarke, Archibald Murray, E. L. Scott, F. M. Soutten and Robert P. Whitworth, Walch was a professional writer who combined playwriting with journalism, which gave him access to the topical detail required for comical and musical stage works. Like many of these writers, he began by localising foreign texts. He also created original plays, as the market required. The texts of about 20 of his works have survived.

As a theatrical journalist, and as an editor who created outlets for Australian fiction, Walch sought to promote the local product to visibility alongside the imported. Economic pressures on the theatre made this difficult during his career, which coincided with the rise of J. C. Williamson's chain and the long-running imported play, the economic depression of the 1890s and the consolidation of international copyright laws. Walch's first collaborations were with Rosa Cooper, Charles Young and the scene painter Alexander Habbe at the Adelphi Theatre in Sydney. He adapted the burlesques *Love's Silver Dream*, *Conrad the Corsair* and *Prometheus* (1870). For George Darrell at the Royal Victoria Theatre, he wrote an Australian pantomime, *Trookulentos, the Tempter* in 1871. In August 1872 he supplied comic sketches for Carrie and Harry Rickards, for whom he later wrote the burlesques *Pygmalion and his Gal (a Dear!)*—plus a second edition a year later—and *The Babes in the Wood* and the musical sketches *Bric-a-brac* and *Spoons*.

By the end of 1872 Walch was working in Melbourne as a localiser and comic writer. *The True Blue Beard*, a 'Christian Grotesque' with Lachlan McGowan, was followed by his adaptation for W. S. Lyster of Offenbach's *opéra-bouffe Geneviève de Brabant*. For Lyster's *opéra-bouffe* company he wrote also his pantomime *Australia Felix*, which incorporated in its action the first match of the Australian tour of W. G. Grace's all-England cricket team. Lyster also produced *Adamanta, the Proud Princess of Profusia, and her Six Unlucky Suitors*, a pantomime starring Eleanor Carey.

Walch wrote five elaborate pantomimes to display the stars of Harwood, Stewart, Greville and Coppin at the Theatre Royal: *A Froggee Would a Wooing Go*; *Hey-diddle-diddle, the Cat and the Fiddle, the Cow Jumped Over the Moon*; *Jack the Giant-Killer and his Doughty Deeds*; *The Babes in the Wood* with Bland Holt as Clown; and *Sinbad the Sailor* with Richard Stewart and his family. Some of Walch's pantomimes were locally adapted to other cities and his *Beauty and the Beast* had its premiere in Sydney.

For the Stewart family Walch also wrote *Rainbow Revels*. For Alfred Dampier and his daughters Lily and Rose he dramatised a popular American novel, *Helen's Babies*. During the 1870s Walch also wrote *Humble Pie*, a three-act comedy for Dampier's farewell to Australia, and two other comedies, *Perfidious Albion* and *If*. He localised *Pluto*, a burlesque, for Horace Lingard and Alice Dunning, and in 1878 he wrote *Lohengrin in a Nutshell*, a spoof on Richard Wagner's opera *Lohengrin*, which had its first Melbourne performance in 1877. During the 1870s and 1880s Walch created comic sketches incorporating sheet-glass 'ghost' effects for the magician Alfred Silvester, who performed as the Fakir of Oolu at St George's Hall in Melbourne.

In 1881 Walch moved into more dramatic forms, incorporating the wreck of the ship *Loch Ard* at Port Campbell (Vic.) into *Her Evil Star*, a comedy-drama for Mrs G. B. W. Lewis. For Christmas 1881 he supplied Melbourne with two pantomimes: *Gulliver* for Mrs Lewis's infant pupils at the Academy of Music, and *Dyk Whyttyngtonne and hys Wonderfulle Catte* for the English comedian Fred Marshall at the Princess's Theatre.

After a severe illness, Walch announced his recovery with a short comedy, *Proof Positive*, in 1883. Then he sailed to Madagascar, where he reported for the *Argus* on the Franco-Malagasy War. In 1885 Walch resumed theatrical work in Australia for Harry Rickards but he did not write at his hectic pace of the 1870s. He turned to melodrama, a form with a strong comic element, in collaboration with Alfred Dampier in a season which began at the Alexandra Theatre in Melbourne in 1890. *The Count of Monte Cristo* was followed by *Robbery Under Arms*, a popular adaptation of Rolf Boldrewood's novel. In 1891 Walch and Dampier continued to cater for local taste with *The Miner's*

Right, also from Boldrewood, and *This Great City—Melbourne*. They also wrote THE SCOUT and *The Trapper*, westerns for the American star W. F. CARVER and his Wild America troupe, with LILY DAMPIER as heroine. A second *Jack the Giant-Killer* pantomime and two more melodramas, *Wilful Murder* and *Help One Another*, in 1892 marked the end of the struggle against the depression at the Alexandra Theatre and of Walch's collaborations with Dampier. Walch's final stage works were his comedy-drama *Silver Chimes* in Adelaide in 1892 and *Sinbad the Sailor*, a pantomime for J. C. WILLIAMSON in Melbourne in 1893. After writing an operetta libretto with John Grocott, *Kismet*, he lived in retirement for 20 years. ❦*Veronica Kelly*

published stage works

Adamanta, the Proud Princess of Profusia, and her Six Unlucky Suitors—or Harlequin Riddle-me-ree and the Transit of Venus from a new Point of Observation pantomime (1874). Melbourne: Azzopardi, Hildreth 1874.

Australia Felix—or, Harlequin Laughing Jackass and the Magic Bat pantomime (1873). Melbourne: Azzopardi, Hildreth 1873. Brisbane: University of Queensland Press 1988 (ed. Veronica Kelly).

Beauty and the Beast—or, Harlequin King Glorio the Millionth, the Island of Apes and the Fairies of the Magic Roses pantomime (1875). Sydney: G. E. Hooke 1875 (adapted by Samuel Lazar).

Dyk Whyttyngtonne and hys Wonderfulle Catte—or, Arlekyn Lyttel Bo-Peepe and ye Faerie Chimes of Bowe-Bells, pantomime (1881). Melbourne: McCarron, Bird 1881.

A Froggee Would a Wooing Go—or, Harlequin Al Kohol, the Bad Djinn, the Pretty Princess, and the Fairy of the Dancing Water pantomime (1875). Melbourne: Azzopardi, Hildreth 1875.

Geneviève de Brabant, opéra-bouffe libretto after Adolphe Jaime and Etienne Tréfue (1873). Sydney: A. W. Beard 1873.

Hey-diddle-diddle, the Cat and the Fiddle, the Cow Jumped Over the Moon—or Harlequin Sing a Song of Sixpence, a Pocketful of Rye, and the Four-and-twenty Blackbirds Baked in a Pie pantomime (1876). Melbourne: Azzopardi, Hildreth 1876.

Jack the Giant-Killer and his Doughty Deeds—or, Harlequin Hop o' My Thumb and the True Version of Who Killed Cock Robin pantomime (1878). Melbourne: Azzopardi, Hildreth 1878.

Kismet—or, the Cadi's Daughter operetta (with John Grocott). Nottingham: 1894.

Pygmalion and his Gal (a Dear!)—or, The Celebrated Living-Stone of Ancient Athens (No Relation to the Doctor) burlesque (1873). Melbourne: Azzopardi, Hildreth 1873.

Robbery Under Arms play with Alfred Dampier (1890). Sydney: Currency Press 1985.

Sinbad the Sailor, Little Jack Horner and the Old Man of the Sea pantomime (1893). Melbourne: William Marshall 1893.

True Blue Beard, An Old Friend in a New Dress burlesque *(1872)*. Melbourne: McCarron and Bird 1872.

The White Fawn—or, The Loves of Prince Buttercup and the Princess Daisy burlesque (1874). Melbourne: Azzopardi, Hildreth 1874.

Trookulentos, the Tempter—or, Harlequin Cockatoo, the Demon of Discontent, the Good Fairy of Contentment and Four-Leaved Shamrock of Australia pantomime (1871). Parramatta (NSW): Cumberland Times 1871.

further reading

FOTHERINGHAM, RICHARD. Introduction. *Robbery Under Arms* by Alfred Dampier and Garnet Walch. Sydney: Currency Press 1985.

FOTHERINGHAM, RICHARD. Sport and nationalism on the Australian stage—from 'Australia Felix' to Gallipoli. *Australasian Drama Studies* 1/1 (Brisbane, October 1982).

KELLY, VERONICA. Garnet Walch in Sydney. *Australasian Drama Studies* 9 (Brisbane, October 1986).

LOVE, HAROLD. *The Golden Age of Australian Opera—W. S. Lyster and his companies 1861–1880*. Sydney: Currency Press 1981.

RICHARDSON, PAUL. Garnet Walch's 'Australia Felix'—a reconstruction. *Australasian Drama Studies* 1/2 (Brisbane, April 1983).

RICHARDSON, PAUL. Harlequin in the Antipodes *Southerly* 42/2 (Sydney, June 1982).

RICKARD, JOHN. Garnet Walch. *Australian Dictionary of Biography* 6. Melbourne University Press 1976.

Kerry Walker

Actor, dancer, singer. Born 29 February 1948 in Sydney. Grew up in Melbourne. Began acting at high school and in amateur theatre. Studied acting at National Institute of Dramatic Art (Sydney) 1972–74. Professional debut 1974. Foundation member of Hunter Valley Theatre Company (Newcastle NSW), 1976. Lighthouse Company (Adelaide) 1982–83. Australian Artist's Creative Fellowship 1990–92. Closely associated with purchase and establishment of Belvoir Street Theatre (Sydney).

An actor with a range from classical drama to slapstick comedy, Kerry Walker has made her mark with trailblazing bravado. A character actor not known to fail a challenge, she is not afraid of the unprepossessing role—like the retarded Mog Figg in PATRICK WHITE's *Netherwood* or a red-nosed Tom Snout in the slapstick of *The Popular Mechanicals* by Keith Robinson and TONY TAYLOR in 1987. She has been a key participant in several notable experiments. She was a leading actor in the team that founded the HUNTER VALLEY THEATRE COMPANY, for which she created the dashing Breda Mulcahy in JOHN O'DONOGHUE's *A Happy and Holy Occasion*. Other roles included Irene in John Romeril's *THE FLOATING WORLD* and Laura in Tennessee Williams's *The Glass Menagerie*.

Walker acted frequently with the NIMROD THEATRE COMPANY in the 1970s. She played Mother in George Whaley's adaptation of *ON OUR SELECTION* in 1978 and created Frieda Lawrence in DAVID ALLEN's *Upside Down at the Bottom of the World* in 1979. REX CRAMPHORN selected her for his avant-garde Shakespeare experiment in 1980. She was also in his production of Jean Racine's *Britannicus* at Sydney University in 1980. JIM SHARMAN chose Walker for the Lighthouse Company in Adelaide, where her roles ranged from Bertolt Brecht's Mother Courage to Feste in *Twelfth Night*.

She also created two roles in plays by PATRICK WHITE—the Female Being in *Signal Driver* in 1982 and Mog Figg in *Netherwood* in 1983—with Lighthouse. She became a friend of White and a key support and stimulus in his final playwriting. She played Ivy in *Signal Driver* at the BELVOIR STREET THEATRE in Sydney in 1985, created Queenie in *Shepherd on the Rocks* with the State Theatre Company of South Australia in 1987 and gave a notable performance as Mrs Lusty in a revival of *The Ham Funeral* by the SYDNEY THEATRE COMPANY in 1989.

Other roles created by Walker include Eileen Fitzgerald in Stephen Sewell's *THE BLIND GIANT IS DANCING* and multiple roles in Michael Gow's *Furious* with the Sydney Theatre Company in 1991. She performed her own *Knuckledusters—The Jewels of Edith Sitwell* at Belvoir Street in 1989 and later in Melbourne. She achieved a remarkable resemblance to the subject. Walker received a three-year Australian Artist's Creative Fellowship to find Asian works for production in Australia. The first, *The Cockroach Opera* by the Indonesian writer Nano Riantiarno, was presented at the Belvoir Street Theatre in 1992. ❦*Katharine Brisbane*

George Wallace

Comedian. Born 4 June 1895 at Aberdeen (NSW). Son of George Wallace, vaudevillian. Grew up in Sydney. Worked in country. Began stage career touring in 'Happy' Harry Salmon's troupe in north Queensland c.1914. Returned to Sydney after four years' country touring and worked for Harry Clay. In Dinks and Onkus act with Jack Patterson 1919–24. Toured Fullers' Australasian vaudeville circuit with his own revue company 1924–30. Starred in operettas and Efftee and Cinesound films in 1930s. Moved to Tivoli circuit in late 1930s. Died 19 October 1960 in Sydney. Father of George Wallace jnr, comedian in Brisbane.

One of Australia's best-loved comedians, George Wallace sometimes outranked ROY RENE. He was an all-rounder, successful on stage, screen and radio, writing sketches and songs, directing and producing. Wallace's comic character was a blissful innocent with large, expressive eyes and a happy rotund face who stumbled over malapropisms. Known as 'Mr Five-by-five'—he was only 1·63 metres tall and nearly as wide—Wallace was always famous for the physical side of his humour. He frequently fell over, to the great delight of his audiences. In HARRY CLAY's suburban vaudeville in Sydney he quickly built up a loyal following and became one of Clay's highest-paid performers. A critic described him as a 'shriek at first sight'.

Wallace was born in a tent in rural NSW, but his background was distinctly urban. His parents separated when he was very young and he lived with his mother in Sydney. *People* magazine of 28 February 1951 recounted that as a child on the Pyrmont waterfront he busked for passing sailors and down-and-outs, until his mother remarried and they moved to Manly. On leaving school Wallace was apprenticed to his stepfather's ink factory for four years before he decided to go bush. He then worked on the land for a few years, including a stint as a cane-cutter, before joining a travelling troupe. The dry wit of the outback nurtured his comic sense and timing, he claimed.

Adorned in a checked shirt and a battered felt hat, reputedly from his cane-cutting days, Wallace was for many the rural counterpart of Roy Rene's Mo. His essential humour was no more rural than Mo's was Jewish, however. Far from being confined to country scenes, the themes and settings of his revues were routine vaudeville fare, exploiting the colour places like Spain and Honolulu and his stage characters were not necessarily rural in origin. His most popular creations included 'Sophie the Sort', a tough bus conductress, and Drongo from the Congo. He was less deliberately Australian in his language than many other comedians of his era. Wallace energetically projected the image of a well-meaning innocent whose limited comprehension of evil enabled him to survive the onslaught of conmen, nagging wives and the pathetic consequences of falling in love with someone who barely noticed him. In the acrobatic knockabout comedy of DINKS AND ONKUS he was apparently immune from injury.

During the 1930s Wallace worked for F. W. THRING, beginning a successful film career in 1932 and starring in the musical comedies *COLLITS' INN* in 1933 and *The Beloved Vagabond* in 1934. In the late 1930s he went to the TIVOLI CIRCUIT. Throughout the Second World War he teamed with JENNY HOWARD. From 1949 the *George Wallace Road Show* on radio centred on George 'Wallaby' Wallace, the leading identity of an outback town called 'Bullamakanka'—hence the sobriquet 'the boy from Bullamakanka'. He spent time in London in the 1950s, until HARRY WREN brought him back for *Thanks for the Memory* in 1953. His last show was *The Good Old Days* in 1957. Ill health forced him into retirement. ❦*Victoria Chance*

further reading
SAYERS, STUART. George Wallace. *Australian Dictionary of Biography* 12. Melbourne University Press 1990.
People (Sydney) 1/25 (28 February 1951).
Daily Mirror (Sydney) 16 August 1957.
Sun-Herald (Sydney) 23 October 1960.

Charles Waller

Magician. Born 8 December 1879 at Benalla (Vic.). Died 30 May 1960 in Melbourne.

Charles Waller made his mark by inventing and writing about magic, and his books on original magic made him well known to magicians outside Australia. He wanted to become a magician when he saw a magic show by George Waldo Heller in 1890. In Melbourne from March 1895 he pursued a successful business career and performed magic as a hobby. He wrote for overseas magic magazines and his first book was published in 1920. His *Magical Nights at the Theatre*, describes the act of every magician, juggler, ventriloquist and protean artist who visited Melbourne from 1854 until 1948. ❦*Gerald Taylor*

writings
For Magicians Only. USA: Floyd Thayer 1924.
Happy Magic. England: George Johnson 1932.
Magic from Below. England: George Johnson 1929.
Magical Nights at the Theatre. Melbourne: Gerald Taylor 1980.
Up His Sleeve. USA: Floyd Thayer 1920.
Waller's Wonders. England: George Johnson 1926.

Doreen Warburton OBE

Actor, director. Born 22 March 1930 in London. Began professional acting on tour with Joan Littlewood's Theatre Workshop in late 1940s. Emigrated to Australia in March 1953. Toured with Young Elizabethan Players 1959–61. Directed four Shakespeare productions for Australian Elizabethan Theatre Trust. Artistic director of Q Theatre Company (Sydney and Penrith NSW) 1963–1989. Taught voice production at National Institute of Dramatic Art (Sydney) 1965–66. Married actor Ben Gabriel 1969. Member of Australia Council 1974–77. Sydney critics' awards for best actress 1963 (Nola in *The Season at Sarsaparilla* by Patrick White), 1969 (*Daughter in Law* by D. H. Lawrence, *Snowangel* by Lewis Carlino and *Mrs Dally Has a Lover* by William Hanley); for direction 1984 (*The Sentimental Bloke* and *On the Wallaby*). Acts in film, radio and television. OBE 1972.

Throughout her long Australian career Doreen Warburton has been acclaimed as a versatile actor, a skilled director, and a woman of dedication and indefatigable energy. She has always been committed to theatre that is created by an ensemble of actors, is accessible, reflects its society and is reasonably priced. With £30 and five other actors in 1963 she established Q THEATRE, giving lunchtime performances in Sydney. In 1977 she moved the company to Penrith on the western fringe of Sydney. As its artistic director she emphasised the importance of living and working in the community. Australian plays were an important part of her repertoire. She herself directed David Williamson's TRAVELLING NORTH in 1980, BOB HERBERT's *No Names … No Pack Drill* in 1981 and STEVE J. SPEARS's *Send Me Three and Fourpence* in 1987. She also directed the Australian musicals *On the Wallaby* in 1983, *Better Known as Bee* in 1984 and *Zilch* —a rock opera about homeless children by herself, Martin Sharman and the cast—in 1985. While with Q Theatre Warburton also acted for other companies. She played in two plays by Patrick White—THE SEASON AT SARSAPARILLA in 1962 and *A Cheery Soul* for the Union Theatre Repertory Company in Melbourne in 1963. For the OLD TOTE THEATRE COMPANY in Sydney she was Emilia in *Othello* in 1965 and Mrs Mossop in Arthur Wing Pinero's *Trelawney of the Wells* in 1971. She played Mrs O'Dare in the musical *Irene* for J. C. WILLIAMSON's in 1974. Since she retired from Q Theatre she has been a freelance actor and director. ❦*Pamela Payne*

Hugh J. Ward

American actor, dancer, entrepreneur. Born in Philadelphia (USA) 1871. In minstrel shows from 17. In Australia 1899–1903. Returned 1906. Toured Asia and Australia with his own company. Director of J. C. Williamson Ltd 1911–22. Hugh J. Ward Theatres Pty Ltd 1922–26. Died 20 April 1941.

Hughie Ward, as he was known in the profession, seems to have been a performer at heart, with no taste for the machinations of management. A splendid dancer and comedian, he came to Australia from the USA in 1899 in the Harry Connor Theatrical Company, playing in *A Trip to Chinatown* and *A Stranger in New York*, both by Charles H. Hoyt. In the latter play the 28-year-old Ward stole the notices as an octogenarian. By the end of 1899, he had been taken into J. C. Williamson's Royal Comic Opera Company and he remained there for four years as a featured performer.

After playing in London, Paris and New York, Ward was back in Australia by 1906, heading Willoughby and Ward's New London Company with George Willoughby. Later Ward formed his own company, including Celia Ghiloni, Rose Musgrove and GRACE PALOTTA, and toured India, Burma and China in 1908 with popular dramas and operettas. Back in Australia, Ward continued to lead his own company until early 1911, when he said farewell to performing and joined J. C. WILLIAMSON's as a director.

After J. C. Williamson Ltd bought J. and N. Tait Ltd in 1920, Ward became dissatisfied with the new direction, resigned and sold his shares—for £120 000, according to Viola Tait. In 1922 he went into partnership with BENJAMIN FULLER in a company called Hugh J. Ward Theatres Ltd. Ward presented spectacular musical comedies at the Princess Theatre in Melbourne and played dramas and musical comedies at the Grand Opera House in Sydney until the St James Theatre opened in March 1926. Seven months later he retired, at the age of 55. ❦*John West*

further reading
RUTLEDGE, MARTHA. Hugh J. Ward. *Australian Dictionary of Biography* 12. Melbourne University Press 1990.

Frank Waters

Actor. Born 1915 in Broken Hill (NSW). Grew up in South Australia. Trained with Adelaide Repertory Theatre and in revue with Rex (Wacka) Dawe. Military service 1941–46. Became leading freelance radio actor in postwar Sydney. Gave outstanding stage performances until early 1960s. Shakespeare Memorial Theatre Company (Stratford-upon-Avon, England) 1954. Sydney Critics' Award 1956. Died 5 May 1972 in Darwin.

A fine actor during the formative years of present-day Sydney theatre in the 1950s, Frank Waters was a volatile personality with high nervous energy, great good humour and larrikin charm which he sometimes restrained, sometimes released to great effect. The larrikin charm shone when he played the opportunistic Mr Horner in *The Country Wife* by William Wycherley for METROPOLITAN THEATRE. Waters joined this group out of need to work on stage after the Second World War. He was also outstanding as the poetic Joe Byrne in Douglas Stewart's NED KELLY in 1947. For the JOHN ALDEN COMPANY in 1950 he played Edmund the Bastard in *King Lear* with an edgy, engaging braggart flair.

In 1953 Anthony Quayle saw Waters give a splendid performance for INDEPENDENT THEATRE as Willy Loman in Arthur Miller's *Death of a Salesman*, and engaged him for the 1954 season at the Shakespeare Memorial Theatre. In 1956 Waters gave a haunting study of an actor on a hopeless drunken slide in Clifford Odets's *Winter Journey* for Independent Theatre, winning the Sydney Critics' Award, and he was again an outstanding Joe Byrne for the AUSTRALIAN ELIZABETHAN THEATRE TRUST. His containment in this role contrasted with his fiery Starbuck, a foil to LEO MCKERN's gentle old father in *The Rainmaker* by N. Richard Nash. Waters also acted for the Trust in the premiere of Richard Beynon's THE SHIFTING HEART, conveying the essential 'Australianness' of Clarry Fowler's conflict. In the Trust's 1958 production of Eugene O'Neill's *Long Day's Journey into Night* he played the dark, complex James Tyrone with great insight, revealing hidden warmths like shafts of sunlight. Waters then retired from acting for health reasons and went to live in Darwin but he returned to make his last appearance, playing the lead in Archibald MacLeish's *J. B.* at the 1962 Adelaide Festival. ❦*Lynne Murphy*

John Waters

Actor, singer. Born 8 December 1948 in London. Experience in England in theatre, film and pop music. Came to Australia in 1968. Worked briefly as jackeroo in Queensland and returned to pop singing. In cast of *Hair* 1969. Many film and television roles.

John Waters has interspersed his screen career with straight acting and singing parts in the theatre. In 1978 he starred in a dramatisation of Bram Stoker's novel *Dracula*. Waters's suave vampire and black-and-white designs from New York by Edward Gorey were the best things in the show. From 1980 to mid-1982 he co-starred with JACKI WEAVER in a tuneful musical *They're Playing Our Song*. An Australian cast album of the songs was released, a rare accolade then. In 1984 Waters learned sign language for the role of a speech therapist in love with a profoundly deaf girl, in *Children of a Lesser God* by Mark Medoff.

When HARRY M. MILLER revived the musical *Jesus Christ Superstar* in concert 20 years after its first Australian production, Waters played Pontius Pilate, replacing Anthony Warlow, who was forced by illness to leave the cast before the opening on 4 August 1992 at the Sydney Entertainment Centre. In March 1992 at the Tilbury Hotel in Sydney Waters and his accompanist Stewart D'Arrietta performed

Looking Through a Glass Onion, a homage to John Lennon written by Waters. They toured the show to Melbourne, Brisbane and provincial towns. A year later Waters and D'Arrietta toured an expanded version, to critical approval. They began a three-month West End season in London in August 1993. Legal objections by Lennon's widow scuttled Waters's hopes for New York. ❧*John West*

F. B. Watson

Actor, manager. Began theatrical work in Hobart 1836. Became prompter and actor. Leased and managed theatres in Hobart and Launceston in 1840s and 1850s.

During the difficult 1840s and 1850s, F. B. Watson helped to maintain theatrical performances in Tasmania. He seems to have begun his career as a ticket-seller and usher at the Theatre Royal in the Argyle Rooms in Hobart. On 17 February 1837 the *True Colonist*, remarking that Watson and a Mr Butler were to take a benefit at the theatre, praised 'the great civility and attention with which those two young men behave to every decent person'.

While ANNE CLARKE was in London recruiting new performers, the Royal Victoria Theatre in Hobart reopened under the joint management of Watson and ARTHUR FALCHON on 23 March 1841, but when the season ended on 16 August Watson was the sole lessee. In September Watson's company moved to Launceston and played in the OLYMPIC THEATRE at the Steam Packet Tavern until 24 November. The *Launceston Courier* praised Watson on 1 November 1841 as an actor of more than ordinary talent. His company opened in Hobart on 1 December 1841 with SAMSON CAMERON as stage manager.

In April 1842 they were back in Launceston, playing in THE ROYAL OLYMPIC THEATRE at the London Inn. Soon, however, Samson and CORDELIA CAMERON quarrelled with Watson and set up a rival theatre, the Royal Victoria. Newspapers repeatedly condemned this stupid rivalry but both companies performed—often the same play on the same night—until September, when Cameron was bankrupt. Watson continued until the end of October. On 14 December 1842 the Royal Olympic Theatre reopened, after redecoration. Both companies were now united under Watson. Unlike Cameron, he had gained a licence under the new Licensing Act, which gave the Van Diemen's Land government control of the number of theatrical companies. The season continued until 15 May 1843, with frequent complaints about poor management. When the Olympic reopened on 5 June 1843 there were further complaints, despite a company studded with such stars as Cordelia Cameron, CONRAD KNOWLES, HARRIET JONES and FRANCIS NESBITT. Newspapers complained of poor performances and condemned Watson for allowing irregularities, such as prostitutes in the boxes. The *Cornwall Chronicle* thundered on 7 October 1843 that there was little difference between the Olympic and performances in a brothel.

After one more season at Launceston in the first half of 1844, and continued criticism of his management, Watson rejoined Anne Clarke's company as actor and prompter. On 21 October 1844, in partnership with Falchon again, he reopened the Albert Theatre in Hobart for a brief period. By December he was back with Anne Clarke. When GEORGE COPPIN took over her company in 1845, Watson accompanied it to Melbourne as prompter but soon returned to Van Diemen's Land. In 1853–56 he leased the Royal Victoria Theatre in Hobart in partnership with JOHN DAVIES. Nothing is known of him thereafter. ❧*Elizabeth Webby*

further reading
WINTER, GILLIAN. A colonial theatrical experience—The Royal Victoria Theatre, 1837–1857. *Tasmanian Historical Research Association Papers and Proceedings* 32/4 (December 1985).

Jacki Weaver

Actor. Born 25 May 1947 in Sydney. Went to drama school at six. Debut at Phillip Street Theatre (Sydney) 1962. In Old Tote Theatre Company (Sydney) 1966–68. Nimrod Theatre Company (Sydney) from early 1970s. Melbourne Theatre Company. Sydney Theatre Company. Many film and television roles. Married to television journalist Derryn Hinch.

'Blessed and cursed with lasting youthfulness', as the *Bulletin* described her in 1987, Jacki Weaver is one of Australia's most popular actors. She is petite, blonde and has a voice of deceptive innocence. She began as a singer, as a child on television in *Bandstand* with Johnny O'Keefe and in variety shows. She made her first professional appearance on stage at 15 as Cinderella in Sydney. The *Daily Telegraph* critic commented upon her 'small but sweet and sharply focused piping voice'. *Jack and Jill* in 1963 and *Peter Pan* at the INDEPENDENT THEATRE in 1966 followed.

With the OLD TOTE THEATRE COMPANY she played in Arthur Wing Pinero's *The Schoolmistress*, Molière's *The Imaginary Invalid* and George Bernard Shaw's *You Never Can Tell*. For the NIMROD THEATRE COMPANY she made her mark as an innocent Fiona in JOHN BELL's landmark production of David Williamson's THE REMOVALISTS and later recreated the role in a film. Between variety shows and television comedies she played Susan in ALEX BUZO's *Tom* for Nimrod in 1973, and Rosaline in *Love's Labour's Lost* in 1974 and Natasha in Anton Chekhov's *Three Sisters* in 1977 for the Old Tote company. The *Nation Review* critic Greg Curran called the latter 'the most original casting' and drew attention to her potential as a dramatic actor: 'Ms Weaver would appear at first blush too vulnerable, too soft-edged. [But] this is Natasha with dimples of iron.'

After 20 years in the business her first major break came when she was partnered with JOHN WATERS in the two-hander musical *They're Playing Our Song*, which ran from 1980 to 1982 around Australia. In 1983 she made a further hit as the clever-dumb blonde Billie Dawn in Garson Kanin's *Born Yesterday* for J. C. Williamson's and the SYDNEY THEATRE COMPANY. 'Adorable', 'simply gorgeous', 'irresistible', exclaimed reviewers. 'With virtuoso skill she can screech like a buzz-saw, murmur tantalising lovetalk, cut through political knavery with deadly zeal and yet provoke laughter with every change of mood', wrote Frank Harris in the *Daily Telegraph*.

From 1984 she worked steadily for the Melbourne and Sydney Theatre Companies, was seen widely as Felicity in NICK ENRIGHT's comedy *Daylight Saving*; and partnered John Bell in two notable dramas, Tom Stoppard's *The Real Thing* in 1985 and William Nicholson's *Shadowlands* in 1991. As the tough-minded American wife of C. S. Lewis in *Shadowlands* she demonstrated her strength and status as a mature dramatic actor. ❧*Katharine Brisbane*

Bettina Welch

Actor. Born 1922 in New Zealand. Won elocution championship in Sydney Eisteddfod 1939. Began stage work at Minerva Theatre (Sydney). Many roles for J. C. Williamson's. Sydney Critics' Award 1968 (*Wait Until Dark* by Frederick Knott). Died 1993.

For more than 50 years Bettina Welch acted in lead or featured roles, mainly in commercial theatre. She built this career upon a long association with J. C. WILLIAMSON'S. With long red hair, green eyes, secretive smile and husky voice, she first captivated audiences in 1946, when she played a wickedly witty Elvira in Noël Coward's *Blithe Spirit* in Sydney. In 1949 she played opposite Robert Morley in his play *Edward, My Son* in Sydney, Melbourne and New Zealand for the Firm. She clearly became a favourite of Morley, for she played opposite him on his two later tours of Australasia—in Alan Ayckbourn's *How the Other Half Loves* in 1973 and in Alan Bennett's *The Old Country* in 1980.

She played in Coward's *Nude with Violin* with ROBERT HELPMANN in 1958, and toured with JOHN McCALLUM and Googie Withers in Alan Melville's *Simon and Laura* and Terence Rattigan's *The Deep Blue Sea*. In the musical *Camelot* Welch played the enchantress Morgan le Fey for two and a half years. In Sydney she appeared in PHILLIP STREET REVUES in the 1950s and did notable work for INDEPENDENT THEATRE, especially as the blind woman in *Wait Until Dark* in 1968. In 1990 Welch appeared for the SYDNEY THEATRE COMPANY in Luigi Pirandello's *Six Characters in Search of an Author*, and in the musical *A Little Night Music* she was a worldly and still beautiful Mme Armefeldt. ❦*Richard Lane*.

Barbara West

Actor. Born in 1930s in Manchester (England). Graduated from London Academy of Music and Dramatic Art in early 1950s. Worked for BBC television. Married an Australian. Lived in West Africa before settling in Australia. Theatre '62 (Adelaide) 1967. Has acted regularly for State Theatre Company of South Australia (Adelaide). Performed solo show *Miles Franklin and the Rainbow's End* at San Antonio Festival (Texas, USA) 1986. Also film, radio and television roles.

A versatile, restrained actor, Barbara West has distinguished herself in Shakespeare (*The Winter's Tale*) and Henrik Ibsen (*The Seagull* and *Hedda Gabler*) for the State Theatre Company of South Australia—now called STATE THEATRE. She has been equally at ease in new works. These have included Edward Albee's *A Delicate Balance*, Michael Gow's *Away*, Christopher Hampton's *Les Liaisons dangereuses* and Peter Nichols's *A Day in the Life of Joe Egg*. ❦*Murray Bramwell*

West Theatre Company

Community-theatre company in Melbourne, founded in 1979 as West Community Theatre by Jan McDonald, Ian Shrives, Phil Sumner and Linda Waters. Changed name 1983. **venues** 1979–83 various. 1983–90 Incinerator, Moonee Ponds. **artistic directors** 1979–83 Jan McDonald. 1983–86. Neil Cameron. 1988–90 Wanda Dopierala. **first major production** *Riff Raff*, rock musical devised by Jan McDonald and Phil Sumner with Men at Work band, 1979. **last production** *Cards and Flowers* by Rosemary Fitzgerald, November 1990.

For 12 years the West Theatre Company was the only subsidised professional company in the western suburbs of Melbourne. It facilitated community involvement in workshops and classes and in creation of some vigorous local theatrical events. These included *Xenophobia*, about high-rise housing estates, in 1981 and *Vital Signs*, a play about nursing, in 1985. There was a popular street-theatre offshoot, the so-called Essendon Policewomen's Marching Band, which did circus–comedy–cabaret routines, partly in drag, from 1984 to 1988. After the founding members left the company its plays were mostly commissioned and of uneven quality, and subsidies were gradually withdrawn after 1989. ❦*Geoffrey Milne*

further reading
CAMERON, NEIL. *Fire on the Water*. Sydney: Currency Press 1993.

Western Australian Academy of Performing Arts

In its short life the Western Australian Academy of Performing Arts has enriched the cultural life of Perth. Founded in 1979, the academy comprises the School of Dramatic Arts, the School of Visual Arts and the Western Australia Conservatorium of Music. It provides special courses, such as instrumental tuition, and general courses. Among the latter is musical theatre, which includes classes in acting, dance and music. Students in all courses benefit from a diverse creative environment in the single-campus, multi-disciplinary academy, which is part of Edith Cowan University. The School of Dramatic Arts prepares performers for theatre, dance, film and television and offers courses in arts management and production and design. Fundamental to the academy's success have been policies established in the years after its foundation in 1979 by Geoffrey Gibbs, formerly dean of dramatic arts and director of the academy since 1993. These policies include recruitment by audition, excellence in performance, strong liaison with industry and appointment of eminent practitioners to the teaching staff. Because most theatrical, film and television production occurs in Melbourne and Sydney, the graduating class each year takes a 'production' to Sydney so that agents, producers and directors can see the graduates performing.

The standing of the theatre and musical-theatre departments, headed by LISLE JONES and John Milson respectively, can be gauged by the demand for places. In 1988, 200 applied for the theatre course and 22 were accepted, and 16 out of 80 applicants were accepted into the musical-theatre course. The early graduates of the theatre course established its reputation. Notable graduates include Marcus Graham and Robert Taylor in the early years and Camilla Sobb and Nicki Wendt in the 1980s. The production and design course provides training in scenery, costume, sound, lighting and stage management with the opportunity to specialise in one of these fields. All the courses prepare students for transition to the professional world.

Much of the academy's achievement in the late 1980s and early 1990s was facilitated by the former director, Robert Vickery, whose personality and administrative expertise were assets in establishing a harmonious working relationship between the academy and the state government. ❦*Ken Willis*

Western Australian provincial towns

Theatre in provincial Western Australia has developed in parallel with the opening up of new and usually remote areas, principally for agriculture, grazing or mining. Even now, much theatre is produced by local initiative in small service towns that have limited cultural amenities and are distant even from their provincial centres.

Western Australia occupies the Australian continent west of 129° E, covering about 250 million hectares. Despite the size of the state, its population is among the most urbanised in the world and its rural land is among the most sparsely populated. Only about 28 per cent of the 1 665 945 people recorded by the 1991 census did not live in the Perth metropolitan region and the great majority of them lived in the widely separated provincial cities of Albany, Bunbury, Geraldton, Kalgoorlie and Port Hedland, each of which has 20 000–25 000 inhabitants.

Rural settlement was rapid in the first decade of British colonisation to 1839, scattered as far south as Augusta, but it slowed drastically until development of a railway system, mining and opening of new farming districts induced the state's greatest expansion of settlement from 1889 to 1918. In the decade from 1890, the non-Aboriginal population almost quadrupled from 48 500 to 180 000, and the provincial proportion of it became larger. Since the 1950s growth in mining and service industries, especially tourism, has produced another major expansion of the provincial population. The metropolitan population has grown so much in the last two decades that new satellite cities of Mandurah and Rockingham to the south of Perth and Joondalup to the north have absorbed rural areas that once had their own amateur theatres.

Before the gold rushes

Amateur theatre in the provinces before the gold rushes of the 1890s tended to reproduce the mixture of musical items, short comedies, farces and operettas that had dominated the theatrical life of Perth and adjacent Fremantle in the 50 years since the first performance in Perth in 1839. Productions in small country towns, separated by long distances and bad roads, had to be mounted in makeshift venues with scant technical resources. Even where a local group of players had been formed there was no regular season. A play, generally chosen for entertainment value from British acting editions, was usually only part of an evening's entertainment.

Much research is needed on the foundation of amateur theatrical groups in the larger country towns before the gold rushes. A good number of dramatic performances were given, but minstrelsy seems to have been the most widespread form of public performance in the new towns. Minstrelsy required less resources than plays and could be performed exclusively by men if necessary, and it died hard as popular entertainment in Western Australia.

The port of Albany, 400 km south of Perth, was typical. It had its own Amateur Minstrels in 1886. The completion of the Albany Town Hall in May 1888 gave the town its first permanent performance venue, and the Albany Amateur Dramatic Club offered its 'third entertainment', *Ben Bolt* and *The Artful Dodge*, there in June 1888. Albany, the major port of call in Western Australia until Fremantle Harbour was completed in 1897, had been visited by overseas touring companies at least as early as the 1870s. An account of a tour by the Towers Company, which landed at Albany on the way to Perth in December 1876, makes no mention of performing in Albany, 'truly the city of the dead'. It scathingly draws attention to the 400 km of dirt tracks, flea-ridden accommodation and uncomfortable transport to Perth. After playing to 'the poorest, slowest, dullest people', the Towers troupe started back on 'that dreadful six-days overland trip' to board ship at Albany.

Entertainment on Eastern Goldfields

The major impetus for development of provincial theatre came with the opening of the Eastern, Murchison and Pilbara goldfields after the discovery of gold at Coolgardie, about 560 km from Perth, in 1892. Transport, accommodation, even water, were wanting at first. In the Coolgardie of 1894, where the principal building materials were timber, iron and calico, theatre performance conditions were necessarily informal and often rudimentary. Mrs Mack's Variety Company performed in a room adjoining Mr Paisley's Coolgardie store in April 1894. The Coolgardie Minstrel and Dramatic Club, founded in 1894, met in De Braun's Great Western Hotel, and sometimes ended its evening by performing a farce there. But within three years of the discovery of gold the theatre was booming. Coolgardie's first purpose-built theatre, the Theatre Royal, a building of wood and galvanised iron with movable seating for up to 1000 opened in 1895, equipped with overhead gaslight, footlights, flies, stock scenery and a backdrop. Harry Moran appeared there in 1895, with others drawn from 'the best Artists to be obtained from the Eastern Colonies'. They were followed in 1896 by the Gaiety Pantomime Company at the end of an 18-month Western Australian tour, the TAYLOR–CARRINGTON COMPANY in Dion Boucicault's *The Shaughraun* and the Ettie Williams Happy Hours Vaudeville Company from the CREMORNE GARDENS in Perth.

Professional Australian and overseas companies continued to tour the Eastern Goldfields, despite discomfort and dirt and the need to reduce existing sets for small stages at Coolgardie, Kanowna and Kalgoorlie. HARRY RICKARDS played the Theatre Royal in Coolgardie in 1897 and was at Kanowna in the following year. The ALFRED DAMPIER Company extended its Perth season of *East Lynne*, *Royal Pardon* and *Hamlet* to Coolgardie in 1897, and WILLIAMSON AND MUSGROVE toured the Royal Comic Opera Company there in June 1898. Virgie Vivienne played both Hamlet and Ophelia on the same program at the Cremorne (later Palace) Theatre in Coolgardie in November 1898. The Tivoli Theatre in Coolgardie came to the end of a short life when it was destroyed by fire in March 1898.

The Banvards, an acrobatic and vaudeville troupe, played for 11 months at mining camps and towns on the Eastern Goldfields, eventually suffering heavy loss from a fire in Menzies, 130 km north of Kalgoorlie, in 1898. Another acrobatic troupe, the Flying Jordans toured the Eastern Goldfields extensively in 1898.

The American illusionist Carl Hertz undertook perhaps the most extraordinary tour of the Eastern Goldfields. In 1897 he chartered 20 camels to transport his company and apparatus over 600 km of rough terrain from Perth 'inland to Boulder City Kalgoorlie, stopping at a dozen mining camps on the way'. His manager went in advance to prepare brushwood theatres with walls over three metres high, and capable of seating up to 1000 at a time, each spectator paying for admission with gold dust worth up to 24 shillings. Hertz lucratively circumvented goldfields by-laws against performances on Sundays by offering a 'Grand Sacred Magical and Cinematographic Entertainment', including a Biblical illusion called 'Noah's Ark', to a theatre packed to suffocation.

The gold rush gave economic stimulus, increased populations, and brought new life to theatre in Albany and Esperance, distant ports of entry to the Eastern Goldfields. Hertz, Professor Mackay's National Concert and Burlesque Company, Lucifer's Athletic and Specialty Company, and Davis's Fantastiques all began tours of Western Australia from Albany between March and August 1897. The Alfred Dampier Company, under Mrs Dampier's management, began its 1897 tour at Albany and performed in the port before re-embarking after its visits to Fremantle, Perth and the goldfields. FITZGERALDS' CIRCUS wintered in Albany as Fitzgerald's Zoo in 1897, while Dan Fitzgerald toured Europe in search of new acts.

Edward Reynolds opened the outdoor Cremorne Gardens in Albany in 1896 and imported Perth artists to play vaudeville there in the summer months. He roofed the building and reopened it in September 1897 as the Garden, an indoor proscenium theatre seating up to 700. William (sic) Gordon was brought from Melbourne to paint the proscenium, and a Mr Tassell painted the inner walls with Australian bush scenes. The stimulus given to Albany by the gold rushes also saw the Princess Theatre, adjoining the George Hotel, open in 1898.

Albany had its own satellite theatre in surrounding districts. At Katanning, 180 km north of Albany, a local cast played *Honey Moon Experiments*, along with an exhibition of American axe-swinging, in April 1897. Esperance, a small port 475 km east of Albany and 450 km south of Coolgardie, was gazetted as a municipality in 1895 and by 1896 it had enough people to support the Bijou Theatre, newly built of corrugated iron as part of a two-storey general store. It had a drop curtain and inner walls decorated with local scenes of sailing ships in the bay. Amateurs staged H. J. Byron's comedy *Our Boys* there in July 1897.

Amateur performance

The significance of the Eastern Goldfields as a destination for national and international touring companies peaked in the decade before the First World War. During this period the goldfields acquired the Hippodrome and the Majestic Theatre at Kalgoorlie and the Boulder Town Hall, which was used by touring opera and ballet companies. The rapid development of theatre on the Eastern Goldfields for a time stimulated the growth of amateur performance in new satellite settlements. In May 1898 the Banvards, on their way south from Coolgardie to Esperance, became the first professionals to perform in Norseman, half way along the desert track. Their visit coincided with the formation of Norseman's own amateur musical and dramatic group, later known as the Owls. In the same month a noted scenic artist, Gough Hamilton, also travelling to Esperance, painted scenery for the Owls to use in Krakover's new galvanised-iron Royal Hall.

The development of railways and coastal shipping services in the 1880s and 1890s seems to have permitted more efficient and extensive touring. Perth was linked to Albany by the Great Southern Railway in 1889 and by the Eastern Railway to Coolgardie and Kalgoorlie in 1896. In March 1896 the Silvester Family variety troupe left the Mechanics' Hall at Guildford, on the eastern edge of Perth, to tour 'all of the principal towns' on the Great Southern Railway to Albany. The Great Southern Railway carried FitzGeralds' Circus back and forth between Albany and Perth in 1897.

In 1905 Hyland's Circus arrived by ship from the east, played at Albany and then travelled some 890 km by rail through Katanning and Narrogin to Kalgoorlie and Boulder. From 1907 to 1911, Hylands' Circus played in Geraldton, Day Dawn, Cue, Sandstone and Northampton in the Murchison goldfields, before going by sea to Broome, 2200 km north of Perth. After the disappearance of Tom Hyland in the outback in 1912, the company toured by sea and rail to Geraldton, the Eastern Goldfields and via the Albany region to Perth, before disbanding in 1920.

With the onset of the First World War provincial theatre declined, almost as rapidly as it had grown in the 1890s. Small-scale professional touring and self-reliant provincial amateurs, as dramatised by Dorothy Hewett in the musical *THE MAN FROM MUKINUPIN*, seem to have prevailed.

Amateur movement

In the postwar decade and during the Great Depression provincial theatre was shaped, in response to a virtual drying up of professional touring, by the development of a strong amateur movement under the aegis of the REPERTORY CLUB of Perth, to which 18 country groups were affiliated by 1933. For example, the Bridgetown Repertory Club was founded in the southwest in 1930, GARRICK THEATRE opened in Guildford and the GOLDFIELDS REPERTORY CLUB was established in Kalgoorlie in 1931, and the Roleystone Repertory Club began in the Darling Ranges in 1933. These and other amateur groups from the 1930s remain important providers of theatre in the provinces.

The Repertory Club's policy of training amateur actors and playwrights had ramifications in the provinces. Members of the Perth club, working as the Ramblers under the direction of Ralph Stoddart, toured four one-act plays to the Mechanics' Hall at Pinjarra in the southwest in September 1929, and they returned at least in March 1930, when they played *Summer Lightning*. Other members of the Repertory Club took their skills with them when they moved to the country. One such was NITA PANNELL, whose production of *Ambrose Applejohn's Adventure* by Walter Hackett opened the Repertory Club at Goomalling in the wheat belt in 1930. ALEXANDER TURNER wrote and produced one-act plays and the full-length *Royal Mail* for the players at Carnamah, another wheat-belt town, 270 km north of Perth, while he lived there from 1935 to 1939. Jack Bishop, longtime chairman of the Repertory Club, transferred his Perth production of George Bernard Shaw's *The Inca of Perusalem* to Moora, in the central Midlands, to assist in the opening of the Repertory Club there in 1938.

In October 1933, the Repertory Club invited its country affiliates to Perth and discussed a plan to include them in an annual festival along the lines of the English repertory societies. In August 1934, the club sponsored a country week in Perth, during which members and affiliates saw its production of *The Mask and the Face* and clubs from Bruce Rock, Guildford and Northam presented one-act plays. The first State Drama Festival was held at His Majesty's Theatre in Perth in 1936 under the auspices of the Repertory Club. The THEATRE COUNCIL OF WESTERN AUSTRALIA took over responsibility for the annual festival in 1949, and the last festival was held in 1974. The Repertory Club also formed a country clubs committee in 1936; it began by organising a tour of Arthur Schnitzler's *Farewell Supper* to Carnamah. The annual country week also continued. From 1950 the Adult Education Board of the University of Western Australia sent actors such as NITA PANNELL to teach stagecraft in country towns and sponsored tours by the COMPANY OF FOUR.

Larger groups such as the Goldfields and Bunbury Repertory Clubs produced full annual programs of plays, provided training similar to that in Perth and worked to build their own theatres. Smaller groups have generally relied on local halls, but some have impressively restored old theatre buildings. In 1972 the Esperance Theatre Guild redesigned and modernised the Bijou Theatre, which had not been used for its stage since 1946. In April 1993 the theatre group in the wheat-belt town of Merredin reopened the Cummins Theatre, built in 1928, with *One Day Short of an April Fool*, a new play by Di Day, based on the life of Alice Cummins.

The nexus between the provincial groups and their Perth 'parent' weakened decisively after the Repertory Club amalgamated with the Company of Four in 1956 to form the professional NATIONAL THEATRE COMPANY. This toured country towns for some time in the 1960s but in the 1970s much of the responsibility for touring by professional companies fell to the then Western Australian Arts Council.

Festivals continue to provide a focus for much provincial theatre in Western Australia. Country groups take part in an annual festival organised in Perth by the Independent Theatres Association, to which some 60 provincial amateur groups are affiliated. Other important annual festivals include the Bunbury Festival and—the venues rotating annually—the North-West Drama Festival, the North-Eastern Districts Drama Festival, the South-West Drama Festival and the Central Midlands Drama Festival. Venues also rotate annually among the smaller district festivals.

Regional arts centres with performance spaces have been established through local initiatives, and with some government support, at Albany, Bunbury, Carnarvon, Esperance, Geraldton, Kalgoorlie, Karratha and Port Hedland. These centres have provided the infrastructure for country tours through the Western Australian Association of Regional Performing Arts Centres and the Performing Arts Touring Information Office in Perth. Several country towns have appointed regional arts officers. Provincial theatre has also been encouraged since the 1980s by the Western Australian Department for the Arts, which has funded selected performances through a short-term artist-in-residence scheme and its regional-arts and community-arts panels. The department's regional touring fund and the Playing Australia touring fund established in 1993 by the Australia Council also facilitate tours by major professional companies.

The combined effect of these local and governmental actions has been to give provincial theatre groups in Western Australia greater independence in initiating projects and developing local resources than they have ever had previously. Many groups prefer to mount musicals, comedies or music-hall, but there has been steady diversification into other theatrical forms. Bunbury, the largest provincial town in the state, supports the Repertory Club and MESH Youth Theatre. Albany supports three amateur groups—the Light Opera and Theatre Company, the Spectrum Theatre, and the much-toured Coco Youth Theatre. Spectrum and Coco have their own premises.

Perhaps the greatest success to come out of provincial Western Australia has been Jimmy Chi's BRAN NUE DAE, which has toured nationally since it had its genesis in Broome and was presented by the Black Swan Theatre Company at the 1990 Festival of Perth. *Bill Dunstone*

Frank Weston

American comedian, manager. Came to Australia with Cooke, Zoyara and Wilson's circus 1866. Presented minstrel shows at Weston's Opera House, Melbourne, 1869–70. Managed minstrel troupes for remainder of career.

In 1869 Frank Weston anticipated the direction of the Australian popular stage a decade later by establishing a theatre that focused exclusively on MINSTRELS. Originally a blackface performer of comic ballads, he took over St George's Hall in Melbourne, refurbished it and renamed it Weston's Opera House. It was the first theatre in Australia 'devoted exclusively to Ethiopianism, the theatre not also being a drinking and smoking room'. Its success was modest and after some months Weston was forced to relinquish the lease and take his company on the road in search of an audience. He reopened his Opera House in June 1870, but by August he had gone broke and he again surrendered the lease. He was tenacious, however, and he continued to organise minstrel parties for the remainder of his career. In 1885, for example, he teamed up with FRANK HUSSEY, a member of the original troupe at Weston's Opera House in 1869 to stage concerts by Hussey and Lawton's Minstrels at the Nugget Theatre in Melbourne. *Richard Waterhouse*

Raymond Westwell

Actor, director. Born c.1918. Trained at Royal Academy of Dramatic Art (London). Made stage debut 1939. Directed first shows for army during Second World War. Acted in West End, London. Married actor Joan Macarthur. Toured Australia with Shakespeare Memorial Theatre Company as assistant director 1953. Drama director of Central School of Speech and Drama (London). Toured Australia with Old Vic Theatre Company 1955. Director of Dundee Repertory Theatre (Scotland) 1956–60. Artistic director and administrator of National Theatre Company (Perth) 1960-62. Settled in Melbourne 1962. Acted with Melbourne Theatre Company 1967–69. Left Australia 1969. Died 1979 in England.

Raymond Westwell's inaugural directorship of the NATIONAL THEATRE COMPANY was a productive and adventurous but unhappy period in the theatrical life of Perth. A grant of £2250 from the AUSTRALIAN ELIZABETHAN THEATRE TRUST achieved his appointment to the four-year-old Playhouse Theatre, and local expectations were high. Nor did his work disappoint them. His debut, an open-air production of Molière's *The Miser* for the 1961 Festival of Perth, was described as 'a whiff of the West End'. It initiated rapid change in the company from the amateur structure of the former REPERTORY CLUB to British professionalism. Until then the theatre had been administered by volunteers and performers, mostly amateurs. Westwell took executive control with the aim of making a permanent company—no easy task. A disciplinarian with a sharp tongue, he soon alienated the theatrical hierarchy. Nevertheless, as a journalist put it, his appointment to the company marked 'a new step on its relentless road towards professionalism.'

In 1962 Westwell visited Melbourne to direct *The Aspern Papers* by Michael Redgrave for the Union Theatre Repertory Company and settled there with his wife. Westwell directed Terence Rattigan's *Ross* in 1962 and PETER BATEY's bush comedy *The No-Hopers*. In 1963 he directed the musical *Camelot* for J. C. WILLIAMSON's, with Paul Daneman as King Arthur, and Peter Luke's *Hadrian the Seventh*, with the television star Barry Morse, in 1965.

As an actor, Westwell was particularly noted for two courtroom dramas. He portrayed the British statesman Sir Charles Dilke in *The Right Honourable Gentleman* by M. Bradley-Dyne; and the Nazi accused in Robert Shaw's *The Man in the Glass Booth*. Westwell toured to Perth with the Melbourne Theatre Company in 1969 as the King in *Henry IV—part 1*. His last Australian production was Arthur Miller's *The Price* in 1969. ❦*Katharine Brisbane*

further reading
BRISBANE, KATHARINE. Westwell and mass media madness. *Australian Theatregoer* 4 (May-July 1961).

Chris Westwood

Administrator, producer. Born 14 December 1946 in Adelaide. Graduated in German from University of Adelaide and became teacher. Education officer for Adelaide Festival Centre 1973–78. On South Australian Department of Education curriculum committee 1973–78; executive officer of department's performing-arts advisory council 1974–78. Development committee of Carclew Youth Arts Centre 1975–78. Youth and writers' week committees of Adelaide Festival of Arts 1973–78. Churchill Fellowship 1977. Goethe Institute travel award 1978. Project director of Nimrod Theatre Company (Sydney) 1980–82. Formed Understudies Pty Ltd with Sue Hill 1983. General manager of Company B at Belvoir Street Theatre (Sydney) 1984–88. Member of Australian government women's delegation to China 1985. Director of arts for ABC radio 1991. Executive producer State Theatre Company of South Australia 1993–. Sydney Myer Performing Arts Award 1987.

Over 20 years Chris Westwood has established herself as one of the most capable, creative, inspirational and rigorous administrators in the arts. In Adelaide in the 1970s she fostered participation of youth by initiating youth-arts promotions such as Alternative to Football and Dollar Theatre Passport. As co-ordinator of a mass celebration for International Women's Day in Adelaide in 1975 Westwood revealed an enduring commitment to enhancing the status of women in the arts. As project director of the Nimrod Theatre Company in Sydney she co-ordinated the first Women Directors' Workshop in 1981 and the Women and Theatre Project. The latter, which involved 140 female theatre workers in 16 projects throughout 1982, ran in conjunction with the month-long NSW Women and Arts Festival. She also introduced corporately sponsored free performances for the unemployed. In 1983 Westwood left Nimrod and formed Understudies Pty Ltd with Sue Hill to provide professional arts services, including consultancies and production. Understudies involved Westwood in three notable productions—Robyn Archer's *THE PACK OF WOMEN* in 1983, *Whore in a Madhouse* by Franca Rame and Dario Fo in 1985, and *Gertrude Stein and a Companion* by Win Wells in 1987. In 1984 Understudies initiated and co-ordinated the formation of a syndicate of performing-arts workers to buy and refurbish the Nimrod Theatre, which reopened in 1985 as the BELVOIR STREET THEATRE. ❦*Bob Evans*

George Whaley

Actor, director, teacher, writer. Gained degree in engineering at University of Melbourne. Became prominent as actor and associate director at Emerald Hill Theatre (Melbourne) 1961–66. Acted with Melbourne Theatre Company 1966–68. Director of Union Theatre, University of Melbourne, 1969–73. Resident director with Old Tote Theatre Company (Sydney) 1973–75. Head of acting course at National Institute of Dramatic Art (Sydney) 1976–81. Artistic director of Theatre ACT (Canberra) 1981–83. Also acts and directs for film and television.

George Whaley has probably left his greatest mark as a director and teacher at the EMERALD HILL THEATRE, the NATIONAL INSTITUTE OF DRAMATIC ART and Theatre ACT, where he pioneered a wide range of professional styles. His influence on student drama at the University of Melbourne was far-reaching. As director of the Union Theatre he founded the Student Union's Theatre Department, which encouraged and produced student productions and is still vibrant. As an actor, his Hotspur in *Henry IV—part 1*, Vershinin in Anton Chekhov's *Three Sisters* and Proctor in Arthur Miller's *The Crucible*, all for the MELBOURNE THEATRE COMPANY in 1968, were distinguished. Many performances for other companies will be rated equally highly, not least his Maniac in Dario Fo's *Accidental Death of an Anarchist* for the NIMROD THEATRE COMPANY in Sydney in 1981. Whaley's adaptations of stories by STEELE RUDD—*On Our Selection*, first performed in Sydney in 1979, and *The Selection*, in Melbourne in 1991—have had great success. ❦*Geoffrey Milne*

Wharf Theatre

Theatre in Hickson Road, Walsh Bay, Sydney, opened 13 December 1984, seating 319. Architect: Vivian Fraser.

When maritime freight went to containers many wharves became redundant, including Pier 4/5 at Walsh Bay, a double-decked finger wharf projecting 222 metres into Sydney Harbour. The NSW government gave the upper deck of this fine timber warehouse, built in 1920–22, to the SYDNEY THEATRE COMPANY with $3·7 million to convert it into a home. The resulting complex contains the thrust-stage Wharf Theatre; a versatile studio space, renamed Wharf Theatre 2 in 1994; rehearsal rooms; scenery and costume workshops; administrative offices and a restaurant.

The company schedules the Wharf Theatre year round for smaller-scale productions in its subscription seasons and conducts experimental work in Wharf Theatre 2 and occasionally in its rehearsal rooms. Since 1991 it has also sometimes converted warehouse space on the lower deck into a rough open-stage auditorium, named the Blackfriars

Theatre because of Shakespeare performances given there. At the Wharf the company also assembles and rehearses productions for performance in the Drama Theatre at the Sydney Opera House. On the lower deck, Arts Council of NSW has its offices, the Australian Youth Theatre has premises and the Sydney Dance Company has rehearsal and administrative space.

VIVIAN FRASER's conversion retained the material and structural qualities of the wharf. It is built of ironbark, a hard timber which is so fire-resistant that fire regulations required only sprinklers and an internal emergency exit tunnel to the street from the restaurant at the farthest end. The Wharf won the Sir John Sulman Award for architecture in 1985 and the Royal Australian Institute of Architects' President's Medal for the best recycled building in Australia in 1984–85. *Ross Thorne*

further reading
FRASER, VIVIAN. Designing for 'found' spaces. *Australian Theatre Design* (ed. K. Spinks). Sydney: Australian Production Designers' Association 1992.

Sidney Wheeler

English actor. Born c.1890. Began acting 1910. Served with armed forces and in diplomatic service during First World War. Acted in London and South Africa after war. Came to Australia under contract to J. C. Williamson's 1931. Leading character actor in Williamson musicals to 1948, and on radio. Died 1951 in Sydney.

In 1936 the J. C. Williamson's magazine described Sidney Wheeler as one of the finest character actors on the Australian stage. He had a deep, powerful voice and was a master of accent. Russian, German, Swedish and especially Yiddish all came perfectly from him. He was the leading character actor in countless musicals for J. C. WILLIAMSON'S, from *Dearest Enemy* in 1931 to *Annie Get Your Gun* in 1948, in which he had perhaps his greatest stage triumph as Sitting Bull. Serious ill-health then forced Wheeler into retirement, but he returned to radio in 1949. *Richard Lane*

Albert Whelan

Comedian, singer. Born 4 May 1875 in Melbourne. Originally Albert Waxman. Became star of British music-hall. Last performance 1960. Died 19 February 1962 in London.

It is generally held that Albert Whelan was the first performer to use a theme tune. He whistled 'Die lustige Brüder' as he began and ended his singing act, for which he wore elegant formal attire. Like many successful Australian vaudevillians, Whelan began a stage career after an unsettled time in other employment. He was the son of Aaron Waxman, a successful Melbourne banker of Polish origin, and he first engaged in accountancy, with excursions into amateur theatre.

This experience helped him to support himself as half of a comic musical duo, Whelan and Wilson, in 1898, when he was unsuccessful as a miner on the goldfields at Kalgoorlie (WA). Professional work followed, initially in the WILLIAMSON AND MUSGROVE production of the musical comedy *The Belle of New York* in 1899. Whelan spent most of his long career in the Northern Hemisphere, but his numerous sound recordings ensured him popularity in Australia. In the last two decades of his life he made brief appearances in a wheelchair after he had had both his legs amputated. *Jeff Brownrigg*

further reading
MANDERS, JOE and RAYMOND MITCHENSON. *British Music Hall*. London: Studio Vista 1965.

Richard Wherrett AM

Director. Born 10 December 1940 in Sydney. Graduated in arts from University of Sydney 1961. Became schoolteacher. Went to United Kingdom 1965. Taught at E15 Acting School and London Academy of Dramatic Art 1966–69. Returned to Sydney 1970. Associate director of Old Tote Theatre Company and director of productions for Australian Theatre for Young People. Involved in Nimrod Theatre Company from 1970; artistic director 1974–79. Director for 1976 Australian National Playwrights' Conference.
Off-Broadway Obie (New York City) for best direction 1979 (*The Elocution of Benjamin Franklin* by Steve J. Spears). Director and chief executive of Sydney Theatre Company 1979–91. Australia Council theatre board 1985–87; performing arts board 1987–88. Artistic director of Melbourne International Festival of Arts 1992–93. Sydney Critics' Circle Award for best director 1977 (*The Elocution of Benjamin Franklin* by Steve J. Spears). Green Room Award 1986 for directing *The Life and Adventures of Nicholas Nickleby* by David Edgar. AM 1984.

Under Richard Wherrett the SYDNEY THEATRE COMPANY became perhaps the most successful in Australia. His appointment in 1979 was a surprise, but he was well qualified. He had directed classics and modern European works. He had launched new Australian plays and had encouraged new writing as a member of the AUSTRALIAN NATIONAL PLAYWRIGHTS' CONFERENCE committee. Wherrett's taste for elegance and pleasure, combined with cool intelligence and a capacity for work, made him a singularly successful leader. The company's seasons in the Drama Theatre of the SYDNEY OPERA HOUSE both drew the town and attracted tourists, with such success that for many Wherrett seemed to embody aspects of Sydney itself.

The opening of the WHARF THEATRE as the company's home in 1984 allowed Wherrett to let the Drama Theatre subsidise riskier adventures in the smaller theatre. He also directed numerous plays and musicals. They included Edmond Rostand's *Cyrano de Bergerac* in 1980, the musical *Chicago* in 1981, JUSTIN FLEMING's *The Cobra* with ROBERT HELPMANN in 1983, David Edgar's *The Life and Adventures of Nicholas Nickleby* in 1983, Michael Gow's *AWAY* and David Williamson's EMERALD CITY in 1987, and Arthur Miller's *The Crucible* in 1991.

In earlier years in Sydney Wherrett's notable productions were Bertolt Brecht's *The Resistible Rise of Arturo Ui* for the OLD TOTE THEATRE COMPANY in 1971, and *Hamlet* and Peter Handke's *Kaspar* for the NIMROD THEATRE COMPANY in 1973. When he became a joint artistic director of Nimrod he showed that he was diplomatic and encouraging with actors and staff. He chose plays well and his work met the enthusiastic approval of critics and audiences. In 1976 he directed Gordon Chater in Steve J. Spears's THE ELOCUTION OF BENJAMIN FRANKLIN in the tiny Downstairs theatre and the production went on to great successes. *Ron Blair*

further reading
HOWIE, ANN C. (ed.). *Who's Who in Australia 1991* 27th edn. Melbourne: Information Australia.

White Australia

—or, The Empty North. Play in four acts by Randolph Bedford. **premiere** 26 June 1909, King's Theatre, Melbourne. Cast: Bert Bailey, Walter Dalgleish, Harry Diver, Edmund Duggan, Laurence Dunbar, Temple Harrison, J. H. Nunn, Roy Redgrave, Helen Vigors, Stirling Whyte. Designer: Rege Robins. Director: J. H. Nunn. Producer: William Anderson.

An extraordinary mixture of chauvinist speeches and sensational effects, *White Australia* was RANDOLPH BEDFORD's attempt in 1909 to rouse his countrymen from sport and sloth to prepare to repel Japanese invasion. Like his fellow *Bulletin* writers, Bedford was outraged by a defence agreement between Japan and the United Kingdom in 1902. Bedford himself chose the less racist title *For Australia*, and the subtitle *The Empty North* appears to have been the producer's. Bedford saw the north as the prize rather than the site of an attack. 'Our rich and empty land is a permanent temptation to the poor and overcrowded world and if we would hold Australia we must be strong,' he wrote.

White Australia contrasts desperate efforts by a squatter and a scientist to prevent a Japanese invasion with the indifference of fellow Australians. Bedford made the squatter's son an English-educated traitor. In a telling and much-praised scene, the operator at the Katherine telegraph station, trying to warn Sydney and Melbourne that Japan has declared war, is murdered by 'A Jap and a white man [the son] and a Chow'. Meanwhile a horsebreaker and a half-asleep swagman—'two representative Australians', the Melbourne *Age* called them on 28 June—argue about which year Malua 'won the Oakleigh Plate'.

WILLIAM ANDERSON took up *White Australia* and gave it the full spectacular staging of popular melodrama, with the heroes' airship rising into the clouds, flying over Sydney Harbour, dropping bombs to repel the invading Japanese fleet, and then descending into Macquarie Street. There the hero Jack harangues the grateful crowd:

> … *No more mad devotion to vicarious sport—arm yourselves and think, get guns and resolution.*
>
> CROWD: *Hooray!*
>
> JACK: *Cheer today but remember tomorrow. Down with the time servers, the men who look far off for snobbish rewards … Listen to our country's voices, crude and raw but young and strong, self assertive but manly, intolerant but kind.*

After three weeks of propaganda about 'the wondrous nation that it is yet to be' *White Australia* disappeared. Several other plays and films prior to 1914 shared its alarmism, however. ❦*Richard Fotheringham*

reference
For Australia is in the Australian Archives (Canberra), listed as TS, CRS A1336/2 item 931. A later typescript is in the Library of Congress (Washington DC).

Henry E. White

Architect, engineer. Born 21 August 1876 in Dunedin (New Zealand). Designed theatres in Australia 1912–29. Died 3 March 1952 in Sydney.

In less than two decades Henry E. White designed or redesigned dozens of theatre and cinemas and other large structures in Australia, such as the Bunnerong power station in Sydney. He followed structural principles, developed overseas in the 1890s, that allowed balcony-supporting columns in theatres to be reduced from a dozen or so to one or two. He came to theatre design from engineering. On leaving school in Dunedin he went into his father's building business and studied architecture and engineering at night school. At 16 he became dissatisfied with the business, and signed on as a seaman. He landed in Fremantle in November 1893 and spent some time on the West Australian goldfields before returning to rejoin his father as a partner. In 1896 White, only 19, began business on his own, accepting small design-and-build jobs and then a major engineering work, a mile-long tunnel from a river to a hydroelectric plant. This won him a reputation and he was given major commissions in Christchurch, where he developed a love of theatre. A barn-like old theatre in Christchurch made White wonder how the audience could absorb the true atmosphere of the drama when so many people had to peer through a forest of posts and experience poor sound. He ruminated on a design for a perfect theatre.

At the end of the century, the entrepreneur John Fuller snr employed the 23-year-old White to design and build a theatre in Christchurch. In 1911 Fuller's sons decided to build the biggest and best theatre in New Zealand. White designed the 2355-seat Her Majesty's Theatre in Wellington, epitomising all his ideas on theatre design. Now called the St James Theatre, this is now the only survivor of the many theatres in Australasia built or altered by White until the early 1920s in a personal heavily modelled Louis XV decorative style that he called 'Louis Seize'.

In 1913 the entrepreneur HUGH D. MCINTOSH engaged White to design theatres in Australia. The first was the twin TIVOLI THEATRE in Brisbane in 1915. Its principal auditorium was very similar to that of the Wellington theatre. So were the auditoria of theatres to which White made major alterations—the Adelphi Theatre in Sydney in 1915, and FULLERS' NATIONAL THEATRE in Sydney, the MAJESTIC THEATRE in Adelaide and the PALACE THEATRE in Melbourne in 1916—and of the Majestic Theatre in Sydney in 1917.

For his next major batch of theatre designs White changed his decorative style to the more restrained 18th-century classicism of Robert Adam. This style had been favoured in the late 1910s by the American theatre architect Thomas Lamb. White reproduced it in rebuilding the THEATRE ROYAL in Sydney in 1921, in the auditorium of the PRINCESS THEATRE in Melbourne in 1922, in reworking the auditorium of the Palace Theatre in Melbourne in 1923, in rebuilding the ATHENAEUM THEATRE in Melbourne in 1924 and in the luxurious new St James Theatre and office block for Fullers' in Sydney in 1926.

In the meantime White had designed many cinemas. Some in country towns—including Bundaberg, Ipswich, Maryborough and Rockhampton in Queensland—had a stage for touring theatrical companies. So did the PALAIS THEATRE at St Kilda in Melbourne. In the late 1920s Union Theatres commissioned White to design two great picture palaces with fly-tower stages in Sydney—the CAPITOL THEATRE and the State Theatre. White visited the USA in 1927 and was highly influenced by a flamboyant American cinema designer, John Eberson. After he saw Eberson's work White was able to eliminate all posts supporting balconies, and the interiors of both Sydney theatres exhibit the American's influence in an eclectic richness that contrasts with the subdued Adam style of White's live theatres of the early 1920s. White's architectural practice collapsed during the Great Depression and he closed his office. He had designed more than 120 theatres for stage or screen. Some of his former employees, including Cowall Ham, G. N. Kenworthy and Guy Crick, continued to specialise in designing theatres, mostly cinemas. ❦*Ross Thorne*

further reading
THOMAS, JULIAN. Henry E. White. *Australian Dictionary of Biography* 12. Melbourne University Press 1990.

Patrick White

Dramatist. Born 28 May 1912 in London to Australian parents. Grew up in Sydney. Went to school in England at 13. Returned to Australia and worked as jackeroo 1929. Studied languages and literature at Cambridge University. Began writing in London. Royal Air Force intelligence officer in Greece and Middle East during Second World War. Settled in Sydney with lifelong companion Manoly Lascaris 1948. Awarded Nobel Prize for Literature 1973. Published eight plays, 13 novels, two collections of short stories, articles and one collection of poems. Died 30 September 1990 in Sydney. Withdrew from Order of Australia in protest against federal government policies 1976.

The first Australian dramatist to offer a serious alternative to the naturalistic theatre in the 1960s was Patrick White. His plays were in the forefront of increasing innovation, from which playwrights such as DOROTHY HEWETT, LOUIS NOWRA, JOHN ROMERIL and STEPHEN SEWELL emerged in the next two decades. Rather than focusing on domestic reality, White saw everything human in relation to the forces and cycles of nature. Through his characters' spiritual quests, he explored the myths and rituals that make up society, using non-naturalistic forms but realistic characters who become larger than life. A Brechtian emphasis on theatricality allows the world of the plays to be as real and as imagined, as ordinary and as fantastic, as only life in the theatre can be. Through a combination of vigorous vernacular and heightened poetic language White created a new dramatic language and gave it life, colour and energy never previously experienced on the Australian stage. His dramatic power lay in his ability to convey theatrically the intricacies of human nature regardless of time and place, and portray this through a particular society—Australia.

His early work for the theatre has been lost: the comedies *Bread and Butter Women* and *School for Friends*, produced at BRYANT'S PLAYHOUSE in Sydney in 1935; *Return to Abyssinia* (1947) and revue sketches and lyrics performed in London. In 1947 he wrote THE HAM FUNERAL, about the spiritual quest of an artistic young man in London. It won public and critical acclaim when it was first performed in 1961, after it had been rejected for the 1962 Adelaide Festival of Arts.

In less than three years, White wrote three more plays, all of which had mixed receptions. The Adelaide University Theatre Guild performed THE SEASON AT SARSAPARILLA, a harsh but comic and highly theatrical satire on suburbia, and *Night on Bald Mountain*, White's only attempt at a modern tragedy. In the latter work NITA PANNELL played one of Australian theatre's richest and most extraordinary creations, the goat woman Miss Quodling. JOHN TASKER directed all the Adelaide productions. In Melbourne, JOHN SUMNER directed the Union Theatre Repertory Company in *A Cheery Soul*, which also deals with Sarsaparillan destructive insularity. It had a cast of 24 sharing 34 roles, with Pannell as the 'cheery soul' Miss Docker, a do-gooder who spreads disaster. The theatre was then dominated by naturalist traditions and White's innovative use of epic structures, style and form in these plays aroused distrust of what some called 'intellectual' and 'experimental' theatre. The critics rejected what they saw as bitter and hateful satire on the Australian middle class in the plays set in the fictitious suburb of Sarsaparilla. The play received best was the only one set outside Australia, *The Ham Funeral*.

The Season at Sarsaparilla had a mixed reception in Adelaide in 1962 and generated much critical comment in newspapers and journals. It also inspired later playwrights to experiment with theatrical forms. Revivals by the SYDNEY THEATRE COMPANY and the STATE THEATRE Company of South Australia confirmed the play as an Australian classic. In Sydney, JIM SHARMAN directed *The Season at Sarsaparilla* for the OLD TOTE THEATRE COMPANY on 3 November 1976, and *A Cheery Soul* for the SYDNEY THEATRE COMPANY on 17 January 1979. ROBYN NEVIN's Miss Docker was a *tour de force*. The critics praised these productions and interest in White's drama revived. White was himself inspired by Sharman's production of *The Season at Sarsaparilla* to write his first play in more than 13 years, BIG TOYS, a small but ambitious work about corruption and political games. Sharman directed it for the Old Tote company in 1977.

Signal Driver, with a small cast but epic dimensions, followed in 1982. 'A morality play for the times', *Signal Driver* spans 60 years of love (of a kind) and marriage. NEIL ARMFIELD directed the first performance, by the Lighthouse Company in Adelaide, and productions with different casts and differences in staging in Brisbane in August 1983 and Sydney in May 1985. Sharman directed the Lighthouse Company in *Netherwood* in 1983. Set in an isolated farm house, this play dramatises the ways in which a group of outcasts can represent a threat to 'normal' society simply because they are 'different'. *Shepherd on the Rocks* is about magic, dream and love. It takes its 28 characters (played by a cast of 13) from the church establishment, the red-light district of Kings Cross in Sydney, small-town middle class, high society, and a travelling circus. It was the sixth of White's plays to have its world premiere in Adelaide. Armfield directed the production by the State Theatre Company of South Australia in 1987. Critics varied greatly in their views of White's last four plays and he remained controversial to the last. Most recognised, however, that he had played a large role in developing an imaginative and colourful national theatre. He also adapted his short story *The Night the Prowler* as the screenplay for a film of the same title, directed by Sharman in 1976. ❦*May-Brit Akerholt*

published plays
Big Toys (1977). Sydney: Currency Press 1978.
A Cheery Soul (1963). Sydney: London: Eyre and Spottiswoode 1965. New York: Viking Press 1966. Melbourne: Sun 1967. Sydney: Currency Press 1985 in *Collected Plays* 1.
The Ham Funeral (1961). London: Eyre and Spottiswoode 1965. New York: Viking Press 1966. Melbourne: Sun 1967. Sydney: Currency Press 1985 in *Collected Plays* 1.
Netherwood (1983). Sydney: Currency Press 1983.

Night on Bald Mountain (1964). London: Eyre and Spottiswoode 1965. New York: Viking Press 1966. Melbourne: Sun 1967. Sydney: Currency Press 1985 in *Collected Plays* 1.

The Season at Sarsaparilla (1962). London: Eyre and Spottiswoode 1965. New York: Viking Press 1966. Melbourne: Sun 1967. Sydney: Currency Press 1985 in *Collected Plays* 1.

Signal Driver (1982). Sydney: Currency Press 1983.

further reading

AKERHOLT, MAY-BRIT. Biographical note. *Collected Plays of Patrick White* 1. Sydney: Currency Press 1985.

CARROLL, DENNIS. *Australian Contemporary Drama from 1909* 2nd edn. Sydney: Currency Press 1993.

MARR, DAVID. *Patrick White—A life*. Sydney: Random House 1991.

SYKES, ALRENE. In *Contemporary Dramatists* (ed. D. L. Kirkpatrick) 4th edn. London: St James Press 1988.

Whitehall Theatrical Productions

Professional dramatic company in Sydney, founded in 1940 by Alec Coppel and Kathleen Robinson. **venue** Minerva Theatre 1941–50. **directors** 1940–44 Coppel and Robinson. 1944–47 Robinson and Roland Walton. 1947–50 Richard Parry, Robinson and Walton. **first production** *Mr Smart Guy* by Alec Coppel, 10 May 1941, Minerva Theatre. Cast: Harvey Adams, Catherine Duncan, Nigel Lovell. Designer: William Constable. Director: Alec Coppel. Music: Sefton Daly. **last production** *Dream Girl* by Elmer Rice, directed by Fifi Banvard, April 1950. **landmark production** *The Man Who Came to Dinner* by Moss Hart and George S. Kaufman, December 1941.

For ten years Whitehall Theatrical Productions mounted long-running productions in the luxurious 1000-seat MINERVA THEATRE in Sydney's Kings Cross. ALEC COPPEL and KATHLEEN ROBINSON, both recently returned to Australia after successes overseas, founded the company in 1940 and called it Whitehall because Robinson's last season in London had been at the Whitehall Theatre. This was also where in 1938 Coppel had his first success as a dramatist. He wrote and directed the first Whitehall production at the Minerva, *Mr Smart Guy*. It had a gala opening, which was filmed by Fox Movietone and broadcast by radio 2GB.

Whitehall aimed to 'produce good commercial plays continuously' at a time when the only other professional theatres in Sydney were the Tivoli, presenting revue, and the Theatre Royal, given over largely to ballet and operetta. The Minerva ran a play for three weeks at 8.30 nightly plus matinées at 2.15 p.m. on Wednesday and Saturday, then presented it at 6 p.m. nightly while a new play took over at 8.30. Theatregoers who were unwilling to stay out late in the wartime brownout liked the 6 p.m. sessions.

The Man Who Came to Dinner by Moss Hart and George S. Kaufman was a runaway success from December 1941, playing for more than 100 performances. Edwin Styles, an accomplished actor who worked in many subsequent productions by Coppel, headed an all-star cast. Later successes included *I Killed the Count* by Coppel himself, *You Can't Take it with You* by Hart and Kaufman, and *Arsenic and Old Lace* by Joseph Kesselring in 1942; *The Amazing Dr Clitterhouse* by Barré Lyndon, and *George Washington Slept Here* by Hart and Kaufman in 1943; and *Rope* by Patrick Hamilton in 1944. Coppel left Australia in 1944 and Roland Walton, a Sydney accountant, replaced him as codirector with Kathleen Robinson. The Welsh actor and director RICHARD PARRY became the third codirector in 1947.

The company held auditions for each production, and also offered professional work to the most talented students of the Whitehall Academy of Dramatic Art, which was established in 1944 with Frederick Blackman as principal. Some students went on to successful careers, including Vincent Ball, Doreen Harrop, Gordon Glenwright and William Redmond. Whitehall Productions sent touring companies to Melbourne, Adelaide, Perth, New Zealand and, under the direction of FIFI BANVARD, to Japan in 1948 to entertain occupation forces.

In 1949 Metro–Goldwyn–Mayer bought the Minerva Theatre and gave Whitehall Productions six months to vacate the premises. ❦*Jessica Noad*

reference
The Mitchell Library (Sydney) has a small collection, the Joy Lewis Papers: Whitehall Productions, 1947–50, MSS 2924.

Robert P. Whitworth

Actor, dramatist, manager. Born 1831 in Torquay (England). Emigrated to Australia 1855. Particularly active in Queensland, Victoria and New Zealand. Died 31 March 1901 in Melbourne. Father of actor–manager Robert Hollyford Whitworth.

Robert P. Whitworth and GARNET WALCH were the two great survivors of 19th-century Australian journalism and theatre. They survived by writing short stories, plays, light verse, novels and historical works and editing anthologies and cyclopedias. Whitworth also acted on the professional stage, ran his own theatre company, rode in steeplechases and broke horses. He acted with G. V. BROOKE in the late 1850s, and in 1862 he utilised some New Zealand experiences to thrill Sydneysiders with three plays he wrote featuring a group of Maoris. His farce *Catching a Conspirator* was successful in Melbourne in 1867. Next year he costarred with a champion New Zealand horse in his racecourse play *Flying Jib*, a huge success in Auckland.

For many years Whitworth mixed acting and writing with other activities. His last known play was *Fortune's Wheel—or, Captain Ginger Married and Settled*, a comedy staged in Victoria in 1885. In 1886 he published *Velvet and Rags*, a collection of humorous stories based on his theatrical memories. Of these *The Old Man's Story*, about a scratch company performing *Mazeppa* to miners at the Deep Lead Diggings in the 1850s, and *The Prompter's Story*, involving a dog dressed as a lion which barks at the wrong moment in *Androcles and the Lion*, are the funniest, and suggest the improvised character of the early Australian stage.

Whitworth was associated with his friend MARCUS CLARKE's banned localisation of THE HAPPY LAND in 1880, and both Whitworth and Garnet Walch seem to have tinkered with Clarke's unfinished comedy *Reverses*. These three were remembered as old Melbourne Bohemians. Whitworth was 'of the spontaneous type, not the factitious', said the *Bulletin* in its obituary on 13 April 1901. 'His wide knowledge embraced the best in Art, Literature, the Drama, Heraldry and Sport', claimed *Table Talk* on 4 April 1901, but he was more accurately a prolific lightweight raconteur and populist, whose greatest achievement was that he supported himself and his family principally by his pen, perhaps earlier than any other Australian playwright.

One of his three children was Robert Hollyford Whitworth, who was born in 1859 and acted from about

1894 to about 1917. As Robert Hollyford he was a leading actor in the DAN BARRY Dramatic Company in 1899. By 1906 he was BARRY's partner and for at least a decade after Barry's death in 1908 he managed the famous troupe, which gave the outback lurid melodramas and stirring national pieces. He may have been the unidentified actor who played Ned Kelly in the 1906 film *The Story of the Kelly Gang*, on which he and Barry registered copyright. ❦*Richard Fotheringham*

further reading
ALMANZI, HELEN K. Robert Percy Whitworth. *Australian Dictionary of Biography* 6. Melbourne University Press 1976.

Wild West shows

American-style Wild West shows, developed from mid-19th century hippodrama, became popular in Australia in the 1880s and 1890s. They merged with indigenous bushranging plays, which had developed from mid-century adaptations of melodrama to Australian circumstances like the gold-rushes, bushranging, pioneering and exploration. After the First World War the Wild West show rapidly became assimilated into carnival items and circus acts, and sensational bushranging dramas gave way to the homely bush comedy. For the most part Wild West shows were standard fare—trick riding, shooting displays and cowboy costumes—interspersed with and interpolated into bushranging dramas and plays of the American west. They usually featured sensational scenic effects such as waterfalls or flooded rivers. Particular favourites were tales of the Kelly Gang and Thunderbolt and of the Americans Little Star and Texas Jack, who was both a touring performer and a fictional hero. ALFRED DAMPIER relied heavily on Wild West elements in his adventure melodramas at the Alexandra Theatre in Melbourne. He had a sensational hit in 1891 with *THE SCOUT*, starring 'Dr' W. F. CARVER, an American sharpshooter who resembled 'Buffalo Bill' Cody. Another Buffalo Bill lookalike, E. I. Cole headed the BOHEMIAN DRAMATIC COMPANY, a Wild West and bushranging tent show. ❦*Barbara Garlick*

Allan Wilkie CBE

> Actor, manager. Born 1878 in England. Educated and apprenticed to merchant in Liverpool. Went to London to become actor 1899. Performed melodrama and Shakespeare in companies run by Ben Greet, Frank Benson and Herbert Beerbohm Tree. Toured English provinces, India and East Asia with own company 1905–14. Married Frediswyde Hunter-Watts 1908. Arrived in Australia 1914. Headed George Marlow Grand Shakespearean Company, touring Australia and New Zealand with Shakespeare, 18th-century comedy and melodrama, 1916–19. Formed Allan Wilkie Shakespearean Company 1920. Made extensive tours of Australia and New Zealand until 1930s, playing leading roles opposite his wife. Founded *Shakespearean Quarterly* 1922. Toured in modern comedies and scenes from Shakespeare 1930–31. Left Australia in May 1931, and toured New Zealand, Canada, USA and Britain in scenes from Shakespeare. Died 1970 in Scotland. CBE 1925.

In 1920 Allan Wilkie made the first serious attempt to establish a permanent touring Shakespeare company in Australia. He worked for a decade to maintain it and he left the memory of an honest attempt to provide thoughtful, fluid productions of Shakespeare's plays. The ALLAN WILKIE SHAKESPEAREAN COMPANY was all the more remarkable because it was an independent venture. Wilkie brought his love of Shakespeare to an entire generation of Australasian theatregoers and schoolchildren. He was awarded the CBE at least partly in recognition of his contribution to education. He also contributed to the establishment of a tradition of classical acting in Australia. From his earliest provincial tours in England, Wilkie established a repertoire and production style which he retained throughout the 1920s, switching rapidly between popular melodrama and classical plays. The Shakespeare plays he staged most frequently were *Hamlet*, *Macbeth*, *The Merchant of Venice*—in which he played Shylock—and *Twelfth Night*. Wilkie was a traditionalist in style and approach, rooted firmly in the England of Henry Irving, Frank Benson, Ben Greet and Herbert Beerbohm Tree. He deplored the fashion of presenting Shakespeare in modern dress, and took an interest in preserving traditional stage business. His favourite comedy part in Shakespeare was Malvolio, in which he imitated Tree's performance. Wilkie's large build and big voice best suited him to big, blustery parts that permitted broad, robust delivery—Falstaff, Bottom in *A Midsummer Night's Dream*, Caliban in *The Tempest*, Mathias in Leopold Lewis's *The Bells* and Parolles in *All's Well that Ends Well*.

After his arrival in Australia in 1914 Wilkie found work playing 'heavy' roles on tour with NELLIE STEWART in 1915, and then for J. C. WILLIAMSON's. In 1916 he reached an agreement with the melodrama specialist GEORGE MARLOW to head a touring company, presenting Shakespeare at popular prices. Marlow provided financial backing and publicity, while Wilkie had a free hand in selection of plays, casting and production matters. His concern was to put together a company capable of performing the classics, and able to deal with the demands of blank verse. Many young actors learned their craft with Wilkie. The Australasian tour of the Marlow company covered Melbourne, Sydney and Adelaide as well as smaller centres, and Wilkie discovered that a varied program was essential to maintain the interest of the audience. He used the experience he had gained in his tours when he founded his own Shakespeare company in September 1920. Wilkie announced his intention to produce all 37 of Shakespeare's plays but he only managed 27 before the company folded in 1930. These, however, included the rarely-seen *Antony and Cleopatra*, *Coriolanus*, *Cymbeline*, *Henry VIII*, *King Lear*, *Measure for Measure* and *The Winter's Tale*.

The last play the company produced was *Governor Bligh* by Doris Egerton Jones. Wilkie commissioned this play and on 6 August 1930 the *Sydney Morning Herald* congratulated him on his enterprise and courage 'in presenting for the first time on any stage a play written by an Australian author and dealing solely with Australian history'. In 1931, Wilkie rallied with an attempt to present modern comedy. He opened the first professional production in Australia of Noël Coward's *Hay Fever* at the Tivoli Theatre in Melbourne on 21 February 1931. It transferred to Brisbane, where it was followed by John Drinkwater's *Bird in Hand*. A tour of Queensland followed, but there was insufficient support during the Great Depression and Wilkie disbanded the company. He left Australia with his wife in May, and never performed here again. ❦*Lisa Warrington*

further reading

MARSH, NGAIO. *Black Beech and Honeydew*. London: Collins 1966.

RICKARD, JOHN. Allan Wilkie. *Australian Dictionary of Biography* 12. Melbourne University Press 1990.

STRONG, ARCHIBALD. Allan Wilkie and Shakespeare. *Australian Quarterly* 11 (1930).

WARRINGTON, LISA J. Allan Wilkie in Australia—The work of a Shakespearean actor–manager. University of Tasmania MA thesis 1981.

WILKIE, ALLAN. All the World My Stage—The reminiscences of a Shakespearean actor-manager in five continents. Unpublished ms., revised c.1959, in Latrobe Library (Melbourne).

Billy Williams

Comedian, singer. Born 7 February 1878. Originally Richard Isaac Banks. Began as amateur singer in Melbourne in 1890s. Performed as Curly Banks, William Williams and William 'Billy' Holt Williams. Became clown in professional theatre. Went to England 1899. Became vaudeville singer and recording artist. Toured Australia 1910. Died 1 March 1915 in Shoreham (England).

The vaudevillian who styled himself Australia's Billy Williams, 'the man in the velvet suit', possibly entered the professional theatre as a jockey in BLAND HOLT's spectacular productions. In an interview in 1909 he claimed to have toured with the Williamson and Musgrove production of the musical comedy *The Belle of New York* in 1899 and *The Forty Thieves*. Contemporary program notes show a Mr Williams as Ah Bung in the former and a Mr J. Williams as L. S. Dee in the latter. Late in 1899 George Adams, owner of the PALACE THEATRE in Sydney, gave Billy Williams a ticket and £100 to pursue his career in Great Britain. After a short period as a clown he gradually specialised in performing songs with catchy choruses. He adopted a 'bubble cut' hairstyle and usually performed in a well-cut velvet suit. Between 1906 and 1914 he made more than 500 recordings. As a result he found himself well known in Australia when he returned in 1910.   *Jeff Brownrigg*

further reading

MANDER, RAYMOND and JOE MITCHENSON. *British Music Hall*. London: Studio Vista 1965.

Peter Williams

Entrepreneur. Born 21 October 1947 at Yass (NSW). Acted in amateur theatre in Yass and Sydney. Revived and ran Phillip Street Theatre (Sydney) 1979–86. Ran suburban Glen Street Theatre (Sydney) 1987–90. Works in partnership with wife Ellen Williams.

Peter Williams impressively achieves his aim of satisfying the general public, though he seems to be less adventurous than in the 1970s, when he attracted attention by presenting plays by the South African playwright Athol Fugard. As a young man, Williams acted, directed and produced for the Yass Repertory Society and sold tickets at his women's hairdressing salon. The director ROBIN LOVEJOY saw his work when adjudicating in drama festivals, and urged him to try his luck in Sydney.

In 1971 Williams took the advice. He worked at the Independent Theatre, on radio and television and at Amy McGrath's Australian Theatre in Newtown. Then he presented several of Fugard's challenging plays, some of which were also seen at Adelaide Festivals. In 1979 Williams recreated the PHILLIP STREET THEATRE in Sydney. The home of intimate revue had been demolished and replaced by a grand office building which contained a small, flat-floored hall of considerable discomfort, with a small stage. Williams took it over and ran it as a theatre until 1986. In 1987 he began three years running the Glen Street Theatre in Frenchs Forest on the northern fringe of Sydney. In 1990 Williams began using the Playhouse Theatre of the Sydney Opera House for his productions. He chose popular plays and cast them with audience-attracting performers, often with television reputations. In 1991 Williams and his wife and indispensable partner, Ellen, staged seven productions and toured them nationally. The years since have seen similar activities.   *John West*

David Williamson AO

Dramatist. Born 24 February 1942 in Melbourne. Brought up in Bairnsdale (Vic). Graduated from Monash University (Melbourne) in mechanical engineering 1964. Worked as design engineer for General Motors Holden 1965. Lectured in thermodynamics and social psychology at Swinburne College of Technology (Melbourne) 1966–72. First play performed 1968. Writer and actor with La Mama Company and Australian Performing Group 1970–72. Member of Australian Council for the Arts 1972–75. Visiting associate professor of drama at Aarhus University (Denmark) 1978. Member of Australian Broadcasting Commission 1978–79. President of Australian Writers' Guild 1979–93. Also writes for film and television. Major Awgie awards 1972 (*The Removalists*), 1978 (*The Club*). Awgie awards for best stage play 1973 (*Don's Party*), 1980 (*Travelling North*), 1988 (*Emerald City*). George Devine Award, London, 1972 (*The Removalists*). London *Evening Standard* award 1973 (*The Removalists*). AO 1983. HonDLitt 1988 (University of Sydney), 1990 (Monash University).

David Williamson has achieved greater popularity than any other Australian playwright. After more than two decades he continues to chart the manners and morals of his audience to an extent that has set the direction in which the Australian theatre has developed.

As a student at the University of Melbourne and later at Monash University Williamson wrote subversive sketches for student revues on such subjects as conscription, Aborigines, imperialism and sexuality. He also wrote sketches for the EMERALD HILL THEATRE COMPANY. His first play was *The Indecent Exposure of Anthony East*, a three-act comedy about a corporate executive who writes romantic fiction. The TIN ALLEY PLAYERS, directed by Christopher Bell, presented it at the Union Theatre at the University of Melbourne on 28 August 1968.

In 1970 Williamson's career began to move with the performance at the LA MAMA THEATRE of three short plays and his first full-length play, *THE COMING OF STORK*. This was quickly followed in 1971 by *THE REMOVALISTS* at La Mama and *Don's Party* at the Pram Factory. In 1972 he resigned from teaching. Williamson was now placed at the centre of a new movement of aggressive Australianness by a chain of events that included protest against Australian involvement in the Vietnam War, which created a rebellious, anti-authoritarian mood; establishment of the Australian Council for the Arts and of the publisher Currency Press; rebirth of the film industry; and emergence of entrepreneurs who reflected the climate of the time.

Sydney theatres took up *The Removalists* and *Don's Party*, which both moved rapidly into the mainstream and achieved further commissions for the young writer. *The Removalists* won an award in London. Both plays and *The Coming of Stork* were published and made into feature films and Williamson began a parallel career as a screenwriter. His early style was comic, confrontatory and irreverent, deriving from and contributing to the political and social criticism of the AUSTRALIAN PERFORMING GROUP. *The Coming of Stork* deals with the sexual and social habits and material ambitions of a group of young graduates who share a house in Melbourne and the favours of one woman. *The Removalists* is a black comedy about domestic confrontation and abuse of privilege, as two predatory policemen interfere in a marital dispute. *Don's Party* traces the fading ambitions and compromises made by a once-close group of student radicals in parallel with the fading hopes of the Australian Labor Party during an election night reunion.

These were the plays that established Williamson's reputation. They were followed at a steady craftsmanly pace by *Jugglers Three* (1972), about the effects of the Vietnam War upon a group divided by conscription; *What If You Died Tomorrow?* (1973), about the traumas of deserting regular employment for the life of a writer and married life for greater fulfilment; *The Department* (1974), which criticises the trivia of academic politics; *A Handful of Friends* (1976), about a writer's friends who see themselves betrayed by a work of fiction; and *The Club* (1977), which describes the conflict within a football club as old loyalties are replaced by market forces.

These plays, all intensely personal and domestic, contributed substantially to the self-examination that preoccupied Australians in the 1970s as the disillusionment of Vietnam and other social changes induced national independence. While providing the new audiences of the recently established state theatre companies with characters to whom they instantly related, Williamson's plays also charted with uncanny accuracy—even prescience—the changed emotional climate brought to the country largely by his baby-boom generation.

A member of the Australian Labor Party, Williamson experienced the euphoria of its victory in November 1972 after 23 years of conservative government, the avalanche of change that followed, the mounting fear at the pace of change, the inexperience of the decision-makers, the relief at the landslide conservative victory in 1975 and the enthusiasm with which the nation gave itself from the idealists to the managers. Williamson's metaphor is always domestic but his characters hold in their hands the heart of Australian politics.

His next major play, *Travelling North* (1979), was a threnody for the 1970s. It is the story of an elderly Communist who resolves to leave the harsh climate of Melbourne for the earthly paradise of the Queensland coast. With him goes his lover, a single mother who leaves behind two married, unhappy and ungrateful daughters. As Frank faces the unexpected prospect of death the couple find themselves confronted with the real values of life and a realisation of the emotional cost of principle upon those closest to them. Williamson's adaptation of *King Lear* in 1978—an experiment later suppressed—had its realisation in *Travelling North*, which many regarded as his finest play.

His family's six months in Denmark in 1978 bore fruit in 1982 with *The Perfectionist*, a domestic drama about the complexities of accommodating career and marriage, reason and emotion. This play was followed through the 1980s by a series of exploratory works on disparate subjects with an increasingly moral subtext. *Sons of Cain* (1985) is about investigative journalism and political corruption. In *Emerald City* (1987) a screenwriter teeters between the demands of national integrity and international aggrandisement. In *Top Silk* (1989) an ambitious legal couple clash over the divisions between head and heart. *Siren* (1990) is a moral tale in farce form about undercover police attempting to catch a local government official on a bribery charge. *Money and Friends* (1991) is a recession comedy in which a well-heeled group who have long shared their beachside leisure, are confronted with the unsavoury dilemma: 'Would you lend a friend $10 000?'

Brilliant Lies (1993), deals with the conflicting emotions and power plays of a sexual harassment case. It makes a tightly argued case for the damage caused by selfishness in the amoral world of the 1990s. The play is suffused with a sense of material and spiritual failure and is less comic and more prophetic in its implications for the future of human relationships than any of his plays since *Travelling North*. The theme is taken up again in *Sanctuary* (1994), a head-to-head confrontation between a public figure and a young critic. Here Williamson returns to the comic accusatory violence of *The Removalists*.

He has been more widely produced in the world's theatre centres than any other Australian playwright. He visited London for a season of *The Removalists* in 1973, and later for seven further plays. He went to the USA for *The Club* in Washington DC and on Broadway in 1978, and since then he has worked periodically in Los Angeles. His success overseas remains moderate, however. This is related to the intensely Australian quality of his writing rather than to any alien form or character.

The 1992 success of *Money and Friends* in Los Angeles may be a sign not of change within Williamson's role as storyteller but of the increasingly homogeneous quality of middle-class values in the 1990s. Since *Don's Party*, a play then mysterious in the United Kingdom for its portrait of the upwardly mobile, he has continued to chart the public pretensions and private fears of the new middle class. The worldwide hectic exchange of money and power in the 1980s has deprived the older nations of wisdom that was once inherited; and rendered the world of David Williamson more familiar to outsiders than it had ever been in the past. ❦*Katharine Brisbane*

published plays
Brilliant Lies (1993). Sydney: Currency Press 1993.
The Club (1977). Sydney: Currency Press 1993 in *Collected Plays* 2.
The Coming of Stork (1970). Sydney; Currency Press 1986 in *Collected Plays* 1.
The Department (1974). Sydney: Currency–Methuen 1975.
Don's Party (1971, revised 1972). Sydney; Currency Press 1986 in *Collected Plays* 1.
Emerald City (1987). Sydney: Currency Press 1987.
A Handful of Friends (1976). Sydney: Currency Press 1993 in *Collected Plays* 2.
Jugglers Three (1972). Sydney; Currency Press 1986 in *Collected Plays* 1.

Money and Friends (1991). Sydney: Currency Press 1992.
The Perfectionist (1982). Sydney: Currency Press 1993 in *Collected Plays* 2.
The Removalists (1971). Sydney; Currency Press 1986 in *Collected Plays* 1.
Sons of Cain (1985). Sydney: Currency Press 1984.
Top Silk (1989). Sydney: Currency Press 1989.
Travelling North (1979). Sydney: Currency Press 1993 in *Collected Plays* 2.
What If You Died Tomorrow (1973). Sydney; Currency Press 1986 in *Collected Plays* 1.

further reading

CARROLL, DENNIS. *Australian Contemporary Drama*. Sydney: Currency Press 1995.

KIERNAN, BRIAN. *David Williamson—A writer's career*. Melbourne: Heinemann 1990.

MOE, CHRISTIAN M. In *Contemporary Dramatists* (ed. K. A. Berney) 5th edn. London: St James Press 1993.

J. C. Williamson

American actor, dramatist, entrepreneur. Born 26 July 1844 in Mercer (Pennsylvania, USA). Joined stock company in Milwaukee (Wisconsin) as junior assistant and actor 1861. In stock company of Royal Lyceum Theatre, Toronto (Canada) 1862–63. Junior comedian at Wallack's Theatre, New York City, 1863–71. Leading comedian at Californian Theatre, San Francisco, 1871–74. Married Maggie Moore in San Francisco, 2 February 1873. Toured Australia, co-starring with Maggie Moore, 1874–75. Toured Great Britain, Ireland and USA 1876–79. Returned to Australia with Australasian rights to *HMS Pinafore* 1879. Formed Royal Comic Opera Company 1880. Leased Theatre Royal, Melbourne, 1881. Senior partner in Williamson, Garner and Musgrove, 1882–90; Williamson, Garner and Co. 1890–91. Separated from Maggie Moore 1891, divorced 29 May 1899. Senior partner in Williamson and Musgrove 1892–99. Married Mary Weir in Sydney, 14 August 1899. Senior partner in Williamson, Tallis and Ramaciotti 1904–11. Governing director of J. C. Williamson Theatres Ltd, 1911–13. Died 8 July 1913 in Paris.

James Cassius Williamson founded a firm that remained the dominant theatrical organisation in Australia and New Zealand until the mid-20th century. A measure of its influence was that it came to be known throughout the theatrical industry as 'the Firm'. Williamson replaced slapdash, makeshift stagecraft with international professionalism and a colonial society that was rapidly growing in affluence and education eagerly accepted the quality of theatrical production he offered.

He also gambled on extending popular taste, by presenting with flair and showmanship Shakespeare and Sarah Bernhardt. Other international artists whose tours he organised included GEORGE RIGNOLD in 1882, Jennie Lee and GEORGE S. TITHERADGE in 1883, Genevieve Ward and HOWARD VERNON in 1884, DION BOUCICAULT in 1885, Nance O'Neil in 1900, Margaret Anglin in 1908, H. B. Irving and Dorothea Baird in 1911.

Williamson's own tastes were rooted in the popular taste of his period. He was unimpressed by the new movements that boldly redefined the role of theatre in society in the 1890s. To Williamson the theatre was always a place of simple entertainment and profitable livelihood, not a forum for debate on contemporary moral, social and political issues. Like most 19th-century managers Williamson judged the success of a production not by the intensity of social commentary but by the box-office returns. Williamson and the firm he founded have been accused of cultural imperialism, and of contributing to the view long held in Australia and New Zealand that the best in arts and entertainment had to be imported. This is a quite unfair accusation against Williamson himself. He used and fostered local performers in all theatrical activities and, by exposing them and their audiences to the world's best, gave them a supreme yardstick against which to measure the evolution of the performing arts in Australasia.

Williamson saw his first play at the age of 11 and was stage-struck for the rest of his life. At 16 he became apprentice actor and all-purpose assistant with a stock company playing at the Academy of Music in Milwaukee, where he went to high school. At 17 he obtained a similar position with the Royal Lyceum Theatre in Toronto. In 1863 he began an eight-year engagement as juvenile comedian at Wallack's Theatre, then the leading popular theatre in New York City. His versatility in handling comic character roles brought him acclaim and by the age of 26 he was the theatre's leading character actor.

In July 1871 Williamson moved to San Francisco, as leading comedian at the Californian Theatre. He found a perfect stage partner in MAGGIE MOORE and married her. He also acquired the rights to a one-act comedy-melodrama, *Struck Oil* by Sam W. Smith. Revision and expansion by Clay M. Greene made the play into an ideal starring vehicle for Williamson and his wife. From its premiere at Salt Lake City (Utah) on 23 February 1874, *Struck Oil* brought the couple the applause and affection of audiences around the world. The Williamsons embarked from San Francisco to tour Australia under GEORGE COPPIN's management.

They opened in Melbourne on 1 August 1874 in *Struck Oil* and Melbourne adored it. Its mixture of comedy, villainy and pathos, and homely songs and dances epitomised the popular theatrical taste of the era. Over 43 record-breaking nights 93 000 tickets were sold in a city of 110 000 people. The season continued with established favourites such as *The Old Curiosity Shop*, *Rip Van Winkle* and *Uncle Tom's Cabin*. After Melbourne the Williamsons triumphantly took their repertoire to Geelong, Bendigo and Castlemaine in Victoria and to Sydney and Adelaide.

They left Australia in October 1875, played in Bombay for five weeks and then went to London to open *Struck Oil* at the Adelphi Theatre on 17 April 1876. The critics praised the Williamsons but not their play. The London public, however, flocked to 100 performances of *Struck Oil* before it was withdrawn to allow the Williamsons to star in Dion Boucicault's *Arrah-na-Pogue* and *The Colleen Bawn*. The Williamsons ended their world tour by playing in Liverpool, Manchester, Birmingham, Glasgow and Dublin. When they returned to the USA in June 1877 they had travelled 64 000 km and played 605 performances.

Two years of touring the USA followed, mostly in *Struck Oil*, which proved a hit wherever it was played. During 1878 New York theatres booked three return seasons of the play, though New York critics shared their London counterparts' reservations about *Struck Oil*, while applauding the Williamsons' talents. Williamson hoped to find a superior vehicle that would displace *Struck Oil* in the affections of audiences, but he never succeeded. The Williamsons began a second Australian tour in Melbourne in July 1879, performing *Struck Oil* and *The Chinese Question*, a one-act farce by Clay M. Greene.

Much of Williamson's energy was soon given to litigation to establish that he had exclusive rights to stage GILBERT AND SULLIVAN's operetta *HMS Pinafore* in the Australasian colonies. Successful actions in New South Wales, Victoria and South Australia established the validity of British COPYRIGHT law in the colonies. He subsequently secured performing rights to all Gilbert and Sullivan works in Australasia. The vast superiority of his production of *HMS Pinafore* over earlier pirated versions also won public sympathy for his cause.

In 1881 he triumphantly introduced *The Pirates of Penzance* to Australia within a year of its London premiere. He then took both Gilbert and Sullivan works and *Struck Oil* to New Zealand, playing to full houses in Dunedin, Christchurch, Wellington and Auckland. This began Williamson's connection with New Zealand.

Williamson was now moving rapidly into management. He formed the Royal Comic Opera Company in 1880, and next year he leased the THEATRE ROYAL in Melbourne. He soon established his position as head of a theatrical firm that he controlled for the next 32 years, alone or with various partners. With Arthur Garner and George Musgrove in 1882 he formed WILLIAMSON, GARNER AND MUSGROVE. 'The triumvirate', as it was soon dubbed, began the Williamson policy of bringing international celebrities to the Australian stage and providing the finest theatres to house them, beginning with the PRINCESS THEATRE in Melbourne. Musgrove departed in 1890 and next year WILLIAMSON AND GARNER organised Sarah Bernhardt's tour of Australia.

Williamson found Australasia a huge and rewarding field for his talents but the early 1890s proved to be a time of professional and personal upheaval. In 1891 he lost Garner as a partner, but in 1892 re-established his association with Musgrove. They worked together in WILLIAMSON AND MUSGROVE until 1899, Musgrove latterly managing the firm's affairs in London. Williamson and Maggie Moore separated in 1891, and the rift became bitter when the courts, over Williamson's objections, upheld Moore's right to stage her own production of *Struck Oil*. Williamson never again mounted or performed in *Struck Oil*.

Equally critical was the economic depression of the 1890s, which threatened Williamson's livelihood. He saved himself and his firm by collaborating with Bert Royle, a New Zealand author, on the pantomime *Djin Djin the Japanese Bogie Man*, a delightfully satirical adaptation of a Japanese fairy tale. With lavish sets and effects it proved immensely popular. The cast of *Djin Djin* included Mary Weir, a dancer who became Williamson's second wife in 1899. They had two daughters.

With no business partner from 1899 to 1904, Williamson pressed on with his by now celebrated policies. He presented the American actor Nance O'Neil in 1900 and in 1902 he staged *Ben Hur*, his most costly, elaborate and technically impressive production. Only weeks after the opening in Sydney, on 23 March fire destroyed the production and HER MAJESTY'S THEATRE. Williamson rapidly organised a Shakespearean season elsewhere for the huge *Ben Hur* cast. With the stricken theatre's owner Cecily McQuade, he set about giving Sydney a superb new theatre, which opened on 1 August 1903.

From 1904 to 1911 Williamson was partnered by GEORGE TALLIS and GUSTAVE RAMACIOTTI. Their most striking production was *PARSIFAL*, a verse play with spectacular effects, in December 1906. Ramaciotti retired in 1911, and Williamson then became governing director of his last and largest company, J. C. Williamson Ltd. His partners were Tallis, HUGH J. WARD and Clyde Meynell as managing directors, with Sir Rupert Clarke overseeing the firm's affairs in London. Failing health limited Williamson's activity in his last years, but he accompanied Nellie Melba on several European trips to select singers for the Melba-Williamson Opera Company of 1911.

In 1913, while his wife and daughters stayed in France, Williamson paid a three-month visit to Australia. At Her Majesty's Theatre in Sydney on 22 February 1913 he made his last stage appearance at a matinee to raise money for families of the members of Captain Robert Scott's disastrous Antarctic expedition. He played his favourite character, a nonagenarian Irish servant in Dion Boucicault's *Kerry*, and received thunderous applause. He rejoined his family in Paris, where he died. Williamson had never renounced his American citizenship and his body was buried in the family plot in Oak Woods Cemetery in Chicago. *Ian G. Dicker*

writings
J. C. Williamson's Life-story in His Own Words. Sydney: NSW Bookstall Company 1913.

further reading
BEVAN, IAN. *The Story of the Theatre Royal*. Sydney: Currency Press 1993.
DICKER, IAN G. *J.C.W.—A short biography of James Cassius Williamson*. Sydney: Elizabeth Tudor Press 1974.
FANTASIA, JOSIE. J. C. Williamson's vision for Australia—*Australis; or the City of Zero* (1900). *Australasian Drama Studies* (Brisbane, October 1993).

Williamson and Musgrove

Entrepreneurial management founded in 1892 by George Musgrove and J. C. Williamson. Dissolved December 1899.

GEORGE MUSGROVE and J. C. WILLIAMSON, reunited as partners, launched their new firm in the Princess Theatre in Melbourne with the London Gaiety Burlesque Company in the pantomime *Ali Baba and the Forty Thieves*. The new management, with Musgrove in London and Williamson in Australia, pursued a policy of presenting acclaimed overseas and Australian artists in their most notable pieces. Its productions included Edith Crane and A. M. Palmer's New York Company in Paul Potter's *Trilby* in 1896; *Djin Djin the Japanese Bogie Man*, a pantomime written by Williamson and Bert Royle and given a spectacular production in 1896; JULIUS KNIGHT in Anthony Hope's *The Prisoner of Zenda* and ADA REEVE in the musical comedies *The Gay Parisienne* and *The French Maid* in 1897; Wilson Barrett with Maude Jeffries in his own plays *The Manxman* and *Ben My Chree*, from a story by Hall Caine, in 1898; and the Australian actor Henrietta Watson in *The Christian* by Bernard Espinasse and *The King's Musketeer* by Henry Hamilton in 1899.

In 1899 the Williamson and Musgrove production of the musical comedy *The Belle of New York* in Melbourne was less successful than Musgrove's original production in London. Williamson accused Musgrove of concentrating on his own London affairs at the expense of the partnership's Australian interests and the partnership was dissolved in December 1899, when its lease on the Princess Theatre expired. ❦*Ian G. Dicker*

Williamson, Garner and Co.

Entrepreneurial management founded by J. C. Williamson and Arthur Garner in 1890. Dissolved 1891.

After GEORGE MUSGROVE withdrew from 'the triumvirate' of WILLIAMSON, GARNER AND MUSGROVE in 1890 J. C. WILLIAMSON, the senior partner, and ARTHUR GARNER continued the management as Williamson, Garner and Co. This firm controlled the PRINCESS THEATRE and THEATRE ROYAL in Melbourne and the THEATRE ROYAL in Adelaide. It brought SARAH BERNHARDT to Australia in 1891 for a ten-week tour in a repertoire of ten plays in Melbourne, Adelaide and Sydney. Straitened financial circumstances led Garner to withdraw from the firm at the end of 1891. ❦*Ian G. Dicker*

Williamson, Garner and Musgrove

Entrepreneurial management founded by J. C. Williamson, Arthur Garner and George Musgrove in July 1882. Dissolved 1890.

Williamson, Garner and Musgrove rapidly gained a name for presenting renowned overseas artists in their most celebrated roles. These included GEORGE RIGNOLD in 1882; GEORGE S. TITHERADGE and Jennie Lee in *The Silver King* by Henry Arthur Jones and Henry Herman in 1883; HOWARD VERNON in 1884; the tragedienne Genevieve Ward in *Forget Me Not* by Grove and Merivale, *The Queen's Favourite* by Sydney Grundy, *Macbeth* and *Henry VIII* in 1884; Florence Trevelyan and ROBERT BROUGH in *Iolanthe* in 1885; and DION BOUCICAULT in his own plays *The Shaughraun*, *The Colleen Bawn* and *Arrah-na-Pogue* in 1885.

Three young entrepreneurs, who had all jointly leased the Theatres Royal in Melbourne and Sydney since November 1881, contributed equally to the £3000 initial capital of Williamson, Garner and Musgrove. J. C. WILLIAMSON, aged 37, was the senior partner; ARTHUR GARNER was 31 and GEORGE MUSGROVE was 26. The partnership, soon dubbed 'the triumvirate', launched itself with the Melbourne premiere of Gilbert and Sullivan's *Patience* on 1 July 1882. A week later in Sydney it opened a season of plays starring Rignold, including *The Lights o' London* by G. R. Sims, *Youth* by Paul Merritt and Augustus Harris, *The Two Orphans* by John Oxenford and *After Dark* by Boucicault.

In 1886 the firm gained control of the THEATRE ROYAL in Adelaide and the Princess's Theatre in Melbourne. The architect WILLIAM PITT JNR rebuilt the Princess's. The new PRINCESS THEATRE, the most handsome and up-to-date of its day, opened on 16 December 1886 with a revival of *The Mikado* starring NELLIE STEWART as Yum Yum. Musgrove's brother Harry wrote in 1926 that Garner had been 'the financial pillar of the firm. JCW handled the acting end of it and George Musgrove the productions'. Musgrove withdrew from the partnership in 1890, after disagreements with Williamson, but by then the three had firmly established an enterprise that continued as WILLIAMSON, GARNER AND CO., later became J. C. WILLIAMSON'S, and remained the leading theatrical organisation in Australasia until the mid-20th century. ❦*Ian G. Dicker*

further reading
MUSGROVE, HARRY. Stage secrets. *Table Talk* (Melbourne) August 1926.

L. Peter Wilson

Puppet-theatre director. Born 3 December 1943 in Hobart. Trained in classical dance. Became interested in puppetry at high school in 1958. Formed Tasmanian Puppet Theatre with Peter Oldham, former schoolmate and puppeteer, 1969. Artistic director 1970–80. Artistic director of International Festival of Puppetry in Hobart, January 1979. Studied with PUK Puppet Theatre of Tokyo and National Theatre of Japan 1980. Artistic director of Spare Parts Puppet Theatre Company (Fremantle WA) 1981–. Artistic director of Oz Puppet Festival in Fremantle 1988. BHP Award for Excellence in the Arts 1988. Shared Sidney Myer Performing Arts Award 1988.

L. Peter Wilson is one of two puppet-theatre directors who both bill themselves as simply Peter Wilson, which has been a source of much confusion. He has been artistic director of two major puppet companies, TASMANIAN PUPPET THEATRE from 1970 to 1980, and THE SPARE PARTS PUPPET THEATRE Company since 1981. He began with marionettes but he has been at the forefront in the move away from traditional puppet theatre forms. He has been strongly influenced by overseas developments, especially in eastern Europe and Japan, and has arranged for overseas puppeteers to work with his companies.

Wilson has also been responsible for recruiting visual artists, composers, designers and writers to work in puppet theatre. He provided an introduction to puppetry for Nigel Triffitt when he invited him to take charge of *Momma's Little Horror Show* for Tasmanian Puppet Theatre. For this company he also created *Kidstuff*, which played at the Asian-Pacific Puppet Festival in Tokyo in September 1979. *Faust*, a Spare Parts production which he directed, was part of the 1981 Perth Festival. His production of *The Pied Piper*, seen in eastern states in 1987, was presented at North American children's festivals in 1988.

The Overcoat is a semi-autobiographical work based on early influences in Wilson's life. It was originally performed in 1987 by David Collins, assisted by Noriko Nishimoto. Wilson himself took over the main role in 1988 for a tour of China, Korea and Japan, where it was performed at an international festival of puppetry in Nagoya. Wilson co-directed a puppet play for the Drak puppet theatre of Hradec Králové (Czech Republic) in 1989. For the New Zealand Puppet Theatre, in conjunction with Spare Parts, he created *Paper Ladders*, a solo show with the New Zealand performance artist Nick Blake, in Auckland in 1992. He directed Peter Jagger in the same role for Spare Parts in 1994. ❦*Richard Bradshaw*

Peter J. Wilson

Puppeteer, puppet-theatre director. Born 18 April 1953 in Perth. Qualified as accountant. Trained in modern dance and mime for five years. Joined Parry Marshall Puppet Theatre (Melbourne) 1976. Founding member of Handspan Theatre Company (Melbourne) 1977. With Polyglot Puppets (Melbourne) 1978. Joined Tasmanian Puppet Theatre (Hobart) 1979. Returned to Handspan 1980. Directed plays for Polyglot, Handspan and Skylark Theatre Company (Canberra) from 1989. Artistic director of Skylark 1993–.

The younger of the two Peter Wilsons is a sensitive performer whose dance experience has strongly influenced his technique of puppet manipulation. He won public recognition as the visible lead puppeteer in the HANDSPAN THEATRE COMPANY's *Cho Cho San* in 1984. He recreated the role for the Playbox Theatre Company in Melbourne in 1987 and again in 1988 on tours of Australia and China. In 1983 Wilson had a major role in NIGEL TRIFFITT's *Secrets* for Handspan, and toured with it in 1984 to the Spoleto Festivals in Italy and Charleston (West Virginia, USA) and gave performances in 1984–86 in London, Paris, New York, Quebec, Edinburgh, Belgium, Germany and Italy. In France in 1985 he studied with the puppeteer Philippe Genty and co-devised *Smalls* for Handspan. Wilson has trained puppeteers for Handspan and Terrapin Puppet Theatre in Hobart and taught puppetry in educational institutions.

In 1988 he directed *Almost a Dinosaur* for Polyglot in Melbourne and he has directed several puppet shows since. As co-artistic director of Handspan in 1990 he devised and directed *Reading Boy* with the playwright JOHN ROMERIL. In 1992 he directed *Charlotte's Web* for a national tour by the Skylark Theatre Company. As artistic director of this company he directed *Inside Dry Water* in 1993 and *Almost a Dinosaur* and *Tadpole* in 1994. ❦*Richard Bradshaw*

Strella Wilson OBE

Soprano singer. Born 19 December 1894 at Broken Hill (NSW) to English mother and American father. Grew up in Melbourne. Pupil of Nellie Melba at Albert Street Conservatorium. Professional debut in Rigo Grand Opera Company 1919. Married tenor Ralph Errolle 1920. Went to North America with Errolle after appearances in light opera. Divorced, and returned to Australia. Sang in musical comedy and opera in England. Returned to Australia 1934 for *White Horse Inn*. Entertained troops during Second World War. Official hostess at Australia House in London, 1952–68. Died 10 February 1989 in Sydney. OBE 1950. Daughter Pauline Garrick sang with Australian Opera.

Strella Wilson had her greatest successes in operetta, though she began her career as an opera singer. Her father opposed a stage career but became immensely supportive when, as an understudy, she had a chance to sing a leading role with the Rigo Grand Opera Company in Melbourne in 1919. She made a strong impression. Some new singers were brought in to strengthen the company in Sydney, where it was under the management of J. C. WILLIAMSON's. Wilson married one of them, the French-American tenor Ralph Errolle, in 1920. They starred in the first Australian production of the operetta *Merrie England* in 1921.

The couple went to New York, where he sang at the Metropolitan Opera House but she was, she said, 'just Mrs Errolle with two little children'. Later she sang in Canada and sometimes in grand cinemas in New York. Back in Australia after divorce from Errolle, Wilson sang the leading role in the first Australian production of *The Vagabond King* in 1928. In October 1931 she played the disguised Princess Mirabelle in the original production of Noël Coward's *Cavalcade* in London. She was recalled to Australia to sing the leading role of Josepha in the J. C. Williamson's production of *White Horse Inn*.

During the Second World War Wilson, like other favourites, found fruitful employment in many operetta revivals, including *White Horse Inn*. She also sang for Australian forces at home and in New Guinea, which brought her the OBE. She returned to Australia in 1968, after 16 years at Australia House in London, and became a familiar figure in J. C. Williamson first-night audiences in Sydney. She died after breaking a femur in a fall. ❦*John West*

W. J. Wilson

Actor, manager, scene-painter. Born 24 December 1833 in London. Son and grandson of scenic artists. Worked with father at Theatre Royal, Drury Lane. Exhibited at Society of British Artists and Royal Academy. Arrived in Melbourne March 1855. Worked at Queen's Theatre Royal, Olympic Theatre and Theatre Royal. Went to Sydney 1861. Visited New Zealand 1863. Partner of Alexander Habbe from 1863. In partnership with Eduardo Majeroni operated Bijou Theatre, Melbourne, and Opera House, Sydney, from 1885. Died 20 June 1909 in Sydney. Father of scene-painter William Wilson and actors Frank Hawthorne and Carden Wilson.

In many ways William John Wilson was Sydney's equivalent of Melbourne's JOHN HENNINGS. He painted for operas, Shakespeare plays, melodrama and pantomime. He specialised in architectural illusions and, like Hennings, also painted MOVING PANORAMAS. *The Ocean Mail to India and the Storming of Delhi*, for example, was exhibited in Sydney in 1873. At CREMORNE GARDENS in Melbourne, Wilson designed and painted a three-dimensional modelled panorama of Sevastopol, 122 metres long by 15 metres high. He formed a partnership with ALEXANDER HABBE as decorator for the new PRINCE OF WALES THEATRE in Sydney in 1863. They also worked at Our Lyceum and the Adelphi Theatre and they leased the Royal Victoria Theatre in 1870. As an actor, Wilson described himself in an interview in *Old Times* in 1908 as a specialist in dialects. ❦*Mimi Colligan*

reference
W. J. Wilson's scrapbooks are held in the Performing Arts Museum (Melbourne).

Olive Wilton OBE

Actor, director, teacher. Born 17 April 1883 in Bath (England). Mother was amateur actor. Attended Ben Greet's acting school in London. Married Benjamin Arthur Cornell, actor, 1906. Toured Australia with husband in Grace Palotta company and Willoughby and Ward's New London Company 1906, for William Anderson in 1910–11, and for J. C. Williamson's. Returned with other companies. Settled in Australia 1914. Member of Emelie Polini company 1918. Settled in Hobart in 1920 and formed her own company and school. Principal director of Hobart Repertory Theatre Society 1926–33. Active as teacher, examiner, and administrator until 1950s. OBE 1959. Died 8 June 1971 in Hobart. Mother of Junee Cornell, radio and stage actor.

Olive Wilton came to Australia as a touring star and remained to become a driving force in amateur theatre in Hobart. She had her first success in the title-role of the New York production of Arthur Wing Pinero's *Sweet Lavender*, which led to major roles in London and the English provinces and her first tour of Australia. Wilton was tall, commanding and beautiful, with red-gold hair. In her youth she alternated bad women with outback roles and was renowned for equestrian feats on stage. In 1910 she played the leading role in a film of *THE SQUATTER'S DAUGHTER*, but no copy of it has survived. She created the role of Jessie Moreland in Edmund Duggan's MY MATE in 1911. Wilton was always concerned for the welfare of fellow-actors and in Melbourne in 1910 she attended a meeting called to consider ways to protect Australian actors from exploitation. By 1914 she had decided to remain in Australia, touring for J. C. WILLIAMSON's and other managements.

When she settled in Hobart she formed her own company, aiming to provide regular, high-quality theatre with fine actors performing for a knowledgeable, discerning audience. She was a perfectionist in every aspect of her work and she inspired others. Influential citizens helped her to found the HOBART REPERTORY THEATRE SOCIETY in 1926. ❦*Gillian Winter*

further reading
MOORE, JOHN. Olive Wilton. *Australian Dictionary of Biography* 12. Melbourne University Press 1990.
Hobart Repertory Society Golden Jubilee 1926–1976. Hobart Repertory Society 1976.

The Winning Ticket

Play in four acts by William Anderson and Temple Harrison. **premiere** 10 September 1910, King's Theatre, Melbourne. Cast: Bert Bailey, Edwin Campbell, Max Clifton, George Cross, Eugenie Duggan, Roy Redgrave, Olive Wilton, Stirling Whyte, and Kookaburra. Designer: Rege Robins. Director: J. H. Nunn. Producer: William Anderson.

A triumph of stage machinery more than story, *The Winning Ticket* was a sporting melodrama remembered mainly for two great sensations. In one a train carrying the champion racehorse Kookaburra to Melbourne is approaching a swing bridge when the operator who is closing it suddenly sees his child being thrown into the river by the villain. He leaves his post but, remembering his 'duty', he falls back across the levers. The bridge revolves and the squatter's daughter dives from a cliff and surfaces with the child in her arms just as the train roars safely across.

The other sensation was the Melbourne Cup race, with horses galloping on a moving platform in front of a revolving back scene of the Flemington racecourse. Kookaburra forged ahead as the finishing line flashed by. A moderately successful six-week season ended abruptly when J. C. WILLIAMSON opened an even more spectacular production of a London play, *The Whip*, from which *The Winning Ticket* had obviously borrowed. It proved twice as popular as the Australian play, which retreated to Sydney for a short pre-Christmas season. ❦*Richard Fotheringham*

reference
A manuscript copy of *The Winning Ticket* is in the Australian Archives (Canberra), CRS A1336/2, item 1656.

Eliza Winstanley

Actor. Born *c.*1818 in England. Daughter of scene-painter William Winstanley. Came to Sydney with family May 1833. Debut at Theatre Royal, Sydney, 31 October 1834. Played 11 Shakespearean roles in Sydney and Hobart, 1834–36. Married theatre violinist H. C. O'Flaherty in Sydney, February 1841. Managed Australian Olympic Theatre, Sydney, with O'Flaherty in 1842. Left for England 1 April 1846. Debut at Theatre Royal, Manchester, 28 October 1846. Said to have performed for two years at Wallack's Theatre, New York City. Joined Princess's Theatre, London, November 1851. Became prolific novelist after O'Flaherty's death *c.*1854. Editor of family fiction weekly *Bow Bells* from 1865. Returned to Australia 1880. Died December 1882 in Sydney. Elder sister of actor and singer Ann Winstanley (Mrs Ximenes).

Eliza Winstanley has been hailed as the first Australian-trained actress to be successful overseas, but she had a fairly ordinary career in her native England. She does, however, typify a purely Sydney-trained 'native talent'. She made her stage debut in 1834 at the Theatre Royal in the title-role of John Howard Payne's *Clari—or, The Maid of Milan*. It was performed without the music by Henry Bishop that brings it classification as an opera. Eliza Winstanley was not a singer, unlike her younger sister Ann, another prodigy-performer for Barnett Levey at the Theatre Royal, where their father was a scene-painter. Early praise for Eliza was mixed with adverse comment on her 'insufferable affectation' and her habit of aspirating—pronouncing 'order' as 'horder', for instance. The sisters were also assailed for anti-colonial snobbery by native-born 'cabbage-tree hat boys' in December 1840. But all acknowledged the 'rapturous applause' that Eliza won in such mature parts as Belvidera in Thomas Otway's *Venice Preserv'd* at Sydney in March 1842, and she was hailed as 'unrivalled in this part of the world in the tragic style'.

She shocked critics by playing Richard III in May 1842, when she and her husband were managing the Australian Olympic Theatre in Sydney after the failure of LUIGI DALLE CASE. At that time her growing obesity made for some odd casting, such as Desdemona in June 1842. She played Isabel of Valois in a play written for her by her husband in August 1842. A critic in the *Australasian Odd Fellows Quarterly* magazine of July 1845 indicated that she had a distance to go by writing that 'when we look upon her beaming, intelligent countenance we feel satisfied that, by careful study … her triumphs would be mightily enhanced'.

After her husband became insolvent they left for England in April 1846. Eliza Winstanley made her English debut at Manchester in 1846 and critics complained of her 'whining' in tragedy. One mentioned that she was new to the English stage but she was never taken in England for anything but a provincial English actress. In the northern hemisphere she had no scope to play the temperamental and erratic 'Siddons of the South' and she never advertised her Australian past. The high points of her English career were roles like Mistress Quickly in *The Merry Wives of Windsor*, which she played at CHARLES KEAN's Princess's Theatre in London in November 1851. She played comic roles especially in afterpieces.

History may come to record Eliza Winstanley as a chronicler of early days in Sydney theatre rather than a star performer. Her 1859 novel *Shifting Scenes in Theatrical Life* almost certainly portrays CONRAD KNOWLES, and she wrote several other novels with Australian settings which require examination for historical sources. ❦*Helen Musa*

writings
Bow Bells (London) 21 December 1864. Erratic autobiography.
further reading
ROBINSON, N. M. Eliza O'Flaherty. *Australian Dictionary of Biography* 2. Melbourne University Press 1967.
The Misses Winstanley and the natives. *Sydney Monitor* 1 January 1841.

May Wirth

Circus equestrian. Born 6 June 1894 at Bundaberg (Qld). Began circus training with father, a gymnast. Adopted by Marizles Wirth Martin of Wirths' Circus when her parents separated. Trained as equestrian in Wirths' Circus. Toured USA in Barnum and Bailey circus 1912–13. Toured with own equestrian troupe in Europe 1913–15. Troupe performed in Wirths' Circus as Royal Martin Wirth Family 1915–16. Performed in USA 1917–37. Worked with husband Frank White in theatrical booking agency from 1937. Died 18 October 1978 in Sarasota (Florida, USA).

Acclaimed in the USA as the greatest circus equestrian of her time, May Wirth was ignored and finally forgotten in Australia. Her equestrianism was extraordinary for its grace, artistry, spectacle and technical precision. At the time of her American debut in 1912 she was one of the few female riders capable of executing a backwards somersault on horseback and she was the only woman capable of the even more difficult feat of flinging a forward somersault on a bareback horse.

She continually added to her repertoire such extraordinary feats as the 'back across' in 1912—a somersault from the back of one horse to the back of another running behind it. In the same year she also developed the 'back-backward' somersault, which required her to stand on her horse's hindquarters, facing its tail, before throwing her body over and making a half-twist in the air so that she came out of the turn facing forward as her horse continued its steady canter around the ring. In 1917 she introduced a forward somersault while blindfolded and her famous basket stunt, in which she made all manner of leaps from the floor of the ring on to her horse's back with her feet encased in wicker market baskets.

May Wirth was only 1·5 metres tall—the most adroit circus artists are short—and striking in appearance, perhaps because of a mixed ancestry. Her father, John Edwin Zinga, a gymnast, was a native of Mauritius, while her mother, Dezeppo Maria *née* Beaumont, born at Schnapper Point, (Vic.), may have been of Anglo-Indian ancestry. Her father began to train her as a circus performer, but her parents separated before her eighth birthday and she was given for adoption to Marizles Wirth Martin, an accomplished rider and horseback juggler and a sister and partner of the Wirth brothers in their large circus. May Wirth's training for a career as a circus artist began in earnest in WIRTHS' CIRCUS. Years of practice as a contortionist, trapeze artist, wirewalker and acrobat developed her strength. She was taught dancing to develop grace. Her accomplishment in all these disciplines enabled her to graduate with ease to bareback riding, the most difficult and demanding of the circus arts.

She began training as a rider when she was about ten years old. In a large circus there were fine riders as tutors, such as her adoptive mother, her adoptive uncle Philip Wirth, the renowned English rider John Welby Cooke, Gus St Leon and his son Philip. She was also able to observe and learn from the fine riders that the Wirths annually imported from the USA and Europe. Wirths' Circus reserved pride of place for these overseas stars, so May Wirth was not prominent on the program although her superlative ability was clearly evident. She was often billed under other names such as Mayazel, May Martin and even May Ringling. Another reason why she attracted only passing attention from the Australian press and public during her early teens was a decline in appreciation of equestrianism, which had been increasingly evident since the 1890s. May Wirth's appearances during the Easter season of Wirths' Circus in Sydney in 1911 were confined to a three-minute sequence at the beginning of the evening program, in which she rode and drove eight ponies at once, and a five-minute somersault equestrian act during the second half. The *Sydney Morning Herald* gave the 'remarkably pretty' young equestrian passing notice on 3 April 1911.

Less than a year later, on 21 March 1912, May Wirth made her American debut at Madison Square Garden in the enormous three-ring Barnum and Bailey circus, billed as 'the astounding Australian equestrienne' and as 'the world's greatest lady bareback rider, exhibiting feats of equestrianism never before attempted by a woman'. She became famous in the USA overnight. She toured the USA with the Barnum and Bailey circus, one of two large circuses owned and operated by the Ringling brothers, during the 1912 and 1913 seasons. From December 1913 to June 1915, Wirth and her troupe of riders appeared throughout England and in Paris.

She made her only return to Australia in 1915–16, for a season with her troupe in Wirths' Circus. They were given star billing as the Royal Martin Wirth Family—because of an appearance before royalty during their English tour—but their reception was largely indifferent throughout Australia and New Zealand. May Wirth engaged PHILIP ST LEON as a comedy rider for the troupe's appearances in the USA from early 1917. She spent the rest of her equestrian career in the USA, with the occasional visit to Canada or Europe. She was one of the principal stars engaged by the Ringling circuses in the years 1917–20 and 1924–27. She appeared with the Walter L. Main Circus during the 1921 and 1923 seasons and performed with her troupe in London during the summer of 1922. During the winter months, when large circuses in the USA laid up, the Wirth troupe usually performed in vaudeville and indoor circuses and it restricted itself to these engagements and county fairs after its last season with the Ringling circus.

May Wirth married Frank White, whom she had met in Wirths' Circus in 1907, in New York City on 24 November 1919. He operated a substantial theatrical booking agency during the 1920s. After a seven-year hiatus, he resumed this activity in 1937 and May Wirth retired from riding to assist him in the business. White, who adopted the name Wirth for professional purposes, remained active in the field until his death in 1965.

May Wirth received the supreme honour of American circus on 23 February 1964, when, she was admitted to the Circus Hall of Fame in Sarasota, a small Florida city where many American circus people retire. She was only the second person to be honoured in this way while alive. Only two other artists of Australian origin, the wirewalker CON COLLEANO and his sister the trapeze artist Winnie Colleano, have been similarly honoured. *Mark St Leon*

further reading
KIRK, RHINA. *Circus Heroes and Heroines*. Maplewood (New Jersey, USA): Hammond 1972. Contains interview-based chapter on life and career of May Wirth.

ST LEON, MARK. May Wirth. *Australian Dictionary of Biography* 12. Melbourne University Press 1990.

Wirths' Circus

Australia's own 'greatest show on earth' was Wirths' Circus, the 20th-century successor to BURTON'S CIRCUS, FITZGERALD BROTHERS' CIRCUS and ST LEON'S CIRCUS. It was founded in 1882 by the four sons and two daughters of Johannes Wirth, a Bavarian musician who arrived at Melbourne aboard the ship *Merlin* in 1855 with his brothers Jacob and Peter. These three brothers had spent time in England, apparently during the troubled years after the revolutions throughout Europe in 1848. Numerous German musicians seem to have found their way to Australia during the gold rushes for the early annals of the Australian circus record musicians bearing such names as Beileiter, Gilcher and Koehler. The three Wirth brothers, however, appear to have made their living by playing music on the goldfields and in the streets and public houses of Melbourne and Sydney.

The first known professional association of the name Wirth with circus is in a large advertisement for John Jones's National Circus in the *Yass Courier* of 18 December 1858. Included in the array of talent billed to visit the town were Mr and Mrs 'Werth'—probably Johannes Wirth and his English wife Sarah. The 'Herr Londervink' who headed Jones's band at that time was also probably Johannes Wirth. His son Philip said he was 'a musician of great ability and versatility and would play any instrument from a Jew's harp to a clarinet or double bass'.

During the 1860s the three brothers and their families wandered round the goldfields, dance halls, country race meetings and agricultural shows of northern NSW and Queensland, a pleasant if not bountiful existence. Late in the 1860s they settled at Dalby (Qld), and constructed a 'huge barn-like dance hall' almost entirely from bark. In this they gave music and dancing lessons. About 1869, the Wirth musicians were 'bailed up' north of Tamworth (NSW) by the infamous bushranger Thunderbolt.

In 1870, Johannes Wirth joined Ashton's Circus but soon returned to Dalby to collect his two eldest sons, John and Harry, to train them as musicians in the circus band. The Wirths considerably improved Ashton's band and gave it new tunes. Later they were joined by the two younger sons, Philip and George. Throughout the 1870s the Wirths played in other circuses, including those of William Barlow in 1872 and John Ridge in 1879–80. They also played at balls, parties, picnics and open-air occasions such as the festivities for the opening of the railway line to Tamworth.

Johannes Wirth died in Sydney on 10 July 1880, and his four sons rejoined Ashton's Circus as bandsmen and performers. In addition to being fine musicians, the brothers could sing comic songs, dance on stilts, perform on horizontal bars and with Roman rings, and perform the customary equestrian, acrobatic and clowning feats. They left Ashton's company for the last time after a 'rough-up'—presumably a brawl—at Goulburn (NSW), probably during the visit of the circus on 14–15 February 1882. They came to Sydney and gave circus and musical performances in a small tent in the Haymarket, apparently for six months, perhaps billed as the Star Variety Troupe.

By late 1882 the four brothers appear to have begun to travel as a circus in their own right. They had their first financial success when they struck a township on the Castlereagh River at the time of the annual races. The brothers were later joined by their mother and sisters Madeleine and Marizles, an American clown, two acrobats and another circus identity.

The Wirths' circus grew in size and status. It visited Melbourne for the first time in 1885 and toured New Caledonia and Tasmania in 1888. Early in 1889, the Wirths discarded their covered wagons in favour of the railway, and relied upon it thereafter. They began their first tour of New Zealand at Invercargill on 18 December 1889. During this tour, Harry Wirth and the circus agent, George Alexander, sailed for the USA to engage a Wild West show. They returned to New Zealand with this show—probably the first American Wild West show seen in Australasia—and brought it to Australia in 1890. Other performers engaged with Wirths' Circus during the New Zealand tour included Gus and Alfred St Leon.

Wirths' Circus toured the Australian mainland extensively during 1890–93, making two visits to Western Australia to capitalise on the gold rushes there. In the early 1890s the Wirths employed a two-ring format, a trademark of the American circus. Economic depression led the Wirths to ship their circus to SOUTH AFRICA late in 1893. This was the first leg of a seven-year odyssey that took the circus to South America, England, South Africa again, India and southeast Asia—a journey unparalleled in Australian circus. The eldest brother, John Wirth died while the circus was in South Africa in 1894. Harry Wirth did not accompany his brothers but organised his own circus, Wirth's Pacific Circus, in 1895, and took it on tour throughout the Far East. He died of sunstroke on the ship that was taking his circus into Hong Kong in July 1896.

The main Wirths' Circus returned to Australia at Fremantle in late July 1900, and the Wirths never again ventured overseas for a long period. To Philip Wirth there was no country on earth to equal Australia 'either for climate or for resources'. The circus faced the problem of restoring its name and reputation with the Australian public. There was intense competition between the Wirths and the FitzGerald brothers, Australia's pre-eminent circus showmen, during the early 1900s. Only with the premature deaths of the two FitzGeralds early in 1906, did Wirths' Circus assume the position of Australia's premier circus.

Imported performers

The Wirths built upon many of the FitzGeralds' innovations, such as routing, annually importing overseas acts, and promoting token acts of public benevolence. They imported such famous artists as the Flying Jordans, trapeze artists, in 1911; Hilary Long, 'the champion head balancer of the universe', in 1912; the Flying Codonas, a Mexican trapeze troupe, in 1913–15. There were many others from many different parts of the world but few Australian artists. Members of the Wirth family who performed in the ring were customarily subsidiary to the imported acts—even MAY WIRTH, although her equestrian artistry was so exceptional that she was later acknowledged in the USA and Europe as the finest female bareback rider of all time.

For some years from April 1916 Wirths' Circus played its annual Sydney season in the Hippodrome, now the CAPITOL THEATRE. In Melbourne a building suitable for its activities was erected in 1916 on the site of the old Olympia building used by the FitzGeralds. In the 1920s and 1930s other circuses, particularly Perry Brothers' Circus, may have rivalled Wirths' in size but the quality of the Wirth program appears to have been unexcelled. Recorded music began to accompany the performance between the wars, but the circus still employed full-scale brass bands for city seasons. Wirths' Circus continued to tour during the Second World War, although petrol rationing limited its daily advance at the height of the war.

After the war it needed two trains to convey it throughout Australia and New Zealand. The company, comprising 70–80 artists and a similar number of supernumeraries, performed in a single ring. During the 1950s the circus adopted a multi-ring format, chaired seating and many other characteristics of American circus. These bold but inappropriate steps were typical of the mismanagement that now plagued the company. It also had to cope with strong opposition, particularly from the newly organised BULLEN BROTHERS' CIRCUS. Wirths' Circus came to an end in 1963. The spread of television was cited as the reason for its demise. ❦*Mark St Leon*

further reading
ST LEON, MARK. *Spangles and Sawdust*. Melbourne: Greenhouse 1983.
ST LEON, MARK. Australian circus reminiscences. Ms., 1984. Copies in major public and university libraries throughout Australia, national libraries of United Kingdom, Wales, Scotland and New Zealand, and in several libraries in USA. Includes an edited and annotated transcript of a lengthy autobiographical record of Marizles Wirth Martin.
WIRTH, GEORGE. *Round the World with a Circus*. Melbourne: Troedel and Cooper 1925.
WIRTH, PHILIP. *A Lifetime with an Australian Circus*. Melbourne: Troedel and Cooper 1930.
Circus romance—Mr Phillip Wirth's career. *West Australian* (Perth) 9 September 1931. Interview with Phillip Wirth.
Romance of a great circus—George Wirth in a reminiscent mood. *Theatre* (Sydney) 1 April 1922.
The circuses of the world—Seen and compared by George Wirth. *Theatre* (Sydney) 1 April 1922.
The Wirths and their circus. *Theatre* (Sydney) 1 May 1911.

Eleanor Witcombe

Dramatist. Born 20 September 1923 in Yorketown (SA). Trained in Sydney under Dorothy Hemingway of Mosman Theatre Guild and at Mercury Theatre School. Began working with Mosman Children's Theatre and New Theatre in 1940s. Initiated Australian Theatre for Young People 1963. Writes for film, television and radio. Lives in Sydney.

A pioneer of theatre for young people, Eleanor Witcombe launched her professional career with the production of her full-length play for children *Pirates at the Barn* in 1948. She wrote extensively for the young in the 1950s and 1960s, including the plays *The Bushranger* (1949) and *Smugglers, Beware!* (1950). After five years in England, Witcombe culminated her study of theatre for children and young people by writing *The Runaway Steamboat* with John MacKellar and Dot Mendoza for AUSTRALIAN THEATRE FOR YOUNG PEOPLE. It was first performed at the 1968 Adelaide Festival. Since then she has principally written for screen and radio. In her pioneering work she sought to introduce young audiences to 19th-century working-class life through traditional, recognisably Australian characters and themes. She is well known for adaptations of Australian literature, including Norman Lindsay's *The Magic Pudding* for the MARIONETTE THEATRE OF AUSTRALIA. ❦*Rachel Healy*

published plays
Pirates at the Barn. Sydney: Currency Press 1989.
Smugglers, Beware! Sydney: Currency Press 1989.

Women in the theatre

Since professional theatre began in Sydney in the 1830s women have been prominent as actors, managers, directors and playwrights. Despite social prejudice and the constraints of domestic life, they have written, danced, sung and acted with talent, versatility and resourcefulness and sheer hard work. They have initiated and administered theatrical ventures with flair and success.

In the 19th and early 20th centuries women were considerably better off in the theatre than in almost any other occupation. Social restrictions did not operate within the theatre, but outside there was social stigma. The waspish Colonial Auditor G. T. W. B. Boyes of Hobart noted in his diary on 13 February 1847: 'To apply the word "class" however in its ordinary meaning to Miss Young's pupils, she being a *danseuse* at the Theatre, would not be over and above reputable seeing that Ladies in her line have acquired, whether deservedly or not, a classification *de sui generis* [of its own kind]'. Sometimes a woman was the professional partner of her husband and often more active and successful, like CORDELIA CAMERON in the 1830s. She set standards of female dramatic acting in Australia from the time her husband, SAMSON CAMERON, opened the first professional theatrical season in Hobart in December 1833. Male actors had no comparable model until G. V. BROOKE toured the colonies in 1856.

Nor did women succeed in the theatre at the cost of domestic life. Martha Thomson in the 1830s and 1840s was a favourite with the public and the press as an actor of merit and a person who 'in private life bears a most exemplary character'. Her daughter Jane was a successful actor and dancer, usually billed in Australia as MRS CHARLES YOUNG. Theatrical dynasties were common from the 1840s, the time of THEODOSIA STIRLING, whose daughter NELLIE STEWART had exceptional talent, a long career and the respect and affection of countless audiences.

The versatility of early colonial women is exemplified in the demands of the leading role in THE CURRENCY LASS, which Edward Geoghegan wrote for the popular Sydney performer TILLY JONES. It required her to undertake three widely different roles, acting, singing and dancing. ANNE CLARKE, a talented singer and actor, demonstrated entrepreneurial and administrative ability during the 1840s in Hobart. She imported able performers from England, under contract to limit defections to rival companies. She also offered to train local theatrical aspirants. Her disciplined rehearsals, well-run theatre and programs, which included opera and melodrama, set new performance standards. She attracted an audience of people who had previously disapproved of the factional and debt-ridden companies that presented under-rehearsed performances of burlesque and farce with players of often dubious talent.

Australian theatre continued to receive infusions of new talent—women who were not afraid of the challenge presented by a new country where theatrical centres were widely dispersed. MAGGIE MOORE is a notable example. Women proved adaptable to the nomadic theatrical life, marrying and bringing up families while acting, singing, dancing and assisting with the administration of companies. They travelled to wherever work was available. Some, like Katie Towers, in the Towers family company in the 1870s and 1880s, travelled to England, South Africa and India. KATE HOWARDE, 'the Tent Theatre Queen', travelled throughout New Zealand and South Africa as an actor-manager and playwright from 1900 to the 1930s.

To gain experience and recognition women have had to be enterprising, courageous and sufficiently confident of their abilities to travel beyond Australia. ELIZA WINSTANLEY in 1846 was perhaps the first in a line of *emigrées* that included JUDITH ANDERSON, CORAL BROWNE and ZOË CALDWELL. Their successes and those of visitors inspired actresses of later generations. Despite limited access to financial backing—always a problem for women in business—women showed entrepreneurial ability, even when big firms developed early in the 20th century. NELLIE BRAMLEY, for example, competed tenaciously with J. C. WILLIAMSON'S in the 1920s.

Between the wars AMATEUR THEATRE gave opportunities to actors, directors and playwrights and sustained audiences that sought modern drama. Throughout Australia women maintained serious and innovative drama at a time when the embattled professional theatre was retreating into operetta revivals and West End and Broadway hits.

In Adelaide, PATRICIA HACKETT ran her own Torch Theatre in 1934–35 and 1952–55. AGNES DOBSON ran Independent Repertory Theatre from 1936 to 1940. She taught JEAN MARSHALL, who has been an influential actor, director and teacher in amateur, community and semiprofessional theatre, especially in the ADELAIDE THEATRE GROUP, since 1933. In Brisbane, BARBARA SISLEY founded the BRISBANE REPERTORY THEATRE SOCIETY in 1925 and directed it until her death in 1945. Two other women founded breakaway groups in 1936 and controlled them for many years. RHODA FELGATE ran TWELFTH NIGHT THEATRE until 1961. JEAN TRUNDLE was chief producer of BRISBANE ARTS THEATRE until she died in 1965. OLIVE WILTON established the HOBART REPERTORY THEATRE Society in 1926 and impelled it to become the first amateur group to own its theatre.

In Melbourne, two women were in the forefront in maintaining theatre during the Second World War. LORNA FORBES founded amateur companies. IRENE MITCHELL was a pillar of the semiprofessional Melbourne Little Theatre Company, and from 1962 to 1977 of its professional successor the ST MARTIN'S THEATRE COMPANY. In Perth, ANITA LE TESSIER was an independent producer, and amateur theatre was largely supported by female actors and directors, including Ida Beeby of PATCH THEATRE. After the war, JEANA BRADLEY was a mainstay of drama at the University of Western Australia, which gained an array of theatres largely through her efforts. In Sydney, CARRIE TENNANT founded Community Theatre in 1929 to produce Australian plays. DORIS FITTON founded INDEPENDENT THEATRE in 1930 and directed it until 1977. BERYL BRYANT ran BRYANT'S PLAYHOUSE from 1932 until 1943. In the later year MAY HOLLINWORTH founded METROPOLITAN THEATRE. In professional theatre, QUEENIE PAUL and her husband Mike Connors formed Con-Paul Theatres to revive variety in 1931. In 1940 KATHLEEN ROBINSON co-founded WHITEHALL PRODUCTIONS, which presented plays at the Minerva Theatre in Sydney until 1950. After the Second World War, FIFI BANVARD struggled to establish a stock company playing regularly at the Theatre Royal in Hobart.

Few female dramatists emerged in colonial Australia but the 1920s produced some notable, if insufficiently recognised, talents through amateur theatre. Among them were Marguerite Dale, HENRIETTA DRAKE-BROCKMAN, KATHARINE SUSANNAH PRICHARD and BETTY ROLAND. From the 1940s, the political left produced prolific writers such as MONA BRAND, DYMPHNA CUSACK and ORIEL GRAY, but in the resurgent professional theatre of the 1960s ALMA DE GROEN and DOROTHY HEWETT stood almost alone until active consciousness-raising within the theatre in the 1980s encouraged recognition of women's work. Subsidy and a new outlook have not only supported new-generation playwrights, including Joanna Murray-Smith, HANNIE RAYSON and KATHERINE THOMSON, but increasingly provided better roles for female actors and opportunities for the employment of women as directors and designers.

In 1993 two women were appointed to head state theatre companies for the first time—CHRIS WESTWOOD as executive producer of the State Theatre Company of South Australia and Chris Johnston as director of the QUEENSLAND THEATRE COMPANY. ❦*Gillian Winter*

further reading
BRISBANE, KATHARINE (ed.). *Entertaining Australia*. Sydney: Currency Press 1991.
HECKENBERG, PAMELA PAYNE. Women of the Australian theatre. *Australasian Drama Studies* 12–13 (Brisbane) 1988.
PORTER, HAL. *Seven Cities of Australia*. Sydney: John Ferguson 1978. Chapter on Hobart.

John Wood

Actor, dramatist. Born 14 July 1946 in Melbourne. Trained at National Academy of Dramatic Art (Sydney). Nimrod Theatre Company (Sydney) 1971–72. Melbourne Theatre Company 1973–75. South Australian Theatre Company (Adelaide) 1980–83. Nationally known in television series *Rafferty's Rules* 1988–89.

The physically imposing John Wood makes an immediate connection with audiences, which respond to his projection of amiable probity, shy melancholy or coarse vigour. He displayed his versatility at the Nimrod Street Theatre in Sydney, where his activities ranged from nine parts in the present writer's ballad opera *Flash Jim Vaux* (1971) to slapstick humour in his own play revisiting the Marx Brothers, *On Yer Marx* (1972). He played Swiss Cheese in Joachim Tenchert's notable MELBOURNE THEATRE COMPANY production of Bertolt Brecht's *Mother Courage and Her Children*. As a member of the Lighthouse Company in Adelaide he created Theo Volks in PATRICK WHITE'S *Signal Driver* (1982) and Royce Best in White's *Netherwood* (1983), and played Rodrigo in *Lulu*, LOUIS NOWRA'S adaptation of works by Frank Wedekind, in 1980 and Sir Toby Belch in NEIL ARMFIELD'S modern-dress Caribbean production of *Twelfth Night* in 1983. ❦*Ron Blair*

further reading
SADLIER, KEVIN. Reflections on *Rafferty's Rules*. *Sun–Herald TV Magazine* (Sydney) 15 January 1989.

Workers' Art Guild

Amateur dramatic company founded in Perth, by Keith George, Katharine Susannah Prichard, John Gilchrist and Betsy Linton, February 1936. Dissolved 1940. **directors** Victor Arnold, Keith George, Howard Smith, Jerold Wells, Tom Wignall, Sydney Woodbridge. **first production** *Till the Day I Die* by Clifford Odets, 19 June 1936, Assembly Hall, Perth. Director: Keith George. Design: Harald Vike. Cast: Alan Cuthbertson, Gwen Duggan, John Gilchrist, Phyllis Harnet, Bert Vickers, George Wignall. **landmark productions** *Bury the Dead* by Irwin Shaw. *Till the Day I Die* and *Waiting for Lefty* by Clifford Odets. *Hinkerman* by Ernst Toller.

With the motto 'art is a weapon in the people's struggle', the Worker's Art Guild presented pro-Soviet and anti-fascist plays throughout its six-year existence, but it drew performers and supporters from all sectors of society and politics. It was founded by left-wing, middle-class actors, artists and writers as a centre for radical practice of all the arts, an alternative to frivolous bourgeois theatre and as a club for the unemployed. It was the first left-wing theatre group in Western Australia, though Workers' Theatre had been loosely drawn together in 1935 to produce *The Thief* and *Forward One* by KATHARINE SUSANNAH PRICHARD. If nothing else, the Workers' Art Guild showed the conservative theatregoing public of Perth that there was much more to theatre than drawing-room comedy. It initially presented short plays and agitprop pieces. Its landmark productions were almost entirely due to the creative ability and dynamic direction of Keith George, a devotee of Vsevolod Meyerhold and Konstantin Stanislavsky. He ran a rigorous workshop on drama technique and was known to spend up to a year on productions of Anton Chekhov. He directed the American left-wing plays presented in other states by NEW THEATRE. His work was noted for its driving force, startling effects and imaginative use of lighting. It earned him glowing reviews from PAUL HASLUCK, theatre critic of the *West Australian*. The quality of performance declined when George quit the organisation after political differences. After the Communist Party was banned in 1940 the guild was dissolved. It had a successor after the war in the New Theatre League. ❧*Terry Craig*

further reading
BROMFIELD, D. (ed.). *Aspects of Perth Modernism, 1929–1942*. Perth: University of Western Australia 1986.
CRAIG, T. A. Radical and conservative theatre in London and Perth in the 1930s. University of Western Australia dissertation 1988.
GODDARD, H. and L. LAYMAN. *Organise*. Perth: Trades and Labour Council 1988.
GOODING, J. *Western Australian Art and Artists 1900–1950*. Perth: Art Gallery of Western Australia 1987.
WELLS, J. The political commitment of Katharine Susannah Prichard. Murdoch University dissertation 1987.

Harry Wren

Entrepreneur. Born 1916. Worked in cinemas. Presented revues from 1940. Died 30 August 1973 in Sydney.

An entrepreneur of the old school, a spiritual descendant of the 19th-century showman who would send out a second company if he had a spare quid, Harry Wren made his most significant contributions with nostalgic revues in the 1950s and 1960s. He was flamboyant but an artist who often worked in his shows and had no great cause to like him summed up his secret: 'He had charm'.

Wren began as a call boy and sweet-seller in 1930 and worked his way up to chief projectionist in Hoyts cinemas, according to the *Sydney Morning Herald*'s obituary. NANCYE BRIDGES recalls him as a boy tap-dancer who flirted with film exhibition before staging revues featuring GEORGE SORLIE at the Cremorne Theatre in Brisbane in 1940. He was certainly launched as a variety entrepreneur by the Second World War. By 1949 he was staging *Hellzapoppin*, the zany Olsen and Johnson show, not with its American originators but with ROY RENE as star comedian. Rene did his last stage work with Wren in 1949–50.

In 1953 Wren began his nostalgic revues with *Thanks for the Memory*, which brought back many much-loved artists of previous decades, including Morry Barling, JIM GERALD, GEORGE WALLACE and QUEENIE PAUL, who also directed the show. A new nostalgic show seemed to arrive whenever Wren was in trouble. Sooner than most, Wren began importing artists from Japan, Australia's wartime enemy. These presentations were not always successful. *The Cherry Blossom Show* in 1958 was said in 1973 to have lost more than $100 000. Other exotic companies—Spanish, Mexican, black—were temporarily under his wing. In 1967 Wren converted the MAJESTIC THEATRE in Adelaide into the Celebrity Theatre Restaurant, with a show headed by JUNE BRONHILL. The venture quickly failed. Wren's health now began to desert him. ❧*John West*

further reading
Sydney Morning Herald 31 August 1973.

Joseph Wyatt

Entrepreneur. Born c.1788, probably in England. Haberdasher in Sydney until 1833. Became joint lessee of Theatre Royal, April 1835. Sole lessee May 1836 to May 1837. Opened Royal Victoria Theatre, March 1838. Left for England March 1841. Recruited performers and returned January 1843. Lost control of Royal Victoria Theatre 1854. Built Prince of Wales Theatre in Sydney and ran it 1855–58. Died 20 July 1860 in Sydney.

Joseph Wyatt, a retired haberdasher, imported 'stars' to Sydney, possibly dealing the death blow to early attempts at a local style of theatre that had been begun by BARNETT LEVEY. Wyatt, who was perhaps an emancipist, had no theatrical experience. He prospered as a haberdasher in Sydney as early as 1813 and retired in 1833. In April 1835 he joined a group who took on the lease of Levey's THEATRE ROYAL and in May 1836 he became the sole lessee. The theatre was back under Levey's control in 1837 but he soon died. Wyatt meanwhile was building the larger ROYAL VICTORIA THEATRE. Just before it opened on 26 March 1838 Levey's widow closed the Theatre Royal.

Wyatt left for England in March 1841 and sent out a batch of English performers whom he had contracted for two years—John Gibbs, leader of the orchestra, and his wife Louise Gibbs, a singer; J. B. James, actor, and his wife Mme Louise, dancer; ANDREW TORNING, actor and dancer, and Louise Torning, dancer. When Wyatt returned in January 1843 he brought with him five more actors—HENRY DEERING and his wife, J. G. GRIFFITHS, and Mrs and Mrs Mereton. Controversy and riots over Wyatt's 'cockney imports' coincided with the opening of JOSEPH SIMMONS's unsuccessful Royal City Theatre.

Wyatt constantly ignored press warnings about the need to strengthen the acting in his company. He sacked Royal Victoria favourites like Simmons and ELIZA WINSTANLEY in 1843 because they were not on written contracts. He had no understanding of the nature of verbal contracts with actors. Nor did he understand audience loyalties, theatre buildings, or benefit nights. He took the best benefits for himself as proprietor in March 1844 though he had denied one to Levey in 1837 in similar circumstances.

Wyatt frequently landed in court when he tried to cut his losses at the expense of others. His lack of concern for the human side of the theatre earned him many enemies, one of whom tried to burn down the Royal Victoria on 25 September 1844. Wyatt sold this theatre and leased it back in 1849, but in 1854 he was unable to renew the lease. He built the PRINCE OF WALES THEATRE in Castlereagh Street for £30 000 and opened it in 1855. Three years later he sold it for just £10 000. After this he gave up the theatre to speculate in property. ❦*Helen Musa*

further reading
OPPENHEIM, HELENE. Joseph Wyatt. *Australian Dictionary of Biography* 2. Melbourne University Press 1967.

Charles Young

Actor, manager. Born 5 April 1819 at Doncaster (England). Had some training and theatrical experience. Joined navy. Arrived in Australia 1843. Debut at Theatre Royal, Hobart, 30 October 1843. Married dancer Jane Thomson at Launceston (Tas.) 6 June 1845. Joined George Coppin's company 1845. Acted in England 1857–61. Divorced by wife, May 1862. Married Ellen Curby. Died 29 January 1874 in Sydney.

According to GEORGE COPPIN, Charles Young was 'a very versatile actor; in his early days equally good in tragedy, comedy and burlesque'. He was also a talented dancer and singer. He received his early training in his father's company in England and later played in London, appearing as Noah Claypole in an adaptation of Dickens's *Oliver Twist* at the Surrey Theatre in 1838. He joined the navy shortly afterwards and as a ship's officer he reached Hobart in 1843. There he was reunited with his sister Emma, an actor in ANNE CLARKE's company and the wife of G. H. ROGERS. She persuaded him to remain in Tasmania and return to the stage. He made his debut as Michael in Friedrich von Schiller's *William Tell* with Francis Nesbitt.

In March 1845, he joined Coppin's company in Launceston. In June he married the dancer and actor Jane Thomson and they went to Melbourne with Coppin. She now performed as MRS CHARLES YOUNG. After a disagreement with Coppin in October, the Youngs rejoined Mrs Clarke in Tasmania. A further disagreement saw Young and his mother-in-law, the veteran actor Martha Thomson, set up a rival company in Hobart in September 1846. By June 1847, he was stage manager of Hobart's Royal Victoria Theatre, with G. H. Rogers as acting manager. From 1849, Young worked mainly in Melbourne as manager and later lessee of the QUEEN'S THEATRE ROYAL and afterwards as a member of G. V. BROOKE's company.

In 1857 Young and his wife returned to England, where he achieved considerable success as a burlesque actor. Jane, now known as Eliza Young, made an even greater name for her acting, however, and this led to their separation and Young's return to Australia in 1861. They were divorced in 1862 and he later remarried. He appeared in Melbourne and Sydney with many leading companies and with overseas stars, including CHARLES MATHEWS, WALTER MONTGOMERY and BARRY SULLIVAN. ❦*Elizabeth Webby*

further reading
RUTLEDGE, MARTHA. Charles Young. *Australian Dictionary of Biography* 6. Melbourne University Press 1976.

David Young

Actor, director, dramatist. Born 6 September 1943 at Sidford (England). Emigrated to Australia at 30. Artistic director of Arena Theatre Company (Melbourne) 1973-75. In England as writer–researcher for Belgrade Theatre theatre-in education (Coventry) 1975–77. Artistic director of Toe Truck Theatre Company (Sydney) 1984; Salamanca Theatre Company (Hobart) 1985–90. Married to Sandi Young, playwright and community arts worker.

David Young has worked largely in theatre for children and young people. His best-known plays include *Eureka* (1974), *Wasting Away* (1985), and *Copping It Sweet* (1988), which he devised with the SALAMANCA THEATRE COMPANY in Hobart. Young has worked with many other companies throughout Australia, including TROUPE in Adelaide and the NATIONAL THEATRE COMPANY in Perth. ❦*Rachel Healy*

published plays
Eureka (1974). Sydney: Currency Press 1978.
The Price of Coal parts 1 and 2 (1976). Sydney: Methuen 1979.
Wasting Away. Sydney: Currency Press 1985 in *Learning from Life* (ed. John Lonie).

further reading
White man comes—black man goes—An interview with David Young on Salamanca Theatre Company's production of *Num Lagger* by David Gerrand. *Lowdown* 8/4 (Adelaide, September 1986).

Florence Young

Actor, singer. Born 2 October 1870 in Melbourne. Debut 1890 in Nellie Stewart Opera Company. Became J. C. Williamson operetta and pantomime star. London engagements 1897–99. Studied singing with Mathilde Marchesi in Paris. Musical-comedy star in Australia 1901–20. Died 11 November 1920 in Melbourne.

From her first appearances for J. C. WILLIAMSON in Gilbert and Sullivan operettas in the early 1890s Florence Young's voice and tiny figure delighted audiences. She played the principal boy in Williamson's pantomime *Djin Djin the Japanese Bogie Man* in 1895–96 and Dick Whittington in a London suburban and provincial production in 1898–99. On the London stage in 1897–99 she had limited success and George Meudell, who called her 'the most remarkable of all the attractive and clever women I have known', surmised that this was because of her excessively 'sweet' nature. She could not fight and trample like Nellie Melba.

Reviewers often commented on her vocal power, however. The *Sydney Morning Herald* called her 'the artist who sings in comic opera with a grand opera voice'. Young studied singing with Melba's teacher, Mathilde Marchesi but, for reasons never satisfactorily explained, she gave up the prospect of a career in opera in Europe and returned to Australia to star in Williamson's Royal Comic Opera Company. She began as Poppy in *San Toy* in 1901. In 1903 she was O Mimosa San in *The Geisha*. One of her biggest successes was *Our Miss Gibbs* in 1910, when she was the 'recognised prima donna of the Australian stage', according to the *Stage Year Book*. She played in *Our Miss Gibbs* for seven years. By 1917 her supremacy was being challenged by her rising co-star GLADYS MONCRIEFF. She retired from the stage in November 1920, and died just weeks later, aged only 50. ❦*Richard Fotheringham*

further reading
MASLEN, JOAN. Florence Young. *Australian Dictionary of Biography* 12. Melbourne University Press 1990.
MEUDELL, GEORGE. *The Pleasant Career of a Spendthrift*. London: Routledge 1929.
The Stage Year Book 1910.

Mrs Charles Young

Actor, dancer. Born 1827 in Bath (England). Originally Jane Eliza Thomson. Daughter of Martha Thomson, English actor. Came to Australia with family in 1837. Debut in Sydney 1842. Married actor Charles Young 6 June 1845. Returned to England 1857. Successful on London stage for several decades. Divorced Young 1862. Married actor Hermann Vezin 1863. Died 1902 in Margate (England).

Jane Thomson learned to act and dance in the Australian colonies and performed here for 15 years, mostly billed as Mrs Charles Young. Then she returned to her native England and began a long career on the London stage. She arrived in Hobart in 1837 with her parents and two older sisters, Eliza and Mary Christina. Her mother was the star of the opening night of the THEATRE ROYAL in Hobart on 6 March 1837. A local paper referred to her as 'in her youth ... a favourite performer on the London boards'.

The family moved to Sydney, where Mrs Thomson appeared at the Royal Victoria Theatre in 1838–40. They returned to Hobart at the end of 1840 but were back in Sydney again in 1841–44. Jane received most of her theatrical training from her mother but in Sydney in 1841–42 she studied dancing with a visiting French dancer, Monsieur Charrière. After the Thomsons returned to Hobart in 1844, Jane danced and acted minor roles in ANNE CLARKE's company. In Launceston in 1845 she married the English actor and dancer, CHARLES YOUNG, and on the same day both sailed for Melbourne with GEORGE COPPIN's company. After a disagreement with Coppin in October 1845, the Youngs returned to Hobart and rejoined Anne Clarke's company. They went to a rival company in Hobart in 1846. From 1851 Jane Young concentrated on acting. She played Emilia to G. V. BROOKE's Othello in Melbourne in 1855.

In 1857 the Youngs returned to England by way of the USA. They performed at the Walnut Street Theatre in Philadelphia in September. Also in the cast was the American actor Hermann Vezin, later to be Jane's second husband. Upon reaching London in October, the Youngs joined Samuel Phelps's company at the Sadler's Wells Theatre. Jane—who now acted as Eliza Young—received considerable critical acclaim, particularly as Lady Townly in *The Provoked Husband* by Colley Cibber and John Vanbrugh. In 1859 she played Lady Macbeth and many other roles at the Surrey Theatre. She subsequently moved to the Haymarket Theatre. In 1862 she divorced Young, from whom she had been separated for at least a year, and in 1863 she married Vezin. As Mrs Herman Vezin she remained a popular performer in Shakespearean and other roles until the 1880s. ❦*Elizabeth Webby*

further reading
Mrs Jane Elizabeth Vezin. *Dictionary of National Biography, 1901–1911*. London: Oxford University Press 1912.

Young people's theatre

Subsidy, government intervention and a few remarkable individuals have shaped young people's theatre—a movement that includes children's theatre, theatre-in-education and youth theatre. There has been theatre for children since early colonial days but only since the 1970s have activities for, by and with young people developed with financial support from government arts or educational authorities. The AUSTRALIA COUNCIL has supported high-quality theatre for young participants and audiences in all states. State governments have emulated its leadership, particularly in South Australia and Tasmania. After a burst of energy in the late 1970s and early 1980s progress has been erratic and new directions are sought. Theatre for schools is accepted, although there is ample room for expansion, but children's theatre seeks an audience. Annual youth and performing-arts conferences are influential in shaping its future. In the nationalist cultural movement young people's theatre has been significant. Up to 80 per cent of the repertoire of young people's companies is Australian. Other trends include the emergence of Aboriginal playwrights and themes and acknowledgment of the diverse parental cultures of young Australians. Nearly a quarter of them were born overseas or have parents who were, and nearly 20 per cent have parents whose first language is not English. Many companies are trying to reflect the concerns of these people and to develop an Australian self-image that is multicultural rather than English.

Professional theatre for children and young people in Australia began after the Second World War. In 1955 there was only one organisation performing programs related to school studies—the Shakespeare in Jeans Company of the Young Elizabethan Players. There was also Australian Children's Theatre, founded in Melbourne in 1948 by the sisters JOAN AND BETTY RAYNER to tour productions throughout the country. During the 1960s children's theatre companies sprang up, among them AUSTRALIAN THEATRE FOR YOUNG PEOPLE in Sydney, the ARENA THEATRE COMPANY in Melbourne and PATCH CHILDREN'S THEATRE and the CHILDREN'S ACTIVITIES TIME SOCIETY in Perth. By 1975 more than 20 full-time companies were touring schools and performing in the community.

The prevailing view that Mother England was the source of culture influenced the earlier companies' repertoires. Theatre-in-education came to Australia from England in the early 1970s with, for example, the work of Barbara Manning and her SALAMANCA THEATRE COMPANY in Hobart. Some of the founders of English theatre-in-education also came to Australia. The playwright DAVID YOUNG was artistic director of the ARENA THEATRE COMPANY in Melbourne in 1973–75, spent a time with the TOE TRUCK THEATRE COMPANY in Sydney and took over at Salamanca on Manning's retirement in 1984. Another Englishman, Roger Chapman set up the MAGPIE THEATRE COMPANY in Adelaide in 1977 and went on to become director of CARCLEW Youth Performing Arts Centre. These and similar companies began to focus on Australian content and style, and with other artistic movements began to shape a conscious Australian identity.

In 1975 the Australia Council's theatre board experimented by giving general grants for theatre-in-education to five major adult companies—the MELBOURNE THEATRE COMPANY, the NATIONAL THEATRE COMPANY in Western Australia, the QUEENSLAND THEATRE COMPANY, the STATE THEATRE Company of South Australia and the Tasmanian Theatre Company. Many theatre-in-education companies no longer label themselves as such and many perform beyond schools. Social issues such as peace, equal opportunity, racism, sexual relationships and old age predominate. The styles and working methods of theatre-in-education have influenced COMMUNITY THEATRE, which emphasises co-operative creation based on issues relevant to a particular audience. In theatre-in-education, however, commissioned plays outnumber group-devised works. Adaptations of children's literature, particularly contemporary Australian works, have also become most successful.

Youth theatre—performed and often created by young people, usually in collaboration with professional adult directors—is growing. About 20 companies receive federal subsidy to pay the professionals. Several youth-theatre companies have developed comprehensive training and workshop programs, and the best produce work that expresses young people's ideas. There has also been strong development of young playwrights. Youth theatre flourished after education departments began to include AUSTRALIAN DRAMA IN SCHOOL CURRICULA during the 1970s. In 1977 Anne Godfrey-Smith wrote, in a report commissioned by the Australian Youth Performing Arts Association, that youth theatre and theatre-in-education were the main points of growth. Some education departments supported existing theatre-in-education teams or set up their own.

Children's theatre—by adults for children, excluding theatre-in-education—provokes debate about what is appropriate for children. There is no repertoire of Australian traditional stories or fairy tales. Occasionally there have been new and well-made productions for children. Most productions are conservative in content and played during school holidays. Costs work against experimentation in children's theatre—it may be as expensive as adult theatre, but the box-office income is much less. No major subsidised company consistently produces theatre for children. The repertoire of children's theatre has always been deeply indebted to British theatre, though JACK DAVIS, Anne Harvey, DOROTHY HEWETT and other playwrights have contributed enormously towards an Australian style.

PUPPETRY has enormous potential in Australia because of the variety of European and Asian influences here. About half the puppet repertoire still comprises traditional children's stories from Europe. Several companies experiment with content and technique. Numerous unsubsidised individuals and pairs travel the country and perform in schools and shopping centres.

Youth festivals encourage creation of new works, permit exchanges between young artists and take their work to a wider public. Adelaide's COME OUT YOUTH ARTS FESTIVAL has become a major festival. Youth festivals were held throughout Australia in 1985—International Youth Year. This year also saw the birth of Melbourne's Next Wave Festival, for 12-to-25-year-olds. The Queensland Youth Arts Festival provides professionally led workshops that culminate in performances. The fourth Interplay international festival brought 52 young playwrights from 22 countries and 42 tutors from 15 countries to Townsville (Qld) in 1994 for workshops, readings and performances of works by writers aged from 14 to 22. These festivals have encouraged new young groups and promoted collaboration between established professional artists and young people.

Notable influences on young people's theatre include, as well as those mentioned above, the playwrights Peter Charlton, DAVID HOLMAN, Graeme Pitts and RICHARD TULLOCH; the directors Errol Bray, Angela Chaplin and ANDREW ROSS; the Magpie designers Richard Roberts and Ken Wilby; and the pedagogues John Lonie and CHRIS WESTWOOD. Outstanding distinctly Australian productions include *Eureka*, written and directed by David Young for Arena; *I'll Be in on That*, written and directed by Anne Harvey for Salamanca; *Strike at the Port*, group-devised and directed by Roger Chapman for Magpie; *Year 9 Are Animals*, written and directed by Richard Tulloch for Toe Truck; *Wolf Boy*, written and directed by Peter Charlton for Arena. Also noteworthy are Jack Davis's plays NO SUGAR and *Honey Spot*, directed by Andrew Ross; and *Mesh* and *Memo* by Graeme Pitts, directed by DON MAMOUNEY for the Sidetrack Theatre Company. These were the first successful plays dealing with ethnic issues.

SHOPFRONT THEATRE FOR YOUNG PEOPLE in Sydney, CANBERRA YOUTH THEATRE, UNLEY YOUTH THEATRE in Adelaide and the ST MARTIN'S YOUTH ARTS CENTRE in Melbourne have been leaders in youth theatre. As well as group-devised works, they have especially nurtured young professional writers, directors and designers. Their work has provided outlets for the artistic expression of young people and allowed their voices to be heard. CARCLEW YOUTH ARTS CENTRE, unique in Australia, works in Adelaide to promote the arts for young people throughout the country.

The Australian Youth Performing Arts Association, established in 1975 under the inspired leadership of Margaret Leask and Joan Pope, was an early driving-force in national promotion and development of theatre for children and young people. It was the Australian centre for the Association du Théâtre pour l'Enfance et la Jeunesse (ASSITEJ) and in 1981 it became ASSITEJ Australia, operating from Carclew. It has promoted Australian young people's theatre overseas. Australia has been a member of the 17-country ASSITEJ executive committee since 1981. In 1993 the present writer was elected world president of ASSITEJ for three years and in 1987 the ASSITEJ world congress and general assembly were held in Adelaide.

The Australian Script Centre in Hobart, established in 1980 as the Salamanca Script Resource Centre, and the Carclew Scripts Library, set up in 1978 and based on the library of STATE THEATRE, list Australian material, published and unpublished, for performance by and for young people. ❦*Michael FitzGerald*

further reading
GODFREY-SMITH, ANNE. *Youth Performing Arts in Australia, 1975–1977*. Sydney: Australian Youth Performing Arts Association 1977.

Radvan, Mark. *Youth Theatre*. Sydney: Australian Youth Performing Arts Association 1980.

Salamanca Theatre Company. *Annie's Coming Out—A study of a residency program*. Hobart: Tasmanian Education Department 1982.

National Theatre-in-Education Study. Sydney: Australian Youth Performing Arts Association 1980.

Support for Young People's Theatre. Sydney: Australia Council 1982.

Theatre, Childhood and Youth. April 1987. Special edition dealing exclusively with Australia, published by French centre of Association du Théâtre pour l'Enfance et la Jeunesse to coincide with ASSITEJ world congress and general assembly in Adelaide, 8–16 April 1987.

William Zappa

Actor. Born 13 October 1948 in Hadleigh (England). Played first major role at Marlowe Theatre, Canterbury. Graduated from Central School of Speech and Drama (London) 1971. Actor, movement coach and choreographer at Dukes Playhouse, Lancaster, 1972–75; began directing there 1976. Came to Australia to teach at Victorian College of Arts (Melbourne) May 1976. Australian acting debut 1977. Married actor Cathrine Lynch 1983. Has worked extensively in film and television. Mo Award for best supporting actor in a musical 1992 (*The King and I*).

William Zappa is a generous and adventurous actor. His craggy face and athletic bearing, together with an ability to speak classical dialogue, make him open to casting as the bluff soldier or the sophisticated villain. His dramatic range is wide, extending from the sinister Clay in Leroi Jones's *The Dutchman* to the brooding young Edmund in Eugene O'Neill's *Long Day's Journey into Night*, and encompassing Valmont in Christopher Hampton's *Les Liaisons dangereuses* and another voluptuary, Molière's Don Juan. He was outstanding as Gethin Price in Trevor Griffiths's *The Comedians* for the Playbox Theatre Company in 1980. Other performances for this Melbourne company include Clay in 1977, Edmund in 1982, Eddie in Sam Shepard's *Fool for Love* in 1984, and Brecht in Roger Pulvers's *Bertolt Brecht Leaves Los Angeles* in 1979. Zappa gave strong support to the surreal works of Pulvers and others of the avant garde when he was with Playbox. He directed several productions in its Upstairs theatre, which he founded with Carrillo Gantner and Nancy Black in 1978.

Zappa played the title-role in *Don Juan* in 1984 for Australian Nouveau Theatre and the Adelaide Festival, to much critical acclaim. With the State Theatre Company of South Australia he played title-role in *Richard III* in 1985 and Benedick in *Much Ado About Nothing* and Valmont in 1987. In Sydney he has played Trigorin in Anton Chekhov's *The Seagull* for the Sydney Theatre Company in 1986 and Hummel in Václav Havel's *The Increased Difficulty of Concentration* at the Belvoir Street Theatre Downstairs in 1990. His roles in musicals include Thénardier in *Les Misérables*, the Kralahome in *The King and I* and Julian Marsh in *42nd Street*. ❦*Katharine Brisbane*

Zootango

Professional dramatic company in Hobart, formed in 1985. **venue** Peacock Theatre 1987–. **artistic directors** Richard Davey 1986–92. Louise Permezel 1994.

A young company with a name devised in a word game and an innovative approach to contemporary works, Zootango has been acclaimed by critics for high standards of stagecraft. It was established as a co-operative to present a broad range of theatre to the widest possible audience and to provide work and training for resident writers, directors, actors and production staff. In 1986 it became Tasmania's principal production company in a joint venture with the Theatre Royal and the Tasmanian Arts Advisory Board. In its first five years Zootango presented 30 productions—half of them original works—from cabaret, clowning and Theatresports to major plays. Since 1990 it has operated independently as the state theatre company, taking many productions to country towns. By 1990 experiment had given way to a more conventional program demanded by the public and the funding bodies.

A change from an annual grant to project funding in 1992 was accompanied by expressions of concern about the long-term viability of the company and its recent artistic standards. A major criticism was that the company was dominated by Richard Davey, who has since acknowledged that his ambition to produce his own work is not entirely compatible with the artistic directorship of a company. Zootango was a vehicle for Davey's own plays and for some productions he doubled as director and designer. His *A Bright and Crimson Flower* was successful in 1992 and went on interstate tour in 1993. Other popular productions have been Christopher Hampton's *Les Liaisons dangereuses*, Peta Murray's *Wallflowering* and Shakespeare in the Botanical Gardens in summer. A report on adult theatre in Tasmania by Roger Hodgman in 1993 said Zootango should be a 'small scale company of excellence … drawing on local and interstate resources and producing at least one work which is uniquely Tasmanian and capable of touring interstate'. ❦*Gillian Winter*

Index

Bold type indicates articles and the pages on which they begin. Page numbers in *italics* refer to illustrations.

A

A la carte 211
Aarons, Joseph 87
Aarons, 'Mo' 16
Ab Intra Studio Theatre 11, 27, 33, 42, 83, 261
Abbey Theatre 211, 298
Abbie and Lou, Norman and Rose 413
Abbott, John 76
Abdullah 144
A'Beckett, Gilbert. See *The Happy Land*
Abell and Klaer's circus 612
Abermain Society 405
Abnett, Leslie 582
Aboriginal National Theatre Trust 97
Aboriginal Women's Art Festival 224
Aborigines and theatre 12, 46, 71, 139, 143, 361, 452
Aborigines' League 400
Aborigines Woomera 13
About Marie Stopes 224
Abraham Lincoln 112
Absurd Person Singular 168, 233, 254, 318
Acacia Avenue 28
Academy of Music: Adelaide 25; Ballarat (Vic.) 268, 443, 590, 591, 593; Launceston (Tas.) 584; Melbourne 87; Sydney 605
Access Arts Theatre of the Disabled 194
Accidental Death of an Anarchist 216, 618, 635
Accidental Poke, The 276, 508
Achard, Marcel. See *Patate*
Achimovich, Lois. See *Meekatharra*
Achurch, Janet 15, 205, 214, 490
Ackland, Rodney. See *Strange Orchestra*
Acrobatic Arts Community School 144, 232
acrobatics 16
ACRONYM Theatre Company 150
Across the Board on Tomorrow Morning 621
ACTEST 598
acting 17
Acting Out 247
Action Poetry 219
Active Casting 34

Actors' Agency 35
Actors' and Announcers' Equity Association of Australia 23, 296. *See also* Actors' Equity
Actors' Association of Australia 295, 600
Actors Company 124, 498
Actors' Development Stream 444
Actors' Equity 23, 45, 161, 177, 190, 302, 321, 442
Actors' Federation of Australia 23, 296
Actors' Theatre 103
Acworth, Elaine 223
Adam and Eva 263
Adamanta, the Proud Princess of Profusia, and her Six Unlucky Suitors 626
Adams, Arthur H. 19, **24**, *172*, 404, 452. *See also Doctor Death; The Minstrel;* **Mrs Pretty and the Premier;** *Pierrot in Australia; Tapu; The Wasters*
Adams, Francis 449
Adams, George 423, 641
Adams, Harvey 24, 639
Adams, John 258
Adams, Peta 508
Adams, Phillip. See *A Funny Thing Happened on the Way to The Front*
Adamson, Lois 124
Adcock, Dan 119
Add a Grated Laugh or Two 320
Adding Machine, The 50
Adelaide 25
Adelaide Festival Centre 29, 109, 216, 433, 590, 595
Adelaide Festival Centre Trust 29, **30**, 317, 557
Adelaide Festival of Arts 28, 29, **30**, 54, 68, 84, 89, 120, 144, 154, 166, 190, 195, 215, 225, 227, 228, 237, 257, 258, 260, 276, 279, 282, 290, 291, 297, 298, 306, 309, 332, 337, 344, 363, 368, 369, 386, 404, 407, 416, 418, 421, 432, 433, 459, 462, 470, 482, 510, 514, 525, 527, 555, 556, 557, 573, 579, 616, 629, 638, 650, 656
Adelaide Literary Theatre 26, 32, 39, 613, 619
Adelaide Musical Comedy Company 28
Adelaide Repertory Theatre 20, 26, 27, 28, **32**, 40, 79, 207, 215, 257, 268, 525, 614
Adelaide Theatre Group 27, 28, **32**, 43, 79, 198, 344, 418, 651
Adelaide University Theatre Guild 27, 28, 31, **33**, 79, 81, 83, 98, 109, 173, 198, 258, 306, 519, 577, 619, 638
Adelaide Women's Theatre Group 223
Adele, Barvar 483. *See also* Bill Reed

Adele, Ethel 234
Adelphi Theatre 238, 342, 605, 637
Adeson, Lilias 417
Adler, Larry 603
Adler, Stella 440, 575
Adman, The 272
Admirable Crichton, The 489
Adrien, Lesley 286
Adrienne Lecouvreur 86
Advanced Vaudeville Entertainers 79
Adventures of Brer Rabbit, The 271
Advertiser (newspaper) 173
Advocate (newspaper) 174
Aeolian Hall 581
Aeschylus. See *Oresteia*
Afford, Max 33, 74, 207, 452, 478. *See also* **Awake My Love;** *Colonel Light—The Founder; Dark Enchantment; Lady in Danger; Laughter in the Dark; Mischief in the Air*
Afford, Thelma 33, 76
Afinogenov, Alexander. See *Distant Point*
Africa—A savage musical 538
Africa—Tales from a drum 538
Africaine, L' 115
African Theatres 535
After Dark 645
After Dinner 95, 617
After My Fashion 315
After Sunday 365
After the Fall 157
After-Life of Arthur Cravan, The 187
Aftermath, The 359
Aftershocks 109, 156, 290
Age (newspaper) 170
agents 34, 42
Agnes 581
Agnes of God 137
Agnew, Philip 101
Agnew, Steve 74
Ah Goon 135
Ah, Wilderness! 34, 81
Ahearn, Johnny 434
Ahon, Lucy 608
Aiglon, L' 41, 47, 111, 482, 549, 574
Airey, Walter 151
Airlie, Ella 114. *See also The Bunyip*
Aitken, John. See *Daisy Bates and the Dancer; Watershed*
Akabah Arabs 143
Akerholt, May-Brit 73, 217
Akersten, Donna 164
Akhurst, W. M. 35, 115, 170, 425. *See also L'Africaine; The Battle of Melbourne; Colonial Experience; Harlequin Robinson Crusoe; The House that Jack Built; The Rights of Women; The Siege of Troy; Tom Tom, the Piper's Son*
Akins, Nancy 469

Akins, Robert 469
Akins, Zoë. See *The Greeks Had a Word for It*
Akon, Kosta 95
Aladdin 91, 162, 271, 285
Aladdin and Company Limited 605
Aladdin and the Boss Cocky 84
Alaya 356, 386
Albany (WA) 632
Albany Town Hall 109
Albee, Edward 574. See *The American Dream; The Ballad of the Sad Café; A Delicate Balance; Tiny Alice; Who's Afraid of Virginia Woolf?*
Albert, Stephen 14, 97
Albert Hall 584
Albert Names Edward 411
Albert Theatre 57, 146, 630
Albertazzi, Emma 287
Albrecht, Cordula 97
Alchemist, The 231
alcohol 65
Alden, John 36, 159, 308, 321, 332, 491, 498, 524, 527
Alderdyce, Scott 504
Aldgate Pump, The 288
Aldous, Allan 67, 481
Alexander, Bill 440
Alexander, Bob 24
Alexander, Fred 225
Alexander, George 649
Alexander, Hal 24, 296
Alexander, Neill 462
Alexander, Scott 41
Alexandra Theatre 180, 269, 443, 449, 626
Alford, Mark M. See *Turned Up*
Alfred Dampier Company 490, 507
Alfred the Great 115, 147
Alhambra Minstrel Company 460
Alhambra Theatre 601, 604
Ali Baba and the Forty Thieves 644
Alice in Wonderland 325
All Aboard for Happiness 469
All Diggers 191
All for Gold 36, 180, 181, 284
All for the Love of a Lady 420
All My Sons 198
All Out Ensemble 29, 432
All Stops Out 251
All the King's Horses 622
All Those in Favour 337
Allan, Maud 348
Allan Wilkie Shakespearean Company 36, 66, 150, 172, 250, 278, 290, 523, 563, 611, 640
Allan's Music Warehouse 298
Allen, Arthur W. 300, 576
Allen, Christopher 432

657

Allen, David 29, **37**, 58, 614. See also *Cheapside*; *Coppin and Company*; *Crunchy*; *Gone with Hardy*; *If I Ever Get Back Home Again I'll Stay*; *Joseph Conrad Goes Ashore*; *Meat*; *The Professor*; *Upside Down at the Bottom of the World*; *Zen and Now*
Allen, Elizabeth 37
Allen, Fred 294
Allen, John 175
Allen, Marilyn 37, 336
Allen, Jack and Cottier 521
Alleycat Alice and Friends 509
Allgood, Sara 47, 296, 298, 300
Alliance Française 216
Allnut, Robert 422
All's Well that Ends Well 157, 200, 256, 305, 315, 412, 466, 480
Almost a Dinosaur 646
Almost Managing Company 34, 498
Alpha Children's Theatre 122
Alsop, Donald 599
'Alta' 345, 504, 518
Altmann, Karin 508
Altona 365, 395
Amadeus 200, 208, 234, 365
Amateur Comedy Company 38
Amateur Dramatic Club 278
Amateur Dramatic Corps 436
amateur theatre 34, **38**, 50, 173, 473, 474, 491, 567, 634
Amateur Theatrical Association 511
Amateur Theatricals 38, 436
Amazing Dr Clitterhouse, The 639
Amazing Johnsons, Nine 135
Amazons, The 110
Ambassador, The 459
Ambrose Applejohn's Adventure 633
America Hurrah! 53, 132, 137, 193, 317, 401, 403, 577
American Dream, The 568
American Independence Hour, The 54
American influences 46, 208
American Theatre of the Deaf 582
Amery, Phyllis 199
Amherst, J. See *Michael Howe, the Terror of Van Diemen's Land*
Amiel, Leonie 153
Amor, Christine 194
Amorous Prawn, The 186
AMP Theatrette 471
Amp-i-theatre 470
An Inspector Calls 209
Anatassiades, Chris. See *Legends*
And Here Comes Bucknuckle 284
And So to Bed 233, 386
And so to Bedlam 98
Andeganora 12, 212
Anderson, Colin 125
Anderson, D. J. 92, 312
Anderson, Florence 282
Anderson, Gaye 178

Anderson, James 25, 170, 205, 373, 522, 552
Anderson, (Dame) Judith 27, 28, 31, **54**, 72, 200, 248, 290, 344, 651
Anderson, Kingston 73, 290
Anderson, Lindsay 285
Anderson, Mary 55
Anderson, Maxwell. See *Elizabeth the Queen*; *Winterset*
Anderson, Michael 519
Anderson, Oswald. See *Jinker, the Grafter's Mate*
Anderson, Robert. See *Tea and Sympathy*
Anderson, William 54, 101, 197, 233, 245, 281, 316, 450, 474, 490, 497, 498, 533, 539, 637. See also **The Winning Ticket**
Anderson, 'Wizard' 397
Andorra 215, 555
Andrews, E. B. 583
Andrews, William 55, 154
Androcles and the Lion 357
Andros, Billy 186
Angell, Barbara 498
Angels in America 574
Anglin, Margaret 600, 643
Angus, Rohanna 97
Angus and Robertson 467
Anketel, Christine 429
Anketell, Margaret 351
Anna Christie 24, 81, 350, 623
Annese, Maurice 308
Annie 150, 200, 386, 395, 435
Annie Get Your Gun 52, 67, 124, 264, 302, 384, 386, 636
Annie's Coming Out 184
Anniversary 179
Anniversary, The 104
Anoli—the Blind 453, 607
Anorexia Sometimes 309
Anouilh, Jean. See *Antigone*; *Colombe*; *The Lark*; *Point of Departure*; *Ring Round the Moon*
Anstead, Flora 553
ANT. See Australian Nouveau Theatre
Anthill. See Australian Nouveau Theatre
Anthony, C. L. See *Autumn Crocus*; *Touch Wood*
Anthony, Julie 55, 128, 304
Anthony A. Williams Management 34
Antigone 124, 198, 228, 257, 371, 417
Antonio, Adeline 229
Antony and Cleopatra 27, 61, 63, 96, 165, 185, 194, 363, 428, 551, 557
Anything Goes 50, 318, 386, 409
Aorta 273
Apocalypsis cum Figuris 459
Apollo Music Hall 162
Apollo Theatre 237, 422
Apple Cart, The 305, 367

Appleton, F. C. 117, 197, 518
Appleton, Mr 481
Apprentice Theatre 279, 322
Arabin 12, 131, 447
Arabin, Gustavus 55, 335, 340
Arabin, Mrs 335
Araluen Arts Centre 433, 590
Arbor, The 337
Arbuzov, Aleksey 515. See also *Old World*; *The Promise*
Arcadia 208
Arcadians, The 124, 149, 386
Archdale, Alexander 56, 236, 341, 569
Archer, Robyn 56, 98, 125, 224, 240, 342, 422, 497. See also *Cafe Fledermaus*; *Kold Komfort Kaffee*; **The Pack of Women**; *Scandals*; *A Star is Torn*; *The Three Legends of Kra*
Archer, William 15
Archibald, Professor Douglas 336
Archibald Prize 367
architectural awards 472, 636
Archives Office of NSW 328
Archway Motif 83
Arden, Cecil 281
Arden, John 208. See *The Business of Good Government*; *Serjeant Musgrave's Dance*
Arden, Kate 281, 307
Ardrey, Robert. See *Thunder Rock*
Are You Lonesome Tonight? 439
Are You Now, or Have You Ever Been? 347
Are You Ready, Comrade? 506
Arena Management 126
Arena Theatre Company 57, 154, 224, 508, 653, 654
Aren't We All? 94, 622
Argue, David 573
Argyle Rooms (Adelaide) 25, 113;
Argyle Rooms (Hobart) **57**, 85, 121, 249, 278, 364, 430, 592, 630
Aristophanes. See *Lysistrata*
Arizona 490
Arlecchino e gli altri 217
Arlen, Albert 497, 519. See *Girl from Snowy River*; **The Sentimental Bloke**
Arlen, Michael. See *The Green Hat*
Armadillo 119
Armfield, Neil 57, 86, 90, 178, 194, 245, 308, 407, 411, 514, 515, 519, 526, 556, 573, 574, 638, 651
Armitage, Mary 174
Armoured Train, The 403
Arms and the Man 319, 376
army entertainment units 58
Arnhem Land Dancers 13
Arnold, Chick 409
Arnold, Victor 400, 401
Arnold, Villiers 114

Aronson, Linda 60, 223. See also *Dinkum Assorted*; *Reginka's Lesson*
Around the Loop 88, 516
Arrah-na-Pogue 645
Arrighi, Luciana 550
Arrow Theatre 60, 106, 331, 356, 408, 549, 597
Arsenic and Old Lace 166, 234, 240, 458, 639
Art and Working Life 337
Art of Speech Association 102
Art Studio Players 28, 198
Art Theatre Players Company 41, 234, 514
Arthy, Judith 418
Artrage 60, 226, 438
Artreach 194
Arts Access 194
Arts Council Ballet 61
Arts Council of Australia 43, **60**, 67, 79, 497; NSW 498, 563; Queensland 105; South Australia 28, 80, 536; Victoria 83; Western Australia 438
Arts in Action 194
Arts Theatre: Adelaide 32, 595; Brisbane 44, 103, 595
As Dorothy Parker Once Said 512
As It's Played Today 310
As Time Goes By 242
As We Are 198
As Ye Sow 478
As You Desire Me 258, 317
As You Like It 19, 61, 80, 258, 349, 366, 412, 510, 512, 518, 577, 596
Ascent of F6, The 27
Asche, Oscar 19, **61**, 63, 207, 490, 523, 596
Ashbolt, Allan 363
Ashby, Jeff 73
Ashes 240
Ashikawa, Yoko 440
Ashton, Annie 509
Ashton, 'Captain' Fred 63
Ashton, Dorothy 520
Ashton, Doug 63
Ashton, Dougie 520
Ashton, Ethel 62, 509
Ashton, Fred 62, 63
Ashton, Freddy 62
Ashton, James 62, 509
Ashton, James Henry 62, 138, 142, 477
Ashton, Joe 63
Ashton, Mervyn 509
Ashton, Queenie 497
Ashton and St Leon's Combined Circus 62
Ashton's Circus 62, 137, 138, 306, 434, 498, 509, 613, 649
Ashtons, Seven 520
Asia and the Australian theatre 63
Ask No Questions 364
Aspects of Love 317
Aspen Tree, The 11
Aspern Papers, The 599, 635

Aspinall, Ric 76
Asplin, Wilfred 615
Asquith, Anthony. See *Ten Minute Alibi*
ASSITEJ Australia 655
Association du Théâtre pour l'Enfance et la Jeunesse 655
Association of Community Theatres 310
Association of Fringe Theatres 45
Astley's Amphitheatre 106, 465
At Cripple Creek 490
At Last the 1984 Show 403
At Least You Get Something Out of That 367
At the Desk of Eugene Flockhart 411
At the Silver Swan 275
Atacama 217
Athenaeum Hall 64
Athenaeum Theatre 64, 591, 637
Atherden, Geoffrey. See *Hotspur*
Atkins, G. 421
Atkinson, Roslyn 462
Atonement, The 598
'Atticus' 147
Atwell, Winifred 152
Atzala 43, 216
Auden, W. H. See *The Ascent of F6*
audiences 65, *101*, *300*, *301*
Aussie Kiddies 135
Aussie Smart Set Diggers 511
Australasian (newspaper) 170
Australasian Drama Studies 468, 496
Australasian Publishing Company 467
Australasian Theatre Record 175
Australia Council 45, 69, 73, 75, 76, 90, 104, 105, 108, 155, 160, 175, 200, 216, 220, 241, 242, 250, 310, 341, 433, 468, 563, 569, 572, 634, 654; Art and Working Life 166, 337, 359, 562
Australia Felix 35, **70**, 131, 256, 287, 425, 447, 626
Australia Hall 604
Australia Magazine 172
Australia Majestic 468
Australian (national newspaper) 175
Australian Aboriginal Theatre Company 119, 517
Australian Aborigines' League 371
Australian Actors' Union 295
Australian and New Zealand Theatre Record 405
Australian and New Zealand Theatres Ltd 301, 507
Australian Archives 70, 72, 84, 118, 191, 245, 287, 463, 497, 637, 647
Australian Artists' Creative Fellowships 77, 251

Australian Authors' and Writers' Guild 422
Australian Ballet 70, 72
Australian Broadcasting Commission 72, 74, 150, 393, 478
Australian Broadcasting Company 478
***Australian Bunyips, The* 71**, 447
Australian Capital Territory: Council of Cultural Societies 497; Playwrights' Festival 598
Australian Children's Theatre 96, 482, 498, 654
Australian Contemporary Theatre Company 71
Australian Council for the Arts 38, 69, 73, 95, 159, 174, 241, 250, 341, 433, 458, 518, 563. *See also* **Australia Council**
Australian Cultural Development Office 250
Australian Drama Company 72, 290, 331
Australian Drama Foundation 69
Australian drama in school curricula 71
Australian Drama League 42
Australian Dramatic Company 518
Australian Elizabethan Theatre Trust 20, 33, 36, 44, 56, 68, **72**, 73, 77, 84, 85, 88, 128, 159, 174, 175, 195, 196, 201, 204, 208, 217, 225, 250, 258, 276, 278, 281, 289, 304, 326, 330, 331, 341, 342, 394, 395, 396, 418, 421, 454, 465, 469, 497, 510, 524, 528, 555, 557, 563, 565, 568, 570, 581, 582, 615, 629, 634
Australian Free Theatre Troupe 248, 259
Australian Hoax, An 484
Australian Marionette Theatre 83
Australian Music Examinations Board 42
Australian Musical Productions 275
Australian National Black Playwrights' Conference 73
Australian National Memorial Theatre Ltd 396
Australian National Playwrights' Centre 72, 103, 570
Australian National Playwrights' Conference 69, 76, 91, 148, 153, 202, 208, 216, 230, 264, 271, 456, 497, 575
Australian National University 122, 621
Australian Nouveau Theatre 22, **74**, 215, 216, 220, 355, 356, 363, 515, *549*, 656
Australian Olympic Theatre 179, 213, 466, 647; Sydney 566

Australian Opera 70, 72, 208, 244, 245, 511
Australian People's Theatre 286, 574
Australian Performing Group 13, 22, 54, 68, 69, **74**, 91, 98, 110, 145, 184, 191, 195, 209, 215, 218, 223, 276, 321, 345, 355, 454, 492, 498, 507, 515, 520, 538, 562, 588, 613, 614
Australian Puppet Festival 96
Australian Quarterly (magazine) 173
Australian Radio, Television and Screen Writers' Guild 76
Australian Script Centre 516, 655
Australian Security Intelligence Organisation 401, 598
Australian Stage Company 492
Australian Theatre for Young People 75, 240, 417, 568, 636, 650, 654
Australian Theatre Record 175
Australian Theatre Society 39, 105, 354, 451
Australian Theatre Studies Centre 175
Australian Theatre Workshop 122
Australian Theatrical and Amusement Employees' Association 23, 296
Australian Theatrical Choristers' Association 294
Australian Variety Artistes' Association 76
Australian Variety Company 535
Australian Vaudeville Artists' Association 294
Australian Vaudeville Artists' Federation 295, 296
Australian Writers' Guild 75, 456, 458
Australian Youth Performing Arts Association 655
Australis 426
Authors and Artists' Association 93
'Autolycus' 170
Autumn Crocus 525
Autumn Manoeuvres 111, 596
Available Light 187
Awake My Love 33, 34, **76**, 435, 452
awards **76**, 453, 458
Away 57, 71, **77**, 222, 251, 254, 260, 557, 573, 636
Awful Rose, An 262, 313
Ayckbourn, Alan. See *Absurd Person Singular; Bedroom Farce; How the Other Half Loves; The Norman Conquests; Season's Greetings; Woman in Mind*
Ayr, W. H. 158
Ayr, W. J. 92
Aztec Services Pty Ltd 104, 129, 237, 304

B

Babes in the Wood, The 162, 380, 626
Babicci, Sam 91
Baby's Luck 147
Bacchoi 102
Back From the Grave 183
Back to Bourke Street 580
Back to the Burgh 291
Backhouse, Benjamin 590
Backhouse, Clarence 423
Backhouse, Elizabeth. See *Mirage*
Backhouse and Backhouse 338, 605
Backhouse and Laidley 168
Backstage 584
Backus Minstrels 370
Backyard 80, 148, 570
Bad Girl of the Family, The 343, 606
Baddeley, J. M. 68
Baden-Powell, Frank 77, 110, 157, 280, 395, 588
Bader, Valerie 308, 622
Bagge, C. F. Ohlfsen 416
Baggs, S. A. 270
Bagnini, Jorge 124
Bagnold, Enid. See *The Chalk Garden*
Bah Humbug! 615
Baigent, Harold 44
Baile, Debbie 199
Bailey, Bert 17, 24, 55, **78**, 118, 163, 197, 199, 392, 417, *450*, 497, 513, 532, 554, 637, 647. See also *The Man from Outback; The Native Born;* **On Our Selection; The Squatter's Daughter**
Bailey, James 225
Bailey, Robin 416
Bailey, 'Tim' 78
Bailey and Grant 78
Bain, Bill 318
Bain, J. C. 79, 99, 485
Bain, Keith 326, 393
Baird, Dorothea 299, 643
Baird, Maie 504
Bakaitis, Helmut 79, 126, 399, 470, 471, 544, 555. See also *The Incredible Mind-Blowing Journey of Jack Smith*
Baker, John Simms 401
Baker, Lorraine 271
Baker, Philippa 531
Baker, Walter E. 98, 232, 283, 296, 345, 504
Balalaika 386, 406
Bali: Adat 64
Ball, Valerie 362
Ball, William 440
Ballad of Angel's Alley, The **79**, 386
Ballad of Billy Lane, The 291
Ballad of Lois Ryan, The 95, 359, 508, 562
Ballad of the Sad Café, The 83
Ballantyne, Cedric 268

Ballantyne, Colin 27, 28, 32, 41, **79**, 172, 215, 497, 514
Ballantyne, Elspeth 79, 599
Ballantyne, Guy 79
Ballantyne, Gwenneth 80, 514
Ballantyne, Jane 79
Ballantyre and Hare 423
Ballarat Players 234
Ballet, Arthur 73
Balls 276
Balodis, Janis 73, **80**, 217, 456. See also *Backyard*; *Heart for the Future*; *No Going Back*; *Too Young for Ghosts*; *Wet and Dry*
Balos, Rowena 440
Banana Bender, The 190
Bananas 96
Bancks, J. C. 90
Bandicoot on a Burnt Ridge **80**, 196, 405, 454
Bandit of the Rhine, The **81**, 121, 214, 278, 297, 325, 446
Bandmann, Daniel 213
Banjo 458
Banks, Curly 641. See also Billy Williams
Banks, Judy 129
Banks, Ron 176
Bankside 621
Bankside Theatre 581
Bankside Theatre Productions 96
Bannon, Anne 178
Bannon, John 28, 587
Banvard, Fifi **81**, 101, 128, 278, 394, 639, 651
Banvards, the 632, 633
Barbara Gange Management 34
Barbara Leane and Associates 34
Barbe-bleue 386, 533
Barbour, Lyndall **81**, 528
Barclay, C. J. 584
Barclay, David 584
Barclay, Edmund 130, 478
Barclay, Helene 130
Barclay, Peter 123, 399, 504
Barker, Arnold 407
Barker, Don **81**, *102*
Barker, Howard 208. See also *No End of Blame*
Barling, Morry 652
Barlow, Billee 233
Barlow Family, The 88, 446
Barmaids 189, 597
Barnard, Flo 428
Barnes, Brian D. 398
Barnes, Frank 345
Barnes, Michael 515
Barnes, Norman 153
Barnet, Nahum 269
Barnett, Alice 244, 382
Barnett, Morris 538. See also *The Serious Family*
Barnett, Pat 97
Barningham, John 242
Barnstormers 334, 600
Barnum 330, 386
Barone, Monica 123, 124

Barr, Margaret 393
Barr, Rosemary 395
Barr Smith Theatre 39, **82**
Barrett, Ray **82**
Barrett, Wilson 205, 214, 299, 644. See also *Ben My Chree*; *The Manxman*; *The Sign of the Cross*
Barretts of Wimpole Street, The 27, 342
Barrie, (Sir) James M. See *The Admirable Crichton*; *Half an Hour*; *The Little Minister*; *Mary Rose*; *Peter Pan*; *Quality Street*; *What Every Woman Knows*; *The Will*
Barrington Prologue 495
Barry, Dan **82**, 197, 281, 449, 490, 640. See also *The Kelly Gang*
Barry, Dennis 37
Barry, John 140
Barry, Philip. See *Hotel Universe*; *The Philadelphia Story*
Barry, Stephen 339, 395
Barry, Tara 384
Barrymore, John 47
Barrymore, W. See *Trial by Battle*
bars in theatres 353
Bartlett, J. J. 160
Barton, John 510
Barton, Roy 62
Barton's Circus 62
Barton's Follies 62
Baruch, Kester 11, **83**, 577
Barungin (Smell the Wind) 185, 196, 509
Basically Black 13, 347, 569
Basquette, Lina 50
Bass, Eric 538
Bastard Country, The 157, 276, 454, 616
Bastard from the Bush, The 228, 480
Bastardy 13, 507, 508
Batchelor, Don 153
Bate, Michael 539
Bates, David 122
Bates, Mr and Mrs F. M. 47
Bates, Sandra 168, 210
Batey, Peter 44, **83**, 87, 125, 330, 395, 555. See also *The No-Hopers*
Bathroom 334
Bathurst, Peter 363
Battersby, Jean 250
Battle of Hastings, The 35
Battle of Inkermann, The 35
Battle of Melbourne, The 35, 538
Battler, The 212, 442, 451
Bauble Shop, The 108
Bauer, Irvin 73
Bauer, Mina 11
Bauerle, Adolf. See *Die Falsche Catalani in Krahwinkel*
Bausch, Pina 31
Bax, Clifford. See *The Poetasters of Ispahan*; *Prelude and Fugue*
Baxter, Keith 133

Baxter, Virginia 241. See also *Just Walk*; *Tokyo Two*
Baxter, Warwick 122
Bayaertz, C. N. 172
Bayless, L. M. 46, 605
Bazaar and Rummage 482
Beach Blanket Tempest 79, 386, 399
Bear Dinkum 96
Bear, The 237, 371, 515
Beaton, Cecil 548
Beaton, Hilary 223, 405
Beattie, James 365, 395
Beattie, Joy 415
Beatty, Harcourt 149
Beatty, Maud 460
Beatty, May 460
Beaumarchais, Pierre. See *The Marriage of Figaro*
Beautiful Mrs Portland, The 271
Beautland 190
Beauty and the Beast 282, 308, 337, 626
Beauty Shop, The 429
Beauty Spot, The 386
Becher, Alan 439
Beck, Ron 28
Beck, Syd **84**, 441, 603
Beckett, John 177
Beckett, Rutland 392
Beckett, Samuel. See *Footfalls*; *Happy Day*; *Krapp's Last Tape*; *Waiting for Godot*
Beckett Theatre 177
Bed Before Yesterday, The 285
Bedbug Celebration, The 75
Bedfellows 412
Bedford, Randolph **84**. See also *The Boss Cocky*; *White Australia*
Bedford, Vera 84
Bedlam Autos 190
Bedroom Farce 168
Beeby, Bruce 396
Beeby, Edward 43, 428
Beeby, Ida 43, 428, 651
Beef Trust 429
Before the Dawn 533
Beginning of the End 80
Behan, Brendan. See *The Hostage*
Behn, Aphra. See *The Rover*
Behrman, S. N. See *No Time for Comedy*
Belasco, David. See *At Cripple Creek*; *Du Barry*; *The Girl I Left Behind Me*; *The Girl of the Golden West*; *Sweet Kitty Bellairs*; *Zaza*
Beletso Revue Company 441
Belfield, Francis **84**
Belinda 622
Bell, Andrew 422
Bell, Christopher 195, 216, 641
Bell, David 104
Bell, Hilary 84, 223, 626

Bell, John **84**, 89, 136, 193, 203, 260, 317, 326, 393, 407, 413, 432, 476, 497, 524, 544, *569*, 573, 574, 613, 622, 626
Bell, June 306
Bell, Lucy 84, 626
Bell, Mary Haley. See *Duet for Two Hands*
Bell, Ron 135
Bell, Book and Candle 166
Bell Shakespeare Company 23, 84, 209, 524, 570, 610
Bella Donna 319
Belle and the Bushranger 252
Belle Hélène, La 124, 244, 382, 386
Belle of Brisbane, The 100
Belle of Mayfair, The 386
Belle of New York, The 46, 379, 386, 636, 644
Bellew, Kyrle 214
Bellingham, Lois 124
Bell's Life in Victoria (newspaper) 170
Bells, The 96, 299
Belmore, Daisy 96
Belmore, James **85**, 121, 364, 531, 583
Belmore Market 126
Beloved Vagabond, The 386, 628
Belphegor the Mountebank 181
Belvoir Street Theatre 58, **85**, 178, 208, 215, 216, 222, 227, 235, 260, 282, 286, 308, 328, 398, 514, 515, 526, 544, 551, 570, 580, 595, 596, 627, 635, 656
Belz, Maurice 600
Ben Bolt 561
Ben Hur 270, 299, 490, 644
Ben My Chree 644
Benhamo's English Circus 228
Benison, Louis 49
Benjamin, Peter 330
Bennell, Eddie. See *My Spiritual Dreaming*
Bennet, Harold 398
Bennett, Alan 208
Bennett, George 65, 327
Bennett, John 313, 405
Bennett, Kevin. See *St Marys Kid*
Bennett, Roger. See *Funerals and Circuses*
Bensky, Roger-Daniel 470
Benson, Jennie 384
Benson, Jenny 507
Benson, Lucy 278
Bent 577
Bent, Roxxy 223, 625
Benyon, Lissa. See *Pennies Before the Holidays*
Berenice 166, 432
Bergin, Brian 258
Berkman, Chris 345
Berkoff, Steven 83, 208. See also *East*; *The Fall of the House of Usher*; *Greek*; *One Man*; *Salome*
Bernard, Jean-Jacques. See *Martine*; *The Unquiet Spirit*

660

Berney, William. See *Dark of the Moon*
Bernhardt, Sarah 86, 214, 566, 645
Berrell, Lloyd 296, 515, 564
Berry, Graham 260
Bert and Maisie 405
Bert Bailey Dramatic Company 78
Bertie, C. H. 495
Bertolt Brecht Leaves Los Angeles 99, 444, 468, 656
Bertram, Arthur 417
Bertram, Charles 336
Berwick, Kester 83. See also **Kester Baruch**
Besieged at Port Arthur 63, 283
Best, Christine 516
Bester, Rudolf. See *The Barretts of Wimpole Street*
Better Known as Bee 79, 322, 386, 471, 629
Better 'Ole, The 484
Betting Book, The 283
Betty 387
***Betty Blokk Buster Follies, The* 83, 87**, 330
Betsy Can Jump 75, 223
Between Engagements 190
Bevan, Alfreda 417
Bevan, Ronald. See *Stalag 17*
Beware of Imitations 412
Beyer, Elsie 308
Beynon, Richard 87, 497, 519. See also *The Shifting Heart*
Beyond the Labyrinth 429
bhuto 31
Bibby, Peter 97
Bid Me to Love 51, 464
Big and Little 215
Big Boat, The 440
Big Hand for the Limbs, A 379
Big River 85, 119, 234, 248, 368, 387
Big Sister 83, 330
***Big Toys* 87**, 230, 456, 526, 596, 638
Biggins, Jonathan 234
Biggles 88, 91, 234, 407, 492, 544
Bijou Theatre (Esperance, WA) 633, 634
Bijou Theatre (Melbourne) **87**, 108, 238, 338, 353, 594, 601, 603, 646
Bill of Divorcement, A 325
Billbar Puppet Theatre 613
Billinghurst, Rick 44, 104, 508, 617, 618
Billings, Malcolm 564
Billington, John 607
Billington, Michael 176
'Billy Barlow' **88**, 446, 447
Bing Boys Are Here, The 331
Binks, the Photographer 501
Birch, Carroll and Coyle 128
Bird and Taylor's Great American Circus 116
Bird in Hand 161, 253, 350, 640
Birds of the Moon 429

Birdwood-Smith, Gloria 104
Birman, John 225
Birnie, Richard 170
Birth of Space, The 219
Birthworks 189
Bishop, Jack 633
Bishop, John 30, 362
Bishop, Pat 508
Bisley, Steve 573
Bisset, O. D. 445
Bit o' Petticoat, A 252, 387
Bitter Tears of Petra von Kant, The 215
Bitter-Sweet 387
Bjørnson, Björn 61
Black, Don. See *Song and Dance*
Black, Elton 286
Black, John 465, 585
Black, Nancy 656
Black, Ollie 223, 625
Black and White Minstrel Company 604
Black Cargo 359, 508
Black Diamonds 261
Black Flag, The 181
Black Horse, The 423
Black Inc. 123
Black Rabbit 374
Black Rainbow 241
Black Sheep, The 337
Black Swan Theatre Company 149, 412, 438, 509, 536, 634
Black Theatre 517
Black Theatre of Prague 31, 470
Black-Eyed Susan 113, 205, 309, 327, 335, 364, 382, 487, 566, 585
Blackfriars Theatre 635
Blacklock, Wendy 72, **88**
Blackman, Frederick 49, 90, 639
Blackman, Madeleine 519
Blackwell, Paul 308
Bladon, Douglas 396
Blahova, Dasha 217
Blainey, Geoffrey 70
Blair, Ron 76, **88**, **91**, 258, 298, 407, 497. See also *Biggles*; *The Christian Brothers*; *Flash Jim Vaux*; *Marx*
Blake, Julia 97
Blake, Leila 89
Blakemore, Michael 89, 168, 440
Blaxland, Antoinette 75
Blaxland, Audrey 342
Blay, John. See *The Bedbug Celebration*
Blaylock, Malcolm 104, 243, 310, 497
Bleak Dawn 453, 607
Bleedin' Butterflies 147, 614
Blenkinsop, David 225
Bless the Bride 124
Blewett, Dorothy 90, 452. See also *The First Joanna*; *Quiet Night*
Blinco, Maggie 245
***Blind Giant is Dancing, The* 54**, 58, **90**, 178, 222, 252, 262, 307, 309, 520, 627

Bliss, Charles 151
Blister, The 196
Blithe Spirit 302, 346, 458, 631
Blocksidge, Bruce 90
Blocksidge, Jennifer 44, **90**, 104
Blondin 213, 509
Blood and Honour 242
Blood Knot, The 13, 402, 536
Blood on the Wattle 265
Blood Orange 155, 188
Blood Relations 317
Bloomfield, Peter 405
Blue Beard 31, 530
Blue Bird, The 489
Blue Folk Community Theatre 122
Blue Freckle, A 374, 466
Blue Mazurka, The 387
***Blue Mountain Melody* 90**, 384, 387
Blue Roses 201, 387, 504
Bluebell in Fairyland 387
Bluett, Belle 91
Bluett, Fred 91, 380, 485
Bluett, Gus 90, **91**, 331
Bluett, Kitty 535
Blundell, Graeme 74, **91**, 191, 219, 345, 444, 497, 520. See also *The Sentimental Bloke*
Blunden, Camilla 123, 224
Blythe Waterland Minstrels 116, 370
Boat, The 526
Bob and Joe Show 369
Bobadil 387, 535
Boccaccio 382, 559
Boddy, Michael 91, 381. See also *Biggles*; *A Cloak, a Crown and a Sword*; *The Cradle of Hercules*; *The Legend of King O'Malley*; *Meet Mr Brutus*
Bodill, Olive 536
Boesman and Lena 536
Bohemian and Texas Jack Company 18
Bohemian Dramatic Company 48, 65, 67, **92**, 126, 158, 333, 421, 449, 490, 581, 610, 640
Bohemian Girl, The 561
Bokor, Pierre 124
Bol, Lorna. See *But I'm Still Here*; *Treadmill*
Boland, Bert 603
Boland, Bridget. See *The Prisoner*
Bold Girls 280
Boldrewood, Rolf 163, 180
Bolonkin, Nicholas 124
Bolt, Christine 410
Bolt, Robert. See *A Man for All Seasons*
Bolton, Heather 308
Bolza, Joe 369
Bombastes Furioso 100, 204, 365, 436
Bon-Bons and Roses for Dolly 150, 233, 271, 387, 395, 417

Bond, Edward 208. See also *Narrow Road to the Deep North*; *Summer*
Bond, Grahame 95, 259, 422
Bondi Pavilion Theatre 575
Bondman, The 503
Bones 468
Bones of My Toe, The 346
Bonham, Gillian 124
Boom of Big Ben, The 98
Boomerang Show 58
Boomeroo! 439
Booth, Edwin 46, **92**, 312, 553
Booth, Junius Brutus 92
Booth, Lancelot. See *Outlaw Kelly*
Booth, Paul 242
Boothe, Clare. See *The Women*
Boothman, Alfred 232, 345, 504
Bopha 31
Borderland 481
Born Yesterday 157, 258, 317, 630
Borny, Geoffrey 124
Borovansky Ballet 384
Borradale, Harry 93, 102
Borthwick, Nellie 326
Borzell, Adrian 125
Boss Cocky, The 84, 491
Bostock and Wombell's circus 141, 306
Bostock, Gerald. See *Here Comes the Nigger*
Boswell for the Defence 349
Botsman Report 621
Bottomley, Gordon. See *Suilven and the Eagle*
Boucher, Ken 125
Boucicault, Dion 35, **93**, 94, 297, 643, 645. See also *After Dark*; *Arrah-na-Pogue*; *The Colleen Bawn*; *The Corsican Brothers*; *Flying Scud*; *Kerry*; *London Assurance*; *Louis XI*; *The Octoroon*; *The Shaughraun*; *The Streets of London*
Boucicault, Dion jnr 18, **93**, **94**, 107, 110, 112, 622
Boucicault, Nina 93, **94**, 107
Boulder (WA) 633
Bourgeois gentilhomme, Le 147
Bourke, Governor Sir Richard 131, 249, 327
Bourke, Max 70
Bourne, Robynne 90, 607
Bovell, Andrew 94, 359. See also *After Dinner*; *The Ballad of Lois Ryan*; *State of Defence*
Bovis, Charles and Will 99
Bowden, Harald 95, 293, 302
Bowl Music Hall 381, 409, 587
Box and Cox 409
Boy Friend, The 291, 331, 387, 512
Boy Meets Girl 621
Boyce, Ian 97
Boyce, Raymond 405
Boyd, Arthur 420
Boyd, Grace 324
Boyd, Robin 204, 514

Boyd, Thomas Spencer 335
Boyer, Richard 250
Boys from Syracuse, The 387
Boys in the Band, The 53, 68, 132, 193, 368, 444, 551, 575, 577
Boys' Own McBeth **95**, 387
Bracy, Henry 382
Bradley, David 96
Bradley, Jeana **95**, 399, 412, 619, 621, 651
Bradshaw, Richard **96**, 128, 342, 469
Brady, Graeme 297
Brady, Terry 539
Braham, D. D. 172
Braham, Leonora 244, 382
Brainrot 272
Brame, James 509
Bramley, Adele 97
Bramley, Nellie **96**, 101, 392, 651
Bramwell, Murray 175
Bran Nue Dae 14, 64, **97**, 387, 412, 456, 494, 509, 612, 634
Brand, Mona **97**, 403, 453, 497. See also *Here Under Heaven*; *On Stage Vietnam*; *The Pirates of Pal Mal*; *Strangers in the Land*
Brandon, Dorothy. See *The Outsider*
Brandon, John G. See *The Silent House*
Branscombe, Ronald 337
Brass Hat, The 157, 258
Bray, Errol 528. See also *The Choir*
Bray, John 28
Bray, Theodore 70
Brayton, Lily 61, 63, 490
Breach of Trust 622
Bread and Butter Women 112, 638
Bread and Puppet Theatre 470
Break in the Music, A 521
Breaker Morant 536
Breakfast with Julia **97**
Breaking a Butterfly 15
Breaking of the Drought, The 26, **98**, 199, 283, 312, 450
Breaking the Code 320, 342
Breaking Through 582
Breaking Up in Balwyn 595
Breath of Spring 185, 514
Brecht, Bertolt 22, **98**, 186, 208. See also *The Caucasian Chalk Circle*; *Galileo*; *The Good Woman of Setzuan*; *The Mother*; *Mother Courage and Her Children*; *The Resistible Rise of Arturo Ui*; *Señora Carrar's Rifles*; *The Seven Deadly Sins*; *The Threepenny Opera*
Breeze from the Gulf 106
'Brek' 174, 316
Bremen Coffee 215
Bremner, Marie **99**, 535
Bren, Frank 321
Brennan, Harry 99
Brennan, James 99, 239
Brennan, Kevin 76, 396

Brennan, Peter. See *Conspiracy*
Brennan vaudeville circuit **99**, 238, 239, 583
Brennan–Fuller vaudeville circuit 99, 306
Brennan's Amphitheatre 99, 422
Brennir, Albert 226, 382
Brenton, Howard 208
Brereton, Austin 171, 449
Brethren 469
Brewer, F. C. 171, 495
Brewster's Millions 107
Bric-a-brac 626
Bridal Suite 190, 373
Bride of Gospel Place, The 212, 227, 260, 305, 442, 491, 556
Bridge Theatre 201
Bridges, Babe 99
Bridges, Cliff 99
Bridges, Michael 104
Bridges, Nancye **99**
Bridges Trio 99
Bridgetown Repertory Club 633
Bridie, James. See *Daphne Laureola*; *Jonah and the Whale*; *Tobias and the Angel*
Bridson, Leigh 59
Brigadoon 62, 387
Briggs, Marcia 110
Brighouse, Harold. See *Hobson's Choice*
Bright and Breezy, Clean and Wholesome Vaudeville 525
Bright and Crimson Flower, A 656
Brighton, Pam 422
Brilliant Lies 82, 360, 476, 642
Bring Down the House 508
Brisbane **100**
Brisbane, Katharine 69, 73, **102**, 175, 412, 420, 428, 497
Brisbane Actors' Company 102, **103**, 150, 232
Brisbane Amateur Theatres 42, 102, 103
Brisbane Arts Theatre 43, 44, 102, **103**, 615, 651
Brisbane Biennial 557
Brisbane College of Advanced Education 618
Brisbane Courier (newspaper) 174
Brisbane Repertory Theatre Society 41, 44, 70, 82, 90, 93, 102, **104**, 137, 182, 215, 216, 223, 292, 408, 492, 509, 531, 557, 615, 651
Brisbane Shakespeare Society 93
Brisbane Theatre Company 90, 102
Brisley, Stuart 431
Bristol, D. M. 141
Britannicus 166, 185, 230, 258, 363, 627
British Council 255, 340, 414, 510
British Drama League 42, 43, 207, 599, 607
British Hotel 121, 509, 577

Briton and Boer 535
Britto, Anne 24
Britton, Aileen **104**, 302, 321
Britton, David. See *Landlovers*
Brodney, Spencer. See **Leon Brodzky**
Brodrick, R. H. 126
Brodziak, Kenn **104**, 368, 515
Brodzky, Leon 19, 39, **105**, 450
Broinowski, Anna 64
Broken Dreams 184
Broken Home, The 96
Broken Pitcher, The 363
Brolgas **105**, 224, 475
Bromley-Smith, Ivor 515
Bronhill, June **105**, 129, 458, 497, 652
Brook, Anthony 599
Brook, Peter 31, 208, 510
Brooke, Bunney 60, **106**, 396, 587
Brooke, G. V. 63, **106**, 130, 162, 297, 398, 417, 472, 522, 523, 552, 566, 585
Brookman, Anne 625
Brookman, Rob 30
Brooks, Elsa 617
Brooks, Kevin 164
Brooks, Richard 471
Brooksbank, Anne 202. See also *Down Under*
Broome (WA) 633
Broomhall, Joan 402
Brophy, Noel 588
Brosnan, Graeme 307, 515
Brough, Mrs Robert 17, *18*, **107**, 490
Brough, Robert 17, *18*, 94, **107**, 112, 231, 490, 645
Brough Comedy Company 107, 108, 531
Brough–Boucicault Comedy Company 66, 87, 94, **107**, 205, 214, 490, 600, 605, 622
Brough–Flemming Company 107, 231
Brown, Bille **108**
Brown, Bryan 148, 574
Brown, Dave 429
Brown, David 328
Brown, Frank. See *Mates*
Brown, Garth 345
Brown, Joe E. 53, 303, 491
Brown, Morris 116
Brown, Nancy 497, 519. See also *The Sentimental Bloke*
Brown, Noeline 168
Brown, Paul **108**, 188, 328. See also *Aftershocks*; *Cafe Hakawati*; *Coal Town*; *Murray River Story*; *Two Cities*
Brown Potter, Cora 214, 553
Brown, Ros 345
Brown, Rupert 153
Brown, Tom 70, 80, **109**, 393, 413, 433, 472, 568
Browne, Ada 603
Browne, Coral **109**, 150, 253, 651

Browne, George 268, 584
Browne, Lindsey **109**, 174
Browne, Marie 283
Browne, Pattie 94, **110**, 270, 501
Browning, Mike 255
Brown's Mart 184, 409, 595
Bruce, Brenda 510
Bruce, Clarence 140
Bruce, Joan 28, 77, **110**, 258, 341
Bruce Rock (WA) 634
Bruce, S. M. 37
Bruce, Vera 140
Bruch, Max 116
Brudder Humphrey 508
Brumby Innes 13, 51, **110**, 451, 457, 464
Brune, Clarence M. 600
Brunswick—The musical 387, 544
Brunton, Dorothy **111**, 334
Brunton, John 98, **111**, 503, *546*
Brutus 120, 263
Bryant, Beryl 41, **111**, 112, 362, 651
Bryant, George 41, 111, **112**
Bryant's Playhouse 41, 111, **112**, 281, 638, 651
Brydon, Glenna 97
Bryer, Lillie 118, 245, 392, 539
Brylcreme and Maggot Pies 466
BSA Players 226
Buchanan, McKean 46, 553
Büchner, Georg 215
Buckingham, George 25, 35, **113**, 511
Buckingham Family Entertainers 113
Buckler, Hugh 40, 329, 490, 511
Buckley, Arthur **113**
Buckley, Ethel 342, 606
Buckley's 387, 579
Buckstone, J. B. See *Jack Sheppard*;
Buffaloes Can't Fly 184
Builders' Labourers Federation 577, 586
Bulbo 101
Bulgakov, Mikhail. See *The Crimson Island*; *Molière*
Bull, Hilda 211. See also Hilda Esson
Bull 'n' Bush 588
Bullen, Gregory 114
Bullen, Ken 114
Bullen, Percy 113
Bullen, Stafford 114
Bullen Brothers' Circus **113**, 141, 542, 650
Buller, George 197
Bulletin (magazine) 171, 449, 450
Bullie's House 13, 262, 313, 347, 517
Bulwer-Lytton, Edward 516. See also *The Lady of Lyons*; *Money*; *Richelieu*
Bummerz 505
Bunbury Light Opera and Theatre Company 634
Bunbury Repertory Club 634

662

Bunch of Keys, A 501
Bunch of Ratbags, A 387
Bundaberg (Qld) 612
Bungaro and Itchi 306
Bunraku Puppet Theatre 32, 470
Bunraku Theatre of Japan 306
Bunster, Grosvenor. See *Class*
Bunyip, The 114, 238, 426, 429, 441, 490, 491, 561
Bunyip and the Alien, The 598
Bunyip and the Satellite, The 387, 420
Burbury, Governor Sir Stanley 279
Burdekin House Little Theatre 227
Burford, Charles 114, 154
Burford, Mr 481
Burgess, Lewis 32
Burgess, Marie. See Marie Carandini
Burglar, The 375, 463
Burgoyne, John. See *The Lord of the Manor*
Burgoyne, Marcella 116
Burgoyne, Mrs G. L. 494
Buried Treasure 96
Burke, Alan 125, 330, 454, 497
Burke, Brandon 102, 439, 607
Burke, Elisabeth 211
Burke, Marie 114, 127, 240, 275, 603
Burke, Simon 308, 573
Burke's Company 200, 483, 555
burlesque 115, 220, 382, 383, 385, 424
Burn, David 115. See also *The Bushrangers*; *The Queen's Love*
Burn This 263
Burn Victim 360, 520
Burnand, F. C. See *Ixion*
Burnett, Jim 95
Burns, Carolyn 442. See also *Once Upon a Ruby Red*; *The Red King*
Burns, J. R. 584
Burrell, John 192
Burroughs, Maria Watkins 161, 340. See also Maria Coppin
Burrum 13
Burst of Summer 13, **116**, 252, 453
Burstall, Betty 219, 223, 320, 497
Burton, Brian 116
Burton, Henry 116, *139*
Burton, Marie. See *Why the Innocent*
Burton, Marion 559
Burton and Taylor's Grand United Circus Company 116, 540
Burton's circus 116, 139, 509, 612
Burwell, F. W. 315
Bus Stop 198
bush drama 117
Bush Fire 598
Bush Girl, The 118, 533. See also *The Bushwoman*
Bush King, The 117
Bush, Shirley 89
Bushelle, Shirley 275
bushranger plays 131
Bushranger, The 650
Bushrangers, The (by David Burn) 12, 115, **117**, 361, 446
Bushrangers, The (by Charles Harpur) 550
Bushrangers, The (by Henry Melville) 12, 57, **118**, 188, 278, 325, 446, 487
Bushwackers Band 483
Bushwoman, The 48, 55, **118**, 451, 482, 533
Business of Good Government, The 420
Bussell, Jan 342, 518
Busted 166
… But I Wouldn't Want to Live There 83
But I'm Still Here 90
Butavicius, Al 122
Butcher, Elizabeth 70, 146, 393, 572, 573
Butler, Rosemary 519
Butley 378
butoh 64
Butterflies are Free 53, 577
Butterflies of Kalimantan 145, 237
Buttrose, Larry. See *Pallas*
Buy Me Blue Ribbons 202
Buzo, Alex 73, **118**, 209, 422, 455, 497, 544. See also *Big River*; *Coralie Lansdowne Says No*; *Macquarie*; *Makassar Reef*; *The Marginal Farm*; *Martello Towers*; **Norm and Ahmed**; *Rooted*; *Stingray*
Buzzacott, Martin. See *Carnival in Kingaroy*
By Candlelight 292, 427
By Wireless Telegraphy 55
Byakkusha 306
Bye Bye Birdie 52, 387
Byndor, Wayne 196
Byrne, Fay 485
Byrne, Gerald. See *The New Bridge*
Byrnes, Michael. See *The River Jordan*
Byron, Annie 622
Byron, H. J. See *Our Boys*; *Our Girls*
Byron, Lord. See *Sardanapalus*
Byzantine Flowers 517

C

C and G Minstrels 370
Cabaret 217, 290, 387, 416
Cabaret dell'emigrante, Il 195
Cabaret Girl, The 50, 387
Cabaret Passé 56
Caesar and Cleopatra 484, 551
Caesar, Carmen 539
Caesar, J. 504
Cafe Fledermaus 56, 177
Cafe Hakawati 109, 155
Cage aux folles, La 217, 367, 387
Caine Mutiny Court Martial, The 53, 221, 481
Caine, Peggy. See *Who'll Come A-Waltzing*
Cain's Head 79
Cairo 19, 61, 387
Cake Man, The 13, **119**, 178, 347, 456, 493, 517, 569, 575
Calaroga Players 27
Calder, Douglas 32. See also *No Triangle This*
Calderón, Pedro. See *Life is a Dream*
Caldwell, Zoë 28, 56, 60, 76, **119**, 357, 497, 519, 543, 616, 651
Calendar, The 263
California Minstrels 46
Call Me Madam 52, 264, 384, 387, 435
Call Me Madman 288
Call of the Wild 71
Call Up Your Ghosts 179, 329, 400, 403
Callaghan, Master 62, 143
Callaghan, Rex 466
Callas—The Woman 284
Calone, Pio 95
Calouste Gulbenkian Foundation 305
Camelot 52, 177, 217, 387, 615, 635
Cameron, Cordelia 81, 113, **120**, 121, 539, 630, 650
Cameron, David 326, 432
Cameron, Jane 34
Cameron, Megan 179
Cameron, Neil 155, 631
Cameron, Reginald 120
Cameron, Samson 25, 57, 85, 113, 120, **121**, 236, 278, 335, 364, 487, 509, 511, 539, 577, 583, 620
Cameron Cresswell Agency 34
Cameron's Management 34
Camille 16, 46, 214, 490, 566. See also *La Dame aux camélias*
Camm, Frank 116
Campbell, Christine 105
Campbell, Edwin 245, 392, 647
Campbell, J. A. See *The Little Breadwinner*
Campbell, Jock 345
Campbell, Ken. See *Old King Cole*
Campbell, Peggy 483
Campbell, Thomas 33
Campbell Howard Collection 188, 212, 497, 599
Campbell Jackson, Beverley 121, 469, 538
Campion, Richard 80, 405
Campus Amateur Dramatic Society 124
Can-Can 52, 387, 525
Canary Cottage 201, 387
Canberra 122
Canberra Amateur Operatic Society 122
Canberra Children's Theatre 122, 126
Canberra Critics' Circle Awards 77
Canberra Philharmonic Society 122
Canberra Repertory Society 41, 43, 44, 83, 122, **125**, 126, 421, 464, 519, 520, 521
Canberra Theatre Centre 44, 122, **125**, 318, 433
Canberra Theatre Company 123
Canberra Theatre Trust 123
Canberra Times (newspaper) 174
Canberra University Theatre Society 124
Canberra Youth Theatre 122, **126**, 179, 224, 241
Candida 315
Candide 85, 217, 285, 387, 512
Cannonade of Bells 236, 341
Cannot, Jack 331
Canterbury Hall 511
Canterbury Tales 387
Canterville Ghost, The 330
Cantril, Ken 52
Cape Forlorn 263, 451
Capek, Josef and Karel. See *The Insect Play*
Capelin, Steve 562
Capelli, Bettino 238
Capitol Theatre 126, 567, 570, 590, 637
Caporn, Kevin 59
Capriccio's 242
Caprice 173
Capricornia 411, 517
Capron, Robert 226
Captain Hayes 378
Captain Lazar and His Earthbound Circus 96, 342
Captain Midnight, the Bush King 117
Captain Midnight VC 273
Captain Moonlight 92
Captain of the Vulture, The 222
Captain Swift 449
Carandini, Gerolamo 146
Carandini Opera Company 409
Caravan 230, 334, 577
Carboni 507
Carclew Scripts Directory 655
Carclew Youth Arts Centre 29, **126**, 154
Carclew Youth Performing Arts Centre 655
Cardamatis, Raoul 41, 228
Cardella, Harry 143
Carden, George 330
Cardignans 298
Cardini 336
Cardoza, Signor 62
Cards and Flowers 631
Cardus, (Sir) Neville 110, 174
Caretaker, The 153, 371

Carey, Dean 393
Carey, Eleanor 353, 528, 626
Carey, W. G. 17, 421
Cargher, John 396
Carle, W. 421
Carleton, Moira 60, **127**
Carlin, David 57. See *Frankenstein's Children*
Carlisle, Richard Risley 16
Carlotta and Maximilian 79
Carlton (magician) 336
Carmen 538
Carmen Up To Date 240
Carmo the Great 127
Carmody, John 176
Carnamah (WA) 633, 634
Carnival 387
Carnival in Kingaroy 558
Carnivale 226
Carousel 53, 387
Carouselle 459
Carpenter, Alisa 376
Carpenter, Freddie 127
Carpenter, Kevin 508
Carpenter, Kim 128, 407, 562. See also *Swimming in Light*
Carpenter, Tikki 324
Carr, Andrew 599
Carr, Diana 179
Carr Glyn, Neva 128, 308, 528, 531, 615
Carr, Howard 153
Carr, William P. 396
Carrington, Ella 18, 117, 580
Carroll, Bruce 605
Carroll, Dan 128, 380
Carroll, E. J. 128, 380
Carroll, Garnet H. 52, 53, 72, 97, **129**, 186, 230, 237, 247, 465, 515
Carroll, Peter 102, **129**, 136, 308, 456, 574
Carroll Freeholds Pty Ltd 465
Carroll–Fuller Theatres Pty Ltd 129, 237, 465
Carroll-Musgrove Theatres 380
Carshop 184
Carson, Cecil R. 292
Carter the Great 502
Cartwheel Theatre 328
Carver, W. F. 48, **129**, 181, 518, 627, 640
Caselotti, Adriana 50, 603
Casey, Lloyd 164
Cash! 92, 387
Casimiro, Maria Alice. See *Death at Balibo*
Casino Girl, The 326, 387
Cassidy Album, The 314, 317, 577
Cassim, Mahomed 144
Casson, John 519
Casson, (Sir) Lewis 67, 72, 77, 207, 301, 314, 408, 491, 524, 567, 586
Caste 329, 341
Castle of Andalusia, The 409
Casualty 60
CAT 57. See also **Arena Theatre Company**

Cat Among the Pigeons 332
Cat on a Hot Tin Roof 320
Catch that Dove 337
Catching a Conspirator 639
Cathcart, Fanny 130, 162, 564
Cathcart, James 130, 311, 564
Cathcart, Rowley 130
Cathcart, Sarah 224. See also *The Serpent's Fall*; *Walking on Sticks*
Cathedral, The 517
Catherine 526
Catlin, John. See *Children of War*
Cats 30, 386, 387, 439, 511
Catspaw 233, 272, 396, 399
Catto, Max. See *They Walk Alone*
Caucasian Chalk Circle, The 33, 98, 146, 237, 367, 405, 466, 573
Caust, Jo 462, 530
Cave, Colin 70
Cavenagh Theatre Group 409
Cavill, Edward 362
Ceberano, Kate 368
Cece 195
Cecil, Lawrence H. 130, 396, 478, 580
Cedar Chest, The 85
Cedar Tree, The 130, 237, 372, 373, 384, 387, 597
Cedoona 468
Celebrated, The 347
Celebrity Theatre Restaurant 338, 652
Cellier, Alfred 244, 353, 559
Celluloid Heroes 13
censorship 131, 328, 400, 421, 446, 447, 515
Centenary Dance, The 614
Centre International de Créations Théâtrales 225
Centrestage (magazine) 175
Centurion 617
Chairs, The 103, 371
Chalk Garden, The 314, 408
Chalkie 337
Chamber Made Opera 220
Chamber of Horrors, The 222
Chambers, Haddon 449. See also *Devil Caresfoot*
Chambers, Sidney 515
Champion, Stephen 307
Change in the Weather, A 597
Changeling, The 621
Chanti, George 324
Chapel Perilous, The 71, **133**, 233, 271, 396, 399, 455, 620
Chaplin, Angela 57, 189, 224, 336, 337
Chaplin, George D. 47
Chapman, Alan 28
Chapman, Colin 405
Chapman, John. See *Move Over, Mrs Markham*; *Simple Spymen*
Chapman, Patty 311
Chapman, Roger 29, 127, 336, 556, 654
Chapman, Russell 233
Chapman, Sammy 223
Chappelle, Albert 59, 60

Chapple, Ewart 99
Charbonnet-Kellermann, Alice 312
Chard, Kate 382
Charisse, Cyd 617
Charles, Jack 13, 92, 347, 402, 536
Charles Napier Theatre 268
Charles Sturt University 504, 620
Charley's Aunt 56, 94, 409, 471, 474, 489
Charlie Girl 325, 387
Charlier, Paul 211
Charlotte's Web 646
Charls, Rod 122, 123
Charlton, Alan 97
Charlton, Peter 57, 544. See *Cosme*; *Wolf Boy*
Charrière, Madame 213
Charrière, Monsieur 213, 654
Charrington, Charles 15, 214
Chase, Chaz 604
Chase, Mary. See *Harvey*
Chatelaine, Stella 211
Chater, Gordon 133, 202, 420, 519, 568, 636
Cheal, Betty 608
Cheap Living 409
Cheapside 37, 439, 476, 544
Checkout 310
Cheek by Jowl 209
Cheery Soul, A 174, 190, 424, 526, 572, 596, 629, 638
Chekhov, Anton 83. See also *The Bear*; *The Cherry Orchard*; *Ivanov*; *A Jubilee*; *Platonov*; *The Proposal*; *The Seagull*; *Three Sisters*; *Uncle Vanya*; *The Wood Demon*
Chekhov, Michael 42, 83, 261
Cherry, Frank 284
Cherry, Wal 22, 53, 68, 98, **134**, 203, 208, 218, 357, 555, 620
Cherry Blossom Show 652
Cherry Orchard, The 84, 137, 150, 193, 215, 230, 237, 257, 260, 276, 320, 334, 344, 357, 360, 413, 416, 476, 500, 514, 568
Cherry Pickers, The 13, **134**
Chester, Nellie Pollard 460
Chi, Jimmy 97, 509. See also *Bran Nue Dae*
Chiarini's Royal Italian Circus 140
Chicago 50, 53, 265, 317, 387, 573, 636
Chicago, Chicago 54, 507, 508
Chichester Festival Company 305
Chidley 187, 444, 614
Chifley, Ben 43, 125, 159, 249, 255, 340, 394
child companies 134
Childermas 146, 313
Children in Uniform 27, 253, 350
Children of a Lesser God 629
Children of War 439

Children's Activities Time Society 135, 184, 654
Children's Hour, The 50, 543
children's theatre 655
Chilpéric 559
Chilperic, King of the Gauls 287, 387
Chiltern Theatre 135, 592
Chilvers, Simon 135
Chin Foo Lam Boo 144
Chinchilla 227, 260, 317, 573, 596
Chinese opera 66
Chinese performers 135, 144, 246, 306
Chinese Question, The 63, 644
Chinese Youth League 136
Chirgwin, G. H. 233, 501, 566, 601
Chisholm, Robert 136, 153
Cho Cho San 64, 311, 469, 618, 646
Chocolate Frog, The 262, 352, 466, 471, 505
Chocolate Soldier, The 372, 387
Choir, The 527, 618
Chord is Struck, A 189
Chorus Line, A 53, 386, 387
Christian, Beatrix 223
Christian, The 644
Christian Brothers, The 71, 85, 88, 129, **136**, 230, 373, 455, 456
Christie, Alan 124
Christie, Michael 345
Christina's World 396
Christmas Bridge 401
Christmas Carol, A 108
Christy's Minstrels 35
Chrome 562
Chronicle of Macbeth, The 241, 306, 356, 369, 444
Chu Chin Chow 61, 63, 383, 387, 429, 489
Chung Ling Soo 336, 502, 601
Church. See **Australian Contemporary Theatre Company**
church and theatre 136
Church Theatre 355
Churchill, Caryl. See *Cloud Nine*; *Fen*; *Serious Money*; *Top Girls*
Chynoweth, Neville 59
Cibber, Colley 522. See also *The Provoked Husband*
Cilento, Diane 137, 474, 475
Cinderella 91, 331, 426, 603
Cinema Star, The 331, 387
Cingalee, The 326, 387
Cinquevalli, Paul 310, 501, 601
Circle, The 200, 332
Circle Company 243
Circle of Chalk, The 42
circus **138**, 461, 612
Circus Archaos 32
Circus Hall of Fame 152
Circus Oz 16, 22, 75, **144**, 219, 223, 478, 613
Circus Royal 25, 477
Cirkidz 537

Ciszewska, Barbara 57, 223, 224, 367
City of Angels 89
Ciulei, Liviu 85, 221, 332, 515
Civic Playhouse 290
Civic Theatre: Albury (NSW) 433, 593; Newcastle (NSW) 405; Orange (NSW) 433; Townsville (Qld) 399, Wagga Wagga (NSW) 433
Claire, Jennifer **145**, 223. See also *The Butterflies of Kalimantan*; *Siestas in a Pink Hotel*
Clambake 177
Clamp, Burcham 441
Clancarty 600
Clancy, Meg 345
Clare, Ada 474
Clare, Cyril. See *The Duchess of Coolgardie*
Claremont Theatre 89
Clarence Theatre 510
Clari 647
Clark, Brian. See *The Petition*
Clark, Elaine 57
Clark, Frank 116, 375, 517
Clark, Joan. See *Home Brew*
Clark, John 64, **145**, 305, 393, 568, 569, 572, 573
Clark, Liddy 338
Clark, Manning 58
Clark, Maud 155
Clark, Melisande 328
Clark, Owen 336
Clark, Stephen 183
Clarke, Anne 57, **146**, 162, 278, 288, 378, 510, 583, 650
Clarke, Anne Theresa 147
Clarke, Doreen 29, **147**, 223. See also *Bleedin' Butterflies*; *Farewell Brisbane Ladies*; *Missus Queen*; *Roses in Due Season*
Clarke Hall, Janet 599
Clarke, John. See *The Royal Commission into the Australian Economy*
Clarke, Marcus **147**, 169, 206, 232, 497, 528. See also *Alfred the Great*; *Goody Two-Shoes*; **The Happy Land**; *Reverses*; *Twinkle, Twinkle Little Star*
Clarke, Marian Marcus 147, 148, 233
Clarke, Maude 223
Clarke, Michael 146, 506
Clarke, Sir Rupert 149, 644
Clarke, Sylvia 97
Clarke, Terence 73, 88, **148**, 209, 290, 622. See also *Henry and Peter and Henry and Me*; **The Venetian Twins**
Clarke and Meynell 148, 299
Clarke, Meynell and Gunn 61
Class 448
Claudel, Paul. See *Partage de midi*
Clay, Harry 149, 191, 485, 511
Clay's vaudeville circuit 534

Clayton, Faith 149, 621
Clayton, John 587
Clayton, W. H. 584
Clean Sweep 478
Cleary, Frank 186
Cleary, W. J. 478
Clemen, Harald 215
Clendinning, David 103, **150**, 153, 217
Cléopâtre 86
Cleveland, Louisa 552
Cleveres 535
Clewlow, Frank D. 37, 109, **150**, 357, 453, 478, 608
Clifford, Colleen 150, 429, 471, 497
Clifton, Jane 231, 422
Clifton, Marshall 399
Clifton, Max 118, 243, 245, 392, 647
Climax, The 111
Clint, Alfred 150
Clint, Alfred T. 150
Clint, George 150
Clint, Sydney 150
Cloak, a Crown and a Sword, A 105
Cloches de Corneville, Les 559
Close of Play 227, 573
Cloud Nine 512, 618
Clouds 347
Clovelly Puppet Theatre 378, 469
clowning 151
Clowns in Clover 397, 485
club entertainment 151
Club, The 21, 52, 71, 85, 89, **151**, 227, 252, 255, 332, 352, 455, 642
Clutterbuck 128
Clyde Company Station 367
Coad Canada Puppets 470
Coady, Joe 226
Coal Town 109, 156, 188, 474
Cobra, The 267, 292, 317, 636
Coburn, Anthony. See *The Bastard Country*; *Fire on the Wind*
Coburn, D. L. See *The Gin Game*
Cockatoo Farm 117
Cocking, Rae 28
Cockroach Opera, The 64, 627
Cocktail Party, The 618
Cocky of Bungaree, The 616
Coco Youth Theatre 634
Cocteau, Jean. See *The Eagle Has Two Heads*; *The Human Voice*
Cody Versus Cody 478
Cogdon, John 246
Cohan, Josephine 47
Cohen, Paul 396
Cohen, Peter 396
Coke, Peter 185. See *Breath of Spring*
Colbert, Kenneth 515
Colchester Warehouse 585
Colchin, Be 57
Colocott, Eileen 395
Coldwell, Tim 145
Cole, Belle 158

Cole, Charmaine 408
Cole, E. I. 92, 158, 449, 640. See also *Hands Up!*
Cole, Jedda 408
Cole, Michael 395
Cole, William Washington 140
Cole's Concorporated Shows 140
Cole's Players 101, 473
Coleby, Robert 176
Coleman, Elizabeth. See *It's My Party (and I'll Die If I Want To)*
Coleman, G. A. 421
Coleman, Peter 159
Coleman, W. R. 153, 427
Coleridge, Damien 345
Coli, Ross 439
Colin and Gwynneth Ballantyne Performing Arts Collection 80, 497
Colla Family Marionettes 356
Colladetti, Eric 116
Collard, Dorothy 408
Colleano, Bonar 152
Colleano, Con 62, **152**, 509
Colleano, Winifred 143, 152
Colleano's All-Star Circus 143, 152
Colleen Bawn, The 93, 246, 297, 540, 645
College Players 102, 150, **153**, 619
Collie, Therese 562. See *Out of the Blue*
Collier, Willie 47
Collingwood, Peter 153, 341, 555
Collins, Archie 622
Collins, Arthur Childs Dubourg 473
Collins, David 529, 645
Collins, Lottie 26
Collins, Richard 379
Collins, Wilkie. See *The New Magdalen*
Collinson, Lawrence 196
Collis, June 476
Collits' Inn 91, **153**, 177, 372, 373, 384, 387, 451, 497, 597, 628
Colman, Charles 88
Colman, George the younger. See *John Bull*
Colman, Hugh 154
Colocott, Eileen 77
Colombe 221, 357, 491
Colonel Light—The Founder 32, 33, 457. See also **Awake My Love**
Colonial Experience 55, 114, **154**, 160, 285, 447
Colosseum 443
Colton, John. See *Rain*
Colville, Florence 285
Colville, Samuel 294, 464, 512
Colvin, Win 539
Combo Combo 62, 139, 143
Come Back Little Sheba 81, 200
Come Hell or High Water 387, 410

Come Out Youth Arts Festival 29, 127, 154, 307, 607, 655
Come Over Here 500
Comedian, The 137
Comedians, The 656
Comédie-Française 216
Comedienne 296
Comedy Cafe 551, 588
Comedy of Errors, The 71, 225, 413, 442, 555, 556
Comedy Opera Company 313
Comedy Store 551
Comedy Theatre 301
Comedy Theatre Restaurant 588
Comets Soon Pass 51, 179
Comin, Toni 217
Coming of Christ, The 33
Coming of Stork, The 155, 539, 641
Coming, The 607
commedia dell'arte 216
Commitment 273
Common Humanity 286
Commonwealth Copyright Office 163
Commonwealth Games 226
Commonwealth Literary Fund 249, 453, 467
Communist Party of Australia 400, 401
Community Players 41, 122
Community Playhouse 112, 265
community theatre 21, **155**
Community Theatre 41, 153, 236, 341, 569, 581, 651. See also **Marian Street Theatre Company**
Community Theatre Company 56
Company 124, 387, 573
Company A 86
Company B 58, 86, 266, 363, 407, 635
Company of Four 44, **156**, 233, 395, 437, 634
Company of Players 28, 79
Compton, Athol 134
Compton, Fay 301
Compton, Jennifer 405. See also *No Man's Land*
Computicket 368
Con Man, The 587
Con-Paul Boys 429
Con-Paul Theatres 157, 429, 603, 651
Conabere, Sydney 599
Condon, Coralie 77, **156**, 376, 588. See also *The Good Oil*
Condon, James 97, **157**, 257, 395
Confederation of Australian Professional Performing Arts 70
Conference of the Birds 31, 208
Congreve, William. See *The Way of the World*
Conley, Boris 379
Connelli, Judy 422
Connery, Jason 137

665

Connolly, Gerry 297
Connolly, Patricia 615
Connolly, Richard 326
Connor, Barry. See *The Patsy*
Connor, Harry 270
Connors, Mike 49, **157**, 429, 486, 602, 606, 651
Connors–Paul Revue Company 486
Conolly, Patricia 157, 330, 418, 531, 573
Conquest of the South Pole, The 215
Conrad the Corsair 626
Considine, Tom 367
Conspiracy 466
Constable, William 158, 161, 363, 498, 639
Constant Nymph, The 41, 293, 427, 517
Constant Wife, The 408
Consuelo 382
convicts and theatre **158**, 566
Conway, Ken 183
Conyers, Addie 240
Coo-ee 92, **158**, 421, 447, 449, 490
Cook, Carole 265, 435
Cook, Clyde 159
Cook, George Cram. See *Suppressed Desires*
Cook, Patrick 275, 444
Cook, Penny 254
Cooke, Peter 393
Cooke, Zoyara and Wilson's circus 140
Coolgardie Minstrel and Dramatic Club 632
Cooma Kitchie 306, 435
Coombs, H. C. 72, **159**, 250, 255, 394, 510, 563
Cooney, Marcus 259. See also *Biggles*
Cooney, Ray. See *Move Over, Mrs Markham*
Cooper, Bert 613
Cooper, Daniel 585, 586
Cooper, Gordon 345, 604
Cooper, Melody 95, 328
Cooper, Rosa 154, **160**
Cooper, Walter 160. See also *Colonial Experience*; *Foiled*; *Fuss*; *Hazard*; *The History of Kodadad and His Brothers*; *Sun and Shadow*
Cooper, Warwick 29
Cooper and Bailey's circus 126, 137, *140*, 141, 461
Coordah 14, 517
Coote, Robert 49, 384
Coote, W. 583
Copeau, Jacques. See *The House into Which We Are Born*
Copelin, Campbell 161
Coppel, Alec 161, 240, 505, 639. See also *I Killed the Count*; *Mr Smart Guy*

Coppin, George 17, *25*, 88, 106, **161**, 167, 183, 189, 205, 246, 266, 324, 336, 340, 353, 381, 417, 443, 465, 471, 472, 487, 498, 506, 510, 512, 523, 534, 536, 552, 559, 561, 582, 585
Coppin, Maria 88, 161, 213. See also Maria Watkins Burroughs
Coppin and Company 147, 614
Coppin in Cairo 35
Copping, David 178
Copping It Sweet 653
copyright 38, **162**, 244, 446, 644
Cora, Madame 579
Coralie Lansdowne Says No 119, **164**
Corcoran, Paul 123
Coriolanus 240, 252, 286, 398, 556
Corn is Green, The 43, 233
Cornall, Jan 613
Corneille, Pierre. See *The Theatrical Illusion*
Cornelius, Patricia 223, 359. See also *The Aftermath*; *Dusting Our Knees*; *Taxi*
Cornell, Benjamin Arthur 646
Cornell, Junee 41, 528, 646
Cornerstone 364
Cornerstones 147
Corpse! 133
Corrigan, Peter 164, 231, 444
Corroboree 61
corroboree 12, 436
Corrugated Iron Youth Theatre 147, 224, 410
Corsican Brothers, The 319
Corvin. See *Les Danicheff*
Cosgrove, John 462
Così 81, 222, 410, 422
Cosme 544
Costanduros, Mabel. See *Acacia Avenue*
Costello, Billy 50, 603
costumes 547
Cotter, Jim 339, 600
Cotterell, Ralph 510
Cottrell, Richard 407
Coughlan, Frank 59
Could Do Better 606, 616
Coulter, W. J. 474
Coulter Dramatic Company 474
Council for the Encouragement of Music and the Arts 43, 61, 67, 340
Count Hannibal 61
Count of Monte Cristo, The 626
Country Girl, A 299, 326, 383, 387
Country Wife, The 43, 178, 480, 557, 573
County Fair, The 336
Couple of Kids 337
Courier–Mail (newspaper) 175
Courtneidge, (Dame) Cicely 207, 321
Courtney, Vince 114
Cousin From Nowhere, The 114, 387
Cousin Joe 299

Cousin Vladimir 182
Cousins, John 515
Cousins, Reuben 62, 540, 612
Cousse, Raymond. See *Kidstuff*
Covell, Roger 317, 413
Covenant of the Rainbow, The 468
Covert, Earl 275
Coward, (Sir) Noël 208, 415. See also *Blithe Spirit*; *Fallen Angels*; *Hay Fever*; *Nude with Violin*; *Operette*; *Point Valaine*; *Present Laughter*; *Private Lives*; *A Suite in Three Keys*; *Tonight at 8.30*
Cowardy Custard 291, 542
Cowl, Jane. See *Smilin' Through*
Cowper, Murphy and Appleford 465
Coyne, Joseph 49. See *The Queer Subject*
Crackers 165
Cracknell, Ruth 134, **165**, 203, 308, 440, 497, 556, 573, 622
Cradle of Hercules, The 13
Cradle of Thunder 396
Craig, Diane 348
Cramphorn, Rex 165, 193, 217, 219, 230, 245, 326, 328, 411, 428, 432, 444, 471, 497, 515, 524, 543, 572, 627
Crane, Edith 299, 644
Crann, David 429
Cranney, P. P. 166, 337, 562. See also *The Logan City Story*; *Nuovo Paese/New Country*; *Site*; *The Yallourn Story*
Crawford, Jim 402. See also *Billets and Badges*; *Rocket Range*
Crawford Productions 34
Craydon, James 166, 602
Craydon, Letty 166, 302, 408, 525, 603
Crazy Days Show 58
Crazy Show 285, 428
Crea, Teresa 195, 216, 224
Creighton, Michael 342, 470
Cremorne Gardens 167
 Albany (WA) 633; Melbourne 106, 162, 443, 646; Perth 436
Cremorne Theatre (Brisbane) 49, 101, 102, 167, 337, 472, 476, 603
Cremorne Theatre (Coolgardie, WA) 632
Creswick, William 17, **167**, 205, 552
Creyton, Barry 133, **167**, 380, 587
Crick, Guy 369
Cricot 2 31
Crimson Island, The 363, 515
Criterion Theatre (Bendigo, Vic.) 465
Criterion Theatre (Sydney) **168**, 301, 566, 592, 601
Critic, The 17, 356
criticism **169**
Croft, Annie 384
Croft, Colin 59, 73, **176**
Croft, George 100, 138, 508

Croft, James 405
Croft, Joseph 365
Croggon, Alison 176
Crome, Robert 515
Crompton, Robert. See *Rak Awin*
Crosby, Don 24, 70, **177**, 454, 519
Crosby, Liz 177
Crosby, Marshall 153, **177**, 502
Crosby, Matthew 177
Crosby, Michael 24, 177
Crosby, Pat 177
Croser, Rob 29
Cross, George 539, 647
Cross Section 83, 352, 516
Crossroads Theatre 332
Crothers, Rachel. See *Let Us Be Gay*
Crouse, Russel. See *The Great Sebastians*
Crow 279, 410
Crowhurst, Geoff 166, 310, 337
Crowley, Anthony. See *Vincent*
Crowley, Mart. See *The Boys in the Band*; *Breeze from the Gulf*
Crown Matrimonial 516
Crucible, The 135, 232, 241, 257, 261, 285, 286, 367, 514, 517, 558, 574, 614, 635, 636
Crucified, The 607
Cruickshank, Laurie 587
Cruikshank, Margaret 116
Crunchy 614
Crystal Dewdrops 379
Crystal Theatre 238
CUB Malthouse Theatre 177, 444
Cullen, Hedley *28*, 258
Cullen, Max 21, 87, 119, **178**, 203, 338, 569
Cultural Development Council of Western Australia 437
Cuming, Robin 245
Cummings, Alice 634
Cummins, Peter 74, 90, 110, 155, **178**, 231, *455*, 485, 562
Cummins Theatre 246, 634
Cunningham, Joseph 481
Cunningham, Lloyd 396
Cuocolo, Renato 217
Cup of Tea, a Bex and a Good Lie Down, A 186, 330, 440
Cup Winner, The 361
Curley on the Rack 454
Curnow, William 171
Curran, Lynette 110
Currency Lass, The 12, 169, **178**, 205, 243, 254, 305, 310, 387, 447, 471, 531
Currency Press 428, 456, 467
Current Affairs Bulletin 174
Curtain, Frank 515
Curtains for Cocky 341
Curtin, John 159, 249, 394
Curtin, Lorna 73
Curtin, Peter 194
Curtis Brown 34
Curtis, Stephen 90, **178**, 622

Curtis's Afro-American Minstrels 347
Cusack, Dymphna 179, 452. See also *Anniversary*; *Call Up Your Ghosts*; *Comets Soon Pass*; **Morning Sacrifice**; *Pacific Paradise*
Cushing, Peter 414
Cushman, Frank 313
Customs and Excise 273
Cut and Thrust 56
Cuthbertson, Alan 320, 494, 652
Cyrano de Bergerac 41, 55, 85, 317, 376, 411, 480, 573, 636
Czajor, Ewa 224

D

D. D. O'Connor Pty Ltd 414
Da 318
Dags **179**, 606
Dai Rakuda Kan 306
Daily Grind 156, 359
Daily Mail (newspaper) 174
Daily Mirror (newspaper) 174
Daily Telegraph (newspaper) 174
Daily Telegraph-Mirror (newspaper) 176
Dairymaids, The 323, 326, 387
Daisan Erotica 306
Daisy Bates and the Dancer 557
Dale, Jessie 462
Dalgerie 454
Dalgleish, Walter 637
Dalkeith Opera House 315
Dalle Case, Luigi 16, 57, **179**, 213, 278, 467, 508
Dalley, J. B. 172
Daly, Augustin. See *Under the Gaslight*
Daly, Sefton 639
Daly, Timothy 575
Dame aux camélias, La 86
Dames at Sea 265, 387
Demper and Tea 458
Dampier, Alfred 18, 36, 48, 63, 66, 117, **180**, 197, 267, 345, 448, 490, 511, 523, 534, 626, 632, 633, 640. See also *Briton and Boer*; *The Bush King*; *For the Term of His Natural Life*; *Jess*; **Marvellous Melbourne**; *Robbery Under Arms*; *The Scout*; *To the West*; *A Transvaal Heroine*; *The Trapper*
Dampier, Alfred jnr 180
Dampier, Lily 36, 180, **181**, 232, 267, 345, 504, 505, 507, 518, 606, 627
Dampier, Rose 36, 180, **181**, 197, 267
Dampier's Ghost 196, 494
Dance in the Ashes 71
Dance of Death, The 368, 468, 526
Dancing at Lughnasa 232, 298
Dancing Demons 64
Dancing Girl, The 318

Dancing in the Dark 57
Dancing Years, The 384, 387, 415
Dandies 93
Dane, Clemence. See *A Bill of Divorcement*; *Granite*
Daneman, Paul 177, 635
Danicheff, Les 488
Daniell, Helton 357
Danielson, Ron 22
Dann, George Landen 182. See also *Fountains Beyond*; *In Beauty it is Finished*; *No Incense Rising*
Danny and the Deep Blue Sea 60
Dante the Magician 168
Daphne Laureola 600
Darbyshire, Iris 263
D'Arc's Marionettes 468
D'Arcy, Eamon 182, 607
Darcy, Marita 97
Dare, Eric 83, 87
Dargon, Augusta 552
Dark Brother 27, 194
Dark Enchantment 33, 34, 452, 480
Dark Heritage 557
Dark Lady of the Sonnets, The 33, 621
Dark of the Moon 177, 494
Darley, Eileen 308
Darling, Governor Sir Ralph 131, 136, 204, 585
Darling Downs Youth Theatre 475
Darlinghurst Nights 222, 573, 597
Darmont, M. See *Pauline Blanchard*
Darrell, George 48, 66, 130, **182**, 448, 535, 585. See also *Life for Life*; *The Pakeha*; **The Sunny South**
Darrell, Mrs George 130. See also **Fanny Cathcart**
Darrell, Rupert 182
D'Arrietta, Stewart 629
Darwin Amateur Musical Comedy Society 409
Darwin Community College Theatre Group 410
Darwin Performing Arts Centre 410
Darwin Theatre Company 45, **183**
Darwin Theatre Group 80, 183, 409
Dasborough, Walter 11
Daughter in Law 628
Daughter of Eve, A 147, 148
Dauguvietis, Xana 216
Davenport, Lizzie 346
Davey, Kathi 184
Davey, Richard 135, **184**, 280, 656. See also *The Servants of Vaucluse*
David Copperfield 222
David N. Martin Pty Ltd 344, 369
Davidson, Jennifer 578, 582
Davidson, Jim 58, 59

Davies, C. E. 184, 377, 584
Davies, E. Harold 33
Davies, Gordon 539
Davies, Hubert Henry. See *Outcast*
Davies, John 184, 278, 584, 630
Davies, Lindy 22, 74, **184**, 195, 345, 556
Davies, Paul 595
Davis, Allan 185, 514
Davis, Des 587
Davis, Dot 485
Davis, H. H. 154
Davis, Jack 13, 14, 77, 97, **185**, 196, 408, 456, 457, 497. See also *Barungin (Smell the Wind)*; **The Dreamers**; *The First Born*; *Honey Spot*; *Kullark*; *No Sugar*; *Wahngin Country*
Davis, Judy 186, 237, 395, 471, 515, 573
Davis, Margaret 504
Davis, Michael 316
Davis, Sidney 428
Davis, Syd 401
Davis's Fantastiques 633
Davis Morley 228
Davys, Fred 469
Dawe, Clem 199
Dawe, Eric 199
Dawe, George 19, 197, 442
Dawe, Rex 270
Dawes, George 376
Dawn, Gloria 21, 98, **186**, 260, 341, 440, 497, 519, *568*
Dawnay, Eve 481, 543
Daws, Gavin. See *The Dolphin Play*
Dawson, Dagmar 600
Dawson, Janet 326
Dawson, Smokey 59
Day, Beatrice 231
Day Before Tomorrow, The 401, 454, 598
Day, Di. See *One Day Short of an April Fool*
Day in the Death of Joe Egg, A 89, 422, 480
Day Like Any Other, A 216
Day, Margaret 32
Daybreak 396, 453, 528
Daylight Saving 154, 209, 230, 248, 368, 527
Dayman, Leslie 187, 555
Days of the Commune 98
Days of the Land Boom, The 82
Days without End 50
de Basil's ballet companies 548
de Burgh, Celia 573
De Carlo, Yvonne 617
De Gaetani, Thomas 29
De Groen, Alma 187, 223, 405, 456, 651. See also *Chidley*; *The Girl Who Saw Everything*; *Going Home*; *The Rivers of China*; *Vocations*
de Jong, Sarah 211
de Loitte, Vinia 623
De Luxe Annie 298, 350, 458

de Pinna, Herbert 114
De Rullecourt 115
De Saxe, William 286
de Tisne, Eddie 81
de Vries, Beppi 384
Dead Bird (magazine) 171
Dead Class, The 31, 459
Dead Timber 212, 357, 375, 451
Dead to the World 255
Deakin, Alfred 188, 249, 467
Deakin University 22, 620
Deamer, Dulcie 188
Dean, Basil. See *The Constant Nymph*
Deane, J. P. 57, 158, **188**, 278, 364
Dear Brutus 350
Dear Charles 56
Dearest Enemy 50, 111, 387, 636
Deas Thomson, Edward 131
Dease, John 481
Death and the Maiden 124, 240, 376
Death at Balibo 63, 184, 410
Death Defying Theatre 108, 155, 156, 166, **188**, 474, 570
Death of a Salesman 104, 234, 236, 239, 243, 332, 344, 352, 371, 395, 484, 629
Death of a Traveller 273
Death of Minnie, The 89, 190, 237, 373
Death Warmed Up 273
Deathtrap 89, 200, 318, 527
Deave's Manikins 469
Debnam, Brian 263
Decenoski 305
Deckchair Theatre Company 156, **189**, 224, 438, 597
Deep Blue Sea, The 167, 347, 484
Deering, Henry 88, **189**, 283, 652
Deering, Olly **189**, 260
Dees, Mary 50
Defence Forces Academy 75
Definitely Not the Last 508
Degraves, Henry 583
Degraves, Peter 583
Del Sarte's Rooms 278
Delaney, Shelagh 208. See also *A Taste of Honey*
Delavigne, Casimir 213
Delicate Balance, A 233, 332
Dellit, C. Bruce 316, 344, 369
Delphiniums 528
Delysia, Alice 161, 240, 275
Democrat, The 197
Demon's Mask 11
Dempsey, E. J. 172
Dence, Maggie 519
Dench, Judi 510
Denes, Oskar 384
Denham, Arnold 82, 163
Denham, Arthur 449
Denham, Reginald. See *Ladies in Retirement*
Deniehy, Daniel 169, 495
Dennis, C. J. See *The Sentimental Bloke*

Dennis Wolanski Library of the Performing Arts 312, 407, 498
Denniston, Reynolds 329
Denson, Ronald 280
Deorwyn, Alice 281
Department, The 227, 230, 642
Derby Winner, The 283
Derham, David 358
Derum, John 259, 474, 497
Derwent Dramatic Company 278
Desert Song, The 50, 99, *301*, 302, 383, 387, 415
Desire of Spring 61
Desmond, Lorrae. See *The Jesus Christ Revolution*
Desmond, Therese 287
Desperate Game, A 283
Dessaix, Robert 217
Devenish, Luke. See also *Vincent*
Devil Caresfoot 16
Devil to Pay, The 204
Devil Wear Black 598
Devil's Advocate, The 264
Devil's Disciple, The 471, 572
Devils, The 158, 365, 395, 427
Di Marne, Dennis. See *Jack the Ripper*
Diablo 410
Diaghilev, Sergey 42
Diakoff, Valentina 407
Dialogue Between a Prostitute and Her Client 216
Diamond, Arthur. See *Prince Enterprise*
Diamond Cuts Diamond 363
Diamond, Dick 190, 483. See also **Reedy River**, *Under the Coolibah Tree*
Diamond Lil theatre-restaurants 588
Diary of a Madman 57, 58, 86, 282, 308, 420, 474, 514, 515
Dibden, Anne 258
Dibdin, Charles Alexander. See *The Barlow Family*
Dibdin, Robert L. 473
Dick, Judy 555
Dick Turpin 92
Dick Whittington 375
Dick Whittington and His Cat 606
Dickens Fellowship 93
Dickenson, George 603
Dickins, Barry 190, 456. See also *Bridal Suite*; *The Death of Minnie*; *Lennie Lower*
Dickins Christmas, A 190
Dickinson, Peter. See *Your Number's Up*
Dicks, Arthur 242, 471
Dickson, Bettie 27
Dickson, Wendy 190
Diehard Productions 422
Dieter's Dilemma, The 625
Different Drummer, A 82
Digby, Desmond 190, 519
digger companies 191
Digger Dandies 59
Digger Pierrots 191

Diggers Company 191, 405
Diggers' Rest 212. See also *The Battler*
Dighton, John. See *The Happiest Days of Your Life*
Dignam, Arthur 87, 412
Diller-Anderson, Gai 242
Dillon, Charles 205
Dimboola 45, 117, 123, 184, **191**, 273, 320, 410, 445, 539, 588
Dimmed Lights 607
Dingo, Ernie 196, 408
Dingo Flat 117
Dining Room, The 618
Dinks and Onkus 191, 628
Dinkum Assorted 60
Dinkum Bambino, The 470
Dinkum Diggers 191
Dinnelli, Mel. See *The Man*
Dinner at Eight 50
Dinsdale, James 100
directing 192
directors 181, **192**
Dirty Dick's 157, 588
disabled people's theatre 194
Disappeared, The 336
Discipline and Punish 188
Distant Point 500
Ditrichstein, Leo. See *The Great Lover*
Diuguid, Nancy 215
Diver, Harry 637
Diving for Pearls 74, 178, 237, 398, 597
Division Bell, The. See **Mrs Pretty and the Premier**
Divvy Show 59
Dixon, Ian 308
Dixon, Les 59
Dixson, Wendy 615
Dixson Library 497
Djin Djin the Japanese Bogie Man 374, 426, 535, 644, 653
Dlask, Charles 342
Dobbie, John 153
Dobbin, Claire 22, 345
Dobson, Agnes 11, 42, **194**, 201, 497, 651. See also *Dark Brother*
Dobson, Collet 194
Doctor Death 24
Doctor Faustus 263
Doctor Pygmalion 422
Doctor's Dilemma, The 112, 258, 567
dogs on stage 180
Dolia Ribush Award 76
Dolia Ribush Players 20, 215, 500, 514
Doll Trilogy, The 165, **194**, 248, 323, 357, 392, 455, 573
Doll's House, A 15, 86, 157, 214, 286, 451, 490, 566
Dolphin Play, The 367
Dolphin Theatre 96, 426
Dombroskis, Lisa 223
Don, Lady 35
Don, Sir William 35
Don Giovanni in London 146, 309

Don Juan: by Molière 166, 210, 556, 656; by Dacia Maraini 216
Don Quixote in La Mancha 275
Donald, Ann 275
Doncaster Theatre Restaurant 420, 588
Dong Rang Theatre for Young People 154
Donovan, Gerry 420, 440
Donovan, Terence 151
Don's Party 71, 88, 89, 146, 184, 193, **195**, 262, 305, *355*, 455, 569, 580, 641
Don't Piddle against the Wind, Mate 176
Doody—The Progress of a Stripper 224
Doone, Allen 50
Dopierala, Wanda 631
Doppio Teatro 29, 156, **195**, 216, 224
Dorfman, Ariel. See *Death and the Maiden*
Dorothy 387, 559
Double Act 168
Double Bass, The 575
Double Event, The 183
Douglas, H. N. 154
Douglas, Tiny 535
Douglass, Stephen 266
Doust, Paul. See *Lady Bracknell's Confinement*
Dover Road, The 104
Dowdle, Len. See *Song of '54*
Down an Alley Filled with Cats 332
Down Under 202
Down Under Chelsea 97
Downer, David 194
Downer, Sid 173
Downes, Cathy 224
Downing, Desmonde 195, 396, 498
Downing, Vanessa 77
Downs, Annette 582
Downstairs 85, 521
Dr Floyd's Fly by Night Medicine Show 188
Dr Homer Speaks 54
Dracula 629
Dracula's Theatre Restaurant 588
Draffin, Robert 22, 337, 595
Dragged Screaming to Paradise 410
Dragonet Club 532
Dragon's Teeth 27
Drake-Brockman, Henrietta 196. See also *Dampier's Ghost*; **Men Without Wives**
Drama Education And Fun 582
Drama League of Australia 498
Dramatic Hall 25
Dramaturgical Services Inc. 262, 363, 428, 551
Draper, Ruth 27, 49, 301
Dream Girl 81, 639
Dream of Peter Mann, The 198
Dream Play, A 240, 328, 555

Dreamers, The 13, *14*, 71, 185, **196**, 412, 456, 509
Dreams in an Empty City 58, 240, 241, 307, 359, 368, 493, 520, 556
Dreamtime 468
Dresser, The 228, 258, 371
Drew, Con. See *Jinker, the Grafter's Mate*
Dreyer, Marien 80, **196**. See also **Bandicoot on a Burnt Ridge**; **Marien Dreyer's World**
Dreyfus, George 520
Drink the Mercury 530
Drinkwater, John. See *Abraham Lincoln*; *Bird in Hand*
Driscoll, Willie 417
Drive a Hard Bargain 252
Drop Drill 468
Drovers, The 12, **197**, 212, 451, 491
Drunkard, The 114
Du Barry 558
du Feu, John 528
Du Maurier, Daphne. See *September Tide*
Du Maurier, Guy. See *An Englishman's Home*
Dubarry, The 387, 427
Duchess of Coolgardie, The 12, **197**, 283, 490, 585
Duchess of Malfi, The 621
Duckworth, Billy 229
Duckworth, Eric 420, 440
Dudders 507
Dudley Goldman Pty Ltd 326
Duel of Angels 415
Duellist, The 131, 531
Duenna, The 165
Duet for One 376, 577
Duet for Two Hands 475
Duggan, Edmund 54, 55, 78, 118, 163, **197**, 417, 418, 497, 513, 532, 637. See also *The Man from Outback*; *My Mate*; *On Our Selection*; *The Squatter's Daughter*
Duggan, Eugenie 54, **197**, 245, 392, 539, 647
Duggan, Gerry 260
Duggan, Gwen 652
Duggan, P. J. 197
Duhig, Archbishop 114
Duke of Edinburgh 373
Duke of Edinburgh Assassinated, The 202
Duke of Edinburgh Theatre 594
Duke, William 197
Dukes, Ashley. See *Jew Süss*; *Josef Süss*; *The Man with a Load of Mischief*
Duke's Motto, The 319
Dumas, Alexandre *fils* 230. See also *Camille*; *La Dame aux camélias*; *Les Danicheff*; *The Lady of the Camellias*
Dumas, Sir Lloyd 31
Dumb Type 32, 306
Dumb Waiter, The 470
Dunbar, Laurence 118, 539, 637

Duncan, Alastair 341
Duncan, Catherine 198, 207, 480, 497, 639. See also *Soak the Rich*; *Sons of the Morning*; *The Sword Sung*
Duncan McClure 473, 513
Duncan McClure and the Poor Parson 512
Dunn, Anne 410
Dunn, Beverley 198, 471. See also *To Botany Bay on a Bondi Tram*
Dunn, Carmel 74, 358, 564
Dunn, Charles 296
Dunn, John 35, 147, 260
Dunn, Louise 41
Dunn, Marian 35, 147
Dunn, Nell. See *Steaming*
Dunne, Brendan 458
Dunning, Alice 626
Durno's Journey 336
Dunsany, Lord. See *Fame and the Poet*
Dunstan, Don 28, 29, 80, 126, 555
Durack, (Dame) Mary 454. See *Swan River Saga*
Durban, Kim 224
Dürrenmatt, Friedrich. See *The Physicists*; *The Visit*
Dust is the Heart 557
Dusting Our Knees 359
Dutchman, The 656
Dutkiewicz, Wladyslaw 28, 33, **198**
Dutton, Geoffrey 69
Duval, Dorothy 435
Dwyer, Jill 223
Dwyer, Kerry 74, 195, 219, 224, 345, 613
Dyer, Charles. See *Rattle of a Simple Man*
Dyer, Ralph 318
Dyk Whyttyngtonne and hys Wonderfulle Catte 626
Dyson, Edward 98, **198**, 497, 532. See also *Fact'ry 'Ands*; *The Golden Shanty*

E

Eager Hope, An 314
Eagle Has Two Heads, The 43
Earl Arts Centre 578
Earle, Kevin 30
Earle, R. 599
Earle, Tilly 35, 260
Early Childhood Drama Project 90
Earth, Air, Fire and Water Show, The 507
Earth Players 31
Earth Remains, The 228
East 209
East Lynne 66, 92, 96, 168, 201, 361, 380, 470, 474, 587, 632
Easter 188

Eastern, Hosea 274
Eastwood, Laurence 136, **199**, 202, 203, 260, 407
Eberhard, Josie Composto 195
Eberson, John 126
Echoes 526, 581
Echoes of Ruby Dark 312
Ecstasies 83
Eddington, Paul 244
Eden House 90, 462
Edgar, David. See *The Life and Adventures of Nicholas Nickleby*
Edgley and Dawe 28, 199
Edgley and Dawe Attractions 199, 437
Edgley, Edna 199
Edgley, Eric 199
Edgley, Michael 114, **199**
Edgley, Phillip 199
Edgley Ventures Pty Ltd 199
Edith Cowan University 621, 631
Edmiston, Phillip 469
Edmund, John 28, 44, 408, 586. See also *Great Expectations*
Edmunds, Albert 78. See also Bert Bailey; Edmund Duggan
Edmundson, Keith 196
Educating Rita 417
Edward, Bryan 200
Edward, Marion 200, 231
Edward, My Son 303, 378, 491, 631
Edwards, Alan 193, **200**, 393, 475
Edwards, Allen 96, 399, 412
Edwards, Gale 86, 194, 224, 254, 286, 368, 556
Edwards, George 554
Edwards, Jimmy 604
Edwards, Rowland G. 49
Edwards, Vivian 427
Effect of Gamma Rays on Man-in-the-Moon Marigolds, The 200
Efftee Films 597
Efftee Players 350, 597
Egerton, Leonard 599
Eggington, Barry 588
1841 251
84 Charing Cross Road 200, 342
Eijsma, Bettina 379
Einstein 200, 392, 427
Einstein on the Beach 431
Eklund, Kay 260
Elder Conservatorium 26, 32
Electra 258
Elephant of Siam, The 283
Elg, Taina 270
Eliot, T. S. See *The Cocktail Party*; *Murder in the Cathedral*;
Elisha, Ron 200, 456. See also *Einstein*; *Esterhaz*; *In Duty Bound*; *Pax Americana*
Elizabeth the Queen 50
Elizabethan Theatre 72, **201**, 528, 616
Elizabethan Trust News 175
Ellerton, Sam 417
Elliott, Gertrude 49

Elliott, Madge 90, **201**, 238, 301, 302, 312, 491, 498, 503
Elliott, Sumner Locke 202, 207, 454, 497. See also *Interval*; *Invisible Circus*; **Rusty Bugles**
Ellis, Bob 91, **202**, 544. See also *The Legend of King O'Malley*; *Meet Mr Brutus*
Ellis, James 167
Ellis, John 22, 71
Ellis, Lois 22, 71, 223, 320
Ellis, Lynne 549
Ellis, Walter W. See *A Little Bit of Fluff*
Ellwood, Sid 60
Elocution of Benjamin Franklin, The 85, 133, 199, **202**, 373, 444, 538, *568*, 636
Elston, Glenn 203
Elston, Hocking and Woods 64, **203**
Embassy Theatre 605
Emerald City 85, 165, 199, **203**, 398, *569*, 573, 636, 642
Emerald Hill Theatre 218, 595
Emerald Hill Theatre Company 22, 134, **203**, 354, 454, 498
Emerson, Billy 46, 370
Emigrants, The 60, 459
Emigrés aux terres australes, Les 12
Emily Soldene Opéra-Bouffe Company 382
Emissary, The 400
Emma 156, 410
Emmerson, Darryl. See *The Pathfinder*
Emmett, Joseph 47, 553
Emperor Jones, The 50, 335
Emperor Regrets, The 64, 478
Emperor's Nightingale, The 538
Empire Minstrel and Variety Company 511
Empire Talkies Ltd 270
Empire Theatre: Brisbane 101, 238; Launceston (Tas.) 584; Port Pirie (SA) 238; Sydney 238, 270, 511, 567, 593, 604
Empire Theatres Ltd 270
Empress Theatre 396
Emu Plains convict theatre 158, **204**, 382, 545, 589, 616
Enchanted Tryst, The 349
Enduring as the Camphor Tree 43, 371, 411, 453
Enemies, The 515
Enemy, The 481
Enemy of the People, An 574
Enemy Within, The 215
Enemy's Camp, The 233
England's Hope 482
English, Jon 209
English, Thomas 582
English influences 205
English Shakespeare Company 209, 356
Englishman's Home, An 491
Ennery, Philippe d'. See *Don César de Bazan*

Ennis, J. J. 117
Enright, Nick 148, **209**, 393, 456, 498, 555, 556. See also *Daylight Saving*; *Mongrels*; *St James Infirmary*; *The Venetian Twins*
Ensemble Company 210
Ensemble Studios 247
Ensemble Theatre 208, 328, 577, 595
Ensemble Theatre Company 53, 70, 158, 168, 176, **210**, 217, 224, 230, 247, 248, 259, 291, 332, 334, 515, 568, 573
Ensemble Theatre Project 123
Enter a Free Man 176
Entertainer, The 297, 341
Entertaining Mr Sloane 68, 146, 317, 458
entertainment taxes 37, 67, **210**, 249, 296
Entr'acte (magazine) 171
Entr'acte, L' (magazine) 171
Entr'acte Theatre 211, 432, 369, 621
Eora Centre 569
Equus 133, 200, 208, 233, 395, 435, 475, 527, 619
Erdmann, Nicholas. See *The Suicide*
Eroni, Charles 435
Eroni, George 509
Eroni and Sole's Circus 62, 434
Eroni Brothers' Circus 137, 306, 434, 461, 533
Eros 538
Erris, Fanny 118, 245
Errol, Leon 211
Errolle, Ralph 646
Ervine, St John. See *Robert's Wife*
Esperance Theatre Guild 634
Espinasse, Bernard. See *The Christian*; *England's Hope*
Essendon Policewomen's Marching Band 631
Essington Entertainment 85
Essington Lewis: I Am Work 290, 397, 412
Esslin, Martin 73, 215
Esson, Hilda 400, 402
Esson, Louis 12, 19, 51, 105, **211**, 297, 422, 423, 442, 451, 497. See also *The Bride of Gospel Place*; *Dead Timber*; *The Drovers*; *Mother and Son*; *The Sacred Place*; *Shipwreck*; *The Time is Not Yet Ripe*; *The Woman Tamer*
Esterhaz 201, 221
Estrella 387, 535
Ettie Williams Happy Hours Vaudeville Company 632
Eureka 653, 655
Eureka Rebellion, The 421
Eureka! Theatre 123
Euripides. See *Medea*; *Orestes*; *The Trojan Women*; *The Women of Troy*
Europe 251, 254, 309
European influences 213

669

Evangeline Burlesque Company 336
Evans, Bob 176
Evans, Joan 376
Evans, Ken 259
Evans, Roger 442, 588
Evanson, Anny 539
Evening Standard award 641
Everest Theatre 521
Everett, George 311
Everett, Jimmy 13
Evers, Francis 175
Every Night, Every Night 374
Everybody's Doing It 484
Everyman 490, 621
Everyman's Theatre 481, 543
Evita 30, 386, 387
Ewar 305
Ewing, Jon 217, 265, 622
Examiner (newspaper) 170
Excuse I 289
Exit 179
Experimental Art Foundation 431
experimental theatre 218
Explorers, The 342, 469, 519
Exquisite Eight 429
extravaganza 220, 382, 385, 424
Eye of the Law 188
Eyes of the Whites, The 64, 562
Eyes of Youth 458
Eyre, Edward John 25
Eyre Peninsula Regional Cultural Centre Trust 263

F

F.F.F. 348, 388
Faassen, John 381, 587
Fabre, Jan. See *The Power of Theatrical Madness*
Fabulous Apron Parade, The 625
Face of Crime, The 473
Face to Face 616
Faces in the Street 261, 263, 419
Factory Girls of Melbourne 82
Fact'ry 'Ands 199, 491, 580
Faggetter, Robert 97
Fair and Tender Ladies 291
Fair Go 89, 468
Fairfax, George 221, 334, 357, 543
Fairlea Drama Group 155
Fairy of the Lake, The 364
Faithful Heart, The 111
Fake, The 376
Fakir of Oolu 626
Falchon, Arthur 221, 630
Falk, Ronald 221
Falka 388
Fall of Sebastopol, The 35
Fall of Singapore, The 356, 614
Fall of the House of Usher, The 209
Fallen Angels 198
Falling from Grace 482

Falsche Catalani in Krahwinkel, Die 213, 446
Falsettos 265
Fame and the Poet 33
Family Album 624
Famous Diggers and Lady Artists 191
Famous Diggers Company 191
Fanatics, The 542
Fane, Maude 312
Fanny's First Play 329
Fanque, Pablo 509, 542
Fantasticks, The 388, 527, 575
Farewell Brisbane Ladies 147, 317
Farewell Supper 634
Farley, Edward 533
Farley, Tom 528
Farnham, John 368
Farquhar, George. See *The Recruiting Officer*
Farr, Judi 222, 458
Farrelly, Gilly. See *Dancing in the Dark*
Farren, Nellie 240
Farwell, George. See *The House that Jack Built*; *Sons of the South*
Fassbinder, Rainer Werner 215. See also *The Bitter Tears of Petra von Kant*; *Bremen Coffee*
Fat Lady, The 468
Fatal Card, The 553
Fatal Gap, The 378
Fatal Wedding, The 148, 490
Father, The 56, 165, 198, 435, 555
Father We Loved on a Beach by the Sea, The 102, 520
Fatinitza 388
Faucit, J. S. See *The Aldgate Pump*
Faulkner, George 608
Faust 32, 180, 525, 538, 559, 645
Faust and Marguerite 181
Faust Up To Date 240
Fawcett, George 222
Fawdon, Michele 222, 308, 422, 519, 599
Feber, G. R. 43
Federal Minstrels 291
Federated Stage Employees' Association 294, 296
Federation of Italian Migrant Workers and their Families 155, 166, 216
Fédora 86
Feet of Clay 506
Feet of Daniel Mannix, The 402, 411
Felgate, Rhoda 43, 44, 102, 104, **223**, 617, 651
Fellows, Effie 223
Female Parts 216
Feminine Gender 89
Feminine Plural 89
feminist theatre 223
Fen 615
Fennell, Willie 224, 498, 622
Fenoglio, Edmo 217
Fenton, Mr 178
Ferber, Edna. See *Dinner at Eight*
Fergus, Helen 245

Ferguson, Nellie 606
Fergusson, Babette 557. See also Babette Stephens
Fernande 147
Fernando Tiscornia, Nelly. See *Made in Argentina*
Ferrier, Noel 126, **224**, 341, 408, 564
Ferrier, Ron 471
Festa di nozze, Una 195
Festival of Australian Drama 125
Festival of Perth 14, 44, 75, 96, 97, 149, 166, 198, 208, 217, **225**, 227, 257, 286, 365, 367, 395, 396, 399, 420, 424, 428, 435, 437, 438, 538, 557, 620, 621, 634
Festival of Sydney 209, 226, 263, 291, 298, 379, 469, 536, 557, 569, 577, 606
Festival Theatre 29
festivals 225, 655
Fewster, Jack 27
Feydeau, Georges. See *Cat among the Pigeons*; *A Flea in Her Ear*
Fiala, Oliver 582
Fiander, Lewis 375, 418
Ficky Stingers 124
Fiddler on the Roof 52, 124, 245, 247, 266, 304, 388, 624
Fidess, Buster 226
Field, Amanda 126
Field, David 308
Fielding, Henry. See *The Mock Doctor*; *An Old Man Taught Wisdom*
Fielding, Janet 462
Fields, Gracie 59
Fields of Heaven, The 227, 272, 570
Fields, W. C. 47, 310, 502
Fierstein, Harvey. See *Safe Sex*; *Torch Song Trilogy*
Fifi Banvard Productions 322
50-50 Show 59
Fighter, The 311
Filiki Players 156, 216, 333
Fille de Madame Angot, La 388, 533
Fille du tambour-major, La 226, 256, 379, 382, 388, 489, 559
Filling the Silence 195
Fillis, Frank 141
Filthy Children 579
Filthy Lucre 184
Filumena 258
Finamore, John 467
Finch, Peter 20, 59, **226**, 363, 415, 435, 497, 554, 623
Findlay, Jean 135
Finian's Rainbow 388
Finley, Don 41, **227**, 228, 348
Finney, Alan 155
Finney, Ron 539
Finucan, M. D. 100
Fire on the Snow, The 51, 467, 479, 483, 558, 580

Fire on the Wind 616
Fire Raisers, The 146, 215
fires in theatres 88, 594
Fires of St John, The 41
Firing Squad 83, 330
First Born, The: (by Christopher Fry) 27
First-Born, The: (by Jack Davis) 185, 196, 357, 509
First Class Women 209
First Four Hundred Years, The 366
First Joanna, The 90, 352, 366, 452
First National Black Playwrights' Conference 13, 134
Firth, Kenneth 519
Fischer, Colin 124
Fischer, Margaret 223, 625
Fischer, Mrs Carl 171, 498
Fischer, Sara Jenny 171
Fish, Ernie 318
Fisher, Rodney 151, 193, 225, **227**, 341, 413, 480, 555, 556, 573, 574
Fisher, Thomas. See *The Face of Crime*
Fisher's Ghost 558
Fisher Library 499
Fisk Jubilee Singers 347
Fitton, (Dame) Doris 41, 42, 76, 193, 215, **228**, 292, 321, 407, 476, 497, 498, 506, 514, 515, 572, 651
Fitzball, Edward. See *The Flying Dutchman*; *The Inchcape Bell*
Fitzgerald, Catherine 337
FitzGerald, Daniel 228
FitzGerald, Michael 154, 655
Fitzgerald, R. 464
FitzGerald, Thomas 228
FitzGerald Brothers' Circus 62, 137, 139, **228**, 306, 461, 542, 612, 633
Fitzpatrick, Kate 27, 87, **229**, 259, 326, 519, 572
Fitzpatrick, Neil 230, 330, 615
Five Arts Club 98
Five Times Dizzy 587
Fix It, Alice 57
Flanagan, Francis 27, 32, 418
Flanagan, James 362
Flanagan, Patsy 418
Flash Jim Vaux 88, 148, 240, 318, 385, 388, 651
Flash Rat 223
Flaw, The 309, 451, 459, 490
Flea in her Ear, A 260
Fledermaus, Die 388, 415
Fleeced 361, 378
Fleeting, Claude 362
Fleets of Fortune 189
Fleming, Justin 230. See also *The Cobra*; *Harold in Italy*
Flemming, Claude 130, 153, **230**, 296
Flemming, Herbert 107, 108, **231**, 404

Fletcher, Charles Brunsdon 172
Flett, Peter 599
Flexitime 404
Flexmore, J. H. 542
Flight Path 475
Flinders University 208, 620
Flinders University Drama Centre 482
Floating Palais, The 615
Floating World, The 63, 71, 148, 164, 178, 182, 200, **231**, 263, 290, 304, 348, 455, 505, 507, 508, 527, 539
Flood, The 259
Florence Who? 310
Florodora 270, 299, 323, 374, 383, 388, 424, 484
Flower, Cedric 231, 403
Flower, Pat 231
Flowers 209
Flowers, Jennifer 103, **232**
Flying Codonas 649
Flying Dutchman, The 278, 512
Flying Fruit Fly Circus 16, 144, 145, **232**, 379, 613
Flying Jordans 141, 632, 649
Flying Pieman 100
Flying Saucery 97
Flying Scud 93, 488
Flying Squad, The 248
Flying Trapeze Cafe 442, 588
Flynn, Leo 137
Flynn, Margaret 116
Fo, Dario 216. See also *Accidental Death of an Anarchist; Whore in a Madhouse*
Foans, J. M. 473
Focus 30
Fogg, Ellis D. 219
Foiled 160, 361, 447
Foley Troupe 542
Folies-Bergère Company 604
Follies 322, 388
Follies in Concert 265, 330
Follow That Husband 168
Follow the Girls 406
Folson, Bobby 223
Food 562
Fool for Love 656
Fool's Gallery 122, 223
Fool's Shoe Hotel 190
Footbridge Theatre 248
Footfalls. See *Happy Day*
Footrot Flats 404
Footsbarn Theatre 209
For Australia 84, 637. See also *White Australia*
for colored girls who have considered suicide when the rainbow is enuf 53
For Instance 463
For Love of Appin 404
For Richer, For Poorer 97
For the Term of His Natural Life 148, 163, 181, **232**, 361, 449, 511, 534
For Valour 454, 598
Foran, Barney. See *Come Hell or High Water*

Forbes, Lorna 37, **233**, 356, 618, 651
Forbes, Meriel 72
Forbes, Wilson 233
Forbes-Robertson, Lady. See Gertrude Elliott
Forbidden Fruit 147
Ford, John. See *'Tis a Pity she's a Whore*
Ford, Margaret 133, **233**, 339
Ford, Mrs 421
Forde, Florrie 233, 497, 502
Forde, John 197
Foreman, The 526
Foreskin's Lament 405
Forged 378
Forget Me Not 645
Forlorn Hope, The 183, 448
Formby, George 604
Formosa 18, 605
Forrest, Alexander 585
Forster, Jill 551
Forster, William 467
Forsyth, Julie 549
Forsythe, Drew 234, 556, 622
Fortunate Life, A 248, 427, 494, 509
Fortune and Men's Eyes 178, 575
Fortune Capital Theatre 123, 339
Fortune Theatre 122
Fortune's Wheel 639
Forty Lounge Cafe, The 177, 333
Forty Thieves, The 334, 380, 437
42nd Street 388, 265, 322
Forward One 464, 652
Foster, Lynn. See *The Lost Generation*
Foster, Mike 619
Foul Play 147
Foundation for Australian Cultural Development 70
Foundation South Australia 537
Fountains Beyond 13, 51, 182, 221, **234**, 400
Four Lady Bowlers in a Golden Holden 316
Four Little Girls 579
Fowler, J. Beresford 40, **234**, 599
Fowler, Mrs Fanny 234
Fowles, Kenneth 321
Fox, Len 97
Fox, Mem. See *Wilfred Gordon McDonald Partridge*
Foy, Murray 105
Foyer (magazine) 43
Francart, Yvonne 403
France, Anatole. See *The Man Who Married a Dumb Wife*
Francis, Gordon. See *God's Best Country*
Frank Neil Comedy Company 397
Frank Thornton Company 430
Frankenstein's Children 29, 482
Frankie 307
Franklin, Benjamin 77
Franklin, Governor Sir John 537

Franklin, Miles. See *Call Up Your Ghosts*
Frankly Thring 597
Franquin 235
Fraser, Anne 194, **235**, 418, 543, 549, 564, 615
Fraser, Susie 595
Fraser, Vivian 85, **235**, 573, 635
Frasquita 114, 388
Frawley, John 622
Frayn, Michael 89. See *Noises Off; Wild Honey*
Frazer, Ronald 515
Frederick, Pauline 49
Fredrickson, Kristian 236
Free, Colin 236
free-and-easies 381, 461
Freeman, Ethel 140
Freeman, Freddy 140
Freemason's Tavern 121, **236**, 278, 592
Freewheels 209, 405
French, Anna 236
French Maid, The 388, 644
French Without Tears 24, 59, 293
French's Acting Editions 42
Fresh Fields 321
Friedel, Martin 236, 261, 562
Friedl, Jan 99, **236**
Friel, Brian. See *Dancing at Lughnasa; Philadelphia, Here I Come; Translations*
Friels, Colin 186, **237**, 371, 515
Friend, Gwen 81
Friends 214, 331
Friends of the Soviet Union 402
Frisby, Terence. See *There's a Girl in My Soup*
Frisch, Max. See *Andorra; The Fire Raisers*
Frith, Alfred 130, **237**, 312
Fritz Our Cousin German 47, 553
Frog Promotions 34
Froggee Would a Wooing Go, A 626
From Morning to Midnight 42, 371, 543
From Smike to Bulldog 83
From the Fourteenth Floor You Can See the Harbour 557
Front Lawn 405
Front Page, The 89, 332
Front Room Boys, The 118
Frost, John 248
Frou Frou 86
Fry, Christopher. See *The First Born; The Lady's Not for Burning; A Phoenix Too Frequent*
Fry, Garry 263, 528
Fryer's Circus 141
Fryer Library 33, 34, 83, 89, 90, 182, 196, 223, 309, 408, 419, 497, 606, 619
Fuente Ovejuna 356

Fugard, Athol 31, 536. See also *The Blood Knot; Hello and Goodbye; The Island; 'Master Harold' … and the Boys; The Road to Mecca; Sizwe Bansi is Dead*
Fujian Puppet Theatre 241
Fulfilment 83
Full House 475, 543
Full House—No Vacancies 595
Fuller, (Sir) Benjamin 99, 129, **237**, 238, 414, 465, 485, 606
Fuller, John jnr 237, 238, 465
Fuller, John snr 238
Fuller, Luke 196
Fuller, Lydia 238
Fuller, Michael 196
Fuller, Walter 238
Fuller Dramatic Players 343
Fullers' 48, 66, 88, 96, 99, 201, **238**, 239, 338, 340, 380, 405, 409, 461, 478, 507, 567, 590
Fullers' National Theatre 99, 238, **239**, 637
Fullers' Theatres Ltd 237, 239
Fun on the Bristol 489, 553
Funerals and Circuses 337, 356
Funny Face 50, 388
Funny Girl 52, 265, 266, 337, 385, 388, 435
Funny Side Up 199
Funny Thing Happened on the Way to the Forum, A 52, 337, 385, 388, 527
Funny Thing Happened on the Way to The Front, A 204
Furious 251, 627
Furse, Bruce 369
Furtive Love 187, 314
Fuss 48, 161

G

Gaal, Mark 75
Gabriel, Ben 239, 471, 628
Gabriel, Ethel 240, 471, 564
Gaden, John 21, 28, 179, **240**, 412, 555, 556, 573
Gage, Mary 223
Gaiety Amateur Dramatic Company 278
Gaiety Girl, A 240, 383, 388
Gaiety Pantomime Company 632
Gaiety Theatre: Launceston (Tas.) 584; Melbourne 88, 99, 238; Zeehan (Tas.) 593
Gaiety Theatre companies 240, 327, 379, 383
Gaiety Theatres Ltd 129, 237, 316
Galahad Jones 24
Gale, Myra 485
Gale, Sadie 485, 603
Gale, Sam 294, 485
Galileo 240, 597
Gallacher, Frank 151, **241**, 260

Gallasch, Keith **241**, 555, 556, 614. See also *Tokyo Two*
Gallipoli Bill 24
Gallipoli Strollers 191
Gallop, James 316
Galsworthy, John 208. See also *Loyalties*; *The Pigeon*; *The Silver Box*; *The Skin of Our Teeth*
Game of Billiards, A 264
Game of Love and Chance, The 398
Gamester, The 311
Ganthony, Richard. See *A Message from Mars*
Gantner, Carrillo 176, 177, 193, **241**, 444, 656
Garcias, the 142
Garden of Granddaughters, The 257, 521
Garden Party 365
Gardener's Dream, The 334
Gardiner, Evelyn 244, 301
Gardiner, Robyn 34
Gard'ner, Dorothy 535
Gardner, Phil. See *Clyde Company Station*
Garner, Arthur 242, 330, 338, 340, 644, 645
Garner, Bill 74, 276, 345. See also *Sunday Lunch*
Garner's Theatre 242, 247, 338
Garrick, David 561. See also *The Lying Valet*
Garrick, Pauline 646
Garrick Club: Chiltern (Vic.) 38; South Australia 38
Garrick Players 277
Garrick Theatre (Perth) 42, **242**, 633
Garrick Theatre (Sydney) 501, 602, 605
Garson, Barbara. See *Macbird*
Gary Penny Productions 221
Gaskill, William 264, 440
Gates, Bill. See *The Earth Remains*
Gatliff, Frank 330
Gauntlett, Frank 176
Gay and Lesbian Mardi Gras Festival 226, 242
Gay Divorce 50, 388
Gay Lord Quex, The 329
Gay Mardi Gras Festival 242
Gay Parisienne, The 388, 484, 644
Gay Rosalinda 388, 415
gay theatre 242
Gay Theatre Company 242
Gayler, Charles. See *Fritz Our Cousin German*
Geach, Edwin 474
Geelong Repertory Company 221
Geelong Theatre 378
Geisha, The 383, 388, 654
Gell, Heather 33
Gemelli veneziani, I 216, 304
Gems, Pam. See *Piaf*
General Macarthur in Australia 342, 444, 468
General Motors Holden 72

General, The 478
Genesians 42, 137, 298
Genet, Jean. See *The Maids*
Geneviève de Brabant 382, 388, 533, 626
Gennaro, Aldo 123, 598
Gentleman in Waiting, The 422
Gentleman Joe 241, 388
Gents 241, 614
Genty, Philippe 216, 470, 646
Geoghegan, Edward 242, 297, 615. See also *The Currency Lass*; *The Hibernian Father*; *True Love*
George, Bruce 79
George, Carrie 233
George, Colin 28, 30, 248, 555
George, Keith 172, 215, 514
George, Rob 243, 455, 587. See also *Percy and Rose*; *Sandy Lee Live at Nui Dat*
George and Margaret 28
George Devine Award 77, 85, 485, 641
George Fairfax Studio 624
George Marlow Grand Shakespearean Company 640
George Marlow Ltd 343
George Rignold Company 531
George Washington Slept Here 639
Georgeson, Tom 555
Georgeson, Tony 258
Georgia Minstrels 46, 274, 370
Georgia Minstrels and Alabama Cakewalkers 47, 347
Geraghty, Bob 337
Gerald and Duff Company 473
Gerald, Jim 58, 239, **243**, 429, 652
Gershe, Leonard. See *Butterflies are Free*
Gertrude Stein and a Companion 635
Geschiedene Frau, Der 383
Gestures 582
Get Big or Get Out 263
Getting Married 305, 350, 572
Geyer, Siegfried. See *By Candlelight*
Ghéon, Henri. See *The Comedian*
Ghost of Dog-Leg Creek, The 252
Ghost Train, The 28, 200, 458
Ghosts 57, 85, 86, 207, 232, 301, 360, 363
Ghosts! 190
Gibbs, Geoffrey 631
Gibbs, John 652
Gibbs, Louise 652
Gibbs, Mrs 615
Gibbs, Paige. See *Something Blue*
Giblin, L. F. 394
Gibson, Brenda 107
Gibson, Bunny 352
Gibson, Mel 243, 271, 573
Gibson, Robin 472
Gibson, William. See *Two for the Seesaw*
Gielgud, (Sir) John 192, 399

Gilbert and George 430, 431
Gilbert and Sullivan 27, 205, 214, **244**, 245, 313, 353, 382, 384, 623, 644.
Gilbert and Sullivan Society (Newcastle, NSW) 405
Gilbert and Sullivan Society of Western Australia 244
Gilbert, Bert 484
Gilbert, Ernie 143
Gilbert, Kevin 13. See also *The Cherry Pickers*
Gilbert, Lynette 134
Gilbert, Tony 85
Gilbert, (Sir) William S. See *The Happy Land*; *The Palace of Truth*; *Pygmalion and Galatea*
Gilchrist, John 652
Gild the Mask Again 173
Gilgul Jewish Theatre Company 22, 220
Gilham, George 116, 139
Gill, John 77, 280, 438, 588
Gill, W. B. See *Harlequin Man in the Moon*
Gillette, William. See *Held by the Enemy*; *The Secret Service*
Gillies, Max 22, 74, **244**, 276, 345, 412, 497, 613
Gillies Report, The 244
Gillies Republic, The 244
Gillies Summit, The 244
Gillot, Venetia 615
Gimme Shelter 58
Gin Game, The 165
Ginger 320
Ginger Man, The 254
Ginn, Stewart 76
Gioconda Smile, The 322
Giorza, Paolo 147
Gipps, Governor Sir George 409
Giraudoux, Jean. See *Duel of Angels*; *Tiger at the Gates*
Girl Behind the Counter, The 383, 388
Girl Friend, The 50, 388
Girl from Kay's, The 241, 326, 383, 388
Girl from Outback, The 333
Girl from Snowy River 388, 520
Girl I Left Behind Me, The 19
Girl in the Taxi, The 388
Girl of the Golden West, The 112, 490, 600
Girl of the Never Never, The 245, 451, 533
Girl on the Film, The 388
Girl on the Train, The 383, 388
Girl Who Saw Everything, The 187, 334, 359
Girl with Odd-coloured Eyes, The 271
Girl's Frolic and What Came of It, A 448
Girl's Good Luck, A 96
Girls of Gottenberg, The 323, 326, 388
Girls Please 27
Giroflé-Girofla 388, 533

Give and Take 485
Gladbags 626
Gladstane, Mary 147, 552, 605
Gladwin, Joe 468
Gladys Moncrieff Library 497
Glaspell, Susan 50
Glass Menagerie, The 53, 304, 360, 527, 616
Glaucus 284
Gleitzman, Morris. See *Skin Free, Two Weeks with the Queen*
Glen Street Theatre 641
Glengarry Glen Ross 57, 58
Glenny, Dennis 363
Glenright, Gordon 422
Glide Time 404
Globe Trust 524
Glory 538
Glover, Keith 59
Glugs 76, 315
Gluth, William 183, 599
Glycerine Tears 273
Goatcher, Philip W. 245, 423
Goblin of the Gold Coast, The 447
Godayou family 306
Godfrey, Charles 501, 601
Godfrey, Julie 77
Godfrey-Smith, Anne 122, 125, 655. See also *Ulterior Motifs*
God's Best Country 286
Godsend 323
Godspell 386, 388, 475
Goers, Peter 176
Goethe, Johann von. See *Faust*
Goetz, Ruth and Augustus. See *The Heiress*
Goggin, Dan. See *Nunsense*
Gogol, Nikolai. See *Diamond Cuts Diamond*; *Diary of a Madman*; *The Government Inspector*; *The Marriage*
Going Home 187, 266
Going Up 201, 388, 504
Gold, Horace 336
Golden, George Fuller 502
Golden Age, The 245, 410
Golden Girls, The 179
Golden Goldenbergs, The 190
Golden Journey, The 617
Golden Legion of Cleaning Women, The 106, 284
Golden Lover, The 404, 479
Golden Oldies, The 200, 271, 368, 444
Golden Pathway through Europe, A 367
Golden Shanty, The 491
Golden Valley 71, 272, 336
Golden West, The 436
Golden Years, The 470
Golder, John 217
goldfields 246
Goldfields Players 246
Goldfields Repertory Club 246, 625, 633, 634
Goldie, Albert 188
Golding, Robert. See *Brylcreme and Maggot Pies*
Goldman, Dudley 420

672

Goldoni, Carlo 216. See *I gemelli veneziani*; *The Servant of Two Masters*
Goldsmith, Oliver. See *She Stoops to Conquer*
Goldsworthy, Reginald 27
Goldwyn Brothers' Circus 63
Gombrowicz, Witold 459. See also *The Marriage*
Gondoliers, The 244, 388, 623
Gone with Hardy 37, 614
Gonsalez Opera Company 238, 343, 606
Good Morning 464
Good Morning Dearie 50, 362, 388
Good Oil, The 157, 388, 438
Good Old Days of England, The 61
Good Old Days, The 429, 628
Good Ship Walter Raleigh 330, 388
Good Woman of Setzuan, The 33
Goodbye Judas 459
Goodbye Ted 273
Goodbye to the Music 202
Goodes, Joyce 122
Goodsall, Arthur 37
Goodwin, Percy 158
Goody Two Shoes 334
Goody Two Shoes and Little Boy Blue 148, 425
Goomalling (WA) 633
Gordon, Ashley 248
Gordon, Barry J. 395
Gordon, Charles 246
Gordon, George 247, 331
Gordon, Hayes 52, 53, 210, **247**, 265, 266, 303, 497, 514, 568
Gordon, John 247, 427
Gordon, Lee 368
Gordon, Leon 248
Gordon, Ludovick 617
Gordon, Marie 260
Gordon Frost Organisation 85, 569
Gore, Sandy 194, **248**, 338, *354*, 508, 599
Gore, Walter 509
Gorey, Edward 629
Gorky, Maxim. See *The Enemies*; *The Lower Depths*; *Vassa Zheleznova*
Gorman, Clem 219, **248**, 259. See also *A Manual of Trench Warfare*
Gorrick, Ivy 78
Gorton, John 159, 250
Gossip from the Forest 313
Gougenheim, Adelaide 48, 249, 553
Gougenheim, Joey 48, 246, **249**, 553
Gould, Mark 95
Gould, William Buelow 249
Government Expenditure Committee 563
Government Inspector, The 178, 515

government policy 249
Governor Bligh 37, 309, 451, 640
Governor General, The 31
Governor's Pleasure 466
Gow, Michael 251, 263, 456, 574. See also *Away*; *Europe*; *The Kid*; *On Top of the World*; *Grab Me a Gondola* 167, 525
Graduate Dramatic Society 621
Graham, Burton 97
Graham, Ron 252, 409
Graham, Sybil 440
Grand Chief 105
Grand Duchess of Gerolstein, The 382, 388
Grand Empire Theatre 278
Grand Opera House 238, 343, 603, 606, 629
Grand Pavilion Theatre 101
Grand World Circus 65
Gran'dad Rudd 512
Granite 81
Granite Peak 452, 506
Grant, A. K. See *Footrot Flats*
Grant, Bruce 174
Grant, Julius 78
Grant, Sean 135
Grant Street Theatre 235
Grantleigh, Ada 421
Grant's Music Hall 473
Granville-Barker, Harley. See *The Voysey Inheritance*
Grass, Günter. See *The Plebeians Rehearse the Uprising*
Gration, Steven 336, 337
Graupner, Flora 374
Graves, Peter 129
Gray, Daphne 243
Gray, Donald 586
Gray, Ernie 71. See *Clyde Company Station*; *Fix It, Alice*
Gray, John 252, 471, 483
Gray, Oriel 116, **252**, 452. See also *Burst of Summer*; *Had We But World Enough*; *Lawson*; *Let's Be Offensive*; *Sky Without Birds*; *The Torrents*
Gray, Sandy 119
Gray, Simon. See *Butley*; *Close of Play*
Gray, Trixie 481
Grayson, Richard 431
Graznya, Monvid. See *The Enemy Within*
Great American Cirque and Equescurriculum 141
Great Dragon troupe 305
Great Expectations 28, 586
Great God Mogadon, The 412
Great Kellino Family 152
Great Levante 252, 498
Great Lover, The 376
Great Macarthy, The 445
Great Man, The 51, 463
Great Moscow Circus 199, 232
Great Rescue, The 26, 117, 283
Great Sebastians, The 53
Great United Three-in-One Circus 229

Greater Union Organisation 369
Greater Union Theatres 478
Greek 439
Greek Tragedy 209
Greeks Had a Word for It, The 543
Green, Caroline. See *Janus*
Green, Harry 485
Green, Kristin 485
Green Bay Tree, The 27
Green Hat, The 27, 54, 248
Green Pastures 335
Green Room (magazine) 171
Green Room Awards 76
Greene, Clay M. See *The Chinese Question*; *Struck Oil*
Greene, Gene 348, 602
Greene, J. H. 163
Greenroom Theatre 395
Greenwood, Charlotte 49
Gregan McMahon Play Company 350, 357
Gregan McMahon Players 20, 41, 109, **253**
Greig, Karyn 376
Grenfell, Joyce 440
Gresham, Ida 551
Grey, Daphne 253
Grey, Jessie 226
Grey, Katherine 319
Grey, Sylvia 240
Grey Faced Bandits, The 598
Grieve, Ben 179
Griffin, Benjamin 88
Griffin, Elsie 362
Griffin Theatre Company 77, 220, 242, **254**, 332, 376, 407, 539, 544, 569
Griffith, Pat 258
Griffiths, Annie 254
Griffiths, Emily 254
Griffiths, Fanny 254
Griffiths, Freda 469
Gray, Oriel — see above
Griffiths, J. G. 178, **254**, 652
Griffiths, N. 117
Griffiths, Raeburn 469
Griffiths, Trevor 73, 208. See also *The Comedians*; *Occupations*
Grin and Tonic Theatre Troupe 153, 341
Grindlay, Ian 466
Grosvenor, Dennis 203
Grotowski, Jerzy 54, 184
Ground Rules 478
Grounds, (Sir) Roy 624
Grove (playwright). See *Forget Me Not*
Grove, D. P. 364, 583
Groves, Edward. See *The Warden of Galway*
Grubb, Robert 90, **254**
Grundy, Sydney. See *The Queen's Favourite*; *A Village Priest*
Grupo Teatro Macunaima 225
Gruppo Teatrale Napoletano 216
Guangzhou Acrobatic Company 136, 232

Guarding the Perimeter 184
Guardsman, The 395
Gubarev, Vladimir. See *Sarcophagus*
Guerin, James 561
Guerin, Mrs 561. *See also* Theodosia Stirling
Guerin, Renée 129, *386*
Guernon, Charles. See *Eyes of Youth*
Guhl, Sher 376
Guildford (WA) 633, 634
Guildford, Ada 539
Guinness, (Sir) Alec 528
Gulgong (NSW) 246
Gullet, Henry 523
Gulliver 626
Gulliver on his Travels 35
Gulliver's Travels 95
Gulls 272, 346, 392
Gulpilil, David 13
Gum Tree Gully 117, 286
Gunn, John 148
Gurney, A. R. jnr. See *The Dining Room*
Gurney, Robyn 539
Gurr, Michael 255. See also *Sex Diary of an Infidel*
Gurr, T. Stuart 153
Gurton, Shaun 151, **255**, 442, 544, 556
Gus St Leon's Great United Circus 284, 434, 533, 541, 542
Guthrie, (Sir) Tyrone 19, 67, 96, 200, 207, 221, 250, 255, 305, 315, 332, 366, 412, 426, 440, 466, 480, 592, 608
Guthrie Report 67, 159, 173, **255**, 394
Guys and Dolls 200, 265, 388
Gypsy 186, 388, 516
Gypsy Love 388

H

H. M. Tennent 72, 303
Ha Ha Performing Human Beings 86
Haag, Stefan 44, 72
Habbe, Alexander 70, 214, **256**, 646
Habbe, Nicholas 256
Hackett, Patricia 11, 27, 28, 42, 172, **256**, 651
Hackett, Ron 539
Hackett, Walter. See *Ambrose Applejohn's Adventure*; *The Invisible Foe*; *Road House*
Had We But World Enough 183, 252, 401, 409, 452
Haddrick, Lynette 257
Haddrick, Ron 21, 27, 33, 70, 165, 231, **257**, 418, 615
Haddy, Anne 157, **257**, 341
Hadrian the Seventh 200, 635
Haeburn-Little, Michael 73
Hafner, Dorinda 538

673

Hagan, Jennifer **258**, 613
Haggard, H. Rider 61
Hail Tomorrow 423
Hair 21, 53, 64, 68, 133, 330, 368, 385, 388, 423, 525, 596, 614, 629
Hairy Ape, The 50, 335
Halévy, Ludovic. See *Frou Frou*
Half a Sixpence 388, 416
Half an Hour 622
Halinbourg, Lea 599
Hall, Dick. See *The Duke of Edinburgh Assassinated*
Hall, Edward Smith 262
Hall, Ken G. 78
Hall, (Sir) Peter 70, 571
Hall, Rodney 70
Hall, Roger. See *Flexitime*; *Footrot Flats*; *Glide Time*; *Middle Age Spread*
Hall, Stephen 72
Hall, Thurston 49
Hall's Australian Juveniles 535
Hallelujah Lady Jane 184
Halliday, Robert 49, 384
Halliwell, David. See *Little Malcolm and His Struggle Against the Eunuchs*
Halloran's Little Boat 264, 313
Hal's Belles 356, 396, 597
Ham Funeral, The 28, 33, 44, 58, 68, 72, 110, 120, 178, **258**, 328, 416, 421, 454, 568, 577, 596, 617, 627, 638
Hamilton, Gough 633
Hamilton, Henry. See *The Derby Winner*; *The King's Musketeer*; *The Whip*; *The White Heather*
Hamilton, Julie 258, 586, 613
Hamilton, Patrick. See *Rope*
Hamlet 18, 84, 85, 92, 96, 150, 153, 178, 185, 190, 199, 237, 254, 281, 290, 319, 325, 328, 332, 363, 373, 399, 420, 459, 487, 514, 523, 524, **539**, 552, 579, 632, 636
Hamlet controversy 170, 373
Hamlet on Ice 88, 91, 230, **259**, 388, 396
Hamletmachine 215
Hammer 230
Hammerstein, Oscar II 52
Hammerstein, Ted 52
Hammond, 'Happy' 58
Hammond, (Dame) Joan 70
Hampton, Christopher. See *Les Liaisons dangereuses*; *The Philanthropist*; *The Portage to San Cristobal of A. H.*
Hampton, Paul 485
Hanaford, Maude 49, 50, 263
Handful of Friends, A 227, 240, 255, 258, 642
Handke, Peter. See *Kaspar*; *My Foot, My Tutor*; *The Ride Across Lake Constance*
Handly, Isabella 599
Hands Up! 18, 92
Handsome Ransom, The 388, 436

Handspan Theatre Company 259, 311, 469, 508, 579, 646
Hang Your Clothes on Yonder Bush 557
Hanger Collection 259, 497
Hanger, Eunice 44, 68, **259**. See also *A House is Built*
Hankin, St John. See *The Two Mr Wetherbys*
Hanna, Kim 622
Hanna, Pat 191
Hannan, Bill 276. See also *Not With Yours Truly*
Hanneles Himmelfahrt 41
Hansel and Gretel 518
Hansen, Andrew 259
Hansen, Morton 408
happenings 259
Happiest Days of Your Life, The 558
Happily Never After 80, 388
Happy and Holy Occasion, A 148, 290, 405, 413
Happy Days 89, 165
Happy Family, A 424, 442
Happy Husband, The 422
Happy Land, The 131, 148, 163, 206, **260**, 313, 639
Happy Prince, The 128
Harbour Lights 318
Hard God, A 71, 85, 148, 186, 259, **260**, 314, 346, 455, 527, 544, 570
Harders, Jane 21, **260**, 308
Hardgreaves, Vic 42, 102, 103, 615
Harding, Alex 242
Harding, Lionel 160
Harding Women, The 249
Hardingham, Dres 548
Hardman, Elma 127
Hardwick, Paul 510
Hardy, Frank 260
Hardy, Jonathan 261
Hardy, Mary 260
Hardy, Sara 223
Hare, David 208. See *A Map of the World*; *Pravda*; *Racing Demon*
Harewood, Lord 30
Harford, Alfred 98, 417
Hargreaves, John 21
Harkness, Alan 11, 83, **261**
Harland, Julia 285
Harlequin Arabian Nights 35
Harlequin Blue Beard, the Great Bashaw 378
Harlequin in Australia Felix 261, 487
Harlequin Jack Sheppard 35
Harlequin Man in the Moon 425
Harlequin Robinson Crusoe 35, 425
Harlequin Separation 425
Harlequin Shuffle, The 562
Harlequin Tu-mut-chu, Prince of Wiving-hoe 425
Harlequin Valentine and Orson 35
Harmer, Wendy 551

Harmston's Circus 141, 229, 274
Harnet, Phyllis 652
Harold in Italy 176, 230
Harp in the South 483
Harper, Ken. See *The Wonthaggi Celebration*
Harpur, Charles 262. See also *The Bushrangers*; **Stalwart the Bushranger**; *The Tragedy of Donohoe*
Harris, Augustus. See *A Million of Money*; *The Prodigal Daughter*; *A Run of Luck*; *Taken from Life*; *Youth*
Harris, Elmer. See *Johnny Belinda*
Harris, Frank 174
Harris, Joan 427
Harris, Lionel 165
Harris, Martin 21, 178, **262**
Harris, Max 173
Harris, Richard 228. See *Stepping Out*
Harris's Circus 473
Harrison, Henry Towle. See *Bulbo*
Harrison, Temple 55, 118, 392, 637. See also **The Winning Ticket**
Harrison, Wayne 262, 428, 572, 574
Harry Connor Theatrical Company 629
Harry Rickards Tivoli Theatres Ltd 268
Harry Wirth's Pacific Circus 540, 612
Hart, Francis 436
Hart, Moss. See *George Washington Slept Here*; *The Man Who Came to Dinner*; *Once in a Lifetime*; *You Can't Take it with You*
Harte, Bret. See *The Luck of Roaring Camp*
Hartley, Graham 195
Harvest 27
Harvest Theatre Company 263, 376, 515, 537
Harvesters, The 281
Harvey 53, 156, 233, 303, 491
Harvey, Allen 122, 125, 126
Harvey, Alton 519
Harvey, Anne 73. See also *I'll Be in on That*
Harvey, Benita 396
Harvey, Frank (actor) 161, **263**, 296, 309, 343, 350, 451. See also *The World Against Her*
Harvey, Frank (journalist) 174
Harvey, Frank jnr. See *The Poltergeist*
Harvie, Don 381
Harwood, Henry Richard 263, 585
Harwood, Ronald. See *The Dresser*
Harwood, Stewart, Greville and Coppin 626

Harwood, Stewart, Hennings and Coppin 264
Hasker, J. 154
Hasluck, (Sir) Paul 42, 172, 173, **264**
Hassell Pty Ltd 29, 109
Hastie, Hilda 292
Hastings, Basil Macdonald. See *The New Sin*
Hastings, Cuyler 299
Hastings, Guy 417
Hastings, Hugh 452. See **Seagulls Over Sorrento**
Hastings, Michael. See *Tom and Viv*
Hate 57, 58, 178, 309, 520
Hating Alison Ashley 337, 606, 616
Hatton, Frederick and Fanny. See *The Great Lover*
Hauptmann, Gerhart. See *Hanneles Himmelfahrt*
Havel, Václav. See *The Increased Difficulty of Concentration*; *Protest*
Hawthorne, Frank 646
Hawthorne, Ursla 179
Hawtrey, William 350
Hay, Alexander 33, 146, **264**, 393, 586
Hay, Ian. See *Tilly of Bloomsbury*
Hay, Ronnie 603
Hay Fever 158, 233, 640
Haybittel, A. S. 599
Hayes, Catherine. See *Skirmishes*
Hayes, Evie 49, 50, **52**, 67, **264**, 302, 337, 384, 435, 603
Hayes, Nancye 265, 308, 375, 385, 520, 573
Hayes and Benhamo circus 228
Haylen, Leslie 265, 457. See also *Two Minutes' Silence*
Hayman Hall 426
Haymarket Theatre (Melbourne) 161, 162, **266**
Haymarket Theatre (Sydney) 429, 603
Haynes, J. E. 117
Hayward Scott Productions 408
Haywood, Chris 21, **266**
Hazard 48, 55, 160, 448
Hazlehurst, Noni 266, 271, 339, 438, 573
He Can Swagger Sitting Down 54
Head, Shirley 539
Healey, Ken 73
Healy, Kevin 515
Healy, Richard 328
Heart for the Future 80, 359
Heart of Australia, The 491
Heart of the Midlothian 85
Heartbreak House 178, 179
Hebert, Fred 52, **266**, 385, 435
Hecht, Ben. See *The Front Page*
Hedda Gabler 16, 158, 186, 232, 234, 237, 258, 398, 490, 510, 573, 618
Height, Max 306
Heinemann Educational 468

Heir, Mrs Robert 130, 182. See also Fanny Cathcart
Heir, Robert 130, 162
Heir of the Sept, The 447
Heiress, The 367
Held by the Enemy 100, 281, 490
Helen's Babies 48, 180, 181, **267**, 626
Helleman, Christian 427
Hellenic Arts Theatre 216
Heller, George Waldo 628
Heller, Robert 336
Hellman, Lillian. See *The Children's Hour*; *The Little Foxes*; *Watch on the Rhine*
Hello and Goodbye 89
Hello, Dolly! 200, 265, 389, 435, 570
Hello Down There 166
Hello Everybody 331
Hello Mimi Entertainers 191
Hellzapoppin 652
Helmrich, Dorothy 61, 497
Help One Another 627
Helpmann, Max 267
Helpmann, (Sir) Robert 11, 28, 30, **267**, 331, 413, 415, 497, 498, 524
Helpmann, Sheila 267, 309
Hemensley, Kris 321
Hemer, Liz 124
Hemingway, Dorothy 112
Henderson, William 367. See also *Clyde Company Station*
Henkel, Cathy 528
Hennings, Fanny 441
Hennings, John 214, 245, **267**, 443, 546, 585
Hennings, John Henry 267
Henry, Robert 474
Henry IV 221, 349, 357, 363, 366, 412, 466, 480, 510, 522, 597, 635
Henry V 84, 190, 200, 502, *523*, 614
Henry VIII 347, 645
Henry and Peter and Henry and Me 291
Henry of Navarre 319
Hepburn, Katharine 28, 267, 415, 524
Hepple, Edward 178
Hepworth, John 252. See also *The Beast in View*
Her Evil Star 626
Her Imperial Majesty's Opera House 100, 268
Her Majesty's Opera House 604
Her Majesty's Theatre (Adelaide) **268**
Her Majesty's Theatre (Ballarat, Vic.) **268**, 443, 593
Her Majesty's Theatre (Brisbane) 100, 101, **268**
Her Majesty's Theatre (Melbourne) **269**, 299, 303
Her Majesty's Theatre (Sydney) **269**, **270**, 299, *300*, 301, 303, 304, 443, 502, 566, 592, 594
Her Only Mistake 381

Her Place 463
Her Soldier Boy 389
Herald (newspaper) 170
Herald and Weekly Times 304
Herbert, Andrew 229
Herbert, Bob 270, 410. See also *No Names … No Pack Drill*
Herbert, F. Hugh. See *The Moon is Blue*
Herbert, John. See *Fortune and Men's Eyes*
Herbert, Tommy 229
Herbert, Victor 383
Herbert, Wanda 396
Here Comes Kisch! 97
Here Comes the Nigger 13
Here Under Heaven 97, 453
Here We Are! 606
Herman, Henry. See *The Silver King*
Herstory 595
Hertz, Carl 336, 501, 601, 632
Hertz, Morris 429
Herweg, Kurt 363, 600
Hesford, May 117
Hesling, Bernard. See *My Life with an Interval for Aspirin*
Hetherington, Margaret 271
Hetherington, Norman 271, 469
Hewett, Dorothy 77, 128, 133, 223, **271**, 342, 422, 455, 457, 524, 621, 651. See also *Bon-Bons and Roses for Dolly*; *Catspaw*; **The Chapel Perilous**; *Christina's World*; *The Fields of Heaven*; *The Golden Oldies*; *Golden Valley*; **The Man from Mukinupin**; *Mrs Porter and the Angel*; *The Rising of Pete Marsh*; *This Old Man Comes Rolling Home*
Hewett, Robert 272. See also *Gulls*
Hewitt, Hope 174
Hewitt, Robyn 367
Hey-diddle-diddle, the Cat and the Fiddle 626
Hibberd, Jack 74, 219, **272**, 320, 497. See also **Dimboola**; *The Earth, Air, Fire and Water Show*; *A Man of Many Parts*; *Marvellous Melbourne*; *The Overcoat*; *Peggy Sue*; **A Stretch of the Imagination**; *A Toast to Melba*
Hibernian Father, The 243, **274**, 398, 447
Hick, Jacqueline 32
Hickey, Phillip 531, 615
Hicks, Charles B. 46, **274**, 370, 517
Hicks, (Sir) Seymour 111. See also *The Man in Dress Clothes*
Hicks–Sawyer Minstrels 46, 274, 370, 460, 517
Hickson, Mary 104, 183, 516
Hickson Associates 34
Higginson, Tracey 376

High Jinks 201, 237, 389
High Society 389, 442, 476
Highland, George 275, 362, 372
Highwayman, The **275**, 384, 389, 409
Hilary Linstead and Associates 34
Hildebrandt, Stanley 618
Hill, Alfred 40, **275**. See also *Tapu*
Hill, Barry. See *William Buckley and the Wathaurong Tribe*
Hill, Catherine 280
Hill, David 339
Hill, Jennifer. See *Legends*
Hill, Lex 426
Hill, Nancy 376
Hill, Patricia 396
Hill, Ross **275**, 342, 469
Hill, Samuel Prout **276**, 466
Hill, Sue 86, 421, 422, 635
Hills Family Show, The 22, 75, **276**, 580
Hilly, J. F. 464, 586
Hilton, Collins 396
Hilton, Margot. See *Potiphar's Wife*
Hilton, Tod 275
Hinder, Frank **276**, 498, 615
Hippodrome: Kalgoorlie (WA) 633; Sydney 126, 139, 567, 649
Hira, Arapeta 275
His House in Order 94, 329, 622
His Lady Friends 111
His Last Legs 106
His Little Widows 331, 389, 429
His Majesty's Moving Theatre 101
His Majesty's Theatre (Brisbane) 268
His Majesty's Theatre (Hobart) 278
His Majesty's Theatre (Melbourne) 269, 301, 384, 543, 597;
His Majesty's Theatre (Perth) 109, 238, 245, **277**, 426, 433, 437, 439, 498, 590, 592, 593
His Natural Life 148, 180, 232, 326, 449
His Royal Highness 177
Hiscock, Betty. See *Desire of Spring*
Hiscock, Dorothy 599
Hiscocks, Frank 274
History of Kodadad and His Brothers, The 160, 447
History of the Naga Tribe, The 64
HMS Pinafore 163, 244, 299, 313, 372, 375, 382, 389, 460, 489, 490, 559, 561, 643
Hoad, Brian 175, **277**
Hoban, Maie **277**
Hobart 277
Hobart Operatic Company 278
Hobart Operatic Society 584
Hobart Repertory Theatre Society 41, 146, 278, **279**, 528, 584, 647, 651

Hobson's Choice 570
Hochhuth, Rolf. See *The Representative*
Hocking, Clifford 30, **279**, 289
Hocking, Greg 203
Hocking and Woods 35
Hodge, Christian 77
Hodge, Merton. See *The Wind and the Rain*
Hodge, Thomas 511
Hodge, William 519
Hodgeman, Edwin 28, 33, 80, 254, **279**, 409
Hodge's Hotel 436
Hodgkinson, Steve 515
Hodgman, Roger **279**, 357, 376, 516, 607, 625
Hodson, Georgina 333
Hoffe, Monckton. See *The Faithful Heart*
Hoffman, Elizabeth 110
Hoffman, Monica 110
Hogan, Ernest 347
Hogarth Puppets 469
Hold Everything 389
Hold My Hand 201, 389
Hole, Quentin 154
Hole in the Roof Theatre 280
Hole in the Wall 466
Hole-in-the-Wall Theatre 184, 365
Hole-in-the-Wall Theatre Club 588
Hole-in-the-Wall Theatre Company 70, 77, 132, 215, **280**, 396, 417, 438, 439, 492, 556, 570, 581
Holland, Jane **281**, 349
Holland, Jim 408
Holland, Leslie 331
Holland, Ted 101
Holledge, Julie 29, 482, 614
Hollinworth, May 41, 43, 81, 90, **281**, 290, 366, 396, 445, 481, 528, 574, 607, 619, 651
Hollinworth, W. H. 281
Hollo, Nick 119
Hollow Crown, The 474, 510
Holloway, Beatrice 281
Holloway, Charles 197, **281**
Holloway, E. J. 296, 302
Holloway, Edmund 154, 345, 504, 518
Holloway, W. E. 281, 535
Holloway, W. J. **281**, 307, 416, 474, 535
Hollywood Theatre 605
Holman, David **282**, 307, 456. See also *Diary of a Madman*; *Drink the Mercury*
Holman, W. P. 578
'Holofernes' 170
Holt, Bland 17, 63, 66, 98, 162, 222, **282**, 283, 449, 497, 498, 503, 553, 626
Holt, Clarance 222, 282, **283**
Holt, Florence 553
Holt, Harold 159, 250
Holt, Mary 283

Holt, Tom 484
Home 103
Home (magazine) 172
Home and Beauty 156
Home Brew 401
Home Cooking Theatre Company 223
Home of the Brave 580
Home on a Pig's Back 462
Home, William Douglas (Lord) 208. See also *Lloyd George Knew My Father*; *The Reluctant Debutante*
Homecoming, The 357, 371, 574
Honest Hearts and Willing Hands 336, 564
Honey, Alfred 284
Honey, Golda 284
Honey, W. R. 284
Honey Moon Experiments 633
Honey Spot 185, 517, 655
Honeys, the 284
Honolulu Theatre for Youth 154
Hood, Marion 240
Hooke, Geoff 136, 183
Hooker, Jack 201
Hooper, Minnie 504
Hoopla Productions 91, 99, 241, 444, 468
Hope, Anthony. See *The Prisoner of Zenda*
Hope, Madge 333
Hope, Minnie 226
Hopgood, Alan 76, 80, 330. See also *The Golden Legion of Cleaning Women*
Hopkins, F. R. C. 284, 448, 467. See also **All for Gold**; *Reaping the Whirlwind*
Hopkins, Harold 151, 573
Hopkinson, Simon 183. See also *Buffaloes Can't Fly*
Hopping to Byzantium 176
Hordern, Anthony 300
Hordern, Sir Samuel 300
Hordes from the South 622
Horin, Ros 74, 195, 223, 224, 254
Horizons 350
Horler, Ken 88, 164, 407, 466, 497, 544
Horler, Lilian 544
Hormones 242
Hornby, Faye 227
Horne, Donald 70
Horne, Kenneth. See *Yes and No*
Horne, Liz 539
Hornery, Bob 202, 259
Horror of the Suburban Nature Strip, The 190
Horrortorio 389, 580
Hort, Major. See *Love à la Militaire*
Horváth, Ödön von. See *Tales from the Vienna Woods*
Hoshino, Takeshi 470, 538
Hoskins, William 150, 154, 205, **285**
Hostage, The 317, 570, 616

Hostile Witness 257, 517
Hot Centre of the World, The 463
Hot Gold 196
Hotel. See *America, Hurrah!*
Hotel, The 487, 529
Hotel Sorrento 360, 482
Hotel Universe 81
hotels 592
Hotspur 165
Houdini, Harry 47, 336, 502
Hough, George Scott 170
Houghton, Don 76
Houghton, Mary 69, 70
Hour Before My Brother Dies, The 311
House into Which We Are Born, The 11
House is Built, A 617
House that Jack Built, The 35, 70, 162, 233, 425, 447
Housewife-Superstar 289
How Could You Believe Me? 304
How Does Your Garden Grow 85, 262, 351, 352, 466
How He Lied to Her Husband 567
How the Other Half Loves 375, 631
How to Succeed in Business without Really Trying 52, 127, 389
Howard, Bert 463
Howard, Brian 411
Howard, Carolyn 595
Howard, Caz. See Carolyn Howard
Howard, Jenny 265, 270, **285**, 497, 603, 628
Howard, John 263, **285**, 573, 574
Howard, Kevin 164, 608
Howard, Leslie. See *Tell Me the Truth*
Howard, Sidney. See *They Knew What They Wanted*
Howard Serenaders 370, 371
Howarde, Kate 17, **286**, 497, 610, 651. See also *Gum Tree Gully*; **Possum Paddock**
Howarde, Lydia 70, **287**
Howe, J. B. 205
Howe, Jack 62
Howell, Edward 287
Howell, Lewis 287
Howell, Madeleine 287
How's Tricks 253
Howson, Emma 146, 287
Howson, Frank 146, **287**
Howson, Frank A. 287
Howson, Henry 287
Howson, John 146, 287
Howson, John Jerome 287
Hoyts Theatres 597
Hsu Kung-hsiao 136
Hub Theatre 149
Hubbard, Moya 124
Hudson, Thomas 338
Hudson's Bijou Theatre 338, 501
Huelin, Frank 402
Hugard, Jean 288

Hugh J. Ward Theatres Pty Ltd 239, 629
Hughan, F. W. 170
Hughes, Billy 502
Hughes, Fred 59
Hughes, Hamish 599
Hughes, Nick 263, 462. See also *Once upon Inala*
Huguenots, Les 214
Hullabaloo Productions 242
Hullo Paris 397
Human Body 259
Human Spider 392
Human Voice, The 89
Humble Pie 626
Hume, Fergus 12
Humphries, Barry 21, 83, 279, **288**, 420, 455, 497, 498. See also ***A Nice Night's Entertainment***
Hunan Puppet Theatre 241
Hunchback, The 487
Hundred Year Ambush, The 255
Hungerford, Mary 350
Hunt, Albert 455, 462. See also *The White Man's Mission*
Hunt, Christopher 30
Hunt, Hugh 72, 193, **289**, 297, 332, 393, 454, 476, 497, 568, 615
Hunt, William 124
Hunter, Governor John 131, 530
Hunter, Ian 31
Hunter, John 318
Hunter Valley Theatre Company 148, 185, **290**, 352, 396, 405, 413, 527
Hunter-Watts, Frediswyde 37, 207, **290**, 640
Huntley, G. P. 241
Hurt 241
Hurt, Maurice. See *Record of Interview*
Hussey, Frank 48, 160, **291**, 634
Hussey and Lawton's Minstrels 291, 634
Hussey and Weston's Minstrels 291
Hussey, Kelly and Holly's Minstrels 291
Hutchinson, Garrie 70, 444
Hutchinson, George **291**. See also *No Room for Dreamers*
Hutchinson, Ivan 204
Hutchinson, Mary 223. See also *Birthworks*; *Salt, Mustard, Vinegar, Pepper*
Hutchison, Neil 72
Hutton, Geoffrey 174, **291**
Hutton, Ric 104, **291**
Hwang, David Henry. See *M. Butterfly*
Hychka, Igor 216, 469, 518, 600
Hyde, Rosemary 125
Hyland, Agnes 292
Hyland, Tom 633
Hyland's Circus 62, 292, 633
Hyrons, B. 509

I

I Am Whom You Infer 224
I Do, I Do 266, 389, 435
I Don't Know What To Do With You 483
I Don't Know Who to Feel Sorry For 184, 507, 508
I Hate Hamlet 570
I Have Been Here Before 287
I Killed the Count 32, 161, 491, 639
I Love, You Love 89
I Married an Angel 49, 50, 389
I Remember Mama 198, 458
Ibsen, Henrik. See *Brand*; *A Doll's House*; *An Enemy of the People*; *Ghosts*; *Hedda Gabler*; *John Gabriel Borkman*; *The Lady from the Sea*; *Master Builder*; *Peer Gynt*; *The Wild Duck*
Ice 468
Icy Tea 562
I'd Rather be Left 403
I'd Rather Be Right 389
Ideal Husband, An 108, 154
Idinji Dancers 13
Idiot's Delight 50, 369
Idler's Dramatic Company 278
If 559, 561, 626
If I Ever Get Back Home Again I'll Stay 614
If Only We Had a Cat 606, 616
Iffland, Max. See *Paradise Regained*; *St Marys Kid*
Ignatians 137
I'll Be in on That 655
I'll Go to Australia and Wear a Hat 333
Illawarra Performing Arts Centre 433
Illustrated History of Rock 'n' Roll 614
Illustrious Stranger, The 531
I'm Not Rappaport 257
Image in the Clay 458
Imaginary Invalid, The 20, 311, 363, 415
Imaginary Life, An 128, 264
Immaculate Deceptions 482
Imperial Opera House 592
Imperial Theatres Ltd 344, 369
Importance of Being Earnest, The 94, 108, 134, 165, 200, 346, 412, 458, 514, 558, 614
Imposter, The 63, 136, 356
Impressionist Theatre 41
Imps, The 267
In Australia 512
In Beauty it is Finished 51, 104, 137, 173, 182, **292**, 452, 491
In Cahoots 482
In Duty Bound 200, 201, 368
In Mizzoura 417, 490
In Our Town 185
In Praise of Love 258
In the Field Where They Buried Peter Pan 413
In the Heart of a Woman 188

In the Mind of a Child 188
In the Next Room 481
In the Pink 242
In the Ranks 503
In the Secret Room 598
In the Soul of a Man 188
In Town 240, 383, 389
Inadmissible Evidence 83, 332, 420
Inca of Perusalem, The 633
Ince, Wesley 603
Inchcape Bell, The 38, 436
Incident at Vichy 466
Increased Difficulty of Concentration, The 656
Incredible Mind-Blowing Journey of Jack Smith, The 57
Indecent Exposure of Anthony East, The 600, 641
Independent Children's Theatre 106
Independent Players 42, 77
Independent Productions 198
Independent Repertory Theatre 27, 42, 194, 651
Independent School of Dramatic Art 228, 293
Independent Theatre 20, 24, 33, 36, 41, 43, 45, 50, 53, 67, 81, 89, 98, 104, 106, 130, 132, 193, 215, 228, 239, 240, 281, **292**, 305, 320, 321, 332, 346, 348, 407, 435, 439, 457, 459, 476, 483, 484, 506, 514, 515, 524, 567, 577, 580, 599, 607, 608, 629, 630, 631, 651
Independent Theatre Company 29, 498
Independent Theatre for Children 292
Independent Theatre Ltd 293
Independent Theatres Association 634
industrial relations 294
Industries Assistance Commission 250, 304, 563
Inescort, Irene 194, **297**
influenza epidemic 101
Informer, The 98
Inge, William. See *Bus Stop*; *Come Back Little Sheba*
Ingleton, Sue 224, 276, **297**, 613
Inman, Robert 606
Inner Voices 410, 527
Innkeeper of Abbeville, The 436
Insect Play, The 34, 335
Inside Dry Water 123, 646
Inside the Island 58, 237, 410, 527
Insignificance 165, 230, 241
Interact 123
Intercolonial Circus 138
International Association of Theatre for Children 127
International Casting Service 34
International Centre of Theatre Research 208
International Festival of Puppetry 645

International Theatre Institute 69, 73, 476
International Women Playwrights' Conference 29
Interplay international festival 655
Interval 32, 202
Intervarsity Drama Festival 225, 621
intimate revue 500
Intimate Theatre 89
Into the Woods 263, 389, 527, 574
Invisible Circus 51, 202, 480, 597
Invisible Foe, The 458
Iolanthe 107, 244, 382, 389, 489, 645
Ionesco, Eugène. See *The Chairs*; *The Lesson*
Ipswich Little Theatre 474
Iredynski, Ireneusz. See *Goodbye Judas*
Ireland, David. See *Image in the Clay*
Ireland, G. R. 170
Ireland, George 154
Ireland, Harrie 98
Irene 55, 127, 168, 304, 318, 389, 629
Irene Mitchell Award 76
Iris 61
Irish American Comedy Company 375
Irish Detective, The 490
Irish influences 297
Irish Players 298, 572
Irish Pluck 92
Irishman in London, The 327, 566, 586
Irvin, Eric 298
Irving, Dennis 433
Irving, Ellis 37
Irving, H. B. 270, 299, 643
Irving, Margery 306
Irving, S. R. 362
Is the Girl to Blame? 96
Is This Where We Came In? 398
Isaacs, Myers David. See *The Belle of Brisbane*
Isherwood, Christopher. See *The Ascent of F6*
Isidora 389, 535
Island on the Rocks 291
Island, The 13, 536
Islanders 59
Isle of Bong Bong, The 389
Isle of Swans 311
Isolated Case of Heterochromia, An 271
Italian theatre 217
Italo-Australian Theatre Company 217
It's a Chocolate World 411
It's M.A.D. 419
It's My Party (and I'll Die If I Want To) 280
It's Never Too Late to Mend 12
Ivak, Katerina 440, 606
Ivanov 417, 515

Ivanov, Vsevolod. See *The Armoured Train*
I've Come about the Assassination 305
Ixion 35, 115, 282

J

J. Albert and Sons 478
J. and N. Tait Ltd 40, 46, 191, 192, **298**, 300, 301, 340, 357, 458, 567, 571, 576
J. and N. Tait's New Repertory Company 298, 567
J. B. 580, 629
J. C. Williamson Films 597
J. C. Williamson Gilbert and Sullivan Opera Company 362, 576
J. C. Williamson Italian Opera Company 302
J. C. Williamson Ltd 299
J. C. Williamson Shakespeare Company 36, 332, 408, 420
J. C. Williamson Theatres Ltd 302
J. C. Williamson's 19, 24, 27, 28, 33, 36, 40, 48, 52, 53, 55, 61, 66, 67, 68, 90, 94, 95, 104, 106, 114, 149, 183, 185, 191, 199, 207, 217, 232, 248, 253, 265, 266, 268, 270, 275, 291, 294, 296, 298, **299**, 315, 318, 321, 326, 330, 340, 347, 348, 362, 369, 376, 377, 384, 404, 435, 437, 457, 484, 485, 497, 498, 500, 504, 507, 510, 513, 514, 517, 519, 535, 569, 576, 602, 625, 629, 643
J. C. Williamson's Tivoli Vaudeville 380
J. S. Battye Library of West Australian History 498
Jack 352, 466
Jack and the Beanstalk 559
Jack Charles is Up and Fighting 13, 347
Jack Juan 273, 389
Jack Sheppard 100, 189
Jack the Giant Killer 190, 489
Jack the Giant-Killer 501, 627
Jack the Giant-Killer and his Doughty Deeds 626
Jack the Ripper 32
Jackey Jackey 131, 447
Jackey Jackey the NSW Bushranger 131
Jackson, Enderby 501
Jackson, Glenda 510
Jackson, Lesley 321
Jacobi, Derek 510
Jacobs, John Lewis 25
Jacobs, Wizard 336
Jaeger, Walter 600
Jaffer, Melissa 231, **304**
Jagger, Peter 645
Jago, June **304**, 564

James, Brian **305**, 519
James, Christine 539
James, Des 429, 504, 614. See also *Crunchy*
James, J. B. 652
James, John Stanley 180
James, Mr 178
James, Sid 511
James, Ted 34
James Dossier, The 202, 389
Jameson, Damien 504
Jamieson, J. 511
Jamison, Sir John 204
Jammal, Mishline Yasmine 224
Janaczewska, Noelle. See *Blood Orange*
Janauschek, Francesca 213
Jane My Love 528
Jane Street Theatre 68, 146, 193, 219, 224, 291, **305**, 317, 326, 359, 367, 393, 414, 455, 476, 508, 568, 620
Janus 167
Japanese performers 144, **305**
Japanese theatre 11
Japanese Village 306
'Jaques' 397. *See also* J. E. Neild
Jarrett, Russell 588
Jarry, Alfred. See *Ubu-roi*
Jay, Phil 318
Jean 598
Jean Trundle Players 615
Jeanne d'Arc 86
Jeans, Ursula 352, 408
Jedda 13
Jeffers, Robinson. See *Medea*
Jefferson, Doris 376
Jefferson, Joseph 46, 162, **306**, 488, 553
Jeffrey Joynton-Smith Award 76
Jeffries, Maude 319, 644
Jeffries, William 79
Jellicoe, Ann 208. See also *The Knack*
Jemmy Green in Australia **306**, 447
Jenkins, Rodney 539
Jennings, Essie 243, 502
Jenyns, Essie 18, 183, 281, **307**, 490, 552, 565
Jerrold, Douglas. See *Black-Eyed Susan*
Jerry's Girls 248
Jess 535
Jesus Christ Revolution, The 386, 389
Jesus Christ Superstar 68, 126, 166, 209, 222, 368, 385, 389, 423, 480, 525, 596, 629
Jew of Dresden, The 243
Jew Süss 376
Jewell's Marionettes 469
Jewess, The 121
Jigsaw Theatre Company 122
Jillett, Neil 175
Jilt, The 93
'Jim Crow' 370
Jinker, the Grafter's Mate 491

677

Jo 553
Joan 271, 389
Joan of Arc 240
Job, William 28
Joe 468
Johannsen, Mechthild 261
John, Alan 90, **307**, 508
John Alden Company 24, 36, 43, **308**, 441, 505, 568, 623, 629
John Blake 442
John Bull 204, 364
John Edmund Theatre 470
John Fuller and Sons 237, 238
John Gabriel Borkman 298, 567, 581
John of Austria 213
John Oxley Library 497
John Tasker Memorial Award 76
Johnny Belinda 77
Johns, Marion 568
Johnson, Chris 224, 336, 337
Johnson, Eva 13, 224
Johnson, George 87, 168, 465, 582, 585, 604
Johnson, Gertrude 395
Johnson, Jack 47
Johnson, Patricia. See *Gladbags*
Johnson, Roma 80
Johnson, Terry. See *Insignificance*; *Unsuitable for Adults*
Johnson, Tim 430
Johnston, Chris 475, 651
Johnston, Frank 33
Johnston, George 519
Johnston, Kevan 435
Johnston, Philip. See *Lover's Leap*
Johnston, Roma 564
Johnston, Todd 435
Johnston, Trudy 435
Johnstone, Downs 40
Johnstone, Paul 95
Jolley, Elizabeth 315. See also *The Newspaper of Claremont Street*
Jolly Roger 389
Jolt 579
Jonah 148, 260, **308**, 389, 413
Jonah and the Whale 158
Jonah Jones 308, 317, 389, 508, 573
Jones, Avonia 46, 106
Jones, B. N. 36
Jones, Barry 159
Jones, Billy 116, 139, 143, 509
Jones, Charles 308
Jones, Dennis 116
Jones, Doris Egerton 309, 451. See also *The Flaw*; *Governor Bligh*
Jones, Emma 310
Jones, George 585
Jones, Gillian 21, 90, **309**, 326, 432
Jones, Harriet 309, 319, 516
Jones, Henry Arthur. See *The Bauble Shop*; *The Lie*; *The Silver King*

Jones, John 138, 143, 541
Jones, Leroi. See *The Dutchman*
Jones, Liz 223
Jones, Lyndal 431
Jones, Marilyn 70
Jones, Morna 429, 519
Jones, Rebecca 308
Jones, Rosemary 210
Jones, Stephen 310
Jones, Tilly 178, **310**, 650
Jones, Wilf 124
Jonson, Ben. See *The Alchemist*; *Volpone*
Josef Süss 49
Joseph, A. S. See *Thunderbolt*
Joseph and His Brethren 263, 469, 558
Joseph Conrad Goes Ashore 570
Joseph of Canaan 111, 490, 503, 546
Joske, Joan 11
Joss Adams Show, The 187
journalism 169
Journey, The 333
Journey's End 24, 27
Joyce, Arthur 417
Joyous Pageant of the Holy Nativity 395
Jubilee, A 515
Jubilee Singers 347
Judgement 411
Judgement Day 83, 600
Jugglers Three 148, 248, 357, 555, 642
juggling 310
Juke—A milk bar romance 606
Julius Caesar 19, 61, 81, 111, 130, 234, 442, 616
Julius Knight Company 623
Jumpers 240, 332
Junction Theatre Company 29, 147, 156, 166, **310**
Junior Theatre 27
Junior Theatre League 227, 599
Juniper, Robert 97
Juno and the Paycock 334, 335, 475, 618
Juno, Eloise 147
Jupiter's Casino 152
Jureidini, Khail 306
Jurisic, Melita 90, 245
Jury, Charles 28
Just … One Last Dance 272
Just Before the Honeymoon 273
Just Call Me Jo 195
Just Ruth 165
Just Walk 241
Just Write 310

K

Kaberry and Chard 604
kabuki 31
Kabul 89
Kaczmarek, Kristof 216, 459
Kaczmarek, Marta 216, 459
Kafka Dances 254

Kaguyahimet 538
Kai Tai Chan 64. See also *Dancing Demons*
Kaiser, Georg. See *From Morning to Midnight*
Kakadu 342
Kalevala 538
Kalgoorlie (WA) 590, 633
Kalinski, Tomi 320
Kalmaras, Vasso 217
Kammerspiele 43
Kangaroo Flat 117
Kani, John 13, 536
Kanin, Garson. See *Born Yesterday*
Kantor, Tadeusz. See *The Dead Class*
Kanze troupe 306
Karen 37
Karge, Manfred. See *The Conquest of the South Pole*
Karinska and Vardi 296
Karlovy-Vary Puppet Festival 96
Karnak Playhouse 137
Kaspar 215, 636
Katanning (WA) 633
Katayev, Valentin. See *Squaring the Circle*
Kate Howard Company 286
Katherine Mansfield 224
Kathner, Paul 310
Katinka 371, 389
Katja, the Dancer 114, 127, 389
Katona Joseph Theatre 31
Katz, Leon. See *The Three Cuckolds*
Kaufman, George S. See *Dinner at Eight*; *George Washington Slept Here*; *The Man Who Came to Dinner*; *Once in a Lifetime*; *You Can't Take it with You*
Kavanagh, Lily 149, 156, **310**
Kay, Charles 510
Kay, Sydney John 311, 363, 568
Kaye, Fred 241
Kean, Charles 17, 162, **205**, 297, **311**, 488, 522, 552, 564
Kean, Ellen 162, 205, 297, **311**, 488, 522, 552, 564
Keane, Robert 153
Keane of Kalgoorlie 421, 491
Kear, Shirley-Ann 155
Keating, Paul 70, 77, 251
Keays-Byrne, Hugh 510
Kedrova, Lila 395
Keefe, Barrie. See *Gimme Shelter*
Keene, Daniel 311. See also *Cho Cho San*
Keene, Laura 46, 92, **312**, 553
Keepers, The 337
Keiley, Henry 147
Kekwick, Brenda 27
Kellar, Harry 336
Kellaway, Alec 312
Kellaway, Cecil 312, 535
Kellaway, Leon 312
Kellaway, Nigel 211
Kelleher, Jacqueline 323

Keller, Bruce 74, 211, 328, *549*. See also *Monkey See, Monkey Do*; *Puppy Love*
Kellermann, Annette 98, **312**, 498
Kellermann, Frederick William 312
Kelly, Boris 123, 124
Kelly, Caroline 581. See also Carrie Tennant
Kelly, Edwin 312
Kelly, Walter C. 48, 502
Kelly, Gail 123, 126, 179, 224
Kelly and Leon Minstrels 163, 260, **312**, 370
Kelly and Leon's Opera House 313
Kelly Dance, The 507, 508, 614
Kelly Gang, The 82, 163, 361, 449, 474, 490
Kelso, Ken. See *Fleets of Fortune*
Kelton, Fay 608
Kelvin Grove College of Advanced Education 621
Kemble, Myra 313
Kemp, Jenny 220. See *Call of the Wild*; *The White Hotel*
Kemp, Lindsay 83, 209
Kemp, Robert 77
Kempinski, Tom. See *Duet for One*
Keneally, Thomas 313. See also *Bullie's House*; *Childermas*
Kenna, Peter 53, 186, 209, 298, **313**, 497. See also *The Cassidy Album*; *Furtive Love*; *A Hard God*; *The Slaughter of St Teresa's Day*; *Trespassers Will Be Prosecuted*
Kennedy, Margaret. See *The Constant Nymph*
Kennedy, Patricia 277, **314**
Kennedy, Peter 430
Kennedy, Philip 269
Kennedy, Spruhan 11
Kennerdale, Rosalind 130
Kenney, J. See *Raising the Wind*
Kenney, J. R. 325
Kenny's Coming Home 79, 304, 389, 471
Kensington, George 417
Kenyon, George 153
Kerr, Bill 59
Kerr, Deborah 315
Kerr, William 327
Kerry 299, 644
Kershaw, Robyn 86
Kesl, John 183, 410
Kessell, Norman 73, 76, 174, **315**, 497
Kesselring, Joseph. See *Arsenic and Old Lace*
Kessler, Lyle. See *Orphans*
Kester, Paul. See *Sweet Nell of Old Drury*; *When Knighthood was in Flower*
Kevin, Jeff 508
Kevin Palmer Management 34
Kickett, Colin 408

Kid Stakes 194, 297, 323, 346
Kid, The 251, 360
Kid's Convoy 410
Kidstuff 578, 645
Kiefel, Russell 90
Killer 98
Killing of Sister George, The 367
Killjoys, The 197
Kimber, Robert 183
Kimbrough, Emily. See *Our Hearts were Young and Gay*
Kimmins, Anthony. See *The Amorous Prawn*; *While Parents Sleep*
Kinchela and Ricketts 606
Kinetoscope 336
King, Achilles 465
King, Aldo 328
King, C. E. 101
King, Maggie 570
King, Mervyn 530
King, Morton 120, 121, **315**
King, Percy 285
King, Philip. See *See How They Run*
King, Philip Gidley 408
King, Tom 27
King and I, The 30, 53, 248, 317, 389, 615, 656
King Arthur 35
King Carnival 152
King Hal's Divorce 27
King Lear 96, 120, 121, 150, 165, 186, 200, 217, 241, 286, 308, 324, 336, 363, 371, 408, 412, 420, 444, 475, 513, 524, 527, 539, 608, 629, 642
King Oedipus 165, 221, 305, 332, 413
King of Coolgardie, The 183
King of Country 263
King O'Malley Theatre Company 622
King Richard 538
Kingdom of the Earth 556
King's Hall 278
King's Musketeer, The 644
King's Royal Dramatic Company 181
King's Theatre (Adelaide) 238
King's Theatre (Fremantle) **315**, 437
King's Theatre (Hobart) 278
King's Theatre (Melbourne) 55, 237, 301, **316**, 443
Kingsmill, John 515
Kingston, George 338
Kingston, Peter 77, 254, 539
Kingston, Thomas 427
Kingston Butter Factory Community Arts Centre 474
Kinsela's Cabaret Theatre 91, **316**, 595
Kiosk Theatre 542
Kippax, H. G. 68, 174, 175, 281, **316**, 497
Kipste, Egil 470
Kiraly, Eulea 124
Kirby, Jack 462

Kirk, Beverley 178
Kirk, G. 599
Kirk, Roger 308, **317**, 422
Kirke, Basil 494
Kirkpatrick, Maggie 21, **317**
Kismet musical 124, 247, 389, 489; operetta 627; play 61, 63
Kiss Me, Kate 52, 67, 247, 265, 303, 389
Kissing Time 389
Kitchen Table, The 508
Kite, The 526
Kitts, J. E. 70
Kitty Grey 241, 389
Kiwis revue company 191, 270, 302, **318**, 405
Klaer, James 310
Klag 273
Kleist, Heinrich von. See *The Broken Pitcher*; *The Prince of Homburg*
Klimek, Alf 613
Knack, The 413
Knappett, Bruce 175, 195
Knez, Bruno 29
Knight, Julius 54, 205, 214, 299, **318**, 644
Knight, Tony 393
Knoblock, Edward. See *Kismet*; *My Lady's Dress*
Knowles, Conrad 113, 120, 131, 180, 213, 309, **319**, 327, 340, 511, 516, 586, 647. See also Salathiel
Knowles, Harriet. See **Harriet Jones**
Knowles, Sheridan. See *The Hunchback*; *Virginius*; *William Tell*
Knox, Sir Robert 395
Knuckledusters—The Jewels of Edith Sitwell 627
Koca, Bogdan 216, 459
Koch, Peta 176
Kodamas' United Circus 306
Kold Komfort Kaffee 56, 85, 240
Kolle, Nellie 114, **319**, **604**
Kominos. See *Eye of the Law*
Kontakthof 31
Kookaroos 59
Kopit, Arthur. See *Oh Dad, Poor Dad, Mama's Hung You in the Closet and I'm Feeling' So Sad*
Kops, Bernard. See *The Dream of Peter Mann*
Korchman, Jean 376
Kornweibel, A. H. 516
Kosky, Barrie 22, 220
Kott, Jacqueline 73, 146, **319**, 440, 621
Kotzebue, August von. See *The Stranger*
Kovner, Leonard 216
Kowalski, Henri 148
Krantz, Dorothy 156, **320**, 376
Krantz, Harold 320
Krape, Evelyn 22, 74, 195, 216, 272, 276, **320**, 345

Krapp's Last Tape 56, 341
Krausmann, Rudi 217
Kremer, Thomas. See *The Fatal Wedding*
Kroetz, Franz Xaver. See *Request Program*; *Stallerhof*
Krofta, Josef 538
Krummel, John 320, 341
Kuckles 97
Kullark 13, 185, 509
Kullener—The Story of the Tasmanian Tiger 538
Kunoth, Ngarla 13
Kuring, Jude 164
Kursaal Theatre 41
Kurt, Bert and Jan 99
Kushner, Tony. See *Angels in America*
kyogen 64

L

L. M. Bayless Dramatic Company 274
L.S.D. 285, 448
La Boîte 44, 90, 102, 104, 595
La Boîte Theatre. See Brisbane Repertory Theatre Society
La Luna Theatre 399
La Mama Cellar Theatre 29
La Mama Company 22, 69, 74, 91, 218, 321, 538
La Mama Theatre 22, 54, 190, 218, 223, **320**, 355, 454, 595, 614
La Roche, Mary 52
La Rosiere, Mme 116, 139, 540
La Trobe Library 55, 75, 287, 356
la Varre, Marie 321
Labor Youth Theatre 401
Ladd, Pearl 114, 372
Ladies Bring a Plate 337
Ladies in Retirement 240, 247, 406, 505
Ladies' Night 405
Ladies of Fortune 223
Lady Audley's Secret 66
Lady Bracknell's Confinement 134
Lady Dolly 275
Lady in Danger 33, **321**, 452, 491
Lady of Lyons, The 92, 318
Lady of the Camellias, The 230, 415
Lady of the Rose, The 389
Lady Windermere's Fan 107, 108, 377, 494
Lady's Not for Burning, The 618
Ladysmith Black Mambazo 225
Laing, Andrew 123
Laing-Peach, Jenny 254
Lake, Tom 363
Lalla Rookh 246
Lalor of Eureka 483
Lamble, Lloyd 24, **321**, 403
Lamond, Stella 322, 527
Lamond, Toni 186, 266, **322**, 385, 497, 527

Lamshed, Max 30
Lancashire Lads 199
Lanchbery, Michael 125
Land of Gold, The 183
Land of Heart's Desire, The 32, 39
Land of Morning Calm 401
Land of Smiles, The 389
Land of the Moa, The 326, 404
Landeck, Benjamin. See *Woman and Wine*
Landlovers 60
Landray, Laurie 175, **322**
Lane, Richard 377
Lang, James 137
Lang, Matheson 149
Langdon, Harold 49
Lange, Eleonore 469
Langford, Barney 619
Langham, Michael 156, 225, 437
Langley, Vivian 462
Langridge, Lena 539
Langton, Eila 362
Lanser, Edith 469
Lanskoy, Yevgeny 440
Lap of the Gods 61, 350
Laraski, Boris 123
Larbey, Bob. See *A Month of Sundays*
Large, Diana 322
Larger than Life 408
Lark, The 198
Larra, Mary Anne 213
Larsen, Oda 406
Lascelles, Charles 70
Lashwood, Hal 24, 535
Lasseter 330, 389
Last Circus, The 211
Last, Wilfred 195, 231, 345, 613
Last Cuppa, The 352, 466
Last Day in Woolloomooloo 89
Last Drive-In On Earth, The 615
Last Laugh Theatre Restaurant and Zoo 442, 551, 588
Last of Lands, The 153
Last of the Knucklemen, The 150, 261, 357, 392, 463
Last of the Ogres, The 35
Last Wake at She-oak Creek, The 271, 389
Late Arrivals 263
Latham, David 625
Lathouris, Nicos 95, 326, 432
Latin America Live 124
Latona, Joe 59
Lauder, (Sir) Harry 298, 300, 484
Laughter in the Dark 491
Laughton, Verity 223
Launceston Players 41, 578
Laurent, Arthur. See *Home of the Brave*
Lauri, George 17, 299, **323**
Lauri, Robin 223
Laurie, John 36, 524
Lavender Bags 273
Laverne, Pattie 226, 382
Lavery, James 318
Law, Myra 124
Lawford, Ningali 224

Lawler, Ray 53, 74, 315, **323**, 356, 357, 395, 497, 564. See also *Cradle of Thunder*; **The Doll Trilogy**; *Hal's Belles*; *Kid Stakes*; *The Man Who Shot the Albatross*; *Other Times*; *The Piccadilly Bushman*; *Stars in the Home*; **Summer of the Seventeenth Doll**;
Lawman, Joe 322, 441, 525, 527
Lawrence, Ada 233
Lawrence, George 585
Lawrence, L. 539
Lawrence, Raymond 309
Lawson 231, 252, 400, 401
Lawson, John Howard 51
Lawsons, The 364
Lawton, Frank 166
Lay of Sir Orfeo, The 79
Laye, Evelyn 166
Lazar, John 25, 121, 162, 189, **323**, 340, 365, 471, 536, 586
Lazar, Rachel 323, 324
Lazar, Samuel 323, **324**, 582, 586. See also *Prince Enterprise*
Le Blanc, Bert 48, 226
Le Brun, Bobby **324**, 405, 474, 497
Le Brun, Grace 497
Le Brun Brothers 324
Le Joke 442, 588
Le Roy, Talma and Bosco 127, 336
Le Tessier, Anita **325**, 651
Leader (newspaper) 170
Leading Lady 607
Leamar, Alice 240
Learner, Tobsha 223
Lease of Life, A 532
Leask, Margaret 655
Leave It to Jane 50, 389
Lecocq, Charles 214
Lee, Alan David 308
Lee, Baayork 386
Lee, Clara 325
Lee, Donna 186
Lee, J. Clarence. See *Out on the Castlereagh*
Lee, J. H. S. 113, **325**, 370, 477
Lee, Jennie 342, 553, 643, 645
Lee, Margo **325**, 420, 440
Lee, Robert E. See *The Night Thoreau Spent In Jail*
Lee, Will 252
Lee Gee 135
Lee Joo For, John. See *The Propitious Kidnapping of a Pampered Daughter*
Lee Murray Radio Players 321
Lees, Allan 409
Lees, Frederic 365, 395
Leete, Jack 501, 601
Left Book Club Theatre Group 400, 401
Legend of King O'Malley, The 68, 76, 84, 91, 184, 193, 202, 229, 305, **326**, 385, 389, 410, 432, 455, 492, 544, 569
Legend of the Losers 557

Legends 265, 507, 508
Legouvé, Ernest. See *Adrienne Lecouvreur*
Legs on the Wall 241, 570
Leigh, Euston. See **The Duchess of Coolgardie**
Leigh, Mike 209. See also *Greek Tragedy*
Leigh, Vivien 43, 207, 363, 414, 415, 491, 584, 621
Leighton, Harold 402
Leitch, George 18, 214, **326**. See also *His Natural Life*; *The Land of the Moa*
Leith, Susan 376
Lemon, Andrea 223, 224. See also *The Serpent's Fall*; *Walking on Sticks*
Lennie Lower 190, 373
Lennigan, John 59
Lennon, Jack P. 417
Lennon, Hyman and Lennon 238
Lenton and Smith's Great Dragon Japanese Troupe 305
Leon, Francis 312
Leon and Cushman Minstrels 313
Leonard, Doug 32
Leonardo Group 276
Leong Chan-Kwong 135
Leopold, George 70
Lerner, Tobsha. See *Mistress*; *Witch Play*
Les Darcy Show, The 273
Leslie, Fred 240, **326**, 498
Leslie Brothers 327
Leslie, Michael 97
Lesson, The 420
Lesson from Aloes, A 536
Lesson in English, A 411, 412
Lesson in Love, A 147
Leston, Harry 232
L'Estrange, Harry 509
Let Us Be Gay 24
Let's Be Offensive 252, 400, 403
Let's Face It! 50, 389
Letter, The 622
Levey, Barnett 38, 158, 262, 319, **327**, 335, 340, 382, 487, 522, 531, 566, 585, 589, 652. See also *The Stage-Struck Tailor and the Trickish Youth*
Levey, Sarah 327, 586
Levin, Ira. See *Deathtrap*
Levine Comedy, The 201
Levings, Nigel 328
Levis, Robert 73, 396
Levity's Royal Marionettes 468
Levy, Benn W. See *Clutterbuck*; *The Rape of the Belt*
Levy, Jerome 231, 363, 403
Lewis, Alan and Kay 469, 470
Lewis, Eva. See *Ficky Stingers*
Lewis, George 35, 87, 465
Lewis, Jamieson 614
Lewis, Monk. See *Raymond and Agnes*
Lewis, Mrs G. B. W. 19, 626

Lewis, Robert 573
Lewis, Rose 147
Lewis's Georgia Jubilee Singers 274
Liaisons dangereuses, Les 240, 258, 317, 512, 551, 656
Liars, The 623
Liberty Hall 329
Licensed Victuallers' Gazette (newspaper) 170
licensing of plays 446
Lie, The 406, 459
Lie of the Mind, A 526
Life and Adventures of Nicholas Nickleby, The 110, 165, 208, 217, 221, 240, 286, 389, 511, 551, 573, 580, 636
Life and Death of Captain Cook, The 180
Life and the Idiot 607
Life for Life 404
Life in Australia 441
Life in Sydney 131, **328**, 446
Life is a Dream 356
Life of Galileo, The 98
Life of the Party, The 346
Lifeguardsman, The 319
Light is Dark Enough, The 315
Lighthouse Company 58, 90, 178, 304, 410, 520, 526, 555, 638. See also **State Theatre**
lighting 139, 448, 545, 589, 605
lighting design 328
Lights of London, The 59, 206, 645
Lilac Domino, The 389
Lilac Time 99, 296, 389
Lilies of the Field, The 32
Liliom 366
Lillian 145
Limelighters, The 458
Limit, The 286
Limited Life Shakespeare Company 258
Lincoln, W. J. 112. See also **The Bush King**
Lind, Letty 240
Linden, George 158
Linden, Vene 92, 158
Lindesay, Vane 329
Lindsay, Howard. See *The Great Sebastians*
Lingard, Horace 626
Lingwood, Tom 498
Linstead, Hilary 34
Lion and the Mouse, The 319
Lion in Winter, The 320
Lion Tamer, The 196
Lipscombe Hannam, 'Tookie' 112
Liquid Amber 273
Liquor Act (NSW) 590
Listen Closely 314
Listener In—TV (magazine) 174
Little, Mark 551
Little, W. 427
Little Bit of Fluff, A 275
Little Breadwinner, The 281
Little Fella Bindi 342, 469, 518
Little Foxes, The 50, 228

Little Lady Steps Out, The 79
Little Lord Fauntleroy 474, 489
Little Malcolm and His Struggle Against the Eunuchs 260, 280
Little Me 389
Little Michus, The 326, 389
Little Minister, The 270, 501
Little Miss Muffet 393
Little Murders 332
Little Nellie Kelly 389
Little Night Music, A 228, 263, 270, 389, 435, 514, 574, 631
Little Patch Company 429
Little Red Riding Hood 567
Little Redinka 284
Little Round House, The 34
Little Sheep Run Fast, The 202
Little Theatre (Adelaide) 27, 28
Little Theatre (Melbourne) 542
Little Theatre (Sydney company) 40, 112, **329**, 511, 594
Little Theatre Guild 457
Little Theatre Laboratory of Dramatic Art 42, 481, 542
little theatre movement 40
Little Tich 502, 601
Little Women 27
Littlemore, David 571
Littlest Theatre 406, 469
Live-Could-Possibly-Be-True-One-Day Adventures 56
Livermore, Reg 83, 87, **329**, 440, 555. See also **The Betty Blokk Buster Follies**; *Ned Kelly*; *Reg's Show*
Livesey, Roger 352, 408
Living Newspaper 51, 188
Living Room 588
Living Rooms 595
Livingstone, Minnie 98
Llewellyn, John 564
Llewellyn-Jones, Tony 599
Lloyd, Frank 396
Lloyd, Marie 26, 502, 601
Lloyd, Sue 326
Lloyd, Tim 176
Lloyd George Knew My Father 291, 332
Lloyd Webber, (Sir) Andrew 208, 596
Lock Up Your Daughters 200, 389, 471
Locke, Edward J. See *The Climax*
Lockwood, Johnny 330
Lockwood, Rupert. See *No Conscription*
Loco 156
Loft, The 544
Logan City Story, The 155, 166, 474, 562
Lohengrin in a Nutshell 626
Lola Montez 72, 230, **330**, 384, 389, 454
London after Dark 114
London Assurance 605
London Comedy Company 17, 205, 214, 247, **330**, 333

London Gaiety Burlesque Company 240, 644
London Gaiety Company 26, 424
London Pavilion Theatre Company 238
London Theatre Group 83
Lone Hand (magazine) 171
Lone Woman, A 60
Lonely without You 346
Long, Hilary 649
Long, Joan 73
Long, Sumner Arthur. See *Never Too Late*
Long Day's Journey into Night 27, 158, 200, 227, 257, 342, 527, 573, 616, 629, 656
Long Long Time Ago 432
Long Tack Sam 602
Long View, A 227
Long Way Home, A 445
Lonie, John. See *Kullener—The Story of the Tasmanian Tiger*; *Wanted—Dead or Alive*
Lonnen, E. J. 240
Lonsdale, Frederick. See *Aren't We All*; *On Approval*; *The Fake*
Look Back in Anger 82, 208, 427
Looking Through a Glass Onion 630
Lookout Theatre 216
Lopian, David 44, 437, 494
Lord, Pauline 49
Lord, Robert. See *Bert and Maisie*
Lord of the Manor, The 146
Loreda 115
Lorgnette (magazine) 171, 495
Lorna Forbes Repertory Players 233, 296
Los Trios Ringbarkus 203, 442
Lost Generation, The 480
Lost in Yonkers 254, 317
Lost Weekend 63, 508
Lotus Flower, The 506
Louis XI 299
Louise, Mme 178, 310, 652
Love, Herbert 197
Love, Minnie 331, 377
Love, Robert 606. See also *Outpost*
Love à la Militaire 38, 436
Love and the Single Teenager 254
Love from a Stranger 56, 128
Love Letters 318
Love of Four Colonels, The 165, 281, 435
Love on the Dole 403
Lovejoy, Robin 53, 178, 193, 230, 239, 305, **331**, 393, 413, 415, 418, 497, 531, 568, 580, 615, 641
Lovell, G. W. See *The Wife's Secret*
Lovell, Nigel 481, 639
Lovelock, Jeremy 328
Lovely, Louise 128
Lover's Leap 366
Love's Awakening 389
Love's Labour's Lost 264, 420, 630

Love's Silver Dream 626
Lovett, Barry 332, 381, 622
Lowdown 127
Lowe, Stephen. See *Tibetan Inroads*
Lower, Norene 306
Lower Depths, The 85, 198, 221, 318, 332, 344, 500, 515, 575
Loyal, George 542
Loyalties 109, 350, 357, 599
Lu Guang Rong 232
Lu Yi 136
Lucas, Betty 332, 440
Lucid Interval, The 188
Lucifer's Athletic and Specialty Company 633
Luck of Roaring Camp, The 474
Luck of the Navy, The 343
Luckham, Claire. See *Trafford Tanzi*
Lucky Streak, The 262
Luhrmann, Baz 194
Lukashima troupe 306
Luke, Peter. See *Hadrian the Seventh*
Lulu 186, 328, 573, 651
Lumer, Rodney 74
Lupino, Barry 296, 298
LuPone, Patti 386
Luscombe, Edna 199
Luton, Lew 73, 418, 599
Luxor Theatre 605
Lyall, Dorothy 437
Lyceum Hall 584
Lyceum Theatre (Launceston) 510, 584
Lyceum Theatre (Sydney) 294, 566, 592
Lye, Reginald 418
Lying Valet, The 204
Lynch, Cathrine 656
Lynch, David 77
Lynch, John 170
Lynch, Michael 70
Lyndon, Barré. See *The Amazing Dr Clitterhouse*
Lyndon-Gee, Christopher 124
Lyne, Allen 462
Lynn, Fred 179
Lynton, Mayne 309, **332**, 558
Lyon, Nicolas 95
Lyons Mail, The 299
Lyric Theatre: Brisbane 102, 472; Melbourne 238
Lysistrata 304
Lyssiotis, Tes 216, 224, **333**, 456. See also *The Forty Lounge Cafe*; *A White Sports Coat*; *Zac's Place*
Lyster, W. S. 333, 353, 379, 464, 489, 566, 605
Lytton, Philip 19, 65, 101, 181, **333**, 473
Lytton's Moving Theatre 473

M

M and L Casting 34
M. Butterfly 368
MacArthur, Charles. See *The Front Page*
Macarthur, Joan 83, 634
Macartney, Keith 69, **334**, 344, 453, 600, 619
Macbeth 31, 36, 80, 84, 150, 207, 237, 241, 301, 306, 310, 317, 332, 334, 344, 363, 421, 432, 487, 491, 524, 527, 580, 645
Macbird 32
MacCallum, Mungo. See *Misrepresentations*
MacColum, Joe 393, 475
MacCunn, Andrew 90, **334**
Macdonald, Donald 334. See also *Caravan*
MacDonald, Fred 17, 78, **334**, 417, 450, 462, 513
Macdonald, Graham 475
MacDonald, Ian 556
Macdonald, Robert David. See *Chinchilla*
MacDougall, Duncan 40, 50, **334**, 394, 498
MacFarlane, Gay 386
Macfarlane, Tim 30
MacGregor, Royston 59
Machiavelli, Machiavelli 165, 373, 622
Mackay, Allan. See *Cain's Head*
Mackay, Angus 169, 335
Mackay, Cyril 245
Mackay, Frances 55, **335**
Mackay, George 143
Mackay, Kenneth. See *To the West*
Mackay, Mary 531
Mackay, Tim 126
MacKellar, John. See *The Runaway Steamboat*
Mackellar, John. See *Crackers*
MacKenzie, Phillip 123
Mackie, Georgina 418
Mackintosh, Cameron 23, 30, 208, 465, 511
Macky, Stewart 442. See also *John Blake*; *The Trap*
MacLeish, Archibald 51. See also *J. B.*
MacLeish, Charles 335
MacMahon, James 335, 405, 474
MacMahon, Joseph 335
MacMahon Brothers 335
MacMillan, Nance. See *Christmas Bridge*; *Land of Morning Calm*
Maconochie, Alexander 409
Macpherson, Ken 60
Macquarie 71, 118, 221, 257
Macquarie Auditorium 444
Macquarie Radio Theatre 227
Macquarie University 621
Macunaima 31
Mad, Bad and Dangerous to Know 89

Mad Jean 538
Mad Scene, The 622
Madame Bovary 506
Madame Butterfly 299
Madame Favart 226, 389
Madame Mao 478
Made in Argentina 124
Madeline Clifton 284
Madman and the Nun, The 459
Madonna and Child 527
Madonna emigrante, La 195
Maeterlinck, Maurice. See *The Blue Bird*
Mag and Bag 190
Magdalen. See also *Foiled*
Magic Pudding, The 83, 96, 342, 469, 518
magic shows 336
Magistrate, The 112, 413
Magnetic North 255
Magpie Theatre Company 29, 127, 224, **336**, 356, 513, 537, 556, 597, 655
Maguire, Fenella 564
Maguire, Gerard 151, 338
Mahabarata 31, 208
Mahoney, Beverley. See *Flight Path*
Mahoney, Will 49, 50, 186, 264, **337**, 603
Mahy, Margaret. See *The Man Whose Mother was a Pirate*
Maid of the Mountains, The 60, 136, 371, 372, 383, 389, 415
Maids, The 264
Mainstage 279
Mainstreet Theatre Company 166, **337**, 537
Mainwaring, Karin 223. See also *The Rain Dancers*
Maione, Osvaldo 217
Majeroni, Eduardo 87, 213, **337**, 489, 503, 646
Majeroni, Giorgio 337
Majeroni, Giulia 213, **337**, 489, 503
Majeroni, Mario 337
Majestic Theatre (Adelaide) 25, 238, **338**, 637
Majestic Theatre (Kalgoorlie, WA) 633
Majestic Theatre (Sydney) 72, 201, 238, 590, 591, 637
Major, Bessie 107
Major, Bradshaw 37
Major Barbara 32, 551
Makassar Reef 118, 119, 248, **338**, 346, 397
Makeshifts 572
Making of the Documentary D'Arcy Conran, The 248
Malade imaginaire, Le 420
Malarky Barks 273
Malavolti 56
Malcom's Royal Australian Circus 62
Malden, Joan 135
Malini, Max 336
Malleo Man of Salt 124

681

Malleson, Miles. See *The Fanatics*
Maloney, Billy 339
Malouf, David. See *An Imaginary Life*
Maltz, Albert. See *Rehearsal*
MAM 35
Mame 124, 248, 389
Mameena 61
Mamet, David. See *Glengarry Glen Ross*; *Speed the Plow*
Mamouney, Don 123, **339**, 530
Man and Superman 329, 357, 616
Man and Wife 183
Man for All Seasons, A 27, 310
Man Friday 606
Man From Chicago, The 507
Man From Mukinupin, The 227, 233, 237, 257, 260, 266, 271, 328, **339**, 360, 389, 395, *438*, 573, 587
Man from Outback, The 55, 78, 197, 450, 482
Man From the Bush, The 196
Man from Toronto, The 122
Man in Dress Clothes, The 111, 397
Man is Man 98
Man Must Live, A 198
Man of Destiny, The 32, 39
Man of La Mancha 221, 304, 389
Man of Many Parts, A 273, 417
Man of Respect, A 271
Man of Sorrows 386, 390
Man on the Box, The 329
Man, The 210, 217
Man They Could Not Hang, The 333
Man to Man 316
Man Upstairs, The 248
Man Who Came to Dinner, The 50, 166, 284, 639
Man Who Married a Dumb Wife, The 357
Man Who Shot the Albatross, The 323, 349, 358, 466, 512
Man Whose Mother was a Pirate, The 429
Man with a Load of Mischief, The 56
management 339
Mandel, Frank. See *His Lady Friends*
Manderson, Roland 126
Mandrake 390
Manila Yellow 37
Manly Ferry 103
Manners, J. Hartley. See *Peg o' My Heart*
Manning, Barbara 516, 654
Manning, Bernard 244
Manning Clark's History of Australia 390, 505, 508
Mannix, Jack 422
Manolis, Michael 97
Manson, Diana 422
Mantell's Marionettes 469
Manton, Guy 396
Manual of Trench Warfare, A 230, 237, 248

Manxman, The 644
Many Happy Returns 243, 285, 373, 429
Maoris 404
Map of the World, A 208, 573
Maraini, Dacia 216. See also *Dialogue Between a Prostitute and Her Client*; *Don Juan*; *Mary Stuart*
Marcin, Max. See *Eyes of Youth*
Marcus 284
Marcus, Frank. See *The Killing of Sister George*
Marcus, Royston 32
Marcus Show 49
Margaret of the Red Cross 96
Marginal Farm, The 119, 397
Marian Street Children's Theatre 342
Marian Street Drama School 342
Marian Street Theatre 341, 378
Marian Street Theatre Company 208, 222, 224, 227, 230, 258, 304, 318, 332, 334, **341**, 376, 458, 527, 551, 569, 570, 572
Marien Dreyer's World 458
Marin la Meslée, Edmond 100
Marina and Ulay 431
Mariner 193
Marini, Yvonne 195, 345
Mario Lanza Story, The 284
Marionette Theatre of Australia 69, 72, 96, 121, 128, 271, **342**, 469, 498, 518
Maritana 561
Marivaux, Pierre. See *The Game of Love and Chance*
Mark Twain 588
Marks, Alfred 185, 517
Marks, Naomi 57
Marli Biyol Company 30, 408
Marlow, George 36, 237, 238, **342**, 606, 640
Marlow, May 238
Marlow–Rolls Theatres Ltd 270
Marlowe, Christopher. See *The Tragical History of Doctor Faustus*
Marlowe, Mary 343, 417, 498
Marmondelle the Moor 534
Marriage of Figaro, The 221, 421
Marriage, The 459, 515
Marriner, David 465
Marriner, Elaine 465
Marsh, Berys 164
Marsh, (Dame) Ngaio 404
Marsh, Vic 110
Marsh King's Daughter, The 165, 432
Marshall, Fred 331, 626
Marshall, Jean 28, 32, **344**, 418, 586, 651. See also *Little Women*
Marshall, Mrs Harry 606
Marshall-Stoneking, Billie. See *Sixteen Words for Water*
Marsupials 412
Martello Towers 119, 237

Martin, David N. 104, **344**, 369, 486, 567, 604
Martin, E. C. See *Ostracised*
Martin, Faith 34
Martin, Florence 344
Martin, Helen 342
Martin, J. H. 504
Martin, Jane 330
Martin, Kathleen 344
Martin, Lloyd **344**, 604
Martin, May. *See* **May Wirth**
Martin, Zac 13, 119
Martin and Shanahan 34
Martin Artists 34
Martine 11
Martinettis, the 16
Marvellous Melbourne by Alfred Dampier and J. H. Wrangham 180, **345**, 361
Marvellous Melbourne by Jack Hibberd and John Romeril 74, 184, 273, **345**, 492, 507, 580
Marx 89, 221, 230
Marx, Chico 604
Marx of Time 252
Mary 223, 390, 482, 595
Mary Latimer—Nun 606
Mary Queen of Scots 27
Mary Rose 543
Mary Shelley and the Monsters 505
Mary Stuart 216
Mary's Own Paper (newspaper) 173
Mascot, The 390
Mascotte, La 559
Masefield, John. See *The Coming of Christ*
Mask and the Face, The 634
Maskelyne and Devant 336
Mason, George B. 100, 473, 583
Mason-Cox, David. See *Paradise Regained*; *St Marys Kid*
Mason–Miller Theatre Company 412, 417
Masonic Hall 278
Mason's Concert Hall 100, 583
Masque (magazine) 175, 496
Masses and Man 335
Massinger, Philip. See *A New Way to Pay Old Debts*
Master Builder 86, 198, 260, 328, 551
Master Class 129, 135, 228, 416
'*Master Harold' … and the Boys* 165, 536
Masterman, Kay 69
Masters, Edgar Lee. See *Spoon River*
Mastodon Minstrel Party 313
Mastrantone, Lucia 195
Matarese, Raffaele 216
Mates 314
Matesek, Petr 538
Mather, Dibbs 408
Matheson, Alan 127
Mathew, Ray 345. See also *A Spring Song*; *We Find the Bunyip*

Mathews, Charles 17, 205, **346**, 552
Mathews family circus 141
Mathieson, Graeme 519
Mathy, Marianne 105
Matilda Awards 77
Matilda Mine 390, 579
Mating of Ulrich Dooley, The 440, 586
Matsa, Queen of Fire 426
Matthews, Bernie. See *The Other Side is Greener*
Matthews, Jessie 167, 408
Maugham, Somerset 81. See also *The Circle*; *The Constant Wife*; *Home and Beauty*; *The Letter*
Maughan, Monica 330, 338, **346**
Maver, Neil 604
Mawer, Allan 508
Maxwell, Ian 396
Maxwell, Max 98
Maxwell, Miles 483
Maxwell, Rene 153
May, Dave 613
May, Frederick 215
Mayakovsky, Vladimir. See *Vladimir Mayakovsky, a Tragedy*
Mayazel. *See* **May Wirth**
Mayfair Theatre 239
Maytime 390
Maywald, Elizabeth 285
Maza, Bob 119, **347**. See also *Mereki*
Maza, Lisa 119
Maza, Rachel 347
McAdoo, Orpheus 47, **347**
McCackie Moments 485
McCallin, Clement 393
McCallin, Tanya 89
McCallum, Charles 396
McCallum, Joanna 347
McCallum, John 52, 59, 167, 303, **347**
McCallum, John N. 167
McCarten, Anthony. See *Ladies' Night*
McCaughey, James 22, 273, 367, 444
McClements, Susan 379
McCluskey, Bill 60, 408
McColl, Colin 280
McCombie, Thomas. See *Jackey Jackey*
McConnell, Betty 407
McCrae, Hugh 348. See also *The Ship of Heaven*
McCreery, Stuart 90
McCutcheon, Sandy. See *Dance in the Ashes*; *The Truce*
McDonagh, Donagh 42
McDonald, Donald 72, 573
McDonald, Garry 348, 497, 508, 573
McDonald, Helen 376. *See also* Helen Neeme
McDonald, Ian 442
McDonald, Meme (Jan) 223, 631

682

McDonald, Robert. See *Chinchilla*
McFadden, Allan 271
McFarlane, John 304
McFarlane, Joyce 123
McGee, Greg. See also *Foreskin's Lament*
McGillick, Paul 175
McGillivray, Joan 598
McGlone, Carmel 308
McGowan, G. 158
McGowan, Lachlan 626
McGrath, Amy 73, 497
McGrath, Frank 73
McGrath, John 73, 208
McGrath, Kevin 134
McGregor, Brent 216, 290, 562
McGregor, Jennifer 622
McGregor, Mary 376
McGregor, Ross 125, 290
McGuire, Betty 265
McHenry, Judy 613
McHilton, Louis 462
McIlwraith, Bill. See *The Anniversary*
McIntosh, Hugh D. 48, 61, 268, **348**, 370, 461, 484, 489, 502, 601, 604, 605, 637
McIntosh, Madge 149
McIntyre, Margaret Edgeworth 578
McIntyre, Shane 196
McKay, Adam 172
McKay, Claude 334, **349**, 560
McKellar, John 83, 316, 420, 440
McKenzie, Alick 481
McKenzie, George 539
McKenzie, (Sir) John 301 404, 576
McKenzie, Sally *102*
McKenzie, Sandra 304
McKern, Abigail 349
McKern, Harriet 349
McKern, Leo 281, 323, **349**, 396, 453, 510
McKinnel, Norman 622
McKinnon, Cath 224. See also *Immaculate Deceptions*
McLachlan, J. R. See *Arabin*; *Jackey Jackey*
McLaren, Mike 263
McLaughlin, Eugene 33
McLaughlin, Michael 528
McLeay report 250
McLeish, George 268
McLeod, Marjorie 349. See *Within These Walls*
McMahon, Gregan 19, 40, *41*, 50, 66, 108, 109, 110, 112, 192, 228, 248, 253, 296, 298, 319, 340, **350**, 354, 356, 375, 377, 451, 458, 567, 571, 599
McMahon, (Sir) William 160
McManus, Mark 306
McMaster, Anew 19, **351**, 372
McMenamin, Mary 337
McMillan, Hec 124

McMillan, Nance 402. See also *Christmas Bridge*; *Land of Morning Calm*; *The Painter*
McMinn, Tom 617
McMullen, Jim 124
McNae, Jenny 280
McNamara, Kate. See *In the Secret Room*
McNamara, Shane 408
McNeil, Jim 119, 209, **351**, 398, 455, 497. See also *The Chocolate Frog*; *How Does Your Garden Grow*; *Jack*; *The Last Cuppa*
McNeill, Anne 476
McNiven, Donald 153
McPhee, Hilary 70
McQuade, Cecily 270, 299, 644
McTernan, John 622
McVicker, Norman 43, 458. See also *Banjo*; *Damper and Tea*; *The Limelighters*
McVilly, Fiona 124. See also *Spanner in the Works*
Me and Me Mum and Dad 579
Me and My Girl 390, 525
Meadows, Garry 395
Mearing, Christine 135
Measure for Measure 36, 166, 258, 267, 286, 363, 441, 524
Meat 614
Mechanics' Institute (Hobart) 278; Launceston (Tas.) 584
Medea 31, 36, 46, 54, 72, 120, 207, 290, 315, 332, 344, 359, 491, 624
Media, Entertainment and Arts Alliance 23
Medlin, Brian 28
Medlin, Harry 28, 33
Meehan, John 386
Meekatharra 509
Meering, Chris 224
Meet Mr Brutus 105
Meg and the Castaway 375
Meikle, Richard 481
Meilhac, Henri. See *Frou Frou*
Meillon, John 308, **352**, 516
Melba, (Dame) Nellie 99, 357, 372
Melba–Williamson Opera Company 201, 299, 301
Melbourne 353
Melbourne Comedy Festival 297
Melbourne Concert Hall 624
Melbourne Fringe Festival 223
Melbourne International Comedy Festival 442
Melbourne International Festival of the Arts 226, **356**, 636
Melbourne Italian Arts Festival 217
Melbourne Little Theatre 20, 42, 43, 50, 67, 90, 116, 198, 221, 354, 371, 411, 453, 481, 498, 542, 543. See also **St Martin's Theatre Company**
Melbourne Mechanics' Institute and Hall of Arts 64

Melbourne Repertory Theatre 233, **356**, 498
Melbourne Repertory Theatre Company 40, 109, 150, 192, 350, 354, **356**, 375, 572, 624
Melbourne Spoleto Festival 87, 217, 226
Melbourne State College 22
Melbourne Theatre Company 22, 45, 64, 68, 69, 74, 79, 80, 82, 89, 91, 98, 106, 118, 128, 129, 135, 151, 154, 158, 165, 178, 186, 190, 193, 194, 198, 200, 215, 216, 231, 236, 241, 248, 255, 256, 257, 258, 261, 279, 284, 285, 310, 315, 323, 332, 338, 346, 354, **357**, 363, 365, 367, 368, 392, 412, 413, 441, 463, 466, 480, 492, 505, 508, 514, 520, 526, 527, 538, 544, 551, 565, 570, 599, 607, 614, 620, 624, 655. See also Union Theatre Repertory Company
Melbourne University Dramatic Club 20
Melbourne Workers' Theatre 94, 156, 223, **359**, 508
Melbourne Writers' Theatre 74, 273, 374
Melbourne Youth Theatre 22
Melbourne's Mystery Murder 580
Meldrum, Max 258, 341
Meldrum, Rob 231, 276
Melfi, Leonard. See *Bird Bath*
Mellen, James 97
Mellor, Aubrey 102, 105, 193, 217, **359**, 393, 407, 444, 475
melodrama 360, 451, 461, 490
Melrose Theatre 238
Melville, Alan. See *Dear Charles; Simon and Laura*
Melville, Emily 382
Melville, Frank 361
Melville, Frederick. See *The Bad Girl of the Family*
Melville, Henry. See *The Bushrangers*
Melville, James 361
Melville, Josie 362
Melville, Neil 549
Melville, Walter. See *The Worst Woman in London*
Memo 655
Memoirs of a Carlton Bohemian 273
Memory Room, The 211, 369
Men Without Wives 196, **362**, 452, 494
Menmuir, Raymond 418, 615
Menotti, Giancarlo 226, 356
Menzies, Archie 452
Menzies, Ivan 244, 301, **362**, 384
Menzies, Robert 363
Menzies, (Sir) Robert 159, 256
Menzies Hotel theatre–restaurant 247, 588
Merce Cunningham Dance Company 431

Mercenary Mary 390
Mercer, David. See *Cousin Vladimir*
Merchant of Venice, The 16, 17, 27, 36, 61, 63, 85, 93, 112, 153, 258, 315, 324, 376, 416, 420, 435, 441, 579
Mercury Mobile Players 311, 363, 415
Mercury Theatre 20, 42, 81, 89, 165, 226, 311, **363**, 441, 527, 568
Mercury Theatre School 20
Meredith, Gwen 364, 479. See also *Shout at the Thunder*
Meredith, John 57, 81, 85, 121, 146, 278, 335, **364**, 522, 583
Meredith, Louisa Anne 278
Meredith, Peter 306
Meredith, Richard 379
Mereki 13
Mereton, Mrs 278
Meriamie Company 13
Merlin, Henry Beaufoy 365, 377, 405, 468
Merlyn Theatre 177
Mermaid Players 357
Merrie England 390, 646
Merriman, G. 126
Merritt, Daisy 114
Merritt, Paul. See *The New Babylon*; *Youth*
Merritt, Robert J. 119, 497. See also **The Cake Man**
Merry Widow, The 105, 374, 390, 415, 430
Merry Wives of Windsor, The 36, 291
Merry-Go-Round 420
Merton, Julia 518
Mervale, Gaston 149, 427
Mervin, Fred 226, 382
Mesh 655
Mesh, Frank 588
MESH Youth Theatre 634
Mess Hall Players 466
Message from Mars, A 350, 489
Messel, Oliver 518
Messenger, Barbara 587
Messenger, The 188
Messenger Boy, The 326, 390
Metaphysics of the Two-Headed Calf, The 459
Metcalfe, Edgar 193, 280, **365**, 395. See also *Alleycat Alice and Friends*
Metro Theatre: Melbourne 422; Sydney 369
Metropolitan Artists 233
Metropolitan Merry-Go-Round 440
Metropolitan Players 366
Metropolitan Theatre 43, 90, 281, 317, 331, 352, **366**, 377, 651
Metz, Phillipa 57
Mews Playhouse 455
Meyerbeer, Giacomo 214
Meynell, Clyde 148, 298, 299, 644
Meynell and Gunn 149, 490

Mezger, John 57
Mice and Men 279
Michael, Brooke 408
Michael and Mary 228, 293
Michael Edgley International Pty Ltd 199
Michael Howe, the Terror of Van Diemen's Land 361
Michael Strogoff 284
Michell, Helena 366
Michell, Keith 27, 105, 129, **366**, 497, 510
Michinton, Mark 613
Mickey's Moomba 507
Mico, Domenic 122, 123, 124, 598
Middar 13
Middle Age Spread 404, 405
Middle Stages 90
Middleton, Thomas. See *The Changeling*
Middy Ashore, The 512
Midnight Frolics 27, 199
Midnite 509
Midsumma Festival 242
Midsummer Night's Dream, A 33, 36, 200, 203, 247, 258, 264, 280, 304, 334, 344, 352, 408, 417, 420, 476, 490, 510, 555, 579
Mignon, Jean-Pierre 22, 74, 216, 515, 556
Mikado, The 244, *303*, *383*, 390, 489, 623, 645
Miles, Kevin 396, 519
Milestones 252, 319
Milgate, Adam 367
Milgate, Rodney 367, 497, 531, 615. See also *A Refined Look at Existence*
Mill Theatre Company 22, 223, **367**, 482
Milland, Ray 257, 517
Millar, Maggie 367
Miller, Arthur. See *After the Fall*; *All My Sons*; *The Crucible*; *Death of a Salesman*; *Incident at Vichy*; *The Price*; *A View from the Bridge*
Miller, Dennis 110
Miller, George 380, 409, 497, 587
Miller, Harry M. 35, 53, 68, 126, 230, 265, **368**, 369, 385, 404, 444, 497, 526, 569, 577
Miller, Lorna 380, 587
Miller and His Men, The 38, 327, 436, 566, 581, 586
Millhouse, Carmel 519, 555
Milligan, Patrick 422
Million of Money, A 283
Millionairess, The 253
Milliss, David 403
Mills, Frank 245
Mills, Hayley 248
Mills Brothers 50, 603
Milne, A. A. See *The Dover Road*; *Michael and Mary*; *Mr Pim Passes By*; *The Truth About Blayds*
Milne, Lorraine 191, 320, 345

Milroy, Austin 96
Milson, John 103, 280, 341, 617
Mime Spectrum 211
Mimini's Voices 337
Mine A Sad One 350
Minear, Harold 306
Miner's Right, The 180, 626
Miner's Trust, The 451, 482, 532
Minerva Theatre 33, 161, 344, 352, **369**, 555, 567, 594, 623, 639
Ministry for the Arts (NSW) 569
Minstrel, The 26
minstrels 46, *48*, 325, **370**, 461
Mirage 412, 417
Misanthrope, The 103, 150, 230, 232
Mischief in the Air 33, 104, 452
Miser, The 56, 634
Misérables, Les: musical 125, 390, 439, 465, 511; play 180, 449
Misrepresentations 122
Miss Esmeralda 240
Miss Hook of Holland 383, 390
Miss Julie 234, 368, 468
Missus Queen 147, 614
Mistero buffo 216, 217
Misto, John. See *Sky Mistress*
Mitchell, Adrian. See *Man Friday*
Mitchell, Alastair 304
Mitchell, Heather 573
Mitchell, Irene 45, 60, 97, 116, **371**, 481, 498, 542, 543, 615, 651
Mitchell, Marion 460
Mitchell, Patrick 104, 183
Mitchell, Warren 371, 395, 475, 574
Mitchell Library 15, 18, 34, 55, 78, 92, 97, 118, 159, 181, 188, 221, 232, 326, 344, 351, 498, 512, 529, 596, 599, 639
Mitchener, Michael 544
Mixed Grill 598
Mixed Kill 337
Miya Studio 401
'Mo' Awards 76
Moby Dick 356, 614
Moby Dick Rehearsed 357, 551, 597
Mock Catalani in Little Puddleton, The 131, 213, 446, 531
Mock Doctor, The 382, 390
Modern School of Speech and Drama 277
Modern Theatre Players 441
Modest Expectations 37
Moiseiwitsch, Tanya 497, 556
Mokotow, Fay 74, 276
Molière 515
Molière. See *Le Bourgeois gentilhomme*; *Don Juan*; *The Imaginary Invalid*; *Le Malade imaginaire*; *The Misanthrope*; *The Miser*; *A Physician in Spite of Himself*; *Scapin*; *Tartuffe*
Mollison, Ethel Knight 299
Molloy, Thomas 277, 585
Mollusc, The 332

Molnar, Ferenc. See *Liliom*; *The Guardsman*; *The Play's the Thing*; *The Wolf*
Momma's Little Horror Show 469, 578, 614, 645
Monash Teachers' College 22
Monash University 620
Monash University Library 498
Moncrieff, Gladys 111, 130, 153, 239, 296, **371**, 384, 478, 497, 535, *554*, 603, 654
Moncrieff, William. See *Tom and Jerry*
Mondo marionetta, Il 538
Money 331
Money, Bob 174
Money and Friends 89, 129, 240, 360, 398, 476, 642
Mongo Mongo 62, 139, 143
Mongrels 209, 285
Monk, Varney 130, 153, **373**. See also **Collits' Inn**
Monkey King, The 538
Monkey See, Monkey Do 606
Monkhouse, Harry 241
monodrama 373
Monsieur Beaucaire 263, 319
Monsieur Tonson 327, 382
Montagu, Helen 73, 228, 258, 371, 573
Monte Cristo Junior 240
Monte, George 343
Montefiore, Jacob. See *John of Austria*
Monteiro, Jose. See *Death at Balibo*
Montezuma Theatre 38, 268
Montgomery, Faye 587, 597
Montgomery, Walter 18, 170, 205, **373**, 488, 522, 552
Month in the Country, A 258, 515, 558
Month of Sundays, A 200, 257, 305
Monvid, Grazyna. See *The Enemy Within*
Moomba 226
Moon, George 191
Moon, Gerald. See *Corpse!*
Moon for the Misbegotten 320
Moon is Blue, The 53, 238
Mooney, Ray **374**, 455, 466. See also *A Blue Freckle*
Mooney, Thomas 465
Mooney's Kid Don't Cry 403
Moonshine 350
Moonstone, The 147
Moor, Andrea 77, 203
Moora (WA) 633
Moore, Carrie 299, 323, **374**, 383, 606
Moore, Decima 241
Moore, Denis 607
Moore, James E. 374
Moore, John 97
Moore, Maggie 63, 162, 340, **374**, 474, 488, 553, 566, 643, 651
Moore, Malcolm 154, 336, 556
Moore, Mary 308, 614

Moore, Red 318
Moore, Rod 195, 345, *355*
Moore, William 172, 264, **375**, 497, 581
Moorish Maid, A 275
Moorli and the Leprechaun 185
Moorman, Charlotte 431
Moran, Harry 632
Moran, Vince. See *Manly Ferry*
More Than a Sentimental Bloke 474
Morell and Kemp 269
Morgan, Robert 245
Morgan, Sally. See *Sistergirl*
Morgan, Terence 414
Morgillo, Antonietta 195
Morley, Michael 175
Morley, Robert 321, 375, 631. See also *Edward, My Son*
Morley, Wilton 375
Morning 506
Morning Sacrifice 51, 179, 297, **376**, 452, 491
Morning's at Seven 378
Morrell, Geoff 77, 587
Morris, Ces 318
Morris, Mary. See *Two Weeks with the Queen*
Morris, Phyllis. See *The Rescue Party*
Morris, Royston 292
Morris, T. B. See *Gild the Mask Again*
Morritt, Charles 336
Morse, Barry 635
Morse, Helen 376, 413, 497, 573, 577
Mortensen, Kevin. See *Why People Go to Traffic Accidents*
Mortimer, Ian 379
Mortimer, John. See *Cat among the Pigeons*; *A Voyage Round My Father*
Mortlock, Joyce 376
Mortlock Library 34
Morton, Frank 172
Morton, J. M. See *Box and Cox*
Morton, Thomas. See *Speed the Plough*
Mo's Merry Monarchs 485
Moscovitch, Maurice 49, 215, **376**
Moscow Art Theatre 356
Moscow Circus 114, 144
Moses, Charles 72, 159
Moses, J. 364, 583
Moses, Jack *172*
Moss, Warwick. See *Down an Alley Filled with Cats*
Motel. See *America Hurrah!*
Mothballs 273
Mother, The 164
Mother and Son 212, **376**, 442
Mother Courage and Her Children 90, 98, 186, 258, 427
Mother Goose 330
Mother of Pearl 240, 390
Mothers and Fathers 404
Motivators, The 249

Mount Gambier Theatre Group 537
Mourning Becomes Electra 43, 67, 89, 228, 285, 293, 325, 398, 435, 476
Moustique 148
Mouth Show, The 259
Move Over, Mrs Markham 150
moving panoramas 377, 547
Mr Big the Big Big Pig 54
Mr Pim Passes By 406
Mr Potter of Texas 183
Mr Siggie Morrison with his Comb and Paper 483
Mr Smart Guy 24, 161, 491, 639
Mrozek, Slawomir 459. See also *The Emigrants*
Mrs Dally Has a Lover 628
Mrs Klein 90, 222, 297, 570
Mrs Mack's Variety Company 632
Mrs Porter and the Angel 271, 396
Mrs Pretty and the Premier 24, **377**, 452
Mrs Thally F 507, 508, 614
Mrs Warren's Profession 110, 341
Much Ado About Nothing 84, 93, 192, 199, 234, 240, 258, 263, 286, 348, 490, 527, 626, 656
Mudrooroo Nyoongar 13
Muffs Dramatic Club 578
Muir, Christopher 543
Mulcahy, Lance 316, 420, 440
Mulder, John 83
Mulgan, Alan. See *For Love of Appin*
Müller, Heiner. See *Hamletmachine*
Mullett, Jane 232
Mullinar, Liz 34
Mullinar, Rod 168
Mullins, Mike 431
Multi-Coloured Umbrella, The 103, 623
Multicultural Theatre Alliance 156
Mummenschanz 215
Mundey, Jack 586
Munro, Charles 59, 60
Munro, Rona. See *Bold Girls*
Munyard, Ella 376
Muppet Show 96
Murcutt, Glen 316
Murder in the Cathedral 28, 31, 77, 137, 252, 264, 276, 290, 344, 527
Murderer 137
Murdoch University 620
Muriel 193, 432
Muriel, Henry. See Henry Beaufoy Merlin
Muriel's Virtues 314
Murlin, Henry. See Henry Beaufoy Merlin
Murphet, Richard 22, 367
Murphy, Frank 174
Murphy, J. W. B. 377
Murphy, Jennifer 386

Murphy, Lynne 377, 481
Murphy, Morris 116
Murray 378
Murray, Archibald 378. See also *Fleeced*; *The Imps*; *The Scarlet Letter*
Murray, Dinah 81, **378**
Murray, Douglas. See *The Man from Toronto*
Murray, Edith 96, **378**, 469
Murray, Peta 223, 328. See also *Spitting Chips*; *Wallflowering*
Murray River Performing Group 22, 109, 155, 223, 232, **378**, 625
Murray River Story 109, 155, 379
Murray Smith, Joanna 224
Musaphia, Joseph. See *Mothers and Fathers*
Muschamp, Thomas. See *The Brass Hat*
Musgrove, Arthur 380
Musgrove, Frank 168
Musgrove, George 46, 226, 240, 299, 340, **379**, 382, 383, 558, 605, 644
Musgrove, Harry 380
Musgrove, Harry G. 348, **380**, 602
Musgrove, Jack 380, 602
Musgrove, Mr 481
Musgrove, Rose 379
Musgrove Theatres 380, 603
Music Hall 278
Music Hall Company 77, 157
Music Hall Theatre Restaurant 91, 167, 332, **380**, 385, 569, 587
music halls 381
Music Hole 588
Music Loft 420, 588
Music Man, The 52, 390
musical comedy 115, 383, 461
musical plays 383
musical theatre 66, 240, **382**
Musicians' Union of Australia 294, 296
My Fair Lady 30, 52, 200, 228, 303, 371, 385, 390
My Foot, My Tutor 215
My Lady Frayle 390, 429
My Lady Molly 323
My Lady's Dress 263, 406, 459
My Life is My Affair 252
My Life with an Interval for Aspirin 470
My Mate 197, 392, 447, 482, 647
My Note Book (magazine) 170
My Pal Ginger 117
My Shadow and Me 291
My Spiritual Dreaming 14
My Three Angels 36, 77
Mykyta, Anne-Marie 217
Myles, Bruce 194, *354*
Mysteries of Sydney, The 84, 114
Mysterious Potamus, The 271, 342

N

Nagel, Charles. See *The Mock Catalani in Little Puddleton*; **Shakespericonglomorofunnidogammoniae**
Naked Possum, The 623
Naked Truth, The 183
Nanjing Acrobatic Troupe 16, 136, 145, 232
Napier, Hector 392
Napier, Valantyne 392
Napier and Cartledge 393
Naracoorte Drama Club 337
Narkle, Lynette *14*, 196, 408
Narkle, Maxine 196
Narrow Road to the Deep North 420
Nash, N. Richard. See *The Rainmaker*
Nash, Wally 59
Nason, Bryan 102, 153, 184, 341, 410, 475, 617
Nathan Juvenile Troupe 160
Nation (magazine) 174
National Amphitheatre: Melbourne 99, 238, 422, 590; Sydney 99, 239, 590
National Black Theatre 13, 347, 569
National Capital Development Commission 125
National Critics' Circle 76
National Festival of Australian Theatre 124, 125
National Film and Sound Archive 393, 497
National Gallery of Australia 195
National Health, The 200, 258
National Institute of Dramatic Art 20, 72, 98, 109, 148, 178, 200, 208, 220, 245, 290, 305, 385, **393**, 411, 413, 432, 459, 498, 514, 550, 568, 616, 620
National Library of Australia 24, 72, 78, 179, 265, 283, 309, 315, 317, 392, 480, 497, 533
National Professional Theatre Awards 76
National Sporting Club 239
national theatre 393
National Theatre (Balmain, Sydney) 286
National Theatre and Fine Arts Society 278, **394**, 584
National Theatre Company 69, 77, 83, 95, 148, 149, 156, 196, 233, 236, 339, 365, **395**, 396, 412, 417, 438, 494, 498, 509, 556, 570, 614, 616, 634, 655
National Theatre Movement 43, 315, 349, **395**, 498, 615
National Theatre of Great Britain 209
National Theatre of Papua New Guinea 13
National Times (newspaper) 175

National Young Playwrights' Weekend 528
Native Born, The 78, 197
Nattrass, Sue 329
Naughton, Bill. See *Spring and Port Wine*
Navarro, Renald 124
Naylor, Rufe 270, 507, 535
Neagle, Anna 325
Near Ms's 297
Neary, Nick 582
Ned Kelly (musical) 330, 390;
Ned Kelly (play) 192, 195, 349, 366, **396**, *453*, 500, 558, 581, 629
Ned Kelly and the City of Bees 313
Neeme, Aarne 73, 133, 259, 280, 290, 338, 341, 395, **396**, 399, 405, 412
Neeme, Helen 133. See also Helen McDonald
Neil, Frank 50, 92, 201, 239, **397**, 485, 486, 603
Neild, J. E. 169, *170*, 306, 373, **397**, 528
Neill, Rosemary 176
Neill, Wilfred. See *The Web of Steel*
Nell the California Diamond 48
Nellie Stewart Opera Company 559
Nelson, Sydney 35
Nepean College of Advanced Education 621
Nesbitt, Francis 17, 56, 121, 180, 243, 254, 274, 297, 315, **397**, 472, 487, 653
Neskovski, Blagoja (Bill) 217, 587
Netherwood 627, 638, 651
Never Too Late 161
Neville, Augustus 37
Nevin, Robyn 102, 179, 203, 224, 326, 351, **398**, 519, 556, 572, 573, 638
New Babylon, The 222, 282, 283, 490
New Blood 432
New Circus 145
New Comedy Company 350
New Crime, A 160
New Dan Barry Company 101
New Dramatic Company 100
New England Theatre Centre 398
New English Opera Company 149
New Ensemble Circus 145
New Fortune Theatre 96, 149, **399**, 428, *524*, 594, 620
New London Company 229
New Magdalen, The 16
New Men and Old Acres 331
New Moon, The 99, 321, 390
New Moon Theatre Company 79, 137, **399**, 474
New Opera House 502
New Princess's Uncle Tom's Cabin Company 274

685

New Queen's Theatre 25, 162, 189, 323, 419, 487, 534
New Rocky Horror Show, The 614
New Sandhurst Theatre 465
New Sin, The 511
New Stages 574
New Sydney Repertory Society 41, 441
New Theatre 50, 67, 208, 215, **400**, 452, 516; Adelaide 42, 252, 401; Brisbane 13, Hobart 583; Melbourne 13, 51, 79, 158, 190, 198, 329, 354, 401, 402, 457, 483, 515; Newcastle (NSW) 401, 402; Perth 401, 402, 464, 652; Sydney 53, 79, 97, 98, 132, 172, 215, 216, 234, 252, 261, 317, 400, 403, 498, 506, 515
New Theatre Daytime 402
New Theatre League (USA) 400
New Theatre Royal 278, 583
New Theatre Singers 402
New Theatre—Australia (magazine) 175, 496
New Tivoli Minstrel and Grand Specialty Company 501, 601
New Tivoli Theatre Adelaide 26; Sydney 429, 486, 603, 606
New Triad (magazine) 211
New Way to Pay Old Debts, A 254, 487, 488
New World Productions 203
New York Serenaders 370
New Zealand Pierrots 191
New Zealand Playwrights' Conference 73
New Zealand theatre in Australia 404
Newcastle (NSW) **405**
Newcastle Dramatic Art Club 405
Newcastle Marionette Theatre 292
Newcastle Repertory Theatre 405
Newcastle Theatre 365, 405
Newcastle University Student Players 402
Newman, Bill 385
Newman, John 588
Newman, Paul 588
Newman, Robert 164
Newman, William 266
Newspaper of Claremont Street, The 315
Next Wave Festival 655
Ney, Marie 240, 343, **406**, 505
Niblo, Fred 47, 489
Nice Goings On 91, 390
Nice Night's Entertainment, A 279, 289, **406**
Nichols, Peter 208. See also *A Day in the Death of Joe Egg*; *The National Health*
Nicholson, Derek 621
Nicholson, William. See *Shadowlands*
Nicol, Beth 406

Nicol, Don 296, **406**
Nicol, W. D. **406**, 469, 518
NIDA Company 146, 258, 305, 393
Nidjera 359
Night and Day 208
Night in the Arms of Raeleen, A 248
Night Must Fall 81, 321
Night of January 16th, The 227, 555
Night of National Reconciliation, A 244
Night of the Ding-Dong, The 440
Night of the Iguana, The 32, 318, 378
Night of the Party, The 329
Night on Bald Mountain 28, 33, 577, 638
Night on the PS, A 124
Night Out, A 89, 312
Night the Prowler, The 638
Night with the Right, A 244
Nightbirds 390
Nightfall 98
Nightmare, The 535
Nightmares of the Old Obscenity Master 236
Nimmo, Heather 224, 247. See also *One Small Step*
Nimrod Street Theatre 328, 407, 455, 544, 569, 595. See also **Stables Theatre**
Nimrod Theatre 85, 199, 407, 455, *550*, 569, 595. See also **Belvoir Street Theatre**
Nimrod Theatre Company 23, 53, 58, 68, 77, 79, 84, 88, 98, 148, 164, 178, 186, 187, 199, 202, 209, 215, 216, 218, 219, 223, 234, 237, 240, 243, 244, 245, 252, 257, 258, 259, 262, 285, 304, 318, 325, 326, 348, 359, 363, 385, 396, **407**, 411, 459, 485, 492, 498, 512, 515, 520, 521, 524, 527, 544, 562, 569, 570, 573, 580, 620, 622, 626, 627, 630, 635, 636
Nindethana Theatre 13, 110, 134, 402
Ningali 224
Niobe 108
Nishimoto, Noriko 538, 645
Nixon, Arundel 321
No Conscription 403
No End of Blame 179
No Going Back 80, 359, 368, 570
No Incense Rising 182, **407**
No Man's Land 182
No Mercy 180, 447
No Names … No Pack Drill 243, 266, 271, 573, 595, 629
No Room at the Inn 377, 458
No Room for Dreamers 71, 210, 291, 439
No Sugar 14, 71, 185, 196, **408**, 456, 509, 517, 655
No Time for Comedy 406, 427
No Time Like the Present 273

No Triangle This 32
No Worries 263, 282, 337
No! No! Nanette 127, 239, 321, 383, 390, 435, 525, 570, 617
No-Hopers, The 83
Noad, Jessica **408**
Noah 27
Noble, Buster 59
Noble, J. S. 138, 461, 605
Nocturne 526
noh 31, 64
Noises Off 168
Nolan, (Sir) Sidney 195, 396
Nolan, Steve 408
Noonan, Helen 224
Noonan, Michael. See *A Different Drummer*
Noongar Theatre 13
Norfolk Island 158, **408**
Norm and Ahmed 63, 118, 133, **409**, 455, 617
Normal Heart, The 263
Norman, Albert 98
Norman, Charles 275, **409**
Norman Conquests, The 208, 395, 477
Norris, Terry 97
Norseman (WA) 633
North American Circus 141
Northam (WA) 634
Northcote, H. Stafford 28
Northern Territory **409**
Northside Theatre Company 168, 198, 257, 262, 305, 320, 341, 527. See also **Marian Street Theatre Company**
Not Even a Mouse 557
Not in the Book 230, 408
Not Now, Darling 304
Not the Six Hundred 617
Not with Yours Truly 203, 204, 390, 492
Nothing Personal 242
Nott, Lewis 41, 122, 125
Novak, Jan 538
Novello, Ivor. See *Full House*
Nowell, C. 599
Nowhere to Hide 217
Nowra, Louis 215, 271, **410**, 456, 497, 556. See also *Byzantine Flowers*; *Capricornia*; *Così*; *Crow*; **The Golden Age**; *Inner Voices*; *Inside the Island*; *Lulu*; *The Precious Woman*; *The Prince of Homburg*; *Spellbound*; *Visions*; *Whitsunday*
NSW Archives 88, 446
NSW Theatre of the Deaf 582
NSW Writers' Centre 73
Ntshona, Winston 13, 536
Nude with Violin 81, 267, 331, 631
Nugent, Colin 133, 135
Nugget Theatre 291, 634
Nunn, J. H. 118, 245, 392, 539, 637, 647
Nunn, Trevor 510
Nunsense 168, 390, 570

Nuovo Paese/New Country 155, 166
Nutter, Lynda 97
Nyitray, Emile. See *His Lady Friends*
Nyungar theatre 14

O

O 273
Oakes, Russell **411**. See also *Enduring as the Camphor Tree*
Oakley, Barry 75, 175, **411**, 497. See also *The Feet of Daniel Mannix*
Oakley, John 126
Oates, Jan 462
Obey, André. See *Noah*
O'Brien, Francis Belfield 84
O'Brien, Julianne 224. See also *The Rainbow Warrior*; *The Women There*
O'Brien, Richard 596
O'Brien, Stuart 154
O'Brien, Terry 245, 326, 432
O'Brien Girl, The 239, 390, 465
Obscene Fables, The 216
O'Casey, Sean. See *Juno and the Paycock*; *The Plough and the Stars*; *The Shadow of a Gunman*
Occupations 227
O'Connell, Geoffrey. See *Brunswick—The musical*
O'Connell, Terry 342, 399, 474, 504
O'Connor, Anna. See *Birds of the Moon*
Octagon Theatre 96, 256, **412**, 426, 594
Octagon Theatre Company 240, 621
Octoroon, The 46, 48, 361
O'Day, Anne 470
Odeon Theatre: Adelaide 127; Hobart 278
Odets, Clifford. See *Paradise Lost*; *Till the Day I Die*; *Waiting for Lefty*; *Winter Journey*
O'Doherty, Patrick 27
O'Donnell, Frank 515
O'Donnell, Marilyn 74
O'Donoghue, John **412**, 456. See also *Essington Lewis: I Am Work*; *A Happy and Holy Occasion*
O'Donoghue, Rory 95, 259
Odyssey of a Prostitute 273
Oedipus 555, 556
Oedipus at Colonus 555, 556
Oedipus Rex 33, 96, 149, 190, 256, 412, 440, 577, 608, 621
Oedipus the King 30, 257, 417
Of Mice and Men 50, 403
Off the Wall 241
Offenbach, Jacques 214
Officers' Mess, The 429
Offord, Colin 211

Offshore 166, 310
O'Flaherty, H. C. 647
Ogier, Tony 418
Ogilvie, George 22, 28, 193, 216, 236, 330, 358, 367, **413**, 497, 555. See also *A Long View*
Ogle, Bill 92
O'Grady, Governor Sir James 279
Oh, Calcutta! 133
Oh Dad, Poor Dad, Mama's Hung You in the Closet and I'm Feeling' So Sad 81
Oh Killara! 341
Oh, Lady! Lady!! 50, 111, 390
Oh, What a Lovely War! 200, 221, 390
Oh! Oh! Delphine 390
O'Halloran, Sheila 376
O'Hara, John D. 49, 50
O'Hara, Lyle 420, 440
O'Hearn, Dinny 74
Ohlin, Bjarne 95
Oikawa, Miki 64
O'Keefe, Jack 608
Oklahoma! 51, 52, 124, 265, 303, 384, 390
Old Allegiance, The 617
Old Corporal, The 338
Old Country, The 631
Old Curiosity Shop, The 643
Old Familiar Juice, The 352, 466
Old King Cole 556
Old Man Taught Wisdom, An 382, 390
Old Mill Theatre 95
Old Mrs Wiley 598
Old Players and Playgoers Association 495
'Old Playgoer, An' 532
Old Time Music Hall 77, 78, 157
Old Time Music Hole 280
Old Tote Theatre Company 13, 23, 68, 69, 75, 84, 87, 88, 89, 92, 98, 109, 128, 133, 146, 153, 157, 165, 190, 193, 200, 208, 215, 221, 230, 234, 235, 239, 240, 256, 257, 264, 276, 290, 304, 315, 318, 319, 326, 331, 332, 367, 378, 404, 407, 409, 412, **413**, 417, 420, 435, 440, 458, 476, 480, 498, 514, 519, 527, 568, 569, 572, 575, 595, 608, 620, 629, 635, 636, 638
Old Vic Theatre Company 20, 28, 43, 67, 110, 192, 207, 267, 278, 340, **414**, 491, 524, 548
Old World 515
Oldaker, Max 296, 308, 384, **415**, 440
Olde English Fayre, Ye 436
Olde King's Music Hall 588
Olde Time Music Hall 588
Oldham, Peter 469, 578, 645
Oleanna 514
Olive Tree, The 195
Oliver, Annie 167
Oliver, Maggie 246, **416**

Oliver! 200, 322, 330, 390, 527, 570, 617
Olivette 390, 559
Olivier, Laurence (Lord) 20, 43, 96, 192, 207, 278, 290, 363, 414, 435, 491, 524, 528, 584, 621
Olley, Margaret 363
O'Loughlin, Paul 76
Olsen, Dennis 27, 243, **416**, 497
Olsen and Johnson 49
Olympia 139, 229
Olympic Circus: Adelaide 25; Sydney 62, 138, 605
Olympic Theatre (Launceston) 121, 325;
Olympic Theatre (Melbourne) 106, 161, 162, **416**
O'Malley, John 321
O'May, John 57, 573, 607
Omodei, Raymond 280, 395, 412, **417**, 556
On Approval 94, 622
On Archeology 211
On Grubb's Selection 93, 473, 513
On Our Selection 67, 78, 117, 118, 177, 197, 239, 266, 285, 305, 334, **417**, 427, *450*, 471, 491, 512, 532, 567, 627, 635
On Sibley Settlement 513
On Stage Oz 526
On Stage Vietnam 97, 390
On the Line 216
On the Spot 263
On the Wallaby 209, 390, 471, 628, 629
On the Whipping Side 360, 419
On Top of the World 222, 251
On Yer Marx 332, 651
Once in a Lifetime 317, 527
Once Upon a Mattress 186, 390
Once Upon a Ruby Red 429
Once Upon a Time there were Two Kings 443
Once Upon Inala 155, 562
One Dam' Thing After Another 604
One Day of the Year, The 28, 32, 68, 72, 87, 106, 157, 177, 178, 208, 224, 233, 239, 344, **418**, 424, 454, 474, 521, 568, 616
One Day Short of an April Fool 634
One Hundred Guineas 617
One Man 209
One of Nature's Gentlemen 273
One Small Step 557
One Woman Shoe 190
O'Neil, Nance 47, 299, 490, 567, 643, 644
O'Neill, Errol 419, 462. See also *On the Whipping Side*; *Says Who?*
O'Neill, Eugene 212. See also *Ah, Wilderness!*; *Anna Christie*; *Days without End*; *The Emperor Jones*; *The Hairy Ape*; *Long Day's Journey into Night*; *Mourning Becomes Electra*; *SS Glencairn*;

O'Neill, J. P. 82
Ongley, Byron. See *Brewster's Millions*
Only a Fool 284
Only Heaven Knows 242
Oodgeroo Noonuccal 13
Oopla, We Live! 98
Oops! 310
Open City 241
Open Couple, The 216
Open Spaces 452, 598
Open Stage 184
Openshaw, Charles. See *All the King's Horses*
Opera Comique 604
Opera House: Melbourne 338, 443, 601, 604; Sydney 590, 646
Opera Theatre 268, 592
opéra-bouffe 115, 205, 213, 382, 489
operetta 383
Operette 415
Opie, Edward 25, 197, **419**
Orange Grove, The 182
Orchid, The 323, 326, 383, 390
Orcsik, John 164
Ord, Duncan 97, 329
Ordell, Tal 17, 24. See also *Kangaroo Flat*
Order of the Day 196
Oresteia 42
Orestes 432
Oriental Circus 612
Original Ballet Russe 344
Orlandi, Alex 143
Ormandy, Eugene 159, 249
Orphans 237, 371
Orphel, Phyllis 32
Orpheus Descending 210, 557
Orpheus in the Underworld 390
Orr, William 186, 366, **420**, 440, 500, 568, 588
Orton, Joe 208. See also *Entertaining Mr Sloane*; *What the Butler Saw*
Osborn, Paul. See *Morning's at Seven*
Osborne, John 73, 208. See also *The Entertainer*; *Inadmissible Evidence*; *Look Back in Anger*
O'Shanassy, Blanche 343
O'Shannessy, Annie 408
O'Shaughnessy, Peter 36, 175, 289, 306, 308, 351, **420**, 474
O'Shea, Two-Ton Tessie 270, 604
Ostoja-Kotkowski, Stanislaus 258, **420**
Ostracised 361, **421**
Ostraka 211, 369
O'Sullivan, E. W. 158, **421**. See also *Coo-ee*; *Keane of Kalgoorlie*
Oswald, Debra 224, 456. See also *Dags*
Othello 19, 25, 36, 43, 61, 93, 121, 254, 281, 283, 286, 305, 328, 335, 340, 349, 365, 366, 377, 404, 420, 487, 503, 512, *523*, 539, 586, 629

Othello Transvestie 25
Other Side is Greener, The 466
Other Side of the Moon, The 598
Other Times 194, 323
Otto, Barry **421**
Otto, Miranda 421
Otway, Thomas. See *Venice Preserv'd*
Ouida. See *Puck*
Our American Cousin 46
Our Boys 633
Our Country's Good 209, 313, 363, 494
Our First Lieutenant 115
Our Girls 100
Our Glad 470
Our Hearts were Young and Gay 77
Our Lyceum 566
Our Miss Gibbs 326, 334, 383, 390, 429, 654
Our Town 157, 228, 281, 292, 293
Out of the Blue 562
Out of the Dark 371
Out of This World 390
Out of Time 286
Out on the Castlereagh 67
Outback 581
Outcast 111
Outlaw Kelly 26
Outpost 606
Outsider, The 376
Outward Bound 161, 621
Overcoat, The 273, 505, 515, 645
Overcome by Chlorine 184
Owen, Gillian 104
Owen, Harrison **422**
Owen, Taffy 318
Oxenford, John. See *The Two Orphans*
Oyston, Peter 22, 155, 208, 444, 625
Oz Puppet Festival 538, 645
Oz Theatre Company 291
Oznost 442

P

Pacific Overtures 390
Pacific Paradise 179, 401, 452
Pacific Rape 32
Pack of Women, The 56, 317, **422**, 635
Packer, Doris 49, 50
Packer, Sir Frank 61
PACT Theatre 455
PACT Youth Theatre **422**
Paddington Red 332
Paddlesteamer 483
Paddy 189
Padmore Hill, Cecilia 397
Page, Louise 208. See also *Salonika*
Page, Robert 175
Pageant of the Love Tree, The 79
pageants 33
Pagel, Oscar 229, 535

Paget, Violet 40, 329, 490, 511
Paige, Eric 59
Paint Your Wagon 390
Painter, The 402
Pair of Claws, A 255
Pajama Game, The 52, 266, 322, 390
Pakeha, The 404
Pal Joey 390
Palace Gardens Theatre 101
Palace of Truth 579
Palace Theatre (Coolgardie, WA) 632
Palace Theatre (Melbourne) 96, 238, **422**, 591, 637
Palace Theatre (Sydney) 237, 245, **423**, 566, 601
Palais Theatre **423**, 637
Pale Sergeant, The 264
Pallas 60
Palmer, A. M. 644
Palmer, Howard 174
Palmer, Kevin 555, 556
Palmer, Vance 211, 422, **423**, 442, 497
Palmerston, Edith 135
Palmerston Dramatic and Musical Society 409
Palotta, Grace 241, **424**, 484
Pandora's Cross 272
Pannell, Nita 156, 395, 418, **424**, 438, 633, 638
Panozzo, Dina 224
Pantheon Theatre 443
pantomime 220, 324, 382, **424**, 447, 461, **489**, 547
Pantomime Kiddies 135
Paolo and Francesca 428
Paper Ladders 645
Paper Moon 124
Parachute Productions 375
Parade Theatre 620
Paradise Lost 543
Paradise Regained 471
Paramor, John 326
Paramount Arts Centre 433
Parfitt, Trevor 196
Paris the Prince and Helen the Fair 35
Paris Theatre Company 145, 166, 230, 498, 572
Paris, Virginia 52
Parish Priest, The 92
Park, Ruth. See also *Harp in the South*
Park Entertainments 203
Parker 462
Parker, George D. 376
Parker, Louis N. See *Joseph and his Brethren*
Parkes, Lizette 319
Parkinson, Charles 232
Parkinson, Peter 96, 277, 412, **426**
Parnell, Wallace 397, **426**, 486, 603
Parnham, Diana 50
Parr, Bruce 103
Parr, Mike 430

Parramatta Theatre 592
Parrott, Chrissie 538
Parry, Richard 426, 639
Parsifal 137, 214, 220, **427**, 490, 644
Parslow, Frederick 231, 275, **427**, 599
Parsons, Fred 427
Parsons, Nicholas 103, 428
Parsons, Philip 103, 263, 396, 399, 412, **428**, 497, 524, 577
Partage de midi 417
Particular, The 478
Pascoe, Richard 510
Pascoe, Timothy 70
Passengers in Overcoats 309
Passing Show, The 334
Passionate Pianist, The 623
Pastrymaker, The 363
Patate 332, 358
Patch Children's Theatre 654
Patch Theatre 43, **428**, 651
Patch Theatre Company 29, **429**, 470
Pate, A. J. 122
Pate, Michael 59, 497
Paterson, Jack 191
Paterson, Trixie 191
Paterson's Printing Press 467
Path of Thorns, A 283
Pathfinder, The 71, 128, 356
Patience 244, 382, 390, 489, 559, 623, 645
Patrick, John. See *The Teahouse of the August Moon*
Patrikareas, Theodore 217
patronage 562
Patsy, The 78, 168
Patten, J. G. 117
Patterson, Jack 628
Paul, Queenie 49, 114, 157, **429**, 486, 602, *603*, 606, 651, 652
Paul Jones 256, 383, 390, 559
Paul Pry 17
Paula 429
Pauline Blanchard 86
Paulton, Harry and Edward. See *Niobe*
Pavilion Theatre 25
Pavlova ballet company 548
Pax Americana 201, 417
Payne, John Howard. See *Brutus*; *Clari*
Payne, Stephen 359
Payne, Steve 126
Payne Steel Bellringers 535
Paynton, Jennifer. See *Balancing Act*
Payten, Gloria 34
Peach Melba 478
Peachey, Christine 182, 535
Peacock's Feathers 147
Pearce, Vera 348, **429**
Pearl Divers, The 214
Peart, Charles O. 229
Peck, George 430
Peddie, Brian 189
Peddle Thorp and Walker 441
Peel, Dennis 562

Peel, Pauline 562
Peer Gynt 112, 290, 332
Peers, Lisa 89
Peg o' My Heart 47, 81, 111, 298, 300
Peggy Sue 273
Peking opera companies 136, 225
Pelham, Meta 430
Pell, John 408
Pell, Kelton 408
Pember, Ron. See *Jack the Ripper*
Penalty Clause 464
Penberthy, James 454
Penguin Books 467
Pennies Before the Holidays 297
Penny, Gary 58, 569
People Keep Giving Me Things 538
People Next Door 123
Percy, Edward. See *Ladies in Retirement*
Percy, Hal 42, **481**, 542
Percy, W. S. 430, 460
Percy and Rose 29, 243, 253, 544
Peregrinations of Pickwick, The 539
Perfect Strangers 89
Perfectionist, The 129, 200, 227, 255, 398, 556, 642
Perfectly All Right 187
Perfidious Albion 626
performance art 430
Performance Centre 393
Performance Space 431
Performance Syndicate 165, 219, **432**, 459, 524
Performers' Management 35, 203
Performing Arts Museum 75, 195, 253, 256, 285, 498, 646
Performing Arts Workshop 439
Performing Lines Ltd 88
Performing Puppet Company 578
performing-arts centres 20, 109, **432**
Périchole, La 390, 533
Pericles 236, 258, 413, 432, 480
Permezel, Louise 379, 656
Perrier, Robert 232, 378
Perrin, Mil 122. See also *Is This Where We Came In?*
Perry, Albert 435, 509
Perry, Bridget 434
Perry, Charles 434
Perry, Charles Henry 434
Perry, Edward ('Teddy') 435
Perry, Henry ('Dummy') 435
Perry, James 435
Perry, Jim 435
Perry, John. See *The Life and Death of Captain Cook*
Perry, Mealia 434
Perry, Robert 509
Perry, Virginia 99
Perry, William George 434
Perry Brothers' Circus 435, 650
Perry family circuses 434

Perry's Jubilee Circus 434
Perry's Young Queensland Circus 434
Perryman, Diana 308, **435**
Perryman, Jill 52, 266, 270, 365, 385, 395, **435**, 440, 497
Perryman, William 435
Persan, Igor 459
Persecution and Assassination of Marat, The 215
Perth 436
Perth Concert Hall 439
Perth Dramatic Club 436
Perth Entertainment Centre 439
Perth Festival Fringe Society 60
Perth Theatre Trust 437, **439**, 498
Perth Town Hall 436
Pete McGynty and the Dreamtime 367
Peter and the Wolf 342
Peter Pan 94, 281, 390, 489, 630
Peter Rix Management 35
Peter Scriven Puppets 518
Peter Summerton Foundation 319, **439**, 575
Peters, Anne 35
Peters, Dorothy 525
Peters, Lance 73
Petersen, Keith 266, 385
Peterson, Ralph 59, 332, **440**, 515. See also *The Mating of Ulrich Dooley*; *The Night of the Ding Dong*; *The Square Ring*
Petherbridge, Edward 510
Petit, Philip 509
Petition, The 332
Petrov 284, 390
Pettitt, Henry. See *The Black Flag*; *In the Ranks*; *A Million of Money*; *The Prodigal Daughter*; *A Run of Luck*; *Taken from Life*
Phantom of the Opera, The 30, 390
Phantom Ship, The 511
Phelan, Martin 155
Philadelphia, Here I Come 475
Philadelphia Story, The 286, 292
Philanthropist, The 287
Philip-Harbutt, Lisa. See *Pigs Might Fly*
Philipina, Senorita 541
Phillip, Governor Arthur 131
Phillip Productions 420, 444
Phillip Street Revue 88
Phillip Street revues 20, 88, 165, 385, 420, **440**, 500, 516, 568
Phillip Street Theatre 440, 641; Sydney **441**
Phillip Street Theatre Company 441
Phillip Theatre 440, 498
Phillips, Alfred 441
Phillips, Anna 165
Phillips, Barbara 376, 539
Phillips, Elizabeth. See **Mrs Alfred Phillips**
Phillips, Hans 441
Phillips, Harold, Leon and Hermann 423

688

Phillips, Jacqy 90, 429. 519
Phillips, Malcolm 599
Phillips, Mrs Alfred 441
Phillips, Nat 114, **441**, 485, 490, 525, 561. See also *Cinderella*
Phillips, Simon 60, **441**, 526, 555, 556
Phillips, Stephen. See *Paolo and Francesca*
Phillips, Teddy 119
Phipps, Max 21
Phoenix Too Frequent, A 56, 60, 341, 527
phonograph 336
Physician in Spite of Himself, A 329, 403
Physicists, The 215
Piaf 395
Picasso, Pablo. See *Four Little Girls*
Picasso and Françoise 60
Piccadilly Bushman, The 68, 323
Piccolo Spoleto 356
Piccolo Teatro di Milano 217
Pickard, John 478
Pickett, George. See *The Silent House*
Pied Piper, The 538, 645
Pielmeir, John. See *Agnes of God*
Pier, The 305
Pierrot in Australia 24
Pigeon, The 350, 567
Piggin, Lindy 328
Piggin, Tony 328
Pigs Might Fly 429
Pilawuk. See *Rak Awin*
Pilbeam Theatre 475, 593
Pilgrim Puppet Theatre 71, 469
Pilgrim Theatre 422
Pinder, John 22, **442**, 588
Pinero, (Sir) Arthur Wing 94. See also *The Amazons*; *His House in Order*; *Iris*; *The Magistrate*; *The Second Mrs Tanqueray*; *Trelawney of the Wells*
Pinjarra (WA) 633
Pink Lady, The 331, 390
Pinkney, John 196
Pinocchio 271, 342
Pinter, (Sir) Harold 89, 208. See also *The Caretaker*; *The Dumb Waiter*; *The Homecoming*
Pioneer Players 19, 211, 227, 354, 424, **442**, 451, 463, 491
Pipi Storm Children's Circus **443**, 498
Pippin 285, 390
Piquo 223
Pirandello, Luigi. See *Cece*; *Six Characters in Search of an Author*
Pirates at the Barn 650
Pirates of Pal Mal, The 622
Pirates of Penzance, The 105, 209, 317, 330, 390, 489, 644
Pits Theatre 122
Pitt, Helen 110

Pitt, William jnr 268, 269, 299, 316, **443**, 465, 582, 583, 584, 590, 601, 604, 645
Pitt, William snr 417, **443**
Pitt-Morison, Margaret 135
Pitts, Graham 530. See also *Death at Balibo*; *Emma*; *Memo*; *Mesh*
Pizarro 398
Place in the Present, A 89
Platonov 515
Play a Tune For Me 538
Play Society 581
Playbox Art Theatre 188, 227, 334
Playbox Society 40, 334, 567
Playbox Theatre (Adelaide) 27, 42, 464
Playbox Theatre (Melbourne) 176, 368
Playbox Theatre (Sydney) 27, 368, **444**, 569
Playbox Theatre Centre 177, 241, 359, **444**, 505
Playbox Theatre Circle 335
Playbox Theatre Company 53, 91, 145, 165, 190, 193, 200, 221, 230, 236, 242, 245, 254, 261, 272, 333, 342, 347, 355, 356, 360, 363, 444, 468, 478, 492, 493, 505, 544, 595, 624, 646, 656. See also **Playbox Theatre Centre**
Playboy of the Western World, The 27, 28, 88, 177, 587
Players' Club 42
Players, The 89. See also *The Club*
Playgoer 333
Playgoer's Co-operative Ltd 341
Playhouse: Adelaide 29; Bundaberg (Qld) 595; Canberra 125; Hobart 41, 279, 594; Melbourne 624; Perth 395, 437, 438, 439, 494, 498; Sydney 511; Wagga Wagga (NSW) 620
Playhouse Theatre 357
Playlab 74, 456, 468
Plays and Players (magazine) 42, 208
Play's the Thing, The 156
Playschool 96
Playworks 74, 223
Playwrights' Advisory Board 40, 228, **445**, 453, 457, 483
playwrights and the screen 445
playwriting **446**
playwriting competitions 13, 33, 61, 72, 76, 80, 87, 90, 91, 103, 105, 110, 116, 134, 179, 182, 196, 198, 252, 259, 271, 292, 313, 362, 364, 408, 440, 445, 451, 452, 453, 454, **457**, 464, 475, 480, 483, 506, 521, 528, 532, 557, 565, 622, 623
Please Return to Sender 595
Pleasure and Repentance 510

Pleasure of His Company, The 408, 504
Plebeians Rehearse the Uprising, The 215
Plews, Barry 614
Plimmer–Denniston Company 107, 268
Plot! 147
Plough and the Stars, The 290, 297, 332
Plumb, Gwen 321, **458**, 604
Pluto 626
Po An Toy 135
Pocket Children's Theatre 458
Pocket Playhouse 43, **458**, 498
Pocock, Isaac. See *The Miller and His Men*; *Rob Roy*
Podrecca, Vittorio 469
Poetasters of Ispahan, The 11
Pogson, Roland 124
Point in Time 253
Point of Departure 56
Point Valaine 91, 115
Pokey's 242
Policy and Passion 484
Polini, Emelie 263, 298, 309, 406, 451, **458**. See also *The Flaw*
Polish influences 459
Politics 412
Pollak, Linsey 195
Pollard, Charles 460
Pollard, Henry 460
Pollard, James Joseph 460
Pollard, Tom 460
Pollard, May 460
Pollard opera companies 81, 409, 437, **460**
Pollock, Channing. See *The Enemy*
Pollock, Ellen 376
Poltergeist, The 56
Polyglot Puppet Theatre 469
Polygon 279
'Polygon' 173, 264
Pomeroy, Louise 47, 552
Pommies 37
Poole, Charles 294, 464
Poole, John. See *Paul Pry*
Poole, Mrs Charles 481
Poole, Sam 447
Poolman, Alan 363
Poor of Melbourne, The 35
Poor of New York, The 35, 93
Poor Soldier, The 382, 390
Pop Mex 2 514, 580
Pope, Brian 135
Pope, Charles 274, **460**, 517, 534
Pope, Joan 135, 655
Poppie Nongena 536
popular entertainments **461**
Popular Front 419
Popular Mechanicals, The 514, 580, 627
Popular Theatre Troupe 102, 155, 419, **461**, 474, 620
Porch, The 332
Port Adelaide Theatre 25
Port Essington (NT) 409
Port Lincoln Players 537

Portage to San Cristobal of A. H., The 422
Porter, Carol 231
Porter, Dan 258
Porter, David. See *Clyde Company Station*
Porter, Hal **462**, 499. See also *Eden House*; *Home on a Pig's Back*; *Parker*; *The Professor*; *Toda-San*; *The Tower*
Portlock, Harry 324
Possessed/Dispossessed 211
Possum Paddock 117, 286, **450**, 451, **462**, 610
Post, Guy Bates 49, 111, 298
Post, Sue Ann 297
Pot Luck 486
Pot of Message 231, 403
Potiphar's Wife 237
Potter, Dennis. See *Son of Man*
Potter, Paul. See *Trilby*
Pounder, Betty 266
Pounds, Courtice 244
Poverty Point 34, 151, 294, **463**
Power, Tyrone 299
Power, Val 110
Power of Theatrical Madness, The 31
Powers, Carmel 323
Powers, John **463**. See also *The Hot Centre of the World*; *The Last of the Knucklemen*; *The Reluctant Rebel*; *The Second Story*; *Shindig*
Pownall, David. See *Master Class*; *Pride and Prejudice*
Prairie King, The. See **The Scout**
Prairie Scout, The 48
Pram Factory 75, 355, 595
Pratt, Ambrose. See *Thunderbolt*
Pratt, James 321, 528
Pratt, Richard 564
Pratt, Valma 599
Pravda 240
Pravda, George 76
Pravda, Hanna 76
Precious Woman, The 266, 410
Prelude and Fugue 33
Premier Nigger Minstrels Troupe 127
Present Laughter 106, 237, 491, 513
President Wilson in Paris 89, 320
Preston, John 544
Preston, Mary 330
Pretty Peggy 560
Prévert, Jacques 574
Prey 89
Price of Coal, The 653
Price, The 416, 635
Prichard, Katharine Susannah 110, 400, 402, 451, **463**, 652. See also *Bid Me to Love*; **Brumby Innes**; *The Burglar*; *Forward One*; *The Great Man*; *Solidarity*; *The Thief*
Prictor, Wally 318
Pride and Prejudice 366
Prider, Jack 464

689

Prider, Joy 464
Prider, Lloyd 27, **464**
Priest, Joanne 342
Priestley, J. B. See *An Inspector Calls*; *I Have Been Here Before*; *They Came to a City*; *When We Are Married*
Prime of Miss Jean Brodie, The 346
Primrose 50, 390
Prince, Arthur 485
Prince, Elsie 239, 384
Prince, Hal 386
Prince, The 368
Prince Enterprise 220, 425
Prince of Homburg, The 304, 363
Prince of Wales Opera House: Gulgong (NSW) 246, 249; Melbourne 333, 501, 591, 604; Sydney 333
Prince of Wales Theatre (Adelaide) 238, 268
Prince of Wales Theatre (Hobart) 278, 590
Prince of Wales Theatre (Melbourne) 604
Prince of Wales Theatre (Stanthorpe, Qld) 473
Prince of Wales Theatre (Sydney) 254, 288, 294, **464**, 547, 566, 594, 608, 653
Prince Patrick Hotel 588
Princess Charming 391
Princess Theatre (Albany, WA) 633
Princess Theatre (Bendigo) **465**
Princess Theatre (Brisbane) 100, 102, 617
Princess Theatre (Forbes, NSW) 416
Princess Theatre (Fremantle, WA) 238
Princess Theatre (Grenfell, NSW) 416
Princess Theatre (Launceston, Tas.) 433, 590
Princess Theatre (Melbourne) 129, 238, 247, 443, **465**, 591, 593, 629, 637, 645
Princess's Theatre 222, 333, 465
Pringle, John Douglas 72
Prins, Richard 466
Prinsep, Henry 436, **466**, 540
Prisoner, The 421, 424
Prisoner of Zenda, The 318, 644
Prisoner's Country 424
prisoners' theatre 466
Pritchard, Bill 587
Private Lives 232, 238, 317, 320, 406, 427, 504
Private Yuk Objects 284
Privates on Parade 310
Probasco, Ellsworth 229
Probasco's circus 542
Prodigal Daughter, The 283
Producers and Directors' Guild of Australia 146, 221, 347

Producers, Authors, Composers and Talent. See **PACT Youth Theatre**
Professional Drama Council 498
Professor Mackay's National Concert and Burlesque Company 633
Professor Quack's Travelling Medicine Show 166
Professor, The by David Allen 468; by Hal Porter 64, 462
Proi 147
Prometheus 626
Promise, The 515, 586
Promises, Promises 52, 391
Prompt 243
Prompt Theatre 122, 455
Proof Positive 626
Proper, John 129
Property of the Clan, The 209
Prophète, Le 214
Propitious Kidnapping of a Pampered Daughter, The 136
Proposal, The 103
Pros and Cons Playhouse 266
Prospect Theatre Company 440, 586
prostitutes 353, 503, 630
Protest 421
Prout, John Skinner 179, **466**
Prout, Samuel 466
Provoked Husband, The 654
Provost, Marie 46, 553
Prunella 441
Prunes 108
publishing 467
Puck 430
'Puck' 343
Pugno di terra, Un 195
Puig, Manuel. See *The Kiss of the Spiderwoman*
Pullen, Ru. See *Curley on the Rack*
Pulteney Hotel 121, 327
Pulvers, Roger 99, 368, 459, **468**. See also *Bertolt Brecht Leaves Los Angeles*; *General Macarthur in Australia*; *Witold Gombrowicz in Buenos Aires*
Punch and Judy 468
Puntila 98
Puppet Guild of Australia 406
Puppet Power 96
puppetry 468, 655
Puppetry Guild of NSW 378
Puppy Love 223
Pure Puppet Adultery 96
Purple Onion 242
Purse, The 409
Puss In Boots 334
Pygmalion 200, 233, 322, 420
Pygmalion and Galatea 319, 331
Pygmalion and his Gal (a Dear!) 626

Q

Q Theatre (Adelaide) 28, 497
Q Theatre (Perth) 42
Q Theatre Company (Penrith and Sydney) 56, 79, 89, 222, 230, 239, 332, 413, 420, 459, **470**, 505, 515, 570, 572, 626, 628
QED 582
QTC Tangent Productions 476
Quaker Girl, The 326, 391
Quality Street 108
Quantock, Rod 551, 588
Quarry Amphitheatre 439
Quayle, Anthony 303, 510
Queen Elizabeth II 61, 72
Queen of Coolgardie 183, 585. See also **The Duchess of Coolgardie**
Queen Venus 147
Queen's Favourite, The 645
Queen's Love, The 115, 169
Queen's Park Theatre 426
Queen's Theatre (Adelaide) 25, 113, 121, 323, 419, **471**, 534
Queen's Theatre (Ballarat, Vic.) 38
Queen's Theatre (Melbourne) 269
Queen's Theatre (Sydney) 324, 566, 608
Queen's Theatre Royal 121, 197, 419, 447, **472**, 506, 653
Queensland Cultural Centre 433
Queensland Festival of Arts Society 226
Queensland Marionette Theatre 292, 469
Queensland Performing Arts Complex 109, **472**, 595
Queensland Performing Arts Trust 200
Queensland Playwrights' Laboratory. See Playlab
Queensland provincial towns 473
Queensland Theatre 100, 416, 579, 583
Queensland Theatre Company 53, 69, 82, 90, 98, 102, 105, 108, 120, 137, 150, 153, 175, 193, 200, 215, 232, 234, 261, 286, 320, 325, 326, 332, 356, 359, 371, 458, 474, **475**, 515, 516, 526, 527, 551, 557, 577, 651, 655
Queensland Theatre of the Deaf 582
Queensland University Dramatic Society 93
Queensland University of Technology 618
Queensland Youth Arts Festival 655
Queensland Youth Theatre 475
Queenslanders 59
Queer Subject, The 436

Quentin, Robert 43, 68, 193, 208, 219, 228, 290, 293, 305, 393, 413, **476**, 497, 568, 620
Quentin Massys 188
Quest, The 51, 212
Quick Quick Slow 562
Quiet Little Dinner, A 421
Quiet Night 90, 396, 452
Quilley, Denis 89, 519
Quin, Betty 28, 470. See also *The Dinkum Bambino*
Quin, Don 28, 470
Quin, Shirland. See *Dragon's Teeth*
Quinn, Anna Marie 278
Quinn, John 508

R

Rabe, David. See *Sticks and Bones*
Rabe, Pamela 279, 607
Racine, Jean. See *Berenice*; *Britannicus*; *Phedra*
Racing Demon 178
Radford, Basil 624
Radford, Robert 138, 278, **477**
Radic, Leonard 175, **477**
Radic, Thérèse 224, **478**. See also *The Emperor Regrets*; *Some of My Best Friends are Women*; *A Whip Round for Percy Grainger*
radio 20, 32, 67
radio and theatre 478
Radio Players 24, 113, 287
Rae, Betty 608
Ragged-Trousered Philanthropists, The 403
ragtime 347
Rahilly, Agnes 19, 102
railways 473
Rain 81
Rain Dancers, The 574
Rainbow Revels 559, 561, 626
Rainbow Serpent Theatre 255
Rainbow Warrior, The 57
Rainbows Die at Sunset 182
Rainer's Ethiopian Serenaders 370
Rainhill Murders, The 82
Rainmaker 538
Rainmaker, The 149, 349, 629
Rains, Claude 287
Raising the Wind 436
Rak Awin 429
Raleigh, Cecil. See *The Derby Winner*; *The Whip*; *The White Heather*
Ralph Wilson Theatre 598
Ramaciotti, Gustave 299, **480**, 586, 644
Ramaciotti, Vera 480
Ramblers 59, 633
Rame, Franca. See *Female Parts*; *The Open Couple*; *Whore in a Madhouse*

690

Ramsay, Molly 362
Ramsay, Robin 261, 330, 357, 480. See also *Bastard from the Bush, The*
Ramsey, Robin 57
Ramsey, Tamasin 480
Rand, Ayn. See *The Night of January 16th*
Randall, Brett 34, 42, 481, 506, 542
Randall, Carl 275, 302
Randall, Peter 481, 543
Randazzo, Nino 217
Randolph, Clemence. See *Rain*
Random, Margo 422
Rape of the Belt, The 427
Raphael, H. P. 141
Raphael, John N. See *Madame X*
Rapunzel in Suburbia 128, 342
Rats of Tobruk 227
Rattigan, (Sir) Terence 208. See also *The Deep Blue Sea*; *French Without Tears*; *Ross*; *Separate Tables*; *The Sleeping Prince*; *The Winslow Boy*; *While the Sun Shines*
Rattle of a Simple Man 352, 516
Raun Raun 31
Ravenswood, David 599
Rawil Productions 123
Ray, Joseph 531
Raye, Carol 613
Rayment, Colette 75
Rayment, John 225, 328, 341
Raymond and Agnes 204
Raymond, Linda 189
Raymond, Lord of Milan 114, 378, 481
Rayner, Betty 481
Rayner, Joan 481
Raynor, Joseph 294
Raynor, Molly 482
Rayson, Hannie 224, 456, **482**, 595. See also *Hotel Sorrento*; *Mary*; *Please Return to Sender*; *Room to Move*
Read, W. See *Formosa*
Read and Barnes 87
Reade, Charles. See *Masks and Faces*
Reading Boy 508, 646
Real Inspector Hound, The 527
Real Thing, The 85, 240, 317, 556, 630
Real Time 241
Really Interesting Gypsies, The 188
Reaping the Whirlwind 63, 285
Rebel Smith 105
Recital 224
Record of Interview 466
Recruiting Officer, The 131, 158, 209, 332, 363, 466, 487, 545, 566, 589
Red and Gold 526
Red King, The 429
Red Like the Devil 195
Red Mill, The 326, 391
Red Riding Hood 299, 330

Red Shed Company 29, 220, 223, **482**, 615
Red Sky at Morning 179, 452
Reddy, Helen 322
Reddy, Max 59, 322
Rede, Reg 504. See also *The Kelly Gang*
Redemption 319
Redfern Dramatic Society 416
Redgrave, (Sir) Michael 318, 408, 510. See also *The Aspern Papers*
Redgrave, Roy 55, 118, 392, **482**, 637, 647
Redmond, Bill 413, 617
Redpath, Martin 399, 428
Redshaw, Marie 97
Reed, Bill 483. See also *Burke's Company*; *Truganinni*
Reedman, Mark 310
Reedy River 190, 391, 401, 402, 403, **483**
Rees, Leslie 68, 74, 173, 256, 394, 445, 453, 478, **483**, 621
Rees, William 228, **483**
Reeve, Ada 253, 285, 348, **484**, 601, 644
Reeve, Edward. See **Raymond, Lord of Milan**
Reeve, F. B. 377
Reeve, Goodie 484
Reeve, William. See *The Purse*
Reeve, Wybert 82, 242, **484**
Reeves, Melissa 223. See also *In Cahoots*; *Sweetown*
Refined Look at Existence, A 13, 54, 262, 332, 367
Refractions 211, 220
Regan, Alec 27
Regent Theatres 597
Reginka's Lesson 60, 198
Reg's Show 87
Reid, Don 73, 210, 577
Reid House Theatre Workshop 122, 126
Reid Library 498
Reidy, John 318
Reiman, Eric 125, 281
Reimers, Monroe 338
Reiniger, Lotte 469
Reluctant Debutante, The 352, 408
Reluctant Rebel, The 463
Remans, Anne. See **Anne Clarke**
Removalists, The 71, 81, 85, 230, 262, 266, 321, **454**, **485**, 526, 544, 641
Rendra, W. S. See *The History of the Naga Tribe*
Rene, Roy 27, 91, 114, 370, 380, 426, 427, 429, 441, **485**, 502, 561, *603*, 652
repertoire 487
Repertorian 351
Repertory Club (Bunbury, WA) 634
Repertory Club (Goomalling, WA) 633

Repertory Club (Moora, WA) 633
Repertory Club (Perth) 20, 42, 44, 156, 225, 362, 395, 437, **494**, 498, 633
repertory movement. See **amateur theatre**
Representative, The 83, 146, 215, 264
Reprieve, The 581
Request Program 215
Rescue Party, The 543
research 495
Reservoir by Night 190
Resignation of Mr Bagsworth, The 526
Resistible Rise of Arturo Ui, The 85, 98, 413, 636
Resurgents 466
Rettick, Justine 330
Return Fare 83, 288
Return to Abyssinia 638
ReUnion Show, The 562
Reveille, The 533
Revenge, The 487, 529
Revenger's Tragedy, The 432
Reverses 147, 148, 639
revue 67, 370, 461, **500**
Revue Of The Absurd, A 574
Rex, Tony 318
Reynolds, Vicki 359. See also *Daily Grind*
Rhapsodies 486
Rhodes, W. B. See *Bombastes Furioso*
Riantiarno, Nano. See *The Cockroach Opera*
Ribush, Dolia 20, 41, 192, 344, 498, **500**, 514
Rice, Elmer. See *The Adding Machine*; *Dream Girl*; *Judgement Day*
Rice, Tim 596
Richard, Monsieur 71
Richard II 96, 234, 240, 331, 527
Richard III 20, 85, 149, 166, 225, 233, 278, 310, 328, 396, 398, 399, 409, 414, 428, 437, 465, 487, 491, 510, 522, 524, 539, 656
Richards, Lloyd 73
Richards, Max. See *Cripple Play*
Richardson, Howard. See *Dark of the Moon*
Richardson, (Sir) Ralph 72, 77, 291, 319, 332
Richardson, Sally. See *Picasso and Françoise*
Richardson, Wendy 501. See also *Windy Gully*
Richbrooke Theatre 420
Richelieu 114
Richmond, Gwenneth 79
Rick Raftos Management 34
Rickards, Harry 47, 205, 336, 338, 340, 381, **501**, 601, *602*, 605, 632
Rickards, Helen 259
Rickards, Kate 601
Rickards, Madge 601

Rickards, Noni 601
Rickards Tivoli Theatre 268, 602
Rickards Tivoli Theatres Ltd 604
Rickards's New Tivoli Theatre 338
Ricketts, Charles 548
Rickie, Nellie. See *The Emissary*
Ricordi 195
Ride Across Lake Constance, The 215, 626
Ride, Edwin 519
Rider, Sue 224
Ridge's Royal Tycoon Circus 434
Ridgeway brothers 116
Riding St Leons, Five 140, 542
Riding to Win 283
Ridley, Arnold. See *The Ghost Train*
Rienits, Rex 457. See also *Lightning Strikes Twice*
Riff Raff 391, 631
Riggs, Grattan 47, **502**
Rights of Women, The 447
Rignold, George 12, 18, 162, 205, 206, 233, 270, 490, **502**, 523, 643, 645
Riki-Tiki 391
Ring Round the Moon 81, 233, 317, 363
Ringbolter, The 261
Ringer, The 376
Ringling, May. See **May Wirth**
Rio Rita 371, 383, 391, 507
Riogoku troupe 306
Rip Van Winkle 46, 299, 488, 535, 643
Rising of Pete Marsh, The 271, 396
Ristori, Adelaide 213, 489, **503**
Ritchard, Cyril 90, 201, 238, 301, 302, 312, 408, 491, 497, 498, **503**
Ritchie, Jack 376
Ritz Theatre 605
Rivals, The 331, 332, 527, 574
River Jordan, The 466, 505
Riverboat Show, The 379
Riverina Playhouse 504
Riverina Theatre Company **504**, 620
Riverina Trucking Company 504
Riverland Youth Theatre 147, 537
Rivers of China, The 187, 286, 359, 363, 573
Riverside Theatres 434, 570
Road House 111
Road to Mecca, The 297, 536
Roadknight, Margaret 422
Roadwork 105, 475
Roar, China! 403
Roar of the Greasepaint, the Smell of the Crowd, The 391
Rob Roy 204, 511
Robbers, The 214

691

Robbery Under Arms 12, 163, 180, 181, 361, **448**, 449, 482, 490, **504**, 626
Robbins, Jerome 53
Robe of Yama, The 11
Robert and Elizabeth 105, 129, 366, 391
Roberta 50, 321, 391
Roberts, Alastair 515
Roberts, Doug 33
Roberts, Harry 374, 474
Roberts, John W. 270
Roberts, Laura 417
Roberts, Sue 328
Roberts, Vic 561
Robert's Wife 115, 240
Robertson, Agnes 93, 94
Robertson, Cathryn 469
Robertson, Henry 464, 512, 589
Robertson, Janet 105, 224
Robertson, Malcolm 36, 466, **505**, 544
Robertson, Tim 75, **505**. See also *Manning Clark's History of Australia*; *Waltzing Matilda*
Robertson, Tom. See *Caste*; *Home*; *Ours*; *School*; *Society*
Robey, George 603
Robin, Gertrude. See *Makeshifts*
Robins, Rege 392, 637, 647
Robinson, Cathryn 538. See *Faust*
Robinson, Gerry 328
Robinson, Kathleen 161, **505**, 639, 651
Robinson, Keith. See *The Popular Mechanicals*
Robinson, Governor Sir William 38, 436, 540
Robson, Allie 377
Robson, Diane 422
Roche, Hattie 47
Rock and Reel 288, 420
Rock 'n' Roll Circus 102, 562
Rocket Range 401
Rockhampton Dramatic Society 473
Rockhampton Little Theatre 475
Rocks Players 515
Rocks Theatre 342
Rocky Horror Show, The 230, 260, 386, 391, 525, 596
Rodger, Mick 306
Rofe, Thomas 343
Roffey, Jack. See *Hostile Witness*
Rogers, G. H. 506. See also *Transportation and the Demon Discord*
Rogers, Meredith 223, 224
Rogers, Paul 290, 524
Rogers's California Troupe 291
Roland, Betty 402, 497, **506**. See also *Granite Peak*; **The Touch of Silk**; *War on the Waterfront*; *Wedding Bells*
Roleystone Repertory Club 633
Rolfe, Alfred 181, 504, 505, **507**, 606

Rolfe, Des 396, 531, 615
Rolfe, Michael 412
Rolfe, Patricia 69
Rolls, Ernest C. 27, 49, **507**, 301, 397, 486
Roma 223
Romance 560
Romanian National Theatre of Craiova 356
Romanoff and Juliet 83
Romeo and Juliet 33, 85, 90, 96, 243, 341, 349, 366, 476, 487
Romer, Elizabeth 107
Romeril, John 54, 74, 276, 321, 356, 359, 457, 505, **507**. See also *Bastardy*; *Chicago, Chicago*; *The Floating World*; *The Great Macarthy*; *I Don't Know Who to Feel Sorry For*; *The Imposter*; *Lost Weekend*; **Marvellous Melbourne**; *Mrs Thally F*; *Reading Boy*; *Top End*
Roof-Garden Theatre 604
Rooklyn, Maurice 508
Room to Move 185, 332, 482, 595
Rooney, Rose 462
Roos 96
Rooted 118, 248, 455, **508**
Roots 198
Rope 20, 639
ropewalking 508
Rory O'More 55
Rosa Ribush Awards 76
Roscians 197
Rose, Julian 502
Rose of the Wilderness, The 81
Rose Tattoo, The 81
Rose-Marie 50, 81, 300, 383, 391, 415, 623
Rosenberg, Pam 125
Rosencrantz and Guildenstern are Dead 230, 332
Rosenwax, Nathalie 153
Roses in Due Season 147, 570, 614
Ross 635
Ross, Andrew 14, 97, 104, 196, 408, 412, **509**
Ross, Frances 98, 283
Ross, Gregory 508
Ross, Kenneth. See *Breaker Morant*; *Don't Piddle against the Wind, Mate*
Rostand, Edmond. See *L'Aiglon*; *Cyrano de Bergerac*
Rothwell, Geoffrey 497
Rough Crossing 221
Round Earth Company 135, 184
Round the Moon 156
Rouse, Graham 260, 613
Rover, The 286
Rowan Brothers' Circus 152
Rowbotham, David 175
Rowe, George Fawcett. See George Fawcett; *The New Babylon*
Rowe, Joseph Andrew 141
Rowe, Thea 98
Rowell, Kenneth 509
Rowell, Ruth 376

Rowett, Edith 292
Rowley, William. See *The Changeling*
Rowse, Dick 600
Roxburgh, Richard 574
Roxy Theatre: Leeton (NSW) 433; Sydney 239, 397
Roy Murphy Show, The 118
Royal Academy of Dramatic Art 287
Royal Adelaide Theatre 25, 189, 419
Royal Albert Theatre 605
Royal Alexandra Theatre 100
Royal Amphitheatre (Hobart) 508; (Launceston) 62, 151, 325; (Melbourne) 35, 465
Royal Assembly Rooms 585
Royal Australian Comic Opera Company 460
Royal Australian Equestrian Circus 116, 541
Royal Australian Opera Company 535
Royal Circus (Hobart) 62, 278; (Launceston) 16, 62, 138, 434, 477, 541
Royal City Theatre 65, 85, 325, 365, 398, 531, 566, 592
Royal Clarence Theatre 577
Royal Comic Opera Company 246, 299, 331, 559, 629, 632, 643, 653
Royal Commission into the Australian Economy, The 86
Royal Court Theatre Company 209
Royal Divorce, A 318
Royal English and Italian Opera Company 100
Royal Foresters' Hall 511
Royal Hawaiians 152
Royal Hotel 113, 319, 327, 335, 364, 585
Royal Hunt of the Sun, The 102, 120, 153, 252, 475, 555
Royal Mail 617, 633
Royal Marionette Theatre 365, 468
Royal Marionettes 468
Royal Martin Wirth Family 648
Royal Olympic Theatre 189, **509**, 577, 630
Royal Pantheon Theatre 278
Royal Pardon 632
Royal Pavilion Saloon 65, 511, 592
Royal Princess's Theatre 465
Royal Queensland Theatre Company. See Queensland Theatre Company
Royal Shakespeare Company 31, 209, 225, 474, **510**. See also Shakespeare Memorial Theatre Company
Royal Show 411
Royal South Street Society 268
Royal Standard Theatre 238, 329, 566, 594, **511**

Royal Theatre 465
Royal Uyeno troupe 306
Royal Victoria Theatre (Adelaide) 25, 323, 419, 471, 534
Royal Victoria Theatre (Bendigo, Vic.) 465
Royal Victoria Theatre (Brisbane) 100, 579
Royal Victoria Theatre (Hobart) 146, 180, 189, 278, 419, 506, 583, 630
Royal Victoria Theatre (Launceston) 121, 510, 630
Royal Victoria Theatre (Melbourne) 113, 121, 319, **511**
Royal Victoria Theatre (Newcastle, NSW) 592
Royal Victoria Theatre (Norfolk Island) 409
Royal Victoria Theatre (Sydney) 160, 206, 254, 285, 294, 319, 323, 335, 364, 382, 461, 464, 487, 506, **512**, 530, 531, 539, 545, 566, 589, 590, 591, 592, 593, 594, 646, 652
Royalists 38
Royboys 190
Royle, Bert. See *Djin Djin the Japanese Bogie Man*; *Matsa, Queen of Fire*
Royle, Milton. See *The Squaw Man*
Rube Redmond 48
Rubenstein, Deidre 512
Rubinstein, Gillian. See *Beyond the Labyrinth*; *Paula*; *Space Demons*
Rudd, Steele 12, 305, 417, 473, 497, **512**, 635. See also *Duncan McClure*; *On Grubb's Selection*; **On Our Selection**; *The Rudd Family*
Rudd Family, The 55, 197, 491, 512, 513
Rude, Rodney 551
Rudelhoff, Dinah. See Dinah Murray
Rudkin, David 240. See also *Ashes*
Rudrick, Paul. See *I Hate Hamlet*
Rule, Jean 429
Rum Do!, A 200, 391, 475
Run of Luck, A 282, 490
Run of the Mill 337
Runaway Girl, A 326, 391, 424
Runaway Steamboat, The 650
Rundle Rita 615
Rusden State College 22
Rush, Geoffrey 86, 90, 243, 336, **513**, 515, 574. See also *The Popular Mechanicals*
Russell, Anna 177, 185, 270, **514**
Russell, Fred 348, 426, 502
Russell, Katherine 180, 197, 345, 504
Russell, Willy. See *Educating Rita*; *Shirley Valentine*
Russell Street Theatre 514

Russian influences **514**
Rusty Bugles 20, 41, 51, 68, 132, 239, 440, 454, 491, 498, **515**
Rutenas, Paul 600
Rutenis, Paulius 216
Rutherford and Son 350, 557
Rutherford, (Dame) Margaret 82, 558
Ruthven, Margaret 407
Rutter, Chris 123
Ruttledge, Frances 98
Ryan, Madge 564
Rydge, Norman B. 277, 316
Ryley, Madeleine Lucette. See *Mice and Men*
Ryton, Royce. See *Crown Matrimonial*

S

Sabrina 604
Sacred Cow 83, 330
Sacred Cow II 83
Sacred Place, The 212, 375
Sad Song of Annie Sando, The 147
Sadka, Donna 174, **516**
Sadler, Bill 34, 151, 561
Sadler's Wells Opera Company 105
Sadlier Vidette 152
Safe House 201
Safe Sex 60
Sagar, J. T. 582
Sailor Beware 318
Sailor's Girl 598
Sainken, Sol 156, **516**
Saint Denis, Marie 397
Saint Joan 27, 28, 31, 56, 207, 257, 291, 301, 491, 616
Saint or Sinner 181
Sainthill, Loudon 357, 498
Sakuragawa Troupe 305
Salad Days 153, 233, 391, 409
Salamanca Script Resource Centre 516, 655
Salamanca Theatre Company 279, 291, **516**, 653, 654
Salathiel 319, 398, **516**
Salici's Marionettes 469
Salisbury College of Advanced Education 37
Salisbury Teachers' College 29
Sally 50, 362, 391
Salome: by Steven Berkoff 209; by Oscar Wilde 60, 172, 257, 597, 621
Salonika 458, 614
Salsbury, Nate 129
Salt, Mustard, Vinegar, Pepper 189
Salter, Boyd 598
Salter, June 352, 365, 497, **516**
Saltzer, John 393
Salzburg Marionettes 470
Salzer, Adam 582
Same Time, Next Year 375
Sammers, Christine 188, 328

Sammut, Saviour 338
Sammy at Sea 518
Samson, Lynne 462
Samuels, Edmond. See *The Highwayman*
San Francisco Palace Circus 141
San Quentin Theatre Workshop 203
San Toy 299, 326, 374, 391, 654
Sanctuary 254, 445
Sander, Sally 408
Sanders, Wendy 539
Sandford's American Players 460
Sandgate Amateur Dramatic Society 182
Sandhurst Amateur Dramatic Club 38
Sandinista 402
Sandow 502
Sandy Lee Live at Nui Dat 243, 544
Sankai Juku 31, 306, 369
Sansom, Clive 517
Sara, Mlle 382
Sarcophagus 515
Sardanapalus 63, 267
Sardou, Victorien. See *Fernande*; *Friends*; *La Tosca*
Saroyan, William. See *Across the Board on Tomorrow Morning*
Sartre, Jean-Paul. See *Altona*
Sas, Igor 90, 519
Satsuma troupe 305
Saunders, Hal 342, 600
Saunders, John 504
Saunders, Justine 13, 119, **517**
Savory, Gerald. See *George and Margaret*
Sawyer, A. D. 274
Saxby, David 396
Say It With Star 330
Sayer, Philip 510
Sayles, Irving 274, 460, **517**, 534
Says Who? 419
Scandal 50, 263
Scandals 56, 86
Scandinavian Hall 381, 605
Scandinavian Music Hall 605
Scanlan 412
Scanlon, Valerie 362
Scapa! 452
Scapin 432
Scarlet Letter, The 518
Scarlet Pimpernel, The 319
scenery 589
Scenic Studies Pty Ltd 310
Schall, Ekkehard 203
Schemers, The 27
Schiller, Friedrich von. See *The Robbers*; *William Tell*
Schilling, Ivy 326
Schneider, Alan 440
Schnitzler, Arthur. See *Anatole's Wedding*; *Farewell Supper*
Schofield, Leo 356
scholarship 495
Schonell Theatre 102
School 353

School for Friends 112, 638
School for Scandal, The 81, 83, 153, 329, 356, 414, 556, 564, 585
Schulz, Peter 215
Schumacher, Colin 504
Schwezoff, Igor 344
Scollay, Clive 508
Scott, Clement 15
Scott, Dulcie 292
Scott, Edwin Lewis. See *A Tale of the Transvaal*
Scott, Ian 367
Scott, Maurice. See *The Con Man*
Scott, Phillip 234
Scott, Russell 130
Scott, Thelma 517
Scott-Siddons, Mary 517, 552
Scout, The 48, 86, 129, 180, **518**, 627, 640
Scribe, Eugène. See *Adrienne Lecouvreur*
Scrimgeour, Colin 363
Scriven, Peter 121, 216, 342, 469, **518**, 600. See also *The Tintookies*
Scudamore, Daisy 118, 482
Scullin, James 249
Scully, Sean 608
Sculthorpe, Peter. See *Ulterior Motifs*
Seaborn, Broughton and Walford Foundation 254, 544
Seagull, The 85, 286, 356, 363, 514, 555, 570, 656
Seagull Theatre 587
Seagulls Over Sorrento 177, 305, 452, **519**
Seamer, Gillian 549
Searchlights 607
Searelle, Luscombe 535
Season at Sarsaparilla, The 28, 33, 58, 87, 120, 187, 190, 200, 230, **519**, 526, 556, 557, 577, 628, 629, 638
Season's Greetings 168, 342
Seasprite it's Dynamite 337
Seaton, Rose 599
Second Mrs Tanqueray, The 107, 108, 622
Second Story, The 463
Secondary Teachers' College 22, 184, 355
Secrecy 581
Secret Service, The 490
Secrets 259, 469, 614, 646
Sedley-Smith, William. See *The Drunkard*
Seduction Opera Company 236
See How They Run 332
Sefton, Queenie 417
Seidler, Harry 586
Selection, The 363, 635
Selective Artists Management 34
Sells Brothers's circus 141
Selwyn, Mr 481
Semi-Detached 224
Senator from California, The 468
Send Me Three and Fourpence 629

Senior, Mary 429
Señora Carrar's Rifles 98
Sensational South Yarra Show, The 544
Sentimental Bloke, The: musical 125, 186, 232, 384, 391, 471, **519**, 628; play 78, 420, 491, 525
Separate Tables 72
September Tide 166
Serious Family, The 538
Serious Money 241, 574
Serjeant Musgrave's Dance 29, 614
Serpent's Fall, The 224, 373
Servant of Two Masters, The 234, 367, 562
Servants of Vaucluse, The 606
Servo di due padroni, Il 217
Seton, Beryl 275
Seven Ashtons 16, **520**
Seven Deadly Sins, The 56, 435
Seven Little Australians 491, 532
1776 291
Seventh Heaven 263
Seventy Times Seven 466
Sewell, Stephen 90, 208, 445, 456, **520**. See also *The Blind Giant is Dancing*; *Dreams in an Empty City*; *The Father We Loved on a Beach by the Sea*; *Hate*; *A Long Way Home*; *Traitors*; *Welcome the Bright World*
Sex Diary of an Infidel 64, 255, 279, 392
Sexton, Timothy 367
Seymour, Alan 196, 497, **521**. See also *A Break in the Music*; *The Float*; **The One Day of the Year**; *Swamp Creatures*
Seymour, Everest York 521
Seymour Theatre Centre 85, 434, **521**, 594, 595
SGIO Theatre 475, 619
Sha Yexin. See *The Imposter*
Shackleton, Ernest 128
Shackleton, Molly 396
Shadow and Splendour 237, 526
Shadow of a Gunman, The 298
Shadow of Light 198
Shadow of the Glen, The 298
Shadowlands 574, 630
Shadows of Blood 79
Shaffer, Anthony. See *Murderer*
Shaffer, Peter. See *Amadeus*; *Equus*; *The Royal Hunt of the Sun*
Shaftesbury Theatre 605
Shafto, Thomas 605
Shairp, Mordaunt. See *The Green Bay Tree*
Shajiabang 136

693

Shakespeare, William 28, 84, 333, 488, **522**, 566. See also *All's Well that Ends Well*; *Antony and Cleopatra*; *As You Like It*; *The Comedy of Errors*; *Coriolanus*; *Cymbeline*; *Hamlet*; *Henry IV*; *Henry V*; *Henry VIII*; *Julius Caesar*; *King John*; *King Lear*; *Love's Labours Lost*; *Macbeth*; *Measure for Measure*; *The Merchant of Venice*; *The Merry Wives of Windsor*; *A Midsummer Night's Dream*; *Much Ado About Nothing*; *Othello*; *Pericles*; *Richard II*; *Richard III*; *Romeo and Juliet*; *The Taming of the Shrew*; *The Tempest*; *Titus Andronicus*; *Twelfth Night*; *Two Gentlemen of Verona*; *The Winter's Tale*
Shakespeare Club 325
Shakespeare Company 166, 363
Shakespeare in Jeans Company 654
Shakespeare in the Park 476
Shakespeare Memorial Theatre Company 192, 257, 281, 341, 349, 415, 491, 510, 524. *See also* **Royal Shakespeare Company**
Shakespeare tercentenary celebrations 183
Shakespeare Tercentenary Memorial Library 499
Shakespearean Quarterly 523, 640
Shakespeare's Women 406
Shakespericonglomorofunnidogammoniae 254, 446, **525**
Shakuntala 432
Shall, Theo 32, **525**
Shallow Cups 179
Shamus O'Brien 92
Shanahan, Bill 34
Shanahan Management 34
Shand, Ron 166, 396, **525**
Shange, Ntozake. See *for colored girls who have considered suicide when the rainbow is enuf*
Shanghai 391
Shanley, John Patrick. See *Danny and the Deep Blue Sea*
Shann, Edward 621
Shape of Time, The 211
Sharman, Jim 28, 30, 53, 69, 87, 98, 166, 193, 215, 230, 309, 409, 411, 471, 497, 519, **525**, 555, 556, 572, 596, 638. See also *Shadow and Splendour*; *10 000 Miles Away*
Sharman, Martin 629
Sharp, Andrew 260, 519
Sharp, Bob. See *Come Hell or High Water*
Sharpe, Diana 75
Shaughraun, The 93, 632, 645
Shave, Lionel 526
Shaw, Di 189

Shaw, George Bernard 208, 253, 564. See also *Androcles and the Lion*; *The Apple Cart*; *Arms and the Man*; *Caesar and Cleopatra*; *Candida*; *The Dark Lady of the Sonnets*; *The Devil's Disciple*; *The Doctor's Dilemma*; *Fanny's First Play*; *Getting Married*; *Heartbreak House*; *How He Lied to Her Husband*; *The Inca of Perusalem*; *Major Barbara*; *Man and Superman*; *The Man of Destiny*; *Mrs Warren's Profession*; *Pygmalion*; *Saint Joan*; *You Never Can Tell*
Shaw, Irwin. See *Bury the Dead*
Shaw, Margery 153
Shaw, Robert. See *The Man in the Glass Booth*
Shaw, Roderick 403
Shawn, Ted 429
She Stoops to Conquer 413
Shearer, Jill 442, **526**. See also *Shimada*
Shearing, Dinah 308, 367, 497, **527**, 528, 531, 615, 616
Sheldon, Edward. See *Romance*
Sheldon, Frank 322, 527
Sheldon, Tony 260, 322, 497, **527**, 622
Shellcove Road 119
Shepard, Sam 368. See also *Buried Child*; *Fool for Love*; *A Lie of the Mind*; *The Tooth of Crime*; *True West*
Shepherd, Catherine 527. See also *Daybreak*; *Lalor of Eureka*
Shepherd, Wayne 124
Shepherd on the Rocks 58, 596, 627, 638
Sheppard, Hattie 353, 397, **528**
Sher, Antony 510
Sheridan, John F. 553. See also *Fun on the Bristol*
Sheridan, Noel 431
Sheridan, R. B. See *The Critic*; *The Duennae*; *Pizarro*; *The Rivals*; *The School for Scandal*
Sheridan, W. E. 47
Sheridan Theatre 32
Sherlock, Maureen 243
Sherman, Martin. See *Bent*
Sherriff, R. C. See *Journey's End*
Sherrifs, Mark 378
Sherwood, Amy 158
Sherwood, Robert E. See *Idiot's Delight*
Shiel, Graham. See *Bali: Adat*
Shields, Ella 397, **528**, 602
Shifting Heart, The 72, 81, 87, 128, 276, 281, 290, 357, 424, 454, 457, 492, 527, **528**, 629
Shillingsworth, A 350
Shimada 63, 442, 526
Shindig 258, 463
Ship of Fools 95
Ship of Heaven, The 41, 275, 348
Ship that Never Was, The 184
Ship's Whistle, The 412

Shipwreck 51, 212, 366, 453, 558
Shiralee Theatre 426
Shirley, Arthur 283. See also *The Boom of Big Ben*
Shirley Valentine 258, 417, 438
Shop Girl, The 241, 383, 391, 484
Shopfront Theatre for Young People 528
Short, Harry 161
Shota Rustaveli Company 31
Shotlander, Sandra 223
Shoulder the Sky 179
Shout at the Thunder 408
Show Boat 50, 67, 301, 384, 391
Sidaway, Robert 158, 339, **529**, 566
Sidaway's theatre 131, **529**, 589
Side by Side by Sondheim 391
Sideshow 478
Sidetrack Performance Group 156, 166, 223, 431, **530**
Sidetrack Theatre Company 166, 210, 216, 339, 530, 570
Sidney Myer Performing Arts Awards 77
Siege of Troy, The 35, 115
Siestas in a Pink Hotel 145, 297
Sign of the Cross, The 137, 318, 490
Signal Driver 58, 71, 304, 555, 579, 627, 638, 651
Silberer, Geza. See *Caprice*
Silent House, The 376
Silent Partner 311
Silver Box, The 32
Silver Chimes 627
Silver King, The 263, 319, 437, 551, 585, 645
Silver Lining 304
Silverdome 578
Silver's Circus 141, **530**
Silvester, Alfred 626
Silvester Family 633
Simcox, Cliff 475
Simes, Thomas 327, **530**, 586, 615
Simmonds, James 465
Simmons, Joseph 131, 178, 327, 446, 516, **531**, 586, 653
Simon, Neil. See *Brighton Beach Memoirs*
Simon and Laura 167, 347, 408, 484
Simonsen, Fannie 214
Simple Spymen 106
Simpson, Alan. See *Mariner*; *Muriel*
Simpson, Helen 207
Simpson, J. P. See *Alone*
Simpson, J. 202 87
Sims, G. R. See *Blue-eyed Susan*; *In the Ranks*; *The Lights of London*
Sin 273, 391
Sinbad the Sailor 334, 559, 626, 627
Sinclair, Stephen. See *Ladies' Night*
Sing a Rainbow 538

Sing for St Ned 346
Sippe, George 585
Sir Benjamin Fuller's Royal Grand Opera Company 237
Siren 445, 642
Sirius Cove, A 526
Sisley, Barbara 41, 104, 292, **531**, 581, 615, 651
Sister Mary Ignatius Explains It All for You 326
Sistergirl 149, 509
Sisters 466, 521
Sitarenos, Mary 607
Site 155, 166
Sitting Ducks 98
Six Characters in Search of an Author 215, 258, 317, 404, 435, 573, 631
Sixteen Words for Water 135
Sizwe Bansi is Dead 13, 536
Skelta 311
Skevington, Patricia 621
Skewes, T. 599
Skin Free 606
Skin Game, The 61
Skin of Our Teeth, The 53, 317, 414, 491
Skinner, Carole 194, *454*, *568*
Skinner, Cornelia Otis 408, 504. See also *Our Hearts were Young and Gay*
Skinner, Phyl 28
Skirmishes 60
Sky 575
Sky Without Birds 252, 401, 452
Sky Wizard, The 128
Skylark Puppet and Mask Company 123
Skylark Theatre Company 123, 645
Slade, Bernard. See *Same Time, Next Year*
Slater, Florence 382, 533
Slaughter of St Teresa's Day, The 72, 157, 186, 313, 341, 454, **531**, *568*, 570, 615
Slaves of Sydney 345
Sleeping Prince, The 72, 458
Slice 128, 264, 562
'Sly, Christopher' 171, 397. See also **J. E. Neild**
Small Craft Warnings 570
Small Poppies, The 282, 337
Smalls 646
Smart, Jeffrey 33
Smart Set Diggers 58, 59, 191
Smash Hit 273
Smiles Away 96, 342, 469
Smilin' Through 104
Smith, Beaumont 334, 417, 513, **532**, 535. See also **On Our Selection**; *Seven Little Australians*; *While the Billy Boils*
Smith, Clay 602
Smith, Eddie 59
Smith, Edward 396
Smith, Frank 511
Smith, Georgie 16

694

Smith, James 106, 169, 306, 373, 499, **532**
Smith, Jill 444
Smith, Jo 118, **532**. See also *The Bushwoman*; *The Girl of the Never Never*; *The Miner's Trust*
Smith, John Thomas 472
Smith, Lindzee 231
Smith, Robert 402, 403
Smith, Rod. See *Seventy Times Seven*
Smith, Sam W. See *Struck Oil*
Smith, Shirley 420
Smith, William 362
Smith, Winchell. See *Brewster's Millions*
Smith's Weekly (newspaper) 137, 173, 292
Smugglers, Beware! 616, 650
Smythe, John 110, 195, 599
Snapshots of 1926 581
Snowangel 628
Snowden Picture Theatre 594
So Long Letty 201, 391
So This is Hollywood 226
Soak the Rich 190, 401
Soapbox Circus 145
Society for Arts and Literature 41, 122
Soft Sands 13
Soft Targets 254, 615
Soldene, Emily 382, **533**
Sole, Bill 435
Sole, Mary 434, 509, **533**
Sole Brothers' Circus 139, 435, 535, 542, 613
Sole family 434, 534
Solidarity 437, 464
Solomon, Emanuel 25, 471, **534**
Solomon, Vaiben 471, 534
Solomon and the Big Cat 337
Solomons, John 168
Some Night at Julia Creek 347
Some of My Best Friends are Women 478
Somers, Thomas 511, **534**. See also *For the Term of His Natural Life*
Somerville Auditorium 620
Something Blue 60
Son of Betty 330
Son of Man 230
Song and Dance 386
Song of '54 401
Song of the Seals 272, 336
Song Room, The 411
Song to Sing O, A 416
Songs My Mother Didn't Teach Me 83
Sons of Cain 82, 90, 178, 217, 255, 642
Sons of the Morning 198, 281, 400, 453, 480
Sons of the South 401
Sophocles. See *Antigone*; *King Oedipus*; *Oedipus*; *Oedipus at Colonus*; *Oedipus Rex*; *Oedipus the King*
Sorcerer, The 244, 391

Sorgato, Anton 60
Sorlie, George 405, 490, **534**, 581, 652. See also *My Pal Ginger*
Sorlie's tent show 324, 534, 581, 611
Sorrows of Satan, The 482
Sort of Chimera, A 147
Sothern, Lytton 333
Sound of Music, The 53, 55, 105, 129, 225, 386, 391
Souper, Gerald Kay 309, 329
Soutar, G. H. See *The Good Losers*
Soutar, Jack 462
South, Dorothy 49
South Africa 397, **535**, 611, 649
South Australian Performing Arts Centre Inc. 126
South Australian provincial towns 536
South Australian Regional Cultural Council 537
South Australian Theatre Company 28, 33, 44, 69, 79, 81, 83, 88, 89, 154, 165, 187, 193, 198, 209, 216, 227, 236, 240, 254, 255, 332, 413, 440, 515, 525, 555, 562, 577. See also State Theatre
South Australian Youth Arts Board 127
South East Performing Arts Collective 337
South Pacific 52, 391, 570
South Polar Expedition 537
South Sea Gold Bay 598
South Street Memorial Theatre 268
Southern Cross, The 197, 212. See also *The Democrat*
Southern Maid, A 61, 391, 478
Southport Street Theatre 280
Southward Bound 473
Soutten, F. M. 538. See also *The Battle of Melbourne*
Sowerby, Githa. See *Rutherford and Son*
Space 29
Space Demons 429, 616
Spangles 379
Spanish Main, The 19, 61
Spanner in the Works 126
Spare Parts Puppet Theatre Company 121, 438, 469, **538**, 578, 645
Spark, Muriel. See *The Prime of Miss Jean Brodie*
Sparklers 93
Sparring Partners 562
Sparrow, John 339, 529
Speaight, Robert 290
Spears, Steve J. 243, 455, **538**. See also *The Elocution of Benjamin Franklin*; *Young Mo*
Spectrum Theatre 634
Speed the Plough 583
Speed the Plow 58, 618
Spellbound 304, 411

Spence, Bruce 74, 155, 195, 231, **485**, 505
Spencer, Albert 539
Spewack, Sam and Bella. See *My Three Angels*
Spinks, Kim 188, 328
Spirit of the Bush, A 197, 391
Spirit of the Goldfields, The 447
Spitting Chips 606
Splinters 124
Spoiled Child, The 583
Spoleto Melbourne Festival 356, 615
Spong, W. B. 107
Spoon River 458
Spoons 626
Sport from Hollowlog Flat, The 67
Sporting Chance, A 337, 597
Spring and Port Wine 185, 517
Spring Chicken, The 326, 391
Spring Song, A 230, 346, 458, **539**
Spring-Heeled Terror of Stepney Green, The 332
Springle 108
Spring's Awakening 335
Spunner, Suzanne 184, 223. See *Dragged Screaming to Paradise*; *Ingkata's Wife*; *Overcome by Chlorine*
Spurr, Mel B. 231
Spy, The 403
Square Ring, The 60, 440, 480
Squaring the Circle 401
Squatter, The 183
Squatter's Daughter, The 55, 78, 197, 361, 450, 491, **539**, 646
Squaw Man, The 112
Squeaker, The 248
Squibs 274
Squirts 244
SS Glencairn 81, 130, 580
St George and the Dragon 271
St George's College Dramatic Society 621
St George's Hall (Melbourne) 634;
St George's Hall (Perth) 436; **540**
St George's Leagues Club 152
St James Hall 381, 441
St James Infirmary 209, 222, 471
St James Theatre: Melbourne 422; Sydney 239, 372, 567, 590, 637
St Joey's Local Club 374
St Leon, Alfred 540, 542, 649
St Leon, Cassimer 541, 542
St Leon, Clyde 542
St Leon, Daisy 284, 541, 542
St Leon, Dimpi 542
St Leon, Elsie 540
St Leon, George 540
St Leon, Gus 229, 540, 541, 542, 649
St Leon, Ida 540
St Leon, Mathew 541
St Leon, Norman 542
St Leon, Philip 140, **541**, 542

St Leon, Reginald 541, 542
St Leon, Sylvester 541, 542
St Leon, Walter 62, 142, 540, 542
St Leon's British-American Circus 542
St Leon's Circus 116, 461, 612
St Leon family circuses 138, 533, **540**, 541
St Leon Troupe 540, 541, 542
St Leons, Five 16, 284, 542
St Leons, Five Riding 140, 542
St Mark's Gospel 505
St Martin's Theatre 498, 542, 543, 544
St Martin's Theatre Company 45, 217, 221, 252, 310, 371, 432, 481, **542**, 551, 614, 615, 651
St Martin's Two 544
St Martin's Youth Arts Centre 79, 505, **544**
St Marys Kid 471
St Peters Community Players 458
St Thomas More 27
Stable, J. J. 104
Stables, Gerry 619
Stables Theatre 202, 210, **544**, 569, 595
Stace, Rose 376
Stacey Testro Management 35
Stafford-Clark, Max 209
Stage 122
Stage Company 29, 30, 70, 81, 129, 243, 254, 291, 332, 416, **544**, 607
Stage Crisis Day 70
stage design 545
Stage Door 474
stage effects 545
Stage-Struck Tailor and the Trickish Youth, The 446
Stagemaster 124
Stages 74
Stainton, Bette Bailey 380, 587
Stainton, Philip 587
Staircase 305
Stallerhof 215
Stalwart the Bushranger 214, 262, 446, **550**
Stamford, Wybert 596
Stammers, Blanche 242, 330
stand-up comedy 551
Standard Theatre 511
Standish, H. A. 174, **551**
Stanford, C. R. 437, **551**, 585
Stanislaus, F. 107
Stanislavsky, Konstantin 20, 227
Stannard, Peter 330
Stansfield, Mary 179
Stanton, John 551
Stapleton, Terry 418, 519
Star Company 151
Star Dramatic Company 246, 249
Star is Torn, A 56, 224, 228
star system 552
Star Theatre: Adelaide 338; Chiltern (Vic.) 135, 592
Star Variety Troupe 649

695

Stark, James and Sarah 46, 553
Starke, Russell 586
Starlight Express 386, 391
Starr, Muriel 48, 49, 263, 481, **555**
Stars in the Home 396
Startrick 462
Stasis 297
State, William 362
State Archives of NSW 274
State Drama Festival (WA) 494, 634
State Government Insurance Office Theatre 102. *See also* Suncorp Theatre
State Library of Queensland 497
State Library of South Australia 472
State Library of Tasmania 377, 498
State Library of Victoria 498
State of Defence 95, 359
State of Shock 13, 562
State Opera of South Australia 265
State Theatre 28, 30, **555**.
State Theatre: Melbourne 624; Sydney 590, 637
State Theatre Company 555. *See also* **State Theatre**; State Theatre Company of South Australia
State Theatre Company of South Australia 28, 53, 79, 80, 81, 147, 178, 185, 190, 194, 215, 217, 221, 240, 241, 255, 258, 260, 286, 304, 308, 309, 317, 328, 346, 398, 416, 441, 442, 508, 519, 520, 526, 551, 555, 596, 627, 635, 638, 651, 655, 656. *See also* **State Theatre**
State Theatre Company of the Northern Territory 184, 410
State Theatre Company of Western Australia 280, 417, 438, **556**
State Theatre of Lithuania 31
Statements after an Arrest under the Immorality Act 536
Steaming 228, 570
Stebbing, Frank 138
Steel, Anthony 30, 70, **557**
Steele, Rob 119
Steele, Tommy 604
Steele-Scott, Kathleen 258
Steinbeck, John. *See Of Mice and Men*
Stelarc 430
Stellmach, Barbara 74, 137, 497, **557**
Stephen 526
Stephens, Adrian Consett. *See Echoes*
Stephens, Babette 44, 104, 557, 617
Stephens, Barbara 102
Stephens, Bill 124
Stephens, Jon 508

Stephens, Tom 557, 617
Stephensen, Clara 154
Steppenwolf Theatre Company 225
Stepping Out 228, 325
Sterke, Jeanette 366
Stern, Sam 535
Sterne, Laurence 84
Stevens, Cliff 243
Stevens, Jon 368
Stevens, Samuel. *See A Girl's Frolic and What Came of It*
Stevenson, Janet and Philip. *See Counter Attack*
Stevenson, Ross. *See The Royal Commission into the Australian Economy*
Stewart, Docie 263, 558, 560, 561
Stewart, Douglas 207, 404, 453, 497, **558**. *See also The Fire on the Snow; The Golden Lover; Ned Kelly; Shipwreck;*
Stewart, Grace 534
Stewart, Innes 33
Stewart, Maggie 267, 558, 560, 561
Stewart, Nancye 26, 308, 309, 332, 379, 396, **558**
Stewart, Nellie 48, 213, 267, 379, 382, 450, 489, 497, 498, 533, **558**, 561, 567, 596, 645, 650
Stewart, Richard 298, 299, 558, **560**, 561, 585
Stewart, Sophie 413, 476
Sticks and Bones 297
Stiffy and Joe 441
Stiffy and Mo 238, 426, 441, 461, 485, **561**
Stigwood, Robert 30
Stingray 397
Stirling, Theodosia 146, 558, 560, **561**, 650
Stirrer, The 89
stock companies 487
Stoddart, John 70
Stoddart, Ralph 633
Stombucco and Son 268
Stone, Leonard 52
Stone, Louis 413, 497. *See also Lap of the Gods*
Stoneham, William 326
Stoppard, Tom 208. *See also Arcadia; Enter a Free Man; Jumpers; Night and Day; The Real Inspector Hound; The Real Thing; Rosencrantz and Guildenstern are Dead; Rough Crossing; Travesties*
Storey, David. *See Home*
Stork 539
Storming Mont Albert by Tram 595
Storming St Kilda by Tram 595
Storr, John 59
Story of the Kelly Gang, The 640
Strachan, Tony **562**. *See also The Eyes of the Whites; State of Shock*
Strand Theatre 278

Strange Orchestra 27
Stranger in New York, A 629
Stranger, The 120, 121, 213, 236, 278, 539, 577, 579
Strangers in the Land 97, 401
Stransky, Helen 248
Strauss, Botho. *See Big and Little*
Strauss, Johann II 388
Stravaganza 216
Strawhan, Gavan. *See Bah Humbug!; The Floating Palais; The Last Drive-In On Earth*
Stray Leaves Opera and Theatre Company 580
Street Arts Theatre Company 102, 155, 166, 474, **562**
Streetcar Named Desire, A 53, 297, 376, 398, 491
Streets of London, The 160
Strehler, Giorgio 217
Stretch of the Imagination, A 60, 71, 117, 178, 241, 273, 367, 373, **455**, **562**, 614, 624
Strike at the Port 655
strikes 294
Strindberg, August. *See The Dance of Death; A Dream Play; The Father; Miss Julie; The Stronger*
Stripper, The 596
Strode, W. Chetham. *See The Guinea Pig*
Stronger, The 83
Struck Oil 47, 374, 474, 488, 497, 566, 643
Strutton, Tony 429
Stud 538
Student Prince, The 50, 391
Student Theatre 400, 401
students' theatre 122
Studio 228 80
Studio Australia 89
Stuffed Puppet Theatre 613
Styan, Arthur 98
Styles, Edwin 408, 554, 603, 639
Sub-Editor's Room 483
Subiaco Theatre Centre 280, 439
subsidy 456, **562**
Suburban Mysteries 241
Suburban Requiem 598
Such is Life 439
Sudermann, Hermann. *See The Fires of St John*
Sugar 391
Sugar Babies 348
Suicide, The 310
Suilven and the Eagle 11
Suite in Three Keys, A 104, 291
Sullivan, Barry 205, 297, 498, 510, 522, 541, 552, **564**
Sullivan, Cornelius 152
Sullivan, John L. 336, **564**
Summer 618
Summer Lightning 633
Summer of the Aliens, The 410, 411

Summer of the Seventeenth Doll
20, 52, 53, 68, 71, 72, 87, 193, 194, 199, 208, 222, 224, 235, 239, 240, 255, 260, 290, 304, 323, 355, 358, 445, 454, 467, 471, 483, 492, 498, 515, 536, 549, **564**, 573
Summer Rain 148, 209, 317, 391
Summer Shadows 87
Summerland 80, 391
Summers, Alison 606
Summerton, Peter 53, 439, 497
Sumner, John 22, 68, 69, 157, 193, 194, 208, 323, 330, 354, 357, 396, 405, 427, 491, 497, 564, **565**, 638
Sumner, Phil. *See Riff Raff*
Sun (newspaper) 174
Sun and Shadow 160, 361, 447
Sun Books 467
Sun News–Pictorial (newspaper) 174
Sun on Our Backs, The 402
Suncorp Theatre 102, 475
Sunday 600
Sunday Lunch 241
Sunken Garden Theatre 149, 594, 620
Sunny 50, 186, 270, 391
Sunny South, The 71, 183, 361, 448, 490, **565**, 572, 585
Sunrise 411
Sunshine Girl, The 383, 391
Suppressed Desires 50
Sur le pont 252
Surplus, Sean 125
Surtees, Miss 578
Susannah's Dreaming 272
Süsskind, Patrick. *See The Double Bass*
Sutherland, Peter 462
Sutherland-Williamson International Grand Opera Company 304, 341
Suttor, Lloyd 378
Suzuki, Tadashi 64, 306, 369, 444. *See also The Chronicle of Macbeth*
Swamp Creatures 521
Swan Down Gloves, The 108
Swan Gold Theatre Awards 77
Swan Hill National Theatre 349
Swan Hill Shakespeare Festival 349
Swan Hill Theatre Group 349
Swan Players 96, 621
Swan River Saga 424
Swan River Stage Company 196, 509
Sweatproof Boy, The 187
Sweeney, Harry 392
Sweeney Todd 127, 217, 265, 391
Sweeping Statements 562
Sweet Bird of Youth 320
Sweet Charity 265, 266, 385, 391
Sweet Kitty Bellairs 560
Sweet Lavender 329
Sweet Nancy 501

Sweet Nell of Old Drury 48, 379, 489, 560
Sweetest and Lowest 133, 440
Sweetown 482
Swimming in Light 222
Swinburne, Mercia 414
Sword Sung, The 400
Sybil 391
Sydney 566
Sydney, Dorothy 329
Sydney, Joan 148, 424, **570**
Sydney, Juliet 281
Sydney, Maie 149
Sydney Corporeal–Mime Theatre 211
Sydney Coves 342
Sydney Critics' Circle 76, 315, 577
Sydney Delivered 115
Sydney Entertainment Centre 109
Sydney French Theatre 216
Sydney Front 220, 431
Sydney Mail (newspaper) 171
Sydney Marionettes 469
Sydney Morning Herald (newspaper) 171, 403
Sydney Opera House 210, 433, 498, **571**, 590, 592
Sydney Opera House Trust 344
Sydney Players' Club 40, 362
Sydney Repertory Theatre Society 40, 66, 112, 172, 275, 350, 357, 567, **571**, 599
Sydney Rocks 405
Sydney Stage Employees' Association 294
Sydney Stage Society 441
Sydney Street Theatre Space 422
Sydney Theatre Company 53, 69, 72, 85, 128, 129, 145, 146, 148, 157, 158, 165, 178, 183, 186, 193, 199, 203, 215, 217, 221, 222, 230, 231, 234, 236, 237, 240, 243, 251, 252, 257, 258, 260, 262, 265, 267, 285, 292, 304, 308, 316, 317, 328, 332, 334, 348, 363, 371, 376, 398, 410, 411, 413, 414, 428, 480, 511, 515, 517, 524, 526, 527, 551, 556, **572**, 596, 607, 627, 630, 631, 635, 636, 638, 656
Sydney Union Repertory Theatre 399
Sydney University Dramatic Society 38, 41, 58, 81, 84, 281, 396, **574**, 607, 619
Symes, Mrs P. J. 292
Symon, Arthur. See *The Harvesters*
Synge, J. M. 211, 297. See *The Playboy of the Western World*; *The Shadow of the Glen*
Syron, Brian 13, 73, 119, 187, 497, **575**
Szeps, Henri 575, 613

T

Table Talk (magazine) 170
Tadpole 646
'Tahite'. See **J. E. Neild**
Taiichi troupe 306
Taijin Municipal Beijing Opera 136
Tait, Arthur 575
Tait, Charles 298, **575**
Tait, E. J. 298, 299, **576**
Tait, (Sir) Frank 298, **576**
Tait, John 298, **576**
Tait, Nevin 298, 300, 415, **576**
Tait's Concert Bureau 575
Takahashi, Yasunari 306
Take a Bow 270
Taken for Granted 337
Taken from Life 283
Talbot, Frank 64
Tale of a Tiger 216
Tale of Mystery, A 325
Tale of the Transvaal, A 535
Tales From Noonameena 342
Tales from the Vienna Woods 33, 215
Talk to the Moon 314
Talking to Grandma While the World Goes By 337, 616
Tallis, (Sir) George 48, 298, 299, **576**, 644
Tally's Folly 577
Tame Cat, The 24
Taming of the Shrew, The 61, 96, 137, 234, 267, 279, 406, 410, 475, 524
Tanaka, Min 306, 369, 431
Tangled Skein, A 532
Tango 459
Tango 160 124
Tannaker troupe 305
Tanner, Les 403
Tannett, Thomas 443
Tantrum Press 468
Taphouse, Lucy 379
Tapu 24, 275, 391, 404, 460
Taqa 224
Targett, Ellen 267
Tarkington, Booth. See *Monsieur Beaucaire*
Tartuffe 150, 618
Task Force 13
Tasker, Ian 242, 422
Tasker, John 44, 53, 193, 242, 258, 368, 405, 440, 516, 519, 555, **577**, 586, 608, 638
Tasmaniacs 59
Tasmanian Arts Advisory Board 656
Tasmanian provincial towns 577
Tasmanian Puppet Theatre 275, 469, 470, **578**, 614, 645
Tasmanian Theatre Company 53, 278, 394, 516, 584, 619, 655
Tasmanian Theatre in Education 516
Tasmanian Theatre Trust 291, 584

Taste of Honey, A 68, 616
Tata Goonight Goonight 28
Tate, Frank 523
Tate, Harry 502
Tate, John 128
Tate, Nick 128
Tatler (magazine) 170
Tatty Hollow Story, The 264, 271
Tavares, Morton 100, 416, **578**
Taxi 359
Taylor, Ariette 259, **579**
Taylor, Charles 580
Taylor, Frank 519
Taylor, Grant 531, 615
Taylor, H. Vivian 269
Taylor, John 579
Taylor, Maria 531, **579**
Taylor, Robert 116, 310, 542
Taylor, Samuel. See *Beekman Place*; *The Pleasure of his Company*
Taylor, Stan. See *Victor Hara, Companero*
Taylor, T. Hilhouse 214. See also *Parsifal*
Taylor, Tikki 266, 588
Taylor, Tom. See *Clancarty*; *Our American Cousin*
Taylor, Tony 22, 195, 276, 345, 393, 573, **580**, 622. See also *The Popular Mechanicals*; *You and the Night and the Housewine*
Taylor, 'Toso' 427. See also *Parsifal*; T. Hilhouse Taylor
Taylor–Carrington Company 117, 580, 632
Taylor's Royal Amphitheatre 25
Tchinarova, Tamara 227
Tea and Sympathy 53, 230
Tea For Three 248
Teahouse of the August Moon, The 53, 395, 424, 438, 458
Teale, Leonard 422, 497, **580**
Tearle, Conway 299
Teatro dell'IRAA 217
Teatro Settimo 217
Teede, Neville 396, 399, **580**, 621
Telegraph (newspaper) 173
television 20, 51
Tell Me the Truth 103
Tell Tales 557
Telling Mrs Baker 424
Temperance Hall 278
Tempest, (Dame) Marie 207, 263, 406, 558, 623
Tempest, The 36, 86, 150, 165, 193, 200, 240, 308, 332, 432, 476, 524, 579
Temple, Emma 107
Temple, Joan. See *No Room at the Inn*
Temple, The 411
Tempo Theatre 123
Ten Minute Alibi 517
10 000 Miles Away 193, 219, 432
Tenkei Gekijo 306
Tennant, Carrie 41, 457, **581**, 651

Tenschert, Joachim 98, 427
tent shows 92, 209, 361, 473, **581**
tents 138
Terrapin Puppet Theatre 147, 279, 578, **582**
Territory North Theatre Company 410
Terror Australis 219, 526
Terror, The 376
Tetsuwari–Tachibana troupe 306
Texas Jack 92, 640
Thalia Theatre 216
Thanks for the Memory 285, 429, 628, 652
That by which Men Live 188
Thatcher, Charles 246, 498
That's Murder 526
Theatre (magazine) 171, 333
Theatre 61 77. See also Hole-in-the-Wall Theatre
Theatre '62 28, 44, 240, **586**
Theatre ACT 123, 216, 635
Theatre Arts 42
Theatre Arts Productions 113
Theatre Australia 496
Theatre Australia (magazine) 175
Theatre Collection 498
Theatre Council of Western Australia 42, 225, 437, 457, 634
Théâtre de Complicité 209, 215
Theatre East 515
Théâtre en Spirale, Le 459
Theatre Erumu 154
Theatre Exchange 29
Theatre for Children 311
Théâtre Française de Melbourne 216
Theatre Freeholds Ltd 293
Theatre Guild and Drama School 150
Theatre Laboratory 459
Théâtre Nouveau 216
Theatre Now 279
Theatre of Image 128
theatre of the deaf 69, 72 582
Theatre of the Disabled 194
Theatre of Youth 482
Theatre Players 122
Theatre Project 190
Theatre Research Group 459
Theatre Royal (Adelaide) 25, 26, 324, 443, 533, **582**, 591, 592, 645
Theatre Royal (Ballarat, Vic.) 285, 592
Theatre Royal (Bendigo, Vic.) 38
Theatre Royal (Brisbane) 100, **583**, 592, 601
Theatre Royal (Broken Hill, NSW) 590, 593
Theatre Royal (Castlemaine, Vic.) **583**
Theatre Royal (Coolgardie, WA) 632
Theatre Royal (Geelong, Vic.) 189, 419

Theatre Royal (Gulgong, NSW) 246
Theatre Royal (Hobart) 57, 81, 85, 184, 377, 394, 433, 443, **583**, 590, 591, 592, 593, 594, 619, 656
Theatre Royal (Launceston, Tas.) 510, **584**
Theatre Royal (Melbourne) 106, 161, 162, 263, 267, 285, 338, 373, 443, 511, **584**, 590, *591*, 592, 593, 594, 645
Theatre Royal (Newcastle, NSW) 405
Theatre Royal (Perth) 238, 380, 437, 551, **585**, 601
Theatre Royal (Rockhampton, Qld) 473
Theatre Royal (Sydney) 65, 205, 309, 319, 323, 324, 327, 379, 380, 461, 480, 499, 508, 530, 531, 539, 545, 547, 566, 577, **585**, **586**, 589, 591, 592, *593*, 594, 603, 637, 652
Theatre Royal (Townsville, Qld) 473
Theatre Royal Adelphi 160
Theatre Royal Company 394
Theatre Royal Light Opera Company 394
Theatre Royal Management Board 395
Theatre Royal Musical Comedy Company 394
Theatre Royal Opera Company 394
Theatre Royal Workshop 394
Theatre South 156, 501, **587**, 597, 620
Theatre Workshop 621
Theatre Workshop and Actor's Studio 134, 204
Theatre Zart 216, 459
theatre-in-education 21, 224
theatre-restaurants 21, 77, 356, **587**
Theatrefest 225
Theatregoer (magazine) 174
theatres 589
Theatres and Public Halls Act (NSW) 594
Theatres Associated 28
Theatrescope (magazine) 175
TheatreWorks 22, 223, 431, **595**, 625
Theatrical Employees' Association 296
Theatrical Illusion, The 166
Theatrical Producers and Managers' Association of Australia 296
Théodora 86
There's a Girl in My Soup 280
Thérèse Raquin 112
Therry dramatic societies 27, 42, 77, 137, 298
These Cats Are Dangerous 98
They Came to a City 600
They Knew What They Wanted 50, 376

They Walk Alone 24, 81
They're Playing Our Song 391, 629, 630
Thibaudeau, Pierre 211
Thiersch, Marlis 69
Thief, The 652
Third Degree, The 319
Third Secretary, The 332, 440
Thirlwell, George 517
Thirst 516
Thirteen Dead 51, 198
Thirteenth Chair, The 26
This Dying Business 310
This Great City 627
This Great Gap of Time 273
This Old Man Comes Rolling Home 77, 178, 262, 271, 332, 399
This Sceptred Isle 84
This Year's Model 310
Thomas, Al 595
Thomas, Arthur H. 173
Thomas, Augustus. See *Arizona*; *In Mizzoura*
Thomas, Brandon. See *Charley's Aunt*
Thomas, Dylan. See *Under Milk Wood*
Thomas, Evan Henry 81, 297. See also *The Bandit of the Rhine*; *The Rose of the Wilderness*
Thomas, Geoffrey 346
Thomas, Julian 180. See *No Mercy*
Thompson, Chris 544
Thompson, Dot 402
Thompson, Gerald Marr 171, 172, **596**
Thompson, Jack 422
Thompson, Phil 189, 379. See *Fleets of Fortune*; *Paddy*
Thompson, Ross 178
Thomson, Brian 497, 526, 550, **596**
Thomson, Helen 175
Thomson, Jane Eliza. See Mrs Charles Young
Thomson, John 124
Thomson, Katherine 456, **596**. See also *Barmaids*; *Darlinghurst Nights*; *Diving for Pearls*; *Tonight We Anchor in Twofold Bay*
Thomson, Lloyd 519. See also *The Sentimental Bloke*
Thomson, Martha 650, 654
Thomson, Mary Christina 308
Thomson, Pat 376
Thomson, Russell 606
Thorndike, (Dame) Sybil 67, 72, 77, 207, 293, 301, 314, 319, 408, 491, 524, 567, 586
Thorndyke, Louise 93, 94
Thorne, C. B. 46
Thornett, Kenneth 519
Thorneycroft, Bob 369
Thornton, Eric 330

Thoughts of Chairman Alf, The 371
Three Beatings of Tao Sanchun, The 136
Three Cuckolds, The 216, 555, 556
Three Good Witches and the Bad Bad Prince, The 252
Three Legends of Kra, The 137
Three Little Maids 241, 391
Three Men and a Baby Grand 234
Three Months Gone 346
Three Old Friends 273, 321
Three Sisters 32, 85, 215, 233, 236, 257, 359, 367, 413, 422, 477, 512, 514, 556, 626, 630, 635
Threepenny Opera, The 56, 98, 186, 230, 391, 480
Thring, F. W. 130, 153, 240, 269, 384, 451, 465, **597**
Thring, Frank 60, 106, 356, 357, 573, **597**
Throssell, Ric 463, 497, **598**. See also *The Day Before Tomorrow*; *Dr Homer Speaks*; *For Valour*; *Ulterior Motifs*
Through Art, Unity 123, 216, **598**
Thumbs Up 199
Thunder Rock 156
Thunderbolt 55, 92
Thurbon, Anthony 178
Thurston, Howard 336, 378
Thurston, Robin. See *Record of Interview*; *Sisters*
Tibetan Inroads 614
ticket prices 66
Tier, Athol 90
Tiger at the Gates 235, 543
Tighe, Harry 292, **598**. See also *Open Spaces*
Tikki and John's 588
Tikki and John's Crazyhouse 588
Tildesley, Beatrice 42, 207, 445, **599**
Tildesley, Evelyn 207, **599**
Till the Day I Die 27, 51, 132, 400, 652
Tilly, Grant 405
Tilly of Bloomsbury 107
Tilton, Webb 302
Time Flits Away 621
Time is Not Yet Ripe, The 71, 212, 354, 357, 451, 491, 595, **599**
Time's Wing'd Chariot 56
Timlin, John 74, 273, 497. See *Dudders*
Timorese Association of the Northern Territory 410
Tin Alley Players 334, **600**, 619, 641
Tintookie Man, The 519
Tintookies, The 72, 391, 469, 518, **600**
Tintookies 2000 342, 519
Tiny Alice 239
Tiny Town 532, 535
Tip-Toes 50, 391
Tippett, Naomi 469

Tipping the Scales 337
'Tis a Pity she's a Whore 279
Tischbauer, Alfred 345. See also 'Alta'
Titheradge, Dion 600
Titheradge, George S. 18, 107, 149, 295, 331, 441, **600**, 643, 645
Titheradge, Madge 149, 422, 600
Tittell Brune, Minnie 47, 214, 299, 427, **600**
Titus Andronicus 36, 356
Tivoli Celebrity Vaudeville Pty Ltd 603
Tivoli circuit 50, 52, 66, 101, 300, 302, 344, 348, 380, 397, 409, 534, **601**, 606
Tivoli Circuit Australia Pty Ltd 603
Tivoli Follies 348, 429, 602
Tivoli Gang 186
Tivoli Theatre (Adelaide) 26, 268, 338, 590, 592, 601
Tivoli Theatre (Brisbane) 101, 591, 602, **604**, 637
Tivoli Theatre (Coolgardie, WA) 632
Tivoli Theatre (Melbourne) 380, 498, 602, **604**
Tivoli Theatre (Perth) 594, **605**
Tivoli Theatre (Sydney) 380, 498, 501, 568, 569, 601, 602, **605**
Tivoli Theatres Ltd 344, 603
Tjinderella 224
TN Theatre Company 80, 102, 232, 617, 618. See also **Twelfth Night Theatre**
TN2 618
To Botany Bay on a Bondi Tram 198, 373
To the West 606
Toast to Melba, A 272, 320, 580
Tobias and the Angel 36
Toda-San 462
Todd, Edna 407
Todd, Lionel 571
Todd, Richard 233, 395
Toe Truck Theatre Company **606**, 616, 653, 654
Tokyo Two 64
Tolano, R. 512
Toller, Ernst. See *Masses and Man*; *Oopla, We Live!*
Tom 118, 630
Tom and Jerry 65, 328
Tom and Viv 165, 292, 422
Tom Thumb, General 46, 535
Tom Thumb Theatre 188, 335
Tom Tom, the Piper's Son 35, 425
Tomholt, Sydney 453, **607**. See also *Anoli—the Blind*; *Bleak Dawn*
Tomkins, Max 466
Tommy 391
Tomoe Shizune and Hakutobo 306
Tonight at 8.30 302, 491, 504
Tonight Lola Blau 56

Tonight We Anchor in Twofold Bay 587, 597
Too Young for Ghosts 80, 148, 456, 544, **607**
Toohey, Angela 77
Toole, J. L. 205, **607**
Toorak Players Children's Theatre 57
Tooth of Crime, The 199, 266
Toowoomba Town Hall Theatre 474
Top End 63, 106, 368, 508
Top Girls 208, 615
Top of the Bill 420, 440
Top Silk 176, 227, 255, 286, 445, 642
Toppano, Enzo. See *The Jesus Christ Revolution*
Toppano, Peggy. See *The Jesus Christ Revolution*
Torch Song Trilogy 527
Torch Theatre 11, 27, 28, 256, 651
Toreador, The 299, 383, 391
Torning, Andrew 464, 512, 545, **608**, 652
Torning, Louise 652
Torrents, The 252, 401, 445, 458
Torres Strait Island Dance Company 13
Tosa, Yoshi 608
Tosca, La 86, 214
Totem Theatre 409
Totos, Christine 223
Tottenham, E. Hyacinth. See *The Golden West*
Touch of Midas, A 247
Touch of Silk, The 32, 150, 491, 506, 577, **608**
Touch Wood 617
'Touchstone' 532
touring 138, 473, **609**, 610, 633, 649
Tourmaline 509
Tourneur, Cyril. See *The Revenger's Tragedy*
Tower, The 462
Towers, Katie 651
Towers Company 632
Townsend, Peter 429
Townsend, Sue. See *Bazaar and Rummage*
Trafford Tanzi 228, 544, 615
Tragedy of Donohoe, The 262, 446, 550
Tragical History of Doctor Faustus, The 124, 286
Traitors 58, 222, 237, 244, 266, 297, 421, 520, **613**
Trans-Tasman Theatre Exchange 405
transformation scenes 547
translation 217
Translations 363, 577
Transportation and the Demon Discord 447
Transportation versus Emigration 158
Transported for Life 182, 559

Transvaal Heroine, A 535
Tranter, Neville 470, **613**
Trapper, The 48, 129, 181, 627
Travail 350
Travellers 424
Travelling North 85, 89, 110, 222, 258, 332, 445, 575, **613**, 629, 642
Travers, Ben. See *The Bed Before Yesterday*
Travers, Maurice 396
Travesties 240, 421
Treadmill 90
Tree, (Sir) Herbert Beerbohm 319
Tree Players 27
Treharne, Bryceson 26, 32, 39, 613, 619
Trelawney of the Wells 622, 629
Treloar, George 417
Trespassers Will Be Prosecuted 224, 314
Treteau de Paris, Le 216
Trethowan, Pamela 574
Tretyakov, Sergey. See *Roar, China!*
Trevai, Winnie 152
Trevelyan, Florence 107, 645. See also **Mrs Robert Brough**
Trevor, Alan 621
Triage or the Fortunates 367
Trial by Battle 477
Trial by Jury 244, 382, 391
Trial of Bardell and Pickwick 409
Trials of Hilary Pouncefortt, The 381, 588
Triangel 470
Tribe 219
Triffitt, Nigel 63, 469, 578, **614**, 645. See also *The Fall of Singapore*; *Juke—A milk bar romance*; *Moby Dick*
Trigg, Rev. 136
Trilby 299, 376, 560, 644
Trinder, Tommy 28, 322, 604
Trio in Gunshot 32
Trip to Chinatown, A 270, 629
Tripp, Helen 614
Tripp, Tony 338, **614**
Tristram Shandy 84, 505
Trojan Women, The 96, 306
Trollope, Anthony 297
Trookulentos, the Tempter 55, 70, 256, 287, 626
Troupe (Adelaide) 29, 37, 215, 241, 492, **614**, 620
Troupe (Canberra) 123
Truce, The 89
True Blue Beard, The 626
True Love 447, **615**
True St Joan, The 27
True West 165
Truganinni 13, 483
Trumbo 106
Trump Card, The 182
Trumpets and Raspberries 216
Trundle, Jean 42, 102, 103, 104, **615**, 651

Truscott, John 116, 356, 543, **615**, 624
Trust Players 20, 53, 72, 157, 276, 331, 367, 457, 568, **615**
Truth About Blayds, The 622
Tsoutas, Nicholas 29, 211, 431, 432, 459
Tucker, James 204, **616**. See also **Jemmy Green in Australia**
Tucker, Lilian 49
Tucker, Sophie 604
Tudor, Carrie 501
tufff… 108
Tuggeranong Playgroup Theatre 124
Tulloch, Peter 57
Tulloch, Richard 128, 339, *438*, 606, **616**. See also *Hating Alison Ashley*; *Year 9 Are Animals*
Tunis, Irene 310
Tuohill, Pat 407
Tur, Simone. See *Rak Awin*
Turgenev, Ivan. See *A Month in the Country*
Turnbull, Sydney 356
Turned Up 94, 107
Turner, Alexander 617. See also *Royal Mail*
Turner, David. See *Semi-Detached*
Turner, Eardley 296
Turner, Geraldine 24, 308, 520, 573, **617**
Turner, Hastings. See *The Lilies of the Field*
Turner, Richard 242
Turret Theatre 41, 227, 499
Twain, Mark 47
Tweedie, Jeana 95, 621. See also **Jeana Bradley**
Twelfth Night 31, 44, 58, 80, 109, 178, 200, 222, 281, 290, 413, 415, 421, 435, 510, 527, 617, 651
Twelfth Night Complex 44
Twelfth Night Theatre 43, 90, 102, 154, 223, 259, 346, 539, 557, **617**, 651. See also **TN Theatre Company**
Twelve Moons Cold 526
24 Hour Art 431
22 Hits and a Miss 59
Twinkle, Twinkle Little Star 148, 313, 425
Two 200
Two Cities 109, 155
Two for the Seesaw 435, 484
Two Gentlemen of Verona 96
Two Minutes' Silence 41, 240, 265, 491
Two Mr Wetherbys, The 357, 572
Two of Us, The 258
Two Orphans, The 160, 645
2 Till 5 Youth Theatre 619
Two to One 88
Two Weeks with the Queen 263, 574, 606
Twopenny, Richard 139, 169

U

Ubu-roi 208
Ulterior Motifs 391
Un-named Players 277
Uncle Tom's Cabin 46, 48, 92, 274, 347, 360, 409, 643
Uncle Vanya 31, 57, 129, 241, 359, 422, 514, 515, 574
Under Milk Wood 81, 254
Under the Coolibah Tree 190, 391, 401
Under the Gaslight 160
Underhill, Jeff 79. See also *The Bunyip and the Satellite*; *A Funny Thing Happened on the Way to The Front*
Understudies Pty Ltd 86, 422, 635
Underwear, Perfume and Crash Helmet 255
Unicomb, John 515, 584, **619**
Union Internationale de la Marionnette 378, 470
Union Theatre Repertory Company 20, 21, 22, 53, 60, 68, 83, 106, 119, 127, 134, 157, 193, 196, 200, 208, 224, 235, 284, 315, 330, 354, 357, 413, 418, 424, 483, 514, 549, 564, 565, 616, 619, 629, 638. See also **Melbourne Theatre Company**
United States Circus 434
Unity Dance Group 402, 483
Unity Theatre 400. See also **New Theatre**
Universal Theatre 203
universities 68, 355, **619**
University Dramatic Society 437, 620, **621**
University of Adelaide 455, 621; Performing Arts Library 497
University of Adelaide Theatre Guild 28, 44
University of Melbourne 68, 354, 565, 600, 619
University of New England 309, 497, 620
University of Newcastle 406, 620
University of NSW 68, 208, 290, 305, 393, 619
University of Queensland 68, 455, 497, 618
University of Queensland Press 467
University of Sydney 68, 73, 211, 521, 619
University of Tasmania 578
University of Technology 68
University of Western Australia 44, 68, 95, 156, 225, 396, 412, 437, 620, 634, 651
University of Western Australia Dramatic Society 96
University of Wollongong 587, 620
University Players 42
Unjustly Condemned 580

Unjustly Sentenced 580
Unknown Soldier and His Wife, The 421, 466
Unley Youth Theatre 29, 537, **622**
Unquiet Spirit, The 198
Unsuitable for Adults 185, 230
Up the Ladder Again 347
Upfront Theatre 598
Upside Down at the Bottom of the World 37, 58, 421, 627
Upton, John 622. See *Machiavelli, Machiavelli*
Upward, George 548
Ustinov, (Sir) Peter. See *The Love of Four Colonels*; *Romanoff and Juliet*; *The Unknown Soldier and His Wife*
Utzon, Joern 571
Uys, Pieter-Dirk 536

V

'Vagabond'. See *No Mercy*
Vagabond Camp 212
Vagabond King, The 392, 646
Valentine, Alana 224
Valley of the Shadows 598
Valli, Joe 191
van Amstel, Pamela. See *Are You Lonesome Tonight?*
Van Dieman's Land 12
Van Druten, John. See *Bell, Book and Candle*; *I Remember Mama*
van Eyssen, Louis 30
van Itallie, Jean-Claude. See *America Hurrah!*
van Macklenberg, Robert 395
van Raay, Tina 598
van Roosendael, Eddie 231
Vanbrugh, (Dame) Irene 94, 207, 607, 622
Vanbrugh, (Sir) John. See *The Provoked Husband*
Vanbrugh–Boucicault Company 94, 161, 207, **622**, 623
Vane, Dorothy 299
Vane, Lance 243
Vane, Sutton. See *Outward Bound*; *The War of Wealth*
Varda che bruta ... poretta 224
Variations 148, 209, 392
Varieties 604
Varona, Olga 622
Vassa Zheleznova 515
Vaude, Charlie 502
vaudeville 66, 67, 149, 370, 461, 500
Vaughan, Edward 197
Vaughan, Robert 417
Vaughan, T. See *The Hotel*
Vaughan, Terry 124, 318
Vega Carpio, Lope de. See *Fuente Ovejuna*; *The Pastrymaker*

Veiller, Bayard. See *The Thirteenth Chair*; *Within the Law*
Vela, Irene 359
Vella, Maeve 259, 470
Venetian Twins, The 85, 148, 178, 209, 216, 217, 234, 357, 392, 527, 573, 580, **622**
Venice Preserv'd 56, 647
Verge, John 585
Vernon, Barbara 623. See also *The Multi-Coloured Umbrella*
Vernon, Howard 383, **623**, 643, 645
Vernon, Isabel 117
Vernon, Lou 623
Vertelli 509
Very Good Eddie 298, 392
Vezin, Hermann 654
Vezin, Mrs Herman. See **Mrs Charles Young**
Vickers, Bert 652
Vickery, Robert 631
Victor Hara, Companero 466
Victor, Leslie 623
Victoria Concert Hall 583
Victoria Hall 443
Victoria Regina 301
Victoria State Opera 105, 200, 228, 318, 330
Victoria Theatre: Adelaide 25, 121, 487; Ballarat 268; Brisbane 583; Newcastle (NSW) 238, 405
Victorian Arts Centre 109, 433, 591, 592, 595, **624**
Victorian Arts Centre Trust 221
Victorian College of the Arts 22, 208, 223, 355, 379, 595, 620, **625**
Victorian Drama League 43
Victorian National Theatre Movement Ltd 396
Victorian Socialist Party 211
Victorian Theatre of the Deaf 582
Victory 188
Victory Theatre 396
Vielier, Bayard. See *Within the Law*
Vietnamese Water Puppets 32
View from the Bridge, A 77, 570
Viewpoint 76
Vigo, David 279
Vigors, Helen 637
Vike, Harald 652
Vile, Jim 104
Village Priest, A 108
Village Theatre 396
Villanova Players 42, 137, 557
Villiers, Laura 318
Vincent 544
Vincent, Frieda 246
Vincent, Seddon 247, 625
Vincent Report 247, **625**
Vine and Valantyne 392
Vinegar and Brown Paper 365
Virginian, The 112
Visions 230, 411

Visit, The 56, 215, 222, 293
Vital Signs 155, 631
Vitalstatistix 29, 223, **625**
Vivian, May 421
Vivienne, Virgie 632
Vladimir Mayakovsky, a Tragedy 515
Vocations 187, 237
Vogues of 1935 27
Voices of the Night 345, 534
Volpone 85, 279, 328
Volska, Anna 84, 178, **626**
Vosper, Frank. See *Love from a Stranger*
Voyage Round My Father, A 318, 408
Voysey Inheritance, The 571, 572

W

Wade, George 331
Wade, Mike 87
Wagner, Lucy 175
Wahngin Country 14
Wait Until Dark 631
Waites, James 175
Waiting for Godot 243, 289, 363, 420, 424, 570
Waiting for Lefty 50, 401, 402, 403, 621
Waiting for Rupert Murdoch 622
Wakefield mystery plays 30, 323
Wakyn, Arthur. See *Not in the Book*
Walch, Garnet 425, 559, 561, **626**, 639. See also *Australia Felix*; *Helen's Babies*; *The Miner's Right*; **Robbery Under Arms**; *The Scout*; *Sinbad the Sailor*; *The Trapper*; *Trookulentos, the Tempter*; *Wilful Murder*
Waley, Arthur. See *The Demon's Mask*
Walk Among the Wheeneys, A 236
Walk, Maree. See *A Lone Woman*; *Casualty*
Walkeley and Hollinshed 269
Walker, George Leitch 326
Walker, George Ralph 326
Walker, John. See *Paddy*
Walker, Kath 13. See *Burrum*
Walker, Kerry 64, 90, 497, **627**
Walker, Thomas 534.
Walking on Sticks 224, 373
Walkley, Byrl 153
Wallace, Edgar. See *The Ringer*; *The Terror*
Wallace, George 28, 153, 191, 497, 597, 604, **628**, 652
Wallace, George jnr 59, 583, 628
Wallace, Mrs 178
Wallace, Nellie 602
Wallace, Rowena 24, 168
Wallace and Firmin company 47

Wallace–Dunning Troupe 382
Waller, Charles 628
Waller, Daniel 46
Waller, Emma 46
Waller, Lewis 149
Wallett, Jim 440
Walley, Richard 13, 196, 408. See also *Coordah*
Wallflowering 435
Walls, Tom 149
Walsh, Leonora. See *Why the Innocent*
Walsh, Mr 481
Walsh, Russell 359
Walsh, Stanley 381, 588
Walters, George. See *Joseph of Canaan*
Walton, Alice 462
Walton and O'Rourke 469
Walton, Henry 260
Walton, John 151
Walton, Roland 639
Waltz Dream, A 392
Waltzes of Vienna 392, 409
Waltzing Matilda 505, 507, 508
Wandor, Micheline 208
Wanted—Dead or Alive 538
War and Peace 367
War of Wealth, The 283
War on the Waterfront 400
Warana Festival 226
Waratah Spring Festival 226
Waratahs 59
Warburton, Doreen 239, 470, 572, **628**
Ward, Bruce 369
Ward, Dudley 604, 605
Ward, Frank 519
Ward, (Dame) Genevieve 552, 643, 645
Ward, Hugh J. 237, 239, 298, 299, 343, 372, 465, 606, **629**, 644
Ward, Peter 175
Ward, Rachel 176
Warden of Galway, The 274, 447
Warhorse, The 622
Warlow, Anthony 587
Warner, Cora 462
Warner, H. N. 512
Warner Theatre 338
Warnock, John 587
Warren, Barry 306
Warren, Kenneth 564
Wars of the Roses 356
Wasters, The 24, 26, 614
Wasting Away 606, 653
Watch on the Rhine 50, 104
Water Babies, The 342
Waters, Frank 27, 396, 528, 531, 615, **629**
Waters, John 629, 630
Watershed 60
Waterworth, Noel 59
Watkins, Maurine Dallas. See *Chicago*
Watkins, Will 238
Watkyn, Arthur. See *Not In The Book*

Watson, Don 505. See also *Manning Clark's History of Australia*
Watson, F. B. 121, 510, 584, **630**
Watson, Henrietta 644
Watson, Ian 254, 376, 556
Way, Brian 57
Way of the World, The 234, 570
Waybacks at Home and in Town, The 333
Wayside Theatre 89
WBK 124
We Can't Pay? We Won't Pay! 216
We Find the Bunyip 346, 454
WEA Little Theatre 27, 79
Weatherly, Queenie 186
Weatherly, Zaida 186
Weatherly, Zilla 186
Weaver, Jacki 454, 574, 629, **630**
Web of Steel, The 32
Webb, Charles. See *Belphegor the Mountebank*
Webb, Charles and Mrs 468
Webb, Irene 37
Webster, John. See *The Duchess of Malfi*
Wedding Bells 400
Wedekind, Frank 186, 215, 328. See *Spring's Awakening*
Weekly Times (newspaper) 170
Weihl, Maria von 525
Weill, Kurt 56
Weingott, Owen 36, 308, 580
Weintraubs, the 311
Weir, Johnson 197, 462
Weir, Mary 643
Weir, Peter 422
Weiss, Peter. See *The Persecution and Assassination of Marat*
Welch, Bettina 302, **631**
Welcome the Bright World 58, 182, 222, 244, 422, 520
Weller, Archie 13, 359. See also *Nidjera*
Welles, Orson. See *Moby Dick Rehearsed*
Welling, Sylvia 384
Wells, Jerold 494
Wells, Peter 339
Wells, Win. See *Gertrude Stein and a Companion*
Weltzel, E. 605
Wendt, J. M. 582
Werder, Felix 444
Wertenbaker, Timberlake. See *Our Country's Good*
Wesker, Arnold 208. See *Roots*
Wesley-Smith, Martin 63
West, Barbara 631
West, Bob 143
West, Mr 481
West, Obed 589
West, Timothy 510
West Australian (newspaper) 173
West Australian Theatre Company 439
West Community Theatre 631

West of the Black Stump 330, 392
West Side Story 52, 53, 129, 385, 392, 615
West Theatre Company 223, 625, **631**
Westbrook, Jane 75
Western Australian Academy of Performing Arts 208, 438, 620, 621, **631**
Western Australian Arts Council 634
Western Australian Drama Festival 42, 90, 264, 437
Western Australian Playwrights' Consortium. See Stages
Western Australian provincial towns 632
Western Australian Theatre Company 97, 247, 280, 286, 395, 408, 412, 438, 557
Western Australian Young Playwrights' Workshop 439
Western Limit 252
Weston, Frank 291, **634**
Weston, Mrs 335
Westwell, Raymond 395, **634**
Westwood, Chris 29, 86, 223, 407, 422, 555, **635**, 651
Westwood, Faye 528
Wet and Dry 80, 184
We've Taken Gardiner 35
Whaite, Harry 462
Whaley, George 123, 134, 203, 204, 393, 418, **635**. See also *On Our Selection*
Whalley, Joan 44, 102, 154, 617, 618
Wharf Theatre 569, 573, 595, **635**
Wharmby, Denise 580
What Every Woman Knows 560
What If You Died Tomorrow? 165, 221, 234, 257, 455, 527, 642
What the Butler Saw 365
Whatever Happened to Realism? 132
What's New 168
Wheeler, Anthony 536
Wheeler, Ben and Frank 535
Wheeler, I. W. 535
Wheeler, Philip 508
Wheeler, Sidney 636
Wheezily Distinguished 189
Whelan, Albert 502, **636**
Whelan and Wilson 636
When Knighthood was in Flower 558, 560
When the Tide Rises 286
When the Wind Blows 259
When They Send Me Three and Fourpence 538
When We Are Married 156
Where Did Vortex Go 236
Where's That Bomb? 403
Wherrett, Richard 176, 193, 199, 202, 203, 308, 407, 411, 497, 569, 572, **636**
While Parents Sleep 24

While the Billy Boils 491, 532
While the Sun Shines 59, 227, 555
Whip Round for Percy Grainger, A 346, 478
Whip, The 485, 490, 647
Whipping Boy, The 275
Whitaker, David 73
Whitbread, Don 124
White, Desmond 344
White, Dick 199
White, Dorothy 199
White, Frank 648
White, Fred. See *Cockatoo Farm*; *Dingo Flat*
White, Henry E. 64, 126, 201, 239, 405, 422, 423, 465, 586, 590, 604, **637**
White, George 73
White, Lee 602
White, Leslie 199
White, Michael 359
White, Patrick 87, 166, 174, 208, 220, 317, 454, 456, 526, **638**. See also *Bread and Butter Women*; *Big Toys*; *A Cheery Soul*; *The Ham Funeral*; *Netherwood*; *Night on Bald Mountain*; *School for Friends*; *The Season at Sarsaparilla*; *Shepherd on the Rocks*; *Signal Driver*;
White, Penny 135
White, Ruth 112
White Australia 63, 84, 482, 491, **637**
White Cargo 248
White Fawn, The 627
White Heather, The 283
White Horse Inn 321, 384, *385*, 392, 409, 646
White Hotel, The 297
White Justice 13, 400
White Man's Mission, The 462
White Paper Flowers 337
White Slave Traffic, The 286
White Sports Coat, A 333, 373
White With Wire Wheels 273, 274
Whitehall Academy of Dramatic Art 639
Whitehall Theatrical Productions 53, 81, 129, 158, 161, 166, 344, 369, 427, 505, 568, 624, **639**, 651
Whitehead, Robert 120
Whiteley, Dorothy 407, 531
Whitemore, Hugh. See *84 Charing Cross Road*
White's Rooms 25, 242, 338
Whitfield, David 604
Whiting, John. See *The Devils*
Whitlam, Gough 160
Whitsunday 58, 411
Whitworth, Robert Hollyford 639
Whitworth, Robert P. 147, 170, 495, 626, **639**
Who? 273, 274
Whole Town's Talking, The 114
Whoopee 397

Whore in a Madhouse 216, 297, 635
Who's Afraid of Virginia Woolf? 88, 146, 184, 193, 264, 305, 319, 357, 413, 414, 551, 568, 570
Why Girls Leave Home 286
Why People Go to Traffic Accidents 431
Why the Innocent 137
Whyalla Players 537
Whyte, Stirling 118, 637, 647
Whyte, W. Farmer 61
Widdop, Bruce 508
Widow's Victim, The 511
Wife's Secret, The 311, 564
Wignall, George 652
Wilcox, Dora 375
Wild About Work 310, 337
Wild America 48, 129, 518, 627
Wild Duck, The 198
Wild Honey 85, 240, 254, 512, 515
Wild Stars 614
Wild West shows 92, **640**, 649
Wildcat 322
Wilde, Oscar. See *The Happy Prince*; *The Importance of Being Earnest*; *An Ideal Husband*; *Lady Windermere's Fan*; *Salome*; *A Woman of No Importance*
Wilder, Elizabeth 95
Wilder, Thornton. See *Our Town*; *The Skin of Our Teeth*
Wildflower 114, 275, 321, 392
Wilfred Gordon McDonald Partridge 429
Wilful Murder 181, 627
Wilkie, Allan 19, 36, 207, 290, 309, 451, 490, 498, 523, *524*, 606, **640**
Wilkins, Peter 124, 307
Will Mahoney Company 281
Will, The 622
Willard, Pemberton 306
Willett, John 98
William Buckley and The Wathaurong Tribe 367
William Moore's Annual Drama Nights 39, 354, 375, 451
William Street Management 34
William Tell 398, 653
Williams, Alan 210
Williams, Billy 497, 502, **641**
Williams, Doris 362
Williams, Ellen 641
Williams, Emlyn. See *The Corn is Green*; *Night Must Fall*
Williams, James 170
Williams, Leslie 362
Williams, Michael 510
Williams, Peter 441, 516, 569, **641**
Williams, Rod 338

Williams, Tennessee. See *Cat on a Hot Tin Roof*; *The Glass Menagerie*; *Kingdom of the Earth*; *Mooney's Kid Don't Cry*; *The Night of the Iguana*; *Orpheus Descending*; *The Rose Tattoo*; *Small Craft Warnings*; *A Streetcar Named Desire*
Williams, William. See Billy Williams
Williamson, David 73, 74, 209, 398, 497, 556, 588, **641**. See also *Brilliant Lies*; *Celluloid Heroes*; **The Club**; **The Coming of Stork**; *A Dangerous Life*; *The Department*; **Don's Party**; *Emerald City*; *A Funny Thing Happened on the Way to The Front*; *Gallipoli*; *A Handful of Friends*; *The Indecent Exposure of Anthony East*; *Jugglers Three*; *Money and Friends*; *The Perfectionist*; **The Removalists**; *Sanctuary*; *Siren*; *Sons of Cain*; *Top Silk*; **Travelling North**; *What If You Died Tomorrow*
Williamson, J. C. 15, 19, 24, 41, 46, *47*, 82, 86, 93, 94, 112, 162, 163, 214, 244, 245, 269, 299, 313, 333, 340, 374, 382, 417, 427, 429, 451, 460, 488, 489, 546, 552, 566, 611, **643**, 645. See also *Djin Djin the Japanese Bogie Man*; *Matsa, Queen of Fire*
Williamson, Pippa 224
Williamson and Musgrove 240, 268, 282, 299, 374, 379, 383, 643, **644**
Williamson Comic Opera Company 299
Williamson, Garner and Co. 86, 183, 607, 643, **645**
Williamson, Garner and Musgrove 15, 226, 240, 340, 353, 379, 382, 463, 553, 559, 576, 585, 586, 643, **645**
Williamson Juvenile Comic Opera Company 460
Williamson, Tallis and Ramaciotti 299, 480, 576, 643
Williamson-Edgley Theatres 304
Willoughby, George 343, 606, 629
Willoughby and Ward's New London Company 629, 646
Wills, Nance 402. See also Nance McMillan
Wilson, Carden 646
Wilson, Dennis 155
Wilson, Frank 151, 330, 613
Wilson, J. Plumpton 37
Wilson, J. R. 158
Wilson, John 141
Wilson, Judy 365, 395
Wilson, L. Peter 469, 538, 578, **645**
Wilson, Lanford. See *Tally's Folly*

Wilson, Peter J. 123, 259, 469, **645**
Wilson, Ralph 122, 123, 125
Wilson, Rod 307
Wilson, Snoo 73, 208
Wilson, Strella 27, 384, **646**
Wilson, Viola 302, 576
Wilson, W. J. 256, 443, 546, **646**
Wilson, William 646
Wilson's San Francisco Palace Circus 126
Wilton, Olive 41, 118, 207, 245, 278, 279, 392, 528, **646**, 647, 651
Wiltshire, John 363
Wimble, June 363
Wimmins Circus 223
Winchester, Jone 439, 497
Wind and the Rain, The 32
Wind in the Willows, The 271, 342, 469
Windeyer, Richard 41
Windy Gully 501, 587
Wineera, Stan 318
Wines, William 362
Winning, Fiona 189
Winning Ticket, The 55, 482, **647**
Winskills, the 142
Winsloe, Christie. See *Children in Uniform*
Winslow Boy, The 352, 491
Winstanley, Ann 180, 310, 647. See also Mrs Ximenes
Winstanley, Eliza 120, 180, 310, 324, 340, 516, **647**, 651, 653
Winstanley, William 545, 647
Winston, Jeanie 70
Winter Journey 352, 435, 629
Winter's Tale, The 31, 36, 240, 408, 420, 510
Winterset 27, 43, 366
Wirth, George 649
Wirth, Harry 649
Wirth, Jacob 213, 649
Wirth, Johannes 213, 649
Wirth, John 649
Wirth, Madeleine 649
Wirth, Marizles 648, 649
Wirth, May 140, *142*, 152, 541, **648**, 649
Wirth, Peter 213, 649
Wirth, Philip 649
Wirth family 62, 126
Wirth's Pacific Circus 649
Wirths' Circus 26, 139, 213, 229, 306, 434, 473, 535, 541, 542, 612, **649**
Wish No More 196
Wish You Were Here 330
Wissler, Rod 617
Witch Play 373
Witcombe, Eleanor 497, **650**. See also *Smugglers, Beware!*
Withers, Googie 167, 303, 347, 366, 515
Withers, R. 599
Within the Law 48, 81, 555
Within These Walls 350, 396

Witkiewicz, Wladyslaw Ignacy 459
Witold Gombrowicz in Buenos Aires 459, 468
Witt, Freddy 157
Witzenhausen, Where Are You? 321, 411
Wives Have Their Uses 364
Wizard of Oz, The 106, 458
Wogs Out of Work 64, 203
Wolf, William 277
Wolf, The 480
Wolf Boy 57, 655
Woman and Wine 283
Woman in Mind 317, 570, 573
Woman Mary, The 607
Woman of No Importance, A 107
Woman Song 83
Woman Tamer, The 32, 212, 375
Women! 273
Women, The 49, 50, 166, 233, 332, 371, 491, 543
Women and Arts Festival 223
Women and Theatre Project 223, 635
Women Directors' Workshop 635
women in the theatre 650
Women of Importance 89
Women of Spain 464
Women of Troy, The 222
Women on a Shoestring 123
Women There, The 57, 154
Women's Circus 223
Women's Dreaming 14
Women's Own Work 410
Women's Theatre Group 75, 223
Women's Theatre Workshop 123
Wonder Woman 83, 330
Wonderland City 55, 469
Wong, Anna May 603
Wonthaggi Celebration, The 155
Wood, Coralie 124
Wood, Jane 422
Wood, John 90, 259, 308, 556, **651**
Wood, Nici 606
Wood, Robin 59
Wood, Wee Georgie 602, 604
Wood Demon, The
Woodcock, Christine 259
Woodlochs' American Circus 306
Woodlock, Tilly 326
Woodrow, Carol 122, 123, 126, 224, 307
Woods, Alfred 606
Woods, Leslie 462
Woods Theatrical Agency 34
Woods, Tim 203
Woodward, Joe 122, 123, 307
Woodyear, William 116
Wool Game, The 367
Wooldridge, Alice 70
Woolly Jumpers 367
Woolpack Inn 364, 592
Work Girl, The 233

Workers' Art Club 400, 403, 567
Workers' Art Guild 42, 172, 400, 437, 464, 598, **652**
Workers' Educational Association dramatic societies 43; Adelaide 27, 41; Newcastle (NSW) 405
Workers' Theatre 652
Workers' Theatre Group 190, 400, 402
Working Out 508
Workman, Charles 244, 429
World Against Her, The 66
World Expo '86 408
World Expo '88 60, 102, 128, 226, 265, 618
Worlds Apart 255
Worrell, William 141
Worst Woman in London, The 332, 490
Wouk, Herman. See *The Caine Mutiny Court Martial*
Wragge, Maibry 102
Wran, Neville 569
Wrangham, J. H. See *Jess*; *Marvellous Melbourne*; *A Transvaal Heroine*
Wreck Ashore, The 608
Wren, Harry 53, 316, 429, 628, **652**
Wren, John 149
Wright, Arthur. See *Keane of Kalgoorlie*
Wright, Nicholas. See *Mrs Klein*
Wright, Walter 362
Write Me a Murder 257
Writer's Cramp 242
Writers' Theatre 74, 76
Wrong Side of the Door, The 35, 392
Wu Zuguang. See *The Three Beatings of Tao Sanchun*
Wuhan People's Art Theatre 136
Wushu (Martial Arts) Group 136
Wyatt, Joseph 56, 121, 254, 324, 340, 365, 464, 512, 531, 566, 586, **652**
Wyatt, Rachael 512
Wycherley, William. See *The Country Wife*
Wyndon, Barbara 440
Wynn, Patricia 70
Wynne, Watkin 504
Wynyard, Diana 510

X

Xenophobia 631
Ximenes, Mrs 647. See also Ann Winstanley

Y

Yackandandah Playscripts 456, 468
Yagan 12
Yallourn Story, The 155, 166
Yamashita 468
Yang, William 326, 432. See also *10 000 Miles Away*
Yarraroos 59
Yates, Theodosia. See **Theodosia Stirling**
Yeamans, Annie 62
Year 9 Are Animals 336, 606, 616, 655
Yeats, W. B. 211, 297. See also *The Land of Heart's Desire*
Yellow Brick Roadshow 614
Yeomen of the Guard, The 124, 382, 392, 623
Yerbury, Di 70
Yes and No 408
Yes, Madam? 321, 392
Yes, Uncle! 111, 392
Yevtushenko, Yevgeny 200
York Theatre 521
Yorricks 38
Yoshitsune Sembon Zakura 305
You and the Night and the Housewine 512, 527, 580
You Can't Take it with You 50, 166, 260, 595, 639
You Never Can Tell 112, 630
Young, Amelia 576
Young, Charles 506, **653**, 654. See also *The Goblin of the Gold Coast*; *Transportation and the Demon Discord*
Young, David 57, 516, 606, **653**, 654. See also *Eureka*; *Wasting Away*
Young, Edward. See *The Revenge*
Young, Eliza. See also Mrs Charles Young
Young, Emma 506, 653
Young, Florence 18, 111, 299, 372, 374, **653**
Young, John 519
Young, Mrs Charles 650, **654**
Young, Sandi 653
Young, W. See *Ben Hur*
Young Australian League 135, 536
Young Elizabethan Players 72, 105, 474, 524, 654
Young Mo 187, 348, 486, 538
Young People's Guide to the Orchestra 342
young people's theatre 654
Young Person in Pink, A 325
Young Tote 568
Younge, Frederick 63, 100
Younge, Richard 100
Your Number's Up 57
Your Obedient Servant 202
Youth 490, 645
youth theatre 224, 655
You've Never Had It So Good 403
Yuncken Freeman 125
Yunnan Provincial Acrobatic Troupe 136

Z

Zac's Place 57
Zappa, William 556, **656**
Zavistowski Sisters 48
Zaza 560
Zeal of Thine House, The 264
Zen and Now 439
Zeneto 152. See also Con Colleano
Zeplin, F. 70
087 337
Zilch 392, 629
Zindel, Paul. See *The Effect of Gamma Rays on Man-in-the-Moon Marigolds*
Zinga, John Edwin 144, 648
Zootango 184, 279, **656**
Zwar, Charles 90

Sources of illustrations

Page **11**: Mitchell Library. **13**: Currency Press (*photo* Peter Holderness). **14**: Currency Press (*photo* Geoffrey Lovell). **18**: Mitchell Library. **21** upper: Currency Press; lower: Currency Press (*photo* Robert McFarlane). **25**: National Library of Australia. **26**: State Library of NSW. **28**: Currency Press. **39**: Mortlock Library of South Australia. **40**: Mitchell Library. **41**: State Library of Victoria. **42**: Dennis Wolanski Library. **46**: State Library of NSW. **47** upper and lower: Mitchell Library. **49**: Mitchell Library. **51**: Dennis Wolanski Library. **52**: Denis Wolanski Library. **100**: John Oxley Library. **101**: John Oxley Library. **102**: Currency Press (*photo* Sesh Raman). **138**: State Library of NSW. **139**: National Library of Australia. **140**: National Library of Australia. **142**: Dennis Wolanski Library. **143**: Mitchell Library. **170**: State Library of Victoria. **172**: Fisher Library. **205**: Mitchell Library. **206**: Mitchell Library. **207**: Performing Arts Museum. **299** upper: Mitchell Library. **300** upper: Mitchell Library. **301** upper: Mitchell Library; lower: National Library of Australia. **302**: Dennis Wolanski Library. **303**: Dennis Wolanski Library. **353**: State Library of Victoria. **354**: Melbourne Theatre Company (*photo* David Parker). **355** upper: Currency Press (*photo* Ian McKenzie); lower: Currency Press (*photo* Harold Love). **383**: Mitchell Library. **385**: Mitchell Library. **386**: Dennis Wolanski Library. **388**: Mitchell Library. **437** upper and lower: Western Australian Performing Arts Museum. **438**: Currency Press (*photo* Sally McConnell). **448**: Mitchell Library. **450** left: State Library of Victoria; right: Performing Arts Museum. **453**: National Library of Australia. **454**: Currency Press (*photo* Robert Walker). **455**: Currency Press. **456**: Currency Press. **489**: Mitchell Library. **490**: Mortlock Library of South Australia. **523** upper: State Library of NSW; lower: Mitchell Library. **524** upper: State Library of NSW; lower: Currency Press (*photo* Ray Irvin). **546**: Mitchell Library. **547**: Mitchell Library. **548**: Mitchell Library. **549** upper: Melbourne Theatre Company; lower: Currency Press (*photo* Jeff Busby). **550**: Currency Press (*photo* Max Dupain). **552** upper and lower: State Library of Victoria. **553** upper: Dennis Wolanski Library; lower: Mitchell Library. **554**: Denis Wolanski Library. **566**: National Library of Australia. **568** left: Currency Press (*photo* Peter Holderness); right: Currency Press (*photo* Leon Gregory). **569**: *photo* Branco Gaica. **590**: Mitchell Library. **593**: National Library of Australia. **601** left and right: Mitchell Library. **602**: Currency Press. **603** upper: Performing Arts Museum; lower: Dennis Wolanski Library. **609**: Mitchell Library. **610**: Mitchell Library. **611**: John Oxley Library. **612**: John Oxley Library. Endpapers: Currency Press (*photo* Dennis Del Favero).

Printed by Southwood Press Pty Ltd, 80–92 Chapel Street, Marrickville NSW 2204

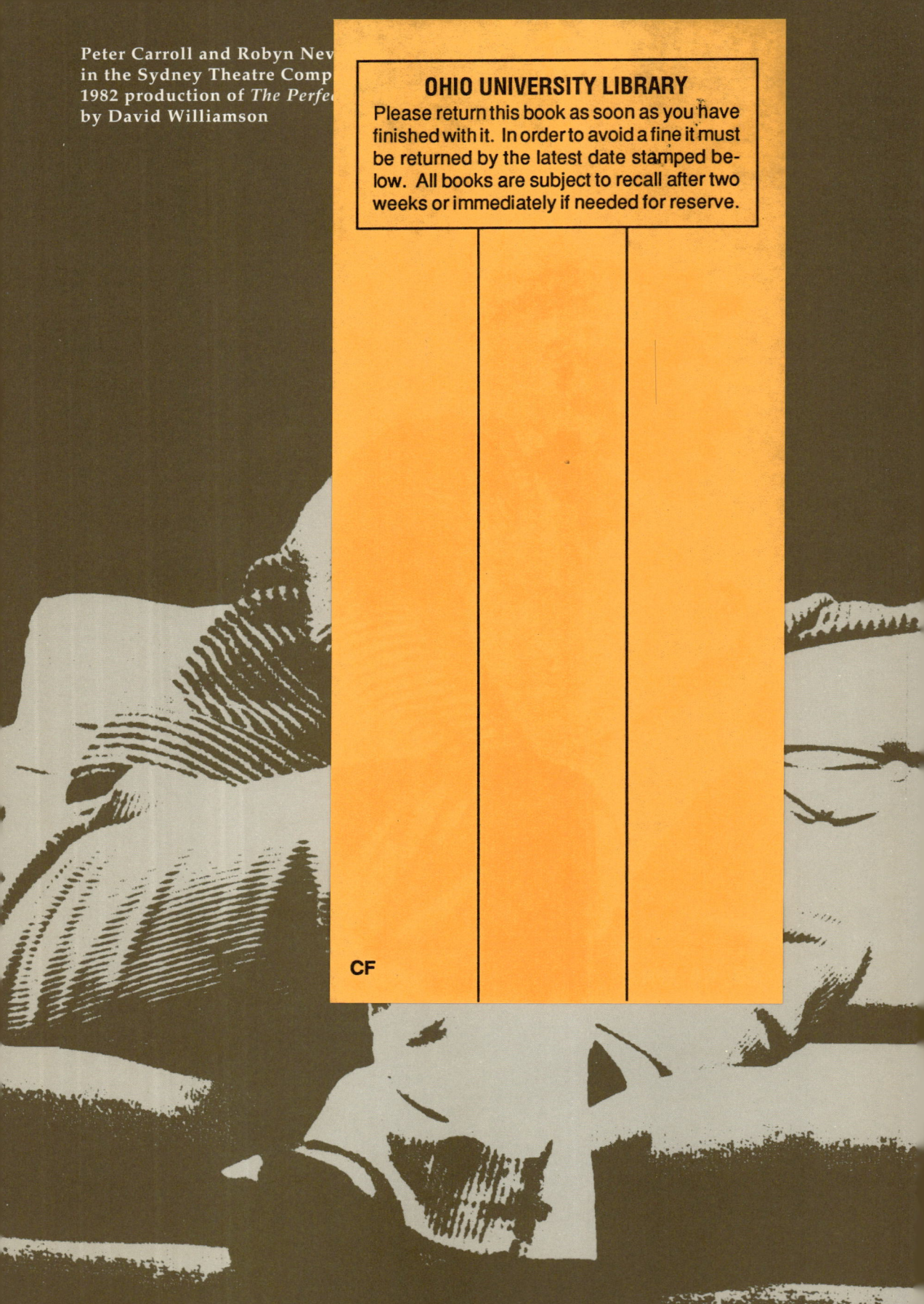

Peter Carroll and Robyn Nev[in] in the Sydney Theatre Comp[any] 1982 production of *The Perfe[ct]* by David Williamson